FOUR DECADES
IN
PARLIAMENT

FOUR DECADES IN PARLIAMENT

VOLUME II
STATE OF THE ECONOMY

Atal Bihari Vajpayee

Edited by Dr. N.M. Ghatate

SHIPRA

(2021 PoD, 2018, 2000, 1998 twice, First Published 1996)

Rs. 9000, US$ 360
Set Price

ISBN: 978-81-85402-69-7 (Set)
978-81-85402-70-3 (Vol. 1)
978-81-85402-71-0 (Vol. 2)
978-81-85402-72-7 (Vol. 3)

2024 Impression PoD

Four Decades in Parliament

Published by:
SHIPRA PUBLICATIONS
LG 18-19, Pankaj Central Market,
I.P. Ext., Patparganj, Delhi 110092, India
91 11 47322068; 9650028065, 9810522367
info@shiprapublication.com
www.shiprapublication.com

VOLUME II

Contents

I Budget and Planning

II Corruption In High Places

I BUDGET AND PLANNING

Common Man Crushed by Budget

Hindi Agitation

Sir, before I express my thoughts on the budget proposals I would like to express regrets over the Hon'ble Prime Minister's reference in his speech to the Hindi agitation in Punjab. In my opinion the Hindi agitation in Punjab is in no way related to the budget proposals before the House. There can be a difference of opinion on the Hindi agitation, but it was most inappropriate on the part of the Hon'ble Prime Minister to have raised this issue in this House. The leaders of the Arya Samaj had approached the Prime Minister for a compromise, but the Prime Minister could not evolve such a compromise, and possibly this may have forced them to place their demands before the Punjab Government by way of a *Sadbhavana Yatra.* I would not like to say anything more on this matter for the present. I would request the Hon'ble Prime Minister to intervene in the matter, because intervention even at this stage could save the situation. There is none in the country who does not want all Indian languages to develop. Punjabi too is our language, in fact it is one of India's national languages, but differences crop up when Hindi and Punjabi are treated differently. I feel that if this discrimination was ended and everyone given freedom to learn both the languages the situation that has risen in Punjab could be resolved. And for this situation the Central Government is responsible and the Prime Minister cannot absolve himself from that responsibility.

Burden on Common Man

The budget proposals before us are being debated for the last some days. I had hoped that the Prime Minister would say something in his speech that could justify the taxes that are being imposed on the common man. But after listening to him *(interruption)* I would like to say that almost all parties have opposed the tax burden proposed in the budget. It cannot be denied that the common man to whom an appeal for greater sacrifice is being made is not capable of bearing it. I am happy to see that in his speech the Prime Minister has accepted that the Five Year Plan is not something sacrosanct and is open to change. Everyone will agree that the Plan is not the end but a means to the end. Our end is a happy life, but the new budget proposals impose an

Lok Sabha on May 30, 1957 during discussion on the General Budget

unbearable tax burden on the common man. Success in planning depends upon popular enthusiasm. Today the people are gripped by a sense of pessimism. There is a certain discontent. Can planning succeed without enthusing the people and are these tax proposals capable of enthusing the people ? This needs to be considered. I regret to see that the Finance Minister does not seem to agree with what the Prime Minister says. If the Plan is not sacrosanct why is it not amended in accordance with national resources and the people's capacity to bear the burden ? The election manifesto of the Congress had accepted that it is possible to amend the Plan from time to time. On page 10 it says :

> "It is a flexible Plan and it will have to be adjusted from time to time as circumstances demand and as resources of the country permit."

This is the Congress party's assurance to the people. But the Finance Minister's speech in the Rajya Sabha says exactly the opposite. He said :

> "I am afraid the Plan is not a piece of India rubber. I mean it is not something which has certain flexibility and I can elongate it."

I do not believe election manifestoes are meant only for elections and can be shelved afterwards. If a manifesto is for the people we would have to give thought to the prevailing conditions—our resources and the people's capacity to bear. And Sir, I would respectfully submit that the common people cannot today bear the burden you are imposing upon them. Day by day the production cess on essential commodities is being raised, and all things like tea, sugar, matches, tobacco, vanaspati have been made more expensive.

Raising Price will not Curtail Sugar Consumption

The price of sugar has been raised from 13 annas to a rupee per seer. You would say—and the Finance Minister has actually said — that you want to control consumption of these things and increase their export. I submit you can't achieve both the objectives. These commodities are not articles of luxury. Their demand has not grown so much that it can be reduced substantially.

People do not gobble up sugar. Sugar is not an addiction. When one can make do with one spoonful of sugar how much can he cut down on its intake ? And I would like to point out that there is so much sugarcane production in the country that with proper crushing arrangements we would not only be able to meet domestic demand but also make stocks available for export. But I have doubts—I am not sure—if in view of our production cost our sugar can find a market outside the country. This too needs to be considered.

Costlier Rail Travel

Sir, an American expert who visited this country had suggested that overcrowding in trains could be controlled by raising railway fares. At that time his proposal had been considered immoral, but the Finance Minister has decided to raise rail fares and the people would now have to pay more. The Government is not prepared to give the assurance that in return the travelling public would get more facilities. If you want to increase fares increase First Class fares. At present first class passengers enjoy First Class facilities on paying Second Class fare. The Third Class passenger cannot bear an increase in fares.

Post and Telegraph Rates

Post and telegraph rates are also being raised, and this increase is being justified in a very strange way. That is the Government is running these services at a loss. In fact the Finance Minister has brought the Government down to the level of a petty shopkeeper. To argue that public services be curtailed because they are running in loss does not become of a Government claiming to establish a welfare state. Public utilities are run for the service of the public. They have to be run even at a loss, and the posts and telegraphs are one of them.

The price of a post-card has already gone up by half a paisa because of the Naya Paisa. Now it is being raised still further. All in all there would be a 33 percent price increase. There is no justification for this. Perhaps the Finance Minister does not want people to share their joys and sorrows with others through letters or travel, so he wants to deny them even this.

Finance Minister's is Full of Contradiction

As for bringing down the income tax limit I would like to know if the Government feels that a person earning Rs. 250 per month saves enough to be able to pay the saving by way of tax. The House does not so far have a report on how much progress the Five Year Plan has achieved, but it may be acknowledged that there has been 'progress' in some fields—for instance, unemployment has increased, commodity prices have gone up, and today the common man, the labourer, the farmer and the middle class are being ground between the millstones of price rise brought about by taxation and inflation. If you bring down the tax limit you would have to think of other relief measures. These days a Wage Commission is being demanded and demonstrations are being held. The Central Government employees are demanding additional allowances. You do not want to appoint a wage commission but want to lighten their pockets. The two cannot be done at the same time.

The Finance Minister has said if the income tax is reduced it might arrange allowances, and there would be an allowance for those with large families. When it was asked in the Rajya Sabha if this would not adversely affect the family planning programme the Finance Minister said that small matters like family planning should not be considered when we are thinking of big things! Sometimes family planning becomes a big thing, sometimes it is a small matter! We should have a clear stand on this. I regret to say the Finance Minister's speech is full of contradictions. When it is said that the First Plan has not resulted in any appreciable elevation in the common man's level of life, the Finance Minister argues that this is not possible with just one plan, but when it is said that our economy is not capable of bearing the burden you are imposing on it he attracts our attention at the common man's condition, which needed to be improved!

It is alright to think of the future, but to completely sacrifice the present for its sake might not be correct. It is only on the foundation of the present that the edifice of the future can be built. The future will take care of itself; you should think of the present. And, in view of the present conditions of the country no one, I feel, can seriously suggest that the new tax burden imposed on the people should be continued. But the question is, what is to be done ? Yesterday I had said that this House had accepted five year planning; this House can change it also. Perhaps many of my friends did not appreciate this talk of change. Now the Prime Minister says we neither want to curtail it, nor to expand it. What is the third way ? Is it to keep to the way we are going ? You are in a majority and can keep to that way. But the people, whom you want to take with you, should be convinced that they are capable of extending the co-operation and sacrifice that are expected of them.

Self Example Reduce Expenditure

Many Members of the House have pleaded that the Government should reduce its expenditure, practise economy and simple living and our ministers and high officials should set an example before the people by their own conduct. This is essential for creating public enthusiasm for the Plan. But although everyone agrees on this yet no progress is seen in this direction.

Yesterday an Hon'ble Member mentioned Chandigarh. I heard it even in Bhopal that a new Chandigarh is coming up. A new capital will be built at a cost of Rs. 2-3 crores. But tall mansions of the capital cannot bring benefits to the seven lakh villages of India and inspire their hearts giving them the will to sacrifice. A new legislature house is being built in Chandigarh at a cost of about Rs. 10 lakhs. You can stop it. You could and should also put a stop to the plan of building the capital at Bhopal. If there are not enough buildings in Bhopal you can shift the capital to Gwalior. There is a need to change the entire outlook.

Sir, a major reason of public apathy for the Plan is also that it is being conducted on party basis. This is not national planning. The effort has not been made to secure the participation of all parties and classes in it. As a member of Parliament I have been inducted into the District Planning Committee. But while it was to meet on May 10, I received intimation of the meeting on May 16. There is a flood control committee in my district. Its meeting was fixed on the 26th, but I was informed about it on the 29th. Now I am not in a position to say if this was due to the inefficiency of the Posts & Telegraphs Department or of the District Officers, but so long as people at every level are not invited to participate in planning and the Plan is not implemented in a genuinely national form, popular enthusiasm necessary for the success of the Plan cannot be generated. The new taxes have adversely affected this enthusiasm still further. There can be no difference of opinion on the need to develop the country in a planned manner but it is necessary to preserve the national character of the Plan while designing and implementing it. May I hope that the tax burden in the new budget proposals would be reduced, and while determining the priorities of the Plan — what the Finance Minister calls 'rephasing', I shall not use the word 'pruning' if he feels bad about it — we should put first things first and the Plan would be implemented in consonance with the country's resources and the people's capacity.

The Plan should be Labour and not Capital Intensive

My basic objection to the Plan is that it is capital-intensive while it should be labour-intensive. Manpower is our greatest asset. If we provide work for all and put the maximum manpower to work as per the Plan we can certainly make progress in the direction of economic reconstruction despite a lack of greater capital. Unfortunately the Plan has been so prepared that it pays less attention to manpower and more to capital. Today we have a foreign exchange problem, and the food problem is getting serious. I do not think there is a shortage of food stocks in the country, but the distribution is faulty. This deficiency in distribution cannot be remedied even by keeping aside a separate fund of Rs. 25 crores.

I have seen during election days that at a place in Deoria District in U.P. only those people were given rations at government shops who brought a Minister's slip showing a pair of bullocks. The location of shops is also decided from the party point of view. Distribution too is not properly done. You may set aside Rs. 25 crore, still the economic problem would not be resolved. You should make proper distribution arrangements and secure the co-operation of all.

Agricultural Production Ignored

The policy to ignore agriculture is on the rise. It is hoped that there would be greater agricultural production with a lesser investment, and the adverse results are before us. Agriculture is the basis of India's economy, it is our principal industry. We ignored agricultural production and the result is the food problem facing us today. And now in the name of the food problem such burdens are being imposed on the people as they cannot bear. I urge that the priorities of this plan be considered afresh and an effort made to secure public support for it in every field.

I do not wish to say anything more and thank you.

The Second Five Year Plan
Beyond Resources

Sir, before I express my thoughts on the difficulties that have arisen in connection with this Plan I would like to say something about the opening speech the Prime Minister made today. The people at large and this House had hoped that in his speech the Prime Minister would indicate the way to solve the difficulties that have arisen in fulfilling the Five Year Plan, strive to dispel the pessimism prevailing in the country and create an atmosphere of enthusiasm. I have no hesitation in saying that the Prime Minister's speech was a great disappointment for me. While listening to it I felt he was not speaking in the Parliament of the Republic of India but in a public meeting organised by a Yogashram, where people are taught not how to stand on their feet but on their head.

Today the country expects that the Government unambiguously spell out the means that have to be adopted to fulfil this Plan. The difficulties in its implementation are not divine impediments. We cannot absolve ourselves of responsibility by blaming the nature or the Suez Canal conflict or our bickerings with Pakistan. Those who are more concerned with the strife in Indo-China and Korea cannot take it for granted that there would be peace in the world. We also have floods and droughts off and on. To say that they damaged the crops and so the Plan could not be fulfilled would not be an acceptable excuse to the people.

Self-sufficiency is a Joke

The Prime Minister has just now advised the people to become self-sufficient. What greater joke could there be than that the Prime Minister of a country whose Finance Minister wanders all over the world with a begging bowl in his hand and auctions the prestige of India in the market places of Washington, London and Bonn should preach self-sufficiency to the people. If any one needs to learn the lesson of self-sufficiency it is the Government.

When the Second Plan was formulated foreign assistance to the tune of Rs. 800 crores was estimated for it. Are we under the impression that America is full of embodiments of generosity like Karna ? Are we unaware of the U.S. policy towards India ? This policy is not a matter of a year or two. If we want to pursue an independent foreign policy we should not expect so much from America. If the U.S. gives us some small assistance and then gives Pakistan

Lok Sabha on November 20, 1957 during discussion on the review of the Second Five Year Plan and current economic conditions

arms in that proportion the financial aid given to us would be cancelled out, as we would have to spend that much on defence. Today it is being said that we had no idea we would have to spend so much on defence. If that is so who is to blame ? Pakistan's anti-India policy is not a new thing, nor the U.S.-Pak military alliance. I am doubtful about how those who are not so far-sighted can build the country.

Our Prime Minister is a dreamer, but he does not have around him people who can translate those dreams into reality. The result is, *'Vinayakam Prakurvano rachayamasa Vanaram*—we set about making a Ganesh idol but end up making the likeness of a monkey. It is argued that there was just a small mistake—the trunk that was to be attached at the front got attached at the back. Yes, it was a small mistake, but see the result. Before thinking of ways and means of making the Second Plan a success we must go into the basics and ponder over the difficulties that confront it.

Who is responsible for the foreign exchange problem today ? The Planning Commission that formulated the Plan was not far-sighted. Now we are told that during his tenure as Commerce Minister, the present Finance Minister gave away import licences indiscriminately. The Ministry of Commerce issues licences but the Reserve Bank and the Finance Minister do not know about them till the bills come in. And neither the Commerce Ministry itself nor the Planning Commission knows how many of those licences were actually used. It is the Economic Committee of the Cabinet that decides the import policy, so I charge the Central Cabinet is collectively responsible for it.

Issue of Licence to the Private Sector

What after all was the basis on which licences were issued to the private sector ? Is it not true that more than necessary foreign exchange was used in the private sector, and if that was so was it for the fulfilment of the targets of the Second Plan ? Fixing targets is the responsibility of the Planning Commission. Then were they fixed wrongly ? The Economic Committee of the Cabinet determines the import policy. It is for the Committees of senior officials of various ministries, the Licensing Committees, to take decisions on various projects, and it is the business of the savings banks and the Reserve Bank to make foreign exchange available for them. I doubt if there is any co-ordination among all these bodies.

We are told that a warning of the emerging foreign exchange crisis had been given 15 moths in advance. Then why was it not heeded ? It is time to identify those who are responsible. We say this not because we want to cry over spilt milk but to avoid mistakes in future. So I suggest that the Planning Commission be reorganised. It includes both the Prime Minister and the Planning Minister. They are omnipresent—from the Planning Commission to the Sadhu Samaj. It also includes Shri Krishna Menon who can be used for foreign co-operation. But I feel the Planning Commission should have experts who can give frank, fearless and impartial opinions. I am doubtful if anybody can say anything in the presence of the Prime Minister. But the net result is that we have formulated a plan for which we do not have the required resources.

We are told there is nothing wrong if the Plan is ambitious, even over-ambitious. But it is necessary that we should have the resources for whatever plan we prepare. Recently an American expert who visited this country observed that so far as the needs of the country are concerned the Plan is not ambitious. May I respectfully submit that we do not need an American expert to tell us this. Even a child in this country would be able to say if our Plan is realistic, this should depend upon our resources. Today we lack resources. We should cut our coat according to our cloth. Our feet is sticking out of our blanket.

Unnecessary Imports were Made

In respect of imports I would like to say that iron and steel were imported more than necessary. Available figures indicate that during the past 18 months 4.3 million tonnes of steel was imported. In 1956-57 iron and steel worth Rs. 3.25 crores imported. There was also an increase in the import of essential commodities and the imports were to the tune of nearly Rs. 95 crores. The present foreign exchange problem in the country is the result of last year's increase in the import of consumer goods.

We also have a shortage of trained workers. The recent report on Bhilai says that there is a shortage of civil engineers of about 30 per cent than the requirements. There is no Chief Mechanical Engineer nor a Chief Electrical Engineer, and there are insufficient senior divisional engineers, and yet the plant goes on.

We had hoped that the Rourkela plant would be the first to start production. It should have started partial steel production in the final year of the First Five Year Plan, but even the furnaces are not yet ready there. Who is responsible ?

Along with this there is a continuous rise in the prices of commodities. I do not want to repeat the figures Mr. Masani has placed before the House, but to put it briefly, if we want to get out of the difficulties in which we find ourselves today it would be necessary to change and amend the basic premises of the Second Five Year Plan.

Foreign Minister's Opportunism

We want to bind the country in the straitjacket of an ideology, and the fun of it is that when our Finance Minister goes to the U.S. he becomes a capitalist but when he returns to India he becomes a socialist. For foreigners we are capitalists, for our countrymen we are socialists. In other words, it is necessary to be socialists for our countrymen's votes and to be capitalists for foreign aid. Today we are like *Trisanku*, hanging between two worlds.

There can be no difference of opinion where it is a question of advancing the life of the country, of ending inequality, and of equality of opportunity for all for the development of personality. But it would not be right to bind the country within a rigid frame to achieve this. Moreover it is a fact of history that such an attempt does not succeed.

I am not talking about China. I have not been there. Those who have have talked about things there. But the fundamental principle of our plan is re-construction on the basis of democracy. If we give up democracy during planning it would be akin to decking a corpse with ornaments. I must make it clear that we cannot support efforts to rebuild the country on the basis of dictatorship. The ways of China and India are different. We should build our country in accordance with its genius and its traditions.

Hence the amendment I have tabled demands that we should take seven years to complete the Five Year Plan. Let us extend the period a little, and let not the government take up projects that it should not. But we see on page 420 of the Second Plan document that the government proposes to set up plants to make textiles, sugar and earthenware factories. I say nothing would be lost if the government does not make earthen pots. Let us leave it to the private sector and let us give priority to food production.

There is one more thing. My respected friend Shri Govind Das has appealed to all parties to co-operate in making the Plan a success. We do want to cooperate but nobody wants to accept our co-operation. We are putting an end to untouchability in the social sphere but please start it in the political sphere. The Bharatiya Jana Sangh has passed a resolution offering co-operation in the government's small savings schemes. We sent intimation of the resolution to State Governments as well as to the Centre, but our letters have not even been acknowledged.

Bharat Sevak Samaj became Congress Sevak Samaj

The Bharat Sevak Samaj which was set up to secure the people's co-operation is also gradually becoming Congress Sevak Samaj. It is not I who says this but an article by Shri Ram Narayan Choudhary in the July 1957 issue of the Bharat Sevak Samaj magazine. The title of the article is, 'Are we loyal ?' He has raised certain questions and also answered them. He writes :

> "I am myself not satisfied with these answers, so it is clear that those who put the questions would not be. After all this loud thinking, a seeker again and again asks himself— are we loyal ?"

SHRI L.N. MISHRA, Parliamentary Secretary to Minister for Labour, Employment and Planning : It is his personal opinion.

SHRI VAJPAYEE : This is the organ of the Bharat Sevak Samaj. I cannot accept it as his personal opinion. It is the opinion of those who work for the Bharat Sevak Samaj. The Bharat Sevak Samaj needs to be made more broad-based. We want to work in it but cannot.

SHRI L.N. MISHRA : You are welcome.

SHRI VAJPAYEE : If you want the people's co-operation you will have to create a congenial atmosphere for it. The government has failed to do so. The country's reconstruction is not a party affair, however big that party may be. For that you have to awaken the latent might of crores of arms. Only then is national regeneration possible. What we need is realism in planning. The result of forsaking realism is before us.

I hope the crisis we face today will compel the government to do some re-thinking in this direction and the people of the country will extend full co-operation to the government in implementing nation-building plans. On this note of hope I close my speech.

Lesser Efficiency, Greater Expenditure

Sir, it cannot be denied that economically we find ourselves in a difficult situation. To a certain exent it is a concommitant of growth, but to a greater extent it is the result of the way the Plan has been prepared and is being implemented.

The budget presented by the Prime Minister as interim Finance Minister and the *Economic Review* accompanying it give us a glimpse of the difficult economic situation. He has admitted that the food procurement position is critical. The increase in industrial production this year is nominal as compared with some previous years. The stock market is on the decline. Equity shares have come down by 25 per cent in value as compared to August 1956. The index of gilt-edged securities has declined by 0.7 per cent. There is a net decline of 0.7 per cent in the value of government securities. Foreign reserves with the Reserve Bank have come down from Rs. 530 crores at the end of 1956 to Rs. 298 crores by end of 1957. In small savings there is a shortfall of Rs 14 crores as compared to the previous year. The net gain in the last ten months of this year has been Rs. 37.6 crores while in the same period last year it was Rs. 44.8 crores.

The Prime Minister has also made it clear in the Rajya Sabha that there would be heavy repayments of our foreign debts in 1960 and 1963. In 1958-59 we have to pay slightly more than Rs. 23 crores. In 1961-62 this sum will rise to Rs. 123 crores. During the period from 1960 to 1963 it will rise from Rs. 62 crores to Rs. 123 crores.

How do we pay our Debts ?

He has admitted that repayment of more than Rs. 100 crores would be difficult for us. But his speech does not clearly indicate how we are going to repay this debt. We have to think of how much debt is from what area—how much from the dollar area and how much from Europe and how we are going to repay it.

Shri Ashok Mehta has said we shall step up steel production and export it. The point is, would these areas where we have borrowed need our steel ? There is also another aspect to this matter. The Americans say a recession is coming and Shri Bhagat has agreed in the Rajya Sabha that this is so. What effect would this recession have on our economy ? In Europe too Common Market schemes are being discussed. They adopt a resolution there, but we have to think of what consequence that resolution will have for our country. There is no such indication in the Finance Minister's speech. The result is that

Lok Sabha on March 18, 1958 during General Discussion on General Budget

the budget proposals fail to inspire the confidence in the people that the government would be able to successfully tackle the developing economic crisis.

First Deficit Budget

This year we have a deficit budget. The deficit is in excess of Rs. 27 crores. If I am not mistaken this is the first time after 1947-48 that a deficit budget has been presented. This makes it clear that even the Government has reached the conclusion that no more taxes can be imposed. Perhaps this is why a deficit has been kept in the budget. Last year's experience in this respect has also not been good. Many of Prof. Caldor's tax proposals were made applicable in the country in spite of the resentment they created among the people, but they did not yield the expected returns. The Prime Minister has admitted that tax revenue is much below the expected extent. Now we have a Gift Tax which is expected to yield Rs. 3 crores. I would not be surprised if next year this comes down to one crore. For figures presented by the Government in respect of revenue from wealth tax and rail fares prove past estimates wrong. This has on the one hand spoiled the climate of investment and on the other failed to raise the resources required for the Five Year Plan. In other words, we are neither here nor there. If we look to Government expenditure we see it continuously rising. The picture presented before us on actual expenditure account is quite disappointing. The revenue from new taxes is spent on administrative and non-Plan items. The result is that the revenue budget is also transformed into a tax budget. I have collected some figures showing how government expenditure is going up. In 1953-54 Rs. 64.17 crores were spent on civil administration. In the budget estimates of 1958-59 this rose to Rs. 200.44 crores. Under the head of police we spent Rs. 3.16 crores in 1953-54. In 1958-59 this went up to 8.27 crores. The Foreign Ministry's expenditure has also substantially increased. In 1953-54 it was Rs. 4.56 crores, now it is Rs. 7.50 crores. The rise in Defence expenditure has gone up so much that almost all Members have commented upon it. If we work out a percentage with 1955-56 as the base year civil expenditure has gone up by 113 per cent and Defence expenditure by 62 per cent. The Taxation Inquiry Commission had calculated that in every rupee spent by the Government on civil expenditure nine annas and six pai were spent on non-government expenditure, three annas on social services and only three and a half annas on economic development. This expenditure is being made in the name of development, taxes are being imposed in the name of reconstruction, but the result is that expenditure is going up on taxes that have nothing to do with development.

The Prime Minister had once said files get lost in the jungle of bureaucracy. I would say a large part of the Plan also gets lost in the same jungle.

Economic Policy not in Right Direction

The Finance Commission's Chairman Mr. Santhanam said in a recent speech in Madras, "There is a tendency in New Delhi to equate public expenditure with development." The Government thinks the more we spend the more there is reconstruction. But the Government has failed to bring down expenditure not being incurred on reconstruction works. The Taxation Inquiry Commission has also brought this to the attention of the Government. At one place it writes : "Efficiency in administration and economy in public expenditure which make far more effective use of public funds and secure a better return on investment of tax proceeds should at least diminish people's unwillingness to suffer an increase in tax burdens."

But today neither is efficiency in administration being increased nor is expenditure being brought down. Appeals are being made to the general public to make sacrifices. I would say that the people have not cooperated a little during the three years of the second Plan. If we tally the figures we would find that the people have paid the taxes that were imposed. In 1955-56 tax revenue was to the tune of Rs. 406.97 crores. In 1956-57 it rose to Rs. 486.75 crores. In the revised estimates for 1957-58 this sum went up to Rs. 553.85 crores, and in the budget estimates for 1958-59 to Rs. 562.51 crores. Thus we have had additional tax revenue of Rs. 375.20 crores. As per estimates for the five years of the Plan this sum should have been Rs. 225 crores. Tax collections amount to Rs. 25 crores every year of the five years. If we add up this sum, it comes to Rs. 850 crores. The second Plan estimates also put tax collection at Rs. 850 crores. So the people have paid the money expected of them, but the government has not been able to fulfil the people's expectations of it. This is why you see discontent in the country during the Plan. This discontent is not the creation of opposition parties. Rather, we want to assist in the creation of an atmosphere of enthusiasm in the people. But government policies are not leading the country in the right economic direction. The result is before us.

Planning without considering Defence Requirement

In respect of the increase in defence expenditure too it is being said we had not thought of that beforehand. I am surprised that we make a plan for the nation without taking defence into consideration. There can be no bigger proof of our shortsightedness. Defence is a must in a plan for the nation's development, but we prepared a plan in which national defence was ignored. Pakistan was not created yesterday. Its alliance with the U.S is no new thing. We should have been warned in advance of the danger that this poses. We could have foreseen it and provided for it. Today expenditure on the armed forces is on the increase, but this does not mean the country's defence is getting stronger. For, so far as I can guess, the increased expenditure is being incurred on replacing old weapons with new ones. I doubt if this increases the country's defence potential. Normally when defence expenditure goes up employment goes up with it, but we do not see this happening here. It is necessary to make a realistic assessment of the difficulties that have arisen during the Plan. The Plan is not a matter of prestige for any particular party, but if it is really a national Plan, as the ruling party claims, it should not be linked with the prestige of any party. Whatever difficulties have arisen should be accepted and a realistic policy adopted to try to overcome them.

Faulty Tax Structure

The new budget provides for a Gift Tax. I have welcomed it. Prof. Kaldor's taxation system suffered from this deficiency and we have made it up. But Prof. Kaldor had also said Estate Duty should be completely abolished. He has called it an antiquated tax. He says, "The true incidence of inheritance tax falls on the recipients of the inheritance and not on the deceased." We have an expenditure tax, a wealth tax, and now we have also added a gift tax to them. But we have not followed Prof. Kaldor's recommendation about amending the estate duty. We have diminished the limit from one lakh rupees to fifty thousand rupees. The result will be that the number of estate duty payers to be caught in the tax net will go up, and if the net is more widely spread government expenditure on it will also go up. In view of this expenditure I very much doubt if lowering the limit would be of any benefit to us. I also fear that the limit of ten thousand rupees in marriages in the Gift Tax may promote the dowry system. We want to put an end to this system in the country, but I feel this concession of ten thousand rupees in the Gift Tax may encourage it in some states. One more thing. Charitable institutions and government companies have been exempted from the Gift Tax, and along with them exceptions have also been made of public companies or companies conducted by six or more persons. I am unable to understand the reason for this. If a company run by six or more persons is exempted from Gift Tax it could possibly misuse its funds. Such companies would help political parties with funds, which would not be of any use for gift tax. I think the exception in the case of private companies run by six or more persons is also not desirable. This concession can be misused.

People Want Concrete and Not Paper Results

The point is, what measures do we adopt in the third year of the Plan that can promote national development ? I suggest the government bring down its undevelopmental expenditure. If this is properly done I think there could be an annual saving of at least Rs. 50 crores in the expenditure of the Central and State governments together. If we put a brake on the rate at which we are spending and go slow on establishing and staffing new departments it would not be a major problem to save fifty crore rupees annually. There should also be a check on the travelling expenditure being incurred in the name of public relations. Most important of all, there is scope for curtailment in the expenditure on publicity and propaganda. The Second Plan has a provision of Rs. 13 crores under this head. I would say that at least half this amount could be saved. Every ministry has its own magazine, in which it advertises itself. All this expenditure is so much money down the drain. Today we have *Bhagirath, Social Welfare* and *Yojana.* What is more surprising, we also have a monthly *Digest of Articles* and a monthly *Digest of News*, which have nothing in them. They are distributed among Members of Parliament.

Those who read the day's paper do not need a news-digest. Its publication can be stopped. The Plan has been well publicised in the country. The people do not want paper propaganda. They want to see concrete results of the Plan, so the expenditure in this respect can be curtailed.

Introduce Housing and Ration Bonds

There is one more thing. I would like to place two proposals before the government. One is that if the government issues housing bonds to the people, develops three to four lakh flats with the funds thus raised and sells them, preference being given to those who are prepared to buy them on a no-profit-no-loss basis, the Government could raise a lot of funds. Along with this the housing problem could also be solved. The government should give serious thought to this.

Another proposal is issuing ration bonds. If official ration bonds were issued to urban government employees with limited incomes and rations were assured to them at a certain price eight to ten crore rupees could be raised this way too.

The small savings scheme did not achieve the expected success. The need is for new techniques to attract funds. I feel if the government could give houses and arrange foodgrains for the people at fixed prices it could raise substantial funds. I hope the government gives serious thought to this matter.

Advance Financial Year to Suit Economic Conditions

Finally, I would like to say that the system of beginning the financial year on April I and ending it on March 31 was introduced by the British and has no relation to the economic and social conditions in this country. We have the Rabi crop at Diwali time. By that time we also know about the monsoon. So we should change the financial year a little and present the budget in October. Then it would not be necessary for the government to present supplementary demands, which the government has to do because crop estimates are not available by budget time. In my opinion changing the financial year to Diwali time would be more useful from the point of view of crops.

SHRI M.P. MISHRA (Begusarai) : Traders too would be happy.

SHRI VAJPAYEE : If traders are happy about it that would be very good, but I am talking about the farmers. The government and the Congress Party too are already thinking of the traders, and it is quite necessary to think of them. But even otherwise, in my opinion, this proposal is beneficial.

Future Mortgaged for Present Prosperity

Sir, the Budget the Finance Minister has presented has a capital B, a capital D and also a capital T. B is for borrowing, D for Deficit and T for Taxation. I would like to assess this budget on these three tests. The figures presented by the Finance Minister show that public debts are mounting—there is a rapid rise in government borrowings here and abroad. In March 1959, this figure stood at Rs. 4066.82 crores and if liabilities—unfunded debts—are added it would rise to Rs. 6023.20 crores on March 1, 1960. Calculations will show that our public debt is 50 per cent higher than our national income. A matter of still greater concern is that an unproductive sum of Rs. 1001 crores has been left uncovered. At the same time our foreign borrowings are also on the increase. By the end of 1959-60 they stood at Rs. 681.75 crores. The Finance Minister has not made it clear how this is to be repatriated. There is also another aspect to this debt. The Centre has given loans to various state governments for development works, and Shri Bhagat, Deputy Minister for Finance, has informed the House that so far the amount of these loans has come to Rs. 1295.80 crores. The question is, will the Centre get this money back from the states ? Events in Punjab make one feel that the Centre may lose both capital and interest. Rs. 170 crores were given as a loan for Bhakra Nangal, the interest on which comes to Rs. 16 crores. The Punjab Government has levied a betterment levy for this purpose. Now, not only are our communist friends agitating against it but elected Congress members from Punjab are also trying to get the Centre to waive the interest. In view of the political pressure being exercised I feel this payment may be waived. But the question is, will the loans given to the states be recovered ? And how are we going to repay our foreign debts ? Future prosperity is being mortgaged in order to get over present economic difficulties. Neither the Economic Review by the Finance Minister nor his budget speech indicates how we are going to make our way out of this situation.

Deficit Financing

So far as deficit is concerned there is a shortfall of Rs. 28.32 crores on the revenue side. The Finance Minister wants to wipe it out by imposing new taxes to the tune of Rs. 23.35 crores. I say the shortfall would exceed the estimate. In the budget presented last year by the Prime Minister as interim Finance Minister the revenue deficit was put at Rs. 29.2 crores, but when the revised figures came in it rose to Rs. 59.95 crores. I feel this year too the

Lok Sabha on March 12, 1959 during General Discussion on General Budget

shortfall would far exceed its estimate. In order to fill it up deficit financing is being resorted to. A deficit economy is being adopted. From Shri Deshmukh to Shri Desai every Finance Minister has said that deficit financing should not exceed requirement. But at the time of budget making he is like the drunkard who swears every morning not to touch the bottle but takes to it every evening. In our speeches we advocate keeping deficit financing at a safe distance, within a safe limit, but our entire economic structure is in the grip of ever increasing inflation. A deficit economy is being adopted to the maximum extent.

The Planning Commission has provided for a total of Rs. 1200 crores by way of deficit financing for the Second Five Year Plan. Now the total outlay on the Plan has come down from Rs. 4800 crores to Rs. 4500 crores, but there has been deficit financing of Rs. 655 crores in three years and there will be further deficit financing of Rs. 260 crores next year. If we leave the later years the deficit of Rs. 1200 crores will be made up, but if deficit financing exceeds this limit it will exert adverse pressure on the country's economy. Then a vicious circle sets in—the Government prints currency notes, the value of the rupees goes down, prices go up, Government employees demand bigger salaries and greater allowances. It is a vicious circle that we cannot breach. I urge great caution in this respect.

Taxation Proposals

Now I would like to say something about the tax proposals. So far as direct taxes are concerned the Finance Minister has done away with the wealth tax payable by companies. I think even when this tax was in force it was said that levying wealth tax on companies was not right, but the Government took two years to realise this. I would not thank the Government for this, for my objection is that when the Government has set up an inquiry committee for a probe into the direct taxation administration why did it not avail of the recommendations of that committee before carrying out any changes or amendments ? Whatever changes have been made could have waited till the committee's report was submitted. If the government was to take its own decision what was the need of the committee at all ?

As for the committee itself I would say enough care has not been taken while selecting its members. Its chairman should have been a High Court judge or some eminent personality. For instance when the Calvin Commission was set up in the U.K. with 22 members they were all experts in direct tax administration and had personal experience. In the present committee of five members no member, with the exception of Shri K.S. Sundarrajan, who is a member of the Board of Revenue, has expertise in the field.

SMT. TARAKESHWARI SINHA, Deputy Finance Minister : Even the chairman has it.

SHRI BRIJRAJ SINGH : As minister you too will have it.

SHRI VAJPAYEE : I can say a lot about the person who has been appointed Chairman, but I would not like to say it, as he is not present here. But if the Deputy Minister forces me I am prepared to say something.

DEPUTY CHAIRMAN : There is no need.

SHRI VAJPAYEE : I submit the members of this Committee should have been selected in a different way. Somebody else should have been the Chairman of the Committee. Shri Mahavir Tyagi's performance in the Finance Ministry and the policy he adopted in respect of income tax do not make him suitable for the position of Chairman of this Committee. Even the terms of reference of the Committee cannot include measures for improving administration for preventing income tax evasion.

Inadequate Training of Tax Officers

There is another small matter. I would like to point out how income tax officers are trained. An income tax officer, by name Shri Venkatacharya, who is from the South and who is in service for 25 years, was posted in a district of Bengal that had a large number of Marwaris.. He just could not understand their account books. When the Finance Minister was asked about training arrangements he replied there was a training centre in Nagpur, and it was necessary to learn two languages in addition to the mother–tongue, income tax law, book-keeping as well as office procedure. I do not know how all this is possible. The result is that those who are appointed income tax officers cannot do justice to their responsibilities.

There were high hopes that this committee would make recommendations on proper tax collection and improvements in administration. Prof. Kaldor has estimated that income tax evasion occurs to the tune of Rs. 200 to 300 crores. Even if we do not impose additional taxes but adequately collect income tax we would be able to raise funds that we feel are needed for the Five Year Plan.

As for indirect taxes, I submit, Sir, that the Finance Minister who, it was hoped, would advocate home industries, village industries, has struck them a big blow. About the levy on khandsari I would like to say that at a time when we are trying to secure a stable foreign market for granulated sugar it would be inadvisable to take any step that would adversely affect sugar production in the country and raise the price of sugar.

AN HON'BLE MEMBER : The price of granulated sugar would not go up.

SHRI VAJPAYEE : It has gone up. In what world are you living Mr. Member ? The levy on khandsari has resulted in the price of sugar going up.

Charge Licence Fee

While speaking on the excise duty imposed on khandsari the Finance Minister explained in the Rajya Sabha that the present profit on khandsari would continue in future. The government wants a cut of Rs. 5 on Rs. 13, so Rs. 8 would still remain. I say, give also some thought to how these 8 rupees would be divided. It is to be divided among the farmer, who produces it, the labourer who works in its production, as also the seller. If you want to give protection to mill-made sugar this is not the way to do it. The most objectionable aspect of the whole matter is that those who have set up small-scale industries will have to pay excise duty and fill any number of forms and maintain a large number of registers. Excise duty inspectors will collect whatever they deem fit. If the Finance Minister does not wish to cut down excise duty I would suggest the charging of licence fees that may be collected once a year at one place, so that khandsari producers scattered in the villages are saved the botheration of filling many forms.

Another point is about vegetable non-essential oil. The concession of 125 tonnes that had been given to producers when a duty was imposed on it in 1956 was brought down to 75 tonnes. This time the concession has been altogether withdrawn. I say the big oil mills are not in competition with the village ghani. The ghanis are in a separate field; they have a separate market. The big mills are competing with the small mills of Agra, Kanpur and Bareilly that do not run on steam and whose power rates are higher. If you do not provide for these small mills as against the big ones they will close down. I would like to know from the Finance Minister what the government definition of cottage and home industries is ?

Don't Differentiate between Charkhas

This definition keeps changing. The Central Government refused assistance to the home industry on the ground that it runs on the traditional charkha instead of the Ambar Charkha. The government says the Ambar Charkha is a cottage industry, the old, traditional charkha is not.

SHRI MORARJI DESAI : Who says so ?

SHRI VAJPAYEE : The Central Government says so.

SHRI MORARJI DESAI : That is wrong.

SHRI VAJPAYEE : The facilities for home industries that are available to other states are denied to U.P only on the ground that there they use the traditional charkha, not the Ambar Charkha. And now for the sake of the big sugar mills and oil mills khandsari units and small oil mills are placed in a position where they are unable to compete. In such a situation they would close down. If competition does not lead to development, and if we go in for western type of industrialisation, in which big industry is given more importance than small industry and the machine more importance than man, the speech the Prime Minister made yesterday on the creation of a decentralised economy will never come true. There would be centralisation of power, of capital and of labour. Most unfortunately the Finance Minister's speech is a pointer in this direction. That is all I have to say. Thank you.

Crowded Planning Commission

Mr. Deputy Speaker, while thinking about the Finance Bill it is natural that we should give some thought to the present situation in the country and to the direction in which economic reconstruction of the future is sought to be made. Currently the third Five Year Plan is being discussed. Its shape will have to be determined by the Planning Commission. The Estimates Committee has made some recommendations about how the Planning Commission should be constituted. It had expressed the opinion that the Commission should not have too many ministers. If the Prime Minister, Defence Minister, Finance Minister, Planning Minister are all included in the Planning Commission and then the plan prepared by the Commission placed before the Cabinet for consideration the Cabinet would not be able to make any comprehensive amendments or changes in it. It is to be regretted that this recommendation of the Estimates Committee was not accepted. Rather, efforts are being made to ensure that the Planning Commission should indirectly function more and more under the control of the ruling party. What ought to have been done was to reduce the number of ministers in the Planning Commission and non–party economic experts taken into it. But recent appointments to the Planning Commission include a member of this House and a former Secretary of the A.I.C.C. I do not want to say anything about their eligibility, but the point is that if we want to enthuse the entire nation to make a success of the Plan having a majority of individuals from the ruling party is not going to help.

There is one more thing. Shri V.T. Krishnamachari, Deputy Chairman of the Planning Commission, attends AICC meetings. This is most objectionable. The AICC controls the congress. But in a democracy there has to be a demarcation line between party and government, and any attempt at obliterating it would be detrimental to democracy. I would like to know if the Deputy Chairman would attend meetings of the Working Committees of other parties, if invited to do so, and address them, or he thinks it proper to attend only Congress Working Committee meetings. I hold that if you really want to enthuse the people for reconstruction plans you have to stop making the plan a party forum. You will have to try and secure popular co-operation not only for chalking out the plan but also for implementing it.

Recently an all-party committee has been set up to consider the Third Five Year Plan, but it has not met so far and I am doubtful if it will meet in future. It would meet only when the Plan has been given its final shape. I suggest the Government should change this attitude.

Lok Sabha on April 22, 1959 during debate on Finance Bill

There is one more thing to be said in this connection. This House has extensively debated the need for the Government to curtail its expenditure. The growing civil expenditure should be cut down a little. But I read in the papers that the Congress Party has set up a Committee for bringing down Government expenditure and Shri Feroze Gandhi is its Chairman. I also heard that this committee is going through Government files, investigating how Government expenditure has increased and making recommendations on how it can be brought down. The Congress Party has the right to suggest how expenditure can be cut down and is welcome to do so, but if a committee of the Congress Party goes into official files, interviews government officers and discusses how government expenditure can be curtailed it indicates the desire of the ruling party to completely control the life of the nation. I feel there is a lot of scope for bringing down government expenditure, and whatever curtailment has been effected can be extended still further, but for a committee of any party to involve itself so much in government administration would not be in the interest of democracy.

SHRI MORARJI DESAI : May I give some information in this connection ? They are not allowed to see any papers or anything of that sort. They do not go and see them. If they ask for any information that is supplied to them. If the Hon. Member wants any information that also is supplied. Therefore there is no question of treating them in a special way or giving them a special position.

SHRI VAJPAYEE : Is it not a fact that they are asking officers to appear before them ?

SHRI MORARJI DESAI : No Sir.

SHRI VAJPAYEE : Sir, I stand corrected.

Refugees and Official Claims

The Government also claims that all refugees from West Pakistan have been fully rehabilitated and so the West Pakistan Division of the Ministry of Rehabilitation will be closed down.

Sir, this is clearly a big claim and I urge the Government to accept the setting up of an impartial commission to test its veracity. There is no doubt that many people have been rehabilitated, but there are still many more who are not. Crores of rupees have been spent. Has all this money been put to good use ? It must be examined if every pie has been rightly used.

Many refugees are currently staging a *dharna* in front of the Prime Minister's house. No one likes to stage a *dharna,* but their grievance is that the houses and shops built by the Ministry of Rehabilitation are being auctioned instead of being given on a no-profit-no-loss basis. Auctions increase their prices and refugees with limited means cannot get them. What ought to have been done was to give the houses and shops to the refugees at the cost the government incurred on building them. But the Government is extracting a profit from the refugees. Their demand that the loan given to them be recovered in instalments has also not yet been accepted.

Shore up the Public Sector, Don't Expand It

There is talk of expanding the public sector in the country. I am not against the public sector, but we have not shown much efficiency in running whatever sector we have entered. Accounts of 13 public sector undertakings have been placed before this House. They show that excepting the Sindri fertilizer factory no public sector undertaking is doing well. The profit of the Sindri factory is also due to the fact that farmers are made to pay a high price for its fertilizer. If the fertilizer is sold at a proper price even that profit would be wiped out. I suggest that instead of extending the public sector the Government pay attention to the proper functioning of industries it has taken into its hands and run them successfully, as well as control and regulate private industries and check profiteering in them. But if the Government takes all powers into its hands the present situation is that it would not succeed, nor will it be desirable for democracy.

Mr. Deputy Speaker, I would now like to say something about excise duty. The Finance Minister has brought it down a little, but that is not enough, and it will not provide as much relief to small industries as they need. The real problem is about the collection of excise duty. Will small factory-owners be required to maintain separate registers ? Won't excise inspectors harass them ? Will the expenditure on collection not exceed the collection itself ? I suggest that the collection system be simplified and collection be made in one down payment. And those in the oil, khandsari and synthetic silk industries should not be involved in this. This would serve the purpose of collection and simplify its procedure as well. Thank you.

What is the Limit for Direct Taxes ?

Sir, before saying anything about the tax proposals I would like to say something about the talks that are currently going on between the Prime Ministers of India and China. I would like to congratulate the Prime Minister on the sentiments he expressed at the airport and in his speech at the State banquet yesterday. His words have echoed the sentiments of the entire nation, and I am confident he will show the same firmness to the end of these talks. The Chinese Prime Minister is trying to play down the whole controversy. I would like to say just one thing to him—if Mr. Chou-en-Lai does not succeed in arriving at a compromise with our present Prime Minister his prophecy about establishing friendship with India—the friendship that has been lost due to the Chinese aggression—for thousands and lakhs of years will not be fulfilled. It is possible that a future Prime Minister may not share our present Prime Minister's desire for friendship with China. The Chinese leadership should exploit this opportunity and try to correct the mistakes our Prime Minister has pointed out.

The Finance Minister has announced some cuts yesterday. In my opinion they are not enough. A tax on bicycles cannot be justified in any way. While the Central Government impose a tax on bicycles, all parties in the Delhi Municipal Corporation, including the Congress, are demanding that there should be no such tax. It is the common man's vehicle. On the one hand, the Finance Minister is reducing the excise duty on cars and on the other levying a new excise duty on bicycles. I do not think there is any justification for duty on bicycles.

SHRI TYAGI : Remove it.

SHRI VAJPAYEE : He has also announced some cuts in respect of aluminium sheets and rolls. But the announcement does not explain why those who make sheets and utensils out of used aluminium should have to pay excise duty. Big factories making aluminium sheets and rolls are charged a one-time excise duty. Once the product gets old it has already paid that duty. The Finance Minister says duty will be charged at Rs. 200 per metric tonne. I feel he should reconsider the matter. Aluminium utensils are used by common people, not by the rich. So it does not seem proper to charge a double duty on it.

Duty has also been imposed on all types of internal combustion engines. I request an explanation from the Finance Minister in this connection. As per a recent directive of the Finance Ministry the price of all engines has been fixed at Rs. 4,400, but actually there are engines made in Ghaziabad,

Lok Sabha on April 28, 1960 during debate on Finance Bill

Punjab and Delhi that do not cost more than Rs. 2,300. But even the manufacturers of these engines are told that the price of their engines is Rs. 4,400. And they will have to pay duty accordingly. I do not know how this directive was issued. Their price had been fixed at Rs. 2,300 by the U.P. excise department on the basis of their sale records for the past 12 months. These engines are bought and sold at Rs. 2,300. It is true that some big factories like Kirloskar, Kapur make engines for Rs. 4,400. These are sold at a still higher price in the black market. But engines made on a small scale in Ghaziabad, Punjab and Delhi are sold for Rs. 2,300, and yet you tell them duty will be levied on a price of Rs. 4,400 per engine. Some manufacturers met Revenue Board officials and protested against it. I was surprised to learn that an officer said to them: If we do not levy a duty on your engines how will the engines of Kirloskar and Kapur sell ? I do not know if this is true.

SHRI MORARJI DESAI : I do not think that would have been said.

SHRI VAJPAYEE : The manufacturers who met the officer have said this. I hope this is wrong. They should not be charged duty on an engine of Rs. 4,400. This has no basis, and the Finance Ministry should think about this.

Amend Definition of Cut-piece

Excise duty has been imposed on cut-pieces. I understand this has been done to prevent mill-owners from selling good cloth as cut-pieces. But small traders in cut-pieces have to pay for the sins of the mill-owners. The Finance Minister has now relaxed the limit from two yards to two and a quarter yards. I think it would have been better if it had been made two and a half yards. Two and a half yards is a measure that can suffice for an average person's garment. If the mills play mischief the control should be at the mill end. It is a crime to release good cloth in the market as cut– pieces, and it should be stopped. Some other new duties too have been imposed. I feel there is a need to amend the definition of cut pieces. There was nothing very objectionable if we had watched the effect of the duty for a year and thought about it the next year. However the Finance Minister has given some concession. It would be better if this concession was increased from two yards to two and a half.

For the past many years excise duty has been going up. In 1948-49 the Central Government's revenue from this duty was Rs. 50.63 crores. But this year the estimate has been put at Rs. 380 crores. All essential commodities, kerosene, sugar, matches, vegetable, coffee, tea and cotton textiles have come within the purview of excise duty. There is also a separate sales tax on these commodities, and when excise duty goes up the incidence of sales tax also goes up, the ill-effects of which have to be borne by the common man.

What Is the Limit of Direct Taxes ?

On the one hand the Finance Minister says more direct taxes cannot be imposed because they have reached the limit. May I know what this limit is ? Is it not a psychological limit ? And if it is, there is still scope for augmenting the revenue from direct taxes. For this the taxation administration needs to be strengthened. The Committee set up under the chairmanship of Shri Tyagi says at one place in its report, 'Determined efforts are being made' to realise old outstandings. But the figures given in the report do not indicate that the new government is going all out in that direction. The task is so big, the work force so small and the personnel so inexperienced that they cannot even make new assessments, let alone realise old dues. The result is that the government has no income from direct taxes.

I would like to say one more thing. According to the economic review of four years of the last Five Year Plan, commodity prices have gone up by 20 per cent. This price rise tendency is seen not only in the case of foodgrains but in all other fields like industries and services. If the Government cannot check price rise it would not be possible to fulfil the targets fixed for the Five Year Plan. Prices are rising because the government is indulging in excess expenditure and we are faced with inflation. So long as civil expenditure does not come down inflation will not be contained. But we see civil expenditure going up. In 1948-49 it was Rs. 35.56 crores while in 1960-61 it rose to Rs. 267.76 crores. This expenditure is not related to Plan projects, and if we utilise taxes realised from the people non-developmental items there can be no justification for such taxes.

Sir, may I submit that total planning and democratic institutions cannot coexist. What is our problem ? It is that in the economic field we want total planning, but in the political field we have adopted democratic institutions, which we cannot give up. The biggest problem for the Government is how to reconcile the two.

State Trading

Now the government has decided to go in for state trading. I think no democratic approach is necessary in this. The government has decided to take over food-grain trading, but that is not possible because it would mean going to the extent of rationing, and if it is not prepared for rationing there would be no meaning to the governmentalization of the food-grain trade. It is necessary to reconcile total planning and democratic institutions, and if one of the two has to be jettisoned I would say the government should preserve democratic institutions. If it is necessary to amend the approach to planning for this we should do it. There is scope for it. Thank you.

The Third Five Year Plan

Industry must also Contribute

Sir, the Third Five Year Plan will be our third step in the direction of economic reconstruction. While taking this third step it becomes necessary to see how much success we have achieved in the first two steps. What difficulties confronted us, and in order to overcome them what changes and modification have to be effected in the draft of the Third Plan ?

What we see from our experience with both the previous plans is that we have not been able to rouse adequate enthusiasm among the people for their implementation. National reconstruction, economic reconstruction cannot be achieved on the strength of the official machinery alone. No one party can shoulder this responsibility. For this the latent might of the entire nation has to be harnessed in a cooperative effort. Our plans fall short in this respect. I believe this is because we have not been able to base our economic planning on a philosophy of life. We have tried to achieve physical targets, we have also increased production, and I do not agree that we have made no progress during the first two plans. We have made progress. It is a different matter that this progress is not satisfactory. But does planning mean only fixing physical targets and striving to fulfil them ? Or do we want to base them on a way of life that would establish economic equality and social justice in the country in a democratic manner. This great country of India wants to make economic progress in a democratic way. We are making a new experiment and showing the way to the newly independent countries of Asia and Africa. We are showing them that economic progress is possible not only through dictatorship but also by way of democracy. This is a big responsibility that we shoulder. But I feel we have not been able to present a philosophy of life along with economic progress—a philosophy that could unify the people, a message that our workers could take to the people in the villages and place before them a veritable picture of heaven on earth, a picture that is related to the noble values of our ancient culture.

Yesterday the Prime Minister said money is not everything, there is also spirituality, morality. Then is it not possible for us to formulate national planning in such a way that it combines *artha* (money) with *dharma* ? Here I use *dharma* not in a narrow, sectarian sense but in the broad meaning of 'that which sustains life'. So far we have not been able to achieve this blend, and hence our planning has remained confined to the physical level. It has not touched the heart-strings of the people. We have not been able to instil an

Lok Sabha on August 23, 1960 during debate on Draft Third Five Year Plan

intense will among the people and among parties believing in planning to forge ahead. This is a big challenge for us, and we have to meet it. Communism is one way of life. Can we adopt another way ? From this point of view it is important to relate our planning to our spiritual values.

Everyone for His Own Socialism

Now we are told our goal is socialism. Conditions in our country are such that there are many who believe in socialism, but there is no definition of socialism. One socialist says to another: you are not a genuine socialist but a fake one. Here in this House we have as many as four socialisms and it is difficult for us to determine which one is the real one and what it looks like. The various prevailing ideas of socialism create confusion in the people's mind. We do not have the clear and forceful ideology that we need for successful planning. There are misunderstandings. Then we are told socialism is just a slogan; we do not really want to establish it. I say that at least those who believe in socialism should finalise its definition. It is another matter that I may not agree with it, but clarity is necessary in the nation's thinking.

Yesterday the Prime Minister also referred to cooperative farming. There are many parties in this House as well as in the country at large that support cooperative farming. There are very few who oppose it. But when those who support cooperative farming in the House go out into the field they say cooperative farming is desirable but under the present government it would ruin the farmer. They say cooperative farming is good, but this government cannot do it, we can. I do not think this indicates their belief in cooperative farming. In India we need a unity of thought and concreted action. Planning has ignored this need.

Planning and National Defence

Secondly, this planning has no reference to national defence. I agree that while preparing a plan of economic reconstruction we cannot directly discuss arms production. But the situation on the northern frontier is worsening which is not in our hands, and if we have to face a new crisis, if our talks for a compromise with China fail, as seems likely, then we should need additional funds to regain Indian territory under Chinese occupation and to face a new Chinese aggression. Have we thought of this while determining the resources for this plan ? I hope in the event of a new crisis on the northern frontier our plan does not have to be shelved. Economic reconstruction is necessary, but the nation's security must be given the first priority. We need to be aware of this danger while fixing the target of economic progress and provide for adequate resources in case we have to face a critical situation on the northern border.

Thirdly, we are increasing national income and production. This is of course necessary, for without production there can be no distribution. The question of proper distribution comes only later. But there are two methods of production, and we have to give thought to which one we should adopt.

Two Methods of Production

One method of production is to use big machinery in both industry ana agriculture. This way we can increase production, but is this method suited to the conditions in our country ? Today our production is on the increase but the people do not find employment in that proportion; they are not being equipped with the power to purchase these products. We have not adopted production by the masses in the place of mass production, and so unemployment is not being contained. Everyone is agreed that unemployment must end.

We also need to produce machines for small industries. At the same time we must think about what sort of structure we want for our industries and agriculture. Our biggest objection to cooperative farming is that with big farms the tendency to use big machines would increase, and then what will the masses depending on small farms do ?

We have not been able to develop small industries adequately and consequently we have a situation in which production is increasing but not the hands that produce. Unemployment is thus growing. I know it cannot be ended overnight, but at least let our planning aim at optimum employment. If unemployment grows in a democracy it will put our economic planning in the doldrums even if we fulfil production targets. It will pose a danger for our democracy. So we must adopt such production method as would give employment to the maximum number of people both in industry and agriculture.

I am not against new methods of agriculture. Technology suitable for small-scale application can also be developed. Conditions in our country require that we develop technology that can provide maximum work to our growing population.

Fourthly, our Plan gives top priority to foodgrain production. This is proper. Industrialisation is necessary. But I am not one of those who believe that industrialisation requires exploitation of the farmer. Some people believe that so long as farmers are not exploited the proper ground for industrialisation cannot be prepared.

Self-sufficiency in Food Production

It is essential to make the country self-sufficient in food production. But the Plan does not indicate any concrete efforts in this direction. What is to be done about it ? Even as it is, we had kept excess targets, which we could not achieve. Why ? Could we not set up the necessary organisation ? What defects did it have ? Was there insufficient coordination between the States and the Ministry of Agriculture ? Will the deficiencies be remedied this time ?

Wheat imports from the U.S. may perhaps prevent foodgrain prices from escalating, but I fear that they may generate the feeling that with wheat coming from the U.S. we do not have to produce more of it here— a feeling of complacency that when America is ready to give and our Agriculture and Food Ministries prepared to take, no concerted efforts to increase food production are called for. It would not be good if this sort of feeling is generated. But for this we must have a concrete plan of food production.

It was once asked in this House if it was possible for the Government to ask every farmer in the country why his food production was not increasing. What did he lack ? Was it water or fertilizer or loans ? Or was he being harassed by the police under Sections 107 and 117, adversely affecting food production ? In reply the Food Minister said it is not possible for us to contact every farmer. But if that was not possible some region of the country should be selected where the farmers should be contacted to find out the difficulties in the way of higher food production.

This Plan mentions a betterment levy. It is true that where water has been made available and the farmer has made use of it food production has increased, but there are areas where water is not yet available and yet the betterment levy is being charged. The result is that the State Governments cannot collect the levy from the farmers and the Central Government cannot collect it from the States. The revenue from the betterment levy therefore falls short of the target. And still we have already started talking about a betterment levy in the Third Plan.

AN HON. MEMBER : There are still three years for it.

SHRI VAJPAYEE : Not three years. In some States it is being already charged, although there is no water. This situation must be corrected. Even three years after water is made available, the State Governments are unable to collect revenue from the farmers, and because they are unable to collect it they are unable to pay to the Centre. This matter needs attention.

While determining the resources for the Third Plan a lot of caution has been exercised as compared to the previous plan. Deficit financing is a step in the right direction. But if deficit financing goes beyond limit a price spiral cannot be prevented, and if commodity prices rise there will be a demand for higher wages and allowances, and that in turn would necessitate still more deficit financing. Hence deficit financing should be kept within the limits that the economy can bear.

Prices of Essential Commodities

At the same time it is necessary to maintain stable prices of essential commodities. If we fail to develop a stable fiscal policy within the period of the Third Plan, if we cannot fix prices of essential commodities and prevent them from escalating this development plan would be shattered on the rock of inflation, discontent would spread in the country, political selfishness will raise its ugly head and an atmosphere conducive to planning will not be created. Hence the Government needs to formulate a clear policy about fixing prices of essential commodities and to follow it firmly.

So far as resources are concerned it is hoped that the public sector undertakings will raise Rs. 440 crores. It is proper to expect that they should make us profit and this profit may be invested in other things. But while determining the prices of the product of these public sector undertakings it is necessary to ensure that they do not have an element of taxation in it. It is right to earn profit by increased efficiency, lessened expenditure and greater production, but it would not be proper to have an element of taxation in the prices of public sector undertaking products simply for greater profits. To make a profit is not objectionable, but not in a way that would affect all market prices. It is necessary to exercise caution in this respect.

Build People's Confidence in the Government

Finally, one more thing before I close. Our economic planning depends upon how far we can implement it. And this is related to the administrative structure. The people do not see any socialist structure being set up. What they would like to see is that they get a fair deal and get justice when they deal with the village policeman or a small court or a local government functionary. If those limbs of the administration that come into contact with the public are not made honest and free from corruption it would be difficult to convince the people that the administration we want to set up in the country would be responsible for the development of all. The success of the Third Plan would depend upon making the administration efficient, honest and responsive at the local level. I hope efforts will be made to ensure the cooperation of all in the implementation of the Third Plan, and that when the debate in this House is over whatever changes and amendments are found to be necessary would be carried out. Thank you.

Planning will have to be Village-oriented

Sir, economic planning is necessary for an undeveloped and underdeveloped country, so that maximum benefit may be derived from deploying limited resources in the shortest possible time.

Those individuals and parties who do not believe in planning are perhaps not bothered about fulfilling the minimum needs of crores of people. If we look to the conditions in the country no one can deny that we must have a definite plan of economic development. The annual budget is our economic plan for the year. This economic planning can be for five years and even beyond that.

What should be the basis of this economic planning ? Along with material prosperity how far should we preserve our life values ? We have decided to achieve economic progress by democratic means. We have launched a great experiment. The future of democracy in Asia and Africa will depend upon how far India can achieve economic progress through democratic means.

We have made some progress in this direction, and every citizen should feel proud of it. But we also have to bear the other side of the picture in mind.

Cooperation from Parties and the People

The Prime Minister has called for cooperation of all parties in implementing the Plan. May I point out that there would have been no hesitation in extending such cooperation if it had been invited before preparing the Plan. But the Plan was prepared on a party basis. Consensus of all parties was not obtained while preparing the Plan, but now that it is ready all are invited to participate in its implementation. This method is not proper in view of the fact that the success of the Five Year Plan requires the creation of an atmosphere of popular cooperation in the country.

The Prime Minister had set up an All-Party Committee at the Centre in which almost all parties had been represented. But this committee was not given the chance to function properly. It was not given the opportunity to put forth decisive opinions on the Plan. And when the demand was made that such all-party committees be also set up in the States the Government's response was not positive.

Planning is not only a Central subject. For the people's cooperation we will have to go right up to the villages, so it is necessary to strive for securing popular cooperation at every level, and to make planning an all-party exercise. At present the National Development Council includes Central Ministers as well as all State Chief Ministers. The Government should

Lok Sabha on August 22, 1961 during General Discussion on the Third Five Year Plan

consider whether it would not be advantageous to also include in it some members of Parliament and Legislatures, elected on the basis of proportional representation. As it is, development plans are finalised in the meetings of the National Development Council, and if elected representatives of the people could express their opinions and influence the economic plan an atmosphere would be created in the country in which national reconstruction plans could be kept aloof from party politics.

The Estimates Committee had recommended that Ministers be removed from the Planning Commission. The Commission should be a body of experts, as its recommendations go before the Cabinet. So it is not necessary to have Ministers in the Commission. For reasons unknown this recommendation has not so far been implemented.

It is expected of the opposition parties that they would keep Five Year Plans away form the coming elections. The Prime Minister has even expressed such sentiments in an interview. I suggest that the Congress Party first decide its own policy in this regard. Will the Congress Party not ask for the people's votes in the coming general elections on the basis of achievements of Five Year Plans ? If it does not solicit votes on this basis and if the improvement in the national income and the progress in development works are presented as a national endeavour and a national achievement it would be possible to keep the plans away from the election. But if the Congress Party presents the achievements the opposition parties would be constrained to place the deficiencies in the Plan before the people. So if the Plan is to be kept away from the election the Congress Party should clearly decide its policy in this regard.

Plan for whose Benefit ?

So far as the people's prosperity through planning is concerned the increase in national income is a matter of happiness for all of us. But we must take into account the fact that there are two distinet regions in the country — the rural areas comprising five lakh villages, where 85 per cent of the population lives, and the urban area, with the remaining 15 per cent. To which area is the prosperity we see limited ? Have we been able to make the expected progress in the rural area, where 85 per cent of the people live ? In this respect our plan suffers from a basic infirmity. The way we are going about industrialisation tends to expand the area of the urban population while the industries of the rural area, with 85 per cent population, cannot stand up to the competition, thus putting us in a double difficulty. On the one hand, because of lack of employment in the villages there is an influx of population into the cities and towns and we are faced with the problems of providing it with civic amenities, housing and food. On the other hand, the large-scale western-type concentration of big industries in big cities is proving fatal for our cottage and small industries.

Figures of per capita income show that the villager's income and that of the city-dweller are not the same.

In Uttar Pradesh an attempt was made to estimate how much the per capita income in rural areas had gone up. It showed that on the basis of prices in 1948-49 it had remained around Rs. 197 from that year to date. In 1949-50 it was Rs. 197 and 63 Naye Paise, while in 1958-59 it is Rs. 183.47 Naye Paise. The situation would be basically the same in other provinces, perhaps with some small difference. Per capita consumption figures indicated by a survey carried out in U.P. in 1959-60 are also an eye-opener. They indicate that in Eastern U.P. the consumption is 8.81 chhatak (519.6 grammes), and in Western U.P. 10.62 chhatak. There is also no rise in the per capita consumption. Again, there is no change in the per capita income in the rural areas as compared to the urban areas. The Third Plan gives no indication as to how this growing gulf between the urban and rural populations is going to be bridged. If our economic planning and our industrialisation, which is a part of it, continue with the same speed in the same direction this gulf will further widen instead of getting bridged. So the need of the hour is to reorganise the rural economy and pay attention to a decentralised economy.

Neglect of Cottage and Small Industries

The Third Five Year Plan has a provision of Rs. 84 crores for industries running on small machines. If we take into account the outlay on small industries in the second and third plans we see that the outlay in the third plan is not enough for revitalising small and cottage industries and handicrafts. And so long as we do not enable village industries to stand on their feet our efforts at economic development of the country cannot succeed.

For this it is also necessary that we adopt a firm land reform policy. The size of land-holdings has been determined, but nowhere has an effort been made to implement it. Certain States have extended the time-limit for determining the maximum land-holding limit to such an extent that those possessing excess land have distributed the excess among the members of their families and there is no land left for distribution among the landless or those with non-economic holdings. Available land distribution figures show that at present 40 per cent families have less than an acre per family and the land with them comes to just one per cent of total land. On the other hand four per cent families own one-third of the total land. It is therefore necessary to implement land reforms with firmness. Those who own more land than they can look after cannot achieve the objective of intensive farming. Their excess land should be taken away from them and distributed not among co-operative societies but among the landless. But State Governments are not implementing Central directives in this respect. They seem to be influenced by vested interests. This has proved a hindrance in land distribution, and the result is that we cannot enthuse the common farmer to toil more for greater food production and intensive farming....

Villager's Income

SHRI VAJPAYEE : I had briefly talked about the situation regarding the villager's income. A recent survey has showen that 45 per cent families spend less than Rs. 80 per cent per month per family, 50 per cent spend Rs. 150 per month, and only 5 per cent spend more than Rs. 150. If we examine the claim about the increase in the actual income in the light of this fact we would see that justice is not being done to the rural sector of the economy. In the final analysis it is in the villages that India lives. If we cannot bring economic well-being to the villager by way of adequate supply of essential commodities we cannot enthuse 85 per cent of the population to contribute to the great endeavour of nation-building.

Economic Planning and Defence

This economic planning has not been related to defence needs. The Prime Minister said if anybody anywhere in the world lit a torch it would set our planning on fire. Let us hope there is peace in the world, but I cannot understand how our economic planning can completely ignore defence requirements. It is necessary that along with our economic plan we should also have a defence plan and it should be a part of the economic plan. The two need not be mixed up, but the people should be assured that along with economic planning our frontiers are also being guarded well. We should have before us a clear picture of what we propose to do for it and how much we intend to spend. Sometimes when there is a question of resisting a foreign aggression we are told that we would not act in this matter because doing so would jeopardise our economic planning. Perhaps the possibility of having to face such an eventuality is not taken into account while preparing the economic plan. I submit that economic planning cannot be divorced from the defence of the country. Careful thought needs to be given to this.

People's Capacity to Bear Tax Burden

I would now like to say something about the targets of new taxes that have been fixed in this Plan. If we want to take up new development works it would mean a greater burden on the people. But it is necessary to see which section of the people will have to bear this burden. If we arrive at the conclusion that there is no more scope for direct taxes, as the Finance Minister had declared, we would have to procure funds for economic planning by imposing such taxes as would have to be borne by the common man. The result would be that we would find it difficult to raise the living standard of those whose standard we are talking of raising. Figures for the last some years would show that imposition of indirect taxes is gradually increasing and that of direct taxes decreasing. Excise duty is also increasing. Further, it is not only the Central and State Governments that levy taxes. We also expect that local bodies like municipalities and Zilla Parishads would raise resources to match government aid. So we must think of the total burden on the people. Then we would see that our economic targets fall short of the people's needs but exceed our resources. We must also bear in mind the people's capacity to bear the burden, because we must not forget that we have adopted democratic planning. Our goal is not only economic well-being, it is also preserving moral and spiritual values.

Plan Fulfilled, Unemployment Grows

We must keep growing unemployment in mind. The framers of the Third Plan have accepted the fact that there would be greater unemployment than now at the end of the Plan. It is not only that unemployment means unfruitful labour of some people. Unemployment would create social and political problems for us. Educated unemployment is dangerous for the stability of the State. But our planning promotes unemployment. The way out is that our plans should be less capital-intensive and more labour-intensive. We have great man-power, which is our biggest asset. If we put it to proper use we can fulfil our development plans to a substantial extent. God has given man not only a stomach, which needs food, but also hands to work with, so that we can earn food. But we are not using those hands.

The reason is that the structure of our industrialisation follows that in countries which are perhaps not faced by the problem of providing work for a growing population. The right to work is the biggest right. We call our land *'karma-bhoomi'*, the land of action, of work, but today there is no work in this land. If we adopt such production techniques as increase production but save labour they would not succeed in today's conditions in the country. Adopting automation is meaningless in prevailing Indian conditions. If we make machines work but keep man unemployed where will we get the market for the goods produced by the machines ? We cannot depend upon foreign markets long enough to give stability to our economic structure. If we want a strong and stable base for it we will have to develop a domestic market for growing production. This is not possible without strengthening the common man's purchasing power. For this every able-bodied person has to be provided work. This the Five Year Plans have failed to do.

The Plan and Government Undertakings Workers

No one will deny that those working in industries and in government offices have worked very diligently to implement the Five Year Plan. The public sector is growing. The Government is taking up more and more work in its hands. But now the time has come to determine the rights of government employees and workers of government undertakings. Will they or will they not have the freedom to form unions ? Since recognition of workers' unions was withdrawn one cannot say with confidence that their enthusiasm for the success of the plans has grown. Yet, far from restoring recognition, the Home Ministry has issued a directive prohibiting Central and State Government employees from participating in election meetings. I fail to understand how an employee can be prohibited from attending an election meeting or listening to an election speech. Government employees should keep away from active politics, but they have the right to vote, and for the proper exercise of that right it is necessary that they attend meetings of political parties to examine what economic programme they place before the country and what future for the country they envisage. Here, however, is a directive of the Home Ministry of which I have a copy and I would like to draw the attention of the Speaker to it....

SHRI K.D. MALAVIYA, Minister for Mines and Petroleum : Your remarks give the wrong impression that a Government employee does not have the right even to listen to a public speech. So far as I know no such directive has been issued by the Home Ministry.

SHRI VAJPAYEE : If you would bear with me I would explain everything. I and Shri Surendra Nath Trivedi had put starred question No. 657 to which the Minister had given the following reply :

> "But on a reference from the Ministry of Works, Housing and Supply, received in June last, the Home Ministry advised that government servants should not participate in election meetings organised by any political party."

What does this mean ? If a political party holds an election meeting would you not permit a government employee to attend it and listen to the speeches ? This is what it says here. If this is wrong the Home Minister should issue a contradiction. If you do not approve of government employees attending electon meetings of political parties you should deny the right to vote to two million employees. But if you want to keep that right you cannot prevent them from attending election meetings and listening to election speeches. It is understandable that they should not participate in organising election meetings, addressing them, and in taking part in any election activity, but it is beyond comprehension that they should not be allowed even to listen to election speeches. Perhaps you have not yet forgotten your defeat in New Delhi. But remember, if you rob government employees of their fundamental rights New Delhi will repeat itself all over the country. Thank you.

Economic and Political Discipline must for Plan Success

Madam, we in this country are engaged in a great experiment, the experiment of bringing about economic prosperity through democratic means. For the success of this experiment it is necessary that there should be a consensus in the country on the basis of economic progress and that the reconstruction endeavour be conducted with the cooperation of all. Yesterday Shri Khandubhai Desai said we should look upon the Plan as a national plan. It would have been very good if we had been able to create this sort of atmosphere in the country. But so long as the Congress Party does not feel the need to secure the cooperation of the opposition parties in the formulation and implementation of the Plan it would not be possible to give it a national form.

People's Cooperation a Must

Democracy imposes certain restrictions, and if we transgress those restrictions we cannot accelerate economic progress even if we want to. We cannot impose a burden on the people that they would be unable to bear or for bearing which they would have to make sacrifices to an extreme extent. Every five years we have to go to the people. So the only way is to make the plan a national plan. Let an effort be made, as far as possible, to secure the co-operation of all parties, and let the Congress Party stop asking for votes in the name of progress achieved through the plan. If this is a national plan a single party cannot claim credit for its fruits. If that party lays such a claim other parties would naturally tend to criticise it, whether that criticism is constructive or destructive. Normally the criticism is more destructive than constructive, and I also hold opposition parties responsible for this. But when the biggest and oldest party is not prepared to discharge its responsibility in this hour of crisis not much more should be expected of small parties.

For the success of the plan we need a certain political and economic discipline in this country. We have not been able to create this discipline, and so long as we do not create it we cannot achieve our targets, nor can we secure voluntary cooperation of the people. I am happy about Shri Ashok Mehta's appointment as Deputy Chairman of the Planning Commission. I would not go into the crisis that this appointment has created in his party, but Shri Ashok Mehta's appointment is a step in the right direction. I wish more such persons were inducted into the Planning Commission—persons who are not

Rajya Sabha on February 26, 1964 during discussion on the Mid-Term Review of the Third Five Year Plan

only economic experts but who have an urge to change the situation, who will go all out to build a new society, and whose personality would inspire the people to extend willing cooperation in this task.

Composition of Planning Commission

The number of Ministers in the Planning Commission should be reduced. If Gandhian economists could find a place in the Commission it would be possible to bring economic planning from the high heavens down to earth. But I request an explanation in this connection. Shri Ashok Mehta has continued his connection with a political party even after the appointment as Deputy Chief of the Planning Commission. Will other members of the Commission have this freedom ? Members of Parliament appointed to the Planning Commission had to resign from Parliament, as membership of the Commission was considered an office of profit. Will the same rule not apply to the Deputy Chairman ? If it has been decided to give this freedom I would welcome it, but it should be applied equally. Making an exception of a particular individual would not be proper.

Our targets for the Third Plan were self-sufficiency in food production, development of basic industries, full utilisation of the country's manpower, growth in employment and equality of income and opportunity. But the past two years hold no assurance that we would be achieving these objectives. On the food front we have failed completely and I fear the situation will worsen in the next two-three years. The rabi crop has been destroyed by blight. Wheat and pulses will not be grown adequately. In sugar too the targets we had fixed would not be fulfilled. Sugar mills are closing down for want of sugarcane. The government should give a thought to the situation that would arise when these targets remain unfulfilled. The Food and Agriculture Ministry has proved to be the nemesis of many a Minister. We must think of how we can progress if the monsoon does not cooperate. Certain elements in the country want to indulge in agitation over this question of foodgrains. In Uttar Pradesh grain shops have been looted in many cities. This is not a spontaneous public resentment; there is a plan behind it. The matter of maintaining law and order is also involved. If we do not organise proper distribution of whatever foodstuffs we have the situation will worsen and the government will find it difficult to control it. We must keep a strict watch on elements which seek to exploit a difficult situation and take the people towards anarchy.

Why no Increase in Food Production ?

There can be no two opinions that our problems will not be solved so long as food production does not increase. But why does it not increase ? There are various opinions on this. If we want production to increase it is not enough to have an agricultural production board at the Centre or a sub-committee of Ministers in the States or appoint an agriculture commissioner. All these things should be done, as they are necessary for coordination, but the real problem is how to enthuse the farmer for greater production. According to a note circulated by the Planning Commission to the members arrangements are being made to provide credit to farmers, extend irrigation facilities, cut down power rates and provide good seeds. There is also the problem of loans. Cooperative societies give loans but demand a deposit in return. Not many farmers can give it. Only the big farmers can, and they get the loans. But if agriculture is to progress the small farmer should be enabled to invest more, labour more and enjoy the fruits of his labour. This confidence should be awakened in him. This the government has not been able to do. If we fail do it even in future our failure on the farm front will continue.

Gram Sevaks Embroiled in Party Politics

It would be highly beneficial if we could fully utilise the gram sevak for increasing food production. But the gram sevaks are embroiled in party politics. They are busy with everything except farming. Politics at lower levels is so dirty that production targets are relegated to the background. So I submit that the key to the successful achievement of plan targets is the cooperation of all not only at the Centre but at every level, including the village level. If we do not answer these difficult questions we may not succeed in this great experiment of economic planning through democracy. It is obvious that our economic progress has to be speeded up. This is not possible so long as we do not increase the investment rate. We should not hesitate to accept foreign aid for this purpose.

If economic development is to be accelerated we would have to invest more funds. And in such a situation we cannot do without foreign aid. I regret to say the proposals of the Communist Party of India are contradictory. On the one hand, it wants to step up the pace of economic progress, but on the other it seeks to create an impediment in the way of raising resources for such acceleration.

Nationalisation of Some Companies

Nationalisation is being talked about. A demand is being made about the nationalisation of the oil companies. If we do that we would not get foreign funds, and if we do not get them can we, in a democracy, impose on the people a burden they cannot bear and yet would be required for economic development ? So I would submit that instead of extending the public sector the government should first efficiently manage the plants and factories that it has already taken over.

We have a shortage of trained personnel. With a few exceptions our plants do not run properly. If we have a techno-economic service and the right, trained personnel to run the plants, and if we show profits the misunderstanding about the public sector would be removed. No one is opposed to the growth of the public sector—no one should be—but what happens when a job that can be done well privately is taken over by the Government ? I shall give an instance of what happens and close. There was a fire in the heavy machine building plant of the Heavy Engineering Corporation at Ranchi. The Minister estimated the loss at Rs. 45 lakhs.

According to an official estimate the damage to property is to the tune of Rs. 1 crore. The most surprising aspect of the matter was that when the fire broke out the operator at the Dhurva telephone exchange informed the Director of the Corporation about it and asked what was to be done. The Director replied that it was not necessary to bother the Chairman or Director of the Corporation about such small things as fires. The telephone operator has written this in his log book, which is now in the possession of the police. I demand a judicial inquiry into this fire. In this respect we cannot trust a Director or a Chairman there. They have left property worth crores of rupees lying in the open. This is misuse of public funds. If we misuse funds like this in public projects we cannot secure public sympathy for these projects. After all funds for them are raised by the Government by levying taxes on the people. Naturally the people want proper use of those funds and good returns for themselves. This is just one example to show that all is not well with our public sector projects and so we cannot make the expected profit. You expect a profit of Rs. 450 crores from public projects in the Third Five Year Plan. How is this profit possible if these projects are run the way they are being run ? I hope the Minister will ponder over this.

The most important point that I would like to reiterate is that we lack the economic and political discipline that is a *sine qua non* for the success of economic planning. If the government, the Planning Commission, could create this discipline we would be able to place an unprecedented example before the world—an example of how economic disparity can be ended and property ushered in without ending individual freedom. Thank you.

Budget as Complex as Finance Minister

Madam, before I say anything about the budget I want to register a protest. Every year this House used to discuss the budget first, and then it was taken up in the other House. Party leaders have decided on the adoption of this system. I am unable to understand why this system has been changed this year. The Constitution is quite clear on this point. Articles of the Constitution do not prevent this House from discussing the budget, nor does the Constitution prevent the Finance Minister from announcing cuts in his tax proposals in this House if he so wishes. But even if he does not want to announce amendments in the tax proposals here that cannot deny this House the right to be the first with the debate. The fact of the matter is that the other House has discussed the budget and the Finance Minister has expressed his reaction on the criticism there. Now if he has a closed mind and he is not prepared to amend the budget in the light of whatever is said in this House the whole discussion would in a way become meaningless.

Mahalanobis Committee Report

Another point I would like to make is that during the discussion on the budget many members referred to the report of the Mahalanobis Committee. I was surprised to see members quoting at length from that report. These quotations have been taken from a daily newspaper. But when a demand is made in the House for placing the report on the table the reply given is that the Government has not yet received the report and so it cannot be placed on the table of the House. If the report has not reached the Government how was it published in the newspapers ? Are some members of the Mahalanobis Committe responsible for the partial publication of the report ? Are some members in touch with some newspapers ? How was it that certain newspapers came to know about a report which members of the House did not know. This is a very serious matter. I would urge the Government to place the report of the Mahalanobis Committee on the Table of the House without delay. If the report is published in the newspaper without the Government releasing it an inquiry should be made into how it reached the papers. The published facts are very serious.

Madam, no Minister of the Ministry of Finance is present in the House. What is the use of speaking ? Only the Minister for Irrigation and Power present here. He is not going to reply to this debate.

SHRI C.B. PANDE (U.P.) : The Government is represented by Dr. K.L. Rao.

Rajya Sabha on March 11, 1964 during General Discussion on General Budget

SHRI A.B. VAJPAYEE : There are three Ministers in the Ministry of Finance and one of them should be present here.

THE DEPUTY CHAIRMAN : I thought Mr. Bhagat was here. Was he not here ?

DR. K.L. RAO, Minister for Irrigation and Power : Government is indivisible.

THE DEPUTY CHAIRMAN : I know that.

SHRI C.D. PANDE : The Government is represented; there is joint responsibility.

THE DEPUTY CHAIRMAN : I think one of the Ministers from the Ministry of Finance should be here also.

SHRI C.D. PANDE : He is here; he has come.

SHRI B.R. BHAGAT, Minister of Planning : I am sorry, Madam. I had to make an urgent phone call. I was there in the lobby. I just went out for a minute.

SHRI VAJPAYEE : As I was saying, the budget that has been presented is as complex as the Finance Minister's personality. He has attempted to reconcile the partly contradictory tasks of accelerating the pace of progress and ending inequality. But he has not succeeded. For me the budget is not just a statement of income and expenditure. The budget should be an effective instrument of achieving the national goal that we have set in the economic field. Our goals are increased agricultural and industrial production, equitable distribution and lessened disparity. When tested against these criteria the budget does not seem capable of fulfilling our economic needs.

No Relief for the Common Man

Fortunately the Finance Minister has not burdened the common man with new taxes, but he cannot be congratulated on this. The tax revenue target fixed for the five years of the Third Five Year Plan has been fulfilled. A collection of Rs. 1100 crores by way of tax revenue was expected in five years, but within three years Rs. 1900 crores have been realised from taxes. Obviously there has been excess collection of Rs 800 crores with two years of the Third Five Year Plan still to go. In such a situation new taxes were not called for. One the other hand, the Finance Minister could have been congratulated if he had tried to lighten the common man's growing burden. The argument he had put forward yesterday in the Lok Sabha for not bringing down excise duty is not convincing. He says if the excise duty on kerosene or coarse cloth or match boxes was cut down the benefit would not go to the consumer, to the common man, it would be pocketed by the middleman. If this argument were accepted there is no possibility of the success of the steps to contain prices that are being stressed. Last year when the excise duty on kerosene was raised the revenue from it was estimated on the lower side. Actually it was higher. It is possible to give relief to the common man, but the Finance Minister is not prepared to do so.

If we compare the direct and indirect taxes for the last some years we would find that direct taxes are declining and indirect taxes increasing. The burden of the indirect taxes falls on the common man. Even if it was not possible to extend any concrete benefit a psychological atmosphere could have been created in the country to make people feel that the budget has some relief for the common man.

Rate of Increase in Excise Duty

Madam, it is necessary to keep track of the rate at which excise duty is increasing in the country. The revenue from excise duty was Rs. 67.54 crores in 1950-51, which rose to Rs. 145.25 crores in 1955-56. In 1960-61 this amount went up to Rs. 490 crores and the budget for 1964-65 has estimated it at Rs. 603 crores. When we ponder over increased prices and everyone says the Government has failed to bring down prices, we have to give thought to what new taxes lead to their escalation. Excise duties play a large part in this. If basic duties were cut down and the States told not to levy sales tax and other taxes on essential commodities it could help to stabilise or somewhat bring down prices.

I am surprised to see that in his speech the Finance Minister expressed concern at price rise, but he does not seem to have clear ideas on what steps are required to prevent it. I do not agree with his statement that there is in general an eight per cent increase in wholesale prices. The common man's life is governed by retail prices, not wholesale prices. If we look at retail prices they have gone up by 25 per cent. I am surprised to see that in his speech he has used a sentence that can be used any time anywhere, but which was no meaning. Replying to a question on what the government would do to contain prices, he said: "The problem is being examined at the highest level with the greatest care."

SHRI B.R. BHAGAT : And that is necessary.

SHRI VAJPAYEE : We quite agree that whatever the level it would be the highest, and whatever the care it would the greatest, but what is the result of the high level and great care ? How will price rise be controlled ? If we do not control it all our plans will be dashed to pieces on the rock of price rise. There are many countries where revolts have started in the market-place. If we want to prevent such a possibility in our country we would have to take effective steps to stabilise prices. For this we have first to see why prices rise and how far the Government is responsible for it.

Increased Purchasing Power, Empty Markets

I submit that our production of goods and increase in services are not keeping pace with any substantial investments in development and defence. People now have increased purchasing power, but goods are not proportionately available. At the same time it would not be enough to say that an increase in production is necessary for a decrease in prices. There can be no difference of opinion on this. But the point is, are government policies conducive to escalation in prices ? I have referred to excise duties. I would also want thought to be given to how far the increase in railway freight or road transportation charges have affected prices. The excise duty on petrol and diesel has gone up, road transport has become expensive, railway freight has gone up by as much as 12 per cent. Such policies help price rise. If the government wishes to check them from going up it should refrain from taking such steps in the remaining two years of the Third Five Year Plan.

The biggest reason of price rise is our failure on the food front. Those responsible for this should be identified. We cannot blame the weather and trumpet the success of economic planning. At a time of crisis Parliament and the Central Government can make a law on a subject in the State list, but this extraordinary power was not exercised. The prices of raw materials have also gone up, affecting prices in general. There is a power shortage in the country, a shortage of indigenous raw materials, and a foreign exchange crisis prevents us from importing raw materials in adequate quantities. All this has also had an impact on industries and prices of whose products have gone up. A growing population also contributes to a rise in prices, because there is growth in consumption without a corresponding increase in production. We should also examine how far the policies adopted by the State Trading Corporation have caused prices to go up. Will the STC's rate of profit not affect the market and market trends ? There is no limit to the rate at which the corporation is making a profit on such things as betel nut, camphor and coconut oil. I am not against the STC making a profit but the impact of that profit on the market should be kept in view.

Neglect of Consumer Goods

The most important point regarding price rise that we should bear in mind is that the structure of economic planning that we have accepted does not adequately stress production of consumer goods. We have neglected consumer goods and emphasised heavy industries. We have the example of Communist countries before us. They are feeling the need of stepping up production of consumer goods. In a democratic country like ours, where success in economic planning requires popular cooperation, we cannot afford to neglect production of consumer goods. Available figures indicate that while production of producer goods has gone up by 14 per cent that of consumer goods has increased by only two per cent. This policy needs to be changed. In the next seven years we should therefore concentrate on increasing production of agricultural produce and consumer goods.

Controls are suggested for checking price rise. Yesterday the Finance Minister also stated in the other House that the Government would have to impose strategic controls. He should clarify what he means by strategic controls. If he means by them that the Government would buy the crops at proper prices, store them and at critical times release the produce to the market, thus preventing prices from rising, no one could have a quarrel with him. If he means that the farmer should take care of his produce, take loans against it and then sell the produce at his own free will, that too is a good arrangement and should be done. But if he means we should adopt a policy of controls from procurement to distribution, from godown to consumer, I warn that such controls would not work. We know the type of administration we have in this country. The experience with war-time controls was not good, and there is no reason to believe that our national character has very much improved since then. If the Government means to take over all the food-grain trade—wholesale as well as retail— as it has indicated, the result would not be good. We should beware lest the remedy proves worse than the disease. I am not against partial control, but we cannot afford to ignore the capacity of the society, of the system in which we work.

Further, I am not prepared to agree that prices must rise in a developing economy. We have the example of other countries before us, where they have accelerated the pace of development and also successfully stabilised prices. In Italy the rate of development has gone up by eight per cent and still prices have gone down. In Japan too the national income has grown but the price rise has not exceeded two per cent. In our country we accelerated the rate of development in the First Five Year Plan but kept prices stable. So let us get rid of the notion that we cannot keep prices stable because we are engaged in a developing economy. Difficulties in the way of increasing production should be removed. The Government must ensure that the urban population —especially those with fixed monthly salaries—get essential commodities at the right price. It is also necessary to see that there is a proper proportion in the prices of agricultural produce and factory-made goods. Today the farmer's produce is sold cheap, but what he buys is not cheap. It would not have been so objectionable if the benefit of the price rise had gone to the farmer, but it is the middleman who gets the benefit. The proper arrangement in this regard should be considered.

Greater Invitation to Foreign Capital

Madam, in the budget the Finance Minister has talked of inviting more foreign capital. In the present condition of our economic development we cannot do without foreign capital. At the same time we cannot ignore the dangers posed by large-scale influx of foreign capital. The conditions on which we would like to invite foreign capital have not yet been spelt out. The Finance Minister said yesterday that in industries and factories foreign capital will have a minority share. This explanation was necessary, but the conditions on which even this minority share would be accepted should have been explained. The conditions of repatriation of foreign capital should also have been clarified. If we decide to nationalise what would be the conditions for nationalisation ? Further, as compared to other countries there is greater profit on foreign capital here, and there is ample encouragement for foreign capital to come here to make a profit. The Commerce Department of the U.S. has stated that American capital invested in India makes a greater profit than that in other countries. The profit rate in this country is 20.6 per cent, while in Western Europe it is 11.5 per cent, in Australia 7.1 per cent, in North America 4.3 per cent, and in neighbouring Pakistan 3.5 per cent, and still we have decided to extend greater facilities to foreign capital. It is necessary to exercise caution in this matter. If, while formulating the plan, we could lessen its foreign exchange component and base economic development mainly on internally available resources we would not need so much foreign capital.

Publish the Mahalanobis Report

The Foreign Minister has suggested that a commission be set up to probe the concentration of wealth in the country and the monopoly that prevails in the industrial sector. I am surprised to see that the Mahalanobis Report has not yet been published. It just hangs fire. Members of Parliament have not even had a glimpse of it, and already the Finance Minister has announced a new commission. A commission or a committee is set up whenever something is to be avoided.

Nobody can deny that there is concentration of wealth in the country. The remedy on it is also known. But the question is : is the Government serious about wanting to prevent the sources of wealth from getting concentrated in the hands of a handful of people ? If the Government is serious about it, no commission is necessary.

Madam, the appointment of this commission has provided an instance of the style of working of this government. The same day that the Finance Minister presented the budget in Parliament the Commerce and Industries Minister was asked in the other House during Question Hour if the government was thinking of setting up a commission to prevent monopoly, and the Minister had replied that there was no such proposal. This answer was given during Question Hour and at five o'clock in the evening the Finance Minister announced that the Government proposed to set up a commission. When asked how two Ministers gave two different answers the Finance Minister said this was an example of how budget proposals were kept secret from members of the Cabinet. The appointment of a commission does not fall within budget proposals. This is not a question of raising or lowering a tax. If a commission was to be set up to probe monopoly other members of the Cabinet could have been taken into confidence.

But I feel the Finance Minister does not consult anybody while formulating the budget, nor, perhaps, can any other member of the Cabinet influence him. The whole world is laughing and the whole country is feeling surprised at one Finance Minister levying an Expenditure Tax and praising it fulsomely, while another Finance Minister abolishes it on the strength of his experience. When the Finance Minister imposing the Expenditure Tax returns the tax is levied again. Why was this tax imposed in the first place ? Then why was it abolished ? And why was it imposed again ? Is this the result of the Government's economic understanding and farsightedness ? Does the Finance Minister have the freedom to levy any tax and abolish any tax ? Does the Government not take a comprehensive view of the matter ? Experience showed that the Expenditure Tax did not yield the expected revenue and so it was abolished, and yet it is being reimposed. What Shri Morarjibhai did has been stood on its head and the Finance Minister has taken the burden on himself. I think what Shri Morarjibhai had sown Shri V.T. Krishnamachari is reaping, and who will eat what he has reaped only time can tell.

Last year more than necessary taxes were imposed, as a result of which popular discontent grew, and with it grew the unpopularity of the administration. Today it has become easy for the Finance Minister to go ahead on the strength of the substantial revenue from these taxes. When the Expenditure Tax was imposed I had supported it on the ground that no individual in the country could be permitted to indulge in unbridled expenditure, as such expenditure vitiates the savings situation and adversely affects the need to lead a simple life. But it seems that the revenue from the Expenditure Tax was negligible, perhaps it was all spent on collecting the tax, and so it was abolished. Now the same tax is being reimposed. Madam, the situation today is such that if one earns an income he has to pay income tax, if he makes money he has to pay wealth tax, if he spends it he has to pay expenditure tax, if he gives it in charity he has to pay gift tax and if he dies without giving it away in charity there is an estate duty to be paid.

We have in this House a member named Shri Karmarkar. I like his name very much. With apologies to him I would like to explain his name like this — the Government imposes a *'kar'* (tax), then even if you *'mar'* (die) it still imposes *'kar'* (tax). In 'Karmarkar' I can understand *'kar'* but not the *'mar'*. I am not against taxing people who can pay taxes. They should be taxed. But let this government clarify its own thinking on whether accelerating the rate of development and ushering in socialism in accordance with the Bhubaneswar resolution are not contradictory things. As I see it the Finance Minister's difficulty increases because he wants to mix the two. If the pace of development is to be speeded up we will have to invest more, and if we have to invest more we will have to save more, but if the Government collects all the savings through taxes or excise duty how can economic development be accelerated ?

Great Burden of Central Debt on States

Madam, the Finance Minister's budget makes a very serious point and it is that the economic condition of the States is worsening. Last year too I had said in my speech on the budget that the economic condition of some States has become much worse. The Constitution empowers the Central Government to declare a financial emergency in such States and strive to improve their economy. But perhaps the Central Government has not tried to discipline them because all States have Congress Governments. As a result the Central debt burden on the States is increasing. To date it stands at Rs. 3600 crores. There is no question of repaying this amount. If repayment is demanded the State Governments ask for new loans to repay old loans. They want to incur debt to repay debt. The Central capacity to give loans is not unlimited. How long will we keep giving loans to the States, and how long will we make up for it by taking foreign loans ? We take loans from abroad and the States take loans from us. *'Rinam Kritwa ghritam pibet'* ("Borrow money and drink ghee, that is enjoy life") is an old saying, but here there is no possibility of 'drinking ghee', enjoying life. The situation we see is, borrow money, incur losses, incur debts, increase taxes and misuse money. The Central Government must take serious notice of this economic condition of the States. If some State Governments are not prepared to increase their income and lessen their debt burden and if they spend money given for planning on things that have not even a remote connection with planning, the Centre should stop giving them loans, and whatever loans have been given should be strictly recovered. If necessary, the Constitution should be invoked to declare a financial emergency in such States. If today the Central Government does not interfere because the States have Congress Governments it would not be able to intervene even when governments of different parties are in office in the States. So the tradition of intervention should be set right now, and I am confident that in view of the worsening economic condition of the States the Finance Minister would take some strict steps.

Public Undertakings are Failing

I agree with the Finance Minister that public undertakings should make a profit, but they are not making it. The profit is not in proportion to the outlay. In 1962-63 the profit was Rs. 1.3 crores, in 1963-64 it was Rs. 2.32 crores our investment was Rs. 800.47 crores share capital, on which the return was only 0.25 per cent. The *Explanatory Memorandum* tells us that our public projects are not running well. But let us not fix the prices of products of these enterprises so as to increase the common man's tax burden simply because we want to make a profit. What is the principle behind fixing these prices ? At what price should the consumer get these products ? How much profit should public projects make and at what rate ? None of these things is as yet clear. I referred to the State Trading Corporation. It is making a 400 per cent profit. If the element of taxation enters price fixation for public sector products this profit would not be a real profit. These projects should make a profit through efficient management. But everyone agrees that they are not running efficiently. The Japanese expert who recently visited this country has also criticised bureaucratic mismanagement. He has charged that India's iron ore trade has gone down because of the bureaucratic style of management. The recent report of the Estimates Committee on the National Development Corporation is also quite serious. It states that in two years a sum of Rs. 1.90 crores was spent on repairs and maintenance of plants. The Public Accounts Committee's 19th report has referred to a building of the Tea Board which was constructed at a cost of Rs. 39.36 lakhs. The Committee opined that it was not necessary to spend so much money on the building, that the Tea Board did not need such a big building, and yet it was built. The story of the Rourkala steel plant is known to all. The lock-out there caused a loss of Rs. 76 lakhs to the Government — that is, to the people, because the management was not prepared to give a bigger allowance to skilled labour. An example of a cycle factory in Mysore is also quoted. It is said this factory made 18 cycles in two and a half years. This is a government factory, and the price per cycle came to Rs. 16,000.

SHRI BAIRAGI DWIVEDI (Orissa) : For one cycle ?

SHRI VAJPAYEE : Because only 18 cycles were manufactured in two and a half years. The expenditure on running the factory on wages, on allowances....

SHRI BAIRAGI DWIVEDI : Who buys them ?

SHRI VAJPAYEE : They are displayed in exhibitions.

My point is, let the government run the projects in its hands efficiently. What the public projects, the public sector needs is not expansion but consolidation. For those who demand nationalisation I have a question: are nationalisation and socialism interchangeable terms ? Yesterday the Finance Minister said no member of an opposition party should discuss the Bhubaneswar resolution and he also told Congress members that if they wanted to speak against the budget they should do so in party meetings, not in the House. I do not think he can say such a thing to members of the House —but objecting to it is the Congress members' job, not mine, though as a Member of the House I am not prepared to accept any such restriction.

SHRI C.D. PANDE : There is no restriction.

SHRI VAJPAYEE : The representatives of the Congress are also representatives of the people, and they should express the feelings of the people. They may say whatever they like within the party, but if the Party takes the place of Parliament the future of democracy is dark. It is also not proper for the Finance Minister to say that he would not accept the remedy of the opposition parties because the opposition parties want to finish us. We do not want to finish anybody. We want to improve them, we want to change them. But if there is no common ground between the ruling party and the opposition it becomes meaningless to talk about everyone's support for national reconstruction.

The Bhubaneswar Resolution and the Budget

Madam, I do not want to test the budget against the Bhubaneswar resolution, because there was a political motive behind passing that resolution and the Finance Minister needs to have his feet on the ground of reality. For me socialism is not a complete philosophy of life because I do not consider man a slave of money or a creature of carnal desire. Man's physical needs should be fulfilled, but there are also certain moral and spiritual values that need to be protected. Socialism does not take those values into consideration. But what is the philosophy of life on which socialism is based ? When Communists talk of socialism there is a Marxist philosophy behind it, a materialistic view of life. But if we are not prepared to accept materialism fully what is the philosophy of life behind our socialism ? Does socialism mean the nationalisation of banks, augmenting the public sector and government control over as many things as possible ? Do some programmes collectively mean socialism ? I do not agree. If there is a need, the Government should take something into its hands, if there is no need, it should not. But Socialism cannot mean doing some programmes collectively. There has to be a philosophy of life behind it. The Government has not been able to do it, the Congress Party too has not been able to do it. That is why I say the Finance Minister has a difficult job. He wants to increase the pace of progress and also contain disparity, he wants to set up a commission to probe monopolies but also admits that in the prevailing circumstances increasing the pace of development would not be possible without some monopolies. At the same time he also says that the nature of monopolies is changing, controls are a separate thing, management is separate and share-holders are increasing.

I think the Finance Minister is doing tight-rope dancing. As a result the budget he has made could not satisfy all, rather, could not satisfy anybody. The capitalists are dissatisfied because although there is a complaint that they are given facilities they would be made to shell out eleven crores of rupees more. The common man is dissatisfied because there is no relief for him, although it is true that he has not been burdened with more taxes. So I urge the Government to bring clarity into its thinking. The country's economic problems can be solved if the government decides its policies on the basis of realism without giving in to political or economic pressure.

The budget has no concrete suggestion on how to bring down government expenditure. The reports of the Estimates Committee and the Public Accounts Committee say that with determined efforts a saving of Rs. 100 crores is possible in government expenditure. But the recommendations of these committees were not acted upon. Civil expenditure is on the increase. Taxes are imposed in the name of the Plan but the revenue from those taxes is not spent on plan projects....

I submit that there is ample scope for cutting down on government expenditure, but the administeration has not been able to take any step in this direction.

And Corruption ?

The final topic I would like to discuss is corruption. Eradication of corruption is necessary if we mean to create political and social discipline in the country. But there are some things that raise doubts as to whether the Government really wants to put an end to corruption. The nexus between Ministers and capitalists is reaching fearful proportions. I shall not discuss facts that have not seen the light of the day. But I would like to know why no commission has yet been set up for a judicial inquiry into the Sirajuddin affair. I do not want to refer to how much money he gave to which Minister, but it seems Sirajuddin's net is spread pretty wide, and it includes highly placed people not only at the Centre but also in the States. It is necessary to set up a commission to go into the whole affair, so that the people's suspicions are allayed. The gur scandal here in Delhi under the very nose of the Central Government has still left a bitter taste in our mouth. The Delhi Police wants to take action against the management of that cooperative comprising members of Parliament, but the Law Ministry has put spokes in the wheel. I cannot understand how the Law Ministry comes into the picture. No one can deny that there was a gur scandal and the Home Minister declares in the House that action will be taken even against the top-most people, but when the time for action comes the Government drags its feet. This is not the way to end corruption. This is not the way to rouse the confidence in the people that the administration really means to end corruption. The opposition is willing to extend cooperation in eradicating corruption. But first the Government will have to prove that it would not cover up any act of corruption of any corrupt person for political considerations. The Punjab Chief Minister has not resigned, in Delhi no legal action is taken against Choudhary Brahma Prakash, and no inquiry commission has been set up for the Sirajuddin affair. These things do not indicate that the Government is prepared to rise even above political considerations for ending corruption.

Madam, with these words I close my speech and express the hope that the Finance Minister would amend his tax proposals in accordance with the sentiments of the people and arrange for some concrete facility or concession for the common man. Thank you.

Gathering Clouds of Corruption

Madam, I had no intention of expressing myself on the Finance Bill, but I feel it necessary to throw some light in connection with the observations made during the debate by Kumari Shanta Vasistha, member from Delhi. I had requested her to be present when I spoke in the House, but it seems she is not present here as she has gone to attend some meeting.

In her speech Kumari Vasistha had made two charges. The first relates to the Government and also to the Congress Party, to which I would like to draw your attention. She said many Central Ministers collected funds for the elections but neither deposited them in the account of the Congress Party nor gave their account. Madam, when she was levelling this charge you reminded her that she was making a very serious allegation, and she had reiterated her charge and said she was making it in all seriousness.

Madam, these charges have been made by a member of the Congress, not by an opposition member. The charge is quite clear : some Ministers of the Central Government collected funds at election time but did not account for them to the Party. I would like to ask Kumari Vasistha—although she is not present in the house—which Ministers she is charging. She should name the Ministers, otherwise the whole Council of Ministers would come into disrepute. If the Ministers are not named every Minister would become the object of suspicion. This would not be desirable either for the Ministers or for the party of which they are members and of which the lady making the allegations is also a member. The Home Minister is trying to put an end to corruption, so when a member makes such charges in the House the Government cannot keep mum. She should be asked who these Ministers are, from whom they collected funds, whether they misused their position in collecting them, if there was any official *quid pro quo* involved, if any licences for industries and commerce were given in return. All these facts should come to light. I hope that while replying to this debate the Finance Minister would say what he proposes to do about these serious allegations made by a Congress member. The Home Ministry should collect the necessary information and lay it on the Table of the House. This is not an internal affair of the Congress Party, because the charges have been made not in a Congress meeting but in the House. Now every member of the House has the right to know if there is truth in these charges. If there is not Kumari Vasistha should be asked to withdraw them. The prestige of the entire Cabinet is at stake. If Congress members go on making such charges and they are not asked either

Rajya Sabha on April 27, 1964 during General Discussion of Finance Bill

to substantiate them or to withdraw them all loud declarations about eradicating corruption would be in vain.

The Jana Sangh versus the Delhi Administration

Madam, the other charge Kumari Shanta Vasistha made concerns my party, the Bharatiya Jana Sangh. In her speech she charged officers of Delhi with being partial to the Jana Sangh. To quote her :

> "The Congress party in Delhi somehow is treated by the Delhi Administration in a very unhappy manner. They are very much interested in the Jana Sangh. They go out of their way to help the Jana Sangh party."

At an other place in her speech she has said that the Chief Commissioner and other senior officials of Delhi listen to the Jana Sangh, not to Congressmen. For the first time it has been stated in the House that Government officers—the Administration—favours an opposition party and does injustice to the ruling party. So long charges were being made against the opposition, but I think this charge has been made deliberately. So far as partiality towards the Bharatiya Jana Sangh is concerned, we have been complaining that in spite of the Jana Sangh being the main opposition in Delhi, we are not being treated fairly. When Committees are set up they are filled with people from the ruling party. The opposition is not taken into confidence, nor any effort made to secure its cooperation. And yet the Chief Commissioner and the officers of Delhi are charged with ignoring the Delhi Congress. Does this mean Miss Vasistha wants the officers of Delhi to dance to her tune ? Does she want the Delhi Administration to become an instrument of partisan interests of the Congress ? Does she want that the Administration should become a plaything in the hands of a certain group within the Congress which she represents ? If it does not become a plaything of that group does it mean she can stand up in the Hose and slander the Delhi Administration, level charges against it, threaten the officers and try to break their morale ?

Congressmen Saw Red when the Black Market in Gur was Exposed

Madam, I charge that whatever Kumari Vasistha has said was for threatening the Delhi Administration and the Chief Commissioner. This criticism must be taken very seriously. Since the time the matter of a black market in gur in Delhi—of selling gur brought from U.P. at a profit—has come up a group within the Delhi Congress has become hostile to the Chief Commissioner and the officers here, and the present allegations are a link in the propaganda being made by that group. I want the Home Minister to probe these charges. It is most unfortunate that such charges should be levelled in the House against officers when they do not have the freedom to refute them, and that too by a member of the Congress Party. We do not expect any favours from any officer in Delhi, rather it is our complaint that we are not treated fairly. But when such charges are levelled against these officers in the House I would expect the Central Administration to investigate them, and if they are proved false *(interruption)*–

SHRI BANSILAL (Punjab) : On a point of order, the Hon. member has just complained that whenever the Chief Commissioner sets up any committee only people of the ruling party, of the majority, are taken into it. Will the Hon. Member name the Committees in which members of the Congress majority have been taken ?

DEPUTY CHAIRMAN : That is a point of information, not a point of order. There is no point of order.

PROF. M.B. LAL : May I ask Mr. Vajpayee whether he would be prepared to support my idea that an impartial inquiry is needed in the affair ? Kumari Shanta Vasistha says that Ministers are conspiring with officials of the State against the ruling party, and Mr. Vajpayee, on behalf of the Jana Sangh, says that though the Jana Sangh is the main opposition party it is not being treated fairly by the officials of the State. I feel that there should be an impartial inquiry into the matter so that the public may be able to know how the administration is being carried on in Delhi. We cannot ignore the Administration of Delhi, particularly because it may have repercussions on the Central Government also. The Central Government is responsible for the Administration of Delhi.

SHRI VAJPAYEE : Madam, I was going to say the same thing that Prof. Mukut Bihari Lal has said. The charges levelled are quite serious and their truth or otherwise should be investigated. Delhi does not have a legislative assembly. Parliament is responsible for the administration of Delhi, so when such allegations are made in Parliament the Central Government cannot afford to ignore them.

Why Should Delhi's Fate be in Congress Hands ?

Another point Kumari Shanta Vasistha has made is that the Delhi Corporation has a Congress majority, so whatever is done in Delhi should be done in consultation with the Congress Party, not any opposition party. I would like to remind her that there was a time when the Congress was in a minority in the Delhi Corporation and the opposition in the majority. We never said don't talk with Congressmen because the Congress is in a minority in the Corporation. We did not try to intimidate officials in Delhi. But the Congress is fostering fascist tendencies, and Kumari Vasisha's speech is an instance in point. She says don't talk to the opposition at all, Congressmen alone will decide Delhi's fate. This is not democracy. In a democracy the opposition too is a part of the administration. I am sure the Finance Minister will refute the charges or clarify the position. The Home Ministry too should view these charges seriously and arrange for an impartial judicial inquiry into them, so that the truth is revealed and the attempt to break the morale of Delhi's civil services foiled. Thank you.

Gold Control Ordinance

Failure in Basic Objectives

Sir, I stand to oppose the proposal before the House. I want that the Rajya Sabha returns this Bill to the Lok Sabha and refuse to include any of its members in a Joint Select Committee. The Gold Control promulgated during the crisis under the Defence of India Rules has completely failed in its objective. The Administration had claimed that immediately on the introduction of gold control smuggling of the precious metal from abroad would come down and the domestic price of gold would decline. If we examine the gold control ordinance against these two tests we would have to honestly admit that it has failed in its basic objective. Gold is being smuggled into the country without let or hindrance. Perhaps Finance Minister Shri T.T. Krishnamachari may not admit this today. It is not as easy to accept a fact while one is a Minister as it is to accept it when one has ceased to be a Minister. When Shri Morarji Desai got the Gold Control Act passed and Shri T.T . Krishnamachari was not the Finance Minister, he (Shri Krishnamachari) had stated that the smuggling of gold into the country had increased—a statement that he did not later retract. But today something very different is being said, although the Government can prove anything with the help of statistics. But there is no evidence to convince the House and the people that smuggling has gone down. If it has to be brought down the steps for it have to be taken on the borders. Government machinery must be strengthened enough to prevent it. But smuggling from outside continues and the market price of gold has not declined. Perhaps Shri Bhagat had said in the Lok Sabha that even if the price of gold did not come down it has stabilised, but what is the difference between the domestic price and the international price of gold ?

SHRI B.R. BHAGAT : A lot of difference.

SHRI VAJPAYEE : How can this difference be lessened ? Could the gold control ordinance bring the market price down ? And if it could not be brought down in the last year or a year and a half there is no guarantee that making the directive permanent would be able to do so. On this it is argued that we want to cut down the use of gold. No one can quarrel with this objective. In olden days, when other means of safeguarding money were not available, people used to make gold ornaments, as they could be safeguarded and also became useful in times of difficulty. Ornaments could be pawned any time to raise cash. In those days not every town had a bank and adequate arrangements for keeping cash were not available. The *Mahajan*, the

---

Rajya Sabha on June 6, 1964 during discussion on the Motion opposing the Gold Control Bill, 1963

money-lender, took the gold as collateral security and lent money, though the interest rate was high. Still, when a daughter had to be married off, when cattle died, when the villager, the kisan, was in difficulties he could make use of the ornaments of the gold that he had earned with his labour. Now things have changed. Now we are making arrangements to enable people even in the countryside to save money in banks and post offices, although these arrangements are not as extensive as they should be. The people's habit to hoard gold and make ornaments needs to be changed. But can law change a tradition so quickly ? Can a stroke of the pen change the people's way of thinking, of living ? Weddings are taking place. Many weddings took place during the last some months. Ask those whose daughters got married. No one likes to part with gold, but when there is no gold, not gold ornaments to give, the bride's father buys smuggled gold and makes ornaments. No one is prepared to accept ornaments of 14-carat gold. The fathers of the grooms are not willing to accept them. They want full value for their sons. This is a social evil. Old traditions have to be changed but the method adopted for it—that of issuing a *Firman* of the Delhi Darbar—is not the right method. Law cannot change society. If after independence we had done this propaganda, to change the people's mentality and instil in them the attitude to gradually give up their fascination for gold a situation was possible in 17 years in which gold consumption could have gone down. But till the Chinese agression we gave no thought to improving this tradition. Only with the Chinese aggression did we realise the need to change this old tradition. Better late than never, so I shall not oppose it, but is the method right ?

Sir, things were not so had so long, but now clause 17 proposes to provide that the Administrator can issue a directive, a *Firman,* whenever he likes, asking for an accounting of the ornaments in one's possession. And it has not been made clear to whom this directive would be issued. It can be issued to anyone. But the Bill is silent on a directive on who should have how much gold in sornaments. I can understand that you pass a law saying if you have even old gold ornaments you should not have them beyond a certain limit, and if they exceed this limit....(*interruption*)

SHRI B.R. BHAGAT : What is your opinion ?

SHRI VAJPAYEE : I am expressing my opinion on what you are saying. The Administration cannot be given such wide powers : they could be misused. It would create a turmoil in our family life, and discontent among the people. One can understand it if you ask big people, who have ample gold ornaments, to account for them. But it does not seem necessary to give the Administration such wide powers, and that too in such vague terms. It seems the administration is gradually tightening its stranglehold. To begin with what started as a temporary regulation is being made permanent by law. Now an administrator is being introduced and it is said he can ask for an accounting of the gold ornaments you possess. One should not be surprised if as the next step the government says if you have gold ornaments beyond this limit deposit them with the Treasury and they will be paid for at the international market price.

The Poor Will Become Suspicious

The government should realise that such a law would create a suspicion in the minds of those poor people who have spent their hard-earned money in making a couple of ornaments. There is no reason why we should equip the administration with such wide and vaguely worded powers, but this law shows the direction in which the government wants to proceed.

One thing the Minister too would admit—and no one can honestly deny —is that even today 22– carat and 24–carat gold is being clandestinely used for making ornaments and gold is being sold in the black market. Those excise people who are charged with the task of supervision in this matter have earned crores of rupees during the past year or a year and a half. If the Minister gives the assurance of stern action I can quote examples of employees who have a nexus with goldsmiths and who collect fixed monthly sums. This way gold ornaments are being made clandestinely, because they know there is money in it.

Gold Control has posed the problem of unemployment before the goldsmiths and it has opened up an avenue of earning for excise employees. Everybody knows the type of bureaucracy we have in this country. As it is a part of our society we should be aware of its faults as well as its merits. But the stronger the hold of the Government over the life of the people is getting —even though with the best of motives—the more miserable the life is becoming. We cannot deny that this expansion of powers would have serious consequences. Has the assurance about the rehabilitation of goldsmiths been fulfilled ?

SHRI B.R. BHAGAT : To a considerable extent.

SHRI VAJPAYEE : I say not at all. The goldsmiths have been taken for a ride. They have been made fun of and their life ridiculed. The Central Government has left this responsibility with the States. But the State Governments have no time to understand the problems of the goldsmiths and take concrete steps to solve them. It does not become of the Government to say we have made very good arrangements for them. It is like rubbing salt on a wound. Those working in goldsmith's shops are now unemployed. It was announced that they would be given priority in new jobs.

Job for Goldsmiths

I would like to know from the Hon'ble Minister how many children of goldsmiths have been given priority in Government jobs at the Centre and in the States and what means of livelihood have been made available to them. I know about my area. There are half a dozen children of goldsmiths who had learnt the art from their childhood but whose art has now been killed. Today even peons are expected to be matriculates. I had forwarded their applications with the plea that this rule should not be applied in their case because they were goldsmiths and had lost their livelihood due to the government's policy. But nobody is prepared to listen. They are going from pillar to post, they are committing suicide. We are making goldsmiths unemployed, but we have not been able to prevent gold from being smuggled into the country, nor to bring down its market price.

So far as changing the tradition is concerned, it has not happened in the past year and a half. Shri Bhagat is from Bihar. I had the occasion to go there for a wedding. Had an excise inspector been there it would have been an eye-opener for him. And if eyes were not open at least his pocket would have been closed. This is what is happening. Are we opening up an avenue of earning for the excise people ? I urge that the problem of gold be reconsidered, because the objective with which gold control was introduced has not been fulfilled. The Government should not hesitate. If it does not admit its mistake and does not formulate a new policy in the light of the old mistake it would mean the Government wants to continue on the wrong path, Not only this, it wants to tighten its hold. So I oppose this Bill and would ask the House to return it to the Lok Sabha. At the same time we make it clear that we are not prepared to include our members in the Select Committee and in the present circumstances gold control should be abolished. Thank you.

The Budget
Optimistic But Not Realistic

Madam, before I say anything on the budget I would like to draw the attention of the House to the speech that Shri Nausher Ali made here yesterday. I regret I was not present at the time, but I was shocked when I read the report later. It is most unfortunate that a citizen of India—that too a member of Parliament—should make a statement on the floor of the House that would be helpful to Communist China. He said China is not our enemy. He also said that the India-China border has not been demarcated. He even went to the extent of siding with China and saying that our forces that were massed on the border could be construed as intending to invade China. He denied that China had made an aggression on India and said no Communist country can invade another country. Expression of such sentiments in the House is most objectionable. He is not present here. He is a senior citizen. I do not want to use harsh words, but I must say the sentiments he has expressed do not denote love for the country. His speech justifies the need of the steps the Government took against the Leftists. Even if we do not discuss the facts given in the Home Minister's speech and even if we ignore the facts that the Home Minister claims he has in his possession but which he has not revealed before the House and the country, Shri Nausher Ali's speech yesterday makes it clear that there is a class in this country that has a nexus with the aggressors and which, when the time comes, would not hesitate to actively conspire against our independence and our integrity. The Administration as well as the House would have to take serious note of the speech and the danger signal it gives.

So far as the budget is concerned it bears a clear stamp of the Finance Minister's personality. Like a clever magician he has tried to spread his magic net and to create the illusion that the country has crossed the valley of crisis and reached the plateau of progress, and now the pinnacle of prosperity is not far. In a way I can understand the Finance Minister's magic, for at present there is a crisis of confidence in the country, and the Finance Minister has presented a budget that would restore that confidence. However the difficulty is that the budget is not in consonance with realism.

Economically and financially the current year was quite unbalanced. A grave food crisis, exceptionally high prices, depletion of foreign reserves, a declining market and inadequate investment of capital show that our economy is still in a state of crisis, and the hopes that the Finance Minister seeks to give have no concrete basis.

Rajya Sabha on March 16, 1965 during Discussion on General Budget

The Finance Minister has claimed that the national income has gone up by four and a half per cent, and as compared to the growth by two and a half per cent for the past three years this could be called satisfactory. But a four and a half per cent growth is not enough. It will neither meet our needs nor fulfil the people's expectations. Four and a half per cent would be just enough to repay our loans. We cannot use this growth to build a society in which there is prosperity and equality. In Japan there has been a 15 per cent growth in the national income and in Italy and Germany 11 and 14 per cent per annum respectively; but even if we do not compare ourselves with such advanced countries we would need an annual growth rate of minimum seven per cent if we are to guarantee every citizen a minimum standard of life. Yesterday Shri Bhagat said we will have a five per cent growth and would wipe out the deficit of Rs. 3000 crores in the Fourth Five Year Plan. I am doubtful about it. The Planning Commission's Memorandum on the Fourth Five Year Plan that is before us makes one feel that the Commission is not prepared either to learn anything or to forget anything. It is a victim of its own failures and is not ready to acknowledge its mistakes. According to this memorandum Rs. 3000 crores will be realised through new taxes and the same amount....

SHRI B.R. BHAGAT, Minister for Planning : Not through taxes.

PROF. M.B. LAL : Then there will be a gap.

SHRI VAJPAYEE : I have talked about this gap earlier. You may call it foreign aid and arrangement for new resources. It is three thousand crores of rupees. The memorandum has talked of raising this much. I have already discussed the gap. Now I am talking about something else. Everyone agrees that efforts to raise resources on such a big scale would bring the economic system under pressure. It is said India is the world's most taxed country. The Finance Minister has also said he would not go in for a deficit economy, but I do not think the Planning Commission or the Finance Minister would be able to live up to this assurance.

Nature of Development

The biggest problem is that we have tried to partition development time into periods. Development is a continuing process. Distributing it into five sections would be neither logical nor useful. The whole attention of the Administration is concentrated on fixing targets for five years and striving to fulfil them even if adequate resources are not available and even if the administration required for fulfilling those targets cannot be set up.

Madam, I suggest that the matter of preparing five-year development plans be reconsidered. There is nothing sacrosanct about five years. Even now we take up projects that would bear fruit after five years. If we fix broad planning objectives, indicate basic policies, fix priorities and leave out details our planning would come to have a pragmatic approach and it would be more fruitful.

The Finance Minister has sought to create the impression that he has given relief to the people. In some respects this is true—the production duty has been lowered, income tax too has come down, but this relief is only to the extent of Rs. 42.99 crores. The Finance Minister has also estimated how much revenue would accrue from the 10 per cent regulatory duty levied on imported goods from February 17. Madam, I feel it is wrong to increase the import duty 10 days before presenting the budget, not taking the people and the House into confidence over how much revenue it would yield, and then ten days later create the illusion that people have been given relief, that no bigger burden has been put on them. The Finance Minister should clarify how much revenue would be raised by increasing the import duty. My estimate is that it would be at least Rs. 100 crores. We also cannot forget that a few days ago the Railway Minister has imposed a fresh burden of Rs. 21 crores.

SHRI T.T. KRISHNAMACHARI, Minister of Finance : Will the Hon. Member make a bargain ? I will accept Rs. 70 crores from him.

SHRI A.B. VAJPAYEE : Madam, it is very difficult for me to bargain with the Finance Minister.

SHRI AKBAR ALI KHAN (A.P.) : One hundred crores must be based on some basis.

PROF. SATYBRATA SIDDHANTALANKAR (Nominated) : Let him come forward.

SHRI A.B. VAJPAYEE : Let the Hon. Minister give his own figures.

PROF. M.V. LAL : It is his duty to give us that information.

SHRI VAJPAYEE : Madam, my complaint is that revenue is estimated on the lower side and expenditure on the higher side. This year's budget also makes this clear. The revenue surplus for 1964-65 was estimated at Rs. 83 crores, but it rose to Rs. 229 crores while the expenditure was less than the estimate by Rs. 42 crores. This is our saving now. And the point to note is that when last year's budget was presented the Finance Minister had not taken into account the fact that an additional sum of Rs. 38 crores will have to be disbursed to government employees by way of incresed dearness allowance, rehabilitation would involve greater expenditure and we would also have to give more assistance to the states, and still, after all this, there was a saving of Rs. 104 crores.

SHRI B.R.BHAGAT : What about the shortfall of Rs. 70 crores ?

SHRI VAJPAYEE : That is for now. I shall come to that.

SHRI B.R. BHAGAT : No, it is an old thing.

SHRI VAJPAYEE : I think if the income is not estimated realistically the Finance Minister would not be able to do justice to the scope for lowering taxes.

The income-tax concession that has been given benefits the upper classes more than the lower ones. An additional surcharge was levied on income tax in 1962-63 after the Chinese aggression. The new facilities given by the Finance Minister make one feel that the higher-income group would get a five per cent concession, but for those within the 7,500–10,000 bracket the additional surcharge would become a permanent feature. Actually it was this class that ought to have been given greater facilities.

Production Duty should be Lowered Still Further

The Finance Minister has expressed the hope that the benefit of the lowered production duty will reach the consumer, but the present market trend does not seem to indicate that this would happen. Even as it is, production duty is increasing at such a rate that it should have been lowered still further. In 1950-51 the duty was Rs. 63.43 crores, in 1955-56 Rs. 145 crores and in 1964-65 Rs. 770 crores. The Finance Minister could have given still more relief in taxes. because a sum of Rs. 2550 crores has been collected within three years of the Third Five Year Plan—or even if we add the fourth year, while the estimated revenue for all five years of the plan period was half of this. During the 13 years of planning the proportion of taxes to national income has risen from six per cent to 14 per cent. The Finance Minister has proposed taxing urban property. In some quarters the proposal has been welcomed as socialistic. I do not know what socialism it contains. But let us bear in mind the practical difficulties it would create. The Railway Budget had also increased freight on building materials like lime, stone, iron etc. The Railway Minister has sought to make them expensive. Let the Finance Minister ponder : will the proposal to tax urban property not further slow down house-building activity in the country, which is already going very slow ?

Madam, this year we have seen an exceptional price rise, and the *Economic Review* has admitted that while in 1963-64 the rise in wholesale prices was 9.1 per cent, in 1964-65 it rose to 14 per cent. If we want to make a success of economic planning we will have to take effective steps to stablise prices. The key to price stabilisation is agriculture, because agriculture not only provides the raw material for our economic development but also meets half the expenditure of the population, which is on food. But food production is not keeping pace with the traget. For the last some days the situation seems to be improving, but I would warn the Government against complacency on the food front. It is true that we have had a good wheat crop and prices have somewhat gone down, but we could again have an uncertain situation in June, July, in the monsoon. The farmer now wants to keep more foodgrains with him than he needs. The Government will have to come up with a concrete plan for greater foodgrain production, for if we cannot control food prices the low income group would certainly be in difficulty.

National Price Stabilisation

Madam, it has been suggested that we should have a national price stabilisation board, which would fix prices keeping the interests of both producers and consumers in view. We already have a Food Corporation and a Tariff Commission, and various wage boards are also set up for employees, but this is piecemeal thinking on the price problem. For comprehensive thinking on the subject the Finance Minister should give serious thought to the proposal of a national price stabilisation board.

SHRI AKBAR ALI KHAN : There is a commission appointed under Prof. Daruvala to look into this matter.

SHRI A.B. VAJPAYEE : Only agricultural prices. It has nothing to do with industrial prices and wages. I want the whole problem in its various aspects to be taken into consideration.

Madam, the Memorandum on the Fourth Five Year Plan says it would be satisfactory if public enterprises make a 12 per cent profit. I do not know on what basis this 12 per cent rate of profit has been fixed. But the Audit Report reveals that the profit our public enterprises are making is much higher than 12 per cent. If public sector enterprises make a profit or a bigger profit we should welcome it, but this profit should not be based on a price policy that has an element of taxation in it. Take, for instance, the State Trading Corporation. It has earned a profit of over 51 per cent. I am not complaining about it. But the price at which it is importing fertilizer and the price at which it is selling it to the farmers is certainly objectionable. When the State Trading Corporation took over the import and distribution of chemical fertilizers it was said that this would be done on a no-profit-no-loss basis, but now there is profiteering—I have no other word for it. I have with me the figures given in the Audit Report (Commercial). They show that the State Trading Corporation is making a profit of over Rs. 300 per metric tonne of fertilizer.

SHRI C.M. POONACHA (Mysore) : May I by way of explanation inform the Hon. Member that it is not so ? I have personal knowledge about the working of the S.T.C. The S.T.C. acts as an agent to the Food Ministry, and the disposal of the fertilizers so imported is entirely in the hands of the Food Ministry, while the S.T.C. is paid a nominal commission to meet out of pocket expenses.....

SHRI VAJPAYEE : The Hon. Member may try to see the Audit Report (commercial) to which I have referred. It is not enough to say that the S.T.C. is not making a profit but the Food & Agriculture Department is making it. The point is at what price is the agriculturist getting the fertilizer ? If there is a profit it is on the price to the farmer and at the cost of the plan to increase food production. No one wants our public sector projects to run at a loss. They should make a profit. But the profit should not be at the cost of the consumer.

Foreign Influence

Madam, the Finance Minister is opening the door wide to foreign capital. I am not against foreign capital if it comes in on our terms and conditions, and if it helps the country to become economically independent. But the policies being adopted make one apprehensive that the door is being opened so wide for foreign capital that it may prove the exit for our independence, our independent foreign policy and our great goal of national economic self-sufficiency. From olden times we have seen what happens when the fulcrum of the trader's balance becomes the staff of authority. We do not face the danger of political slavery in that sense. But it cannot be denied that foreign capital promotes foreign influence. I am surprised to see that facilities not available to domestic capital are being extended to foreign capital. It is also difficult to say if foreign capitalists really want India's economic or industrial progress. Their main aim is to make a profit, and so adequate capital from abroad is not available to us for the development of basic industries. Our friends in Britain and America are ready to give us wheat, but not steel plants. Machine-making industries, which can lay the foundation of economic progress, are not able to attract adequate foreign capital. Most of the foreign capital is tied up in the production of consumer goods. All the profit goes out in the form of foreign exchange and to that extent hinders our economic development.

What will be the Form of the Amendment in the Patent Law ?

The Government proposes to amend the Patent Law. We would like to know what the form of that amendment would be. We must remember that 90 per cent of the patents registered so far in India are foreign. In their agreement with our companies they put the condition that the technique, the process, would be kept secret. A similar condition was imposed when we entered into an agreement with a foreign firm for antibiotics. When the Government wanted an agreement with a foreign company for manufacturing raw film that company was also given the assurance that 40 high posts of the joint company would be given to foreigners. But that company did not come. *The Economic Review* says the system of licences for new plants would be changed and letters of intent would be issued to private foreign investors who wish to invest in India in collaboration with Indian partners. The change in policy would go against domestic small and medium capitalists. So long the Government used to give licences to Indians and they would try for foreign collaboration. Now the licences would be given directly to foreign capitalists, as a result of which they would come to India and find out with which party they should have an alliance. This would benefit those 18 or 20 multi-millionaire families in the country who control the whole economy and who have amassed great wealth due to economic planning; it would not benefit small and medium capitalists and industrialists. As I see it, Government policy is aimed at preventing the concentration of economic power and economic resources. But the new change in the licensing policy would go against this policy.

Foreign Capital Growing in the Country

Madam, during the period 1946 to 1961 American capital in the country grew from Rs. 11 crores to Rs. 96 crores. In 1957 there were collaborations with 81 foreign companies, out of which only six were American. In 1964 this figure rose to 78. British capital too is rapidly growing in the country. In 1948 it was Rs. 226 crores and in 1961 it became Rs. 447 crores. In 1964 there were 105 collaboration agreements with British firms. I do not want to misconstrue these figures, but we have to be cautions in inviting foreign capital. Perhaps the Finance Minister may have read an article by a certain Australian economist. He has sent a note to the Planning Commission. His name is E.L.

Wheelwright. He has warned the Government of India. He is not a communist and wishes India well. According to Wheelwright foreign capitalists want to make enough profit in five years to repatriate their capital. If this is true no long-term development plan that depends upon foreign capital can bear fruit. We should use foreign capital, but it should not come the Coca Cola way, it should come the heavy industry way.

Unaccounted Money

Madam, I shall make one more point before I close. I have taken more time, for which I apologise to you. The Finance Minister is trying to trace unaccounted money. He has not estimated how much income this search would yield. Does the Finance Minister think these raids would not have greater results and would not yield more hidden wealth ? Still the wealth traced so far should have been accounted for in the budget and the wealth expected to be traced should also be indicated. But the Finance Minister is silent on this.

His silence is eloquent, but we shall construe it our own way. It should be accepted on all hands that raids would reveal unaccounted wealth. It would be good if people voluntarily disclose their unaccounted wealth, but I have no hope that they would do so by depositing 60 per cent and being content with 40 per cent. Further, this 60 :40 proportion is applicable only to big capitalists and industrialists. This tax rate does not apply to small and medium capitalists. Does the Finance Minister expect that small and medium capitalists, who too may have unaccounted wealth, would also deposit 60 per cent of it and remain content with 40 per cent ? If he does he should realise that small and medium capitalists would not be motivated to disclose their assets.

So far raids have yielded a total of Rs. 35 crores, while black money is estimated at Rs. 15 to 20 thousand crores. What steps are being taken to bring out the rest of the money ? The Finance Minister has admitted that black money is generated through tax evasion or by flouting price regulations. Then can taxes not be so modified as to lessen the temptation to evade them ? If a person honestly pays all taxes he cannot manage his expenditure. So he tends to evade them, and police raids cannot curb this tendency. Even as it is, it is the small people who have been raided while big people have been spared. The Government net catches small fish but big crocodiles escape.

Madam, I suggest that the Finance Minister should give serious thought to exempting married people with two children from paying taxes. This would entail a loss of only Rs. 2 crores, but five lakh people would be exempted from income tax. The total number of income-tax payers is 14 lakh. Along with it there is a 60 per cent arrangement for tax on companies. We would have to promote capital investment if we want to raise resources, invest them in industries, increase the pace of progress, bring prosperity to the country, arrange more equal distribution and make everyone happy. Seven months ago company tax was 25 per cent, now it is 60 per cent. Can the Finance Minister think of making it 50 per cent ?

Injustice to Bachelors

Finally I shall say something about bachelors, you may call them unmarried people. On the one hand the Government talks of family planning and wants to promote it, while on the other hand bachelors have to pay more taxes. The amendment in the income tax law that has been made....

SHRI MAHAVIR PRASAD BHARGAVA (Uttar Pradesh) : They have less expenses.

SHRI VAJPAYEE : No, they spend more because there is no lady in the house to manage the expenses.

SHRI MAHAVIR PRASAD BHARGAVA : If you think so, why not bring one ?

SHRI VAJPAYEE : But I want to contribute to family planning. I urge the Finance Minister to give sympathetic consideration to the matter of the income tax on bachelors. I shall make concrete points when the Finance Bill comes up, but we must realise that we are not doing justice to them.

With these words I thank you and express the hope that the Finance Minister would make amendments in the budget he has presented in a new direction in consonance with the hope he has built, so that our progress becomes still faster and we reach our goal.

Pitfalls of Foreign Collaborations

Madam, the country is going through conditions of war. This war is not of our seeking, it was thrust upon us. Our forces have crossed into Pakistan, but our aim is not to conquer Pakistan, not to occupy it. We want to live in peace with Pakistan. But today war has become inevitable for the preservation of peace. If Pakistan gives up its aggressive designs on India, lives in peace, and lets us live in peace there would be no reason for us to wage war. One thing the whole world, including Pakistan, must understand, and it is that India is not prepared to bow down in any way in the matter of Jammu and Kashmir. Jammu and Kashmir is a part of India and will remain a part of India.

It is regrettable that those who are our friends and also allies of Pakistan are not being fair to us. Today Britain, the United States and some other countries blame us for sending an army into West Punjab for our security, for preventing a future Pakistani aggression, but when Pakistani invaders openly violated the ceasefire line and entered Jammu-Kashmir these countries were silent, they did not think it necessary to condemn Pakistan. Had Pakistan not clandestinely sent its armed invaders in large numbers into Jammu-Kashmir the present situation would not have arisen. Every step that we took was defensive, not aggressive. Britain is the head of the Commonwealth and both India and Pakistan are members of it. We can understand Britain's desire for peace. We hold peace dear, but there would be no peace in this subcontinent so long as Pakistan does not give up its intention to force us to accept its improper and unjust demands through use of force. We hope Britain and the United States would not do anything that would adversely affect India's relations with them.

Madam, at this time of crisis the whole country is united as one. Party divisions have disappeared. Our differences should come to an end. The whole country has to firmly and unitedly meet this challenge. Today there is no place for agitations or direct actions. If meetings are to be held, processions taken out, demonstrations to be organised they should all be meant for raising the morale of the people, for strengthening the war effort. It is also the duty of the Government to strengthen people's cooperation with the war effort by setting up committees at every level in New Delhi, in the States and in the districts. The food situation is critical and proper distribution arrangements will have to be made, but let not the people take the law into their own hands. We cannot allow anti-national elements to indulge in violence. While the political parties would have to observe certain restraints

Rajya Sabha on September 7, 1965 during discussion on the Finance Bill

the Administration on its part will have to ensure that if the people's difficulties cannot be completely removed and it would be difficult to do so in a day—they could at least be minimised. The people's resentment should be kept in view and sympathetic policies adopted.

It is also necessary that except for pro-Peking communists those who have been arrested under Defence of India Rules should be set free. I am not happy that my friend Dr. Ram Manohar Lohia should be in jail today. He is a patriot and if freed would inspire the people to win the war. It is also necessary to release many political leaders and workers who have been arrested in connection with the food agitation in Maharashtra. We have to create an atmosphere of cooperation in the country. All those who need not be kept in jail without jeopardising defence should be released.

Madam, it is very necessary to maintain communal peace in the country. So far as the Bharatiya Jana Sangh is concerned, we are ready to extend full cooperation to the Government in this respect. When our jawnas are staking their lives on the front to win the war we cannot make the mistake of promoting communal strife or animus within the country. Some Pakistani elements may be bent upon mischief and may incite the people, but however grave the provocation, the people must exercise restraint, control themselves.

The Economy would Influence the War Too

Madam, when we think of our economy at this critical juncture we feel that in the past our economic planning did not take into consideration the possibility that we may even have to fight a war and win it. For many years we have been demanding that the aspect of defence be given priority in our economic planning. We had also demanded—and we repeat that demand that the Planning Commission should have a member who is an expert in defence matters, who can keep defence requirements before the commission during economic planning. A war is not fought only on the battle-front, it has also to be won on the domestic front. For this it is necessary to put the economy in proper shape, increase production, arrange proper distribution and motivate people to control consumption. But today we find ourselves in the midst of an economic crisis. The Finance Minister has admitted in his speech that the money market is sluggish and loan realisation would be Rs. 20 crores short of the target. Small savings have slowed down, and there too there would be a shortfall of Rs. 10 crores. The annual collection is expected to fall short probably by Rs. 15 crores. It is clear that the Government has miserably failed in stablising prices. When the Prime Minister took office he had declared in his broadcast to the nation that the problem of stabilising prices would be given priority and efforts would be made to see that if prices cannot be brought down they would at least be kept stable. But the Administration has not succeeded in this efforts.

The foreign exchange problem has become very serious. When the budget was presented—I mean the main budget, now we have two budgets in a year, I hope we don't have a quarterly budget—the Finance Minister had announced some stern measures for saving foreign exchange. He had said we would increase our balance by augmenting exports and curtailing imports. Restraints were placed on foreign travel, as also on the propaganda work of our embassies abroad. An attempt was also made to have some control on their expenditure. In spite of all this the foreign exchange position continues to be serious. We have to seriously think about why this is so.

Sometimes I feel the present freedom of unbridled collaborations with foreigners in the industrial field has also led to an outflow of foreign exchange, and of domestic capital being attracted abroad. There are certain areas where collaborations are necessary, where we need foreign exchange, where we also need know-how. There is no opposition to such collaborations, but Madam, I cannot understand foreign collaboration for making chocolate and face powder and children's gripe water and the freedom to repatriate their profits. I was amazed to see the account of Cadbury's whose name is well-known. I would ask the Foreign Minister to explain the royalty of Rs. 10,87,316 that it got last year. I cannot definitely say all that money went out, but I would like to know what happened to it, where it was invested, whether it was used for the economic development of the country. In 1964 their profits were still higher and the royalty they got was Rs. 13,83,964.

Cadbury and Krishnamachari

Now there are people who say and you cannot stop people from talking that T.T. Krishnamachari and Company are the sole selling agents of Cadbury and Company. The Finance Minister has no connection now with T.T. Krishnamachari and Company, but the name is there. I am not raising that question, but I had warned even in my budget speech that our foreign collaborations are on the increase, and I had proved with facts and figures that we have had more collaborations with Britain and the U.S. in the last two-three years than in the ten years before that. Is this an index of the country's economic progress in the right direction ? I am doubtful. Further, we have collaborations with different countries in the same field, for making the same goods. Their plants are different, their spare parts problems are different, there is no standardisation.

Is it not possible for the Government to specify different areas for different foreign collaborations ? There should be collaboration with a country in one specific area, so that there is no problem of standardisation and we face no problem in respect of spare parts. Collaboration with many countries in one and the same field, with different types of spare parts create problems for us. This matter should be looked into. The more foreign collaborations we have the more will be the outflow of our capital; no one can stop it.

Exports Increased

Madam, our exports have gone up. The Finance Minister has stated that he wants them to increase still further. In some areas there is scope for curtailing imports, but there are certain areas in which cutting down imports would affect the rate of economic development. For instance we want good steel, our defence effort depends on it, efforts to make machinery are linked to it, so it is not advisable to think of curtailment in it. Where curtailment is possible the country should be prepared for it. But I am surprised to see that our export earnings have not fully reached the Reserve Bank. It is said that there is a difference of opinion on this matter between the Commerce Ministry and the Finance Ministry. Reserve Bank figures indicate that about a hundred crore rupees that the Commerce Ministry claims it has earned through exports have not reached the Reserve Bank coffers. This is a gap in export earnings that have not been deposited with the Reserve Bank. I would like to know the reason to this gap. Is this not an indication of the Government's inefficiency, of the malpractices going on in the export- import field ? I want that the Finance Minister throw light on this gap in his speech and explain its reason.

Because of a fall in the value of the Rupee Indians living abroad, who used to send money to India, now tend to deposit it in London and Hong Kong. In exchange for it some people here pay them in cash and use the deposited foreign exchange for their own purposes. If this is true it is a most serious situation. The country should benefit from the earnings of Indians living abroad, but it would be the loser if this tendency of keeping their earnings abroad increases among them and if some elements enter into dubious agreements with them to pay cash to their families and relatives here in lieu of the foreign exchange kept abroad. This too is a matter for consideration for the Finance Minister.

There is also a complaint that when we order machinery we pay some earnest money, but the machinery does not arrive, as a result of which a lot of our earnest money is blocked abroad. So there should be careful investigation into why there is delay in ordering machinery and how long the earnest money would remain blocked, as this affects our economy.

One Occasion, Two Statements

Madam, I wish the Finance Minister were present in the House, as I want to raise a point related to him. Yesterday too there was a reference to this matter and in his speech on the no-confidence motion on March 11, 1965 Law Minister Shri Ashok Sen had stated in the Lok Sabha that the Finance Minister had severed all connection with T.T. Krishnamachari and Co. in 1942—I am quoting Shri Sen. "All connection" means both direct as well as indirect, but this proved wrong. Speaking on this same Finance Bill the Finance Minister said in the Lok Sabha, "On April 27, 1946 my youngest son became a major, and with that my responsibilities came to an end."

There is no reason to disbelieve his words. But it is difficult to reconcile what the Law Minister said with what the Finance Minister said. The Law Minister said all connection was severed in 1942 and the Finance Minister says all connections were severed in 1946. Between the two who is telling the truth ? Both are Honourable Ministers, one is a legal expert and the other a financial expert, but they could not agree on the year.

SHRI LOKNATH MISHRA (Orissa) : Both are wrong.

SHRI VAJPAYEE : A third fact that has come to my notice, which was perhaps referred to yesterday, is that according to evidence with the Registrar in Madras Shri T.T. Krishnamadari's son had not become major on April 24, 1946. The notice of his becoming a major was given on April 5, 1952. It is clear that the Finance Minister did not sever his connection in 1946. A photostat copy has been given to the Finance Minister. Thus there is a big difference in the dates and the position should be clarified. Of course it is not objectionable if he remained his son's guardian till 1952, but why this confusion in dates ? This sort of thing creates suspicion. Members of Parliament may come to feel that facts are being hidden. I wish the Finance Minister would clarify the position in his speech. Possibly 1946 was mentioned by mistake, but evidence is available that in 1952 he was connected as guardian. So I want the position to be clarified.

Minister's Image

Madam, we are passing through a crisis, and at such a juncture a responsible minister should be above suspicion. This is not the time to settle old scores or to ask for somebody's resignation, but if there is a suspicion in anybody's mind that policies are determined in a discriminatory manner and their implementation depends upon who are close and who are not, the people cannot come to have the required confidence in the Government. We do not want such an atmosphere at such critical times; we must cleanse it.

For the last some days the Finance Minister has come under a cloud—I wish he would emerge through that cloud and formulate the country's economy in the proper manner. He should therefore clearly and fearlessly place the facts before the House. With these words I close. Thank you.

The Planning Commission
Plagued by on Bookish Principles

Sir, in a developing economy the budget is not just a statement of income and expenditure, it is an effective and powerful instrument for the achievement of economic and social goals. Our objective is to build a society in which there is prosperity and equitable distribution of that prosperity with everyone a sharer in it. Tested against this criterion the budget is a disappointment. It does not provide for an arrangement that would increase the rate of development and enable us to move faster towards prosperity. As compared to other developing countries we have a very low development rate and we would have to give thought to improving the economy so as to increase it.

The budget proposals are not conducive to increasing investment in setting up plants so that production may increase and proper distribution of the increased production may fulfil the basic needs of the people. At the same time the budget has tax proposals that would be a burden for the common man. It will be admitted on all hands that the majority of the country's population lives in a situation of scarcity. It is true that everyone has to make sacrifices for a golden future, but the downtrodden and the depressed among us should also have a share of our achievements. Increasing excise duty on essential commodities cannot enthuse people to save. The Government intention may be that people should spend less, buy less, and without doubt the savings rate should go up, so that those savings could be invested in development works. But not every commodity has an elastic demand. Sugar and textiles are not commodities whose demand can be brought down. The common man does not use them more than required. In such a situation an increase in the excise duty on commodities increases the common man's burden.

In respect of income tax what the Finance Minister has given with one hand he has taken away with the other. The budget proposals do not give any hope to the common man. Neither are they helpful in solving our economic problems. The country is caught up in a serious economic crisis. Production is going down, there is a shortage of raw materials, there is the foreign exchange problem, unemployment is going up and our dependence on foreign countries increasing. At the same time the common man is losing confidence in a planned economy, because even after three five year plans we could not fulfil his basic needs. In order that this confidence may not be completely lost it is necessary to lessen his burden. He should be given some

Rajya Sabha on March 23, 1966 during discussion on the General Budget

relief. The Finance Minister has completely failed in this objective. He seems to have become a prisoner of economic planning. The Finance Ministry has become a part of the Planning Commission and the Planning Commission is trying to go ahead on bookish principles that are unrelated to reality. This is why our economic progress is not as fast as we want it to be.

Sir, prices are going up and this Government has failed to check them. So long as economic, financial and fiscal policies are not changed it would not be possible to check dearness. But increasing dearness decreases the income and the purchasing power of the fixed-income group. How can that be made up ? The dearness allowance of Central Government employees has been increased, but not that of State Government employees. They would naturally feel resentful. The States and the Centre should together find a solution to this problem. This difference in dearness allowance cannot continue for long. Otherwise 60 lakh State Government employees would be forced to take to the streets. No one among us would want that to happen. If the Central Government helps the States they would be able to adequately increase the dearness allowance of their employees.

Sir, there are also some other points that I would like to make. According to tradition all matters can be included in the discussion in the budget. I would refer to them because they are very much in my mind.

Dicourtesy to Israel President

A few days ago the President of Israel was on a visit to neighbouring Nepal. In order to go to Nepal you have to pass through India. India permitted this. It is a different matter that we do not yet have full diplomatic relations with Israel, but there is an Israeli representative in Bombay. There was no reason why, when the Israeli President was on his way to Nepal, our Government could not extend even common courtesy to him. He was visiting a country that is friendly to us, he was a guest of Nepal, and it would have been in keeping with our etiquette to treat him as the President of a nation; but there was no senior official of the Foreign Ministry to receive him at the airport. The result was that he sat in the plane for 45 minutes. He also has a complaint about the way he was treated in Calcutta. The Foreign Ministry should clarify its position. Can we not even behave with proper manners ? This does not help to promote our international prestige. I do not want to enter into a lengthy debate at this juncture, but why have we not established full diplomatic relations with Israel ? Whose fear is it that prevents the Government of India from taking such a step ? Those who swear by Gandhiji's advice of fearlessness should explain their mental difficulty in establishing diplomatic relations with Israel. Possibly some countries may take it amiss, but we could reason with them. Many countries in Africa have set up full diplomatic relations with Israel. Many West Asian countries that are friendly to Israel are also friends with Egypt, with the United Arab Republic. Israel is a fact. For some it may be a bitter truth, but we cannot assume that there is no Israel on the map. It is true that we have to look to our own interests while deciding a policy, but it is neither in our interest that we should not extend even common, human courtesy to the President of Israel.

Nationalist China

I may say one more thing in this connection. Some Ministers of Nationalist China, Taiwan, are also on a visit to our country. Nationalist China is a member of the United Nations and a permanent member of the Security Council. There could be occasions when we might need their help, their sympathy, their support. They are here to participate in the ECAFE meeting being held here today, and they have brought with them some seeds of good quality rice. We get these from the Philippines, but Taiwan is ready to give them to us. They have brought a hundred tons of seeds with them but no one in the Government of India is ready to take them. This is a very low-level exhibition of the untouchability policy in the international field. Do our Ministers' hands get dirty on shaking hands with them ? What mentality is this ? I can definitely say that this is not in the country's interest.

Reorganisation of Punjab

Sir, one more thing. The Home Minister has made a statement about the reorganisation of Punjab. I welcome his statement that the reorganisation would be based on language, not on religion. The question is, why is a big section in Punjab suspicious ? Why did those suspicions erupt in the form of a big agitation ? The Government and the ruling party should think about this. The Congress Working Committee decided to have a State in Punjab on the basis of language, but the very next day Congress President Shri Kamraj told correspondents that Kangra would go to Himachal Pradesh. On the one hand it is said an expert committee would decide the demarcation line, on the other, decisions are declared, fiats are issued. I cannot understand this. It has to be determined what the language of Kangra is. The Experts' Committee can decide this. I and my party have an open mind. If the experts' committee opines that the language of Kangra is Hindi it can go to Himachal Pradesh. But giving a decision without waiting for the experts' opinion smacks of communalism.

When the regional formula came into being Kangra was joined to the Hindi region. There is no geographical continuity between the Hindi region and Kangra. Kangra could have gone to the Punjabi region, but the calculation behind joining it to the Hindi region was that the proportion in population in the Punjabi region should be such that it could satisfy the Akalis. Will that same consideration be used again now ? If the linguistic principle has been accepted it should be acted upon firmly. The Committee of Members of Parliament had recommended the setting up of an expert body, but it too took a decision on Kangra. It is said that the population of Kangra does not want to live in the Punjabi Suba, it wants to go with Himachal.

Sir, if we were to take the people's opinion we would land in a big mess. Then the people of Pathankot would say they do not want to be with Punjabi

Suba, the people of Gurdaspur would say they do not want to be with Punjabi Suba—there would be no end to it. Then we would have to make Punjabi Suba out of only two districts, Jalandhar and Amritsar. Do we want people there to say whether they want to live here or other ? We do not want to open a Pandora's box. So we emphasised and the Government agreed to it—a linguistic basis. But before acting upon it with firmness the fate of Kangra is being decided. This is not proper. If the Home Minister's assurances are sincerely implemented there could be a new beginning in Punjab, but new difficulties would arise if unprincipled decisions are taken under influence and under pressure.

Now there will be a new Punjab and a Haryana—and let there be no doubt about Haryana. The same principle that you accepted in respect of the reorganisation of Punjab is also applicable for Haryana. It is necessary to clearly understand that Haryana would be a full-fledged state. Had the people of Haryana accepted Punjab it would have been good; the integrity of Punjab would have been preserved. But for this neither did the Centre try nor even the Committee of Members of Parliament. But if reorganisation is to be based on language there should be no doubts about Haryana. Haryana has been treated most unfairly. The people of Haryana are unhappy. This too is one of the reasons why they want to separate from the rest of Punjab. However, once a decision is taken on the principle of language there should be no pressure, no doubt in the mind.

I hope those arrested in Punjab would be set free, seized assets would be restored to their owners, those who have suffered loss of property would be compensated on the lines of Delhi, and there would be a judicial inquiry into the whole Punjab affair, including police excesses. The Government of India will have to put pressure on the Government of Punjab to restore normalcy at the earliest, to assuage people's hurt feelings and not to do anything that would again produce a misunderstanding in the people's minds and incite them. Thank you.

Devaluation of the Rupee

This is Just the Beginning

Madam, while speaking on the budget in the last session of the House I had warned the Government against devaluation. My warning was ignored and the Rupee has been devalued. When was the decision to devalue taken ? Was it taken while Shri Ashok Metha was in Washington, or was it taken in Delhi under pressure from Washington after he left ? In Delhi Shri Metha told the correspondent of an English-language newspaper that he had not undertaken a journey of thousands of miles to devalue the rupee. I want that all documents relating to Shri Ashok Metha's talks in Washington be published, so that the House and the people may know how much pressure the United States exerted for devaluation and to what extent the Government of India resisted that pressure.

It cannot be denied—and it should not be denied—that the unfortunate decision of devaluation was taken under foreign pressure. The note circulated to members of Parliament by the Finance Minister on June 8 has made this clear. It has already been quoted, and I am quoting it again. A sentence in that note says : "The action could not be postponed, as all further aid negotiations hinged on it." In other words, all hopes of aid depended on whether or not we devalued the Rupee. Is it not a fact that ten days after the devaluation decision the U.S. released the economic aid that had been blocked ? For the sake of appearances the State Department said we want peace in the subcontinent and we have released aid because there is now peace. But there has been peace for nine months. Even nine months after the war ended American aid was not released, and for six months after the Tashkent Declaration foreign exchange was not made available to our industries. But ten days after it was decided to devalue the Rupee the resumption of American aid was announced.

Madam, it is not only the Rupee that is under American pressure but also the Pound. Some days back I had the opportunity to visit the U.K. After attending sessions of the House of Commons and talking to some other representatives I felt that the U.S. is trying to get the Pound also devalued. On July 20 Prime Minister Wilson said in the House of Commons : "For several weeks there has been an increasing pressure on liquidity in the world's financial centres." And on the 27th he had clearly said and I quote : "It had to be recognised that in the past some years, some of these companies

---

Rajya Sabha on August 23, 1966 during discussion on the Calling Attention Motion on Devaluation of the Rupee

with American roots had been under pressure from their own government to transfer profits more rapidly to the U.S."

I say the time has come for India to join other countries in demanding a refixation of the price of gold. We should demand that the international price of gold be brought down. It is really surprising to see that the question of bringing the price of gold down has been taken out of the purview of the ten-nation committee set up to consider improvement in the international monetary system. If the price of gold falls the value of the Dollar would fall. This will save the Pound as well as the Rupee. I do not see any other way to increase international liquidity. The question is, could we not resist the American pressure for the devaluation of the Rupee ? Britain could succeed in saving the Pound; was it not possible for India to save the Rupee ? After all, this was a political decision and we could have saved the Rupee had we declined to bow before political pressure.

During my foreign tour it was my experience that many countries wondered how India decided to devalue the Rupee in such a hurry. West Germany and France were not so eager about this devaluation. Britain was worriedly watching whether or not India could withstand the pressure. As it is, the demand for devaluation is not something new. Since the Bell Mission of the World Bank submitted its report there has been demand for devaluation of the Rupee. But we stood our ground and succeeded. We should have shown the same firmness that we showed two years ago, but this Government could not stand American pressure : It could not stand pressure either from Washington or from Moscow. It devalues the Rupee under pressure from Washington and it commits the mistake of signing the Tashkent Declaration under pressure from Moscow. If this Government does not muster the courage to firmly stand up to international pressure it would head for a deep pit and take the country with it.

Obtaining Assistance was Possible Even Without Devaluation of the Rupee

Madam, even if we had declined to devalue the Rupee the U.S. would have been forced to think about continuing economic aid. That we should be a strong nation is also in the interest of those countries who help us. It is true that they do not want a first-class nation, but they would certainly want that somehow we should be in business and so would have come forward to help us one way or the other.

The truth is that the devaluation decision was taken in such a hurry that the Government had no time to think of the steps in its wake. Devaluation was decided upon, but how were prices to be checked ? What alternative arrangement would there be in the place of the export incentives that had been given and the curtailment to certain imports that had been decided upon ? How far would our decision of import liberalisation be taken ? In none of these matters did the Government of India have any clear thinking or any action plan. And this shows that the Government was not ready for devaluation. It had to act under foreign pressure, and it should admit this honestly. But it is not easy to accept the truth.

Madam, I do not agree that the Government ought to have informed Parliament or taken the opposition parties into confidence before deciding upon devaluation. This is a ridiculous demand. A decision like that on devaluation is not presented in advance for consideration. It is necessary to keep it confidential. But was it really kept so ? Is it not true that some industrialists of Calcutta had advance information about it ?

MANY HON. MEMBERS : No, no.

SHRI VAJPAYEE : Reports to that effect have been published, and I would like to know if the Government has investigated them. The way spies are being caught it does not seem impossible. Spies are not caught only in the office of the A.I.C.C., undesirable persons may also be present in the Secretariat. Here I would like to make a particular reference. The intelligence department had prepared a report on a certain officer and sent it to the Government, but it fell into the wrong hands. I demand an inquiry into whether or not this charge is true. The report was written by a responsible person and was sent to a still more responsible person. But the report got published and parts of it appeared in the press. How did this happen ? Such things should not be covered up.

Singing Praises of Devaluation

Madam, now poems of praise are being sung for devaluation and it is being claimed that it would infuse a new vitality into our economy. Our exports would rise, imports of raw materials would keep our industries going, and the lethargy that had overtaken the economy would vanish. If devaluation is so good why did we wait so long ? Why did we wait for American pressure ? Why did we not decide upon the devaluation of our own accord ? The examples of Yugoslavia and France are being quoted. Argentina went to the extent of having five devaluations within a year, but they did that to meet their own needs, not under any pressure.

Can the Government really swear devaluation would solve our problems ? The fact of the matter is that the same problems that led to devaluation would face us again. Commodity prices are going up; it is not necessary to go into the percentage of the price rise. How will they be checked ? There is not much scope in exports. Fifty-eight per cent of our exports are traditional. There is a possibility of exporting engineering goods, but such exports form only three per cent of total exports. That is why the Commerce Ministry had opposed devaluation in its recent report. Where is that report ? It should be published. At least it should be made available to members of Parliament. The Commerce Ministry report says devaluation is not in our interest. But it is on this very report that devaluation is being praised.

On the one hand it is argued that the international value of the Rupee had already declined and we only accepted the reality. When did this value decline ? I recollect that when I was in Hong Kong in 1962 the pound was worth Rs. 20 there and the Dollar worth Rs. 10. But at that time we did not devalue, because we did not consider devaluation in the interest of the nation. Today have the domestic and international values of the Rupee become one and the same ? In London a Pound fetches Rs. 30.

AN HON. MEMBER : Even today ?

SHRI VAJPAYEE : Even today. There are certain centres in the world where a Pound is worth upto Rs. 40. Does the Government not know this ? Are we going to devalue the Rupee still further to bring it on par with the reality ? These arguments do not hold water. Madam, the only reason is that we could not manage our economy well, could not make our plans realistic, could not motivate our labour force for enough production to fulfil our needs, and could not introduce financial and administrative discipline. Shri Ashok Mehta says administrative and financial discipline is required to combat the post-devaluation situation. Had there been administrative, financial, physical discipline in this country, in this government, devaluation would not have been necessary in the first place. Today we are faced with the same problems that faced us before devaluation.

Devaluation A Challenge

Madam, something good can also come out of anything bad. Devaluation is a warning, a challenge. A warning that if we do not open our eyes even now we may be in for still further devaluation. A challenge to set our house in order. But I do not see any eyes opening in the wake of devaluation. Is financial discipline being maintained in the States ? Are the States being forced to keep their expenditure within their means ? I had suggested in the budget session that constitutional provisions be resorted to for declaring a financial emergency in some States. They keep overdrawing on the Reserve Bank. They are taking the country to an economic abyss. The Constitution empowers the Centre to declare a financial emergency. But the Central Government is not ready to touch any State. This devaluation would prove no remedy if the State Governments do not curtail their expenditure, the Centre does not bring down its non-plan expenditure, if we do not put a stop to deficit financing, and, most important of all, if we do not overcome the present crisis of confidence in the country. This remedy would then prove worse than the disease.

Government Still Floating in the Air

Madam, the Government's eyes have not opened. This is proved by the fact that the outline of the Fourth Five Year Plan that has been presented shows the government is still floating in the air. It does not show that the Government has its feet firmly planted on the ground. Our dependence on foreign aid is still increasing. How are we going to repay this debt ? Are we in a position to repay it ? We had inherited a Sterling balance of Rs. 1700 crores. We finished it. Today our foreign debt is to the tune of Rs. 4300 crores and devaluation has increased it still further. Our plans are still formulated on the expectation that substantial foreign aid would be forthcoming. I am not against foreign aid in principle. But no one can deny that it comes with strings attached. The U.S. is putting the condition that there should be peace between India and Pakistan. If there is unilateral violation of peace, if Pakistan plays mischief, aid would stop, and the Fourth Plan would be in jeopardy. Can we not formulate a plan in accordance with our resources ? We should. I am not in favour of a small plan. Let us have as big a plan as possible, but let us depend upon our own resources. Foreign aid should be accepted only within digestible limits.

Madam, we have neither socialism nor capitalism in this country, because it would have progressed even if we had genuine capitalism. I say genuine because genuine capitalism would have put new scientific progress to use for agriculture, there would have been healthy competition, and the atmosphere in the country would have been conducive to maximum production through maximum investment. Capitalism can even be tolerated during the transitional period, but at present we see a conspiracy between corrupt politicians, greedy capitalists and useless bureaucrats. It has neither scope for individual initiative nor for honesty nor for diligent officers.

Corrupt Bureaucracy

I shall quote two examples, which are just small specimens. There is open land near the Santa Cruz airport of Bombay which is given for grass-cutting on an annual contract. A certain person has been bagging this contract for 17 years. It is said the contract is given in accordance with the tender, but no one except this person knows when tenders are invited and passed. He takes the land on contract for 20 or 30 thousand rupees and then passes it on to cowherds for grazing for two lakhs rupees. This time the cooperative society that took the land on contract from this person came to now about this. Thereuopn it sumbitted a tender for Rs. 51,000. It was a bigger tender and so had to be passed. But strings were pulled from Bombay and political pressure exerted. The tender had been accepted and the cooperative society notified accordingly; still it was cancelled and fresh tenders invited. They contained this person's tender and he was given the contract.

SHRI BABUBHAI M. CHINOY (Maharashtra) : For how much ?

SHRI VAJPAYEE : That the Government will have to say.

SHRI RAJ NARAIN : Two thousand extra. Initially it was given for Rs. 51,000. Later the contract was given to the same person for Rs. 53,000.

SHRI VAJPAYEE : The older party, the one who had sumbitted a tender for Rs. 51,000, ought to have been informed that fresh tenders were being invited. The land that was given for Rs. 53,000 would be given to the same cooperative society for Rs. two lakhs. This is a matter of the Civil Aviation Ministry, not the State Government. There should be an inquiry into it. The Government claims that formation of cooperative societies would bring down prices, but if the cooperatives are robbed of their rights like this the people would lose their faith — they are already gradually losing it. This is dangerous.

The Bargaining between Private Bus Owners and the Congress

There is another matter. It is a matter of political corruption. The Delhi Transport Undertaking (DTU) runs some private buses. They are used for peak hours. Formerly Congress leaders used to claim that all buses must be government buses, there was no place for private buses under socialism. I do not know what their definition of socialism is. People wait at bus stops, but if socialism prevents buses from plying who would care for such socialism ? And this is not socialism in the first place. At first it was decided that private buses will not ply, then the decision was reversed. There was a bargain for this. It was between the Delhi Pradesh Congress Committee and private operators, and the bargain was that for every private bus that plied the DPCC would get Rs. 50 per month.

SHRI LOK NATH MISRA : Socialist consideration.

SHRI VAJPAYEE : I am making a charge with a full sense of responsibility, and I am ready to be punished if it proves false. I demand that this charge be investigated. Every month the private bus operator pays the Delhi Pradesh Congress Committee Rs. 50 and he gets a receipt for the amount. You would say this is not corruption, this is a donation to the Congress Committee. Then how does this donation fluctuate ? It depends upon the number of buses that ply. When there are more buses it is bigger, when less, it is smaller. And this payment is made through the operators' association, the Delhi Contract Carriage Bus Association. The account books of the bus association as well as the Delhi Pradesh Congress Committee should be seized. Every month the amount is deposited by cheque in the Naya Bazar branch of the Punjab National Bank. I can prove that Rs. 50 are paid for every bus that runs. The number of buses does not depend upon the number of passengers, does not depend upon the needs of the citizens of Delhi, it depends upon how much money the Congressmen of Delhi want. I am not happy to make this charge, but I would be failing in my duty if I did not expose this fact.

Corrupt Triplets

Corrupt politicians, greedy capitalists and useless bureaucrats—these three are leading the country to its downfall. Still the saying about something good coming out of bad would prove true if devaluation could open our eyes and give us a shock treatment, if we could realise the country's bankruptcy and gird our loins to fight the dangers ahead. The people of Britain, led by Prime Minister Wilson, are fighting the economic crisis by avoiding devaluation. What Britain is doing should not be impossible for India. It is not the people who fall short, it is the leadership. What is wanting is the adoption of realistic policies. Merely bookish principles cannot solve our problems. It would have been possible to save the situation if we had put a stop to misuse of funds, if we had controlled prices and concentrated all our efforts on saving, and then we could have found a way out of our economic crisis. We do not yet see that way. And I am warning that this devaluation would not prove the final devaluation. If the Government continues with its policies like this the country must prepare itself for more devaluations in future. Thank you.

Finance Minister is Sharpening His Knife

Sir, the Deputy Prime Minister's budget speech has revealed to us a new facet of his personality. A budget speech is a dry affair, but the Deputy Prime Minister has laced it with humour at some places and sarcasm at others. The speech has some smears of colour as well as a touch of *gulal.* He has referred to actors and actresses and made fun of their yearning for immortality. He has accepted the delicacy of the husband-wife relationship but also shown the adroitness of not entering it.

SHRI D.C. SHARMA (Gurdaspur) : The Hon. Member does not know anything about it.

SHRI VAJPAYEE : But his biggest joke is about plastic surgery. He said he did not want to undertake a major operation, just some minor plastic surgery, in which a little skin from one place would be grafted at another. Plastic surgery involved the taking out of skin from a place where it can be taken out without being noticed and grafted at a place where it can be seen and can make up some deficiency.

Facilities for Corporate Sector

The Finance Minister has made some skin grafting in the area of corporate taxes. He has acted generously. It was necessary to give some relief in corporate taxes. The facilities that have been given in order that the country may shed its financial lethargy, capital formation may grow, the capital market may come alive and the people may accelerate the rate of pace of development through greater swings, are proper, and no one should grudge them. For instance, ending the dividend tax on additional distribution of the dividends on ordinary shares, the scaling down of the additional tax on company profits from 35 per cent to 25 per cent, abolishing the various surcharges on earned and unearned income, and abolishing the annual deposit scheme in the area of individual income,—all these are steps in the right direction and we may hope that they would have the proper impact and would help to remove financial lethargy in the country.

But for giving so many facilities to the corporate sector was it necessary to add such taxes to direct taxes as would directly affect income ? Now it may be argued that if indirect taxes were not levied at all the budget deficit would go up. During the budget discussion the Finance Minister was again and again reminded of his old speeches and told that he was committed not to go in for a deficit economy, and yet this budget had left an uncovered deficit of Rs. 250 crores. In this regard I would submit that a deficit economy

Lok Sabha on March 4, 1968 during discussion on the General Budget

encourages inflation. No one can deny this. But it would not be right to adopt the rigid, inelastic stand that in no circumstances would we have a deficit economy. Adopting such an economy by way of a cure is understandable. We have only to be careful so that it does not increase inflation beyond a certain limit and does not adversely affect prices.

According to the Government spokesman, out of Rs. 290 crores Rs. 140 crores have been provided for building up food stocks, and Rs. 100 crores for making up the shortfall in the PL 480 wheat that we used to import. I hope the Finance Minister will clarify these matters in this reply. If what the Government spokesman says is true the so-called deficit budget just amounts to book transfer of funds. It cannot be called a dangerously deficit budget.

The Plastic Surgery

Sir, I think the budget is like an iceberg floating in the sea, with only its tip being seen. I am afraid the Deputy Prime Minister is preparing to present a supplementary budget. That is why he is content with plastic surgery this time. But he is preparing for a major operation. The plastic surgery is just for assessing the patient's reaction. Can he bear the plastic surgery ? And if the Finance Minister concludes he can, he will prepare for a major operation. Very frankly, he said in his speech, that such a big deficit called for his sharpening his knife for a major operation for marshalling additional resources, and he is doing that. If this time we can force him to give relief in the burden on the people we might be able to save the common man in the coming supplementary budget as well. If we lose this time I am afraid there is a distinct possibility of a major operation for claming a big chunk of the flesh.

Loss in P & T Department

Sir, it is estimated that there would be a deficit of Rs. 22 crores in the revenue of the Posts and Telegraphs Department this year. So the budget has proposed an increase in the postal rates. There is no justification for this increase. The Finance Minister will point to the recommendations of the Mahavir Tyagi Committee to justify it. Certainly Shri Tyagi is a very lucky person. He gets the opportunity to head many important committees and commissions. But if we look to the terms of reference of this committee we would see that when the Government set it up its intention was to raise P & T rates. It wanted some committee to recommend such a raise, and the Tyagi Committee obliged it.

The question is, should the postal and telegraph services be run on profit-making commercial lines, or should they be considered essential services which it is necessary to continue even at a loss ? Both types of examples are available in the world. But the Tyagi Committee has mentioned only those instances that are in its favour. Other examples have been ignored. I say rail and postal services cannot be viewed piecemeal. When the Railways were contributing to the general revenue the Railway Minister did not restrain the temptation to increase passenger fares and freight charges on the ground that Railways were making a profit. Postal and telegraph rates were increased even when they were making a profit. The present justification of increasing rates in the name of losses is an attempt to view the problem piecemeal, which would never help us arrive at the right decision. The bitter truth is that increasing P & T rates is tantamount to encouraging the inefficiency, waste of money and mismanagement of these services and penalising the people for them. The Tyagi Committee has made some startling revelations, although they relate to minor officials. Still the Committee has made a small effort to show what is burning under the chair in the empire that Dr. Ram Subhag Singh rules.

The Tyagi Committee's Facts

Sir, I would like to quote two examples from the Committee's report. The first is that a certain postman in the Rs. 75-95 salary scale collected Rs. 2220 in September 1967 by way of reimbursement of medical expenses and Rs. 460 in October 1967. There is another example. A clerk drawing a monthly salary of Rs. 240 collected Rs. 975.20 as overtime allowance in October 1967 and Rs. 5552 as the same allowance for the first ten months of 1967. The Tyagi Committee has also given other examples. If minor employees are misusing facilities to such an extent what officers may be doing can be easily guessed. There is scope for curtailing unnecessary expenditure in the post and telegraph services. Losses entailed in strengthening the services can be made up, but there is no justification for increasing the rates.

And on what are the rates being raised ? On post cards and inland letters. A post card is a thing of the common man's use. Neither does the Government use it for a letter of dissent nor a person for a love letter. People use it to write about their woes in brief and finish it. I appeal to the Finance Minister to exempt the post card and inland letter from this increase. We would not complain if those who want to use an envelope pay a little more.

The Tobacco Rates Anomaly

Sir, the Finance Minister has proposed a 10 per cent increase in the present rates of all types of unmanufactured tobacco and putting them all on the same level, has proudly declared—I am quoting him : "On this occasion I have decided to be impartial to different lovers of nicotine, whether they are lovers of the ordinary bidi, hukkah or chewing tobacco or cigarette, cigar or pipe." This is the Finance Minister's impartiality—putting the bidi and the cigar in the same class and claiming impartiality. Actually this is being unfair to both. It is unfair to the bidi because it cannot bear so much burden and it is unfair to the cigar because it can bear a still bigger burden. Now if the Finance Minister puts Shri Jagannath Pahadia of his ministry and Shri Piloo Mody of the opposition in the same class and says he is putting an equal burden on both it would break Shri Pahadia's back but would be a less than enough burden for Shri Piloo Mody. The tobacco used for making bidis and chewing tobacco should be exempted from the new taxes. I trust the Finance Minister will seriously think about this. It would not be a matter for worry if those who smoke cigarettes, good quality cigarettes, have to pay a little more, but it does not look good if those who want to forget their worries by chewing tobacco or smoking a bidi cannot escape the Finance Minister's whip.

Public Sector and Private Sector

Sir, during the discussion on the budget frequent references have been made to the public sector and the private sector. It looks as if a cold war is going on between the two sectors in the country. When the critics of the public sector speak they see nothing good in it, and when those critical of the private sector open their mouth they find all sorts of evil in it. This is not a healthy outlook : to a certain extent it is vitiated, it is perverted. We must look upon the public sector and the private sector as two parts of one and the same national sector. In the present situation every one should have a full opportunity to develop according to his capacity and potential. It is necessary to end the cold war between the two sectors. It is also natural that when the strife between the public sector and the private sector escalates the people's sector, the sector of self-employment, which covers small businessmen and those earning by their own labour, suffers. We should adopt a healthy attitude in this regard.

One more thing and I shall finish. Sir, I am not one of those who look upon nationalisation as the panacea for all ills. When the need arises the Government can expand its sphere of authority. But in the circumstances prevailing today the Government should first run the factories in its hands efficiently, increase their production, operate them at their designed capacity, and enable the public sector to set a model in respect of the labour force. Then the criticism of the public sector would substantially decline and expansion can be taken up. The need today is to consolidate this sector. So long as we do not create a management cadre the unbridled expansion of the public sector cannot benefit the country's economy.

Contributions, Privy Purses and Partisan Politics

It is also necessary not to drag in politics while nationalising an industry. I suggest that there should be a judicial commission to go into the condition of an industry, and only on its recommendation made after taking all aspects into consideration should the Government take it into its hands. Unfortunately the fact of the matter is that important decisions are taken for political considerations. Take, for instance, the matter of contribution of companies to political parties. My friend Shri Minoo Masani, who is sitting here, was also a member of the Lok Sabha when he first introduced a bill disallowing companies from contributing to political parties. I had also brought a similar bill in the Rajya Sabha, but in reply the then Finance Minister Shri T.T. Krishnamachari had said it was not possible, it was not necessary. Now you are talking about prohibiting companies from contribution — is this not for a political purpose ? Now that the opposition parties too have begun getting some contributions a law is being talked of. Sir, so long as the princes were siding with Congress, giving privy purses was all right, but now that they are slightly turning their face away they are being threatened with stoppage of privy purses.

Sir, this is not the way to improve the country's economy. Our viewpoint has to be realistic, practical—one that would accelerate economic growth through marshalling of the country's resources and strengths. If the Finance Minister makes such amendments in the budget we would welcome them. Thank you.

Budget in a Developing Economy

Sir, before I say anything about the budget I would like to draw your attention to the wrong report of what happened in the House yesterday that has appeared in the press today.

Yesterday the opposition had raised the question whether or not the Deputy Prime Minister had consulted the Attorney-General while levying a tax on agricultural produce and the Deputy Prime Minister had replied in the affirmative. But the papers have reported that he has consulted the present Attorney–General, while my information is that it was the former Attorney–General that he had consulted. It is necessary to put the record straight in order to obviate the possibility of any misunderstanding that the press report may create and I hope the Deputy Prime Minister will clarify the position in his reply to this debate.

Budget an Effective Instrument

Sir, in a developing economy the budget is not merely a statement of income and expenditure. The budget should be an effective instrument of implementation of the policies, strategies and programmes to be adopted for economic reconstruction. Does the present budget stand this test ? In other words, will the budget proposals increase production and productivity ? Will employment opportunities increase ? Will savings and investment be promoted ? Will there be relief for the common man who is being ground between the millstones of high prices ? Will the widening gulf of disparity be narrowed ? There are the tests on which I want to assess the budget and these are the questions to which I seek answers in the budget proposals.

In my opinion the picture of the economic situation that the Finance Minister has painted in his speech is not realistic. There is an element of exaggeration in it. He has presented only the bright side of the picture, while the darker aspects are out of sight. In the Finance Minister's words the food crop this year is expected to be satisfactory, but the Deputy Prime Minister forgot to say that most of the credit for the good crop goes to the weather. So far our agriculture has depended upon the heavens. The year the monsoon is not merciful we may again have to face a food crisis. Even today shortage of water has led to a drought in many parts of the country, and at some places the people and cattle are actually wandering in search of food and water.

Lok Sabha on March 7, 1969 during discussion on the General Budget

Impact of Devaluation

The Deputy Prime Minister has said exports have gone up, but the fact of the matter is that the increase has not come up to expectations. It is also the bitter truth that previously, due to devaluation, we could earn more with exporting less, but now we cannot earn that much even by exporting more. Tea, jute and cotton textile markets are slipping out of our hands. As compared to other countries our prices are higher, and our quality is also not high enough to stand competition. Our prestige is going down.

The Finance Minister has admitted that as compared to 1967-68 our repayment obiligations are higher and foreign aid has been utilised less. As a matter of fact our economic dependence on foreign countries has reached dangerous proportions. The situation is such that New Delhi looks to foreign capitals, State Governments look to New Delhi, and the people look to the State Governments. During the freedom struggle we had dreamt of a self-reliant, self-respecting India, but the picture before us today is that of a dependent, disabled India. We have to face this bitter truth.

In the colourful picture of the economic situation that the Deputy Prime Minister has painted there is no place for those crores of unemployed people who are willing to work but have no opportunities to do so. Growing unemployment, especially educated unemployment, is a matter for serious concern. It is not only a proof of the failure of the Government's economic policies and planning but it can also pose grave danger to our political and social structure.

Visionless Budget

The Government estimates that this year the rate of development would be three per cent, but in view of the rate at which our population is growing a development rate of three per cent cannot remove our economic bakwardness. Whatever development we achieve is swallowed by this growing population. So there are no signs of economic backwardness being removed. We would have to accelerate the pace of progress for a happy present and a bright future. There are no visible signs that the present budget would help this process. The present budget can neither be called a development budget nor a regeneration budget, although it was hoped that it would be a development-oriented budget and would regenerate the economy. This is a disappointing budget, devoid of clear thinking, realistic understanding and a vision of the future.

Now I shall come to the budget proposals. Before dealing with them one by one I would like to say that in some areas the Deputy Prime Minister has given relief, while in some others he has imposed new burdens. It seems that the relief that has been given has been given very reluctantly, because of compulsion, while the new burden has been imposed callously, perhaps without caring for the consequences. The House should give serious thought to this reluctance to give relief on the one hand and callousness in imposing burdens without caring for the consequences on the other.

For example the Deputy Prime Minister has very kindly relaxed the present taxable profit margin of Indian companies from Rs. 500 to Rs. 1000. This step would have been welcome. This is a step in the right direction, and the Finance Minister would have been congratulated on it, but while he has taken one step in the right direction he has taken two in the wrong direction.

I shall now discuss those wrong steps.

Anti-Middle and Rural Class

Sir, as I was saying, the Deputy Prime Minister's relaxation of the profit margin of Indian companies from five hundred rupees to a thousand is a step in the right direction. But along with it he has taken two steps in the wrong direction. In the first place the progressive increase proposed in individual income tax rates is a retrograde proposal and it will directly hit the middle class, which is already pressed down by the economic burden. The proposal to increase the tax rate on income from Rs. 10001 to Rs. 15,000 by two per cent and from Rs. 15001 to Rs. 20,000 by three per cent cannot be called considerate. It should be taken back. Is it not surprising that the Finance Minister and Deputy Prime Minister should be harbouring an animus against the middle class for a long time ? Whenever some new experiment is done in respect of taxes the middle class is invariably made the target, whether it is the compulsory savings scheme or the annual deposit scheme. The class that is the backbone of the society is being burdened with new loads. This weakens its capacity to save, and consequently it cannot adequately contribute to economic reconstruction.

Now I come to production duty. Here the Finance Minister has spread his net far and wide. Not only has a production duty been imposed on old commodities but new ones have also been brought within its purview. Now the end-product tax on cement, vanaspati, electric fans, bulbs and tubes, soap, soda ash, caustic soda and sodium silicate would be changed into ad valorem. The Finance Minister has expressed the hope that this change would encourage the manufacturers to increase investment and decrease prices. There are, however, no signs that this hope would be fulfilled. Whatever the change, the consumer will have to pay for it. He will have to pay more for these commodities.

A production duty of 23 per cent has been imposed on granulated sugar. It is unnecessary and improper. It is neither in the interest of the cane-grower nor in the interest of the sugar industry. It is argued that an increase in the production duty on granulated sugar would bring uniformity in the regulated price and the open-market price of sugar. But the fact of the matter is that the market-price of sugar has risen still higher. This will force the common man to spend still more on sugar, as regulated sugar is not sufficiently available to all. The Delhi Administration deserves to be congratulated on making adequate stocks of sugar available to the urban and rural areas of Delhi, but this is not so in other states. The rural population cannot meet its need with the sugar available on regulated prices. For that it has to buy in the open market and pay more. Surprisingly enough the Finance

Minister has said in his speech — I am quoting him : "Hon. Members should not oppose a production duty on sugar simply because it would incidentally yield additional revenue of Rs. 27.45 crores."

Sugar has Become Bitter

Incidentally, the Deputy Prime Minister has no desire to increase the duty, he has a clean conscience, but if the policies he has adopted incidentally make a profit of Rs. 27 crores he would not say no to it!

Now I want to know, if there is a profit, into whose pocket will it go ? And who will bear its burden ? I respect his capacity for humour and congratulate him on it, but let him not forget that it has made sugar somewhat bitter.

Another question is, how much of the increased production duty on sugar will go to the cane-grower ? Before the midterm election the Food and Agriculture Minister had declared that nowhere would the price of sugarcane be less than Rs. 10 per quintal. This announcement has not been acted upon. The mills have not been fair to cane growers. The cane grower sells his cane cheap, but he will now pay more for sugar. This cannot be called a balanced point of view. There should be some balance between the price of farm produce and that of factory products. The Government has failed to strike this balance. By increasing the production duty on granulated sugar the Deputy Prime Minister has aggravated this imbalance still further.

It is true that removing the duty on grey cloth would give relief to some textile mills. But by increasing the per square metre duty on fine and superfine printed cloth by 5 paise and on all other types of printed cloth by 2.5 paise what the Minister had given with one hand he has taken away with the other. Not all mills make grey cloth. Those that will get the relief are small in number, those who will bear the burden are bigger in number.

SHRI S.R. DAMANI (Sholapur) : Those mills that will get the relief are nore in number.

SHRI VAJPAYEE : Does the Hon. Member not know that the mills of Ahmedabad will benefit very little from the relief ?

SHRI S.R. DAMANI : I may sumbit for the information of the Hon. Member that 88 per cent of the production is of coarse lower medium and high medium cloth and 12 per cent of fine and superfine.

SHRI VAJPAYEE : I am talking of grey cloth. The relief has been given only on grey cloth, not on any other type. The Hon. Member will agree that not all mills make grey cloth.

The question is that by imposing a 15 per cent price-proportional duty on suiting, furnishing, decorative textiles and Tukish towels a blow has been struck at this class in the hope of greater saving, and the Finance Minister hopes to invest this saving in reconstruction.

As I do not smoke I cannot say for sure, but those who do—I wish the Finance Minister would clarify this point—claim that the burden of the production duty on cigarettes that has been raised from 10 per cent to 18 cent would fall on those who smoke medium quality and low quality cigarettes, not on those who smoke high class cigarettes. If this is so it is necessary to reconsider this matter.

Increase in Duties Unimaginative

The increase of seven paise per litre in the production duty on motor spirit would create problems for road transport, in which small and middle-class people have invested their money. If motor spirit becomes costlier bus fares would go up and goods transport rates would rise. All this together would push prices up. Instead of earmarking funds for improving the condition of the roads the Government keeps making money out of road transport. This is not a far- sighted policy. This would frustrate long-term objectives for the sake of short-term gains.

It must also be remembered that only the other day the Railway Minister increased freight rates by 10 per cent without obtaining the sanction of Parliament. This increase in railway freight and in the production duty on motor spirit would together lead to a price-rise.

So far as the question of imposing a 10 per cent price-proportional production duty on chemical fertilizer and of 20 per cent on power pumps is concerned, it cannot be justified. I am surprised to see that this duty contradicts what the Finance Minister himself said in his speech. I would like to draw the attention of the House to the third paragraph of the speech. It says :

> "Although food production has increased we have still to make great efforts to make satisfactory arrangements for the growing population of the country. We still import raw agricultured produce and foodgrains on a large scale. Hence our first priority is to invest our limited resources in agriculture, which includes such essential agriculture-related inputs as research, chemical fertilizers and water resources."

The point is, if the farmer comes forward of his own accord to fulfil this need for capital should he be discouraged ? There is no propriety in imposing a production duty on fertilizers. There is already a shortage of chemical fertilizers in the country. The demand is greater than the supply. Further, not all farmers have become used to chemical fertilizers. We have to persuade more and more of them to use it. The Government has withdrawn the subsidy on chemical fertilizer. Now imposing this 10 per cent production duty is not being fair either to agriculture or to the agriculturist. This will not only disrupt food production efforts but also kill the farmer's enthusiasm.

I agree that the tendency to save should grow among wealthy farmers. Conditions should be created in which this saving could be invested in new products. But this purpose will not be served by taxing chemical fertilizers and electric pumps. Is it not possible to motivate wealthy farmers to invest their capital in digging borewells so that other farmers could be provided borewell water at a reasonable rate ? Can we not create an atmosphere in which savings of farmers could be used for digging borewells ? This would put the excess money that has entered the rural sector to good use and it would also prove to be a matter of satisfaction for the farmers.

Encourage Agro-based Industries

Prosperous farmers could be encouraged to start small and medium scale agro-industries in the rural areas. Such industries could start if the Government could extend necessary facilities. Then the prosperity we see in the rural areas could be put to use for industrialisation in the rural region itself. It is very necessary that the Government prepare a plan for this. By proposing to tax agricultural wealth the Finance Minister has put his hand in a wasps' nest. Now these wasps are surrounding the Deputy Prime Minister on all sides. There are wasps in the Council of Ministers and also in his party!

SHRI MORARJI DESAI, Deputy Prime Minister and Finance Minister : We will escape them.

SHRI VAJPAYEE : Well, you can escape if you have a thick skin. The question is not about escaping. The question is, is it necessary to tax agricultural wealth ? And if it is, should it be at the Centre or in the States ? Yesterday I heard on the radio that the Kerala Chief Minister Shri Namboodiripad and the Andhra Pradesh Chief Minister Shri Brahmanand Reddy have supported the imposition of a tax on agricultural wealth. If that is true why are they not taking steps to impose it ?

SHRI MORARJI DESAI : It is not within their powers.

SHRI VAJPAYEE : There could be an agriculture tax.

SHRI DESAI : That is a different matter.

SHRI VAJPAYEE : They want to transfer their headache to you. There are already many points of dispute between the Centre and the States. It is not necessary to add a new controversy on this point.

SHRI MORARJI DESAI : You are doing it.

SHRI VAJPAYEE : That is because you are giving up the opportunity. We won't let an opportunity go. I mean a tax on agricultural wealth is unconstitutional, illegal. This is a State subject. It should be imposed by the States, not the Centre.

Agricultural Tax

The Finance Minister has estimated a revenue of some five crores rupees from this. This estimate has been put on the lower side. But if it is right, if there will be a revenue of only five crores, and if even these five crores the Finance Minister is going to give to the States, why involve the Centre at all in the controversy ? The States could be advised to try to meet their expenses by raising such resources, but the imposition of such a tax by the Centre cannot be justified. We also cannot forget that the present prosperity in the rural areas has not yet settled down. No steps should be taken in the beginning itself that would kill enthusiasm, generate public discontent and create economic and political problems. Differences within the Central Cabinet and in the Congress Parliamentary party have come to the fore. The Finance Minister has certainly tried to soften the blow by promising to exempt genuine agriculturists from this tax, but that would not solve the problem. If and when you go into who is genuine and who is not government officials would be equipped with powers that can be misused. It could also mean greater harassment for genuine and honest agriculturists. So this sort of tax on agricultural wealth needs to be withdrawn.

The export duty on tea is being reduced from 20 per cent per kg to 15 per cent per kg, and the rebate on it has been raised from 35 paise per kg to 55 paise. Export duty on tinned tea has been completely abolished. This is a step in the right direction, but it is late and is not enough. The production cost of tea is going up, and it will go up still further. The Deputy Prime Minister will have to think about it. The decrease in the export duty will be exploited by the traders. But if the growers are to be given relief the production duty on tea will have to be brought down.

About jute I may say that even after bringing down the duty our exporter would not be able to stand the competition from Pakistan. It has been estimated that Pakistani exporters make a profit of 600 rupees per ton on the export of hessian, while an Indian exporter loses 300 rupees. The jute market is constricting for us. The jute industry is in a crisis. The Deputy Prime Minister's decision to put it in the priority list is the right decision. But this much help cannot solve the present jute crisis.

Reduce Non-Plan Expenditure

Every year excise duties and production duties are being raised, and if we look at the history of the last many years this increase amounts to a hundred crores of rupees. The burden of this falls on the common man. The point is, is it necessary to increase the production duty ? On the one hand we are told that we are emerging out of an economic slump. If we are to fully come out of it the market demand for goods has to grow. But dearness is being promoted by imposing new taxes and production duties. There is also such a thing as consumer resistance. If demand does not grow production will not grow. Financial lethargy cannot be completely removed. But let us not increase commodity prices so much that consumer resistance sets in. The Deputy Prime Minister would have to keep this in mind.

It has been said—and I want to repeat it—that the budget has no reference to efforts at cutting down non-Plan expenditure. The reasons put forward for increase in non–Plan expenditure are well known. If dearness increases dearness allowance will increase. That increase cannot be avoided. Still there is scope for curtailing government expenditure. The Government could save a hundred crore rupees if wasteful expenditure is prevented and economy is practised. The Deputy Prime Minister has not given any assurance about saving this money.

I would like to discuss two things that I liked about the budget. So long there was a debate on how we should decide about the Fourth Plan—should we first decide upon the outlay and then think about the ways and means of collecting that much money ? That was a wrong method, and it created problems for us. But the budget speech makes it appear that the controversy on this point within the Central Government, especially between the Finance

Minister and the Planning Commission, has ended with the victory of the Finance Minister, and in his speech the Deputy Prime Minister has explained this year's total investment for the Fourth Five Year Plan. May I expect that this method would be adopted in future too, and that the Plan would be decided upon the resources available ? I would welcome this if it is adopted as a matter of policy. There is no other way of making economic planning realistic.

Need for More Consumer Goods

The Deputy Prime Minister's acceptance in his speech of the need to promote industries producing consumer goods is also to be commended. We need heavy industries, we want a self-sufficient economy, but we cannot forget that our economic planning has to proceed on democratic lines. If we deny the people basic needs we cannot fill their minds with the enthusiasm needed for economic planning. I would like to refer to what the Deputy Prime Minister has said in his speech :

> "It is necessary that along with agricultural production industries producing consumer goods should have greater efficiency and productivity. Giving attention to these industries is specially necessary, because doing so would motivate increased productivity and this also augments Government revenue."

The need for consumer goods is accepted on all hands. The Deputy Prime Minister has accepted it. This also is an indication of a slight change in the old policy. This change should have already taken place. But increasing the production of consumer goods and then making them more expensive by imposing an excise duty on them are contradictory policies and it would be difficult for the Deputy Prime Minister to reconcile them.

Who is the Villain ?

Sir, in his speech the Finance Minister has called himself the Sutradhar. He said, "This time I am present before you only as a Sutradhar. The job of the Sutradhar is to be present on the stage for some time before a play begins and rouse the spectators' interest in it." But I would like to know, who is the play-wright of this play, who has written it, who are its hero, heroine, and above all, who is the villain ? Is the Sutradhar's job only to rouse the interest of the audience, or does he also want to become the director ? This is not a play, this is life. This is not acting, this is reality. The wheel of time has chosen the Deputy Prime Minister to play an important role on the stage of the play that is life of 50 crore people. This is not just a play to watch; the very destiny of India is being decided. The country is going through a process of political transformation, and at this juncture it is necessary that our economic thinking should be clear, our goal realistic, and our proposals conducive to greater production, equitable distribution of increased production, saving-oriented and a motive force for an accelerated growth rate. I doubt if the present budget can fulfil those objectives.

The Deputy Prime Minister will listen to the debate in the House and he will also have the opportunity to amend his budget proposals in the light of the discussion. But he should withdraw the tax proposals that would prove a burden for the middle class and so burdensome for the rural population that they would hinder agricultural production. We would have to keep these criteria in mind when taking the final decision on the budget proposals, and I trust that keeping in view the reaction of the House and of the country the Deputy Prime Minister would carry out amendments that would make the budget acceptable to the people.

A Bigger Outlay No Criterion of Planning

Sir, after achieving a thumping majority in the mid-term elections the Finance Minister had presented an interim budget. I would like to quote what he had said in it :

> "We shall accelerate the pace of development and fulfil the needs of the weaker sections of the society."

I also quote what he had added :

> "We are now waging a new war on poverty and injustice. I have no doubt that the people of India will win again and this great democratic country will soon see the dawn of social and economic freedom."

No one can disagree with these words of the Finance Minister and the sentiments they express. But his new budget does not stand this test. The new budget holds out no assurance that the pace of development would be quickened. There is also no concrete proposal for affording relief to weaker sections of the society. Now it is argued that this budget is not socialistic because one budget cannot bring in socialism. It is also being argued that the Finance Minister has no magic wand to remove poverty. Sir, I submit that this is an anti-development budget. It does not promote savings. This budget does not reduce inequality, nor does it even make a courageous attempt to marshal possible resources for stepping up the rate of development.

Sir, I am surprised to see that every budget talks of a bigger and bigger outlay in the Plan. In the present budget too the Finance Minister has said in his speech that an additional amount of Rs. 155 crores has been earmarked for this year's Fourth Plan. Many Hon. Members clapped when the Finance Minister said this. I would like to know if the test of the Plan, its success in the achievement of its target is confined only to the outlay on it. If you look at the interim budget and the *Explanatory Memorandum* accompanying it you will be surprised to see that the amount earmarked under many heads in the last budget were not spent. The public sector outlay in the total Plan expenditure was Rs. 2122 crores, but the amount spent was Rs. 1953 crores. The shortfall was Rs. 169 crores. The money was earmarked but could not be spent. You would be surprised to see the amounts earmarked, the heads under which they were earmarked and the amounts that remained unspent.

Incompetent Administration

Rs. 25 crores were set aside for rural works (drought areas), but only Rs 6 crores were spent, Rs. 19 crores remained unspent. Today we have famine

---

Lok Sabha on June 9, 1971 during the debate on General Budget

conditions in many parts of the country. Parliament had made a provision for it. But this administration is so useless that it could not use that money, could not spend it. When another budget is presented more money is demanded. There is a shortage of fertilizer in the country. We import it. Fertilizer is sold to farmers at a high price. But we had provided Rs. 27 crores for it, out of which Rs. 19 crores were spent and Rs. 8 crores remained unspent. Government companies and corporations had planned to spend Rs. 241 crores, but Rs. 191 crores were spent and Rs. 50 crores remained. I cannot understand the reason why less money is spent. This time too the Finance Minister has stated that out of the amount of Rs. 155 crores that has been provided Rs. 18 crores are being set aside for food collection. If he looks at previous figures he would find that the amount provided for the Food Corporation was not fully spent. Now I would like to know, who apart from the Food Corporation collects food ? If the State Governments do it the Central budget does not have to provide for it. It is definite that this amount will go under the head of Food Corporation, and the Corporation could not spend last year's outlay.

The *'garibi hatao'* slogan was raised. Nobody says one budget would remove poverty. But it should at least be decreased. Will the taxes that have been imposed not add to the common man's burden ? Before the Finance Minister the Railway Minister presented his budget and increased fares. A burden of Rs. 11 crores was imposed on third class passengers and freight rates increased. Will this not affect commodity prices ? And then the price of petrol has been raised. Just now the Finance Minister was saying taxi and autorickshaw drivers would be paid more. And who will pay ? Those who use the taxi. And remember, if taxi fares go up it will also affect the number of taxi-users. Ultimately this loss would have to be borne by the taxi-drivers. If transport gets expensive—diesel prices too have gone up—in the final analysis the burden will fall on the common man. Is the common man in a position to bear that burden ?

What did the Common Man Get ?

What inspiring message have we given to the common man through this budget ? What steps have been taken to remove disparity ? What effective steps have been taken to provide relief to the weaker sections ?

In his speech on the interim budget the Finance Minister has himself voiced concern at rising prices. It is strange that even after increased food production prices are rising. Last year's reasons for rising prices are still applicable. Except for sugarcane there is a shortage of cash crops. This will affect prices. The tax proposals in the budget will together result in commodity prices going up by eight to ten per cent. The Finance Minister may well say we are increasing the price by half a paisa, but in the open market situation in which we live this increase changes into five paise by the time it reaches the consumer.

SHRI HARI SINGH (Khurja) : The Hon. Member is talking about rising prices, but in the Mandis of Uttar Pradesh Jan Sangh activists and appointed purchasing agents are harassing the farmers. They buy foodgrains at less than proper prices and then sell them to the Government at higher prices *(Interruption).*

SHRI VAJPAYEE : Sir, what reply can I give to such a senseless point ? Here I am not in the dock, the Government is in the dock. If the Jan Sangh workers are indulging in rowdyism they should be prosecuted (*Interruption*). The Hon. Member does not know that this is a discussion on the budget; it is not a question of Jan Sangh and Congress workers. Are Congress workers as pure as snow ? I am also coming to them.

SHRI HARI SINGH : The Hon. Member can agitate against the budget but he cannot tell the mandi traders to sell to the farmers at prices determined by the Government.

SHRI VAJPAYEE : Sir, this is the Hon. Member's first time here. Please stop him. I am not used to such taunts. This House is not meant for discussing what Jan Sangh workers are doing (*Interruption*). This representative of farmers is talking nonsense. Is this the way ? If he has not been taught manners it is time he learnt them.

SHRI HARI SINGH : Telling the truth is good manners.

SHRI VAJPAYEE : The question is not what the Jan Sangh workers are doing, the question is what the Finance Minister is doing. The Government is not in our hands, it is in their hands. They cannot even bear to listen.

Sir, I regret he tried to derail me in the middle.

Unprecedented Tax Burden

This budget has imposed taxes to the tune of Rs. 220 crores, not Rs. 170 crores. If the States' portion is included the new burden comes to Rs. 280 crores. The Finance Minister will agree that except for the year after the Chinese aggression never had such a big burden been imposed. Had it resulted in an increased development rate, a means of employment for every able-bodied person, a greater acceleration of neglected classes and neglected areas towards development, the attempt to build a golden future even by burdening the common man could have been justified. But, as I have said before, the burden will fall on the common man. Who is happy with this budget ? Big industrialists are happy as their corporate sector has not been touched. Big agriculturists are happy as they have a large number of respresentatives in the ruling party and the Finance Minister had not shown the courage to touch them.

SHRI K. N. TIWARI (Betia) : That is not so. They to have been touched.

SHRI VAJPAYEE : Profiteers are happy with this budget, as they will get the opportunity to fleece the consumers. And who is unhappy with the budget ? It is the middle class, the Dalits, the backward classes and the fixed-income group, whose burden has increased and who will have to face the fearful calamity of price rise.

But even the Government would not be able to escape that calamity. There is a demand to raise the dearness allowance. The index is said to be 225 points. The moment it reaches 228 points the dearness allowance will have to be raised. If the Central dearness allowance goes up the employees of the States will not keep silent. The demand for equality in the dearness allowance is going to grow, whether the employees belong to the Centre or the States. A vicious circle will set in, and there seems to be no way to come out of it.

Import Licences can be Sold

It may be asked how else can we raise resources ? And no criticism of the budget will be meaningful so long as we cannot suggest alternative resources. We should think seriously about whether import licences cannot be auctioned. And if auctions are not useful can import licences be sold to people at ruling market prices ? The Finance Minister cannot deny that import licences have a large profit margin. Licences for certain commodities are selling in the market at a two hundred, three hundred per cent profit. The actual user buys raw material at a high price. The middleman is making a profit. Why should not this profit go into the Government's coffers ? Why should not an import licence be given to the highest bidder ?

As I have pointed out, prosperity is coming to a certain class in the rural areas—to those who have used new techniques of farming and who possess means of irrigation. The big agriculturist is becoming a sharer in national prosperity, but the nation does not get an adequate share of his prosperity. I remember, when the Finance Minister was the Home Minister he had warned that if we are not on our guard the green revolution may turn into a red revolution. But this budget has not tried taxing agricultural produce.

I read in the papers I do not know how far it is true—that the wedding feast given by some Minister of Maharashtra was attended by only one and a half lakh guests. The power connection of an entire neighbouring village was cut off so that the wedding pandal could be lit up, so that there could be light in one house. This is ostentation in bad taste. I regret that the Finance Minister was also present there. I can appreciate his difficulty. When he reached there and found one and a half lakh people present there what could he say to those who had invited them ? But he will agree that the nation should have a share in the wealth and income accumulating in the hands of some people in the rural areas. At the same time ostentatious exhibition of wealth should be curbed. So we demand.... (*Interruption*).

AN HON. MEMBER : Brahmins were fed.

SHRI VAJPAYEE : Sir, I do not know if he was there or not.

Impose a Consumption Tax

Our third demand is that those who spend above a certain limit—it could be five thousand rupees per month, though we would like it to be two and half thousand, those who spend two and a half thousand Rupees per month—should have to pay a heavy consumption tax. If that money is invested in reconstruction it should be welcomed. But if it is spent on purchasing consumer goods and in procuring luxury items it should be taxed heavily. This would on the one hand procure resources and on the other promote an atmosphere of simplicity. But such an atmosphere of simplicity cannot be promoted in the country when newspapers report that Rs. 25,000 were spent to repair a circuit house for a one-day tour of the Prime Minister.

Shares of Public Enterprises

The fourth point we have proposed, and which deserves serious consideration by the Finance Minister, is a joint sector. An attempt is being made to acquire equity shares in those private industries that receive loans from the Government, banks and financial institutions in lieu of those loans. No one will object to this. But on the other hand can we not allow people to buy shares in public enterprises—not majority shares, but 30 per cent, 35 per cent...

SHRI PILOO MODY (Godhra) : Who will buy ?

SHRI VAJPAYEE : The people would. It is wrong to hold that all enterprises are running at a loss, some are making a profit. Their employees could be induced to buy shares. A limitaion could be imposed against any one firm buying many shares, but if small people buy a large number of shares the public sector could really become a public sector. This could help to raise resources. Further, if employees become small share-holders their elected representatives could keep an eye on the bureaucracy and help to increase the productivity of that enterprise. This too needs to be seriously thought about.

Taxation Law

The Finance Minister has tried to slightly amend the taxation law. I feel the entire taxation law needs to be reconsidered. I am in agreement with Dr. V.K.R.V. Rao's suggestion that a taxation inquiry committee should be appointed to go deep into the whole matter.

SHRI Y.B. CHAVAN : He had talked of an expenditure commission, not a taxation commission.

SHRI VAJPAYEE : That too could be considered by this commission. You could even amalgamate the two commissions....

SHRI CHAVAN : I am not agreeing even to that.

SHRI VAJPAYEE : You are not agreeing to either ? You are opposing my proposal ?

The More the Taxes, the Greater the Dishonesty

You will agree that the direct tax should not be so big as to promote dishonesty. According to our calculations, in the present situation a man earning two and a half lakh rupees per year will have Rs. 49,325 left with him after paying taxes. But if the same man earns seven lakh rupees from two and a half lakh rupees he would be left with Rs. 16,875. I would request the Finance Minister to get these figures checked. Shri Salve has also said something like this. Today there is large-scale tax evasion. Income tax to the tune of seven hundred crore rupees remains in arrears. Every earner is considered dishonest. This atmosphere needs to be changed. It can be changed. Let us on the one hand adopt the right tax collection system and on the other see if there is scope for some lowering in the highest note. I would not however like a decision on this to be taken on some political basis.

There was a Bhoothalingam Committee that had suggested that there should be no income tax upto seven and a half thousand rupees. In the Public Accounts Committee we have seen that the income tax people spend more time, resources and energy on investigating small tax-payers than big ones. As a result big tax-payers easily escape, while all attention, all resources are concentrated on the small ones. This recommendation should be accepted and the tax collection machinery should be strengthened enough to prevent the big fish from escaping the net. Today big crocodiles escape and small fish are caught. This morning there was some talk about hanky panky in direct dialling. Somebody's line is connected to somebody else's. Somebody makes a call but somebody else pays for it. The Minister for Communications said in his reply we have caught a linesman and a chowkidar. Can a linesman and a chowkidar indulge in all this hanky panky ? Certainly there must be somebody above them. But crocodiles escape while small fish are caught. This is a strange way to spread the net. It is necessary to change it.

Educated Unemployed

A sum of Rs. 25 crores has been mentioned for the educated unemployed. The Finance Minister will agree that this is not enough. The Rs. 50 crores previously earmarked for the rural sector is also not enough. The need of the hour is large-scale provision of work for the educated as well as uneducated unemployed. Again the question is, where are the resources ? The Finance Minister says give me the resources and I can provide a hundred crores.

Financial Discipline and States' Overdrafts

In this connection I want to ask, is there or is there not any financial discipline for our States ? We are living under a planned economy. We expect sacrifices from every individual. We hope a few hardships in life at present would lead us to a bright future. But the State Governments are not prepared to live under any financial discipline. In the interim budget the Finance Minister had expressed the hope that the State Governments would go slow with overdrawing, and in this budget too he has said the same thing. But is any state Government prepared to listen ? The situation is such that all state budgets are deficit budgets. State Governments do not have the courage to raise new resources. They are worried about the coming assembly elections. So they seek the simple way out—that of drawing funds from the Reserve Bank. Today India is borrowing from abroad and the State Governments are borrowing from the Centre. There is no limit to the State Governments' borrowings. The Finance Minister's appeals are not enough.

In his budget speech he has admitted that in 1970-71 special assistance worth Rs. 195 crores was given to the States, and yet overdrafts continued. By the end of March last at least 14 States had together overdrawn Rs. 260 crores. But there is no supervision over how this money is spent. It can also be used for non-Plan expenditure as well as on items that have no economic priority. But the Central Government cannot do anything except give advice. I submit that if the Government so wishes it can use the Constitution in this matter and declare a financial emergency under Article 360. I quote :

> "If the President is satisfied that a situation has arisen whereby the financial stability or credit of India or of any part of the territory thereof is threatened, he may by a proclamation make a declaration to that effect."

The Constitution further says :

> "During the period any such proclamation as is mentioned in Clause (1) is in operation the executive authority of the Union shall extend to the giving of directions to any state to observe such canons of financial propriety as may be specified in the directions and to the giving of such other directions as the President may deem necessary and adequate for the purpose."

So far we have not used this provision. I was looking at the figures of the overdrafts by the State Governments and I feel some stern action is called for in this direction. But action is not possible till we give a direction to the States, and directions can be given under Article 360. The Finance Minister should seriously ponder : has the time come for such a direction to be given to the states ? So long as we do not bring the states under some financial discipline we cannot achieve our goals, whatever the resources we marshal at the central level. In this matter the states will have to march in unison with the Centre, but this is not possible so long as we do not force the states to put whatever resources are available with them to proper use.

It is true that the Finance Minister has appealed for greater marshalling of resources and for cutting down non-Plan expenditure, but these appeals are not going to have any effect. The centre needs to take some stern steps, and one of them is issuing a direction to the states under Article 360.

Inadequate Sum for Bangladeshis

Sir, only Rs. 60 crores have been set aside for refugees from Bangladesh. The Finance Minister will admit that this sum is unrealistic and inadequate. The Prime Minister has herself said then we will have to spend Rs. 180 crores in six months. So we can easily calculate the total amount that would be spent in a year as a whole. Let us not depend too much on international assistance. According to reports this morning the maximum aid we have received is perhaps worth Rs. 23 crores, which is in the form of medicines, milk tins and other things. Most of the burden would have to be borne by ourselves. Already the Finance Minister has left an uncovered deficit of Rs. 220 crores. This deficit is going to go up. There will be expenditure on refugees, which would generally lead to inflation, prices would rise, discontent would spread, and this Government would become a prisoner of its own slogans. Sir, economic problems cannot be solved without facing reality. A consensus will have to be brought about in the country also on the question of economic reconstruction. Merely making attractive economic policies cannot change economic principles. Slogans cannot change reality. Now that the elections are over and the ruling party has secured a big majority the Finance Minister should...

SHRI PILOO MODY : They have got a massive mandate.

SHRI VAJPAYEE : Yes, they have got a massive mandate which has now changed into a massive burden.

We would have to find out a middle class that would quickly achieve our goals of economic and social independence by democratic means, but this is not possible so long as a new wave is not created in the country. Sir, this is a 60-lakh-rupee question—will this new budget create a new wave ? I am talking of 60 lakhs because there is an American expression of something serious being a 64–million–dollar question. Our country is not America, we do not have dollars here, we have rupees. There they talk about dollars. Here when any important question comes up it should be called a 60-lakh-rupee question. So Sir, whether or not this budget creates a new atmosphere is a 60–lakh–rupee question.

Now that we are talking of 60 lakh rupees I would close by asking the Finance Minister to also tell us in his reply the head under which these 60 lakh rupees have been withdrawn. No light has been shed on this matter so far. It is also not *sub-judice*. Mr. Nagarwala withdrew Rs. 60 lakhs and Mr. Malhotra paid Rs. 60 lakhs. The House wants to know, the country wants to know the head under which this amount was withdrawn from the State Bank. I trust the Finance Minister will not whitewash this matter but place the facts before the House. Thank you.

Budget—A Clever Exercise

People Taken for a Ride

Sir, before I say anything about the budget I would like to congratulate Shri Sathe, whom I know well, on a fine speech. He is a new entrant to this House, and I am sure he would enhance the prestige of this House with his cogent speeches and would make a significant contribution to the process of the debate.

Sir, the budget presented by the Finance Minister is like an iceberg—the invisible portion is much bigger than the visible one. To put it briefly, it is a clever exercise in taking the people for a ride. I am prepared to congratulate Shri Chavan on the cleverness, but this attempt at deceiving the people will not succeed. This is a deceptive budget, this is an attempt at deceiving the people. I wish the House takes a serious view of it.

In the first place many members have said in their speeches on the total revenue expected from the new taxes that there was a fear of heavy taxation but the Finance Minister has left off tax-payers easily.

This is contrary to facts. This time's budget has imposed new taxes of Rs. 183 crores, but while giving the figures the Finance Minister has not tried to explain the impact that last year's additional taxes will have on the common man this time. The 1971-72 budget had estimated the revenue at Rs. 3,607.86 crores.

In the 1972-73 budget this figure rose to Rs. 4,228.50 crores. There has been a similar rise in non-tax revenue. In the 1971-72 budget the revenue was estimated at Rs. 4,670.37 crores while according to 1972-73 budget it came to 5,348.77 crores. This means an increase of Rs. 160.64 crores in tax- revenue and of Rs. 678.40 crores in non-tax revenue. The total comes to Rs. 731 crores.

But Shri Chavan has cleverly estimated the revenue on the basis of the revised estimate instead of on the original estimate, which cannot be called proper. The revised estimates include the revenue accrued from last year's burden. If we look at them we find that the tax revenue comes to Rs. 323 crores, not Rs, 731 crores. He has sought to create the impression that the additional resources that have been deployed have yielded Rs. 368 crores. The truth of the matter is that the revenue is higher than this.

Rate of Development is Decreasing

The point I want to make is that the taxes now imposed will place a burden of Rs. 332 crores on the common man. The additional import and customs duty to the tune of Rs. 118 crores imposed last year will have to be paid by

Lok Sabha on March 24, 1972 during discussion on General Budget

the common man this year. The additional excise duty of Rs. 31 crores will also have to be paid this year. All told, taxes to the tune of Rs. 332 crores have been imposed. Along with this an uncovered gap of Rs. 242 crores has been left. I feel this deficit will increase. It is also doubtful if the Finance Minister will present a supplementary budget to make up this deficit. Immediately after the elections, basking in the sunshine of victory, he has played with figures and wants to create the impression that this time the Government does not want to burden the common man any more. But this is a wrong impression. The burden has grown and it is likely to grow further in future.

Sir, a reading of the budget makes it clear that it will hinder progress, not accelerate it. For the last three years the rate of development is slackening. The rate of national development is decreasing. It is not enough to say, as Shri Chavan has said, that a slight sluggishness has set in. The truth is that since 1968-69 the pace of development is continuously going down. This budget holds no assurance that it will pick up. Plan objectives have been drastically curtailed. This budget is being praised on the ground that it has earmarked substantial funds for public sector development. But is it enough to set aside funds ? The Finance Minister has himself agreed in his speech that it is not. If the funds are not accompanied by proper planning of a programme and efforts at implementing it the money will bring no benefit. The Finance Minister says, I quote :

> "Our experience this year has reinforced the truth that merely provision of funds cannot keep up the tempo of progress. Equally important for this is timely preparation and selection of projects and their quick implementation."

Has this realisation dawned on the Finance Minister after earmarking Rs. 75 crores for the eradication of poverty in last year's budget ? A sum of Rs. 50 crores was provided for the eradication of rural poverty, out of which only Rs. 1.5 crores have been spent. Out of Rs. 25 crores provided for educated unemployed only Rs. 9 crores were spent. There is no shortage of resources. Taxes were imposed on the common man in order to raise them, and Parliament sanction was also obtained for expending them, but the Government could not spend the money. This budget cannot be praised merely for providing funds under a variety of new heads. It does not indicate whether or not there have been in-depth studies of those areas and special, concrete plans prepared. I do not think this budget will accelerate the pace of progress. Neither will it promote savings nor encourage investment. Then how can there be growth in the rate of development, which has fallen even behind Fourth Plan targets ? If the rate of development does not improve how can the people's standard of life improve ? How can the *garibi hatao* slogan come true ? How can employment opportunities increase ?

Consumption of Essential Goods is Going Down

Just now I was looking at the *Economic Review*. It shows that in 1970-71 the consumption of edible oils was less than in 1964-65. The per capita consumption of coffee was less in 1970-71 as compared to 1967-68. The consumption of essential goods is going down and prices are going up. The burden of the new taxes is falling on the common man. What hope has this budget to give him ? How will he have the confidence that under the new political dispensation some concrete steps would be taken to raise his standard of living ? This is a hollow budget. It is a disappointing budget. It does not even attempt to solve grave economic problems. This morning it was being said we want to end dependence on foreign aid. There should be some consonance between the Government's words and deeds. How long will this hypocrisy go on ? We defeated Pakistan and a sense of pride in victory spread in the country. To be in tune with that feeling we are being told we can do without foreign aid, but all plans are so made that it would increase. I charge that the Government is conducting behind-the-scene talks with the U.S. for increasing foreign aid. When today the *Explanatory Memorandum* was placed before the Finance Minister he said these were old figures. I want to know the new figures. This year foreign aid will be bigger by Rs. 75 crores as compared to last year and we are talking of self-sufficiency. Whom are we deceiving ? Are we deceiving ourselves or are we deceiving the country ? If we do not now pledge ourselves to self-sufficiency, if we do not now put to use the spirit of self-reliance that has been roused in the people we would never become self-sufficient. But the budget figures do not give any indication.... *(Interruption)*.... Shri Damani knows that the growth that has taken place in agricultural production is now creating problems, and when official aid is curtailed it will not benefit the producer and the consumer will have to pay more.

I am not saying we have not become self-sufficient in food. We have become self-sufficient in food, but we should not remain under the wrong impression that just this self-sufficiency would fulfil our effort to make the whole economy self-sufficient. The truth is that in the industrial field our dependence on others is increasing.

Sir, in this *Economic Survey* the Government has admitted, I quote :

> "Recent events have made it clear that the diplomacy of economic aid is another means that can be used against us in delicate times of extreme need."

Now we are told we would only accept that economic aid which has no strings attached. Conditions are sometimes visible, sometimes not. But they come to light when the nation gets into difficulties. Economic aid is then used for making us change our decisions. This was what happened in 1962, and it was repeated in 1965. In 1971 we had the same bitter experience, and yet today we are not taking to the way of self-reliance.

Let us Vow not to Take Foreign Aid

The *Economic Review* also says that a major portion of the foreign aid we receive is used up in repaying our loans. The *Review* further says war-time economic aid in 1970-71 is Rs. 248 crores. I say let us vow not to take foreign aid. If we want a loan we can take it in the international capital market. It is true that it will have some difficult conditions. It is also true that we would have to repay it somewhat more quickly. But it will be without conditions. It will not be conditional aid. The *Economic Review* has said 90 per cent of the aid we are given is conditional. We have to purchase goods from the countries that give us aid, at the prices prevailing there, and for the repayment too we have to look to the convenience of the donor country. The need of the hour is to determine to carry on without foreign aid. If the Government so determines the people can be motivated for sacrifices. But raising slogans of self-reliance on the one hand and conducting negotiations—sometimes direct, sometimes indirect—for foreign aid on the other amounts to creating confusion in the nation's mind. It splits the nation's personality. It will not create a will in the people, and without a will we can never stand on our own feet.

Sir, even if neither production targets are fulfilled, nor savings targets, the Government has nonetheless made considerable progress in three fields. The target of Government expenditure has risen from two per cent to nine per cent. The target of printing currency notes was seven per cent, which has gone up to 13 per cent. It was said there would be a marginal rise in commodity prices. But what is a marginal increase ? The Government does not know. I saw in the reply to a question that the funds provided for aid to the marginal farmer was not spent. Why ? Who is the marginal farmer ? We still do not know. The rise in prices is not marginal. Last year it was 10 per cent. I think the taxes now proposed would raise prices by 8 per cent.

A tax on kerosene is not at all called for. Do we want to spread darkness in homes ? Making kerosene more expensive because it is mixed with petrol is like making water more expensive because it is mixed with milk. This will not stop the mixing but it will make water expensive for the people.

Bungling in Distribution of Fertilizers

There is also no propriety in raising fertilizer prices. I was going through a report of the Public Accounts Committee. Fertilizer prices have gone higher than before. We expect the new taxes to yield an additional sum of Rs. 12 crores but during the past three years we spent Rs. 10.50 crores on inter-State transport of fertilizer. Is it not surprising that fertilizer for Madras goes from Orissa and fertilizer from Andhra goes to Bihar ? Crores are spent on this. Who is responsible for it ? As it is, our fertilizer is more expensive as compared to other countries. In Pakistan the price of ammonium sulphate is Rs. 1282 per metric ton and that of urea Rs. 1035 per metric ton, but here it is Rs. 2340 per metric ton for ammonium sulphate and Rs. 1822 per metric tone for urea. Even as compared to the U.S. our fertilizer prices were already high and now they are being raised still further. Small farmers will now not be able to use fertilizer. They would not be able to share in the green revolution. This will promote disparity in the rural areas.

I cannot understand whose interests have been kept in view while imposing taxes on fertilizer and power-driven pumps. Along with this the Government should take the House into confidence over the mysterious rise in tractor prices. Who knows what all has happened in these election times ?

On February 11, the prices of tractors were suddenly raised. Already farmers did not have tractors, and now tractors will be beyond their reach. According to my estimate tractor manufacturing companies have made a profit of Rs. 10 crores. Who took this decision of raising prices ? Everything that the farmer needs is being made expensive. In food purchase State aid is being curtailed. This is an anti-farmer budget. This will neither increase production nor decrease inequality. But an illusion has been created that the common man has escaped. The fact is that he has not. These taxes will have long-term repercussions....

Tax Evasion and Political Nexus

At present there is large-scale tax evasion in the country. This is known to everyone. The Wanchoo Committee has made recommendations, and in my opinion many of them are realistic. It is not only a question of drawing out black money, it is also a question of how to prevent its formation in future. If a little tax evasion is more profitable than to toil and earn, would people work to earn or evade taxes a little for a life of comfort and luxury ? I wish the Government makes a serious study of the Wanchoo Committee's recommendation. I read in the papers that an Hon. Member said the Wanchoo committee report is a third class report. What he does not like is third class. This is not how decisions are taken on economic questions.

But I want to say something important about tax evasion. In Delhi a big case of tax evasion has been exposed. The evasion is of lakhs of rupees, but the person who gave the information is now threatened with death. I have with me a letter from the Deputy Director, Income Tax Intelligence, Income Tax Department to the Home Ministry saying this person should be given protection, but so far the police have not taken any step. On the basis of information provided by this person the Intelligence Branch of the Income Tax Department had carried out a raid there, in which they have got hold of many account books, 250 smuggled watches have also been seized. But it is felt that if the police do not protect this person the whole thing could be hushed up. I would request the Minister to find out what the Home Minister is doing. When that person went to the police he was told his safety lay in leaving Delhi. Now if the police cannot protect people complaining against tax evaders all claims of checking tax evasion become hypocrisy and deceit. I wish the Minister personally gets information on this matter. Political considerations should not prove any impediment in his way. Whoever is the tax evader, he should be brought to book, and he who provides information should be rewarded. But far from being rewarded he finds his life in danger. This is not the way to check tax evasion.

All I can say is that this budget does not fulfil the common man's hopes. It will push up prices. It will force the class already harassed by rising prices to demand higher wages. Then a vicious circle would set in, and the economy will be still more jeopardised. Hence it is necessary to amend the tax proposals radically.

The Bangladesh Cess

I demand that the cess being collected in respect of Bangladesh be abolished. We are happy that Bangladesh has been formed. Refugees have returned. Now there should be no tax in our country in the name of Bangladesh. It is also not proper for the self-respect of the people of Bangladesh. We too accept aid from other countries but there are no postal stamps in the name of India saying this aid is being given to India. This situation needs to be changed. The excise duty imposed on kerosene, fertilizers and power-driven pumps should be withdrawn, and serious thought should be given to lowering the duty on steel. Have we accepted that there will always be a black market in steel ? If steel prices rise by 30 per cent the rise will affect every field.

It is also necessary that the Government do some basic thinking about taxation. Small-income groups should be given relief and the tax system should be so amended that those with big income are not inclined to evade taxes.

With Every Budget per capita Income and Consumption Declined

Sir, if we test this budget on the criterion of development and view it against the background of the budgets presented so far we have to regretfully say that not only has our development come to a halt but in some areas we are even going backward. The national growth rate has fallen. The value of the rupee has come down. When, in the sixties, Prof. Dandekar and Prof. Rath estimated the people living below the poverty line it was found that 40 per cent of the people were living a life of poverty below this level. Now this figure has officially risen to 44 per cent. The per capita income has gone down. Even the per capita consumption of essentials has declined. It is strange but true that in our country the per capita consumption of foodgrains fertilizer, oil and coarse cloth has gone down.

According to Prof. Shenoy, *dal* is the best source of protein for the common man. In 1961 the per capita per day consumption of *dal* was 2.43 oz., but in 1972 it has come down by 32 per cent.

Shri Bhagat may differ with Prof. Shenoy's opinion, but he cannot differ with the figures. The figures may be right or wrong. Hon. Members may challenge the conclusions derived from the figures, but there is no point in quarrelling with facts. It is clear that our budgets cannot stand the test of growth.

The second test the Finance Minister has talked of is maximum social justice. But how can we give in when the disparity between income and expenditure is widening ? It is really surprising that the number of agricultural labourers in the country is going up. I have figures for Uttar Pradesh. There in 1951 the number was 22 lakhs, while in 1971 it rose to 52 lakhs. This means marginal farmers do not find it possible to live on agriculture and have become labourers.

We are discussing land reforms and making declarations of distributing excess land among the landless. Still the number of farm labourers is on the increase, which proves that the poor are increasing in the rural areas. In the urban areas too the urban poor, as Prof. Dandekar calls them, are increasing. If this number increases how can the Finance Minister's objective of maximum social justice be achieved ?

The number of unemployed registered with employment exchanges are as follows : 51 lakhs in 1971, 69 lakhs in 1972, 81 lakhs in 1973 and 95 lakhs in 1974. Everyone knows the actual figure is much higher.

SHRI D.M. TIWARI (Gopalganj) : The population is growing very much.

Lok Sabha on March 15, 1974 during discussion on General Budget

SHRI VAJPAYEE : Does a person become unemployed right from birth ?

The Finance Minister's third test is self-reliance. Self-sufficiency is our national goal. We keep taking of self-sufficiency. When the World Bank Report exposes our dependence our national ego is hurt. But I was surprised to see that this year's budget speech of the Finance Minister estimates greater foreign assistance than last year. According to him we are expecting more than Rs. 144 crores worth of foreign aid. According to knowledgeable circles even these figures are not right. They do not include the wheat loans from Soviet Russia and the aid from oil-producing countries. If we add these the foreign aid figure may possibly go up to Rs. 1200 crores. Now if foreign aid goes up how can the objective of self-sufficiency be achieved ?

I am not one of those who will rest content with an agreement being reached on PL-480, but will not refer to the other form of PL-480 that has come to the fore by way of our developing economic relationship with Soviet Russia. What will be the price of the wheat we are receiving from Russia ? What will be the rate of the oil we are importing from Soviet Russia ? What is the price of the fertilizer we are getting ? And also of the steel ? We also want newsprint from Soviet Russia. It is necessary to take the House and the country into confidence over Soviet prices as compared to international prices. Self-sufficiency cannot mean less dependence on the U.S. and more dependence on the Soviet Union. Dependence is dangerous, whether it is on this big power or that. It is wrong to assume that foreign aid comes without strings. The conditions are at times visible, at times not. But when a crisis develops they come to light and close our national options. At least our dependence on them cannot indicate our self-sufficiency.

SHRI SATPAL KAPOOR (Patiala) : Take a delegation there.

SHRI VAJPAYEE : It is you people who get the chance to go in delegations.

Sir, in spite of the expectation of prices becoming stable the fact cannot be denied that all the tax proposals would lead to rise in prices. It is true that the Finance Minister finds himself between two grinding stones. On the one hand there is realism, which prompts him to adopt practical policies, which will encourage capital investment for greater production, generate savings by the people for investment in more and more industries, and create an atmosphere conducive to growth, and on the other there is radicalism.

AN HON. MEMBER : Socialism.

SHRI VAJPAYEE : Socialism has now become somewhat old. Now we are in the age of radicalism. It prevents them from becoming realistic. The reaction to this budget makes the Finance Minister's embarrassment clear. He has taken some steps that are conducive to increased production. I cannot definitely say if there will be increased production. He has brought down income tax from 97.50 per cent to 77 per cent. The period of the development rebate for industry, which was to expire in 1974, has been extended. These steps have been welcomed in the stock exchange. Yesterday even our friend Shri Piloo Mody was praising them. But the difficulty for the Finance Minister is that the more Shri Piloo Mody praises his steps the more our friend Shri Indrajit Gupta will condemn them. In such a situation what should he do ?

I say this terminology of socialism and capitalism has become old....(*Interruption*).....

SHRI PILOO MODY (Godhra) : Bring in Akhand Bharat.

SHRI VAJPAYEE : For Akhand Bharat Shri Piloo Mody would have to prepare his friend Zulfie.

SHRI PILOO MODY : Only he can save you.

SHRI VAJPAYEE : He could not save you. How can he save us ?

Sir, even in those countries where there are what we call capitalist governments they are changing into welfare governments. It is the duty of every administration to fulfil the basic needs of the common citizen. Whatever the ideology to which the powers that be may be tied, they will have to discharge the responsibility of fulfilling the basic needs of the citizen. The administration that does not do so cannot last, however high its proclamations.

Socialist Governments being Defeated

On the other hand in those Scandinavian countries that had socialist governments for the past 25 years the people have expressed their desire for a change. Socialist governments are being defeated in the elections. A political system caring for the citizen from cradle to education makes the people dependent and lazy, and obstructs their will to achieve. Obviously we will have to take the middle road. This government is also trying to take to such a middle road, but politics is proving an impediment.

The difficulty with the present government is that it wants political solutions for economic problems. These political solutions serve the purpose for a few days, but in the final analysis they cannot strengthen the economy.

I was greatly surprised to learn that the 14 banks which we had nationalised with such fanfare cannot stand the profitability test that had been laid down. We took over banks and gave compensation in return. It was hoped that they would make a profit of at least 5.5 per cent, as compensation had been paid on this basis.

But what is the history of those 14 banks, what are their achievements ? In 1971 this profitability was 5.1 per cent, but in 1972 it came down to 4.8 per cent, and in 1973 to 3.8 per cent. As I recall, in an election meeting in Moradabad, Defence Minister Shri Jagjivan Ram had plainly admitted that nationalisation of banks had failed because those classes of people who should have benefited from it were not benefitted. Some banks are actually in grave difficulties. The Allahabad Bank's profit, which was 4.2 per cent in 1971, came down to 2.2. per cent in 1972. In the case of the Bank of Maharashtra it was 7 per cent in 1971 but was reduced to zero per cent in 1972. With the Central Bank there is no difference in the profit in 1971 and 1972, it is 1.9 per cent, but it is very low according to the profitability test that has been laid down. The profit of the Indian Overseas Bank was 3.2 per cent in 1971, which has come down to 0.5 per cent in 1972. The profit of the Union Bank of India has also been reduced.

The Customs and Manners of Nationalised Banks

Sir, I know that in reply the Finance Minister would say the banks have their reserves, on the basis of which they can claim that there is no crisis for them. But I want that serious thought be given to the customs and manners of nationalised banks, their achievements and the absence of achievements. I know many examples where deposit collection targets are set for nationalised banks and then the employees and officers are forced to fulfil those targets by whatever means possible. I have an example before me. If the Finance Minister wants I can give the details. A certain person was asked to deposit money in the bank. He was made to deposit Rs. 20,000, but a fixed deposit document was prepared for two lakh rupees. In exchange of the fixed deposit of two lakh Rupees he was given a loan of one lakh 80 thousand Rupees. The amount of 20,000 Rupees he had deposited was black money, but in exchange he got a loan of one lakh 80 thousand... *(Interruption)*....

SHRI SAT PAL KAPOOR : What bank is this ?

SHRI VAJPAYEE : This amount of one lakh eighty thousand rupees is also black money—there are so many such incidents.

SHRI SAT PAL KAPOOR : It is not a theoretical matter. Name the bank. Don't just tell a story.

SHRI VAJPAYEE : It is the misfortune of the country that you think this is just a story.

SHRI SAT PAL KAPOOR : It is also unfortunate that you just tell a tale and walk away.

SHRI VAJPAYEE : I am not walking away anywhere. I am staying here to harass you.

Sir, what will be the banking system now ? Will the banks be allowed to be used for turning black money into white ? Will we permit the efficiency of nationalised banks to go down ? Shall we promote irregularities by fixing figures as targets ? If the Finance Minister wants to know more about this he can call for the reports of the inspectors who examine the accounts of nationalised banks. If necessary I can also give him more information on this.

SHRI Y.B. CHAVAN, Finance Minister : I would like to have the information.

SHRI VAJPAYEE : I am not saying this from a narrow point of view. Today no political party is saying that nationalised banks should again be privatised. It can also not be denied that nationalised banks have started giving loans where previously loans were not available, such as agriculture and small industries. Nationalised banks have progressed in the direction that we felt necessary. But we should not ignore the irregularities that we see today, we should ceaselessly try to correct them.

Sir, it is also necessary to stop this system of the government taking loans indiscriminately from banks. Not only the Government even big industrialists and businessmen are getting bank loans. In course of time this liberal loan process would promote inflation. Loans are given in excess of deposits collected. I would like to quote a sentence from a report by some economists :

> "During the end of 1969 and of the third week of January 1974 bank credit has increased by 87 cent."
>
> Another part of the report says :
>
> "Whereas the percentage of government expenditure available through bank loans in 1968-69 has gone up by 13 per cent in 1972-93".

The *Economic Review* has plainly admitted that our economy is in the grip of inflation. Production of goods and services has not grown adequately. Money supply has gone up. The money supply made in the form of loans should also be counted in this. For example, last year we were told that there would be a deficit of Rs. 87 crores but finally it came to Rs. 650 crores. I say it is still bigger, it is Rs. 1643 crores, because we would have to add net credit to it. It has not been added here, and the deficit has been shown on the lower side.

This year too the budget estimates a deficit of Rs. 125 crores. I do not know on what hope it has been shown less, it is actually going to increase. It is going to increase because we will have to pay the farmer more for foodgrains. The Agricultural Price Commission has agreed to a higher price. The State Governments have even gone two steps ahead. The Finance Minister has himself suggested a price of Rs. 105 per quintal for wheat in his State of Maharashtra. A meeting of Chief Ministers has been called. We hope it will decide upon a common price policy.

Don't Think Farmers Know Nothing

Now the truth cannot be ignored that the Indian farmer will not accept a low price. It is not necessary for anybody to invite him. I am grieved that my party has been charged with inciting farmers, and so they are asking for a higher price. Let us not think our farmers know nothing. When the farmer sees that goods are being bought from him at lower prices and the same goods are being sold in the market at higher prices he cannot be forced to sell at lower prices.

As a matter of principle no one can oppose a levy on big farmers, but it is seen that they form a nexus with officials and escape it, while small farmers get caught in its noose.

Sir, last year we had arranged a subsidy of Rs. 130 crores but it rose to Rs. 151 crores. Even if prices had not risen this subsidy would go up to Rs. 160 crores. But it seems prices will have to be raised. The result will be that on the one hand we will have to pay the farmer more and on the other we may also have to raise the issue price. This will make foodgrains more expensive. A major portion of the common man's budget is spent on foodstuffs. If foodgrain prices and edible oil prices go up—the Government is itself raising Vanaspati prices—If sugar prices go up, nothing can prevent the common man's life from becoming more miserable.

National Food Policy Necessary

I submit we should decide upon a national food policy. I agree that in the prevailing circumstances foodstuffs cannot be a matter for partisan politics, because even if we decide to import foodgrains they are not available abroad. It is also doubtful if we can afford the price on which they are available. But policies should not be decided under the influence of slogans. Then the question arises : do we adopt a practical policy or do we take steps to achieve cheap popularity—steps that would eventually fail and make our problem more serious ?

Sir, we were against State trading in foodgrains. We felt it was not practical. Ultimately the Government too came to adopt the same viewpoint. State trading in rice had to be given up. Now restrictions on the movement of coarse grain have been removed. May I say that in the present circumstances controls create artificial hindrances, promote corruption and encourage smuggling.

Sir, I sometimes feel that the country today needs Rafi Ahmed Kidwai. The Prime Minister is searching for an economic wizard. It is not a question of an individual, it is the question of a policy.

Successful Controls Depend Upon Stocks

Controls cannot be successful unless the Government has enough stocks to make up the artificial scarcity that they would produce. The situation today is such that the moment controls are imposed goods vanish from the market. Prices go up. Controls can possibly succeed if the government has sufficient stocks for the people's requirements, otherwise they are a remedy that is worse than the disease. I urge a practical point of view on this matter. Radical realism, not radical unrealism, should be the true guide. Hollow realism would only maintain the *status quo.* At the same time unrealism does not have the potential to bring about a revolution. Its attractive form may well win our hearts. What we need is radical realism and a realist revolution. If we can make this our guide in the economic field we could progress with change. Change is necessary. Disparity should decrease. But today lethargy seems to have gripped life. The will for revolution has become violent and is dancing the *Tandava* on the streets of Gujarat.

Sir, I have seen that every evening large numbers of hungry people gather before the hotels in the Jama Masjid area. There is a crowd in front of every hotel. They do not ask, they do not put forth their hand, but they certainly wish that a customer coming out of the hotel would arrange a little food for them. I wish the Prime Minister went and saw the scene. I am saying this because I went there yesterday. On the one hand we have this scene, on the other there may possibly be no vacant seats in five-star hotels. This gulf is widening. This widening gulf would endanger our entire democratic framework. But an authoritarian economy cannot succeed. We cannot take dictatorial decisions in a democratic structure.

Need for Fiscal Discipline

Sir, what is the position with our fiscal discipline ? Can the Finance Minister compel the States to stay within the overdraft regulations made by the Reserve Bank ? I am afraid these regulations would not be abided by.

SHRI Y.B. CHAVAN : They are being observed to a certain extent.

SHRI VAJPAYEE : To a certain extent is not enough. Look at the States. They are deficit budgets. Budgets for Haryana, Punjab, Jammu and Kashmir have been presented. They think the Centre has funds and Central assistance would be available even if they do not raise their own resources, even if they do not cut down on their expenditure. In view of the flood of new construction projects in Uttar Pradesh at election time there can be no hope of fiscal discipline on the part of the States. Now that you allow the State to start new projects worth Rs. 550 crores, elections are coming up in Gujarat too, and there again you will have to spend more money. It is necessary to try to impose fiscal discipline on the States. They should be clearly told that if they to not open up development avenues with their own resources their plan outlays would be cut.

This time the Finance Commission has given them good assistance. With the funds and resources available they should not find it difficult to develop. But States do not have fiscal discipline. We will have to introduce it.

Sir, the Finance Minister has tried to combine the budget with the first year of the Fifth Plan and establish an accord between the two, but I think there is no accord. Only the hard core of the Plan has remained; the rest of the whole Plan has disappeared.

In respect of agriculture the provision is one crore rupees less than last year. There is a shortfall of Rs. 39 crores in water and power, and of Rs. 90 crores in social and community services. The Central outlay for drought-prone areas is very small. I have doubts on how much the States would get under these heads. The rural employment plans that were inaugurated with so much fanfare are now in a shambles. In Uttar Pradesh only sign-boards remain for the projects initiated by the Prime Minister; there will be no construction work there. Even those arrangements that we had at first made in rural areas for minimised programmes have been done away with. On the one hand the outlay on social and community development services has been curtailed and on the other, the outlay on the Central Reserve Police is on the increase. In 1966-67 it was Rs. 7 crores, in 1970-71 it was Rs. 17 crores, in 1971-72 Rs. 23 crores and now it has exceeded Rs. 40 crores.

Finance Minister's Tax Proposals

I would now conclude my speech. One of the Finance Minister's tax proposals is wholy objectionable. It is about 50 per cent rise in the price of postcards. He should withdraw this proposal. According to the report of the Posts and Telegraphs department their profits have gone up and telephones are yielding higher revenue. Postcard prices cannot be viewed separately. It is surprising that the price of a postcard has gone up by as much as 50 per cent, but not that of envelopes. It is possible—I do not know—that the Finance Minister may not wish to put an equal burden on all. There should be rethinking in respect of the postcard.

Secondly, the rebate given in income tax is very late and very little. It should have been Rs. 7,500. The Minister says that there is only a minor rebate, upto Rs. 6,000. If you take prices into account this rebate should have been Rs. 10,000. I request the Finance Minister to reconsider this matter.

The rebate in income tax is not the same at every level. For instance a person earning Rs. 10,000 gets a rebate of Rs. 22, but one who earns 70,000 gets a rebate of Rs. 4,000. A person earning two and half lakh rupees gets a rebate of Rs. 22,000. For those with a high income the rebate is 11 per cent, for middle income it is five and a half and for small income earners it is 22 per cent. No one can object to small income earners getting a bigger rebate, but look at the difference in the rebates on high and middle incomes. It is not proper that middle income earners have been given a small rebate. This also needs to be looked into.

Fourthly, let the Government decide not to let the money supply increase by more than five per cent per year. Economic experts have also made such a recommendation. In case the Finance Minister wants to exceed this limit he should get Parliament's sanction. There is no doubt that indiscriminate printing of currency notes would lead our economy to the brink of ruin.

Finally, the Government must curtail its expenditure. This time the Finance Minister has not discussed this. If the country is in difficulties every section must see that the Administration and the society are aware of the situation. The Prime Minister appeals for solving problems on a war footing. Appeals are made to the people to lead a life of greater austerity. I think we can overcome this economic crisis if we cut down on Government expenditure, non-productive expenditure and promote an atmosphere of simplicity. But for this the Government would have to rise above all controversies. Thank you.

Undeclared Devaluation of the Rupee

Madam, the encouraging picture of the country's economy that the Finance Minister has painted does not fit in with the reality. Last year he had said that the stock market was bullish, so the situation was improving. This year he cannot even make that claim. It is good that the maximum number of people are buying company stocks, but the numbr of buyers cannot exceed 13 million. It is also good that an atmosphere conducive to investment in industries prevails, and if the policy of liberalisation has been adopted for this it should not be opposed. But the indiscriminate freedom to import that is being given in the name of liberalisation is creating difficulties for us. On this I shall say something later.

Madam, the Finance Minister has given a lot of figures in this speech. I too would like to place some figures before him. Figures speak and remove the curtain covering reality.

Can anyone deny that prices are rising ? Last year at this time the consumer price index was 619, now it is 700. The Finance Minister cannot get away by calling it just a seasonal increase. I think the whole season is getting spoilt for the Finance Minister. Autumn has set in even before Spring.

Is it not true that the purchasing power of the Rupee is steadily on the decline ? In March 1985 the real value of the Rupee was 17 Paise, in September 1986 it has been reduced to 14.79 Paise. There has been an undeclared devaluation of the Rupee. The Government has not declared it. Is it not true that the value of the Rupee has come down by 20 per cent as compared to the Pound, by 30 per cent as compared to the Deutsch Mark and by 40 per cent as compared to the Yen ?

Country's Debt Increased

Is it not true that the country's indebtedness has increased ? It would not be an exaggeration to say that the country is sinking in debt. In 1984-87 the amount of public debt has reached one lakh eight thousand sixty-five crores of rupees, which is 48 per cent of the GNP. This includes domestic as well as foreign loans. One-fourth of this is foreign. Repayment of the loan of fifty thousand million rupees taken from the IMF five years ago will begin this year. It seems 30 per cent will go toward debt servicing. This means if we step up exports—and it is necessary to increase exports, we shall support proper steps taken in this direction—out of one Rupee we earn through exports 29 or 30 paise will go for payment of interest on the loan.

Rajya Sabha on December 12, 1986 on the occasion of a Review of the Country's Economy

There is also no likelihood of a decline in the loss of foreign trade. In 1985-86 the loss was to the tune of Rs. 8600 crores. Foreign goods were indiscriminately imported. Now our industrialists have started complaining against them. So long the same person was Foreign Minister and Commerce Minister.

SHRI V.P. SINGH, Finance Minister : I would like to inform Shri Vajpayee that according to import figures of September the Commerce Secretary showed us for the six months of this year, the import increase is only 1.1 per cent.

SHRI CHATURANAN MISHRA (Bihar) : It is not the same policy as before. You have put restrictions on many things. VCR is not to be allowed in. You have restricted it.

SHRI V.P. SINGH : I am telling the result.

SHRI CHATURANAN MISHRA : I said you have changed the old policy. We can say you have become alert. But I have to say you said a wrong thing.

SHRI VAJPAYEE : Madam, we do not mind if there is some slight improvement in the patient's condition. But let not the Finance Minister labour under the illusion that the patient has fully recovered and is ready to run on the path of progress. He is talking of six months, but he cannot say with confidence what will happen after six months. In spite of being Vishwanath Pratap Singh he cannot say with *vishwas* (confidence).

Madam, a problem cannot be viewed in parts. Was it not a wrong decision to amalgamate the Foreign and Commerce Ministries ? How was this decision taken ? It proved wrong and had to be changed, but the damage was done. This is however a political problem and I do not want to inject too much politics into this debate.

Unemployment Increasing

Madam, unemployment too is increasing. In 1985 the number of those registering their names with employment exchanges rose by 11 per cent. In reply to my Unstarred Question No. 1334 the Minister for Labour has admitted that this figure, which was 226.7 lakhs in December 1985, rose to 288.5 lakhs in August 1986. The Labour Minister added that even those who have jobs register their names. At the same time it is also true that there are those who are unempolyed who do not register their names. It cannot be denied that unemployment is on the increase.

Madam, it is also clear that government expenditure is increasing. The Finance Minister had given assurances and he also took some steps in an attempt to cut down non-Plan expenditure, but the attempt has not succeeded.

There is also a continuing process of supplementary demands. We had the first instalment in July, now the second instalment is ready. In the first instalment a demand for Rs. 64 crores was made, now a sanction for Rs. 3038.54 crores is being sought. Madam, if we add the two the total exceeds Rs. 3200 crores. This year's budget had an estimated deficit of Rs. 3600 crores and the supplementary demands are for Rs. 3700 crores. The deficit is bigger than the estimate, the expenditure is also bigger than the estimate. The Government will have to provide for a deficit of Rs. 7500 crores.

The Finance Minister has admitted in his speech that the debt servicing expenditure would now rise to Rs. 10,150 crores. Defence expenditure is expected to rise by Rs. 11,900 crores. Clearly, the Fourth Pay Commission has placed a bigger burden on the government, leading to problems being created in the states. I hope the Finance Minister is not unaware of them.

Now inequality will not be tolerated in the salaries of those employed in public enterprises, Central Government offices and State Government offices. Where are the resources for this ? This is a big question-mark. But if we increase salaries at the Centre and give more facilities to its employees but deny them to the employees of the States and Municipalities it would be against the call of the times. I would like to know from the Finance Minister what the difficulty is.

SHRI V.P. SINGH : Are you talking economics or politics ?

AN HON. MEMBER : Both ....(*Interruption*).

SHRI VAJPAYEE : Madam, the question is, what is the Government going to do ? How will non-plan expenditure be cut down, and by how much ? Yesterday Dr. Jha had raised the question of waste. It is a very important matter. The non-Plan expenditure involves waste and the Plan expenditure too is not being incurred in the proper manner and on proper things. Is there no scope for saving in the defence expenditure ? But the problem is, there is no an atmosphere of austerity, of avoiding waste, in the country. If we have a series of *tamashas* in Delhi there cannot be an atmosphere of austerity.

Foreign Collaborations

Madam, at the rate collaboration agreements are being made with foreign firms and doors are being opened to multinational companies there is a possibility of the national goal of self-reliance being jeopardised. Are foreign companies anxious for our development ? Is it not true that their eyes are on their profit, not on our progress ? They do not want development, they want a market, they want our cheap labour. I have read some portions of the speech of the chairman of the multi-national company Coopers & Lybrand. They are really surprising. I quote :

> "A hundred million people classified as middle-class, living largely in four cities, suggest a highly targetable market for American industrial goods and services. In many ways India ranks among the top five markets in the world from the perspective of attractiveness and growth for the U.S. manufacturers."

The Finance Minister may consider it a recommendation, but for me it is a danger signal. They are building bridges of praise for us, but it is not only impossible to cross over them, it seems difficult even to pass under them. It is said :

> "India should be able to maintain an average 15-year growth rate in excess of seven per cent annually. This puts it among the fastest growing countries in the world."

The average of our growth rate is 3.5 per cent. It seems as if our food production has stagnated at 150 million tons. The industrial growth is not satisfactory, but multinational companies think it could be seven per cent for 15 consecutive years. Such optimism is not in evidence either in the Finance Ministry or in the Planning Commission. I want to know the secret behind this. Now there is a race between the Americans and the Japanese for capturing Indian markets. Grady Means says : "Aggressiveness of the Japanese corporation in Indian markets is a matter for concern".

How is Japan entering ? Why has America lagged behind ? There is a race going on. If we are under the impression that they are anxious for India's development we are not doing justice to the country.

The Cabinet Controversy

Madam, I would like to raise a rather delicate matter. Is there full accord between the Prime Minister and the Finance Minister ? Or is there a communication gap ? On September 19 (*Interruption*)....

SHRI V.P. SINGH : Come over and become the link.

SHRI VAJPAYEE : Now that our friend Arjun Singh has become the Communications Minister it is no wonder there is a communication gap. But on September 19—I am saying this in all seriousness — the talks the Prime Minister had with industrialists in Calcutta and the report that Shri Bajaj gave of those talks indicate that the Finance Minister did not abide by the guidelines which the Prime Minister had laid down in respect of raids on big houses. Is this true ? If it is, it is most regrettable, it should be corrected. The Finance Minister first went in for liberalisation, reduced taxes, and gave an opportunity to those with ill-gotten wealth to declare it and pay the due tax on it. This was all right in the beginning. It would have been better if at first time had been given and then raids made. But will there be selective raids now ? Will the raiding activity be guided by political considerations ?

The second point I want to ask about is the public controversy that is going on between two ministers, two members of the Cabinet, who are talking about expanding the public sector and who are calling each other Don Quixote and Sancho Panza—how far is this proper ?.... (*Interruption*)....I don't want to make them fight, I want to end the fight. The government should have a clear point of view regarding the public sector. We are against its indiscriminate expansion—neither are we against it today nor have we been aginst it from the start. We said there should be consolidation, not expansion. Show us that it makes a profit. But the Government has an uncertain policy. The entire structure of the Seventh Plan rests on the profit from the public sector. It is not enough to make a Bajaj or a Tata the head of the Indian Airlins or Air India. I cannot understand what difficulty stands in the way of your strengthening the public sector and making it an instrument of the country's development.

The undertakings of the States are in a still worse condition. Their power houses are in darkness. Their buses do not run. There is corruption everywhere. These States will approach you tomorrow for bigger salaries for their employees. They will demand amendments in the recommendations of the Finance Commission. Please sit with them and think about how this loss could be reduced, how financial resources could be marshalled.

The Finance Minister Deserves Congratulations but...

One more thing. You have been talking with industrialists. It is good to meet them. The Finance Minister has come with an open book. I welcome it. I would like to congratulate him, but I cannot do so because my congratulation could go against him. Somebody might report to the Prime Minister that Vajpayee was praising the Finance Minister, and that would be taken to mean something was definitely wrong somewhere. Openness is a good thing, but why don't you talk with farmers and consumers as openly as you talk with representatives of commerce and industry ? Do the farmers get the right price for their produce ? If prices rise does the benefit reach the farmer ? Or does the middleman pocket it ? Cannot the middleman's profit be reduced ? Further, can your discussions with industrialists not help you to assess the investment on factory products, the various taxes on them and the generally proper profit on them ? Cannot such information be placed before the country ?

We had got such a study made by a group of professors of Nagpur. A popular company's scooter sells for Rs. 12000. Including the investment expenditure, adding tax and even including 4 per cent profit the scooter should in no circumstances cost more than Rs. 7 to 8 thousands. Is not this price of Rs. 12000 high ? A cake of soap that costs Rs. 1.25 to make sells for Rs. 5. We want to know the amount of tax on it. The buyer should know the amout of the central tax, the provincial tax and the profit. There has to be adequate profit. Without proper profit no one will run an industry, but it should not be indiscriminate. It should not be excessive on the price that the common man of this poor country pays. I request the Finance Minister to consider this aspect of the matter. Thank you.

What are the IMF Conditionalities ?

Sir, I had made some points while speaking in this House on the Motion of Thanks on July 18—by that time the Budget had not been presented. I had said that the biggest reason of the balance of payments crisis was the illegal expatriation of capital out of India. In this connection I had referred to gold smuggling. I had put the responsibility on under-invoicing and over-invoicing. If we calculate the wealth flowing out of the country in this manner it would come to 56 billion dollars in the last 10 years.

The Finance Minister has called it flight of capital. It is not flight, it is theft, plain theft. The country's wealth is leaving the country and we cannot stop it. When we are faced with a serious economic problem and need the funds deposited abroad we give it amnesty, and then a process of converting black money into white starts. Sir, how long will it go on ?

Sir, in my speech I had made some concrete suggestions, but I am sorry to say they were not paid heed to and the budget proposals were not formulated in their light. The Government is still not prepared to say what steps are being taken to prevent such illegal expatriation of capital in future. Unless we take effective steps capital would keep flowing out and the country would keep sinking in an economic crisis. If the Government has thought of something in this matter it should take the House into confidence.

Sir, I had also demanded that the House and the people should also be taken into confidence about the basis on which we are holding discussions with the International Monetary Fund. I had demanded that copies of correspondence conducted by two previous Finance Ministers and the present Finance Minister with the Board of Directors and Managing Director of the IMF be placed on the Table of the House, but the Government is silent on this point too.

In the meanwhile, borrowing from the IMF continued. Everyday we read in the papers about IMF delegations coming and going and having discussions. There are 30 countries in the Board of Directors. They know the conditions of borrowing. Our Shri Gopi Arora also knows those conditions, but we do not know, Members of this House do not know. Is this a satisfactory situation ? The Government should think seriously about it. We should at least know what is cooking with the IMF.

Sir, in an interview to the *Economic Times* on July 26, 1991 the Finance Minister had said and I quote:

> "There will be a tremendous revolt on the streets of the country if all the conditionalities are accepted."

Lok Sabha on August 5, 1991 during discussion on General Budget

All right, the Government of India is not going to accept all conditions—neither should it, but what are these conditions that the IMF wants to make us accept ? Are they so humiliating that they would cause a revolt on the streets of the country ? This is what the Finance Minister himself says. In the light of these words it becomes all the more imperative that all things are made clear to the House. What are the conditions ? Which of them have we accepted and which have we rejected ?

Sir, this is necessary also because the IMF has dealings not only with us, but also with other developing countries. So far as we are concerned, during the 40 years of independence we have set up an industrial framework, we have become self-sufficient in food and progressed in other directions as well. Although the country has been entangled in economic difficulties because of wrong policies we are in a position to face up to the IMF at least to a certain extent. But will the humiliating IMF conditions not apply to those countries that are worse off than us ? Should those conditions not be discussed ? If the House is not taken into confidence in this respect the country would not know the whole picture.

Role of State Bank in Foreign Borrowing

Sir, I had also demanded information regarding the role of the State Bank in taking foreign loans. It is not the State Bank's business to raise foregin loans. That is the business of the Reserve Bank. How did the State Bank come into the picture ? It seems the Government is misusing the State Bank. The news has just come that efforts are on to remove the State Bank Chairman and the Managing Director too in a hurry, although their tenures are not yet over. The reason is that the Government wants to cover up certain things. In his interview to the *Economic Times* the Finance Minister had also said: "I am worried about the banking system which is burdened with many strains." What are these strains, these pressures ? The Finance Minister is not present in the House, nor is Shri Potdukhe. His name means 'stomach–ache.' I don't want to give him a headache.

The 1991 report of the State Bank has just been published. It is an annual report. According to it the State Bank incurred foreign loans of Rs. 18,000 crores which rose by Rs. 8000 crores during the period March, 1989 to March, 1991. This is a serious matter, a matter for concern. In this respect the role of the State Bank should be clarified.

Sir, thought should also be given to the role of our officials in the balance of payments crisis. During 1985-1991 the situation went on worsening every month. Did any of our officials give a warning about this ? Did they discharge their responsibility ? Is it not their duty to tell the Government, tell the concerned Minister about any step that they might think wrong ? It is true that the policy will be determined by the Cabinet, by the political leaders. The political leaders fight elections. They have to be responsible to the people. The people can defeat them in the elections. But what was the role of the senior officials responsible for financial and economic matters ? This needs to be seriously looked into.

In the course of a seminar Shri Vimal Jalan had said: "Bureaucrats do not care as to what the consequences of their actions are." If the report of this seminar, which is published, is true, it is quite sensational. Now the Government is formulating some policies. This same administration, this same apparatus, will be chargec with implementing the new policies. Will they be successfully implemented ?

Industrialist–Leader–Bureaucrat nexus

I want to say something about industrialists too. Industrialists demand liberàlisation but there are industrialists who are used to a protected market in India, who fear competition, who want that controls and regulations should continue and who line their pockets by way of a nexus with corrupt leaders and the bureaucracy. Now they too will have to face competition. Are they ready to face the challenge ?

I would like to quote a small instance in point. Recently there was a discussion with the Prime Minister about how far the present subsidy on fertilizer was called for, and if it is to be scaled sown, how much.

Sir, do we know that we spend foreign exchange on importing urea and we want to set up five gas-based fertilizer plants to make up the shortfall ? According to the promoters of three out of five plants, construction work has virtually ground to a halt for want of a green signal from the Government in some matters. Everyday we are losing foreign exchange worth Rs. 4 crores while the matter on which the green signal has not been given is quite small. But who will give the green signal, and why should he give it ? If this situation continues the liberalisation of the economy that we are talking of will not yield the expected benefit.

Expenditure Tax on Small Hotels

Sir, now I would like to speak about some tax proposals. The Government has talked of amending the Expenditure Tax Act, 1987. So long the expenditure of five-star hotels was being taxed. But now the Finance Minister wants to extend the tax limit to include even small hotels with just one air-conditioner. The number of five-star hotels is small and the tax levied on them can be easily realised. If the small eating places spread all over the country are brought within the net of this tax it may not lead to an increase in Government income. What is definite is that corruption will increase. Proprietors of small hotels will be subjected to harassment. I urge the Government to rethink over this matter.

Increase Income-Tax Exemption Limit

So far as the question of individual income tax limit is concerned the limit of Rs. 22,000 really makes no sense in view of inflation. The prices may rise still further in future. We have been demanding that this limit should be Rs. 40,000. I demand that this budget fix it at least at Rs. 30,000.

Sir, one thing that repeatedly bothers me is, has any gentleman evading taxes, ever been punished in this country ? I say gentelman because he is not convicted. I cannot charge such a *Sajjan* with being a *Durjan*. Cases were filed and suits were conducted but I do not remember if ... any member can refresh my memory. . . Shri Indrajit Gupta may help in this matter.

SHRI INDRAJIT GUPTA (Midnapur): Why do you need help ?

SHRI VAJPAYEE : Has any tax-evader ever been punished in this country ? Do you recollect any such example ?

SHRI INDRAJIT GUPTA : There is no proof of tax-evasion

SHRI VAJPAYEE : This means they can evade taxes and yet flaunt their innocence. They were so smooth with the evasion that they could not be caught. But I know about an instance in England. There was a jockey of the Queen called Sir Lester Pigot.

SHRI ABDUL GHAFOOR (Gopalganj) : He was a good jockey.

SHRI VAJPAYEE : Ghafoor Sahib has good knowledge about horses. But I am talking of a species that is lower than horses.

Sir, Sir Lester Pigot was given a prison sentence of two and a half years and taxed heavily. It is necessary that people should pay taxes honestly, but it is also necessary to see that the tax burden should not be so heavy that it is more profitable to evade taxes and a losing bargain to pay them.

In his speech the Finance Minister has quoted Prof. Caldor to the effect that the tax limit should not exceed 45 per cent. But he has not implemented it this time; he has not shown the courage to do so. He says wait for five years. Who knows where the Finance Minister will be, we all will be, five years from now ? Let him not ask us to wait so long.

We really feel that the taxation limit should not exceed 40 per cent. Whatever the tax you impose, realise it honestly. In that be firm, don't give any concession. But if tax evasion is to be stopped the tax-burden must not be unbearable for the tax-payer.

The budget has talked of bringing down the depreciation allowance. It has been reduced from 33 per cent to 25 per cent.

SHRI INDRAJIT GUPTA : They are bringing it down.

SHRI VAJPAYEE : That is what I am saying. I say the budget has reduced the depreciation allowance to 25 per cent. This is a big cut. I suggest it should be stabilised at 25 per cent. There is now a new Industrial Policy, in the light of which an attempt should be made to give some stability to industrial houses.

New Avenues of Income

The Finance Minister has said he is one of the most harassed Finance Ministers. We sympathise with him. Even, we are not only talking about tax concessions; I would also like to suggest some new avenues of income. The Finance Minister has announced the application of the Modvat Scheme to fibres and yarn. His intentions are good but the result is wrong. The Government would lose an income of Rs. 230 crores. But the Finance Minister expressed the hope in his budget speech that this would benefit the consumer. This is not happening. Fibre and yarn industries have hiked their prices. They not only absorbed the yarn concession, they also raised prices to

11 rupees per kg. or Rs. 11000 per ton. If the consumer is not benefited the whole purpose of the Finance Minister fails.

Sir, in this connection I would like to point out that the same sort of situation had developed in 1988. The 156th Report of the PAC had strongly criticised giving concessions that neither benefit the consumer nor bring income to the Government. That report had created a lot of commotion in the House. I think the manufacturers of fibre and yarn should be clearly told to give concession to consumers, otherwise this concession should be withdrawn. Things cannot go on like this.

Sir, the Finance Minister has admitted large-scale tax evasion in the country. They want to give the evaders one last chance to bring out black money. He has said this in his speech. According to one estimate black money to the tune of Rs. 80,000 crores is generated in the country every year. Now an attempt is being made to change this black money into white, for which the Finance Minister has proposed three plans.

Under the first plan those who deposit their black money before November 30 will be given a pardon, they will not be prosecuted, but they will have to give up 40 per cent of the black money. The second plan is to improve th balance of payments position. It gives the freedom to any individual to bring in foreign exchange in terms of rupees. There will be no gift tax on it. There will also be no inquiry into where the money came from. Under the third plan the State Bank will issue India Development Bonds in dollars. These can be purchased by Non–Resident Indians. I am surprised. Why did not the Finance Minister look at these plans as a whole ?

Hawala Premium Rate Going Up

In order to bring out hidden black money he has urged people to deposit it, let 40 per cent go, and has assured that you will not be asked where it came from. You will not be penalised. But his second and third plans have made a mess of all the plans. If on deposit of 40 per cent black money with the Government one can get the facility to convert the rest of the black money into white why will there be no efforts to send the money out by way of hawala premium and then bring it in dollars instead of depositing it with the Government ? Such attempts are going on. Hawala premium rates have gone up. I do not think people will deposit money with the National Housing Bank. These plans should have been kept separate. All the three should not have come together. Perhaps the Finance Minister did not receive the right advice.

As you know, the hawala premium rate has now risen to 30 per cent. The Government wants 40 per cent deposited. Crores of Rupees flow out of the country every day by way of hawala transactions. Now the Finance Minister has opened the way for its return in dollars. This is a grave situation and should be seriously looked into. Why would people incur a loss by paying a double tax ?

Excuse me, but those who have taken the money out are very clever people. We may well try to rouse the sentiment of patriotism in them, but they are greedy. They have not done justice to the interests of the country, and if they are to be persuaded to bring the money it is possible only after plugging all types of holes and then giving them adequate incentives. The question is does the Government want to check flight of capital or does it want to promote it ? I suggest that the Government reconsider all these three plans.

There can be other plans, other techniques by which Indian capital that has gone abroad can return. The Government is itself ready to give equity shares in some public sector companies. The Finance Minister has talked of 20 per cent. They are preparing to invite some foreign companies for a 51 per cent partnership and some even for 100 per cent. I suggest that the government assess the net worth of some good public sector companies. Their share-holding should be kept in a national renewal fund and their price fixed as per evaluation. Every share should have a face value of Rs. 10 and the shares should be sold to the public. It is not necessary to ask where the money came from. This will on the one hand procure money and on the other save us from the ill-effects of the other plans.

Gold Smuggling

Sir, I now come to gold smuggling. So far, one lakh six thousand tons of gold have been mined all over the world. Out of this we have ten thousand tons, out of which 5000 tons is hoarded gold, 5000 tons smuggled gold. If we arrange to take from the people 2000 tons of this gold—I am suggesting 2000 tons, not talking of 5000 tons, it is necessary that this gold should not only be in the form of ornaments, but in the form of biscuits too. If, in view of the serious situation, we can acquire 2000 tons of gold for the nation and acquire it on the basis of gold bonds at two and a half per cent maturing in ten years, it would be possible to open up a new avenue for solving the present problem. I recollect that after the Chinese aggression, when Pandit Nehru was alive, we had appealed for gold donations. Gold had come in big quantities. We had returned it with interest. The present economic problem is no less serious. The gold lies buried underground, we have to bring it out. We should find a way to solve the present problem with its help. The Finance Minister is quite silent on this.

SMT. GITA MUKHERJEE : What is the difficulty if we trade in rupees and in silver ? What is the need for gold ? For dowry ? Don't take gold as dowry.

SHRI VAJPAYEE : We are not at the age where we should talk of dowry.

SHRI SANTOSH MOHAN DEO, Minister of State in the Ministry of Steel : You are underestimating yourself.

SHRI VAJPAYEE : I will take your expert advice in this matter.

Sir, if we can succeed in acquiring 2000 tons of gold it will be worth 36 billion dollars. Now gold has lost its glitter in the world. Even during the Gulf War the price of gold did not rise—only slightly, not much. Now people want to keep wealth in other forms. In our country too we should motivate people for this; it is necessary to motivate them. At the same time we should assure them that their gold is safe, and if it does not remain safe they will be provided with resources in place of the gold so that they can fall back upon on a rainy day. I have many proposals for this, but again the Finance Minister is absent.

AN HON. MEMBER : The Minister of State is present.

SHRI VAJPAYEE : Yes, he is there.

Give Land in Lieu of Gold

If we sell gold worth 25 billion dollars for paying off our debts and invest the rest at 10 per cent profit it would help us to solve the economic problem facing the country. If we so wish we can assure the donor of the gold that after 10 years he would be given a good plot of land in a big city. Along with gold the attraction for land is growing a lot. Land is dwindling. People are ready to spend anything for land. The Government will have to take the responsibility. It has a lot of land that is lying idle. Shri Jaswant Singh, who is present here, was the Chairman, and he has found out that lakhs of acres of land are lying in Army Cantonments. The Army should have the land it needs, and we should also bear future expansion in mind, but if the Government so wishes it can promise to give land in big cities in lieu of the gold as well as interest. This would motivate the people to give gold. The Government should go deeply into this.

SHRI INDRAJIT GUPTA : Who knows what government would be there after 10 years ?

MANY HON. MEMBERS : The country will be there.

SHRI VAJPAYEE : Now people are taking Vikas Patras, some for five years, some for 10. Nothing is possible without trust, Comrade. At least some trust is necessary.

I suggest that NRIs be permitted to import gold into the country, but it should be only in the form of biscuits, in no other form. There should be a flat rate duty on it and it should be realised either in dollars or in gold. This will stop smuggling and also fulfil domestic demand for gold to a certain extent. At the same time the hawala business will also slacken.

Return of Indian Capital from Abroad Necessary

Sir, other steps are also necessary for the return of Indian capital back home. As I said earlier we are inviting private capital, foreign capital for partnership in the public sector under the new Industrial Policy. If the Government so wishes it can give serious thought to this matter and prepare a plan. But so far the Government has not been able to make up its mind. This is because while everybody realises the seriousness of the problem, but the problem is how to find out a way through the political pressure. I say let the ruling party make up its mind and then approach the Opposition. At present there is no communication. Policies have been determined and have also been placed before the House. The alternative before us is either to reject those policies or adopt them. This is not a satisfactory situation.

The point I made earlier in my speech and which I would like to repeat in conclusion of my speech is about long-term changes in our policies for overcoming the serious economic difficulties facing us. As I said in the beginning, we gave amnesty to black money—it was given earlier too—it changed black money into white and the black money-makers went back to their old ways. Ten years from now black money will again become a problem for us. It will have to be stopped, its generation will have to be stopped. So if the economy is freed from rules and regulations and from the stranglehold of the bureaucracy we should welcome it.

It is proper and necessary that the Government should pay more attention to neglected classes and neglected regions. The Government of today cannot rest with only maintaining law and order, it has to be concerned with the welfare of the society. Many things it will have to do itself, but while doing them it will have to take care not to misuse our limited resources and to chalk out the right direction for the future.

I trust that in his reply to the debate the Finance Minister will also answer to these basic questions and try to take the House into confidence. Thank you.

Public Awareness Needed to Revolutionise Economic Policies

Sir, now that this discussion is about to end and the Finance Minister is about to reply to it I shall not stand for long between him and the House.

He has been quite plain in painting the economic situation of the country in his speech. I would like to congratulate him on it. The speech makes it clear that although we may have got over the temporary difficulty regarding foreign borrowings we are not yet out of the woods.

Economic Reforms

During the last six months many changes have been brought about in economic policies, in industry, in trade and in finances. They are long-term changes and from some points of view they are basic changes. I am not one of those who say the old structure has failed. After independence we adopted a mixed economy. It was the right decision, but later, due to political reasons, the area of state authority expanded. Our industrialists too did not do justice to the country. Their eyes were not so much on development as on profit. They wanted a protected market, not competition.

What happened in Europe has made it clear that there can be no economic development without competition. A monopoly, whether of the Government or of industrialists, proves an impediment in the way of economic development. I am not finding fault with the concept of public sector enterprises. Such enterprises were set up for the good of the people, but we could not run them properly because we could not manage them professionally. We left public sector enterprises to the mercy of IAS officers. They got training in administration, not in running an industry. Now these industries are running in losses. What should we do ? We raise prices of their products. This becomes a tax on the people, it does not solve the problem. But if industries are to be closed down on a big scale—a big list that has been published indicates this—has the country been prepared for this ? My complaint is that, in fact, the situation is such that the Finance Minister had to take some decisions in a hurry. The country was not mentally prepared for the long-term changes of liberalisation and privatisation that we made. In particular the labour class was not at all prepared. If the plants close down where will they go ? I fear the new economic policies may dash against two rocks and break into bits. One of the rocks is Inflation. Prices are rising.

The Finance Minister can provide immediate relief by importing oil, but that would increase the losses in foreign trade. Still oil will have to be

---

Lok Sabha on December 18, 1991 during discussion on the Economic Situation

imported, people would raise a hue and cry for oil because we want to bring about a change within the democratic framework. This framework makes for very competitive politics. There is a race on, and elections might take place any day. This is the people's feeling.

A national consensus should have been developed on these reforms and this process should have taken place before implementing the reforms. This was not done. There is a general feeling that these reforms have been made under pressure from the IMF. This is another difficulty. Lack of mental preparedness for this has led to some disorder. I see that during the past two-three years prices and unemployment are on the rise. I was looking at some figures of the International Labour Organisation. According to them by 1992-93 there would be one to three million people wandering about in search of jobs, and in 1993-94 this figure would rise to four to six million. It is possible that industrial production may grow but employment opportunities will decline.

We are talking of new technology. We do need new technology, production must increase, productivity must rise, the quality of our goods must improve. We have to sell them in the world's market. Who will buy inferior goods ? But when new technology comes employment opportunities will decline. Then where will people go ?

Losses in Public Sector Industries

Public sector enterprises that run in loss have to be closed down. Where will the retrenched labour go ? On this point we need a general consensus among all political parties. That general consensus is absent. Just now there was a reference to the strike of the 26th. I am not blaming our leftist parties, they are just doing their duty. There is a certain way in which they think. Now either there is an in-depth debate on this....(*Interruption*).

SHRI BHOGENDRA JHA (Madhubani) : Vajpayeeji, your stand has never been that public sector industries should be closed down, that the patient should be killed. Why don't you say that their working should be improved and workers should be made partners in running them ?

SHRI VAJPAYEE : Efforts must be made to improve the working of public sector industries. I know there are some industries that cannot run. What do we do about textile mills ?

SHRI BHOGENDRA JHA : They are also in the private sector.

SHRI VAJPAYEE : That is true. What are we to do about them ? I may also refer to the Government's attitude. There is a jute mill called New Central Mills Company in 24-Parganas, South. As many as 13,000 workers work there. The owners declared a lock-out in April, 1986 but the workers came together and said we would contribute from our earnings. The workers were prepared to give as much as Rs. 6 crores. They actually gave the amount, but the BIFR delayed its report and the financial agencies did not give money. This was perhaps the only plant that the workers undertook to run in spite of its being sick, but because of the Government's wrong policies the plant could not start. There may be other examples as well, where sick industries could be run with the workers' help and improved management. I am not in favour of closing them down, but we now have some white elephants on our hands and they need a remedy. At the same time some exit policy needs to be formulated.

If mill workers come on to the streets because of the mills closing down—excuse me, but if there is corruption in allotting mills under privatisation to industrialists the workers would never tolerate it. This is what is happening in the Dala cement factory. Excuse me, but the public sector has become a cesspool of corruption.

Misuse of Public Sector Industries

I would like to give an example. I shall give no names. The Central Government had changed and V.P. Singh's government was in office. We were not a part of it, we were supporting it from outside. A certain gentleman came to see me with a high official of a public sector industry. I shall not give his name, but if the Finance Minister wants I could give it to him later. They told me that a new chairman, a new managing director was to be appointed for that industry. They took a name and said if I helped the appointment of that person they could arrange for a donation of one crore rupees every year from that industry to our party. I was amazed. Are public sector industries meant for this ? But this was how they were misused. This was another reason for their losses. Now the public sector cannot be run like this. These distortions have set in. Controls were imposed as an aid, but they led to artificial scarcity, corruption increased, and the competitive spirit died. There should be no unnecessary controls, no unnecessary regulations. But this will lead to cut throat competition. How to save the small man, the small entrepreneur, the small farmer from it ? This is the challenge. I submit that although the Finance Minister is very intelligent he cannot find an answer to this challenge without arriving at a consensus. The decisions may be right, but for their implementation we need the right atmosphere in the country. It is not yet there. Neither is an effort being made to create it.

Need for a Consensus

There is a shortage of electricity. Excuse me—this will be published against me—farmers are getting it at a nominal rate and even that is not realised. There is unlimited power theft, but you cannot stop it.

SHRI BHOGENDRA JHA : Is there less power theft in the cities ?

SHRI VAJPAYEE : Yes, it is there too. You cannot stop it. As for rates, You cannot hike them. Electricity boards are running at a loss. Just now our friend suggested that the Centre should take them over, but a Central take over would not solve the problem. It is the same malady everywhere. There is no work-ethic in this country. We have to work extremely hard in these critical times if we have to resolve the crisis. This feeling is absent. The Government is unable to create this feeling. So I fear inflation will go up and people would come out into the streets. As our friend said, unemployment will grow, the youth would come on to the streets, and a political duel would start. The decision to lower the subsidy on fertilizer was basically right. How much subsidy, and for how long ? This country cannot depend upon subsidies. But who will lower them. And if you lower them we shall accept it here and oppose it outside. Then what happens ? There is still time. Arrive at a consensus.

You have talked of curtailing government expenditure. Excuse me, there has not been much curtailment. There is no atmosphere of simplicity. There is no realisation that the country is in difficulties. There is no determination to unitedly resolve this crisis. How will you overcome it ? If there is a political competition let it be so. I do not wish to say anything more, but if the Finance Minister wants his changes to succeed, prepare an atmosphere for success. Develop a general consensus. This is my submission. Thank you.

The Economic Crisis : Who is to be Blamed ?

Sir, I rise to initiate a discussion on the budget proposals. This is the Finance Minister's second budget. I have no hesitation in saying that he has shown great diligence and intelligence in preparing the budget proposals. That day it almost seemed as if Dr. Manmohan Singh had lived up to his name and bewitched the House by his *mohini*, his spell. Those who saw the budget on television were also highly impressed. But this spell like any spell, does not last long. When realisation dawns the charm breaks. When the people emerged out of the charm created by his speech they realised that the actual situation was not only different, it was very serious.

Any budget presented in the prevailing circumstances would naturally be tested against two main criteria : inflation and growing unemployment. No one can deny that inflation, which had gone down a little in the meanwhile, is again growing. During the last 25 days it has increased by 0.1 per cent. It is likely to increase further. People are apprehensive about it.

So far as the question of removing unemployment is concerned, the budget speech is mostly silent on it. An exit policy has been discussed, but there is no provision for an entry policy. It is feared that people might lose their jobs. There would be a new labour force in the market, searching for jobs. We want to compete in the world market. For that competition we want to make the best possible goods. We want to use new technology. The net result will be that the number of people working in the organised sector would come down. Sick industries are being closed down—with some industries that is the only way. I shall come to that later, but clearly the people there would lose their jobs.

The Finance Minister has announced a renewal fund. This is a step in the right direction. But danger looms ahead, and the Finance Minister has himself admitted that although the economic boat of the country has weathered the storm it has yet to reach the haven of safety. He wants time for it, he wants three years. Who will give three years to come out of the crisis ? Unemployed youth wandering all around in search of jobs, the labourer who has lost his job, the toiling peasant, Dalit, those members of Scheduled Castes who have suffered from deprivation for long years and are groping in the dark—none of these see any hope in this budget. Will they wait for three years ? I do not know why the Finance Minister has talked of three years. Can this period not be shortened ? This is a democratic country, price-rise and unemployment

Lok Sabha on March 23, 1992 while initiating discussion on General Budget

would generate social discontent and the people would come out on the streets. On what basis will they be asked to have patience ?

An Open Debate on Economic Policies : A Good Beginning

Sir, one good thing is that we are now openly discussing economic policies which are now being looked at as economic policies, not as a part of politics. So long politics was dominant. For some time the Finance Minister had fallen a victim to that politics when, in the other House, he held the V.P. Singh and Chandrashekhar Governments responsible for all economic ills. When he said in his first speech that we were all guilty I had said we were all guilty but those who were the longest in power were the most guilty and those who were never in power not guilty at all. But why this apportioning of blame ? Today the Finance Minister can be asked—during the days of the Janata Government you were the Finance Secretary, and a good Finance Secretary. and so in the decade of the seventies the country made progress. Things went wrong in the eighties. At that time the Finance Minister became Governor of the Reserve Bank and the Chief Economic Advisor. He used to advise my friend Shri Chandrashekhar. What sort of advice did he give ?

SHRI CHANDRASHEKHAR (Ballia) : He can himself say.

SHRI VAJPAYEE : You could say a little too.

Now Dr. Singh is the Finance Minister. What was his stand so far ? Does the whole blame for the economic crisis go to the V.P. Singh and Chandrashekhar Governments, which were formed with your support and sustained with your support ? This cannot be accepted. The situation deteriorated because of unbridled expenditure and unbridled borrowing.

I have with me the portion of a letter by Shri Venkataraman, then Finance Minister and now President. I do not want to read it out. In it he had said that till the seventies the country was making rapid economic progress. He pointed to the growth in food production and industrial production. Later the situation deteriorated. Don't blame anybody, for in a way our borrowings and our politics have made a mess of our economy. I am talking of politics from a narrow point of view, not in its broad meaning. Really speaking economics is a part of politics, but partisan politics, hunger for cheap popularity and the tendency to take important economic decisions with the coming elections in view have caused the situation to deteriorate.

I am surprised how can anyone decide to spend more than his income ? The State Bank was put to borrowing from abroad. This was not necessary. What is the present condition of our banking industry ? I do not want to go into whether nationalisation was right or wrong, but it was done in such haste that now the banking system has become the home of inefficiency. Neither is it easy to withdraw our money nor to avail of a loan sanctioned by the Government.

SHRI BHOGENDRA JHA (Madhubani) : You are not given to making a lot, what is the problem in withdrawing ?

SHRI VAJPAYEE : But some of my voters make money, they come and complain. If those working in banks do not feel it is a nationalised bank, that the Government took it over for achieving some broad social objectives, nationalisation will not succeed. This is what has happened. Thus decisions were taken that have brought us to the brink of insolvency.

Now the Finance Minister claims the situation is better than before. On comparing his present speech with the previous one one does feel that the attitude had changed, now there is a willingness to do battle. But as I said the other day during the discussion on the President's Address, there is no need for a battle between us. The Finance Minister's speech and his budget proposals have no answer for the economic crisis before us.

What would Happen to Small Industries ?

What about growing unemployment ? Small industries play—can play—an important role in providing employment. If we look to the capital investment process small industries provide six times more employment as compared to big industries. Even in exports they contribute 40 per cent. With the introduction of the New Economic Policy the *licence-permit quota raj* has come to an end and we have welcomed this step as in the right direction, but what will now happen to small industries ? Now foreign companies are coming in, and they are demanding that there should be no product reservation for small industries.

For years our policy has been to reserve some products for them. It is a different matter that that policy was not honestly implemented. For instance, take soap. Can soap not be made in small industries ? Do we need a very big industry for it ? George Sahib may recollect that once a decision was taken that soap would be made in small industry, but big industries were not prevented from making it. A phased programme could have been chalked out for such prevention. They could have been told—you are big industrialists, don't make small things like soap, generate electricity, set up steel plants, machine-making plants, leave soap to small industries, and gradually phase out. This did not happen. Now there is no restraint whatsoever. Now there is doubt about reservation itself.

SHRI MANI SHANKAR AIYER (Mailaduturai) : May I ask a question Sir ?

SHRI VAJPAYEE : Sure.

SHRI MANI SHANKAR AIYER : In this very field of soap a small producer Shri Karsan Bhai Patel makes Nirma soap. He challenged Lever and cut down Lever's Surf soap. Karsan Bhai Patel actually captured two-thirds of the market. He defeated a multimillionaire. Then what is the need of reservation ? Help all, so that the small people would come up themselves.

SHRI VAJPAYEE : Sir, is the Government going to adopt a policy in which Indian big business will take the place of foreign big business and play havoc with small industries ? That day I had said we do not want a monopoly... (*Interruption*)...

SHRI MANI SHANKAR AIYER : This is not monopoly, it is a small industry.

SHRI VAJPAYEE : Sir, Shri Aiyer has a wide outlook, so he cannot understand such a small thing. I agree that small industries should be ready to face competition, but they should first be made capable enough to face competition. The necessary means should be made available to them. Ninety-five per cent of the small industries are tiny industries. It looks as if medium industries have swallowed small industries. Now you will say it is a good thing if medium industry is developing. It has an investment of Rs. 65 lakhs. But what happens to the person investing Rs. 5 lakhs ? What happens to self- employment ? Will a network of small industries remain just an idea ?

Even small industries are becoming sick. Lakhs of them are closing down. No one cares for them. There is capital blocked in them and land occupied by them. Their workers cannot find employment at other places because the production techniques adopted at those other places are the same as those of the industries against which they want to put up a fight. How will small industries prosper ?

Is the Government going to decide that liberalisation should mean leaving small industries to the mercy of God and letting them die ? We should beware of the social consequences of such a policy. If the weaker sector is forced to commite suicide the country will be on fire. But that is happening today.

Hence though change is necessary continuity with change is also necessary. Change has a certain rhythm. It is a wave, there should be no jerk in it. I know the Finance Minister prefers *jhatka*, not *halali*, but the rhythm of development should not break; it is breaking, it is getting disturbed. The Finance Minister's shrill voice and shriller policies are intermittently breaking the waves of music.

I am sometimes surprised the country finds itself in such economic difficulties. Is no one responsible for it ? After all, who decides the economic policy ? Certainly the political leaders are guilty, but are the economic experts, who are in permanent service, also not to blame to a certain extent ? It seems there are half a dozen people—sometimes some of them go from North Block to Prime Minister's Office, from there back to North Block and from there to Yojana Bhavan.

SHRI SOMNATH CHATTERJI : And to IMF.

SHRI VAJPAYEE : Yes, to IMF.

SHRI NIRMAL KANTI CHATTERJI : How did you forget them ?

SHRI VAJPAYEE : I left them out so that you should remind me.

SHRI N.K. CHATTERJI : That won't save me.

SHRI VAJPAYEE : I want to take you with me.

SHRI SOMNATH CHATTERJI : Everyone wants that—they as well as you.

SHRI VAJPAYEE : Excuse me, Sir, you are negotiating with GATT. You are also trying to get the World Bank and the IMF to agree with you.

Who are the people who are talking ? What is the negotiating strategy ? We are not among those who say don't talk, who say reject the Dunkel proposal without looking at it, without giving it a thought. As I said the other day there are certain things in the proposal that we cannot accept. The U.S., for instance, cannot agree to open its door for Indian textiles. If they have the right to shut their door we too have the right to take steps for our development. But I am talking of the negotiating strategy. The strategy is not right. We should have a strategy of offence and defence. Where we can press them, we should do so, where we have to accept, we should do that. But this is not happening. Are the officers who are talking the same people who would later go looking for jobs with the World Bank or the IMF ? I am not accusing anybody, but I regret to say our administrative apparatus contains many talented people, many intelligent people (*Interruption*)...but the country did not get justice at their hands. Now every Finance Minister is not an economic expert like Dr. Manmohan Singh, he is a representative of the people.

SHRI MANMOHAN SINGH, Finance Minister : It is most unfortunate if you mean that those officers who have served the Government of India have their loyalty to some institution outside the country. I can say with full confidence that I know most of the officers who have served this country. I think this is very improper charge...(*Interruption*)...

SHRI BHOGENDRA JHA : Not all. Only a majority of them.

SHRI VAJPAYEE : Sir, I am not accusing anybody, but I am making a general point which cannot be ignored. Mr. Finance Minister, political leaders are certainly responsible for this economic crisis, but are not those officials who act as yesmen also responsible ? We see how the public sector is being run—I had referred to how it is run in Uttar Pradesh, in Rajasthan and in Madhya Pradesh. I am not doubting the patriotism of the officers, but flattery is a part of this country's culture. They should be warned against wrong things. I am not saying the officials will not protect our interests, but sometimes the way of thinking is so different that overall interests get ignored.

Change Intentions Before Changing Policies

Sir, now we have liberalisation, a new tax system, structural changes as well as changed Government policies. But have the people been prepared for these changed policies, this new tax structure ? Does the Finance Minister have the confidence that the industrialists, capitalists and moneyed people who were so long playing the game of tax evasion and justifying it on the ground that in view of high taxation rates there was no other go, stop playing the same card ? Will taxes be paid honestly now ? Will the Administration strengthen the apparatus for honest collection of taxes ? There is no reason why this big country of ours should not have made any economic progress all these years. Yet in such a big country there are only 5000 people who fall in the above-lakh bracket as tax-payers. A big industrialist actually said he had paid only Rs. 95,000 by way of taxes in a year. A similar situation prevailed in Mexico and Brazil, but there was a change in Mexico and the new President took stringent steps. Mexican money used to be deposited in American banks and the figures that these banks gave were eye-openers. He jailed ten big industrialists. I am not talking about jailing anybody here, but what happens if the industrialists do not respond to liberalisation, to 40 per cent lowering of the tax limit ? How will the tax collection system be made stringent ? Now there should be no amnesty. Setting up an industry in the country is not obliging the country. It is one's duty to contribute to the country's economic development. I had read somewhere that when the Finance Minister had some discussion with Swiss bank authorities and referred to the shortage of foreign exchange the Swiss bankers said your problem is not shortage of foreign exchange, your problem is that your funds are flowing out and being deposited here. And now there is open freedom. Will the industrialists , traders and capitalists exploit this open freedom ? Now we have a tiger unchained and I am afraid he might become a man-eater. The Government should be on guard.

What Is the Total Number of Tax-payers ?

Sir, I had told you that the rich are not prepared to pay taxes. What is the number of tax-payers ? In 1990-91 five thousand people have declared an income above Rs. 5 lakhs but Tatas have produced a new car, which is priced at Rs. 5 lakhs and 6000 people have registered their names as buyers and paid an advance of Rs. 25,000. Now I cannot understand this situation ...*(Interruption)*...

Sir, I had said three things in my speech of August 5, 1991. I had said three factors are responsible for the present economic crisis—over-invoicing of import, under-invoicing of export and gold smuggling. So far as over-invoicing of import and under-invoicing of export are concerned the Government did not act upon my suggestions. The Government would say we have opened up everything, and yet the need would remain. There should be no confusion about how much we should import and how much we should export. Some steps should be taken to conduct export-import business with honesty.

I am happy that the Finance Minister has accepted our suggestion to issue gold bonds. He has tried to explain why it was not accepted a year ago, but I refuse to understand. I cannot understand. But it was very necessary to stop gold smuggling. Those NRIs who want to return to India and bring gold with them should be allowed to do so. Only a reasonable duty should be charged. I had made this suggestion a year ago, and it has been accepted now. Well, better late than never. I only fear it might be too late.

There are Heavy Gold Stocks in the Country

Sir, there are large gold stocks in the country. Now gold bonds have been issued and full freedom has been given to bring in gold from abroad. There is a crisis in the hawala market. The places from where gold was being smuggled are in a turmoil. Gold prices have fallen abroad, and they will fall still further. We have calculated that an Indian now pays 800 rupees less on every ten grammes of gold. This fall in prices took place in 25 days. This comes to a saving of Rs. 8 crores per ton. About 150 tons of gold are in use in the country. If we calculate this amount, the possible savings come to Rs. 1200 crores. There are various estimates of how much gold there is in the country. One of them is 7500 tons. We say it is 10,000. If 2000 out of this comes within the bonds—and I think it will, as the Finance Minister has given enough facilities—if we can collect 2000 tons of gold the economic crisis would be substantially resolved. But this would need a campaign.

Mobilisation of Gold

I had suggested that it was very important to involve the society, to involve all organisations, in this gold campaign. It should not be conducted only on an official level. It could be made a people's movement. Our present target is to see that India is not a defaulter. Our national goal should be to establish a debt-free India. We want a debt-free India, and we have to reach this goal as fast as we can. Currently we are paying out Rs. 32,000 crores by way of interest. This includes both domestic and foreign debts. India can be freed from debt. This is not impossible. There is capital in the country. The country also has the potential to stand up with full might in times of crisis. The need of the hour is for us to inspire the country, but for that we have to adopt the right policy.

BIFR's Role

I have referred to small industries. Big industries are also sick. I do not want to go into the causes. But all these sick big industries are being left to the mercy of BIRF. Is not the BIRF itself sick ? Is it able to discharge its responsibility properly ? Does it have full membership ? Does it have an office, a staff ? Should more members not be appointed ? This agency has been given the responsibility of 56 sick big industries. How can it do justice to it ? It is the public sector, it is not a question of the private sector. Where are the people ? I feel this agency first needs to be streamlined, to be organised.

One more thing should be done. While determining the price of agricultural produce we think—and should think—of the investment. But when we think of the prices to industrial goods, does it have no connection with investment ? Do we pay attention to this ? Should limitless profits be allowed ? I am not talking of controls, but what should be the basis of the price of an industrial product selling in the market ? I ask questions in Parliament and the Government has been replying that the inquiries being made and figures being collected will not be made public. Why ? There are also cooperative societies in agriculture and their accounts are kept and audited. They are also published. Why can't this be done in the case of factories ?

Unlimited Consumerism

The makers of cosmetics are making a 1400 per cent profit. I know the Finance Minister is concerned about it. He has even said it in his speech. He said we should not ape the unrestrained consumerism and luxurious life-style of rich Western countries. Ostentatious consumption should be effectively discouraged. The quality of thrift should be emphasised. The sentiments of the Minister are very good, very noble. One cannot imagine where unlimited consumerism would lead this poor country to. But what is the way to check it ? Government television, the newspapers and advertising agencies that depend upon advertisements of big companies— all these are propagating unlimited consumerism. This is the position when television is under Government control, and now cable TV, Star TV are coming—have come. They will sell luxury articles. People will watch them in their huts. Even if the children do not have milk to drink, shampoo will be bought. The shampoo which will be shown on colour TV with an attractive face will reach the poor man's home.

SHRI N.K. CHATTERJI (Dumdum) : You should distinguish between shampoo and champagne.

SHRI MANORANJAN BHAKTA (Andaman & Nicobar) : You said champagne.

SHRI VAJPAYEE : I did not say champagne. Those who love champagne thought I said champagne.

"Jaki rahi bhawana jaisi, Prabhu
moorat dekhi tin taisi"

(A devotee sees God in the image he wants to see)

SHRI BHOGENDRA JHA (Madhubani) : At least we should care for those who are not snared by an attractive face.

SHRI VAJPAYEE : There is no effective strategy for this. This is not a matter of the ruling party only. There is now a middle class made up of crores of people. They have their hopes, their demands, their expectations. If, on top of this, there is no thrift, no continence at the leadership level, if there is no firm resolve to cut down government expenditure and no strategy to implement that resolve, then nothing can be done.

Income-Tax Limit Relaxed, Concessions Curtailed

Sir, the other day the Finance Minister admittedly drew a lot of applause. He gave some thanks, but received many more. But he has shown great miserliness in giving income tax concessions. If the limit was to be changed from Rs. 22,000 to Rs. 28,000 but at the same time concessions like 80-CCA, 80-CCB, 80-L were to be withdrawn it would have been better not to relax the limit.

This reminds me of Manmohan Krishna. Gopis went to him to ask for something, but his magic was such that they even lost their clothes. Now we have the modern edition of this 'Cheer-haran', 'Choube' went away to become 'Chhabbe' but remained "Dubey" and 'Dubey' got drowned. What is the propriety of this ? You may recall that at first the concession limit was Rs. 15,000, then it became Rs. 18,000. It changed with the times. Now dearness has increased, the price index has risen high. Now it would be proper to demand concession upto Rs. 48,000. But the Finance Minister says he has a problem. He says, honestly there is a problem, I would give concession but what would happen to the States ? We do not want to deplete the financial sources of the States. So the Finance Minister should sit down with us and think of what way can be found. It is essential to find out a middle way, a way to increase the limit without cutting down the States' share.

Sir, there is one more thing. The Finance Bill presented by the Finance Minister contains 115 amendments to the Direct Tax Laws. An amendment of a few months ago contains 163 amendments to them. Actually this should not be a part of the Finance Bill at all, it should be a separate bill. If necessary it could also be sent to a select Committee. There are many things in the Finance Bill that need to be discussed in depth. For instance, is it proper to club the income of minors with that of their parents ? It has never happened before. Secondly, is the partnership amendment in order ? People also have suggestions about the capital gains tax and the wealth tax. I say if all these things are included in the Finance Bill there would be problems. This House would not be able to do justice to such a large number of amendments.

Ways to Bring Down Budget Deficit

Sir, In his speech the Finance Minister has mentioned many ways to bring down the deficit, one of which is disinvestment in public undertakings. I know this is very much an open question, but everyone will agree that if there is to be disinvestment it should be on the best possible terms in the best possible manner. It is all right that the disinvestment so far has been through the UTI and mutual funds, but it has not been on the right price. Of course there is a long queue in the share market. The common man also wants to buy shares. This is good, but if the Government sells the shares of public enterprises to make money it would not be acceptable if the price is not good. I do not know on whose advice this was done. Somewhere there has been lack of caution in this. It should not happen in future.

Sir, restructuring is being talked of. Not only economic restructuring but social restructuring is also necessary. Are people ready for a change ? After coming to power the Prime Minister had called a meeting and fashioned a general consensus. Is that general consensus still operative ? Is it not necessary to try and join it again ? We have taken a big step. There are dangers in it. How the powers of the world behave is also one aspect of it. But another aspect is how we behave at home. Will the game of politics allow a general consensus to be formed ? I would like to draw the Finance Minister's attention to what he has said in his speech:

> "Our long–term objective is to develop a labour-intensive production process, so that maximum employment avenues may be opened up for high productive income and the disparity between rural and urban income and wealth is minimised."

This is certainly a very good objective. We too want that industrialisation should be labour-intensive, disparity should be minimised and employment opportunities increased. But why three years ? Will the present economic reforms mean that today's labour–intensive industries would disintegrate but when the Government's restructuring succeeds new industries would start that would make labour- intensive, productive employment available ? Certainly this cannot be the intention.

Who will Give Three Years, and Why ?

I had raised the matter of three years before, and I would like to raise it again. The Finance Minister has further said, "For at least three years hard efforts will be needed." I had asked, who will give three years, and why ? People can be asked to wait if there is an atmosphere of simplicity in the whole country, if there is realisation of a national calamity, and if the leadership placed a model before the people, not only in speeches. The Finance Minister said in his speech that industrialists should be trustees of the society, they should consider themselves trustees of the wealth they have. This is Gandhiji's thought and it is a very good thought. Really trusteeship can be an Indian concept of ownership. There have even been some experiments in this direction in other countries, but Gandhi's country did not make progress in this matter. I doubt the Finance Minister's speech would lead to this progress. For becoming a trustee one has first to give up greed, give up the tendency to exploit, bid goodbye to the fine art of tax evasion. Those who have stashed money abroad can never be forgiven. Now they have a chance—let them bring it back. How much money is lying abroad ? But I must say one thing. If we expect capitalists to consider themselves trustees of their wealth should not political leaders and those in power consider themselves trustees of the power they have ? How did the country get into the difficulties in which it finds itself today ? I am not discussing other problems. This is a country at the mercy of the IMF and the World Bank. No one had dreamt of such an India.

Now the Finance Minister says imports should come down, for which *Swadeshi* awakening is necessary. It is true, we cannot live in separate camps, but if we have to accept World Bank aid why accept it for education, for water ? We can understand taking aid for something big. We neglected education, we did not worry about health. We are earmarking Rs. 1500-1700 crores for education and health, which also includes family planning.

I would like to say one more thing. The Education Minister is not present in the House. The adult education propaganda is very good, but the programme for the universalisation of primary education must not slacken. I am afraid that adult education is being discussed more from the propaganda point of view, people are learning to write their names, but what about new-born boys and girls ? If they cannot learn to read in their childhood will they do so when they are grown up ? Do we need foreign resources for this ? Every State Government, whatever the party forming the State Government—pardon me, even the West Bengal Government wants to take up projects with the assistance of the World Bank. What are those projects ? I can understand it if it sets up some big industry or helps us in generating electricity, transport or communication and comes forward to help this country to build up an infrastructure.

We are standing at crossroads. It is necessary that the Finance Minister should create optimism, but it is also necessary that he should not fall a victim to that optimism himself. We should have the lowliest citizen of this country before us. This was the test laid down by Gandhiji. He said I would tell you a magic trick—whatever the steps you take, whatever the policies you adopt, think of what impact they would have on the smallest person, on the person on the lowest rung of the ladder, the one whom we want to raise through

Antyodaya. Mr. Finance Minister, you had closed with a 'sher', so I shall also do the same. The Finance Minister is talking of three years—

"Aah ko chahiye, ek umr asar hone tak,
Kaun jeeta hai, teri zulf ke sar hone tak ?"

Which means—by the time my grief reaches you, a life-time would go by. Sardarji actually has *zulf*, so we do not know what would happen to us by that time. Thank you.

Implications of Dunkel Draft

Mr. Speaker, Sir, the present session of Parliament is coming to an end today. A few hours have been allotted for the discussion on this important issue. The issue has been pending for the last one year. There is no Cabinet Minister of Commerce in the Council of Ministers, there is only a Minister of State in the Ministry of Commerce. This proposal is the talk of the world today.

A paper for discussion was also issued by the Government. I have seen it, that is not sufficient. What was actually required on the part of the Government was to publish a White Paper and Parliament should have been provided with an opportunity to hold discussion. Later on, a committee of Ministers was constituted. It was, in a sense, an effort to put aside Parliament from the scene. I ask, what was the achievement of that committee of Ministers. A discussion is going on on GATT and 'Uruguay Round' throughout the world. The Government has changed in America. President Clinton is making a strategy in connivance with Prime Minister Major. France has, however, expressed its dissent but we need to consider the proposal in the backdrop of the situation of our own country as also from the point of view of our own interests. The proposal is comprehensive enough including all the affairs of life. It includes the areas of medicine, cotton cloth, agriculture, industry, services, investment, technology, employment, environment, and culture etc. and along with all these the trade of India is also included in the list. The Dunkel Draft is such a document that either it will have to be accepted fully or will have to be rejected fully. If there is something good in it and if we want that part to be accepted, then there is no permission for that.

Refer Dunkel Draft to J.P.C.

With regard to the Tokyo Round there was some relaxation. Had we wished, we could have made selection keeping our interests in view. But, now the door for that is closed. The most objectionable thing is that the 'Dunkel Proposal' is adversely affecting the 'Indian Patent Law' which has been giving permission to us for manufacturing medicine and we have made tremendous advancements in that field. The Dunkel proposal creates difficulty. There is no solution to the problem of the likely increases in favour of liberalisation within the country. Unnecessary control is there and the bureaucracy is creating obstacles. There are not as much opportunities as are

Lok Sabha on December 23, 1992,. during discussion on the motion regarding implications of the Dunkel Draft

required because the industrialist of India does not want to compete. The foreign companies want a safe market. They have developed a habit of earning undue profits. But there must be a competition in the market. However, India has to think over its interests before involving itself in the competition with the foreign companies.

It would have been better if a Joint Parliamentary Committee had been constituted and this Dunkel Proposal referred to it. I am not an expert. We should have sought the opinion of experts, if necessary. If there was a need we should have asked for the required material from abroad ? Still there is time, I would like to request the hon. Minister to constitute a Joint Parliamentary Committee in this regard. It is not a case of embezzlement. The Joint Parliamentary Committee may continue to do its work. It is relevant with that.

SHRI RAM NAIK (Bombay North) : We are doing excellent work.

SHRI VAJPAYEE : I would like to congratulate you. As soon as you make somebody a scapegoat, they will realise the position .... (*Interruptions*). A Joint Parliamentary Committee can be constituted and this matter can be referred to it. In this matter, the State Governments should also be consulted. It is correct that you dismissed some State Governments. Even though I am speaking to protect the rights of those State Governments which have not yet been dismissed. That is why I repeat that the State Governments should also be consulted in this regard. My colleagues of West Bengal should congratulate me that I do not indulge myself in such type of politics as they are doing.

SHRI SOMNATH CHATTERJEE (Bolpur) : You have no Government but your opinion is still there.

SHRI VAJPAYEE : Our opinion will always be the same. When we will form the Government at the Centre, we would say good bye to the Dunkel Proposal.

Sir, my suggestion is that the meeting of the National Development Council may be convened for discussing the Dunkel Proposal.

SHRI SOMNATH CHATTERJEE : Sometimes you speak very well.

SHRI VAJPAYEE : The Government should make up its mind first. The resolution moved by the Government does not show a clearcut picture of the Government's views as well as its thinking. The Ministers have also not taken any clearcut decision in this regard and they should not do so. If we accept the Dunkel Proposal as it is, the Government will have to bring comprehensive changes in national activities which may have far-reaching consequences. These cannot be changed without the consent of Parliament. But the Government should at least place the material before Parliament. Therefore I repeat my two proposals. Firstly, a Joint Parliamentary Committee should be constituted and the Dunkel Proposal may be referred to it, and secondly, a meeting of the National Development Council may be convened. Alongwith this the Government should hold negotiations with other countries too. If a big country like India does not espouse the cause and interests of developing countries then who will speak ? I have read the paper prepared by the Government, which says that if any big country seeks an amendment, then our Government would also avail the opportunity for pressing for an amendment. Such language does not befit the dignity and the prestige of India. I admit that we are facing financial problems and these problems have also been created by the Congress Government. But I am not making it a party issue at this juncture. If we too cannot take a stand on the objectionable aspects of the Dunkel Proposal, how will other developing countries face it ? The Government should hold consultations and negotiations with them and explain the difficulties which are being faced by it. If there is some difficulty in European countries about agriculture, even then America is not ready to provide us a safe market there. It has also introduced a quota system under the Japanese economic pressure. These countries do not hesitate in taking steps to protect their interests. We should also not hesitate to do so. We should hold negotiations with developing countries and value a proposal which would not only safeguard the interests of our country but also boost our image in the international arena.

I reiterate that the issue of medicines is a complicated matter. The pharmaceuticals would be the worst affected and if the prices of medicines rise, the people will never spare the Government.

What is our Identity and Where are our Roots ?

Mr. Deputy Speaker, Sir, President's Address is an important event in the Joint Session of Parliament. This time the Budget Session started with the President's Address. I wished to be present on the occasion but could not. The reason is evident. At the end of his speech the Hon. President referred to democracy to be a living thing. He admitted that the country is faced with crises. He has also admitted that there have been remarkable levels of cooperation as also strong areas of dissent last year. He said that our democracy is very lively. I do not understand the extent to which the Hon. President's views and the Government's actions are complementary to each other. Is it not that the President's Address is written separately and the Government acts differently ?

Sensitive Matters Ignored

My hon. friend Shri Mani Shankar Aiyar is not present here. Once he wrote in an article as to how President's Address should be drafted. I do not know as to what procedure is being followed now and who prepares the Address. Mr. Deputy Speaker, Sir, it is true that we wished to be present at the time of joint Parliament Session but we decided to abstain. Shri Advani wrote a letter to the Hon. President and informed that we are sorry that we are not coming and also clarified that it was not a disrespect to the office of the President. We do respect the office of President and since he holds the office we respect him. However, the Government is creating a situation due to which we would respectfully abstain from the Joint Parliament Session. We used the word "respectfully abstain." It is true that attention is not paid to minute things today. Sensitive matters are neither taken into consideration nor evaluated. Next day I read newspapers and the news was that Bharatiya Janata Party boycotts the Joint Parliament Session. Though very minor but there is certainly a difference between the word "boycott" and "respectfully abstain." However, that difference is not being taken into consideration. We were very agitated. It was but natural for us to be agitated for the way in which our rally was banned. But we did not create any obstacle in passing the Railway Budget. The Government crossed all limits in controlling the rally. We also lost patience. But we did not create any problem while presenting the General Budget.

I have very long association with this House. I remember the days when Shri Morarji Desai used to be the Hon. Minister of Finance. He was going to

Lok Sabha on March 2, 1993 during discussion on the Motion of Thanks on the President's Address

present the Budget but some of the Communist members were agitated. So they continued to raise a hue and cry while Morarji Desai continued his Budget speech. We could have also created such a situation. But we did not do so because our conscience did not permit it.

We want that democracy should prevail in the real sense and dignity of the House should be preserved. However, the dignity of the House is not preserved inside the House. Who knows what happens outside the House ? Will the same not be reflected here ? Therefore, when the Hon. President refers democracy to be lively, it should be reflected outside too. Farmers are holding a rally. What is the need to stop them ? The Government asked them to hold the rally near the Red Fort. Cannot the citizens of the country gather in front of Parliament and knock the doors of Parliament ? All the rallies have been banned. Our leftist friends are also complaining, because there will be oppression. Everyone, big and small, will suffer. Therefore, oppression should not take place. The other day I had pointed out that the hon. Minister of Home Affairs could hold talks. I read in the newspapers that farmers were given permission to hold their rally near the Red Fort. But we were not even asked whether we wanted to hold the rally at some other place. It is altogether different that we would not have agreed.

SHRI NITISH KUMAR (Barh): On the top of Qutab Minar ?

SHRI VAJPAYEE : We would make you climb on it to deliver your speeches.

Is the Government Anti-religious ?

Mr. Deputy Speaker, Sir, the incident of 6th December is the first reference in the President's Address. That was but natural. The matter has already been discussed and will be discussed again. I will say afterwards what I want to say with regard to it. However, I was going through the English and Hindi versions of the Address, its English version is as follows :

"The basic premise of secularism and the rule of law has been threatened."

But in the Hindi version of these lines it has been stated that secularism and law have been threatened. What is the threat and who gave the threat is the matter of discussion. There is a lot of difference in it. But I am referring to the specific word. In English it is said that ours is a secular country and it should remain secular. There is no objection to it. But the difficulty arises only when the specific word is translated as *'Dharam nirpeksh'* in Hindi. Not only in my opinion but in common man's opinion ours is a religious country. To be religious or having good qualities mean the same thing these days. However, emphasis is laid on to safeguard the *'Dharam nirpeksh'* and I would like to submit to the so-called custodians of secularism that *'Dharam nirpeksh'* is not the equivalent of the word 'secularism'. It is creating confusion among the people. Is the Government anti-religious ? Does the Government want to make the country non-religious ?

Nehru's Definition of Word "Secular"

Mr. Deputy Speaker, Sir, I have already made a mention of it and today I would like to repeat the same. I am talking of the years 1949-50. When the

Constitution of India was framed there was no reference to the word 'secular' in it. Everybody agreed that our country should be secular. It was not at all a matter of controversy. Even after the formation of Pakistan, nobody ever raised the demand to declare India a religious state. However, the Constitution-makers did not use the word 'secular' in the Constitution, because they were apprehensive that it might create confusion. When the word 'secular' is translated as *'Dharam nirpeksh'* it is certainly likely to create a confusion. Nehru ji realised this problem in 1961. I am referring to Nehruji because most of the Hon. Members refer to him again and again when they talk of secularism. Nehruji had written the preface of a book called *'Dharam Nirpeksh Rajya* by an M.P. Shri Raghunath Singh in Varanasi in 1961. The book is available in the Parliament library and can be borrowed. I am reading out an extract from the book : "Perhaps the word 'secular' in English. Some people think that it relates to anti-religion and obviously it is wrong to have such a notion. It means that it is a state which gives equal respect to all religions."

Mr. Deputy Speaker, Sir, if taken in this context, India has always been and will remain a secular country and the incident of 6th December has not at all created a threat to secularism. Let us use the proper word. In the latest Hindi version of the Constitution of India, the word 'secular' stands for *'Panth Nirpeksh"* and not for *'Dharam Nirpeksh'*. India should follow the concept of *'Panth Nirpeksh'*. The word religion is used in a wider term. If at all the people of this country have to be encouraged to move ahead, work hard and make as much sacrifice as possible, then religion cannot be isolated.

Shri Indrajeet Gupta is not present here. An incident referred to by Shri Durga Das in his book named *India from Curzon to Nehru* is worth reading. I would like to place it before the House. I quote :

> "I asked Gandhi how he would counter Jinnah's charge that his was a pseudo-religious movement likely to lead to a reactionary revivalism. Gandhi replied that his own idiom was the only one that the masses could grasp. Villagers responded to his call, for they lived nearer to God than the townsfolk, and understood his message as a call to self-abnegation and self-purification. As for revivalism, Gandhi said he certainly wished to see among the Hindus a revival of spirit of resistance to evil and a shedding of their cowardice. Anyway, Hindu-Muslim unity was to him an article of faith and he could never be so foolish as to inaugurate a movement likely to harm this cause. The Muslim masses instinctively understood the religious issue and would feel brotherly towards non-Muslims who espoused their cause."

What is Our Identity ?

Today, it is said that religion and politics should be separated and that religion and politics have no relation. In order to convey the correct idea of it to a common man if we say that communalism should not be associated with politics and that religion should not be misused to fulfil the political motives, I can understand the sense. But the Government does not say this.

It says that religion has no relation with politics and those who try to bring religion into politics pose a danger to secularism in the country. A common man does not accept this idea. I have not, so far, been able to understand why stress is being laid on defining the word 'secular' as *'Dharam nirpeksh'*. Are we not able to make people understand by translating secularism into *'panth-nirpeksha'* or *'sampraday nirpeksha'*.

Roots of the Ancient Country

Mr. Deputy Speaker, Sir, firstly, before taking up other issues, I would like to submit a point in this regard. What is the identity of this country which we call as Bharat, Hindustan or India. Where are the life roots of this country ? From which roots the nationality of this country gets the stream of life ? No new nation was born in the year 1947. The nations which emerged in Europe after the Second World War are in a process of disintegration at present. But this country has remained united for centuries. There were different states and they had sometimes used to indulge in wars with each other. Even then the country was one. What were the reasons for its unity ? Please excuse me. I would like to state that at that time, Islam or Christianity had not reached our country. The believers in Islam did not come with Ghori or Ghazni. First of all, the traders from Arab countries came here and constructed the first mosque in South India by taking permission from the Hindu ruler there. None objected to the construction of that mosque and the ruler also permitted happily. Never before any such fight has taken place in the country. Is it not an evidence that this is an ancient nation ? Only a new chapter was opened in the year 1947. Our intellectuals who are influenced with Western education, will say that : the concept of the nation is a modern concept.

Discuss the Problem

So, they cannot accept our country as an ancient nation. If you do not want to accept it, it is your own wish, but no one can deny about its ancientness. I do not want to quote Nehruji again. He had also said : "since thousand of years, a chain of life is continued and I am proud that I am also a link of that chain. I do not want to separate myself from that chain. "Which is this chain ? Is it not Hindu ? But an objection has been raised on the word 'Hindu' after independence or after the division of the country. Why the effort to give Indian colour to everything, after independence was not fully successful. I have said it earlier also and would again like to repeat that we should discuss this question as to what is the national pride of this country. If this is not a Hindu country or if it is not integrated by the Hindu culture, then what other factors are responsible for the integrity of this country ? Who were those great men who inspired the people for making sacrifices at the time of foreign invasions. It was Shivaji and not Aurangzeb... Why Maharana Pratap inspires the people of this country even today ? I agree that the Muslims, who came from the other countries and settled here, became part and parcel of this country. They should also be treated equally. Our Constitution provides such guarantee. There is a need to bring it into practice also. There is no difference of opinion in this regard, but the people are being misled by creating imaginary differences of opinion. It is necessary to have clear-cut opinions and we are ready for a discussion in this respect.

Mr. Deputy Speaker, Sir, the Hon. Home Minister stated that day that the R.S.S. members consider Hinduism as nationalism. He should understand that Hinduism is not used as Hindu religion. No adjective was used before religion. It was always preached to follow the religion. Later on, sects were formed and ways of worship were developed. But this land has enough strength to take everyone along. Why are we giving less importance to this strength ? If it is said that politics should not be communalised, then this rule should be applicable to all. One should not adopt double-standard.

Apply One Standard

Mr. Deputy Speaker, Sir, I do not want to repeat the same points. I am expressing a point. I am happy that Shri Chandra Shekhar is present here. It is necessary to have clarity in thoughts. You accuse us of being communalists and responsible for dividing the country and we accuse you of dividing the country in 1947 and again you are doing the same. Thus, this discussion will lead us to nowhere. One should have clear-cut views on this issue. We should have same opinions and should speak same language on the basic issues. It is true that we will always have difference of opinion with the persons who say that India is not a nation or India is a group of nationalities. Our Communist friends had been expressing their views till recently that there is no such thing like Muslim communalism. There is no such thing as.. .(*Interruptions*).

Dada Bhupesh Gupta has given these speeches in Rajya Sabha in my presence. I can quote those speeches.

SHRI SAIFUDDIN CHOUDHURY (Katwa) : He would have been afraid of you.

SHRI VAJPAYEE : Please do not say like this, I have a great regard for Dada. There is no question of his being afraid of me. I know when the Constitution was changed and the word "secular" was included, Shri Indrajit Gupta was present there. He had said at that time as to why this word is being included. Our country is already secular.

SHRI INDRAJIT GUPTA (Midnapore) : The word "socialist" has also been included in it.

Dr. Ambedkar Quoted in Parts

SHRI VAJPAYEE : No discussion was held on it. This motion was moved by Sardar Swaran Singh and he had said that the word "secular" means that there will be no religion of the State and it will have no system of worship and its attitude towards all religions will be equal. Some of the members did not speak at all. But when Shri K.T. Shah tried to get included the word "socialist" in the Constitution, Dr. Ambedkar did not accept it. The argument given by Dr. Ambedkar shows his farsightedness. In the Drafting Committee he rejected the amendment. He said that socialism is a hypothesis of an economic set-up and I do not want to include it in the Constitution because economic system and hypothesis keep on changing. A time may come when a better economic system than socialism may come into being and the same is accepted by the people. I do not want to put limitations for the future generations. To say at that time ....

Today the ideas of Dr. Ambedkar are mentioned in parts only, while the need of the hour is to see him in totality. I am not going to discuss that issue.

Mr. Deputy Speaker, Sir, I am expressing a point of view. A discussion is going on seeds under the Dunkel Proposal. The Government is trying to defend the indefensible Dunkel Proposal. The root is more important than the tree and that root has come out from the seed. There is enough matter to consider, but please do not level allegations. You can accuse us and we can accuse you. Where will this dialogue lead us to ?

SHRI SAIFUDDIN CHOUDHURY : We go upto genes.

SHRI VAJPAYEE : Because you are materialistic. That is why, you go upto genes.

Ayodhya and Neighbouring Countries

Mr. Deputy Speaker, Sir, a mention has been made in the President's Address about our relations with neighbouring countries. We all want that we should have good relations with our neighbouring countries, but despite all efforts, our relations with Pakistan and Bangladesh are not improving. The incidents which happened in these countries after 6th of December give a serious warning to our country. It is a matter of grave concern. After all, the issue of Ayodhya is an internal issue of our country and it is our responsibility to solve it properly. We cannot allow our neighbouring countries to make any interference in the issue and demolish temples, burn down the houses of Hindus making thousands of them homeless and burn our National Flag and all this has been done at the Government level. In Faislabad, a Minister of the Federal Government in Pakistan kept looking on and a temple was demolished before him. In Lahore, a temple was demolished through bulldozer. This is totally wrong.

SHRI NITISH KUMAR : In 1984, the same has happened with the Sikhs also.

SHRI CHANDRA SHEKHAR (Ballia) : Sir, the thing is that the Federal Government was responsible there and here the State Government was responsible for it.

SHRI VAJPAYEE : And, who demolished Hindu temples in Bangladesh ?

SHRI CHANDRA SHEKHAR : There is federal set-up there.

SHRI VAJPAYEE : Neither the Federal Government nor the State Government did anything, but 490 temples have also been demolished there. Is it an ordinary incident ? What did our Government do there ? I am taking of only temples here, but shops and industrial units were set ablaze there. Should it not be mentioned ? That is why the Prime Minister of India had to cancel his Dhaka visit and moreover threats are still being given that the Indian Premier will not be allowed to airdash in case he goes there to participate in the SAARC Summit.

A mention was made during his address by His Excellency the President of India that the talks with Premier of Bangladesh were held in a very cordial manner when the latter was on a tour of India. Tin Bigha has been given, well the Government may give something more if it wants so, but there should be cordial relations. Dialogue with neighbouring countries is needed to be carried firmly and in clear terms. We want that our relations with the neighbouring countries should improve. Now, the rest of the world have considerably changed, but the countries of West Asia are still entangled in tensions.

I had told you that we would solve the Ayodhya tangle, but we cannot allow any Islamic country to become the protector of Indian Muslims. It is wrong.

Immigration Problem

Mr. Deputy Speaker, Sir, the immigration of people from Bangladesh who are coming in great numbers is yet another issue concerned with this issue. Many citizens of Bangladesh have succeeded in getting their names entered in the voters' lists even though a voice of protest was not raised against it in Delhi. Their names should be deleted soon. Can it be called a communal demand ? Should any country allow people from its neighbouring country to immigrate illegally ?

Mr. Deputy Speaker, Sir, after an inquiry was conducted in Delhi, names of several thousand Bangladeshis were deleted from the lists of voters. The inquiry is still going on.

I had been to Assam recently. The proposed rally of our party to be held in Guwahati was initially banned. However, it was allowed later on. But, I would like to submit that this House should pay attention to the situation arising in Assam. Issues are generally allowed to linger on. How matters are allowed to linger on for politics of votes was seen by us on Ayodhya issue.

But another type of situation is emerging due to the inflow of a large number of people from Bangladesh. The Election Commission no longer remains to be our institution but the Election Commission has issued directives. Today the members of the Janata Dal and the left parties had raised the issue of Tripura. We agree with them on this score. If inquiry is not held in accordance with the directives of the Election Commission and if the officers in question are not removed, will it then not tantamount to the mockery of the Election Commission ? There is no justification of care-taker Government by the same State Government in Tripura.

It is being stated that the report of the Government has not been received, but it is no secret that the Union Government can get the Governor's report any time of its own choice. You got the reports from the Governors of the four States and dismissed those Governments. It means what you think right is right.

The Central Government may be interested in allowing the corrupt State Government of Tripura to remain in power. The Tripura Government which indulged in electoral irregularities may be allowed to continue in power, even though comments and strictures have been passed by the Election Commission against the State Government. Mr. Deputy Speaker, Sir, yet another drama is being enacted in Assam.

Directions of Election Commission

An order to review the voters' lists throughout the country was given on the 25th November, 1992 by the Election Commission keeping the date of 1st January 1993 in mind. They had written in their report that foreign nationals had come to India in large numbers and they had succeeded in getting their names entered in the voters' lists. The scrutiny of voters' lists should be made keeping in view the date of 1st January, 1993. The names of foreign nationals should be deleted from those voters' lists.

Now I want to quote what the Election Commission has stated. I am having a copy of the entire directive given by it. The Election Commission has stated :

> "AND WHEREAS, being aware of the presence of a substantial number of foreign nationals in some States in India the Commission, in full consultation with the Ministry of Home Affairs, issued a direction with its letter No. 23/92 dated 21 Aug., 1992 to all the State Governments and Chief Electoral Officers containing a special enumeration procedure for areas having a substantial presence of foreign nationals."

The Commission has also written that the direction being forewarded by it has been endorsed by the Ministry of Home Affairs, that is to say the Ministry is agreeable to it. The Commission added that in accordance with the new procedure it is the responsibility of the State Governments to identify foreign nationals in every Assembly Constituency and at every polling booth. It was also stated by the Commission that the work of identifying the foreign nationals and counting their number should be finished by 31st August, 1992. The Commission added that in case there was any doubt about the citizenship of a person, the district collector should decide it by 7th October, 1992. Later on, this date was extended from 7th to 17th of October.

Assam Government's Opposition

But the Government of Assam did not comply with the direction. It said that the counting would be conducted as per the voters' list of 1990. Those who had come up to 1990 would not be removed, whether they are the citizens of India or not. This was the purport of what it said. The State Government made it dear that it was not ready to abide by the new direction. It also issued directives to its officials that they have to ensure this much whether the person whose name was entered in the voters list was of 18 years of age in 1990 or not. Now there is a tug of war between the Government of Assam and the Election Commission.

Now I would like to shift your attention from the situation of Tripura to the situation of Assam. The Election Commission did not accept the objections raised by the Government of Assam. It again issued direction that it should be followed. The Ministry of Home Affairs also reminded the State

Government of its responsibilities, but the Government of Assam adopted adamant posture. A meeting with the representatives of the Government of Assam was held in Delhi on 13.11.92 in order to persuade them to arrive at an agreement in this regard. Now I quote from the order of the Commission.

> "It became further evident that the State Government had knowingly and without any plausible reason disregarded the direction of the Commission issued in full consultation with the Ministry of Home Affairs relating to this matter of grave importance."

The State Government is not ready to abide by it. The Election Commission has stopped the work of preparing new voters' lists in Assam. What will happen ? To make proper arrangements for holding of free and fair elections, to revise voters' list and to add new voters in the voters' lists, all come under the jurisdiction of the Election Commission. But the State Government is bent upon violating the directions of the Election Commission openly. It is also violating the directive of the Ministry of Home Affairs.

10 per cent Annual Increase in Assam Population

When I went to Guwahati I came to know that there are 105 such constituencies in which 10 per cent population has increased during the last one year. How can there be an increase of 10 per cent of population in one year ? But when the Assam Government takes any step, the vote-politics comes in the way and the matter concerning the security and integrity of the country is held up. This is really a serious issue. We do not want to make it an issue of Hindus and Muslims. People in large numbers have come from Nepal. They are creating a number of problems. The Government cannot accept illegal entry.

America is also not allowing foreign nationals to settle there. In America when Mr. Clinton was fighting election, he declared that his attitude would be sympathetic towards the persons who were coming from Haiti to take shelter in America. President Bush had stopped their entry. Now when Mr. Clinton has assumed office, as the President of America, he says that he cannot be sympathetic towards them and that their entry will have to be prevented. That is on the Mexico border. America is trying its best to prevent illegal entry. But in our country every issue is given a communal colour and vote is linked with every issue. When the situation goes out of control, the Government makes desperate attempts to control the situation but even then nothing happens.

Avoid Discontent on Ayodhya Issue

Mr. Deputy Speaker, Sir, there was also a mention about the Ayodhya issue in the President's Address. That the case has been referred to the Supreme Court has also been mentioned. I do not know whether the Supreme Court would give any decision in such case or not. It can both reject the case or give its decision thereon. The decision may favour one side only and the decision may also lead to the state of indecision. Can this issue not be solved even now through cordial talks outside the court of law ? Can Parliament not play any role in it ? If Parliament had played its role earlier, if the judiciary had been a bit fast in pronouncing its decision and if the political parties would have contributed to finding solution rising above vote politics (*Interruptions*).

Mr. Deputy Speaker, Sir, I have not mentioned the name of anybody.

SHRI MOHAN SINGH (Deoria) : And you call it a mandate (*Interruptions*).

SHRI VAJPAYEE : There is a little change in the Muslim opinion. This is not so out of any fear. There is a change in them because they have come to realise that it is really a matter of deep sentiment of the people. Now I would like to submit that the Government should take advantage of this change in their attitude and make all efforts to find a solution to the problem. If the Government remains adamant there may be difficulties in finding the solution to the problem. There is enough time now and I wish what Chandra Shekharji had initiated should be taken up again. Later on, he lashed out at us.

Still there is time. If the court gives its verdict on the basis of the evidence, documents, inscriptions, archaeological material that there was a Mandir then the demand of mosque should be dropped. But it is a different question whether the court gives such a verdict or not. I am also presenting the other side of the picture. Whatever may be the verdict of the court one of the two sides would remain discontent. I do not want that this discontent should be there.

SHRI ABDUL GHAFOOR (Gopalganj) : Many things can be tolerated. You also know how we are exercising restraints.

Mr. Deputy Speaker, Sir, I am offering a viewpoint. You have to assess its weight. Still there is time. All the people of this country have to live together. The politics of vote has disturbed the situation much (*Interruptions*). We joined this game much later. The debate on the vote of Thanks to the President's Address is providing this opportunity (*Interruptions*).

SHRI CHANDRA SHEKHAR : The suggestion made by Shri Atal Bihari Vajpayee is a right suggestion. If a dialogue in the matter is to be resumed, will the Members of Bharatiya Janata Party and other people associate themselves with it. Will they take any initiative in it so that negotiations could be resumed again ? I fully agree with their opinion that this problem cannot be sorted out through court and Government alone. It can be resolved through dialogue only. So I would like to request Atalji to make the people prepared for it and pave the way for holding talks.

Solution Lies in Dialogue

SHRI VAJPAYEE : Mr. Deputy Speaker, Sir, if any such effort is made we are ready to participate in it but it should be done with a goodwill and with an eye for finding a solution to the problem. Till now many efforts have been made but each step raised a new problem, so in disgust we suggested that the matter should be referred to the court. Now the matter is in the court. Hearing will start and verdict will be given. Whatever be the verdict, it would leave one side dissatisfied and that will not be an ideal one. But I think if any matter is not sorted out through mutual negotiations, we should approach the court and accept its verdict. But this is a question of creating goodwill in the country and Shri Chandra Shekhar can discuss this matter with his friends and find out a solution. We have been isolated. BJP has been .... apolitical.

SHRI NIRMAL KANTI CHATTERJEE (Dumdum) : Will that root be strengthened if you recognise Shivaji and Rana Pratap only and not Tipu Sultan.

SHRI VAJPAYEE : Sir, this is an effort to distort my version. I had raised a question. Please put it up in a correct way. It should conform to facts in history and thoughts of the minds. Things took an ugly turn because various aspects of the related dispute have been dealt with separately. It is not enough to say that the Hindus and Muslims should live together. Who are our great men and what was their conduct ? That is why I have raised a question and I would like to know your view in the matter. We do not want to leave anyone. We want to take all together but in this effort we do not want to distance ourselves from the main root. He made a reference to Rana Pratap and Shivaji. Please turn to earlier events. It is being said that the patriots had fought against Muslims but in reality they did not fight against Muslims. They fought against the regime. The problem arises when our Muslim brethren associate themselves with the aggressor of that time ? What is the need to put Ram and Babar as rivals ? What parallel is there between the two ?

SHRI EBRAHIM SULAIMAN SAIT (Ponnani) : Nobody does so, it is wrong.

SHRI VAJPAYEE : It is so nice of you that you are not doing so. If we go into these details the debate will become lengthy and would create a lot of bitterness. If you do not do, it is good.

SHRI EBRAHIM SULAIMAN SAIT : Nobody does.

SHRI VAJPAYEE : Sulaiman Saitiji you will say that you do not oppose Vande Mataram...(*Interruptions*). Please get up and say that you do not oppose Vande Mataram.

SHRI EBRAHIM SULAIMAN SAIT : Please stick to one point only. There is no use in complicating the matter. Why do you connect Babar with Vande Mataram.

SHRI VAJPAYEE : I did not raise this issue. Our communist friends got up. Please be cautions of them; they will continue to do such things.

SHRI SAFFUDIN CHAUDHARY : We had asked some other thing. Vajpayee ji, why it is necessary to cut the roots to take all together. Why does this thing arise.

SHRI VAJPAYEE : Where is the question of cutting the roots ?

Mr. Speaker, Sir, I have taken much time. There are many other speakers from my party. Kindly do not be strict to them. I would like to thank you... (*Interruptions*). Mr. Speaker, Sir, you have come but after a long time. I would like to submit one more thing. I am going to conclude. A White Paper has been published. The paper is white no doubt but whatever has been written contains no substance.

SHRI NITISH KUMAR : I would like to know for my own information. Why it is called White Paper. It is written in black.

MR. SPEAKER : We will do some research on that.

SHRI VAJPAYEE : Shri Advani can make you understand better. This is British tradition. Sometimes papers of other colours are also printed. But I would like to submit one thing that it was charged that all that took place on 6th December was the result of a deep conspiracy and the Government said that it was investigating the matter. But the White Paper does not throw any light on it. Therefore, it is clear that there was no conspiracy in it. If the Government wants to prove it by a CBI enquiry, we are prepared to wait for that also. But the White Paper does not say anything in this regard. The various incidents that the Government has referred to speak that there was no conspiracy. It was wrong. Thank you.

No Justification for Price Hike Before Budget

Mr. Speaker, Sir, before you call for laying the papers on the Table of the House, I want to make a submission to you.

Sir, this is the Budget Session. The common man looks for the Budget with much expectation as well as apprehension. The Budget Session has got its own importance. Budget proposals have got some sanctity in themselves. However, before we assembled here for the Budget Session, the Government put a heavy burden of taxes on the people. Essential commodities which are used by the common man have been made costlier, their prices have been raised by an executive order. Wheat and rice have become costlier. The sweetness of sugar has been reduced. The price of a cylinder of cooking gas has been increased by Rs.15.

Mr. Speaker, we were referring to 'Agni' just now and praising our scientists for their achievement. Whom should we praise for making the gas cylinder so costly ? The price of petrol has increased, the price of high speed diesel has increased.

Sir, according to one estimate, a burden of Rs. 3,000 crores has been imposed. How far this burden is justified—that needs to be debated. I want your intervention. Is it justified to saddle the people with so much burden through administrative orders ? I emphasize the word 'justified'.

Mr. Speaker, this matter cannot be set aside by saying that the Government has got the power to do so. The Government has no right to resort to high-handedness, although it might have attained majority by hook or by crook. We would not allow them to perpetrate this kind of high-handedness.

Mr. Speaker, Sir, it is a point of order. Are such shocks justified before the Budget session ? The Finance Minister is not present in the House. At first he hiked the prices of cooking gas and sugar, then of wheat and rice and thereafter of petrol and high speed diesel. What is the need to wait for the Budget on the 28th now ? Has the session of Parliament no meaning ? The sky would not have fallen if the Government had not hiked the prices. They could have waited for the House to meet, but the House is being devalued. They have destroyed the value of Budget procedure.

Mr. Speaker, Sir, if the Government is allowed such a long rope, the House would become irrelevant and Budget meaningless. We want your intervention in it. You have been giving advice to the Speakers of Parliaments of the whole world, but can't you advise this Government ? What is the

Lok Sabha on February 21, 1994 Point of order raised opposing the decision of the Government to increase the prices before Budget

justification for raising the prices in this way before the presentation of the Budget ? Could the Government not wait for the Budget, was it necessary to make a mockery of Parliament ? Mr. Speaker, we want your ruling on it.

Mr. Speaker, Sir, the Budget session is meant for the purpose of discussing issues like this. You may discuss it later on.

(Other Members also expressed their objection to it)

SHRI VAJPAYEE : Mr. Speaker, Sir, we oppose the policy of the Government and walk out of the House.

Budget Fails to Satisfy the People

Mr. Chairman, Sir, I have got two speeches of the Finance Minister before me. Both are on the Budget. One was delivered here and the other was distributed among the members in the form of a booklet. But there is a difference between the two speeches.

A few Urdu couplets which were recited by the Finance Minister while presenting the Budget in the House are missing in the printed speech. The people have got his printed speech, but the speech made by him in Lok Sabha will serve as a record and, for that a search or a research will have to be made. The coming generations should know that there was a Finance Minister in India who talked not only of Finance, but also of poetry. The Finance Minister said in the couplet "Centuries had to suffer for the faults of Moments......" We are afraid the Moments which committed the mistakes are these very moments, for which the coming centuries would have to suffer.

Change in Direction of Wind Needed

Sir, the Finance Minister wants to create heaven from the present circumstances, but let not our feet go off the ground while gazing heavenward. Today there is danger of such a situation developing. The Finance Minister even wants to change the direction of the wind. We must appreciate his manhood. Really, a change in the direction of the wind is needed. But, Sir, can it be said with confidence whether the change of direction of the wind will help in rowing the boat to the shore or will lead it to a whirlpool ? The Finance Minister has also recited another couplet saying that "the great civilisations of Greece, Egypt and Rome have disappeared from the earth...." It would have been better if the Government had rejected GATT and after that recited the couplet which says—"Many countries have disappeared, but we stand firm and will remain so in future." At times it appears that the couplets recited by the Finance Minister were not so appropriate. However, he recited them and it is good. It is a different thing that our friend Shri Somnath Chatterjee did not relish the couplet ... (*Interruption*)...

SHRI SOMNATH CHATTERJEE (Bolpur) : Before I could understand by tuning to the translation, he came to another topic. I said, enough is enough. It is impossible to keep pace with that, and he was not coming to the Budget at all, because he had nothing to say on that. (*Interruptions*)

SHRI VAJPAYEE : Mr. Chairman, Sir, the Finance Minister had recited the couplets in extenso and if our comrade wanted to understand them through

Lok Sabha on April 25, 1994 during discussion on the Budget

translation, he could have done so .... (*Interruptions*).... He would not understand what the recitation of poetry has to do with the Budget. But as another comrade has said just now, there is a philosophy behind the Budget, it reflects the economic philosophy. It is another thing that we have a difference of opinion about that philosophy, and the philosophy of the party in power, but about what kind of India we want to build .... (*Interruption*).... We must have an inkling of that in the Budget.

SHRI A. CHARLES (Trivandrum) : Poetry is the music of the heart, which can have a fine expression in the Budget. (*Interruptions*).

SHRI VAJPAYEE : Now I want to come to the Budget, because the time at my disposal is short.

I have a complaint that the discussion on the Budget has taken place in two parts. The piecemeal discussion can neither do justice to the Budget, nor can express the sentiments of the House in their totality. In the other House, the discussion is over and the Finance Minister has given his reply, but here the discussion is being prolonged. Had the discussion taken place earlier, perhaps the Finance Minister might have amended some of his taxation proposals in the light of our suggestions. This matter was also kept pending. The Budget should not be treated in such haphazard manner. I hope this would be kept in mind while discussing the next year's Budget.

Sir, the expectations raised by the Finance Minister while presenting the Budget do not conform to the reality. As stated by Comrade Indrajit Gupta, warnings were given after the Budget that it would lead to inflation, prices would rise, but the government did not accept it and now it has been proved. Inflation has crossed the double digit. I do not want to repeat what the Finance Minister had said about inflation. His 1991-92 speech is there ... (*Interruption*)....

SHRI SOMNATH CHATTERJEE : Leave that aside, they have admitted that things have gone wrong ... (*Interruption*)....

SHRI VAJPAYEE : There are no indications now that inflation would be curbed in the near future, because your present estimate as well as your estimate of the last year's Budget have all proved wrong, excepting in regard to the foreign exchange reserves. Fiscal deficit has increased, revenue deficit has increased, the amount of interest on loans has increased, although the Finance Minister had criticised these things in his speech at that time and had said that these too had effect on inflation.

Transparency in the Formation of Budget Required

It is good that foreign exchange reserves have increased, and if the Finance Minister wants to be congratulated for that, we will not be miserly in congratulating him. But, as Shri Indrajit Gupta asked, what are the details of the foreign exchange reserves, from which sources the foreign exchange has been augmented ? As compared to last year, the foreign debt has increased and the internal debt has also doubled. I shall be happy if the Finance Minister contradicts it. We draw our conclusions on the basis of the data available with us. From which sources the foreign exchange reserves have been augmented ? There must be some transparency about it. Now-a-days there is a lot of talk that there should be openness, that there should be transparency. I would like to say that there should be transparency in the formulation of the Budget also. Please leave aside the taxation part, where customs duty has to be increased, where excise duty has to be reduced, but there should be open discussion on Budget allocations in this Parliament and in the whole country, and this discussion should go on continuously. This is the practice in the other countries of the world. If it happens in Japan, why can't we have it here ? After all in respect of the amount of money to be given for poverty alleviation, can't we discuss what is the allocation and how much allocation should be made ? Could it not have been estimated and discussed before the presentation of the Budget ?

Other Aspects of the Economy Need Attention

Mr. Chairman, Sir, I was talking about foreign exchange. Let the Finance Minister take the House into confidence about the detailed account of the foreign exchange reserves. Out of it, how much is real investment ? I have got some information according to which the total foreign investment during 1993-94 is touching $3 billion mark, but out of this $ 425 million is in the form of direct investment. In 1992-93 the amount of direct investment was $ 343.5 million. From this point of view, no claim for a substantial increase in foreign investment can be made. The remaining foreign capital has come in the form of portfolio investment. This amount is of the order of $ 1.36 billion, out of which $ 1.1. billion have been received during the three months of October, November and December. This has come mostly in the form of finance capital, not in the form of productive capital. If these figures are correct, then the approach that foreign exchange reserves have increased and therefore, we need not worry about other aspects of the economy, I think, would not be proper.

Presumptions by the Finance Minister

In the Budget presented by the Finance Minister, he has made certain presumptions. His first presumption is that this year also the monsoon would be good as it has been during the last six years. It is true that our agriculture depends on monsoon. But it is a bitter truth that this aspect must be kept in mind while formulating the Budget. Even now, many parts of the country are facing famine and scarcity conditions. I had been to Rajasthan. Sixty thousand labourers are working there on relief works and a demand has been made that the number of labourers should be increased to one lakh. Similar conditions prevail in many areas. The Finance Minister should regard it as a good fortune of the country, that we got six good monsoons in a row due to which there were good crops. He is proceeding on the presumption that in future too the monsoon would be good. He is also proceeding on the presumption that the tax reliefs given by him to the domestic and foreign industries would raise the rate of industrial development by six to eight per cent. He is also proceeding on the assumption that the law and order situation in the country would remain normal and social tensions would not occur. He is also proceeding on the presumption that the international price of oil would not rise, and would remain stationary at today's rate. He is also proceeding on the presumption that as a result of the reliefs given by him to the middle class, demand would pick up and because of this increase in demand, industries will flourish and the industrial recession would recede, leading to utilisation of unused capacity. The Finance Minister also pressumes that the investment of foreign capital would increase.

Creation of Social Tensions to be Avoided

Mr. Chairman, Sir, ours is a vast country. It has complex problems. Efforts should be made whereby no social tensions are created in the country. But if social tensions occur, well, the Finance Minister refers to them saying that the deficit increased because of the Ayodhya incidents, or due to bomb explosions. This is not proper. No doubt, such things have their impact, but in a vast country some incidents may take place anywhere, and fiscal policy and taxation proposals should be decided by making a guess about them ! Nobody knows what turn the relations with the neighbour might take. It is not known how much serious a situation might arise in Uttaranchal and at what time. If the entire structure of the Budget is based on the presumption that all the circumstances will be favourable, and accordingly the country would make fast economic progress, that would not be realistic. The problem is not so simple and the situation is not so easy. Therefore, it is essential to take care of all these things whoever the Finance Minister might be.

I would like to put it to the Finance Minister as to why these social tensions are allowed to be created ? Why an attempt is not made to resolve them before hand ? Has not the Finance Minister to play any part in it ? Is the Finance Minister concerned with the Ministry of Finance only ? The Home Ministry is independent, it may do any thing it likes. Is every Ministry independent ? There was delay in resolving the issue of Ayodhya. Now the Finance Minister is referring to it. This is a matter which relates to religion, to culture and to nationalism, but it does and will affect you and, therefore, social tensions should not be allowed to be created. I do not know whether this matter is ever discussed by the Cabinet.

Expectations Belied

Mr. Chairman, Sir, in the Budget presented by the Finance Minister we have expected that he would bring such taxation proposals as a result of which prices will stabilise, employment opportunities will increase, inequality will be reduced and the country will march forward towards self-sufficiency. But the taxation proposals do not indicate this.

There is recession in the industry. Several industries are standing in queue before the B.I.F.R. for assistance. They want to take loans. If the government is taking loans, why should the private industries lag behind ? Along with recession, reduction in opportunities for employment may cause social tension. If factories are closed down on a large scale, the people will come out on the streets and if you could not control the price rise along with it, then a situation of social tensions may arise. The Finance Minister himself would be responsible for that situation.

Employment Opportunities Reduced

The Finance Minister has stated at one place in his speech that the number of unemployed registered in the employment exchanges has come down a little—by one per cent. We know that if one gets one's name registered in an employment exchange once and if he does not get employment within a fixed period, he has to renew his registration. It is not registered for all time to come. You are saying that employment opportunities are available with the employment exchanges. There has been a reduction in the queue of the unemployed. How much the employment opportunities have increased, please give details ? The Statistical Organisation does not suply these figures. Don't you have the statistics of how many employment opportunities were made available, how many new persons were given employment ? That would be a true criterion. Do not go by reduction in number on the register. I have collected some statistics. There has been a reduction in the million man days under the Jawahar Rozgar Yojana. There has also been a reduction in the allocation of money for other schemes of poverty alleviation. I have got the statistics about how many families were to be helped under I.R.D.P. In 1989-90, 3.35 million families were given help. In 1990-91 this figure came down and only 2.90 million families were given help. In 1991-92, 2.54 million, and in 1992-93 2.06 million families were given help. The same is the story of Jawahar Rozgar Yojana. We would like to know from the Finance Minister how the figures of employment are increasing ? The way the capital is being invested would give impetus to big industries. Foreigners are also interested in big industries. In fact, their schemes are proving fatal for the small industries. Organised sector cannot provide more opportunities of employment in this country. We want new technology. This is the age of automation. Industrialisation would increase, but employment opportunities would recede—these are the conditions that would be created. In such a situation the Finance Minister has imposed excise on small industries. Shri Indrajit Gupta has rightly said and I too had used these very words yesterday in Gorakhpur, that the Finance Minister has declared war against small industries.

Declaration of War Against Small Industries

Centuries had to suffer, for the faults of moments; small industries provide more employment, they have a hand in foreign trade, they do not allow concentration of power, they also do not allow concentration of the capital. True, there may be some industries among them which misuse the facilities provided to them. Are there no such cases among the big industries ? From thread to umbrella the Finance Minister has cast his net so widely that big sharks got away and small fish were caught in it. Factories have closed down. I have myself met the Finance Minister several times along with the delegations and I feel that the Finance Minister has made up his mind. The supporters of GATT think that small industries are wasteful junk-yards. They are not in tune with globalisation. In small industries, poor people sitting sometimes in hovels, sometimes under tinsheds, are manufacturing something. What is the need of it ? I hope the Finance Minister will make some announcement in his Budget reply and give some relief to the small industries. Serious studies have been made about small scale industries. P.A.C. had also analysed that some people are misusing facilities in the name of small industries. The argument given is that if small industries are earning money and are not prepared to part with the government share, then the matter has to be considered. But the small industries say that they do not shirk in depositing the government share in its treasury and they are prepared for it, but they need to be saved from the Inspectors' rule.

The Finance Minister did not say many things in his speech, but notifications were issued overnight. Inspectors were present outside the factories in the morning. The factory was locked and he was sitting on the chair outside. People were looking to Parliament and Parliament was looking to the Finance Minister. Do you want to bring back the Inspector *Raj* ? An income of only Rs. 100 crores has been estimated. A way could be found for tax recovery by talking to the small industries so that the government's income is assured, the botheration of keeping accounts is avoided and they are relieved of the corruption of Inspectors. It is necessary to have such a system. Otherwise, if by treating the small industries in a shabby manner, we expect that no tension would be created, that there will be judicious distribution of wealth, that all will get their share in the prosperity, our expectations are not going to be fulfilled.

More Allocation Required for Defence

Mr. Chairman, Sir, Hon'ble Finance Minister has made nominal increase in the Defence Budget. That should not have happened. The security atmosphere is getting vitiated. Our neighbour is trying to obtain increasing number of lethal arms. We have to keep ourselves ready. We have long sea boundaries. All of us are proud and feel elated at the progress made by our scientists in the field of ballistic missiles and space technology and we offer our felicitations to them. But this progress must not be stopped under pressure from anybody. Defence is a primary necessity.

Budget estimates for the year 1993-94 were Rs. 19,800 crores but the Revenue expenditure amounted to Rs. 21,000 crores. The revised Budget estimates for 1994-95 are Rs. 23,000 crores. This increase is only one per cent, which is insufficient. If inflation is added to it, there would hardly be any increase. We are standing where we were and the government knows this. The Finance Minister must be knowing that whatever Budget we sanction for the Defence forces, 65 per cent of that is spent on the establishment. Research and Development, manufacture of new arms or purchase of new weapons and modernisation are extremely important. Those responsible for the operation of our forces know it. From where will they get money for it ? Our

Defence experts tell us that if today we decide to acquire some missile, it takes several years to induct it and to give training for it. It could be utilised after a number of years. We will have to review the matter from this angle. This House will have no objection in granting money for Defence purposes. But where there is scope to save money to reduce expenditure, it should be looked into.

Service Tax Imposed

The Finance Minister has how imposed a new tax—the service tax. There is apprehension that it will increase in future. What is the need of this service tax ? The service on which this tax has been imposed has nothing to do with utility, capacity and efficiency. You wanted a service tax, so you imposed 5 per cent tax. It is feared that while today a small window has been opened, tomorrow a big door would open. It is not a right step. To reduce customs duty and to increase the excise duty is not the way to encourage competition. Just now, Shri Indrajit Gupta was saying that competition does not mean that foreign companies start swallowing our companies. Actually what should happen is that some day Indian companies should become international companies, they should go to foreign countries on the basis of the quality of their products, but your present policy does not give any such hope. So far, the process of swallowing Indian companies is continuing. This must be stopped.

Foreign Capital not for Stock Market

It is not proper to allow foreign capital to be invested in the stock market. There is anarchy in the stock market today. It appears that the government has no control over it. There is need to regulate it, otherwise some big scam, like the banking scam, may happen again and it will not be possible to find out where the big amount of five thousand crores had gone even after the constitution of a J.P.C. ? Constitution of another committee will be suggested for that.

Mr. Chairman, Sir, let people earn money, let them save money, but it should be invested for production, not in the stock market. Today the tendency of making quick money by investing in the stock market is increasing. Should we encourage even foreign capital for this ?

More Transparency Required about Loans

Mr. Chairman, Sir, a part of the loan taken by us from I.M.F. has been returned. That is very good. That would improve our credibility abroad. But I want that there should be more transparency about the loans that we take from I.M.F. or the World Bank, about how much loan are we taking, on what conditions it is being taken. Could a consensus not be arrived at about these loans ... (*Interruption*)... What do we do with the loan, that should also be looked into. However, the entire procedure of taking loans is kept in the dark, it takes place in secrecy, and that creates apprehensions. This should not happen. Whatever the trade and dealings we have with the World Bank and I.M.F. should be somewhat open; there should be a consensus on such issues.

Reserve Bank to be an Independent Monetary Authority

It is very necessary to develop the Reserve Bank of India as an independent monetary authority. The Reserve Bank did not play a very salutary role in the bank scam. Sometimes it appears that the Reserve Bank is an adjunct of the Ministry of Finance. At other times, it appears to be a part of the Prime Minister's Secretariat. In many countries, the Reserve Bank acts as an independent monetary authority. It hardly makes a difference that the Governor of the Reserve Bank is an able person. It is important that the Reserve Bank should work in a manner that it may even give the right advice to the Government, if necessary. The Reserve Bank should not succumb to whatever the Government wants.

The Finance Minister has taken one more step by proposing to fix the limit of borrowing from the Reserve Bank. But he is not prepared to impose that limit for himself. Whoever becomes the Minister of Finance after Dr. Manmohan Singh would be bound by this limit. If the proposal to set a limit to the borrowings from the Reserve Bank of India is good, why is it not being implemented with immediate effect ?

SHRI MANMOHAN SINGH, Minister of Finance : From this very year.

SHRI VAJPAYEE : It is very good if the Finance Minister proposes to implement it from now. But from this Budget speech it sounds as if it will not be implemented just now, but from a future date.

Raise Income Tax Exemption Limit

Mr. Chairman, Sir, I want that the Finance Minister should also tell something about increasing the income tax exemption limit in his speech today... (*Interruption*)...

I have already referred to it. You have come late. This limit has been raised from Rs. 30,000 to Rs. 35,000. In real terms it is not Rs. 5,000 but also Rs. 2,000, because there is the effect of inflation. The purchasing power of Rs. 30,000 last year has today come down requiring Rs. 32,750. What is the relief then that you have given ? You have not stopped the flowing tears. You have only given a handkerchief to wipe out the tears. That will not stop the tears to come out. The Finance Minister says that he is prepared to raise the exemption limit, but it would adversely affect the fiscal position of the States. Could some other way not be found to compensate the States ? Well, it is possible to find one and if the Finance Minister is willing he can himself find it out. You are talking of creating the sky out of the dust of the land, but you are not prepared to make up the deficit that is going to accrue to the States ?

Relief to Hindu Undivided Family

Mr. Chairman, Sir, I want to make one more point. For an individual, the exemption limit is from Rs. 30,000 to Rs. 35,000, but for a Hindu Undivided Family the exemption limit is still Rs. 18,000. What should be the attitude of the Government towards a Hindu Undivided Family, so far as the tax is concerned ?

Does the joint family in our country not act as a social security system ? Does the unit of the society consist of an individual or a family ? The Government can never provide social security to all the persons. In a joint family, even today everybody is looked after. There is mutual concern for each other. Why this discrimination against them in the matter of taxes ? If there are four brothers and they live in one house, then they will have to pay more tax, but if all four of them live separately in four houses, they will have to pay less tax. If they live in one house, they leave the other three houses for others. Really, they should be rewarded for this, but here they are being penalised. Therefore, the existing tax policy towards the joint family needs to be reviewed.

Mr. Speaker, Sir, the Minister of Energy is creating difficulty for me. The Finance Minister has done great injustice to the working women also, I am told. One thousand rupees have been reduced from the standard deduction. Is it correct ? If it is not correct, very good. He says it is not correct. I have been told like that and a delegation also met me in this connection. I fail to understand whether I should accept the statement of the delegation or draw my own conclusion from the nodding neck of the Finance Minister.

So far as the limited companies are concerned, there should be no discrimination between the small and the big ones. Forty per cent tax applies to all, big and small. If a company produces more, increases its productivity, it must be encouraged. Investment allowance can be given on setting up of a plant or machinery.

Government has given facilities for setting up industries in ten backward States of the North-East. But this facility has been given only for five years. Those who are connected with industries say that 5 years are not sufficient because 3-4 years are taken away in establishing the industry. This facility should thus be for 10 years instead of 5 years and it should be extended to the backward regions of other States too. No such provision has been made in this Budget.

Mr. Speaker, Sir, I want to conclude my speech. The apprehensions expressed at the time of presentation of the Budget have come true. The expectations of the Finance Minister have failed to awaken a new hope. It is another thing that in the conferences and seminars which the Finance Minister attends he comes across glowing faces and it would not be surprising if a misunderstanding is created in the mind of the Finance Minister due to this.

If the patient's face gets a glow, at the sight of the beloved, the latter thinks that the patient's condition is good.

Mr. Speaker, Sir, the people are waiting for the Finance Minister's reply. I do not know to what extent the Finance Minister is ready to go. But his Budget has failed to satisfy the people. The subsequent events have proved the apprehensions of the people. There is still time. The mistakes committed can be rectified and an atmosphere could be created in the country in which no new social tensions are caused due to economic reasons. Thank you.

GATT is Discriminatory

Mr. Speaker, Sir, I object to the statement of the Minister of Commerce that we want to stage a walk-out. We do not want to stage a walk-out, at least not of our own will. If we are compelled, then we will have to carry out our duty.

I have just now returned after participating in the final session of the Conference of G-15 countries. The document adopted by G-15 countries expresses the sentiments of the developing countries, but it also indicates the apprehensions that the prosperous countries, the rich countries, are on the one hand going to sign the GATT and, on the other, creating new obstacles in the way of trade.

Shri Manmohan Singh had admitted that this is a world of inequalities. The question is whether this inequality would increase or decrease ? After signing this document, will our fight against inequality become stronger, or will our hands and feet be tied down ?

Agreement under Duress

I had raised this question in the afternoon as well and I am raising this question again now. If Shri Pranab Mukerjee is not in a position to reply to it, that is a different thing. Shri Pranab Mukerjee has admitted in an interview with a Hindi daily *Dainik Jagaran* that "We are entering into this agreement under duress; otherwise, this agreement is not a very good agreement." It is true that we cannot remain isolated in the world, we have to move as part of the international trade. But if in the course of next six months we feel that it is not protecting our interests—well, Mr. Jakhar is not here, I would like to say to him that if we feel that the GATT treaty is not protecting the interests of the farmers, shall we get out of the GATT treaty, taking advantage of the withdrawal clause ? I want a straightforward answer. This is a serious matter, please reply.

SHRI PRANAB MUKERJEE : It has not yet come into force. Let it come into force then we will see.

MR. SPEAKER : He says that he will cross the bridge when he reaches there.

SHRI VAJPAYEE : He will be drowned in the river before crossing the bridge.

SHRI PRANAB MUKERJEE : Let us go to the bridge. We have not yet reached the bridge. We are far away from the bridge. Let us reach the bridge and then we will see.

SHRI VAJPAYEE : This is not a satisfactory reply. I would also like to say that you have admitted that for this purpose you will have to frame a law and for that you will have to come before Parliament. Our battle has not ended, it would not end with a walk-out. This battle would continue. We walk out of the House by making this declaration.

Lok Sabha on March 30, 1994 during the discussion on the Dunkel Proposals

Renegotiate GATT Treaty

SHRI ATAL BEHARI VAJPAYEE : Mr. Speaker, Sir, really, a deadlock has arisen and this deadlock can be resolved in the Chamber.

MR. SPEAKER : That is why I had held three meetings.

SHRI VAJPAYEE : Three meetings were no doubt held, but if it was agreed upon that this motion will be taken up under Rule 184, then the solution to the problem could have been found. It was stressed there that the motion will not be taken up under Rule 184. Mr. Speaker, Sir, this motion that the statement made by the Minister of Commerce on his return from Marrakesh be taken into consideration could be taken up under Rule 184 and an amendment could have been moved to that motion to the effect that after consideration of the statement the House advises the Government to reconsider its position. The House can say this. We have been asking the Government every day to move forward in the matter. The Government can say 'no', but to stall the discussion and debarring the House from expressing its opinion through vote by taking recourse to procedure, would create difficulties.

Mr. Speaker, Sir, according to the legal position it is not even necessary for the Government to get the approval of the House after signing such a document, but do the rules permit that if an amendment like this is brought it may not be taken up ?

Mr. Speaker, Sir, I want to ask you a question.

MR. SPEAKER : Instead of asking me a question, it should be addressed to the Government.

SHRI VAJPAYEE : No, Mr. Speaker, it is a matter relating to procedure. Suppose you do not allow it under Rule 184, but my name comes up in the ballot of Private Members' Resolutions and I move the Resolution, "that this House do reject GATT," would you have ruled out the Resolution ? You could not. That would have been discussed in the House and we could also demand voting on that and the Government could have rejected that on the strength of its majority. But how can you stop me from moving that Resolution ? And if I can do this as a private member, why can't I create the same situation by moving another motion under Rule 184 ?

I do not understand why Government was adopting such an attitude in this matter. You get the seal of Parliament and then go before the country, and say, "look here, we have defeated the Opposition, we have managed to get the majority, whatever the way we might have done it. The majority is with us, though the country might not be with us.

Lok Sabha on April 26, 1994 during a short duration discussion regarding the GATT Treaty

SHRI SOBHANADREESWARA RAO VADDE (Vijayawada) : Mr. Speaker, Sir, the point I wanted to make has been placed by revered Shri Indrajit Gupta. My submission is such a situation has never occurred earlier because the issues have never figured where the powers of the Government of India and the constitutional jurisdiction pertaining to the States have come into conflict. Apart from agriculture, even health care is also in the States' authority and here is a situation where the Government of India have signed the agreement and apart from the States where the Opposition Parties are in power, even in the State of Andhra Pradesh where the ruling party is in power, the Andhra Pradesh Legislative Assembly has unanimously passed a resolution urging the Government not to sign the Dunkel Draft in the present form because the agreement is contrary to the interests of the people of this country. The situation is such that the present attitude of the Government of India will weaken the Centre-State relations and also it does not help in strengthening the unity and integrity of this country. Whatever the Government says, we, the Members of the Opposition, are strongly convinced that this Government has not taken the interests of the people of this country to the developed countries, particularly the USA and other countries. (*Interruptions*).

SHRI SOBHANADREESWARA RAO VADDE : You express your viewpoints. Let the Hon. Speaker give you an opportunity. (*Interruptions*).

SHRI SOBHANADREESWARA RAO VADDE : We hold this view strongly. (*Interruptions*)

SHRI SOBHANADREESWARA RAO VADDE : We humbly urge upon you to give us an opportunity to register our protest and to register our disagreement with the signing of the final agreement.

SHRI VAJPAYEE : Mr. Speaker, Sir, when the House rose for lunch, there was a deadlock between the Opposition and the ruling side on how to discuss the statement by the Minister of Commerce. The discussion could be held under Rule 184 as well as under Rule 193, but we stressed the point that the discussion should be held under Rule 184. The House should get an opportunity to express its sentiments, and the Members should also be given an opportunity through division to apprise the country what was the attitude of the parties and their Members who were present in the House on this momentous occasion.

An attempt was made in that direction. We met in your Chamber and tried our level best to make the Government understand that there should be no difficulty in admitting a motion under Rule 184. But it is regrettable that we have not been able so far to bring round the ruling party. We are also firm on our stand that the discussion must be held under Rule 184 and not under Rule 193. It was also decided to have further exchange of views on this matter. If we could bring round the ruling side to accept our viewpoint by spending some more time, we are ready for that and the ruling side could convince us, because we are keeping an open mind and have not closed it. But we want that matter should be settled in the light of the points made on this question in the beginning. If the aim is to avoid voting then the voting could not be put off for ever in the House. Suppose a cut motion is moved emphasizing the same issue and we demand a division, could it be avoided ? But we can make an effort to understand the viewpoint of the ruling party.

Therefore, I urge upon you that in case the House so desires and all are agreed, you may please postpone the discussion on this matter for the time being. Let us have another opportunity to have a dialogue so that we may convince the ruling party and bring them round to our viewpoint.

SHRI NITISH KUMAR : While rising for recess, you had mentioned Rule 193. You may say that the rule may be relaxed.

SHRI SHARAD YADAV : Mr. Speaker, Sir, we are firm on Rule 184. If we are to debate it, let it be under Rule 184. While rising, you had referred to Rule 193, but Members have doubt whether you said so or not. Therefore, there is still deadlock on this question. You have not said anything, nor you have given any ruling. If it is made clear, we can be sure.

SHRI NITISH KUMAR : Some time may be taken to make the ruling party understand. But discussion must be held under Rule 184. (*Interruptions*)

SHRI SOMNATH CHATTERJEE (Bolpur) : Sir, so far as I have been able to understand, you did not give your final decision before the House was adjourned for the recess. Now, certainly I hope .the Government also keeps an open mind so that there can be some utility in this discussion.

Sir, I am prepared to request my party member, Prof. Malini Bhattacharya, not to move it and it can be postponed until we can have discussions to find out whether there is any change of mind of the Government. (*Interruptions*).

MR. SPEAKER : Shri Bansal, do you want to say anything ?

SHRI PAWAN KUMAR BANSAL (Chandigarh) : Nothing. (*Interruptions*).

MR. SPEAKER : If it has to be put off, the Railway Minister should be in the House.

SHRI VIDYA CHARAN SHUKLA, Minister of Water Resources and Minister of Parliamentary Affairs : Sir, I welcome the suggestion given by the Leader of the Opposition. We will certainly explore the ways and means of trying to bring divergent viewpoints together and find out a way in which we can have a thinking which will be in the best and long-term interests of the country.

II Corruption In High Places

Das Commission Report

Madam, the question of corruption is not a question of any one party. The future of democracy in the country is linked with whether we can keep the Government free of corruption or not. Everyone will agree that if we have to end corruption we must begin at the top. If the conduct of ministers is doubtful we cannot expect Government servants and the services to discharge their responsibility honestly.

The appointment of the Das Commission has initiated a new chapter in the political life of the country. This has proved two things. One is that even persons occupying high positions are not free from corruption, and the other is that Indian democracy is alert, effective. People's opinion is awake, active, and however highly placed a person who indulges in corruption, the people's opinion will not forgive him. He will be punished may be by the people's court.

More corruption charges are also being levelled. No one should be affraid of them. They need to be inquired into, and a commonly accepted method of inquiry should be found out. Charges are being levelled against many Chief Ministers, although there are more Chief Ministers against whom there are no charges; so the Congress party should not think we want to topple some Chief Minister by levelling charges against him. If the charges don't hold water no Chief Minister will fall. He will be acquitted with honour. His reputation will grow and the prestige of the Congress party will also go up. But if the charges have substance in them if someone's conduct is suspect, he should be punished. If Chief Ministers can not provide models of conduct democracy would be struck at the roots. Like Caeser's wife Ministers must be above suspicion. Can anyone say Sardar Pratap Singh Kairon's conduct was above suspicion ? It is not a question of how many charges were proved and how many were not. In a democracy Ministers' conduct cannot be tested against the narrow test of law. After all moral values will also have to be borne in mind. In order to strengthen people's faith in the government it is also necessary to see that if fingers are pointed there is a proper inquiry, and if the inquiry shows that conduct is not above suspicion, the person concerned is removed from office.

Lok Sabha on December 21, 1961 on the resolution regarding the Das Commission's report about corruption charges against Sardar Pratap Singh Kairon and other Ministers

Madam, this is the country of Lord Ram, who had left Sita on the complaint of an individual. That person had not submitted a memorandum. Had Lord Ram so wished, he could have suppressed that person's voice, but what he said is so memorable that our Ministers should frame that Shloka and hang it in their offices :

"Sneham dayam cha soukhyam Cha
yadi va Jankim api,
Aradhanaya lokanam munchato
nasti me vyatha."

I shall give up love forsake compassion, I shall not care for personal happiness, if need be I shall leave even Sita. Why ?

To keep the people happy. In order to leave no scope for public criticism Lord Ram left Sita who had proved her blemishless character in an ordeal of fire. The question is not that of law. The question is what ideal we place before the people.

No one can deny that taking advantage of Sardar Pratap Singh Kairon's Chief Ministership his sons earned estates. The Commission is also clear on the point that Sardar Pratap Singh was aware of it had been brought to his attention that his sons were doing so. He cannot escape by saying that I have nothing to do with my sons. A person occupying the seat of power must become ruthless. He must sever bonds of affection. He must behave differently with his sons and his relatives. If our Ministers cannot live up to such an ideal I see danger for the development of democracy.

This report has left action against four categories as yet. One is Sardar Pratap Singh Kairon himself, the second is his family, the third is the non-official people mentioned in the report, who include some Ministers and at whom some friends have also pointed fingers. Then there are some Government officials who collaborated in the misuse of authority, who indulged in irregularities for allowing Kairon's son to benefit. We want to know what action the Home Ministry is taking against all these four categories. I do not advocate a witch hunt, but justice will not be served if the guilty are not fully punished. Of course those who have been named should be given an opportunity to defend themselves. They should be formally charged, they should be given the opportunity to defend themselves, there should be an inquiry, and if the inquiry proves that they deliberately misused their position they deserve to be punished. And what happens to the wealth that has been wrongly amassed? The Finance Ministry wants to take action against those who have made black money, and we welcome the action, but there should also be an inquiry into how wealth has been earned in Punjab through the misuse of power. They may defend themselves, but if they cannot prove that the estate was lawfully earned it should be confiscated. No one is to be chased with a stick. At the same time there must be no concession in matters of corruption.

All Inquiries Should be Equal

One more thing and I shall conclude. All inquires into the charges against Chief Ministers and Ministers should be conducted in the same manner. If we do something in Pubjab, adopt another method in Orissa and still another in respect of charges in Mysore we would not be able to create the right atmosphere in the country. The Government should accept the Santhanam Committee's recommendation that a national panel should be set up and if 10 members of a Legislative Assembly or Parliament present charges to the President the matter should be sent to the panel. The Home Minister and the Prime Minister should not take this responsibility on themselves. They belong to the ruling party. I do not doubt their integrity, but there is no doubt that one day some Congressmen will doubt integrity. They will be charged with behaving in different ways in different matters on the basis of groupism. Such charges are being made in respect of Orissa. I think we should adopt the same procedure.

My friends Shri Choradia and Shri Mani have also said the charges should be sent to the Attorney General, he should see if there is a prima facie case or not, and if there is, a commission of inquiry should be set up. If this proposal is not acceptable to the Government it should accept the Santhanam Committee's recommendation that there should be a national panel of leading citizens and the charges that are levelled should be sent to two or three members of the panel. Congress members should not be afraid of these charges. Democracy and corruption have a deep connection, so we must be extra careful about corruption charges.

It is not a question of the ruling party or the Opposition party. Parties will come and parties will go. Governments will be formed and Governments will go. But the issue now on test is whether or not there will be democracy in India. If we do not act firmly to eradicate corruption the coming generations will never forgive us. Thank you.

Question of Inquiry Against Ministers

Sir, the resolution on special powers that has been moved is a separate thing, because I think Shri Nanda has sought to differentiate between an 'inquiry' and 'looking into'. He has also admitted that a CBI team went there, examined the documents and prepared a report, which is with the Home Ministry. But he had denied that a report of the inquiry has been received. But now that it is befdore the Cabinet Sub Committee it cannot be denied that the CBI went there, looked into the charges, examined documents and reached some conclusions, which are before the Cabinet Sub-committee. In such a situation if we want to play with words we may say the CBI did not make an inquiry, it looked into the papers. But Shri Nanda should honestly admit that he had asked the CBI to go and look into the papers and submit its report. Was not the CBI told ?

AN HON. MEMBER : He has already said so.

Shri Vajpayee : I mean the inquiry. If the CBI did not go to make an inquiry how did the question arise about whether or not the CBI should conduct an inquiry into charges levelled against Ministers ? There are members of the council of Ministers who have publicly stated that CBI should not inquire into charges levelled against Ministers. Therer is a difference of opinion in the Cabinet on this. So it is clear that the CBI went and inquired and its findings support this point. And I, Sir, also want to say to you that both reports have been tabled in the House and have become public property. They have been published in the papers, but your decision is binding on us. But if the report has been placed in that House while we cannot refer to it here....

CHAIRMAN : Who says so ?

SHRI VAJPAYEE : Then the question that arises is, — and Congress members have also said — does Shri Nanda deny that the tabling of the report in the Lok Sabha is not right ?

Rajya Sabha on March 14, 1965 in connection with notice on the question of special powers regarding inquiry into charges made against Ministers

Steel Minister Exposed

Mr. Chairman, Sir, I would like to congratulate my friend Shri Gujral on demanding that the whole affair be proved under the Commission of Inquiry Act. Had my friend Shri Dharia too supported this demand it would have enhanced the prestige of the Congress Party. The Prime Minister has agreed to conduct an inquiry as the report of the Public Accounts Committee has established a *prima facie* case. Shri Dharia is not right when he says there is no *prima facie* case. The question is what should be the form of this inquiry ? All will agree that the inquiry should create confidence in all concerned circles, be impartial and high-powered, and should not be influenced in any way. Obviously it should be headed by a Supreme Court judge. In order that all documents, all relevant facts and all witnesses are presented before it is necessary that the inquiry should be done under the Commission of Inquiry Act. If the Prime Minister accepts that and makes an announcement to that effect she could assure this House and the people to a substantial extent that she genuinely wants to eradicate corruption from India's public life.

Sir, the question is not whether a particular minister resigns or not. Actually a resignation should not have been demanded. The concerned minister should have resigned of his own accord. If we want a clean public life, if we want to set standards of conduct in the country, Ministers, like Caesar's wife, should be above suspicion. In fact it is not enough to be above suspicion, they must be seen to be so. Can Shri Subramaniam's conduct stand this test ? It would be wrong to say that the Public Accounts Committee has absolved him. Even after cross-examining him, listening to whatever facts Shri Subramaniam could produce and going deeply into all of them the Public Accounts Committee says in its Second Report :

However, the reason for this review, even after the detailed examination by the Committee, still remains somewhat obscure."

SHRI C. SUBRAMANIAM : This is the first part.

SHRI VAJPAYEE : I am coming to the second part also. In the second part the Committee has not said it is satisfied with whatever clarification has been given.

SHRI I.K. GUJRAL : Neither has it said it is dissatisfied.

SHRI VAJPAYEE : Will you go only by what has not been said ?

SHRI MUKUL GOVIND REDDY : Mr. Gujral is not in his seat, Sir. He has moved towards the Treasury Bench.

Rajya Sabha on August 27, 1966 in the context of the Auditor-General's Report on the Steel Minister's conduct

SHRI VAJPAYEE : Sir, as I was saying, will the whole thing be considered from a narrow point of view, or will it be so treated that no doubts remain in the people's mind ?

Sir, Shri Subramaniam has not thought it necessary to put his Deputy Steel Controller and Chief Controller beyond suspicion. He has suspected them. But he does not want others to suspect them. What was the basis of his doubt ? I would like to place a portion of his statement before you. When he issued a directive on June 28, it was not a draft, it was the final order. It should have been immediately acted upon, as the July 23 directive was immediately acted upon. The House should note that Jitpal met the Minister on July 20, his letter was received on July 22, the directive was drafted on July 23, and the Secretary signed on July 24. The whole thing was done with great dispatch. Do files move so quickly in Government offices ? If they do there is no need to set up an Administrative Reforms Commission. Now you have to go into when the July 28 directive was sent to Calcutta, why the Chief Controller's Office did not act upon it, why a letter was sent on July 12 and yet another on July 17, and why the firm was given the chance to get in touch with the Minister and exert influence ?

Minister's Admission

As I was saying, in the cross-examination by the Public Accounts Committee the Minister has admitted that there were two reasons for changing the order. One was that he—his Ministry—was asked twice by the Controller's office. At first the Deputy Controller enquired if the directive would apply to rolling mills— at that time the Controller was on a foreign tour. When he returned, instead of implementing the directive he asked for yet another clarification. He asked if the directive would apply to Apeejay too. When the Committee asked why, instead of carrying out the order of June 28, the Controller's office sent these letters, the minister said he could not say there was a nexus between the Chief Controller and the Deputy Controller, as there would have been cause for suspicion had there been only one letter, but it was difficult to suspect both. Still he added :

> "Therefore two persons had made these references and my own impression is that I do not think that both of them would be guilty. If one had done this there is room for suspicion. Even now I would not say that it is free from suspicion."

In order to save his own skin the Minister is ready to point the finger of suspicion at his officials. Then he should not blame the country, the Parliament and the Opposition parties if we want to point a finger at his conduct for the purpose of establishing standards of conduct. Sir, the question is, why was the order of June 28 changed ? The Minister said in the other House that there was a letter from the Transport Ministry. The Public Accounts Committee was told that in the meanwhile a man from the firm met him (the Minister) and the firm had apologised. Neither of the two things may be right. Now the Minister is trying to reconcile them. Even if a directive had come from the Transport Ministry was it not necessary to exempt only

Apeejay from it, the only firm related to shipping from it ? There was no need to exempt all Ministries from it.

Why and How did the Man from the Firm Meet ?

So far as the man from the firm is concerned the Minister could not explain why and how he met, who arranged his meeting, whose recommendation he had brought. He does not even remember who else was present in the room during the meeting. Why can't he positively say there was no one else ? He could have said it, but perhaps his conscience may have pricked him, perhaps he may have thought it was not good to tell such a lie. So he said he does not know who was there. When we listen to a Minister saying such a thing and when we take the background into consideration it increases suspicion instead of lessening it.

It cannot be denied—and the Public Accounts Committee has also pointed it out—that the only difference between the very first order and the one of July 23 is that while the first one was for an indefinite period, by the order of July 23 the Minister limited the period to two years. The first order could have increased the period, the second one curtailed it. The firm of Amichand Pyarelal did some hanky panky in the meanwhile, but instead of punishing it the sentence for the previous offence was commuted. Why ? The Minister wanted to give one more chance to Amichand Pyarelal,—the firm which has been dealing with Government departments since 1950-51, which has kept in touch, against which the Public Accounts Committee has submitted its report, and against which an order has already been passed in the past.

What was the need of giving this chance ? Did the Minister feel confident that it would reform them ? But the Government does not give them the freedom to give chances for reforming sinners. That task would be entrusted to the Sadhu Samaj; it is not the responsibility of the Steel Minister. It is natural to suspect that he did this either under pressure or for other reason. Now the opposition parties are asked to give the reason—are they saying the Minister accepted money from Amichand or Jitpal ? It is for the Minister to prove he did not do so. That is not the responsibility of the opposition parties. All we say is that the Minister's conduct is suspicious and one whose conduct is suspicious is not worthy of remaining a minister.

Subramaniam close to the Prime Minister

It is said that Shri Subramaniam is very close to the Prime Minister. If that is true the only way he can save her from an embarrassing situation is by tendering his resignation of his own accord instead of leaving the decision to her. Ministers are wont to say they have confidence in their leader, if she says so I would step down. This is not being fair to the Prime Minister. Shri Subramaniam should resign ? After both the reports of the Public Accounts Committee and after the debate in Parliament, his conscience is roused and he wants to set standards of conduct. But if he does not resign the Prime Minister will have to decide. It is generally said in the country that the corruption eradication campaign that was going on has slowed down after

Shri Shastri's passing away, has even stopped, because it is apprehended that those close to the Prime Minister may be caught up in it. This impression would gain strength if Shri Subramaniam is not asked to resign. This would not be good either for the Prime Minister or for the country.

An HON. MEMBER : It would be beneficial to you.

SHRI VAJPAYEE : Shri, I am not talking about benefit. This is not a party matter. It was our democracy that gained in strength when action was taken against some corrupt Ministers. The credit for that also went to the Congress Party. If Shri Subramaniam resigns it would not benefit the opposition. Rather, it would be of benefit to the opposition if he continues as Minister, as we can them keep saying to him, 'if you have a sense of shame, resign'. Here the Congress should look to its own interests. It is in the interest of the Congress to ask for Shri Subramaniam's resignation. There is a high-power inquiry going on. Shri Subramaniam can resign, present himself before the inquiry, and if cleared, can return with enhanced enthusiasm, enhanced prestige. This would enhance the prestige of democracy and of the Prime Minister and would also benefit the Congress Party. Our benefit lies in corrupt Ministers continuing and our continuing to raise the matter before the public.

Sir, I am about to finish. The question is not what Shri Subramaniam's conduct has so far been. The question is not how he contributed in the freedom struggle. The question is not even how he served as a Minister in Madras. The question is that he has taken a wrong step. The question is whether his conduct causes suspicion. Vishwamitra spent his whole life in penance, but a single sin set all his penance at naught. Yudhishthir never told a lie. But the only lie he told brought his chariot, which was always above the ground, down to the ground. The question is not about the life so far, it is about a conduct, a conduct that is full of doubt, as everyone will agree, democracy demands, parliamentary democracy demands, that a Minister who is not above suspicion should not remain a minister. Thank you.

The Kanti Desai Controversy

Sir, I would like to congratulate my friend Shri Madhu Limaye. While listening to him, I was constantly reminded of Dr. Lohia. Dr. Lohia was an iconoclast. He believed in destroying before building. Shri Limaye has tried to carry on Dr. Lohia's iconoclastic tradition. Sometimes I envy his enthusiasm and dedication. However weak a case he presents it most forcefully, and even if the verdict goes against him he cannot but impress the spectators. Sir, it is a matter of coincidence that today too Shri Limaye has made the Deputy Prime Minister his target, although, as he just said, he has great respect for him. Actually Shri Limaye's intention is to topple this government. For this he is ready to use any weapon. But in the present motion he has involved the Prime Minister along with the Deputy Prime Minister. This may cause difficulty to some of his friends who are always gunning for the Deputy Prime Minister but are afraid of even touching the Prime Minister.

Sir, most of the facts placed by Shri Limaye before the House have been published in a Bombay weekly. This weekly is engaged in a regular campaign against the Deputy Prime Minister. This campaign can even be called character assassination. This weekly has even stooped so low as to indirectly involve the Deputy Prime Minister in Gandhiji's assassination. This is a matter for investigation and I do not wish to say anything about it. What is surprising is that this weekly has the support of a number of Ministers. It frequently honours them with special interviews. Political circles in Delhi openly aver that some Ministers are behind the weekly's poisonous propaganda against the Deputy Prime Minister. A new weekly titled *The Indian Monitor* recently got together in Bombay and discussed collective leadership in the Congress are behind it. Have they lost confidence in the Prime Minister's leadership ? I would like to quote from the New Delhi correspondent's dispatch published in the first issue of this new weekly :

> "So the Prime Minister's priorities shifted to undermining Mr. Desai and Mr. Nijalingappa. This was sought to be done through yellow journals raking up Kanti affair and through a controversy about Mysore Government's agent in London. Mr. Dinesh Singh and the over ambitious Commerce Minister of State Mr. Raghunath Reddy worked overtime putting on data about these controversies."

Government a Divided House

I do not know how far these reports are true. But one thing needs to be probed—how is it that facts not available to reporters in general and even to

Lok Sabha on August 19, 1968 during discussion on the motion on Deputy Prime Minister Shri Morarji Desai's statement on his son's business connections

members of Parliament reached a certain newspaper ? Did some Ministry pass on the facts ? It seems the present government is a house divided. In a parliamentary democracy the Council of Ministers should work on the principle of collective responsibility. This principle has now gone with the wind. Ministers are working against each other. The Cabinet is divided into groups. The freedom of the country and the security of its frontiers are not safe in the hands of this Cabinet.

Sir, I would like to make a point that has been touched upon by Shri Shantilal Shah. It should be clarified further. It is said that in his speech at the time of the budget the Deputy Prime Minister said his son is miles away from business. This is not true. Members sitting in the House will have to accept the sanctity of facts. Comment is within our freedom. The question is of preserving purity in public life. If there is a mistake on anybody's part it should be pointed out. But we must save ourselves from making false allegations. I do not want to read out that part of the proceedings. When the Deputy Prime Minister was replying about his son he was discussing the leakage of the budget and referring to the investigation carried out by the police. He never said his son was miles away from business. He made it clear that his son was miles away from such irregularities. But it is being spread among the people; this should be refuted. We cannot preserve the purity of democratic life by spreading falsehoods, nor can we place good standards before the people.

Public Life is a Double Edged Weapon

It cannot be denied that there is some difference in the statements made by the Deputy Prime Minister in the House about his son. I am willing to accept that Shri Morarji Desai did not want to mislead the House, but he should accept that his son certainly misled him and did not bring all the facts before him. In view of the high position of the father it was Shri Kanti's duty to place all facts before him, so that they could come before the House. But sir, this is not the first time when an unworthy son misled his worthy father, when a public figure fell in the esteem of the people because of near relatives. Sardar Pratap Singh Kairon is being mentioned, but I would praise him. He had severed his connection with his son and talked about it openly. Nobody can object to a son helping his father in his old age and relieve his hardship, and no one has the right to object if Shri Morarji Desai even appointed his son as his private secretary when he was not Deputy Prime Minister. Every father has the right to take his son's help and the son to help his father. But after his appointment as Deputy Prime Minister he should have drawn the line somewhere. Ministers should not only be beyond suspicion, they should seem to be beyond suspicion. In this debate nobody has doubted the Deputy Prime Minister's integrity, nor can there be any doubt about his patriotism. But public life is a double edged weapon. In it you have to be strict with your relations, you have to sever all bonds of love. This is the land of Lord Ram, who once discarded Sita, the mother of the world, at the instance of an individual. In Bhavbhuti's words he said : "I shall leave love, compassion, happiness, even Sita, without grief if it is necessary to do so to please the people." See what he said — not to punish the people but to please them. He told his father not to grieve. This is our ideal. Not all of us can reach it, but our leaders will have to keep it before them, as they have to guide the people, as politics has become the focus of life and because people look to political leaders for inspiration. Lord Krishna has said in the Gita that small people follow in the footsteps of the great. Today the issue is not that of a party. It is not even that of the Opposition and the government. The level of public life is falling in this country. The influence of money on politics is on the increase. An unholy alliance is shaping up between politicians and corrupt capitalists. The tendency to misuse power is getting entrenched. Public leaders must be on guard lest some relative sully their status.

Limitations in Public Life

Sir, in his statement the Deputy Prime Minister has admitted that he placed before the House the facts that he was told and he tried to take the House into confidence in respect of the facts that came to his knowledge later. I know this is a very difficult thing. Shri Kanti is his support, his only son, whose mother does not keep good health and there has been a grade by in the family. We cannot ignore the humanitarian aspect. Man is fallible, and a man who admits his mistake rises a little above humanity. If Shri Morarji is willing to decide the limit for his son so far as public life is concerned I think this chapter can come to a close and the door can be closed on any such possibility in future. Shri Kanti has slightly furnished Shri Morarji's *Kanti* (lustre), for which we are all very sorry. We do not want this lustre to lose its shine. If he keeps his son within limits the limits of democracy could be preserved.

SHRI MORARJI DESAI : The Hon. Member has said that I should make limitations. I have already said that there is a limitation—he does not do any government work. Beyond that limitation what have I to do ? If anybody shows that he has done it and can prove it, I shall certainly be prepared to receive any penalty.

The Steel Scandal Investigation Shield for the Guilty

Sir, before I say something on the matter I would like to congratulate Shri Madhu Limaye on his promptness and vigilance and on his sense of duty. He did not leave a matter raised as many as ten years ago. Many members raise matters, but I envy him, his qualities of taking matters to their logical conclusion, of keeping a vigilant eye on the bureaucracy and of making Parliament an effective check. It is a different matter that I cannot agree with him 100 per cent, but this does not mean we should not appreciate the way he raises a matter, keeps chasing it and stands the guilty in the dock. His effort is commendable, and it can be said with confidence that in this respect he is following in the footsteps of his leader Dr. Lohia.

Now I would like to turn to this matter. I am closely connected with it. Fortunately or unfortunately I was a member of the sub-committee which the Public Accounts Committee had set up in 1960 for investigating this steel scandal. Later the matter was entrusted to the Sankar Committee. This Committee's report has a note of dissent. Shri Madhu Limaye caught hold of it and on the basis of that information raised the matter again.

The Public Accounts Committee is an important Committee of the House. It can summon officials and they are expected to give true information. It is hoped that they would not hide facts and mislead the committee. If Parliamentary Committees are misled by officials or if they deliberately hide facts parliamentary committees would lose their utility. Then the House would not be able to function effectively. So if it is revealed that in some matter an official had indeed misled a parliamentary committee it becomes a very serious matter.

Shri Madhu Limaye kept an eye on this matter. It was entrusted to the Privileges Committee. Had this Committee wanted, it could have summoned both officials, questioned them and arrived at an independent decision. In this event it was not necessary for the Public Accounts Committee to come into the picture again. But perhaps the Privileges Committee felt that the Public Accounts Committee that had started the whole thing should be consulted. The Public Accounts Committee, of which I am currently the Chairman, set up a Sub-Committee to probe the whole matter. This Sub-Committee consisted of Prof. Hiren Mukherji, Shri Kaushik, Shri Sonawane and Smt. Sushila Rohatgi. This sub-committee summoned Shri Wanchoo and also interrogated Shri Mukherji. The conclusion of this

Lok Sabha on December 2, 1970 during discussion on the Calling Attention Motion on report of Steel Scandal Investigation Committee

Sub-Committee was accepted by the Public Accounts Committee and forwarded to the Privileges Committee for consideration. Had the Privileges Committee not been satisfied with our findings it would have made an independent investigation. It would have again summoned these officials. That would have been better, for then my friend Shri Madhu Limaye would not have had the chance of saying I have a soft (*Narm*) heart.

AN. HON. MEMBER : It is *Komal* (delicate).

SHRI VAJPAYEE : There is not much difference between *Komal* and *Narm*. But my heart is neither soft nor hard.

AN. HON. MEMBER : It is *Atal* (indomitable).

SHRI VAJPAYEE : There is Behari joined to Atal. But it is not proper to say that Shri Wanchoo has been let off because he is an ICS officer. If Shri Limaye can believe it, I knew from his face that he is a Kashmiri. When we considered Shri Wanchoo's conduct we did not consider whether he was an ICS officer or a Kashmiri. We took no decision in that light. Our decision was taken in the light of the facts before us. Everyone has the right to differ with it honestly, but the PAC report has also explained the reasons for our decision.

For instance one of the reasons is that when this matter happened Shri Wanchoo was not Secretary to the Steel Ministry. Secondly, so far as the instructions that were issued are concerned, Shri Wanchoo was asked about them six years later. Possibly he may have forgotten some facts by that time. Hence the Committee arrived at the conclusion that he did not deliberately mislead the Committee. But the Committee has commented that Shri Wanchoo had not read the whole file. This is not an ordinary matter, it is a very serious matter. It may not be a breach of privilege, but if our senior officials appear before parliamentary committees without equipping themselves with full information, testify before them, do not read files fully, they do not do justice to their duties, and to that extent Shri Wanchoo is guilty of not properly discharging his duty.

Steel Scandal Continuing for a Decade

As Shri Madhu Limaye said this is a very important matter. This steel affair is going on for the past ten years. The Sarkar Committee has come out with its report. The PAC also came out with its comment in 1960 about who is responsible for this loss, this '*gol-mal*'. The Government has not yet taken any action against the guilty officials. This is the Government's failure, and it should be held responsible for it.

As for Shri Mukherji, the Committee went deep into the matter. At some places we gave him the benefit of the doubt, at some others we concluded that he did not deliberately suppress facts. But so far as the bank guarantee is concerned we conclude that he misled the Committee.

A person who misleads a parliamentary committee is not fit to remain in Government service; he should be dismissed. Had it been within our powers and had there not been constitutional difficulties in the way we would have certainly recommended Shri Mukherji's immediate dismissal. Such a person cannot remain in service. He is not only guilty of insulting a parliamentary committee, he is guilty of showing disrespect for the entire democratic process. When he comes to testify he gives the assurance that he would speak the truth, and yet he tells lies. He cannot be forgiven. But Sir, you are a constitutional expert. You know that before removing a Government official from service many processes have to be gone through. He is given a charge-sheet...(*Interruption*).

SHRI S.M. BANERJI : I was removed without a charge-sheet.

SHRI VAJPAYEE : Perhaps you deserved it. Sir, that was just a joke. I know that his removal was also wrong.

Strong Sentences Required

Sir, the Constitution is in our way. There is a process that will have to be undergone. For this we have tried to find a way out. Shri Limaye has proposed to the House that Shri Mukherji should be sentenced to seven days. But if he is to be sentenced at all, why only for seven days ? It seems Shri Limaye is also soft- hearted. That means softness is only a matter of degrees. Instead of seven days the sentence could have been for fifteen days as well. But he has not suggested a sentence of fifteen days. Obviously he too feels more than seven days would not be proper. As for us we feel even seven days would not be proper. Thus there is no basic difference. I can understand his anger. Perhaps he wants to hand down a punishment that would be an example for other officials. But I do not agree to his proposal of seven days. Is it logical to argue that sometimes a demonstrator in the visitors' gallery is punished, so this matter also calls for punishment ?

SHRI MADHU LIMAYE : It is a serious matter.

SHRI VAJPAYEE : I know Shri Limaye was not in favour of punishing who has been punished. But if that is so how can he advocate punishing somebody else ? I agree this is a serious matter, and so we should give a serious punishment. But for someone even flogging may not be punishment and for someone else even a couple of insulting words would be a big punishment. We would have to draw a line between penalties. When we call a government officer before the House to reprimand him and then, by an amendment presented by Dr. Ram Subhag Singh and prepared by our able friend Shri Nath Pai, we recommend that the government may not pursue the matter any further it does not mean the House is abdicating its responsibility. We are saying to the Government that keeping the Constitution in view and undergoing the legally required processes you may give the maximum punishment. We also said that the House be informed of what the punishment was. The House wants to keep the door open for deciding whether or not the punishment was adequate.

If Punishment not Adequate Matter will Open Again

I warn the Government that if the punishment is not adequate the matter will be opened again; the House will again take it into consideration. The Government acts as our agent. We are not abdicating any responsibility.

Shri Bhandare has tabled an amendment to Shri Limaye's resolution. I accept the propriety of that amendment. The Privileges Committee contains all parties. It is a parliamentary committee. It....(*Interruption*)...

SHRI R.D. BHANDARE (Bombay Central) : I shall explain.

SHRI VAJPAYEE : Let me explain it first. The other day my friend Shri Limaye said we should listen to the Rules Committee. Then should we not listen to the Privileges Committee ? But I feel the Privileges Committee has not gone deep enough in this matter. So we have found a golden mean between Shri Bhandare's amendment and Shri Limaye's resolution. It is that Shri Mukherji be summoned before the House and reprimanded, the Government directed to give him the maximum punishment in keeping with constitutional processes and report to the House what that punishment is, and then the House would decide if it is adequate or not. In view of the joint amendment I would request my friend Shri Limaye not to press his resolution. I would also suggest to the House that the joint resolution to which the ruling party is also a party—better late than never—be adopted. Thank you.

Maruti Car Scandal

Sir, while considering the Government's policy on cars what we have to think about is—what, after all should be the priorities of the Government in the field of industrial production ? At first there was a proposal to make a small car in the public sector, but the Planning Commission, when Dr. Gadgil was its Deputy Chairman, did not approve of it. Then it was decided to make the small car in the private sector. A few days back the Industrial Development Minister had himself said that in view of the limitations on resources in the country we cannot spend on the small car, so it will not be made in the public sector; it can be made in the private sector. Is it proper to adopt such a point of view in respect of the country's resources ? The question is, does the country need a car today ? There I have basic differences with the Government. We are expanding the production of luxury goods, while 30 crore people are living even below the poverty level. If the Government says, we are allowing production of the car in the private sector, not in the public sector, that does not take the full picture of economic planning into consideration. After all there is a national sector, we have limited resources, how should we use those resources ? Recently a watch factory was inaugurated with an investment of four crore rupees, which would make automatic watches. Television has been set up in Bombay-Poona which would cost Rs. 75 crores....(*Interruption*).... Bombay-Poona TV has been inaugurated and not 75 but Rs. 100 crores will possibly have to be invested in the development of that complex.

SHRI I.K. GUJRAL, Minister of State in the Ministry of Information & Broadcasting : I never like to interrupt my Hon. friend, but I think he gets his figures wrongly.

MR. DEPUTY SPEAKER : That is irrelevant.

SHRI VAJPAYEE : That is not irrelevant.

MR. DEPUTY SPEAKER : If you want to know how it is irrelevant, I will explain it. We are talking about the car policy. We are not talking about the television policy. That way, if you want to expand the scope of discussion you might go into the entire economic policy of the Government. Time is very limited. I am drawing the attention of the Hon. Member to it. When your remark has diverted the discussion and drawn another Minister into the discussion, that is not relevant here.

SHRI VAJPAYEE : I very much regret you do not want to allow this discussion to go on properly.

MR. DEPUTY SPEAKER : But you are going into the broader economic policy matters.

Lok Sabha on December 22, 1972 during discussion on Government policy vis-a-vis car production

SHRI VAJPAYEE : The question is, what should be the priorities of our planning ? ...(*Interruption*)... I repeat, recently the Government refrigerator factory in Hyderabad, which is doubling its production of refrigerators, has been asked to make coolers. Is it not being done in the public sector ? In what direction does the Government want to take the country in respect of industrial development ? Who can buy a car these days ? A small car is being very much talked about, but I have seen it in Haryana, it won't be so small. The cars being currently made are themselves quite small. How smaller than them can a car be ? It may be calculated that a small car can be had for eleven thousand rupees but how many in India can buy a car for eleven thousand ? How many per cent ? For which people is our planning meant ? (*Interruption*).

When the question of fixing priorities arises, will it be the need for TV in Bombay or will it be arranging drinking water supply for slum dwellers ? So far we have not been able to equip the people with the capacity to buy even a bicycle, but we are spending our scarce resources on luxury goods. In respect of consumption we are going into the category of the most modern countries, but in respect of production we are in a pitiable condition. For people who cannot keep body and soul together is a car a necessity or is the fulfilment of basic needs ?

I would like to draw your attention to what the Prime Minister had said after the Lok Sabha elections. I quote :

> "Whatever resources are committed to luxury goods, it is not possible to convert them into commodities of mass consumption like transport or houses for the people."

This is the speech at the F.I.C.C.I. Now this is the basic public transport that will be developed. Recently my friend Shri Chandra Shekhar, whose status as a progressive is impeccable and who is a member of the Congress Working Committee, wrote in an article that in the coming Five Year Plan Rs. 250 crores have been earmarked for public transport but Rs. 280 crores for loans to Government employees and officers to buy cars. Is this the purpose of setting aside Rs. 280 crore rupees ... (*Interruption*) ... I can show you the source, the Minister may refute it.

SHRI B.R. BHAGAT (Shahabad) : It cannot be true.

SHRI S.N. MISHRA : This came out in the *Financial Express* also.

SHRI VAJPAYEE : You may find out.

The question is do we develop public transport or do we provide a still bigger amount for giving loans to employees for buying cars ? If my figures are wrong the Hon. Minister may correct me. I would like to know if they are right or wrong.

Maruti Car

This discussion has dwelt at length on the Maruti. Maruti is the name of Hanuman's mother. It is said about *'Pawan-Putra'* Hanuman that he does not walk, he flies or leaps. Now if the son possesses this quality the member cannot be bereft of it. The way the Maruti car is fast progressing it seems it does not run on the street, it leaps in every matter. The rapidity with which land was acquired—we know how difficult it is to acquire land, had not the Haryana Government deceived the farmers, had it not thrown all rules to the wind, it would never have been possible to acquire land like this. Those farmers whose land was acquired themselves say that it was acquired for Rs. 11,000 per acre while adjacent land is being sold at Rs. 40,000 per acre. They have given affidavits to that effect. My friend Shri Salve says the farmers are free to approach the court. But does he know that the farmers who complain are threatened that if they go to court it would be made difficult for them to live in the State ?

SHRI SATPAL KAPOOR (Patiala) : Some have gone to court, the rest you can take to court.

SHRI VAJPAYEE : Whether or not some have gone, you won't do anything, you will plead for Maruti...And, it is not only a question of irregularities in acquiring land, ...(*Interruption*)...

AN HON. MEMBER : You are talking of Birlaji.

SHRI VAJPAYEE : You are the people who sit in Birla's lap and come to this House with his patronage; why are you talking like this ?

This Maruti Leaps

Now it is argued that not Maruti alone has been issued a letter of intent, others can get it too and make cars. They too will get licences when their road-worthiness is proved. Does my friend Shri Salve know that a private firm has repeatedly written asking that the conditions of road worthiness be made known to it ? It was told that it would not be told those conditions, yet it should first make the car and then we shall see if it meets those conditions. Is this not objectionable ? If you want private parties to make a small car you should publicise the conditions of road-worthiness, so that they can make cars accordingly. But so far these conditions have not been stated. That is because they would be those that Maruti fulfils. That is why they are not being revealed. I would ask the Hon. Minister to clarify this. Why is there no public declaration in respect of road worthiness ?

Secondly, the speed with which Maruti Ltd. got 6000 tons of steel is really an example of official promptness. If the Government starts working with such dispatch there would be no difficulty in solving any problem facing the country. But this speed is not in evidence in respect of others. This is Maruti, it leaps. It leaps from one office to another, from one city to another. No Ministry can obstruct its course. No Minister has the guts to raise any objection. No nationalised bank can refuse it a loan, for this car runs on a different power altogether.

I would also like to know if Maruti Ltd. has so far been given 35 rakes of coal. Maruti Ltd. has one oven. If the Hon. Minister does not know he can get the information.

AN HON. MEMBER : Coal is not a controlled commodity.

SHRI VAJPAYEE : It is not controlled, but who gets it ? I know it is available at controlled rates, but the coal that has so far been given to Maruti Ltd. 35

rakes—would perhaps not be needed for brick-making even for a hundred years. Have they been asked what their real requirement is ? Why have they been given so much extra coal ?

That is not the only thing. If you telephone Gurgaon you have to go through the exchange, but there is a direct line from Delhi to Maruti Ltd. You can phone whenever you like.

Another small thing. If you go on to that road you find it has been widened from Delhi, but only upto where the Maruti Ltd. factory is located, not beyond that, I know these are small matters, but such small matters ...(*Interruption*)....

SHRI TYAB HUSSAIN KHAN (Gurgaon) : Rani Sahiba has also a telephone line. The road is from Delhi to Jaipur.

SHRI VAJPAYEE : I know, I telephone every day.

There can be no objection if a young man becomes an entrepreneur and sets up a factory with his own labour, but can it be denied that the capital invested is in excess of the expenditure precisely because the young man is the Prime Minister's son ? There is no shortage of enterprising young men in this country, but no one among them can open a car factory, because no one has the good fortune of being born in the Prime Minister's family. Why are people investing ? Because those who are doing so are being benefited by the Government elsewhere. Those who are Directors are being given licences to open industries. In U.P. a private industrialist who invested his capital was given such a licence. Raunaq Singh was also given a licence like this. Is this not due to the influence of the Prime Minister's position ?

The purpose of this discussion cannot be to sully anybody's image.

SHRI SATPAL KAPOOR : What else can it be ?

SHRI VAJPAYEE : But if there are some things that sully the image it cannot be stopped. This is not Maruti Limited, this is corruption unlimited. This is the century's biggest scandal, and it sullies the Prime Minister's image. I am incapable of comprehending it. The Prime Minister enjoys the people's confidence, she has much influence, and yet for the sake of a small factory of a son she has given the people the chance to point a finger at her. This is not an instance of mother's love. It is an instance of disregard for the limits of public life. Those who are in power must take care to ensure that nobody has the chance to point a finger at them. Justice should be done to the son. This is not justice, this is an attempt to throw all rules and regulations to the wind for furthering the son's interests and decking him with riches.

SHRI R.V. SWAMINATHAN (Madurai) : Is it a crime to have such an intelligent son ?

SHRI H.K.L. BHAGAT : How can Mr. Vajpayee answer it ?

SHRI VAJPAYEE : This is not a small matter. In other countries this is not an offence, it happens there, but it cannot be permitted here.

SHRI RAJ BAHADUR, Minister for Parliamentary Affairs, Maritime and Transport : Vajpayee has gone below the limits of decency.

SHRI VAJPAYEE : What I am saying is not below the limits of decency, what was done is below the limits of decency. We can have a difference of opinion.

There is still a chance for you to accept carrying out an investigation into whatever irregularities have taken place in this regard. I do not want to say anything against this young man. I have not even seen him. But no one can deny that the way this factory is being set up shows misuse of the Prime Minister's office, her prestige and her influence. I do not say she wants to do so. But those who are helping to set up the factory want to exploit her influence elsewhere. This is not a good tradition. This is not going to enhance the Prime Minister's prestige.

Ministerial Malpractices

Sir, the motion before the House is based upon the report of the Kapur Commission. This report was submitted to the Government on July 14, 1963. This huge report of 13,000 pages is about Bharat Sevak Samaj. Sir, it would have been in the fitness of things if the Government had informed the House what decision and what action it had taken in respect of this report under Sections 3 and 4 of the Commissions of Inquiry Act. According to law this should have been done within six months. The report was given in 1963 and we are discussing it in 1974. Perhaps it would not be before 1975 that we know what action the Government has taken on the report.

Sir, Bharat Sevak Samaj was registered in 1950. No one can have a quarrel with the aims and objects with which it was set up. It was quite necessary to set it up in order that the society should voluntarily participate in development work. I would even say that if we are to save ourselves from statism we would have to develop a system by which the society can stand on its own legs. The establishment of Bharat Sevak Samaj was a right step in this direction.

But Sir, as you know, many good projects fall into bad hands and become bad. Today the name of Bharat Sevak Samaj is not taken with respect. This situation does not make me happy, it makes me sad. But how did it happen ? In 15 years the Government had given the organisation three crore rupees through various Ministries as aid and grant for various activities all over the country. Was it not the duty of Bharat Sevak Samaj to keep an account of these funds ? They are the fruit of the people's toil. Bharat Sevak Samaj is a voluntary organisation. But this does not mean it is not responsible to anybody. Rather, it is responsible to the whole country and will have to discharge this responsibility by accounting for every pie. Those who are pledged to social service will have to face a stiff test. In their case even a small speck becomes a big blemish. These are the ideals we have set in this country.

Affairs of Bharat Sevak Samaj

But Bharat Sevak Samaj could not live up to these ideals. In the beginning the Public Accounts Committee took up the matter of Bharat Sevak Samaj in 1965. At that time I was a member of the Committee and Shri Morarka its Chairman. In the Committee we do not think on party lines. But it cannot be denied that Congress members are in a majority in it, even if Shri Jyotirmoy Basu is its Chairman. But we do not think on the lines of majority and minority. It was necessary for the Committee to consider the comments passed on Bharat Sevak Samaj by the Comptroller and Auditor-General. We

Lok Sabha on December 18, 1974 on charges of malpractices against Shri L.N. Mishra

were shocked when we probed the grants given to it by various ministries. At that time Shri Lalit Narayan Mishra was not in the limelight. Shri Gulzari Lal Nanda was certainly somewhat in the news. But it is not a question of personalities. It is a question of a system of organisations. I quote from page 153 of the PAC report on the Samaj :

> "In view of the large transactions and amounts of Government funds made available to the Bharat Sevak Samaj preparation of consolidated annual accounts duly audited by the C. & A.G. giving an overall financial position of the organisation should be insisted upon."

The Committee adds :

> "Here the Committee would like to reiterate the following observation made in para 51 of their eighth report (Third Lok Sabha) :
>
> "It would be advisable for the Government to lay down certain broad and healthy conventions to be observed by the persons holding high official posts when they are either participants or patrons of non-official organisations which have any financial dealings with the Government.

The Committee further says :

> "No minister of the Central Government should be associated with a private organisation which enters into contracts with departments of Central Government. The same principle should normally apply in the case of private organisations receiving grants. If any exceptions are to be made they should be made only with the approval of the Cabinet...."

Kapur Commission

Sir, when this report was placed before the Cabinet it appointed the Kapur Commission for an inquiry.

SHRI L.N. MISHRA, Railway Minister : Vajpayeeji, your memory is at fault, when the matter was being discussed by the PAC and Shri Nanda's name was mentioned he voluntarily offered the suggestion that there should be an inquiry by a commission.

SHRI VAJPAYEE : Sir, I quote from a copy in my hand :

> "At their meeting held on 12.11.68 the Union Cabinet considered the summary dated 22.11.68 and approved the proposal for appointment of a commission to inquire into the affairs of the Samaj."

SHRI L.N. MISHRA : He demanded a commission.

SHRI VAJPAYEE : What I am stressing is that a commission was set up by a decision of the Cabinet and Justice Kapur became its Chairman. He is a respected personality and even today he is Chairman of the Delimitation Commission. The Government did not show its apathy towards him. Now the commission is drawing flak because some members do not like its report, recommendations and some results of its inquiry. This is not because of any Hon. Member.

Sir, it would have been good if the scope of this motion were wider and only Shri Lalit Narayan Mishra had not been made the target. But the mover of a motion is free to use the words of his choice. My difficulty, however, is that whatever I say the motion will bring me back where it wants me.

Involvement of Shri L.N. Mishra

Sir, Congress members have tried to casually laugh away the matter by saying that Shri Mishra has said where the amount of Rs. 203, 840 with him came from and to whom he gave it. But can we ignore what the commission has said ? Perhaps my friend Shri Jyoti Basu has quoted this, but I am forced to repeat :

"According to the statement made by Mr. L.N. Mishra in Parliament on June 2, 1971 he had resigned from the convenorship of the Kosi project of the Bharat Sevak Samaj in May 1957. He also stated that this amount was sent to the various people concerned for the purposes it was meant on the recommendations of the Committee duly constituted for the purpose, and there was no unaccounted money left."

Now the commission asks :

"Who formed the Committee and what authority it had is not shown by anything on the record nor whether the payees were persons who could properly be the recipients of these moneys. Table 29.1 sets out in figures what was stated by Mr. L.N. Mishra."

Now look at Chapter 29 which shows who were given the money : Shri L.H. Jha Rs. 1.36,306; Shri D.N. Jha, Shri J.P. Mandal, M.P. Shri Jagannath Mishra, Shri Murlidhar Kejriwal, Shri Devi Prasad Kejriwal, Shri Radha Kant Mishra, Shri Tej Narayan Singh, *Indian Nation*, Patna—these too have received Rs. Rs. 589; Secretary, Madhopura, High School, Shri Bind Dev Jha—advances given to Eastern side Kosi on different dates for Community Savings Scheme and Bharat Sevak Samaj work, bank charges, postage, stationery etc. The question is, when did Shri Mishra get this money ? How long was it with him ? ...(*Interruption*)... Since when did Mandal become Mishra ?

Shri Y.P. MANDAL : Since you became Dronacharya.

SHRI VAJPAYEE : Have all Mandals run to the rescue of Shri Mishra ?

SHRI MANDAL : What can we do when Dronacharya has stood up ?

SHRI VAJPAYEE : The Commission has further commented. This comment may also have been quoted. I too quote what the Commission has further said :

"Unfortunately the records have not been produced before this Commission to show the persons to whom these moneys were paid or the personnel of the Committee which had made the authorisation and the details of the works for which these amounts were disbursed are also not there.

"(4) Mr. L.N. Mishra had said in his statement that he had given full accounts of the Western Embankment in 1963 and the accounts had been accepted. Whether they were audited or not is not shown. But in the absence of any contradiction of this statement by Government the Committee is unable to adjudicate on the correctness or otherwise of this statement."

Wasteful Expenditure

Sir, this matter did not come before the Kapur Commission alone. The Bihar Legislative Assembly had also considered the report of its committee on the Kosi project. This report was placed before the Assembly on August 24, 1973. I quote a portion from it :

> "Before approving the 50th report on the Kosi project on May 26, 1973 the Estimates Committee had inquired if there was enough information on the guide bund, flood control and silt removal, as a lot of wasteful expenditure has been incurred on all these three heads and mostly persons belonging to one family have been benefited. Shri Vinayak Prasad Yadav, convener of the project sub-committee, explained the situation by saying that due to lack of time the sub-committee could not give a detailed report on these three heads, but references have been made frequently. On this the report was accepted and a special sub-committee was unanimously set up for the three heads, with Shri Vinayak Prasad Yadav as Chairman.

SHRI KRISHNA CHANDRA PANDEYA : You are reading from Legislative Assembly proceedings. What is the connection between the Legislative Assembly and the Lok Sabha ?

SHRI VAJPAYEE : What is the connection between Shri Pandeya and Shri Mishra ? Now, Sir, I quote from what the sub-committee has said :

Mishra Family Benefited

> "So far as the question of benefiting a particular family by giving most of its members contracts in the Kosi project is concerned the sub-committee has reached the conclusion on the basis of direct and available testimony by local engineers and local residents that most of these contracts were given to the members of the Mishra family of Balua Bazar or its nominees. These are all sworn testimonies.

SHRI D.P. DHAR, Planning Minister : The Hon. Member may excuse me—the motion before us at present is on what the Kapur Commission has said. In my opinion bringing any resolution passed by the Bihar Assembly or the Bihar Government into the present debate would be against rules and regulations and also improper. As Atalji has himself said the scope of this discussion is limited to Shri Jyoti Basu's motion. It would be an injustice if we go out of it and quote from proceedings of the Bihar Assembly or the U.P. Assembly or the British Parliament.

SHRI VAJPAYEE : Whatever the Kapur Commission has said about Shri Mishra relates to the Kosi project, and I am referring to what the Bihar Assembly report on the project said. Look at page 114 of the Kapur Commission report :

> "The appointment of Dutta Commission by the Bihar Government to inquire into the Community Savings Committee, Kosi Project Construction Committee and the advances given to the union leaders."

The Kapur Commission has itself referred to the proceedings of the Bihar Assembly in this matter.

SHRI D.P. DHAR : Absolutely not.

SHRI PILOO MODY : Are you challenging the ruling of the Chair ?

SHRI DHAR : I am not challenging the ruling at all. I also do not want Mr. Mody to provoke a discussion on this question.

SHRI JYOTIRMOY BASU : Let me make it clear that Shri L.N. Mishra wanted the Bihar Government to scuttle the Datta Commission and with the help of Shri Bhola Paswan Shastri he accomplished it.

SHRI L.N. MISHRA : What are you talking ? It is nonsense.

Shri D.P. DHAR : I might agree that the Hon. Member is entitled to draw any conclusion about the dissolution of the Datta Commission, but we are not competent to discuss any dissolution or make it the basis for any of our discussion here.

SHRI JYOTIRMOY BASU : This is a motion involving Mr. L.N. Mishra. Mr. D.P. Dhar is nobody to reply on his behalf. The Minister is present and he should reply. (*Interruption*) No, no. This is a motion against Shri L.N. Mishra, his misconduct and improprieties in connection with Kosi project. Therefore the only person who can speak as far as the Cabinet Ministers are concerned is Shri L.N. Mishra. We would tolerate his atrocious language, but he should speak.

MR. SPEAKER : I have given the ruling. If there is any reference to the Bharat Sevak Samaj from anywhere I cannot prevent it. But please be kind enough not to bring in anything not related to it.

SHRI VAJPAYEE : The Planning Minister should speak, because the maximum money to the Bharat Sevak Samaj was given by the Planning Ministry or the Planning Board. The Samaj has squandered that money. So I wanted to attack them too. But Shri Bosu has confined the motion only to Shri Mishra. He has held only Shri Mishra guilty of corruption. This is the report of the Estimates Committee of the Bihar Assembly. Has it no meaning ? Is it worth the waste paper basket ? This matter had been raised there. It relates to the Kosi project and Shri L.N. Mishra is connected with the project.

SHRI D.P. DHAR : If the Estimates Committee has referred to the Bharat Sevak Samaj you can certainly do so.

Kosi Project

SHRI VAJPAYEE : The Bharat Sevak Samaj took up the Kosi project. Shri Mishra was connected with the project. He committed irregularities in it. The Bihar Assembly considered them. The report of its committee is before us. Everything can be connected if you want to, but if you do not want to know the truth nothing can be connected.

SHRI DHAR : Shri Vajpayee's anger is quite improper. Your ruling perhaps meant that if anything about the Bharat Sevak Samaj was said in the Bihar Assembly—whether right or wrong, good or bad—we are prepared to listen to it. But the matter referred to does not concern the Bharat Sevak Samaj.

MR. SPEAKER : I have already said that I cannot prevent any reference to the Bharat Sevak Samaj.

SHRI VAJPAYEE : Did or did not the Bharat Sevak Samaj take up the Kosi project ?

SHRI DHAR : If, as you say, it did and if the Bihar Assembly referred to the same you can certainly say so.

SHRI VAJPAYEE : I shall convince you. I shall do so by extracting what the report itself says. Are we or are we not discussing unit leaders ? Shri Jyotirmoy Bosu has talked of unit leaders and it is also there in the report. The report contains all the details of the payments made to the unit leaders. Can it not be referred to ? Please do not raise a pointless quarrel. This is a printed report. You cannot suppress the truth by saying I cannot refer to it in the House.

SHRI L.N. MISHRA : The reply also is printed.

SHRI VAJPAYEE : Read it. I shall not stop you. Shri Dhar does not know. He is in a hurry to leave Delhi.

SHRI DHAR : So far as hurry is concerned both Atalji and I are thinking about it. If he so wishes we can fix the same date.

That he imposes on me, that he is angry with me is another matter. But what he is quoting now is improper, it has no connection with the Kapur Commission. The terms of reference say that the monies received by the Bharat Sevak Samaj from the Government of India should be gone into. So your ruling is quite right. The Kapur Commission inquired into these amounts. The Bihar Assembly should not be brought into this. That there is a relation of mine in it is another matter. But that is no reason for connecting Bihar Assembly proceedings with the Kapur Commission.

SHRI VAJPAYEE : I think Shri Dhar himself does not know what he is saying. He has not seen this report, nor has he fully read the Kapur Commission report. The discussion has been on clause numbers 1, 2 and 3 on page 128. The reference is to how much money was spent and who had been appointed. And all these matters have been discussed in the report of the Estimates Committee. Both deal with the same thing.

MR. SPEAKER : I would again assure Shri Vajpayee that I shall allow every reference to the Bharat Sevak Samaj, but let him not try to extend the discussion by saying that Shri L.N. Mishra was involved in it and now he is Railway Minister.

SHRI VAJPAYEE : Sir, please do not say such a thing from the Chair you occupy. The Railway Ministry is not being discussed. Has not the Kosi project been a matter of inquiry for the Kapur Commission ? Why cannot other reports about it be referred to ? (*Interruption*). They can certainly be referred to (*Interruption*). They will be referred to (*Interruption*).

MR. SPEAKER : I wish to tell Shri Vajpayee very respectfully that I do not wish to enter into a discussion with him on this point.

SHRI VAJPAYEE : You gave your ruling once but changed it at their instance. Does the Kapur Commission deal wholly with the Bharat Sevak Samaj ?

MR. SPEAKER : The Kapur Commission report deals with the Bharat Sevak Samaj. It is before me — *Report of the Commission of Inquiry into the Affairs of the Bharat Sevak Samaj*. I request you to give all references to the Bharat Sevak Samaj, but please do not raise an unnecessary controversy. I know you have so much material about the Bharat Sevak Samaj that you can say a lot about it and have already said a lot.

SHRI VAJPAYEE : I have said in the beginning that the scope of this motion is quite restricted. I wish that the whole of Bharat Sevak Samaj should be discussed. At that time Shri Dhar kept quiet. Now he says bring in the whole Bharat Sevak Samaj but do not speak about the Kosi matter in which comments have been passed on Shri Lalit Narayan Mishra.

SHRI DHAR : The Kosi project is a State Government project. The Estimates Committee there can inquire into the amounts that relate to the Bihar Government. The Kapur Commission was set up to inquire into the funds received by the Samaj from the Central Government. The project to which Shri Vajpayee refers was a project of the Bihar Government.

SHRI VAJPAYEE : Both are one and the same.

SHRI DHAR : Both are the same, but the jurisdiction of the Kapur Commission does not extend there. Its jurisdiction is over the amounts received by the Bharat Sevak Samaj. So in a way the Hon. Member has fallen into a misconception from which I wish to extricate him.

Frauds are Everywhere

MR. SPEAKER : Before giving my opinion I would like to know if the Kosi Project to which Shri Vajpayee refers was or was not constructed under the supervision of the Bharat Sevak Samaj.

SHRI DHAR : The fact of the matter is that the Kosi project was a state project. Parliament does not pass a State budget, although the Centre provides funds to the States. A State project comes within the jurisdiction of the State Assembly, and its Estimates Committee can come into it. Bharat Sevak Samaj is a voluntary organisation, to which the Centre gave some money. According to it the Bharat Sevak Samaj worked on the Kosi project (*Interruption*). I do not say there may have been no fraud. (*Interruption*). There are frauds everywhere.

SHRI JANESHWAR MISHRA (Allahabad) : To say there are frauds everywhere is a strange argument. Shri Mishra should be forgiven because there are frauds everywhere. Wherever he goes there are frauds.

SHRI DHAR : I am taking the liberty of talking to a reasonable member of this august House and that is why I want him to draw the distinction between the affairs of the Bharat Sevak Samaj and the affairs of the Kosi project as they fall within the jurisdiction of the State Government of Bihar and therefore State Assembly. The two are different. There would be no difficulty if he accepts this.

MR. SPEAKER : If Shri Vajpayee accepts the responsibility of saying that the Kosi project to which he refers was constructed through the Bharat Sevak Samaj he can certainly speak about it.

SHRI VAJPAYEE : I am speaking with full responsibility. The motion under consideration contains allegations against Shri L N. Mishra. These allegations are supported not only by the Kapur Commission report but by other material as well.

I quote further :

> "During the course of the inquiry the sub-committee arrived at the conclusion that most respected local individuals are frightened of the Mishra family. This has been proved by the meeting on August 6, 1973. Three private individuals have given sworn statements. Others were either unable to be present before\the sub-committee or were prevented from doing so."

Friends of the Congress may say a matter of 2 lakh 10 thousand rupees is not a big thing for Shri Lalit Narayan Mishra. I agree. Shri Mishra is at present a favourite of Goddess Lakshmi. He plays with crores. But this was not so when he was rising in public life in 1950. I have no hesitation in saying that when I came to know him at that time I began to respect him as a young man who was motivating people to work hard, but I regret to say he could not maintain that respect. I like him still and will continue to do so. I want to give the assurance that I am not interested in anybody's character assassination. But one thing is clear—a person active in public life must keep a standard of behaviour. After all we are in politics. There can be licence scandals. Now if you say we cannot discuss them I shall not do so.

AN HON. MEMBER : No, no. Connect it to Bharat Sevak Samaj and go on.

SHRI VAJPAYEE : It is a Swayam Sevak Samaj, a self-serving society. There would have been no problem if it had been Bharat Sevak Samaj, a society for services to India.

SHRI N.C. PARASHAR : Say Swayam Sevak Sangh.

SHRI VAJPAYEE : So far you did not get an opportunity to discuss Swayam Sevak Sangh. They do not prosper on government funds. They live by the sweat of their brow.

After all what do one fraud after another indicate ? Do they add to Shri Mishra's reputation ? Can this battle be won only with legal ploys ? I do not agree with Shri Jyotirmoy Bosu that he should be removed. Rather I would appeal to Shri Mishra to resign from the Lok Sabha in the present circumstances and save his party and his party's leader Smt. Indira Gandhi from all blame. Thank you.

The Kuo Oil Scandal

Sir, I listened very carefully to Petroleum Minister Shri Shiv Shankar and also read his speech with great care later. The matter to which he has referred does not belong to his time, he has inherited it. He cannot decline his inheritance. He is an able lawyer. He has tried to make a good presentation of a weak case. For this he has gone through these newspapers of 1980. It is perhaps for the first time that the Government had to take the help of two-year-old newspapers to support its case. I shall also throw light on what the newspapers say. He has also discussed international prices. All in all his effort is to somehow wash away the oil spots on the Government's sleeve. But his statement has made those spots still more prominent. I remember an Urdu *sher*. As it is, there are not many left in this House who quote Urdu *sher*—

PROF. MADHU DANDAWATE : He will become the President one day.

SPEAKER : He has said it for me.

SHRI VAJPAYEE : The *sher* says a garment that is torn cannot be darned. If you sew a torn sleeve it tears all the more. If you wash it looks all the dirtier. One crime stresses another.

Shady Oil Deal

The Hon. Minister stood up to explain away, but he has had to admit certain things because he cannot completely deny the truth. He has attempted some whitewashing, but he has not succeeded. He has admitted that in the beginning of 1980 — when the people there were all too busy celebrating their victory and when their members thought that their victory in the elections would not only mean a pardon for their old offences but would give them full freedom to commit new crimes — the Petroleum Ministry brushed aside the Indian Oil Corporation and entered into a contract for oil. He has also admitted that the deal caused a loss of crores. He has also admitted that the file connected with the deal is missing. This is the type of working government we have, in which a file sent by a Minister to the Prime Minister for advice goes missing and cannot be traced for a year.

PROF. MADHU DANDAWATE : For two years.

SHRI VAJPAYEE : It remains untraceable for two years.

I do not stand here to level charges against anybody, but there cannot be a compromise with corruption. The Hon. Minister has admitted that tenders had been called for. The notice issued for it had specified the quantity and quality of the oil and the mode of payment. But, I quote : "It did not specify

Lok Sabha on July 28, 1982 during discussion on the statement of Minister of Petroleum regarding purchase of H.S.D. from Kuo Oil Company

whether quotations should be on a fixed price basis or on a variable price basis."

Why was this not fixed ? Why was it left open ? If the Petroleum Ministry and the then Petroleum Minister Shri Sethi, who is present here, were sure that oil prices were going to rise in the international market and buying oil at variable prices would be a losing bargain for us, we should buy it at a fixed price, why was the matter of fixed price not made clear in the tender notice that was issued ?

SHRI K.P. UNNIKRISHNAN : It was. I will prove it.

SHRI VAJPAYEE : I am discussing Shri Shiv Shankar's statement. Fourteen firms made offers, out of which four were willing to sell at fixed price. It has also come to light that the Hong Kong firm that was later authorised to supply oil had submitted both types of tenders. It was certainly very smart. Some companies submitted fixed price tenders, some others variable price tenders. But the Hong Kong company, which has powerful supporters in New Delhi, tried to close both doors. It ensured that the Minister would fall into its lap whichever way he tilted. But if this company was given the opportunity to revise its tender why was this opportunity not given to the other firms ? But according to my knowledge—and you too, Sir, will agree that full information in this connection has not been placed before the House, nor before the country. Why a certain company was favoured can only be known through a high level inquiry. I shall come to that later.

Sir, oil bargains are made by the Oil Corporation, not by the Oil Ministry. Does the Minister have the final word on whether oil prices would rise or not ? What experts does the Ministry have ? What is the Oil Corporation for ? It includes experts. It is an autonomous body. Most of the deals are made by the Oil Corporation. In this matter the Oil Corporation was not even consulted. Had it been consulted it would have clearly advised a decision to purchase oil at variable prices as prices were going to fall in future. But the Hon. Minister was not in favour of such a decision.

Oil Corporation not Consulted

Shri Shiv Shankar says it was an error of judgment. He further says the Janata Government had also made an error of judgement. Maybe. It may be an error of judgement. But there are some established procedures to avoid the possibility of errors of judgement. There are some techniques, some systems, some processes. One of those processes is for the Oil Corporation to make these deals, and for it to be consulted. What did the Oil Corporation experts say ? *The Financial Express* has been quoted, the *Economic Times* has been quoted. I know how this news was got published in them, but I would like the Petroleum Minister to tell us in his reply what the opinion of government experts was. Who decided to disregard that opinion and why ?

Is it not true that the Janata Government had constituted a high-level committee ? It included officers of the Oil Corporation, the Ministry and also the Finance Ministry. Why was this committee bypassed ? Why was this decision taken in the Ministry ?

Had experts been consulted and decisions taken after undergoing a fixed procedure what the Minister calls an error of judgement could have been avoided. But there were some ulterior motives. So this decision was not taken by mistake. It was a deliberate decision, taken for the benefit of some people. Only a high level inquiry can bring the facts to light.

Shri Shiv Shankar said in his statement that the file was lost. Sir, I must thank him for bringing in the matter of the file. Now we have the opportunity to tear up the file. By that time Shri Sethi had left and Shri Virendra Patil had come. The oil deal had been struck. Shri Shiv Shankar says the file was sent to the Prime Minister's Secretariat for advice on what policy should be adopted for future deals.

Shri Sethi did not think it necessary to seek the Prime Minister's advice. In his time the matter did not go to the Cabinet. But Shri Virendra Patil was afraid he might be at the receiving end in this mess, so his PA passed the file on to the Prime Minister's S.A. It was an important matter relating to oil purchase. There was a crisis in the world. Saudi Arabia was going to change its policy, there was no knowing at what price oil would be available, whether it would be available at all, and agriculture and industry would be jeopardised. Shri Virendra Patil was worried and eager to consult the Prime Minister. He did not send the file through the office. He said to his PA this is an important matter, go and hand it over personally to the Prime Minister's S.A.—and the file went missing from the Prime Minister's Secretariat. Is this how this Government is working ? What is the condition of the Prime Minister's secretariat ?

I object to that part of Shri Shiv Shankar's statement in which he said—I quote :

> "There seems to be no reminder about the file from anybody for nearly a year or so until early 1981."

This statement is not based upon facts.

Is it not true that in December Audit was looking for this file ? At that time the file was not searched. Is this the seriousness with which this Government will take Audit ? Audit said the file is not to be found. Why was it not searched at that time ? But had it been found then it would also have been placed before the Public Undertakings Committee. It would have been an unmasking. Audit was also prevented. But it can be proved from the record that in December Audit was looking for the file. Shri Shiv Shankar has tried to mislead the House.

Kuo Oil Company

The Government directed the Oil Corporation to purchase oil at the lowest fixed price. This directive is dated February 22, 1980. The London company was asked to dispatch 30,000 tons of HSD at 350 dollars per metric ton. Another directive of the same date said 500,000 tons of HSD should be bought from Kuo Oil Company of Hong Kong at 353.50 dollars per metric ton. The same day's order marked up the price for the Hong Kong company. Could the Hon. Minister tell us from the records if the London company was told we accept the offer of 30,000 tons, but we need more HSD, can you give it ? Were other firms also asked ?

What is this Hong Kong Company ? Is it well-known ? How much paid-up capital does it have ? What is its credit ? Who are its partners ? Is it not true that it is just a sign-board company, a fraud ? Did we deal with this company in the past too ? The Hon. Minister should throw light on these facts. The truth is that a company from Hong Kong was to be favoured, so this company was chosen.

Underhand Deal

There was another established procedure. An agent or agency is not required for purchasing oil from abroad. We have been dealing directly. There was also a government decision to that effect. Now who is this Indian agent ? This agency, which is said to be a company dealing in spare parts for bicycles, was told that we want to buy oil from a Hong Kong company. Why did not the Government negotiate directly ? In an underhand deal you feel a little ashamed to talk directly, you need a middleman. The truth is that the whole deal was finalized by a middleman. Who is this Indian agent ? Has it been involved in oil deals before, or was this its first deal ? What is its standing and its credit ?

Shri Shiv Shankar has referred to the *Financial Express* and the *Economic Times*. According to my information these news items were planted by those who wanted to benefit from the whole deal. I also have a copy of the *Economic Times*. *The Hindustan Times* has also published similar news. A certain newspaper refused to print the news under a byline, it just said 'from a correspondent'. This was because the proprietors knew that the news was expected to serve some vested interests. They refused to accept the responsibility. But look at the news. It is the same — prices can go up, so it would be profitable to buy at a fixed price.

High-Level Probe Demanded

This is a scandal. It is a question of a loss of crores. The matter is under consideration of the Public Undertakings Committee. But it cannot give its verdict so long as there is no 'Action Taken' report. I demand the setting up of a parliamentary committee to probe this whole mess. It should go into this specific deal. You may constitute such a committee. We are not making this demand with any political motive. But if there is an attempt at a cover-up it would not strengthen democracy. If corruption is promoted it would not strengthen parliamentary democracy. Let a high-level committee be set up and all facts placed before it.

Finally, I would like to make one more point. In last week of April, my friend Shri Rakesh had tried to raise this matter during question hour. Shri Shiv Shankar was replying. Shri Rakesh asked if it was true that a file had gone to the Prime Minister. What was Shri Shiv Shankar's reply ? On reading the reply I feel like calling him Bhola Shankar. I quote :

"SHRI SHIV SHANKAR : Prime Minister's House ? I think your information is just a figment of the imagination or not based upon facts, for there is no file that Prime Minister's House called for."

Now Shri Shiv Shankar may say it was not called for so I said it was not called for. Will he play with words ? Was action taken against anybody in the Prime Minister's Secretariat for losing such an important file ? Or was white-washing being tried there too ? A Special Assistant who is responsible for the loss of such an important file is not fit to remain in his position. But this is not carelessness. It is an attempt to cover up corruption. But, as I said before, the more you suppress this matter the more it will spring back. These oil stains will not be cleaned easily.

The Churhat Lottery Scandal

Sir, I beg to move :

"That this House resolves that the government notification No. 2242 published in the Government of India Gazette on June 14, 1986 in accordance with Clause 296 of Income Tax Act, 1961 and placed on the table of the House on July 18, 1986 be withdrawn and a recommendation be made to the Lok Sabha to approve of this motion."

Sir, a notification was published in the Gazette on June 14 in which the Churhat Balkalyan Society had been named for tax assessment years 1986-87 and 1988-89 under Income Tax Act, 1961. Other amendments were also published in this gazette. But, as you see, the resolution has been placed before the House after cancelling only the notification relating to the Churhat Bal Kalyan Society.

Sir, the Society has been given this concession under Section 23(C) of the Income Tax Act, 1961, which refers to—I quote:

"Any income received by any person on behalf of:

(1) the Prime Minister's National Relief Fund, or
(2) the Prime Minister's Fund for Promotion of Folk Art, or
(3) the Prime Minister's Aid to Student Fund, or
(4) any other fund or institution established for charitable purposes which may be notified by the Central Government in the official Gazette having regard to the objects of the Fund or institution and its importance throughout India or throughout any State or States."

Clearly, this concession is being given to the society because it claims to work for children's welfare, is a non-government organisation and the Government has always desired to extend income tax concessions to non-government efforts to assist children, women and the handicapped.

Why Union Carbide Chose Churhat for Donation

But since this society became a topic of discussion has the Finance Ministry kept an eye on its accounts and its activities ? This notification published in the Gazette on June 14, 1986 was placed on the floor of the House on July 18, 1986. Had the opposition not been alert it would have been approved by the House.

Sir, you will agree that the Churhat Society has become a matter of a lot of discussion. The first time I heard about it was at the time of the great

Rajya Sabha on June 14, 1986 during discussion on the Motion regarding income tax exemption to Churhat Lottery

Bhopal tragedy in which more than two thousand people died due to leakage of poisonous gas at the plant of Union Carbide. It came to be known that Union Carbide had donated a lot of money to the Churhat Society. I do not have the figures to show how much. The Finance Minister should give that information to the House.

Union Carbide is a multinational Company. The Churhat Bal Kalyan Society is in Churhat. Churhat is the native place of the former Chief Minister of Madhya Pradesh. He is the whole and sole of this society. (*Interruption*). Sir, why did Union Carbide choose Churhat for a donation ? Did it donate money to other bodies also ? But I do not want to go into that now. It was at that time that I heard about this Society for the first time. Now it has become a topic of discussion. While thinking about the income tax of any Society the Finance Ministry would naturally see if it functions according to society regulations, if its accounts are audited annually and if its office-bearers are properly elected. Did the Finance Ministry do so in this case ? Was it brought to its notice that this society is flush with funds ? It went into the lottery business. Lottery tickets worth crores were printed and sold. In one of its raffles the first price was one crore rupees. The guidelines laid down by the Central Home Ministry were thrown to the winds. Now the matter is being explained by saying that the prize of one crore rupees was announced first and the guidelines came later. Were there no guidelines before this society's lottery ? To whom was that first prize of one crore rupees given ? The society declared that it was given, but nobody knows the name or whereabouts of the winner. The second prize was 77 lakhs. To whom did it go ? There was a Contessa car as a prize. Who got it ?

Has the Finance Ministry found out if the office of the Churhat Society is in Churhat ? I have postal proof. When a citizen wrote to the Churhat post office asking for the address of this society the post office wrote back saying there is no such society in Churhat. Then where is it ? The first prize winner deposited the ticket in his bank in Madras to get the prize money by getting in touch with the bank in Churhat, but he got no reply. Letters were written but they were returned with the noting that there was no such society.

Fraud of Crores of Rupees

Churhat is in Sidhi district, but the printed tickets mention Rewa district. Those who went to collect their prizes were asked to go to Rewa district. Giving the name of another district while announcing a lottery is against rules, but it was done. The prize winners wandered here and there, but they could not get the prizes because they could not fulfil the condition of claiming them within 40 days. Is it the business of a children's society to deceive people and commit a fraud of crores of rupees ? Had the Finance Minister and the Finance Ministry examined all these aspects while giving concessions to this society ?

Sir, that day the matter of the lottery had been raised during Question Hour. This was on July 24. That time the Chairman had directed the Home Minister to collect full information about the irregularities in the lottery and place it on the floor of the House as early as possible. Today is August 22. About a month has passed but there is no report before the House. Today the House will be adjourned. Is the whole thing being whitewashed ? Why ? Is it because the former Chief Minister of Madhya Pradesh is connected with it ? Is it because his son is involved in it ? And also his son-in-law ? Is not everybody equal before the law ? The Finance Minister had himself given an assurance. Shri Nand Kishore Bhatt, a member from Madhya Pradesh had stated that there were many complaints of frauds in lotteries. But if a Society engaged in children's welfare gets involved the whole welfare activity comes to naught. But unfortunately this society is involved. At that time the Finance Minister had given an assurance and Shri Advani had read it out. The Finance Minister was not present in the House. The Home Minister said I cannot make a statement as the matter relates to the Finance Ministry. Today the Finance Minister is present. He must explain this today. I quote his words :

> On March 11, 1985 the Director (Investigation) of the Income Tax Department has been asked to take a survey of lotteries with a view to ascertaining details of organiser, details of lotteries organised, amount collected, amount of prize distribution per lottery, amounts and details of expenses, tax deduction and payment. Appropriate action will be taken depending on the evidence."

Children's Welfare or Family Welfare ?

Did the Finance Minister bear his assurance in mind while notifying the Children's Society of Churhat under the Income Tax Act ? Were the irregularities committed by this society in organising the lottery investigated ? If he did and was satisfied that there were no irregularities and concessions were consciously given, I would like him to take the House into confidence. We would not want to unnecessarily cast aspersions on this non-government organisation if it is really engaged in children's welfare. We shall fight our political differences in the political field. But children's welfare is being used as a cover for a particular family's welfare. In the name of children's welfare fraud of crores of rupees is being committed. And the only reason why the Finance Minister is not investigating is that those engaged in the noble work of children's welfare are connected with him. I say if the Finance Minister does not do justice to this House he is also not doing justice to the country.

SHRI V.P. SINGH, Finance Minister : You may know that A.A. Enterprises, who were in the lottery, were raided by the Income Tax Department.

SHRI VAJPAYEE : I know and I was going to ask about it, what did the raid at their office yield ? And when the government knows that the real business of this society is something else .... (*Interruption*).

SHRI V.P. SINGH : I shall give the full reply ...(*Interruption*)... I do not want to interrupt you while you are speaking, but I would like to say before that.

SHRI VAJPAYEE : Then why was this society given a concession under the Income Tax Act ? Why was it notified ? This is the main question and we want a satisfactory reply to it.

So I demand that the notification should not be acted upon so long as this society is not fully investigated and all facts do not come to light. And this investigation should be such as would satisfy both parties in the House and reassure the people as well. I would call upon the House to support my motion and cancel this.

SHRI N.K.P. SALVE (Maharashtra) : Mr. Deputy Chairman, Sir, it is very satisfying ....

SHRI DIPEN GHOSH (W. Bengal) : Salve is pressed for salvaging.

SHRI VAJPAYEE : Operation Salve.

SHRI N.K.P. SALVE : Sir, it is extremely satisfying to see that Shri Atal Bihari Vajpayee while moving the motion has used the language with restraint and he has avoided an acrimonious debate.

SHRI VAJPAYEE : I always do that.

Bofors Scandal

Disclose Information

Sir, I am grateful to you for giving us an opportunity to obtain a clarification regarding a statement made by Shri Shivraj Patil, Minister of State for Defence, in the House on August 14, 1987. Shri Shivraj Patil's statement of August 14 was for correcting the reply he gave in the House on August 12. When did Shri Patil find out that he had made a mis-statement on August 12 ? When did he realise that he had made such a big mistake that in order to expiate for it he had to suddenly appear in the Rajya Sabha on August 14 on the eve of Independence Day and make a statement, for which the House had to extend its sitting, which would otherwise have been over at five o'clock ? He gave his statement at two minutes past five and the House adjourned at three minutes past five, which gave no opportunity to any member to ask for an explanation.

After all Shri Shivraj Patil's senior colleague Shri Krishna Chandra Pant was present in the House when Shri Patil was speaking on the 12th. If Shri Patil was making some mistake Shri Pant could have pointed it out and immediate correction would have been possible. But Shri Pant thought no mistake was being made and what Shri Patil was saying was right. After the 12th the House met on the 13th. Shri Patil did not come to the House on the 13th. Even on the 14th he did not arrive till 12 noon, or even after Question Hour. He came at five o'clock. What is the mystery behind this ?

My first question is, when did he find out he had made a mistake ? Actually there was no mistake. He has said, "Some misunderstanding seems to have been created in some quarters in regard to my statement of 12th August 1987." Some quarters, some misunderstanding. What misunderstanding ? In whose mind ?

SHRI A.G. KULKARNI (Maharashtra) : You have also been Foreign Minister. You too may have said so. This is diplomatic language.

SHRI VAJPAYEE : The statement of the 12th was quite clear, to the point. There was no scope for any misunderstanding in it. I would like to quote. A discussion was going on here. The question was being asked— what happened when Shri Bredin of Bofors came to India ? At first Patil admitted that a Bofors delegation was here. He also admitted there were talks with it. He also admitted that it was willing to part with information. But Shri Patil said we told the representative we do not want oral information, we want it in writing. I quote his words :

Rajya Sabha on August 20, 1987 during discussion on the Bofors Guns Purchase Scandal

"We said : 'Give us the information in writing and if you are not going to give us the information in writing, well, we do not want information which can create problems for us'."

I admit that here Shri Patil did not have only the Congress Party, the Government in mind. Perhaps he meant the whole country would be in difficulty. So Shri Patil said—no verbal accounting, bring it in writing.

Sir, just now Shri Kulkarni was talking about diplomacy. Is it not the tradition that when there are talks with foreign countries or foreigners they are oral and later they can be supported in writing ? It is not that at the time of talking with foreigners everything is in writing. On that very day I had realised that the Government did not want to know the truth, did not want to discover the facts, was covering up the reality....

SHRI A.G. KULKARNI : This was your mistake.

SHRI VAJPAYEE : Kulkarni, now don't make any more mistakes yourself. That day Shri Patil said one thing, and repeated : "We wanted the information. The information was not given in writing."

He repeatedly stressed writing. This means Bofors was willing to give information orally. This is what Shri Patil said and this is what it meant. I have a report of the *Indian Express.*

"When Mr. Patil referred to the Bofors stand that it would convey the information sought only orally and not in writing. Mr. Upendra retorted, will anybody believe this cock and bull story ?

You may say you do not believe the *Indian Express* because it is opposed to the Government. I also have a report of the *Times of India.*

SHRI R.A. SINGH : That is Shri Rajiv Gandhi's paper.

SHRI VAJPAYEE : The *Times of India* is publishing a lot these days. It says :

"In reply to an Opposition question regarding the visit of Mr. Bredin, Vice-President of Bofors, to India on July 3, it was stated that Mr. Bredin was willing to orally give the names but the Government did not accept it."

Do you have different meanings for words, and do those meanings change from day to day ? The meaning that the word had on the 12th did not remain the same on the 14th. Those who were to understand it were all under an illusion. You are capable of creating so much illusion that even the Opposition was deluded, the newspapers were also taken on to the wrong track. You did not yourself know about the mistake that day. You did not know about it on the 13th, you did not know about it the whole day on the 14th, and in the evening you suddenly realised you had made a terrible mistake and you should come to the House to correct it.

Sir, what happened on the 14th afternoon ? Is it true that Shri Shivraj Patil came to the House to make a statement on this day because that day the Prime Minister talked to some press reporters in the Rashtrapati Bhavan and different versions of the talks have appeared in the press, including a report of the UNI or some other agency according to which the Prime Minister said Bofors is not ready to give any information orally ? Now what could poor Shri Shivraj Patil do ? He had to run to the House. All right, he came on the

14th evening. He said his statement has created some misunderstanding. Some misunderstanding in some quarters—not your misunderstanding but only quarters. Then Shri Patil said in his statement : "The fact of the matter is that Mr. Bredin did not give any convincing information."

What is this convincing information ? What is the test of convincing ? Can this test keep changing ? On the 12th there was one test of convincing, on the 14th there was another test. Take us into confidence. What did Bofors want to tell ?

Is it true that when Shri Bredin came and you had talks with him Shri Bredin said—we are prepared to invite your senior officers to Sweden and give you information in writing, but on condition that all the written information would be kept in a sealed envelope, which would be given only to the Prime Minister and none else ? Is it true that you have not acquainted the House with all the information you possess on Bofors ? Is it true that you have kept the House in the dark ? What the Prime Minister said to the media that day has not removed doubts, on the contrary doubts have been strengthened, old doubts became stronger and new doubts arose. I have already said that the Prime Minister's press conference has been reported in different ways. According to one report–

> "The Prime Minister on Friday said that Bofors had given some information but not the full details of the gun deal. In the Swedish Audit Bureau report also there were names of some institutions but not individuals."

You know institutions have names. What are those institutions ? Why have you not informed the House about this ?

> "The Prime Minister said Bofors was willing to tell us something orally, but not in writing."

This is a PTI report. According to another agency the Prime Minister said they were not ready to give information even orally. Now whom should the people believe ? That day a letter from Bofors was presented in the House quite dramatically. Bofors has written other letters too. Will the Government place on the Table of the House the letter Bofors wrote to our Ambassador on April 24 ? Will the Government place the entire correspondence with Bofors on the Table of the House and take the House and the country into confidence ?

Sir, I would like to conclude. If mis-statements are made like this, if contradictory statements are given, if in the name of removing doubts new doubts are created the people would be driven to only one conclusion—that the Government does not want to unmask the real culprits, because it fears that if they are unmasked the Government itself would be unmasked.

Sir, a small question arises. They were really to give information on the 12th, but orally, not in writing. Now we are told they were not ready to give even oral information. May I know why you did not get the information they were ready to give ? And what was that information ?

Bofors Inquiry

The Guns Will Continue to Boom

Madam, I stand to initiate a discussion on the report of the Joint Parliamentary Committee on the Bofors deal. During a long parliamentary life of 27-28 years I have initiated discussions on many important subjects. I have participated in many discussions. But to date I have never found myself in such a strange situation.

Madam, this is the first time in India's parliamentary history that a Joint Committee does not represent joint Houses but divided Houses. This is the first time that the Opposition is not represented in a Joint Committee.

SHRI M.I. BEG (Gujarat) : We had invited you, but you did not accept the invitation.

SHRI VAJPAYEE : This is the first time that no one from the ordinary members of Parliament was selected for the chairmanship of a parliamentary committee. A person occupying a ministerial position was made to resign and then made Chairman of the Committee.

This is the first time the Chairman of a parliamentary committee rejected the right of members of the Committee to give a note of dissent. Had there not been a lot of noise outside and had no one knocked on the Lok Sabha Speaker's door my friend Shri Alladi Arun would have been deprived of his fundamental democratic right to register his dissent.

SHRI M.L. FOTEDAR, Steel Minister : Since when did he become your friend ?

SHRI VAJPAYEE : Since your friendship with him soured a little.

Image of Parliamentary Committee Tarnished

Madam, this is the first time a note of dissent was presented not as a note of dissent but as a post-script. I have been a member of many joint committees. I have been giving notes of dissent. A note of dissent should be given as a note of dissent, not as a post-script. This is a new form. This is really India's own contribution to the world's parliamentary development. The report will be received, there will be no dissent of dissent, just a post-script.

Still the Committee's Chairman did not sit quiet. After the post-script he even added a comment of his own. What is that comment ? Does a Committee add a comment after a note of dissent ? It never happened before.

Madam, just imagine, if we had all become members of the Committee and if we had added separate notes of dissent they would all have been given

Rajya Sabha on May 11, 1988 while initiating discussion on the Bofors Guns deal.

as post-scripts and every note of dissent would have had a separate reply. This is a ridiculous situation.

Madam, the way the parliamentary committee was set up, the way its terms of reference were fixed, the way the Committee conducted its business—and I thank Shri Alladi Arun for his note of dissent on the committee's proceedings—all this is an eye-opener for us on the one hand, but on the other it tarnishes the prestige of the parliamentary committee. The members of the Committee were ill-treated. They were not given all the documents, and even from the documents that were furnished some portions were deleted. There was no information on the witnesses to come. We were told the Attorney-General was coming, but it was the Bofors officials who came. I would like Shri Alladi Arun to throw light on this. I do not want to bother him but these aspects of the matter have pained us. Will a joint parliamentary committee appointed for an inquiry behave like this ?

The Committee accepted depositions but declined to take some important ones, and it rolled out the red carpet for the Bofors officials. Win Chaddha was let off lightly. I do not want to go deep into what conditions he had put forward and on what conditions he had come to India. And the biggest thing is that the Committee ignored the documents published by the English daily *Hindu* although its report had not been finalized by that time.

'Hindu' and Hinduja

Madam, the *Hindu* is not only a South Indian newspaper, it is a national daily. Its Chief Editor is considered to be one of the Prime Minister's friends. He is invited for exclusive interviews. We see him on Doordarshan—we have his Darshan from *Door*—from a distance. He published some documents. They are important documents and a new revelation. They again put Bofors in the dock and also involved the Hindujas in the whole affair. Was it not the responsibility of the Committee to also consider new documents, new proofs, when they came to light ? Had the Committee so wished it could have obtained from the Lok Sabha an extension of its tenure. But the Committee was in a hurry–God knows what invisible power was moving it, was inspiring it to finish its job immediately. Perhaps it feared what would happen to it if there was some new exposure, if some more facts came to light from Sweden. so the Committee thought—come on, let us wind up things fast, let us somehow submit a report. But has this not put a question-mark on the committee's credibility ? Even if we leave other things, so far as this parliamentary committee is concerned—I am sorry to say so, it is a parliamentary committee and they are our colleagues—this one thing has unmasked it.

Madam, for some time past democratic institutions are gradually being eroded, being devalued. Now we have one more link in that chain. So far a joint parliamentary committee had escaped this devaluation, at least one parliamentary democratic institution was safe, at least one institution was without blemish, but with this report even that institution has become an object of public suspicion.

Madam, I would not take your time by reading out newspaper comments on this report, nor do I want to discuss the reaction of the intellectuals. I also do not want to point my finger at the conclusion of the opinion poll conducted by MARG and the *Sunday Observer*. But one thing is clear, and it is that the public mind will not accept the findings of this parliamentary committee.

Madam, the Committee had been appointed to find out who the middlemen were. That there was a commission is definite. The Committee was appointed to find out who took it. The Committee was appointed to find out, not to cover up. After the Committee's report the real culprits should have been in the dock. But the Committee did its job in such a way that it itself stood in the dock.

Madam, the doubts the Opposition parties had expressed before the Committee was set up have come true. We had said an inquiry was needed after the Audit Bureau's report, catch Bofors by the neck on the basis of the facts given by the Audit Bureau and the facts that have been hidden. Pressurise Bofors. Tell them, you said no commission would be paid. The Audit Bureau's report shows a commission was paid. The Audit Bureau is Sweden's national bureau. It is an independent body. After its report what was the need to set up a separate committee ?

Madam, when we were demanding a committee the Government did not accept the demand, and when the Government set up a committee we did not accept it. We did not accept because in our opinion it was not necessary to involve this matter in a parliamentary inquiry. What was needed was prompt action. What was needed was not inquiry but action.

The Mountain and the Mouse

Madam, this report has proved that the inquiry committee could accomplish nothing. Sometimes a mountain is dug up, but a mouse is produced. In this case not even a mouse was produced, because the mountain was not dug up at all. The mountain was just circumambulated and a report produced.

Madam, the Committee's Chairman is Shri Shankaranand. I recollect a tale from the Puranas. Lord Shankar had two sons—Kartikeya and Ganesh. Once there was a wager between them—who was the greater devotee of the father ? The age apart, who had the sharper intellect ? A race was decided upon to decide the matter. Whoever went round the earth was the greater. Kartikeya immediately set out for the circumambulation. He thought he could finish it quickly. Ganesh did not set out to do so. With his generous stomach how could he undertake such exertion ? But he had a very sharp intellect. Kartikeya was on the move. Ganesh thought—let him go, I shall go round Lord Shiva and claim that Shiva permeates all the three worlds, so why bother with going round only the earth ? Madam, while the Bofors charges were being discussed and like Kartikeya Jethmalani, Jaswant Singh, Arun Shourie, George Fernandes, Indrajit were going round the world, Shankaranand thought—let me just go round the mountain and give a report.

Madam, a committee of 30 members, more than 40 meetings, proceedings that went on for 200 hours, examination of 500 files—how much labour–but what was the result ? Why there was no result should be seriously thought about. Either there was no result or the Committee did not want a result.

I am sorry the inquiry committee spent more time than necessary in proving that Bofors guns are good. Even if the guns are good does it mean the scandal associated with them is also good ? The real question is not about the guns. After the report of the National Audit Bureau there was only one question—to whom did Bofors pay Rs. 64 crores ? But instead of concentrating its attention on finding an answer to this the Committee spent time in showing that the Bofors gun has a longer range. We know the range is long. The gun fires in Sweden and the boom is heard in India. It fires on the border of Rajasthan and shakes up Delhi. But one thing is certain—Bofors did not have its own arrangement for manufacturing ammunition at the time the agreement with it was made. There was talk about bringing in an Italian company named Semel. And from this point of view the French gun was better.

I do not want to involve former Army Chief Sundarji in the debate. He has a right to change his opinion. He can change it even within 15 days. If the perspective changes the opinion may change. But now we are told Pakistan had acquired Radar. Is radar a new American invention ? Was it not used before ? Did we have no idea of the Pak-U.S. relationship ? Could a far-sighted view of this not have been taken ? Was the French company asked for a solution in the new circumstances that had arisen ? Obviously the Government did not act with foresight.

Madam, we are told the country's security would have been jeopardised if the Bofors agreement had been cancelled. I do not agree. I have definite information that the Defence Ministry had expressed the view that security would not be endangered if the bargain was called off; only we would have to change our programme for 6-8 months.

This has been the Defence Ministry's opinion. And it was not just oral, the Defence Minister had given it in writing. But it was ignored. Why ?

There was only one way to extract the truth from Bofors. It should have been told—you have broken the conditions of the agreement, you will have to tell us the truth. You will have to come out with who has pocketed Rs. 64 crore earned by the people of this country with the sweat of their brow. If you do not spill the beans the agreement will be cancelled. I see that the Defence Ministry has been doing plain-speaking with Bofors. When Vohra and Banerji, officers of the Defence Ministry, met Bofors they did not mince matters. The correspondence of the Defence Ministry to which this report refers also indicates that the Defence Ministry wants to know the truth and in its opinion there is no problem in having an inquiry. I would like to quote from the report. The Foreign Ministry has also apparently been firm. An *aide memoire* of the Indian ambassador to Sweden dated August 21 says :

> "Keeping in view the gravity attributed to the statements of the Swedish public officials, the Swedish Government is requested to give the

complete report of the Swedish National Audit Bureau, including the portion that have so far not been made available to Government of India, without any further loss of time. This information is vital to the work of the Joint Parliamentary Committee which is being set up by the Indian Parliament to investigate the matter."

On paper the Government shows the Defence Minister has spoken very plainly. I was reading Bhatnagar's deposition. At one stage Bhatnagar said we are threatening Bofors to tell the truth. But Bofors ignored the Defence Ministry's threat. Bofors did not answer the questions the Defence Ministry asked. The Defence Ministry's threats shake neighbouring countries, big powers are forced to reconsider a matter. This is the Defence Ministry of a big country, it threatens Bofors and Bofors just ignores the threat !

Madam, Bofors is a shop-keeper, we are a purchaser. Bofors is a salesman, we are a customer. We have obliged Bofors by making a Rs. 1700 crore Defence contract with them. This armament factory was closing down, there was a hue and cry, they needed a contract, and we gave them one. We did them a good turn but they betrayed us. We could not put pressure on them. Why not ? I charge that Bofors had a contact, a contact with the Defence Ministry, a contact with our ambassador in Sweden, some invisible contact somewhere in New Delhi, and whenever Bofors was in difficulties this contact patted it on the back and said—don't worry, my boy, I have you under my wing. No one is asking me who this invisible contact was. Is the attitude of Bofors in keeping with this great country's prestige ? (Bell). For the present ammunition is being collected. Let the time to fire the gun come. They have to be finished.

Madam, is it not a sorry joke that your certificate about the good quality of Bofors guns, which you flaunt, comes from Opposition members ? General Aurora and Jaswant Singh are in the Opposition but they have been Army Officers.

SHRI K.C. PANT, Defence Minister : Have you any objection ?

SHRI VAJPAYEE : No objection. But these officers who are commending Bofors guns also say the guns are good but a big commission has been paid. You are not discussing that.

Who is the Middleman ?

Madam, as I said, after the audit report it has been proved that Rs. 64 crores were paid. At first they said no payment was paid. When it came to light that payment was made they said payment has been made but there is no middleman. This morning the question arose—I do not want to repeat it—how do you define a middleman ? I can show many statements of the Prime Minister and the Defence Minister in which middleman, agents and representatives—all these three terms have been used together in one breath. The Attorney-General may well adopt a narrow legal definition, but the Prime Minister had said after assuming power—now there would be no middlemen in defence contracts. What a clear conscience ! There would be no middlemen, no agent ! But can anyone say there is no middleman now, no agent ? That we don't know who the agent is a different matter. Three companies have been named. But their addresses were not given. Who conducts them, who is behind them ? No light was thrown on this. Three Indian investigating agencies were brought into the field to find this out. Kumar went one place, Katre went another, another Kumar went yet another and a third Kumar went some place else. They went all over the world but returned empty-handed.

There are two companies in Panama. They have three ladies who have nothing to do with Bofors. They are just not in a position to provide consultancy services. We do not know if there is even an agreement with them. I had said Bofors will escape by naming such companies. There is, however, a company called A.E. and E. Services. Whose company is this ? It is located in London. Is it in some way connected with Swraj Paul ? Is it true that Bofors made an agreement with this company even after it was decided in October that there would be no middleman, no agent ? And then the agreement was wound up in three months. Ten .crore rupees were paid. Ten crores is not a small sum. Had Shri Tiwariji got ten crore rupees he would have lighted a lamp in every hut. He would have made water flow in a desert, perhaps in a big desert. But just one company took away ten crores.

Madam, this is a strange thing. When the Prime Minister took office he said there would be no middleman, Bofors was told and by October the Company knew about it. And yet agents continued to be there. The proof of this is contained in the report of this Joint Committee. Defence Secretary Shri Bhatnagar was loudly claiming that he had been successful in bringing down the price of the Bofors gun. Perhaps he may be looking for the Committee's congratulations for that. But what he said in the course of this praise is revealing. I quote his words :

> " Bofors had quoted on the 10th February a price of Rs. 1,620 crores and came down to Rs. 1,427 crores on the 21st March, which means that within a period of one month and ten days, there was a reduction of near about Rs. 200 crores."

Within one month and ten days the price of Bofors guns came down by Rs. 200 crores. Then should we say the previous quotation was exorbitant ? But there was a miracle. This miracle happened within one month and ten days. Shri Bhatnagar has also thrown light on how it happened, and it is remarkable—

"Such was the intensity of the competition generated."

All right, the competition was exploited. There is no objection to that.

Shri Bhatnagar adds :

> "As a result of negotiations and as a result of fresh conditions such as the elimination of agents, there was a massive and unexpected reduction in the price."

As a result of negotiations and as a result of fresh conditions such as the elimination of agents !

Between February 10 and March 21 prices came down by Rs. 200 crores, and that was because new conditions were imposed. The new condition was elimination of agents. Does this not mean there were agents till March 21 ? Who were these agents ? Were their names given to the Joint Committee ? I would like the Defence Minister to throw light on these names. The Defence Secretary has admitted that till March 21 there were agents. Who were they ? And if the Prime Ministers of Sweden and India had agreed in December that there would be no middleman, no agent, is it not open transgression of Government policy that there were agents till March 21 ? I would like the Defence Minister to clarify the motivation behind the Prime Minister's declaration, which he made after assuming power, that in defence contracts there would be no agent, no middleman. Did the Prime Minister come to know some facts that made him feel that there was a lot of irregularity in Defence deals and so middlemen should be kept away from them ? Is it true that commissions and irregularities had been reported in the case of previous purchases of submarines from West Germany and the Prime Minister was worried because of them ? But it is a matter of regret that the Prime Minister laid down a policy but could not get it implemented. Even to date agents are active.

What was the Role of the Marconi Group ?

That day I had asked a question about the Marconi group and the Defence Minister had given the reply that there were no agents and middlemen. I can produce documents to prove that the Marconi group has a middleman. They may ask, what do you mean by middleman ? We would like to call the Attrorney-General to tell us what a middleman means. Words should be given the right meanings. The meaning should be clear and right, then alone can it be proved that there is no irregulariy'. The Committee could not prove this.

Madam, on April 17, 1987 the Swedish Radio made the revelation that there has been transfer of money in the Bofors deal and leading Indian political leaders and persons connected with the Army have been bribed to get the contract. That very day the Prime Minister of India should have come before Parliament and before the people of the country, and said our policy is not for middlemen's commissions in such deals, what the Radio has said is a serious matter and it has caused us worry. But he did not say so. It was claimed that the radio broadcast was false, mischievous, baseless. Without making any inquiry it was also claimed that this is a conspiracy to destabilise, to degrade the Government of India. What sort of a reaction is this when you say the powerful government of a great country, elected by the people, can be destabilised by one radio broadcast ? That day we felt there was something fishy. Now it seems the whole thing is fishy.

After this Bofors sent a letter to our ambassador in Stockholm on April 24. It agreed money had been passed and a Swiss company was involved. This was before the audit report was received. But even after this the Prime Minister said in a meeting with high-level commanders that there was no middleman and no payment was made. Was the Prime Minister not aware of the Bofors report given to the ambassador ? If he was, how did he make such a statement ? But this thing was repeated over and over again, which only strengthened suspicion.

Martin Ardbo's Taped Admission

Madam, I regret the Committee did not call our ambassador in Stockholm Shri Oza for a deposition. I have listened to a tape of Martin Ardbo, in which he says he went to India many times in connection with the deal and met the Prime Minister. He has also said he used to go to Pakistan from India as he was a director of a company in Pakistan. We are buying guns against Pakistan in view of their preparations, and we are buying them from Bofors, whose official was the director of a company in Pakistan. He says so himself, and I can produce the tape. Was it not necessary to call Martin Ardbo ? Should the Prime Minister not have appeared before the Committee ? If the Swedish Prime Minister can appear before a parliamentary committee there why can't the Indian Prime Minister do so here ? My friend Shri Arun Singh was not called....

Why Shri Arun Singh resigned is still a mystery to me. I cannot accept a minister of his calibre leaving the cabinet for personal reasons,—and that too when his friend's boat is rocking. Whenever there was a shower of corruption charges in India, whenever that shower became a downpour, whenever new facts came to light from Sweden the process of covering up began. The setting up of a parliamentary committee was also a part of the process. Hand it over to a parliamentary committee, it will struggle with it for months. The storm will die down and lips will be sealed. But if a Committee was set up it should have called all. The Committee's report says we said whoever wants to come may come, but nobody came, then what could we do ? Do Parliamentary Committees work this way ? Could a public notice not have been given ? You had only to find out the facts and you had to convince the people of the country that you are really interested in finding out the facts. Even here the Committee has failed.

Madam, how did the Committee conclude that money was given ? It admits that money was given, but it was not given to Indians—neither to resident Indians nor to non-resident Indians. When you do not know at all to whom it was paid and to whom it was not, how did you know it was given ?

Sir, Shri Shankaranand is a great scholar. The Vedas have defined Brahma, Godhead, as *'Neti, Neti'*—it is not this, it is not that. It seems Shri Shankaranand has become 'Brahma-Gyani', has acquired supreme knowledge. They are not Indians, they are not non-resident Indians. They who they are ? We do not know. They do not remain Brahma-Gyanis here. They get entangled in *'Maya Jaal'*—wordly temptations.

What I regret is that a commission is taken, a commission is given, the huge amount of Rs. 64 crores change hands, but no Indian benefits from it. This situation cannot be accepted. It is our birthright to take and give a commission. Who is this third party who robbed us of our right and made away with Rs. 64 crores ? He must be caught. Who will catch him ? They say bring proof. Is not the report of the National Audit Bureau proof ? The way Bofors has been changing its stand—is that not proof ? Where can we get proof ? The Government has to find out. The policeman cannot tell the family–I admit there has been a murder, but you have to produce the proof, and this is what the Government is saying. This is what the Prime Minister said. At one stage he said even evidence is not needed, just bring proof. The proof is with Bofors. There was one proof in the form of the Audit Bureau's report. I have referred to the documents published by the *Hindu*. Who is this 'Pitco' ? When did it manifest itself ? How many *Avataras* did it have ? What is this matter of a *'Śangam'*, an accord, between Pitco and Hinduja's company ?—*'Bol Radha bol, Sangam hoga ki nahin...*

Sir, Hindujas say these documents are forged. If that is so there should be legal action. We shall not ask the Joint Committee, but we shall and the Defence Minister—what is the Government's opinion about these documents published by the *Hindu*, these photo copies ? Was *Hindu* asked about it ? Were Hindujas asked about it ?

I have read—it may be true, it does not look otherwise— that the Defence Minister said even if it is supposed to be true the most that is proved is that Hindujas and Bofors are connected. Sir, the documents prove the connection between Hindujas and Bofors. The connection between Hindujas and Bachchan is already established. No one can deny that. Bachchan is the Prime Minister's friend. Now there is one more link in that. The new ambassador being sent to Sweden has been selected carefully. He is a childhood friend of the Bachchan family. The Government is afraid of what exposures might come from Sweden and when. It is not necessary to see what the Swedish officers have been saying. The Public Prosecutor said we could not find out the truth because the Indian Government and the Swedish Government did not cooperate with us.

Do not be under the impression that with this report the guns affair has cooled down. These guns will remain hot. They will remain not so long as the culprits are not exposed. The task of finding out the truth will go on. It is to be regretted that the Government's credibility has gone down. It is painful for all of us that a parliamentary committee fell in public esteem. But do not forget, this matter will not be suppressed. Finally, truth will triumph—*Satyameva Jayate, nanritam'*—truth alone triumphs, not falsehood. Thank you.

HDW Submarines and the Middlemen

SHRI N.D. TIWARI, Minister of Finance and Commerce : I have respectfully noted the points that have been made by the distinguished leaders of the Opposition. Reference is to the photostat copies published in *The Hindu* on HDW submarines deal, and to a letter reportedly written by the Secretary of Defence Ministry to the Chairman of HDW, and the reply that the Chairman HDW sent to the Defence Secretary. It is correct that the other day my esteemed colleague Mr. Gadhvi did answer a question as to what steps are being taken by the Enforcement Directorate and the question was that he did not have adequate and competent officers to examine the matter, and in (c) part, Mr. Advani mentioned : It has been referred to that the information conveyed to the Government of India is incorrect and possibly the result of a misunderstanding. Now, the concluding line of the reply is : the matter is being pursued with the Government of the Federal Republic of Germany. Now, Mr. Advani has said that no mention has been made regarding Globetech. I will certainly look into whether this correspondence had been exchanged or not. I will go back and will certainly go through the file and if the answer needs any correction.....

SHRI VAJPAYEE : This is not a question of correcting the reply. You have kept the House in the dark. You have hidden the facts.

SHRI N.D. TIWARI : The point is, I do not have all the facts just now. I do not know about the letter reportedly written. But as I said I will go and look up the file and see whether the question needs certain corrections....

I would say to Shri Atal Bihari Vajpayee that I have been listening to all things most respectfully. I am not. that type of person. I am parliamentary by nature. I would urge him to be calm in whatever he has to say, and I have faith in his parliamentary temperament. If something is not being done deliberately....

SHRI VAJPAYEE : They are indulging in corruption and teaching us parliamentary behaviour.

SHRI N.D. TIWARI : We are as much worried about corruption as you are.

SHRI VAJPAYEE : No, you are not. Madam, I am sorry I lost my temper a little. I was not angry with Shri Tiwari. But he said he would correct the reply. Had this matter been so simple it would not have been necessary to get so upset. Even when the matter for a parliamentary committee was under consideration in the House I had said that the matter of the submarines be handed over to a parliamentary committee for inquiry. Now I know why that was done.

Rajya Sabha on August 31, 1987 during discussion on Submarine Purchase Scandal

Madam, this is a matter of suppressing the facts. This is a matter of middlemen in the matter of purchase of submarines, and the government has been claiming that there were no such middlemen. It has been proved that there was a middleman. Now there is a question-mark on the honesty of the whole government, it is not a question of correcting a reply.

SHRI N.D. TIWARI : I am deeply grateful to Hon'ble Shri Vajpayee for returning to his parliamentary temperament. That was expected of him. Hon'ble Shri Vajpayee knows well that this is a question of August 27 and it is the convention of the House that if a reply is incomplete the House always has the right to correct it. I would like to assure that we had absolutely no intention of suppressing any information, nor is there any question of doing so. The question is that a couple of matters had already been given to the Enforcement Directorate for inquiry and it is investigating them.

What Happened to the Submarine Inquiry ?

Madam, on March 11, 1987 Shri Vishwanath Pratap Singh, the then Defence Minister, had directed the Directorate of Enforcement to inquire into the information received about the commission of Rs. 30 crores involved in the purchase of submarines from the Federal Republic of Germany. Some days back it was stated in reply to a question that the Directorate had completed the inquiry, but so far the House has not been taken into confidence about its report. The matter is not only about the inquiry of the Directorate. The Central Board of Direct Taxes will also be connected with the inquiry, as was stated by the then Defence Minister Shri Arun Singh. He had also said that the Committee set up under the Chairmanship of the Defence Secretary would go into what types of contracts agents, whether Indian or foreign, were active in the deal. So he said that the Economic Intelligence Bureau would also be involved in the inquiry. I would quote a portion of what Shri Arun Singh said that time :

> "The Economic Intelligence Bureau of the Ministry of Finance were also desired by the then Defence Minister to carry out a systematic study of the *modus operandi* of the agents, Indian and foreign. The Defence Secretary has written to the Finance Ministry in pursuance of these directions as per the draft letter approved by the then Defence Minister. A committee under the Defence Minister to study the *modus operandi* of agents has also been constituted and has begun its work."

I regret the reply was not for a starred question, so a supplementary could not be asked on it. Consequently it cannot be known if the inquiry that was made was as comprehensive as was assured. Secondly, as I said, the inquiry was ordered on March 11, 1987. This is a departmental inquiry and the Defence Secretary is conducting it. Our proposal that the submarines deal should also be referred to the Joint Parliamentary Committee was not accepted. It was stated—let us first receive the Defence Secretary's report, then we would decide about this. But in this matter too Parliament is not being taken into confidence. We do not know when the report was received. The Government has reluctantly admitted that the report has been received. We would like to know when it will be placed on the floor of the House and before Parliament, and we would also like to know if the inquiry was really carried out in the manner ordered. Thank you.

Rajya Sabha on March 30, 1988 during discussion on the irregularity regarding Submarines purchase

Reported Allegations of Pay Offs by Harshad Mehta

Mr. Speaker, Sir, I want to raise a serious matter with your permission which is not only concerned with the dignity of the House, but is also connected with an incident challenging the credibility of a respectable member.

The Statesman has been publishing a report for the last two days. *The Statesman* is a respectable and responsible newspaper, it tries to put forth the facts after investigation. Yesterday, there was a news report on the front page. I am reading out the heading.

"Attempt to implicate Advani, Joshi in Harshad Mehta Pay-off."

When we read this news report, we apprehended that a conspiracy was being hatched to deliberately implicate Shri L.K. Advani, Shri M.M. Joshi and the Bharatiya Janata Party. But we did not take it very seriously: we neither raised it in the House, nor any other Hon'ble Member thought it necessary to raise it, because the story was so baseless, so mischievous, and without any foundation that nobody would believe it after going through it. But we took one step, which is quite adequate to show that if such allegations are made, then we are prepared to face any kind of enquiry. Therefore, Shri Advani, Shri Joshi and Shri Pramod Mahajan wrote a letter to the Chairperson of the J.P.C., Shri Mirdha, and sent a clipping of the news report along with it, saying that they were prepared for enquiry into this matter. If the Committee wanted to call them, they were ready to appear before the Committee.

SHRI NIRMAL KANTI CHATTERJEE (Dumdum) : Are these communications made public ?

SHRI VAJPAYEE : Yes. They have been made public.

SHRI INDRAJIT GUPTA (Midnapore) : Are these allegations made by *The Statesman* or somebody else ?

SHRI VAJPAYEE : I am coming to that. But the news which has been published today gives the entire episode the shape of a dangerous conspiracy. A foreign national is behind it. The scope of this conspiracy is not confined to India only, but it extends upto London. Geneva is also coming into its orbit. A criminal businessman is involved in it, and that businessman has been provided special security. Perhaps he is apprehending danger. Danger from whom ? Or because the deal in which he has been included is

---

Lok Sabha on August 27, 1993 regarding the news report published in The Statesman about alleged pay off by Harshad Mehta to Shri Advani and Shri Joshi

not only a deal, but a conspiracy as well as a deal, a plot and a deal, and perhaps the danger is due to that.

This foreign national says that he has connections with Harshad Mehta and he looks after the wealth of Shri Mehta abroad. He offers him services for repatriation of his money. An affidavit has been prepared by that foreign national which has been quoted extensively by the newspaper, I would come to that later on. But this businessman is of Indian origin and here the Indian Government comes into the picture. It appears that there is some department under the Government, some people in the Government encouraging this conspiracy and operating this conspiracy. After all, what is the necessity of providing security to this person ? (*Interruptions*).

SHRI VAJPAYEE : This gentleman, named Shri Randhir Jain, is the person who has been provided special security. He is an advocate, claims to be an advocate. Whose advocate is he, I do not know, but he has been provided security and, while providing security, what has been noted by the Intelligence Bureau has been quoted by the newspaper. Mr. Speaker, Sir, I want to read out this portion of *The Statesman* :

> "A letter from Dr. K.K. Paul of the Intelligence Bureau, who handles only V.V.I.P. security and interacts with the Prime Minister's Office tells the story."

The following is the text of the letter written to Mr. P.S. Bawa, then Additional Commissioner, Administration and Co-ordination, in Delhi Police, on June 25. This date of June 25 is to be kept in mind. The paper quotes :

> "In view of the sensitive information having a bearing on security, it is requested that Shri Randhir Jain, resident of P-448, New Friends Colony, New Delhi, may be provided security guards in uniform for a period of two weeks.
>
> It is also requested that before actual deployment, we may kindly be informed so that an officer can suitably bring the guards and also introduce them to the protectee."

Who is this Randhir Jain ? What danger is he facing ? In what conspiracy he was involved ? Not only a foreign national is involved in it, not only an Indian criminal is involved in it, but a former Foreign Secretary, who is occupying a high post, is also involved in it. Mr. Speaker, I do not want to name him, you know that I do observe the etiquette of the House.

MR. SPEAKER : You not only observe the etiquette, but also promote it. I am sure about it. I am not saying this simply because you are there and I am here.

SHRI VAJPAYEE : If you want to say anything else, then I can go out of the House. You may be feeling embarrassed in saying that before me. (*Interruptions*).

SHRI VAJPAYEE : This is a very serious matter. This has caused me immense pain. There could be difference of opinion with Shri Advani and the Bharatiya Janata Party, but Shri Advani is a clean leader and an attempt is being made to assassinate his character and he is being linked with Harshad

Mehta; Harshad Mehta is reported to have paid Rs. 2 crores to Shri Advani and Rs. 40 lakhs to Shri Joshi through these persons. Will Shri Joshi take that money on a day when he was admitted to an intensive care unit in a hospital? February 25 ... (*Interruptions*).

SHRI VAJPAYEE : The shooting of water through water cannons by Shri Pilot, of which our communist friends have also had a taste recently, and as a result of which Shri Joshi was in the I.C.U. is said to have been paid money there?

The most objectionable thing is that the Ministry of External Affairs is being used in it. What was the need for a former Foreign Secretary to write a letter to the officials of the Ministry of External Affairs ? What help had he sought from them ? Where is the affidavit prepared and filed by the Swiss national ? Is it with the Government ? What is this story ? This is an attempt towards character assassination.

If allegations are made against the leaders, let them give the explanation, this is the straightforward method. Here the history of St. Kitts is being repeated, once a story was concocted to involve the former Prime Minister Shri V.P. Singh. In that too officials of the Ministry of External Affairs were involved. Are they also involved in it ? That story was proved wrong, but nobody was punished. The officials involved were promoted instead. Is it the way to conduct the public life in the country ? Come into the field by challenging the ideology to fight a political battle. Mr. Speaker, Sir, this is a very serious matter and I want that the Government must make a statement on it.

SHRI RAJESH PILOT, Minister of State in the Ministry of Home Affairs : Sir, Mr. Atal Bihari Vajpayee has mentioned about the security specially given to a citizen. I do not have the correct information at the moment. But as Mr. Vajpayee has mentioned, I will certainly inform the House before the House rises today why security was given, who has recommended security, on what grounds we have given security—the way Mr. Atal Bihari Vajpayee has said is something like it has been planned in that manner—so that that impression is removed.

I will put the whole facts to the House before the House rises today.

The J.P.C. Report on Securities Scam A Historical Document

Mr. Speaker, Sir, I rise to raise a discussion under Rule 193 on the Report of the Joint Committee to enquire into Irregularities in Securities and Banking Transactions, presented to the House on December 21, 1993. It would have been better had this discussion taken place under Rule 184, which provides that after the discussion the House can also express its opinion. It is evident that another occasion would have to be found for this purpose. I want to make the best use of the opportunity that is now available.

Unanimous Report—An Achievement

Mr. Speaker, Sir, 30 members of both the Houses of Parliament, belonging to different parties have presented this Report after 16 months of hard labour. As I have said earlier, it is a historical document. The Committee included members holding different viewpoints. It included members of the party in power as well as those of the Opposition. The Committee was to consider the securities scam. It was to discuss different Ministries. The Boards and Corporations connected with those Ministries were also under consideration. In a way, the entire Government was subject to inspection and investigation. There are differences of opinion in the Joint Select Committees. Appending of notes of dissent is a common practice in such reports, but a new story has been written and a new chapter has been added. All the Members working in this Committee have prepared a report with general consensus in the direction of strengthening the parliamentary traditions. This is an important event in itself. It is an achievement.

Mr. Speaker, Sir, this report has restored the lost prestige of a Joint Select Committee, which is an important organ of Parliament. The prestige was lost when a similar Committee was constituted on Bofors issue, in which the Opposition had refused to participate and the Committee under the Chairmanship of Shri Shankaranand presented a report whitewashing the matter. Then, the institution of Parliament was hurt. I am happy that this report has proved to be a concrete step in the direction of restoration of the prestige of the institution of the Parliamentary Committees. This report would enhance the prestige of Parliament. Democracy will be strengthened, authenticity will be revived and credibility of the Members of Parliament will be enhanced.

Lok Sabha on December 29, 1993 during discussion on the Report of the Joint Parliamentary Committee to enquire into irregularities in securities and banking transactions

Mr. Speaker, Sir, I hope and trust that the way the Members of the Committee, inspite of being affiliated to different parties, have succeeded in forming an unanimous opinion, so also an unanimous opinion would evolve on certain important issues during the discussion. If this security scam, which is the biggest scandal of the century, could shake up this House, this Parliament and this country, if it could awaken us towards our responsibility, then I think that even out of this most horrible scandal some good indications could be had for the future of the country.

(Mr. Deputy Speaker in the Chair)

Mr. Deputy Speaker, Sir, first of all I would like to congratulate the Chairman of the Committee Shri Ram Niwas Mirdha as also its other members for the hard labour and devotion to duty shown by them, but this does not mean that I am fully satisfied by the Report of the Committee. I am not in agreement with the approach of the Committee in leaving aside the most controversial issues, in order to achieve consensus. There are several shortcomings and defects in the Report. These relate to the institution of Parliamentary Committee. In matters, in which Ministers are involved, Ministries are involved. Reserve Bank is involved, public undertakings, banks, nationalised banks, foreign banks are involved, in which failure has to be pinpointed, punishment has to be recommended after investigation, is a Parliamentary Select Committee an effective instrument for enquiry into such complicated and sensitive issues ?

The Report presented, as I said before, is unanimous. I thank the Hon'ble Members for this Report. But Parliament will have to consider this question because we do not want that any such scandal may be repeated in future. However, I am not prepared to under-rate our capacity to generate scandals. God forbid if some scandal occurs again, then how to investigate into it ? The experiences of this Committee should be kept in mind by all.

Mr. Deputy Speaker, Sir, a Committee is constituted by the House. However, nobody knows where the Chairman of the Committee would sit, wherefrom his staff will come. A few from here, a few from there that is how the staff is collected. There is no dearth of staff, the staff did very good work, I am prepared to vouch for it. Parliament has got a number of Committees, the staff and the officers working in these Committees are dedicated and do their work dutifully. I do not have to worry about it. But they have got their own limitations, if for example the CBI does not cooperate, if any witness refuses to part with all the facts that he or she possesses. In spite of all these difficulties, the Committee did its job.

An Alarming Situation

Mr. Deputy Speaker, Sir, during my 23 years of Parliamentary career I have raised discussions and participated in debates on reports of several select Committees. We have seen many scandals. But the picture brought out by this securities scam of the entire economy, of the entire Administration is alarming. I do not want this matter to be considered on the basis of party politics. Where are we going, what all this is happening in the country ? It is not known how much money was siphoned off, how much money was involved in the scam. Different figures are being given, but, Mr. Deputy Speaker, do these figures not alarm us ? Is not the amount involved in this scam sufficient to pass sleepless nights ?

I had referred to Bofors. The range of guns manufactured by Bofors is long, but the amount appropriated fraudulently in that gun deal, investigations about which are still going on, and God knows how long will they continue, does not go beyond Rs. 162 crores. The amount of Rs. 162 crores is peanut as compared to the amount involved in the securities scam. According to reports, the public undertakings made available a colossal amount of Rs. 36 thousand crores for the securities scam. Please see Question No. 114, Para 14.21 of Committee Notes. I Quote :

> **Para 14.21 :** "The Committee note that the PSUs were the single largest source of surplus investible funds of around Rs. 36,000 crores between April, 1990 and December, 1992 only."

While our Defence Budget for one year is only of the order of Rs. 18,000 crores, Rs. 36,000 crores were made available for the scam from Public Undertakings alone. Now they will say that they did not give it for the scam, they had invested it in order to earn more money, so that the Public Sector may reach the peak of success. But it went down the drain. However, Rs. 36,000 crores were available for this. If you say that the amount of Rs. 36,000 crores is exaggerated, that the entire money did not go down the drain, some money must have been retrieved and come back, then I would like to ask a question. How much money was lost in the securities scam ? Janaki Raman Committee says that Rs. 4,024 crores were lost, the CBI's estimate is higher. They say that the amount lost is Rs. 8,338 crores.

Loss Sustained due to Scam

If we make a compromise at Rs. 5,000 crores, even then we will have to admit that the estimated amount of expenditure provided in the last year's Central Budget for social services, such as education, health, broadcasting etc. was not even half the amount of Rs. 5,000 crores lost in the securities scam. It was only Rs. 2,373 crores. For education and health in the whole country—I do not know why broadcasting has now been tagged to it in the Budget and if Broadcasting is also included in it, we had provided Rs. 2,373 crores only under these heads. But here Rs. 5,000 crores disappeared and were lost. Where has this money gone ? Now the Committee has recommended constitution of another Committee to find out where that money has gone. That Committee would investigate the matter and perhaps the Government has taken a decision about it and it is a right decision. It has to be taken by the Government. Even without constituting an Action Taken Committee, the Government has to show its reaction to the recommendations made in this Report that it has taken steps that something concrete is being done, and this is a step in that direction.

Enemies of Society

Mr. Deputy Speaker, Sir, such a huge amount of money was lost. The complaint was that this should have been announced inside the Parliament. But, the amount of money is only one aspect of it, although without doubt it is important. In this country where more than 48 per cent of people live below the poverty line, those who have fiddled with Rs. 5,000 crores are nothing but enemies of the society.

Morality the Greatest Asset

Mr. Deputy Speaker, Sir, more than the money, the question is that of integrity, of authenticity and of morality. Morality is an asset on the strength of which we have survived till today, on the basis of which we mobilise our capacity to face the external and internal pressures. What is the inner strength of this country ? In poverty too we moved keeping our heads high, since we have got the moral strength. We commanded respect in the world inspite of being backward, because we made morality as the touchstone, a standard of our character. The most painful side of this entire scam is that it has hurt our credibility of those moral values. I want to quote an extract from the Report of the Committee :-

> "What is extremely worrisome to the Committee, however, is an unhappy side effect. Amongst all the witnesses that appeared before the Committee, in all the many hours of evidence taken, the Committee seldom came across an instance where responsibility for wrong was forthrightly accepted. Further, and more worrisomely, the Committee found that as of routine through the entire apparatus of Governmental machinery, a very damaging approach seems to pervade, that of transferring responsibility downwards. This distressing lack of fibre in the apparatus of governance can only debilitate the state. This persuades the Committee to briefly comment upon the third dimension of this entire matter, which is moral. No system can work through regulations alone. Of course, it cannot work if they be flouted, but much more than that, if a system be devoid of the moral quotient, of a common sense appreciation of right from wrong, of a sense of public duty particularly when entrusted with public funds, then it cannot work".

Will the discretion to judge what is right and what is wrong be given a go by, and the public money be treated as a plaything ? Please read the whole Report, each and every page of this Report is full of stories which cause immense pain in the heart.

Systemic Failure

It is meaningless to say that it is a systemic failure. An argument is being forwarded that it was a 'systemic failure'. Who comprises the system ? Are individuals not responsible for making the system a success ? So, it is not a failure of the system. Warnings have been issued since many years. In 1986

Shri Augustine P. Kurias gave a warning in his report, counted the points. I can quote him if you so desire :

> "The Committee have noticed that the kind of irregularities that have recently surfaced can be traced back to as early as October 1986. This had been pointed out in a letter by a Joint Chief Officer of the DBOD, in RBI, Shri Augustine P. Kurias, way back in 1986, on the basis of special scrutiny of securities transactions in Andhra Bank and Syndicate Bank. The irregularities then noticed were ...."

If you see these irregularities, they are the same irregularities which later on ... (*Interruption*).

DR. KARTIKESWAR PATRA (Balasore) : It has already been said that it is a systemic failure.

SHRI VAJPAYEE : In our country we have the Ministry of Finance, the Reserve Bank of India, the Banking Department and the SEBI. They have been regularly issuing circulars. There is a mention of those circulars in this Report and it has been pointed out that they were not followed by anybody. Not only were they not followed, but there was nobody to check whether they were being followed or not. This is the failure of the system. The system says that a watch must be kept. The system says that there should be continuous inspection. But inspection was not done, a watch was not kept, circulars were sent; they appear to have been thrown into the waste paper basket. Can the officers be acquitted from their responsibility, could they be exonerated ? What was the role played by the Ministry of Finance ?

Openness and Scandal Cannot go Hand in Hand

Mr. Deputy Speaker, Sir, our Finance Minister and his colleagues regarded the unprecedented boom in the share market during the securities scam as a salutary outcome of the introduction of economic reforms. I had given a warning at that time. Please read my speech. I had said that the energy which had been released from the chains of bondage might turn into a man-eater, be careful. Sufficient care had to be taken along with liberalisation. The Committee has observed that when there is transparency scandal cannot take place. Our communist friends have not been able to comprehend so far that openness and scandal cannot go hand in hand.

Mr. Deputy Speaker, Sir, this was the thinking of the Finance Minister, but inspite of that the Finance Ministry should have been alert, they should have taken action. There is a mention in the Report that the Minister of Finance had called a meeting of the Presidents of the Stock Exchanges. I have gone through its proceedings. There is no reference there of an unprecedented or abnormal rise in the prices of shares. They discussed other subjects, but this particular subject was not discussed. Steps could have been taken at that time and the situation could have been retrieved but this was not done.

Emergence of Culture of Non-accountability

Mr. Deputy Speaker, Sir, the facts revealed by the Committee, while trying to find out the source of the money used in the securities scam, are alarming.

I have already stated that the money was received from the PSUs and the foreign banks. There is a reference to the figure of Rs. 36,000 crores. What was the idea behind establishing the public undertakings, what was the philosophy ? The objective was to strengthen the national economy, to make ourselves self-sufficient. While setting up the public undertakings, did it ever occur that we could be involved in such a scam ? The philosophy developed is, don't do your work, earn maximum profit by giving money for the stock market. Maybe, the Central Government was telling them that it was not proper to run these units in loss. But the Central Government could have said that it was O.K. to run in loss, but it would be happy if they showed profits. After all, there was the Department of Public Enterprises and the Banking Department was there to see how the money was being squandered by the public undertakings by handing over huge sums to the stock brokers. The schemes formulated to mobilise additional resources were misused, because the interest was less and so the money went directly into the hands of the stock brokers. It is stated at one place in the Report that public undertakings meant for production, but they gave up production and resorted to stock-brokering. The gambling that is going on in this country is not with the money, but with the fate of this country. How could they behave in this manner—those who run the public undertakings ? But they were behaving like this due to their meagre intelligence and to earn some quick profits and there was none to check them, there was nobody to keep a watch over them. 'Emergence of the culture of non-accountability'—these are the words used in the Report of the Committee.

Mr. Deputy Speaker, Sir, a culture of non-accountability is developing in the country. Can any reform work, can any state perform its duty in this situation ? How did this culture develop ? The Finance Minister is not prepared to take the responsibility. He is not prepared to say that his was wrong judgement, that he committed a mistake. He does not even say that he is prepared to atone. It is not known what did he say to the Prime Minister and what the Prime Minister told him ? But he has taken a right step by tendering his resignation. He has followed the Parliamentary tradition.

AN HON'BLE MEMBER : But you people did not do so.

Finance Minister Must Own Moral Responsibility

SHRI VAJPAYEE : I am not making an allegation that the Finance Minister has made any pecuniary gain out of it. He has not made any money, there is no doubt about its authenticity. But he is the Minister of Finance and the Finance Minister will have to take moral responsibility for the failure of the Ministry of Finance, for the failure of the Reserve Bank of India and for the stagnation of the entire system and I do hope that the Prime Minister would take a right decision. As a matter of fact, the whole Government is involved in this scam.

Mr. Deputy Speaker, Sir, a very horrible picture has emerged before us. I am not saying this as a member of a party, but the malaise has become so serious that the parties have become minor in this matter. Take each chapter one by one. The Reserve Bank is issuing circulars, but nobody bothers to implement them. Every Board has a nominee of the Reserve Bank of India in it, but he does not attend its meetings. He is an officer of the Central Government. He has been sent to the Board of the Bank, but he is not prepared to attend the meetings of the Board. He does not ask for the facts in the meetings. Out of 49 meetings, the representative of the Reserve Bank of India attended only 15 of them and that too only cursorily. What is this ? Is it accountability ? You go to the Board meetings, you represent the Reserve Bank of India, you do not attend the full meeting. If you attend the meeting, you do not take the trouble of knowing as to what is going on in the meeting. If the report of the meeting comes, then nobody looks at it, as though it was a pleasure trip. Can the Hon'ble Minister shirk the responsibility ? No Minister can say that he had no hand in the decision that his officer took. If your officer had taken a wrong decision, you could reject that decision, but you will have to take the responsibility, this is the parliamentary tradition, this is the norm and today all of you have to pass this test.

System on Test

I do not want to refer to those whose names are mentioned in the Report. Our Shankaranand is accustomed to drinking poison. His capacity to drink poison must not be under-estimated. But at the time of the churning of the ocean, not only poison came out, but Laxmi, the Goddess of wealth and the wine had also come out. Today he is going round and asking why should he resign ? If Shri Shankaranand's conscience tells him not to resign, I cannot offer any comment on it. I can say only that had I been in Shri Shankaranand's place, I would have resigned immediately. It is not the time to apportion blame. It is not the time to account for gram and miligram. The whole system is on test and by failing in our duty we cannot improve our future.

Mr. Deputy Speaker, this Report has raised many issues and when I was a student I did not read my course books so carefully as I have read this Report. However, as I said each and every page of this Report tells a story which leaves a bitter taste in the mouth. We wonder, which aspect should we raise here ? However, I must refer to the aspect relating to foreign banks, because among the foreign banks there is a bank, whose name I shall not disclose, but when the discussion on this scam started, some of its representatives approached me by appointment. I was very much impressed by their appearances, white shining colour of their skin, Englishmen's manners, correct pronunciation of English language surpassing even the Englishmen, ready to answer each and every argument with documentary proof and they had all the details with them to show how that bank has made progress in a short span of period. Besides this they had a diary and video cassettes also by which an ordinary man like me was naturally bound to be impressed. I thought many scandals have taken place, but after hearing these gentlemen it appeared that these people were innocent, but later on I came to know that maximum bungling had been done by that very bank.

SHRI VILAS MUTTEMWAR (Chimoor) : You get impressed very soon, Atal ji.

SHRI VAJPAYEE : Mr. Deputy Speaker, Sir what is the role of these foreign banks ? How do they deal ? Do they observe the rules ? If they observe the rules more in their violation, they are violating the rules of this country. They are not only not following the rules of this country, but they are violating the rules of the country to which they originally belong. The Committee has passed very strict strictures against these banks. The licences of these banks should be cancelled. The profit earned by them by joining the scam should not be allowed to be repatriated to their parent company in the foreign countries. I am not in favour of sending back or closing down all the foreign banks. There are so many foreign banks, but these are some selected banks. This is a very strange thing, which is not only true in case of banks, but also in case of brokers. Very special, selected people, selected banks, selected brokers, selected officers all are involved in this big scandal. They have power to create such a scandal and the nationalised banks and the financial agencies go along with them, all involving themselves in it. Millions of people have invested their money in the stocks and when the Finance Minister said that this is the result of economic reforms, then the people invested all their money which they had, even by selling their ornaments and utensils they purchased shares. Dr. Manmohan Singh said the rates are likely to go up, the country is running fast towards the direction of economic reforms. But the people were ruined. Many committed suicide. Bank of Karad and the Metropolitan Co-operative Bank disappeared from the scene. What relief has been given to those who had deposited money in these banks ? If they are victims of the system, even then they must get compensation. But they are not the victims of the system alone. They are the victims of the carelessness and the criminal negligence on the part of the big people occupying high posts and they are the victims of the policies pursued by people who have no sympathy, no pain for public funds.

Most Painful Aspect of the Scam

Mr. Deputy Speaker, Sir, I am coming to that point again and again. The most painful aspect of the scam is that when the scam occurred and, it came to light and the time for taking action came, we know from the Report itself what kind of action was taken. Smaller officers, and even bigger ones, went on leave, retired, were transferred, asked explanation. No strict action was taken, no exemplary punishment was given, only whitewashing was done, whitewashing from top to bottom. This system of whitewashing must be stopped.

Cannot this Report make us conscious even about this aspect ? I do not want to read out all the names. Among them, there are some persons who commit a scandal at one place, appear at another place, then they become Managing Directors somewhere, they become Chairmen elsewhere. With whom are these selected persons connected ? With whom are the brokers connected ? How did they play so freely ? Loot is going on in the country and nobody is there to check this loot. Those who are responsible for checking it have failed in performing their duty. There is the Department of Public

Enterprises, earlier it was a part of the Prime Minister's Secretariat. Later on, it was sent to Industry Minister. And now the entire Ministry of Industry is under the charge of the Prime Minister. The failure of this Department is so evident. What was the Department of Public Enterprises doing, what did it supervise, why did it not ascertain how the money was being pumped into the Stock Market, what did it do to ensure that it should not reach the speculative market, that it should be invested for the development of the country, that it should be used for the benefit of the undertakings ? Who did it and in what way ?

I thought SEBI was a good institution, it must be doing some useful work. But after going through the Report and after having some talks, I came to know that SEBI was indulging in double talk. On the one hand, it was writing letters to the Ministry of Finance and the Reserve Bank of India that the sudden spurt in the Share Market was not good. But in the replies prepared for Parliament, it was saying that this boom in the Share Market was due to economic reforms. Did it not have the courage of plain-speaking ? Will the big officers say only what suits their masters ? Do the higher officers not possess the moral courage to say to the Minister that what he was doing was wrong although 'you may issue the orders, we would obey them.' Should not the officers possess that much of courage ? However, one comes across very few officers who have that courage; most of them would say, 'we are on the verge of retirement, let us make hay while the sun shines'.

Mr. Deputy Speaker, Sir, I do not know what steps the Government proposes to take, whether the Prime Minister proposes to take any bold decision or not ? We are at a delicate turn. The position of the Prime Minister has now improved in his party, he has won the elections. Now he is in a position to take firm steps. It is good that a decision has been taken to make a recommendation about Goldstar; it must reach the bottom. If Harshad Mehta fails to prove his allegations, action must be taken against him too. It is not proper to let a person go scot-free if he fails to prove the allegations made by him.

Appointment of Lokpal

I have been continuously pointing out that the Administrative Reforms Commission had recommended the appointment of a Lokpal. When allegations of corruption are made against the leaders of high stature, which system of investigation should be followed ? The Administrative Reforms Commission had recommended the appointment of a Lokpal, someone like the Ombudsman, high powered, completely unattached, who could investigate the charges against the highest placed person. Not only he could investigate, but also have his own investigating machinery. The C.B.I. cannot be relied. The credibility of the C.B.I. has been eroded. The C.B.I. refused to answer the Committee and the Committee could not do anything. The C.B.I. stated that it could not supply the requisite information because it would affect the matter under investigation. What would happen to that inquiry which is underway ? The C.B.I. did not co-operate, its reorganisation is necessary.

But I was making another point before you. Howsoever of high stature the person might be, if allegations of corruption are made against him, a special system must be evolved for investigation and that Ombudsman should have the authority to requisition people from any of the investigating agencies. A new machinery cannot be set up for each and every inquiry. But the machinery should be honest and find out the truth. The appointment of that machinery and the promotions of its personnel should not depend upon the Government. After all, there must be one, two or five thousand such honest people in the country who may speak the truth even at the cost of facing difficulties themselves. Only then this country can have some expectations for its future.

I want to assert again that we are standing on a trijunction. This Report is just not a document on the Banking Scam, it is a very bitter comment on our national character. It will put us all in the dock. It demands a reply from the entire Government. It is an unanimous Report, I want to reiterate this fact.

Our friend Shri Jena was raising this question with a view to point out that since this is an unanimous Report, should not the House form an unanimous opinion about it ? The notes which are appended separately, in which some other points are mentioned, I do not want to refer to them at present. They are important in themselves. But about the Report, to which no note of dissent has been appended, can't the whole House form an unanimous opinion ? The unanimous opinion could be that those who have been accused under the Report, against whom adverse comments have been made, action should be taken against them. If he is a Minister, he should resign, and if he is an official he must be put in the dock. Only that can restore to some extent the faith lost by the people. Thank You.

Action Taken Report is Sham

Mr. Speaker, Sir, I apologise for reaching a little late in the House.

You are aware that our Party is generally in favour of not dispensing with the Question Hour. Our efforts have always been in that direction, but I can very well understand the excitement caused today and you can understand it as well. A Report has come and the greatest scandal of the century has been white-washed in that Report, the concerned Ministers have been declared innocent, officers have retired, the enquiry continues. This enquiry will continue until this Government is retired by the people, until it is changed. Hence this excitement.

J.P.C.'s Report was unanimous and the Parliamentary Committees do not work on party-basis. What has been the fate of that Report ? This Report is humiliating. It violates the dignity of Parliament. You have given a clean chit to everybody and the rest of the enquiry is continuing. How long will this enquiry continue ? The Prime Minister has now opened his mouth against corruption, and this is the result.

Mr. Speaker, Sir, I agree with you that the Question time is our time. But today that time appears to have become frightening. We have also given notice of an adjournment motion. We want a discussion on it under Rule 184, we do not want a short duration discussion. We want to record our vote under Rule 184. Let the House record its opinion and let the ruling party make up its mind about it.

A short duration discussion can be talked out, we do not want such a discussion. It is no reason that if the discussion is held under Rule 184 and voting takes place, the ruling party cannot express its views freely. The ruling party members had expressed their views about Assam and we want them to search their conscience in this matter also. I do not think that they would also support this Report or would associate themselves with it. If the J.P.C. members read this Report, they cannot but shed their tears over it. This Report cannot be accepted. We want you to give your ruling, taking into account both the excitement caused among the Members as well as the importance of the subject matter. If you so desire, I am prepared to tell my friends to let the Question Hour continue and you may listen to us thereafter....

Mr. Speaker, Sir, during the discussion in the Business Advisory Committee meeting with the Minister of Parliamentary Affairs it was decided as to how the debate would take place on the Action Taken Report. It is also

---

Lok Sabha on July 27, 1994 on the demand for discussion under Rule 184 on the Action Taken Report presented by Government on the J.P.C. Report

notable that the ruling party had constantly insisted that the debate should be held under Rule 193 and not under Rule 184. I welcome the change in the attitude now, but, Mr. Speaker, this meeting took place before the Action Taken Report was received. We had not seen it, but we thought that the recommendations made by the Joint Parliamentary Committee unanimously would by and large be accepted, some Minister would be removed or some officer would be put in the dock or arrested, because we would like to see a slight reflection of what is being done against corruption which is so rampant all around today. But Mr. Speaker, after going through the Report, the discussion has no meaning at all. Therefore, the Government must withdraw the Report and let its reaction be made known. Thank You.

Action Taken Report Must be Withdrawn

Mr. Speaker, Sir, the Minister of Parliamentary Affairs has just now read out the motion, which the Government had placed in the meeting called by you. I would like that the motion of Shri Indrajit Gupta in response to which this motion had come, should also be brought before the House, because Shri Indrajit Gupta had tried to find a way out of that impasse. However, the Government did not allow it to succeed.

Sir, the record must be complete.

MR. SPEAKER : Yes, please carry on.

SHRI VAJPAYEE : I want to read it out. The motion put forth by Shri Indrajit Gupta, before the meeting of the leaders of the parties, is as follows :

> "After consultation with the various opposition parties about the Action Taken Report laid on the Table of the House on such and such date pertaining to the Report of the JPC, since the decisions in some respects are not comprehensive enough to satisfy the expectations of the Members of Parliament, the Government is now willing to have the Action Taken Report amended, augmented and to bring the Report so revised before the House at an appropriate stage. In the meanwhile, the present Action Taken Report may be treated as an interim report and the approval or disapproval of the final report may be decided by the House at an appropriate time."

This motion was from Shri Indrajit Gupta. We were asked to consider this motion forthwith today morning. We wanted to put it in the meeting of our Parliamentary Party, but could not do so, because we were asked to take a decision on it immediately. But if we compare both the motions, the allegation made by the ruling party that the Opposition was not adopting a reasonable attitude would prove wrong. Shri Indrajit Gupta had tried to find a way out and the Government did not accept even that limited toned down motion, because the Government does not want to have an agreement. The Government has adopted an attitude of obstinacy...

As I said, Shri Indrajit Gupta... (*Interruption*)...

MR. SPEAKER : Yesterday Shri Vajpayee was not present, so let us hear him.

SHRI VAJPAYEE : As I said earlier, it is connected with that, and therefore, I want to make it clear. I said that Shri Indrajit Gupta's motion came before us this morning for the first time and we had to consider it at the party level, hence we have not accepted it. But I want to invite the attention of the House

---

Lok Sabha on August 2, 1994 on the new motion of agreement moved by Minister of Parliamentary Affairs Shri Vidya Charan Shukla on the Action Taken Report on the JPC Security Scam

towards the sudden change brought about in the attitude of Shri Shukla. We decided to resign from the membership of the committees, and then he accepted the motion of Shri Indrajit Gupta. You might recall, Mr. Speaker, now you will have to stand witness to it, that when in your Chamber...

MR. SPEAKER : Whether it may be wrong or right. I think that if you will put pressure, then he will accept it, and if he makes a request to you, then you will accept it.

SHRI VAJPAYEE : That is why we are putting a little more pressure, so that he may withdraw the Report. If he does not withdraw it, then we too will have to walk out of the House along with other friends ... (*Interruptions*)...

(Thereafter Shri Atal Bihari Vajpayee and some other Hon'ble Members walked out of the House).

Non-cooperation by Opposition the Only Way Left

Mr. Speaker, Sir, an unprecedented situation has arisen in Parliament. I have been connected with Parliament since 1957 and I have spent most of my time in the Opposition. We have all along emphasized that the Opposition in its conduct must maintain the dignity of Parliament. However, as I said on the first day of the Monsoon Session, we feel sorry and pained at what happened.

Government's Negative Attitude

The negative attitude of the Government on the reports of Parliamentary Committees is also an important factor in the credibility of the parliamentary system. It has created a feeling of lack of faith among the people in the parliamentary system. On that day this Report had not come. We never imagined that this kind of Report was in the offing. But before this Report was submitted, the people of the country were having a feeling, they were expressing their view, that Parliament was not carrying out its responsibility properly. The people had started asking us as to what do we do in Parliament ? Whenever allegations of corruption are made, no enquiry is held. If an enquiry is held, no action is taken, only whitewashing is done.

There has been a deadlock in the House for so many days. Mr. Speaker, we are beholden to you for trying again and again to find a way out to resolve the deadlock. The proceedings of the House must continue. You have tried to bring together the Opposition and the Government in order to find a way out, but the Government has taken no initiative. Why it has not done so ? Will you have to be a medium always between the Government and the Opposition ? Will there be no direct dialogue ? Has the Government discounted all possibilities of direct talks ? How can then the parliamentary system work, how will democracy survive ? Mr. Speaker, there should be no need to involve you in every matter. We are all grateful to you for the contribution you have been making in this matter.

Let the Government ponder over what after all is that thing which has united the entire Opposition. Today opinion was sought separately from all the smaller parties who hail from North-East and the South. All were speaking in unison that the Action Taken Report on the J.P.C. Report was not proper and the Government must withdraw it.

Lok Sabha on August 2, 1994 informing about the decision of the Bharatiya Janata Party to resign from all the Parliamentary Committees and to boycott the House for the rest of the Session in protest against the Action Taken Report

It is not a political issue. What kind of a Report has come ? Mr. Speaker, you might recall that when J.P.C. was constituted, we had demanded on behalf of the Opposition that the Chairman should be from the Opposition, because after becoming a member of the Parliamentary Committee one does not conduct himself on party lines. It is an important matter. It is a scandal, the biggest scam of the century. Where did Rs. 5000 crores go ? The common man is affected by it. Small people purchased shares and all their shares were sold dirt cheap. Who created such a big scam ?

You accepted the demand for the Parliamentary Committee. The party in power accepted it. A suggestion was made that the Chairman should be from the Opposition, because everybody knew that the discussion that would take place in it, the decisions that would be taken by it, will have far-reaching effects and heads of some people might roll on the road. Therefore, a senior member of the Congress Party Shri Ram Niwas Mirdha was appointed as the Chairman of the Committee. We did not raise any objection. We have faith in him. Congress had majority. We do not work on party basis in the Committee. Proofs and facts were submitted, evidence was taken. Moving from the convention, you yourself gave an opportunity to the Ministers to appear before the Committee to present their case. When the Committee was constituted, the Prime Minister himself had stated that action would be taken against the guilty. Hard labour was put in for 18 months. It was in the news both inside as well as outside the country. The Report came, but the Action Taken Report which has come is such that the Government itself thinks that this kind of Report should not have come. It was, therefore, suggested that some words may be deleted. Besides that, a proposal was also being discussed that this Report may be treated as an interim report and another report may be submitted because the Government thinks that a mistake has been committed. If a mistake has been committed, then there should be no hesitation in admitting it openly. The other day, in the meeting summoned by you, the Prime Minister had stated that they had an open mind. There is a difference between the open mind and a vacant mind. The mind is open and you come... (*Interruption*)....

SHRI VILAS MUTTEMWAR : But what to do when it is a closed mind ?

SHRI VAJPAYEE : Closed mind "*Ughudun pahayache*". When I am speaking Marathi, why do you laugh ? ...(*Interruption*)... I have said in Marathi that a closed mind requires examination after opening it, but a closed mind would not serve the purpose. This united and stubborn Opposition has had its effect on the Government. The Government have realised that its case is weak. Now the Government can take one more step forward.

Mr. Speaker, Shri Chidambaram is sitting here. He offered his resignation unnecessarily. He should also have continued. Had the Report made adverse comments against him even then he should not have moved, but followed in the footsteps of Shri Shankaranand and remained in the Government. But the good man in him resigned and the resignation was accepted forthwith. The Prime Minister would not ask for resignation from anybody else, because he fears that perhaps in this process he himself may be asked to resign. What

Shri Shankaranand has stated in the House is amazing. He said that whatever bungling he had done is under the rules, but that some Ministers have bungled by violating the rules and therefore, if no action has been taken against them, how he can be penalised ? I am telling the essence of what he said. I am not quoting his words.

Mr. Speaker, corruption is eating into the vitals of our public life as well as our political life. It would endanger democracy. Is political power a means to earn money ? All sorts of allegations are being made outside. It would become difficult for political leaders to move out on the roads. Therefore, we are demanding with great anguish in our hearts : set an example, don't be greedy, don't stick to power. Power will ultimately go, but purity of life has to be maintained in this country and in public life. Even though it may not remain completely pure, we have to check it from getting more polluted and this is an opportunity. The Report of J.P.C. had given a chance. It was an unanimous Report. You could have taken action. Even now you can take action. We want to persuade you for some action.

This is not the first case of neglecting the recommendations of a parliamentary committee. Please execuse me, there is the Railway Convention Committee. Shri Jaffer is sitting here, people say there is only one Sharif in the Cabinet. I am not making allegations against others. The unanimous report of the Railway Convention Committee was thrown into the waste paper basket, why ?

The people ask us : what do you do in the committees ? If an unanimous report of a committee does not get due respect how can democracy survive? I do concede that the Government can say that it has such and such difficulties in accepting the report. The members in the Committee can consider it and take a decision by raising themselves above party politics, but in the House it is not possible. Either a whip will be issued or a hundred other restrictions would be put. Hence the report of the committee should be given much more importance. This Report received is an unanimous report. Now the Government is recounting how many recommendations have been accepted. There is a difference of opinion about it too. Action has not been taken against anybody. Please remember that unless action is taken against some Minister how the people would know that an attempt is being made to remove corruption. The people would not understand it. Action should not be limited only to government officials. I am not talking about any criminal offence. Is there no moral responsibility ? The Finance Minister is a good Minister of Finance. We have no doubt about his personal integrity. But the Ministry of Finance has failed during the entire scam. When the enquiry was going on, the Finance Minister was supporting the Governor of the Reserve Bank all along. At that time also, we had objected to it. Dr. Manmohan Singh himself had tendered his resignation, having been affected by the Report and having admitted the impact of its recommendations. Shri Chidambaram's resignation was accepted, but Dr. Manmohan Singh's resignation was not accepted. I am not prepared to accept the plea that without him economic reforms of the Congress Party would not materialise. Dr. Manmohan Singh's resignation could have been accepted for the sake of a sacred principle. This would have raised the prestige of Dr. Manmohan Singh as well as that of the party. When Dr. Manmohan Singh had tendered his resignation and his resignation was returned to him, how would Shankaranand then resign ? Elections are due to be held in Karnataka, it is not known what may happen. Where the public life is going ?

Mr. Speaker, I am afraid that after receiving the Action Taken Report, which indicates the Government's reaction to the J.P.C. Report, it would be impossible to work any more in a parliamentary committee above party lines. A beginning has been made.

The Public Accounts Committee was enquiring into the sugar scandal. The Food Secretary had been called to present himself before the Committee ... (*Interruptions*)... This is a fact. Today when we are deciding to resign from all the committees, can't we make a mention as to what kind of treatment is being meted out to the committees by the Government ? Obstructions are being created in the way of the Public Accounts Committee. I can understand the difficulty of the members of the Congress Party. If Shri Shukla would call them one by one and ask what a mess they had made, what would the members do ? ... (*Interruptions*)...

Mr. Speaker, how the committees would work ? I am telling an old story, I am leaving aside the present context, because I am not in a mood of confrontation.

MR. SPEAKER : Well, if you have said something and someone wants to make a correction in that, he can do so.

SHRI VAJPAYEE : I have no objection, but after I have completed.

MR. SPEAKER : All right.

SHRI RAM VILAS PASWAN : If some one tries to make a correction, he would be entangled further ...(*Interruption*)...

SHRI VAJPAYEE : A report of the Public Accounts Committee about sugar import had come earlier. Serious allegations were made in it. Sugar was purchased abroad at higher prices. We enquired into it. There was no difference of opinion among the parties. I was the Chairman. We had made recommendations. Now Shri Kalp Nath Rai claims that he is following the same recommendations. However, we had made a recommendation in that that a high level enquiry must be held. The C.B.I. investigated the matter. After investigation, the C.B.I. held guilty the then Sugar Minister, Shri Sukh Ram. I am prepared to lay that Report on the Table of the House. That Report was not allowed to be placed before the House till I was the Chairman, till that Public Accounts Committee lasted. Even now, it is not being allowed to be placed before us. However, the Government knew about that report. Was any action taken against Shri Sukh Ram ? He was included in the Cabinet and now he is preparing to involve himself in some other scandal. We do not want that he may be involved, but who would like to go to the P.A.C. now ? What would he do there ?

I asked the Prime Minister the other day whether he had seen the C.B.I. report. Now the Action Taken Report on J.P.C. report has come. It is being said in various quarters that the C.B.I. is investigating the matter. What is it investigating ? Will action be taken on its findings ? Our faith has been shaken, and this is the result of a process which has continued for the last three years. An attitude has been adopted to cover up the scandal. All this opposition and all this resentment is a result of that. You might recall, on the day when this session began, we had said that we will not only forcefully put our views, but also act, if necessary. You had asked, will it be done simultaneously ? This Government has blown a wind that has united everybody inside the House. Sometimes the winds bring the clouds together, and the result is that the deadlock continues to increase. In such circumstances we do not see any way out ? (*Nanyah Pantha Vidyate Ayanay*) there is no other way to escape. There is only one way, that of non-cooperation, the way to resign from the committees. What further steps are to be taken, we will inform you after consideration. You may continue your efforts, but we have no hope from this Government. It appears that we are treading on different paths. Thank you.

Unusual Rise in Sugar Prices—Something is Fishy

Mr. Speaker, Sir, I have got in my hand the Rules of Procedure and Conduct of Business in the House and today I want to make use of one of the rules of these Rules of Procedure. That rule authorises the Members to demand an adjournment of the business of the House in order to debate a particular issue. I want to move an adjournment motion to adjourn the business of the House because Government could not check the prices of sugar from rising and therefore, the business before the House must be adjourned to discuss it.

Mr. Speaker, Sir, I have given notice, which is under your consideration. The question is of public importance since it is connected with the life of the common man. Sugar is selling at the rate of Rs. 16.50 per kg. in the open market (*Interruptions*). I want to amend what I have said. The sale price of sugar has reached up to Rs. 20 a kilogram. Why this has happened ? Did the Government not know that there would be less production of sugarcane and there will be shortage of sugar ? Should not the import of sugar have been arranged earlier ? Who would import, even this could not be decided by this Government. One Ministry accuses the other. A Minister rebukes his secretary publicly. Nothing is known what the Prime Minister's Secretariat does.

The way the prices of sugar have risen in the open market involves dealings of crores of rupees. The sugar mill owners have earned huge profits and the traders also have made good profit. This is summer season; there is more consumption of sugar during these days. It is also the marriage season. Moreover, the aspect of importing sugar from abroad also needs to be investigated. But we are asking you that before investigation, this matter should be debated thoroughly. The sugar scandal has not taken place for the first time. In 1989, I was the Chairman of the Public Accounts Committee and Pandit Sukhram, who hails from Himachal Pradesh, was the Minister concerned. He has not forgotten so far the serious consequences which he had to face as a result of the sugar scam.

The consequences of sugar scandal are not always sweet, sometimes they leave a very bitter taste in the mouth and today such a situation has arisen in the country . This is a very serious matter. It is connected with the life of the common people, it is a matter of urgent public importance. Please do not

---

Lok Sabha on June 13, 1994 while giving notice for Motion of Adjournment regarding rising prices of sugar

reject my adjournment motion on the plea that the prices keep on rising and why was this matter not raised earlier.

Mr. Speaker, Sir, my submission to you is to give a chance to the House to debate this matter of urgent public importance (*Interruptions*). Let the Government also have an opportunity to defend itself. (*Interruptions*).

SHRI INDRAJIT GUPTA (Midnapore) : We have also given an adjournment motion about sugar (*Interruptions*). I hope you are going to admit it. (*Interruptions*).

SHRI NIRMAL KANTI CHATTERJEE (Dumdum): We have also given notices for adjournment motion.

SHRI NITISH KUMAR (Barh): We have also given notice for adjournment motion (*Interruptions*).

SHRI VAJPAYEE: Mr. Speaker, there are other members too who are supporting my motion (*Interruptions*).

MR. SPEAKER: I have received notices from twelve members.

SHRI VAJPAYEE: Mr. Speaker, please do not delay your ruling on it. Certain matters require quick decision and this is such an issue. Today the entire country is looking towards this House. I know, you will say, this is a special session, we have to amend the Constitution, we have to amend the Representation of People Act.

MR. SPEAKER: I think you need not predict what I am going to say.

SHRI VAJPAYEE: No, no—these arguments will be put forward on behalf of the Government, I am not saying this about you. An attempt will be made to avoid the issue by saying so. Any discussion on other subjects could be stopped, other topics can wait, but it is very essential to raise the issue of public discontent caused due to rising prices of sugar today. We want to censure the Government for that and only discussion would not serve the purpose.

The One Thousand Crore Sugar Scam

Mr. Speaker, Sir, the Adjournment Motion on which our friend has initiated the discussion does not concern one Ministry only. The responsibility for delay in importing sugar which led to sharp rise in its price rests not only on the Ministry of Food, but on the Commerce Ministry as well. Prime Minister's Secretariat was also active in this matter. The Cabinet Secretary, too, has a role in it. But I find that only the Minister of Food is present here. It is such a serious matter, it has affected the public life so widely, that a detailed explanation is required in this matter from the Government, and this could be done only by the Prime Minister, since allegations have been made against the Food Minister himself.

Sir, now when the role of the Cabinet Secretary is going to be discussed, who will reply to that ? Who will give an explanation about the orders issued from time to time or the decisions taken by the Prime Minister's Secretariat ? This work cannot be handled by our friend Shri Kalpanath Rai. Therefore, I would say that if justice is to be done to this Adjournment Motion the Prime Minister should be present in the House. As I have said before, this matter does not pertain to one Ministry alone.

An estimate had already been made that there would be a shortfall in the production of sugarcane and consequently lesser sugar would be produced. Why then suitable steps were not taken to augment the supply of sugar, whether in the open market or through the Public Distribution System ? It was known beforehand that the sugarcane production would be less, yet steps were not taken in time to meet the situation. The facts and the statistics in this regard are not only alarming, but also create suspicion in the mind. Unfortunately, the atmosphere in the country is such that in everything there appears to be a scam, and hence there is need to have transparency. It is necessary to place all the facts before the House, but this is not being done.

Decision to Import Sugar Delayed

Mr. Speaker, Sir, on 24th January, the Food Minister sent a note to the Cabinet in which it was stated that there is likelihood of a shortfall of one million tonnes of sugar. When was action taken on it ? For 6-7 weeks, no decision was taken in this matter; why was it not done ? Was it not apparent that there would be shortage of sugar ? The rising prices of sugar were a warning and when the prices of sugar did not come down even after the festival season, the danger bell tolled. During the festival season, the price of sugar rises slightly in the open market, but after the season is over, it reverts

Lok Sabha on June 13, 1994 during the discussion on the Adjournment Motion moved on the rising prices of sugar

to its normal position. However, this time it did not happen. I can quote figures. It was a danger signal. According to it, immediate arrangements should have been made for the import of sugar. I am referring to the letter dated January 24, a meeting was held on March 8, in which it was decided to import sugar under O.G.L. But this decision "leaked". I am making this allegation seriously. India would import sugar under O.G.L.—this news reached the international market. Otherwise too, the international sugar market is confined to London. It is dominated by some companies and they got a din into their ears that there is shortage of sugar in India and it will be imported under O.G.L. why did the Government not decide to import by itself ? The decision "leaked", as a result of which the price of sugar rose by Rs. 50-60 per tonne in the international market. I can quote earlier figures. At that time the price was less. Sugar could have been imported at that time without making any noises. The sugar could be purchased from the international market at cheaper rates after making an estimate of the shortfall. But there was delay, and the information about delayed steps reached abroad too, resulting in instant rise in the prices of sugar.

I hold the view that there has been a bungling of Rs. 1000 crores. Rs. 300 crores extra were paid abroad—there could be slight variation in it and if we calculate the extra amount of money which the consumers inside the country had to pay, that comes to Rs. 700 crores. What was the rate of sugar and at what rate it is being sold ! A loot is going on. It is the marriage season now, and summer is there when people drink more *sharbat*. So, all this was done in a planned way. This also needs to be investigated. The doubts that are being harboured cannot be removed by any explanation.

Loss to Consumers and Gain to Foreign Dealers

Mr. Speaker, Sir, I would like to repeat again that there was a delay of 6-7 weeks. Who is responsible for it ? The Food Minister would say that he had written a letter to the Cabinet. Why did the Cabinet not take any decision thereon ? The explanation for this must also come from the Cabinet. The consumers inside the country lost and the dealers outside gained.

Mr. Speaker, Sir, it was estimated that, along with the open market, there would be a shortfall of one million tonnes of sugar in the Public Distribution System. When we were considering import of sugar, we did not take P.D.S. into account. There was lesser production of sugarcane which was due to drought to a considerable extent. The sugarcane was diverted from being supplied to mills to the production of *Gur* (Jaggery) resulting in shortfall in the production of sugar and receipt of less levy sugar. Sugar which is purchased by the poor is a part and parcel of the Public Distribution System. Sugar is counted as an essential commodity.

I remember that the price of onion had once risen. There was a public outcry. Our friends sitting on the treasury benches were shedding tears by cutting onion into pieces and applying them to their eyes. One gets tears into one's eyes while making slices of onion. But, how about the bitterness of sugar and this sugar crisis, the pain a housewife feels while purchasing sugar at Rs. 20 per kilogram ? If this is mismanagement, then whose mismanagement it is, or is it a scandal ? Wherever the Government puts its hand it becomes a scandal. Like whatever was touched by Gandhiji turned into gold. Now this Government is turning everything into scandal. This is not a propaganda made by the Opposition. This is an expression of public resentment.

How to Meet Shortfall of Sugar for P.D.S. ?

Mr. Speaker, Sir, will sugar have to be imported for P.D.S ? Was this factor not considered ? Which agency should have considered it ? Why was it not thought of ? I was looking at the figures supplied by the Food Ministry. Sugar is released by the Ministry of Food by directing the Mills to release a particular quantity for the month. Sugar released during the month of May was less, why was it so ? More sugar should have been released in the month of May. This is the summer season, this is the marriage season, the result was that even the shops under Public Distribution System could not supply enough sugar to the people. Even if a poor man marries his daughter, he cannot serve *sharbat* made from *Gur* to his guests, he will have to offer *sharbat* made of sugar. He also had to purchase sugar at higher prices from the open market. Why there was not enough sugar available even at P.D.S. shops ? If it was necessary to import sugar for supplying it to the P.D.S. shops, why was it not estimated beforehand ? Whose responsibility it was ? We supply sugar at the rate of Rs. 9 per kg. under the P.D.S., which includes Rs. 3 as subsidy.

Who will Pay the Subsidy ?

Mr. Speaker, Sir, ever since our love affair has become thick with the World Bank and the International Monetary Fund, this subsidy comes into our way at every step and our decisions get vitiated. When it was decided that sugar had to be imported and this sugar will be supplied to the common people through P.D.S., it should also have been decided as to who would pay the subsidy, since sugar is supplied at subsidised rates at the P.D.S. ? The Finance Minister had been indicating that he would not pay the subsidy. However, if the S.T.C. and the M.M.T.C. were to import sugar and sustain a loss, they would be pulled up. An explanation would be called for from those who would supply sugar at cheap rates. Should not these questions have been attended to simultaneously that sugar will be imported and who will pay the subsidy ? This should have been settled beforehand. This was not done and hence delay was caused in importing it. Therefore, its prices abroad as well as inside the country rose. You may please look at the date, it was decided at the end of April that the sugar would be imported for P.D.S. But no action was taken after the decision. There was no decision as to who would pay the subsidy and what would be its amount. The Prime Minister's Office was seized of this matter and the Cabinet Secretary came into the picture and then, on 14th May, when the Prime Minister was going on a foreign trip, he took the Cabinet Secretary aside before emplaning and holding his hand told him,

I have read it in newspapers, I was not present there, something will have to be done in regard to sugar. The Prime Minister was going on an important trip. Which issues would arise during that trip, how they would be disposed of, how they would be answered—instead of thinking about all these matters, he thought that after his departure there would be a hue and cry about sugar, and that would end the sweetness of his entire trip, and with that in view, he took aside the Cabinet Secretary and told him something. It was now for the Cabinet Secretary to move in the matter and have discussions with the Ministries of Food and Commerce. Our Food Minister has a complaint, he was touring Ghazipur area. He was worrying for votes, so was I. It is being said that the Food Minister could not be traced. This could be understood had there been some small, insignificant and thin fellow. But the Food Minister cannot hide himself, he cannot hide himself even behind someone else, making it difficult to find him out. The Government says that the Food Minister could not be contacted. Anybody could be contacted in any corner of the country through the District Magistrate. If the Government could not contact its own Minister at the time of an emergency, its inefficiency becomes all the more apparent. Perhaps it would not be able to contact even the Minister of State in the Ministry of Defence when the need arises. A decision was taken without his consent and when the Food Minister returned, he cancelled the decision. He has referred to the report of the Public Accounts Committee, whose Chairman I am, for cancelling the decision.

SHRI MOHAN SINGH (Deoria) : In order to please you.

Episode of 1989 Repeated

SHRI VAJPAYEE : In order to save his skin. I have got that report with me. It shows how history repeats itself. The situation in 1989 was repeated in 1994. The Public Accounts Committee had given its report after careful investigation. If I read out some extracts from the report, you will think it to be the report not relating to year 1989 but to 1994 :

> "Initial delay of about three months in according approval to the import of sugar."

Earlier, there was no need to import sugar in such a large quantity. It was only a matter of one or two lakh tonnes, even then a crisis had arisen. At that time also, Pandit Sukhram had come within bounds of allegations. That is why he could not reach Lok Sabha at that time. But a similar scandal had taken place at that time as well. Delay was caused in importing sugar. Who should import was the subject of contention even then. Those who were responsible did not import it in time, the reason given being :

> "First tender enquiry floated on 23rd August, 1989 proved infructuous due to the failure of telex machine."

The Telex machine failed. Later on the officer disclosed that there was no paper in the macine. The machine was working, paper was missing, so it was not indicating the rates. Whose tender it was, who was the purchaser, the machine was not telling this and the Government was going on, preparations were being made to import sugar. Times have changed, but the ways of the

Government have not changed. This time, the scam is bigger. A huge quantity of sugar is involved. This time, the people have suffered more. But the 1989 PAC report and Action Taken Report are there. No report this time has yet come, but the information received so far indicates that FCI said that it did not want to involve itself in this matter and PAC had also recommended that it was not the work of FCI. FCI's work is to distribute sugar in the country. If it is to be imported from abroad or a deal is to be struck in the foreign market and if the deal has to be settled skilfully on the basis of equality with the big sharks sitting in London, then experts are required and those experts could be available with the STC and the MMTC. Services of the Commerce Ministry officials could be requisitioned. But it should be done through an open deal. However, this was not done.

Task Force Needed to Resolve Sugar Crisis

We are now being told that sugar is coming. These figures are also with me. The quantity of sugar that has reached the ports is less. The quantity of sugar which has reached the market is even less and the quantity which has reached the shops is lesser. Can't it be accelerated ? Could not a Task Force be set up to follow up this matter so as to overcome the sugar crisis ? It appears to me that the Government did not take this matter seriously and made no preparations.

Bungling All Around

Again, Mr. Speaker, the PAC in its earlier report had recommended that un-registered companies should not be allowed to partake in this deal. They have no background, no credibility, but the decisions taken in this regard at the initiative of the Cabinet Secretary also brought un-registered companies into the picture. How did they come ? What were the reasons behind it ? Who will reply to that ? As I said in the beginning, the Food Minister cannot answer this, the Prime Minister can. This was the decision of the Cabinet Secretary. What was the necessity to bring in the unregistered companies ? Registered companies can settle this deal, can give their opinion. Again, it was decided to import sugar in the open market under O.G.L. The prices went up here as well as in the foreign countries. Difficulties arose here. The Food Ministry did not release sugar for the open market properly which also caused rise in prices.

No Co-ordinated Policy About Sugar

Mr. Speaker, Sir, unfortunately, I have to say that no co-ordinated policy about sugar could be formulated so far. Sometimes the production of sugarcane increases, sometimes it decreases. I remember that Acharya Vinoba Bhave had said that sugarcane and foodgrains are at war with each other. You may sow sugarcane or you may sow foodgrains. We need foodgrains more than sugar. But now the demand for sugar is rising. *Gur* cannot serve the purpose. Now even *gur* is selling at the rate of Rs. 20 per Kg., but it is not possible to gulp the tea prepared from *gur*. How much *gur* would be manufactured, how much *Khandsari* (raw sugar) would be produced and how much sugarcane would be required for manufacturing sugar ? Is it not possible to form a co-ordinated policy by having a proper estimate of all these things ? The States will have to cooperate in the exercise. Since the increase in the prices of sugar, how much profit the Mill owners have earned and how much the traders have earned should be estimated. The loot is going on. The common man and the poor man has to pay through his nose. He does not like paying so much, but there is no alternative. It is true that the people are not condemning the government so vehemently by coming out on the roads in large numbers, as it should have been the case. But it is a scam and a burning proof of the inaction on the part of the government. There is another question, whether licences for opening new sugar mills should be issued or not, and if they were to be issued, then how many ? Licences were granted, then withdrawn. The Uttar Pradesh people went on demanding licences, but the Punjab people got them. How to decide how many licences would be issued, how much sugar would be required ? There is one government, but it is a divided government, it is asking decisions in divisions. The Ministers are accusing the officers, the officers are speaking ill of the Ministers behind their backs and the purchasers of sugar were being crushed under the burden.

High Level Enquiry Needed in Sugar Scam

Mr. Speaker, Sir, we are, therefore, forced to bring this Adjournment Motion. It is necessary to have a high level enquiry into the entire gamut of this sugar scam. At first a satisfactory explanation should be given before the House. All the figures and facts must be placed before the House. Everything should be stated very clearly. This is the second time that sugar scam has taken place after 1989. I wanted to say that a system should be evolved so that this kind of scandal is not repeated in future. But I do not feel like saying so, because during the regime of this government a second scam has taken place and if this government continues a third one will also take place. This government has to go in some scam, but that is a separate subject. I want that the members of the Congress Party should also ponder over the question under consideration a bit seriously. If we have brought the Adjournment Motion, that does not mean that your consumers, your voters, your supporters are not suffering due to the rising prices of sugar. Somebody must be answerable for it. Somebody will have to be put in the dock, somebody's head must roll on the road. How long would it be kept behind the curtain ? How long the misdeeds of certain people would be condoned, how long will the eyes be closed towards these misdeeds ? However big a Minister, howsoever big an officer, he must be put in the dock to answer the charges, and if this Adjournment Motion could motivate this Government a little to move in this direction we would consider that it has succeeded in its mission. Thank you.

III Rising Prices And Consequences

Starvation or Malnutrition: Quibbling with Words

Madam, I wanted to congratulate the Prime Minister on her personally going to Orissa to see the situation for herself. But her speech makes one feel that she is trying to whitewash the whole affair. She said those who came to see her were smiling, and what did that lead her to conclude ? A *sher* comes to my mind:

> "*Unke dekhe se jo aa jati hai munh par raunaq,*
> *Woh samazte hain ki bimaar ka hall achha hai.*"
> "Her sight lights up the face with pleasure, but she thinks the patient is in good condition."

Whether or not there were starvation deaths is still being debated. This neither enhances the prestige of the Government nor that of the country. No one should hesitate to accept the fact that we could not foresee the crisis in Orissa, nor take effective steps to overcome it. Weaving a web of words is not going to help us. It is claimed that there were no starvation deaths but malnutrition deaths. Now it is difficult for me to distinguish between starvation and malnutrition, to draw a line between the two. What is the situation in Orissa that has affected 60 lakhs people and forced five lakh of them to leave their hearth and home ? Mothers left their children on the street, and these children were bought and sold for a rupee each. Husbands left their wives. Upper caste Hindus were forced to eat beef. Even today people are living on Pipal leaves and Mahua flowers. We do not expect journalists to be partial. Just now the *Times of India* was quoted. The report on Orissa that has appeared in the *Indian Express* on May 9 makes one hang one's head in shame. The Government should honestly admit its failure. There should be no hesitation in admitting that the Orissa Government and the Central Government have failed. If the Opposition talks of these things from a political motive it is wrong on its part, and if the Government says things to hide facts that too is equally wrong.

Rajya Sabha on March 2 and 8, 1966 during discussion on situation arising out of famine conditions and alleged starvation deaths in Orissa

Madam, the question is why such a situation arose in Orissa. The Government of Orissa knew that there was a drought and it was going to affect lakhs of people. In August 1965 there was a debate on the drought condition in the Orissa Legislative Assembly. There was another discussion on the subject in December 1965 and yet another during the debate on the budget, but what steps did the Orissa Government take ? It is not enough to simply know that a crisis is developing. The administration has to take steps to prevent it from developing or, if it does develop, to contain it. Obviously the Government of Orissa did not act. Had it acted such a serious situation would not have arisen.

The Central Government too cannot absolve itself of responsibility. Can the Central Food Minister deny that large amounts of rice were dispatched from Orissa to Kerala and West Bengal ? He may say Orissa is a surplus State, but had the State Government honestly informed the Centre that drought had adversely affected crops and there were famine conditions, rice would not have been sent out of the State.

Madam, the Food Minister had stated in this House that nobody would be allowed to die of starvation, and on this ground he had justified food imports. But we could not prevent starvation deaths. Even with massive imports of wheat and rice we could not avoid the crisis in Orissa. We should therefore realise that merely importing foodgrains is not enough. You also have to arrange proper distribution. If we leave this to State Governments Orissa has shown what happens. What surprises me is that neither has the Prime Minister said nor is the Food Minister prepared to say that punishment will be given to those Government officers and bureaucrats in the drought-affected region who failed to do their duty. Their sins are being covered up. On the political level the leadership has failed and on the administrative level government machinery has failed, otherwise such a situation would not have developed in Orissa. If we feel that with importing foodgrains our job is done what happened in Orissa could repeat itself in other States. The administrative apparatus has become heartless, it is stone-hearted, it does not feel for the people. I have noticed during the past some months that the control of the political leadership over the Government machinery is slackening. Government officers have become willful, defiant and apathetic. Not only in Orissa, and not only in the field of food, in every sphere Central and State Officials are exhibiting apathy. The Prime Minister should bear in mind that gradually control over the bureaucracy is slackening, gradually the bureaucracy is dominating the government, dominating the political leadership. This is a very dangerous situation for the country, and Orissa is a warning for us.

Madam, in February a Planning Commission team had visited Orissa. It has submitted a report. But the Food Minister admitted in that House and will admit here too that it was in April that steps were taken to prevent the situation in Orissa from worsening. Can the State Government of Orissa explain why there was so much delay ? Is the Central Government satisfied that relief works were taken up in Orissa in good time ? If not, why not ? To date there is no answer to this question. I would say the situation is still not under control. The Food Minister says "the situation is under control" and the Prime Minister also repeats that "the situation is under Control." What situation ? What is the situation that is under control ? There are now more problems facing us. There is the problem of electricity supply to farmers. How is the cattle problem going to be solved ? I do not think the Orissa Government by itself can control the situation. The Centre too would have to shoulder its responsibility. Along with electric power there is also the problem of procuring farm labour. Because of food shortage people cannot work for eight or six hours, they get exhausted in four hours. So they get paid less. Now the labour charge has been made on rupee, but that too is not enough.

SHRI BANKA BEHARY DAS : It is 61 Naye Paise, as reported by the Central Team.

SHRI VAJPAYEE : Now they have increased it to Re. 1. That is what the Prime Minister has stated.

SHRI BANKA BEHARY DAS : It is on a contract basis.

SHRI VAJPAYEE : But there will be the problem of farm labour for future crops. Where are the bullocks ? How will they be put to the plough ? It is said 54,000 cattle were sold there. A panchayat made a profit of Rs. 14,000 on the sale.

I suggest the appointment of an officer on special duty in Orissa by the Central Government. Not everything can be left to the State Government. This House and this Government should accept the responsibility of ensuring that no one dies of starvation. So it is necessary to appoint a special officer of the Centre to see whether the relief works there are going on properly.

Secondly, those local officers who failed to do their duty should be punished. They should at least be transferred. I cannot understand the argument that at present we are paying to contain the crisis, later we would see who is to blame and who should be punished. This is the same argument we put forward in the days of the India-Pakistan conflict, and again we are using the same whitewash technique in the case of Orissa. Those officers who failed in the performance of their duty should be immediately transferred. There should be an investigation in their functioning and they should be asked to explain why they could not discharge their responsibilities...

One more thing and I shall finish. The food position will worsen in June-July. Every year during the monsoon the food situation becomes critical in some parts of the country. This year the situation will be particularly acute, because there is a drought all over. At such a time the Central Government must not be caught off guard. It is necessary to ensure that before the situation becomes serious in any area we arrange food supply there, provide for milk for children and start relief works.

We are faced with a serious crisis. At this juncture the Central Government, the State Government and all political parties have to work unitedly. This is not a political problem, it is a humanitarian problem. But I regret that the Prime Minister did not take any opposition MP with her.

Could she not have done so ? Shri Surendra Nath Dwivedi could have accompanied her. Maharaja Kalahandi could have accompanied her. Congress members could also have accompanied her.

Shri N. PATRO : Maharaja Kalahandi was with her.

SHRI VAJPAYEE : The Food Minister too could have asked the opposition for suggestions.

SHRI C. SUBRAMANIAM : Raja of Kalahandi was there.

SHRI VAJPAYEE : Not at the invitation of the Prime Minister but of his own accord.

SHRI C. SUBRAMANIAM : Why should he be invited ? He belonged to that constituency.

SHRI VAJPAYEE : But the Prime Minister should have shown the courtesy of inviting the opposition members to accompany her. This is the peculiar attitude that stands in the way of the Government, and if the ruling party with its large majority cannot rise above party politics it should not accuse the opposition parties. This should apply as much to the ruling party as to the Opposition parties. Thank you, Madam.

Rise in Prices of Essential Commodities

Sir, I call the Finance Minister's attention to the following matter of urgent public interest and request his statement on it :

> "Recent rise in the prices of various essential commodities like Soap, Vanaspati, Medicines, Steel and so on."

Sir, I regret to say that the information given by the new Finance Minister is not correct. Information available from official sources contradicts the Minister's statement that there has been no rise in the prices of most of the essential Commodities. Here is the Commissioner's report— I draw the Finance Minister's attention to some of the details he has collected on prices in Delhi. He has admitted that the price of rice has not gone down. Rather, it has gone up...(*Interruption*)... It has risen both before and after the budget. Butter has become 33 per cent dearer and milk 7 per cent. The price of 500 gm of tea has gone up by upto 33 per cent, that of Vanaspati Ghee by 16 per cent, that of Mustard oil by 26 per cent and of washing soap by 7 per cent. Are not these essential commodities ? Can the common man do without them ? When the Prime Minister presented the Budget the *Economic Survey* accompanying it had admitted that last year commodity prices had gone up by 7 per cent. After that prices of miscellaneous articles had gone up by 15 to 20 per cent. The point is, does the Government have any price policy or not ? Listening to or reading the Finance Minister's speech does not make one feel it has. I would like to submit one more proof in this regard. The Fourth Plan is big tome but it has no chapter on a price policy. Previously there used to be such a chapter in the Plan, which used to analyse how prices rose in the previous five years and indicate the steps proposed to be taken to control them, but this time the Planning Commission has deleted the chapter on a price policy from the Fourth Five Year Plan.

Finance Minister Speaks Like Home Minister

When traders mark up prices they are called profiteers, but when they do so with the consent of the Government what should we call the Government ? The Finance Minister just now said he has permitted a slight rise in the price of soap. Does the Finance Minister know that soap is not selling at that price but at a still higher price ? Then what is the point in having an understanding with soap manufacturers ? The Finance Minister says the price of washing soap has been raised by 14 paise per kg. Before the budget it was selling at Rs. 280 per quintal, then it went up to Rs. 290, and now the price is Rs. 303.50. This price rise is not 14 paise, it is more than that. It is the same with steel

Lok Sabha on August 5, 1970 on a Calling Attention Motion on rise in prices of essential commodities and the new Finance Minister's speech

and medicines. It is claimed that drug prices have been brought down, but actually medicines are not available at lower prices, and in some cases the manufacturers have not informed the chemists how much the prices have been lowered. Is the Finance Minister's function merely to lower prices ? It is argued that the price of soap had to be raised because tallow is imported, and the price of Vanaspati had to be increased because there is a shortage of groundnut, but does the Government have no machinery that would collect information on how much investment there is in what commodity, what is the proper quantum of profit and at what price that particular commodity should be sold ? When tallow was cheaper soap prices had not been lowered. At that time soap manufacturers did not cut their profits but now with a slight rise in the price of tallow the consumer's pocket is being picked. Vanaspati prices are continuously being raised. I do not want to make an allegation, but the people say that these prices are being raised for political ends. The Finance Minister will have to refute the charge and endeavour to make essential commodities available to the common man at proper prices.

I ask the Finance Minister, is it enough to express anxiety ? At first the Prime Minister said prices would not be allowed to go up, but now they have gone up. Now it is said we are watching them. Sir, I feel Shri Chavan may well have shifted from the Home Ministry to the Finance Ministry but his terminology has not changed : "Rising prices will be checked. A strict watch will be kept." This is the Home Minister's language, not the Finance Minister's. The speech has no concrete proposal. Sir, I would like to know what steps the Finance Minister is taking to see that the common man gets things at proper prices.

When he talks of informal control does it mean he sits with the manufacturers of oil, Vanaspati, soap and so on and discusses with them how much their profit should be raised ? What is that machinery in the Ministry ? Is it a Deputy Secretary or an Under Secretary ? Is it not possible to set up an experts' committee for this, which would decide the investment on these things, the quantum of profit on them, and what price would be right for the consumer ?

Same Statement, Same Minister Only Prices Differ

Sir, the point is, the Finance Minister cannot be let off lightly. When everything has become so expensive how can he be let off cheaply ?

SPEAKER : You do not let off anybody.

SHRI VAJPAYEE : No, Sir, I have nothing against you. I only pray for your kind consideration when the matter of the Shimla Agreement comes up. I would like to read out the introductory portion of the Finance Minister's statement. He has made another statement today, but I would like to go through an earlier one. I quote.

> "I share the anxiety of this honourable House regarding increase in the prices of essential commodities in the recent months and the hardship caused to the people belonging particularly to the lower income and fixed income groups."

Now I would read out today's statement and you can compare the two:

> "The recent pressure on prices has become a matter of concern and I share the anxiety of the Honourable House regarding the rise in the prices of essential consumer goods, particularly food articles, and the consequent hardship caused, specially to the lower and middle income groups."

This is today's statement and the first one was of November 16, 1971. Today we are in 1972, and not in 1971. It is not November, it is July. But it is the same statement, the same anxiety, even the same Finance Minister; only prices are going up.

SPEAKER : I stand corrected that this is a continuing matter.

SHRI VAJPAYEE : Sir, it would have been better if you had listened to me fully and then given your verdict. Does this Government think its duty is done by merely expressing anxiety on rising prices ? Or is it enough for it to repeat what it has once said ? Here is also something else that calls for your attention, I quote :

> "The ultimate solution lies in increasing production both in the agricultural and industrial sector, and this is being attempted through planned development."

No one can disagree with what has been said. Production will have to be increased .....

SHRI RAM SAHAY PANDE (Rajanandgaon) : Suggest a readymade solution.

SHRI VAJPAYEE : You will be serving more if you keep quiet at this time.

SPEAKER : That is difficult for him.

Lok Sabha on July 31, 1972 during discussion on the Calling Attention Motion on price rise

SHRI VAJPAYEE : But all this is long-term talk. The Finance Minister could be asked why production has not increased. What was the target of the Plan and what is the achievement ? Industrial production was to increase by 7 per cent, it has increased by 1.5 per cent. Will merely changing the Industrial Development Minister increase industrial production ?

People Harassed by Price Rise

Sir, this is a disappointing speech, it will create discontent and anger in the mind of the employed and labour classes, who are already harassed by rising prices. It is proof of the Government's failure on the price front. The Government has neither a short-term plan nor a long-term one to contain prices, let alone lower them.

SHRI R.D. BHANDARE (Bombay Central) : This is not an adjournment motion, but a calling attention motion.

SHRI VAJPAYEE : Sir, he sometimes becomes the Chairman but has not forgotten old habits. Even when he is just a member he continues with his chairmanship.

Sir, when prices go up the purchasing power of the rupee goes down. The fixed-income group is harassed. He does not consider the value of the rupee. The value of the rupee is assessed on how much it can buy in the market. As compared to 1950 the value of the rupee has been reduced to 25 paise in 1972. He gets 100 paise but in return gets goods worth only 25 paise in the market. Imagine how much dearness has increased. When the Finance Minister speaks he talks of wholesale prices. The common man does not buy wholesale. He lives his life by buying at retail prices. If the Finance Minister paid a visit to the market he would learn the prices of dal and atta.

What is the position with retail prices ? We have stocks of wheat rotting in the open and its price has gone up by Rs. 5 to 13 per quintal. This is not benefiting the farmer, it is benefiting the middleman. The consumer has to pay more. Gram has gone up from Rs. 94 to Rs. 118. Sugar has gone up from Rs. 314 per quintal to Rs. 340. No vegetable is available for less than Rs. 2 per kilo.

Open Market Cheap, Super Bazar Expensive

The surprising thing is that the Super Bazars that have been opened for keeping prices stable are selling goods at higher than market prices. I have here a letter to the Editor of the *Times of India* from one Smt. Vijaya Laxmi. She has given comparative figures and says til oil sells in the market for Rs. 27.20 per kg. but at the Super Bazar for Rs. 32.70.

It is the same with white jeera : in the Super Bazar it sells at Rs. 7 and in the open market at Rs. 6. Black pepper sells at Rs. 7.60 in the open market and Rs. 9 in the Super Bazar. She has written the same thing about Ovaltine and Bournvita. It is a different thing that Super Bazars which were opened to keep prices stable are running at a loss, but the prices of many commodities are higher there than in the open market.

The Finance Minister has talked of fair price shops in his speech. I know this is a State subject, but the Finance Minister will admit that essential commodities are not available to the common man at the right price in adequate measure. This was why Super Bazars were opened. It is necessary to regulate prices. It is also necessary to open more fair price shops, ensure proper distribution through them, and see that they receive supplies properly. What is the Finance Minister doing in that direction ? I am not in favour of the government taking the whole trade into its hands. This sort of remedy would be worse than the disease. You may see the result if you want to. I shall not become an obstruction in your way and in the way of the Communists. They are your friends and can advise you. You can accept their advice. But politics and the economy cannot be conducted with slogans. You will have to arrange production and distribution of food on the criterion of practicality.

Deficit Financing has a Hand in Price Rise

I want to know something from the Finance Minister. Is it true that deficit financing, which has gone up, has a big hand in the price rise ? This year we have exceeded the target fixed for deficit financing. We have exceeded the limit. We have arrived at double the figure fixed for deficit financing for the fourth Five Year Plan. If money is pumped into the market at this rate but goods supply does not increase, a price rise is inevitable.

I wish the Finance Minister would assure the working class and labour that although dearness has increased due to unsuccessful policies of the government, whenever there is a Pay Commission report he would give it retrospective effect and thus make up all their losses.

Is the Finance Minister also prepared to give the assurance that in the case of those with a monthly income of less than Rs. 300, basic commodities would be made available to them at subsidised rates and the Government would take concrete and effective steps for this ? If the Finance Minister does not give a satisfactory reply we would again table an adjournment motion. Thank you.

Price Situation is Grim

Sir, in the month of August there was a discussion on the price rise in this House. That time the Finance Minister had said, I quote :

> "Naturally we shall be on trial in this matter. We cannot say that we have taken a decision and, therefore, our responsibility is over. Ultimately the test of a decision is in its implementation."

He had also said that members would have to have patience for some months and that the decision taken would not be merely legal but will be backed by political solutions. Months have gone by, let alone weeks. How much more patience does the Finance Minister want us to have ? The Government has been tested and has failed the test.

No one can deny that our economy came under pressure because of inclement weather, the War and the influx of refugees. But is the rise in prices in proportion to that ? If there is a drought we should have had an adequate buffer stock to meet the resultant situation. The Government claims there was a buffer stock of 80 lakh tons. That figure was wrong. I think the buffer stock did not exceed 50 lakh tons. But with this buffer stock in hand why should grain prices have gone up so much ? Refugees came. For them we imposed a tax on the people. The Finance Minister claims he could collect more revenue than was expected from the tax. When he is looking for plaudits who will take the blame ? In our country 70 per cent of the common man's expenditure is on foodgrains or foodstuff, so when food prices go up the common man's domestic budget gets upset and dearness prevails in every field. The Finance Minister had said they would open cheap grain shops, but did not say how many of them are running efficiently. And, if you claim that all those shops have been opened and are running well you will have to admit that merely opening fair price shops will not solve the price rise problem.

The fact is, the main reason for a rise in prices is an increase in money supply. It is not only the War. At the rate the Government is resorting to deficit financing no other outcome was possible. In the First Plan deficit financing was to the tune of Rs. 330 crores, in the Second Plan Rs. 454 crores, in the third Rs. 1133 crores, in the Fourth 850 crores and in 1971-72 we have deficit financing for Rs. 700 crores. Now if there is a proportionate increase in the production of goods and services this deficit economy will not put us into difficulties. But on the one hand money supply is increasing. The Reserve Bank reports that money supply is increasing at the rate of 15 per cent per annum, while goods production is increasing only by three and a half per cent annually. Last year there was even a steep fall in production. I can understand that it is the monsoon that has created the crisis in the field of food, but who

---

Lok Sabha on November 14, 1972 during discussion on the Adjournment Motion on the price situation

is responsible for the fall in industrial production ? Here the Government cannot escape by blaming Indra. At first the rate of industrial production was four and a half per cent. Then it came down to 1.5 per cent. And now we are told that the rate of national growth is zero, and so figures are not given. The Prime Minister's Secretariat was to give these figures, but it is sitting tight over them. They were to be given two months ago but are not yet given. I want to know, what, after all, are the impediments in the way of industrial production ? Are they not related to price rise ? What has the Government done to remove those impediments ? Is it not surprising that the production of refrigerators and air-conditioners has gone up by 200 per cent, 400 per cent, but that of salt, textiles, edible oil has gone down ?

If there is a fall in the production of essential commodities and if money is spread around in the market you cannot prevent prices from rising due to inflation. Pardon me, but the remedy suggested is worse than the disease. Our Communist friends have been stressing from the start that the Government should take all trade into its hands, but the Finance Minister had told this very House that this was not practical. But in Indu Chacha Nagar —people say it was Indu Chachi Nagar, I do not want to enter into that controversy—it was decided to take wholesale grain trade into our hands. Sir, it is a matter of principle. If it is in the interest of the nation trade can be taken over, but the question is of what is practical. What happened to that decision ? One after the other the Chief Ministers are saying they cannot take over the trade because there is a drought in the State, because they do not have distribution machinery. If we take over trade we would buy from the traders, so what is the point in talking big ?

What I am saying is that if you take on the responsibility of the wholeseller you will have to put more money in the market, purchase foodgrain, pay for it, arrange for its storage and also set up a distribution machinery for it. At what cost is the Food Corporation storing foodgrain ? Is that cost not high ?

Sir, I had read somewhere that the Public Accounts Committee of some States had found that the keeper of a cat was paid from the State Exchequer. The members were concerned that the State should keep a cat, but it was found that its food godowns were interested with mice and the cat was employed to catch them, and it was paid from the State Government.

This problem will not be solved by adopting an impractical and unrealistic point of view. The rise in prices cannot be checked so long as production and services do not increase. All impediments in the way of increasing production should be removed. But they can be removed only when a pragmatic approach is adopted and ideological considerations are not allowed to intervene.

The Commerce Minister has arranged for a lot of cloth. The Foreign Trade Minister has also arranged to import readymade garments in place of rags. Now there should be no shortage of clothes in the country—this is a different matter, I do not want to raise it now...

SHRI L.N. MISHRA, Foreign Trade Minister : That is finished.

SHRI VAJPAYEE : Even there you are discriminating. As many as 26 companies have been given permission.

SHRI L.N. MISHRA : You will come to know in a couple of days.

SHRI VAJPAYEE : It is necessary to increase production, to stop money- supply and to severely curtail non-developmental expenditure. Preaching simplicity to the people and living a life of luxury cannot go together. A certain ICS officer has imported an airconditioner for his residence. There is scope for curtailing non-Plan expenditure. It is also necessary to run the public sector efficiently. I was talking about nationalisation—what is happening at the Durgapur Steel Plant which is a government enterprise ? Nationalisation is not a panacea. It cannot be said with confidence that when the Government takes over an industry it will start running efficiently. So the takeover of industries should be decided on the basis of realism.

Sir, we are now blaming the government. It could do not prevent prices from rising. But when the government itself raises prices what can we say ? Parliament was to meet and it was announced that sugar prices would be raised. They say we are giving bonus to the workers, we are paying for the sugar-cane, but could this burden not be placed on the mill-owners ? The mill-owners are selling sugar in the open market and making multiple profits. Could they not make up this loss ? When it was a question of paying for the sugar-cane they were allowed to sell sugar in the open market, but now you want to burden the consumer. I do not want to introduce politics into this controversy, but people say the sugar mill-owners have been given this opportunity to fleece the people because they sided with you in the elections.

Sir, the talk of nationalisation has also a political motive behind it. In the Bombay Session the nationalisation resolution was passed— in Uttar Pradesh sugar mills would be nationalised, because Shri C.B. Gupta was benefiting from them. Nationalsiation was proper then, but now that Pt. Kamlapati Tripathi has come nationalisation is not proper...

AN HON. MEMBER : This is called double standards.

SHRI VAJPAYEE : Do not talk of double standards. I say a discussion on nationalisation is worse than nationalisation itself. If you want to do it, do it at once. You discuss how mill-owners do not invest money and have left machinery to rot. If you want to go in for nationalisation with the mills of Uttar Pradesh in view it is not going to be of much benefit. We have more mills than necessary but less production. The Government may take them over if it wants to, but nationalisation is being announced, not acted upon, while the burden falls on the consumer.

Sir, the rise in the price of vegetable oil is not at all called for. If the common man can be burdened, so can the mill-owner. Why should the burden not be distributed ? But it was not done and prices are going up. The rising of prices is a symptom, not a disease. The economy is mired in a serious crisis and still more difficult times are ahead. Foreign aid is stopping and we will have to make the country stand on its own feet. There will have to be motivation for maximum production in every field, equality in distribution and a model of consumption before the people. But this Administration could not do so and the result is that the people's discontent is erupting on the streets. The atmosphere in the country has changed. Now any agitation can become violent.

The people would lose patience. If your tall assurances are not acted upon the people's patience would break the dam and they would be inclined to solve their problems in the streets. India's victory in the War, the creation of Bangladesh and the defeat of Pakistan should have aroused self-confidence, but why is that self-confidence not in evidence in the country today ? Why can we not harness the people's enthusiasm for the reconstruction of the nation ? ...(*Interruption*).... Do not give us so much credit. We have let that self-confidence get depleted. We have let pessimism overcome the people. We have not properly assessed the people's discontent. I say the price rise is a danger signal. In order to save the Government from failing still more on the economic front in times to come it is necessary to change policies right from today. Today is Pt. Nehru's birthday, so back to Nehru, back to the Vedas. I sincerely say this. For the Planning Minister what would be the new proposal, the new slogan of back to Nehru ? It should mean 'look to the future'.

There is another thing I would like to say. Our communist friends want to take you on a downward slide from which you would not be able to return. Of course if you want to go downhill I cannot prevent you. But be sure that whatever economic solutions we want to find would be within the democratic framework. The solution they are suggesting does not fit the democratic framework. Our decision will have to be in accordance with the type of administration we have. We have seen the situation in the Food Corporation. Corruption charges are being investigated. I want to know whom you want to entrust the task of food distribution up to the village level. Think of the problems it will create. In Communist countries it is possible to see people line up, buy bread and meekly go away without a word. But this is India, and we still have democracy here. You may change policies, but do it within the democratic framework, with the people's free consent. You have lost one chance, and there won't be another. The Government should introspect and heed the warning bell of rising prices.

Effective Remedies for Scarcity and Price Rise

Sir, the scarcity and inordinate rise in prices of essential commodities are an index of a serious economic crisis. While taking over wholesale trade in wheat the Government had claimed that the governmentalisation of trade would bring down prices and promote availability. Both these objectives have failed. Previously when the crops came in ample wheat used to be available in the market. This time wheat is not available. Nor does the Government have enough stocks to meet consumer needs.

It is completely false to charge that the Indian farmer is reluctant to take his wheat to government purchase centres due to incitement by political parties. The farmer is an intelligent person. He knows his profit and loss. So long as he can earn more by selling *Chinas, Jou* and *Lahi* he will try to keep wheat as long as possible. The Government can persuade him to bring wheat into the market by offering competitive prices. As it is, the Government is going to buy wheat abroad. It will have to be paid for in foreign exchange. Will that not be a burden on the country ? So the Government should not hestiate to give the farmer a slightly higher price.

Now the imposition of a levy is being talked about. I warn that imposing a levy would mean creating widespread discontent among the farmers and leaving them at the mercy of an administrative set-up that is corrupt, incompetent and insensitive. If force is used, the law and order situation would deteriorate in the countryside, which the Government would find difficult to control. Today blackmarketing in coal has gone up to such an extent that if a factory-owner in Ferozabad obtains a rake of coal he does not run his factory with it but sells the rake in the black market and makes a bigger profit than what he would make by running the factory. The Government can find out about this. When factories do not run, production goes down and less goods arrive in the market, how can you prevent prices from rising ?

The problem will not be solved by the Government taking over more and more things. In order to check price rise production will have to be increased. Increased production is the key to it.

In respect of the food problem the Government wants to escape responsibility by blaming the weather. Is it not true that food-grain production is declining for the last three years ? Why ?

AN HON. MEMBER : Fertilizer is not available.

SHRI VAJPAYEE : Who is responsible for the shortage of fertilizer ?

Lok Sabha on May 15, 1973 during Debate on scarcity and rising prices of essential commodities

AN HON. MEMBER : God.

SHRI VAJPAYEE : God is responsible ! God will set up fertilizer factories! God will run to full capacity the Government factories that have been set up ! We can have the *Darshan* of such a God right here in this House!

Shortage of power cannot be explained away just by blaming it on the drought.

AN HON. MEMBER : To some extent.

SHRI VAJPAYEE : I agree to some extent, but not to this extent. Why could the target of power production from coal not be achieved ? Why have the targets fixed for nuclear power production not yet been fulfilled ? Take Dalda, I wish the Minister for Foreign Trade were present here ... (*Interruption*) ... Production of Dalda has fallen. The Government delayed in importing its oil requirements. For the oil that was imported there are no transportation arrangements to take it from one corner of the country to the other. Imported oil is not available where Dalda is used. It is sent where not Dalda but coconut oil or *Sarson* oil or *Til* oil is used. As a result Dalda has become expensive and it is not available.

Sugar has become scarce. It is not to be seen in the villages. Will sugar production go up with the governmentalisation of sugar mills ? Mere governmentalisation is not the solution of the problem.

The Government took over the distribution of cotton yarn. But there were no distribution arrangements. It was announced in the Lok Sabha : we are taking over the distribution. The directive was not sent to the mills. It was sent five days later. The mills entered into fake deals and sold all cotton yarn. They did not ask State Governments how much yarn they wanted. The situation today is such that on the one hand cotton yarn is lying unused in the mills while on the other hand the weaver is unemployed. The shortage of yarn has put him in a grave economic difficulty. The Government could not increase production where it should have increased. Where distribution was needed it could not do so properly. The Government has failed on the economic front.

Rate of Development

If you take a long-term view, our development rate is three and a half per cent, our population growth is two and a half per cent. Our prices are going up by 15 per cent. How can we overcome the economic crisis ? Slogans will not solve the problem. The triple key to the solution of the economic problem is increased production, equal distribution and restrained consumption.

But production is increasing not of essential commodities but of refrigerators and air-conditioners. A small car is being produced. The production of luxury goods is on the increase. Production of oil, salt, coarse cloth has declined. There is an indiscriminate expansion of the luxury sector. A luxury sector has come into being in the country which wants to introduce here the consumption level of advanced and progressive countries of the West. Twenty-two crore people are leading a life of poverty. They do not need television and refrigerators. They can do without air-conditioners. They do not need a small car. They want food to eat, clothes to wear, medicines in illness and education for their children. I want to know if the Government wants to control why does it not control the luxury sector ? But the luxury sector is not being controlled.

You will also have to bring about equality in distribution, for which you will have to solve the black money problem.

SHRI Y.B. CHAVAN, Finance Minister : What has the third thing you said ?

SHRI VAJPAYEE : I said increase in production, equality in distribution and restraint in consumption...(*Interruption*)....You do not have to become a Sadhu. I shall also come to who have to restrain consumption.

Sir, this is not the way to have equality in distribution. Equality cannot be brought about by imposing controls and creating artificial scarcity. The Government will have to recognise its limitation. We have to conduct ourselves within the democratic framework. Merely opening fair price shops is no guarantee that things available there would be priced fairly and would really reach the consumer. Today the goods vanish midway. Sugar does not reach the villages. Farmers line up in long gueues for diesel but do not get it. So you will have to develop a distribution system that would take the average Indian's conditions and temperament into consideration and would succeed democratically.

Restraint in Consumption

The third point is restraint in consumption. The ideal of restraint will have to be presented from above. There is more expenditure on Rashrapati Bhavan and less on Parliament. How do our Governors live ? Do those called leaders of the society present an ideal of simplicity and straightforwardness ? Are we making it clear that if a new economic system is brought about in India its basis will be non-covetousness, not incontinence ? We have roused the hunger for acquiring more and more. By raising slogans at election time we have brought about a revolution of expectations. Now arguments cannot calm this revolution. The people's hunger has been roused. Scarcity has agitated the people. Even at such a juncture the Government does not aim at securing the cooperation of all parties for the formulation and implementation of national policies. When there is a crisis the cooperation of all opposition parties is demanded. This only means that opposition parties should share the responsibility of creating the crisis and also present themselves before the people as the culprits. What could be more ridiculous than charging that the farmer does not bring foodgrain because the Bharatiya Jana Sangh is inciting him ? Sometimes it is said the Jana Sangh has no farmers with it, that it has no work in the villages. When foodgrains do not come and you need a scapegoat you think of the Bharatiya Jana Sangh. This is all right for propaganda, but it is not going to bring foodgrains to the market. This is not going to remove scarcity. It is not going to lessen dearness.

Implement Wanchoo Committee Recommendations

If prices are to be stabilised the Finance Minister has to limit deficit financing. The net credit secured from the banks is also substantial. It too will lead to inflation. It should also be brought down. The money supply should be linked to the growth rate. It is not so now. There is uncontrolled money supply. Essential commodities should not be taxed. They are being taxed. Dearness is having its impact. Courageous demonetisation is required for bringing out black money. At the same time an atmosphere needs to be created in the country which would prevent black money formation in future. Implement Wanchoo Committee recommendations. Reduce the rates of direct taxes. Encourage the people to save. Motivate them to invest capital. This air of uncertainty must end. It will neither allow agricultural production to grow nor allow people to invest in industries. By holding up the sword of governmentalisation you cannot achieve economic development of the country in the democratic framework. So I say, the country stands at a crossroad. This is not a question of the rise in the price of some articles. Neither is it a question of scarcity in some commodities. We have to decide the direction in which we want to go. If you want to go in the direction of government trade be sure it will culminate in total rationing. There is no half-way house. If you want total rationing how will you manage it ?

SHRI Y.B. CHAVAN : You want equality in distribution. Show how is that to be brought about ?

SHRI VAJPAYEE : If you had not taken over trade wheat prices would have fallen and the consumer would have got it at lower prices. But when I talk of equality in distribution ...*(Interruption)*....

SHRI Y.B. CHAVAN : What was the position even before the take-over decision ?

SHRI VAJPAYEE : The situation was that when the crops came in prices fell.

SHRI CHAVAN : It was the same position then. It was the same even when there was a good crop. We agree with your principle of equality in distribution. But you have not said how to bring it about. We want to know it from you.

SHRI VAJPAYEE : Proper equality in distribution is not possible with official control. It will lead to goods vanishing from the market. How can there be equality in distribution ? The way to do it is to increase production and arrange to provide essential commodities to the weaker sections of society at fair price shops at subsidised rates. But only weaker sections should get this facility, it is not necessary for all. So it is not necessary to take over all the trade. Take over part of the trade and control prices through it. You will not be able to manage a monopoly. You do not have the apparatus, you do not have the manpower. You cannot build a new economic system by putting the country into difficulties. Thank you.

Crisis of Commodity Prices Crisis Also of Life Values

Madam, I am grateful to you for letting me start a brief discussion on the rice situation in the country.

No one can deny that there is a price crisis in the country. It is a double crisis. On the one hand we are faced with a crisis of values of life and on the other with the crisis produced in the rise in prices of essential commodities. Here I shall not discuss the crisis in life values. That is a different subject, and it will be a different debate. My purpose this time is to attract the attention of the House to the situation created by rising prices.

No one can deny that the economy inherited by the present government was in a deplorable state.

SHRI SURESH KALMADI (Maharashtra) : How long will you say that ?

SHRI VAJPAYEE : I was going to come to what you say.

SHRI S.S. AHLUWALIA (Bihar) : The expelled Congress leaders he found were quite inferior. They could not run the Government.

DEPUTY CHAIRMAN : Hon. Members, we have taken up this discussion at the instance of a leader of the opposition. If you feel the price rise situation is serious let us discuss it in a calm atmosphere, so that something could come out of it. Please do not disturb anybody.

SHRI SYED SIBTE KAZI (U.P.) : His reference to the previous government... (*Interruption*) ... He should tell us why prices are rising so much.

DEPUTY CHAIRMAN : You may refer to the later government, somebody else may refer to the previous government, but please do not disturb.

SHRI VAJPAYEE : Had the opposite party not interrupted me I was going to come to that same point after laying the background, but you did not give me the chance. First, you will have to accept that the situation was not good. But we cannot ignore what happened during the last 8-9 months because of it. When the Government gave the assurance that rising prices would be controlled it had done so taking into consideration the situation it had inherited. This was not just an election promise that we gave. After the Government was formed its Finance Minister and Prime Minister too wrote letters to Chief Ministers and members of Parliament. They expressed concern over rising prices and indicated what steps were being taken. I wish to quote a portion of the Finance Minister's budget speech :

> "The first task of the new Government was to contain the rise in prices. A Cabinet Committee on prices was formed and effective steps were taken to increase the supply of essential commodities to remove the

Rajya Sabha on August 7, 1990 initiating discussion on price rise inflationary psychology and contain inflation. The price situation, however, remains a matter for concern, and the management of inflation is one of the priority areas of this Government."

Madam, the Government that came to power on the mandate of the people was worried over the price situation. It had promised to take steps. Some steps were indeed taken, but it is a fact that prices are rising despite those steps. Figures, official figures, support this. These figures have been obtained from official sources. *Commodities group percentage change increase in wholesale price index as of June 13, 1990 over end December, 1989 :* Pulses 10.7, fruits and vegetables 55.1, cardamom 21.1, other food articles 15.0, oilseeds 22.6, sugar, Khandsari and gur 10.0, edible oils 17.5, beverages, tobacco etc. 11.8.

Wholesale prices have gone up. I have the figures with me. But wholesale prices do not reflect the real position. The common man has to buy goods at retail prices. But the rise in wholesale prices is abnormal, serious. It has caused dearness that the common man finds back-breaking. What is the cause of this dearness ? Without doubt it is the economic situation, the inflation that this Government inherited. But what it inherited was only after the elections ...(*Interruption*)....

SHRI JAGESH DESAI (Maharashtra) : Just a minute, Vajpayeeji.

DEPUTY CHAIRMAN : Mr. Desai, please don't disturb. Let him speak.

SHRI DIPEN GHOSH (W.B.) : They have their own speakers.

DEPUTY CHAIRMAN : Please don't interject. I would not allow.

SHRI VAJPAYEE : Madam, I am not against interruption, but against prevention.

Madam, I submit that the steps that the Government has taken are not enough, because the situation the Government has inherited is pretty serious. This time I was not interrupted. Thank you. But saying so is not enough, what is needed is steps to improve the situation that has come down.

Taxes Imposed in the Budget

It is the policies that have been adopted, and among them a major reason is the tax burden imposed in the budget. The Central budget had new taxation to the tune of Rs. 1790 crores. In the Railway Budget Rs. 470 crores were realised by way of passenger fares and freight rates increase. Retail prices of petroleum products were hiked. The import duty on crude oil was also raised, as a result of which the Government earned Rs. 834 crores. Then State Governments have imposed taxes. Different electricity boards have increased power rates. This too has had an impact, although at that time the claim was made by the Finance Ministry that the price rise would be nominal. The Railway Board Chairman went so far as to calculate zero, zero, zero and present some figures. But the Government will admit that this too has affected the rise in prices.

It is true that the Government will say we inherited a big deficit; deficit causes inflation, and this was necessary to control inflation and reduce the deficit. But if prices rose and taxes were increased, other steps ought to have been taken to see that prices of essential commodities did not rise. I am repeatedly raising the question of prices of essential commodities, commodities used by the common man. I have figures with me, but I do not want to weigh down my speech with them. Pulse prices have gone up. A small tin of edible oil has become costlier by ten rupees. Cement has become more expensive. So also tea. The rise in the price of these articles is upsetting the common man's budget and playing havoc with family life. Salt too has become costly. I was talking about *Dal* (pulses), because *Dal* is the food of the poor, it contains protein, and it has the capacity to satisfy unexpected guests with a little addition of water. No other food article has this capacity.

SHRI V.P. SINGH, Prime Minister : Sometimes there is *'Dal mein Kala'*.

SHRI VAJPAYEE : Yes, but I am afraid of the whole *Dal* getting black.

SHRI MAKHAN LAL FOTEDAR (U.P.) : There is also salt.

SHRI VAJPAYEE : Shri Fotedar is talking of salt, but after a certain age less salt is more advisable.

Common Articles also Expensive

Madam, articles of the common man's use are also getting expensive. It is true, as I said, that the Government has taken steps, the Prime Minister is concerned, but what has been the result of the letter he wrote to the Chief Ministers ? There is a talk of curtailing Government expenditure, and in respect of prices we are told someone is monitoring how much they are rising.

Madam, Newton's Law does not apply to prices. By Newton's Law what goes up come down. But that is not so with prices. Once they go up they always remain up. What is the result of this monitoring ?

About sugar I know the Government has decided that if sugar released for free sale is not sold out it should be changed into levy sugar. What was the result. The Government had taken steps about cement. Cement producers had given the assurance of bringing down prices, but I was surprised to see that in Delhi's Super Bazar cement sells for Rs. 80 per gunny bag and elsewhere in the market for Rs. 91 but the consumer buys it for Rs. 91. Is this because there is a long queue at the Super Bazar. The problem of distribution is also relevant here, and I want to bring this to the notice of the House.

Madam, the Finance Minister had assured that the Government would think about a limit on how much the Government could borrow at home and abroad. He had also assured about thinking of applying the limit under Article 292. But so far no steps have been taken in this direction.

I am told that everyday our country is incurring a debt burden of Rs. 120 crores. These are Shri Nani Palkhivala's figures, and I think they are right. How is indebtedness increasing so much ? Should there be no limit to borrowing ? Should not the Government present itself before Parliament in this matter ? We have no objection if funds are spent in productive works, but what if they are spent on unproductive things ? So I wish that while replying to this debate the Finance Minister should tell us how far the Government has succeeded in cutting down unproductive expenditure during the past some months. He should place figures before the House, take the House into confidence.

Deep Economic Crisis

Madam, a deep economic crisis faces us today. I would now like to rise above politics. Charges and counter-charges will continue, but in the changing global scenario foreign aid for us is going to decline. For the industrialised nations the whole of Europe has become a market. They will not be much attracted to investing capital in this country. So, competition for our goods in foreign markets would grow. Hence it is necessary to keep a vigil on production of goods, on productivity, on quality, so that we can earn foreign exchange and cut down losses. But we do not yet have the economic discipline that is required for this.

Shri Salve, who is sitting opposite me, was Chairman of the Finance Commission. The demands of the States are increasing, their responsibilities are also growing. They impose new taxes, but they do so with reluctance. Here I would like to say that there has to be a change in the way the electricity boards of the States are working. I am told their payment to the Railways is in arrears to the tune of Rs. 800 crores. The coal that the Railways carry to the power houses produces electricity, on which industries run in the States and their agriculture goes on, but the Boards are not paying Rs. 800 crores that they owe to the Railways. How can this go on ? The electricity boards will have to be improved. The railways' dues will have to be settled. Everyone will have to discharge his responsibility towards the other. For this we need economic discipline, but we are so immersed in partisan politics that we tend to ignore some important problems.

Madam, I want to raise a basic point about prices. The entire House wants, the country wants, that justice should be done by the farmer, that he should get a beneficial price for his produce. This is not any one individual's policy, this is our collective policy, and with this in view the prices of wheat and rice have risen, but the farmer is not only a producer, he is also a consumer. Whatever he has gained with a little increase in wheat and rice prices is set at naught by the rising prices of other consumables.

Less investment, Higher Price

Now we have an Agricultural Cost and Price Commission. At first there was only price, not cost. The name was changed. The commission was entrusted a responsibility, and it is discharging it. It goes into details. Its report is placed before Parliament, and becomes public. But I ask you, is there any accounting of the investment of big industrialists manufacturing commodities of daily use, their price and the profit earned on it ? On the other day the Finance Minister was saying on an open platform—and I was amazed to hear—that the prices of industrial products are determined very carefully. I could see no proof of this.

I have been raising this question for a long time—what is the investment—price of a scooter that sells in the market for 12-13 thousand rupees ? Those companies ......(*Interruption*)..

SHRI V.M. JADHAV (Maharashtra) : Not more than four thousand ....(*Interruption*)....

SHRI VAJPAYEE : No, not four thousand. Jadhav Sahib, you have not calculated. Adding a 20 per cent profit its price should not be above Rs. 7000. We have worked on this. If anybody says your figures are not right, we are ready to place our balance sheet before him for being looked into. But industrialists are not prepared to present their balance sheets and the Government is not ready to force them to do so. This was what the old government was doing, and this is what the new government is doing. Sometimes I feel all governments work the same way... (*Interruption*) ....

AN HON. MEMBER : Sweet words !

SHRI VAJPAYEE : I am still not sure ...(*Interruption*)....

AN HON. MEMBER : You are responsible ...(*Interruption*)....

SHRI VAJPAYEE : Look, you have again started interrupting, Madam, as I was saying, in some matters governments behave the same way.

SHRI S.P. MITTAL (Nominated) : No, Sir, listen

"Khoob parde hai ki chilman se lage baithe hai,
Aap chhupte bhi nahi, samne aate bhi nahi."

"You are sitting behind a curtain in such a way that neither you are well hidden nor visible."

SHRI VAJPAYEE : Once more, once more.

AN HON. MEMBER : You can put up with interruptions, but a cover up.... (*Interruption*)....

SHRI VAJPAYEE : If somebody has made a mess you have to have a whitewash.

Madam, I want to raise a serious matter and request your support in it. Forget what the old government did. On what basis will the prices of industrial goods be determined ? On what basis will they sell in the market ? How is a tooth-brush with an investment of a rupee and ten paise on it sold for three rupees ? I have more figures with me — for tea, for cement. Madam, when the figures for tea and cement are arrived at even the small irregularity done in them produces a long-range impact. There is a Bureau for Industrial Costs and Prices, but its report is not made public. We demand that that report be made public...(*Interruption*)....

Don't Allow Excessive Profit

Will it not be proper to have a commission for industrial goods on the lines of the Agricultural Prices Commission that has been set up ? Adequate profit should be earned, but there must be a stop to excessive profit. We have the freedom to loot in this country. Even the Government is not discharging its responsibility in this matter. The price of wheat was raised—how much ? But there is no relationship between the rise in the price of wheat flour and that in the price of wheat. It is the same with Government- run flour mills. The

Government may say we have to go by market rates, otherwise there would be a loss. If there is a loss there would be one more difficulty. We have been caught in a vicious circle from which there is no escape. I submit the farmer should get a profitable price, but commodities of daily use should be priced properly. There should be a profit, without profit no industry can run, but not excessive profit.

Companies making beauty aids are making a 500 per cent profit and declaring it in their reports. They also advertise on television. Should not the advertisement be accompanied by the price ? Television advertising is promoting consumerism so much that even those harassed by prices cannot check their sons and daughters from buying shampoos widely advertised on TV. When the son or daughter goes to buy he or she does not inquire about the price, because they think of the beautiful face on television.

SHRI S.S. AHLUWALIA : You are lucky you have not married. The problem is for us, who have to face daily demands from our children.

SHRI VAJPAYEE : Is it just a problem for you or is it also a pleasure ?... (*Interruption*)....Madam, may I say that since long there has been a demand that there should be some parity, some relationship, between the prices of agricultural produce and that of industrial goods. Today there is no such relationship.

I had written to the Finance Minister about rising prices. He wrote back saying we have a committee of members of the Cabinet which is seized of the problem. Very good. But where is the report of the Committee ? What steps has the Committee suggested, and what has been their impact in reducing prices.

SHRI JAGESH DESAI : In raising prices ?

The Government's Shortsightedness

SHRI VAJPAYEE : The situation is serious. Its correction needs long-term as well as short-term steps. I have a complaint against the Government. You have to reduce the foreign exchange deficit, so you are being a little strict about imports, but was it necessary to declare in advance that you will not import edible oil ? Has this not assured the hoarders and profiteers of oil that there would be no such imports ? Domestic supplies of oil are not enough, so why sell at proper prices ? Even if the Government had taken a decision internally traders and industrialists should be under the apprehension that if they exploited the situation to harass the consumer more than necessary the Government would not hesitate to import. This should have been done at least as a strategy. But the Government says it won't import. How will the requirement be met ? The demand for edible oil has increased and the people's habit has been spoilt. Previously they used to use *Sarson* oil, *Til* oil, groundnut oil, but now they want refined oil.

Improve Distribution System

I would like to quote an instance of irregulity in distribution. Prices of edible oil have gone up and the Government is importing Palmolein oil.

SHRI M.S. GURUPADASWAMY, Minister of Petroleum and Chemicals : Vajpayeeji, may I just say, it is not true that we are not importing oil. We are importing palm oil.

SHRI VAJPAYEE : I was coming to that, but Palmolein oil is being imported, which is cheaper than vegetable oil, but the distribution arrangement for it is not good. Instead of reaching the consumer it is reaching the Dhaba-owner, the hotelier. I am myself one of the victims. For the last three weeks I have been trying to buy Palmolein. Every time my servant goes they say no stocks. When did they arrive, and when were they over ? How can they be finished when they did not arrive at all ? If they did arrive where did they go ? I told my servant don't tell them where you have come from, just stand in the queue and find out. We too do some monitoring, because we wish this Government well.

SHRI FOTEDAR : The Government or the people ? ..(*Interruption*)....

SHRI VAJPAYEE : We want both, you want one...(*Interruption*).... When they found out they told me just give a phone call and we shall send to your place whatever you want. This is not good. The Government should make the distribution arrangement more effective.

Open shops where there are no shops, and increase their stocks of goods. Include pulses, include edible oils, include soap and make it a permanent arrangement. This should not be like some fireworks—the fire is out but the shop is closed, the shop is open but it does not run properly. There should be good arrangements. We see slackness. One of the reasons for slackness is that when production increases and there is no shortage, distribution arrangements tend to be neglected. It should not be so. In the phase of the economy we are passing through anything can become scarce. I had just been to Lucknow. There is an oilseeds research organisation there. They say they have not been able to achieve a breakthrough in pulses. How high *Chana* (gram) prices have gone. How can the poor manage ? See to it that the distribution machinery is strengthened and shops run properly. I would like to know what suggestions the Chief Ministers have made.

Madam, when the country is faced with a price crisis we hold demonstrations and raise demands. They have a place in a democracy. But it is also necessary that if the Government wants some constructive cooperation it should say so. We are ready for constructive cooperation too in this matter. I am sure my friends in the opposition will also join us in this respect. There is a crisis. Any carelessness would prove fatal. The people need immediate relief. Take such far-sighted steps as would reduce deficit, reduce inflation and successfully resolve the crisis gripping the country.

The recent Iraq-Kuwait conflict naturally causes concern. Although Government spokesmen say it will have no impact on supplies but it will. What if this conflict escalates ? From the global perspective our economic situation depends upon many factors but we need to take firm steps, effective action in respect of forces and elements that are our basic strength. I trust the discussion here will be in an amicable atmosphere. If necessary the Government should be hit soundly. I shall also not lag behind in doing so, but at the same time a constructive attitude is also necessary.

Madam, I am thankful to you for permitting me to speak.

IV Taxation and Banking

Impose Expenditure Tax and Practise Economy

Sir, I support the basic objective of this Bill. Unrestrained expenditure is against our tradition and culture. Indian culture believes in restraints, and these restraints should apply to individual expenditure also. Unrestrained expenditure by an individual produces social tendencies that shake the very basis of the society. From this point of view it is necessary to put constraints on expenditure.

At the same time we are also engaged in the *Yagya* of national regeneration. I am not in complete agreement with the Five Year Plan that has been presented. I had submitted that it should be amended in view of the resources of the country and the people's capacity to pay taxes. I do not want to harp on the same thing, but we all want that the development plans we have taken up should succeed. Building the nation is not a question of any one party. Today the whole world is watching us to see if we use all our might to successfully implement reconstruction plans, or if we fail to do so. For these plans we need funds, and an expenditure tax would help us raise funds, so from that point of view too it should be welcome. But there is a 'but', and with this 'but' I would like to place before this House my doubts about this Bill.

The Finance Minister has himself admitted that history has not so far supported this type of tax. I quote : "This is a form of taxation which has no backing as yet of historical experience."

I agree with my friend Shri Bharucha that if it has not been imposed in other countries that is no reason why we should not impose it. We need not imitate others. We can use our own intelligence. That there is no such tax in other countries and we are imposing it only in our country could create problems. Suppose a person deposits money abroad in order to evade this tax and then goes abroad to spend that money ? There is a neighbouring country that was a part of us and has now become a new State. I suggest that this possibility should be seriously considered. It is necessary to prevent our citizens from making money here and spending it elsewhere.

Lok Sabha on July 17, 1957 during discussion on the Calling Attention Motion on Expenditure Tax Bill

USA Considering Expenditure Tax

During the War an expenditure tax was considered in the U.S. and Prof. Fisher had placed some proposals in this regard before the U.S. Government. The then U.S. Government was considered more progressive as compared to the present one. But due to practical difficulties the U.S. Government did not accept Prof. Fisher's proposals and an expenditure tax was not imposed in the U.S. I think our situation is entirely different from that in the U.S. At the same time we cannot ignore the practical difficulty in levying and collecting the tax. The Finance Minister has admitted in his speech that we need an effective administrative machinery for taxes.

The point is, can we set up such a machinery ? The experience so far is not encouraging, and I doubt if things will improve in future. We know very well the type of people we have. It cannot be said with confidence that when they are given the power to collect this tax there would be no problems, no harassment.

Privacy of Tax-payer's Family would be Violated

The wide powers this tax would give the State to enter personal life, family life, its sanctity and its secrets really create apprehensions in the mind. Dr. A.K. Krester of Cambridge University makes this point clear. He has asked whether the State should be given such powers to enter personal life : "Whether it is reasonable for the State to require such a degree of information as would be needed from the tax-payer about his activities."

In view of the type of tax-collection machinery that we have and the type of people we have it is necessary to guard against its misuse. Prof. Kaldor has himself admitted that if such a tax was imposed there would be many problems in the interim period. It is possible that people in the area where the tax would operate might withdraw their money from the banks. So he has indicated that current bank notes may have to be recalled.

Demonetisation of Existing Bank Notes

I do not think the Finance Minister proposes to take the serious step suggested by Prof. Kaldor. Neither should he do it. But it is necessary to give thought to the problems this tax would lead to in the interregnum.

It was really sad to see that Jammu-Kashmir was not included in the purview of the tax. It was not kept apart in the wealth tax proposed yesterday, but it has been removed from the purview of this tax. I do not know the special reasons for which this has been done. If you can have a wealth tax why not a tax on the expenditure of that wealth ? This matter should be reconsidered. I hope the Select Committee would not differentiate in respect of Jammu-Kashmir.

One more important point, to which my honourable friend Pt. Thakur Das Bhargava has called attention and which Shri Bharucha has also supported. I would like to draw the Finance Minister's attention to it. The joint Hindu family system is the best social security system, which has stood the test of time since ages. This system should continue so long as the State cannot provide food, clothing, shelter and medical treatment to every old person, every widow and every handicapped person. There should be no attempt to break it up. I agree that it is breaking up with the passage of time. But I can never agree to the adoption of an economic policy that would completely destroy it instead of saving it and strengthening it. Thank you.

Gift Tax

Full of Loopholes

Sir, apart from some exceptions almost everybody has welcomed the gift tax proposed by the Prime Minister as interim Finance Minister. We have accepted a gift tax as an integral part of the taxation system that we have accepted since last year. It would have been better if, along with an expenditure tax and a wealth tax, we had introduced a gift tax too last year. Still, better late than never. A step in the right direction has been taken, though belatedly, and so almost everybody has welcomed it.

But there are many shortcomings in the proposal as it has come before us, and I hope the select committee will think seriously about them. All possible steps should be taken to prevent a rich person or a capitalist from evading taxes. But care should be taken not to spread the net more widely than we intended.

First of all I want to draw attention to the exemption contained in the bill. As many Hon. Members have said, there are many institutions in the country— schools, hospitals— that may be limited to a certain sects but whose purpose is the good of the people and who want to contribute to the building of the nation in their own way. In this respect Section 15 B of the Indian Income Tax Act, which is limited to a certain sect, does not extend to charitable organisations. Here the argument is secularism. I think the whole country is agreed that religion should not be mixed with politics. But in the case of charitable institutions, even if they are confined to a certain section of the society, donations to them should not be taxed in any way at present. The Income Tax Act provides that an institution confined to a sect cannot avail of the concession available under Section 15 B. In my opinion this Bill should be amended so that all types of charitable institutions could be brought within its purview.

Gift Tax not Proper on Donation above Hundred Rupees

This gift tax would apply to all those who give more than a hundred rupees by way of donation. There are many people who help students with their education by giving them annual assistance, and looking to the rapidity with which educational expenses are going up it would not be just to fix the limit at a hundred Rupees. That would not cover even a year's fee of the student. We should not do something through this Bill that would adversely affect the charitable tendency which has prevailed in the people of this country because of age-old *Samskaras*. That would not be proper. In contrast

Lok Sabha on April 24, 1958 during discussion on the Calling Attention Motion on Gift Tax Bill

to other countries we had developed a social system and an economy in which it would not be necessary to depend upon the Government for everything and in which a person would help another person and the society of his own accord. If this gift tax results in affecting the old tradition of charity in this country the purpose of its farmers would not be served.

Gifts given on the occasion of marriages have also been discussed here. The Bill says : "...... female relatives dependent upon him for the necessaries of life on the occasion of the marriage."

I think the scope here is very much restricted. There may be girls who may be earning their livelihood in some small way till the time of their marriage and thus, according to this wording, may not be dependent nor may be partly dependent upon the person giving her the gift. According to the provisions of this Bill even such girls would be denied gifts, and if somebody gives them a gift he would be liable to pay a tax which he would like to evade. So I submit that those who earn their livelihood with some small or part-time work should not be included in this. They should be completely exempted.

Loan Waived, Waive Tax

Section 4 of this Bill mentions some transactions that would attract the Gift tax. It further adds that the purpose of the Section is that if a person gives a loan to another person but, for some reason, is unable to recover the full amount of the loan, and if, in exasperation, he decides to waive the remainder or if the borrower is not in a position to make full repayment, the amount waived by the lender will attract the gift tax. This means we would be encouraging litigation between the borrower and the lender and if even a suit does not result in repayment the officer concerned would decide the amount of gift tax to the imposed. It would be left to his discretion to determine if the loan can or cannot be fully recovered. I feel this discretion is very wide and can be misused. It is also possible that the officer may accept three-fourths of the waiver to be proper but one-fourth liable for tax. I feel this Bill should be amended in such a way that if any person wants to waive a loan or any such transaction and if the person for whom he wants to waive is not within the family or related, indicating the intent to evade the tax, he should not be forced to pay a gift tax. It is necessary for the Select Committee to go deep into this matter.

There is also another provision in the Bill. If a person keeps a joint bank account with his wife and if the wife withdraws some money from that account, even if for domestic purposes, the amount withdrawn would be gift-taxable for the husband. It is provided that this Bill would cover all joint tenancies or bank accounts in existence from April 1, 1957. I think such retrospective effect would not be necessary after the section is amended. Now this bill is being passed and those husbands and wives who hold joint bank accounts have been warned. Now they will open separate accounts. But in order not to make any difficulties for those who have had such accounts for the last one year this amended section of the Bill should be made applicable from April or May 1, 1950.

Attractive Incentive

The provision in the Bill for a rebate on advance payment is very good and everybody has welcomed it. If we could come up with such incentives also in respect of other taxes, tax collection would become quick. But here too I have two objections. One, it is possible that tax-offficers may take more than a year for assessment. We also see that in respect of things for which advances are made there is a tendency to take more time for assessment, as happens with income tax collection. In such cases rebate payment does not remain very attractive.

Another thing, if a person makes a gift of Rs. 50,000 there would be tax of Rs. 2000 at 4 per cent, and if he makes an advance payment there would be a gain of 100-200 rupees. I think this is a big gain and the people would want to pay taxes quickly. But if a person gives a gift of two lakhs of rupees he would have to pay Rs. 30,000 by way of tax at 15 per cent, while according to this Bill he can make an advance deposit of Rs. 16,000, which means he will get a rebate of only Rs. 1600. This is a small rebate. He would earn much more by investing his money outside. So it seems an amendment is necessary to make early payment attractive also for those who receive gifts.

Collection of the Tax

The final point is about the collection of this tax. The same arrangements that have been made for collecting income tax, wealth tax or expenditure tax would be applicable here. This would be a heavy burden for the employees and officers concerned and would lead to a number of administrative difficulties. The Taxation Inquiry Commission has also drawn attention to them. We shall again face those difficulties. This Bill estimates an annual revenue of Rs 3 crores for the Government. I think this is on the high side and I would not be surprised if it is seen to be much lower after a year. This is what has happened with other taxes. But if really Rs. 3 crores are collected the Government has provided for an expenditure of Rs. 8 lakhs on the collection of this tax. I think as an incentive for higher efficiency it would be better if we could give some more facilities to the employees and officers collecting the tax. The tax collection administration should also be improved to make their efficiency more useful and to enthuse them to discharge their responsibility with honesty.

With these words I give general support to this Bill and close my speech. Thank you.

Delhi Sales Tax Bill
An Exercise in Shortsightedness

Sir, great care is required in any bill regarding Delhi that is presented in this House. Delhi is a Union Territory, which has no elected legislature. Parliament is the only place where the feelings of Delhi should be genuinely represented and a law made after taking all aspects into consideration. It is a matter of regret that when this important matter relating to Delhi is being discussed members except the Hon. Member elected from Delhi could not spare the time to be present in the House.

CHOUDHARY RANVIR SINGH (Rohtak) : They do not know.

SHRI VAJPAYEE : Then it is all the more necessary that there should be no haste in passing this Bill and all possibilities should be taken into consideration. It is also necessary to bear in mind that Delhi has a special place in the field of commerce and industry. It may be a Union Territory but it is a very small territory. The flow of commerce and industry breaks its borders with adjoining States and buyers come to Delhi in large numbers. For all of them Delhi is a market-place and they are the basis of Delhi's economic prosperity. Any step that would adversely affect Delhi's trade would be very dangerous. So while preparing any legislation we should keep in view not only Punjab but also Uttar Pradesh, which adjoins Delhi, and the rules and regulations operating there.

Before placing this Bill on the floor of this House did the Minister consult the Advisory Committee for Delhi ? I have already said Delhi does not have a legislature. But an Advisory Committee has been formed in which all parties and classes are represented. While making any law concerning Delhi we should set the tradition of consulting this Advisory Committee either formally or informally. Its advice should be given all due weight and Bills presented in this House in the light of that advice. Has the minister consulted the Committee on this or has he not ? If he has, what is its opinion about the present sections of this Bill ?

Sales Tax versus Purchase Tax

It cannot be denied that a sales tax is basically a reactionary tax which mainly affects the consumer. It is called a sales tax but in practice it becomes a purchase tax which directly falls on the buyer. Hence there has always been a general demand that essential commodities should be free from sales tax. Secondly, a sales tax should be a one-point tax. Thirdly, the sales tax

Lok Sabha on April 30, 1959 during discussion on the Calling Attention Motion on Sales Tax (Delhi Amendment) Bill

collection system should be so simple that there would be no scope for tax evasion and administrative corruption.

Tested on these criteria this Bill is somewhat disappointing. I have no hesitation in saying that with the exception of the provision to withdraw sales tax from newspapers I am opposed to all other sections. I welcome the removal of sales tax on newspapers because it is basically wrong to tax newspapers. Other States do not have this sales tax. That it was in operation in Delhi so long was itself wrong. It is good that this mistake is being rectified. Now if newspaper prices have gone up, as it is now argued, it is not due to the sales tax, it is due to the Information and Broadcasting Ministry's failure to implement the price page schedule so far. If the government determines the number of pages of a newspaper and their price there would be no danger of the readers being charged more. But the Government has not been able to reach a final decision in this matter. As a result readers are being charged more and small newspapers are falling victims to unhealthy competition from big ones.

Other sections of the Bill mention a tax of two to four Naya Paisa and seven per cent on some material. I say how much tax you increase is not that important. But when we increase taxes even the increase of a single Naya Paisa in taxes badly affects the whole economy. There is a wave in the market that taxes are going up and the consumer has to suffer the consequences. The economic system we have is of our own making, and we cannot disown it. The list of things on which a seven per cent tax is proposed includes many articles of daily use directly or indirectly, and the burden of the increased tax on them would have to be borne by the common man. In my opinion this list should be re-examined and an attempt made to make it still shorter.

Another point which is under discussion is that under section 5 A the Chief Commissioners of Delhi would have the power of direct imposition of the tax at any one point. This has been defined in two ways. Perhaps the Minister may say that under Section 5 A the Chief Commissioner can direct that the tax be charged at only one place.

SHRI B.R. BHAGAT : That is the intention.

SHRI VAJPAYEE : But I would like to draw his attention to section-B wherein it is stated: "The burden of proving that in respect of any sale effected by a dealer he is not liable to pay tax under this tax shall lie on him."

I think giving this type of concession and then asking the dealer to prove that he is liable to pay tax at only one place amounts to opening up a way to catch him. This makes it appear as if those who collect taxes possibly feel that there should be multi-point taxation. If they make any such recommendation it would be the dealer's business to go to court and prove that the tax should not be levied at more than one place. If the Minister is clear in his mind that the tax would be applicable at only one place section 5 B would have no utility; it should be removed. If you do not want to extend any new facility, if you want to save the trader from litigation and if your intention is not to collect the tax from more than one place, as it should be, then this Bill has no need of section 5 B.

SHRI B.R. BHAGAT : By way of explanation I would like to say that so far as the law and the government are concerned it is quite clear that there would be a one point tax. So far as section 5 B is concerned...

DEPUTY SPEAKER : It should not be charged at all, neither one-point nor two-point. According to him 5 B means if the trader says he should not be charged at all, at no place, then the responsibility is his.

SHRI VAJPAYEE : This should not be used for charging at two places. If what you say is right there is no cause for objection.

Traders' Account Books

Another thing mentioned here is that the power given to traders to keep accounts for 30 days could be misused. No one can deny that traders' account books should be inspected and if necessary also used, but the authority given under section 12 is very wide and the major complaint about sales tax is that the law is misused. It would not be proper to equip the government with a weapon that could be used against traders.

This Bill does not provide for the safeguards that are required to see that sales tax is not evaded and those collecting sales tax do not get an opportunity to act as they please. There are many traders who are illiterate and cannot keep accounts. Now if their income is up to Rs. 10,000 they will have to register themselves, and keep accounts. If they cannot maintain accounts they will have to employ somebody to do it for them, and even after that, it seems, they would be at the mercy of the sales tax inspector.

The Bugbear of the Sales Tax Inspector

I have seen in the market-places that when a Sales Tax Inspector arrives the dealers run out of their shops shouting he has come, he has come, as if an evil spirit is coming. If you want to collect a tax, by all means do it—you should do it—but it would not be proper to create a feeling of uncertainty in the minds of the traders, which would encourage them to evade taxes, and to give government employees a chance for corruption. I am of the opinion that the whole sales tax system needs to be considered. In Delhi it is common to see that there is a heavy sales tax on watches but if you want to save yourself from it the dealer will show you the way—he will not give you a cash memo and you can buy a watch without paying sales tax. What is the meaning of this sort of sales tax on watches ? Without issuing a cash memo the dealer becomes dishonest and unfortunately the law as it is encourages him to be so. The dealer is so clever that he encourages the buyer to be dishonest. In such a situation there is full scope for government employees.

I think the way the Sales tax is imposed and collected in different parts of the country is defective. We had hoped that in the light of that system a Bill would be presented in the Lok Sabha that would remove all those shortcomings and would be in accordance with Delhi's requirements. But in its present form this Bill does not fulfil Delhi's requirements. It has not benefited from old experience and it has been proposed without taking Delhi's special position into consideration. This would create difficulties for industry and commerce, foster dishonesty among traders and give government employees a chance for corruption. I am very much disappointed with this Bill. I think the government should still give it some more thought. Thank you.

Nationalisation of Banks Will Impede Pace of Development

Sir, I stand to oppose this resolution not because I advocate an economy in which capitalists should have all freedom to make profits. The days of full freedom are over and those who talk of full freedom are not in tune with the times. But while I am not in favour of full freedom, I am also not a supporter of an economic system in which the administration has full control, all powers. The Government has accepted the goal of socialism. I am not opposed to socialism, but I do not consider it a complete philosophy of life. Man is not merely a slave of lucre, nor is he a creature of carnality. We cannot violate moral and spiritual values of life. We should build a society where there is not subordination but discipline, not control but continence, not licence but liberty, not a conflict of rights but a competiiion of duties. The picture of socialism that has emerged before us cannot satisfy the Indian people. There is a certain wave in the country, according to which nationalisation is presented as a panacea for every national malady. Nationalisation should be resorted to where necessary, but whether it is needed or not should be decided on practical considerations, not on ideological or theoretical predilections. Nationalisation is considered synonymous with socialism and it is felt that if the Government takes over an industry or trade or commerce, socialism would arrive and the people would become happy. In our country nationalisation has come to mean governmentalisation and, although not in the field of banking, in other fields governmentalisation has not been able to make the people happy.

So far as the question of nationalisation of banks is concerned we should use the test of practicality and see if it is necessary today. We talk of the public sector and the private sector. I do not like this terminology. As a matter of fact there is only one sector in the country, and it is the national sector. If we do not decide to eliminate the private sector, to leave no scope for private initiative, if we do not decide that all means of production, exchange and distribution would be in government hands, then we cannot oppose efforts to invest capital in private enterprises, trade and commerce. Either the Government or the House decides that there would be no scope for individual initiative in this country, the government will do everything — it is running the railways, it will run cars, run hotels, banks, it will do trade and run factories, it will farm the land...(*Interruption*)...

SHRI C.D. PANDE (U.P.) : Will distribute sugar.

Rajya Sabha on December 6, 1963 on the resolution to nationalise banks

SHRI VAJPAYEE : If we take all these decisions we have to take one more decision — that there will be no democracy in the country.

SHRI SHEEL BHADRA YAJEE : There will be.

SHRI VAJPAYEE : No economic policy can be determined by ignoring the democratic values of life. It is true, those democratic values require that in the economic field we should have control to the necessary extent. If private banks misuse their funds and the power derived from those funds they should be strictly controlled. Even today the Reserve Bank has a lot of controlling authority—all such matters as what types of loans the banks should give, whether or not advances should be made, what the interest rate and interest tax rate should be, are decided in consultation with the Reserve Bank. All shareholders have the right to vote. If necessary this control can be tightened. But the argument that the Government should take over the entire banking industry because there are some evils cannot be supported.

There is also the question of compensation. Shri Yajee has gone to the extent of saying that Tata and Birla do not need compensation. Then it would not be possible to give compensation even to the small farmer, the small shopkeeper. The Government has calculated that compensation to the tune to Rs. 100 crores will have to be paid. The amount will not be just in thousands. Where will we find a hundred crores ? In 1962 the Banking industry had made a profit of Rs. 6.5 crores. If we have to pay the entire profit by way of compensation we would have to do so for sixteen years. Deposits of 2100 crores are lying with different banks, out of which the State Bank and other government banks have Rs. 700 crores. Out of the remaining, Rs. 1400 crores with private banks 30 per cent are in government securities. I do not think an extreme step like nationalisation is required only for acquiring what remains.

We are told that we need financial resources for development and construction. So let us calculate. In 1962 the total profit from the banking industry is Rs. 28.8 crores. Out of this Rs. 14.4 crores went towards taxes and Rs. 4.06 crores towards bonus for employees and shares of shareholders. After nationalisation there would be no question of reducing the bonus of employees, it will have to be increased, and shareholders too will have to be given their share.

SHRI C.D. PANDE : Income tax will also have to be paid.

SHRI VAJPAYEE : There will also be other burdens. It cannot be denied that whatever the Government does, it does expensively. And the biggest point is that after nationalisation interest at 6 per cent will have to be paid on bonds worth Rs 80 crores which comes to approximately Rs. 4 crores. It should be calculated—and we should be told—how much would remain after discharging these obligations.

The biggest point is that we have adopted a mixed economy for the development of the country. We give scope for private enterprise, we also go on increasing the public sector, for which we get economic aid from abroad and also take foreign loans. We cannot take any step that would have an adverse psychological reaction here and abroad. The question of ending private enterprise is also linked to the question of foreign capital. I am not in favour of achieving economic progress with so much foreign capital. If plans depend upon foreign loans, foreign aid, would nationalisation of banks create an atmosphere conducive to capital accumulation within the country that we need today ? Like a new daughter-in-law capital is shy. I want it to come out into the open. Would nationalisation of banks not drive this shy capital still more behind the veil ? We also depend upon foreign aid. I can understand what the Communist Party wants—they want to nationalise oil companies, they may even try to jeopardise our relations with friendly countries in the economic field and in other fields.

If Shri Sheel Bhadra Yajee can talk of nationalising newspapers we had better dissolve Parliament and ban Opposition parties. Then do not talk of socialism, of dictatorship. We cannot have democracy in the political field on the one hand and keep all resources, all authority in the economic field in Government hands on the other. So we have to adopt the middle way, and the middle way requires that we do not take any extreme step. We need more capital for development, but this step would prove an impediment in development, it would reduce our credit abroad and slacken the pace of our progress. The need is to step up this pace, and possibly those who support this resolution also have the same intention. But the result will be opposite of what is intended. Whatever the intention, the test of the success of any work lies in its result. There can be no two opinions about the result.

Private banks have also rendered service, their funds have been invested in trade, industry and factories, and they have motivated the people to save. They took the saving system right up to the villages. In 1952 there were 2671 savings offices, while in 1962 there are 4611. In 1952 there were 32 lakh savings accountings, now their number is 6.5 lakhs. These funds belong to common people, and the shareholders are also common people. If there is accumulation of capital anywhere it should be checked, but it is not necessary to take a step which would impede economic progress, concentrate power in the hands of the Government and produce an adverse psychological reaction. Such a step is not desirable at this juncture. The question should not be looked at from an ideological point of view. The only test is the test of practicality, and this test would show that in the prevailing circumstances this step is neither necessary nor desirable. Thank you.

The Bank Nationalisation Ordinance : Parliament Ignored

Sir, according to the agenda of business now the Prime Minister is to speak on bank nationalisation. The Minister for Parliamentary Affairs has already placed a copy of the Bank Nationalisation Ordinance on the floor of the House. This morning I had met you and submitted that the House should get an opportunity to discuss the manner in which this Ordinance was issued.

SHRI J.M. BISWAS (Bankura) : Quite proper.

SHRI VAJPAYEE : I am not going into the merits and demerits of the Ordinance. The question is not whether bank nationalisation is right or wrong. There can be a difference of opinion on that, and when the ordinance is presented to the House for approval, Hon. Members would have the opportunity to express their opinion. The question now is only of propriety. It was announced that Parliament would sit on the 21st. The President had already summoned Parliament. But 40 hours before it met, the Acting President issued an Ordinance on the advice of the Prime Minister.

SEVERAL HON. MEMBERS : Shame, Shame.

SHRI RANDHIR SINGH (Rohtak) : That was a revolutionary step, Sir... (*Interruption*).

MR. DEPUTY SPEAKER : May I request Hon. Members to be calm ? He is only raising an issue of propriety. Beyond that he is not supposed to go into the merits of it. It is only the question of propriety with regard to the promulgation of an ordinance.

SHRI VAJPAYEE : Sir, according to the Constitution if Parliament is not in session ...(*Interruption*)

SHRI BAL RAJ MADHOK (South Delhi) : Sir, I want to make one thing clear. If they do not allow him to speak we will not allow the Prime Minister to speak. Let it be made very clear to them.

SHRI CHINTAMANI PANIGRAHI (Bhubaneshwar) : Sir, I want to raise a point of order. (*Interruption*).

MR. DEPUTY SPEAKER : Under the Rules of Procedure and Conduct of Business, and under the Constitution, he is within his rights to question the propriety of the promulgation of an ordinance. That is all.

SHRI CHINTAMANI PANIGRAHI : What is the rule ?

MR. DEPUTY SPEAKER : He is pointing out the rule.

SHRI VAJPAYEE : Sir, the Constitution gives the power that if Parliament is not in session...(*Interruption*).

AN HON. MEMBER : We know.

Lok Sabha on July 21, 1969 during debate on the Bank Nationalisation Ordinance

SHRI VAJPAYEE : They have yet to know a lot more, Sir. There can be no calm debate in this atmosphere. If the Congress members are bent upon creating a scene in the House they would be taught a lesson. Sir, please check them.

SHRI HUKAM CHAND KACHHWAI (Ujjain) : Sit down.

MR. DEPUTY SPEAKER : May I request Hon. Members to resume their seats ? As I said, the Hon. Member is perfectly within his rights to raise the question of propriety. Beyond that he cannot go. Please resume your seats.

SHRI VAJPAYEE : Sir, I submit that this is not a party matter. It is related to the prestige of the whole House. It is related to the process of parliamentary democracy. This is not the first time that the House has discussed the Government's powers to issue an ordinance. As you know, some correspondence on the Government's powers to issue an ordinance had taken place between Shri Mavlankar, Speaker of the First Lok Sabha, and our first Prime Minister, Shri Jawaharlal Nehru. I would like to quote a portion from it. Some parts of it have been given in a book by Shri Kaul and Shri Shakdhar. I quote :

> "Speaker Mavlankar, in his letter of July 17, 1954, to the Prime Minister, stated : 'The issue of an ordinance is undemocratic and cannot be justified except in case of extreme urgency or emergency'."

Shri Mavlankar further said :

> "He expressed that Lok Sabha carries a responsibility of laying down the tradition. It is not a question of present personnel in the Government but a question of precedent, and if this ordinance-issuing is not limited by convention only to extreme and very urgent cases the result may be that in future the Government may go on issuing ordinances, giving Lok Sabha no option but to rubber stamp the ordinance."

I would like to place before the House a part of the reply Panditji gave to this. In reply he wrote on July 19 :

> "We have issued in the past a very limited number of ordinances and we have always placed before Parliament the reasons for having issued each one of them".

And perhaps the Prime Minister is about to say the same thing. But please see what Panditji says further :

> "I am myself unable to see why this should be considered undemocratic. Of course this power, like any other power, may be abused, and Parliament will be the ultimate judge as to whether the use of this power has been right or wrong."

Ordinance Issued at Improper Time

So I place before this House ...(*Interruption*)... Sir, please hear me out. This is clear. During an emergency, when Parliament is not in session, an ordinance can be issued, but nowhere has it been said and never has it happened, that Parliament was summoned, it was to begin proceedings within 40 hours, and an ordinance was issued.

Now I would like to know—what is the emergency about the nationalisation of banks ? Or was the country facing an economic crisis ? What was that crisis ? If there was a crisis at all, it was a crisis of the Congress Party. If there was a crisis at all, it was a crisis of the Prime Minister...(*Interruption*).

MR. DEPUTY SPEAKER : The Hon. Member is going beyond the scope of the discussion. He cannot question the propriety of a decision. I have permitted him only to question the propriety of the promulgation.

SHRI VAJPAYEE : I am questioning the timing of the promulgation.

Crisis not of the Banks but of the Party

The decision is a different thing. It has been stated in this discussion, which Speaker Mavalankar had also accepted and you will accept, that an ordinance can be issued if there is a crisis. The Prime Minister will have to explain what that crisis was. So far as we can see, there was a political crisis, a party crisis.

Sir, I would like to close. I would only like to say that protection of the rights of this House depends upon you. The prestige of this House is in your hands. Was it proper to issue this ordinance 40 hours before Parliament met ? Is this democratic ? Is it in keeping with Parliamentary traditions ? Please permit Parliament to discuss this. Thank you.

Foreign Accounts of Indian Companies

Madam, it is a serious offence for any Indian or Indian company to have foreign account in foreign currency. The Government claims that it wants to end economic offences and stringently punish such offenders under the law. But today a certain matter has come to light which not only gives the lie to this claim of the Government but provides evidence for the charge that the Government tried to hush up such matters.

Madam, there is a company called Stillal Ltd. in Calcutta. Since 1980 the E.M.C. Stillal Ltd. has been keeping an account in Dubai. On September 9, 1991 an amount of 650,734 Dinars was deposited in this account. This matter was brought to the notice of the Government. I have with me a letter from the Reserve Bank of India dated November 10, 1991. My information is not based only on a report published in the *Indian Express*. I am prepared to place the documents on the floor of the House proving that the company has a foreign account. This was done without the Reserve Bank's permission. When the Government came to know about it it carried out some investigation, but under pressure from above that investigation was closed down.

I want to quote. This is an official communication. I am prepared to authenticate it and place it on the floor of the House.

DEPUTY CHAIRMAN : You cannot place it on the floor of the House.

SHRI VAJPAYEE : This is the letter the Controller wrote on November 10, 1991 to the Assistant Director, Enforcement Directorate (FERA), Government of India, Calcutta Zonal Office :

"Dear Sir,

> With reference to your letter dated 13th Oct. 1991, we advise that we do not appear to have given permission to the captioned company to maintain foreign currency account abroad. Nor does it appear to have declared the same to us."

The letter following this has been written by Shri A.K. Rai Choudhary, Deputy Director to Shri M.S. Bindra, Director, Enforcement Directorate. It is dated January 2, 1992. I am prepared to place it on the floor of the House. I take full responsibility for it.

DEPUTY CHAIRMAN : You can send it to the Minister. There is no law requiring it to be placed on the floor of the House.

SHRI VAJPAYEE I would like to quote from it :

> "We have received information through secret source 'X' to the effect that E.M.C. Stillall Ltd., 51, Canal East Road, Calcutta, has been maintaining Account No. 59283 with the Algmene Bank, Nederland

Rajya Sabha on March 14, 1988 during discussion on the Calling Attention Motion on the foreign accounts of Indian companies

N.V., Dubai. We have ascertained from the Reserve Bank of India, Bombay, that the captioned company have not been given any permission to maintain such foreign currency accounts.

"Our inquiry reveals that Company belongs to Shri O.M. Khosla and Mahendra Nath. Shri Mahendra Nath is the father of...."

I won't read further. The letter further says :

"I forward herewith copies of the secret source report and Reserve Bank of India's letter dated 10th November, 1981 for your kind perusal and further inspection in this matter."

Madam, an Indian company maintains two foreign accounts in which crores of rupees in foreign exchange have been collected. This has been going on since 1981. The Government had come to know about it, raids were conducted at the office of the company, and the residence of a person connected with the company was also raided, but New Delhi began exerting pressure and the whole thing fizzled out, the whole investigation was wound up. This is a serious matter. I am grateful to the *Indian Express* for raising this matter. I too have some documents. I want the Government to explain why no action was taken against this company and its officials when the matter was within its knowledge.

V Industry And Working Class

Right to Work A Birthright

Sir, no one can deny that unemployment is increasing in the country. That it should increase despite Five Year Plans is really a matter for concern. In no country of the world has it happened that constructive planning and unemployment have gone together. It was at first etimated that eight million people would be provided with jobs under the Second Plan. But even there the Planning Commission had accepted that nine million new unemployed would be created during these five years. Now this figure of eight million has been brought down to six, and I doubt if even that would be fulfilled.

Why is unemployment on the rise in spite of the Plans ? We want to increase production during the plans. For that increased production we need a market within the country. Gradually it is becoming clear that you cannot develop the country's economy very much through exports, because we are facing keen competition in the market-place of the world. Clearly we need a domestic market for increased production. This means we have to increase the people's purchasing power. In my view increasing production and increasing the common man's purchasing power are complementary to each other in a five year plan. But today the situation is such that we keep emphasing increase in production but the common man's purchasing power is on the decline. The biggest reason for this is that crores of people have no work and lakhs of people who have work do not find it an adequate means of livelihood.

If we want to develop our economy and establish a domestic market for increased production we would have to find jobs for the people. If we do not do that there would be no lasting foundation for our economy.

Now, how can this be done ? I suggest that the government change its industrial policy. Adopt a policy that emphasises maximum employment generation. We have more people and less land in this country. In Europe and other countries there may be more land and less people. Here we have the opposite. Here we have a bigger population and less hand. There are more lands and less work. If we want to provide work for crores of young

Lok Sabha on November 21, 1958 during discussion on the Calling Attention Motion regarding setting up a committee to study the unemployment problem

men—and the Prime Minister does say *'Aram haram hai'*—we would have to adopt a different policy. What would be a bigger joke than raising slogans of *'Aram haram hai'* before those who are sitting idle, or standing in queues before employment exchanges or fighting like cats and dogs outside the Delhi station for carrying a holdall ?

Our plans emphasise big machine-run industries. I am not saying we should boycott machines. But if it is possible to give more work to people we should do it. If man is hungry it is not proper to work a machine, I have not had an opportunity to visit China. Those of my friends who have been there say they too are building big dams, but without big machines. Lakhs of Chinese are working like ants to build them. The wage would be small, and capitalist countries may call it forced labour, but let us not be deluded. If you can provide work only through these development plans I feel it would be nothing very wrong if you showed them down a little. After all for whom are these plans meant, for whom these big dams ? Are they not for people ? These same people, for whom this is being done, need work. The right to work is a birthright. This land is *Karma Bhoomi*. We are born to work, and I say the right to work should be included in our fundamental rights. Today we have the right to speak, the right to write, the right to fight an election, but not the right to work.

SHRI S.M. BANERJI : We have the right to die.

SHRI VAJPAYEE : We do not have the right to a livelihood. I wish the right to work was included among the fundamental rights in the Constitution, and we realised our responsibility of providing work to every individual. How work can be provided has been indicated in a proposal I have placed before you. I urge a change in the industrial policy and an emphasis on small industries.

Secondly, our education system also needs to be overhauled. Those who come out of the mint of a university reach the unemployment market. There is no dignity of labour. No one wants to do manual work. Foreign rulers had worked this education system only to produce clerks. They are gone and their education system should go with them. We should have an education system that gives dignity to labour, that teaches us to work with our hands, and which takes our educated classes to the villages instead of to offices.

Today villages are falling empty and cities are filling up. There are no people to live in the villages and there are no houses to live in the cities. Our industrial policy does not increase the people's purchasing power. As a result cloth is lying in the market and textile mills are closing down. There are naked people in the market and also cloth in the market. The naked want cloth and the cloth dealer wants such naked as have money. But there is no money because there is no work and the administration cannot provide work. We are faced with a serious situation. This is not a matter for any one party. It is also not a question of inciting the unemployed for political ends. But this problem can be solved if we bring about a basic transformation in our industrial policy and our education policy. The Government should include the right to work in fundamental rights, accept it, and progress towards this goal. Then alone can the unemployment problem be solved.

It is not enough to set up a committee to accomplish this, though I am not against the committee. Thank you.

Industrial Policy

CHAIRMAN : Resolution of Shri Tangamani moved :

"This House calls upon the Government to appoint a Committee consisting of 30 members of both Houses of Parliament to review the working of the Industrial Policy Resolution of 1956 and to suggest changes in the policy and its implementation in the light of the necessity for rapid industrialisation of the country and to prevent the inroads into our national economy of foreign private capital in collaboration with Indian interests or otherwise."

Some amendments have been tabled. Are they moved ?

SHRI VAJPAYEE : I beg to move :

In the resolution, after the words "of the country" insert —

"Simultaneously guaranteeing by an appropriate dovetailing of heavy and small-scale industries : that industrialisation does not bear adversely on the employment situation in the country" (1)

In the resolution, for the words "to prevent the inroads into our national economy of foreign private capital in collaboration with Indian interests or otherwise" substitute —

"and safeguarding against the possibility of foreign capital being able to influence the internal affairs of the country." (2).

SHRI AUROBINDO GHOSHAL : I beg to move :

In the resolution, after the words "of the country" insert —

"through public sector." (3)

CHAIRMAN : Now the resolution and the amendments are before the House.

SHRI VAJPAYEE : Sir, I welcome Shri Tangamani's resolution not because I support the demand in his resolution or because I agree with what he has said in support of his resolution but because it gives us an opportunity to reconsider the Industrial Policy Resolution of 1956. The Draft Third Five Year Plan is before the country. The Second Plan is about to end. It is necessary that before marshalling efforts for the Third Plan we should see how far the industrial policy we have adopted has proved right in the situation in the country and in accordance with its genius or whether it needs to be amended, and if it needs to be amended, in what direction. I have moved two amendments. The Industrial Policy Resolution of 1956 had discussed small industries and cottage industries along with big industries, but the progress in that direction is far from adequate. In the Second Plan we had earmarked an amount of Rs. 200 crores for the development of small industries, and I

Lok Sabha on August 5, 1960 during discussion regarding review of Industrial Policy Resolution

am surprised to see that in the Draft Third Plan the Government is thinking of providing only Rs. 250 crores. The question is not of the amount. The question is, what type of industrialisation do we want ? What picture do we have before us ? Is that of Russia or America where big industries push small industries back in the competition and go ahead ? Or do we want an industrialisation based on village and cottage industries ? In spite of the declaration that there should be an accord between big and small industries the administration has not yet been able to bring about that accord. There is a competition between the Gur and Khandsari industry and the sugar industry and the Gur and Khandsari industry cannot stand the competition. The government's policy in this regard is also discouraging. Similarly, the government has not been able to strike a balance between the production of Khadi and handloom and mill-made cloth. It is not enough to assist small industries, their areas should also be demarcated, so that an exclusive area is available for small industries for production. I could give an example. Textile mills can be prevented from making Dhotis or Saris, and if they made these they would be reserved for export. The handloom industry could be fully entrusted with the job of making Dhotis and saris. The point is to base our production on small industries. On the one hand, we want to develop small industries, but on the other, handloom weavers do not get yarn. They have to depend upon the mills for it. The Government has not been able to earmark separate areas for big and small industries so that they could develop without competition. The Industries Policy Resolution has accepted the utility of small Industries. They prevent concentration of wealth, as well as concentration of labour and decentralise industrial power. But in actual practice this is not seen. Small industries have not yet been able to stand on their own feet.

Neglect of Small-Scale and Cottage Industries

The Government gives them assistance, but it is as if a full plate is placed before big industries while some small crumbs are thrown to small ones. This industrial structure is not in accord with the situation in the country, because even if we increase production by setting up big industries, we would have to find a domestic market for that increased production, for which we would have to increase the purchasing power of the common man. If we do not develop small industries we would not be able to provide work to our increasing population and then the production of big industries would become a major problem for us. We should lay stress on exports, but we see that export possibilities are declining. As the slave countries of Asia and Africa go on becoming independent they will stand on their own feet, develop industrially, and thus our export area would get all the more restricted. Then we will have to find a domestic market for our products, but this would not be possible unless we find work for everyone. On the basis of experience with the Second Plan we can say that even with increased industrial production we have not been able to lessen unemployment. In my opinion the only way out is to change the method of industrialisation. Instead of laying stress on big industries we should spread a network of village and cottage industries. Thus the maximum number of people would be able to get work. Their purchasing power would increase. Then our increased production would find a domestic market and we would be able to elevate the people's standard of living.

The industrial policy should be so amended as to make small industries the basis of our industrialisation, and then we should strike an accord between small and big industries. So far all facilities are aimed at big industries and small industries have to depend upon them. The Government should give a thought to this aspect.

So far as foreign financial aid, whether official or private, is concerned, we have no objection provided there are no strings attached. But in the present situation large-scale foreign aid could create political difficulties for us. I do not agree with Shri Tangamani when he says official aid can be accepted but not private aid. Foreign aid will have its political impact, whether it is official or private. If Russia helps us to set up Bhilai—for which we are grateful to them — it will have a political reaction too. If Soviet experts work with Indians at Bhilai even that has a reaction. And if things are different at Rourkela even that has a reaction. In this matter I am not prepared to accept a distinction between official and private. If we have the strength we can digest foreign aid. But our digestion has become weak, so foreign aid can create difficulties for us. We must be on guard against strings attached to foreign aid. If our people have patriotism foreign aid cannot distort their mindset. But for this it is necessary that there should be a foreign policy consensus among all parties in the country. Aid received from any quarter can be used for nation building, but it would create problems for us if one party says we should join this bloc, another says we should go to that bloc. We must be on guard against that.

Pay Commission Report A Disappointment

Madam, the recommendations of the Pay Commission have greatly disappointed more than two million Central Government employees. As they were being ground between the millstones of increasing dearness and increasing taxes for the past many years they had hoped that the Pay Commission would increase their salaries and allowances in keeping with the country's economic condition, so that they could lead a proper life. This was necessary for a proper discharge of their duties and was also in accordance with the objective of our five year plan to raise the standard of life. But the report of the Commission has caused deep resentment among them. The terms of reference that the Government placed before the Commission put big limitations on it. But some of its recommendations have not been accepted by the government in toto. Even the labour organisation affiliated to the Congress party has criticised the fact that the Government accepted those recommendations that were in its favour but changed those that were in the interest of the employees. One way before the Government was to accept the Commission's report in toto and implement it. But if it wanted to make any changes in the recommendations it is very necessary that it should discuss them with representative organisations of the employees.

There is the question of holidays. Everyone wants that every citizen of India should put in maximum work, maximum labour, and Government employees are as industrious as anyone else. But the Pay Commission's recommendation even in respect of increasing working hours on Saturday has not been fully accepted by the Government. Holidays were cut down. The total number of holidays was cut down. This would increase the employees' workload. They would be prepared to shoulder the responsibility of this load provided, in exchange, the facilities they have been enjoying so far are not curtailed and more facilities are given to meet the demands of the situation, but the Pay Commission recommendations have resulted in more work and less facilities.

Just now there was a reference to Railway employees. Now the rental of the quarters allotted to them will be calculated on the basis of the land on which they stand. If the land was acquired at high rates that price would be recovered from the employees by way of rent. Present medical facilities have also not been extended. Those employees for whom the Government could provide accommodation are very small in number, the rest are suffering from shortage of accommodation and are forced to pay high rent for it.

Lok Sabha on February 11, 1960, during discussion on the Report of the Pay Commission

Government pass and P.T.O. facilities have also been reduced. And I have come to know that the Railway Ministry has issued a directive that free passes and PTOs should be issued only as per cuts recommended by the Commission till March. It is argued that even those railway employees who are not in service are given travel facility, and that too from their homes. But there should be some consideration for the conditions in which railway employees work. So long as the terms of their services do not change they should not be robbed of the facilities they have obtained after years of struggle. Even today, under Rule 148, a railway employee can be removed from service with one month's notice without showing cause. These conditions of service do not apply to other employees. Their work is also different. Employees of the Post and Telegraph Department also do a special type of work. They work day and night and they need the facilities they have secured with their organised might for the proper performance of their duties. The Government is going to reduce them too. Instead of gaining something the employees are losing something. 'Choube' was going to become 'Chhabbe' but became 'Dubey'. The employees were looking forward to some gains but are faced with the problem of diminished facilities. I must tell the Hon. Minister that the recommendations of the Pay Commission have caused dissatisfaction among the employees. If present facilities are reduced there will naturally be a reaction, and if the employees take some steps for their continuance which indicate to the Government that they are not prepared to give up those facilities, it would be quite justified.

Successful Plan, Hard Life for Employees

In a speech at a public meeting in New Delhi on January 30, the Prime Minister has appealed to the employees to keep the country's broad interests in mind. I think the credit for the success of the Five year Plan does not go to any one as much as it goes to the employeas. The Government also claims that the plans are succeeding. But it is really surprising that despite these plans the employees' standard of life is going down. Dearness is on the increase. And in view of the economic policy the Government is adopting, it would not be improper to hope that it would decline further. There are clear signs of inflation. Prices of foodgrains, textiles, daily necessities are all going up. The class that is most affected by this increase is the fixed-income group of government employees. And it is claimed that they can get a meal for 56 Naye Paise in Delhi. The Commission may reach that conclusion, but those Ministers who live in Delhi and are at least a little acquainted with the dearness in Delhi, let them honestly ask themselves is a 32-ounce meal available for 56 Naye Paise ? It may be enough to keep his body and soul together, but it cannot motivate him to work more.

It was also expected that the Pay Commission would make some changes in the service conduct Rules. It seems that the facilities of Government employees are now on the decline and the restrictions on them are on the increase. Even recognised unions are being told that they should not have outsiders as office-bearers. They cannot even hold meetings within office premises. Efforts are being made to gradually cut down their work motivation. Once the Government accepts that employees' unions are necessary for promoting their efficiency and maintaining their relationship with the Administration they should be given all encouragement. Had the Pay Commission so desired it could have suggested such amendments in the Service Conduct Rules as would facilitate the employees' participation in the surrounding social and cultural activities. But I have come to know that the Home Ministry has prepared a black list of some such organisations and even if a minor functionary of the intelligence department reports simply on the basis of a doubt that a certain employee seems to be in touch with a certain organisation he is removed from service. I am of the opinion that in view of the changed circumstances in the country the terms and conditions of the employees' service should also be amended.

Pay Commission Does not Pay, It Pushes Back

The Pay Commission did not even accept the basis determined by the previous Varadachari Commission for fixing dearness allowance. On the one hand, the Commission admits that it would not be easy to bring down dearness in the near future and on the other it does not want to revise even the basic salary upwards as it feels educated, able-bodied people are available in this country for Rs. 80. So the Commission is not ready to increase the basic salary. In my opinion the Government should not apply this supply and demand rule while fixing the salaries of its employees. The situation in the country is such that educated people would be ready to work for even less, but the government should behave like a model employer. When we demand that private employers of industrial workers should give them higher salaries and bigger allowances it is necessary that the Government should pay its employees adequately and increase their dearness allowance in step with the growing dearness. From this point of view the recommendations of the Commission are still more backward as compared to the basis determined by the previous Pay Commission.

So far as the proposal to fix the basic salary at Rs. 120 to 125 is concerned, I do not think the government should have any objection to accepting it in the present situation. It is said that accepting all recommendations of the Commission would mean an expenditure of 31 crores for the government. But if we add up the employees' facilities that are being reduced, the income that is being generated through making them work for extra time, the savings that would be effected by reducing their passes and PTOs and the addition to the Government exchequer the employees would be making through additional working hours, I do not think an expenditure of Rs. 31 crores would be a loss for the government. The employees' unions also made their own calculations. Railway employees claim that they would give the Government at least Rs. 26 crores by working extra. This is their claim and I think it is valid.

SHRI HARISHCHANDRA MATHUR : Have you examined it ?

SHRI VAJPAYEE : Yes.

SHRI HARISHCHANDRA MATHUR : That is what I want to hear.

SHRI VAJPAYEE : If Railway employees work more and their facilities are cut down, as is being done as per the Pay Commission's recommendations, clearly the government exchequer would save money, and that would be the employees' contribution. But if the Government has to contribute something from its funds to the employees' salaries and funds, it should be prepared for that too. In the final analysis it is the employees that keep the administration going. We expect them to be honest and to work with dedication. Appeals to this effect are also made. But we must take care that the standard of living of the employees does not go down despite Five Year Plans. This is the danger that looms.

Pay Commission and Pay Scales

The Pay Commission has also not properly fixed the pay scales for the categories of various services. It does not seem as if any scientific system has been used for fixing pay scales. There are different grades for different categories in the Post and Telegraph Department, and especially in the Railways, and they are uneven. Thus they sometimes clash with each other and create resentment in the employees' mind, adversely affecting their efficiency. It was hoped that the Commission would consider all categories and recommend pay scales for them.

Take the Railways. There are the Station Masters and the Assistant Station Masters. Their eligibility conditions are higher, their work is bigger, but their grades are not in keeping with their responsibilities. More such examples can be given. A big job for the Commission was to go into different categories of services and fix their salaries and allowances in accordance with their responsibilities. But what the Commission did not do the Government could do. Some recommendations are currently under consideration of the Government. I suggest that before taking a final decision on recommendations that would diminish the present facilities of the employees the Government should invite their unions, talk to them, and take them into confidence about the situation in the country. If they are invited and talks are held, a way could be opened up so that the employees would be satisfied and at the same time the Government would also be able to explain its stand to them. But if the Finance Minister talks from a distance, does not take the employees into confidence, emphasises only the burden on the Government, and does not pay heed to the employees' reactions, then the discontent among them would grow still further. In order to prevent such a situation from arising the Finance Minister should take the Employees' unions into confidence before it is too late. Thank you.

Very Important to Promote Small Industries

Sir, I support Shri Thangamani's resolution. Not because I support the demand made in it or because I agree with what he said in support of it, but I welcome it because it gives us an opportunity to re-examine the Industrial Policy Resolution passed in 1956. The draft Third Five Year Plan has been presented to the country. The Second Plan is about to end. Before organising our efforts for the Third Plan it is necessary that we review how far the policy we adopted in the industrial field has proved true to the situation and the genius of the country, if there is a need to amend it, and if so, in what direction.

I have given notices of two amendments. The Industrial Policy Resolution of 1956 had discussed small income industries and cottage industries along with big industries. But the progress made so far in that field is totally inadequate. In the Second Plan we had earmarked an amount of Rs. 200 crores for the development of small industries, and I was surprised to see that in the draft Third Plan the Government propose to provide only Rs. 250 crores. The question is not about funds. The question is what type of industrial structure we want in this country. What is the picture before us ? Is it Russia or America, where big industries progress at the cost of small ones ? Or do we want in this country an industrial structure that will have small, village industries and cottage industries as its basis ? It was declared that a consonance should be brought about between big and small industries, but the Administration has not yet been able to do so. There is a competition between the *Gur* and *Khandsari* industries and the sugar industry, and the *Gur* and *Khandsari* industry cannot stand the competition. The policies of the Government also tend to discourage them. Similarly, the Government has not been able to establish any consonance between the Khadi and handloom cloth on the one hand and the mill-made cloth on the other.

I say it is not enough only to help small industries, you have to determine production areas, and thus make an unrestricted production area available to small industries. For example, textile mills can be prevented from making Dhotis and Sarees, and if they do make them they should be reserved for export. The making of Dhotis and Sarees could be completely entrusted to the handloom industry.

Make Small Industries the Basis of Production

It is necessary to make small industries the mainstay of our production. On the one hand we want to develop small industries, but on the other handloom weavers do not get yarn. For yarn they have to depend upon mills.

Lok Sabha on August 5, 1960 while moving amendment to the motion on Industrial Policy Resolution

The Government could not set aside separate production areas for small and big industries so that they could develop without competition. In the Industrial Policy Resolution the Government has accepted the utility of small industries. They prevent concentration of wealth and concentration of labour and lead to decentralisation of industrial power, but in actual practice this is not seen. Small industries are still not able to stand on their feet.

The Government helps them, but this help can be compared to a few morsels thrown to them as against a full meal served to big industries. This type of industrial structure is not in keeping with the condition of the country, because if we increase production by promoting big industries we would have to find a market for their products within the country, and for that we would have to strengthen the purchasing power of every citizen. If we do not develop small industries we would not be able to provide employment to our growing population, and if we cannot provide employment the products of big industries would land us in trouble.

We must emphasize exports. But we see that export possibilities are declining. As the slave countries of Asia and Africa go on becoming free they will stand on their own feet and achieve industrial progress, in the process restricting export areas still further. Then we shall have to find a market for our goods within the country. This market cannot come up so long as we do not arrange work for everybody. The experience of the Second Plan shows that despite increased industrial production we could not bring down unemployment. The only way out of this situation is to change the method of industrialisation. Instead of laying stress on big industries let us spread a network of cottage industries in every village. This would give work to the maximum number of people. Their purchasing power would increase, and by selling increased production within the country we would also be able to elevate their standard of living.

It is necessary to amend the industrial policy so as to make small industries the basis of our industrialisation and then big industries may be given their appropriate place. So far all facilities are oriented towards the big industries and small industries have to depend upon them. The Government should think about this.

So far as foreign economic aid is concerned, whether it is official or private, we can have no objection to it if it has no strings attached. But in our present condition large-scale foreign aid would create political difficulties for us. I do not agree with Shri Thangamani when he says official aid is acceptable but private aid objectionable. If foreign aid is to have a political impact on the country it will be there, whether the aid is official or private. If Russia helps us set up Bhilai—for which we thank them—it has a certain political reaction. If Soviet experts working at Bhilai do so in cooperation with Indians that too has an impact. And if there is a different experience at Rourkela that too has a reaction. In this respect I am not prepared to distinguish between official and private. If we have the power we can digest foreign aid. It is a different matter that our digestion has weakened and consequently foreign aid is creating difficulties for us. We have to guard against accepting conditional foreign aid. If the country develops, if people are patriotic foreign aid will not distort their thinking. But for this it is necessary that there should be a consensus among all parties on foreign policy. Then foreign aid may come from any quarter. We can use it for national reconstruction. But if every party wants alignment with a particular bloc foreign aid would become a problem for us. We should beware of this. Thank you.

Central Employees' Strike Government Responsible

Sir, it cannot be denied that the Central Government is largely responsible for the Central employees' strike. After the Pay Commission's report was published such changes were carried out without consulting responsible employees on matters which were detrimental to the Employees' interests. Now it is argued that the Pay Commission's report was the award of a tribunal. Had it been so there should not have been unilateral changes in it. Take such things as the Saturday holiday or facilities to the Employees from July 1. The Government made changes at its own sweet will. The Pay Commission had recommended alternate Saturdays to be full working days and full holidays but the Government changed it. The facilities that were to come into effect from July 1 were postponed till December 31. I do not think the Central Government has started work by accepting the report as an award. And even if it is accepted that the Pay Commission's report was an award there are instances where the Government has amended awards. Shri Giri had resigned in protest against the change in the Bank Award. If an award can be changed in the interest of banks, mill-owners, there is no reason why this particular award cannot be changed in the interest of 22 lakh employees.

Pay Commission's Report an Award ?

My complaint is that the Government has not treated it as an award, and INTUC leaders complain that some of the Commission's recommendations go against the previous commission's report. Some recommendations curtail the facilities that the employees had secured after years of struggle. Was it not natural that before implementing those recommendations the Government should have held talks with the representatives of Central employees ? Was the previous Pay Commission's report not an award ? Did the Government implement its recommendations in respect of dearness allowance ? Did the Government set up the machinery required for such implementation ? The Government put the First Pay Commission's report into cold storage because it favoured the employees and accepted the Second Commission's report as *'Panch Parameshwar'*. If there was a difference of opinion in the two commissions and if the second commission recommended cuts in the present facilities for the employees there should be no objection

---

Lok Sabha on August 8, 1960 during discussion on the Central Government employees' strike and the related Ordinance

to meeting with Central employees' representatives in that regard. The Joint Council of Action was set up later.

When this House considered the Pay Commission's report and the Finance Minister was asked if he would meet Central employees' representatives he had clearly replied in the negative. He said whatever talks were necessary had taken place; now the report is there and we shall implement it. This was a very wrong attitude and it was an invitation to the strike. The Joint Council of Action was set up later. I feel the Prime Minister was aware that the Finance Minister had declined to meet Central employees' representatives. There was no question of a strike then. Perhaps the people had not even thought of it. Had the Government talked with the Central employees' representatives at that time there would not have been a strike. But the Government adopted an obstinate attitude and the result is an unfortunate strike. It is unfortunate both for the Central Government and for the Central employees' leadership. But had the Government so wished, it could have avoided the strike.

The Employees' Demands

I talked to the leaders of Central employees. They did not think a strike would be necessary. They had not even prepared for it. Neither had they incited the employees for it. Had they prepared the employees for a strike you would not have claimed, as you do now, that only 20 per cent employees have gone on strike. And even if 20 per cent have gone on strike their demands have the backing of all Central employees. They had thought saner counsels would prevail and the Prime Minister would at least not refuse to see them. And even if they set up a Joint Council of Action was it such a calamity ? The Prime Minister says for the last forty years he has been willing to meet any person any place. Now these Central Employees' representatives are his followers and are trying to rebuild the country under his leadership. If they made a mistake in setting up a struggle committee the Prime Minister should not have made another mistake by refusing to meet them. By this refusal the Government has closed the door on talks. This has created resentment and also a state of confusion among the leaders of the employees. In my opinion circumstances forced them to decide upon a strike.

A day before the strike I met Shri Nath Pai and suggested that Shri Feroze Gandhi's formula should be accepted. Although it did not fully support the Central Employees' demands I had suggested this in view of the Government's obstinate attitude and its preparedness to suppress the strike with all its might. But the striking leaders feared that if they agreed to anything that was not acceptable to the employees they would be in difficulties. In my view this is not a question of leadership. The powers that be should also understand the situation. But they failed to do so, and the striking leaders found themselves in a situation from which there was no escape.

I had suggested to Shri Nath Pai that if a strike was a must it should be for one day. If the employees of the Central Government wanted to express their anger against the policies of the administration they should go on a one-day token strike, that would demonstrate their opposition. This would save us from the serious repercussions of an indefinite strike. But it looks as if things slipped out of his hands and the strike took place.

Sir, the Prime Minister's speech on the radio was emotional and it had a deep impact on the employees. He painted two pictures in it. One was that of the labourers and Jawans as the heights of the Himalayas, and the other was that of employees fighting the battle on the plains and in the offices with the sword of the pen. I regret to say he painted these pictures in such a way that a gulf was created between the Jawans of the Army and the civilian employees. This was most unfortunate for the country. They are all employees of the Government, servants of the country. We should not discriminate between them like this. And it is not that these two pictures contrast Jawans stationed on mountain-tops and civil employees working on the plains. We can see both the pictures on the plains. The wide difference between the salaries of the Jawans and officers can be seen both on mountain-tops and on the plains.

Ratio of Minimum–Maximum Salaries

If the Government feels that the minimum salary of an employee should be Rs. 80 I say his maximum salary should be Rs. 800. Do not all parties agree that the ratio between minimum and maximum salaries should be 1:10 ? And even if you say that it should be 1:20 in the present circumstances the maximum salary cannot exceed Rs. 1600 when the minimum is Rs. 80. But a grade four employee may draw Rs. 30-40, while a senior officer may get three or three and a half thousand. This is what causes resentment among the employees. If this discrimination continues the Government cannot stop a strike by making a law. In the Mahabharat Kunti had said : I do not mind my sons going hungry, but my mind fills with anger when I see the Kauravas living in royal splendour.

This is a natural feeling, Sir. The Central Government should endeavour to minimise this difference. No maximum salary was fixed and no restraint placed on profits. An ordinance was passed against Central employees but it cannot be passed against millowners who raised cloth prices. I say this was not an attempt at a civil rebellion. The Prime Minister has used a most unfortunate phrase. But today the explosive of discontent has spread everywhere in the country. It is the third and fourth grade Central employees and students who could not get admission to universities. Any spark would be enough for this discontent to become a configuration. What is required is for the strike to give us a shock. This strike should be welcomed as shock treatment. It would be good for everybody if the country, the Government benefits from it and if we use it to adopt policies that can prevent an increase in dearness.

If Prices Rise, Salaries and Allowances would have to Go Up

If the Government is unable to check the prices of essential commodities there would be a demand for increased salaries and allowances, and no law of the Government can prevent it. Why does the Government work only when threatened with a strike ? The Pay Commission's report was gathering dust for a year without being implemented. Only when the calamity of a strike loomed did ordinances begin to be issued. Even the Prime Minister regretted in his broadcast the delay in implementing the Pay Commission's report. Who is responsible for this delay ?

AN HON. MEMBER : The Government.

SHRI VAJPAYEE : If the Government is responsible it should change its ways. It is not necessary to pass a law to prevent the strike. It is necessary to remove the factors that cause a strike. The strike is not the cause of a disease, it is its manifestation, and if the cause is removed the manifestation can cease. I suggest that the Government set up a machinery for joint consultations with Central employees in case of a difference of opinion, so that matters could be resolved, and if the difference persists it should be referred to a tribunal for compulsory arbitration. Then a strike would not be necessary. In the present case too, had the Government so wished, it could have virtually banned the strike under Section 10 of the Industrial Disputes Act and referred the whole matter to a tribunal. But perhaps the Government wanted to assert its might. And I regret the way the INTUC behaved. When the strike was withdrawn and the Railway employees at the Lucknow workshop reported back on duty INTUC people stood at the gate the decided who could go in and who could not, and the departmental head did as he was told.

SOME HON. MEMBERS : Shame, Shame.

SOME HON. MEMBERS : That is wrong.

SOME HON. MEMBERS : **That is right.**

SHRI KASHI NATH PANDE : That is quite wrong. The Hon. Member cannot prove that the INTUC did anything there.

SHRI VAJPAYEE : Sir, I was in Lucknow that day. I was an eye-witness. The INTUC should restrain its leaders. This is not the way to gain the trust of the Central employees. A feeling of revenge cannot get you the employees' trust. What happened was a bad dream, we should forget it and start a new relationship. But for this those who have been jailed should be set free and those who have been removed from employment reinstated. And going on strike should not be construed as violence and removing coal from an engine before going off work should not be called sabotage.

SHRI JAGJIVAN RAM, Railway Minister : Then what is it ?

SHRI VAJPAYEE : Then could the employees have left the coal in the engine ? That too could have been sabotage, for it could have damaged the engine. Let the definition of sabotage and violence not be so involved that the Government is entangled in it. Thank you.

Conditions of Domestic Servants Law Needed

Sir, I heartily welcome the sentiment behind the Bill moved by Shri Valmiki. It would be natural to give thought to the terms and conditions of services of domestic servants, their hours of work and their wages and to see that their wages are properly paid to them. We have a very large number of them in the country. They will be there so long as the administration cannot provide work to every able-bodied person, and the question of determining the terms and conditions of their service would also remain before this House and before the country.

But while considering this question mere sentiment cannot take us far. It would also not be proper to compare our country with other countries. We cannot compare with conditions in our country the conditions in those countries where not much manpower is available, where there are no coolies at stations and where keeping a domestic servant is very expensive. It is true that we want to reach a condition where a person could get a wage of five or seven rupees per hour, as in other countries and because of which it is not possible to keep domestic servants, but it would not be practical to implement such rules today. So this Bill should be considered from the practical point of view.

Different conditions prevail in different parts of the country, and I do not agree with the mover of the Bill that there should be a uniform law for the whole country, which should be enforced without giving thought to local conditions. I would suggest that the Central Government should prepare a model Bill in this regard, which could be sent to the State Governments for their consideration and approval and which could be implemented in accordance with the conditions there.

Law Made, Difficulties Increased

So far as this Bill is concerned there are certain matters that need to be thought out. It is quite right that domestic servants should have a weekly off. But my own experience is that my domestic servant does not want even a day's holiday. For he is the cook, and taking a holiday would mean there would be no cooking. Then he would have to arrange for his own food somewhere else. Now I can understand it if the mover of the Bill were to provide that on the domestic servant's holiday his employer should cook for him, but he has not made any such provision. That means even he is not prepared to go that far.

Lok Sabha on May 5, 1961 during discussion on the Domestic Servants

SHRI S.M. BANERJEE (Kanpur) : You are a bachelor, that is why difficulty arises. Otherwise the wife will prepare the meals.

SHRI VAJPAYEE : That is true, and that is why the domestic servant does not want a holiday. So before making a regulation in this regard let us see that a law that we want to pass for their benefit does not actually work against them. The sentiment is of course laudable, but if we make a law there will be difficulties for the domestic servants and the purpose of the mover of the Bill will not be served.

As for the wage it is very small as compared to the conditions today. It provides for a monthly salary of Rs. 30 for those below 18 and Rs. 40 for those above. Does this include meals or no ? If not how can it be a part of the salary and if the domestic servant has to arrange for food at his own cost how can he manage within these thirty Rupees ? At present domestic servants in Delhi take a monthly salary of 30-40 rupees with food. So the matter of food needs to be clarified. As for hours of work it can be 10 hours provided the servant is called at both meal times of the family and arranges his own meal outside.

Police Inquiry a New Hassle

Even if 10 hours are arranged like this there could be a difficulty for the servant. Today if there is not enough work for 10 hours he can relax or do something else. But once we determine the employer-employee relationship on the basis of trade unionism the domestic servant will have to be on duty for full 10 hours.

The powers the police have been given in this matter would also not prove to be in the domestic servants' interests. The police will make inquiries and would find where they come from. Now there are some domestics who are forced to come down to the plains by conditions at home, some leave home without telling their families, while some want to return on earning some money. If the police inform their families where they are it is possible that their families may force them to return. And how many servants would be ready to give full information to the police ? And if the police collect information I do not think it would be good for the domestics.

As for the employer he would have to pay Rs. 25 if he does not get the servant registered. This is a very small fine.

I submit this Bill does not go as far as it should but seeks to progress in the direction of increased difficulties for the domestic servants. So I urge the setting up of a Parliamentary Committee to examine this matter and consider what steps other than a law should be taken to improve their condition. Let it take all things into consideration and develop a system whereby the domestics could lead a comfortable life and yet the law may not create unnecessary difficulties in their way. Thank you.

Trade Union Bill

Let Recognition not be the Issue

Sir, no one can deny that it is necessary to strengthen the trade union movement and develop it on healthy lines. If it becomes strong it will not only satisfy labour, it will also contribute to the maintenance of industrial peace. It is necessary for the Government as well as for proprietors to encourage trade unions and create conditions in which workers' interests could be reconciled with the nation's interests for the sake of progress.

Recognition of Trade Unions

At present the government has no fixed policy on recognising trade unions. This morning's Question Hour had also discussed this and that problem is also related to this Bill. There are many industries where the Government has recognised more unions than one. The Railways are an instance in point. Defence workers, with whom Mr. Banerjee is connected, also have two all-India trade unions. Hence the question arises : if there are to be more than one trade union what should be the basis of recognition ? The present Bill says only one union should have the right to take to or negotiate with the proprietor or the Government, as the case may be, as an organised body. This looks all right as a matter of principle, but it would lead to practical difficulties. Take Railway employees. In the Post & Telegraph Department there are gradewise employees' unions and they are recognised. They can place their demands before the Administration, and the confederation of such recognised unions can negotiate at the level of the Central Government. There are many scales in the Railways. They have their problems and they have their interests, but there is no provision for recognising them. For instance I am connected with the organisation of Station Masters and Assistant Station Masters. You have attended their meeting at Poona and have also inaugurated their convention. Now who will place before the Government the difficulties of their grades, and how will they be solved ? Will they be considered untouchables in the field of trade unions ? Central unions have not been able to do justice by them. So the system that has been adopted for Post & Telegraph will also have to be adopted in the Railways. What rights un-recognised unions should have needs also to be thought about.

Lok Sabha on April 11, 1969 during discussion on Trade Union Bill

Trade Unions are Free to Change

Recognition is a changing thing. Employees can turn away from a union because of its policy. If a trade union does not function democratically or may prove a security risk at a time of national calamity employees and workers may turn away from it. They can decide to join another trade union. Then will that union not have the power to talk on their behalf so long as it is not recognised ? I submit that the Government may bargain with recognised trade unions but the way should be kept open to maintain lines of communication with those unions that have been registered and which represent any section of the working class.

SHRI MADHU LIMAYE : This Bill does not have any such restraint.

SHRI VAJPAYEE : The Hon. Member Shri Madhu Limaye says there is no such restraint in the Bill. I say it does not restrain, but neither does it say so clearly. This is its deficiency.

The Labour Minister will admit that there are some labour unions whose recognition is currently under consideration of the Government. For instance I would like to mention Bharatiya Mazdoor Sangh. Why is it not being recognised at the Central level ? What is the problem ? Even in the States it is being discriminated against. I would welcome the formulation of rules and regulations about recognition, but care will have to be taken that interests of unorganised labour or labour not connected with a recognised union do not suffer. Our effort should be to bring the maximum section of the labour class within the organised trade union movement, but we all know that workers join many unions at one and the same time and contribute to them. If they want something done they approach the INTUC. and if they want to fight they go to some other labour unions.

Labour, Labour Unions and Bargaining

This does not mean the INTUC is more powerful. It only means that by colluding with the Government or with the owners it can do some successful bargaining. But while granting recognition to labour unions we would have to keep in mind that the interests of those who are not yet directly connected with the trade union movement but who have genuine problems are not overlooked and they too get an opportunity to have their say.

The present Bill has some good suggestions. For instance labour unions should keep their doors open to all. We cannot make the mistake of dividing workers on religious or communal lines. It is essential that labour should fight for its rights as labour and work with camaraderie. In the field of labour there can be no place for communalism or narrowness.

It is also necessary that trade unions should have annual meetings and office-bearers elected properly. I agree that trade unions do not hold meetings or if they do the notice does not reach all. Some individuals have made trade unions their fiefdoms and they do not want their empires to end. It is very necessary that the workers should have the opportunity to proceed against such people and elect office-bearers of their choice.

Creation of Union Authority

This Bill proposes the setting up of a trade union authority which would consider and decide matters of recognition. At present the question of recognition is left to the Government or to the proprietors. In my opinion this suggestion merits careful consideration by the Labour Minister. The question of recognition cannot be left to the proprietors or the Government. But the Government would have to think of what arrangement there should be for those who are not recognised.

While replying to questions today the Labour Minister had said the National Labour Commission is considering these aspects. I commend Shri Madhu Limaye's suggestion that this Bill be circulated for public opinion, trade unions to express their various reactions on it and then it should come to this House. By then the Commission's report may also be before the House and the House would be in a position to decide properly. Thank you.

Threatened Railway Strike

Sir, the scope of this adjournment motion is quite limited. The Railway Minister cannot deny that the leaders of railwaymen who were negotiating with him were arrested last night. He also cannot deny that they were to meet him this morning. The meeting was fixed for 10 O'clock this morning, and Shri George Fernandes was to leave for Delhi, then why was he arrested during the night ? This House wants to know, 20 lakh railwaymen want to know, 56 crore countrymen want to know. But there has been no satisfactory answer so far. Friends of the Congress may pardon me, but the arrest of railwaymen's leaders last night has placed them in a false position ... (*Interruption*)... who made the arrest ? Did the opposition parties arrest George Fernandes ? ...(*Interruption*)... They say he might have got himself arrested. This is not a laughing matter. If you laugh this matter away you cannot secure the people's support on a serious matter like this strike. You will have to satisfy the people about what happened from last night to this morning that made it necessary to arrest Shri George Fernandes at 3 O'clock in the morning at Lucknow and other leaders of railway employes in Delhi.

Arrests and Victimisation

If you say they were preparing for the strike, that was nothing new. They were doing it openly. You too were preparing to prevent the strike. Then what was the provocation for the arrest ? The House should be taken into confidence about this. The Railway Minister's silence makes a mystery that creates doubts about the government's intention. I doubt if the Government sincerely wants to negotiate. His doubt has been strengthened ...(*Interruption*)... your conduct speaks loudly, Sharmaji.

SHRI A.P. SHARMA : Serious efforts are being made for a compromise.

SHRI VAJPAYEE : Why were George Fernandes and other leaders arrested last night ? ...(*Interruption*)...

Sir, Shri Sharma has himself admitted that when the coordination committee was negotiating with Shri Qureshi the first point of discussion was victimisation. Did this not mean there was victimisation ? Railwaymen were being arrested before the talks. They were being transferred as punishment. Who started this provocative action ? If there was no victimisation how did it become the first point of discussion ? The Railway Minister was ready for talks because there was victimisation, and that victimisation led to arrests. Right from the beginning the Government was not sincere about a solution through talks.

Lok Sabha on May 2, 1974 during discussion on the Adjournment Motion of Threatened Railway Strike

Secondly it was said that the matter of bonus would be taken up after the review committee's report was received. This is an afterthought. When Shri Sharma was abroad—God knows where—INTUC President Shri Bhagwati and some other leaders met the Prime Minister ....(*Interruption*)...

SHRI A.P. SHARMA : After that there were regular talks and this was decided upon during negotiations.

Government not Sincere

SHRI VAJPAYEE : INTUC leaders told the Prime Minister the bonus demand was legitimate. Now Shri Sharma says the demand for bonus was made even before. But on the day INTUC President Shri Bhagwati met the Prime Minister it was not said we are ready to wait till the Bonus Review Committee's report. It was said the bonus demand is legitimate and the Government should accept it. If it does not discontent would spread among railway employees.

Sir, you will recollect that there was a Banking Commission and it was functioning, but when the Government had to decide upon nationalisation it did not care for the commission's report, it did not care for it. This talk about the Bonus Review Committee is just an excuse. There is no sincerity in it too... (*interruption*)... Now our Congress friends are worried about the bonus payments. They had not thought about money when they made the law that even loss-making factories would have to pay bonus.

SHRI M.R. REDDY (Hyderabad) : That was wrong.

SHRI VAJPAYEE : If the Railway Minister and the Labour Minister admit that it was a mistake we are willing to reconsider our position.

SPEAKER : Hon. Reddy ji, please do not interfere.

SHRI VAJPAYEE : Once a law is made that employees of loss-making enterprises would also receive bonus no industry would escape payment of it. You are caught in your net. You have accepted a demand on which you cannot go back. An employee in the Tata Locomotive Works receives a bonus, while an Indian citizen working in a government factory making engines does not get it. This position will not now be acceptable to anybody. Nobody will tolerate this injustice. Understand this. The day you made the Bonus Act you opened the door for all. Now no window can be closed. The railwaymen's demand for bonus is legitimate.

Cat is Out of the Bag

I would like to know if really... (*Interruption*)... But the Railways should be an ideal employer. If the matter of bonus was related only to the Bonus Review Committee what was the need for the Prime Minister to write to the Chief Ministers that the Government was not in a position to pay bonus ? Suppose the Bonus Review Committee said railway employees should get bonus what then would happen to the Prime Minister's letter ?

SHRI L.N. MISHRA, Railway Minister : We reserve our opinion.

SHRI VAJPAYEE : That means even if the Committee says bonus should be given you will not give it. Then don't talk of the Bonus Commitee... (*Interruption*)...

Shri Sharma says the bonus matter is before the Review Committee... (*Interruption*)...Why was it necessary for the Prime Minister to write a letter saying the Government is not in a position to pay bonus ? Has this not created doubts in the minds of the employees ? If the matter is to be left to the Bonus Commitee leave it to it. But now you want the power to say the final word if the Bonus Committee recommends payment.

SHRI L.N. MISHRA : This is so everywhere.

SHRI VAJPAYEE : If you have the final authority labour is now going to take the final step. I cannot stop them. The present discussion has made it plain that whatever the railway employees got they got after collective bargaining. Shri Sharma has discussed the Miyabhai Tribunal at length. When did it give its award ? It was in July 1972 and now we are in May 1974. To date the Railway Ministry did not take any action on the award.

SHRI A.P. SHARMA : It has been substantially implemented.

SHRI VAJPAYEE : You thought it fit to accept the demands of labour only when they were forced to decide upon united action. But now the Miyabhai Tribunal recommendations have no meaning. Loco workers have already decided upon a strike for decreased working hours. It was only after the strike that you thought their demands were proper. This has made workers of every category feel that the Government will not listen to their demands, however legitimate, unless they threatened a strike. This is exactly what they are doing now. I do not want a strike. A strike would lead to conditions that in the present situation in the country we would not be able to face. But arresting leaders while talks are on is not the way.

Release Arrested Leaders

Shri Chavan is sitting before me. I recollect an instance from history. Emperor Aurangzeb had invited Shivaji through Ram Singh for talks, but when he came he was put in prison... (*Interruption*).

History is repeating itself, Aurangzeb is no more, nor is Chatrapati Shivaji. But Aurangazeb is born in every age. The question is of the attitude. There is still time. The strike is scheduled for May 8. Today is May 2. The situation can be prevented from deteriorating. Arrested leaders should be released unconditionally and efforts made to find a solution through negotiations. I am not prepared to believe that railwaymen are not ready to appreciate financial difficulties, if there are any. They are patriots. They stood shoulder to shoulder with you during the war, and during every crisis they contributed to the success of your plans. You should rouse patriotism in the employees. Do not use the sword of suppression on them. Talk with them with cordiality. Do not show dishonesty. The leaders of the employees can still be released and talks held with them.

SPEAKER : Is it not true that when talks with the employees were going on and when it was proposed that the financial implications of their demands should be discussed the Railway Ministry said there could be no discussion ?

SHRI A.P. SHARMA : There was a discussion for four hours.

SHRI VAJPAYEE : It is not open to discuss that railway employees may show how expenses can be cut down, income increased, and funds marshalled for fulfilling their legitimate demands ? I want to know from the Railway Minister, not Shri Sharma. Is this topic still open for discussion ?

SHRI A.P. SHARMA : A committee has been set up for this.

SHRI VAJPAYEE : Whenever you want to avoid something you entrust it to a committee.

[Shri Ishaq Sambhali in the Chair]

Welcome, Sir, I am now less afraid of the bell.

We were discussing how many crores are required to fulfil the employees' demands. The radio, the media and all official means of propaganda are busy misleading the people by saying that fulfilling employees' demands would cost Rs. 500 crores.

SHRI A.P. SHARMA : Four and a half crores.

If There is a Will There is a Way

SHRI VAJPAYEE : The leaders of the emloyees say these figures are not correct, this much would not be required. Can you not arrive at one figure ? Can this not be resolved through talks ?

The Railway Minister may say we are not in a position to pay bonus. Your demand for bonus is legitimate, but today we cannot fulfil it. If you accept the bonus in principle, 50 per cent can be paid now and 50 per cent added to the provident fund. If there is a will for a solution any number of ways can be found. But if there is no will all roads are closed. There is still time. The situation can be saved. Provocative action can be taken back. The country can be saved from falling into a deep economic crisis. But the Government has made two big mistakes. The first is the publication of the Prime Minister's letter and the second is the arrest of leaders. This has created doubts about the Government's intentions. Now you cannot convince the people about your sincerity in negotiations. Yesterday's arrests have queered the whole pitch. I hope at this time there would be members in the ruling party who would give evidence of intelligence and perspicacity, pressurise the government to correct its mistake, release the leaders, talk with them, and resolve the issue. This is the only way to avoid the strike, otherwise railwaymen would be forced to go on strike and the whole country would have to suffer its consequences.

Assault on Rights of Workers

Sir, I listened to Shri Sukhadiya's speech very attentively.

SHRI MOHANLAL SUKHADIYA : Now I shall listen to yours.

SHRI VAJPAYEE : It was good that he did not go to Calcutta, otherwise we would have been deprived of his speech. But I am surprised to see that under this ordinance his services were not compulsorily availed of for West Bengal. If you felt West Bengal has the most dictatorial regime he should not have been made the Governor at all there. Perhaps the proposal to make him Governor was prompted by such a feeling about the West Bengal Government. Sir, I am surprised to see that even the Home Minister is not present in the House today.

SHRI P. VENKATASUBBAIAH, Minister of State in the Ministry of Home Affairs and Department of Parliamentary Affairs : He is having a Calling Attention on an important matter in the Rajya Sabha. He will be coming here soon.

SHRI VAJPAYEE : The Labour Minister seems in no way connected with this matter. It seems it is the Home Ministry that deals with labour, with public sector employees and Central employees. The biggest problem before the Home Ministry is how to tackle these workers. The Home Ministry is not concerned with how to provide relief from rising dearness, which is resulting in a daily diminishing of their real income and which has made it difficult for them to maintain their families. After all what is the Government's economic record of the past 18 months ? When this government came to power the wholesale price index was 223, now it is 289. Every month there is a rise of more than four points. How are fixed-income workers and employees affected by this ? Central employees should have been given three instalments of dearness allowance. During the Janata Party government employees did not have to agitate for dearness allowance. Should the Central employees sit quiet ? Today you are robbing them of their voice. Now the Government is preparing to impound half the dearness allowance. How can the Central employees manage their expenses ? They are not responsible for the dearness allowance. They do not want a dearmess allowance, they want stability in prices. If this Government brings prices down to the 1978 level discontent would diminish. But prices are going up and the Government is unable to check them. Now it is preparing to freeze wages, suppress demands for bonus, force Central employees to hand over half their dearness allowance to the Government Exchequer, and jail all those workers who raise their voice for their legitimate demands necessitated by a worsening economic situation.

Lok Sabha on September 15, 1981 on the Essential Services Bill and the related Ordinance

Sir, contradictory arguments are being made in this House. I saw the Home Minister's interview on television. He was asked what was the need to issue an ordinance at the very time Parliament was to meet ? With great simplicity he replied it was the business of the Parliamentary Affairs Minister to decide the time when Parliament should meet. I am the Home Minister, my business is to see that everything is all right in the country. On the one hand, the Government says we have not used this ordinance, this black ordinance, this ordinance that is an assault on the rights of trade unions, then what was the need to issue it ? Should the Government not have waited till the session of Parliament ?

Sir, I am reminded of Speaker Mavlankar. He had once ruled that the House would not be prorogued, and because it will not be prorogued the Government cannot issue an ordinance. Ordinances should be issued in exceptional circumstances, but they are being issued to cover up Government's failure to check inflation, to cover up the fact that it has failed to keep its word that if elected it would do something. This sword of an ordinance is taken out in panic, in fear of future doubts. The Finance Minister had promised an anti-inflationary package. Where is that package ? This black ordinance has come out of that package.

Satisfy the Employees, Don't Suppress Them

Are any other steps, any concrete steps, being taken to check prices ? You may suppress the employees' discontent, but suppression cannot remove it. I cannot understand the compulsion behind the issuance of this ordinance. We do not what labour to go on strike. A strike should be the final weapon. But instead of robbing them of the right to strike it was necessary to find a way that would obviate the need for a strike. But in view of what the Government did to the employees, of how they behaved with the loco workers of the Railways the employees and workers cannot be blamed for suspecting that the Government wants to rob them of their right to collective bargaining.

We do not want the Railways to come to a halt, but you cannot bring about industrial peace in the Railways by falsely charging railway workers of sabotage. It is the Railway Minister, the Railway Board, that is responsible for accidents. Shri Tripathi was removed because the railways were not running properly, and in Shri Pandey's time they are sinking in the river. Now Shri Pandey will not be touched. Nor is the Railway Board Chairman being held responsible for accidents. An attempt is being made to make the employees the scapegoat. Loco workers are being transferred from one railway to another, from one corner of the country to another. You may say a transfer is not punishment, but many of us know how difficult it is to find accommodation in a new place. An attempt is being made to harass them.

And if their discontent rises, this ordinance is ready. There can be arrests without a warrant, there can be a summary trial, and there can be imprisonment for six months. Do you believe these steps will be effective ? They will not. Neither had they been in 1974. It seems the cycle of events is gradually turning to 1975, turning towards Emergency. I cannot say what the country's condition would be. I do not know what the future has in store for the country, but gradually the cycle of events is going that way. All thinking and far-sighted people can see this. An assault on the workers' rights is no solution to the problem.

DEPUTY SPEAKER : You are going to come back to power if it is like this. Why should you oppose this Bill ?

SHRI VAJPAYEE : I am afraid for you. I hope when we come to power again you will be with me.

DR. KRIPA SINDHU BHOI (Sambalpur) : He is not saying anything about agricultural labourers.

SHRI VAJPAYEE : I leave that to you. My time is limited.

DR. BHOI : He is saying so much about 10 per cent people, he does not talk about 90 per cent people.

SHRI VAJPAYEE : You have brought forward this Bill for 10 per cent people, so I am talking about them. We would be with you if you bring a Bill saying if agricultural labourers do not get the minimum wages fixed for them the land-owners would be prosecuted and those governments that do not enforce the law would also be proceeded against.

DR. BHOI : You should also say something about them.

SHRI VAJPAYEE : Should he tell me what I should say ? Sir, the Government's wrong economic policies and growing corruption are responsible for dearness. In Punjab wheat was procured from farmers at Rs. 130 per quintal and in Bombay wheat is selling at Rs. 3.30-Rs. 3.50 per kilo.

AN HON. MEMBER : The Lok Dal is responsible.

SHRI VAJPAYEE : No Dal, party is responsible, by the *Daldal*, the bog. in which this Government is caught. Grain transport is prohibited from one district to another—not because of any strike, not because of an agitation by workers, but because you want the power to issue permits and make money with those permits.

Sir, I wrote a letter to the Prime Minister a month back, but it has not even been acknowledged yet. She is so busy she does not have the time to attend Parliament.

SHRI RAM GOPAL REDDY (Nizamabad) : What you say is wrong. She replies within three days.

SHRI VAJPAYEE : I am talking about my own experience. If you have a different experience you are fortunate, I envy you.

Have Labourers no Share in the Profit ?

In my letter to the Prime Minister I have demanded that there should be an investigation in the circumstances in which certain companies were given edible oil import licence. The import price of these oils is Rs. 5000 per metric ton, while their market price is Rs. 9,000-10,000 per metric ton. There is a profit of Rs. 4000-5000 per metric ton. There is a company called Prabhat Solvent Reconstruction Company Pvt. Ltd. On April 9, 1980, it was given a licence to import edible oil worth Rs.2,12,78,400. Initially the company was rejected the licence. The company approached the Delhi High Court against the Government's decision, but the Court rejected the writ and ruled that the Company had no right to a licence as it had applied after the date of application was over. The writ was cancelled but the licence was issued. A licence of two crore rupees means a profit of Rs. 4 crores. Who pocketed this profit ? Don't the employees of that company know ? Did the profit go only to the proprietors of the company, or was it shared ? Who were the sharers?

There is another company called Associated Oil Industries, Coimbatore. Its application for a licence was also rejected. On February 6, 1979 the Controller of Imports & Exports wrote a note on its application. I quote :

> "That your application recorded in this office only on 23rd December 1978, that is, after the expiry of the last date of receipt of applications dated 18th December 1978. Hence your application is hereby rejected as time-barred."

Still this company was given an import licence—a licence of Rs. 29 crores, just to import edible oil. I had told the Prime Minister to investigate this matter. If imported edible oil sells at a high price in the country and if the common man comes to feel that there is an unholy alliance between the political leaders and the industrialists, then you cannot appeal to labourers and employees to work honestly, and even if you appeal to them not to go on strike it will have no effect. Who does not want workers to work properly? But if workers are to work properly are not officers also to work properly? If the officers work properly what will the political leaders do? The way we are conducting Parliament is not the way to strengthen democracy.

AN HON. MEMBER : You are responsible for it.

SHRI VAJPAYEE : We are responsible for it, we are also responsible for dearness, we are responsible for the strike that is going to be broken, we are responsible for Lala Jagat Narain's murder and we are also responsible for your coming to power. Is that not true ? Understand one thing — it would also be due to us that you will have to go. But you will not admit this ... (*Interruption*)...

Dictatorship Cannot Contain Chaos

Sir, you have rung the bell. I would like to appeal. For me this ordinance is not something sacred. It is true that today the country is in difficulties, in grave difficulties. It is gradually sliding into chaos, but dictatorship is not the way to prevent this. This weapon will no more do. A weapon can be used once, but gradually it becomes blunt. If this country is to be built up it will have to be run with the people's consensus, with the consensus of all. But I would like to give an instance of how the Government operates.

There are canteens and tiffin rooms in Government departments. On December 11, 1978 we had declared that employees of these canteens would be considered Government servants by the Home Ministry. They would get all the benefits of Central employees. But that ordinance is still not being acted upon. The canteen workers are not getting dearness allowance at

Central scales. For them it has been fixed at Rs. 95 per month, neither more nor less. Dearness would rise, but not their allowance. How can you satisfy them ? They had held a rally at the Boat Club. I did not advise them to go on strike, but nobody is prepared to talk to them.

Sir, if workers' problems are not solved by a recourse to compromise, by talks, if necessary by arbitration by third parties, problems would worsen, they would aggravate, but by wielding this stick Gyaniji ... (*Interruption*)...

SHRI ZAIL SINGH, Home Minister : The stick will come later.

SHRI VAJPAYEE : The stick will come later 'Gyaniji', you do not hide your intentions.

SHRI INDER JIT GUPTA : First they will take vitamin pills, then they will show the stick.

Reconsider the Bill

SHRI VAJPAYEE : I would urge you to reconsider this Bill. Do not view the looming national crisis in pieces.

In 1977 a situation prevailed in which we had stopped importing foodgrains. In four years you have again stood India in the market-place of Washington with a begging bowl in hand. This is not because we have grown less wheat but because your useless government could not procure it. In Punjab and Haryana the Chief Ministers were busy defeating Bahuguna in Garhwal and had taken the police with them instead of procuring wheat.

I have just returned from a tour of Punjab. There is a drought there, the grain is getting yellow, the standing crop is drying up, there is no electricity for the farmers, there are again queues for diesel oil. The farmer too may lose his temper. This Bill cannot control him. The country is sitting on top of a volcano. You cannot solve problems by bringing in Bills like this and creating tension. It is first of all necessary to look at a national difficulty from a national point of view. But it seems this Government is incapable of it. It is destined to go to perdition. Whatever we say they won't listen. This we know for sure. Thank you.

Privatisation in Power Sector

Mr. Chairman, Sir, I did not want to speak on this Bill but when I saw that Shri Kalp Nath Rai has presented an important Bill, I thought that I must congratulate him. It is true, as just now our friend was saying, that it is a new beginning. It appears that the time has completely changed now. You can call it cycle of time. Earlier it was decided that power generation and distribution would remain under public sector because it is the backbone of industries. But now, the private sector is being allowed to enter in this sphere. It is being done because of the experience we have gained over these years. Had power generation and its distribution been proper under public sector, the country would not have faced the present power crisis. There has been a constant demand to allow private sector in power generation but it was not accepted. But now we have reached a point where there is no alternative except to allow the private sector. All State Electricity Boards are running at loss, generating less electricity as compared to their capacity and large scale pilferage in distribution is taking place. Many States are facing serious power crisis.

Inefficient Public Sector

I would speak particularly of the situation in Uttar Pradesh. In the rural areas of Uttar Pradesh electricity remains cut off continuously for many days. The people have started *gherao* of Ministers of the State Government. A new Government has assumed office there and they have inherited this situation from their predecessors. The Government is under debt and the State Electricity Board is also under debt. The Centre says that coal will not be supplied to the State so long as debt is not cleared. From where they will clear their debt ? If coal is not supplied to them, electricity cannot be generated. It will further aggravate the power crisis. Shri Kalp Nath Rai is very well aware of the situation.

Now the Central government is saying that Thermal Power plant of Unchahar should be handed over to it and its cost will be adjusted against the debt. How a State Government can hand over its Thermal Power Plant to others when it is itself in difficulty. I know that the Centre is also in difficulty.

Lavish Expenditure

Himachal Pradesh has many rivers where electricity can be generated. Besides its own requirement, Himachal Pradesh can fulfil the requirements of neighbouring States to a great extent. But the State Government does not have money to undertake new projects. Industrialists are interested to invest capital. Therefore, they should be given a chance to invest. We cannot restrict

---

Lok Sabha on September 17, 1991 during discussion on the Electricity Laws (Amendment) Bill

ourselves to one particular philosophy. If we realise that there is a need to make new experiments in economic sphere, we should not hesitate to do so. Recently, the Soviet Union and East European countries had to face serious financial crisis because of their commitment to a particular ideology. We should learn by this experience. On the one hand the State Electricity Boards are in the red whereas on the other hand, I have seen the rest houses of these Electricity Boards which are lavishly furnished and one feels shy to touch things lest they may get dirty.

MR. CHAIRMAN: Do you suggest auction ?

SHRI VAJPAYEE : Mr. Chairman, Sir, I do not know what to do with them. All the money has gone down the drain. Does public sector mean this ? Should this be the attitude towards public money ? The question is of the attitude of the management, besides the wasteful expenditure. Shri Mohan Singh is right in saying that even the private sector is dependent on Government financial institutions. This is a strange situation. I do not have time to go into the details but if there is professional management there is no reason for losses in the generation of power. We are giving opportunity to the private sector on the ground that they would not only bring capital but also professional management in the industry. I would like to say that we should go a step further. If we want to set up new industries we should encourage these industrialists to set up captive plants for power generation and give them relief in that.

Solution to power crisis is very essential. If there is no electricity there will be no agriculture, no industry and the cities would be plunged in darkness and incidence of crimes would increase. I had gone to Manali some time back. Everyday when there was maximum rush in the markets the power went off. The shopkeepers used to literally weep. I had gone to the Somnath temple also. There the people told me that when it is time for *Aarti* (evening prayer) the power goes off.

SHRI SAIFUDDIN CHAUDHARY (Katwa) : It seems there is a conspiracy behind it.

SHRI VAJPAYEE : No, I am not saying that.

SHRI SYED SHAHABUDDIN : I may add that power goes off during *Iftar* and *Sahri* in Srinagar, Kashmir.

SHRI RAM NAIK (Bombay North) : This point has become a good meeting ground for all the cultures.

SHRI VAJPAYEE : I would like to appeal to Shri Kalp Nath Rai to help the Uttar Pradesh Government in overcoming the power crisis in the State. This impression should not gain ground that the U.P. Government will have to face some difficulty because Congress is in power at the Centre and BJP is in Uttar Pradesh. I know that Shri Kalp Nath Rai is seized of the matter but unless concrete steps are taken in this direction it will not serve any purpose. We are supporting your Bill. Please help our Government.

VI FOOD AND AGRICULTURE

The Food Crisis

Sir, if we think about the reasons for the food situation currently prevailing in the country we would see that the reason for the crisis is our neglect of agriculture in the Second Plan. The Second Plan laid more than necessary stress on industrialisation. Agriculture is India's biggest industry, and if we aim at economic development our self-sufficiency in food production can alone be its basis. I do not agree with the view of the Ashok Mehta Committee that we cannot be self-sufficient in food. If efforts in the right direction are made the country can certainly stand on its own feet in this respect, but the right point of view is necessary for it. I am happy that the Food Minister agrees with us that instead of big irrigation projects we should concentrate on small ones. Better late than never. I hope we do not stray again.

The Ashok Mehta Committee has thrown light on the conditions in the eastern districts of Uttar Pradesh, which shows that out of the amount of about Rs. 9 crores earmarked for flood control and irrigation arrangements only Rs. 40 lakhs were spent. Small irrigation projects have remained incomplete due to labour shortage and inefficiency of government officials. By and large the adverse food situation is due to natural causes, but human efforts have also been inadequate. It is now clear that the situation cannot be saved without food imports. But the point is, what are we doing to see that whatever increased production we have reaches the common man at the right price ?

Ashok Mehta Committee Failed

The Ashok Mehta Committee has made a strange suggestion. I cannot but call it strange. It is that there should be neither full freedom nor complete control in foodgrain trade. It recommends full socialisation of wholesale trade. I do not know whether or not the government is going to adopt this policy. But it is necessary to clarify the practical form of this so-called socialisation. If we agree that in the present situation in the country complete control cannot succeed, talking about socialisation of trade is pointless. In my opinion this suggestion about socialisation is neither practical nor beneficial, and whether the government accepts it or not it will certainly have an adverse

Rajya Sabha on December 3, 1957 during discussion on the Motion on the Food Situation

effect. People will hoard foodgrain and it would become difficult to bring it into the market so that it could reach the common man at the proper price.

There is another strange thing that the Ashok Mehta Committee has said. My knowledge of English is limited. I would like this thing to be clarified. Page 54 of the Committee's report, where food prices have been discussed, says :

> "It has to be recognised that in a developing economy a secular tendency to price-rise will exist."

What is this 'secular tendency' ? I would request the Food Minister to explain. Now we have secularism in food problems and a secular tendency in the rise and fall of prices. What does it mean ?

There is yet another strange thing that the Ashok Mehta Committee has said. On the one hand it suggested ways of making up the food deficiency in the country, while on the other it has suggested decrement of the country's cattle-wealth that it considers useless. In this connection I would say that no food policy that does not adequately provide for the protection and development of cattle wealth can succeed in India. If we want to be self-sufficient in food we cannot separate our food policy from the protection and development of cattle wealth. I say milkgiving cattle, specially cows and buffaloes, never become useless. They can be used in some way or the other. But the 'goshals' for which the government made provision in the Second Plan have not yet been set up. Here the Government has failed in its duty. We need milk as a nutrient, and so what the Ashok Mehta Committee has said need not be taken seriously.

As for resolving the present food situation both long-term and short-term measures are called for.

So far as the Ashok Mehta Committee's suggestion about sending food out of certain districts is concerned, what is the Food Minister's reaction ? Newspapers report that the U.P. Government has written to the Centre about this. If that is so immediate steps need to be taken. Export of foodgrains from these 14— not 10— districts should be stopped and in order to resolve the adverse situation there not only the U.P. Government but the Centre too should fulfil its responsibility. According to newspaper reports the reports from the U.P. Government are playing down the seriousness of the situation. A little inattention in this regard would have serious consequences. We should realise the seriousness of the situation and this national problem should be solved with the cooperation of all parties and all sections of the society. I have nothing more to say.

Sugarcane Ordinance
A Wrong Step

Sir, the Food Minister's speech does not clarify two points. The first is, if the area under sugarcane is to be restricted why was it not done before the sowing ? Everyone will agree that we cannot give unrestricted freedom to sugarcane growers to grow sugarcane on still more cultivable land. Some limit will have to be placed somewhere. So the real question is not about the principle of such a limitation. The question is did the Food and Agriculture Ministry take the right step at the right time from the practical point of view ? The situation today is that the sugarcane crop is standing in the field and the farmer is greatly worried. I was very much surprised to hear the Food and Agriculture Minister say that the shortfall would not be more than four per cent. So far as my area is concerned there are two sugar mills in it, one at Balrampur and the other at Tulsipur. The figures about the Tulsipur sugar mill that I have received indicate that last year it had crushed 45 lakh tons of sugarcane but this year it is being told to crush 30 lakh tons. This means the cut will not be 10 per cent, it will be 20 per cent. The Hon'ble Minister may either ask the U.P. administration about these figures or get information directly. Sir, now if a mill is to have a 20 per cent cut in crushing sugarcane what will be its impact on the farmer growing sugarcane ? This needs to be taken into consideration.

SHRI S.K. PATIL, Food and Agriculture Minister : If there is anything outside ten per cent, it is outside the scope of this Bill.

SHRI VAJPAYEE : How can it be outside the scope of the Bill ? It is for the Government to explain how a particular sugar factory had been asked not to crush cane beyond a certain limit.

SHRI S.K. PATIL : Beyond 10 per cent ? If it is more than ten per cent, there is evidently a mistake. That can be gone into and corrected.

SHRI VAJPAYEE : The second point the Food Minister made was that had efforts been made to increase the per acre cane crop this problem would not have arisen, but we are in difficulties because the cane area has increased. I say it is not proper to raise here the question of increasing the per acre yield. This is because had the per acre yield gone up we would have been faced with the problem of increased sugar production. Whether the farmer increases per acre production or increases the area, the problem has been caused by excess cane production. How the production has increased is not the main question. Raising this question in this context is meaningless,

Lok Sabha on November 28, 1961 on the resolution regarding Sugar (Regulation of Production Ordinance and Sugar (Regulation of Production) Bill

because whether more sugarcane is produced because of growth in per acre production or because of a greater area the net result is that more cane goes to the sugar mills, more sugar is produced, and because domestic demand is limited the problem remains as it is. So I fail to understand how the Food Minister has introduced the question of raising per acre cane output into this controversy. The problem relates to the increasing production of sugarcane. And even if you reduce the area under cane cultivation and prevent the area from expanding will there not be a problem before the country if, as a result of the restriction, the farmer uses better methods of cultivation on the available land and produces more cane on it ? This is not a question of intensive and extensive cultivation. The question is that the use of cane for sugar production has reached the saturation point. Now we have to think of how we can promote the consumption of sugar.

SHRI MAHAVIR TYAGI (Dehra Dun) : Eat *Halwa*.

SHRI VAJPAYEE : While thinking on this matter we will have to see how many people in the country consume sugar. Can their number not grow ? In the villages many people have to go without it. It is so expensive that they cannot afford it.

Controls Removed, Prices Fell

Now controls have been removed. Sugar prices have also somewhat come down. As a result its consumption has picked up. It would have increased still further had control been removed in the summer, which is the marriage season. So the effort should be to increase sugar consumption. For this the Government would have to consider some reduction in the excise duty. For the past some days the newspapers have been reporting that the Government is thinking along these lines. If that is so I would welcome it. I hope that in his reply to this debate the Food Minister will make some clarification in this regard.

Here we have to bear one more thing in mind. It is true that the farmer is quite willing to sow sugarcane, as it gives him good returns. But there are areas where the very livelihood of the farmer depends upon his sowing cane. Take, for instance, the Terai area. In the constituency that has returned me paddy and wheat crops have been destroyed for three years running, either because of floods or drought or hail. In this area the farmer cannot survive if he does not sow sugarcane. I know that because of the floods in Bihar the Hon. Minister had assured the farmers there that their cane crop would not be left standing in the field. I urge that in the flood-hit eastern districts of Uttar Pradesh too, where farmers have suffered tremendous losses, special efforts should be made to see that all their cane is sold out.

So far as the question of making Khandsari and Gur is concerned the Government has been making the mistake of imposing a tax that greatly harmed the khandsari industry. But now they are surrendering before it. In my opinion adequate attention has not been paid to the development of the khandsari industry. But the big problem is that much of the sugarcane is produced where sugar mills are located and by law khandsari industry cannot be set up near a sugar mill. Now a new problem has arisen. There is no buyer for the cane. Nor can he make Khandsari. There is also no possibility that he can use it only to make gur. I cannot say about other areas but on extensively touring my own constituency I have concluded that if the sugarmills do not buy the cane and if it is left standing in the field the hope that the farmer will use it to make Gur will not be fulfilled and the farmer would be put to great hardship.

Comprehensive Policy Needed

This House has many times discussed the need for the Government to formulate a coordinated all-India policy for sugar, Khandsari and Gur production, so that the right place could be fixed for each. But so far the Administration has not taken any steps in this direction. Last year, in the expectation that there would be a good cane crop farmers were not given adequate incentive to make Gur. As a result not enough Gur was made, and what was made was sold at a very high price. The farmers want to take their sugarcane to the sugar mills, but they would be willing to make Gur if they get timely assistance for its production and if they are assured that their Gur would fetch a good price in the market. But in the present circumstances it would not be proper to expect that the farmers would be able to use up all the cane for making sugar. Such an expectation would not be fulfilled.

Thought should be given to how this matter of four per cent that the Food Minister has talked about could be applied to sugar mills. I have learnt from the sugar mill at Pilibhit that the cane supply to it would be made not from the farmers who grow it near the mill but from the Government farm in Terai. Then why will there not be resentment among the farmers ? If the Government has a farm there it should not be allowed to sell its cane to the Pillibhit mill at the cost of the farmers. The interests of the farmers should be kept in view. But this ordinance fails to do so. The Food Minister has neither confirmed it nor denied it. There is a doubt that Government powers may not be properly used.

Central Government should not Leave Matters to States.

In this connection the Government should address itself to some questions : How much sugarcane will the sugar mills buy from the farmers? How much will be left ? Does the farmers have the resources to crush this remainder ? If they need assistance to do so it should be given. It would not do to leave matters to the State Governments. There they mix policies with sugar. I cannot say so about the Centre. But if everything is left to the States the interests of the growers and the consumers would be ignored and politically-motivated facilities would be extended to the sugar mills which would in the final analysis harm the people's interests.

So I would urge the Food Minister to clarify why this ordinance was not promulgated before the cane was sown, why the farmers were not intimated in advance and why the Government did not act with farsightedness. It is not proper to penalise the cane-growing farmer for the Government's mistake. Now the cane crop stands in the field and if the sugar mills do not buy it there would rise a wide wave of discontent in the crane-growing region. That would not be good for anybody. I do not think even the ruling party would want to create such a situation. But the Government's directive has given rise to such a suspicion in the minds of the farmers. And what is the basis of this 4 per cent test of the Food Minister ? Has he separately consulted the States in this regard ? Will every region be considered separately ? I wish the Government gives the assurance that in the flood-hit eastern districts of Uttar Pradesh no farmer's sugarcane would be left standing in the field and all arrangements for crushing it would be made. Thank you.

Ushering Economic Imperialism in the Name of Co-operatives

Madam, it is most regrettable that the Administration is playing down the gravity of the food crisis. It must be accepted that we have failed very badly on the food front. Production has gone down, it has not been possible to achieve targets, prices have gone up, distribution has not been properly organised and a food policy or agricultural policy is not being determined for the future that would enable fulfilment of the production targets of coming plans.

It is most surprising that when food production increases the Government praises economic planning and pats itself on the back but when production declines it holds the weather responsible. The two cannot go together. The purpose of planning is to fulfil the shortfall and meet the tension caused by the weather. But the weather should not be used to cover up every failure. The reasons for the decline in food production should be seriously considered. In my opinion a major reason is that we have not given adequate importance to agriculture in the Second Five Year Plan. We emphasised industry more. And this we did despite knowing that so long as agricultural production does not increase we cannot procure the raw materials required for industries. We have a shortage of cotton, a shortage of jute, a shortage of sugarcane, and these shortages have also affected related industries. We are spending foreign exchange to import cotton. Cash crops are supposed to fetch good prices and the people are eager to sow them, but we have not been able to increase their production and meet the country's requirements.

Now an attempt has been made to show as if more importance has again been given to agriculture in the Third Plan. But here the question is of implementing the Plan. In respect of agriculture there is no coordination between the Centre and the States, nor between the various ministries of the Central Government. The Community Development Minister should have been present here today. Community Development is related to agriculture, and so is irrigation. But in the States these ministries are in the hands of different ministers and there is no coordination between them. They are not able to unite all these efforts on the food front and motivate the farmers for greater production.

Secondly, whenever there is a food crisis we want to adopt techniques that neither fit a democratic structure nor pass the test of practicality. In respect of agriculture we look to communist countries and want to adopt communist methods, while the truth is that agriculture has not yet been properly

Rajya Sabha on December 6, 1963 during discussion of a Resolution on Food Crisis

organised in communist countries. Even the Soviet Union imports wheat from the U.S. and wants to import it to the tune of Rs. 250 crores. In China the food position is not good, they too import. We cannot increase food production by introducing Communist techniques here.

The slogan of cooperative farming has been raised and it has created a sense of uncertainty in the minds of the farmers. Land reforms are needed. Land should belong to the tiller. Once he owns the land he should be assured that under no circumstances would he be deprived of it. If propaganda is being carried on against the Seventeenth Amendment of the Constitution the Food Minister should take this opportunity to declare that wherever land ceiling has been applied and the size of land-holding determined, under no circumstances would agricultural land be acquired. Land within the ceiling would belong to the farmer and if it is acquired he will be compensated at market rates. Just one declaration would end the whole propaganda. But in case you entertain the hidden hope that one day you would rob the small land-holders of their land, bring it together and do cooperative farming on that land the people would never accept it. The farmer is attached to his land, he would even tear open his chest ... *(Interruption)*...

SHRI AKBAR ALI KHAN : We do not want to deprive the small workers.

SHRI VAJPAYEE : That is what is being done.

SHRI M. GOVINDA REDDY : That is to be assured.

SHRI VAJPAYEE : Yes, let there be a declaration from the Government.

SHRI LOK NATH MISHRA : But their declaration does not mean anything.

SHRI P.L. KUREEL URF TALIB (U.P.) : They are not true to their word.

Let the Land Belong to the Farmer

SHRI VAJPAYEE : There is one more thing. You may make a declaration today but you may change it tomorrow. So in the coming constitutional amendment fix the ceiling and give the assurance that the farmer would not be deprived of land within the ceiling. The farmer should own the land. Introducing cooperative farming by the back door would not motivate the farmer, it will not increase production and it will strengthen the hands of the bureaucracy. Boundary delineation is a very good principle, all parties are agreed on it, but when it is put into practice it proves a source of harassment for the farmer and a situation of confrontation is created. We should decide our policy within our limits.

So far as distribution is concerned the Government has adopted the middle way. Some of our friends suggest that the Government should completely take over the grain trade. I do not agree with them, because this will neither give the farmer the right price for his produce, as the Government would fix a low-price for its purchase, nor will the consumer get it at the right price. The Government should have stocks for times of emergency and should open fair price shops, but the open market and the fair price shops should go together. If we take over the whole grain business from production to distribution it would lead to discontent in the country. The experience with controls is quite bitter. The people's temperament did not change, the bureaucracy's style of work did not change. And do not forget this is a democratic country. Every five years you ...

SHRI TARAKESHWAR PANDEYA (Uttar Pradesh) : I have a question.

SHRI VAJPAYEE : I submit time is very short.

SHRI PANDEYA : Please extend by a minute. My question is, if this Parliament can run the affairs of such a big country, conduct its administration, keep a police force, can it not undertake state trading and send to jail profiteering middle-men ? This is my question to you.

SHRI VAJPAYEE : Steps will have to be taken to eliminate the middlemen's profit. But these steps should not lead to difficulties that would be bigger than the difficulties caused by profit-earning. What sort of State trading are we talking about ? Today official agencies are being promoted and we are being told cooperatives will take the place of traders. But Delhi has recently provided an example of how cooperatives work. My friend Shri Bhupesh Gupta has referred to it. I shall place it before you at length.

There are cooperative stores in Delhi and they are authorised to bring in 500 tons of Gur from Uttar Pradesh. Now there is a ban on bringing in Gur from Uttar Pradesh. The Government should not have grudged if the farmers were getting a better price. But on the one hand Gur was stopped and on the other co-operatives are issued permits to bring in 500 tons of Gur. At what price was it purchased and at what price is it being sold in Delhi ? The other House was told the matter was being investigated. There is no need for an investigation. Those who conduct the cooperative stores have themselves admitted that they indulged in profiteering in Gur. They bought it cheap and sold it at a high price, making a profit of Rs. 17 per quintal.

Is profiteering bad for businessmen but not for cooperative stores? Recently some businessmen have been arrested. They did not display the rate list or some item was left out of the list, so Defenee of India Rules were invoked. Can DIR not be used against office-bearers of co-operative stores ? Why does the Home Ministry not strictly see at what rate the Gur was purchased and at what rate sold ? Receipts are available for this. But we are told a 'show cause notice' has been served. I say a *prima facie* case exists, there is no need for a show cause notice. The police and Central Intelligence should be brought into the picture in this matter. I charge that the figure in the receipt for Gur purchased in Muzaffarnagar was shown high. The Gur was brought cheap but the receipt has shown a high price. And in Delhi it was shown still higher. The managers of the stores cannot deny this. But no one will try to touch them, because they are Congress leaders and members of Parliament. They can resort to profiteering. In this regime they have the liberty to do so. But if anybody else displays a wrong list he would be arrested under the Defence of India Rules.

To whom will Cooperative Stores Sell ?

I would also like to know to whom these cooperatives would sell goods. Is it their business to sell their goods to businessmen or to the consumers ? This cooperative store ordered Gur through a businessman and sold it through a businessman. This cooperative store sells half the coal in Delhi. But it does not sell to the people, it sells to traders and makes a profit of Rs. 3,50,000 per month.

The question is not only of Gur, it is also of rice. The Food Ministry had given rice to these cooperative stores. On August 13, 1963 the Ministry gave a quota of 500 tons of rice to the co-operative store. Rice prices were rising in Delhi. The quota was given for the purpose of bringing in rice and selling it to the people at proper prices. But this co-operative store did not sell the rice; it deposited 4180 gunny bags of rice with the Central Warehousing Corporation. Is this not hoarding ? What was the need for a co-operative store to hoard rice ? That rice was given for selling to the people. Even today 1960 gunny bags out of 4180 are lying with the Warehousing Corporation. Is this not hoarding ? Will any action be taken against it ? What is the Government policy in this regard ?

The Food Minister told the Lok Sabha an investigation is being made. What is to be investigated ? It has been proved that they have made a profit. They also said something else. They said they sold Gur dearly because they had to give bribes to get Railway wagons. They have even challenged the Railway Minister. Whether they challenge the Railway Minister or not the Home Minister goes about declaring that corruption would be ended in two years. He says not only taking a bribe is an offence, giving it is also an offence. The Manager of a cooperative, a member of Parliament and a big Congress leader, stands in the House and states that he had to give a bribe to get a Railway wagon. Will there be no action against him? Where did he get the bribe money ? Was it his own ? Was it shown in the accounts of the cooperative store ? The question is, why should he not be proceeded against for bribery ?

If the Government is serious about checking prices from rising it should take strong action, it should give stern punishment. It is not a question of one individual or one party. If you want to create the right atmosphere in the country you should make a beginning at home. It is most undesirable that corruption should continue in Delhi under the very nose of the Government, that an economic empire should be established in the name of cooperatives and that a cooperative should be given a monopoly in coal, camphor and Gur. There is a 400 per cent profit in camphor and this cooperative store has been given monopoly rights to import it into Delhi. This cooperative also orders wrist-watches. And whom does it sell them ? Not to the people, but to traders, for making a profit. You say you will end corruption, but this is not the style to do it. I demand strict action against the office-bearers of this co-operative store. Just one example—and not a declaration about setting up a vigilance commission—would show if the Government is serious about checking profiteering and black-marketing.

Just one more thing and I shall conclude. I have given an amendment to the effect that in Uttar Pradesh and Bihar the sugarcane price should be Rs. 2 per maund. Fixing it lower has generated a lot of resentment there. And even if this democratic government does not care about discontent, the mills will not get good cane if it does not fetch a good price. Then whatever the restriction you put on Khandsari and Gur, the sugar mills will not get enough cane for their intended sugar production and the production target of 33 lakh tons will not be fulfilled. You should think of fixing cane prices at least Rs. 2 per maund. As it is, the farmers of Uttar Pradesh and Bihar are financially in a bad position. It would be very proper if the Government helped them in this way and did justice by them. Thank you.

Uniform Ceiling Law

Sir, the form in which the Joint Select Committee has presented this Constitution Amendment Bill is quite different from its previous form. When reference to the Select Committee was proposed it had been feared that even those farmers would be deprived of their right to own land whose land was included in the maximum ceiling Act. It is a matter of satisfaction that the Joint Select Committee has amended the Bill to the effect that in case a farmer owns land within the maximum ceiling laid down by law it would be acquired only at market rates. This amendment deserves to be welcomed.

Bharatiya Jana Sangh is in favour of a maximum ceiling on land. We cannot make the mistake of joining this question to that of urban propety. There is intense hunger for land in the country. From the social point of view the concentration of land in a few hands would neither help to increase production nor help in the fulfilment of our objective of minimising disparity. From this point of view land ceiling should be welcome, but there is a difficulty here. It is the States who decide the maximum land-holding. If the States so wish they can lower the ceiling and create uncertainty in the farmers' mind. There is no guarantee against this in the Bill. The Select Committee had proposed that the ceiling laws in the States should not be changed for at least 10-15 years. For increasing production it is necessary that the land should belong to the tiller, that he should get full returns for his labour and contribute in increasing production. At the same time it is also necessary that he should be assured that in the near future he would neither be deprived of the land he owns nor would the ceiling on it be lowered.

It is true that it is the States that make these laws, but formulating a common policy for the States should not be difficult at least today, when the same party rules all States and the ruling party is in a position to make all States amenable to its policies. If we protect the ceiling laws—as this Bill does by saying that they cannot be challenged in a court of law—we would also have to ensure that the State laws on ceiling are not amended in the near future.

The Orissa Congress had passed a resolution to the effect that the maximum land ceiling should be six acres. If the Congress Government of Orissa implements this resolution of its party the law there would have to be changed. As a result a feeling of uncertainty would be created in the farmers' minds, they would become doubtful about the future, and in such a mental condition they would not be able to put in the efforts and the resources that would be required for increasing production.

Rajya Sabha on June 5, 1964 on Constitution (Seventh Amendment) Bill relating to land reforms

I demand that even if the Central Government cannot make a constitutional provision to prevent change in the ceiling laws in the near future it should declare that the land that vests in a farmer and his family as per present ceiling laws would not be taken away from him in the near future. There would be no objection if changes in these laws are considered after 10-15 years to suit changing circumstances. But for the near future the farmers should be fully assured that the land with them will belong to them and they can invest money in it, adopt improved techniques of farming and improve their own condition besides making up the shortage of food in the country.

What will be the Maximum Ceiling ?

I hope the Government would give serious thought to this matter. We cannot leave it to the States, and if it was to be left to the States, there was no need for this amendment in the Constitution. If we give protection to State laws we can demand that the States should not play with the ceiling laws.

Sir, there is another aspect of this matter—what should be the maximum ceiling, and what are the factors that should be kept in view while implementing it? The Planning Commission had laid down some guidelines in this connection. They were sent to the States so that the States could make their ceiling laws in accordance with them. But in the Joint Select Committee we were surprised to see that the States adopted different policies in respect of the ceiling. Some States left sugarcane farms outside the ceiling while some others brought them within it, with the result that Parliament has had to protect both types of laws. Representatives of Maharashtra in the Joint Select Committee complained about this.

Personally I feel—and my party is also of the opinion—that a ceiling law should cover all types of crops, but if the Planning Commission recommends that sugarcane farms, tea and coffee plantations and efficiently run mechanised farms should not be covered by a ceiling the Commission should have made all the States agree to this policy. At present the States have various policies. In such a situation when all States ask for protection for their laws there is a possibility of discrimination against the citizens of one state and in favour of those of another, and of injustice, and Parliament is being asked to put its stamp of approval on this discriminatory policy.

I think the Central Government and the Planning Commission should still try to bring about uniformity in the ceiling laws of all states, for if they are not uniform there would be difficulties. The tendency of people to speak against each other would be strengthened. From this point of view uniformity in the laws of all States is necessary.

Thirdly, when the Bill was presented to the House for the first time there were 124 enactments, which were to be placed in the Ninth Schedule. Later their number was reduced, and from the way this was done it seems the Law Ministry has not thought about which ceiling laws need constitutional protection and which do not. Had the Law Ministry given proper thought to this it would not have had a long list of 124 laws in the previous Bill before sending it to the Joint Select Committee. Later, the Committee was told the number is being reduced and it was reduced to 88. Again, a new list was drawn up and we were told to include 8-9 new laws in it. All this shows that the Law Ministry does not give serious attention even to the important business of deciding which laws need protection and which do not.

Land Reforms—We Want No Delay, No Laxity

We want land reforms to be expeditious. We are not against giving special parliamentary protection to a law that the High Court or the Supreme Court may have struck down if there is a possibility of the Court verdict affecting many people. But this Bill includes laws whose legality has not yet been challenged and which have not been struck down by a Court, a High Court or the Supreme Court. Perhaps the Law Ministry apprehends that one day this law may be challenged and so wants to give it protection right now. This is not the right way to think. Except for a couple of clauses the ceiling laws have been accepted by the High Court and the Supreme Court. Putting a ceiling on land-holding is not against the Constitution, nor against the fundamental right to property.

It is argued that this Bill strikes at the fundamental right to earn and keep wealth. I agree that an individual should have the right to earn and keep wealth, and in a democracy we cannot take away this right. But there can be no right without a limit. Whenever we give a right it is always accompanied by a limit. We do not want to give anyone the freedom to have limitless wealth. When the society—especially a large section of it—is denied even basic needs of life, the right to property will also have to be restricted. There is no difference of opinion on putting a limit. The difference is on whether there should or should not be limiting big property and taking away the small earnings of hard toil. We did not oppose when Princely states and Zamindaris and Taluqadaris came to an end. Neither was there a need to oppose. A system should change in accordance with the times and those who try to stop the flow of time may be thrown aside. But I am afraid that even the small farmers may be deprived of their small pieces of land. Will they be given full compensation ? We cannot forget how the farmers have been banging the doors of Parliament for compensation.

Bill Raises Doubts

We cannot give full compensation to big people for all their property. We would scale it down in public interest. But it is necessary to fully ensure that the small farmer, the small shopkeeper, who lives by his labour, can earn property and has his property protected. But the types of laws protected in this Bill raise doubts. The Government thinks that as an amendment is being made in the Constitution, even those laws that are not related to land reforms should also be given protection.

For example, this includes a law from Mysore which deals with the removal of 12000 people from jobs. It is true that these traditional jobs have been going from father to son and from son to grandson. We do not think it proper that in a free and democratic India there should be such hereditary jobs. But I ask, how is this 'Mysore Village Offices Abolition Act', which has been included in the Bill for protection, related to land reforms ? It is possible that it would not be possible to end the jobs of 12000 people if this law is not passed or if Parliament does not give it protection. But if the jobs of these 12,000 people continue will that halt land reforms in Mysore? How can we protect that law when this is an exceptional arrangement ?

Now law can be challenged by the exercise of fundamental rights enshrined in the Constitution. Hence this special arrangement is being made and the Constitution amended, so that laws cannot be challenged. But we cannot use this opportunity for including in this Bill laws that are not related to land reforms. But perhaps the Government of Mysore thought : this is a good opportunity, the Constitution is being amended, this law is a harassment for us.

SHRI M. GOVINDA REDDY (Mysore) : May I say a word about it ? It was perhaps because some of the village officers had land grants as their remuneration that this Act has been included. That is all.

SHRI VAJPAYEE : If they had grants and they are to be paid in cash.

SHRI M. GOVINDA REDDY : They were Inams.

SHRI VAJPAYEE : Even then it is an entirely different matter. It relates only to 12,000 persons. It should not have been brought into this Bill.

SHRI M. GOVINDA REDDY : But they were by way of Inams. That is why they had to be resumed.

SHRI VAJPAYEE : But I fail to understand how the process of land reforms is retarded. Even if we say that these 12,000 persons are allowed to keep their land how is the process of land reforms retarded ? It might affect to some extent.

SHRI M. GOVINDA REDDY : Those Inams had to be resumed.

SHRI B. RAMAKRISHNA RAO (A.P.) : If that is not included in the Schedule it will not be applicable to the tenants of those lands. That is why that law is being protected.

SHRI VAJPAYEE : Do they have land above the ceiling limit ?

SHRI BIBHUDENDRA MISHRA, Deputy Minister in the Ministry of Law : It relates to land reforms in the sense that all these people were granted land in lieu of services. They no longer perform the services. How do you take away the land ? You pass an Act saying that since the services are not performed the lands had to be taken away. They are no longer performing the services. In that way it has been done.

SHRI VAJPAYEE : Even now I am not convinced. If they are not performing the services, still they possess the land. If they are prepared to cultivate the land and if the area of the land is under the ceiling limit, then there is no need to deprive them of their land.

SHRI BIBHUDENDRA MISHRA : In the Act also provision for compensation is there.

SHRI VAJPAYEE : There is a doubt that has been expressed with regard to amending the Constitution. It is a strong doubt and should be removed. Many doubts have been removed by changing the ceiling, but an assurance needs to be given that the ceiling law would not be used for forcing the farmers to join cooperative farming against their wishes. It is widely feared that the Nagpur session of the Congress has decided upon co-operative farming. There are two opinions about co-operative farming and there is no reason to believe that once co-operative farming is implemented all our land problems and production problems would be solved. Even in communist countries where co-operative farming has been introduced the experience is not good. To put it plainly,by adopting the technique of communist countries we can neither increase our production nor preserve individual freedom.

Let Co-operatives not be Forced on Farming

There can be no objection if some farmers want to work jointly, plough and irrigate jointly and sell their produce jointly. They are free to work together and the Administration may encourage them to do so. But if a farmer does not want to include his land in the common land of the village, wants to retain ownership of his land, wants to till it himself and wants that it should go to his sons on his death he should not be forced to join co-operative farming. There is a doubt that the Government is going to do this. This doubt should be removed.

The Central Government should make it clear that co-operative farming would be voluntary. It will be introduced only when the people want to farm together. It will not be forced on them. If it is forced it will not be *'Sahakari'* (co-operative) farming but *'Sarkari'* (official) farming. If the law is used to force co-operative farming on the farmers and deprive them of their land you cannot check their resentment with constitutional amendments. A widespread agitation would be launched and the Government would have to bow before public opinion. But there should be no scope for doubt in the farmers' minds. This doubt is still gaining strength.

The Bill includes a law from Gujarat under which any farmer's land can be changed into a co-operative farm and he cannot challenge it in a court of law. We are giving that law protection by this Bill. If the ceiling laws of some States can be exploited for introducing co-operative farming by the backdoor, I say do it by the front door, not by the back door. We cannot give protection to any law for co-operative farming, because there is a wide difference of opinion in respect of co-operative farming. Even the Government would agree that co-operative farming should not be forced on the farmers against their wishes. But the law in Gujarat that we are protecting provides that farmers' lands can be transferred to a co-operative but the farmer cannot approach a court of law.

Another way of having cooperative farming would be for the farmer to be the owner of the land on paper, by law, but he should hand it over to a cooperative for farming. But this would not be a good system. So if even those laws are given protection which create doubts in the farmers' minds it would not be possible to check the propaganda that the Government wants to deprive the farmers of their land. I believe the Government does not have such an intention, nor can it be allowed to do so. But if you do not want it and if your declared policy is that the farmer may join the type of farming of his choice what is the need of making such a law, and what is the need of Parliament's protection for laws that create the apprehension in the farmers' mind that they could be deprived of that land any time ?

Sir, I do not hope that the Law Minister will give satisfactory replies to the questions I have raised, because he is bent upon amending the Constitution and implementing the amendment as early as possible. I am not against amending the Constitution. I am not one of those who consider the Constitution something to be worshipped, something that should not be changed. We are living in revolutionary times. Circumstances have changed since the Constitution was passed in 1950. The people's feelings are changing. Their hopes and aspirations are increasing. In comparison our achievements fall short. If the gap between rising expectations and our accomplishments went on increasing it would endanger not only democracy but the very existence of the country.

So we should amend the Constitution, if need be in the interest of social justice, in order to bring about a social system that is not based upon exploitation but upon equal opportunity of progress for everyone. But it is not proper to include in this Constitution, under cover of amendment, laws whose legality has not yet been challenged nor those that have not yet been struck down by the High Court or Supreme Court. This is not a good tradition. If a State Government or a State Legislature makes a law that transgresses the present limits of the Constitution it should be challenged in a court of law, and if the court strikes it down the legislature should amend it. We can make exceptions, but we cannot make it a practice of affording Parliament's protection under pressure of the Congress majority to any laws passed by State Legislatures and State Governments that may go against the sentiments of the Constitution and are struck down by the High Court and the Supreme Court.

Which State Governments Want Land Reforms ?

After all we live under a federal system in which it is the function of the legislatures and Parliament to make laws and the function of the judiciary to interpret them. It would indeed be a black day for Indian democracy if we promote the tendency of legislatures and Parliament to make any laws and then limit the right of the courts to criticise those laws, to strike them down, by amending the Constitution. We can make an exception of some laws, as land reform cannot wait. It is already very much delayed. I even doubt the sincerity of the State governments about implementing land reforms. The ceiling law was made only when people distributed all their land among the members of their families. The purpose of making the ceiling law is to see that excess land is given to those who are landless. We want that those who are prepared to toil but have no other resource can own land and contribute to increasing production. As it is the ceiling laws have come late, and they have been made in such a way that no excess land remains. All the land was distributed among members of the family. Well, I am not against it. Although it has been distributed it has not been concentrated in one hand. But what have the State Governments done about the land that is lying with them and with the Central Government, the fallow land that can be made arable and distributed among the landless as their own ?

The Law Minister may say this problem has nothing to do with him. That is true. It is not a matter of law. But the State Governments and the Central government which keep tomtoming about land reforms and even stress that the Constitution should be amended in the name of land reforms, should be asked what steps they have taken to see that the fallow land lying with them, which can be made arable, is distributed among the landless. What the State Governments have done in this regard is not satisfactory. The Central government too has not been able to take revolutionary steps in this regard in the Union Territories ruled by it. The result is that hunger for land remains, and there is not enough incentive for farmers and workers to produce more.

I hope the Central Government will give serious thought to my proposals, and even if it is not possible to include them in this Bill it should clarify the following points as a matter of policy :

1. No farmer would be forced against his wishes to join cooperative farming.
2. No change in the present maximum ceiling laws made by the States will be made for the next 10-15 years.

This would assure the farmers that they would not be deprived of their land and land reforms would help us achieve the twin objectives of social justice and increased production. Thank you.

Cause of the Food Crisis Not the Farmer but the Government

Sir, Opposition parties are being charged with wanting to make political capital out of the food crisis. Should the Government and the parties supporting it expect that opposition parties should renounce politics, forget their duty and sit idle when the people cannot get essential commodities at reasonable prices and when their life is adversely affected ? We too have a sense of responsibility towards the people of this country, and when the government fails in its duty, when its food policy gets into difficulties and when it cannot successfully overcome those difficulties, it becomes the responsibility of the opposition parties to peacefully express the resentment and anger of the people.

Sir, when a hungry man becomes angry and his anger is suppressed, he revolts. When anger is silent, it produces a revolution. You should thank the opposition parties for peacefully and unitedly expressing the anger of the people. Had it been suppressed and had it seethed inside, peace and order in the country would have been put in great danger.

SHRI DEVKI NANDAN PANDE : You would have been responsible.

SHRI VAJPAYEE : The responsibility lies with the Government that created the food crisis.

AN HON. MEMBER : Who created the crisis ?

SHRI VAJPAYEE : The Government did. The *Review of the Food Situation* had admitted that signs of pressure on it were already apparent in the first half of 1963. The Government also knew that the wheat crop had gone bad and probably 19 lakh tons less wheat had been produced. Then why did the Government not take a farsighted view of the coming crisis? The Government may not expect crops to go bad, but when that happens demand for wheat would increase and prices would go up. Why did the Government not keep enough stocks to meet this situation ? The Food Minister should place figures before the House. How much of a buffer stock of wheat did the Government have when Sardar Swaran Singh became Food Minister and how much of it was there when he left the Ministry ?

Is it not true that he was very generous, very kindheated in releasing buffer stocks but did not care to replenish them ? Today we hear that ships sailing from Australia are being called to Bombay. The Governments of the USA, UK and Canada are being asked to direct their ships and feed the poor of this country. When the Government was all the time declaring that it would not allow a food crisis to develop, that if it did develop there was so much

Rajya Sabha on September 17, 1964 on the Calling Attention Motion on Food Problem

foodgrain in stock that the market would be flooded with it, why was it not done ? We are importing foodgrains on a large scale. Why were they not available in the market in times of need ? Why were our godowns not filled up ?

There is one more question I would like to ask. There was great difficulty in unloading the ships at Bombay harbour, the ships had to lie at anchor for months and the foodgrain could not reach scarcity areas. Could not the Food Ministers who preceded you make sure that the ships would not have to be at anchor longer than necessary and that there would be no difficulty in unloading the foodgrains and reaching it to scarcity areas ? I say both these problems were ignored.

One may disagree with Shri S.K. Patil's food policy. But by building up ample stocks he created a sense of confidence in the country's markets. Later this confidence diminished, was shaken and a feeling spread in the country that Government godowns did not have enough foodstocks. Then prices went up. People started hoarding, and the result is today's crisis. This crisis is the result of the Government's wrong policies. Opposition parties cannot share only the blame. Did the Government look at this crisis as a national crisis? Congress members now say this difficulty should be overcome by mutual consultation. I may inform them that it was at my instance that a meeting of opposition leaders at the Centre was called. The Prime Minister did not suggest it. The Food Minister too did not think it necessary to call a meeting of Opposition leaders. I wrote to him saying the situation was serious and suggested that a meeting of Opposition leaders be called. You are not prepared even for an exchange of views.

Government should Create a Crisis and We should Leave our Duty ?

Sir, when the Government creates a problem should we leave our duty at such a time in the name of nationalism ? That cannot be. Of course if there is a flood or an earthquake or danger of foreign aggression we shall stand behind the Government. But in the event of an internal crisis resulting from the Government's wrong policies we shall certainly serve the people by peacefully organising them. Demonstrations and strikes are components of democracy. You should congratulate the opposition parties and the people on the fact that except for Amedabad there were no incidents of violence anywhere. We also assure you that we do not want a violent agitation. But after all, patience has a limit. Ask the people of Uttar Pradesh and of Maharashtra who cannot pay the increased prices of things and cannot buy enough foodgrains.

What was the need to divide the country into separate zones ? In Europe national barriers are breaking down, a common market is coming up, and in our country we are building walls between States. Wheat from the U.S. can reach Bombay quickly, but wheat from Punjab cannot go to U.P. quickly. Why were these zones made ? Do they not strike at nationalism ? Do they not impede the easy flow of trade ? The opposition parties were agreed that these wheat zones should be abolished. What is the difficulty in doing so ?

Is not politics in Punjab and Madhya Pradesh involved in this ? I agree that if the zones were abolished and free flow of foodgrains allowed the Government would have to see that the traders do not exploit the situation and there is no unchecked price-rise in the scarcity-hit areas where wheat is sent, but this zonal scheme has no propriety.

For Everyone His Own Shame

I regret it was observed during this discussion that we should be ashamed that we are importing wheat from the US. Kakasaheb Gadgil is ashamed that rice comes from Punjab. Shri Bhupesh Gupta is ashamed that wheat comes from the U.S. But nobody is ashamed that we cannot give enough food to the people. I do not want to present figures. That is not the point at issue. But it is true that there have been starvation deaths in Uttar Pradesh and Bihar. It is a matter of shame that because food is not available people eat mango stones and roots of trees. We buy wheat from the U.S., we do not beg for it. When we take rice from Pakistan we pay for it. This is not to be ashamed of. But when we cannot step up food production in the country adequately what other way is there to allay the hunger of the people except to import it ? Mere sentiments do not allay hunger—and, as the Sanskrit saying goes, what sin does a hungry man not commit ? It was cheap sentimentality that had prompted the late Prime Minister to declare in 1948 that the country would be self-sufficient in food in a couple of years. We should have self-sufficiency as our objective but we should not fall prey to this cheap sentimentality and stop importing foodgrains. This could still create an internal crisis which we may perhaps not be able to handle.

Some long-term steps also need to be taken. It is said that agriculture has an important role in our economy. Last night the Planning Commission circulated a note among members saying 70 per cent of the people in the country directly depend upon agriculture. About 50 per cent of the national income comes from agriculture. Agriculture provides the raw materials for industrial development, and people connected with agriculture provide the market for industrial products. Two-thirds of our people depend upon agriculture. Without agricultural development industrial development is not possible. But merely saying so would not develop agriculture. Some other figures in the same note reveal that while our food production target for the Third Plan was 10 crore tons we could not produce more than 9 crore 20 lakh tons. There is a shortfall of 80 lakh tons. How will it be made up ?

Why did Agriculture Fall behind the Target ?

Our targets from irrigation, for improved seed and for fertilizer have not been fulfilled, and the Planning Commission thinks that this shortfall in target achievement would lead to a shortfall of 49 lakh tons in food production. May I know if the opposition is responsible even for the shortfall in the achievement of all these targets ?

AN HON. MEMBER : Or is the weather responsible?

SHRI VAJPAYEE : Or is the weather responsible . It is the administration that is responsible. The administration should own its mistakes.

The most important thing is that the annual food production rate in the Third Plan is the same as in the First Plan. In the First Plan the annual growth rate was 2.5 per cent. In the Second Plan it went up to 3.5 per cent. Now in the third Plan we have come back to 2.6 per cent. Our population is growing by 2.3 per cent. People are migrating from the villages to the cities. Their food habits are changing. When people earn more they want to eat better food. The farmer's condition has also improved and he wants to keep the foodgrains for himself. At this rate how can we solve the food problem ?

Two other things have led to the food crisis. One of them is the Congress Party's policy of raising hollow slogans. The Nagpur slogan of cooperative farming has created a sense of uncertainty in the farmer's mind. We accepted the principle that land should belong to the tiller, but by raising the slogan of cooperative farming we have made him apprehensive that he might lose his land any time. Once he fears this he will not invest in land development, sinking wells and adopting new techniques of farming. We need to remove this fear from the farmer's mind. It is easy to say farmers should come together to farm, but it is difficult to farm together. When Congress leaders cannot serve the country unitedly how can we tell the farmers to farm unitedly ? When even the government and opposition parties cannot work together in times of national crisis we cannot expect only the farmers to work together. We cannot close our eyes to practicality.

SHRI CHANDRA SHEKHAR : The cat is out of the bag.

SHRI VAJPAYEE : It is not enough to raise a slogan, you have to have adequate arrangements to implement it. We have had land reforms and it is necessary to carry them through for the sake of food production. We have imposed a land ceiling, and this too needs to be implemented firmly. Those States where the land reform process is not yet over should complete it. At the same time it should be declared that there would be no change in the ceiling laws in the next 10-15 years. This suggestion has been made by Shri Sriman Narayan, member of the Planning Commission, and it is a very proper suggestion. We did land reforms, we passed a ceiling Act and we fixed a ceiling limit under it. Now we should tell the farmers that the land within that ceiling will remain with them, that would get an incentive price for the maximum foodgrain they can produce in it, and that this would benefit them as also resolve the national crisis posed by the shortfall in food.

The Government should go into the Market as a Buyer

Sir, some parties in the country demand that the Government should take over foodgrain trade. Some parties want the government to take over wholesale trade, some others want it to take over retail trade. I say this is not a matter of principles, this is a matter of practical considerations. I would like the Government to go into the market as a buyer, and from this point of view I welcome the Food Minister's plan for a corporation. But those who advise the government to take over the entire food distribution arrangement, from godown to kitchen, are no friends of the Government. They do not know what difficulties this will mean. Does the government have enough funds to buy foodgrains ? Does the government have a distribution machinery ? If the government does not have all these things it will first have to set them up, then alone can it think of taking over the whole trade. If the government takes over this responsibility today the food situation would become still more serious. There should be a partial take-over by the Government and it should build up ample stocks by paying the farmers remunerative prices—stocks not only of imported foodgrain but domestic as well, which the Government could release to the market in order to check a price- rise. Today had the Government enough food-grain stocks in its godowns—whether imported or domestic—food prices and prices of other things would not have risen so high. If finally, the government decided to take the whole trade over I would not stand in the way. But whenever the Government takes over anything the people's hardships increase. Controls bring corruption with them. We cannot close our eyes to the type of government machinery that we have. We also cannot close our eyes to the human material that we have. So let not the Government go in for a monopoly, let it go in for a partial take-over of trade, so that, when the need arises, it can influence the market.

Foodgrain Prices

One more thing and I shall conclude. There is the question of foodgrain prices. It cannot be divorced from the rest of the economy. The Third Plan document has a sentence in it—I quote : "The success of a price policy depend upon a successful farm price policy."

This farm policy has not yet been fashioned, and yet the Finance Minister is now trying to develop it and we wish him success. He should adopt a practical point of view and proceed in the direction he has taken. I do not want to praise him more, as that too would create difficulties for him. He would be told that as the Jana Sangh is praising him there must certainty be something wrong with his policies. But the question of prices needs to be seriously considered. Prices do go up in a developing economy, but they should do so within a limit. Rising prices should go hand in hand with an increasing purchasing power. Today the increase in prices does not have the capacity to buy foodgrains at that price. So the whole economic system has to be reconsidered.

Policies should be Dynamic, Not Static

I am sorry to see that time and again the late Pt. Nehru is mentioned and the government is made to swear that it would not change his policies. May I know if there would be no changes even if circumstances change ? Policies are either static or they are dynamic. They have to be changed in keeping with the circumstances. At present it is not necessary to change the basic policies, but if circumstances demand a change no government can deny them, with all due deference to the departed leader. How will we fulfil the people's need for essential commodities? Industrial development is necessary, and for that we need heavy industry too, but we cannot ignore the people's basic needs. After all we are a democracy, not a dictatorship. Every five years you have to go to the people, and if you make a mistake we are here to exploit it.

In a democratic system economic planning cannot ignore the people's immediate needs. Having laid a firm foundation for industrial development we should concentrate more on agriculture and the production of consumables, change our economic, material and fiscal policies, cut down government expenditure, print less currency notes and make our policies more realistic. Then alone can we contain this crisis. The situation is not only difficult, it is also serious. If proper steps are not taken, proper plans not made, it can get out of control, so the government must wake up and act. Thank You.

Legislation—No Solution to Food Problem

Madam, on November 5, the Government issued an Ordinance. Now a Bill is being presented to make that Ordinance into a law. The question is, when Parliament was to meet from November 16 why was the Ordinance issued on November 5 ? The Food Minister should tell the House how many people were proceeded against under the Ordinance during the 11 days from November 5, when the Ordinance was issued, and November 16, when Parliament session started. So far as I know, except for a couple of cases no action was taken under the Ordinance. Was it not possible to met out punishment in these couple of cases with the powers that the Government possesses ? Was it necessary to issue an ordinance 11 days before Parliament met ? Was the food situation to worsen seriously during these 11 days ? Had some serious crisis developed on November 5 that could not have been foreseen by the Government during the last Parliament session, and to resolve which the Government did not think its present extraordinary powers were enough ?

Madam, in a parliamentary democracy an ordinance should be issued only when it is essential and when there is an apprehension that in the absence of such an ordinance a situation might develop which the Administration may not ordinarily be able to contain. So far the Government has not explained why it had become necessary to issue the Ordinance on November 5. Had the Government so wished, it could have brought about such an amendment in the law in the last session of Parliament, when it was warned that the food situation would deteriorate still further. But at that time we were told that the situation is certainly serious but we have taken care of it and within a few days it would be under control. The issuing of the Ordinance shows that the Government could not act with foresight. We shall not hesitate to arm the Government with powers provided it can prove that without them it cannot successfully solve the food problem.

Why Ordinance ?

At the same time we have to look at the reasons given for issuing the Ordinance. The statement issued along with it is laughable. It says there is an Emergency in the country. Defence of India Rules are in force, but this situation is not lasting, it could change and Defence of India Rules will not be always there, so it is necessary to amend the Essential Commodities Act.

Rajya Sabha on December 15, 1964 on the Essential Commodities (Amendment) Ordinance 1964 and the Bill

What I want to know is — was this Administration under the impression that the Emergency would end before Parliament session began on November 16 and Defence of India Rules would be abrogated ? It is true that this situation would not always prevail, but in the situation that prevails today the Government is equipped with extraordinary powers under Defence of India Rules which it can use for stern action against grain dealers, and hoarders. But the Emergency will not continue, so the issuance of the Ordinance cannot be justified. The statement that has been issued does not make it clear that this Ordinance will have an impact in two ways. In the first place it provides for summary trials, and secondly, in some cases the right to appeal has been denied. The statement only reveals one truth but hides the other. I cannot understand the reason for this.

Even if the ordinance had not been issued on November 5, the Food Minister could have immediately presented the amendment when Parliament began its session on November 16 and secured the approval of the House. Then what made the Central Government issue the Ordinance on November 5 ? Can the Food Minister satisfy the House that there was no other go ? He should say in how many cases proceedings were launched under the Ordinance. Perhaps no cases were filed except for one in Delhi. On December 2 it was asked in the other House how many matters had come before the Government under this Ordinance. The reply given was that so far no matter had come up. If, perhaps the Food Minister has come to know some facts after December 2 he should take the House into confidence and say in how many matters action was taken under the Ordinance. But there cannot be many such matters.

The Government's Ulterior Motives

It would have been better if the Government had not issued this Ordinance. Sometimes one suspects that the Government may be arming itself with more and more powers in order to cover up its failures on the food front. As it is the Government does not lack powers. It is not that the Food Minister wants a couple of arrows because the Government's quiver is empty. The bitter truth is that the Government could not take care of the food situation by effectively using the powers that Parliament has given it. The Detention Act could be used—has been used—the Defence of India Rules are there, and even without the Essetial Commodities Act being amended the Government had powers that could be used. But perhaps the Government thinks the problem can be solved simply by adding to its powers. I beg to differ. So long as powers are not firmly used the purpose for which this Ordinance was issued or for which the Government is bringing forward this Bill will not be served.

No one can deny that the food situation is serious and despite warnings the Government is not acting farsightedly. I agree there are difficulties in the Government's way. It is easy to provide for summary trials of traders. The Government can also arm itself with the power to punish them without their having the right to appeal against the punishment, but that is no guarantee that the government machinery would act precisely in those matters that need action. The experience is that when the bureaucracy is re-equipped with wide powers those powers are misused and even honest traders and small traders suffer.

There can be no two opinions about the need for the Government to act sternly against profiteers. Those who hoard foodgrains are making a profit out of scarcity and do not deserve mercy. They are enemies of the society and deserve the most rigorous punishment, but so far the government has failed to bring them to book. This failure is not due to Government not having the power to punish. Nor because they get away on appeal. Nor even because there are no summary trials. It is because action is not taken against those who deserve to be proceeded against, and because some politics intervenes. And those who should not be acted against are proceeded against under extraordinary powers. I can quote an example of Delhi.

Reason for a Raid

There is a leading businessman of Delhi — I do not want to name in the House, but if the Food Minister wants to know I can tell him—who was raided only because he is connected with an opposition party and is against the ruling party. It is a different matter that the raid revealed nothing. At the same time strict action was not taken against those at whose places raids were conducted and those raids yielded evidence, because they are connected with the ruling party.

It is not necessary to tell the House how the Central Cooperative Store of Delhi is indulging in irregularities. Its Chairman was not proceeded against because he is a member of Parliament and is connected with the Congress, although those working under him have been arrested and the police are taking them to court. If politics comes in the way the problem is not going to be solved, whatever the powers the Government acquires. When we are reluctant to arm the Government with more powers here it is not because we support the profiteers but because we fear those powers would be misused and a discriminatory policy adopted on political considerations.

We also fear that small and honest businessmen will also be caught along with big and dishonest businessmen. We also fear for the farmer—what will be his condition ? If he wants to store grain at home and thinks of selling it when the time comes will he not come within the category of dealer under the proposed Bill ? Will he not be proceeded against ?

The Food Minister has admitted that foodgrains are being hoarded and there is a nexus between big businessmen and big farmers involved in this. How will this nexus be eliminated ? These days big dealers do not store foodgrains in their godowns, they have paid money to the farmers and in exchange for that money the foodgrains are stored in the farmers' granaries. It is not possible for the Government to carry out raids from village to village and bring out the farmers' stocks from their granaries. If the traders are raided the raids will not yield foodgrains. They will go scot-free because the farmers have stored them on behalf of the traders. How will this ordinance solve this problem ? Those who deserve stern punishment should be punished, but summary trials and no right to appeal are not things that can be welcome. Of course profiteering can also not be welcome. When starvation stalks the land no one can be allowed to store more foodgrains than necessary. But is it enough only to strengthen the law or to amend it ?

What was the Outcome of Previous Amendments?

Had amending the law been enough to solve the problem, it would not have arisen in the first place. This is not the first time the Essential Commodities Act is being amended. There have been amendments in the past. But in how many cases was action taken on the basis of the amendments ? It is the same administrative machinery and the same political situation. I for one do not think the Government would triumph over the food crisis merely by taking over powers.

It has been suggested that the provision for a minimum sentence of one month and no appeal should be extended to three months' sentence, so that this amendment could be brought to the level of the Criminal Procedure Code. Even Congress members had made this suggestion, but perhaps the Food Minister could not accept it. It was also suggested that the sentence for technical offences should be less, as they should not be considered as important as major offences, but the present amendment does not make any distinction between the two. If anyone forgets to display a list he would merit as severe a penalty as is given to a big hoarder.

Madam, a solution of the food crisis besetting the country requires both short-term and long-term measures. As yet the Government has not been able to decide upon the long-term steps. I cannot avoid the temptation to refer to a cartoon in an English - language newspaper this morning. In it the Food Minister is shown asking the Prime Minister — what is our food policy today ? It indicates that the food policy changes from day to day. Sometimes, we are told that the food situation, the food crisis, is under control, sometimes that it would continue for years. Sometimes they say we have made a law that would work like a panacea—prices would come down and there would be ample foodstocks available. But no steps have proved effective.

Ridiculous Advice

At times I am surprised to see that these days wherever the Prime Minister goes he advises students to go to the villages and explain to farmers how to grow more foodgrains. The students should be busy with books, examinations are near, it is meaningless to tell them to go to the villages. And what will they do there ? They would prove a burden for the villagers. They cannot distinguish between an ear of wheat and an ear of Jau. They have not studied agriculture. Even agriculture graduates do not really help the villagers. Does it mean anything when you tell students to go to the villages and tell farmers to grow more food ? But the Government is doing everything haphazard. It seems it is losing its grip, it is not able to decide what policy it should firmly follow to face the crisis. The result is that at times there is a two-year plan, at times there is talk of ten years. This is not the way to solve the food problem. If the Food Minister acquires more powers we shall not stand in the way, we shall not give the Government the chance to say we had asked for powers but you did not give them, and so we could not overcome the food crisis.

The late Prime Minister used to say if anyone indulges in profiteering and blackmarketing we would hang him by an electric pole—at that time the British were ruling here. When freedom came and the general of the freedom-fighters became Prime Minister we waited for 17 years to see someone hanging by an electric pole, but in vain. Now there is no talk of hanging anybody, nor is such talk proper. We are a democracy, we have a constitution, we have fundamental rights and we have a judiciary to protect those fundamental rights. We want that whoever is punished is punished under the law and he should have the right to appeal. I do not approve of this law, as it does not provide for freedom to appeal. But if the Minister wants such a law I shall not stand in the way. He may have such a law and punish whomsoever he wishes. Even if you grind the worm with the wheat we shall not raise our voice in times of crisis. But if, even after grinding the wheat and the worm together the administration could not bring down prices and could not provide enough food for the people the administration will not have the right to administer the country.

The Minister's Haste

I may repeat that there was no need to promulgate an ordinance on November 5. The Minister could have waited for Parliament to meet. But on the one hand he did not act with foresight, and on the other, he acted in haste. The heavens were not going to fall in these 11 days. It is not very democratic to rule by ordinance, so I have moved that this Ordinance should be withdrawn, because the proposed Bill talks of punishment with retrospective effect. Nothing very much wrong would happen even if the House agrees with me and annuls the Ordinance. The Minister's Bill can be passed. The only difference would be that in the couple of matters in which action has been initiated under the Ordinance it would not be possible to give punishment with retrospective effect.

DEPUTY CHAIRPERSON : Vajpayeeji, that is for them to answer.

SHRI VAJPAYEE : Madam, the discussion on my resolution and on the Food Minister's Bill, in which members of all parties participated, makes one point clear — it is that the whole House is agreed that the Government does not need more powers. What is needed is for the Government to firmly exercise the powers it has. Justifying the issuance of an ordinance 11 days before Parliament met the Minister had said some time would be required for a machinery to be set up in various States and hence it was considered useful to promulgate an ordinance on November 5. Tell me, when did the States set up their separate machineries ? Is it not true that for many days after the ordinance was issued the States did not think of setting up any sort of apparatus ? I would draw the Minister's attention to a report from Patna that appeared in the *Hindustan Times* of November 19 :

> "The Bihar Government will soon set up its machinery for the enforcement of the Anti-Hoarding and Anti-Profiteering Ordinance providing for the summary trials of traders and officials."

Bihar and other States

The Government of Bihar has announced that this machinery would be set up on November 13. Now when there was no machinery in the States and it was not set up even after the Centre's caution — and I believe Bihar is not alone in this respect, other States would not lag behind — what was the point in promulgating an ordinance in the States? If there was no machinery in the States till the 13th and the State was thinking of setting up such a machinery the Food Minister could have waited till Parliament met. This Essential Commodities Bill could have been given priority over other Bills and it would not have been necessary for the Government to issue an ordinance. But I am still not sure if the Government did any serious thinking before issuing the Ordinance. Had it done so the Prime Minister would not have stated in a speech at Allahabad on November 12 that the food crisis would soon be over. I quote the press report that appeared on November 13 :

> "Food crisis near end," says Shastri.
>
> "Allahabad, P.T.I., November 12, Prime Minister Lal Bahadur Shastri today said that the Government would tide over the present food crisis in a few days."

This report was not rebutted. Did the Prime Minister really think so, or was the speech aimed at the election then taking place at Phulpur ? Were the food crisis to be over in a few days there was no point in issuing the Ordinance on November 5, and then what is the need to bring forward a Bill ? After issuing the Ordinance you should have created an atmosphere in the country to the effect that profiteers and black-marketeers would be severely dealt with, for which the people and the opposition should cooperate with you. But the Prime Minister made a speech saying in a few days the food crisis would be overcome. Such speeches sour the atmosphere. A speech like this raises doubts about the Government's intentions. It creates the suspicion that the Government takes the situation lightly or plays it down or wants to play it down.

In the last session I had said and now many Congress members have repeated that the food crisis is going to get still more serious. Things would go from bad to worse. What has happened in Punjab should open our eyes. We should learn from what has happened in Kerala. Yesterday the Food Minister rushed to Chandigarh — I must compliment him for rushing to wherever there is a problem and trying to solve it. But it is not a temporary crisis, a momentary crisis, it is a long-term crisis, a serious crisis, and we must heed foreign experts' warning that the food situation is going to worsen still further.

Arrests In Calcutta

Even after this Ordinance was issued some traders of Calcutta were arrested under Defence of India Rules, not under this Ordinance. I would like to place before you some portions of the editorial of the *Hindustan Standard* of November 15. Traders were arrested there, but not under the new ordinance. Commeniting on this the paper asked : if the Government does not want to enforce this Ordinance why was it promulgated? I quote :

> "It is not known why the Anti-Hoarding Ordinance promulgated last week is being allowed to rust in the Government armoury. Friday's arrests in Calcutta were not made under the new enactment".

SHRI C. SUBRAMANIAM, Minister of Food and Agriculture: May I point out that this does not provide for the arrest ? This provides for procedure in the trials. The arrests will have to be made either under the Criminal Procedure Code or the Defence of India Rules. I do not think there is anything wrong in that.

SHRI VAJPAYEE : Was it not open to the West Bengal Government to have made a declaration according to the Ordinance and then to have proceeded against the traders according to these provisions ?

SHRI C. SUBRAMANIAM : This is only for the purpose of changing the procedure for summary trials. For arrests they will have to use other laws.

DEPUTY CHAIRMAN: The common laws.

SHRI VAJPAYEE : I entirely agree with the Hon. Minister, but why was not summary trial resorted to in this case ?

SHRI C. SUBRAMANIAM : That does not deal with summary trials. They will have to be arrested under the Defence of India Rules or the Criminal Procedure Code. That is some misinformed criticism.

DEPUTY CHAIRMAN : This deals only with the procedure.

SHRI VAJPAYEE : Why then was the Ordinance promulgated? If the Ordinance provides for an amended procedure, before action was taken, why did not the West Bengal Government issue a notification in the Gazette and take action under the Ordinance ?

Who Demanded the Amendment ?

Madam, I do not know if this amendment in the law is being made at the instance of the States or at the instance of the Chief Ministers or if the Central Government is doing it of its own accord, for its implementation will also lie with the States. Their officials will take action if they choose, and the State Governments would have to provide with a Gazette notification for summary trial under this Act. Have the State Governments suggested such a law ? And will they honestly take action under it ? Whatever has happened now shows that they will not take such action. I would like to know how the Central Government would overcome the food crisis by making new laws one after the other if the State Governments do not cooperate.

We must not forget that all provinces have Congress Governments. The same party is in power in all of them. If it is so difficult to coordinate State and Central policies even in such a situation and the Central Food Minister cannot make the Chief Ministers agree with what he says, think how difficult it would be to put a Central policy into practice when the States will have Government of different parties.

The Food Minister had agreed that from the point of view of foodgrains there should be no zones, the whole country should be considered one unit, but he left his position under pressure from the Chief Ministers. Now every province is a separate zone. Now walls are being raised between the districts within the States. This is not the way to solve the food problem.

Then again the Government does not have clear ideas from the long-range point of view. The Food Minister had said he was thinking of setting up an agriculture commission, but the Government has not been able to take any decision in this regard. Then how will hoarded grain come out ? Will it be taken out from the farmers too ? If yes, what steps will be taken for it ? Will the Government risk unpopularity ? On all these matters the Government should take a clear stand. But it seems its failure is egging it on to acquire more and more powers.

Let Government Look for Real Solutions

Madam, we do not mind giving powers to the Government, but not for a moment are we ready to accept that the problem would be solved by its acquiring such powers right now. The situation is serious, it may go out of control and the Government should take steps and prepare a plan right now. I hope the situation does not worsen by the time Parliament meets again and there is no scope for the Government to ask the House for more powers.

I had welcomed the Food Minister on his appointment. The policies he has adopted seem to go in the right direction, but we do not see their results. There is certainly something lacking somewhere, and it should be identified. If the situation worsens the Government would not be forgiven. You are getting all the powers you are asking for. I shudder to think of what would happen if you could not check rising food prices and could not make adequate food available to the people on exercising these powers. Even Congress members have warned, and I wish even if the Food Minister does not listen to the opposition he listens to these warnings. Let him read the writing on the wall. The Government's failure on the food front may endanger law and order, economic planning, even democracy. It would be the government's misfortune and the country's misfortune if the administration could not read the writing on the wall. Thank you.

Do not Frighten the Farmer, but Gain His Support

Madam, the country is faced with a serious food crisis. It should not be played down, nor should it be blown up. Had the situation been normal, had the country not been entangled in a war, there would have risen a big agitation. Opposition parties are inspired by a feeling of patriotism. Our people realise the gravity of the situation. So in spite of famine-like conditions in many parts of the country the people are patiently waiting for the Government to take effective steps to overcome the crisis. While nature is partly responsible for the present food crisis the Government's policies are also the cause for it.

The Food Minister has presented a plan of how food production would be increased in future. Plans have been presented in the past too, but they were confined to paper, not implemented. There is no solid basis to believe that they would be implemented, because we have the same administrative set-up at the Centre and in the States. The Food Minister expects that with the same apparatus, the same system, his long-term plans which have so far proved a failure on the food front would succeed. The question is, what steps are being taken to tackle immediate difficulties ? However attractive the long-term plans, they cannot allay the people's hunger. Some strong Government action is needed for this.

For the past many months we have been hearing that rationing would be introduced in cities with a population of one lakh and more. Will the Food Minister succeed in making the provinces implement this policy ? Are all State Governments preparing to introduce rationing ? There are some States that do not wish to do so—not for economic reasons but for political reasons. Some State administrations are against rationing because it goes against vested interests and because there is a nexus between them and big grain dealers.

In the capital city of Delhi itself we see that rationing is to be introduced from December 15 but preparations are not complete and cards have not been distributed at all places.

SOME HON. MEMBERS : It has begun from today.

SHRI C. SUBRAMANIAM, Minister of Food and Agriculture : It has been introduced from today.

SHRI MULKA GOVIND REDDY (Mysore) : Sugar from the 15th.

Rajya Sabha on December 8, 1965 on the Food Problem

Rationing

SHRI VAJPAYEE : Yes, sugar too would be included from the 15th and grain rationing has begun today, but there are no preparations for it and I doubt if the Delhi Administration is serious about succeeding with it. If the Food Minister wants the rationing policy to succeed we must act firmly. Our party was so long against rationing, not as a matter of principle but because the experience with rationing so far has not been very happy. It leads to black-marketing, fosters corruption and encourages smuggling. But in the present critical situation there is no alternative to rationing. If we want to fight and win the war and if we want to make a definite quantity of foodgrains available to the people at proper prices we would have to go in for rationing. We are prepared to support rationing. I had said before and I would like to repeat on behalf of my party that we shall back whatever steps the Government takes to overcome the present food crisis and cooperate in implementing it, but politics must not come in the way of the ruling party. If the opposition parties are expected not to make the food crisis a political issue we expect the same of the ruling party. I do not have a complaint against the Centre, my complaint is against the State Governments. They are still not serious about introducing rationing. Sometimes it is said if it is implemented the people would have to pay for it and then people would have to buy foodgrains at a high price. Sometimes it is said they would recover the expenses from the Centre. It seems the State Government have no realisation of the gravity of the situation. We are going through an explosive situation. In some parts of the country the situation is terrible. How the common man lives there is a big question for me. How people can manage a living when foodgrains sell for a rupee a kilo or more is a very big question. If the State Governments do not rise above the situation it would be difficult to overcome this crisis.

National Food Policy

One thing that is clear is that we would have to formulate a national food policy for the whole country. The Food Minister has already said that when rationing is introduced in cities with a population of one lakh there should be no place for food zones. At present provinces with more produce are not prepared to care for provinces with less produce. There are barriers between State and State, and between one district and another in the same State. I have recently been to West Bengal. There foodgrains from surplus districts cannot go to deficit districts. The result is difficulties at both places. The West Bengal government has introduced rationing in Calcutta and the Food Minister is all praise for it, but I have a lot of complaints against the West Bengal Government's food policy. One complaint I would like to place before the Food Minister relates not only to West Bengal but to other provinces as well.

Remunerative Price

You charge the farmers a levy, requiring them to deposit their produce, whether rice or wheat, in Government godowns at a price fixed by the Government. But on what basis is this price fixed ? Take West Bengal. There the price of paddy has been fixed at Rs. 14.40 to Rs. 16 per maund, but according to the West Bengal Government's figures themselves the production cost of the paddy ranges from Rs. 5 to Rs. 21. If that is the production cost how can you ask for it at Rs. 16 per maund ? That is the maximum price. In such a situation how will the farmer be motivated to sell his produce ? It is true that he will sell it to the Government as there is no go for him. But his tendency will be to hoard to hide it, so that he can get a good price in the market. If we want that after keeping the foodgrains he requires for his own use the farmer should sell all the rest to the Government the price should be attractive, it should take the production cost into consideration, and it should also motivate him to invest in agriculture for greater production in future. In West Bengal jute fetches a better price than paddy, then why will the farmer not sow jute rather than paddy? The farmer is attracted to cash crops because he hopes for better returns from them. If we want to prevent him from going in that direction his foodgrains should fetch a remunerative price.

The Heavy Levy

There is also another thing. The levy for every farmer is so heavy that it would be beyond his capacity to give. Take West Bengal. A farmer with 10 acres of land will be required to give 128 maunds of paddy by way of levy. This means the Government expects 12.8 maunds of paddy per acre. But West Bengal's average is 10 maunds of paddy per acre, then how can he pay 12 maunds ? If he does not give he will fall in the clutches of the bureaucracy and would be harassed. Our heartless bureaucracy would terrorise the farmer in the name of levy. This would not enthuse the farmer to cooperate for greater food production. We know it is a difficult choice. We have to make do with whatever Government machinery we have and carry out our programme, but while fixing the limit of the levy we must ensure that the farmer can keep the grain he needs. There is a similar complaint from Bihar. Can we not launch an official as well as popular movement to awaken the patriotism of the farmer and tell him to keep the grain he needs and hand over all the rest to the Government? Can all parties and all leaders not come together to create such a wave in the country ? I believe it can be done, but it has not been tried. If we went from village to village and conducted a mass movement telling the farmers that there is a serious food crisis in the country, that it is not necessary to hoard at such a time and that he should give it to the Government for the proper price we would be very successful, but if you resort to coercion and arm the government machinery with powers—I am terrified at the thought of its possible misuse—how far would we succeed ? In Bihar the rice mills were charged a levy. It was not a happy experience.

Later it was withdrawn. Now it is the farmers who are charged the levy. If its implementation is left to petty bureaucrats the Government would be a loser politically and the purpose of acquiring foodgrains would also not be fulfilled.

Madam, there is a competition among the State Governments about who will tax the farmer most. At places there is talk of hundred per cent land revenue, at others it has been increased. In Bihar an increase is being discussed. It is being argued that the tax on farmers is being increased because there is a war going on and we want funds for the war effort. I would like to know if the Central Government has given the State Governments any advice in this regard. I suggest that if you want funds for the war impose a levy, a tax on behalf of the Central Government, but when the State Governments impose a tax on farmers it naturally generates resentment. It is true that grain prices have gone up, and the condition of those farmers who produced more has improved, but when a tax is imposed no distinction between big, small and medium farmers is made, there is an effort to involve them all. The result is that the atmosphere gets vitiated. The State Governments should be advised to first consult the Centre, the Planning Commission, before increasing the rental. It would be better to charge a direct war tax if we want funds for the war. People would give and it would be difficult for anyone to oppose. At present taxes are increased for the Plan, but it has not yet been determined what is necessary in the Plan and what is unnecessary.

I think the Central Government should keep an eye on the steps the State Governments are taking to increase the land revenue.

Land Reforms and the Ceiling

Madam, it is also necessary to declare that those States that have not yet fully carried out land reforms should do so. At the same time farmers should be assured that there would be no change in the ceiling laws for the next 15-20 years. I am in favour of a ceiling. Most States have made laws fixing the maximum limit of land holdings. Where they are not made they should be made and strictly applied. But if we want that in future people should be able to invest in agriculture and develop it with modern techniques we will have to create the confidence in the farmer's mind that the farm would not be touched for the next 15-20 years. If there is a feeling of insecurity and worry he would leave farming and rush towards industries, and then it would prove difficult to develop agriculture.

The P.L. 480 Wheat

Madam, these days a debate is going on in the country about whether we should or should not import wheat under P.L. 480. Yesterday the Food Minister said in the Lok Sabha not everything that comes from America is bad. No one says so. But can we deny that large-scale import of wheat has proved detrimental to our agriculture ? Whether we should or should not import wheat is not a big issue. The hungry will have to be fed and no ideology, no principle must come in the way. The Food Minister cannot escape the responsibility of providing food to everybody, and for this American wheat can be procured. But it is not necessary for the Food Minister to say something that would ignore and even denigrate the popular feeling that we shall free ourselves from foreign wheat. I was very sorry to read his statement in the papers. We import foodgrains because we are helpless. But we can make an adamantine resolve not to depend upon foreign foodgrains. Such a resolve should not be harmed in any way. We have been importing foodgrains on a large scale. The result is that we have not been able to pay the farmer the proper price for his wheat, because imported wheat was cheaper and so our wheat also sold at a lesser price. The farmer left wheat and was drawn to other crops. Then again nobody would like the way P.L. 480 funds are used. All in all there is an inflationary effect which affects our economy adversely.

I am sorry to say that the Americans are now thinking of sending monthly shipments of wheat. In the Fourth Five Year Plan we have an estimated import of 60 lakh tons of wheat. During the Third Plan too we had calculated the import of American wheat while making the plan. But when we do not know how much American wheat we shall receive the Food Minister would find it difficult to fix production targets. I cannot understand what the U.S. would gain by sending wheat from month to month. The Democratic Party, to which President Johnson belongs, has announced in its election manifesto that it would give India long-term aid, not only wheat but economic aid too. They believe in long-term giving. During election days I had the opportunity to visit the U.S. I had also met the late President Kennedy. At that time he had said the difference between the Republican Party and the Democratic Party was that while the Republican Party wanted to give aid from month to month and year to year the Democratic Party believed in long-term aid and wanted to keep India on that basis. I do not know if the Democratic Party has now changed its policy or if wheat is being used as an instrument of political pressure on us. We are very happy to hear the Food Minister say no one can pressurise us. But there are many ways of putting pressure. It can be put without saying so, it can be put indirectly. It is most unfortunate if wheat is being made a matter of politics. This will not strengthen the friendly relations between India and the U.S. Today we may import wheat from the U.S. to feed four hungry people a couple of morsels, but the time has come for us to free ourselves from imported wheat. 'Freedom from foreign food' should be our slogan. And if today people are calm, they do not take the law in their hands athough they are hungry, it is because they have a feeling of nationalism. If this national feeling reaches the farmer and the village official we can achieve unprecedented progress. So although we are forced to import foodgrains from the U.S., we must stick to our target and keep up the people's self-respect. American wheat is against our self-respect and one day we would have to free the country from this shame.

Bring Fallow Land under Cultivation

Madam, it is also necessary to chalk out a nationwide programme of bringing under the plough the land that is lying tallow but is arable. If it is possible to give it to landless peasants that should be done, but if the Government thinks it would be more profitable to have a government farm on it, I would not oppose it. Available figures show there is a lot of cultivable land that is lying fallow. In the forests too there are areas that are being farmed. We have to protect the forests, but there too land should not lie fallow. It is also necessary to stop ejectments. If the Government is doing it or if the farmers are being dispossessed of their holdings in some provinces where land reforms have not been fully implemented it is not at all proper. Edjectments should be stopped by law.

The Cabinet Camaraderie

The Food Minister is laying great stress on chemical fertilizers. It is good that on this point the Finance Minister agrees with him. We are deeply grieved when the papers report that members of the Council of Ministers are not on speaking terms. And the reports appear in papers that are reliable. If the Central Cabinet cannot work with a sense of camaraderie and brotherhood, if the Food Minister and the Finance Minister cannot sit together and resolve their differences it would be idle to expect that at this critical juncture the whole country would work with unity and cooperation.

This is also not possible. It is necessary that the Congress puts its house in order. It is necessary that New Delhi's decisions are applied in the capitals of all provinces of the country. Firmness is the need of the hour, going beyond party interests is the need of the hour. But I regret to say that we are not able to do what we should have done on the food front. Why ? Perhaps we are still not free of our old lethargy, of our old ways of thinking, of the habit of making plans but not putting them into practice. Agriculture is being ignored in the provinces. There is no coordination between agriculture, irrigation and the cooperative movement in the rural areas. We had hoped that community development would help to increase food production, but we do not see that picture. Motivating the farmer from village to village and preparing the people to the self-reliant depends upon whether we are prepared to learn from the present food crisis. If the Food Minister could implement the plans to which he has referred we can overcome the food crisis. Otherwise plans have been made in the past too, and have remained on paper. So far we have tried to make the country self-sufficient by tilling the land of paper with the plough of the pen, making canals of ink and sowing the seed of assurances. But self-sufficiency is not in sight. For that we have to take firm, strict and revolutionary steps. Then alone can we successfully overcome the present food crisis.

Let us hope the Government succeeds in overcoming this crisis and makes the country self-sufficient in food. Thank you.

Neither Bullets nor Barriers would Solve Food Crisis

Plea of Unfavourable Weather

Sir, I move "that the food situation in the country be taken into consideration." It cannot be denied that at present we do not have the type of food system, that we require for overcoming the situation through which the country is passing. A national calamity faces us, and it was necessary that when our Jawans are bravely fighting on the front we keep a satisfactory situation on all fronts and share their burden. But due to the wrong policies of the Government and also due to inclement nature the food situation deteriorated. It seems the administration does not have a national food policy to tackle the situation. We make, change and spoil our food policy from monsoon to monsoon, year to year, State to State, and from Food Minister to Food Minister. The weather cannot be controlled, and the Food Minister can prove with examples of advanced countries that the weather affects food production even where agriculture has been developed with scientific and technological means. We cannot remain untouched by the effect of the weather. But planning is meant for the very purpose of lessening the adverse impact of natural calamities. Production as per need should be the aim of the food policy. The Food Minister may claim that food production has increased in the country. This is partly true. Especially this year there has been record production. But this production is not in accordance with our growing needs. Our needs are growing because of the growth in population and also because of the change in the food habits of the people due to industrialisation. When the people leave villages and come to the cities in large numbers, when they will have money due to planning, their food habits will change. This is what we see today to some extent. The question is, why can we not produce enough to fulfil our common needs ? Production should be enough for our needs even when the weather is bad, and there should not be a food problem even when, as today, we are faced with a war.

No one can deny that in some parts of the country the food situation is very serious. Foodgrains are not available in adequate quantities, and whatever is available is not available at proper prices. Delay in the monsoon has greatly damaged the kharif crop and the hoarders and profiteers have the chance to exploit the situation. This includes big agriculturists as well as traders. The result is that the consumer is in great difficulties. What step is the Administration taking for him ? Do we have a national policy, or do we

---

Rajya Sabha on September 8 and 9, 1965 while initiating discussion on the Calling Attention Motion and replying to debate on the 'Food Crisis and its Solution'

have a hotch-potch of bits and pieces of the food policies of different States ? Has the Government been able to view the country as a whole and offer an effective solution for the problems of production and distribution ?

Zonal Restrictions

The present policy provides for zonal restrictions, every State is a separate zone, rice and wheat cannot go from one State to another, and there are also barriers between different districts of the same State. The country has been cut up into hundreds of bits for food purposes. Is this a good situation ? Neither is it politically good nor is it economically beneficial. If we do not consider the whole country a single unit from the food point of view it would not be possible to prevent resentment among the people of States with less production. Nor can surplus States be prevented from pursuing selfish polices. It seems one State is not prepared to understand the problems of another. It seems we have failed to formulate a food policy that encompasses the whole country. Different States put pressure, and I am sorry to see that the Central Government succumbs to it. I can understand the Food Minister's desire to take everyone with him, but that does not mean that the country has to be cut up into different bits from the food point of view. It does not mean a wall should be erected between surplus States and deficit States, benefiting neither.

What is the condition of the so-called surplus states ? At what price is wheat selling in Madhya Pradesh ? Export of wheat out of Madhya Pradesh has been banned for fear that there would be crisis in that State and the traders would exploit the situation. So every State was made into a different zone. But has this brought down foodgrain prices in Madhya Pradesh ? Wheat sells at a rupee a kilo there. The common man cannot buy it. It is difficult to imagine how people carry on. When we say the per capita per day income in the villages is 27 or 23 paise how he may be carrying on becomes a matter of concern for us. And the House should realise the serious situation in the deficit States. Foodgrains are not available even in Bihar, Maharashtra and Rajasthan. The administration has failed to make them available to the people at proper prices. The States complain against the Centre and district collectors plead helplessness. Where can the consumer go ? How can he allay his hunger ?

Figures do not Fill the Stomach—Treat Agriculture an Industry

Sir, figures do not fill the stomach. Even the prophecy that in the Fourth Five Year Plan we shall make the country self-sufficient in food cannot lessen the intensity of the present food crisis. For that we have to take concrete steps, and while taking them we have to take the long-term as well as short-term view. Increasing production is a long-term problem and it should be considered realistically. We have made the farmer the owner of the land, and we have also made ceiling laws. Those laws should be strictly enforced and the farmers assured that for the next 15-20 years the maximum limit of land holdings would not be changed in any way. This would create confidence in their minds and they would invest in agriculture. Agriculture will not develop so long as capital is not invested in it, so long as it does not become an industry. In our country farming has become a way of life. A farmer's son becomes a farmer, whether or not he can earn a livelihood and whether or not he can contribute to a solution of the country's food problem after meeting his needs. He is a born farmer. His ancestors were farmers, so he is a farmer. It is not because of his own will but because of the hand of destiny that he is a farmer. This should change. Agriculture should not remain a way of life, it should become an industry. It should yield profit. It should be done for one's own prosperity and for participation in the nation's prosperity. Our way of looking at agriculture must change. We must so arrange that agriculture attracts capital. The farmer would not be able to invest in it if he is beset with uncertainties and doubts. To enable him to spend on seed, fertilizer, irrigation and new techniques of farming it is necessary to assure him that the ceiling laws would not be changed for 15-20 years, the land he owns will remain with him, and that he will get all facilities for increasing production.

Secondly, the farmer should be given full guarantee of his produce. He should get full value for his labour. In this respect the right policy has been adopted. For the first time the farmers are getting the right price for their produce. There is also a difficulty involved here, as it increases his capacity to keep his produce with himself. To a certain extent we cannot avoid this. But we can motivate the farmer to bring his produce into the market by paying him a fair or competitive price. He may hoard today, but he will bring it out tomorrow. He cannot hoard for long. But these days' arrivals into the market are declining. This creates short term difficulties for us. But if the Government pays remunerative prices the farmer would bring his produce into the market. Then an effort could be made to induce him to ignore the trader and sell directly to the Government.

Food Minister's Claim

The biggest problem is distribution. There was a good crop this year. It was a bumper crop of 88.5 million tons and there was also a bumper import. In very few years have we imported so much — 6.3 million tons. The Food Minister claims the per capita availability is 15.5 oz — higher than during the last 2-3 years. And yet foodgrains are not available and they are not available at fair prices. How do we have such a contradictory situation ? How do we have such a paradox ? Why this absence of prosperity ? Is it not because the distribution system is faulty ? As I have submitted, the restrictions imposed on distribution create artificial scarcity. The purpose of imposing restrictions is to see that grain does not fall into the hands of anti-social elements and they do not exploit the situation for undue profiteering. But the situation is the opposite of this. It makes difficulties for the common man. I would like to quote an instance of how the States behave when deciding and implementing the food policy is left to them.

The States were told to fix the maximum price to the consumer, and they did it. But foodgrains are not available at that price. So the States told their district collectors to allow the traders to sell at a price higher than the fixed price but to issue receipts for the fixed price, not for the price at which they sold. I can place before you what I actually saw in Sujangarh in Rajasthan. The price of wheat has been fixed at 58 paise per kilo there, but no trader was prepared to sell it at that price. The Government did not have enough stocks, either of domestic wheat or of imported wheat, to meet every person's need at every place. It has to depend upon the traders. But while fixing the maximum price it did not take this aspect into consideration.

When the traders of Sujangarh said they would not sell foodgrains for 58 paise per kilo the collector there called them and said — all right, you may sell for 70 paise per kilo, but issue a receipt for 58 paise per kilo.

Now foodgrains are available in Sujangarh, people pay 70 paise per kilo for it but get a receipt for 58 paise per kilo. The Government loses on income tax and sales tax and is deliberately encouraging dishonesty and corruption. I would like to know on what basis these maximum prices were fixed. Why was it done ? Was it necessary ? The Agricultural Prices Commission has given its opinion on this. It has also been criticised. But in today's circumstances we are aggravating the problem by fixing the maximum price, not solving it. If the trader does not sell at the price fixed by us he should be penalised, the fixed price should be forcibly implemented, and then the people's requirements met from our own stocks. If we can do neither what is the point in fixing the maximum price ? In my opinion it is not good to fix the maximum price at this time. When Bajra is selling for 62 paise per kilo in Sujangarh how can wheat sell at a fixed price of 58 paise a kilo ? Clearly while fixing the price attention was not paid to the prevailing conditions in the market.

At the same time the Government too is making a profit. Those traders and shopkeepers who exploit the situation and make profits — since yesterday I have received some complaints in Delhi regarding *Atta* and rice—are guilty of treason. The Food Ministry should appeal to them not to exploit the situation. The Government should also warn them that any trader hoarding foodgrains or profiteering in them during the present critical time would be severely dealt with under Defence of India Rules.

Government made a Profit

But the record of the States is not good in this respect. This was discussed during Question Hour. I shall give the example of Rajasthan. *Chana* (gram) was selling there at Rs. 22 to 28 per maund. The Government of Rajasthan told the traders that they would be permitted to send *Chana* out of Rajasthan and make as much profit on it as they wished provided they gave 20 per cent of it to the Government at Rs. 16 per maund. The market rate was 22 to 28 rupees, but the Rajasthan Government wanted to purchase at Rs. 16. The traders agreed, sold 20 per cent to the State Government at 16 rupees a maund and made excessive profit on what they sent outside. It was sold to the people in Madras at Rs. 32 per maund. Where did this profit go ? Under what rules was the *Chana* that was sold at 16 Rupees per maund in Rajasthan sold in Madras at 32 Rupees ? Maharashtra has the same complaint, the Governments of Madhya Pradesh and Maharashtra are making a profit of 30-40 per cent on the coarse grain that goes to Maharashtra. This is not the way to stabilise prices, this is not the way to create the confidence in the people that everyone would get enough foodgrains at the right price. In my opinion, so far as foodgrains are concerned pressure should be put on the State Governments not to think of their States alone but to decide upon a policy that would be in the interest of the country as a whole. I suggest that the State Governments should deal with food production, but its procurement from the farmers, stocking and distribution should be taken over by the Central Government. As it is there is a Food Corporation. One of these days we would have to set up its branches from place to place and the Government would have to accept the responsibility of feeding more and more people. I do not think the State Governments can do this efficiently. I charge that a majority of State Governments is under the influence of profiteers and black marketeers. It is political influence. I do not want to discuss it today. But I know about Uttar Pradesh. If stern action is taken there political persons intervene and the State Government is unable to do justice to the consumer. So I suggest that the States should be entrusted with food production and the Central Government should take over procurement, stocking and distribution.

I have also suggested that from the foodgrains point of view the country should be considered one unit. So long as the Government cannot successfully discharge the responsibility of feeding all, any type of restraint creates an artificial scarcity. Secondly, at some places the Government resorted to monopoly procurement while at some others it imposed a levy. In Bihar the levy was expected to yield 3 lakh tons but actually it was 30,000 tons. Other States too have fixed similar targets but they could not achieve them. The Food Minister has himself acknowledged in his speech that the food procurement targets in Andhra Pradesh, Madras and Orissa were not fulfilled. It is the same in U.P. The Government has not been able to procure foodgrains to the desired extent. Then what is the use of putting impediments in the normal channels of trade ?

Nationalisation of Foodgrain Trade

I and my party would not stand in the way if the Central Government has reached the conclusion that the production, procurement and distribution of foodgrains from farm to kitchen should be in the hands of the States. We are not in favour of the nationalisation of the foodgrain trade, and in the prevailing circumstances it is an impractical policy. It is true that you do not say so, but if you want to engage in the whole grain trade we shall not prove an obstacle. But I think you will not take over the grains trade and will not block the normal channels of trade. You have chosen the middle way for combining the good points of both. But the result is the opposite and the bad points of both come together. As a result you obstruct the normal channels of trade and are not ready to accept the responsibility of providing food for all. The Central Government also did not keep the promise of providing a quota of imported wheat to the States. Now what will the State Governments feed the people ? There is informal rationing in the States. What is this thing called informal rationing. I cannot understand. Does informal rationing mean it is not the Government's responsibility to provide food ? The Government is not ready to accept such a responsibility and is creating this sort of difficulty. The people also cannot get foodgrains from where they are available. I do not think this is the middle way. If the Government wants the State to engage in foodgrain trade it may let it, but is the Government also prepared to accept the risk involved ? This sort of policy would encourage blackmarketing, smuggling and corruption, and fan popular discontent. We are afraid of it because you do not have the administrative apparatus that you should have. There are no political ends standing in our way, but if the State cannot engage in foodgrain trade you should help the present channels of trade completely.

Food Corporation Should Enter Open Market

After all the levy imposed in Bihar was not realised nor was the target fixed for Uttar Pradesh fulfilled despite Central Government pressure. The Government should take all these facts into consideration and decide a policy in their light. I suggest that the Food Corporation should enter the market as a Competitor and make purchases in the open market. If because of competition it has to pay more for the grain, that additional price would reach the farmer, would again get invested in agriculture and in some way or the other reach the Government. You cannot build up stocks if you do not pay competitive prices for the foodstocks that the farmer has with him. Then I doubt if the decision to introduce rationing in cities with a population of a million could be implemented. At first the Chief Ministers were prepared to introduce rationing in cities with a population of 3 lakhs, but now they have come upto 10 lakhs. It is argued that cities with a population of 3 lakhs would also be covered when an administrative machinery is set up. But I doubt if such an administration would be set up.

We welcome the Government decision to introduce statutory rationing in cities with a population of a million. Accept the responsibility of feeding the labourers who live in large numbers in big cities. But how much foodgrain will you give them? The daily per capita quota is 6 oz. People in Maharashtra are complaining that they get one kilo of foodgrains per fortnight. It is true this is for the rural areas, but has the government calculated how much foodgrain it would need ? If you introduce statutory rationing and if it cannot meet the people's needs how will you meet them ? In this connection I would like to make a suggestion, though I do not know how it would fit in. If anybody requires more foodgrains that you would give him under statutory rationing he should be free to buy them in the open market, for which some such shops should be arranged. These two are contradictory things, but they would have to be reconciled. Otherwise I doubt if you would be able to meet the needs of all through statutory rationing ...

Sir, in the prevailing circumstances we should not stop foodgrain imports, because the government is running one lakh five thousand fair price shops, for which foodgrains are needed, and the government would not be able to build up enough stocks. So continuing imports for some time is necessary. Our objective should be to minimise our dependence on imports as early as possible. But this cannot be done with mere sentiments. The need of the hour is for the Government to formulate a realistic, logical and all-India policy for a solution of the problem.

Hungry Needs Food

People ask for food but get bullets. What happened in Bihar, in Kolhapur is deplorable. What the hungry need is food, not bullets, not assurances for the future. Sir, you will be surprised to learn that when there was trouble and violence in Kolhapur the Maharashtra Government directed that foodgrains be sent to Kolhapur and distributed, but news is reaching us from many districts that there is no grain for distribution. What will they do ? Where will they go ? In the village, there are landless labourers who have to pay for foodgrains. In the cities too there are labourers and workers with small incomes whose life has become a hard struggle because of rising foodgrain prices.

It is true that the present food scarcity should not be exploited for fanning public discontent, and I believe all parties are alive to their national duty. We want that there should be no disturbance in the country on the question of food, but it is for the government to accept the responsibility for this.

SHRI ABID ALI (Maharashtra) : Why do they burn the godowns ? Then foodgrains cannot be stocked.

SHRI VAJPAYEE : They burn godowns because the administration is in your hands and you are not doing a good job of it.

SHRI ABID ALI : Will the food shortage be made up by burning godowns ?

SHRI VAJPAYEE : Nobody is justifying the burning of godowns. But your administration is so useless, no other country may have officers with such a bureaucratic mentality.

SHRI ABID ALI : Food stocks would not increase by burning godowns like this.

SHRI VAJPAYEE : Even a foe knows it and you too should know it. Foodgrains do not increase by burning them, but when there is a fire in the stomach one loses control on the brain. Mr Abid Ali has been a labour leader and he should know this. Nobody will justify violent activities. And there is still less scope for them in the present circumstances. But the Government too cannot be so heartless. So there should be committees at the Centre, in the States and in the districts which would resolve people's difficulties in getting foodgrains. If people's problems are solved without agitations they won't agitate. But the Government has failed in this. The Food Minister had called a meeting of Opposition leaders, but there was no meeting after that.

We are not eager to attend meetings, but in today's circumstances there is a pressing need to resolve people's difficulties.

REPLY TO DEBATE

Sir, the discussion on the food situation in this House has again made it clear that in times of crisis this House and all parties represented in this House can meet the need of the hour and can rise above the occasion. We shall extend cooperation even if the Government does not want it, because we realise our duty to the country. It is a matter of pleasure that the Government wants it too. There should be no doubt that it will get it in ample measure.

It would have been good if those persons arrested in connection with the food agitations had been released without our demanding their release. Actually it should not have been necessary to make such a demand. Circumstances have changed. In the context of the challenge we are facing such agitations and the arrests made in their connection should now pose no problem for us. The need of the hour is to solicit effective public cooperation at every level to resolve the food crisis. The Chief Ministers can be told to form all-party committees in which all political parties could place the people's difficulties before the administration and strive to remove them. Even at the Centre such a permanent committee could be formed. The late Pandit Nehru had also set up a Food Committee in which MPs of both parties used to come together to think about the food situation and suggest solutions. It is also necessary to place some concrete programme on the food front before the people.

The Hon. Food Minister has appealed that gardens at bungalows should grow vegetables instead of flowers, but what programmes are we setting for the rural areas in the present war times ? Is it not possible to set up a big volunteer corps, a food army, to immediately assess arable land lying fallow, and allot it for cultivation ? There is a monsoon on, there would be no problem of irrigation. If the people are given some specified land and implements of agriculture the enthusiasm being created in these times of war can be put to effective use.

Minister's Reply Incomplete

I was sorry to see that in his reply the Food Minister has not clarified what efforts should be made to correct the situation of less grain arrivals in the markets, which are causing difficulties for us. It is claimed that big agriculturists and traders have hoarded foodgrain. It is possible that the sentiment of patriotism may bring some of it to the market. Reports from some places, however, are just the opposite. Even small people may tend to hoard. Apart from appealing to patriotism what steps is the administration taking to see that hoarded foodgrains come to the market and reach the people ? In this regard does the Food Minister's silence not show that the administration is unable to determine its policy ? If that is so, it is a matter for concern, because if we cannot step up market arrivals of foodgrains our present difficulties would greatly increase.

My friend Shri Bhupesh Gupta has given instances of how banks are giving advances against grain. We are told that banks have stopped giving advances against foodgrains, but he gave figures—including figures for 1965—to show that banks are still giving such advances. This is giving traders the facility of hoarding grain. There should be no concession in this respect. In the situation that has come about efforts should be made to solve the food problem on a war footing. If we prepare a definite programme on the food front at the Centre as well as in the States and put the people to carrying out that programme this catastrophe of war can be transformed into a great opportunity. This is a challenge as well as an opportunity. If the Government is clear in its mind and if it can set the people to a definite programme we can achieve on the food front what we could not do in the past 17-18 years.

I thank all Hon. Members who participated in this discussion and hope that the Government would formulate its politics in the light of the suggestions placed before it. Thank you.

They Asked for Food but Got Bullets

Madam, I move "that the food situation in the country be taken into consideration."

Madam, the *Review of the Food Situation* published by the Government shows that the food situation is very serious. Drought has caused great damage to the crops in many States. Some parts of Maharashtra, Gujarat, Rajasthan, Madhya Pradesh, Mysore, Andhra Pradesh and Orissa have been badly affected by it. The gravity of the situation can be guaged from the fact that two million people in different States are engaged in relief works at present. According to Government estimates this figure would reach five million in the month of March.

The situation is, has the Government been able to make the right estimate of the shortage of foodgrains in the country ? In some areas the complaint is that the Food Minister keeps continually scaling up the shortage estimate. According to the *Review* the shortage figure may reach 140 to 150 lakh metric tons. Are these figures right ? All will agree that the system of collecting figures is faulty. Then again, the situation is not as serious as it is made out to be. People ask—if there is really a shortage of foodgrains in the country how is it that as much foodgrain as you want is available even in scarcity areas if you buy it in the black market at high prices ?

Extent of Food Shortage

Madam, perhaps even the Government is not unanimous on the extent of food shortage in the country. Today's newspapers have reported the interview that Prime Minister Smt. Indira Gandhi gave to the *Evening Standard* of London. The Prime Minister said India is not so much deficient in food as in a proper distribution system. At present food is not being distributed equally. She also said that there is a shortage of food in the country but not starvation conditions. The shortage estimate has been blown up highly.

From the way the Government is trying to obtain foodgrains or milk powder from various countries—from the governments and non-official organisations there—it seems the situation is alarming. Clearly it is necessary to reach firm estimates of the real shortage and then to give thought as to how it can be removed.

Madam, one thing is clear—the problem of food shortage cannot be solved by making it a law and order problem. From what happened in Kerala, what is happening in West Bengal and what may happen elsewhere it is clear that

Rajya Sabha on March 2 and 8, 1966 initiating discussion on the Food Situation

if the State Governments try to suppress public discontent with *lathis* (sticks) or bullets the results would not be good. There is a food shortage in the country, improper distribution makes it hurt all the more, there is discontent among the people and the discontent on other matters is also trying to find ways of expressing itself. The problem is all the more compounded when State Governments resort to repression.

The Repression

The people of Kerala naturally resented the fact that they are getting less rice as compared to Madras and Andhra. Even the former Governor there incited the people against the Centre. It is a different matter that when the people rose in anger they were threatened with still greater repression, which led to still further deterioration in the situation.

What recently happened in West Bengal is deplorable. In Basirhar on the 16th some people were going to the officials to present a memorandum. Had an official accepted it and given the assurance that the people's demands would be sympathetically looked into the situation would not have deteriorated, but I was surprised to learn that no official was present there to accept the memorandum. This is an example of how State Governments work. Local residents say there is a shortage of rice in those areas for the last three months. It is not that there is no rice in the government godowns. But it was not brought out for distribution. Along with rice kerosene is also in short supply. It was natural for the people to get upset, but had the officials tried to control the situation intelligently unfortunate incidents could have been avoided. Firing was resorted to for suppressing the people's voice, and as a protest against the firing the students of Swarupnagar took out a procession the next day. Again firing took place and a ten-year-old boy fell a victim to police bullets. His name was Nurul Islam. He was buried in the school ground and the headmaster of the school said with tears in his eyes, "on this boy's grave we shall write the epitaph—'here lies Nurul Islam who asked for rice but got bullets instead'." It is a heart-rending event. The Food Minister should clearly explain to the State Governments that when there is a food shortage in the country and the government is not in a position to make enough foodgrains available to the people they should behave with intelligence and understanding if the people get upset. I am clearly of the opinion that so long as there is no danger to the life of an official or policeman firing should not be resorted to. If the police open fire on a little stone-throwing—and that too when no magistrate is present to order it—it would be difficult to control the people's feelings. We should deal with the situation very sympathetically.

The Question of Distribution

The main problem at present is food distribution. Is the food available within the country and imported from abroad being distributed properly? When we discuss this question our attention is drawn to zonal restrictions.

Whether or not to do away with these zonal restrictions has become a matter of contention.

The Food Minister stated in the Lok Sabha that he has set up a committee of experts which will give its report soon. Who are these experts? Are they connected with the Food and Agriculture Ministry or are they of an independent mind ?

Pardon me, Madam, but we can get experts to give every type of advice. Like lawyers who are available to argue on either side of a suit, expert opinion can be available to support any side. If the experts are connected with the Ministry they will give a report in accord with the Minister's inclination, and the Minister's inclination is clear. He is not in favour of removing zonal restrictions.

SHRI AKBAR ALI KHAN (Andhra Pradesh) : Then they would not be experts.

SHRI VAJPAYEE : I submit that where food is concerned we should not look at things from the point of view of an ideology, whether it is socialism or the Swatantra Party's *laissezfaire*. In the present circumstances we can solve the food problem only if we free ourselves from ideological prejudices and think realistically.

The Surplus and the Deficit States

Sometimes it is said we have pledged ourselves to a socialistic pattern of society in the country, then how can we leave foodgrain trade in private hands ? I think this is not the right way to think. In Japan there is no socialism, but the government is successfully doing official grain trade. It is not a question of ideology, it is a question of what is practical in the prevailing situation. The Hon. Minister has been justifying zonal restrictions on the ground that there is no better alternative before him. But we will have to consider the evils that these restrictions have brought in their wake. We have two types of States—surplus States and deficit States. There is a barrier between the two. Surplus States are not willing to give foodgrains to deficit States. The Madhya Pradesh Chief Minister has clearly said we shall not allow our foodgrains to go out. It was difficult to send rice from Andhra and Madras to Kerala. It is true that the Food Minister is trying to keep all Chief Ministers with him. But I submit that the tendency of keeping their crops with them that the surplus States have acquired is very dangerous. Today the same party is in power in all States, but if tomorrow different parties are in power how can we solve this problem ? The Hon. Minister may silence me by saying there is no possibility in the near future of different parties forming governments in different States. But farsightedness demands that we should also take this aspect of the problem into consideration. Zonal restrictions create an artificial scarcity in deficit areas, there is an extraordinary rise in prices, and the consumer is put to great hardship. On the other hand, in surplus States the farmer does not get full value for his labour and he is attracted to cash crops instead of wheat and rice.

Madam, I have collected some figures which show that the area under sugarcane, jute, tobacco is expanding. Nehruji once said that in our country there is a race between *'ganna'* (cane) and *'galla'* (produce). It seems *ganna* has won the race and *galla* has fallen behind. In 1950-51 cane was sown in 42.17 lakh areas, and in 1961-62 this area grew to 59 lakh 45 thousand acres. The under tobacco is also expanding. In 1950-51 tobacco was sown in one crore 11 lakh 6 thousand acres of land, which has now grown to one crore 58 lakh 40 thousand acres. For jute the area has grown from 19 lakh 11 thousand acres to 25 lakh 59 thousand acres. In Punjab the farmers—especially the big farmers who have the capacity to store food grains—now complain that because of zonal restrictions they are not getting full value for their crops. It is true that if restrictions are removed traders would try to make a profit. I do not want to close my eyes to this fact. But now the Government has to decide—will or will not the foodgrain that is likely to rot in surplus areas be allowed to go to deficit areas ? If the trader makes a little profit we would have to be ready to take that bitter pill. I have figures that show that right now in Punjab 15 lakh maunds of wheat, 40 lakh maunds of *chana*, 25 lakh maunds of maize and Bajra are lying in the market but there is no outlet for them. The people are not ready to sell at the rates at which the Government wants to buy. The result is that this grain is going bad. Madam, this morning I was given some *chana* grains. I have them but I cannot place them on the floor of the House. This grain is highly rotten. What can we do with it ?

It is the same situation in other States. Rajasthan too has the *Chana* problem. About 50 lakh maunds of *Chana*, 10 lakh maunds of maize, 5 lakh maunds of Jowar are lying there, but there is no permission to send them out. In Madhya Pradesh 5 lakh maunds of *Chana* are lying idle, when a new crop is about to come. There would also be a new wheat crop. I would like to say this to the Hon. Minister—in view of the new crops that would be coming would it be wrong to remove the present interdistrict and inter-State restrictions on the movement of foodgrains ?

We claim that our country is one. Today Madam Prime Minister said if there is a shortage in the country we should all share it. Sharing diminished misery and sharing increases happiness. But equitable sharing is conditional on our trying to fix a common price of foodgrains in all parts of the country, which is not possible because of zonal restrictions. There is a wide gulf in the prices. The wheat that sells for Rs. 56 per quintal in Punjab is selling for Rs. 150 per quintal in Maharashtra and Rs. 160 per quintal in Madras. It is the same with *Chana*. In Punjab *Chana* is selling at Rs. 54-55 per quintal, but in Bengal it is selling at Rs. 145 per quintal. In Madhya Pradesh *Chana* is selling at Rs. 50 per quintal, but in Kerala and also in Madras it is selling at Rs. 150 per quintal. Such wide disparity in prices encourages smuggling of foodgrains. We can see this smuggling going on if we stand at the border between Uttar Pradesh and Punjab or Punjab and Delhi. This encourages corruption among the employees, and we give them the opportunity to let trucks go by taking Rs. 250 per truck. Those who take 5 kg with them are caught, while loaded trucks pass through as the policemen and employees at the checkport want to line their pockets, and we are trying to spread this tendency from State to State by imposing zonal restrictions.

It is also clear that before zonal restrictions food prices were less, but after they were imposed prices rose. Even if we do not take into consideration the situation created by the drought it cannot be denied that restrictions have resulted in a price-rise.

State Governments' Profiteering

Strangely enough, at this critical juncture not only traders but even the governments—especially the State Governments—are busy making a profit. The Hon. Minister may have noticed from the figures that they do not want to let their foodgrain go out, and if they do let it go out they indulge in profiteering. I have no objection to their recovering their expenses. I am also not against government transportation of foodgrains if it can be done successfully from a practical point of view. But the Government has to decide some price policy. In the present circumstances, we cannot permit the Government to indulge in unchecked profiteering in respect of food. But it seems there is no check on the State Governments. I would like to again give the example of *Chana*. Punjab gives Maharashtra *Chana* at Rs. 58 per quintal, and there it sells for Rs. 100 per quintal. *Chana* from Punjab went to Gujarat at Rs. 54 per quintal, where it sold at Rs. 80 per quintal. Similarly, *Chana* went from Punjab to Madras at Rs. 65 per quintal and there it sold for Rs. 128 per quintal. *Gulabi Chana* from Madhya Pradesh went to Maharashtra at Rs. 90 a quintal, where it sold for Rs. 170 a quintal. Similarly, Rajasthan is also making a profit in its area. The Government of Rajasthan purchased maize at Rs. 40 per quintal and sold it to Bihar at Rs. 71 per quintal. The Government of Maharashtra sold rice at Rs. 100 per quintal when its wholesale price was Rs. 75 to 90 per quintal. Profiteering is permitted in the name of cooperatives. The Government of Rajasthan sells *Chana* to cooperative societies but makes a profit of Rs. 9 per quintal. The Government of Madhya Pradesh beats them all. It has given the monopoly of sale and purchase of *Gulabi Chana* in the State to the Apex Marketing Society. No one else can buy *Chana* in Madhya Pradesh or send it out. A Minister stated in the Madhya Pradesh Assembly that the Apex Marketing Society purchases *Gulabi Chana* at Rs. 95 per quintal and sells it to some All-India Federation in Bombay at Rs. 130 to 150 per quintal. Purchase at Rs. 95. Sale at Rs. 150—a profit of Rs. 60 per quintal, that too in foodgrains and that too in today's critical condition. Can the State Governments not be brought to their senses ? In Madhya Pradesh only cooperative societies are permitted to send *Chana* out, but not every district has a cooperative society. Whatever societies there are, are in the hands of a handful of people. How they run we have seen in Delhi. The Government of Rajasthan had promised the people that if *Chana* was sold to the Government at Rs. 40 to 50 per quintal an equal amount of it would be allowed to be sent out. But later this concession was withdrawn and the Government went back on its promise.

In respect of foodgrains there are barriers not only between provinces but even within provinces. As a result deficit areas are isolated, as are surplus areas. In Rajasthan at some places maize sells at Rs. 40 per quintal, at others it sells at Rs. 65 per quintal. Jowar sells at Rs. 42 per quintal at one place and at Rs. 62 per quintal at another. I submit that in view of the new crop a decision should be taken to abolish zonal restrictions. Ministers should not depend upon experts. They should act with commonsense. There is certainly some danger, but we should show the courage to face danger. It is not only a foodgrain scarcity problem, it is also a psychological problem, which would be substantially solved by removing zonal restrictions.

Amend the Constitution

Madam, I submit that the Constitution should be amended to entrust the States with the responsibility of food production. The Central Government should take over the procurement and distribution. For this a constitutional amendment is required. The Hon. Minister may say that it is doubtful if the State Governments would allow such an amendment to be made, but in the wider interest of the country and from a long-range point of view such a decision is necessary. There are no prospects of the food problem being solved in the near future. But the final authority should vest in the Centre in order to ensure that the State Governments do not endanger law and order in the country by adopting differing policies in this matter. I have already said that this is the situation when one and the same party is in power all over the country. In future the situation may change. To meet it the Constitution should be changed for entrusting the States with responsibility of production and the Centre should accept the responsibility of procurement and distribution.

Abolish Food Zones

Food zones should be abolished and all restrictions on foodgrain movement removed. Branches of the Food Corporation should be set up in all States. This needs funds. Yesterday I read in the papers that the people are ready to sell rice but the Food Corporation does not have money. It needs Rs. 300 crores. The Centre should fulfil this need, so that it can make largescale purchases in surplus areas and arrange proper distribution.

In big cities rationing should be strictly enforced. Those State Governments that are not willing to do so should be forced to do so. The wheat that comes from outside for small farmers and landless labourers should be distributed in adequate quantities.

From the long-range point of view we should pledge ourselves to the country's self-sufficiency in food within five years and take effective steps for it. All arable land lying fallow, whether belonging to the Government or local units, should be brought under the plough. Cultivable forest lands should also be ploughed. At present there is a total land mass of 49.23 million acres that is arable but is not being cultivated. Farming should be organised there on a large scale.

Land reform and the land ceiling law should be strictly implemented. There should be no new taxes on farmers. Increased subsidy should be withdrawn. Irrigation rates should be such that the farmer may be able to utilise irrigation facilities. Serious thought should be given to freeing uneconomic holdings from taxes.

The food situation is serious. We want this problem to be solved with the cooperation of all. The Government talks of getting the cooperation of all but takes no effective step in that direction. Although the situation is serious we can triumph over it if all-party committees are set up from the Centre to the district level and ways and means found to allay the people's anger. But perhaps it is too much to expect the present administration to show such sagacity, firmness and intelligence.

With these words I move my resolution.

REPLY TO DEBATE

SHRI VAJPAYEE : Madam, many suggestions for the solution of the food problem have been put forth during the discussion. The whole House is agreed on two points. One is that we have no option but to import foodgrains to solve the current serious food problems. My friend Shri Bhupesh Gupta too has not opposed imports; all he has said is that we should make our own efforts to the maximum extent and then import if necessary. No Government can let people die of hunger. Howsoever opposed we may be to foodgrain import from the sentimental and ideological point of view we have no other option in the prevailing circumstances. But the point is—should we present the need of wheat imports in such a way that it harms our own food production efforts ? The Food Minister will agree that when we go in for large-scale imports—and today we have no other option—it adversely affects the sentiment behind greater food production within the country. That should not be done. We must see that our efforts for greater food production do not slacken.

New Agricultural Techniques

The House is also agreed that if we are to increase food production we must adopt new agricultural techniques. Nobody is against using chemical fertilizers, it has only been said that we might not be able to reach fertilizer to every farmer in the near future. The demand is greater than our production. So the programme of making fertilizer in the villages should not be stopped. We should try to increase the production of fertilizer, but at the same time the complementary effort at making green manure in the villages should continue.

Madam, the Food Minister has made a fighting speech. He is discharging a difficult responsibility and our good wishes are with him. Perhaps he did not have enough time, otherwise he would have also thrown light on how he can remove the shortcomings in distribution caused by zonal restrictions. As it is, the weakest part of his speech was the one that dealt with zonal restrictions.

SHRI SYED AHMED : It was at the very end.

SHRI VAJPAYEE : It was the final part but it could not impress. It does not make sense to say that even if we end State zones district authorities would not allow foodgrains to go out. They would impose restrictions and there would be an informal ban. This means we would never be able to formulate a national food policy and firmly implement it. In view of the new crops we will have to give serious thought to removing zonal restrictions.

SHRI AKBAR ALI KHAN : Nothing is definite.

SHRI VAJPAYEE : I had asked in my speech who these experts are who are considering zonal restrictions, but he did not give out their names. I hope they are independent experts and will give the Government proper advice after taking the whole situation into consideration and some decision about removing zonal restrictions would be taken before the new crop comes in.

SHRI P.N. SAPRU (Uttar Pradesh) : The problem is with the Chief Ministers.

SHRI VAJPAYEE : Yes, so persuade them. I had said if today we could not persuade all the Chief Ministers to adopt a common policy there bould be still bigger difficulties in future.

SHRI AKBAR ALI KHAN : But they too have quite a few problems.

SHRI VAJPAYEE : Madam, the Central Government would have to keep an eye on the food shortage situation prevailing in various parts of the country. What happened in Kerala is being repeated in West Bengal. Now the Food Minister says the food situation in West Bengal is not so serious, but he will admit that due to faulty distribution the people are experiencing a shortage at some places. In such circumstances it is natural for them to hold demonstrations and take out processions, although it is true that demonstrations do not increase food production, nor do they speed up distribution. Taking out a procession is a democratic method of expressing one's views and we all adopt it. State Governments should be urged to exercise caution in order to prevent the situation from deteriorating anywhere. For example, if there is firing anywhere ...

SHRI AKBAR ALI KHAN : There should be no violence.

SHRI VAJPAYEE : If there is firing anywhere there should be no objection to a demand for a judicial inquiry. If the police resort to firing and if anyone is killed there can be a judicial inquiry. We would not be able to control the situation prevailing today if the State Governments make it a prestige issue.

SHRI P.N. SAPRU : But when there is firing there is immediately a magisterial inquiry. There is a provision for it in the Criminal Procedure Code.

SHRI VAJPAYEE : Sapru Saheb will agree that there are occasions when there was no magistrate to give the order and the police resort to firing in the name of self-defence. Who will inquire into whether the firing was justified or not and whether it was necessary to use the force that was used ? Such things can come to light in a judicial inquiry and can substantially remove public resentment. It is true that we should rise above politics while thinking of the food problem. But your Chief Ministers are not prepared to do so and this is creating problems. There was naturally some temptation for opposition parties—the Minister also pointed it out—as this is the year preceding the election. So if the Government makes a mistake, if the distribution is faulty and if the people do not get enough food at the right price opposition parties will discharge the responsibility of expressing the people's anger. In my opinion the problem would be largely solved if all these factors are taken into consideration while formulating a food policy and if the State Governments can be persuaded to honestly implement the policy adopted by the Centre. Thank you.

Starvation Deaths

Sir, the whole country's attention is focussed on this discussion. It is a matter of life and death for lakhs of people. I hope the House will consider the food situation with great seriousness.

I regret the Food Minister has refused to admit that there have been some starvation deaths. He says these deaths have not been confirmed, so he is not ready to acknowledge them. I submit this is not the time to play with words.

AN HON. MEMBER : Now we have your governments there.

SHRI VAJPAYEE : What I am saying applies to both parties, and if we do not rise above party considerations we would not be able to prevent lakhs of people from dying.

I have recently been on a tour of Bihar, and I met people who told me there were starvation deaths in the families. What figures is the Food Minister talking about ? If people are dying of hunger it should be accepted as a fact. This is a shame not only for any one government but for the whole country, and no party no region, can escape the responsibility for this. We can achieve nothing by covering up facts.

SHRI VIBHUTI MISHRA (Motihari) : Is any Minister starving there ?

SHRI VAJPAYEE : Were some areas in Bihar declared famine areas ? In reply we were told this would damage our prestige in the world, it would spread panic.

SHRI JAGJIVAN RAM : Whoever said so, the Hon. Member may say so to him. Why is he saying it here ?

SHRI VAJPAYEE : It was said on behalf of some people sitting here. I did not name the Hon. Minister.

AN HON. MEMBER : That is what the Hon. Member meant.

SHRI VAJPAYEE : Why does the Hon. Member think I meant that ? He should listen to my words.

If State Governments confirm starvation deaths what will be the position of the Central Food Minister (*Interruption*)...

SHRI K.N. TIWARI : What is the responsibility of the region ?

SHRI KANWARLAL GUPTA : Sir, why are these people disturbing ?

SMT. TARAKESHWARI SINHA : We shall listen to the Hon. Member but those who are creating a disturbance on that side should also be told.

SHRI VAJPAYEE : We must accept the bitter truth that there have been some starvation deaths, and if the situation is not brought under control there would be large-scale starvation in the coming couple of months.

It has been charged — and the Food Minister has yet to reply to it—that the quantity of foodgrains allotted by the Centre to the States has not reached

Lok Sabha on May 22, 1967 during discussion on the Food Situation

them. The problem is not about the demand of the States, it is that the amount the Centre has decided to send to them after considering their demand is not received by the States.

The reasons given by the Minister for this are true. The amount of rice expected from Burma did not arrive. There were strikes at Bombay and Visakhapatanam ports, as a result of which unloading the ships and loading the foodgrains on to rail wagons became difficult. But this does not disprove the fact that the promise to give a certain amount of foodgrains was not kept. It is also surprising that this breach of promise has taken place mostly with States that have non-Congress governments. I do not want to give a political colour to this problem.

SHRI JAGJIVAN RAM : The Hon. Member did not want to know about other States.

SHRI VAJPAYEE : The Hon. Minister should tell me.

AN HON. MEMBER : The Hon. Member should not have spoken without knowing things.

SHRI VAJPAYEE : I shall present only what I know. If he knows something else, if he has also figures about other States he may place them here.

AN HON. MEMBER : The Hon. Member is going by hearsay.

SHRI VAJPAYEE : I am not going by hearsay. He too is not talking of some *Brahma Gyan*.

My point is that there should be no difference of opinion between the Central Food Minister and the Food Ministers of the States in respect of how much foodgrain the Government has, how much it can order or procure, and how it will be distributed in the States. A new government has taken office after the General Election, a new Food Minister has been appointed at the Centre, non-Congress governments are functioning in eight States, but on the food front no revolutionary transformation is as yet in evidence, either in distribution or in production.

Zonal Restrictions on Foodgrain Movement

It has been said — and I would like to repeat it — that it is easier to bring wheat from the U.S. than to take it from a surplus State to a deficit State. Movement of foodgrains from one district to another has been prohibited. This causes disparity in prices. At one place justice is not done to the producer, at another place injustice is done to the consumer. In this connection I would like to place some figures before the House. Madhya Pradesh is one State, yet there is so much difference in the food prices within it.

In Indore wheat is selling at Rs. 75 per quintal, but the same wheat sells in Sagar and Jabalpur at Rs. 150 per quintal. *Chana* is priced at Rs. 60 per quintal in Indore but the same *Chana* is priced at Rs. 140 per quintal in Raipur and Raigarh. I fail to understand why restrictions placed on the movement of coarse grains all over the country cannot be withdrawn. If it is not possible to abolish zonal restrictions at one stroke because doing so would harm the interests of the States, still restrictions on coarse grain should be removed.

SMT. TARAKESHWARI SINHA : The Hon. Member's party is in many governments. Will they help ?

SHRI VAJPAYEE : I have said this is not a party matter.

SMT. TARAKESHWARI SINHA : If they help we can make some efforts.

SHRI VAJPAYEE : Efforts should be made.

SHRI P.C. VERMA (Hamirpur) : They are in office in Punjab and Haryana, but these governments are not helping us. We are starving.

SHRI VAJPAYEE: Our governments too are facing difficulties.

SMT. TARAKESHWARI SINHA : The Hon. Member is a leader of the Jana Sangh and there are Jana Sangh governments in Haryana and Punjab. May I request Shri Vajpayee to tell his governments to change their attitude towards the zonal system, because U.P., Haryana and Punjab were once one zone but Haryana and Punjab broke it and converted it into single-State zones.

Shri P.C. VERMA : Himachal Pradesh should also be added to it.

SHRI VAJPAYEE : Sir, how can I answer all these questions in such a short time ?

I agree that all States and all political parties will have to formulate a national food policy. If today it is difficult for non-Congress governments it is because when all States had Congress governments how did they behave ?

SHRI K.N. TIWARI : This is a hollow argument.

SHRI VAJPAYEE : All these zones are not a new creation. They have been there all the time.

SHRI P.C. VERMA : When there was a Congress government in Punjab there was a joint zone with Himachal.

SHRI VAJPAYEE : A lot of *Bajra* is lying in Mysore. The people there do not eat it much, and it sells there at Rs. 50 or 55 per quintal, but in U.P. *Bajra* is priced at Rs. 125 per quintal, in Bihar at Rs. 130 and in Delhi at Rs. 98.

SHRI P.C. VERMA : Talk about Punjab.

SHRI VAJPAYEE : The States, whether they have Congress governments or non-Congress governments, would have to be persuaded to formulate and implement a national food policy.

I would like to suggest that production of food should be left to the States and the Central Government should take over procurement and distribution. Branches of the Food Corporation should be set up in all States and arrangements should be made to purchase adequate stocks of produce from farmers at proper prices. I know that in the past Opposition parties were criticising procurement and now Congressmen are doing so.

SMT. TARAKESHWARI SINHA : That is good.

SHRI VAJPAYEE : This is not good. It won't solve the problem. We will have to appeal to the farmers and the traders. All parties together should do this. At a time when we are passing through a crisis, when we are standing before the world with a begging bowl in our hand and when we are also repeating that lakhs of people are in danger of dying of starvation it is time for the cuntry and the political parties to rise to the occasion. We will have to appeal to the traders and farmers to keep with them only enough stocks for a couple of years and sell the rest to the governments at proper prices. If appeals do not work you will have to act. But action will not be possible so long as there is not an understanding on the political level that no one will exploit the food situation for selfish ends. In this respect the Congress will have to take the lead. Thank you.

Tardy Implementation of Land Reforms

The topic before us is important enough to merit a serious discussion. No one can deny — and the members sitting on that side will also agree—that the Government has failed to implement land reforms with firmness and effectively. The story of this failure is 23 years old. After ending Zamindari, Jagirdari and the Inami practice the laws passed for giving the land to the tiller, determining the maximum limit of land holdings and protecting the interests of the ryots were not implemented. In some States there are no land ceiling laws at all. For instance Punjab. In PEPSU the old maximum land holding law is in operation but in the rest of the area there is no such law. In Bihar there is a law but it was not implemented. No land limit was fixed.

SHRI K.N. TIWARI : It has been fixed.

SHRI VAJPAYEE : It has been fixed only by law. I know about Bihar. Let the people of Bihar not to be too smart. The limit decided by law has not been implemented on the ground. It is still to be implemented. These people are interrupting without understanding.

Land Reforms not Implemented

In a conference of Chief Ministers held a year ago it was decided to implement land reform laws by the end of 1970. August is about to end. How many months remain for the implementation ? The matter relates to State governments. If they do not want to implement the laws what can the Centre do ? Are political parties ready to take it up on a political level ? Had they been ready we would not have seen the situation that has lingered on for 23 years. I charge that land reforms are not being implemented because power is in the hands of big agriculturists. The land that should have been left after the fixation of the maximum landholdings was actually not left, and what was left was not distributed. People did *benami* occupation of land. The Zamindari Abolition Act of U.P. was a progressive piece of legislation as compared to laws of other States. But the land that was left surplus as a result of the law was given to the *Gaon Sabha* and in the *Gaon Sabha* those who dominated it forcibly occupied the land. No party has refrained from doing so, not even those parties that are still carrying on a forcible occupation agitation. Can the land be recovered from them ? Can it be done peacefully? Can the Government be pressurized into prompt implementation of land reforms ?

SOME HON. MEMBERS : No.

SHRI VAJPAYEE : Members of the ruling party are saying no. Were our agitating friends to launch a satyagraha against the Government because the

Rajya Sabha on August 19, 1970 during discussion on land reforms and occupation of lands movement

government did not implement the laws, because the laws are defective, and because fallow land has not been made cultivable and distributed among the landless, we could also have supported the agitation. But this demonstration should have been held before the residence of Prime Minister Smt. Indira Gandhi, not at someone's farm.

SHRI RAM SEVAK YADAV : There were peaceful demonstrations against the Government in 1957 and 1960.

SHRI VAJPAYEE : You still claim that those demonstrations were peaceful.

SHRI SAMAR GUHA : On August 9 hundreds of people of the Praja Socialist Party have offered satyagraha before the Prime Minister's residence.

SHRI VAJPAYEE : The claim is still being made that the agitation is peaceful. The agitators still declare the date and time of their arrival and court arrest. The question is, why can the satyagraha not be offered before the government instead of at someone's farm ?

Do not Awaken Bhasmasur

All farms existing today have been formed according to law. You may say the law is wrong. You may say it needs to be changed. But can you say that all these farms—such as the Birla farm—have not been set up according to law ? Who made the law ? Who implements it ? Today the call is being given to occupy land. I read in the papers that someone has advocated occupying empty houses in the cities. Will there be a limit to this or not ? Where is that limit ? It is for Parliament to fix it. This problem would not be solved by fighting over land. Do not awaken Bhasmasur. You are awakening him for cheap popularity, but one day he will burn you down too. Can it be denied that there have been attacks on small farmers' holdings too ? Land is being made an instrument of revenge in the countryside. This is not the way to bring about social transformation. Sir, you are yourself known as sober communist. Through you I would like to remind my communist friends that there had been an intense debate between Lenin and Rose Luxermburg on whether or not there should be forcible occupation of land and Rose Luxembourg had said that if farmers were incited to occupy land forcibly communism could not be introduced. Usurpation cannot be the basis of equality and of an equalitarian society.

Sir, constraints are breaking down today, laws are being broken, systems are scattering and there is violence in the air. In such a situation anything that helps people to transgress constraints would take the country towards chaos. This would endanger not only independence but also the tiller's right to the land.

It is necessary for the government to declare that it would firmly implement land reforms in so many months. The maximum land-holding law must be implemented. At this time I am not in favour of decreasing the land holding limit. If you create uncertainty in the farmer's mind capital would not be invested in agriculture. Then production would not grow. Is land distribution the main aim ? Is it not the country's self-sufficiency in food ? We have to keep both objectives in view.

We have also to look to how much land there is for distribution. The hunger for land is greater than the available land. Even while stressing land distribution we cannot satisfy this hunger. We have to bring down the present pressure on land and divert people to industry. From this point of view a movement that binds the people to land and promotes hunger for land is a reactionary movement. We must implement land reforms firmly, increase per acre production, make fallow land cultivable and distribute it among Harijans, Adivasis or the landless, and at the same time spread a network of small and medium industries so that lakhs of unemployed villagers may get work.

Green Revolution would become Red Revolution

Sir, as you know, the Dhebar Commission set up in 1960 had gone into the problems of tribals. According to a law then in force no land belonging to a tribal could be given to a non-tribal without permission from a government official. But this law has been broken. Lakhs of acres of land have slipped out of the hands of the tribals and gone into the pockets of non-tribals. This is an explosive situation. The Government set up the Dhebar Commission in 1960. Shri Dhebar is a senior leader. He recommended that all land gone into the hand of non-tribals should be recovered. The government should pay compensation and again distribute the land among tribals. Ten years have passed but this recommendation has not been acted upon. There is no shortage of intentions and of sentiments, but this government is unable to act. This is perhaps because it has to depend for its power on those in whose hands land has been concentrated and who wield the stick in the countryside. There is till time. Let the government listen to the warning of time.

The Home Ministry had said if land reforms were not firmly carried out the Green Revolution would change into a red revolution. It would not be so, because the farmer would protect his land. But those who are landless must either have land or have jobs. If we can give, neither would we be able to develop this country nor secure freedom and democracy.

Don't Extract Political Mileage

The present movement has failed... (*Interruption*). The problem will not be solved with an agitation. The problem is deep and complex. Let nobody try to extract political mileage out of it. But it should be solved on a political level. The hopes and aspirations of crores of people have risen. If we cannot satisfy them the situation will worsen.

This movement can prove as a warning, unless the government takes the right steps. But it would have been better if there had been no such movement. (*Interruption*). There should have been a peaceful satyagraha against the Government, not a movement of forcible cultivation. It should have contained not a programme of occupying land but also a programme of providing a means of livelihood to every youngman.

Land Ceiling—Slogan and Reality

Sir, the debate going on in the ruling party on the question of bringing down the maximum limit of land holdings is not a controversy between kulaks and small farmers; it is a controversy between slogans and reality. It is easy to say in the election manifesto that the maximum land holding should be 10 acres or 12 acres or at the most 18 acres. But problems arise when it is sought to be implemented.

Defective Ceilings

So far I have been unable to understand one thing—what is the basis of this talk of acres ? Why at least 10 acres, why not 8? Why maximum 10 acres, why not 30 ? Do these figures have any scientific basis ? Has the production per acre been actually calculated ? There are various types of land and there is a difference in their productivity. So different States made different laws. I feel if we go in for per acre calculations we would not be able to reach the right conclusion. So, the starting point should be—how much income do we want to give a farmer for the livelihood of his family ? Do we not want that the farmer's son should get university education ? Do we not want that the farmer's son should obtain the standard of life of a city-dweller ? I say let us talk of rupees rather than of acres. Some have said, our party has said ...(*Interruption*).

SHRI AMRIT NAHATA: Fifteen thousand.

SHRI VAJPAYEE : Don't say fifteen thousand, say what you want to say.

SHRI AMRIT NAHATA : Your party said fifteen thousand.

SHRI VAJPAYEE : We said a ceiling should be imposed with a minimum monthly income of fifteen hundred in view.

Ceiling Law has become a Joke

Secondly, we are talking of lowering the ceiling. Is it because we want to cover up the failure in implementing the present ceiling laws ? Are there no ceiling laws ? I it true that they were not implemented ? I was greatly surprised to learn that at some places the ceiling was on individuals, not on families. There were separate plots of land for the husband, wife and children. Today the ceiling law has become a joke. At some places there are no records at all. They have not been collected. No efforts were made to collect them. The ceiling law was not honestly implemented. The ruling party should admit that it failed to implement the ceiling law and is now raising the slogan of lowering the ceiling in order to cover up its failure.

Lok Sabha on May 19, 1972 during discussion in connection with the determination of the Ceiling for Land Holdings

I would like to know the purpose behind lowering the ceiling. I was reading *Poverty in India* by V.M. Dandekar and Neelkant Rath. Nobody can call them reactionary economists. Read their articles. They say lowering the ceiling would not solve the problem of rural poverty. How much land would be left to give to the people ? Is it enough just to give land ? Would it not be necessary to give water with the land ? Some figures in *Indian Agriculture in Brief* tell their own tale. Figures speak. During the past some years the number of the landless has increased. Those who have uneconomic holdings are selling them off, because cultivating them is not gainful. Do we want to give land to those who cannot farm it ? Where will the resources come from ? How will irrigation be arranged ? Does the Government have enough financial resources ? So the farmer is afraid. Today we are talking of a ceiling of 10 acres, tomorrow it could be still lower. Is creating uncertainty in the farmer's mind the way to increase food production ?

The Lowering of the Ceiling

The farmer is also afraid that since the Congress has now an alliance with the Communist Party it wants to revive cooperative farming, bring about collectivisation, make the farmer dependent upon the Government. I agree that we want the maximum yield from farming. Intensive farming is the solution to our problems. So no maximum ceiling on land holding can be sacrosanct for ever. If production increases the ceiling can come down. We want to diminish the people's dependence on land. But distribution of land alone will not do it. And where is the land that can be distributed? There is more hunger for land than there is land. There is already great pressure on land. We can solve the problem if we can spread a network of agriculture-related industries and provide industrial jobs to those landless people who are dependent upon agriculture, otherwise this lowering of land holding would go to ridiculous lengths, and a situation would develop in which not only would agriculture be spoilt, the farmer would also lose his land. Collectivisation will not work in the country. The Indian farmer will give his life but not his land. Even the communist government of Poland could not take away the farmer's land. We still have democracy in the country, but I feel we are playing games with agriculture. I submit that this problem cannot be solved with slogans. Solve it with your feet firmly on the ground of reality.

It is not a question of only lowering the land ceiling. Even after lowering it jobs will not be available in the rural areas. People from the villages are coming into the cities. Slums are increasing. If they are to be provided jobs there, agriculture related industries will have to be developed. This the Government could not do and it is looking for a solution to the problem the wrong way ... (*Interruption*).

SHRI PILOO MODY : It is a *Bekar Sarkar*.

SHRI VAJPAYEE : You will have to distinguish between farmers who have made their own irrigation arrangements and those who get water through Government means. A farmer spent money on sinking a well ... (*Interruption*).

SHRI SAT PAL KAPOOR (Patiala) : How much distinction ?

SHRI AMRIT NAHATA : Where did the money come from ?

SHRI VAJPAYEE : He earned it with his own labour. He got it where Malviyaji got it. But there is no limit to Malviyaji's income and on his expenditure. We have to decide whether we want or do not want the farmer to invest in agriculture. The farmer should develop his own irrigation facilities where the Government cannot provide them. The situation today is that people are doing away with wells. Was this the meaning of lowering the ceiling ?

One thing more. The Government should announce that there would be no more lowering of the ceiling for the next 10 years. This would end the atmosphere of uncertainty and the people would exert for maximum production...(*Interruption*).

SHRI S.N. MISHRA : Is it in their hands ? One has to do what the situation requires. You have given them a document for ten years ... (*Interruption*).

SPEAKER : He believes they will remain in power for ten years.

SHRI VAJPAYEE : Mishraji is right. What I mean is that whatever policy is formulated will have Parliament's approval. The uncertainty in the farmer's mind will have to be removed. He will have to be assured that laws will not be made again and again to diminish his land. Otherwise he will lose interest in agriculture. If there is no personal interest in agriculture it will not grow. We must realise this difference between industry and agriculture. Agriculture cannot prosper without the farmer's personal attention. So there should not be any uncertainty in his mind. The present debate has created it.

One last thing. Some of our Communist friends are preparing for a new split in the Congress party. I wish before you decide on a ceiling ... (*Interruption*).

SHRI AMRIT NAHATA : How very concerned you are about our party!

SHRI VAJPAYEE : I have to feel concerned. When you join hands with them it is a matter for concern. This calf of the Communist party is milking the Congress cow. Let our Congress friends beware. Thank you.

Burning Stomachs versus Burning Hearts

Sir, the Hon. Minister has tried to paint a very colourful picture in his statement. If it is true then no one would object to rejoicing. But I am afraid the Government is making the same mistake it had made while tomtomming about the Green Revolution. In the name of the Green Revolution the Government got lost in the greenery of the revolution and the country had to face the tragedy of a famine. It is true that some regions have had a good monsoon. But the next four months—till the new crops come in—are crucial. I would like to know how much foodgrain the Government has in its godowns, how much is in the pipeline, how much has been ordered from abroad, and how much it needs for the public distribution system.

More and more grain shops are being set up but there is no grain in them. Today I have received by mail a specimen of the grain these shops have. It was sold at Shop No. 22 on Gadra Road. You cannot decide if it is Jowar or Bajra or a mixture of the two, if it is fit for human consumption or if it is for animals. I wish the Minister looks at it. If people eat the foodgrain sold at ration shops they are bound to die and then you will say they died of illness, not of hunger. This foodgrain will certainly lead to illness. According to the memo of the Gadra Road shop the Government gives 3 oz. of rice. Four kilograms of foodgrains were given in three months. How can people live on four kg. in three months ? In the open market foodgrain prices are sky-rocketing. As compared to wheat, jowar, Bajra, Maize are selling for as high as Rs. 210 per quintal. How can the poor afford such prices ? There has been a good monsoon but it has not improved the poor man's purchasing power. What is the minimum quantity of rations that the Government has decided upon ? There is a demand that the minimum monthly quota should be 12 kg of wheat. How much can the Government give through the public distribution system ? Does the vulnerable section of the society have the capacity to fulfil its needs with foodgrain purchase in the open market ? If not, how can you save them from dying of hunger ?

Centre Stopped Aid

Shri Limaye has raised the right questions. After Maharashtra got rains relief works are being wound up. The Central Government has stopped its matching contribution of fifty paise per rupee. Not more than two people in a family can work. That is the rule being made. Not all people are ready to

---

Lok Sabha on July 24, 1973 during discussion on Famine and Relief Works

take up agriculture. There are no resources for it. There are those who are prepared to stay in relief camps and work— Why don't you give them freedom to work ? Why is the Central Government closing down relief works ? As compared to Maharashtra an equally—if not more—terrible famine is spreading in eastern U.P. and Bihar. The situation is serious. There is an apprehension that law and order may break down. What sin does a hungry man not commit ?

If, in order to combat this famine, the Centre does not start relief works in Bihar, U.P. etc., does not sanction enough of them, and does not arrange food distribution where relief works are going on, it is feared that there would be an influx of people from the villages into the cities. The entire population of Mirzapur tehsil is on its way to Varanasi. The same situation prevails in Bihar. The same thing is happening in many parts there. There is no indication of this frightful situation in this statement. It is an exercise in self-praise. I do not undervalue whatever efforts have been made to fight the famine. But let not the Central Government make the mistake of being off guard.

Relief Works on Large Scale

I would like to repeat that the next three months are going to be crucial. Rains have made it still more difficult to reach food to the villages. Means of transport break down. Villages do not have shops. Where will landless labourers get food ? For their sake relief works will have to be taken up on a large scale. Arrangements will have to be made there for distributing food. People would have to be provided with work. There is no assurance of such relief here. It is not enough to say that people are not dying of hunger. I know they are dying. This is not a party question. Yesterday too the Finance Minister had appealed for cooperation. The Prime Minister is inviting opposition leaders to discuss the economic situation. But why can we not come together to fight the famine ? Why cannot a parliamentary committee tour eastern districts of Uttar Pradesh and Bihar to assess the extent of the food shortage, how serious the situation is, and what effective steps need to be taken ? Why cannot the Hon. Minister approach the Speaker with the proposal to set up such a committee ? Wherever possible political ends are sought to be served. I regret the Minister has either refused to throw light on the seriousness of the situation or to see it. I want to know what steps are being taken to provide relief work to people in U.P., Bihar etc. Is it true that in Maharashtra the Central Government closed down relief works by declining the grant of fifty paise and thus again created a food problem for the people ?

Government Should Feed 56 crore People

The Government has taken over wheat trade. Now that the Government has gone into business it should also accept the responsibility of feeding 56 crore people. There is no way to escape this. You cannot escape your responsibility by blaming the opposition. The *Far Eastern Economist* has written: "If scapegoats were edible, there would have been no starvation in India." But they are not. People's hunger is getting more and more severe and if you cannot give enough food at the right price the situation would get out of hand. What will then happen only time can tell.

SHRI FAKHRUDIN ALI AHMED : The statement placed before the House on behalf of the Government has stated what the Government did during the drought last year and what assistance it gave to the people. In my statement I have said that we are taking steps to continue with this work in U.P. and Bihar and to give substantial aid to the affected people ... (*Interruption*). So far as eastern U.P. is concerned. I have just received information that 10,000 quintals of foodgrains from surplus districts are being dispatched and arrangements being made to distribute them to the people through fair price shops.

SHRI VAJPAYEE : How much will an individual get per week at the fair price shops ?

SHRI FAKHRUDIN ALI AHMED : The Hon. Member has raised the right point. Today there is no uniform rate for the whole of India. At some places it is less, at some it is more...(*Interruption*). I said the whole country does not have uniform rates. The quantity of foodgrains to be distributed through fair price shops is determined in consultation with state Governments....(*Interruption*).

SHRI S.N. BANERJEE : He should reply to the question. The question was raised by Shri Vajpayee about the quantity of ration which has been given in Uttar Pradesh. It was reduced last week. Let him reply to the question ... (*Interruption*).

SHRI FAKHRUDIN ALI AHMED : I have said this depends upon how much foodgrain is available in that State, how much is available free, and how much we can give through ration shops. We fix the quota for every State after taking this into consideration. So far we have not fixed any uniform rate.

Poverty of Food Corporation Prosperity of Officials

Sir, I move that this House take the functioning of the Food Corporation of India into consideration.

Objectives of the Corporation

The Food Corporation was set up on January 1, 1965. At that time the Corporation was entrusted with some serious responsibilities. The Act passed in this connection said the Corporation would purchase and store foodgrains, arrange their movement, would be responsible for their distribution and at the same time would also promote food production. It was also said that the Corporation would either take over rice mills or assist in setting them up and would take steps to ensure proper distribution of foodstuffs.

These objectives are good in themselves and no one can have a quarrel with them. In our country we cannot develop an economy that would not protect the interests of both producers and consumers. If the farmer produces more and prices fall because of greater production, causing loss to the farmer, it is necessary for the corporation to buy foodgrains, stock it properly and bring it to the market, so that prices are stabilised and the people, especially the poorer sections, get enough food at proper prices.

Extraordinary Powers to the Corporation for Corruption

But the problem is that we have armed the Food Corporation with extraordinary powers and responsibilities. The governmentalisation of the wholesale trade in wheat was itself not the right decision. Now that it has been implemented through the Food Corporation it has totally failed. Today the corruption in the Food Corporation, the inefficiency, misuse of public funds, wilfulness of officials and the injustice to both the farmer and the consumer have become a matter of public debate. Things have come to such a pass that even Central Ministers are constrained to speak against the corruption prevailing in the Food Corporation. As the House is aware, a few days back Shri Shinde had said in an interview to the press—I quote : "Corruption in the Food Corporation of India knows no bounds...".

SHRI ANNASAHEB SHINDE, Minister of State in the Ministry of Agriculture : I would like to say that I did make a statement on some of the malpractices in the Food Corporation of India, but the words that have appeared in print are not exactly an honest reproduction of my views. I did refer to the

---

Lok Sabha on December 12, 1973 on Functioning of the Food Corporation of India

malpractices. I did refer to corruption in the Food Corporation. But the words which the Hon. Member is reading now, I must say in fairness to the House and to the Hon. Member, are not exactly the words I have used. They have been put in my mouth.

SHRI VAJPAYEE : Sir, now I am in difficulties. The Hon. Minister has not refused what has appeared in the press. He is also not willing to say what exactly he said. If he tells us that I am prepared to sit down.

SHRI ANNASAHEB SHINDE : I did refer to some cases of medical bills which were deliberately inflated by submitting false bills and more money was extracted from the Food Corporation. I also referred to the fact that in some areas the workers are resorting to illegal gratification.

SHRI JAGANNATHRAO JOSHI (Shajapur) : The tip of the iceberg.

SHRI VAJPAYEE : Sir, in Bombay port for every truck the Government of Maharashtra ... (*Interruption*).

SHRI ANNASAHEB SHINDE : I did refer to the statement of the Chief Minister.

SHRI VAJPAYEE : Sir, Shri Shinde has confirmed corruption. There may be some slight difference in the wording of the press reports. He has quoted the Chief Minister of Maharashtra — when trucks from Maharashtra leave Bombay port with imported foodgrains a bribe of Rs. 35 per truck has to be paid. I have read about the Chief Minister of Maharashtra asking : we pay the bribe, but please tell us in which account it is to be included.

Shri Shinde has also confirmed that medical bills have been greatly inflated. The medical bill of the Calcutta unit has grown from Rs. 12 lakhs to Rs. 82 lakhs. He also said the matter has been handed over to the C.B.I. and the Income Tax department is also inquiring into it.

Sir, it is not only the matter of the medical bills of the Calcutta unit that has been handed over to the C.B.I. I have read that the C.B.I. is inquiring into some charges against a former Chairman of the Food Corporation who was once a member of this House, later became a minister, later lost an election and then became Chairman of the Food Corporation. Let the Minister say what those charges are. What are the parameters of the C.B.I. inquiry ? I would also like to know when the inquiry would be completed.

So far the situation about the period of a C.B.I. inquiry is not satisfactory. I know of a matter where the C.B.I. took seven years to investigate. If so much time is taken for inquiring into corruption charges the very purpose of the inquiry would be defeated.

Sir, there are all sorts of complaints against the Food Corporation. There are complaints that at many places the fixed price of Rs. 76 per quintal for wheat was not paid to the farmer, it was returned on the ground that it was of poor quality, and later the same wheat was purchased from the traders at high prices. If the Minister wants to know the names of such places I can tell him.

Another complaint is that the Food Corporation's handling charges are continually going up. At first it was also said that these charges are from Rs. 22 to Rs. 32 per quintal for the storage of the wheat. But I have read press reports saying these charges have now risen to as high as Rs. 56. I wish the Minister throws light on this.

SHRI ANNASAHEB SHINDE : Rs. 56 which cost is he referring to ?

SHRI VAJPAYEE : Overhead charges per quintal for handling wheat.

SHRI S.D. SINGH (Chatra) : Per quintal.

SHRI VAJPAYEE : Yes.

Sir, there is also the serious charge that the Food Corporation incurs losses of crores of rupees every year because it wants to oblige contractors and benefit them. On May 10, 1973 the employees of the Food Corporation held a press conference in Calcutta in which they said :

> "Pilferage and corruption was rampant in the F.C.I. The detention of wagons at railway sidings had gone up, whereby the FCI has been sustaining a huge loss due to demurrage on wagons and pilferage of foodgrains to the tune of 40 per cent."

It is also well-known that the Food Corporation's own godowns lie empty while private godowns are taken on rent. This is done so that owners of private godowns should benefit and the officers of the Food Corporation could share the profit.

Sir, many such matters have come to my notice — for instance at Hathras the Food Corporation's own godown is lying vacant and a private godown has been rented to keep sugar. I fail to understand the propriety of this. In Hapur, Alipur the Food Corporation is paying a rental of Rs. 15,000 per month for land for which the rent could be Rs. 5,000.

Cost of Gunny Bags not Recovered from Mill Owners

Sir, it has already been discussed in this House that the Food Corporation gives foodgrain in the gunny-bags of flour mills. The price of these gunny-bags is not recovered from the mill- owners,. There is an attempt to give grain to the mills for grinding at cheap rates. The total cost of the gunny bags comes to Rs. 20-22 crores per year. The Food Corporation can recover this cost from the mill-owners. The Public Undertakings Committee had also made some recommendations in this regard, but so far as I know—the Hon. Minister may correct me if I am wrong—the cost of gunny-bags is not being recovered and the Food Corporation is incurring losses so that mill-owners may benefit. I have figures for 1972—the Food Corporation incurred a loss of Rs. 24 per quintal. I would like to know—what was the loss for 1973 ?

Sir, there is great irregularity in the movement of foodgrains. The Public Undertakings Committee has given some figures in this regard. In 1969-70 there was a loss of Rs. 8.83 crores. In 1970-71 it was 8.40 crores. We do not have figures for this year, because the Committee is yet to submit its report. But a certain matter has just been brought to my notice—eight wagons of wheat came to Varansi from Bihar, the Varanasi depot manager unloaded them by making out a fake receipt, and the grain was sold—it never reached the godown. It was distributed right at the railway station...(*Interruption*).

The Missing Bags

In Ludhiana 1600 bags were found to be missing at the Khanna depot. There are more complaints like this. It seems the Food Corporation is not inspired by the noble sentiment that every single paisa of the people, earned by hard labour, every single grain of food that is the product of the farmer's labour, should be taken care of and put to good use.

The situation today is such that the State Governments are setting up separate agencies of their own — call them corporations, call them food departments. Has the Central Government agreed to the setting up of separate agencies ? Has the Government accepted that if this job is entrusted to the State Governments it would be done cheaply ? Does the Centre feel that if the States do it there would be no corruption ? Does it feel that the moment this job is entrusted to the States all corruption, inefficiency and wilfulness of the officials would come to an end ? It seems the Centre wants to escape its responsibility and pass the buck.

Retrenchment of Staff

At present retrenchment is the order of the day in the Food Corporation. Employees are being removed. In Uttar Pradesh 924 employees have been removed. As many as 1200 employees have been demoted... (*Interruption*)...Shri Banerji says the number is 1242. I accept it. But I am surprised to see that while small employees are being retrenched the horde of officers is being augmented. During these very days 53 Deputy Managers and 10 Financial Advisors have been appointed and 80 Senior Assistant Managers have been made Deputy Managers. Junior employees recruited for the Rabi campaign were immediately removed when the campaign ended, but officers appointed for the same campaign have been absorbed by the Food Corporation. They have been accommodated.

Will the Food Corporation work for accommodating officers ? Will conditions of service be changed for some particular officer ? A certain matter has been brought to my notice—I shall not name names—where a gentleman was Quality Control Manager in the grade of Rs. 1000- 2000, but the grade was revised upward from Rs 2000 to 2500 because he is to retire in June 1975. The moment he retires the grade will again be brought down. Does a grade go up and down with an individual ? If this person possesses exceptional ability Shri Shinde can take the House into confidence, otherwise I cannot understand the reason for changing the grade like this.

The Economy Paradox

Sir, you will be surprised to learn that economy is being talked about in the Food Corporation. Propaganda is being made to the effect that 43 lakh rupees will be saved. But no efforts are being made to recover the outstandings of Rs. 291 crores that the States owe to the Food Corporation. The Food Corporation has borrowed this money from the banks and is paying interest on it. In two and a half years the Food Corporation has paid

Rs. 45 crores by way of interest and now Rs. 43 lakhs are being saved. Can the State Government not be persuaded to return the Food Corporation's money ? Can they not be forced to do so ? If the State Governments want to do the Food Corporation's work they should at least return the Corporation's money. Because of their not doing so the Food Corporation is losing in interest payments and looks impoverished, and in the name of economy small employees are being retrenched. Can the Centre not recover Rs. 291 crores from the State Governments ?

Sir, there is scope for difference of opinion on whether or not the Government should engage in grain trade. It is not only a matter of principle, it is also a matter of practical considerations. Through which agency do we want the farmer to get the right price and the consumer to get foodgrains at the right price ? We condemn traders by calling them middlemen. No one can deny that among traders there are elements that exploit scarcity conditions to make a profit. But what is the Food Corporation doing ? Has it not itself become a middleman ? Are its handling charges not high ? Is it not responsible for adulteration ?

In Punjab wheat was sent from Doraha to Monghyr, not by some trader but by a government agency, and it was found to contain iron pieces. Where did they come from ? Milo and *Dhatura* can be found together, because according to American friends they grow together and may be cut together in the machine, but has iron started growing in the field under the present dispensation ? If not, how were iron pieces found in the wheat sent to Monghyr ?...(*Interruption*). It was sent by a government agency, unloaded by a government agency and was transported by the Government's railway...(*Interruption*).

SHRI ANNASAHEB SHINDE : Some traders may have purchased some of our officers.

SHRI VAJPAYEE : Then they can purchase your Ministers also.

Reorganisation of Corporation Necessary

Sir, what I want to say is that entrusting the States with the Food Corporation's work will not solve the problem. It should not surprise anyone if doing so increases expenditure, slackens maintenance and promotes corruption. Nor will the problem be solved by retrenching employees. What is needed is to organise the Food Corporation on the lines of Life Insurance Corporation. Instead of having one organisation for the whole country there could be zone-wise organisations. That could also help to establish coordination with the State Governments. Stern action should be taken against corrupt elements—pardon me, they are more among officers.

In view of the interests of both the farmer and the consumer an agency would always be needed that would give a remunerative price to the farmer and make foodgrains available to the consumer at the proper price. It is necessary to strengthen such an arrangement. But the Government should not have a monopoly either in sale or in purchase. Monopoly is the source of evils. We should strengthen the distribution system still further but at the same time rid it of corruption and make it alert. Now-a-days the Food Corporation is known as food corruption, and it is the small employees who are blamed for this. When a net is spread to snare the corrupt small fry get caught but big crocodiles get away. This is not the way to eliminate corruption.

I wish the House discusses this matter seriously and comes up with suggestions that could provide guidance to the Central Government. Thank you.

Rampant Irregularities in the Name of Land Reforms

Sir, our first priority is to make the country self-sufficient in food. Steps taken in the field of agriculture will have to be tested against this criterion. Zamindari abolition and fixing the maximum ceiling on land holdings are necessary steps. We have to see that the person who takes personal interest in production from land and whose future is linked with land becomes the owner of the land. From this point of view land reforms are necessary.

Land Reform Laws not Implemented

But is it enough to make a law ? In our country we talk a lot about land reform, but we have not acted very effectively for it. If courts come in the way of implementing land reform laws those laws should be given proper protection. We have clearly given protection to 66 laws and yet land reforms have not been implemented. The Hon. Minister should explain this. For example there are two Acts of Uttar Pradesh. The U.P Zamindari Abolition and Land Reforms Act, 1950, and the U.P Ceilings on Land Holdings Act 1958.

We have protected them. The present Bill does not mention any law of Uttar Pradesh.

The means in U.P. the Court is not an impediment in implementing land reforms and yet what is their plight ?

Sir, the U.P. Government had set up a land system investigation committee. It was headed by Shri Mangal Dev Visharad. This Committee submitted its report on March 30, 1974. If you read it you will find it hard to believe that land reforms have been implemented in U.P. Appendix 18 mentions some important cases in which ways and means to escape the ceiling regulation have been given. One of them relates to the Majithia family of Gorakpur. It says :

> "The Majithias are a family of big farmers. Its four main figures are Sarvashri Gurjit Singh, Surendra Singh, Gurnihal Singh and Dalip Singh. Before the ceiling regulation came into effect these four together had 3,131.71 acres of land."

The report further says after the Act came into force only 29 acres of land were declared excess. According to the Committee, "somehow the family saved its entire land-holding to be declared excess." How did this happen ?

Another case is of Ramgarh Farm and Industries, Calcutta. Here the committee says : "This party's total land holding area is 5,548 acres."

Lok Sabha on August 26, 1974 on Constitution Thirty-fourth Amendment Bill relating to Agriculture

According to the Committee this farm was also wrongly favoured. It too has excess land.

Another instance is that of Sardar Jogender Singh, resident of Bhangaha, district Bahraich. In this connection the Committee says :

> "The party's total land-holding was 2260.60 acres. He asked for a waiver on a very large area under the excuse of an orchard, on which the Committee ruled that it was not proved that the trees were planted before May 1, 1959. Only two acres were set aside for an orchard."

The Committee further observed that a large area of this land is lying unattended.

I would like to place one more example before you. It is of Gopalpur Farm, district Mirzapur. About it the Committee writes:

"In district Mirzapur there is a big farm of 4532 acres named Gopalpur Farm in Gopalpur. According to land records the names of 14 persons were registered for this land, most of whom are residents of Varanasi. If every one of these parties is said to have an equal share everyone's share of land comes to 323.71 acres. On making inquiries with the district office it was learnt that no ceiling proceedings were undertaken in respect of these landholders under the U.P. Maximum Ceiling Act of 1960 when even with this farm every party had land in excess of the maximum ceiling. It is said these landholders have a cooperative agriculture committee. But even if such a Committee was formed it could not have been given concession under the old section 6 (15) of the Act. Even the land records prove this. This whole holding was registered in the name of 14 persons, not in that of any cooperative agricultural society. The Committee says :

> "Another interesting fact that has come to notice regarding this farm is that on the basis of orders by the judicial officer dated April 17, 1972 the names of 63 other persons were registered as partners for the whole land of Gopalpur Farm. According to information given by the district office this claim was registered before January 24, 1971. The result of this would be that it would not be possible to declare any land of such a big farm to be excess. When the question comes up, the farm is one unit and exists for the benefit of the family. The names of the people of many districts of the State and of Bihar and Nepal have been falsely registered in the farm so that it could escape the provisions of the Ceiling Act."

These instances given in the report make fun of our land laws. In Punjab instances of forcible occupation of such lands have been highlighted by the Harchand Singh Committee .

Sir, if there is no sincerity in implementing land reforms no laws can achieve the government's objective.

Rather, too much debate on land reforms has the adverse effect of creating uncertainty in the farmer's mind. I would forcefully urge the Minister of Agriculture to implement land reforms honestly. Once that is done, announce that for the next 10-15 years that there would be no change in the land-holding, so that the farmer would invest more in land and adopt modern techniques of food production, making the country self-sufficient in food.

Talk of Reforms Decreased Production

These days too much talk of land reforms has created uncertainty in respect of agricultural production. If you want that land reforms should be implemented honestly and agricultural production should increase it is necessary to remove this sword of uncertainty. So I am opposing this bill. At the same time I know that all these laws that you want to keep outside the jurisdiction of the courts would not be implemented, because those controlling the reins of the administration lack the will- power.

Secondly, we want the landless to have land. A majority of Harijans and Vanvasis is in great need of land, but it would not be enough to give land. They need agricultural tools and they need loans. We have seen in the Terai region of Uttar Pradesh that land has been given to those who are not used to farming. The result was that they sold it. If people have land but not the implements of farming they would not be able to cultivate it and later they would again become landless. So it is necessary that if you give people land you should form them into a cooperative farm and give them agricultural tools so that they can together engage in farming. If anyone wants to farm on his own he may do so, but merely giving land would not solve the problem.

Sir, we have aroused a hunger for land but we do not have enough land to satisfy it. What we should rather do is to lessen the pressure on land, divert people from land to industry. We could not spread a net-work of agriculture-related industries. It is not enough to give the example of Japan. In Japan the farms are small, but every farm is connected with a factory.

I had been to a Communist country. It is not necessary to name it. The farmers there have three times the land specified by our land ceiling. Nobody there wants land because the country has been industrialised. We do not have industrialisation here, so people are more dependent on land. We cannot give land to everybody. But we are raising hopes in their minds. The problem of the rural population would not be solved so long as we do not develop agriculture-related industries along with land reforms.

Maximum Land-holding

It is necessary to have a maximum ceiling on land-holding. It would have been better if the ceiling had been in terms of income rather than acres. But I have seen that money laws are silent on the minimum limit. Do we want to cut up land into pieces ? Do we want to increase uneconomic holdings ? You have laid down the maximum limit in the name of social justice. I doubt how much production this will increase. But the Minister of Agriculture will agree that if the maximum limit is small and if the land is distributed among many sons of a landholder a limit should be laid down below which distribution of land would not be permitted. But here we are giving blanket powers. It is not possible for the House to examine every law in all its details. The Chief

Ministers have decided upon a policy for exceptions. Is that policy being implemented equally in all states ? What is the policy about tea plantations and what is the policy for sugarcane farms ? What is the policy regarding making exceptions of cooperative societies formed by families ? It is necessary to go deep into these questions.

No Land Records

A strange situation prevails in some States. In Bihar there are no land records at all. How will the land reform law be implemented ? In Andhra land reforms have been much discussed, but big farmers are still in existence there. Ministers are planting vineyards. Now what to do with these grapes ? So wine distilleries are being opened. And in Haryana sign-boards saying *'Pio aur jio'* are being put up. Can the Minister of Agriculture say if our policy regarding vineyards is the same everywhere ?

SHRI DARBARA SINGH (Hoshiarpur) : The signboards are for milk—drink and live.

SHRI VAJPAYEE : Since when did grapes start giving out white juice ?

Do not be under the impression that you have won on the food front by passing the laws that we have put outside the jurisdiction of the courts, and that your duty has come to an end with giving land to the landless. This is a complex problem. Actually it is bound up with our entire social system. Making laws will not be enough. If land is to be distributed will the landless have majority representation on the Committees set up for this purpose ? Will the Government machinery be effective enough to see that those who have been given land can actually take possession ? In Uttar Pradesh the U.P. Government announced in Lucknow that Harijans would be given land in the Balrampur region. I went to see where the land was and they told me we have been given it but we have not got it. I came to Lucknow and asked where the land was given and I was told we have sent it from here, it will reach shortly.

The land you are giving is in somebody else's possession. They not only own the land, they are eminent people. They wield the stick. They also have the vote. Who will now dispossess them of land ? The courts will be sidelined and *'Danda Raj'* will prevail. You may pass this law — there is no difference of opinion on that. But do not start feeling that with this you have triumphed on the land reforms front. Thank you.

Drought Stalks the Land

Sir, I want to raise a discussion under rule 193 on a statement made by the Minister of Agriculture in this House on July 20, 1982 on drought conditions.

The Hon. Minister made not one but two statements on July 20—one in the Rajya Sabha and the other in the Lok Sabha. The first was made before lunch and the other before dinner. The first showed worry and despair, the other had a glimpse of hope. How did this change come about in a matter of hours ? In the meanwhile he received reports of some rain in Rajasthan, Haryana and Punjab. It is natural to be gladdened with the news, but the Agriculture Minister should be on guard against swinging between hope and despair. We have to look at the situation neither pessimistically nor optimistically but realistically. Our perception should be realistic.

According to what the Minister said that day the present situation is more serious than even the drought of 1979. About that drought it was said that there had been no such drought for the past 100 years. Do they feel this time's drought would outstrip any old drought ? According to a forecast of the meteorological department—I do not know if it can be relied upon—there would be less rain this time than in 1979. If it proves right the drought would spread and the situation would worsen.

Situation is Explosive

That day the Hon. Minister admitted that out of 243 districts of nine States there has been less rain in 146 districts. These States stretch from Gujarat to West Bengal and Orissa. Even Maharashtra has not escaped.

AN HON. MEMBER : Even Rajasthan.

SHRI VAJPAYEE : In Rajasthan the situation is very serious. Reports from Madhya Pradesh and West Bengal make me apprehensive that unless there are immediate rains or immediate effective steps by the Government looting would start there. People are leaving their homes in search of work. Reports like this are coming from many States.

This is happening in Chhatisgarh in Madhya Pradesh. The paddy crop has wilted for want of rain. In West Bengal there was no paddy sowing at all. The seed beds of paddy have also been destroyed. Newspaper reports from West Bengal indicate that people have started *gheraoing* government officers for foodgrains. Districts like Burdwan and Bankura which used to be called rice granaries have also been affected. I quote a *Statesman* report—

> "The Block Development Officer of Raipur II in Bankura was gheroed for eight hours while touring the block. The demonstrators demanded

Lok Sabha on August 3, 1982 while initiating discussion regarding drought conditions in various parts of the country

> work and food. The next day another large group ghearoed him in his office for several hours and heckled him. The BDO, Indpur was also gheraoed by 4000 people recently."

There is also a report that a truck carrying grain from Midnapur was stopped and looted. I do not know how far this news is true. I am only saying what has been published.

In Chhatisgarh people are leaving their homes in large numbers. This is because there is no rain and there is no food. People are in great difficulties in Palamu, Chhota Nagpur and other parts of Bihar.

Sir, what should farm labour do ? Nature has turned its back on them, the land is parched and work has stopped in the fields. How can those working on daily wages allay their hunger ?

The Hon. Central Minister became hopeful with a little rain. The Rajasthan Government is pleased no end. A *Patriot* report says —

> "Finding the first monsoon showers to be 'adequate' the Rajasthan Government has decided to discontinue all famine relief work in the State from July 31."

Look at the promptness with which the Government takes a decision. No one can charge it with laxity. But how dangerous this decision is need not be told.

Rajasthan has been in the grip of drought for the past five years. Thousands of villages have been affected. People have no water to drink. There is no fodder and water for the cattle. Just a little rain, and Government stopped all relief work. The report further said :

> "Announcing the decision taken by the State Government yesterday, the official spokesman said that with these showers the farmers had become busy in the fields and there was no need to continue the relief work in the State."

Is it on the strength of these State governments that preparations are being made to fight the drought ? I do not say all State governments behave the same way but if there is even a little optimism it would spread to some areas. State governments would forget their duty. The rains have come now, all's well, and there is no cause for worry.

On the other hand, I would like to warn against ...

CHAIRMAN : Is optimism also contagious ?

SHRI VAJPAYEE : Yes, both happiness and grief, hope and despair are contagious.

Secondly, I am apprehensive that attempts may be made to blow up the situation. State governments have to depend upon the Centre. The Centre goes on in the same old way. It will send a study team to study the situation. To how many States has it gone ? Then there will be reports. Then the State Governments would say the reports do not present the real situation. The Chief Minister says another study team should be sent for a correct assessment. Then there will be a debate on it. New Delhi has delayed a decision. How can such a serious crisis be overcome ?

Bengal Famine of 1943 Remembered

If the situation is more serious than in 1977, if people in West Bengal are reminded of the famine of 1943, if thousands of people are forced to leave their hearths and homes and trek to towns, clearly the situation needs to be tackled on a war footing. If the Centre shifts its responsibility to the States and the States just rely on district officers we cannot do justice by the famine-affected.

Shri Rao is not present in the House, perhaps he is busy monitoring.

SHRI R.V. SWAMINATHAN, Minister of State in the Ministries of Agriculture and Rural Development : He will come. I am here.

SHRI VAJPAYEE : You are here but he is not here.

SHRI R.V. SWAMINATHAN : He is coming.

SHRI VAJPAYEE : But I want the Cabinet Minister. They are not taking the discussion seriously.

SHRI R.K. SWAMINATHAN : We are very serious.

CHAIRMAN : He will be coming, I think.

SHRI VAJPAYEE : It is a question of propriety. I know there is no sense of urgency on their part. But at least parliamentary propriety should be observed. He did not write to you.

I do not want a heated discussion on this. This is not a party matter. A very serious situation has arisen. I do not know what is going to happen. If you are not alive to your duty...

SHRI R.V. SWAMINATHAN : May I give you some information about the rainfall in the country ?

SHRI VAJPAYEE : Not now, whatever rain there has been, canalise it properly after the discussion.

SHRI RAMAVATAR SHASTRI (Patna) : Have an umbrella.

12–Point Programme only on Paper

SHRI VAJPAYEE : That day the Agriculture Minister repeatedly discussed the Prime Minister's Twelve-Point Programme in his speech. In 1980 the Prime Minister had prepared a 12–point programme to fight the drought. I have seen that programme. It is a good programme. It looks good on paper. The test will be how far it is implemented.

According to this programme how many full-time relief officers have been appointed in drought-prone areas ? Let the Agriculture Minister give the details to the House (*Interruption*). Yes, the States have to do it, but the States together make up the Centre.

The second point is that there should be daily monitoring of food stocks, employment opportunities, starvation deaths and availability of drinking water. In how many drought-prone areas is this daily monitoring going on ? According to the Prime Minister's suggestion there should be buffer godowns in affected areas. How many such buffer godowns have been set up ?

There is a food shortage at the Centre. Stocks of 15 million tons are not enough. But these stocks should be available in affected areas for immediate distribution to the people. There are transportation problems. So the Prime Minister has suggested that buffer godowns should be located there. Has this been done ?

The 12-Point Programme also said there should be a fair price shop per 2000 population. It also said banks should give assistance in this.

Is it not true that the whole grain distribution machinery of the government has broken down ? There were already no shops in the villages. Wherever there are shops they do not receive enough supplies. The Centre says we have given foodgrains but they do not fully reach the States. Where does the grain go on the way ?

Then there is the problem of reaching it from the States capitals to the villages. In these nine States you will have to arrange foodgrain distribution at proper prices in the villages. Has a survey been made about how many shops would be required to be opened per 2000 population, as suggested by the Prime Minister, and how many of them have been opened ? Will the Centre not do this ? Is it enough to prepare a 12-Point Programme and end it ? I said the project is good, but the real test . . .

SHRI R.V. SWAMINATHAN: Let me inform you, Mr. Vajpayee ...

Drought Relief Money Spent on Construction of Godowns

SHRI VAJPAYEE: Sir, the Agriculture Minister has referred to drought-prone areas in his speech. This programme has been going on for years. Some commendable work has been done in it. But I was looking at an audit report on drought-prone areas. According to this report of 1980-81 the Centre has to give 50 per cent and the States 50 per cent. But the report says the Centre gave 50 per cent while the States did not. I am coming to the financial position of the States. Even the amount given was not spent. This audit report is full of examples where funds earmarked for this programme have not been spent. In Bihar three agencies were given Rs. 1247 lakhs but only Rs. 1000 lakhs were spent. Unspent amounts remain in Madhya Pradesh and Uttar Pradesh. The situation in Andhra is such that they have not given any account of Rs. 9 crores 63 lakhs. In respect of the drought-prone areas programme the Centre has clearly directed that unless works in hand were completed no new work was to be taken up. The States disregarded this. Many incomplete works of the Fourth Plan were not included in the Fifth Plan. In Andhra Pradesh seven projects were left incomplete after spending Rs. 50 lakhs, 280 irrigation projects were taken up in the Fifth Pan in Andhra, Orissa, Madhya Pradesh. Of them 86 were left incomplete. Seven crore rupees went down the drain.

There are also examples where money was spent and potential created but that potential is not utilised because there is no command area for irrigation. Now that there is a drought and nature is adverse we can well imagine how much we are suffering because of the deficiencies in this programme. There are also examples of money given for drought relief being spent on godown construction. Instead of fighting the drought houses were built.

Sir, let the Agriculture Minister take the House into confidence about the current situation. How much rain was there after July 20 ? How much intensity of the drought did it mitigate ? Did it at all mitigate or not ? And what is the picture today ? Let the House know.

Insufficient rainfall has also created difficulties for hydropower generation. How much power are we providing for agriculture ? What efforts are being made to make up the shortfall in power supply ?

Migration to Urban Areas

What is the situation in Uttar Pradesh ? The Power Minister is not here. Both the Power and Agriculture Ministers should have been present here, but when the Agriculture Minister himself is absent (*Interruption*)... I do not have eyes at the back, I can see only ahead of me. Sir, what is the situation in U.P. ?

"Thermal generation is about 525 MW against an installed capacity of 2267 MW, while hydel generation is around 485 MW against an installed capacity of 1212 MW."

On top of it shortage of rainfall and the water table going down. How can we make up the suddenly increased demand for water for irrigation?

Let the Agriculture Minister also say how much money the State Governments asked for tackling drought and how much of it the Centre has been able to give. I feel some States may have inflated their demands. This is natural, but the Centre should not discriminate against any State only because it does not get on with it. If drought is a national problem no discrimination against any State or party will be tolerated.

Hon. Members from West Bengal will tell you that the overdraft has been stopped, there are no foodgrains in the villages and the distribution system is breaking down. In such a situation the Centre's behaviour should be such as to create confidence in the minds of all States.

I also want to know what projects the government is going to take up for providing work to agricultural labour. If there is a large outflow of labourers from villages into the cities the results would be disastrous. Reports of looting are coming in. Already the law and order situation in the country is bad. If effective steps are not taken in time this drought will have unimaginable consequences. Agricultural labour has to be provided work on a large scale in the villages and it should not be restricted to road building.

Drought is not a Party Problem

Sometimes a drought proved a blessing for the ruling party. There was a by-election to a Lok Sabha seat in Jaipur. Before the day of polling 80,000 people were provided work in that constituency and a few days later it was stopped.

SHRI G.L. VYAS (Bhilwara) : It is still going on.

SHRI VAJPAYEE : I demand an inquiry. We are ready to prove our charges. We do not worry about your victory in the elections, but do not starve people to death.

I request the Central Agriculture Minister to call a meeting of Chief Ministers in New Delhi. By that time the Prime Minister would have returned from abroad. She too should participate in that meeting. Thought should be given to and decisions taken on what steps need to be taken at the level of the Centre, the State, the district and the village, and implementation of the decisions should be monitored (*Interruption*). The Centre has sent a study team, but another study team is being demanded.

Today the States want funds and foodgrains, agricultural labourers want work, cattle want fooder and water, and all this needs to be done on a war-footing. I have also suggested to the Minister for Parliamentary Affairs that the Agriculture Minister should keep in constant touch with Members of Parliament from drought-affected areas.

I would like to repeat that this is not a party problem. But there are many States where the Administration has been paralysed, where the Chief Minister is more concerned with what the newspapers say against him. He does not care for what the people think of him. Administration in Bihar is going to the dogs, but the Chief Minister is not worried about it. He only wants that no news should be published against him. Is this the time to fight the opposition by bringing in a Bill against the freedom of the press ? This internecine warfare will go on. If you want cooperation in fighting the drought this is not the way to do it. But I see no concern for the drought, I see concern for power. That is what the Chief Ministers are concerned about.

Shri Rao has arrived ......

Sir, I do not see the urgency that is needed to tackle the situation. But if we do not work with a sense of urgency the country would be caught up in a grave crisis. My purpose in initiating this discussion was to acquaint the Hon. Minister with the sentiments of the House so that he could take it into confidence about the Government's plans. We do not want the country to be caught up in a major crisis.

RAO BIRENDRA SINGH, Minister of Agriculture : You can pray.

SHRI VAJPAYEE : I can pray and I can also bless, but my blessings have the opposite impact.

SHRI G.L. VYAS : Then please excuse.

SHRI VAJPAYEE : I am not giving my blessings. Prayers would not be of use. Those who are Ministers should not talk of praying. Let *Pujari* talk about it. Ministers should talk about administration. The hungry will pray. But if the Government cannot give food, water and work to the drought-affected, prayers cannot save it. It will burn down in the flames of the people's hunger.

VII Railways And Transport

Listen to the Railway Employees

Sir, I welcome the Railway Minister's announcement regarding ending the distinction between Class III and Class IV employees but I would like to know from the Deputy Railway Minister if this facility would be extended to the artisan staff too. The Railway Ministry and the Railway Board should also consider the condition of employees working in railway sheds and workshops, which is bad. I regret to note that the Hon. Minister has not said anything about the demands of other classes of railway employees. Commercial clerks draw very poor salaries, but in the announcement made by the Railway Minister on February 10, 1957, which is known as the New Deal, commercial clerks were not given more facilities on the ground that they would get Inspectorate posts by way of promotion, but in reality these posts are not filled from their ranks and they stand to lose.

I would like to draw the Minister's attention to Station Masters and Assistant Station Masters. They have important posts and also big responsibilities. They control and supervise everything. But the announcement of February 10 does not seem to have benefited them. A railway employee becomes a signaller after ten months' training and receives a salary of 60 rupees. After working as a singaller for four years he becomes an Assistant Station Master and in these four years his salary becomes Rs. 75. The only benefit given to Assistant Station Masters by the announcement of February 10 is that instead of Rs. 76 they will now get Rs. 80 per month. A monthly benefit of four rupees in these days of high prices and rising dearness cannot be called satisfactory. It is the same case with Station Masters. An Assistant Station Master becomes a Station Master after 15 years of service. According to his grades his salary comes to Rs. 114 per month. The benefits given by the Railway Minister would not be available to those Station Masters who will retire by 1960, and so this cannot be considered immediate relief.

Obviously Station Masters and Assistant Station Masters are dissatisfied with their lot. They have also expressed their resentment. They had observed July 1, 1956 as Demands Day. On February 1, 1957 they had a salary strike and 92 per cent of the Station Masters and Assistant Station Masters did not draw their salaries. They did not take these steps to pressurise the Railway Ministry or the Railway Board. They want their demands to be given

Lok Sabha on July 19, 1957 on the Demands for Grants of the Ministry of Railways

sympathetic consideration. But the Railway Minister is not ready even to talk to them. What sort of democracy is this where you refuse even to talk to an employees' association ? That association has not yet been recognised, but that is a different matter. You should talk to them, understand their difficulties and explain your difficulties to them. If you do this some way out would certainly be found. But when all doors for talks are closed they will be left with no option but to take some drastic step. I do not want these people to take any such step.

This does not depend upon them alone. If the Railway Board and the Ministry force them to take a serious step there would be no option left for them but to take a step that would not only adversely affect our development plans but disrupt the life of the entire nation. I hope such a situation would not arise and some way would be found.

Just now the Railway Minister said something about recognising unions. I want to express my disagreement with it. His claim that the Railway Board or the Railway Ministry does not interfere with employees' unions appears confined to mere words. I have before me the Northern Railway Mazdoor Union's case. It has been going on for some two years. Those who control the Northern Railway Mazdoor Union have lost the confidence of the members and if they continue in office it is only because the Railway Board supports them and wants to help them to continue in office. There is widespread resentment among these workers and it has also been expressed. Wherever the General Manager of the Northern Railway goes demonstrations are held against him. I do not know how such a situation can continue for long. If you do not want to recognise new unions, withdraw the recognition of the unions that have lost the confidence of their members. If the only reason for continuing their recognition is that they are supported by the ruling party, then the hope of establishing peace in the Railways will never be fulfilled. Conflict is then inevitable.

Think About Railway Unions

In this connection I would like to submit that everybody wants that there should be one union of all railway employees and that there should be no dissension in it—at least I want it. But I don't think splitting elements are present only in opposition parties. When partisan and selfish sentiments are generated all talk of unity remains empty talk, it is not acted upon. The Railway Board should think about the Northern Railway Mazdoor Union. It is not a good situation — and no one likes it — that there are demonstrations against the General Manager, that he should have to travel by night and not by day and he should be greeted with black flags wherever he goes. Friendly feelings and cooperation between officers and employees are a *sine qua non* for the efficient running of the Railways. Railway employees had great expectations of Shri Jagjivan Ram. But I would very respectfully say that those hopes have become somewhat blurred. There is still time. The situation has not deteriorated, it can be improved. I do not have anything more to say in this regard.

The Centralisation Move

For the past some days an inclination towards centralisaton has been noticed in the Railway administration. The new divisions that are being set up are being headquartered at places that already have a number of offices. The headquarters at Bandikui are being taken to Jaipur and the headquarters at Gonda to Lucknow. I do not think this centralisation would help administrative efficiency or increase Railway employees' benefits. We should have decentralisation along with operational efficiency. The Railway Ministry should think from this point of view.

As for pilferage on the railways a protection force has been set up and this House is aware of the objections raised on it. If we want to check pilferage we should not entrust the protection of railway property, which is the nation's property, to people who do not prove upto the job.

There is also the problem of railway wagons. Nizamuddin is under the very nose of the Railway Board. It is a big transit point. I have seen that just because of labour shortage wagons are not loaded here, they lie idle. If labour is in short supply the contractors are responsible for it and they could be penalised. If the Railway Minister were to call for figures for the last two months to see how many wagons were lying idle and how much loss the Railways have incurred because of this some startling facts would come to light. It is a matter of surprise that this labour shortage has been dismissed as a shortage of Railway employees.

Railway employees are ready to work more and they have given full cooperation in making the Five Year Plan a success. But vested interests are forming a nexus with some officers and employees whose loyalty is suspect. This creates difficulties. In order to resolve these difficulties all such centres should be kept under close observation, and the suggestions of those workers who are working sincerely and who want to improve the situation should be seriously considered.

That is all that I have to say. Thank you.

The Railways are in Shambles

Sir, before I express my thoughts on the Railway Budget I express my disagreement with my hon. friend Seth Govind Das's statement that the Railway Minister deserves sympathy for the accidents that have taken place.

SETH GOVIND DAS : I did not say about this.

SHRI VAJPAYEE : Our sympathies should be not with the Railway Minister but with those thousands of people who have lost their lives because of the inefficiency, incapacity and laxity of the railway administration.

SETH GOVIND DAS : Sir, a personal explanation. I did not say I sympathise with the Minister for the accidents, I said I sympathised with the difficult conditions under which all this goes on.

SPEAKER : He knows it.

AN HON. MEMBER : Like the accidents that are taking place.

SHRI VAJPAYEE : The sympathies are there, but they are with those who were killed.

SETH GOVIND DAS : Mine too.

The Increasing Railway Accidents

SHRI VAJPAYEE : It is not the Railway Minister but a weak person with whom one sympathises. The Railway Minister is not weak. If he wants, he can bring about such changes in the railway administrations as would substantially bring down the number of accidents. I do not agree that some accidents have taken place due to natural causes. Whatever reasons have come to light on inquiry indicate that many accidents could have been avoided if caution and foresight would have been exercised and if every Railwayman would have been motivated for dedication to duty. Last year's accidents had claimed 4,322 lives while the number of deaths this year is 5045. This year 32,341 people were injured while last year the number was 28,770.

This does not include employees killed or injured while working in the workshop. These accidents have created a sense of insecurity in the travellers. When they travel they throw themselves on the mercy of God. They do not hope that they would return alive. Our Railway Minister has both *'Jag'* and *'Jivan'* in his name but travellers lose both *'Jag'* (the world) and *'Jivan'* (Life). They are left, only with Ram, the last portion of the Railway Minister's name.

The steps so far taken to prevent accidents are neither adequate nor effective. I shall not demand the Railway Minister's resignation on the basis of these accidents although the tradition of tendering such a resignation for an accident in the interest of a healthy constitutional tradition has been set in this House. But resignations cannot prevent accidents. They need effective

Lok Sabha on February 27, 1958 during General Discussion on the Railway Budget

steps. The Hon. Minister has acquainted the Rajya Sabha with what was decided in this regard in the General Managers' meeting. What is needed here is operational efficiency and awakening, up to high levels of a sense of responsibility among the people entrusted with the job. In my view the Railway administration has not been able to awaken this sense of responsibility in every employee at every level. During the past decade this has been its greatest failure despite Independence. If we go to the root of the problem we find that the employees—including the officers, who are more to blame — are not yet as alive to their duty as they ought to be. The Railway Minister will have to reassure the people that their life and property would be safe during a journey. Last year's accidents have shaken this confidence. It will have to be restored.

Railways' Labour Policy is Reactionary

Views for and against the current policy of the Railway Ministry have been expressed here yesterday and today. If our Communist friends say anything in favour of labour it cannot be dismissed by asking—what is the position of labour in countries where the Communist Party is in power ? I have no hesitation in saying that the Railway Ministry's policy regarding labour and recognition of labour unions is reactionary. It smells of partisanship. It cannot develop healthy trade unionism in Railwaymen. I see that in the North-Eastern Railway the Northern Railway labour union has been recognised even when it has lost the workers' trust. If elections were held today it would not get a majority. But the General Management and railway officials are propping it up. This is why the employees feel disappointed, and an employee suffering from pessimism and dissatisfaction cannot be expected to work well.

Recently a large part of the Northern Railway labour union has been amalgamated with the Northern Railwaymen's union. In other fields too two unions have been recognised. But in the North Eastern Railway only the union recognised by the ruling party is being officially propped up. I hope this policy will be changed. If labour unions go in the right direction, if they keep national interests in view they can be of assistance to the railway administration. They will not be a hindrance. It is wrong to feel that railway unions are against the administration. It is necessary that the two should work in cooperation. But cooperation can be based on justice, not on serving party ends. So I call upon the Ministry to reconsider its policy.

Pension Scheme and Provident Fund

In his speech the Hon. Railway Minister has referred to a pension scheme for all Railwaymen. According to him it would be compulsorily applicable to those employees who join after November 15, 1957 and voluntary for those in service before that date. But even for those for whom it has been presented as voluntary it has been made compulsory that they should say before March 31, 1958 whether they would like to opt for it or continue under the provident fund plan. In my view this is too short a period. It should be extended. Not every employee can decide by March 31, 1958. The scheme envisages a radical change in the system. It will have far-reaching consequences. Every employee's future is linked with it. He should be given enough time to examine every aspect of the problem. So I suggest an extension of the period by six months beyond March 31, 1958 and the rules of the pension scheme should be given to every employee in his own mother tongue in printed form. The Railway Minister has indicated how Hindi is being increasingly used in the Railways. I would like to point out to him that all employees have not received the pension scheme rules in their mother tongue. Minor employees cannot use rules printed in English to decide if they should join the scheme.

One more thing. The benefits of the scheme have not been publicised enough. The employees are beset with doubts and cannot decide which way they should go. So extending the period and giving them enough time for a decision are necessary. So far as I can see the Railway Ministry has decided upon the pension scheme, because it will be compulsorily applicable to those employees who joined after November 15, 1957. In my opinion both options should be open to the employees even later. The provident fund plan should be open even to those who joined after November 15, 1957 if they do not want to be covered by the pension scheme.

Corruption and Victimisation

Many members have stressed the eradication of corruption in the Railways. Our experience is that the more the efforts in this direction the more varied and formidable the forms that corruption assumes. All the recommendations made in this regard by the Acharya Kripalani Committee have not so far been implemented. Cases of corruption come to light from place to place. Attempts are made to cover them up. I know that the case of appointment of Khalasis at Lucknow has recently come up. The Selection Board recruited some other people in place of those selected for recruitment. When a complaint was made to the Senior Vigilance Officer he made an inquiry into the cases of a hundred Khalasis out of 500 and found that seven had not been selected. One of them was working in another's place. A person named Mohammed was selected but a person named Gulab was appointed in his place. This fraud was exposed and I am afraid it is being hushed up. I hope firm steps will be taken in all cases of corruption that come to light and railwaymen would not be made to feel that the railway administration is in any way interested in suppressing corruption cases.

Another point I would like to make is that railway employees are being harassed on trifling excuses. Charges are levelled against them and they were removed from employment even when those charges cannot be proved. An employee at the hospital in Jabalpur was charged and removed from service in 1950. He took the matter to the Court and the Court ordered his reinstatement. He resumed duty, but within three hours he was again suspended and later dismissed. He took the matter to the Bombay High Court and the Court struck down the dismissal. But when the man again resumed duty he was again suspended and is still suspended. Sir, such instances do not redound to the prestige of the railway administration.

The Imperialist Hang Over

The conduct rules laid down for railwaymen also smell of imperialistic administration. I would call the Minister's attention to their Hindi copy. On page 2 it says, 'It will be the duty of every railway employee to assiduously try and prevent his family members to participate in any movement or activity aimed at covertly or overtly overthrowing a constitutional government, contribute to such activity or in any way assist it." I want to know how it can be objectionable to overthrow the Government by constitutional means. How can overthrowing a legally constituted government be wrong ? Every citizen of the country has the right to contribute to a change of government by constitutional and peaceful means. The language used is incorrect and should be corrected.

SHRI BHAKTA DARSHAN (Garhwal) : It is an error of translation. I think it is a translation of "government as constituted by law".

SHRI VAJPAYEE : Do not create misunderstanding by using such language. There too caution is called for.

On the North-Eastern Railway telegraph offices are being removed from stations. Telegraph offices at Gonda, Gorakhpur and Banaras city have been removed far away into town and now there are no arrangements for sending telegrams at the stations. Why this has been done should be made clear. It is argued that on the North Eastern Railway more importance is being given to wireless than to telegraph offices. I feel wireless is more expensive and there is no guarantee that the message sent would remain confidential. Whatever the reasons, telegraph offices are a must at railway stations.

Konkan Railway Needed

Many proposals have been given about new railway lines. I think there is also a proposal about laying a line from Madhopur to Udhampur. It should be given priority. A road from Madhopur to Udhampur has been built, and now there should be no difficulty in laying a railway line. It is also strategically necessary. I am happy that yesterday in the Rajya Sabha the Railway Minister has assured consideration of this.

Similarly, serious thought also needs to be given to the Konkan line that would link Goa.

The backward areas of Madhya Pradesh also need attention. The States Reorganisation Commission has stressed that all the regions of the State should be linked with a transportation network.

Finally, Sir, I would like to talk about my constituency. The Uttar Pradesh Government had placed before the Centre a proposal to lay a railway line by Balrampur, Utraula, Dumariaganj, Bansi and Sahajnawa. Hon. Shri Shastri had given an assurance about this when he was Railway Minister, but the present Minister does not seem to believe in carrying out old assurances. I would like to draw his attention to the assurance given by his associate. This railway line would cover an area of 82 miles including Gonda and Basti. This area produces large amounts of foodgrains and rice but has no means of transportation. The railway line is about 15-20 miles away. I would be very happy if this matter could be considered.

The railway line of Rohtak - Gohana-Panipat had been uprooted. Now it is being again started. I suggest it should be extended up to Panipat instead of terminating it at Gohana. In the beginning it was already laid up to Panipat. It had been removed in the last war. So now it should again be extended up to Panipat.

Profit for Ministry of Transport Humiliation and Loss for Travellers

Sir, in this controversy...

SHRI BHAKTA DARSHAN (Garhwal) : Not controversy, debate.

SHRI VAJPAYEE : Many members have stressed the point that the pressure on the Railways during the Five Year Plan due to greater passenger traffic and greater freight load has not been relieved to the desired extent by water transport and road transport. The policy adopted for the expansion of water transport leaves much to be desired. No effort has so far been made to spread a network of roads all over the country. I trust that the Government would try to formulate a national transportation policy in which rail, water and road transportation means will have balanced positions.

Censorship of Letters

A few days back an amendment to the Post & Telegraph Act had been tabled in this House. At that time some Opposition members had brought it to the notice of the Government that provisions of that Act relating to censorship of letters are being misused. That day I was not present in the House, otherwise I would have joined these members and said...(*Interruption*).

SHRI RAJ BAHADUR : I may submit that the Act does not give any censorship authority at all to the Department.

SHRI BALRAJ SINGH : This was discussed.

SHRI RAJ BAHADUR : There was a discussion but I do not think it was justified.

SHRI VAJPAYEE : Well, if it was not justified that day it is justified today. I charge that about *'Virodhi'* (Opposition) parties, so far as my party is concerned...(*Interruption*).

SHRI RAMAM (Narsapar) : Sir, the word *'Virodhi'* is unparliamentary. In Sanskrit, Telugu and other languages it means an 'enemy'. The Opposition is not an enemy. The proper word here would be *'Pratipakshi'*.

DEPUTY SPEAKER : When he says *'Virodhi'* everybody understands it as opposition.

SHRI VAJPAYEE : I am also *Virodhi*.

The Government censors letters of Opposition members, especially of prominent workers of political parties. This is my clear charge, and if the Hon. Minister promises indemnity to those employees who are engaged in doing this, I am prepared to prove it. Even the rules regarding censorship

Lok Sabha on March 27, 1958 during discussion on Demands for Grants of the Ministry of Transport

that are contained in the Act are flouted. The Intelligence Department sends some names and letters received in those names which are opened and delivered late. I do not know why this is done. In a free country it is the duty of the Government to guarantee that parties working for a peaceful and constitutional change of government should have the freedom to conduct their activities.

But the laws of the British days still prevail. Let alone amending them, undemocratic ways and means are being adopted. The government should clarify its position in this regard. If the Government wants to censor the letters of opposition leaders it should do so openly and also tell us about it. We are not doing any secret work. Whatever opposition there is, it operates within constitutional bounds. If you suspect that we are indulging in secret activities you should act according to the censorship provisions in the Act. I charge that even those provisions are not acted upon.

Delhi's Transportation System

Many Hon. members have referred to the shortcomings in the means of communication all over the country. Sir, in this connection I would like to draw the Hon. Minister's attention to the problems of Delhi and New Delhi. According to the report placed before us no satisfactory transportation arrangements could so far be made in Delhi. As many as 534 buses ply to carry only 29,475 passengers at a time. In view of the rate at which the population of Delhi is growing and people are coming into the capital from every nook and corner of the country the present bus arrangements are extremely inadequate. It is necessary to augment the fleet. You cannot be sure of catching a bus even after waiting for half an hour.

Along with this children below 12 are not given half-ticket concession. According to the report the Delhi Transport Authority is making a profit. A big profit has been shown of Rs. 1957.58. It would be good if children are given this facility.

Some days back my friend Shri Naval Prabhakar had asked what difference there is between the bus fares in Bombay and Calcutta and those in Delhi. The reply to this question that was placed on the floor of the House shows that the fares here are higher. The reply does not make it clear why bus fares on all routes here cannot be brought on par with those in Bombay and Calcutta.

There are also other difficulties that bus passengers face. If a passenger asks for the complaint book he is not given it, and if at all a complaint is written it is not inquired into. It is my personal experience—I had made two complaints in writing but I have no knowledge of what happened to them. If DTS officers ignore the people's complaints like this one day a situation of conflict may arise.

The report mentions a courtesy week to be observed by DTS employees. Courtesy weeks are observed every year but there is an absence of courtesy among the employees.

There is also a lot of corruption in the DTS. Shri Datar, Minister of State in the Ministry of Home Affairs has admitted that when he travalled in DTS buses *incognito* like Harun-al-Rashid he found that many students made long trips with little money. This saved the students some money and some went into the conductor's pocket. A firm policy should be adopted in this regard. This lowers the students' moral standards and gives the employees an opportunity for corruption.

There are some request stops for buses. They are called "by request". But I have seen with my own eyes that buses pass by such stops even when empty without halting although people are waiting at the stop and signal them to halt. When buses are few in number the employees should be given strict warning about this.

Confirmation of Staff in P&T Directorate

Finally, I would like to say what I have indicated in my cut motion. Some confirmations have been made regarding clerks of the second division grade in the Post & Telegraph Directorate. Neither do the employees understand the basis of the confirmations nor perhaps those who made them are able to explain them properly. Those who have long service behind them are ignored and those who are taken into the Directorate after 10 or 12 years' service are not confirmed on the ground that their service will be counted from the time they joined the Directorate. Now they did not start service in the Directorate. They were working in small post offices and were called to the Directorate on grounds of merit. Those appointed after them were confirmed.

The promotion policy that has been adopted is also against the regulations laid down by the Home Ministry. I urge the Hon. Minister to conduct proper inquiries into such difficulties and the resentment among the employees, and try to remove it.

Shri Datar has admitted that six of the confirmations in the Directorate were wrong and assured that they would be corrected, but they were corrected in such a way that these six new people who were confirmed were not confirmed on seniority basis. If old employees are ignored we cannot expect them to work well. With drawing the Hon. Minister's attention to this matter I close my speech. Thank you.

Neither Job Security nor Travel Comfort

Sir, the financial condition of the Railways as reflected in the Railway Budget cannot be called very encouraging. Two aspects of the picture that come to special notice are that income is going down and administrative expenditure is going up. I regret to say not enough caution and farsightedness have been exercised in formulating the Railway Budget. The result is that estimates do not come true, income falls short of the estimate and the expenditure exceeds it. On the 24th, I had asked—and other members had joined me — if the working expenses of the railways had risen in proportion to income from passenger fares and railway freight. The Railway Minister said no, working expenses have not risen. But in this connection, I would like to draw his attention to a letter addressed by the Railway Board to General Managers which quotes a letter of November 8, 1958 as follows :

> "The Board considers that it is imperative to arrest immediately any tendency for a rise in the working expenses which are disproportionately high compared to the growth of traffic and railway earnings."

The Hon. Minister's reply was accompanied by a statement that contains a lot of figures. One would get so lost in the jungle of trees that it would be very difficult to figure out the real situation. As the saying goes, there are lies, white lies and statistics.

Now there is a clear discrepancy between the Minister's figures and the Railway Board's letter that I have mentioned. Where does the truth lie ? The adverse effect of the depletion in the Railway's income is that there is a minus balance in the Railway Development Fund and we are borrowing something from General Revenues. Sir, I cannot understand how the Railways contribute to the General Revenues beyond their capacity and then borrow from the same General Revenues for the Development Fund. I believe the proportion in which the Railways contribute to the General Fund should be brought down. In this connection the Railway Minister has said the convention of 1954 would be extended by a year. I say extension of the period would not solve the problem. It is necessary to bring down the contribution of the Railways. This year the Railways' net income from revenue is Rs. 75.60 crores out of which they have to contribute Rs. 54.41 crores to the General Revenues. The result is that the Railways have only about Rs. 21 crores left with them.

I doubt if even that saving would be possible, for last year's estimate fell short by Rs. 13.1 crores. The result of the shortfall in the Development Fund was cuts in the allocation for passenger amenities or labour welfare. I can

Lok Sabha on February 27, 1959 on the Railway Budget

place the relevant figures before you, but that is not necessary. The Hon. Railway Minister will agree that because of the shortfall in the Development Fund there have been some minor cuts in the passenger amenity and labour welfare schemes. So long as the Railways' contribution to the General Revenues is not scaled down you would not be able to extend the desired amenities on the Railways.

One of the reasons given for the decline in income is more or less a bogey — the bogey, that there is war between rail and road transport. This is on the same lines as the apprehension that there would be a battle between *'Galla'* and *'Ganna'*. It looks as if there is also going to be a war between rail and road in our country, but I do not think we have to be too much worried about it. There are two main reasons for the decline in the railways' income. One is inefficiency of the railways, and the other is the law of diminishing returns in freight charges. Now we are told restraints would be put on road traffic to give the railways an opportunity to progress and increase income.

In my opinion all such proposals would put a premium on inefficiency. Our country is big enough to have enough scope for rail, road and all other types of transport. Let the Railway Ministry put its own house in order so that it may know why people prefer sending goods by road. Is it because the goods reach the doorstep, there is less pilferage or there are other facilities ? From the economic point of view the railways carry goods a greater distance at a lesser cost. Then why do people still prefer motor transport ? Putting restrictions on road transport is not the answer to this problem. The Hon. Minister has expressed the hope in his speech that as steel mills get going and the economy improves the deficiency in rail transport would be made up and enough goods would be available for transportation by rail.

Goods Trains have Slowed Down

In this connection I would like to point out that the average speed of goods trains has come down, and that too in spite of the fact that express goods trains are run. On the broad gauge the average speed was 10.8 in 1950-57 but it came down to 9.28 in 1957-58. On metre gauge the average was 9.58 in 1949-50 but it came down to 8.23 in 1957-58. A goods train takes 10 and sometimes even 16 hours to cover the distance from Agra Cantt. to Tundla, although the distance between the two points is only 19 miles. If that is going to remain the speed of goods trains, whatever restraints we impose on road transport traders will not use rail transport. There is another danger. It is that if we place restrictions on road transport motor cars may replace bullock carts. Bullock carts have a major role in our economy and in goods transport. In my opinion all these three systems should be complementary, not contradictory. We should adopt a balanced point of view.

Railway Accidents

Now I would like to say something about railway accidents. The Hon. Minister has admitted that for some time past unfortunate accidents due to collisions or derailments had somewhat increased. I have collected figures of this increase. During the period January 1, 1958 to December 31, 1958 there were 18 major railway accidents in which 80 people were killed and 424 injured. Railway property worth Rs. 6,90,000 was damaged and Rs. 3,72,199 were paid out by way of compensation to the injured or the dead. This is a serious situation and I would like to know from the Hon. Minister what effective steps have been taken to prevent accidents in addition to setting up a safety organisation and appointing safety inspectors. It is well known that most accidents occur because rules are not properly observed. Now have the employees been properly trained in the new unified general rules ? I have received complaints that officers approach the employees and make them fill forms saying they know the rules and can work according to them. If you have made new rules it is very important that you should give proper training in them. If this aspect is ignored and employees are made to say they know the rules although they do not know them but are reluctant to say so to the officers, the results would be disastrous and there would be no possibility of railway accidents going down.

In this connection, zonal general managers have been given extraordinary powers, and in the name of preventing accidents railway employees are removed from service with one month's notice in accordance with Rule 148 of the Railway Establishment Code. Under Rule 148 the employee is not asked to explain, not given a chance to explain.

In the Rajya Sabha some members had asked the Railway Minister how many employees had been removed like this. I can give their names. Everyone wants that railway accidents should end. Railway employees also want that there should be less accidents and the Railway Minister has also admitted that exceptional circumstances prevail, as a result of which the employees sometimes make mistakes. If the mistakes are only sometimes made they should not result in dismissal from service. I submit that Rule 148, under which summary powers have been given, should be withheld for the present. In fact it should be removed from the Railway Establishment Code, but if you are not going to remove it you should not use it.

Punished for being Alert

The Railway Minister says that the steps we are taking will establish a sense of safety in the employees. I say it creates a sense of insecurity about their job in them. If an employee makes a mistake, find out why he made it. I can enumerate instances where employees were removed from service not because they caused accidents but because they prevented them.

AN HON. MEMBER : Should a person making a mistake not be punished ?

SHRI VAJPAYEE : The guilty should be punished, but here that is not enough. You should find out why the accident occurred, and how much the human element was involved in it. The Minister said the person alone is not responsible. I say everyone should be given a different responsibility. The Station Master at a wayside station sells tickets, operates the signal, replies to people's inquiries, fills forms, and at the same time it is expected that he should also set the point. All this he cannot do. If this is the system it is impractical, deficient. Different persons should be given different responsibilities. Joint responsibility will not benefit us.

Then again when an accident occurs an inquiry is instituted against railway employees. The Australian Railway Act provides for representatives of railwaymen's unions to be summoned. If we are to prevent accidents we have to gain the trust of the employees. The Railway Minister needs to pay a great deal of attention to this.

The labour policy of the Railways has been discussed at length here. I appreciate the Railway Minister's difficulty here, for the All India Railwaymen's Federation is connected with INTUC, and INTUC is the beloved of the ruling party. So some temptation is natural. Still I have seen that they have given some recognition to the National Federation of Railwaymen. But they have downgraded it slightly, they love it a little less. I think this deficiency will also be made up. So far as railway workers' unity is concerned the sincerity with which the Hon. Minister desires it is laudable, but propping up a tottering federation is not the way to unity. The Northern Railway Mazdoor Union is a branch of the Federation. The registration of this union has ended, but its recognition continues. There is no registration because their accounts are not in order. There are irregularities in it, still it has recognition. This is not an impartial policy. There should be free elections and the union or federation that secures the trust of a majority of railwaymen should be recognised. It is time some decisive steps were taken in this direction. Then alone can confidence be created in the employees.

There is another thing. The Railway Ministry is such a big concern and the number of its employees so big that one association or federation cannot fully look after their interests. There is also the question of Station Masters and Assistant Station Masters. The promotion system of the British days still continues. It used to give preference to Anglo- Indians. The same channel of promotion still continues. They approached the Railway Minister but did not get justice. Now they have approached the Supreme Court. This is against the spirit of the Constitution of India, but it is a tradition that continues.

There is also the question of their security. Dacoits attacked a train near Jindpur station between Shahjahanpur and Pillibhit. They looted Railway property and even wounded the Station Master. Another person was also wounded. The dacoits robbed him of ornaments. What security arrangements have been made for people who are lying in the jungles ?

SHRI SHAHNAWAZ KHAN : There are dacoities even on the roads.

SHRI VAJPAYEE : We are not talking about dacoities on roads, Mr. Minister. What are you doing about the dacoities at your stations, and about your employees who get wounded and cannot protect your property ? You cannot escape responsibility by giving the example of dacoities on the roads. If there are dacoities like this your people cannot feel secure. If railway employees come under essential services and if it is essential for them to live in their quarters can you not waive the rent of the quarters, or can you not allow them to live where they please ? They can live in the villages where their property and families would be safe. But if your rules require they must live at the station arrangements should be made for their safety. The State Governments say that is the railways' field, but in the railways' field there are no arrangements for their safety. This is a real problem. You cannot avoid it by giving some reply. You have to find some solution. Station Masters at some wayside stations have proposed that they could be given gun licences. A railway protection force could also be organised. I agree that this is a big problem and there is a large number of wayside stations, but something must be done about it.

Government Catering : Sweet Illusions

The Hon. Minister has said departmental catering is getting popular. I beg to differ. Departmental catering is not getting popular. So it has been closed down at Varanasi, Katni and other stations. It is also running at a loss. In 1957-58 there was a loss of Rs. 21.98 lakhs. According to budgeted estimates for 1959-60 the net loss would be Rs. 18.38 lakhs. The total loss to Railways in departmental catering so far is to the tune of Rs. 35 crores.

DEPUTY SPEAKER : Thirty five crores or 35 lakhs ?

SHRI VAJPAYEE : The loss in lakhs is just for one year. I do not have time. If you could give me time I would place all figures before the House...

DEPUTY SPEAKER : I shall accept them without knowing them.

SHRI VAJPAYEE : It is no use making such experiments. You should have tight control and you should end this deparmental catering. The common traveller has not benefited from it, except for some selected people whose good comments are deliberately written down in the remark books saying they got good food. But so far as the general public is concerned there is no benefit.

One more thing. The Railway Minister has indicated in his budget speech that metre gauge lines would be converted to broad gauge. I beg to differ, because I claim that the metre gauge is functioning better than the broad gauge, and we should invest funds in laying railway lines in neglected areas like some areas of Bundelkhand and Vindhya Pradesh, not in gauge conversion. I have nothing to say about ending narrow gauge, but in view of the prevailing situation and the resources position it would not be right to take up the programme of converting metre gauge to broad guage.

Electrification of Railways

So far as electrification is concerned I must say the Government has not planned properly. Even before the Bhopal factory turns out engines and parts you are talking of electrification. Now if electrification and the Bhopal plant are interdependent and if the plant lags behind while you forge ahead with electrification you will have to import engines and parts, and this will create a foreign exchange problem. But electrification is necessary, because more power is being generated, what shall we do with it ? And how can we save the coal that is being lost in the Railways on such a big scale ?...

DEPUTY SPEAKER : The Hon. Member may now conclude.

SHRI VAJPAYEE : All right, I shall conclude. But you need engines and parts for electrification. That is why I say this is not an example of good planning. It is necessary to give serious thought to the current financial position of the Railways. The Railway Ministry and especially the Railway Board should adopt a new point of view for securing the cooperation of Railway employees and the public at large. Thank you.

Railway Employees in Bondage

Sir, the picture of the railways' financial position as painted by the Railway Minister's budget speech is very serious. The increase in the Revenue Reserve Fund is negligible and the Development Fund is completely depleted. The Depreciation Fund had Rs. 103.47 crores in 1955-56 and 1956-57 out of which Rs. 17.75 crores was left in 1960-61. If we compare it with capital- at-large, which stands at Rs. 1563.29 crores, it looks totally disappointing. It also means the Railways will not have enough funds to replace outdated stock with new stock. Like last year this year too the income has fallen short of the estimate and the expenditure has exceeded the estimate. It is necessary to take special care while formulating the railway budget. In 1958-59 the income from traffic fell short of the estimate by Rs. 4.17 crores. The revised estimate of net saving has also come down from Rs. 13 crores to Rs. 8.63 crores. The Railway Minister has increased railway fares. In 1959 there was a 4 per cent increase and it came to 5 per cent. It looks as if the income from freight is the result of competition by road transport, and this has been accepted. A Committee has also been set up to consider how railway traffic and road traffic could be coordinated. I cannot understand how Railway fares were increased before the Niyogi Committee made its recommendations. It would have been better if operational efficiency had been increased and expenditure decreased, so that more road traffic could turn to railways and the income of the railways increased. The increase in railway fares can only result in a price rise. I cannot understand the propriety of raising Railway fares when the Finance Minister wants to help the Railways indirectly by taxing diesel in his budget and controlling road transport. Even now, if the Railway administration wants it, it can bring down expenditure and meet the financial burden that has gone up because of the recommendations of the Pay Commission. But there are no indications of a cut in expenditure. I shall give an example.

Uneconomic Shifting of Office

The Deputy Minister had stated in reply to a question that all branches of the RDSO will be brought together in Lucknow. This may take a couple of years. But for the present one branch is being shifted to Simla. The part at present in Chittaranjan will also have to move to Simla and after two years it may possibly have to move from Simla to Lucknow. All this will entail an annual recurring expenditure of at least Rs. 5 lakhs.

Lok Sabha on March 1, 1960 on the Railway Budget

There is a shortage of accommodation in Simla. From the point of view of centralisation also Simla is not the right place. I have come to know that an officer had recently been there. He has also expressed his disagreement in his report. If after two years the whole organisation is to be taken to Lucknow why does it have to be taken to Simla in the interim period ? Here in New Delhi too a sky-scraper named Railway House is under construction. It was said that railway offices would be accommodated in it. Now we are told offices not connected with the railways in any way would also be accommodated in it. On the other hand the RDSO will be taken to Simla and two years later to Lucknow. This can be stopped and money saved.

Meaningless Display of Time Tables at Stations

At all stations we see big time-table posters displayed in frames. They are printed in such small type that you need a magnifying glass to read them. Hardly a traveller would read them. These posters are printed in lakhs just to decorate railway stations. I do not see any need to print them. Every station has a smaller board displaying the timings of local trains. Then why is this all-India time-table displayed at all stations ? This money can be saved. The Railway Ministry should be specially careful about this.

Separate Wage Board for Railwaymen

The Pay Commission's recommendations have to some extent increased the financial burden on the railway administration. But that has not satisfied the employees. I think it is necessary to set up a separate wage board for fixing the salaries and allowances of railwaymen. For argument's sake railwaymen are a part of Central employees, but their terms and conditions of service are so different that when they are considered all together justice is not done by them. Sir, you will be surprised to learn that railway employees are still bound by a contract system. They are called government employees, but they appear a contractor's employees. Even today they are contracted. Any railway employee can be removed by giving one month's notice without showing cause. He cannot approach the Court. He cannot ask the reason for his removal, nor can he compel the railway administration to give it. The companies have ended, the British have left but railwaymen are still treated like contract labour.

We had hoped the Pay Commission would give thought to these terms and conditions. Rule 148 of the Railway Establishment Board and Article 311(2) of the Constitution prevent railway employees from working properly. No one will say they should take part in politics, but even government servants passing a resolution on foreign aggression is considered objectionable. You will be surprised to learn that when government servants passed a resolution against the Chinese aggression and intimated to the government that in order to fight this aggression they would fulfil their responsibilities with determination the Government objected to their passing such a resolution.

The Government says passing a resolution against foreign aggression is interfering in politics. I do not know how politics is defined. If government servants declare their pledge to protect the nation in the face of an invasion the government should welcome it. But the terms and conditions of service are so narrow and restrictive that they prevent the employees from doing their duty. It is time we reconsidered them.

Serious and Non-Serious Accidents

The Railway Minister has expressed satisfaction over no major accident having taken place this year. What is the definition of a major accident ? A review of accidents published by the Railway Ministry does not distinguish between major and minor accidents; it distinguishes between serious and non-serious accidents. According to definition a serious railway accident is that which involves loss of life or serious injury to passengers or which causes damage to property in excess of twenty thousand rupees. When the Railway Minister says there was no big accident does he mean a big accident by this definition ?

Accidents are Caused

He further said the decrease in the number of accidents was either due to chance or to ceaseless efforts of railway employees. What is this chance ? Is it chance that cause accidents ? And should we understand that when accidents occur they are due to chance and railway employees were not responsible for them ? Sir, if luck causes accidents it is not necessary to arm General Managers with summary powers. On the one hand the Railway Minister says most accidents are caused mainly by workers' negligence, on the other he says accidents are going down, either by luck or because of railway employees' constant efforts. When railway accidents go down the element of chance is brought in, but when they increase railway employees are caught by the neck. It would be better not to bring in luck and give serious thought to why accidents take place. I do not believe accidents happen. I say accidents are caused. And so long as the cause is not removed accidents cannot be prevented. This review says accidents happened due to workers' negligence. But if the terms and conditions under which the employees work are such that the employees cannot but cause accidents cannot be prevented. So we should think about the terms and conditions of work for the employees.

At Rahuri Station in Sholapur division an accident was narrowly averted. It was an aborted collision. Two goods trains came on the same track and the Assistant Station Master there was dismissed under summary powers. But the Assistant Station Master says the slide instrument in the Station Master's cabin had no meter-key and they were asking for it for months. The accident almost happened because the master-key was not available, and yet the Assistant Station Master was thrown out of employment.

In my last budget speech, I had complained that the employees were not trained in the new rules. The inspectors made the employees sign forms saying they knew the rules when actually they do not know them. And if employees do not know the rules and do not go by them, accidents will happen. You cannot decrease accidents by giving summary powers to General Managers, which are being misused. Creating insecurity for railway employees cannot guarantee security of railway passengers. I would urge the Railway Minister to consider all such cases very sympathetically. If they cannot be reinstated they may be taken into some other employment on fresh consideration of merit. If there are any clear cases of negligence or carelessness no one would plead for them. This Parliament would strengthen the Railway Minister's hands in taking action against such employees. But there are a number of cases where accidents have occurred not because of the employees' negligence but due to rules and due to faults in the equipment with which they work. Such cases should be viewed sympathetically.

By and large, our employees work well. The railways have progressed. During the Second Plan foreign exchange to the tune of Rs. 90 crores has been saved. For this the Railway Minister deserves to be congratulated, but there is still a lot of scope for improvement. That needs to be taken into consideration. Thank you.

Emancipate Railwaymen

Sir, it cannot be denied that during the last year the Indian railway system has made remarkable progress in many directions. We now have before us a picture of progress in the spheres of self-sufficiency efforts involving stock and other equipment, safer railway travel through lesser accidents, construction of bridges over the Ganga, the Gandak and the Brahmaputra, and more amenities for third class travellers.

But the picture also has another side, and we must look at it. This Railway Ministry could not fulfil the targets fixed for the Second Plan, whether related to laying a double track or to electrification. Efforts in these directions fall much short of the targets.

The Unfulfilled Plan Targets

The target for broad gauge wagon building could also not be fulfilled. And the biggest thing is that the estimate of increase in passenger traffic has proved wrong. The traffic has exceeded the estimate. The railway administration should make true estimates. Even the estimates for the Third Plan appear short of present targets. It is the responsibility of the Railway Ministry to make proper estimates of increase in passenger traffic and make proper arrangements for it. There is at present a controversy going on in the country between rail and road transport, and in spite of saying that there should be coordination between the two it has not yet been possible to make proper arrangements for it.

Rail-Road Competition

The recommendations of the Niyogi Committee should be given serious consideration, although no one will favour unchecked competition between rail and road transport. The two should be coordinated in the interest of the nation . But one thing that we cannot forget is that in all countries of the world road transport is increasingly dominating railway transport. Gradually, for goods movement people prefer road transport, and it cannot be denied that there are reasons for it.

If we look to the figures for other countries we find that in the U.S. there are 43 lorries to a mile, in France 22, in the U.K. 21 and in India 3 so far. In the U.S. railway transportation has in a way stopped, and it is being replaced by road transport. As it is, we can see that the investment in the development of the railways does not give adequate returns, and this would be proved by some figures that I would like to present. In 1947-48 the Indian Railways had

---

Lok Sabha on March 2, 1961 during General Discussion on Railway Budget

a mileage of 33,985, which rose in 1958- 59 to 35,081, that is, by one per cent, but if, in comparison, we look to the capital-at-charge and the working expenditure we find that the increase is from Rs. 742 crores in 1947-48 to Rs. 1382 crores in 1958-59, that is, the former increased by 84 per cent and the latter by 110 per cent.

According to the Renuka Ray Committee the cheap movement of iron ore puts the railways to a loss. I do not think the railways should start transporting government goods cheaply. The government should be charged the same rates as others, and if there is a loss it should be shown as a part of the total loss of the government. Forcing the Railways, to move goods cheaply and thus making it lose in the competition with roads is not a good situation for us.

Railwaymen's Strike

Sir, the Railway Minister has referred to the railwaymen's strike in his speech. It was without doubt an unfortunate strike. It has now ended, but its adverse effects have still to be made up. The Railway Minister and the Railway administration have adopted a very generous attitude. It is true that those who did not indulge in violence and destruction of property should not be penalised. The definition of gross misbehavior is also in favour of the employees, but it is a matter of regret that the directives of the Railway Board are not properly implemented by the lower echelons.

I know about Lucknow. There was no violence there, no destruction of property, but employees are being given notices, and that too in a very strange manner. There are also employees who did not participate in the strike and kept working. When the strike ended, within a week's time they were issued 'show cause' notices. There is even an employee who was on duty during the strike, who was not a member of the union or a delegate and yet was arrested on a complaint by a rival union, but because the police had no case against him he was released. After 61 days he was reinstated but was transferred from Lucknow to Bikaner. In another case an employee was charged with not working on the 10th nor allowing others to work. When inquiries were made and witnesses called, it came to light that July 10 was a Sunday, and the workshop was closed, so there was no question of the man's absenting himself or preventing others from going to work. When it became known that the date on the charge-sheet was wrong as it was a Sunday, the date was changed instead of withdrawing the chargesheet.

A complaint was made against an employee on November 17, 1960 that he had participated in a meeting on July 11, 1960. Now a complaint against his participation in a meeting on July 11 should not be made on November 17, 1960, and anyway there is a Railway Board circular that participation in meetings is no offence. The Railway Minister has very generously issued this directive, but the Divisional Superintendent at Lucknow is not obeying it properly. I submit that before removing any employee from service the Railway Minister should personally go into every case.

On February 24, there was some trouble in the Carriage and Workshop at Lucknow. There was some internal trouble with the Railway Protection Force. There have been arguments on both sides. I would say even if there was some trouble it was not necessary to call the police. Departmental action could have been taken. If, however, the junior officers are bent upon vitiating the atmosphere, it is most unfortunate. It is the Railway Minister's duty to warn Railway officials in this regard and do justice by those who have been wronged.

Railway Catering

The Railway Minister referred to departmental catering in his speech. I would ask for a clarification about it, and it would reflect adversely on him. He said in his speech that the direct loss on catering in 1958-59, which was Rs. 11 lakhs, was reduced to about Rs. 4 lakhs in 1959-60. For 1960-61 the estimated loss is around Rs. 4 lakhs. In this connection I would like to draw his attention to the 21st report of the Public Accounts Committee, which says that in 1957-58 the loss was Rs. 21.48 lakhs, in 1958-59 Rs. 18.61 lakhs and in 1959-60 Rs. 18 lakhs. Which are the true figures — the Railway Minister's or the Public Accounts Committee's ? The Railway Minister may please clarify. But one thing which I would like to say is that loss estimates for departmental catering are not true and the figures presented are misleading, because departmental catering is entrusted to a contractor, and the loss does not include the licence fee he is charged, the sales tax collected from him and the power and water expenses recovered from him. It does not even include the rise in prices of food articles since departmental catering was handed over to him. This puts the travelling public to hardship. In the beginning it was said we want to conduct departmental catering on a no-profit-no-loss basis. Does that mean prices of food articles should be raised ? I would place some pricelists before you. So long as we had private vending purees were sold at Rs. 1.50 a seer. But since departmental catering began, the price of Purees went up to Rs. 2 per seer. The price of Jalebi was Rs. 1.50 a seer; it was raised to Rs. 2. Milk used to sell for 75 paise a seer, now it is 87 paise. Petha sold at Rs. 1.50 a seer, now the price has been raised to two rupees. Is it proper to charge the travelling public higher prices and then say departmental catering is not running at a loss ? After all, if the Government wants to go in for departmental catering its final objective should be to provide to the traveller good things at reasonable prices. But prices have already been raised. The question of quality should also be given a little thought.

It has now been made a rule that food articles of departmental catering are to be sold to hawkers or vendors against a cash memo and are not returnable. If the hawker cannot sell them the same day he sells them the next day. When there was private catering unsold foodstuffs were taken back. Even for the workers the food arrangements are not good. Neither from the point of view of quality of foodstuffs nor from that of prices has departmental catering benefited the traveller.

The Committee set up for this had recommended that both systems should continue side by side. I don't think this means we should have one system in Agra and another in Tundla. Is it not possible to have both systems at the same place ? There is no propriety in the government taking up catering arrangements where facilities do not exist. The loss is recovered from the people by way of taxes. Prices of things have gone up, but not the sense of service, because there is not the same hope of profit. Still free passes are issued for departmental catering. They can come to Delhi to fetch commodities. There are also other expenses that the railways have to bear. There are losses in licence fees, and sales tax is not recovered. Despite all this the system is running at a loss. I say the figures for loss that have been presented are not correct. It is not necessary to expand departmental catering; it is necessary to make it successful where it is functioning. The old shopkeepers and other small people who were there before departmental catering have become unemployed and no arrangements have been made to settle them.

I know of instances where a single caterer operates at as many as four stations while the other people, the old people, are without a job. No arrangements have been made to settle them. I say under the present circumstances departmental catering should not be a subject of expansion. And in the figures given thought should also be given to the loss caused to the Government by rise in prices and non-recovery of dues.

The Regional Demands

Sir, this discussion has thrown up a number of regional demands. I am not talking about my region. But a railway line should extend upto Jammu. This is very necessary. I was hoping that the Railway Minister would make some announcement in this regard, but he has not done so. Whether from the point of view of security or from that of bringing Jammu-Kashmir emotionally closer to the rest of India, this work should be taken up without delay. It is also necessary to bring Chandigarh on to the main line. According to newspaper reports the Prime Minister has given some assurances in this connection. I would like to know the position. The Defence Minister has recently announced that Chandigarh would be made a big base for spreading a network of roads in that hilly region. In view of the growing importance of Chandigarh it is necessary to bring it on to the main line.

Similarly, there is a station called Kounch between Kanpur and Jhansi. An engine takes two carriages from here and returns with them in the evening. It would not be a big loss if bringing this station on to the main line could also be considered. A survey about this has already been made and it was seen that this would not involve a very big detour. It would be profitable if the main line passed Kounch. It is a big mandi and this would help to develop the region. As it is Bundelkhand is a backward region. You can help its development by bringing Kounch on to the main line. This too may be considered by the Hon. Minister.

Pay Commission Recommendations

The Pay Commission's recommendations have also not been fully implemented. There are also some categories that are dissatisfied. It is not that the Railway Minister is not acquainted with their discontent. But no active step has been taken to remove it. Eight thousand Station Masters and Assistant Station Masters have sent a memorandum to the Railway Board in which they have individually represented that their workload is far in excess of their salaries. If they are to be given the same salaries and the same benefits it would be better to give them some other work. I know it would not be possible for the Railway Ministry to accept their demands. But this will show you the conditions in which they work and the pessimism and hopelessness that have made them go to such extremes. I urge that their case should be considered sympathetically.

Recognition of Unions

Now you are going to set up a Whitley Council. The recognition of labour unions that had been withdrawn will have to be restored in some form or the other. The Railway Minister may see if it would not be better to recognise category-wise unions as in Post & Telegraph. At present whatever the trade union, workshop people dominate it. As they are greater in number this is natural in a democracy. But because of this situation the interests of other categories are not properly represented. Now that we are thinking of reorganisation we should also think about whether we should not try to have a representation system that could represent all interests.

One more thing and I shall conclude.

Readymade Uniforms

Employees complain that the ready-made uniforms they are given do not fit them. This is because they are procured wholesale, while workers are not made wholesale. Naturally they do not fit. The employees have to get them altered for a proper fit. Is it not possible to give the workers the cloth or its price so that they could get their own uniforms stitched ? They are prepared to pay the tailoring charges. But it is not proper to force them to pay them. The say we already pay for the alterations, so it would be better if you give us the cloth so that we can arrange our own tailoring. So if you give them the cloth and the tailoring charges they would welcome the Railway Minister in smart uniforms when he visits them instead of loose fitting clothes, that do not look nice. Please give this a thought. Thank you.

Railway Accidents

Sir, I move the following amendment :

"The original motion be amended as follows : 'This House recommends that the Government consider the desirability of a judicial inquiry into these accidents'."

The Railway Minister's speech has referred to three major accidents. They have occurred within a period of 20 days, causing 75 deaths and serious injuries to 240 people. These accidents have shaken the faith of the travelling public in the capacity of the Railways to take them to their destination safely.

The Railway administration has not been able to provide them seats, has failed to transport goods properly and has also not been able to provide enough facilities to railway employees, but it is hoped that it would at least reach the traveller to his destination. This main job the Railways have not yet been able to do.

The Ranchi Express Accident

I was surprised at the figures of the Ranchi Express accident that the Railway Minister has given. They do not tally. The statement says 45 people died and six died later. Apart from this 11 were seriously injured and 184 slightly injured, out of whom 71 were allowed to go after first aid, 92 were discharged after hospital treatment, while 32 were still in hospital on the day of the statement. If we add up these figures of 32 people, 71 people and 92 people, the total comes to 195, not 184. Even if we add people who are in the hospital, the total comes to 195, and the Railway Minister says the number of the injured was 184, including those who received minor injuries. On what basis were these figures given ? They do not tally with the figures given ? They do not tally with the figures given by the Railway Minister. How can we accept what the Railway administration says about these accidents ?

The Ranchi Express accident is said to have been the result of sabotage and the Railway inspector's testimony is cited for this. It is said the Railway inspector is not connected with the Railway but with the Transport and Communications Ministry. I would very respectfully submit that the Railway inspector's belonging to another ministry does not make his report right. So far the Railway Minister has not explained the purpose behind the sabotage. There were no subversive activities in this region before. They have indeed taken place in the region of Punjab near the Jammu-Kashmir border, in which some people could be suspected of subversion. But so far as the region in which the Ranchi Express accident occurred is concerned, there is no reason

Lok Sabha on December 2, 1961 while moving Amendment during discussion on a motion regarding Major Railway Accidents

to suspect subversive activities and if there is, the Railway Minister cannot allay the people's suspicions by showing the inspector's report. The only way to allay them would be to institute an inquiry by a High Court judge into the accident.

Newspapers have reported that the people are not ready to accept the subversion theory. I do not want to express an opinion on this, but I would say that merely saying that it was an accident cannot satisfy the people. If there was subversion, by whom ? What was its purpose ? It should be proved beyond doubt that it was the result of subversion, otherwise people would not believe it.

I would like to say something about the accident that took place near Manipuri. I have personally collected some information at site. I have talked to the Railway employees. The high speed of the train has been given as the cause of this accident. The Railway Minister says according to regulations the engine should not have run at a speed of 30 miles. He says it was running at a high speed, but he does not say how high. So far as my information goes — and I have gained it by talking to the Railway employees — the train was running at a speed of 12 miles per hour. You will know everything if you calculate how many hours the train took when it arrived at the station and at what time it had departed. This accident did not take place at any railway station, it occurred in between.

In any case, the question that arises is, if the train was running at a high speed, why ? Even if we accept that it was running at a speed of 30 miles, why ? Was it late ? How late ? Was the driver ordered to run at high speed ?

Eyewitness for the Train's Speed

I have talked to people on board the train and they said the train was not running fast. People working in nearby fields at the time of the accident also say it was not running fast. As for passengers on board the train it is not difficult for them to see whether it was running very fast as compared to a speed of 30 miles per hour. But they say it was not running fast. Even if we accept that it was running fast, why was it running fast ? Then the Railway Minister says the driver applied the brake. Why ? Was there some obstruction on the track ? Was there somebody, or a bullock cart or some other obstruction ? Why was it necessary for the driver to apply the brake ?

The AWC engine was discussed here. Is it not true that if this engine is suddenly braked such big accident cannot happen ? I have talked to the drivers who drive these engines and they say even if the brake is suddenly applied — although it is not clear why that was done, but even if we accept it there is no reason for such a big accident. Let the Railway Minister explain this. It is not enough to say the train was running fast, the driver applied the brake and the train jumped the rails. The Railway Minister's statement does not bring out the facts. We cannot remain content with relying on the inspector's inquiry.

Further, is it not true that railway drivers are encouraged to drive fast ? The Railway Gazette shows that they are rewarded for fast driving. I even know a case where action was taken against a driver because the train was late. When he was told to drive fast he said I am now old, I cannot drive fast. So action was taken against him. If you encourage railway drivers to drive fast we cannot avoid accidents.

The Track and the Engine Load

Then again, is it not true that the track on which this engine was running cannot bear the load ? This was a 90-pound track, while this type of engine needs a 120-pound track. Was this track properly inspected ? I have come to know that for the last three years there has been no track recording on this line. The track recording machine examines the track, but for the last three years this has not been done. There has also been no DS special on this line for the last many months. What is the truth ? If the track was bad the Railway Minister and the railway administration cannot escape their responsibility by putting all the blame on the driver who was killed.

Sir, if the train was running fast and if the driver had to apply the brake we must not forget that he was an experienced person. If there was a possibility of the train derailing and the passengers and the driver getting killed on the engine being braked he would never have done so. No driver can feel unconcerned about his life and that of the passengers, and if there was a possibility of the train derailing because of sudden braking the driver would know about it.

Further, before taking the train on to this track had not the driver complained that the track was not good and he had experienced difficulty ? It is easy for you to say now that there was no such complaint. But on inquiring I have found out that previous drivers had made similar complaints but no action was taken, the track was not inspected, and the disastrous result is before us.

Complain and be Punished

Then again is it not true that engine failure is not properly reported ? Are not defective engines issued from the shed, and if a driver complains that an engine is defective and he will not drive it, is not action taken against him ? I know that a certain driver was charge-sheeted because he made a complaint like this and refused to accept the engine.

SHRI JAG JIVAN RAM : I would like to know about the case.

SHRI VAJPAYEE : I shall place the matter before you.

SHRI S.M. BANERJI : There are many such complaints.

SHRI VAJPAYEE : In conclusion I would demand a judicial inquiry into these railway accidents. A departmental inquiry or an inquiry by an official connected with some other ministry would not remove the people's doubts.

I have not said anything about the Ranchi Express, although there are many things that can be said. But on the basis of the information about the Manipuri accident that has come to light I can say that the Railway administration is trying to cover up the facts. It does not want the facts to come to light and wants to hide its sins. So I say that so long as there is not a judicial inquiry into this matter the railway administration cannot escape the blame for playing with the lives of the people.

My friend Shri Rajendra Singh says the present Railway Minister should emulate the example of Shri Lal Bahadur Shastri and resign. But we have no such hope of him, although this is the time to resign, as elections are coming. When Shri Shastri resigned the resignation was tomtommed about and it was claimed that healthy democratic traditions were being set. That time the Prime Minister rose in the House and said :

> "I do feel, from constitutional propriety, that we should set an example in this matter."

When Shri Shastri resigned it was said we are making an example, although the Prime Minister said Shri Shastri was not personally responsible if some bridge broke down. Where are those democratic conventions now ? Why does the Railway Minister not follow that example for the deficiencies of the railway administration and railway employees and for playing with the lives of the travelling public ? The only honourable course for the Railway Minister is to resign now and order a judicial inquiry into these accidents before that. Thank you.

More Trains, More Passengers But More Deficit

No National Transportation Policy

Sir, the Railways are an important part of our transportation system. They are spread over an area of 57,000 square km. As many as 10,000 trains run every day, and they carry 5 lakh passengers and 5 lakh metric tons of goods. So we have to think of how we can coordinate the railways with other means of transportation. It is a matter of regret that so far the government has not been able to formulate a national transportation policy that includes road transportation and shipping in addition to railways, so that we could reorganise our transportation system in accordance with the needs of national development. The railways have to compete with road transport. A committee had also been set up to consider as to how this competition could be avoided, but Shri Niyogi resigned from it and it seems some pressures are preventing us from taking the right decisions regarding the formulation of a national transportation policy. If the railways are to survive the competition they would have to give a better performance as compared to road transport. The progress we see this year should not go to our head because this year economic development was slow and so the railways could carry goods. If the economic conditions improved, the pace of progress picked up and our targets of industrial and agricultural production achieved, then the railways would have to carry more goods. We cannot remain content with the progress made by the railways this year. It is really a matter of surprise that on the one hand the railways are earning bigger profits while on the other hand freight rates have been increased. The reasons given for this are not satisfactory. There is no justification for the increase in freight rates. In all there will be a 12 per cent increase. If any increase was to be effected a freight structure committee should have been set up and a policy formulated in the light of its recommendations. All in all, this rate increase will lead to inflation, price-rise and growing dearness. We cannot play down the adverse effects of the rate increase by saying it is only 2 per cent because the economy is currently in such a condition that an increase of even a single Naya Paisa grows to many Naye Paise by the time commodities reach the consumer.

Under-estimated Income and Over-estimated Expenditure

It is also argued that employees are being given more allowances, so more income is needed. I say the annual income estimate of the railways is put on the lower side while the actual income is higher. The expenditure is estimated

Rajya Sabha on March 2, 1964 on Railway Budget

on the higher side while the actual expenditure is less. Figures would show that we have saved more than the saving estimate. In 1962-63 the net saving was Rs. 42.06 crores while the revised saving estimate was only Rs. 23.20 crores. In 1963-64 also an excess saving of Rs. 6.75 crores has been shown. This year's saving estimate is also low, and when the revised estimate comes next year the income will be seen to exceed it. Hence there is no basis for an increase in freight rates. If you want funds for other increased expenditures there is also scope for cutting down railway expenditure to which not enough attention has been given. If we look at the figures for working expenses they go on increasing every year. It would not be good to think it is impossible to cut them down. Coal pilferage is causing losses of lakhs of rupees every year. So far the steps taken to prevent this pilferage have had no effect.

Coal freight has been increased in the name of rationalisation. What is this rationalisation ? If you want to increase the rate it is not necessary to make excuses. Let the Minister explain the basis on which coal freight has been rationalised. Now coal would become expensive for regions away from the coal mines. This is not the way for the railways to contribute to the country's industrial and economic development.

Irregular Increase in Contribution to General Revenue

One more thing. The railways contribute to the general revenue. A Convention Committee is set up for it. It had recommended that from April 1, 1961 the railways' contribution should go up from 4 per cent to 4.25 per cent. But when the Emergency came the railways increased this contribution from 4.25 to 4.50 per cent without setting up a committee. Was this increase called for ? If it was thought necessary to increase the contribution due to the emergency the process of setting up a Committee should have been followed and its approval for the increase obtained. This was not done and the railways increased the rate from 4.25 per cent to 4.50 without taking the Parliament or a Committee into confidence. There is no objection to this increase, but the way it has been done is wrong and it is not in accordance with the policy we have formulated.

SHRI D.N. NARAYAN : Now it has been increased from 4.50 per cent to 5.75 per cent.

Less Accidents, More Deaths

SHRI VAJPAYEE : Sir, the statement we have been given claims that this year there have been less railway accidents. They may be less in number, but there is no decrease in deaths and damage to railway property. There have been more deaths in 1962-63 as compared to 1961-62. That year 120 people had been killed, while in 1962-63 the number was 187. For the injured too the number was 491 before, it is 504 now. Property worth Rs.15 lakhs was destroyed before, in 1962-63 the loss was Rs. 23 lakhs. The explanation given for the accidents is infuriating. I would like to draw the attention of the House to a particular accident. This time the passengers were travelling on the roof of the train and it dashed into a bridge, killing 28 and injuring 2. This accident happened on November 11, 1962. An inquiry was made into this accident and its report said that those travelling on the roof of the carriage did not know there was a bridge ahead and so they would die when the train dashed against it. But the Railway Ministry did not accept the report and the Ministry and the Railway Board said — I quote :

> "The Railway Board did not accept this conclusion of the Additional Commissioner, Railway Safety. In the opinion of the Railway Board the accident was the result of the rowdiness and negligence of the passengers, because they violated Indian Railway Regulation 118(2) and insisted on unauthorised travel on the carriage roof."

It is against the regulations of the Railways to travel on the roof, but what regulation says that if passengers are sitting on the roof you have to run the train without getting them down and kill them by dashing on a bridge ?

SHRI SHAH NAWAZ KHAN, Deputy Minister in the Ministry of Railways : They were repeatedly made to come down.

SHRI VAJPAYEE : Even then it was not proper to run the train, you could have stopped it there.

SHRI SHAH NAWAZ KHAN : When the train started they again rushed and climbed in the dark.

SHRI VAJPAYEE : The train could have stopped again. You explain away, but your explanation cannot cut ice with anybody.

SHRI L.N. MISHRA (Orissa) : What is your Railway Police for ?

SHRI H.C. DASAPPA : That was night.

SHRI VAJPAYEE : If we run extra trains during pilgrimages such accidents could be avoided.

AN HON. MEMBER : Not many trains run, except for the Kumbh Mela.

SHRI VAJPAYEE : The Railway department should see that even if the passengers disobey the rules they should not be allowed on to the roof and the train should not run. If there are complaints they can be removed, but those who are killed cannot be brought back to life.

SHRI RAMASWAMY, Deputy Minister in the Ministry of Railways : The train was stopped three times.

SHRI VAJPAYEE : Why was it started at all ?

VICE-CHAIRMAN (Shri M. Govinda Reddy) : The trouble, Mr. Vajpayee, was that the train was moving and they got on to the roof. It was pitch dark. They could not see. That is the case.

SHRI VAJPAYEE : I say if we have to run the train we cannot do so with anyone on the roof. The report we have received about this accident is that the train was started even when there were passengers on the roof of the carriage. Perhaps even those who ran the train may have thought that there would be no collision with a bridge. But the Railway Board's report says the passengers rowdily sat on the roof. This attitude of the Board towards the accident is inhuman. When the railways sell a ticket to a traveller but cannot give him a seat is that not the inefficiency of the railway administration ? Does that not show that the administration is useless ? If we give the traveller a ticket but not a seat we should stop issuing tickets. And if it is necessary for the traveller to travel with a ticket but without a seat we should not hesitate to accept the blame. Had the officials present at that station acted with care this accident could have been avoided. Maybe there would have been some other complaints, but 28 lives could have been saved. The railway administration cannot escape the responsibility for these deaths.

Where is the Inquiry Commission's Report ?

Then again, where is the report of the commission set up to inquire into the accident at Dumrao ? Why is it delayed ? A lot of time has elapsed since the accident took place, but its report is yet to come. The Kunzru Committee has taken exception to the fact that inquiries into accidents are not conducted properly. The Railway Inspectorate makes inquires only to fill forms, but it has not been able to contribute to the prevention of accidents in future. In the opinion of the Kunzru Committee 70 per cent accidents occur due to human failure. Railway employees can make mistakes and those mistakes should be brought down. But we should also give some thought to the conditions in which they work. I know of an example in which a roadside Assistant Station Master, whose wife had died, could not go for the funeral because another Assistant Station Master did not come as relief and the dead body lay in the house for 24 hours. There was nobody to cremate it and the Assistant Station Master could not leave his place so long as there was no other person to take his place. The Railway Minister should find out how many cases there are where leave is not given because relief is not available. According to the figures we have collected there are nearly a thousand vacancies of Assistant Station Masters on the Southern Railways that have not been filled up.

I do not know if the situation has changed in the past some months.

If you do not give employees leave in time, if you force them to work beyond necessity will they not find the work beyond their capacity ? We have about 27,000 Assistant Station Masters in the country and the Railway Minister had said the other day that he would look into their scales. But neither the Railway Budget nor his speech gives any indication of it. We should realise under what difficult conditions railwaymen work. Station Masters and Assistant Station Masters working at small stations—they are station masters only in name—sell and check tickets, book goods, attend to the telephone, receive and flag off trains and thus do all sorts of jobs. For one man to look after so many things how developed his capacity has to be ! What salary, what allowance and what benefits should he get in return for such a responsibility ? There are many categories in the Railways that bear the major part of the responsibility for running them but proportionate justice is not done to them.

Recognise Workers' Unions

The Railway Minister is new to his job and I would like to place a new thought before him. The present system of recognising labour unions should be reviewed. We could have categorywise recognition on the lines of Post and Telegraph Department and all employees could be told to bring these unions together in a confederation. The employees who run the present unions do not represent all categories, they do not even know about all categories. As a result there is resentment among various categories like station masters, assistant station masters, guards, commercial clerks, telegraph employees and so on. Their voice is stifled because their unions are not recognised. They are not given an opportunity to meet with the Railway Board. If the Railway Minister would not spare time for them who will listen to them and resolve their difficulties ? Their difficulties could become difficulties in the way of running the railways. At present there are two all-India labour unions in the railways and they cannot meet the needs of all railwaymen. They are embroiled in party politics. They are not aware of employee's difficulties. How can they represent them truly ? I would urge you to recognise category-wise unions on the model of the Post and Telegraph Department. Later these unions could be brought together in a confederation which could present employees' complaints at the level of the Railway Ministry or the Railway Board, which could then listen to the problems of employees of different categories. We should have this sort of arrangement.

Sir, there is an incentive scheme in the workshops. I am in close touch with the Lucknow workshop, so I can say on the basis of personal knowledge that although it has succeeded to a limited extent the scheme is spreading resentment among the employees. The resentment is due to three things. First, posts are being surrendered and employees rendered surplus. Secondly, there is talk of teaching them another trade. You should give a little sympathetic consideration to how difficult it is to teach a new trade to someone who has been doing a particular job for 30-35 years. This scheme has also stopped the upgradation of workshops and new appointments. All in all the employees do not feel enthusiastic about the scheme. So in the light of experience so far it should be reconsidered.

Reinstatement of the Corrupt

In 1956 I had raised in the House a matter relating to the recruitment of Khalasis in the Stores Department at Alam Bagh, Lucknow. I had charged that there was corruption in the recruitment. Later there was an inquiry and the Chief Clerk was suspended for four years. Later he was demoted and transferred to Jodhpur. This penalty was quite light as compared to the extent of corruption. But under pressure this penalty too was done away with, and he was transferred back to the Lucknow workshop where he had been charged with corruption in the appointment of Khalasis. Will political pressure soften the stringent steps required to be taken against corruption ? I know of a case at Lucknow where an employee was transferred for taking part in the strike. His wife was ill. The doctors had advised that he should stay in Lucknow. But his transfer was not revoked. On the other hand the person who was sent to Jodhpur on charges of corruption was brought back. Even today there is corruption in the recruitment of Khalasis in the Lucknow

Division. It will continue so long as the Government does not keep officers under tight control.

Management–Employee Relationship

I regret that the Railway Minister has dismissed in one sentence the important topic of the relationship between the employees and the management. It was a long speech but employees did not merit more than one sentence in it. On page 42 he said :

> "All in all there was a friendly relationship with the Railway employees."

Do they have no other problems ? In their view the two-rupee increase in the dearness allowance is not enough. Prices have risen more. How is relief possible ? The Railway Minister should think about opening shops for making essential commodities available to the employees at the right price. The administration will not be able to check dearnes in the near future. But in order to prevent the employees' standard of life going lower due to dearness it is not enough to just increase the dearness allowance. Availability of essential commodities at proper prices has also to be ensured. At first the Railway department had opened some shops for the employees but some defects in them were noticed. If we correct these faults fair price shops could be run for the employees.

New Verdict of the Supreme Court

The Supreme Court's new verdict was discussed today during Question Hour. The verdict was given on December 5 and now we are in March. This is an example of the speed with which the Government works during the Emergency. The Supreme Court's verdict is quite clear. In this House we have always been saying on this side that clauses 148 and 149 of the Railway Establishment Code are against the spirit of the Indian Constitution. We cannot remove any employee from employment without giving him the reason, without asking him to explain and without an opportunity for an inquiry. During the British regime railwaymen were kept on a different level. The railways had not employed them. They had a contract with the railways. A condition of that contract was that they could leave service or the railway administration could terminate their service with one month's notice. After independence this system should have changed. We cannot put railway employees in a different category from other Central employees, and if any employee is to be removed from service it is necessary to give him the show–cause notice and an opportunity to explain. But hundreds of railway employees have been removed from service without giving reason or making an inquiry. The Supreme Court has struck down both these clauses of the Railway Establishment Code as *ultra vires*. Now the Railway Ministry has no option but to reinstate these employees. Where does the Law Ministry come into this ? Are we asking the Law Ministry to find out a way of not taking them back ? This would be quite serious. If we do not implement the Supreme Court's verdict promptly we cannot preserve its prestige. Even if it is necessary to go into every case, departmental action can be taken. For this implementation of the Supreme Court verdict should not be delayed.

Administration's Interference in Unions

Sir, the Eastern Railwaymen's Union is an example of how the railway administration interferes with employees' unions. There was some difference of opinion among the office-bearers of this union, but for that reason it was not proper to withdraw the facility to compromise and negotiate with the administration. Which union has no conflict between the office-bearers ? But the administration's attitude towards the conflict in the Eastern Railwaymen's Union strikes at the root of workers' interests. I had asked if the recognition of the Eastern Railwaymen's Union had been withdrawn and the Minister had replied in the negative. Technically this is true, but the power to negotiate that goes with recognition, the power to vent grievances, cannot be exercised by the Union. If keeping recognition means the union does not have the power of representation and negotiation, the recognition should be withdrawn. The administration should not interfere in workers' quarrels. It should find out which group has the majority and deal with it. The employees' interests should not be affected.

Sir, there is no uniform policy regarding the night allowance. Telephone employees complain that they do not get it. Commercial Clerks complain that they do not get it. Northern Railway Station Masters say they have been given a night allowance but it is conditional upon a certain number of trains passing the station. Does that mean we expect the employees to sleep between two trains ?

SHRI SHAH NAWAZ KHAN : If there is time they may sleep.

SHRI VAJPAYEE : Would you allow them to sleep ?

SHRI SHAH NAWAZ KHAN : Certainly. If there is an interval of eight hours between two trains they may sleep.

SHRI VAJPAYEE : There cannot be an interval of eight hours, and even if there is you cannot allow them to sleep.

SHRI SHAH NAWAZ KHAN : Why not ? He can sleep. There is no objection.

SHRI VAJPAYEE : But if there is an accident ?

SHRI SHAH NAWAZ KHAN : He should wake up before the train arrives and be on duty.

SHRI VAJPAYEE : I say the question of overtime should not be linked with the number of trains. If the employee is on duty for more hours he should get a night allowance irrespective of the number of trains.

I shall finish in two minutes. A lot of sympathy has been shown for Third Class passengers but there is no possibility of improving their lot in the near future. At the rate railway traffic is growing and at the rate rolling stock is being manufactured it seems even for 15 years one cannot guarantee a seat for the traveller whom we give a ticket.

SHRI R.K. BHUWALKA (West Bengal) : The number of people is increasing more than that.

SHRI VAJPAYEE : This is a serious situation. Arrangements should be made to increase the number of trains and to press into service third class passenger carriages being used here and there.

Officer–Staff Relationship

In this connection I have a complaint. I am not sure if I should voice it. It is that it does not look nice in the year 1964 that officers of the Railway Ministry and the Railway Board should insist on travelling by special saloons and obstruct the track for it. There are reserved carriages for other ministers, so it should be the same for the Railway Minister. The Government has also other officers. Why should a Railway officer have special facilities and a special saloon—and he uses abusive language for minor employees. This is not a good thing. Railway officers still think like bureaucrats. You should rid them of this bureaucratic mentality. Otherwise we would not be able to motivate the employees to put in maximum work. I know about an incident on the Candausi station platform, when the Northern Railway Divisional Superintendent stood on the platform and abused the employees because joining his compartment was slightly delayed. Employees may make mistakes, and for that they should be punished, but if the Railway Police or an officer of the Division stands on the platform and abuses the Station Master or Assistant Station Master it does not add to the prestige of the Railways, nor can it create a good opinion about the Railways in the people's mind. But Railway officers still insist on throwing their weight about. A good relationship with the employees can be based only on equality, not on a servant-master basis. Thank you.

Corruption in Reservation

Madam, this Bill has been presented to combat a major evil prevalent in the Railways. But it cannot satisfy us. Perhaps the Railway Ministry thinks that crimes will not be committed if there is penalty for them or if, in case the penalty is light, it is increased. I am not in agreement with this way of thinking. As it is, the present law provides for punishment. The guilty can be sentenced to three months' imprisonment or a fine of Rs. 250 or both. Now section 144 of the Act is being amended. But now many people have so far been punished under the prevailing law for selling tickets or for selling half of a return ticket to somebody else ? Does the Government have facts and figures that would go to show that people were punished under the law in force but it fell short, the punishment that could be given under it was insufficient and so the law is being amended and the punishment being increased ? No facts and figures have been placed on the floor of this House that would enable us to conclude that the prevailing law is not enough and needs to be amended.

Corruption in Reservations

In his introductory speech the Hon. Minister had said that the present law deals with a season ticket or a return ticket, and other types of tickets are not included in it. I would like to know about the corruption that is going in reservations. Seats and berths are reserved in fake names and a genuine traveller is told that there is no seat, but on the platform he is approached by people who offer him a seat for consideration. Is there no law that can stop this evil ? Is this evil continuing because the law does not provide for punishment ? Even under the present law penal action can be taken against such people. If they are not punished it is not because there is no provision for punishment. It is because reservation of seats and berths has become a big racket in which railway employees are colluding with outsiders. The present Bill does not guarantee that railway employees would not ally with or encourage such corruption. Then how can we check this evil ?

Madam, at the Delhi Station people queue up when reservations begin, but some agents approach them and tell them there will be no reservation for you as we have already reserved the seats but we can arrange a seat for you if you want it. Such agents regularly move about on the platform. Should I understand that neither the officials at the Delhi Station nor the Railway Police are aware of such agents' activities ? Are they being not caught because there is no provision in the law ? We have an Emergency now and the

Rajya Sabha on April 21, 1964 Amendment resolution on amendment 114 bill on the Railway Act

Government has armed itself with extraordinary powers. Will they be used against political opponents ? Cannot fake travellers who hinder genuine travel be booked under the common law ? Railway officials know that such people mislead travellers, because they are in league with them. The reservation staff is in league with them and shares the booty. So long as the Railway Ministry does not put its own house in order, does not motivate its employees to do their duty honestly and gives severe punishment to those against whom there are complaints, merely passing a law will not check this evil.

Madam, I would place an example before you. I was travelling from Lucknow to Delhi. For some reason I could not reserve my seat. I was very much doubtul if I would get a seat. There was a passenger with me. He too had no reservation, but he was not worried. Quite proudly he said, I never reserve a seat, every time I go to the platform and get a seat. We both reached the platform. I wandered around, looking for a seat. This gentleman made a round of the platform and returned, saying he got a seat. He got a seat without reservation. I too had no reservation but I did not. When I asked him about his magic trick he said a fiver did the trick.

Had I so wished I could have created a scene against the Railway employee who accepted the fiver. If we are bent upon it we can create an incident where we might well miss the train but we could force such officers and employees to face punishment. Do the Railway Ministry and the Railway Minister propose to see that employees participating in such corruption are properly punished ? I was surprised to see that a person making an illegal sale of a ticket is given the same punishment as the person making an illegal purchase of it. He who sells a ticket does so for profit, he who buys it does so because he is helpless. How can the two be treated on par and given the same punishment of three months ? This new system makes both giving and taking a bribe a crime.

Should a person who buys a ticket by mistake be punished or the person who sells it for profit ? It is not necessary to punish the buyer, you should find out who he bought it from, you should secure his cooperation and create circumstances in which no one would have to buy a ticket in such a wrong way. If an illiterate villager who is in a hurry cannot get a ticket, should he be punished for buying a ticket like this ? It would be enough to confiscate his ticket. He will have to travel with a new ticket. But is it necessary to punish him with three months' imprisonment or a fine of two hundred rupees or both ? In my opinion an amendment is called for here.

One last thing. As I have said, there is a countrywide racket in reservation and sale of tickets. The Railway Minister should appoint a committee — he may include Members of Parliament if he thinks it necessary under the chairmanship of a member of the Railway Board. He should visit all major stations, meet travellers, listen to their complaints, and if necessary move *incognito* to see how corruption goes on. One type of corruption is quite common. That is getting a sleeping berth in a third class compartment. If you travel from Delhi to Bombay you need a sleeping berth, but as berths are insufficient in number they are allotted on a first-come-first-served basis. Others have to pay three rupees for it. But in the case of a passenger who boards the train in between at wayside stations there is a general type of corruption. He is given a seat on payment but is not given a ticket, and at the destination he is allowed to detrain in collusion with the officer or employee who stands at the door. The amount shelled out by the passenger is pocketed by the Railway staff. This matter needs to be looked into. There is so much corruption in the reservation of seats at Delhi, Lucknow and other big stations that merely making a law would not check it. I urge the Railway Minister to set up a committee under the chairmanship of a member of the Railway Board which should tour these stations, contract travellers and determine what administrative and disciplinary steps need to be taken to weed out this sort of corruption among railway employees. Thank you.

Where is the Relief for Passengers and Staff ?

Madam, I regret to say the Railway Budget does not bear the stamp of the Hon. Minister but a clear imprint of the bureaucracy. This old, traditional, worn-out Budget neither reflects the needs of a developing economy nor is concerned with the means of transportation required for economic regeneration. Every year we see that the Budget shows the expenditure estimate on the lower side. The result is that every year the saving exceeds the estimate. It is the same with this year's budget. In 1963-64 there was excess income of Rs. 5 crores from passenger traffic, of Rs. 3 crores from freight, and a saving of Rs. 1.3 crores in suspended accounts. The total saving has been to the tune of Rs. 10 crores. But this was not estimated in advance. The revised saving estimate is for Rs. 49.24 crores. Estimating income on the lower side and expenditure on the higher side would never help the Railway Minister or the Railway Board to arrive at the right conclusions.

When income is estimated on the lower side and expenditure on the higher side there is a temptation to increase passenger fares and freight rates. This has been done this year again. The House should raise its voice against this rise, for if we let the Railway Minister easily make these increases there is no knowing how many increases we would have to face by February 27. This Railway Budget shows the way the wind is blowing.

There is no loss in the Railways. The Railways are contributing more and more to the General Revenue. As yet it has not even been properly determined how much this contribution should be but it is on the increase, and then it is said the dearness allowance given to the employees would be made up from the increase in passenger fares and freight rates. At some point or the other the House, the Parliament, would have to put a check on how much the Railways should contribute to the General Revenue. There should be some principle behind it. Madam, you will see that the contribution was 4 per cent from the year 1950 to 1960. In 1961 it rose to 4.25. In 1963 it went up to 4.5 per cent and in 1964 to 6. What was the basis of this increase ? The Government borrows money at a rate of less than 4 per cent but the Railways are made to contribute at a rate of 5.75 per cent. What is the propriety in this ? No one opposes the Railways making a profit, contributing more to the General Revenue and sharing in economic reconstruction. But when it is argued that this contribution causes loss to the Railways and this loss is made up by increasing passenger fares and freight rates, this cannot be justified.

Rajya Sabha on February 24, 1965 on the Railway Budget

Madam, there has been a 30 per cent increase in passenger fares during the past ten years from 1955 to date. In 1955 the fares had increased by 10 per cent and in 1957 the tax on fares was also 10 per cent. The Railway Minister said in his speech that this tax goes to the States, not to the Railways' coffers. I accept that the Railways do not get it. But it is the same pocket that shells it out. Whether it goes to the States or to the Railways, it is the same person who pays. Whether you put the knife to the fruit or the fruit to the knife, it is the fruit that gets cut.

SHRI RAM SUBHAG SINGH, Minister of State in the Ministry of Railways : It was a reverse cut.

SHRI VAJPAYEE : Even then it was the fruit that got cut. I cannot understand how the increase in railway fares should not be called an increase because that part goes to the States. And even now an increase of 10 per cent is being made in Third Class fares upto 800 kilometres. Even those travelling 50 km have not been spared. The result is that during the past 10 years railway fares have gone up by 30 per cent. Was this increase necessary ? The economy of the Railways does not say you should go on increasing your contribution to the General Revenue and then justify that increase by increasing passenger fares and freight rates.

A definite policy needs to be formulated in this connection. The share of the Railways in the General Revenue should be determined on the basis of some principle, keeping in view the developmental needs of the Railways themselves. No proper policy has been adopted in this regard.

Freight Rates Again Increased

Freight rates have again been increased. The rate of increase has also been increasing during the past many years. On October 1, 1958 the rate had increased by 4 per cent; on April 1, 1960 by 5 per cent. On July 1, 1961 also there was some increase and last year we increased it by 2 per cent. What ought to have been done was that a freight structure committee should have been set up and a freight rate increase considered only if it was necessary in the light of its recommendations. Such a committee was not set up and the Government took a unilateral decision. The freight for iron, steel, cement, stones, lime and unrefined metals is being raised by 7 per cent and that of crude petroleum by up to 8 per cent. We would have to look at it against the background of the national economy. Our economy is under pressure. Prices are rising, there is inflation, and nothing that promotes these two things can be justified. When Shri Shastri formed his Cabinet he had announced that rising prices would be his government's biggest problem and steps would be taken to bring them down. But prices are not falling. Perhaps that is also not easy. This is a complex problem that cannot be solved in a couple of months. But if the Government does not take any effective steps to bring down prices it should at least not do anything that would hike prices and promote inflation. Today the economy is in such a state that however modest the tax that you may increase on things and however small the fare increase, a wave spreads in the market and by the time the increase of five Naye Paise reaches the consumer it grows to 20-25 paise. If we bear this background in mind it would not become necessary to increase the fare or freight. But I feel all this has been deliberately done. For the present the Railway Minister has come forward with a proposal for an increase and later the Finance Minister may also come forward with some proposal, and possibly the people, the Parliament, are being readied for it. This will aggravate the economic situation.

After all there is competition between rail and road transport. You now claim that the goods movement capacity of the Railways is being adequately utilised and some more capacity could also be brought into use. I have no hesitation in accepting that the Railways have really performed well in the field of goods movement and they should be praised for it, but what is the propriety of increasing fares ? After all you have to stand the competition from road transport, and in such a situation if you want to keep your customers with you it would have been better not to increase fares. It is also argued that employees are being paid dearness allowance, expenditure has gone up, prices of things have also gone up. Do these things not apply to road transport ? There too prices of vehicles and parts have gone up and employees have to be paid more, but has road transport increased passenger fares and freight rates in the same proportion as the Railways have done ?

SHRI N. PATRA (Orissa) : They are also increasing the fares.

SHRI VAJPAYEE : Not so much.

SHRI RAM SUBHAG SINGH : Quote.

SHRI VAJPAYEE : I am prepared to quote and if the Railway Minister so wishes his Ministry can itself provide these figures. If we collect even the figures of goods movement from Delhi to Calcutta we would see that the increase made by road transport is not in the same proportion as that effected by the Railways. Still it is making a profit, giving people better service, there is less fear of pilferage, there is door–to–door delivery, and so road transport is making progress. The Railways should not envy that progress. Healthy competition would help the country's economy, but if you increase freight without improving your service, income will go down and the purpose of increasing it would not be served. Passenger traffic is on the increase. If the Railways can carry all of it, if it can attract those who are forced to travel by bus, income can go up without raising fares.

The Railway Accidents

Madam, a separate review of railway accidents has been presented. It has been claimed in it that as per the record so far the number of accidents in 1963-64 has been the least. Some supporting figures have also been given. Now figures can prove anything, and there is a technique of presenting them. The figures in this review make it clear that collisions of passenger trains have increased. There were 24 accidents in 1962-63 and 30 in 1963-64. There were 160 mishaps due to derailment in which 34 people were killed and 301 injured. In 1963-64 there were nine major accidents in all while there were 11 in 1964-65 till December, in which 20 people were killed and 186 injured. I say accidents do not happen, they are caused. I cannot say about accidents happening due to storms or natural causes, but this review admits that 67.2 per cent accidents are caused by human failure. A total of 14-18 per cent accidents were caused by collisions or derailment. Of these 953 were caused by negligence on the part of the railway staff.

Kunzru Committee Recommendations and Accidents

Man is not a machine. He can make mistakes. But has the Railway Ministry arranged such facilities for work for the employees as would substantially minimise the possibility of accidents. The Kunzru Committee's recommendations on the deficiencies relating to accidents are yet to be implemented, and those faults continue. The Committee had held that there is a shortage of personnel in the categories of Station Masters, Assistant Station Masters, Firemen and Permanent Way Inspectors. Can the Hon. Minister say with certainty that there are no posts of Station Masters and Assistant Station Masters lying vacant ? I am connected with this category and I know there are vacancies, employees cannot go on leave because there is no relief, and on top of this employees at stations are being retrenched.

I can give an example. The Southern Railway General Manager has recently issued a directive to retrench the Assistant Station Master at every station on the Mangalpet-Renigunta line. He has also ordered that every employee will now work twelve hours a day, that is, 72 hours a week, not 48. The Hon. Minister should find out about this. If an employee has to work 12 hours a day and cannot get leave when he wants it exhaustion would overtake him and the possibility of accidents will increase. All vacancies should be filled up and employees should be given leave when they need it. The rules for minimising accidents should also be reviewed. There are many of them that are not practical. Even members of the Railway Board are aware of the fact that if Assistant Station Masters and Station Masters were to strictly abide by all the rules that are written down and which they are expected to follow trains would grind to a halt. The rules have not been framed with the reality in view; they have been made sitting in an office. It is true that there are provisions for penalising erring employees and we also see their result. At the same time it is necessary to amend those rules that are found to be impractical.

The terms and conditions of the employees' service and their benefits should also expand. The Railway Minister says they have a good relationship with the two federations of railwaymen. But I may point out to him that these two federations do not represent all railway employees. Once you recognise two federations you have accepted that it is wrong to have only one labour union in one industry. If you can have two federations why cannot categorywise labour unions be recognised ? There are 27,000 Station Masters and Assistant Station Masters. They have their own association. There is an All-India Commercial Clerks' Association. And there are separate organisations of stenographers and the running staff. This is because the two existing federations can neither represent workers' interests nor protect them.

Patil Sahib has been with P & T. I ask him — why not organise railway employees on the same lines as Post and Telegraphs ? There should be a separate union for every category and a confederation above them all to jointly represent all employees. After all the Railway Ministry and the Railway Board should know about the complaints and difficulties of every category. There is scope for improvement in the present system. If you cannot keep all employees, all categories, satisfied even a bad bolt would bring a train to a halt. I am happy to see that the Railway Ministry has attended to the difficulties of Assistant Station Masters and Station Masters and increased their scales. But the increased payments have not been made and the increase has not been so made as to benefit every employee. I know of an instance where a senior worker's pay was cut and a junior worker's increased. The result of the scales that have come into effect from April has been that those whose increment fell due on different dates stood to lose. The Railway Ministry has decided to introduce the new grades from April 1, 1964. As a result those whose increment fell due on April 4, 1964 lost it. Actually they should get two increments—one because of the upgradation and the other because their increment was due on April 4. But the new grade has brought them a benefit of only 4-5 naye paise. What ought to have been done was to give a one-time increase of Rs. 20 to every employee. If a new employee gets more and old ones do not get an increase it would lead to discontent. So this should be considered afresh.

Madam, the Kunzru Committee had recommended that 25 per cent vacancies in the railway department should be filled with railway employees' children. Has the Railway Ministry accepted this recommendation ? If that is done they will feel secure about their future, their morale would rise and they would work still better. To date the Railway Minister is silent on this recommendation.

I would like to mention an incident which typfies the way the Railway Board works. The stores staff of the North-Eastern Railway are being told to give applications for the 48 days' leave that they had so far availed of. They had been given these holidays along with the workshop staff of the Railway; they had not asked for them. There was some mistake somewhere, because they could enjoy 48 holidays. They did not report on duty because it was a holiday. Now the Railway Board has found that the stores staff was not entitled to these holidays; only the workshop staff was. So the stores staff are being asked to submit applications for leave and are told that if leave is not due their salary would be cut. What is this ? Should the stores staff of the North-Eastern Railway pay for the Railway Board's mistake ? This order should be withdrawn. The stores staff was given holidays and they enjoyed them. If you now tell them their pay would be cut for being absent it would be an injustice to them and they would have to oppose it. I wish the Railway Ministry keeps in touch with Railway employees at every level. If the recognised unions write to the Railway Minister that he should not meet with unrecognised ones he hesitates to do so. This is not a good system. You are not a Minister only for the employees of recognised unions, you are the protector of the interests of all railwaymen. You should be ever ready to listen to and redress the grievances of people wherever they are.

There is much scope for improvement in the Railways. Not that the work they are doing deserves less praise. We have probably the world's largest railway network. It runs 10,000 trains every day and carries 50 lakh passengers. This huge task can be performed still better.

Withdraw Passenger Fare Hike

Finally, I would pray—for God's sake withdraw the passenger fare hike. It is not called for and cannot be justified. It is not proper to burden even short-distance travellers with this increase. It was hoped that under Shri Patil's leadership the Railways would make greater progress, but this budget does not bear the stamp of his personality. The Railway Board's stamp, however, is clear. It would have been so nice if his dominating personality could have brought about some charge in the Railways which would have shown the people that the old ways have somewhat changed. But sometimes I feel he feels cramped in the Railway Ministry and needs some more elbow room to spread around. But if the available time is properly utilised a lot of improvement could be brought about. Something is already being done. The situation can change still more if attention is paid to improving the conditions for third class travellers increasing their amenities and establishing closer relations with the railway staff. Our railway system can confidently stand comparison with any railway system in the world. But there are some shortcomings and deficiencies that are jarring. Efforts should be made to remove them. With these words I conclude my speech. Thank you.

Road Transport Derails Railway

Sir, the Railway Minister has presented a deficit budget for the first time in 25 years. It is a red signal to warn us that the Railways are falling in a financial pit and that the country's economic crisis is worsening.

The Railway Minister has given less goods movement as the reason for the deficit. The actual movement fell short of the estimate by nearly 80 lakh tons. Who is responsible for this estimate ? The responsibility for the mistake lies with the Planning Commission and another ministry, but surprisingly enough the mistake is now sought to be corrected by increasing passenger fares and freight rates.

How the Railway Ministry itself arrives at the estimate we have seen in the budget presented in March and May. In the March budget the total loss had been estimated at Rs. 15 crores, but in the May budget this rose to Rs. 24 crores. Now if the Railway Ministry can make such a big difference in its estimates within a period of two months it is clear that neither is income rightly estimated, nor are goods movement targets fixed on a realistic basis.

It has been argued that there was less movement of goods because there was a drought and less production of foodgrains and other agricultural produce. But it cannot be denied that the Railways had to transport a lot of wheat imported from U.S. Had there not been a drought and scarcity it would not have been necessary to import so much wheat. It is also claimed that less coal movement caused losses. Sir, you will be surprised to learn that on the one hand there is the complaint that less coal was handled while on the other it is being carried by ship in Saurashtra. The Railway Minister would find that between Bhavnagar and Kandla coal is not being moved by rail but by ship, involving a big detour. If the Railways have idle wagons, for which there are no goods to carry, what is the end to send coal by ship ?

Another reason for the loss that the Railway Minister has given is less movement of materials to and from steel mills. I cannot believe that such a big loss would be incurred by carrying raw materials to steel mills or finished products from them. What is surprising is that on the one hand less goods have been moved, causing a loss, and on the other freight rates are being hiked, with the additional levy being increased from 3 per cent to 6 per cent. Is this the way to attract more goods to the railways ?

The Railway System of Goods Movement

It cannot be denied that the Railways have fallen behind in the competition with road transport and road transport is dominating the scene. By increasing freight rates the Minister may perhaps earn Rs. 15 crores but he is not making

Lok Sabha on March 30,1967 on Railway Budget

the railways more attractive for goods movement. Everyone knows that goods movement is expensive because more transportation costs are involved. Still we prefer road transport to railways, especially for more expensive goods because in the first place goods reach the destination in time, secondly they are not damaged on the way and further the customer who sends the goods is satisfied. But what is the railway system of goods movement ? Have the railways tried to improve it in order to enable it to stand competition with road transport ? I say no. I can give an example. I have just been to Patna. Sand from river Sone is sent out from there. It is used for making cement and for other purposes. When the railways were a company this sand was sent at a low rate, but now the freight rate for it is the same as that for foodgrains. There may be a slight difference, but not much. The result is that this sand is now transported by truck. The position with goods trains is such that a goods train laden with fruits took 20 days to cover the distance from Faridabad to Jalandhar. During this period the fruit went bad, the trader suffered a loss, and when he claimed damages a full year was spent in conducting an inquiry, which finally ruled that the period of 20 days for travel from Faridabad to Jalandhar was quite right and a goods train cannot reach earlier. Then who will send fruit by rail and why, and why will wagons not lie idle ?

Empty Wagons, Scarce Wagons

There is a third example. On the one hand the railways complain in that wagons lay idle, they had no goods to carry, while on the other traders have been complaining that their goods lay idle as they did not get wagons. I find it very difficult to believe the figures of the Railway Ministry. I cannot say where they are loaded up. But sometimes figures are cooked with which Parliament and the people are taken for a ride. In this connection I want to level a very serious charge. The Railway Ministry claims that there is continuous progress in the timely running of trains and many trains now run on time. But Sir, do you and does this House know that the scheduled time of trains is not indicated but the time they actually arrive at a station. A train reached Shahdara two and a half hours late and arrived at Delhi Station in time. How did this happen ? An engine left the loco shed at Mughalsarai at two o'clock but its train left at 11.30. How did it leave at 11.30 when its engine had not arrived ? There is a different time of departure, a different time of the Station Master, a different time of the Guard and a different time of the Controller. The Station Master says the train has arrived two hours late. The Controller says no problem, show the train as arriving right time, and that is done. This is a very serious charge. Parliament is kept in the dark, the country is deceived. I am prepared to prove this charge. If a committee of MPs is set up I can prove that so long the Railway Board and the Railway Ministry have been leading the Parliament and the people up the garden path. The arrival time of the train is not shown in the Controller's chart. There can be a similar irregularity with other figures as well. It should also be investigated whether the Railways had a shortage of goods or a shortage of wagons.

How Many Wagons to a Goods Train ?

I was giving you an example of how the Railways serve their consumers. There was a shortage of wagons in the Delhi Division of the Northern Railway. At the Khanna Station traders were asking for wagons so that they could take foodgrains out of Punjab — they knew the Punjab Government was going to ban the movement of foodgrains out of the State. But there were no wagons, so sick, non-waterproof wagons were given which could leak. The traders accepted some of them and refused others. The Station Master there was told you did not give wagons, you are responsible and he was transferred. He had been posted there four months back. I placed his case before the Minister. Can the Railway administration force traders to accept useless, sick and leaky wagons ? Let the Railway Minister clearly explain in his reply how many wagons were in demand all over the country and how many lay idle. If different wagons, different types of wagons are made for the movement of coal and for steel mill materials I am ready to exclude them from this calculation. But I cannot accept the Minister's claim that goods movement is mainly responsible for the loss. There are also other factors that are responsible.

There are different railways and they have different divisions. Where two different divisions of two different railways meet, a goods train lies for a number of days. There is a conflict between division and division and a battle between railway and railway. The goods transporter suffers a loss, the trader suffers a loss. The result is that they leave the railways and take to road transport.

The Railway Minister has claimed that the least number of accidents took place in 1965-66. But in the same report he has also admitted that there were more such accidents in 1966-67 in which the Commission of Railway Safety inquired and the number of casualties in them was also bigger. So far we have not been able to make our railways safe. Why do accidents occur ?

Accidents Don't Happen, They Are Caused

I say accidents don't happen, they are caused. They can be avoided. An accident claiming a large number of lives in the South had been referred to on the very day the Hon. Minister was presenting the Railway budget. Not only this, an accident took place on the light narrow-gauge railway between Gohad to Bhind, where we had never heard of an accident to date. It was between Gohad and Nonera. Three people died in this accident and 32 were injured. Whenever the question of accidents is raised the Minister claims most of them take place because railway employees do not do their duty properly. He calls it failure of the human element. In this report too he has claimed that railway employees are responsible for 688 incidents out of 1046, that is, 60.58 per cent of them. But who is responsible for the conditions in which railwaymen work ? They can make mistakes, but is it not the responsibility of the Railway Ministry to create an atmosphere in which they would not make them and provide them conditions of work in which they would perform well ?

Sir, if railway employees are solely responsible for railway accidents it would not have been that there was not a single accident during the period from December 1 to December 21, when Station Masters and Assistant Station Masters had conducted a work-to-rule campaign. During the 21 days of this campaign there was not a single accident.

Railway accidents happen because railway employees are forced to disregard rules and take short-cuts. Higher officers force them to do so in order to show their own efficiency and have a good record for themselves.

I can give you two examples of this. At Agra a Station Master was suspended because he refused to allow a train to leave because it had no vacuum and no Guard. Have you ever heard of a train running without vacuum and without a Guard ? When this Station Master said the train cannot run as there was no Guard and no vaccum he was threatened with action for insubordination if he did not allow it to run. Action was taken and later it was also withdrawn. But the question is, why are employees forced to transgress rules ?

No Vacuum in the Train

On May 4 a goods train on its way from Haridwar to Doiwala met with an accident, in which five people including the Guard were killed. The train was not inspected when it left Haridwar. There was no vacuum in the whole train; only in the engine. So it could not climb towards Doiwala. The wagons got disconnected from the engine and ran down the slope and were later smashed to pieces. There was a preliminary inquiry by the D.M.E. The Railway Minister should find out if this preliminary report seeks to make out that the accident happened by itself and no one was responsible for it. A special inquiry should be made into this matter, because a member of the D.M.E. inquiry committee that submitted this preliminary inquiry report is threatening employees not to tell the truth.

The engine driver of that train had been on duty for more than twelve hours. The engine—its number is CUD 1249—was useless. After the Duiwala accident it got into difficulties at Dehradun, and later at Moradabad. An engine in such bad condition was given. The driver was forced to work for more than twelve hours and there was no vacuum in the train. So the goods train was smashed to pieces and five people including the driver were killed.

The Hon. Minister may say this too is failure of the human element. But was action taken against any officer in connection with this accident ? Was any officer called to explain ? Accidents can be averted, but for that you have to take the small employees into confidence. Accidents cannot be averted just by setting up a big safety organisation and appointing safety inspectors. Crores of rupees are being wasted on the safety organisation, but nobody calls the human element, on which the Railway administration depends for work, for a discussion. Nobody asks it how many working rules are impractical, unimplementable and outdated and need to be changed.

Thirty-thousand Station Masters and Assistant Station Masters conducted a work-to-rule campaign so that working rules should be observed and short-cuts not adopted. But Railway officers force them to take short-cuts. There was no accident during the work- to-rule campaign. The then Railway Minister Shri Patil had given the assurance that the demands of thirty thousand Station Masters would be considered and action would not be taken against any employee. But in Danpur Division three employees are still under suspension. They have still not been taken back. All transfers have still not been cancelled. There are charge-sheets against thousands of Station Masters.

Former Railway Minister's Assurance Set Aside

Those charge-sheets have not been withdrawn. I feel the Railway Minister is reluctant to carry out the former Railway Minister's assurance. That assurance was given to me and to my association. This is a matter of prestige for us. If these suspensions, transfers and charge-sheets are not withdrawn I and my association would have to do something. I am not threatening. I want peace and discipline in the Railway. Nobody should misunderstand me. But if the terms and conditions decided upon at the time of suspending the agitation are transgressed I, as a servant of railway employees, cannot sit silent. I will have to take stern action.

I still have faith in the Railway Minister. He is new to the job but he is getting entangled in the Railway Board's clutches. It is very difficult for any Railway Minister to escape the bureaucracy that prevails in the Railways. Sometimes I have doubts about who presides over the fate of the Indian Railways. Is it the Minister, who is responsible to this Lok Sabha, or is the top brass of the Railway Board ? It is necessary to establish a good relationship with Railway employees. The Railway Minister had also claimed that there is a very good relationship with the all-India unions. But what about those who are not a part of these unions ?

Category-wise Unions

By recognising two labour unions the Railway administration has thrown the 'one industry one union' principle to the winds. If two unions can be recognised, why not three ? Why not four ? Who will protect and promote the interests of category-wise employees, whether they are booking clerks or commercial clerks, Station Masters or Guards, or those who do not work in workshops but play an important role in keeping the wheels moving ? Two all-India organisations could not do it, so category-wise unions on the lines of the Post & Telegraph Department should be recognised in the Railways. It is true that there are more categories in the Railways but they could be grouped and these unions could be brought together in a confederation like the confederation in P & T. Then the complaints of employees of every category could be heard. The Railway Minister should reconsider his labour policy.

Increase in Fares and Freight in the Budget

Sir, I would not take more time. There is no propriety in the increase in passenger fares and freight rates in the budget. It should be withdrawn. Perhaps the Finance Minister has shifted his burden to the Railway Minister's shoulders. The Railways are not running in loss. They are regularly contributing to the General Revenue. Had it been slightly decreased it would have been possible to prevent passenger fares from going up and to keep freight rates as they are, but the Railway Minister did not do so. If he reorganises the Railways, stops wasteful expenditure and adopts thrift policies the loss of Rs. 20 crores can be made up without increasing fares. I would like to give some concrete suggestions in this regard.

1. Railway officers have the authority to waive demurrage and wharfage. The bigger the officer the bigger the amount he can waive. This power is being used for giving concessions to big companies, mills and big industrial houses. Railway officials form a nexus with the mills and industrial organisations who should be charged demurrage and wharfage and waive the charge. Crores of rupees are thus waived. I want the Hon. Minister to place before the House details of how many crores of rupees the officers have waived by way of demurrage and wharfage during the year for which we are at present discussing the budget. This authority should be withdrawn. That would increase the income of the Railways.
2. Employees are given charge-sheets without reason, cases are conducted and government funds are wasted, as is the employees' time. Sir, you will be surprised to learn that in Kota Division about 300 railway employees were suspended and later taken back with a warning. This is the case with just one division. If employees in all divisions are suspended like this there would be a lot of expenditure as well as discontent among the employees.
3. Serious thought should be given to whether or not safety organisations should be set up. I think accidents have increased even after the safety organisation. Steps taken on paper would not decrease accidents. It is not necessary to set up a whole army of officers. Funds spent on the safety organisation would also be saved.
4. It is said that ticketless travel causes loss of Rs. 9 crores. It can be substantially reduced if the Hon. Minister takes the cooperation of all political parties and student organisations. Ticketless travel is an offence, but we would have to create an awareness for it, and checking arrangements will also have to be strengthened. That alone, I feel, can the number of ticketless travellers be reduced. Effective action is called for in this direction.
5. It is also necessary to stop the saloons given to officers. Saloon travel by Railway officials is not in tune with the times. Railway Officers should be on par with officers of other ministries. If those officers can travel by ordinary trains, so can Railway Officers. I am told there are

900 saloons at present. If these 900 saloons are converted into trains you can run at least 50-60 new trains. This year the Railway Ministry has introduced a total of 67 new trains. If all these saloons are converted into trains an equal number of additional trains can be run.

6. It is also necessary to cancel the gold and silver passes of Officers. Members of Parliament can make do with card passes, but for officers gold passes, silver passes ...

SHRI ONKARLAL BERWA (Kota) : Tokens have been given.

SHRI VAJPAYEE : His talking about tokens is a *'tok'* (Interruption) for me. I say there is no need for a gold pass and a silver pass. This is a very old system, continuing from British days. Now Railway Officers will have to change their ways and their style of working. When officers reach a station red carpet is rolled out for them. That they should be given a British-type salute and common people should be shoved away does not accord with democracy. This atmosphere will have to be changed.

Sir, I hope the Railway Minister will consider the points I have raised in the time you allotted to me and will implement the assurance given in connection with the work-to-rule campaign. Thank you.

Cut Expenses, Don't Hike Fares

Sir, I move that "this House rejects Presidential Ordinance of October 22, 1971 on Railway Passenger Fares (Ordinance Number 17 of 1971)."

We have just given the House's approval to an ordinance. Now another ordinance has been placed before the House for consideration. As many as 13 Ordinances were issued in the last inter session. Not since the Constitution was adopted were so many ordinances issued. The Constitution empowers the President to issue ordinances, but it does not give him the authority to misuse them. If there is an extraordinary situation and if public interest demands it, recourse to an ordinance can be taken as an exception. But now it seems this government wants to rule on the strength of ordinances. The ruling party has a two-thirds majority in the House. It can do anything on the strength of this majority, and yet it does not wait for this House.

Sir, it is greatly surprising that ordinances have been resorted to for hiking taxes, railway fares and postal rates. What Speaker Mavalankar had said in this regard has already been referred to in this House. I quote :

> "The procedure for the promulgation of ordinances is inherently undemocratic. Whether an ordinance is justified or not, the issue of a large number of ordinances has psychologically a bad effect. The people carry an impression that government is carried on by ordinances. The House carries a sense of being ignored and the Central Secretariat perhaps get into the habit of slackness which necessitates ordinances and an impression is created that it is desired to commit the House to a particular legislation, as the House has no alternative but to put its seal on matters that have been legislated upon by ordinance. Such a state of things is not conducive to the development of the best parliamentary traditions."

After this Speaker Mavalankar said that imposing a tax by ordinance is simply incomprehensible. In this connection he wrote a letter to Prime Minister Shri Nehru on July 17, 1954, from which I would quote a portion :

> "I may invite your attention to one more aspect, namely, the financial aspect involved in the amendment of the Indian Income Tax Act, 1922. It is not directly a taxation measure, but it is intended for the purpose of collection of taxes. Indirectly it affects the finances and it would be a wrong precedent to have an ordinance for such a purpose."

Speaker Mavalankar was not in favour of an ordinance issued in connection with an indirect system of tax collection but now new taxes are being imposed by ordinance.

Lok Sabha on November 24, 1971 while moving a Resolution seeking rejection of the Railway Passenger Fare Ordinance, 1971

A Deplorable Tendency

This is a deplorable tendency. The Government says—and it has been stated in the objectives of this Bill—that in a meeting of Governors and Chief Ministers of States held on October 12, it was resolved that the expenditure being incurred on refugees from Bangladesh should be made up with a hike in railway fares. On October 22 this ordinance was promulgated. It is being implemented from November 15 and the session of this House has begun from November 15. The Governors and Chief Ministers suggested the promulgation of an ordinance, but they did not say what other steps should be taken to mobilise resources for helping the refugees without putting a new burden on the common man.

Has there been any curtailment of government expenditure ? Has wasteful expenditure been stopped ? Have such loopholes been plugged that enable the money earned by the people by the sweat of their brow to pass into the wrong hands by unfair means ? We have a duty towards refugees from Bangladesh. We cannot close our doors to them. It is our moral duty to look after those who take refuge with us to save themselves from dying from hunger in East Bengal, and if the Government wants more funds for it this House will not refuse them. But to whom should this money go ? Is it called for to increase even third class passenger fares in the name of refugees ? Do these persons travelling by this class have the capacity to pay more ? During the past years railway fares have been hiked many times. But seats and amenities for third class passengers have not increased in proportion to the increase in the fare. They are packed like sardines and travel standing. Now they are being forced to pay more in the name of Bangladesh refugees. On top of it there will be a passenger tax even on a one-rupee ticket. A one-rupee ticket and a passenger tax on it — is this a part of the *Garibi hatao* campaign ?

Refugees and the Tax Burden

While more resources need to be mobilised for the refugees only seventy crores of rupees have been arranged through these taxes. Actually five-six hundred crores rupees would be required for the year. In the beginning we were told the refugees will go back in six months. Eight months have gone by, and their number is growing instead of going down. In a way this problem is of our own making. Had we recognised the local government of Bangladesh in April itself and given it large-scale military aid the *mukti vahini* would not have had to pile up so many martyrdoms and we would not have had to face the problem created by such a heavy influx of refugees. At that time the Government kept waiting for the right time and kept trying to build up world opinion.

Eight months have elapsed, but there are no signs of the refugees going back. The question is, how to mobilise resources for them ? I suggest that more than seventy crore rupees could be raised if you impose additional charges on foreign liquors, rooms in big hotels, horse-racing, shares of big companies and, if you like, on lotteries. This Bill has estimated an income of seventy crore rupees for the year. This year the amount stands at only Rs. 2.6 crores. The Railway Minister is present. Pilferage of coal on the Railways itself amounts to Rs. 7 crores per year. No steps have been initiated to prevent it. Lakhs of people travel without ticket. If arrangements are made to catch them, if there is strict management and if employees work sincerely the income of the Railways can go up and it would not be necessary to impose new taxes. But the travelling public is being burdened with fresh taxes and no efforts are being made to increase income and cut down wasteful expenditure. I could have appreciated the propriety of this Bill if, along with it the Railway Minister had explained that in view of the Emergency more funds are needed for the refugees and so attempts are also being made to cut unnecessary expenditure of the Railways. Sir, you are Chairman of the P.A.C. You know the situation. A report has been presented in the House to the effect that there is over-capitalisation in the railways as well as underutilisation of capacity.

Income, Expenditure and Loss of Railways

In 1969-70 the total income of the Railways was a thousand crore rupees. Even with a ten per cent cut in expenditure there can be a saving of a hundred crores. I read in the newspapers—I do not know how far it is true—that the Central Government has asked everybody to economise. In such a situation seven crores is peanuts. Much more than that can be saved by the Railways cutting down on their expenditure. But no such effort has been made. Instead of raising more resources the Minister and the Railway Board Chairman are busy with their own affairs. The old Chairman of the Railway Board is gone. If his words mean anything he wanted to save the thirty thousand crore rupees being lost due to corruption. Shri Ganguly was not allowed to do so. So he was derailed.

Sir, I stand to oppose this bill because in my opinion there is no propriety in imposing a bigger burden on the common man. If you want resources take them out of the pockets of those who travel in air-conditioned carriages. I shall not object to that. First class passengers can also contribute something to the government exchequer. But burdening third class passengers and forcing those who buy a one-rupee ticket to pay a bigger tax are anti-people steps. This will neither raise the morale of the people nor fulfil the Government's declared objective of checking dearness. The country is also a victim of inflation. Prices are going up. The fixed-income group is harassed, and on top of it a bigger burden is being imposed in the name of the refugees. I urge the Minister to amend it. Free third class passengers of it. Assure the House on behalf of the Railway administration that efforts would be made to cut down expenditure and practise economy. A target for such saving should be fixed and the House informed of it.

I have said, and I would like to repeat, that resources can be mobilised for the relief of the refugees without putting a bigger burden on the common man, but for that the government will have to give up its anti-people form and put a burden on those who have a capacity to bear it. I feel this aspect has been completely ignored while imposing taxes by this ordinance. Hence this opposition. This opposition will spread up to the people and it will create unnecessary bitterness in this hour of crisis.

Before closing I would like to make one more point. The Government says the refugees from Bangladesh will go back. After how many refugees going back will the tax be revoked ? There is no possibility of all of them going back. Will this tax be for ever ? Let Smt. Sushila Rohatgi clearly say how long it will continue temporarily. The experience so far is that taxes imposed in the name of Emergency are never revoked. The refugees may go back, but the tax will not be taken back. This is a very serious situation and a clear assurance in this regard is needed. Thank you.

Employees Participation Needed

Sir, I did not wish to participate in this debate. But on hearing Shri Bhagwat Jha Azad's speech I think it is necessary to say something.

SHRI D.N. TIWARI : There has been some revelation.

SHRI VAJPAYEE : No one can deny that the Railways have some achievements to their credit. The Hon. Minister takes the credit for them, but for the deficiencies it is the officers who are held responsible. This is not good logic...(*Interruption*).

SHRI D.N. TIWARI : It was said because officers say so.

SHRI VAJPAYEE : It is not necessary to defend the Railway Board ...(*Interruption*).

SHRI BHAGWAT JHA AZAD : Let him save red-tapism. It makes no difference.

SHRI SATPAL KAPOOR (Patiala) : You are pleading as well as defending. What is your politics ?

SPEAKER : You have had your say. Now let him have his.

SHRI VAJPAYEE : We have demanded in this House that the Railway Board should be wound up.

We have also demanded in this House that railway employees should have representation on the Railway Board. The Railway Board is necessary, but members of the ruling party are not supporting this demand.

In parliamentary democracy the Cabinet is responsible to the House. We hold the Minister responsible for the Ministry's failure and we also congratulate him on its success. If it is necessary we may also go into the details of the Ministry's working and level criticism. The House can never be denied this right. But our tradition has been that so far as possible we do not drag officers into our affairs. A serious situation prevails in the country. There was a plane accident and a serious situation was created in the country. The Civil Aviation Ministry's failure has been exposed, but nobody thought it necessary to level a charge directly at the Secretary to the Ministry. We did not do so because the Minister is present to explain. If his Ministry indulges in any irregularity the Minister is there to discipline it. But this does not mean the Railway Board is not criticised. When we discuss the Railway Budget and the Railway Board is roundly attacked the House points out its deficiencies. But if the Railway Board does anything good there should be no hesitation in praising it...(*Interruption*).

Pardon me, I am in the opposition and I have hundreds of complaints against the Railway Board, but I have also watched its work from close quarters — at first in the Public Accounts Committee and then as a member

---

Lok Sabha on August 23-24, 1973 during discussion on Railway Ministry's supplementary grants demands

of the Railway Convention Committee. I know that when the Bangladesh problem arose the whole Ministry, including the Railway Board, put up a good performance in keeping the wheels moving. This House had congratulated it on this...(*Interruption*).

The Wagon Shortage

Today the problem is there is a shortage of wagons in the country. Just now an Hon. Member from Kerala raised this question. We had gone deep into it. I say there is no shortage of wagons in the country—if there is anything, it is mismanagement. The railways did not get enough goods to transport. Still wagons fall short, because they lie here and there. Sometimes labour agitations create problems. Sometimes there is pilferage of goods. Here I would like to quote what the Railway Convention Committee has observed in this regard :

> "It would appear that the Railways have sufficient surplus lines and wagon capacity to handle additional traffic. The constraints would appear to be mainly the law and order problems, thefts of parts, labour troubles and operation inefficiency."

It is also clear that there is slackness in the manufacture of wagons. An eye will also have to be kept on the private manufacturers. If the Railway Ministry so wishes it can set up its own plant. This House is willing to authorise it for this purpose. But we would have to look to the question of shortage of wagons as a part of the whole picture. I call upon the Railway Ministry to meet the needs of the country in this respect.

Recognition of Labour Unions

I have opposed the policy the Railway Ministry has been pursuing in connection with recognising labour unions. Now this policy has completely failed. It is said there would be one union in one industry. Then why do the Railways have two unions in one industry ? And if there are two, why can't there be three ? There should be one union, but it should be on the lines of the P & T confederation, in which representatives of different categories should also have a voice, there should be someone to listen to their woes, discuss matters with them and remove their legitimate complaints.

The feeling behind the strike of the Loco Workers was that nobody listened to them. It is the same with commercial clerks, Station Masters and Guards. I appreciate the Hon. Minister's difficulty. There are hundreds of categories and it is not possible to recognise them all. But those categories can be regrouped, they could be brought together in a confederation of category-wise unions on the lines of P & T, and they could be given an opportunity to voice their complaints and be heard.

The Hon. Minister is new to this Ministry. He wants to work with enthusiasm. Let him look at the problem of recognising labour unions from a new point of view. The Railway Ministry and the Railway Board have both fallen in a rut. The old style cannot prove effective in the new circumstances. Whenever there is a strike we have to listen to the Minister and the work grinds to a halt. We do not want a strike in the Railways. We do not want *'Pahiya Jaam'* (halted wheels). We want the trains to run, move the maximum goods, and fulfil the people's needs. But the Hon. Minister and the Railway administration will have to assure workers of every category that if they have some genuine complaint somewhere there would be a door to knock on for ventilating their grievance. Today all doors are closed, because they are not recognised. The Government may not recognise their union but it can at least serve as a channel of communication. The Government can meet with its representatives, consider their representations and give replies. I say even the question of recognition should be considered afresh.

SHRI N.K.P. SALVE (Baitul) : Does the Hon. Member want two unions ?

SHRI VAJPAYEE : Sir, he is interrupting me. I will have to reply to him.

SPEAKER : You should think of the situation into which you put him when you interrupt him.

SHRI VAJPAYEE : The 'one industry one union' principle has already been given up. When the Railways can have two unions why not three ? There should be one union, but it should have scope for category–wise representation. It should not be a federation but a confederation. Today only the workshop workers' union is invited. Those categories that are scattered, that are busy running the trains and cannot come together at one place cannot plead their case effectively. The Hon. Minister should think about this. Thank you.

Loco Workers' Strike : Who Forced Them ?

Sir, it cannot be denied that the Railways are in the grip of a grave financial crisis. But it is of its own making. Other Ministries and government departments are also responsible for it. There was a time when the Railways made a profit. Now they run in loss. It is not necessary to describe the plight of third class passengers. In spite of the fact that Rs. 4000 crores from public funds are invested in the Railways they have become a losing enterprise. The Railway Convention Committee, of which I too was a member, gave some relief. The Railways got Rs. 107 crores. But this was like transferring money from one pocket to another. If the Railways' contribution to the General Revenue is reduced it may well show a lesser loss for the Railways on paper, but it cannot make the railways contribute adequately to the total financial condition of the country.

The biggest thing is that the Railways do not get enough goods and passenger traffic as compared to the development of its carrying capacity. In the Fourth Plan the financial provision for the Railways was Rs. 400 crores which is going to go up by Rs. 40 crores. And yet there is going to be a loss in the number of 32.5 million passengers. I wish great care is taken while formulating the Fifth Plan. The Planning Commission lives in an ivory tower. It forces the Railway Ministry to put the passenger and goods transport estimate on the high side. Accordingly, the Railways extend their capacity. But there is neither enough goods nor enough passengers. The result is a loss for the railways. What is needed is a realistic assessment of how much capacity should increase in the next five years and whether goods and passenger traffic would match the increased capacity.

In British times they started the practice of presenting the Railway budget separately. I cannot understand why it has to continue. Either we could make the Railways an autonomous corporation or we could treat them on par with other ministries. But the Railways have a separate budget and a separate Convention Committee. I cannot understand this. It needs to be radically changed.

Railwaymen Ignored

We were just discussing the Loco Workers' strike. No one wants the railway service to be disrupted. But I am not prepared to accept—no one will accept—that railway employees go on strike for fun. Those who have the

Lok Sabha on December 17, 1973 during discussion on Loco Workers' Strike and Report of the Railway Convention Committee

sword of retrenchement hanging over their heads and for whom the future is a question mark are not incited by someone to go on strike. The truth is that there is no one to listen to the various categories of railwaymen. The 'one industry one union' principle is universally accepted. If you too accept it why are there two unions in the Railways ? Wind up both of them. Give railwaymen a chance to say by secret ballot what type of union they would like to join...(*Interruption*).

SHRI A.P. SHARMA (Buxar) : Who will wind them up ?

SHRI VAJPAYEE : Those who have recognised them can also derecognise them. How did the INTUC union come ? By the back door ? The Hon. Minister says category-wise unions cannot be recognised, but saying so is not enough, you will have to admit that the present all-India organisations do not represent the common railwaymen. There are 27000 Station Masters. Who will listen to their complaints ?

SHRI A.P. SHARMA : We will.

SHRI VAJPAYEE : Wrong. Who will determine if the Railway Minister's assurances to the loco workers were carried out or not.

SHRI L.N. MISHRA : You do it. We will accept it.

SHRI VAJPAYEE : Call a meeting of opposition leaders and place the facts before them. Loco workers' representatives could also be called ... (*Interruption*).

SHRI JAGANNATH MISHRA : What the Minister says should be accepted.

SHRI VAJPAYEE : He is not an incarnation of truth. The employees may have some legitimate grievances ... (*Interruption*).

SHRI S.M. BANERJEE : Here is a telegram which has been received from Mr. Sabapathy. It reads thus :

> "RAILWAY MINISTER'S FAILURE TO IMPLEMENT DEMANDS.
> As per August agreement and railway officers' convenience with recognised unions resorting to mass victimisation afresh resulted Western and Northern Railway present agitation. Pray immediate intervention to implement agreement."

DEPUTY SPEAKER : He could pass it on to the Hon. Minister.

SHRI S.M. BANERJEE : It further reads :

> "Cancel all victimisations including present agitation within forty-eight hours in interest of nation and industrial peace otherwise other railway Loco running staff will be compelled to join the agitation."

Reconsider Railwaymen's Unions

SHRI VAJPAYEE : The Railway Minister should accept the facts that the Railways too need a labour union like the one in the Post & Telegraph Department, which is not just a federation but a confederation and in which category-wise labour unions are also recognised. But on behalf of all of them the confederation negotiates with the Government. There should be a similar arrangement in the Railways. You should reconsider this matter. This problem is not confined to the Loco staff. Whether they are Station Masters, running staff or Loco workers, if an all-India union does not represent them they keep feeling discontented, and one day or the other this accumulated discontent finds an expression. You have been kind enough to send these papers. Here you ask, who is responsible ? And you reply 'left adventurism and right reaction' are responsible. By borrowing this communist phraseology you cannot solve the Railways' problems, Mishraji. You may abuse anybody...(*Interruption*).

SHRI A.P. SHARMA : It is true.

SHRI VAJPAYEE : In my opinion, to avert this calamity you could proceed with what you had said about the meeting of January 17. Proceed with it. There should be an agreement about a 10-hour shift. If you do not want to give negotiating facility to labour unions you should at least give them a channel of communication. Giving a channel of communication does not mean giving recognition. If the employees do not come to feel that there is somebody in Delhi who would listen to them nobody can prevent them from going the wrong way.

Gauge Conversion—When, Where, How ?

The Railway Minister should carefully listen to what the Finance Minister of Uttar Pradesh has just announced. He said it has been decided to convert the metre gauge line linking Kumaun to broad gauge. That day too I had raised this matter with the Speaker's permission. I have seen the supplementary demands, I have gone though the whole Railway budget, but nowhere did I come across financial provision for such conversion. How did the Finance Minister of U.P. make this announcement ?

AN HON. MEMBER : He has demanded it.

SHRI VAJPAYEE : He has not demanded it. He has said : "The Union Government has accepted the proposal to convert the metre gauge into broad gauge". Let the Railway Minister explain this. Either railway lines at places of strategic importance are being converted or new lines are being laid there. The Railway Minister also pays special attention to backward regions. But I have heard that the narrow gauge line from Gwalior to Shivpuri is being taken off. On the other hand the small line between Shahdara and Saharanpur which had been closed down is being converted to broad gauge, because there are going to be elections in Uttar Pradesh...(*Interruption*).

AN. HON. MEMBER : Has all work in Uttar Pradesh been closed down ?

SHRI VAJPAYEE : In Uttar Pradesh new lines are being laid, they are being converted to broad gauge, while in our Madhya Pradesh they are being taken off. I request the Hon. Minister to convert them to broad gauge. It is a backward region and should be linked ahead. The broad guage line can be extended from Shivpuri to Guna. This would help the development of the region.

When Shri Mishra had just taken charge of the Railway Ministry the Railway Board had agreed in principle that the Taj Express, which reaches Agra at 11.00 o'clock and lies there till 6 in the evening, should be extended upto Gwalior and Jhansi. I was a member of the Railway Convention Committee.

SHRI B.P. MAURYA (Hapur) : The Hon. Member should see the Minister in private.

SHRI VAJPAYEE : This is not a question of meeting privately. It is these people who meet privately. We speak openly.

The Central Railway General Manager had said in Bombay, there is just a problem with the platform at Gwalior. Once that is solved we shall take the Taj Express up to there—we even want to take it up to Jhansi. But in reply to my letter the Hon. Minister has said there is no question of taking the Taj Express further because it is meant for foreign tourists. It reaches Agra at 11 o'clock and lies there till 6 in the evening. Is this proper utilisation of railway staff and rolling stock ? The Hon. Minister can take it further. This would help the development of the region as also ensure full utilisation of rolling stock. I would request the Railway Minister to call for all relevant papers and reconsider the matter. Thank you.

For Whom Our Railways Run ?

Sir, it cannot be denied that our railway system has been plunged into a deep financial crisis. There are many reasons for this crisis but the chief among them is lack of proper understanding between the Railway Ministry and the Planning Commission. The Planning Commission urges the Railways to build up capacity that cannot be used. The finances of the railways suffer from the twin maladies of over–capitalisation and under-utilisation of capacity. Some efforts have indeed been made in this direction, but there should be proper assessment of the amount of goods the railways would move and the number of passengers they would carry, and there should be complete understanding between the Planning Commission and the Railway Ministry.

Sometimes I wonder for whom our railways run. Is it for the Railway Minister who can get down at any station he chooses ? Or is it for the railway officers, who can keep hundreds of saloons ? Or for those who travel by Rajdhani and air-conditioned trains ? In my view the most important person for the Railways is the Third Class traveller. But there is nobody to listen to him. If the Railway Minister really wants to make some basic changes in the railway system there can be only one change— there should be only two classes, those who travel by day sitting and those who travel by night sleeping.

If the railways start giving as many seats as the number of tickets sold their losses would increase and the difficulties of travellers who suffer being packed like sardines for reaching their destination would increase. But once in a while we should see the scene in the Third Class compartment of some important train. As a member of Parliament I am entitled to First Class travel, but the adjoining scene is a hair-raising experience.

Passengers Packed Like Sardines

The other day, on the eve of Holi, I was travelling to Bareilly. Some people were travelling on the roof of the compartments. They had also entered the corridors of First Class compartments. Can no special arrangements be made for Third Class passengers on the occasion of a festival like Holi ? Can separate arrangements not be made for festivals ? Pardon me, but a time will come when Third Class passengers will not let First Class passengers travel in peace. We have raised people's expectation so much and repeated the *mantra* of socialism so often that those who do not get a seat look at First Class passengers and wonder what sort of socialism it is when they have to

Lok Sabha March 12, 1974 during General Discussion in on the Railway Budget

hang on to footboards while First Class passengers sit in comfort. I urge the Minister to think about this from a basic point of view.

Is it not possible for us to provide berths to all passengers travelling by night ? Is it not possible to provide seats for those who travel by day ? Is it not possible to provide as many seats as tickets sold, or sell only as many tickets as seats are available ? The Hon. Minister may estimate the loss. I would not be surprised if railway passengers refuse to be packed like sardines and launch an agitation for seats for the tickets they have bought. What reply would the Railway Minister have for such an agitation ?

A train journey has three parts. The first is the waiting.

SHRI MOHAMMED JAMILURRUAHMAN (Kisanganj) : Waiting is a big pleasure.

SHRI VAJPAYEE : When pleasure is stretched too long it is lost. The train does not arrive and passengers keep waiting. When its arrival is intimated the second stage begins, which is restlessness and where the train arrives the battle is joined.

The Railway Minister can even arrange that the passenger should be able to locate the conductor. He has no fixed place to sit. It should be fixed. As the train arrives at the station an electric signal from a compartment should indicate where he is. Is this a very big thing to arrange ? But no attention has been so far paid to it. People rush to find seats. Sometimes the conductor is found asleep. It is a big problem to wake him up. This small thing could be a big addition to passenger amenities. But this has not yet been thought about.

Gulf Between Railwaymen and the Railway Board

Sometimes I wonder if the Railway Ministry is really serious about providing amenities to passengers. Amenities cannot be measured by the greater amount of money spent. It is also possible that more money would be spent but less amenities may reach the passengers. For this it is necessary to motivate the whole structure. It is regrettable that no one right upto the Railway Minister has been able to do this. The speaker before me said that the Railway Minister had announced on the auspicious date of May Day that workers would have full participation in management. Will this full participation go to the extent of giving railway workers representation on the Railway Board ? Can that not be done ? Are railwaymen not worthy of contributing to the administration of the railways ? Can we not make this experiment in the country's biggest public sector undertaking ? Today there is a gulf between the railwaymen and the Railway Board. It is widening. It has to be bridged.

The fact that railway service commissions have been set up in many places has also been praised. I say this is not enough. The problem is that the commission replaces its own selectees with other candidates. Many such cases have come to me and I have written to the Railway Minister. A certain candidate was selected but not appointed and the commission advertised the post again. New candidates were invited and the old ones pushed aside. The one who was initially selected was left out. This was a great injustice to him. Merely setting up commissions at different places is not the solution to the problem. This may provide jobs to some members of the commission but the basic problem would remain.

One more thing I am not 48, but there has been no increase in the number of trains from Delhi to Bombay *via* Jhansi. Will all trains to Bombay go by the west ? Has the Railway Ministry seen the Ratlam-Baroda line ? There are only two trains that go to Bombay *via* Jhansi. The crowded conditions in these trains cannot be described. It is difficult to get in, and once in, it is difficult to get down. This aspect needs to be taken into consideration.

Extend Taj Express to Jhansi

The old Gwalior State had a narrow gauge line. It still goes from Gwalior to Shivpuri. What is its future ? (*Interruption*). If it is dark we will have to fight for it. You can convert it to broad gauge. You can link it with Guna. You have taken a broad guage line from Bina to Guna. You can link this too. Do not shower all your favours on Bihar alone. I am not making any charge. I am only advocating my backward region. Out of the shower of favours on Bihar our Madhya Pradesh, especially the Gwalior region, should also get a few drops.

I would like to raise the Taj matter again. Our Railway Convention Committee had a meeting with the Central Ministry. In it the General Manager had agreed that it should be extended upto Jhansi. It reaches Agra at 10.30 in the morning and lies idle there till it leaves in the evening. As the Rani Jansi train it could be taken from Agra to Jhansi and could return by evening.

Expenses Have Increased but so has Inefficiency

Sir, within a year passenger fares and freight rates have been raised by 30 per cent. This is an extraordinary rise and the Hon. Minister had justified it by saying that fuel expenses have gone up and employees will have to be paid more. It is true that fuel expenses have increased, but so has inefficiency in the Railways.

But why is the consumption of and expenditure on coal increasing ? All efforts are concentrated on dieselisation and later on electrification. If we look at the figures we find we are spending more on coal than before. What is this mystery ? It should be unravelled. Sir, if you look at coal consumption per 1000 km of passenger and goods services you will see that the figure of 59.0 per cent per thousand in 1970-71 became 70.25 per cent in 78-79. How is this possible ? Now look at Goods trains. In 1970-71 it was 60.3 per cent while in 1979-80 it became 81 per cent. This is how coal consumption has increased. I think there is something fishy about coal. Is someone blackening his hand in underhand deals in coal ? A strict watch is called for. The Hon. Minister will have to prove with facts and figures why increased expenditure on coal is justified when we are working for dieselisation and going towards electrification.

Electrification was discussed. In 1981-82 we want to electrify 1418 km of railway line. In five years you will need 45 electric locomotives. We have a capacity of 300 or 350 electric locomotives, not more. From where are the remaining locomotives going to come ? Or what steps are being taken to manufacture them ? In fact the opposite is happening. You are giving more attention to producing diesel Locomotives. Even there wasteful expenditure can be avoided. Currently production of diesel components is being increased at Patiala with an investment of Rs. 30 crores. Was it not possible to step up this production by utilising the excess capacity of the DLW plant at Varanasi where excess capacity is still lying idle ? Then why was the Patiala plant necessary ?

Inter-Departmental Rivalry

Sir, there was a meeting of Secretaries to the various Ministries of the Government of India. It had taken the decision that in view of the energy policy we have adopted we should give priority to electro-locomotives and extend electrification. But the Railway Ministry does not seem to have paid enough attention to this. Is this because members of the Railway Board

Lok Sabha on March 3, 1981 during general discussion on the Railway Budget

belong to the Mechanical Engineering Department ? All electrical work comes under mechanical engineering. When expansion is being talked of, whether of engine manufacture or of electrification, is it perhaps that the whole electrification programme is falling a victim to the internal competition that is going on within the Railway Ministry ? It was recommended that a representative of the Electrical Engineering Department should also be on the Railway Board. I do not know what happened to that recommendation, but I do know that there is departmental rivalry. Those who think in sections instead of comprehensively cannot serve the railway administration, nor can they do good to the country. The Minister must attend to putting an end to this rivalry.

Sir, we want to bring in new technology. An instance of how the Railway Ministry brings in new technology has been brought to my notice. A plant for the manufacture of cast-steel wheels was set up in Banglore in collaboration with the U.S., a decision taken to manufacture the wheels was taken, but there is as yet no decision on where these cast-wheels would be used.

SPEAKER : What is not known ?

SHRI VAJPAYEE : Sir, we make two types of wheels. Under the new technology cast-wheels would be made but how they will be used is not yet known. There was to be an estimated investment of Rs. 34 crores on this plant. Now it has reached Rs. 132 crores, and by the time the project is completed it will have reached Rs. 200 crores. But where will this wheel be fixed ? Will it be fixed in the engine. It will not be fixed in the engine, nor will it be fixed in passenger bogeys. The Hon. Minister has mentioned box cars, but the wheel will not be fixed in them either. So I want to know where the cast wheel will be used. I want a reply to my question.

Gauge Conversion

Sir, gauge conversion is being discussed a lot. What we have seen is not a change of gauge but a change of Ministers. We thought Pandit Kamlapati Tripathi will be the guard of the Railway Ministry train for five years. But there was an accident on the way. Shri Tripathi went and Shri Pandey came. I am not concerned with it, but this change of Ministers within a year is beyond comprehension. Either Shri Tripathi's appointment was wrong or his removal was wrong. Both cannot be right. But I shall not discuss this. It is an internal matter of the ruling party.

AN HON. MEMBER : You are discussing it and yet say you won't discuss it.

Political Pressures

SHRI VAJPAYEE : Sir, I was just mentioning it. I am saying something else. The Hon. Minister has made the very important announcement—I welcome it—that it should not be necessary to convert metre gauge to broad gauge. What is priority work is to lay railway lines in many parts of the country where there are none. We have to promote road transport. Our resources are limited. I say why did we not take this policy decision before ? It is true that this decision will not be popular. Those members or Ministers whose regions do not have broad gauge will demand it.

SPEAKER : This has been criticised and will be criticised in future too. A paper like the *Hindu* has criticised it in its editorial.

SHRI VAJPAYEE : You are a great Pandit and a scholar too.

SPEAKER : Not a Pandit.

SHRI VAJPAYEE : Sir, there is *'Shreya'* (good) and *'Preya'* (pleasing) and there is a constant conflict between the two. The Hon. Minister has taken a beneficial step but it will not be popular. I am saying something unpalatable. If you have decided against gauge conversion what was the need to carry out a survey for the purpose of gauge conversion in eleven sections ? Are these two things not contradictory ? Is it not being done under political pressure ? Under whose pressure is the survey in the Mhow-Shahgunj section being done ? Whose note was received for it ? Has the Planning Commission sanctioned it ? A certain Secretary of the ruling party—I do not want to name him—showed interest in this connection and the Hon. Minister had to give in. But the Railway Ministry or the Railway Board or some other department has not prepared any estimate for it. Another connection is from Bangalore to Mysore. It is also under political pressure.

AN HON. MEMBER : Shri Dandavate had done it.

SHRI VAJPAYEE : He who did it is present here. But now a new policy has been adopted. A change in policy has also been announced. But devising a policy is one thing, actual action is another. This will not help the Railway Minister's credibility, nor that of the Railway Ministry. I can understand if gauge conversion is advocated for operational or financial reasons, but there should be no political pressure at all.

The Sikri Committee's Report

Accidents are increasing. Serious thought must be given to the why of it. The Sikri Committee had been set up to inquire into them. It had made some recommendations. Why were they not acted upon ? Was it not possible to act upon them on a couple of zonal railways just to see ? While discussing the accidents the Committee had passed a comment. I would like to draw the Minister's attention to it.

SPEAKER : Please finish with it.

SHRI VAJPAYEE : I shall finish if I am not finished.

SHRI R.L. BHATIA : Let us not have an accident on top of an accident.

SHRI VAJPAYEE : The Sikri Committee wrote :

> "The Safety Organisation should be manned by officers from any of the five major Departments, namely Operating, Civil Engineering, Mechanical Engineering, Signal and Tele-communication Engineering, and Electric Section, who are mainly concerned with safety in train operation."

So far all safety matters were looked into by the Traffic Transportation Department. Is it not necessary to change this in the light of the Sikri Committee recommendations ? In this matter departmental rivalry must not be allowed to dominate. It must be ensured that railway travellers must reach their destination safely, even if late. But our Railways have become so efficient that a passenger buying a ticket for one destination is taken somewhere else. At least do not take him to a place from where it would be difficult—even impossible, for him to return. Thank you.

Index

FOUR DECADES IN PARLIAMENT

FOUR DECADES IN PARLIAMENT

VOLUME III
FOREIGN AFFAIRS

Atal Bihari Vajpayee

Edited by Dr. N.M. Ghatate

SHIPRA

(2021 PoD, 2018, 2000, 1998 twice, First Published 1996)

Rs. 9000, US$ 360
Set Price

ISBN: 978-81-85402-69-7 (Set)
978-81-85402-70-3 (Vol. 1)
978-81-85402-71-0 (Vol. 2)
978-81-85402-72-7 (Vol. 3)

2024 Impression PoD

Four Decades in Parliament

Published by:
SHIPRA PUBLICATIONS
LG 18-19, Pankaj Central Market,
I.P. Ext., Patparganj, Delhi 110092, India
91 11 47322068; 9650028065, 9810522367
info@shiprapublication.com
www.shiprapublication.com

VOLUME III

Contents

Shri Atal Bihari Vajpayee : *A Biographical Sketch*
(refer at the end of the book)

and Atalji told the legislators meeting held in July 1995, "Prepare to strike when the iron is hot."

This work is by no means an exhaustive compilation of all that Shri Vajpayee spoke in the Lok Sabha and the Rajya Sabha from 1957 to 1995. Only important speeches are included in this publication.

I owe an incalculable debt to Shri Atal Bihari Vajpayee, who despite his heavy schedule found time to go through the manuscript and agreed to write about his overall views about the institution of Parliament, democracy in action, role of the Government and Opposition and Prime Ministers during the last four decades. In fact this work starts with his signed article—"I Recollect".

This work is in three volumes and each subject is organised chronologically. Hindi speeches of Shri Vajpayee and also comments made in Hindi during the debates are translated to maintain homogeneity.

Speeches of Shri Vajpayee on general national problems facing the country are included in Volume I—*State of the Nation*; economic issues and related subjects are given in Volume II—*State of the Economy*, and Volume III—*Foreign Affairs* deals with topics such as international situation, neighbouring countries and super powers.

I am sure this publication would be of abiding interest to the general reading public particularly the elite opinion makers, the legislators, journalists and students of Social Sciences.

Shri Vajpayee's speeches are a poetry in prose and at times I felt that it was almost an impossible task to translate his words without diluting their flavour and charm. But Shri Sudhakar Raje and Shri O.P. Khosla have put in their best possible efforts and I am thankful to them.

I am indebted to Mrs. Namita Kaul Bhattacharya who collected indexes and in making useful suggestions. I am much obliged to Shri Shiv Kumar, P.L. Sharma and T.N. Maken who were ever willing to help whenever help I needed it and to Shri P.V.C. Kutty, Shri Abraham Varghese and Shri Dwarka Prasad Aggarwal for rendering assistance. I wish to record my appreciation to Shri D. Kumar of Shipra for hard work he has put in to bring out this book. Needless to say I accept all responsibility for any omission and mistakes.

DR. N.M. GHATATE

I International Situation

Foreign Policy Too Foreign Oriented

Mr. Speaker, Sir, it can't be denied that the foreign policy we have been following for the last ten years has enhanced the prestige of India in the world. Crores of people come out to welcome our Prime Minister wherever he goes. He is addressed as the prophet of peace. When he is honoured, each and every Indian, to whatever party he or she may belong, feels proud. But I regret to point out that our international difficulties have also increased in the same proportion. If we consider the problems facing our country, we see that our problems are getting more and more complicated. Take the question of Kashmir or that of Goa or the problem of the Indians settled abroad, the prestige and the respect of our Prime Minister has not been as helpful in solving these problems as it should have been.

Our mission was to make every country of the world our friend, but the position today is that we find ourselves totally friendless. The countries from which we expected support over Kashmir issue have not extended the expected support. We helped some countries and tried to solve their problems, but even those countries are not extending their firm support to the Indian cause over the Kashmir issue. On the issue of the Suez Canal the attitude we adopted in favour of Egypt resulted in the apprehension that our ties with Britain may snap. But the same Egypt and its President Col. Nasser have not so far supported the just cause of India on the Kashmir issue.

It is the same with Communist China. Time and again we advocated China's entry in the United Nations Organisation; and it was also proper to admit her in the U.N. We also ignored the Chinese attack on Tibet, but Chinese leaders have not so far extended us their open support on the Kashmir issue.

Not only that, Pakistani newspapers report that Mr. Mao Tse-tung, President of China, has expressed the view that Communist countries should remain neutral on the Kashmir issue. I don't know how far it is correct, but Pakistani newspapers are engaged in such propaganda and it is the duty of the Government to bring out the truth in this regard.

In this connection we must look at Russian policy also. When Pakistan attacked India on Kashmir and we took this issue to the United Nations, Russia did not support our cause until Pakistan openly came out against

Lok Sabha ... September 2, 1957 during discussion on the motion for consideration of the International Situation

Russia by making a military alliance with the U.S.A. Our cause in Kashmir was just even before that, but Russian leaders chose to keep silent on earlier occasions. Still they are now speaking in our favour, and we welcome that. It is but natural that the silence still being maintained by the Chinese leaders over this issue should raise apprehensions in our minds. I would request the Prime Minister to dispel these fears, if he deems it proper.

In this respect there is another aspect that has become clear. It is that international politics does not work on the basis of morality. There is no place for selfless dedicated work. We may burn our hands while performing *'havan'* (part of worship of Hindus) and also create new problems for ourselves while solving the problems of others. Our foreign policy needs to accord with the realities of international politics but this is to be done carefully in view of the current situation, when we badly need the co-operation, help and support of all countries. As regards Indian policy of not aligning with any bloc, we fully support it. As far as my party, Bhartiya Jan Sangh is concerned, we agree with the policy that we should not join either the American or the Russian bloc, as doing so is in the interest of the country.

Policy of Non-Alignment

Today we are engaged in the task of nation-building. For the present we are not in a position to annoy any one by getting ourselves aligned with any bloc. At the same time it is equally important that we should not involve ourselves in the disputes of other countries. When we are not directly concerned with those disputes we can keep silent over them. In politics it is sometimes necessary to keep quiet, and we should speak only to further the interests of our country. In this connection it is my submission that there are many problems facing the world and we do have a definite attitude towards them, but it is not necessary that our attitude should be expressed openly. I shall quote only one example. We have a *Panchsheel* agreement with Russia. According to this agreement Russia cannot interfere in the internal affairs of our country and we also do not have the right to interfere in her internal matters. During the last few months there were some internal changes in Russia. Some Ministers were changed and some were removed from their posts. This was an internal matter of Russia, but our Prime Minister expressed his opinion about that. It is just a co-incidence that this change in Russia would, perhaps, be useful from our as well as the world's point of view, but tomorrow there might be some internal changes in Russia which might be harmful from our point of view or for democracy or world peace. How shall we express ourselves at that time ? If we keep silent at that time our present utterances become meaningless and if we give our views now, we might be compelled to speak at that time also. Whatever changes are introduced in Russia are their internal affair. We should not speak on them.

But whatever issues crop up in the world, we do not control our urge to speak about them. The difficulty with us, and particularly with our revered Prime Minister, is that he is so engrossed with the creation of world history that some chapters of Indian history skip his notice. There is no doubt that the coming generation will remember our Prime Minister as the maker of world history, but it is also possible that it may remember the fact that we got ourselves entangled in world problems to such an extent that we could not solve our own problems, properly; rather, some more difficulties were added to them. I am of the view that in case we modify our policy from this angle and try to win the friendship of all we could come out of the difficulties that we face at present.

The Overseas Indians

At the very outset I have referred to the issue of Indians settled abroad. I regret to say that we have not paid as much attention to them as we should have done. There are about 50 lakh Indians living abroad. In Burma there are eight lakh Indians, and their number is constantly declining. We are providing every type of assistance to Burma. We provided them a loan. Our Prime Minister even donated guns for protecting the Government of Burma. But Indians settled in Burma are not being treated properly. There are ten lakh Indians in Sri Lanka. They are being deprived of their right to citizenship. In view of the activities of the Government of South Africa we have snapped our ties with them. But by doing so we have left the Indians settled there at the mercy of that Government. The problems of the Indians there cannot be solved only by snapping ties. In Mauritius 64 per cent of the people are Indians. They can come closer to us. But I am pained to observe that all our Commissioners who are posted there got engulfed in party politics of the local people. Local newspapers level all sorts of charges against our Commissioners. Those charges were also published in an esteemed newspaper of India. In this connection I had asked a question but the reply given was that the charges were incorrect. If they were wrong our Ministry of External Affairs should refute them officially and should remove the misunderstanding that has risen about our Commissioner. The number of Indians in British Guiana and Fiji is 44 per cent and 45 per cent respectively. All of them are the sons of Mother India and are the inheritors of the same Indian culture. We should try to bring them closer to us, but we have not been able to pay as much attention to them as we should have. These people are so far away from us and their difficulties are so great that today we hardly have the power to overcome those difficulties and solve their problems.

The Middle Eastern Countries

In today's discussion mention has been made about the Middle Eastern countries, and it has been said that since last evening a new crisis is developing in Syria. We should do whatever is possible to prevent the emergence of this crisis. But the one noteworthy thing is that all countries of the Middle East region are weak. They have been economically exploited because of their slavery for a number of years. Now the Prime Minister says the countries of that region should themselves fill the vacuum that has been created there. As a matter of principle this is correct, and it should so happen. But practically this is not possible. Those countries don't have the power to stand on their feet. From the population, military and industrial point of view they are so backward that they need support from outside. This support could be given either by Russia or America. But if these countries try to give support it would create further difficulties. The third alternative is that the United Nations Organisation could prove to be of some help in filling this vacuum that has been created there. This alternative needs to be considered. I would like to tell Mr. Prime Minister that it would not suffice to say that the people of those countries should fill the vacuum there. There are practical problems. The United Nations Organisation and the Afro-Asian countries could jointly make some arrangements through which the backward nations of the Middle East could be given the chance and the facilities to achieve their political, economic and industrial development. This issue needs to be considered from this angle.

When we talk of Middle East countries the problem of Israel also comes to the forefront. No one can deny the fact that there could be no peace in the Middle East until the Arab countries accept the existence of Israel. If the Arab countries are bent upon annihilating Israel there would always be the danger of a war breaking out in the Middle East. Occasionally there would be peace, but again feelings of unrest would flare up, acquiring a most violent form. In this connection the Government has not so far discharged its duty. We have established diplomatic relations with all countries of the world but we do not have ambassadorial-level relations with Israel. I would like to know why such diplomatic relations have not been established. They should have an ambassador in Delhi and there should be an Indian ambassador in the capital of Israel, so that we could get direct information about the events taking place there. I feel that our Prime Minister can create goodwill between the Arab countries and Israel by using his good offices, and he should do so. But before doing that we must take steps to establish ambassador-level relations with Israel. This is the need of the hour.

The Goa Problem

Now I would like to say something about Goa. Whenever there is a discussion on the Goa issue it is said that our policy is the policy of peace and non-violence and we would not use any type of military force. The Goa issue is not an issue of a particular political party. It would not suffice to say that Goa is a part of Indian territory. The people of Goa have been crushed between slavery and atrocities for the last four hundred years. More than ten years have elapsed since we achieved independence, but they are still slaves. The difficulties of the residents of Goa are not going to be removed by our merely saying that the Indian revolution will not be complete till Goa is liberated.

The question is, what are we going to do for Goa. During the discussion on Goa sometimes the example of Macao is given. It is said that Communist China did not use force in Macao and we should also not use force in Goa. My submission is that the situation in Goa is somewhat different from that of Macao. Goa being situated in the mainland is the part of the mainland while Macao is isolated and Communist China has kept it open for illegal trade. Do we want that the illegal trade that is going on through Goa should continue ? Look at what is happening in Delhi. Shops in Delhi are flooded with watches brought here illegally from Goa, and it is adversely affecting our economic interests.

Our Goa policy is bringing down the morale of the Goan people. We should have no cause for complaint if the people of Goa feel that the people and Government of India have betrayed them. What have we done to alleviate their suffering and difficulties. And, if we can't do anything we should express our inability in clear terms and lift the economic sanctions that we have imposed. We should do something that could bring some respite to the residents of Goa who are reeling under the tyranny of the Portuguese. Even if we keep hoping till doomsday that just like a fruit getting detached from a tree and falling to the ground Goa would also fall into our lap after getting detached from the Portuguese tree, that hope of ours will never be fulfilled.

In this connection it would not be proper to quote the examples of Britain and France. Portugal is a dictatorship. There is no opposition party and the Government cannot be criticised there. In that country public opinion cannot be roused against the rulers, whereas this is not the case with Britain and France. I would like to know how Goa is going to be liberated in such a situation. I remember that our Prime Minister had once made a forecast that not only Goa would be liberated but the rule of Salazar in Portugal would also end. Our Prime Minister does not believe in astrology. Perhaps, that is the reason why his forecast has not turned out to be true. Goa has not got rid of slavery and the termination of the Salazar rule in Portugal still remains a far cry.

Panchsheel and Non-Alignment

In this connection, Mr. Speaker, I would like to say that when we talk of non-violence and peace the world expects that these principles would be practised within our country too. If we preach '*Panchsheel*' to the world and make proclamations about peace and non-violence why do we use the stick and the bullet to suppress the people in our own country ? In such a situation the world would naturally laugh at our proclamation of *Panchsheel*. It is not their fault and we cannot blame them for that. In a country where small children are made victims of police firing and where peaceful people offering *Satyagrah* in prison are done to death by lathi charge there could be no bigger irony than the talk of peace and non-violence by the Prime Minister and Members of Parliament. *Panchsheel* should be observed outside as well as within the country. If we believe in non-violence it should not be observed only with respect to Pakistan and Portugal but the same policy of peace and nonviolence should be followed with respect to our own people also.

The whole country supports the Prime Minister on the question of foreign policy. Our differences are internal differences. But efforts are not being made to elicit co-operation and to arouse the power of the masses which could be an asset for the forceful implementation of foreign policy.

We want to remain non-aligned. The world *'tatasth'* (neutral) literally means to remain on the bank of the river. The man standing on the edge is called *Tatasth*. But who can keep on standing on the bank ?

A small country and a weak person cannot keep on standing on the edge. A small plant will float away even with a single wave. One violent storm will blow away a small stone mid-stream in a river and break it into pieces. Only those can stand firmly on the edge whose roots go deep. Only that country can remain non-aligned which has the support of its masses and advances with its own dignity, and possesses national power, character and discipline. The need of the hour is that if we want to adopt and follow a non-aligned policy we should be strong and we should adopt it in the real sense of the term.Thank you.

Lopsided Norms for Entertaining the Foreign Dignitaries

Mr. Speaker, Sir, I have moved two Cut Motions on the demand for Supplementary Grants. One of them is concerned with the excessive expenditure incurred on foreign dignitaries during their visits to Delhi.

At least I am not satisfied with the clarification given just now by the Prime Minister in this regard. This Cut Motion has been moved not only with the objective of drawing attention of the Government to the excessive expenditure, but also to the receptions or entertainment of such visitors (*Interruption*).

MR. SPEAKER : On what demand ?

SHRI VAJPAYEE : Ministry of External Affairs, demand No. 24.

MR. SPEAKER : You may continue.

SHRI VAJPAYEE : Whatever has been said in that regard, no reply has been given with respect to the arrangements that are required to be made for such welcome—entertainment ceremonies etc. There was great disorder and indiscipline in the functions held at Red Fort not only on the eve of the visit to India by the Shah of Afghanistan, but a similar situation prevailed here even when the Shah of Iran visited India. The Central Government cannot escape its responsibility by just saying that the functions at Red Fort were organised by the Delhi Municipal Corporation. The Delhi Municipality also seeks grants from the Centre for these functions and the Government introduces its demand in Parliament. I would like to know whether it is necessary that the Delhi Municipal Corporation should welcome every foreign visitor by giving him a welcome address. Whenever a guest visits us it is natural that we should welcome him. We have our old tradition of honouring our guests.

SHRI RAJ BAHADUR, Minister of State in the Ministry of Transport and Communications : It is not only natural but also necessary.

SHRI VAJPAYEE : Nature has more force than need. What is natural comes out spontaneously and expresses itself spontaneously, whereas need has the element of something brought from outside. The feeling of honouring our guests is ingrained in the very nature of Indians.

SHRI DEEP CHAND SHARMA (Gurdaspur) : Are you opposing that ?

SHRI VAJPAYEE : I am not opposing that, Sharmaji. Please listen carefully. I am of the view that we should have certain standards for welcome which should be in conformity with our present-day position and our old traditions.

Lok Sabha on February 21, 1958 while moving cut motion on the Supplementary Demand of the Ministry of External Affairs

The Delhi Municipal Corporation should present a welcome address and that alone should constitute the welcome. If we think that by illuminating Delhi Gate with lights and fixing electric bulbs on each and every leaf of the trees in Asaf Ali Park we have discharged our duty of welcoming our guests it is not correct and I am not ready to accept that. Our present day welcome should also conform to the atmosphere of renunciation and sacrifice that we want to build up for the success of our Five Year Plan. If these functions smell of pomp and show, and if the common man also feels that we can express our love for our guest even without organising such welcome functions, I feel that some change must be brought about in the manner of organising these functions.

Change the System

Recently President Ho Chi-Minh visited India. A chair embedded with gold and silver was kept at Red Fort to seat him. Dr. Ho Chi-Minh enhanced his prestige manifold by not sitting in that chair and everybody praised him for that act. But the faces of all those who had placed that chair for him fell. Is it necessary that a poor country should adopt the same tradition of pomp and show to welcome foreign guests that was once adopted by the British in New Delhi on some occasions ? The monarchical system has been replaced by democracy, but this tradition has not undergone any change.

Our foreign guests should be welcomed with simplicity and without any fanfare. If, in their receptions, they could have a glimpse of the fight that the country is making for its reconstruction, they will go back to their countries more impressed than by showing them that the leaves of trees are illuminated with electric bulbs. But the people who are lying in their shade don't even have warm clothes to wear in winter. The darkness hides poverty. So darkness looks good in New Delhi, but wherever the bright lights start illuminating that dark place to welcome foreign guests it looks as if our poverty is laughing at us. The purpose of this Cut Motion is to draw attention of the Government to the present manner of holding receptions.

Small children are brought to show their performance on these occasions. It is good that they should show their physical fitness. But this time, on the eve of Dr. Ho's visit here, I saw that the children who were brought from Shakur Basti were collected at 6 a.m. although they were to give their performance at 9 a.m. No arrangements were made to provide them water or any refreshment. Physical performances are alright but at the same time they must not be put to unnecessary hardship. Also, such functions should be organised within the limits of our resources.

When members of Parliament ask for one more copy of their speech they are told that the Government is exercising economy, but I have seen that hundreds of bundles of welcome addresses that are offered at Red Fort in Delhi lay in the scrap shops in the vicinity of Jama Masjid near Red Fort. They are sold as waste paper. It is obvious that we can make savings in this field.

SHRI MEHAR CHAND KHANNA : What were you doing at Jama Masjid ?

SHRI VAJPAYEE : I can go to Jama Masjid which is within our country.

SHRI B.R. BHARGAV : Good.

SHRI VAJPAYEE : It is true that we should establish foreign relations and should whole-heartedly welcome all guests who visit our country, but it is not necessary that to express our sincere love to them we should incur huge expenditures. I feel that the Government should examine this issue in detail and consider what changes should be made in organising such welcome functions keeping in view our resources and capacity and our need for reconstruction of the country.

Plight of Government Employees

Through my Cut Motion I have also drawn the attention of the Government towards another aspect. As per the Report of the Pay Commission Central Government employees have got an increase of five rupees in their pay. Looking to the present-day situation and the increasing burden of high costs and taxes, this increase is inadequate. But there is another aspect to this issue. Central Government employees got this interim relief, but State Government employees have received nothing so far. In many cities Central and State Government employees work together, and the prices of the commodities and other expenses there are the same for both of them, but the allowances paid to the State Government employees are not equal to those received by the Central Government employees; they are paid less.

There is paucity of funds with the Government, but it is not proper that on this account alone the pay of Central Government employees should be increased but State Government employees should be deprived of that. To avoid discrimination and also to create among all employees a uniform feeling of devotion to their duty, whatever interim relief has been given should be extended to the State Government employees also, and the Central Government should provide to the States the necessary assistance for this purpose, so that State Government employees could also benefit. If we start increasing dearness allowance or interim relief at one place, it is but natural that a similar demand would be raised at other places also. It may also be considered as to how the interim relief granted so far could be increased till the submission of a complete report by the Pay Commission. Thank you.

Do We Have to Speak on Every Issue

World Peace and National Interests

Mr. Speaker, Sir, it can't be denied that the foreign policy of keeping ourselves away from the two power blocs of the world and of not getting ourselves involved in the disputes of other countries that we have adopted during the last ten years is the right policy. It has not only resulted in securing the welfare of the nation, it has also helped in maintaining world peace in the present-day situation. Our national interest and world peace are interlinked. If there is peace in the world it would serve our national interests; and if Indian interests are protected and promoted the forces of peace in the world would also be strengthened. Therefore, if anyone says that we should give up this policy and join either the Russian or the American bloc he says so either due to a lack of understanding or he has developed a tendency of acting on the signals given by some other countries. Our national interests demand that we should follow this policy firmly.

I have said that if there is peace in the world it would be important for our national interests also. We are engaged in the task of nation-building; we are performing a *'Yagna'* and in this *'Yagna'* we need help and support of all nations. But there is also another aspect. Because of our continuous struggle against imperialism for the last one hundred and fifty years and the great sacrifices we made to achieve our independence, democracy and nationalism have become our second nature. We, therefore, understand the importance of independence for others also. Whenever foreign forces land on the soil of any country of the world it shocks us and we cannot remain silent.

Too Much Talking Impedes National Interest

The point is whether in the contemporary situation we can promote our national interests by speaking more on international politics. It is true that we cannot remain in isolation and the world will also not allow us to remain so. We may like to keep ourselves isolated but events would take us in their grip. However, the question is whether we can discuss in some details the policy of keeping ourselves actually aloof from the disputes of other countries. One requires a voice to speak, but to keep quiet one requires both a voice and wisdom. In the international sphere we have developed a tendency of speaking a little more than necessary, and it is my submission that we should learn and practise the art of keeping quiet.

This task is, of course, difficult for our Prime Minister, who always thinks in terms of world politics but this is the need of our national interests, and,

Lok Sabha on August 19, 1958 during discussion on International Situation

therefore, I was happy when the Prime Minister, speaking about the internal developments in France, said that it was an internal matter of France and he would not like to speak more on that subject. Of course there are certain people in our country who were bent upon making him speak on this subject also. We hardly need to give our views about the Indonesian dispute, which is their internal matter. It would, therefore, be better for us to speak as little as possible and follow the policy of keeping quiet on issues which are not directly related to us.

The Summit on West Asia

In this connection I would like to refer to the Summit Conference (on West Asia). When the newspapers came out with the news that our Prime Minister was going to participate in the Summit Conference it was natural that every Indian felt proud about it. From the geographical, population or any other point of view India occupies a definite place in the international forum, and accordingly in such a Summit Conference we should be rated along with big countries. Weapons don't make a country big or small, but the situation in which the proposal for the Summit Conference was made and the way the news about the government's acceptance was published from New Delhi created the impression that we were a little too eager to participate in it. This impression was caused by the newspapers and is not in conformity with our position.

SHRI C.D. PANDE : This was an illusion.

SHRI VAJPAYEE : Yes, but we should not have afforded any opportunity for creating such an illusion. If all countries invite us we should attend the Summit Conference with everybody's consent. But looking at the circumstances in which the Summit Conference was being held I feel that it would have been more useful if instead of India, some other country of West Asia, Egypt with its President Nasser, had attended the Summit Conference. But Russia proposed the name of our country and it was but natural that we welcomed that move. Other countries however created hurdles and the result was the emergence of the feeling among the Indian masses that Russia liked us while America did not. In short, it meant that Russia, in her cold war, made us their pawn in her publicity fight and we allowed ourselves to be used as such.

AN HONOURABLE MEMBER : No, we didn't

SHRI VAJPAYEE : It is good that we didn't, but it appeared so.

SHRI C.D. PANDE : We avoided that.

SHRI VAJPAYEE : No, we could not avoid that. But we should avoid it and should remain alert about the misgivings that have developed.

The Need and Trends of the Age

Whatever events take place in West Asia, they are naturally the cause of concern for every Indian, and these events clearly show that there cannot be peace in the world till the big powers accept the fact that every nation has the right to be independent and to mould its life according to its own ideals.

Nationalism and democracy are the strong currents of this age and whosoever stands against them will have to sooner or later accept defeat in spite of being the biggest power. The cause of concern is that Western countries, which are headed by America, talk of democracy and are really democratic within their own borders, but beyond them, they want to protect tottering thrones. Monarchy won't do now, as it is against the trend of this age.

The thrones of kings and 'Nawabs' would be washed away by the strong wave of democracy, and if anyone tries to stop the spread of so-called communism through those thrones he would never succeed. I regret to say that the democratic countries of the world are adopting such measures to stop the spread of Communism, while these very measures are ultimately leading to the spread of Communism. Democracy cannot be protected by supporting monarchy. It should be recognised that the people of every country have the right to achieve independence and to regulate their life according to democratic principles. Unless and until Russia and America accept this fact they cannot be helpful in establishing world peace even if they make innumerable announcements on *'Panchsheel'*. I am sure that the leaders of America will reconsider their policy in this regard. By supplying arms to our neighbouring country Pakistan they want to check communism. If anything can check the spread of communism in Asia it is only the democratic force. Where the government of a country changes after every six months and where within 24 hours the Chief Minister of a province, the Governor and their whole government undergo change, such a country is based on feudalism and is a promotor of communalism. It is far away from democracy, and it cannot check the rise of communism by getting help from America.

The American policy has created a difficulty in our country also. We are being compelled to spend a large amount of our revenue on the purchase of arms when actually we should fully engage ourselves in the task of nation-building. What is required is that American leaders should act with wisdom.

Incidents of Border Violation on the Rise

There are numerous incidents of border violation on the eastern frontier of our country. Pakistani soldiers intrude into our territory and resort to round-the-clock firing. I would request the Government to take these incidents seriously.

It has been hinted that talks are going to be held with Pakistan. I hope that before these talks are held Pakistan would vacate all Indian territory in its possession. But if our land remains in their possession and we still go to them for peace talks it would only strengthen their adamant attitude and audacity. They should vacate every inch of our land and should assure us that they really want peace on the border. Sometimes I feel that we do not talk to Pakistan in the language that it understands. We speak in a language that might be correct from our point of view but Pakistan cannot understand that language.....

AN HONOURABLE MEMBER : Because we talk in difficult Hindi.

SHRI VAJPAYEE : We also speak in English, but they fail to understand. I feel that the sense in which I am talking would be understood by all. Nobody in the country wants war. There is no one in India who wants war with Pakistan, there should be peace with honour. Peace should be established on strong foundations. If in the face of such heavy firing we do not take adequate steps that could create confidence in the people they may become apprehensive and feel that if we cannot face this occasional firing what shall we do if Pakistan, after being equipped with American arms, becomes determined to put into practice the slogan of *Jehad* that they keep on shouting. We are quite capable of meeting their challenge, but we should also create this confidence in the public and for that purpose we should take some more steps for defending our eastern borders. If necessary, arms could be supplied to the people of border areas. They could also be given military training. We could form a National Militia and the confidence should be built in the public that Pakistan cannot have its own way on the eastern border. I believe the Government would act in a determined way in this respect also.

Excessive Show of Internationality

I shall conclude my speech by referring to the fact I had mentioned at the outset. We cannot remain isolated from events that take place in the world. But another important aspect is that all the might of our people should be directed towards nation-building. In fact we are over-obsessed with internationalism. Our newspapers and our political parties are less bothered of the events that are taking place within the country. We look more towards the world outside. I do not say that outside events are not important but today there is a tendency to be more extrovert than introvert. If we pay more attention to the disputes pertaining to other countries of the world the attention of our masses towards the task of nation-building would be diverted. I would like to say that if we have not been able to create the spirit of making maximum sacrifices for the task of nation-building, one of the major reasons is that our attention remains diverted to so many issues. The Prime Minister should see how it could be possible that we do not go into isolation and our energies are directed towards the task of nation-building. Our newspapers should draw the attention of our people towards the task of nation-building and they should give a prominent place to developmental news.

Sir, as I have already said, I feel that we should practise the art of keeping a bit quiet in international politics. If we adhere to this practice our efforts for establishing world peace would be successful to some extent. The Prime Minister had said peace does not prevail because of us. We should make efforts to establish peace, but at the same time we should not allow our effort in the task of nation-building to slow down. For this purpose the people will have to devote themselves to this task unitedly and the Government will have to take the initiative in this field. With these words I conclude my speech. Thank you.

Parliament Not Taken into Confidence

Mr. Speaker, Sir, the people of the country and members of Parliament expected the Prime Minister to let them know how far we are prepared to face the danger created to the independence and security of India due to the establishment of a military dictatorship in Pakistan and the supply of American arms to that country. In this regard this House and through this House the people of this country expected that they would be taken into confidence. But I am pained to observe that in this respect the Government has not so far discharged its duty. The danger is there and if we close our eyes like a pigeon before a cat or ignore the truth like an ostrich burying its head in the sand the impending danger would not vanish. It is true that the U.S. Secretary of State Mr. Dulles had once assured us that they would help India in case Pakistan attacked us. On the one hand they go on supplying arms to Pakistan, and on the other they go on saying that America would help us if Pakistan attacked India. It is very difficult to decide whether we should believe the country which is supplying arms or the country who is being supplied these arms. The fact is that arms and ammunition are reaching Pakistan. At present there is a military dictatorship in Pakistan. The Government of Pakistan is now in the hands of those people who have been defeated by us in Kashmir and they would never forget that defeat. Political leaders may forget their defeat but it is very difficult for a soldier or a General to digest defeat. It would not be surprising if the rulers of Pakistan, with a view to diverting the attention of their people from their internal difficulties, become a potential danger to our freedom after being well-equipped with American arms. What would be our response at that time ?

Don't be Carried Away by American Assurances

I agree that we need not be panicky. But the required degree of readiness, preparedness and of being well-equipped has not so far been achieved by this country. The need to take the public into confidence in this regard is still wanting. As regards the American assurance that if Pakistan attacks us first America would come to our help I would like to say that it is always very difficult to decide as to who started a war. Even about Kashmir it has not so far been possible to decide this issue. About Korea also charges and counter-charges about starting the war were made by South and North Korea against each other. So it won't do to just believe the American assurances. We should keep ourselves fully prepared, although I believe that no thinking person in India wants war with Pakistan. But peace is not something that can be

Lok Sabha on December 8, 1958 during discussion on the International Situation

purchased in the market. Stable peace depends upon strength and strong policy. The people of Pakistan are like our own people. The country has been divided but the people still remain the same. The difference in religion does not change nationality. We have all sympathy for the people of Pakistan.

We fought the Britishers for independence. Under the leadership of the Muslim League the people of Pakistan also aspired to get independence. But their independence was put to auction in the market place of Washington. It is but natural that our heart goes out to them. Yet we should not make a mistake in understanding the Pakistani rulers, who did not take any part in the freedom struggle and who are ready to sell the interests of their country to others. Their intentions are not good. One should observe their speeches and simultaneously see their acts. Our Prime Minister is very liberal. He can accommodate the whole world in his large heart, but the problem is that our Pakistani counterparts want to keep in this heart a small knife also. We should be vigilant about them. The purpose for which the Agreement with Malik Firoze Khan Noon was executed was that there would be peace on the East Bengal frontier, the firing would stop, and the Pakistani people would not intrude into our territory. Parliament was in session but ignoring that session the Prime Minister entered into this agreement without taking Parliament into confidence.

Indian Land Given in Donation

The Constitution of India does not empower anybody to give away Indian land to others. According to our Constitution we can annex territory belonging to others, we can extend our boundaries, but we cannot give away our land to others. Our Prime Minister is very liberal. Our country is witnessing a *'Bhudan'* movement. Perhaps he was also overwhelmed by the spirit of *'Bhudan'* and gifted away some of our land about which there was no dispute at all. Just now my friend Shri Tridib Kumar Choudhury talked about the Berubari Union Territory. There was no dispute with Pakistan about that. It was given to them and along with it the nationality and citizenship of ten thousand Indian citizens is also being terminated.

Nobody, not even the Prime Minister, has the right to deprive any Indian citizen of his nationality and citizenship. But the Prime Minister entered into an agreement—he first ignored Parliament and then, after entering into the agreement came and said before Parliament that it was upto us to accept it or not and if we don't accept it he would offer his resignation. What would Parliament do if the sword of resignation hangs over it ? But the agreement that has been entered into is against the interests of the country. We should not accept that agreement. Let us also see whether Pakistan complied with that agreement. Have the border disputes come to an end ? Have the border incidents stopped ? No sooner the agreement was made than its violation started. Pakistan metes out the same treatment to every agreement. It complies with the agreements by violating them. Even the ink on the agreement was not dry before they renewed the attacks. The Prime Minister says these are seasonal attacks related to crops. Why is this crop always harvested on this side ? Let it sometimes be harvested on the other side too. Why is this an one-sided affair ?

My friend Shri Alva was just now talking about the border police that he saw in the Russian Parade. We too have police on our border and on 6th August our Lakshmipur post manned by the police was attacked. Pakistani troops attacked that post and took six police personnel including a commandant to Pakistani territory as prisoners. One of them was kept lying there in a paddy field throughout the night, groaning and crying for water, but nobody gave him water. The next day evening that wounded police man was removed from there. Lakshmipur might have been captured by the Pakistani troops. Who is in possession of Tukergram ? It is stated that the Pakistani Flag has been removed. Their flag has been removed, but their authority still remains there.

Who Occupies Tukergram and Lakshmipur ?

The Prime Minister should tell us whether Tukergram is in our possession or not and why Pakistani troops have not vacated Lakshmipur. Mr. Noon has stated that the Nehru-Noon agreement allows the Pakistani people to use the water of the river Ichhamati. Indo-Pak borders meet downstream in this river, but its upper part is such that the Indian border extends even across the river and there are about 100 villages in this territory which are inhabited by one and a half lakh people. The area of this territory is 100 square miles. The Pakistani Radio has claimed that even this area has come under Pakistani control. Delhi has refuted this claim, but the situation is not clear yet. In case we have allowed them to use the waters of river Ichamati does it mean that through the stream of this river they would also go to the area where Indian territory extends across the river ? This would create many difficulties. They could illegally enter that area and would gradually demoralise the people living there whose morale is actually being shattered. We could be pacified on being told that there are seasonal firings or attacks, but what do the people living on the border feel. They fear about what would happen in case Pakistan makes a surprise attack. Would we be capable to defend them ? I believe we would be quite capable of doing that, but the government should satisfy this House as to why we are bound by the Nehru-Noon Agreement when Pakistan has not complied with it.

My submission is that the Prime Minister should reconsider this agreement. The matter regarding the right given to Pakistan over the Berubari Union Territory and for using the waters of the Ichhamati river should be reconsidered. We gave some land to Pakistan in Tripura for a railway passage, but we did not demand some land from Pakistan for going to North Bengal from West Bengal and for going to Assam *via* East Bengal ?

We neither demanded nor did we take anything, and we also did not insist on anything. We had just gone to Mr. Noon with a liberal mind and a sense of only giving. But the purpose for which this agreement was executed has not been fulfilled. The disputes are still there and it has been stated that they would keep on going. When this is the situation why was the Nehru-Noon

Agreement concluded ? There should be a permanent arrangement on the border. If the State Government is unable to defend the borders I would request the Centre to recruit its own police and take up the defence of Indian borders in its own hands.

Paper Protests Can't Save Self-Respect

It is true that we should not attack others or enter or illegally occupy territory belonging to others. But we are attacked and we remain content with sending only letters of protest. It cannot be a matter of pride for any self-respecting independent country. I am not in favour of war with Pakistan, but peace would not be established by yielding to them. We should talk to Pakistan in the language it understands and I need not say what language the new rulers of Pakistan understand, because every intelligent person knows it.

During this debate on foreign policy it has also been said that the policy of remaining isolated from both the power blocs that has been adopted by us is somewhat incorrect and the policy being adopted by Nehruji which is called the Nehru Policy is more correct. I for one cannot understand this semantics. The foreign policy being followed by our country does not belong to a particular person and it should not be. The decision taken by us to keep away from the two power blocs of the world and to assess every global issue impartially is in conformity with our old tradition, the background of our freedom struggle, our anxiety for establishing world peace, dignity of the individual, our political freedom and our faith in economic equality. We have laid down this policy only after taking into consideration all these factors. It is not proper to link this policy with any particular person. Any attempt to link it with our Prime Minister would be an injustice to him. This policy is in the interest of India and is also helpful in maintaining world peace. That is why we have followed this policy. There is no element of compulsion in it. Nobody has compelled us. We could have joined the Russian bloc if we so desired. Our communist friends have been trying to persuade us to do that.

AN HONOURABLE MEMBER : What is the policy of the Jan Sangh ?

SHRI VAJPAYEE : The Jan Sangh people say what they mean. We could have joined the Russian or American bloc. The way to join the American bloc was open to us. But we refused to join either of the two blocs because we know that our national interests and the welfare of the world both compel us to adopt this policy. This is not like remaining neutral to evil. After all foreign policy cannot be formulated only on the basis of idealism; it has to take into consideration the ground realities. It is the same with the problem of national development. We cannot ignore reality. We followed this foreign policy and found that it has enhanced the prestige of the country, protected its national interests and has made all possible contribution towards establishing world peace. Not even for a moment should we be under the illusion that world peace prevails because of our faith and strength. We can only make a small contribution in this field. At the same time we should not forget the fact that whatever the ultimate Indian position in the international politics, it would depend upon the might of the country and our resources. From this point of view I feel that we should strictly follow this policy.

Sometimes it appears that we are more inclined towards a particular bloc. We should be careful to see that such an impression is not created. I do not agree with people who demand that we should join a particular bloc. Our policy should be to keep away from both the blocs, get the cooperation of everyone and keep ourselves engaged in the task of nation-building. The foreign policy we are developing is meant for achieving this objective and I feel we are getting substantial success in that.

Diplomatic Relations with Israel

I would like to say one thing in this context. There was a reference about China. We have friendly relations with China and that is necessary. China is our biggest neighbour and we have been demanding in the United Nations Organisation that this country should get its proper representation on this forum. This demand is justified, but at the same time it is rather strange that the Government of India has not so far even accorded recognition to Israel. Why have we not recognised Israel ? The people who have been neglected in West Asia, who were suppressed and oppressed for thousands of years have now been able to form a small country of their own. Those who return after visiting Israel are full of praise for that country. They say one could have a real glimpse of socialism in Israel. I would like to know why the Government of India has not established diplomatic relations with Israel. Just a few days back newspapers published a photograph showing Vijay Laxmi Pandit sitting with Dictator Franco. When we have established diplomatic relations with Spain, what makes us hesitate to establish relations with Israel. In case it is argued that it would adversely affect our relations with the Muslim countries of South-East Asia or Middle East, I would submit that we should not refuse to accept the truth just for fear of such adverse consequences...

SHRI RAGHU NATH : Should we recognise all countries ?

SHRI VAJPAYEE : There may be some bitterness in America if China gets entry into the United Nations Organisation or when a demand for its entry in it is made. But we do not stop advocating this cause only for this reason. Sometimes it works as if the advocate is more keen than the plaintiff, but even then if we can keep on advocating that why not accord recognition to Israel.

I would, therefore, request that the Government should reconsider this issue and Israel should not be made to feel that a new government that is being established in West Asia, a new society that is in the process of formation, is being treated like an outcaste. We have eradicated untouchability in our country, and we should not treat Israel like an untouchable one. Thank you.

India's Security Linked with That of Its Neighbours

Mr. Speaker, Sir, today's newspapers carry a report that out of the Tibetan refugees being sent from Misamari camp to Dharamshala five died in the train while the whereabouts of 30 Tibetan refugees are not known. It has also been reported that no arrangement for their medical treatment was made by the Government. On the way they did not have any interpreters who could understand and try to remove their difficulties.

When it was decided to resettle the expatriates in Dharamshala and the administration was asking Parliament for funds for this purpose appropriate arrangements should have been made so that nobody would have a chance to complain.

Plight of Tibetan Refugees

Struck by misfortune, the Tibetan refugees have come to our country. I feel we cannot take our task to be over just by settling them. A lot of discussion is going on about the Tibetan Convention going to be held in Delhi in this regard. I am pained to observe that the Government, particularly the Prime Minister, has expressed annoyance at this Convention. It is true that the Convention is being organised by the people. The Government may not realise its duty towards Tibet, but the people of this country realise their moral duty towards Tibet. Having come out of the shackles of slavery, India cannot but express sympathy for countries that are being trapped in a new type of slavery. The Prime Minister has, perhaps forgotten, and I would remind him of what he said in this very House on 7th December, 1950. I quote his words:

> "It is not right for any country to talk about its sovereignty or suzerainty over any area outside its own immediate range. It is a right and proper thing to say, and I see no difficulty in saying it to the Chinese Government, that whether you have suzerainty over Tibet or sovereignty over Tibet, surely according to any principle—principles you proclaim, the principles I proclaim—the last voice in regard to Tibet should be the voice of the people of Tibet and nobody else."

These words cannot be forgotton, but the present conduct of the Government of India regarding Tibet is very much at variance with them. The Prime Minister has been struggling against imperialism and colonialism throughout his life. It is possible that after occupying the office of Prime

Lok Sabha on March 17, 1960 during discussion on the demands for grants of the Ministry of External Affairs

Minister he might be feeling some difficulties which may prevent him from expressing his real views openly. But I don't believe he is not perturbed when humanity itself is under attack or human rights are violated anywhere, as is happening in Tibet, where efforts are being made to annihilate the very identity of Tibet.

If he cannot speak for or support the demands of the Tibetan people he should at least not express his annoyance when the people of India want to organise a convention to express the sympathy of Afro-Asian countries towards Tibet. We can well understand the policy of the Communist Party, because this party raises the slogan of self-determination and on the basis of this very slogan they supported the communal demand of Pakistan. But that same party is now unwilling to apply this principle of self-determination to Pakhtoonistan, or to speak about Tibet. They are at liberty to do so but the difficulty is that they also don't want us to raise our voice. They praise the Prime Minister only because he cannot express his open support for the people of Tibet on account of difficult circumstances.

As far as feelings are concerned, I am never prepared to accept that the Prime Minister does not feel for the people of Tibet. China had assured Tibet that it would respect its autonomy and on the basis of this very assurance Tibet had surrendered a part of her sovereignty to China. But when China violated this agreement the part of sovereignty that Tibet had surrendered reverts back to her and as such even from the legal point of view it is incorrect to say that Tibet cannot demand autonomy.

In case the Government has some difficulties because of which it is helpless, it should at least not say something that could hurt sentiments of those people who have sympathy for the plight of Tibet.

Tibetan Autonomy and India's Defence

I feel the security of India is linked with the autonomy of Tibet. If we can support Algerian independence and the Communists can take a leading part in that crusade no one should raise a voice against the demand for Tibetan autonomy. But China claims that Tibet is a part of China just as Portugal claims that Goa is a part of Portugal. We can't accept this claim of Portugal, and similarly this claim of China can also not be accepted. China removed Tibet from the world map. I was pained to see that Tibet has not been shown in the latest maps printed by the Government of India also. Tibet has been erased from the map. The name of Tibet does not figure on these maps. They show only China. If China has removed Tibet, does it mean that we should also accept that Tibet is gone ? I don't feel that this policy will lead to any good result. From a moral point of view this policy is not at all fair for India, and even from the point of view of our narrow national interests annihilation of Tibet in this manner cannot be in the long-term interest of India.

Mr. Speaker, the Prime Minister of China is visiting India on an invitation extended by our Prime Minister. We don't know the basis on which talks would be held with him, because no basis for these talks has been laid so far. Previously it was said that we would hold talks but would not enter into any agreement. Now it is being said that we will make an agreement but not bargain our interests. In this connection, I would like to draw the attention of the Prime Minister to a speech of Shri Krishna Menon, Defence Minister, that he delivered in Hyderabad on 7th March. I quote :

> "Addressing a mammoth public meeting under the auspices of the Hyderabad City Congress Committee, Mr. Menon said that in view of the impending visit to India of the Chinese Prime Minister Mr. Chou En-Lai he would speak with restraint..."

Mr. Menon added :

> "While we shall not tolerate violation of integrity of our country, and while we shall not be humiliated, we are not to be so weak as to say that we will not talk. While we shall not allow anybody to think that we can be intimidated, we shall negotiate but not bargain."

Agreement with China Yes, But No Bargain

Previously it was said that we shall talk but not negotiate, but now it is being said that "we shall negotiate but not bargain". If we interpret these words in Hindi they would mean we shall negotiate but not 'give and take'. This is the correct meaning of the word 'bargain'. Now if we shall not give and take does it mean we shall only give and take nothing. The invitation extended by the Prime Minister was a bolt from the blue for the people. It has caused apprehensions which are increased by such statements.

In case the Prime Minister persuades Mr. Chou-En-Lai to make their troops retreat after vacating Indian territory and the bitterness that has been created between the two countries as a result of the Chinese attack—termed as a betrayal by our President—is removed, every Indian would welcome that. But I doubt whether such a thing can happen. In a press conference the Prime Minister stated that in case the talks between the two Prime Ministers failed it could worsen the situation. I fear that just to prevent the worsening of the situation we may enter into an agreement that is against the interests and dignity of the country. Are we bound to make the talks successful at any cost ?

If the Prime Minister participates in the talks with the attitude that he must reach an agreement at any cost it is not going to have a good result for the country. The Prime Minister is bound in oath to undo the Chinese attack. He has made this commitment to the nation. The Chinese attack on Indian territory must be undone. Nobody would have any objection if it could be done through talks. But it hardly seems possible because no basis for the talks has been laid so far. The Chinese Premier accepted our invitation. But after accepting the invitation on 20th December they have sent a note on 27th December. I would urge the Prime Minister to observe the language of this note. After sending the invitation our Prime Minister did not say anything inside or outside Parliament and avoided saying anything that could hurt China. But the note written by China on 27th December, after accepting our invitation on 20th December, conveys the impression that China is not ready to change its attitude. Perhaps they want time through a protracted dialogue.

China would not lose anything by sitting at the negotiation table. China is the agressor country and they are occupying our territory. In case the talks fail they are not going to lose anything. So China has nothing at stake, whereas we could be the losers and our experience so far has not been good.

Peace not Required at the Cost of Unrest

We want peace, but for this peace we should not pay a price which could become a cause for creating unrest in future. Anxiety for peace has often led to the execution of agreements which have not been in keeping with our national interests. Negotiations are being held in Delhi. The history of Delhi is the history of yielding. It has been the history of bowing before the aggressor. Once the Prime Minister of Pakistan visited Delhi at the invitation of our Prime Minister and we left the Hindus of East Bengal at their mercy. The Pak Prime Minister paid another visit and he had almost taken the Berubari Union Territory. Thanks to the Supreme Court, the transfer was prevented at the nick of time. And once again the Home Minister of Pakistan came and he wanted to take away the five villages of Pathria.

Now the Chinese Premier is visiting us and it is very difficult to say what he would take away from us. But the people of India would not accept any negotiation which is against the honour and interests of this country. Our Prime Minister is well aware of these feelings and he should participate in the talks resolutely. Although we have differences with him the Prime Minister may have talks with Shri Chou En-Lai, his counterpart, with the fullest confidence that the entire country is behind him in respect of the Chinese aggression. We would express our reaction according to the results of these talks, but for the time being we pray to the Almighty to give to our Prime Minister the strength and will to conduct a dialogue in conformity with the feelings of the country.

How should Chou En-lai be welcomed ?

I will take one minute more. There has been a discussion regarding the welcome that should be accorded to Shri Chou En-lai. I think we have invited him and he is coming on our invitation. Mr. Chou En-lai came in 1954 and Mr. Chou En-lai is coming in 1960. I hope our Government will not try to convey to the people the impression that he is the same Chou En-lai who visited India in 1954. People see between these two visits the dead body of Tibet writhing in agony. There are as many as three white papers between the two countries that are big hurdles in the way of friendship between them and we should not hesitate to accept that no such welcome should be accorded that could hurt the sentiments of the people and weaken their morale. Mr. Chou En-lai could be taken to Rashtrapati Bhawan from the airport and talks could be held with him there. But collecting small children, army jawans and raising the slogan of *'Hindi-Chini Bhai-Bhai'* would not be allowed till the Chinese aggression continues on our territory. To ask the people tc give such a welcome to an aggressor would not be in keeping with the prestige of the country and I think that the Government would keep in mind these sentiments of the people. That is all I have to say. Thank you.

False Propaganda by Communists

Mr. Speaker, Sir, the Deputy Leader of the Communist Party Professor Hiren Mukherji, for whom I have great respect...

SOME HON'BLE MEMBERS : Since when ?

SHRI VAJPAYEE : For his learning and not for his views. In his speech he has thrown a challenge to the Prime Minister. I believe he will get a befitting reply. The Central Government must have received from the State Governments and the Hill Districts news that could prove that the Communist Party is making false propaganda on the question of the Chinese aggression. I would like to draw the attention of my communist friends to the *Blitz* published this week from Bombay. Nobody can charge that *Blitz* is an anti-communist magazine. If any charge could be levelled against it at all, it would be that it has a leaning towards the Communists. But this week, the *Blitz* has stated :

> "In upper Garhwal, there are two villages—Chanyee and Thanyee. The communists have gone round to tell the people that the area belongs to China because the names of villages sound like Chinese. In other hill districts of U.P., local Communists are accusing the Government of India of raising the bogey of China's aggression just to divert the public attention from other pressing problems like unemployment and rising prices."

My submission is that in case this news was false our respected Communist members should sue this journal and compel it to tender an apology. But some more similar news has also poured in. During my visit to Almora last year the local people had told me that there was a cultural organisation connected with the Communist Party which attracts people through plays in the border areas and that organisation staged a drama there in which the Chinese army was shown to have come there as a liberation army. I would like the spokesman of the Communist Party to give a correct reply to these allegations. The point here is not that of the *New Age* which has been referred to by the Prime Minister. There is a Hindi edition of the *New Age* by the name *Janyug* which is published from Lucknow. That magazine had published an advertisement of the Uttar Pradesh Government. When the aggressive activities of China started increasing the Government of Uttar Pradesh gave an advertisement in all Hindi newspapers of the State. I am reading out that advertisement to you :

Lok Sabha on August 31, 1960 during discussion on the motion regarding International Situation

"The residents of Uttar Pradesh have a special responsibility in protecting the northern borders of the country. We can face the aggressive activities of China only by mutual co-operation and combined efforts. The State Government is implementing many schemes for the development of the entire State and particularly for the border areas. By making these schemes successful you will show your patriotism and contribute in increasing the national strength."

This advertisement was published in all Hindi newspapers, and the *Janyug*, a Communist newspaper, also published it. But after several days the editor of *Janyug* published in the newspaper a letter of apology. It said : "We committed a blunder by publishing this advertisement; we have committed a sin and we should not have called China aggressor and we have hurt the sentiments of our people, we shall never repeat such an act. This time we should be forgiven..."

SHRI RAGHUNATH SINGH : Did they repent also or not ?

SHRI VAJPAYEE : I would like to read out to you the English translation of this letter seeking an apology :—

"Many readers sent indignant letters drawing attention to the anti-China advertisement of the Uttar Pradesh Government. The attention of the paper had been drawn to the 'lying and mischievous' contents of the advertisement even before these letters were received. There was no doubt that an advertisement of this kind should under no circumstances have been published by the paper."

The Communists Support China, Not Our Country

The point is, when the advertisement of the Uttar Pradesh Government mentioned only aggressive activities and not the Chinese aggression, and it was also not a policy decision of the Communist Party but a mere advertisement, what was the need of seeking an apology ? Does it not show that the Communist Party does not support the country on this issue ? They may be having internal differences about China, which I can understand, but once Parliament and the Union Government have determind that China has committed aggression, I do not understand how parties or groups in the country could be given the liberty to dispute the aggression. Whether aggression has been committed or not will be determined by the Government and once it is so determined, it becomes the duty of each citizen in this country to abide by that decision. But I regret to say that the Communist Party is not showing patriotism on this issue. Whenever our Prime Minister expresses concern he or the people of this country feel about the communist attitude on this issue, the communist leaders challenge him to prove it. I ask them what could be more convincing proof. If China has not committed aggression, have Chinese troops entered India on a goodwill mission ? Have not 12000 square miles of Indian territory been occupied by them ? If the country and the people of this country remain divided over this issue, this country cannot defend its freedom. The Communist Party should change its policy. They may hold any view about economic issues, and one may have no objection if it wants to be kept wedded to the hackneyed philosophy of Marx. But when the question of independence and security of the country is involved, how could a party be allowed to function in India if it does not support India ? I want a reply to this question. But instead of realising its mistake the Communist Party throws a challenge and this challenge is not against the aggressor but in favour of the aggressor.

I feel the time has come when we should tell the Communist Party in clear terms to change its policy, and if it does not respond favourably, we should not allow its workers to enter the border areas. These areas are facing poverty and starvation. We got independence after a thousand years of slavery. Our Government has also not paid as much attention to the Hill Areas as it should have. Now if somebody goes there and tells them they are poor but right across the Himalayas people in the Chinese empire are leading a highly prosperous life it would not be patriotic. But this is being done and Government should be alert in this regard.

China's Entry in UN

I welcome the decision of the Government that in the ensuing session of the U.N. General Assembly our Government will not initiate the move for admitting China. Until now in every meeting of the UN our delegation raised the demand that China should get an entry in the organisation. We know China should get an entry, but if in view of our dispute with that country, if we do not take the initiative in the matter, it will show to some extent our anguish towards China, and this would be a step in the right direction.

But one thing I fail to understand, and it is why are talks going on at the official level being kept secret ? Shri Ranga had raised a question which was replied to by the Prime Minister, but it does not mitigate the apprehension that we have made our entire border a matter of dispute. For example, when we have a dispute only about Barahoti there is no need to scrutinize the entire Uttar Pradesh border that touches Tibet.....

SHRI JAWAHARLAL NEHRU : You are absolutely correct, I agree with you.

SHRI VAJPAYEE : I am happy that the entire border is not being subjected to scrutiny. But so far there has been an impression that must be removed. The reason is that it would not be in our interest if we make the entire border a disputed issue. But the real problem is that these officers have to submit their report in September. It is obvious that they cannot take any decision and they have simply to submit the report. I would like to know what would happen if they report that there would be no agreement.

SHRI JAWAHARLAL NEHRU : There is no question of an agreement at all.

SHRI VAJPAYEE : My submission is what would happen if they interpret that we have failed to agree on dates ?

SHRI JAWAHARLAL NEHRU : I don't know what they would say. But they have been told to report on the nature and type of documents from either side. They would examine all those documents and report after scrutiny on whether they were proper or not. By proper I mean whether they are worth consideration or not. They would give only their views. How can they take decisions. It is obvious they can't enter into any agreement irrespective of anything in their mind.

SHRI VAJPAYEE : It is true they can't make any agreement, but if there are differences even about the papers and documents at what stage would the talks be resumed again. If the officers could not be unanimous in their views and if their documents and papers support totally opposite border lines from which point shall we start these talks. And will the problem of the Chinese aggression not get prolonged as a result, so that we may gradually forget the aggression and get trapped in minor border adjustments by making them the subject of our discussion ? Now everyone agrees that China has occupied Indian territory and is strengthening its hold there. The Government has admitted that roads are being built in the occupied territory and a military build-up is taking place in Tibet. In these circumstances if this problem is not solved through negotiations are we preparing ourselves for a situation in which we could regain the territory that China has captured forcibly ?

The Prime Minister has talked of Algeria in his speech. When more and more Asian countries are achieving independence it is but natural that our attention is drawn towards Algeria. But if we pay attention to Algeria and human rights in neighbouring Tibet continue to be violated, serious charges of man-slaughter and other atrocities continue to be made and our government adopts the policy of keeping quiet over Tibet; and if, when a question is raised in the UNO to discuss this issue, our Government does not even support such a move, then our declarations regarding imperialism, colonialism and human rights become meaningless. On the one hand, western colonialism is receding and the colonised countries are becoming independent, but on the other hand a new kind of imperialism is raising its head in our neighbourhood.

This type of imperialism is more lethal than the earlier imperialism, because it comes in the garb of freedom. It raises the slogan of individual liberty, it promises to counter slavery with an economic philosophy. Hence, while we are happy over the devastation of Western imperialism and welcome the newly independent countries of Asia and Africa we should also pay attention to Tibet. Thailand and Malaya have decided to raise the issue of Tibet in the U.N. Actually this issue should have been raised by India itself, but if we can't initiate this move ourselves we should atleast support these countries.

As regards the question of human rights there can be no difference of opinion that China is also bound to enforce them. China had participated in the Bandung Conference, and in that conference the Geneva Convention on Human Rights was adopted, whereby all countries agreed to protect human rights. But now human rights are being trampled upon in China itself. If this question is raised in the United Nations the Government of India should participate in that discussion wholeheartedly; and it should fulfil its moral responsibility.

Now it can be argued that Tibetans would not be benefitted if the Tibet issue is raised there. I feel this line of argument is not correct. Only Tibet can decide how Tibetans are going to be benefitted. If we start deciding that there would be no difference between India and China, because China also speaks in similar terms and says Tibet will be benefitted only by remaining with the Chinese. What is required is that the Tibetans should themselves decide how they are going to be benefitted. If they want that the issue of Tibet should be raised in the United Nations the Government of India should not avoid its moral responsibility.

Prime Minister's Pak Visit

The Prime Minister is visiting Pakistan. I am not against his visit to that country. But this House should have been given some more details of the Canal Water Treaty that is going to be signed with them. So far we have been kept in dark and the agreements are being made behind the curtain of secrecy and today the Prime Minister also said that there would perhaps be an interim *status quo* period of 10 years. The point is, what amount will we have to pay to Pakistan or how long shall we continue to supply water to them. How long will the desert of Rajasthan be starved of water. Shall we get the money that Pakistan owes us for the supply of water, and if so how much ? Whatever the treaty, this House should be taken into confidence and we should be informed of the terms and conditions of the agreement which is going to be signed with Pakistan.

It is also said that the talks would be held on Kashmir. I don't know what talks would be held on Kashmir, because if there are going to be any talks on Kashmir they could only be on when Pakistan was going to vacate that portion of Kashmir which is still in their occupation. The Kashmir problem has been created only due to the Pakistani attack; there is no other problem about Kashmir. I disagree with members who say that the Chinese attack is an aggression but the Pakistani attack is not an aggression. Aggression is aggression, whether the aggressor is China or Pakistan. If we are friendly with Pakistan it is good, but as long as one-third of Kashmir remains occupied by Pakistan there could be no friendship. The question of providing joint defence does not arise. But I welcome the move that Pakistan should make a 'no war' pact with us. The Prime Minister had made this suggestion even earlier. India and Pakistan should declare that they should solve all their problems peacefully and should not resort to war even over Kashmir. If we could get back Pak-occupied territory of Kashmir through negotiations I would welcome such talks.

I would like to say one thing to those who talk of joint defence. They say that in case we have joint defence with Pakistan our army engaged on the Pakistani border would be relieved from that front and deployed on the Chinese border. My submission is that as long as the Government policy of not using military force holds the field deploying a huge army against China is not going to make any difference and the joint defence with Pakistan will not alter the situation. First of all the Government policy should change to the effect that we shall use military force if necessary.

Military collaboration between India and Pakistan is not possible so long as both the countries have divergent foreign policy objectives. We do not want to get involved in disputes. This is the right policy and we should keep following it firmly. The question of changing this policy arises only when some people feel that in the present circumstances we cannot defend our country. When Pakistan made an alliance with America voices were raised that we should join the Russian bloc, and today when China has violated our territory it is being argued that we should unite with Pakistan. I don't think it is a sign of confidence in ourselves. And it clearly shows that in case the Government is unable to defend our borders, it would become difficult to keep public opinion in favour of our policy of keeping away from either bloc. Gradually a voice would be raised that the defence of the country is supreme and we must join either of the blocs for the sake of our country. If thinkers like Professor Ranga and Shri Chakravarti Rajagopalachary advise us to give up the policy of keeping away from both the blocs they are perhaps having apprehensions about further Chinese attacks. But I am not in favour of inviting the Pak army to India in order to face the Chinese invasion. President Ayub says India needs their help, but I would like to say that Pakistan also needs our help, because the events taking place in Afghanistan also pose a danger to Pakistan, and so circumstances are not favourable for fruitful negotiations. But if we are to take a firm stand against China in any negotiations we must exhibit same firmness against Pakistan too. If the problem of aggression is solved through negotiations it would be most welcome. But if we change our policy of keeping away from both the blocs just on the basis of a threat of foreign invasion it would be against our national interest, and I don't agree with such a proposition.

I believe that the visit of our Prime Minister to Pakistan would be successful in the sense that we will get that one-third portion of Kashmir that is occupied by Pakistan and the acts of sabotage going on the border will also come to an end. On the one hand, Pakistan wants friendship, but on the other it is indulging in acts of sabotage on the cease-fire line. Where is the need of such subotage ? Now they say they don't want a referendum in Kashmir. There was no question of a referendum in the first place, then do they want that we should yield to their invasion ? Once we do so in we would not have the moral courage to face another invasion. Both invasions are invasions and must be treated as such, and my submission is that we should have a clear policy in this regard. Thank you.

Don't Burn Your Hands

Mr. Speaker, Sir, in the international sphere we have decided to keep away from both the power blocs and to consider every issue on its merits. This policy not only serves our interests but it is also correct from the point of view of the global interest; we should follow it firmly. We should try to keep ourselves away from those international disputes with which we are not directly concerned. We may have the best of intentions, but in this world divided into power blocs we cannot operate successfully on the basis of honesty alone.

I had the privilege to hear the Prime Minister deliver a speech in the General Assembly session of the United Nations on the 4th October. I was not only happy but felt proud of his speech. Amidst the tension of the cold war his voice, which had come from the core of his heart and which overwhelmed the audience, was the voice of peace, the voice of reason and restraint. It was as if the soul of India was finding expression through him. In his speech I saw a glimpse of the ancient Hindu sages whose life mission was peace. In spite of being in the opposition party I can say this although I differ with so many things in his speech. And I shall place those differences before you.

It would have been better if the New York visit of the Prime Minister had terminated after that speech. We should not have got ourselves involved in issues that are beyond our control. If we involve ourselves in them, we can get only a bad name. Let us take the example of Congo. The Prime Minister gave very constructive proposals. He believes in democracy and India has parliamentary democracy. He said the United Nations should help the establishment of the parliamentary system in Congo. But how are the difficulties involved in such a recourse going to be overcome ? Will United Nations troops fight the forces of Mobutu ? Shall we take part in the internal war of Congo ? Will the United Nations undertake the responsibility of maintaining peace and order in Congo ? Military dictatorship has been established in many countries after dissolving the parliament. It is true that the situation in Congo is different, but we should consider to what extent we could go.

Situation in Congo

Our officers who have gone to Congo are doing very good work, but the situation there is such that not only the U.N. but we too have been trapped in Congo. Belgium, which has almost been dislodged from Congo, wants to

Lok Sabha on November 22, 1960 during discussion on the motion regarding International Situation

stage a comeback there. Keeping in view the fertile land of Africa the communist countries also want to seek entry there on the pretext of Congo. The U.S.A. is also trying to maintain capitalism in Congo by supporting Belgium. All this is happening because the people of Congo are not united and also because their President and Prime Minister are opposed to each other. How could we successfully solve this riddle ? My submission is that we should keep aloof from such questions.

I know it is very difficult for us because the new African countries, which have gained entry into the United Nations, look up to us for leadership. It would be a matter of pride for us if India leads these non-aligned countries, but although this leadership might be dear to us it can't be in our interest. It might satisfy our ego but it would not be in the interest of India. When I heard the Prime Minister say that we do not want to form a third bloc, I felt happy. As long as our policy is against alignment how could we form the third bloc even if that bloc consists of countries which are not aligned with any bloc. But the countries that are non-aligned look to us and naturally our Prime Minister has become their leader.

The Bid to Arbitrate between Two Big Powers

Although five countries jointly moved a resolution in the U.N. calling upon the leaders of the Eastern and Western blocs to hold a summit conference the President of Yugoslavia left and President Nasser also departed from New York leaving our Prime Minister holding their baby.

I don't think the circumstances under which that proposal was made were suitable. Our wish that the leaders of U.S.A and U.S.S.R should meet each other is commendable but under what circumstances should they do so ? Neither is the Russian Prime Minister ready to do so because he wanted America to apologise nor is the U.S. President ready to meet his counterpart because he wanted to get his airmen released. We tried to arrange the meeting of those who were not prepared to meet each other and the basis for making such an attempt was the thought that a big crisis might develop if they did not meet. I don't think there was any imminent danger of war breaking out. The Russian Prime Minister knew that elections were going to be held in the U.S. and he had also stated that he would talk to the newly elected American President. The present U.S. President had become ineffective because of the coming elections and he was not in a position to talk on behalf of the American people. But still we made a proposal on behalf of the five countries and that proposal was taken to mean that we wanted to embarrass America.

I know that this was not our intention, but we should understand that if we do want to arbitrate between the two power blocs we can pick only those points on which both of them have identical views. We should not touch points on which they have differences. We embark upon doing good, but get only a bad name. We should not burn our hands while performing *havan*.

Problem of Disarmament

Even in the proposal for disarmament made by us precautions have not been taken about how the danger of a surprise attack on Western countries by communist countries would be met.

During my visit I happened to go to Pearl Harbour where Japan had made a sudden attack in December, 1941 and consigned more than 2,000 American naval personnel to a watery grave. During my visit to the U.S.A. I observed that despite their desire for peace that country is obsessed with the fear of a sudden attack. This fear may be unfounded, but if we want disarmament in the world we should also make efforts to dispel this fear and for that purpose there should be some sort of control and inspection. Democratic countries are open countries where it is easy to carry out this work but Communist countries are closed behind a strong iron curtain. There should be some arrangement to ensure compliance of disarmament agreements. If we work cautiously and also keep in view the apprehensions and fears being felt in this regard, it would open the way for disarmament in the world.

The Prime Minister has told us about the type of speeches and gestures that are made in the General Assembly of the United Nations. I was surprised and even pained to hear all that. We have respect for the Russian Prime Minister because he is the Prime Minister of a great country. But the way he conducted himself there is not going to enhance his prestige and it would also not add to the image of the Russian people. It is a matter of shame if the representative of a country holds up his shoe while addressing an international forum. Time has come for the nations of the world to make efforts for evolving a code of conduct for the General Assembly of the United Nations. To interrupt speaking members and to use abusive language to convert the United Nations into a propaganda forum, are tendencies that should be condemned and I hope India will raise its voice against such tendencies. But when on returning to New Delhi the Prime Minister called a Press conference and the correspondent of a newspaper, drawing his attention to the criticism made by a newspaper of some words spoken by Shri Khruschchev, asked him whether it would not adversely affect Indo- Soviet relations, surprisingly enough the Prime Minister instead of saying there was democracy in India and the press enjoys freedom, uttered some words condemning that newspaper. I don't think this attitude is consistent with the non-aligned policy.

What the Russian Prime Minister did in the U.N. must be condemned. But in case the Prime Minister does not think it proper to do so it is wrong to say that the person or the newspaper making such condemnation wants to spoil Into-Soviet relations. I want friendship with Russia...*(Interruptions)*.

SHRIMATI RENU CHAKRAVARTI : Oh ho !

SHRI VAJPAYEE : Saying oh ho wouldn't do. We want friendship with Russia, we don't want the mastery of Russia. My other friends may want that. I for one want friendship with all, but the basis of that friendship can't be support for uncivilised behaviour. I was expecting that our Prime Minister would present an ideal form of conduct before the U.N. General Assembly by his restrained behaviour.

China's Entry into U.N.

In his speech delivered before the U.N. General Assembly, our Prime Minister talked about representation of China in the United Nations. I have no complaint against that. China should get representation in the United Nations and it would get it though it may be delayed.

SHRI A.M. TARIQ (Jammu & Kashmir) : But doors cannot be closed for an indefinite period.

SHRI VAJPAYEE : For that the United Nations should itself open its doors. But my complaint is that issues relating to our conflict with China and pertaining to the situation that has arisen as a result of the Chinese attack have been shelved by them by calling them only a controversy. Is the situation that has arisen as a result of the Chinese attack a mere controversy ? If China has invaded Indian territory the Prime Minister, while talking about admitting China to the United Nations, should have said that although China has attacked India and has occupied 12,000 square miles of its territory we still advocate its admission to the United Nations because all nations should get admission to this forum. Had he made a reference to the Chinese attack our argument for providing a place to China in the United Nations would have been further strengthened as in spite of their attack we were advocating their cause for admission to the United Nations. But perhaps the Prime Minister did not think it proper to use strong words. Perhaps his harsh words are reserved only for the opposition parties in the Lok Sabha. I think the right signals should have been given. We had a chance to influence world opinion. We could have explained to other countries the nature of our conflict with China. Unless we do so repeatedly other countries would not be in a position to understand the gravity of the factual position about it. They think there is no big dispute and so India advocates admission of China in the United Nations. We had a chance to educate the public and create world opinion in our favour.

It is a matter of regret that we have decided not to support the complaint moved by Thailand and Malaya about violation of human rights in Tibet. It could have been appreciated if India did not recognise the right of self-determination of Tibet because India has inherited from the Britishers the notion that China has suzerainty over Tibet. But so far as the issue of violation of human rights is concerned India should not adopt a no-comment policy. To say now that this question relates to the cold war and we don't want that a cold war should start on this or to say that it is meaningless to raise this question when China was not represented makes no sense to me. What should we do if China is not represented there ? But we do have the responsibility of expressing Indian sentiments about the people of Tibet. If we talk of putting an end to imperialism and colonialism, if we are against French imperialism in Algeria, we can't shut our eyes to the new imperialism that is raising its head on the Himalayan heights touching our frontiers. My submission is that the Government of India should review its policy in this regard.

It may be that no solution is going to be evolved by raising the issue of Tibet in the U.N. But we have already raised several issues in that forum that have not been solved, but by doing so we at least got the satisfaction of having done our duty. When we claim that we raise our voice against imperialism and colonialism throughout the world, we can't close our eyes to the developments that are taking place in Tibet.

Sir, I have also felt that our publicity system in foreign countries is weak and deficient. It needs to be made more efficient. During my visit to the U.S.A I observed that people there had misconceptions about the Kashmir issue and these misconceptions relate to facts. I happened to meet many Americans who don't even know that after partition of this country crores of Muslims are still living in India and are enjoying equal rights with others. They think the country was partitioned, Pakistan was established and all Muslims migrated there. Therefore, as Muslims, according to them, are in a majority in Kashmir it should also merge with Pakistan. When I told them that crores of Muslims are still living in India and, therefore, we are not prepared to accept the communal argument over the Kashmir issue they appreciated the point. But in an interview in New York our Prime Minister said that we would not try to get back that part of Kashmir which is occupied by Pakistan. We accept this status and we will not disturb it.

I don't agree with this policy. If we give up our right over that part which has been taken away by aggression it would further strengthen the plea that we should relinquish our right over other territories too that have been taken away from us by force. This policy would not be correct in the present situation. Even otherwise the Pakistani attitude still requires to undergo a great change. We did not keep in view India's interest when we agreed to supply them canal water. But instead of being thankful to us the rulers of Pakistan say that while we had done a very good thing by supplying them water they should also get Kashmir, from where this water comes. My submission is that we should improve our relations with Pakistan, but to achieve this objective we are not prepared to bow before Pakistani aggression. Aggression is always an aggression whether it is of China or of Pakistan. We should try to regain our land which has been occupied. In case we can't regain that territory at least do not raise the question of giving it away.

So far as China is concerned we have, perhaps, not properly explained even to our neighbouring countries the facts about our dispute with that country. The Prime Minister of Burma had come to India. I read his statements. Time and again, he lauded the sincerity of the Chinese Prime Minister. It sounded as if he did not repose equal confidence in our sincerity. There is a quotation in Sanskrit which says that if a man has two wives and it is said one of them is faithful it would naturally imply that the other is not. His repeated utterances that the Prime Minister of China is honest and he wants a settlement suggest that he had doubts about the intentions of our

Prime Minister. I don't think there should be reason for such an assessment, but if it is so, then it is most unfortunate for us.

Perhaps we have not been able to make even the Burmese Prime Minister fully understand our attitude towards this dispute. The very objective of the talks that are going on is to solve the dispute but China does not want to settle it. Our Communist leader Professor Mukherji says that they want a settlement. There is only one way for a settlement of this dispute and it is that China should vacate the Indian territory that has been occupied by them and go back. No other settlement would be acceptable to India because that would not be a settlement; it would be surrender. We too want settlement but not by surrendering to them. China has no maps and documents. That is why it was talking of accepting the "actualities". I don't think the talks that are going to be held in Rangoon would be successful. But if they are not successful what will India do to get back the Indian territory that is under Chinese occupation ? There is need to think about that and to start preparations in that direction right now. Thank you.

India Should Take Initiative for German Unification

Mr. Chairman. Sir, while considering the international situation and Government of India's policy about it, it is but natural that our attention is drawn towards the factors that have created tensions and endangered world peace. There is no denying the fact that world peace is in India's self- interest. Our efforts to build the nation would not wholly succeed unless peace prevails in the world. Therefore, it is necessary to exert our influence in the maintenance of world peace while protecting our own interest. It is heartening that the Indian Government is pursuing a policy in the international sphere which strengthens world peace, reduces international tensions, and enables our country to help those nations that do not see eye to eye to come closer.

Today the attention of all of us is attracted towards the Berlin problem. We should declare in unambiguous terms that we do not like the division of Germany to continue and I am glad that the Prime Minister has also given an indication to this effect in his speech. The imperialist countries' solution for such problems is to divide the country. But our own experience bears testimony to the fact that division does not solve the problems, rather it only complicates them further. France wants to divide 'Algeria'. We are opposed to it, because it would not fulfil the national aspirations of the people of Algeria. If the people of Germany wish to have a united German nation their sentiments should be respected. We had expected that the leaders of the Communist Party would also express their views on unification of Germany through a free election, but the Communist leaders of East Germany and their partners and Indian supporters are afraid of free elections being held in Germany. It is not difficult to find out the reason behind this. But if there could be a democratic solution to the German problem it is free and fair elections there under the supervision of the United Nations. If both Germanys want to unite and wish to stand as a unified German nation they should be given full opportunity to do so. After that Germany can decide to join any bloc if she so desires, although I would like Germany to remain aloof from international groupings. If an agreement could be arrived at to the effect that the German nation emerging out of free elections would not join either the American or the Soviet bloc, and both the blocs would respect its freedom and neutrality, many problems of Europe could be solved.

Lok Sabha on August 16, 1961 during the discussion on the motion regarding International Situation with particular reference to the Prime Minister's Visit to the U.S.A.

Prime Minister should take Initiative

It is good that doors for a dialogue on the German question have not been closed completely. I think our Prime Minister can contribute a lot to further the prospects of talks for an agreement. He is going to visit Soviet Russia in the near future. Thereafter, he will pay a visit to U.S.A. at the invitation of the new American President. I hope taking advantage of this visit he would make efforts to bring an accord on the German-Berlin question, so that the world may be saved from the danger of a war.

The brightest facet of the international situation is that colonialism is gradually coming to an end. On the one hand, Western nations are being forced to retreat as a result of struggles for freedom, and on the other a large number of non-aligned nations are emerging on the international horizon. The entire world felt the strength of the non-aligned nations during the last meeting of the United Nations General Assembly. It is a strong sign of peace that small nations independently ponder over the problems facing the world without becoming camp-followers of anybody. India stands in the front rank of such nations, and we should be proud of it. Those who are demanding that we should also become a camp-follower of somebody, accept arms from someone with strings and thereby restrict our freedom do not take into account the present situation prevailing in the country as well as in the world.

A Forum of Non-Aligned Nations

It is necessary to have a forum of nations that are not members of any bloc, that can put forth their views on each and every international issue without fear or favour and try to cultivate the friendship of all. Our Prime Minister is going to take part in a conference of such non-aligned nations. He has rightly said that this conference should not become an instrument for formation of a third bloc. But there is one more thing to take care of— it is that we should have an appraisal of how far we could influence their decisions in such a conference.

From newspaper reports of the Cairo meeting in which our Secretary-general took part, it appears that we have been able to take with us the countries of South-East Asia to a considerable extent. But our relations with the countries of Africa that have recently become independent are not as close as they should have been. It is necessary to make special efforts to take them with us. We hope this conference of non-aligned nations would strengthen the cause of peace. Let us expect that a third voice would emerge in the international sphere as a result of this conference,—a voice that would speak of freedom, of the right of self-determination and of equality of mankind in the din of weapons.

There are certain problems that are directly connected with our country. It is but natural that we should give some serious thought to them. Whatever has been said by the Prime Minister regarding our border conflict with China cannot solve this problem. I am opposed to sending the Secretary-General to Peking for talks with the leaders of Communist China. It is not in keeping with the dignity of India that our Secretary-General should visit Peking and knock at the doors of Communist China in order to find out the reaction of the leaders of that country on the report of the talks that were held between the officers of the two countries. No reply has been received from China; China has not even published that report. Can't we understand their reaction from this ? Was it necessary to send the Secretary-General to Peking for this purpose ? When no leader of Communist China was available in Peking he had to proceed to Shanghai to have talks with them. We should understand the mentality of the leaders of Communist China. They are asking as to why we published the report, which also shows that we should not exepct China to reach an agreement with us.

We shall not Resort to War ?

The Prime Minister has said that "we shall not resort to war". But if you will not resort to war what will you do ? India has no answer to how it will recover its territory occupied by China. A policy of inaction neither protects the interest of the nation nor raises the morale of the people. It does not even create confidence among our neighbouring countries about our capability. The need of the hour is to adopt a certain dynamic policy and for that we have to look at our strength. We should consider what steps could be taken against China in the present circumstances and move accordingly.

SOME HON'BLE MEMBERS : Let Hon'ble Member suggest the steps.

SHRI VAJPAYEE : Some of our Congress friends are interrupting to ask what the Government should do. I want to tell them that at least the Government should not send persons like the Secretary-General to knock at the doors of Chinese leaders. If it cannot do anything, let it not; but it should not let the self-respect of India be kicked like that. If it cannot recover the territory belonging to India....

SOME HON'BLE MEMBERS : It can.

SHRI VAJPAYEE : It cannot. But it should not do anything that weakens our case and lowers the morale of the people. The explanation given by the Prime Minister for sending the Secretary-General to Peking is very weak and has no substance. We are told that we wanted to know the reaction of the Chinese leaders. That could be ascertained from the Chinese Ambassador in New Delhi. A letter could be written to Communist China for this purpose. There was no need to send the Secretary-General for this purpose. We are quite categorical that if military action is needed to drive out the Chinese from Indian soil that should be done. We are not in favour of war; but it does not mean that we would not resort to war for recovering our land from the enemy. That we are not in favour of war only means that we would not invade the territory of any other country. But a war of aggression and a war of liberation are not the same thing. If we send troops to Goa, it would not constitute an attack and it would be in pursuance of our policy of peace. If there was scope for the use of the sword in Mahatma Gandhi's non-violence the Prime Minister's policy of world peace should also include military action to liberate Indian territory from aggression. Otherwise, if we talk of peace and let our land remain under the occupation of foreigners it would be considered a sign of weakness, and it goes against our national interest.

Reason Behind the Birth of Pakistan

The Prime Minister has also referred to Pakistan and has admitted that the foundation of Pakistan was based on opposition to India. Hatred towards India is the genesis of the birth of Pakistan. He has also stated that if the problem of Kashmir is resolved the rulers of Pakistan will raise some other bogey to continue tensions between the two countries. This analysis of the situation is perfectly correct. Then how could we deduce from it that we should become extra liberal in cultivating friendship with Pakistan ? An agreement was reached about canal water with the hope that it would create goodwill between the two countries. Berubari was given to Pakistan in the hope that it would improve relations between us. But what was the result of all this ? Experience shows that Pakistan always raises new obstacles in order to get some undue advantage. In such circumstances should we not review our policy towards Pakistan ? The day Pakistan will end its enmity towards India, Pakistan's existence would come to an end. The very foundation of Pakistan's existence would come to an end. The very foundation of Pakistan is hatred of India. The day its hatred towards India ends this wall of division would automatically tumble down, because although the states have separated the people are one, and a mere difference of religion cannot change nationality. We have never accepted the two-nation theory.

SHRI A. M. TARIQ (Jammu and Kashmir) : The Hon'ble Member is speaking very vociferously today.

SHRI VAJPAYEE : Shri Tariq always listens to sensible talk, but when he attended the Muslim Convention he was not even allowed to speak.

SHRI A. M. TARIQ : I have become wiser after that.

SHRI VAJPAYEE : Mr. Deputy Speaker, Sir, I want to submit that in spite of this political division the people of both the states have the feeling of oneness. The day relations between India and Pakistan improve this political division will disappear as there would be no need for it. Those leaders who demanded Pakistan, who agitated for Pakistan, who became puppets in the hands of the British, would never like relations between India and Pakistan to improve.

So far as we are concerned, I agree with the observation of the Prime Minister that we wish Pakistan well, we want friendship with Pakistan, we want to improve our relations with Pakistan. But we are not in favour of granting undue concessions to Pakistan. We should adopt a reciprocal policy towards Pakistan, because reciprocity is the one answer to such questions.

American Intentions

So far as the question of American aid to Pakistan is concerned, I am not satisfied with the observations of the Prime Minister. American intentions might be good, but once the arms are out of their hands they shall not listen to what the U.S.A. says. We would then have to listen to what the recipient of the arms says. It is not written on the arms that they would go off only towards the Soviet Union and not towards India. The arms received from the U.S.A. could well be used against India, and it is most regrettable that in spite of there being a change of Government in the U.S.A. Pakistan continues to get more military aid. When the Democratic Party came to power it was expected that instead of giving military aid it would lay stress on giving economic aid. But not only aircraft but even submarines are being given to Pakistan. There is no communist country touching Pakistan's territorial waters and therefore, there is no need to supply submarines to Pakistan. These submarines could be used against us. We should also beware of the obnoxious alliance of which both Pakistan and Portugal are members. In Goa efforts are afoot to separate it from India, for making Goa a separate colony. We should also remember that increasingly close relations between Pakistan and Portugal may create further impediments in the liberation of Goa.

The Prime Minister is to visit the United States of America. Nobody has demanded that he should give an ultimatum to the U.S.A. But American leaders must be told in unambiguous terms that by supplying arms to Pakistan they were not strengthening peace and democracy in this region. How would a country that did not have democracy strengthen democracy ? If in this region, in South-East Asia, democracy is to be strengthened, India with its 440 million people could make its contribution towards that end. The USA cannot protect democracy by giving military aid to tottering thrones and shaking crowns. It should put pressure on Pakistan to change its anti-India policy. The U.S.A. should be told in clear terms about this.

I think our foreign policy is being conducted in the right direction insofar as the question of safeguarding world peace and raising the prestige of India is concerned. This policy does not belong to a particular person or party, this is the policy of the entire nation. But so far as the interests of India are concerned, there is need to make our foreign policy more firm, more dynamic and more forceful. Thank you.

Self-respect Cannot be Auctioned in World Market

Sir, I move :

9. "That at the end of the motion, the following be added, namely :

'and having considered the same, this House regrets—

(i) that Government's attitude towards China continues to be ludicrously unrealistic and consequently its China policy, inept and ineffective

(ii) that nothing has been done to educate world opinion in general, and opinion in our neighbouring States in particular about the expansionist designs of China;

(iii) that as a result of this lapse, Government has failed to checkmate effectively China's bid to drive a wedge between India and Nepal;

(iv) that our Nepal policy has not yet succeeded in lessening strains between India and this neighbour of ours;

(v) that Government has failed to realise that the recent outbursts against Hindus in Dacca, Rajshahi, and other parts of East Pakistan are not just sporadic outbursts of communal frenzy but are clear indications that it has become impossible for non-Muslims to live in the Islamic State of Pakistan with peace and honour, and so the situation there warrants a more radical and realistic approach on India's part than the lodging of mere protest notes; and

(vi) that in their representation of India's case for Kashmir at the U.N., our delegates have failed to reaffirm India's rights over the Pak-occupied portions of Kashmir and her determination to recover them'."

3. "That at the end of the motion, the following be added, namely :

'and having considered the same, this House recommends—

(i) that as a first step towards a realistic reorientation of our China policy, diplomatic ties with China be severed;

(ii) that the primary objective of all diplomatic and defence policies and postures *vis-a-vis* China should be clearly accepted as the early recovery of lost territory;

(iii) that a conscious and concerted effort should be made at international forums and in our neighbouring States to expose China's perfidious conduct towards India and its imperialist designs in general;

Rajya Sabha on June 23, 1962 during discussion on international situation

(iv) that efforts towards lessening of Indo-Nepalese strains should be intensified;

(v) that in view of the fact that Pakistan has failed to assure to the Hindu minorities in Pakistan a secure and honourable living, Pakistan must be called upon to cede territory to India to rehabilitate the heavy influx of displaced persons coming over from Pakistan; and

(vi) that Government should make it clear to the United Nations that the only function it has to perform in respect of Kashmir is to help in securing vacation of Pakistan's aggression and that if, instead, members of the Security Council suffered Pakistan to exploit this international forum for a continued slander against India, India would be constrained to dissociate from all U.N. discussions on Kashmir."

Mr. Chairman, Sir, while discussing the international situation, it is but natural that our attention is drawn towards the nuclear tests that are being conducted nowadays. We are living in a strange paradoxical world where nuclear tests are being conducted and at the same time peace conferences are also being held. But what is amazing is that a peace conference is being organised by the Soviet Russia, which was the first to violate the moratoriam signed to suspend the nuclear tests. We should condemn whosoever conducts the nuclear tests, because today the humanity has only two options left before it, prosper or perish. The entire human race would either live on this planet on the basis of goodwill, or it would be enveloped by destructive forces in persuit of arms race.

Soviet Peace Conference a Mockery

A conference was held in our country recently in protest against proliferation of nuclear arms. While attending that conference I felt that even though we raise our voice against armament, yet the circumstances of today have forced us to equip ourselves with arms, and when we preach other nations not to store arms they must be laughing at us—that India which is eager to purchase arms for its security from all the countries of the world and is actually purchasing them, does not lag behind whenever there is an opportunity to sermonise. In that conference, it was also said that we should unilaterally decide and act not to arm ourselves. Those who said so were imbued by noble sentiments. This is the eternal voice of India which is heard amidst loud noises and rattling of arms. However, that is an ideal situation which does not fit in the practice of today and the Hon'ble Prime Minister has done well in stating in clear terms that irrespective of what the saints may say, the ruler has to tread the path of ground realities.

I would like to tell those gentlemen who are going to attend the Peace Conference in Moscow that if there was ever an opportunity to put moral pressure to stop nuclear tests, it is this and we should refuse to attend the Moscow Peace Conference and tell them that it is a mockery to hold the conference in the Soviet Russia which was the first to break the agreement on nuclear tests and the people of India are not prepared to join it. However, I do not know how far this request of mine would be accepted.

The biggest problem is that if we resort to disarmament, then how to face colonialism, aggression and injustice ? We could not resolve the problem of Goa peacefully and I do not think we can recover the Indian territory which is at present under the occupation of Pakistan and China through peaceful means. The alternatives are that either we surrender before the aggressor or defend ourselves bravely against the aggression. I fail to understand how would we do without arms in such a situation.

U.N.'s Role on Aggression in Kashmir

In the final analysis we have to shape our foreign policy having the interests of India in mind and nobody can deny that India's interests are in jeopardy today. We may raise our voice in support of world peace, but at the same time it is essential to safeguard the interests of our country. The Kashmir problem is pending before the Security Council and we have not been able to convince many countries of the world that Pakistan is an aggressor in Kashmir and that they should pressurise Pakistan to withdraw its forces from Kashmir. Pakistan raises the issue of Kashmir in the Security Council first for the sake of publicity, and then to defame India. For her, Kashmir may just be a piece of land, but for us it is a symbol of our sovereignty, our secularism and our democracy.

We have integrated Kashmir with India, not to use the issue by inciting the feelings of our people every now and then. But Pakistan is actually adopting such tactics and some member countries of the Security Council, it is difficult to say whether knowingly or unknowingly, are toeing the line of Pakistan. Perhaps a situation has come when we should tell the Security Council in clear terms that it has only one thing to do in respect of Kashmir and that is to get the Pakistani aggression vacated. If it does not do so, we should tell it that we would not allow ourselves to become a party to Pakistan's attempt to use the Security Council as a forum to conduct anti-India propaganda and that if the Security Council starts a debate on Kashmir, India would be compelled to dissociate itself from that debate.

China's Border Strategy

We cannot forget that part of Kashmir which is under occupation of Pakistan. The Prime Minister has done the right thing in withdrawing the proposal to negotiate with Pakistan on the basis of the cease-fire line. However, I have not been able to understand one thing. We have a border dispute with China as well and China is sitting pretty after occupying almost fourteen and a half thousand square miles of our territory. The Prime Minister had also suggested to China a withdrawal of forces in accordance with each other's maps. This suggestion was first made in 1959. The offer has been repeated again. China rejected this proposal on both occasions. I want to invite the attention of the House to the language used by the Chinese while rejecting our proposal this time. They doubt even our bona fides. They have said that 'there are reasons to believe that the Indian Government has not put forth the above proposals seriously.' They have further stated as to 'how could one assume that the Government of China would accept such degrading conditions imposed unilaterally ? Is China a defeated country ? China has used this language in its note dated June 2nd and has imposed the condition that India should withdraw from the area in NEFA which has been claimed as Chinese territory. Only then they would consider withdrawing their forces from Ladakh, not otherwise. It means that China has rejected the proposal made by the Prime Minister, I would like to know whether this proposal still stands or has been withdrawn ? There is no meaning in persuing it. It is clear that when China is not prepared to have a dialogue, how a compromise could be reached with her and how the Indian territory under Chinese occupation could be recovered.

Communists Silence on Chinese Aggression

I am pained to note that there are certain parties and some individuals in the country who exaggerate our conflict with Pakistan, but when the question of China comes, they keep quiet. My colleague, the leader of the Communist Party Shri Bhupesh Gupta, has given notices of many amendments, but not one of them refers to our conflict with China, as if China has not committed any aggression against us, as if we are having very friendly relations with China. (*Interruptions*) This is not an imperialist game, our patriotism demands that every citizen of India, each individual who calls himself a patriot, should condemn these aggressions whether they are committed by China or Pakistan. But the Communist Party far from condemning the Chinese aggression, gives an opportunity to China to publish anti-India literature in its Press. The Ministry of Home Affairs may not like to take any action, but I want to know why the Communist Party allows the printing of "*China Today*" in its Press, when its copies had been proscribed ? This newspaper has recently started publishing Chinese notes in which India has been abused and filthy language has been used against us. Our own land is being used for anti-India propaganda and the Indian Government cannot escape responsibility by giving an excuse that the newspaper published by the Chinese Embassy can print the notes sent by the Chinese Government. Should we take such a legal view ? What facilities are being provided to the Indian Embassy in China ? Should we not have some reciprocal policy in this matter ? Numerous restrictions have been imposed on our Embassy staff in China, what treatment was meted out to our staff in Tibet ? Compared to that, how much relaxation we are giving to them ? The House should seriously ponder over these matters.

India Not a Purchasable Commodity

Madam, the House need to consider one more thing which is connected with foreign aid. India has decided not to join any bloc. This decision is correct and we should strictly adheres to this policy. We are taking economic aid from all the countries, but we have never accepted aid with strings.

However, the type of comments that have been made in the United States of America about our purchase of Mig aircraft from Soviet Russia and the way in which an attempt has been made to effect a cut in the economic aid that we receive from America is not conducive to promote democratic values in the world. When strings are attached to economic aid—they are not in the form of thick ropes, they are thinner even than a thread and are not visible they could be felt at the time of crisis. If the American leaders think that they have purchased India by giving economic aid, they are sadly mistaken. We are accepting economic aid from all the countries in order to remove our poverty and to bring economic prosperity in the country. But we are not prepared to auction India's self-respect in the markets of Washington for the sake of economic aid. The observations made against our Prime Minister and the leaders of our country could easily create resentment in the minds of anybody. I do not look at this question from the viewpoint of the Communist Party. I look at it from a patriot's point of view. We sent our forces to Goa, which was our own decision. We did not try to air drop our troops in the darkness of night like America did in Cuba. Whatever we did, we did openly, in broad day light, although it might not have been in conformity with our moral pronouncements. But what right America has got to point its finger towards it ? However, those who live in glass houses think it wise to throw stones at others.

America Should Review Its Foreign Policy

The policy adopted by America on the issue of Kashmir cannot be helpful in restricting the growth of communism in this region. The Americans say that they are giving arms to Pakistan in order to stop the spread of communism in this part of the world. However, recently when the question of sending troops to Thailand under the "SEATO" pact came up, according to American aims this was being done to stop the march of Communism. Pakistan did not send its troops to Thailand. I do not want that armed forces be deployed in Thailand or Pakistan should send its troops there. However, by refusing to send its troops to Thailand, Pakistan has made it clear that she has no interest in stopping the spread of Communism, its sole purpose is to accumulate arms for use against India. Those countries who want us not to purchase aircraft from Soviet Russia, must stop supplying aircraft to Pakistan. Why do they go on supplying aircrafts to Pakistan. Actually, they are to be blamed for disturbing the military balanced in this region. If we can get good aircraft from Soviet Russia at cheap rates, we must buy them. Aircraft is not communist or non-communist just as there are no capitalist and non-capitalist arms. However, the countries which want that we should not purchase arms from Russia should review their policy of supplying arms to Pakistan. If they go on supplying arms to Pakistan, we would have to purchase arms from whatever source they are available for our security, and if anybody speaks against this, we would regard it as an interference in our internal affairs.

I would like to tell the American leaders that the economic aid they have given us would lose its value in a such a situation. They cannot understand the sentiments of the people of India about Goa. If they cannot understand our policy about Kashmir, if they cannot understand why we have been forced today to buy aircraft from the Soviet Union, then the future of democracy in the world does not appear to be safe in their hands. Democracy cannot survive in the world by supplying arms to hollowed thrones and shaking crowns. If America wants to stop the onward march of Communism in this part of the world by supplying arms to the military dictatorship in Pakistan, they are committing a great mistake. Communism is a philosophy of life and if it is to be faced, it must be confronted with a more effective philosophy of life. Light can face Light, darkness cannot efface it. If the Americans think that the spread of an ideology can be stopped by erecting a wall of weapons, they should better review their policy. There is unanimity in the whole of India—excepting perhaps the Communist Party—over the policy of not joining any bloc. However if a situation comes when we are forced to accept arms from anywhere to safeguard our freedom, we would do so and my party will fully support the Government of India in whatever steps it may take in this connection....

MR. DEPUTY CHAIRMAN : Only three minutes remain in the time allotted to you.

SHRI VAJPAYEE : Please give me five minutes more.

MR. DEPUTY CHAIRMAN : Twenty minutes were allotted to you.

SHRI BHUPESH GUPTA : Give him five minutes, Madam, because he is supporting the Government of India.

SHRI VAJPAYEE : But I am attacking the Communist Party.

I want to draw the attention of the Prime Minister to certain smaller matters. Like the Chinese Embassy, the North Vietnamese Embassy also sometimes indulges in anti-Indian propaganda. Recently, they have published a note in which India has been criticised in regard to the International Commission. But before that the North Vietnamese Ambassador had criticised the policies of India in a speech delivered by him at a press conference held in July, 1961. I do not think that it is a healthy practice and in keeping with diplomatic etiquette that the heads of foreign missions in Delhi should indulge in propaganda against us. We should think over it seriously.

Question of Israel

I would also like to invite the attention to another thing. One of our special secretaries had visited Jordan. He attended a Press Conference there and described India's policy of not granting recognition to Israel as "pro-Arab." He used the words "Pro-Arab" and this was broadcast from Aman Radio. I do not think that it would be proper to describe India's policy in that manner. I have not been able to understand why we have not established full diplomatic relations with Israel. It has got a Consulate at Bombay. We should not have any objection if they want to bring the Consulate at New Delhi. As a matter of fact, we should establish full diplomatic relations with them, because many foreign tourists who want to visit India straightway from Israel cannot get *visa* directly for coming to India due to absence of the Indian Embassy in Israel. They have to obtain a visa through Britain which takes a month's time. Therefore, many foreign guests who want to come here have to return without visiting India, because they have no way to come over here from Israel. I am unable to understand why the Government of India has not been able to alter its policy regarding Israel.

India's Representative at U.N.

I would like to make one more point. I cannot understand the basis of selection of our representatives for the United Nations Organisation. I have had an opportunity to go to the U.N. two years ago and what I am saying today does not apply to our representatives at that time. However, I have felt that some caution should be observed while selecting these representatives so that they may not fall ill due to the extreme cold of New York or fracture their legs due to the slippery snow there or go to bed just after the fall of the evening. Such people cannot represent the interests of India properly.

I would also like to say a word about the leader of our delegation. He possesses a keen intellect and sharp wisdom. But when he speaks his tongue works like scissors and his expressions are very provoking. He put forward India's case on Kashmir very forcefully. However, I felt, when I was in the United Nations, that our sentiments could have been expressed in a better way. Can the facts not be narrated in a sugar-coated manner ? Is it necessary to say things which hurt the feelings of the people ? I have read somewhere that a good diplomat is one who puts his case in such a nice manner that if he wants to tell a person to go to hell he would say it in a way that the person would himself offer to go there. But in the case of the leader of our delegation, even if he asks somebody to go to heaven he would say it in such a rough manner that the person would never agree to go to heaven. This does not mean that Shri Krishna Menon should not lead the Indian delegation now and then. It is for the Government of India to decide as to who should lead the Indian delegation. But there is no dearth of persons in our country who can present India's policies nicely and in a more sophisticated manner which could be attractive. They can stick to their point, but can make it without hurting others. We need such a type of leader in the United Nations.

There are similar other small issues which require to be mentioned and I have indicated them in my amendments. Thank you.

Adjust Foreign Policy Needs to Our Security Requirements

Madam, Deputy Chairman, when we appeared on the international stage as a free country, the world was divided into two opposite blocks with a Cold War going on between them, and an arms race and it was being pulled towards another war. It was but natural and necessary for us to adopt a foreign policy of keeping aloof from both the power blocs. The first and foremost question before us was the economic and social reconstruction of the country for which we needed peace. We could not afford to commit the mistake of involving ourselves in the quarrels of other countries.

Non-alignment is Not Genuine

In spite of our claim of having a foreign policy of non-alignment and of judging each issue independently on its merits, we could not stick to it in the true sense. Instances of Tibet and Hungary are given in this connection and I may add a few more such examples. India has not established diplomatic relations with Israel so far, our effort is to have friendly relations with all the countries of the world. We have accepted this policy, and nobody can deny the existence of Israel. Why then do we not have diplomatic relations with Israel ? We do not have our ambassador in the capital of Israel and we are not prepared to give permission to the representative of Israel who is in Bombay to shift to New Delhi. I am amazed at the arguments that are advanced in support of this policy which makes our position ridiculous, and which lowers us in the eyes of the world. I would like to invite the attention of the Hon'ble Prime Minister to the observations made in the United Nations Organisation on July 20 by our permanent representative Shri B.N. Chakravarty. This is what he said while explaining why we did not have diplomatic relations with Israel, I quote his words :

> "Mainly because of our inability, there are a number of countries where we have not been able to send envoys, and there are other considerations such as the sentiments of our Muslim population in India which is a very big population—fifty millions—and they feel somewhat more sympathetic on religious grounds to the Palestine Arabs."

I think if this is the reason for adopting that policy, then this is a matter of very grave concern. Ours is a multilingual country, inhabited by people professing various faiths, and we have given them equal rights. But if the faith of a particular section of people becomes an obstacle in the formation

Rajya Sabha on September 2, 1963 during the discussion on the International situation

of our foreign policy, this would neither be in conformity with the secular nature of our policy, nor can it give a healthy content to the development of our foreign policy. Marshal Tito established diplomatic relations with Israel. Ghana and Nigeria established diplomatic relations with Israel. That did not adversely affect their friendship with the United Arab Republic. Burma and Nepal have established diplomatic relations with Israel. What kind of a fear is this which debars us from establishing diplomatic relations with Israel ? If we are afraid, we cannot follow a right policy. So far no explanation has been given about this matter.

Armaments are Neither Communist nor Captalist

The international situation has changed and it goes on changing. Should we not review our independent foreign policy according to the changed circumstances ? So far, need has not arisen to give up its basis and I hope that no such need would arise. But if such a need ever arises, then I would not be prepared to listen to it that we are ready to sacrifice even the interests of our country merely to protect our policy. A policy is for the country, the country is not for the policy. It is not imperative for us today to join the American bloc and nobody is making a demand for that also. We are getting military arms aid that we want. We are facing danger not only from China, but a good deal of danger from Pakistan as well. Therefore, we should be firm. From whatever source we may get arms, our policy would remain the same. Arms are neither capitalist nor communist. They do not belong to the East or the West. The arms belong to those who wield them. If those arms protect our border and safeguard our freedom, they are sacred for us. When the arms are stained red with the blood of the sons of the soil, they become holy and when they are soaked in the blood of the enemy, they become holier. The representatives of the Communist party are opposed to the acquisition of arms from the United States of America. But we have never opposed acquisition of arms from the Soviet Union and we need not also do so. However, we have to compare the utility of arms supplied by each side and to see of how much use they would be for us in the changed circumstances.

The Changing Global Power Balance

My submission is that the international situation is changing, the pace of cold war has slowed down, Moscow and Washington are coming closer to each other and the gap between Soviet Russia and China is widening. There is a wave of freedom among the countries which where slaves earlier, and since the formation of the United Nations, 55 new countries have attained freedom whose voice could be heard in the U.N. The suppressed and the oppressed nations are standing up. The Blacks in America are fighting for the right of equality and there is a wave of resentment against *apartheid* in the whole world.

France is getting out of the American bloc and showing signs of following an independent policy. Now there are not only two poles in the world, namely, Moscow and Washington, two new poles have come up as a result of the Sino-Indian war. One is at New Delhi and the other at Peking. New Delhi is attracting the nations towards it and Peking is also trying to do so.

In such a changed situation, we cannot repeat non-alignment as a mere *Mantra*. If adoption of non-alignment means that we should have a policy of friendship with all, that we should accept aid from wherever it comes, I would support such a policy. However, if non-alignment comes in our way of building military power, or tries to belittle the danger from China or becomes a weapon in the hands of our Communist friends in order to weaken India, then I would like the Prime Minister to reiterate those words which he had uttered in the wake of the Chinese invasion that so far as China is concerned we are not non-aligned. Whatever steps we may take in order to defeat China and to get back the Indian territory occupied by it, from whatever source we may acquire arms, whatever game we may play on the chessboard, would be right. That would be the proper policy and that policy cannot go against non-alignment.

The Government have entered into an agreement with great Britain and U.S.A. about Air exercises. The entire country has welcomed this agreement excepting some of our Communist friends. Our Communist friends say that we should not accept aid from Britain and America and that China would not attack until we start manufacturing those arms in our own country. I can understand their predicament to some extent. But howsoever close some of them might be to China, they cannot give such an assurance on behalf of China.

Politics of Military Aid

We want aid from Soviet Russia, but it is not forthcoming in the quantity we want. I would like to know from the Hon. Prime Minister if any new agreement has been entered into with Soviet Russia ? Are any negotiations going on ? Is the Soviet Union prepared to come forward to help us ? We have put up the MIG factory with the assistance of Soviet Russia. We had sent some pilots to Russia for training in flying the MIG aircraft. I am not disclosing any secret when I say that the pilots who have returned after training have not come back with a good experience. They were not allowed to take notes of the training which was imparted to them. They were given a copy book, the pages of which were numbered, on the day of training and in the evening it was taken back from them. When our pilots were on their way back home and they requested the Soviet authorities to return their notes, because they would need these notes in India, they were told that those notes would be delivered to them in Delhi. But they have not received those notes so far. These pilots had gone at the end of September and their training was due to start at that very time. The plan was that these pilots would demonstrate the flight of MIG Aircraft during the Republic Day Parade on January 26. However, due to Sino-Indian war in October, their training was stopped and it was resumed only after the ceasefire between India and China. In case there is another war with China, will the military aid from Russia not be suspended ? Could the Hon'ble Prime Minister assure the country and the

House that in case China attacks India again or any military action is taken in order to recover the Indian territory occupied by China, we would continue to get full support from Soviet Russia ? If he could make this announcement, then the support extended to the policy of non-alignment in the country would get further impetus. However, if an apprehension takes root in the minds of the people in this country that we have to depend solely on Western countries to fight China, then one should not be surprised if some chicken-hearted people start demanding that we should completely join the American bloc. The Prime Minister must not get angry with them, because if this demand has been raised, it is entirely due to our own weakness. It has been raised because we can not protect our borders. If the Government can demonstrate by taking some positive steps that we would be able to protect our borders, then the people of India would never give their consent to becoming a satellite of anybody else.

What is Our China Policy ?

What is our policy regarding China ? I was expecting that the Prime Minister would announce in his opening speech today that China has not accepted the Colombo Proposals and now these Colombo Proposals are no more valid; the facilities extended by us to China would not be available now. That the Chinese stay put in Ladakh and we start negotiating with them for an agreement, this position would not be allowed to continue any more. We had given in to some extent under the persuasion of Colombo Countries, but if China remains adamant, then we would withdraw our support to the Colombo Proposals. After all the Prime Minister has done the same thing in respect of Pakistan. When negotiations broke down, the Prime Minister stated that we withdraw the concessions earlier granted by us. I welcome this announcement although I would like to know what were those concessions ? You have withdrawn the concessions alright, but let it be known what those concessions were. I hope the Prime Minister would throw light on it. We have withdrawn those concessions it is all right, because we do not want to give another opportunity to Pakistan to demand fresh facilities on the basis of those that were granted earlier. However, what we are prepared to do with Pakistan, we are not prepared to do in the case of China. The Prime Minister has reiterated this morning the same five-point programme in his statement. My submission is that he had stated in Lok Sabha that if China does not accept the Colombo Proposals, Colombo Proposals fall to the ground. I am quoting from what he stated on February 25:

> "The Colombo Proposals fall to the ground if China does not accept them in toto."

Colombo Proposals

China did not accept the Colombo Proposals. Now how long would these proposals be binding on us ? China has not even accepted the suggestion made by the Prime Minister that this question may be referred to the International Court. China is not even prepared for mediation in this matter.

In any case the Prime Minister has not been in favour of mediation so far as the question of sovereignty is concerned. He had rejected the question of mediation. This is what he had stated on September 12, 1959 :

> "There can be no mediation, conciliation or arbitration about those demands of the Chinese about large chunks of territory. It is quite fantastic and absurd basing their demands on what happened in the past century."

However, he suddenly advanced a proposal for mediation. China did not accept it as well. Now we should withdraw from these proposals and tell the Colombo countries that we waited for their efforts to bear fruit, but they could not bring round China. We are no more bound by the Colombo Proposals.

After all, on the question of China, we should somewhere gain an initiative in our own hands. Would it always be that if there is a war it would be started by China, if there is a cease-fire China would take the initiative for it, if the forces are to be withdrawn, China would withdraw the forces ? Once again the initiative rests with China as to whether she should accept the Colombo Proposals or not, and we are waiting for her nod. She is accumulating her forces on the border and we are waiting for her next move. Will China always act and we would only react ? Will the initiative never come in our hands ? Can't we have military, diplomatic, political initiative in our own hands in this conflict ? India's statesmanship is on trial and if we go on repeating the same proposals which have been rejected by China, we would never be able to resolve this problem in conformity with our self-respect.

Will U.N. Membership Contain China ?

I would like to make one more point about China. We have been stressing that China should get a seat in the United Nations Organisation and for this an argument is advanced that if China becomes a member of the U.N.O., she could be influenced by the world opinion, she would act under the control of the United Nations Organisation. But the policy we are following in U.N.O. as well as outside it on the question of South Africa and Portugal belies this argument. We could not wean away South Africa from its policy of *apartheid* while she was a member of the U.N.O. and the influence, the power, the moral force of U.N.O. could not inspire South Africa to return to the path of equality of human beings. The U.N.O. could not make Portugal quit its colonies. Then how can we say that it is necessary to have China as a member of the U.N.O. and if she is admitted into it she would accept the decisions of the U.N.O. and would give up its aggressive designs ? I think we are still living in a dreamworld. If China would become a member of U.N.O. she would then also wield a Veto. China would get a worldwide platform to propagate against India.

Even now she is misleading the newly independent countries of Africa and Asia against us. Are we not creating another danger for ourselves by sponsoring China into the United Nations Organisation ? The Prime Minister says that we would stick to the right policy. But this policy is neither right for there is need to stick to it. At least we should not support the entry of China into U.N.O. If China becomes a member of the United Nations Organisation with the votes of other countries, then we will have to accept it as a bitter pill. But we should maintain at least this much self-respect as not to espouse the cause of a country which has committed aggression against us.

Cracks In Sino-Soviet Relations

Madam, differences are cropping up between Russia and China and these differences would be far-reaching and we cannot ignore them merely as superficial. However, we must not forget one thing that these differences are about the means, not about the aim, these are about the path and not about the destination. Both of them want to paint the entire world red. The difference is only about how the world should be painted red. We should not forget that if India per chance becomes a communist country, of which there is little possibility for we would not allow this to happen and would fight against it, but we cannot ignore this possibility, then the question would arise under whose influence should India be. There might be a difference of opinion between Russia and China at present, but they cannot differ with each other about India becoming a communist country. Obviously, so far as the question of meeting the aggression by China is concerned, we will have to depend upon democratic countries. This does not mean that if some countries want to remain neutral in the Sino-Indian conflict we should ask them to go to the Chinese side. That would not be wise. We should never commit such a mistake. But we cannot forget that the borders of India and China are adjacent. The other day the Home Minister had told the Lok Sabha that the House would be stunned if he disclosed the number of members of a particular party who are the supporters of China. Whatever foreign policy we may adopt it should secure and promote the interests of the nation. Today, the nation faces a danger from the armed forces of Communist China which are massed on our borders. There is no doubt that we are facing a danger from Pakistan too and we should also guard against it, but there are some Western countries who could control Pakistan at present while China is out of anybody's control. China is challenging its earlier leader, the Soviet Russia. It is not difficult to imagine what she would not do to destroy our democratic fibre.

Panchsheel No Shield Against Aggression

I am sorry to note that a debate is going on in the country as to whether the Chinese forces would attack India or not. Predictions are being made, the politicians in their speeches say both the things—may attack or even may not attack—in a single breath. My submission is that this debate is useless, because the attack has already taken place, the aggression continues, China has laid its foot on our chest and we feel humiliated and defeated. The debate should be on what we are going to do to recover our land from the Chinese clutches. The Prime Minister said that his policy is two-pronged : firstly, to resolve the problem peacefully, and secondly, to increase the military might of the country at the same time. My submission is whether there are any indications on the part of China of resolving the problem peacefully or we just go on mentioning peace as a matter of policy, but in our heart of hearts we feel that China is not amenable to peaceful means ? Who has convinced us, what are the indications which suggest that China is amenable to peace ? We should change our policy according to changed circumstances. Let us remember that at the time when we developed an independent foreign policy, we had no apprehensions about Chinese danger. It is necessary to make the country strong both militarily and economically in order to have a successful non-aligned foreign policy. But we have ignored the power aspect. We could have increased our military power even while remaining non-aligned with both the blocs. Indonesia and Egypt are following that path. But we thought that if war comes we would go to the battlefield wearing the armour of *Panchsheel* and the enemy will retreat seeing that armour. There is nothing wrong in the principle of *Panchsheel* and if my friends do not take it ill, I would say that India alone could give the principle of *Panchsheel* to the world.

PROF. MUKUT BEHARI LAL (Uttar Pradesh) : That was some thing new.

SHRI VAJPAYEE : There was nothing new in it. However we forgot that power is needed even for safeguarding peace, power is needed for successful operation of the policy of non-alignment too. The word " *Tatastha* " means neutral. Being neutral is like standing on the shore. Only a strong person can remain standing on the shore, not a weak one. Even plants that stand on the shore must have their rootes firmly placed deep into the earth drawing sustenance of life in order to survive the tumultous waves and protect their existence. Only then it can protect its borders and its honour. We did not match our foreign policy with measures of security and that is why our foreign policy failed and we could not also protect the country. We must make constant efforts to improve our defence capability, regain initiative in the diplomatic sphere and understand the actual import of the Chinese danger while remaining firm on the policy of non-alignment according to the changed circumstances. Thank you.

Friendship Not at Cost of Kashmir

Madam, as per convention, all subjects could be discussed while considering the Appropriation Bills. Taking advantage of this convention I would like to place some issues before the House for consideration.

There is almost unanimity in the country that the State of Jammu and Kashmir has become an integral part of India and no power on earth can separate it from us. But since the release of Sheikh Abdullah and the publication of his speeches in the newspapers views are being expressed that if we are prepared to reach an accord on Kashmir after putting aside the line adopted by us so far it may perhaps be possible to bring Sheikh Abdullah and his colleagues round and our relations with Pakistan would also improve.

PANDIT SHYAM SUNDER NARAYAN TANKHA (Uttar Pradesh) : No responsible person thinks so.

SHRI VAJPAYEE : In New Delhi, the rumour is afloat that when Sheikh Abdullah comes here for talks with the Prime Minister he would lay stress on the point that Government of India should accept the constitutional position as it existed in 1953, under which Jammu and Kashmir had become a part of the Indian Union only for three subjects. All other Indian princely States had joined the Indian Union under this very agreement. All of them gave up their separate entity. This applies to Jammu and Kashmir as well; but Sheikh Abdullah and his colleagues are not agreeable to it. It is said that if the Government of India is prepared to bend a little and accept the accession of Jammu and Kashmir only for three subjects an agreement could be reached. Although there is no reason for me to believe this rumour, looking to the way the Government of India is behaving at present, looking to its behaviour, it has become imperative to issue a warning. The people of India would not accept any agreement that may thwart the process of integration or reverse it or make any alteration in it, in the matter of integration of Jammu and Kashmir with India.

Jammu and Kashmir is not merely a piece of land for us; it is a symbol of certain ideals and principles. Sheikh Abdullah says that the country of Mahatma Gandhi should not try to keep Jammu and Kashmir with it by taking recourse to falsehood. I do not want to keep Jammu and Kashmir with India on the basis of falsehood. But is it not true that the Maharaja of Jammu and Kashmir, and later its people, had decided to accede to India ? Sheikh Abdullah can go back upon this decision, but the people of Jammu and Kashmir are committed to it. Furthermore, when Jammu and Kashmir has

Rajya Sabha on April 22, 1964 during discussion on the Appropriation Bill

become a part and parcel of India, its fate would be decided not only by the people of Jammu and Kashmir, but also by the people of the rest of India.

India Cannot be Divided Again

If supporters of an independent Dravidistan stand up tomorrow and say that the residents of so-called Tamilnadu do not want to remain in India and for this purpose a referendum should be held will we accept this anti-national demand of theirs ? Today a handful of armed Nagas are challenging the Government of India. We have decided not to bow before them. We cannot repeat the mistake of dividing India again. But if a wrong step is taken in regard to Jammu and Kashmir it would have an adverse reaction throughout the country. The forces of disintegration would get an opportunity, separatist demands will raise their ugly head and our resolve to build a united, invincible and impregnable India will come to naught. I want that the Government should fully acquaint itself with the feelings of the people on the question of Kashmir and firmly take steps necessary to bring Jammu and Kashmir on par with other States.

Abrogate Article 370

Article 370 of the Constitution should be abrogated. It is a temporary provision. But now an attempt is being made to put the clock back. An effort is being made to reverse the tide of time. Sheikh Abdullah may be a great man, I respect him, but he cannot be greater than Jammu and Kashmir and the rest of India.

The Prime Minister hails from Kashmir and the Prime Minister of Jammu and Kashmir also belongs to Kashmir. The former Prime Minister of that State was a Kashmiri too. Will the Kashmiris always create crises for us ? There are two Prime Ministers in this country and both of them belong to Kashmir. In other States there are Chief Ministers not Prime Ministers. The Bill brought in the Legislative Assembly of Kashmir to change the name of the Prime Minister and to designate Sadar-e-Riyasat as Governor has also been postponed. I want to know where has the prestige of New Delhi gone ? Madam, I wish to make the position of my party clear. When I think of Kashmir I always think of Dr. Shyama Prasad Mukherji and the circumstances in which he died. We would not allow the Government of India to enter into any such agreement about Kashmir and I hope the Government would not sign any agreement that would nullify all that we have done during the past sixteen years.

Sheikh Abdullah Indulging in Undignified Propaganda

I am sorry to say that Sheikh Abdullah, after his release from jail, has started indulging in talking in a way that we had never expected. He had promised to start on a new slate. He told those who had gone to see him that he had no bitterness in his heart, that he would like to start his life afresh. But whatever he has said after his release from jail is not a new start. He has again started harping on the issues that had been raised in 1953. Let him come to Delhi and have talks with the Prime Minister. But he should take care that we cannot even think of Kashmir's accession to Pakistan. Similarly, this House and the country cannot think of an independent Kashmir or establishment of special relations with Kashmir on the pattern of Sikkim or Bhutan.

It is said that if we want friendship with Pakistan Kashmir will have to be given to Pakistan. It is also said that friendship is valuable. We have no objection to establishing friendship with anybody any time. We want to have friendship with all, but friendship at what cost ?

SHRI N.M. ANWAR (Madras) : Who said Kashmir should be handed over to Pakistan ? You might have dreamt it. Let it remain a dream.

SHRI VAJPAYEE : It was not a dream. There are certain parties and individuals in the country who are saying such things. You also know it as well as we do.

SHRI SYED AHMED (Madhya Pradesh) : We do not know.

SHRI N.M. ANWAR : Even Sheikh Abdullah has not said this. He is talking about his independence.

SHRI VAJPAYEE : Whose independence ?

SHRI N.M. ANWAR : His own.

SHRI VAJPAYEE : What do you mean by his own ?

SHRI N.M. ANWAR : Ask him.

SHRI VAJPAYEE : Since you have said it, you must be knowing.

SHRI N.M. ANWAR : Who said Kashmir should be handed over to Pakistan ? No fool is saying this.

SHRI VAJPAYEE : Fools are not saying this, very intelligent men are saying this. Those people also who are under pressure from Britain and America are saying this.

SMT. ANEES KIDWAI (Uttar Pradesh) : Perhaps they whisper this into your ears.

SHRI VAJPAYEE : They are not whispering this into my ears, they are openly saying into my ears, they are openly saying this. You have to read between the lines, but....it is very good if they have not said so. If there is any misunderstanding in somebody's mind that....

SMT. ANIS KIDWAI : If you want this it is another matter.

SHRI VAJPAYEE : Leave aside what I want or do not want. It does not behove Congress members to interrupt like this. I did not even want Pakistan, you have made it. Had I been in power the country would not have been divided, the problem of lakhs of migrants from East Bengal would not have arisen, the question of Kashmir would not have come up. But those who swore by nationalism divided the country, caused bloodshed in the country, and partitioned the motherland. We did come to an agreement with the British in 1947, it was Congress leaders, with greed for power, who made that accord. They should not make the mistake of taunting us. We saved Kashmir, otherwise it would have gone in 1948. The tricolour would not have been flying there today, the Pakistani or American flag would have been there. When Bharatiya Jan Sangh launched an agitation for complete integration of

Kashmir with India we were dubbed communal. During that agitation Dr. Mukherji's life was sacrificed and that is how Kashmir was saved. Please do not try to incite me. The question of Kashmir is not a party question. My submission is that under the delusion of attaining friendship with Pakistan we should not take any steps which may further worsen the situation.

Our relations with Pakistan cannot improve unless the leaders of Pakistan change their mentality. Pakistan has been set up on the foundation of hatred for India and that Pakistan could subsist on this hatred alone. Once they change their mentality of hatred neither Kashmir, nor any other issue could stand in the way of friendship between our two countries. But if this hatred continues and we try to reach an accord by making some concessions fresh difficulties would arise. After all, what is the reason of infiltration of Pakistanis in such large numbers into Assam ? Suppose the problem of Kashmir is resolved, how will the question of deportation of Pakistanis from Assam be resolved ? How will the question of oppression of minorities in East Bengal be resolved ? If these questions are to be resolved let us not take them up piecemeal. Let us have a package deal.

Do not Look at the Questions Piecemeal

While talking to Pakistan at government level we have so far been committing the mistake of looking at every question piecemeal, be it the question of canal waters or the question of Pakistan's debt to us or the question of minorities in East Bengal. We have failed in making a package deal with Pakistan comprising all issues. Nor have we ever pressed them for such a deal. The result is that although we may solve a particular problem by paying a heavy price, new problems crop up in the meantime.

Madam, the happenings is East Pakistan have caused considerable disquiet in the country. It is regrettable that the government has so far failed to adopt any effective and firm policy. I am sorry to say that the facts are either being concealed from the House or are presented in a distorted manner. There are no two opinions that whatever might happen in East Pakistan, peace must prevail. All must live together.

SHRI SYED AHMAD : Thank you, thank you. I thought you were going to say something else.

SHRI VAJPAYEE : There is need to work together. But the government should also do its duty towards the minorities in East Pakistan. I was amazed to see that when in the other House a complaint was made that two girls who were coming to India by railway train were molested by a Pakistani driver, who is a railway employee. Smt Lakshmi Menon, who is fortunately present in the House, said these were exaggerated news reports and that no such incident took place. I want to ask her if it is not a fact that these girls were produced in court ? Is it not a fact that these two girls made statements in the court ? Is it not a fact that both the girls have confirmed their statements that the Pakistani Railway employee had raped them ? So this matter was taken to court. They made statements. Can the Ministry of External Affairs or the Government deny this ? Who is at fault ? Truth cannot be suppressed by putting a cover on the sins. I am surprised, why should Pakistani Railway employees enter Indian territory with the trains ? Where our border starts Indian Railway employees should take over and come with the trains. There is no need for Pakistan to bring trains into our country. There is deterioration in the situation, there is emotional upsurge, some people are also bent upon committing mischief...

Abduction of Girls from East Bengal

Madam, there is another issue connected with it on which the Ministry of External Affairs has adopted a wrong attitude. An allegation was made that some Hindu girls were abducted from East Bengal and sold in some countries of West Asia. Shri Dahyabhai Patel had also asked a similar question yesterday, in reply to which the Minister of External Affairs stated that the Government had this matter investigated by the Deputy High Commissioner and that no such complaint was received. But a statement by a renowned physician of Calcutta, Shri Arun Ganguly, was published in the newspapers the day before yesterday. He has mentioned a girl named Padma, who met him during his tour of West Asia and narrated the tragic tale of how she was abducted from East Pakistan and then sold to a Sheikh, who sold her to another Sheikh. A full statement of the renowned doctor of Calcutta, who has no connection with any party, has been published in the newspapers. I want to know how our Deputy High Commissioner, who is not allowed to visit the streets of Dhaka and cannot even find out about the atrocities being committed there, could ascertain that no girl was abducted or sold outside the country ?

SHRIMATI LAKSHMI N. MENON : Madam, the Hon'ble Member is making an allegation here. When *Sanmarg*, a Hindi paper of Bengal, published that about 1200 girls....

SHRI VAJPAYEE : It has appeared in all the papers.

SHRIMATI LAKSHMI N. MENON : It first appeared in *Sanmarg*. Evidently, the Hon'ble Member has some interest in this paper.

SHRI VAJPAYEE : No, I have no interest at all.

SHRI DHAYABHAI V. PATEL (Gujarat) : Even if he has, is that a crime ?

MADAM DEPUTY CHAIRPERSON : Interest or no interest, this thing appeared in the paper.

SHRI VAJPAYEE : Madam, I had no desire to raise so much controversy. If no contradiction is issued immediately about what appears in the newspapers it would aggravate misunderstanding and it will be difficult to maintain communal peace and harmony in the country. Moreover, if the Government should not exaggerate the danger it should also not commit the mistake of minimising it. If doubts are not removed immediately they persist in the minds of the people and lead them to believe that the Government wants to hide certain facts deliberately.

Original Issue Missing in Home Minister's Talks

In this controversy reference has also been made to the talks between the Home Ministers of India and Pakistan. These talks were proposed to consider the situation arising out of squeezing out of the minorities from East Bengal. But we were amazed to see that this issue was completely missing and the question of infiltration of Pakistanis into Assam, West Bengal and Tripura came to the fore. In fact the Government of India should have refused to discuss the question of those Pakistanis who had illegally intruded into India. There are two reasons for this. Firstly the meeting was not convened for this purpose and secondly, because it has ultimately to be decided by the Government of India as to who among those living in India are Indian citizens. This is our sovereign right and we are not prepared to hand over this right to anybody else. But the Government agreed to talk about it and Pakistan got us entangled into a wrong controversy. At first it was said that riots took place in East Pakistan because a hair of Hazarat Mohammed was stolen, which had its reaction there. Well, the Home Minister of Pakistan did not refer to the stealing of the hair and tried to justify the happenings in East Pakistan by referring to squeezing out of Pakistanis from Assam. It is claimed that the meeting of the Home Ministers of the two countries has not failed but has yielded very good results. I am still trying to understand what those good results are.

Nehru-Liaquat Pact Still Awaiting Implementation

During the meeting we should have stressed that Pakistan must fully implement the Nehru-Liaquat Pact. It has been laid down in the Pact that whosoever wanted to come should have freedom to do so, but the Home Minister of Pakistan went back on the Pact and said they would allow only' 'genuine refugees' to come and not anyone else. When he was asked at the Press conference who were genuine refugees, he said that if a gentleman lives in Karachi and his wife is in Delhi or vice-versa then we can allow them to come and go; but we cannot allow people to go in such large numbers from East Bengal. It means that Pakistan was not prepared to implement the Nehru-Liaquat Pact.

When Pakistan was not prepared to accept the old pact why are you going to sign a new pact ? What is the guarantee that Pakistan would honour the new one ? If you have the strength to get the Pact implemented why not have the Nehru-Liaquat Pact implemented ? Why is a new pact needed ? Our experience is that Pakistan has broken all agreements which we made with her and we become bound by the agreements unilaterally. We honestly observe those agreements and Pakistan violates them. Our position becomes difficult, while Pakistan is having the cake as well as eating it too. She puts us on a wrong track by entering into an agreement but acts as it likes, without honouring the agreement.

I am glad that the Home Minister refused to yield in any manner on the question of Pakistani infiltrators. I welcome his statement that all Pakistani infiltrators will have to go back from India. Indian citizens, irrespective of what religion they follow, could not be sent back from India against their will. It is not necessary for the Government to deport them. The people are also not demanding it.

There are only two demands being made in the country at present. One, those who want to migrate from East Bengal be allowed to do so safely. Pressure should be put on Pakistan to pay compensation for the property left behind by them. Secondly, those Pakistanis who have infiltrated into India, in whatever part of India they might be, should be deported from India. I hope the Government would not adopt a vacillating attitude on these issues.

Suspicious Activities of Pak Commissioner

But today the situation is that one Ministry of the Government of India pulls in one direction and another in a different direction. The Cabinet should follow the principle of collective responsibility. But it appears that the present Government is not working on this principle. The Home Minister went on a tour of Assam. On his return he made a statement to the effect that the office of the Deputy High Commissioner of Pakistan in Shillong was indulging in objectionable activities. This is the statement made by the Home Minister. This is not the statement of a member of the Opposition or a Member from Bengal or Assam. But the Ministry of External Affairs was not prepared to close down the office of the Pakistani Deputy High Commissioner at Shillong. Is this the way to act during an Emergency ? It cannot be that the Home Minister has made a wrong statement saying the office of the Pakistani Deputy High Commissioner was indulging in objectionable activities. If he was right why does the Ministry of External Affairs not take any action ?

Three central Ministers have spoken unambiguously about Kashmir. I want to congratulate them. But their tune is different from that of the Prime Minister. This is not a good situation for the country. If the Government cannot show the firmness and efficiency expected of it, it would be very difficult for it to take the boat of the nation to the shores of security and prosperity during this period of crisis.

Dialogue with China

Madam, I will say one more thing and close. For some time there has been talk about getting ready for a dialogue with China. The Prime Minister has stated that if the proposal, in which China in a letter written to the Prime Minister of Ceylon has suggested *suo motu* withdrawal from the seven posts in the Ladakh area, is directly received from China by New Delhi, it could be considered. It is not of much importance whether the seven posts should remain in Ladakh or not. The point for consideration should be the motive of China behind attacking India. Do we think that China has abandoned her objective and now wants to live peacefully with India, observing the principle of co-existence ? After all, what is our assessment of the situation ? What is our evaluation about China's intentions ?

I want to know—how did the Prime Minister, without taking permission from Parliament, without taking the country into confidence, give a commitment to the Prime Minister of Ceylon that Indian forces would not be sent at the moment to the MacMahon Line ?

SHRI G. RAMACHANDRAN : That has been denied.

SHRI A.D. MANI : But that is a one-sided denial.

SHRI G. RAMACHANDRAN : But it is the denial from our side.

SHRI VAJPAYEE : Even in the denial it has been admitted that the Prime Minister did say 'at the moment'. "At the moment we have no intention..." The Prime Minister has no business to give such a commitment to the Prime Minister of Ceylon.

During the discussion on the question of China in this House the Prime Minister had stated that no dialogue will be started with China until the Colombo Proposals are accepted in toto. It has been asked several times in the House why our army does not go upto the MacMahon Line. The Prime Minister's reply is that it was for the army generals to decide. When the Prime Minister has made a commitment to the Prime Minister of Ceylon, could our Chief of Staff send our army upto the MacMahon Line against the advice of the Prime Minister ? It is not for the generals to decide where the army should go and where it should not. This is for the Government to decide, for the civil authority to decide. But the civil authority, the Prime Minister, has bound himself with a commitment. It is surprising that we were not informed about it. The country was to fight a war, to achieve public support to win the war. The Prime Minister should apologise to the House that he made such a commitment to the Prime Minister of Ceylon while keeping us in the dark. Thank you.

Cracks Within the World Blocs

Madam, today when the House is considering the international situation, it is but natural that our thoughts go back to late Pandit Nehru, who was the architect of the foreign policy of free India. When he formulated independent India's foreign policy he laid stress that we should follow such a policy which may protect national interests as well as promote world peace while keeping ourselves aloof from both the power blocs. At that time the world was divided into two blocs which were engaged in a cold war and there was apprehension that the cold war might take the shape of a world war any moment. But there has been a perceptible change in the international situation during the last few years and we will have to recast our policy keeping that change in view.

Cracks are developing in these power blocs. Differences between the Soviet Union and Communist China have reached a flashpoint. In the Western bloc France appears to be treading a different path. Many countries in the world have attained freedom. A mighty wave has arisen against imperialism and colonialism. About 113-114 countries are now members of the United Nations Organisation and want to discharge their responsibility towards world peace.

Emergence of New Power Centres

There were two centres of power so far in the world, Washington and Moscow. Now some new centres are emerging, which are attracting attention of many countries. One of these centres is Peking. Another could be New Delhi, if we so desire. For this purpose there is no need to give up the policy of non- alignment. It has become clear from the way we are getting military and economic aid from America as well as the Soviet Union that we must firmly adhere to the policy of non-alignment. Those friends who advocate our joining the American bloc perhaps do not understand what they are saying. I have the *New York Times* of 13 September before me. I would like to read out a few lines of its editorial. While commenting on the military aid that is being given to us by America the paper says :

> "Now the obsolete cold war stereo-type no longer explains this kind of co-operation between capitalist United States, neutralist India and Communist Russia against the imperialist designs of Communist China".

But we will have to assess the danger from Communist China very seriously. Communist China wants to swallow the entire South-East Asia. Those who think that if we present Aksai Chin to Communist China on a

Rajya Sabha on September 22, 1964, during discussion on the motion regarding International Situation

platter we could win their friendship are living in a fools' paradise. They refuse to understand the intentions and ambitions of Peking. Peking wants its hegemony over South-East Asia. Moreover, the policies pursued by Peking have today become a source of danger for the whole world, including the Soviet Union. The leaders of Peking believe in the inevitability of war. They are dreaming of creating a great culture on the bedrock of destruction of culture by nuclear war. The danger of Communist China hovers not only on India, but also in all peace-loving countries of the world, including Soviet Russia and America.

I want that the government of India should take the initiative in organising a worldwide front against Peking including the Soviet Union, the U.S.A., and all peace-loving countries of the world. The aim of this front would not be to take any action against the Chinese people. It would not also be against communism. It is for the people of China to decide which political or economic system should prevail in their mainland. They could stick to their achievements in the economic sphere, if they so desire. This front should be against the policies pursued by Communist China today and not against the people there, nor against the system prevailing there. This front should not have before it the question of restoration of the old political and economic order on the mainland of China. It should be formed with the limited objective of liberating the people of China from the clutches of those leaders who do not believe in world peace, who want to throw the entire world into the turmoil of war in order to establish their hegemony over the world and achieve their ambitions.

How to Tame China

It is a difficult task, but I do not see any other way of stopping world war. I had an opportunity to tour South-East Asia recently and I found the dark shadows of Communist China cast upon the entire region. So far two policies have been pursued towards China. One was to boycott it, not to establish diplomatic relations with it, isolate it and then try to contain and control it by isolation. This policy was followed by the United States of America and many other countries of the world.

The other policy was to establish diplomatic relations with Communist China, bring her to the United Nations Organisation, make her a member of the Security Council and by treating her well try to persuade it to behave like other civilised nations of the world. New Delhi set the example in this regard. My submission is that both the experiences have come to naught. Communist China could not be contained. She has taken over North Korea, has established its hegemony over North Vietnam, and is creating trouble in Laos and South Vietnam. It has grabbed territories belonging to India, having occupied 14,500 sq. miles of our land. The objective of keeping Communist China under control and its containment has failed. The other policy of bringing round the Chinese leaders to follow the right path by advocating China's case has also failed. Now there is no way out except to formulate and follow a new policy. This policy would be to constitute a front of the countries of the world aimed at ousting the present leadership of China and trying to emancipate the people of China from the clutches of their present rulers.

Madam, for this purpose we have to examine the present situation prevailing in South-East Asia. South-East Asia is the storehouse of rice; rubber is grown in abundance here; it produces tin. And China is looking at this fertile region with an avaricious eye. About 15 million Chinese live in South-East Asia. The rulers of Peking want to utilise these people of Chinese origin also for fulfilling their expansionist designs. It is, therefore, necessary that so long as such a front of countries of the world is not constituted we should take it for granted that there is not one China but two Chinas—Communist China, and Nationalist China. One China has faith in the Charter of the United Nations Organisation, while the other one does not have any. Do we want that the Chinese living in South-East Asia should have their loyalties only for Peking ? Are we determined to see them lined up with the Communist Government of Peking ? If they are prepared to accept Chiang-Kai Sheik as their leader they should be encouraged to do so and should not be pushed into the lap of Peking. If the Chinese living in South-East Asia start working as agents of Peking a serious internal crisis would be created for the governments of this region. We should keep in mind the happenings in Malaysia. I do not say that we should establish diplomatic relations with the government of Taiwan, but I must say that we should not forget the fact that if we want to reduce the power of Peking we must be prepared to follow the policy of pulling out the thorn with the help of another thorn.

Sino-Pak Collusion

Madam, it is said that if we have to face the Chinese danger we must reach an agreement with our neighbour Pakistan. Nobody would like to fight on two fronts, but one cannot have friendship and goodwill just by wishing for it. When China attacked India if Pakistan had come to our succour by forgetting all past rancour an atmosphere would have been created in India which could have made the solution of any problem easier. But we are advised to have friendship with Pakistan in order to ward off the Chinese aggression. When Pakistan is in league with China the talk of friendship does not hold much substance.

I am sorry to say that neither the Prime Minister nor the Minister of External Affairs has so far unambiguously contradicted the misleading propaganda being carried out by the Sarvodaya leaders. It is not enough to say that we are not alarmed at the efforts that Shri Jayaprakash Narayan is making. You might not get alarmed, you might not be perturbed, but what are the effects that the visit of Shri Jayaprakash Narayan to Pakistan, his statements about Kashmir, the long rope given to Sheikh Abdullah are having on the people of Jammu and Kashmir ? What is its impact on world opinion ? Jammu and Kashmir is an integral part of India and the question of bartering it away for the friendship of Pakistan does not arise at all. In fact, we should tell the rulers of Pakistan to understand that if there is friendship between the two countries a solution to the Kashmir problem could also be found. I can give an example, but it should be taken only as an example. There was much bitterness over Saar between Germany and France. But when Germany and France became friends there was no difficulty in resolving the question of Saar.

Kashmir First or Friendship First ?

Kashmir first or friendship first ? That is the question. Let it be remembered that Kashmir is not a disease, but only the symptom of a disease; it is not a sickness, but only the manifestation of sickness. The disease is whether the rulers of Pakistan want to live in friendship with India. Could those individuals or parties who are stressing that we should come to an agreement with Pakistan on the question of Kashmir give a guarantee that if an agreement is reached on the question of Kashmir no fresh problems would arise between India and Pakistan ? After all, what is the relationship between the question of Kashmir and the situation in East Bengal ? Why does shooting take place on the cease-fire line ?

President Ayub Khan talks of friendship, but the exodus of minorities from East Pakistan continues unabated and the ceasefire line is being violated continuously. It does not show that Pakistan really wants friendship. If our relations could improve a solution to the Kashmir problem could also be found, which, while safeguarding our integrity, would be helpful in maintaining friendship. I would like the Minister of External Affairs to make a clear statement on this matter. Shri Jayaprakash and the Prime Minister have a very close relationship. They talk for hours. Therefore, it is not unnatural that some misunderstanding might be created among the people. No misunderstanding should be allowed to remain so far as the question of Kashmir is concerned.

Madam, Malaysia and Indonesia have also been mentioned during this debate. With both these countries we have friendly relations. But if a country sends armed soldiers into another country, violating its borders, and admits in the Security Council that it has done so, then in spite of our friendship we must condemn those aggressive actions of Indonesia. We should try our best to see that this conflagration does not grow. We should make efforts to resolve the conflict between the two countries by bringing them to talk across a table. But if a country's sovereignty is challenged, its borders are violated, force is used against it, then, in spite of being friends, we cannot keep quiet. When at the time of Communist China's aggression against us, a country which is friendly both towards China and India spoke against that aggression we can also not remain silent against aggression on Malaysia. Just as there is danger for Indonesia from the British base in Singapore Malaysia also has the right to allow another country to have a base in its territory. And if Malaysia has allowed a British base in her country that does not give another country the right to send its armed forces to its borders. There are several countries which are members of military alliances. East Pakistan has become the base of Western powers. Then should we send our troops there because this has endangered our security ? But if it is impressed upon the leaders of Indonesia that if they had friendly relations with Malaysia and the leaders of Malaysia were convinced that they had no danger from outside and their independence was secure, it could be easier to remove the British base from there. Now what Indonesia is doing would further strengthen the fears and doubts of Malaysian leaders and they would like to cling to the British base for their security.

Right Step by Swaran Singh

I have welcomed the appointment of Sardar Swaran Singh. Nobody should infer from this that there is a collusion between the Jan Sangh and the Congress. Dr. Ram Manohar Lohia has made this allegation and I was amazed to read it. An English daily of New Delhi has also written a similar story in its 'political diary'. We as an opposition party want to perform our duty in this House as well as outside it. Opposition does not mean opposition just for the sake of it. The person conducting our foreign policy should be one who has no tilt towards this bloc or that, whose heart is neither in Moscow nor in Washington–his heart should be in Delhi–and in whose mind the interest of India remains uppermost. Sardar Swaran Singh is such a person. We wish him success in his mission. He has taken the right step in visiting neighbouring countries. We have ignored these countries so far. We have been looking far and wide, but have overlooked countries that are nearest to us. However, what is the net result of the visits to these countries ? Is it not a fact that Sardar Sahib has retuned empty-handed from Burma ? Goodwill, no doubt, has increased, we don't deny that. But if we could find a reasonable solution to the existing problems between Burma and India and Ceylon and India, safeguarding at the same time Indian interests, only then would we consider his visit successful.

SHRI AKBAR ALI KHAN : It will take time.

SHRI VAJPAYEE : I welcome the improvement in our relations with Nepal. Communist China is increasingly exerting its pressure on Nepal. An officer of the team that had come from Communist China for road-building fled from there. The revelations made by him should be an eye-opener for all. The road-builders are actually soldiers in plain clothes. There are spies along with them and they want to build road in Nepal so that in future they may annex Nepal. I trust that Nepalese rulers would understand the increasing pressure from China. We do not want interference in the internal affairs of Nepal. But the question of our security is related to Nepal, Sikkim and Bhutan. If the pressure of Communist China increases on these countries we cannot sit silently.

How to Improve Publicity in Foreign Countries

Madam, one more point, and I shall finish. The Minister of External Affairs had mentioned how our publicity machinery in foreign countries could be improved. I want to make a concrete suggestion in this regard. Our embassies cannot properly handle our publicity work, they have their limitations. When

I was in Saigon the Associated Press distributed an article which was published by the newspapers there. It said India was looking for disturbances to take place in Bhutan so that it can send its forces there immediately. In that article India and China were placed in the same category. I want to read out one or two lines from it which are as follows :

> "A mutiny or serious revolt could create a political and military vacuum which both Communist China and India would be anxious to fill."

We have special relations with Bhutan. We are responsible to some extent for its foreign policy as well as its security. We cannot be placed on the same level as China. But when this article was published in the newspapers of Saigon I asked our representative there : What would you do about it ? He said nothing could be done. Could he not issue a contradiction to that article ? The French News Agency in Cambodia is guilty of circulating anti-India news there. It has tried to vitiate our relations with Cambodia and the Combodian Embassy has received several complaints against this Agency for presenting distorted facts and a distorted version of our viewpoint. This French News Agency has also connections with the P.T.I. It gets Rs.15,000 worth foreign exchange from the P.T.I. The Governments of Cambodia and Laos buy news from this Agency and do not accept news from any other source. How could we contradict ?

Pakistani Propaganda is Better

In Britain too, during the Commonwealth Prime Ministers' Conference, although our Minister of Information was present Pakistan won the battle of propaganda between India and Pakistan and India had to cut a sorry figure. Pakistan fired a propaganda salvo to the effect that the question of Kashmir was discussed in the Commonwealth conference, and our propaganda machinery came to know after three hours that wrong news had been published and it was no use contradicting it at that stage. I want to suggest that an Indian Information Service be organised on the pattern of the British Information Service or the United States Information Service, which may not be attached to the embassies, which may be free. Funds may be provided to it for requisitioning the services of journalists who may present a picture of India before the world independently of the embassies. Thank you.

What is Our Response to China's Atom Bomb ?

Madam, it would have been better if the Prime Minister were present during this debate. Criticism has been heard for some time past that officers of the Ministry of External Affairs were playing a major role in deciding the foreign policy of our country. Parliament is in session and there is no justification for going to Shantiniketan at this time. I could understand the trip to London, but the dates for Shantiniketan could have been so decided as to enable the Prime Minister to be present during this debate, so that he could listen to whatever Hon'ble members have to say about foreign policy. True, Sardar Swaran Singh is the Minister of External Affairs, but as head of Government the Prime Minister is ultimately responsible for our foreign policy and it would, therefore, have been helpful to him to get acquainted with various views in the matter.

We can discuss international situation and foreign policy in the context of our own country also. The aim of foreign policy is to safeguard and promote national interests, but it cannot be denied that today our interests are being adversely affected. There is already great danger from Communist China which has occupied a large chunk of our land. Now it has created a critical situation for us by exploding an atom bomb. It is being debated throughout the country whether we should manufacture an atom bomb or not. I want that this question should be discussed with an open mind. But certain arguments are being advanced for not manufacturing the atom bomb, which are ridiculous. It is argued that we are the adherents of non-violence, that we are the heirs of Gandhiji, so how could we manufacture an atom bomb ? A country which can keep a large army, which can spend Rs. 800 crores every year on its maintenance, which can ask for military aid from all countries of the world to equip that army, which can use that army for the liberation of Goa, and which is committed to use that army for recovering the land occupied by China, that country is not able to form its opinion in favour of or against manufacturing an atom bomb, and the slogan of non-violence or Mahatma Gandhi is being raised to evade the issue. Gandhiji was against all kinds of weapons. But we cannot ignore the world in which we live, the neighbours surrounding us and their evil intentions. China has not manufactured an atom bomb for keeping it in an exhibition. The Chinese leaders intend to use that bomb. A delegation of the French Parliament had recently met Chou En-Lai and the Government should read the report submitted by it after

---

Rajya Sabha on December 22, 1964 during discussion on the motion regarding International Situation

returning from China. Chou En-Lai told them that they were manufacturing the atom bomb to use it, and that they knew it would kill crores of people. Chou En-Lai then cited an example from history that there was a king in China during whose rule a war was fought in which four crores Chinese were killed. But, Chou En-Lai said, ultimately China came out victorious; so, what if four crores Chinese were killed ? Now they are 65 crores. It is thus evident that they are manufacturing the atom bomb to use it. They cannot use it against America, because America has got atom bombs. They are manufacturing the atom bomb to use it against us.

Answer to Atom Bomb is Atom Bomb

What is the answer to the atom bomb ? The answer to an atom bomb is an atom bomb, nothing else. Today the Soviet Union and America both have got atom bombs and, therefore, it is possible that an atomic war may not take place. But when America alone possessed the atom bomb and Japan did not have it, it was used against Japan. Had Japan too possessed an atom bomb at that time perhaps America would not have dared to drop one on Japan. The Allied nations as well as Germany had poisonous gases and hence they were not used by either party.

If China possesses an atom bomb, as a result of which it gains prestige and browbeats the smaller countries of South-East Asia, thereby disturbing the military balance, such a situation would not be good for us. We will have to examine this question on practical considerations. If the Government says there are difficulties in manufacturing the atom bomb because our economic condition is not good, because we have to develop our country and, therefore, we cannot utilise our resources for manufacturing an atom bomb, then I am prepared to think about these arguments. But do not talk of morality, non-violence and Gandhiji. The country must be saved. The Government must acquire the weapon that can save the country. I am not prepared to accept the logic that a small weapon is better than a big weapon. I want the government to seriously consider manufacturing the atom bomb. Although it is said that we can manufacture an atom bomb in 18 months, if we so desire, this government has not been able to do so many things during the last eighteen years, and I doubt if it could accomplish such a big job in eighteen months. I have doubts because our atomic establishments have failed to record at first the atomic explosion made by China. We could know only from foreign countries that China has detonated the bomb. Our Prime Minister had promised to find out why our atomic establishments failed to record the atomic explosion by China. But he has gone to Shantiniketan, leaving us behind to discuss war and peace. I want the Minister of External Affairs to throw some light on this situation. If we could not even find out when China exploded its atom bomb I very much doubt the government's claim that we can manufacture an atom bomb in eighteen month's time if we so desire.

Understand the Difference between France and China

My friend Shri Sapru is not present here. Whenever the question of the Chinese atom bomb is raised he mentions France. I want to tell him that the leaders of France do not believe in the inevitability of war as the Chinese leaders do. The French leaders do not dream of global domination as the Chinese leaders do. France has not attacked its neighbouring countries. But we were also against France manufacturing the atom bomb. If some communists and their fellow-travellers bring in the name of France in order to conceal the hazards and dangers from China's atom bomb they do no service to the country, they create confusion, they try to create a delusion which may be used for our deception, but is far from truth.

Madam, the question whether Communist China should be made a member of the United Nations Organisation or not has come up again. The Minister of External Affairs stated today that the Government will stick to its old stand. I would like to know how long will it continue to stick to its stand. News reports about the shifting Government stand have not come from the heavens. They have emanated from the Ministry of External Affairs. Can the Minister of External Affairs deny the fact that at one time what stand should be taken regarding the entry of China into the U.N. was being considered ? Did not the Ministry of External Affairs think about whether it should be by a two-thirds majority or a simple majority ? Were the published news reports baseless ? Why then were the decisions changed ? I do not believe that the Government should take shelter behind procedural wrangling. I am of the opinion that in today's circumstances we should not support the resolution for the entry of China in the UNO. Communist China has attacked us, it constitutes a danger to world peace, it has challenged humanity by manufacturing the atom bomb. Are we so naive as to think that there would be a complete metamorphosis of China if she becomes the member of the U.N. ? The Minister of External Affairs just now said that we want to discipline her.

SHRI C.D. PANDE (Uttar Pradesh) : We would bind her, bind her with a rope.

Intentions of Portugal have not Changed

SHRI VAJPAYEE : Let the United Nations Organisation first discipline Portugal and South Africa. Portugal is a member of the U.N.O., but it has not abandoned its policy of colonialism. South Africa is also a member of the United Nations Organisation. Resolutions have been passed against it and a demand was also made to boycott it. Even then it did not give up its policy of apartheid. If small countries like Portugal and South Africa did not change after becoming members of the United Nations Organisation could Communist China change ? We should not indulge in self-deception. If Communist China enters the U.N.O., becomes a member of the Security Council, receives the right of veto, gets the world forum to make propaganda against us, it will not be in the interest of India. Perhaps we may not be able to stop her from becoming a member of the United Nations Organisation. But we must have enough sense of shame in us not to plead the case of a country which has committed aggression against us. We should oppose its entry into U.N.O. Let us not take shelter behind the question of procedure.

My complaint against this Government is that though it wants to take the right step, it fights shy of it and hesitates. Had Shastriji been here I would have told him to be firm. It is not necessary to always follow in others' footsteps. Circumstances change and the changed circumstances demand a change in policy. Let Shastriji not think even for a moment that he is short-statured, that he is weak. He represents 45 crores people of India. Stature does not consist of one's height. One should speak with confidence and take unambiguous decisions on a question. That firmness is lacking. I wonder if the decision on Tibet has been changed. The Government has announced that it would support the question of violation of human rights that is being raised in the United Nations Organisation by other countries. I hope the Government stands by it. This is the only right decision which the new government has taken. I want to congratulate it on it. But congratulations would have been complete if we had taken a decision on the question of Communist China's entry in U.N.O. in conformity with our self-respect.

Soviet Policy towards India

Madam, our leaders as well as the Russian leaders go on repeating that there has been no change in the policy of the Soviet Union towards India. New Delhi may feel some satisfaction, but there are some straws in the wind that force us to think otherwise. When our President went on a visit to the Soviet Union—Smt. Lakshmi Menon also accompanied him—a public function was held in his honour in the grand Kremlin Palace. In the speech delivered on that occasion by the Russian President some countries with which we have friendly relations were criticised. Did it not amount to violation of diplomatic etiquette ? Our President was a guest of Russia. We have friendly relations with the Soviet Union and we want to strengthen them. But if in the presence of our President any foreign leader criticises countries with whom we have friendly relations that could not be acceptable. He criticised Malaysia and also said certain other objectionable things. No answer was given on our behalf. Had our President said that Communist China has committed aggression against India, that Communist China was guilty of committing a crime against humanity, perhaps a voice might have been raised against it and the Russian leaders also might not have liked it. We should draw the attention of the Soviet Union towards this violation of diplomatic etiquette.

Another violation was also committed. Comrade Khruschev has gone. This is an internal matter of the Soviet Union. Whom they bring forth and who is made to disappear is their own affair, we do not come into the picture at all. But when our President visited the Soviet Union a joint communique was issued by him and the Soviet President. There was a reference to

Comrade Khruschev in that communique. The booklet brought out by the Soviet Embassy in India about that visit contained the full text of the joint communique. But a few days back a new booklet has been issued. I have no objection against the publication of a new booklet, but I certainly object to the fact that the Soviet-Indian communique printed at the end is not the same that was signed by Dr. Radhakrishan. They could summarise the communique if they so desired, but they cannot put a caption on the communique in a manner that may create the wrong impression that the communique published in the new booklet was issued in Moscow. Was this done with the consent of the Government of India, and if not, will it be brought to the notice of the Soviet Union ?

There is yet another thing. Our Minister of External Affairs had also visited Moscow, as he mentioned in his speech. He held a Press conference there and we are told that he made certain observations, but Soviet magazines published only that material which suited them and did not print what he wanted to convey to them. In Russia newspapers do not have freedom as in India, and the Soviet Government cannot escape by saying that newspapers there have freedom to publish what they like. The news coverage of his Press conference was not adequate. Could some meaning not be read into it ?

Objectionable Article by Indian Leader in Russian Press

Recently an article by a communist leader of India was published in *Pravda* in which the Government of India has been criticised. Our opposition parties are free to criticise the Government, but it is objectionable that a Government paper of the Soviet Union should publish an article by an Indian criticising his own government. We want to have friendship with the Soviet Union, but that friendship does not mean that some parties and individuals should work in our own country at their behest and we should tolerate them. The two things are quite different. Our friendship with communist countries is one thing, but what our attitude towards the parties in our country should be is our internal matter. If there are any parties here that are being controlled by Peking or Moscow and, in spite of our knowledge that their loyalties lay outside the country and they are working here at their behest we do not take any action against them so as not to incur the displeasure of either Moscow or Peking, it is not the right thing as it could endanger the freedom and security of the nation.

The United Arab Republic maintains friendly relations with the Soviet Union, but they have declared the Communist Party illegal. Algeria too maintains relations with the Soviet Union, but the leaders of Algeria have not allowed free play to the communists due to this reason. I do not say that you should ban the Communist Party, but I do say that our relations with the communist countries and our attitude towards the communists inside the country are two separate things. The attention of the Soviet leaders should be drawn as to why any article by an Indian communist leader containing criticism of the Government of India was published in *Pravda*. They cannot escape by saying that it is a private newspaper since it is a Government paper. That is why I have raised this question, otherwise I would not have raised it.

China–Pakistan Collusion

The question of our relations with Pakistan is before us. It would not suffice to say that we had made a 'No-War Pact' offer but Pakistan did not accept it. Did not Pakistan create further problems for us ? Pakistan is colluding with China and the embassies of Pakistan, China and Indonesia in New Delhi are working hand in glove with each other and co-operating in creating an atmosphere against us. Recently some Pakistani spies were caught. The Second Secretary in the Pakistan High Commission was asked to quit India. On that day we could not get a reply, because the Minister of External Affairs was not present. Today all three are present. I would like to ask him why our Foreign Secretary agreed that the orders issued regarding the expulsion of the Second Secretary of the Pakistan High Commission from India would not be published for the next 24 hours. Was a similar assurance taken by our High Commissioner at Karachi from the Government of Pakistan ? This is not the first time that the Ministry of External Affairs has fallen in the trap laid by Pakistan. On the question of the Air Attache also the Government of India had shown lack of wisdom. Why should we give a chance to the world to place both Pakistan and India on the same level ? In propaganda too we have been left behind. Large-heartedness does not mean not protecting the interests of the country and not projecting a proper picture of our country in foreign countries. Stringent action should be taken against spies. Simultaneously, there is need to keep a strict watch on the employees of the embassies of Pakistan, China and Indonesia. If they work against our interests by taking undue advantage of our friendship necessary action should be taken against them.

There has been considerable discussion on how our propaganda machinery should work in foreign countries. I want to give an example of how our officers in the Ministry of External Affairs work. When our President visited Moscow some journalists accompanied him. A banquet was held in honour of the President where he made a speech. Mr. Mikoyan also spoke on the occasion. The Indian journalists requested the Press Attache of our Embassy to get a copy of the speech of our President. But he said it could not be made available that day; it could be had the next day. When they asked for it the next day they were told that they could be supplied a summary of the speech of President Mikoyan and so far as the speech of our President was concerned it had been published in *Pravda* and they could have it from there. But the Indian journalists were not familiar with the Russian language and they did not even want to have the speech of President Mikoyan. They needed the speech of the President of India, but the Press Attache did not take the trouble to make it available to be published in our papers. He did not even come to meet the journalists. I do not know who is our Press Attache there, but our Minister of External Affairs should investigate this matter. If such Press Attaches are sitting in Moscow, London and Washington how could they properly project our case before the world ?

What China is Going to Give ?

One more point and I have done. Shri Sudhir Ghosh is not present here at the moment. He made some good points, but in the case of certain other points he got derailed and said that an agreement could be reached with Communist China on the basis of 'give and take'. I want to know from him what China is going to give ?

AN HON'BLE MEMBER : The atom bomb.

SHRI VAJPAYEE : China can give the atom bomb, China can raze our prestige to the ground, China can offer insults, what else can we get from China ? What more do we want now from China ? Is not what we got from China enough ? There is no question of an agreement on this question. The sovereignty and integrity of India cannot be bargained. China is an aggressor. Let it first vacate Indian territory. If it has any claims regarding our border we are ready to discuss them and consider them. But the aggressor has changed the complexion of the quarrel by using force. It must first vacate our territory. Shri Sudhir Ghosh says if he is given the authority he can find a non-military, political solution. The Ministry of External Affairs should take his desire into consideration. He has made several rounds of Washington and Moscow.

AN HON'BLE MEMBER : He wants to go to Peking.

SHRI VAJPAYEE : If he wants to go to Peking he should have full freedom to do so, so that he could make the Chinese leaders understand. But it seems there are some members of this Parliament who fly in the air, who are not ready to walk on earth. We did not invite a war from China. War was thrust upon us. There is no proof that China wants friendship. If we talk of give and take at this juncture it would only mean that we are ready to surrender Indian land to China. Those who want us to come to an agreement with China by offering it Aksai-chin are not aware of the intentions of China. We wanted to have China's friendship by handing over Tibet to them but the consequences of this are before us today. History would not be allowed to repeat and the Government of India would not be allowed to bow before China. The earlier we understand the fact that we will have to confront China to safeguard our security and to protect democracy, the better it would be, for then we may build the required military power and develop our industries and make effective publicity in foreign countries. The Government in New Delhi should decide its foreign policy with determination and implement it with firmness. The Prime Minister goes about somewhat scared, somewhat hestitant and groping of something. This is not proper. He should formulate his foreign policy with the same self-confidence that he exhibits while speaking in the House, and implement it. That is the need of the hour, Thank you.

Do Not Tie Hands of Troops

Mr. Chairman, Sir, on 3rd May, when the House was declaring its resolve not to rest until the territory belonging to India was vacated by the aggressor, I had said that this country was never defeated on the battlefield, but always in the *Durbar* of Delhi. I am sorry that my warning appears to be coming true. On that day the Prime Minister had assured this House that until Pakistan agrees to *status quo ante* a cease-fire would not take effect. We were not satisfied even with that proposal. We said that so long as the troops of the aggressor remained on Indian soil we should not agree to a cease-fire. But by accepting the British proposals the Prime Minister has gone back on his words. Pakistan has not yet agreed to withdraw its forces, but we have issued orders to our troops not to take any action. Does it not amount to deceiving the country ? Does it not amount to throwing dust into the eyes of the House ? It is possible that we may not have accepted the cease-fire formally, because it would be announced from New Delhi and Karachi simultaneously. But does our order to the troops not to take any action until provoked by the Pakistani side not amount to a cease-fire ? Does it not amount to tying the hands of our troops ? On that day it was said that full freedom had been given to the army, that the army could strike not only in Kutch but also at any other suitable spots on the Indo-Pakistan border. The Government was considering giving that latitude. But now restrictions have been put on the army on the Kutch border and they have been asked not to take any action until Pakistan indulges in some new provocation. Is the presence of Pakistan in Kutch not sufficient provocation ?. Is the presence of the aggressor on Indian soil not sufficient ? What more provocation do we want ? I am sorry to say that this government is not fulfilling its promises given to the country. It is not in the interest of the country to make tall announcements, to rouse the sentiments of the people, to provoke them and then, as an anti-climax, enter into an agreement which would adversely affect the morale of the army.

In the case of Communist China we did not accept the cease-fire offer, China itself declared a cease-fire unilaterally and to date we are not a party to it. It is another matter that we have not tried to violate the cease-fire although we are not a party to it. But in the case of Pakistan we took one step backward and offered a cease-fire from our side. The Prime Minister could have waited until Pakistan was prepared to accept *status quo ante*. The cease-fire could take effect if Pakistan accepted it.

I want to ask the Congress members if yesterday's announcement was necessary. Already there is a cooling down of the war due to water-logging

Rajya Sabha on May 6, 1965 during discussion on the Appropriation Bill

of the area. Why then was such an announcement made ? Does it show statesmanship ? This is taking the country and the House too lightly and is so surprising.

The Prime Minister had stated on 3rd May that there was no territorial dispute regarding Kutch. We had welcomed the statement. But if we accept the British proposals, about which the government appears to be eager, what would be the result ? Pakistan would dig up the Sheikh-Swaran Singh Pact and raise a dispute over half of the Kutch region comprising 3,500 sq. miles, on which it has already laid its claim. Was the Prime Minister unaware of that Pact ? He should have known about it. Who were his advisors ? Has this not weakened India's position ? Accepting the British proposals has further weakened our position. We should have firmly said that unless Pakistan withdrew its army from our territory we will not accept a cease-fire.

Pakistan's Claim Unacceptable

The second point I want to make is that we cannot accept Pakistan's claim on 3,500 sq. miles. On the Sind-Kutch border 40-50 miles of the boundary has been demarcated and talks could be held with Pakistan regarding demarcation of the rest of the border. But these talks should not be held until Pakistan fully vacates the aggression committed by it. Pakistan is not only raising a border dispute, it is also demanding a large chunk of Indian territory. How could we refer this question of Pakistan's claim on 3,500 sq. miles for arbitration or mediation ? India's sovereignty cannot be a subject for mediation or arbitration. The circumstances under which the Hague Tribunal was set up do not apply to the case of the Sind-Kutch border. The question to be decided here as per the August 15, 1947 agreement, is where to demarcate the border. But now the circumstances have changed. We have been in that area since 1947. Pakistan has never been in possession of that area. And Pakistan is now demanding 3,500 sq. miles of land. The Prime Minister is not present here today, otherwise I would have reminded him. I restrained myself on that day, but today I will not accept any restrictions. Pakistan has its eyes beyond the 3,500 sq. miles. President Ayub had visited the United States of America about two or two and a half years ago. He held a Press conference there in which a map of Pakistan was distributed showing the entire Kutch area and half of the Saurashtra region as part of Pakistan. The proprietor of the daily *'Aaj'* published from Varanasi, was present at that Press conference. He brought that map with him and handed it over to Shastriji. Shri Lal Bahadur Shastri was our Home Minister at that time and it is said that he sent that map to the Ministry of External Affairs. Nobody knows what happened to that map thereafter.

SHRI ABDUL GHANI (Punjab) : God knows.

SHRI VAJPAYEE : If we agree to mediation or arbitration can we then stop Pakistan from extending its claim further ?

SHRI BHUPESH GUPTA (West Bengal) : Shall we have to approach some soothsayer for this ?

SHRI VAJPAYEE : Do we want to be caught in the net being spread by Pakistan with the help of Britain ? If Britain really wants to resolve the conflict between India and Pakistan and help both countries she should not insist on our accepting the cease-fire and asking our troops not to fire until Pakistani troops completely vacate the Indian territory. Pakistan has still not agreed to 'restore' the *status quo*. Reports coming from Karachi indicate that Pakistan would not accept that position. Pakistan attacked us, we are the victims of aggression, and even then we are being forced to accept insulting conditions while the aggressor sitting across the border is reluctant to accept even those conditions that are favourable to it. The British Prime Minister has failed to exert his influence on Pakistan. I want that this question be discussed openly in Parliament. If Pakistan does not agree to cease-fire in Kutch and does not withdraw its forces, then it is neither in our interest nor necessary for us to accept a cease-fire or an insulting agreement. For some time the area would be filled with water and a major battle could not take place there.

The Prime Minister is committed to dislodging the Pakistanis from there in five-six months. What is the hurry about accepting the British proposals ? Why were orders issued to our troops so hurriedly ? It appears that this government lacks the resolve which it expects from the people of this country. This is a very unfortunate moment for the country and if we do not remain steadfast at this unfortunate moment it would be difficult to maintain the morale of the people.

Prime Minister's Announcement

Mr. Chairman, Sir, the Prime Minister has announced that the country would rather starve than compromise its honour. He has also stated that if need be we would cut down some projects and step up the nation's defence preparedness. We want to ask the Finance Minister what changes are being effected in the Fourth Five Year Plan, which is being finalised, in view of defence requirements ? Due attention has not been paid to our security requirements while deciding our overall plan programme. I doubt if the Ministry of Finance or the Planning Commission has any concrete policy in the financial sector to implement the Prime Minister's anouncement. Emphasis should be laid on the development of industries that have a direct bearing on defence. Those works should be given priority which are essential for achieving economic self-sufficienty and the works that can be given up for the present may be left out. The Planning Commission and the Finance Ministry do not appear to be aware of the exigencies of the situation. I hope that while replying to the debate the Finance Minister would declare that if need be we would give up some project in view of the danger created by China and Pakistan and in keeping with the announcement made by the Prime Minister. He should tell us what changes are being contemplated in the financial sector strategy and the outline of the Fourth Five Year Plan. If we could not make an adjustment between our defence requirements and developmental needs we would neither have proper development nor could we perform our prime duty of safeguarding national security.

Language Controversy

Sir, unfortunately the country is involved in a language controversy. Whether the Official Language Act should be amended or not continues to be discussed. However, orders are still being issued by various ministries that are contrary to the status given to Hindi in the Constitution on January 26, 1965. The Director-General of P&T has issued an order on 29th March. I have its copy with me. I was surprised to read it. Instead of making an effort to promote Hindi gradually he has issued a *firman* that English would continue to be used for purposes for which it was being used before January 26, 1965. He did not even issue an order that Hindi would also be used along with English. After all the Official Language Act provides simultaneous use of both languages.

SHRI NAFISUL HASSAN (Uttar Pradesh) : Hindi should be included.

SHRI VAJPAYEE : Yes, Hindi should really precede English. But I do not want to say this, because I am considered to be a protagonist of Hindi and nowadays it has become a curse to be pro-Hindi. It is considered a sin. Have we committed any crime because our mother tongue is Hindi ? Today one can plead the case of all languages except Hindi. Where is Satya Narayan Singhji ? He is considered to be a great champion of Hindi and is considered a scholar of Tulsi literature. His opponents even accuse him of being a devotee of Hindi, a Hindi enthusiast. Being a Hindi enthusiast is considered to be a great crime. But I want to ask how was this order issued that only English will continue ? This is wrong. This order is against the Constitution, against the Official Language Act, against the decision of Parliament. It puts the clock back. How can we allow it ?

The Home Ministry is also guilty. They have also issued an order. It says the Centre should use Hindi with the Hindi-speaking States. It does not say that Hindi should also be used along with English with the non-Hindi speaking States. Why ? If after 1956 the Centre has become bilingual for some time under the Official Language Act what is the justification for corresponding in English alone ? If Hindi is to be brought in sometime later and not at once preparations for that will have to be made from today. This direction of the Home Ministry goes against the Constitution. What is the need to provide for progressive use in the case of Hindi-speaking States ? Correspondence with the Hindi-speaking States in Hindi should start immediately. There should be no hurdle in it. But it appears that the Home Ministry is also wavering. Many allegations were made against Nandaji and some of our friends even went to the extent of saying that the subject of official language should be withdrawn from Shri Gulzari Lal Nanda and the Prime Minister should himself take it over. Is it out of this fear that Nandaji has distanced himself from the decision that has been taken by the government and confirmed by Parliament ?

Controversy about Urdu

Mr. Chairman, I shall finish within two minutes. In the controversy on languages a controversy about Urdu is also going on. Urdu was born in India, it is an Indian language, we want it to flourish. But whether Urdu should become the State language or not is a separate question with which I shall not deal at present. I want to know a small thing. Some conveners of the Urdu Convention which was held some three-four days ago in Delhi are sitting in the House. I want to ask them what connection this Urdu Convention had with Pakistan. If it did not have any connection with Pakistan how did the Deputy High Commissioner of Pakistan attend this convention ?

SMT. ANIS KIDWAI (Uttar Pradesh) : He might have come to listen to Urdu poetry, not to attend the Convention.

SHRI VAJPAYEE : That is wrong. He did not come to listen to Urdu poetry. The Deputy High Commissioner attended the Convention, we had seen him sitting there. He was present there.

SMT. ANIS KIDWAI : That is wrong.

SHRI VAJPAYEE : Mr. Chairman, you can deny what I am saying, but it has been published in all newspapers. People who had seen him with their own eyes said this. You cannot dub *Patriot* as anti-Urdu.

SHRI M.R. SHERWANI (Uttar Pradesh) : If the King of Nepal could attend the session of the Hindu Mahasabha as chief guest does it become objectionable if somebody comes to listen to Urdu poetry ?

SHRI VAJPAYEE : Mr. Chairman, he came to attend the convention, not to listen to Urdu poetry. The poetry session was attended by the Press Attache of the Pakistan High Commission.

SMT. ANIS KIDWAI : Nepal was also invited.

SHRI M.R. SHERWANI : You are saying that you object to it.

SHRI VAJPAYEE : Yes, I do object to it. I am objecting to it, because with Nepal our relations are not inimical. Nepal has not attacked India. Nepal is not defiling the prestige of India. Pakistan is acting like an enemy. Moreover this was a question of Urdu, not of Muslims. Why should Pakistan interfere in the question of Urdu ?

SMT. ANIS KIDWAI : He did not come to interfere.

SHRI VAJPAYEE : Then why did he come ? Why was he invited ?

SMT. ANIS KIDWAI : He must have come to see the *tamasha*.

SHRI VAJPAYEE : He was invited.

SMT. ANIS KIDWAI : Look, what you are saying is absolutely wrong.

SHRI M.R. SHERWANI : Mr. Chairman, in this very conference the Pakistani attack was censured.

SHRI VAJPAYEE : I want to refer to that too. I know what happened there, I have my own sources too. When the resolution to condemn the Pakistani attack was brought forth it was not an open session, not an open meeting, those who were present there opposed it, in the beginning, it was opposed. A Maulvi of Urdu Bazar said Pakistan has not committed aggression, it is India that has committed aggression.

SMT. ANIS KIDWAI : Absolutely wrong.

SHRI VAJPAYEE : I say let the Central Intelligence Department find out the truth. The resolution was passed when Mir Mustaq Ahmed and Shri Jamna Das Akhtar threatened to walk out if it was not passed.

It was not proper for the Deputy High Commissioner to attend the Convention. Please do not spoil the case of Urdu. It was not proper to invite the Deputy High Commissioner of Pakistan and to give him a V.I.P. treatment was still worse.

SHRI M.R. SHERWANI : The symposium on Urdu poetry was open.

SMT. ANIS KIDWAI : No invitation cards were sent to anybody.

SHRI VAJPAYEE : Mr. Chairman, my allegation is not against the Urdu Poetry Symposium. My allegation is against the convention. Let the government deny that the Deputy High Commissioner of Pakistan attended it. Our friend Shri Sherwani says he did attend and if the Nepalese King could attend a function why not the Pakistani High Commissioner ? We wish we could place Nepal and Pakistan in the same category. We want to maintain similar relations of brotherhood with Pakistan. But when the situation on the border is deteriorating and Pakistani elements are indulging in activities like removing railway lines and are bent upon killing our Jawans, the presence of the Deputy High Commissioner of Pakistan in any convention might create misunderstanding. Please do not spoil the case of Urdu. Thank you.

India Becoming A Second Rate Power

Mr. Chairman, Sir, the aim of foreign policy is the protection and promotion of the nation's vital interests. These interests are permanent. But foreign policy, which is the instrument of protecting these interests according to the changing circumstances in the world should be flexible. I have not the least hesitation in saying that our policy has not been able to protect our wider interests.

After independence we have four times been the victim of aggression. Both our neighbours succeeded in annexing large chunks of our territory. On the sacred occasion of the late Pandit Nehru's birthday the previous Parliament whose successor this House is, had taken the pledge after the Chinese aggression that this country and the House would not rest till the land occupied by the aggressor is liberated from its clutches. Today nobody even talks about that pledge. There seems to be no plan to recover the land lost by us. We must admit that we have failed to make our foreign policy an instrument of building a strong India, protecting our borders and shaping India into a centre of power in the world.

Mr. Chairman, world peace, *Panchsheel*, co-existence, international brotherhood are all noble sentiments. We have a very close relationship with them. But these high-sounding attractive words cannot be a substitute for a well-considered foreign policy. The world of today is not what we would like it to be. And we will have to keep the world as it is today in view while framing our foreign policy.

We arrived at an agreement with Communist China on *Panchsheel*, Communist China stabbed us in the back. We tried to develop friendly relations with Pakistan, but in return Pakistan attacked India. Today, U.S.A. and Communist China are coming closer to each other. This is an unprecedented development. It is proof of the changing situation of the world. When we framed our foreign policy China was not in the picture. A cold war was going on between the Soviet Union and U.S.A. We did not want to involve ourselves in that cold war. Our policy of non-alignment with any bloc was correct to that extent. But when the situation in the world changed, and not two but several centres of power emerged—France separated itself, Peking became a centre of attention—the cold war between the Soviet Union and the United States ended as both came closer. Even then we did not bring flexibility to our foreign policy, we made no changes. We continued to recite the *mantra* of non-alignment. If non-alignment means that India will follow an inde-

Lok Sabha on July 19, 1971 during discussion on the demands for grants of the Ministry of External Affairs pendent foreign policy nobody would have any quarrel with it. But if nonalignment means we go on aligning ourselves with one country or the other in turn—previously we were with America, now we are with Russia and are reduced to a second rate, low grade power—then this policy of nonalignment could neither protect our national interests nor could achieve the objectives of foreign policy.

Failure to Win Friends

Mr. Chairman, the case of Bangladesh has again proved that during the past 23 years we have failed to muster friends. Today we find ourselves totally bereft of friends. Displaced persons are coming in large numbers to India to take refuge here. The Government was not prepared to admit it. With great difficulty they have admitted that the number would cross 30 lakhs. Now the Rehabilitation Minister says that their number may be higher. Famine conditions are prevailing there. Pakistan Government can neither supply them food nor would like us to do so. Lakhs of displaced persons are expected to reach India. The issue of East Bengal is not only a matter concerning democracy, the future of democracy in India has also become interlinked with East Bengal.

I do not blame other countries of the world. Perhaps they are protecting their own interests. We kept our friendship with the Arab countries even at the cost of displeasing Israel, for whose birth the Soviet Union was equally responsible with America. We supported the Arab countries. Today they are keeping quiet. Their silence is more vocal than their speech. It is possible that they might be having their own difficulties. They are not coming forward to help us. They are not even prepared to condemn the holocaust in East Bengal.

The Soviet Union is our friend. We are grateful to it for the support it extended to us on the question of Kashmir in UN. But the Soviet Union too has been doing things in its own interest which we do not like and which could not be justified on the ground of propriety. For example, the supply of arms to Pakistan. Can the Soviet leaders or any one of their supporters inside or outside this House say from the heart of his heart that arms supplied by Soviet Union to Pakistan are not being used in Bangladesh ? They are being used there, although Soviet leaders had supplied arms to Pakistan on the ground that Pakistan may not fall in the trap of China. And the United States was supplying arms to Pakistan on the ground that Pakistan may not fall into the clutches of the Soviet Union. And we are the victims of this situation.

Their Own Interests

Every country looks to its own interest. Do we also have any self-interest or not ? The Soviet Union, the champion of democracy, sent its troops to Czeckoslovakia. Nobody in the world raised a little finger against it.

America is doing in Vietnam whatever it likes. Nobody is doing anything about it except condemning it. If we had tried to acquire more power after independence and made our foreign policy an instrument for strengthening our industrial, military and social base, if we had awakened among the 50 crore people of India the spirit that India had either to live as a great nation or will be finished into some corner of the world as a third-rate power, this situation would not have arisen today. Shri Amrit Nahata is not present in the House at the moment. He said that the fact that China possesses an atom bomb or that China has a very large population was of no consequence. Then what is of consequence ? I want to read out an extract from the statement of the Press Secretary of President Nixon :

> "It was China's possession of nuclear power and her huge population which made Mr. Nixon anxious to improve relations with that country."

SHRI S.M. BANERJEE : That is to say we should increase our population.

SHRI VAJPAYEE : Well, you are already increasing it without my saying so.....

Mr. Chairman, China cannot be ignored. One wishes it could also be said about India that a country with 50 crores population full of natural resources, placed in a geographically important position cannot be ignored by anybody. But Moscow ignores us whenever it so desires. The attitude of Washington towards Pakistan is no more a secret. China has committed aggression against us. Where do we stand on the world map ? Where has our foreign policy brought us ? Could we still call it a successful foreign policy ?

What Kind of Foreign Policy ?

Mr. Chairman, it is essential that India should follow an independent foreign policy, but it should be flexible, not rigid. India's foreign policy should be realistic not hypothetical. Our eyes were opened when Communist China committed aggression against us in 1962. We then gathered strength and also slightly showed it in 1965. But Shri Lal Bahadur Shastri passed away and the country again fell into a state of inertia.

Today we are not in a position to take any effective action in regard to Bangladesh. I am tired of listening to the statements of the Minister of External Affairs that recognition will be granted when the time comes. When will that time come ? Is that time to come or is it lapsing ? After all leaders of Bangladesh know whether granting of recognition would benefit them or not. But our government is a greater well-wisher than the leaders of Bangladesh themselves. We say granting of recognition to Bangladesh will not be in the interest of Bangladesh. I vividly remember that Pandit Nehru used to say the same things about Tibet. When we said in the House that the case of Tibet should be raised in the United Nations and an effort made to liberate Tibet, Pandit Nehru said that raising the Tibetan issue was not in the interest of Tibetans. I have with me a statement of Dr. Mazr-ul-Islam, a close associate of Sheikh Mujibur Rehman. I would like to read it out :

> "He urged India to recognise Bangladesh soon. Lack of *de jure* recognition was hampering the efforts of the freedom-fighters to obtain arms from abroad."

He made one more observation. Let me read it out also :

> "He welcomed the proposed campaign of the Jan Sangh for recognition of Bangladesh."

This is not a certificate (*Interruptions*).

Why Delay on Decision about Bangladesh ?

Mr. Chairman, we will have to stand on our own feet on the issue of Bangladesh. Nobody says we should fight a war with Pakistan, and send our troops to Bangladesh. But it is our duty to extend all assistance to the Bangladesh government after granting it recognition. Not only for the sake of protection of democracy, but in order to protect our own interests also it is an imperative requirement of our national interest that recognition is granted to the Government of Bangladesh. It is essential in our national interest that Pakistan breaks up and disintegrates, and the process that has begun should be strengthened by us. The refugees are not going to other countries of the world, and therefore other countries do not bother about what is happening in Bangladesh. They are trying to make their own moves on the chessboard. I was amazed to listen to the speech of our Marxist Communist leader just now who said that everybody has improved relations with China, but we have not. Has China committed aggression against any one else except us ? Of course, it is also trifling with the Soviet Union.

SHRI S.M. BANERJEE : It has attacked Tibet.

SHRI VAJPAYEE : Tibet is our companion. When we talk of aggression against us, it includes Tibet as well. But China has not attacked America, it has also not committed aggression against Britain. We are the only victims of China. We tried to have friendly relations with other countries. When Mao Tse-tung smiled New Delhi also started looking a little happy, but later all hopes were dashed. If China is prepared to return our territory, if it keeps the sanctity of our borders like a civilised country, if it respects our sovereignty, relations with China could be improved and if India could play a role in the meeting that is going to take place between President Nixon and the leaders of Communist China it could try to make the meeting somewhat broadbased. Recently some American senators have said that President Nixon should also pay a visit to the Soviet Union. It is necessary to remove the impression that one angle of the triangle consisting of China, Pakistan and the United States of America would be pointed at our chest and the other at Soviet Russia.

SHRI S.M. BANERJEE : It would be a grand alliance.

SHRI VAJPAYEE : If this triumvirate works in the wider interest of world peace and China is brought on the right path making it abandon its theory of inevitability of war I can understand it. But if China wants friendship, it would have to give proof of it. I am not one of those who think that a meeting between Nixon and Mao Tse-tung would solve all problems. This is not going to happen. The problems are difficult and complicated. We can try to open the door to resolve them, a window could be opened. But one thing is clear that this triumvirate could become a cause of worry for us and the solution to this is not to go and sit in the lap of Soviet Russia.

China Ahead of Us on Several Fronts

There is only one solution. We should stand firm on our feet, become self-reliant and decide to make the atom bomb. We became independent in 1947. Twenty-four years have passed since then. In China the revolution took place in 1949, *i.e.* two years after our independence. Still Communist China has reached a stage where everybody seeks friendship with it. We will have to seriously think what is wrong with our policies, why cannot we become a focal point in the world. Today even a small neighbouring country like Pakistan appears to be outmanoeuvring us (*Interruptions*). It has surely befooled us. I want that we should review our foreign policy in the context of the changing world. We should ensure that our foreign policy maintains flexibility with the changing world situation. We should also examine whether our foreign policy has helped us to make friends.

Leave aside the big nations, we have not been able to maintain friendly relations even with neighbouring countries. The Government of Burma expelled the P.T.I. special correspondent after giving him nine hours' notice. He was the only Indian correspondent in Rangoon. He was called to the immigration office at 2 p.m. and asked to leave the country alongwith his wife by 2 a.m. Then, he was not allowed to meet his wife, he was not allowed to go home. Does any friendly country treat the correspondent of another country like this ? I do not know what the Minister of External Affairs did in this matter. I do not know whether this matter was taken up or not. We are being meted out such treatment in Burma.

We are not having as strong a relationship with Nepal as we should. My friend Hiren Mukherjee was just now talking about Ceylon. We extended help to Ceylon, but Ceylon did not stop Pakistani troops from going to Bangladesh.

Foreign Policy Made Us Friendless

Who is with us ? Who is our friend ? Our foreign policy has made us friendless. This foreign policy has failed in protecting our national interest. It should be reviewed. We are not so small that we should join any bloc. But we should proceed on the assumption that at the time of any conflict we will need friends. These friendships will not be formed on principles, but on the basis of self-interest.

It is time we came out of a world of make-believe and determined our foreign policy after assessing whose interests are tied with ours and whose interests clash. Then alone could the objectives of our foreign policy be achieved, not otherwise. Thank you.

Asian Security Pact Not So Innocuous

Mr. Chairman, Sir, the aim of foreign policy of a country is to protect and promote its vital national interests. There is scope for ideals, principles and intentions but it is formulated and conducted on the basis of reality. It cannot be framed on the basis of idealism alone. A country seeks peace if it is in its national interest but if its national interests so require it takes to war also. Our policy has been to have friendly relations with all countries. We have not allowed ideology to come in the way. Ours is a democratic country and Nepal is a monarchy, but we want to strengthen our relations with Nepal. We are a secular nation while Islam is Malaysia's state religion, but this does not come in the way of our relations with Malaysia. Our political and economic system is different from that of Soviet Russia and other countries of Eastern Europe, yet we have established cordial relations with them keeping in view our self-interest and are trying to further strengthen those relations.

Mr. Chairman, I was amazed to hear the following words from our Prime Minister. I quote :

> "We do not make our policy according to who did or did not support whom, but on certain principles."

Principles do have their importance in the international sphere, but foreign policy cannot be decided unilaterally. Is it not a fact that since the change of the U.S. attitude to India our tone has also become harsher in condemning American action in Vietnam ?

SHRI DINSEH SINGH : That is right.

SHRI VAJPAYEE : Right or wrong, I am not discussing that, but whatever is happening in Vietnam is not a new development. However, our tone in condemning it was not so sharp, whatever the reasons. It has happened now and therefore the reasons are also clear. If Washington stands up against us openly we will also have to criticise its policies strongly.

Where is Reciprocity ?

In this very context I want to say that in the light of the policy adopted by Arab countries on the question of Bangladesh and the wrong manner in which our cooperation with the liberation struggle there is viewed by them we should review our policy towards the Arab countries too. It is natural to have a desire to maintain friendly relations with them, but in the international sphere reciprocity is of the essence. If Arab countries could be friendly to both

Lok Sabha on April 25, 1972 during discussion on the demands for grants of the Ministry of External Affairs

Pakistan and us at the same time there is no reason why we should not make efforts to establish diplomatic relations with Israel while maintaining friendly relations with them. This does not mean we should overlook the aggression committed by Israel. An aggressor would not be allowed to enjoy the fruits of its aggression. We will apply this in the case of Israel too, but our relations with Israel could still be improved while keeping our demand intact. India can at least play the role of a mediator or peace-maker in the Middle East.

So far we have been discussing international affairs. Efforts are going to be made from tomorrow to woo Pakistan. A large Indian delegation has left for Pakistan today. What work has been assigned to it ? If we could believe President Bhutto the delegation would only prepare an agenda for the summit. Was it necessary to send such a high-powered delegation for this purpose ? I have a complaint—all reports relating to the summit talks have emanated from Pakistan, not from New Delhi. What do we want to achieve in these talks ? Is there no need to take Parliament and the country into confidence ? (*Interruptions*).

President Bhutto wanted to start the summit right away, but we thought it fit to have talks first at the official level. But what do we want to achieve in these talks ? This has not been explained clearly so far. If friends of Pakistan learn some lesson from the formation of Bangladesh and the defeat of Pakistan, and if foreign powers stop using Pakistan as a tool in their hands peace could be established permanently in this region. India and Pakistan could bind themselves in the bond of permanent friendship and brotherhood. But Pakistan has been used by certain foreign powers since its inception as a tool to contain India. I do not see any possibility that those powers would give an opportunity to Pakistan to initiate a new chapter of friendship. Pakistan is dependent upon America and China for economic and military aid. President Bhutto would like to have the support of the army to have full power in his hands. General Tikka Khan has taken over the command of the armed forces. Pakistan is not prepared to get out of those treaties that have instigated it to attack India four times as a result of supplies of arms to it.

Jeddah Conference

The conference of Foreign Ministers of Muslim countries held recently at Jeddah would also result in diverting Pakistan from following the right path. The message sent to the U.S. Congress by President Nixon and the joint communique issued after President Nixon's visit to Peking strengthen the apprehension that China and the U.S. would not persuade Pakistan to normalise its relations with India. I am afraid America wants to enter Bangladesh in a big way. Peking would try to incite disturbances in Kashmir against us. We may extend our hand of friendship, but we should be cautious. We should desire peace, but if that desire is not fulfilled we should not be caught napping.

Mr. Chairman, I was surprised to see the speech of the Minister of External Affairs delivered by him on December 21, 1971 in the United Nations, which is printed in the report of the Ministry. I would like the Ministry of External

Affairs to explain the position. It is likely to create misunderstanding. Our Marxist friend Shri Dashrath Deb has quoted the speech and advocated that the Kashmir issue should be settled by making some adjustments in the cease-fire line. I would like to bring before you what the Hon'ble Minister said :

> "There is thus need to avoid the repetition of such incidents by making some adjustments in the cease-fire line in order to make it more stable, rational and viable. This we propose to discuss and settle with Pakistan."

Pak-Occupied Territory to be Presented on a Platter ?

I know that it was said in some other context. But today, when a dialogue is going on between India and Pakistan and when even during this dialogue President Bhutto has only one aim, namely, to get his prisoners of war released, the observation of the Minister of External Affairs could be used against India. Does this not amount to saying that India was prepared to present Pakistan-occupied Kashmir on a platter to President Bhutto ? The other day the Minister of External Affairs said entire Jammu and Kashmir was an integral part of India, and this is true constitutionally as well as legally. We have kept 25 seats vacant for the people of Pakistan-occupied Kashmir in the Jammu and Kashmir Legislative Assembly.

I think we should not talk of entering into an agreement with some adjustments on the cease-fire line. This would amount to betraying the integrity of India. This would amount to allowing the aggressor to have the fruits of aggression. Pakistan is an aggressor in Kashmir and that aggression should be vacated. India should get the entire State of Jammu and Kashmir. There is need to announce this in unambiguous terms.

I agree with the viewpoint of the Government that the question of release of prisoners of war cannot be separated from other questions. Pakistan is receiving arms from China and the United States of America. There are also reports of fresh recruitment. President Bhutto has declared his intention of making his army the best fighting machine in Asia. If he does not adopt a reasonable and practical attitude towards other questions we cannot allow him to achieve his objective of getting the prisoners of war released and create danger to us by equipping his armed forces with weapons received from foreign countries. True, Pakistan is not in a position to become a source of great danger to us single-handed. But the intentions of its foreign friends are also not clear. We have to frame our policy keeping in view their intentions.

New Balance of Power in Asia

With the formation of independent Bangladesh and the emergence of India as a power a change has been brought about in Asia, a new balance of power has been established. Some foreign powers do not like it. We have to see to it that we do not try to ensure the security of this region by depending on some foreign power. Sufficient misunderstanding has been created. It is said that comrade Brezhnev had initiated the Asian Security Pact. I have just now heard a Congress friend that it was initiated by our Prime Minister in 1968 while she was on a tour of Japan, Indonesia and other countries. Where the suggestions of Comrade Brezhnev's Asian Security Pact and Prime Minister Smt. Indira Gandhi's treaty or agreement of cooperation among the countries of Asia coincide and where they differ from each other should be clarified. That Asian countries should feel secure, that they could defend their integrity, that they could be saved from the influence of foreign powers are any good objectives in themselves. But when such a proposal comes from Moscow it creates suspicion. The statement of the Minister of External Affairs is also self-contradictory. On return from his Moscow trip he stated that there was no such proposal before him. But it has appeared in the *New Times* published from Moscow, and the following words have been put in the mouth of our Minister of External Affairs :

> "The idea of an Asian Security Pact had not yet assumed concrete shape, but as a proposition its objective was good."

What is the objective of the Asian Security Pact which has emanated from Moscow ? Which countries are to be included in it ? Will it take the form of a defence treaty ? If any outside power would endanger the security of Asian countries will any other foreign power intervene ? I want that the position regarding this controversy should be clarified.

Recently a conference of some of our ambassadors was held in New Delhi. The conference was held with much pomp and show.

SHRI SWARAN SINGH : There was no pomp and show.

SHRI VAJPAYEE : The Ministry of External Affairs is setting a new precedent. The manner in which the decisions of the ambassadors were publicised this time is unprecedented. It appears that this time they have been assigned some job.

SHRI SWARAN SINGH : It was a business gathering. Further, even now nothing has been published.

SHRI VAJPAYEE : They have been asked to contact the governments in their respective capitals and to mobilise public opinion there on the Prime Minister's plan for the security of Asian countries, which includes, on the one hand, the Brezhnev doctrine and, on the other, the Indira doctrine. This is what has appeared in newspapers, unless the Ministry of External Affairs contradicts it : "India will support a move towards guaranteeing the sovereignty, independence and territorial integrity of the countries of the region through an international convention and agreement."

AN HON'BLE MEMBER : What is objectionable ?

SHRI SHASHI BHUSHAN : It is against the Atal Bihari doctrine.

SHRI VAJPAYEE : I am seeking a clarification. Who would give the guarantee ? Against whom this guarantee is ?

SHRI SWARAN SINGH : Something has appeared in your party's paper about it. Please read that.

SHRI VAJPAYEE : My submission is that the Minister of External Affairs may please keep it in safe custody till his reply to the discussion. This is not an issue relating to our party or his party. The country wants to know what is the origin of the Asian Security Pact ? Which countries will be included in it ? What will be the form of this agreement ? These aspects should be explained by taking us into confidence. So far these things have not been made clear.

The Indian Ocean

For the past some time, I should say for some years, the Indian Ocean has become a naval base of big powers. The American fleet is there, the Soviet fleet is there, the Chinese are also active there and France too is sending its ships to the Indian Ocean. But where is Hind (India) in this ? *Hind Mahasagar* (Indian Ocean) ?

SHRI SHASHI BHUSHAN : Is it *Hindu Mahasagar* or *Hind Mahasagar* ? (Hindu Ocean or Indian Ocean).

SHRI HUKUM CHAND KACHCHVAI : You may have the intelligence to know.... (*Interruptions*).

SHRI VAJPAYEE : When these two intelligent persons speak I can't follow anything.

Our friend Shri Shashi Bhushan was speaking just now. He was praising the officers of the Ministry of External Affairs. There is no convention of praising officers in the House. Officers are neither criticised in the House nor given testimonials. Whatever has to be said is addressed to the Minister of External Affairs. One has to make observations in the name of the Ministry of External Affairs. But, Mr. Chairman, after the elections an atmosphere has been created in which only praises are showered. We can't understand how this maintains the dignity of the House. This is not the way. Had Shri Shashi Bhushan not interrupted me I would perhaps not have said all this. Where is India in the Indian Ocean ? The littoral states of the Indian Ocean are also nowhere in the picture. A resolution was passed in the United Nations Organisation with the efforts made by Ceylon. India was also a party to it. It was stated in that resolution that the Indian Ocean will be a zone of peace. No big power was prepared to act on this resolution. What did we do to get that resolution implemented ? Can New Delhi not take the initiative in this matter ? Could not all the big powers be asked to quit the Indian Ocean and to let it remain a zone of peace ? May I know what objection New Delhi has to calling a conference of all the littoral states of the Indian Ocean ? If this conference cannot be called formally at least an atmosphere should be created in the capitals of all these countries by having informal contacts so that the Indian Ocean could really become a zone of peace.

Our Ignorant Ambassadors

I want to say one more thing. A renowned Hindi writer Shri Sachchidanand Hiranand Vatsyayan was on a foreign visit. He met our Ambassador there. The Ambassador organised a function in his honour and while introducing him said that he was Mr. Vatsyayan, who had written the *Kamasutra*. No doubt the *Kamasutra* was written by Vatsyayan. But Vatsyayan, the writer of *Kamasutra*, is no more with us. It appears that the

Ambassador is so busy that he could not distinguish between Vatsyayan, the writer of *Kamasutra*, and the present-day Vatsyayan.

Our ambassadors must have some knowledge of our culture, traditions and literature. I am not talking of all ambassadors. But there is a need to start some process of training in the Ministry of External Affairs so that Indian ambassadors could become true representatives of the nation abroad. They should also have a modern outlook. I would like to relate an episode in this regard also.

I was on a visit to a European country. A function was organised in our Embassy there. The weather was very cold outside, but inside the Embassy lime water was being served to the guests. Has the Ministry of External Affairs issued instructions to the Embassies that only lime water should be served to guests even during snowfall ? No foreign guest would visit our embassies in such circumstances to participate in the programmes.

SHRI BHAGWAT JHA AZAD : They must have done so for fear of you.

SHRI VAJPAYEE : It was at my instance that serving of lime water was discontinued and some wine was served. My friend Shri Bhandare was with me.

SHRI R.D. BHANDARE (Bombay Central) : But not in drinking.

SHRI VAJPAYEE : There should be prohibition in the country, I have no objection. But in foreign countries in order to make the Indian embassies a place of meeting of various shades of people, for their participation in our functions, there should be some modernism. Our efficiency lies in having a good synthesis of ancient tradition and modernism. Thank you.

Limitations in Pursuing Non-Aligned Policy

Mr. Chairman, Sir, when we ponder over Indian policies in relation to the international events that took place last year mixed feelings of satisfaction and disappointment cross the mind. Satisfaction, because we enhanced the country's prestige by contributing to the great war of liberation of Bangladesh. Disappointment, because we have been unable to keep up that prestige.

I would like to quote from the report of the External Affairs Ministry which says :

> "India feels that if lasting peace is to be established in the sub-continent Pakistan should accept the reality of the new situation and recognise Bangladesh as an independent, sovereign country. This would help in resolving the issue of the return of war prisoners who had surrendered before the joint command of India and Bangladesh".

Surrender or Initiative

It is clear that when this report was prepared the Government's stand was that Pakistan should first recognise Bangladesh and then only would India negotiate about the release of war prisoners. But our Foreign Minister has now taken a new 'initiative', which in fact is a new surrender. There is the talk of a package deal now. During the Indo-Pak war period also the question of a package deal was raised. Before the Summit Conference at Simla it was emphasized that all issues would be solved together and India will not fall into Pakistan's trap of solving them in parts. But at the summit we entered into an agreement which could not be called a package deal. It was a piecemeal agreement, because several issues were left undecided. And again there is talk of a package deal on the issue of prisoners of war.

I want to know what would happen to the question of recognition of Bangladesh. True, it is a human problem; but is it a human problem for us only and not for Pakistan ? At Simla Pakistan took back its territory, but we could not take from Pakistan the territory of Kashmir. So much so, we did not insist even on retaining the Chhamb area. We could well have said that we would vacate that area only if they were prepared to leave the chicken-neck. But we were trapped into the mirage of peace and compromised to the advantage of Pakistan. And now Pakistan is going to take back the prisoners of war. I am afraid Pakistan will not stick to this

Lok Sabha on April 23, 1973 during discussion on the demands for grants of the Ministry of External Affairs

package deal also. They are already asking for clarifications; Mr. Bhutto's statement is creating doubts. We should decline to have bilateral talks with Pakistan on this issue. Pakistan wants bilateral talks to the exclusion of Bangladesh as a party. Pakistan will never like our friendly relations with Bangladesh to be strengthened.

Pak Threat Exists

We had arrived at the Simla Agreement with the hope of a lasting peace. But the Government spokesman is now giving the warning that the danger from Pakistan is not yet over. Its intentions are not good. It is accumulating arms and increasing its expenditure on defence. Our assessment of Mr. Bhutto should not be based on what our friend Mr. Mody says about him. Mr. Bhutto may be a friend of Mr. Mody. But he is also the President of Pakistan. We must not commit the mistake of mixing personal friendship with national interest. So long as Mr. Bhutto does not decide to extricate Pakistan from the clutches of China and USA and encourage interference of world powers in this region our desire for a permanent peace cannot materialise. For this Pakistan will have to make a basic change in its thinking, but there are no indications of such a change. On the other hand, indications are that Iran is not being groomed to emerge as a strategic power in this region, so that Pakistan is able to wield influence on our territorial waters and help the Americans to play their game. The assurance that is being asked for from USA that their arms would not reach Pakistan *via* Iran is meaningless. What has been the value of the assurance the U.S.A had given us that their arms will not be used against India ? There is no substance in the American assurance about what Iran will or will not do. I am afraid Pakistan will increasingly associate itself with the powers of West Asia, its relations with Iran will grow closer and then it will try to influence the entire region. In this situation its policy of keeping alive tensions with India may prove advantageous to it.

Some of our friends have expressed the opinion that since Pakistan has not adopted a democratic system we should try to help it strengthen democracy. I had the occasion to meet some Pakistani journalists who had recently come here and they were also talking in the same vein. I asked them, and I want to ask those of my friends here who swear by democracy, should we interfere in the internal affairs of Pakistan ? Whether they have or do not have democracy in Pakistan is their internal affair. We should not be under the illusion that Pakistan will not adopt an anti-Indian attitude merely because there was democracy there. If Pakistan's interpretation of its interests is that maintaining tensions with India is to its advantage conflict between the two countries will continue irrespective of the form of government there. It will not be in our interest to give some new concessions, or to give in to the Pakistanis' demand in the name of democracy.

Great Powers are Averse to Strong India

Mr. Chairman, the report says that we do not basically have any conflict with the U.S.A., and whatever conflicts appear are a result of the policies pursued by the United States and India in respect of the third countries. I agree with this analysis to an extent. But there is another side to it also. Do the great powers really want India to emerge as a big power ?

Our land-mass, our man-power, our natural resources, our strategic position provide us an opportunity as well as a challenge to emerge as an independent centre of power. Soviet Russia, the U.S.A., China, West Europe and Japan are five emerging centres of power. India must also count among them. Our power should never be to terrorise our neighbours, but to help them. From times immemorial our mission has been to punish the wicked and protect the good. India should carry on this mission in future also. It should be the national objective of our foreign policy to emerge as a centre of power. America does not like it. It is also doubtful whether Soviet Russia wholly supports it.

Sir, we have friendly relations with Soviet Russia. They have helped us in times of need. We are bound by a treaty. That treaty also lays down that Soviet Russia would not interfere in our internal affairs. But their interference in our internal affairs is continuing. The latest example is the 50th anniversary of the birth of the Soviet Union, which was celebrated from 19 to 22 December at Moscow. It was an official function to which India was also invited. India was represented by our Vice-President and the Minister of External Affairs. The declarations of Indo-Soviet friendship made on that occasion cannot be a matter of controversy for anybody. But to seat Shri Dange, the Chairman of the Communist Party of India, next to the Vice-President and to have him deliver a speech amounts to indirectly putting at par the Communist Party of India with the Government of India.

Interference in Domestic Affairs

The speech delivered by Shri Dange on that occasion was even more objectionable. Referring to the United Front Government in Kerala he wanted the Soviet Government to assist India in setting up a Government at the Centre on the model of Kerala. Is that not an open invitation to Soviet Russia to interfere in the internal affairs of India ? Has not the Soviet Government disregarded the Government of India by equating the Vice-President of India with the Chairman of the Communist Party of India ? Let them maintain their relations with the Indian Communist Party and let the Communist Party follow Moscow's dictates. But I would like to ask, what would have happened if a similar situation had arisen in the United States of America ? If the Indian Vice-President and a leader of an Indian party were seated on the same forum and the leader was made to say that America should assist us in setting up a coalition Government of democratic forces what would have been the reaction of the self-respecting people of India ? We would never have tolerated such interference from America, and we must not tolerate this interference from Soviet Russia too. But the Foreign Minister says that he had no objection and that this was an expression of our love for democracy; this is an exposition of our weakness in the international arena and the pitiable situation in which we find ourselves.

Mr. Chairman, in the present context talking of non-alignment is meaningless. A country that has reached a stage of dependence on imports of foodgrains from America and arsenic is being imported with that foodgrain, a country that meets its defence requirements from the Soviet Union cannot follow a truly independent foreign policy. We must recognise our limitations and try to build up the country's industrial and defence power by following a foreign policy within these limitations. Only an industrially developed and militarily self-sufficient India can pursue a truly independent foreign policy.

Commonwealth Membership

Mr. Chairman, India continues to be a member of the Commonwealth. Even earlier the Commonwealth did not have much utility, and whatever of it there was came to an end with the formation of the European Common Market. Now there is no reason for us to remain in the British Commonwealth. We should quit it.

Reconsider Our West-Asia Policy

We should also reconsider our policy towards the Arab countries. Our friendship with the Arabs cannot be one-sided. We have been crying hoarse that Israel should vacate occupied Arab territory. But no Arab country has said that Pakistan-occupied part of Kashmir or China-occupied Aksai Chin should be liberated. Our policy should be based on the principle of mutual co-operation. If the Arab countries can be friends of India and Pakistan, and India and China at the same time, why cannot we also be friends of Arabs and Israel at the same time ? We have given recognition to Israel, but have not established diplomatic relations with it. I fail to understand this. We must not discriminate with any country in setting up diplomatic ties. We should forge diplomatic ties with both the Koreas. As with North Vietnam, let us also have ties with South Vietnam as well as with Israel. There should be no difficulty in establishing diplomatic relations with a country that exists on the map of the world and where an effective Government is in control of it.

Sir, Sikkim has also been mentioned during the debate. Many of our members belonging to the Marxist Communist Party are not present here at the moment. For China they have a soft corner, but about Sikkim they say that India made a blunder in sending her army there. Under the relations that we have with Sikkim we were bound to send our army on its request. We have only discharged our responsibility by sending the army. There can be no question of our having any expansionist ambitions in Sikkim. When our Marxist friends speak of Sikkim's independence it sounds as though we are keeping Sikkim a slave. Their speeches can be used against us by China. It is for Sikkim to decide what kind of relations it wants to have with India. We do not want to impose anything on Sikkim. But one thing is clear : Sikkim cannot remain untouched by the rising wave of democracy. We would be happy if conditions were created in Sikkim whereby it adopted the course of a constitutional set-up.

Reference was made in the House to the Prime Minister's speech in the One Asia Conference. The speech she made was good. I know there was nothing in her mind about racial discrimination. But can anybody deny the fact that America dropped an atom bomb only on Japan ? It could not have dared to do so on any European country. Only Asia was to be used as a laboratory for testing such destructive weapons. Either the Prime Minister should not have said anything of this sort in the One Asia Conference, or, if she said it, she should have stood by it with courage.

I want to submit again that we are under pressure from the U.S. as well as Russia and still we claim to follow a policy of non-alignment. We will have to remould our foreign policy into a more elastic, more practical one that takes care of protecting and promoting our national interests. Today our foreign policy sometimes gets dull, sometimes inelastic, and that is why we could not retain the prestige that we had earned last year in the world. If we are able to protect our national interests and promote world peace through necessary changes in the conduct of our foreign policy, then alone will it be successful. In the present context it cannot be called a success. Thank you.

Foreign Policy of the Janata Government

Mr. Chairman, Sir, in the last 20 years I have often had to participate in foreign policy debates. But it is for the first time that I shall have the salutary experience to be at the receiving end of the volleys of criticism. This is an indication that times have changed and the people of India have put the responsibility of running the government on the shoulders of those who were thus far called reactionaries, and have given the responsibility of constructive opposition to those who considered themselves indispensable.

First of all I would like to express my gratitude to all my predecessors—from Pandit Jawaharlal Nehru to Shri Yashwantrao Chavan each one of whom has in his own way contributed to the framing and implementation of foreign policy. Pandit Nehru was, of course, the great architect of our international relations. I feel it my duty to express my gratitude to all of them.

Truly speaking, whether one is in the opposition or in the government, the question of foreign policy naturally connects us to the promotion and protection of national interests which, detached from the play of domestic politics or the cut and thrust of parliamentary debates, provides a quality of permanence to foreign policy, which is not static but dynamic and which does not go unconcerned of the given situation but takes it into account.

I hope, with the confidence which comes from the support of the people and the sensitivity to the broad national consensus in our international attitudes which we all share, I will be able to earn the support from all sides of the House in the discharge of my present responsibilities to guide our foreign policy.

The recent Lok Sabha elections were mainly contested on domestic issues. Foreign policy was not a question in debates. The Janata Party had said that in the international field it will pursue a genuinely non-aligned policy. One can very well ask why is Janata Party so emphatic about genuine non-alignment ? My humble submission is that India should not only remain non-aligned but must also appear to be so. If anything that we say or do gives rise to the feeling that we have leaned towards a particular bloc and have surrendered our sovereign right of judging issues on their merit it will be a deviation from the straight but difficult path of non-alignment. The Janata Government would never allow this to happen.

Lok Sabha on June 29, 1977 initiating discussion on the demands for grants of the Ministry of External Affairs

Non-Alignment : An Ideological Crusade

Non-alignment is not the policy of an individual or a party. It is based on national consensus. After freeing itself of the clutches of imperialism a great country like India could not possibly become a camp-follower of some great power. This would have been a negation of the ideals of our struggle for independence and also against our national self-respect. The policy of non-alignment is, in fact, a logical and essential extension of national independence in the field of international affairs. What has happened during the past three decades has, undoubtedly, proved the relevance of the policy of non-alignment in the context of the contemporary international scene.

Non-alignment is no longer a lonely cry for peace in a global battle-ground of armed camps convinced that they were embarked on an ideological crusade which they thought would overwhelm or contain their adversaries. Now the voice of non-alignment has become the trumpet of more than half the total membership of the international community. As the House is aware, the new Government did not hesitate for a moment to confirm the meeting of the Non-aligned Bureau, even though it was scheduled to be held within a fortnight after we assumed office. The Bureau meeting provided us with an occasion to assure the Non-aligned fraternity that India remained committed to independence of judgement and to political attitudes and the economic programmes which had been chalked out at the last summit meeting in Colombo.

We reaffirm this old tenet of policy because non-alignment recognises that in today's nuclear world war or its inevitability must be ruled out. We cherish our national independence but reject the need to consign national defence to a committed or dependent military or ideological arrangement. Non-alignment frees a nation from the pressures to borrow foreign models or adopt other ideologies which may be alien to a nation's civilisation or its ethos.

Co-existence : The Only Alternative

Today all ideologies are getting domesticated and every country's development strategy has a character of its own. Non-alignment gives freedom of flexibility and yet enables a country to join with like-minded nations who face similar economic and political odds. As it happens today, all major powers, including those who belong to military alliance systems, accept that there is no alternative for the international community but to accept the logic of peaceful co-existence. Most nations, and non-aligned are in their forefront, go further and believe that international peace can only be secured through positive cooperation across ideological, political and military frontiers. We cannot but commend the declaration of the President of the United States that anti-communism will not be the test or drive of America's policies, and we are likewise convinced that the Soviet Union is deeply committed to the search for international detente and the easing of tensions amongst nations.

With the world accepting that peace and interdependence demand international cooperation India is well placed to pursue a policy of simultaneously safeguarding its own interests and supporting the enlightened goals of international social justice.

I must, however, be quick to add that whatever success we may achieve or the weight of influence which we may carry in international affairs will not merely be through a rational foreign policy but will depend on our internal cohesion and the pace of our economic progress. This House reflects the strength and sagacity of our people. This ancient land draws vitality from its rich civilisation, its tradition of tolerance, its vast wealth of resources, its people who have the mental capacity to master science and a physical capacity for hard work and inner discipline.

Our other great asset is that India has never lived by hate; we have no history of conquest or expansionism. We have always tried to win the heart and not the body. Our culture gives us no ground for a sense of inferiority or dependence.

Mutual Benefit

As a nation we can be self-confident enough to clasp the hand of friendship everywhere and welcome cooperation which is based on dignity and can be judged on the touchstone of national and mutual benefit. Today we are in a better position to give shape to our own willingness to cooperate, wherever there is proof of beneficial complementarity, with nations who have a like-minded approach to international stability. It is in this spirit that we will continue to participate with the United Nations, the Non-aligned, the Group of 77 and the developing nations. It is in this spirit of mutual benefit entirely of a benign nature that we have and will seek to forge bilateral links with other nations regardless of their ideologies, level of development or their political system.

Since we assumed office we have, with this background and approach, held high-level conversations with the Kings of Nepal and Bhutan and the Soviet Foreign Minister, the Foreign Minister of the Federal Republic of Germany, with several Ministers who attended the conference on International Economic Cooperation in Paris, and more recently with the Shahenshah of Iran, with the Prime Minister and Foreign Secretary of UK, other Heads of Government and Ministers at the Commonwealth Conference in London. It was gratifying to find that the rationale of our policies was never questioned. In fact we can claim that not only have we been able to bring credibility to the continuity of old policies, we have discovered a positive desire to seek closer friendship with India. The world, I believe, has confidence in India. Enlightened nations everywhere have given us the assurances of their goodwill towards the Government of India under a new captain like our Prime Minister and a new crew to take command of the ship of State.

While making it quite clear that we stand by the broad outlines of our foreign policy and will respect all inherited obligations, let it not be mistaken for a policy of rigid immobilism. As I mentioned earlier, the world situation is changing. India itself is developing new industrial, technological skills, new dimensions to its commerce and new horizons for its economic capacities. As a new Government with a fresh mandate from the people we consider it our duty, indeed our responsibility, to bring to bear a fresh scrutiny on the tasks and international problems as they may present themselves.

Our Neighbours

We have recognised that our first priority must be to promote a relationship of cooperation and trust with our immediate neighbours. We share with them a common history and a great deal of common culture, but we also recognise their own right to determine their separate national fulfilment. We shall be vigilant about our territorial integrity but pose no threat to their national personalities. Overlooking any suspicions of the past and not denying that some problems will always arise with close neighbours, we believe it is in our separate and common interest to forge, on the basis of our geography, the sinews of economic cooperation in the subcontinent. If we succeed we could ease the burdens for all our peoples so that some of the swords can be turned into ploughshares and the entire region can better tackle the common enemy of poverty and inherited degradation. If the Indian sub-continent remains free of tensions it would command unique weight in the counsels of the world. It can be an example of how our ancient heritage can be transformed to modern progress. It can be a bridge to link the economic chasm which divides the world, and if we work together we can be a powerful group of nations contributing to international stability.

It is with this vision that we have been directing our policies towards Pakistan, Bangladesh, Nepal, Sri Lanka and Bhutan. We can claim that in some measure the climate for such trust and cooperation with our neighbours has already shown significant improvement. Some old suspicions and irritants have been removed; with sustained diplomacy and reciprocal response we hope we can move steadily forward.

I am aware that some members of the House have been exercised at reports that Bangladesh nationals have been denied refuge in India. After seeing these reports some senior officers were specially deputed to enquire into these allegations. After full scrutiny they have concluded that no force or compulsion has been used or hardships inflicted on Bangladesh nationals who were in India. The House is no doubt aware that the Prime Minister had made it clear in his conversation with President Ziaur Rahman and in public statements that no Bangladesh nationals will be compelled to return to their own country. But the constitutional right of political liberty which we enjoy will not be extended to permit the use of Indian soil for hostile activities against our partner nation. If we were to permit such freedom we would be going against the fundamental principles of co-existence and non-interference.

Our Government has also made progress in reaching the basis of an understanding with Bangladesh on the question of sharing Ganga waters. We have yet to reach a comprehensive settlement. These waters are the lifeblood of our national economy, for our agriculture and our industry. In our approach we see the problem as one of development—of sharing sacrifices by taking into account the competitive needs and entitlements in the short run, so that we may make optimum use of the waters available for benefit to both our countries in the longer span of time.

Shared Interest

Though our first concern is for our neighbourhood we know we have a shared interest in the friendship, welfare and the search for self-reliance and progress by our friends in the wider circle of Asia and in the continents of Africa and Latin America. The Prime Minister has already spoken of a brief visit to Teheran and his conversations with His Imperial Majesty the Shahenshah of Iran, during which a gratifying reaffirmation of friendly relations emerged. With Afghanistan as well as the entire Arab world we shall not only continue to seek to maintain old links but further strengthen our economic cooperation. We have assured the Arab world that we shall continue to lend full support for a just settlement of the West Asian problem based on the UN Resolutions which require the vacation of occupied territory. We hope that in the near future the process of negotiations at Geneva will get under way so that there is peace based on justice and security for the States in the West Asian region.

With Africa our old bonds are based on a common commitment against colonialism and racialism. We have been second to none in our principled support for majority rule in Zimbabwe and Namibia. Along with enlightened opinion everywhere we are pledged to the eradication of the evils of apartheid or institutionalised racialism. But beyond this we shall maintain the momentum to become partners in the effort of African nations for their national development. With countries like Tanzania, Zambia and Mauritius we have already forged such many-sided economic links that one can almost claim the relationships to be models for cooperation among developing countries. Our developmental experience is relevant and appears complementary to the needs of Africa in manpower and economic expertise. These beginnings are still confined largely to the Eastern Seaboard, but we hope to overcome the disadvantage of geography to extend it further to West Africa.

Ups and Downs in Sino-Indian Relations

With South-East Asian countries India has very old links and no serious bilateral problems. We follow with interest their efforts to find the answer for national integration and economic development within the framework of regional stability. From our side we shall lay greater emphasis and make more sustained efforts to develop even closer political, economic and cultural relations with all the states of the region. We will also be ready to respond to any initiative in which we can contribute bilaterally or on a regional basis in the search for stability in this vital area. During the visit of the Foreign Minister of Vietnam we had occasion to reaffirm our willingness to respond positively to the immense tasks faced by Vietnam and Laos in the reconstruction of their ravaged economies. We would also like to strengthen our relations with Australia and other countries in the South Pacific and have responded positively to the idea of periodical consultations amongst Asian and Pacific members of the Commonwealth.

The House is familiar with the ups and downs of the story of our relations with China and the problems still remaining unresolved, which complicated our relations. However, our Government welcomed the normalisation of our diplomatic relations and took the initiative to resume the severed trading links with that country. Based on the old Five Principles, we must have as our goal the forging of beneficial relations as is appropriate between two large Asian countries like India and China.

We have a feeling that India has in the past been slow to recognise the vitality and importance of Japan, which now commands the third most powerful economy in the world. We hope to repair this hesitation not merely through trade, or greater technological exchange, but through closer rapport with this dynamic country.

Indo-Soviet Ties

Members are already aware of the prompt initiative taken by our Government to invite the Foreign Minister of the Soviet Union to India soon after assuming office. The conversations with Mr. Gromyko were friendly and forthright and gave reasons for satisfaction to both countries. We believe the Soviet Union recognises fully that the new Government in office enjoys the full confidence of the Indian people. Both our countries accept and recognise the sincerity of the mutual desire to maintain a beneficial relationship covering so many diverse strands of cooperation. We have in fact no reason to doubt that the quality of relations between India and the socialist countries of Europe have in any way suffered with the change of Government; on the contrary, the logic of mutual benefit and a common interest in peaceful co-existence and international stability promises even closer economic cooperation in the future.

USA and Western Europe

I come now to the relations with the developed continents of Europe and North America. Unlike the apparent judgement of the previous Government, in our perception we do not see the relations with the socialist countries in any way inhibiting the search for improved relations with the USA and Western Europe. There were undoubtedly hesitations on the part of Western democracies in their attitude towards India, particularly after the developments which took place when the Emergency was proclaimed. Many well-motivated friends in Europe and USA expressed their concern and raised their voice in protest at the degeneration of India into authoritarianism.

The credit for the resurgence of democracy in India goes to no one else but the people of India. Our people have given the lie to those political scientists who thought that the successful practice of parliamentary democracy could take place only in affluent Europe and the Anglo-Saxon world. On the other hand, there were other social democrats, statesmen and the people in the communication media who had maintained faith in the democratic strength of India. I would like to express my gratitude to those people who kept faith in democratic resilience of the Indian people. Anyway, be it in the media or the people at large, there is a new fund of goodwill and respect abroad for India which, we feel sure, will help to improve relations with Europe and North America.

Our relationship with Western Europe is valuable not merely because the European Economic Community is the biggest trading partner of India but because there is scope for obtaining technology and resources which could be oriented for our own economic development. Besides the diversity and mutually-beneficial nature of our ties with the countries of EEC we also enjoy cordial relations with the other countries of Western Europe. Many of them have taken an enlightened interest in our problems and have extended their whole-hearted cooperation in our developmental efforts. There is no hesitation on our part to have a better dialogue with Europe. If anything, it is for Western Europe to decide to what extent in its own perspective of the world, a mature, self-reliant, non-aligned, non-disruptionist India can be looked upon as a worthy partner in the quest for international stability and cooperation.

Time does not permit me to dwell on a host of problems which confront the international community.

Like with Western Europe, we have reason to believe that after the recent developments in India the climate for the restoration and improvement of relations, based on dignity and self-respect, with Canada and the USA is also more propitious. The new administration in USA is taking a fresh look at the world to find a new balance between their own national interest and a more cooperative world order. The diplomatic exchanges between the Prime Minister and President Carter have been characterised by warmth and understanding and augur well for the future. We hope the USA in its policies will assist the process of stability in South Asia, which is the goal of our national policies.

Role of Indians Abroad

On this occasion, when I speak on foreign policy for the first time from Government benches, I would like to send a message of greetings to the millions of sons and daughters of India who are working or residing in different parts of the world—be they under governmental cooperation or as private citizens. Each one of them in his way is a messenger of India and a symbol of our ancient civilisation and culture. Though they may have chosen to go to work or reside abroad we shall never disown them or fail to appreciate and reciprocate their loyalty to the culture and heritage of their motherland. Wherever they are, they carry the stamp of India's heritage. We must, however, advise them to prove worthy of the traditions of tolerance and the capacity for adjustment characteristic of the land of their forefathers. In their own interests, as also for the fair name of India, we hope that even when they work for their own benefit, they will seek to identify themselves with the enlightened interests of the country of their domicile and abide, as required, by the laws of the land of their residence.

We believe India is well placed and the political climate in the world is propitious for pursuing within the framework of non-alignment the twin basic objectives of our policies—national interests and international cooperation. In the last two years, for the first time since World War II, the world is free from international conflicts. Never before has the logic of detente been so widely recognised. All responsible nations acknowledge that no nation can today expand and dominate or even insidiously seek to better its neighbours. No nation can survive or prosper alone, and peace, we know, is only the twin brother of nuclear annihilation! Have the nations any alternative but to make a more positive effort to cooperate for international social justice ?

So far as India is concerned we are committed to making sacrifices for the enlightened well-being of the whole world. We are gratified at the pledges of friendship which we have received. If we persist purposefully in our domestic endeavours we are confident that in our external relationships we shall command respect and obtain reciprocal goodwill from the community of nations as never before. Thank you.

Foreign Policy Cannot be Conducted on Party Lines

Mr. Chairman, Sir, I shall first speak in Hindi and later on in English. Ours is a multilingual country and it is true that I had spoken in Hindi in the United Nations Assembly. But at times I have to use English in this House because I think that language is important; but language is only a means and not an end in itself. If we abuse anybody in our language will he relish it ?

MR. M. RAMGOPAL REDDY (Nizamabad) : Should we abuse anybody in his language ?

SHRI VAJPAYEE : It is not necessary to abuse anybody. Mr. Chairman, Sir, I would like to congratulate all those Hon'ble members who have participated in the discussion. Yesterday the debate was rather listless, but today it became exceedingly lively. I want to thank those who have appreciated the conduct and execution of foreign policy during the last one year, but more than that I would like to thank those who have criticised it. In Marathi there is a proverb that one should always have a critic as one's neighbour. But in a democracy one need not be a neighbour—they may be facing each other. However, it is essential that praise is free from bias and criticism is free from rancour. With due apologies to Mr. Mavalankar I beg to differ from him with regard to today's debate. It is clear from this debate that there is a broad consensus in the country about foreign policy. There are certain aspects of foreign policy which have been criticised by members of my own party and there are certain other aspects which have been admired even by the members of the Opposition. But foreign policy is neither decided nor conducted on party lines. I am sorry that the issue of non-alignment has created some bitterness.

Nehru and Indian Policy of Non-Alignment

Mr. Chairman, Sir, in 1957, when I was first elected to the Lok Sabha, Pandit Jawaharlal Nehru was our Prime Minister as well as Minister of External Affairs. I had said at that time in his presence that even if, after independence, there had been any party in power other than the Congress and any person as Prime Minister other than Panditji, we would have had no option but to follow the policy of non-alignment. Could India afford to join any bloc after attaining independence ? Could we afford to mortgage our national sovereignty in the international sphere. It is true that the world is not divided precisely into two blocs at the moment. There are several blocs,

Lok Sabha on April 18, 1978 as Minister of External Affairs while replying to the discussion on the demands for grants of the Ministry of External Affairs

several centres of power are emerging, but that does not render the policy of non-alignment irrelevant.

Our friend Swamiji wants that we should not call it a policy of non-alignment, but a policy of self-dependence. He may excuse me self-dependence is the basis of non-alignment. How could we be self-dependent if we join some bloc and become dependent on some big power ? The essence of non-alignment is that we would take a decision on every international issue on the basis of merit, independently and fearlessly, and strike a balance between national interests and international requirements.

Mr. Chairman, Sir, while discussing foreign policy of India it is but natural and in fact inevitable that the name of Pandit Nehru should be mentioned and mentioned with admiration. I know my friend Swamiji differs from me in this matter. In a democracy differences of opinion are bound to be there, and to some extent they are necessary. But we have to consider their relevance. When I took over charge of the Ministry of External Affairs and delivered my first speech in the House as Foreign Minister I paid tributes from Pandit Jawaharlal Nehru to Shri Yashwant Rao Chavan and expressed my appreciation for them. It is a part of our tradition for the past thirty years and it has been our history. I too had differences with Pandit Nehru and I never tried to conceal them, but whenever there was occasion to admire him I never minced my words. After achieving independence it was essential for the freedom and economic development of the country, as also for the world peace, to follow an independent foreign policy, keeping aloof from the two power blocs.

Achievements of One Year

The question is asked as to what are the achievements during the last one year ? Mr. Chairman, Sir, it is not proper to blow one's own trumpet, but in a democracy a little bit of self-aggrandisement is excusable. When I look back to the scenario of the last one year I am overwhelmed with a small sense of satisfaction. Ever since 1962 India never enjoyed the prestige that it has today in the world community. Relations between India and its neighbours have never been so cordial as today since independence. In the international sphere India's trustworthiness was never so high in the last eleven years as now. All capitals of the world now cherish the faith that India will do what she says and whatever she says she will say with a full sense of understanding. The gap that existed between our words and deeds during the past some years, which was not only creating a conflict in the internal policy but was also hampering a clean and efficient execution of foreign policy, has been removed today. Now our neighbours feel assured. Our relations with friendly countries have improved further and we have also succeeded in bringing closer those countries that were at loggerheads.

Change in Foreign Policy

Mr. Chairman, Sir, it is no use asking whether there has been a change in the foreign policy or not. May I ask, if the situation changes should the foreign policy remain static ? Sticking firmly to the basic principles of foreign policy we effected alterations, variations, modifications wherever necessary according to changed circumstances. But where continuity was required we have succeeded in maintaining it with freshness.

Shri Stephen is not present at the moment in the House. He was asking me what changes had been made in the 'content' and the 'style'. Sir, I would like to give two examples in that regard. Nepal is one of our neighbouring countries. We have extraordinary relations with Nepal. Our border with Nepal is open. Nepal is a land-locked country. It was demanding separate treaties for trade and transit. The previous Government did not accept this. I fail to understand why ? If there was smuggling due to trade both the countries should strive to stop it. The terms and conditions of trade could be changed, but Nepal should get transit facility, because it is a land-locked country. Had we been a land-locked country what would we have done ? We accepted two treaties and also executed an agreement to stop smuggling. Here there is a little difference in the content, but it is a significant difference. Thus we succeeded in earning the trust of Nepal. Our friends in the opposition should not have any objection to it.

SHRI VAYALAR RAVI : Are you accepting the suggestion for a corridor ?

SHRI VAJPAYEE : No corridor, my dear friend, Mr. Vayalar Ravi, that is why I said I would like to say something in English.

Visit to Pakistan

Mr. Chairman, nobody can deny the fact that although the previous Government had also tried to normalise relations with Pakistan no Indian Minister had ever visited that country in the last twelve years. I was the first Minister of the Janata Government who visited Pakistan for the first time. This is a difference in style. (*Interruptions*). Mr. Swaran Singh had visited Pakistan but I am talking of the last 12 years.

SHRI VAYALAR RAVI : Simla was the beginning

SHRI VAJPAYEE : I admit you made a beginning, but that was also the end.

We have tried to make our relations with all countries meaningful and qualitatively better on the basis of mutual advantage. We have given new dimensions to foreign policy and new vistas have opened up before us. We have been successful in developing economic relations and have succeeded in increasing technical cooperation irrespective of social and ideological differences. Certain small factors had been creating tensions in our relations with some of the neighbouring countries. We have achieved success in removing them and our mutual relations have improved.

The main objective of the foreign policy of India is to promote world peace, stability and international co-operation. For protection and promotion of our national interests it is essential that peace prevails not only in our neighbourhood but throughout the world. Development is possible only in a peaceful atmosphere. Without new constructive activity political freedom is incomplete. We wish the process of detente which has started in Europe would spread to all parts of the world. We also wish that the talks about disarmament proceed at a rapid pace, so that the limited resources of the world could be utilised for conquering hunger, disease and illiteracy instead of being used for acquisition of deadly weapons.

Genuine Non-Alignment

During the debate a question was also raised—non-alignment was understandable, but what does this 'genuine non-alignment' mean ? Outside the House it is being said that it is not non-alignment at all. I would like to submit that the matter is not so simple. We believe in democracy. But the happenings in India during the past nineteen months have confirmed that Janata Party believes in genuine democracy. Whatever has happened during this period has happened in the name of democracy. Somebody may ask : Why do you talk of genuine democracy ? A democracy is a democracy. What is genuine and what is fake ? To this I would like to say that we have seen with our own eyes what genuine democracy is and what sham democracy is. If autocracy could be resurrected in the name of democracy, an attempt could also be made surreptitiously to join a power bloc while outwardly adhering to non-alignment. It is not enough to be non-aligned; the world should also accept that we are non-aligned.

Today there are some countries on whose soil foreign armies are stationed and yet they want to become new members of the Non-Aligned Movement. Should we enrol them ? There are several countries in the world that are not members of any military bloc but are mentally aligned with some bloc. In this context too we have to say that we should stick to integrity and firmness and to a commitment to the principles of the Non-Aligned Movement.

At the time when India decided to become non-aligned non-alignment was considered immoral. My friend Swami would recollect that courage was needed in those days to call oneself non-aligned and only those freedomfighters could talk of non-alignment who had passed through the fire of self-sacrifice during the freedom struggle and come out burnished like pure gold. We have adopted their policy of non-alignment. I want to emphasise that this policy does not belong to any individual or to any particular party. This belongs to the entire nation. When those countries that have newly found their freedom insist on becoming members of the Non-Aligned Movement and the number of non-aligned nations has almost reached ninety, if any voice is raised against non-alignment in our own country it becomes necessary to look into our foreign policy a bit more deeply. I want to state that the policy of non-alignment is not a negative policy, but is a positive and constructive policy. It is not only an extension of our sovereignty in the international arena, but also an instrument of building a new country, a country that will be free from political discrimination and economic exploitation, where the status of a person would not be decided by the colour of his skin or by his birth.

In this context it would perhaps be worthwhile to consider what does not constitute non-alignment. We should understand that non-alignment does not mean neutrality.

India cannot remain neutral between freedom and slavery, justice and injustice, apartheid and non-discrimination, international co-operation and international tension, a world order based on economic exploitation and a new economic order free from exploitation. We favour freedom, we want peace, we are participants in the struggle for racial equality and we continue our struggle for a new world economic order.

Mr. Chairman, a new voice is nowadays heard about our foreign policy almost everyday. A voice so familiar, yet so full of irritation that it has become fearsome. In the midst of tumult this voice sometimes sounds like a shriek, a shriek that comes when all is lost.

Opposition is Welcome, Grateful for Criticism

Sir, I welcome opposition and am grateful for criticism, but the voice of opposition to which I am referring has less of criticism and more of anger, less of substance and more of intolerance, less of light and more of heat. It would not be wrong to say that the voice that I am referring in the context of foreign policy is a deliberate attempt to create misapprehensions inside as well as outside the country.

What is surprising is that these known voices have changed so much within a span of one year. Those who preferred to speak in this House in measured tones and considered that to be a sign of nobility and looked down upon those who indulged in shouting are today themselves indulging in shouts and shrieks. Day in and day out, whether stationary or on the move, whether asleep or awake, whether eating or drinking, they have only one topic to raise that the Janata Party Government is hell-bent on selling out India. Could there be a bigger lie than that ? Could there be anything more unreasonable ? India is not so cheap that anyone may purchase it, we are not the bad sons who would bargain the prestige of the nation. Patriotism is in our veins, national prestige is our invaluable heritage. We would rather sacrifice our lives than bargain for the country's honour and prestige.

Mr. Chairman, Sir, this is what is being said about us : "The Janata Government is dependent on the west. India is leaving the non-aligned path. The present Government is moving away from non-alignment in a way that would please western countries. Janata policy may trigger war in the Indian Ocean. Non-alignment has been diluted to suit U.S.A. India's stock is ebbing among the non-aligned."

SHRI VAYALAR RAVI : Whose quotation it is ?

SHRI VAJPAYEE : You might have understood now. My submission is that while in the Opposition we also had severely criticised the Government, but where appreciation was called for we expressed it profusely. So much so that later on during the elections we had to pay for it.

Do not Divide the Country on Question of Foreign Policy

I do not expect from the Opposition that they would be as liberal as I have been to them. But my submission is that it should not try to divide the country on the question of foreign policy. There are several other issues for controversy, for quarrel, for approaching the people, but there should at least be one area in which, if we have not brought about any fundamental change, we should be able to work together. It is essential to maintain that atmosphere.

SHRI VASANT SATHE : Please tell us something about the secret donation.

SHRI VAJPAYEE : I am coming to that.

Concentrate Improvement in External Relations

Now, I would like to say a few words in English. The price of our democratic freedom will always be eternal vigilance. We can, however, claim that without any sacrifice or short-sightedness India today has less reason than ever before to apprehend threats which would distract us from bending our best efforts towards constructive endeavours. The sub-continent, as a whole, pulsates with a new desire and confidence in peace and cooperation. We have moved a long way, indeed faster than anyone thought was possible, to arrest the corrosion of suspicion and rediscover the incontrovertible logic of the geographical compulsions of good-neighbourly cooperation and the vision of regional stability. Having visited or met the leaders of all our neighbouring countries I can assert that the confidence of a new era in relationships with India is shared by their leaders. These new perspectives are, of course, as much due to their leadership as our own. We can all feel more confident that if we can sustain these efforts towards mutual understanding the sub- continent will remain free from the play of malevolent politics as it affects many other parts of the world.

The House is aware that the year under review has been an unusually exacting and intense period for our diplomacy; and concrete improvement has been made in the wide circles of external relations. The House is familiar with the number of high-level visitors from different continents representing different social systems who have either visited our capital or have invited our leaders to their own countries. These visits have been mostly at the suggestion of high dignitaries and are proof enough of the regard in which India is held. I cannot think of any other country—in fact, even our own in the past—which in such a short time has been honoured by so many important Heads of State and Government.

The interest which these leaders have shown in our country is a tribute to this land and its people. Whatever their own social systems, our demonstration of a mature commitment to democracy has earned their respect for the political wisdom of our people. Our partner nations have also been impressed that however poor we may be, in statistical terms, our potential in the field of agriculture, industry, technology and science is significant.

These visits and contacts have not been for purely ceremonial or protocol purposes. Each visit had a character of its own and all of them deepened understanding and identified new potential of bilateral economic complementarity with our own developmental dynamism. The occasional criticisms that the Government policies were tilting in one direction or tilting away in other directions are often based on an antiquated understanding of the world situation.

Consistent with non-alignment our purpose has been charted within a conceptual framework of promoting and enriching relationships based on beneficial bilateralism. We have, with full confidence, carried Indo-Soviet friendship and economic cooperation to levels well beyond what existed before. At the same time we have restored mutual confidence in our relations with the United States. Problems, no doubt, exist or may arise, but Indo-US relations are no longer clouded with unwarranted and acrimonious mistrust. Without pretending to overlook the existence of difficult problems and the ups and downs of our past relations we have created the basis for improved bilateral exchanges in the economic, commercial and cultural fields with China.

We have truly broken new grounds in responding with sincerity and alacrity to co-operate with Vietnam in the immense task which that brave country faces in its national reconstruction. We feel proud that India may be the first country outside the socialist bloc with which such links are being forged with the Democratic Republic of Vietnam. We are poised for improved relations bilaterally and regionally in our sub-continent. We have prepared the ground for closer rapport and greater economic and collaborative relations with Japan.

There is a new warmth of understanding in our relations with Australia on the one hand and, at the other end, with the United Kingdom. We have concluded far-reaching agreements for new fields of economic cooperation with Iran. Our public sector undertakings have, during the year under review, forged new economic links in Libya, Iraq and the Gulf States. We are hopeful of higher technological and scientific and trade co-operation with the Federal Republic of Germany and France, as with Western and Northern Europe. Our strong ties of technical co-operation with many countries, notably Afghanistan, Mauritius and East Africa, continue to grow in diversity and scope. The thrust of our foreign policy has moved on a broad front, and everywhere our diplomatic effort has gone hand in hand with an integrated effort to strengthen our economic links.

Nuclear Weapons

May I, at this point, say a word on the national problem of international co-operation in the field of peaceful use of nuclear energy ? Our policy on this has been made clear by the Prime Minister. Our entire foreign policy is one which has always recognised the need for discipline on all matters which may be a threat to international peace. As such, we strongly believe that the world should not make use of nuclear energy for destructive purposes and should aim not only at non-proliferation but the elimination of existing weapons.

Our problem arises out of a contractual obligation by which the Tarapur reactor was planned on the presumption of a pledged supply of enriched fuel for its functioning. We have adhered to our side of the contract. We have noted the recent American domestic legislation on non-proliferation, which seems to imply that even past contracts may be sought to be re-negotiated with new conditions. While willing to adhere to our side of the obligations and while continuing the dialogue with the US Government, we certainly hope that such long-standing co-operation will not come to an end. But we will have to face the contingency if it should arise.

MR. SPEAKER : Just one minute, I will ask the House to extend the time of the House till the Demands are voted, because, under the rules, I have to do it 15 minutes before the scheduled time of adjournment. Is it the pleasure of the House to extend the time ?

SEVERAL HON. MEMBERS : Yes.

SHRI VAJPAYEE : Thank you.

SHRI K. GOPAL (Karur) : You should thank us.

MR. SPEAKER : All of us, not excluding me.

SHRI VAJPAYEE : May I say that we do not believe in the use of the option of nuclear weapons ? We cannot but maintain that it is unrealistic that these chances of nuclear war can be averted and sensitive technology can be exclusively preserved for peaceful uses unless there is a universalised discipline against nuclear weapons.

Some hon. members referred to our poor performance in the field of external publicity. I have been all too aware of the need to re-orient and give a more purposive content to the efforts made by our Missions abroad and the organisational structure in India to project the correct image of contemporary India, the policies and programmes of the Government and the hopes and aspirations and traditions of our people.

Cultural Diplomacy

The Report of the Ministry of External Affairs alludes to some of the efforts which have been made in the past year to give a meaningful content to our publicity efforts abroad. I must say that whereas I am gratified at some of the progress which has been made I fully recognise that there is scope for improvement. A committee headed by Shri Chanchal Sarkar was recently set up to go into the various aspects of our publicity efforts. The Chanchal Sarkar Committee has made far-ranging recommendations not only on strengthening and reorganising the institutional framework of the external publicity organisation, but has made recommendations on equipment, formulation of publicity literature, training, liaison with Indian organisations and a number of other related matters. I would like to assure the House that we are carefully evaluating the recommendations made by the Committee and Government will take expeditious decisions to streamline and improve our publicity efforts abroad.

It has long been recognised that cultural heritage evokes considerable interest and fascination among the scholars and intellectuals and indeed the public at large abroad who see in our cultural heritage the panacea for many of the ills which affect present-day civilisation. It is recognised that our national ethos which stems from this cultural heritage has an abiding rationale in a world which is beset with increasing materialism and neglect of the values of yore. It is for this reason that we have long recognised the importance of our cultural diplomacy as a vital arm of our foreign diplomacy.

Non-Aligned Movement

Apart from bilateral relations we have continued and indeed intensified our participation in the United Nations and other international organisations and in the gamut of multilateral diplomacy. It would be pertinent to recall the success of the meeting of the Non-aligned Bureau which took place in Delhi soon after we assumed office. We are at present engaged in consultation with friendly Afghanistan for the preparation of the Kabul Bureau meeting. This will be followed by a meeting of the Foreign Ministers and the entire movement which will take place in Belgrade where it will be recalled the first major meeting of the movement took place in 1961. These meetings are coming at a time when the Non-Aligned Movement faces many challenges. They will demand sober judgment and careful adherence to the spirit of the movement.

Commonwealth Conference

It was, I believe, well recognised that our Prime Minister's contribution played a significant role in the success of the Commonwealth Heads of Government meeting in London last year and the first ever Regional Commonwealth Conference in Sydney two months ago. In all these and other international meetings our approach is one not of trying to seek leadership—and here I would like to draw the attention of my friend, Shri Subramaniam Swamy—but responding with whatever expertise and capability we possess to fulfil the ideals of constructive inter-dependence and beneficial solutions to international problems. We have consistently sought to play an active and responsible role to help fashion a new economic order and joined the developing countries in their quest for development and correcting economic imbalances through international co-operative effort and the promotion of economic collaboration within our fraternity.

Notwithstanding the consensus in favour of peaceful solutions the international scene today is beset with grave problems. We still have to see the vacation of aggression and the fulfilment of the rights of the Palestinian people, so that the serious efforts and hopes to see peace and stability established among the States of Asia are fulfilled.

We have been active directly and in international forums striving to underline the urgency of bringing about majority rule and democratically granted independence for Zimbabwe and Namibia. We are alarmed at the diverse conflict between fellow non-aligned countries such as in the Horn of Africa whereas we have counselled the end of conflict and respect for established frontiers.

Indian Ocean A Zone of Peace

Though the U.S. and the U.S.S.R. have made a beginning we have yet to see a genuine breakthrough towards making the Indian Ocean a zone of peace. Here I would like to correct the impression—I do not know from where he got that impression— of my friend, Shri Unnikrishnan. India is opposed to all foreign bases in the Indian Ocean. All foreign bases including Diego Garcia must be eliminated from the Indian Ocean. There is no change in our stand. But we are living in a strange world. The problem of Indian Ocean is being discussed by two big powers without the participation of any of the littoral countries. But we have been exerting our influence in the United Nations and outside to see that the pace of the talks is accelerated and an agreement takes place between all big powers to make the Indian Ocean a zone of peace. We do not believe that if big power rivalry is eliminated there will be a vacuum. The littoral and hinterland countries are in a position to guarantee freedom of navigation. The Indian Ocean will be free for all countries provided they do not indulge in military rivalry and we propose to accelerate the efforts in this direction in the United Nations at the forthcoming session.

While I do not pretend to catalogue all the world's problems I can assure you that on the basis of our well-established policies of independent judgment, non-alignment and international cooperation we shall strive vigorously and play a constructive role wherever possible as a responsible member of the international community.

A Secret Understanding ?

Now I come to the question, a delicate question, about whether there was some secret understanding between Mrs. Gandhi and Mr. Bhutto in Simla or not. When I was in the opposition I had made an open charge. But now when I speak I speak as Foreign Minister of India and I am in possession of all the records.

SHRI K.P. UNNIKRISHNAN : You must lay it on the Table.

SHRI VAJPAYEE : Not necessarily. All the records cannot be placed on the Table of the House. I would like to take the House into confidence.

SHRI K.P. UNNIKRISHNAN : This is an important issue.

SHRI VAJPAYEE : I do not speak on unimportant issues. Let us have the discussion in a cool and calm atmosphere.

Ever since I took charge of the Ministry of External Affairs I have been trying to know the circumstances in which the talks between Smt. Gandhi and Mr. Bhutto in Simla in 1972, which had run into serious difficulties, suddenly culminated in the Simla Agreement.

I myself was present in Simla when the talks were going on between the two sides and it was common knowledge there that the negotiations had run into rough weather. Therefore, it puzzled me and I am sure it must have puzzled many other observers of Indo-Pak relations at that time, how all of a sudden an agreement had emerged. Several journalists, some of whom had interviewed Mr. Bhutto, have given stories of a sudden change in the course of events after a post-dinner meeting between the two leaders. In fact the country at large was surprised that a reference to "final settlement of Jammu and Kashmir" had been included in the Simla Agreement.

Since assuming charge of the Ministry of External Affairs I have made an effort to acquaint myself with not only various documents relating to the discussions but also have held personal discussions with a number of knowledgeable individuals. Piecing together all the evidence from different sources I cannot but reaffirm that some sort of secret understanding was reached by Smt. Gandhi in her confidential conversation with Mr. Bhutto....

SHRI K.P. UNNIKRISHNAN : Is he telling us from the minutes ? Were any minutes kept, I would like to know. He is saying this on the basis of...(*Interruptions*).

SHRI VAJPAYEE : I have not yet completed.

Let me add straightaway that in drawing attention to this I am looking at it as an internal matter...

SHRI VASANT SATHE : That does not make any difference.

SHRI VAJPAYEE : So far as external policies are concerned, contrary to what has been suggested by certain interested quarters, we have maintained continuity and adherence to the broad parameters of our non-aligned foreign policy. Perhaps, it was being hoped that India's image will have a setback after the Janata Party came into office. This may be the reason for annoyance and disappointment in some quarters.

Improvement In Indo-Pak Relations

As far as Pakistan is concerned, whatever may have been my differences with the Government in power at the time of the Simla Agreement we have accepted in letter and spirit the obligations undertaken by India in that accord. We have indeed managed and improved the climate of relations with Pakistan. We have assured Pakistan that we would continue to follow a policy of strict non-interference in Pakistan's internal affairs. In fact, the House knows, even with regard to the legal processes affecting Mr. Bhutto, we have observed scrupulous detachment.

Keeping in view the fact that our foreign policy, which is strictly and transparently in tune with our national interests and has been based on a broad national consensus, I would urge that any discussion we may have on this subject should not weaken our efforts for peace in this subcontinent.

Mr. Speaker, our foreign policy, I believe, has conceptual coherences and transparent logic from the point of view of both national interest and international stability. Indeed I would hope that India, along with its neighbours, can continue to be both an example of stability and a force which stands for a cooperative world order, I would beg of the House not only to approve the modest demands put forward on behalf of my Ministry but also give its blessings and support so that the standing of India continues to rise and commands respect in the comity of nations. Thank you.

Non-Aligned Conference at Belgrade

Mr. Speaker, Sir, as Honourable Members are aware, the Conference of Foreign Ministers of Non-Aligned countries was held in Belgrade from 25-29 July, 1978. Though the 25-Member Coordinating Bureau of the Non-Aligned countries had met twice at Foreign Ministers' level first in New Delhi in April 1977 and in Havana in May 1978 this was the first meeting of the Foreign Ministers of all the Non-Aligned countries since the Fifth Summit Conference held in Colombo in 1976. An important highlight of the Conference was the inaugural address delivered by His Excellency Joseph Broz Tito, President of the Socialist Federal Republic of Yugoslavia.

Eighty-six member-countries of the Movement, 10 countries and 12 organisations with observer status as well as 9 countries with guest status attended the Conference. Djibouti was admitted as a new member and Pakistan and San Marino as guests. Welcoming Pakistan as a guest we expressed the hope that it will go on to detach itself from the military alliance system. In my statement at the Conference I also stated in general that while welcoming nations who seek association with the Movement we expected them to move on rapidly to repudiate totally their dependence on military blocs and multilateral military alliances.

India Unanimously Elected Chairman

India was unanimously elected Chairman of the Political Committee. India also presided over the Drafting Committee set up by the Political Committee to finalise the Political Declaration. I also utilised the opportunity for talks on bilateral as well as international questions with many Foreign Ministers. On the eve of the Conference India organised a special cultural performance of Indian artists which was widely appreciated.

The Conference adopted unanimously a Declaration at the end of its deliberations consisting of a political and an economic section and an Action Programme for Economic Cooperation. The general debate in the Plenary provided the forum for a review of the international political and economic situation, and the role which the Non-Aligned Movement has played and should continue to play in strengthening peace and promoting cooperation on the basis of justice and equality. The common theme in the general debate was the need to preserve the unity and solidarity of the Movement and to reaffirm the fundamental principles of non-alignment which were proclaimed at the First Summit Conference of Non-Aligned countries held in

Lok Sabha on August 3, 1978 as Minister of External Affairs on the Conference of Foreign Ministers of Non-Aligned Countries held at Belgrade

Belgrade in 1961. Our stress that no attempt, either from inside or outside, can weaken or deflect the Movement if we remain genuinely non-aligned found wide support.

Problems Faced by the Conference

The Conference was held in the midst of a great deal of speculation regarding the ability of the Movement to maintain its unity and cohesion in view of the emergence of sharp differences and even conflicts between some of the Non-Aligned countries and of foreign military presence in some of these countries having potentiality of involving them in the vortex of cold war politics.

The Conference faced these problems squarely and addressed a special appeal to the Non-Aligned countries involved in mutual disputes to make every effort themselves to reach peaceful settlements, primarily by bilateral means. In addition, it recognised that Non-Aligned countries could render assistance to the parties concerned by bilateral means and through various forms of good offices for reconciling and resolving disputes peacefully. The possibility of establishing informal *ad hoc* groups for providing good offices to parties to the disputes, should they so desire, was also examined and recommended to the parties directly concerned.

The Summit Conference of the Organisation of African Unity held in Khartoum just before the Conference of Foreign Ministers of Non-Aligned countries greatly facilitated the task of the latter Conference and constituted an important contribution towards its success. The Conference admired the courageous stand of the African States in Khartoum in their decision to be exclusively responsible for Africa's defence and security by considering the possibility of establishing an inter-African force within the framework of the OAU. It also noted that the OAU summit has totally rejected all attempts aimed at involving Africa in the cold war politics and its condemnation of any foreign interference on the internal affairs of African States.

Recommendation

The Conference recommended that in order to avoid the emergence of such conflicts the relations between the Non-Aligned countries must be guided by the basic principles of Non-Alignment, the Charter of the United Nations, strict mutual respect for independence, sovereignty and territorial integrity of each Non-Aligned State and the inviolability of legally established international frontiers. It was also recognised that the interest of unity and cohesion of the Movement can be best served if narrow national, regional and ideological issues are kept outside the forum of the Movement as far as possible and Non-Aligned countries devoted their attention and energies principally to what unites them in the task of restructuring the world economic and political order and promoting mutual cooperation based on collective self-reliance.

Of particular significance was the concern expressed by the Conference at the setback which the process of detente has suffered recently and at the recent disconcerting tendencies towards a revival of certain cold war manifestations. The Conference called upon the world community to redouble its efforts to avert the aggravation of tensions and for a deepening and broadening of the process of detente in order to encompass all the spheres of international relations in all regions.

The political part of the Declaration reflects the views of the Non-Aligned countries on the major international issues as well as issues facing the Non-Aligned Movement itself. The Declaration and the Programme of Action together constitute a comprehensive platform and a concrete programme of joint action by Non-Aligned countries in international affairs. The Declaration contains the united stand of Non-Aligned countries on such major international issues as Southern Africa, West Asia and the Palestine questions, Indian Ocean as a Zone of Peace, Disarmament, etc.

The House is aware of the position of Non-Aligned countries on these issues and that, by and large, they coincide with those of the Government of India, which I have had the honour to state on the floor of the House a number of times in the past. I would, however, highlight the decisions taken at the Conference on some of the major issues.

Decisions Taken

Reiterating the known stand on the West Asia and the Palestinian questions, the Conference called for preparatory work during the forthcoming Thirty-third Session of the U.N. General Assembly to convene a Special Session to be devoted exclusively to the consideration of the Palestinian question. In regard to the situation in Southern Africa, the Conference endorsed the recommendation of the Ministerial meeting of the Coordinating Bureau held in New Delhi in April, 1977, to send a Non-Aligned Solidarity Mission to the frontline States and the liberation movements of Southern Africa.

The Foreign Ministers also endorsed the decision of the Ministerial Bureau meeting in Havana held in May 1978 to convene a Special Ministerial Meeting of the Coordinating Bureau in Maputo (Mozambique) to review the situation in Southern Africa.

In regard to Namibia the Conference, while welcoming the decision of the Security Council at its recent meeting, observed that while taking practical measures to bring about the independence of Namibia, it was necessary to exercise absolute vigilance in the new phase of efforts for bringing genuine independence to the people of Namibia.

On Zimbabwe the Foreign Ministers rejected and totally condemned the so-called "internal settlement" in Southern Rhodesia and characterised it as a sham attempt to consolidate the racist minority regime in Zimbabwe.

On disarmament the Conference expressed regret at the negative attitude of some nuclear-weapon States on two major aspects of the problem of which India, together with other non-aligned countries had, taken initiative at the Special Session of the U.N. General Assembly devoted to Disarmament. These were: adoption of measures necessary to prohibit the use of nuclear weapons, and a moratorium on their testing pending conclusion of a comprehensive Test Ban Treaty.

The Declaration contains a new section reaffirming the commitment of the Non-Aligned countries to the furtherance of human rights and stressing the need for the world community to adopt an integral and comprehensive approach to human rights which would include not only civil and political rights but also social and economic. The Conference stressed that human rights and the fundamental freedoms of the individual and of the people are inalienable. The emphasis in this section on the rights of the individual and on ensuring the full dignity of the human person as one of the principal objectives of human rights, was incorporated at the initiative of India.

The economic section of the Declaration reviews the recent trends in the world economy and the position and prospects of the developing countries in it; sets out the positions and recommendations of the Non-Aligned countries on the major issues in international economic cooperation and development; enunciates the role of the Non-Aligned countries in this field and reviews the implementation of the Programme of Action for Economic Cooperation among the Non-Aligned countries and other developing countries. The general conclusion of the Foreign Ministers on the implementation of the Action Programme is that while economic cooperation among the Non-Aligned countries has grown steadily during the recent years, the available opportunities for such cooperation have by no means been yet utilised. Among the recent major developments covered in the Action Programme, mention has been made of the adoption of the Statute for establishing a Council of Associations of Developing Countries, Producers–Exporters of Raw Materials, the formation of a Trade Information Service in Georgetown, and the acceptance of the offer of India to open a Centre for Science and Technology for Non-Aligned and Developing countries in India.

New International Economic Order

As regards the role of Non-Aligned countries in the field of international development cooperation, the Conference recommended that the movement should continue to play a central and catalytic role in the Group of 77. It was recalled in this connection that it was mainly at the initiative of Non-Aligned countries that a number of issues such as the establishment of a New International Economic Order have been made the principal concern of the international community as a whole.

An Assessment of the Conference

The brief review and assessment of the Conference which I have just given will indicate that the Conference has eminently served the purpose for which it was called. At this Conference the Non-Aligned Movement has once again exercised its undoubtedly great influence on the side of world peace and stability. The Conference is yet another milestone in the long journey undertaken by the Non-Aligned countries to reorder the world economic and political relations, to establish a New International Economic Order and to achieve collective self-reliance as an important means towards this end. The prophets of gloom who predicted that the Conference would end in disorder and bitter controversy were once again proved wrong. The Non-Aligned countries at this Conference did not make any effort to avoid the problems besetting them, but went ahead and faced them squarely and sincerely and assiduously tried to find means of solving them and made appropriate recommendations to this end. They reaffirmed the need for unceasing vigilance to preserve intact the essential character of the movement and for maintaining its unswerving fidelity to its basic principles and policies. They also attached paramount importance to the exercise by the Non-Aligned countries of the independence of action and judgment as one of the fundamental principles of the Movement.

The Conference proved that no single country or group can deflect the Movement in a narrow sectarian direction, so long as the members adhered scrupulously to the fundamental principles of the Movement. Though the public platform provided by the Conference was used more than before for airing bilateral differences the Declaration representing the final outcome of the Conference amply reflects the essential unity of purpose of the Non-Aligned Movement in the midst of its rich diversity of socio-economic systems, political philosophies and cultural ethos of the individual member-countries and sets out the key role which the movement has to play in meeting the challenges and the problems of this growing interdependent world.

Before concluding I would like to take this opportunity to express my sincere appreciation for the meticulous preparations and excellent arrangements made for the Conference by the Government of Yugoslavia, which contributed a great deal to its success.

India Cannot be Neutral between Freedom and Slavery

Mr. Deputy Chairman, I heartily thank the members who have participated in the discussion.

SOME HON. MEMBERS : Please speak in English.

SHRI VAJPAYEE : I shall speak in English as well as in Hindi. Of course, not at the same time. Sir, I am grateful to the Hon. members who have participated in this debate. I have heard their speeches with deep interest and considerable benefit. I must say that my friend Shri Bipinpal Das and Smt Alva are more effective in Opposition than while they were on the Treasury Benches.

SMT. MARGARET ALVA : Sir, I could return the same compliment to you also. You were much better on this side.

SHRI VAJPAYEE : So, if there are no fireworks in my reply and if I do not reply with any passion friends sitting in the Opposition can very well understand my position.

Genuine Non-Alignment

Sir, I do not understand why a strong objection has been taken to the use of the word "genuine". How can anybody oppose genuineness ? Would anybody like us to follow a policy of non-alignment which is fake, which is spurious ? Certainly not. Sir, the policy of non-alignment is not a policy of an individual or a party. It has been evolved as a result of national consensus. When I was elected in 1957 to Parliament for the first time—Panditji was alive; he was our Foreign Minister—and when I spoke for the first time in the Lok Sabha in the debate on the subject—though I was elected on a ticket of the erstwhile Jan Sangh—I said: We accept this policy of non-alignment because this is the only policy which India could have adopted after becoming free.

SHRI BHUPESH GUPTA : But, Mr. Vajpayee, we never heard you saying that "we accept the policy of non-alignment subject to its being made genuine".

SHRI VAJPAYEE : Sir, we continue to stick to the policy of non-alignment, because it is in the best interests of the country, because it is a policy for peace. It is a positive policy and not a negative framework. Non-alignment is not neutrality. We can never be neutral between peace and war. We stand for peace and those who would like to...

SHRI BHUPESH GUPTA : Between imperialism and national liberation.

Rajya Sabha on August 8, 1978 as Minister of External Affairs while replying to the discussion on the Working of the Ministry of External Affairs

SHRI VAJPAYEE : Of course I am coming to that. We cannot be neutral between freedom and slavery. We stand for freedom. We fought for our freedom and we have been helping freedom-fighters in South Africa since the days of our freedom struggle. There can be no question of supporting the racist white regime either in Namibia or in Rhodesia or in South Africa. Apartheid is a crime against humanity and we are fighting against this crime shoulder to shoulder with other non-aligned nations, with other countries. We are committed to a world order in which there will be no political domination, no racial discrimination. Sir, we are not neutral if freedom is imperilled, if injustice is perpetrated, if a war is thrust upon us by those who would like to make profit because they are engaged in the trade of armaments. But non-alignment has to be followed with regard to changing world situation; it cannot be static policy. Of course, we have to stick to certain principles, but if conditions change we have to adjust and that adjustment cannot be ruled out.

Sir, I am inclined to agree with the analysis of the world situation which was made by my friend, Prof. V.P. Dutt. The international situation today presents a curious mix. So much of the familiar framework of the international relations is in a flux in the great power context, not the super-power context. Peace has prevailed since the end of the war, but the search for stable and confident international relations is bedevilled by lingering suspicions and diversity of national and international objectives. The confidence in the logic of *detente* has recently come under a shadow. Power politics and ideological and bloc relationships have changed virtually out of recognition. Today a new debate is taking place on the forms of rights and wrongs of intervention. Unfortunately, continuing or incipient conflicts are occurring in various parts of the developing world.

Mr. Deputy Chairman, since India joined the international community as a free nation we have been guided by non-alignment and independence of judgement. We have sought to pursue our own developmental path and strategy and respected the right of others to do so. But with that right we never doubted that independent nations, regardless of their economic or political systems can, indeed must, co-operate with each other. Our guidelines have been clear and consistent. But steering a foreign policy which serves our national interest and takes into account the events which erupt to the surface of the tidal currents of economic, political and strategic changes which are under way below the waves and storms, demands a careful appreciation and shrewd judgement.

Mr. Deputy Chairman, these are the broad parameters within which we function. Our policies have sufficient flexibility to adjust to change and turmoil. We have the national resilience to see the opportunities to give positive thrust for advantage of bilateral and multilateral co-operation. We have reason to believe that the entire world community has a clearer and more favourable understanding of the objective of our foreign policy than in the past. Some misapprehensions and misunderstandings which had existed have been assuaged, established friendships have been preserved and strengthened, bilateral relations where they had been lukewarm have gained a measure of confidence and warmth.

SHRI BHUPESH GUPTA : This is the trouble. The moment you are speaking *extempore* you are talking understandable sense. The moment you start reading you start rigmarole, absolutely rigmarole. This is the proof. Produce it. Present it before the House. This is the trouble with him. I was listening very carefully. When you are speaking *extempore* you are making some sense. Now it is obvious that there is not a word of imperialism not even colonialism in the high-flown lecture. You have put them aside.

SHRI VAJPAYEE : Have I to keep on repeating what I have said ? I am sorry, Sir, my friend, Mr. Bhupesh Gupta, can repeat his speech every year, I cannot.

SHRI K.K. MADHAVAN : Sir, the Hon. Minister said that there is a clearer understanding of our foreign policy than in the past. Would he explain it ? (*Interruptions*)

SHRI VAJPAYEE : I would like to assure my friend, Mr. Bhupesh Gupta, that there is no conspiracy to change the foreign policy, there is no deviation, no distortion. We firmly adhere to the basic postulates that have governed our foreign policy since we became independent. Sir, we have to function in a complicated and complex world. When the non-aligned nations met at Belgrade...

SHRI BHUPESH GUPTA : No, no, don't read.

SHRI VAJPAYEE : This is a document, the Belgrade Document, Sir, he is very much afraid of any paper in my hand. At the Belgrade meeting we emphasised that the distinct identity and the authentic character of non-alignment must be preserved (*Interruption.*) What did my friend Mr. Sharma say ?

SHRI ANANT PRASAD SHARMA : No. I did not say anything. Prof. Ranga was saying something.

SHRI VAJPAYEE : Sir, I would like to quote further from the document :

> "As an independent, vital force, the Non-Aligned Movement has given its whole-hearted commitment to the struggle against imperialism, expansionism, colonialism, neocolonialism, apartheid, racism including Zionism and hegemony, in other words, the rejection of any form of subjugation, dependence, interference or pressure, be it economic, political or military."

Can any exception be taken to this ? And we are a party to this Declaration. I am inclined to agree with my friend, Prof. Rasheeduddin Khan : "hegemony" was included at Algiers.

PROF. RASHEEDUDDIN KHAN : Mistakes have to be removed and not repeated.

SHRI VAJPAYEE : If the word is used in a proper context, then we should not quarrel over words. Let there be no wordy duel or squabbles. Sir, we have to see whether the substance is being preserved or not.

Now people say that we are tilting towards one particular bloc. No, we are not. We will never do that. Non-alignment does not mean that we have to adopt a policy of equidistance. No. Soviet Russia has been our friend.

Indo-Soviet friendship has stood the test of time. I was in the Opposition when the treaty with Soviet Russia—the Treaty of Peace, Friendship and Co-operation—was signed. And while belonging to the Opposition I had supported that treaty. Whenever India was in difficulty Soviet Russsia came to our assistance. In building the infrastructure of our industrial base Soviet Russia has been of immense help to us. More than 70 projects are functioning in our country with Soviet assistance. So there is no question of equating one power with another power. But I would like to claim that we have succeeded in developing a more balanced relationship with all the powers in the world.

A lot has been said about our agreements with our immediate neighbour. We have been accused of appeasement. It has been said that we are guilty of sacrificing our national interests. Sir, I cannot accept this charge. The Salal agreement contains nothing new. We have not made any new concessions. It has been arrived at on the same basis on which the previous Government wanted to conclude that agreement. Even then we are being accused. I know there are differences on the Farakka Agreement. But let nobody say that we have betrayed India's interests. What was done for one year by the previous regime...

SHRI L.R. NAIK (Karnataka) : Sell-out.

SHRI VAJPAYEE : ...has been formalised in an agreement. Nothing new has been done even in the case of distribution of the Farakka waters. One might differ on whether there should be two separate treaties, one for trade with Nepal and another for transit or whether there should not be two different treaties. But to say that because we have agreed to have two separate treaties we have sacrificed national interests is beyond the mark. We have succeeded in building bridges of confidence, of understanding, with some of our immediate neighbours. We have strengthened our ties with Soviet Russia. In this connection I would like to consult the records. My friend, Mr. Bhupesh Gupta, should not object to it...

SHRI BHUPESH GUPTA ; Oh, no. I will not take objection if you say good things. Why should I ?

SHRI VAJPAYEE : My friend Dr. Mahavir referred to the Soviet maps depicting our boundary, our northern boundary. I know, when I was in the opposition I used to raise this question. This question has been raised from time to time...

SHRI N.G. RANGA : We marched together against it.

SHRI VAJPAYEE : Then we assumed responsibility, we again raised this question and I am glad to mention to the House that the Soviet Union has informed us that in future the cartographic delineation of Sino-Indian frontier in Soviet publications will more closely correspond to the delineation in our maps. But we have been informed that the border in the western sector will be delineated by the conventional sign of an unestablished border but in the middle sector and the eastern sector the new delineation will correspond with our own. For years the erroneous delineation had been the subject of representation by our Government. It was pressed again after this

Government assumed office. This significant response in the light of our repeated requests is an improvement which should be welcomed.

Nuclear Non-Proliferation Treaty

A beginning has been made for improving our relations with the United States of America. There are differences. Some differences are of a very vital nature. But as we are wedded to the policy of resolving all differences through negotiations, we have adopted the course which is best suited to our interests. I would not like to take up the question of atomic energy because the matter is being dealt with by the Prime Minister. But we have refused to sign the nuclear non-proliferation treaty and we will continue to refuse to sign it because this treaty is unequal and is discriminatory and, therefore, we can never accept the treaty in its present form.

India has unilaterally decided not to manufacture atomic weapons. But those who continue to pile up atomic weapons day in and day out have no moral right to tell India to sign a treaty which is against our self-respect. Nor are we prepared to open our indigenous atomic installations for international inspection unless the non-nuclear weapon States get similar facility to inspect the nuclear installations owned by the nuclear weapon States. Unless all nuclear installations are opened for international inspection we are not going to submit to any such arrangement. It is yet to be defined what full-scope safeguard really means.

How did South Africa get fissionable material ? Who supplied the material to Israel ? Obviously the material has gone from those countries who would like us to tighten our security arrangements so far as atomic energy installations are concerned.

The West Asia

Sir, on West Asia I need not reiterate the Government's policy. We would like Israel to vacate all the Arab territory that it has occupied. The inalienable right of Palestinians must be restored including the right to have a separate homeland and separate State. This stand is based on principles. Aggression is aggression..

SHRI BHUPESH GUPTA : How to arrive at that ?

SHRI VAJPAYEE : By convening the Geneva Conference.

SHRI BHUPESH GUPTA : Say so.

SHRI VAJPAYEE : That I have been saying. I am prepared to repeat it. We did not welcome the new initiative taken in West Asia. Unless our Arab friends stand united and if the attitude of Israel continues to be intransigent there will be no just solution to the West Asia problem.

Our stand on South Africa is well known. We are helping the freedom-fighters morally and materially. But if there is a negotiated settlement and a peaceful transfer of power, then we would certainly welcome such a development.

SHRI N.G. RANGA : What is the material assistance we are giving ?

SHRI VAJPAYEE : It is not to be disclosed, Acharya Ranga. But I can tell you in private, if you so desire. Certain other points were raised. In the case of the Belgrade conference I was asked why India did not oppose Pakistan's participation as a guest. After the Colombo Summit the doors were wide open. Rumania was admitted as a guest and so also Portugal and Philippines. Pakistan wanted to come as an observer which was resisted. We also resisted the same demand. But India decided to go along with the consensus in Colombo. So, we also decided to accept...

SHRI BHUPESH GUPTA : CENTO and Pakistan's participation in CENTO are there.

SHRI VAJPAYEE : I know it Dada. That is why Pakistan cannot become an observer. But if Pakistan wants to leave CENTO, if Pakistan wants to join the fraternity of the Non-Aligned nations, if Pakistan has come to realise that military alliances are not going to pay, then we should help Pakistan in that process. As a guest Pakistan will have no right to reply. They will not participate in the decision-making. They will be there just as a guest and I said it in my speech so very clearly and categorically that "I hope that Pakistan would detach itself".....

SHRI BHUPESH GUPTA : Two things are there. The US military pact and CENTO. These are the two things.

SHRI VAJPAYEE : If there were no pacts like this, then Pakistan could have become a full-fledged member. But even the observer status was denied. There is a move to make it conditional for those who want to come as guests, the condition being that they should make a declaration of their intent to leave military alliances. We have supported this move and I hope, before the Havana summit, something will be finalised on this question.

Sir, there is a lot of controversy as to whether I should go to Peking or not. I don't understand it...

SHRI HARKISHAN SINGH SURJEET : What happened to Zaire ?

SHRI VAJPAYEE : It was surprising indeed that my friend, Mr. Das, asked as to who has invited me. I have received a formal invitation and the invitation has come from the Foreign Minister of the Republic of China. Can I go uninvited ?

SOME HON. MEMBERS : No.

SHRI VAJPAYEE : But why should this doubt be raised ? After all, I know what our relations are. (*Interruption*).

SHRI BHUPESH GUPTA : The doubt arose because Mr. Subramaniam Swamy was telling us that there was difficulty. (*Interruptions*). Then he left and before leaving he said that he had no quarrel with Mr. Vajpayee any more.

SHRI VAJPAYEE : May I clarify that Prof. Swamy has gone on his own ? He is nobody's emissary.

SHRI BHUPESH GUPTA : How ?

SHRI VAJPAYEE : You are free to go to China and also to Soviet Union if you like.

SMT. MARGARET ALVA : The doubt arose because of what has appeared in the newspapers. (*Interruption*).

SHRI VAJPAYEE : Yes Mrs. Alva, go on.

SMT. MARGARET ALVA : Don't go on contradicting what your free Press says. (*Interruption*).

SHRI VAJPAYEE : Our free Press ? I know that you would not like the Press to be so free.

SHRI BHUPESH GUPTA : I am very glad that...(*Interruption*).

SHRI VAJPAYEE : But the freedom of the Press has come to stay and I cannot go on contradicting everyday.

SMT. MARGARET ALVA : I believe what the Press says. I believe them.

SHRI VAJPAYEE : No. Please take them with a pinch of salt.

SMT. MARGARET ALVA : Yes in future.

SHRI VAJPAYEE : Recently, a newspaper in Delhi published something....

SHRI BHUPESH GUPTA : Sir, I am very glad that Prof. Swamy has gone on his own. Now, Sir, the meaning and definition of "own" will begin to change. Something has to be written into the Oxford English Dictionary as to what "own" means.

SHRI VAJPAYEE : He is not the Government's emissary, and he has not taken any message from me. He decided to go and he has gone.

SHRI BHUPESH GUPTA : There will be a revolution if he goes with a message from you. Angel of peace...!

SHRI VAJPAYEE : There are allegations, I am sorry to say. Whatever good has been achieved during the last 17 months was begun by the former regime. I do accept that the process of improving relations with Pakistan was initiated by the former Congress Government. But I have taken that process further. Am I to be complimented or to be decried ? I know you would not compliment me (*Interruptions*). You are a miser. I know how I praised the former Prime Minister in 1971, without any reservation though I did not call her Durga or Kali. No I did not. I praised her. I stood with the Government. Let foreign policy be a field in which party considerations should not be allowed to vitiate our outlook. There might be some differences.

SHRI BIPINPAL DAS : This point was raised only because the Prime Minister had said—not once but several times— that it is they who have succeeded in creating a new climate of peace and friendship.

SHRI VAJPAYEE : If there is a new climate, what is wrong in it ?

SHRI BIPINPAL DAS : That is not the point. The point is that it is not you who have done it.

SHRI VAJPAYEE : No, no. You started the process, and we have...(*Interruptions*).

SHRI K.K. MADHAVAN : I am quoting what he said now; there is a clear....(*Interruptions*)...a more balanced relationship with the powers. Is it the presumption that the previous Government were not balanced, nor clear ? (*Interruptions*).

SHRI VAJPAYEE : There was a clear understanding. Now it is clearer...(*Interruptions*). Let us not fight over trivialities. If and when I go to Peking the border problem will be uppermost in my mind...(*Interruptions*). And I would like to assure the House that we will not have friendly relations with any country at the cost of any third country...(*Interruptions*). If there is to be a solution, if has to be on the basis of maintenance of our territorial integrity and keeping in view our national self-respect. But when we have ruled out the use of force, then there is no alternative but to talk. We will not talk out of fear; but we are not afraid to talk...(*Interruptions*).

SHRI BIPINPAL DAS : Will you also raise the question of Chinese helping and training the Naga and Mizo hostiles and their stand on Kashmir ?

SHRI VAJPAYEE : Every problem will be raised.

SHRI BHUPESH GUPTA : You remind them about *Panchsheel* and the Bandung spirit.

SHRI VAJPAYEE : Of course. There can be no normalisation of relations unless all oustanding problems are solved. And the problems can be solved on the basis of the five principles of peaceful co-existence. That I have said so many times. And I hope I will succeed in my mission. But rest assured, there will be no bartering away of India's vital interests.

Foreign Policy must be Result-Oriented

Sir, there has been criticism about why we have emphasised that foreign policy should be such as bears fruit. Foreign policy is formulated, conducted and implemented to achieve certain objectives. A country's foreign policy cannot be based on high-sounding declarations; it should be based on the realities of the situation. We may keep our objectives high, but our feet should be firmly planted on the ground.

Safeguarding national interests is the main goal of foreign policy. We are actively pursuing that goal. A foreign policy based on certain principles would have to be followed to achieve national interests. There is no difference of opinion about that in this House or in the country. Some little doubts as expressed by Prof. Rashiduddin Khan may sometimes arise. Let all doubts be shed from our minds. The people of India will not tolerate any government that may make the mistake of sacrificing the interests of the country. Foreign policy is not merely a question of policy followed by the Government, the future of 60 crore people of India is bound with it. No party can exist if it ignores national honour and national interest.

SHRI BHUPESH GUPTA : That is our only hope, only safeguard against you.

SHRI VAJPAYEE : It is right that we want results. I want to give an example. We support a new economic order in the world. The gap between the industrialised and the developing countries is widening. The developing countries, most of which are members of the Non-Aligned Movement, are poor. Colonialist countries had exploited them. They have not been able to utilise their own resources for their development. That this gap is increasing is a cause for concern. We should state our views clearly, but, Sir, I want to ask whether we can realise the aim of a new economic order merely by making strong speeches against the industrialised countries ?

SHRI BHUPESH GUPTA : Which peace-making is more difficult, Charan Singh-Morarji Desai or India-China ?

SHRI VAJPAYEE : Peace-making between the Communist Party of India and the Communist Party (Marxist). Now you have got it. Mr. Bhupesh Gupta, I am younger to you. I am junior to you. But I have also learnt a few tricks of the trade from you while I was in the Rajya Sabha.

Sir, I was saying that strong words alone cannot bring about a solution to all problems. Today industrialised countries are also afflicted with internal economic conflicts. Inflation and unemployment are on the rise. I was surprised to find in some western countries that the labour unions there, which should have been in the forefront of executing the new economic order, were demanding a barrier so that the goods of the developing nations may not enter their countries and render them jobless.

Paris Conference

I had the opportunity to participate in the Paris Conference. Our effort was that something should come out of it; our duty did not end by delivering speeches only. Therefore, I did not merely say that our policy should be result-oriented. I also said that we cannot go about posturing. Is our aim achieved by expressing our views on a problem and then packing off ?

India did play a role at the Belgrade Conference. It is not self-praise. There was an apprehension at Belgrade that the Non-Aligned Movement may get divided and I am happy that all countries realised it. India alone cannot take the credit for that. It is also not true that we wrote something at the instance of Yugoslavia. I had my speech prepared here. It is not that Yugoslavia had told us beforehand to incorporate such and such matter. Prof. Rasheeduddin has been going to international conferences. I do not think he writes his speech at the instance of someone......

PROF. RASHEEDUDDIN KHAN : I do it.

SHRI VAJPAYEE : But our foreign policy tries to forge unity and avoid division where there is danger of disintegration due to differences of opinion. It is essential to preserve the integrity of the Non-Aligned Movement. Certain powers are out to create dissensions among the countries of Non-Aligned Movement that follow different ideologies and have different social systems. Our aim is to carry them forward unitedly towards the common objectives. When I say that our foreign policy should be fruitful, that is what I mean. We cannot cast aside our principles and move in a void. May the Almighty not make us that senseless. If the House is awake and I get the affection and confidence of all I am sure the foreign policy of India will move on the right track and, incorporating national interests, it will side by side assist in creating a world full of peace and free from fear and hunger. Thank you.

Change with Continuity

Mr. Speaker, Sir, if any member of this House says that I have sold the prestige and dignity of this country as Foreign Minister he either suffers from insanity or has lost control and balance over his tongue. Foreign policy is decided by the Cabinet, not by me. Shri Raj Narain, who has left the House, was also a member of the Cabinet. At that time the foreign policy was all right. But since he came out of the Cabinet all kinds of charges are being levelled so much so that we are being accused of selling this country to others. No Hon'ble member has the monopoly of being a patriot. We are also patriots and are formulating and conducting the foreign policy keeping the interests of the country in mind. There might be mistakes, there might be differences of opinion, but intentions must not be doubted. I also had the occasion to sit in the opposition for twenty years.

Today, I recollect 1957 when I was first elected to this House. Pandit Jawaharlal Nehru was the Prime Minister and also the Foreign Minister at that time. You can see my first speech delivered in the House. I had welcomed the decision of our country to pursue an independent foreign policy, free from the influence of the two power blocs. I had said that there could not be any other course to follow for a free India. This policy is associated with our fight for freedom. When the world was divided into two power blocs, when the cold war was going on, the only course for us to adopt was to strengthen our political freedom, to use our limited resources for economic development and to expand the area of peace in the world by remaining aloof from the power blocs.

I know, when I mention the name of Pandit Jawaharlal Nehru some members of my own party make comments on it. But I had criticised Pandit Nehru also. Whenever there was a difference of opinion on some international issue I never hesitated to express my views. But when the foreign policy of India is discussed it cannot be that while other countries refer to Pandit Nehru we may not mention him. I had said it earlier and want to reiterate it again today—to differ from Nehru is one thing, but he is a part of India's heritage.

Mr. Speaker, Sir, my partymen are not displeased with me. When in the case of Bangladesh some achievement was made under the leadership of Smt. Indira Gandhi I had praised her....

AN HON. MEMBER : You had called her Durga.

SHRI VAJPAYEE : That's wrong. I had not called her Durga.

Lok Sabha on April 2, 1979 as Minister of External Affairs while participating in the discussion on the demands for grants of the Ministry of External Affairs

SHRI SHYAMANANDAN MISHRA : She has recently stated that you had called her.

SHRI VAJPAYEE : My speech is there.

SHRI RAMDEV SINGH : You had called her *'Rana-chandi'*.

SHRI VAJPAYEE : I do not want to go into that controversy. Presently we are debating the international situation and India's foreign policy in that context. I am happy that the Leader of the Opposition has come. And I would like to congratulate him for making a very sober speech on this occasion. He began his speech by quoting Jawaharlal Nehru. He quoted from the last speech made by Panditji in 1964 in this very House .Panditji had said:

> "In the light of the changing situation, how far our non-alignment must be adjusted with the changing events is a matter of consideration."

That is what we are trying to do, continuity with change. Where continuity is necessary, the same policy is being adopted, but where change is desirable it is being made. No policy can be static, it has to be dynamic.

We are living in a fast-changing world. Some members rightly pointed out that the world is no longer bipolar, it is a polycentric world. Military alliances are collapsing like houses of cards, and efforts are being made to forge new alliances against old adversaries. That is not going to help.

We are happy that some of our neighbours have decided to withdraw from CENTO, but here is Mr. Unnikrishnan who said that India was aligning herself with the United States of America. Iran, which was aligned with the United States of America has withdrawn from CENTO. Pakistan is eager to join the Non-Aligned Movement. Why should India align herself with the United States of America ? Is there any valid reason ?

There are people who pay lip service to non-alignment, but their attachment or commitment to non-alignment is superficial, it is skin deep. They would like India to be aligned with this bloc or that bloc. I would not like to point out...

SHRI K.P. UNNIKRISHNAN : You have become the Mullah of non-alignment now!

SHRI VAJPAYEE : I am a champion of non-alignment.

SHRI K.P. UNNIKRISHNAN : High priest.

SHRI VAJPAYEE : Non-alignment has become more relevant in this fast-changing world. That is why the membership of the Non-Aligned Movement has gone up to 88. The majority of African countries which have achieved independence after 1961 have joined the Non-Aligned Movement.

We are playing an active role, a constructive role. I had been to many Non-Aligned conferences. The first meeting of the Bureau of the Non-Aligned, after the formation of the Janata Government, was held in New Delhi, and there were prophets of gloom and prophets of doom who had deliberately created misunderstanding, saying that after the advent of the Janata Government Indian foreign policy would be in a mess, the ideals of non-alignment would be abandoned, India would antagonise the Arab world, India would align herself with the West. But what is the situation now ? Our policy is being appreciated by Non-Aligned nations.

Recently I was in Maputo, capital of one of the frontline States which is facing aggression from the racist regimes and as a member of the Non-Aligned Movement, India pledged its full support to liberation movements. May I inform the Leader of the Opposition that within two years our assistance to liberation movements has been doubled! He rightly said that India should not send its forces. He also said that we need not supply arms. But I would like to inform the House that we are supplying material and equipment. I would not like to go into the details. But our commitment....

SHRI C.M. STEPHEN (Idukki) : I did not say that we should not supply.

SHRI VAJPAYEE : It is there on record. Please correct it.

Our commitment to the liberation of Zimbabwe and Namibia and for the establishment of majority rule in South Africa is total. We have expressed our solidarity with all frontline States. We are giving them assistance, political, material.

SHRI K.P. UNNIKRISHNAN : Including Centurion tanks.

SHRI VAJPAYEE : I would like to deny that. I will come to that. It has already been denied. But Mr. Unnikrishnan is in the habit of repeating the same thing over and over again.

Genuine Non-Alignment

Sir, objection has been taken to the use of the word 'genuine'. Last year also the same objection was raised. Of course, I cannot give a different reply. Non-alignment must be genuine if it is to serve the cause of peace and the interests of the non-aligned countries.

Now there are countries in the world which have foreign forces on their soil, but which would like to join the Non-Aligned movement. Should they be allowed to do so ? Certainly not. Then there are countries which claim to be non-aligned but which are mentally aligned with a particular bloc (*Interruptions*)....not in the military sense. It is the duty of the non-aligned countries to steer clear and to preserve and promote unity by adhering to the basic principles which were enunciated in 1961 when Prime Minister Nehru had attended the Belgrade Conference. I know that Dr. Lohia had a world vision of his own. He was a great leader in his own right. But to put Nehru against Lohia or Lohia against Nehru will not be in the interest of the country.

On foreign policy there has always been a national consensus.

SHRI C.M. STEPHEN : That is what we are asking for.

SHRI VAJPAYEE : I would like to appeal to the Opposition not to destroy or disown that consensus because of domestic politics. Have we changed the policy ? The charge that India has tilted towards the West, and the charge should come from my friend sitting behind the Leader of the Opposition, Mr. Mohsin...

SHRI F.H. MOHSIN : There is evidence for that.

Indo-US Relationship

SHRI VAJPAYEE : Can you cite a single example of such a tilt ? I challenge you here and now. Don't make baseless allegations. Undoubtedly, our relations with America have improved...

SHRI F.H. MOHSIN : If I am given a chance I can speak out. But he will not.

SHRI VAJPAYEE : He wants another chance to make another charge. He will require a third chance to make another charge.

Our relations with the United States have improved. May I know who had initiated the process ? After the tilt in 1971, who had invited Mr. Kissinger to India ? We were not here on the Treasury Benches then.

SHRI F.H. MOHSIN : What is wrong there ?

SHRI VAJPAYEE : The invitation to Mr. Kissinger was not wrong. We should have friendly relations provided friendship is based on mutuality of interest and we do not sacrifice our own vital interest. As a result of Prime Minister Morarji Desai's visit to Washington and President Carter's visit to India, a personal rapport has been established. It does not mean that there are no differences. On the supply of enriched uranium, there are difficulties. We have received one more instalment; we hope to receive another instalment.

Then there is the question of sale of arms to Pakistan. We have emphasised that what Pakistan needs is internal stability and economic development. We wish them well. We want a strong, stable Pakistan. But no amount of arms is going to create that stability.

A charge is made that we are equating our friendship with the Soviet Union with our relations with the United States of America. That is not correct. Every relationship stands on its own footing. Every relationship has its own quality. As a result of Prime Minister Kosygin's visit to India Indo-Soviet relations have been further strengthened. They have acquired a new dimension, a new depth. We have a long-term programme for economic cooperation. We have decided to have joint ventures in third countries. One of my friends pointed out, perhaps Dr. Subramaniam Swamy, that the Government keeps on saying, 'We won't allow established friendships to be affected in trying to seek new relationship.' His complaint was that we do not say that in our quest for new relationships we will not allow established friendship to come in the way. If I may point out, I am sorry, he did not do his home work properly, after the visit of Prime Minister Morarji Desai to Moscow a joint communique was issued; there was no joint communique after my visit to Peking. The former Foreign Minister is not here: I know he had an important meeting to attend.

But after Prime Minister Desai's visit there was a joint communique which clearly stated that India's friendly relations with Soviet Russia will not come in the way of India developing or normalising relations with other countries. I was in the Opposition when the Indo-Soviet Treaty of Peace, Friendship and Co-operation was entered into and, as a member of the Opposition I had supported the Treaty. But that Treaty does not debar India from having similar treaties with other countries.

SHRI HARI VISHNU KAMATH : Why not such a treaty with China ?

The China Visit

SHRI VAJPAYEE : Whether such a treaty should be made with China is a moot question. (*Interruptions*). I am glad you have reminded me of China. I have no regrets for having visited Peking. My conscience is clear. I am not a fence-sitter: I believe in taking risks: I believe in taking initiatives. But nothing has been done against the honour of the country. Now members would like to say... and it has been said in the debate—that the timing was not right. I was invited in the month of March.

SHRI SAMAR GUHA : Not your going.

MR. SPEAKER : The next time you go, take some of them also!

SHRI VAJPAYEE : Now the Leader of the Opposition took objection to the fact that the invitation was conveyed by the Leader of the Goodwill Mission.

AN. HON. MEMBER : What is wrong in that ?

SHRI VAJPAYEE : Nothing wrong. And the Goodwill Mission was not so unimportant: otherwise Mrs. Gandhi would not have gone to the Chinese Embassy to meet the Leader of the Delegation.

I accepted the invitation in principle but I said that I will come after adequate preparation and at the proper time. No objection was taken in the House nor outside...

SHRI C.M. STEPHEN : Is it a fact that the initiative was from you ? You said initially that 'if I am invited I will be prepared to go' and then the invitation came. It is not that the invitation came and you considered and accepted it. It is not so. You made an initial announcement that if an invitation comes I am prepared to go' and then the invitation came—and the invitation came in this manner. That is not the way to treat a country like India.

SHRI K.P. UNNIKRISHNAN : Let him not mislead the House. When he says that no objection was taken....

SHRI VAJPAYEE : I am not yielding.

SHRI K.P. UNNIKRISHNAN : You may or may not yield: I will leave it to you. Now he should not be allowed to mislead the House.

MR. SPEAKER : You can put your question at the appropriate time.

SHRI VAJPAYEE : I would like to clarify the position. When I came back from Islamabad I was asked a question by a correspondent whether I would be willing to visit Peking if an invitation is extended. I said 'yes' let the invitation come: I will consider the matter.

SHRI F.H. MOHSIN : That is asking for an invitation.

SHRI VAJPAYEE : That may be your interpretation, but I don't agree with you.

The dates were fixed and I was to go in the month of October. Then I fell ill and then my illness was described as something diplomatic or political. Then the dates were renegotiated. Then I decided to go. Having postponed the visit once and having fixed another dates I thought it proper to go. When the second set of dates was fixed the Kampuchean developments had not taken place. There were reports that something might happen between China and Vietnam. Our own agencies informed us. Let them not be criticised. But nobody could say with certainty that on this particular day something would happen.

SHRI F.H. MOHSIN : What about your intelligence ?

SHRI VAJPAYEE : I would like the former Deputy Minister to use some of his intelligence in this matter.

SHRI F.H. MOHSIN : You were devoid of intelligence. That is why you failed. (*Interruptions*).

SHRI VAJPAYEE : Questions have been asked about whether I raised the Kashmir issue. Yes, I did. Whether the question of arming the Naga rebels was taken up. Yes, it was taken up. (*Interruptions*). Mr. Stephen, perhaps you have not gone through the statement which I made after I came back from China.

AN HON. MEMBER : He has no time.

SHRI VAJPAYEE : When the Chinese decided to mount a massive attack on Vietnam I cut short my visit and came back. Before I reached Delhi the Prime Minister had issued a statement calling for complete withdrawal of the Chinese forces from Vietnam. So my visit to China did not prevent us from taking a principled position on the question of Vietnam. The withdrawal must be complete; it must be total.

AN HON. MEMBER : He is not prepared to say that they were the aggressors.

SHRI VAJPAYEE : Again you are repeating the same thing. Say something new for a change.

The Kampuchea Question

Some Hon. members have raised the question of Kampuchea. They say we have not recognised the new regime in Kampuchea. We have not done so in order to please the Chinese. This is something baseless. We did not wait when the question of recognising the new Government of Afghanistan was raised.

SMT. PARVATHI KRISHNAN (Coimbatore) : You wrote to Mr. Bakhtiar and he was out before your letter reached.

SHRI VAJPAYEE : That was a routine message, Mrs. Parvathi Krishnan. There was no change of Government in Iran at that time. In the case of Iran we have accorded recognition. But the situation in Kampuchea is a bit complicated....

AN HON. MEMBER : No, no.

SHRI VAJPAYEE : The fighting is still continuing. There is a qualitative difference. Foreign forces were not involved in Iran. I know an analogy is being drawn with Bangladesh. Yes, Indian forces went to Bangladesh. But we sided with Bangladesh nationalism and we withdrew our forces. India would like the Kampuchean Government to be on its own....

AN HON. MEMBER : It is already on its own.

MR. SPEAKER : I do not know who had gone there and come back.

SHRI VAJPAYEE : They have a direct link. May be they have a hot line but we have our own sources of information. We have nothing to do with the Pol Pot regime. India had no diplomatic relations and I may inform the Opposition that the former government wanted to establish diplomatic relations with the Pol Pot regime but the Pol Pot regime did not agree....(*Interruptions*).

SHRI C.M. STEPHEN : A great secret !

SHRI VAJPAYEE : Don't raise questions which will create unnecessary controversies.

SHRI P. VENKATASUBBIAH : That was a legally constituted government.

SHRI VAJPAYEE : Please listen.

When an important dignitary of the Pol Pot regime called on the Prime Minister when he was in New York—which has not been publicised till now—the Prime Minister was angry with him....

SHRI C.M. STEPHEN : As usual.

SHRI VAJPAYEE : Not as usual. He had come to plead for the establishment of diplomatic relations but he had to cut short the talks and had to leave in a hurry because the Prime Minister was full of righteous indignation, and now, we are being blamed for nothing.

Sir, I hope the situation in Indo-China will be stabilised. We have friendly relations with the Republic of Vietnam. The other day the whole House joined in paying a tribute to the brave people and we have forged closer links with Vietnam. But, at the same time, we have started a dialogue with ASIAN countries. Sir, only 17 countries have so far recognised the government of Kampuchea...

SHRI KANWAR LAL GUPTA : Out of them how many non-aligned ?

SHRI VAJPAYEE : India would like a constructive role and we cannot play that role if we decide to recognise the government of Kampuchea now. We would like to act as a bridge....

SMT. PARVATHI KRISHNAN : A narrow bridge.

SHRI VAJPAYEE : The non-aligned fraternity consists of 88 members and the question is likely to come up at the Colombo meeting.

Sir, many Hon. members referred to...

SHRI DINEN BHATTACHARYA : *Oh, sab chod-deejiye.* (Oh, leave all that)

The West Asia Situation

SHRI VAJPAYEE : ...the situation in West Asia. Members have made a reference to the Israeli-Egyptian treaties which were signed in Washington last week. Since then 16 Arab States meeting in Baghdad have unanimously expressed their strong reactions against the treaty and have decided to break off diplomatic relations with Egypt.

I cannot but share with the House our anxiety at the situation which is developing in the Middle East. We are concerned lest these treaties should actually heighten tensions in the region as also between the Arab States.

Our own position on the West Asian problem is well known. We endorse the view that the constituent elements of the unanimously accepted Resolution of the United Nations must be satisfied if peace is to be durable. These elements, it may be recalled, are:

(1) total vacation of Arab lands which had been under occupation since the conflict in 1967;

(2) fulfilment of Palestinians' aspirations for determination of their own future in their homeland; and

(3) if these conditions were satisfied there should be security in well-established frontiers for all the States in the region.

Sir, the treaties signed fall short of these conditions. The likelihood of a comprehensive solution remains doubtful. Therefore, durability of any peace may also be in question. The future of East Jerusalem does not even figure in this agreement. While no doubt the West Asian problem is, above all, a matter of primary concern to the Arab countries, it cannot be overlooked that it is one of the gravest international problems. It could jeopardise international peace and adversely affect the world economy. We believe that the international community must bring to bear its weight in favour of a comprehensive solution.

Sir, at one stage the United States and the Soviet Union had both agreed on a framework for the solution of the West Asian problem. In the present tense situation the super powers and the comity of nations must, in practical wisdom, take a hand in bringing pressure on the Israelis for a more far-reaching solution which is in keeping with the basic elements mentioned above. A just and comprehensive solution cannot be postponed.

Treaties with Nepal

Sir, unfortunately our policy of good-neighbourly relations had been questioned. The Leader of the Opposition took objection to India's having separate treaties— one on transit and the other on trade with Nepal. Perhaps he has not seen the treaty which was signed in 1971. The treaty had two parts—the first part related to the trade and the other related to transit.

SHRI C.M. STEPHEN : That was subsequently.

SHRI VAJPAYEE : We have two treaties.

SHRI C.M. STEPHEN : If you do not find the difference between the two, then I have nothing to say.

SHRI VAJPAYEE : There is a difference. We have correctly done it. I need not be apologetic. Nepal is a landlocked country, so the terms and conditions of trade may vary. Don't they have the freedom ? Should they not have the opportunity to trade with other countries ? In one breath, the Leader of the Opposition said that we have to identify ourselves with the people of the smaller countries but when we decide to do so, he takes objection in another breath.

Sir, as a result of this development a new confidence is created between India and Nepal. For the first time, during thirty years, some concrete progress is being made in regard to river water projects.

Relations with Bangladesh

Our relations with Bangladesh have also improved.

PROF. SAMAR GUHA : You can't talk like that on Bangladesh. I know what exactly is taking place there. Thousands of men were being pushed back. Don't talk like that—that our relations with Bangladesh have improved. We have great respect for you on many matters.

SHRI VAJPAYEE : Sir, if my Hon. friend Prof. Guha has the freedom to say that the relations have not improved I have equal freedom to say that they have improved.

PROF. SAMAR GUHA : They have not improved. Hundreds of men, women and children have been pushed back. The houses of the minorities have been burnt. We only see this Islamic fanaticism there.

SHRI VAJPAYEE : Sir, I know my friend is emotionally attached with the problem of Bangladesh. He hails from that part of the world.

AN HON. MEMBER : World ?

SHRI VAJPAYEE : I cannot say 'country'. Sir, I do not accept that as a result of the Farakka agreement the Calcutta port is being starved. I have the latest figures. In regard to Farakka (*Interruptions*). I have the latest figures about the sharing of the Ganga waters at Farakka between India and Bangladesh from March 1 to March 10. Total cusecs flow at Farakka are 99,436. It is not just 22,000.

SHRI DHIRENDRANATH BASU : You have betrayed us.

SHRI VAJPAYEE : Here is a Congress member who talks of betrayal. May I remind him that when Mrs. Gandhi was in power she had accepted a lesser quantity of water in regard to Farakka. (*Interruptions*).

I know the problem. The problem is how to augment the flow of water so that the water will be enough for Bangladesh as well as India. That is why we are discussing long-term schemes. That is why we would like river water projects to be expedited in Nepal. I know this problem has to be solved.

India's Strength

Our relations with Sri Lanka have improved. (*Interruptions*).

Sir, when I visited Islamabad there was no objection. Why was that so ? Has it got anything to do with domestic politics ? If we can have friendly relations with all countries why only a single country should be singled out ?

SHRI C.M. STEPHEN : Which was it ?

SHRI VAJPAYEE : You know, Mr. Stephen, I am not afraid of anybody. Sir, I am afraid of one thing. The ultimate success of foreign policy will depend on our internal strength. And at the moment India is on the threshold of an economic breakthrough as Dr. Subramaniam Swamy rightly pointed out. (*Interruptions*).

Sir, let us not underestimate India's strength and India's potential. Let us not suffer from an inferiority complex. If I decided to go to Peking I decided to do so with the self-confidence that comes from the vast population, the industrial infrastructure, political stability and internal cohesion...

AN HON'BLE MEMBER : And unity in the Janata Party.

SHRI VAJPAYEE : ...and disunity in the Congress Party! Sir, we are in the same boat.

But let there be a national consensus so far as foreign policy is concerned. I welcome your decision to have a debate on the International Situation in every session. I welcome criticism. I would like to be benefited by it, if there is constructive suggestion. But please don't impute motives.

I would like to repeat what I said in the beginning: We might commit mistakes. But we will never be dishonest so far as India's interests are concerned.

I wish my friend Mr. Raj Narain was here...

I do not see Shri Sharad Yadav too. I would not like to say anything behind somebody's back because these things have to be said face to face. Sir, some of our friends who are in the ruling party have not understood the reality so far. When I was in the opposition I had opposed the Simla agreement, but now I am implementing it. However, nobody is complaining about that. But if I go to China to take back our land lost to them, motives are imputed. My visit to China was not undertaken at the instance of America. When the previous Government took the initiative of sending our ambassador to China nobody said that we should not take the initiative, that China should take that step first...(*Interruptions*)

SHRI K.P. UNNIKRISHNAN : It is entirely different.

SHRI VAJPAYEE : That means that their standards of judgment are different.

SHRI VASANT SATHE : How are the two things comparable ?

SHRI VAJPAYEE : Mr. Chou En-lai had come to India in 1960. This time somebody had to go from India. But had India insisted that some Chinese leader should come first....

SHRI VASANT SATHE : That was not the thing.

SHRI VAJPAYEE : He has not understood me, nor will he.

Mr. Speaker, I have taken enough time of the House. A number of Cut Motions have been tabled, but I hope they will not be pressed. Thank you.

Non-Aligned Movement Passing Through Crisis

Mr. Vice-Chairman, Sir, I am grateful...

SHRI PREM MANOHAR : It will be good if you speak in Hindi.

SHRI VAJPAYEE : Please do not start language controversy.

SHRI M. KADERSHAH : You leave it to the Minister. Don't instruct him.

SHRI VAJPAYEE : I am grateful to all the members who have participated in this debate. On the whole the level of the debate has been high, and it reflects the national consensus on the basic principles that govern our foreign policy. Sir, as I stand to reply to the debate my thoughts go back to the year 1957 when I was first elected to the Lok Sabha. In my maiden speech I had emphasised that as a newly independent nation India has to adopt the policy of non-alignment because we require peace to consolidate our freedom, we require peace for socio-economic transformation, and the cause of peace cannot be served if we decide to join multilateral military blocs. Sir, my friend Dr. Rafiq Zakaria said that while I was in the Opposition I was for the policy of non-alignment, but since I have become a Minister that policy has been given a go-by. Sir, I am sorry if that is the impression which has been created. Dr. Zakaria belongs to the Opposition. It is his duty to criticise. But criticism should be constructive. During the last two years nothing has been done to deviate from the policy of non-alignment. Sir, may I request the House to raise its sights a little above the din and dust and debate of domestic politics and to consider the question of foreign policy in a non-partisan manner ?

Sir, the elections were fought mainly on domestic issues. The Janata Party did say that if elected they will adopt the policy of genuine non-alignment. Now, an effort has been made to ridicule the use of the adjective "genuine".

SHRI CHARANJIT CHANANA : More genuine.

DR. RAFIQ ZAKARIA : By implication you mean that ours was not genuine. That is all.

SHRI VAJPAYEE : I do not imply anything.

DR. RAFIQ ZAKARIA : Why ?

SHRI VAJPAYEE : If you have a guilty feeling that your policy was tainted I cannot help.

DR. RAFIQ ZAKARIA : You have used the word "genuine".

SHRI VAJPAYEE : Because genuine has to be used not only in the national context but also in the international context.

Rajya Sabha on May 16, 1979 as Minister of External Affairs while replying to the discussion on the International Situation

Sir, the Non-Alignment Movement is passing through a crisis. The difficulty is that Hon'ble members will not go through the document which was adopted at the Belgrade Conference. The entire movement is laying emphasis on the fact that non-alignment must be genuine. It must be real and in the garb of non-alignment the basic principles which were enunciated in 1961 when Pandit Nehru had attended the Belgrade Conference should not be thrown away.

DR. RAFIQ ZAKARIA : Ours was also genuine and yours is also genuine.

SHRI VAJPAYEE : Something happened in between which created a wrong impression.

SHRI CHARANJIT CHANANA : That is your own complex, your own psychology.

SHRI VAJPAYEE : Sir, I can claim that our national policy of non-alignment stands vindicated. Some of the major powers have gone through the process of agonising reappraisals and readjustments in their approach to external relations. In contrast India's policy is marked by a continuity, a continuity where it served the national interest, but it is flexible enough to adjust to the changing world situation.

Detente should be Universal

Sir, old adversaries have become new allies. But one thing is clear that multilateral militarism has failed. The idea to reshape the world on a single ideology does not hold good any longer. It has been rightly stated by many Hon'ble members that the world is no longer bipolar. Still the Soviet Union and the United States of America are two super-powers. There is no question of equating them. Sir, our relations with each country stand on a different footing. We would like that the international situation should change for the better. There are signs of relaxation of tension. We welcome the proposed SALT II agreement. We hope talks on the Indian Ocean will be resumed very soon between the United States of America and the Soviet Union. As a Non-Aligned nation, as a littoral country, we are playing our part in making the Indian Ocean a zone of peace. But there are disturbing signs also. There is *detente* in Europe. But we would like *detente* to be universal. There are tensions in Africa, in Asia. But due to our policy of good-neighbourliness our region, the region to which we belong is comparatively tranquil and tension-free. Sir, as a result of our policy there is less threat, there is less danger, of foreign intervention. There is less possibility of bilateral issues assuming international proportions.

My friend Dr. Dutt is not here. He criticised even the Salal agreement with Pakistan. Sir, we did not make any new concession to Pakistan. The agreement has been arrived at on the same conditions which were offered by the former Government but which Pakistan did not accept at that time. We have succeeded because India's credibility has enhanced, because neighbouring countries know that though India is big in size, in population, in resources, India has a Government which will deal with all its neighbours on the basis of equality and will try to further common interests.

Sir, it is not correct to say that we have decided to bring in Nepal so far as the question of river waters is concerned. The other day my friend Shri Barnala made the position clear. The short-term agreement has been in the interest of both Bangladesh and India. We have succeeded in securing more water than what was conceded by the former Government of Bangladesh. But even then we are condemned, we are criticised. We do not mind it. I was on the Opposition benches for the last 20 years. Now I am at the receiving end. But on the question of foreign policy let us try to evolve, as far as possible, a common approach. Can anybody deny that our relations with Pakistan have improved ? As a result of the visit of the President of Sri Lanka to India and Prime Minister Desai's return visit the friendly ties between India and Sri Lanka have been further strengthened. In spite of the change of Government in Iran—and the Government has been changed by the people—our relations have not been adversely affected. On the contrary the economic cooperation which was going on with Iran is still continuing and we hope that it will further expand. Changes have taken place in Kabul. We did not wait to accord recognition to the new Government. India was one of the first countries to recognise the new Government in Kabul. Our traditional ties of friendship with Afghanistan are gaining from strength to strength. Many honourable members mentioned about our relations with China, especially in the context of my visit to that country and China's attack on Vietnam. I have already made statements in the House on the results of my visit to China and our viewpoint on the Chinese attack on Vietnam. We did not hesitate to express our strong feelings at China's attack ~~and the~~ persistent differences which are still manifest in Sino-Vietnamese relations. But we hope that the talks between China and Vietnam will succeed. I would like to pay a tribute to the brave and valiant people of Vietnam who have been fighting for their freedom for the last thirty years; they have made great sacrifices. But I pay a tribute to them that they are prepared to settle differences at the negotiating table. If war is to be ruled out as a means to settling disputes there is no other alternative but to talk. Talking does not mean that vital national interests should be sacrificed or that we should adopt a policy of appeasement. Dr. Dutt accused me and the Government....

DR. V.P. DUTT : You are confusing between the two doctors.

SHRI VAJPAYEE : I am unfortunately a patient. What am I to do ? I am under attack from doctors, Sir...

MR. VICE-CHAIRMAN (Shri G. Lakshmanan) : You can attack the doctors also.

SHRI VAJPAYEE : The initiative for talks came from China. Now a reference was made by my friend that I announced my visit to China in America. The news was already published in India.

SHRI CHARANJIT CHANANA : I can give the dates.

SHRI VAJPAYEE : I can also give you the dates. While I was addressing a meeting of Indians in America I was given a chit by a pressman who was in the Prime Minister's party that something has already been published in New Delhi that you are visiting China. Would you confirm or deny it ? Then I said I have decided to visit China. It had nothing to do with the American authorities. He said that my visit to China was announced in America and then the agenda was also drawn up in America. This is grave injustice.

SHRI CHARANJIT CHANANA : My source of information is Indian newspapers. The only unfortunate thing probably is that the Hon. Minister forgets the date-line in New York or Washington, wherever he spoke.

SHRI VAJPAYEE : Wherever I spoke I spoke in a meeting which was attended by Indians.

DR. RAFIQ ZAKARIA : You should make such important announcements on the soil of India.

SHRI VAJPAYEE : There was a leakage. The news was already published here. I wanted to make the formal announcement here. But when I was confronted whether the news was right or wrong, I said I have decided to visit China. It had nothing to do with our relations with America. Are we going to be dictated to by any other country ?

SHRI CHARANJIT CHANANA : That should not happen.

SHRI VAJPAYEE : No, no. That will never happen, Dr. Chanana.

DR. RAFIQ ZAKARIA : You used to accuse us of worse things.

SHRI VAJPAYEE : So you are doing the same thing. Please do something better. We did not have the experience of running the Government, which you had.

We still hope that on the basis of the five principles and recognised right of independence of policies and objectives of the two countries Sino-Indian relations will continue to be free from friction and hopefully, at a moment considered convenient and opportune by both the countries, the exploratory dialogue could be resumed.

DR. V.P. DUTT : Please speak from heart. Don't speak by looking at papers.

SHRI VAJPAYEE : You also spoke referring to the papers in your hand. Don't you teach your students holding a book in your hand ?

Sir, the Non-Aligned Movement is passing through a critical phase. There are serious problems and these may come up at the forthcoming meeting in Colombo and later at the summit meeting in Havana. Many countries have been in consultation with us. Indeed the House must be aware that the question of non-alignment came up in discussions during the visits of the Vice-President of Egypt, Mr. Hosni Mubarak, the Foreign Minister of Yugoslavia and the Education Minister of the Socialist Republic of Vietnam. With all of them and with other non-aligned countries we have sought to emphasise the imperative of preserving the strength of non-alignment. But though there are, no doubt, different approaches and even different priorities between different countries of the Non-Aligned Movement, our approach will be to focus on maintaining the consensus and solidarity of the movement in the spirit of its original concept and its original criteria of membership. Non-alignment has come a long way, and at the moment of its widening appeal, it must not be splintered or its strength weakened by countries seeking to use the forum for narrow national priorities or for ideological considerations. The strength of non-alignment is that it provided a basis for independence, peace and diversity among nations. At the time of deep international confrontations it made the five principles a valid and fundamental basis of inter-State relationships. Great wisdom, restraint and dedication to the five principles would be necessary. If the movement is splintered by divisive or ulterior purposes, it will only give mocking comfort to those who have no faith in our principles. For our part, so far as India is concerned, we have never used the forum of non-alignment for bilateral disputes or ulterior objectives. We ourselves cannot prevent such tendencies. Our full weight will be for not permitting the bonds which unite us to be weakened by the attitudes which may be brought up in the forum.

Recognition of Kampuchea

Sir, many Hon. members demanded recognition of the new Government of Kampuchea. In this connection a reference was made to the statement made by our Permanent Representative in New York. Sir, I would like to inform the House that the Permanent Representative in New York did not refer to Kampuchea at all in his speech. In fact the question of Kampuchea cropped up after his speech. What he said was that the question could be decided by the Foreign Ministers at Colombo. The report which appeared in the Press here was not correct. If the Hon. members want, I can give them a copy of his speech. We did not take any initiative.

DR. V.P. DUTT : Do you recognise the Pol Pot regime at present or not ?

SHRI VAJPAYEE : We do not have any diplomatic relations with the Pol Pot regime. The Pol Pot regime is a member of the United Nations. The Pol Pot regime is a member of the Non-Aligned Movement.

DR. V.P. DUTT : Kampuchea ?

SHRI VAJPAYEE : Kampuchea is represented by Pol Pot.

DR. V.P. DUTT : The question is, who represents ?

SHRI VAJPAYEE : This question will be decided in Colombo. So far as India is concerned, we are not in favour of the Pol Pot regime being invited (*Interruptions*) to represent Kampuchea in Colombo. But let us not shut our eyes to the realities of the situation. Only 17 or 18 countries have so far recognised the new regime in Kampuchea. Many of the non-aligned nations had diplomatic relations with the Pol Pot regime. Now it has become a ticklish question. India will try to play a constructive role. Now members say: You recognise the new Government now, otherwise how are you going to lead ? Sir, I do not believe in a spectacular foreign policy. I do not believe in a melodramatic approach. We have explained to our Vietnamese friends and they appreciate it. While others appreciate, for domestic politics some of our friends sitting on the side opposite—they pretend they do not appreciate. There is no confusion in our mind. Where has our friend Mr. Bhattacharya gone ? Sir, we have not recognised the new Government because it is still not in effective control. The fighting continues. The criterion is the same. We have not yet recognised the new Government of Uganda.

DR. V.P. DUTT : So much the worse.

The West Asian Question

SHRI VAJPAYEE : We do not have double standards. But the situation in South-East Asia and in West Asia is disturbing. Sir, many Hon. members referred to the peace treaty between Egypt and Israel. Strong reactions had been expressed by 16 Arab States and in addition to breaking of diplomatic relations, various economic and other measures have also been taken against Egypt. Only recently two non-Arab Islamic States—Iran and Afghanistan—have also severed diplomatic relations with Egypt. The Vice-President of Egypt, Mr. Hosni Mubarak, was in New Delhi on the 3rd and 4th of May. He came at his Government's initiative. He had earlier been to Indonesia, Malaysia, Singapore and Bangladesh. He had a detailed exchange of views with the Prime Minister. The purpose of the visit was to explain the Egyptian point of view. It is their belief that the treaty only marks the beginning of a peace process. This should eventually lead to the full implementation of the provision of the Security Council Resolution 242. The Yugoslav Foreign Minister was also in India. Among other subjects we exchanged views on the West Asian question. In our discussions with the Egyptian Vice-President and the Foreign Minister of Yugoslavia as also in various statements which have been made by me in Parliament and elsewhere, we have constantly maintained that only a comprehensive solution which is acceptable to all the concerned parties would be durable and lead to lasting peace. The reactions which have been evoked since the signing of the Egypt-Israel peace treaty only support this conviction. The treaty and other documents exchanged do not give adequate assurance or hope that all occupied Arab territories would be vacated and the problem of Palestinian front solved. The recent escalation of hostilities in Southern Lebanon regarding Israeli settlements in occupied territories casts further doubts on any expectations that the peace treaty and discussions between Egypt and Israel can finally lead to an acceptable settlement. The best assurance for the security of Israel would be under conditions where she no longer occupies territories which belong to others and continues to deny them their rightful hearths and homes from where they have been driven and the future of which they alone have the right to determine. Peace is best secured not through force or the threat of the use of force, but by removing the very causes which lead to misunderstanding, conflict and war. As such the full weight of world public opinion must be brought to bear upon Israel to accept the implementation in its entirety of the relevant UN Security Council Resolution.

No Pro-West Tilt

Sir, when the Janata Government was formed apprehensions were expressed that there will be a pro-West tilt in the foreign policy of the Janata Party. It was also said that India's relations with Soviet Russia will be adversely affected. All these prophets of gloom have been proved wrong. Our relations with Soviet Russia have acquired new strength, a new quality and a new dimension. Recently the Soviet Prime Minister, Mr. Kosygin, was in India. He had a free and frank exchange of views with our Prime Minister. On many international issues India and Soviet Russia hold identical views. If there are any differences we would not allow them to come in the way of our growing co-operation. The Prime Minister will be visiting Moscow next month. He will be paying a visit to some other countries in Europe—Yugoslavia, Poland and Czechoslovakia. Sir, I entirely agree with Hon. members when they say that India-Soviet friendship has stood the test of time. And that friendship does not depend on a single individual or a particular political party. But our relations with the United States of America have also improved. Now, somebody said that I went to Washington and came back empty-handed. Sir, I did not go there to bring back with me a bagful of enriched uranium. I had gone to attend the meeting of the Indo-American Joint Commission. The meeting took place; the meeting was successful.

AN HON. MEMBER : The member said some other good things also.

SHRI VAJPAYEE : There are differences. But there are common ideals which we share. Both are open societies. Differences are on Tarapur. Now, my friend Mr. Bhattacharya has gone away.

DR. V.P. DUTT : Conveniently.

SHRI VAJPAYEE : So far America has not violated the contractual obligation to supply enriched uranium to Tarapur. And we hope that the legislation passed by the Congress will not be applied retrospectively.

DR. V.P. DUTT : Do you really believe that ?

SHRI VAJPAYEE : As the Prime Minister said, if there is violation of the contractual obligation India will be free to make its own arrangements. We told our American friends that they should not think in terms of evolving a new military arrangement in this region, nor is induction of new arms going to help any country. Sir, there was no paucity of, no dearth of, arms in Iran, but the Shah had to abdicate. Some of the countries in this region are facing problems of economic development, problems of political instability and these problems cannot be solved by supplying more arms...

SHRI CHARANJIT CHANANA : Excepting the sellers.

SHRI VAJPAYEE : ...which will generate new tensions and which will be used to put down their own people. I hope better sense will prevail.

Sir, on the whole, we have done well so far as the international relations are concerned. But as my friends, Shri Ladli Mohan Nigam, Shri Sadashiv Bagaitkar and Shri Pranab Mukherjee...

SHRI PRANAB MUKHERJEE (West Bengal) : It is Shri Pranab Chatterjee.

SHRI VAJPAYEE : ...pointed out—when I heard their speeches I was reminded of Dr. Ram Manohar Lohia, whose contribution to these debates was great, it has yet to be evaluated—that they would like me to do something different. I wish I could do something of that sort. But I do not have a clean slate to write upon.

DR. V.P. DUTT : That is our only hope.

SHRI VAJPAYEE : We are living in a complex and complicated world, Shri Ladli Mohan Nigam has said one thing which I would like to underline, namely that unless we are strong internally we cannot maintain our high prestige abroad. But we are not that weak internally. India is a force to be reckoned with. Our size, our population, our natural resources, industrial infrastructure, our political stability, our skilled manpower they all help us in playing a more positive and more dynamic role. But my friends' complaint is that while I was in the opposition I was more dynamic but now I have become less dynamic. I do not know what is that touchstone. If I announce the recognition of Kampuchea tomorrow I will become dynamic, and if I delay, then I am not so dynamic.

Nuclear-Free World

Sir, now I have to implement a policy and I have to safeguard India's vital national interests. But my friends sitting opposite are now in the same position in which I was before coming to these benches. Those who were opposed to atomic weapons now have become supporters of atomic weapons and they remind me of my old speeches. Sir, I made speeches as a member of the Jan Sangh Party. The Jan Sangh Party does not exist now. We have accepted a common programme. And India would like the entire world to be nuclear weapon-free. We are asking for total and complete disarmament. And if that happens there will be no need to have more arms so far as India is concerned. But so long as it does not happen we have to be careful. We have not neglected our security. We have succeeded in striking a balance between defence and development, and our foreign policy is trying to serve our national goal.

Sir, I am grateful to the Hon. members...

DR. V.P. DUTT : Sir, the Hon. Minister has not replied to the basic question that we raised and that was about Pakistan's atomic bomb. What is going to be the response of India towards this developing trend ?

SHRI VAJPAYEE : The Hon. member knows the answer. We observed restraint when China decided to manufacture atomic weapons. Every effort is being made to dissuade Pakistan from joining this disastrous race. Militarily, they do not require atomic weapons; economically, they cannot sustain atomic weapons. They have nothing to be afraid of us. The Prime Minister is in correspondence with President Zia. Other countries are also trying to exert their influence. But let us not get panicky.

DR. V.P. DUTT : Sir, this is also another extreme, words like panic: what is panic ?

SHRI VAJPAYEE : Simply because there are reports that Pakistan is engaged in the manufacture of atomic weapons should we throw away our entire atomic policy ? A new situation is developing...

DR. V.P. DUTT : That is what we are asking. What is your atomic policy ?

SHRI VAJPAYEE : I am not prepared to enter, at this late hour, into an argument and describe what is our atomic policy. Let my Hon. friend address his question to the Prime Minister and he will get a befitting reply.

DR. V.P. DUTT : He does not reply; it is only unilateral.

SHRI VAJPAYEE : With these words, Sir, I thank the Hon. members.

Agreement Between Two Super Powers A Good Omen for the World

Mr. Deputy Chairman, Sir, today, when I rise to initiate a discussion on the working of the Ministry of External Affairs, my mind goes back to the period between 1962 and 1967. At that time I was a member of this House. Our first Prime Minister was also in charge of the Ministry of External Affairs. The international situation used to be discussed regularly in the House. Pandit Jawaharlal Nehru himself used to take the initiative for a discussion. That tradition appears to have been lost now. The international situation and the Indian Government's policy in that regard is a subject which is closely connected with our national interest. And national interest binds us together, whether we may sit on the treasury benches or in the Opposition. There could be some difference of opinion as to what constitutes national interest in a particular situation, but when common interests bind us they provide stability to foreign policy—a stability that is not static but dynamic, in which there should be continuity, not lack of direction. I find that the occasions for discussions of foreign policy have now become rare. It is not enough to discuss it in the House. It is a subject on which there should be constant exchange of views even outside the House.

Constant Interaction Required

I had, therefore, requested Shri P.V. Narasimha Rao, Minister of External Affairs, to call a meeting of the Consultative Committee attached to the Ministry of External Affairs to discuss the crisis that has erupted in Indo-Nepal relations. I wanted that meeting to be held before the demands and the working of this Ministry came up for discussion in the House. But I am sorry to say that Shri Narasimha Rao did not accede to my request. He sent me a reply to the effect that there is going to be a discussion on the Ministry. Of course, the Ministry would be discussed in the House, but why have relations between Nepal and India suddenly deteriorated so much ? It is necessary to have an informal discussion on this matter. An attempt has been made to explain the Nepalese version to me. The Nepalese Ambassador in New Delhi has been meeting people, telling them the Nepalese side. But I do not know the full version of our own Government. It is not a happy situation.

Rajya Sabha on April 27, 1989 while initiating discussion on International Situation

Non-Alignment

We want to know the background of the problems, we should be in constant touch with each other in regard to the foreign policy of the country. Shri Natwar Singh was right. I was going through his speech in which he has stated that, broadly speaking, there has been a national consensus in regard to foreign policy. It is true that there have been some people who wanted us to join this or that bloc. But the majority of the people in India, the mainstream of thought in India, including the Opposition parties, has supported this policy of not joining any military bloc and deciding each and every question on its merit. Today that policy stands vindicated.

Non-alignment means not only acceptance of the fact of existence of diversity in the world, but also promotion of a spirit of co-existence between various social and economic orders.

Dramatic Change in International Situation

The changes that have come about in the international situation are soothing. There have been amazing and dramatic changes. Sometimes it is difficult to recognise the changed world, but the world has undoubtedly changed. The two super powers have reached an agreement. For the first time an agreement has been reached between them in which they have consented not to control but to reduce the number of certain kinds of nuclear weapons, and that is being actually done. A provision for inspection has been made for this purpose. Soviet representatives have visited the U.S.A. to see whether inter-continental missiles have been dismantled or not, and U.S. representatives have visited Russia for the same purpose. It was not imaginable sometime back.

The Soviet Union has unilaterally declared a reduction in its armed forces, and they are implementing it. The I.N.F. Accord is a historic agreement. And it is really surprising that the agreement was signed by none else than President Reagan, who used to say that 'the Soviet Union is an evil boy and the leader of the Soviet Union is out to convert the whole world into red'.

Nehru's Contribution

Just as Pandit Jawaharlal Nehru showed great courage and far-sightedness by evolving the policy of non-alignment during the cold war period in the world, so is President Gorbachev going ahead with great fortitude. This agreement has had its side-effects the world over. Regional disputes have been resolved. The Iran-Iraq war has come to an end. The Gulf area is quiet. The Soviet army has quit Afghanistan. In fact, there should have been no Soviet intervention in Afghanistan. I do not want to go into the entire history now. At that time I was in New York. There was no need for military intervention, but the Soviet Union took that decision and later realised that they had committed a mistake. Now Cuban forces are withdrawing from Angola. A serious dialogue is afoot for the withdrawal of Vietnamese forces from Kampuchea. The P.L.O. has recognised the existence of Israel. The

U.S.A. has initiated a dialogue with the P.L.O. It is true that Israel is adamant but it should change its attitude. There is no justification for Israel to continue occupation of the Arab land. Israel has to quit that area. If an international conference is called to resolve the question of West Asia, for which India is insisting, a way could be found to resolve the impasse. New combinations and permutations are being evolved in the world. Old differences are being eroded, new friendships are being forged.

Foreign Policy Responding to Challenges ?

In view of these changing alignments our foreign policy as well as our diplomacy should be more dynamic. Sometimes it appears that our diplomacy is not suitably meeting the challenge. Was serious thought given to the situation arising after the departure of Soviet troops from Afghanistan ? I admit that the Geneva Accord is being observed faithfully by the U.S.A.The way the Mujahideens are being aided is not indicative of the will to bring peace in Afghanistan or let it emerge as a non-aligned country. But nobody is in a position to do anything. We are also feeling helpless, except that we could present our point of view forcefully in the Security Council. What role do we have to play ? Perhaps we had thought that the Soviet Union is not going to pull out so soon.

India has to Take Initiative

Shri Natwar Singh has been meeting the ex-ruler of Afghanistan, King Zaheer Shah, but I do not think that we are playing any substantive role in Afghanistan at the moment. It is all right that we extend our support to the Government of Afghanistan, but we are also demanding that the Government should be broad-based. Have we established any contacts with the other elements or groups that are likely to join the broad-based Government ? They are not anti-Indian, but we count them as our opponents. This is not justified. Similarly, tomorrow the Soviet Union and China may improve their relations; they should. But that creates a new situation for us. Today a new situation has arisen before the entire Non-Aligned Movement. So long as the cold war existed there was competition between the super-powers, there was hostility between them and we thought we had a mission. Now we feel as if there is nothing left to be done. Recently I was at the United Nations Assembly. During the meeting of the General Assembly I found that the non-aligned nations were looking for a new role. Now India has to take the initiative to give new relevance to the Non-Aligned Movement. Non-alignment is not a *mantra* it is a guiding light.

There does not exist as much South-South cooperation as there should be. Efforts for a new international order are inadequate. Those who talk of peace do not appear to be fulfilling their commitments to peace when it comes to their involvement.

A Dynamic Approach Needed

I remember, it was in 1986 that Soviet leaders had come here. They had to say in their speeches that rumours were being spread that the Soviet Union would desert India, but it was baseless since our friendship stood on the foundations of certain permanent ideals. In certain quarters in the Soviet Union a question is being asked as to what would happen to us in the scenario of changing policies. In case the Soviet Union resumes friendly relations with China, where do we stand ? We have been highlighting this from the very beginning and we will without doubt have to stand on our own feet; we too have to seek new alignments. In this changing world, we have to pursue a dynamic diplomacy which could turn these changing alignments into an opportunity. We have to use this situation as a challenge to mould the world according to our dreams and carry out our national objectives. Mr. Deputy Speaker, Sir, ultimately the aim of foreign policy is to safeguard the freedom of the nation, to preserve the inviolability of the borders and to create conditions in which our country could march ahead without hindrance on the path of development as chosen by us. There could be no two opinions about these aims and objectives.

The Prime Minister had visited China and Pakistan. These countries are our neighbours. There is an extremely bitter chapter of our relations with China. I myself had visited China in 1979. The talks proceeded very well, but in the meantime China invaded Vietnam, with the result that the visit came to naught. I am happy that no such incident took place this time. But the success of my foreign visit could not be measured in terms of the time taken in shaking hands by a particular leader. Where there was no handshake and only an 'Adab Arj' should we take it that the visit or the talks were a complete failure ? If two heads of State—Presidents or Prime Ministers—call each other by their first name it also does not indicate closeness of their relations. If, for intance, instead of saying Shri P.V. Narasimha Rao, I say, 'Narasimha Rao, how do you do ?' and Shri Narasimha Rao replies, 'Atal, I am all right', how are you ?'

SHRI SATYA PRAKASH MALAVIYA (U.P.) : He is not treating properly.

SHRI VITHALRAO MADHAVRAO JADHAV (Maharashtra) : Treatment should be *atal* (firm).

Tibet and Nehru's Blunder

If the interests of the country are at stake the attitude of co-operation is missing, relations sour. One question has not been answered so far in regard to the Prime Minister's visit to China. I had raised this question the other day even at the meeting of the Consultative Committee. During the Prime Minister's visit to China, when the Chinese leaders themselves raised the question of Tibet, they offered us an opportunity to speak out our views on Tibet. I am an admirer of Pandit Nehru, but by accepting Tibet as a part of China he had committed a Himalayan blunder. I do not want to go into the details of why this blunder was committed. Tibet has a right to be free. But the blunder was committed. Tibet was recognised as an 'autonomous region' of China. Where is that autonomy today ? Human rights are being violated. Martial law has been declared. There is suppression on a large scale. Terror is let loose. So when an opportunity was provided to us by the Chinese leaders themselves by raising the Tibet issue why did we not take advantage of it by raising the question of violation of human rights in Tibet and discussing it with the Chinese leaders in a friendly atmosphere ? There has been a change in the viewpoint of the Dalai Lama. Peking should have welcomed that change. But Tibetans are fighting for their identity, for their existence. China is trying to rectify the mistakes committed during the 'cultural revolution' in the domestic field. China should also rectify the mistakes commited by it in foreign affairs. We should also urge them to do so. But if we keep quiet in the matter of Tibet we shall not be doing justice either to Tibet or to us.

Pakistani Interference

Sir, the question of human rights is not confined to one country. Democracy has been restored in Pakistan. We are happy about it. It is good that our relations may improve further. But, in my view, there is only one test of whether there has been an improvement or not in our relations with Pakistan. And that is whether Pakistan has stopped interfering in our internal affairs, including Punjab and Jammu and Kashmir. I do not understand why Pakistan continues to meddle in Punjab, though this has come down. What does it indicate ? Sometimes it is said that Begun Benazir wants to reduce it, but other elements do not allow her to do so. Shall we have relations with the Government of Pakistan, or will we go about in search of other elements ? Then there is fresh infiltration in Jammu and Kashmir. Pakistan continues to aid terrorists in Punjab. You know how much furore was created in the House today on the question of their continued activities in Jammu and Kashmir. It is necessary to put this matter before Pakistan forcefully.

India-Nepal : An Example in Close Relations

Mr. Chairman, I will now like to take up Nepal, our neighbour. The Minister of External Affairs has rightly stated that our relations with Nepal are unique. No two countries in the world could be so close as Nepal and India are. We are bound with each other by history, geography, tradition, culture, religion and rivers. Nearly 1700 km long length of our border is open, no passport or visa is required. Indians work there and lakhs of Nepalese work here. Gorkhas have been associated with our Armed Forces and still have links with them. Now suddenly what has happened ? I have received a letter from Kathmandu. It is dated April 10. The letter is addressed to Shri Advani, and endorsed to me. I am quoting a portion from it :

> "Nepal is facing an acute shortage of essential commodities after the expiry of trade and transit treaty on March 23. Nepal feels that India has put economic blockade against it. The people in the kingdom are not getting salt, kerosene, sugar, petrol, diesel, cooking gas, medicines and

other items. Rationing has been introduced and whatever is available is being distributed among people standing in big queues in every ward of the Panchayat of the town."

This is a letter from an Indian who resides there. Now it is quite all right for the Government of India to say, let the Government of Nepal decide what kind of relationship they want to maintain with India. The difficulty is that the people of Nepal are suffering as a result of this. Here in India the people are partners in the functioning of the Government, because we are a democracy. If the Government is not good then the people will have to suffer, because they elected it. But we cannot say this about Nepal. Nepal is a monarchy. The Nepalese people have no say in the Government. They are asking, they can ask only their rulers, they are asking us too, what has happened, how has this come about ? It is alleged that Nepal had started this discrimination against India since 1987. They had issued a notification to the effect that Indians should be treated as foreigners. Objection was also being taken to the employment of Indians by the companies of the third world countries. It is also said that something more happened in 1982. I want to know why this matter was allowed to hang on for such a long time. The trade and transit treaties expired on March 23, I was looking at the statement of Shri Narasimha Rao, it took five long months to prepare a package after that.

I do not know who is at fault. Maybe Nepal is at fault. Nepal then did not adhere to the package deal made with the Nepalese Ministers and the situation deteriorated further. I think some lacuna must have remained there. I do not have the full facts before me. But I know one thing—the only one way to achieve success in diplomacy with Nepal is to have rapport with the King of Nepal. He is all-in-all. There has always been an element in the King's palace that has been anti-Indian, that brings in a third country between India and Nepal. Even in the present crisis there is the shadow of a third country. Our mistake is that previously we used to send some heavy-weight political leader as our ambassador to Kathmandu, who used to be a very high dignitary and who succeeded in establishing a direct contact with the King of Nepal, but this time it has not been so. The present ambassador to Nepal has worked with me. He is an able officer. But requirements of the palace are different. The palace has different demands, and if it is the King's Court the situation is still more different. But nowadays there are courtiers in a democracy also. One has to see who has an approach there. In the case of Nepal that was not done.

It is correct that the 1950 treaty was an instrument to give legal shape to our traditional relations. We had old relations. The ambassadress of Nepal had seen me. She had told me that they wanted to follow the 1950 treaty, that they were bound by the treaty of 1950. We did not say that we wanted to revise the 1950 treaty. It is, of course, for Nepal to decide whether it wants to have special relations with us or the 'most-favoured nation treatment'. I was going through the speech of Shri Narasimha Rao. The legal position is that we have not ratified those international agreements under which Nepal could take advantage of being a land-locked country.

Nepal is not a member of GATT and India has not ratified the International Convention on Transit Trade of Land-Locked Countries. India has also not ratified the United Nations Convention on the Law of the Sea. Therefore India has no legal responsibility. But this matter is not so legal, not that narrow. We have our own responsibility in it. We have a responsibility towards the people of Nepal and we should carry out that responsibility. It is necessary to resolve this stalemate at the earliest. As I said, Nepal has to take a firm decision as to what she wishes. If she does not want to have special relations with us she would have to get herself ready for ordinary relations. But our diplomacy is on test here. And its success would be observed in its application. Now it is being propagated in the world— recently a gentleman had come back from Europe and told us that it is being propagated—that India has effected economic blockade against Nepal. They do not know the facts. The fact is that India cannot effect economic blockade against Nepal even if it wanted, because our borders are open. Smuggling is going on unabated, traders are making hay and prices are rising. People are unhappy. There is need to find a way out in view of the miserable condition of the people.

MR. DEPUTY CHAIRMAN (Shri Jagesh Desai) : Mr. Vajpayee, how much more time do you require ?

Relations with West Germany

SHRI VAJPAYEE : There are two or three small issues. Sir, our relations with West Germany have been very cordial. We have co-operation with them in the economic field. We have cultural exchanges. But certain incidents that are taking place raise certain questions regarding West Germany. First, there is the case of submarines. Sir, you might recall that a United Nations Committee is investigating as to how West Germany provided to South Africa the blue-print of the submarines on the basis of which we had purchased them from it. No country is allowed to provide such material to South Africa. West Germany has violated that, and, indirectly, we also have got entangled in it.

When the question of setting up of a chemical gas factory in Libya was raised, again the name of West Germany figured. The report in *Wall Street Journal* says :

> "The West German companies have admitted supplying nuclear weapons-related material to Pakistan, the material being zirconium, and disclosed that one of their unwitting sources was India."

Today an Indian Government spokesman has admitted that such material was sent :

> "It was officially stated here today that the Nuclear Fuel Complex in Hyderabad sent a small quantity of zinc alloy tubes to a company in West Germany in 1983-84. The West German firm said that they needed the tubes for certain tests and gave an undertaking that these would neither be re-exported nor resold."

But they supplied it to Pakistan. This is a serious matter. It is necessary to raise this matter firmly at higher levels with Germany. Exchanges would no doubt take place between the two countries, but if they are providing material to our neighbours which may endanger our safety we must be prepared to review our relations with them.

Withdraw Army from Sri Lanka

Elections have been held in Sri Lanka. The President has been elected. Parliament has been constituted. A North-East Council has been set up. There is no justification now to keep the Indian Army there any more. There is no need for it. Howsoever close a neighbour might be, howsoever close a friend might be, if a need arises to send the army there it is also necessary to ensure that the withdrawal of the army is carried out at the earliest. If a foreign army is stationed in a country antagonism is created amongst the people against the people whose forces are stationed there.

Even the superpowers have started doing it, but after paying a heavy price. The U.S.A. had intervened in Vietnam but had to withdraw after a great deal of humiliation. It is true that we had not intervened, we had gone there at their invitation.

Our jawans tried to help them by sacrificing their own lives. But if the people of Sri Lanka do not want to live in peace our armed forces cannot establish permanent peace there. We have played our role. Even otherwise the jawans are being used now for police work. The army is not meant for that purpose.

Minorities in Bangladesh

Since the declaration of Bangladesh as a Islamic State there is unrest among the minorities there. Earlier, people had already been infiltrating into India from Bangladesh, now there is an exodus of Hindus from there on a large scale. Its consequences will not be good.

The formation of SAARC was a step in the right direction. This region is compact. Nature has made it so. History has brought it together. The environment has united it. Now its economic needs are uniting it. But if bitterness is created in mutual relations multilateral co-operation is bound to be adversely affected. It is essential to tell Bangladesh that it cannot throw its burden upon us. They should face their own problems, they should create conditions in their country so that people may live there with dignity. India has created such conditions here, but such conditions do not prevail in Bangladesh.

Namibia

Sir, you have been pleased to give me time, I thank you for that. (*Interruption*). My friend Shri Verma is reminding me that I forgot Namibia in the flow of my speech.

MR. DEPUTY CHAIRMAN (Shri Jagesh Desai) : Please do not repeat.

SHRI VAJPAYEE : I have caught it. I cannot let it go now.

The whole world has been asking for the liberty of Namibia. All countries have been raising their voice in support of it. We hope that Namibia marches forward with a quick pace in the direction of independence.

Concept and Conduct of Foreign Policy

I will say only one thing and finish. India is a great country. We have a status and we have got responsibilities in conformity with that status. We occupy a respectable position befitting our status. We have also conducted our foreign policy accordingly. One thing in foreign policy is concept, the other is conduct. There has been some disturbance in the conduct at certain places, but the basic concept is all right. Our foreign service is an able diplomatic service. But it should get proper guidelines from New Delhi. At times I fail to understand where this foreign policy is formulated in New Delhi. Who formulates it ? Where are the decisions taken ? Why are there delays ? Why does it sometimes look immature ?

SHRI SATYA PRAKASH MALAVIYA : There is a foreign hand behind the foreign policy too.

SHRI VAJPAYEE : Foreign policy is something which binds the entire nation and all parties since it involves national interests. It is necessary to protect national interests by joining hands. Though it is a difficult task in an election year we have to accomplish this difficult task too. Thank you.

Mr. Prime Minister Don't Succumb to American Pressure

Mr. Speaker, Sir, the Prime Minister has accepted the invitation from the President of the United States of America. The date of his visit to U.S.A. has also been fixed according to the convenience of the Prime Minister. The heads of both the countries, the U.S. President Mr. Clinton and Prime Minister Mr. Narasimha Rao, have not met each other anywhere so far. Therefore, this meeting has become all the more important.

The apprehensions that are being expressed about this meeting need to be removed by the Government. Some of them have been removed, but that is not sufficient. Even if this visit had not materialised, the pressure that U.S. has been putting on us would increase further. This pressure is not only about N.P.T. This Treaty is going to be revised. We have told them that a discriminatory treaty is not acceptable to us. The pressure would increase because America wants to put Pakistan and India at par, while India's security requirements are different.

China is our neighbour. China has accumulated a large stockpile of nuclear weapons. Our relations with China are improving, that is a good thing. Efforts should be made to further improve the relations. Shri Bansal was referring to my China visit. As a matter of fact this improvement in relations with China started at that time and it was agreed that peace should prevail on the border. China had attacked Vietnam, not India. But it was made a big issue due to political reasons in order to scuttle the success of my visit, I do not want to go into that.

Mr. Speaker, Sir, our security perceptions are not confined to Pakistan alone. If Pakistan acquires F-16 aircraft, we know how to face them and our forces are capable of giving a befitting reply to that. But the question is, why should America supply F-16 planes to Pakistan ? At present there is a strike in the Lockheed factory. Lockheed is running in losses. They have to sell their planes, so why not give them to our neighbour ? The aircraft and the weapons given to our neighbour so far have been used against us, not for fighting against communism. Although the arms were supplied for use against Soviet Russia, but they were used against us. For whom does Pakistan want F-16 planes ? America says that if we want to purchase arms, they are ready to supply F-16 planes to us also. Is an arms race going to be set into motion in this region ?

Lok Sabha on May 2, 1994 during the Zero Hour discussion on the proposed visit of the Prime Minister to U.S.A.

Mr. Speaker, the real point of contention is whether N.P.T. relates to South Asia or the whole world ? Soviet Union has disintegrated and nuclear weapons have spread out along with that. Now independent republics have been set up in Asia, they have got atomic weapons. There are other countries in the world which have the capability of manufacturing nuclear weapons. They are called as threshold countries. America is making all efforts to make India and Pakistan agree to settle this issue between themselves, otherwise they may be pressurised to come to a settlement. China is not ready to agree to disarmament and nobody is prepared to put pressure on China in this matter. America is ready to have trade with China and it is prepared to sidetrack the issue of human rights. The position that China should sit as a judge over us is not acceptable to us.

However, America is putting pressure on us for arriving at an agreement covering South Asia. The Government is opposing it, but it seems to me that the Government may succumb to the pressure and change its policy.

Whatever discussion takes place about non-proliferation, the countries which are on the threshold must be included in it. North Korea and Israel must join the discussion. It is necessary to include those countries of Latin America in the discussion which claim to have developed atomic weapons' technology. But America does not bother about it. When the Prime Minister visits Washington, intense pressure is likely to be put upon him. We hope that pressure would be resisted. After all, the Prime Minister has to report to the Parliament of this country on his return. This Parliament would demand a reply from him. But the apprehensions have become deep that it is being suggested that the Prime Minister should cancel this visit. I do not think that the Prime Minister can do so because things have gone too far. I had also given an interview to the Voice of America earlier in which I had suggested that the Prime Minister should not go. But now the invitation has come, the date was changed, all preparations are underway. Therefore, now we will have to tell our Prime Minister that the entire Parliament and the whole country would support him, but he must not budge from the role which India has to play in such important matters. We have to give this message to the Prime Minister.

A good suggestion has come from Shri Chatterjee in this regard that the Government should remove all misconceptions by reiterating and again declaring that it stands firmly by its commitment. A comprehensive statement should be made in Parliament before the Prime Minister's visit, which may satisfy the House as well as remove all misconceptions that have crept into the minds of the people. Thank you.

II Neighbouring Countries

Tibet

Why Tibet Cannot Remain Independent ?

Mr. Deputy Speaker, Sir, it cannot be denied that the happenings in Tibet have caused strains in the relations between India and China. But India is not responsible for these tensions.

Notwithstanding the fact that India had very cordial relations with Chiang-kai-Shek, when the Communist regime came to China we welcomed it and tried harder than China itself to get her a respectable place in the comity of nations. Looking at our zeal, sometimes it looks as if we were more eager for that than China itself. We pleaded for China because we thought that even though we had differences with Communism, it was for the Chinese people to decide whether to follow the path of Communism. China and India could remain friends though they had different lifestyles.

China's Occupation of Tibet

But the first blow was struck to that friendship on the day Chinese armies 'liberated' Tibet. Our Prime Minister had asked at that time from whose cultches Tibet was being 'liberated', because Tibet was not under the control of any other country. India is the closest neighbour of Tibet. Our past history shows that if we had desired to amalgamate Tibet with India we could have done so. But the Chinese leaders who are levying charges of expansionism against India forget that we never tried to amalgamate Tibet with India. Tibet is small but we respected its independent existence. We honoured Tibet's freedom and we had expected that China would do the same. But Communists have their own methods. Their words have different connotations. When they want to enslave they say they were going to liberate. Today, when they have let loose suppression, they say they want to reform. If one wants to bring reforms those supposed to be reformed should have an inclination for reforms. Reforms could not be imposed from above.

Whatever is happening in Tibet cannot be called reforms. China should have respected the autonomy of Tibet as per agreement. But China intervened in the internal affairs of Tibet. Lakhs of Chinese were brought to

Lok Sabha on May 8, 1959 while discussion on situation in Tibet

Tibet for resettlement so that Tibetans themselves were reduced to a minority in their own country and subsequently Tibet could become an integral part of China. Thousands of Tibetan youths were sent to China to learn the new religion. But when they returned home and the Chinese leaders found that their brain-washing was not having the desired effect on them, that their spirit of being Tibetans could not be washed away, that their zest to maintain their distinct identity and protect their way of life continued unabated, they tried to destroy the Tibetan way of life. The present conflict has arisen due to the lust of a big nation to swallow a small nation.

Recognition of Chinese Suzerainty over Tibet was a Blunder

Mr. Deputy Speaker, Sir, my submission is that we committed a great blunder by accepting Chinese suzerainty over Tibet. It was the most unfortunate day. But the blunder was committed. And perhaps we thought that this matter would be resolved, a new conflict would not be created. We did not want that others should get an opportunity to take advantage of our differences with China. But what was the result ? China not only violated their terms of agreement with Tibet, but also violated the terms of agreement entered into with India in the background of that agreement. Where is the *Panchsheel* declaration ? Some votaries of *Panchsheel* claim that democracy and dictatorship can co-exist under *Panchsheel*. If the peaceful and religious minded people of Tibet cannot protect their particular lifestyle under communist empire it is meaningless to say that communism and democracy can co-exist in this wide world. We do not want to interfere in the internal affairs of China. But Tibet is not an internal affair of China. China is bound by agreement to respect autonomy of Tibet and not to interfere in the internal matters of Tibet. But that agreement has become null and void, and I think it is time the Government of India also review its position. Agreements should be respected by both the parties, they should be followed by both the sides. If China has violated the agreement we have a right to review our position. What is the reason for depriving the Tibetan people of their liberty ?

Jan Sangh Supports Independence of Tibet

Why can Tibet not remain independent ? They say it was not independent before. Cannot a country which was not independent previously have a right to become independent ? Should slavery continue where it was prevailing previously ? If we can support the call for the independence of Algeria, and that support does not amount to interference in the internal affairs of France, then how could support for the independence of Tibet be construed as interference in the internal affairs of China ? Just now my friend Mr. Khadilkar said that there is no party in the country which supports the independence of Tibet. I differ from him. I represent a small party, but my party supports the independence of Tibet. It is not the number of people who raise their voice in support of independence of Tibet that makes this demand right or wrong. Chinese colonialists can suppress the voice for the independence of Tibet today with their muscle power, but the hunger for independence cannot be suppressed. Suppression would lead to fanning that fire and, if not today, tomorrow Tibetan people would win their freedom.

But the question is what can we do about it ? I submit that we committed a blunder in 1950. Now we are reaping the harvest. But it is time to repent and recognise our blunder. I expect the Prime Minister to correctly express the wishes of crores of people of this country on this occasion. Barring a few friends India is united in saying that whatever is happening in Tibet must stop. But is it possible that Tibet can enjoy its autonomy in the Chinese State ? It appears to me that autonomy and the Communist system are antagonistic to each other. There cannot be any autonomy in a Communist State. In 1930 Mao Tse-tung had said that they had framed a constitution under which if any one wanted to secede he could do so. Tibetans did not talk of secession. They wanted to maintain their separate entily but they were not allowed even this.

Mao also said that he wanted to see a flower bloom with thousands of petals. Let alone thousands, even the dainty bud of Tibet is being stifled. The colonialists in Tibet are making allegations against us. We never tried to annex Tibet with India. When we pleaded the case of China for membership of the United Nations we could have pleaded for admitting Tibet too. Ukraine is a part and parcel of the Soviet Union, but it occupies a separate seat in the United Nations. Could Tibet then not occupy a separate seat in the United Nations even though allied to China ? But we did not do so in order to earn the friendship of China. What did we get in return ?

China's Friendship not Required at the Cost of Tibet

We require China's friendship even today, but the palace of that friendship cannot be built on the corpse of the independence of Tibet. We cannot shut our eyes to injustice. This has been the tradition of India, and our Prime Minister has conducted the foreign policy of this country according to this tradition. Wherever there is injustice, violation of human rights or oppression, we will raise our voice against it, we will speak the language of truth, and we will fearlessly protect the rights of the oppressed. Today Tibet is the acid test of Shri Nehru's statesmanship, Tibet is the test of the Government of India's firmness, Tibet is the test of China's adherence to *Panchsheel*. Mere declarations of *Panchsheel* cannot bring respect to the spirit behind *Panchsheel*. The test of *Panchsheel* lies in its implementation.

However restrained our Prime Minister may be, if that does not solve the problem of Tibet we will have to admit that there is need to bring some firmness, some dynamism in that policy.

Whether the Dalai Lama should live in Tibet or leave it is not such a crucial question. This would be decided by Tibetans themselves. But Tibet is a test case of annexation of a small nation by a big nation. If small countries were to be annexed in this manner peace could not prevail in the world. There are so many countries in South-East Asia where the Chinese live in large numbers. A wave of panic has gripped all these countries because of Tibet. So far as India is concerned China is casting an evil eye on us. Indian territory has been shown as belonging to China in Chinese maps. Chinese Communists have thrown away Chiang Kai Shek, but have retained his maps. Had they so desired, they could have discarded his maps too. Our Communist friends have not even seen those maps, though I do not believe them. These maps constitute an indirect attack by China on India. The Chinese have occupied two places in Uttar Pradesh. These incidents are indicative of future danger. We need not become panickly, but we should adopt a firm policy.

Don't Restrict Dalai Lama's Freedom

I want to make one more submission. The Dalai Lama has come to India. He is a fighter for freedom. He is struggling for the independence of his country, as a result of which he had to quit his country and come to India. I want that he should have a right to fight for the freedom of his country from Indian soil. The restrictions imposed upon him, although they are for security purposes, need to be relaxed. If our own patriots could fight for the freedom of India from foreign soil during the British days and could become the cynosure of our eyes there is no reason why the Dalai Lama should not have the liberty to do so.

Nothing could make the people of India happier if Dalai Lama succeeds in reaching an agreement with China and our Prime Minister could act as a mediator between the two. But if the Chinese leaders are not amenable to reason, cannot be made to see reason through political or diplomatic pressures, and cannot be influenced through an effective mobilisation of public opinion in Burma, Lanka and Indonesia and a clear expression thereof, then no other option is left except to give liberty to Dalai Lama to make efforts for the freedom of his country.

We Know the Pangs of Slavery, We Know the Price of Freedom

The youth of India consider Tibet's freedom invaluable, not because they have close relations with Tibet, but because we have experienced slavery, we know the pangs of slavery, we know the price of freedom. Hence he should have freedom to work. If the Tibetan people struggle for their freedom the people of India would always be with them. We would extend our sympathy to them and we expect China too not to talk in terms of imperialism. The days of imperialism are over, but this is a new type of imperialism. The danger in it is that it comes in the guise of revolution, with slogans for a new order; but it is colonialism, it is stark imperialism. In the past we had been fighting with white imperialism, but now yellow imperialism has raised its ugly head on the roof of the world. We should firmly face it too. Thank you.

Refer Tibet Issue to the U.N.

Sir, I beg to move :

"This House is of opinion that Government should refer the Tibetan issue to the United Nations."

Sir, the General Assembly of the United Nations is going to meet from the 15th September, 1959. The Government of India have decided to raise the question of China's admission into the United Nations. By this Resolution I want this House to recommend to the Government that the Tibetan issue should also be raised in the United Nations.

India has been a strong champion of the United Nations, and that is the only ray of hope in a world threatened with nuclear wars. We have all along maintained that international conflicts should be settled by sitting round the table, the use of force should not be resorted to and that all disputes should be settled by negotiation. We have adopted an independent policy in the international sphere away from the warring groups, because we think that it is the only correct policy not only in the best interests of our nation but also in the interests of world peace. By this policy India has achieved a certain stature. We command respect. The peoples of the world look to our Prime Minister when they are in distress not because we are militarily stronger, not because we have armaments, but because we try to adopt a policy based on moral considerations in the international sphere. This moral force which India has come to possess demands that whenever there is any aggression we should support the just cause; and in the past, when the independence of any nation was threatened, India did not keep quiet. We also supported the right and the just cause without being afraid of any power.

You are aware that the question of Tibet was raised in the United Nations in 1950 when the armies of China marched into that country. On 25th October, 1950, the Chinese army entered Tibet and on 7th November, 1950 the leaders of Tibet sent a complaint to the United Nations against the Chinese aggression. On 18th November, 1950, the representative of El Salvador moved the United Nations formally and asked the General Assembly to create a special committee to study what measures should be adopted by the United Nations General Assembly to assist Tibet against the unprovoked Chinese aggression. But when the Steering Committee of the United Nations met the, Indian representatives asked the Committee to drop the whole matter and gave the assurance that the Chinese forces that were advancing had stopped and that the Committee need not go into tnis matter.

Lok Sabha on August 21, 1959 while moving the Resolution seeking Reference of the Tibet Issue to the United Nations

Nehru's Advice to Dalai Lama

The Government of India wanted that China and Tibet should settle the issue by peaceful negotiations and our Prime Minister advised the Dalai Lama to come to an agreement with Communist China in view of the assurances given by the Prime Minister of China, who visited India during those days. As a result of our assurances the Dalai Lama came to an agreement, the 17-point agreement, with China.

I need not go into that history now. What has happened in Tibet is clear. It is clear that the Sino-Tibetan agreement of 1951 has been violated. The Dalai Lama has been forced to leave his country and to seek refuge in India. With him, thousands of Tibetans have come to our country. Even then the Government of India wanted the situation to calm down in the hope that wisdom would prevail and a satisfactory solution of the Tibetan problem found.

What is happening in Tibet is very painful to all lovers of freedom and to all those who believe in human dignity. They are aghast at the fate of the Tibetans. Now it is not a question of Tibetan independence or autonomy. The question now is whether Tibet will remain an entity, whether Tibet's distinct personality will survive or the Tibetan people will be annihilated. We are aware, and the Dalai Lama has confirmed, that a large number of Chinese are being settled in Tibet. Five million have already been settled and four million are in the process of being settled. Besides this, there are a large number of army officials.

Sinister Aims of China

The whole aim of China is to reduce the Tibetans to a minority in their own country and thus to destroy the Tibetan personality. It is a new phenomenon; it is a new type of imperialism. Except in South Africa, the western countries, I mean the imperialists, subjugated other races, but they never tried to outnumber them in their own country so as to wipe them out completely from the map of the world. France has subjugated Algeria, but the Government of France respects the distinct personality of Algeria. But it appears that the people of Tibet will have to go the way of Inner Mongolia. Outer Mongolia, though not truly independent, has something of its own, but Inner Mongolia has been annexed and it has ceased to exist as a separate entity. That is happening in Tibet. The Human Rights Charter, to which Communist China is a party—because the Charter of Human Rights was approved at the Bandung Conference of Afro-Asians attended by China—these human rights are being violated in Tibet. According to the International Commission of Jurists the people of Tibet had been denied, and are still being denied, the right to life, liberty, and security. Forced labour has been inflicted on the Tibetans; torturous, cruel and degrading treatment is being inflicted on them; rights of home and privacy have been violated; freedom of movement within the state and the right to leave and to return to Tibet have been denied; marriages have been forced upon unwilling parties;

property rights have been arbitrarily violated and freedom of religion and worship has been systematically denied. If human rights are to be violated in this manner and by a nation which is seeking admission to the United Nations, the world, and especially our country, cannot and should not remain a silent spectator.

Violations of Human Rights by China

In addition to the violation of human righs the International Commission of Jurists has come to the conclusion, and they have evidence to show a *prima facie* case of a systematic intention to destroy in whole or in part Tibet as a separate nation and to put an end to Tibetan interest. A *prima facie* case of genocide according to the Convention of 1948 has also been made out by the Commission. I need not go into these charges. Unless a commission of independent countries can go into Tibet and find out for themselves what is happening, nothing can be said. In addition to this the Dalai Lama has stated that during this upsurge 65,000 people have perished and the people of Tibet have been denied freedom to frame their future according to their own ideas and conceptions.

Now the question is raised that since China is not a member of the United Nations no useful purpose will be served by referring this question to this august body. May I submit that India joined the nations who branded North Korea as an aggressor though North Korea was not a member of the United Nations ? We did not say at that time that since North Korea is not in the United Nations we are not going to join in condemning North Korea as an aggressor. We want that China should be admitted to the United Nations because we have faith in the United Nations and we think that whatever the form of Government the people of China may have, since the Government of China is the actual government and is actually in possession of the administration of that country China should be admitted to the United Nations. But everything does not depend on us. China is not there. But it does not mean that we should not refer the Tibetan issue to the United Nations.

Question of Existence of Smaller Countries

Another point made out is that if the Tibetan issue is referred to the United Nations it might intensify the cold war. When the Anglo-French invasion of Egypt took place the whole world joined in denouncing that aggression and no country, including ours, raised the apprehension or the fear that the Anglo-French aggression should not be denounced because it would become a part of the cold war. It is a question of the rights of man. It is a question whether smaller nations can exist in this world or not or will they have to lose their entity, will they have to be wiped out ? India has a moral duty to the people of Tibet. We have a moral responsibility. Apart from the considerations of India's security, with our age-old relations with Tibet, how can India remain silent when before our own eyes a nation, the personality of the people of Tibet, is being destroyed ?

Suppose India does not refer the question to the United Nations; some other country may raise it. I would like to know what our policy will be in that case. We cannot prevent other nations from raising that issue. What would be the policy of our Government ? All our attempts for a peaceful solution of the Tibetan tangle have failed. In spite of the best wishes of our Prime Minister Chinese communist leaders are not prepared to heed the voices of wisdom, reason and justice. On the contrary they are branding India and also the Indian people as imperialist. India relinquished its extra-territorial rights that accrued to us from the Britishers. The other day our Prime Minister objected to the boundary line between India and China being called as the MacMahon Line. He actually objected; he said, he disliked it, I think because the very name MacMahon smacks of British imperialism. As Shakespeare has remarked, there is nothing in the name. But it showed how deep our feelings are against imperialism. But then the Chinese communists are branding us as imperialists !

Chinese Propaganda against India

Propaganda against India, against the people of India, has been let loose by China. A journalist has estimated that in seven days from April 23 to 30, China, through its official newspapers, news agencies and radio has published, distributed and broadcast 77 articles, commentaries and editorials, totalling more than 40,000 words, condemning India in the most unrestrained imaginable language. Indians in Tibet are being harassed. Police are still posted in front of our Mission in Lhasa. Indian currency has been declared illegal. Cartographic aggression including 30,000 square miles of territory of India is still there. Our protest notes are not even replied to. Do we think that, in the present circumstances, China can be induced to accept the just demands of the Tibetan people ? The Dalai Lama has clearly stated that he and his fellows are not against social or economic reforms in Tibet. But now that stage has passed and I do not think there is any other course left for India but to mobilise world opinion in favour of the Tibetan people. I am sure something good will come out of it. As a nation that has faith in the United Nations, that is the only course left open for us.

Now that the Government of India have decided to raise the issue of China's recognition and admission into the United Nations, in spite of all that is being done and said against India by the Chinese Communists, I think it is but proper that the Tibetan issue should also be raised by our Government in the forthcoming meeting of the General Assembly of the United Nations. Government will have the benefit of knowing the wishes of the House in this matter, and I am sure my resolution will get wide support, and Government will accept it and will discharge the moral duty to the people of Tibet as a free nation.

With these words, I move the resolution.

MR. DEPUTY SPEAKER : Resolution moved :

> "This House is of opinion that Government should refer the Tibetan issue to the United Nations."

What is Our Policy in the Context of Tibet ?

Mr. Speaker, Sir, I have heard with rapt attention what the Hon'ble members have said on my resolution. I want to thank those members who have supported it, but while thanking also those who opposed it, I would like to say that I could simply not understand what their point of view was.

The problem of Tibet is before us. As the Hon'ble Prime Minister has said, when the question of Tibet was raised for the first time in the United Nations our representative there had expressed the hope that the problem of Tibet would be resolved peacefully through negotiations with China. But the history of the last nine years bears testimony to the fact that no effort was made to resolve the Tibetan problem peacefully. China used force in Tibet. China tried to abolish the free status of Tibet. I had said in my previous speech that the question now is not that of Tibetan autonomy or independence but the question was whether Tibet would survive as a separate country with all its characteristics ? If the hope of the Government of India that the question of Tibet would be resolved peacefully had materialised, India and this House would have been very happy. But indications so far are that there are very dim chances of resolution of this problem through mutual dialogue. The Prime Minister has also not expressed any such hope in his speech. We gave shelter to the Dalai Lama and his compatriots in India. That is indeed good, and all have welcomed it. But has India fulfilled its obligations towards Tibet just by offering shelter to the Dalai Lama ? Will the Dalai Lama and his colleagues be able to return to Tibet with honour and dignity ? Will the autonomy of Tibet, which was guaranteed by China, ever be restored ? Will Tibet be able to save its existence ? No answer was forthcoming to these questions.

What should be the Basis of Friendship

The Prime Minister said that his policy was to have friendship with China. The entire country is in agreement with this policy. Not only with China, we also want friendship with Pakistan. We want friendship with all the countries of the world. But the question is what should be the basis of that friendship ? At what cost shall we have that friendship ? We want friendship with France, but on that account we cannot refuse supporting freedom for Algiers. We also want friendship with Portugal but we cannot give up the demand for liberation of Goa for that reason. We want friendship with South Africa, but we did not desist from raising the question of the non-whites of South Africa

Lok Sabha on September 4, 1959 while replying to the discussion on the Resolution moved on August 21, 1959 regarding raising the Tibetan issue in the U.N.

in the United Nations. We raise the question of Indians in Africa in the United Nations every year. Every year South Africa refuses to comply with the decisions of the United Nations. But we raise this question because we think that there is no other way to resolve these questions apart from mobilising the public opinion throughout the world.

When I moved the resolution to take the Tibetan question to the United Nations my clear stand was that since we have faith in the United Nations we should raise the Tibetan question there. Moreover, we also believe in the genuineness of the complaint of Tibet. Hence we should raise this issue in the United Nations.

Raise the Tibet Question in the U.N.

Whether raising the issue of Tibet in the United Nations would be beneficial or not, may better be left to the wisdom of the Dalai Lama, the supreme leader of the Tibetans. Can any one else besides the Dalai Lama judge what is good for Tibet ? He has himself issued an appeal on 30th August to all the civilised nations of the world, including India, to raise the question of Tibet in the United Nations. If the Hon'ble Prime Minister refuses to accept my resolution it means that he refuses to accept the appeal of the Dalai Lama too. If the Dalai Lama thinks that it would be beneficial for Tibetans to raise the problem of Tibet in the United Nations. I think India should do so. The Prime Minister has also made it clear as to what our policy would be if any other country raises the question of Tibet in the United Nations. We cannot debar any other country of the world from raising this issue in the United Nations, Shall we say at that time that this question should not be raised ? Clear instructions should be issued in the matter to the Indian delegation which is going to attend the General Assembly session. I doubt if the leader of the Indian delegation to the General Assembly would be able to correctly represent the feelings of India on this question. On a previous occasion too he could not express the true feelings of the Indian people on the question of Hungary. The Prime Minister said one thing while the leader of our delegation said something else. I am afraid history may repeat itself on the question of Tibet. Therefore, if the Government of India itself does not raise the question of Tibet, then as proposed by the Congress member Dr. Gohokar in the amendment moved by him, if any other country raises this question India should support it. Last time we did not extend our support and so no other country came forward. After all, we have the greatest interest in Tibet; being its neighbour we have great sympathy with Tibet.

AN HON'BLE MEMBER : Why does not Chiang Kai Shek raise this question ?

MR. SPEAKER : Order, Order. This is not the first time that the Hon'ble member is moving this motion. He has moved his motion and spoken on it. If any explanation has to be given to what has arisen out of the speeches that have been made for or against, he can do so by explaining a few points. He cannot make a second speech like the one he made while moving the resolution.

SHRI VAJPAYEE : I am only explaining a few points.

MR. SPEAKER : The Hon'ble member is not doing that. He has reopened the whole thing.

SHRI VAJPAYEE : I want to ask, if any other country raises the question of Tibet what would be India's policy ? I want to know the reaction of the Government to the amendment moved by the Congress member. That is not my amendment. And the Prime Minister has not clarified the Government's stand in that regard.

Appeal to the Conscience of the World

It is true that there are practical difficulties on the issue of Tibet. But apart from raising the problem of Tibet in the United Nations there does not appear to be any other tangible solution to it. It is true that there would be a heated debate on this subject. But if we have faith in the United Nations Organisation, and China wants to become a member of it then the world public opinion must have some influence on China. Now India has only one choice before it and that is that we appeal to the conscience of the world and appeal to its sense of justice. We should moboilize world opinion against the violation of human rights in Tibet. And if that does not have any effect on Communist China we would at least have the satisfaction of having done our duty. We want to know what the policy of the Government of India is towards Tibet. Is-it to sit idle ? Is it a policy of indecision and helplessness ? What steps are we taking to resolve the Tibetan problem peacefully ? As I submitted merely by offering shelter to the Dalai Lama would not solve the Tibetan problem.

India Should not Raise Question of China's Membership in the U.N.

I want to say one thing more. India has recently decided to again move the motion for admitting China to the membership of the United Nations. We have been raising this question for the last seven years. But should we raise this issue in the circumstances of today ? China may like to join the United Nations, but keeping in view what is happening between India and China should we take the initiative to get China admitted to its membership ? I think the time has come for the Government of India to drop the proposal for admission of China to the membership of the United Nations. We could support the motion if any other country of the world raises this question. If we are not prepared to raise the question of Tibet in the world body why should we take an initiative to get China admitted to the membership of the United Nations Organisation in view of what China is doing to us ? After all, as I said before, we should not cultivate friendship with China at the cost of our self-respect. China is an aggressor. China has violated our borders, she is knocking at our doors, but the Prime Minister says we are not prepared to talk about the borders.

I think we should not now raise the question of U.N. membership for China. I appeal to the House to accept my resolution and to prove to the world that though the Government of India may not raise the question of Tibet due to certain international difficulties yet the feelings of the Indian people are with the people of Tibet and with the Dalai Lama. There is only one way out of this and that is to accept this resolution. Thank You.

China

Withdrawal of Police from Bara Hoti Border ?

Mr. Speaker, Sir, my adjournment motion on the reported withdrawal of the Indian border police from Bara Hoti has not been admitted on the ground that the matter can be raised in the discussion on the 25th instant. I am prepared to wait, but I am afraid that the Chinese may not like to wait till the 25th. This House is entitled to know why the border police is being withdrawn from Bara Hoti and why Government have not made sufficient arrangements for our troops to stay there during the winter season.

MR. SPEAKER : All that will be discussed.

SHRI JAWAHARLAL NEHRU, Prime Minister and Minister of External Affairs : There has been for some time past an agreement with the Chinese Government in regard to Bara Hoti, that is, that Bara Hoti being a disputed area no party should send any armed troops there. No armed troops have been sent there accordingly. Civil personnel have gone; this year, our civil personnel went there. They went there on the 27th of May this year, and they withdrew six weeks ago; there is no question of withdrawing them now. They withdrew on the 13th September, conditions becoming very difficult. The Chinese sent as their representative, I suppose, of civil personnel, a Tibetan official, but no Chinese came this summer there at all, so that we are functioning in terms of that agreement which said that no attempt will be made by either party to change the status of this Bara Hoti area unilaterally.

There are, of course, quite considerable difficulties about either the Chinese or the Indians remaining there during this period. It was the high Himalayas from this side, and in view of that, we may, and we shall naturally consider afresh whether we should erect any permanent structure there which are capable of withstanding climatic conditions. For the present we have abided by the treaty or arrangement arrived at with the Chinese, and insofar as we know, they are abiding by it too.

SHRI VAJPAYEE : Why has Bara Hoti been treated in an isolated manner ? When the Chinese have not vacated their aggression on other territories why should we refrain from sending our men to the place which belongs to us from time immemorial ?

SHRI TYAGI : Should we leave it to them until the whole thing is decided ? (*Interruptions*).

Lok Sabha on November 17, 1959 while moving the adjournment motion regarding the reported withdrawal of the Indian Border Police from Bara Hoti

SHRI VAJPAYEE : What is the guarantee that they will not do in this place what they did in Ladakh ?

SHRI JAWAHARLAL NEHRU : I am sorry I am not personally acquainted, as the Hon. member appears to be, with 'time immemorial'. But I deal with historical periods. As regards this particular place, it is a minor dispute with the old Government of Tibet. About this little area it has been going on. We think our case is a good one and, therefore, we hold by it. But it has been a disputed area and long before the other incursions of the Chinese took place this matter was being argued.

SHRI TYAGI : I wish to make a suggestion. In respect of the border area disputes, questions of a nature which seek to elicit information about the location and deployment of the armed forces may by convention not be asked of the Minister. If they are asked at all, I think it is in the interest of the security of the border that the Prime Minister should not reply to such questions in a manner....

SEVERAL HON. MEMBERS : No, no.

SHRI TYAGI : The deployment of the armed forces is a matter which should be kept secret.

SHRI NATH PAI : What secrecy ?

SHRI JAWAHARLAL NEHRU : What the Hon. member, Shri Tyagi said is, in spite of the protest of Opposition members, the obvious rule followed in every country.

SHRI BRAJ RAJ SINGH : Nobody is asking for it.

SHRI VAJPAYEE : Nobody has asked for secrets to be disclosed.

SHRI JAWAHARLAL NEHRU : I am not saying that the Hon. member asked. I am saying that what Shri Tyagi said is the obvious rule followed everywhere, especially in a moment of crisis.

SHRI VAJPAYEE : We never asked for any information that will not be in the public interest to give. There is no need for making a suggestion like that.

SHRI JAWAHARLAL NEHRU : The Hon. member need not think that he is being attacked in any way. Nobody is attacking the Hon. member. Shri Tyagi made a suggestion that we might be treading delicate ground if repeatedly questions are asked about these matters. So far as these matters are concerned we have put the army authorities completely in charge and we abide by their advice, as our specialist-advisers, in this matter.

Construction of Airfield by China in Ladakh

MR. SPEAKER : I have received notices of five adjournment motions, all relating to the construction of airfield by the Chinese in Ladakh.

SHRI VAJPAYEE : The subject-matter of this adjournment motion raises a very important issue. Large chunks of Indian territory are under forcible occupation of the Chinese. Do we have any means to know whether war preparations, through construction of airfield are or are not being made by the Chinese on Indian territory ? Secondly, supposing these reports appearing in the press are correct and the Chinese are making airfields on our territory, may I know if the basic attitude of the Government of India towards these border incidents will change and the Chinese will be asked not to make war preparations on our territory ? Otherwise our negotiations will not run smoothly.

MR. SPEAKER : The Hon. Prime Minister.

SHRI JAWAHARLAL NEHRU, Prime Minister and Minister of External Affairs : The question raised in these adjournment motions is about a report that the Chinese authorities have built an air-strip in the Aksai Chin area. That is one thing. In some reports it is further mentioned that such an air strip has been constructed near Chusul. In the third set of reports, to which the Hon. member Shri Braj Raj Singh referred, it is said that something was happening in the Malikshah region.

Now the question is one of fact. I shall reply with such factual information as I have got. The inferences to be drawn from it naturally depend upon the correctness of the facts. I shall not go into inference. Hon. member will have a chance in four or five days' time to discuss this entire matter more fully.

So far as the Aksai Chin area is concerned we have received no information about the building of an airfield. We have tried to find out what we can, and this report has not been confirmed. I cannot at the same time absolutely say that it is not so, because none of our people has been there. My information is that some travellers and others have said this in Srinagar. I do not know on what their information is based. The utmost I can say is that I cannot give any precise information about the rumour that an airstrip has been constructed at Aksai Chin. We are still trying to get as much information as possible. So far as the report about an airfield near Chusul is concerned that is definitely incorrect. There is no such thing.

Lok Sabha on November 19, 1959 while moving the adjournment motion regarding the Reported Construction of an Airfield by China in Ladakh

So far as Malikshah is concerned Malikshah is not in Ladakh at all. It is well within the Sinkiang region of China.

SHRI NATH PAI (Rajapur) : I want a small explanation. The Prime Minister has been kind enough to tell us that he cannot either confirm or deny whether such an airstrip has been built. We are told and we hold the view that Aksai Chin is an integral part of India. Now, do you not think it is an extraordinary state of affairs that we do not know what is happening on our own territory ? Either we are being prevented from getting that information by foreign forces or we are not watchful enough. We would like to know what is it that prevented us from knowing what is happening on our own territory.

SHRI JAWAHARLAL NEHRU : It is a fact, which we may deplore, that in the Aksai Chin area there is no representative of the Indian Government. Neither is there now nor has one been there for sometime. Except that occasionally patrol parties have gone in past years we are not there. We can go there only, more or less, at the present moment after some kind of conflict and after exhibiting high mountaineering skill etc; we can, no doubt. There is a question of controversy and dispute now. Anyway the only possible way of discovering that would perhaps be flying over it and taking a picture at low flight. It is a matter for our military authorities to see if that is a right course to adopt in the circumstances or not.

SHRI VAJPAYEE : Is it not a fact that the Indian border police have stopped patrolling the traditional border in Ladakh after the ultimatum given by the Chinese on the 26th October that if they continue to patrol on the traditional border they will violate the MacMahon Line and come into India ?

SHRI JAWAHARLAL NEHRU : The Hon'ble member referred to an ultimatum by the Chinese Government. I am not aware of any ultimatum. But it is true that in one of their communications they said something like what the Hon'member has said. But it has no bearing on this matter at all. This is something which has no effect on our actions and on whatever decisions we take.

RAJA MAHENDRA PRATAP : This is only Anglo-American propaganda going on...*(Interruptions)*.

SHRI VAJPAYEE : I strongly object to what my Hon. friend has said. Let him withdraw his words.

ACHARYA KRIPALANI (Sitamarhi) : On September 12th in my speech I said that no mention was made of the airstrip built in our territory and the Prime Minister in his answer said :

> "Some Hon. member mentioned or enquired if the Chinese had built an airfield in Indian territory. There is no such thing."

At that time the Prime Minister said positively that there was no such thing. Today he is very uncertain.

SHRI JAWAHARLAL NEHRU : My answer will stand.

ACHARYA KRIPALANI : I have not mentioned the place but it was the same place. There was no question of the place. There was only the question of an airfield.

SHRI JAWAHARLAL NEHRU : My answer would still be that so far as my knowledge goes there is no such airstrip on Indian territory. About the place near Chushul which I have seen recently, I can definitely say that it is not there. But about places where I have not been or any of my informants have not been for sometime, I cannot be equally definite. That is why I answered in that way. But so far as we have been able to trace, there is no reliable information to the effect that there is such an airfield. We have not been able to get any person who can be considered to have any knowledge of it. This report is sometimes circulated by travellers in the mountains. I cannot absolutely deny it. May I also say that the so-called airfields or airstrips here cannot be compared with any other airstrips ? Nothing is done there except the removal of stones and boulders. It is a concealed thing and without any preparations something can land there. No one could deny that it may not have landed but I have no knowledge of it.

SHRI JADHAV : Sir, before having a discussion on the border issue may I know whether the Defence Minister will have a tour for an on-the-spot study of the situation as it is very difficult to get any information. We do not have this information. Let him go and study the situation there.

SHRI JAWAHARLAL NEHRU : If some Hon. members wish to go to these areas we shall facilitate that.

SHRI VAJPAYEE : We are ready to go provided the Defence Minister accompanies us.

SHRI JAWAHARLAL NEHRU : If the Hon. member wants in addition to the Defence Minister a company of our army to go with them to protect them all the time it would rather upset our arrangements. May I say, Sir, that I hope to lay on the table of the House tomorrow the answer that has been sent to Premier Chou En- lai to his letter...

MR. SPEAKER : All these matters will be discussed in the debate that we are going to have. In view of this I am not allowing these adjournment motions.

What if Chou En-Lai does not Agree to Nehru's Proposals ?

Mr. Speaker, Sir, a national crisis has been created as a result of the Chinese attack on the northern border. It is imperative for us to consider it from a national viewpoint in order to resolve this crisis. But I regret to say that the Prime Minister made certain observations during his speech yesterday which have unwittingly provided a setback to the national consensus that was emerging on this issue. There is no party in the country which would like to use this national crisis to its advantage.

But we have certain differences, honest differences, with the Government on this issue, and we would like to place them forcefully before the country. I would urge upon the Prime Minister not to think that we want to exploit this national crisis for the advantage of our party.

The other day, the same people whom he had described as a motley crowd supported the Prime Minister when the Central Government dismissed the Communist Government in Kerala. At that time, he did not call us a motley crowd. If our support at that time was just, then our criticism today is also justified and he should calmly ponder over it. When we supported the action of the Central Government in Kerala the Communists accused us of being partisan. But we did not have any partisan view before us.

There was danger to democracy in Kerala. So we stood united against that danger, forgetting our mutual differences. Today our country is facing a danger due to the Chinese attack. So, we stand united, forgetting our differences again.

The Prime Minister has appealed that in such matters we should speak with one voice. I am sorry to say that when we try to speak in unison he gets annoyed. I could not understand why did he get annoyed yesterday. He was annoyed because.....

SHRI JAWAHARLAL NEHRU : I did not get annoyed at all.

SHRI VAJPAYEE : I am very happy to know that you were not annoyed. But I would like you to consider our point of view.

House should have been Informed

The Prime Minister had stated that he wanted to know the opinion of Parliament, that he wanted guidance from Parliament, but I have a complaint against him. A letter was received from Mr. Chou En-Lai on November 7 and a reply to it was sent on November 16 and the sitting of the Lok Sabha also

Lok Sabha on December 22, 1959 regarding discussion on Sino-Indian relations

commenced on the same date. In case he really wished to know the opinion of Parliament in regard to the proposals sent by Mr. Chou En-Lai he could have sent the reply after two days. If the reply could be delayed by two days because of his visit to Dehradun it could also be delayed for two days because of the sitting of the Lok Sabha. On that day, when we moved the adjournment motion, the Prime Minister informed us that he had already sent the reply and that when the reply reaches its destination it will be considered. My submission is, had the Lok Sabha been provided an opportunity on that very day to consider the proposals sent by the Chinese Prime Minister the alternative proposals suggested by our Prime Minister in his letter might have taken a different shape. Till now our Government has been emphasising that our border is already settled–it has been settled through treaties, settled by age-old traditions, settled by use and the question of re-settling it afresh does not arise at all. The entire country has supported this stand of the Government.

The Prime Minister has also been stressing the point that we would not have any talks so long as the Chinese aggression continues on Indian soil. The country has supported this stand too. The Prime Minister has also stated that we may negotiate some agreement, but only regarding some minor matters; the entire border cannot be made a point of dispute afresh. This has also been accepted. But I have the grudge that the Prime Minister in the letter has come down a little bit from that principle. Now he has agreed that if the Chinese forces withdraw from our land then we too would not send our men in our own territory. Why has such a thing been proposed ? Why should we not send our men into our own territory ?

Is this the price being paid to China for committing aggression ? I think this is wrong. It is against the sovereignty of our country. If a firm policy is not adopted against the Chinese aggression it would not be possible to force the Chinese to behave with us properly. There appears to be a plan behind the Chinese attack. These cannot be overlooked as small incursions.

New China no More the Same Old China

China has expansionist designs. The Defence Minister had recently said in a Congress Party meeting that we have had 2000 years' old friendly relations with China, while our Prime Minister says that China has been expansionist from the very beginning. We do not know whom to believe. But I would like to say that the China with which we had friendly relations for 2000 years is no more. The Communists have wiped out that China which our Buddhist monks had visited carrying with them the message of Lord Buddha. The China from where Huentsang and Faihan had come here with the message of friendship is dead. A New China, an imperialist and expansionist China, has emerged on the ashes of that China. We should not forget to what extent China has expanded its borders during the past years. Manchuria which ruled over China till 1911 has been obliterated from the map; it has become the North-Eastern part of China, Turkistan has become Sinkiang, Inner Mongolia has lost its existence. Religious-minded Tibet has also fallen a prey to China's ever-increasing hunger. China's own territory consists of only 14 lakh square miles, but China has occupied 22 lakh square miles of land belonging to Manchuria, Inner Mongolia, Kansu, Chinghai, Sinkiang and Tibet. Now it has set its eyes like a vulture on 48 thousand square miles of land belonging to India.

A refugee Lama has revealed the sensational news that the Chinese are propagating that Tibet is like the palm of the hand of China and Ladakh, Bhutan, Sikkim, Nepal and Assam are its five fingers. It is obvious that if suitable counter-action is not taken against the incursions of China into Ladakh and Longju China would get encouragement and our security would be jeopardised.

Chinese Road in Aksai Chin

The Prime Minister while addressing the newsmen somewhere has said that if the road constructed by China in the Aksaichin area is used for civilian purposes we would allow that. I want to ask him what would happen to the Indian territory through which the road passes ? How is it to be decided whether the road was being used for military purposes or civilian purposes ? Who would decide it ? Today it is a total war. It is not possible to differentiate between civilian or military uses.

I have carefully gone through the White Paper. I have tried to find in it an answer to whether China really wants friendship with India. I have found the reply in the negative. China does not want to have friendship with India. I would like to invite the attention of this House in this connection to the note given by the Chinese Embassy to our Foreign Secretary on March 16, 1959. It says :

> "China will not be so foolish as to antagonise the United States in the east and again to antagonise India in the west....We cannot have two centres of attention, nor can we take friends for foe. This is our State Policy."

It says further :

> "....Friends, it seems to us that you too cannot have two fronts. Is it not so ? If it is, let this be the meeting point of our two sides."

China has not said that peace is essential for the world. Peace is essential for the development of 100 crore people; it is essential for the progress of India and China. For China peace in India is a part of its strategy. Since China does not want to fight on two fronts it wants friendship with India, and it is also trying to convince us that since India cannot fight on two fronts we should maintain friendly relations with them in our own interest. I would like to ask the Prime Minister whether this is a constructive, emotional and justified basis for friendship between India and China. For them friendship is opportunistic. When in 1954, they entered into agreement on *Panchsheel,* raised the slogan of co-existence , they had only one objective in mind, that we should not interfere in Tibet and let Tibet's independence be tampered with. And perhaps our Prime Minister thought that if Tibet was sacrified the hunger of the Chinese dragon might be satisfied and we may not have to face any danger. But he forgot the lessons of history.

By giving in to the aggression one cannot satisfy the hunger of the aggressor; it gets further stimulated. Perhaps it is the result of Tibet's annihilation that today our borders are being intruded upon by China. I want to ask those who had gone to Peking to attend the celebrations of the Chinese Republic Day by trampling upon the honour and prestige of India as to whether the treatment meted out to our Trade Agent in Yangtse, the inhuman behaviour meted out to him, denotes the friendly attitude of China towards India. On the one side the Soviet Union is resuming its old trade ties with its enemy of yesteryears, the United States of America and on the other China is destroying our old trade ties with Tibet with the sharp edge of its sickle and hammer. This shows that China does not want to have friendship with us. I would submit that we should realise the seriousness of the danger in order to face it. On August 25, 1959, while speaking on the Kerala debate the Prime Minister had stated that India would not remain India if per chance it becomes communist. The same thing applies to China as well. China is not the same China any more. We have before us imperialism incarnate. The Prime Minister is a historian himself, he has written history, he is making history and in future history he would occupy a place of honour. But China is expansionist. Has this been revealed to us just now ? Could we not have known it ten years ago ? Could we not have made arrangements for the security of our borders ? I am sorry to say that we have bungled in this matter. We depended more on China's friendship instead of depending upon our own strength, and today we are facing despondency.

Defence Minister's Leanings

Mr. Speaker, Sir, the Defence Minister spoke today. He has a doubtful past, and his present conduct is dubious. He is neither popular among the people nor has he any credibility in the Congress Party. He has Communist leanings by nature and that is why he has failed to faithfully implement the Prime Minister's policy of keeping aloof from both the blocs. In his message on the Territorial Army Day he made a peculiar observation. He said that India should not keep a large army, because keeping a large army was not compatible with our morality, that it was contrary to our moral values. If he considers keeping a large army as immoral, he might consider the conduct of such a large army even more immoral. If a person in charge of the Defence Ministry regards keeping a large army immoral I think our country's security is in danger. If he really regards it immoral then he must resign from the post of Defence Minister, join the Bharat Sadhu Samaj and take up the work of moral awakening. Keeping a large army is not immoral. When the enemy is knocking at our borders it is immoral not to have a large army and the Minister for Defence is guilty of that.

General Thimmayya's Resignation

I want to make one more submission. The Prime Minister said that there should be plain-speaking. I wanted to ask the Defence Minister a question, but you Mr. Speaker, did not allow it. My question was whether it is a fact that in the evening on the day a storm was raised in the Lok Sabha on the resignation of General Thimmayya–and the very next day that storm subsided due to intervention of the Prime Minister–a Colonel of our armed Forces visited the Defence Minister's bungalow and congratulated him on his victory!

Mr. Speaker, Sir, if there is any feeling in the country today against the Defence Minister the main apprehension behind it is that he was creating a cadre of officers in our Defence Forces who are loyal to him. There is an apprehension too in the minds of the people that the Defence Minister was making preparations that may enable him to snatch the reigns of power in the country, with the help of Defence officers loyal to him, whenever Prime Minister Nehru is not present here. It is just possible that this apprehension might be wrong, and I wish it is wrong, but it persists and our Prime Minister should not ignore it just by saying that he is still a young man of 70 years. We wish him long life, but this apprehension is there, and it must be removed. The Defence Minister cannot be trusted and today when the country is under foreign attack, the need of the hour is to hand over the Defence Ministry to a person who is above suspicion, like Ceaser's wife, and who may exhort the entire country to make the greatest sacrifices. That cannot be done by our present Defence Minister. I hope the Prime Minister would not allow personal friendship to come in the way of national interest.

During this debate the question of foreign policy has also been raised. I do not think that the question before the House today is whether we should join either of the two blocs or not. The aggression being committed on our borders today does not have much relevance to our foreign policy. Barring the Communist Party the entire country agrees with the policy of the Prime Minister that we should not join any bloc. I have named the Communist Party because it has always been trying to get us into the Soviet bloc. These people who have been the greatest opponents of our foreign policy till sometime back are its greatest supporters today, but those who have been its greatest supporters are being dubbed by the Prime Minister as its opponents. I want to make it clear that no enlightened person would like us to join any bloc. It is not in the interest of our country. It is against our self-respect to join any bloc and ask for military assistance on the ground that some foreign forces are stationed on our soil.

Need for PM's Call to Oppose Aggression

This would weaken our nationalism. Ultimately we have to march forward on the basis of our nationalism and fight for our own safety. Therefore, the question of our entering into a military pact with any country does not arise at all. There is no need for us to join any bloc. But whether we join any bloc or not, a doubt arises in our mind and the people of this country. Would like the Prime Minister to remove it ? The people expect from the Prime Minister to repel this aggression. But strength has to be acquired to repel it and if we do not have that strength, a call should be given to the people of the country to come forward and fight out the aggressor. If the Prime Minister gives a call the country would extend all cooperation to him. But this call should be to fight out the Chinese aggression, not to surrender before it.

We want to strengthen the hands of the Prime Minister. The entire country wants it. The question of a difference of opinion does not arise in this matter. But our self-respect should be protected, the borders of the country should be defended. I would like to know from the Prime Minister what the Government would do if Mr. Chou En-Lai does not accept his proposals. Even the Prime Minister has doubts, if he would accept his proposals *in toto*. The Prime Minister stated in the Press Club that he may not accept them *in toto*, but some sort of dialogue would continue. The Prime Minister has this doubt, and if his doubt comes true what would the Government do ? What would happen if China does not accept our proposals ? If China declares that it would not accept our proposals and if the problem is not resolved through dialogue also, will military action be resorted to ? We want to liberate our land from the aggression and, therefore, the country demands a straight forward answer from the Prime Minister. This is my submission.Thank You.

China Creates New Complications

Mr. Speaker, Sir, the fresh letter received from the Prime Minister of China has created a new situation before us. The Prime Minister had put forth certain alternate proposals before China in his letter of November 16, according to which China was required to vacate the Indian territory in Ladakh. At the same time it was also proposed that India too would not send its personnel in that area. The proposal made by the Prime Minister of India was criticised in this House. We had regarded it objectionable and had said that this would encourage China in its aggression. It would give her an opportunity to substantiate its old claims and put forth new ones. This has been confirmed by the reply received from the Prime Minister of China.

In order to keep the dignity and honour of China our Prime Minister had proposed that China should vacate Indian land, but they replied that this proposal should not be confirned to the Ladakh border alone. If they vacate the land shown in the Indian maps Indians should also vacate the NEFA area shown in their maps.

Mr. Speaker, Sir, I would submit that the attempt to maintain the honour of China resulted in bringing dishonour to us. Instead of accepting the hand of goodwill extended by the Prime Minister China has further extended its claim. The places belonging to us in Uttar Pradesh, Punjab and Himachal Pradesh by virtue of geography, history, tradition and treaty have been claimed by China. They are asking a price for their withdrawal from Ladakh. We are being asked to give up our rights over other areas. When this is China's attitude, what is the basis of our expectation that an agreement with China would materialise ? There should be an agreement between the two. Nobody in the country wants war, but if Indian interests are sacrificed, if we strike a deal with China, if we cannot protect India's honour, then this kind of peace would not be desirable, nor would it last long.

Why the Meeting in Rangoon ?

The Prime Minister of China has replied to our communication after a lapse of one month. They want this correspondence to go on for a long time, so that they would in the meanwhile build roads and aerodromes on the land occupied by them and thus consolidate their aggression. Shri Karam Singh too has stated in his statement that motorable roads have been constructed in the area where he was arrested. War preparations are going on on the land belonging to India. China requires time for it. Therefore, it is indulging in

Lok Sabha on December 22, 1959 during discussion on the motion regarding the Sino-Indian relations as a result of the situation created by the letter received from the Prime Minister of China

prolonged correspondence. China took one month to reply and expects from our Prime Minister to leave for Rangoon bag and baggage as soon as he gets their letter. I do not know how the Chinese Prime Minister can expect such things from us ? I am satisfied that our Prime Minister has turned down the proposal to go to Rangoon. That was not a proposal to go to Rangoon, that was not an invitation to Rangoon, that was an invitation to Munich. The Chinese Prime Minister wants to repeat this Munich drama in Rangoon. It is gratifying to note that our Prime Minister has rejected the proposal to go to Rangoon. But he said in the Rajya Sabha this afternoon that he greatly appreciated the eagerness expressed by the Prime Minister of China to see him. Is the Chinese Prime Minister really keen to have an agreement or has he expressed his desire to see our Prime Minister just as a propaganda stunt ? He wants to show to the world that China wants peace even though it has attacked India, whereas India does not want peace because we are not prepared to meet them. There is a great deal of similarity between the proposals put forth by the Prime Minister of China and the line adopted by the Communist Party of India. They have also raised the slogans in Calcutta that both the Prime Ministers should meet, and the Chinese Prime Minister also says we should meet. What to do after the meeting ? What is the meeting ground between the two ? What is the basis for a dialogue for agreement ? If both the Prime Ministers are to meet why should they meet in Rangoon or in China ? Why not in Delhi ?

I object to the allegation made by the Chinese Prime Minister that an atmosphere is being created in India against Chinese friendship. Mr. Speaker, Sir, there is no such atmosphere against friendship in India, there is an atmosphere against aggression in India. So long as this aggression continues such an atmosphere would prevail. We are a live nation, we value our independence, we have self- respect, and if there is transgression on our land, our reaction is inevitable. Nobody can stop it. But the Chinese Prime Minister wants to indulge in propaganda, he wants to become an apostle of peace, he wants to put our Prime Minister in the dock. Now Communists would say that Mr. Chou En-Lai wants to meet, but Panditji does not want to meet. If he does not want to meet he is right. After all what is the basis for the meeting ? When there is no agreement about the facts, when there is no unanimity about principles what shall we do at the meeting ? And if there is a meeting and subsequently the meeting fails the result would be all the more disastrous. Therefore, this viewpoint of the Government is correct. Preliminary modalities should be settled before the Prime Ministers of the two countries meet. The basis for an agreement should be settled. But so far as the preliminaries are concerned there is no indication in the letter that the Chinese want an agreement, except that they have repeated *Panchsheel* and have harped on peace.

SHRI JADHAV (Malegaon) : They have a knife in their pocket.

SHRI VAJPAYEE : Ours is a backward country, we have to build our economy, this has been referred to in the letter. But they are not prepared to vacate the land belonging to India, occupied by them. Our Prime Minister has stated that India's northern border is settled. It might not have been demarcated on the map. We can talk about some minor border disputes, but India's entire border cannot be made a subject-matter of dispute. However, the Chinese Prime Minister is trying to bring the entire border under dispute. He wants to dictate our border. Clearly the Government of India and the people of India cannot tolerate this situation.

But now what should we do ? The Prime Minister asked in the Rajya Sabha, what should be done, should we fight ? Nobody wants you to fight. But I want to ask, what will you do if the Chinese start further incursions in Longju or Ladakh ?

An HON'BLE MEMBER : Negotiations.

Restriction on Chinese Needed

SHRI VAJPAYEE : There cannot be a compromise with aggression. Therefore, we must be prepared for a war. We may not begin the war from our side, but if the other party is bent upon fighting then a war could not be avoided. There are other alternatives to war. Our trade with Tibet has almost stopped. China has put restrictions on trade between Tibet and India. In spite of this we have not done so. We have only set up a guard post in front of the Chinese Trade Agency in Kalimpong. There are other Chinese Trade Agencies in India whose activities could be restricted. Similar restrictions as have been imposed on the Indian Embassy in Peking have not been imposed on the Chinese Embassy in New Delhi. It is time to take this step.

An HON'BLE MEMBER : India is democracy.

SHRI VAJPAYEE : Today we are facing a dangerous situation due to the Chinese aggression. The friends of China cannot make us close our eyes to this danger by raising the slogan that India is a democracy. We can adopt other methods without resorting to war. Where there is a will, there is a way. We can sever our diplomatic relations with China if we so desire. I think the entire country, except the Communists, is unanimous on the point that the Chinese challenge should be met firmly. It is obvious that we will have to fight, but unless we take our steps in time an atmosphere to meet the challenge unitedly cannot be created.

External Affairs Ministry's Lapse

One thing more. The Ministry of External Affairs is not working properly. The Prime Minister stated in the Rajya Sabha that there is a place named Pulin Samado. A mistake was committed and it was wrongly printed. It is located in China, but we claimed it as our own and he has expressed his regret for that. Such a mistake should not be committed. I think the Ministry of External Affairs should work cautiously. The Chinese detect such minor mistakes and make our case weak. The Ministry of External Affairs has not been able to rise to the occasion during this dangerous period. It should come up to expectations. Thank You.

Land Occupied By China Shall Be Retrieved

Sir, I move :

3. "That at the end of the Motion, the following be added, namely : 'and having considered the same, this House is of the opinion—

(i) that Government's China policy has been a dismal failure inasmuch as full eight years after China committed its first act of blatant aggression on Indian soil by constructing the Aksai Chin highway across our territory, Government has not merely failed to redeem. Chinese-occupied territory, but has been unable to check-mate China's continuing forays and encroachments and, more deplorably still, continues to betray an utter confusion of mind and suicidal illusions in respect of Chinese objectives and intentions, with the result that our attitudes very often seem humiliatingly incongruous with the situation, provide positive encouragement to the aggressor in its misdoings and undermine our prestige and credit in the eyes of world opinion and particularly of our neighbouring countries in Asia;

(ii) that the policy enunciated by the Prime Minister recently in respect of unconditional talks acting as a prelude to further negotiations, constitutes a major and retrograde departure from the hitherto avowed Government policy about negotiations;

(iii) that the Note of July 26, 1962, sent to China seriously compromised India's position because the Note, as drafted, impliedly committed India to acceptance of China's claim-line of 1956 and was, therefore, tantamount to a virtual offer to cede a major part of the occupied area; but welcomes the Prime Minister's subsequent affirmation that India would not accept anything other than the traditional international boundary as the basis of any talks;

(iv) that the continuing acts of aggression by China and the content and tone of its communications to India make it amply clear that China has not the slightest intention of relenting its hold on the Indian territory it has surreptitiously or forcibly seized;

(v) that in the face of the Chinese attitude, Government's present probings for opening of talks, whether in the form of the Defence Minister's parleys with the Chinese Foreign Minister, or as indicated by the Prime minister's recent pronouncements, reflect

Rajya Sabha** on August 22, 1962 while moving the Motion regarding Situation along the Indo-China **Border

adversely on India's self-respect, smack of a policy of abject appeasement and serve only to whet the aggressor's appetite; and this House, therefore, calls for an abandonment of this policy and a categorical declaration by Government that vacation of aggression by China is an absolute pre-requisite for negotiations'."

How to Retrieve the Land Occupied by China

Madam, there is not much difference of opinion in the country about the question of China and, as stated by the Prime Minister in Lok Sabha, it is not a party issue nor do we want to bring the cold war at our borders on this issue. However, there are surely some people in the country who are not prepared to accept the fact that China has attacked India, who do not even admit that our case is genuine and the land occupied by China belongs to us and we should recover it.

We have just now listened to the speech of the spokesman of the Communist Party. They claim that they agree with the policy of the Prime Minister. But the Hon'ble Prime Minister has stated in unambiguous terms that China has attacked us, that the territory occupied by China belongs to us and until that territory is vacated by China no negotiations would start. Does the Communist Party agree with this viewpoint of the Prime Minister ? It is obvious that the Communist Party does not agree with it. It is then meaningless to say that the Communist Party agrees with the policy of the Prime Minister and wants to extend its support to this policy.

Prime Minister Wants Free Hand

The Prime Minister wants a free hand on the question of China. I have not been able to understand the purpose for which he wants a free hand, because he is bound by whatever declarations he has made and the assurances he has given. He has declared that we would rather face destruction than enter into a humiliating agreement with China. He has also stated that no negotiations would take place until and unless China returns to the traditional international boundary. In such a situation, I would like to know for what purpose he wants to have a free hand. Where is the scope for manoeuvring now ? He has tried to make a subtle distinction that we may talk to the Chinese, but would not negotiate with them. My submission is that the talks are going on even today, it is not that we are not on talking terms with the Chinese; the letters that are being exchanged is also a way of talking. And so far as China is concerned, this is the right way because China can go back on its words. It has in fact done so and, therefore, it is better to have talks in writing.

Moreover, we are having talks orally as well. The Prime Minister had despatched Shri R.K. Nehru, Secretary-General, to Peking to probe the mind of the Chinese. Recently, our Defence Minister had held talks with the Chinese Foreign Minister at Geneva and the Prime Minister had himself talked to the Chinese Ambassador by inviting him to his house for dinner. When these talks are going on, what fresh talks he wants to hold now ? It is said that these talks will be held in order to create a congenial atmosphere. I would like to know humbly from the Hon. Prime Minister as to what will be his touchstone to judge that the atmosphere has become congenial. Would he like the Chinese to withdraw to the traditional international boundary, or to the Chou En-Lai Line, or that China should accept his proposal that both the countries withdraw their forces from the disputed area ? When will it be presumed that a proper atmosphere has been created to hold the negotiations ? What are its conditions ? The country should be taken into confidence in this matter. Nobody is opposed to talks with China and I have submitted to you that the talks are going on even today. However, it is not clear as yet as to what would be the basis of the talks. I hope the Hon. Prime Minister would throw some light on it.

Country Kept in Dark

I was amazed to see that no information was given to the country about the firing resorted to by the Chinese troops on 27th July in Pegong Lake area and again on 29th July in the same area and on 4th August at Daulat Baig Oldie. The Prime Minister had also called a meeting of the leaders of various parties. Even in that meeting, when a query was made whether any incidents of firing had occurred on the border after the firing reported on the 20th last, no information was given. Not only that, the protest notes we have sent are about the firing incidents that took place on the 27th and 29th July; we have not sent any protest note about the firing on August 4 at Daulat Baig Oldie. I would like to know the reason.

I would also like to know why did the Indian Government put this proposal before the Chinese Government that until both the countries agreed to publish the notes exchanged between them, China should not make its notes public. Is it aimed at keeping the people and the Parliament of India in the dark about such incidents that occur on the border ? We should forthwith publish the notes exchanged between China and India. If we expect the people of this country to keep awake against this aggression and if the Prime Minister requires the people's support on this question, then it is imperative to keep the people constantly informed about the incidents that take place on the border. Supposing China does not agree to publish the notes because it has a different kind of structure—it does not have as much of freedom as is allowed in India and it has no Parliament—shall we also in that case not publish the notes until China permits us to do so ? Shall we keep the country and the Parliament in the dark about the incidents that take place on the border until China allows us freedom to make them public ? I do not think that this is a healthy tradition. The Government should reconsider its viewpoint in this matter.

I have not been able to understand so far why the note that was sent on July 26 was couched in the language it was. The Prime Minister knows that the note has created apprehensions in the minds of the people. It is not that we want to oppose the Government on the question of China. There are many other issues on which we can oppose the Government. But the Prime Minister should have some faith in the patriotism of the people sitting on the Opposition benches. If the note sent on July 26 is criticised, it is because it gives an impression that the Government of India is considering a change in its old stand. After all, what was the need to tell the Chinese to at least withdraw upto the Chou En-Lai boundary line of 1956 ? So far we have been saying that the Chinese forces should withdraw up to the international border. The Prime Minister has tried to explain away the contents of the note of July 26, but that will not do. Every word of a note should be carefully examined before it is sent. The pros and cons of a statement that is made should be carefully weighed. Sino-Indian relations are at a delicate stage. Every wrong word used, and wrong step taken would on the one hand jeopardize the morale of the people and, on the other, strengthen China's aggressive intentions.

We Do Not Know What China Wants

In this connection, I would like to draw the attention of the House to the speech made by the Defence Minister in Geneva. He said: "These are largely unoccupied areas." About Ladakh area he says: "These are largely unoccupled areas." On the one hand, we describe those areas as belonging to us and say that we would not rest till the Chinese vacate those areas and, on the other, we describe these areas as "unoccupied areas." Can we describe any part of our land as "unoccupied area" ? But our Defence Minister had talked earlier about 'administered or unadministered territory'. I want to know as to why such a statement was made ? Could the Prime Minister vouch for the propriety of such a statement ? When it comes to the question of Kashmir, nobody raises his finger at the statement of the Defence Minister. When he speaks on Kashmir in the meeting of the Security Council, he expresses the sentiments of the entire country. But what is the reason that when he speaks about Ladakh and China he talks things which hurt our feelings ? We are not opposed to the Defence Minister. We do not even want to create an anti-government atmosphere on the question of China. But patriotism demands that if aggression has taken place against India, and things are said which do not express the resentment of the people against the agression it causes suspicion. We have no objection to the Prime Minister inviting the Chinese Ambassador for dinner. We have no objection to the meeting of our Defence Minister with the Chinese Foreign Minister. We have also no objection to having a dialogue with them. But objection arises because when people see these things in the context of the statements of the spokes-persons and find a different meaning. After all, what is the need to say that China does not want war ? Do we know what China wants ? Have we still not understood the Chinese intentions ? After all why has China intruded into Ladakh ? Is it because there was a rebellion in Tibet ? Is it because we had given asylum to the Dalai Lama in our country ? We would be deceiving ourselves if we say that China had attacked Ladakh due to these reasons and history would never forgive us for having taken such a view.

China Wants to Humiliate India

China has committed agression, because she wants to humiliate India, because she has got expansionist designs over the South-East Asia. The Chinese troops are sitting inside our borders, because China wants to subjugate us in her zest for becoming a big power. This hunger for power is not only manifest against us, but is visible towards all our neighbours too. It is this aspect that has created a chasm between India and Nepal. This big brother attitude, this arrogance of power, is affecting Burma as well. That is why the official newspaper of Burma writes that the Chip Chap Valley belongs to China. I am not talking of any non-governmental newspaper. This paper is published by the Information Department of the Burmese Government and it writes such false things. Have we put our case before the people of Burma, the Government of Burma in a correct perspective ? What is the reason that not a single country of South-East Asia has openly supported us on the question of China ? I do not agree with the proposition that we should call a conference of South-East Asian countries and enter into some kind of a military pact with them. However, if the proposal for a pact comes up, then the language in which the Prime Minister has opposed the pact is not the language of a statesman.

South–East Asian Countries Should Not Be Belittled

I can understand that the Prime Minister was unhappy with the leader of the Swatantra Party in Lok Sabha and used a language in anger which he should not have used. But when he was questioned at the Press Conference even then he gave the same reply. I want to read that out:

> "In reply to a question whether he would consider calling a conference of non-Communist countries in South-East Asia to discuss the question of containing Chinese expansionism, the Prime Minister said,

I quote:

> "I should like to see the list of those countries and know how much strength they have to contain anything including themselves."

What is this language ? The countries of South-East Asia may be small and may not be powerful. But we want their friendship, we require their goodwill, we need their moral support on the question of China. And when the question of Kashmir comes up in the General Assembly of the U.N.O., we want their votes. Will we be creating goodwill in their hearts towards us by saying that they have got no power and that they cannot even save themselves ? If we want that the people living in South-East Asia should have friendly feelings in their hearts towards us, our Prime Minister could reject this proposal in some other way. However, to use such a language which hurts the sentiments of the people living in these countries and of which China may try to take undue advantage, at least we do not expect it from our Prime Minister. But such language was used and I think there is need to be cautious about this matter.

SHRI BHUPESH GUPTA : The Prime Minister wanted a list. Let us have that list. He wanted a list of those countries.

SHRI VAJPAYEE : The Prime Minister has got the list of those countries. He may or he may not convene a conference of those countries, but he should not refer to those countries in such a contemptuous language. That is my objection.

SHRI BHUPESH GUPTA : Madam, on a point of order, it is not contemptuous language.

SHRI VAJPAYEE : There is no point of order. It is a question of opinion. I hold my opinion. The Hon. Member has no business to interrupt me.

THE DEPUTY CHAIRMAN : Mr. Vajpayee, he can raise it as a point of order, and it is for me to give my ruling. *(Interruptions)*

SHRI VAJPAYEE : Is it not for me to make my submission ? I am quite right in saying that there is no point of order.

MR. DEPUTY CHAIRMAN : Anyway you have five minutes more, and you may have your say.

SHRI BHUPESH GUPTA : That five minutes may be utilised for supplying the list.

SHRI VAJPAYEE : I thought that the leaders of the Communist Party would show some wisdom, but they want to go to such an extent in support of the Prime Minister which does not conform to the policy of their party.

Anyhow, I leave this matter here. I would like to say that the situation on the border is serious and no effort should be spared to retrieve it. Just now our Congress friends were saying that we are not in a position to fight. Then what should we do ? My submission is that if we cannot fight to safeguard our freedom, our borders and our honour what would we fight for ? This does not mean that we should fight today.

SHRI AKBAR ALL KHAN : They did not say that we are not in a position to fight.

SHRI VAJPAYEE : It is but natural that if we find that it is favourable to us from the military point of view to fight today, we would fight. But if we are not in a position to fight, does it mean that we should bow before China ? Should we change our old policy ? Is there no other way out ? There is a way.

Alternatives are There

If we so desire we can adopt other ways to pressurise China. We can severe our diplomatic reations with China, we can refuse to accept Chinese suzerainty over Tibet, and wherever we find an opportunity we can warn the South-East Asian countries against the Chinese intentions and ask the countries of the world to beware of the Chinese designs. However, when our representatives speak about China in the United Nations Organisation, they say that we have a "controversy" with China; but when the same thing is written by a Burmese newspaper and is said by the leaders of Burma, then we do not relish it and say that we have not only a "controversy" with China but China has attacked us. Obviously several other steps excluding war could be taken through diplomatic channels. Can these steps not be taken ?

The other point is that we should strenghten ourselves militarily. We should build roads, develop our communication network and create an atmosphere in the country so that, if not today then tomorrow, we retrieve our land that has been occupied by China. But I shudder to think what might happen if the matter goes on lingering on for long, and there are signs of its lingering on and on. It is being said now that the situation on the borders is delicate. But the situation has become delicate because we have moved forward and it would become more delicate if we retrieve our land occupied by China. Does creating a favourable atmosphere mean that China may withdraw a little, but we shall not move forward ? If this happens, then we would never be able to retrieve our land occupied by China. Could it be retrieved through negotiations ? So far China has not given any such indication. Whatever proposals we have put before China have been rejected by it. China claims our land as its own and is not prepared to withdraw from it. My submission is that if it is possible through peaceful negotiations, let us have them; but if the use of the military might is required, let us recover our land even by use of force. If it cannot be retrieved today, let us kindle a fire in the hearts of 440 millions of our people telling them that a country which has signed with us the treaty of *Panchsheel*, a country for which we went out of our way to get her a respectful place in the comity of nations, has kicked at our honour, is trying to bend the Himalayas and has stabbed us in the back and we would not rest in peace until the humiliation inflicted upon us is wiped out.

Don't Sign Humiliating Agreement

I would like to end my speech with a word of caution to the Prime Minister. If this Government is not in a position to recover our land today from the clutches of China, let it not, for God's sake, enter into any humiliating agreement with her. I do believe that the Prime Minister will not do so, but at times doubts arise in our mind and therefore, it is necessary to declare in unambiguous terms that if not today then tomorrow we shall retrieve our territory. If this Government is not in a position to do so, its successor Government will. Thank You.

Communists' Loyalties ?

Madam, the statement made by the Home Minister regarding the anti-national activities of the Communists owing allegiance to Peking has confirmed that these elements are active in our country in the guise of leftist communists and constitute a danger to the freedom and security of the country. I have a grudge against the government as to why did it take so much time to expose the designs and misdeeds of these anti-national elements ?

Revolutionary Ideology of Communism

Communists believe in a revolutionary ideology. But if that ideology remains confined within the borders of the country and does not adopt violent methods to bring about change in the society it could be fought. However, communism is not a philosophy of life. It is a worldwide conspiracy to deprive the people of their freedom and dignity by hook or by crook, by the use of force and arms. And that is the reason why, when one should feel ashamed of treason and using the language of a traitor, our Communist friends, drunk with revolution are not prepared to accept anti-national activities as treason. We heard the speech of Shri Nausher Ali the other day. That speech was made deliberately. It was a challenge thrown to the House, to the country. Even if the Ministry of Home Affairs had not published this booklet his speech alone was sufficient to prove that their loyalties lay beyond the Himalayas and they would not hesitate to betray the country in the garb of revolution. Not only this, they would rather deem it their duty and would feel elated in doing so. What should be done with such elements ? Let no Hon'ble member take me otherwise, but I would like to give an example. If a party is formed in India–I am not talking of individuals, I am talking of a party–which says that Pakistan had not attacked Kashmir, and its members display pictures of the President of Pakistan and shout slogans in their processions asking people not to worry, saying that Pakistan would be coming here in four months' time, what attitude would be adopted by the people and the government of this country towards them ? I am not in favour of placing China and Pakistan in the same category. Until recently Pakistan was a part of our country and we want to improve our relations with Pakistan. But if any group of people with their loyalties centred elsewhere, outside the borders of India, tries in an organised manner to shatter the morale of the country during this period of crisis and makes an

Rajya Sabha on March 25, 1965 on Calling Attention Motion regarding anti-national activities of pro-China Communists

attempt to bolster the strength of the enemy the government cannot sit silently and watch. The surprise is not why the government woke up now, but why it kept mum so long.

Leftists Display Portrait of Mao

The left Communists had displayed the portrait of Mao Tse-tung in their Conference at Tenali. A war-like situation is prevailing between China and India. China has occupied a large tract of our land, an emergency has been declared in the country, and the country and this House are bound by the sacred resolution that we would not rest till the last inch of our land is liberated from the Chinese clutches. Does the hanging of Mao Tse-tung's portrait on this occasion not show where their loyalties lie ? And it was not only in the Tenali Conference alone, Mao Tse-tung's portraits were also displayed at Bagdogra, Darjeeling, Berhampur, Murshidabad, and in Maharashtra in Bombay, Guntur and Nadia district as well. At the time of the Calcutta Conference also Mao Tse-tung's pictures were hung at the venues of the Press Conference. When the Press people were called, the portrait was removed and when the mediamen pointed out to the vacant space and asked whose picture was put up there the Communist leaders had no answser.

SHRI BHUPESH GUPTA : It is just possible that Shri Nanda's picture might have been displayed there.

SHRI VAJPAYEE : Madam Chairperson, there was a time when Shri Nanda was praised sky-high and our friend Shri Bhupesh Gupta did not see any other person who was as progressive and as committed to the economic development of India as Shri Nanda was. Today the situation has changed.

SHRI BHUPESH GUPTA : I am sorry for him.

SHRI VAJPAYEE : You need not be sorry for him, because Shri Nanda took action, even though belatedly, against the communists. Therefore Shri Nanda has now become a reactionary, an autocrat and what not. I want to tell my Congress friends to beware of their friendship.

SHRI BHUPESH GUPTA : Here is my friend. Congressmen too can have as their friend a Jan Sangh member.

SHRI VAJPAYEE : Do not talk of Jan Sangh. Our assessment of a person, our assessment of a Congressman does not depend upon his attitude towards us. Sardar Vallabhbhai Patel had banned Rashtriya Swayam Sewak Sangh. Thousands of people were put behind bars on the basis of false allegations. All of them were released later on. But we never said that Sardar Patel was not a great man or that he was not the chief architect of national integration.

SHRI ARJUN ARORA : On a point of order. Is not the word *Jhutha* (false) unparliamentary ?

SOME HON'BLE MEMBERS : No, No.

SHRI VAJPAYEE : Madam, so long as the interests of the Communist Party get promoted this government's policy, this governments' Ministers are all right for them but as soon as the policy of the government goes against them they change their assessment immediately, and this is the reason for the opposition to Shri Nanda today. Otherwise, Shri Nanda continues to be the same person as before. The question is why did the Ministry of Home Affairs take belated action ? The second question is, why did they take action half-heartedly ? Some Communists were arrested, but their supporters and followers were not arrested. They have been left free in order to break the morale of the people. Shri Namboodiripad and Shri Jyoti Bosu have not been touched. Only the government makes distinction between the Left and the Right although this distinction has come down and among the Leftists also the government has released two leaders. They have been allowed to contest the elections and make election propaganda. The government has to be criticised for this weakness, and not for arresting them.

Communists' Loyalties Lay Outside India

I submit that those whose loyalties are not with India, who are out to strengthen the hands of our enemy and who can revolt at the behest of Peking could never be treated leniently. More of their workers should be arrested if the need arises. Their newspapers have been allowed to be published freely. I have never seen you dub the party as anti-national and indulging in pro-Peking activities, and you allow its newspapers to continue to be published. Action should have been taken against them as well. An impression should have been created in the country and among the people that you really mean to take action against them. But if you take action with a wavering mind and hesitatingly it could not be called action. The government has only attempted to tinker with the problem that is not enough. Those who are not patriots should not be treated lightly, they should be dealt with firmly. Only that could protect our freedom and security.

Do Leftists get Money from Chinese Embassy ?

The Home Minister had stated in the other House that Leftist Communists were getting financial help from the Chinese Embassy. This should be thoroughly investigated. The Bank of China accounts have been referred to in this connection. We have already demanded in this House that the result of examination of the accounts of the Bank of China should be made public and should be made known to the House. Communists have alleged that certain Congressmen have taken money from the Bank of China. To the best of my knowledge the big guns of the Communist Party withdraw money from the Bank of China and huge amounts were withdrawn before the elections through blank cheques and no account has been kept. Where has that money gone ? Who are the recipients of that money ? After all, why is the government hesitating to put forth the report about the accounts of the Bank of China before the House ?

SHRI DAHYABHAI V. PATEL (Gujarat) : Because Congress has a share in it ?

SHRI BHUPESH GUPTA : Madam, they must be eating chicken tandoori in Moti Mahal Restaurant.

SHRI VAJPAYEE : I would like to make a suggestion in this regard, although it has got a wider implication. A restriction should be placed on all foreign embassies here that they should get all their printing work–advertisements etc.–done only through the government, through the Ministry of Information and Broadcasting. The embassies that are financially helping those elements or forces do it through distributing printing work and advertisements in the newspapers belonging to their party. Why should not the Ministry of Information and Broadcasting, in consultation with the Ministry of External Affairs inform the foreign embassies that whatever printing work or advertisements are given should be routed through them ? They were influencing the politics of our country by giving them money through printing work and distribution of advertisements.

Sending Communists to Jail not Enough

Madam, after all, it is not enough to put the communists behind the bars.

SHRI BHUPESH GUPTA : Shoot them. We might be the target, but they will miss it.

SHRI VAJPAYEE : I am not advocating that they be shot. We have to think about this problem a bit deeply. We have Defence of India Rules during the Emergency and we may arrest them and put them behind the bars. Merely because some communists have won the elections in Kerala does not change the seriousness of this problem. It is true that they have won. But if they have won the election they cannot be allowed to play with the security of this country.

AN HON'BLE MEMBER : Absolutely correct.

SHRI VAJPAYEE : Who should form the government in Kerala is a different question. But I would like to go deeper into the matter. It is well known that the Communists have their loyalties outside the country. But how to resolve it, let Shri Nanda explain it. Why has a ban not been imposed on the Left Communists, the Communist Party (Marxist) ? Why has it not been declared unlawful ? They are with China. They do not believe in democracy. They are against a peaceful change and nobody should have any doubt that if they get an opportunity they would try to bring a change in the country with the help of arms, because this is their philosophy, this is their ideology, there is no need to collect proof in favour of it. If a communist does not believe in an armed revolution he is not a communist in the true sense.

I pity Shri Bhupesh Gupta. If anybody has to be a communist in India why should he become pro-Moscow ? Why should he not be pro-Peking ? Peking is our neighbour. Peking has a revolutionary ideology, Peking can supply arms. The defeat of the Right communists in Kerala and the victory of the Left communists over them is not only a warning to them but a warning to the entire country. This quarrel between Moscow and Peking...(*Interruptions*).

I am closing. This quarrel between Moscow and Peking is over ideology. But we should not forget that looking at the geographical position of India only Peking supporters could be more effective. The position in Europe is different. The position in South-East Asia is quite different. That entire area is sitting on dynamite. He who ignites it would attract notice. Therefore the government should seriously ponder over the question, which has far-reaching consequences.

It is one thing to have friendly relations with communist countries, and quite another to adopt a particular policy towards the Communist Party. I had said this earlier too, and I repeat it again. President Nasser has maintained friendly relations with the Soviet Union, but has not allowed the Communist Party to grow in his country. Algeria has maintained friendly relations with Communist countries but has declard the Communists in the country unlawful. We maintain relations with communist countries but are allowing such communists to function in our country whose loyalties are outside India and who would not hesitate to conspire against our freedom during a period of crisis. Thank you.

Karakoram Highway: Sino-Pak Axis Established

SHRI SAUGATA ROY (Barrackpore) : I call the attention of the Minister of External Affairs to the following matter of urgent public importance and request that he may make a statement thereon :

"Reported construction of Karakoram Highway by Pakistan and China in the Pakistan-occupied territory of Jammu and Kashmir."

SHRI VAJPAYEE : Sir, as the House is aware, a road called "Karakoram Highway" linking Pakistan with China, and passing through Pakistan-occupied Kashmir, was inaugurated on the 18th June, 1978 by Pakistan's Chief Martial Law Administrator, General Zia-ul-Haq and Chinese Vice-Premier Keng Piao at Thakot. Plans for this road were mooted sometime around 1963, soon after China and Pakistan entered into an agreement in accordance with which 2100 square miles of Indian territory in Jammu and Kashmir, under Pakistan's illegal occupation, was handed over to China. Construction of the portion of the road between Gilgit and Mor Khun was undertaken in accordance with an agreement reached in 1966 and was completed in 1969. The portion of the Highway from Mor Khun to Khunjerab has been built following an agreement between the two countries which was signed on October 21, 1969. The road became fully operational on 18th June 1978.

According to reports the 800-kilometre long Highway starts from Haveli, a rail-head 60 miles north of Islamabad, and follows the general course of the river Indus from Thakot to Gilgit. From Gilgit onwards, it runs along the Gilgit, Hunza and Khunjerab rivers upto the Khunjerab pass which is 15,800 feet above sea level. Beyond Khunjerab Pass this Highway is connected with the Chinese road network in Western Tibet which links with Kashgar in the Sinkiang Province. The elevation of this Highway varies from 2000 to about 15,000 feet.

The Government received confirmed news about the construction of the road in June 1969. A strong protest was accordingly lodged on 25th June, 1969 with both Pakistan and China. To Pakistan, we pointed out that the whole of Jammu and Kashmir was part of Indian territory and neither Pakistan nor China had any *locus standi* in Kashmir, and therefore, whatever action the two countries were taking singly or jointly against this territory of India was wholly illegal. In our protest note to the Chinese Government we questioned

Lok Sabha on July 21, 1978 as Minister of External Affairs in response to the Calling Attention Notice regarding Construction of Karakoram Highway by Pakistan and China in Pak-occupied territory of Jammu and Kashmir

their undertaking construction of a road in a territory lawfully belonging to India.

Neither Pakistan nor China formally replied to our protests. However, an official spokesman of Pakistan Foreign Office stated on 11th July, 1969 that India's complaint was based on premises which were not acceptable to them. The question was raised in Parliament and a statement was made by the then Minister of External Affairs on July 23, 1969.

When we came across press reports, stating that the Highway was inaugurated on 18th June, 1978 the Chinese Ambassador and Pakistan CDA in New Delhi were called to the Ministry of External Affairs and apprised of our position on the illegal construction of the road in a territory which is an integral part of India. It was made clear to the two envoys that India cannot acquiesce in the legal implications of the construction of this road.

In reply, the Government of Pakistan have stated that consistent with their position on Jammu and Kashmir they could not accept the validity of our protest. As regards China, while there has been no response so far from Peking the Chinese Ambassador referred to his country's position in response to India's protest against the conclusion of the Agreement between China and Pakistan on 22nd March, 1963 ceding 2100 square miles of Indian territory in the Pakistan-occupied Kashmir in China. He recalled that the Chinese Government had stated at that time that the boundary agreement was a "provisional" one and hence the construction of the road would have no bearing on the status of Kashmir. It may be pertinent to recall that this agreement does include a provision according to which the boundary question is open to re-negotiation. I may mention here that the Karakoram Highway does not pass through the territory in Kashmir ceded by Pakistan to China.

Apart from the illegality of the construction of this Highway, this development also has serious strategic implications for this region. While we are fully alive to these implications, I would like to express the hope that these neighbours of ours, with both of whom we are trying to normalise our relations would see to it that this communication link is not used in a manner that runs counter to the search for good-neighbourliness and stability in this area.

SHRI SAUGATA ROY : Sir, the External Affairs Minister has taken particular interest in normalising relations with Pakistan for which he has received due appreciation from the country. We have concluded the Salal Project Agreement even if it had not been so good for the interests of the country. He himself flew down to Islamabad. Our whole question is that on this plea we see that after the coup in Afghanistan a new effort is being made to open the Chinese-Pakistani axis, reopen the question of Kashmir, and the question of Kashmir has been reopened at the Islamic Summit by Pakistan. I would like the External Affairs Minister to take note of this, and that is why on this very important issue I would like to ask the Minister: (a) why there was this time lag of 12 days between the reports appearing in the Indian press about the arrival of Keng Piao in Islamabad and the actual lodging of our protest note; and (b) whether, in view of the fact that the Chinese have made references, without any right, about the territorial intergity of Jammu and Kashmir, the External Affairs Minister is going to cancel his proposed visit to China as a protest.

SHRI VAJPAYEE : There has been no undue delay in summoning the envoys of China and Pakistan. We wanted to take action simultaneously. We had to inform our High Commissioner in Pakistan and our Ambassador in Paking. Protests may be lodged there also.

AN HON. MEMBER : When ?

SHRI VAJPAYEE : I cannot tell the exact date.

PROF. MADHU DANDAVATE, Minister of Railways : At an appropriate time.

SHRI VAJPAYEE : At appropriate time. The Railway Minister has come to my rescue. (*Interruptions*). That explains the delay. All political parties have their problems. The Janata Party is no exception. But we have never allowed party considerations to come in the way, or internal disputes in the party to come in the way of dealing with national and international issues.

SHRI K. GOPAL : Then why did you cancel the trip to Geneva ? (*Interruptions*).

SHRI VAJPAYEE : I wanted my colleague to go to Geneva. I am so accommodative.

My friend asked why there is no reference to the Chinese statement that the people of Jammu and Kashmir should be given the right of self-determination.

MR. SPEAKER : This question does not arise (*Interruptions*).

SHRI KANWAR LAL GUPTA : The main problem is about Kashmir and the agreement of China with Pakistan. These are national issues. (*Interruptions*).

SHRI VAJPAYEE : I am prepared to state India's position. The position is well-known. Jammu and Kashmir is an integral part of India and there is no question of giving the right of self-determination to a part of the country. But to say that I have deliberately avoided saying something will not be fair. (*Interruptions*).

So far as the question regarding my visit to Peking is concerned, whether that visit will be cancelled or not, the Hon. member made a suggestion. But I am not inclined to agree with that suggestion.

DR. VASANT KUMAR PANDIT (Rajgarh) : Out of the statement of the Hon. Minister of External Affairs, three main issues arise. First is about the legality of the road: second the logistics, *i.e.* the strategic position of the road, and the third issue is our Government's policy of having friendship with all our neighbouring countries.

As far as the first issue is concerned since 1962 and then again in March 1969, I would like the Hon. Minister to tell us how many times written protests were given. It has always been an oral dialogue.

SHRI VAJPAYEE : No, No.

DR. VASANT KUMAR PANDIT : Except in 1969, where the word 'Note' is mentioned, *i.e.* "Note was sent." Is it a legal note ? I would like to know whether our legal position with regard to this road was maintained by sending a written protest; and whether our Government will consider—if not now, at some appropriate time—lodging a written, legal protest against it.

With regard to the second point, *viz.* about logistics of the road—it is a road with which goes all round the old established traditional Silk Route. And, therefore, when our Hon. Minister goes to China will he get an assurance that this road will not be used in such a manner or fashion that it will endanger the security of our country ?

MR. SPEAKER : The rule says 'a question'. There are two from you.

DR. VASANT KUMAR PANDIT : Thirdly, since the Janata Government came to power, they are following a positive policy of genuine non-alignment. That policy has given some results. With regard to both these countries it has given good results. But there are certain recent events. One, which I have just now mentioned, is about the issue of self-determination. The second is that there is a pronouncement by Chinese Deputy Prime Minister that they are considering putting Pakistan on nuclear parity with India. The third is the Asiatic Islamic Conference which was recently held, where a resolution on plebiscite in Kashmir was passed. In view of this, could we hope that the Minister of External Affairs, with all his dynamism, charisma and diplomatic personality—when he goes to China in October—will bring about some sort of a rapprochement, so that we can go ahead with our genuine non-alignment policy.

SHRI VAJPAYEE : It will not be correct to say that the Government of India has not lodged written protests. On 10th June, 1962, a note was given by the Ministry of External Affairs to the Embassy of China in New Delhi regarding Sino-Pak boundary negotiations. And I have a long list of dates on which written notes and protests were submitted. Let us not think that if we say something orally, it is less important than that what is given in writing. But written protests have also been given.

So far as the question of the use of this road is concerned, I have already stated—and perhaps the Hon. member was not attentive....

MR. SPEAKER : The question was: when you go to China, will you take up this question and see that this road is not used....

SHRI VAJPAYEE : If I go to China I will take up many problems including this (*Interruptions*).

MR. SPEAKER : In international matters, might is right—in actual practice.

SHRI VASANT SATHE (Akola) : I am really surprised that the Hon. External Affairs Minister, who has been so proudly proclaiming that since he took over this important portfolio India's relations have been improving with all our neighbours and with everyone around, I find that while he is living in this happy illusion of improving relations, there is a systematic erosion of our interests, our national interests, with our neighbours. Any person who has the slightest vestige of patriotism left in his veins will feel shocked at this inroad into Indian territory by this road.

AN HON. MEMBER : You are responsible for this.

SHRI VASANT SATHE : I find some persons, even today, are trying to defend the construction of this road. Kindly see the last para of the statement of the Hon. Minister. It reads :

> "...this development also has serious strategic implications for this region. While we are fully alive to these implications, I would like to express the hope that these neighbours of ours with both of whom we are trying to normalise our relations would see to it that this communication link is not used in a manner that runs counter to the search for good-neighbourliness and stability in this area."

Now what is this, Mr. Vajpayee ? You are giving up your case in this manner. Although you have said earlier in protestation that this is an illegal road, that they have no right to have this road, this land does not belong to them and it is none of the business of Pakistan to make a gift of it for the construction of a road to China, having said all this, in the last paragraph you have given up everything. Sir, you have been a judge and you know how a lawyer can, by one such sentence, give up even a good case. You have given up your case. This is the biggest tragedy. If you go to China tomorrow, you will be caught by your own sentence. They will tell you "don't worry, Mr. Vajpayee, we will use this road only for peaceful purposes to promote good-neighbourliness". Then will you come back satisfied ? I am really shocked at the attitude of the Government.

When the Prime Minister went to Washington, a more serious thing has emerged. According to a report dated 11th June from Washington, sent by the Special Correspondent of *New York Times*, the well-known columnist, Mr. David Binder :

> "Prime Minister, Morarji R. Desai of India, indicated in an interview broadcast today, that his Government was prepared to accept Chinese seizure of 14,000 sq. miles of disputed territory between 1957 and 1962 and to acknowledge the present boundaries formally to normalise relations with China."

Is this the price you are going to pay ?

I will recall your words, Mr. Vajpayee, when you were on this side, what protestations you were making about even an inch of territory. They were your words. Are you suggesting that merely because you have gone to that side now, you agree that this is your policy that the entire 14,000 sq. miles occupied by China are going to be surrendered, compromised and gifted away for friendly neighbourly relations for a smile from Hua ?

I can understand those persons who were trying to normalise their relations with masters, because they got a rebuff when they sent a message of condolence on the death of Mao and that was rejected and returned to them. I can understand their trying to be good boys and to make up their relations, but why should you as a Government do this in the name of normalisation of relations ?

There is another aspect. Yesterday's *Times of India* refers to Loy Henderson's secret negotiations about having an independent Kashmir. So, there is a triple alliance, China and USA having come together, now with

Pakistan, they are trying to pressurise the Government of India in the name of normalisation to acquiesce in this. Is this your concept of genuine non-alignment, to give up Indian interest, give away territory ? Is this what you are trying to do ?

AN HON. MEMBER : We are hearing another voice, somebody else is speaking.

PROF. MADHU DANDAVATE, Minister of Railways : Mr. Sathe is speaking in two voices.

SHRI VASANT SATHE : I hope there is no bugging here now.

SHRI A. BALA PAJANOR (Pondicherry) : I protest at his remark. It was the exclusive right of the previous Government, not of this Government.

SHRI VASANT SATHE : You do not know, your phone is being tapped.

MR. SPEAKER : There have been enough doubts, let us go to the subject.

SHRI VASANT SATHE : I have asked two questions of the External Affairs Minister about the policy of the Government of India. In terms of your statement, are you going to concede and compound the illegality by accepting the normal use of that road as you say in your statement ? Are you going to surrender the interests of India in terms of the reported statement of the Prime Minister ? These are my two questions.

SHRI DINEN BHATTACHARYA (Serampore) : Please tell them that this road was not built in a day.

SHRI VAJPAYEE : My friend, Mr. Sathe has reminded me of what I used to say when I was in the opposition. Should I remind him what he used to say when he was here on the treasury benches (*Interruption*).

SHRI VASANT SATHE : You were saying the same thing which I said today.

SHRI VAJPAYEE : This road has not been built in a day. But it does not mean that we are going to compromise with the illegality of the road. (*Interruptions*).

SHRI VASANT SATHE : What is the meaning of the last para of your statement ? Otherwise, delete it.

SHRI VAJPAYEE : I am not prepared to delete anything. This statement has been made after careful consideration. You may or may not agree; that is your view. (*Interruptions*). Let not the opposition accuse us of betraying the interest of the country. (*Interruptions*). You are responsible for giving one-third of Kashmir to Pakistan. You did not have the courage to say anything at that time. Now, you are accusing us. (*Interruptions*).

SHRI K. LAKKAPPA : When Mr. Sathe called the attention of the Minister of External Affairs...

SHRI VAJPAYEE : Mr. Sathe did not call the attention.

SHRI K. LAKKAPPA : Over and above the statement the Minister of External Affairs made a remark which is not warranted. He has made such a derogatory remark....(*Interruptions*).

MR. DEPUTY SPEAKER : Please take your seat. There is absolutely no point of order.

SHRI K. LAKKAPPA : He made a remark that one-third of Kashmir was given to Pakistan...(*Interruptions*).

MR. DEPUTY SPEAKER : If you go on like that it will go off the record.

SHRI K. LAKKAPPA : He should withdraw that.

MR. DEPUTY SPEAKER : He will not withdraw anything. Mr. Sathe has asked a question and he is replying. You cannot get up on a point of order and go on giving your opinion.

SHRI VAJPAYEE : I am sorry if I retaliated in strong words. I did not mean that any part of India had been handed over to Pakistan, because the stand of the previous Government and the present Government on the question of Kashmir is the same. But when insinuations are made...

SHRI K.P. UNNIKRISHNAN (Badagara) : You made an allegation.

SHRI VAJPAYEE : I do not want to go into that question.

SHRI K.P. UNNIKRISHNAN : You go through the record. You made an allegation.

SHRI VAJPAYEE : You accused the Government.

SHRI C.M. STEPHEN (Idukki) : You made an allegation that it was handed over by the previous Government to the other Government. If it was really handed over then you are confirming the position that Pakistan is *de jure* in possession of that. If it was handed over—that was the allegation that you had made (*Interruptions*).

SHRI VAJPAYEE : What I meant was that you ordered the ceasefire without complete liberation of Jammu and Kashmir (*Interruptions*).

MR. DEPUTY SPEAKER : Well, he has corrected himself.

SHRI VAJPAYEE : I do not understand why there should be so much of excitement on a question on which the whole House stands united.

SHRI P. VENKATASUBBAIAH (Nandyal) : He must be careful in choosing his words.

SHRI VAJPAYEE : It applies to both sides.

SHRI P. VENKATASUBBAIAH : You made that accusation.

SHRI VAJPAYEE : The process of normalisation of relations with Pakistan as well as China was initiated by the former Government and we have accelerated the process.

SHRI VASANT SATHE : We are not against that.

SHRI VAJPAYEE : Now, Mr. Sathe has put an interpretation on the last sentence of my statement which is not correct, which is unwarranted. We have challenged the legality. We say that the whole of Jammu and Kashmir is an integral part of India, including that area which is under illegal occupation of Pakistan. If and when that area comes back to India (*Interruption*). India will be in a position to use this road.

SHRI K.P. UNNIKRISHNAN : Obviously (*Interruptions*)...

SHRI K. GOPAL (Karur) : They cannot take the road away.

SHRI VAJPAYEE : Are you disputing this statement also ?

SHRI K.P. UNNIKRISHNAN : Mr. Minister, why do you give a suggestion about how to use this road ? Please read this sentence again.

SHRI VAJPAYEE : I have read the sentence. It has been put after a good deal of thought

SHRI K. GOPAL : By whom ?

SHRI VAJPAYEE : Of course by me.

SHRI K.P. UNNIKRISHNAN : I hope so.

SHRI VAJPAYEE : I run the External Affairs Ministry. There is a world of difference, Mr. Unnikrishnan. I would not like to go into detail. I will not be here for a minute if I do not formulate the policy.

SHRI VASANT SATHE : I am sorry, the impression in the country today is that the Prime Minister makes the foreign policy, Mr. Jagat Mehra implements it, and you only translate it in Hindi.

SHRI VAJPAYEE : Thank you very much. Foreign policy is not formulated or implemented by any particular Minister. It is the collective responsibility. But I would not like to go into that question.

Mr. Sathe has also referred to the story by Mr. David Binder in the *New York Times* about the interview given by the Prime Minister to the NBC in the 'Meet the Press' programme. In this case also the correspondent put his own interpretation.

SHRI VASANT SATHE : He has quoted.

SHRI VAJPAYEE : He has not. In this case also the correspondent put his own interpretation on what the Prime Minister has said. An official denial was issued the same day...

SHRI K.P. UNNIKRISHNAN : Where ?

SHRI VAJPAYEE : In New York as well as in New Delhi. It was widely published. It was made clear...

SHRI VASANT SATHE : Why are you misleading ? In quotes, he says : "Questioned on NBC-TV's 'Meet the Press' Programme Mr. Desai said..." In quotes, he says : "...All depends on China. But we are determined not to go to war on that issue. We do not want to take back the area which, we say, they have taken from us by force. We do not take by war, we have sufficient..." What does this mean ?

SHRI VAJPAYEE : Where is the position that India is prepared to hand over that territory to China ? The only statement that the Prime Minister made was that India would not go to war in order to recover that territory. But our claim stands, Mr. Sathe.

Mr. Speaker, Sir, I want to speak in Hindi now because Shri Sathe does not understand my English and I cannot understand what he says. It is not a question of language, but of ideas. What the official spokesman said that day, I would like to quote :

> "What the Prime Minister said in the interview was that India would not go to war with China on the boundary issue or try to take by force the Indian territory occupied by China and the boundary issue could be solved between the two countries by negotiations."

There is no question of surrendering Indian territory. We have not compromised our stand. The Prime Minister the other day made the position clear in this very House.

SHRI K.P. UNNIKRISHNAN : Declaration of peaceful intentions!

SHRI VAJPAYEE : Which you share, I hope.

Mr. Deputy Speaker, Sir, our Government has earlier given an assurance, and I am prepared to repeat it that we are making efforts to recover by peaceful methods our territory which is under Chinese occupation. I don't think there is any need to demand any such assurance.

SHRI KANWAR LAL GUPTA : We should not surrender it.

SHRI VAJPAYEE : Nobody should even imagine that we might purchase peace by bargaining our territory. Peace is not purchased, peace has to be maintained on one's own strength. (*Interruptions*). If they do not return it, we will formulate our policy in consultation with you.

Taking advantage of the Calling Attention Notice members of the House have expressed their sentiments and the Government's policy will be formulated and implemented by keeping them in mind.

SHRI KANWAR LAL GUPTA : My last question was whether the Government was alert, because China constructed such a long road and the story of 1962 should not be repeated. What machinery have you devised to ensure it while extending the hand of friendship ? I want a categorical answer.

SHRI VAJPAYEE : We are cautious, we are on our guard. We have learnt our lessons from the past events and are determined to ensure that they are not repeated in future. This is all I have to say.

Sino-French Agreement to Transfer Nuclear Technology to China

SHRI BRIJ BHUSAN TEWARI (Khalilabad) : Mr. Deputy Speaker, Sir, I beg to draw the attention of the Minister of External Affairs to the following matter of urgent public importance :

"Reported agreement between China and France and supply of Nuclear Plant and Technology to China by France under authorisation of USA."

SHRI VAJPAYEE : As the House is aware, press reports have recently appeared stating that France and China have signed an economic agreement in Peking on December 4, 1978 regarding trade between the two countries over the next seven years. This agreement is reported to include a provision regarding the sale of nuclear power reactors to China by a French firm.

It has also been stated that the nuclear power reactors in question are based on technology originating in the U.S.A. While Government have seen newspaper reports that it is likely that the US Government would give their clearance, which would be necessary for their export to China by France it is understood that the question of their clearance is still under the consideration of the US Government.

Government do not yet have confirmed details and information on the scope and conditions of the reported sale of nuclear power equipment to China. In the absence of these it is not possible to comment on the precise implications of this transfer of technology which, further, is the immediate concern of the three parties involved. However, I would like to reiterate the Government's well-known views on the peaceful utilisation of nuclear energy and the necessity to ensure that any safeguards that may be eventually applied in the matter of the transfer of nuclear technology should be uniform and non-discriminatory covering all activities of nuclear and non-nuclear weapon states.

The Hon. member has raised a very important issue. If the United States supplies to China through France, the technology that it does not normally give to other countries and, if it does so, puts the condition that the atomic reactors of the recipient country will be covered under full-scope safeguards then any discrimination in regard to China will be wrong and we will not accept that. China possesses an atom bomb. It had carried out the first atomic explosion in 1964. China has made considerable progress in the direction of weapons. However, we are not on this question at the moment. If China

Lok Sabha on December 19, 1978 as Minister of External Affairs in response to the Calling Attention Notice regarding the reported agreement between China and France and Supply of Nuclear Plant and Technology to China by France under Authorisation of U.S.A.

wants nuclear energy for modernisation it is the duty of the supplier country to ensure that the recipient remains under full-scope safeguards, as in Tarapore, so that the atomic information may not be used for producing such elements or converting uranium into plutonium, which may lead to expansion of weapons. I would like to take the House into confidence in this matter. The Hon. members might have seen the statement of Senator Frank Church, Chairman of Foreign Relations Committee. I want to quote him :

> "There is a real possibility of selling commercial nuclear reactors to the Chinese. Remember that since the Chinese have already developed a full capacity to manufacture nuclear weapons the normal concern that we have about proliferation of such weapons is not present in the Chinese case".

Mr. Deputy Speaker, Sir, this is a ridiculous situation. On the one hand, the USA wants to stop proliferation and, on the other, it wants to impose all the conditions of non-proliferation on those countries that have already decided not to manufacture nuclear weapons. I think the Hon. member's allegation that the USA is adopting a double standard on this issue is correct. India will oppose this double standard.

SHRI OM PRAKASH TYAGI : Mr. Deputy Speaker, the Hon. Minister has not replied to my question. I wanted to know whether such accord is likely to have adverse effects in the international field and on India and , if so, what efforts are being made to neutralise the same ?

SHRI VAJPAYEE : India is fully alert to its security. We constantly review our security arrangements. Keeping in mind the happenings in our neighbourhood, whenever any shortcoming is detected it is removed.

Mr. Deputy Speaker, Sir, as I have already said, there are two aspects of this question : one, China possesses nuclear weapons and is further developing them, and is busy in improving its technology from whatever sources possible. Secondly, the USA–in contravention of the condition which it has imposed upon us for supplying enriched uranium for Tarapore–waives that condition for China on the ground that China already possesses nuclear weapons. This is not only a matter of concern for us, but also of displeasure, and we are conveying our sentiments to them in no unambiguous terms. Full-scope safeguards cannot apply only to those countries that do not possess nuclear weapons. We have already declared that...

SHRI KANWAR LAL GUPTA : You also manufacture them.

SHRI VAJPAYEE : Would America like it ? I don't think America likes it. But it is doing just the opposite of what it does not like.

SHRI BRIJ BHUSAN TEWARI : You bring it from Russia, then it will like.

AN HON. MEMBER : You may express your feelings to that effect.

SHRI VAJPAYEE : It is not a question of expressing feelings. The policies of the Government are announced. In Parliament we only express our feelings. As a spokesman of a big country like ours, which is a strong country with so many men of calibre, if I say something that would not merely be an expression of a feeling, that would be the voice of the whole country.

DR. KARAN SINGH : Feelings lend strength to duty.

SHRI VAJPAYEE : When the moment of doing our duty arrives we will not lag behind.

Mr. Deputy Speaker, Sir, Shri Ugrasen asked about the various kinds of preparations being made by China. He brought in Pakistan also, and mentioned about international competition. Well, all these things are important, but they do not arise out of the question that is before us now. As I said, we are going to have a discussion on the international situation day after tomorrow when all these matters can be raised.

Mr. Deputy Speaker, the Hon. member has expressed serious concern over the entire episode. We are in constant touch with our embassy in Paris to acquire information from the French Government. According to it political, financial and technical details have not yet been finalised, and so long as that is not done, no agreement should be supposed to have been reached.

America is also a party in this matter because the technology has to go from America. China is a communist country and if American technology goes to China via France there must be American clearance for it. Yesterday too, we had a talk with the US Embassy here and they said no clearance had been given so far.

The Hon. member has raised some other issues also. I think they are not directly connected with this matter. There would be a debate on foreign policy and the international situation day after tomorrow when all these issues could be considered in depth.

Mr. Deputy Speaker, Sir, the agreement that we have with America about Tarapore has to be honoured. The legislation passed by the American Congress later cannot apply to the agreement made earlier. We have received one instalment and hope that the second one will come. We know that the attitude of President Carter is helpful about it. But there are other agencies also there, which object to it. America is a democratic country and we hope that, in spite of all this, it will honour the commitment made to us. But if it does not, we will be free to run Tarapore by making arrangements from other sources. The Hon. member asked whether a letter will be sent to President Carter. Well, exchange of letters between our Prime Minister and President Carter always goes on, in which views on the international situation and bilateral matters are expressed. I believe that when this matter will take a final shape it can be raised at a higher level also:

> "There is a real possibility of selling commercial nuclear reactors to the Chinese. Remember that since the Chinese have already developed a full capacity to manufacture nuclear weapons the normal concern that we have about proliferation of such weapons is not present in the Chinese case."

Mr. Deputy Speaker, Sir, when I go to Peking all these issues will be discussed and this question may also come up. But I want to repeat that this question relates more to America, because through France they are giving to China a technology about which they talk of full-scope safeguards before giving the same to others. If the statement of Senator Frank Church is correct, the USA is not prepared to press for these safeguards in the case of China.

As I have already said, we are in contact with the American Embassy and if this agreement is finalised we will take necessary diplomatic steps.

The Hon. member also observed that sometimes hurdles are created in the way of our efforts to develop friendly relations with our neighbours. Well, it is the duty of India and her neighbouring countries to cast aside these hurdles and improve and strengthen our relations. The present Government is eager to improve relations with our neighbours. But one thing is clear...if we want to normalise our relations with some country we do not want to do so at the cost of a third country. Therefore, this process of normalisation would not be to weaken our relations with other countries. We want to normalise relations with our neighbouring countries while maintaining close relations with others. Thank you.

Visit to China

Mr. Speaker, Sir, I wish to report to the House on my visit to the People's Republic of China, which had to be postponed at the last minute in October 1978 on medical advice. The mutually convenient dates for the visit had been fixed over six weeks ago. The House will recall that I had made clear that I was accepting the invitation of Foreign Minister Huang Hua to visit China in the spirit of adherence to our Government's policy of non-alignment and to explore the possibilities of improving bilateral relations with all countries without jeopardising well-established friendships. My visit and my conversations were entirely in keeping with this declared policy and objective. While exchange of views on international issues was always intended to figure in the discussions the primary focus of my visit was on the difficult and complex questions which beset relations between India and China.

Our foreign policy and its endeavours and successes in promoting positive improvements in bilateral relations and India's national strength gave me a measure of confidence in my mission. My anticipation that these resumed ministerial-level bilateral contacts at this time might prove worthwhile in securing a better understanding of each other's viewpoint has been borne out from my visit.

Situation in the Sub-Continent

It was my first visit to China. From my brief stay in Shanghai and Hang-chow I got vivid impressions of the very strong cultural and historical links between our two large and ancient Asian countries and the similar problems confronting them. The temple in Hangchow which I visited is a beautiful historical monument to the message of the Buddha which went from India to China. In Shanghai I got some idea of the achievements of China as well as the similarities of our developmental problems.

Of primary importance, however, were the conversations which I had with the Chinese leadership in Peking. The three sessions of talks I had with Foreign Minister Huang Hua and a long conversation with Vice-Premier Teng Hsiao-ping and finally the meeting with Premier Hua Kuo-feng were all characterised by an atmosphere of cordiality. The discussions were wideranging in content and both sides were frank in the presentation of their respective viewpoints. In these talks all major issues of common concern to the two countries were covered. In dealing with the international political and economic scene we focussed on problems in Asia, Africa and Europe and

Lok Sabha on February 21, 1979 as Minister of External Affairs on Visit to China

exchanged respective assessments on the prospects of war and the difficulties which cast their shadow on world peace and stability. We discussed in detail the situation in and around the Indian sub-continent and, more important, the issues affecting India-China bilateral relations.

Both sides agreed on a few issues, such as the vital importance of supporting the struggle for liberation in southern Africa and the need for a comprehensive settlement in West Asia which must include the fulfilment of Palestinian rights. We agreed that for the progress of the developing countries it was necessary to create an international environment of peace and tranquillity. However, both sides clearly recognised that we had differing assessments on the inevitability of war, the logic of disarmament and the prospects of detente. I naturally affirmed our well-known positions on such subjects.

I explained in detail how, in keeping with India's traditional and continuing policy of non-alignment, our Government had made strenuous efforts, and with gratifying success, in preserving well-established friendships, and at the same time in improving relations with others. I explained that in our view the world order, with its enlarged membership of nation States, must be made safer and stabler so that independent nations may be able to exercise their right to progress in their own way. A new economic order must be fashioned which would correct the dangerous imbalances which have developed and made more just so that impediments faced, notably by the developing world, are removed and international economic relations are structured.

On the subject of the situation in the sub-continent, which was discussed at considerable length, I explained that, with full deference to the independence of our neighbours, we have sought assiduously to resolve outstanding problems. I spoke of our attempts to create a climate of confidence between the nations south of the Himalayas, which, on the one hand, will lead to an optimisation of our respective national development and cooperation between neighbours, and, on the other, could reduce hopefully, the long story of great power involvement and competition in the problems of our region. A stable and cooperative South Asia, I urged, can be an example and an asset to the world.

Non-Interference

Against this background I described in detail our strict and scrupulous policy of non-interference in internal problems and the steps taken to improve relations with Pakistan. Even while we do not object to normal bilateral relations between Pakistan and China the prospect of improvement of India- China relations would be impeded if their relations adversely affect our legitimate interests.

In this context I summarised the origin and the long history of our differences with Pakistan on the question of Jammu and Kashmir. I informed the Chinese leaders that under the Simla Agreement, to which both countries are parties, we are committed to the final settlement of the Kashmir question through bilateral discussions. It has been the considered view of the Government and all sections of the people in India that unlike the stand taken by the Chinese in the fifties the attitude adopted by the People's Republic of China in the last decade and a half had been an additional and unnecessary complication to the prospect of Sino-Indian relations. In this connection I also reiterated our concern at the construction of the Karakoram Highway across territory which formed part of the State of Jammu and Kashmir.

The Chinese Government showed understanding of our policy towards Pakistan and our neighbours and expressed, both in public and in our conversations, appreciation of our efforts, and indeed, the rationale and success of the policy. The Chinese leaders noted the facts of improved bilateral relations between the countries in this region and the propitious climate of co-operation which now prevailed in the sub-continent.

Boundary Question

I come now to the major bilateral issues between India and China. I underlined to the Chinese leadership the fundamental importance attached by the Government and people to a satisfactory solution of the India-China boundary question. Parliament and public opinion in India consider that its resolution is vital to the resolution of confidence and full normalisation in the climate of our relations. There was recognition of the importance of this issue amongst the Chinese leadership.

As the House is aware, the India-China boundary question is an old problem. While the cartographic positions of the two countries are well-known the discrepancy in the effective control on the ground and the diplomatic position has remained where it was since 1962. I had made it clear that mine was an exploratory mission. It was not my purpose, nor was it, indeed, the expectation on the Chinese side, that my visit to Peking could resolve this difficult problem which concerns differences between the two countries involving approximately 50,000 sq. miles of territory.

Frank Exchange

Our conversations did provide an opportunity for the first time in 19 years to have a frank exchange of views on this complex and politically vital issue. I made clear that the unresolved boundary question must be satisfactorily settled if relations of mutual confidence are to be established between India and China. These exploratory preliminary contacts have at least unfrozen the issue and both Governments are agreed on the need to reflect further on the possible ways to resolve this crucial question. The common willingness to recognise it as such is not an insignificant step forward.

My conversations with the Chinese leaders also covered other past irritants to our relations. I drew attention to the fact that rebels or disaffected elements from Nagaland, Mizoram and Manipur who had managed to reach China had received moral and material support for their insurgent or anti-constitutional activities inside our country. I was glad to learn from

Chinese leaders that such support which may have been given—the last instance was some time ago—was looked upon as a thing of the past.

The Tibetan Question

When the question of the Dalai Lama and Tibetans was referred to I informed the Chinese leaders that we had made it clear that it was in deference to the Dalai Lama's spiritual position and in recognition of the needs of the Tibetan refugees, who voluntarily came to India, that asylum and resettlement facilities were extended by India. If the Dalai Lama and the Tibetans consider that the conditions are suitable for their return to the places of their origin we, from our side, would not stand in their way.

Pilgrimage Facilities for Kailash and Mansarover

I also invited the attention of the Foreign Minister of China to the fact that millions of Indians looked upon Kailash and Mansarover as sacred and that the devout have for centuries visited the places on pilgrimage. No one from India has been able to go to Kailash and Mansarover for nearly two decades. It is true that the Agreement between India and China pertaining to trade and intercourse with the Tibet region expired in 1962 and has not since been renewed. Nevertheless it was our hope that the Chinese Government would consider facilitating pilgrimages to those holy places. Should such facilities be granted I have no doubt that the people in India would look upon it as symbolic of the improved relations between the two countries. We, on our part, are ready to consider similar facilities for pilgrimage to India.

From this brief account Hon. members will observe that international problems and specific questions of concern to the two countries figured squarely in our discussions. Our relations with other countries, which did not in any way affect our relations with China, did not come up in our discussions. Where there was a reference to differences between great powers and areas of tension I expressed the hope that they would be resolved peacefully.

Deteriorating Situation in Indo-China

I might add in this connection that there was a discussion on the situation in Indo-China. The Chinese leaders expressed their viewpoint on the deterioration of their relations with Vietnam. I clearly expressed my concern at the prevailing tension and stressed that each of the countries in the region must be enabled to maintain their independence and were entitled to respect for their sovereignty and territorial integrity. This recquired adherence to the principle of non-interference. I cautioned that there should be no further developments which could lead to a dangerous deterioration of the situation. It is a matter of regret that in the course of our frank exchanges, where we clearly recognised that we had differing perspectives on the international situation, the Chinese leaders did not inform me of the possibility of developments on the China-Vietnam border.

Tranquillity has existed along our border and this, we agreed, in any case should be maintained. Following the restoration of our diplomatic representation to ambassadorial level in 1976 restrictions on trade, banking and shipping had been removed and functional contacts and exchanges of delegations had already started. Since the present Government assumed office this process has continued and the scope for possible bilateral functional cooperation has been identified. The Chinese Government are now embarked on a gigantic programme of modernisation. The Chinese leadership hinted that in many fields it would be of reciprocal advantage for the two countries to share each others's experience and expertise. Trade could improve further and scientific and technological knowhow in various branches could be exchanged. It remains for the officials and experts of the two sides to study more closely and work out areas and forms of advantageous co-operation where real bilateral complementarity exists.

India-China Relations can Improve

Mr. Speaker, we have not slurred over setbacks of the past or the out-standing problems which remain. India and China have different perspectives on internal and external policies. We are confident of India's strength and need not be diffident of our ability to safeguard our interests in our diplomacy. It is not too far-fetched to believe that neither China nor India can profit from an attitude of hostility or even detachment of a kind which characterised our relations for many years. I believe there is a new respect for our policy of genuine non-alignment and independent rationale in our judgement on international issues and notably for our policy towards South Asia as well as economic and technological progress of India. We for our part, cannot but equally recognise the importance of the People's Republic for its ancient past and its achievements in the last 30 years, and its position in the world. Given mutual respect based on equality and dignity, India-China relations can also improve bilaterally and fit into the web of positively oriented and advantageous relationships, which is the essence of our foreign policy. Just as I would caution against euphoria I would also urge a measure of self-confidence that any effort at improvement in relations need not mean the sacrifice of our national interests and aspirations. We have made a beginning and I come back satisfied with the decision to undertake the mission. But I also know it would be a long haul demanding maturity and reciprocal efforts by both Governments if, in the path ahead, satisfactory results are to be obtained.

I must acknowledge that the official delegation and the large party of journalists who had decided at their own expense to cover the visit were shown great hospitality and courtesy. I have extended an invitation to Foreign Minister Huang Hua to visit India at his convenience to enable us to continue the dialogue. Premier Hun Kuo-feng asked me to convey an invitation to our Prime Minister to visit China at a mutually convenient time in the future.

Goal of Full Normalisation of Relations

I went to China with the confidence that I had the broad support of a national consensus. I know for every Indian, whether in Government or outside, national interest and honour must be supreme. I vividly remember that in the late fifties and early sixties I gave expression to my strong feelings when the hopes of India-China friendship suffered a serious setback. With the burden of responsibilities I now carry my concern for national interest and honour remains the same. All those who were alarmed at the fear of adverse consequences and almost cautioned against my undertaking the visit should rest assured that our dignity, independence and our national interests have not been allowed to suffer in any way.

India and China are not only two important members of the international community, they are also neighbours. With full respect to each other's personality and guided by the principles of peaceful co-existence the two countries must strive for the goal of full normalisation and work for a world order which is just and equitable and where all nations big and small can, in peace, develop in their own way. Thank you.

Violation of Indian Airspace by China

Mr. Vice-Chairman, Sir, I am sorry that the Hon'ble member did not listen to my statement carefully. I had made it clear that we have not made any concession to China. No Chinese aircraft has violated the air-space of India. Even before the programme of my visit to Peking was finalised China informed us on their own on June 15, 1979 that they wanted to undertake reconnaissance flights for the maintenance of the pillars put up on the border under their treaty with Nepal and India does not come in the picture, Therefore, the question of our giving any concession to China does not arise. Had we given any concession we would also have asked for something in return; hence this question also does not arise. I do admit that the international relations require *quid pro quo.* But the question of *quid pro quo* arises only when somebody asks for something from us and we in return demand some concessions.

No Concessions

But so far as the flights are concerned we have not given any concessions. The second point raised by the Hon'ble member was regarding China's attitude towards the world. Obviously India and China think differently about the world. I made it clear in my speech in Peking that we do not believe that world war is inevitable, that we are in favour of peace and all the countries must cooperate in establishing peace. The Hon'ble member referred to a letter. I would like to clarify further that the initiative to normalise the relations with China was taken by the previous government with the exchange of ambassadors. We have taken that one step further. But we have made it clear that in our eagerness to normalise our relations with China our relations with old friends which are based on a stable footing will not be disturbed in any way. I think China too should realise this.

SHRI NAGESHWAR PRASAD SHAHI (Uttar Pradesh) : Sir, I have a point of order. Hon'ble Minister is talking of the same peace in the same vein in which Shri JawaharLal Nehru used to talk with China.

MR. VICE-CHAIRMAN : This is not a point of order. Please let him speak....There is no point of order.

SHRI NAGESHWAR PRASAD SHAHI : China does not believe in peace at all.

MR. VICE-CHAIRMAN : This is not a point of order.

SHRI VAJPAYEE : Sir, the Hon'ble member also wanted to know whether our policy towards China would be decided piecemeal or we would take an

Rajya Sabha on March 6, 1979 as Minister of External Affairs regarding violation of Indian airspace by Chinese Aircraft

overall view. My submission is that we do not take decisions piecemeal in regard to any country or about any situation. We take decisions keeping in view the entire picture before us. This also applies in the case of China. But as I said in the beginning, Nepal is also a party to these flights. With Nepal we have very cordial relations. It has entered into a border agreement with China. Pillars have been put up to demarcate the border. Now if they remain within their air-space for the maintenance of these pillars the question of taking permission from us does not arise. I would like to clarify that this matter, which was settled in June 1978, has no connection whatsoever with my recent visit to China. I have also seen the report published in the *Times of India*. Our friend Shri Bagaitker has interpreted it in one way, while I have put a different interpretation of it. Newspapers are free. We should not draw our conclusions on the basis of newspaper reports. I do admit that the Ministry of External Affairs should have denied it as soon as the report was published....

SHRI SADASHIV BAGAITKER : Will the Hon'ble Minister be pleased to state why this report was not denied ? Secondly will the Hon'ble Minister be pleased to state whether Nepal has also approached for granting such permission to China, because he has mentioned Nepal in this connection ? This should also be clarified.

SHRI VAJPAYEE : Sir, I have already explained that no permission was required. Neither any permission was sought, nor any given, China had informed us on its own. This gave us the advantage of keeping a watch on whether our air-space was being violated or not. I have already admitted the lapse about the denial.

But I would like to point out one thing to the Hon'ble member. So many reports are published in the newspapers, and if we start issuing denials for each and every report hardly any time would be left to the Ministry of External Affairs to attend to its normal work.

SHRI SITARAM KESRI (Bihar) : Hon'ble Minister for External Affairs wants to get away by making allegations against newspapers....(*Interruption*).

SHRI VAJPAYEE : I have not made any allegation.

SHRI SITARAM KESRI : There is no justification behind it.

SHRI RAMESHWAR SINGH (Uttar Pradesh) : On a point of order. Hon'ble Minister has admitted...(*Interruptions*).

MR. VICE-CHAIRMAN : Please let them whose name has precedence in the list of speakers speak first. You cannot speak simply by raising a point of order...(*Interruptions*)

SHRI VAJPAYEE : I may state that when this news report appeared, the government spokesman had clarified the position, but that was not published.

Pakistan

Berubari Agreement : Treaties Should Be Ratified by Parliament

Mr. Speaker, Sir, yesterday I had submitted that this House was not taken into confidence by the Prime Minister before signing the Nehru-Noon Pact. Earlier too there have been several occasions when this House was not given an opportunity for considering various important issues relating to foreign countries.

Amend Constitution to Restrict the Right

The question is not that of Berubari alone. We relinquished our rights in Tibet which we had got after the British Government left India, and that matter was never brought before Parliament for its approval. While relinquishing our rights in Tibet we did not care to link that question with the border question so as to get our permanent border confirmed by China. Our Prime Minister is guilty of granting undue advantage to Burma as well. When India became independent Burma owed us Rs. 48 crores. Parliament was not taken into confidence before remitting that debt. The question of property of Indians there, about which difficulties have arisen, was not even taken into consideration. Later we even granted a further loan of Rs. 20 crores to Burma. I think the time has come to restrict the right of the Government to enter into international treaties and agreements. If necessary, the Constitution should be amended to restrict the Government in executing treaties etc. so that treaties could not be considered valid unless approved by Parliament. The right given to execute treaties was being misused and it is time to restrict that right. Whether it is the question of transfer of Berubari, or the question of entering into an agreement with Pakistan regarding canal waters or the question of running a railway train between West Pakistan and East Pakistan, passing through India, the Government should execute all these only after knowing the views of Parliament.

The other thing I would like to say is about the maps that were placed in the Library yesterday after the direction of the Hon'ble Speaker. Members went there and saw the maps. There was one map prepared by the Government of West Bengal and another map which Justice Radcliff was reported to have signed. When we read the explanation given in the Radcliff Award with those maps we were unable to understand why the Prime

Lok Sabha on December 20, 1960 while participating in the discussion on the Border Treaties and the Constitution (Ninth Amendment) Bill

Minister had agreed to hand over Berubari to Pakistan. I would also like to know which map was placed before the Prime Ministers of India and Pakistan during their talks. Which was the map on the basis of which it was decided to divide Berubari ? It should also be made clear as to what impelled us to believe that if the Berubari dispute raised by Pakistan was referred for international arbitration the entire Berubari area would go to Pakistan ? What was the difficulty in our case ? Yesterday, after seeing the map and going through the Radcliff Award we came to the conclusion that India had a strong case and we should not be prepared to hand over half of the Berubari area to Pakistan under any circumstances. Had the matter been referred to international arbitration there was a hundred per cent possibility of the judgement going in our favour. What are the reasons which impelled the Government to hand over Berubari to Pakistan ?

When it was decided to hand over half of the Berubari area to Pakistan the Prime Minister knew that the displaced brethren from East Bengal were settled there, and they would once again be rendered homeless. It should be clarified whether this fact was brought before Pakistan ? Was any assurance sought from Pakistan that their properties would be safeguarded or full compensation would be given to them in lieu thereof ? The Prime Minister has stated that if they decided to remain in East Pakistan they would be treated well. I would like to know whether any guarantee has been sought from Pakistan that they would be treated well. Did the two Prime Ministers consider what would happen to those six thousand people who would be affected by the implementation of this agreement ?

The statement of the Prime Minister that the people who are going to be displaced as a result of this agreement would be welcomed by us has no substance in the present circumstances. The Government of India has not been able to perform its duty towards the displaced persons who have come from East Bengal.... (*Interruptions*).

SHRI BIBHUTI MISHRA (Bagaha) : It has done its duty. Forty thousand displaced persons have been resettled in my district Champaran alone. I can tell you.... (*Interruptions*).

SHRI VAJPAYEE : I want to know how many displaced persons are still to be resettled apart from those who have already been resettled. And if you take them to Dandakaranya for resettlement that cannot solve their problem. But what would happen to the property of those displaced persons who will now come to India ? How much compensation will Pakistan give for that ? Has any demand been put before Pakistan regarding this ? Will they be allowed to bring their assets with them or not ? If they decide to remain in Pakistan what kind of treatment would be meted out to them by Pakistan ? Were these things raised with Pakistan while entering into an agreement with it ? If not, on what basis is it said today that they can live in Pakistan even as Indian citizens if they so desire ? If they could live in Pakistan they would not have come here as displaced persons.

My submission is that before implementation of this agreement a referendum should be held about it. I have moved an amendment that these

Bills should be circulated for elicting public opinion. The general elections are approaching. If the implementation of the Nehru-Noon Pact could wait for one and a half or two years the enactment of these Bills could also be postponed for some time. The Prime Minister had stated yesterday that there was no deadline to implement the Nehru-Noon Pact, there is no fixed date by which this Pact has to come into force. My submission is that the House would commit a great mistake, it would belie the faith reposed in it by the people, if a decision is taken on such a crucial question without eliciting opinion. Therefore, I appeal to the House to accept my amendment to circulate the Bills for eliciting the opinion of the people. Thank you.

Pakistani Infiltration in Assam

Mr. Speaker, Sir, there is one adjournment motion by Shri Vajpayee. I want to know what exactly is the matter. There is also a Starred Question about it given notice of by Shri Harish Chandra Mathur. I have admitted it for answer on the 9th. It is about the grave peril to India's security and integrity posed by planned, large-scale infiltration of Pakistani nationals into Assam and the Government's failure to take effective measures in this regard. May I know what is the position ?

SHRI JAWAHARLAL NEHRU, Prime Minister and Minister of External Affairs : In so far as I can recollect, there has been no large-scale infiltration in recent months; probably there was some. There has been, I believe, some infiltration during the last 12 years on a relatively small scale. We have tried to stop it; we have succeeded to some extent; occasionally they come through the border. The Assam Government and the Government of India are taking more effective steps to stop this kind of thing. But I think it will not be correct to say that there has been large-scale infiltration.

SHRI VAJPAYEE : May I make a submission ? According to a conservative estimate, during the last few years more than six lakh Pakistani Muslims have infiltrated into Assam, and the Hon. Prime Minister, in his Press Conference, stated that if during the last 12 years even five lakhs have come to Assam, that is not large-scale infiltration. May I know the definition of 'large-scale' ? Are we to understand that even if lakhs of people come from across the border into Assam and concentrate themselves into Cachar, Goalpara and Nowgong, the districts which already have a large Muslim population, and that too with a view to make these districts Muslim-majority areas, no serious action will be taken by the Government ? Even the Chief Minister of Assam had stated that he was thinking of creating a barbed wire fence on the border. That shows the seriousness of the situation.

SHRI JAWAHARLAL NEHRU : May I respectfully submit that in the guise of asking for information all kinds of insinuations should not be made; such as the Hon. member is making ?

SHRI VAJPAYEE : What sort of insinuation have I made ?

MR. SPEAKER : He will say it.

SHRI VAJPAYEE : Sir, I seek your protection. It is for you to define 'insinuation'. I have not made any insinuation.

SHRI JAWAHARLAL NEHRU : I may point out that it is an insinuation that people are coming there in order to upset the Government and to add to a

Lok Sabha on August 7, 1961 regarding the Alleged Pakistani Infiltration in Assam

certain majority of a certain community, etc. These are insinuations which I say, to my knowledge, have no basis in fact in the slightest.

I do not know factually how many have come in. The Hon. member has given certain figures. I do not know where he has got them from. I am not prepared to accept it. I would rather wait for further enquiries and further examination in detail for the census figures and others. Then we shall accept that figure, whatever it is, I do not think that figure is accurate.

But may I just remind the House of the long-term background of all these areas ? I should imagine that for the last 60 or 70 years—I do not know how long, and it may be more—and that is long, long before partition—there has been a continuous movement from the overcrowded parts of old Bengal into Assam. I remember reading in the census report of 1911, *i.e.* exactly fifty years ago, about the movement from I think, the district of Mymensingh, like an army of ants marching, because Assam was relatively under-populated while this area was terribly populated.

This has been happening all this time for the last sixty or seventy years and all kinds of devices were adopted in those days—the so-called line system etc—to stop this. To some extent they succeeded; to some extent not. Sometimes the Government of Assam was more vigilant; sometimes it was not. This is a very old problem of population flowing over from an over-crowed area to a less crowded area. Since partition, of course, this over-flow has stopped. An attempt has been made to stop it and it has largely been stopped. It may be that some of it still flows where there is a chance and we are still trying to stop it.

As to the actual facts, after examining the census figures and such other information we may get we shall know the position. But anyhow, it is our purpose and intention to stop this.

SHRI HARISH CHANDRA MATHUR : I would like to invite the attention of the Prime Minister to the census report and the alarming figure given in the census report itself. The percentage of increase in Assam, in particular early this year, has been enormous and has not been explained by any other factor except that there is infiltration.

SHRI JAWAHARLAL NEHRU : I do not think that necessarily follows to the extent that the Hon. member thinks. The census people have themselves told us that they want to look into this in greater detail before they can express any opinion. Certainly all this has to be kept in mind.

SHRI VAJPAYEE : May I know whether the Government of Assam has approached the Central Government for additional funds so that effective measures can be taken to stop this infiltration ?

SHRI JAWAHARLAL NEHRU : No question of funds has arisen in this matter. But obviously it is the interest of the Government of India and it is of the Government of Assam to deal with this situation.

Inhuman Treatment Meted Out to Minorities in East Pakistan

Madam, whatever has happened and whatever is happening in East Pakistan has once again made it clear that there is no place for non-Muslims there. Along with Hindus, Buddhists are also being expelled from East Pakistan and atrocities are being committed against Christians too. The question is not only of Hindus and Muslims, but that of forcing Pakistan to treat its minorities with humaneness. It is essential to give full freedom to those who want to migrate to India. But the aim of our policy should be to create such conditions in East Pakistan that those who want to live there may live with security and dignity.

At the time of partition the leaders of India and Pakistan had given assurances to the minorities. The leaders of Pakistan are not prepared to abide by their assurances. But what are our leaders doing ? What policy does our Government have to ensure justice for the minorities in Pakistan ? There are no two opinions that peace should prevail in the country, that the safety and dignity of the life of every citizen in the country should be ensured. But is that all that is necessary to secure the safety of minorities in Pakistan ? We have tried to tread on the path of secularism in our country during the past 16 years, but we have not been able to force Pakistan to change its policy of communalim. It is evident that we will have to take further steps in this direction and, as I have submitted, the aim of these steps should be to ensure justice for the minorities of East Bengal in their homes. India should be prepared to go to any length to achieve this objective. The future of our country is linked with the minorities of East Bengal.

It we look at the riots in East Pakistan against the background of the obnoxious alliance between Pakistan and China, we would come to the conclusion that these riots were started in a pre-planned manner. The riots may subside or calm down today, but Pakistan would incite these riots again whenever it so desires. It is feared that Pakistan is intending to create tension on the cease-fire line in Kashmir.

Imagine how dangerous for our country's security it would be if, on the one side some disturbance is created on the cease-fire line and, on the other, there is squeezing out of the minorities in East Pakistan resulting in lakhs of displaced persons coming over, to take refuge. Our attention will be divided. Questions of maintaining peace and law and order inside the country would arise. The refugees from East Bengal will put pressure on our economic

Rajya Sabha on March 4, 1964 during discussion on the motion regarding Communal Disturbances in East Pakistan

structure also. Can we find out a way to ensure the security of the minorities in their own homes in East Pakistan ? I do not want to overlook the danger involved in it. But there is danger in closing our eyes to the problem also.

In 1950, the Nehru-Liaquat Ali Pact was signed, but the riots did not stop after that. Today riots are taking place again. It is being suggested that the Home Ministers of both countries should meet, the Presidents of both the countries should issue appeals. Is this the way to bring back Pakistan on the right path ? Those who suggest such means and ways perhaps refuse to understand the psychology behind these riots, to understand why people were incited to indulge in riots and why they would be incited to do it again. The political situation in Pakistan is not good. Shri Ayub Khan is becoming more and more unpopular. The people of Pakistan are fighting for their democratic rights and the military dictatorship is gradually losing its hold. This unrest is greater in East Bengal because East Bengal has just become a colony of West Pakistan. There is widespread unrest in East Bengal against the domination of West Pakistan. The rulers of Pakistan want to divert the attention of the people from the internal problems by creating these riots.

Secondly, they want to pressurise us on the question of Kashmir. As the leaders of the Congress had capitulated before the demand of Pakistan after the Calcutta massacre the rulers of Pakistan today think that if a massacre of minorities is committed in East Pakistan the deities in New Delhi will come under pressure and surrender Kashmir. But Pakistan should not remain under such an illusion. The people of India would rather prefer death than giving in to force and atrocities. We can make an agreement with Pakistan on any issue on friendly terms. An Agreement could be made on a give-and-take basis, but if the rulers of Pakistan think that they could make us agree on the question of Kashmir by use of force and other barbaric methods they are living in a fool's paradise. But their intention is to pressurise us by squeezing out the minorities from East Bengal.

Pak Intention to Drive out non-Muslims from East Bengal

They also want to bring about "parity" between West Pakistan and East Bengal. If all non-Muslims are driven out of East Bengal the population of West Pakistan and East Pakistan would equalise. There would then be no obstacle in crushing East Pakistan. It would help in suppressing the protests of the people in East Pakistan. When this is the aim of the policy of Pakistan can peace be established in East Bengal by a meeting of Home Ministers or appeals of the two Presidents ? Such peace would only be the peace of the graveyard. Today the fire may be extinguished, but tomorrow or at any other time it might be rekindled. Those who did not migrate in 1950 under the belief that they might be able to live in East Pakistan were forced to migrate in 1964. I do not want to repeat the story of their woes in this House. It is easy for Shri Bhupesh Gupta to sermonise that we should maintain peace in our own country and that peace should be maintained at all cost. But if the neighbouring house catches fire, while it is necessary to make arrangements to secure your own house from the fire, it is necessary to put out the fire in the neighbour's house also. If the neighbour's house is on fire and we make arrangements to safeguard our house by closing our door we cannot stop the fire from reaching our house. Therefore, the problem is not confined to maintaining peace in our country. The problem is how to create conditions so that the minorities could live in East Pakistan with honour and dignity.

Madam, I said that it was not a Hindu-Muslim question. After all, why are Buddhists being expelled, why are Christians being expelled ? The exodus of Christians in such large numbers from East Pakistan had never taken place. We should not forget that certain aspects of the riots this time are very clear. The first aspect is that instead of killing people more attention was paid to driving them out. This second aspect is that Pakistan wants to get the area adjoining the border vacated by all non-Muslims. Why is this being done should be seriously taken note of by defence experts. Was Pakistan preparing for some military adventure on the border of East Pakistan ? Does Pakistan want to create disturbance on the Kashmir front as well as on the border of East Pakistan at the same time ? After all, what was the reason behind removing non-Muslims from the border areas ? All Christians and Buddhists who have been driven out were settled on the Indo-Pakistan border.

Third Aspect of the Riots

There is a third aspect of the riots too, which is that women have been molested on a mass scale. Those people who have migrated to India after leaving their sisters and daughters behind cannot put out the smouldering fire of anguish and anger in their hearts by applying the balm of secularism. Some of our workers had interviewed a Christian missionary. The report received from them is an eye-opener. On February 5, an American missionary, 'Father of Borodokuni' was stabbed and wounded because he wanted to save the fleeing Hindus and their womenfolk from the Ansars. Women were abducted by Pakistanis, but this American missionary had a 13-year-old girl with him. The Ansars tried to molest her as well. The missionary was crying and wailing, but those people did not listen to him. They wounded him and in front of him 27 persons gang-raped that 13-year-old girl. One Christian gentleman, Mohendra Master, who had brought a letter from the Sisters of Bori Mari Mission, narrated what he saw there. I want to read out the letter of Sister M. Emanuel written by her to Indian missionaries :

"Dear Fathers,

> Please take care of our driver Robert Ritchie, and all the family and all our Catholics. Mohendra Master will tell you about it. I do not know what will be for us next."

Italian and American missionaries were killed in the riots. What have we done to invite the attention of the world to these atrocities ? When questions were raised in this House as well as in the other House and the Ministers were asked to make a statement a statement was made about how Christians were being driven out of Pakistan. But what have we done to put the true version of the communal riots that have taken place in East Pakistan before the countries of the world, especially before the governments and the people of those countries who claim to be friends and allies of Pakistan ?

Take the Issue of East Pakistan to U.N.O.

Madam, I suggest that we should raise the issue of treatment of minorities in East Pakistan in the United Nations Organisation before Pakistan again raises the issue of Kashmir in the Security Council. Pakistan's diplomacy demands that it should draw the attention of the world towards Kashmir, India's diplomacy demands that we should draw the attention of the world towards East Pakistan. But the Government has failed to do so. It is still not too late. We should knock at the door of the World Court and should take our complaint to the U.N.O. against the violation of human rights and the Charter of Human Rights. Can we not draw the attention of the entire world to the inhuman atrocities being perpetrated in East Pakistan ? Apart from this it is also essential to collect the statements and the painful stories of those Buddhists and Christians who have been forced to migrate to India from East Pakistan. These should be translated into all languages of the world and distributed in the form of a booklet. It is also necessary to prepare a documentary film on the refugees coming from East Pakistan, a small documentary which could be exhibited by our embassies in foreign countries. This film need not be shown within the country, as the results of doing so could be disastrous and we want to avoid them. But we should show to the world and the friends of Pakistan how mistaken they are in putting India and Pakistan in the same category and show them what is happening to non-Muslims in East Pakistan. I am again and again using the word non-Muslims, but this does not mean that all Muslims in East Pakistan have abetted the rioters. There have been cases where Muslims have saved them from death and prevented the murderers from killing them. Muslims saved Hindus in the same manner as Hindus had saved Muslims in Calcutta. But how long would these lamps of goodwill and humaneness survive the poisonous guns of communalism and guide our future ? We should multiply such instances. If we could not take any step at the Governmental level to ensure justice to the minorities in East Pakistan the wave of unrest that is rising fast inside the country cannot be suppressed.

China-Pakistan Collusion

Madam, I have referred to the alliance between China and Pakistan. China and Pakistan have colluded to defeat us in the diplomatic field. It would not cause any surprise if the two collude at some time to take joint action against India. This possibility cannot be ruled out. I am surprised at the Western friends of Pakistan who have been giving arms to it in the hope that it would fight communism. Today the same Pakistan was making friendly gestures to Communist China. Chou En-Lai is playing a very dangerous game and he wants us to fight with Pakistan. China's game is that if differences of opinion between India and Pakistan increase the conflict, then it would not be possible for Western countries to provide us military aid in substantial quantity, as a result of which India would remain weak, and that is what China wants. Western countries are pressurising us to come to an agreement with Pakistan on the Kashmir issue, but why are they not prepared to use strong language against the Sino-Pakistan alliance ? Are we to take it that they have no words to use against what is happening there ? Since when do they believe in the adage silence is golden ? They speak even where they need not do so; but in this case their silence is not beyond suspicion.

American Ambassador and General Ayub Khan

Madam, I want to give an example. Late Dr. Raghuvir, when he was a member of the Congress Party—he joined Jan Sangh later—paid a visit to Pakistan. He met President Ayub and had also seen the American Ambassador in Pakistan. He has written a travelogue about his visit. If I make a revelation now I shall not be doing injustice to him. Dr. Raghuvir has written that before meeting General Ayub he had met the American Ambassador Whatever the American Ambassador said about India-Pak relations was repeated in full the next day by General Ayub, right up to the comma and full stop. I am not prepared to admit that Washington cannot put Pakistan on the right path if it so desires; but perhaps they are committed to back Pakistan on Kashmir. But they should understand the adverse consequences arising out of it. Only India can act as a bulwark against the expansion of communism in this part of the world on the basis of democracy. But the issue of Kashmir is such that if the Western countries extended their cooperation to Pakistan, as they are doing now, then in spite of existing cordial relations between us on the basis of democracy, in spite of the help given by them so promptly at the time of the Chinese aggression, the relations between India and Western countries would weaken. This would neither be good for them nor for us. But the responsibility to stop it lies with them, not with us. We want to have friendship with Pakistan, but it cannot be one-sided. So far friendship has been understood to be weakness. We cannot have friendship with any country by bowing down before it.

Plight of Hapless Refugees

I was sorry to see that no Minister went to meet the refugees belonging to the minority community who have migrated from East Pakistan and enquire about their welfare. Perhaps their misfortune is that they belong to the Hindu community. There is none in this country to look after the Hindus. This is a secular Government and the Ministers of this Government claim to be secular in outlook. Only Prof. Humayun Kabir and Shri Shahnawaz Khan went to see what happened in Calcutta. They visited the Muslim localities but did not visit the Hindu localities. Could any one of these Ministers not go to listen to the woes and painful stories of Hindu, Christian and Buddhist refugees ? Could not Shri Nanda go there ? Shri Nanda also believes in secularism. Is this the love that we have for the refugees ? Is this the sympathy we have for them Our workers who visited the refugee camps have seen their plight. There are no doctors there. An epidemic is likely to spread. There is no space to live, no clothes; cereals are given for two meals a day, but there are no utensils to cook Can nobody go there from here to apply balm to their wounds ? Shastriji went to Calcutta to perform the opening ceremony of the Rifle Club, but could not go to Garo hills. He could not visit the border area. Shri Mehar Chand Khanna who has been entrusted with the responsibility of looking after the minorities also did not go.

Madam, I too believe in the ideal of a secular state. But I am not prepared to forget that Hindus have no other place to live except India. Josh Malihabadi can migrate to Pakistan, Phizo can migrate to London, but I have no other place to live and die that way. You should not draw from this the conclusion—I want to repeat it again—that we want to establish a theocratic state in India. It is wrong to allege that we want to set up an administration based on religion. We have never discriminated against anybody on the basis of religion. We have never linked nationality with religion. The rights of citizenship should be uniform. But how can we keep mum when atrocities are being committed in East Pakistan ? The Hon'ble Minister should indicate what other steps the Government propose to take apart from raising the slogan of secularism and keeping the door open to receive them.

Organise World Public Opinion

One more point and I have done. We must make diplomatic moves. It is necessary to organise world public opinion in our favour. At the same time we have to take vigilant action on the East Pakistan border keeping in view the defence aspect of the situation. Could Shri Bhupesh Gupta deny the fact that slogans of 'Pakistan Zindabad' were raised during the riots in Calcutta ? Could anybody deny the fact that Pakistani flags were hoisted and slogans of 'Pakistan Zindabad' were raised at several places in Assam ? The Hon'ble Minister has admitted these facts in his statements. There can be no place for those in India who raise the slogan of 'Pakistan Zindabad' and hoist the flag of Pakistan. They should go to Pakistan. Those who have infiltrated into Assam, Tripura and West Bengal should be expelled. They could endanger our security at any time. They would serve as an instrument in the integration of Assam with East Pakistan. We cannot rely on the Government of Assam in this matter. The Government of Assam is weak and powerless. It was formed on political considerations. The Centre should itself take the responsibility to safeguard the border of Assam, Tripura and West Bengal. Shri Chettiar was just now reading out a statement in which it was said that Pakistanis infiltrate into Tripura, change the direction of the stream of the river and abduct people because there are no proper arrangements on our border. The governments of Tripura, Assam and West Bengal are unable to make suitable arrangements. The Centre must take over the security arrangements of this area. If we cannot send the Army let the Centre entrust the security arrangements of the border to the Central Reserve Police.

There are people settled along the border whose loyalty is doubtful, about whom it is suspected that they are in collusion with Pakistan. We will have to consider removing such people from the border areas.

Nobody can say what the intention of the leaders of Pakistan is. I fear they may try to create disturbances inside Kashmir or incite riots in East Pakistan again as soon as the debate in the Security Council is resumed. We should be ready to face that situation and the only way to get ready is for the Central

Government to make up its mind to do something in the matter. But the Central Government does not appear to be in a mood to take any decision. This situation must change. Our nation is passing through a critical time which is perhaps unprecedented. It is our foremost duty today to safeguard the borders and the freedom of our country against the joint conspiracy of China and Pakistan. We should understand the seriousness of this situation and prepare ourselves to give a strong and far-sighted leadership to the people.

Calcutta Riots

Madam, the days's debate would end. The refugees would continue to pour into India from East Pakistan. If we cannot do anything for them let us at least admit that we are not in a position to do anything for them. But I do not think the Government would not be in a position to do anything. If our objective is clear we can take proper steps. Today we must clarify our objective. It is not the work of a single party, although Shri Bhupesh Gupta has deemed it necessary to condemn certain reactionary and communal elements for the riots that took place in Calcutta. The resolution adopted by the Communist Party of West Bengal has come in handy for Pakistani propaganda. No effort has been made to throw light on the real position in Calcutta. To say that what happened in Calcutta was not a reaction to the happenings in East Pakistan, but was engineered by certain communal and reactionary elements would be too naive. What are those reactionary and communal elements ? If a riot takes place in Madhya Pradesh or in Uttar Pradesh and even if Jan Sangh is not remotely connected with it the Communist Party blames our party. But in West Bengal our party has only a negligible presence. Does Shri Bhupesh Gupta see our ghost even there ? I want to let him name those parties and elements who started riots in Calcutta. If he would name my party I would challenge him to prove the allegations made by him against the people of my party.

SHRI BHUPESH GUPTA : I said what I had to say. Those who indulged in rioting did so because of communal reaction. Otherwise they would not have done it. I have not ventured to give any name or party, because I am not concerned with that, I am concerned with the description. Madam, Mr. Vajpayee need not take upon himself.....

SHRI VAJPAYEE : Here is a copy of the resolution adopted by the West Bengal Communist Party which says specifically that the disturbances in Calcutta were not a reaction to what happened in East Pakistan but certain communal and reactionary elements fomented the trouble. Who are those elements ?

SHRI BHUPESH GUPTA : If the Communist Party wanted to mention your name it could have done it.

THE DEPUTY CHAIRMAN : Mr. Vajpayee, please continue.

SHRI VAJPAYEE : Madam, it has become clear from the discussion that has taken place just now that Communist leaders have no names. But if they have no names why did the Communist Party of West Bengal adopt a resolution which was printed by the *Dawn* on its front page and which put us in an embarrassing position in the world ? Perhaps neither the Communist Party nor the Congress Party have a detached outlook, free from internal politics of the country, on the question of minorities of East Bengal. This is not a question of politics. This is a question concerning the defence of India and safeguarding the honour and dignity of minorities. We cannot make the mistake of considering this question on partisan lines and with a narrow outlook. We should concentrate our attention on the clouds of danger that are hovering over us. We should jointly consider how to ward off the danger successfully. The Government should create confidence among the people that it really wants to do something in the matter.

Strict Reciprocity with Pakistan is needed

Madam, I will finish in one minute. So far as diplomacy is concerned we should adopt a policy of strict reciprocity towards Pakistan. There is no need to have any long debate on this matter. If they have closed our Consulate in Rajshahi we can close their Consulate in Shillong. If they do not allow our Deputy High Commissioner to go out in Dhaka we cannot allow their Deputy High Commissioner to go out in Calcutta. But during the Calcutta riots the Pakistani Deputy High Commissioner had visited the Lal Bazar Police Station. What was the need for a Pakistani Deputy High Commissioner to visit a Police Station in Calcutta ? He took a round of *bastis* (settlements). Several other allegations have been made against him. It is not a matter on which we may create a crisis, but we should be ready to adopt a tit-for-tat policy against Pakistan. However, our behaviour is different. So much rioting took place in East Pakistan yet the Indian High Commissioner at Karachi did not visit Dhaka. If he did visit Dhaka, on what date ? Is he not responsible for looking after East Pakistan ? Why did he stay put in Karachi ? Should he not have gone to Dhaka ? Similarly, when Shri Chagla had gone to the United Nations Organisation to speak on the Kashmir issue, neither our Ambassador there nor his number two was present in the Embassy. The news about the riots in East Pakistan was not published at all in the newspapers of U.S.A. Such news should be published so that the American people could know about the situation in East Pakistan. What did our Embassy do in this connection ? If the newspapers there are not ready to publish such news we must get it published on advertisement rates. We can get time on television there on payment. What did we do to educate the American public opinion about it ? The Home Ministry could not do anything for the minorities of East Bengal. And the Ministry of External Affairs cannot even give publicity to their plight. This Government lacks leadership, it lacks direction, that is the misfortune of the country. But we have to change this misfortune and safeguard the fortune of India. Today this work appears difficult, but whatever Government is there, we can only make an appeal to it. I hope and trust that the reply to be given to this debate by the Home Minister would be clearer than his earlier replies. Thank you.

The Kutch Fiasco : Who is Responsible ?

Mr. Chairman, Sir, we congratulate the Jawans and officers of our army who are battering the enemy in the battlefield of Kutch endangering their own lives. We salute the pilot who has brought the photographs of the American battle tank. We are grateful to the Army Officer who, with the help of a single machine gun, defeated an entire platoon of the Pakistani Army and was successful in creating a situation in which four Pakistani Officers fell into our hands and brought to Delhi. Those officers were lying on the ground with their faces downwards. They were not dead, but were feigning as dead, and on close inspection were found alive. Our Army and the officers of our Armed Forces deserve compliments of this House and the country.

We congratulate our Army for showing exceptional bravery in the battlefield where there are no roads, not enough water to drink, and where they are short in number as well as in armament as compared to the enemy. We have full faith in our Armed Forces and its officers. One wished one could say the same thing with confidence in respect of our political leaders.

People ask, why were roads not constructed in Kutch ? Why were cantonments not set up ? Pakistan had given an indication of its unholy intentions by intruding into the Chharbet area in 1956-57. Why did the Government then ignore that border ? Why were we caught unaware ? Was the lesson learnt by us in 1962 not sufficient to open our eyes ? Have we to learn the same lesson *de novo* ? Do we still have to realise that weakness is a curse and an invitation to aggression ? In this cruel world if we have to safeguard our independence and integrity it can be done only through power and armed might and not through imaginary principles. We were defeated on the northern border. We blamed the height of the Himalayas. Shall we blame the depth of the sea today ? At that time snow became an obstacle in our way. Shall we blame the desert and the marshy land this time ? One Mr. Kaul was blamed then, who will be blamed now ? Then, Mr. Krishna Menon had to resign, who will resign today ?

SHRI DAHYABHAI V. PATEL : Chavan will resign.

SHRI VAJPAYEE : Mr. Chairman, Sir, according to the Government of Pakistan, they have been intruding into the borders of Kutch since January. Pakistan at first intruded into Kutch in January, but when were Parliament and the country informed about it ? Does the concealment of facts about a foreign invasion from Parliament and the country not amount to shirking of responsibility ? When I and my other friends asked in the Rajya Sabha and the Gujarat Assembly whether Pakistanis had occupied 13,000 acres of land

---

Rajya Sabha on May 3, 1965 during discussion on the motion regarding situation on Kutch Border

the Government replied in the affirmative. But even then full information was not placed before the House. The Home Minister said there was no land in occupation of Pakistan. Pakistan had constructed only standing posts. Nandaji's statement is there as evidence. He will have to answer. In the map distributed three days ago the entire 20 sq. miles of area has been shown under occupation of Pakistan and three posts have been shown instead of two. Why were we not taken into confidence ? Today appeals are being made for unity. We will support these appeals for unity because the country is greater than the Congress Party, the country is greater than this kind of leadership. But unity cannot be achieved by keeping us in the dark. Even today there is no definite and permanent arrangement for consultation with opposite parties. Could the Prime Minister not set up a committee consisting of members of the Congress Party and opposition parties, whose sittings could be held daily in the evening and who may be kept informed about the daily developments on the border ? What is the difficulty in this ? Or, does he think that opposition parties do not deserve it ? I would like to tell him that there is still time to do so. Please do not hesitate to put before the people, the House and the Opposition parties the entire situation openly in all its seriousness.

American Weapons in Pakistani Hands

Mr. Chairman, Sir, Pakistan is using American weapons against us. It is a matter of serious concern to us. When the Pak-U.S. Millitary Pact materialised we had warned America that Pakistan was asking for arms in the name of fighting against Communism but those arms would be used against peace-loving India. America did not pay any heed to our warning, but our apprehensions proved true. The arms supplied by America are today piercing the chests of Indian Jawans. Is that the way to save democracy and stop expansion of communism in South-East Asia ? And when the Government of India complained that Pakistan was using American arms against India President Johnson did not think it proper to warn both the countries that the supply of military aid would be stopped to either using American arms in this war. The United States of America could have issued such a warning, if it so desired and that would have had a salutary impact. America could cancel the invitation to our Prime Minister to visit America in a crude and uncivilised manner, but could not issue even a warning to Pakistan not to use arms supplied by it. After issuing the warning the matter about who was using the arms and in what quantity would have been investigated. The manner in which the invitation to our Prime Minister was cancelled has hurt friendly Indo-American ties. But the way in which Pakistan was using American arms against us and the failure of U.S. not to take prompt action against their use could cause so much damage to Indo-U.S. relations that it would be difficult to repair it. American leaders should decide about who would act like a rock against the expansion of communism in South-East Asia. We want to become their friends, we cannot become their satellite. But a true friend who would even criticise in a polite language and would also keep in mind the wider interests of a friend is better than a camp-follower who would stab in the back.

Sir, President Ayub has threatened us. Ater committing aggression he is threatening a full-scale war and speaking of a new attack. The Prime Minister has replied to him firmly in his statement, but we should understand the intention of Pakistan. It can create a crisis at some other place on the border in order to divert our attention. We should be prepared for both the eventualities. If Pakistan creates any problem on a new front we should be able to thwart it successfully. To avenge with interest the open attack made by Pakistan on Kutch we should also find some spot of our choice. The border of India and Pakistan is one and it cannot be divided into pieces. The border is indivisible like peace and freedom. If they intruded into Kutch taking advantage of our weakness there we should avenge the attack by defeating them at a place where they are weak.

I welcome the announcement of the Prime Minister that if Pakistan did not come to its senses our Army would be given liberty to decide its own strategy. But I would like to know one thing. They intruded into Kutch, then was it not possible for our Army to attack from behind from the Khakkhar side in Kutch ? Was any such suggestion put up before the Cabinet by the Army ? Has the Cabinet really given liberty to the Army or is it just for Parliament's consumption ? Has our Army full liberty to decide its own strategy ?

Freedom Demands Sacrifice

Mr. Chairman, Sir, we are passing through a critical situation. But this critical situation is continuing since 1962. Freedom demands sacrifice. What is the reason that this Government and the Parliament could not sustain the national awakening that arose among the people after the Chinese attack ? China and Pakistan are our natural enemies—we do not want to measure them with the same yardstick. But they are forcing us to do so. If per chance both of them jointly attack us we should keep ourselves ready to succesfully ward off the danger. For this purpose we need an army of at least 20 lakh soldiers. The decision taken by the Defence Ministry after the Chinese attack to reduce the strength of the Army—and the same has been approved by the Cabinet—needs to be reviewed. We need at least 20 lakh soldiers, equipped with modern weapons. The arms should be obtained from wherever available. In such circumstances the Government should not hesitate in any manner to take full help from countries, professing any ideology, who come forward to extend a helping hand. A strict watch should be kept over fifth-columnists within the country. In today's papers reports have been published to the effect that fifth-columnists have been arrested in Silchar, Punjab and Kutch. If the Government is alert there is no need to say anything more. It is the duty of the people to maintain peace in the country. Whatever the incitement be we cannot play into the hands of the agents of the enemy. Pakistani elements can incite communal riots in collusion with the supporters of Peking. We should not get excited, nor should we be caught napping. We have to protect our freedom while safeguarding the integrity of the country.

Expand the National Defence Council

I would like to request the Prime Minister to expand the National Defence Council. It is not sufficient to include only Atulya Babu in it. He cannot inspire among the people the courage to fight and to face the crisis. However close he might be to the capitalists his relations with the public are nil. Why should not Acharya Ranga, Shri Surendra Nath Dwivedi and Shri Deendayal Upadhyaya be included in the National Defence Council. If the National Defence Council is to be expanded it should be done in the right manner.

Sir, I would make one more point and finish. The war has not begun yet but talks about cease-fire have started. We have not started fighting so far. We have not made a strike yet. Our Jawans have not yet got the opportunity to show their mettle. How can there be a cease-fire ? And if the British Prime Minister wants a cease-fire please tell him to advise Pakistan to leave the Kutch border and the Kutch region. Then the cease-fire would become effective automatically. We will not fire at Pakistan in its territory. But if we accept a cease-fire in our own land and cover up this act by saying, let us first accept the cease-fire and then they will go away, I have to say : Please reverse the process—let them go first, then there would be no need for a cease-fire. The cease-fire could not be effective in today's position. Let us not ignore what impact such a cease-fire would have on the morale of the army as well as the country. Although I am in broad agreement with the attitude adopted by the Prime Minister in this regard, and I have also given my amendment to this effect, I hope the Government will have no objection to accepting my amendment.

Mr. Chairman, I have referred to the duties of the Government. Members of Parliament too have some duty cast upon them and I would particularly like to address the Opposition parties. The country is at war and we want to win this war. Is bringing an adjournment motion the way to win the war if one post falls ? And to walk out if you do not get an opportunity to speak and demand resignation of the Prime Minister ? I am not a great admirer of the Prime Minister. I am sitting in the opposition. But if the resignation by the Prime Minister could solve the problem there would be no need to ask for his resignation—the Prime Minister himself would not hesitate to tender his resignation. But the Prime Minister's resignation is not a panacea—that he would resign in Delhi and the Pakistani troops that have intruded into Kutch would withdraw automatically. This is neither an occasion for political publicity nor for acquiring cheap popularity. The country is on severe test and so are the opposition parties. We have to maintain the morale of the nation.

We could understand retreat of our Army in front of China, but retreat in the face of Pakistan is inconceivable. Sir, we have never been defeated in the battlefield, but always in the Durbar of Delhi. We have never been defeated in war, but always in peace. We have never been defeated in conflict, but always in treaty. I am glad that Shri Yashwant Rao Chavan has come. I was recently on a tour of Maharashtra and the people of Maharashtra were asking : What was Defence Minister Chavan doing ? What is Sahyadri which had gone to defend the Himalayas doing ? Where is he whom you described as the incarnation of Chhatrapati Shivaji doing ? I told them, Chavan could not do anything single-handed in Delhi. In Delhi, one cannot hear the sound of the running of real horses, because paper horses run there. But there are hopes and aspirations. People are seething with anger to avenge the defeat and dishonour. And Yashwant Rao Chavan had said that the Army was seething to avenge the defeat at the hands of Pakistan. There should be no hesitation in avenging the defeat we had suffered at the hands of Pakistan. The entire country is with the Government. The need of the hour is for the leadership to rise to the occasion. We have lost ground, but not the battle. And we will not give up the battle until it is converted into a victory. The entire country is resolved to win. What is required is leadership. Please march forward and we will follow you. If you waver, we will never forgive you. Thank you.

Entire Kutch Belongs to India : Why Arbitration ?

Mr. Chairman, Sir, I have some objections. I have mainly three objections to the consideration by the House of the motion moved by the Prime Minister.

My submission is that a motion for consideration has been moved in the House regarding the statement which contains the agreement about Kutch. This agreement is against our Constitution. As per Clause (2) of article 3 and Schedule I of the Constitution the borders of India are definite and settled. According to these borders the entire Rann of Kutch is a part of India. The Government of India has no right to secede any part of India. The Government has agreed to refer the claim of Pakistan over 3500 sq. miles of area of Rann of Kutch to foreign arbitration. This agreement has been made behind the back of Parliament. This violates the articles of the Constitution. I think this agreement cannot be debated in the House.

At the same time reference has been made in it to the agreements made with Pakistan in 1959 and 1960. I will not say here that Pakistan has broken those agreements by launching an attack on Kutch, because that would not constitute a point of order. But I would certainly like to say that the Government has entered into an agreement about Kutch which goes far beyond the agreements made earlier in 1959-60 with Pakistan.

My objection is that the executive has overstepped its rights. The Government had stated that under the 1959-60 agreement only the question of demarcation of border was to be settled and it was not a question of determination of the border. This is what the Prime Minister had said in this House as well as in Lok Sabha :

> "So far as India was concerned the difference involved is the boundary alone. We do not accept that there is any kind of territorial dispute, but in regared to boundary the matter can be discussed."

But the agreement entered into with Pakistan in case of Kutch does not relate merely to the question of demarcation of the border. In this case the border has to be determined and in determining the border the judge, who would be a foreigner, may accept the preposterous claim of Pakistan and could give 3,500 sq. miles area belonging to India to Pakistan.

The 1959-60 agreement also provided how the tribunal would be constituted. A judge proposed by India was also to be included in the tribunal. I do not want to go into details in this matter.

Rajya Sabha on August 19, 1965 during discussion on the motion regarding the agreement on Pak-occupied land in Kutch

Mr. Chairman, Sir, I am raising separate points of order. I am saying that according to the 1959-60 agreement one judge should be proposed by us. The Government has decided that the judge would not be proposed by us, he will be a foreigner. This would be going outside the 1959-60 agreement. The Executive has taken a decision which it was not empowered to do.

My third objection is most serious. It is that our Constitution is a federal constitution. It is not a unitary constitution. It is true that Parliament is empowered to increase or decrease the area of the States and we can also change their borders, if we so desire. But according to article 3 of the Constitution whenever the border of a State was to be changed the Centre would have to write to the State Legislature and the Administration concerned to give an opportunity to them for considering the matter.

Yesterday the Prime Minister had stated in the Lok Sabha that the Government of Gujarat was not consulted before entering into an agreement about Kutch. This is a very serious matter. The Lok Sabha had approved of that agreement. If this is the Council of States, *i.e.*, Rajya Sabha, we are representatives of the States, we have been elected by the States, we have to safeguard the rights of the States here. Can the Central Government enter into such agreements without consulting the State governments and the legislatures concerned as would change the borders of the States or would give away a part of the State to foreigners ? My submission is that the Central Government is not empowered to execute this agreement. If this agreement will be executed without consulting the State Government concerned it would be a blow to the foundation of the federal system. Today there is a Congress Government in Gujarat. It fears the High Command and it cares for the prestige of the Party. Suppose there had been an opposition Party Government in Gujarat, what would have happened then ? It would have risen in revolt against the Centre and would not the country have broken into pieces then ? I would like this House to safeguard the rights of the States and keep the sanctity of the Constitution intact. We cannot bring a no-confidence motion against the Government here, but we can tell the Government that the agreement entered into by it violates the rights of the States and we are not prepared to consider this agreement in this House.

Mr. Chairman, Sir, I would request you to please give your ruling in this regard. The Rajya Sabha should protect its rights. We are looking to you in regard to this issue that has arisen before us today. You are the custodian of this House and, therefore, you must protect our rights. You can tell the Prime Minister that this agreement violates the rights of the Rajya Sabha and that it should not be debated. The debate should be adjourned until the opinion of the Law Ministry or the legal experts is taken on this question of law that has been raised.

SHRI LAL BAHADUR SHASTRI, Prime Minister : I would like to state in regard to the constitutional point raised by Shri Vajpayee that there is nothing in the agreement entered into by us which goes against the Constitution, because the Government has a right to enter into such agreements.

Secondly, I would like to say that we have not seceded any part of our country, nor do we propose to do so now. It is not true that we have handed over any part of the country.

SHRI GOWDE MURAHARI : But the Tribunal would give its judgement.

SHRI LAL BAHADUR SHASTRI : The Tribunal can also give the judgement that there should be no change in the present boundary.

SHRI BHUPESH GUPTA : Suppose the Tribunal decides otherwise ?

SHRI LAL BAHADUR SHASTRI : If any such situation arises then we will have to amend the Constitution for which we will come to the House. But I think we will not have to amend the Constitution in this case. If the situation which you are contemplating arises, then the law to separate Gujarat from Bombay State would have to be amended. Therefore there is no substance in the question raised by Shri Vajpayee and other colleagues.

SHRI VAJPAYEE : Madam, a Resolution was adopted by this House unanimously on May 3. I would like to read out the last part of that Resolution :

> "With hope and faith this House affirms the firm resolve of the Indian people to drive out the aggressor from the sacred soil of India."

Today when we are discussing the Kutch agreement the first litmus test of that agreement is whether the agreement is in tune with our resolve expressed in the Resolution adopted on May 3 ? Has Pakistan completely vacated the Rann of Kutch ? Is there no Pakistani presence in the Rann of Kutch now ? Have we fully established our authority over Rann of Kutch ? Only this morning the Prime Minister stated that the entire Rann of Kutch has been vacated. Does the Rann of Kutch not include the 20-mile stretch of land in which Pakistan has been given a right to patrol ? Does it not constitute a part of Rann of Kutch ? Is it not sacred ? The Prime Minister had said :

> "There is no question of surrendering any part of our land, not an inch of it."

The same language was used by the Home Minister Shri Gulzari Lal Nanda. On May 14, when the sitting of the House was going to be adjourned he said :

> "We will not succumb to pressure. There is no question of succumbing to any force, to any aggression and there can be no question of our surrendering an inch of our sacred soil to anyone else."

Are 20 miles less than an inch ?

Why Withdraw from our Own Land ?

Nobody can say that our resolve to liberate the last inch of our land from the clutches of the aggressor has been fulfilled. The Prime Minister says Pakistani forces have been withdrawn from the Rann of Kutch. Our troops too have withdrawn. Pakistani forces have been withdrawn because they were the aggressor forces, that had intruded into the Rann of Kutch. But why did our troops withdraw from the area ? If Rann of Kutch belongs to us, if it is a part of India, why have our troops withdrawn from there ?

It is said that our troops were not there on January 1, 1965. How this date came up I shall discuss later. It is a fact that our troops were not there on January 1, 1965, but I would like to ask, had we no right to keep our troops there ? Has this right come to us today ? Can we send our troops to Rann of Kutch today, if we so desire ? There are several tests to determine whether a piece of land forms part of a country or not, one of them being whether a country can station its army there or not. This is a sign of its sovereignty. The Rann of Kutch belongs to us, but we cannot station our army there. We have abdicated our right. After Pakistan's aggression we will not station our army there. Does this condition of the agreement not constitute a violation of our sovereignty ? Is it not against the pledge taken by us on May 3 ? At that time we did not station our army there because we did not think it necessary to do so. That decision was out of our own free will. It was a decision taken by a free country, it was not taken under pressure of anybody, it was not taken by succumbing to somebody's pressure. But today's decision is not our own. Pakistan committed aggression against Kutch. Instead of punishing it for the aggression we are covering the sin committed by it, abdicating our sovereign right, and the Prime Minister wants us to close our eyes to that situation!

Why Pakistani Police in Kutch ?

The Prime Minister has stated that our Police is there in the Rann of Kutch. But Pakistani Police is also there. The only difference is that Pakistani Police occupies a small portion of the land and our Police occupies a larger chunk of land there. Why are they in occupation of our land ? How did we give them the right to patrol that area ? Then, we cannot keep as much Police force in the Rann of Kutch as we may like to. This derogatory agreement provides that we can keep as many Policemen in Chharbet as were present on January 1, 1965, not more. We cannot set up a post in Kanjarkot, although we can send our men for patrolling. A post cannot be set up because there was no post earlier. It was our own decision not to have a post there, Pakistan was not a party to it. Now we cannot set up a post anywhere except Chharbet. We cannot keep as many policemen in Chharbet as we would like to. We cannot set up a post in Bearbet. Our brave soldiers had wrested the Sardar and the Wigkot posts, but now we cannot set up posts there! The Prime Minister unfurled the national flag on Red Fort on 15th August. I want to ask whether the tricolour was unfurled in Kanjarkot ? There should have been some brave son of Mother India to unfurl the National Flag at Kanjarkot. The Prime Minister says we have recaptured Kanjarkot. In what sense has it been recaptured ? We cannot set up a post there, we cannot hoist the tricolour there and we have also given the right of patrolling Kanjarkot to Pakistan.

What is the position today ? Pakistani forces are stationed at the international border, they have not retreated, they are ready for war and our troops have vacated the Rann of Kutch and are stationed away from the border. If the situation worsens and aggression is committed again, will we not have to suffer the same punishment that we had to undergo at the time of the previous attack on Kutch due to not stationing our troops there ?

Madam, this agreement is objectionable on another ground too. The Prime Minister says that he had made a commitment that he would not have talks with Pakistan until the position that existed on 1 January, 1965 is restored, and the position of January 1, 1965 was restored. How did the date of 1 January, 1965 come into the picture is still a mystery to me. It was because the Government has said that Pakistan intruded into Rann of Kutch for the first time on January 25. I regard this as the only explanation for restoring the position of 1st January, 1965. That was the date on which aggression was initially committed. Before 1 January, 1965, there was no aggression from Pakistan on Kutch, it was not patrolling the area, it had not intruded there. It was stated by the Government in the House that the intrusion began on January 25, and hence we did not object to the date of 1 January, 1965. We wonder why the Prime Minister is repeating the date of 1 January, 1965 again and again. But when a statement was made by the Government that Pakistanis made the intrusion for the first time on January 25 we did not object to it and we thought the *status quo ante* as existed before the aggression would be restored. But this did not happen.

Today we cannot station our army there. This is being supported by invoking the date of 1 January, 1965. The right of Pakistan to patrol the area is being advocated on the plea of 1 January, 1965 and it is being said that the Prime Minister has fulfilled his commitment. The Prime Minister has not fulfilled his commitment. The date of 1 January, 1965 was referred to in the context of the intrusion by Pakistan beginning on 25th January. If the *status quo ante* as on 1 January, 1965 was restored Pakistani presence would not remain in Kutch in any form. But I would like to know whether the Government of Gujarat was consulted before announcing the date of 1 January, 1965 ? Before signing this agreement was the Government of Gujarat asked to contradict all those proofs which Pakistan had produced about patrolling the area before January 1, 1965 ? The Prime Minister had stated yesterday in Lok Sabha that our officers did have a talk, but we did not consult the Gujarat Government at the time of signing the agreement. I want to know whether the Prime Minister had placed the proofs submitted by the Gujarat Government before them while giving his preliminary consent to the agreement in London and when had the Government of Pakistan submitted the proofs to the Government of Great Britain regarding its claim over Kutch ?

Fake Register, Fake Records

I have some information with me which I want to place before the House and which would make it clear that Pakistan's right to patrol the area in Kutch, for which an agreement has already been signed is not substantiated by the records produced by Pakistan. I do not know which records were produced by Pakistan. It is said that they had shown some registers of patrolling. Could these registers not be fake ? Those people who are in business know how registers are prepared and how they are changed. And if their register was examined was our register also examined ? What were the dates on which the Border Reserve Police of Gujarat had been patrolling that area ? These dates are no more a secret now, these have been revealed. I will not recount all the dates. I will point out only one date. On February 5, at the request of India, a meeting of an Inspector of Pakistani Rangers and an Officer Commandant of our garrison at Chharbet was held in which the Pak Officer admitted that the wheel marks there were fresh marks and he also admitted that some camels had passed before that. But there were no wheel marks on the road of Ding Surai or on the roadside. On January 7, our patrol went there and found no road there. Our Assistant Commandant of the garrison had visited that place, he did not report the existence of any road there. A Head Constable had gone there for patrolling later, he also did not see the marks. That is why our Government had stated that there was no patrolling by Pakistan in that area before January 25. Pakistan had not intruded into that area. I want to know why the Prime Minister did not stick to this proof. Why did he not say that whatever patrolling was there had begun on the 25th January or after, not before January 1 ?

Even if it is admitted that Pakistan was patrolling that area before January 1, it was done surreptitiously. That patrolling constituted an act of aggression, it was against the 1960 agreement, because in the ground rules framed under that agreement it is stated that :

> "Each side will inform the other about actual patrol by it or any change thereto if it falls within fifty yards of the boundary."

Pakistan should have informed us even if the patrolling was done with 50 yards of the border. This patrolling was done after crossing our border. They committed violation of the ground rules which amounted to an act of aggression on our land. This continued surreptitiously and the Government did not know about it or if it knew, it did not tell us. On both these counts there was inaction on the part of the Government. If Pakistan was patrolling in the Rann of Kutch area this Government is not fit to hold office. It is not capable of guarding the borders. This Government is not fit to take an oath saying we will protect every inch of our land. If this Government has any self-respect it must resign. Or let Shastriji say that he did not know about it. This would also amount to self-condemnation. And even if he did not know he could have stuck to that point in London . A trespass cannot be legalised; an intrusion cannot be accepted as a right. They had intruded into the Rann of Kutch by keeping us in the dark. We cannot accept it as a right in broad daylight. If Pakistan did not vacate the Rann of Kutch we should have been ready to face the consequences. But Shastriji yielded. I doubt if this agreement was signed in Delhi or London. Has it been signed in the Cabinet room or in a room of the Buckingham Palace ? How much pressure was exerted by Britain regarding this agreement ? Why did the Prime Minister not remember the commitment made on May 3 ? Why did he not remember the assurances given to the country ? If you want to maintain the morale of the country it cannot be done by going back on the commitment.

The Agreements of 1959-60

Madam, the Prime Minister has repeatedly said in this House that we would not recognise any territorial dispute in the Rann of Kutch. It is the Opposition which reminded him about the 1959-60 Agreement and not Sardar Swaran Singh who is responsible for signing this insulting agreement. He should tell this House how the agreement of 1959-60, which is now being quoted in order to cover up the violation by Pakistan in Kutch was entered into ? It is written nowhere in the agreement that Pakistan had laid its claim to over 3,500 sq. miles, otherwise we would have objected to that. But Sardar Swaran Singh knew what was the claim of Pakistan. Pakistan has expressed its claim by other means too. Two years ago, when President Ayub visited America, the Pakistani Embassy had distributed a map showing not half of Rann of Kutch but the entire Rann of Kutch as part of Pakistan. This map was brought to New Delhi by the proprietor of *Aaj* published from Varanasi. The present Prime Minister was a not a Minister at that time, he had resigned under the Kamraj Plan. He saw that map and sent it to the Ministry of External Affairs. But nobody knows what the Ministry of External Affairs did about it. The Prime Minister did not recall the 1959-60 agreement. When we reminded him about it he said that we did not recognise it as a territorial dispute in that agreement, that our border is already determined, it is determined on the map, the only thing to be determined is where it should be demarcated on land as depicted on the map. Thus only the demarcation was to be done, not determination of the border. Shastriji has repeatedly said that we would not recognise any territorial dispute. Then why did he not stick to it ?

It is said that the 1959-60 agreement came as a hurdle in our way. Did Pakistan follow the 1959-60 agreement ? I have given an example of how it broke the ground rules. There was a condition in the agreement that no one from India and Pakistan would use force, no one would disturb the *status quo*. But Pakistan committed aggression openly in the Rann of Kutch. Our representative Shri Chakravartty wrote a letter to the United Nations Organisation describing it as open aggression. Pakistan's claim is preposterous and it is using force to get its preposterous claim recognised. There was no territorial dispute about Kutch. Why did we not disregard the 1959-60 agreement ? Are the agreements to be observed unilaterally ? If the other party does not observe the terms of the agreement and goes on violating them could we continue to bind ourselves with it ? The entire country would have supported the Prime Minister; all the Opposition parties would have approved the policy of the Government if it had said that since Pakistan had broken those agreements by attacking the Rann of Kutch there was no reason for us to be bound by those agreements. But this was not done.

I want to repeat what I said this morning. The Prime Minister has gone even beyond the 1959-60 agreement. The issue is being referred to the Tribunal. But this Tribunal was not the same as was envisaged under the agreement between Sardar Swaran Singh and the Sheikh. All the three judges would be foreigners, their verdict would apply to us, we would be bound by that verdict and on no ground could it be challenged. Nowhere in the world are such Tribunals formed. What would happen if a member of the Tribunal violates his terms of reference or transgresses his authority or the entire Tribunal violates the terms of reference ? What would happen if a member is misled, or is corrupted ? Suppose the Tribunal refuses to look at the evidence—there is a condition in the agreement that it would look into the evidence—could the Tribunal not give its verdict without going through the evidence ? I would like to state my fears. These proofs, these registers submitted by you would remain uncared for. Pakistan would say this is not land, this is a 'sea-way', this is a passage to sea and in the sea the border is demarcated midway. Let the map of India remain as it is. It may argue, India had its sovereign right over the Rann of Kutch, but you have to demarcate the border and this is a sea-way and the border is demarcated in the middle of the sea-way.

Even if perchance, the Tribunal accepts the contention of Pakistan and refuses to take into account our evidence we cannot reject its verdict, because we have committed ourselves, we have bound ourselves. The Tribunal will continue until the decisions of the agreement are implemented and would monitor the implementation of its verdict.

Reject the Derogatory Agreement

Did the Prime Minister have the right to enter into any such agreement ? It is open defiance of the Constitution, an affront to democracy and breach of privilege of Parliament to refer the territorial integrity and sovereignty of India for foreign arbitration behind the back of Parliament and without taking the country into confidence. The Prime Minister had no right to enter into such agreements. Is this House, the Parliament, taken as a stamping machine on erroneous agreements made by the government ? Today we are told that we may reject the agreement if we do not like it. Does the Prime Minister think as he has the majority with him—Congress Party members are present here in a large number—he can enter into any kind of agreement, even by going back on his words, and nobody would speak against him ? It is true that nobody spoke against him in the Lok Sabha. That is why I am apprehensive about the future of democracy. The next election is approaching. Tickets are to be distributed. A big Congress leader said in Bangalore that Congressmen are suppressing the voice of their conscience today, they cannot open their mouths before the High Command, because the High Command would not give them tickets for the next election. I would not make such an allegation. But one should not commit the mistake of calling this kind of agreement an honourable agreement. It is being imposed on us by defying the Constitution, by ignoring the Parliament and by openly violating one's own commitments. You can say mistakes were committed, the Prime Minister was taken in by the pomp and pageantry of London, he got entangled in British diplomacy and perhaps could not properly follow the clauses of the agreement.

Madam, you would be surprised to know that the opinion of our legal experts was not sought on this agreement. When this agreement was finalised our Law Minister was not present in the Cabinet meeting. Our Attorney-General was in Moscow. This is a legal agreement and every clause of it should have been studied thoroughly. But a political decision was taken and today the House is being asked to approve it. How can we approve it ?

Madam, this agreement has been supported on the ground that as a result of it friendship would be established between India and Pakistan, that it will promote goodwill and open a new chapter of mutual relations. Which chapter has been opened you can see in Kashmir. When this agreement was being written, when this agreement was being signed in New Delhi, Pakistan was chalking out a plan to invade Kashmir and was despatching its armed troops to Kashmir. Is this the proof of Pakistan's honesty ? The ink on the agreement had hardly dried up and the seal of approval by Parliament was not even put on it when Pakistan invaded Kashmir. The Prime Minister asks, what is the relationship between Kutch and Kashmir ? So far as the question of negotiations with Pakistan is concerned I am prepared to admit that we will not have any negotiations about Kashmir, but Kutch and Kashmir both are parts of the same country. One and the same country has committed aggression against Kutch and Kashmir and the 45 crore people who have to be mobilised, awakened and put into action to face the aggression are also the same. A cease-fire in Kutch and opening a war-front in Kashmir! Courtship with Pakistan on Kutch and shower of bullets in the Kashmir Valley! War and peace cannot go together. The talk of love and the din of weapons cannot be heard together. It is proper that the meeting of the Foreign Ministers has been postponed but can we bind ourselves with such a derogatory agreement ?

Suppose a majority of members were in favour of this agreement. The reasons could be personal, partisan and even ideological. But what is our duty in view of the new situation created in Kashmir ? Should we stick to this agreement ? Whatever happens in Delhi affects the people of Kashmir.

We talk with the Foreign Minister of Pakistan in Delhi and listen to Pakistan, but Pakistanis try to put Kashmir on fire and make our Jawans targets of their bullets. Such things cannot be allowed to go on. This is not the way to prepare the country for war. This is not the way even to establish unity in the country. The Government will have to take a decision, and I want to appeal to the Members of Parliament that they should look at this agreement in the light of the new situation created in Kashmir. We cannot bind ourselves with this agreement unilaterally. It is argued that this is an international agreement. I want to ask whether the agreement with the 'Voice of America' was not an international agreement and whether we did not dissociate ourselves with that agreement ? Professor Mukut Behari Lal has just now given an example of an agreement between Germany and the Soviet Union. When Germany invaded Soviet Russia the Russians terminated the agreement. No agreement could be binding only on one party. One cannot clap with one hand. As two parties are required to fight, so also two parties are required to establish peace. If the other party is bent upon committing aggression war becomes unavoidable.

The way we gave ourselves up, surrendered in Kutch, was not conducive to safeguarding peace. What happened in Kutch did not raise the morale of our Jawans, did not enhance the prestige of our country. It hurt the dignity and honour of the nation. But the mistake committed can be rectified. The agreement about Kutch could be put into cold storage for ever and Pakistan could be told that no agreement would be made until it gave proof of good faith. If an agreement is made only to be broken it becomes meaningless. We doubt the intentions of Pakistan. The Prime Minister has also said that it appears that Pakistan does not want peace. Why should then we bind ourselves with the agreement on Kutch ?

Article 51 of the Constitution vis-a-vis the Agreement

The Prime Minister says article 51 of our Constitution provides that we will try to resolve international problems through arbitration. We are doing the same in Kutch. But we will not resort to it in Kashmir, because Kashmir problem is different. I admit that the issue in Kashmir is different, but why do you recognise an agreement which could be used against us in Kashmir ? There are certain people abroad who say that the same procedure should be adopted for Kashmir issue. In fact there are some people inside our own country who say the same thing. But I would like to tell them that we cannot enter into such agreements anywhere whether it is Kutch or Kashmir.

Have we not maintained our integrity and sovereignty after rejecting international opinion on Kashmir ? I am amazed to see that newspaper editorials and world opinion are quoted to assert that the agreement on Kutch was welcomed by all. It is said that this agreement was accepted by America, Britain and even by the Soviet Union.

DEPUTY CHAIRPERSON : You have taken more than half an hour.

SHRI VAJPAYEE : Madam, I am concluding my speech. This is a subject on which I have intense feelings and I should be given full opportunity to express my views.

There are certain countries in the world which would like to see that peace is established at the cost of others. Nobody will ask us to fight with Pakistan. Nobody will come between our fight. I have no doubt that if we maintain peace with Pakistan at any cost, our Prime Minister would be called an incarnation of peace. I am not against resolving problems through peaceful means. If international problems could be solved through peaceful means that must be done. But had any international problem cropped up in Kutch, or is Kashmir an international issue ? Aggression was committed in Kutch. If Pakistan had not attacked the officers of both the countries could have met and held talks. Surveyors would have met, proofs would have been seen, maps would have been examined and the problem might have been resolved as per the agreement of 1959-60 which though in my view is wrong, is binding on us. I would not have opposed observance of those agreements. But the aggression today must be removed completely. Pakistan must be punished for committing it. We have put a cover on the aggression. Both the aggressor and the victim have been put on par by this agreement. If the people of the world put us in the same category we feel aggrieved and say they are refusing to declare Pakistan an aggressor. But what have we done ourselves ? We have also put ourselves and Pakistan on the same level. This is not the way to establish peace.

Those who Run Away from War are Chased by War

Madam, those who run away from war are chased by war. Surrendering before the aggressor feeds his hunger for power. One way to establish peace is the Chamberlain method—he wanted to appease Hitler by offering him land, but that laid the foundation of the great World War. Another way to establish peace is the one which was adopted by Kennedy who regarded the Russian missiles installed at a distance of 90 miles from American border in Cuba as a challenge to his country and forced the Soviet Union to withdraw them. That established peace and war was avoided. The agreements made with Pakistan bring the war nearer, stimulate Pakistan's aggressive mentality, and therefore a line has to be drawn somewhere. The time has come now to do so.

Madam, the Prime Minister has appealed for unity. Who has broken the unity ? Who has destroyed the morale of the country ? When we oppose the agreement it is not because of political reasons. Please read my speech of May 3. All members had listened to it. I had wholly supported the Government. I had condemned those Opposition parties that were putting obstacles in the way of the Government. But I had said one thing that if our Government falters we shall strongly oppose it. That is why our movement is going on against the Kutch agreement. This is not a partisan movement. National unity is a matter of devotion to us. We have faith in democracy. If the Prime Minister wants to maintain unity I would ask him to redeem his pledge to the nation. That is the way to keep up the morale of the country. Today there is unrest in the country, people are angry, the situation is explosive, there is shortage of food at some places, at other places prices of commodities are rising, at some places provincialism and at other places communalims are raising their ugly heads. In such a critical period only nationalism can keep the country united.

Lakhs of people came to Delhi from every nook and corner of the country, but not a single incident took place. The Home Minister was so much worried that we were bringing lakhs of people and something untoward may happen. But not a single incident occurred. The disciplined and patriotic people came here to knock at the door of Parliament, because they believed in peaceful means and had faith in the democratic way. But if Parliament does not fulfil its duty and the Government enters into undignified agreements behind the back of Parliament, overlooking the feelings of the people, those feelings cannot be controlled. We welcome the appeal for unity, but the Prime Minister should know the way to establish unity. Thank you.

Indo-Pak War of 1965 and U.N. Double Standard

Mr. Chairman, Sir, I rise to discuss the resolution adopted by the Security Council of the United Nations Organisation on September 20 for effecting a cease-fire between India and Pakistan and the Prime Minister's statement thereon on September 22. Before saying anything on the resolution and on the Prime Minister's statements I want to congratulate the brave soldiers of our Armed Forces who have paid the price in their blood to safeguard our freedom. The Jawans of our Air Force and the Army have brought glory to the nation by sacrificing their lives. Their names will be written in letter of gold on the pages of history. We will remain indebted to them for ever. I want to assure them that their sacrifice will not go in vain and the victory achieved by us in the battlefield would not be allowed to be frittered away in the court of diplomacy.

It is regrettable that the Security Council in its Resolution of September 20 did not condemn Pakistan for committing aggression on August 5 against the Jammu and Kashmir part of India. The date of August 5 has been mentioned in that Resolution, but being the guardian of world peace the Security Council should have openly condemned Pakistan. This is not the first time that Pakistan has attacked Jammu and Kashmir. During 1947 too a similar aggression took place and after a lapse of 18 years Pakistan is exhibiting the same attitude. But it is regrettable that during the past 18 years there has been no change in the Security Council. There has not been any change either in the aggressive posture of Pakistan or the mental attitude of the Security Council. Pakistan was not condemned earlier for committing aggression against Kashmir, and this time too the Security Council wants to close its eyes to the Pakistani attack. When India sent its troops across the international border in her defence from Pakistan, suddenly the Security Council became active, its meetings were called, there was immediate exchange of views and letters in the capitals of the world. But when, on August 5, Pakistan violated and openly flouted the cease-fire agreement, sent armed militants into the State of Jammu and Kashmir which is an integral part of India, no heed was paid by the Security Council, not a ripple was raised in the capitals of the world. The cease-fire agreement of August 13, 1948 between India and Pakistan was effected at the instance of the United Nations and it was the responsibility of both the countries to follow that agreement.

Rajya Sabha on September 24, 1965 on the Resolution by the Security Council of the United Nations for effecting Indo-Pak Cease-fire

Agreement Torn to Shreds

A cease-fire line was drawn under that agreement, Pakistan violated that line, tore the agreement to shreds, sent armed militants into Kashmir to create unrest, but the U.N. sat idle in the U.N. building and did not think it necessary to intervene.

Mr. Chairman, this situation would not have arisen had the Security Council become active after August 5, called meetings, condemned Pakistan for sending the militants and directed Pakistan to withdraw the raiders from Jammu and Kashmir. But it failed the test and closed its eyes on the initial attack by Pakistan which resulted in the spread of war in this region. Peace was violated and India was forced to cross the cease-fire line in Jammu and Kashmir in self-defence. After all, the raiders were coming into Kashmir by crossing the cease-fire line, creating disturbances in the State and inciting people to revolt. They wanted to overthrow the legally constituted government to grab a part of India. India had no other way left but to cross the cease-fire line and send its forces to the valleys and the mountains from where the raiders were coming.

But even then the Security Council did not wake up. When Pakistan attacked Chhamb by crossing the international border, even then the guardian of world peace did not become alert. But when we decided to send our forces towards Lahore and Sialkot for self-defence, only then did the Security Council become active and its meeting was called. How long would the Security Council adopt such a partisan attitude ? Can world peace be maintained in this manner ? Can justice be assured in the world in this way ? The Security Council cannot escape its responsibility in the situation that has been created today.

Sir, the cease-fire agreement has been executed and 20th September, 1965 will be remembered for ever. But a cease-fire agreement was signed on August 13, 1948 also. Who broke that agreement ? Who violated it ? According to that agreement Pakistan was to withdraw its forces from Jammu and Kashmir and was also to withdraw those tribals sheltering behind whom Pakistan was fighting a proxy war and the entire Jammu and Kashmir was to be brought under a single authority. But Pakistan refused to accept that agreement. Will Pakistan accept the present agreement ? Does Pakistan really want a cease-fire ? Will Pakistan stick to the cease-fire ?

The cease-fire agreement had not even become fully operational when Pakistan commenced aggressive action. Those members of Parliament who were present at Ferozepur yesterday are witness to it. Pakistanis had started shelling Ferozepur at 10 o'clock in the morning resulting in the death of one of our Jawans and injuring two. In Jammu area too Pakistan has occupied our land and dug in trenches. Pakistani leaders are threatening us and forecasting a long-drawn battle. Will the Security Council be effective in getting Pakistan to implement the cease-fire agreement ? If Pakistan violates the cease-fire agreement the Security Council had to be informed about it, but we must be clear in our mind that if Pakistan did so, we would give them a befitting reply. We may lodge a complaint but our army, our Air Force must be told to get ready to answer in case Pakistan intrudes into our land after committing a violation of the cease-fire.

In the Resolution of the Security Council a mention has been made of August 5 and it has been stated that all the armed personnel must go back. What will happen to infiltrators who are present in Jammu and Kashmir ? Pakistan does not take responsibility about them and Pakistan is not ready to take them back, then what solution is the Security Council going to have about them ? We have the right to deal with them, and we will deal with them, but my suggestion is that the Government of India must insist that Pakistan should take the responsibility of taking back the raiders since it had sent them to Kashmir. We are ready to prove, we have got proofs and evidence with us, that these raiders were sent by Pakistan, they are a part of the Pakistani Army, they have been directed by Pakistani commanders and were sent to Jammu and Kashmir in a planned manner with arms and Pakistan cannot escape this responsibility.

Pakistan Sent the Raiders

We should put pressure on the Security Council, and tell the U.N. Secretary-General that Pakistan had sent the raiders.

Even earlier Pakistan had deceived the United Nations Organisation when it stated that its forces were not persent in Jammu and Kashmir, but when the Observers began reaching there it admitted the presence of its army. We should insist that the raiders were sent by Pakistan and it should call them back. If the Security Council cannot make Pakistan admit that the raiders were sent by it, if the Security Council cannot make Pakistan accept the responsibility for calling the raiders back, if the Security Council cannot get a commitment from Pakistan that in future Pakistan would not send armed raiders to create disturbances in the valley of Jammu and Kashmir, India's duty is very clear. We cannot accept any arrangement whereby Pakistani raiders could again intrude into Jammu and Kashmir. The position is clear—the question of vacating those valley and mountain tops which are under our possession does not arise. We cannot trust Pakistan any more.

The Security Council is not in a position to ask for any guarantee from Pakistan. If it takes a guarantee how far would it be able to get it implemented ? We will have to see all this in the light of our past experience. Our experience so far has not been good, because it was at the instance of the United Nations that we had vacated the posts at Kargil. Kargil is our defence life-line for the road leading to Leh where we have to face the Chinese. There is a collusion between Pakistan and China and China is ready to jump into the fray in order to help Pakistan in the war. We vacated the posts at the behest of the U.N. and Pakistan has again started interrupting our supply lines, as a result of which we had to reoccupy those posts. Now those posts should not be vacated.

The question of retreating to the cease-fire line of August 5 does not arise at all. And why the line of August 5 ? The whole of Jammu and Kashmir belongs to us, the entire Jammu and Kashmir State forms a part of India. Pakistan has occupied a portion of it by aggression. We should, therefore, have demanded that Pakistan withdraw from the whole of Jammu and Kashmir. But since we did not raise the question of return of the Pak-occupied area of Kashmir Pakistan got an opportunity to make the preposterons claim over our part of Jammu and Kashmir. We should not take up that old question. We should demand that we have the legal, constitutional and moral right over that area and the Pakistani army must vacate it.

We should now ask the Security Council to declare Pakistan an aggressor and get that aggression vacated. But I doubt if the Security Council would be able to do so. I even doubt if Pakistan would be able to fulfil its commitments to the Security Council. Therefore India should make it clear that we do not consider it necessary to go back to the old cease-fire line of August 5 as Pakistan has violated that line. Pakistan has betrayed and deceived the Security Council by violating the cease-fire line agreement and sending in the raiders. Now our forces, our Jawans, would stay put on the hill-tops where they are and we would not vacate those posts. We have to keep in mind the Chinese danger, and if we vacate the posts at Kargil how could we save Ladakh from China ?

China could create a dangerous situation for us at any time and nobody could say what China's designs are. Let no political pandit make a wrong prediction about Chinese designs, because it has the capacity to falsify all predictions. China's relations with Pakistan have become clear. Now it is our duty, it is our *dharma*, that in order to defend Ladakh we should hold on to those posts which we have taken into our possession.

Sir, a reference has been made in the Resolution of the Security Council about a political solution. What would that political solution be ? So far as we are concerned, the question of Jammu and Kashmir has already been resolved and if any solution remains it is about that part of Jammu and Kashmir which is under the occupation of Pakistan. Pakistan has to be removed from there. The Maharaja of Jammu and Kashmir had decided to merge his State with India and the people of Jammu and Kashmir had put their seal of approval to it during several elections and had expressed their opinion in clear terms. During this war also when the dictator of Pakistan was expecting revolt in Jammu and Kashmir, the people of Jammu and Kashmir, including the Hindus and the Muslims, have shown what they wanted and what was in their heart by opposing the Pakistani raiders, by getting them arrested and by passing on the information about their arrival to the government of Jammu and Kashmir. The people of Jammu and Kashmir do not want to go to Pakistan. There might be some who may be toying with the idea of having an independent State of Jammu and Kashmir. But even Pakistan has proved that Jammu and Kashmir cannot be an independent unit. The leaders of Pakistan have been saying that Pakistan cannot survive without Jammu and Kashmir. I want to quote from the speech of the President of Pakistan. President Ayub Khan says :

"Kashmir is vital for Pakistan, not only politically, but militarily as well. Kashmir is a matter of life and death."

Pakistan has other Intentions

Pakistan does not want Kashmir for the Kashmiris. In fact it does not care for its trumpeted concern about their right of self-determination. It wants Kashmir for Pakistanis. It wants to make the Kashmiris as sacrificial goats. It wants to make Kashmir a pawn on the chess-board in order to fulfil its political ambitions. I want to tell those few Kashmiris who are in favour of an independent Kashmir that their eyes should be opened by Pakistan's attack. Pakistan would not allow them to remain independent, Pakistan would not honour any guarantee. Pakistan would not allow its ambition of grabbing Kashmir by force to remain unfulfilled. Jammu and Kashmir can progress and bloom as a part of India. The people of Jammu and Kashmir can achieve their objectives only by remaining in India. Therefore, we should make it clear that Jammu and Kashmir is a part and parcel of India. We have kept Jammu and Kashmir with us legally, constitutionally and with our blood. Our Jawans have shed their blood and put a seal of the decision of the people. I want to read out an extract from the letter dated 14th September of our Prime Minister to the Secretary-General of the United Nations :

"Let me make it perfectly clear, Mr. Secretary-General, that when consequent upon the cease-fire becoming effective further details are considered we shall not agree to any disposition which will leave the door open for further infiltrations or prevent us from dealing with the infiltrations that have taken place. I would also like to state categorically that no pressure or attacks will deflect us from our firm resolve to maintain the sovereignty and territorial integrity of our country of which the State of Jammu and Kashmir is an integral part."

I am quoting this extract from the Prime Minister's letter lest the Government forgets the assurances given by it while dealing with the manoeuvring now being done on the diplomatic front. Pressures would be exerted on the Government. Several big countries would adopt a partisan attitude and would try to convert our victory achieved in the battlefield into a defeat in the diplomatic field. But I have faith in our leadership who have faced the entire situation with strong determination and fortitude and hope that they would not deviate an inch even now and would remain steadfast to the last. The entire country stands behind them. A new awakening has taken place among the 47 crore people of India. A new chapter has been opened in our national life and we must take care that it is not undone, that the blood of the martyrs is not allowed to go waste and a new blot may not besmear our face. So long as our leaders remain firm on their commitment the whole country would stand behind them.

Our True Friends

Mr. Chairman, I shall soon finish. When the question of Kashmir was discussed in the Security Council we got the opportunity to know who is our true friend is, who is our enemy, and who is neutral. When diplomatic manoeuverings take place in the times to come we shall know it further. The number of our friends is not very large, and this cannot be construed as a proof of the success of our foreign policy. We are grateful to the Soviet Union which has constantly supported us on the question of Kashmir. We would like to thank them. But we have a complaint against Britain. The other day when the Communist leaders spoke against Britain in the Ramlila grounds I had told them that was not the opportune moment to speak against the British Government as we may require their help against China. But now patience also is nearing exhaustion.

The attitude of Britain is hurting us. If they cannot extend their support for justice, if they cannot speak in favour of the victim of aggression, they could at least remain neutral, being a prominent member of the Common-wealth. But they support Pakistan. They created Pakistan and nurtured it. They tightened their grip over Pakistan in order to maintain their influence on the oilfields of the Middle-East, but the leadership of Britain forgets that if they want to keep democracy and secular values in South-East Asia alive that cannot be achieved at the cost of India. The time has come when we should seriously think whether India should continue as a member of the Common-wealth or not. I agree with Shri Chagla that we should not take any decision in haste or in anger. But we can't remain silent over the indifference shown by Britain towards the interests of India and its policy of discrimination against India.

Our Publicity Machinery Abroad

Mr. Chairman, there is need to put our publicity machinery abroad in the right gear. A friend of mine has recently arrived from Europe. He says that upto 16th September it was being publicised that Pakistani forces were advancing and Indian troops were retreating. Who made this publicity and how ? It is amazing that our embassies there did not issue a contradiction. Now after 16th September they have come to know that the retreating forces were those of Pakistan and not of India. But why did our publicity machinery fail ? In this wide world all are not opposed to us. Perhaps we are not able to make some people understand us and in the case of some we are not able to convey the information properly. It is time now to review our foreign policy and at the same time to look into our publicity machinery.

Mr. Chairman, I will finish in one minute. Cease-fire does not mean peace and our Prime Minister had said that he would not go from one cease-fire to another. We have reached the second cease-fire, but we should not get trapped into an illusion of peace. The leaders of Pakistan are threatening with another and bigger confrontation. Mr. Bhutto has already talked of a 1000-year war. We do not want to fight with Pakistan. We do not want to conquer Pakistan. But I would like to say that if Pakistan is bent upon breaking India, cutting her to pieces, disrupting the Indian Union, then we too will have to think about the future of Pakistan. We cannot allow Jammu and Kashmir to secede. If Jammu and Kashmir secedes India cannot remain united, the entity of the Indian Union will come to an end. If we accept religion, communalism as the basis at one place we cannot fight disruptive forces at another place. Hence the integrity of the Indian nation from Kashmir to Kerala must be preserved. We should tell the rulers of Pakistan that if they were not fed up with the fight of so many days they may do whatever they like. India will face their challenge with fortitude and firmness. We will have to maintain unity and communal harmony in the country, give a fillip to our war efforts, increase the number of the armed forces, accelerate production of aircraft and tanks and comply with all the requirements of the armed forces by acquiring weapons from foreign countries or by producing them within the country. Political parties should forget that the elections are due in 1967.

The country is passing through an acid test. Elections could be postponed, but not the moment of decision by the nation. Being the largest party the party in power has the overall responsibility, but we too have to discharge our responsibility. We should be ready for a war. We are not warmongers, we are not eager for war, but if anybody challenges us to fight we have to accept the challenge. Please remember that we have the responsibility to get this country of 47 crores ready not only to face Pakistan but also China—to face the combined might of China and Pakistan. Perhaps God Almighty has entrusted us with this responsibility. If the House, Parliament, the Government and the Opposition fail to discharge this responsibility properly history would record a blot on our face that would not be wiped out by blood or tears or sweat. I conclude with the belief that we would not let ourselves besmeared with such a blot. Thank you.

Pakistan Radio's Venomous Propaganda against Jan Sangh

Mr. Chairman, Sir, before the Prime Minister leaves the House I would like to invite his attention through you to a matter of urgent public importance. I have also given a notice about it.

Pakistan Radio is propagating day in and day out that the Government of India has distributed arms to the workers of the Jan Sangh with which they are massacring the Muslims of Kashmir. I heard this news while I was in Africa and on my return also I heard that Radio Pakistan keeps on repeating this charge. At the same time the permanent representative of Pakistan to the United Nations Mr. Amjad Ali has written a letter to the Chairman of the Security Council in which the allegation has been repeated that Jan Sangh workers have been supplied arms with which they are killing the Muslims of Jammu and Kashmir.

Mr. Chairman, I would like to know why the Government has not contradicted this news report so far. Why is All India Radio keeping mum ? Why is the Ministry of External Affairs keeping quiet about it ? The whole world knows that the question of supplying arms to Jan Sangh does not arise at all.

We have not received any arms and the question of killing somebody with those arms also does not arise. But Pakistan is propagating this and the Government is keeping quiet as a result of which an impression was created in the country as well as outside that Pakistan's propaganda might be true.

Refute Pak Propaganda

I would like the Prime Minister to refute this propaganda and declare that no arms have been supplied to Jan Sangh workers and not a single Muslim has been killed in Jammu and Kashmir. This is totally wrong. We want that all Muslims in the country including those in Jammu and Kashmir, should live here safely and participate in the work of constructing the country. If the Government keeps mum the venom spread by Pakistan would gradually take effect and worsen the position of the Government of India as well as the Jan Sangh abroad.

SHRI LAL BAHADUR SHASTRI, Prime Minister : Mr. Chairman, Sir, what Shri Vajpayee has said is not something new because Pakistan has become habituated to such ways. If we listen to their broadcasts daily and read what their newspapers write this propaganda would appear petty in comparison.

Rajya Sabha on December 7, 1965 while moving a Calling Attention Motion regarding the Propaganda launched by Radio Pakistan against Jan Sangh

They indulge in false and baseless propaganda. There is no doubt that it is totally wrong and baseless to say that Jan Sangh workers are supplied any arms. It is also totally false that Muslims are being attacked in Jammu and Kashmir or their life is in danger. Pakistan has always been trying to create dissensions between Hindus and Muslims in our country so that they may fight each other. They may have been disappointed at having failed in their design, but it is a matter of great happiness for us that we have maintained communal harmony in the country in a dignified manner. We wish that this communal harmony may continue.

We supply arms to individuals on a licence basis. We do not discriminate against anybody in this matter on the basis of Hindu, Muslim, Christian, Parsi or Sikh. And our intention is to specially make arrangements for training in the use of arms to people who live in the border areas. This training would be imparted to those living on the border irrespective of their being Muslims, Sikhs or Hindus.

SHRI VAJPAYEE : Please excuse me. I would like that this should be made clear in a letter from the Ministry of External Affairs to the Chairman of the Security Council of the United Nations Organisation as a rejoinder to Mr. Amjad Ali's letter. Thank you.

After Tashkent Declaration What ?

Madam, in the words of President Dr. Radhakrishnan, the Tashkent Declaration was not a legal document, nor a political agreement, not even a declaration of any moral responsibility. In his own words, the Tashkent declaration is a call to conversion of heart. I want to put all that has happened after the Tashkent Declaration through this litmus test.

I would not discuss now what has been done by Pakistan during the past 18 years and what has been her conduct before the Tashkent conference. But the House will have to pay attention to Pakistan's behaviour after signing the Declaration at Tashkent. No agreement could be unilateral. If an agreement is not binding on both the parties, and if it is not implemented honestly by both of them, then it is not worth the paper on which it is written. If the paper is blank it could be used to write something else. But an agreement which the other party is not prepared to honour and which has already been written down makes that paper worthless.

Madam, just three hours after signing the Tashkent Declaration the Foreign Secretary of Pakistan Shri Aziz Ahmed said in Tashkent itself that the Tashkent Declaration did not apply to Pakistani infiltrators. Shastriji was alive at that time. This news must have reached him and I believe that the statement made by the Foreign Secretary of Pakistan must have shocked him. If Pakistan is not prepared to accept that this declaration also applies in the case of infiltrators, if it is not prepared to agree to the proposition that it will not send infiltrators in future and does not accept the responsibility of having sent the infiltrators, then one pillar out of the three on which the Tashkent Declaration rests falls down.

Our Foreign Minister had said on January 16 in a broadcast :

> "The late Prime Minister and the entire Indian delegation felt that conditions laid down by the Prime Minister had been completely met by Pakistan's agreement not only to withdraw all armed personnel but also to respect, after withdrawals, cease-fire terms on the cease-fire line."

Thus the Minister of External Affairs had stated that Pakistan had agreed to withdraw the infiltrators. Pakistan says that it has not agreed to any such condition. Whom to believe ? We want to believe our Minister of External Affairs.

SHRI ARJUN ARORA (Uttar Pradesh) : This is reasonable.

SHRI VAJPAYEE : But if the other signatory party to the Declaration interprets it as it suits it, then the value of that Declaration is reduced. The Government should tell us how many infiltrators have been withdrawn by

Rajya Sabha on February 21, 1966 during discussion regarding the Tashkent Declaration

Pakistan so far. Has a single infiltrator gone back ? The other day the Defence Minister had stated in reply to a question that some infiltrators had been arrested, some were killed, but some of them were still there in Jammu and Kashmir. Has Pakistan announced their withdrawal ? Have they gone back after listening to the Pakistani announcement ? After all, we have to judge the Declaration by its implementation. Shastriji had said on September 24, 1965 :

> "Pakistan must own and discharge the responsibility of withdrawing the infiltrators from our State of Jammu and Kashmir."

A reference is made repeatedly to the letter written to the Secretary-General of the United Nations, but I would like to ask if even according to the letter Shastriji had agreed in the Tashkent Declaration to withdraw from Haji Pir, Kargil and Tithwal, what is the conduct of Pakistan after signing that Declaration ? I want to know whether Pakistan had agreed to withdraw the infiltrators. If it did how did it go back on its words, and, if it went back, why did New Delhi keep quiet ? Even now Sardar Swaran Singh goes on repeating that the Tashkent Declaration applies in the case of infiltrators, I have not been able to understand this. Madam, until Pakistan is prepared to apply the Tashkent Declaration to infiltrators there is no reason for us to abide by the decision to withdraw our troops from Haji Pir, Tithwal and Kargil. You can say that we had agreed in Tashkent to withdraw our troops. Although that was a wrong decision—I will discuss that later—but we had agreed because we thought that by doing so Pakistan would accept the responsibility of sending the infiltrators and ensure their withdrawal. But Pakistan has breached the trust we reposed in it. Pakistan has murdered the Tashkent Declaration on the very first day. We must also not withdraw our troops from Haji Pir, Kargil and Tithwal. What is the objection to adopting this attitude ? But we are not ready to adopt it.

Shastriji's Worry

Before going to Tashkent Shastriji was worried that Pakistan may not admit that the infiltrators were sent by it and was prepared to withdraw them. Shastriji had told me and other leaders of the Opposition parties that we would be in difficulty if Pakistan did not agree to the suggestion that the infiltrators were sent by it and did not give a guarantee to withdraw them. But in Tashkent Pakistan did not accept the responsibility for sending the infiltrators. The Government should have remained adamant on it. On an earlier occasion too, in 1947, Pakistan had said that its troops were not fighting in Kashmir, but later on admitted that its forces were there. For Pakistan it is not a new thing to admit its guilt, but we could not get Pakistan agree to it.

Shastriji's assurances about it were clear. When the cease-fire was accepted leaders of the opposition parties had asked him, "Are you accepting the cease-fire ?" He said, "I am accepting a 'simple cease-fire'. We said to him that today you are accepting a 'simple cease-fire', tomorrow you may agree to withdrawal of forces from Haji Pir, Kargil and Tithwal. We told him that pressure would be put on him on that issue. Other leaders of the Opposition are witness to that. Shastriji had thumbed the table and said, "I may remain or not, this Government may continue or change, nobody in the world may support us, but our forces would not withdraw from Haji Pir, Kargil and Tithwal." Then somebody among us had said if our forces would not withdraw from Haji Pir, Pakistan would not withdraw its troops from Chhamb. Shastriji replied that if Pakistan would not withdraw from Chhamb we would not withdraw from Lahore and Sialkot. Today we are told that had we not withdrawn from Haji Pir Pakistan would not have withdrawn from Chhamb. This thing was raised at that time too, but did the Government give those assurances just to shut the mouths of the Opposition leaders ? Were those assurances given just to play with the sentiments of the people ? Does the Government want that the country should not believe its assurances ? This is a very serious situation.

Will Pakistan Accept Responsibility for Sending Infiltrators

Madam, there is another aspect too. Haji Pir, Kargil and Tithwal are part of India legally and constitutionally. Haji Pir is as much a part of India as Srinagar. Why should we vacate it while no clear-cut assurance has been given to us about infiltrators ? Sardar Swaran Singh says Pakistan has agreed to respect the cease-fire and if infiltrators are sent, it will be a violation of the cease-fire. But Pakistan would not admit that it was sending the infiltrators. You could not get it admitted when the report of the observers of the United Nations Organisation was in your favour. When General Nimmo clearly stated that the infiltrators came on August 5 Pakistan did not accept that they were sent by it. In future too if it sends infiltrators it will deny it and say that they were Mujahids of Jammu and Kashmir.

When our troops reached Haji Pir our Jawans showed great valour, the people there welcomed our armed forces. Smt. Gandhi is not in the House. She had given assurance to the people of Haji Pir that it would not now be handed over to Pakistan. Today we are handing over to Pakistan over 15,000 people who are citizens of India, who have a right to get protection from our army and police. Our civil Administration had been set up in Haji Pir. We are not doing justice to those people. Shri Pathak has forgotten even his own words since he took charge as the Law Minister. He is not present in the House, I wish he were here. The other day, when I raised a point of order Shri Pathak said there was nothing in withdrawing from Haji Pir, Kargil and Tithwal. But when he had not become a Minister and was sitting on this side he delivered a speech on September 24. I want to read out an extract from that speech. He said :

> "Another problem may be whether we can be asked to give up those strategic positions, those territories which we have taken, without which it will not be possible to have the security of the territory which is in our possession. Out of sheer necessity, on the ground of our sovereignty, these should not be allowed to be vacated."

These are the words of Shri Pathak. On becoming a Minister he forgot his own words, he forgot his own speech. We are weakening our authority over the whole of Kashmir by withdrawing our troops from Haji Pir, Kargil and Tithwal. We are strengthening the claim of Pakistan without any rhyme or reason. But Smt. Gandhi said that one has to surrender a small thing for a big thing. So we surrendered Kargil. I want to know what is that big thing which we got ?

Pakistan's Commitment not to Use Force

It is said that Pakistan has promised not to use force. We wanted that Pakistan should sign a No-War Pact, but Pakistan did not do so. Pandit Nehru had suggested a No-War Pact in 1949. Did he not know that Pakistan was a member of the United Nations Organisation, did he not know that Pakistan was bound by the Charter of the United Nations Organisation ? Even then he was insisting that Pakistan should enter into a No-War Pact independently of the Charter of the United Nations Organisation. Nehruji knew that the Charter was not sufficient. Pakistan had attacked Kashmir in spite of its being a member of the United Nations. Shastriji too knew this, and he talked about the No-War Pact because Pakistan had committed aggression against Kutch at the time of Shastriji. Pakistan committed aggression in Kashmir at first through infiltrators and later by attacking Chhamb openly.

Madam, I submit that the Tashkent Declaration does not fulfil our demand of having a No-War Pact with Pakistan, because the reference to the U.N. Charter under which a provision has been made in the Tashkent Declaration prohibiting the use of force already applied to Pakistan and in spite of that Pakistan attacked India thrice. There is another aspect to which I would like to draw the attention of the House. It is provided in Article 2 of the United Nations Charter. I quote :

> "To develop friendly relations among nations, based on respect for the principle of equal rights and self-determination of peoples."

Pakistan has so far been creating disturbances in Kashmir by harping on the principle of self-determination. Article 2 of the Charter of the United Nations Organisation says that relations among nations should be based on the principle of self-determination. Tomorrow Pakistan could say that it had vowed not to use force under the Charter of the United Nations Organisation, but the Charter also provided that relations among the nations should be determined on the basis of the principle of self-determination and since India was not prepared to apply that principle in the case of Kashmir it dissociated itself from this Declaration.

I would also like to invite the attention of the House to Article 33 of the U.N. Charter which says :

> "Parties in a dispute the continuance of which is likely to endanger international peace and security shall, first of all, seek a solution by negotiation, enquiry, mediation, conciliation, arbitration, judicial settlement, resort to regional agencies." etc. etc.

Pakistan has a clear-cut game-plan. As soon as the withdrawal of forces is completed Pakistan would ask India to discuss Kashmir. Our Government claims that Pakistan has agreed not to interfere in the internal affairs of India and the Government also says that Kashmir is our internal affair. But Pakistan says Kashmir is not India's internal affair. On February 13 a spokesman of Pakistan stated that "the article referring to non-interference in each other's internal affairs did not apply to Kashmir because it was a disputed territory and was not an internal affair of India."

Pakistan's intention could also be gauged from the fact that even before the completion of withdrawal of forces it has sent a letter demanding that the first question on the agenda at the meeting of the Ministers of both the countries should be Kashmir. India had opposed the proposal to bring Kashmir on the agenda when Sardar Swaran Singh and Mr. Bhutto met in Tashkent. I do not know what feelings Sardar Swaran Singh might be having in his heart at the time of meeting Mr. Bhutto who had called us 'dogs'. But Sardar Swaran Singh had stated that Kashmir cannot be included in the agenda. I repeat his words :

> "Sovereignty of India over Kashmir was not a matter for mediation or arbitration or discussion."

Is the Government of India firm on this attitude ? I hope it is. But I want proof in this regard, and the only proof is the letter dated February 3, which has been sent by Pakistan, in which it has asked to include Kashmir as number one item in the agenda of the meeting of the Ministers of the two countries. In reply the Government of India should clearly state that Kashmir cannot be included in the agenda. That letter was received on February 3, but no reply has been sent so far. May I know the reason why ? The reply should be clear-cut—Kashmir will not be discussed. But as soon as the Government would say that it was not prepared to discuss Kashmir Pakistan would immediately approach the Security Council and say, look there has been a cease-fire as per the resolution of September 20, troops have been withdrawn to the position of August 5, now the political questions involved in the conflict between India and Pakistan may be resolved. Pakistan can put forth the proposal that the question of Kashmir may also be referred to for arbitration as was done in the case of Kutch. At one time there was talk that Pakistan would demand constitution of a Tribunal consisting of three persons, namely, the Secretary-General of the United Nations, Chairman of the World Bank and Chairman of the International Court of Justice. Pakistan would say : Let the Tribunal consisting of three persons decide as to whose case is right in regard to Kashmir. India cannot accept arbitration. On this Pakistan would say that India has closed the door for peaceful resolution of the question of Kashmir and, therefore, Pakistan has no other way except the use of force, to send infiltrators or resort to disruptive activities in Kashmir. Thus we will reach where we were.

Is the Blood of Jawans so Cheap ?

Shri Yashwant Rao Chavan, Defence Minister, was asked in Jaipur what he would do if Pakistan again sent infiltrators and created disturbance ? The Defence Minister replied we will do what we had done earlier. It means we will reoccupy Haji Pir, Tithwal and Kargil. I want to ask : Are we doing justice to our armed forces ? Our Jawans have captured these posts by shedding their blood, but we are giving away these strategically important posts, these valleys, by being trapped in an illusion of peace—only so that we may recapture them ? Is the blood of our Jawans so cheap ? Mothers will lose their sons again, sisters would lose their husbands and children would become orphans only because our Government was deceived by Pakistan. President Ayub has clearly stated that they would not sign a No-war Pact until the problem of Kashmir is resolved. President Ayub has also said that they had not executed a 'No-War-Pact' in Tashkent, they have only said that so long as the doors are open to resolve the Kashmir problem peacefully they would not take to arms. His meaning is clear—if Pakistan gets Kashmir peacefully it will not take the trouble of fighting. But we cannot offer Kashmir to it. So it will search for some way to use force.

What Happened at Tashkent ?

Madam, what happened in Tashkent that made us sign such a Declaration ? So far I have not received any reasonable answer to this question. Pakistan did not take the responsibility to withdraw the infiltrators, it did not accept Kashmir as our internal affair, it is not even ready to sign a No-War Pact until the Kashmir problem is resolved to its own satisfaction and still we signed the Declaration. The simple answer to this is that we did it under Soviet pressure. The Soviet Union said if an agreement was not reached in Tashkent India would have to go to the Security Council. The unanimous resolution of the Security Council is that forces should withdraw to the line of August 5, hence it is better for India to agree to it in Tashkent. The Soviet Prime Minister has also said that if India does not sign the agreement here, then it would become difficult for the Soviet Union to help India and India would thus be isolated.

SARDAR SWARAN SINGH, Minister of External Affairs : To whom did he say so, to you ?

SHRI VAJPAYEE : To you people.

SARDAR SWARAN SINGH : This is absolutely wrong. You are saying all sorts of things which have no end.

SHRI VAJPAYEE : Look here, I have also got some information; I do not want to disclose the names here, because whatever I was told was in confidence.

SARDAR SWARAN SINGH : So you are keeping the confidence by telling it here.

SHRI VAJPAYEE : No, I am not disclosing the name. I am keeping it confidental. I would like to ask—if they did not put pressure on you why did you agree to it ? Then this Declaration, this agreement, becomes worse. One more explanation is given about this Declaration.....

SHRI M.M. DHARIA : Please disclose the name.

SHRI VAJPAYEE : Please leave it to me. Take it as my guess. There is no need to disclose anybody's name. The Soviet Union put pressure. Please read the report of the Indian journalists who had gone to Tashkent in this connection. I would like to read it out.

Shastriji was adamant on a 'No-War Pact but Mr. Kosygin said at midnight—this report is from *Times of India,* I want to read it out :

"Mr. Kosygin and his officers came forward with the suggestion at about midnight last night that the U.N. Charter to which both India and Pakistan were signatories offered an appropriate basis in this context for them to reaffirm their obligation to each other not to have recourse to force in settling their disputes. The Indian plea for an independent declaration by the two countries was thus bypassed. When Pakistan accepted this advice, India was left with no choice, except to fall in line."

It was stated earlier that there would be no talks about Kashmir in Tashkent. It was also stated that when Mr. Bhutto had visited Moscow he told them that President Ayub would not be able to say anything about Kashmir in Tashkent and Russia had agreed to it. But as soon as the Pakistani delegation reached Tashkent they began saying that they had come to talk about Kashmir.

I want to ask—when the meeting of the Foreign Ministers was deadlocked over the question of agenda who forced Shastriji to talk to the President of Pakistan informally on the Kashmir question ? Did not Mr. Kosygin ask him ? Were both of them not pressurised by the Soviet Union to talk about Kashmir ? If the newspapers are giving wrong reports the Minister of External Affairs.....(*Interruptions*).

SARDAR SWARAN SINGH : No newspaper has reported that the Chairman of the Council of Ministers of the Soviet Union had asked both of them to talk about Kashmir. In a moment of great heat you may say whatever you like, but you should state the events correctly.

SHRI VAJPAYEE : Madam, all the newspapers have written this.

SARDAR SWARAN SINGH : No Government has said that the Chairman of the Council of Ministers of the Soviet Union asked both of them to talk about Kashmir. No newspaper has published such a report.

SHRI VAJPAYEE : Did you get ready to talk about it on your own ?

SARDAR SWARAN SINGH : I was only replying to your point.

SHRI VAJPAYEE : I have no copies of the newspapers with me here, I have no files. All the journalists were standing there. Shri Krishan Bhatia, Shri Rangaswami, Shri Swaminathan, all these persons had gone to Tashkent and all of them have sent the report from there that when the Foreign Ministers' talks failed the Soviet Prime Minister came into the picture and said : All right, if you do not want to keep Kashmir in the agenda it does not matter, but you may talk informally. You have not contradicted it till today.

SARDAR SWARAN SINGH : There is no mention of it anywhere.

SHRI VAJPAYEE : It is strange. You will reply tomorrow. I shall have to put the newspapers before you and ask you whether the Soviet Union pressurised you ?

Russia Supports Pakistan

Madam, Russia supported Pakistan at every step in Tashkent. I had praised the Soviet Union in this very House when my friend Shri Dahyabhai Patel had criticised her. At that time Russia was acting in our interest which nobody can deny. But today Russia's attitude has changed. It is natural. Russia has changed its attitude in her self-interest because it wants to isolate Pakistan from China. It wants to keep Pakistan away from America. We may have sympathy with the Soviet Union in their mission, but we want to tell them—please do not do so at our cost. But they are doing it. Shri Rangaswami is the correspondent of *The Hindu*. He has filed a report in *The Hindu* dated January 14. Shri Rangaswami is not an irresponsible correspondent. He has written that Shastriji had said that three months' time is required for the withdrawal of troops, because Shastriji thought that if that much time was made available we would come to know whether Pakistan wants to implement the agreement or not. But the Russian Prime Minister said that three months' time was too long and when you have agreed to withdraw the forces, withdraw them quickly. And now the forces are being withdrawn.

Won In the War, Lost In Treaty

I want to say that Pakistan's intention is not unambiguous. The Congress Working Committee has stated in its resolution that if the Tashkent Declaration is implemented honestly the way to peace could be opened between the two countries. But Pakistan is not prepared to implement honestly, and hence the Tashkent Declaration has opened the way for surrender. It is becoming a topic of discussion in the country. A person like Shri Jagjivan Ram, who is a member of the Cabinet, is saying we should arrive at an agreement on the basis of the cease-fire line by giving away 10-12 miles of area. When Shri Krishna Menon says that the entire Jammu and Kashmir belongs to us members of the Congress Party clap, but when a member of the Cabinet, Shri Jagjiwan Ram, says let us make an agreement with Pakistan on the basis of the cease-fire line by giving away some area the Prime Minister does not contradict him and even the Minister of External Affairs keeps mum.

Since our signing the Tashkent Declaration the supporters of surrender have become stronger and the people are now saying that if an agreement can be reached with Pakistan by offering her something why not have a peace-deal with China also by offering it Aksai-Chin ? I am afraid if this attitude continues the country would again fall into a crisis. What our Jawans have achieved in the battle-field by sacrificing their lives will all be lost while sitting at the table. We had won the war, but have lost in the treaty.

I am not against having friendship with Pakistan. The entire country wants to improve relations with Pakistan, but peace cannot prevail till Pakistan insists on its claim on Kashmir, till leaders of Pakistan want to have an agreement on Kashmir on their own terms. We should not get trapped in the illusion of peace. The country would again be in danger in case we commit the mistake of closing our eyes to the looming danger.

Madam, I would request the Minister of External Affairs to contradict the wrong interpretation put by the leaders of Pakistan on the Tashkent Declaration. Why has he not done it so far ?

SARDAR SWARAN SINGH : You might not have seen it. I have stated this in the other House also.

SHRI VAJPAYEE : We will now see what you say tomorrow.

SARDAR SWARAN SINGH : But first I have to see what you are saying today.

Increased Armed Activity by Pakistan in Kashmir

Mr. Speaker, Sir, I want to draw the attention of the Minister of Defence to the following matter of urgent public importance and request him to make a statement thereon :

> "Firing by Pakistani troops on the Indian border Patrol on 19th May, 1967 in the area south-west of Akhnoor and concentration of Pakistani troops in Daggar area."

SHRI SWARAN SINGH, Minister of Defence : Mr. Speaker, Sir, at about 8 a.m. on 19th May our police patrol moving in the area between 4 to $5^1/2$ miles south-west of Akhnoor inside Indian territory was fired upon by Pakistani troops. The Pakistani troops fired LMGs and threw grenades and also used MMGs and 81 mm mortars. Our Security Forces had per force to return the fire. Firing died down by and large by 9.15 a.m., but thereafter sporadic firing continued till about 4 p.m.

Earlier on 17th May, for the first time our police patrol party moving in the same area had been challenged by the Pakistani troops who objected to its patrolling, claiming that the track used by our patrol party was within Pakistani control. Since our patrol had all along been using this track, which also is within Indian territory, the Pakistani claim was not accepted. It appears that the firing by the Pakistani troops on our police patrol on 19th May was a premeditated one, designed to establish by force their so-called claim to the track.

In the firing by the Pakistani troops, one Indian police head constable was killed and two ORs wounded. Injuries were also caused to two civilians. It appears that the Pakistanis have also suffered casualties.

Under the aegis of the U.N. Field Observers' Team Pakistan asked for a cease-fire and for a Sub-Sector Commanders' meeting. This was agreed to on our side. The meeting was held at 5 p.m. on the same day. It was agreed to maintain the ceasefire. Further meetings held at the Sub-Sector Commanders' level failed to produce any further agreement. The Sub-Sector Commanders have agreed to refer the matter to their Commanders.

Protest has been lodged with the Government of Pakistan. It may be added that the agreed procedure is that in the case of such differences the matter should be referred to higher authorities and no firing should be resorted to. For reasons best known to them the Pakistani forces did not adopt this procedure and resorted to use of force.

Lok Sabha on May 25, 1967, while moving a Calling Attention Motion regarding Firing by Pakistani troops on Indian border patrol near Akhnoor

Government is aware that since the firing incident, Pakistan has moved some additional Army units into the Daggar area on their side across the Akhnoor border. Without wishing to increase the tension that the unfortunate Pakistani firing has caused I would like to assure the House that all necessary measures are in hand to deal with any development that may take place in this area.

U.S. Rearmament of Pakistan

SHRI VAJPAYEE : Sir, is it not a fact that ever since the U.S. decision to resume military aid to Pakistan it has, on the one hand, intensified the propaganda war against India and, on the other, warned us by attacking our patrol near Akhnoor that it is in search of some excuse to raise the Kashmir issue in the Security Council again ? I would like to have the assessment of the Hon'ble Minister about Pakistani intentions.

Secondly, the firing started at 8 a.m. and ended at 4 p.m., but how is it that the world came to know about firing from Pakistan first ? Pakistan has claimed that the Indian patrol intruded into its territory and fired on its troops. So much so that even Indian newspapers first published the news emanating from Pakistan. That means that publicity was put into motion the world over that Indian troops had entered Pakistani territory and were attacking their troops. I would like to know why delay occurred on our part to disseminate the news that the first attack was made from the Pakistan side and we only fired in defence. It appears that this time also we are left behind Pakistan in the publicity campaign.

SHRI SWARAN SINGH : On the question of the United States Government having decided to resume the supply or sale of spare parts to Pakistan the Government position has been clarified more than once. We think that this step of the United States Government will definitely act to our prejudice, as most of the Pakistani equipment is of United States origin.

So far as the present incident is concerned we should view it as an incident which took place at the border. I do not think that there is any direct connection between this incident and the desire that Pakistan may have to raise the matter in the U.N. Security Council. They have not made any secret of their desire to go to the Security Council; they have already stated that it was the intention of the Pakistan Government to raise the question of Jammu and Kashmir in the UN Security Council. This is a matter which the External Affairs Ministry will deal with. About the other question, that news about this was given for the first time from the Pakistani sources, that is not quite correct. Our version also appeared in the newspapers.

SHRI VAJPAYEE : Only the next day.

SHRI SWARAN SINGH : They may have circulated it but our version, which was the correct version, was there. Our version is that the firing took place inside our territory and it appeared in the Indian newspapers.

Foreign Minister Ill-informed

SHRI VAJPAYEE : I am sorry to say that the Hon. Minister is not well informed and is not prepared to ask for time to get the information. The day the firing took place Delhi newspapers displayed this news on the news-stand : "Pakistan Claims Border Clash". But the spokesman of the Indian Government did not say anything about it to Indian newspapermen. The Hon'ble Minister should ponder over this and if there has been delay he should try to mend things.

SHRI SWARAN SINGH : It is a suggestion for action; I will certainly look into it.

SHRI VAJPAYEE : Will he enquire whether there was delay ?

MR. SPEAKER : He says he will look into it.

SHRI VAJPAYEE : He says it is a suggestion for action. He is keeping mum.

SHRI SWARAN SINGH : I am not keeping mum. The Hon. member says that I should check up if that has appeared in certain newspapers and I say I will look into it. But the correct version put out by us did find its place in the morning newspapers on the following day.

Government Misled the Country on Kutch Issue

Mr. Speaker, Sir, I am grateful to you for giving me this opportunity to beg leave of the House to move a motion of breach of privilege of the House. I had given the notice of the motion on May 4. I had included the Minister of Home Affairs in the original motion, but today, with your permission, I want to extend the scope of my original motion and bring the Prime Minister, the Deputy Prime Minister and the Minister of Home Affairs within the purview of this motion.

Sir, you might recall that on February 28, a motion of no-confidence moved by Professor Balraj Madhok against the Government was discussed in the House. The discussion was mainly confined to Kutch. The verdict given by the Tribunal about Kutch was criticised and, while replying to the discussion or intervening in the debate the Prime Minister, the Deputy Prime Minister and the Minister of Home Affairs made certain statements. While I will be quoting extensively from those statements in the House I would like to say, in order to save the time of the House that all the three Ministers expressed their regret on the land being handed over to Pakistan as a result of the verdict of the Kutch Tribunal. The Home Minister stated that he had personally visited the area that was being handed over to Pakistan and had himself seen how bravely our Jawans had defended that area. He also stated that we had a cast-iron case regarding Kutch, but the verdict had gone against us and now there was no way out but to accept the verdict. The Deputy Prime Minister said that we are not happy in handing over the land because it belonged to us, but we were bound by the commitment and hence we could not challenge the verdict of the Tribunal. More or less similar words were used by the Prime Minister. Before that day, whenever the matter of Kutch was raised in this House, whether it was during the period of Shastriji or thereafter, whenever Government publications were issued about Kutch issue, only one thing was said. It was that the entire Kutch belongs to us, constitutionally, legally as well as by tradition, but Pakistan wants to create difficulties before us by trying to forcibly occupy it. Shastriji had stated that there was no territorial dispute involved in the case of Kutch, only the border was to be demarcated, and the Government spokesmen had also repeated time and again that Kutch belonged to us and we had left no stone unturned to save it.

Lok Sabha on May 10, 1968 while raising a question of breach of privilege against the Minister for allegedly misleading the House about giving Indian land to Pakistan

Affidavit by Government

But, Mr. Speaker, Sir, if what has been stated in the affidavit filed by the Government of India in the High Court of Delhi in reply to a writ petition filed by a citizen, Shri Shiv Kumar Sharma, is taken to be true, and there is no reason to take it otherwise, it is clear that the Prime Minister, the Deputy Prime Minister and the Minister of Home Affairs have deliberately misled Parliament and this House about the position of Kutch and its status in the Indian Union. They have concealed facts, they have refused to divulge the truth and therefore they are guilty of breach of privileges of Parliament and of this House.

Yesterday my friend Shri Madhu Limaye had read out a portion of the affidavit filed by the Government. Can a Government in its sense file such kind of affidavit in a court of law ? But what should not have happened has been done and the Government cannot escape its responsibility. The proper course was the removal of the Government for filing such affidavit. The House should have expressed its want of confidence in this Government. We wanted to censure the Government, but you did not permit us. Therefore we have adopted the course of bringing a motion of breach of privilege.

It is said in the writ petition by Shri Sharma that our land was being handed over to Pakistan, but it cannot be handed over without passing a law. It is necessary to amend the Constitution for this purpose. The Government was doing something without undergoing legal formalities for which it has no authority. Honesty demanded that the Government should have introduced a Constitution amendment Bill in Parliament in order to implement the verdict on Kutch, but the Government did not do so. To cover up one sin several sins are being committed. The Government is playing with the interests of the country in order to conceal its mistake. The affidavit filed by the Government of India is tantamount to present India as an aggressor in Kutch. Mr. Speaker, Sir, I quote :

> "It is also denied that the territory which the Tribunal has held to lie on the Pakistan side of the alignment of the boundary belonged to Kutch District of Gujarat State under the Bombay Reorganisation Act, 1960 or that it was recognised as Indian territory by the Constitution of India."

Implementation of a Black Verdict

The land which is being handed over by us did not belong to us, it never belonged to us. Therefore, there is no question of handing over any land—this is the black verdict which we are implementing. Is any value attached to the statements given in this House by the Prime Minister, the Deputy Prime Minister and the Minister of Home Affairs ? Does this affidavit not go against all the claims made by Government spokesmen all along ? Does this affidavit not vitiate the position of India ? Shri Shiv Kumar has in his writ petition referred to the statements of the Prime Minister, the Deputy Prime Minister and the Minister of Home Affairs made in this House, and in the Government, reply affidavit is worth reading. It should open the eyes of this

House and serious thought over the position of the Government should be given. He is an officer of the Ministry of External Affairs and the Ministry of External Affairs is under the charge of the Prime Minister. Referring to the statements one by one the affidavit says :

> "In reply to para 2 of the petition I say that the statement purported to have been made by the Hon'ble Union Home Minister is not material to the issue. It is denied that a very important part of territory or any territory of India is being given to Pakistan and that too for fear of war. A mistaken claim to territory which was in the adverse possession of India does not have the effect of converting such territory into territory of India and demarcation of the red boundary does not amount to cession of territory."

It is thus being taken for granted that our land actually belonged to Pakistan and we had forcibly occupied it. The second para of the affidavit is about the statements of the Prime Minister and the Deputy Prime Minister. I quote:

> "The statements purported to have been made by the Prime Minister of India are equally not material to the main issue. It is denied that any part of the territory of India is being given to Pakistan simply on the false hope of improvement of relations with Pakistan. The statement purported to have been made by the Deputy Prime Minister of India is also not material to the main issue. It is denied that the Union of India has taken any decision to transfer the territory of India which is recognised by Indian Constitution as Indian territory."

Mr. Speaker, Sir, such are the affidavits.

Contradiction in Words and Deeds

Mr. Speaker, Sir, I welcome the ruling given by you. The statements or speeches made in the House become the property of the House and to bring a motion of breach of privilege on these is the prerogative of the members of the House. The Government has not controverted the extracts being quoted from the affidavit filed in the High Court. The complete affidavit was placed on the table of the House yesterday. This House is fully competent to consider whether the Prime Minister, the Deputy Prime Minister and the Minister of Home Affairs have deliberately misled the House. From the extracts which I have quoted it has become quite clear that even those who have been saying certain things in this House about the position and the status of Kutch were themselves not convinced about the propriety of those things. They had something in their hearts and something else in their mouths. Their words and deeds contradicted each other. It is evident from the affidavits filed in the Delhi High Court that the Prime Minister, the Deputy Prime Minister and the Minister of Home Affairs are guilty of breach of privilege of the House. This is not the first time when facts have been concealed from the House. The other day the Prime Minister got very much annoyed when Shri Kanwar Lal Gupta alleged that an aircraft had landed in Nagaland and that the Prime

Minister was deliberately concealing this fact. The Prime Minister became angry and said that such allegations should not be made.

Similarly, some members of this House are witness to the fact that when China built a road in Aksai-Chin the Government concealed that fact from the country and the Parliament and the Prime Minister had promised in the House not to repeat such a mistake in future. But when Pakistan attacked Kutch in 1965, again the fact about the attack was concealed. The fact of occupation of 1300 sq. yards of land by Pakistan was concealed from the House and now the Government has refused to bring all the facts of Kutch before the House. Untrue and wrong information has been given. I, therefore, urge you to give me permission to seek the leave of the House to move a motion of breach of privilege in order to find out the facts by referring the matter to the Committee of Privileges of the House so that the grain is sifted from the chaff. Thank you.

Soviet Arms to Pakistan

Mr. Chairman, Sir, it cannot be denied that a new and serious situation has been created by the decision of the Soviet Union to supply arms to Pakistan. We will have to face this situation with firmness and self-confidence. The Prime Minister told the House in her statement today that the security of the country will receive top priority at the hands of the Government. She has also expressed the confidence that it will be possible to face the new situation successfully with the support of the people of India. Would it not have been better if along with exhorting the people to face the new situation unitedly, this House had condemned the Soviet decision with one voice and declared its resolve that India would henceforth stand on its own legs, and would not compromise its future by reposing its confidence in the cooperation and support of a super power ? If we in this House cannot speak with one voice who will inspire the nation to speak in one voice ? The Prime Minister said that there was no convention of passing this kind of resolution. My submission is that this kind of situation had never arisen before. When America supplied arms to Pakistan we could have relied on Soviet Russia. But Russia has now created a situation where our position has become vulnerable. Secondly, at that time nobody had suggested moving of such a resolution. I am confident that Pandit Nehru would not have opposed such a suggestion if it were made at the time. He himself had taken the initiative for a campaign against American arms aid to Pakistan. Is the Prime Minister prepared to take a similar initiative ? Nehruji issued instructions to the Congress Party to mobilise public opinion in the entire country against the improper step taken by America and to give it an effective expression. Is the Congress of today prepared to initiate such a move against the decision of the Soviet Union ? Is the Prime Minister prepared to take the line adopted by her father ?

Russian Arms would be Used Against India

While Pandit Nehru had taken the initiative against American arms aid to Pakistan the present Prime Minister called a meeting of the editors and correspondents of newspapers and gave tacit advice to suppress the resentment of the people against Soviet Russia. This country has a free press and I am sure it will perform its duty, but I am only pointing out the difference in the Government approach.

Lok Sabha on July 22, 1968 during discussion on the adjournment motion regarding Soviet arms supply to Pakistan

One more thing. The United States had supplied arms to Pakistan in the hope that it would check expansion of communism and become a part of the world-wide U.S. strategy. However, it should not be difficult for the leaders of Soviet Russia to understand that the arms received by Pakistan will not be used against any one except India. American arms were given to an ally, but Russian arms are being given to Pakistan that never had a military alliance with Soviet Russia. On the other hand, Pakistan is still a member of SEATO and CENTO. The aim of the foreign policy of Soviet Russia is to break these military alliances. It was on this premise that the Russian leaders had been giving statements against Pakistan which led us to believe that there would be no drastic change in their policy towards Pakistan.

Mr. Chairman, on 14th February, 1962 a top leader of the Soviet Communist Party Comrade Suslov made a statement before the Central Committee of the Party from which I would like to quote. Let this House see for itself how it is relevant to the changed context. Mr. Suslov was criticising China for helping Pakistan against India and arming it against India. Commenting on that he said :

> "While allowing relations with India, which everybody knows is not a member of military blocs, to deteriorate sharply, the Chinese leadership at the same time actually leagued together with Pakistan, a member of SEATO and CENTO, which are threatening peace and security of Asian peoples. It is a fact that having discarded their revolutionary pharisee-mongering Chinese leaders have in reality adopted a line that can hardly be dovetailed with the principled position of the countries of the socialist commonwealth with regard to imperialist blocs.... the approach of the Chinese leaders to the choice of friends and allies is strange, to say the least".

Comrade Suslov went on to say :

> "How is it possible, it may be asked, to fling mud at socialist countries, at communist parties, and at the same time, with the whole world watching, shower compliments on the reactionary regime in Pakistan ? That is simply unthinkable....can anyone believe that the rapprochement with Pakistan has been dictated by the interests of the development of the revolutionary struggle of the peoples of Asia against imperialists that the Chinese leaders talk so much about ?

This was the reaction of Moscow when Peking entered into league with Pakistan, but the same Moscow is now going to arm Pakistan. Have things in Pakistan changed ? Has it come out of the imperialist camp ? Is it not now a member of SEATO and CENTO ? Is the Communist Party no more banned in Pakistan ? The fact is that the framework in Pakistan has not changed, but the policy of the leaders in Moscow has changed, and we must properly assess it.

Russian Assurance Is Worthless

The Prime Minister says that she is not aware what kind of weapons are being given. She does not even know whether arms delivery has begun or will start at a later date. But we are told that Soviet Russia has assured us that those arms will not be used against India. My submission is that such assurances have been tried by us earlier too. These assurances are not worth the paper on which they are written. A blank paper has some worth, but it becomes a waste paper after writing an assurance on it. Assurances are given by those very people who give arms. These have no substance. It is the intention of the recipient of the arms that matter. If America could not stop Pakistan we are not prepared to be allured by the mirage of Soviet assurances. On the one hand it is said that Russian arms given to Pakistan will not be used against India and on the other it is argued that they are meant for defence. These two things are contradictory. No line can be drawn between arms meant for attack and for defence.

When Soviet Russia took the decision to supply helicopters to Pakistan our Government had tried to plead in favour of that decision in this House. At that time we had received an indication of the change in the policy of Soviet Russia and we want to know from the Government what they did to stem the Soviet decision after such a clear indication. The Prime Minister says that every country has the right to supply arms to any other country. But do we not have the right to protest ? If they have the right to change their policy do we not have the right to review our policy in the changed circumstances and to recast it accordingly ? When American arms find their way to Pakistan through Italy or Iran we sent a protest knowing that they have a right to sell arms. When these arms affect our interest we denounce it and send a protest note. Then why has no protest been made to Russia so far ? The Prime Minister may say that we are writing to them. But if this communication does not properly reflect the sentiments of the people, its language and content must be changed.

Pakistan has Become Belligerent

Mr. Speaker, Sir, the question is not how many and what sort of weapons are being given by Soviet Russia. The issue is that their policy has changed, and we will have to keep that in view and act accordingly. What the effect of receiving these weapons on Pakistan can easily be imagined. The decision of supplying arms has changed the tone of the Pakistani leaders. The Hon. Prime Minister has referred to this in subdued tones. As soon as Moscow decided to supply arms the Foreign Minister of Pakistan declared that his country did not recognise the international cease-fire line. Thereafter, Shri Arshad Hussain gave another statement on 13th July :

> "The Pakistan Foreign Minister warned yesterday, the 13th July, that if India remained obdurate over Jammu and Kashmir and other disputes Pakistan was ready to meet any situation."

That means if India does not step down on Kashmir they are ready for any situation. We are being threatened with war. Pakistan has been emboldened by getting Russian arms. Its leaders are full of hatred against India. It has not forgotten the defeat of 1965. Is Soviet Russia supplying arms to Pakistan for bringing it nearer to India to create stability in this area and to reduce tensions ? Let us make an effort to understand the aims of Soviet Russia. But there should be no difference of opinion in the country about the effects on us and we should decide what we should do to undo these effects.

So far Pakistani leaders were harping on Kashmir, but now they have added the issue of Farakka Barrage to it. President Ayub has said that Kashmir and Farakka Barrage are basic questions and so long as they are not solved properly—properly means as per the desire of Pakistan—there would be no peace. At the same time a letter from Premier Kosygin is received about the Farakka Barrage. That indicates which way the wind is blowing.

Defuse Threat to Czechoslovakia

The Prime Minister has said that she would not succumb to any pressures. If our Government has so much firmness the communique issued at the time of the President's visit to Russia would have been somewhat different. We could have made a reference in it about the Soviet arms supply to Pakistan. We could have expressed our apprehensions, and Soviet leaders could have added a sentence removing that apprehension. We have been advised in the communique to settle our disputes with Pakistan peacefully. We could have pressed Russia to settle her dispute with Czechoslovakia peacefully and not interfere in the internal affairs of other countries. But our representative did not press these things. The small Czechoslovakia is becoming a prey to the expansionist policies of Soviet Russia. What will be the reaction of our Government if Soviet armies enter Czechoslovakia ? The blame that attached to the Government for keeping quiet in the case of Hungary has not so far been washed away. Before Russian armies enter there New Delhi should extend a warning, invoking the United Nations Charter and the principles of *Panchsheel,* that Soviet Russia should not take any step which may endanger peace and violate the independence of any other country. But our Prime Minister is silent on Czechoslovakia. Russia can advise us to settle our disputes peacefully, then can't we talk to them of justice, policies and principles ? When we could not resist Russian pressure in the preparation of the joint communique I cannot believe, in spite of my best efforts, that New Delhi will be able to resist when Russian pressure is exerted about Kashmir, Ganga waters and Farakka Barrage.

Government's Indecision

I am not afraid of the Russian arms. This country was not afraid when American arms were given to Pakistan. The People of India, the entire manpower, our resources and, if we could properly utilise them, the strength born therefrom can face any outside challenge. The worry is not the arms of Russia, but the attitude of indecision of New Delhi. Sir, just look at the strange situation. Our President was on a goodwill visit of the USSR and was speaking on Indo-USSR friendship at every place he visited and at the same time our Prime Minister was analysing the dangerous situation that had arisen out of Russian arms supply to Pakistan. If it was known before the President's USSR visit that the Russian leaders had decided to arm Pakistan the President's visit could have been postponed. The Russians would have felt sore about it, but at times it is necessary to let the people of the world know that India also feels sore and our sentiments should also be respected. Sometimes situations do arise in the international field when it becomes necessary to take a strong stand in some form or the other. We might not have cancelled the visit, but could have postponed it. However, that was not done and the President went ahead with the visit. After his departure the Prime Minister could have refrained from criticising the Russian decision. Being a responsible Government its official spokesman could have said that we have received information that Soviet Russia has taken such and such a decision but we will not comment on it till the President's return. There the President was making speeches of mutual goodwill, and here the Prime Minister, while surveying the floods in Gauhati, was analysing this dangerous situation trying to play it down so that the strong feelings of the people may not aggravate.

I am sorry to say that some officials of the External Affairs Ministry are interfering in politics. How the Russian decision to supply arms to Pakistan reached the newspapers should be inquired into. I will not blame the newspapers. It is their job to search for news. But how the secrets of the External Affairs Ministry leak to foreign countries needs to be investigated. The Prime Minister should put her house in order.

Curse can Become a Boon

The decision of Soviet Russia is dangerous. But some good can come out of evil, a curse can become a boon, if it opens our eyes to the fact that we cannot trust anybody. Ultimately we have to stand on our own feet. But I feel sorry at some reactions. Some people have suggested that we may align with America in view of the Russian arms supply to Pakistan. If we do that or think on these lines it means we have not learnt our lesson from the Russian decision. The present times are not for seeking alignment with somebody. Nobody will continue to coddle us also. Every country is making its own moves nowadays. Russia has its eyes on the Indian Ocean. Russia wants to have access to the sea through Pakistan and Afghanistan. It may also try to fill the vacuum created by the US defeat in Vietnam and British withdrawal from Singapore.

Take the House and Country into Confidence

The Prime Minister should take this House and the country into confidence and tell us what kind of talks we are having with Russia. Russia is giving assurances of friendship and, if it is honest about it, these assurances can be given the shape of a treaty. Is Russia prepared to sign a formal treaty with India incorporating all the assurances and promising future support ? Can Russia make this commitment to us ?

The other thing is whether the Government is prepared to declare in unambiguous terms that it will not come under any international pressure and will not take any decision that may adversely affect the interests of India on any issue—whether it is Ganga water, Farakka Barrage or Kashmir. We will have to review our foreign policy. Having been kicked at one place we cannot take shelter in another place to be kicked there too. Our policy should be elastic and realistic. The Russian decision has opened new avenues for us. We can look to Western Europe. We can expand our relations with South-East Asia. International politics of today looks more to regions rather than the world as a whole. If we could restructure and implement our foreign policy so as to take with us the people of the region where we live and with whom our relations are good, at the same time establishing relations with different countries in accordance with our different interests and protecting our wider interests, the Russian decision would have given us a blow which, instead of creating frustration, may awaken us to a new resolve for the future. But this Government is incapable of resurrecting that resolve. For a new resolve , a new Government is necessary. Therefore, I support this motion of censure.

Simla Accord : Case of Broken Promises

Mr. Deputy Speaker, Sir, the Minister of External Affairs has praised the Simla Agreement in his statement and has expressed the hope that, if implemented faithfully, it can open a new chapter in Indo-Pak relations. I want to draw the attention of the House to the words "if faithfully worked out". It is clear that the Hon. Minister himself has doubts about whether Pakistan will honestly carry out the responsibility expected of it under the Simla Agreement. Sir, today, when the Minister of External Affairs stood up to make his statement, it was a pathetic scene in the House. At that moment I was reminded of 4th December when we had assembled in this House after the Pakistani aggression on 3rd December. At that time the House was united. Why this division now ? That day we were full of enthusiasm; today we are full of resentment. That day the entire country was united in facing the Pakistani aggression; today there is division. We were one at that moment of danger. We were one at the time of war. Is it not the responsibility of the Prime Minister to maintain unity in the time of peace also ? I want to ask the Prime Minister, who has broken this unity in the House ?

SOME HON. MEMBERS : Your party.

SHRI VAJPAYEE : Sir, the hirelings will have the opportunity to reply to my points. They should have patience to hear what I have to say.

I want to say that the responsibility of dividing this country and this House rests on the Prime Minister.

SOME HON. MEMBERS : It rests on Jan Sangh.

Not the Promised Package Deal

SHRI VAJPAYEE : Before going to Simla the Prime Minister had assured the House that this time the problems with Pakistan will not be solved piecemeal and that there would be a package deal. I want to reproduce her words. This is what she said in an interview broadcast on 14th May in the U.S. and it has been printed in the paper published by the External Affairs Ministry of the Government of India, otherwise the External Affairs Minister would have denied that the Prime Minister ever said so :

> "We had been trying to have a step-by-step approach all these years, but this obviously has not worked."
>
> "Indo-Pakistan problems could not be looked upon piecemeal".

The word as used by the Prime Minister is PIECE and not PEACE. But you have returned from Simla not with peace, but with a piecemeal agreement. This is not a package deal. The Prime Minister has broken her word.

Lok Sabha on July 31, 1972 during discussion on the motion regarding Indo-Pakistan Agreement

SHRI SATPAL KAPOOR : It required intelligence to understand.

SHRI VAJPAYEE : You think all the intelligence is concentrated in you. Those who interrupt in this manner do not exhibit intelligence.

Mr. Deputy Speaker, Sir, even on returning from Simla the Prime Minister said in her press statement that our experience of settling each issue separately had not been good and we wanted to solve all the problems once for all. I want to judge the Simla Agreement on this ground first. A step by step approach was the policy of Pakistan. To enter a package deal was our declared policy. But the Government was defeated at Simla. Mr. Bhutto outdid our Prime Minister in diplomacy. Can anybody say that the Simla Agreement is a package deal ? Have all problems between India and Pakistan been resolved ? This is what has been said even in the statement :

> "The agreement is the first step towards establishing durable peace in the sub-continent."

We Always Take the First Step

So it is the first step. The expectations we had and the assurances that were given to the country were that it will not be the first step but the last step that will be taken at Simla. During the past 25 years we have always been taking the first step. When the Nehru-Liaquat meeting took place the first step was taken. Nehru and Noon met, Nehru and Ayub Khan met, and later on Ayub and Shastri met. Then also, the first step was taken. But there was no need for the first step after what had happened in 1971. A last step was needed for establishing permanent peace between the two countries. A thing well begun does not always end well.

I am not inspired by any political motive in opposing this agreement. It is not something to laugh at. During the war, when I praised the Prime Minister and supported the Government, causing embarrassment to my party I was a patriot. Now, when I am speaking against the Government, these people do not have the patience to hear me. We did not indulge in politics then. Today also we are not doing politics. We will have to examine the Agreement on merits. Does the Simla Agreement provide for lasting peace ? My submission is that the Simla Agreement does not stand this test. It is not a package deal. It looks at the issue in pieces.

Kashmir Is Made the Subject of Dispute

We accept the fact that Kashmir has been the main contention between India and Pakistan. There have been four wars between the two on this issue. There was a cease-fire agreement every time, and yet the war broke out again. Has the Kashmir issue been resolved at Simla ? Far from it, it has been reopened anew. The portion of Kashmir that is with us has also been a subject of dispute at Simla. So far we had been saying that Kashmir is a part of India, that its accession to India is final. I read the speech of Shri Krishna Menon delivered in 1954 in U.N.O. He is present here. This is what he said :

> "Kashmir is a situation created by Pakistani aggression"

Was Kashmir not made a subject of dispute at Simla ? What is meant by a "final settlement of Jammu and Kashmir" ? We have undone all that we had been asserting at the United Nations. We have covered with dust what our own advocates had argued. At Simla our Government deviated from the country's stand on Kashmir. We have become a laughing stock in the world. What is after all meant by a "final settlement of Jammu and Kashmir ?" We had said that Pakistan is an aggressor in Kashmir, that it had no *locus standi* in Kashmir, that it must vacate Kashmir and go. I would again like to quote from the speech of the leader of the Indian delegation before the Security Council in 1954 :

> "Therefore, our country has faced with the position that part of our territory was invaded and the invasion had to be resisted, and, more important, it had to be rolled back."

This was India's stand so far. Is it not a fact that the Indian side had presented before Pakistan a proposal which accepted the division of Kashmir along the cease-fire line with minor adjustments ? Is it also not true that at Simla India did not even once tell Pakistan that it was the aggressor and must withdraw from Kashmir ? Those who partitioned India in 1947 in the hope of peace but could not achieve it, those who pushed the country into four wars now want to purchase peace at the cost of one-third territory of Kashmir!

We had said in the United Nations that our sovereignty, our rights, in Kashmir were not negotiable. How did then Kashmir become a subject of negotiations ? What is the meaning of a "final settlement of Jammu and Kashmir" ? Nobody has the right to give away one-third of our land in Kashmir to Pakistan. In 1962 we had taken an oath in this House that we will not rest in peace so long as our territory was not freed from the aggressor. This oath was taken at the time of Pandit Nehru, when Chinese invasion took place. The same words were repeated in the time of Shastriji : The aggressor will have to vacate its aggression. But today the aggressor is being told that we will negotiate the final solution of Kashmir with him. Is that the success of our Prime Minister's diplomacy at Simla ? Is that the way of establishing a lasting peace ?

Mr. Bhutto Achieved His Three Objectives

Sir, Mr. Bhutto had come to Simla with three objectives : recovery of lost territory, release of war prisoners and to make Kashmir again a subject-matter of dispute. Mr. Bhutto was successful in his first object, since our Government accepted to return the territory it had occupied. What happened to the declaration that the land we had taken will not be returned ? The Prime Minister can say that she had never said so. Today the supporters of the Prime Minister are declaring all over the country that she had said that we did not want an inch of Pakistani land. We also do not want an inch of land belonging to Pakistan, but Pakistan cannot be allowed to sit pretty on the 30,000 square miles of our territory it has occupied in Kashmir. You are telling it to take back its land, but are not asking it to return our land. We had taken its territory after it attacked us on 3rd December. Pakistan was also an aggressor in Kashmir. If our Prime Minister wanted to be very liberal and project herself as the apostle of peace in the world she could have returned the land won in the war of 1971, but could have at the same time asked Pakistan to vacate our territory in Kashmir for which our people have made sacrifices and which is a part of India under the law and the Constitution.

It is argued that such a stand would have broken the negotiations and built up tensions. Should we alone care for tensions ? Does Mr. Bhutto not care for tensions ? Can peace be one-sided ? I had said it in Simla, and I reiterate it again, that there was no need to break the negotiations. We could have told Mr. Bhutto, without parting with the land, that we were happy to meet him and will be glad to meet him again; but the land we had won will not be returned until Pakistan vacated our land in Kashmir. Why was this not done ?

Is it Easier to Keep Land or War-Prisoners ?

It is now being said that we have returned the land but the prisoners of war will not be returned till permanent peace is restored. This is the Prime Minister's statement at the Press conference. I want to ask whether it is easier to keep the land or the prisoners of war. The land which is under our occupation has displaced 10 lakh people of Pakistan. This has become a headache for Pakistan. Therefore, recovery of land was a priority for Mr. Bhutto and we accepted that priority by giving away that land under the Simla Agreement. In the words of the Prime Minister the first step has been taken. Negotiations are going on, air services will also be resumed, a beginning of new relations is being made, then how can you keep the prisoners of war ? Mr. Bhutto has already declared that he would mould world opinion for release of prisoners, that is, he will try to build up world opinion against us. Further, when there is cessation of hostilities you cannot continue to detain prisoners of war. You can argue that the prisoners belong to Bangladesh, not us. But when the Prime Minister is trying to tie up the issue of prisoners with permanent peace it would have to be admitted that Simla did not bring an agreement of permanent peace, and that is why we are opposing it. We have returned the land, we will have to return the prisoners of war and the pandora box of Kashmir has been opened again !

Is there a Secret Understanding ?

A state of uncertainty has come into the minds of the people of Jammu and Kashmir, particularly those in the valley, as a result of the Simla Agreement. There was lull in Kashmir Valley for two or three days. Those who were supporters of India were crest-fallen while the separatists were in high spirits. I want to know what decision was taken about Kashmir at Simla. I am sorry to say that some secret agreement has taken place. I want to know whether Mr. Bhutto has given some assurances to the Prime Minister or the Prime Minister has given any assurance to Mr. Bhutto. My doubts are strengthened because Piloo Mody who is Mr. Bhutto's friend says there is nothing that they have not shared between themselves. I don't know of what things he is talking about. But one statement of his is significant and also indicative. He says that there should be a softening of the border, that is, let people come and go, let trade and commerce go on, let this generation forget Kashmir and leave the matter to the next generation.

SHRI PILOO MODY : Only then you will be able to go.

SHRI VAJPAYEE : I have been there only recently.

Softening of the border means leaving Kashmir to the mercy of infiltrators. But I want to know whether such an agreement has taken place. What transpired in Simla behind the curtain ? It is said that Pakistan has agreed to solve all issues peacefully. This is being trumpeted about. Our External Affairs Minister said: " It is virtually a no-war pact." So, it is "virtually", not actually, a no-war pact. Mr. Bhutto says he has not made any no-war pact. The truth is that we have given up our stand about a "no-war pact" at Simla. Pandit Nehru wanted a no-war pact, but Pakistan did not accept the proposal. Shastriji said there should be a no-war pact, but that too was not accepted by Pakistan. Smt. Indira Gandhi in her speech also stated that there should be an agreement on avoidance of war which was also rejected by Pakistan. Even then we say that Pakistan has accepted it, while Pakistan says it has not. Now a controversy has started on the interpretation of the Simla Agreement. But this kind of thing has not happened for the first time. Whenever there was an agreement between India and Pakistan, Pakistan had said that it will not take to arms and will solve the problems in a peaceful manner. Here I want to quote from article 3 of the Simla Agreement which was arrived at on 3rd July, 1972 :

> "In accordance with the charter of the United Nations they will refrain from the threat of the use of force against the territorial integrity or political independence of the other."
>
> The Tashkent Agreement signed on 10 January, 1965 says :
>
> "They affirm their obligations under the charter not to have recourse to force and to settle their disputes through peaceful means."

Thus in 1965 also Pakistan had accepted that it will not use force. Then why did it use force ? Before that, on 23rd October, 1959, there was an agreement between India and Pakistan, from which I want to reproduce a few lines :

> "Both Governments affirm their determination to solve border disputes by negotiations and agree that all disputes, if not settled by negotiations, be referred to an impartial tribunal."

Nehru-Noon Agreement

Thus it says settle the dispute by negotiations or refer it to tribunal. Now it is said it will not be referred to a third party for mediation. I will talk about that also, but it was said in 1959 that disputes should be solved by negotiations. A year before that, on 12th September, 1958, the Nehru-Noon Agreement said :

"The Prime Ministers further agree that pending the settlement of unresolved disputes there should be no disturbance of *status quo* by force."

The history of 25 years tells us that whenever Pakistan wants to acquire something it speaks the language of peace. But it continues to prepare for war while speaking the language of peace and instigates the people for war immediately after achieving the objective. Therefore, there should have been a guarantee that old history will not be repeated. If Pakistan said it will not resort to use of force it should have been asked why it was accumulating arms. Why this defence budget of Rs. 446 crores ? Pakistan was partitioned, Bangladesh got independence, Pakistan's defence requirements were reduced. The borders of Pakistan shrank and the size of its army should also be reduced and there should be reduction in arms as well. If the assurance regarding use of force has any substance there must be curtailment in the armed forces and weapons and, above all, Pakistan should come out of the military alliances of SEATO and CENTO. Did we emphasise this in our talks ? Did we say that there was no meaning in not taking recourse to force so long as Pakistan continued military preparations ? The Defence Minister is not in the House, but can he deny that recently Pakistan received 30 MIG aircraft from China and 36 aircraft including Mirage from France and other Muslim countries ? Our Government claimed that 70 Pakistani aircraft had been destroyed in the war, but Pakistan has now acquired more than 70. It has also added two divisions in the army. Mr. Bhutto had gone on an arms purchase mission. Two new divisions have been formed and two more are under way. (*Interruptions*)....I accept that Mr. Anthony is a defence expert, he is confiring what I said.

Pakistan Still Wants Arms

What is the meaning of non-use of force ? Can we forget that while fighting elections Mr. Bhutto had declared that Pakistan will leave military alliances ? He won the elections, came to power, was talking of peace at Simla, but is not prepared to implement the assurances of his party. He must severe ties with SEATO. Why does he want arms, against whom he wants them ? India is now becoming his friend, India wants a relationship of brotherhood with Pakistan, Afghanistan is his friend, China and America are his friends, he has recently visited Moscow also. Who then is his enemy ? It is argued that if we had asked Pakistan for reduction in arms, it could also have asked us to do the same. But we could have told it that in view of our size, our borders, our expanse, our defence problem and danger from China it is not possible for us to effect a reduction in arms or our armed forces. I have heard that at Simla it was argued that Pakistan is backward and it should not spend much money on arms and that one of our representatives rolled out statistics to that effect before Pakistan delegates, rendering them tight-lipped. But what was the outcome of all this eloquence ? Only that Pakistan said it will solve all problems with India peacefully. It is not a new thing. Every time Pakistan has said the same thing. Every time it has spoken of a peaceful solution and every time it has broken that promise. The history of Pakistan till today is not the history of honouring agreements; it is a history of violating them. At Simla we did not merely want an agreement, we wanted something solid, not these paper assurances. Our Government has failed to achieve anything solid.

No Third Power Interference in the Sub-Continent

Another thing being said is that Pakistan has agreed for a peaceful solution of disputes between the two parties. What does that mean ? We do not want any interference of third powers. These third powers through their interference have not only made us fight, weakened us, vitiated our position, but also prevented India from emerging as a great power. We do not want interference of third powers in this sub-continent, but Pakistan has not severed its relations with the powers that have supplied it arms. So far as solving the issues mutually is concerned Pakistan has not said that it will not raise the question of Kashmir in the United Nations. Things are happening just the other way round. Mr. Bhutto says that Kashmir can be raised there. Not only that, he is inciting the people of Kashmir to revolt against India. He is giving them assurances that if they rise in revolt against India, against their own country, Pakistan will shed the last drop of blood in their support (*Interruptions*). Is that the way of keeping third powers away from this part of the world ? The Indian delegation should have demanded the withdrawal of the Kashmir issue from the United Nations. Far from that, when our Government said there was no need for the United Nations observers Pakistan officially declared that the observers would remain, that the UN resolution remained effective, and if there was no agreement on Kashmir Pakistan would raise the issue in that forum. Even if Pakistan does not raise it who can stop China from raising the Kashmir issue in the United Nations ? Being a friend of Pakistan China can oblige it (*Interruptions*)...What will then happen to bilateral talks ?

SHRI S.M. BANERJEE : Tell us what should be done.

SHRI VAJPAYEE : For the present, you allow me to continue.

Tashkent is Repeated at Simla

Mr. Deputy Speaker, Sir, we have arrived at an agreement at Simla, but it must be reconsidered in the light of what Mr. Bhutto has said about it, particularly about Kashmir, in the National Assembly. The root of the trouble is Kashmir and Mr. Bhutto says that if they revolt against India, Pakistanis will shed their blood. He is inciting them to revolt. Is it not an incitement against the territorial integrity of India and interference in our internal affairs ? The ink on the agreement has not dried when Mr. Bhutto violated it. Are we unilaterally bound by the agreement ? The Prime Minister could say that we had extended the hand of goodwill but he had vitiated the atmosphere by his speech in the National Assembly and that talks will have to be held again for implementing the agreement...(*Interruptions*)...I want to know from the government whether Mr. Bhutto's speech in the National

Assembly is in tune with the spirit of the Agreement. The Prime Minister had to say at her press conference, "not exactly" ? What is the meaning of this "not exactly" ? What responsibility has Pakistan accepted in regard to Kashmir ? Who started the trouble in Kashmir can never be decided. Pakistan can send infiltrators and say that the people of Kashmir are fighting for their rights and Pakistan was bound to support them. You may say that they were Pakistanis, not the people of Kashmir, but the situation will deteriorate and we will again be where we were. What is left of the Simla Agreement then ?

In this connection I want to give an example from the speech of the then Foreign Minister, Shri Chagla, after the Tashkent Agreement. Look how much similarity there is :

> "It was emphasised in Tashkent Declaration that one country will not interfere in the internal affairs of another country. All differences should be solved through peaceful means and contacts at various levels should be established. Mediation by a third country was considered unnecessary under this Declaration and it was emphasised that the two countries should solve the dispute by mutual talks."

On going through the Tashkent Declaration I found so many similarities—the same praise and felicitations, the same song of peace, tall statements and expressions of goodwill. We had expected that Tashkent will not be repeated at Simla and the Prime Minister also in one of her foreign visits had said that the people of India will not tolerate repetition of Tashkent. My submission is that this agreement is worse than Tashkent because it is not 1966 but 1972. We had emerged victorious and Pakistan was defeated. You may call it proud talk. But did Mr. Bhutto not proudly talk after 1962 ? When a member of the Indian delegation, Shri Gundevia went to talk to him, Mr. Bhutto said : " Mr. Gundevia, don't forget that you are a defeated country." It was not necessary for us to say so. But we should have taken our steps in a manner consistent with the achievement of our Jawans in changing history, changing geography, defeating Pakistan, liberating Bangladesh—all of which provided a golden opportunity for establishing permanent peace. We could have told them that it was not 1966, now all questions will be properly resolved, all old accounts will be settled.

The Government was Trapped in Mirage of Peace

But we were trapped in a mirage. The speech that Mr. Bhutto made in the National Assembly of Pakistan was hardly necessary for him to make. In fact Pakistan is happy because under the agreement it got its land back. It will also get the prisoners back and the way to raise a hue and cry over Kashmir is opened. What more does Pakistan want ? But the Pakistani President perhaps tried to show at Simla that a crisis may overtake him if he returned empty handed, and pleaded for filling his bag, and *Devi* Indira was pleased and filled his bag. The Prime Minister may please excuse me for using the words *Devi* Indira. But what did she bring for the country from Simla ? This country was united during the war; it was the duty of the Prime Minister to keep up this unity during peace also (*Interruptions*). Even if there is a single dissenting voice it means the country is not united. Do not forget that this is not my lone voice, there are lakhs of voices behind me (*Interruptions*). Mr. Deputy Speaker, I do not want to get involved in this controversy. I want to know why this kind of agreement was arrived at in Simla.

What Happened on Last Day of Talks ?

I went to Simla, not on the invitation of the Prime Minister, but on my own. Mr. Bhutto had brought leaders of opposition with him. Our Prime Minister did not have time to meet the opposition leaders here. Hon'ble Shri Lal Bahadur Shastri had met the opposition leaders before going to Tashkent. For two days I was in Simla. I also know what happened on the third day. A deadlock had occurred. The representative of the Indira Government was taking a tough stand. What happened was that the Indian representative sent a draft and asked them to sign. Shri T.N. Kaul made a statement : "If the President of Pakistan wants to meet the Prime Minister she is available". That was the language. This was the language of the last day. Let alone talking, Pakistan was not prepared to bend on the Kashmir issue. But the Indian Government bent down. I want to ask the Prime Minister what transpired during her 15 minutes' talks with Mr. Bhutto. How was the attitude of the Indian Government changed ? Now Sardar Swaran Singh says Mr. Bhutto changed. When did he change ? On the first day, the second day or the third day ? On the first day Mr. Bhutto's face was on one side and Smt. Indira Gandhi's on the other. Press people were present. Or, is it that Mr. Bhutto did not change but Sardar Swaran Singh's glasses changed ? With which glasses did he see Mr. Bhutto on the last day ? What colour was there on those glasses ?

SHRI RAJ BAHADUR, Minister of Parliamentary Affairs : Hearts are changing.

SHRI VAJPAYEE : Yes, hearts are changing nowadays. It is not a joke, it is a matter of hearts.

Mr. Deputy Speaker, there is a curtain of mystery on what happened on the last day. This mystery should be disclosed. How did the failing conference suddenly turn successful ? How were the talks which were on the verge of breaking down, saved ? Is It true that a representative of Soviet Russia was present at Simla ? Is it true that the Soviet Ambassador at Dacca was present in Simla during the talks ? (*Interruptions*). Even before that is it true that when Mr. Nixon and Mr. Brezhnev met in Moscow they discussed the problems between India and Pakistan, particularly the war of 1971 and its outcome ? Is it true that when the Soviet President Podgorny was going to Hanoi he got detained at Calcutta for talks ? Is it not a fact that the weather was perfect and the sky was clear for a flight, but since talks had to take place weather was described to be bad ? There were so many people present who could vouchsafe that the weather was good. I want to know what transpired during the talks at the airport. I also want to ask whether there was a talk on the hotline with the Kremlin on the last day of negotiations at Simla.

An All-Party Committee Should Inquire

Mr. Deputy Speaker, Hon'ble Speaker is not present here and I, therefore, request you to set up an all-party committee to enquire into the allegation that on the last day the Government of India, which was not prepared for the agreement, consented to agree due to direct intervention of Soviet Russia and indirect intervention of the USA. But it is necessary for the enquiry that you take in your possession all the files of the Ministry of External Affairs relating to this matter. Further, please also allow the telephone operators at Simla to appear before the Committee and tender free evidence...(*Interruptions*)...

Sir, it cannot be denied that both Russia and America want that India and Pakistan should arrive at an agreement. Is it not true that Russia wants to reestablish its lost influence in Pakistan ? Is it not true that Russia wants to go up to the borders of Burma ? It is not a new objective of Russia's foreign policy. It is an old objective dating from the times of the Czar. Mr. Bhutto praised Russia at the Lahore airport. It was not merely an expression of courtesy. It was an expression of gratitude for a favour and that favour was the Simla Agreement.

Mr. Deputy Speaker, I would like to finish now. There were four wars. In every war we have won, but in every peace, we have lost. We have won in the battle-field, but have lost at the negotiating table. We have won in the strategy of war, but have lost in the strategy of diplomacy. We had thought that a new history will be written at Simla after the war of 1971, but what has been written is shameful history. It is history that has washed away the sacrifices of our Jawans. This Simla agreement is a betrayal of the country's interests.

Blunder at Simla

Prime Minister Indira Gandhi and President Bhutto are made of the same stuff, and represent a class of people, who are not interested in ending disputes. They want some issue or the other to remain alive. This was an opportunity for permanent peace which we let slip. The statement of the External Affairs Minister is proof enough that permanent peace depends on how Pakistan implements the agreement. The rulers of India and Pakistan have so far been putting the people of the two countries at loggerheads. They have been saying that there should be no foreign interference. But both of them have been inviting foreign interference. The Simla Agreement has confirmed that the mental frame of both Smt. Indira Gandhi and Mr. Bhutto is the same. We have seen its evidence. A language dispute is going on in Sind, that the language of that province is Sindhi and Urdu should not be thrust on it. Shri Bhutto gave the decision that it would neither be Sindhi nor Urdu, but English. It is the same here. Hindi will not come. If there is dispute between Hindi and Tamil neither Hindi nor Tamil, nor any other Indian language will prevail. Sir, you may ask what this has got to do with the Simla Agreement. The Prime Minister is concerned with Simla and what I am saying concerns the Prime Minister.

I say we have committed a blunder at Simla. There is still time to undo that wrong. Talks should again be held with Pakistan before vacating the territory. In fact, for a meaningful debate on this subject we should have been given a copy of Mr. Bhutto's three and a half hours' speech. We do not know the details of what Mr. Bhutto said in his speech. All that we know is what is being broadcast by All India Radio. He can be asked for a clarification, and vacation of land can be stopped.

Things will Now be Said Frankly

I would also like to say that the territory won by us cannot be returned without amending the Indian Constitution. Indian territory has been defined as territory acquired.

We have conquered that territory. Territory can be acquired by conquest. We have established civil administration and unfurled the tri-colour there. The Chief Minister of Rajasthan has also visited Chachro and assured the Sindhi refugees and its residents that this land will not be returned. He not only asked that farming be started but also distributed land to them. Today one lakh refugees are facing death and to save their lives they have come to India.

SMT. INDIRA GANDHI : Why do you say this ?

SHRI VAJPAYEE : It is necessary to say this. We have had enough of it, now no more. Things will now be said frankly, not behind the curtain. You are openly saying that the Sindhi refugees will be pushed into Pakistan. We sent our army to save Bangladeshi refugees and here we want to pull back our army to let these people be killed. I request you to reconsider this agreement and not send back the refugees who have come here. If the Prime Minister thinks that this agreement has the approval of the people let her have a referendum on it. Give every major citizen an opportunity to express his opinion on this Agreement. We will accept the judgment of the people. Thank you.

Madam Prime Minister, Don't Misquote Me

Mr. Deputy Speaker, Sir, I rise to make a personal explanation with your permission. I was not present in the House yesterday when the Prime Minister made her speech. Even if I were present it would not have been proper to interrupt her. I want to quote a sentence from the Prime Minister's speech yesterday. She said :

> " How dare he say that we are leaving the people of Kashmir to the tender mercies of the Pakistanis" ?

I did not use any such phraseology in my speech. I made a mention of Kashmir at two places. At one place I said that as a result of the Simla Agreement....

MR. DEPUTY SPEAKER : The Hon. member can read it out. There can be no debate on it now.

SHRI VAJPAYEE : But what I had said should be heard.

MR. DEPUTY SPEAKER : In the first place the Hon. member should have been here and protested and that would have gone on record. The Hon. member had requested the Speaker and the Speaker had agreed. But under the rules no debatable matter should be allowed and no speech can be allowed. He can just read out what he has given to the Speaker.

SHRI VAJPAYEE : I am reading out what I actually said. I did not speak the words the Prime Minister has attributed to me—how can I explain this unless I tell what I had actually spoken ?

MR. DEPUTY SPEAKER : That is not exactly contained in what he has given to the Speaker. Then it becomes a debate....

SHRI K. MANOHARAN (Madras North) : Let him clarify the position.

MR. DEPUTY SPEAKER : If I allow him, then I would be violating the rules ?..

SHRI VAJPAYEE : What rule ?

MR. DEPUTY SPEAKER : The rule under which he has written to the Speaker. He can only read that out and he cannot go into the details.

SHRI VAJPAYEE : Am I to read out only the portion of the speech delivered by the Prime Minister or should I not read out from my speech also ?...

MR. DEPUTY SPEAKER : He can read out only what he has written to the Speaker.

SHRI VAJPAYEE : Not exactly. You have to allow me.

MR. DEPUTY SPEAKER : No

SHRI VAJPAYEE : It is not in the rules. There are no such rules.

Lok Sabha on August 1, 1972 while making personal explanation

SHRI R.V. BADE (Khargone) : Kindly read rule 353.

SHRI VAJPAYEE : You have allowed me to give my personal explanation.

MR. DEPUTY SPEAKER : The Hon. member may kindly resume his seat for a minute...

SMT. INDIRA GANDHI, Prime Minister : May I submit, Sir, that you allow the Hon'ble member to state what he had said, if you have no objection. It is up to you, Sir.

SHRI VAJPAYEE : I think now you are prepared to waive the rules...

MR. DEPUTY SPEAKER : The Hon. member should not anticipate what I am going to say.

The rule says :

"A member may, with the permission of the Speaker, make a personal explanation although there is no question before the House, but in this case no debatable matter may be brought forward and no debate shall arise."

SHRI K. MANOHARAN : Here there is no debate. He will only read out from his own speech.

MR. DEPUTY SPEAKER : Let me finish what I was going to say. The Hon. member has written to the Speaker and his letter has been accepted and this is to be read to the House. But if a debate arises from this, then...

SHRI MUKHTIAR SINGH MALIK (Rohtak) : He is only making a personal explanation.

MR. DEPUTY SPEAKER : If he is going to start reading out what he said yesterday and what he did not say yesterday, then it becomes a kind of debate.

SHRI R.R. SHARMA (Banda) : He is only giving an explanation.

SHRI MUKHTIAR SINGH MALIK : He is only explaining the position. What does explanation mean ?

MR. DEPUTY SPEAKER : It is the convention that first of all the Speaker must assure himself that no debate would arise...

SHRI VAJPAYEE : I met the Speaker in his Chamber and I convinced him...

MR. DEPUTY SPEAKER : On the basis of this letter...

SHRI VAJPAYEE : On the basis of this letter I sought his permission to offer a personal explanation. How can you prevent me from quoting from my own speech ? It was not perhaps correctly understood by the Prime Minister and that was why she had made that remark.

MR. DEPUTY SPEAKER : The Hon. member should have incorporated all that in his letter to the Speaker, but he has not done that.

SHRI VAJPAYEE : It is not needed. I have sought his permission to make a personal explanation.

MR. DEPUTY SPEAKER : I am in the hands of the House.

SHRI K. MANOHARAN : The House has already agreed.

MR. DEPUTY SPEAKER : I have to take the sense of the House. I am in the hands of the House. If the House would like me to depart from this well-laid rule, I have no objection...

SHRI VAJPAYEE : There is no rule...

SHRI K. MANOHARAN : You may put the question, then.

MR. DEPUTY SPEAKER : I shall take the sense of the House.

SHRI SWARAN SINGH, Minister of External Affairs : We cannot certainly be a party to your departing from the rule, and you, Sir, are in the Chair now, and you are the best person to interpret that rule. From the letter that he has sent it is evident that it was only a limited matter and he has quoted one sentence from the Prime Minister's speech. While making his personal explanation he cannot go over the whole speech.

SHRI VAJPAYEE : I am not going over the whole of my speech.

MR. DEPUTY SPEAKER : He says that he has not said that. He can say that he had not said that. What more does he want now ?

SHRI MUKHTIAR SINGH MALIK : That is the only explanation that he wants to give.

MR. DEPUTY SPEAKER : Let us not lose time over this now. In the first place the Hon. member should have been here. It is necessary that every member who participates in the debate should be present in the House when another member speaks so that if the other member says something which he says he has not said he can protest and that could go on record.

SHRI R.V. BADE : But there was interruption.

MR. DEPUTY SPEAKER : The Hon. member should have protested then, and that would have gone on record. It is an unusual thing that when a speech is made the member is not here and then he comes forward the next day and says that he never said that and, therefore, he has to offer a personal explanation. This by itself is unusual...

SHRI VAJPAYEE : It is not unusual. This has been done here many times.

MR. DEPUTY SPEAKER : I would say this that this is an exception and it is not a precedent. If we start this convention every member will say that he must be given on opportunity for personal explanation and to say that he never said this, or he never said that. Then there would be no end to it. Even so, the Hon. member went to the Speaker with the written document and the Speaker has agreed, and I assume that he had permitted him to make a personal explanation on the basis of what he had written to him.

SHRI VAJPAYEE : Will you please read out my letter to the Speaker ? Then I will be satisfied.

MR. DEPUTY SPEAKER : Yes. He has written :

> "Under Rule 357, I seek your permission to give a personal explanation in regard to the speech made by the Prime Minister. While intervening in the debate on the Simla pact the Prime Minister said :
>
> > How dare he say that we are leaving the people of Kashmir to the tender mercies of the Pakistanis ?"
>
> "I never said anything like that in my speech. Either the Prime Minister did not listen to my speech attentively or she has deliberately attributed thoughts and words which were never expressed by me.
>
> "As I must make my position clear I seek your permission to make a personal explanation."

The Hon. Speaker has permitted it.

SHRI VAJPAYEE : I am satisfied now.

Simla Accord has Solved Nothing

Sir, I want to draw the attention of the Hon. Foreign Minister to the following matter of urgent public importance and request him to make a statement thereon :

"Pakistan's continued intransigence in respect of delineation of the Line of Actual Control in Jammu and Kashmir"

SHRI SWARAN SINGH, Minister of External Affairs : Mr. Speaker, Sir, Hon'ble members would recall my statement in the House on August 30, at the conclusion of the meeting between the representatives of India and Pakistan, wherein I had conveyed the agreement of both sides to the delineation of the line of control in Jammu and Kashmir along its entire length. I had also stated that maps showing this agreed line would be exchanged by both sides and that delineation of the line would be completed by the 4th September, 1972 and withdrawals to the international border would be completed by the 15th September. In accordance with the Simla Agreement the line of control had to be mutually respected. Therefore its delineation has to be agreed so that its inviolability may be ensured by both sides.

The Senior Military Commanders of India and Pakistan, who were entrusted with the task of delineating the line of control on maps, have so far held nine rounds of discussions. By the seventh round which was completed on 18th October, an agreement was reached on 19 maps delineating the entire length of the line of control from the Chhamb area on the international border to Partapur sector in the north. These maps were to be signed in the eighth round. On that occasion, however, Pakistan's senior Military Commander raised a fresh controversy over a pocket approximately $1\frac{1}{2}$ square miles in area which is in Pakistan's occupation but separate from the line of control. Several messages have been exchanged between the Chiefs of the Army Staff of India and Pakistan on this issue and as a result further meetings took place between the Senior Military Commanders on November 7 and 9. However, these discussions failed to iron out the differences. It is now being considered whether the stage has been reached for a meeting at another level to resolve this question. Hon. members would appreciate that as the talks are still in progress, it would not be in our national interest to discuss this matter in greater detail. The major task of delineation of the line of control in Jammu and Kashmir in terms of the Simla and Delhi Agreements has been completed on maps. It is hoped that the remaining problem will also be resolved by

Lok Sabha on November 13, 1972 while moving the calling attention motion regarding Pakistan's intransigence in Delineation of the Line of Actual Control in Jammu and Kashmir

further bilateral discussions. After the delineation of the line of control is approved by the two Governments the withdrawal of troops to the international border will be completed in the shortest possible time. We hope the Pakistan Government will view this matter in a realistic and constructive manner.

SHRI VAJPAYEE : Mr. Chairman, Sir, the Foreign Minister's statement has not done justice to the objective for which this Calling Attention motion was moved. Its purpose was that this House and the country should know on which mountain or plain the Simla Accord is derailed and what is the dispute that has now erupted between the two countries. The Foreign Minister has said that it is not in the national interest to discuss the matter in greater detail. I do not agree with his definition of national interest. Discussion with Pakistan can go on, but this House and the country must be taken into confidence on the points on which the discussions have come to a halt. National interest demands that we are informed that the work of delineation of the line of control is stopped.

Take the House into Confidence

I have read in the newspapers that on this issue there has been correspondence between the Prime Minister and the President of Pakistan. Parliamentary convention requires that such correspondence is tabled in the House and we are taken into confidence. From the correspondence we would have known what the point of dispute is and what is being done to resolve it. There has been correspondence between the Army Chiefs, and that is also not disclosed. It is difficult for me or any member of the House to know what is going on behind the curtain of secrecy.

I am reminded of July 31, when I raised a lone voice of caution about Pakistan's intentions. Now even the Prime Minister is saying that the Pakistani attitude has hardened.

SHRI PILOO MODY : Great similarities.

SHRI VAJPAYEE : Since when has it hardened ? This Calling Attention Notice is on a limited subject. I would like that an opportunity may be given to discuss Indo-Pak relations in the House.

The Minister of External Affairs has admitted in his statement that the Delhi Agreement which was arrived at to save the Simla Agreement—an agreement on agreement—provided that the line of control in Jammu-Kashmir will be demarcated. To quote him :

> ".....wherein I had conveyed the agreement of both sides to the delineation of the line of control in Jammu and Kashmir along its entire length."

It was a question of delineation of the entire border. There was talk among the Commanders. It is said that an agreement on the maps was reached and a date for signing it was fixed. But Pakistan backed out. I want to ask when Pakistan had backed out, why did our Chief of Staff tell Pakistan that if there was no meeting of minds on the $1\frac{1}{2}$ mile territory let it be left out, we are prepared to call back our force from there. Does the dispute here not come under the agreement of delineation of the entire border ? Where was the question of going back upon the decision of delineation of the entire border ? But our Government told Pakistan that discussion on this issue will continue and we will withdraw our forces.

Pakistan Trying to Rewrite Simla Agreement

Pakistan did not agree to this. Pakistan is accusing us of trying to rewrite the Simla Agreement. The President of Pakistan is claiming that it is a matter of principle with them. Well, is it not a matter of principle for us ? After all, the armies of both countries have to return to the international border. Thathu Chak or Thakur Chowk is our area. That must be returned to us and Pakistani forces must withdraw from there. But we are prepared to keep that dispute open and withdraw our armies from the border. Is it not a change in the stand of the Government of India ? What are the reasons for this change ? So long as Pakistan does not vacate that area the work of delineation of the border will not be completed, and so long as the work of delineation is not completed how can we withdraw our forces ?

Whether Pakistan had approved of any agreement or not about this area is also a mystery. At first it was said on behalf of our Government that the Pakistani Commander had agreed and only signatures were left to be affixed to the agreement. Pakistan was also informed that we will not discuss this issue and if they want to meet for signing they may send their representative to Delhi. But the Government backed out from this stand also. Now it is being said that we are prepared to talk. This has made us a laughing stock in the international field. It is being alleged that differences have arisen on questions of fact. After all, when the commanders meet a record of their discussions is kept. What does that record say ? Did Pakistan agree or not ? If Pakistan had once agreed why did we not stick to the stand that only signatures were left to be affixed and no more talks would be held ? If Pakistan does not want to honour the agreement the armed forces will also not be withdrawn because the border had not been demarcated.

We Surrendered Our Territory

The issue of the return of the armed forces to the international border not only involves return from Thathu Chak, which is also known as Thakur Chowk, but also from the Chhamb area. The Pakistani army had entered Chhamb after violating the international border. The posts of Lipa Valley belonged to us, which were occupied by Pakistan after 17 December. We gave away Chaknod for exchange of these posts. We surrendered our territory to Pakistan. We bargained for our land, we did not protect it.

Today we feel distressed for the one million displaced people of Pakistan. The Government of India is worried that they should be able to sow and harvest the rabi crop. But what about those people of Chhamb who have been displaced and rendered homeless ? The Indian Government can demand vacation of Chhamb area because under the Simla Agreement the armies must withdraw from wherever they have crossed the international border.

I would like the External Affairs Minister to give a clear answer to these questions. Ministers in the Government are speaking in different words which is creating a great deal of confusion among the people. Sometimes it is said that Pakistan is going to attack and at other times they say there is no danger from Pakistan. We want to know from the Hon'ble Foreign Minister whether Pakistan is following the Simla Agreement with the same earnestness in which we had entered it and, if not, the reasons for the change in the attitude of Pakistan. If the attitude of Pakistan has changed will India make one-sided efforts for peace ? Can one-sided peace efforts succeed ? Thank you.

American Arms to Pakistan

Sir, The Government of India have seen press reports based on *the Washington Post* of USA of March 29, 1977, to the effect that the US President has approved the sale of over 2 billion dollars worth of arms to a number of countries including Pakistan. Until the proposal is formally submitted for approval to the US Congress the precise list of materials to be available for sale to different countries will not be known. We understand, however, that the sales pertain to an ongoing programme going back several years for refurbishing of equipment previously supplied by the US to Pakistan.

As the House is aware, India is fast normalising its relations with Pakistan and seeks to explore the possibilities of increasing beneficial cooperation between the countries of this region in order to make our sub-continent free from tension and a region of stability. This, we believe, is in the wider interests of peace in Asia and should be welcomed both by positive encouragement and restraint by the powers who have expressed their satisfaction at these trends.

Dangers of Arms Sale

We have often in the past and more recently brought to the notice of the US Government our concern at the dangers of arms sales which could upset this process. The Government of India have noted with satisfaction reports of President Carter advocating restraint in the transfer and sale of arms to developing countries. As recently as on March 17, addressing the Special Session of the UN General Assembly, President Carter said, "There must be a wider effort to reduce the flow of weapons to all the trouble spots of the globe. Accordingly, we will try to reach broader agreements among producer and consumer nations to limit the export of conventional arms, and we will take initiatives of our own, since the United States has become one of the major arms suppliers of the world." It is, therefore, our hope that arms sale policies by the USA would not reverse the trend towards normalisation, or contribute to revival of tensions, stimulating an arms race and imposing greater economic burden on the people of the sub-continent. That is all I have to say. Thank you.

Rajya Sabha on April 4, 1977 as Minister of External Affairs

Visit to Pakistan

Mr. Deputy Chairman, Sir, ever since the Janata Party assumed office last year the major thrust of the Government of India's foreign policy has been towards fostering the development of friendliest possible relations between India and her neighbours. It was on the basis of this policy that I have earlier visited Afghanistan, Nepal, Bhutan and Burma. The same policy motivated my goodwill visit to Pakistan from February 6 to 8, 1978.

I went with no agenda for discussion. My intention, as an emissary of good-will, was to make clear India's desire for a relationship of peace and friendship with Pakistan on the basis of respect for sovereignty, territorial integrity, non-interference in internal affairs and mutual benefit.

The past history of the relations between the two countries has created some problems which both sides have to recognise, to face and to attempt to resolve. I mentioned to Mr. Agha Shahi, Adviser on Foreign Affairs, Government of Pakistan, that while it is true that India happens to be a big country we want to improve relations between India and Pakistan on the basis of equality, understanding and goodwill. This clearly implies respect not only for the sovereignty of each country but the right of each country to determine its own political and social system. One of the most heartening features of our general elections last year was the absence of any controversy over our relations with Pakistan. During 1977 there were far-reaching political changes in Pakistan also. The fact that despite political upheavals in both countries the climate of Indo-Pakistan relations did not receive a setback is a tribute to the maturity of our two peoples. This encouraged me to undertake this mission of goodwill.

During my visit, I had discussions with Gen. Zia-ul-Haq, Chief of Army Staff and Chief Martial Law Administrator and Mr. Agha Shahi, Adviser on Foreign Affairs. Our discussions were held in a very cordial atmosphere. They covered bilateral relations, and also international issues such as the North-South dialogue and the U.N. General Assembly's Special Session on Disarmament, on which we had a broad similarity of approach. During our discussions, the Pakistan side referred to the Simla Agreement. We assured them that the Janata Government stands by this Agreement. In this context, the Pakistan side made a mention of Kashmir. Both of us stated our respective position. while recalling that the Simla Agreement commits both countries to abjure use of force.

During my discussions with Gen. Zia we noted that there has been a significant growth of our trade relations and recognised that they should and could grow in a balanced manner to our mutual advantage. Trade teams of

Rajya Sabha on February 28, 1978 as Minister of External Affairs

the two countries are to meet shortly to review the Trade Agreement of 1975 and to study how two-way trade can develop.

The two sides also had discussions on the need to facilitate a freer flow of people and information between the two countries. In this context, the Government of India are happy to note that there has been some exchange of artists, scholars and sportsmen. We were also happy to welcome Dr. Amir Mohammad, Adviser on Agriculture, Government of Pakistan on February 20, 1978. He is visiting a number of our projects during his stay in India. We hope that his visit will mark the beginning of exchange in the field of science and technology so that experts in both countries can learn from each other's experience.

During my discussions it was also agreed that we should complete the process of exchanging detenus held in either country with utmost expedition. This is a humanitarian problem and we are interested in seeing it resolved as soon as possible.

Another point of agreement was that we would resume talks on the Salal Dam project from where they were left off in October, 1976. A delegation from Pakistan is expected to come here for this purpose shortly. Dates will be fixed according to our mutual convenience.

On behalf of our Prime Minister I transmitted a letter to the Chief Martial Law Administrator formally inviting him to visit India. He accepted the invitation in principle.

Climate of Trust

Sir, there was widespread speculation in the press about my visit before it took place. My own belief is that public opinion in both countries has welcomed the normalisation of our relations and the restoration of the severed links. It is also my belief that there is a recognition in both countries that the pace in the development of our relations can and should be accelerated. We on our part are ready to go ahead. However, we recognise that such acceleration and further cooperation can be possible only with the consent of both the countries.

In conclusion, I would like to state that I am convinced that good relations between the two countries of the sub-continent are in our separate and common interest, and in the interest of the region as a whole. My visit to Pakistan was based on this conviction. I do not think I would be wrong if I say that the discussions I had with Pakistani leaders have led to a better understanding and have helped in the task of removing mis-apprehensions, promoting greater goodwill and better understanding between the two countries. With greater contact between the two peoples and the established Governments there can grow a climate of trust and confidence in which problems can be solved and good-neighbourliness can be patiently fostered. India stands ready to cooperate in the growth of such relations to the extent Pakistan is willing to go.

SHRI SHAYAM LAL YADAV (U.P.) : There should be a debate on the statement made because it contains a sentence which according to me is not correct and that is there were some differences in Indo-Pak relations. Indo-Pak relations have improved for better because of the Simla Agreement. It is not true that there was no difference of opinion as has been stated by Shri Vajpayee. Use of such words only to highlight the success of his visit is not proper. It is therefore necessary to have a debate on the statement made by the Hon. Minister regarding his visit. The main controversial point between India and Pakistan which was solved is again revived; and from your statement it appears that Indo-Pak relations are not good. That is why I submit that there should be a debate on this statement.

SHRI VAJPAYEE : Mr. Deputy Chairman, Sir, I am prepared for a debate. I do not agree with the view expressed by the Hon. member that I made all these statements to highlight the success of my visit. Individuals come and go, relations between countries are not dependent on personalities. The Simla accord was signed by the previous Government. I have said as the Foreign Minister that the present Government is bound by it. When this agreement was signed we were in the opposition and we had opposed it. But when the new Government was formed we said the country is bound by the Simla accord and we are obliged to take steps according to this agreement. It is not correct to say that I had raised a new issue. You have kept certain issues alive in the Simla Accord and have compelled us to take steps in accordance with the Agreement.

SHRI SHYAM LAL YADAV : According to me the use of words "severed relations" in your statement is wrong.

SHRI KHURSHID ALAM KHAN (Delhi) : Sir, I have a clarification to seek. This is from the humanitarian point of view. This is about the visa facilities for going from India to Pakistan and coming from Pakistan to India. There have been difficulties in getting visas for going to Pakistan. I would like to know whether the Hon. Minister had particularly taken up this point—and what are his views— and whether any facilities will be provided in this regard.

Reciprocity Needed

SHRI VAJPAYEE : Sir, this question was taken up in Islamabad. We have already liberalised the rules regarding issuing of passports. We are giving more visas to those people...

SHRI KHURSHID ALAM KHAN : I am afraid I am not asking about them but about...

SHRI VAJPAYEE : We have offered to Pakistan that if they allow us to open an office in Karachi they can open a similar office in Bombay, so that all people will not have to come to Delhi to secure visas. There is a rush, I know. I would like the problem to be solved, but it cannot be done unilaterally. We have increased the staff. But in Islamabad there is a problem about accommodation and we have approached the Government of Pakistan to help us in this matter, and I hope that more and more people will be able to visit the other country so that families are not divided, they can go in times of distress or death. I am here determined to see that the rules are further liberalised and conditions created in which travel between India and Pakistan is made easier. Thank you.

The Historic Salal Agreement

Mr. Chairman, Sir, the House will recall that the Indus Water Treaty of 1960 provided for exclusive use of the three eastern rivers (Sutlej, Ravi and Beas) to India while Pakistan was allowed the exclusive use of the waters of the three western rivers (Chenab, Jhelum and Indus). Exclusive use meant that except for some limited uses for domestic and agricultural purposes, the waters of the western rivers could not be removed except for non-consumptive purposes such as the generation of hydro-electric power. However, under the Treaty, Pakistan, as a lower riparian, was entitled to study the design and raise objections on the ground that the design did not, in their opinion, conform to the criteria laid down in the Treaty. The Salal Hydro-electric Project on the Chenab in the State of Jammu and Kashmir was planned by the Central Water and Power Commission which, when completed, will generate 345 megawatts of power and provide significant increase in the availability of power for the State of Jammu and Kashmir and other States of the Northern Region. The designs were first sent to the Pakistan Commissioner for Indus Waters in 1970. Pakistan raised various objections to the design and urged in brief that the design was not in accordance with the provisions of the Treaty. It was also suggested that it would give India the capacity to manipulate the flows of the river which may cause harm to Pakistan. As a consequence discussions had been going in the Permanent Indus Commission since 1974 and were continued at the Foreign Secretaries level since 1975.

Pakistan Agrees

These discussions did not resolve the differences, and as a result, at one stage it was being discussed that the question might be referred, under the provisions of the Treaty, to a neutral expert. However, following the agreement for the restoration of diplomatic relations and the other severed links and in keeping with the understanding reached in the Simla Agreement of 1972, we took the initiative to invite Pakistan to resume bilateral negotiations to resolve this problem. Pakistan agreed to the suggestion and two rounds of discussions were held at the Foreign Secretaries level in October 1976 at New Delhi and Islamabad. These negotiations succeeded in narrowing the differences and a broad understanding was reached on the points at issue pertaining to the design. However, no agreement could be finalised.

Lok Sabha on April 14, 1978 on the Salal Agreement regarding Hydro-Electric Plant on the river Chenab; as Minister of External Affairs

When I went to Islamabad in February this year the Pakistan Government indicated their willingness to resume the negotiations on the Salal plant. I am glad to report to the House that as a result of the present discussions it has been possible to reach and sign an agreement on the design of the Salal Electric Plant today. In terms of this Agreement the height of the spillway gates shall be 30 feet and all the sluices shall be closed within one year of the date of first filling of the reservoir up to the full pondage level or within three years of the date of the first filling of the reservoir up to the crest of the spillway, whichever is earlier. Adequate provision has been made to meet any unforeseen emergency if the safety of the plant might be endangered. In essential respects the specifications of the design are the same as were informally agreed in Islamabad in October, 1976.

Thus an important and a most difficult problem which has been bedevil ling relations between the two countries has been resolved to the satisfaction of both the countries.

The discussions were held in an atmosphere of understanding and cordiality which reflected a desire to foster friendly and good-neighbourly relations on the basis of sovereign equality and mutual benefit in order to usher in an era of cooperation and confidence between the two countries.

Past Obligations Respected

The Agreement once again demonstrated that the Janata Government respects inherited obligations and seeks to build with greater vigour cooperative relations with our immediate neighbours. We hope this Agreement will be a significant step to consolidate and to reinforce these policies and to make our subcontinent an area of stability and thus enable the nations of the region to optimise their natural resources and spur their development and promote the well-being of the peoples in the countries of the region.

Sir, I beg leave of the House to lay on the table a copy of the Agreement between India and Pakistan regarding the design of the Salal Hydro-electric Plant on the river Chenab Main. Thank you.

Pakistan Entering Nuclear Age

SHRI YADVENDRA DUTT (Jaunpur) : I call the attention of the Minister of External Affairs to the following matter of urgent public importance and request that he may make a statement thereon :—

"The reported situation arising out of Pakistan going nuclear with the help of China and other foreign countries."

SHRI VAJPAYEE, Minister of External Affairs : Mr. Speaker, Sir, a number of reports have come to the attention of the Government regarding the efforts of the Government of Pakistan to purchase equipment which could be used for a programme to develop nuclear explosive capability.

As the House is aware, Pakistan concluded an agreement with France in January, 1976 to secure a nuclear reprocessing plant. It was reported that US Government had urged that the Pakistan-French programme for reprocessing should be supended. Some months ago reports appeared that the French Government had decided to suspend further supplies under the agreement. It is not known what equipment and design had already been supplied. In addition, it was reported that the Government of Pakistan also imported from United Kingdom "Variable Frequency Inverters", an equipment which is used both in synthetic fibre manufacture as well as in gas centrifuges for uranium enrichment. This matter was brought up in the House of Commons in July, 1978. We understand that the UK Government have taken steps under the Export Control regulations to stop further supplies to Pakistan. We have, however, no information of China giving assistance for Pakistan's nuclear programme.

In any case, in the light of these reports it was felt that the matter was grave enough to be brought to the attention of the Government of Pakistan. The Prime Minister accordingly took the initiative to write to President Zia on February 8, 1979, expressing India's concern over Pakistan's effort for acquiring nuclear technology to the point of explosion capability. A reply to this letter has since been received from the President of Pakistan. In his reply dated 3rd March, President Zia has stated that Pakistan's entire nuclear programme is geared to peaceful uses of atomic energy and that Pakistan has no intention of acquiring or developing nuclear weapons.

The policy of the Government of India on the nuclear question is well known and has been reiterated on several occasions in this House as well as outside. We have unilaterally announced our intention to gear our nuclear programme only for peaceful purposes. The possibility of Pakistan developing explosion capability is of understandably grave concern to India.

Lok Sabha on March 30, 1979 as Minister of External Affairs in reply to the Calling Attention motion regarding reported situation arising out of Pakistan going nuclear

We earnestly hope that the assurance given by President Zia in his letter to the Prime Minister would be adhered to in the acquisition of nuclear technology.

SHRI YADVENDRA DUTT : Sir, I have heard with rapt attention the statement of the Hon'ble Minister and I would like to ask him a very pointed and a clear-cut question. I hope he will give a clear-cut answer in view of Gen. Zia's reply of 3rd March. An American scientist has given an interview on the radio national hookup on 17th or 18th March that he was approached by high Pakistani officials with the request that he should help Pakistan to make an atomic bomb. Is it a fact or not ? If so, whether the government will take this thing into consideration for rethinking on the preparedness on nuclear power ?

SHRI VAJPAYEE : Sir, I would like to give a clear-cut reply. It is true that an American scientist John Aristotle Phillips who appeared on ABC network on the 16th March was asked by a correspondent about Pakistan's approach to have the plan from the American scientist. I would like to quote what transpired between them :

> "*Q*. I understand that the Pakistani Government wanted to get a hold of your plan.
>
> *A*. : Yes. I got a call about three months after the publicity started from a representative of a foreign government—the Pakistani Government—and he wanted to buy the plans from me and I refused. Of course, I notified FBI and Senator Proximire. At that very moment the Pakistani government was attempting to acquire some very sensitive technology from France and they had promised the French and promised the rest of the world that they had no interest in using it for bomb building purpose. Just when the deal was about to go through the Pakistanis are caught trying to get a bomb...designed from an American under-graduate and I would say the nicest thing that has happened from this whole experience is that the fact that the Pakistani-French deal has fallen through."

Sir, it is clear from the interview that some Pakistani had approached the American student who is an under-graduate but who claims to be an expert in making crude atomic bombs.

AN HON. MEMBER : Maybe crackers.

SHRI VAJPAYEE : I do not know.

To the latter part of the question I would like to assure the House that the Government's nuclear policy is constantly under review.

SHRI V.M. SUDHEERAN (Alleppey) : I have carefully gone through the statement of the Hon. Minister. Here he says we have however no information of China giving assistance for Pakistan's nuclear programme. About a year back it was reported, on 15 August, under the caption "China offers N-technology to Pakistan" and the report says :

> "Peking had offered to provide Pakistan with nuclear technology to reprocess spent nuclear fuel and extra-pure plutonium, according to reports here. *The Financial Times* quoting the authoritative New York

newsletter *Nucletonics* said today that the offer was made by the Chinese Vice-Premier Mr. Keng Piao, in Islamabad recently."

This was stated last year. While our Foreign Affairs Minister was in Peking, a high-level Pakistani military mission headed by their chief of military staff was also there; the chairman of the Pakistan's atomic energy commission also visited China very recently. Those delegations were accorded a warm reception and attention was given to them in the Chinese Press also, much more than to our Foreign Affairs Minister. This report created great anxiety and poses a threat to the security of our country. The present military regime under General Zia is following the same nuclear policy of Mr. Bhutto who was determined to have atom bombs even if Pakistan was forced to live on grass. Pakistan has been trying to knock at various doors for help. In this connection there were reports that they were trying to get French help and Libyan money because President Gaddaffi of Libya was very much interested in making the so-called Islamic atom bomb; because he says that the Jews, the Christians, the Hindus and all those people had bombs; so we should have an Islamic bomb. But the most important thing is the Chinese collusion with Pakistan. It is reported that China was providing nuclear knowhow to Pakistan and that there had been exchanges of experts between the two countries. Even our Foreign Affairs Minister admitted while replying a question that the Government had received reports of Pakistan embarking on a nuclear programme which might not be for peaceful purposes. Though the Pakistani military delegations visiting China seem to be goodwill missions, actually they were negotiating military deal with the Chinese. In the circumstances I charge the External Affairs Minister for giving up our security consideration by following a very submissive policy in relation to China. Our Government has not even come forward to recognise the Kampuchean Government. The Foreign Affairs Minister's statement on the Chinese aggression on Vietnam has given another notice to China to do anything. In view of all this may I know what the Government's reaction is to the reported move of Pakistan for further strengthening its nuclear programme with the help of China and other countries ? The Prime Minister has made a statement earlier that there would not be any nuclear explosion even for peaceful purposes. Now the Minister says there will be nuclear explosion for peaceful purposes. I want to know which is true. I also want to know whether the Foreign Affairs Minister has sought any clarification from the Chinese Government about China-Pakistan atomic nuclear collaboration and whether he is taking up the matter at the international level to build up strong world public opinion against arms race ?

SHRI VAJPAYEE : I would reply to the nuclear part only. Other questions will be discussed during the debate on the demands. When reports appeared in the press about China's assistance to Pakistan in the development of nuclear energy we got those reports verified and those reports have not been confirmed so far.

Bangladesh

East Bengal Under Occupation

Mr. Speaker, Sir, the reply given by the Hon'ble Minister is not only disappointing but also causes resentment. This House had unanimously passed a resolution that we will express our sympathy towards the brave people of East Bengal, who are fighting for their independence and extend our support to them but let alone helping the people of Bangladesh we are not even able to protect our own borders. We are not able to stop the violations of our border by Pakistan, we are not able to stop the violations of our air space. They intruded into our territory and took away our Border Security Force personnel. They have taken two of our journalists as prisoners, they have violated our border 47 times. When Pakistani troops committed violation of our border did we arrest any one of them ? We have not been able to arrest even a single Pakistani soldier, we have not been able to shoot down a single Pakistani aircraft. It is not enough to say that sufficient security arrangements have been made on the border. If the arrangements are sufficient they must also appear to be sufficient also.

I do not want to ask any question of the Hon'ble Minister. Mr. Speaker, Sir, I want to make a request to you.

MR. SPEAKER : Please make the request to him only.

SHRI VAJPAYEE : I will ask him the question but make the request only to you. My question is whether in government's view the Border Security Force is capable of answering violations by Pakistan. The Border Security Force is doing a good job. I myself have seen this on the border. But when Pakistan has brought its army on the border then army alone can face the army. It would be difficult for the Border Security Force to face the Army. We cannot expect the Border Security Force to shoot down Pakistani fighter planes. They have no anti-aircraft guns. When Pakistan has brought its army on the border should we not take our army also to the border to answer the violation by the Pak army ? Have clear orders not been issued to our armed forces to give a befitting reply to the aggressive actions of Pakistan ?

The Defence Minister has just returned after inspecting whatever arrangements are there on the border. He has stated that the countries of the world must do something to meet the situation that is developing in Bangladesh. I want to ask what our own country is doing in regard to what we are expecting from other countries of the world. If we do not take the initiative in the case of Bangladesh and go on waiting for other countries of

Lok Sabha on May 24, 1971 regarding violation of Indian border by Pakistani Army in East Bengal

the world we will not be performing our duty towards the people of Bangladesh.

My question was regarding granting recognition to Bangladesh, but it could not be reached. I have given notices of adjournment motions.... (*Interruptions*).

Mr. SPEAKER : We will see that later.

What happened to Journalists ?

SHRI VAJPAYEE : I will club them together. I want that our Minister of Home Affairs—'Affairs' have gone now, only 'Home' remains—let the Home Minister state unequivocally whether he is confident that the Border Security Force is capable of replying to the aggressive action by Pakistan. If not, what is he doing to further strengthen the borders ? If we had shot down a single Pakistani plane within our borders we would have helped Bangladesh without saying anything. But we have not been able to shoot down a single Pakistani aircraft so far. We could not get those B.S.F. men back who were arrested. I want to ask what happened to those journalists who were caught by Pakistanis ? Does Government have any information as to how these journalists are being treated ? This is a question that must be answered. Patience, Patience, Patience—that is what the government has been advocating. It has said that we would not watch silently what is happening in Bangladesh. Shall we then watch it vociferously ? Is it now time to show patience or to show that we have the power to stop it ?

SHRI RAM NIWAS MIRDHA : So far as the question of sending the army there is concerned, the Minister of Defence has explained the position to the House just now. As for the Border Security Force being competent or not to face the Pakistani army, I have already stated that it is competent, it is competent to meet the situation which prevails at present on our border. If need arises, the army could also be sent there and further action could also be taken. But it would be unfair to say that the Border Security Force was incapable of doing the job entrusted to it.

As for the Hon'ble member's question whether any Pakistani was arrested....(*Interruptions*)

SHRI VAJPAYEE : I will have to make it clear. I did not say that the Border Security Force was incompetent. What I meant was that the Pakistani army has come on the border and from experience it appears that the Border Security Force was not adequate. Thank You.

Exodus from East Bengal

Mr. Deputy Speaker, Sir, we are discussing an important topic today. Historic change is in process before us. Twenty-three years ago India was divided on the basis of religion. Today the clock appears to have come full circle and it is becoming clear that religion cannot be the foundation of a nation.

There are several aspects of the problem of Bangladesh, and even though they are related to each other it would be better to look at them separately. One aspect is that Bangladesh is our neighbour. Till yesterday it was a part of our country. Its people are the blood of our blood and the flesh of our flesh. Politics divided us. But even then we are bound by an unbreakable tie of common history and culture. Genocide is now going on in Bangladesh. Attempts are being made to exterminate an entire race. The United Nations charter speaks against genocide, against elimination of a race or a specie. However, the United Nations have not so far reacted to the genocide that goes on in Bangladesh. But we have to do our duty as a neighbour.

Genocide must Stop

Lakhs of people have been massacred in Bangladesh. Women have been subjected to mass humiliation. Intellectuals have been annihilated. The Pakistani army is behaving in Bangladesh in the same manner in which imperialist armies used to behave in their colonies. In fact all crimes committed against humanity so far have paled into insignificance in Bangladesh. This genocide must be stopped. If the United Nations and the big powers of the world refuse to interfere they are always moving their pawns on the chess-board of power politics—India will have to perform its duty.

The other aspect of the problem of Bangladesh is that democracy has been murdered there. Pakistan came into existence in 1947 and we hoped that it would be easier for us to develop friendly relations. But so far Pakistan did not have either a constitution or free elections. The army grabbed power. We felt happy when it was decided that elections would take place there. In the elections that took place the Awami Party got a majority. Sheikh Mujib-ur-Rehman who is perhaps in prison now—we do not know whether he is safe or not—should have been the Prime Minister of entire Pakistan. But he was put behind the bars and his life is in danger. Instead of handing over power to the elected representatives of the people the army crushed their democratic right. For us, a democratic country having unshakable faith in

Lok Sabha on May 25, 1971 while participating in the discussion regarding Influx of Refugees from East Bengal

democratic values, this tyranny on democracy in our neighbourhood, this attempt to throttle democracy there, is a challenge and we must face it.

I remember—and those who are elder to me may remember very well—that when an effort was made to entrust power to Franco in Spain after the end of democracy the youth of this country decided to send a batch there under the leadership of Pandit Jawaharlal Nehru. We were not an independent country then, and could not take a decision in the capacity of a free country, yet our sympathy was with the people who were fighting for democracy in Spain. Today we are a free country. Today we have the army of a free country. The Government has the backing of the entire country on the question of Bangladesh, which is not a party issue. If the government takes some courageous step for restoration of democracy in Bangladesh the entire country would support it. But these are not the times to send volunteers. If need be, army squads can be sent.

Pakistan's Problem has Become Our Problem

There is also a third aspect to the Bangladesh situation that is intimately connected with us. As the Prime Minister rightly said, what was Pakistan's problem has become our problem. More than 35 lakh people have been expelled. They have come to our land in search of shelter. Men, women and children, rendered homeless and deprived of every grain of food, are seeking shelter with Mother India for protection of their life and honour. Their number may go up to one crore. The Pakistan army will not let any Hindu remain there. Muslims are also being expelled in large numbers. Yesterday the Prime Minister said that Buddhists and Christians were also coming. To rehabilitate one crore people and to take their responsibility is a very serious problem. I would say that these people are being forced out in a planned manner. In a way Pakistan has declared a war against us. By sending one crore people to India it wants to disrupt our economy, endanger the north-eastern region, and incite communal disturbances in our country.

I remember—I would again like to refer to Pandit Nehru—that in 1950, when there was no question of the independence of Bangladesh nor any question of suppression of democracy, and refugees were being turned out from there, Pandit Nehru had declared in this very House that if the pushing of people into India was not stopped we would have to adopt other methods. And the result of that threat was that the then Prime Minister of Pakistan, late Liaquat Ali Khan, came running to Delhi. Today people in much larger numbers are being pushed out. Pakistan wants to win a war against us without firing a shot.

Recognise Bangladesh

The Prime Minister has said that the people who have come here should return. But will they go back ? If the situation in Bangladesh remains unchanged, if life is not secure, if women's honour is violated, if discrimination on the basis of religion continued, if the army continues to commit such inhuman and barbaric atrocities, nobody is going to return in spite of our keen desire. If we really want them to go back there only one way is left, and that is to recognise Bangladesh as a free country and, if she so desires, to provide her active assistance.

We do not want this question to develop into a problem between India and Pakistan, but can we fully assist Bangladesh without giving recognition to it ? Countries the world over are with Pakistan in this matter, but this is not surprising. That has been the politics of big countries. Those who brought Pakistan into existence, those who are nursing it, those who support it in every struggle, have now been exposed in this struggle against humanity. They will always continue to pat the back of Pakistan in order to weaken India. The demand of the time is that we stand firm on our legs.

It is regrettable that even our friends are not expressing their views in this matter with the clarity they should. The President of Soviet Russia had said something in the beginning. I am not able to understand why he is silent now. The countries of West Asia whom we had supported against Israel by going out of our way are maintaining silence in this matter. Those who became vociferous even at a small communal riot in India are sitting with sealed lips at the genocide and slaughter of human beings in East Bengal.

Let us Awaken World Conscience

But, Mr. Deputy Speaker, Sir, the countries of the world say what India is doing about Bangladesh ? Let us awaken the soul of the world, let us continue our efforts to create world opinion in favour of Bangladesh. The Government has achieved some success in this effort, but the future of Bangladesh cannot be left to the fond hope of the outcome of this effort. We will have to take a bold decision and perform our duty. The moment for decision has come. The Prime Minister is on trial. The credentials of the Government of India are at stake. The power of this country is being challenged.

May I ask, if Bangladesh is not given recognition and the Pakistani army crosses the border, creating a situation of war, what will happen ? No doubt there is the danger of China coming into the open, but this country must be prepared to face dangers. I am confident that if the Government takes a courageous decision the people of this country, as the Prime Minister appealed yesterday, would not lag behind in any sacrifice. But if the Government remains passive and frustration overtakes the people some elements may take advantage of the situation. It may become difficult to manage the economy, and peace may be endangered. Hence the challenge of Bangladesh is before us. This House will have to face this challenge with courage. I hope when the Prime Minister replies to this debate it would be a reply that would satisfy the House and give confidence to the country that the Government does not depend on mere words but, when action is called for, it can also act boldly. Thank You.

Raise Bangladesh Issue in Security Council

Mr. Chairman, Sir, I want to congratulate Shri Samar Guha, who has given an opportunity to this House to consider the latest situation in Bangladesh by bringing this resolution. The resolution also gives an opportunity to the Government to explain its policy in the light of the new situation. I was very much disappointed to listen to the speech of Shri Bibhuti Misra. It appears that the ruling party is not able to decide which speaker to field on which subject. When a resolution regarding Bangladesh is being discussed in the Lok Sabha the discussion should take place in a serious atmosphere which could portray the true feelings of the nation and convey to the world that the patience of India has now reached its limit and if world opinion fails to put Islamabad on the right track it would become impossible for the Government of India to reject the demand of 55 crores of its people. But Shri Bibhuti Misra's speech does not meet this requirement and is not helpful in creating such an atmosphere in the world. Who fought for independence is not the subject matter for discussion ? Those who wanted to fight for the independence of the country were members of the Congress at that time, but there were people outside the Congress as well at that time who fought for the independence of the country who did not have faith in non-violence, who fought against the British with arms. Not only members of the Congress Party are patriotic (*Interruptions*). I was in jail in 1942, where were you, please tell us ?

MR. CHAIRMAN : Please leave aside individual cases.

SHRI VAJPAYEE : Mr. Chairman, Sir, a strange unrest is prevailing in the country since the publication of an article in the *Indian Express* by Anthony Mascaranes about massacre in Bangladesh. I want to congratulate Shri Anthony. He was the Karachi correspondent of *Sunday Times* published from London and also Assistant Editor of *Morning News*, which is published from Pakistan. He had accepted the citizenship of Pakistan. Originally he belongs to Goa. He has been in Pakistan so far and he was one of the few selected journalists who were taken to East Bengal by the Government of Pakistan to show round the situation there. On his return he could have written a story which suited Pakistan if he so wanted. But what he saw in Bangladesh was that the blood that flowed there was so deep red and so thick that his own conscience pricked him and I want to quote what he has said. These words of a journalist would be recorded in the history of journalism :

Lok Sabha on June 18, 1971 while participating in the discussion on the Resolution moved by Shri Samar Guha for Raising the Bangladesh Issue in the Security Council of the United Nations

"Either I would write the full story of what I had seen or I would have to stop writing. I would never again be able to write with any integrity."

Shri Mascaranes knew that he cannot write the true story while he was in Pakistan, so he shifted to London, he took his family with him and wrote this story, the story written in blood, the story submerged in tears—I have not been able to control myself since I read this story. We are talking of political solutions here, but there is a solution in the mind of Islamabad too. Do we guess it or not ? These are the words of a Pakistani journalist. We should read them carefully. Mascaranes says that Pakistan has two plans about East Bengal. One is massacre, killing and the second is colonisation. I want to quote an extract from his article :

"The Government's policy for East Bengal was spelled out to me in the Eastern Command Headquarters at Dacca. It has three elements:

(1) The Bengalis have proved themselves "unreliable" and must be ruled by West Pakistanis.

(2) The Bengalis will have to be re-educated along proper lines. The "Islamisation of the masses"—this is the official jargon—is intended to eliminate secessionist tendencies and provide a strong religious bond with West Pakistan ; and

(3) When the Hindus have been eliminated by death and fight their property will be used as a golden carrot to win over the underprivileged Muslim middle class. This will provide the base for erecting administrative and political structures in the future."

Mascarnes writes : Today Bengalis are not found in the cities of East Bengal. Lull prevails in the villages. Crops are not being grown in the fields. Terror reigns supreme, people have been done to death.

I want to quote his words again :

"Where are the Bengalis ? I had asked my escorts in the strangely empty streets of Dacca a few days earlier. 'They have gone to the villages', was the stock reply. Now, in the countryside, there were still no Bengalis. Comilla town, like Dacca, was heavily shuttered. And in 10 miles on the road to Lakshani, past silent villages, the peasants I saw could have been counted on the fingers of both hands."

The rulers of Pakistan were proceeding according to a definite plan in regard to East Bengal, and this plan was of massacring and creating famine conditions there. I want to quote Mascaranes again :

"Discussing the problem in his plush air-conditioned office in Karachi recently the Chairman of the Agricultural Development Bank, Mr. Qurni, said bluntly : 'The famine is the result of their acts of sabotage. So let them die. Perhaps the Bengalis will come to their senses'."

We want to help East Bengal. We have passed a resolution unanimously for them. Even the legislatures of the States have demanded that Bangladesh should be granted recognition. It is not clear in which direction the speeches of the Prime Minister want to lead the country today. Shall we get time for the political solution about which we are thinking ? Will Pakistani rulers accept it ? My friend Shri Samar Guha is saying that the Awami League will not accept it. It will be difficult for Bangladesh to live as a part of Pakistan after so many atrocities. But I am not referring to that. Has it been possible to bring Pakistani rulers on the right track ? Has the world public opinion been able to compel Pakistan ? I want to know what the Ministers' caravan, which had left New Delhi on a world tour, has brought back. What is the reaction in the capitals of the world ? Are they only prepared to give money for helping the refugees and ready to express their oral sympathy ? The political solution about which we are talking means that the Government of elected representatives of Bangladesh should be established there, Bangladesh should cease to be a colony, the refugees who have fled Bangladesh could return back and their life, property and honour may remain secure. Will the countries of the world help us to achieve this solution ? We do not see any possibility of their going to help us in this task. We would like to hear what the Hon'ble Minister has to say about it.

Mr. Chairman, Sir, the volume of discussion that has taken place in the British Parliament on Bangladesh is perhaps more than the discussion in our own Parliament. I want to congratulate those 120 Members of Parliament belonging to the British Labour Party who have demanded that the Bangladesh issue should be raised in the Security Council. But I would like to ask—why should not the Government of India raise this matter in the Security Council ? I have read today that 18 members of the Swatantra Party have sent a telegram to the Secretary-General of the United Nations Organisation that this matter be raised in the Security Council. If the Secretary-General replies that instead of sending him a telegram they may ask their Government to raise this issue in the Security Council what face will we have ?

Nobody can deny that a massacre is being done there. Can the issue of the massacre not be raised in the UN ? Let the Government of India raise it. It is not necessary that we would get the support of the world, but by doing so we would get satisfaction on the one hand, and the position of some other countries of the world would become clear on the other. Subsequently it would be easier for us to decide our policy. There can be only one policy, and that is of making a firm resolve not to compromise with the present position and to create conditions in Bangladesh whereby the displaced persons could return to their homes and democracy could be established there. And for that, if there is no alternative except war India should get ready for war.

A war had taken place between India and Pakistan in 1965. It cost Rs. 50 crores. Today Pakistan was disturbing our economy without firing a single shot by sending lakhs of displaced persons into our country. Shri Chavan said that it would involve an expenditure of Rs 60 crores. The Prime Minister says Rs. 180 crores will have to be spent, and today the Minister of Labour and Rehabilitation has stated in his statement that it would cost us about Rs. 300 cores. War is costly, but not that costly. We may not go to war, we may help East Bengal. We may give an ultimatum to Pakistan that the massacre that is going on in East Bengal must stop and conditions should be created to discourage people to seek refuge under the benevolent shelter of

Mother India in order to safeguard their life, property and honour. Otherwise India will have to take strong steps in its own interest and in the interest of security of the country, and that strong step could even be going to war. The country which wants to avoid war is chased by war. We may not invite war, but if we are going to lose this battle without fighting a war then the Government must get ready for every eventuality.

Explosive Situation in Calcutta

I have referred to the economic aspect. What other consequences would follow it ? Shri Chapala Kant Bhattacharya has come from Bengal today. He says that conditions prevailing in Calcutta are such that an explosion may occur any day. It is possible that the people may *gherao* the Writers Building. There is no water available. Life has become disturbed, the law and order situation is at breaking point, the minds of the people are agitated and the Government of West Bengal is thinking of declaring an emergency.

The question is not only that of Bengal. The whole of India is concerned about Bangladesh. We have already delayed the matter considerably. Had the mind of the Government been clear, and had we decided upon our policy on March 25 when Pakistani forces had started the atrocities, perhaps the situation in Bangladesh might have been different.

We have missed it. But even now the delay could be changed in our favour. I am not opposed to mobilisation of public opinion in the world. That work may continue, but New Delhi's mind should be clear. The fate of Bangladesh, and for that matter of the displaced persons from Bangladesh, would not be decided in Washington, London, Bonn or Moscow. It will be decided in New Delhi. And if New Delhi takes a bold decision a new chapter could be written in history. Today we have to judge whether the Government has got the power to create new history or not. Thank You.

Holocaust in Bangladesh : Liberation the Only Solution

Mr. Speaker, Sir, The External Affairs Minister has returned after visiting a number of countries. Evidently he is happy with the outcome of his visits. He has claimed that he explained to the Governments of these countries the situation in Bangladesh, as a result of which he was able to mould their opinion and get their support for a political solution of this problem.

Sir, other Ministers are also proceeding on world tours. It appears as though our embassies in all the countries have failed to provide proper information to the people and the Governments there. The External Affairs Minister asks, how could our embassy get the information about supply of arms to Pakistan reported in the *New York Times* ? He also says that espionage is not a function of the embassy. Is then espionage a function of newspapers ? The correspondent of *New York Times* could find out that arms are going to Pakistan, that the ship will leave on such and such a date, as also what was the material that it was carrying. This information should have been available to our embassy also. If our embassies cannot acquire this kind of information then one is compelled to say that our Foreign Ministry as well as our Foreign Service have failed to do their duty.

What is Meant by Political Solution ?

Mr. Speaker, Sir, the Governments of the countries which our Foreign Minister visited have said that there should be a political solution to the problem of Bangladesh. Our Government also says the same thing. A little while ago Shri Bhagwat Jha Azad also pleaded for a political solution. I would like to know what is meant by a political solution. The Foreign Minister visited various capitals of the world. In Moscow he discussed the general world problems including China, disarmament, the situation in West Asia etc. His visit was not limited to the issue of Bangladesh. I want to ask him whether, along with these matters he also discussed in Moscow the shape of the political solution which is being so much talked about. Did he ask these countries what form this political solution would take ? If he did not, then we would like to ask our Government whether the political solution that is being suggested in the context of Bangladesh would be acceptable to the people there.

The six-point programme that is being mentioned was prepared before 25th March. Much water has flowed down the Padma since then, and not

Lok Sabha on June 28, 1971 during discussion on the visit of the Minister of External Affairs to several countries and supply of arms to Pakistan

only water but so much of blood and tears have flowed. Will the people of Bangladesh accept any solution that conceives it as a part of Pakistan even after the atrocities that are being perpetrated since 25th March and the massacre that is being done there ? Pakistan may make the cunning move of a political solution. It can form a puppet Government in Bangladesh. A sham Government could be formed with the support of parties like the Muslim League and Jamat-e-Islami and some 'frightened people'. Those in authority in Britain and America can then say that a Government has now been formed in East Bengal, the military dictators of Islamabad are now trying to normalise the situation, a beginning has been made, and with the passage of time the problem would be solved. The acting President of Bangladesh, Shri Nazrul Islam, has also put forth some conditions. Has our Foreign Minister seen those conditions or not ? He has put four conditions which are : release of Sheikh Mujibur Rehman and other representatives of the people; withdrawal of the Pakistani army, which is keeping Bangladesh under forcible occupation; recognition of a free, sovereign Bangladesh; full compensation for the atrocities undergone by the people of Bangladesh.

Does the Government of India keep in mind these terms when it talks of a political solution ? Or will it like to thrust on Bangladesh a Government which the people will not accept ? If the Pakistani army continues to remain in Bangladesh and if it remains a part of Pakistan no displaced person will go back.

Pushing People into India is Invasion

What is the basis of the Prime Minister's optimism that the displaced persons who have taken refuge in India will go back in six months ? Since the partition of the country one crore eighty lakh people have come to India from East Bengal. Earlier, only Hindus had come; now, Muslims and Christians are also coming along with Hindus because of fear and terror People have been slaughtered on a mass scale. Fields have been destroyed Houses have been burnt. Young girls have been gang-raped. Small childrei were flung in the air and caught on bayonet points. So long as Pakistan tha has committed such sins remains there can any displaced person return Nobody will go back and we can only imagine what will happen to thi country.

Nobody is asking you to go to war with Pakistan. But Pakistan has startec a war against us. There is no question of our attacking Pakistan, but we mus at least reply to the Pakistani invasion. Displacing six million people and pushing them into India is an invasion on India. These people will ruin our economy and endanger our political stability. They will create problems for communal peace.

The Legislative Assembly of West Bengal stands dissolved and President's rule is going to be imposed. Tripura does not have the capacity to absorb the displaced persons. The number of displaced people who are coming is more than the population of Tripura. Another kind of tension is building up in Assam. We cannot shut our eyes to the situation in Meghalaya. Immigration of six million people, which may go upto 10 million, is an invasion on us. We must reply to it.

I want to know from our External Affairs Minister what kind of political solution he has in his mind. Did he ask the countries of the world what they would do if Pakistan did not accept this solution. The US reply is there. I do not have any misunderstanding about Britain also. Mr. Duglous Hume says one thing to our Foreign Minister and another in the House of Commons. Those countries that have agreed to delay the decision on economic assistance to Pakistan also say that Pakistan should try to find a political solution to the Bangladesh problem. Today the President of Pakistan is going to make a broadcast. He will put up a puppet Government in Dacca.

Britain is the Father of Pakistan

I have no misgivings about the attitude of Britain and the US. Britain is the father of Pakistan. The US has been nursing it. I do not agree with Shri Bhagwat Jha Azad's view that they have disturbed the balance between the two countries by supplying arms. It is the policy of America and Britain to maintain a balance between the two countries, put Pakistan on leash, so that they may keep a control and restraint on India. That is why military assistance was given to Pakistan. That is why, whenever India was attacked, we found Britain and America patting Pakistan. London and Washington are playing the same game as Peking. They cannot be depended upon for a solution of the Bangladesh problem.

We have some hope from Soviet Russia, but the statement of the Foreign Minister does not throw enough light on it. Some expectations arose when President Podgorny made a statement and sent a letter to Yahya Khan. But the Foreign Minister should take the House into confidence and tell us what else transpired in his talks and which countries will support us.

It is a matter of regret and resentment that Pakistan is getting arms. But even if it did not get these arms was there any dearth of arms with it for suppressing the unarmed people of Bangladesh ? America, Russia, China—all these countries have already filled the armouries of Pakistan. If Moscow changes its policy we will welcome it. The two faces of America are not hidden from us. I do not agree with my communist friends that America is not a democratic country. It is very much democratic, otherwise the *New York Times* could not have published these news. *Izvestia* and *Pravda* can never publish such news. But should we depend upon these countries to solve the problem of Bangladesh ?

SHRI K.D. MALAVIYA : You will know more about them after some time.

SHRI VAJPAYEE : Shri Malaviya had gone to Damascus and whatever he has learnt there is enough.

Delay Helping Pakistan

If we want a satisfactory solution of the Bangladesh problem let it be understood that no such solution is going to come out by depending on the other countries of the world. We will have to stand on our own legs. The situation would perhaps have been different if our Government had given recognition to Bangladesh. History would perhaps have taken a different course if New Delhi had taken this decision on 25th March. We must not forget that the time now is in favour of Pakistan. It is indulging in intimidation and suppression. The memory of the atrocities committed in Bangladesh will gradually fade away from the world capitals. Attention from the main issue will be diverted and search for a political solution will begin. The people of Bangladesh would find it difficult to swallow that solution.

If the leaders of Awami League are not released, or if power is not entrusted to them, or if they do not accept the Pakistani political solution then what will India do ? I do not think there is any other way before India except to help Bangladesh, and it should not only be moral but material help also. Pakistan has thrust a war upon us and we must react to it. It is necessary to give recognition to Bangladesh, because recognition would make the help legal. We can easily give recognition, but if there is any other alternative with the Government let it make it clear and take the House into confidence.

Country's Patience is Breaking

It is a state of crisis today, for which the country has to be mentally prepared. But to prepare the country the Government itself should first be prepared mentally. I have the issue of *Patriot* before me. It is a paper belonging to those who are supposed to be near the Prime Minister. In its editorial the *Patriot* says :

> "Answering them to the satisfaction of the people, however, will be difficult as long as divided counsels continue to confuse the Government."

It is being said that the Foreign Minister is deadly against any stringent action on the Bangladesh problem because he is afraid that the war will not be limited to Bangladesh but would be taken to Punjab by Pakistan. The issue of Bangladesh is also being used to make propaganda against the Defence Minister. This House must be given an assurance that all-out efforts will be made to awaken world opinion, but if we have to go it alone we will go ahead. Bangladesh is a country of Rabindra Nath Tagore and Kazi Nazrul Islam. Poet Ravindra had told us :

> *"Ekla chalo re*
> *Yadi tor dak sune keu na ashe*
> *Tabe ekla chalo re".*

So let us walk alone on the path of duty, go alone for the defence of democracy in Bangladesh. We are not bound to preserve the unity of Pakistan. India was divided in 1947. Today the clock has gone full circle, and Pakistan is on the verge of disintegration. We do not have any hand in this partition. but if the people of East Bengal want to secede from Pakistan we cannot force it to remain a part of Pakistan.

We will have to help Bangladesh on our own strength. If other countries of the world join us, then jointly with them, and if they remain mute observers, then in spite of them we should go ahead with full assistance to

Bangladesh in its struggle for freedom. If the Foreign Minister can remove the doubts of this House during this discussion, well and good; otherwise I want to warn that the patience of the people of this country is at the breaking point. The stories that are pouring in are full of blood and tears and are agitating the people of India. The only way to calm down the people is to assure them that the Government will not step back, that it will not betray weakness in the garb of a political solution, that it will do everything possible for the liberation of Bangladesh. This assurance from the Foreign Minister can calm down the people; otherwise they will be obliged to force the Government to take the right step. Thank you.

Recognition to Bangladesh

Mr. Speaker, Sir, though delayed, a right step has been taken in granting recognition to Bangladesh. The process of change of history is going on before our eyes, and the destiny has brought this Parliament and the country to an important moment, when we are not only fighting shoulder to shoulder with those who are sacrificing their lives in this war of liberation but are trying to give a new direction to history as well. Today the blood of the fighters for their freedom in Bangladesh and of Indian Jawans is flowing together. This blood would evolve a relationship that would not snap under any kind of pressure, nor would it fall prey to any diplomatic manoeuvring. The liberation of Bangladesh is coming closer and I feel that our troops are now reaching the doorsteps of Dacca. The Government of India, by granting recognition to Bangladesh, have not only helped the liberation battle but have given international status to Bangladesh. They will now go to the Security Council as representatives of a free Bangladesh. Therefore our recognition to them at this juncture has become more meaningful.

I think our Prime Minister really deserves congratulations on this occasion. We hope to hear some more such news in the days to come. Thank you.

Lok Sabha on December 6, 1971 on the Government of India according recognition to Bangladesh

The Farakka Agreement

SOME HONOURABLE MEMBERS : Please speak in Hindi.

SHRI VAJPAYEE : There is arrangement for simultanious translation. Please use the ear-phones.

SMT. PRATIBHA SINGH (Bihar) : Hon'ble Minister, you spoke in Hindi in the U.N. Why are you speaking in English here ?

SHRI KALYAN ROY (West Bengal) : This is not U.N.O. Let him go on.

DR. V.P. DUTT (Nominated) : There is nothing wrong in reading a statement in English. What is wrong with it ?

SHRI VAJPAYEE : Sir, obviously there are differences in the Congress Party, and on the question of language, there is always a differences.

SMT. SAROJ KHAPARDE (Maharashtra) : It would be better if the Hon'ble Minister speaks in Hindi.

SHRI VAJPAYEE : Sir, the Hon'ble members of this House would have gathered from the press that an agreement between India and Bangladesh on the sharing of the Ganga waters at Farakka and on augmenting its flows was finally negotiated and signed at the Ministerial level in Dacca on the 5th November, 1977. I place on the Table of the House a copy of the Agreement which, in accordance with the understanding reached with the Bangladesh Government, was released upon its signature. I must crave the indulgence of the House for the length of this statement. Apart from the importance and the complexity of the problems raised during the negotiations I have to cover in it most of the criticism which has been voiced regarding this Agreement and consequently it has become necessary to explain the position in its historical perspective and the facts involved. The historic nature of the Agreement and its extraordinary significance for relations between India and Bangladesh and for sub-continental politics have been recognised almost universally abroad and by broad sections of public opinion in India. With the signing of this Agreement and its simultaneous entry into force a major problem which had bedevilled relations betwen the two countries and vitiated the political atmosphere in the subcontinent for over 25 years has been resolved.

Complicated History

Hon'ble members are aware of the long history and complexity of the Farakka problem. The issue involved in the negotiations of the Agreement affected political, economic and cultural interests and sensitivities on both sides. We were seeking to ensure that while not reducing the flows available

---

Rajya Sabha on November 14, 1977 as Minister of External Affairs regarding the Farakka Agreement with Bangladesh on the sharing of Ganga Waters

for flushing the Hooghly below a reasonable limit, arrangements were made at the same time for augmenting the flows in order adequately to meet our upstream and down-stream requirements. From the Bangladesh side it was argued that they had to protect the existing consumptive uses and avoid adverse effects on the country's ecology and economy in the future. They further contended that in order to preserve the ecological balance the entire flow of 55,000 cusecs during the leanest period of the dry season should be maintained uninterrupted. The negotiations were necessarily complicated and protracted in order to reconcile these disparate and conflicting objectives from both sides.

The negotiating problem was further compounded because international law on the rights of riparians is yet to be codified and thus there is no universally recognised criteria to go by in determining equitable sharing. Even though the Helsinki Rules of 1966, which have received broad acceptance by countries as a model of international law, mention some factors to be taken into account, it has been generally recognised that considering the unique features of each international river, equitable sharing can be determined only through bilateral (or multilateral) negotiations betwen the riparian States concerned. And in bilateral negotiation of this nature it is not possible to arrive at an agreement on the basis of a precise quantitative determination of the rights and entitlements of each co-riparian. A settlement through negotiations is essentially an exercise in the art of compromising from extreme positions taken by the negotiating parties. In this case it involved balancing between differing uses and priorities in the utilisation of waters. The initial position of Bangladesh was the maintenance of the historical flow which amounted to a lower riparian exercising a veto on utilisation of waters by the upper riparian. India's initial position was to be able to withdraw an optimum flow of 40,000 cusecs in order to have maximum beneficial effect for the restoration of Hooghly river to its normal health and thus for the preservation and improvement of the Calcutta port.

Shared Sacrifices and Mutual Accommodation

Moreover, a bilateral agreement cannot be based exclusively on the considerations of rights and entitlements particularly in a situation of the kind that prevails in the lower Ganga basin where during the lean season there is not just enough water to meet the requirements, let alone the entitlements of both the countries. The Agreement, therefore, had to be based on the principle of shared sacrifices and mutual accommodation without affecting the rights and entitlements of either country.

Hon'ble members would also appreciate that the negotiations involved not only the sharing of waters between the two countries—nor only augmentation of its flows—but also the political imperative of improving relations with our closest neighbour, which is an acid test of the effectiveness and credibility of our entire foreign policy and for that matter of the principles which India has always advocated should guide relations among nations.

In its attempt to reach an agreement on the Farakka problem this Government did not have a clean slate to write afresh. The then Government of Pakistan and later the Bangladesh Government never accepted our right to go ahead with the construction and commissioning of the Farakka Barrage Project without reaching an agreement with them on the sharing of the Ganga waters. Inter-governmental consultations and negotiations have been held ever since 1951, when preliminary investigations of the project were in progress. In their Joint Declaration of May 1974 the Prime Ministers of India and Bangladesh noted that the Farakka Barrage would be commissioned by the end of 1974, but at the same time they agreed that a mutually acceptable allocation of the water available during periods of minimum flow in the Ganga should be arrived at before commissioning the Barrage. Thus the Hon'ble members will note that there was already a basic decision taken by the previous government that withdrawal of waters by India would follow agreement on allocations with Bangladesh.

The Barrage was commissioned in April 1975 after an agreement with the then Government of President Mujib for withdrawals by India in the range of 11,000 to 16000 cusecs for the period of 21st April to 31st May. Unfortunately no agreement for the dry season of 1975-76 could be rached. Though the Government of India took the view that the April 1975 Agreement was valid only till the end of May 1975, and did not bind it in any way so far as withdrawals after that date were concerned, the Bangladesh Government's position was that its share covering the period 21st April to 31st May should in no circumstances fall below the quantum *i.e.* 39,000—44,000 cusecs agreed with the previous Government to be released for Bangladesh.

Attempt to Internationalise the Farakka Issue

When no agreement was reached for the dry season of 1975-76 and when India started drawing close to the Feeder Canal capacity the Bangladesh Government made a number of moves to internationalise the Farakka issue, alleging unilateral withdrawal by India. The issue was taken to the Islamic Conference in Istanbul, the Non-aligned Summit Conference in Colombo and finally in the form of a formal complaint to the 31st Session of the United Nations General Assembly. The General Assembly concluded its consideration of the item proposed by the Bangladesh Government with the adoption of a consensus statement which, among others, incorporated the decision of the two Governments to resume bilateral negotiations urgently at the Ministerial level. This was in keeping with the stand all along taken by India that bilateral problems can be best resolved bilaterally, but it placed on us the responsibility to negotiate purposefully. Accordingly, four rounds of Ministerial level talks were held between December 1976 and April 1977. A break-through in these negotiations was reached between the leaders of the Indian Delegation, *i.e.* our Defence Minister and the leader of Bangladesh the details of which were to be elaborated in official-level talks and incorporated in a comprehensive agreement between the two countries. An agreement was finally concluded and initialled at the end of the third round of the official level talks on 30th September 1977. These negotiations had aroused great expectations not only in the two countries but, in view of the previous involvement of the General Assembly and particularly friendly non-aligned countries, also in the international community. The conclusion of the Agreement was, therefore, widely regarded as a vindication of the trust placed on the sagacity and reasonableness of the two countries and an example of how developing countries can negotiate to resolve problems affecting their development.

The Farakka Barrage Project has been designed mainly for the protection and improvement of Calcutta Port. No one in India can minimise the importance of this Port for the city of Calcutta and for the economy of the entire eastern region on which depends a vast segment of our population. This Agreement contains the best possible arrangement for realising the objective of the Farakka Project and at the same time meeting the requirements of Bangladesh during the period of distress.

India's Share

The members of the House are aware that a number of estimates in the past, including the Farakka Barrage Project document which was approved in 1960, had envisaged that the project would be fully justified even after it was possible to withdraw up to 20,000 cusecs of water during mid-March to mid-May. This and other data were exchanged with the then Government of Pakistan even though it was made clear that they were provisional in nature and subject to modifications in the light of further studies and model experiments. The Agreement concluded provides for a withdrawal of 20,500 to 26,750 cusecs during March-May as well as for a progressive increase in India's share when the flows are above the minimum level of 55,000 cusecs during 3 out of 4 years based on 25 years' observed data. The minimum withdrawal by India is also almost the double of the minimum withdrawal which was permissible under the April 1975 Agreement. India has also been able to secure in this Agreement a near-optimum level of withdrawals, that is 35,000 to 40,000 cusecs for 8 months during the year, *i.e.* from June to January. The Agreement also provides for a guarantee to Bangladesh of 80 per cent of its share for each 10-day period. This gives a margin of 20 per cent, which would make for administrative convenience and minimise the problem of daily questioning of variations in the flows arriving at Farakka.

Hydrology is not an exact science and, therefore, hydrodynamic model studies are not capable of predicting effects of withdrawal within negligible margins of error. However, on the basis of both model experiments and prototype studies of actual effects so far carried out by Indian engineers it can be stated that the schedule of withdrawals agreed upon in the Agreement would enable us to arrest further 'deterioration in the Port of Calcutta and, with the help of such other measures as dredging, river training, prevention of soil erosion etc., to bring about improvement in the Port. The need to adopt these complementary measures in addition to ensuring maximum amount of head-water supply has been recognised throughout the period of the formulation and execution of the Farakka Barrrage Project.

The improvement of Calcutta Port as a result of headwater supply from the Farakka Barrage is bound to take time and cannot be achieved too quickly. Meanwhile, as the nation has progressed and as agriculture has modernised, the demand for consumptive and non-consumptive use, particularly for irrigation, of the Ganga waters has increased even more rapidly in future. Therefore, a national arrangement for increasing the availability of water through some long-term scheme is necessary for meeting both our upstream and downstream requirements, even aside from the needs of Bangladesh. A long-term solution is as important, if not more, for India as it is for Bangladesh, and this could best be achieved with the co-operation of both the countries.

In the Agreement the two Governments have not only agreed to study all available long-term proposals but they have also set a time limit of three years to complete such a study. The Agreement provides for the two Governments to select in good faith a scheme or schemes on the basis of the recommendations of the study and to take necessary measures to implement it as speedily as possible.

Short-term Sacrifice for Long-term Gain

We have thus accepted the short-term sacrifice involved in the arrangement for sharing because it is also linked to measures for finding a solution to the long-term problem. The Agreement is valid for an initial period of 5 years and provides for a review after 3 years entailing consideration of the working, impact and progress in its implementation including progress towards long-term solution.

The Agreement, we hope, would not only lead to a solution of the long-term problem of augmenting the flow of the Ganga, but would also pave the way for the optimum utilisation of the water resources of the region as a whole. The activisation of Joint Rivers Commission under the terms of the Agreeement should result in increasing cooperation between India and Bangladesh for flood control and in other problem areas affecting the interests of the other party.

Mr. Deputy Chairman, Sir, in considering this Agreement one should cast one's mind back to the long years of differences, suspicions and even hostility that have prevailed in our subcontinent. One should also remember that India is a nation which by its tradition and the principles that it has upheld both nationally and internationally, is committed to policies of cooperation and friendly relations with other nations. This Government has recognised that for the sake of our own development and the effectiveness of our foreign policy the crucial test is whether or not we could make this subcontinent free of friction, allowing us to concentrate our resources on our primary task of development and the welfare of our people. If we are convinced that India's own interest is also served in the prosperity of our neighbours, then we cannot but make serious attempt to resolve such problems which affect development in both countries.

We were also committed to resolving the Farakka issue bilaterally, without the involvement or interference of a third country or party. In reaching this Agreement through bilateral negotiations and, in particular, by providing for settlement of differences and disputes strictly within bilateral framework we have demonstrated that all issues, howsoever complex, between close neighbours, can be resolved bilaterally in a spirit of shared sacrifice and mutual accommodation.

The approach and spirit which have made this Agreement possible should, if applied to the larger spectrum of our relations with Bangladesh, lead to an ever-widening cooperation between the two countries, both bilaterally and in multilateral forums. This should also contribute to the furtherance of our objectives of promoting peace and development in the subcontinent and of working together towards a better world order.

With anticipated increase in demands for water for diverse uses, it was clear that as time went by the problem would become more complex and intractable. This would have not only resulted in loss of tremendous opportunity for the two countries in not taking timely action to solve the long- term problems, but would have also made it extremely difficult to make arrangements for short-term sharing. Therefore, if an agreement was to be reached, the common interests of the two countries lay in reaching it sooner rather than later.

The Farakka problem has been a national issue in Bangladesh transcending political parties and regimes. All the political parties and groups in Bangladesh have been united in demanding much larger shares and a speedy settlement of the dispute.

In India also the Farakka problem must be seen as a non-partisan national issue. We have gone on to finalise the agreement respecting the commitment made by the previous government. May I seek the indulgence of the House to treat this Agreement in the same spirit as sinking inter-party differences and in the wider perspective of the overall objective of our foreign policy and specifically the well-being of the two countries ?

Influx of Refugees from Bangladesh

Mr. Speaker Sir, I respect the sentiments expressed by Professor Guha. But it was not correct to say that the issue of Bangladesh was being looked after only by the Prime Minister and that the External Affairs Ministry had nothing to do with it.

SHRI SAMAR GUHA : I had said he is specially looking after this problem.

SHRI VAJPAYEE : If that were so his place would not have been vacant today. I am standing here to reply. All the decisions are taken on the basis of joint responsibility and are arrived at after full deliberations.

This Calling Attention Notice has two parts. In the first part it has been stated that people from Bangladesh are arriving here in large numbers, leaving their homes and property behind. My colleague Shri Kundu has said in his statement and this statement is based on the facts received from various agencies of the Central Government and the Government of West Bengal—that it would not be correct to say that there has been a sudden increase in the number of immigrants from Bangladesh.

SHRI SAMAR GUHA : I did not say "sudden". I gave a warning that it may happen in future.

SHRI VAJPAYEE : What is hidden in the future only futurologists like Professor Guha can see. An ordinary man like me cannot look into the future.

SHRI SAMAR GUHA : About 10 years back I wrote a book *Swadhina Purva Bangla* [Independent East Bengal] which was ridiculed a lot. Dr. Lohia and I made speeches at Calcutta Maidan. I spoke for two hours, but no paper published a single line.....perhaps they thought we were speaking nonsense. But what we had said proved to be true after 10 years. What I have said about the future is from the political angle and not from the astrological point of view.

SHRI VAJPAYEE : It is unfortunate that nobody cared for Professor Guha's warning at that time. But he will agree that we are listening to him very carefully. I hope the press will also publish it and he would have no occasion for complaint.

The number of immigrants who came to India from Bangladesh between April and December 1974 is 15, 278. In 1975 this number increased to 38,445. I do not want to go into the situation prevailing in Bangladesh in 1975—Professor Guha can understand that. This number came down to 7, 924 in 1976. This year the number has not increased. But I want to submit that the arrival of even 7, 014 people is a matter of worry for us. Even if a single citizen of Bangladesh has to leave his home and take shelter in India

Lok Sabha on December 1, 1977 as Minister of External Affairs in response to the Calling Attention notice regarding Influx of Refugees from Bangladesh

we feel sorry for it. We are constantly taking up this matter with the Government of Bangladesh. It has been raised in Dacca at the level of Foreign Secretary. The High Commissioner of Bangladesh in New Delhi was called and the matter was brought before him. I discussed it with the Foreign Minister of Bangladesh when we met in New York. When our Prime Minister met the President of Bangladesh, Shri Ziaur-Rehman, he also raised this matter with him. Professor Guha has referred to the statements of Mahatma Gandhi, Pandit Jawaharlal Nehru and Dr. Shyama Prasad Mukherjee. I have the fortune of being a follower of Dr. Shyama Prasad Mukherjee. He died in detention and he had tendered his resignation from the first Government of free India on the issue of minorities. How can we forget this question ?

But this is 1977. A lot of water has flowed down the Ganga and Padma. India was divided in 1947. Pakistan was divided in 1971. Bangladesh has emerged as a free, sovereign country and it need not be reiterated that the role of Professor Guha in the struggle for Bangladesh's independence will be written in history. I understand his sorrow and pain. But he should not think that the Government is not worried. He stated that recently a census was held there and the number of Hindus left in Bangladesh is 60 lakhs. I want to ask him—in which statement of the Bangladesh Government has this number of 60 lakhs been mentioned. ?

SHRI SAMAR GUHA : It has been published in newspapers.

SHRI VAJPAYEE : If you put your faith in newspapers that won't do. There is no such census by the Government of Bangladesh. We have made inquiries about it. The fact is that when a census is held in Bangladesh no data is collected separately for Muslims and Hindus. Therefore there is no way of knowing the basis on which this figure of 60 lakhs is arrived at.

The other thing mentioned in the Calling Attention Notice is that Bangladesh has been declared an Islamic State. My submission is that this has not happened....(*Interruptions.*) I know what has happened. Please allow me to speak.

SHRI SAMAR GUHA : This is the amendment of the Constitution.

SHRI VAJPAYEE : I know an amendment has been made.

After all, when the Prime Minister has entrusted the external affairs to me, I know all these facts, Bangladesh has not been declared an Islamic State. In place of the word 'secular' 'Almighty Allah' has been substituted. We also drew the attention of the Bangladesh Government towards this...

SHRI SAMAR GUHA : Is it not a theocratic State ?

SHRI VAJPAYEE : It has now been provided that Bangladesh will follow the path shown by the Almighty Allah. Please wait a while. It serves no purpose to repeat what has not happened.

SHRI SAMAR GUHA : In the Preamble of the Constitution, in place of the word 'secular', a reference to Almighty Allah has been substituted. Will it not be called a theocratic State ? State-sponsored complexes of mosques are being built. Will you not call it a theocratic state ?

SHRI VAJPAYEE : I do not want to draw interferences like Professor Guha. We should state things only as they are. When our officers drew our attention to it they told us of the statement of President Zia-ur-Rehman that there was no intention to set up an Islamic or theocratic state and that both Hindus and Muslims will have equal rights. The President also said that he was taking care to ensure that minorities did not develop a feeling of insecurity. Professor Guha may complain that there is difference between word and deed. But we will have to consider what has been said.

Mr. Deputy Speaker, if the number of immigrants from Bangladesh is exaggerated, which is not based on facts, its results will be unsalutary. A sense of insecurity will spread, and its reaction in India will not be good. The objective which Professor Guha wants to achieve will not be realised.

SHRI SAMAR GUHA : I have given only one statement in six months.

SHRI VAJPAYEE : It was so good on your part, but it would have been still better if you had given no statement at all.

SHRI SAMAR GUHA : I gave this statement after spending two days with Shri Jayaprakash Narayan and discussing with him, not before that.

MR. DEPUTY SPEAKER : Mr. Guha, this dialogue may be stopped so that others may say something.

SHRI SAMAR GUHA : I shall stop here.

SHRI VAJPAYEE : This allegation is false and I want to deny vehemently that immigrants from Bangladesh who had taken shelter in India were pushed back into Bangladesh against their will. This allegation was levied earlier also and we got another inquiry made into it. Not only the officials of the External Affairs Ministry but officials of other Ministries also went to the border and came to the conclusion that the immigrants had returned of their own will (*Interruptions*). If anybody did not want to go back the alternative of asking the Indian Government for political asylum was open to him. But we had put two conditions on it—first, he would not be allowed to stay at the border and second, no political activity in India against Bangladesh will be permitted (*Interruptions*).

SHRI CHITTA BASU : Let us know what you are going to do.

SHRI VAJPAYEE : Chitta Babu is unnecessarily interrupting me. Those who have not returned are living in India. Nobody has been sent back against his wishes nor will ever be. It is our moral duty to give shelter to those who have come to India and we have fulfilled that duty and will fulfil it in future also. No matter what pressure is used, we will not send them anywhere against their wishes. Professor Guha has also admitted that ever since this was brought to the notice of the Government...

SHRI SAMAR GUHA : I accept that nothing has happened after that.

SHRI VAJPAYEE : It is our wish and desire that those who have gone of their own may live there in security.

SHRI SAUGATA ROY : A secret deal took place in London.

SHRI VAJPAYEE : The Government that entered into the secret deal has been thrown out by the people. Whatever we do we do openly....(*Interruptions*). Dr. Karan Singh may please not interrupt me. I had praised in this House the role played by that Government, but please do not put the blame of secrecy on me. We have the strength to pay them in their own coin. I do not want to place before the House what was happening on the Bangladesh border surreptitiously.

SHRI VAYALAR RAVI : Please do not be emotional.

SHRI VAJPAYEE : It is a question of the country's interest, but to accuse the Prime Minister of making a secret deal in London is not to understand his personality. He will die, but make no secret deal.

I am sorry, Mr. Deputy Speaker, that I got a little agitated. As Minister of External Affairs I should not have been agitated, but old habits die hard.

Professor Guha also said that laws directly affecting the minorities are being enacted in Bangladesh. In this connection he has referred to a law relating to property. I would like to draw his attention to the fact that no basic difference has been brought into the ordinance issued, so that action can be taken immediately.

SHRI SAMAR GUHA : Don't try to convince me. I have gone through the matter very deeply. You are aware with whom the talks took place. It is difficult to mention all the names.

SHRI VAJPAYEE : However, there could be complaints about the manner in which that law is being implemented, and Professor Guha has indicated these complaints. We have also drawn the attention of Bangladesh towards the implementation of this law. I do not stand here to defend Bangladesh. I heard a voice from behind. Both sides are attacking. But we have to debate the situation as it is and the House may take a decision in the light of that. It is also not correct to say that we are not watchful about the situation in Bangladesh or are not able to wield enough influence to ensure the safety of minorities living in Bangladesh. Mr. Deputy Speaker, we are putting an example before our neighbours by giving a treatment of equality, justice and to an extent liberalism to the minorities in our country. A proposal to exchange population on the basis of religion was mooted at the time of partition, but that was not accepted because it was acknowledged that it could be the constitutional, legal and moral responsibility of the Government of the respective country to protect the lives and properties of its minorities. India has tried to conduct herself according to this, and we want that Bangladesh should also do the same. However, Professor Guha will agree, and he has himself said this, that he does not want any direct interference in this matter in Bangladesh. The House and Professor Guha may rest assured that we are trying to influence Bangladesh in this regard to the extent that the situation which we are trying to improve may not deteriorate.

Nepal

Trade Difficulties with Nepal

Mr. Speaker, Sir, it is not necessary to reiterate that Nepal is our neighbour and we want to have most friendly relations with it. But if, as a free and sovereign country, Nepal can develop its relations with Pakistan and China, keeping in mind its interests, our relations should also be decided by giving prominence to the interests of India. The Hon. Minister has said in the last sentence of the first paragraph of his statement that "they helped identify the issues." What are these issues ? He has given some indication that we do not want to put any restrictions so far as the goods produced by Nepal are concerned, but if the goods manufactured by third countries are dumped into India indiscriminately that would create difficulty. Is that the issue or are there other issues as well ? Will the Hon'ble Minister please throw light on this ?

Take Opposition into Confidence

Secondly, I want to know whether the Hon. Minister is ready to take the Opposition parties into confidence regarding Indo-Nepal relations. Tomorrow you are going to have talks. After the talks you would invite the opposition parties. It is necessary to take the Opposition parties into confidence about such things as what the Government's view-point is, what the points being stressed by Nepal are and what points India cannot accept so that no misunderstanding remains. We would like to protect the interests of India while maintaining friendly relations with Nepal. If the Hon. Minister takes the Opposition parties into confidence many misunderstandings would be cleared.

SHRI L.N. MISHRA : So far as the question of India's interests is concerned there can be no two opinions about what Shri Atalji has said. This is what we are saying, first of all we have to look to India's interests. It is also in the interest of our country that Nepal should progress and develop. Nepal is our neighbour and you know India is a very large country.

We can bear a bigger burden, Nepal can bear less. But this does not mean that India should be used to dump third countries' goods. We cannot accept the proposition that goods manufactured in third countries should be exported to India through Nepal and we should look on helplessly. This cannot be allowed.

Lok Sabha on November 12, 1970 during the discussion regarding Trade Difficulties with Nepal

He asked what issues were identified. As I said before, I did not want to analyse those things even on that day. But the Nepalese Minister made a statement after reaching Kathmandu which the Hon. member might have seen. Even now we do not want to spell out the points of difference and would bear with it, because that would facilitate talks. Although he has mentioned certain things and the Hon. member might have seen that, I want neither to contradict nor to affirm them. I do not want to give my opinion on the advice tendered by him. But this much I have already said, and I would reiterate it, that we will not do anything which harms the interests of India, and we cannot be a party to that.

Whether the Opposition parties should be taken into confidence or not about the agreement that may be executed between India and Nepal is a political matter. This has not happened in the case of trade agreements executed so far, and it appears to be rather inauspicious to start this practice with Nepal. I would request him to bless us so that we may succeed in our effort and we trust that we shall succeed. Opposition parties must concede that we are as much committed to protect the interests of the country as they are and I do not want to say anything more.

SHRI VAJPAYEE : The Hon. Minister has taken my suggestion in a wrong light. We do not want to discuss the trade agreement. I come from an area which is contiguous to Nepal. I know the position. But what is being done to resolve the difficulties that have arisen with Nepal by inviting the Opposition parties ? What is the objection to it ?

SHRI L.N. MISHRA : This has never happened so far in regard to trade relations and, Mr. Speaker, I am not free in all these matters. I will also have to talk about it and only after having a talk I can say anything about it.

SHRI RANGA (Srikakulam) : Are they not working in close co-operation and consultation with their Foreign Minister ?

SHRI R. BARUA (Jorhat) : It appears from the Nepalese statement that they, being a land-locked country, are not given international facilities for transit of trade by India. That is the general complaint and main propaganda against India. What are the facilities that we are not in a position to offer them according to the international code ? Secondly, how is it that these two friendly countries have not been able to iron out their mutual differences through diplomatic channels ? And, how is it that, on the other hand, we have allowed Pakistan and China to come so much closer to Nepal ?

SHRI L.N. MISHRA : According to the international convention any land-locked country has a right to have access to the sea, and that we have given. They have access to the sea through Calcutta, and there cannot be any two opinions on this matter. About other matters which are political I would not like to say anything, but about transit I can positively say that Nepal will have free transit of goods originating from Nepal to go to any third country that they may like to send them to, and they will have access to the Calcutta port.

Visit to Nepal

Mr. Speaker, Sir, as the Hon'ble members are aware, I recently paid a visit to Nepal on the invitation of His Excellency Professor Krishna Raj Aryal, and I stayed there from 14th to 16th July, 1977. I visited some other countries also in order to participate in the international conferences as Foreign Minister as per the schedule fixed earlier. But I am very glad to say that I paid my very first visit to Nepal in the context of bilateral relations. This fact denotes our excellent relations, which are based on history, culture, religion and social as well as economic contacts. The visit was paid mainly to promote the existing goodwill between India and Nepal and to continue the dialogue initiated at the highest level by the new Government, which was inaugurated in early April during the visit to India of His Majesty the King of Nepal.

I called on His Majesty the King of Nepal in Kathmandu. We discussed various subjects of mutual interest in a cordial atmosphere. I also met the Prime Minister Shri Tulsi Giri. During the talks it was natural that an interest in the recent developments in India was shown. I reiterated that we in India are committed to a democratic way of life and I also told them that the Government of India would not interfere in the internal affairs of Nepal or for that matter any other country.

Two rounds of talks were held with the Foreign Minister of Nepal, during which officials of both the countries were present. All matters pertaining to relations between the two countries were discussed in an atmosphere of friendship and amity, which is a special feature of Indo-Nepal relations. I am fully confident that our talks have led to the recognition of the fact that for strengthening our friendship and increasing our co-operation for mutual benefit uniformity of interests is most important. Both India and Nepal are equally interested in establishing stability, harmony and cooperation among all the countries of this sub-continent.

Entire Sub-Continent should be a Zone of Peace

We discussed the views of the Nepalese side on the issue of a zone of peace. I explained to our host that it is the heart-felt desire of the Janata Government that the entire sub-continent should constitute a zone of peace and the government was taking steps with a view to improving its relations with all the neighbouring countries of India. So far as the question of Nepal was concerned, I gave an indication that keeping in view our friendly relations we would consider with an open mind any suggestion that may be put forth by the Government of Nepal. I reaffirmed the fact that there existed

Lok Sabha on July 26, 1977 as Minister of External Affairs on the Visit to Nepal

a treaty of peace and friendship between India and Nepal in which it has been accepted that both the countries would ever live in peace. This treaty and the subsequent action taken by us fully reconfirm the freedom, sovereignty and territorial integrity of Nepal. It gave me great pleasure to learn from the Foreign Minister of Nepal that Nepal would continue to honour this treaty as well as all other commitments which both the countries have made to each other.

During the talks held with the Foreign Minister of Nepal, and also in talks held in a meeting with H.E. Pitambar Dhoj Khati, Minister of Commerce and Industry of the Government of Nepal, the question of a new treaty between India and Nepal was raised for consideration, as it was pending since August, 1976. Both sides put up their cases. The Nepalese side made certain proposals on which we indicated our initial reaction and both the sides agreed that the viewpoints of each would be considered carefully. Until a new agreement is reached regarding trade and transit the provisions of the old trade and transit treaty, which ended in August, 1976, would continue to be operative. This is proof that the Government of India was very eager to avoid any difficulty in the way of trade between India and Nepal or in the way of transit trade of any other country with Nepal. Our experience shows that this treaty has not proved to be an obstacle in the ambitions of Nepal in the direction of increasing its trade and in finding new markets for its goods. Both the countries will have to take care of reasonable concerns of each other and will also have to see that transit arrangements do not harm the interests of either.

Consideration of Joint Projects

Various projects that are under way between the two countries for using the large potential of water resources of the Himalayas for mutual benefit were also discussed. It was also agreed that the pending work of a joint study of future projects for intelligent utilisation of these resources in the interest of environmental problems and promotion of social as well as economic development of the peoples of both the countries should be undertaken early.

I am satisfied with the visit and the reasons for my satisfaction are that being close neighbours, whose borders are contiguous for long distances and also open we will resolve our problems, which naturally arise between countries, through mutual negotiations and for the benefit of the peoples of the two countries. The essence of my talks reflects that both the countries are eager to maintain our multifarious and excellent relations for all times. Both the sides felt that this visit has strengthened our friendship and reconfirmed the desire of both the sides that our mutually beneficial relations should further improve in the interest of the two countries.

I want to express my gratitude on this occasion for the hearty welcome extended to me by His Majesty's Government of Nepal and the warmth and cordiality shown to me as well as to the delegation accompanying me during our stay there.

SHRI UGRASEN : Mr. Speaker, Sir, when the Hon'ble Minister of External Affairs returned from his goodwill mission to Nepal he made a statement before journalists on the 16th. I want to have a clarification from him on what he stated then.

The first thing he said was that both the countries have committed themselves to discuss the Karnali River Valley Scheme and have agreed to take steps regarding the Pancheshwar Dam Project, the Rapti River Scheme and the Daulal Ghat Nakara Road Project.

The Hon'ble Minister has referred to them in indicative terms but has not clarified the same.

While talking to journalists, he also stated that he had talks with the Maharajadhiraj of Nepal, the Prime Minister of H.M's Government, Dr. Tulsi Giri, and other leaders there about democracy, human rights and freedom, and he was satisfied that these talks would benefit both the neighbouring countries.

India is the largest democratic country. During the last Lok Sabha elections a very great experiment of democracy has been made here, which has not been done anywhere in the world. Even President Carter of the U.S. admired it. While it is the duty of India to see that democracy should prosper in our country, it should also support democratic forces in neighbouring countries, whether it is Bangladesh, Pakistan or Sri Lanka. We are glad Shri Jayawardhane has won in Sri Lanka. I want to know in clear terms whether during the course of the talks he held with the leaders of Nepal about human rights, democracy and freedom, did the question of Shri B.P. Koirala also come up.

SHRI VAJPAYEE : During the talks the projects of Karnali, Pancheshwar and Rapti were discussed. It is proposed to build a hydro-electric project at Karnali, which would generate 2000 Megawatts of power. It appears that Nepal and India would not be able to complete this project with their own financial resources. Therefore it would be necessary to obtain international funds. Nepal wants to set up a Board for this project. They have asked us to nominate four Indians on this Board. We are going to make these nominations and we have urged upon them that, in the meantime, they may inform us about the terms of reference and the jurisdiction of the Board, so that a final decision could be taken about the constitution of the Board.

Pancheshwar Scheme

The Pancheshwar scheme is concerned with the river called Mahakali in Nepal and Sharada on our side. The experts of both countries are considering this scheme jointly. We have decided to complete this consideration early. This project will be built on the borders of both the countries and, therefore, the question of acquisition of land is also before both the countries.

So far as the question of the Rapti river multi-purpose scheme is concerned the Hon'ble member will accept the fact that in this House I have been a representative of the Balrampur constituency which is a victim of devastating floods in the Rapti river every year. Naturally I was personally interested in this scheme. We have received the project report from Nepal. Indian experts have completed their study of it. Now we have constituted a Joint Committee which will finalise this scheme This scheme will benefit Nepal for irrigation and power.

The Karnali project would also generate power. We have told Nepal that India would be ready to purchase surplus power.

Shri Ugrasen has asked one more question. If he had read my complete statement given to the newspapers, or had quoted it, he would have got the answer to his question. We discussed many matters with the King of Nepal and the leaders of Nepal. It would not be proper to mention all the matters here. If our friend Shri Ugrasen wants to have any particular information I can give it to him separately. Thank you.

Sri Lanka

Attacks on Tamilians

Mr. Chairman, I do not want to widen the scope of this discussion. Sri Lanka and India have very old and close relations. Both have faith in the ideals of non-alignment. Besides, we are bound with each other by many ties of cultural and geographical proximity. Occasionally, ups and downs in relations do come. I also remember that day when the Sri Lankan Government had permitted Pakistani aircraft to land there for flying onwards to Bangladesh. At that time the country had Smt. Bhandarnayake's Government, and India had to raise its voice against this step. Later there was a change of Government there, and in India also the Government changed. In the democratic system Governments may change, but change in Government should not bring about a change in the basic principles of foreign policy of the countries. At least I can say that in the formulation and conduct of foreign policy I never allowed party politics to enter, because in 1977, we fought the elections on domestic issues. But I regret that Smt. Gandhi— she has just now left the House—brought foreign policy for the first time in the election arena in 1980.

Mr. Chairman, the situation that has been created today is serious and delicate. The concern expressed by the Minister of External Affairs in this matter is the concern of the entire House and the entire nation and there is no scope for party politics in it.

I agree with him that the unity and integrity of Shri Lanka should be preserved. Sri Lanka is already so small geographically. If she takes any steps for maintaining her unity and integrity, that is within its jurisdiction. If Indian citizens are affected by these steps we can take up this matter with Sri Lanka at the diplomatic level, and I want to draw the attention of the External Affairs Minister to it. In his statement he has referred to the Public Security Ordinance. This Ordinance provides for the method of disposal of the dead bodies of people killed by police firing. I have a copy of the ordinance with me. Under it there would not be any *post mortem* of the dead bodies now. They will either be cremated or buried. Their relatives will not be informed. I agree it is a harsh step. Our embassy has protested against it.

I would like to put two questions to the Hon. Minister. Is he aware that similar ordinances were also issued in 1959 and 1971 also ?

SHRI RAMGOPAL REDDY : Where ?

Lok Sabha on July 27, 1983 during discussion regarding the Attacks on the Tamil-speaking people in Sri Lanka

SHRI VAJPAYEE : We are talking of Sri Lanka, not of Andhra Pradesh.

Did we make a protest at that time ? Is the Hon. Minister aware that the wordings of the ordinances of 1959 and 1971 were exactly the same except with one difference ? The difference made in the Ordinance this time is that if any such step is taken, the permission of the Defence Ministry would have to be obtained. This is the little amendment or improvement over the old Ordinance. I am not justifying the Ordinance. The relatives of the dead would at least like to be shown the dead bodies and to know what is going to be done with them. I would like to know whether, at the time of protesting, our embassy knew that such ordinances had been issued earlier also. Did the embassy know that there was a slight difference between this Ordinance and the old ones ?

Secondly, we made a diplomatic protest and we have, of course, a right to do so. But how did the news of this protest get published in Sri Lankan newspapers ? There is an anti-India lobby in Sri Lanka—a newspaper. I do not want to mention it by name, against which the Bhandarnayake Government had taken action. This newspaper is bent upon spoiling the relations between Sri Lanka and India. Somebody informed it about the Indian protest and it published the news in bold headlines. The intention was to create an impression among the Sinhalese that India was interfering in the domestic affairs of Sri Lanka, that India had no business to interfere in how Sri Lanka disposed of the dead bodies. And things got worse.

Publication of Anti-India News

I want to know if a protest was to be made why was it disclosed to the press. How did anti-India news got published in Sri Lankan newspapers ? It is possible that it was leaked to the press by the Sri Lankan Government. Our External Affairs Minister should look into it as to how did it happen. Was it known before making the protest that such an Ordinance had been issued earlier also and did we protest or not at that time and what effort was to be made to stop it from going to the newspapers ? Why were Tamilians made a target in Colombo ? I can understand about Jaffna, because it has been a scene of skirmishes and is a disturbed area. So is Trincomali. A new incident has taken place there. Fighting has started in the Sri Lankan Navy between the Tamils and the Sinhalese working there. They are fighting with each other and a Tamilian working in the Navy has been killed. If their mutual feuds spread to the Navy and the Army it would create a very difficult situation. Who will then protect life and property ? It is true that the number of Tamil-speaking people has increased there, but never before have disturbances on such a large scale taken place in Colombo. Even today it is difficult to say how wide-spread the disturbances were. I have just now read the headlines in newspapers. The Minister of External Affairs has not been able to supply much information in this matter. I can understand his difficulty and that is why I was not very keen for a discussion on it today. But I must say one thing. Sri Lanka is our very close neighbour, but in spite of that there is no Indian news agency there. I want to know how many Indian newspapers have their representatives there.

The news published today in Delhi newspapers has been taken from the newspapers that look at news through their own glasses and do not care for relations between India and Sri Lanka. The distorted version which the Western newspapers, Video, T.V. and radio presented about Assam events is known to us. We should not trust that media. *The Hindustan Times* has reported today that there was wide-spread arson, but the policemen stood by as onlookers. The report further says that the fire-brigade which wanted to go to put out the fire was prevented by people who threw stones at it. Police was just looking on, and the army did not want to perform its duty, but the fire-brigade people wanted to do their duty. They wanted to go to put out the fire but were prevented by the people! I wish to tell our newspapers, I know it is not the responsibility of the Government, but at least the newspapers in the capital should send their representatives to Colombo. Our news agencies are subsidised by the government. They also should have their representatives in Colombo. We should get correct information.

Question of Stateless

One more point and I will conclude. No misunderstanding of any kind should be created between Sri Lanka and India. A small misunderstanding had erupted. I called for a report and went through it. The Annual Report of the External Affairs Ministry says that during the year under review relations between India and Sri Lanka continued to be cordial. Thereafter, it says that talks have been held on the question of stateless people of Indian origin in Sri Lanka. My submission is that it is for the people of Sri Lanka to decide whose Government should be there. Our Government has to deal with the Government that is in power there. Governments will change, rulers will change, but relations between the two countries should continue to be stable and friendship should be perpetual. We must not permit any issues to sour that friendship.

No doubt people would raise their voice if there was violation of human rights, whether in India or in Sri Lanka. I know Amnesty International has been sending its reports. I have read them. They have said that those people might be reactionary or extremist, but they cannot be subjected to torture in jails. They are being tortured. Jayawardane cannot escape by saying that Amnesty International is communist. Our Government's attitude about its reports is also not very good. But I do not want to go into that. Protection of human rights is necessary in Sri Lanka also. If need be, we should speak about that too.

However, as the Hon. Minister of External Affairs has said, nobody wants to interfere in their domestic affairs. The Government there is passing through a difficult phase, and we wish it success in getting over it. We want it to protect the life of every citizen and every stateless citizen in that country. I think the statement given by the Hon. Minister is not merely a Government statement, it also expresses the sentiments of the whole House, and I am fully in agreement with it. Thank you.

III SUPER POWERS

Russian Interference in India's Elections

Sir, so far we used to talk of American interference in the internal affairs of this country. Now some evidence of Soviet interference is appearing. The entire House will agree that being a free and sovereign country we cannot tolerate this kind of interference, from whatever quarter it might come. But I am greatly disappointed and surprised to hear the statement of the Home Minister in this regard. He has no doubt referred to the reports published in newspapers in this matter, but he has not taken the trouble of saying anything about the veracity of the report. It says :

> "Mr. Loginov has described how a high-ranking K.G.B. officer whose real name was Mr. Lyudin was sent last year as a political counsellor in the Soviet Embassy in Delhi where, under the assumed name of Mr. Yuri Modin, he organised the Soviet Union's election campaign".

Does the Home Minister accept that there was a counsellor in the Soviet Embassy in New Delhi by the name of Mr. Modin ? I have a booklet published by the External Affairs Ministry of the Government of India which carries the names of the staff of foreign embassies. On page 93 of this booklet, under the head "Union of the Soviet Socialist Republics", this is given: "Counsellor : M. Yuri I. Modin, Flat No. 16, House No. 4, Residential Buildings of the USSR Embassy, Chanakyapuri, New Delhi - 21 "

The allegation made is that Mr. Modin was a high ranking K.G.B. Officer. He came to Delhi during the time of elections, remained here between summer and spring, and indulged in activities that would affect our elections.

Has it also come to the notice of the Home Minister that Mr. Modin's name is being associated with certain fake documents ? This is a very serious matter. I want the Home Minister to give a clear and straightforward reply on the basis of solid information. A fake letter was written on behalf of the Counsellor-General of the US Consulate in Bombay to the US Ambassador. Another letter on behalf of the British High Commissioner was written in which serious charges have been made against Shri Patil and other leaders. Has the Ministry of Home Affairs made any inquiries to find out who wrote these fake letters ?

The Home Minister has stated that we are making inquiries into the alleged interference. What is this "alleged" ? The "Radio Peace and Progress"

Lok Sabha on December 7, 1967 while moving the calling attention motion regarding the Russian interference in general elections programme is broadcast from the Soviet soil. Can anybody deny this ? Nobody can deny this.

MR. SPEAKER : But the Hon. Minister has said that the Government have already protested and written to that Government.

SHRI VAJPAYEE : When the Government is protesting what is the point in saying "alleged interference" ?

SHRI YASHVANT RAO CHAVAN : I have not said it in that connection.

SHRI VAJPAYEE : I want to submit that even if the Hon. Minister does not go into any other evidence the "Radio Peace and Progress" programme is an open interference in India's domestic affairs and goes against the principle of co-existence. Instead of sending a protest why does the Indian Government not tell Soviet Russia that if this programme was not stopped it would be considered an unfriendly act and adversely affect our relations with them ?

I want to make it clear that we want friendship with the Soviet Union and are grateful for the help they have given to us. But they cannot assail our freedom, our sovereignty and our self-respect. Nor will we allow America to do it.

SHRI Y.B. CHAVAN : I entirely agree with the Hon. member about the sentiments that he has expressed in the last part of his statement. I did not talk about the alleged interference as far as the radio was concerned.

I have said that we have taken up this matter with them but about the other matter, naturally, when I do not have the text of the statement with me, I just cannot say anything about it.

It is a fact that an officer of the name of Mr. Yuri Modin, mentioned in the news items etc. was an officer designated Counsellor, and he was in India between 12th July, 1966 and 22nd April, 1967. That is a fact. But that fact would not authorise me to say whether what is alleged is right or wrong. This fact is true and we know about it.

Certain other allegations also are made, but unless we come to any conclusion with proper evidence, I think it would be very unfair, in view of our relationship with other countries, friendly countries, both America and Soviet Russia, to make any authoritative statement on the floor of the House. That is my main difficulty.

SHRI D.N. PATODIA : On a point of order ....

MR. SPEAKER : There is no point of order now.

SHRI VAJPAYEE : Mr. Speaker, Sir, my question has not been replied. Is the Government of India prepared to tell the Soviet Union that this interference should stop, otherwise it would be considered an unfriendly act ?

MR. SPEAKER : The Hon. Minister has already said that it should stop whether it be from America or from Russia.

SHRI RANGA (Srikakulam) : It is an omnibus answer which he has given. But the Hon. member had asked a specific question.

MR. SPEAKER : He has already said that it should stop, whether it be from America or from Russia.

SHRI Y.B. CHAVAN : I did say that.

SHRI D.N. PATODIA : Information is being concealed.

SHRI KANWAR LAL GUPTA (Delhi-Sadar) : Is the Hon. Minister prepared to say that it is an unfriendly act ? Let him stand up and say it.

U.S. Interference in India's Elections

Sir, my party is being accused of having taken money for elections from America. This indeed is a very serious charge. A few days back a Congress member had ......

MR. SPEAKER : What did I do about Shri Ramamurti ? Did I not ask him to write to me ? I will give a chance to explain if you write to me.

SHRI VAJPAYEE : Let them speak as they wish and do the mischief they like. But we want that this matter should be properly investigated. On the one hand we are accused of taking money from America, on the other hand *Young India* has published an article accusing us of taking money from Soviet Russia. I want to make it clear ....

SHRI PILOO MODY : It is wrong to take money from both sides.

Taking Foreign Money for Election is Treason

SHRI VAJPAYEE : We don't take money from any side. Instead of taking money from foreign countries to fight elections, we would prefer to renounce politics. If it is proved that Jan Sangh has taken money either from America or Russia I will severe my ties with Jan Sangh. It is treason to take money from foreign countries and we can never be a party to any treason.

But I also submit that the investigation that is being conducted by the Intelligence Bureau is inadequate; it cannot gain credibility in the country. I would like a Supreme Court Judge to be appointed to conduct the enquiry and we are prepared to face it. Let the Government level allegations against us and we will give our reply. If the charge is established we are prepared to suffer the highest publishment.

Lok Sabha on December 12, 1967 during the discussion on the calling attention motion regarding U.S. interference in the General Elections.

Russian Radio Propaganda Against Indian Political Parties

Mr. Deputy Speaker, Sir, I beg to draw the attention of the new Minister of External Affairs to the following matter of urgent public importance and request him to make a statement thereon :-

> "Propaganda by Radio Peace and Progress, Moscow, against certain political parties in India, which constitutes interference in the internal affairs of the country."

SHRI DINESH SINGH, Minister of External Affairs : Sir, Radio Peace and Progress located in U.S.S.R., has from time to time criticised Indian political parties and personalities in its broadcasts. The Government have drawn the attention of the Soviet Government to such references by the Radio Peace and Progress. The Soviet Government have taken the position that this Radio Station is not a Government concern but an independent organisation. They have drawn our attention to many statements and publications appearing in India which are critical of the Soviet leaders and Soviet policies and stated that their official radio stations and newspapers do not criticise our Government or make references to which Government could take exception.

The Government have noticed that in the critical references towards India Radio Peace and Progress make considerable use of quotations from the Indian newspapers.

In view of some of the critical broadcasts on Radio Peace and Progress during the recent elections the government have again brought the matter to the notice of the Soviet authorities.

SHRI VAJPAYEE : Does the Government of India agree with this assertion of the Soviet Government that Radio Peace and Progress is an independent organisation and that the Soviet Government has no control over it ? All those who are familiar with the system of government and social structure in Soviet Russia know that whatever happens in Soviet Union is under the control and direction of the Government. Is the Government of India unaware of this fact, and if it is not, why has a protest not been lodged by the Government of India so far instead of simply drawing the attention of the Government of the U.S.S.R. ? We are friends of Soviet Russia and want to strengthen relations of friendship, but the basis of such friendship cannot be open interference in our internal affairs. If the Government of the Soviet Union interferes in this manner we will have to protest against it, and if our government does not protest against that interference we would be forced to

Lok Sabha on February 19, 1969 while moving the calling attention motion on propaganda by 'Radio Peace and Progress' against certain political parties in India

say that this government appears to have become a satellite of the Soviet Union.

Mr. Deputy Speaker, Sir, the question is not merely that of 'Radio Peace and Progress'. The fact is that during the elections, Moscow Radio has made broadcasts in which political parties in India were criticised. I want to give an instance. On January 23, 1969, Moscow Radio in its news Bulletin broadcast in Bengali at 4-30 made certain allegations against the Bhartiya Jan Sangh. I was criticised by name and it was stated that we want to change our foreign policy, favouring imperialism. So far, the Government of the Soviet Union had been interfering in our internal affairs behind the curtain of 'Radio Peace and Progress', but now it has exposed itself and such broadcasts are being made on Moscow Radio. Another broadcast was made on January 27, 1969 at 4 o'clock in which Shri Shankaracharya was named and it was said that reactionary forces want to launch an agitation in the name of cow before the mid-term poll.

I want to know whether the Hon. Minister has these broadcasts by Radio Moscow in view ? Allegations are being made not only against Jan Sangh. Radio Peace and Progress relayed a broadcast on February 10, 1969 in which Congress President Shri Nijalingappa was attacked. Once Shri Morarji Desai and Shri Patil had been attacked, and now Shri Nijalingappa has been selected for the attack. I want to quote the words :

> "At a pre-election meeting in Patna (India) Mr. Nijalingappa has made a speech which has infuriated all honest people"

Where do these honest people reside ? After this has it not been said in Russia about Shri Nijalingappa that he too wants to change the foreign policy of India and that he wants to reverse all what late Shri Nehru wanted to do ?

Mr. Deputy Speaker, Sir, my question is clear and I would like to repeat it : Does the Government of India agree with the assertion of the Soviet Government that Radio Peace and Progress has nothing to do with the Soviet Government ?

Secondly, has the broadcast made by Radio Moscow come to his notice ?

Soviet Russia goes on making announcements about non-interference into the internal affairs of other countries. It is an advocate of the policy of non-alignment based on the principle of respect for freedom and sovereignty of every country and non-interference in their internal affairs.

I want to know why the Government of India is not willing to formally lodge a protest with the Soviet Union and why does it not give a warning that if such interference continues it will create tension in the relations between India and Soviet Russia ?

SHRI DINESH SINGH : I agree with the question of principle referred to by the Hon. member, that a country should not interfere in the internal affairs of another country. But so far as the expression of our views is concerned there is some difference. The Hon. member knows that many countries that are close to us express their views through their Radio and newspapers that are not in conformity with our views. Or, they talk against our institutions or our political structure and say many things which we do not like. But different countries have their own ways and we have to keep that in mind while reacting. So far as the relations of one country with another country are concerned we have to observe restraint and have to behave in a particular manner. It is not the question of our liking or disliking what the other country does. The question is what we can do and what we cannot do according to certain norms and practices. When the government of a country tells us that they have no control—I am not talking of relations, I am talking of control—over that Radio, how can we say, 'no, you have control over that', whether we may or may not like it .... (*Interruptions*)

SHRI RANGA (Srikakulam) : Are there political parties there vying with each other as they are doing here ? Are there newspapers which are criticising their Government as is the case in this country ? Why does he shut his eyes to the fact ?

SHRI DINESH SINGH : We are not discussing the Soviet system here, nor the Indian system; we are discussing a particular fact, a statement made by a government and how we deal with these statements so far as government-to-government relations are concerned.

SHRI SURENDRANATH DWIVEDY (Kendrapara) : Do you accept what China says, namely, that they have occupied their own territory ?

SHRI DINESH SINGH : So far as the views of Hon. members are concerned they have already been fully expressed and will be taken note of everywhere. ... (*Interruptions*)....

SHRI VAJPAYEE : The Hon. Minister has not replied to my question. I said that Radio Moscow is broadcasting. I do not accept that the Government has no control over Radio Peace and Progress. But what does the Hon. Minister have to say about the Government broadcast ? Has he got any spirit of national dignity or not ? Here governments of other countries abuse us and the Minister of External Affairs keeps mum. This situation will not be tolerated.

SHRI SHASHI BHUSHAN (Khargone) : Mr. Deputy Speaker, Sir, when the Voice of America speaks against the government institutions of India why is no demonstration held against them ? We should protest against whosoever speaks against our country.

SHRI VAJPAYEE : If the Voice of America does so a protest must be lodged against that too. This is also wrong.

SHRI BALRAJ MADHOK (South Delhi) : The question is about Russia, not America. If America does it, we can take up that also. Russia has a particular system of government. There is no democracy there. Let him deny that ...... (*Interruptions*)......

Russia Violates Indian Air Space

Mr. Speaker, Sir, I beg to draw the attention of the Minister of External Affairs to the following matter of urgent public importance and request him to make a statement thereon :

> "Reports that Russian aircraft carrying arms to North Vietnam are flying from Moscow to Hanoi via India and the reaction of the Government of India thereon."

SHRI DINESH SINGH, Minister of External Affairs : No Russian planes carrying arms and military equipment have been permitted to fly over India to North Vietnam or to any other destination. Civilian aircraft, however, do fly over India to Hanoi and back with the clearance of the Government of India. Such civilian flights are of 11-18 aircraft and they land at Calcutta (Dum Dum) airport on their way to Hanoi. These aircraft carry passengers, baggage, mail and cargo but no military equipment.

SHRI VAJPAYEE : Mr. Speaker, Sir, on 18th March, the Budapest Radio announced that passenger aircraft of the Soviet Union are flying over India and Pakistan on way to Hanoi as an experimental measure so that later on their fighter aircraft may carry weapons to Hanoi by this air route. Subsequently this was broadcast by London Westinghouse. I want to know whether any clarification has been sought from the Soviet Union whether this will be confined to the flights of civilian aircraft only or later on they will ask for permission to fly arms to Vietnam. Sir, as you know, relations between Russia and China have deteriorated with the result that it is no more possible for Russia to send aid to North Vietnam which it used to send, through China. Russia is now in search of another route and wants to use this route.

The External Affairs Minister will agree that India wants that the talks going on in Paris about Vietnam may be successful. We want a peaceful solution to the problem of Vietnam and India would not like anything to be done that may increase tensions and the war between North and South Vietnam may aggravate. But if India allows its territory or air-space to carry arms to North or South Vietnam its international objective about Vietnam cannot be achieved. I want the Hon'ble Minister to give an assurance to the House that India will not allow any country, whether it is the USSR or the USA, to use her air space for carrying arms to Vietnam.

SHRI DINESH SINGH : I agree with the Hon'ble member that we have to make efforts for a peaceful settlement and solution of the Vietnam problem, and we are trying for that. I also fully agree with him that we should not do anything that may adversely affect the peace talks that are now going on and

---

Lok Sabha on March 31, 1969 while moving the calling attention motion regarding the flight of Russian Planes to Hanoi over India

there is no reason for anybody to worry on that account. No aircraft carrying weapons for North Vietnam or South Vietnam are flying over India.

SHRI VAJPAYEE : The question is not whether they are flying at present. If a country makes a request to us in future to allow it the use of our air space for this purpose will the Government refuse such a permission ?

MR. SPEAKER : It is a general question, not pertaining to the call attention and, therefore, not relevant just now.

SHRI VAJPAYEE : It is a question about Vietnam only. The Hon'ble Minister should declare in unambiguous words that we will not allow our air space to send arms to Vietnam.

SHRI DINESH SINGH : What can one say now about something that may happen in future ?

SHRI KANWARLAL GUPTA (Delhi-Sadar) : This is no reply. The Government must spell out their policy.

SHRI DINESH SINGH : We have already clarified our policy.

SHRI PILOO MODY (Godhra) : Perhaps after the Russian take-over he will say.

SHRI VAJPAYEE : Mr. Speaker, Sir, I want your protection. The calling attention motion was on the issue that there were reports that Soviet Russia wants to use our skies to send arms to Vietnam. The External Affairs Minister has given only half reply. He has said that no Russian aircraft is carrying weapons at present. It is not a question of today. What will be the reaction of the Government if they ask for such permission tomorrow ? Will the Government take day-to-day decisions ? Have they not seriously considered such an important issue and made up their mind ?

SHRI DINESH SINGH : I have clearly said what our reaction will be. We want a peaceful solution of the problem there and we do not want any arms to go through Indian territory. I have clearly stated that.

Blood Bath inVietnam
A Challenge to Humanity

Mr. Speaker, Sir, the people of Vietnam have been fighting for their freedom and sovereignty for centuries. At first they fought the Chinese, then they fought the Japanese aggressors, thereafter they defeated the colonialist France and today the Vietnamese are facing the mightiest power of the world. In their struggle, apart from America, which has directly become a party there, other great powers have failed in performing their duties. It appears that there is a secret unwritten agreement among the great powers of the world about Vietnam, as a result of which no step has been taken to resolve the issue of Vietnam either in the United Nations or after the Geneva Conference outside the UNO.

The people of Vietnam, whether in the north or in the south, are passing through a terrible struggle, and paying the greatest price. Blood bathed Vietnam is a challenge to the entire humanity, but the big capitals of the world are content with either supplying arms or just wishing success to Vietnam and thinking that their duty ends there.

The Geneva Accord

The Geneva Conference was held in 1954, where an agreement was reached under which Vietnam was partitioned. The 11th parallel was drawn as the boundary line. It was decided in Geneva that elections will be held after two years. But elections were not held. America started giving military aid to South Vietnam. Someone who was doing the job of washing clothes in America was brought back to South Vietnam and made its President. He did not have the support of the people of South Vietnam. Elections were not held there. The people of Vietnam have not so far been given the opportunity to decide their fate with their free will.

India was the Chairman of the Control Commission. The Control Commission was responsible for guarding the cease-fire line and to hold elections in Vietnam. I feel that the Control Commission has failed in carrying out its responsibilities. It is possible that it might not have been given an opportunity to work. But then there was no need to maintain the Control Commission. India could have withdrawn from it by resigning. The Control Commission is only a Commission without having any control in its hands. It is not even known yet who started violation of the Geneva accord. Contradictory reports have been received about it.

Lok Sabha on April 17, 1972 in the context of American invasion of Vietnam

US Involvement

Reports of such activities have been received from North Vietnam as a result of which the U.S. Administration got an opportunity to involve itself in the Vietnam conflict by throwing dust into the eyes of the American public. Pentagon papers have been published. It is no more a puzzle now as to why America got involved in it. The struggle of Vietnam is primarily a struggle for national independence. Whether Vietnam should become a Communist State or not is a minor question. Firstly, Vietnam should be fully independent. Secondly, India would like to see not only Vietnam but also Laos and Cambodia to be free, neutral, non-aligned countries not allied to any bloc and which could contribute in establishing peace in this region. Such a Vietnam would not come out of war.

War in Absentia must Stop

My submission is that the super powers should not try to conduct the Vietnam war as a war in absentia. America has got itself involved in it. America wants to get out of it, but wants face saving while getting out. But there does not appear to be any possibility for this. Soviet Russia is supplying arms, but has not become effectively active in resolving this issue inside or outside the U.N. The leaders of Peking are very clever. Taking advantage of the Vietnam conflict they are trying to improve their relations with America and extract the full price of their friendship. My submission is that India can take initiative in the matter. There is no propriety in not raising this issue in the United Nations. I was greatly surprised to hear Dr. Sharma make the point that somebody may use the veto. Was not the issue of Bangladesh raised there in spite of the veto ? This will disclose the intentions of all countries. The U.S. is a member of the United Nations, so are Soviet Russia and China. At least we can raise our voice in the Security Council demanding that war in Vietnam must stop forthwith. The U.S. should stop bombing and North Vietnam should promise not to indulge in any inciting acts until an agreement is reached.

America Entangled

Secondly, a date must be fixed by which American troops should leave Vietnam and all prisoners of war released. India should also try to have a date fixed by which free and fair elections could be held in Vietnam and the Vietamese people could decide their own fate. We would be glad if Vietnam resolves to develop itself as a non-aligned and neutral state. At the same time the work of mobilising world opinion should be undertaken. As stated just now, a very large section of the American Administration has got itself entangled in a crisis from which there appears to be no escape.

President de Gaulle had warned the U.S. that if America committed the mistake of involving itself from where France is coming out it would become difficult for America to get out of it. American leaders, not President Nixon alone, started committing mistakes in the case of Vietnam ever since America decided to keep itself aloof from the Geneva conference. America did not bind itself with the Geneva Conference and subsequently made such attempts in Vietnam due to which the dividing line between the battle for national liberation and the war with the Communists became very thin.

I got a chance to visit Vietnam. After my visit I had stated that the American people should understand that Vietnam was fighting for its independence and it will not accept colonial status. It would continue its fight for independence and we should respect its desire for freedom. America will have to quit Vietnam one day. If the Government of India takes any concrete and effective action in the international sphere to reduce the anguish, pain and hardships of the people of Vietnam, I think a way could be found out of this knot. This is the test of statesmanship of New Delhi whether it can really prove to be of any active assistance or not in this matter. Mere expression of sentiments is not enough. The entire House and the whole country are one in condemning the bombardment. But mere condemnation could not solve the problem of Vietnam. For that the Government of India will have to prove itself effective in the field of international statesmanship and diplomacy. I want that the Minister of External Affairs should give a bit of indication while replying to the discussion , whether we are really in a position to do something or not and if we are then what is that we can do.

Asian Security Syndrome

Now the Government of India is talking about Asian security. If we want that our efforts to increase cooperation and goodwill among the Asian countries may succeed it cannot be done merely by expressing verbal sympathy for Vietnam's struggle. So long as the great powers are bent upon interfering in this region, directly or indirectly , the Assian countries cannot come closer, our wish to create cooperation and goodwill among them cannot fructify. I feel that before talking about an Asian Security Pact, we should try to resolve Vietnam conflict peacefully and in the interest of the people of Vietnam India should take initiative in this direction. If it did so an atmosphere could be created in Asia in which smaller countries, assured of their integrity, could run their Government and economy with the consent of their own people, otherwise not. In this direction India too is somewhat failing in its duty along with the big powers. Now we have to see what kind of leadership New Delhi provides in this moment of conflict. Thank You.

Naval Exercises in Indian Ocean

Mr. Deputy Speaker, Sir, I will ask only three small questions. The first: The Defence Minister, who till yesterday was Minister of External Affairs has expressed his concern over the fact that NATO countries including Pakistan are carrying out naval exercieses in the Indian Ocean. He also stated that he had made a speech in a public meeting against this exercise. I want to know if that is enough. Is it sufficient ? will the diplomacy and the Defence policy of a mature country like India be conducted from public platforms ? Had we not brought this Calling Attention Notice, the Hon'ble Minister would have thought that he had done his duty in this matter by speaking in a public meeting. I want to know why, when the government had information about these exercises, it did not call the ambassadors of the U.S., Britain, Iran and Turkey in New Delhi to express its concern and lodge protest against these exercises ? We have no diplomatic relations with Pakistan and, therefore, the question of calling the Pakistani ambassador does not arise, but the ambassadors of other countries are present in Delhi. The Defence Minister considers it as the biggest exercise. Was it then not proper to call the ambassadors of those countries and formally express our concern and lodge a protest ? Why was it not done ?

The second question is : The Hon'ble Defence Minister concedes that participation of Pakistan in this exercise has very serious implications. Pakistan has been bluffing that it has no connection with CEATO. It has been trying to sit in the line of non-aligned countries. But Pakistan has now been unmasked. What have we done to express our displeasure against Pakistan ? Today, when these big countries are creating tensions in the Indian Ocean and Pakistan is acting as their hosts, our representatives are signing agreements in Pakistan to resume air flight and start a telex service! I am not against these agreements. We have to normalise our relations with Pakistan. But if Pakistan makes a move on the chess-board of international politics could we not take the step of postponing the talks by saying that we would not talk till these exercises are in operation. This could have been a way to express New Delhi's displeasure. Now who will take note of our displeasure when we are engaged in love talk by going to Pakistan while Pakistan is making a show of her strength by inviting foreign powers in the Indian Ocean ?

My friend Shri Bhogendra Jha has provoked me to ask the third question. After hearing his speech I sometimes feel as if he was speaking on behalf of Soviet Russia. But he is a representative of the Indian Parliament, he has to protect Indian interests. The Defence Minister said that when one country's

Lok Sabha on November 20, 1974 while participating in the discussion on the calling attention motion regarding the naval exercises in the Indian Ocean by NATO countries

navy comes the other country gets encouragement to send its navy. A report in today's newspapers says that at present there are 12 Soviet warships, 18 supply vessels, one helicopter– carrier named Leningrad in the Indian Ocean, and one warship named Kieve is due to arrive. Besides it has also been reported that Soviet Russia has established bases in Somalia, Aden and Iraq in order to utilise all kinds of services. Soviet Russia is our friend and when it says it is not in favour of creating tensions in this region we believe it. Then can't we advise Soviet Russia to take a unilateral decision not to bring its navy into the Indian Ocean, even though the U.S., Britain, Turkey and Iran, who are also our friends, want to create tensions in this region ? If a war starts the Soviet Union is capable of facing it from anywhere. Will the Defence Minister give this advice to Soviet Russia ?

Crisis in Horn of Africa

DR. BALDEV PRAKASH (Amritsar) : I call the attention of the Minister of External Affairs to the following matter of urgent public importance and request that he may make a statement thereon:

> "Reported presence of Naval Force of the United States of America in the Indian Ocean as a consequence of the explosive situation in the Horn of Africa and the suspension of US-Soviet negotiations over arms limitation in the Indian Ocean."

SHRI VAJPAYEE : Mr. Speaker, Sir, the House is fully aware of the Government's view that the military presence of Great Powers in Indian Ocean is a cause of tension and insecurity in the area. The concept of a Zone of Peace in the Indian Ocean implies elimination of foreign military presence from the area. India, a member of the U.N. Ad Hoc Committee, is also actively participating in the implementation of the U.N. Resolution on Zone of Peace in the Indian Ocean. Preparations for a meeting of the littoral and hinterland States of the Indian Ocean to be convened in New York for implementing the U.N. Resolution are at hand. India has given expression to its belief that for achieving concrete results the participation of Great Powers and major maritime users of Indian Ocean in the proposed international conference is essential.

It is in this context that India has welcomed USA-USSR talks on mutual arms limitation in the Indian Ocean as a step towards the establishment of Indian Ocean as a Zone of Peace although our objective remains that of elimination of all foreign military presence from the Indian Ocean. India hopes that any bilateral understanding/agreement reached by the Great Powers shall incline them to extend increased cooperation to the U.N. in this matter and thus facilitate the establishment of the Zone of Peace.

Explosive Situation

The current explosive situation in the Horn of Africa is a source of deep concern to us. Ethiopia and Somalia, apart from being neighbours linked to us by the Indian Ocean, with whom we have friendly relations, are also developing countries and our fellow partners in the non-aligned fraternity of nations. The continuance of this conflict is vitiating the generally improving climate of international relations and causing a serious setback to detente. This makes it all the more imperative for us to contribute to the search of an

Lok Sabha on February 27, 1978 as Minister of External Affairs in response to the calling attention notice regarding reported presence of U.S. Naval Force in the Indian Ocean as a consequence of the explosive situation in the Horn of Africa

early peaceful and negotiated solution to the problem. This House will recall that as early as August last I had appealed to the leaders of Ethiopia and Somalia through their Charge d' Affaires in New Delhi for exercise of restraint and statesmanship, and had also expressed the hope that a peaceful settlement of the dispute would be arrived at and that the OAU Good Offices Committee on this subject would succeed. I had also expressed our apprehension that the conflict in the Horn of Africa would divert attention away from the burning issues in Southern Africa and that the continuation of the dispute would weaken the non-aligned movement and invite increased Great Power rivalry in the region. To our great disappointment the OAU efforts have not yet succeeded and some of our fears are proving correct.

The differences between Ethiopia and Somalia over the Ogaden province of Ethiopia erupted in the form of a full scale armed conflict last June. Ethiopia ascribed this to the invasion of its territory by Somalia troops while Somalia claimed it as liberation of Ogaden by the Western Somalia Liberation Front. Though the matter came before the OAU Summit Conference in Libreville last August its subsequent mediatory efforts did not succeed. The situation continued to deteriorate. Now there are reports of large-scale external military involvement in the area. Allegations have even been made that Ethiopia with its augmented military capabilities may decide to carry the war across the frontiers. Ethiopia, as the House is aware, has denied these allegations and has gone on record to say that its objective is to get the aggression vacated.

A U.S.-Soviet Restraint Necessary

Our Prime Minister has had an exchange of correspondence with President Carter of USA and President Brezhnev of USSR in which the developing situation in the Horn of Africa has been referred to. He has stated that the conflict in the Horn of Africa required restraint on the part of external powers as it could become more complicated by increasing rivalry and foreign military involvement. He has suggested that ways and means of restraint should be found to bring about a settlement respecting the principle of inviolability of the established frontiers as enshrined in the OAU Charter and urged an acceptable political solution under the OAU, UN or any other mutually acceptable auspices.

Secretary of State Vance had stated in his Press Conference on 10th February 1978 that the Soviet and Cuban involvement cannot help but have an effect upon the relationship between USA on the one hand and USSR and Cuba on the other, and that it is a matter which USA will obviously keep in mind as they proceed with the talks on the Indian Ocean because what seems to be happening there was in his view inconsistent with the limitation of forces insofar as the Indian Ocean talks were concerned. Even then he had observed that USA would continue with those talks, but pointed out that obviously it affected the political atmosphere in which those talks are carried forward.

Terminate Intervention in Ethiopia

There have been some consultations recently about the desirability of convening the Security Council of the United Nations to consider the situation in the Horn of Africa. Both the USA and UK feel that the aim of a debate in the UN Security Council would be to have deliberations and seek negotiations which would contribute to a political solution by reinforcing, through UN involvement, the OAU efforts at mediation. They stress that the purpose of the Council meeting is to seek a settlement and not to engage in a propaganda exercise. They also feel that the respect of territorial integrity of all States in the area should be one of the guiding principles in bringing about a peaceful resolution. In fact, as stated by Dr. Brezinski, the U.S. position is that Somalia ought to withdraw to its territorial frontiers, that the invasion of Ethiopia ought to be terminated, that there ought to be peace keeping arrangements, preferably by the OAU, and, in that context, the reported foreign involvement by the Soviet Union and Cuba ought to be also terminated by the departure of their forces.

The Soviet Union holds the view that the first step is that Somali withdraw from Ogaden. They are at pains to point out that while Western Powers had shown no concern at the time of Somali aggression of Ethiopia they are now voicing their concern about the situation in the Horn of Africa where the Ethiopian side has begun to repel this aggression. They feel that their assistance to Ethiopia in repelling the aggression should not be construed in any way as their being interested in the expansion of the conflict. They are categorical in stating that cease-fire without Somali withdrawal is not possible. They think that once Somali forces have withdrawn the problem could be tackled by the OAU. They have informed the USA that they are opposed to a Security Council meeting as it would only aggravate the situation.

We also understand that the African group is not in favour of discussion in the Security Council. At the same time Nigeria, who is chairman of the OAU Mediation Committee, has been trying very hard to mediate between Ethiopia and Somalia in order to bring the conflict to an end. Nigerian efforts seem at last to be succeeding with their having arranged a meeting, which would take place in Lagos shortly between the special emissaries of Ethiopia and Somalia.

Respect OAU Charter

We have all along felt that the solution to the problem—as indeed for all Intra-African problems—should be sought in consonance with the letter and spirit of the OAU Charter. We therefore believe that the parties to the dispute should respect and observe the letter and the spirit of this Charter. We are in favour of any concrete and agreed initiative that can bring about such a solution. We, therefore, welcome the proposed meeting to be held shortly at Lagos between Ethiopian and Somalian special emissaries and hope that it will have a successful outcome. We would support any move which would reinforce the OAU efforts leading to cessation of hostilities and a mutually acceptable solution, and we hope that the requisite cooperation for the success of such efforts would be forthcoming from all parties concerned.

I would now refer to what certain Hon'ble members seem to regard as a connected move, namely, the reported U.S. Naval presence in the Indian Ocean. There have also been reports of Naval presence of other Great Powers in the area. While it is not possible for us to accurately assess the connection between this development and the situation in the Horn of Africa, we are of the view that such foreign naval presence in the region cannot but act as an impediment to the lessening of the tension in the area, and also to the effort of the international community for establishment of a Zone of Peace in the Indian Ocean.

Suspension of Arms Limitation Talks

There is no truth in the reports that due to developments in the Horn of Africa US-USSR talks on questions concerning arms limitation measures in the Indian Ocean have been suspended.

In fact the last round of such talks was held in Berne, Switzerland according to schedule, from February 7 to February 17. Thus this did not end abruptly nor were they called off prematurely on account of the situation in the Horn of Africa for any other reason. However, we are given to understand that the US Government has informed the Soviet delegation at these talks that it regretted the current Soviet activities in the Horn of Africa and that the increase in Soviet naval forces was inconsistent with the spirit and substance of the negotiations. The Soviet side view this as another instance of the American practice of making use of unrelated situations for political purposes. As regards the substance of the negotiations that ended ten days ago, we understand that concrete progress has been registered. Both USA and USSR have characterised the discussions as "frank and useful" contributing to an understanding of each other's position. Moreover, there is agreement for these talks to be resumed, though unlike the hitherto practice of agreeing upon approximate date and venue of the next round of talks the date of subsequent meeting has been left to be fixed by mutual agreement later on.

India Cannot Afford Tension

Sir, we have always held that the benefits of *detente* should flow to the international community as a whole. We have always been in favour of peaceful solution of disputes bilaterally, or through regional organisations such as the OAU in case of intra-African problems, and if need be through mutually acceptable auspices. Indian Ocean should be a Zone of Peace guaranteeing peaceful maritime activity through which international commerce flows. Meaningful programmes of economic cooperation among its littoral and hinterland States for the benefit and welfare of the people inhabiting Indian Ocean region ought to be developed. Any development which impedes evolution of the course of events in these directions is a matter of serious concern to us. What is more, India can ill afford to have tension-creating presence in the vicinity of its maritime zones. This is how we view the situation to which the Hon'ble members have drawn attention. This House will agree that a just, peaceful and negotiated settlement of the problem in the Horn of Africa is bound to exercise a healthy influence in bringing about an early establishment of Indian Ocean as a Zone of Peace and will be conducive to development of mutually beneficial *inter-se* economic cooperation in the region. All efforts in this direction will have our full support.

SHRI SHYAMNANDAN MISHRA (Begusarai) : May I rise on a point order ? We are grateful to the Hon. Minister for giving a massive information in answer to a calling attention motion. But I address this question to the Chair specifically that in a calling attention you always insist, very rightly so, that it should not occupy more than 20 or 25 minutes or so. This is also the opinion expressed in the Business Advisory Committee. Now, if the Hon. Minister takes so much time in making a statement in response to the calling attention motion then the time necessarily taken would be much longer.

Would you kindly not ask the ministers to so frame their statement in a smaller compass ? He has already read out ten to fifteen pages statement.

SHRI VAJPAYEE : Five pages only.

SHRI SHYAMNANDAN MISHRA : Whatever it may be you pull up any Hon. member if he takes more time.

MR. SPEAKER : I do not pull up anybody. I only request. This might have been much smaller.

DR. BALDEV PRAKASH (Amritsar) : In my calling attention motion, what I stressed was regarding the presence of American war ships in the Indian Ocean. Tension is increasing in this region. The Hon. Minister has also admitted that any kind of presence of U.S. Naval Forces in the Indian Ocean, is hampering the efforts of the reducing of tension in the region. He has said that it is a matter of serious concern to us. I want to ask, if it is so, then whether the Government has undertaken any action or is only watching the situation carefully. This has always been the policy of America. In the 1972 Indo-Pak war also America had sent its war ships in the Bay of Bengal. This policy is greatly responsible for Indo-Pak tension.

The American President says about complete de-militarization of the Indian Ocean but on the other hand U.S. Naval force's are coming there. How can one understand these contradictory stands.

On 20th February, the U.S. Defence Secretary while delivering the speech at the world affair in Los Angles said :

> "USA plans to strengthen its strategic forces in Asia and upgrade it in the Pacific."

Where will this leading to ? Are we only cautiously watching the whole situation or if any protest note is sent ? Or any resentment or displeasure communicated to the American Government ?

The Minister has said that meetings are being held and we wish to resolve the problem peacefully. I am in agreement with this effort. But what step Government is going to take ? This should be clarified.

SHRI VAJPAYEE : The question of making the Indian Ocean a Zone of Peace has arisen out of the fact that the big powers have made it an arena of rivalry. The Hon. member has himself quoted from a statement of the US spokesman. According to it the USA is augmenting its naval power. We are in contact with the USA in this connection and we have expressed our concern over it. The Hon. member should not think that there is no effect of expressing concern in the House or that it does not help in mobilising world opinion. It is being said that there has been no significant increase in our naval power. That means that the existing power is always there. I want to draw the attention of the Hon. member to my detailed statement. I have stated there that if the situation in the Horn of Africa deteriorates it will lead to a power competition both in the Red Sea and the Indian Ocean. Therefore, the problem of the Horn of Africa should be solved quickly. The contention of the Hon. member that talks between the USA and USSR in regard to limitation of weapons in the Indian Ocean have broken down is not correct. I have referred to it in my statement. Talks are going on and will take place in future also.

SHRI SAUGATA ROY (Barrackpore) : The Hon. Minister has made a long-winded, wishy-washy statement in which he tries to give the view of both sides. But there is a sort of silence on the role which the Government of India is going to take. This is not the first time that the U.S. presence has been noticed in the Indian Ocean. It has been noticed in the Indian Ocean whenever there was a conflict. For instance, the US Navy moved in the Indian Ocean during the Bangladesh conflict. I may also remind the Foreign Minister that it was in this Indian Ocean, in the Horn of Africa, that a nuclear base has been set up at Diego Garcia, against which the Government of India had protested at that time. This is gun-boat diplomacy. Now they are moving their Naval Fleet from the Western Pacific Ocean into the Indian Ocean. That is why I said it is a wishy-washy statement. This is a statement of goodwill visit. It does not declare our policy. Sir, with your permission, I want to ask the Hon'ble Minister if the Government of India is going to give an outright condemnation of the United States presence in the Indian Ocean. Whether the Government of India instead of depending on the United Nations is going to take any initiative in calling a Conference of the littoral States to protest against the presence of the U.S. Navy in the Indian Ocean.

SHRI VAJPAYEE : I am sorry I do not agree with the Hon. member that it is a wishy-washy statement. I am making a statement on a situation which is very delicate and India would like to play a constructive part. To be frank, in regard to the Indian Ocean, the Janata Government has not departed from the policy which had been adopted by the former Government.

SHRI SAUGATA ROY : It was good.

SHRI VAJPAYEE : It was good then. Now it has become bad! Sir, we have repeated times without number that we are opposed to all military bases in the Indian Ocean including Diego Garcia. All bases are to be eliminated. But that cannot be achieved simply by making a statement in Parliament or making a speech outside. After all those who have established bases, whose presence is causing tension in the Indian Ocean, we are having talks with them. The talks have made some progress, though we would like the talks to succeed immediately. But it is always good to talk rather than indulge in gun boat diplomacy. India has no intention of calling a Conference of littoral and hinterland States because the United Nations Ad Hoc Committee has already convened a Conference and we are an active member in it. We are an active member of that ad hoc committee and no useful purpose will be served by calling a parallel conference.

SHRI JYOTIRMOY BOSU (Diamond Harbour) : In the meantime what about the details of the build-up at Diego Garcia ? They are equipping it every day with the most modern weapons, ICBMs, etc.

PROF. P.G. MAVALANKAR (Gandhinagar): My questions are : a, b, c, d, and e. Was this question of the Indian Ocean discussed with the United States President when he came here, as because Mr. Vajpayee had assured us in November last year that this question will be discussed threadbare ? I want to know whether it was discussed. Was it a discussion in general terms or in depth ? Did Diego Garcia come in for specific mention. If not, why not ? Is it a fact that the United States has been taking active steps for strengthening the Diego Garcia Island ? In May, 1977 the United States Senate Armed Services Committee approved 7.3 million U.S. dollars for additional construction at Diego Garcia. Was this fact pointed out by our Prime Minister when the US President came here ? Is India satisfied with a freeze at the current level of US and Soviet naval presence ? What is India's initiative in the matter ? Was there a subtle or a significant shift in the Indian position on the Indian Ocean ? What is the response to the holding of a conference of all concerned — littoral, hinterland States and the Big five countries ? Does the Indian coast continue to be under active US military surveillance ?

SHRI VAJPAYEE : I made a long statement in the expectation that there will be fewer questions. I would now like to reply to his questions. The question of the Indian Ocean was certainly discussed when President Carter visited New Delhi. There has been no shift or tilt in India's policy on the question of Indian Ocean being made a zone of peace. I am inclined to agree with the Hon. member. This question was raised by my friend, Mr. Shyamnandan Mishra that during the election, Mr. Carter–not President Carter, he became President afterwards–had stated that Indian Ocean should be demilitarised, but now talks are going on between the two big powers not about demilitarisation, but about limitation of armaments. Obviously there is a sliding back and this is not for the first time that this aspect has been brought to the notice of the House.

SHRI JYOTIRMOY BOSU : Will there be a Control Commission ?

SHRI VAJPAYEE : Which Control Commission ?

MR. SPEAKER : You answer Mr. Mavalankar's question.

SHRI VAJPAYEE : You prevent me from replying to Mr. Bosu's interruptions ? He should be prevented from interrupting. In the interruption I have forgotten....

SHRI JYOTIRMOY BOSU : I am sorry.

SHRI VAJPAYEE : I know and the House is also aware that the United States Senate has sanctioned some extra amount so that the bases in Diego Garcia could be further strengthened. When this question was discussed with President Carter our Prime Minister was very clear and categorical and said that as a result of the talks between the U.S. and the Soviet Union nothing will be left in the Indian Ocean except peace. That means all foreign bases are to be eliminated, no new bases are to be established and there should be no further strengthening of the existing bases. I do not know why there should be any doubt about the policy of the Government in the minds of members like Mr. Mavalankar.

SHRI LAKHAN LAL KAPOOR : Mr. Speaker, Sir, the Minister of External Affairs has made a six-page statement in response to the Calling Attention Notice. But it is like the proverbial mouse coming out after digging the mountain. He has not been able to give a solid reply. Talks are going on since 1972 for making the Indian Ocean a Zone of Peace and every time an assurance is forthcoming that we are aware of it. But all that we do is to protest against the big powers.

SHRI VAJPAYEE : Hon'ble Chairman Sir, we are talking of an Ocean, not a mountain. Only a fish would come out of the ocean. Not a mouse.

The Hon. member said that talks had been going on since 1972 but no result had come out. But that is only a statement of fact by him. We want that a result should come, but that is not in our hands. All the big powers are present in the Indian Ocean with their naval fleets. The Indian Ocean is an open sea, nobody can be stopped from going there. But when their presence there converts into rivalry a crisis is created in that zone. We are impressing upon both sides to conclude their talks soon. We have the support of all littoral countries in this. When President Carter and British Prime Minister Mr. Calaghan came here we talked about the issue with them also, and they agreed that the naval power of all the countries present there should be reduced. Soviet Russia also acknowledges that its naval power there should be reduced. But in actual practice they augment their power.

SHRI KANWAR LAL GUPTA : All the countries

SHRI VAJPAYEE : Yes, all the countries. And the main reason for all this is the Horn of Africa. Therefore, I have stressed in my statement that if the question of the Horn of Africa is resolved, the rivalry can be reduced. Ultimately, the whole issue should be settled through negotiations. So far as the question of mobilising the world opinion is concerned, India is doing so on its part and an *ad hoc* committee of the United Nations is active in this regard.

DR. MURLI MANOHAR JOSHI : The naval force of USA is present in Indian Ocean as a result of the explosive situation created in the Horn of Africa. The situation in the Horn of Africa is very serious. The tension so far prevailing between Ethiopia and Somalia is now taking the shape of world war. Armed forces of Cuba are present there, Soviet pilots are there and arms and ammunitions have been air-dropped. The ships of Soviet Russia carrying arms and ammunition passed through Karachi, where they were stopped and efforts were made to search them, but they were released after diplomatic activities. Ten thousand Cubans are still there. Previously, when Somalia was with Soviet Russia, everything was all right. Port of Barbara was under Soviet control. One who controls the Horn of Africa will also control the Port of Barbara, Aden, Suez Canal and Indian Ocean. Therefore, the problem of the Horn of Africa is the most important problem.

SHRI VAJPAYEE : I agree with the Hon. member that if the situation in the Horn of Africa was not kept under control, it may take a serious turn. The situation is further deteriorating due to foreign interference. This morning, I had separate meetings with the ambassadors of Ethiopia and Somalia. We wish the talks in Lagos to succeed, although there are many hurdles in the way. There is controversy on whether the forces should withdraw first or a cease-fire should be effected first. There is no consensus about a meeting of the Security Council, and we are, therefore, requesting the big powers to exercise restraint. We have asked both our friends– Somalia and Ethiopia–to resolve the dispute through bilateral talks. There should be no use of force under any circumstances because that will only invite foreign intervention, which could create a serious situation. It is not correct to say that India is a mute spectator what I and you are saying here itself clearly shows that India is not silent ......

DR. MURLI MANOHAR JOSHI : I did not say that you are silent.

SHRI VAJPAYEE : At the moment Diego Garcia is not the main problem. The base at Diego Garcia should no doubt be wound up; but if the situation in the Horn of Africa deteriorates it can become extremely explosive. That is why I made a detailed statement, on which Shri Shymnandan Mishra raised an objection. But I hope all members would read this statement in depth, and if they think that something more could be done in this matter and they do not want to give their suggestions in the House, they can give their suggestions to me personally. Thank you.

Super Power Presence in Indian Ocean

SHRI HARSH DEO MALAVIYA (Uttar Pradesh) : Sir, I beg to call the attention of the Minister of External Affairs to the reported serious and tense situation arising out of the increasing naval activity by the Super Powers in the Indian Ocean and the reaction of the Government of India thereto in the context of maintaining the Indian Ocean as a zone of peace.

SHRI VAJPAYEE : Hon'ble Chairman, Sir, the House is fully aware of the Government's view that the military presence of Great Powers in Indian Ocean is a cause of tension and insecurity in the area and total elimination of all foreign bases from the area is a necessary condition for maintaining it as a Zone of Peace. India regards the participation of Great Powers and major maritime users of Indian Ocean in the proposed international Conference of the Littoral and Hinterland States of the Indian Ocean to be convened in New York for implementing the UN Resolution on the establishment of Indian Ocean as a Zone of Peace as essential. It is our hope that any bilateral understanding/agreement reached by the Great Powers shall incline them to extend increased cooperation to the U.N. in this matter. India has, therefore, welcomed talks between the USA and the USSR on arms limitation measures in the Indian Ocean as a step towards its establishment as a Zone of Peace. Our steadfast objective remains that of eventual demilitarisation of the Indian Ocean.

Militarisation of indian Ocean

I may mention that when the question of Indian Ocean was discussed with President Carter, our Prime Minister had stated very clearly and categorically that as a result of talks between the USA and the Soviet Union, nothing should be left in the Indian Ocean except peace. In other words, there should be no further strengthening of existing foreign bases, that no new bases are established and that all existing foreign bases are eliminated.

Our view has been that while the Indian Ocean is open for freedom of navigation, a dangerous situation is created when the presence of big powers gets escalated in the form of rivalry and establishment of bases. That is why we are in favour of complete demilitarisation of the Indian Ocean rather than only stabilisation or freezing of forces there. In this context recent deployment of naval forces of Great Powers in the Indian Ocean has caused us deep concern. We are in no position to accurately assess the increased strength of such presence compared to that in the previous months. We do, however, hold the view that such foreign naval presence in the region acts

Rajya Sabha on March 1, 1979 as Minister of External Affairs in response to the calling attention notice regarding increasing naval activity by Super Powers in the Indian Ocean

as an impediment to the lessening of the tension in the area, and turns the clock back away from progress in the establishment of a Zone of Peace in the Indian Ocean, to which the international community is committed.

A Matter of Deep Concern

As a member of the UN Ad Hoc Committee on the subject India is actively participating in the implementation of the UN resolution on Zone of Peace in the Indian Ocean. All Littoral and Hinterland States also share our view in regard to the elimination of foreign military presence from the Indian Ocean. We will continue to very carefully watch the resultant situation arising out of increasing military activities by the Great Powers in the Indian Ocean.

Having said this let me state that both USA and USSR are keeping us informed about the progress of talks between them on questions concerned with arms limitation measures in the Indian Ocean. In the round of talks held in Berne from February 7 to February 17, characterised by both sides as frank and useful, some progress has been achieved.

Sir, we regard the activities of Great Powers in regard to the establishment of Indian Ocean as a Zone of Peace as a touch-stone for their commitment towards *detente* and for the spread of its benefits for the international community as a whole. We very much hope that the Great Powers would exercise restraint and that the situation in the Horn of Africa would get defused, thereby creating a better political atmosphere for these talks when resumed. On this matter our Prime Minister is in touch with both President Brezhnev and President Carter. In addition, in the framework of the UN Ad Hoc Committee we would continue to strive to build an international climate of opinion conducive to an early establishment of the Indian Ocean as a Zone of Peace. Thank you.

U.S. Naval Presence in the Gulf

Mr. Speaker, Sir, we have read with considerable concern reports that the United States Government are dispatching a carrier-led naval task force to the Indian Ocean and the Gulf Area. Committed as we are to keep the Indian Ocean free from naval presence and rivalry of great powers, we are distressed at this announcement. This is contrary to the spirit of the U.N. resolution on keeping the Indian Ocean as a zone of peace.

The latest move cannot, in our view, assist the process of bringing stability in a region which has seen serious upheavals and is still seething with tensions and uncertainty. Stability in the region will, first and foremost, depend on the countries themselves and the resolution of bilateral problems and regional cooperation between them. The world community as well as the economics of many of the countries which depend on the oil supplies from this region, would like the flow of oil to continue and not threatened, the production not impeded, and peaceful trade to go on across the Indian Ocean.

The Arab League met only a few days ago and agreed upon measures to be taken to bring about cessation of hostilities and an understanding between the People's Democratic Republic of Yemen and the Yemen Arab Republic, following the conflict which has taken place recently between the two countries. In keeping with the spirit of the Arab League recommendations and our own policy, we would urge an end to the hostilities on the basis of non-interference and respect for established frontiers between countries.

Efforts at stability and mutual respect and harmonious relations are shared by all nations of the region and serve the interests of countries outside the region. The increased military and naval presence in the area and fears of involvement of great powers can have adverse political and economic consequences which would not ease but only add to the tensions in this vital region.

Lok Sabha on March 12, 1979 as Minister of External Affairs regarding the presence of U.S. Naval Task Force in the Gulf Area

IV West Asia

Existence of Israel

Mr. Speaker, Sir, before seeking some clarification I would like to stress a point. It is a matter of great regret that the Prime Minister lost an opportunity to formulate a national policy on the question of West Asia. I would like to make it clear that we want to maintain friendly relations with the Arab countries. But whether Arab countries ... (*Interruptions*).

SHRI SIDDHESHWAR PRASAD (Nalanda) : Never.

SHRI VAJPAYEE : Mr. Speaker, Sir, I was saying that so far as my party is concerned we want to maintain friendly relations with the Arabs, we want to strengthen our relations, but if the condition to maintain friendly relations with Arab countries is that we should accept extermination of Israel, then we will have to forgo this friendship.

Arab countries are also saying that they do not want to annihilate Israel. I want to ask what objection the Prime Minister had while making a statement today in this period of crisis, in asserting that if an attempt was made to wipe out Israel India would not be a party to it and we would have no sympathy for those countries who want to do so ?

The statement is silent on this aspect and I think this silence must be broken. It is not enough for the Prime Minister to make a statement in the meeting of the Congress Party alone to the effect that we do not want the existence of Israel to be wiped out. An authoritative declaration to this effect must be made in this House—from the platform of Parliament—that India would not tolerate any attempt to wipe out the existence of Israel.

We Want Friendship With the Arabs

We want friendship with Arab countries, and if we have to choose among the Arab countries I find the United Arab Republic closer to us as compared to Jordan or Saudi Arabia. We should understand that there are some countries in West Asia that have been working at the instance of imperialists and had openly supported Pakistan in the conflict between India and Pakistan. It is true that we did not get as much sympathy, assistance and support from the United Arab Republic as we should have and we will have to keep that in view while deciding our policy.

Lok Sabha on June 6, 1967 while seeking clarifications on the statement by the Prime Minister in response to the Calling Attention Notice about making India's policy clear regarding Israel

But when the din of weapons is being heard, should the voice of peace, co-existence and tolerance be raised more loudly or should we adopt an attitude of accusations. I would request the Prime Minister to lay on the table of the House the entire material and information, indicating the source, on the basis of which she made a statement to the effect that Israel was responsible for starting the war. The Security Council has not passed any such resolution so far. Israel has not been declared an aggressor so far. India's representative is present in the Security Council. In the resolution moved by him no mistake has been committed of making allegations against anyone. But the mistake which we did not make in the United Nations Organisation is being made while sitting in New Delhi. I would like that the House must be taken into confidence and whatever literature, material and information is in the possession of the Government should be placed on the table of the House.

I want to have one more clarification. We mourn the death of all those soldiers who have been killed. But I want to ask whose responsibility it is to bring those soliders from the Gaza Strip. Two weeks have passed since those soldiers were removed from there and the contingent of the United Nations was disbanded. Could they not be brought back from the Gaza Strip to India during these two weeks ? Why did we leave them there to die ? Are arrangements now being made to bring back the remaining soldiers from there or shall we have to mourn their death ?

AN. HON. MEMBER : It is an excellent and historic speech.

Humiliation at Rabat Islamic Conference

Mr. Speaker, Sir, instead of apologising to the people of the country for the national humiliation heaped in Rabat, the Government is only rubbing salt on the wounds. Nobody can deny that what happened in Rabat was due to our own policy; we had invited it. The Conference at Rabat was for Islamic countries, it was called by Islamic countries and the problems of Islamic countries were to be considered there. The propriety of India, which is not an Islamic country, going to attend such a conference officially could not be supported. Even before this Islamic conferences had been held in many countries of the world and some delegates from India had participated in them. But this is for the first time that the Government of India sent an official delegation. The leader of the delegation was a Minister of Cabinet rank. The delegation also included the Minister of State in the Ministry of External Affairs. Our ambassador in Rabat was also included in the delegation— it was a very high-level delegation. Will the Government please explain why we changed the traditional policy of sending non-official delegations to such Islamic conferences ?

Muslims do live in India and their number is considerable. They enjoy equal citizenship rights. They have to observe equal duties towards the nation. We do not discriminate among our people on the basis of religion. We have established a secular state in India. Muslims might have their religious problems, which they can discuss within the country. They can also discuss them outside the country, but there is no need to send an official delegation to such a conference.

Mr. Speaker, Sir, in 1955-56 at the time of the Suez Canal crisis, when the question of sending an Indian delegation to the Islamic Conference organised in Cairo arose, Pandit Jawaharlal Nehru was alive, and I am told that he had said that we should not send an official delegation. Has the present Minister of External Affairs seen that file on which our late Prime Minister had written his note ? It is said that those papers have been removed from that file. Since then many conferences have been held at Mogadishu in 1965, at Bangdung in 1965, at Mecca in 1965 and at Kuala Lumpur in 1969.

I remember that, Malaysian people had come to invite us for the Kuala Lumpur Conference. Dr. Zakir Hussain was the President at that time. He was told that he was the President of India, that he was a Muslim, and he should send a delegation. I also remember that Dr. Zakir Hussain told them

Lok Sabha on November 17, 1969 while moving the Adjournment Motion protesting against sending official delegation of India to the Muslim Conference organised at Rabat

that he was no doubt a Muslim, but he was the President of India, which was a secular country and they were insulting us by inviting us to an Islamic Conference.

No official delegation had gone to the Kuala Lumpur Conference, I want to know why a decision was taken now to change this policy. Was this matter considered by the Cabinet ? Was any memorandum prepared for the Cabinet ?

When policies are changed a memorandum is prepared for the Cabinet. What is this memorandum, on what ground was the decision to change the policy taken ?

Policy of Non-alignment Abandoned

Our policy is to remain aloof from the blocs. We do not want to involve ourselves in military blocs, nor we can commit the mistake of binding ourselves with religious blocs. This policy of non-alignment was also abandoned in Rabat. Our policy has not been to allow formation of an Islamic bloc; now they say our policy is that if such a bloc is formed let us enter into it. Our policy is that military blocs should not be formed, but if they are formed, shall we enter them ? Our policy to stop formation of an Islamic bloc has failed. Our policy of non-alignment, our policy of secularism, also failed when this government decided to go to the Rabat Conference by casting the prestige of India aside.

Invitation was Begged

Mr. Speaker, Sir, we used to receive invitations to attend the conferences held so far, but we hesitated to attend, we talked of attending unofficially. However, in Rabat we had to beg for the invitation. At first it was decided that we would not be invited. Then we knocked at the doors of those countries, we bowed down at the door-steps of their embassies in New Delhi, and urged them to call us also. It is said that we were invited unanimously. I want to ask how this unanimity changed overnight ? The reply given to this is that the President of Pakistan was pressurised by his own people and a telegram was sent from Pakistan to the effect that if they accept inclusion of India in the Conference they will not be spared. There is no democracy in Pakistan, it is dictatorship. Our democratic government cannot be shaken by a telegram. If Shri Pheruman dies, the Government is unmoved, if bullets are showered on the people of Telengana it does not care, we take thousands of people to the door of the Prime Minister and ask for his resignation but the Prime Minister does not oblige. Mr. Speaker, this is the position in a democratic country. And we are being told to believe that the dictator of Pakistan received some telegram and the same dictator of Pakistan who had earlier shaken hands with our ambassador and had unanimously decided to invite us overnight got a message from God that in case India joined the Conference in the morning his dictatorship would come to an end. These are all ridiculous talks, nobody in his senses could believe them.

I have come only to one conclusion— that the decision to invite India unanimously was a trick. It was a noose for humiliating us through invitation and we fell in that noose. There is no meaning in accusing Pakistan for this. Pakistan is our opponent, it has been inimical to us since its birth, it is sitting pretty after committing aggression against our land. It wants to create disturbances inside our country, and does not want to miss a single opportunity to malign us outside. Why should we become a victim to the gameplan of Pakistan ? If we had not gone there we would not have faced this humiliation. If a non-official delegation had gone there it could reply to the allegations made by Pakistan.

Mr. Speaker, Sir, it is also being said that had the riots not taken place in Ahmedabad we would not have to face humiliation at Rabat. The riots took place in Ahmedabad on the 19th and on the 25th, that is, by the time the countries gathered at Rabat unanimously decided to invite us, the riots had been suppressed, and there was peace. Did they not have the news reports about the Ahmedabad riots on the 25th ? Was all the propaganda made overnight ? Pakistan might have tried to use the Ahmedabad riots, but I am not prepared to accept that the entire conference turned against us due to this. It should also be noted that the Ahmedabad riots are being investigated. I do not want to say anything more about it, but is it not possible that the riots in Ahmedabad might have been caused by elements that wanted to vitiate the position of India in Rabat ? There might be such elements in our country, they should be unmasked. But we cannot shirk our responsibility by accusing Ahmedabad riots for our humiliation at Rabat. If the riots had taken place and we had decided not to attend we would not have to face humiliation.

Where were the Friends ?

The most regrettable thing is that even those who claim to be our great friends, and we did not hesitate to change our decided course of policy to fulfil our obligations of friendship towards them, did not come forward to help us in the Conference at Rabat. We have no grudge against Jordan : Jordan is a member of the military bloc. Jordan is still an outpost of imperialism. We do not have any complaint even against Turkey and Iran. We did not have much hope even from Saudi Arabia. But we want to ask the Minister of External Affairs and the Prime Minister as to what did the United Arab Republic do in the Conference at Rabat. Did they stand up and say even once that a country which was invited unanimously could not be expelled, and if they did it then UAR will also have to leave the Conference along with India and then the Conference could not be held ? A friend in need is a friend indeed. But the United Arab Republic did not perform the duties of a friend. I am not saying this in anger, but in great anguish. We know that in West Asia reactionary forces are fighting against progressive forces. But if we want to encourage the progressive forces then those progressive forces must also encourage us.

The Prime Minister said that the Rabat matter is being raised only by those persons who do not want to have friendship with the Arabs. It appears that the Prime Minister alone has usurped the prerogative of seeking friendship with the Arabs at any cost. The whole country wants friendship with the Arab countries, but this does not mean that Israel should be treated as an enemy. If the Arab countries can have friendship with us as well as with Pakistan, if they can have friendship with Pakistan and China, why then cannot India have friendship with the Arabs as well as Israel at the same time ? We want Israel to vacate the area belonging to Arabs which has been occupied by it. But are they prepared to say that Pakistan and China should vacate our territory occupied by them ? Friendship is not a one-way traffic. It cannot be a one-sided affair. Friendship is based on mutual interests and relations.

UNO Weakened

We have weakened the United Nations Organisation by trying to join the Islamic bloc. We have struck at the unity of African and Asian countries. We have also broken the unity of the Arab countries. The Charter of the United Nations Organisation allows regional groupings, not religious groupings or blocs formed on the basis of religion. African countries have an organisation, Arab countries have an organisation. But now a new wind is blowing under which efforts are being made to organise blocs on the basis of religion. We should have resisted it, but our government flew with that wind, got its feet uprooted, and now, instead of admitting that mistake, efforts are being made to whitewash it (*Interruptions*)....

I want to finish my speech by giving an example of a newspaper of Yugoslavia. This *Review of International Affairs* is published by the Federation of Yugoslav Journalists. In this issue an article by a great intellectual of Yugoslavia Lagomir Manovich has been published. Our Minister of External Affairs had visited Yugoslavia before going to the Rabat Conference and the statement published from there said that matters of mutual interest as well as the decisions taken in regard to West Asian relations will be discussed. I want to ask Shri Dinesh Singh whether he asked Yugoslavia if they were invited to the Rabat Conference and are they going to attend it ? In Yugoslavia too there are Muslims .... (*Interruptions*) ....

AN HON'BLE MEMBER : 13 per cent.

SHRI VAJPAYEE : There are more Muslims than in India.

SHRI DINESH SINGH, The Minister of External Affairs : Not more.

SHRI VAJPAYEE : You may please find out. Shri Manovich writes in his article. I quote :

> "If a meeting of the Muslim countries is called to discuss some religious matter, *e.g.* regarding a religious place ...... Akasa or any other sacred place of international level such as any part of Jerusalem, then it could be called reasonable. But here the reason is not clear. The meeting has been called on a religious basis and political problems are to be considered"

Do not Mix Religion with Politics

My greatest complaint is (*Interruptions*).... Please give me one minute more. Secularism means equal regard for all religions inside the country and keeping religion separate from politics. The Prime Minister says that we went to Rabat because political matters were to be discussed there. In these circumstances there should have been greater objection to our going there. That Conference was called by the Islamic countries. In the agenda there was reference to cooperation among the Islamic countries and in the announcement made later the names of Islamic countries were published.

When Islamic countries discuss political questions, we cannot go there—that is against our policy of secularism. If they discuss Islam, Muslims of our country can go there as delegates. But when they mix up politics with religion, Islam with politics, then they close their doors for us. But we gate-crashed into Rabat and came back humiliated from there. Instead of apologising for it, the Government was repeating the mistake, and I am afraid in future they will participate in the Conference of Foreign Ministers. To help in the establishment of a secretariat that is being set up is against our policy of non-alignment and secularism. If the Government has decided to leap in the dark, setting aside all the policies and national interests, then we are prepared to give it one more push. But the people of this country would not tolerate this humiliation. Thank you.

Israel Must Accept Inalienable Rights of Palestinians

Mr. Deputy Speaker, Sir, I want to quote what the Prime Minister has stated at the end of her statement. Indicating what should be done to solve the problem of Lebanon, the Prime Minister said:

> "Such a solution must ensure the sovereignty, independence and territorial integrity of Lebanon, and the inalienable rights of the Palestinian people, including their rights to an independent nation-state".

On both these counts there is unanimity of opinion in the country. An aggression is an aggression, whichever the country that is the victim and whichever the part of the world where it takes place. The attack by Israel cannot be supported. Secondly, the problem of West Asia will not be solved until the issue of Palestinians is solved. How long will they roam about without any shelter ? They might be suppressed today with the power of arms, but to establish an independent State is their just demand, and sooner or later this demand will have to be conceded.

However, I have one complaint against the Government, not because I am in the opposition, but was it necessary for the Prime Minister to wait till the commencement of the sitting of Parliament to give a statement about Lebanon ? Israel attacked Lebanon on 6th June and 33 days have since then passed. Nearly 15,000 people have been killed and 50,000 wounded. Lakhs have been rendered homeless. The atrocities committed were such that even Israel is ashamed of being shown on American television. But the Indian Prime Minister kept mum and there was no statement from the External Affairs Minister either. It is true that a statement was given on the second day of the sitting of Parliament, but by that time Lebanon was devastated.

The statement given has been prepared hurriedly. The choice of words has not been proper. I do not know whether the draft of the statement was prepared in the External Affairs Ministry or the Prime Minister's Secretariat. Nowadays, in the matter of External Affairs, sometimes there appear to be two parallel authorities. The Prime Minister's statement says:

> "Israel's cynical and contemptuous disregard of international opinion, its continuing aggression and its use of military means to seek political objectives provide a very sad precedent for the future".

Are we opposed only to military means ? Do we not have a difference of opinion with the political objectives of Israel ? Why have these wordings

Lok Sabha on July 22, 1982 during discussion on the statement made by the Prime Minister regarding the situation in Lebanon

been used in the statement ? It can create a misunderstanding about our stand.

ACHARYA BHAGWAN DEV : Mr. Vajpayee, this is what you are saying today, but what was your attitude when you were the Minister of External Affairs ?

SHRI VAJPAYEE : Please sit down.

MR. CHAIRMAN : We are discussing foreign policy now.

SHRI VAJPAYEE : Sir, I once said in this very House that while one requires a voice to speak, one has to have both voice and vision to remain silent.

ACHARYA BHAGWAN DEV : It is you who is losing vision. See your face in the mirror.

MR. CHAIRMAN : Vajpayeeji, you may please continue.

SHRI VAJPAYEE : Please call great speakers like him to speak on behalf of the Congress Party.

ACHARYA BHAGWAN DEV : No, you alone are a great speaker left in the House. See for yourself what Jethmalani said and what you are saying.

SHRI VAJPAYEE : What Shri Jethmalani said was his personal opinion.

Mr. Chairman, the time lost in interruptions should not be added to the time allotted to me. The chain of my ideas is broken. Perhaps that was his intention and his aim.

MR. CHAIRMAN : You just ignore him.

SHRI VAJPAYEE : No, Mr. Chairman, it is for you to control him. We also know how to put such obstructions. .....*(Interruptions)*.

ACHARYA BHAGWAN DEV : Why have you stood up in the middle ?

MR. CHAIRMAN : Why are you talking in this manner ? Please let him speak.

SHRI VAJPAYEE : There is a way to conduct oneself in this House.

ACHARYA BHAGWAN DEV : Do we have to learn the conduct from you ?

SHRI VAJPAYEE : Yes, you have to.

ACHARYA BHAGWAN DEV : It is you who will have to learn. You say something, and Mr. Jethmalani of your party says something else.

MR. CHAIRMAN : Why are you indulging in all this ? Please sit down.

SHRI VAJPAYEE : Mr. Chairman, we are opposed not only to military measures. After all, what is the aim of Israel in attacking Lebanon ? To break the unity of Lebanon, to end its independence, to set up a puppet Government there ? The second aim is to finish the Palestine Liberation Organisation. We cannot acquiesce in any one of them. We are against terrorism. Resort to violence against innocent, helpless people cannot be supported. But it is not understandable that the leaders of Israel raise a finger against terrorists. They themselves have not been non-violent. They had taken resort to terrorism for the establishment of Israel. I am also not prepared to accept the theory that it is a retaliatory action to avenge the murder of the Israeli ambassador in London. As the Hon. members have said, preparations for this invasion were made beforehand. An attack on such a big scale cannot be carried out without prior preparations. The Defence Minister of Israel has given a statement on 30th June in Beirut. I have read in today's newspapers that this press conference was held in the same hotel in which our ambassador in Lebanon is staying. I want a clarification from our External Affairs Minister— whether it had become necessary for our ambassador to take shelter in Israeli-occupied territory to save his life ? I am quoting from the newspapers the statement of the Israeli Defence Minister :

> "The Israeli Defence Minister Mr. Ariel Sheron said yesterday we had told Washington of Israel's intentions to invade Lebanon only ten days before the invasion".

This is a proof. But I have another statement of Mr. Reagan in which he has said :

> "The US had been just as surprised by the invasion of Lebanon as anyone else".

Whose version should we take as correct ? One thing, however, is clear. The Israeli action as well as the multi-point suggestions put forth by the USA for the solution of the Lebanon problem both have the same objective.

Israel Must Live Within Its Border

Sir, nobody can have any difference of opinion on Israel's right of existing as a nation within its own boundaries. At least I hold that opinion. However, United Nations Resolution No. 242 which speaks of 'secured borders' has so far not been defined. This concept of 'secured borders' is very dangerous. Golan Heights was occupied because it was considered necessary for the security of Israel. What will happen to East Jerusalem ? The West Bank has gone, the Gaza Strip has gone, Israelis are now talking of Judia Samaria. When pressure is being exercised on PLO to accept the existence of Israel then Israel should also be pressurised to find out a solution of the Palestine problem. Israel should be asked where its boundaries lie. I have also seen what is inscribed on the Parliament building of Israel—that Israel extends from Nile to Euphratus. The leaders ruling Israel say that Israel is not the name of a country; it is a concept, an idea, a dream. But this dream appears to be turning into a danger to world peace. What Israel has done can only be termed as madness. My friend Shri Indrajit Gupta has referred to the fact that at first a 40-km. corridor was asked for but now that has been given up and Israel wants to swallow the entire Lebanon. Sir, I do not have the answer to what should be done. The unanimous resolution of the United Nations could not bring Israel onto the right path. A decision could also be taken to expel Israel from the United Nations. The other day when Prime Minister Begin went to address the United Nations General Assembly almost the entire hall was vacant. What more insult can there be ? But the rulers of Israel are not worried. They understand only one language—the language of force.

For the last few months the world is witnessing the spectacle of 'might is right'. There was a battle in the Falkland Islands, which the British suppressed by the use of force. But the situation in Asia is full of tension today. Iraq and Iran are at war with each other. Previously, the army of Iraq was inside Iran, but now the Iranian army is inside Iraq. What will happen, I do not know. If the Arabs fight between themselves, how can they face Israel unitedly ? The non-aligned countries have not been able to bring an end to the Iran-Iraq war. On the other side tensions are building up in the Indian Ocean. Competition between super-powers is increasing. Afghanistan has lost its independence. When the Prime Minister visited Saudi Arabia she said the security of the Gulf countries and the security of India were tied up with the security of this region. But the danger can be seen clearly. The Arab-Israeli war or the Israeli invasion of Lebanon have also revealed changes in the methods of warfare. It is now time for military electronics. We are now arguing about F- 16. Syria had made a good deal of strategic deployment of forces, but its entire missile deployment was rendered futile by Israel. It is true it could not have been possible without US assistance.

SHRI BHIKU RAM JAIN : Computerised.

SHRI R.L. BHATIA : It was from an organisation.

SHRI VAJPAYEE : Today's newspapers carry a statement of Arafat : Palestine does not want prayers, it wants weapons. The Arab countries are not prepared to supply weapons. After the Cairo Summit there was a proposal to make a Joint Defence Force. But when Lebanon was invaded nobody except Syria came forward. Syria too did not fight the battle. It confined itself to some air combats and then made a cease-fire. Where will the world go with this situation ? What will happen to our security and the security of this region ? This question arises again and again in the mind after this war.

U.S.A. must be Persuaded to Recognise P.L.O.

Mr. Chairman, for the time being PLO has been defeated militarily. Can we convert their military defeat into a diplomatic victory ? Even though indirect, there is already talk of having negotiations with PLO. If PLO is to be persuaded to accept something talks will have to take place. Can the USA be prompted to extend recognition to PLO ? The Prime Minister is going to the USA. I will not demand that she should cancel her US visit, but she would have to use all her tactfulness to bring round the United States. I do not know whether the USA can be brought to the track or not. But the new External Affairs Minister has accepted that so long as the question of Palestine is not solved there could be no permanent solution in West Asia. I would like to know from the Minister of External Affairs what role the non-aligned countries can play in this matter. The routes to Beirut are closed and supplies cannot reach there. However, the move for all the members of the Security Council to go there is a right step. Simultaneously with Washington, the doors of Moscow should also be knocked. My intention is not to criticise Moscow, but the Arab friends of Moscow also have the same complaint. An interview of the PLO ambassador in New Delhi, Mr Avedha, has been published in the *Patriot* from which I quote:

> "Asked about the Soviet role in the wake of invasion he pointed to the initial statements and warnings from the side of USSR, but expressed surprise at the latest silence on the part of Moscow. This silence was inexplicable"

However, one can now say that Moscow is not silent. Only today Moscow has declared that if US forces went to Beirut Moscow will oppose it. The question is not of sending American forces, but of withdrawal of the Israeli forces from Lebanon. When the last war took place Russia gave a threat and it had its effect. I do not know the reasons for what is happening today. But Moscow and Washington and other members of the Security Council should be made to realise that what was being done by Israel could well trigger off a world war. Its hunger is increasing with every aggression.

Israel must Withdraw from Occupied Territory

I know our Congress Party members will ask what did the Janata Government do! The Janata Government did not bring about any change in the country's policy towards Israel. The autobiography of Moshe Dayan confirms it. So long as Israel is in possession of Arab territory and until a peace treaty is signed there is no question of establishing diplomatic relations with it.

It is not a new policy. At that time I was in Bharatiya Jan Sangh. We had then passed a resolution—on 30 June, 1967—on the Arab-Israeli war in which we had demanded :

> "Isreal should withdraw its force from areas it has occupied in the recent conflict."

We had also said that Isreal will have to live with Arab countries on the basis of co-existence. It must forget that it is a country of whites: it must develop an Afro-Asian personality.

Therefore. there are no differences in the country in the matter of principle but what we should do in this situation I do not have any suggestion to put before the External Affairs Minister. But I would like that efforts should be made to convert the military defeat of PLO into a diplomatic victory. The question is how to pressurise Israel. If the world goes on heading in the direction of 'might is right' the situation could worsen.

This tendency would have to be stopped and there is only one way of stopping it that we mobilise world pubic opinion. At the same time we will have to stregthen our own country at the earliest, because if some adversity comes, nobody will come to our support, we will have to fight out the crisis ourselves. Thank you.

Despair in the Gulf

Mr. Deputy Chairman, the entire country is deeply concerned and there is a great deal of restlessness on the press reports being received from Kuwait, Iraq and Jordan about the miserable conditions of Indians stranded there. They want to come back to India, leaving their hearths and homes there due to insecurity. But they cannot leave Kuwait and all routes from Iraq are also closed for them. There is only one route open through Amman. The situation in Amman today is that there are thousands of people, not only from India but also from Sri Lanka, Bangladesh, Pakistan and Philippines, who had gone there as labourers and who contributed a lot to the prosperity of that country. But now they want to return to their homelands. They are living in camps. There are no tents there and they are living under the open sky.

MR. DEPUTY CHAIRMAN (Shri Bhaskar Annaji Masodkar) : What is the temperature there ?

SHRI VAJPAYEE : During the day they feel difficulty due to heat of the sun and during the night due to cold because there is sand. Mr. Deputy Chairman, now a new crisis has arisen there. There is no food for the people to eat, no milk for the children, there are no medicines. There is much scarcity of water. Yesterday we saw it on the television and a news report has also come from Washington that there is a scramble for water bottles that are sent there. There is a cry of desperation all round. Sir, this situation has arisen due to the economic blockade of Iraq by the Security Council. But America and other allied countries are taking this blockade to mean that import of foodgrains, milk and drugs also cannot be allowed, which is wrong. What sin have those Iraqi children committed who are dying without milk ? It is a humanitarian question.

American Blocade

Secondly, although America and its allies concede that Kuwait is an independent country and they have not recognised the occupation of Kuwait by Iraq yet they are not ready to give us permission to export foodgrains to Kuwait. They say that they are blockading Kuwait also. The Government of India are daily sending aircraft to bring back the stranded people. These aircraft go empty. The Government is ready to send foodstuffs in these aeroplanes. Milk could be sent, medicines could be sent. But these aircraft can neither land in Iraq nor in Kuwait. They are landing in Jordan, where the aerodrome is small. If we decide that all internal flights in India would be cancelled and we will send these aeroplanes to Jordan they cannot land there.

Rajya Sabha on September 6, 1990 regarding Return of Indians stranded in the Gulf War and to remove restrictions on Iraq

They cannot bring back the people. This is another difficulty. Therefore, I want that the Government of India should take this matter to the Security Council and raise it in the United Nations. A joint strategy should be chalked out along with the neighbouring countries. This voice must emanate from this House. The United States of America is a democratic country and the voice of this House should go to them. They should be told that economic blockade does not mean that they stop import of foodgrains, milk and drugs.

MR. DEPUTY CHAIRMAN (Shri Bhaskar Annaji Masodkar) : I think the whole House shares your concern.

SHRI P. SHIVASHANKAR (Leader of the Opposition) : I believe that all the members would support it. We all associate ourselves with him.

V Other Countries

Portugal

Portuguese Colonies in India

Mr. Deputy Speaker, Sir, I rise to support the Resolution moved by Shri Banerji. But this resolution is incomplete in its present form, because no date has been specified in it by which Portugal must quit India. If we are to give them an ultimatum it is essential to indicate a date in it, and therefore I have moved an amendment to it specifying that Portugal must quit Goa, Daman and Diu by January 26 next, which is the Republic Day of India.

It cannot be denied that so long as Goa remains slave India's freedom is incomplete. The Prime Minister has also said that so long as Portuguese colonies remain in India the political revolution will not be complete. The question is, what have we done for the liberation of these colonies ? What is the policy of the Government of India about Goa ? We snapped our ties with Portugal, but that did not bring Goa's freedom nearer. We tried to take economic measures against the administration of Portugal working in these colonies, but those measures also did not produce any result. Now it is for the Government to explain how, if its goal is Goa's liberation, it is going to achieve that goal.

So far as the question of world public opinion is concerned, we have raised our voice against Portuguese imperialism in the United Nations and other international fora, and we must continue to do so. But we need not have any illusions that Goa will get its freedom as a result of our protests. Portugal has crossed limits in perpetrating atrocities in Angola. It has been strongly condemned in world forums, but there are no visible indications that this will have any effect on the Portuguese imperialists. If diplomatic and economic moves and attempts to mobilise public opinion have failed what is the other way left through which we may ensure the liberation of these colonies ?

Only Two Ways for Goa's Liberation

There can be only two ways. One is that the Government of India give freedom to the people to take steps to liberate these colonies. The *Satyagraha* movement was started and the people had gone there to participate in the movement from all parts of the country. It is just possible that a situation

Lok Sabha on November 24, 1961 during discussion on the Resolution moved by Shri S.M. Banerjee regarding Liberation of Goa, Daman and Diu

could have developed at that time which might have forced the Portuguese administration to leave Goa, but the administration did not allow the *Satyagraha* to continue. Now if the path of *Satyagraha* is closed and the people cannot take any peaceful steps to free their Indian brethren who are rotting in the jails of Portugal the Government must make it clear what the way out is before it for liberating Goa. It brings no credit to India to say that a wave of resentment is rising in the whole world against the Portuguese empire, that a very powerful movement is going on in Africa and that the days of the Protuguese imperialism are numbered, and if the Portuguese empire vanishes from Africa how long could it sustain in Goa ?

If Goa becomes independent through the independence of African people, through their efforts to attain freedom, would it be a matter of any pride for the people of free India and for that matter for the Indian Government ? We raise our voice in the whole world against imperialism and colonialism. Representatives of India bring resolutions in the United Nations condemning colonialism, and demanding that imperialism must be abolished, but we are tolerating Portuguese imperialism on our own soil. If we want to abolish colonialism we must begin with the liberation of Goa and for this the Government has only one way before it. It has made all kinds of efforts and the way now left is to resort to Police Action. It is necessary to give an ultimatum to Portugal for this purpose. For some time it is being said that if need arises we can even use force for the liberation of Goa. I welcome this. Not only for the liberation of Goa, but also for liberation of any part of Indian territory, which may be occupied by Portugal or by Communist China or Pakistan, if the need arises we must use force. But I am surprised that the Minister of Defence, who talks about using force against Portugal, is not even prepared to concede that the Chinese forces have advanced into Ladakh or that they are advancing there. He says they are not Chinese forces but some Chinese elements. And then it is said that we will settle the issues peacefully. Of course force can be used in Goa.

Non-violence no Obstacle in Liberation of Goa

My submission is that every Government has the freedom to use force. And our resolve to solve all problems peacefully does not mean that we cannot use force even to meet the danger to our sovereignty, our freedom and our security. This is not the meaning of non-violence. Gandhiji used to say that there is room for use of the sword in his non-violence and with his blessings we had sent our army to save Kashmir. Our decision to resolve problems through non-violent or peaceful means cannot become an obstacle in the liberation of Goa.

We have decided not to commit aggression, we would not wreck the freedom of any country, we would not look at anybody's freedom with greedy eyes, we would not cause danger to anyone's security. But this does not mean that we would not face the aggressor. And what are the Portuguese colonies ? An aggression against India continuing for the last four hundred years, and to use force to remove that aggression is not an immoral act. It is legal, it is moral and it is our duty to defend our sovereignty. It is in conformity with our self-respect.

The slavery of Goa renders our freedom incomplete. It is causing danger to our security. Goa's slavery is depriving the people of India of the glow of freedom. It ridicules our declaration against colonialism. Goa's slavery is a challenge for us. It is a challenge to India's manhood. If the Government wants the world to take its declarations against colonialism seriously the only way out is to take active steps for liberating Goa. We have broken diplomatic relations with Portugal, we have even enforced an economic blockade against it, but that has failed. Even by rousing world public opinion we could not change the violence ridden heart of Portugal. Now there is only one way left for us and that is to talk to Portugal in the language it understands. And Portugal understands only one language. Let Portugal be told that either it should vacate our land or we will drown the remnants of its power into the sea. The people of India can no more tolerate the blot on their forehead in the form of these enslaved Indian settlements.

Therefore, I have suggested that January 26, 1962 should be fixed as the date by which Portugal must vacate Indian land and go. The Government should unambiguously spell out its policy about this issue. It is said that force would be used. But there are no indications about it. Some people allege that the bogey of use of force is being raised in order to divert the attention of the public from the Chinese aggression. I do not believe these allegations, but these allegations are being made and are being connected with an election in Bombay. My submission is that the Government should declare its policy in clear terms. It should not be that our Prime Minister says that force could be used, but the Finance Minister says that use of force is not proper. This creates confusion. This also misguides those who have sympathy for Goa's liberation. Our policy should be clear, the Government must declare its policy unambiguously on this issue, taking advantage of this Resolution.

So far as I am concerned. I would like that an ultimatum upto January 26 be given to Portugal and if it does not quit within this period Police Action may be resorted to. That would not be war, but Police Action. Only in this way can Portugal be forced to quit Indian territory. There is no possibility of world war in it, nor is there any apprehension of NATO nations jumping into the fray. There is no such possibility. This is a matter between India and Portugal. It requires firmness on the part of our Government, some boldness and courage to face the challenges of slavery successfully. Thank you.

Czechoslovakia

Russia Invades Czechoslovakia

Mr. Deputy Speaker, Sir, I beg to move under Rule 109 that the debate on the Gold Control Bill be adjourned. The reason for moving this motion is that just now news has been received from the United Nations that the Indian representative did not vote in favour of the resolution moved in the Security Council condemning events relating to Czechoslovakia .... (*Interruptions*) ....

MR. DEPUTY SPEAKER : I shall take a vote just now. It is the Hon. member's responsibility to control his party now...(*Interruptions*) ....

SHRI NATH PAI : What ? We want them to behave like that!

SHRI KANWAR LAL GUPTA : We want the resignation of the Prime Minister.

SHRI VAJPAYEE : When a resolution was moved in the Security Council condemning Soviet Russia and other countries which had violated the Charter of the United Nations Organisation by sending their troops into Czechoslovakia and threatening world peace thereby the Indian representative did not support the resolution and remained neutral. The decision to abstain at the time of voting on the resolution condemning Soviet Russia and others was contrary to assurances given by the Prime Minister yesterday in the House (*Interruptions*).

Can India be Neutral to Aggression ?

Mr. Deputy Speaker, Sir, the Government has not only betrayed this House but this country as well by doing so. Yesterday, a plea was made not to insist on a division on the amendment moved by Smt. Sucheta Kripalani on the ground that India would discharge its duty in the Security Council. The Prime Minister had reiterated her faith in the Charter of the United Nations Organisation, indicating that although the Government of India might not be in a position to accept an amendment here in the House, when the question relating to Czechoslovakia came up in the Security Council the Government of India would respect the sentiments of this House as well as of the country. But we abstained. Can we remain neutral when aggression takes place ? Can anyone remain neutral between good and evil, darkness and light, aggression and peace ? If this Government claims to be following in the footsteps of Pandit Nehru then let us not forget that he had declared that when the question of aggression came up we would not keep quiet, we would not remain silent. The present Prime Minister had also said that the history of

Lok Sabha on August 23, 1968 while moving for postponement of the debate on the Gold Control Bill in order to discuss the situation in Czechoslovakia consequent upon the voting on the relevant resolution in the United Nations

Hungary would not be repeated. When a meeting of the leaders of opposition parties was held regarding the decision of the Soviet Union to supply arms to Pakistan we had raised this matter relating to Hungary. The Prime Minister had then said, let bygones be bygones, now we shall do our duty. But India did not do its duty; it appears that India has been pressurised by Soviet Russia. We have abandoned our freedom, we have given up our self-respect, and since this Government is guilty of doing so, the House must get an opportunity to discuss the matter.

I will not take more time. My submission is that under the Rule the debate on Gold Control Bill be adjourned and the sin committed by the Government of India in the United Nations Organisation must be discussed immediately. Thank you.

Vietnam

Chinese Invasion of Vietnam

Sir, I am grateful to the Hon. members who have participated in this debate. Though the debate was intended to be a short duration discussion, it has turned out to be almost a full-fledged debate.

I need hardly emphasise that there is complete unanimity in the House as well as in the country in our desire to express our solidarity with the brave and valiant people of the Republic of Vietnam who are facing a new crisis. We have nothing but admiration and appreciation for the people of Vietnam who fought against imperialism and intervention, who secured their independence and who have now undertaken the task, if I may say so, the Herculean task, of economic reconstruction.

It is a matter of great regret that at this time when Vietnam and its neighbours, Cambodia and Laos, who were ravished, are trying to utilise every ounce of their energies and every resource available to create a better life for their people, they are facing armed conflict.

AN HON MEMBER : Aggression.

SHRI VAJPAYEE : Just now, my Hon. friend. Mr. Rameshwara Rao, used the word "massive incursion".

SHRI K.P. UNNIKRISHNAN : What you are trying to say.

SHRI VAJPAYEE : I am not trying to say anything.

SHRI K.P. UNNIKRISHNAN : Is it an aggression or not ?

SHRI VAJPAYEE : I am not prepared to deal with the matter in the manner in which the Hon. member would like me to deal with.

SHRI K.P. UNNIKRISHNAN : You answer any question. I am not bothered about the manner in which you deal with it. You will face the consequences. That is a different thing. (*Interruptions*).

SHRI A.C. GEORGE (Mukandapuram) : You expressed admiration for the brave people of Vietnam but you have not expressed indignation against the Chinese aggression. (*Interruptions*).

PROF. SAMAR GUHA : A Foreign Minister has his own language. (*Interruptions*).

SHRI VAJPAYEE : We are raising unnecessary controversies. The People's Republic of China is guilty of committing aggression against the Socialist Republic of Vietnam. But I do not understand the insistence on using a

Lok Sabha on February 22, 1979 as Minister of External Affairs while replying to the discussion on the Chinese invasion of Vietnam

particular word. When we demand that the Chinese forces should withdraw from Vietnam what does that mean ?

The position of the Government is clear and categorical. The world at large has, no doubt, no suspicion. But unfortunately suspicions are being created by some of our friends. They are not helping the cause of Vietnam, they are playing politics. As Mr. Venkataraman rightly pointed out, at least on certain issues we should speak with one voice and this is one of those issues. Yesterday my friend—I do not find him here— Mr. Raj Narain talked of the unanimous resolution adopted by both the Houses of Parliament in 1962. He also criticised Nehru but forgot that the Resolution was adopted under the leadership of Pandit Jawaharlal Nehru.

Ever since I assumed office, I have never approached the question of foreign policy in a partisan manner. Even in China, while replying to the banquet speech made by the Foreign Minister Huang Hua, I expressed the distress, the sense of profound sorrow and personal hurt that Pandit Jawaharlal Nehru had felt, clearly and unequivocally. I did not speak on behalf of any party, nor as an individual, I spoke on behalf of this country.

Vietnam Congratulates India

On the question of Vietnam there is no difference of opinion. Only this morning I met the Ambassador of the Republic of Vietnam. He congratulated the Government of India and the people of India for the massive support that we have extended to the people of Vietnam. May I request the Hon. members to keep this question above party politics ? There are many questions on which we are at loggerheads, but not on this question. (*Interruptions*).

No country, however big, no nation, however strong, has any business to act like a policeman of the world. Gone are the days of punitive expediions. gone are the days of gun-boat diplomacy. Really, I am shocked that those who want to teach a lesson to others forget those very lessons when the time comes for them to act upon those lessons.

Unfortunately, my visit to China has been mixed with the Chinese attack on Victnam....

SHRI KANWAR LAL GUPTA (Delhi Sadar) : Was it a matter of chance ?

SHRI VAJPAYEE : There is room for speculation.

SHRI KANWAR LAL GUPTA : What is your opinion ?

SHRI VAJPAYEE : Various conjectures have been made. For example, Deng Hsiao Ping had come back from abroad. Norodom Sihanouk had arrived in Peking, the Prime Minister of the Republic of Vietnam Pham Van Dong had gone to Kampuchea; but as soon as I came to know about the massive attack, I informed the Chinese authorities in Peking through their Ambassador who was accompanying me that what had been done was a matter of grave concern for us. And I decided to cut short my visit. This is the civilised way to act, to protest.

I would like the Hon. members to consider my visit to China separately on merits. Now there are differences. Some Hon. members said that I should not have gone at all. Then there were others who said that I should not have gone at this juncture. (*Interruptions*). Having accepted the invitation, and having postponed the visit once, not because of any diplomatic illness— my friend, Mr. Satyanarayan Rao said that, perhaps, God wanted then that I should not go to China....

AN HON MEMBER : Which God ?

SHRI VAJPAYEE : The God in which he believes, I know, you do not believe in God.

Does that mean that this time, because I was quite all right, I was hale and hearty. God, had wanted me to go to Peking ? Let us not drag God into this. (*Interruptions*).

Sir, I decided to visit Peking because there are outstanding problems. I do not want to say things which will not be very palatable to my friends sitting on the opposite....

SHRI K.P. UNNIKRISHNAN : What is that ?

SHRI VAJPAYEE : Some of those things were said by Mr. Mandal. What did we do in the last 18 years to get back our territory ? If I may say so, the entire issue was put in cold storage, and now I have brought it to the fore. I am not saying this in order to boast. If there has to be normalisation of relations the boundary question must be solved. You go through my speech and all the press reports. Apart from the boundary question there are other problems also, and we have to talk....

SHRI K.P. UNNIKRISHNAN : That we shall discuss separately.

SHRI VAJPAYEE : All right. But please do not draw the conclusion that the visit was a complete failure simply because China decided to attack Vietnam....

SHRI K.P. UNNIKRISHNAN : It was a great success! We shall discuss the success later. Let us now talk about Vietnam.

SHRI VAJPAYEE : Mr. Venkataraman made a very constructive suggestion. I would like to congratulate him on his speech though....

AN HON. MEMBER : He is in the Opposition.

I am now on the Receiving End

SHRI VAJPAYEE : ... we sit face to face. I used to be there for 20 years. Now I am at the receiving end. I do not mind it. He wanted the government to consider the possibility of convening a meeting of the General Assembly of the United Nations under the uniting for peace provision. That can be done only if the Security Council fails to act. Unfortunately, in this case the Security Council has not yet met. We are not there. We are not a member of the Security Council. Then there are five members with a negative vote. There was a meeting of the Security Council on Kampuchea. All the non-aligned nations who are currently members of the Security Council had voted for a particular resolution but that was vetoed. That may be repeated. But I would like to assure the House that we are in consultation with all friendly countries. Within these two days we have had a meaningful exchange of views with the Ambassadors of Malaysia, Sri Lanka, Indonesia, Nigeria, Zambia, Kuwait, Yugoslavia, Bangladesh, Thailand and also with the

Ambassadors of Japan, Australia, UK and USA. We are constantly in touch with the Ambassadors.

SHRI DINEN BHATTACHARYA (Serampore) : Not of USSR ?

SHRI VAJPAYEE : Yes, with USSR also. But it will not be possible for me at this stage to indicate....

SHRI DINEN BHATTACHARYA : ... their reaction.

SHRI VAJPAYEE : ... whether any initiative can be taken. But we are considering all possibilities.

Sir, the situation has got to be defused. We stand on a precipice. If there is escalation there will be global repercussions. All countries and particularly the great powers have to exercise restraint and put pressure on the People's Republic of China to withdraw from the Vietnamese territory. Sir, an aggressor cannot be allowed to enjoy the fruits of his aggression. If there are any problems....

AN HON. MEMBER : Mr. Unnikrishnan, you get it ?

SHRI VAJPAYEE : I know there are problems.

The problems should be discussed....

SHRI DINEN BHATTACHARYA :... Bilaterally.

SHRI VAJPAYEE : ... bilaterally and in a peaceful manner. They should be solved through negotiations. The use of force must be ruled out and those who want to use force must be condemned universally. May I request the Hon. members that if they have any concrete suggestions to make they should do so ....

SHRI A.C. GEORGE : There was a specific suggestion about sending a medical mission to Vietnam.

SHRI VAJPAYEE : That I have noted. Unfortunately the Health Minister is not here. We have to ascertain from the other quarters also whether such a mission is needed and whether it will be of any use.

We seek to normalise relations with all countries. I went to Peking in pursuance of that policy of improving relations with all neighbours. But, I would like to assure the House that normalisation will not be at the cost of established friendships. The dialogue must continue and a proper climate for such a dialogue has to be created. Unfortunately, what happened on the last day of my visit has been a set-back.

SHRI A. BALA PAJANOR : We sympathise with you.

SHRI VAJPAYEE : I need your support—not sympathy. That won't do. On another occasion, not while we are discussing the President's Address, there will be debate on the demands relating to my Ministry.

SHRI K.P. UNNIKRISHNAN : The debate will be about your visit ?

SHRI VAJPAYEE : I do not mind.

SHRI K.P. UNNIKRISHNAN : It was agreed.

MR. SPEAKER : Don't commit me to anything. All agreements will be on record.

SHRI VAJPAYEE : I thank the Hon. members.

Zimbabwe

A Puppet Black Government in Zimbabwe

Sir, the present problem in Zimbabwe arises directly out of the unilateral declaration of independence in 1965 by the minority government headed by Ian Smith. Notwithstanding a qualitative change in the situation in southern Africa, consequent upon the dissolution of the Portuguese Empire in 1975, this regime continued, largely because of the active support extended to it by the racist regime in South Africa. Meanwhile, national liberation movements in the area have been gaining momentum.

The Geneva Conference on constitutional arrangements convened in 1976 failed to achieve any definite results except the emergence of a consensus that Zimbabwe should attain independence latest by March, 1978. Important disagreements remained, particularly regarding the question of who should control the army and the role of the minority during the transition to independence.

Thereupon the Frontline States coordinated their efforts in assisting liberation movements in Zimbabwe and promoting unity in their rank. The OAU Summit held in Libreville in 1977 recognised the Patriotic Front as the sole liberation movement in Zimbabwe.

It is against this background that the diplomatic efforts of Dr. Owen of UK and Ambassador Young of USA led to the formulation of the well-known seven-point Anglo-US proposals in September 1977 for a negotiated settlement of the Zimbabwean problem.

The Anglo–U.S. Proposals

The Frontline States had welcomed certain positive features of the Anglo-US proposals. The Patriotic Front had reservations with regard to the envisaged presence of UN force as well as about the role and power of the British Resident Commissioner. We had extended support to these proposals if these could lead to the removal of the illegal Ian Smith regime and the formation of a democratically elected government based on universal adult suffrage.

These proposals were taken note of by the Security Council which authorised the UN Secretary-General to appoint a representative to enter into discussions with all concerned parties relating to the military and associated arrangements considered necessary to effect transition to majority rule in

Rajya Sabha on March 20, 1978 as Minister of External Affairs on Situation in Zimbabwe

Southern Rhodesia (Zimbabwe). In pursuance to this Lt. Gen. Prem Chand from our country was named by the UN Secretary-General as his representative. The British Resident Commissioner, Lord Carver and Lt-Gen. Prem Chand held talks with Ian Smith in Salisbury. Talks were held in Malta from January 31 to February 3, 1978 between the British Foreign Secretary, David Owen, US Ambassador Andrew Young and Patriotic Front leaders Robert Mugabe and Joshua Nkommo. Ian Smith did not participate in these talks. Some progress was achieved there in narrowing down the differences on the precise arrangements for transition to majority rule in Zimbabwe.

Meanwhile, Iam Smith conducted talks with African leaders based within Zimbabwe, namely Bishop Muzorewa, Reverend Sithole and Chief Chirau. These talks resulted in the internal settlement which Hon'ble members have rightly characterised as the setting up of a puppet government in Zimbabwe by Ian Smith under the cover of a consitutional settlement.

This arrangement between Smith and a few selected African leaders within Southern Rhodesia (Zimbabwe), apart from excluding any role for the United Kingdom and United Nations, preserves the weighted position for the white minority at least for ten years. It is contrary to UN Resolutions on the subject. Moreover, the elections envisaged under it do not conform to the principle of one-man-one-vote on single electoral roll basis.

Danger of Civil Strife

As the House is aware, when the situation came up for discussion some days ago at the UN Security Council we reiterated that the Ian Smith regime is illegal and that therefore any settlement negotiated by it directly with certain groups inside or outside Southern Rhodesia would *ipso facto* also be illegal; that the *de jure* responsibility for decolonisation of Zimbabwe in conformity with relevant Security Council and General Assembly Resolutions remains with the UK. We stressed that majority rule should be brought about through the free exercise of the right of the people there for self-determination.

We are of the view that the present situation calls for a new approach — a constructive, creative and positive approach —to seek out the elements that are broadly acceptable to all the parties and conform to the principles and purposes of the Anglo-US proposals—and thereafter to achieve the restoration of legality in Zimbabwe. We remain convinced that any attempted arrangement for transition which excludes the Patriotic Front is likely to lead to civil strife in and around Zimbabwe and view the consequences of such a situation as dreadful.

Such an approach is shared by a majority of the members of the UN, as would be clear by the recent Security Council Resolution adopted without dissent which condemns the internal settlement as illegal and unacceptable.

Our Prime Minister has been in touch with the leader of the Frontline States and Zimbabwe leaders as well as with British and US leaders on this matter. Our diplomatic efforts are guided by the belief that greater efforts than those made hitherto are necessary for evolving a common approach acceptable to the Frontline States and African nationalist leaders so as to ensure a time-bound and effective transition to constitutional arrangements leading to genuine African majority rule. Moreover, we will continue our moral, diplomatic, political and material support to our African brethren in eliminating this vestige of colonialism.

Tanzania

Visit to Tanzania

Sir, I have just returned from an official visit to Tanzania and felt that I should take the first opportunity of reporting to this august House on the results of the visit.

My visit to Tanzania was the first by any Minister of the Janata Government to an African country. It, therefore, provided me with an opportunity for reaffirming our desire to forge closer links—political, economic, cultural, technical and scientific with our African friends and also for assuring the liberation movements in Southern Africa of our continued solidarity and support.

My visit to Tanzania fell into two parts. During the first, I was the guest of my friend and colleague, Foreign Minister Mkapa, and we had two rounds of in-depth discussions on the situation in Zimbabwe, Namibia and Southern Africa generally. The tense situation in the Horn of Africa was also reviewed. I took the occasion to explain to my Tanzanian colleague the recent developments in the Indian sub-continent. We also exchanged views on a number of international issues of mutual interest and the discussions were marked by the traditional warmth and cordiality which have always characterised Indo-Tanzanian relations.

President Julius Nyrere was good enough to receive me on July 29. The meeting could not have taken place at a better time as President Nyrere had just returned from a Summit of the Frontline Presidents in Lusaka and was preparing to leave on an important mission to Washington. President Nyrere is a statesman of world stature and his intellect, courage, vision and simplicity have won him universal respect. My talk with him was a stimulating experience and gave me fresh insights into the situation in Southern Africa.

Coincidentally President Nujoma of SWAPO was in Dar-es-Salaam for a brief visit during my stay there. We were able to meet and review the situation in Namibia. He told me about the manoeuvrings which were under way to bypass the UN in finding a solution to the Namibian problem and of the determination of SWAPO to frustrate these designs. He felt that a special session of the UN General Assembly could help in focusing attention on the urgency of the Namibian problem and help in speeding Namibia's march towards independence. We have agreed to support the idea.

Lok Sabha on August 4, 1977 as Minister of External Aftairs on Visit to Tanzania

Mr. Nujoma expressed appreciation of the moral and material support we have extended to SWAPO and said that he is hoping to visit India later this year. I have told him that he would be most welcome .

While my political discussions in Dar-es salaam were timely, rewarding and fruitful, the primary purpose of my visit was the second session of the Indo-Tanzanian Joint Commission which took place from July 29 to august 2. Vice President Jumbe did us the honour of inaugurating the joint commission and the inaugural session was attended by five ministers of the Tanzanian Government. This was symbolic of the importance which Tanzania attaches to strengthening her relations with India and I would like to assure the House that we fully reciprocate this desire.

Expansion of Economic Co-operation

Our co-operation with Tanzania in the economic, scientific and technical fields has grown rapidly and ranges from small and medium scale industries at one end to exploration for oil and gas at the other. About 800 Indian experts are working in Tanzania and our Tanzanian hosts were generous in expressing their appreciation of the valuable services they are rendering in the development of the Tanzanian economy.

My visit to the small Indian Ocean island of Songo Songo, about 200 killometres south-east of Dar-es-Salaam was particularly memorable. It is on this island that our Oil and Natural Gas Commission has succeeded in locating gas in commercial quantities in cooperation with the Tanzanian Petroleum Development Corporation. The present estimate of the gas reserves in Songo Songo is placed at around 30 billion cubic metres and would be enough to meet a large proportion of the energy requirements of Tanzania. Songo Songo is relatively isolated and the conditions of work on it are by no means easy. Despite these difficulties, however, I found that the morale of our experts there was very high. I would like to take this opportunity to compliment them on the excellence of their work and the role they are playing cementing Indo-Tanzanian ties.

Plans for the exploitation of the Songo Songo gas are being prepared by ONGC for consideration by the Tanzanian Government. We shall look forward to intensifying our cooperation with Tanzania in this field and extending it to other related areas such as fertilisers, petrochemicals, etc

Another major industrial project which India and Tanzania have agreed to implement is the Kagera Sugar Plant. This will have a cane crushing capacity of 2,500 tons per day which can be expanded to 3,500 tons per day in the second stage. The import of Indian machinery and equipment for this project will be financed partly out of a Government-to-Government credit and partly out of a credit extended by IDBI/SBI. The project is expected to be commissioned in 1980 and will doubtless mark yet another stage in the development of closer relations between India and Tanzania.

The economic cooperation between India and Tanzania is now so extensive that I could mention a number of other projects in which we are collaborating—industrial estates on the mainland and in Zanzibar, a bicycle plant in Dar-es-Salaam, supply of commercial vehicles to Zanzibar and locomotives, wagons and other railway equipment to Tanzania and development of small-scale and rural industries.

There were also discussions on steady supply of raw cashews to India by Tanzania. The Tanzanian authorities have agreed that, after meeting the needs of their own processing industry, they would give priority consideration to our requirements in view of our traditional position as the largest market for Tanzanian cashews. Prospects of augmenting production of raw cashews through Indo-Tanzanian collaboration are also being explored.

Collective Self-reliance

There has been a great deal of talk lately in various international fora, at non-aligned conferences, in meetings of the Group of 77 and elsewhere about the development of cooperation amongst developing countries as a step in the direction of collective self-reliance. Indo-Tanzanian cooperation, which is non-ideological and non-exclusive, is a model of what can be achieved when there is a genuine political will to cooperate. I have come back confident about the prospects that lie ahead and have no doubt that our cooperation with Tanzania and hopefully with other developing countries, will continue to grow from strength to strength.

May I conclude by expressing my grateful thanks to the Government and people of Tanzania for the warmth of the welcome accorded to us and the courtesy, attention and hospitality which our delegation received throughout its stay in Tanzania. Thank you.

Mauritius

Visit to Mauritius

Mr. Speaker, Sir, I visited Mauritius from 10th to 14th March in response to the invitation extended to me by Prime Minister of Mauritius, Sir Seewoosagur Ramgoolam, to participate in the celebrations of the Tenth Anniversary of the Independence of Mauritius.

The House is aware of the close, friendly and historic relations that have existed between India and Mauritius. Ethnic ties between the majority of the inhabitants of Mauritius and of the people of India have established a relationship which has been sustained over all these years by intense cultural contacts and is acquiring contemporary relevance through increasing functional cooperation in economic, scientific and technical fields between our two countries.

SHRI JYOTIRMOY BOSU (Diamond Harbour) : Did you find out the treasure taken out of the country ?

SHRI VAJPAYEE : Mauritius is our neighbour linked to us by the Indian Ocean. It is an active member of the Organisation of African Unity, and, like us, a member of the Non-aligned fraternity of nations and a developing country facing similar problems. It was, therefore, with a feeling of great happiness and a sense of duty that I accepted the invitation to visit Mauritius.

Before I reached Mauritius, I had a transit stop at Mahe, the Capital city of Seychelles. The Foreign Minister of Seychelles, Mr. Guy Sinon, received me at the airport and we were able to use the short time that was available to us for discussing possibilities of establishing and further strengthening of cooperation between India and Seychelles in the fields of agriculture, education, small-scale industries and health. Specific areas of cooperation had been identified during the recent visit of a delegation from Seychelles led by their Minister of Ports and Works, Mr. Loizeau.

When I landed in Mauritius on the afternoon of Friday, 10th March, I was deeply touched by the presence at the airport of the Mauritius Prime Minister, Sir Seewoosagur Ramgoolam, and Lady Ramgoolam and several of his colleagues in the Cabinet and a large number of other persons representing different walks of life in Mauritius. During a brief statement that I made at the airport, I observed that Mauritius would remain independent so long as the sun and the moon shine in the sky and also that the unbreakable bonds of friendship between India and Mauritius will continue to grow from

Lok Sabha on Much 16, 1978 as Minister of External Affairs on the visit to Mauritius

strength to strength as long as the waters of the Indian Ocean continue to wash the shores of India and Mauritius.

During my stay in Mauritius I had the opportunity to visit practically every part of Mauritius and to meet a very large cross-section of the people of Mauritius who, as the House is aware, have succeeded in forging a nation in spite of the diversity of the cultures, religions and languages of its people. As I mentioned at the banquet hosted by the Prime Minister, Mauritius is the living proof of the basic unity of the family of Man.

I visited the Mahatma Gandhi Institute which was set up in 1975 with our assistance with the objective of developing as a Centre for Indian studies, cultures and traditions. The Institute is already equipped with a good library and a printing press, and is running a Higher Secondary School where the medium of instruction is Hindi. In the very near future, the Institute will have a full-fledged Centre for Indian studies and other oriental studies.

During the course of my visit I had a *tour d'horizon* with the Mauritian leaders on international matters and bilateral relations. There was complete identity of views on the subject of the establishment of the Indian Ocean as a Zone of Peace and the related question of the convening of a conference of littoral and hinterland States for furthering the objectives of the United Nations Resolutions on the subject. Our two countries will co-operate within the framework of the UN *Ad hoc* Committee on the Indian Ocean and endeavour to ensure that all Great Powers and major maritime users will participate in the proposed conference.

The Question of Namibia

We exchanged views regarding the current deliberations in the Security Council on the subject of Zimbabwe and agreed that steps should be taken for an effective time-bound and constitutional transfer of power to genuine African majority rule.

We agreed that all efforts should be made to prevent the development of an internal solution of the Namibian problem as a result of South African manoeuvrings and machinations.

SHRI HARI VISHNU KAMATH (Hoshangabad) : By the end of the year.

SHRI VAJPAYEE : We agreed that non-aligned countries should concert their moves when the Namibian question comes up next month at a Special Session of the United Nations.

SHRI HARI VISHNU KAMATH : I hope you will attend.

SHRI VAJPAYEE : I pointed out to the Mauritian leaders that the continuance of the conflict in the Horn of Africa would, apart from vitiating the generally improved climate of international cooperation and detente, also contribute to the escalation of military presence of the great Power in the Indian Ocean. We agreed that a mutually acceptable political solution should be found and that all possible support should be given to the on-going OAU mediation efforts on this question.

While exchanging views on the West Asian situation we were of the opinion that everything possible should be done so as to facilitate irreversible progress towards a just settlement of this protracted problems.

I explained to the Mauritian leaders our stand on the Disarmament problem and the need for the non-aligned countries to work out a strategy for the Special Session of the United Nations General Assembly devoted to Disarmament and also to ensure that the necessary follow-up action is not ignored. We agreed that the meeting of the Non-Aligned Bureau, scheduled to be held in Kabul in May, should devote special attention to the Disarmament problems.

While reviewing the progress towards the establishment of the new international economic order we agreed that the steps taken so far have been meagre and tardy and that all aspects of the inter-dependence of the world economy should be taken into account.

Co-operation is Mutually Beneficial

As the House is aware, Mauritius has been an important beneficiary under our Technical and Economic Cooperation Programme. There are 49 Indian experts working in different fields. Mauritius is the largest beneficiary of our scheme for admission of self-financing foreign students in technical and medical colleges in the country. A grant of Rs. 13.1 million was made available to Mauritius in 1975 towards the capital assistance and this has been largely utilised by the Mahatma Gandhi Institute, the Industrial Trade Training Centre and the Mauritian Central Electricity Board. In addition to the earlier Government of India credit of Rs. 50 million extended to Mauritius a new credit of Rs. 100 million was recently agreed to. Eighty-four per cent of the credit is proposed to be utilised for purchase of capital equipment and the remaining for the purchase of agricultural commodities. Besides, a commercial credit of Rs. 50 million was extended last year for facilitating Mauritian purchases from India of commercial vehicles, machinery, medicines, etc.

Eleven Indo-Mauritian Joint Ventures have been approved and seven of them are already functioning. In my discussions with the Mauritian leaders, I informed them that we would be glad to provide further assistance in the field of irrigation, ground water resources, power generation, transmission and distribution, urban and rural water supply as well as technical assistance in the agreed rural and animal husbandry areas.

On the morning of the day of my departure from Mauritius, I, together with Prime Minister Ramgoolam, signed the Agreement establishing a Joint Commission on Economic, Technical, Educational and Cultural Co-operation between our two countries. The establishment of the Joint Commission will contribute significantly to the further strengthening of the existing close and friendly ties between India and Mauritius.

I am convinced that continued friendship between India and Mauritius is in the best interests of the peoples of India and Mauritius and will contribute to the establishment of peace and stability in the region to which we both belong. Thank you.

South Africa

Emergence of a Non-Racial South Africa

Mr. Speaker, Sir, today is a day of great rejoicing for the whole world. The emergence of a free, democratic and non-apartheid South Africa on the map of the world is a great moment of victory in the battle of liberation of mankind. Today the last vestige of colonialism has been demolished, the fortress of apartheid has been razed to the ground. As the Hon. Prime Minister said, a barbaric system of evaluation of human beings on the basis of colour of their skin has collapsed.

The people living in Africa have been suffering since 1662, being crushed between the two milestones of slavery and apartheid and were struggling to free themselves for generations. Thousands sacrificed their lives and lakhs suffered atrocities. Their sacrifices have brought success and their sufferings have borne fruit.

Mr. Speaker, Sir, the peaceful transfer of power in South Africa and surrender by the hateful apartheid system is in itself a miraculous event. It is also an indication of the changed world. The seed of *satyagraha* sown by Gandhiji in South Africa decades ago, is in full bloom today and is giving the message of love and equality to the people of South Africa.

The people of South Africa deserve our congratulations and Dr. Mandela our greetings. His whole life was spent in struggle. He spent his youth in jail, but did not lose his fortitude. He did not compromise with the tormentors. He inspired generations. Today, he has been elected as President of South Africa. We offer our felicitations to him and send our good wishes.

We ourselves have tasted the sin of slavery. In our country too, there is considerable discrimination prevalent. Those, who have been the victims of it, know its pain. May South Africa march forward on the path of prosperity on becoming free. Non-whites and whites and the people of mixed colour among whom there is a large number of people of Indian origin, all of them should contribute their mite for building South Africa; this is the need of the hour.

As the Prime Minister stated, we have been extending our cooperation to them in their war of independence from early times. Now we would be ready to offer our resources for the reconstruction of South Africa. You may please convey our good wishes to the people of South Africa and their new President Dr. Mandela. Thank you.

Lok Sabha on May 10, 1994 offering felicitations on the rise of a democratic non-apartheid South Africa

VI MISCELLANEOUS

Liberalised Passport Policy

Mr. Speaker, Sir, in the course of my reply in this House during the debate on Foreign Affairs, I had mentioned that ever since I took office I have been considering the question of how best to reduce delays in the issue of passports. I am fully aware of the importance of this question to which many Hon'ble members have drawn my attention.

I had committed myself to undertaking a complete review of the present procedures for issuing passports in order to determine how far we could simplify existing procedures and reduce to a minimum the inconvenience and hardship to applicants, specifically those from the weaker sections of our people.

I would like to draw the attention of Hon'ble members to the fact that there has been a very extraordinary increase in the number of passports that we have been issuing from year to year. For instance in 1972 we issued only 1.6 lakh passports but by 1976 which is the last year for which complete figures are available the figure almost came up to 6 lakhs. The estimates for the current year are of the order of 8 lakhs, and if this trend continued it seems a reasonable assumption that within the next couple of years we shall be issuing over 1 million passports a year.

It is against this background that I would like to acquaint members with the new simplified procedures which we propose to introduce.

Simplified Procedure

In future, endorsements will be given for travel to all countries with whom India has diplomatic relations. This would naturally exclude countries like South Africa and Rhodesia, whose present Governments we do not recognise because of their illegal or racialist character. Secondly, the present process of verification leads to delays in the issue of passports. Upto now the authority to give a verification certificate has been confined to Government and Judicial officers of a certain level. I feel that Members of parliament who are representatives of the people and are in close touch with the people of their constituencies should be enabled to give such certificates of verification. I, therefore, propose to introduce a system by which Members of Parliament would be fully competent to give verification certificates. However, in this

Lok Sabha on August 8, 1977 as Minister of External Affairs regarding the Revised and Liberalised Policy for Grant of Passports

context may I express the earnest hope that members will take every care and precaution to see that they issue certificates only on the basis of personal knowledge, and further when they are requested by the Passport issuing Authority to confirm that such a certificate has been given they will speedily reply to such queries.

As far as police verification procedures are concerned, we propose to introduce uniform system which will be designed to elicit simple and basic information that there will be no need to probe into an individual's life and his antecedents and thus become a source of harassment. With this end in view we are initiating consultations with State Governments who are primarily responsible for the issue of police verification certificates.

Passport application forms at present are available only from the Regional passport offices and the District Headquarters. We now propose that passport application forms should be available also through the network of post offices against a small fee to cover printing and distribution costs involved in the process. I would like, in this context, to express my gratitude to the Posts & Telegraphs Board who have agreed to cooperate with us to introduce this system on a selective basis as a trial measure.

I propose to introduce the new liberalised endorsement policy with effect from the 15th August. It is possible that there will be administrative delays in bringing about the changeover, but I have given instructions to see that these delays are cut to the minimum and the new procedure is implemented as speedily as possible.

Passport-Holders must not be Duped

I would like to mention, as a matter of prudence, that I propose to watch the effect of the new policy in all its aspects, and ensure that there are no adverse effects on our citizens at home and abroad consequent on the simplified and liberalised procedure for the issue of passports. I, therefore, intend to review the working of the new policy after a year and in the light of the experience gained, changes if required will be made to correct any abuses or difficulties that might come to light.

I would like to close this statement with an earnest appeal to all concerned that the new and simplified procedures should not become a cause for the exploitation of our people by unscrupulous elements. I have issued directions that, when a new passport is issued, the holder is suitably cautioned about the need to familiarise himself with the entry regulations in foreign countries and to get whatever visas are necessary. If the passport-holder seeks to go abroad for employment, he should ensure that he has a firm employment contract or is sponsored by a close relative who will take some responsibility for his maintenance. We must ensure that passport-holders are not duped into travelling abroad on the basis of spurious offers from foreign countries. This is a matter on which public opinion should ever remain vigilant. Thank you.

Privilege Motion Against Foreign Minister

Mr. Speaker, Sir, I will first speak in Hindi and then in English.

Sir, I am standing in the dock but I am not a sinner. For the past twenty years I have been bringing motions of breach of privilege against those who had been sitting on the treasury benches. The clock has turned full circle. Those very people are now bringing motions of breach of privilege against whom such motions were being brought earlier and those who had the habit of attacking are today defending themselves from the attack.

I want to make it clear that I have not committed any breach of privilege, I have not concealed any fact deliberately, and I have not tried to mislead the House.

This House is a temple of democracy for me. I have tried to maintain the dignity of this House for the last twenty years. Even when I was sitting in the opposition, I used to hold the view that the House must run properly and decisions should be taken on the basis of debate and without making any allegations against one's integrity. When I was on the opposite side I held the same view as I hold now, sitting on the treasury benches. Therefore, it is never going to happen that I do not place all the facts before the House and deliberately say wrong things. The day such an occasion arises I will not only not remain a Minister but will also leave the House.

Shri Unnikrishnan has rightly stated that this matter was raised by our friend Shri Shyamnandan Mishra under Rule 377. If I wished I could have kept quiet. But I did not keep quiet, because I do not want to hide anything. I do not want to cover the facts that are before me. I am eager to bring out the facts. I want to unmask those faces that are hiding behind this scandal. If the effort, the labour, the trouble, and the ingenuity which our friend Shri Unnikrishnan has mobilised in preparing material for this privilege motion was utilised in helping us perhaps .... (*Interruptions*)....

SHRI M.N. GOVINDAN NAIR : Since you did not put up those facts Shri Unnikrishnan put them before us.

SHRI VAJPAYEE : His entire speech was based on my statement.

SHRI M.N. GOVINDAN NAIR : What Shri Unnikrishnan has placed before us, you could have told us.

SHRI VAJPAYEE : He did not say any new thing. When Shyam Babu had raised this matter.... (*Interruptions*).

SHRI K.P. UNNIKRISHNAN : Your statement was the cause for raising the privilege issue.

Lok Sabha on May 15, 1978 as Minister of External Affairs while participating in the discussion on the question of breach of privilege

Facts were not Concealed

SHRI VAJPAYEE : So you had to bring this privilege motion. I know that, otherwise you could not raise this matter at all.

On the one hand, Shri Unnikrishnan says that the reply was given after five weeks and on the other he says that it was for the Minister not to reply if he so desired. I decided to reply, decided after five weeks, which makes it clear that I tried to collect the information about this matter. Whatever facts came to my knowledge I placed them before the House. I did not conceal the facts. I confirmed the fact that 5.5 million were deposited in two instalments separately in the Bank of Switzerland out of the Discretionary Fund of the Ministry of External Affairs (*Interruptions*). That is why I said in separate instalments.

AN HON'BLE MEMBER : Why was the money deposited ?

SHRI VAJPAYEE : I wish I could reply to that question.

Now our friend Unnikrishnan says that I had said that it was a cheque, not a Demand Draft. He even said that it was a Demand Draft, not a cheque. My submission is that Rule 80 of the Central Treasury Rules of Government of India provides, I quote :

> "Demand Drafts shall not be distinguished for the purpose of these Rules"

Now I would like to speak in English.

With regard to this Motion of Privilege, may I first state what I think is undeniable and common ground ? These payments were authorised by the previous Government and this Government was in no way involved with them. There were undoubtedly some orthodox aspects in these transactions when 11 million dollars in two instalments were paid in Switzerland from Special Discretionary Funds and by normal bank or book transfers. It is also true that these payments of 5.5 million dollars each were sanctioned by the Ministry of External Affairs in 1976, when I was not here ......

AN HON. MEMBER : When you were in Jail.

SHRI VAJPAYEE : Yes I was in jail.

...... although the transaction was negotiated by an officer of the Finance Ministry, Economic Affairs Department. But the rationale and its unusual features could be explained exhaustively only by the Government of today. There is no reasonable ground for any complaint, constitutional, legal or any other kind against me or my colleague, the Finance Minister.

When the question was raised, careful examination was made to ascertain facts from papers available in piecing together all the relevant details particularly on the rationale of adopting an unorthodox modality of the payments. Our enquiries have been greatly handicapped because the officer who conducted the negotiations has unfortunately passed away. Since I made the last statement to the House on 12th April 1978, we have continued to make further enquiries on facts which may throw light on these payments. Some officers who now happen to be serving abroad and who were at that time aware of the relevant transactions, have provided some relevant information. I have no hesitation in sharing as much information as is now available to me on the points raised by the Hon. members.

According to circumstantial evidence gathered, the payments of 11 million dollars made in two instalments of 5.5 million dollars each in Switzerland, related to a loan Agreement with Iran, signed in November, 1975, for 250 million dollars. The text of the loan agreement is available in the Economic Affairs Department and the facts relating to it were publicly disclosed at the time. The Agreement was signed by the then Ambassador of India in Iran on behalf of the State Bank of India and the proceeds were deposited by the State Bank in the account of the Government of India. This was a soft loan carrying an interest rate of 2.5 per cent per annum together with a management fee of 0.5 per cent per annum and was repayable over a period of 12 years with a grace period of six years. The loan tranches were received in two instalments and corespondingly the payments were made in Switzerland after deposits were received. (*Interruptions*). I am not yielding.

The attempts to negotiate such a loan started in July, 1974. This was at a time when, following a steep hike in oil prices, India was faced with a very severe balance of payments problem. Government was reluctant to make additional drawings from the IMF because of the stiffer conditions attached to drawings from IMF in higher credit tranches. Even taking into account the payments of 11 million dollars, the terms of repayment were decisively advantageous for India, considering the totality of economic circumstances prevailing at the time.

The Indian Ambassador signed the agreement in accordance with Article 299 which provides the necessary authorisation to do so for and on behalf of the President of India.

Discretionary Grants

As regards the specific provisions in the Demands for Grant, it may be mentioned that a sum of Rs. 23.69 crores were voted in 1975-76 under Major Heads—External Affairs Special Diplomatic Expenditure and Discretionary Expenditure. This included provision for payment of US $ 5.5 million which was made in that year. Similarly, in the year 1976-77 a sum of Rs. 16.8774 crores was voted under these Heads. The overall provision under the Head as augmented through the Supplementary Grant obtained in March, 1977 covered the payment of US $ 5.5 million in the financial year 1976-77. From all evidence available, the payments of 11 million dollars in two instalments of 5.5 million each was in full payment of the transaction.

The House will understand that payment of this nature cannot be effected through book adjustments. I may also clarify that under the Treasury Rules of the Government of India, as I have already made it clear, the terms 'cheques' and 'demand drafts' are synonymous.

Further, in order to maintain the confidentiality of the transactions and presumably the nature of understanding reached— about which I do not know—the payments had to be made in Switzerland. I surmise that the Government of the day felt that the confidentiality of a transaction could best be maintained by payments being made out of the Discretionary Grant for which a provision existed in the budget of the Ministry of External Affairs. I may add, this is the only transaction of this nature for which financial privision was made in the Discretionary Expenditure of the Ministry of External Affairs.

SHRI SHYAMNANDAN MISHRA : Was it done under the orders of the then External Affairs Minister or under the orders of the then Prime Minister ?

SHRI VAJPAYEE : I have already stated in my last statement that the expenditure was authorised by the then Prime Minister.

SHRI SHYAMNANDAN MISHRA : He was not in the picture.

SHRI VAJPAYEE : Mr. Speaker, having inherited good relations with Iran, our Government has sought to strengthen them purposefully as we are convinced that they were to our mutual advantage. We do not wish to risk damage to this relationship, and I am happy my friend, Mr. Unnikrishnan also concurred with this view, or allowed any unintended misunderstandings to come between us and Iran. On the basis of mutual confidence and mutual trust, we shall pursue the quest for economic cooperation between our countries as, we believe, it can be a factor in promoting cooperation and stability in the entire South Asian region.

Mr. Speaker, I like to reiterate that there was never any intention nor is there now to suppress information or mislead the House. Indeed, as far as the present Government is concerned there could be no possible reason to do so in the light of these facts, I would state respectfully that no motion of privilege against me or my colleagues the Finance Minister is warranted.

Index

Shri Atal Bihari Vajpayee
(A Biographical Sketch)

Born on December 25, 1926 at Gwalior, then a princely state, as the youngest of the four sons of Pandit Krishna Bihari Lal Vajpayee, Inspector of Education. Shri Atal Bihari Vajpayee had been imbued with an ardent nationalistic spirit ever since his childhood days. Even while at school, writing poems and participation in debates had become his main hobby. Even though Shri Vajpayee came from conservative background, he was exposed to organisations like Arya Samaj and the Rashtriya Swayamsevak Sangh (RSS), which influenced his thinking.

Shri Vajpayee studied at Victoria (now Laxmibai) college at Gwalior and obtained his BA Degree with the highest marks and MA in Political Science from DAV College, Kanpur. He was active in the student movement and was elected as the General Secretary and Vice-President of the Victoria College Students' Union. During that time he came in contact with the Student Federation of India. He, however, parted company when the Communist Party of India opposed the 1942 Quit India Movement. He joined the freedom struggle and was imprisoned in the Bateshawar conspiracy case in 1942. He came in contact with the RSS and became its full-time worker in 1947.

Shri Vajpayee is a bachelor and has dedicated his life to the service of the country. Starting his career as a journalist, he became the editor of the RSS organs *Rashtra Dharma* during 1947-50, the weekly *Panchajanya* during 1948-50, the daily *Swadesh* during 1949-50 and lastly, of *Veer Arjun* (daily as well as a weekly).

Shri Vajpayee was a founder member of the Bhartiya Jana Sangh, a new political party formed under the leadership of Dr. Shyama Prasad Mukherjee in 1951 and closely worked as his associate. Shri Vajpayee was with Dr. Mukherjee at the time of his arrest in Jammu and Kashmir where he died in custody. After Dr. Mukherjee's martyrdom he decided to join politics in a big way to complete Dr. Mukherjee's unfinished task.

Shri Vajpayee was first elected to Lok Sabha from Balrampur in 1957 and became the president of the Bhartiya Jana Sangh in 1967. He was also the leader of the Party's Parliamentary wing from 1957-77.

In the interregnum, he suffered another spell of imprisonment during 1975-77 in the wake of Internal Emergency declared by Shrimati Indira Gandhi. When the Janata Party was formed in 1977, he was among its founders and when the party assumed power after the elections, he was appointed Minister of External Affairs in the Morarji Desai Ministry and held the portfolio for the entire duration of the Janata Government i.e. 1977-79.

After the fall of the Janata Government in 1979, Shri Vajpayee, was among those who founded the Bharatiya Janata Party in 1980 and remained its President during 1980-86. During 1980-84 and again during 1986-91 he was Leader of the Bharatiya Janata Party's Parliamentary Party.

Shri Vajpayee has had almost an uninterrupted Parliamentary career which began in 1957 when he first entered the Lok Sabha having won the Balrampur seat and since then has adorned the Chambers of either the Lok Sabha or the Rajya Sabha. In all, he got elected to the Lok Sabha six times (in 1957, 1967, 1971, 1977, 1980 and 1991) and twice to the Rajya Sabha (in 1962 and 1986). Whatever the office he held in Parliament and whatever the business before the House, he always held Parliament and its rules and procedures in high esteem. As he has said: "The Opposition may be forced to speak a bit louder but points can only be scored by making use of the parliamentary rules and procedures." Not surprisingly, he was honoured with Best Parliamentarian Award for 1994 instituted by the Govind Ballabh Pant Memorial Society by the Prime Minister Shri P.V. Narasimha Rao on August 17, 1994. He was also conferred Padama Vibhushan by the President of India in 1991.

Shri Vajpayee always took keen interest and played useful roles in the functioning of the Parliamentary Committees. In 1966-67 he was Chairman of the Committee on Government Assurances and in 1969-70 and again in 1991-92 of the Public Accounts Committee. He was Chairman of the Petitions Committee of the Rajya Sabha in 1990-91. He made useful contributions as member of the General Purposes Committee (1986), and of Rajya Sabha's Home Committee and Business Advisory Committee during 1988-90.

In the international parliamentary arena, Shri Vajpayee was a member of the India's Parliamentary Goodwill Mission to East Africa in 1965 besides being member of Indian Parliamentary Delegations visiting foreign countries viz. to Australia in 1967, and European Parliament in 1983, Canada in 1987. He was an active member of the Indian Delegation to the Commonwealth Parliamentary Conference held in Canada in 1966, Zambia in 1980, Isle of Man in 1984, Indian Delegation to the Inter-Parliamentary Union Conference held in Japan in 1974, Sri Lanka in 1975, Switzerland in 1984. Besides Shri Vajpayee was also member of the Indian Delegation to the United Nations during 1988, 1989, 1990 and 1991.

Shri Vajpayee led the Indian Delegation to the U.N. Conference on Human Rights held in Geneva in 1994 and staunchly defended India's case on human rights violations in Kashmir. His forceful advocacy of the Indian stand won him laurels, both in the country and abroad.

Shri Vajpayee was a member of the National Integration Committee in 1958. As President of the All-India Station Masters and Assistant Station Masters Association in 1965-70 he tenaciously espoused the cause of the Railwaymen and helped in the solution of several problems being faced by them.

In the social and cultural field, Shri Vajpayee functioned as President of Pandit Deen Dayal Upadhyaya Smarak Samiti during 1964-68 and of Janmabhoomi Smarak Samiti since 1969.

Shri Vajpayee besides being a journalist, has been a scholar and author of several publications, some notable ones being *Kaidi Kaviraj Ki Kundaliyan* (a collection of poems written in jail during Emergency), *New Dimensions of India's Foreign Policy* (a collection of speeches made as Minister of External Affairs), *The Jana Sangh and Muslim, Mrityu Ya Hatya* and *Amar Balidan.* He also has a number of articles and poems published in newspapers, journals and magazines to his credit.

In addition, a three-volume compilation titled *Sansad Mein Teen Dashak* was published in 1992 and an abridged translation thereof in Marathi titled *Sansadetil Teen Tape* was published in 1995. A compilation of Shri Vajpayee's poems entitled *Meri Ekkavan Kavitayen* published also in 1995.

FOUR DECADES
IN
PARLIAMENT

FOUR DECADES IN PARLIAMENT

VOLUME I
STATE OF THE NATION

Atal Bihari Vajpayee

Edited by Dr. N.M. Ghatate

SHIPRA

SHIPRA

(2021 PoD, 2018, 2000, 1998 twice, First Published 1996)

Rs. 9000, US$ 360
Set Price

ISBN: 978-81-85402-69-7 (Set)
978-81-85402-70-3 (Vol. 1)
978-81-85402-71-0 (Vol. 2)
978-81-85402-72-7 (Vol. 3)

2024 Impression PoD

Four Decades in Parliament

Published by:
SHIPRA PUBLICATIONS
LG 18-19, Pankaj Central Market,
I.P. Ext., Patparganj, Delhi 110092, India
91 11 47322068; 9650028065, 9810522367
info@shiprapublication.com
www.shiprapublication.com

Editor's Note

Shri Atal Bihari Vajpayee has been on the central stage of national politics for a period longer than any other leader since independence. His parliamentary career commenced in 1957 and for four decades he has been influencing the politics of India both from inside and outside the Parliament. His every public utterance is a news and his speeches are listened with wrapt attention by his friends and foes alike. If his inimitable oratory, repartee and humour capture the hearts of the people his tolerance, width of vision and reasoning based on the facts and figures influence their minds. But what is more amazing is that in Parliament he has spoken with authority on almost all aspects of Indian life—whether it is international affairs or agriculture, defence or social reforms industry or education, Five Year Plans or Centre-State relations.

Shri Vajpayee does not mince words when criticism is due or warning necessary. But his criticism does not hurt any one. He has never hesitated to support rival's point of view when situation demanded. His approach is consructive and persuasive always emphasizing what is in the best national interest. His contribution in enhancing the standard of debates and maintaining the decorum and dignity of the Parliament is second to none. In recognition of his services to the country Shri Vajpayee was in 1992 awarded Padma Vibhushan by the President of India and the Prime Minister in 1994 decorated him as the Best Parliamentarian.

Shri Vajpayee has fingers on the pulse of the people and has an enviable knack of diffusing tense situation by his humorous comments. His capacity to drive home a point and to inspire workers is unmatched.

Politician thinks of today while statesman thinks of generations. Shri Vajpayee comes in the latter category. This fact repeatedly emerges from his speeches. On reading his speeches one is left with an impression that had his suggestions, warnings, and views been given the due consideration they deserved, the country would not have been in such a grave political, economic and social crisis as it is today.

I have known Atalji since 1957—the year he came to the Parliament and I came to Delhi to study law. It was the beginning of close and treasured relationship nearing four decades. As a man, he is intensely human always willing to do his little bit to those who come for help. He speaks little but whatever he says touches the heart. To Atalji politics is a vehicle to serve his country and its people whom he dearly loves. The underlying current of his thinking which surfaces in his speeches is that we have inherited a glorious civilization and we owe a duty to future generation to leave a better world.

No sooner did he come to Parliament in March 1957 his powerful oratory and thought provoking speeches, ready wit and humour mesmerized the house. In August 1957 Ananthashayanam Ayyangar addressed the students of Delhi University and when I asked him who is the best speaker in Parliament he replied, "Shri Atal Bihari Vajpayee in Hindi and Prof. Hiren Mukherjee in English."

Foreign Affairs has always been his favourite subject. Prime Minister Pandit Nehru was so moved by Atalji's speech in Hindi that he chose to reply to the debate in Hindi instead of his usual English; and fully agreed with Atalji's statement that "to speak one requires voice but to keep silent one requires voice as well as brains." Panditji burst into peals of laughter when replying to his criticism of Jana Sangh. Atalji said "I know the Prime Minister does head-stand every day. I have no objection. But why does he see my Party up side down ?"

After the death of Dr. Shyama Prasad Mukherjee in early fifties, a towering personality who founded the Jana Sangh, Pandit Nehru had remarked Jana Sangh is like a chicken without head, but is still growing. "The sixties saw the steady increase in its influence in all spheres when party suffered another set back. Pt. Deen Dayal Upadhyaya, the President of Jana Sangh succumbed to his death in mysterious circumstances. The party decided to choose Atalji as its President. In this obituary speech he said "Pandit Dendayalji lighted a lamp, we shall convert it into an inferno," which inspired the workers to work for the cause.

Seventies was the most eventful decade. In the Lok Sabha election of 1971, the Jana Sangh strength was reduced from 35 to 22. When I asked Atalji what was Prime Minister Indira Gandhi's reaction, he laughed and said, "Now she looks at us with lot of affection and smiles."

During the 1971 Indo-Pak war Atalji toured the entire country helping to boost the morale of the people. On December 16, 1971 when Bangla Desh became independent Atalji had gone to Gwalior to address a public meeting and I was with him. Since he hailed from Gwalior and was elected to Parliament from there, the workers knew him intimately. Worried Sheetala Sahai, who was then the M.L.A. from Gwalior, said "Now Indiraji will take full advantage of victory in the coming Assembly elections." He kept quiet then. But in the public meeting warned the Congress "Don't try to bake election bread on the funeral fire of our soldiers."

Next day when the Government announced in Lok Sabha that all parties had agreed to cease fire declaration, Atalji opposing the decision said, "This is only a cease fire not cessation of hostilities" and made a fiery speech. When Indira Gandhi met him in the lobby she remarked, "You already seemed to be gearing up for elections."

For a one and a half year, during the black days of Internal Emergency of 1975, his voice was not heard in Parliament as it was silenced by the Government which had mala fide detained him along with all Opposition leaders. Immediately after his arrest at Bangalore I had gone to see him. I was surprised to see him wearing jail clothes, surprised I said "Atalji what is all this ?" and he replied Now Indira Gandhi will feed me and Indira Gandhi will give clothes. I am not going to spend a penny from my pocket." I told him I had drafted a *Habeas Corpus* petition challenging the detention as also the Emergency. But there was difference of opinion amongst the Opposition parties whether we should approach the court. Some leaders thought that like in 1942 Quit India movement, we should not. His immediate reaction was "This is 1975 not 1942. We are in an independent country. Courts are ours. If we do not knock the doors of the judiciary, tomorrow the judges might say we would have given relief. We must make the judiciary face the acid test."

But whatever his personal opinion he believes in decision by consensus and immediately he said let me also consult Advaniji, and other party leaders Shri S.N. Mishra and Madhu Dandavate, who were also with him in the Bangalore jail. They all decided to approach the Court and their *Habeas Corpus* petition was filed in Karnataka High Court. A precedent was set. And hundreds of petitions were filed in almost all the High Courts. High Courts after High Court held that illegal and mala fide detention can always be challenged. But the 5 senior most Judges of the Supreme Court by 4:1 delivered the blackest judgement reversing the view taken by nine High Courts; making sovereign the slave and servant the master.

After the historic election of 1977, his words on the occasion of merger of Jana Sangh with the Janata Party brought a lump in the throat of workers, "During the dark days of emergency our *Deepak* (lamp) was the only ray of hope. But now there is sun rise and time has come to snuff our lamp."

During Janata Government Atalji was the Foreign Minister. This period witnessed an unprecedented improvement with India's relations with her neighbours. It is not difficult to understand reasons. When he went to Pakistan, his words "Now India will defeat Pakistan only on the hockey field," evoked applause from all Pakistanis. Which Indian or Nepali will not be happy to hear, "There are no countries on this globe which are closer to each other than the India and Nepal. History, geography, civilization, religion and the rivers have tied us together."

He placed before the U.N. the towering ideal *Vasudaiva kutumbakam*, which means the world is one family. After the sudden fall of Janata Party Government talking to me about international relations he said, "If I had a full term perhaps dispute with China and Pakistan would have been solved."

The beginning of eighties saw the return of Smt. Indira Gandhi to power and Atalji again reverted to Opposition benches. During that time there was gruesome incident of brutalities against the Harijans in Uttar Pradesh and Atalji's programme to undertake *padayatra* of the area was announced. When I asked him how long his *padayatra* would last, he said "It will continue till the goal was achieved."

The yatra is on. Almost fifty years have goneby. But now there is glimmer of hope on horizon. Due to sheer dedication and hard work of decades by known and unknown workers B.J.P. has today become a national alternative and Atalji told the legislators meeting held in July 1995, "Prepare to strike when the iron is hot."

This work is by no means an exhaustive compilation of all that Shri Vajpayee spoke in the Lok Sabha and the Rajya Sabha from 1957 to 1995. Only important speeches are included in this publication.

I owe an incalculable debt to Shri Atal Bihari Vajpayee, who despite his heavy schedule found time to go through the manuscript and agreed to write about his overall views about the institution of Parliament, democracy in action, role of the Government and Opposition and Prime Ministers during the last four decades. In fact this work starts with his signed article—"I Recollect".

This work is in three volumes and each subject is organised chronologically. Hindi speeches of Shri Vajpayee and also comments made in Hindi during the debates are translated to maintain homogeneity.

Speeches of Shri Vajpayee on general national problems facing the country are included in Volume I—*State of the Nation*; economic issues and related subjects are given in Volume II—*State of the Economy*, and Volume III—*Foreign Affairs* deals with topics such as international situation, neighbouring countries and super powers.

I am sure this publication would be of abiding interest to the general reading public particularly the elite opinion makers, the legislators, journalists and students of Social Sciences.

Shri Vajpayee's speeches are a poetry in prose and at times I felt that it was almost an impossible task to translate his words without diluting their flavour and charm. But Shri Sudhakar Raje and Shri O.P. Khosla have put in their best possible efforts and I am thankful to them.

I am indebted to Mrs. Namita Kaul Bhattacharya who collected indexes and in making useful suggestions. I am much obliged to Shri Shiv Kumar, P.L. Sharma and T.N. Maken who were ever willing to help whenever help I needed it and to Shri P.V.C. Kutty, Shri Abraham Varghese and Shri Dwarka Prasad Aggarwal for rendering assistance. I wish to record my appreciation to Shri D. Kumar of Shipra for hard work he has put in to bring out this book. Needless to say I accept all responsibility for any omission and mistakes.

DR. N.M. GHATATE

VOLUME I

Contents

IV HOME AFFAIRS

V PREVENTIVE DETENTION

VI CENTRE-STATE RELATIONS

VII Kashmir Tangle

VIII Assam and Punjab

IX Judiciary and Fundamental Rights

X Elections

XI EDUCATION

XII LANGUAGE POLICY

XIII SOCIAL PROBLEMS

XIV RELIGION

XV OTHER IMPORTANT ISSUES

I Recollect

Time passes off quickly. Almost forty long years have elapsed. Still it looks as if all this happened only the other day.

It was the year 1957. The second general elections for Lok Sabha were in offing. My Party—Bhartiya Jana Sangh was engaged in the gigantic task of establishing itself. The benign presence of Dr. Shyama Prasad Mookherji was no longer there. Neither was there a distinguished leadership nor was there a wide mass base. Candidates were hard to find to fight the elections. There was none who was willing to spend his own money to face forfeiture of security deposit. Even so elections had to be fought. What better chance could there be to spread the message of the Party to the vast masses to the maximum possible extent ?

It was decided to field me from three constituencies: Lucknow, Mathura and Balrampur. I had earlier fought the bye-election for Lok Sabha from Lucknow. Victory was out of question. Yet I had polled a good number of votes. It helped to boost the morale of the Party. Accordingly, it was decided to field me again from Lucknow. There was hardly any candidate of stature ready to stand from Mathura. The few, who after great persuasion and difficulty were prevailed upon to fight the election, wanted to stand for the Legislative Assembly. Firstly, it involved less expenditure. Secondly, there was hope of saving one's security deposit. Thirdly, if luck favoured one could even get elected. But for Lok Sabha no suitable candidate was forthcoming. I had made some name. People had started to flock around to hear my speeches. In my name funds could also be easily raised to fight the election.

So far as contesting the election from Balrampur was concerned, the position of the Party was relatively better there. Late Shri Pratap Narain Tiwari, first as whole-time Pracharak of Rashtriya Swayamsewak Sangh (R.S.S.) and later as full-time worker of Bhartiya Jana Sangh, had succeeded in raising a strong organisational structure of the Party in Balrampur. The youth, farmers, employees, teachers and shopkeepers were drawn to the Party in sizable number. From the Party's angle here were good chances of winning election from Balrampur. After filing my nomination papers from Lucknow and Mathura I went to Balrampur.

Prior to this I had never been to Balrampur. Neither did I know its geography nor was I familiar with its history. The Balrampur station was located on the metre gauge, which ran from Gonda to Gorakhpur. The train used to leave Gonda at midnight reaching Balrampur in early hours. I was familiar with the metre gauge. Between Gwalior and Bhind there used to be a narrow gauge which was even smaller. The train used to run leisurely and took lot of time to reach the destination. On the same ticket and at the same fare one could experience the joys of a long journey! I boarded the train from Gonda. After spreading my bed on the narrow berth, I went to sleep. When I woke up I found the train standing in the station. When I raised the shutter to have a view, I found that hundreds of crows, perched on nearby trees, were crowing aloud. Their crowing virtually rented the whole sky. I enquired of the name of the station. The answer was "it is Kauwapur."

The Balrampur station situated between Kauwapur and Intiathok was a place of halt for passengers bound for Nepal. The town stood on the banks of river Ghagra. Balrampur was a princely state which was merged with Uttar Pradesh in 1947. People had found in Bhartiya Jana Sangh an alternative to Congress. They were attracted to it. The nationalistic ideology of Jana Sangh made an impact on them. Though monarchy was abolished, the Zamindari still continued. Several landlords were Muslims by faith and besides indulging in economic exploitation also discriminated on religious grounds. During my election campaign I toured many places in my constituency where striking of gongs and blowing of conch shells was prohibited. Although things had considerably changed after independence yet the winds of change had not reached the remote areas. Small and medium level farmers, who lived under the perpetual terror of landlords, gathered around Bhartiya Jana Sangh. As a result thereof I got elected to Lok Sabha from Balrampur. There were in all 4,82,800 voters. Out of them 2,26,948 electors exercised their franchise. I got 1,18,380 votes, while Shri Haidar Hussain lost by nearly 10,000 votes. Had the Congress fielded a Hindu candidate, perhaps I would not have won the election. Shri Haidar Hussain was a reputed lawyer of Lucknow. For him to maintain contacts with people in Balrampur was not easy. He used to win elections on the support of Congress. Resentment against Congress was on the increase. As a result I was successful in the battle of the ballot.

As against this success I lost in the other two constituencies with heavy margins. In Mathura I even lost my security deposit. At the eleventh hour even the staunch supporters of Bhartiya Jana Sangh deserted it and went with the independent candidate Raja Mahendra Pratap. People had great respect for Raja Saheb. He had participated in freedom struggle and had been the first President of the Government of Free India formed abroad. The Prem Ashram founded by him was doing commendable work in the field of education. He succeeded in fully exploiting the anti-Congress sentiment. His being a Jat also helped him. I regret that the local unit of the Party should not have, in the first place, persuaded me to fight the election from there; or if it had fielded me it should have remained firm in its resolve to get majority of votes cast in my favour. The swaying of ardent supporters of the Party in anti-Congress wave can hardly be tolerated.

In Lucknow the Party got good public support. The winning candidate Shri Pulin Behari Bannerji of the Congress polled 68,579 votes, whereas 57,034 votes were polled in my favour. Had the Communist candidate cornered some more votes the Congress could have been defeated at the hustings. It appeared that in a bid to defeat Jana Sangh, voters with pronounced leftist leanings too had cast their votes in favour of the Congress.

In 1957, only 4 candidates of the Party including me, got elected to Lok Sabha. The Party had scored victory in the Hardoi (Reserved) Constituency. Two other members Shri Uttam Rao Patil and Shri Premji Bhai Aasar were elected from Maharashtra. In Maharashtra the Opposition Parties had waged a collective struggle for the formation of united Maharashtra. Jana Sangh was a co-participant in this struggle. It was also decided to fight the elections there jointly. Shri Uttam Rao Patil got elected from Dhulia, whereas Shri Premji Bhai Aasar was elected from Ratnagiri. Shri Patil was an advocate by profession and Shri Premji Bhai Aasar was a businessman. Thus all the four members of Jana Sangh in a way represented the entire society.

In the beginnir of 1957 there were doubts whether the elections would be held or not. It was only a year ago that the states were reorganised and linguistic states had come into existence. Although the general atmosphere was disturbed in many areas yet the elections were held on time. An estimated 20 crore voters had taken part in the elections. Elections to Legislative Assemblies were also held alongwith elections to Parliament. Congress polled 42.8 per cent votes and as compared to the last elections it increased the strength of its members in the House by seven. The Communist Party of India got 8.9 per cent votes and the number of its members rose from 16 to 27. The Praja Socialist Party polled more votes as compared to the votes cast for the Communist Party, but it was successful only at 19 places. Bhartiya Jana Sangh succeeded in retaining its all India recognition, while several other parties, namely, the Hindu Maha Sabha, the Scheduled Caste Federation and the Ram Rajya Parishad failed to retain their recognition for not being able to secure the minimum 3 per cent votes. The Bhartiya Jana Sangh, on the other hand, succeeded in securing 6 per cent votes.

The President of the Hindu Maha Sabha Shri Nirmal Chandra Chatterji and the General Secretary Shri Vishnu Ghanshyam Deshpande lost the election. In Orissa the Gana Tantra Parishad made its appearance on the political scene. The advent of Anna Dravida Munnetra Kazhagam (D.M.K.) in Tamilnadu (Madras) was a significant development. The Sanyukta Maharashtra Samiti, which fought for the creation of a separate Maharashtra State by reorganising the Bombay State and the Maha Gujarat Parishad, which spearheaded the movement for the formation of a separate Gujarat State, achieved notable successes in the elections to Lok Sabha.

After the elections the Council of Ministers formed under the leadership of Shri Jawaharlal Nehru included top leaders like Maulana Abul Kalam Azad, Shri Gobinda Ballabha Pant, Shri Morarji Bhai Desai and Shri Jagjivan Ram. Shri Krishna Menon also became the Minister without Portfolio. The Opposition benches were graced by the presence of veteran parliamentarians and political leaders like Acharya J.B. Kripalani, Shripad Amrit Dange, Shri Narain Ganesh Gore, Professor Hiren Mukherji and Shri Minoo Masani. Smt. Vijaya Raje Scindia, who today sits in the front row of the Opposition in Lok Sabha, was in those days in the Congress. Besides her Smt. Sucheta Kripalani,

Miss Parvati Krishnan, Smt. Tarakeshwari Sinha were very active in the House and used to make significant contribution to the debates.

We all the four members of Bhartiya Jana Sangh had entered into Parliament for the first time. None of us had ever been a member of any legislature. We were quite new to the legislative work. We neither had any previous experience nor any experienced member was there, to whom we could turn for help. Being a few in number we had been allotted seats in the House on the back benches. From there it was difficult to catch the Speaker's eye. During discussions on various issues time was allotted according to the strength of the Party in the House. Members of smaller parties hardly got any time. Even now they rarely get any.

Foreign Policy has been my favourite subject. In those days discussion on international situation used to be an important event. Prime Minister Shri Nehru was also the Minister of Foreign Affairs. When demands for grants to the Ministry of Foreign Affairs were discussed in the House it used to be packed to its capacity. The visitors gallery tended to be overcrowded. There was virtually no space left unoccupied in the Diplomatic gallery. The Communist Party being the major Opposition Party, its leaders used to initiate discussion on international situation and India's policy towards it. The Praja Socialist Party too used to project its viewpoint. But there used to be great difficulty in getting time to speak for the Bhartiya Jana Sangh. The Party hardly got more than 3 to 4 minutes as its share. Discussions often got prolonged. A definite time was fixed for the Prime Minister to reply to the debate.

On one occasion I had to stage a walkout to register my protest against non-allotment of time. Irrespective of this whatever time was allotted to the Party the Jana Sangh members tried to make full use of it.

My very first speech on Foreign Policy attracted attention of the House. English used to dominate the proceedings of the House. Most of the speeches on Foreign Policy were usually delivered in English. Of course Shri Brajraj Singh of the Socialist Party, as a rule, did speak in Hindi. My Hindi was chaste. The members liked my fluent style. On 20th August, 1958 Prime Minister Shri Nehru after concluding his speech in English in reply to the full debate sought the permission of the Speaker to speak something in Hindi. The members welcomed this gesture by clapping their hands. When Shri Nehru after referring to me by name started speaking in Hindi the members once again expressed their happiness over it. Shri Nehru's speech ran as under :

> "One of the many speeches delivered yesterday was that of Shri Vajpayee. During his speech Shri Vajpayee had said one thing. To my mind he had said that in his opinion our foreign policy was correct. I am thankful to him for having said so. But he had also said one thing more. He had said that in order to speak speech is needed but to keep silent both speech and discretion are required, I am in complete agreement with him on this point. You may well be aware that this could work in other councils, but in the councils of world this may not work.

At least so far as our foreign policy is concerned some times we may be caught up in our enthusiasm and at times we may suffer an illusion. But I have always wanted that we should speak the least and interfere the minimum. But our dilemma is that when we do not speak many others say that you have developed cold feet and that that you are afraid. Shri Khadilkar said that you have given the reins in the hands of others, instead you should ride yourself. I fully agree and had once said perhaps here in this House or somewhere else that if all the foreign diplomats of the world observe silence for at least about six months then it would do immense good to the world, will better its lot and will not harm anyone.

Shri Vajpayee said one thing and Acharya Kripalani too had referred to something similar and said that in respect of the summit conference in question we reacted in haste. To some our prompt response gave an impression that we were eager to attend it and to participate in it. I would like to narrate what actually happened.

We have repeatedly said and this has been our policy too for the last several years that if we are invited to attend any conference, we are not particularly keen to participate in it; but if there is any advantage likely to accrue from it and people, almost all the people, invite us then we are willing to go there. If on some such occasion we take an adamant position and say that we would not participate it will surely be a faux pas on our part.

It is just possible that we may not derive any benefit out of it, but outright refusal is also incorrect. In the case of Korea as well as of Indo-China we got involved because it became very difficult for us to decline the invitation, especially so because all the people requested us with one voice to participate in it. No other country was either willing to respond or was favoured for it. By favoured I do not mean that we are the most preferred country in the world, but we are surely among those few countries, which are in a way trusted by both the blocs. That is how a thing like this takes place. For this very reason we went to Korea and precisely for the same reason we went to Indo-China.

We have now made our position clear on this point. In respect of many other conferences as well as the summit conferences, which were held at one time or the other, we have already explained our views. The fact is that for this summit conference I received a telegram from Shri Khrushchev. This telegram came at a time when the situation had taken a critical turn. There was some semblance of peace after the war. At a moment like this even a little indiscretion here or there could start the war again. I could not possibly know what was in the mind of the people. But when the British and the American forces were sent there, then it was obvious that such a step may lead to grave consequences and may escalate into a large scale war. It was just possible that in retaliation the other side launch a bigger offensive.

But after a great deal of deliberation it was thought that we could take this step and war will not start. It was a gamble. But at the same time, it was also very much on our mind that it may start a war for which there was total preparedness on both the sides.

Had even a single provocative action been taken you could have surely witnessed within the next 24 hours the total destruction of scores of cities. The situation was tense on both the sides and things had come to a dangerous pass. Once a decision was reached and a button was pressed the hell would have been let loose. All the strategic plans were already there and the armies knew it well that they had to move from here to there to destroy a particular city and drop atom bombs at such and such place. At such a likely moment mutual consultations would have been out of question. The button could have been pressed at any time. All the time we kept reminding ourselves that the worst may happen. During these agonising moments I got Shri Khrushchev's telegram. This was the same telegram, which he had sent to other countries, the bigger ones. In the telegram it was stated that the proposed conference was likely to be convened within the next two or three days. Perhaps Geneva was suggested as the likely venue for the proposed conference.

I was in a great transfix. Even to reach there in time appeared well nigh impossible except that I start off the next morning. But the deliberations of the last two or three days had made me realise that the matter was serious and if things took a wrong turn it could well start a war. I don't mean to say that our reply would have either added to or lessened the grimness of the situation but the fact is that we had very little time. After considering all these aspects I decided to send the reply at once. As a matter of fact, the reply had been already given. I only reiterated it. The reply was that if at this juncture all concerned so desire and deem it right and we too think that by going there we can be of any service then we are ready to go.

In this way, both these conditions were to be met. This was then our reply. I only reiterated it. By this if somebody draws this inference that we were sitting in readiness to go or we were pretty anxious to be there, it hardly sounds to be convincing. Personally speaking I am weary of attending such big conferences. I feel weary because as a matter of routine whenever 10, 15 or 20 people meet they are accompanied by an army of 200, 300 or 400 secretaries followed by 600 to 700 photographers along with their movie cameras. On such occasions my mind gets boggled. All the time one is surrounded by an array of flash lights and movie cameras while you are at work and tackling the problems of the world. I hardly have any inclination to go and attend such occasions. Nonetheless, I do feel that if men meet in small groups and hold mutual discussions then certain misgivings could be removed and they can be mutually benefited.

In the last few years I got the opportunity to travel all over the world. I have been to several countries. I have also visited countries, which are divided in blocs and are opposed to one another. I have been to both types of places and have received warm welcome there. Wherever I went, whether because of the name of India or because of its reputation, I was accorded a rousing reception and received with great affection and abundant goodwill. I realised in how much high esteem they hold India. Whatever be the views of other governments, their views do have impact on others, yet what India has to say also affects the public opinion there, because irrespective of the fact whether it was right or wrong, at least it was considered there. People there believe that we earnestly desire peace and that we do not accuse one another in rage and also that whatever we say we say after a good deal of deliberation and with a cool mind. Accordingly our presence at such forums may sometimes prove beneficial.

These are then some of my thoughts which I wanted to place before you."

* * *

I was sad at my failure to get elected to the Third Lok Sabha. The span of time from 1962 to 1967 was the most significant period in the life of independent India. During this short period the nation went to war twice. The cruel hands of death snuffed out the lives of our two Prime Ministers. The Chinese invasion left Shri Nehru a shattered man. Their betrayal had shaken him to the core of his heart. Thereafter he never again looked his old lively self. On seeing him one felt as if he had lost his zest. Shri Lal Bahadur Shastri died of a massive heart-attack. He had been a heart patient but the circumstances in which he died naturally led to the suspicion that he was subjected to great pressure to sign the Tashkent agreement and that his heart could not endure it. This eventually led to his collapse.

In the Third Lok Sabha the majority of Congress was slightly reduced. The strength of its members fell from 371 to 361. The Communist Party improved its tally by 2 seats. The fortunes of Bhartiya Jana Sangh registered a long jump. The strength of its members in the House rose from 4 to 14. By winning as many as 28 seats the Swatantra Party ranked second in the Opposition. The Praja Socialist Party lost 7 seats. The strength of its members fell to 12.

The notable feature of the Third Lok Sabha was that Opposition stalwarts like Acharya Kripalani, Lohia and Masani got elected to it through bye-elections. There was a wave of anti-Congressism in the country. The Opposition parties fought the elections jointly. Unfortunately the leader of Bhartiya Jana Sangh Shri Deen Dayal Upadhyaya, who contested the election from Jaunpur, failed to get elected. The void created by his death continues to be still felt by the Party.

My failure in the elections for the Third Lok Sabha was unanticipated. I had looked after my constituency well during my five-year term. In and outside the Parliament I had forcefully represented the Balrampur constituency. Being an Opposition member I had made Government the target of my scathing criticism, and as spokesman of the Bhartiya Jana Sangh had nurtured it and had succeeded in establishing its separate identity. Its detractors were dismayed by its growing influence. They conspired to defeat me at the hustings. It was decided to shift the President of the Sampradayikata-Virodhi Samiti from Haryana to contest against me from Balrampur. She enjoyed the support of all the leftist forces. She also claimed to have the blessings of Shri Jawaharlal Nehru. On reaching the constituency, she launched a vituperative attack on Bhartiya Jana Sangh in general and the R.S.S. in particular. To her, the Sangh was a fascist organisation and its founder Dr. Hedgewar had gone to Germany and the R.S.S. was being organised on the lines and pattern of the Nazi Party. Although such baseless talk did not make the desired impact on the public, yet it provided an issue to the Congress to fight the elections. They were adopting aggressive attitude. They had no shortage of resources. They intimidated the district and local authorities into submission by claiming to have access to Delhi. To influence the election all types of unfair means were used. So much so that on behalf of the Brahmins an appeal was addressed to Brahmin voters in support of the Congress. Planned efforts were made to generate communal tension in the area. On the day of election a conspiracy was hatched to engineer a stabbing incident in the Balrampur city to intimidate the voters, especially the women voters, who had gathered since early morning at the polling booths to cast their votes for Jana Sangh and force them to return to their homes without casting their votes. In some areas polling had to be suspended. Majority of those voters who had gone to their houses did not turn up again for voting.

Still I had a hope of victory, because I enjoyed wide public support. In spite of having brought Shri Nehru to canvass support for the Congress candidate, her chances had not shown any marked improvement. In fact the sentence in Shri Nehru's speech that there are some good people in Jana Sangh had actually helped me. Possibly what Shri Nehru had said was not said keeping me in view, but most of the voters interpreted it as pointing towards me. Almost all people had admitted that had I not stood from Balrampur Shri Nehru would never have taken the trouble to visit it. Good polling was reported to have taken place in favour of Jana Sangh at all other places except the Balrampur city.

But a common complaint received from several places made me apprehensive. The complaint was that the Congress supporters in a bid to cause confusion among the voters had started the propaganda that if they wanted to support me in the Lok Sabha elections then they should put stamp on the election symbol of Deepak (the earthen lamp) on the pink coloured ballot. In those days, elections for Lok Sabha and State Assemblies were held simultaneously. Every voter was given two ballot papers. Both were of separate colours. Seeing the growing popular support for me the Congressmen asked the voters to cast their votes for me on the ballot paper of a different colour. Some officials posted at polling booths also helped to spread this confusion. When counting took place the result of the well-planned and deep-rooted conspiracy came out in the open.

I lost the election by a margin of 2,000 votes. I polled 100,208 votes, whereas the Congress candidate secured 102,266 votes. What intrigued us most was the fact that out of the 5 candidates put up by my Party for Legislative Asembly 4 romped home with handsome margins. Sardar Baldev Singh won from Tulsipur by more than 6000 votes. From Balrampur (S.C.) constituency Jana Sangh's winning candidate Shri Sukhdev Prasad secured 2000 votes more than what the Congress polled. From Atraula also Shri Suraj Lal Gupta was ahead of his Congress rival by 4500 votes. Shri Avadh Narain Singh had also won the Sadulla Nagar seat. The Jana Sangh lost only one Assembly seat, that too by a paper thin margin of 55 votes. Perhaps this constituency was the only constituency of its kind where a Party had won 4 of the 5 seats in the Assembly segment but its Lok Sabha candidate lost the election. This could happen only under two conditions. Firstly, if the candidates for the Legislative Assembly had solicited votes only for themselves and bypassed the Lok Sabha candidate. Secondly, if confusion had been created in the minds of the voters about the colour of the ballot paper and the voters thought that they were casting their votes in favour of the Lok Sabha candidate whereas actually they were the candidates for the Legislative Assembly who cornered their votes. There was hardly any possibility of candidates contesting the elections for the Legislative Assembly seeking votes only for themselves. In reality they hoped to win the elections on the wave of popular support for me. But what happened was that they were able to cross the river, but I was drowned midstream. After the election results were declared many voters met me and expressed shock over my defeat in spite of their having voted for me *en masse*. Obviously the Congress had succeeded in creating confusion in the minds of the voters.

Members of Parliament and Legislatures are expected to look after their constituencies well, to visit them frequently and share the joys and sorrows of their electorates. This expectation is not unjust. I was elected member of the Lok Sabha for the first time from Balrampur. I had always taken good care of my constituency. Ever since my election to the Lok Sabha I had maintained close contacts with my electorate and brought Balrampur in prominence in Parliament. After I lost the election I resolved henceforth not to maintain more than necessary contact. I wanted to give a chance to the Congress candidate to work fully. But I was firmly determined to seek re-election from Balrampur. I had to avenge my defeat. Before the next general election some of the senior leaders of Congress suggested to me that I should leave the Balrampur seat and seek election from elsewhere. Their logic was I could win election from any constituency but for the successful Congress candidate leaving of Balrampur seat would be a disgrace. I turned down their suggestion. I again contested from Balrampur and won the seat. This time I won by a margin of more than 30,000 votes. I had secured 1,42,446 votes, while the Congress candidate polled 1,10,704 votes. Along with me 4 other candidates, contesting the elections for the Legislative Assembly also won on Party ticket.

* * *

In the history of the Parliament, 6th May, 1961 will always be remembered. On that day a joint meeting of both the Houses of Parliament took place for the first time. There is a provision in the Constitution for convening such a meeting. Barring the matters relating to finance and money both the Houses enjoy equal rights. I had the privilege to be a member of both the Houses. Rajya Sabha is the Council of States whereas members of Lok Sabha are directly elected by the voters and represent the whole country. Members of Rajya Sabha too represent the country, but they are also the representatives of their respective States. In certain matters Rajya Sabha has some special privileges, which the Lok Sabha does not have. It is a continous body not subject to dissolution.

It is not surprising that the difference between both the Houses arose on a relatively small issue like dowry. But as a matter of fact, dowry is not a small issue. It concerns with the social structure, old conventions, past traditions and the religious beliefs. In a tradition bound society whenever a social reform is brought about, it creates great controversy. The heat and dust generated by Hindu Code Bill all over the country is quite well known. In fact the convening of a joint session of Parliament on the question of dowry was more surprising because as against Lok Sabha, the Rajya Sabha had taken a more progressive stance. Rajya Sabha is considered to be more mature and is a House of elders. The utility of a second House lies in applying the brake but in the matter of dowry the Rajya Sabha was in favour of taking a rapid stride.

The majority of members in both the Houses were of the view that dowry was a social evil, which must be eradicated. They also did not differ on the necessity of enacting a law to curb this social evil. The main issue on which members differed was that how much stringent the law should be made. The Rajya Sabha was in favour of enacting a rigorous law. Many members were of the view that if at the time of marriage of the daughter, her father and other relatives wished to gift cash and jewellery to her of their own accord in that case such cash and jewellery should be excluded from the meaning of dowry.

But majority was against *Thehrauni* (agreement money). *Thehrauni* means that such part of dowry as is agreed upon as a pre-condition of marriage. Before a marriage is solemnised the father of the girl is made to agree what items and how much cash he will give along with her daughter to the boy's father in lieu of the boy's marriage with her. In short how much the bridegroom will cost ? The law aimed at stopping such type of dowry, but many members expressed the apprehension that if in the law exemption was granted in respect of gifts or presents then the very purpose of enacting a law would get defeated. Their fears were further confirmed by an amendment proposed by the Government. The whole discussion centred round an explanation appended to the main clause. The explanation read as under :

> "To remove the apprehensions, if any, it is hereby stated that at the time of marriage any gifts given to a party to a marriage in the form of cash, jewellery, clothes or other items of use will be excluded from the meaning of dowry under this clause except in case they are given as consideration for the marriage of the contracting parties."

The Government did not concede the demand for dropping the explanation. It was of the view that if in the marriage of a daughter cash, jewellery etc. are given voluntarily, then how it can be stopped. I suggested that a middle path be found out. By way of an amendment I suggested that the total cost of the appliances to be given at the time of marriage be limited to 2000 rupees. In 1960 rupees 2000 was considered a big amount. Now this amount looks like a peanut. Some members suggested a limit of 51 rupees. My amendment failed. The amendment to drop the explanation was also rejected by 192 to 230 votes.

This Bill proposed to make both giving and taking of dowry a penal offence. It also provided for imprisonment upto 6 months. Besides, demanding of dowry was also categorised as a criminal offence punishable with imprisonment upto one month. The strangest thing was that to the expression 'demanding of dowry' words directly or indirectly' were added. The evidence for demanding dowry directly can be produced but how indirect demanding of dowry will be proved ? Will this not be misused ? I proposed the amendment that the addition "directly or indirectly" be dropped. The House did not approve it. Some members desired that in the matter of dowry the police should have the right to intervene. But the Government took the rigid stand that the court will not take cognizance of offence relating to dowry as long as prior approval of the State or an officer appointed by it is not obtained.

There was no doubt that the anti-dowry law was made quite innocuous. But the matter of satisfaction was that both the Houses had, by reconciling their differences over the legislation, taken a concrete step in the direction of social reform. Nowadays the evil of dowry has assumed demoniac proportions. Every year hundreds of newly wed daughters-in-law are sacrificed on the altar of dowry. The dowry-seekers do not hesitate to burn their daughters-in-law alive by dousing them with kerosene oil and putting a match to them. The law has been made quite severe. Still dowry related crimes are on the increase. What is required is that the law should be enforced strictly and honestly. There is also need to awaken the conscience of the people. In my speech I had dealt on it. I had said—

> "What was needed is that the country should make economic progress, education should be spread, the caste barriers should be broken and boys and girls allowed to marry each other without any inhibition. Marriages should no longer be arranged in heaven but should be fixed by mutual consent. This alone can end the system of dowry."

Nearly forty years have gone. There is neither adequate economic progress nor the limited objective of total literacy has been achieved. The caste affiliations instead of weakening have been strengthened. The number of inter-caste marriages is very low. To give away a daughter in marriage is still regarded as a humiliating act. Even the educated people, on joining the bridegroom's procession are seen indulging in unrestrained behaviour. As we get more and more modern we are more and more forgetting the human qualities and values. Perhaps nobody knows where these trends would lead to.

I was elected member of Rajya Sabha twice—first time in 1962 and second time in 1986. In 1962 our Party had only two members in the House. In spite of this the then Chairman of Rajya Sabha Dr. Radhakrishnan had allotted me a seat in the first row. There was hardly any occasion when we were not given a chance to put forward our Party's viewpoint during the course of discussion. Dr. Radhakrishnan used to conduct and control the proceedings of the House with great modesty and dignity. Later, Dr. Zakir Hussain assumed the office of Chairman. He used to get distressed by the unruly noise witnessed immediately after the Question Hour.

The members of the Rajya Sabha, being limited in number, get more time to speak. In accordance with the convention, members could speak on a non-official motion or Bill for as long as they liked. On a similar motion, the Communist member Shri Bhupesh Gupta set a new record by his marathon speech, which lasted for 6 hours.

In 1986 when I got elected to Rajya Sabha for the second time, the constitution and the complexion of the House had changed perceptibly. The young members outnumbered the seniors. Because of the youthful Prime Minister Shri Rajiv Gandhi many young persons connected with the youth Congress got elected as members of Rajya Sabha. The Opposition was less in number but was more effective quality-wise.

Question arises when the founders of our Constitution took the decision to constitute a Rajya Sabha, what was their objective ? Has that objective been realised ? During a discussion in the Constituent Assembly Shri Loknath Misra, a member from Orissa had said that the Rajya Sabha in its present form would be unnecessary. But his plea was not accepted. Shri Anantashayanam Ayyangar advanced three arguments in favour of the retention of the Rajya Sabha. First, there is great enthusiasm among the people for participation in politics, for which they must be provided a chance and they should be given opportunities to make use of their talent. Secondly, the Rajya Sabha can apply the brake of 'go slow' on any legislation passed by Lok Sabha in a haste. Thirdly, the Rajya Sabha will be a standing House, whereas the Lok Sabha will not. Shri Ayyangar concluded that for the progress of the country the second House was a must.

In the matter of providing opportunity to more people for participation in politics the Rajya Sabha has succeeded in its objective. But it has miserably failed in its aim to apply brakes on the haste of the Lok Sabha. The biggest reason for this is that even though the members of Rajya Sabha come as representatives of the States, yet they function as the representatives of their Party. They are tied to the discipline of their Party and project only the policies decided by it. In a situation like this, there is hardly any scope for exercising any control. In the beginning the usual practice was that various political parties used to honour their senior members, who besides being older in age were also more experienced, by nominating them to Rajya Sabha. Nowadays, even this practice is not being observed. The Rajya Sabha is a House of elders only in name. There is no visible difference with regard to the constitution of both the Houses and the categorisation of their members according to their age-group. However, only this much difference is there that for contesting the election of Lok Sabha one should be of 25 years of age, whereas a minimum age of 30 years has been prescribed for election to Rajya Sabha.

To me it looks that the political parties should exercise greater caution in choosing members for Rajya Sabha. The senior leaders of parties can be honoured with the membership of Rajya Sabha, but at the same time, it is as much necessary that they should be quite experienced and knowledgeable. If the political parties, while making selection of their nominees endeavour to give primacy to competent persons of various sections of the society then this will not only give strength to them but also enrich the complexion of the Rajya Sabha in a meaningful way. The retired personnel of armed forces, the educationists, the scientists, the industrialists and the constructive workers can contribute a lot to make the discussions in Rajya Sabha more useful.

* * *

In the general elections of 1984, which were held soon after the diabolical murder of Smt. Indira Gandhi, the Opposition suffered a humiliating defeat. The wave of sympathy towards Congress uprooted the Opposition. The Bharatiya Janata Party in terms of the percentage of votes polled in its favour got the same public support as it had received in 1971. But while in 1971, the Party had secured 22 seats in Lok Sabha, in 1984 the number was reduced to a mere 2. I also lost election. In the north other political parties too suffered heavy losses. The Lok Dal could get elected to Lok Sabha only three members.

The numerical strength of Janata Party too did not reach a dozen. The reason for its securing larger number of seats vis-a-vis Bharatiya Janata Party and the Lok Dal was that the sympathy wave was not as effective in the south as it was in the north.

The impression that if I had, instead of shifting to Gwalior, fought from my old constituency of New Delhi I would have surely won is not correct. The sympathy wave had its impact in Delhi also. The Bharatiya Janata Party could not get a single seat from Delhi. The position in New Delhi was relatively better in 1980 when the Bharatiya Janata Party lost all other seats for Lok Sabha in Delhi, even then it got the New Delhi seat. Perhaps on this ground it was surmised that I could have retained the New Delhi seat even in the face of the sympathy wave.

It is also not correct to say that I had gone to Gwalior in search of a safe seat. The Truth is that being burdened with Party responsibilities, I could not give as much attention to the New Delhi constituency as I should have given. From an organisational angle some areas of New Delhi have always been weak. To win the New Delhi seat more hard work and more time were needed while discharging the responsibilities of an all India campaign it was not possible to give more time to New Delhi and to work more for it. It was in this context that the suggestion to shift to Gwalior was made since. I had earlier also got elected from there. In those days Gwalior was represented in Lok Sabha by Shri Shejwalkar. He was not willing to fight election again. The former Maharaja had been elected from Guna. Before taking the final decision I had one day enquired of him in the lobby whether he intended to contest the election from Gwalior. He replied in the negative. But at the eleventh hour he filed his nomination papers from Gwalior. I did not have enough time to file my nomination papers from elsewhere. The secrecy and cleverness with which the whole strategy to tie me down to Gwalior was planned came to light only after the Janata Dal was formed.

In fact there was a dual policy behind the whole plan. Firstly, to confine me to Gwalior so that I would not be available to tour the whole country to campaign against Congress. Secondly, whatever be the outcome of election it suited the political objectives of a faction in the Congress. If I lost the Opposition would be weakened. If by any chance Shri Madhav Rao Scindia lost, chances for which were least, even then it would have served their limited purpose.

But there was no possibility of the defeat of Shri Scindia. He was contesting the election from Gwalior for the first time. Even now people have great regard for the royal House of Gwalior. Being the only son of his father he has always reaped the benefit of his influence. Rajmata Vijaya Raje Scindia too wields immense influence. The dignified personality of Rajmata and her commitment to principles has attracted the people towards the Party. Whatever success the old Jana Sangh and the New Bharatiya Janata Party have achieved in the Gwalior region is all due to Rajmata Scindia. It is needless to say that her influence has evidently helped the party to a great extent. I do not know what would have been the outcome if in 1984 instead of me Rajmata Vijaya Raje Scindia had taken the decision to seek election from Gwalior and if her election rival had been none other than her own son Shri Madhav Rao Scindia. But I wanted to avoid any such confrontation at all costs. The rift that has somehow developed between the mother and the son has never been liked, least of all by me. Political differences are one thing but because of it generation of bitterness in the inborn, natural and tender relationship between the mother and the son is absolutely another thing.

It is true that Rajmata Scindia had asked me not to go to Gwalior unescorted to file my nomination paper and had expressed a wish to accompany me for this purpose. But I did not think it proper to trouble her. I was also apprehensive that if she herself filed the nomination papers along with me, it may be difficult to withdraw later on. Afterwards when some friends asked Shri Madhav Rao Scindia why did he stand against me to contest the elections, he is said to have replied that after filing his nomination papers Shri Vajpayee had thrown a challenge to me to contest the election against him and find out myself what my real worth was in the eyes of the public. This is absolutely a concocted story. It is not in my nature to behave rudely with my political opponents. I always had a natural affection and respect for Shri Scindia. It was I, who had in the first place, enrolled him as member of Jana Sangh.

Shri Scindia should have acknowledged that he was pressurised to stand from Gwalior and that as a conscientious Congressman he had no other option except to fight from there. Though I would not term the treatment he meted out to me by filing his nomination papers at the last minute as breach of faith, yet after weighing his action in the criteria of mutual relationship I would not either be able to describe it as proper. Today he may even deny that he had said to me anything about his not contesting the election from Gwalior but it is an incontrovertible fact that he was fielded from Gwalior at the last moment only with the intention to defeat me.

Because of the sympathy wave as well as the personal influence of Shri Scindia my defeat was a foregone conclusion. If the former ruler knocks at the door and solicits votes for himself then it becomes very difficult to say 'no' to him. But had there been no sympathy wave in that case, in spite of a sense of respect and loyalty towards the ruler, the Bharatiya Janata Party would have received far wider public support. In Jammu Dr. Karan Singh, who contested election against the Congress, could not score election victory in spite of his being a former ruler of the State.

The Congress was given a dose of its own medicine in Vidisha in 1991 for the treatment it meted out to me in Gwalior. The Congress candidate and his supporters were so much upset by the turn of events that they welcomed me by pelting of stones. Besides, they indulged in false propaganda against me by depicting me as an outsider.

Why did in 1991 I contest the elections to Lok Sabha from two constituencies has a background of its own. In those days I was a member of Rajya Sabha. I had announced that I would not contest the election for Lok Sabha. My term in Rajya Sabha had not as yet expired. But the Party decided to field me from Lucknow. The Party wanted to form its Government in Uttar Pradesh. To boost the election campaign it was very necessary to field from there a person who could muster more public support for the Party. Dr. Murli Manohar Joshi, being the national President of the Party, had already taken the decision not to stand for election. There was also no question of shifting Rajmata Vijaya Raje Scindia or Shri Lal Krishna Advani from the seats they had won. The astrologers too made their contribution. The Party needed a good candidate to contest the Lucknow seat. I had my old contacts with Lucknow and had contested the elections thrice from there. It was because of this that a decision was taken to field me from the Lucknow constituency.

But when it was decided that Shri Advani should contest elections from New Delhi as well as from Gandhi Nagar, I was also called upon to stand for election from two seats. It was already known that the New Delhi seat was not a sure seat. But the victory from Lucknow was a foregone conclusion. Even if the Congress party had fielded a top film star from Lucknow it would not have been easier for him to win the seat. Uttar Pradesh was flooded with Ram wave. The Opposition was not only divided but had earned a bad name in the bargain. The excesses committed in Ayodhya on the *Kar Sewaks* had roused the ire of the people. To defeat Bharatiya Janata Party the Opposition had held several rallies. The presence of the members of the minority community in these rallies in large numbers and the delivering of inflammatory speeches by them helped the B.J.P. all the more. Had the *Kar Sewaks* in Ayodhya not been fired upon and had at these rallies such speeches not been delivered as to hurt the sentiments of the majority community the Bharatiya Janata Party would not have achieved so much success in the elections. The division of anti-B.J.P. votes also helped to carve out this victory.

In the final picture that emerged after the conclusion of the 10th General elections to Lok Sabha, the Bharatiya Janata Party by securing 119 seats became the main Opposition Party in the House. The Congress by winning 227 seats emerged as the largest single party. When the President Shri Venkataraman invited Shri P.V. Narasimha Rao, the leader of the Congress Parliamentary Party to form the Government, the Congress Party did not have a majority in the House. In a situation like this, before inviting the Congress to form the Government, the Bharatiya Janata Party too should have been consulted. Perhaps the President was so much disgusted by the political instability of last one and a half years that he did not even think it necessary to have consultations with any other party.

As a matter of fact, in the history of Indian politics the period of 1990-91 will always be remembered as the period of political instability. The Congress got defeated in the General elections, but the National Front, which included the Janata Dal failed to get a clear majority in the House. The Bharatiya Janata Party and the Communists decided to extend support to it from outside without joining the Government. On this basis, the President invited Shri Vishvanath Pratap Singh to form the Government. If in 1984, the Indira wave had given Congress a massive majority in the House, the anti-corruption wave, of which Bofors was a symbol, forced the Congress to lick the dust.

In the elections the non-Congress parties had promised the people that they would not repeat the history of 1979 and this time they will work together. The people had voted on this trust. But the National Front, especially the Janata Dal failed to maintain its unity. The mutual distrust, which developed on the very first day, eventually led to the collapse of the Government itself. The disgraceful history of 1979 was repeated in spite of the assurances given to the contrary. The Congress by extending its support to the group, which separated from Janata Dal under the leadership of Shri Chandrashekhar, ruined the second historical experiment of a non-Congress Government at the Centre. But for this non-Congress leaders were more responsible than the Congress.

Like 1979 this time too the rift in the Janata Dal did not occur on any question of principle or matter of policy. The infinite lust for power was alone responsible for the rift in the party. The recommendations of the Mandal Commission were used as a weapon to give an ideological twist to this rift. Even this was done in hasty and in a clumsy way. The parties supporting the Government were neither taken into confidence nor any effort was made to create within the country a favourable opinion especially among the younger generation. Had it been, announced on day one that along with social and educational backwardness economic backwardness will also form one of the criteria and some posts will be reserved for the younger people of the so called forward classes keeping in view their economic conditions, the anti-reservation movement would not have taken such a violent turn. The younger generation suspected that the announcement to give 27 per cent reservation to the backward classes was not motivated by any sense of social justice but was guided by the sole desire to remain in power.

The issue of reservation is very sensitive. It needs to be tackled with great caution. The maintaining of a balance between the declining number of employment opportunities and the rising aspirations of the younger people demands a wisdom of a very high order. The problem cannot be satisfactorily solved either by fanning the caste prejudices or by linking this question to the politics of vote. While on one side among the younger generation of the backward classes a feeling of resentment is gradually growing against the social injustices, on the other the younger people of forward classes are fast loosing patience. A solution should be found only on the basis of a national consensus on this question. But the Janata Dal, torn by its internal dissentions, had become so much entangled on this issue that not only its Government fell, but also the question of reservation is still not satisfactorily solved.

Because of the internal strife of Janata Dal and its policy to give more weightage to the leftist parties than what their strength warranted, the question of Ayodhya instead of getting solved became more complicated. The objective of Shri Advani's *Rath Yatra* was not to bring down the then Government. It was undertaken with the sole aim to mobilise wider national support in favour of the reconstruction of the Shri Ram Temple. It did succeed in this aim. As the *Rath* rolled on, it became increasingly clear that the question of building a Ram Temple deeply touches the emotional cords of the majority community. During the past 40 years rule of the Congress the policies and programmes adopted by it in the name of secularism have, rightly or wrongly, left an impression on the minds of the Hindus that they are not being treated well.

In the *Case of Shahbano* the judgment of the Supreme Court was first welcomed but later on the Constitution was amended to reverse this judgment. This wounded the psyche of the Hindus. The challenge to the integrity and solidarity of the country in Kashmir and Punjab has also agitated the Hindu mind. The politics of vote persued by the Congress and the Leftist parties has also made adverse impact on them. The *Rath Yatra* became the symbol of their disenchantment. A solution would have been possible if instead of postponing Ayodhya issue Shri Vishvanath Pratap Singh had made sincere efforts to solve it. But he allowed himself to be caught by mutually contradictory pressures and refused to appreciate the acute feelings of the majority community. The Muslim voters had given the Janata Dal wide support. Muslim religious leaders too were, in large number, associated with it. Had the leadership of the Janata Dal tried to convince them about the wisdom of adopting a conciliatory attitude on this issue they would have surely succeeded in finding a solution. But it did not attempt any such thing. It kept itself busy with the equation of votes. It calculated that the minorities and the backward classes together constitute a large vote bank on the strength of which elections can be won. But it did not cross its mind that the question of building a Ram Temple can also affect the backward classes and they could also vote differently.

Due to the rift in the Janata Dal the National Front Government fell on 7th November 1991. The Rashtrapati Bhawan turned into a centre of political activities. Shri Venkataraman started consultations with leaders of various political parties. The President was implored not to encourage switching of partly allegiance. But what was the alternative left to the President ? If Janata Dal breaks and the Congress gives assurance of support to the break away group and on the strength of this support it stakes its claim to form the Government then what can the President do ? He had the apparent option to order fresh general elections but there was also another question before him whether it would be advisable to order general elections so soon ? Whether elections would help establish political stability ? Will any party get absolute majority ?

* * *

Now it is a well-known fact that during the first week of November, 1990 when the fall of Janata Government was imminent and a faction of the Janata Dal was trying hard to form its Government on Congress support, the President Shri Venkataraman felt convinced of the necessity to install a National Government and even held informal discussions with the leaders of different political parties in this regard. He was deeply worried about the future of the country. How will the nation tide over the present crisis in the absence of an eluding political stability ?

I had publicly welcomed the idea of the formation of a National Government. Later on the Bharatiya Janata Party also expressed its agreement with this idea. But the things did not go farther, because other parties were not willing to opt for it. This time the main difficulty was not how to make the Communists and the B.J.P. sit together. That chapter had closed in November 1990 itself. Even the logic of Shri Madhu Limaye did not work, i.e., if in Poland an organisation called 'Solidarity,' which was considered to be an extension of the Roman Catholic Church, could form coalition Government with the Communists then why can't the B.J.P. and the Communists function together on a minimum based programme ? But this time there were other difficulties.

The relations between the Janata Dal and the B.J.P. had become embittered. The anti-Congress attitude of Janata Dal had also hardened. Would the formation of a National Government be possible under these circumstances ? In the event of war the necessity to form a National Government can be understood but in times of peace how far its formation will be justified ? What will happen in the next elections ? Will the parties in the Government fight the elections on a common platform ? If not, will not the preparation to fight the elections on separate identities start while still working together in the Government ? The experiment of coalition Government did not succeed in 1977-79 nor did it succeed in 1990. In what way would the National Government be different from a coalition Government ?

One question which was discussed in those days in whispers and about which there is a lot of misunderstanding even today is that the President Shri Venkataraman himself wanted to be the Prime Minister and the whole exercise of the formation of National Government was in fact directed towards this end. In my capacity as the leader of the parliamentary group of B.J.P. I took part in almost all the discussions held in this connection. On the basis of my talks with the President Shri Venkataraman I can confidently say that when he made the suggestion for the formation of a National Government the idea of becoming Prime Minister had not even once crossed his mind. The truth is that during the discussions if it was ever suggested that none else other than him was better qualified to head such a Government, he summarily dismissed it. He was of the view that a person who was occupying the high chair of the President should not even allow such a thought to enter into his mind. If the question of leadership ever arose, though the truth is that the suggestion for the formation of a National Government never reached this concrete stage, Shri Venkataraman mentioned the name of Shri Shankar Dayal Sharma. In this connection, who-so-ever has accused Shri Venkataraman of being ambitious, has done a great injustice to the former President. They are either ignorant of facts or they are suffering from their own prejudices. Had Shri Venkataraman wished, he could have easily got himself elected President for another term. But the way he relinquished his high office willingly and smilingly, leaving behind all the paraphernalia of Rashtrapati Bhawan is an example for the others to follow.

I am, as in 1990 and 1991, even today of the view that to strengthen and to bring prosperity to this large country with many diversities it is essential to evolve consensus on all national problems. Solely on the strength of Government and administration no single party or group of parties can keep the nation either united or fulfil the demands of its development. We may not have a united Government but we must not be divided in our resolve. This is the message of *"Sam vo manaansi jaantaam."* *(Let there be a union of minds).*

* * *

I have had the opportunity of coming into close contact with all Prime Ministers, from Pandit Nehru to Shri Narasimha Rao. Among them Pandit Nehru was the only one to leave an indelible stamp on Parliament. With his complete commitment to democracy he considered the institution of Parliament a sacred temple and was ever alert about preserving its prestige. He not only attended Parliament regularly himself but encouraged all ministers to take parliamentary business with due seriousness. Be it Question Hour or a discussion on any subject, Pandit Nehru made it a point to be present if his presence was required and listened to the debate attentively. As Leader of the House he discharged his duty diligently and also cooperated with the Speaker in the discharge of his duties. His very presence charged the atmosphere in the House, lending it greater prestige, greater seriousness.

Pandit Nehru was by nature a democrat, but he was also somewhat headstrong. If he thought something was right he would stick by it. His capacity to take the House with him was unparalleled. If and when necessary he did not hesitate to act in accordance with the sentiment of the House.

I recall the time there was great resentment in the House over certain adverse remarks that Shri M.O. Mathai, Pandit Nehru's Special Assistant, had made about members' behaviour. Members of almost all parties had objected to Shri Mathai's statement. A notice of breach of privilege was given against him and the matter of contempt of House was also raised. My resolution was accepted by the Speaker. When it came up for discussion Pandit Nehru sought to save his Special Assistant by arguing that it was not a matter of breach of privilege but of impropriety. But Members did not accept the contention. Even Congress MPs were not happy with Shri Mathai's general behaviour. The unanimous demand was made that the matter be handed over to the Privileges Committee. Pandit Nehru immediately assessed the situation. Sensing the mood of the House he realised that it would be futile to say anything in Shri Mathai's favour. He agreed to hand over the matter to the Privileges Committee. What he said in the House on that occasion is guidance for future Prime Ministers. He said when a substantial section of the House is of the view that something needs to be done in a certain matter it is not proper for the majority to disregard the feelings of that section. He also said nothing should be done here that would lead the people to feel that something is sought to be covered up or hidden from the public eye. This small incident throws ample light on Pandit Nehru's personality.

Shri Lal Bahadur Shastri's election as Prime Minister after Pandit Nehru highlights both the maturity and the apparent contradiction of Indian democracy. Nehru with his regal upbringing on the one hand, and on the other hand Lal Bahadur Shastri fought his way through abject poverty. A barrister who had acquired Western education and imbibed Western culture at Cambridge University on the one hand, and Lal Bahadur who had obtained the 'Shastri' degree at the Kashi Vidyapeeth on the other. Despite this dissimilarity Shri Shastri proved a worthy successor to Pandit Nehru, which shows the inner strength and elasticity of the Indian society.

Before becoming Prime Minister Shri Shastri had impressed everybody with his capacity by working ably in many positions. I still recall the time he presented his budget as Minister for Railways in Hindi. As a protest many members including Dr. Shyama Prasad Mookherji had staged a walk-out. Later Dr. Mookherji explained that he had no intention either to insult Shri Shastri or to oppose the presentation of the budget in Hindi.

Shri Shastri's rose to dizy heights during the Indo-Pak War. Had he lived he would have changed the direction of Indian polity.

The mystery that covered the circumstances of Shri Shastri's tragic death in Tashkent has now been more or less removed. No basis has been found for the suspicion that his death was not natural. I was greatly relieved to read in the book by Shri Shastri's special assistant Shri C.P. Shrivastav that I was not the cause for worry for Shri Shastri that fateful night in Tashkent. What happened was that when the news of the Tashkent agreement reached Delhi, the press asked for my reaction. I criticised the agreement severely and called it a surrender. This news was conveyed to Shri Shastri in Tashkent. When the news of his death due to heart-failure arrived I got the guilty feeling that my harsh criticism may have deeply affected him. But Shri Shrivastav's narration of that fateful night in Tashkent has lifted a big burden off my mind.

During the Indo-Pak War Shri Shastri had made arrangements to keep Opposition leaders posted with news from the front every evening. When necessary he would personally contact them and brief them.

Shri Shastri's sudden death posed before the country the question of a new Prime Minister's choice. There were many claimants for the post. Once again Congress President Shri Kamaraj played a decisive role. He had already decided in favour of Smt. Indira Gandhi. Other senior Congress leaders too did not wish to see a formidable person like Shri Morarji become Prime Minister. In the belief that Indiraji would be pliable in their hands they disregarded abler and more experienced leaders and put the reins of the country into Indiraji's hands.

In the innermost recesses of his heart Pandit Nehru might have certainly wished his daughter to succeed him, but it does not appear that he made any special effort in that direction. He must have certainly liked Indiraji being made Congress President and indirectly he may have even helped in it, but it seems other Congress leaders were more responsible for making her Congress President as they sought to influence Nehruji through her.

The participation of Congress in the "liberation struggle" against the first Communist Government of Kerala and later the Centre's decision to topple it exposes senior Congress leaders' strategy in making Indiraji Congress President.

In contrast to her father Indiraji generally stayed away from Parliament. In the beginning she was so silent that she had been called a dumb doll. But that was unfair to her. She believed in talking little. After listening to all she formed her opinion and expressed it at the end if at all.

Morarji Desai's personality was just the opposite. He expressed himself even before listening to others. He had some firm beliefs, some definite opinions, and he never hesitated to express them. Indiraji was cleverer in this respect. Instead of attending the House she used to turn the levers of power sitting in her office. She kept a sharp eye on what was happening at home and abroad, what was going on in Parliament, what was happening within Opposition parties. She impressed the world by ruling for 14 years and she bested the Opposition many a time.

Wherever I met Smt. Indira Gandhi, I felt she was in the grip of some unknown fear. There was a deep sense of insecurity in some corner of her mind. Watching everybody, not saying anything openly, thinking that the whole world was conspiring against her—all this indicates a mindset that needs to be analysed in depth if we are to fully understand Indiraji's personality and actions.

It was this mentality of hers that made her ensure Shri Neelam Sanjiva Reddy's defeat even after filing his nomination for President's post. She thought if Shri Reddy became President he would not let her continue as Prime Minister for long. Later events proved that this was a baseless fear and President Reddy did not pose any danger for her.

Had Indiraji resigned from the Prime Ministership after her election was nullified in 1975 and taken up leadership of the Congress, there was no one to challenge her within the party. But she had no confidence in herself, and this led her to declaring an emergency. She preferred throttling democracy for the sake of saving her position of power. History will never forgive her for this. Later she did succeed in regaining power, but the blot on her name can never be washed away.

Indiraji's role in the creation of Bangladesh will always be appreciated. The firmness and statesmanship with which she formulated the strategy to defeat Pakistan, as a result of which Pakistani forces were forced to lay down arms, has become a legend full of pride and glory. The then Defence Minister Shri Jagjivan Ram had made a substantial contribution to this success, but it is Indiraji who is given the credit of creating an independent Bangladesh. However, when India was humiliated by China the entire blame was laid at the door of the then Defence Minister Shri Krishna Menon. No one can say how and whom the cycle of events would do injustice in apportioning praise and blame.

I was also one of those who praised Indiraji highly for her successful leadership in the Bangladesh crisis, but the impression is wrong that I once called her *'Durga.'* I had certainly praised her but had not called her *Durga*. I have clarified this fact a number of times, still this impression is so deep-seated that people still praise me by saying that in that hour of crisis I rose above party politics, extended full cooperation to the Government, and described Indiraji as *Durga*. Smt. Pupul Jayakar wanted to mention this when she was writing Indiraji's biography, but though she refrained from doing so on my objecting to it she did make a detailed investigation about it. After going through Parliament's proceedings and newspapers of the time she was convinced that I had not called Indiraji as *Durga*.

Then the question arises — how did the news got spread? I think some leader described her like that at that time and some newspapers attributed it to me. What newspapers these were is still not known.

I often clashed with Indiraji in Parliament, but she never let political difference affect personal relationships. Her dastardly and tragic assassination removed suddenly from our midst a personality that will not only be remembered as the worthy daughter of a worthy father but also for her own ability, dexterity, decisiveness and firmness.

Shri Rajiv Gandhi became Prime Minister at a tragic juncture. He had no administrative experience. He did not even have any interest in politics. He was happy to be a pilot. Once when I alighted from a plane I saw a young man wearing his cap standing below and greeting me with a smiling *Namaskar*. I could not recognise that he was Shri Rajiv Gandhi, son of the Prime Minister. On another occasion, when he was going out of Delhi with his family, there was unexpected delay in the plane's departure. Had he so wished he could have returned home with Smt. Sonia Gandhi and the children, but he decided to spend time in the airport's resting lounge. He kept playing and chatting with his children. But Prime Ministership greatly changed his informal and simple nature.

Shri Rajiv Gandhi was always particular about etiquette. Whenever he met anyone he did so heartily. He would try to understand the other's point of view and make him understand his own. But his lack of experience and absence of proper advice made him commit many grave mistakes. I saw him at close quarters as a pilot, as General Secretary of the Congress, and as Prime Minister, he showed great fortitude in the wake of his defeat in the elections. As Leader of the Opposition he never missed an opportunity to put the Government in a difficult position. But because of lack of adequate experience his decisions at times bordered on impropriety. The way he behaved in Srinagar as a member of the All Party Parliamentary Committee set up for studying the situation in Kashmir was not liked even by his well-wishers. Similarly by being present at the independence celebrations of Nambia he greatly embarrassed not only Prime Minister Vishwanath Pratap Singh but himself as well. He took a long time to realise the fact that he was no longer in power and as the Leader of the Opposition he had to play the constructive role.

India is the largest democracy of the world. Leaving aside the short span of 1975 and 1976 the reign of democracy has remained uninterrupted. Adult franchise, impartial elections, independent judiciary, multi party system and free press are the corner stones of our democratic set up. People change Governments through ballot. In 1977 people had even defeated a formidable Prime Minister like Smt. Indira Gandhi at the hustings. In 1980 the Janata Party Government, which had ascended to the throne of power on the tide of people's wrath against the excesses committed in the emergency and had the blessings of Lok Nayak Jaiprakash Narain was similarly swept out of power by the same people. In 1989 even the Government of Rajiv Gandhi, which just 5 years ago the people had, by conceding 445 seats out of a total of 517 seats, given a massive mandate to rule, was in a similar way swept off its feet by the same electorates. In States also people have changed Governments in this way and demonstrated the decisive power of the ballot.

Does it mean that Indian democracy is inwardly as much strong and mighty as it looks alive and vibrant outwardly ? Are all democratic institutions discharging their responsibilities properly ? Are the democratic values of life being defended in the country ? Has the democracy taken deep roots in our land ? While searching for answers to these questions one is sorely disappointed.

In Parliament there is less discussion but more noise. Elections have been reduced to a farce because of the use of money power on an extensive scale. The party system is getting eroded due to the unethical trend of horse-trading. Accusing fingers are beginning to be raised at the impartiality of the judiciary. The Election Commission has become a target for charges and counter-charges. The politics is becoming increasingly criminalised. The outer shell of democracy is, no doubt, intact but it appears to be moth-eaten from inside.

Democracy is not a game of simple majority of numbers, a majority of 51 versus a minority of 49. Our election system is such in which it is not necessary for the winning candidate of the victorious party to secure even 51 per cent votes. The Westminster system already suffers from the defect of feigned majority on the strength of minority of votes. The multiplicity of parties and more than it the division of vote on account of the presence of large number of candidates in the elections is giving rise to a befalling phenomenon. The parties are forming Governments on the strength of 30-35 per cent of votes and by securing even a lesser percentage of votes candidates are getting elected to Lok Sabha and State Legislatures. This sytem is basically defective.

In India also in accordance with the Westminster system the Leader of the Opposition is accorded a special status and he gets salary, allowances and perquisites equal to what members of the Council of Ministers receive. Following the British convention in India too the office of the Chairman of the Public Accounts Committee goes to the Opposition. So much so the tradition of giving the post of Deputy Speaker to the Opposition is somehow or other being honoured. But at the root of these conventions and traditions lies the genuine respect for the Opposition. It is needless to say that this sentiment is conspicuous by its absence in our country. Far from basic respect for the Opposition even an attitude of tolerance towards it is lacking. The Opposition is treated as enemy. Not only they are treated as such but declarations to this effect are publicly made. In fact the growing intolerance is posing a serious danger to the democratic fabric. As a result of imitating the Westminster model many divisive factors which were already present in the Indian polity became more acute. The society already divided by the considerations of caste, subcaste, modes of worship, languages and different life styles is getting gradually disintegrated. Communalism is at its worst.

The poison of casteism is playing havoc with public life. The factors which once united the people have now assumed a divisive role. The politics has now been reduced to a game of power. To capture power by questionable methods and, after usurping it; to remain in power by whatever means has become the sole objective of politics. In their lust for power the political parties do not refrain from giving encouragement to secessionist forces, so much so that they do not even desist from hobnobbing with anti-national elements.

For the success of democracy it is very essential that the party system should be strong. In a large country like India with diverse traits the two-party system unlike Britain, does not seem to be practicable. Nonetheless, it is imperative that whatever be the number of parties, they should be based on their policies and programmes, should observe democratic norms, have regular membership, hold regular organisational elections and on the basis of their clear-cut manifestos should go before the voters to solicit their support. Due to historical reasons the Congress has acted more as a political platform and less as a political party. From communists to communalists all have played politics under the umbrella of Congress. The Congress has changed with times as much as it hasn't. It may have taken 60 years to journey from the goal of creating a socialistic society to its new haven of free economy but it has from the angle of ideology traversed that distance with great ease. Its flexibility may have been an asset to it, but it has been a source of great embarrassment to other Parties. There is very thin line of demarcation between pragmatism and opportunism. The proverbial saying *"Jaise Bahe Bayar, Peeth Tab Taisi Dijiye"* (As the wind blows so set your sails) may be a sure formula for leading a comfortable life, but it cannot induce a newly independent nation to strive hard for building it anew. For this, a deep commitment for certain values of life is essential.

1.1.1996
New Delhi

A.B. Vajpayee

I NATIONAL ISSUES

The Twin Danger

Sir, I take this opportunity to congratulate the President on his re-election. It is true that the Congress Party has not initiated the democratic tradition of consulting all major parties on the election of the President. But once a President is elected he does not belong to any particular party or province, he is the President of the entire Indian Republic. By electing Dr. Rajendra Prasad to presidentship we have honoured ourselves. It is possible that some of my friends may not approve of this observation of mine....

SOME HON. MEMBERS : We do, we do.

SHRI VAJPAYEE : I stand in the opposition, but opposition for the sake of opposition is not my purpose. Although the number of Bharatiya Jana Sangh members in this House is small we have the ideal of the late Dr. Shyama Prasad Mukherji before us. We shall try to continue to be inspired by that ideal and contribute our mite to the great *Yajna* of the nation's reconstruction.

Memories of Dr. Mukherji bring back memories of Kashmir, and memories of Kashmir bring back memories of the government hospital where he had to sacrifice his life in a corner under police guard for the sake of unity. It is four years since he died, but his death still remains shrouded in mystery. The gentle hands of time have healed the wounds, but the pain remains. And when the Prime Minister or Defence Minister repeats what Dr. Mukherji had said on the Kashmir problem in this House four years ago I feel had we adopted this policy on the Kashmir question right from the beginning we would not have had to pay the price of Dr. Shyama Prasad Mukherji's precious life.

The Government's Kashmir policy is weak and indecisive. We took the complaint to the Security Council, but we did not stress Pakistan being declared as aggressor right from the beginning. Our armed forces were marching from victory to victory and the aggressor was running for dear life, but at such a time we fettered our triumphant forces with the cease-fire line. Whatever was won on the battlefield was lost in the mansion in New Delhi. We won the war but lost the treaty, and now one-third of Kashmir is under the control of the aggressor. How will it be liberated ? In what way will it be done ? What is the Government's policy in this regard ? In the Vedas God has been described as "Neti, neti"—'not this, not that'. God is not this, God is not that.

Lok Sabha on May 15, 1957 during discussion on the Motion of Thanks on the President's Address

Kashmir, Goa, East Bengal—Same Plight

These words, *'Neti, neti'* [(No. No] very well describe the Government's policy in respect of the problem of the Hindus in Kashmir and Goa and East Bengal. Will one-third of the territory of Kashmir be liberated on the strength of arms ? No, no. Shall we gift it to Pakistan ? No, no. Then what shall we do ?

Shall we take police action in Goa ? No, no. Then shall we permit a Satyagraha by the people ? No, no. Then shall we leave Goa to the tender mercies of Portugal ? No, no. It is the same with the Hindus who are being driven out of East Bengal. We are not prepared to pressurise Pakistan into observing the agreement arrived at the time of the Partition and treating Hindus in Pakistan with the same equality and respect as Muslims in India. This was the basis of the partition, and if Pakistan does not accept it we should think of resorting to other means. But we are neither prepared to put pressure on Pakistan nor to demand territory for the resettlement of Hindu refugees. What is our policy ? It can only be defined as *'Neti, neti'*.

The Cease-fire Line

I was speaking about the Kashmir problem. The Prime Minister is committed to liberating one-third of its territory. Not an inch of land must be surrendered to the aggressor. Sometimes there are reports that a compromise has been proposed with Pakistan about the cease-fire line. I am happy that the proposal has been abandoned. I may make it clear that no proposal involving division of Kashmir would be acceptable to the people of India. Kashmir has fully merged with India, and the only problem is when Pakistan would vacate its illegally occupied territory. A few days ago the Prime Minister said we are prepared to talk to Pakistan provided two premises are accepted—one, Pakistan is the aggressor, and two, that one-third territory belongs to India. If both these points are accepted what remains to talk about ? Nothing. If there is at all a point worth talking about it is to ask Pakistan when it is going to vacate one-third of Kashmir. But there are no signs of Pakistan agreeing to this. Let alone getting back Pakistan-occupied territory, even the territory that has merged in India has become a bone of contention.

Preparation for war

There are danger signals. Pakistan is preparing for war. Equipped with American arms it is posing a danger for India's freedom and security. I am not an advocate of war. I am also a supporter of peace—but not peace of the funeral ground but peace of life. The peace we may get by surrendering one-third of Kashmir would not be lasting peace. So let us not continue our weak-kneed policy under the guise of peace. We should learn from the example of Dharmaraj Yudhishthir. Nobody wants war, but others can force it on us. Dharmaraj did not want war, he tried his best to avoid it, he made beseechments, sent messages of peace, even accepted partition, suffered

Draupadi's indignity, but he could not escape war. If you run away from war, war runs after you, but he who prepares to face war with courage not only protects his rights but succeeds in establishing peace.

I am sorry to see that the President's Address does not refer in any way to the danger posed to the security and independence of India by the war-like preparations of Pakistan. This is a real danger. Pakistan has placed us in an adverse position by accepting American aid and by making it clear that this aid would be used against India, while the USA has also indulged in a hostile act against India by providing aid to Pakistan.

Failure of Foreign Policy

We had hoped that the Prime Minister's visit to the U.S. would bring about some change in American policy. But later available signs indicate no change. So from this point of view the Prime Minister's visit to the U.S. cannot be called successful. It is no use blaming others. Instead of blaming others we should rather do some introspection.

Some of my friends have profusely praised the Government for a successful foreign policy. I regret I cannot join this chorus of praise. The objective of our policy was that we would not join any power bloc, but would strive for world peace. And this foreign policy has been so "skillfully" conducted that war itself is knocking at our doors ! It now seems that we cannot but join some power bloc. If this is the success of foreign policy what is failure ? That word failure would have to be deleted from the dictionary.

I would also like to say something on the internal situation in Kashmir. Everyone in the country wants to strengthen Bakshi Ghulam Mohammed's hands, but covering up his mistakes is not the way to do so. The unity of Kashmir with the rest of India cannot depend on any individual, however great, on any party, however powerful, or on any government, however popular. Men may come and men may go, parties will form and break up, governments will take office and change. The relationship between India and Kashmir must not depend upon them. Our good wishes are with Bakshi Sahib, but the people of Kashmir are not satisfied with the way the administration is functioning there. Democracy is yet to take root in Kashmir. It is possible that our neighbour Pakistan may try to exploit what I am saying, but....

SHRI L.N. MISHRA (Saharsa) : And still you are saying it ?

SHRI VAJPAYEE : Truth cannot be hidden for fear that somebody would exploit it. We have already once suffered the consequences of the policy of silence on Kashmir. If we do not want that history to repeat itself we will have to face the truth.

Irregularities in Elections in Kashmir

Elections have recently taken place in Jammu and Kashmir. I visited Jammu during the election. I regret to say there were irregularities in the election. I saw with my own eyes that voters' lists, which had been prepared in Urdu, were illegible on many pages. Curiously enough while Praja

Parishad people could not read them the National Conference people could. There was no advance notice of where polling stations would be located. And in some cases they were changed on the very day of the polling. At many places the ballot boxes were kept with the presiding officers. Praja Parishad Chief Pandit Prem Nath Dogra raised objections before the presiding officers. I have a photo copy of it, which I am prepared to place on the floor of the House. The presiding officer admitted that at a particular place a box was missing while counting was going on.

SPEAKER : I would like to say for the Hon. member's information that rules have been made according to which in case a member has in his possession any document, paper, photograph etc. that he may wish to produce here he should first show it or its copy and then refer to it, so that it could be determined in advance whether it could be permitted or not. So the Hon. member should wait for such advance inspection and permission for an opportunity to make reference.

SHRI VAJPAYEE : Accepted.

Sir, as I was saying, the Praja Parishad fielded 17 candidates from 18 constituents in the Jammu and Kashmir elections. In 12 of these 18 constitutencies ballot boxes were found broken. Such an irregularity cannot be condoned. I appreciate Bakshi Sahib's difficulties, but we have to take Kashmir forward on the path of democracy. For this we need to create an atmosphere in which all parties loyal to India can function freely. I expect to soon see a change in the Government's Kashmir policy that is required for this purpose. The Praja Parishad wants to co-operate with the National Conference, but cooperation cannot be one-sided, it needs the right atmosphere.

Danger of External Aggression

I have just now referred to Pakistan's war-like preparations. In just ten years of India's independence and partition we are faced with the twin danger of external aggression and internal break- up. War is at our doors. If a small country like Israel can make an aggression at the behest of Britain and France it is possible that Pakistan may indulge in the misadventure of a confrontation with India, as Pakistani leaders are guided by others and are willing to auction their starving people in the market place of Washington. I do not want to sound an alarmist, but we should be on guard. It is true that we are engaged in the great *yajna* of national reconstruction that for this we need a well-equipped army, and alert people and an administration devoted to duty.

Fissiparous Reorganisation of States

One more thing. The President has admitted in his address that reorganisation of States has somewhat halted the progress of the Five-Year Plan. Could this not have been foreseen ? Was this reorganisation necessary at this time ? And if it was to be done, why was it not done properly ? This is not reorganisation but a break-up. The legitimate demands of the people of Maharashtra and Gujarat have not been accepted. I hail from Uttar Pradesh and live in Madhya Pradesh but I have moved in Maharashtra and Gujarat and I know about the intense feelings of the people there about a state of their own. These sentiments can neither be ignored nor suppressed. I do not approve of the threats that were given here yesterday. They cannot force their point of view. This is not the right way. But I would like to say to the non-Maharashtrian members especially those from Uttar Pradesh and Bihar, who took the initiative in creating the bilingual Bombay State—I respect them—that their sentiments were noble but they should also bear in mind the prevailing situation. Fissiparous forces would exploit the situation and incite the people. You want unity but you have adopted a method that would promote separation. It is still not too late. This House can reconsider the issue. In the circumstances that prevail the creation of *Samyukta* Maharashtra and *Maha* Gujarat should be considered again.

One of my friends has referred to the Punjab problem. I do not agree that a lasting solution for it has been found. The solution found has complicated the situation still further. The language problem has not been properly solved, and the seeds of separatism have been sown. Thank you.

Threats to Nation's Security

Sir, the state of the nation as painted in the President's Address cannot give the people hopes for a good future. The Address stressed more on what the Administration has done so far, while the House and the people had hoped that it would indicate how the danger before us would be overcome. We see before us the consequences of the policies adopted by the Government in various walks of the nation's life. I was deeply distressed to see that the President's Address has made no reference to the various new dangers that are coming up for the security and unity of the nation.

The other day the Defence Minister said in a speech : "India is not cent per cent secure." When the Defence Minister of a country makes such a public statement the question that arises is, why were adequate efforts not made for the nation's security, which is of paramount importance ? As is well known this danger comes from a neighbouring country, and this country is seeking nuclear weapons. No one has any about against whom these weapons would be used. So far as conventional armaments are concerned are our armed forces capable of successfully facing an aggression ? I know there is no possibility of a big war but Pakistani leaders could at any time provoke a quarrel for inviting international military intervention on the question of Kashmir in order to divert their people's attention from their deteriorating economic condition. Under any circumstances the people want the Government's assurance that India is cent per cent secure. The Government must create confidence in the people's mind in this respect.

Dual Stance on Kashmir

So far as the Kashmir problem is concerned the Government has repeatedly assured that it is not prepared to talk about it in the U.N. or with any foreign power so long as one-third part of Kashmir, which is legally an integral part of India, is not returned to India. Despite such assurance, we learn from newspaper reports that talks on Kashmir are being held with Security Council representatives sent to Karachi and New Delhi. The talks are going on and for many hours. When we have rejected the Security Council resolution under which Dr. Graham has come to India will not the world take it to mean that such protracted talks with him mean that in some form or other we have accepted that resolution ?

It has been indicated that Dr. Graham has been told that India will not hold any talks so long as Pakistan's aggression is not vacated. So much time need not have been taken to tell him this. The talks took place for many hours.

Lok Sabha on February 14, 1958 during discussion on the Motion of Thanks on President's Address

Were they about the weather or for inquiring after each other's health ? So long as we keep talking about the Kashmir problem in the U.N. or with some foreign power the people of Kashmir will continue to suffer from a feeling of instability. The former Chief Minister, released from jail, has not been responsible for creating that feeling. I also do not hold the conspiracies that are going on in New Delhi in this connection responsible for this. For this I hold that government responsible which took the domestic problem of Kashmir to the U.N. and made it a pawn on the chessboard of international politics. It is good that this mistake has been admitted, but it still continues in some form or another. When we talk to Dr. Graham those who are against the merger of Kashmir with India get the opportunity to indulge in the propaganda in the Valley that the future of Kashmir has not yet been decided. If we want to put an end to this instability we have no option but to stop talking on the Kashmir problem with any foreign power and plainly tell the U.N.: you have done injustice to us on the Kashmir problem, so we are withdrawing it from the Security Council. If it is said that a question taken up by the Security Council cannot be taken back we can at least refuse to talk about it there. Pakistan may take the complaint there if it so wishes, but so far as India is concerned we should refuse to say anything on the Kashmir problem.

Sheikh Abdullah Changes Stance

Secondly I would like to point out that the sudden change in Sheikh Abdullah's thinking is most regrettable, though not unexpected. My party, Bharatiya Jana Sangh, had already warned about this. Whenever the Government makes some new pronouncement on Kashmir, on which Dr. Shyama Prasad Mukherji had already insisted in this House, I feel his martyrdom would not have become necessary had we adopted the right policy right from the beginning. Then this new danger facing us today would also not have arisen. The reason for this danger is that we have not fully integrated Kashmir with India. When we proposed a referendum Sheikh Abdullah asked for his price for preparing the opinion of the people of. Kashmir in favour of India, and when we could not fully pay that price nationalist Sheikh Abdullah turned a communalist. If we still keep a gulf between the rest of India and Kashmir somebody will again exploit it and we would have a new problem on our hands. We must fully bridge that gulf. We should fully apply the Indian Constitution to Kashmir. We are spending crores of rupees from Central funds for the development of Kashmir. This is necessary, because Kashmir is an integral part of India. We are responsible for its development. But the Auditor-General should have the powers to see if these funds are properly utilised. The Legislative Assembly of Kashmir has passed a resolution but it has not been implemented. Our Auditor-General has not yet been able to audit the accounts of Kashmir. Elections in Kashmir are not held under the supervision of India's Election Commission. If our Election Commission is so capable and so impartial that it can be invited to Sudan to hold elections there, there should be no objection to inviting it to

Srinagar. On the one hand the Indian Constitution gives our citizens fundamental rights, but on the other the people of Jammu and Kashmir have been denied even those rights.

The Supreme Court does not have full authority to hear the appeal of the citizens there. Such things make a discrimination between the people of India and those of Kashmir and make them feel apart. We need to replace this discrimination, this *Dwaita* with *Adwaita*. Thanks to this *Dwaita* we now see the distorted form of Sheikh Abdullah. There should be no distinction between Jammu and Kashmir and the rest of India. Of course, the country will have no objection if, for some reasons, the special rights of the people of Jammu and Kashmir need to be preserved. So far as the qustion of compensation and the question of Indians buying land in Jammu and Kashmir are cancerned there can be no two opinions. Other parties are now leaning towards the stand that the Jana Sangh has to date taken for solving this controversy. We should be alert to the situation that is developing in Kashmir and the Government should adopt a realistic policy.

Punjab Government incompetent

Challenges to the nation's unity are also developing in other parts of the country. Look at Punjab. No patriot can ignore what is happening there. Nothing can be more sorrowful than a conflict between brothers. But that is the situation in Punjab and the present administration in Punjab has completely failed to contain it. The Indian Constitution has given certain emergency powers to the President. The situation in Punjab demands that these powers be now used, the Cabinet disbanded and President's rule imposed. The administration could not protect the honour of womenfolk, it could not give equal justice to different faiths, it could not implement even a judge's report, it is vitiated with the spirit of communalism and it has alienated the people. All in all it is a blot on democracy. The people of Punjab want deliverance from such an administration. The Centre should intervene before it is too late, otherwise the situation could go out of control. The short-sighted policies are also responsible for what is happening in Punjab. For the sake of winning the election the Congress had made an agreement with the Akali Dal and its consequences are before us.

Tamil Nadu on the Separatist Path

Not only in Punjab, in Tamil Nadu too a fissiparous situation has developed. The government has failed to put down separatist tendencies, as a result of which the danger of the country breaking up is growing. Power politics is being played in the name of language and sect, which are being used as instruments. If we did not face this separatism we would not be able to maintain national unity, which is so necessary for all-round development.

The observations on the economy in the President's Address are not such as to satisfy the common man. Today we are faced with an economic crisis. Starvation stalks many parts of the land. There have been starvation deaths in the eastern districts of Uttar Pradesh but when they were brought to the notice of the State's Food Minister, he said they were not starvation deaths but deaths due to eating mango seeds. But who eats mango seeds ? Those who have no food to eat. When he was asked if there was food in the dying person's house he said not after his death. He was again asked if there was no fair price shop nearby he replied in the negative. If effective and thorough steps are not taken to tackle the adverse situation in various parts of the country due to drought, starvation may spread on a large scale. The Centre can get away with saying this is a State subject. The whole country is one and in a speech during a tour of eastern districts of Uttar Pradesh the President had said even if a single person dies of starvation it would be a disgrace for the administration. There have been not one but many starvation deaths. There is a food shortage, people do not have enough purchasing power and the government has not been able to tackle this situation.

The need of the hour is both long-term and short-term measures. It would not do to sit in New Delhi and fix food production targets. At times the Prime Minister says food production could increase by 70 per cent, but he does not say how. Food production cannot be increased sitting in Delhi so long as figures do not come from the villages, so long as the needs and difficulties of every farmer are not assessed, and so long as targets are not fixed for a family, a village, tehsil, a district and a State. The figures given in the First Five Year Plan were found wrong on examination and I have a feeling that it is all a jugglery of figures.

Figures do not Allay Hunger

The President's Address is full of statistics. But figures cannot allay hunger. The Government claims food production is increasing but as against this we see people dying of hunger. People dying of starvation need food, not statistics. But if there is food in the country people should have the capacity to buy it. I have toured the eastern districts of Uttar Pradesh, Chhattisgarh districts of Madhya Pradesh, districts of Vindhya Pradesh and northern regions of Bihar and seen with my own eyes that hundreds of people have left their hearths and homes for other States in search of work. It was like a wholesale migration of population. This is a very serious situation, but the Government has not shown itself to be as alert to it as one would expect. The food problem is the biggest problem. We are using up foreign exchange for importing food. This has led to a foreign exchange crisis. There are also other reasons for this crisis and a high-power committee should be set up to go into them. I am sure such an investigation would bring to light as sensational facts as the Mundhra affair, if not more.

In 1956 licences were issued for importing many foreign products. I have just learned that in that year a certain firm was issued a licence for importing silver plates for the tea cups and saucers. But that material has arrived only now. The country would not have starved to death if this licence had not been issued in 1956 and these silver cups and saucers had not come. We are devoting a lot of thought to the development of the nation. We have prepared a plan, but we cannot hope to get as much foreign aid as expected in the plan.

The right import policy was not determined and the results are before us. There is still a shortfall of Rs. 700 crores. How will it be made up ?

The figures given by the Finance Minister a couple of days back indicate that the small savings scheme is not being that successful. Last year 37 crores 4 lakhs of rupees had been mobilised during the period April to January. Before that 44 crores some lakhs of rupees had been mobilised during the corresponding period. Now the people do not have enough funds to save. Then again the taxes collected are not being used to make up the shortfall in the external aid and internal resources in the plan. They are spent on defence. Dearness is on the increase, prices are going up and consequently government employees are demanding higher salaries and allowances. That demand too we have to fulfil. There seems to be no well-defined policy on the changes and amendments needed in the Five Year Plan. Sometimes it is said 'the core of the plan' will be completed, sometimes it is said 'the hard core of the plan' will be completed. But in the present situation the people do not know the essence of the plan and the essence of the essence. I am not sure if even the Government understands it.

Pruning the Plan

The Plan is not a prestige issue. If we see that external aid is insufficient and internally mobilised resources cannot make up the shortfall we should not hesitate to prune the plan. If we feel that the targets fixed in the Plan cannot be attained, we should realistically scale them down without delay. We should have no hesitation in doing so. But speeches are made to say, whatever the circumstances the Plan would be fulfilled. The circumstances have now deteriorated, not enough foreign aid is available and optimum taxation has been resorted to for mobilising internal resources. No more taxes are possible. If more taxes are imposed in the coming budget there will be resentment in the people. If there is resentment in the people how will they have enthusiasm for the Plan ? And so long as the people have no enthusiasm for the Plan it will not succeed. For no constructive work can succeed on the strength of the bureaucracy. The machinery on which we are depending for the success of our plans is not representative of the people. It does not properly represent the feelings of the people. If we want the Plan to succeed and to acquire the people's cooperation that is required for it we will have to change our point of view and try to secure the people's cooperation at every level for determining and implementing the Plan. If efforts are made in this direction the whole country would cooperate with the Government. The development of the nation is not only one party's problem. For the sake of success of the Plan the Government should create an atmosphere that would be congenial for every one's cooperation. I have no hesitation in saying that the Government has not been able to create such an atmosphere. On various problems its point of view is not in accord with the people's sentiments. Thank you.

Nation's Prestige at Stake

Sir, the Prime Minister's invitation to Shri Chou En-Lai to visit Delhi has created a new situation. The letter of invitation was sent on the 5th and the Parliament's session began on the 8th. Honesty required that the President's Address should have indicated the Government's decision to change its China policy.

The China Policy

The President is the head of our polity. He addresses Parliament once a year. The Address should have at least indicated a change in Government policy. But the President was made to say that China has taken unilateral action on the common frontier. He also said China has betrayed us. At the same time he also said—my Government is following the policy of peaceful talks in proper conditions and at the proper time and at the same time firm preparations are being made to defend the country. Even before the President was saying this in Parliament the Prime Minister had invited the Chinese Prime Minister to Delhi. The President was thus put in the wrong. The Prime Minister was not honest with Parliament. The invitation to Shri Chou En-Lai is totally against the policies declared so far and supported by Parliament. Like a bomb blast this policy change is sudden, unnecessary and derogatory.

Yesterday when the adjournment motion was moved the Prime Minister said our policy has always been of our willingness to meet anyone to find a solution. In this connection he referred to the last forty years. I do not want to go that far back. I only want to know from him why he had rejected Chou En-Lai's invitation to come to Rangoon. At that time he had said : "How can we reach agreement on principles when there is such complete disagreement about facts ?" In his letter of November 16 he had also stated :

> "While I am ready to meet at a suitable time and place, I feel that we should concentrate our immediate efforts on reaching interim understanding which will help in easing the present tension and will prevent the situation getting worse. Thereafter the necessary preliminary steps might be taken and time and place for meeting could be fixed."

He had also written :

> "It is necessary that some preliminary steps are taken and the foundation of our discussion laid."

Now I want to know—what preliminary steps were taken during December 26 to February 5 ? What interim agreement was made ? Was any

Lok Sabha on February 17, 1960 during discussion on the Motion of Thanks on President's Address

foundation for discussion laid ? I am not one of those who feel there is a difference between our Prime Minister going to Rangoon and the Chinese Prime Minister coming to Delhi.

As a nation we cannot make such a small matter a prestige issue. The point is, if at that time the condition was laid down that preliminary steps should be taken and an interim agreement made before a discussion is held, and if such a condition was proper at that time and so the Prime Minister did not go to Rangoon, then that condition is valid even today. On the other hand, if the Prime Minister feels that it was wrong on our part to lay such a condition then he should clearly say so. He can change the policy. He has a majority in the House and the people of the country also love him. If he wanted to change policy he would not have kept the House and the country in the dark. The President's Address should have indicated that Government policy is changing. But I regret to say no such indication was given. Has he received any signals in the meanwhile ? Has Shri Parthsarathy brought any message from Peking ? Have Soviet leaders given any assurances ? What was that pressure under which the Prime Minister has invited Shri Chou En-Lai to Delhi ? I feel not all facts have been placed before us. Possibly that is why we are against this invitation. The Prime Minister should take the House into confidence. Even in his letter of February 5 he has said :

> "I do not see any common ground between our respective viewpoints. Although any negotiations on the basis you have suggested are not possible, still I think it might be helpful for us to meet."

People's Feelings Ignored

At first he had said so long as there is no interim agreement a meeting would not be useful. Now he says it could be helpful. On what basis does he say so ? Tell us, explain to us. We are ready to understand. But it seems there is no basis because a spokesman of the External Affairs Ministry told press reporters that we sent the invitation because the world was saying we are not willing even to meet. World opinion was turning against us. It is a matter of deep regret that the Ministry of External Affairs cares for world opinion but no attention has been paid to the psychological effect of this invitation on the forty crores people of the country. Before caring for the world we should care for the country. This invitation is not in accord with the people's sentiments. The Government's China policy is gradually changing and the Prime Minister is sliding down from his high pedestal. He has presented two faces to this House. One day, he had discussed 'a nation in arms', in the House. In the Rajya Sabha he had repeated Churchill's words—'blood, toil and tears'. He has two faces. One is that of a national leader, who wants to meet aggression with self-respect. The other is that of a weak person unable to protect the honour of the country. One face reflects Churchill, who brought victory to Britain, the other reflects Chamberlain who gave courage to Hitler with his appeasement policy. I am sorry to say all this, but both pictures are before us. It is as if we are looking at a divided personality.

I had congratulated the Prime Minister when he discussed the 'nation in arms'. I had said to him—I am assured the prestige of the country is safe in your hands. But his recent letter has shaken this confidence and I wish he would re-establish it. For this he has to explain the basis on which he is going to talk to Shri Chou En-Lai. At first it was said there was no harm in meeting, but on what basis ? Now it is said we can meet and even talk but we will not talk of an agreement. I fail to understand where mere talking would end and talking of an agreement begin. If Shri Chou En-Lai is coming to New Delhi he is certainly not coming to discuss the weather here. He is also not coming to explain the Chinese technique of producing rice. For that the Chinese pavilion in the Agriculture Fair is enough. For that Shri Chou En-Lai does not have to bother to come all the way from Peking. Let us not delude ourselves. It is clear that the talks would be on the border dispute. What will be their basis ? How far is the Prime Minister prepared to take this matter ? I fear we want to buy peace with surrender of Aksai Chin.

SHRI C.D. PANDE (Nainital) : Not at all.

SHRI VAJPAYEE : Then let the Prime Minister again dispel the doubts and confusion created in the minds of members of Parliament and the people of the country because of his letter.

Get Indian Territory Vacated

What actually should have happened was that the Prime Minister and the Government should have exploited the winter season and driven the Chinese aggressors out of Indian territory, but here we are preparing for surrender. He declared in a speech that foreign forces would not be tolerated on Indian territory. I hail his declaration. But 42,000 square miles of territory in Kashmir are under Pakistani control. Kashmir is an integral part of India, but the forces in slave Kashmir do not belong to India. Foreign forces are present in Kashmir, as also in Ladakh and Long Ju. If there is a talk in the country about a military alliance with Pakistan I do not support it. But if it is there it is an indication of the fact that the defence and foreign policies of the Government of India have failed to promote the nation's interests. When we realise our weakness we look here and there. Talks of alliance with others would stop if the Government takes courageous steps to free Indian territory from foreigners. But it seems the Government lacks such courage. If the Prime Minister can drive Chinese out of Ladakh and Long Ju he should at least not enter into an dishonourable agreement that would break the nation's morale.

The Prime Minister has written to Shri Chou En-Lai that if he came he would be given an official welcome. The Government may extend an official welcome and, if necessary, a guard of honour may be presented at the airport, school-children of Delhi may be made to stand by the roadside, but this will not be a welcome by the people. So far as my party is concerned—it is a small party—we are opposed to inviting Shri Chou En-Lai to New Delhi and, if necessary, would express our opposition.

AN HON. MEMBER : Black flags ?

SHRI VAJPAYEE : One more thing. We receive many foreign guests. We have set a procedure system of receiving them. It is now time to change that procedure. How much crowd there is for somebody's welcome has become a sort of index of how far we follow a policy of neutrality and whether we want to follow it at all. This is not good. We want and the people of the country want that we should not align ourselves with any bloc, but the procedure of welcoming foreign guests that we have adopted and the crowd we gather indicate to foreign media which way we are tilting. This is like tight rope walking. If it is a working day, if there is no crowd in spite of declaring it a holiday and lining up school children, it is taken as an index of towards which bloc we are tilting. The time has come to change the procedure of welcoming foreign guests. The size of the crowd that is present cannot be an index of our neutrality. It should not be so. A reconsideration of this procedure is called for.

The Corruption Syndrome

Sir, this debate has also discussed corruption. Merely seeing red at the name of corruption is not going to change things. If we are vexed people think there is certainly corruption, that is why we are angry. *"Sesham Kopena Poorayet"*—'when logic does not work a man gets angry'.

PANDIT. K.C. SHARMA (Hapur) : And talks loudly.

SHRI VAJPAYEE : This anger cannot take the place of logic. If corruption is being discussed there is certainly corruption *"yetra yetra dhoomah, tatra, tatra, wannih"*—'wherever there is smoke, there is fire.' The point is that we should not look at the problem of corruption through the eyes of law. It is possible that many things may not come within the grasp of the law but may come within the parameters of good and bad, proper and improper. Every time proof is called for. Shri C.D. Deshmukh should be asked this, as he has levelled various charges, and the Prime Minister's correspondence with him should be published and placed on the table of the House. I am in favour of setting up a commission for inquiring into charges of corruption. I suggest that it should not be like the Election Commission. It should have a separate prosecuting machinery. If it is like the Election Commission and if there is no separate arrangement of inquiring into cases and collecting evidence it would be the same situation as the Nathdwara affair in Rajasthan. Merely setting up a commission at the top is not enough. The prosecuting machinery of the commission should be apart from the Central and State administration and it should inquire into the charges, collect facts and bring forth evidence. Such a commission needs to be appointed.

Partition of Bombay State

Sir, one more thing and I shall conclude. Everyone has welcomed the Centre's decision to bifurcate Bombay province. It would have been better if this decision had been taken earlier and the resultant bitterness avoided. Better late than never. We have come to the right path. But the way it is being done makes it appear as if the bifurcation of Bombay is an internal matter of the Congress party. It is being solved in such a way that new questions and new doubts are arising in the minds of other people. The Bombay-Mysore border dispute has not yet been satisfactorily resolved. It is necessary to give aid to Gujarat but in what form it should be given needs to be thought about. It would not be right if Maharashtra comes to feel that it has to pay a ransom to help Gujarat become a separate State. Whatever aid needs to be given should be given by the Centre, and the people of Maharashtra as well as opposition parties should be taken into confidence while arriving at a decision.

Meaningless Slogan of Maha Delhi

But along with Bombay there is also a call for the division of Punjab. Yesterday a member from Delhi had talked about Maha Delhi and had also said there is no responsible government in Delhi. I thought he was a responsible person but he talked quite irresponsibly. Even if all assemblies in the country are dissolved, the Parliament takes over the administration and a unitary form of government gets established. So even then democracy will remain. It is not necessary that we should have legislative assemblies everywhere. And Delhi does not need it at all. But there are some politicians who think only of themselves and do not care for the good of the country. They say—divide Uttar Pradesh, even if it is not willing, separate Haryana, establish Maha Delhi, and then place us in the seats of power. There is no need of a Maha Delhi. The problem of the neglect of Haryana should be considered. Punjab need not be divided; it should be made bigger. Himachal could be merged with Punjab. The language problem cannot be resolved by dividing Punjab.

Small states cannot help the country's economic progress. As industrialisation grows borders of states lose their importance. Planning is a Central subject that is concentrating more and more powers in the hands of the Central Government. The point is, no linguistic group should come to feel that its language is sought to be suppressed or killed. If there is such a feeling in Punjab it is wrong. Punjabi too is our language. We should learn it too. We speak Punjabi, and there should be no objection to learning it. Hindi should have equal status with Punjabi. The language controversy need not be politicised, so there is no question of a Maha Delhi. It is the disgruntled political leaders who are raising the Maha Delhi slogan. This slogan has no importance. The situations in Punjab and Bombay are different. It would not be proper to apply the situation of Bombay to the situation in Punjab. Punjab has a different problem. It needs to be solved, but it is not necessary to link it with Bombay. We cannot raise demands for small states when we are faced with the danger of external aggression and we have to fight poverty. I hope the Government will have the right approach towards such demands. Thank you.

New Threat to National Unity

Vacate Chinese Aggression

Sir, I welcome the statement the Prime Minister made in the Rajya Sabha yesterday that an agreement with China is possible only on the basis of the Chinese vacating Indian territory, and there is no question of give and take. I also support the Prime Minister's decision not to go to Peking for the present. So long as there is no change in the attitude of the Chinese it would be fruitless to talk to them. But while welcoming these declarations I have failed to find in the Prime Minister's speech an answer to the question as to what steps will be taken to liberate the Indian territory in case the Chinese did not vacate their aggression on it. If it is not possible to take military action it should at least be possible to replace the police with the military at border posts. The Chief Minister of Uttar Pradesh has stated in the Legislative Assembly that the checkposts of Kala Pani and Garbian are still manned by the civil police, not by Jawans. He also said these posts function only for some months, not the year round, and then the police returns. If the Chinese soldiers can work at Tahlakot for all the year there is no reason why we cannot replace the police there with Jawans so that the border could be guarded all the year round.

Along with this there is also another question—apart from military action are we prepared to take some other steps that would show we shall not tolerate the Chinese aggression ? The other day the Deputy Foreign Minister stated in the Rajya Sabha that the Personal Assistant to the Indian Ambassador in Peking was treated in a very insulting manner. We have lodged a protest. But is that enough ? Are we waiting for the day our Ambassador will be treated similarly ? To protest the Chinese behaviour against us we should recall our envoy to Peking, and so long as we do not do so the same restrictions that are imposed on our ambassador and his staff should also be imposed on the staff of the Chinese embassy in New Delhi.

Basis of Tibet Policy

The talks between officials of the two countries make it clear that our policy *vis-a-vis* Tibet is not supported by historical facts. Even the Chinese have accepted Tibet's right to enter into agreements. We too have mentioned that Tibet had the right to sign international treaties. Then how can we accept cent per cent Chinese suzerainty over Tibet ? The facts we have presented and the agreements we have quoted support the fact that Tibet had the right to live as a free country. If for some reason the government is not now willing

Lok Sabha on February 21, 1961 during discussion on the Motion of Thanks on President's Address

to go that far we can at least lend our support to the question of human rights violation in Tibet, which Thailand and Malaya have raised in the U.N. The opinion of the Government of India has been sought on how this resolution should be framed. Efforts could be made to see that the question of human rights violation does not become a question of cold war. This is possible if the Government indicates the form of the resolution. It is not right that the might of China should reduce us to silence in respect of human rights in Tibet.

Along with this we should also endeavour to build up world opinion on the border dispute. Yesterday it was said during the debate that China is isolating us from our neighbours. Nepal and Burma have made treaties with China, and we have no complaint about that. But they should profit from our experience. China's history so far is a history of breaking treaties. The Chinese Prime Minister stated during his visit to Delhi that they would respect India's relations with Bhutan and Sikkim. What he said has been tape-recorded. But *Peking Review* has added the adjective 'proper' to relations. Nepal and Burma might find themselves in difficulties in future if they trust China through fear or because of not understanding Chinese intentions, for which the Government of India too cannot escape responsibility. It is our duty to acquaint our neighbours with China's intentions and propagate throughout the world, especially in Britain where there is a lot of misunderstanding about our border dispute with China. The British are very legalistic. Now our report has made an argument legally quite strong. This report should be published in other countries as well. Those African countries that have newly become independent should also be acquainted with China's intentions. The advent of their freedom should be welcomed and they should be put on guard against the new colonialism that is raising its head in the form of Chinese expansionism.

New Danger for National Unity

The President's Address has made no reference to the new dangers that our national unity faces. Yesterday the Prime Minister said in the Rajya Sabha that national unity is even more important than five year plans. There can be no two opinions on this. But during the past 13 years what steps did we take to strengthen national unity in the country ? Unity does not come about by appealing for unity or making speeches against communalism. What happened in Jabalpur is a matter of disgrace for every Indian. But we are making a big mistake if we think the problem is solved by getting angry, doing some whitewash or putting the blame on somebody. The Jabalpur incident is not a disease, it is the symptom of a disease. Yesterday some people asked—if a girl was being raped by some people why did people see to what religion she and those boys belonged ? I agree with them. An offence is an offence, an evil is an evil, it does not matter what religionist commits what offence. But during the past 13 years have we created an atmosphere in which such problems would not be seen from the Hindu-Muslim point of view ? On the other hand we still think on Hindu-Muslim lines. I hold this

Parliament and this Government responsible for generating this feeling of alienation.

Pass Civil Code

The Constitution says there should be a common civil code for all communities. Then why was a code passed only for Hindus ? Can we not pass a common civil code ? Should marriage laws be different for different sects ? Is bigamy bad for one sect but not for another ? There are instances where a Hindu wanting to marry again leaves the Hindu religion for doing so. Can this sort of thing promote a feeling of nationalism in the country ?

The Government has recently set up a commission to stop the misuse of the properties of Hindu maths and temples. I welcome it but would like to know if only the properties of maths and temples are misused. Are the properties of mosques and churches not misused ? Should a secular state not have a law that is equally applicable to all ? Why can the terms of reference of this commission not be expanded ? Why can't you forget this Hindu-Muslim distinction ? Hindus may be Hindus for worship and Muslims may be Muslims for namaz, but where the State is concerned, where the administration is concerned no one is a Hindu or a Muslim. We want to build up an Indian society, but the unity we profess we want to bring about cannot be established by passing a separate code for Hindus and setting up a separate commission for Hindu maths and temples.

Jobs and Reservations

What I am saying is not my own. It has appeared in the press—I do not know how far it is true—that a Central Minister has written to the Prime Minister that there should be job reservation on religious grounds. I call upon the Prime Minister to refuse the report. Who is the Minister who wants job reservation on religious grounds ? If we have reservation in the services on grounds of religion the national spirit will never grow in the country. Will you ask a candidate his religion before giving him a job ? If you do communalism will spread in the services. The person selected for a job not on grounds of merit but on communal grounds will practise communalism even in his job. There will be a chain reaction of the attitude and thus a vicious circle will set in, shattering our dream of unifying our country. This Central Minister must be asked to resign. He does not believe in our secular democracy. The other day the Prime Minister counselled the Harijans of Hyderabad that reservation was not good and it should go, it is not a sign of health. But we can understand reservation for Harijans and tribals, as they are economically backward and socially discriminated against, but where is the question of reservation on grounds of religion ? But this sort of call is being given and I call upon those who swear by unity to express their opinion on this, so that we could see who stands where. If you want to fight destructive forces, raise this problem above the party and I shall join you. If Hindus become communal they should be opposed, they should be fought but you cannot tolerate the communalism of a particular religion.

Holi, Diwali, Dushehra and Syllabus

For some time past organised efforts are being made to create communalism. Since the alliance with the Muslim League in Kerala this communalism has spread all the more. Believe me, people are saying our religion would be in danger if the text books in schools contain lessons on Diwali, Dashahra and Holi. A demand is being made that such lessons should be removed from the books. Is such a demand proper ? Holi, Dashahra and Diwali are our national festivals, they are not connected with any religion. If there is anybody who does not want to celebrate Holi he may sit at home, but we shall celebrate it, we shall sing. When spring comes and the new crop comes home we shall sing Phagun songs. And if, by mistake, some colour gets sprinkled on somebody will blood have to flow ? This is something that needs to be made clear. What is our Ministry of Cultural Affairs doing ? The problem before us is about developing one homogeneous culture, but we are talking about a variety of cultures.

Unfortunately for us since the creation of Pakistan efforts are being made to send fifth columnists into the country in order to incite communal passions and break up national unity. Many things have been said about the Jabalpur incident. I would like to place a quotation from the *Nagpur Times* on the floor of the House. This newspaper is said to be a supporter of the Congress. It has called for an inquiry into whether Pakistani fifth columnists had a hand in the Jabalpur incident.

Commenting on the Prime Minister's statement the *Nagpur Times* writes :

> "Prime Minister Nehru's statement on Jabalpur disturbances does not differ from what people may have expected of him. He denounced the heinous crime against the girl, and said that events that had taken place later indicated that our health is not good."

Violence is bad. It shows lack of restraint and impatience with the processes of law. Generally viewed, Nehru's reaction to the events is, as it ought to be.

One would have, however, expected Nehru to be in possession of more facts than are available to the common man. But even from what is now known of events in Jabalpur, a platitudinous disapproval of violence would not appear to be enough.

Subversion

Stocking of fire-arms in the mosques, attacks against the police and prompt and detailed relay of broadcasts from Radio Pakistan about incidents in Jabalpur and Sagar within an hour of their occurrence are all facts which point to planned fifth column activities in the heart of the country.

There is no dearth of sermons to those who have been humiliated by the molestation of the helpless girl. We published one such sermon in our letters columns only the other day. But the main question is, what is the Government going to do about the fifth columnists who are preparing for disturbances in the country and have direct wireless contacts with our unfriendly neighbours across the border ? The people would very much like to have an answer to that question from the Prime Minister.

The riots in Jabalpur must be condemned and an inquiry committee set up under the Chairmanship of a High Court judge. Those who took the law into their own hands and indulged in violence and killing must be brought to book. But the problem of national unity is not the problem of a party. We should hold an all-party conference. Efforts must be made to remove all obstacles in the way of national unity. Go to the bottom of the problem and understand it. Then prepare the country to fight communalism whatever its hue. The whole country will listen to you. But you cannot promote the communalism of one and suppress that of the other.

A member of the Communist Party has proposed a resolution of preventing the political use of temples, *Maths,* Gurduwaras , mosques and churches. Is the Congress Party prepared to support this resolution ?

SHRI TYAGI (Dehradun) : Yes.

SHRI VAJPAYEE : Then pass this resolution. Stamp out communalism, whatever its form. We are with you. But nothing will be gained if you adopt the policy of appeasing a particular community. If there is a spark there will be conflagration. If there is action there will be reaction. We do not want this. But could we prevent the Jabalpur incident ? Our friend Shri Ashok Mehta said yesterday we could do nothing. We merely watched. We must see that such a thing does not happen again. Thank you.

Country's Future must not be Jeopardised

Sir, the Address delivered by the Vice-President in the discharge of the President's function is colourless and uninteresting. It has neither clarity nor firmness. It contains no clear direction in respect of the future. It also expresses no firm resolve regarding the fulfilment of targets. Perhaps, this is because the political situation in New Delhi is quite delicate, and this has affected the Vice-President's Address. The President is indisposed, and the Vice-President is shouldering his responsibilities. The Prime Minister is weak and there is no Deputy Prime Minister. The Ministers are fighting over who is number one, number two, three and four.

The struggle for inheritance is in full swing. Everyday new alliances are being formed. New moves are being made on the chess-board. This is having an adverse impact on the country. The people are living in despair, the administration is losing its grip, and India's international image is taking a beating. The danger from China is not yet over and the possibility of a conflict with Pakistan any moment is increasing. At such a juncture the atmosphere of political instability needs to be removed. We need a Deputy Prime Minister. The future of the country must not be jeopardised with a protracted struggle of inheritance.

The Vice-President's Address has referred to the danger facing the country, but there is no direction on how it can be overcome. The danger from China has been discussed but there are no answers to the question—what is our China policy ? How long will we be bound by the Colombo proposals ? The Colombo proposals permit us to send our armed forces up to the international border in NEFA, but so far they have not been deployed. The controversy raised in this connection by the letter of Smt. Bandaranaike has created still more doubts. Has the Government assured Smt. Bandarnaike that India would not send armed forces up to the McMahon Line ? This point should be clarified. We should also be informed when our armed forces would be sent. It is claimed that defence arrangements are in full swing and the country is being readied. The test of our preparations for the past two years would be when we send our armed forces to NEFA. We could not successfully resist the Chinese aggression when we had our forces there. The ice is melting, spring is here and there is no knowing when China may create a disturbance on the border. In such a situation it is imperative for our forces to reach upto the border in NEFA. The

Rajya Sabha on February 13, 1964 during discussion on the Motion of Thanks on the Vice President's Address

Colombo proposals also permit us to do so. Then why are we not sending in the army ?

Colombo Resolutions Ineffective

China did not accept the Colombo resolutions. How long will we wait for their acceptance ? The Government accepted the resolutions although they do not provide for China to vacate the Ladakh area and although we declared that we would not allow the aggressor to enjoy the fruits of aggression. I think it was a concession to the Colombo countries. But the Colombo countries could not persuade China to accept their resolutions. We should take back that concession. We should make it clear that we will not have any talks with China so long as Chinese forces do not vacate the Ladakh region. We should also tell the Colombo countries not to waste time in persuading China. They should support the just position of India. Recently there was a border dispute between Morocco and Tunisia. President Nasser of the United Arab Republic wanted to resolve the dispute peacefully. But his peaceful intentions did not prevent him from calling Morocco the aggressor. The Colombo countries want to resolve the India-China dispute peacefully. I can understand the sentiment of peace, but if countries believing in neutrality remain silent on the question of aggression the moral strength of neutrality would be lost and neutrality would become a form of opportunism.

Hindus being Driven out of East Pakistan

The attention of the whole country and of the House is focused on the Hindus coming from East Pakistan. Apart from saying that they will be resettled the President's Address does not indicate any policy in this regard. At the time of Partition we had assured the Hindus of East Pakistan that we shall never be apathetic to the protection of their life, property and honour. The time has come to live up to that assurance. Dr. Shyama Prasad Mukerji had resigned from the Central Cabinet when there were riots in East Pakistan in 1950 and had prophesied that the Nehru-Liaqat Pact would not be able to protect the Hindus. His prophecy has come true. But today there is no Minister from West Bengal in the Central Cabinet who would kick his chair and force the Government to change its policy. There is also no Central Minister like Sardar Patel who would say if Pakistan cannot protect the Hindus in its eastern part it will have to part with territory to resettle them. Prime Minister Nehru had also declared at that time that if Pakistan did not listen other methods would be adopted. Today the Prime Minister is not in a position to make such a declaration, but what will happen to the Hindus of East Pakistan ?

There are no options open to them except to die or leave their religion or come over as refugees and take refuge in the lap of Bharat Mata. But even the doors are not open to them—they are given certificates of entry for only two days in a week. Our office in Rajshahi has been closed down. Will intending refugees now go to Dhaka for migration certificates ? Who will look after their security ? There are no arrangements for the safety of those who want to come over to India. They are being shot at. Last night I received a telegram from Tripura. With your permission I would like to read it —

> "One lakh refugees crossed in continuous influx of thousands daily. On sixth evening just on the borders Pakistani police fired on four thousand fleeing refugees from three sides. Hundreds shot dead. Many injured in hospitals. Thousands in Pakistan are stranded and being tortured."

Under the Nehru-Liaqat agreement it was provided that they would be safely escorted to India. If the Pakistanis are not ready to abide by that agreement we should be ready to send our armed forces to escort those Hindus who want to come over to India. We cannot leave them to die in Pakistan.

It is not right on the part of Shri T.T. Krishnamachari to say we have only a moral responsibility towards them, not a constitutional and legal one. We are bound by the assurances we gave them. They are political and historic assurances. The partition of the country was done on the basis that justice would be done to the minorities in both countries. We have abided by that assurances. Pakistan has not. In a way the whole basis of establishing Pakistan has been set at naught.

Give Refuge to Refugees Generously

We gave refuge to Parsis who came to our land with the sacred fire. Refugees from Tibet are living in this country. Is there not even that much humanity in our hearts for the Hindus of East Pakistan ? What are we doing for them ? It is said, what can we do ? The first thing we can do is to allow in whoever wants to come and arrange for settling him. Even today the old refugees are lying on the streets of Sealdah. Even they could not be resettled. If necessary the Finance Minister may include a rehabilitation levy in the new budget. No one in the country would hesitate to contribute something for the rehabilitation of these unfortunate brethren.

The administration's attitude in this matter must change. A serious cause for concern is that the riots in East Pakistan had a reaction in Calcutta. There were disturbances in Calcutta too. They should not have taken place. We should not follow in the footsteps of Pakistan. But if the Calcutta police and Pakistani elements had shown some restraint bloodshed in Calcutta could have been avoided. The riots in Calcutta started with a procession of students. It was a peaceful procession and at first did not cause any harm in the city. But it was attacked with soda water bottles. Three students were stabbed and the police entered the Deenbandhu Andrews College and shot a student dead. After this the conflagration of rioting started.

Warn Pakistan

An inquiry should be made into how much of a land Pakistani elements had in the disturbances in Calcutta. Is it true that before the riots in Calcutta began various rumours had been spread ? Is it true that Pakistani elements had taken out advance insurance of their houses and properties ? Is it true that when some Muslims were being moved in a truck from riot affected areas a bomb was thrown from it and another exploded in front of the Praja Socialist Party Office ? Later when the police searched the truck no bombs were found. But when the truck went ahead a fire broke out in it. How did all this happen ? These facts confuse the people. It is vital to remove this confusion. The Central Government should conduct an inquiry. It would be against the truth to allow the impression regarding the riots in Calcutta that whatever was done by the Hindus and nothing was done by elements in league with Pakistan. This would amount to getting entangled in the Pakistani game of discrediting India in the eyes of the world. What happened in Calcutta is disgraceful. Every citizen of the country should have security of life and honour. But one thing we must understand clearly—if we cannot accept the responsibility of protecting Hindus in East Pakistan it would be very difficult to maintain communal peace in India. After all the people are human beings and they have hearts. There were people in the Calcutta Police whose families had been killed in East Pakistan. How can we expect them to discharge their duty firmly ? Still we have to triumph over human frailties. We suppressed the disturbances in Calcutta with firmness, now we must show the same firmness in taking steps against Pakistan.

We have done nothing to educate and mobilise world opinion on this problem. In order to cover up the events in East Pakistan, Pakistan raised the Kashmir problem in the U.N. We have not drawn the attention of any world body to the genocide of Hindus that is going on in East Pakistan.

Let Leaders Go to East Pakistan

We know the number of Pakistanis who are living in India. Why can't we ask them to leave ? Pakistanis are illegally infiltrating and have infiltrated into Assam. We have hesitated to drive them out because that would cause riots in East Pakistan. As it is, there are already riots in East Pakistan. Still we are dragging our feet in driving out Pakistanis from Assam. There are 8 to 10 lakh Pakistanis living in Assam. Their number in West Bengal is 4 lakhs. According to the census of 1961 there are 50 lakhs Pakistanis living all over the country. They could be asked to leave. In the case of those who are Indian citizens there should be no discrimination on religious grounds. But Pakistanis must not be allowed to enjoy the citizenship of two countries. Diplomatic and economic pressure would be brought to bear on Pakistan. We should shut down Pakistani's office in Shillong. We should break the Berubari agreement. Pakistan should be told that if they do not do justice to the Hindus in Pakistan India will take whatever steps are in its interest.

On an unofficial level I would like to say that some of our leaders should go to East Pakistan. The trouble is, this government can neither talk the way Sardar Patel did nor can follow in the footsteps of Gandhiji. Why do the preachers of peace and non-violence not go to Dhaka and Khulna and see the condition of the Hindus there with their own eyes ? Prof. Humanyun Kabir could go. General Shah Nawaz Khan could go, Shri Fakhruddin Ahmed could go and say to the Muslims of East Pakistan—if you do not do justice by Hindus living in Pakistan how can we do justice for Muslims in India ?

But those swearing by Gandhiji are not willing to follow in the steps of Gandhiji. What is the condition of women in East Pakistan ? Why does Dr. Sushila Nayar not go there, why not Governor Padmaja Naidu ? Smt. Indira Gandhi could spare a little time to go there ?

SHRI JOSEPH MATHAINI (Kerala) : Why don't you go too ?

SHRI VAJPAYEE : I am ready to go if anybody is ready to come. But our General Secretary has been externed from West Bengal. Who will allow entry into East Pakistan ? Let us try for this on an unofficial level and seriously try to resolve this problem.

Trouble in Kashmir

Sir, the riots in East Pakistan were linked with Kashmir. New Delhi is doing justice by the people of Kashmir. After long years a call was unitedly given in Kashmir for intervention by the Central Government. Not doing so would be doing an injustice by the people of Kashmir. The present administration in Kashmir has lost the people's trust. This is the time for Central intervention. We sent government officers there, of whom we wanted one to be Joint Secretary to the Jammu-Kashmir Government and the other Information Director. But when they reached Srinagar they were told not to touch any paper. They packed up and returned. It is not just a question of sending some officers there. The shaken trust of the people of Jammu and Kashmir will have to be re-established, and for this stern steps are called for. I welcome Shri Tariq's suggestion that a study team of members of Parliament should visit Jammu and Kashmir. Parliament should also set up a special committee to inquire into how the funds given to Jammu and Kashmir so far by way of loans and grants have been utilised. The P.A.C. and the Estimates Committee cannot do this. There should be a special parliamentary committee for this.

The people of India have been shocked by the speech the British representative made in the Security Council. Their present attitude has deeply affected the strong friendly relationship that had been established when Britain extended military assistance at the time of the Chinese aggression. Pakistan and India are both members of the Commonwealth and Britain is its head. Britain should remain neutral in a quarrel between two members of the Commonwealth. They do not even call Pakistan the aggressor. They refuse to accept the changed circumstances. They do not even want to blame Pakistan for the riots in East Pakistan. The British representative has done great harm to Indo-British relationships. If this attitude continues a demand will rise in India for breaking off with the Commonwealth. For us Kashmir is not a pawn on the political chessboard. It is also not a part of the cold war for us. It seems that the present British Government has not yet been able to dissociate itself from the imperial 'divide and rule' policy. The people of India are waiting to see what the U.S. representative says in the Security Council.

One Day India-Pakistan may Come Together

We do not want to keep quarrelling with Pakistan. No party in the country wants a war with Pakistan. Shri Deoki Nandan Narain is not here. But he mentioned Shri Golwalkar by name and said he talks of *Akhand Bharat*. It is not an offence to talk of *Akhand Bharat*. I dream that one day India and Pakistan would come together. If there can be a dream of a united Germany, a united Korea, a united Vietnam why can't there be a dream of a united India ? But it cannot be fulfilled by force. The army will not bring it about. It cannot be won in a war. It can be achieved by a change of heart. This dream will come true only when the people of Pakistan want it. For that no one's speech should be presented in the House out of context. I foresee a time when India and Pakistan may come together in an elastic confederation and we would come near in respect of defence, transport and foreign relations. Today this is just a dream, but howsoever bitter the reality we cannot stop dreaming. I cannot understand how those who raise the slogan of 'Jai Jagat' can object to the dream of *Akhand Bharat*. But so long as Pakistan is separate we have a firm policy towards it. A weak policy is not called generosity. It is misconstrued. While we are embroiled in a dispute with China we do not want to escalate a dispute with Pakistan. But I feel that in the coming two-three months relations with Pakistan would worsen still further. At that time we must be alert. We must keep an eye on Pakistani elements active within the country, and we must also keep an eye on that section of the Communist Party that is pro-China and is becoming pro-Pakistan because of being pro-China.

Eradication of Corruption

Whatever has been said about the riots of Calcutta is one-sided and makes it appear as if we want to indulge in false and anti-national propaganda. We must be on guard against such propaganda.

Sir, one more thing and I will conclude. The Home Minister has just declared—and it was also discussed during Question Hour—that corruption would be eradicated within two years. I do not know which astrologer was consulted or what almanac seen for fixing this period of two years. Why cannot it be a year and a half ? Why not three years ? Corruption needs to be eradicated, but the melodramatic steps now being taken will not do it. In Delhi we saw drama. Pledges were given. Harijans and sweepers were collected in the Ramlila grounds, the Prime Minister was taken there and the Harijans were made to vow that they would not take bribes. How much of a bribe do they take ? And are bribes taken because those who take them have not taken a vow ? Will they not take bribes after taking a vow ?

Why the Corrupt Have No Fear

There was recently an incident in Delhi. A certain contractor began to give bribes for getting some underhand work done. The officer who had taken the bribe said he could not take it because he had taken a pledge. After some time he said his wife had not taken any such pledge. Does that mean wives would be administered oaths along with their husbands ? Will the pledge be given while tying the marriage knot ? But even if wives take the oath the children would remain. Then bribes would be taken in their name. I have one more doubt—so long as people had not taken a pledge a couple of rupees were enough for getting something done. Now no one would oblige for a couple of rupees, for if they are offered only that much they will say we have taken an oath. Why would they break an oath for a couple of rupees ? They could break it for fifty or a hundred rupees. Thus along with the bribe the job will be paid for and it would become an expensive proposition for the bribe-giver. Clearly this is not the way to end corruption. If corruption is to be ended a model of clear behaviour should be presented from the top. Lord Krishna said in the Gita that small people follow the behaviour of the big people. No one says there is no corruption at the ministerial level. How will it be inquired into ? The Chief Minister of Andhra is going to resign, but the Chief Minister of Punjab sticks on. Should the Supreme Court verdict be honoured only in Andhra not in Punjab ? Why did the Punjab Chief Minister not resign ?

The Home Minister of Punjab has charged the opposition with conspiring with foreign forces. When I threatened in the House that I would go on a hunger strike if this charge was not proved he changed and said he did not say so. If he had not said so he could have refuted the report the next day. Once the charge is levelled, it should be proved, and if it is not proved at least it should be refuted and the matter closed. But the Home Minister of Punjab could not do even this.

Inquiry into Corruption Charges

The facts coming to light before the Das Commission are quite serious. I do not want to discuss them as an inquiry is going on. If the Congress Party shelters the corrupt the vigilance commission's declarations cannot end corruption. The need of the hour is an open inquiry into charges of corruption and in the interim those who are charged should resign. If proved innocent they can return to their posts with honour and dignity. But if eradication of corruption means to catch small fry when big crocodiles go free, the people cannot believe it.

The people of Delhi and of the country are waiting for the outcome of the inquiry being conducted against a cooperative store in Delhi that had indulged in profiteering in Gur and whose manager is a big Congress leader. What action will be taken against it ? This matter is before everybody. This is a test for the Home Ministry. It can take stringent action. Eradication of corruption is not a party issue, and with the cooperation of the people we can cleanse our public life as well as our administration. The beginning of this should be at the Centre, in New Delhi. But New Delhi does not seem to be in a position to take new and firm steps. This must change. Thank you.

The Rightful Place for Hindi

Madam, I regret members of my party could not remain present during the President's Address. We wished that after January 26, 1965 the President would not deliver his address in English. Had he felt some difficulty in speaking in Telugu—and I do not agree with the argument that the Constitution prevents him from speaking in Telugu—he could have asked the Vice-President to read out his speech. This would have also saved the President the trouble caused by weak eyesight. If the Address is to be read by the Vice-President there should be no objection to the text in Hindi to be read first. But let not our absence be misconstrued as disrespect for the President. The President's personality is such that all citizens, whatever their party or class, have respect for him. We wish the operation on his eyes is successful and he regains good health for guiding us.

A high-level judicial inquiry should be instituted into the disturbances that took place in Madras in the name of language. A Congress member has also demanded this, and I think my friend Shri Annadurai would also agree that an inquiry should be made into the source of the inspiration, planning and preparation behind the disturbances. I can understand high passions and we should think about allaying them. But some incidents that took place during these disturbances cannot be called the result of passions alone. The Aurobindo Ashram in Pondicherry was attacked. The windows of the room in which Yogi Aurobindo did penance for 25 years were smashed. Women and children were ill-treated. What was the reason for this attack ? The Aurobindo Ashram is not a government institution. It is also not a symbol of the Hindi language in Pondicherry. Still it was attacked, and the inmates have charged that police and government officers did not take adequate preventive measures although they knew something like this was going to happen. A call had been given for a general strike from the 12th, but the police was nowhere to be seen on the 11th, and the miscreants attacked the Ashram that night. An inquiry should be made into why security arrangements of the police were not adequate.

Opponents of Aurobindo Ashram

Mataji says there are four elements opposed to Aurobindo Ashram. One is the militant Catholics. She did not include all Catholics. She says there are some militant Catholics who are not prepared to tolerate the Aurobindo Ashram. The other is the Communists, who cannot bear to look at the Ashram. But it is to the credit of Mataji that among the Communists she did

Rajya Sabha on March 9, 1965 during discussion on the Motion of Thanks on the President's Address

not distinguish between the Right and the Left, as the Government does. And—my friend Shri Annadurai will pardon me—Mataji has also named the D.M.K. who, she said, "cannot tolerate the presence on their soil of people coming from the north." The fourth is the status-quo-ists, who do not want any change. All these together made the attack.

There were also other incidents during the disturbances. Gandhiji's statues were smashed, the National Flag was insulted, and Dr. Radhakrishnan's library of books in English was torched. Such tendencies are dangerous for the country. If there are any misconceptions in the south on the question of language, any doubts in the minds of the people, the Government should certainly take steps to remove them, and we shall support any proper steps of the administration, but compromising with the miscreants, with those who indulge in violence and murder and those who challenge authority would not lead to anything good.

Multilingual Centre

Madam, Shri Annadurai has suggested that we should have a multilingual centre. Administration should be conducted in 14 languages. I am not against this suggestion, but I fail to understand why he wants to postpone the date of doing so and why he wants to retain English. It should be agreed on all hands that all regional languages are national languages. All Indian languages are our languages, our own languages. They reflect our soul, they are the means of our self-expression. Among them there is no difference of big and small. Many languages not mentioned in the Constitution are also our languages. I have been advocating Sindhi in this House. A bill of mine about it is before the House. But are not all our languages yet developed ? If administration in Bengal can be carried on in Bangla, in Kerala in Malayalam, in Andhra in Telugu, in Karnataka in Kannada why cannot administration of the Centre be carried on in all the fourteen languages ? Is the love Shri Annadurai has expressed for the languages meant for retaining English ? If work is done in languages there will be practical difficulties and we should overcome them, but I cannot understand why English should be advocated for that.

Shri Annadurai is proud of Tamil. I respect his pride. But he should not forget that we too are proud of Hindi. We did not raise slogans of 'Tamil murdabad' in Delhi, but there were slogans of 'Hindi murdabad' in Madras. How has Hindi harmed Madras ? The people of Madras may be against this Government, but the people of Madras should not oppose Hindi. How would my friend Shri Annadurai feel if I raise the cry of 'Tamil murdabad' in Delhi ? But he raised the cry of 'Hindi murdabad'. Hindi was insulted, and he wants that passions should not run high. If we have to respect all languages, they also include Hindi, not only Tamil. Tamil is a rich language, but I am not prepared to accept even for a single moment that Hindi is not a rich language.

The High Court of Madhya Bharat was conducting its business in Hindi before the Constitution came into being in 1950. In Jaipur, Udaipur Hindi was the language of the Court. Hindi can express all sentiments. But can a language be developed without using it ? Can anyone be taught to swim without his entering the water ? English is rich today because administration, education, the business of the court of law, cultural influences—all these have gone on in it for centuries. And if our languages are somewhat less developed than English it is because they were not given the opportunity to develop as compared to English. Once English is removed our languages will develop. Language is first established and then used. If Israel can exhume Hebrew from the grave, carry on administration in it, conduct new scientific research in it, there is no reason why we cannot develop our fourteen languages and make this democracy truly the government of the people.

Listen to Goa's Voice

Madam, the Government has fallen into the habit of avoiding problems, keeping them hanging, making them complicated, and then trying to resolve them. The Government must give up this habit. This is a dangerous situation and it shows the weakness of the leadership. Take the question of Goa. General elections were held there and the people of Goa voted in favour of joining Maharashtra. The Legislative Assembly of Goa passed the resolution but the Central Government is proving a hindrance. Goa is an example of how problems get complicated. I warn that if the decision to merge Goa with Maharashtra is not taken within three months there will be a conflict between the Catholics and non-Catholics there. The seeds of such a conflict are being sown, and they are being nurtured for party interests. Under no circumstances can such a policy be supported. Whatever needs to be done the Government should do without delay, so that problems do not get complicated further.

Madam, today's newspapers have discussed Orissa. The C.B.I. report has been published and the recommendations of the Cabinet Sub-committee are also known. When, with reference to them, we look at the Prime Minister's statement in this regard we feel the whole Orissa affair is being whitewashed. The Cabinet sub-committee held ministers Shri Biren Mitra and Shri Patnaik guilty of 'impropriety'—if Shri Annadurai will permit the use of an English term—but ruled that a judicial inquiry was not necessary, nor an inquiry commission, and that the matter should be closed. On what basis, on what principles, was this done ? Once you accept that Shri Biren Mitra and Shri Patnaik were guilty of impropriety you have in a way accepted that a primary case against them exists. There is some truth in the case against them. In the final analysis it was not possible for the Cabinet Sub-committee to determine the intention behind the promulgation of the circular, of the directive, that caused a profit of lakhs of rupees to Smt. Mitra and an equal loss to the Government treasury. Only the court could decide this. An inquiry commission should be set up and the whole matter be entrusted to it.

Shri Patnaik has challenged the verdict of the Sub-committee. He says the impropriety in the eyes of the Sub-committee is not an impropriety in our eyes. Whatever he did he did for the good of the people and he did not misuse his office. The Central Government should accept this challenge. Incidentally, all members of this Committee are Congressmen and the allegation can be levelled against them that with a view to serving the interests of the party they let off Shri Biren Mitra and Shri Patnaik cheaply with just resignations.

SHRI BHUPESH GUPTA : Deputy Chairman, even the Prime Minister gave an assurance that a Cabinet Minister should be present in the House. They have got to be here because....

DEPUTY CHAIRMAN : Yes, the Prime Minister himself had said yesterday that someone from the Cabinet should be present here all the time. Mr. Singh is here of course but he himself said that somebody from the Cabinet should be here. It would be conveyed to the Government.

SHRI LOKNATH MISRA : That, Madam, is the way the Government is functioning.

SHRI BHUPESH GUPTA : Why not adjourn ? Some of them are having tea in the Central Hall. Why not we also do that ?

DEPUTY CHAIRMAN : Mr. Vajpayee will continue.

SHRI VAJPAYEE : Madam, I am happy that you would like to listen to me, but some Minister should also be here.

SHRI T.N. SINGH, Minister for Industry : I am listening. I am listening to your speech quite attentively.

SHRI VAJPAYEE : Your attention is welcome, but it won't express itself in a reply. Those who have to reply should be present.

Corruption Not Family Issue

As I was saying, the verdict of the Cabinet Sub-committee cannot satisfy the people. Corruption is not a family issue of the Congress party. If high standards are to be set in public life, Ministers should not only be beyond suspicion, they must also seem to be beyond suspicion. The other day the Prime Minister asked—what would be achieved even if we set up an inquiry commission ? The late Sardar Partap Singh Kairon had to resign—what more can we do ? But Sardar Partap Singh Kairon resigned when he was tarnished with corruption. Shri Biren Mitra and Shri Patnaik are challenging the verdicts of the Cabinet Sub-committee, and they are also getting a good conduct certificate from Shri Atulya Ghosh. Those who left office under a charge of corruption should also get the opportunity to prove their innocence. In my opinion by not appointing a judicial Committee the Cabinet Sub-committee has done an injustice not only to the country and to democracy but also to Shri Biren Mitra and Shri Patnaik. It is still not too late—let the whole matter go to an inquiry commission. The other day Shri Nanda had said even if a single member levels a charge against a Minister we are ready for an inquiry. But not only charges were levelled, even a Cabinet Sub-committee found some validity in them. So nothing less than the appointment of an inquiry commission would satisfy us.

National Defence Council Defective

Madam, now that Shri Atulya Ghosh has been mentioned by name I would like to say one thing more. Recently the National Defence Council has been reorganised, some new members have been included and Shri Atulya Ghosh is one of them. The Council does not include Shri Morarji Desai, Shri Jagjivan Ram, Acharya Kripalani. It includes Shri Atulya Ghosh.

SHRI L.N. MISHRA : That is because they are in the Syndicate.

SHRI VAJPAYEE : I am doubtful if the Council has been reorganised on the right lines. The Congress has still more representation and inclusion of such persons does not redound to the prestige of the Council. I am happy that the Prime Minister has arrived....

SHRI BHUPESH GUPTA : Now that the Prime Minister has come, I wish to invite his attention. Yesterday he was kind enough to say that in the House a Cabinet Minister should be present but today when we met in the afternoon nobody came and I pointed out....

SOME HON. MEMBERS : Mr. Chagla was there.

DEPUTY CHAIRMAN : I am told Mr. Chagla was here.

SHRI BHUPESH GUPTA : But then he went away. When he went he saw that there was none. Nobody came afterwards, Madam. Through you I would like Mr. Shastri to make his Cabinet colleagues obey him for the sake of a change.

Prime Minister Shastri's Weakness

SHRI VAJPAYEE : Madam, I would like to repeat a point that was made yesterday. It is eight months since Shastriji assumed Prime Ministership. The atmosphere of goodwill in which he assumed power is deteriorating. A feeling is taking root in the people and in the opposition parties that the Prime Minister is not as firm with senior members of his Cabinet and his party as he should be. I am terrified about what would happen to the country if this feeling spreads. There was a storm in Madras. But if members of the ruling party do not face that storm firmly no compromise on the question of language would preserve the country's unity. Whether we like it or not, today the Congress has the responsibility of making or marring India. Not for a moment should the Prime Minister think that he cannot have his way because he has been educated at Kashi Vidyapeeth, not at Oxford. Not for a moment should he think that because physically he is small in structure and not tall like a palm tree he....

SHRI BHUPESH GUPTA : Mr. Atulya Ghosh did not enter any university.

SHRI VAJPAYEE : He cannot speak out firmly. He is being blamed for his silence in the language controversy, but I would not do so. Listening to all parties and solving the problem with a peaceful mind is not a bad thing. But it is very dangerous to allow the feeling to be spread that the future of India is in the hands of the Chief Ministers; they would decide it or a couple of members of the Congress Party known as the Syndicate—I don't know why—would decide it. Let us overcome this crisis, preserve the unity and integrity of the country, and forge ahead on the path of economic progress. But if New Delhi's authority becomes weak and the Chief Ministers take it upon themselves to make all decisions it would be difficult to maintain unity. Today all Chief Ministers belong to the Congress—what would happen when Chief Ministers of other parties come to power ? In the final analysis the

Central Government, the Parliament, would have to take decisions. There is no objection to consulting the Chief Ministers, because every policy will be implemented through them. But it must be firmly made clear that whatever the decisions have to be taken they would be taken by New Delhi. Of course, they will be taken in consultation with all, but whatever the decisions they would be implemented firmly. The minority should be taken along, but the majority cannot be given the power of veto. No province, no class can be given the veto for any problem. We must always bear in mind this key to democracy.

The Colombo Resolutions

Madam, China did not accept the Colombo resolutions and is repeating its claim on 90,000 sq. km. of Indian territory. In such a situation what is the point in being bound by the Colombo resolutions ? The Government can announce that because communist China has not accepted the Colombo resolutions we would not talk to them so long as they do not vacate all our territory. The Colombo resolutions were a convenience and Colombo powers still say that it is not proper that we should accept these resolutions and China should remain obdurate. The Government of India should be firm in this matter and say that we would not allow the aggressor to enjoy the fruits of aggression. We will not have any more talks with China so long as it does not vacate all our territory. Such a step should be taken by the Government. Thank you.

Sovereignty not Negotiable

Madam, this morning the Communist Party leader Shri Bhupesh Gupta, who unfortunately for me is not present in the House, made the suggestion that we should accept the partition of Kashmir on the cease-fire line. I stand to oppose it. In my view it is a very dangerous suggestion, which would strengthen the hands of the aggressor, make our sovereignty negotiable, and weaken India's right over the rest of Kashmir. Shri Bhupesh Gupta said that in 1956 the late Pandit Nehru had made a similar suggestion to Pakistan, but he did not say what Pakistan's reaction to it was. Pakistan had not accepted it. Pandit Nehru had then withdrawn it and stated in Parliament that the suggestion was no longer open from the Indian side.

I am surprised that there should be this sort of talk even after signing the Tashkent Declaration. The Tashkent Declaration does not prevent us from telling Pakistan to vacate that part of Jammu-Kashmir which it occupies. In fact we should have emphasised this. Had we so emphasised Pakistan would not have dared to lay claim to the rest of Kashmir. But we are such players of the political game that we lay all our cards on the table in advance, so that our opponents can take advantage of them and continue with their demands. What right after all, does Pakistan have on that part of Jammu and Kashmir which is under its occupation except that it has been occupied by force ? Even if we surrender that part for the sake of peace we are not going to get peace. Pakistan has designs on the whole of Jammu and Kashmir, and especially on the Kashmir Valley. Such suggestions would weaken our position and provide Pakistan a means of propaganda against us.

Shri Bhupesh Gupta said a natural corollary of the Tashkent Declaration is that we give one-third of Kashmir to Pakistan and a natural corollary of giving one-third of Kashmir to Pakistan is to give Aksai Chin to China. He did not say so, but he certainly had that in mind. I cannot but praise the loyalty of Marxist Communists who are openly saying that we should make a compromise with China by giving them Aksai Chin.

Surrender before aggression is not the way to end aggression. If we leave territory which is ours by right and by law because somebody has forcibly occupied it we would not be able to preserve the nation's integrity and sovereignty.

National Interest Ignored at Tashkent

Madam, I am surprised to see that our leaders did not suggest at Tashkent that we would withdraw from Haji Pir, Kargil and Tithwal but Pakistan

Rajya Sabha on March 1, 1966 during discussion on the Motion of Thanks on the President's Address

would not enter these areas and they should be declared a demilitarised zone. But it seems we did not care for national interests at Tashkent. And now that declaration is giving strength to people who want a compromise with China and Pakistan at any cost. We should beware of such suggestions.

The Bharatiya Jana Sangh's stand is clear on this issue. We have been opposing the handing over of one-third Jammu and Kashmir to Pakistan and we shall continue to do so. Under no circumstances are we prepared to give up our sovereignty. If anyone does so we shall forcefully resist him.

Madam, the leader of the Communist Party has expressed himself in Vietnam. I would say most respectfully but firmly that in respect of the situation in Vietnam the Government of India should not utter a single word, take a single step that would strengthen Communist Party. We cannot approve of what is happening there. But in international politics sometimes we have to keep mum. We should study the cult of silence.

We have to be very careful about expressing our opinion on questions that directly affect our interests and on a situation that could go against us in the long run. I am not satisfied with the Government's policy on Rhodesia and we should put pressure on Britain to use force there. African countries look to us for an initiative. We are a member of the Commonwealth and we also claim to be a leader of it. On the matter of Rhodesia let us not make the mistake of keeping silent. We should speak on it. It would be in our interest to pressurise Britain into using force.

Allegations against Jayanti Shipping

Madam, serious allegations are being made against Jayanti Shipping Company. The former Managing Director of the Company had presented a 24-page memorandum to the late Prime Minister. The memorandum had demanded that all matters relating to Jayanti Shipping Company should be handed over to the C.B.I. for an inquiry. However, the Government has not taken any action as yet. The Company has a paid-up capital of two crores of rupees but a debt of two and a half crores. I would not mention the circumstances under which the Company was given the loan. The Government went out of its way to give it, but the Company did not put it to proper use. The Company was even reluctant to give ships to India. The Company has been making its ships available for carrying foreign goods for the sake of earning foreign exchange. A high-level inquiry into the affairs of the Company is called for. According to today's press reports more directors of the Company are also resigning.

The Government cannot be casual about such a big company. A constructive suggestion would be for the Shipping Corporation to take over Jayanti Shipping Company and ply its ships for the good of the country.

Controversy over Name of Banaras Hindu University

Madam, the Education Minister has left. I would like to ask him—how long will the Banaras Hindu University run on an ordinance ? It should be given autonomy and a law should be made for it. If there is a difference of opinion in respect of removing the word 'Hindu' from the name the Government should respect the majority and give up the proposal to delete the word 'Hindu'. But that does not mean an ordinance should remain in force there for all time to come. The budget of the Hindu University is bigger than the budget of Nepal. The management of the university has a lot of power which is not being put to proper use. In my opinion the government should bring a Bill so that the ordinance could be replaced by a law.

Partial Radio

I would also like to say something to the Information Minister. He too has left. I would like to give an example of how All India Radio functions. Just now he was talking big about his department and claiming that P.I.B. does justice to all parties. I am under the impression that A.I.R. also comes within this. When the other day Shri Savarkar died All India Radio did not lead the news with it. The Prime Minister keeps giving speeches day in and day out and the All India Radio keeps repeating them every day. That day the lead item was the Prime Minister's speech and the news of Savarkar's death followed. A.I.R. did not even say it was sorry to report Savarkar's death. Does not the Radio have simple manners or a little etiquette ? There can be a difference of opinion about Savarkar's thoughts but his sacrifice for the country is simply incomparable. The Government should be alert to see that All India Radio does not make such a mistake again. Thank you.

Not Dynamism but Beginning of Anarchy

Sir, I am happy to see that Shri Hanumanthaiya is present in the House. Yesterday he had called the President's Address extra-ordinary. I fail to understand why he called it so. But one thing is clear : by calling this Address by the President extraordinary Shri Hanumanthaiya has admitted that all previous addresses were quite ordinary.

It is the same President, it is the same government that drafts the President's Address, and it is the same Prime Minister. Then how was this Address extraordinary ? One reason I see is that this Address was delivered after the division in the ruling party. Does this mean the ruling party will have to split again for another extraordinary Address by the President ?

The truth of the matter is that the President's Address is unrealistic. It presents an incomplete, unrealistic, one-sided and somewhat distorted picture of the situation in the country. The Address makes it appear as if the country is a garden in bloom. But the situation is just the opposite.

The President says the country has become dynamic. He also said that a lot of strength and vitality have been created among the people, and rapid changes are taking place in their thinking, inclinations and attitudes. But what the President calls dynamism is just the beginning of anarchy. We have seen in Punjab and Haryana what sort of strength the people have acquired. On the auspicious occasion of Republic Day the National Flag was insulted in Punjab and Gurdwaras damaged and defiled in Haryana. Ask Chaudhary Randhir Singh who is not present in the House, what strength has been produced in the people—his house was demolished.

Is what is happening in West Bengal an index of the people's strength and enthusiasm ? Political murders, insult of womenfolk, disclaim of the judiciary, apathy of police, gherao of the Vice-Chancellors, attacks on railway stations, rowdyism of students—if these are the signs of *Josh* (enthusiasm) the country does not need *josh*, it needs good sense (*hosh*).

In a speech at Calcutta the Prime Minister had said, "Frustration leads to progress." This is a new principle. If frustration leads to progress more and more progress would need more and more people getting frustrated.

The President's Address reflects this new principle of the Prime Minister. The Address said the changes currently taking place in the country are taking place within the democratic structure. Democracy is not only a structure, it is a feeling, a life-breath. Can any one deny that during the past 7-8 months democracy has been weakened ? Democracy does not mean a government

Lok Sabha on February 26, 1970 during discussion on the Motion of Thanks on President's Address

somehow formed out of a motley crowd. Democracy is a way of thinking, acting, behaving—a way of life. Limitations and traditions are the basis of democracy. Today those limitations are breaking down, those traditions ridiculed, absence of discipline is in fashion, unbridled behaviour is being commended, betrayal is worshipped and the purity of means has gone with the wind in the struggle for power.

Not long ago in Uttar Pradesh legislators were purchased for fifty thousand rupees a piece. I do not have to say who made the bids. A word is enough for the wise, and the Prime Minister and her supporters are quite wise.

After the Supreme Court's historic verdict in the matter of the nationalisation of banks a systematic campaign was launched to make the judiciary fall in the people's esteem. Such an attempt cannot strengthen democracy. As in other matters this campaign too was led by the Prime Minister. I quote what Smt. Indira Gandhi said in Indore : "It shows what obstacles are placed in the way of those who want to bring about any change and do something new."

In short she meant that the Supreme Court is an impediment in the path of progress. What is progress and what is not is for the Parliament to decide. But it is for the Supreme Court to decide whether the steps taken in the name of progress are constitutional or not. The decisions of the Supreme Court cannot impede progress. If we want to save ourselves from such verdicts we will have to be more careful while making laws. But blaming the Supreme Court for our own haste cannot redound to the prestige of the judiciary.

Denigrating Judiciary

Once the Prime Minister launched a campaign against the judiciary how could Shri Khadilkar lag behind ? I quote what he said : "Such judgments do not enhance the prestige of the judiciary". Like Sancho Panza tilting at windmills Shri Khadilkar said : "Such judgements will be treated with more and more respect by ordinary people."

Should a Minister of State make such a speech ? Is this not an attempt to denigrate the judiciary ? If people who are considered responsible make such irresponsible speeches how can the common people be kept under control ?

I quote what a so-called leader of bank employees in Uttar Pradesh said : "We shall not guarantee peace in the bank industry until the entire banking industry was declared under the public sector."

I have no complaint if elements not believing in democracy or wanting to undermine the Constitution from within are involved in the efforts to denigrate the judiciary. But when the Prime Minister and her supporters try to topple the judiciary doubts naturally arise about the future of democracy.

But this is not the first time that the Prime Minister has expressed unnecessary impatience with democratic processes. At first she was talking of the services being committed. What does it mean ? Should there be no dividing line between the party and the government ? Does the Prime Minister want to cross that *Laxman Rekha*? If she does, the Sita of democracy cannot be protected. Do the services being committed mean that the bureaucracy should take leave of its conscience and its intelligence and simply agree with whatever the Prime Minister says ?

It is true that the bureaucracy will have to faithfully carry out the decisions of the Parliament. But so long as the decisions are not taken will the officials not be free to express their honest and independent opinion ? But an atmosphere is being created in the country in which it is a crime to express a difference of opinion. This is not the way to strengthen democracy.

One of the bases of democracy is the freedom of the press. The Prime Minister does not like this freedom. During the Bombay session of the Congress she summoned some editors and correspondents and complained that the session was not given due publicity. She said : I can call your proprietors and bring you to your senses in a matter of minutes. Sir, the press of no other democratic country devotes so much to the speeches and pictures of the Prime Minister as that of India. Still the Prime Minister is not satisfied. Perhaps she wants it to be -*"Ekoham dwitiyo nasti"*—'I am the only one, there is none other'. Such a feeling leads to dictatorship. Let the Prime Minister beware of it.

Right to Property

Sir, I admit that the Supreme Court's decision apropos the banks has created a new and delicate situation. We must consider it seriously. If we decide to take over some property or some industry in public interest and pay for it the compensation as directed by the Supreme Court the very purpose of the takeover would be defeated. When we abolished Zamindari in Uttar Pradesh my party said assistance to landlords should cover only their resettlement. They were also issued cards. But the Supreme Court brought us back to the situation of 1964... (*Interruption*).

SHRI SHASHI BHUSHAN (Khargon) : 1946.

SHRI VAJPAYEE : Sir, we would have to find a way by which it would be financially easy to take over private property in public interest. But, I am against removing the right to property from fundamental rights for doing that. The makers of the Constitution have thoughtfully provided for fundamental rights. Removing the right to property from fundamental rights would mean leaving the common people especially those poor peasants whose lakhs of acres of land is being taken over every year for industries or urban development to the tender mercies of the powers that be. It is not a question of a handful of moneybags, it is also a question of crores of common people.

I admit that the right to property is socially oriented. It is limited by social conditions. But the points on which the framers of the Constitution made the right to property fundamental right need no basic change. It is surprising to see that in the matter of removing the right to property from fundamental rights it needs no basic change. It is surprising to see that in the matter of removing the right to property from fundamental rights members of the ruling Congress are speaking with a forked tongue. A few days ago Congress

President Shri Jagjivan Ram had said that we do not want to take away the right to property. But yesterday Smt. Savitri Shyam said this right should be removed from the Constitution. I cannot understand how this pair of Ram and Shyam can speak in different voices. I call for a referendum on this question. It is a question of a basic change in the Constitution. It will affect the people's life. Before taking any decision the people should be consulted.

AN HON. MEMBER : What is the Parliament for ?

SHRI VAJPAYEE : I shall come to that too. Sir, as it is, after the Supreme Court decision in the *Golak Nath case* fundamental rights can neither be abridged nor ended. My friend Shri Nath Pai wants to re-establish that right of Parliament by tabling a Bill. I say the Bill will not fulfil the purpose. The decision of the Supreme Court will stay so long as it does not itself change it in some matter.

It is fruitless to argue who is bigger—the Parliament or the Supreme Court. Both are big in their own fields. We are big in making laws, the Supreme Court is big in interpreting them, but the Constitution of India is bigger than both. Both have to stay within the limits of the Constitution. The Constitution is not something inanimate. It has to reflect changing circumstances. There is a provision for amending the Constitution. But Sir, there are certain things that cannot be changed with a two-thirds majority. For instance can a two-thirds majority declare the Indian republic to be a monarchy ? It cannot. Can a two-thirds majority in Parliament declare Prime Minister Indira Gandhi to be Maharani Indira Gandhi ? It cannot. A two-thirds parliamentary majority can give legal sanction to untouchability. It cannot also declare India to be a theocracy. Neither can we base the society or the polity on caste, creed or race with a two-thirds majority in Parliament. Sir, a lot can be changed, but there is now provision for changing the preamble to the Constitution. Hence before abridging or ending fundamental constitutional rights we must think very carefully.

Bank Nationalisation was not Necessary

To those gentlemen who consider the nationalisation of banks a revolutionary step I would say it is not as revolutionary as they think it is. Recently there has been partial nationalisation of banks in Malaysia. Do our friends want to follow in the footsteps of Malaysia ? Merely nationalising banks will not lead to an exploitation-less society. The government is running banks in Taiwan, Spain, France and Italy, but those countries give no indication of the social structure we want. We had opposed bank nationalisation. But that was not because we agreed with the structure and tending policies of private banks. There was scope for change in that. That change should have taken place. But nationalisation is not a must for it. The Prime Minister had herself said in the Bangalore session that either three-four banks would have to be taken over or social control laws would have to be strengthened. Her own thinking in this respect was not clear. It is a different matter that when she decided to drop Shri Morarji Desai from the Cabinet she nationalised 14 banks in order to justify his dropping.

Shri Morarji Desai later said he was thrown out like a piece of vegetable. I said to him—what else can you expect of a kitchen cabinet ? Vegetables and kitchen cabinet go together.

Sir, the banks now taken over need not be privatised. Now nationalisation has to be made a success. If nationalised banks are to be run like government departments, the people, whose hopes and aspirations have been aroused, will hold the Government to account. So far there has been no change in the lending policies of the banks.... (*Interruption*).

SHRI SHASHI BHUSHAN : The Supreme Court is too busy.

SHRI VAJPAYEE : The Supreme Court came in later. Had the State Bank wanted, it could have changed its policies in the very beginning. Fresh loans are needed for agriculture and small industries, and if nationalised banks can make them available, accelerate progress and fulfil their declared objectives, today's doubts would be largely dispelled. At the same time we cannot close our eyes to the evil effects of increasing concentration of power in the government's hands.

Sir, Bharatiya Jan Sangh is not opposed to nationalisation in principle. It can be done if it is in public interest but we do not consider it a panacea on all ills of the nation. Now the Prime Minister says nationalisation is not a magic wand that would solve all problems. Then was this magic for the benefit of the Congress ?

Indianisation not a Slogan

Sir, nationalisation is not the main problem before the country. There can be a difference of opinion on nationalisation. In England the Labour Party goes in for nationalisation and the Conservative Party ends it, but both are agreed on not weakening democracy. Even while speeding up economic and social change we must not do anything that would strike at democracy. She says its objective is democratic socialism. If, under democratic socialism, democracy is not more important than socialism it is at least as important as socialism. If democracy ends with the advent of socialism we would also lose the freedom to bring in socialism. So social and economic changes would have to be brought about in such a way that the democratic feeling does not get affected.

Sir, it is to be greatly regretted that the Prime Minister is not present in the House. These days she is very much displeased with Bharatiya Jan Sangh over its Indianisation programme. Wherever she goes she comes down heavily on us and does free publicity for us. We thank her for this. But she has either not understood Indianisation properly or she is deliberately trying to mislead people. Indianisation is not related to Muslims alone. It includes 52 crore people of the country. Indianisation is not a slogan, it is a *Mantra* of national reawakening. Nationalisation means only one thing—all citizens of India, whatever their language, religions or state, have undivided and unflinching loyalty to India. India must come first, everything else afterwards. Is there anything objectionable in this ?

Sir, in this country of 52 crore people we come across Brahmins and Harijans. Sikhs and Jains can be separately recognised, there are Muslims and Christians, there are people divided on the basis of province and language, but those loyal to the whole of India can be counted on the fingers. The Prime Minister asks very innocently—what Indianisation of those who are Indian ? So I said, what nationalisation of what belongs to the nation ? Sir, we are all human beings. But poets and philosophers tell us to be human. We are all men, but we are told to be men, not only in name and form but by heart, intelligence, *Sanskaras* and knowledge. We are all Indians, we are born in India, but we must be loyal to India. What happened in Chandigarh the other day ? What is going to happen in Belgaum ? In West Bengal Mao's mental progeny is declaring him to be President of this country and flaunting his little Red Book, having discarded the *Gita* and the *Gitanjali*. Is it not necessary to Indianise them ?

Sir, secularism cannot be strengthened in the country by promoting Muslim communalism. Secularism is not just in Congress slogan, it is a *Mantra* that has emerged from the country's culture. Could India not have been declared a Hindu State after independence ? Pakistan did it, but we did not. Why ? Because our culture does not permit it, Hindutva itself includes a number of ways of worship. We never said—believe in one book, have faith in one individual, otherwise you will go to hell. Truth is one, but the wise define it variously. God is one, but there can be many ways of attaining Him. But today secularism has come to mean anti-Hindu. Like non-alignment this government's secularism has also become suspect. This suspicion will have to be removed. I take pride in my Hindutva, but this does not mean I am anti-Muslim or have a quarrel with Islam. But communalism gets a fillip when politics is mixed with religion, when efforts are made to get into power on that basis, when you promote separatism and when you decide to attend the Rabat conference. This communalism is a double-edged sword. You cannot fan the flames of communalism on the one hand and put them out on the other. This political bargaining cannot strengthen national unity. Our country is full of variety, this variety is an index of the richness of our life, but at the root of variety lies unity. Indianisation means giving strength to this unity.

The Prime Minister should not get upset. She got angry when my friend Shri Madhok said somewhere that he wanted to Indianise the Prime Minister. She is angry if we leave her out, and she is angry, if we include her. The Prime Minister's complaint was that Indianisation was only against the Muslims. In reply Shri Madhok said it included not only Muslims but all, including the Prime Minister. On this she got angry. When Nehruji was angry he made a good speech. So at times we used to tease him. (*Interruption*). But we cannot make the mistake of teasing the Prime Minister. She gets angry on her own. I am sorry she is not present here. In a public meeting she had said she could deal with Bharatiya Jan Sangh in five minutes. Can any democratic prime minister speak like this ? Can a democratic government adopt the policy of putting us in our place with the help of the police or the army ? We are engaged in an ideological battle. Fight us on that level. If the people are against you we will be defeated. But remember, this matter of Indianisation is taking root in the people's minds. No sober person can have a difference of opinion with the comprehensive form of Indianisation that we have presented.... (*Interruption*)... But when the Prime Minister said 'I can take care of Jan Sangh in five minutes, I said in five minutes you cannot take care even of your hair, then how can you deal with us ?

In the economic field Indianisation means holding up a self-reliant India. When we were engaged in this struggle for independence we chanted the *mantra* of *Swadeshi*, but now foreign capital, foreign resources, foreign technology, foreign inspiration and foreign genius are in fashion with us. Instead of becoming self-reliant we have become dependent on others. Our dependence on Russia and America has reached dangerous proportions. We have to suffer the consequences of this even in the political field. We had to devalue the rupee under American pressure. We had to accept the Tashkent agreement under Russian pressure. We had to hand over to the enemy the territory that our Jawans had won with their blood.

Nation's Self-respect and Self-reliance

The Government must make radical changes in the Fourth Five Year Plan. All foreign aid must stop—whether it is American, Russian or from any other country. If we want foreign exchange let us buy it on the international market on our terms. If we want technology we can buy that too. Nobody is helping China. All countries have stopped aid to China. China too accepts aid from nobody. Still China is progressing. We have become so dependent on foreign aid that we have lost the strength to stand on our own feet. We shall support whatever harsh steps are necessary in the economic field if the nation's self-respect and self-reliance and the people's spirit of sacrifice are aroused. We shall demand those steps. But today this government does not have the picture of self-reliance before it.

The President's Address has no guidance in this direction. In the Fourth Five Year Plan our dependence in foreign aid does not diminish; rather, it increases. The Bharatiya Jan Sangh has placed the outline of a Swadesh Plan before the government. Prof. Subramaniam Swamy, who was for long years a professor at Harvad, has returned to India at our request and has prepared a Swadesh Plan that claims to raise the development rate by ten per cent without foreign aid. The National Development Council should consider it.

It is also necessary to review our foreign ties. For the last 22 years we have been entering into collaborations with foreign countries. The need for such collaborations is increasing, not decreasing. The auditors' report gives some indication of the situation regarding foreign collaboration in the private and public sectors. We demand a high-power commission to go into whether all these collaborations were needed, whether they were entered into on conditions beneficial to the country, and whether they have strengthened our economy and our industry. So long as we do not have the report of such a commission the tendency towards foreign collaboration should be discouraged.

It is also necessary for the government to take over all our rupee trade with Communist countries. This trade is done on government level.... (*Interruption*).

AN HON. MEMBER : All trade.

SHRI VAJPAYEE : In respect of all foreign trade we want a commission to go into the irregularities in export-import. Let the government prepare a case before nationalisation. No such case has been prepared to date in respect of bank nationalisation. The country should be acquainted with the irregularities going in the export-import trade. It should also be decided if the trade should be taken out of private hands and governmentalised. We should decide the issue of ownership. We should develop a system of maximum public ownership. Statism in place of capitalism is no solution to our difficulties. I am happy the Government has talked about developing a joint sector, in which private enterprise and government can come together. If we can decentralise ownership we could save ourselves from the bad features of a concentration of economic power.

Sir, one more thing and I shall conclude.

The Chandigarh Issue

The President has referred to a decision about Chandigarh. This issue created a very unfortunate situation, but, as others have said, the government cannot escape responsibility in this matter. This government is expert at letting matters hang. Like a snake charmer who keeps his snakes in a box this government keeps its problem hidden in a box and thinks they have ended. But when the lid is removed these problems raise their hood. I regret the decision on Chandigarh has not been taken on any principled ground. The border controversy of today should be resolved but before doing that some principle should be decided upon...(*Interruption*)....These principles have to be determined by the Government...(*Interruption*)....We go even further. We demand that border disputes should be arbitrated upon not by a commission but by a tribunal. Shri Patil says the same thing today. The Shah Commission was set up but its report was consigned to the waste paper basket. The Mahajan Commission was set up, but its report is not being implemented...(*Interruption*)....So first decide the principles.

Will the village be a unit, or a Tehsil or a district ? Along with language will geographical contiguity, administrative convenience and all such factors be taken into consideration or not ? Fazilka was given to Haryana and congratulations to Choudhary Randhir Singh for it. He went on a hunger strike, but it was for four days. Had it been longer we might perhaps have seen the result. But on the one hand a decision on Fazilka was taken, and on the other a commission was set up. If you want to set up a commission why the decision on Fazilka, and if a decision on Fazilka was taken why a commission ? Now again we would be opening a Pandora's box, again border disputes will crop up, difficulties will arise and the Commission's decision will not be accepted. So we want not a commission but a tribunal. It will function on the basis of principles and its decision would be acceptable to all. I see similar difficulties coming up on the Belgaum problem, and again the Prime Minister would apportion the cheese between two quarrelling cats. She has found a new way of solving problems, in which principles are given the go-by. She is admittedly very good at political understanding and morality, but all this is taking place at the cost of the country. I say decide the principles, we have a tribunal for river water disputes to whom the disputes are entrusted and its decisions are accepted. Similarly, we should also have a tribunal for border disputes. Then we could prevent a repetition in Belgaum of what happened in Chandigarh. I hope the government takes the proper decision in this regard.

Sir, I thank you most sincerely for allowing me so much time.

President's Eloquent Silence on State of Country

Sir, Shri Bali Ram Bhagat's speech yesterday and Dr. V.K.R.V. Rao's speech today have shown us how talent blooms and obstructed speech flows freely on quitting ministership. If freedom from ministership is so beneficial for health the Prime Minister should give some more colleagues to breathe open air and give the House their thoughts without constraints. It would have been good to hear Shri Gulzari Lal Nanda on the railways. But it seems the railway has been derailed a lot and has still to come back on the track.

Sir, on hearing the speeches of some Hon. members I felt as if this was the first general election in the country. Elections have taken place even before. Then too the people had given their verdict. Members of the ruling party should not forget that their strength in this House before 1962 was greater than their strength today. Obviously the people's verdict will have to be accepted. Those who have won are to be congratulated. But there is no doubt that if this victory goes to their head it will one day bring about their fall. Victory should lead to humility. Victory brings responsibility in its wake.

Sir, it is also clear that never before had government resources been so openly misused during election as in this election...

SHRI K.C. PANDEY (Khalilabad) : Even after losing in Maniram, T.N. Singh continued as Chief Minister. 70 jeeps were plying for him. Still he lost by 1,60,906 votes. Government resources were openly misused. Still the Hon. member is charging us with misusing resources.

SHRI VAJPAYEE : Their spokesman can reply to this. But this shows how majority can make one impatient. But if you do not have the tolerance and the grace to listen to the opposition (*Interruption*).

SHRI SHAMBHU NATH (Saidpur) : We cannot listen to lies.

SHRI VAJPAYEE : You will have to listen. Are you to decide the truth and the falsehood ?

SMT. INDIRA GANDHI, Prime Minister : I appeal to Hon. members to let Shri Vajpayee speak. I would like to tell Shri Vajpayee that we were not responsible for this rowdyism. It was the doing of other Hon. members of the previous Lok Sabha.

SHRI VAJPAYEE : But now we have a new Lok Sabha. A new era has begun. Is the Prime Minister justifying rowdyism by pointing her finger at the old Lok Sabha ?

Lok Sabha on March 31, 1971 during discussion on the Motion of Thanks on the President's Address

Sir, as I was saying, general elections have taken place in this country even before. The people had then given their verdict. But never before were government resources, propaganda machinery including All India Radio, and money power so misused as on this occasion. It is necessary to build up healthy conventions in a democracy. The ruling party has a brute majority. It has the responsibility of setting conventions in which All India Radio and TV would not become the means of propaganda for any one party. Such a recommendation had also been made by the Chanda Committee, but it was not implemented. Today it needs to be reconsidered in all seriousness.

The Constitution charges the Election Commission with ensuring free and fair elections. But no one can deny that this time's voters' lists were faulty. Not that this has only harmed us. At places it has also harmed the ruling party. It is not a question of benefit for any particular party. For an election it is necessary to have correct voters' lists. They should include all eligible persons, who should have the opportunity to exercise their franchise.

Three-member Election Commission

The counting procedure was changed at the eleventh hour. The Election Commission did not consult anyone in this matter. I was told that not even the ruling party was consulted. It is not a question of the ruling party and the opposition. If the procedure of counting votes is to be changed all parties should be taken into confidence. The Election Commission had assured us that it would hold an all-party meeting in which it would invite suggestions about changing this procedure, but such a meeting could not be held. We demand that a single individual should not be the election commissioner. The framers of the Constitution had intended that there should be a three-member election commission. Elections are a big job. Conducting elections all over the country is a heavy responsibility. It is not within the capacity of one individual. Hence it is necessary to appoint a three-member election commission so that the irregularities that took place during this election do not repeat themselves in future.

The *Garibi Hatao* Slogan

It is easy to win elections by raising the slogan of 'quit poverty', but slogans do not remove poverty... (*Interruption*).

Am I to understand that the governments so far in office—and they were United Congress governments—did not want to remove poverty ? Is the removal of poverty some new discovery ? I can understand it if the ruling party says that our efforts for 23 years to remove poverty have failed and if they give the assurance that they would sincerely strike it in future. But completely disowning the history of 23 years of activities does not redound to the credit of the United Congress. Both the President's Address and the Finance Minister's speech are before us, and we can consider not only the professions but also the method of their implementation. We hope that the Finance Minister's budget speech would indicate the policy and programme of the government for a concrete solution of the problems raised by the President in his Address.

We are told poverty should be removed. There would hardly be a party that would want to preserve poverty. But the first step for poverty removal, which the President has also indicated, is to arrange maximum employment. I would like to give a concrete suggestion. The party in office has a two-thirds majority. Let us amend the Constitution to make the right to work a fundamental right. The government should accept the responsibility of providing work for every citizen, and in the case of those for whom it cannot do so it should arrange livelihood for some time. We are not against an amendment in the Constitution. We shall support an amendment in this direction. The right to work should be included among fundamental rights.

But the Finance Minister has allocated Rs. 50 crores for employment. That much would be spent just on making an employment plan.

SMT. INDIRA GANDHI : The Plan is ready.

SHRI VAJPAYEE : Had it been so it would have found a mention in the President's Address and in the Finance Minister's speech. If there is a concrete plan let the Prime Minister tell it in her reply. The House would be happy to know about it.

SMT. INDIRA GANDHI : I have already talked about it.

SHRI VAJPAYEE : A sum of Rs. 50 crores is too inadequate for this plan. It cannot fulfil the objective of providing employment to the maximum number of people.

Need for National Minimum

I agree with Dr. Rao that there should be a national minimum. We should decide upon a daily wage. The minimum income of an Indian citizen should be determined, and that is not enough. If disparity is to be removed the government should clarify the proportion between minimum income and maximum income and minimum expenditure and maximum expenditure—whether it should be 1 to 100 or 1 to 50 or 1 to 20. One person earning 30 paise a day and another spending 30,000 rupees a day, an Indian Airlines Corporation employee getting a monthly salary of 165 rupees while the maximum salary in the country is Rs.10,000—this is not the way to end disparity. It is not a question about whether or not the Address contains the word socialism. The question is whether any concrete steps are being taken to bring socialism into practice. I would invite the Prime Minister to indicate in her speech what, according to the government, the difference between the minimum and maximum income should be. This is the test of removing disparity, and we would like to see how far the government stands that test.

About unemployment the President's Address says, "Social attention will be given to the problem of educated unemployment". Does this mean so far only attention was being paid and now special attention will be paid ? Is unemployment some god that needs to be meditated upon for its removal ? Are we being taught a lesson in meditation ? It is rue that rural unemployment is becoming a serious problem. But let us not play down the seriousness of urban unemployment.

For this factories that are closed down need to be restarted and factories with one working shift should move on to two or three shifts. On the one hand plant capacity is not being utilised to the full extent, while on the other educated and trained people are without employment. If we could run factories to full capacity we would be able to solve at least the problem of educated unemployment substantially.

I was also surprised to see that the President's Address nowhere mentions that a network of power-driven and small agro-industries would be spread all over the country. Full rural employment is not possible without developing agro-industries. Does the Government have any plan for this or not ? If it has, it needs to be implemented, and a special allotment needs to be made for it.

Land Reforms

Land reform is necessary. Land should belong to the tiller...*(Interruption)*....Sir, perhaps he is listening to me for the first time. Those who have come to the Lok Sabha for the first time would take some time. They should show patience. But the number of people depending upon land has to be brought down. It is agreed on all hands that a fallow land should be made cultivable and distributed among the landless. If this has not been done in 23 years the influence of big landlords on the ruling party is responsible for it, not the opposition. Prepare a plan and distribute the land. Make government land cultivable and distribute it. But there is more pressure on land and less of land available. In spite of all efforts and in spite of wanting to do so we cannot give land to all. We have to remove people from land and put them into factories. Agriculture-based industries have to be developed. A concrete plan for this should be made.

The President has discussed rising prices in his address. The Finance Minister has also referred to them. But neither shows the way to resolve the serious situation caused by rising prices. I quote what Shri Y.B. Chavan has said in his budget speech :

> "We propose to take effective steps for stabilising the prices of essential commodities of common use to an adequate extent."

How long will you propose ? When will the proposing end ? We cannot have balanced development of the economy if we cannot stabilise prices. The railways are running in loss. The Finance Minister has presented a deficit budget. State Governments are also presenting deficit budgets. If we have inflation and a deficit budget prices will rise. Then where can we get funds for development ? Today we find ourselves overtaken by this serious situation. The States do not want to mobilise resources by resorting to higher taxation. The Central Government is also reluctant to increase taxes. Then the only way left is to cut down wasteful expenditure, to cut down government expenditure. But there is no indication about this in the budget speech.

Prices cannot be kept stable so long as the government does not adopt a concrete and effective policy about increasing production on the one hand and proper distribution of the increased production on the other. There is a shortage of kerosene. There is a shortage of coal. This shortage is not due to any shortcoming in the export-import policy. It is due to faulty distribution. If we do not correct this fault and if we do not arrange proper distribution of the increased production prices will rise and with them will rise the employees' demand for an increased dearness allowance.

The question of parity between the dearness allowances of Central and State Government employees is bound to arise. The States do not have the resources for this. The Centre should provide them the resources, and the Centre too has a resource problem. But if you concentrate all attention on giving dearness allowance without stabilizing prices you cannot resist a demand for increasing the dearness allowance.

No Magic Wand

In Delhi we opened a Super Bazar for helping the people but during the last four years it incurred a loss of Rs.75 lakhs. Running a Super Bazar at a loss, making heavy losses in government plants, not making a profit even in the rate of interest on the funds invested—are these the ways of putting resources to work ? Is this the way to bring about socialism ? Indiscriminate expression of the public sector is not the way to mobilise the resources we want. Let us first work the public sector we already have, increase its capacity and motivate people to work harder. Along with that their demand for wages based on minimum needs should also be met. But one thing must be made clear to our countrymen—it is that government efforts alone cannot remove poverty. The people will have to work for it too. They think that the Prime Minister has a magic wand; she has just to have it to make poverty disappear. Elections are over. Now I do not want to bring in election politics here. But the slogan to herald a new era can be translated into practice only when 50 crore countrymen would be motivated for hard work and become partners in the nation's prosperity.

SHRI K.N. TIWARI (Betia) : When the Prime Minister visited our place she said poverty cannot be removed by magic.

SHRI VAJPAYEE : Did she say that before the elections or after ?

Sir, it is necessary to take effective constructive steps to remove poverty. At least we want to give the assurance that if the Government takes concrete constructive steps it will have our cooperation. The ruling party has ridden to power on the crest of a wave. Let no one forget that if the people's hopes and expectations are not fulfilled the wave that takes one to the throne of power can also fling one to the ground.

I would like to refer to a particular sentence in the President's Address. This morning we passed a unanimous resolution on the situation in East Bengal. The situation in East Bengal is not a matter for a difference of opinion. But our responsibility does not end with merely passing a resolution. The President said in his Address :

"This government will raise its voice wherever peace is in danger. Countries lose their freedom and efforts are made to bring colonialism back either in the old form or in a new one."

In East Bengal we see the fearful dance of a new colonialism. The people there and their leader Sheikh Mujibur Rehman have our support and I would repeat Shri Indrajit Gupta's demand that if the East Bengal Government stabilised under the leadership of Sheikh Mujibur Rehman approaches India for recognition we should not hesitate to give it.

We congratulate Sheikh Mujibur Rahman. Nationalism cannot be based on religion. This is East Bengal's very first lesson....

SMT. INDIRA GANDHI : You should learn it.

SHRI VAJPAYEE : We never believed in the two-nation theory. It is completely wrong. Sir, when the country was partitioned our party did not even exist. I can accept this charge that we were so powerful that we partitioned the country even before our birth. Partition took place before our birth, and I do not want to point my finger at those who were responsible for it. But the East Bengal problem makes us all think from a new angle. Economic disparity is also becoming a serious problem in our country.

Second States Reorganisation Commission

I wish the Government sets up a second States reorganisation commission. Demands for statehood are being raised in Telengana and Goa. Our brethren in Manipur and Tripura are also agitated. Instead of solving this problem piecemeal we should have another States reorganisation commission and consider the issue on the basis of economic balance, linguistic unity and geographical continuity. Instead of acceding to demands for statehood under political pressure it would be better to entrust the problem to a commission and take a decision on the basis of its recommendations.

Sir, we are being taunted about an alliance. We entered into an alliance and we are not sorry for it. We are happy we did not ally ourselves with those who were responsible for the partition of the country. We allied with those who do not have extra-territorial loyalties. We entered into an alliance with those who believed in democracy, nationalism and economic and social justice. Securing the cooperation of all on the country's problems will be necessary not only for us but even for the Prime Minister. But we accept the people's verdict and we are prepared to discharge our responsibility as the opposition party in Parliament. Thank you.

The Hollow Call of Greatness

Sir, I would like to begin with the words with which the President has ended his Address : "...Greatness beckons this nation—that greatness that springs not from conventional power but from spiritual power."

These are inspiring words that have the power to touch the strings of the heart. The call of greatness through spiritual power sums up in one sentence a glimpse of the glorious past and still more glorious future of India. There is no doubt that India has to become great. It is also certain that greatness is our destiny. Our greatness will not depend upon stockpiles of arms. This also is an immortal truth. But somehow the call for greatness in the President's Address sounds hollow. Somehow the reference to spiritual power sounds a heresy.

Possibly the reason for this is that while the call for greatness was being referred to, the biggest opposition party in this House was calling the Prime Minister a murderer of democracy and a fascist in the Central Hall in the presence of the President himself and of foreign diplomats. The call was of greatness, the exhibition was of shallowness.

What our Marxist friends did that day cannot be commended. Their behaviour was objectionable. We too have received reports of irregularities in the elections in West Bengal. Even elsewhere such methods were adopted as would prevent the elections from being considered free and fair. But if any party had to express its anguish over it the President's Address was not the place for it. Members of that party could have come to the House after the Address and expressed their opinion. In a democracy the *Laxman Rekha* of propriety has to be drawn somewhere.

But did the ruling party not overstep this line of propriety ? Was its behaviour model ? That day in the midst of the President's Address the ruling party exposed itself. There was clapping when Marxist members began to leave, and those who clapped included not only the back benchers but the Leader of this House, the Prime Minister. The claps said—Good riddance ! Those who clapped did not look sad. There was not even the slightest anguish on their faces. There was a proud smile—a smile that did not have the grace to tolerate opposition, let alone respect it.

I shall present two more examples of a call for greatness and conduct of smallness. One dates before the elections, the other after. One is about the hunger for victory, the other about how victory goes to one's head.

Some eminent citizens of Delhi had organised a function to felicitate the Mayor, Lala Hans Raj Gupta. It was to take place in Rashtrapati Bhavan. The

Rajya Sabha on March 29, 1972 during discussion on the Motion of Thanks on the President's Address

sanction for the function had been obtained, invitations had been sent out, preparations were complete, and the function was to take place on February 28. Suddenly the programme was suspended and it was announced that it would take place on March 20 after the elections. But when March 20 approached it was announced that the function would be held in April but no date was set. The organisers realised that the Government did not like the idea of the programme taking place in Rashtrapati Bhavan. Then why was it organised there ? And if it had taken place there would it have polluted the Rashtrapti Bhavan ? This behaviour needs to be tested on the touchstone of greatness.

The other event dates after the election. The Jain Samaj of Jaipur organised a function to felicitate newly elected legislators. Members of many parties participated in it. Later members of the ruling party were hauled up and asked—why did they attend the communal platform of the Jain Samaj ? Why did they sit with Jan Sangh legislators ? Is the Jain Samaj a communal platform ? What can be more ridiculous than those engaged in a love affair with the Muslim League in Kerala calling the Jain Samaj communal ? As for sitting with Jan Sangh members has opposition sunk to such low depths ? Instead of eradicating untouchability from the social field do we want to introduce a new untouchability in the political field ? Have our hearts become so narrow ?

The President has truly said—greatness beckons. But those who lack greatness themselves cannot bring about greatness. The President has rightly said that greatness would be achieved through spiritual power. But those who have used every power except spiritual power to win the election do not have it in them to awaken spiritual power.

Is it not surprising that the violence and excess committed during the elections in West Bengal are being justified on the ground that the Marxists did the same thing ? Why friend Stephen is present in the House—I am sorry I am speaking in Hindi, he may find it difficult to understand, but I quote a portion of his speech. Addressing Marxists he said :

> "When you start stoning you must be prepared for being stoned back. When you start stabbing you must be prepared to receive the stab back."

I was sorry to hear this. I was still more sorry to read a portion of Prof. Hiren Mukherji's speech. He is in the Communist Party but his personality cannot be bound within the confines of any party. Perhaps it was the influence of the atmosphere that made him say what he said. I quote :

> "When violence is practised by certain people it is all right, but when violence is practised by certain other people it does not seem to be all right."

Both Shri Stephen and Prof. Mukherji have said the same thing—that what happened in West Bengal was all right, because the same tactics that the Marxists had adopted before against their opponents were used against them. Does this mean violence will be answered with violence ? Will murder be answered with murder ? Will fire be put out with fire ? Will there be no difference between the followers of the Mahatma and of Marx ? The Shastras talk about the worshipper of Shiva becoming Shiva himself, but now we see those fighting Marxists adopting all the bad characteristics of the Marxists.

Sir, if violence is to conquer violence it is useless to discuss spiritual power in the President's Address. Talk of spiritual power does not become those worshipping brute power. This heresy must stop. Elections have been won, authoritarian power has been established, now what is the need for this empty talk of spiritual power ?

Sir, the President has said that the people of the world were dragging their feet when the life and freedom of the seven and a half crore people of Bangladesh were in danger. But was not the Government of India itself not dragging its feet ? Did it not do anything for eight months ? Is it not true that even before his arrest Sheikh Mujibur Rahman had sent a message to New Delhi that he would declare Bangladesh independent if India was prepared to accord immediate recognition ? I got this information from a Bangladesh leader and I want the Government to clarify its position in this respect.

During the election efforts were made to give the entire credit of the liberation of Bangladesh to the Prime Minister. In that case who will bear the shame of the loss of life of lakhs of people and the dishonour of thousands of people due to delay in action ? In the election the Government took the credit for Mujib's liberation when actually the Prime Minister did not know if he was alive or dead. When news came that Mujib had left in a plane for an unknown destination she even said in Lucknow she had no idea if he was living or not.

Now that the elections are over the Government should not hesitate to admit that it delayed action in Bangladesh. Everyone makes mistakes, big people make big mistakes, but those who give a call for greatness should not hesitate to admit them.

Retired Chief of the Army, General Kumaramangalam is not in politics nor can he be counted among the Prime Minister's opponents. He too says India delayed action in Bangladesh. In an article he said when he thought back on all such matters as last year's events, the heavy influx of refugees, the heavy cost of their resettlement, the large number of innocent people killed in the last eight months, the question of disarming irregular forces, soon he reached the conclusion that it would have been beneficial for us to act in April. The point of view, not inspired by political considerations should be kept in view.

Sir, in reply to the charge of delay in action in Bangladesh it is argued that Bangladesh earned its independence on its own strength; we did not give it on a platter. I do not want to play down the sacrifice of the people of Bangladesh. Had they not raised their voice for freedom and struggled for it we could not have helped them in spite of all our desire to do so. But it is the bitter truth that without the direct intervention of the Indian army Bangladesh could not have become free. A still more bitter truth is that without Soviet support we could not have won this war.

It is also the bitter truth that Soviet pressure was working at the bottom of the unilateral ceasefire. If Soviet pressure was not there why was there so much haste in the ceasefire ? Was it the fear that if the war went on for long a third force would jump in ? How did the Government think about the ceasefire ? What happened in South Block, in Moscow and in Washington in the period between the fall of Dacca and the declaration of a unilateral ceasefire ? What strings were pulled ? What arms were hoisted ?

In order to justify the ceasefire it was said we stopped the war on our own because we did not want territory from Pakistan. This is ridiculous. We did not want even Bangladesh territory. But there we did not stop the war till the Pakistani army laid down arms. Why was the policy not adopted in the West ? On the night of December 17 our valiant forces were preparing to launch the final assault on Shakargarh, but at that very time ceasefire was declared.

Now it is said the danger is not yet over. It is also said people should be on guard. But the question is why was Pakistan left capable enough to pose as a new danger ? Why were steps not taken to defeat it in the West ? If Pakistan indulges in mischief again the responsibility will lie with the government that was in so much of a hurry to stop fighting. General Manekshaw said had the war gone on for 5 more days Pakistan would have shut up for 25 years.

Sir, the armed forces showed their mettle on the battle-ground but the leadership has to pass the test in the field of diplomacy. I call on the government to break its silence in respect of returning prisoners of war and the occupied territory, take this House into confidence and not keep the country in the dark any more. Since the Pakistani President's return from Moscow it is being said that the Kremlin wants India not to link the question of returning POWs with other bilateral problems. I do not know how far this is true. But if it is true it is a very serious matter and it is an indication of the fact that after stacking all its cards in favour of India during the war Russia is again preparing for a game of cards and heading for Tashkent.

Beware of Bhutto

According to the Geneva Convention POWs can be returned only after a peace treaty. But Pakistan is not ready even for a cessation of active hostilities, let alone a peace treaty. Shri Bhutto has turned down the Prime Minister's proposal for a no-war pact. He keeps repeating the self-determination chant on Kashmir. Sometime he threatens war, sometimes he chants peace. He is blowing hot and cold. India should not be taken in by him. The question of returning POWs cannot be seen as apart from other problems. The other problems are :

The return of one-third of Kashmir ending Pakistan's aggression on Kashmir, making good the expenditure on the war and on the resettlement of refugees, and settlement of the old debt of Rs. 300 crores. Along with this Pakistan will also have to bear the cost of the reconstruction of Bangladesh.

At present Shri Bhutto is in difficulties. He wants India to save him. We did not put him in difficulties. He has done it himself. But India cannot put itself into difficulties in order to extricate him from his own difficulties. The Pakistani President is now talking of humanity. Bhutto and humanity ? The two are not even remotely related. Bhutto was with Yahya Khan when humanity was being killed in Bangladesh. Now he wants to prove that he is as pure as snow. In order to understand what Shri Bhutto would do in future it would be enough to recollect what he did in the past.

The question is not whether we should or should not release POWs. The question is, can we release the POWs ? Can we jeoparadise security ? Can we separate the POW question just to save Bhutto even without a permanent peace treaty ? India has every right to link the POW problem with that of a permanent peace treaty. This is a question of our security. International law is also in our favour. The Government must not show weakness at this critical hour. What was won on the battlefield cannot be lost at the negotiating table.

Pakistani POWs are POWs of both India and Bangladesh. They have surrendered before the joint command. The talks on POWs with Pakistan will not be bilateral, they will be tripartite. How can Dacca talk with Pakistan so long as Pakistan does not recognise Bangladesh ?

Article 119 of the Geneva Convention of 1949 gives us and Bangladesh the authority to try those POWs against whom cases have been filed and put them in prison till their sentence is over. If Shri Bhutto really wants to normalise relations he should do at least a small act to prove his bonafides. He should hand over General Tikka Khan to Bangladesh so that this man who put on the role of Halaku Khan and Hitler could be brought to book. If Shri Bhutto does not do that we should know that his peace effort is a sham. The moment the POWs are released and reach Pakistani soil, Shri Bhutto will change colours. We must also make Soviet Russia understand that in order to prevent Pakistan from going under American influence the Soviets should not try to improve its relationship with Islamabad at the cost of India. This is 1972, not 1965. The Government is bound by the pledge not to repeat Tashkent. The Government will not be allowed to go back on its word. The people would not let the sacrifice of the Jawans go in vain.

Chief Ministers Mere Puppets

The election results have placed exceptional power and authority in the Prime Minister's hands. A British newspaper described her as the empress of India. Now all the power is concentrated in New Delhi. The Chief Ministers of the States dance to New Delhi's tunes. Central Ministers have been reduced to courtiers at the Delhi Darbar. I quote what Lala Durga Das, a well-known journalist, has written while commenting on the proposed Cabinet changes. He says :

> "The upper strata of bureaucracy is convinced that whoever be the new master all decisions of consequence will have to get clearance from the Prime Minister's Secretariat."

The Prime Minister's Secretariat has become a parallel cabinet. But this is not surprising. Nothing else is possible when all power becomes concentrated in two hands. But for parliamentary democracy this is not a healthy development. Ministers are the people's representatives. They are responsible to this House. But that cannot be said about their secretaries.

There has developed a gap, a power gap between the Prime Minister standing at the pinnacle and her colleagues lying at her feet. How will it be bridged ? Is this situation not fraught with the dangerous possibility of one individual getting established as a dictator ? The Prime Minister says there is no such danger. I quote her : "We (the Congress) had similar power many years before also. Fascism could have developed then, if it had to, but it did not."

But there is a difference between then and now. Then purity of the means was also stoned along with the ends. Then we had faith that whatever the situation some values of life could not be sacrificed. We believed that whatever the provocation there would be no hitting below the belt. Today things are very different. Now the Prime Minister's camp followers and opponents both know that she can do anything to get what she wants. That is the key to her success. But there also lies the seed of the end of democracy.

These days the atmosphere in New Delhi makes one choke. It is not easy to breath freely. Raising a voice of dissent is looked upon as a revolt. Everyone moves about with the badge of commitment on this lapel. Commitment to whom ? To an individual or to a party ?....

SHRI SHASHI BHUSHAN (South Delhi) : Socialism.

SHRI VAJPAYEE : Or to principles, to ideals ? My friend Shri Shashi Bhushan says commitment is necessary. Commitment to socialism. What socialism ? There is a socialism in Communist countries too, but there is no individual freedom there. There are many great countries in the world where the first thing you are told on arrival is—if you want to criticise the government do not do so in the hotel room, do it in the garden, for in the hotel room your conversation may be taped and recorded. There are also socialist countries in the world where writers are prosecuted, where there is no freedom of expression, where the government cannot be criticised. What sort of socialism we want should be made clear.

Defining Creative Commitment

Some eminent writers and journalists including Shri J. Swaminathan, Nirmal Verma, M. Govindan, Srikant Verma, Ganga Prasad Vimal, Kamalesh, Raghuvir Dayal and so on brought out a statement taking the Ministry of Education left and right for publishing decisions taken in a conference of writers, artists and intellectuals in December 1971 in a distorted form. I would like to quote that statement extensively. The convention was called by the Ministry of Education. Commenting on it the eminent writers said :

"While the invitees to this convention were given to understand that a declaration will be formulated and adopted after a free and frank discussion, they were presented with a readymade draft full of sycophancy and political jargon. Even the amendments proposed and accepted to this draft were not incorporated in it and the draft itself was published and circulated by the Ministry of Education in the name of the participants. The declaration commits the Indian intellectuals to 'a solemn pledge' to write in a so-called broad national cultural front and to use their creative talent for the realization of certain political concepts. This attempt at defining creative commitment and subjugating it to the ideas of a national cultural front is, to say the least, questionable in our democratic and pluralistic society. The use of the State bureaucratic machinery makes it all the more reprehensible ."

In conclusion, the writers say :

> "During the last two decades a coterie of conformist intellectuals has emerged around various committees and cultural bodies and other Government-aided institutions whose interests do not reflect in any way either the creative needs of the mass of intelligentsia or the cultural aspirations of the Indian people."

Is this the shape of things to come ? Will freedom of thought and expression be muzzled in the name of commitment ? If that is so, democracy is certainly in danger.

The Prime Minister had set out to end poverty, but she has succeeded in sending the opposition while poverty remains. Dearness is on the increase, unemployment is getting out of control. The rate of development is falling. Despite self-reliance in the matter of food the industrial field is sluggish.

The question is how will poverty be removed ? Recently the Prime Minister addressed a FICCI Conference. I have read her speech and I quote a portion from it :

> "I must confess the path is not at all clear. We can make the path and bring about a qualitative change through your co-operation."

If this means the Prime Minister does not want to tread a fixed path it could be a matter of satisfaction. But if it means what is to be done is not clear and if nothing was done and the voice of dissent arose it would be taught to be suppressed by dubbing it as reaction this would signal serious danger for democracy.

Opportunity to Show Results

Will there be no difference of opinion in the country on economic and social questions ? Can there be only one way of removing poverty ? Cannot there be different paths to prosperity ? Will there be no scope for an honest difference of opinion in a democracy ? What is this test according to which one who opposes is a reactionary and one who nods in agreement is a progressive ? Is this the terminology of the Congress Party ? I can understand my friend Shri Chandrajit Yadav using it, but it won't do in a democracy.

SHRI SHASHI BHUSHAN : It wont't do in Jan Sangh.

SHRI HUKAM CHAND KACHCHWAI (Morena) : He won't understand.

SHRI VAJPAYEE : It is difficult to say who understands and who doesn't.

In the FICCI Conference the Prime Minister had also said we would have to show some results in 3-4 years, otherwise we would be thrown aside. Already this talk of being thrown aside has started. The Prime Minister has just won the elections. Now she has the opportunity to show some results. Now there can be no excuses. What is the point in telling industrialists about being thrown away if nothing is done ? The people have given to the Prime

Minister and her party the authority to do something. Now show us the results.

But I would like to say one thing. Three-four years is a long time. The people won't wait so long. You will have to do something within a year. There are three things to be done—jobs for the unemployed, land for the landless, and homes for the homeless. If nothing concrete is done in this direction the consequences, as the Prime Minister has said, would be dire. But not dire for democracy, dire for those who are in power. So far as democracy is concerned we shall fight to save it, and we shall consider no sacrifice too big for it.

The ruling party got a tremendous majority, still the game of defection is on. It is time for defections to end. Those who talk of stability should introduce some stability in politics. Even now the process of luring away people of the opposition is going on. In my view so long as we do not have an anti-defection law the ruling party should declare that they would not encourage defections nor admit a defector to its ranks. If the ruling party does not have a vested interest in defections it should not hesitate to make such a declaration itself.

Big money has acquired a stranglehold on politics. Elections have become so expensive that no one can fight them on his own strength. This time it was not only that capitalists provided funds but they were told not to fund a particular party. Otherwise it would not be good for them.

SHRI SHASHI BHUSHAN : Still money was taken.

Radical Change in Election Law

SHRI VAJPAYEE : This is a glimpse of the extent to which we can go to win an election. Radical changes in the election law are called for. A Committee had been set up for amending the election law. It has made some important recommendations. We can adopt the system prevalent in West Germany, where most of the election expenditure is borne by the Government. This is a costly arrangement, but democracy too is not a cheap process. If we want to prevent democracy from being distorted by the influence of big money we would have to think seriously in this direction. It is true that those who have power can collect as much money as they want and those who have money can distribute as much of it as they want. But this would not reflect the people's will. It is also necessary to introduce such healthy conventions as would ensure that the election is between two parties, not between a party and the government. In the elections we did not fight the Congress party, we fought the government. Helicopters, planes, the chanting of the Prime Minister's name on All India Radio from morning to night, saturated propaganda on the Cinema screen—how can those sitting in the opposition fight all this ? Healthy conventions can be set if a voice against this is raised within the ruling party itself. Cannot all parties be given time on All India Radio ? Cannot transportation be made available to all parties ?

Democracy runs on conventions. Today you have all the power in your hands. Monopoly in any field is bad, but will our friends welcome the monopoly of power as something good ? Along with so much power you also have to shoulder the responsibility of setting some good conventions.

Sir, 102 legislators of Haryana had presented a memorandum against the Chief Minister to the President. Members of Parliament also demanded an inquiry into the charges of corruption against him. But no inquiry is being made. In Punjab an inquiry was begun against Akali Dal Ministers. The Prime Minister had publicly made some derogatory remarks against *Bandokar*....

AN HON. MEMBER : She stated in the House that she did not use such words.

SHRI VAJPAYEE : If she has refuted it I take back my words. I was not in the House. I do not know.

But what is the reason for not making an inquiry against Chaudhary Bansi Lal even after all evidence of his corruption was submitted to the President ? Why is corruption crossing the limits of Haryana and touching even New Delhi ? Power should have no scope for corruption. The Prime Minister should be prepared to take stringent action even against somebody from her own party.

DR. KAILASH (Bombay South) : Say at least something on the budget.

SHRI VAJPAYEE : This is not the budget. He does not know what subject is being discussed. This is not the budget, this is the President's Address.

Sir, one more thing and I shall finish. I have received complaints about irregularities being committed in collecting the National Defence Fund in Andhra. I was shown receipt that had no numbers. Money is being collected against receipts without numbers. Is this money going to the National Defence Fund or in somebody's personal fund ? I have also seen receipts on which the signatures of Dr. Sanjiva Reddy and Brahmanand Reddy were cancelled and the signature of the present Chief Minister Shri Narasimha Rao stamped. Can we not print new receipts ? I wrote about this to Finance Minister Shri Chavan. He replied the matter is not within his jurisdiction but in that of the Prime Minister. And the Prime Minister is too busy to reply. I know she has a heavy responsibility. But fate has also placed in her hands the power to make or mar the future of democracy. Now she is being tested. Let us see if this Government can pass the test...*(Interruption)*....

Testing Period for PM

SHRI K. SURYANARAYANA (Eluru) : On a point of information for him.

SHRI VAJPAYEE : I am not yielding.

SHRI K. SURYANARAYANA : Through you I want to tell him for his information ....

CHAIRMAN : He is not yielding.

SHRI VAJPAYEE : He can speak later if he wants to. He broke my chain of thought. Perhaps he was justifying Andhra. But I have left Andhra and come to New Delhi. Do not think of the Chief Minister, speak of the Prime Minister. Fate has placed exceptional power in her hands. She has acquired the power to make or mar democracy. She is being tested. This government is passing through a testing period. What party lost the election, is not important. We are believers in democracy, we accept the election results. But today what is at stake is not the future of some party but the future of democracy. If we can make democracy permanent there would be some meaning to the President's call for greatness. If there is only talk of spiritual power and no practice of it such heresy will not build the nation, it would pen the way to the nation's downfall.

SHRI K. SURYANARAYANA : With your permission I want to enlighten the House on one point. Shri Atal Bihari Vajpayee has referred to the issue of receipts for the National Defence Fund with the signature of Shri Sanjiva Reddy and other friends. The Andhra Government has recently announced that those receipts also were valid. They have already accounted for them. The Chief Minister has also contradicted this, but the House may know that these are accounted for.

SHRI VAJPAYEE : The Hon. Member has accepted that there are receipts without numbers. That was the point that I wanted to make. He has confirmed it.

SHRI C.M. STEPHEN : I wanted to make a submission by way of personal explanation. My Hon. friend Vajpayee ji, when he was speaking has mis-represented me and my speech.....

SHRI VAJPAYEE : I quoted from your speech.....

SHRI C.M. STEPHEN : ....as an attempt to defend violence and conceding that there was violence on our part. I only want to clarify the position so that it is on record. What I said was, "Assuming but without conceding, assuming for argument's sake that there was violence I said that anybody else might have any complaint but the Marxist Communist Party, which is believing in violence (an Hon. Member : No.) and is propagating violence, had absolutely no right to complain about violence. That is what I said. And I said that for the Marxist Communist Party, who say that they stand by Mao's doctrine of power by the barrel of the gun, to come and wail that there was violence against them was cowardice. This is what I said. This is the point I made. I never conceded that there was violence on our part and I never defended the Government for that. I only said, "Assuming but not conceding."

SHRI VAJPAYEE : I accept his explanation.

The Corrupt Foundations of Electoral Success

Sir, the Constitution has placed on the President the responsibility of addressing a joint Session of Parliament. He has been discharging this responsibility with sincerity. At the beginning of the budget session he arrives in a horse-driven carriage, there is a gleaming umbrella on his head, bugles sound, the President reads out a prepared speech and returns.

Some friends have called this a meaningless ritual. To me the whole thing looks like a joke. Not only the President's Address, this House, this Parliament — in a sense this whole scene looks meaningless and cut off from the people's life.

This is the Lok Sabha, the People's House, but it does not reflect the people's power. This House has become an attractive ornament of political power. The opposition is so weak that it can only make some noise. The ruling party is so strong that it is bent with its burden.

In 1971 the ruling party got a two-thirds majority, but how did that majority benefit the country ? What did the common man get ?

The ruling party considering the ending of the privy purses and the nationalisation of banks as the ultimate in progress, but three years later this same party surrendered before the old princes for winning the elections in Bundelkhand. Defence Minister Shri Jagjivan Ram had to admit in Moradabad that bank nationalisation has failed, because it did not bring the expected benefit.

By separating Lok Sabha elections from elections to Legislative Assemblies the Prime Minister not only made elections more and more expensive but forced the party in power to adopt election methods that can neither be called healthy nor good for national unity. The Prime Minister's repeated statement that if the people of U.P. did not vote for the ruling party the development of U.P. would halt was nothing less than political blackmail.

On December 23, 1973 the Prime Minister said in a speech in Dhenkanal that if people did not vote Congress they would be denied Central assistance. A telegram to this effect was sent by Shri Patnaik to the Election Commission. It was later also published in the papers. The Prime Minister has not refuted it. Such threats do not only make a mockery, they also incite feelings against the Centre. This can strike a blow at national unity. We want a strong Centre, but the strength of the Centre flows from the Constitution, not from some party's monopoly of power. If the Centre does not behave with justice, if it

Lok Sabha on February 27, 1974 during discussion on the Motion of Thanks on the President's Address

behaved with partiality with States on partisan bases feelings against the Centre can rise in the States, and that would be a sad thing for the country. This government has taken away the job of cleaning up slums from the hands of the Delhi Corporation. I fail to understand why this was done. Before this the DTU was taken away from the Corporation and handed over to an autonomous corporation. This is being done only because the Jan Sangh has a majority in the Corporation and the ruling party cannot tolerate it.

The glut of pre-election foundation-laying ceremonies in Uttar Pradesh has unmasked the partial nature of the Central Government. Was not the foundation-laying or inauguration of projects worth Rs. 550 crores at election time not meant for influencing the voters ? Is this not misuse of power ? I would like to quote an editorial of the *Hindustan Times*. By no stretch of imagination can the paper be called anti-Congress, but it is impartial and fearless. It says :

> "The series of two special reports entitled 'Foundations of electoral success concluded elsewhere on this page presents a catalogue that does the Prime Minister and the Chief Minister of Uttar Pradesh little credit in larger terms of liberal principles, democratic values, economic discipline or national example. Perhaps some of the electorate too might be more annoyed than flattered by all these blandishments. Not everything that has been done is by any means wrong. But, as the Supreme Court has ruled, energy to do public good should be used not on the eve of elections but much earlier — and, we would urge, elsewhere too. The Central leadership, governmental or party, has had little time for Gujarat or the deepening economic crisis. There is a large grey area in politics. But the grey should not assure a darker side. Even if the Congress is conceivably not guilty of electoral malpractice in U.P., not a few of its actions come dangerously close to unfair practice. And Mrs. Gandhi, also, stands greatly diminished.
>
> Uttar Pradesh goes to the polls within a fortnight. The Congress may win the election, it may not. Whatever the result, this much is certain. India has lost."

A party that begins projects worth Rs. 550 crores at election time proves that it slept for 4 years 10 months and suddenly became active when defeat stared it in the face.

On December 29, 1973 the Prime Minister said during a speech at Supu, Canara :

> "The worst was over in the country's economy and from the next month onwards things will improve for the better. Food shortage will be a thing of the past."

The Suffering Economy

This is the Prime Minister's speech of December 29. I do not know who her economic advisors are. Who gives her the facts is also a mystery. Instead of improving the situation had worsened. The crisis is assuming serious proportions. Food shortage is leading to an explosive situation. There has been a good crop, but wrong policies have created an artificial shortage.

Our economy suffers from three shortcomings— inflation, black money and corruption. The value of the rupee is constantly going down. This is leading to a terrible situation. In this reply on November 27, 1973 the Finance Minister had said that according to calculations based on the 1974 consumer price index the value of the rupee was 99 paise in 1950, 80 in 1960, 44 in 1970 and 36 in 1973. We still get 100 paise for a rupee in the market place but the value of 100 paise is 36 paise. Now our students will have to learn a new arithmetic — one rupee is equal to 100 paise and 100 paise are equal to 36 paise. If the price of the rupee falls like this and inflation grows the common man's life will become still harder. Indiscriminate supply of currency notes is the major reason of inflation. In 1965-66 the people had notes worth Rs. 4529 crores, and in 1971 they came to 10, 061 crores. In comparison the development rate has consistently fallen. In 1969- 70 it was 5.3 per cent, in 1970-71 4.2, in 1971-72, 1.7 and in 1972-73 it is 0.6 per cent.

Black Money

Black money is undermining our economy. There is a parallel black money in the country. Elections are fought with black money. No party is untouched by it. The entire structure of this House, of Democracy, stands in a falsehood. The first thing an MP or MLA does is to present false accounts. We gather here shouting the slogan 'truth alone triumphs', but an untruth is hidden at the base of us all. Can you believe that the Prime Minister has given an election account of Rs. 12000 for her constituency ? Can anyone fight an election by Rs. 12000 ? But the account has been given.

SHRI S.A. SHAMIM (Srinagar) : On a point of order, Mr. Vajpayee has said 'the entire House'. He has not made any exception. He can speak for himself. He can speak for those about whom he knows....

MR. DEPUTY SPEAKER : It has gone on record, No point of order.

SHRI SHAMIM : Will you allow me to clarify, Sir ? He has said the entire House. He must make one honourbale exception, and that is myself.

SHRI VAJPAYEE : I do.

Corruption

Sir, corruption is gaining fearful proportions, but how can corruption be eradicated when the Prime Minister had recently included in her Council of Ministers a gentleman whom ten years ago on the principle of "high principles of parliamentary democracy by which the office of a minister is governed" Shri Jawaharlal Nehru had ....

SHRI K.P. UNNIKRISHNAN (Badagara) : Put the facts straight. He resigned.

SHRI VAJPAYEE : When he resigned he too said he was doing so to protect some values in which he believed. Have those now been devalued ? Have the standards of ministerial conduct changed ?

SHRI D.N. TIWARI (Gopalganj) : Can a person not become good later ?

SHRI VAJPAYEE : Yes, if you say so I have no objection. The Prime Minister complains that opposition parties are trying to exploit the economic difficulties. It is our duty to express and organise the public discontent generated by the wrong and shortsighted policies of the government and we shall discharge it. But such a charge does not become those who did not hesitate to utilise the national victory of 1972 for paltry ends. Those who live in glass houses should not throw stones at others.

Prime Minister's Misplaced Surprise

The Prime Minister is surprised that the poorest of all are silent while those who are better placed are agitating. I quote her :

> "The very poorest were not complaining or non-cooperating or having strikes, but the people who were comparatively better off."

Is a special effort needed to understand this ? The very poor are mute, disorganised, suppressed for centuries, they cannot fight. They freeze to death on the foot path, they cannot loot cloth shops. They may die of starvation but they won't raid godowns. On the other hand, those who are better off are aware, organised. They would adopt new ways of change. Those who are very poor are resigned to their fate, but those who are somewhat enlightened are struggling to change their fate. This is why students, teachers, doctors, engineers are struggling today. Instead of resorting to oppression the government should try to understand their mind.

What are the junior doctors of Delhi demanding ? Yesterday Dr. Karan Singh discussed spiritual values in his long speech. He also presented a picture of the humanity of the doctors sitting outside his house. But this government has become heartless. It does not even speak properly with the junior doctors. How sincerely they attend to workers during working hours is not hidden from anybody. They are asking for a salary of Rs. 500, a city allowance and a non-practising allowance. Is giving them Rs. 650 a great obligation ? The Government does not even say what it wants to give. It is bent on breaking the strike. This would produce seeds of rebellion.

Sir, you will be surprised to learn—I am sorry the Prime Minister is not present in the House, later she would say I was listening to the speech in her room—students in Rae Bareli were arrested by the police because they had made the mistake of inviting me for inaugurating the Feroze Gandhi Memorial College Students' Union. They were arrested during the night, taken to the police station in handcuffs and beaten up. Have you ever heard of students being put under the condition that they should present themselves at the police station every third day ? From students they become criminals. What were they demanding ? That professors should be appointed in time, that books worth Rs. 15000 missing from the library should be accounted for. Receipts should be issued for library fee charged. They want proper use of funds collected for medical and other amenities.

The junior engineers of Uttar Pradesh are also not asking for the moon. They are demanding equal wages for equal work. They are asking for 50 per cent promotion. But they too are being suppressed.

Sir, suppression acts as fire in an agitation. People can be killed with bullets, but their hearts cannot be won with bullets. Gujarat is a warning, Gujarat is a challenge—a warning for those corrupt, power-hungry people who want to grab power with immoral means but who want to ignore the widening gulf between the people's expectations and the government's achievements. Gujarat is a challenge for all those who want to bring about a change with peaceful means.

By dubbing the popular discontent in Gujarat as inspired by capitalists the Prime Minister has not only shown her inability to understand the new forces that change history but has also insulted the people of Gujarat. Crowds may well be hired for hailing the Prime Minister but no one can make them face police bullets. In the words of Gandhian thinker Prof. Amritanand :

> "We can describe the Gujarat popular upsurge as a movement of self-disciplined and non-violent protest directed against a corrupt and inefficient system based on unpopular leadership."

Sir, elections were won by exploiting the Bangladesh victory and on the slogan of political stability. But the Prime Minister could not give to the States an honest and effective administration that would be based not on cheap popularism but on radical realism. The results are before us. Gujarat is burning, there are sparks in Maharashtra, and the whole of India stands on the rim of revolution.

The Prime Minister is not prepared to dissolve the Legislative Assembly of Gujarat. But was not the Legislative Assembly of Kerala dissolved when there was a similar mass upsurge there and the first Communist government toppled ? At that time the Prime Minister was the President of the Congress. But that Legislative Assembly was dissolved because it had a Communist majority. The Gujarat Legislative Assembly is not being dissolved because....

SHRI K.P. UNNIKRISHNAN : Not a single MLA was assaulted in Kerala like this. You are defending fascism now.

SHRI VAJPAYEE : Because Congress is in a majority. These double standards, this double-faced politics, this naked power politics — this is the biggest course today. This makes the Muslim League secular in Kerala and communal in Uttar Pradesh. Shiv Sena is backed in Bombay while a show is made of opposing it all over the rest of the country. In Pondicherry Organisation Congress is befriended while it is scowled at in Uttar Pradesh. A love-hate drama with the Communists goes on at one and the same time.

Sir, in Delhi the Prime Minister gives speeches against communalism but in Uttar Pradesh she openly incited Muslim communalism. I quote what the *National Herald* wrote while reporting her speech in Hardoi on February 14 :

> "The PM said that the Muslims should not divide themselves as in that case they would grow weaker and would not be able to guide their own destiny".

What does this mean ? Is this an appeal for national unity ?

SHRI S.A. SHAMIM : She said so to save herself from you.

SHRI VAJPAYEE : Is it not an incitement to separatism to tell Muslims not to vote as they pleased, nor to vote according to the programme of parties, to vote as Muslims, to vote *en bloc* ?

She even charged that a young Muslim who convened a new Muslim League branch in Delhi was given money by the Jan Sangh. She should know that the Muslim League was not formed in Delhi now, it was set up in 1968. She should also know that its worker Mirza Usman was elected as a member of the Corporation on the ticket of the Prime Minister's party but later joined the Muslim League. Either the Prime Minister should prove her charge or she should take it back.

Sir, I would like to conclude. It is not impossible to come to power by raising attractive slogans, spending money like water and by openly misusing government machinery. But power for what ? Is power for power's sake or is it for transformation of the Society ? Is power only for enjoyment ? Is power for writing your name in the history in the time capsule or for cutting out other people's name ? Is power for satisfying your ego ? Is this the only purpose of power ? Is it for giving your name to some university, port or canal ?

Even 25 years after independence the Indian society is mired in lethargy, superstition, evil customs and untouchability. What have we done to change the society ? India's Prime Minister is a woman, but crores of women are living a hellish life. They are under a veil, under a burqa. The Sarda Act put an end to child marriages. Still lakhs of children are married in the cradle. There is a law against dowry, but it has increased. Young girls even commit suicide because there is no dowry to give. Even today and even in good families the daughters-in-law are ill-treated because the dowry was not enough.

Old Values Discarded

Untouchability is a cognisable offence but Harijans are burnt alive. Their women are publicly branded with hot irons. Can the Prime Minister not launch a campaign against these social evils ? Can she not tell the Hindus and the Muslims that they will have to change with the times ? Can she not remain firm on amending Muslim Personal Law ? But she wants votes.

SHRI M.A. SHAMIM : What is that to you ?

SHRI VAJPAYEE : Sir, these need to be changed first.

Had the Prime Minister spent the time, power and resources that she spent on winning the election in one State on initiating a social revolution it would have been a different picture in the country. It is regrettable that she lost the time that she had. Today the alarm bell is ringing for all of us. A system is breaking up. It is not the question of a party alone, the whole democratic system is at stake.

Old values have been discarded but new values have not yet been established. Old points of faith have broken down but we have not been able to put up new ones. The old era is ending, but new one is not yet born. Today the country stands at the crossroads. This is the hour of decision. Elections, votes, power politics — all these have limitations. If we do not break away from these limitations our dream of a great India will never be fulfilled.

The flood of popular expectations that the Prime Minister has roused is rocking her throne. If she does not wake up in time she may meet the same fate as Chimanbhai Patel.

Government's Immunity to Separatists

Indian Postal Bill

Sir, I am sorry to say that I would not be able to associate you with the Motion of Thanks on the President's Address. I would like to thank the President separately. We commend him on his stand on the Indian Postal Bill, which has gone to him for signature and we hope the Government would amend the Bill in accordance with his objections. The whole opposition was united during the discussion on the Bill, but nobody listened to us. Communications Minister Shri Arjun Singh did not think it necessary even to open his mouth during the discussion. He was content to place the whole burden on Santosh Mohan Dev.

The Prime Minister says again and again—we want to take the opposition with us. Does he want to do so only in those matters where the government gets into difficulties or does he need the advice and cooperation of the opposition in other matters as well ? The entire opposition was one on the question of the Postal Bill. We tabled amendments but they were turned down. I would wish that the President's objections are not made a matter at issue in the cold war currently going on between the Prime Minister and the President. The Postal Bill should be assessed on its merits and demerits. I congratulate the President on his attitude.

So far as the Address is concerned it is unnecessarily lengthy, uninteresting and uninspiring. I was comparing it with his old speech of January 17, 1985. It was made after the general elections. It was also a presidential address, but it was brief, full of vitality and self-confidence. It was an 8-page speech. The present speech is 16 pages long. As the achievements come down the number of pages and paragraphs goes up.

Compare the two speeches and you will see the great change in the country's condition. Today I was listening to a Congress member's speech. When the Prime Minister assumed office two years ago lights of hope lit up people's minds. Whatever the result of the elections, we may have faced defeat, but we and the whole world congratulated the people of India on the organised manner in which they faced the challenge democratically and gave a fitting reply. But now the whole world is asking—what has happened in two years ? Where are we headed ? Why is there discontent in every class and every field ? Have the Prime Minister and his colleagues ever thought about this ?

Rajya Sabha on March 2, 1987 during discussion on the Motion of Thanks on President's Address

Punjab and the Central Government

Yesterday 14 people were killed in Punjab. They included three terrorists. Eleven innocent people were killed. How long will this killing of the innocent continue ? An all-party campaign is all right, but the President had talked about it in his Address last year too. I quote : "It is necessary that all secular and democratic forces combine to conduct a popular campaign on the basis of those national, secular, democratic and socialist values that are the basis of India's unity." A full year has gone by, but there is no such campaign. Was it not possible to hold in the past the type of meeting that was held recently in Chandigarh ?

Opposition parties were prepared to join the Congress in going from village to village. But the Congress did not have a clean mind. The Punjab Congress was saying one thing, the leadership in Delhi was saying another.

I would like to raise an important point. The political situation in Punjab began to deteriorate with Shri Tohra's victory in the election to the Shiromani Gurdwara Prabandhak Committee. What was some Central leaders' role in Shri Tohra's victory ? Do you really want to support Barnala ? There was a person in jail in Tihar. He was released a day before the election, and taken to Punjab for casting his vote. Another voter had come for Canada....

SHRI H. S. HANSPAL : Sir, I may tell you that he was released by the Court.

SHRI VAJPAYEE : Did the Government tell the Court to release him on bail ?

SHRI HANSPAL : I have only to say that he was released by the Court.

SHRI VAJPAYEE : Sir, a person who has settled in Canada is still a member of the S.G.P.C. He came to Delhi to vote. He is now a foreigner. He needed the Central Government's permission to go to Punjab. How was that permission given ? Yet another member was caught up in Baramula in the snow. It was difficult for him to come out. A telephone call was made by the Prime Minister's secretariat. He was brought from Baramula to vote for Tohra. When Tohra won the election he was arrested. This is not the way to tackle the situation in Punjab...*(Interruption)*.... Whatever I am saying I am saying in all seriousness.

SHRI H.S. HANSPAL : Sir, it is wrong to level such a charge against the Government when there is a secret ballot. What proof does he have that the Government managed the voting ?

SHRI VAJPAYEE : Sir, I demand an inquiry into the vote of some Central Government leaders into that election. I would be happy to be proved wrong. But don't play politics in Punjab. Once politics has spoiled Punjab. Pardon me, but religion has not spoiled Punjab as much as power-hungry politicians have. Gurdwaras were taken over after the S.G.P.C. elections. I am including everybody. All of us are guilty. This is not the time for apportioning blame. Let everyone of us look into himself. Barnala is now being praised. The President's Address never praises any Chief Minister by name. This is an extra-ordinary situation. Barnala is still to undergo his final test. We praise the little firmness he showed. Shri Hanspal is here. Barnala was elected by the people and we too have supported him, but the Barnala Government calls itself a Panthic Government. He wants to fight the Panthic Committee and has assumed its form. There is a difference between his policies, and practices. It is necessary to go deep into how these differences could be resolved and the people of Punjab prepared for unitedly fighting terrorism. We had made a serious demand and the Central Government passed a resolution under Article 249, but it is lying without implementation. It is not only the Bharatiya Janata Party that is calling for military help. We want the Punjab police and the para-military force to put down terrorism and stop the killing of innocent people. We would have been happy if that had been done. But why hesitate to call the armed forces if that is required in border areas ? I have with me an article by Communist leader Satyapal Dang, and I quote a portion from it :

> "But when all this is essential use of the army by civilian officers is not prohibited to the necessary extent like flag march, patrolling and other activities."

Shri Dang added that at the time of Blue Star the army was called to Punjab and now it is being charged with misusing its powers. All these charges are not true. He said what the army did also needs to be assessed.

Apart from a people's campaign what more effective step does the Government has to eradicate terrorism in Punjab ? The Prime Minister says the Constitution would be amended. In the past too he made an amendment under Article 249 but did not act upon it. Will now there be another amendment ? First and foremost, the government must stop the killing of innocent people otherwise the people's campaign will not go far.

Sir, fiats are issued and it is natural for objection to be raised against them. We cannot allow politics to be controlled from religious places. Here I am talking about 'religion'. *'Dharma'* has a wider connotation. I do not want to define it. Shri Sathe is present here. Maharashtrians are adept at splitting hairs. All this is not limited to Punjab. Recently I have seen a statement of Muslim Mushawarat. It was published in New Delhi on February 9. It said there are going to be elections in some States and in these States the Muslims should vote in such a way that Muslim identity, Muslim dignity and Muslim security are extended.

Accordingly to a press report :

> "The statement issued by Mushawarat General Secretary Ahmed Ali Khan says that in three States, Jammu and Kashmir, West Bengal and Kerala, Muslims form a large share of the population. It is 64 per cent in J & K, 22 and 21 in West Bengal and Kerala, respectively. The Mushawarat has called on all Muslims to vote for candidates keeping in mind their policies and...."

In policies it has not talked of any economic matters. I quote the last paragraph :

> "The Mushawarat appeals to the Muslim community that in their constituency they should select one candidate carefully and vote him unitedly and solidly so that the candidate of their choice is not only

elected but it is known that he has been elected only due to Muslim support".

Who are in the Mushawarat ?

What organisations are included in this Mushawarat ? What leaders of so-called secular parties are there ? There is a respected leader of the Bohras. I do not want to say anything against his eminence, but there is a struggle going on between progress and fundamentalism in the Bohra society and the situation has deteriorated to such an extent that if somebody disobeys the Syedna he does not have to be buried in the cemetery. There is now an opportunity. Take a courageous decision. There is a reference in the President's Address. I do not know why it is there, but it is really there. A finger has been pointed at the situation that prevailed after Gandhiji's assassination, but nothing more is said. In 1948 the Constituent Assembly had passed a resolution calling upon the Government to take steps to end communalism in the political life of the country. Only two months before that Mahatma Gandhi had been assassinated. That time the memory of brutal killings was fresh in the minds of the framers of the Constitution.

The resolution of the Constituent Assembly was mentioned and the matter was left at that. Can such political parties not be prevented from fighting elections as do not have their doors open for every Indian ? The Election Commission can do this. Those who are confined to a sect should do religious work, cultural work. But when those who make an alliance with the Muslim League in Kerala, revive the Muslim League that was dead, support the Majlis-e-Ittehad-ul-Muslameen in Hyderabad for winning the Lok Sabha seat there and make their man the mayor of Hyderabad, talk of fighting communalism , the talk sounds hallow. There should be equality between precept and practice. Encouraging one type of communalism is not the way to fight another type of communalism.

The tendancies now rising in the Hindu community make me worry. If Hindus leave their generosity and become narrow-minded the future of this country would be plunged into darkness. But a reaction is setting in the Hindu's mind because political parties care for votes. It was also votes that spoiled the case of Punjab.

Who Sheltered Subhash Gheising ?

In Punjab communalism can be blamed to an extent. But what is happening in Gorkhaland ? Shri Gheising is a Hindu and there is no Hindu-Sikh-Muslim problem there. The Central Government mishandled the situation so much that Shri Subhash Gheising became the leader of all Gorkhas, all Nepalis, without anybody making him so. He had become the sole spokesman. I was recently in Siliguri. There is a bandh on alternate days there. Labourers are starving . All work is disrupted. There was attack on a police station and policemen were killed. Gheising is called to Delhi and talks are held with him. On what subject was the talk held ? Could not the conditions have been placed on him before the talks that he should give up violence ? Was it enough to create a headache for the Marxist government of West Bengal ? This is not the way to save the unity and integrity of the country.

Once this method had landed the country in deep difficulty. We thought there is now a new Prime Minister, he will tread a new way—the way of Shri Feroze Gandhi. He did tread some distance. His natural reactions are normal. This morning I had the opportunity to see him. I discussed the matter with him and I saw that his spontaneous reaction was good. I do not know what will happen in that matter. I am not referring to it. I do not know who advises him, how he works, but one by one he is forgetting his promises.

In his old speech of March 17, 1985 the President had declared :

> "The Government are committed to a clean public life. They intend to engage in wide-ranging discussion on electoral reforms with political parties and welcome their co-operation."

Two years have passed but no discussion has started. The Election Commission has not held any meeting of opposition parties and the ruling parties. Does the ruling party have a vested interest in the present election method ? Money power and muscle power are on the increase.

Recently there was a by-election in Haryana. The constituency where the Chief Minister contested the election had the by-election, while all other seats are lying vacant. Why were by-elections not held for all seats ? There was no opposition to the Chief Minister, the opposition parties had boycotted the election. 92 per cent votes were cast. Should there not be an inquiry into who cast 92 per cent votes ? If I raise this matter many members would say file an election petition.

Sir, this is not an ordinary matter, so it is necessary to go into it in some depth. Now there is no talk of clean politics. The same old thing has come back again.

How Long will the Matter of Reservations Hang Fire ?

In March 1985 the Prime Minister said in a speech in Hyderabad that the problem of reservations is quite complex and delicate. He said it was getting out of hand. In respect of reservations in job and educational institutions the Prime Minister said he would consult the opposition parties after the elections and arrive at a consensus. You may recollect that in Madhya Pradesh and Gujarat the reservation percentage was suddenly increased. There were riots. In Gujarat the ruling party gave a communal colour to these riots. Solanki had to go. Two years have passed but the sensitive issue of reservations still hangs fire. The Prime Minister does not have the time—and nobody has advised him—to sit with the opposition and arrive at a consensus. Recently in Kerala the Karunakaran government increased the quantum of reservation of 15 per cent before the election on the basis of poverty. When the Muslim League opposed, it was withdrawn. The Nair Service Society said if you withdraw it we will not be on your side. The Chief Minister said come with us for now, we'll see after the elections. Is reservation too an instrument for garnering votes or is it a means of taking backward people forward ? Will everything be linked to the vote ? In what will this result ? And yet we talk of unity and swear by integrity. This is not the way to save unity and integrity.

Sir, I am worried about China. In respect of Pakistan many Hon. members have expressed their thoughts. I feel the tension of the past some days could have been avoided. I was recently in Ahmedabad. Newspapermen asked me will there be a war between India and Pakistan ? I said leaders of both countries were intelligent and they will not make the mistake of fighting. But later I thought my assessment was not right. A war was barely avoided. When the Pakistan Prime Minister Shri Junejo met the Prime Minister in Bangalore could the whole situation not have been made clear to him ? Pakistan knew that we are conducting an exercise in Rajasthan. There is an arrangement in both countries to keep the other informed. Then how was there a misunderstanding ? Could it not have been avoided by contacting Delhi ? Our Secretary had visited Pakistan before Shri Junejo's visit to Bangalore. This matter could have been raised.

Ministerial Changes

For the last many days I have been hearing that Pakistan is not being charged with sheltering or arming terrorists of Punjab. Has this matter been resolved through talks ? If that is, I am very happy. Still the President's Address says in passing : These anti-national elements are working at the behest and under the control of foreign elements. Who are these foreign elements ? Name them, give some information about them. If it is Pakistan and if relations with Pakistan have improved, who is it ? Is it the U.S.A. ? If it is, was the issue raised with them on a priority basis ? The Canadian Prime Minister was with us. Were there not satisfactory talks with him on this matter ? How long will we keep blaming others ? If conditions at home get worse neighbours would certainly try to exploit the situation. But why are we allowing conditions at home to worsen ? Is it not our responsibility to maintain a good condition ? There was tension on the border, no shots were fired, but the Defence Minister fell a victim. He has been devalued. I am talking about Shri Arun Singh.

The Defence Minister was not changed when there was tension. When the situation was diffused Shri V.P. Singh was entrusted with the charge of the Defence Ministry. How is it that the Prime Minister looks for a new Defence Minister whenever there is tension ? During peace the Defence Ministry *should remain* with the Prime Minister.

SHRI N.K.P. SALVE (Maharashtra) : Please say in detail who was the Defence Minister when tension was at its height and who was there when it lessened.

SHRI VAJPAYEE : You will see that Shri V.P. Singh was made the Defence Minister when the tension was on the decline. There is one more question. Would the Defence Ministry remain with Prime Minister in peace time and is somebody made Defence Minister in times of tension ? Does it add to the Prime Minister's image ?

SHRI N.K.P. SALVE : One thing is sure, he was not downgraded.

SHRI VAJPAYEE : Sir, the budget was going to be presented, preparations for it were going on, Shri Arun Singh was doing good work, the Defence Ministry was with the Prime Minister, then what was the necessity of the change ? The Prime Minister, not here now, said it was a dire necessity. What was that dire necessity ? Could the Prime Minister not bear the responsibility of the defence of the country ?

Is it necessary to change the Finance Minister on the occasion of the budget session ? Why it was done is still a mystery. When we unravel it we shall place our findings before the House. But one thing is clear—this decision is not as innocent as it looks.

Relations With China

I shall conclude with something about China. Two years ago the President had said in his Address on January 17, 1985 :

> "Our relations with China have shown improvement. We shall persevere in seeking a solution to the boundary question."

In two years things have changed. This time the President said :

> "My Government continues to strive for a just and peaceful settlement of the border question with China. The question remains crucial to full normalisation of our relations.

Arunachal and Tamil Nadu Complaints

If relations had improved two years ago why did they deteriorate ? Border talks have been going on for seven years. An agreement was made with China in 1979, according to which *status quo*, peace, would be maintained so long as the border problem is not solved. Why did China first enter Arunachal ? Why was not the country, the Parliament not immediately informed about it ? How much has China infiltrated in Arunachal in all ? A still bigger question is, why did this change take place in China's attitude ? The international scene is changing. We have to keep an eye on it. Let us be alert about Pakistan but there is no reason for fear. If Pakistan has friends India too is not friendless. India should conduct its foreign policy with self-confidence.

I was in Madras for two days. The people of Tamil Nadu complain that New Delhi does not pay as much attention to the problem of Sri Lanka as it should. The Prime Minister says Jayawardane foxed us, betrayed us. Sometimes he says the militants do not listen to us. People stranded in Jaffna are starving without food and have no medicines for illness. They are the flesh of our flesh, the blood of our blood. There is no question of our military intervention, but there are certain humanitarian considerations. Can we not give any help to the people stranded in Jaffna ? The Central Government should think about it. The entire opposition will support it. But there is no firm policy on Sri Lanka. There are too many advisors, and even they are changed. People who came to see me in Madras said they did not know whom to see in Delhi—at first Shri G. Parthasarathi was the advisor, now he is not, at first there was Bhandari, he was on the way to Colombo, but he was stopped on the way at Madras and he was found in the Congress Party's Office. Now he has become the advisor of the Congress party. Sometime back Shri Natwar Singh was in the picture, sometimes Shri Chidambaram makes the decisions.

These are delicate matters and the Prime Minister needs right and logical advice, which is not available. Thus problems are getting more complicated. The picture of two years ago has changed for the worse. This is your doing. Don't devalue democratic institutions one by one.

Vacancies in High Courts

How many judges' vacancies are there in Allahabad ? In reply to this question today the reply was 11 vacancies. How long ? Since 1984. Is there no advocate worthy of becoming a judge ? Or is it that the Chief Justice there and the Chief Minister do not see eye to eye ? Lakhs of law-suits are pending, but judges are not appointed. Will there be discrimination even in appointments ? Will All India Radio and Doordarshan be misused ? The Election Commission has been made a plaything. Should the Chief Election Commissioner be removed from office ?

Elections in States

Why are elections taking place in Haryana ? The Government of Bengal wanted to hold the elections, but they were told—wait, we shall hold the elections together. Now there will be elections in three States, but not in Haryana. The Commission says the law and order situation is not good there. I do not think Chief Minister Bansilal will agree. The situation is normal. If the electoral rolls are not ready the Election Commission is responsible for it. But the elections should not be stopped. You made the old Election Commissioner a Governor, he was rewarded for his services. You cannot strengthen democracy by misusing democratic institutions one by one.

The time has come for the ruling party to review its policies and re-examine its conduct. No one will accept this talk of taking the opposition along. After the elections you had said the opposition parties have been finished. We accepted 10 + 2 + 3. You got more than 400 seats in the Lok Sabha. Now show us how you solve the country's problems. But the country's problems cannot be solved on the strength of one party. One individual, howsoever popular, cannot find a way out of complicated problems. You need political consensus for that. We had hopes when Shri Rajiv Gandhi came to power, but perhaps he thought it would not save the party's interest, let us go back to the old ways. This will have dangerous consequences. That is all I have to say. Thank you.

Economic Crisis—Causes and Cure

Mr. Chairman, Sir, this is my maiden speech. I will not allow interruptions in it ....(*Interruptions*) ....

SHRI GHULAM NABI AZAD : His maiden speech of 10th Lok Sabha.

SHRI VAJPAYEE : Mr. Chairman, Sir, President's Address to the joint sitting of both the Houses is a historic event. If the Address takes place immediately after the elections it is all the more important. There is a need to maintain the solemnity of this occasion. Several members including Shri Sunil Dutt who spoke just now and prior to him Shri Jaswant Singh spoke who mentioned that the members who had assembled in the Central Hall to listen to the President could not listen to his Address. This should not be repeated. The programme is rehearsed and the arrangements are reviewed several times. We invite foreign dignitaries to participate in this event and if the loudspeakers do not function properly, we feel that we are not discharging our duties satisfactorily.

Another incident took place on that day. Some honourable members whose party affiliations are not known to me and I don't know to which House they belong, wanted to say something, and they were feeling extremely restless. They wanted to interrupt the President's Address to express themselves. But there is no scope for such things. Such scenes neither allow us to listen to the President's Address nor the words of the member, are audible to us. It would be better for some members, who are very keen on saying something before the Presidential Address, to meet the President and express themselves after the Address is over, but it would be still better if we avoid to such interruptions.

Right Time to Establish Healthy Conventions

Mr. Chairman, Sir, I wish my suggestion is followed in States also. When the Governor addresses, he simply reads out the speech prepared by the elected government. The Governor is the constitutional head of a State. At times, some Governors had to quit office on account of the Address ....(*Interruptions*) .... but if there is a scuffle, a pandemonium during the Governor's Address, such an incident diminishes the dignity of the Indian democracy. There is a need for preparing a code of conduct and we should take some effective steps in this regard after the Lok Sabha elections are over and this is the proper time for taking some steps, because if the Congress party is ruling here, in some States it is in the opposition and if we are in opposition here, our party is in power in some States.

Lok Sabha on July 18, 1991 during discussion on the Motion of Thanks on the President's Address

This applies to Janata Dal as well as Marxist party. As such if we make an attempt to set up new traditions then democracy can be made stronger and successful.

The National Economic Crisis

Mr. Chairman, Sir, a reference to the national crisis has been made in the President's Address. The crisis is not only financial, but it is political and social also and above all, at present the nation is facing a serious crisis of morality.

I would like to discuss the prevailing economic crisis at length in my speech. The Government has taken certain steps in this regard and the on-going discussion is to ascertain whether the steps taken by the Government are right or wrong. Take for instance devaluation of rupee, which has been done in two instalments. It appears as if something has been done surreptitiously, gold has been sent abroad and that too in instalments and in such a manner as if it is being smuggled out or being sent stealthily. Was all this necessary ?

My submission is to have a discussion on the issue of devaluation of rupee to find whether the move was right or wrong. But the basic question is as to how such a situation arose that we had to resort to devaluation of the rupee. Why and how the country was pushed towards an economic crisis which compelled us to devalue the rupee, sell our gold and make desperate efforts to get foreign aid.

The Hon. President has made a cursory mention of this issue in his Address. He said :

> "The Government recognises that the country is in the midst of an economic crisis of unprecedented magnitude. It has been living beyond its means and adopting soft options. We have been overtaken by events".

He further says :

> "The country must prepare itself to take hard and unpleasant economic decisions."

Our expenditure exceeds our earnings. How it happened and what made us reach this state ? Were our policies faulty or they were not implemented properly or did we hand over our economy in the hands of such persons for whom the interest of the nation was not important.

Excuse me for being harsh. After all the policies that have been formulated will lead the country to total bankruptcy. Could it not be perceived before hand ? All right, our country is democratic and democracy is prone to a certain degree of popularism but popularism of a very less magnitude. If we run after the means and totally ignore the way of achieving it, in that case we should realize that we have the deficiencies somewhere.

Don't Trade Charges

I know that this is not the right time for allegations and counter-allegations. The Prime Minister is not present in the House. During the course of his discussions regarding the crisis he commented on the work done by the previous two Governments but he has not made any comments on the work done by his party's Government which ruled before them. That should also be mentioned. After all among the previous Governments Shri V.P. Singh's Government remained in power for a very short time and the Chandrashekhar Government ruled with the support of the Congress and enjoyed power as long as Congress extended its support. It is true that Shri Chandrashekhar took some important and bold steps. If my information is correct then according to it after assuming the post of Prime Minister when Shri Chandrashekhar called the officers and asked them about the reason behind the prevailing situation in the country, their reply was that "now the situation cannot be retrieved."

Indiscreet Borrowing and Indiscriminate Spending

Did the officers have no role in this ? Are the formulators of the policies not to be blamed ? Taking debits indiscreetly and spending it indiscriminately has brought the country on the verge of economic crisis and as such this issue should be seriously discussed.

Now we are approaching I.M.F. for financial assistance. On what conditions the amount of the loan we propose to take and what have been the conditions imposed in the case of loans that we have taken till date. The other day, my colleague Shri Indrajit Gupta had raised this question. I have also gone through the reply given by the Hon. Prime Minister. He is not prepared to divulge the conditions. What does I.M.F. expect from us and to what extent are we prepared to accept their conditions ? Mr. Speaker, Sir, I urge that the copies of the correspondence between the present Minister of Finance, officials of the I.M.F. and Managing Director should be laid on the Table of the House. Copies of the correspondence relating to the agreements made between the former Ministers of Finance of the previous two Governments and the I.M.F. should also be laid on the Table of the House.

We expect the countrymen to drastically cut expenses to make sacrifices and bear the burden of new taxes. The country has immense power of tolerance. I am not prepared to believe that at the time of any crisis, the countrymen will not rise to meet the situation. They will stand by the country not because of this Government but because they love their country and have a deep sense of patriotism. They are in favour of safeguarding the self-respect of the country. But if we wish to ask for the support of the masses it is very important to win the confidence of the poor who are in majority. Is it not essential to take this House into confidence ? What is the necessity to send gold in this manner, what conditions are being imposed by the I.M.F. and what is the need to conceal it ? But it is very unfortunate that we are being kept in the dark. (*Interruptions*). Mr. Speaker, Sir, we are supposed to return the amount of the loan that we have taken. I would like to know the total amount that is to be repaid in the next ten years year-wise. The country and this House should be informed about it. We are keeping it confidential from our people and even keeping the House in the dark. But the thirty representative countries of the I.M.F. are well aware of the entire situation. How much loan the Government has taken and why it became necessary to take commercial loan ? What was the need to take short-term loan and the reasons for taking this loan ?

Total Liability and Conditions of Loans

As per my information the State Bank has also taken loan from I.M.F. although it should not come into the picture so far as foreign credit is concerned because financial assistance from any foreign source should be sought only through the Reserve Bank of India. As such how the State Bank was involved in it ? There is no discussion on the amount of loan taken by private companies, public undertakings and Defence. Loans are taken for Defence purposes also. What is the total liability ? The terms and conditions of the loan are never disclosed. What is the intention of the Government behind it. I would like the Government to take the House into confidence.

Mr. Speaker, Sir, we are very much worried as to how this loan will be repaid. Our new Minister of Finance is getting weaker day by day on account of it. He has already a weak constitution and now this problem is torturing him day and night. I know that he is not a shrewd politician as he has entered in this atmosphere only recently. I will not be surprised if I am told that he is having sleepless nights. He is losing weight day by day but the share markets of the country are flourishing by leaps and bounds. The manner in which the prices of shares shot up and to what level implies that there is no dearth of wealth, earned through honest means in this country. On the one hand the prices of shares of companies are rising sky-high and on the other hand it is an irony that the country is facing acute financial crisis. I hold the view that the idea of liberalising economic measures has played its role and the result is that the capital is coming out and the people are eager to join the mainstream. Perhaps they were looking for encouragement. But there exists a paradox in our economy. I want the Minister of Finance or the Prime Minister to clear all ambiguities in regard to this issue.

Mr. Speaker, Sir, as I have said earlier there is no dearth of capital, talent and manpower in this country. Perhaps there has been some deficiency in running the administration of the country, there have been some flaws in it. The Indians who go abroad make themselves affluent and make a vital contribution in making that country prosperous. Many Indians migrated to America as farmers, professionals, and small traders. They have reached the stage where they have the capacity of earning 50 billion American dollars and they have earned the same. Local people of Britain are jealous of Indians settled there. Wherever Indians go they try their utmost to earn money and they achieve great success. But it seems that the moment they come to this country their talent is blunted.

No Power Can Purchase India's Prime Minister

We are struggling against our deficit economy. In my opinion if policies are changed the condition of the country can improve. For that we will have to make a new beginning. For a new beginning it is necessary that the leader should have a clean record, Government officials should be accountable and the industrialists should be asked to earn only reasonable profits. They should not be allowed to make excessive profits.

Mr. Speaker, Sir, I am not among those who immediately become defensive whenever the name of IMF is mentioned. IMF is not something like a bug bear. India is an ancient and a vast country. It is not possible for anyone to purchase India. When Shri Chandrashekhar was our Prime Minister I had said that nobody can purchase the Prime Minister of India and I am prepared to repeat the same for the present Prime Minister too. The Prime Minister of this country is an elected representative. It is immaterial whether he is elected by a majority or a minority but it is a fact that he is the Prime Minister of this country and nobody can purchase him. If he sells himself, that is a different thing. But it is not possible for IMF to purchase us. IMF cannot swallow such a big country.

SHRI NIRMAL KANTI CHATTERJEE (Dum Dum) : But this happened in Japan.

SHRI VAJPAYEE : If conditions are being laid down we have every right to analyse the merits and demerits of those conditions. It is not proper on our part to feel frightened whenever the name of IMF is mentioned. Mr. Speaker, Sir, it is not that wealthy countries in the world are very much anxious to invest in India. Actually, they have a number of other better opportunities. The fact is that people lose their senses as soon as they disembark on an Indian Airport. After all they have the market of Soviet Russia, Communist China and Eastern Europe which need investment and they are offering attractive conditions. It is true that we had a bitter experience of the East India Company. But if the country does not act with self-confidence, it would be very difficult for us to overcome this crisis.

Three Aspects of Foreign Exchange Crisis

Mr. Speaker, Sir, there are three aspects of the present problem of foreign exchange. The first is the smuggling of gold on a large scale. On July 12, 1991 the Minister of State of Finance told the Parliament that the Customs Department had seized about 2926 kg gold, *i.e.* about 3 tonnes of gold worth Rs. 102 crores from January to June and everybody knows that only two or two and a half per cent of the total gold smuggled into India is seized. We can guess from it as to how much gold is being smuggled into the country. According to our estimate it is 200 tonnes every year. During the last ten years from 1981-82 to 1990-91 the price of gold has been about Rs. 36 crores per tonne. It means that gold worth about Rs. 7200 crores has been smuggled into the country during the last ten years which comes to about US $ 36 billion.

Another aspect of the foreign exchange crisis is over-invoicing. The Government has come forward with a number of proposals of economic reforms, but nothing concrete has been put forth by it in this regard. We took loan from foreign countries to meet the immediate crisis. That is all right. But what will happen in future ? How can we guarantee that the country will not retread the path which led it to the present catastrophe. Smuggling of gold should be checked. I would suggest some effective measures for this. But besides those, other measures should also be taken.

Mr. Speaker, Sir, we import plants, equipments, spare parts and raw material for industrialisation. During the period 1981-82 and 1990-91 we imported plants, equipments and raw material worth Rs. 2,29,640 crores. Generally, it is believed that importers indulge in 10 per cent over-invoicing. The commission taken in the arms deal is also a part of this over-invoicing. I have consulted the industrialists. Ten per cent is not a high amount. But at this rate of 10 per cent we left about Rs. 22,964 crores in foreign countries during the last ten years, which comes to about US $ 11.4 billion.

The third aspect is that of under-invoicing. We export commodities. During 1981-82 to 1990-91 we exported commodities worth Rs. 1,57,655 crores. Generally, it is believed that the exporter deposits 10 per cent on an average of his exports in foreign countries. However, some exporters are there only for name sake while some are genuine. If we accept that five per cent under-invoicing is done then the deficit comes to Rs. 7,08,883 crores which is equal to 3.9 billion US dollars. It means that we paid about Rs. 1,02,845 crores because of this defective system. I agree that in this process recycling of money takes place. Suppose we allow a margin of 25 per cent on account of it even then that money comes to about US$ 39 billion. If the decades of 'fifties to 'seventies are included then the amount comes to 56 billion dollars. This should be checked. If we fail to check it and continue to meet our immediate requirements by taking loans, then though we may get immediate relief but we will entangle ourselves badly in this crisis again.

Black Money and Gold Smuggling

At present we have not to face elections and there is sufficient black money in the country for the purpose. About Rs. 90,000 crores of black money is generated every year. That day during the Question Hour it was said that one cannot fight election with black money. The President in his Address has referred to the ways to eliminate black money. But its generation should be stopped. Many schemes and proposals are being put forth to bring the black money into circulation and suggestions are being made about the purposes for which it should be used. However, I would not like to go into detail.

We will have to think how the smuggling of gold, under-invoicing and over-invoicing should be checked. A suggestion in regard to issuing gold bonds has been made. The Government can issue bonds or take other measures. There is a great demand of gold in the country despite the fact that due to her weakness for the golden deer, Sita was abducted. Now Sita has been elected to the Parliament and Ravana is also there and there is no fear of abduction. The truth is that the BJP has brought Sita and Ravana together. This should not create any confusion in the 'Vanar Sena sitting opposite us.

Love for gold is always very strong and the people require some gold for domestic purposes. Measures should be taken to ensure that they are not forced to meet their requirements through smuggled gold. Many proposals have been made in this respect. More suggestions and even suggestions to bring about basic changes can be made if the Minister of Finance so desires.

How to Check Under or Over-Invoicing

Suggestions to check under-invoicing or over-invoicing can also be given, as, for instance, in regard to import over-invoicing, the representatives of industry and finance should be called and directed to find out the rates of plants, equipment, spares and raw-material etc. in the international market. They should contact the foreign chambers and publish the price list regularly. A constant watch should be kept on the prices of plants and spares being imported. I think it can be checked to a great extent. No efforts have been made so far in this regard. We can seek the cooperation of foreign chambers and can also invite quotations from authorised dealers by contacting them. Some are of the opinion that it can give rise to corruption. If the persons involved are dishonest they will find out loopholes, despite bringing about lot of improvement in the system. I do not assume that people in our country are corrupt or dishonest. We should have faith in the honesty of the citizens of the country. We should encourage them, provide opportunities to them and see that they are not forced to take wrong steps.

There is also a suggestion to check export under-invoicing. A foreign consultant concern can be appointed to assess the cost and the market price of the commodities being purchased from us. This should be done at regular intervals. Exporters should be made to export their goods at actual prices.

Other developing countries are also facing the similar problem of under-invoicing in export and over-invoicing in import. Indonesia is our neighbouring country. They have entrusted the entire responsibility to look after the customs of their country to a Swiss company. I am not advocating its case. But they have taken such a step. I only want the Government to take immediate measures to check bungling in foreign exchange which may enable the Government to save $ 50 million.

Economic Implications of Uni-Polar World

International situation has changed. It has become more difficult for the developing countries to get assistance from the West. We should understand this fact. Not many days have passed when in December, 1990 a German professor named Hatmat Elsane had visited Delhi and had delivered a lecture. I had chance to go through it. He spoke very bluntly and these blunt things are a challenge as well as a warning to us. It is true that he referred to those countries which get aid. But we should understand what he wanted to convey. I quote him :

> "But this aid will be characterised by conditionality. It will be extended under rather severe conditions because the South no longer has the option of threatening to change allegiance from one power bloc in the North to the other. The argument, if you do not give us aid on the terms we want, we will get it from elsewhere, will no longer be operative."

It is a sort of hidden warning to the developing nations. Now you have no other option and you will have to come to us. It is true that we are not getting aid, rather we are concentrating on trade. It is also true that we took loan and we are paying it in instalments. There may be difference of opinion over the way gold was mortgaged. However, the whole country, including all of us, would like that the country should pay the instalments of the loan at every cost. Yet we have every right to ask as to why the situation was allowed to be deteriorated to this extent. We also want that such a situation should not arise in future. But it should not be taken that we can make the country self-reliant only through words but virtually rejecting it in practice. If the assistance or aid suits the interests of the country we should accept it, otherwise we should reject it. Besides we should create confidence and determination among the people. When I suggested setting up a National Government, my friend Shri Indrajit Gupta said about that. . . .

SHRI INDRAJIT GUPTA (Midnapore) : Whatever you said in the House, has been reported in my name.

Take the Whole Country in Confidence

SHRI VAJPAYEE : They also want that you and we should cooperate. Mr. Speaker, Sir, it is good that the Government has won the Confidence vote. It is a matter of happiness. But Shri Advani also pointed out in his speech as to how long will this arrangement last on day-to-day basis. It is just like digging the well everyday and drinking water. There should be some permanent arrangement. The country is facing crisis and I agree with the Hon. Prime Minister that even if he had full mandate he would not have been able to solve it singlehandedly. I do not want to go into the details of the crisis that the country is facing today. I would like to confine myself only to the economic crisis. The country is in a warlike situation. I am not saying war situation but warlike situation and that situation is even more dangerous than war. The enemy is known and well identified in a war but here it is assaulting us from behind the curtain. We are in deep economic crisis. There is political instability in the country and therefore, the people should rise to the occasion and resolve to stand united. All of us should help in creating this national resolve. But this cannot be done by keeping the Opposition in the dark. We should be taken into confidence and the people of this country should also be taken into confidence. If this Government works on these lines, I am sure we can overcome this crisis. Thank you.

Establish Wholesome Conventions
Need of the Hour

Mr. Speaker, Sir, I want to start from the very beginning. On 24 February the hon. President addressed the joint session of both the Houses. It is an annual feature. He reads out a written speech. In this regard, he can be compared with the Queen of Britain. But the Queen of Britain at least enjoys respect from the members of Parliament. In our country the President's Address is marred by repeated interruptions. At times it is even boycotted. There may be occasions when the situation may go even out of control.

Solemnity of President's Address

Mr. Speaker, Sir, since 1957 I have been listening to the President's Address. The other day, sitting in the Central Hall I was thinking as to whether this Address by the President is really essential ? Has it not been reduced to a mere tradition ? Are we able to maintain the dignity on that occasion ? Should the President's Address be allowed to be interrupted ? It is correct that the President of our country does not address the entire nation like the President of America. His constitutional position is different. However, let us give a thought to the kind of peculiar position faced by our President. In the first instance he read out the address prepared by the V.P. Singh Government. Thereafter, he read out one prepared by the Chandra Shekhar Government and now an address prepared by the Narasimha Rao Government.

Review Conventions

We are not sure what will happen today. I know nothing will happen. Now President will have to read out another Address. I think we should review this situation.

Mr. Speaker, Sir, the situation in States is still worse. When the Governors come to deliver the Address in Legislative Assemblies they come prepared for anything. They are stopped from entering the Assembly, prevented from reading the Address, papers are thrown on them, documents are thrown over their heads. Many of the Governors read out only the first and last paragraph of the speech and go back. This sort of thing is not proper. What is the necessity of putting the Governors in such a difficult situation ?

Lok Sabha on March 7, 1992 during discussion on the Motion of Thanks on the President's Address

Mockery of Democracy

Mr. Speaker, Sir, I am raising a serious matter and would like to emphasise that here is an opportunity to re-establish the previous good traditions and to establish certain new traditions, if necessary. We should not make democracy a subject of mockery. We should not present wrong ideals before the new generation. In case we find it difficult to maintain the dignity and decorum at a particular occasion we should better avoid that occasion. You can convene an All-Party meet and prepare a code of conduct in this regard. The situation in the country at the moment is such that one or the other party is ruling one state or the other and as such it should not be difficult to prepare a code of conduct for such occasion.

Mr. Speaker, Sir, I was going through the President's Address. It is unduly lengthy. An effort has been made to incorporate even the petty things. What is the necessity of doing so in the President's Address ? There are 30 paragraphs in it and it seems that the 30th paragraph has been added at the last minute in a haste. The entire speech has been divided into small paragraphs but the 30th para is a long one and it appears to be on the education policy. It is quite possible that the Education Minister might be busy elsewhere, he may be on a visit from Kukreshwar or Chitrakut and he could not have found the time to see this paragraph. However, it is not coherent and does not fit in the entire Address. But as the customary Address is to be made and every Ministry has sent its note so let it be done. The President's Address should not be treated in such a casual way.

Mr. Speaker, Sir, when the Government assumed power it was hoped and the Government had also given an announcement, and being a minority Government it was also proper to run the country on consensus. Had the Government been in majority even then in view of the crisis being faced these days—those may be the crisis of the unity and integrity of the nation or financial crisis—it would have been very difficult to overcome those crises without determination and consensus approach. We had thought that the Government is in minority. It would take everyone into confidence and try to build up consensus. For some days an effort was made in this direction but later on the situation changed.

Horse Trading in Meghalaya

The same thing had happened with late Shri Rajiv Gandhi also. I do not want to go into that part of the history. Today, no effort is being made towards building up a consensus and even if a consensus is evolved it is not followed properly. After all, what happend in Meghalaya. Mr. Speaker, Sir, you might be remembering, I do not want to drag you into this controversy, it was decided in a meeting with the opposition that the fate of the Government of that State should be left to the Legislative Assembly. It was not followed. Congress Government was formed then by engineering defection. Was it essential ? Meghalaya is an important part of the country. If you want to solve the problems confronted by the country with consensus then was it necessary to enact all this drama in Meghalaya ? No, it was not.

I welcome the newly elected friends from Punjab. However, the objective behind holding elections in Punjab was not to increase Congress strength in Lok Sabha. The objective was rather greater, we wanted to fulfil the need of democracy. For that matter it was initially thought by all parties to contest the election together. Later on, it was decided to contest it separately. At one stage it was said that the Congress Party was not keen to form a Government there. Such a Government should come into power there which could fight terrorism unitedly. Unfortunately Akalis boycotted the elections. Their decision cannot be termed as correct. However, I want to congratulate the Congress Party for this massive victory. Had Congress desired it could have invited Shri Amrinder Singhji to join the Government and could have also invited the members of Bahujan Samaj Party to join the Government.

Does the Punjab problem not demand that this is the need of the hour. After Independence there was no hesitation in including even Dr. Syama Prasad Mookerjee in the Cabinet.

SHRI KAMAL CHAUDHARY (Hoshiarpur) : Atalji, the Akalis did not participate in the Punjab elections and the people cast their votes as they wished. Shri Amrinder Singh's party was able to capture only three seats. Why are you pleading the cause of Akalis ? (*Interruptions*).

SHRI VAJPAYEE : Mr. Speaker, Sir, I am not bothered about votes but if I am interrupted like this, I would raise such matters which should not be raised here (*Interruptions*). This should not have happened there. This is my suggestion and I am putting forth my opinion. There is no question of liking or disliking.

SHRI P.V. NARASIMHA RAO, Prime Minister : I know that the suggestions you have given here are good, but I have my limitations. I cannot divulge it in public. I will tell you later.

SHRI VAJPAYEE : That is the problem (*Interruptions*).

SHRI SHARAD YADAV (Madhepura) : Sir, this is an injustice to all members...(*Interruptions*).

SHRI VAJPAYEE : Mr. Speaker, Sir, the Hon. Prime Minister says he is helpless, we want to see him strong.

SHRI RAM VILAS PASWAN (Rosera) : Mr. Speaker, Sir, the Hon. Prime Minister should not have said that he is helpless, if he did not want to divulge anything...(*Interruptions*).

MR. SPEAKER : Shri Paswan, please sit down.

SHRI VAJPAYEE : I was saying that because there is no need to hide anything (*Interruptions*), the Hon. Prime Minister was saying that he is helpless, but we want him to be strong ....(*Interruptions*).

SHRI P.V. NARASIMHA RAO : Sir, there is an amount of propriety in divulging certain matters, certain negotiations and certain talks which we hold with Leaders of other parties and that is my difficulty. In course of time I would certainly like to take the Leaders of Opposition groups into confidence. I would not like to suppress that. In course of time, if no one concerned has any objection, the story can come out.

Brute Majority

SHRI VAJPAYEE : Mr. Speaker, Sir, it is a universal fact that if a party has clear majority it is good and if it has two-thirds majority which gives it the right to amend the Constitution—it is all the more better. But during the last 10 years of our parliamentary career we have found that this country cannot be run by brute majority alone *i.e.* majority of number. It can take decisions but it cannot inspire the 80 crore population of this country.

Unfortunately the problems have become so complex that the Congress party cannot run away from its responsibility. Repeatedly the Government headed by Shri Vishwanath Pratap Singh and Shri Chandra Shekhar have been blamed for various lapses but the Hon. Prime Minister and his colleagues have never pointed to the circumstances which have led the country to a state of bankruptcy. No proud person will ever like such a situation. Today, we cannot do without debt. There are conditionalities with the granting of loans.

"Rahiman kar par kar karo kar Tar karo no koy
Ja din kar tar kar karo ta din marna hoy"

The saint poet Rahim said that if you give alms to somebody it is good but if you receive alms it is better to die on that day. That is a fact. It is a different matter that the entire country can be brought together on this issue which has not been done so far.

Nobody Can Sell This Country

The Hon. Prime Minister is right when he says what is the other alternative ? I would like to submit to my friends who belong to leftist parties that levelling charges that the country has been sold by vested interests is not proper. Ours is an ancient and great country. Who can sell it ? Who has the courage to do it ? And if the country is sold while we are here, we will have to hang our heads in shame. We would not be able to face the masses. To give a warning that we would not allow anybody to compromise with the sovereignty of the country is good. Nobody can sell this country. Is this a way to boost the morale of the country ? By lowering the morale we cannot make the country strong. I have a grouse with the Hon. Prime Minister. Why doesn't he make efforts now to find new solutions and alternatives. Agreed, that he did not have sufficient time when he was sworn in. He should have taken remedial steps to check devaluation of rupee, getting back the mortgaged gold. But it is never late. Now he has time to do that. He should take immediate steps lest the pendulum goes to the other extreme once again and the situation deteriorates to such an extent that we may have to face hardships again.

Mr. Speaker, Sir, Communism has failed but this is no reason to believe that capitalism has succeeded. America itself is in crisis. When the hon. Finance Minister presented the Budget he was in high spirits and said :

Sarfaroshi ki Tamanna Ab Hamare Dil Mein Hai
Dekhna hai jor kitna Baju-e-Katil Mein hai"

Fight the Problem not the Opposition

Sir, would you fight with us ? If you want to fight with anybody, fight with the crisis that we are facing today. And fight in a way that the country's self-respect and sovereignty is not compromised and India is able to show a new path to the developed and developing nations ? What will happen if we ourselves go astray ? So, if the Hon. Prime Minister had called for a meeting where we could sit together and try to find ways to overcome the crisis it would have been better. He could have said that the Government has taken immediate steps but there is need for long term solutions. But this did not happen. Such a thing ought to have been done. I do not know whether there is a third alternative ? But it is a fact that we never tried to find it out. It should have been found out. The foreign companies want to enter Indian market for making profit. Nobody should have this illusion that they want to work for our upliftment. We should exercise our discretion as to which company should enter into Indian Market, in which sector and to what extent. This all depends on us. The doors are just being thrown open. Any World Bank official is free to meet the Finance Minister. Doors are open and all are welcome. If the door is closed one can get through the window. This was not the practice earlier. Earlier, the World Bank officials could meet only the Secretary or other officials of the Secretariat, but now they have come very close, where will it lead us ?

Some basic changes in the structure of the economy have been made and I agree that these changes were essential but we were not yet prepared for it. We have supported the Government in removing the unnecessary constraints. We have also supported in the removing of obstructions created by the bureaucracy. For progress there is need for competition. This has become clear from the communist countries of Europe. Being in competition there can be monopoly also. If the monopoly of State can create problems, the monopoly by individuals can create more problems.

Encourage Small Industries

The small scale industry feels directionless. Emphasis is being laid to formulate policies for small farmers. They are apprehensive of future. The public sector factories are running in loss. The Bharatiya Janata Party had warned earlier that in principle there is nothing bad in the public sector. In a backward country like India the intervention of State is essential. But it should be done only in sectors where it is essential like the core sectors and efforts should be made to make it successful. We opened factories in public sector, but did not equip them with professional management. We did not develop managerial staff. We left these industries at the mercy of I.A.S. officers. We saw it for ourselves, how these IAS officers functioned in Uttar Pradesh, Madhya Pradesh and Rajasthan.

What is their stake or interest in running these factories ? If the factory goes in loss or gets sick these IAS officers are transferred as Managing Directors of another factory. Their job is safe. How long will this continue ? When these factories were taken over by the public sector, at that time there was corruption and now once again when these are being handed over to private hands, there will be corruption. A factory in Uttar Pradesh was taken over. That produced cement. It was said that it could not run. The previous Government had taken it over. The workers launched an agitation. Workers said they were ready to run the factory. The case was filed in the court. The court rejected the Government decision. Now that factory is running well and running with the cooperation of workers. There is no need to hand it over to private sector. Is the Government ready to think about each such factory with wisdom ? Speaking on the previous Budget I cited an example of the West Bengal Jute Factory. The workers are ready to give Rs. 7 - 8 crore, their total savings, to run the factory. They say you run the factory with some of your assistance. Where there is no way to run the factory without closing it, workers' cooperation should be taken. There should be provision of alternative employment for them. The exit policy is all right. But there is no social security system. The moment a worker loses his job, he will be there on the roads and will start starving. These are some issues that need collective approach. These issues should not be politicised. Elections are not going to be held in the near future.

I have a complaint against the Congress. Was it necessary to break the Shiv Sena to increase its own strength ?

"Kay Sharadrao tumhin sanga Kay sangay che te"

(Sharadrao, please tell us what you have to say.)

SHRI SHARAD PAWAR, the Minister of Defence : There was a need to keep them away from you.

SHRI VAJPAYEE : Only two Members (*Interruptions*).

SHRI ASHOK ANANDRAO DESHMUKH : The B.J.P. too helped in breaking the Shiv Sena. They made Gopi Nath Munde the leader of the Opposition at once (*Interruptions*).

Threat of Consumerism

SHRI VAJPAYEE : If there is any advantage, it is quite insignificant and quite momentary (*Interruptions*). The Janta Dal disintegrated due to its own reasons. But I know well that the *Swamis, Bhu-Swamis* and *Grih-Swamis* related with the ruling party were engaged in playing their role to add to that division. If you manage majority, it is good but keep in mind that only majority cannot solve the problems. Today the country is at a critical juncture. There is a threat from outside, there is internal disintegration. Your determination to adopt new policies in the economic field lacks will and public support. It looks as if the country has become a soft state. Who will sacrifice ? A consumer culture is cropping up due to television and the middle class is hankering after that culture. We have to present ideas if we want this class should learn to face hardships. We will have to create faith in the values of life. I am sorry that we could not do so. We do not accept the Dunkel proposal. It cannot be accepted in the present situation. The Government should make it clear whether there is any scope of amendment or modification in this proposal after negotiations. If the proposal is rigid, it should be rejected. But if scope is there, have a dialogue. Western countries have their own problems. America is carrying on its subsidy programme. Japan has its own difficulties. European countries are trying to find out solutions to the problems of their farmers. The leadership should understand that we have a type of complex in mind. We have been slave for a long time. Today it is the age of interdependence. First independence and then interdependence. It is quite necessary to safeguard our interests. We all should co-operate to find Third Alternative.

But if it is said that the country is being sold out, the people may get enraged. If we have to take recourse to fanaticism, it can easily be said without going seriously into it that the country is being sold out whether the country is being sold out or not. But if it is done, we will have to pay price for it. I would like to give a warning against it. If the country is really being sold out, then this Government, this Parliament and the entire edifice do not have any relevance today. This question is supreme, this is the first and the foremost question. But I do not agree that those, who are ruling the country, are selling it out. I think such an unfortunate moment will never come when a democratically elected Government will sell the country. At last they will have to go to the people. The people will not spare those who will sell the country. But I would like to say that this is not a question of feelings. We should find out a third alternative collectively. The pendulum should not be allowed to move completely to the other side, a balance will have to be struck somewhere and there should be harmony in policies. The Prime Minister wants to carry on the politics of consensus. But perhaps his party is not allowing him to do so. Now he is the president of the party. He should convince his party. Will this game of power once again play with the fate of the country ? I have been a witness. I have been watching this game since 1957. Where we were and where have we reached ? What has been the state of our institutions ? Now a charge-sheet is ready against the Chief Election Commissioner. I thought that the Chief Election Commissioner would be asked to quit. Now the Government says that he is not ready to quit, it is very ridiculous. Make him ready to quit.

Challenge of Tomorrow

Talks are already going on about prosecution against the Supreme Court Judge. Now a case against the Chief Election Commissioner. Keep in mind that this country will start prosecuting the Members of Parliament in open courts. It is not in good taste. So try to have consensus as far as possible. Still time is there. I have come to know that you have made all arrangements to win today's voting. But what would be after it ? Tomorrow we will have to face the same questions. There is a need to give a new shape, a new style to the politics so that we can properly answer the prospective questions. We are fighting for achieving it. Thank you.

MR. SPEAKER : Thank you Vajpayee ji. Efforts will be made to take action on your suggestions in regard to interruptions during the President's Address.

What is our Identity and Where are our Roots ?

Mr. Deputy Speaker, Sir, President's Address is an important event in the Joint Session of Parliament. This time the Budget Session started with the President's Address. I wished to be present on the occasion but could not. The reason is evident. At the end of his speech the Hon. President referred to democracy to be a living thing. He admitted that the country is faced with crises. He has also admitted that there have been remarkable levels of cooperation as also strong areas of dissent last year. He said that our democracy is very lively. I do not understand the extent to which the Hon. President's views and the Government's actions are complementary to each other. Is it not that the President's Address is written separately and the Government acts differently ?

Sensitive Matters Ignored

My hon. friend Shri Mani Shankar Aiyar is not present here. Once he wrote in an article as to how President's Address should be drafted. I do not know as to what procedure is being followed now and who prepares the Address. Mr. Deputy Speaker, Sir, it is true that we wished to be present at the time of joint Parliament Session but we decided to abstain. Shri Advani wrote a letter to the Hon. President and informed that we are sorry that we are not coming and also clarified that it was not a disrespect to the office of the President. We do respect the office of President and since he holds the office we respect him. However, the Government is creating a situation due to which we would respectfully abstain from the Joint Parliament Session. We used the word "respectfully abstain." It is true that attention is not paid to minute things today. Sensitive matters are neither taken into consideration nor evaluated. Next day I read newspapers and the news was that Bharatiya Janata Party boycotts the Joint Parliament Session. Though very minor but there is certainly a difference between the word "boycott" and "respectfully abstain." However, that difference is not being taken into consideration. We were very agitated. It was but natural for us to be agitated for the way in which our rally was banned. But we did not create any obstacle in passing the Railway Budget. The Government crossed all limits in controlling the rally. We also lost patience. But we did not create any problem while presenting the General Budget.

Lok Sabha on March 2, 1993 during discussion on the Motion of Thanks on the President's Address

I have very long association with this House. I remember the days when Shri Morarji Desai used to be the hon. Minister of Finance. He was going to present the Budget but some of the communist members were agitated. So they continued to raise a hue and cry while Morarji Desai continued his Budget speech. We could have also created such a situation. But we did not do so because our conscience did not permit it.

We want that democracy should prevail in the real sense and dignity of the House should be preserved. However, the dignity of the House is not preserved inside the House. Who knows what happens outside the House ? Will the same not be reflected here ? Therefore, when the Hon. President refers democracy to be lively, it should be reflected outside too. Farmers are holding a rally. What is the need to stop them ? The Government asked them to hold the rally near the Red Fort. Cannot the citizens of the country gather in front of Parliament and knock the doors of Parliament ? All the rallies have been banned. Our leftist friends are also complaining, because there will be oppression. Everyone, big and small, will suffer. Therefore, oppression should not take place. The other day I had pointed out that the hon. Minister of Home Affairs could hold talks. I read in the newspapers that farmers were given permission to hold their rally near the Red Fort. But we were not even asked whether we wanted to hold the rally at some other place. It is altogether different that we would not have agreed.

SHRI NITISH KUMAR (Barh) : On the top of Qutab Minar ?

SHRI VAJPAYEE : We would make you climb on it to deliver your speeches.

Is the Government Anti-religious ?

Mr. Deputy Speaker, Sir, the incident of 6th December is the first reference in the President's Address. That was but natural. The matter has already been discussed and will be discussed again. I will say afterwards what I want to say with regard to it. However, I was going through the English and Hindi versions of the Address, its English version is as follows :

"The basic premise of secularism and the rule of law has been threatened."

But in the Hindi version of these lines it has been stated that secularism and law have been threatened. What is the threat and who gave the threat is the matter of discussion. There is a lot of difference in it. But I am referring to the specific word. In English it is said that ours is a secular country and it should remain secular. There is no objection to it. But the difficulty arises only when the specific word is translated as *'Dharam nirpeksh'* in Hindi. Not only in my opinion but in common man's opinion ours is a religious country. To be religious or having good qualities mean the same thing these days. However, emphasis is laid on to safeguard the *'Dharam nirpeksh'* and I would like to submit to the so-called custodians of secularism that *'Dharam nirpeksh'* is not the equivalent of the word 'secularism'. It is creating confusion among the people. Is the Government anti-religious ? Does the Government want to make the country non-religious ?

Nehru's Definition of Word "Secular"

Mr. Deputy Speaker, Sir, I have already made a mention of it and today I would like to repeat the same. I am talking of the years 1949-50. When the Constitution of India was framed there was no reference to the word 'secular' in it. Everybody agreed that our country should be secular. It was not at all a matter of controversy. Even after the formation of Pakistan, nobody ever raised the demand to declare India a religious state. However, the Constitution-makers did not use the word 'secular' in the Constitution, because they were apprehensive that it might create confusion. When the word 'secular' is translated as *'Dharam nirpeksh'* it is certainly likely to create a confusion. Nehru ji realised this problem in 1961. I am referring to Nehruji because most of the Hon. Members refer to him again and again when they talk of secularism. Nehruji had written the preface of a book called *Dharam Nirpeksh Rajya* by an M.P. Shri Raghunath Singh in Varanasi in 1961. The book is available in the Parliament library and can be borrowed. I am reading out an extract from the book : "Perhaps the word 'secular' in English. Some people think that it relates to anti-religion and obviously it is wrong to have such a notion. It means that it is a state which gives equal respect to all religions."

Mr. Deputy Speaker, Sir, if taken in this context, India has always been and will remain a secular country and the incident of 6th December has not at all created a threat to secularism. Let us use the proper word. In the latest Hindi version of the Constitution of India, the word 'secular' stands for *'Panth Nirpeksh"* and not for *'Dharam Nirpeksh'*. India should follow the concept of *'Panth Nirpeksh'*. The word religion is used in a wider term. If at all the people of this country have to be encouraged to move ahead, work hard and make as much sacrifice as possible, then religion cannot be isolated.

Shri Indrajit Gupta is not present here. An incident referred to by Shri Durga Das in his book named *India from Curzon to Nehru* is worth reading. I would like to place it before the House. I quote :

> "I asked Gandhi how he would counter Jinnah's charge that his was a pseudo-religious movement likely to lead to a reactionary revivalism. Gandhi replied that his own idiom was the only one that the masses could grasp. Villagers responded to his call, for they lived nearer to God than the townsfolk, and understood his message as a call to self-abnegation and self-purification. As for revivalism, Gandhi said he certainly wished to see among the Hindus a revival of spirit of resistance to evil and a shedding of their cowardice. Anyway, Hindu-Muslim unity was to him an article of faith and he could never be so foolish as to inaugurate a movement likely to harm this cause. The Muslim masses instinctively understood the religious issue and would feel brotherly towards non-Muslims who espoused their cause."

What is Our Identity ?

Today, it is said that religion and politics should be separated and that religion and politics have no relation. In order to convey the correct idea of it to a common man if we say that communalism should not be associated with politics and that religion should not be misused to fulfil the political motives, I can understand the sense. But the Government does not say this. It says that religion has no relation with politics and those who try to bring religion into politics pose a danger to secularism in the country. A common man does not accept this idea. I have not, so far, been able to understand why stress is being laid on defining the word 'secular' as *'Dharam nirpeksh'*. Are we not able to make people understand by translating secularism into *'panth-nirpeksha'* or *'sampraday nirpeksha'*.

Roots of the Ancient Country

Mr. Deputy Speaker, Sir, firstly, before taking up other issues, I would like to submit a point in this regard. What is the identity of this country which we call as Bharat, Hindustan or India. Where are the life roots of this country ? From which roots the nationality of this country gets the stream of life ? No new nation was born in the year 1947 The nations which emerged in Europe after the Second World War are in a process of disintegration at present. But this country has remained united for centuries. There were different states and they had sometimes used to indulge in wars with each other. Even then the country was one. What were the reasons for its unity ? Please excuse me. I would like to state that at that time, Islam or Christianity had not reached our country. The believers in Islam did not come with Ghori or Ghazni. First of all, the traders from Arab countries came here and constructed the first mosque in South India by taking permission from the Hindu ruler there. None objected to the construction of that mosque and the ruler also permitted happily. Never before any such fight has taken place in the country. Is it not an evidence that this is an ancient nation ? Only a new chapter was opened in the year 1947. Our intellectuals who are influenced with Western education will say that the concept of the nation is a modern concept.

Discuss the Problem

So, they cannot accept our country as an ancient nation. If you do not want to accept it, it is your own wish, but no one can deny about its ancientness. I do not want to quote Nehruji again. He had also said : "since thousand of years, a chain of life is continued and I am proud that I am also a link of that chain. I do not want to separate myself from that chain. Which is this chain ? Is it not Hindu ? But an objection has been raised on the word 'Hindu' after independence or after the division of the country. Why the effort to give Indian colour to everything, after independence was not fully successful. I have said it earlier also and would again like to repeat that we should discuss this question as to what is the national pride of this country. If this is not a Hindu country or if it is not integrated by the Hindu culture, then what other factors are responsible for the integrity of this country ? Who were those great men who inspired the people for making sacrifices at the time of foreign invasions. It was Shivaji and not Aurangzeb... Why Maharana Pratap inspires the people of this country even today ? I agree that the Muslims, who came from the other countries and settled here, became part and parcel of this country. They should also be treated equally. Our Constitution provides such guarantee. There is a need to bring it into practice also. There is no difference of opinion in this regard, but the people are being misled by creating imaginary differences of opinion. It is necessary to have clear-cut opinions and we are ready for a discussion in this respect.

Mr. Deputy Speaker, Sir, the Hon. Home Minister stated that day that the R.S.S. members consider Hinduism as nationalism. He should understand that Hinduism is not used as Hindu religion. No adjective was used before religion. It was always preached to follow the religion. Later on, sects were formed and ways of worship were developed. But this land has enough strength to take everyone along. Why are we giving less importance to this strength ? If it is said that politics should not be communalised, then this rule should be applicable to all. One should not adopt double-standard.

Apply One Standard

Mr. Deputy Speaker, Sir, I do not want to repeat the same points. I am expressing a point. I am happy that Shri Chandra Shekhar is present here. It is necessary to have clarity in thoughts. You accuse us of being communalists and responsible for dividing the country and we accuse you of dividing the country in 1947 and again you are doing the same. Thus, this discussion will lead us to nowhere. One should have clear-cut views on this issue. We should have same opinions and should speak same language on the basic issues. It is true that we will always have difference of opinion with the persons who say that India is not a nation or India is a group of nationalities. Our Communist friends had been expressing their views till recently that there is no such thing like Muslim communalism. There is no such thing as...(*Interruptions*).

Dada Bhupesh Gupta has given these speeches in Rajya Sabha in my presence. I can quote those speeches.

SHRI SAIFUDDIN CHOUDHURY (Katwa) : He would have been afraid of you.

SHRI VAJPAYEE : Please do not say like this, I have a great regard for Dada. There is no question of his being afraid of me. I know when the Constitution was changed and the word "secular" was included, Shri Indrajit Gupta was present there. He had said at that time as to why this word is being included. Our country is already secular.

SHRI INDRAJIT GUPTA (Midnapore) : The word "socialist" has also been included in it.

Dr. Ambedkar Quoted in Parts

SHRI VAJPAYEE : No discussion was held on it. This motion was moved by Sardar Swaran Singh and he had said that the word "secular" means that there will be no religion of the state and it will have no system of worship and its attitude towards all religions will be equal. Some of the members did not speak at all. But when Shri K.T. Shah tried to get included the word "socialist" in the Constitution, Dr. Ambedkar did not accept it. The argument given by Dr. Ambedkar shows his farsightedness. In the Drafting Committee he rejected the amendment. He said that socialism is a hypothesis of an economic set-up and I do not want to include it in the Constitution because economic system and hypothesis keep on changing. A time may come when a better economic system than socialism may come into being and the same is accepted by the people. I do not want to put limitations for the future generations. To say at that time ....

Today the ideas of Dr. Ambedkar are mentioned in parts only, while the need of the hour is to see him in totality. I am not going to discuss that issue.

Mr. Deputy Speaker, Sir, I am expressing a point of view. A discussion is going on seeds under the Dunkel Proposal. The Government is trying to defend the indefensible Dunkel Proposal. The root is more important than the tree and that root has come out from the seed. There is enough matter to consider, but please do not level allegations. You can accuse us and we can accuse you. Where will this dialogue lead us to ?

SHRI SAIFUDDIN CHOUDHURY : We go upto genes.

SHRI VAJPAYEE : Because you are materialistic. That is why, you go upto genes.

Ayodhya and Neighbouring Countries

Mr. Deputy Speaker, Sir, a mention has been made in the President's Address about our relations with neighbouring countries. We all want that we should have good relations with our neighbouring countries, but despite all efforts, our relations with Pakistan and Bangladesh are not improving. The incidents which happened in these countries after 6th of December give a serious warning to our country. It is a matter of grave concern. After all, the issue of Ayodhya is an internal issue of our country and it is our responsibility to solve it properly. We cannot allow our neighbouring countries to make any interference in the issue and demolish temples, burn down the houses of Hindus making thousands of them homeless and burn our National Flag and all this has been done at the Government level. In Faislabad, a Minister of the Federal Government in Pakistan kept looking on and a temple was demolished before him. In Lahore, a temple was demolished through bulldozer. This is totally wrong.

SHRI NITISH KUMAR : In 1984, the same has happened with the Sikhs also.

SHRI CHANDRA SHEKHAR (Ballia) : Sir, the thing is that the federal Government was responsible there and here the State Government was responsible for it.

SHRI VAJPAYEE : And, who demolished Hindu temples in Bangladesh ?

SHRI CHANDRA SHEKHAR : There is federal set-up there.

SHRI VAJPAYEE : Neither the Federal Government nor the State Government did anything, but 490 temples have also been demolished there. Is it an ordinary incident ? What did our Government do there ? I am taking of only temples here, but shops and industrial units were set ablaze there. Should it not be mentioned ? That is why the Prime Minister of India had to cancel his Dhaka visit and moreover threats are still being given that the

Indian Premier will not be allowed to airdash in case he goes there to participate in the SAARC Summit.

A mention was made during his address by His Excellency the President of India that the talks with Premier of Bangladesh were held in a very cordial manner when the latter was on a tour of India. Tin Bigha has been given, well the Government may give something more if it wants so, but there should be cordial relations. Dialogue with neighbouring countries is needed to be carried firmly and in clear terms. We want that our relations with the neighbouring countries should improve. Now, the rest of the world have considerably changed, but the countries of West Asia are still entangled in tensions.

I had told you that we would solve the Ayodhya tangle, but we cannot allow any Islamic country to become the protector of Indian Muslims. It is wrong.

Immigration Problems

Mr. Deputy Speaker, Sir, the immigration of people from Bangladesh who are coming in great numbers is yet another issue concerned with this issue. Many citizens of Bangladesh have succeeded in getting their names entered in the voters' lists even though a voice of protest was not raised against it in Delhi. Their names should be deleted soon. Can it be called a communal demand ? Should any country allow people from its neighbouring country to immigrate illegally ?

Mr. Deputy Speaker, Sir, after an inquiry was conducted in Delhi, names of several thousand Bangladeshis were deleted from the lists of voters. The inquiry is still going on.

I had been to Assam recently. The proposed rally of our party to be held in Guwahati was initially banned. However, it was allowed later on. But, I would like to submit that this House should pay attention to the situation arising in Assam. Issues are generally allowed to linger on. How matters are allowed to linger on for politics of votes was seen by us on Ayodhya issue.

But another type of situation is emerging due to the inflow of a large number of people from Bangladesh. The Election Commission no longer remains to be our institution but the Election Commission has issued directives. Today the members of the Janata Dal and the left parties had raised the issue of Tripura. We agree with them on this score. If inquiry is not held in accordance with the directives of the Election Commission and if the officers in question are not removed, will it then not tantamount to the mockery of the Election Commission ? There is no justification of care-taker Government by the same State Government in Tripura.

It is being stated that the report of the Government has not been received, but it is no secret that the Union Government can get the Governor's report any time of its own choice. You got the reports from the Governors of the four States and dismissed those Governments. It means what you think right is right.

The Central Government may be interested in allowing the corrupt State Government of Tripura to remain in power. The Tripura Government which indulged in electoral irregularities may be allowed to continue in power, even though comments and strictures have been passed by the Election Commission against the State Government. Mr. Deputy Speaker, Sir, yet another drama is being enacted in Assam.

Directions of Election Commission

An order to review the voters' lists throughout the country was given on the 25th November, 1992 by the Election Commission keeping the date of 1st January 1993 in mind. They had written in their report that foreign nationals had come to India in large numbers and they had succeeded in getting their names entered in the voters' lists. The scrutiny of voters' lists should be made keeping in view the date of 1st January, 1993. The names of foreign nationals should be deleted from those voters' lists.

Now I want to quote what the Election Commission has stated. I am having a copy of the entire directive given by it. The Election Commission has stated :

> "AND WHEREAS, being aware of the presence of a substantial number of foreign nationals in some States in India the Commission, in full consultation with the Ministry of Home Affairs, issued a direction with its letter No. 23/92 dated 21 Aug., 1992 to all the State Governments and Chief Electoral Officers containing a special enumeration procedure for areas having a substantial presence of foreign nationals."

The Commission has also written that the direction being forwarded by it has been endorsed by the Ministry of Home Affairs, that is to say the Ministry is agreeable to it. The Commission added that in accordance with the new procedure it is the responsibility of the State Governments to identify foreign nationals in every Assembly Constituency and at every polling booth. It was also stated by the Commission that the work of identifying the foreign nationals and counting their number should be finished by 31st August, 1992. The Commission added that in case there was any doubt about the citizenship of a person, the district collector should decide it by 7th October, 1992. Later on, this date was extended from 7th to 17th of October.

Assam Government's Opposition

But the Government of Assam did not comply with the direction. It said that the counting would be conducted as per the voters' list of 1990. Those who had come up to 1990 would not be removed, whether they are the citizens of India or not. This was the purport of what it said. The State Government made it dear that it was not ready to abide by the new direction. It also issued directives to its officials that they have to ensure this much whether the person whose name was entered in the voters list was of 18 years of age in 1990 or not. Now there is a tug of war between the Government of Assam and the Election Commission.

Now I would like to shift your attention from the situation of Tripura to the situation of Assam. The Election Commission did not accept the objections raised by the Government of Assam. It again issued direction that it should be followed. The Ministry of Home Affairs also reminded the State Government of its responsibilities, but the Government of Assam adopted adamant posture. A meeting with the representatives of the Government of Assam was held in Delhi on 13.11.92 in order to persuade them to arrive at an agreement in this regard. Now I quote from the order of the Commission.

> "It became further evident that the State Government had knowingly and without any plausible reason disregarded the direction of the Commission issued in full consultation with the Ministry of Home Affairs relating to this matter of grave importance."

The State Government is not ready to abide by it. The Election Commission has stopped the work of preparing new voters' lists in Assam. What will happen ? To make proper arrangements for holding of free and fair elections, to revise voters' list and to add new voters in the voters' lists, all come under the jurisdiction of the Election Commission. But the State Government is bent upon violating the directions of the Election Commission openly. It is also violating the directive of the Ministry of Home Affairs.

10 per cent Annual Increase in Assam Population

When I went to Guwahati I came to know that there are 105 such constituencies in which 10 per cent population has increased during the last one year. How can there be an increase of 10 per cent of population in one year ? But when the Assam Government takes any step, the vote-politics comes in the way and the matter concerning the security and integrity of the county is held up. This is really a serious issue. We do not want to make it an issue of Hindus and Muslims. People in large numbers have come from Nepal. They are creating a number of problems. The Government cannot accept illegal entry.

America is also not allowing foreign nationals to settle there. In America when Mr. Clinton was fighting election, he declared that his attitude would be sympathetic towards the persons who were coming from Haiti to take shelter in America. President Bush had stopped their entry. Now when Mr. Clinton has assumed office, as the President of America, he says that he cannot be sympathetic towards them and that their entry will have to be prevented. That is on the Mexico border. America is trying its best to prevent illegal entry. But in our country every issue is given a communal colour and vote is linked with every issue. When the situation goes out of control, the Government makes desperate attempts to control the situation but even then nothing happens.

Avoid Discontent on Ayodhya Issue

Mr. Deputy Speaker, Sir, there was also a mention about the Ayodhya issue in the President's Address. That the case has been referred to the Supreme Court has also been mentioned. I do not know whether the Supreme

Court would give any decision in such case or not. It can both reject the case or give its decision thereon. The decision may favour one side only and the decision may also lead to the state of indecision. Can this issue not be solved even now through cordial talks outside the court of law ? Can Parliament not play any role in it ? If Parliament had played its role earlier, if the judiciary had been a bit fast in pronouncing its decision and if the political parties would have contributed to finding solution rising above vote politics (*Interruptions*).

Mr. Deputy Speaker, Sir, I have not mentioned the name of anybody.

SHRI MOHAN SINGH (Deoria) : And you call it a mandate (*Interruptions*).

SHRI VAJPAYEE : There is a little change in the Muslim opinion. This is not so out of any fear. There is a change in them because they have come to realise that it is really a matter of deep sentiment of the people. Now I would like to submit that the Government should take advantage of this change in their attitude and make all efforts to find a solution to the problem. If the Government remains adamant there may be difficulties in finding the solution to the problem. There is enough time now and I wish what Chandra Shekharji had initiated should be taken up again. Later on, he lashed out at us.

Still there is time. If the court gives its verdict on the basis of the evidence, documents, inscriptions, archaeological material that there was a Mandir then the demand of mosque should be dropped. But it is a different question whether the court gives such a verdict or not. I am also presenting the other side of the picture. Whatever may be the verdict of the court one of the two sides would remain discontent. I do not want that this discontent should be there.

SHRI ABDUL GHAFOOR (Gopalganj) : Many things can be tolerated. You also know how we are exercising restraints.

Mr. Deputy Speaker, Sir, I am offering a viewpoint. You have to assess its weight. Still there is time. All the people of this country have to live together. The politics of vote has disturbed the situation much (*Interruptions*). We joined this game much later. The debate on the vote of Thanks to the President's Address is providing this opportunity (*Interruptions*).

SHRI CHANDRA SHEKHAR : The suggestion made by Shri Atal Bihari Vajpayee is a right suggestion. If a dialogue in the matter is to be resumed, will the Members of Bharatiya Janata Party and other people associate themselves with it. Will they take any initiative in it so that negotiations could be resumed again ? I fully agree with their opinion that this problem cannot be sorted out through court and Government alone. It can be resolved through dialogue only. So I would like to request Atalji to make the people prepared for it and pave the way for holding talks.

Solution Lies in Dialogue

SHRI VAJPAYEE : Mr. Deputy Speaker, Sir, if any such effort is made we are ready to participate in it but it should be done with a goodwill and with an eye for finding a solution to the problem. Till now many efforts have been made but each step raised a new problem, so in disgust we suggested that the matter should be referred to the court. Now the matter is in the court. Hearing will start and verdict will be given. Whatever be the verdict, it would leave one side dissatisfied and that will not be an ideal one. But I think if any matter is not sorted out through mutual negotiations, we should approach the court and accept its verdict. But this is a question of creating goodwill in the country and Shri Chandra Shekhar can discuss this matter with his friends and find out a solution. We have been isolated. BJP has been .... apolitical.

SHRI NIRMAL KANTI CHATTERJEE (Dumdum) : Will that root be strengthened if you recognise Shivaji and Rana Pratap only and not Tipu Sultan.

SHRI VAJPAYEE : Sir, this is an effort to distort my version. I had raised a question. Please put it up in a correct way. It should conform to facts in history and thoughts of the minds. Things took an ugly turn because various aspects of the related dispute have been dealt with separately. It is not enough to say that the Hindus and Muslims should live together. Who are our great men and what was their conduct ? That is why I have raised a question and I would like to know your view in the matter. We do not want to leave anyone. We want to take all together but in this effort we do not want to distance ourselves from the main root. He made a reference to Rana Pratap and Shivaji. Please turn to earlier events. It is being said that the patriots had fought against Muslims but in reality they did not fight against Muslims. They fought against the regime. The problem arises when our Muslim brethren associate themselves with the aggressor of that time ? What is the need to put Ram and Babar as rivals ? What parallel is there between the two ?

SHRI EBRAHIM SULAIMAN SAIT (Ponnani) : Nobody does so, it is wrong.

SHRI VAJPAYEE : It is so nice of you that you are not doing so. If we go into these details the debate will become lengthy and would create a lot of bitterness. If you do not do, it is good.

SHRI EBRAHIM SULAIMAN SAIT : Nobody does.

SHRI VAJPAYEE : Sulaiman Saitji you will say that you do not oppose Vande Mataram...(*Interruptions*). Please get up and say that you do not oppose Vande Mataram.

SHRI EBRAHIM SULAIMAN SAIT : Please stick to one point only. There is no use in complicating the matter. Why do you connect Babar with Vande Mataram.

SHRI VAJPAYEE : I did not raise this issue. Our communist friends got up. Please be cautions of them; they will continue to do such things.

SHRI SAIFFUDIN CHOUDHURY : We had asked some other thing. Vajpayee ji, why it is necessary to cut the roots to take all together. Why does this thing arise.

SHRI VAJPAYEE : Where is the question of cutting the roots ?

Mr. Speaker, Sir, I have taken much time. There are many other speakers from my party. Kindly do not be strict to them. I would like to thank you...

(*Interruptions*). Mr. Speaker, Sir, you have come but after a long time. I would like to submit one more thing. I am going to conclude. A White Paper has been published. The paper is white no doubt but whatever has been written contains no substance.

SHRI NITISH KUMAR : I would like to know for my own information. Why it is called White Paper. It is written in black.

MR. SPEAKER : We will do some research on that.

SHRI VAJPAYEE : Shri Advani can make you understand better. This is British tradition. Sometimes papers of other colours are also printed. But I would like to submit one thing that it was charged that all that took place on 6th December was the result of a deep conspiracy and the Government said that it was investigating the matter. But the White Paper does not throw any light on it. Therefore, it is clear that there was no conspiracy in it. If the Government wants to prove it by a CBI enquiry, we are prepared to wait for that also. But the White Paper does not say anything in this regard. The various incidents that the Government has referred to speak that there was no conspiracy. It was wrong. Thank you.

Parliament Not Government's Puppet

Mr. Speaker, Sir, I support whatever has been said by Mr. George Fernandes. Could the Government not decide beforehand that the matter would be included in today's List of Business ? Why a Supplementary List of Business had to be issued for it ? If the Government can wait, then what is the need of giving a statement for the same ? I would request you to at least sometimes use your authority forcefully and not give your permission for it.

Sir, I have raised the question of propriety and am not going into the merits. We will have to go into it in detail. Heavens would not fall if this policy statement is not placed before the House today or the House is not apprised of the new policy. I want to know the position.

SHRI VIDYA CHARAN SHUKLA, Minister for Parliamentary Affairs : Mr. Speaker, Sir, this was approved in the cabinet meeting held this morning at O'Clock. Hence it could not be included in the Order Paper. I, therefore, requested you in this regard and about 450 copies were sent. If a decision had been taken about it yesterday, it would have been included in the Order Paper. As today is the last day of this session, having full respect for this august House, and being aware of its dignity, this policy statement has been laid on the Table of the House so that Hon'ble Members might know about it. Had it been decided yesterday even then it would have been implemented and we would not have waited. Hon'ble Members may study this policy statement and would find that every word of it is in the interest of the country. There is nothing in it which may jeopardize the security of the country. If the country has to forge ahead expansion would have to take place. I urge upon the Hon'ble members to go through this policy statement and not go by the newspaper reports. They write so many things, but this statement has something contrary to that. Please do read this policy statement. We have placed it on the Table of the House in order to maintain the dignity and honour of the House and whenever I will get an opportunity I will certainly remove any doubt and apprehensions about it.

SHRI VAJPAYEE : Mr. Speaker, Sir, strange things are being produced before the House one after another.... Whether the session will end today or not, this matter is being discussed for at least one week and we have had even a talk with you about the consensus which had emerged and we were told that the session would not be extended.

SHRI SPEAKER : Yes.

Lok Sabha on May 3, 1994 while opposing the Government's proposal to extend the session for adoption of National Communication Policy

SHRI VAJPAYEE : The members have gone to their constituencies. Bye-elections are to be held in several States. There is no question of extending the session now. The Government extends the session whenever it likes, brings a Bill whenever it so desires, keeps aside the rules whenever that suits it and changes the business of the House whenever it so wants. The House cannot be allowed to be made a puppet of the Government. Mr. Speaker, Sir, we are against extending the session of the House.

President's Address Not a Mere Ritual

Mr. Speaker, Sir, when the Bill on Panchayati Raj institutions was introduced in the House, there was great jubilation, everybody was happy at decentralisation of power and there was joy that authority was being vested in the Panchayats. Hope was expressed at that time that if Panchayat elections were held in the States under the State Governments, they would be fair and free and there would not be any kind of rigging in the elections.

Mass Rigging of Panchayat Elections in U.P.

Sir, the reports coming from Uttar Pradesh about the Panchayat elections belie all the hopes expressed in this House. Not only the decision of the House has been negated but the very foundations of democracy are being destroyed. Have you ever come across any election in which the number of candidates is less than the election symbols printed on the ballot papers ? When there is no candidate, when nobody has come forward to contest the election, how all the names of candidates and their election symbols were printed ? There were ballot papers of different colours. Malpractices were resorted to in the delimitation of constituencies, and the electoral rolls were also faulty. If somebody wanted to contest the election against the ruling party, he was called to the police station and was stopped from filling up the nomination form. There were hosts of such incidents. You can assess the situation from the fact that a Minister went on hunger strike to protest against the malpractices of his own Government and a Central Minister, Shri Rahi too decided to go on fast because he could not tolerate the malpractices resorted to in his constituency. Even the Congress Party faced difficulty in pursuading him not to undertake the fast. The Prime Minister assured him that if malpractices had taken place they would be examined and information would be collected in this regard.

Mr. Speaker, Sir, the largest number of our members are elected from Uttar Pradesh. I myself have been elected from Lucknow. Should the members of Parliament remain silent spectators ? Candidates who had won were declared defeated. Election results are not being allowed to be declared. Results were altered. There has been resort to firings. If the roots of democracy are not protected the people would lose faith in democracy. The House and yourself cannot remain neutral in this matter. This is a very serious matter. We want a detailed discussion on it and the House should find a way out so that the election which has been rigged could be declared

---

Lok Sabha on April 25, 1995 on the Motion of Thanks on the President's Address

null and void. A Commission should be set up to enquire into all cases of rigging. It comes under the jurisdiction of Parliament and it can do this.

We want Shri Rahi, to make his statement. The Prime Minister had given him an assurance on the basis of which he broke his fast. His entire statement is with me. Whatever Shri Rahi has written ... (*Interruptions*)

MR. SPEAKER : You should not read out his statement.

SHRI VAJPAYEE : This is strange. It is a public property. Shri Rahi himself made this statement.

MR. SPEAKER : You can authenticate it.

SHRI VAJPAYEE : Mr. Speaker, Sir, this letter is from the Deputy Home Minister of India, North Block, New Delhi. There is no need to authenticate it.

MR. SPEAKER : He will have to do it.

SHRI VAJPAYEE : If you have any doubt I can get it authenticated by him.

MR. SPEAKER : As per rules you cannot read other's statement.

SHRI VAJPAYEE : That is why I am not reading it out, Sir; I have referred to it. However, I want to refer to it in greater detail.

MR. SPEAKER : Please omit the inverted commas.

SHRI VAJPAYEE : It is not so. The letter contains point one, two, three and so on. Wherever electoral rolls were prepared, there is not a single 'gram sabha' in which a large number of voters have not been omitted. Any influential person could bring pressure got the names of voters belonging to his opposite party deleted and the names of his ineligible supporters included in the electoral rolls. Thus the procedure of finalising the electoral rolls was faulty and partisan. Secondly, the Officers and staff employed for election duty at various levels, including the Returning Officers, included names in the voters list—according to their fancies. Those whom they did not like ran from pillar to post with their applications in hand to be included in the voter's list with no result. There are many such instances before us.

Money has played its role in the giving of scrutiny certificates. False certificates have been issued. Nomination papers have been rejected on the plea that they were Presidents or Vice-Presidents of some societies while they were not actually holding an office of profit and were free to contest elections and were eligible. The administrative officers indulged in sale and purchase of polling stations on the day of polling for ensuring victory or defeat of Gram Sabha candidates. Rs. 5,000 to 10,000 were charged for this. An officer was also killed in connection with a booth capture.

SHRI RAJNATH SONKAR SHASTRI (Saidpur) : Rs. 5,000 to Rs. 25,000 were charged.

SHRI VAJPAYEE : So Shri Rahi's information is somewhat incomplete. Mr. Speaker, Sir, this makes a mockery of the entire democratic system. (*Interruptions*). I want your direction in this matter.

MR. SPEAKER : I will. But I do not know whether you would like it or not.

SHRI VAJPAYEE : We will like it, provided you ... (*Interruptions*). That is why I am not saying this, I am asking you what should we do. Please let me know, should I also leave the House like Shri Rahi ? Should I abandon my responsibility as Leader of the Opposition and go to Lucknow and sit on a hunger strike there ? The entire State would get ablaze, I do not want to do this. Then what should be done if conflicts begin in each and every village, firing is resorted to, the people are deprived of their right to contesting elections, the candidates who have won are declared as defeated... (*Interruptions*). My submission is that you may kindly also listen to those Hon'ble members on this matter who have personal experience in this regard.

MR. SPEAKER : All this is being dicussed, there is nothing more to say. You have focused your objection. Now you may please resume your seat. There is no need to go into more details.

Constitutional Break-Down in U.P.

SHRI VAJPAYEE : Mr. Speaker, Sir, our submission is that the Government of Uttar Pradesh is not being run according to the provisions of the Constitution. The Constitution is being openly violated in Uttar Pradesh. The Government which cannot ensure free and fair Panchayat elections has no right to remain in power. We request the Centre to intervene in Uttar Pradesh and improve the situation there. We have a right to demand this.

MR. SPEAKER : You are within your right, I do agree, but you need not go into the details of the rest of the things.

SHRI VAJPAYEE : Details are not so important, but we are expressing our resentment.

MR. SPEAKER : You are right. You can do that.

SHRI VAJPAYEE : The happenings in Uttar Pradesh, the policy adopted by the Central Government in respect thereof and the policy followed by the Government of Uttar Pradesh will wipe out the Congress party from that State. Whether or not it is wiped out, we are walking out of the House in order to express our resentment....

SHRI VAJPAYEE : Mr. Chairman, we have been listening to the speeches of the two Hon. members of the ruling party on the President's Address for the last about two and half hours. Two hour's time is pretty long. I was expecting that though the present Government was living in a make believe world, yet members of the ruling party, who have to knock at the doors of the people along with us after a few months, should express their views with some objectivity. But this has not happened.

Why Congress lost States ?

The Government has stated through the President that "the optimism and self-assurance evident last year has been vindicated. The projections made have been fulfilled in substantial measure and it can be said with confidence now that the country has made the turnaround." The country has made the turnaround no doubt, and the country is also preparing itself for a further turnaround, but I fail to understand what I should say about the Government that claims that the turnaround is due to its policies.

The President has referred in his Address to the elections that had been held in the States and expressed satisfaction that the polls were held in a peaceful atmosphere. But there is no indication what conclusions have been drawn by the Government from the election results. Neither the President's Address, which is an essay written by the Government, nor the long speeches that have been delivered by our friends just now throw any light on this. Why was the ruling party rejected by the electorate in one State after another ? Karnataka and Maharashtra were considered to be the strongholds of the Congress.

The Prime Minister comes from Andhra Pradesh. When the Congress Government was formed at the Centre four years ago, it was on the strength of the members of Parliament hailing from the Southern States. I do not want to go into the question of how those who came in a minority, later converted themselves into a majority, but the loss of one State after another does give an indication of the will of the voter. Does the voter not want to say something to the ruling party ? If every thing is alright in the economic reforms, why are the people displeased ? Why are they drifting away from the ruling party ?

The Human Face

Again, why has a discussion been started in the ruling party that the economic reforms should be given a human face ? What was the face so far ? What is the meaning of human face ? Was there any fault in the policies or the mistakes were committed in their implementation ? There is no self-introspection. There is no attempt to find one's own faults. If the ruling party is satisfied with this position, then I have nothing to say. If my friend Shri Ayyar wants to pat his back on their victory in Orissa and Manipur, then let it be so; but what do the people of those States want to convey which have been liberated from the influence of the ruling party ?

Congress on its Death-Bed

It is true that so far as the number of votes polled by Congress is concerned it did secure more votes in Maharashtra, but got lesser number of seats. Our electoral system is such that sometimes when the number of seats increases, the number of votes is reduced and *vice versa*, but we have been tolerating this system. We are trying to find a way out for the last 50 years, but the fundamental question is as to why the people of Maharashtra and Gujarat rejected the Congress Party. The condition of Congress in Bihar has become very pitiable. We have forged ahead of the Congress in Bihar. The number of Congress members in Karnataka has been reduced so much that we have surpassed it. This is not mere defeat. It is as though the entire party has been wiped out, as if the people have said that we do not want this party any more.

The Congress has a very old history. Is it on its death bed now ? If so, then why those who are in power and who are supporting the ruling party have not been able to understand this ? Should the defeat in the elections not compel them to have a deep self-introspection ? I want to again ask whether the electoral results should not persuade the ruling party to have a thorough self-introspection ? If every thing is alright in the country and every garden is green, the flowers are blooming all around and the koel is cuckooing, then what is the reason for the differences that are cropping up within the Congress. Internecine quarrels are taking place which may turn into a civil war tomorrow and reduce their house into ashes ? What is the propriety therefor ?

We All are Living in Glass-Houses

Please leave alone the Bharatiya Janata Party. The more you dub us communal, the more the people will repose confidence in us because the definition of communalism is changing. Please do understand it. By promoting one type of communalism you cannot fight the other type of communalism. Our alliance with Shiv Sena is being objected to, but what about the close links that you are maintaining with the Muslim League for a long time ? Now, Shri Ayyar would say there is no comparison between Shiv Sena and the Muslim League, that we are talking of remote control. I do not want to drag in the name of Late Sanjay Gandhi. But those who tolerated the remote control of late Sanjay Gandhi, they are today pointing their finger at the so-called remote control in Maharashtra. We all are living in glass-houses. But why criticize at this level ? I object to mention the name of Godse. Shri Ayyar is a learned man. He should know the history of the country. He should also know the background of Godse. Godse was opposed to Rashtriya Swayamsewak Sangh. Godse used to criticize the R.S.S. in his newspaper. Inquiry was held about Mahatma Gandhi's murder, not once, but twice. The conclusion drawn in all the inquiries was that the R.S.S. had no hand in it. Do you want to tell the world that the murderers of Gandhiji are now assuming power in India ? Recently we have won the elections in Gujarat, tomorrow we may come to power in New Delhi too.

We pay our respects to Gandhiji. If you say that this is not respect but only a show of it, then there is no room left for any debate, then there is no meeting ground between you and us. If this disbelief is so deep then why talk about the general consensus ? What is the meaning of a broad consensus ? A broad consensus could be reached only on the ground that in spite of difference of opinion no one should doubt the integrity of the other.

Correct Approach Needed

I have been associated with this Parliament since 1957. I have seen all the Prime Ministers from Nehru to Narasimha Rao. It is difficult to come out of the crisis in which the ruling party is now submerged. Proper self-introspection and a correct approach to the problems faced by the country is the need of the hour. The President's Address looks like a catalogue : Government has done this, Government has done that, this is the projection, such and such was done for this. If you have done all this, it is all right; but then why did it happen to you in the elections ? Now you will say that this has nothing to do with the elections, that we may lose the elections, but we shall go on doing what we think is right and proper. This is also not being said with self-confidence. It is being accepted that there is something wrong, the leadership must be changed. The fight in the ruling party is going on.

Not a Cut-Motion but a Quit Motion

Now the Cut Motion—it is not a Cut Motion, it is a quit motion. It is understandable that we may ask for the resignation of Narasimha Rao. But the ruling party members have now joined this demand. This is a very good thing. If the sailors of the boat are bent upon drowning it, nobody can save it. However, let us have some plain-speaking, some clear talks before the boat capsizes fully. Such talks are not being held. We are ready for a debate. What type of a Government are you supporting in Uttar Pradesh, and to what end ? You are neither prepared to forego Narayan Dutt Tewari nor sacrifice him, because you have to support the Government of Mulayam Singh.

Iranian President's Visit to Lucknow—A Mulayam Singh Show

We are glad that the President of Iran paid a visit to our country. We have cordial relations with Iran. These relations should be strengthened further. However, when the Iranian President, Hashemi Rafsanjani visited Lucknow, do you know what happened there ? I do not know who took the decision to send him to Lucknow and why this decision was taken. Lucknow is my constituency, but the President of Iran visits my constituency, a public reception is held there to honour him and I am not even invited to that, what kind of democracy is it ? Was the entire arrangement left to the discretion of the Chief Minister of Uttar Pradesh ? But I was not invited. The entire show was the demonstration of the Government of Mulayam Singh. Flags were put up on the entire route from Airport to Imambara, but all the flags were those of Iran, not a single Indian flag was fluttering. Inside the Imambara also, there were only Iranian flags, there was not a single tricolour there. A gentleman made a speech there. About Mulayam Singh he said before the President of Iran that he is not only the Chief Minister, but the future Prime Minister... (*Interruptions*).

SHRI BHOGENDRA JHA (Madhubani) : So far as the facts are concerned, the President was our guest. But does the Government deny or accept it that there were only Iranian flags and no Indian flag was put up there as stated by Shri Vajpayee ?... (*Interruptions*) Please say yes or no about the factual position... (*Interruptions*).

PROF. RASA SINGH RAWAT : They do not worry about the country, they are concerned only with self... (*Interruptions*).

SHRI VAJPAYEE : Maulana Kalme Sadiq was present there. He is a great leader of Shiaites, he is respected and revered. I have met him several times. He stated before the President of Iran that our U.P. Chief Minister is a "dynamite" who is not only the Chief Minister of Uttar Pradesh, but the future Prime Minister of India. The function was attended by Congress leaders. They had accompanied the President of Iran. None of them was allowed to speak there. Salman Khurshid was there. Our Mani Shankar Iyer was showering praises on Salman Khurshid in front of me, just before, Salman

Khurshid left me behind and went to Lucknow alone without taking me with him. But the honour he got there was that he was not even allowed to speak in the presence of the Iranian President. Syed Sibte Raza was there, but even he could not speak. Anwar Rizvi was also present. He is our colleague and friend and was accompanying him in the plane, but Mulayam Singh asked him not to sit with them. There was jostling as well, I do not want to go into that. What is all this ? And the most objectionable thing is that the Chief Minister of Uttar Pradesh stated openly in the very presence of the President of Iran that the minorities are being tormented in our country and there is a particular party which wants to oppress the minorities and we seek your help in the matter. What does it mean ? Are we inviting the Iranian Head of State to interfere in our internal affairs ? Was he taken to Lucknow for this purpose ? Had the Central Government no control over his Lucknow programme ? Had the Ministry of External Affairs closed its eye ? Was it not a State function ? What would be the reaction on the people outside it ? I do not think you have any idea about all that. That is my grouse.

Corruption and Criminalisation of Politics

The results of these elections had nothing to do with Ayodhya. Ayodhya was not the issue, corruption was the issue, criminalisation of the politics was the issue. The President has also admitted this in his address, truth had to be admitted. Our friend also mentioned that prices have been rising. There has been a rise of 25 per cent in the prices. The foodgrain prices have increased by up to 100 per cent.

However, not a word has been said about corruption in the address, as if the problem of corruption does not exist at all. How will corruption be wiped out ? How would purity be restored in public life ? The people are not prepared to tolerate corruption. Even at the risk of destabilisation, they would not allow the dishonest to remain in power. And this must happen. This happened in Japan and this happened in Italy. The corrupt Ministers have been put behind bars, some have died by swallowing poison. The people of Japan have taken the risk of destabilisation, but they have voted for an honest Government. We have to amalgamate both. The Government should be stable as well as responsible. However, stability should not rest on immorality. There does not appear any sign of responsibility. Do we not have the problem of corruption ? Should it not be eradicated ?

The Bofors report is yet to come. Shri Shukla had called a meeting of the Opposition parties and said that the entire case was in final stages and the report would soon be received. Where is that report ? Allegations of corruption are associated with the new economic reforms. The banking scam took place during the era of economic reforms. There was sugar scandal also. The way the shares of public undertakings are being sold is stinking. The public undertakings have not been established by some business magnates or private capitalists; they have been set up with the hard earned money of the people of India. Nehruji used to describe them as the new temples, but now their shares are being sold in a clandestine manner. Even those undertakings which are working well with a small investment are being sold. Now the pendulum has swung to the other side.

I have been elected from Lucknow. Deals are being struck there about such factories. Money is being made through the sale of these factories to private people. Where will the employees go ? They will be thrown on the streets.

Disparity has Increased

Poverty has increased. The number of those living below the poverty line has increased. Disparity has increased. The gap between Bharat and India has increased. You are, therefore, worried about the schemes that should be taken up for eradication of poverty. There is mention of about 8 or 9 schemes. Well, the schemes have their own place. They look good on paper. But there is no capital available to implement them. The Finance Minister is not present here. He presented a wonderful Budget this time. It is being said that this is not the Budget of an economist. Dr. Manmohan Singh presented such Budget because the Congress wanted its boat to be saved from sinking. It is all right that this is an election year, but the problems cannot be resolved so easily. It is highly suicidal to let an impression be created in the country that he is working under foreign pressure.

When the new Lok Sabha was constituted, I had said in my speech during the opening session that if an impression is created in the country that our self-respect is being hurt, that would not be good for the country and its future. You have not got majority in Rajya Sabha. The Patents Bill is stuck up. It is not the responsibility of the Opposition to help you in overcoming the hurdle in case your Bill is held up. What will you do now in Rajya Sabha ? Shri Chidambaram is sitting here. He is a master of his subject. Knowledgeable persons tell me that there is no need to get the Patents Bill passed hurriedly. Many countries have not signed it and many are expressing their difficulties. I did not attend the meeting called by the Government in this connection. In that meeting the Government stated that it is our obligation, we have decided to pass it just now. What sort of obligation is this ? Why this obligation ? Whose pressure is there ? I am not going into the consequences of such a step but an impression is developing in the country that in spite of all this our condition is not improving. You have to set this right. It appears to me that the real process of self-introspection would begin after the next elections. But I am also worried about the country.

You may say whatever you like about the Bharatiya Janata Party. Everybody has got the freedom of speech, but if extremism has developed in thoughts, then we have to think where does the root cause lie.

Indecision and Silence

Just now Shastriji was talking about Ayodhya. There is no agitation now. Please resolve the problem of Ayodhya through negotiations. If there is any other way, then resolve it through that. It is now stuck up. It has been left to the court. That was done earlier too. No decision is made : indecision, silence, matter is sub-judice, court proceedings are on are the hallmark of this Government. Everything is pending. The Patents Bill is stuck up in the throat. The issue of Ayodhya is pending, and now nobody talks of it. If a riot takes place again, then accusations would be hurled and there would be a search for scapegoats. Not only the issue of Ayodhya is pending, but the issue of Jharkhand Autonomous Council is also pending. When would it be constituted ? Whether it would be constituted at all or not, what would be its powers, what is going to be the financial arrangement, there is no answer to all these questions.

The issue of Ladakh is pending for years. All the worry is about Kashmir Valley. Ignoring Ladakh and overlooking Jammu will also give rise to communal tension. In Ladakh, there are Buddhists, in Jammu there are Hindus, the time has now come, to talk in these terms. Both have been ignored. They feel that the entire attention is being paid to the Muslims of Kashmir Valley and that they are not being cared for. It is not good if such suspicions arise in public mind about a Government. However, you have agreed to constitute a council for Ladakh but then what is the delay in constituting it ? There has been discrimination against Jammu, why should there be any delay in removing it. I do admit that there has been slight improvement in the situation in the Kashmir Valley. Ultimately, terrorism will be defeated, the youths who have been misled by Pakistan will have to understand that their interest lies in remaining with India, that Jammu and Kashmir can progress and march forward only as an integral part of India. While Muslim countries of the world are now veering round this view, we are indulging in politicking here.

Elections in Kashmir

There is talk of holding elections in Jammu and Kashmir. We too want elections. We have been contesting elections since 1952. We had contested an election in which there was wholesale rejection of nomination papers of our candidates. Now this would not work. In 1977, when there was Janata Government at the Centre, all the people conceded that the elections held in Kashmir were free and fair. Nobody talked of integration with Pakistan, nobody talked of secession from India. Had we conducted elections freely, the situation that has arisen in Kashmir now would not have arisen, Pakistan could not have mislead the youth of Kashmir in spite of its utmost efforts. The money allocated to Kashmir has not been spent properly. The Government in Jammu and Kashmir were changed from New Delhi, there was interference from here. But now preparations are being made for elections. Will this Governor continue ? If you want to hold elections, then first of all the Governor should be changed. A general amnesty should be declared before holding the elections. Where is the administration now ? Who will protect the polling stations ? Who will assure security to the voter after he comes out of his house ? There is no need to take everybody into confidence about it. Shri Chavan and Shri Pilot do not see eye to eye with each other, so the department of Kashmir was taken over by the Prime

Minister under his direct charge. We were under the impression that the entire Government is under the charge of the Prime Minister. But he has particularly taken over the department of Kashmir ! Administration is being run by the same officers. What is new that has happened ?

Situation Not Ripe for Elections in Kashmir

The Government should refuse to come under international pressure. Tell them that we want to hold the elections. Elections have been held throughout the country. In spite of some disturbances in Bihar, elections have been held there. We do want to hold elections in Kashmir. But if Pakistan is bent on creating disturbances in Kashmir with the help of arms, it would be difficult to hold the elections. Whenever elections are held, international observers would come in large numbers. We will have to maintain complete transparency. However, declarations are being made that we are ready. It is good if there is no need to take everybody into confidence in this matter. But I do not think that the situation is ripe for holding elections in Kashmir. This is not the way of solving the problem.

Terriorists are sitting in the Charar-e-Sharief, they have taken possession of it. For how long they have been occupying it ? There are some foreign mercenaries too among them. How did we allow them to enter and occupy it. The Government says that if they want to cross the border and go back we would allow them transit facility. If this is the behaviour with the terrorists, what would be its effect on the morale of our security forces ? The terrorists are inside and the security forces are outside. Charar-e-Sharief must be protected, but this is not the way to do it.

India's case on Kashmir is very strong. However, we are not putting our case before the international community as forcefully as we should. We seem to have a guilty conscience somewhere. There is a feeling somewhere in our sub-conscious mind that Kashmir is a Muslim majority area and we will have to find out some kind of a solution which is acceptable to us, to our neighbour as well as to the people of Kashmir Valley. I am glad that this attitude is now changing. There are some intellectuals in the country who were all for secession of Kashmir from India. The unity and integrity of the nation cannot be compromised, this is what the President has also said in his address. But these observations should be put into practice but this is not being done.

Confused Nuclear Policy

Shri Ayyar has very strongly criticized the nuclear weapons policy espoused by the Bharatiya Janata Party. He has every right to disagree with our point of view and express his own, but we think that for the security of the country, particularly because of the arms race that is taking place in our neighbourhood, India cannot forego its option to manufacture nuclear arms. And, are we not refusing to sign NPT on this very basis ? Because it is a treaty based on discrimination. Again, what has happened to our missile policy ? What would be the fate of 'Agni' and 'Prithvi' ? Now if some State Department official in Washington says that there is no need for anybody to worry, India's programmes relating to 'Agni' and 'Prithvi' are in "hybernation" then should the Government not make the position clear ? The Prime Minister had announced from the ramparts of the Red Fort that "we shall start production of'Agni,' we shall deploy 'Prithvi'." Where shall we deploy it, shall we deploy it at Hyderabad ? It needs to be deployed at Jalandhar, not at Hyderabad. Pakistan is acquiring deadly weapons. It is acquiring missiles. China is our neighbour and we have got disputes with her also. How could it be that we do not become self-reliant ? We are not in favour of atomic war. We want all the atomic weapons to be destroyed. We want a world free of nuclear arms, but has such a world to start from India ? Should it not start from those countries which have got a stockpile of nuclear arms ?

The Super powers are not prepared to destroy or reduce their weapons. What is the need for America now to have Diego Garcia as a base ? They are cautious about their weapons as well as about their security needs. The Warsaw Treaty has been wound up, but the Atlantic Treaty continues. Russia is also joining it; it is not being wound up. They are sermonising us who are not maintaining atomic weapons. We do not want to join an arms race with Pakistan but if the Prime Minister of Pakistan threatens us with atomic weapons should we sit idle ?

No Mockery of Swadeshi

Please do not take Swadeshi and self-reliance in a narrow sense. For God's sake do not make a mockery of these words. Can this country having a population of 900 million people make progress only with the help of foreign aid ? Can't it make progress on its own ? What would happen if the aid is reduced or stopped tomorrow ? They are not coming to India for our benefit, but because they want to earn profits. We are also benefited by it, but this feeling must be ingrained in the country that we can progress only on our own. We have got resources, we have man power, we have got capable scientists and engineers, we can, therefore, progress on our own also. This is the spirit of self-reliance. Who can oppose it ? But it is also being opposed. Since we are pleading for self-reliance, Shri Ayyar was pronouncing the words *Swavalamban and Swadeshi* in such a manner as if everything foreign was all right for him. For us, it is not so.

Bharatiya Janata Party has been talking of removing the control and permit system for long. I have seen those days when they were talking of taking the public sector to commanding heights. I had heard in this House the support being extended for setting up Ashok Hotel. At that time, I was sitting on the back benches. It was argued that a hotel set up in the public sector would earn profits and that profit would be invested in schemes meant for the benefit of the people. But that Hotel is running in losses, it is eating into the hard earned income of the people. But I still give a place of pride to the public sector, because some of the public sector undertakings are running very well. They should be praised, and need to be patted on their backs.

Pious Cbligation of the State

In a poor and a developing country, the State has a special role to play. Everybody cannot be left at the mercy of the market forces. Market forces are very harsh and merciless. What would happen to a poor person, to an unemployed person, a widow, an old person, small and marginal farmer, an artisan whose small industry has been closed ? Should the State not play a role for their sake ? But the State should be free from corruption and be full of compassion. That kind of State is needed. You can neither provide an administration which is free from corruption, nor which is compassionate and kind-hearted. We shall have to start not with a human face, but a humane heart, which is lacking.

There is need for self-introspection now. Not much time is left now, only a few months are left. A wave is on—a wave for change. It does not go by arguments, nor by facts. At places we have received success beyond our expectations and you have failed beyond your imagination. The mill of democracy grinds slowly, but it grinds finely, and the grinding is going on, we should understand that. But there is no indication of this perception in the President's Address. Therefore, although we have utmost regard for the President, yet we cannot support the Motion of Thanks on the President's Address.

Mr. Chairman, Sir, I agree with the remark of Shri Ayyar that the President had delivered his Address on February 13, but it is being discussed on April 25. If the Address is made a mere ritual, it would neither enhance the prestige of Parliament nor give any satisfaction to the President. If we cannot perform this ritual properly, it should better be stopped. Mr. Speaker, Sir, I am highly grateful to you for giving me time. Thank You.

II No-Confidence Motions

President's Rule in Rajasthan A Blow to Democracy

Sir, I move that this House expresses its want of confidence in the Council of Ministers.

I move this resolution with regret. This Council of Ministers was constituted only a few days ago. Today the President threw light on its policies. Obviously intimation of the present no- confidence motion was given to the Council of Ministers before other policies were clarified, so I only indicated the situation in Rajasthan among the reasons I gave for this motion. The first thing members of the new Council of Ministers did after swearing allegiance to the Constitution was to strike at the Constitution in Rajasthan. President's Rule was imposed on Rajasthan. The Legislative Assembly was suspended. The Government that the people of Rajasthan elected was deprived of governing the State. Democracy has been murdered in Rajasthan. The mandate given by the people through elections has been openly flouted. It is a matter of great regret that while ministries have been properly formed in all other States of the country, in Rajasthan and Uttar Pradesh the formation of the ministries has cared neither for the letter nor spirit of the Constitution, nor even for the verdict the people gave in the elections. The events in Rajasthan have had wide repercussions in the country. Apart from the political parties even those who are not connected with politics, who think independently, and who criticise even the opposition when required, have severely criticised the Central Government's promulgation of President's Rule in Rajasthan. Newspapers have with one voice dubbed this step undemocratic and unconstitutional. The question is, why did this sorry state of affairs arise in Rajasthan when immediately after the general elections the people had participated in the voting enthusiastically and peacefully apart from a few incidents ?

Rajasthan Governor's Decision Doubtful

The trouble started when the Governor of Rajasthan decided that he would invite the biggest party in the Legislative Assembly to form the government. The question is, will or will not the Governor bear in mind the result of

Lok Sabha on March 18, 1967 during discussion on the Motion of No-Confidence in the Union Council of Ministers

elections while extending such an invitation ? The question also is, while extending this invitation will only the strength of political parties be taken into account or will independent members also be counted ? There was no propriety in the Governor inviting the leader of the Congress party to form the government. In Rajasthan the Congress got only 30 per cent votes while 70 per cent people voted against the Congress. The people of Rajasthan have rejected the Congress. They have defeated the Congress in the elections.

SHRI R.S. PRASAD (Chapra) : What is their number ?

SHRI VAJPAYEE : I am coming to that too. Will only seats be counted ? Will the verdict of the people expressed through the elections be totally ignored ? Even if we count seats is it not true that all elected non-Congress members have organised themselves into a party ? They elected a leader. They also decided upon a minimum programme. The Rajasthan Governor should have respected the people's verdict and invited the leader of the newly formed party to form the government. One day he had even announced that he would inform the people whom he is inviting to form the government. But when pressmen went to him the Governor said my mental balance is disturbed because the leader of the opposition, who had come to see me yesterday, had said something to which I am not accustomed.

Sir, what was said on behalf of the opposition ? Only that they hoped he would decide impartially. Yesterday too we had said you have been elected Speaker and hoped you would function impartially. What was bad in that ? But perhaps the Governor lost his balance because he has a guilty conscience. The decision he took the next day would go down as a very strange decision in parliamentary history, at least in that of India.

Independent Members are also Legislators

The Governor said he did not think it necessary to count members who have been elected as independents while assessing the strengths of the Congress and the non-Congress parties. But no one can deny the existence of independent members so long as they contest elections, so long as they have the right to contest elections, and so long as they win them and become members of the legislature or Parliament. Is it not a fact that in 1962 the Congress could come to power with the help of independent members in this very Rajasthan ? The Governor is not prepared to apply in 1967 the rule that was applied in 1962.

In 1962 the Congress secured a majority by joining independent members to it. In 1967 the Congress has gone into a minority by such joining. So the Governor gave a strange decision which flouted the Constitution. As a result, the leader of the Congress party was invited to form the Ministry. It was natural that there should be a reaction to this in Rajasthan. It was also necessary that the people should feel incensed. The people cannot be prevented from expressing their anger peacefully when the Constitution is flouted, the people's mandate ignored and the Governor's behaviour smacks of partiality. India is a republic, we are a democracy, we cannot deprive the people of their right to express that opposition peacefully.

What was the need to declare Section 144 in Jaipur ? I pity the Congress members' ignorance, and it is through this ignorance that the ministry took a step that deeply damaged its prestige. In Rajasthan Congress members now find it difficult to show their faces. It is clear that the promulgation of Section 144 was meant to thwart a peaceful demonstration. The people were rendered leaderless by jailing opposition leaders, which aggravated the people's anger in Jaipur.

There was firing in Jaipur on March 7. I am happy that the Central Government has agreed to an inquiry by a High Court Judge on the firing. Was the firing necessary ? The commission would inquire into this, but I feel it is my duty to place the facts before the House. All India Radio announced that section 144 was being withdrawn from Jaipur, but the police on the streets did not know this. On hearing the radio announcement about section 144 being withdrawn crowds began to collect on the streets.

SHRI P. VENKATASUBBAIAH (Nandyal) : On a point of order.

Now that the Government has instituted a judicial inquiry into the police firing, can the hon. member raise that matter during the course of his speech here ?

MR. SPEAKER : Not specifically, but in a general way he has been referring to it.

SHRI VAJPAYEE : It is only a fact-finding commission; nothing is sub-judice.

AN HON. MEMBER : Is it a point of order or point of disorder ?

SHRI VAJPAYEE : Sir, the people came into the streets under the impression that section 144 had been withdrawn and the police used force to disperse them, which resulted in firing. But one thing must be borne in mind—there was complete peace in Jaipur after March 7. Apart from Jaipur the agitation was peaceful all over Rajasthan.

Firing in Bastar

It has been alleged that the opposition wanted to take the decision to form the government not within the Legislative Assembly but on the streets. I forcefully refute this charge. The opposition is not only active in Jaipur, it has influence all over Rajasthan. There was peace all over Rajasthan. Does this not prove that the opposition was not in favour of going into the streets ? Had the Rajasthan Government and the police shown restraint it would not have become necessary to resort to firing.

The firing in Bastar was justified in this House. The Pande Commission has submitted its report. It is not necessary to dwell on it any longer. The firing in Delhi on November 7 had been justified in the former House. Let the Home Minister come out with the findings of the inquiry into it. The firing in Jaipur on March 7 and that in Delhi on November 7 show the Government's failure and its alacrity in trampling over the people's feelings.

When the Congress leader Shri Sukhadia saw that the majority was not with him he informed the Governor that he was not in a position to form the Ministry. It was then the duty of the Governor to invite the leader of the united party to form the government. Why was he not invited ? The reply given was that there was a law and order situation in Rajasthan. What happened after March 7 ? What new situation arose ? Before March 7 Shri Sukhadia was willing to form the Ministry; at that time he did not refer to the law and order situation. At that time he thought he would engineer defection of non-Congress members by fair means or foul—through greed, temptation, terror—and would succeed in forming the Ministry. When he saw these hopes dashed he talked about law and order and expressed his inability to form the ministry. The way was thus open for the Governor. He could have called the non-Congress parties and asked them to form the ministry. But had he done so the present situation would not have developed. Instead of giving the opposition an opportunity to form the Government he wrote to the Centre saying the present situation in Rajasthan is such that the Constitution cannot function and President's Rule should be imposed.

Governor's Report should be Revealed

Let the Rajasthan Governor's report be placed on the floor of the House. Such a tradition has been adopted in the case of Kerala. It was said the Governor had recommended that the Legislative Assembly be dissolved, but the Central Government did not abide by the advice. The Legislative Assembly was not dissolved; it was only suspended. The Rajasthan Legislative Assembly has been rendered unconscious. God knows what Hanuman would come with Sanjivani and bring it back to consciousness. Perhaps the Sanjivani lies locked in some cupboard of the Home Ministry.

SHRI Y.B. CHAVAN, Home Minister : We'll take your help.

SHRI VAJPAYEE : Shri Yeshwantrao is standing guard on that cupboard. It is regrettable that the Governor acted with partiality, and the Central Government aligned itself with it. The way was open for the Central Government. The Governor could have been advised to reconsider his report and again take into consideration the changed and peaceful situation. But the Centre too did not do its duty. The result was that while elected governments are functioning in all other States of the country the destiny of Rajasthan has been taken over by the Central Home Minister.

I am surprised to see that the Home Minister announced that the Legislative Assembly could not be summoned because the opposition parties had announced a big demonstration in front of the Legislative Assembly.

PROF. SHER SINGH, Minister of State for Education : Had prepared for, not announced.

SHRI VAJPAYEE : You came to know about those preparations and on the basis of that information you killed the Constitution. Will the mere announcement of a demonstration be enough to suspend a Legislative Assembly and deprive the people of their democratic rights ? Demonstrations will continue—ought to continue—in a democracy, and if demonstrations are not enough for forming a Government our Congress friends would not allow a non-Congress government in any State.

It is not only a question of Rajasthan. The question of the Central Government and non-Congress Government is also joined to it. Yesterday I said the Congress monopoly on power has ended. There are non-Congress governments in many states. Will the Central Government allow them to function ?

SHRI Y.B. CHAVAN : Certainly.

SHRI VAJPAYEE : Rajasthan is a pointer. It creates a doubt about the intentions of the Central Government. If non-Congress governments could be formed and could function in so many states how were Rajasthan and Uttar Pradesh treated differently ?

Look at the difference. Whenever non-Congress Governments were formed and their formation announced the people rejoiced by lighting lamps, but when the leader of the Congress party in Rajasthan was called to form the Ministry funeral pyres were lit. When non-Congress parties came to power ladies applied tilak to their foreheads, but when in Rajasthan the leader of the Congress party discarded and disdained by the people was invited to form the Ministry their own tilak was wiped off.

SHRI MADHU LIMAYE (Monghyr) : Shame !

SHRI VAJPAYEE : When a non-Congress Government is formed people are happy and when the Congress is called to form the Ministry the people resent it. Has this change been brought about only by the opposition parties ? If you think so it means you are not ready to read the writing on the wall.

The events in Rajasthan have struck a blow at the strength the democratic process had gained after the fourth general elections. It has jeopardised the democratic structure, and for this this Cabinet deserves to be condemned.

Never before in India's history has it happened that members of the Legislative Assembly were paraded before the President and counted to show which side has the majority.

AN HON. MEMBER : They were under pressure.

SHRI VAJPAYEE : No one in his senses would say such a thing. If, as the Home Minister says, he is not concerned with numbers, he does not care on what side the number is bigger and on what side it is smaller....

SHRI Y.B. CHAVAN : I never said so. You were talking about the number, not me ?

SHRI VAJPAYEE : When members of the opposition party were presented before the President and we said look, there are 93 of them, you had said 93 or whatever, we are not concerned. We imposed President's rule because there is a law and order problem there.

SHRI Y.B. CHAVAN : Right. Since you were quoting me, I only wanted to make my position clear. I said who had got what number of people is a matter for the Governor to consider. It is not for the Government of India to consider. I was merely making a reference to the constitutional aspect of it. I was not expressing any view on the merits of the matter.

SHRI VAJPAYEE : It is good that the Home Minister has said it is for the Governor to decide which side has the majority and which side not. But if the Governor takes a wrong decision where do we appeal ?

SHRI Y.B. CHAVAN : In the House.

SHRI VAJPAYEE : The House has not been called.

SHRI Y.B. CHAVAN : It will be when peace is established.

SHRI VAJPAYEE : Contradictory things are being said. What happened in Rajasthan can happen in some other State as well. I would not go into the way Governors are appointed. But a Governor can make a mistake. Then should the Central Government close its eyes and support the Governor's decision ? In that case what way would be open for the people ?

I have seen the Constitution and it needs to be amended in this respect. We can impeach the President but there is no provision for impeaching a Governor.

AN HON. MEMBER : He will be dismissed.

SHRI VAJPAYEE : Finally what way is open for the people ? The Legislative Assembly will be dissolved. On the advice of the Centre the Governor will end the democratic processes, but this House cannot impeach a Governor. A constitutional amendment is necessary in this direction.

I also do not agree that the President had no option but to accept the recommendations made to him by the Central Government based on the Governor's report. This is not how I interpret the articles of the Constitution. I also consulted legal experts on this matter and many of them opined that in such matters the President need not be bound by the Central Government's policies; he can use his own discretion. I regret the President did not use his discretion in the matter of Rajasthan, and if he did—I do not know if he did or not—he took a decision that did not honour constitutional limitations.

Preserve Democracy

There is still time. The action taken to put the clock back in respect of democracy in Rajasthan could be reversed. Is there no peace in Rajasthan ? Does the Central Government want the peace of the funeral ground ? If the Constitution is flouted, if the Central Government is bent upon killing democracy we shall fight this injustice, albeit with full faith in peaceful methods. We do not want that this issue be resolved in the streets. But it is not enough to merely say so to the common man. He has also to be told that we shall see that it does not become imperative for him to come into the street.

What harm would have been done if the opposition parties had been called to form the government ? It is said that the opposition could not have undertaken a trial of strength in the Legislative Assembly if they so wanted. Then could Shri Sukhadia not have done the same ? What applies to the opposition parties applies to Shri Sukhadia too. But Shri Sukhadia was given time to engineer defections.

It took the Governor twelve days to decide about independent members. If the Congress was to be invited as the single largest party that could have been done immediately after the elections. What was the Governor doing for twelve days ? Were twelve days necessary to conclude that the independents wanted to be counted ? Was he waiting for the stars to foretell or consulting astrologers ? What happened in Rajasthan was not good. It should be corrected.

SHRI Y.B. CHAVAN : We too do not think it was good. We too are unhappy.

SHRI VAJPAYEE : You do a wrong thing and you are also unhappy. It was you who did whatever was done. There is still time to change it. There is peace in Rajasthan. Will the Home Minister personally go to Rajasthan to see the situation ? But he should not expect this peace to last long. Perhaps he is banking upon that.

The majority in the Rajasthan Legislative Assembly had come to Delhi and presented before the President. That showed where the majority lay. The excuse made for preventing the majority from forming the government and imposing a majority government—the excuse of peace and order—is no more there. The Governor may not agree, but the Central Government will have to take an independent decision in this respect, and if the Governor is not willing to perform his constitutional duties he will have to be removed.

While appointing new Governors the Central Government must bear in mind that the situation in the States has changed after the 1967 elections. Non-Congress governments are functioning in quite a few States. Persons subserving party ends of the Congress should not be appointed Governors. If they are, there would be no meaning to the Prime Minister's assurance that the Centre wants good relations with the States. Mere professions are not enough, there has to be practice too, but the practice in Rajasthan has created doubts in the minds of all non-Congress parties and ministries.

Sir, I hail from Uttar Pradesh. These two constitutional limitations could have been observed if the Governor had respected the people's opinion and invited the united party of opposition parties to form the ministry. But there too the Congress was given an opportunity. Why was the Congress that won 198 seats out of 425 invited ?

Double Standards

AN HON. MEMBER : There should not be double standards in this respect.

SHRI VAJPAYEE : You are adopting double standards. In Rajasthan the Governor did not include the independents but in Uttar Pradesh independents are being included.

SHRI O.L. BERWA (Kota) : Look at Haryana.

SHRI VAJPAYEE : I submit that this action of the government deserves to be condemned. In the situation prevailing in the country after the general elections, and in view of the seriousness and complexity of the problems the cooperation of all parties is needed for solving them. In a way it is a good thing that non-Congress parties are in power in quite a few places. It seems the people have decided to test all parties, on the same touchstone. If this situation is exploited it would be possible to create, as never before, a congenial atmosphere for the solution of problems before the country. The Central Government has vitiated the whole atmosphere by imposing President's rule in Rajasthan.

So this Central Government should be removed, the House should kick it out. It is with this in view I have moved this non-confidence motion and I hope the House will pass it.

MR. SPEAKER : Only 15 minutes are left. If Shri Vajpayee can conclude in 10 minutes he may carry on.

SHRI VAJPAYEE : Sir, I thank those who have spoken on this motion. I thank both those who have supported it as well as those who have opposed it.

It has been asked if the question of Rajasthan was so big that a no-confidence motion had to be tabled against the new ministry. For Congress members Rajasthan may be a small matter, but for us it is a test of whether the Central Government would justly and dispassionately respect the people's mandate and whether it would live up to its professions of cooperation with non-Congress ministries.

Events in Rajasthan are a signal for non-Congress ministries that they should always be prepared for partial behaviour of the Centre. There was no reason to prevent the formation of a non-Congress government in Rajasthan. Now it is said we have permitted non-Congress Governments in many States, what if it did not happen in Rajasthan ? It is like to say there is only one blemish on our sleeve, so what does it matter ? The rest is clear. Is not one blemish on the forehead not enough ? Is it not enough to kill democracy in one State ?

Different Approaches

Sir, the Home Minister has said a lot of things in favour of the Governor of Rajasthan. It is also expected of him. But one thing that he could not explain was—why was the Rajasthan Governor's decision every time in favour of the Congress and against non- Congress parties ? Even when he decided upon forming a ministry it was the Congress that he invited. Is it not true that in Kerala the Praja Socialist Party, with 19 members had been invited to form the ministry ? At that time the issue of the single largest party was not raised. The Praja Socialist Party ranked third. Perhaps it was thought beneficial for the Congress at that time to invite it. So the Governor of Kerala took a different approach and now the Governor of Rajasthan is taking a different approach. And when Shri Sukhadia declined to form a ministry why did the Governor not invite the non-Congress parties to do so ? He says he did not want to fan violence. The Home Minister also says let there be peace in Jaipur and the Constitution will be back on the rails. But was there violation of peace in Jaipur first, or was the Constitution flouted first ? Let us not make the mistake of putting the cart before the horse. There was peace in Jaipur. But the Governor's wrong decision incensed the people. Today there is complete peace in Jaipur, Section 144 has been withdrawn. Now what is the Governor waiting for ? What almanac is he consulting ? What delay is there in establishing complete peace in Rajasthan ? But has the Central Government surrendered all its responsibilities to the Governor ? Has the Governor made it a prestige issue ? Will the people of Rajasthan be denied the right to have a government of their choice so long as the Governor does not please to allow it ? The Central Government also has a responsibility in this.

Sir, the legislators of Rajasthan had come to Delhi with great hopes. Had they wished to settle this issue on the streets of Jaipur they would not have come knocking on the doors of Rashtrapati Bhavan. They had hopes of justice from the Centre. So long as this hope is alive there is no danger to the unity and integrity of India. But by dashing their hopes you have reduced the people's faith in the Centre as well. The whole country should be Centre-oriented. Justice should be available at least at the Centre, and if there is injustice anywhere it should be corrected by the Centre. I was very sorry to hear a Congress member say that the 93 members of the Legislative Assembly who had come had been brought by force. By saying so he has not only insulted the people's elected representatives, he has also jeopardised the President's prestige. Sir, had the 93 legislators gone to the Rashtrapati Bhavan under police escort ? This is wrong. I have a photograph of these 93 legislators. It was taken at my residence in the presence of journalists and photographers. Was the photograph taken in a police cordon ? Sir, I would request permission to place the photograph on the floor of the House.

Sir, we had hoped that the President's Address would correct the mistake made in Rajasthan. But that hope too was not fulfilled. Even today we were hoping that in reply to the debate the Prime Minister or Home Minister would announce that the situation in Jaipur is now normal, so the normal constitutional process would be revived. Don't take Maharani Sahiba's statement wrongly. Yesterday Shri Khadilkar made the mistake of taking my statement too wrongly. In my speech I had not made any threat. I had only given a warning—a friendly warning in the interest of the country and of democracy.

No Place for Violence

After all there is a limit to the patience of the people of Rajasthan. They will keep up a peaceful struggle. In a democracy there is no place for violence. We will have to avoid violent agitations, but we cannot deprive the people of their right to agitate peacefully. This is especially so when open injustice is being done is Rajasthan and the Centre is putting the stamp of approval on it. There is still time. The partiality can still be prevented. Doubts can still be prevented from rising in the minds of non-Congress governments. It is not enough for the Prime Minister to profess that she would like to cooperate with non-Congress governments. Rajasthan is the test for co-operation. If a non-Congress government is allowed to be formed there we shall acknowledge that the Centre's intentions are good. Otherwise we would be forced to take our own decision.

Sir, one more thing and I shall finish. Congress members are criticising the formation of united governments by the Communists, the Jana Sangh and other parties. Frankly, such criticism does not become them. We are honest about our differences, and we are sitting here as separate parties. But the Congress party is itself a conglomeration of Communists, Socialists and....

SHRI Y.B. CHAVAN : And Jana Sanghis too.

SHRI VAJPAYEE : If you accept that there are also Jana Sanghis among you, you will admit that the Congress is not a party, it is a Khichri, and only power has bound it together.

If we are forming governments, it is to serve the people, not for grabbing power. We are forming governments on minimum programmes. We shall remain in those governments as long as we can serve the people, otherwise we shall quit them. But we are not like the Congress party. That is the reason the Congress has been defeated. It should realise which way the wind blows.

With these words I appeal to the House to pass my motion and drive out this government.

Sir, one more thing. Is the Home Minister aware that the Chief Secretary of Rajasthan still takes files to Sukhadia ? Is he willing to inquire into this matter ? If it is proved is he ready to recall the Chief Secretary ?

SHRI Y.B. CHAVAN : Sure.

SHRI VAJPAYEE : No one can approve of what is happening in Rajasthan. President's Rule has been imposed so that Sukhadia may regain a majority. We shall never allow this. Such scandals will go on so long as this Central Government is in office. So I wish the House passes my motion and drives out this government. Thank you.

Have We Lost the Battle of Democracy ?

Sir, I would like to make it clear that our no-confidence motion is in no way related to Mr. Brezhnev's visit. He has come to India as an honoured guest of the whole country. The whole country wants to strengthen our friendly ties with the Soviet Union. But the country also wants that this friendship be based on equality and respect for each other. It is a matter of regret that India-USSR relations are not on the same level on which U.S.-China relations are developing. The reason for this is that India is neither self-dependent nor has it been able to successfully solve its economic problems. We can only be as friendly as a country that is industrially weak, dependent upon foreign food, and at the mercy of some super power for its security can be. Our friendship is confined within these limits.

Sir, today there is a crisis of confidence in the country. Hence our no-confidence motion. This crisis of confidence was not created by nature. The Government has admitted that food production was affected only to the extent of 4 per cent by the drought. This crisis is also not the dire result of India's armed struggle for the liberation of Bangladesh. This crisis is man-made. It is a matter of regret that this crisis is sometimes blamed on Nature, sometimes on world conditions, sometimes on opposition parties and sometimes even on CIA. Why is the CIA not talked of these days ?

SHRI S.N. MISHRA : Dr. Shankar Dayal Sharma is also silent.

SHRI VAJPAYEE : Dr. Sharma's silence is quite mysterious. Is not the CIA not active in the country these days ? Does it mean the CIA has packed up and gone home ? It is not so. The secret agents not only of the U.S. but also of China, Pakistan, Russia and all other countries are active here. Their activities have even increased, but they are not discussed these days.

Friends in the ruling Congress are in search of scapegoats.

They are looking for excuses to cover up their failures. The people will not tolerate these excuses any more. I quote the Prime Minister :

> "Time will not wait for us. The millions who demand food, shelter and jobs are pressing for action."

What type of speech is this ? It is Smt. Indira Gandhi's. But it is not a speech of 1973, it is a speech of 1970. She needs to be reminded of the very words she used in a broadcast to the nation on All India Radio while dissolving the Lok Sabha. I am sorry she is not present in the House, still I quote her :

Lok Sabha on November 21, 1973 during discussion on the Motion of No-Confidence in the Union Council of Ministers

"It is because we are concerned not merely with remaining in power but using that power to ensure better life to the vast majority of our people and to satisfy their aspirations for a just social order. In the present situation we feel we cannot go ahead with our proclaimed programme and keep our pledges to our people."

So the life of the Lok Sabha was cut short by 14 months and the country made to face the ordeal of mid-term elections. The people supported the Prime Minister. Then what is the propriety in her not fulfilling her election promises ? It is now being complained that the people are indulging in violence, but the Prime Minister herself incited violence. I quote again from a press report :

"Mrs. Gandhi today warned that if the prevailing economic and social inequalities were not reduced soon the people would take recourse to violence to achieve that."

SHRI S.D. SINGH (Culatra) : What quotation is that ?

SHRI VAJPAYEE : First listen to the quotation. Then I'll tell you —

"The march of the economic and social change has a momentum of its own which could not be arrested by anybody. On the contrary, Mrs. Gandhi said, those who had come to lose their patience with the pace of progress had adopted violence as the only way out."

This is a speech delivered at a Congress workers' meeting in Chandigarh on November 65, 1970 .... (*Interruption*) .... At that time progress was slowing down, so it was said people would take to violence. Now that the people are taking to violence they are being criticised and opposition parties are being tarnished. Why has progress slowed down ? Who is responsible ? The Prime Minister is ready to take the credit for all good things, then how can she escape the responsibility of the death-dance of hunger that we see in the country, the backbreaking dearness all round, and the corruption that has spread from top to bottom ?

Some Vignettes

Sir, I shall place some vignettes before you.

August 15, 1973—A certain scholar was invited for an interview on TV on Independence Day. He is blind and is the author of many books. His name is Shri Ved Mehta. During the interview he was asked to say something about conditions in the country. The interviewer thought he would start praising the leadership. He said just one sentence—"It seems the country has no leadership today". That very moment the TV was shut off and the interview was terminated. The viewers had a blank screen before them. This is how TV is used in our country. Is this the medium through which we seek to strengthen democracy ? Today the hungry want bread, not TV. When the demand was made in Poona Shri Chavan said we are giving both bread and TV. But unfortunately the bread they give is not enough to allay hunger and the TV has no food for thought. The Prime Minister had set up the Chanda Committee when she was the Information Minister. That Committee had recommended public corporations for All India Radio and TV, but the decision Smt. Indira Gandhi took as Information Minister she rejected as Prime Minister....

SHRI S.N. MISHRA : Now even Shri Chanda is no more.

SHRI VAJPAYEE : Now I present another scene. This belongs to August 14, 1972. The silver jubilee of independence was being celebrated. Our friends in the Congress proposed to take out a torchlight procession in Delhi, but not enough people could be collected for it, so an official directive was issued to the Home Guards to participate in the Congress Party's procession with torches....

SHRI CHANDRAJEET YADAV : This is absolutely false.

SHRI VAJPAYEE : I can prove it.

SHRI YADAV : I challenge you to prove it.

SHRI VAJPAYEE : Sir, I have correspondence with me....

SHRI YADAV : Lakhs of people of Delhi are ready to go with the Congress. I challenge you to prove it.

SHRI VAJPAYEE : Sir, there was a question in Parliament about this.

AN HON. MEMBER : What will happen if the challenge is proved ?

SHRI VAJPAYEE : If this is proved false I am ready to resign. I accept your challenge. Let Shri Chandrajit Yadav prove me wrong.

SHRI YADAV : I am ready to do so. I am prepared to accept your challenge.

SHRI VAJPAYEE : Sir, there has been a question about this. This Minister has replied in the affirmative. At this time a Jan Sangh member Shri Kanwarlal Gupta had correspondence and this was accepted in it. But if they are not prepared to admit it I can produce evidence tomorrow.... (*Interruption*) ....

Appointment of Chief Justice

There is a third picture I would like to present. The appointment made to the post of Chief Justice of India after keeping the cases of three senior judges hanging has become the subject of a lot of controversy. I am not entering it. In order to protest this appointment the Supreme Court Bar Association wanted to hold a conference in Vigyan Bhavan. They applied for the venue, but it was not sanctioned. Some other lawyers were given it on the ground that their application had come earlier, while the record shows that it had come later. They would not hold the conference in Vigyan Bhavan and held it in Vithalbhai Patel House. The Supreme Court Bar Association had to hold its conference in Ashok Hotel and the Vigyan Bhavan remained unoccupied that day.

One more thing is to be added to this. The lawyers who held their conference in Vithalbhai Patel House were invited for dinner by the Law Minister, the Prime Minister joined them there and they were patted on the back for supporting the Government's appointment of a Chief Justice who was a yesman. On the other hand those who fought for the independence of the judiciary were denied even the Vigyan Bhavan (*Interruption*).

One more picture. On October 24 some employees of the Central Food Squad went raiding shops in South Delhi in order to seize adulterated stuff. The shop-keepers did not let them take samples. There was a quarrel between the two and the Central Food Squad people informed the police control room. A police party reached there, but instead of helping the employees of the Central Food Squad the police took bribes from the shop-keepers and put the Food Squad people in lock-up... (*Interruption*).... This is not a small thing. I have a tape-record, in which the A.S.I. ....

SHRI VAYALAR RAVI (Chirayenkel) : On a point of order. Can a member bring a tape-recorder into the House ?

SHRI VAJPAYEE : Give the ruling later. Let me speak.

MR. CHAIRMAN : We'll give the ruling later. You may continue.

SHRI VAJPAYEE : This tape-record contains the conversation between Shri Jethanand Malik, A.S.I. of police, Shri Ahluwalia, field assistant of the Central Food Squad and Dr. Vinod.

MR. CHAIRMAN : You are naming officers. If you want to introduce this into the House the rules require you to first get the Speaker's permission. I am quoting the rule.

SHRI VAJPAYEE : I am not making any allegation. I am just presenting a conversation. Can I not name any officer ?

MR. CHAIRMAN : But we won't allow a tape-recorder to be played.

SHRI P.R. DAS MUNSHI : If you give a ruling we are not objecting to it. But what Mr. Vajpayee is doing really encourages the House to take into cognisance the faults of the officers. I also demand that they should be brutally punished by the Government. There is no doubt about it.

Use of Tape-recorder in House

SHRI B.P. MAURYA : I have here a point of order. This House can only listen to elected members. If a tape-recorder is played many outside voices would be heard.

MR. CHAIRMAN : He is not using the tape-recorder.

SHRI MADHU LIMAYE : I have two points of order. Shri Vajpayee has mentioned only designations, not anyone by name.

MR. CHAIRMAN : He mentioned names.

SHRI VASANT SATHE (Akola) : Is Shri Vajpayee placing the tape-recorder on the floor of the House ?

SHRI R.K. KHADILKAR : It is a fact....

SHRI SAMAR GUHA : On a point of submission.... (*Interruption*).... On a point of order, Sir.... (*Interruption*)....

MR. CHAIRMAN : Whatever the member says will not go on record as he is speaking without my permission.

SHRI SAMAR GUHA : ..... (Not recorded)

SHRI MADHU LIMAYE : So far as the tape-recorder is concerned nothing in our rules prevents it.... (*Interruption*).... what is the difference between the two ?

MR. CHAIRMAN : Shri Ravi has raised this question. I said I shall give the ruling later. I have not given it yet. Then what is the point of discussion ? I have understood Shri Limaye's points.

SHRI R.K. KHADILKAR : The Hon. Member has referred to an incident when I was holding charge of the Health Ministry. Whatever has been referred to upto now is correct. Our squad went there. Police officials, instead of helping us, are alleged to have arrested them and beaten them. Immediately when the facts came to my notice I contacted the Home Minister Shri K.C. Pant and the Lt. Governor and a magisterial enquiry has been ordered forthwith and the concerned Officer has been transferred. So this is my point of order. It is sub-judice.

SHRI S.N. MISHRA : His allegation is proved now ....

SHRI VAJPAYEE : It is a serious matter. I submit it should not be taken lightly and no ruling should be given in haste.... (*Interruption*).... I have been thrown a challenge. So I have brought this up.

SHRI S.D. SINGH : What is your ruling on the tape-recorder ? Please keep it with you.

MR. CHAIRMAN : Do not force. I shall not give the ruling yet.

Capital's Corrupt Police

SHRI VAJPAYEE : Sir, I would like to place on the floor of the House a portion of the tape-recorded conversation about which the Health Minister also knows. This will bring out the whole matter. I only want to give proof of how corrupt the police administration in the capital is.... (*Interruption*)....

MR. CHAIRMAN : I am not permitting. Nothing will go on record, unless I permit it. Whether it is a tape-recorder or a person....

SHRI VAJPAYEE : If you give a ruling there would be a quarrel. No rule prevents me from bringing a tape-recorder. Quote the rule.

MR. CHAIRMAN : Remove this.... (*Interruption*).... By interrupting you are making my work more complicated.

SHRI VAJPAYEE : Show the rule. At present you are occupying the chair but you are not above rules. Show me the rule that prevents me from bringing a tape-recorder.

SHRI VASANT SATHE : He has got residuary powers to regulate the proceedings of the House. How do you say that he has got no powers ?

MR. CHAIRMAN : I do not permit bringing it.

SHRI S.N. MISHRA : If some rule does not give authority how can we accept your ruling ?

SHRI VASANT SATHE : If there is no rule residuary powers are with the Chair.

MR. CHAIRMAN : In the matter that has been raised rule 389 says :

> "All matters not specifically provided for in these rules and all questions relating to the detailed working of these rules shall be regulated in such manner as the Speaker may, from time to time, direct."

SHRI VAJPAYEE : By using residuary powers like this you are providing an arrangement that does not accord with the rules.

MR. CHAIRMAN : Remove it and then speak. I request you, please remove it.

SHRI VAJPAYEE : It won't be removed.

MR. CHAIRMAN : It will have to be removed.

SHRI VAJPAYEE : It will not go. Please listen to me. No line can be drawn between bringing a book or document and a taped conversation into the House. I have not yet played the tape-recorder. I can do so if you want it.

MR. CHAIRMAN : Remove it.

SHRI VAJPAYEE : It won't be removed. It will go with me.

MR. CHAIRMAN : It is one thing to bring a book or newspaper and another to bring a tape-recorder, a camera, a gun or a pistol. It cannot be allowed.

SHRI B.P. MAURYA : There may be a time bomb in it.

SHRI VAJPAYEE : The other day you saw that the Speaker had brought a watch to the House. He had got it abroad. It can be shown. No one had raised a point of order then. What is the difference ?

MR. CHAIRMAN : What is the purpose of bringing it ? For showing ?

SHRI VAJPAYEE : I have brought it because I have been challenged. I shall keep it down.

I would like to place before the House a couple of portions of the conversation that took place between the police officer, the Officer of the Central Food Squad and a respected citizen. The police officer was saying :

> "Every S.H.O. expects his subordinates, the police officer like Shri Jethanand in catching three or four gambling cases and to enhance his reputation.

I tell you truly that if I do not find any case here...."

"Here" means South Delhi.

"I may get them from Sadar Bazar or any other area, and I must register some cases...."

Look at one more portion.

> "I am sitting on *Gaddi* and by swear of God I tell you that if I were to do alone I would have made Rs. 400/Rs. 500 on that day. My children would have enjoyed Diwali.... *(Interruption)*....

One more portion is like this :

> "You know our quarrel with sub-inspector is always on money. I do all the work and I will take eight annas share. He...."

"He "means his superior officer.

> "has no right to interfere in my work, as I am posted by DSP and SHO and he is posted by SP. DSP and SHO are both pleased with me, and if they say even to break somebody's leg I will break it."

He was asked if he had arrested the Central Food Squad Inspector, if he had misbehaved with him, if he was pushed into the van and if he had been kept in police lock-up for four hours. When this matter was dismissed what did the police officer say ?

"Jethanand understands the meaning of arrest and if he....".

(By "he" he means his superior officer).

"....Says to anybody that 'you are under arrest' then he will put him in the lock-up and may release him on bail. Jethanand understands Section 46 and will definitely put in the Rozanmcha that he has been arrested under Section 54. He is foolish .... It is true if he says he is arrested he should arrest under section 54. Now he should think of getting himself absolved of his actions under Section 54; even Dr. Rahdkarishnan can be arrested..."

The Police Officer does not even know who the President now is. He thinks it is Dr. Radhakrishnan....(*Interruption*)....

SHRI MADHU LIMAYE : Sir, this is a very serious mater. This tape should certainly be played.... (*Interruption*)....

SHRI N.K.P. SALVE : This quotation is from a stupid fellow. It should be expunged.

SHRI VAJPAYEE : The Hon. member is calling them stupid. Today the police have fired at students in Shahdara. Now they will become intelligent.

SHRI MADHU LIMAYE : Jethanand should be placed on the Table.

SHRI VAJPAYEE : In this connection please remember that the Government is launching a big campaign against adulteration. Changes are being made in law to make adulteration punishable with imprisonment for life. But what is the apparatus through which this anti-adulteration law will be enforced ? Food Inspectors will go to collect specimens, shopkeepers will quarrel with them, the police will be called, they will side with the shopkeepers and will lock up the food inspectors. So far the Home Ministry has not taken any action against those officers. Even the inquiry cannot be completed, as police officers are threatening the people of the area that if they gave testimony against them they will have to suffer for it. The Health Minister had very seriously sent the matter to the Home Minister, but his hopes were not fulfilled and necessary action was not taken.

Racket in Sale of Wheat

I present one more picture. A thousand gunny bags of wheat were seized from a big agriculturist in a village in Sonepat district. The wheat was deposited in the warehouse. But the man who owned it had very high-level contacts. He somehow manged to get an order issued that the wheat should be sold as seed to a firm in Maharashtra at two and a half rupees a kilo. The wheat that could be sold at 70 rupees in the open market, that had been seized by the police and deposited in the warehouse was sold to a firm in Maharashtra as seed at two and a half rupees a kilo in Haryana under the Government led by Shri Bansilal.

What do these pictures say ? What picture of India do they present ? They are not of the opposition's making, nor can we blame Nature for them. Those who are responsible for these pictures are in the dock today.

It is repeatedly said in this House that the ruling party has a tremendous majority. Is it necessary to say so ? Had it not been so it would not have been necessary for us to take this no-confidence motion. These people have a majority, but why are they not able to bring about the necessary changes in the country ?

What the Prime Minister scented in 1972 ?

MR. CHAIRMAN : The Hon. Minister may now try to wind up.

SHRI VAJPAYEE : Sir, please do not add to my time the time wasted in shouting. I have yet to say many things.

As I was saying, certain hopes had been roused in the country in the wake of the creation of Bangladesh, and an image of a confident India had emerged on the global stage . Who tarnished this image ?

The Government has failed on the food front. It made the mistake of taking over the grain trade and of giving the farmer a small price. This created an artificial scarcity. An effort has been made to improve the policy regarding rice, but there is not enough improvement, because the ruling party has acquired a vested interest in controls, corruption and black money.

(Mr. Speaker in the Chair)

A demand has been made in this House time and again that big denomination notes be taken out of circulation. A demand has also been made frequently that the Government should restrict the production of luxury goods, whose production has risen by 30 per cent and for the purchase of which black money is used, but the Government has not succeeded in doing so.

Well-known economist Prof. M.V. Dandekar has said that black money remains black for a moment but it turns white the moment it reaches the hands of the ruling party. He has also said that the day black money ends will also be the day the ruling Congress ends.

Black money in the economic field and black politics in the political field. This is the story of the last two and a half years. Today the Constitution has become a plaything. Governors are being used as rubber stamps. If there is a crisis in the Congress party, President's rule is imposed in Uttar Pradesh. The Constitution says Article 356 may be used only in the event of a constitutional crisis. There was no constitutional crisis in Uttar Pradesh, but there was a crisis in the Congress party, so President's rule was imposed under Article 356. When the crisis was over President's rule was brought to an end. Would the Constitution be trifled with this like this ?

At first it was said that President's rule was imposed because there were scarcity conditions in Uttar Pradesh. Then is scarcity now over ? It was said that the law and order situation is deteriorating. Then has it improved now ? Only one thing has happened and it is that the ruling party dare not fight elections without being in power. If you wanted a fair fight let us have an election when neither of us was in office. But you cannot fight that sort of an election.

The policies of this government are neither production-oriented nor distribution-oriented; they are only election-oriented. They have been adopted for cheap popularity. Policies are given up under pressure from big industrialists. Political decisions are taken with votes in view.

For votes the National Integration Council can be sidelined and it can also be revived. For votes an alliance can be struck with the Muslim League in Kerala, and for votes the Muslim League can be opposed in U.P. The Government does not care that communalism is spreading. If Muslims of U.P. side with the Congress the League there would become as patriotic as in

Kerala. They do not like the League there only because it cuts into Muslim votes.

Even in respect of eradication of corruption the Government has different standards. In Punjab an inquiry commission was set up against Akali Ministers because a Communist MLA had filed charges against them. An inquiry is necessary. We are not against it. But how many MLAs and how many MPs made representations against Choudhary Bansilal ? Why was there no inquiry against him ? In Bansilal's regime — yesterday the Chair had permitted this issue to be raised — atrocities are being committed on Harijans. 14000 Harijans have courted arrest in Delhi but the Central Government cannot bring Shri Bansilal to his senses. Is that because he is assisting the corruption that has spread from top to bottom ?

I am happy Shri Lalit Narayan Mishra has arrived. I am using constrained words. Opposition parties have presented charges against him. Even the members of his own party have filed charges. They are serious charges. Should they not be investigated ? Should the life of public leaders not be blemishless ? Should leaders of India not be above suspicion ?

It is a sad state of affairs that in this country one cannot get a licence for setting up a cement factory. Tata has to wait for five years for the Muthapur project, but there is no delay in issuing a letter of intent to the Prime Minister's son for producing a small car. What is this, and when will this car run ? Where is the petrol ?

The Prime Minister had made a speech at the Chamber of Commerce after the elections. I would like to make it clear that we have no personal quarrel with the Prime Minister's son. But does the country need buses today or small cars ? Do we need TV or drinking water ? Essential articles or luxury goods ?

Resentment is spreading all over the country. Every class is suffering. The people are losing faith in democracy. This is not a question for any party. Within the ruling party people are found talking of limited dictatorship. Have we lost the battle of democracy ? Can we not build India in accordance with the people's desire by securing the people's cooperation ? Who will do this job ? The leadership of which we had hopes has failed. It should resign. It should step down and make way for someone else. Thank you.

Vengeance Cannot Resolve Railway Strike

Sir, we just now listened to the discourse of Pandit Keshav Dev Malaviya. He has come to the throne after 10 years in exile. I do not want to go into the circumstances in which he had to resign. But his effort to divide the Opposition on this no-confidence motion is to be condemned; it will not succeed. The British used to be blamed for their 'divide and rule' policy. (*Interruption*). Sir, the dividing process is not only going on within the House, outside the House railwayman are also sought to be divided. Efforts are being made to make the common man stand against the railwayman. The government is trying to create such a situation in respect of the railway strike as may go out of control.

Sir, who is a progressive and who a reactionary is a matter of philosophy. We do not need Shri Malaviya's certificate for it. I do not want to go into this controversy. We have different ideologies but I fail to understand the ideology of a party in which Pandit Keshav Dev Malaviya and Shri Subramaniam co-exist. It is not a party, it is a crowd that has come together for power.

Sir, the serious situation brought about by the railway strike needs to be carefully considered. This discourse was not needed. But Shri Malaviya believes in scientific socialism. He talks of scientific socialism and he is in a party that swears by democratic socialism. Scientific socialism means "communism".... (*Interruption*).... Sir, this opportunity that Shri Malaviya has chosen to create a gulf is not an example of good politics. Yesterday the Prime Minister too wanted to play the same game. I do not want to go into that too. She complained that other parties lining up with the Jana Sangh are forsaking their professed secularism. The divisive technique being practised outside has how become a conspiracy of division inside the House, but this will not solve the problem.

Sir, the problem will also not be solved if political parties want to exploit the situation.

It was said that this strike was motivated by political considerations and it was also said that the parties that lost the elections are creating a disturbance .... (*Interruption*).... Sir, this is not the first time that we have lost an election. We have been losing. This does not have to be hidden. It is wrong to link up victory or defeat in elections with today's burning problems. Today

---

Lok Sabha on May 9, 1974 during discussion on the Motion of No-confidence against the Council of Ministers

dearness is playing havoc with the lives of railwaymen and others. Disparity is creating a gulf between the lives of railway employees and employment of government undertakings .... (*Interruption*)....

Sir, there is a shortage of essential commodities. Does it not agitate railway employees ? Can it be denied that never in the last 26 years had dearness grown so much ? Is it not true that never before in the last 26 years was there so much unemployment as at present ? Is it also wrong to say that the *'Garibi hatao'* slogan has raised the people's expectations ? If they now demand that these raised expectations should be fulfilled what is anti-national about it ? Sir, we have recognised the right to work, and with it also goes the right of not to work, the right to strike work. Now if railwaymen give a regular notice of the strike and then talks go on with their leaders how can the condition now be imposed that there would be no talks till the strike notice is withdrawn ? Why has this new condition been imposed ? On the day of the adjournment motion on railways I had said that it was immoral to arrest George Fernandes and his colleagues during the talks. Sir, even the Britishers had not done such a bad thing with our leaders. It never happened that talks were going on with them and they were put in jail .... (*Interruption*)....

DR. KAILASH (Bombay South) : Was it not a conspiracy that they were planning subversion during the talks ? Would you allow them to ruin the country?

SHRI VAJPAYEE : There is no previous example of main leaders being put in jail while talks were going on. This is the first instance.

SHRI VASANT SATHE (Akola) : Now the British are being praised.

SMT. INDIRA GANDHI : They have always done it. It is not a new thing.

SHRI VAJPAYEE : This is false. But you are outdoing the British in evil deeds .... (*Interruption*)....

Sir, their din and noise should not be added to my time.

MR. CHAIRMAN : You may continue.

SHRI VAJPAYEE : Sir, it is said preparations were going on during the talks. They were arrested on the ground that preparations for the strike were going on. Is it not true that preparations for the strike were going on side by side ? But in what atmosphere ? You were issuing secret instructions preparing to deploy the territorial army, recalling old employees and preparing your defences in case the strike came about ? The employees wanted to ensure a strike in case the talks failed. But once you engaged in talks what is the meaning of arresting them on the basis that they were preparing for a strike ?

SHRI L.N. MISHRA : They were not arrested because they had made preparations.

SHRI VAJPAYEE : Then why ?

SHRI L.N. MISHRA : I'll tell you that.

SHRI PILOO MODY : What is this great secret he is keeping from all of us ? Tell us now.

SHRI VAJPAYEE : Sir, that day we heard a cock and bull story. Shri George Fernandes's speeches were not published in the papers. Sir, he was jailed on the basis of CID reports, which are doubtful. Would it not have been honest to place before Shri Fernandes the next day of the talks the speeches that were considered objectionable ?

SHRI R.S. PANDEYA : It was a conspiracy. You do not have full information about it .... (*Interruption*)....

SHRI VAJPAYEE : This was not done. It was said a plane could have been sent for him to come from Lucknow. You certainly carried on talks but it was necessary to give them a final form. Instead of continuing the talks you put him in jail. This was a big mistake. The same day in the evening, when the adjournment motion was being discussed the Railway Minister announced that there would be no talks so long as the strike notice was not withdrawn. (*Interruption*). Can you solve the problem by resorting to repression and running the trains with the help of the territorial army despite the assurance that it would not be used to break the strike ? I would like to give an example of how trains are run. Yesterday a Congress MP said there was no strike, today he says there is a strike. I found out what train left Delhi yesterday. I was told the Assam Mail had left. How did it go ? It stopped at Ghaziabad and returned from there in the evening. It was claimed the Assam Mail had left. It was also said it had returned (*Interruption*). I can prove this.

I have had close connections with Railway employees. I am connected with the Assistant Station Masters' Association for the last eight years. Hon. members of this House should have some realisation of the difficult conditions in which railway employees work. Lakhs of railwaymen work day and night, in sun and rain, in winter and summer....

AN HON MEMBER : Do not farmers work in the field ?

SHRI VAJPAYEE : Do you want to change the discussion on railwaymen into a discussion on farmers ? When we talk of railwaymen they remember the farmer, but when we talk of giving the farmer a bigger price they say the Jan Sangh people incite farmers with bigger prices.

The conditions in which railwaymen work should be taken into consideration. Is it not true that these conditions are more difficult than those obtaining in other public undertakings and still there is a difference in wages ? The minimum salary in the railways is Rs. 210, while in public undertakings it is Rs. 300 (*Interruption*). I am including allowances. Will this difference not be resented ? Will the employees not compare their condition ? Will those doing the same type of work not come together and discuss that they are getting different wages when they are doing the same type of work, serving the same government and are engaged in building up the same country ?

Had the Railway Minister said it is legitimate to demand job evaluation, there should be parity, we accept it in principle but we cannot accept it for the present due to financial constraints. The leaders of railway employees could certainly have looked at it sympathetically and suggested how resources could be raised, or they could have said accept the demand in principle and implement it in pieces, we won't insist on full implementation right away. But this method was not adopted.

Can railway employees forget that in 1950 capital-at-large was Rs. 827 crores while in 1973-74 it rose five times to Rs. 4000 crores ? During this period the length of railway lines has not doubled, nor has the number of wagons doubled. Obviously profit alone is not the criterion of railway expansion. Security considerations are also there. Railway extension is done on the demand of States. It is said factories need railway lines to haul raw materials. The Railway Ministry arranges for them even at a loss. Some lines are laid on political considerations. Will the losses due to all these factors be bumped together to tell the railway employees that their wages cannot be increased because the railways run in losses ?

(Mr. Speaker in the Chair)

I was a member of the Railway Convention Committee. Time is limited, otherwise I could give any number of examples to show how the railway suffers losses in order to bring profit to businessmen and industrialists. In the Railway Convention Committee I saw an instance of why people prefer to pay demurrage charges. When ordered goods are not unloaded a demurrage is charged on them. I have seen examples where businessmen do not keep goods in godowns because godown rent is higher than demurrage.

SHRI L.N. MISHRA : This is an old thing.

SHRI VAJPAYEE : There are also new things like this. Not one but many. If you sat with railway employees and thought about how wasteful practices could be removed and resources raised for meeting legitimate demands the strike notice could have created a feeling of working together between the railway employees and the Railway Ministry, so that efficiency could have improved, income could have gone up, wasteful expenditure could have come down and railway employees satisfied. But no constructive politics was in evidence. Had the Railway Ministry taken advantage of the fact that all categories of railway employees had come together to request their cooperation and continued talks in a spirit of give and take not only the strike could have been avoided but the door to good reforms in railway administration could have been opened. But, pardon me, the government is bent upon teaching the railwaymen a lesson. Somewhere in the government's thinking an idea seems to be fixed that railwaymen have become so overbearing that they need a thrashing.

AN HON. MEMBER : It is true.

SHRI VAJPAYEE : That is a Congress member speaking (*Interruption*). This is why the territorial army is being called and humiliating conditions imposed on the leaders of railway employees. What is the purpose of saying there will be talks only when the strike notice is withdrawn ?

SHRI K.D. MALAVIYA : This is happening due to you.

SHRI VAJPAYEE : Shri Malaviya sees us everywhere.

SHRI MALAVIYA : What did you say in Indore ?

SHRI VAJPAYEE : It is not what I said in Indore but what you are doing in New Delhi that is being discussed. Is your purpose to insult the leaders of the railway employees ? Do you want the railway employees to surrender in humiliation before the powers that be ? If not, why this condition of no talks without the strike notice being withdrawn ? When 60 per cent of the members of the Action Committee of the strikers are in jail how can they think about any new situation ? They should be released. This talk of withdrawing the strike notice be given up.

No one can deny that there was a strike in the railways. You may be able to partly break it in a few days by resorting to repression, but the time has come to estimate how far the strike that has taken place will disrupt the railway system. Shri Malaviya made a speech on the radio in which he said if railways do not run coal would not be moved, and then what would happen to factories ? But on the day of his speech did he not know that that night Shri George Fernandes was going to be arrested ?

AN HON. MEMBER : He knew about his objectionable activities.

SHRI VAJPAYEE : Had he known he could not have made such a speech.

Whatever happens to this strike one thing is clear — we will have to suffer serious consequences because of it. There is still time, the situation can be managed. We are prepared to talk without conditions with foreign enemies. Shri Nehru used to say that every strike should result in a victory for both parties and defeat for neither.

The Prime Minister has also sometimes repeated it. Can this principle not be applied to the railway strike ? Will you act on Mahatma Buddha's advice only on Buddha Purnima day ? Can a solution not be found in which neither the railway employees' leaders nor the Government will be defeated, both will win. I believe if there is a will such a way can be found.

Three Mistakes

But the Government must admit it made three mistakes. First, it was the Prime Minister saying we cannot give a bonus, then saying the matter could be considered by the Bonus Review Committee, then Shri Sharma saying we too demand a bonus and if we don't get it we will go on strike. If Shri Sharma thinks it is proper to go on strike for a bonus why is it not proper for another federation to go on a strike for the same bonus ? Shri Sharma has said we are only waiting for the Bonus Review Committee. If it says no bonus what will Shri Sharma do ?

The first mistake was that the Prime Minister's letter to the Chief Ministers was published. I said that day and I still say that it is one thing to write a letter and another to publish it. It was published by those who did not want a compromise, who wanted the crisis to deepen. The second mistake was Shri George Fernandes's arrest. The third mistake was to say that talks won't begin until the strike notice was withdrawn. There is still time to correct your mistakes. The purpose of today's no-confidence motion is to tell the Government that there is still time to correct the situation, but that needs constructive politics, not a feeling of vengeance. If you are bent upon teaching a lesson there will be a struggle and its consequences will have to be faced both by the Government and the employees.

Sir, the strike has begun but we have still not reached a situation in which there would be no way out. Ways can be found. This is the purpose of this no-confidence motion. We know its fate. All logic is on our side, but the numbers are with them. They want the decision on the strength of numbers and it is possible only within the House. The common man cannot be convinced that the Government has shown intelligence in handling the strike. Nobody supports Shri George Fernandes's arrest.

Sir, we had demanded that the Emergency should be abrogated. There is friendship with Pakistan. Bangladesh has been formed, which Pakistan has recognised, occupied territory has been returned to Pakistan and POWs have been released. Now what is the point in continuing this Emergency ? Give up the extraordinary powers that you have assumed. Now we know why you want to continue the Emergency. It is not for tackling Pakistan but for suppressing the legitimate demands and the legitimate agitation of the railway employees. Is it proper to arrest them under MISA and keep them in jail under D.I.R. ? Is this not misuse of Emergency provisions ? It seems the Government has not the capacity to resolve a democratic agitation except by suppression. The country is going to face difficult times. There is still time. The Government can show intelligence and prevent the damage due to the railway strike. The railway Minister and the leaders of the railway employees can still sit at the negotiating table and arrive at an honourable compromise. If that is not done the responsibility of the resulting serious situation will lie squarely with the Government and with nobody else.

Covert Plan for Imposing Emergency

Sir, I do not stand to rebut Gyaniji's speech. His argument was unassailable. No one can rebut it.

The Manipur Scenario

Sir, I have just returned from a visit to Manipur. The greenland of Manipur now bears the stains of blood. It is a border State of the North-East. So far 135 people have been killed either in clashes with the police or internecine strife. That people should die in a strategically important area of the country—and this number is bigger than Bihar Sharif— is a danger signal for the whole country. Manipur should not be away from our hearts simply because it is away from Delhi. There is President's rule there. The Centre is responsible for the administration in Manipur. This morning two young men were killed in a clash with the police. I had an opportunity to visit the place. Firing was resorted to right in the middle of a busy area. One of those involved was a top student of the Delhi University. Why was he ready to kill and be killed ?

Sir, this is not a matter for interruption.

I would welcome interruption, but it should be done intelligently. Unintelligent interruption neither redounds to the status of Parliament nor contributes to the discussion.

I would like to draw the attention of the House to a serious matter. In Manipur there are one lakh unemployed in a population of 14 lakhs. Why do young men leaving the University go straight into the underground movement and take up arms ?

The People's Democratic Front claims it has a majority. Why is it not being invited to form the Government ? Why is it necessary to have President's rule ? Will the fate of the elected government be decided in the Legislative Assembly or by the report of Governors who have become puppets in the hands of the Centre ?

Assam

In Assam the Congress-I did not have a majority, still its leader was invited to form the Government. That government lost. It has neither the trust of the people nor of the Legislative Assembly. Such a government was imposed on Assam. Will there be different standards of democracy ? Will the Governor behave one way in Manipur and another way in Assam ? Will you just sit at

Lok Sabha on May 8, 1981 during discussion on the Motion of No-confidence against the Council of Ministers

the Centre and not see the explosive situation it Manipur ? Will you not worry about Assamese young men becoming extremists ? Will you just look to party interests ?

AN HON. MEMBER : The interest of the country was considered. There has been peace since the Congress-I came to power.

SHRI VAJPAYEE : Sir, people can be physically killed on the strength of the army and the police, but their hearts cannot be won. There were corruption charges against the government in Manipur—corrupt ministers, dishonest officers, contractors busy fleecing the people and the youth brimming with resentment. I sympathise with the armed forces on the conditions in which they operate. But suppression, terror, is not the answer to the problems of Manipur and Assam. For that we have to stand firm on the real limitations of democracy and not play proper politics. No one will blame you if the People's Democratic Front is invited to form the Government and that government talks. But you are not ready to invite it.

2000 tons of rapeseed oil sent for Manipur during the old State government did not reach there but were sold in Calcutta. What happened to the paper mill that was set up there ? For every job you need a bribe. The Loktak power project is hanging fire for the last many years.

The Disturbed Youth

So the youth are getting disturbed. There will be a battle of the parties, but the crisis has crossed party parameters. It is not only a party crisis. It is a crisis of confidence, a crisis of administration. Why is the country again standing at the crossroads of fate within fifteen months ? Why has the magic worn off within fifteen months ? Why is that you have a majority in Parliament and in the Legislative Assemblies but no contentment in the country ? Dearness is increasing. Last year it increased by 18 per cent. Within the last four months it increased still further. When the budget was presented it was said dearness would increase a little. How can a worker getting a fixed wage manage ? (*Interruption*).

AN. HON. MEMBER : Talk of the rich, it does not become you to talk of the poor.

SHRI VAJPAYEE : It does not become him to say anything at all. I do not want to comment on his interruption.

Gyaniji talks of law and order. He wanted to prove with figures that crime has gone down in Delhi. Does he know that offences are not registered in the police stations of Delhi ? During the Janata Party Government Smt. Indira Gandhi used to say that it has become difficult for women to move about in Delhi in the evening. The conditions in Indiraji's regime are such that even hale and hearty men find it difficult to step out in the evening (*Interruption*).

Buses are being attacked. Trains are looted. Air travel too is no more safe. If the plane that was to take the Prime Minister in 15 days becomes the victim of subversion what will become of other planes ? This is a matter of great concern for air travellers.

This session of Parliament will be remembered for many things. That day a member of the ruling party staged a *Dharna* in the Lok Sabha. This did not happen in 33 years of Parliament's history. He was not an an opposition member. He was not doing it for propaganda. Why did he not raise the matter in a meeting of the Congress Parliamentary Party ? Why did he not take his grievance to his leader ? Is this not a crisis of confidence in the party, in the leader ? Then he was prevented from speaking. This is a sign of a deep illness.

But one incident took place outside the House. A member of the Council of Ministers was taking his meal in his room. He asked his security man not to let anyone in while he was eating. At that very time a Minister reached there. The security man said Sahib was taking his food and had said not to let anyone in. You know what that Minister did ? He hit the security man in the stomach. The man came weeping to me. What decorum is observed when a Minister hits a sentry ? What standard of behaviour is this ? This is not a small incident.... (*Interruption*)....

I charge in all seriousness .... (*Interruption*)....

One more small incident. I would like to indicate the basis of the charge that the government is tending towards Emergency. A meeting was held in Bombay .... (*Interruption*)....

SHRI ZAIL SINGH : Sir, I submit most respectfully that Shri Vajpayee is President of the Party and has been Foreign Minister. His words will reach far. So he should give us the Minister's name for our information.

SHRI VAJPAYEE : I'll give the name but it will put you into difficulties ... (*Interruption*).... He keeps asking for the name because he suspects the finger might be pointing at him....(*Interruption*).... All right, I shall give one name. The Minister who was taking up meal was Shri Bhishma Narayan Singh. Call him and ask him the other Minister's name.... (*Interruption*)....

Sir, if my charge is challenged the matter should be sent to the Privileges Committee. I shall produce the security man...(*Interruption*)...one more thing....(*Interruption*)....

SHRI ZAIL SINGH : Sir, Shri Vajpayee is an old parliamentarian. This is not a matter for the Privileges Committee. Either you should not have said it, or you should have said it is hearsay, or if you have seen you should give the name....(*Interruption*)....I can assure you somebody has given you wrong information, a Minister has not done such a thing. No Minister has done it. Somebody has told you a lie. Don't believe it.

SHRI VAJPAYEE : Then I repeat the whole matter be handed over to the Privileges Committee. I am willing to produce the security man.

I charge that there is a planned effort to declare an Emergency in the country (*Interruption*)....

SHRI H.K.L. BHAGAT : What he said shall not go on record.

SHRI VAJPAYEE : Sir, I again repeat the charge emphatically that an atmosphere for gradually introducing an emergency in a planned manner in the country is being prepared.

After the amendment in the Constitution an emergency cannot be promulgated till there is an armed rebellion. So there is repeated talk of a foreign hand and foreign danger.

Sir, how are judges being tested ? They are being given extensions like casual labourers, who are given extensions every four months.

Sir, an effort is being made to terrorise the press. What happened in Orissa ? I do not want to mention it. The whole House should feel concerned about how a journalist of Varanasi was attacked ... (*Interruption*).... They are supporting it.

A concrete incident took place in Bombay recently. We wanted to hold a public meeting at Chowpatty to criticise the Government of India's Afghanistan policy. It was disallowed and we told it was not allowed because Chowpatty was within the jurisdiction of the Maharshtra Government.

MR. DEPUTY SPEAKER : Mr. Vajpayee, how is this Government responsible for it ?

SHRI VAJPAYEE : I am trying to show the mentality (*Interruption*).

DEPUTY SPEAKER : You are on no-confidence motion (*Interruption*).

SHRI VAJPAYEE : If others could refer to Kerala and criticise the CPI (M) for political murders in Kerala why should I be prevented from referring to the Maharashtra Government.... ? (*Interruption*)....It is for the Government to see that administration in Maharashtra is carried on according to the provisions of the Constitution.

Another ground for disallowing the meeting was still more laughable. We were told Soviet Russia is our friend, we cannot criticise it, Afghanistan is our friend, we cannot criticise it (*Interruption*).

The Throttled Freedom of Expression

Shri Sathe is one of the supporters and is the Information Minister. I ask him, is there no scope for a difference of opinion between us on foreign policy ? Can we not criticise our friends ? It was on this point that they disallowed our meeting. Then we approached the Court and the Court permitted the meeting. The Government of Maharashtra approached the Bench. The Bench met on Sunday. When the Maharashtra Government saw it would lose it said it would withdraw its appeal. But how did Shri Sathe support this step of the Maharshtra Government ? Are preparations being made to throttle the freedom of expression ? Will we not be allowed to speak in this country for the sake of foreign friends ?

They talk of friendship with Afghanistan. At the same time they betrary the people of Afghanistan.

SHRI P.N. TANDON (Damoh) : Talk about friendship with America. Don't talk of friendship with Afghanistan.

SHRI VASANT SATHE : Sir, I said in Srinagar that Shri Vajpayee and his friends want to hold a meeting here. They want to talk of friendship not with the people of Pakistan but with the rulers of Pakistan. This is against national interest, and if anyone says we want to make friends with enemies of the country this is against the nation's interest. So if the government took some step I cannot object to it. This is what I say. You want to support Zia-ul-Huq, you want to support America. If you want to say that I support you.

SHRI VAJPAYEE : Sir, I am sorry to see that the Information Minister said one thing outside and is saying another inside ... (*Interruption*).....

SHRI VASANT SATHE : I had said this and I have given the explanation also.

SHRI VAJPAYEE : We do not support the military rule there. Our question is, will we have or not have the right to say what we want to say ? Will we have this right only if we agree with what you say ? Shri Sathe can play this role—we cannot.

SHRI SATHE : The right to incite communalism ? The right to incite anti-nationalism ? What freedom are you talking about ? (*Interruption*).

SHRI VAJPAYEE : All India Radio has the permission to sing the praises of Smt. Indira Gandhi for 12 minutes in a news bulletin of 15 minutes. Change the name of All India Radio to All Indira Radio, for its credibility is going down—no one will listen to it.

SHRI SATHE : Sir, BBC should be named Bajpai Broadcasting Corporation.

SHRI VAJPAYEE : I hope All India Radio will give verbatim report of this part of the proceedings.

Sir, if the country is realty in danger is it proper to threaten non-Congress Governments with toppling ? Is it proper for the Prime Minister to say in Jammu and Kashmir ..... (*Interruption*)...

SHRI P. NAMGYAL (Ladakh) : Wrong, absolutely wrong....(*Interruption*).

SHRI VAJPAYEE : The Prime Minister said in Jammu if the Central Government did not help the State Government it cannot last even half an hour.

SHRI H.K.L. BHAGAT : He is wrong. It has been contradicted.

SHRI VAJPAYEE : The same people who set up this Government have also elected non-Congress Governments. We may have a difference with them, an ideological struggle will go on, but the fate of an elected government in a democracy will be decided in the Legislative Assemblies, not in Delhi *Durbar*.

The Home Minister had dwelt upon the quarrel in the Janata Party at length. We quarrelled and separated. But the Janata Party was made up of different parties. You belong to one party. To what state have you been reduced in 15 months ? Triparthi was a *Bhakta* (a devotee). Now he has become *Vibhakta* (separated). Skhula has become *Kirhsna*—has gone dark. *Shukla* means white. Today I did not listen to his full speech. But the Prime Minister's Secretariat said Shri Vidya Charan Shukla's resignation has been accepted because he had committed irregularities in sugar. All India Radio also reported likewise, while the whole House knows, the country knows that it is Rao Birendra Singh, not Vidya Charan Shukla, who is responsible for sugar. Now who is next ? So there is a competition of taking oaths of allegiance.

It was also said that yesterday Parliament made new history. I say new history was written but a dangerous tradition set. If the present Parliament changes the decisions of the old Parliament a future Parliament may change the decisions of the present Parliament.

We thought the Prime Minister's status was re-established the very day the Congress-I won the elections to the Lok Sabha. But your resolution yesterday has tarnished it, has clouded the colour of your victory.

Within 15 months it became necessary to bring in this resolution. Within 15 months it became necessary to call a Kisan rally in Delhi. Within 15 months the *'house arrest'* law came. And Gyaniji says very few people were arrested. Then the law was not necessary. This does not prove the need of the law, it proves the intellectual insolvency of this Government.

AN HON. MEMBER : He is out of mood over everything.

SHRI VAJPAYEE : When you are out of mood how can we be in mood ?

MR. DEPUTY SPEAKER : Now the mood is very good. Please continue.

SHRI VAJPAYEE : Sir, 15 months have elapsed but the Central Government has not yet been fully formed. The country is in danger but there is no Defence Minister. How can the Prime Minister look after every ministry ? There is no Industries Minister. Shri Anjaiah has gone, now there is no Labour Minister. There is no Minister for Steel. If no suitable candidates are available from among so many people we are prepared to lend some people from the opposition.

SHRI ZAIL SINGH : I am grateful to Shri Vajpayee. I think this was the whole cause of the quarrel. Even now he can come over.

SHRI VAJPAYEE : Gyaniji is inviting me. He has invited me once before too. I shall come over, but not at your instance, at the instance of the people.

Sir, Shri Jagjivan Ram said members of the Congress as well as the opposition have been elected. It is true that both have been elected. But there is a basic difference. You have been elected through Indiraji's grace and we have been elected in spite of her opposition. The need of the hour is for at least some people in the ruling party saying the truth loudly and clearly. In Mahabharat when Dronacharya and Bhisham Pitamaha were asked—you are so learned and so intelligent, then how could you side with injustice ? Bhimsha Pitamaha replied *"Arthasya Purusho dash"* 'Man is the slave of money'.... (*Interruption*).

Sir here they do not have intelligence even today. They do not read Mahabharat, they can enact it.

Sir, the no-confidence motion has been tabled because today there is a crisis of confidence in the country. We wished the Prime Minister would return and there would be a discussion on the motion on the 14th. We had no intentions of tabling the motion at her back. But why did you not accept our proposal to extend the session ? What is the need of ending the session today ? Will the people not have the opportunity even to discuss things ? Why are you so much afraid of a debate ... (*Interruption*)....

Sir, the charge was levelled against the opposition parties that they tabled the motion when the Prime Minister had gone abroad, and thus they are trying to tarnish the image of India. This is a baseless charge.

I say, why did the Prime Minister go abroad while Parliament was in session ? (*Interruption*)...

New conventions are being set. When, in the past, any minister left the country he was asked why he was going when Parliament was in session. But the Prime Minister is gone abroad, and now even the Speaker has started going. It is a misfortune for the country that new conventions are being set.

Where are We Taking the Country ?

Sir, in her address on the occasion of the 36th anniversary of Independence the Prime Minister appealed to the countrymen to do some introspection. I wish the Prime Minister starts the process with herself.

In a no-confidence discussion, support on the one hand and repudiation on the other are natural. But the process of introspection seems to have started in the party in power. This is proved by Shri Vasant Sathe's speech. Recently some Congress friends complained why the opposition should table a no-confidence motion. As a matter of fact these days that is the only chance we get in the House to talk to the Prime Minister. Of course there are other ministers, but the Information Minister himself says the Congress Party is like a tent supported by a single pillar. So if there has to be a talk it can be only with the Prime Minister, not with those hiding in the tent.

Actually Shri Vasant Sathe has also made certain other serious observations.

AN HON. MEMBER : He'll lose his job.

SHRI VAJPAYEE : He said :

> "Participation in a discussion organised by the Delhi Study Group here yesterday on 'democracy strengthens units' he said superficial solutions neither solved problems nor ensure the balanced economic growth so essential for the survival of democracy."

Mark the word 'superficial'. He added :

> "He felt there was 'no thinking' on these issues even in the Cabinet or the Congress Working Committee.

When asked to elaborate his observation, he shot back, "Haven't heard me ? "

Asked if he himself did any "thinking" he said he did and that was why he was talking about the problems. He warned about what had happened in Pakistan and Burma. A similar situation could arise in India too.

SHRI SOMNATH CHATTERJEE : He's finished.

AN HON. MEMBER : Have mercy.

SHRI VAJPAYEE : Shri Sathe has not refused this speech. In fact he has clearly expressed his misgivings in a speech on Tilak Jayanti after he went to Poona. I do not want to use the speech to level charges against the Government, but let the Prime Minister reply with her hand on her heart to the question—is she satisfied with the condition prevailing in the country ?

AN HON. MEMBER : Yes, fully.

Lok Sabha on August 16, 1982 during discussion on the Motion of No-confidence against the Council of Ministers

SHRI VAJPAYEE : Two and a half years have passed. Half the time is over. Is it not time for stock taking ? What the Janata Government did is not the subject of discussion here.

AN HON. MEMBER : Why not ?

SHRI VAJPAYEE : They have come into power but do not seem to have fully grasped the fact.

Sir, when rising prices are discussed the Finance Minister says this is a seasonal rise. That a seasoned parliamentarian like Shri Pranab Mukherji calls all price-rise a seasonal phenomenon is not easy for anybody to accept.

SHRI SOMNATH CHATTERJEE : Even Shri Frank Anthony has admitted it.

SHRI VAJPAYEE : I wish it were seasonal. But it is not. It is linked with the changes in the economic policy.

During the last two years the industrial policy has changed, the licence policy has changed, export-import matters have changed. The result of all this is that the common man is put to hardship, foreign debt is increasing, and we are leaving behind the national goal of self-reliance.

When the Prime Minister assumed power the foreign debt stood at around Rs. 10,000 crores. This was in March 1980. In March 1982 this rose to Rs. 15,459 crores. In 1983 it reached Rs. 20,000 crores. We will have to pay 2 billion dollars by way of interest. We are going to suffer trade losses to the tune of 7 to 8 billion dollars. Where are we taking the country ?

AN HON. MEMBER : On the road to progress.

SHRI VAJPAYEE : According to the conditions attached to the IMF loan we are moving away from self-reliance. We have now to look to foreign countries even for food. In such a situation how can we be genuinely non-aligned ? In the U.S. the Prime Minister said the Americans have accepted that we are truly non-aligned.

SMT. INDIRA GANDHI, Prime Minister : So far as I remember I did not say so. Those are not my words.

SHRI VAJPAYEE : These are not my words. This has been published in the papers.

SMT. INDIRA GANDHI : Do not believe everything they say.

SHRI VAJPAYEE : You have not refuted it. You have such a big office, Madam (*Interruption*) and I was not in your delegation. How could I be ? I am not even the Foreign Minister (*Interruption*). But if newspaper reports are not refuted I have no go but to accept them as true. If the Prime Minister says she did not say let her say what she said.

SMT. INDIRA GANDHI : I said we stand erect.

SHRI VAJPAYEE : The Prime Minister said we lean neither this way nor that. We stand erect. When we said the same this in 1977 and 1978 you said we are saying so in order to hide the tilt towards the U.S.

SMT. INDIRA GANDHI : You said you are genuinely non-aligned.

SHRI VAJPAYEE : And you say you are truly non-aligned. What is the difference ? (*Interruption*).

SMT. INDIRA GANDHI : The difference is that the Non-aligned Movement trusts us and looks to us and it did not trust you.

SHRI VAJPAYEE : The Non-aligned Movement does not look to any individual, it looks to India, and it is a matter of coincidence that you are the Prime Minister today (*Interruption*). Look at how Hon. Members are rising to defend the Prime Minister.

SPEAKER : No cross-talking.

The Tarapur Agreement

SHRI VAJPAYEE : Sir, if indeed our relations with America have improved due to the Prime Minister's foreign tour no one would oppose it. But there are certain questions that only the Prime Minister can answer. In respect of the agreement about Tarapur the Prime Minister repeatedly says we have not given up the right to reprocess. It is true that you have not given up the right to reprocess, but you have missed the opportunity to reprocess. Had the agreement broken down—it would have been immoral for the Americans to break it, they are bound by the agreement to supply us enriched uranium for 30 years—we should have told them— if you break the agreement we would go elsewhere, we would depend upon our scientists. But what did we do ? Now we shall get enriched uranium from France, but we shall get it *via* America. Could not have we made a direct agreement with France ?

SMT. INDIRA GANDHI : It will be direct.

SHRI VAJPAYEE : Why was it necessary for India and the U.S. to approach France together ... (*Interruption*). What about spares for Tarapur ? The position about spares is not clear. There is no storage capacity there. We will have to remove fuel. Where will we take it ? We could have had a direct agreement with France. It was not necessary to involve the U.S.

It is true that the American attitude has also changed. But it has not changed only about India. It has changed about Brazil, about South Africa. But the Tarapur problem has not been satisfactorily solved.

What decision has been taken about the arms that Pakistan is getting ? At the Palam Airport the Prime Minister was asked if the U.S. has given any assurance for the future. The Prime Minister said it was not asked for at all, so where was the question of giving it ? Arms will continue to be received. The misunderstanding with the U.S. has been due to the arms supply to Pakistan and to their going back on the Tarapur agreement. Where have we reached in both matters ? I do not want to dwell on this at length, as I also want to discuss some domestic problems.

Corruption at Centre

How is Delhi functioning ? When there are disturbances in the states, Delhi says—what can we do ? It is a State subject. Who is ruling Delhi ? It is the Centre. The Prime Minister ordered that power supply in Delhi be made normal within 24 hours. Had the directive been obeyed the citizens of Delhi would have been happy. We too would have been happy to see that the Prime Minister's word carried weight. 24 hours passed. The hours changed into days and the days into weeks. Some areas in Delhi have no power for five hours at a stretch. I can present figures. The expenditure on DESU is increasing, its production is decreasing. I cannot understand this mystery.

Just now my friend asked—was not a civil supplies corporation set up to give relief to the common man in Delhi ? It had a capital of one crore 90 lakhs of rupees and it incurred a loss of one crore. There was a scam of 80 lakh rupees in a sugar deal. Sugar for Delhi was purchased in Madras at Rs. 850 per quintal. Not one kilo of it reached Delhi. It was sold in Madras itself at Rs. 9.50 per kilo. There was a loss of Rs. 80 lakh. Is there anybody responsible for this ?

In Delhi three railway bridges are proposed to be widened— Azadpur, Naraina and a third one. Earth was needed for it. The Railway Ministry asked the Delhi Administration for it. 8000 trucks of earth were required. Right at that time the Nazafgarh drain of Delhi was being dug and earth was being dug out. But the Delhi Administration said—we cannot give earth for the railway, float your own tender and get the earth. A separate contract was given for digging out the earth from the drain. The railways called for tenders for earth supply. The two contractors met together. The earth from the Nazafgarh drain was given to the railways and a profit of one crore 10 lakh rupees was earned...*(Interruption)*...Can any one believe contractors can do this without colluding with officers ? And can anyone believe an officer can do without signals from above ?

DEPUTY SPEAKER : You have to conclude now.

SHRI VAJPAYEE : How can I conclude ? You have to keep the House in order.

Sir, Angre bought the *Surya*. It was this own decision. I do not support what is being published in the *Surya*. But does it not have the freedom of expression ? Had there been a charge of theft it would have been against Rajmata Scindia, not Angre...*(Interruption)*...

Sir, the Siswa affair has been discussed a lot in this House. Perhaps for the first time such a shameful event has occurred when policemen joined in raping women. A delegation of women from the place met the Prime Minister and perhaps the Prime Minister had assured it that the CBI would inquire into it, but no inquiry has been started. Now things have gone to such an extent that those unfortunate women are being told—we'll give you money, clothes, vessels, whatever, but don't say you were raped. I have received a letter from the residents of the place. I do not have the time to read it....

Sir, in Bihar landless Harijans are being prosecuted and slaughtered because they are demanding the wages fixed by the Government. Unfortunately purely communal riots are being presented as clashes between two goonda gangs. Recently 14 people including women and children were killed in a riot in Monghyr- Jamalpur. May I ask ... *(Interruption)*....

SHRI VIKRAM MAHAJAN, Minister of State in the Ministry of Energy : On a point of order. Are we going to raise State subjects in the House or we should discuss policy matters ?

SMT. INDIRA GANDHI : Can we therefore discuss West Bengal also and there will be no noise from that side ?

SMT. PRAMILA DANDAVATE (Bombay North Central) : Yes, discuss.

SHRI VAJPAYEE : We have been discussing a number of communal riots in this House.

May I seek a clarification ? Are we not entitled to discuss the failure of the Government to maintain communal harmony ?

I say there is a government in Bihar and it could be called to account. I want to draw the attention of the Prime Minister to a special situation. The police and the home guard were on duty there (*Interruption*)... The Prime Minister can stand on the ramparts of the Red Fort and talk of communal riots and minorities. I cannot do so in the House ... (*Interruption*)....There she stands to reply on behalf of the whole country. There she should have said—I'm speaking only for the Union Territories, not for the States...(*Interruption*)....

Sir, on June 19, 1982 seven home guards and a magistrate were on duty there. On 20th June three policemen got themselves declared sick. They kept away their guns and left. Other policemen and the magistrate also left. This is not a coincidence. An inquiry should be conducted into whether these people were mixed up with the rioters.

Sir, one more thing and I shall conclude....

DEPUTY SPEAKER : Please conclude now. I will call the next speaker if you are not concluding in time. You have got to conclude now.

SHRI NARAYAN CHOUBEY : You take more than the members.

SHRI VAJPAYEE : I quote what the Prime Minister had said in this very House while replying to a discussion on September 17 1981 :

> "I do not want to go into the cases against me. But one case I do want to mention. I wonder whether you know about it. I had to go all the way to Imphal, Manipur, on a non-bailable warrant. Do you know what the charge was ? I was supposed to be an abettor to a person who had stolen two chickens and six eggs. This was the highest theme in which the Janata Party had charged character and democracy...."

These words stunned us. Who was it who dragged the Prime Minister to Imphal on such trifling charge ? But later I collected all facts. It is false that a non-bailable warrant was issued against the Prime Minister...(*Interruption*) ...It is not true ...(*Interruption*) ....

SHRI P. SHIV SHANKAR, Minister of Petroleum, Chemicals and Fertilizers : Warrant was issued. (*Interruption*).

SHRI VAJPAYEE : A summons was issued against the Prime Minister.... (*Interruption*) ....

I am perfectly in order. It is not a fact that Mrs. Gandhi was summoned.... (*Interruption*).....

SHRI P. SHIV SHANKAR : I am prepared to resign the seat in Parliament... (*Interruption*) .... Supposing, if you are wrong, the point ...(*Interruption*).... You say that from Imphal ... (*Interruption*) .... that was the Trikha Commission which was inquiring into the whole thing. The bailable warrant against Mrs. Gandhi was not issued, if what you say is correct, then I am prepared to resign the Parliament seat.

SHRI VAJPAYEE : As an accused.

SHRI P. SHIV SHANKAR : If what you say is not correct then you must resign from the Parliament seat.

SHRI VAJPAYEE : There are two things in what I have read ....*(Interruption)*.... The Prime Minister has claimed that a non-bailable warrant was issued against her. I say it was a summons, not a non-bailable warrant.

Let the matter be referred to the Privileges Committee and I will produce the document ....*(Interruption)*....

MR. DEPUTY SPEAKER : You must conclude.

SHRI VAJPAYEE : What about the other point ? Were these summons to Imphal issued to give evidence or was she summoned as an accused ? Now you tell us.

SHRI P. SHIV SHANKAR : If you were to be there at the time she was cross-examined the whole day, right from 10.30 onwards up to six o'clock that was not evidence ....*(Interruption)*....

SHRI VAJPAYEE : Mr. Shiv Shankar has thrown a challenge. I accept that challenge. But how do we decide this matter ? Let the entire issue be referred to the Privileges Committee, and I am prepared to abide by its verdict.

SHRI P. SHIV SHANKAR : Why Privileges Committee ? Let it be decided right here.

Dismissal of BJP Ruled States—Fraud on the Constitution

Mr. Speaker, Sir, I beg to move :

"That this House expresses its want of confidence in the Council of Ministers."

Mr. Speaker, Sir, my No-confidence motion is a motion of one line. I have not given any reasons in it as I know that there is no need of giving reasons. In a Parliamentary democracy the Opposition keeps on bringing No-confidence Motions. When Shri Narasimha Rao was sworn in as Prime Minister then as per the orders of the President he had moved a Confidence Motion here and that time also Bharatiya Janata Party had voted against that Confidence Motion. I have not brought this No-confidence Motion to create problem for anybody. (*Interruptions*) Mr. Speaker, Sir, everybody's position should be clear. No-confidence Motion is not a religious ritual. There has been some incidents in the country on, before and after the 6th December. The nation is again in a dilemma. We are unhappy on whatever happened in Ayodhya on 6th December. (*Interruptions*). Mr. Speaker, Sir, if they interrupt then we cannot discuss it properly because they have also to speak next.

SHRI GHULAM NABI AZAD : I request the Hon. members not to disturb.

SHRI VAJPAYEE : If they disturb us, they would also be treated in the same manner.

We Had Given An Assurance

Mr. Speaker, Sir, when I was coming to the House, I saw something written on a dome which says "A meeting is not a meeting which has no elderman, An elderman is not an elderman until he practices religion, and a religion is not a religion which does not contain the truth and a truth is not a truth if it inspires you towards deception." Today in the House I shall speak only the truth and nothing but the truth. I would like that an open discussion should take place today. If it concludes that we are at fault then we are ready to accept it. We had given an assurance to the Prime Minister, I realise his anguish Arjun Singhji will not realise it. Every effort was made to fulfil the commitment given to the Prime Minister. But the commitment could not be fulfilled. The top ranking leaders of B.J.P., R.S.S. and V.H.P. had been trying to prevent Karsevaks there. Video tapes are evidence of it. At that time many journalists were present there. (*Interruptions*) We have apologised to the

Lok Sabha on December 17, 1992 while moving the No-Confidence Motion against the Council of Ministers

journalists who were beaten there. The journalists were beaten and their cameras were broken because the *Karsevaks* did not want their action to be recorded. If it was recorded....(*Interruptions*)

SHRI CHANDRA SHEKHAR (Ballia) : Mr. Speaker, Sir, will the House be conducted in this way ? Have the leaders of the Congress party no check on their members or they belong to C.P.M. ? Whosoever they are, but when Atalji is speaking and the Hon. Speaker has been constantly trying to resume the proceedings in the House and the efforts are being made to maintain parliamentary tradition on the basis of consensus. (*Interruptions*)

SHRI SHARAD YADAV (Madhepura) : We are preventing them. Everything should not be attributed to us. All of us have to check them.

SHRI CHANDRA SHEKHAR : Then it is right.

SHRI SHARAD YADAV : What do you people want ? Oh, all of you are great personalities.

SHRI CHANDRA SHEKHAR : Mr. Speaker, Sir, I am not talking to these people. I am speaking to you.

SHRI SHARAD YADAV : Oh, you are a great man. I have seen you speaking during the course of discussions violating all the rules.

SHRI CHANDRA SHEKHAR : Mr. Speaker, Sir, it is not going to have any effect on me. I am performing my duties as a Member of Parliament. Others have different concept. Their conduct is different. I do not ask them to adopt my ways. I am merely requesting you if you want to run the House, we should be ready to listen to each and every thing howsoever unpalatable it may be. I am not one of those people who can run the country without Parliament.

MR. SPEAKER : I fully agree with the views of Shri Chandra Shekhar. I, on behalf of all the members, request you not to interrupt when any one of you is speaking here. All of you are well aware that it is the only system by which our Parliament can function. By interrupting the speakers or adjourning the House again and again we cannot do anything. Again I appeal to all the members not to interrupt the speakers.

SHRI VAJPAYEE : Mr. Speaker, Sir, I am grateful to my Hon. friend, Shri Chandra Shekhar. He has tried to come to the help of his *guru*.

SHRI CHANDRA SHEKHAR : I would not be able to help him more.

SHRI VAJPAYEE : It has always been a tradition that "Guru" the teacher should assist his disciple. But now a time has come when the disciple has to come to the rescue of his 'Guru' or teacher.

Mr. Speaker, Sir, I was making a submission that it would be far better if the discussions are held with a sense of sincerity rather with a sense of prejudiced feelings. The C.B.I. is conducting an enquiry into the Ayodhya incidents. The findings of the enquiry are still awaited. I would like that whatever the facts are with the Government, it should place them before the House. Whatever the facts are with us, I am placing these before the House. I am ready to go one step ahead and ask those Karsevaks who were small in number to come forward and openly confess that they have demolished the structure and for that they are prepared to face the music. I would also like to state that there were Karsevaks present in a large number but they all were not involved in the demolition.

Ram Temple Cannot Be Built On Deceit

Ram temple will not be constructed by foul or unfair means. If Ram temple is constructed it would be constructed on the basis of moral strength. There was no need to assemble large number of Karsevaks. Had there been an intention to demolish the structure, it would have been done easily without collecting Karsevaks in large number. Fairs are held after every three-months in Ayodhya. If the structure was to be demolished secretly and according to a plan, it did not require Karseva. So whatever happened there, we regret the incident.

We as well as the Government of Uttar Pradesh had requested the Central Government to get the matter expedited in the Court either way. How long the case would be kept pending ? The representatives of the Central Government met us as well as the Government of Uttar Pradesh; but they refused to say in the Court that the verdict of the Court should be delivered soon. They stated that it was too late. On that day, during the discussion Shri Chavan said that the matter was being postponed till 11th instant. Karseva was scheduled to be resumed on 6th instant. The assembled Karsevaks were of the view that they would get some opportunity for construction work. But they could not get the same. However, efforts were made to control the situation. We had hoped that the Karsevaks would wait for the Court's verdict till 11th instant and our leadership made every effort in this regard. The General Secretary of R.S.S. had been requesting the people in Southern languages that no Karsevak should go towards the structure. He should not take part in demolition activity.

Owning Moral Responsibility Advani and Kalyan Singh Resigned

The press reporters who went there told me that Shri Advani was very sad when the structure was demolished. He was in tears. That is why he sent in his resignation expressing his regret over the incident. Owning the responsibility Shri Kalyan Singh also resigned. If you consider it as a drama, then it is a gross misconception because such type of misconception will neither encourage fair politics in the country nor will it encourage the right secularism.

I would like that all the facts should be brought forward. We would like to know the reality because it is a matter of great sorrow and challenge for us. Our organisation was presumed a disciplined organisation. Our organisation was having an image of a disciplined one. It was its glory as to what they finalise they act accordingly. But the tarnished image is causing trouble for us.

We would like to know who was that group, from where it came and who organised it. I repeat it again that the Karsevaks who took part in demolishing the structure should come forward and reveal their participation in the demolition. If punishment is given they should accept it. The temple of Lord

Rama cannot be built without making sacrifice. At least it will not be built in this manner.

It was a Temple Too

But there are other aspects also of this issue. It was not only a structure which was demolished. There was a temple as well. 'Namaz' was not offered in the mosque. Even the entry to the mosque was prohibited. But prayer was offered in the temple by the orders of the court. Now some Hon. member can object that the mosque already existed there and statues of deities were installed there later on. This is right. Statues were installed there but I do not want to go into the history. I would like to ask the Hon. members whether statues were not kept with this belief that it was the birthplace of Lord Rama ? There was no Jan Sangh, Vishwa Hindu Parishad or Bajarang Dal those days. But the people of that area had a strong feeling. Mr. Speaker, Sir, through you, I am constrained to say that the intensity of the sentiments of the majority community is not being understood.

I too did not understand it earlier. When Shri Advani went on the Rath Yatra, I had my reservations. When I expressed my feelings the press would have said that the Bharatiya Janata Party has worn two faces. Sometimes, it displays its countenance of moderates and sometimes that of hardliners. Mr. Speaker, Sir, excuse me, sometimes I deviate from the issue. I had said earlier that it will not serve any purpose. But the way people supported the cause, the mistakes that were committed by the ruling party, particularly the arbitrary decision by the then Chief Minister Shri Mulayam Singh Yadav to deal with the agitation, the way communalism was incited by the announcement that a particular community had the right to have arms, worsened the situation....(*Interruptions*)

SHRI CHOTEY SINGH YADAV (Kannauj) : The name of a person who is not present in the House, is being referred and it is being said that he is responsible for communalism, whereas he is the only person who saved the country. But it is they who mislead the people.

SHRI VAJPAYEE : Mr. Speaker, Sir, Shri Advani too is not present in the House....(*Interruptions*)

SHRI CHOTEY SINGH YADAV : He had vowed to fight communalism and he was the only person who protected both the temple and the mosque. (*Interruptions*)

SHRI VAJPAYEE : If my Hon. friend is hurt by referring to the name of Shri Mulayam Singh Yadav, I would say that the then Chief Minister who was soft by name (Mulayam) was very cruel in his actions....(*Interruptions*)

Mr. Speaker, Sir, why did the situation deteriorate ? People gathered in a large number there. I understand the crisis of the Central Government and the crisis continued during the Kalyan Singh Government also. If people assemble in a large number and do something violently rash, how can it be controlled ? (*Interruptions*) Shri Rajesh Pilot had rightly said that day, that if such a large number of people assemble there, the situation might go beyond our control. But we did not feel like that....(*Interruptions*)

AN HON. MEMBER : Everyone said that it was wrong.

SHRI VAJPAYEE : Everyone did not say that and it matters little whether you say it or not.

Mr. Speaker, Sir, we had trust in the people. Therefore, we said that if the trust of the Hon. Prime Minister has been betrayed, we too are shocked. Shri Kalyan Singh and Shri Advani resigned but nobody from the Central Government is ready to take the blame for it. Shri Arjun Singh said that he had already warned about it. Why did he not resign from the Cabinet. It was felt that the Hon. Prime Minister is on the right path. The N.I.C. had given a free hand to the Hon. Prime Minister. The Hon. Prime Minister did what he considered right. That day in the evening I met him and I am ready to say even if all the members of my party do not agree, that the Hon. Prime Minister tried his best to stave off any incidents and he tried that Karseva was performed peacefully and the structure also remained safe. But the Prime Minister also cannot escape from his responsibility.

The people who went for Karseva intended to resume it and construct the temple, but when they realized that the verdict of the High Court was yet to come, they were disappointed. They thought that indulging in this fruitless exercise of bringing sand from the Saryu and putting it in pits, bring water and drop it on this platform will not serve the purpose anymore. I think a group out of the mob emerged and they refused to follow the leaders and attacked and demolished the structure. It was very bad.

Over Reaction

But the reaction to the happening in Ayodhya throughout the country and abroad is more or less over reaction. I think that primarily our outlook and the approach of Government to the problem is no less a factor to be blamed for it. We did not point out to the world that it was a disputed structure. It was repeatedly stated that there was a mosque. We never clarified that along with the structure of the mosque there is a temple also in which prayer and worship is being done and this dispute has been going on for the last 500 years. There are umpteen examples like this throughout the world. When Russia occupied Warsaw a church was built there. When Poland became independent the first thing it did was demolition of the church. History bears testimony to this. When Toynbee visited India he taunted us that it is possible in India alone where a mosque has been erected after demolishing the temple. We have allowed wrong propaganda in the world. I attend the General Assembly Session of the United Nations as a delegate every year. It is discussed there also. They do not know the root of the dispute. They do not know whether there was a temple. They do not know that the remnants which have been excavated after demolition now confirm that there was a temple at the site hundreds of years ago. If this fact had been told to the people, then there would have been no uproar to this extent. Had they known this fact that an ancient temple was razed to the ground in order to build this Mosque, then they would have asked the Muslims to settle this issue amicably. If this is the fact, then should not the issue be settled with mutual understanding ?

The Government had brought a Bill, which became law. Mr. Chavan is sitting here. He brought a Bill to this effect that there will be *status quo* in respect of all the shrines and places of worship as on 15 August 1947. What does it mean ? Does it mean that time will stop running and cycle of change will stop. Does it mean secularism is in danger so everything should remain as is where is. These places of worship have been there for centuries. The rocks of stone and the monuments of stone also tell a tale. Many tales are linked with these monuments. They have close links with our feelings. The Government had also to accept this fact so it had put Ayodhya in an exceptional category, it had to accept the truth. It could have included Ayodhya also and said that its position would remain intact as we have passed the law because we are Parliament. But it did not do so. Because it knows that the situation of Ayodhya is somewhat different. The issue of Ram Temple is different but after saying this much what has it done? Even other parties have also left this issue to the Government to settle it amicably. I am also of this opinion that Ayodhya issue is different. Thousands of mosques, temples were constructed. My friend, Mr. Chauhan is sitting here, I had been to his place, Amroha for delivering a speech. I had said on that day that this incident is a misfortune. It is my submission that the rulers who came were not true representatives of Islam. That day I was listening to the radio speech of Shri Ghulam Nabi Azad. He said if temples were being demolished in Pakistan and Bangladesh, they were not being demolished in accordance with the tenets of Islam. Were the temples demolished in the country as per the tenets of Islam ? Even this was also against Islam. That is why I do not consider Aurangzeb or the persons demolishing the temples the true representatives of Islam. Therefore, we were expecting our Muslim brethren to deplore such excesses but they did not do anything. In the meantime, certain incidents have taken place in the country which have shaken the feelings of Hindus as also impinged their psyche, be it in the form of the secessionists of Kashmir or be it the people of Punjab who are bent upon disintegrating the country through violence and raising arms or a crisis in Assam due to infiltration there. All such incidents are creating a feeling in the majority class as to what is happening after all ?

The case of Shahbano has also underlined it. When this had not been there, it was all right. We, in Bharatiya Jan Sangh did not ask for a common civil code. We had wide discussions with our late Sarsangh Chalak Param Pujya Guruji in this regard. We used to say that article 44 of the Constitution under Directive Principles is about uniform civil code. Marriage law should be uniform as it will strengthen the unity of the country. He persuaded that every society has its own law regarding marriage and then he quoted Smritis and said until the society does not itself ask for it or gets ready for it, the king should not intervene in such cases. I also apprised Shri Chandra Shekharji of it. We said that we would not make a demand for it but the intention of the makers of the Constitution was quite conspicuous. I have attentively gone through the Debates of the Constituent Assembly. The present and previous members of Muslim League have all along held that they would not tolerate any intervention by Indian State or Indian Republic or Indian Parliament in the matters of marriage. Why would they not abide by law ? Do they have a different type of citizenship ? Will the family planning also not be implemented for the same reasons ? Will the small family norm change on the basis of religion ? Family Planning is the first and foremost problem, but the main obstacle to it is that Hindus, who do not wish to adopt it, say that others are being permitted for marrying with as many as four women, what does this family planning mean then ? I know they are not marrying with as many as four women because married persons know that it is difficult to maintain even one wife. (*Interruptions*) I watch their plight. Mr. Narasimha Rao is asking how I have come to know about it. Mr. Speaker, Sir, in order to know that fire burns, one does not need to put his finger in fire, one can realise it from others' experiences.

Is This Secularism

That time we did not press the demand for a common civil code but in the meantime a case of an old woman from Indore came up before the Supreme Court. The Supreme Court gave its verdict and on its basis the Congress Party decided to have a common civil code. Mr. Arif Mohammad gave a beautiful speech on that day which was appreciated by the Congressmen, who said that it was a right decision and everybody should be governed by the same rules regarding marriage. Later on, the opinion of the Congress Party was changed. The opinion of late Rajiv Gandhi was changed. Everybody knows what happened to Mr. Arif. Then people felt that it was a policy of appeasement. Do the people of majority not get affected by what is happening in the House and outside the House. Do not they react to it ? Now the world has come closer and by sitting at home we can watch the happenings around the world. We can watch even such happenings while sitting in our bed rooms.

I cite an example of Sharjah. People from Kerala went to Sharjah to earn their livelihood. They formed a club there. They staged a play there. This play has already received prizes from Kerala Government. It is a play written by a good writer but somehow, a rumour spread in Sharjah that this play amounts to an insult to Mohammad Saheb. The play has depicted certain things which are anti-Islam. The actors of this play were arrested. They were awarded 6 years' imprisonment and they are lodged in jail. Will this incident not have its repercussion ? I do not know what happened on the official level regarding this case. There is another example, a person went to a foreign country for doing a job. I do not want to mention the name of the country. I mentioned Sharjah's name in connection with cricket. That person took a copy of 'Satyarth Prakash' with him. He reads it daily. As he is a religious person, he took it with him in order to draw some spiritual force. This nation can neither be an anti-religion nor a non-religious one. People could not understand the correct meaning of secularism. That is why, they developed a wrong feeling about secularism. I had said so on that day and want to repeat it today as well. Mr. Speaker, Sir, Pandit Jawahar Lal Nehru wrote an Introduction to the book by Shri Raghunath Singh, M.P. I do not know how many members have read that book. Panditji wrote in that Introduction that the present Hindi translation for the word secularism, which is *Dharma Nirpeksha* is creating trouble and confusion. This is not a proper translation. He said further that secularism has only one meaning that there shall be no State religion and the State shall not discriminate against any religion. But even today the Hindi translation of the word secularism is *Dharma Nirpeksha*.

SHRI BHOGENDRA JHA (Madhubani) : Mr. Speaker, Sir, the Hindi version of our Constitution since 1982 shows the word *Panth Nirpeksha* instead of *Dharma Nirpeksha*.

SHRI VAJPAYEE : Jha Saheb you are right, it has been modified now but it is not being used. You may see how this word is being used by the All India Radio and Doordarshan. It should be changed. The word "secular" does not expresses our traditions and culture. It was used in some other context which I am not discussing here. Do the events taking place outside the country not effect us ? As I was saying that a gentleman took a copy of "Satyarth Prakash" with him. His baggage was checked at the airport. The copy was seized and that he was put behind the bars. The Ministry of External Affairs knows well that he was got released after a lot of efforts. I do not want to mention the name of the country. We do not want to act in the same manner. But we do get such reports. Does such action their part not aggravate fanaticism ? That structure collapsed. The sorrow for it assuaged ever since the reports are being received that in Pakistan, a Minister himself supervised the demolition of temples by using bulldozers. What was the provocation there for demolishing temples ?

Gross Discrimination Against the B.J.P. Governments

Here, the Government is trying to control the situation through bullets. More than one thousand people have been killed. This is another matter but when one gets opportunity of counting dead bodies, then how many died in Madhya Pradesh ? Now the question arises as to how many persons were killed in Maharashtra, Gujarat and West Bengal. But it should not be ignored that whosoever was killed, he was an Indian. I have sympathy for the bereaved families. The Government banned certain organisations and dissolved the B.J.P. Governments. Why ? What is their fault ? Punishment was awarded before any crime was committed, Capital punishment has been awarded before committing the murder. It has been the record of the B.J.P. Governments that they prevented communal riots that was a normal phenomenon during the period of other parties' Governments. The figures will prove it. If the Hon. Minister of Home Affairs speaks the truth today he will admit that the number of communal riots in Uttar Pradesh, Madhya Pradesh and Rajasthan was very low and the police subdued them sternly wherever they erupted. No discrimination was made between a Hindu or a Muslim. To provide security for everyone is the religion of our Governments.

There can be no communalism in this regard. The ruler cannot make any discrimination on the basis of a community. If he does so, it is wrong and he does not properly discharge the duties of his Government. But today whatever is happening is being done only on the basis of gross discrimination. The B.J.P. Governments were dissolved. Why ? Had the law and order failed there ? In Himachal there was no such incident (*Interruptions*)

SHRI KRISHAN DUTT SULTANPURI (Shimla) : Many people were killed there. (*Interruptions*)

SHRI VAJPAYEE : Nobody was killed there. But Shri Arjun Singh is interested in Bhopal. He and Shri Patwa either do not pull on well together or they pull on very nicely. I do not know. I express my ignorance in this regard. If he wants to throw light on it, he can do so.

SHRI ARJUN SINGH Minister, of Human Resource Development : I too will speak the truth. (*Interruptions*)

SHRI VAJPAYEE : This is very good. (*Interruptions*)

SHRI SURYA NARAYAN YADAV (Saharsa) : It means other Hon. members who have spoken hitherto, have not spoken the truth.

SHRI VAJPAYEE : Mr. Speaker, Sir, it does not mean it. Sometimes the sun of truth is hidden by the clouds of politics. Now the truth needs to be spoken after clearing the clouds. I will see how far the Congress leaders speak the truth. I know that they will not admit their guilt. Why the B.J.P. Governments were dissolved ? Were they dissolved only because some persons in these Governments were members of the R.S.S. ? What makes a difference if they were members of the R.S.S. ? Were not they abiding by their constitutional liabilities ? Were they violating the instructions issued by the Centre ?

Mr. Speaker, Sir, when the Patwa Government closed and sealed the office of an unlawful organisation in Indore the members of the office approached the Court and the Indore High Court ordered that the office cannot be sealed. Please tell me whether this judgement goes in favour of or against the Patwa Government ? But when the pressure was being put on the Government here and the Hon. Prime Minister smelled a rat of the situation that the people are determined to dislodge either him or the B.J.P. Governments, he preferred to dissolve the B.J.P. Governments, *'sarvanas he samutpanne ardham ayajati panditaa."* It means that whenever such a situation is create when one has to loose all, then one should try to save whatever one can and in this process it is immaterial whether one follows the norms of ethics or not. The same case is with you. You have violated the Constitution and run over the norms of ethics and sacrificed all the moral values.

Mr. Speaker, Sir, the State Governments were dislodged because they were ruled by the B.J.P. but why the Legislative Assemblies were dissolved ? Was not it possible to keep them suspended ? Were the assemblies not kept suspended in the past ? What was the need of dissolving these assembles ? If there was any complaint it was against those Governments and that complaint too has no proper ground. Those Governments should have been allowed to work for some time and then have been judged about their functioning. After that if you had any complaint against them, it would have been proper and justified to dislodge them. But the Central Government did give them any such opportunity ? No, at all and dissolved them. Today there are so many articles against the Government's decision appearing in newspapers. I would like to quote one of their parts :

"Dissolution is not the only option. When President's Rule was first imposed in Punjab in 1951, the Assembly was suspended as, indeed, it was in Rajasthan in 1967, Bihar in 1969, UP in 1970, Orissa in 1971, Andhra Pradesh and UP in 1973, Gujarat and UP in 1976, Manipur in 1977 and 1981, Assam in 1979, Punjab in 1983 and Kashmir in 1986 when it suited the Congress."

The author of the above lines is not a B.J.P. man.

Mr. Speaker, Sir, articles have appeared in editorial columns in newspapers—even in pro-Congress newspapers—and criticise the Congress party like any thing. The daily *'Janasatta'* which is not at all happy with the B.J.P., especially with Shri Advani, was compelled to publish :

"An action of the Prime Minister taken under pressure is not effective and credible. Shri Rao was playing politics for avoiding communal confrontation till now, but if the politics of Shri Arjun Singh can overrule his politics, Shri Rao should retire from politics."

Mr. Speaker, Sir, I have the editorial comments of an editor who has played a role in settling the Ayodhya issue. Its comments are very harsh against us, but after the dissolution of the Assemblies, you have compelled it to write such an editorial having the title "Political Nihilism." The paper is *"Indian Express."* You go through its above mentioned article.

SHRI VILAS MUTTEMWAR (Chimur) : But this paper is the mouth piece of your own party.

SHRI VAJPAYEE : I wish you were correct. Had we been able to bring out such a large newspaper, we would have dispelled all the doubts which have been created in the minds of the people. We do not have the capacity to run just more than two or three periodicals; but, truth is universal. Its editor Shri Prabhu Chawla is equally a supporter of the Prime Minister. Everybody knows the role played by Mr. Chawla in the N.I.C. But what is he writing these days ? I do not know whether such news, comments reach the Hon. Prime Minister or not. But this type of news and comments must reach the P.M. too. There are other newspapers too. I would like to read out an extract from an article published in the *"Indian Express."*

There was no breakdown of law and order in these States that could even remotely warrant any Central action against their Governments. While 800 people died in Congress-ruled States, there were only 200 deaths in those under BJP control. Yet President Shankar Dayal Sharma accepted the reports of the Governors that they had apprehensions about maintenance of law and order in these States. The Centre itself is open to the charge of criminal inaction, provoking some politicians to demand its removal. The dance of violence that stupefied Surat and Bombay, generating fears that sense and sensibility had vanished from the corridors of power, was apt to sweep away the moronic ministries in Maharashtra and Gujarat. Mr. Narasimha Rao's protective unbrella that saved them was not available to Madhya Pradesh, Himachal Pradesh and Rajasthan where sanity was never shaken."

Mr. Speaker, Sir, it is not our opinion, rather it is the opinion of an impartial newspaper. It should be taken into consideration. In the light of these comments, we should try to introspect ourselves a little bit.

Mr. Speaker, Sir, now I come to the point of "ban." Mr. Speaker, Sir, some organisations have been banned. What was the ground of banning them ? Before the 6th December, all those organisations were good, patriotic, disciplined but on account of a single incident that occurred on 6th December in Ayodhya, they have been banned. The picture of the incident of the 6th December is not clear as yet. The Government is talking about appointing a Commission thereon and the C.B.I. is holding an enquiry in this regard. But in the meantime, the Government took a decision to ban certain organisations. Any way the reasons given for banning those organisations are very ridiculous.

I was going through this Bill. When the Unlawful Activities (Prevention) Bill was presented in the House in 1967, I was a member of the House. That time Shri Yashwant Rao Chavan had moved the Bill and today it is Shri Shankar Rao Chavan. Both are Chavan; both hail from Maharashtra. I was going through Shri Yashwant Rao's speech which he delivered while moving the Bill. The Bill was discussed thoroughly. Some times I remember my House days in Parliament. Prof. Ranga, Sarvashri Madhu Limye, Hiren Mukherjee, Kamath, Manoharan of the D.M.K., Nath Pai and Tridib Chaudhary were members of the House in those days. A grand debate was held that time. Shri Yashwant Rao Chavan went on assuring the members that it would not be applied against them. He gave an assurance that the Government was seeking a right to take action against those who wanted to disintegrate the country.

Clash and Ideologies

I too delivered my speech. I started my apprehension that the Government would involve all the Opposition Parties in the name of the so-called cause of integrity and declare the Opposition as unlawful. Those who would be declared unlawful would go underground. You want to stop the unlawful activities, but how can you stop these activities, you have the option to arrest them; but do you think that by making arrests can you win the battle of thoughts ?

Sir, I want to raise an important question. Whatever is happening in this country is not the battle for a temple, it is rather a battle of ideologies. What is the nationalism of this country ? Wherein lies the base of this country ? Through what roots this country will have water and life ? It is right that different kinds of people have come to this country for centuries. Many generations of people have settled here. Though there had been different States, yet the country remained one. No passport was needed to move anywhere in this country. There was no need of having any permit for pilgrims for going from one place to another. This country was one. What was the uniting force behind it ? The Ganga-Yamuna culture is often talked about. The place where Ganga and Yamuna flow together is called Sangam. But onwards Sangam, the Ganga flows alone taking all with it.

That day I quoted Shri Nehru. While addressing the students of the Aligarh Muslim University he said, "You are Muslims, I am a Hindu. But does not the cultural heritage of this country thrill all of us ? The word used by Shri Nehru was "thrill." Now the situation of the country is that even the slogan of 'vande matram' is being opposed in this ill-fated country. Should it happen ? There are minor issues associated with that cultural heritage which have no relation with any religion. If *"Sam gachhadhvam Sam vaddhvam, Samwo mananasijantam"* is recited in a State function, how can it be a body of the Hindu rituals ? If we should move together, speak together and live together, does it not express the feeling of nationalism ?

I Am Worried

This country had never witnessed religious discrimination at any stage. But now it probability is being seen. Mr. Speaker, Sir, I am worried about it. I have already spoken to my party. I request you too whether you think that the recent incidents in the Jamia Millia do not affect other youths also. I do not want to mention any names, but it does affect them. If the Government compromises with one kind of fanaticism and promotes it, it cannot suppress another one. I am sorry for the demolition of the structure. I usually come across with such people also who are of the opinion that it was a blot for 400 years and there was no alternative but to remove this blot. I am afraid of such type of sentiments. Such issues should be solved peacefully through dialogue. Issues should not be hung in balance otherwise they become a source of constant trouble. As long as the Ayodhya issue was raised it was all right but now the position is somewhat different. When Sardar Patel reconstructed the temple of Somnath, our first Hon. President Dr. Rajendra Prasad attended the function but Shri Nehru was not happy on this. But Rajendra Babu went there, the temple was constructed and the problems were solved. Ayodhya issue has been kept pending in the court for forty years.

The court could have decided the matter early. The Hon. Prime Minister was requested to refer this issue to the Supreme Court under article 143. But delay was made even in this regard. Then there was a proposal to not to touch the structure and start the construction over 2.77 acres of land. It will take 3-4 years during which some solution would be found. But this proposal was also not accepted. The Government did not bother to understand the changing mood of the people of the country. My friend Shri Shahabuddin is sitting here. I am calling him a friend. My party members would not like this word. However, it is a cultured way of behaviour. When I was Minister of External Affairs, Shri Shahabuddin was working in our Ministry. He was well-known as a progressive Muslim leader because he had perhaps been associated with the Students Federation. We wanted to send him to a particular country. I would not mention the name of the country. The Government of that country asked us to send some one else because that was an orthodox country and Shri Shahabuddin was known as a progressive Muslim leader. Then he left the foreign service and started practising law. My party colleagues blame me for bringing him into Janata Party. I am blamed for bringing another person also into politics. I would not mention his name. But the change that has just taken place in Shri Shahabuddin is surprising. He is bringing out 'Muslim India.' If 'Muslim India' can be published why not 'Hindu India' ? .... (*Interruptions*) The matter is not so simple. I know that Shri Shahabuddin is a very articulate person and would give an impressive reply to it. A lot of matter is published in that newspaper. But on the whole, it is doing nothing but spoiling the atmosphere.

We Have to Live Together

Shri Shahabuddin must be remembering that I had said in a public meeting held in Bombay in 1986 that Ayodhya issue could be solved. I had given two suggestions in this regard. First, Muslims should forsake their claim on the structure in favour of Hindus saying that they were doing so because the sentiments of Hindus were attached to this place. Hindus believe that it is the birth place of Lord Rama and there is an evidence to it. Faith is something very precious. We live in this country with you, we have to live together, if you believe that it is the birth place of Lord Rama, we give it to you. Second suggestion was that the Hindus, after getting the structure should say that their struggle for Ram Janmabhoomi has now ended. This structure now would not be demolished. Pooja will continue to be performed there. The temple would be constructed at some other place. But Shri Shahabuddin did not accept it. He wrote me a letter to hold negotiations on the issue. I have that letter with me. This was no solution.

Country is at Cross Road

Mr. Speaker, Sir, I would like to conclude now. Ayodhya is a tragedy. The country is standing on a cross road. It is not the time to level allegations on each other. The more you level charges on us, the more we would be aggressive. The more you try to suppress us, the more we would retaliate. The Government is not understanding the mood of the people. Government is not realising as to what damage the Hon. Prime Minister has caused by giving the statement that mosque will be built again there. What was the hurry in giving such a statement ? Was this statement given under some pressure from outside ? Was it not necessary to find out first whether there existed temple or mosque earlier ? Now the particular State is under the control of Central Government, so Archaeological Survey of India should be asked to carry out excavation at the site with a view to determine whether earlier there existed temple or not. This dispute should be settled once for all.

Shri Chandra Shekhar wanted to solve it and he also got the cooperation of Shri Rajiv Gandhi. Shri Chandra Shekhar arranged for the talks. The talks were held in a cordial atmosphere and a number of documents were exchanged. Solution was about to be reached. But then his Government went out of power. The present Government also may not go out of power before finding any solution....(*Interruptions*) We are sure that there was a temple. If it is proved that there was a temple and the court also gives same verdict, then they will have to abide by it.

But no effort to this effect has been made. The matter was kept pending. After all we had not performed the *'Shilanyas,'* it was performed during the regime of Congress Government. At that time Congress was in power both at the Centre and in the State. Is it wrong to complete a good work started during the days of Shri Rajiv Gandhi ? We want to complete that good work. Will the Government put us behind the bars only because of this ? What did Shri Advani do ? He was arrested in the morning when the Lok Sabha was going on. Look at the allegations levelled against him. How ridiculous those allegations are ? Advaniji was appealling to the Karsevaks that the structure should not be demolished. You may confirm it from TV reports or enquire it from the journalists whereas the Government have got the reports prepared to the effect that Advaniji was inciting the Karsevaks to pull down the mosque! Will it raise your credibility ? Will it bring credibility to the Government ? He is the Leader of Opposition and he was arrested when the Lok Sabha was in session. He was in Ayodhya. I also wanted to hear from him the sequence of events that took place there. I believe that he is a man of integrity and he is such a big man that he would admit if at all he had committed any mistake....(*Interruptions*) Please don't interrupt me, please be quiet if you do not understand the sentiments, I want to express my feelings. I have always been saying this and most of the members of our party are of the same view. Don't think that some are liberal and some are hardliners. Who is liberal in the Congress Party....(*Interruptions*)....Perhaps Margaretji was saying that she is liberal.

Mr. Speaker, Sir, How can I make any complaint to you when I myself have made a mistake. It has never happened in my 30 years' parliamentary career that I would have gone continue speaking when you are on your legs.

SHRI VAJPAYEE : I would like to tell my colleagues that I had gone to the Hon. Speaker and expressed my desire to resign.

MR. SPEAKER : No, no, there is nothing of this sort, it is all right.

SHRI VAJPAYEE : If we cannot speak in the House and you are not ready to hear me, then what is the use of continuing as an M.P. Sometimes there is a noise from our side too, but that is not a good thing. This should not happen. After all, we are also the citizens of this country. We are bound by the ties of democracy. The bonds of our culture are inseparable. This is just a passing phase. It would pass. I am confident that India would emerge stronger and more prosperous out of this crisis. We are passing through crisis and it would rather help us it we discuss the matter sincerely.

Admit Mistakes

Mr. Speaker, Sir, we did not create any difficulty on the first day. It was alleged that B.J.P. members sat with their heads down. We were sitting quiet and calm. We did not want to indulge into any hullaballoo. Even then we were criticized. Our silence was misinterpreted. We asked for an opportunity to express our views... but that too was not given. We continued to plead not to suspend the Question Hour. Today, I faced a great difficulty to persuade my party members. Advaniji has not been released. I would like to know the difficulty in releasing him ? The Government says that he can be released on bail, why is he not being released ? Heavens are not going to fall, if he makes a speech here. Why the Government is adopting an inflexible attitude, in this regard ? It is clear that they do not want the discussion to take place in normal situation. You do not want Advaniji to express his views and that the facts in regard to Ayodhya to come to light. We are ready to admit our mistake, if we have committed at all in Ayodhya. But at the same time the other political parties sitting here should also admit their fault. Central Government should also admit its mistake. I do not want to go into all those details as to how the Hon. Prime Minister complicated the matter and why he did not take any initiative for two months and how he stated contradictory things before the saints, and how he tried to create rift among them. It is true that the Hon. Prime Minister was very particular even upto the last day that the structure should remain intact. Central Reserve Police was also despatched there. What were they doing there ? Why did the Central Government not interfere and impose President's Rule ? Why did the Central Government not intervene in Ayodhya affair ? The Hon. Minister of Home Affairs may please tell us what was the report of intelligence agencies ? What was the role of the officers present there ? Facts to this effect should be brought into light. It won't do just by accusing us. The Government may take the immediate political advantage, by accusing BJP for it, but it would not solve the problem. There is a need to start a new chapter. Ayodhya incident is a challenge and it should be availed of as an opportunity for solving the tangle. It depends on our intention whether we take advantage of this opportunity or not. I do not think that the present Government would be able to do it because I am unable to understand whether the Hon. Prime Minister is unable to take decision or his subordinates do not allow him to take decision. If Dhritarashtra is surrounded by Duryodhan and Dusshasan, he cannot move on the path of justice even if he intends to move. With these words I conclude.

Reply

Mr. Speaker, Sir, I am sorry that I could not hear the speeches of all the Hon. members and could not remain present here, but I have tried to go through the speeches delivered by them.

Lok Sabha on December 21, 1992 while replying to the discussion on the No-Confidence Motion against the Council of Ministers

I regret that the discussion has not taken place in tune with the feelings expressed by me while initiating the debate. Allegations and counter-allegations were levelled against one another in the House and it will continue also. It is easy to accuse but difficult it make introspection. Had the interpretation of the incidents of 6th December been so easy, as some of my friends sitting here have tried to do, it would have altogether been a different thing. I am looking for Shri Rajesh Pilot. One after the other, Hon. Ministers seemed to be eager to show their loyalty and commitment to the Hon. Prime Minister....(*Interruptions*) They were members of the Council of Ministers and were a party to the decisions taken. (*Interruptions*) I have no objection to it, but am I not entitled to make comments ?

Shri Rajesh Pilot's Allegation

Now I would like to raise a minor issue whereafter I would come to serious ones. That day Shri Rajesh Pilot got up and said that the structure had been demolished in Ayodhya and the people who demolished it had been imparted military training. A camp had been set up in Sarkhey near Ahmedabad to impart training. He also mentioned the name of a Brigadier. Of course, you have not allowed the name to go on record....(*Interruptions*) It appeared in the newspapers the next day that there must have been a conspiracy behind the demolition. It would have been a conspiracy by those people who had received training and the training was imparted by a military officer. Shri Pilot should have found out the truth. There is an institute in Sarkhej which imparts training in internal security and the Brigadier is associated with the Congress party. He had been appointed by the Congress Chief Minister to a post. He has issued a statement. He has been appointed as the Chairman of Water Pollution Board. I am not making any criticism. He was imparting training there. Training on rifle shooting and judo are being provided in the camp. There is nothing objectionable in it. I am making any allegation against neither the Brigadier nor the Congress Chief Minister. He should have found out the facts. After all he is the Minister of Communications. Cannot he communicate properly....(*Interruptions*)

SHRI RAJESH PILOT, Minister of State of the Ministry of Communications : Atalji, even today, you are not prepared to accept that it was pre-planned (*Interruptions*) Please say from your inner conscience whether it was pre-planned or not. Even today I am ready to accept....(*Interruptions*)

SHRI VAJPAYEE : Mr. Speaker, Sir, Shri Pilot had made this allegation in the House. At that time Hon. members from this side had voiced their protest that Shri Pilot should resign if this allegation is proved wrong. He is a friend of mine. So I am not demanding his resignation. But I would like to register my complaint against creating such a turmoil in the House.

The Government has set up an inquiry Commission in regard to Ayodhya happenings. We have welcomed the Commission. We would also like to know the facts. But the Commission is being biased by the Government before it unearths the facts and submits its report. The second point is that the Government is creating a poisonous atmosphere against us in the country. We don't know what would be its repercussions. We are sorry for whatever has happened in Ayodhya. (*Interruptions*) The Hon. Prime Minister says that he had been assured. I accept it. I had also said this earlier. Had the discussion taken place making the atmosphere which I said on that day the basis, we would have reached a conclusion long back.

Slow Motion Justice

I would like to make it clear that the discussion of 2-3 days will not help us to reach the correct destination. The Hon. Prime Minister had believed that whatever they were promising, they would stand by that. We also had the same hope which was shared by the Hon. Prime Minister and the Government that the work of providing protection to the disputed structure as also the work of initiating *Karseva* on the 2.77 acres of land would be separated from each other. We also hoped that Lucknow Bench of High Court would deliver the judgement by then and the *Karsevaks* assembled there would get an opportunity to perform the *Karseva*. We were sure about it. I am afraid, you may say that your expectation was genuine whereas our expectations were not so, it was rather a conspiracy. I would then like to ask as to how can there be two different criteria to measure the same thing. If the verdict of the Court that came on 11th had come before 6th December....(*Interruptions*)

SHRI SOMNATH CHATTERJEE (Bolpur) : How could it happen ?

SHRI VAJPAYEE : I do not want to explain it for Chatterjee Saheb would again say as how could the Court give its verdict earlier. You know, he is a big lawyer and he knows how to indulge into legal manoeuvring in everything. I am, on the contrary, a simple man. We are simply aware of the fact that our simple demand of representing before the Lucknow Bench of the High Court to request for an expeditious decision was not accepted by the Government. Even this petty demand was not accepted.

Mr. Speaker, Sir, these questions call for an early reply and I expect that a reply would be given during the course of the discussion. The Government should make an announcement to the effect that it would not make tall claims and would also not place anyone in the dock unless the inquiry report on Ayodhya happenings is submitted.

SHRI P.V. NARASIMHA RAO (Prime Minister) : Sir, I would like to make one thing clear at this stage. For the information of Atalji, I want to tell him that the Central Government is not a party to the proceedings in the Lucknow Bench. We have been made parties because the Land Acquisition Act happens to be a Central Act. Only to that extent. We are not substantive parties. This may be noted, please. (*Interruptions*)

SHRI VAJPAYEE : Mr. Speaker, Sir, the Hon. Prime Minister is again going into the legality of the issue. We are talking about the 'faith.' I do not want to put some ministerial colleagues of the Hon. Prime Minister into trouble by quoting their names. They assured us that the verdict of the court would come soon. Had the Central Government and the State Government made a united approach to the Court for speedy disposal of the case, then the court might have considered it.

SHRI RAM NAIK : He should stand up and speak. We have heard them, so they should now hear us......(*Interruptions*) What is all this about ?

SHRI VAJPAYEE : Shri Somnath Chatterjee, I am not yielding....(*Interruptions*) I refuse to yield. (*Interruptions*)

C.P.I.(M)'s Double Standard

I do not want to enter into arguments with the political parties which have no principles, particularly with those parties which at one time support repeal of article-356 and on the other day support retention of it in the statute book.

Shri Kalyan Singh resigned following his failure to keep his promise given to the Supreme Court through the affidavit. The Central Government dismissed the Kalyan Singh Government instead of accepting the resignation tendered by him. This was a big achievement for the Government.... (*Interruptions*). The Government of Kalyan Singh was an elected one. If the role played by Shri Kalyan Singh was contempt of Court, then the case in this regard is there in the Court and the Court will decide about punishment. But so far as the question of his being responsible to the public is concerned, he resigned accepting his moral responsibility. But the Central Government did not behave with another elected Government in the manner as is expected of an elected Government....(*Interruptions*)

Mr. Speaker, Sir, two reasons have been given for the dismissal of the Kalyan Singh Government....(*Interruptions*) I would like to know from the Hon. Prime Minister as to what were the reasons for the dismissal of the Governments of Rajasthan, Madhya Pradesh and Himachal Pradesh ? One of these Governments was dismissed under the pretext that the Ministers of that Government had sent *Karsevaks* to Ayodhya. At the time when the *Karsevaks* were sent the *Karseva* was not banned by the order of the Supreme Court. As a matter of fact the Supreme Court had allowed *Karseva* to be performed....

SHRI BASUDEB ACHARIA (Bankura) : The Supreme Court did not allow demolition of the mosque.

SHRI VAJPAYEE : He should not interfere. Mr. Speaker, Sir, the discussion cannot go on like this. (*Interruptions*)

SHRI MADAN LAL KHURANA (South Delhi) : We have already heard the abuses from Shri Indrajit Gupta. (*Interruptions*)

MR. SPEAKER : May I please request you to maintain atmosphere in the House in which the battle of wits can go and not the battle of vices.

MR. SPEAKER : I am disturbing you Vajpayeeji for one more minute. Please your side, this and this side, may I plead with you....

SHRI NITISH KUMAR : Not this side, Sir, we are disturbing the least, we are giving patient hearing. There is no question of disturbing Atalji when we have already heard the Hon. Prime Minister who is actually more guilty.

MR. SPEAKER : You disturb very intelligently.

SHRI VAJPAYEE : Mr. Speaker, Sir, it is being asked as to why I moved this No-confidence Motion. You know our leaders have been put behind the bars, three State Governments ruled by our party have been dismissed and assemblies have been dissolved....(*Interruptions*)

SHRI VIRENDRA SINGH (Mirzapur) : Let it be decided first as to how this House will run.

SHRI VAJPAYEE : Now talks are in the offing to ban the Bharatiya Janata Party. Today I came to know that there is one Ram Lal ji who is the Minister of State in the Ministry of Home Affairs. I wonder Ram has such a son or Lal. He has said that the Bharatiya Janata Party should not be allowed to function as a political party. What does it mean ? Yet the members are asking as to why are we moving the No-confidence Motion ? Should we express confidence in the Government and should we congratulate the Government for all that ? We should be concerned about whatever happened in Ayodhya on the 6th of December and about its fallout in the country. My friends who are in the Government as also those who are not in the Government should know, I am not going to disclose any secret—that at the time when large scale killings in Bihar were being committed the leaders of the Congress party approached me with the proposal that if the Bharatiya Janata Party was prepared to support the dismissal of the Laloo Government then the Government would do....

SHRI INDRAJIT GUPTA : What was your reply ? (*Interruptions*)

SHRI VAJPAYEE : I told them that I did not believe in such actions.. The Hon. Prime Minister says "Article 356 lies in shambles"....(*Interruptions*).... What happened in Lucknow and Himachal ? Why the Government of Rajasthan was dismissed ? Is it an offence to give send off to the *Karsevaks* ? It was prior to 6th of December. The *Karsevaks* were free to come from all parts of the country. Will the Constitution be interpreted like this ? Please see the language of article 356. Shri Soli Sorabji, who is a lawyer of different ideology, has said :

> "The basic condition precedent for imposing President's rule under article 356 of our Constitution is that 'a situation has arisen in which the Government of the State cannot be carried on in accordance with the provisions of this Constitution.' The fact that the Chief Minister who helps the Government in a B.J.P.–ruled State belongs to a banned organisation cannot, by itself, lead to the inference of failure of the constitutional machinery."

SHRI PAWAN KUMAR BANSAL (Chandigarh) : The ban was not being implemented. (*Interruptions*)

SHRI VAJPAYEE : Mr. Speaker, Sir, I am thankful to my colleague comrade Indrajit who had also come forward to speak.

SHRI INDRAJIT GUPTA (Midnapore) : Moral responsibility and the constitutional responsibility are two different things.

SHRI VAJPAYEE : I am at the moment referring to the constitutional responsibility.

SHRI INDRAJIT GUPTA : You also believe in the moral responsibility.

SHRI VAJPAYEE : Indrajit Gupta has advised to move slowly but who will allow the Hon. Prime Minister to move slowly at present ? Someone has fixed his eyes on Madhya Pradesh and others are dreaming of strolling again in the Raj Bhawan of Himachal Pradesh rested in the Himalayas atop high peaks. Has the Centre issued any directive, which have not been implemented by all the three Governments ? Is it not a fact that these Governments were functioning according to the Constitution ? Is it not a fact that these Governments had assured to abide by the directives ? Then why these Governments were dismissed ? Sir, is it not a mockery of the Constitution ? Is it not the misuse of article of the Constitution ? The Hon. Prime Minister is repeating the word federation time and again. In our Constitution there is the word Union instead of federation but the foundation of the Union is getting weak. Not because of the incidents of Ayodhya and not because of what have you done. But those who are sitting in glass houses should not throw stones on others.

Mr. Speaker, Sir, which circumstances had come up in these States ? There was only apprehension that such situation would emerge. The Constitution does not work on the basis of apprehensions, it requires facts. In this case, such drastic steps were taken on the basis of apprehension only. I can very well understand Shri Arjun Singhji. He was expecting the office of the Prime Minister. I am not pointing towards the speech Sharad Pawarji had made. I am distressed at his speech. Perhaps it was his first speech and he wanted to impress all but he forgot that he was speaking in the Lok Sabha of the country and not in the Shivaji Park of Bombay. He had made a complaint that the Government of Madhya Pradesh was asked to seek the help of the military, but it did not. Can an elected Government be dismissed on this basis only ? If a State Government controls the situation without seeking help of the military....

SHRI SHARAD PAWAR, The Minister of Defence : If it can...

SHRI VAJPAYEE : Yes, the State Government had controlled the situation. But, will it be made the basis of dismissing a Government ? Sharad Pawarji himself says repeatedly that the military should not be summoned for controlling internal disputes, there should be its minimum use. The Government of Madhya Pradesh was dismissed but the riots took place even in Bombay and they continued even after calling the military. The people were killed, I have tales about the way people were killed, which don't want to relate since it tarnishes the image of the country. You have said that...(*Interruptions*) the people of Bajrang Dal, dressed in Home Guards uniform had gone to create riots. (*Interruptions*)

SHRI SHARAD PAWAR : Such complaint has been received.

SHRI VAJPAYEE : Do you have any proof ? It is just like repeating a hearsay (*Interruptions*) The fingers are already being raised at Sursawalas. It is a matter of serious concern for all. Sir, now they will say that whatever communal virus has spread is all due to us. All right, if we have done so, then we are the worshippers of Lord Shiva and we will drink this poison and do the welfare of the country. But it is not so easy and who will drink the poison ?

Mr. Speaker, Sir, the ban had been imposed on the parties. On what basis it was done ? (*Interruptions*) What was their fault before 6th December ? Shri Jaffer Sharief Sahib was speaking a short while ago. One of his old speeches made on the 19th December, 1989 in the Lok Sabha is with me. I am quoting from it, and if there is any mistake, it may be corrected. He had said : "I would certainly like to inform my Bharatiya Janata Party friends, present here, that I have also attended the *shakha* of the Rashtriya Swayam Sevak Sangh."

SHRI C.K. JAFFER SHARIEF : I am grateful to Shri Vajpayee who raised this point now because I wanted to speak about it in the afternoon, but I was not able to make a mention about it. I am very clear when I said on the floor of this House before as referred to by Shri Vajpayee I had been to the *shakha* only for three days. It was my classmate who took me there. When they found out that I was a Muslim they left me and thereafter I did not go. Whereas Shri Malkani– there is a report in *The Hindustan Times* dated 20.11.92 I did not know he used it, nobody knew that I went to the *shakha*– he appears to have written in his book that I attended it for six months.

SHRI VAJPAYEE : I accept the clarification given by Shri Jaffer Sharief Sahib. I am not saying so to blame him. I had made a special reference to it since there are so many persons on the other side who were associated with the *shakha* of the Sangh and there is nothing objectionable in it. The Rashtriya Swayam Sevak Sangh is a patriotic organisation. (*Interruptions*) Sir, the Hon. Defence Minister, Shri Sharad Pawar is very well acquainted with R.S.S. He had been with us in the Government. During his tenure, a demand was made in the Legislative Assembly (*Interruptions*)....

SHRI SHARAD PAWAR : I have given clarification.

SHRI VAJPAYEE : Yes, Sir, you have given it today. You have already taken a stand. But what you had said at that time was full of wisdom and you had said it after deep thought. So, be firm on that. (*Interruptions*) Actually the ideological differences cannot be overcome by imposing bans. A ban was also imposed on the R.S.S. in the past. I was shocked when a reference to Gandhiji's assassination was made. I have with me the report of the Justice Kapoor Commission but I would not like to read it out. Sir, Gandhiji should not be brought into power politics. This Commission says that there was no hand of R.S.S. in it. You may read it and the whole of the world knows it. Suppose, those who are associated with his murder confess in the House, outside this House or anywhere else in the country that they had assassinated him and that they had made a mistake and now they want to repent then would you not give them a chance ? (*Interruptions*).*

MR. SPEAKER : This is not going on record. (*Interruptions*)

SHRI VAJPAYEE : Nathu Ram Godse had no connection with R.S.S. He used to criticise the R.S.S. It is a documentary evidence that he used to write against the R.S.S. in his articles in his journal.

---

* *Not recorded.*

I mean to say that if you want to level political charges on each other, then there are so many other issues but do not make a reference to Gandhiji. What Gandhiji had given to the country and what we have to take from him in future like *Swaraj, Swadeshi,* this self-reliance, mother tongue and the proper utilisation of the means for noble cause. (*Interruptions*)....

Now you will ask whether we have faith in Gandhiji and if I ask whether you have faith in him then this discussion will lead us to a blind alley. Gandhi is a personality, do not bring him into controversy in this way.

MR SPEAKER : Shri Vajpayee, you do not have to reply to that.

SHRI VAJPAYEE : Mr. Speaker, Sir, I wanted to congratulate the Telugu Desham as it had condemned the dismissal of three State Governments. (*Interruptions*)

Mr. Speaker, Sir, at that time the speech made by Shri Sharad Pawar in the Maharashtra Legislative Assembly reflected a good amount of far-sightedness.

SHRI ANNA JOSHI (Pune) : At that time you were the Speaker of Maharashtra Legislative Assembly. (*Interruptions*).

SHRI VAJPAYEE : You were holding the office of Speaker at that time.

SHRI ANNA JOSHI : Shri Shankar Rao Chavan was also the member of the Assembly at that time. (*Interruptions*)

SHRI VAJPAYEE : But ideological war cannot be fought like this.

The Prime Minister might recall what had said that day and the Home Minister was also present there that the Government has to fight the B.J.P. one day. But it should not fight Ram. (*Interruptions*)

Imposing ban on the B.J.P., derecognising it, debarring it from contesting election are not the ways to take on the B.J.P. This is an ideological war and you should counter the ideology with ideology. I am giving warning to the Government in this regard. Shri Chandra Shekhar is sitting here. (*Interruptions*)

Shri Chandra Shekharji is realising the matter. He has condemned the arrest of Shri Advaniji. He has criticised the way the State Governments were dismissed. The members belonging to the D.M.K. and A.I.A.D.M.K. were of the same opinion. Many members of the Congress Party met me and told me that the Prime Minister did not want to dismiss the State Governments but the forces, which have endured him forced him to do so.

Mr. Speaker, Sir, the ban has been imposed, but the imposing of ban is being seriously condemned.

'Kerala High Court suspends ban on Jamat.'

The Jamat has been banned. But the High Court revoked the ban orders. Were the imposition of ban on these three organisations not enough ? It is not at all necessary to ban one Muslim organisation alongwith three Hindu organisations just to show the secular image. No supporter of yours raises any objection to your secularism. It is only we who have objected and will object in future too, because your secularism is not the right secularism. It is not a balanced secularism. Your secularism is limited only upto the vote bank. You compromised secularism in the case of Shah Bano. Your secularism has no hesitation in seeking vote in the name of installing a Christian Government in Mizoram. It will not be allowed to go on.

SHRI VILAS MUTTEMWAR (Chimur) : Are you not worried about your vote bank ?

SHRI VAJPAYEE : Now we have started to worry. It is a dangerous game. That is why Shri Advaniji said something but a lot of objection was raised over it. Shri Advaniji has said that whatever was happening in the country, it would benefit his party, but it can damage the country. The people asked him as to why was he indulging in such activities as might harm the country. He said that his party did not want to do so. But this game cannot go on one sided. You are not allowing Shri Advaniji to come here and speak. Advaniji has resigned, but you people are not ready to attach any importance to it.

MR. SPEAKER : The ban has been imposed but it is being criticised like anything. The Government has not given any reason for imposing the ban. A tribunal is to be constituted. You cannot wait for 30 days. The tribunal could have considered the matter. The Government is a great supporter of judiciary. The Government does not want to function arbitrarily. You had been waiting in Ayodhya for hours together. I do not blame the Prime Minister for it. You will say that mock-wrestling is going on. I won elections from Lucknow, but I fail to understand the meaning of mock-wrestling even today. What type of wrestling is it ?

Mr. Speaker, Sir, the same type of confusion was being faced by the Government of Kalyan Singh as well as by the Central Government. Shri Kalyan Singh had already said it earlier that he would not open fire on Sadhus and Saints. It was known to everybody, there was no secret in it.

SHRI SOMNATH CHATTERJEE : Were the persons, who climbed over the domes Sadhus or Saints ?

SHRI VAJPAYEE : You are unable to identify, as to who is Sadhu and who is Saint ?

Mr. Speaker, Sir, Shri Kalyan Singh had already made his stand clear. But it should be investigated as to why tear-gas was not used. Why were the rubber bullets not fired ? How did the entire administration become ineffective. These were not the orders of Kalyan Singh....(*Interruptions*)

MR. SPEAKER : You will not get up again and again. It is not conveying anything. It is not being recorded. Please take your seat.

SHRI VAJPAYEE : Mr. Speaker, Sir, when the news came that the structure was being demolished, the Central Government could have taken over the administration without caring for the Government of Uttar Pradesh. The Government could have asked Shri Pawar Saheb to hand over the situation to the army. Why was it not done ? Because the Government did not think it proper. Use of force could have caused a heavy blood-shed. Perhaps, Shri Chandra Shekhar may differ....

SHRI CHANDRA SHEKHAR (Ballia) : 1200 people died there. At least these 1200 people could have been saved.

SHRI INDRAJIT GUPTA (Midnapur) : In the entire country, the toll has gone upto 2000.

SHRI VAJPAYEE : Whatever has happened there. It was wrong.

AN HON. MEMBER : Bring them back.

SHRI VAJPAYEE : Nobody brings anybody back. Comrade, who can bring whom back ? Who will bring those students back who had been brutally killed by the Chinese army by crushing them under the Chinese tanks at Tiannamen Square ? Will China bring those back who had sacrificed their lives in the struggle for restoring democracy in the erstwhile communist countries. (*Interruptions*)

Mr. Speaker, Sir, what type of ban was imposed ? Was it inevitable ? The Government could not wait for 30 days ? What do they want to do now ? Whatever happened with archaeologists yesterday is also a clear indication of the Government's attitude. Will the press conference of archaeologists not be allowed to be held in Himachal Bhavan, Delhi ?

Much, more evidence has been found in Ayodhya which prove that there was a temple which was demolished later on. Why are you afraid of it ? (*Interruptions*)

If such evidence is found, the Government should challenge them. The Government should go to the court ....(*Interruptions*) It may raise a demand that this should be examined by the court. The Government can constitute a court. (*Interruptions*)

Mr. Speaker, Sir, this proposal was placed earlier. The Prime Minister knows it. The other members of the Cabinet also know it. The discussion was going on to refer this matter to the Supreme Court under article 143 or 138. It was to be decided by the Supreme Court whether there was a temple earlier and by demolishing that temple was the mosque built in its place. (*Interruptions*)

SHRI SHARAD PAWAR : You did not agree. (*Interruptions*)

SHRI VAJPAYEE : We said that there should be a package deal including resumption of *Karseva* on 2.77 acres of land, reference to the Supreme Court and complete protection of the structure, for which you did not agree....(*Interruptions*) The Government did not agree to it. Mr. Speaker, Sir, I would like to know whether the Government is prepared to accept our package deal even now ? What happened in Ayodhya....(*Interruptions*). Mr. Speaker, Sir, I was saying that....(*Interruptions*)

SHRI ANIL BASU : You have lost all credibility. (*Interruptions*)

SHRI K.P. UNNIKRISHNAN (Badagara) : What was that package which you are talking about ? Please explain. Let the House be informed. (*Interruptions*)

SHRI VAJPAYEE : Mr. Speaker, Sir, I have already said that we had held ample discussions with the saints. Shri Sharad Pawar did also participate in some of those discussions....(*Interruptions*)

You want to hear a package discussion and yet you say that a wrong thing has been done. According to the proposal passed in those meetings the issue had to be referred to the Supreme Court for its opinion. Secondly, the saints had been pressing for the right of *Karseva* in 2.77 acres of land and besides, they all held the view that the disputed structure must be fully protected.

SHRI SHARAD PAWAR : We have always accepted your contention about referring the issue to the Supreme Court and providing protection to the disputed structure but the proposal of *Karseva* in 2.77 acres of land was never accepted. (*Interruptions*)

SHRI VAJPAYEE : I am telling the very same thing that the Government did not accept the package as a whole. I would not misguide this House. Now I leave the old topic because now we are in a changed situation. The structure is demolished. Those who demolished the structure considering it to be a Masjid, actually did also demolish the Mandir as well. This pains me. In a state of frenzy they forgot the fact that a Mandir also existed there and 'arti' was being performed. The namaz was not offered. The violence would not have broken out had the people been told the fact by the Government that the disputed structure was more a Mandir than a Masjid. (*Interruptions*)

SHRI SHARAD PAWAR : The Vishwa Hindu Parishad had stated that it was a disgraceful structure.

SHRI VAJPAYEE : I am not aware as to what statement was made by them. (*Interruptions*)

Mr. Speaker, Sir, the discussions were held between Sharadji and the leaders of V.H.P. The Bharatiya Janata Party did not participate in those discussions, so I am not aware of any such statements made by the leaders of the V.H.P.

SHRI SHARAD PAWAR : This is the problem with you, you are not aware of all the things.

SHRI VAJPAYEE : Well, at least you have given me a bit relief. But what does the Government propose to do now ? Why so much confusion is being created ? The Government states that the structure will be rebuilt. The Government states again that there was a dome and there was an arch which was a part of the masjid. There were two more domes where the idol of Ram Lala was installed. There were stone pillars on which the images of statues, 'Kalash' and lotus were carved. Will all they be reconstructed in the same way. Shri Sharad Pawar and the Hon. Prime Minister are making differing statements in this regard. I ask, what will be reconstructed there ? (*Interruptions*)

Mr. Speaker, Sir, I would like to submit that we have still time to solve this problem once for all. If we had thought to gain political mileage out of this issue then in that case we would have asked the saints to wait for *Karseva* because election was still far off. As a matter of fact the saints are not to wait now, their loyalty is with the Mandir not with the votes....

SHRI SOMNATH CHATTERJEE : Are you justifying the demolition in Ayodhya ?

SHRI VAJPAYEE : We simply want to know what does the Government propose to do now. Whatever it does, it should take this House and the people of the country into confidence. There is one more option left and that is the Government should take up further excavation so that it may be confirmed whether a Mandir existed there or not. We have already got some proofs. The things of archaeological importance that have been found there prove that there was a Mandir. The Muslim leaders have already promised....

SHRI SYED SHAHABUDDIN (Kishanganj) : We do not promise anything (*Interruptions*) You have betrayed, there will be no short-cut now. Now only law will take its course and none else will take any decision now.

SHRI VAJPAYEE : It is good that our colleague Shri Shahabuddin said it in this House amidst all. I have a letter written by him on the 4th July 1987. This letter was written to Prince Anjum Kadas who is a leader of 'Shias.' The 'Mucealli' of the Masjid was a 'Shia.' It is claimed that the said Masjid belonged to 'Shias.' Shri Buta Singh may also be remembering the efforts which brought the 'Shias' to agree that the dispute should be resolved. Shias were ready to shift the Masjid if the majority Hindus thought that Ram was born there and that a Mandir was demolished to construct a Masjid. But Shri Shahabuddin did not allow the proposal. He wrote the letter and today his intention is clear to all :

> "Even if shift is permissible under some school of thought, there is no reason at all to opt for shift. In one flash, shift would open Pandora's Box. Please do not pursue this line....I remain absolutely and totally opposed to the mischievous idea of shift proposed by the RSS, which you appear inclined to accept. Please reconsider.

SHRI SYED SHAHABUDDIN (Kishanganj) : This has been in accordance with the Shariat and in accordance with the opinions of all the Ullemas in the country. (*Interruptions*)

SHRI VAJPAYEE : Mr. Speaker, Sir, we also were telling the same thing that we did not want to demolish the mosque, we simply wanted the mosque to be shifted honourably to a different place, different from the birth place of Lord Ram....(*Interruptions*)....the mosque could be constructed at a little distance from there and we were ready to perform *Karseva* for the construction of that mosque....(*Interruptions*) it was, however, not done.

SHRI EBRAHIM SULAIMAN SAIT : A mosque cannot be shifted, the location of it cannot be changed....(*Interruptions*)

MR. SPEAKER : I think the Hon. members will measure their words before they utter. It is not good to use such kinds of words.

SHRI RAM NAIK (Bombay-North) : Sir, he should not only withdraw but also apologise.

MR. SPEAKER : It is not going on record. Please don't disturb. Now, Mr. Vajpayee.

SHRI VAJPAYEE : Mr. Speaker, Sir, we have been listening to all those things since yesterday. The glory of the Constitution is sung. It is always impressed upon that judiciary should be honoured. Nevertheless, it is also almost simultaneously said that the Marriage Acts cannot be uniform because it goes against the Shariat and Shariat is a divine law. I do not intend to offend the beliefs of anyone, but I must ask if ever had it been thought that if some other community sticks to certain beliefs of their society what would we do in that case. In this very context I ask as to what is the special importance of the mosque in Ayodhya for Muslims ? It is as simple a mosque as any other mosque.

SYED SHAHABUDDIN : That has always been a mosque.

SHRI VAJPAYEE : Mr. Speaker, Sir, Ayodhya is a place of pilgrimage for the Hindus. They believe that it is the holy place of birth of Ram. This is not a subject matter evidence, this is a matter of belief in the same way as Muslims believe that their marriage system has been set by their "Khuda." This is their belief....(*Interruptions*)

Mr. Speaker, Sir, I would like to appeal to this House and here I would reassert what I said at the very outset. I said that the country is at the junction of three roads. The Government should not encourage a particular type of communalism or fundamentalism only to fight against the counter-productive fundamentalism. The Government has done the same.

I said in the beginning that we could make use of this opportunity for a new beginning. We agree that the Central Government resorted to the dismissal of the State Governments ruled by our party. When the Government imposes ban, we have then got to go before the public and in this context, I would like the Government to remember that we would come here in greater number than what we are at present. The Government does not have a proper understanding of the mood of the Indian people. If it thinks that our party would be sweeped away, then I dare say that the Hon. Prime Minister should dissolve the Lok Sabha following the No-confidence Motion moved by me and he should then go to the people to seek a fresh mandate. He will then come to know the verdict of the people of the country.

Bank Scam

Mr. Speaker, Sir, it is needless to say that I rise to support the Motion of No-Confidence in the Council of Ministers. The present Government was constituted on 21st June, 1991. More than two years have passed. When this Government was constituted it was not in majority. Even today it is not in majority. But it has succeeded in proving its majority in the House. The Government is running and if my Congress colleagues like, they may consider it a great achievement.

At the time of constitution of the Government the country was fed up with 12 months and 6 month Governments. It was in search of stability. The people of the country wanted to get relief from economic crisis, which was mainly a creation of previous Congress Governments. The people were hopeful with the aged, enlightened and experienced leader, Shri Narasimha Rao, that under his leadership, the new Government will lead the nation in the right direction, because the Congress Party was feeling itself leaderless after the death of Shri Rajiv Gandhi. The people thought that dynastic rule was coming to an end and politics would take a new turn. The people had expectations from the Government. In this optimism the people forget that the Prime Minister had been working as Minister in previous Congress Governments also. It had gone into oblivion that Shri Narasimha Rao was handling the Ministry of Home Affairs when innocent people were being killed after the murder of Shrimati Indira Gandhi. The people forgot the matter regarding the St. Kitts.

The Hon. Prime Minister had proposed to run the entire country on the basis of consensus. Efforts were made to get rid of economic crisis. But this situation could not be maintained for a long time. .

Congress session was held in Tirupati. I do not know whether it was an endeavour to link the politics with religion or not. But in Tirupati people observed with surprise that the former Minister of External Affairs was taking a letter regarding Bofors case to hand it over to somebody. He forgot the man from whom he had taken the letter. But he could not forget the man to whom it was to be delivered. In Tirupati session he had played a pivotal role by presenting a resolution on foreign policy. He had ceased to be a Minister for External Affairs. People were perturbed.

Economic Reforms

Mr. Speaker, Sir, my colleagues belonging to the Congress Party discussed the economic reform, yesterday. They had highlighted the changes which

Lok Sabha on July 27, 1993 Motion of No-Confidence in the Council of Ministers

took place to some extent due to these economic reforms. But they have not discussed the other side—the darker side of the situation. External debt is increasing. I do not want to make my speech difficult by quoting dates. But the statistics are very clear and the country is under debt. The situation is that we will have to take loan just to pay the interest incurred on loan taken earlier. It is a fact that foreign exchange reserve has increased. But proper attention has not been paid to the deteriorating financial position. Debt has increased. Import has increased. As regards export, the position is totally hopeless. Custom's Duty has been reduced whereas it has not been done in the case of excise-duty. Indigenous industries are in crisis. Factories are on the verge of closure. The Prime Minister has said in the statement that if we get fertilisers at cheaper rate why should we purchase indigenous fertilisers. Would the Government allow factories in the country to be closed down.

SHRI P.V. NARASIMHA RAO, The Prime Minister : At the same time I had also aid that the Government would make efforts to make these factories economically viable.

SHRI VAJPAYEE : If any factory is running in loss, closure should be the last resort. If improvement can be made production can be increased and cost can be reduced then it should be done and the Government should not close it down. The Government is saying something and doing something else. The factories are going to be closed down. The labourers are becoming jobless.

On 16th December, 1991 the Minister of Finance had said in this very House that the new economic policy would neither have unemployment nor close down the factories. This assurance has not been fulfilled. I was going through the Report of Parliamentary Standing Commitee on Industry. The Government has allocated a large amount for voluntary retirement scheme. Perhaps it had the intention to spend Rs. 788 crores under this head but where are the alternate opportunities of employment ? These have not been provided. The workers should be given proper training and be engaged in some other useful jobs. The Government has failed to do so. Mr. Speaker, Sir, the basis of industry in the country is not sound. There has been reduction in generation of hydel electricity, production of crude oil and fertilisers. The production of crude has been going down and import of petrol had been increasing. We are spending Rs. 22 crores as foreign exchange every year for the purpose of petrol. Now it has become difficult to understand the economic scenario as explained by the Minister of Finance when there has been reduction in production of hydel electricity, crude oil and fertilisers.

Dunkel Proposals

Mr. Speaker, Sir, the Dunkel Proposals have become the topic of the day in the country. Contrary statements are being issued. The Minister of Food and the Minister of Agriculture are not present here. The Minister of Commerce has retired from the membership of the House. He has been put in trouble. Really he is my old colleague. I have sympathy with him. Some arrangement should have been made for his re-election from somewhere. The Government is solving its purpose by leaving him in the midst. But I was referring to Dunkel Proposals. The statements of Shri Jakhar Saheb and former Minister of Commerce are totally different. The Prime Minister does not speak anything to all.

SHRI MRUTYUNJAYA NAYAK : He will speak afterwards.

SHRI VAJPAYEE : Yes, he will have to break his silence tomorrow. But it is a policy related matter. Could consensus not be achieved in respect of economic reforms ? Whether any such efforts were made ? I do not think that the colleagues sitting on my left do not want economic progress of the country or to get rid of the country from economic crisis. If there are differences in modalities, those could be discussed.

Mr. Speaker, Sir, we had welcomed this new economic policy with the hope that unnecessary controls would be removed, practice of delaying tactics would be stopped, entrepreneurship would be given full opportunity to prosper, and we would be able to face the challenges of the changing world. But what happened ? There was a securities scam. Perhaps the Minister of Finance might remember that I had cautioned about it while speaking on the Budget. At that time when there was the boom in the share market, the Government, the Ministry of Finance, the Reserve Bank of India were busy in self praise and watching that boom in a very happy mood. It was being considered as the success of economic reforms. At that time I cautioned the House that we have no objection in bringing the tiger out of the cage. But we will have to keep in mind that this tiger may not be converted into a man-eater. But it happened so. That man-eater is hunting one after another.

Mr. Speaker, Sir, I do not want to go into the securities scam of Rs. 5000 crores, since the matter has been referred to a Parliamentary Committee. I would like to congratulate the Chairman and the Members of the Parliamentary Committee because they have been discharging their duty properly till now. During the regime of previous Governments we had devalued not only the Parliament but put a question mark on the reliability of Parliamentary Committees. My colleague, Shri Shakaranandji, is present here. The report presented by him is also available here. The opposition did not participate in it. It was our mistake. But the matter was covered up. Now in the light of revelation of secrets being made in the case of Bofors, the Report of this Parliamentary Committee stands nowhere.

We hoped from the present Parliamentary Committee to follow its traditions and thought it has members belonging to different parties and would try to bring out the facts rising above the party line. I hope that this tradition will be maintained and the Parliamentary Committee will not only touch the matter ordinarily but go into it deeply.

Mr. Speaker, Sir, this No-Confidence Motion is not related to the economic condition of the country. I had discussed economic conditions earlier also. Today the corruption that has spread over at the high level is the matter of grave concern for the people of the country.

What is happening in other countries of the world ? I remember that once Shrimati Indira Gandhi had said, "Corruption is a global phenomenon".

Perhaps she wanted to save the country from outside attack. Regarding rampant corruption in India she said that it was a worldwide phenomenon. But today a global challenge is being given against this global phenomenon. A movement is going on to purify the public life in Japan, Italy, Britain, Germany and Mexico. Two industrialists have committed suicide in Italy. Hundreds are in jail. Many are being put in locks on the charges of corruption. In Japan, the 45 years old party had been defeated in elections. That party had played an important role in making Japan stand on its feet after defeat in the war. Corrupt politicians, unscrupulous industrialists and mafia leaders had entered into a nexus there. The process of exploiting the country has been going on for years. In the last, the people have taken up arms and there is insurgency in the Liberal Democratic Party.

A Minister in Britain had to resign and there were similar cases in France and Germany. You cannot, therefore, prevent someone from referring to corruption or you cannot say that this is an exaggerated view of corruption or you cannot say that this is an exaggerated new corruption or that efforts are being made to take political mileage out of it. The question remains as to who is involved in the scam ? The issues related to scam are coming up which are unlikely to be covered in the probe of the Joint Parliamentary Committee. Allegations are being levelled against people occupying high positions. Why is it so that a particular person who says something against another person holding commanding position gets the confidence of the majority of the people of the country ? Why is this crisis of credibility ? It is unfortunate for the country that the people are watching with concern the critical decision whether the Hon. Prime Minister is right or what is being said by a stockbroker is right. On my part, I can say that I believe in what is being said by the Hon. Prime Minister. But my belief is not enough, what is important is what the people think. Why is there so much erosion of credibility ? The fact remains that there has been erosion of credibility and the lesson is that there have been a number of incidents in the last 2 years resulting in loss of faith on the part of the people. Now the country faces a credibility crisis and we have to find out the reasons. I feel anguished while saying it, but now you cannot keep mum over these issues.

The Sirajuddin Affair

Mr. Speaker, Sir, I remember the days, 30 years back when Shri Jawaharlal Nehru was the Prime Minister in 1956. Shri Keshavdeo Malviya then was a Union Minister in the Ministry of Mines and Energy. He had some transaction with Sirajuddin and Company. There was a raid in the office of Sirajjudin and Company in 1956. There was an allegation that the company had indulged in the evasion of income tax and customs duty. The documents that were seized in the raid had the deterrence that money had been given to some Union Ministers. A Calcutta daily published an item in this regard in its news edition of February, 6, 1963. The question was raised in the House and the Prime Minister had assured to set up an inquiry Committee. Shri Malviya accepted in the executive committee meeting of the Congress

Parliamentary Party that he had recommended to Sirajjudin to provide Rs. 10,000 to a candidate who was contesting assembly elections from the Minister's Parliamentary constituency. The Prime Minister consulted the Attorney-General and set up a Committee under the Chairmanship of Supreme Court judge Shri Das. Malviya ji had a complaint that the report of Das Committee was not being shown to him and that he was not being allowed to go before the judge alongwith his lawyer. Nehru ji said that there was no need of that and that he had set up the said inquiry just for his own satisfaction. Report of the Committee, however, came later on and Malviya ji had to quit. This happened 30 years back. The matter involved Rs. 10,000 and subsequently the Minister had to resign. Now after 30 years in almost similar circumstances there is no resignation even though the matter involves millions of rupees.

Now no one asks for the resignation of the Prime Minister. We the Members of Opposition parties make this demand. The Hon. Prime Minister does not ask for resignation from his colleagues nor does the Congress party ask for the Prime Minister's resignation. That is why this motion of no-confidence has been moved.

The Degeneration

We should, however, think of this degeneration. Mr. Speaker, Sir, Nehru ji did not compromise even though the matter involved Rs. 10,000 only. How many of us can say from the core of our hearts that there has been no degradation in political life. There is a nexus between politicians in political life. There is a nexus between politicians and criminals. A news has appeared that perhaps a committee under the Chairmanship of Shri Rajesh Pilot has been set up to trace the aforesaid nexus. Now I would like to know whether any such nexus has been traced and whether any action has been taken. Why so much time was taken to deny the allegation brought forth by Harshad Mehta. This has not been determined so far as to whether the Hon. Prime Minister was present during that time. Contradictory statements are being made and different facts are coming to light. This has aggravated the suspicion. This should not have been so. It should have been clearly denied on the very next day Harshad Mehta did not meet the Prime Minister. The issue of taking money could have been denied automatically. But there was no such denial. There was a complete silence in the beginning. It was perhaps thought that the issue would not last longer. We have to understand that the issue of corruption grips the country today. Corruption has become a part of the system, it has become a way of life. Whenever there have been changes in the set-up of the country—there have been changes on two occasions in the past and third is on the cards—corruption has been the main issue on all those occasions. The clarion call for purification in public life given by Jayaprakash Narayan and the movement for restructuring of Gujarat had been responsible for a change over there. It is different that the change was short-lived, but the fact remains that the people want change. The Bofors issue was the main issue of the elections in 1989. Now once again the issue of corruption tops the national agenda. You may say what it has to do with the common people. It is deeply related to the sentiments of the common people. They have to resort to bribing in matters of daily life. Work is not done without bribing. There are complaints of mass-scale transfers in the President's ruled States. Transfer has become a business. Bribe is not called bribe in Uttar Pradesh, it is rather known as *'Suvidha Shulk'*. The common people are affected by this practice. They indulge in this practice since they have to compromise for getting their work done. They cannot jeopardise their work by resorting to quarrels. They, however, feel pained. They have to go to officers, police stations, courts etc. in connection with their work. Corruption has become general phenomena. So when corruption on high levels is exposed, and when it comes to the notice of a farmer who ploughs the field or to an artisan of Muradabad who makes utensils or to the poor women of my constitutency of Lucknow engaged in chicken work we see a smile on their gloomy faces. It is, however, different that afterwards their smile is shortened and they have to weep later.

Dimension of Corruption

I ask, should there not be a serious consideration over the issue of corruption ? Should we overlook the issue related to Harshad Mehta ? I would say that the allegations made by Harshad Mehta would not have held water had the two colleagues of the Hon. Prime Minister—I fail to understand as to what type of colleagues they are—would not have demanded for political protection to be provided to Harshad Mehta. I am not aware of the situation that made Shri Sharad Pawar make such a demand. It is said that he adopted this stand to escape allegations that were likely to be inflicted on him. Shri Arjun Singh had gone to apprise him and no sooner had he come back than he also demanded that Harshad Mehta be given political protection. When colleagues of the Hon. Prime Minister suggest that the particular stock-broker should get protection, what impression will the common people form ? Did these Ministers ask the Prime Minister before making such a statement ? These contradictory things support the suspicion. There were cases of corruption and allegations were also heaped earlier on high positions. The majority that was mustered by making compromises and horse trading cannot do justice to the country. The Government is buying electric locomotives. The Parliamentary Committee opines that there is no need of buying electric locomotives since the institution of Chitaranjan Locomotives can suffice the requirements. Government is buying electric locomotives. There are requirements. The Chairman of the Parliamentary Committee belongs to the Congress Party and the composition of the Committee has a majority of Congressmen. The Committee is unanimous and I have extracts of the report with me. It has been stated in the report that the Financial Commissioner did not perform his duties. The suggestions of the two former Chairmen were ignored. There was a deal of those engines which we did not require. I am not aware as to what irregularities had been committed there but when the unanimous report of a Parliamentary

Committee is rejected in that manner, it is but natural in the situation that prevails to have a suspicion. How did the situation deteriorate to this extent ? How is there so much erosion in the credibility of political leaders ? I also find myself a part of it. Where have we reached, where are we heading to ? We are not in politics for this. Those who sacrificed their lives and youth in jail for achieving freedom are in docks now. We were destined to witness such bad days that are there now. We are now required to take bold decisions on unambiguous designs. The cahoots of corruption should now be closed and for that certain steps are required to be taken. I may be excused, but must say that this Government cannot take those steps.

Electoral Reforms

The Congress Government could not take any meaningful steps to effect electoral reforms. This issue is there for several years. This issue was raised even during 1977. Can election be fought without black money ? What is the source of black money ? We all are aware of the source. Those who provide us black money for fighting elections want our recommendations when the elections are over. Democracy is disgraced, the faith of the common people is shaken in the system and fingers are being raised against the leaders.

Can we not be serious about electoral reforms ? A Select Committee was constituted under the Chairmanship of Shri Dinesh Goswami. Where are the recommendations of that Committee ? The ruling party is not interested in these matters. They are not concerned about fighting elections through honestly earned money. The election expenditure is increasing manifolds.

Mr. Speaker, Sir, I had contested election for Lok Sabha for the first time in 1957. I had two jeeps at that time. I took one jeep from Lucknow which was provided to me by my party and the other jeep was provided to me by the people of Balrampur. They had collected money to provide me petrol for the jeeps. Can anyone contest Parliamentary elections with two jeeps at his disposal today ? A limit has been imposed through rules which are ridiculous. Are misleading accounts not presented in this regard ? Do we not start our Parliamentary career from that point ? Does it not bite our conscience ? We wake up only at the instance of some big act of corruption and we become oblivious of it only little later. This tendency should be checked. Elections fought with the aid of black money cannot generate pure political atmosphere (*Interruptions*). Mr. Speaker, Sir, if our colleagues of the Congress Party feel that what I am saying is worth objecting, then I have nothing to say. (*Interruptions*). Yes, that is what I am saying. This I have already said. I am also the part of this system, but why should we all not change the system and why not this Government should first be changed before we begin the whole system. This government has completed two years but no steps have been taken by it in this regard. Allegations are being heaped one after the other. I was just referring to the issue of electric locomotives. Similarly, there is an issue related to Goldstar. Family members of Ministers are involved in these cases some where or the other. What is this all ? These are serious things. What is required is to give a fresh thought on it in a new way.

Bharatiya Janata party has decided in its Bangalore Session that it would accept money for elections only in the form of cheques (*Interruptions*).

Our colleague Shri Indrajit Gupta asks whether we were not accepting it earlier. He knows the answer himself. I do not expect such a reaction from him. The matter calls for a unanimous decision. A new initiative can be taken. Better late than never. Let us decide. Expenses of the party are not mixed with the expenses incurred by candidates. The party may resort to undue expenses. What is the source of this income ? This is polluting the public life and political workers are deviated. This should be checked. We can make a beginning. Do we possess the willpower for it ? Can we give a new orientation or should politics go on following power by way of manoeuvring ? This practice should be altered. The issue of purity in public life is here before us with all seriousness. There should be some solution to it : but the question is what is that solution and who is to find it out ?

Political Stability

Mr. Speaker, Sir, it is argued that political stability is required in the country. For achieving that stability, it can also be argued that what is happening should be allowed to happen. All right, stability must be there, but now the country has reached such a juncture that we can take up some basic changes without affecting stability. What I mean to say is that the system is set on the path of development and therefore bold steps should be taken to bring self-reliance. There was a bloodbath in Punjab in the wake of terrorism, but the valiant farmers of Punjab never put down their ploughs. They never shirked from their work. President's rule was imposed, army was delplyed but the people of Punjab remained engaged in their work. They were fighting out terriorism on the one hand while on the other had they kept filling the granaries of the country. Several foreigners asked me that though Punjab is the biggest supplier of foodgrains why was the Government not able to curb terrorism there. What would happen ? I told that terrorism would be contained and the farmers of Punjab would not also put down ploughs. Guns were defeated by ploughs.

AN HON. MEMBER : Who solved the problem ? The Congress Party ?

SHRI VAJPAYEE : I was expecting this question.

SHRI MADAN LAL KHURANA : Who created this problem ?

SHRI VAJPAYEE : When you ask as to who solved the problem. Khuranaji is right to ask as to who was responsible for creating the problem. (*Interruptions*). After creating the problem, they were lost in meditation like sages. We should not go into it. The people of Punjab deserve thanks. I would like to thank the Sikhs of Punjab who are struggling against terriorism and are determined. If you say that the Government is responsible for improving the situation then Khuranaji is very much right to ask as to who ultimately created this problem (*Interruptions*).

Situation in Kashmir

They say that they should similarly be allowed to indulge in corruption which would ultimately enable them to improve the situation in Kashmir as well. Mr. Speaker, Sir, deterioration of situation in Kashmir can also be attributed at length to lack of cleanliness in public life. A sum of Rs. 72,000 crores has been provided by the Centre for the development of Jammu and Kashmir. Yet, there is no change in the life of the poor. The people are deprived of items of essential requirements. Money has been grabbed. This is also one of the reasons why the youth of Kashmir have gone astray. Corruption breeds disintegration. It desecrates all walks of life. This corruption is also a hindrance to the pace of our economic policies. So press control and regulations are better. Our colleagues sitting to my left side should note the point that the practice of providing quota permit will result in the exploitation of the people. It is right that the State has its responsibility in a developing economy. In this regard we do not agree with the policy of the Government. This is a developing country. Here 38 per cent people are living below the poverty line. There should be such Government which may take care of them. It should be sympathetic towards them and have compassion for them. This country has been famous for its humanitarianism, and kindness. But today the source of mercy is going to be dried up. But that is a different aspect and I do not want to go into its details. Some people are distressed. Therefore, whenever any issue of corruption is raised, it should be clarified and contradicted immediately. Immediate action should be taken and the guilty should be punished.

Mr. Speaker, Sir, I have a copy of the interview given by an hon. Minister of State in the Central Government. He is also involved in it. His interview was taken for a Doordarshan programme. There is a 'Pritish Nandy Show' programme of the Doordarshan for which the interview of an hon. Minister of State was recorded. Its cassette is available here and literal reporting has been covered here. This interview was taken after the Ramaswamy episode. Perhaps you might have understood my indication as to who is that Minister of State. He was asked.

> "Do you not feel that this has somehow blurted the morale of your Party position on corruption in high office ?

The answer is quite long. Therefore, I would not like to read it completely. I am quoting from it. Shri Bhardwaji stating :

> "What about the scam : how many of your Ministers are there ? I know personally several people who used to roam about and flaunt around with Krishnamurthy. Chaturvedi and this Harshad Mehta were in everybody's bedroom. Fortunately, I was Minister of Planning. Otherwise he would have come to my house also. He gave lot of money to the people, political people."

MR. SPEAKER : You can give a list. You may not quote it (*Interruptions*).

SHRI VAJPAYEE : I would like to congratulate Shri Bhardwaj for this outspokenness. It projects the position of the internal health of the Congress Party. The Cabinet is divided. They are at daggers drawn. How can they give a new direction to the country if the country is to be inspired. For reconstruction it should have inspiring, pure, selfless leaders. First the hon. Prime Minister had formulated the policy on the basis of pungent but liberal nationalism. The same was the tragedy with Shri Rajiv Gandhi. His speech delivered at Bombay did not comply with the deeds he performed. I do not know what sort of course it is. But I would like to take you to the statement of Shri Bhardwaj.

MR. SPEAKER : No, not like this (*Interruptions*).

SHRI VAJPAYEE : No Mr. Speaker, Sir, it is very essential I am ready to authenticate it. All right I will be brief.

Q. There are lobbies within your Party which have vested interests in the way that decisions go in case of like Arjun Singh, in case like Sharad Pawar ?

A. Arjun Singh is my sworn enemy today. I am not involved in his litigation. He does not rely on me. He is a friend of Shivshankar, Fotedar and Bhajan Lal. This is a big group of very moneyed people. They have seen to it that I remain only a Minister of State and first they succeeded in putting me into the plank that if he remains there, he will not allow this. I have never allowed them succeeding, never. I told Rajiv Gandhi that Bhajan Lal was abusing your mother when I was defending her and then he switched overs lightly coming to Sanjay Gandhi in 1988 brought all his Cabinet. In the open Cabinet, and before the present Prime Minister he scolded me. "What are you saying, why do you speak like this ?" I said we are cheating the ladder. Buta Singh was an Akali and Shivshankar was incarceration actually. I gave him shelter in Delhi but all these are my enemies today whom I helped. Because I did not share their money they had collected, so much money you cannot imagine."

'SHRI BUTA SINGH (Jalore) : I was an Akali, no doubt but this Party never collected the money.

Mr. Speaker, Sir, what do the people say about it ?

SHRI NITISH KUMAR (Barh) : A lie detector test of Shri Bhardwaj ji should be done (*Interruptions*).

SHRI VAJPAYEE : It is not limited to what the political opponents say, it is far beyond this. It has crossed the limit. We are entrapped in a very critical situation and it is necessary to free the country of it. We should think about it. If the successive Governments continue to play with the future of the country and if the leaders are concerned about their vested interests only, then what will happen to this country ?

I know that I have made certain harsh comments. Generally I am not in a habit of making such harsh comments, but today I could not restrain myself. I have been a Member of Parliament for 30 years. I have seen many Prime Ministers one after another, but my viewpoint had never been negative. I have never opposed for the sake of opposition alone. But today I am compelled to speak a truth. If somebody is hurt by my comments I beg his pardon. But we should not do any such thing for which the future generation may not ever forgive us. We should keep this in our mind, this is my request.

Finance Minister Should Apologize *(July 29, 1993)*

Mr. Speaker, Sir, the matter raised by Shri Chandra Shekhar has taken a very serious turn. Yesterday, the No-confidence Motion was being discussed in the House and Shri Chandra Shekhar was expressing his views. The Finance Minister interrupted him. The Finance Minister could have kept quiet, he was to speak later on or he could have come before the House after going through the full record. But he was in a hurry. He wanted to undo the effect of Shri Chandra Shekhar's forceful speech. He wanted to give a turn to the atmosphere of the House in his favour. That is why he interrupted in the middle of the speech and I want to repeate here what he said while interrupting : "If you look at the records, the proposal was approved when you were the Prime Minister."

He was sermonizing to Shri Chandra Shekhar to look at the records and he himself had not come after seeing the records. I do not want to go into the question as to how his own entire record has been. He has been serving the country as a Government official, he should know the traditions of Parliament, he should keep in mind the limitations. But he was confident, he was certain in his mind, and he stood up and interrupted.

It was the large-heartedness of Shri Chandra Shekhar, Mr. Speaker, otherwise who in this country accepts his mistake ? Who would say that if the decision was taken in his time, he was ashamed of it ? Only Shri Chandra Shekhar could do so. Our Congress friends must learn something from him. but I could feel the anguish of Shri Chandra Shekhar and I could also see the derisive smile on the face of the Congress friends. We also felt that if Shri Chandra Shekhar's assent was not there, how the decision to set up a Japanese city could be taken ? Now the whole thing has come out.

Mr. Speaker, Sir, the Finance Minister must be summoned to the House, the Finance Minister should be called here. He is not present in the House at this moment even after having a talk with Shri Chandra Shekhar, while Shri Chandra Shekhar had informed him that this matter would be raised and the Finance Minister should have himself understood the situation. Now he says that a feasibility report was prepared. A feasibility report does not mean approval of the proposal. Government goes on preparing feasibility reports. He might have casually mentioned that such and such proposal had come, and asked shall we call for the feasibility report or not ? Shri Chandra Shekhar might have replied, 'you may'. It was not expected of the Finance Minister to present the issue in a way as to show that Shri Chandra Shekhar was casting aside all his old values and was trying to put the Government in the dock.

The Finance Minister should be called here and he must apologize to the House and to the country (*Interruptions*). I trust that he will keep in mind how Shri Chandra Shekhar had accepted his mistake yesterday showing his magnanimity, and apologize to the House and to Shri Chandra Shekhar. If he does not apologize, then this matter is in your hands, let it be referred to the Committee of Privileges.

Horse-Trading to Defeat No-Confidence Motion

Mr. Speaker, Sir, I do not want to go into the position that prevailed at the time of division on the Motion of No-Confidence. The Government was successful in securing the confidence of the House. But so far as the number of members is concerned, you still have to take the decision regarding the integrity of those seven members.

The vote cast by one member is a matter of dispute. We accept announcement of your decision but so far as the result of the division is concerned, it had not been properly decided. That is why you have invited everyone to express his views but such opportunity was not given to the concerned member and he was made to leave the House.

Mr. Speaker, Sir, it is matter of great concern to me that you are being involved in this matter. Everybody seemed to be under this impression that you are looking into the matter because it was brought to your notice. This was the general impression during the discussion on that day that you are looking into the matter.

MR. SPEAKER : There is a wide reaction to whatever a senior member like you says. If somebody tells me here that no step had been received, it might have come to the office, but I have not seen it. If the same has reached the office, then I will look into it and give a chance to know the views of the aggrieved party. When there is no such thing here how can we proceed in the matter ? If Hon. member goes on discussing about the working in my office, then things become difficult for me.

SHRI AJIT SINGH (Bagpat) : Mr. Speaker, it is not the question of the slip.

MR. SPEAKER : I will have to ask Shri Munda also to confirm the fact as to whether he noted or not.

SHRI VAJPAYEE : Then the matter is under your consideration.

MR. SPEAKER : Mr. Ajit Singh's letter is to reach me.

SHRI VAJPAYEE : No, but the Government says that though no decision has been taken, yet this is merely a formality and will be completed.... (*Interruptions*)

MR. SPEAKER : It is not the question of what is being said by whom....(*Interruptions*)

MR. SPEAKER : What is being said is not the point at issue.

SHRI VAJPAYEE : Mr. Speaker, Sir, all the Congress members are sitting here. Shri Shuklaji was trying to give a clarification in this regard. I do not

Lok Sabha on August 3, 1993, during discussion on the No-Confidence Motion against the Council of Ministers

understand one thing that since the Government have survived and the Motion of No-Confidence has been defeated, what was the urgency in such a horse-trading at this point of time ?

SHRI SOMNATH CHATTERJEE (Bolpur) : Mr. Speaker, Sir, have new seats been allotted to these seven members ? And have new division numbers also been given to these members. (*Interruptions*)

SHRI VAJPAYEE : Yadavji is sitting here, he has been warmly welcomed as if they have achieved something mighty. It really is a matter of shame.

III Defence and Security

Let Indian Army Become Indian Identity

Sir, the question of the security of the nation is not the question of any particular party or class. Whatever our political differences, where national security and protection of freedom are concerned the whole country is one and we shall fight any danger with all our might. No one should have any doubts about this. As my friend said just now we should give the first priority to the nation's security. It is true that we are engaged in nation-building. We have development plans before us, but we cannot also ignore the danger to the nation's security. What is the situation today ? Due to our own fault a state has come up in our land which is equipped with American arms and threatens our freedom and security. We do not want to invade it. We also do not have a tradition of aggression. But there can be an aggression on us, and I submit most respectfully that there is an aggression on Indian soil. One-third of Kashmir and Goa are examples of open Pakistani and Portuguese aggression on our sovereign right on Indian territory. The portion of Kashmir that is under Pakistani occupation is Indian territory constitutionally, historically, geographically, from all points of view. That means there is Pakistani aggression on it. It is the same with Goa. We may not invade anybody, but we should not hesitate to remove anybody's aggression on our territory. Everybody knows that there is a nexus between Pakistan and Portugal, and at times there is a fear that India is sought to be surrounded on all sides. We must have a strong defence to counter this situation. In view of this I do not think the provision of additional Rs. 50 crores for Defence in the new budget to be excessive. If necessary we must be prepared to spend even more.

Stop Wastage of Defence Funds

May I say something in this regard ? Whatever money we spend, whatever grant we sanction it should be used properly. But the report of the Estimates Committee indicates that we are not doing so. The Committee's report on Army Stores shows that during the past five years foodstuff losses have come to Rs. 3,13,924. Our losses in respect of medical stores and A.O.C. Stores are also substantial. In the AOC stores goods worth Rs. 8,60,40,914 have been wasted during the past four years, excluding 1956-57. Why ? Many reasons for this can be given. The Estimates Committee has itself given many reasons,

Lok Sabha on July 24-25, 1957 during discussion on the demands for grants of the Ministry of Defence.

one of which is that there is no covered space for storage. On the other hand, however, the Estimates Committee says 15 lakhs square feet covered accommodation is not being used. On the one hand crores of rupees worth of things go waste because there is no covered space, while on the other there are covered spaces that are not being used. A 'Defence Stores Inquiry Committee' should be set up to go into all this so that money is properly used and wastage brought down to the minimum.

Sir, alongwith national security I would also like to draw your attention to the fact that our military intelligence organisation is not functioning properly. There are active foreign agents in the country. Even small details about our army operations reach them. I would give two examples :

Glut of Foreign Agents

We have a cantonment in Jhansi. At the time our delegation at the Security Council was discussing Kashmir our forces there advanced 15-16 miles towards Bina as an exercise, but surprisingly enough the Pakistani delegate at the Security Council immediately charged India with moving its forces towards Pakistan, and mentioned the normal military movements at Jhansi. This is a grave danger signal for us. It is not an ordinary thing that information of movement of our armed forces at Jhansi should reach Pakistan and be mentioned in the Security Council.

I have another example. Recently a parcel was registered at a post office in Jhansi in a Brigadier's name and a post office employee was persuaded to write the Brigadier's address on it, but when the parcel reached the Brigadier and was opened a bomb was found in it. The Defence Ministry should inquire into this. If our Military Intelligence Organisation cannot keep a strict eye on foreign agents our security information could fall into undesirable hands and we would have to repent later.

I suggest that the Defence Minister should get in touch with the Foreign Ministry and the Home Ministry. The Home Ministry has a separate intelligence department. The States too have their own intelligence departments. All these forces and activities could come together. The earlier we do this, the better.

Indianisation of Armed Forces

One more thing. The British have left, but our armed forces have still not been Indianised. It is necessary to Indianise our army, navy and air force. Elements within them that are non-national, whose loyalties are suspect and who could jeopardise our security at a time of crisis must be weeded out from every department. There are 11,000 non-nationals working in our dock-yards. I do not think they can be trusted in times of crisis.

All branches and the soul of our armed forces need to be Indianised. What I mean is that their outer form as well as the feelings inculcated in them should be conducive to nationalism. It is ten years since the British left but the communal classification of the armed forces still continues. There is a Dongra Regiment, a Rajput, a Jat Regiment and a Sikh Regiment. We have declared India to be a secular state. Then is communal classification of our armed forces in accordance with our ideal of a secular state ?

SHRI SHAH NAWAZ KHAN, Deputy Minister for Railways : These names have a long history.

SHRI VAJPAYEE : I know that history, but that history culminated in the partition of the country. If we do not want that communalism to raise its head again in this country we should remove it from the nomenclature used in the army. Those names have been kept as they are even after independence. I fail to understand the difficulty in changing them. Our armed forces are Indian armed forces. Their function is to protect the whole of India. If we divide them on a communal basis, or, as a friend put it yesterday, the question of North-South is raised in them, our national unity, of which our armed forces are a symbol, would break down and the communal canker would enter the forces. If we have to give names to our regiments we should have a Rana Pratap Regiment instead of Rajput Regiment, a Shivaji or Tanaji Regiment in place of a Maratha Regiment, a Ranjit Singh or a Hari Singh Nalwa Regiment instead of a Sikh Regiment. The names should be such as would inspire bravery and at the same time not create a feeling of communalism.

Sir, as I have said yesterday a friend raised the North-South question. I am sorry to say that this sort of language was being used even during the President's election. We already have too many isms—provincialism, linguism and communalism. Now we have a new ism, which we may call 'directionism'. The North and the South are different directions, but there are eight directions, not two—not only North and South but also East and West. North- East, South-East, North-West and South-West. Where does the North end and the South begin ? In politics these controversies may go on but we should keep our armed forces aloof from them. We do not think of region or religion in recruitment. I admit that persons from those provinces that have so far been denied equal opportunities should be given them, and our backward brethren should be given special concessions, but I feel it is basically wrong to think on regional or 'directional' lines in the recruitment and form of the armed forces. From Kashmir to Kanyakumari India is one, its armed forces are national and will protect the whole country.

Armed Forces Symbol of National Unity

If any of our friends have the complaint that there are more people from Uttar Pradesh in the army, as a representative of Uttar Pradesh I am prepared to tell them—if you want it, you may stop recruitment from Uttar Pradesh for ten years. My friends from Uttar Pradesh may perhaps not agree with me, but what I say is—do not raise the question of how many people from what States are in the army. It is not a question of a State, it is the question of the nation's security. If we allow this poison that has undermined the life of the nation to also penetrate the army, I see no hope for this country. Our armed forces are the symbol of national unity—and we are proud of them—and that unity must be maintained. I will not say more in this connection.

We have an M.E.S., a Military Engineering Service, in the army. What is its job ? I am told it works as a liaison between the contractor and the army and all construction works are done by the contractors. I have received information that 98 per cent of the work is done by the contractors. Can the Engineering Service not be used more in construction works ? Yesterday some of our friends demanded that the barriers set up by the British between the army and the people should be brought down. I think the armed forces would automatically come closer to the people if we use them for construction works without impairing their efficiency and discipline. I would give an example about this.

In Jhansi the parapet of a castle fell down and contractors asked for Rs. 80,000 to repair it but the armed forces did the job on their own. Whoever now visits the fort of the Rani of Jhansi his attention is drawn to the parapet that is a living testimonial to our Jawans' construction. If we utilise our army, especially the Military Engineering Service for such works we would save money, we would prevent contractors from wasting the people's money, and at the same time we would be substantially achieving the purpose of bringing the army and the people closer.

Resettlement of Ex-servicemen

Yesterday some of our friends said something about ex-servicemen. It will be agreed on all hands that we have not been able to make satisfactory arrangements for our ex-servicemen. As compared to other countries our arrangement is quite weak. While our circumstances are also responsible for this, in order to make proper arrangements for the resettlement of our ex-servicemen we should give them such education while in service as would give them a livelihood later. With a view to utilising their services in other walks of life we should train them in such a way that after retirement they would lead a life of comfort and self-respect.

One more thing. So far we are dependent on other countries for arms. This is not desirable. We must become self-dependent in the most modern arms as quickly as possible. Military industries should be developed. It is necessary to produce new and modern arms and train our Jawans in them. The time must soon come when we are completely self-dependent in conventional arms.

Further, during the British regime we used to have Victory's Commissioned Officers. The British left, the Vicerory left, but the only change in the structure of the army was that instead of "viceroys" they became Junior Commissioned Officers. Now we have a junior commissioned officer and a senior commissioned officer in every platoon, every company and every battalion. Can the number of these officers be brought down and the expenditure on them saved without impairing their efficiency ?

I do not want to say anything more. Thank you.

Self-Reliance in Arms Production Essential

Sir, while discussing the demands for grants of the Defence Ministry it is necessary to give some thought to the serious security crisis that the country faces today.

It is agreed on all hands that national security should be our first priority. If we cannot defend our borders, cannot fight foreign aggression all our plans become meaningless. And clearly the country is in danger today. An effort is being made to surround the country on all sides. On both sides of us Pakistan stands equipped with most modern American arms, and in spite of the professions of American leaders that these arms would not be used against India, Pakistani leaders and military dictators do not hide the fact that they are getting them for use against India.

And in Goa Portugal is in power. There is a nexus between Pakistan and Portugal. In the trade agreement between the two Goa has been accepted as an overseas province of Portugal. Portugal is a member of NATO, and Pakistan too is a part of military alliances. In the deep South the British base in Maldweep has no purpose for the security of Britain. In the event of a crisis Maldweep can pose a threat to India's security.

What would Happen in the Event of an Aggression of India ?

The recent events in Tibet have also rendered our northern border unsafe. Tibet was a buffer state between China and India. It has come to an end and 1200 miles of our border now touch China. It is true that we want friendship. We are a peaceful country. We have no intention of aggressing on any country, but we must be alert to our own security. Pakistan invades our border every day. Whenever the Defence Minister gets an opportunity to make a speech he keeps declaring—if anyone aggresses on India he would be given a fitting reply. I say an aggression has already been made on our border. One-third of Kashmir, which is constitutionally Indian territory, is under Pakistan's occupation. Pakistani forces are present in Tukergram and the Prime Minister says Tukergram is ours, but we won't fight. Why won't we fight ? Because we would have to go to war to get it back.

The question is, if we do not want a major engagement with Pakistan what will be our position if one day Pakistan suddenly attacks us ? So far the Defence Minister has not taken the House with regard to our position *vis-a-vis* the growing military might of Pakistan. Can we meet a sudden attack ? Can we stand our ground for 2-3 weeks ? It is a different matter that later there

Lok Sabha on April 8, 1959 during discussion on the demands for grants of the Ministry of Defence

may be international intervention and we may involve our friends, but the question is what will happen for the first 2-3 weeks ?

At the same time we must bear in mind that foreign agents are active in the country. Pakistani agents are installed in high places. The manner in which the news of the Dalai Lama's arrival in India reached China is also a matter for concern. Is our intelligence service strong ? Are we sure there is no hole in it ? Have any undesirable elements penetrated it in order to undermine the country ? What will happen if there is an external aggression and at the same time fifth columnists become active, indulge in subversion and sabotage our defence centres ? The Defence Minister should clarify this position. But the country is not being properly prepared to meet this danger.

Sir, we should militarize the nation—not for aggression on anybody but for our own defence. We should give military training to every young man and woman. This will generate discipline and team spirit, and we can use that force, that army, in times of crisis. Suggestions are currently being made that graduates leaving the university should be sent to villages for six months for social service. I am not against it, but you should also seriously think about making military training compulsory for graduates.

Self-reliance in Arms Production

We also need to be self-reliant in arms production. It is true that we cannot compete with Russia or the U.S. in this matter. We cannot make the atom bomb or the hydrogen bomb, but we should think about how much traditional arms production we have in this country and how much we have to look to others. It is good that production in our ordnance factories is increasing, it should increase still further, but it is not proper to put these ordnance factories to civilian use and depend upon other countries for military ware. Ordnance factories should be fully used for making the country self-dependent in arms. So I disagree with the policy of using the army for civilian purposes.

The Deputy Minister has said the houses built by the army in Ambala have been greatly praised. The job may have been praise-worthy. It was filmed. But when he was asked if such houses were built in Pathankot he replied he could not give the information on security grounds. If it was not proper to say about Pathankot why was there so much propaganda about Ambala ? The two are not different. If the army is used for civilian purpose its discipline would be affected. The function of the army is to defend the country, get military training and always be engaged in it. We have no shortage of manpower in this country. We have large number of labourers to build houses. We can utilise them. We have seen a report saying that when Delhi's water system broke down 200 Jawans were put on it, and this was highly praised. Could these men not have been brought from the police ? Is there no voluntary organisation in Delhi that could have been utilised for this ? What was the need of bringing in the army ? In Jamshedpur the army was called in to suppress the labour strike. This is not a good tendency. All around India military dictatorships are being established and democracy is coming to an end. In such a situation this tendency of using the army more and more for civilian purposes could prove dangerous. There is no objection to the army meeting the people, but it is necessary to discourage the feeling in the people's mind that civilian institutions do not work and in times of crisis we should look to the army.

New Names for Regiments

The British have left. They divided our armed forces on communal lines and gave them communal names. We were under the impression that after the establishment of a secular state communal names of the armed forces would be ended, and there would be no classification like Jat Regiment, Sikh Regiment, Mahar Regiment, Rajput Regiment and so on. Our army should be the symbol of national unity. From the emotional point of view we have it too. But these outer names are not helpful in promoting the national spirit. They need to be changed. We can give the name of great heroes. They will not exhibit communalism, and there will be no possibility of the poison of communalism entering the armed forces. But these old names are being justified. It is said they have a long history. We have had a long history of slavery, but we ended it. Communalism has also been with us since ancient times, and we are fighting it. If we want that communalism should have no place in the nation's life we should not have communal nomenclature in the army. We should bid good-bye to it.

Sir, I was talking about intelligence. We now have a situation in which the Defence Ministry has a separate intelligence service, the Home Ministry has a separate intelligence service and the States too have intelligence services of their own. Who coordinates these three—is there coordination at all ? If there is not, it is a matter for great concern. All our intelligence services and counter-intelligence services should be coordinated, so that an eye could be kept on fifth columnists and our secrets prevented from leaking out in times of crisis. At present we do not have a proper arrangement for this. I have come to know that while our delegates to the Security Council were speaking on Kashmir the Pakistani delegate said Indian forces present in Jhansi were advancing towards Pakistan. How did they get this information ?

Borders Unsafe

Our army was not advancing towards Pakistan and there was no reason for it to do so. It was an exercise in which it went 15-20 miles in that direction. But it seems there is a network of secret agents and some of them have reached high positions. The way the news of Dalai Lama became public shows that even our secret code is not secure. News was sent to New Delhi from the border that the Dalai Lama had entered India, but it reached Peking before reaching New Delhi. How ? Was it leaked from New Delhi ? The Prime Minister says no. Then was the secret revealed at the border ? The third possibility is that it was intercepted while being transmitted from the border to New Delhi, but that means our code was known to those who should not know it. They decodified it. Now the situation is not such as the Defence

Minister says—it is not diplomatic, delicate, as he puts it, and we cannot bring in an adjournment motion.

Sir, the adjournment motion may be nullified, but the truth has come to light that our intelligence department cannot keep secrets. If we cannot preserve state security today what would happen in times of crisis ? The very thought makes one shudder.

I am not an alarmist and I feel in times of danger the whole country will rise as one. Perhaps a handful of people may side with the foreigners but the whole country would stand up as one man to face the aggression. But we need a strong defence system. Our borders touch many states and the State Governments there cannot defend those borders because they do not have the manpower, the police force and funds. The Central Government should take over the security of these borders. If we cannot keep the army there we should recruit a special police constabulary, which would police the border on behalf of the Centre. This would promote self-confidence in the country. People living on the border should have the confidence that any aggression would be effectively met. So the House should be taken into confidence and assured that we are fully capable of meeting the new danger that has arisen for the country. This is essential for raising the morale of the people. I call upon the country and on the Defence Ministry to give thought to this. Thank you.

Defence Ministry has Failed

Sir, it is the function of the Defence Ministry to defend the country, and so far as the primary duty of defending the country from external aggression is concerned it cannot be denied that the Ministry has failed in it. India's borders have become easy for aggression by our neighbours. 42,000 square miles of Jammu and Kashmir are under Pakistani control. It is argued that we were not ready at the time of the Pakistani aggression there, but this does not apply to the Chinese aggression on us. There is a warlike situation in Jammu and Kashmir. Communication there is in the hands of the Defence Ministry. So the people going there required the Ministry's permit. Sometimes there was a ban on issuing these permits. This means that the entire responsibility of protecting the border of Jammu and Kashmir was on the Defence Ministry. But the Ministry had no inkling of the Chinese aggression in Ladakh. We were out to defend Jammu and Kashmir from Pakistan but it became an object of Chinese aggression, and the Defence Ministry is responsible for this.

It is argued that we did not expect aggression from China. But in view of the Chinese aggression we should have made full preparations for the defence of Ladakh. It is not only a matter of the border. The Chinese aggressors penetrated 40-45 miles inside Indian territory.

But the Defence Ministry did not know about it. The things this ministry makes cannot be the measure of its success. An increase in production is welcome. I am not opposed to the Defence Ministry producing all sorts of goods, but its first function is to defend the country. When the Chinese committed aggression in Logju and the Prime Minister said 'it is a clear case of aggression' why were Karma Singh and his comrades sent to Ladakh to fall to Chinese bullets ? The Government knew since 1957 that the Chinese had entered Ladakh and prepared a road there, then why was Karma Singh's party not given protection ? They were not armed and stood on lower ground while the Chinese forces were at the top of the hill. Why did the Defence Ministry not arrange for protecting Karma Singh and his party from the Chinese attack ?

Responsibility for Defence of Ladakh

It is argued that this is a State subject, but in my opinion this does not apply to Ladakh, because the defence of Ladakh has been the Centre's responsibility since the time of the Pakistani aggression there. In the first place the Chinese aggression was not discovered and they were not prevented from coming 40 miles inside the Indian border, and the biggest

Lok Sabha on April 9, 1960 during discussion on the demands for grants of the Ministry of Defence

mistake was that Karma Singh and his comrades were left to be killed by the Chinese army. The Defence Ministry must clarify this situation.

Then again, is it true that Gen. Thimayya had indicated in 1957 that Chinese forces had penetrated Ladakh ? I have a basis for saying so. The *Time* magazine of December 14, 1959 reproduced a conversation between Gen. Thimayya and Shri Morarji Desai. The Defence Minister denied an interview with the *New York Times* correspondent that day. Thank God the Finance Minister has not similarly denied. I don't think he has not read it.

Sir, I place a portion of it before you :

> "Finance Minister, Mr. Morarji Desai, angrily set out to get the facts about the red road."

This is about Ladakh.

> "Cross-questioning India's Army Chief of Staff, Lieut-General K.S. Thimayya, he asked when he first knew about the road."
>
> "In 1957, said the General and he had offered proposals."

SHRI NARAYANAN KUTTY MENON : May I know the name of the magazine from which he is quoting ?

SHRI VAJPAYEE : It is *Time*. You may not like it. But it is here.

SHRI NARAYANAN KUTTY MENON : He need not reply me. I only wanted to know the name of the magazine.

SHRI VAJPAYEE : Sir, I had already informed you of the name of the magazine. If the Hon. Member does not understand Hindi, I am very sorry for him.

> "In 1957, said the General, and he had offered proposals to safeguard the security of India. But they were turned down by the Defence Minister, Mr. Menon. Why ?"

"Why" is in inverted commas.

> "Why ?' asked Desai. 'Because' replied Thimayya, 'he said that the enemy was on the other side and not on this side."

This means the Defence Ministry told Gen. Thimayya the enemy was not in the direction of China, it was in the other direction, that is, in the direction of Pakistan. If this is not true let the Defence Minister refute it. But if it is true the Defence Minister is guilty of exposing the country to Chinese aggression. There is a possibility of aggression from Pakistan. It cannot be denied that Pakistan has committed aggression, but if the Defence Minister directs his attention only to Pakistan and closes his eyes to the other side he cannot do justice to the country's defence. Even now, after the Chinese aggression, it seems it has not been taken seriously.

The other day there was a discussion on air space violation. When there was a question about such violation by Pakistan the Defence Minister replied confidently, but he did not say anything about planes coming from the Chinese side. Later he said those who saw it and heard it say the planes had come from China. Now, can our armed forces not see and hear planes coming from China ? Can they not identify them ? Or if they were identified why does the Defence Minister hesitate to say so in the House ? Why ? And if we cannot identify the planes all this praise of the Defence Minister and the

Defence Ministry is meaningless. 13 years have passed since we became independent and this House has never rejected the Defence Minister's demand for funds, whatever it was. We have always given what was asked for. Last year too the House agreed that more funds needed to be spent on defence. But when the Hon. Shri Tyagi asked for an assurance that in future Chinese planes would not be permitted to violate Indian borders the Minister replied "resources permitting."

China and Pakistan may Attack Together

This report also says "consistent with our limited resources." Do we not have the resources even to identify the foreign planes that violate our air space ? If the Defence Ministry does not have then it can approach the House. Whenever it made a demand we acceded to it, we never declined to give money. The country's security must have the first priority. The northern borders have been ignored, and they are still being ignored. Even after the Chinese aggression the Defence Ministry is not discharging its responsibility properly. This is a very serious matter for the country. Our borders have been subjected to aggression on both sides.

I refer to retired Major-General Shiv Dutt Singh, as what he says he would say on the basis of experience. He says it is possible that China and Pakistan may attack our borders together. Pakistan is receiving arms from the U.S. and China from Russia....

SHRI TYAGI : So the two cannot have an accord.

SHRI VAJPAYEE : I am quoting a retired Major-General, but if Shri Tyagi likes to say something more authoritatively than him I do not mind accepting what he says.

SHRI JOACHIM ALVA : Sir, is it not true that this Major-General did not send articles to newspapers only because the newspapers wanted to add "retired" to his designation while he did not ?

SHRI VAJPAYEE : I do not know what my Hon. friend is saying, and perhaps he himself does not know what he is saying.

SHRI JOACHIM ALVA : I am telling the truth. I submit....

CHAIRMAN : Order, order. Let there be no interruptions of this kind. The Hon. Member does not understand his interruption and does not give way. There is no meaning in his trying to rise and interrupt. He has made his speech already.

SHRI JOACHIM ALVA : I am not making a speech.

CHAIRMAN : There is no meaning in this kind of interruption. The Hon'ble member speaking has a right to say what he wants and the Hon. member has no right to interrupt him.

SHRI VAJPAYEE : Sir, the situation has come to such a pass that no one knows what will happen in future. But we cannot take chances with security and we should be ready for all eventualities. It seems the Defence Ministry still refuses to take the matter seriously, for in this budget only Rs. 20 crores more have been asked for. This does not show an understanding of the seriousness of the danger created by the Chinese aggression.

Shri Chou En-Lai is coming to India. It would be a matter of happiness if the talks are successful, but the new note he has sent does not hold out hopes of success. Now he is asking for the Everest. So long he was asking for land, now he is asking for the sky. So long he was asking for the ground, now he is asking for the mountain. He is asking for the highest peak of the Himalayas. I do not think talks would succeed in such a situation. And what would happen if unfortunately they fail ? Then would these Rs. 29 crores suffice ? Does the Defence Ministry, does the Government have the military might to drive out Chinese aggressors ? This question needs to be answered and the Defence Ministry's demands should be seen in that perspective.

The Nanavati Affair

Sir, the audit report also mentions the Nanavati affair. The Defence Minister should have no objection to discussing it, as Rs.10,000 were spent on defending him. There is a big principle involved here—are Jawans and army officers apart from ordinary citizens ? What Commander Nanavati did he did as an individual, not as a naval officer, and he should be left alone to suffer the consequences as an individual. I hope a wrong convention would not be set. It is said that in Punjab the State Government did not give any aid to D.S. Gill although the charges against him related to the discharge of his duties. I am not prepared to accept that the Defence Minister did not use his influence for Central intervention in the Nanavati case. The Prime Minister said that day that Admiral Katari approached him. I was greatly surprised to know that he bypassed the Defence Minister and directly went to the Prime Minister. He should not have gone and I think he did not. You know how much dust was raised when Gen. Thimayya once went, I do not think Admiral Katari made the same mistake. I guess the Defence Minister used his influence and hid this fact from the House. This is most unfortunate for the country.

Gradually democracy is being throttled in the country. That the army should engage in relief work looks praiseworthy. The army giving relief during floods or the army taking out marches through the market place in order to help the law and order forces is legal and the Constitution provides for it. But in it lies the seed of a weakening of the civil authority. It means we are depending more and more on the army. In view of the events that are taking place in India's neighbourhood, in view of how democracy is getting a beating in Asia and Africa, and in view of how dictatorial forces are raising their head in our country, I do not think using the army more and more like this would be good for the future of the country. So I urge that the Defence potential of the country be strengthened. Let us take foreign aggression into account and increase our military might accordingly. If we find provincialism in the army let us remove it. I feel that in secular India there is no place for communal names like Marathi regiment. Or Jat regiment or Sikh regiment. These names should be removed. The army should not be organised on communal bases. Thank you.

Why the Weapon of Emergency ?

Madam, I welcome this discussion—not because of what Shri Bhupesh Gupta has said in support of his resolution but because in this discussion on the state of emergency....

SHRI C.D. PANDE : You welcome the discussion or the resolution ?

SHRI VAJPAYEE : That you can understand. We should redetermine our attitude to the Emergency and to its promulgation. There is certainly force in what Shri Bhupesh Gupta has said in support of his resolution and it is for the Government to prove to the House and to the country that it is necessary to continue the Emergency for the fulfilment of the objectives for which it was promulgated. When the Emergency was declared it was not the announcement of any one party, it was the whole nation's announcement and it had the backing of all parties. But that declaration was not lived up to. We called China an enemy but we did not declare war on China. We did not sever diplomatic ties with China. We did not even stop our ambassador in Peking from a false show of etiquette. When there was a treaty between Pakistan and China Pakistan gave China a big piece of territory under that treaty. We have been opposing that treaty in the Security Council, but our representative in Peking was asked to be present when that treaty would be signed. The Foreign Ministry gave him that advice. When the Chinese Prime Minister went to Cairo our ambassador was asked to greet Shri Chou En-lai at the airport. Shri Chou En-lai was given permission to overfly Indian territory. He is going to visit Pakistan and again he will be given permission. It is said this is etiquette and we should observe it. This conduct, this policy of the Government has created doubts in the minds of the people, who feel that in spite of declaring an emergency the Government does not want to act according to it.

Madam, if the government's assessment of a crisis and the people's assessment of it are not the same it can only mean the crisis is aggravating. There was a time when the two viewpoints were the same. Now the difference between the two is widening and the people feel that the Emergency exists only in declarations. There is no emergency in implementing policies, in the method of administration and in the behaviour of Ministers. This is a very dangerous situation for the country—and Emergency for the government and no emergency for the people. This is an alarm bell. For if there is really a serious danger we would not be able to make the people realise it and prepare the country to face it. After all every

Rajya Sabha on February 14, 1964 during review of discussion on the resolution seeking announcement of revocation of the Emergency

heart must feel the intensity of a crisis. The administration must make that this intensity has gone down. The government must also say how war efforts would be impeded by the revocation of the Emergency. Jawans are being recruited, the size of the army is being increased, arms production is being stepped up. There would be no difficulty in war efforts if the Emergency is revoked. If the Government apprehends some difficulty it should explain it. That is why I said in the beginning that the onus of proving why the Emergency should continue lies on the Government, not on the opposition parties.

One more thing. It is argued that the Government needs extra-ordinary powers to keep peace in the industrial field. The workers have maintained peace at the present time and they should be congratulated on it, but in proportion to that the employers have not fully complied with the agreement to maintain industrial peace. Do we want to suppress the workers' demand in the Emergency that workers should get a share of the profit ? Does the responsibility of maintaining industrial peace rest only with the workers and not with the employers ? Not with the Government ? What is the situation in the government plants ? A labour organisation related to the Congress party is disrupting industrial peace these days. What is happening in Indore ? INTUC leaders are quarrelling among themselves. They have been arrested and their quarrels have brought production down. The promulgation of Emergency cannot prevent INTUC leaders from quarrelling. In Heavy Electricals in Bhopal the government administrators have formed two unions of their own. The INTUC people are creating a crisis there as well. Neither can the government stop them nor can its extraordinary powers curb their activities.

Controversy Over Union Formation

There was a controversy going on among the workers of the Gopal Paper Mills at Jagadhri. A new union formed there claims the majority is with it. But independent elections are not held to find out where the majority lies. And even if the Labour Commissioner of Punjab wants to solve the problem the INTUC leaders of Punjab, who are also leaders of the Punjab Congress, put pressure on the mill management and the labour commissioner not to have an agreement with any labour union except with the INTUC. A member of Parliament is at present in jail at Ambala because he had to stage a *dharna* there. The Government's extraordinary powers could not suppress the feeling of struggle of the workers of Gopal Paper Mills in Jagadhri.

In Uttar Pradesh Defence of India Rules have been promulgated under which farmers could be forced to supply sugarcane to sugar mills. Later the Food and Agriculture Minister removed this compulsion. But he may know that the Jarwal mill has not yet paid lakhs of rupees to the cane producers. The cane was purchased, sugar made and sold in the market, but the Kisans were not paid. Can the Defence of India Rules not be applied against the proprietors of the mill ? But the law was not applied against the proprietors, against INTUC leaders and against the member of Parliament, Choudhary

Brahm Prakash. If small shopkeepers do not display the price list they can be arrested under the Defence of India Rules, but the office-bearers of the Central Cooperative Stores are not proceeded against for profiteering in gur, corruption in coal and for hoarding of rice.

It is argued that if the Emergency is revoked elements linked with China would become active again. Sometimes these elements are recalled for the sake of continuing the crisis. Shri Bhupesh Gupta said just now that most Communists have been released. Obviously the Communists do not pose a danger. If they did why were they released ? The Government deserves to be criticised for it.

SHRI C.D. PANDE : It was a mistake.

SHRI VAJPAYEE : Shri Pande says it was a mistake. It is his government. His Government keeps making mistakes and he keeps supporting it and saying it was a mistake. This is now a mistake. Perhaps the Government thinks it is not necessary to keep these communists in jail and if it is necessary the cause would have to be shown under the Preventive Detention Act and the detenu produced before a board. Whether it is a Communist or a Pakistani agent we are against detention without trial. The Government will have to produce proof, and if it cannot do so it should be prepared to take some risk. But the country cannot be played with, and the Emergency cannot be continued simply because the Communists have to be kept in jail. The fundamental rights given by the Constitution cannot be suppressed forever only because some Communists have to be kept in jail. After all the China crisis is to go on for a long time and I have no hope that it will be resolved so long as this Government is in office. We are not prepared to send our army as far as the Mc Mahon Line, and we are also not ready to free ourselves from the Colombo proposals. We are not even ready to say to China—you did not accept the Colombo proposals, so we shall not be bound by them and we shall not have talks with you so long as you do not quit Ladakh and NEFA. The Emergency was not declared when the Chinese army was in Ladakh, it was declared when it entered NEFA. Now it has quit NEFA, so why do we need the Emergency ?

Misuse of Emergency Powers

Now the excuse of Pakistan has been given. I think such senseless and illogical talk should not be indulged in. The Congress Party should depute some good man to speak. Reference has also been made to Naga rebels. You are allowing their leader Phizo to come to India. Who said he should be allowed in ? No government makes a compromise with a killer, a rebel, but this government is inviting Phizo to India for talks without conditions. The Government's representatives stand up in the House to say they need the Emergency to arrest communists, but even non-communists have been arrested. Members of the Praja Socialist Party staging a satyagraha have been arrested, and members of the Bharatiya Jan Sangh have also been arrested. You want to use extraordinary powers not for strengthening the country's security but for serving your own political ends. I hope the Home Minister will throw light on the reasons that necessitate the continuance of the Emergency. If he cannot satisfy us we won't support this resolution. The Congress party cannot, just on the strength of its majority, maintain the atmosphere of the emergency in the country. A consensus of all parties should be sought on this, otherwise the Emergency should be revoked. When the crisis deepens it can be declared again. The heavens would not fall if we do that. Even your policies are not strong and firm about resolving the crisis.

I shall conclude with a suggestion. If you really want to continue the Emergency because of the Chinese aggression you could find a via media by continuing it in NEFA, Assam, West Bengal, Jammu-Kashmir and Punjab, and revoking it in other parts of the country. This will also be a test of your sincerity.

Why Continue Emergency

Sir, the framers of the Constitution have provided under Article 352 that an emergency may be declared in the event of an external aggression or internal disturbance. The article also says that the duration of the emergency would be two months, unless Parliament decides to extend it. This makes the intentions of the framers of the Constitution quite clear. They have used the phrase 'grave emergency' not merely emergency—an emergency of external aggression or widespread internal disturbance, and they have laid down a time limit of two months. It is argued that the present Emergency has been approved of by Parliament. But is it in accordance with the intentions of the framers of the Constitution to keep the Emergency going on for five years continuously ? It is clear that the country faces a crisis. But we have to learn to live with crises. In the midst of crises we have to give the people an opportunity to enjoy democratic rights.

When we declare an emergency we suspend for some time the fundamental rights given by the Constitution. Equality before the law does not remain, rights to property are curtailed, individual freedom becomes restricted and a citizen can be taken into preventive detention without showing cause. In an emergency a detained citizen need not be presented before any board. An emergency was declared when China committed an aggression. All the opposition parties and the entire country supported it. But why is it opposed today ? The Home Minister should seriously think about this. The only reason for this is that the country faces a danger, but there is no realisation of that danger, either in the Government or in the administration. Neither in the ruling party nor in the people. Now if there is a danger but no realisation of that danger what is the use of continuing the Emergency by law ? The country's psychology has changed and without changing that psychology again it would not be right to continue the emergency.

Is the common law not enough to tackle this situation ? The Home Minister had indicated it but now wants to go back on his word. I charge him with breach of promise. When the new Lok Sabha was convened he announced on the very first day of the session that from July 1 the Emergency would be limited only to some parts of the country. He had given thought to the matter before making the commencement. The difficulties which he now mentions are not new. They were present that time too. There is only one new difficulty—he had thought he would secure the support of opposition

Lok Sabha on June 20, 1967 during discussion on the proposal to continue the Emergency

parties for amending the Constitution but they are not prepared to oblige him. Is it necessary for us to help the Government ?

SHRI Y.B. CHAVAN : For the Emergency.

SHRI VAJPAYEE : You will have to convince us that there is really a danger and you require powers to overcome it, not for anything else. Is the Government preparing to resist the Chinese aggression ? In 1962 we had taken a sacred pledge that we shall not rest till we liberate every inch of our territory from Chinese control. Are we preparing to live up to that pledge ? If the Government takes steps to liberate that territory we are prepared to support the Emergency. If the Government takes action to liberate one-third of Jammu & Kashmir we are prepared to give it extra-ordinary powers. But the Government does not want to do any such thing. It wants to go back on the pledges made to the country. It wants powers just on the apprehension of a new aggression. Was this apprehension not there when it was announced that from July 1 the Emergency would be confined only to some areas ? If it was not I would say this government is shortsighted. It cannot see beyond its nose. That time too there was the danger of Chinese and Pakistani aggression. This time too it is there. But we cannot deprive the citizens of their fundamental rights for all time to come because of some apprehended danger. If there is an aggression on the country the Government can again declare an Emergency. The Constitution has given it the right and the country would extend voluntary cooperation to it. If some elements prove impediments in the way we shall not side with them. The nation's security is supreme. But we have to blend the nation's security with democratic rights.

A Danger Is Countrywide, not Regional

The Home Minister says the Emergency will continue in some areas, fundamental rights will be suspended, and there will be full freedom in the rest of India. Sir, we are basically opposed to limiting the Emergency and lifting it in the rest of India. What sort of a danger is it that is present in one part of the country but is not felt in another ? What sort of a danger is it that does not face the whole country ? Is the crisis in Jammu and Kashmir not a crisis for the whole country ? Is not China's assault on Assam an assault on the sovereignty, integrity and freedom of the country ? If we believe in nationalism and in raising the whole nation as one from Kashmir to Kanyakumari it would be a delusion to limit the Emergency to some parts. It could prove dangerous. It should be given up.

Sir, the Government has enough powers. Perhaps the Home Minister may want to confine the Emergency to Jammu and Kashmir, Punjab, Assam, NEFA and Bengal. I am deliberately saying 'may want', because he has not yet revealed his intentions. Which are the sensitive areas ? If they are these to which I am referring is it not true that the State Governments there have enough powers to tackle any situation ? There is the Public Safety and Security Act. Does not the government in Jammu and Kashmir have powers ? Is the Public Safety Act not in operation in Bihar ? Is there not a public security act in West Bengal ? The Government has already assumed special powers for NEFA and Nagaland. But what is happening after assuming these powers ?

What happened in Jammu and Kashmir on June 7 ? What happened in Srinagar ? I do not want to go into those incidents. There is a crisis in the country. The Government has also the powers. But on June 7 churches were torched in Srinagar. Women were insulted. A jeep belonging to the National Conference was set on fire. No action was taken against anybody. If you assume powers and do not use them it is useless to assume powers, and if you assume powers and misuse them it is dangerous to arm you with those powers. From both points of view these extraordinary powers are not called for.

Defence of India Rules Misused

Can it be denied that Defence of India Rules were misused ? We can understand catching spies, but under these rules students, government employees and businessmen were arrested. In Maharashtra Defence of India Rules were used to stop a love marriage. The Home Minister may not have forgotten this incident, as he hails from Maharashtra. Those who were given powers misused those powers, so now they do not deserve them. There are enough powers in the border areas where the Home Minister wants to limit the Emergency. The common laws should be capable of tackling a situation. If they are not there is some shortcoming in those who use them. If the laws themselves suffer from some deficiency it can also be removed. If the danger faced by the country can be met without suppression or suspension of the fundamental rights of citizens we would always be ready to think of any such question. If the Government wants powers for itself it should come up with a concrete proposal. We shall give our verdict on merits. But we are not ready to give powers that the Government could not use properly and which do not even seem necessary in the present situation.

One more thing. As I said, the country is in danger, but there is no realisation of the danger. That realisation will have to be created, otherwise every step you take will be misconstrued. It will be distorted for political purposes. After all the powers that the government assumes will be used through the State Governments. Naxalbari is mentioned again and again. There is at present an emergency and there are also special powers, but what will the Home Minister do if the Government of West Bengal is not ready to use them ? After all the powers will have to be used by State Governments, but those Governments are not willing. The Home Minister has still not said how many Chief Ministers he has consulted. How many Chief Ministers agree with his proposal to extend the Emergency ? At first a lot was made of consultations with Chief Ministers. These days the Home Minister does not talk of Chief Ministers. Why ? After all they too are responsible. They too should realise the danger. They should be willing to act accordingly. If they are not those who sit in New Delhi and use extraordinary powers, it would complicate the problem instead of solving it. I call upon the Home Minister to think again. There are still some days to go for July 1. Revoke the emergency. If there is a real crisis again the whole country will support him. Otherwise even in a real crisis he would not be able to rouse the country and secure the people's support. Thank you.

Teach the Aggressor a Lesson

Sir, we have come together in the shadow of a national crisis. Pakistan has forced a war on us. Pakistan has challenged our security, integrity and freedom in order to divert the attention of the world from the continuous success of the Mukti Vahini in Bangladesh and for inviting international pressure in this subcontinent. This is a challenge, and it is also an opportunity. We are going through an ordeal of fire. There is no reason why we should not pass it and shine all the more. There is no reason why we cannot secure our borders and teach the aggressor a lesson they would never forget in their lives.

Today I am not prepared to speak on behalf of the party. Today the whole country is one party. We have to forget political differences, set aside small things and march to victory shoulder to shoulder. This struggle will get all the sacrifices it wants. The country will show all the discipline that is called for. There is no reason why we should not exhibit the national determination that is needed on such occasions.

Pardon me, Sir, let no one say I am inciting passions. If there is a war, if there is an aggression on our borders the people will have to be linked with the war effort. Let us not incite passion, but we have to rouse the patriotism of the people to enthuse them to do their job as best as they can, and stand firm on every front. The Jawans will take care of the front and we shall take care of the domestic front. We shall not allow any disturbance and any type of communal unrest to be created.

Sir, the day for which mothers bear their children has arrived. The day for which sisters tie Rakhis to their brothers' wrists has arrived. If Pakistan thinks it can catch us off guard with a sudden attack, it is mistaken. The world has seen who the aggressor is and our Jawans are giving a fitting reply to him.

We hope the Prime Minister, with whom lies the responsibility at this moment of historic change, will provide leadership to the country. We want this country to become victorious and we hope we create new history under the Prime Minister's leadership.

Sir, during this aggression this Parliament can be used as a weapon against Yahya Khan. There is no Parliament in Pakistan, the Government of the people does not have the support of the people. Here we have respresentatives of the people sitting together and the world sees—and will see in future—that in times of danger this country can give a united reply.

Lok Sabha on December 4, 1971 on the Calling Attention Motion regarding declaration of the Emergency and War Strategy

Let plans be prepared to involve all people in the war effort, responsibilities allocated, and an atmosphere conducive to victory be created in the country.

It is not necessary to say that I support the Emergency that has been declared. I do not agree with my friend Gopalan that this is not necessary. Pakistan has declared war, it has launched a sudden attack. On such occasions there is no question of a faltering policy. This House will fully support the Emergency that has been declared and fully back any step taken for a forceful reply to the aggression. Every citizen of this country will successfully meet this challenge. Thank you.

Special Powers should not be Misused

Sir, this Bill equips the Government with extraordinary powers. But the situation facing the country is also extraordinary. The House will not hesitate to arm the Government with whatever powers it needs to tackle this situation. The only question is, these powers should not be misused. In this respect previous experience is not good. Powers are not used at a high level, they are used by the low-level administration. There is a fear of excesses. This should be fully provided for.

My friend Shri Indrajit Gupta has referred to clause 17-A. I quote Section B of this Clause :

> "Where such person had been detained with a view to preventing him from acting in any manner prejudicial to the security of the State or the maintenance of public order."

Security of the State is all right. Stringent action will have been taken against any individual working against the nation's security, whatever his community or party. But what is the need of including public order in this ? Sometimes a public meeting may be held in which an appeal may be made to the people to contribute to the Government's war effort. If necessary the Government may also be criticised. The right to criticise cannot be denied. It is true that criticism should be constructive, it should not bring down the morale of the people. But what will happen to the people who criticise ? No one can claim that those who have the responsibility of conducting the war will always act rightly. Their assessment may be wrong, they may at times take a wrong step. There can be different opinions on how the people's cooperation for the war effort could be secured, and in a democracy there should be full freedom to express these opinions. As the saying goes, the din of arms cannot still the voice of conscience. Even in the din of arms the voice of law must not be suppressed.

Sir, in view of the present atmosphere in the country let the Government assure that it will not misuse the powers being given to it. It is possible that here and there there may be a mistake in thinking, but for this a good suggestion is to have a parliamentary committee, which could be called a standing committee. It could supervise the implementation of this Act and go into any real complaint about it.

Battle at the Front and Battle of the Ballot

It is also necessary that the Government should decide to call off the by-elections currently being held in the country. The battle at the front and

Lok Sabha on December 4, 1971 during discussion on the Defence of India Bill

the battle of these by-elections cannot go together. In Uttar Pradesh alone 9 by-elections are being held. Many candidates are contesting them. I do not see any propriety in the battle of the parties in these by-elections at this time. We must use all our strength for the war effort, not for winning seats. We have to bring victory to the country. There is no question of any party's victory in a seat or two.

Proper steps need to be taken for securing the people's cooperation and that of the opposition parties. For instance branches of the Central Citizens' Council are being set up in the States. In all of them opposition parties should be fully taken along. This is not a matter for any one party. But so far the structure of the Central Citizens' Council has not created any confidence even in the people, let alone the opposition parties. I do not want to name names but we should have a system that would secure that cooperation of all. This is not the time to think about trifles. I was sorry to learn that the Delhi branch of the Central Citizens' Council does not include the Mayor of Delhi. Can any Committee of the citizens of Delhi be set up without the mayor of Delhi ?

SHRI SHASHI BHUSHAN (South Delhi) : There are two committees the Mayor's and the Lt. Governor's.

SHRI VAJPAYEE : And in the States Chief Ministers' Committees are being set up. In Delhi too we have democracy. There is an administration of Delhi. Will it be a Lt. Governor's Committee ? Why can't there be a Chief Executive Councillor's Committee here ? In other states Chief Ministers' Committees are being set up. We are with them. We have not put any conditions. Whether we are included in the Committees or not, we shall do our duty by the country. But people will want to know what system is being set up for securing all people's cooperation in the war effort. We should have such committees at the Centre and in all States. We should take all parties with us and forge ahead.

PROF. MADHU DANDAVATE (Rajapur) : The mayor is there, but with a different spelling—MARE.

Impose Controls during War Time

This Bill says action will be taken against those who indulge in hoarding or raise prices. But action is possible only if a commodity is controlled and it is sold at a price higher than the controlled price. I suggest that remembering that the war will go on for a long time the Government should take over the supply of essential goods to the people at proper prices. If necessary controls can also be imposed during war time, but there should be trust that they would be sincerely worked and provide relief to the people, not harass them. It is the responsibility of the administration to ensure that every citizen gets essential commodities at proper prices. Then if anybody does profiteering or hoarding strict action should be taken against him.

But for all these things it is necessary to create an atmosphere in the country. I am confident that when such an atmosphere is properly created we can appeal to students not to take the law in their hands, we can appeal to capitalists not to indulge in improper profiteering, not to exploit the situation, and we can also appeal to labour to toil hard for the country. At the same time, the law can also be resorted to where necessary. Let the Home Minister assure that the law that is being passed will be properly implemented.

Sir, time is short. You too do not want a long debate. However you may think if there could be a joint committee of the two Houses that could supervise the implementation of this law. Thank you.

Sanctity of Fundamental Rights

Madam, I had thought that the Government would bring an amendment to the Defence of India Act in the light of the judgment of the Supreme Court so as to take the Parliament out of the predicament in which it finds itself as a result of the judgment. I have not been able to fully grasp the argument put forth by the Law Minister that it had become apparent at the time of declaration of Emergency that Parliament would have to enact a law which would not stand the test of the Constitution. I think if it were known either to the Law Minister or the Home Minister that they were going to enact a legislation which the Constitution did not empower us to make, it should have been made clear at the time of the consideration of the Defence of India Act or the rules made thereunder. When this House or Parliament put its seal of approval on the Defence of India Act, it was with the conviction that in view of the Emergency we were restricting the fundamental rights of the citizen only to the extent of not allowing him the liberty to knock at the doors of a Court.

Law Ministry Misled Parliament

However, I cannot for a moment think that any Hon. Member would have ever imagined that we were going to enact a legislation which was not in conformity with the Constitution and that the Supreme Court would strike it down and give its judgment against it. But after the judgment of the Supreme Court, a situation has developed where the Government as well as the Parliament find themselves in a quandry. The Supreme Court says that we have enacted a legislation which is not in conformity with the provisions of the Constitution.

SHRI R.M. HAJARNAVIS : It has not said so.

SHRI VAJPAYEE : It might not have said it in so many words, but this is the essence of the judgment.

SHRI R.M. HAJARNAVIS : How could it be an essence of a judgment which has not been delivered ?

SHRI VAJPAYEE : I submit that it is void. This law is void under the provisions of the Constitution. Such a law cannot be enacted in violation of article 14 or 22 of the Constitution. This has been clearly stated in the judgment of the Supreme Court. I do not want to repeat the extracts which Shri Bhupesh Gupta had quoted. In whatever legal language or jugglery of words it has been couched, it cannot be denied that as a result of this decision of the Supreme Court the position of this House, the Parliament and the

Rajya Sabha on September 19, 1963 regarding the Judgment of the Supreme Court and continued detention of persons under the Defence of India Act, 1962

Government has become very awkward and this predicament cannot be undone by saying that we should have understood it at the time of declaration of the Emergency that we shall frame a law which would not be wholly in conformity with the provisions of the Constitution, but that its validity could not be challenged under the Emergency rules.

Madam, my submission is that the grounds on which the Law Ministry had recommended the enactment of such a law should have been made clear. This is not the first occasion when the Ministry of Law has been proved guilty of giving a wrong advice to the Government. Its advice has been set aside in many cases by the Supreme Court and when this controversy arose....

SHRI R.M. HAJARNAVIS : I do not think that your contention is correct.

SHRI VAJPAYEE : You may remember that at the time of the transfer of Berubari the Law Ministry had advised that there was no need to amend the Constitution and the Prime Minister can hand over any piece of land belonging to India. But this advice of the Law Minister has proved to be wrong and the Constitution had to be amended in order to effect the transfer of Berubari. The Ministry of Law had also recommended that the Law Minister should act as the Attorney General, but later on that recommendation had to be rejected.

SHRI R.M. HAJARNAVIS : I may tell the Hon. Member that this advice that there was no need to amend the Constitution in respect of Berubari was given by the Attorney General.

THE DEPUTY CHAIRMAN : The time is so limited that you can give a reply at the end, Mr. Hajarnavis ?

SHRI R.M. HAJARNAVIS : Even statements are made without reference to facts.

Attorney General's Advice Not Sought

SHRI VAJPAYEE : Madam, if this advice was given by the Attorney General, then the Ministry of Law should have conceded the fact that they had sought the advice of the Attorney General while framing the Defence of India Act. However, the Ministry of Law had not sought the advice of the Attorney General at that time (*Interruptions*). If the Minister does not know it, would he stand up and deny it ?

AN HON. MEMBER : What is your source ?

SHRI VAJPAYEE : I have many sources, I do not have to disclose the source of my information. My submission is that the Law Ministry has badly let down the Government and Parliament on this question. I had expected that after the judgment of the Supreme Court the Minister of Law would come forward and say that the law framed by them is not such as it should have been and that the Government would make necessary amendment in the light of the judgment of the Supreme Court.

Fundamental Rights Cannot be a Party Issue

I have been greatly disappointed with the speech of the Law Minister delivered just now. I do not see this question from the party point of view;

it is a question relating to the freedom of an individual. If you want to preserve the freedom of the individual in the midst of the clash of arms, then the parameters laid down in the Constitution must be adhered to... (*Interruptions*).

Please do not talk of the independence of the country. A Government which allowed an opportunity to the Communist Party the other day to demonstrate its strength in Delhi, cannot ask for power to crush the Communist Party on the same ground...(*Interruptions*)

Defence of India Act Abused

Please leave these things. There is no consistency in the mind, words and practice of the Government. Sometimes they want to suppress the Communist Party in the name of Emergency and at other times some other group. They want to back a particular group of the Communist Party in order to seek the support of a foreign country. Therefore, I say, please do not bring in the Communist Party here. Not only the Communist Party, but non-Communists and other political workers have also been subjected to harassment under the Defence of the India Act. Two workers of the Jan Sangh were detained, a Bombay leader of the Socialist Party is still under detention. I do not want to go into the question of parties. We have framed a Constitution which bestows fundamental rights on all individuals. The Supreme Court has differentiated between the Emergency and normal times and has ruled that the courts cannot be approached if those rights are violated during the Emergency. But Parliament cannot make laws in violation of the fundamental rights during the Emergency. I think the government should reconsider its position in the light of the Supreme Court judgment and take decisions that are in conformity with the provisions of the Constitution, to safeguard the spirit of the Rule of Law, while at the same time, fulfilling the needs of national security. Thank you.

Reorganisation of Army

Sir, national security is a priority matter. But it is a matter of regret that today that much of India is not independent as was in 1947. We could not prevent Indian territory from going under the control of China and Pakistan, nor are we capable of recovering the lost territory. This House and the whole country have pledged themselves not to rest till every inch of the occupied territory is liberated from the grasp of the aggressor. But we seem to be forgetting that pledge. We are not concerned about recovering our territory.

Sir, this report admits that the nexus between China and Pakistan is strengthening. It has also been admitted that militarily Pakistan is now as strong as it was in 1971. Clearly the possibility cannot be ignored that some day the two might come together to pose a danger to our independence and territorial integrity. Equally clearly our aim should be to acquire as much military might as can face a joint aggression by China and Pakistan. I know that along with military strength foreign policy, diplomatic efforts and the atmosphere in the world also have their effect. But sometimes I feel our dependence on any country in respect of Defence should never grow to such an extent that that country could exploit that dependence to interfere with and influence with the determination of our policies.

We are bound with the Soviet Union in a treaty of friendship. Security has been kept in view in that treaty. But a similar treaty also binds Egypt and the Soviet Union. The experience of Egypt's President Shri Anwar Sadat should have a lesson for us. The Soviet Union will supply arms when it pleases, stop the supply when it pleases. It has become necessary for Egypt to look to the U.S. and other countries for arms. We too should not depend only upon Russia for arms supply. We too should keep other doors open.

SHRI B.B. NAYAK : Shri Sadat betrayed Russia.

SHRI VAJPAYEE : I do not want to go into who betrayed whom. But one thing is clear—the same Sadat who depended upon Russia has now to shop around for American arms. I am giving a warning against India finding itself in such unfortunate position.

SHRI JAGJIVAN RAM, Defence Minister : It will never be so.

SHRI VAJPAYEE : We should not put all our eggs in one basket. That would not be a good strategy and good diplomacy.

Basic Change in Army Organisation

Sir, another point I would like to make is that the basic change expected after the advent of independence has not taken place in the organisation of

Lok Sabha on April 26, 1974 during discussion on the demands for grants of the Ministry of Defence

our army, its dress, its tradition and its conduct. Sometimes one feels our armed forces still remain in the British mould. Some of our regiments celebrate occasions when they had fought successfully on some front in Africa under British leadership. What do these celebrations mean? The President's Bodyguard celebrate the day they had accepted the responsibility of guarding some foreign viceroy. They still celebrate the day in independent India and in Rashtrapati Bhavan. I admit tradition has a place in the army, but tradition should not be taken to such an extent. Sometimes I feel our forces are still too much under British influence. These days many senior army officers think of settling down in England after retirement. There is a certain senior officer who has gone to Tehran. I do not want to name names. He has accepted that country's citizenship and even got married there. He already had a wife here. He divorced her, later he returned here, took her with him and settled in Tehran. He is a senior officer. I am not raising an individual case. I only want that the army should be cast in a *Swedish* mould in respect of tradition, genius, cultural influences, temperament, prowess, and the spirit of sacrifice and martyrdom. It is all there even today, I do not say it is lacking, but its nature needs some change.

Thirdly I sometimes feel our armed force is not one. Its officers live in one world, its Jawans in another. They dress differently and they eat differently. Even their means of entertainment are different. For the Jawans there is Vividh Bharati music but for officers there is rock and roll. Babuji is pledged to bringing about social equality. Is such a gulf necessary in the army? I can understand a little distance for the sake of discipline, but it should be for the discharge of duty. It should not be wide, its basis should not be that the Jawan is for hardship while the officer is for giving orders. I know in the war our Jawans and officers have fought shoulder to shoulder, and we congratulate our army on it, but such a gulf in peace time does not look good. It can create some bitterness in the minds of the Jawans, it is actually creating it in some places. It should be stopped in time.

One final point. We are told atomic power will be used for peaceful purposes. This is government policy. I do not agree. Shri Jawahar Lal used to say we shall never make the atom bomb. Shri Shastri slightly changed this and said we will not make it for the time being. I do not know what is being said now, but one thing I will say—if atomic power is being used for peaceful purposes what is the need of all this secrecy? Parliament is not taken into confidence, the country is not told. What is the need of a veil over what our atomic plants are doing? Peace and secrecy do not go together. Pakistan is exploiting this situation. It is getting more and more aid from the U.S. by frightening the Americans that the Indians are not making the atom bomb for the present but can make it. I hope things do not come to such a pass that we do not derive the benefit from our policy that we should, but suffer the adverse consequences that flow from it.

I do not want to say anything more. Thank you.

What is Our Threat Perception ?

Sir, I have recently returned from a tour of the North-East. There are many problems there because it is a border region. When I went there I felt as if we had forgotten our borders. In the House and outside, we talk of a foreign hand in this region, but we do not go deeply into how we can secure it from the foreign hand and foreign interference.

Autonomy for Tibet

One aspect of the problem is internal, which I will not discuss. But the strategically important Eastern region, which adjoins China, Burma and Bangladesh has now become explosive for us. I shall go into the old mistake of our accepting Tibet as a part of China. We are trying to normalise our relations with China. At the same time we should try to secure for Tibet the autonomy it has lost.

There are reports that some of our people are being given military training in some parts of Bangladesh and Burma. These may be areas where the writ of these governments does not run. But if we strengthen our friendly relations with them we could create an atmosphere in which the aid that these elements receive from there could stop, and if necessary those countries could clear up with India's help the anti-India bases set up within them. I cannot say what the situation in Burma will be a few days from now. If Burma strays from the path of non-alignment and if the elements in that country that are influenced and controlled by foreign forces become powerful the situation would become difficult for us in this region.

Now that we are discussing the North-East, I would like to say that we should suppress the tendency of using the army more and more for maintaining law and order. Maintaining law and order is the job of the police. The army is for defending the borders of the country. The army is for fighting the enemy and finishing him. These days we call the army for flag marches. Today this has an immediate effect, but tomorrow this effect will diminish and the day after it would diminish still more. Let us not make the mistake of blunting the edge of this sword. The army is not for marching in the streets. Let the police do its duty and let the army do its job. I know decisions are taken in unavoidable circumstances, but we must be more and more careful about this, because it applies not only to the North-East but to the whole country.

Lok Sabha on July 18, 1980 during the discussion on the outcome of recent talks held in New Delhi between Foreign Ministers of Pakistan and India

Our Defence Requirements

While discussing the Defence Ministry's demands for grants it would be natural for us to ask what our defence requirements would be in the eighties. We will have to look at these requirements as a whole. We shall also have to give thought to our threat perceptions. I was not present during the discussion yesterday, but the proceedings I read make me feel we are looking at the problem piecemeal. It would not be the right thing if the defence debate of the Lok Sabha concentrates only on whether we should or should not make the atom bomb and should or should not buy the Jaguar. Decide these small matters. Let members express their opinions (*Interruption*). I shall accept it if the Prime Minister says they are major questions (*Interruption*). Although these questions have their own importance they should not dominate the defence question inside and outside the House.

DR. KARAN SINGH : There should be a reference to them.

Atom Bomb and Patriotism

SHRI VAJPAYEE : There should certainly be a reference. I know Doctor Sahib will make it. I too used to refer to the atom bomb a lot. Yesterday I was not in the House. Shri Gadgil said Vajpayee used to talk of patriotism and the atom bomb, but now he does not talk of the atom bomb, then what happened to patriotism ? Is patriotism linked with the atom bomb ?

SMT. INDIRA GANDHI, Prime Minister : You did the linking.

SHRI VAJPAYEE : Not with patriotism. But have you decided to do now what we did in the past ?

SMT. INDIRA GANDHI : No, not at all.

SHRI VAJPAYEE : If Pakistan makes the atom bomb there will be a situation in the sub-continent. We should think about that. I am one of those who want all doors open on this debate, but it should not only concentrate on India making the bomb because Pakistan is making it. China made the atom bomb but we did not and we kept facing the crisis created by a China equipped with an atom bomb. If Pakistan makes the atom bomb we too will make it, but then we will have to decide who will use it first. We cannot. China too says it will not take the initiative. And if we are to use it after Pakistan uses it we will have to develop a second strike capacity. There should be a debate on all these matters and a full picture placed before us. I do not want to go into it further. Pakistan has been mentioned in the discussion. The point is, does the danger from Pakistan spring from its intentions or does it spring from its capacity ? Previous experience is not good. The arms received by Pakistan have been used against India. But Soviet military intervention in Afghanistan has brought about a qualitative change in the situation and now we will have to look somewhat beyond Pakistan. Afghanistan, Iran and Pakistan— all three are in turmoil. Had there not been big powers behind this turmoil we would not have worried much. But big powers are actively seeking to expand their spheres of influence. China is also on the verge of becoming a big power. But we too are a power in our own right in this region.

So let us coordinate our defence and foreign policies with self-confidence and forge ahead.

The Navy

It has been said during this discussion that we should also pay attention to naval power. We are trying to acquire submarines, but even before we do so a controversy has started. Today the British Prime Minister has said something about the Jaguar. I do not say the present government has no right to change the decisions of the old government, but there is need for continuity in such matters.

SMT. INDIRA GANDHI : If it is in the interest of the country.

SHRI VAJPAYEE : If national interests cannot be safeguarded the people have elected a government that cannot do so, and the leaders of such a government....

SHRI MALIK M.M.A. KHAN : According to a statement of those who run the government of Assam, a state of two and a half crore people, has been called a nation. Such government leader....

SHRI VAJPAYEE : Shri Narasimha Rao is present here. In Andhra Andhra is called a nation. In Telugu the word nation is used for province.

SHRI NARASIMHA RAO : So what, it is so even in Maharashtra (*Interruption*).

SHRI VAJPAYEE : Don't fight over words. Sir, you'll have to give me time. I do not like interruptions. The Prime Minister has said something very serious. If it is her charge that the previous government....

SMT. INDIRA GANDHI : I am not at all levelling any charge (*Interruption*).

SHRI VAJPAYEE : Sir, these people do not want me to speak, and they are even interrupting the Prime Minister.

Sir, when we talk of a navy we must see what our concept is—do we not want a blue water navy or do we want a navy that will protect our coast and safeguard our coastal commerce. The Indian Ocean is going to become an arena for big powers. We are making international efforts to make it an ocean of peace. We should speed up those efforts. At the same time we should realise the situation. We should think of how we can prevent this region from becoming an arena for big powers. If we express concern over Afghanistan and criticise the Government's policy the basis of this concern is the feeling that if a big power indulges in expansionism in this region other big powers will get the opportunity to exploit the situation. We have to keep this sub-continent free from the influence of big powers. So an accord between the foreign policy and the defence policy is necessary. We must also see if the work the defence services are doing in research and development is on the right lines.

Sir, my time is limited.

SPEAKER : Your time was very much limited, but 15-20 minutes have already passed.

SHRI VAJPAYEE : I would have finished by now had there been no interruptions.

Sir, I have here the copy of a newspaper published from Delhi. Some expert had made a writ petition to the Delhi High Court. The paper says :

> "He listed many instances of corruption in the Directorate of Aeronautics. The Court however ruled that it was not competent to go into the charges and neither did it have the required expertise."

The Court verdict is all right. But it is most unfortunate if scientists working in defence and research feel that they are being prevented from doing research. We have not yet been able to produce an anti-tank missile. Why we have not been able to do so has been discussed since 1960. In the meanwhile it was claimed the missile was ready, but later it came to be known that it was not. We want to buy fighter planes and are discussing which ones to buy. But why have we not been able to produce them indigenously ? Is it possible that the research and development wings are not working properly ? Are our young scientists dis-appointed ? Are there officers who want to buy equipment from abroad because large-scale purchase of defence equipments serves their vested interests ? All these things should be inquired into. We now propose to purchase tanks. When we produced the Vijyanta tank it was greatly praised. How far have we progressed in it ? If we have not progressed, why not ? This House will never hold its hand back in spending on the armed forces, but the strength of the armed forces is not in numbers, it is in their effectiveness. This effectiveness must increase—on land, in the air, and on the sea. At the same time we should also give thought to where the danger lies and how it can be met.

Need for a Full-Time Defence Minister

Sir, one more thing and I shall conclude. I am sorry to see that the discussion is going on and the Prime Minister is present in the House because she has to be present. Had we a Defence Minister she could have used her time for some other and more important work. We have not had a Defence Minister for the past six months. I cannot accept that the Congress-I has no member who is fit to become Defence Minister. But we have no full-time Defence Minister so far.

I had made a mistake—I will explain it as Shri Narasimha Rao is present here. I had gone to Udaipur to address an election meeting. I had raised this point there. I had said if the Prime Minister so wished she could have made Shri Sukhadia the Defence Minister. Some news agency reported that Vajpayee said Narasimha Rao should be removed and Sukhadia appointed Foreign Minister. I refuted it but nobody published the refutation. The Foreign Minister will certainly be annoyed with me, but I do feel we should have a full-time Defence Minister. The Prime Minister may supervise ....(*Interruption*) .... She is supervising all ministries. But this is not a part-time job. The country's defence problems cannot be solved on a part-time basis. Thank you.

Credibility Gap in Defence Matters

Sir, we are discussing the country's security. We are going to spend about Rs. 4,000 crores on defence, but the Lok Sabha discussion has been allotted only six hours, and my share of it is only nine minutes (*Interruption*). No one can do justice to an important subject like defence in 9 minutes.

Security is a national matter. We have to see that our independence endures. Our borders must remain impregnable. We have to bring about circumstances in which we would be able to develop without impediment the life-style we want. The main responsibility for this is on the defence services. I have no hesitation in saying that these services have come up to our expectations. The entire country is proud of their valour. The whole House supports them in this.

The Prime Minister has always been vigilant about external danger since she shouldered this responsibility. But it seems there is a credibility gap. This is dangerous. If we do not see eye to eye on the dangers that face the nation how can we agree on the means to overcome them ?

It is necessary to keep the defence services away from politics. In a democracy governments will change. The loyalty of the defence services should be to the country, not to some individual or party. In this connection I would like to mention two events.

The Prime Minister had visited the Mazagaon Docks in Bombay to make a speech on some occasion. This dockyard is managed by the Navy. The Governor of Maharashtra had also been invited to participate in the function. The Chief Minister was also invited. It is natural that the Governor and Chief Minister should accompany the Prime Minister wherever she went. But later the officers of the dockyard were told to withdraw the invitation to the Governor. Why ? Was it because he had been appointed by the Janata Party ? (*Interruption*).

SMT. INDIRA GANDHI : The Chief Minister did not belong to the Janata Party.

SHRI VAJPAYEE : Yes. I am coming to that too.

Then the officers at the dockyard said it would not be possible for us to withdraw the Governor's invitation, so we won't invite the Chief Minister as well.

SMT. INDIRA GANDHI : May I interrupt here ? I will explain. There is some misunderstanding here ....

SHRI VAJPAYEE : Misunderstanding on whose part ?

Lok Sabha on April 8, 1981 during discussion on the demands for grants of the Ministry of Defence

SMT. INDIRA GANDHI : On our part. When I was initially invited I said time was short and if it was a very formal function perhaps it would not be possible. So it was decided that I would attend it without a lot of noise and ceremony. Later they said we have invited everybody, and I said this was why I was not willing. But had I been told the Governor and the Chief Minister had been already invited I would have said it was all right. But this was not brought to my notice, and as I had said I could not attend a big function it was cut down. I thought otherwise the arrangements would become more elaborate—not because of the Governor. I had suggested a sort of departmental affair.

AN HON. MEMBER : Now take back your allegation (*Interruption*).

SHRI VAJPAYEE : The Prime Minister has explained, so I will leave it. But it would have been better if such an incident had not occurred.

SMT. INDIRA GANDHI : I agree.

SHRI VAJPAYEE : The other thing is rather delicate.

Shri Sanjay Gandhi is no more with us. Our differences with him ended the very day an accident removed him from our midst. But one thing I did not like. Why were the Chiefs of the three services present at this funeral in full uniform and wearing medals ? .... (*Interruption*) ....

DEPUTY SPEAKER : Please sit down.

SHRI VAJPAYEE : Sir, if there are interruptions .... (*Interruption*) ....

DEPUTY SPEAKER : They are sensitive about it. It is their feeling. You do not worry if they say anything .... (*Interruption*) ....

SHRI VAJPAYEE : What is this going on ? (*Interruption*).

DEPUTY SPEAKER : I have requested him.

AN HON. MEMBER : We did not expect a man like you to say such a thing .... (*Interruption*) ....

DEPUTY SPEAKER : That is all right. Please sit down. (*Interruption*).

SHRI VAJPAYEE : No one among these people say it was wrong to go and they should not have gone .... (*Interruption*).

DEPUTY SPEAKER : Order please, order.

SHRI VAJPAYEE : If it is not wrong I shall have my say in the House .... (*Interruption*) ....

Why this interruption ? If you cannot understand my feeling it is unfortunate for you as well as for me .... (*Interruption*) .... Sir, this time will not be added .... (*Interruption*) ....

DEPUTY SPEAKER : I have told him.

SHRI VAJPAYEE : They are speaking of humanity. Many of you would equal the tribute that I paid to Sanjay Gandhi on his death. But what is wrong will be said. You cannot prevent me from saying it (*Interruption*).

SHRI SATISH AGRAWAL (Jaipur) : What is this ? How can the House be conducted if you do not allow him to speak ?

SHRI SHIVRAJ PATIL, Minister of State in the Ministry of Defence : We are discussing a very serious matter here and we expect that whatever the side the members are on, they would say things that would strengthen our security. We are short of time and nothing much can come out of discussions on such subjects. He has said our three service chiefs were present there in uniform. But that is their working dress, they wear that dress in the office as well as outside. They attended a ceremony for tributes to a great son of India who had departed. It would not become us to use time which is short, to say things that would demean him as well as the officers of the armed forces.

Cold War at Doorstep

SHRI VAJPAYEE : It cannot be denied that the international situation is deteriorating. The cold war has reached our door-step. This is a matter of great concern for us as well as for the whole world. The process of diffusing tension that is going on in the world has received a setback. A race for lethal weapons has begun in right earnest. All efforts at disarmament have come to naught.

We want that the arms race should halt, armaments, especially nuclear arms, should be cut down and disarmament should proceed. What is happening in the neighbouring country ? But that is not the only question. Other countries of the world have also joined the nuclear club. We had rightly decided against signing the Non-proliferation Treaty. It is a discriminatory treaty. But if the race for nuclear arms continues and if more and more countries join it a democratic country like India, where the final decision rests with the people, will have to keep its options open.

Sir, in this report of 155 pages if you leave the first page and half the second page there is no realisation of the danger that we apprehend at present. How big is the danger and from what direction ? The Prime Minister had said in some speeches that danger is possible from the old sources, from which it had come in the past, as well as from new directions. There may be new alliances. We may be in danger from land, sea and the sky. But neither Parliament nor the country has been taken into confidence. Even the Prime Minister has not thought it fit to discuss the matter with opposition leaders. After all, if we have to defend the country we have to take with us not only the armed forces but all the people. It would be most unfortunate for the country if there is a crisis of confidence in this respect.

Interference and Intervention

The first page of this report says for the last some years the security atmosphere in the neighbourhood of India is getting very tense. It further says the events in Afghanistan at the end of 1979 were the culmination of a variety of events. What events in Afghanistan before the Soviet intervention justify it ? Can interference and military intervention be put on the same level ? Russia sent its army into Afghanistan. The U.S. is strengthening its military bases, entering into new military alliances and deciding to supply lethal weapons in the neighbourhood. In this situation our defence policy needs the support of our foreign policy. It does not receive it. Nobody wants a military solution in Afghanistan. No one is going to give his life for the Afghans. Brave Afghans became slaves before our very eyes. Poet Rabindra Nath's 'Kabuliwala' died before our eyes. Tagore's country did nothing. If

Soviet soldiers continue to be present in Afghanistan a vicious circle of action and reaction would set in which would pose a danger for us in future and which is posing a danger even now. The Prime Minister should explain what events had taken place that necessitated Russian intervention.

There was a suggestion that on the one hand there should be no external intervention in Afghanistan and on the other the Soviet army should leave the country. Non-aligned countries could have taken the initiative in this matter. They could have sent armed contingents to supervise the borders. I do not know why the Government of India did not push this proposal, and if it did what the Soviet reaction to it was.

Sir, the Defence Ministry has a planning committee. I do not know for how long a period it is planning. The international situation is changing fast, but we cannot take *ad hoc* decisions. Perspective planning for 10-15 years is called for. A question before us at present is how far we should increase our armed forces. We have an army. How much should we strengthen the air force ? Danger from the sea is also possible. What are our prime military requirements ? As I have been in the government only for a few days I cannot claim much experience ....(*Interruption*)....

AN HON. MEMBER : It was by mistake.

SHRI VAJPAYEE : The same people who brought you in also bought us in. But when you came it was right, when we came it was by mistake.

Need for Perspective Planning

Sir, the time has come to consider whether some organisation is needed that could undertake perspective planning and take an integrated view of the requirements of the three branches of the armed forces as well as the challenges before the country.

For instance, the answer to a tank is a tank, but those who are knowledgeable in defence matters say that the answer to a tank is an anti-tank missile. No one can say how different the things would be five years hence.

The international situation can also change. At present the Soviet Union is our friend. We hope it will remain a friend, but we must take all possibilities into account. The relationship between China and Russia is not good at present. But it can improve. No one knows how far the internal changes in China will go. We are talking of the decade. What challenge will face us in ten years' time and what options will we have to face them ? It would not be enough to keep just one door open. It is dangerous to depend too much on a super power.

I submit the Government may consider the setting up of a commission of defence to consider all these issues.

AN HON. MEMBER : There are already many commissions.

SHRI VAJPAYEE : This very morning you have announced an economic reforms commission. Talk some sense.

Secondly, the Government should publish a white paper on defence. Members of Parliament need to know many things. Security is one thing, secrecy is another. With us everything that relates to the armed forces is secret. How much money is being spent ? Is there misuse of money in the army ? We should know.

I would also like to refer to research and development. In this budget we have allocated Rs. 70 crores for it. So far we have spent crores of rupees on research and development. How far we have progressed in it should be evaluated. We have to make the country self-sufficient in military equipment. When it became necessary we decide to buy the Jaguar. If we need tanks we go to other countries. Why has the Vijayanta tank not been adequately developed ?

In 1972 we had decided to launch an 'aircraft development project' and we had hoped it would fulfil our domestic requirements—but it did not. In 1970 we had set up Bharat Dynamics Ltd., but there is no information on what it produced. We import missiles. As for silicons some official was even given a Padma Shri for it, but I am told we still import them. The Hon. Minister may kindly correct me if I am wrong. There was a question in the Rajya Sabha, Shri Patil was giving the reply. There were two replies to one question in one day.

SHRI SHIVRAJ PATIL, Minister of State in the Ministry of Defence : It was necessary to understand it. It was a scientific matter.

SHRI VAJPAYEE : That is the difficulty. All knowledge is concentrated on that side. This side is full of ignoramuses.

Joint Security of Subcontinent

We must strengthen research and development and be able to produce all the equipment we need within the country. The style of the super powers is that they give equipment but they do not give spares, and if they give spares they give them for 2-3 weeks. As a result when there is a war between India and Pakistan it ends in 2-3 weeks. Neither they nor we have the arms. This is a testing time for both Pakistan and India. The security of this subcontinent is a joint thing. The country was partitioned, but we cannot view security in pieces. It is unfortunate that neither Islamabad nor New Delhi has understood the challenge posed by the qualitative change that has taken place in the situation in this subcontinent, and consequently they both have lost a valuable opportunity. Pakistan does not need arms. Pakistan cannot fight the Soviet Union with them. 16 Pakistani divisions have not been deployed on the Afghan border, they have been deployed on the Indian border. Pakistan needs political stability and economic development. But we must admit that we are not able to take all countries of the subcontinent with us. I would like to refer here to a small incident. I hope it does not become a big incident. The President of Sri Lanka had come to India to participate in a conference relating to countries of the Commonwealth. Arrangements were made to interview him on All India Radio and TV. The interview was recorded for TV but it was not telecast.

AN HON. MEMBER : Why ?

SHRI VAJPAYEE : That is for the Information Minister or the Prime Minister to tell us.

SHRI INDRAJIT GUPTA (Basirhat) : You tell us.

SHRI VAJPAYEE : Perhaps he said something that New Delhi did not like. Is this how we should behave with the President, the leader of a neighbouring country ? There is freedom of thought in this country. We should also be prepared for criticism. How will Sri Lanka react to this ? It is a small incident, but it leads to tension. We must be extra careful in our behaviour with our neighbours. They are small in size, manpower and armed strength and even more backward than us economically. They also harbour baseless suspicions. It is our responsibility to take them along with us. It is true that we cannot sacrifice national interests to take them with us, but even while keeping national interests in view our style of functioning should not be that of belittling a neighbour and getting his support.

SHRI RAM GOPAL REDDY (Nizamabad) : Vajpayeeji, we have never done that. Why do you say so ?

An Enemy for Ever ?

SHRI VAJPAYEE : I have now come to the last point. In 1973 Shri D.P. Dhar, Deputy Chairman of the Planning Commission, wrote a letter to all Chief Ministers. I quote some lines from it :

> "We must look to the whole broad spectrum of international relationships to identify our foes and our friends. Is a policy of detente with everyone in our national interests ? It would, on the other hand, appear that for years to come the U.S.A. will remain our most powerful enemy."

I do not know if this letter was written with the Prime Minister's consent. If that was then our assessment of friends and foes, what is our assessment in 1981 ? Is it proper to consider a country our enemy on a permanent basis ? What is wrong with establishing friendship with all ? It is true that we would be greater friends with those with whom we share our interests. As a big power and a big country we cannot divorce the problem of defence from foreign policy. The Shah of Iran collected all arms, but when the people turned against him he was toppled.

In our neighborhood too arms would not save anybody.

The Prime Minister had said in a rally that one son of the kisan was a Jawan and the other son a Kisan. Clearly the Kisan and the Jawan are joint. We cannot separate defence and development. So while drawing up a long-term plan for the security of the country we cannot ignore full development of the country and reaching its benefit to the maximum number of people. We should have a national mind on it. It is for the Prime Minister to say how far she is ready for this.

Last year I had said the Prime Minister should not take charge of the Defence Ministry, but now I feel we see her at least on the demands of the Defence Ministry.

IV HOME AFFAIRS

Delhi—Victim of Neglect

Sir, I welcome Shri Shastri's appointment to the post of Home Minister. There is a Marathi saying which goes—*'Murti lahan pan kirti mahan'*, which means "little figure, big capability". We hope in accordance with the tradition of Sardar Patel and Pandit Pant Shri Shastri will capably handle the internal administration of the country.

The Home Ministry has specially to bear the responsibility of maintaining national unity and promoting national strength. At present national unity faces many dangers. I shall discuss them later. Before that I want to say something about the Union Territories—Delhi, Himachal, Tripura and Manipur. I would say that the Home Ministry has so much pressure of work that it cannot do justice to the Union Territories. They do not have state governments. Not even legislative assembles. Only Parliament represents their interests and protects them. But even Parliament is burdened with so many national and international problems that the interests of these small territories tend to be neglected. The people of Himachal Pradesh and Manipur are not completely satisfied with the present administrative structure. The late Shri Pant had given the assurance that increasing their administrative powers would be considered. But so far the Government has not presented any concrete plan. The case of Delhi is still more disappointing. The Central Government is located in Delhi. The Parliament also functions in Delhi. But Delhi's interests are ignored. There is darkness below the lamp. I suggest that there should be a separate Minister of State or Deputy Minister at the Centre to supervise the Union Territories and ensure that they are not neglected.

Delhi does not have a legislative assembly, but the Government has set up some committees to secure the people's cooperation. These committees are not discharging their duties properly. There are some advisory committees, an industrial advisory board and a public relations committee, but they have been so constituted that they do not properly represent public opinion. I do not understand. There is an elected corporation for Delhi. If we set up advisory committees all parties elected to the corporation on a large scale should be represented in those committees. If the government can set up such committees it would be better to wind up those that have been set up for show and are without public support.

Lok Sabha on March 27, 1961 during discussion on the demands for grants of the Home Ministry

I am also not able to understand why the New Delhi Municipal Committee has not been democratised. Its members are nominated by the Government. How responsibly they function was seen on the day when the Committee's budget was to be presented but there was no quorum in the meeting. Telephone calls were made, budget papers were distributed to the officers, but members were nowhere to be seen. So the meeting was adjourned. This is most shameful. The Central Government should dissolve this municipal committee.

An election of representatives for Delhi's electoral college was held when a member was to be elected to the Rajya Sabha. At that time the Home Minister was made the request that those members elected to the electoral college should be allowed to function as New Delhi's Municipal Committee. But those elected members worked in the election, then they were sent home. The New Delhi Municipal Committee continues to be manned by the Government's nominees. This is not conducive to democracy.

There is a big housing shortage in Delhi. The administration has taken over 34000 acres of land, but no houses are being built there. Neither does the Government build houses there nor allows anybody else to do so. As a result unauthorized construction is going on. This promotes corruption and the tendency to break the law. The other day a Minister declared that the Government would develop the land it had acquired and then auction it. If there is an auction of land those who have no houses and those who have fixed monthly salary would not be able to get it with high bids. The government should not acquire land, develop it with the people's money and then auction it on high bids. Rather it should build cheap houses and give them to the lower and middle classes so that their difficulty could be resolved.

There are at present 39,000 Central government employees in Delhi who have no accommodation. Some houses have been acquired on Minto Road. Four years ago it was said they are not habitable, but now it is said they are. I cannot understand the policy of the Ministry.

Congestion Growing in Delhi

It had been decided that no new office was to be opened in Delhi, that congestion would be reduced and offices that need not be located in Delhi would be sent out. But no final decision has been taken in this respect, and in the meanwhile congestion is increasing in Delhi. Along with congestion problems of peace and law and order are also increasing. In this respect the Home Ministry's administration in Delhi is less than satisfactory.

The number of policemen is increasing, but the number of crimes is also increasing. There is equal progress in both directions. There is no progress so far in the scientific investigation of crimes. The Home Minister should reply to this—for the last two years bomb explosion incidents have been continuously taking place in the capital of India, but no one has been caught and no one punished. There seems to be a well planned conspiracy behind these explosions. They occur when the Prime Minister goes to attend a conference of the British Commonwealth. They also took palce when the Queen of England came on a visit to India. It seems some elements in the capital are actively trying to bring India down in the esteem of the world and tarnish its image. If the inelligence department cannot track down those causing the explosions what is it for ? But sometimes I suspect that the Government does find out but it does not tell. Perhaps it does so because it is not in 'public interest'. This is the standard reply that is always given. But actually it may be that the coming into light of such facts is not in the interest of the ruling party. Such a policy cannot overcome the danger created to the country's internal security.

Glut of Foreign Agents

At present there is a large number of active foreign agents in India—not only agents of Russia and China but also of Pakistan. The Prime Minister has now admitted that some of our employees have been arrested for passing on to other countries some secrets of the Foreign Ministry, Defence Ministry and the Planning Commission. What steps is the Home Ministry taking to prevent a repetition of such incidents ? I have some suggestions in this respect. Can we not make a rule by which foreign legations will be required to consult the Government of India while recruiting Indian personnel ? Today they appoint anybody. They can get material printed in any press they want. High payments are made for small jobs. They can issue big advertisements. Can they not get printing jobs done in the Government's press ? Can their advertisements not be issued through the Ministry of Information and Broadcasting ? We must admit that so far we have not created a situation in the country in which every citizen born in this country would be a patriot and cannot be bought at any price. That day is still far off. So we must keep an eye on fifth columnists. At the same time we have also to keep an eye on the friends and relatives of Foreign and Defence Ministry employees who have to know confidential matters.

Justice has also not yet been done to the employees of the Central Home Ministry. Some members said more than 700 employees have not yet been reinstated. And there is talk of bringing a Bill that would take away the right to strike. I call upon the Home Minister to reconsider this Bill. The right to strike is a democratic right and linked with the right to work. If you accept the right to work you have also to accept the right to strike work. Actually we should create circumstances in which it will not be necessary to go on strike.

It was announced that Whitley Councils would be set up, but no outline has so far been presented. There is no negotiating machinery to consider complaints and demands of central employees. Such a situation gives strength to those who want to take undue advantage of the employees' demands for political ends. We hope the setting up of Whitley Councils would be announced soon and Central employees taken into confidence before giving them the final form.

Communalism Again Gaining Strength

So far as the question of fissiparous forces raising their heads is concerned it cannot be denied that gradually we are again being drawn into that atmosphere which we had conquered to open up the way to economic and social reconstruction of the nation. But as I had said in a debate it would not be enough just to condemn communalism. What we must think of is—have we taken any constructive steps to put an end, after independence, to the two-nation theory that led to the partition of the country ? Have we tried that all sects should lead the same social life and celebrate common festivals ? Communalism cannot be removed if we apply double standards for its eradication.

A lady member of the Congress has just complained that no judicial inquiry has as yet been made of the disturbances in Assam. The Home Minister and the Home Ministry should reply to this. The Jabalpur incident is being inquired into, and that is as it should be. But what is the reason for not inquiring into the disturbances in Assam. Covering up the facts is not the way to fight communalism. And how long are we going to let this business of majority and minority to go on ? National unity will never be created so long as we keep alive this feeling of majority-minority in the political field. Even among Hindus there are many modes of worship. There are Arya Samajists, Jains, Sikhs, Shaktas, Shaivas and Sanatanists. Are they not minorities on today's standards ? In Punjab some people are complaining that Hindus are a minority in Jalandhar district and their interests are not being protected.

I met a certain big leader. When I placed before him the difficulties of the Hindus of Punjab he said—don't worry, all your problems would be over once Punjabi Suba is formed. I said I don't understand, and he replied in Punjabi Suba Hindus will be in a minority and then the Government would take care of them. They will not be cared for so long as they are in a majority.

What Is a Religious Minority ?

After all what is the meaning of a religious minority ? I can understand a linguistic minority. If there are Kannada-speaking people in Maharashtra and they do not have the right even to get primary education in the mother tongue the Central Government should intervene. If anybody has any difficulty in practising his religion it should be removed, but this concept of a religious minority, and that too in politics, is beyond my comprehension. If we want to keep it up we may talk all we want about national unity but actually we do not mean to bring it about.

We must forget who are the majority and who the minority. We are all the children of India. We have pledged ourselves to the establishment of a secular state. Religion is a personal matter. It has no relationship with the community. But today a feeling of separatism is being created in the name of a minority, in the name of the language of a minority. If we do not suppress this separatism in time it will undermine our body national and will never allow our efforts for national unity to succeed.

I wish the Home Ministry adopts some constructive policy in this respect. Police action is not the answer. The problem is to correct our thoughts, our hearts. We have to develop culture in the country. It would not do to blame a particular religion. Of course, if there are riots and if communal passions are incited it should be condemned. Those who do such things should be punished.

Delhi's *Al Jamiat* and *Nai Duniya* have written all sorts of things about the Jabalpur incident. Does the Home Ministry take note of such journals ? If there is no communal disturbance in Delhi the credit goes to the people of Delhi, not to the Home Ministry. Some communal Urdu papers have tried their best to spread the fire of Jabalpur to Delhi. I have their cuttings but there is no time to read them.

AN HON. MEMBER : Hindi papers have also done it.

SHRI VAJPAYEE : Not any paper of Delhi. If Hindi papers have done it they should also be criticised—and they are. The Hindi journal *Yugdharma* of Jabalpur printed a small news item and that is enough for the Communist Party to keep after it. But I ask the Communist Party—has any one ever criticised the way Muslim communal papers of Delhi and Bombay have described the riots of Jabalpur ? No one does it. There is a race on among all parties to please a certain religion. A spokesman of the Praja Socialist Party says communal parties should be banned. I support such a ban, but when you enter into an alliance with communalists in Kerala but say in Parliament that communalists should be banned the two things cannot go together. If we want to fight communalism there should not be such a gap between precept and practice. If you really do not allow communalism, whoever may indulge in it to grow, you must be ready to fight it. Otherwise it cannot be eradicated. Thank you.

Amendment in Penal Code
A Blow at Fundamental Rights

Sir, I move that this Bill should be published for eliciting public opinion till March 15, 1962.

The objectives explained in the Bill indicate that it has been presented as one of the many steps that the Government proposes to take for the eradication of communal and fissiparous tendencies in the country. In it section 156 of the Indian Penal Code has been extended to include religion, caste, language and sect. The definition has been widened and penalty of three years instead of two has been provided.

While presenting the Bill the Home Minister referred to national integration, discussed the relevant decisions of the Committee set up by the Congress party, referred to the Chief Ministers' decisions, and argued that for the sake of national integration some penal steps need to be taken along with constructive and emotional steps. Actually, taking of legal steps for national integration in the fifteenth year of independence speaks of the failure of whatever we have done for national integration during the past fifteen years. Neither the present government nor the party in power can disclaim responsibility for this failure.

PANDIT K.C. SHARMA (Hapur) : That is why this Bill has been tabled.

SHRI VAJPAYEE : In the fifteenth year of independence we propose to take steps for national integration. Are we clear about what we mean by national integration ? Is national integration merely a problem of law, the police, a penalty ? Was not the provision of the Indian Penal Code enough ? If the penalty is raised from two years to three does it mean disruptive tendencies will not raise their head ? Will our objective be achieved by just widening the *definition* ? I hope the Home Minister will place before the House cases where punishment could not be given because the definition was narrow as it did not include religion and language, and therefore fissiparous tendencies increased and national integration was endangered. He has not presented any such cases. Then what will be the benefit of extending the definition ? Could the old definition not punish anyone discriminating between man and man and producing strife in the name of religion ? Could it not penalise anyone inciting disharmony between one caste and another in the name of language ? Had such cases been brought before the House it could have appreciated the utility of this Bill, but no such cases were presented. So I submit that this amendment is not necessary.

Lok Sabha on August 30, 1961 during discussion on the Indian Penal Code Amendment Bill

Why Widen the Definition ?

In the process of widening the definition it has become less than clear. Everyone agrees that the relationship between man and man should be good, there should be communal goodwill, religion should not be exploited, and the tendency to look down upon people on the basis of caste should not be encouraged. But may I ask the Home Minister—what is the reason for deleting the explanation contained in the old Section 153A ? Under the new amendment one cannot honestly demand that conditions favourable for producing communalism should be removed. Under the new amendment he would be liable for penalty. At present there are many elements in the country that make national integration difficult, if not impossible. I would like to place before you an instance in point. In this connection a Bill has also been introduced in Parliament.

There are certain places of worship that have been forcibly taken over from the original worshippers by believers in another religion during the past one thousand or five hundred years—be it Krishna Janmasthan, Ram Janmasthan or Kashi Vishwanath temple. It is not necessary to go into those circumstances, but if we want national integration after independence is it not in the interest of national integration to demand that all such places as have been destroyed and desecrated, to whatever religion they may belong, should be restored to the original worshippers through mutual consultations and with goodwill between the two communities ? Will this not be required for communal unity and national goodwill ?

It is true that it is wrong for anyone to exploit this question for vitiating the relations between religions and it should be condemned. But if anyone honestly makes this demand—when Dr. Kailash Nath Katju was the Home Minister he had written an article demanding that all such places of worship should be restored to the original worshippers. It had also produced a reaction. If any organisation or class honestly feels so he would not be able to demand it after the explanation. This law is being made so comprehensive that a person's intention will not be tested, his objective will not be examined; he will be liable for punishment under this law.

So far as widening the definition is concerned language too has been added to religion. Language is today a matter of controversy in the country—partly it has become a controversy, partly has been made a controversy. An instance in point is the English-Hindi controversy. The Constitution of India had provided that Hindi should replace English by 1965, but this change did not take palce within the stipulated period. Now if it is demanded that Hindi should get its rightful place and should be used for official purposes and inter-state communication will it be an offence under the new amendment ? We know the language controversy in Punjab. The language problem of Assam is before us. After passing this amendment it cannot be demanded that Bangla should also have a place in Assam. It is not a question of Hindi or Bangla. If any one honestly believes English should continue till doomsday I would certainly disagree with him but I shall want him to have complete freedom to propagate his views. But your amendment on the question of language could make even an honest opinion on the language problem an offence. You may say it would not be normally applied, so long as there is no strife, so long as there is no bitterness between communities because of it, it would not be brought within the purview of the amendment. But I see that at times bitterness is created of its own accord, sometimes it is produced. But if law and order are disturbed the Indian Penal Code has a special provision for it, under which punishment can be given. If anyone takes the law in his own hands, causes injury or damage to anyone else's life or property, there is a separate penal provision for him. Does not the widening of this definition produce the suspicion that it may be misused ?

Unnecessary Amendment

Sir, it is not at all desirable to make such an unnecessary amendment six months before the elections and to equip the Government with such wide powers as can be misused. The Minister of State had referred to some conference of Chief Ministers and the decisions taken in it. According to press reports the Chief Ministers had decided that it would also be an offence to demand the secession of any part of India.

MR. SPEAKER : I think a copy of the proceedings or the decisions was placed on the Table of the House ?

SHRI LAL BAHADUR SHASTRI, Minister of Home Affairs : Yes.

MR. SPEAKER : It was placed on the Table of the House, and hon. members had copies of it. They wanted to have copies. The Hon. Prime Minister said the whole thing has appeared in the newspapers, why give copies. Copies were circulated also.

SHRI VAJPAYEE : That decision of making the demand of secession of any territory of India an offence will not be implemented for the present, it will be implemented after the general elections.

SHRI N.G. GORAY (Poona) : That is what the Chief Minister of Madras said.

SHRI VAJPAYEE : That is because he suspects that perhaps this law is being made to create difficulties in the way of opposition parties in the general elections. I think it is a very big offence to demand the secession of any part of the country. But if the implementation can be stopped with the general election in view....

SHRI TYAGI : Is that a fact ? I would like to ascertain. Have they taken a decision that this should be held over until the elections are over ?

SHRI VAJPAYEE : It may be verified from the hon. Minister. This is what appeared in the papers.

MR. SPEAKER : The Hon. Member will have this opportunity.

SHRI TYAGI : I wanted a clarification.

MR. SPEAKER : Such a kind of interruption.

SHRI TYAGI : Too serious a charge.

MR. SPEAKER : Order, order. The Hon. member Shri Vajpayee has only been saying that one of the Chief Ministers or so said that so far as making an offence the demand for making any Indian territory separated from India is concerned, that need not be given effect to until the elections are over.

SHRI TYAGI : Is that so ?

SPEAKER : Very well. Why should he not wait ? Immediately shall I go on examining one statement after another ? What is the hurry ? Will an experienced parliamentarian go on interrupting like that ? Let him go on. If it is false, if it is incorrect, it will be replied to.

SHRI VAJPAYEE : My point is, if the decisions taken by the Chief Ministers can be suspended in any particular State because of some special situation there or in view of the general election there is no reason why public opinion should not be sought on the new amendment being made in the Indian Penal Code. In the final analysis communalism, casteism or linguism cannot be eradicated with law or force. For it the narrowness that has entered people's hearts due to a variety of factors needs to be removed. We have to rouse public opinion for this. Educate the people in all the meanings these amendments may have, so that they do not knowingly or unknowingly transgress them and become liable for punishment. Let us use them for educating public opinion in respect of national integration. Just getting the opinion of the Chief Ministers does not meet the need for educating public opinion. The Home Minister has just admitted that we will have to take other constructive steps as well. For this purpose an all-party conference is being planned. I think we should have a conference only for rousing and educating public opinion. So I do not think the Government would have any difficulty in accepting any amendment. This would serve both of our objectives. People would also learn about the extension of the definition that we propose, the increased penalty we want, and of the inclusion of caste, creed, language etc. along with religion. Their hearts and minds would be prepared for those requirements without which national integration is impossible.

My amendment will also rebut the allegaton that the administration proposes to take steps that could create difficulties in the way of opposition parties in the general elections, but one cannot view this amendment apart from the amendment being made in the Representation of the People Act. We have made the definition comprehensive. Anyone who incites passions in the name of language, caste, religion etc., even if honestly, would be liable for punishment and can be jailed. If he is a people's representative he might even lose that status. Before taking any such decision the administration should bear in mind that there are still six months left for the election. The powers the government had to date were quite enough for tackling fissiparous tendencies, but it could not use them. So it is not necessary to give new powers. There are some instances that prove that the Government was guilty of misusing such powers.

I shall give an example and conclude. There was recently a Muslim conference in Delhi and the Congress, the Communist Party and the Praja Socialist Party allowed their Muslim members to participate in it. Are they Congressmen first or Muslims first ? Permission was given without worrying about whether they were Muslims first or Indians first. The conference took place. It made charges that Muslims are considered second class citizens and are discriminated against as a community in administration, education, commerce and business. Will or will not the speeches made in this conference and the resolutions passed in it promote communalism ? The Home Minister must give a clear answer on this. And, if that conference promoted communalism why was no action taken against its conveners ? Why were the provisions of the Indian Penal Code looked awry ?

Now there is talk of a Hindu conference. We do not agree with it. Bharatiya Jan sangh has decided that there should not be a Hindu conference. It is not necessary. But the Home Minister has given a veiled threat, saying the government is seriously thinking whether it should or should not permit such conferences. It is being whispered into the ears of the convenors of the conference that it was possible that the Government could prevent it and they could be jailed. It is possible that this new amendment may be brought into use against the convenors of the proposed Hindu conference. May I know if the Muslim conference did not promote communalism ? In that conference the charge was levelled that the majority government of this country discriminates against a particular religious community. A former Minister of the government gave a speech at the conference and charged his government with such discrimination. Will a conference held to rebut such a charge promote communalism ? Can the government eradicate communalism by adopting double standards for the purpose ? Can we bring about national integration by encouraging the separatism of a particular religious community ? But the votes of that community are needed, not only by the Congress but by other parties too. So the communalism of that community is being covered up and no action will be taken against the convenors of its conference. But if in reply a conference is held to refute the charges levelled in it the Government would raise the bogey of communalism and the powers now being acquired will be misused. I say communalism cannot be eradicated by law or by force of the police. For that the party running the government will have to change its attitude. This talk of majority must stop.

Bharatiya Jan Sangh is an advocate of a secular state. We advocate a state in which there will be no discrimination on religious grounds. The doors of the Jana Sangh are open to every citizen of the country. But this does not mean that if anyone makes a demand on religious grounds, if separate powers would be demanded in the name of the minorities and special concessions given, if a central Minister demands reservations for a particular religious community in the services and threatens in a speech that if this community is not appeased India would become Spain....

SHRI TYAGI : A Central Minister ?

SHRI VAJPAYEE : Yes, a Central Minister, Shri Humayun Kabir said in a conference in Hubli that if the problem of this community is not solved India would become Spain, there would be civil war in India. This is a Central Minister's speech. This is an invitation to civil war, it amounts to inciting the people, but the provisions of the Indian Penal Code will not be used for them; they are being laid down for us. The Congress Government wants to divert people's attention from its failures by raising the bogey of communalism. If it really feels this Bill is necessary it should welcome our suggestion to elicit public opinion. If it does not want to do so it can itself table a proposal to the effect that the Bill may be sent to a select committee where representatives of all parties represented in the House may sit together and give thought to extending this definition.

AN HON. MEMBER : That will take a lot of time.

SHRI VAJPAYEE : My friend says it will take a lot of time. But if the country did not fall to pieces in 15 years it will not do so in a couple of months. So I submit that this Bill be either publicised for popular opinion or referred to a select committee, and this proposal should come from the government. If both these are ignored this attempt at acquiring wide powers with the general elections in view will not be considered honest. Thank you.

Centre Sheltering Anarchist Elements

Sir, after the general elections the political map of the country has undergone a big change. Non-Congress governments are functioning in eight States. So far as the Centre is concerned the majority of the ruling party in the Lok Sabha has gone down to such an extent that it will need the support of the opposition for an amendment of the Constitution.

The Home Ministry has to do its duty by the country in this changed situation. The Home Minister or the Home Ministry must be on guard against doing anything that would adversely affect Centre-State relations, weaken national unity, and strengthen elements seeking to create anarchy in the country. Shri Y.B. Chavan is not present in the House. I would like to remind him that he is occupying Sardar Vallabhbhai Patel's seat. Sardar Patel had brought the country together by merging 500 princely states. Let not this unified India fall to pieces through some mistake of the Home Ministry.

I was sorry to learn that the Central Home Minister was sheltering elements that had a hand in smuggling with Pakistan, because of which they had to part with the ruling Akali Dal in Punjab.

Shri Chavan is a senior Congress leader. It is natural for him to keep Congress interests in view, but if, when party interests and national interests clash, the Home Minister of the country cannot rise above party interests, it would be difficult for national interests to be safe in his hands.

Twenty years after independence Punjab now has an atmosphere of brotherhood among all communities and sects. A non-Congress government has done in Punjab what the Congress Party and the Congress Government could not do in 20 years. But the Home Minister is sheltering and abetting elements that want to topple the non-Congress government but which do not deserve such encouragement.

I was also sorry to learn that the Home Minister is displeased with the non-Congress government of Haryana because its Chief Minister refused to accept the Prime Minister's mediation on the question of Chandigarh. Whether Chandigarh goes to Punjab or to Haryana or remains a Union Territory makes little difference to me. So long as Chandigarh remains in India there is no reason for anybody to worry. But if the Haryana Government does not want the Prime Minister to be a mediator should the Home Minister make it a prestige issue ? Should the Home Ministry try to topple the Haryana Government for this reason ? Now that Shri Chavan has come I would repeat myself ....

SHRI Y.B. CHAVAN : I have heard.

Lok Sabha on July 5, 1967 during discussion on the demands for grants of the Ministry of Home Affairs

SHRI VAJPAYEE : He is a senior Congress leader. It is natural for him to care for Congress interests. But now Congress interests and national interests are not the same. Sometimes there can be a clash between national interests and party interests and at such a time it is to be hoped that the Home Minister will not give preference to small party interests.

Sir, what is happening in Delhi ? Delhi is the capital of India. Delhi is a Union Territory. The people of Delhi have given the Jan Sangh a chance to serve. But impediments are being created in the way of the Delhi administration. I am not saying that the Home Ministry is directly responsible for creating those impediments, but I cannot but say that under the Delhi Administration Act law and order have remained with the Centre and the President empowered to take over all matters he chose by issuing a proclamation. The President was just given that power. But alongwith law and order the Central Government has also taken over the services. It has also taken over housing. Was this necessary ? Now the services in respect of matters which the Metropolitan Council has powers are also under Central control. No administration can go on like this.

One good thing the Home Ministry has done is to delegate its powers to the Delhi Administration. But the Delhi Administration does not have to keep in touch with the Home Ministry alone. It has to keep in touch with the Education Ministry for educational matters, with the Ministry of Transport for transport matters, with the Railway Ministry for railway matters, with the Health Ministry for health matters. Could other ministries not be persuaded to delegate their powers to the Delhi Administration as the Home Ministry had done ?

AN HON. MEMBER : Even the Railways ?

SHRI VAJPAYEE : It is not a question of the railways. My friend has been elected from Punjab. Perhaps he does not understand that if the railways are to be extended and developed in Delhi the overall control will be in the hands of the Railway Ministry, but there should be no objection to entrusting the Delhi Administration with the responsibility of making suggestions and finally implementing them.

AN. HON. MEMBER : That is already there. Who will deny the right to make suggestions ?

SHRI VAJPAYEE : Sir, how restless Congress members become when we talk of Delhi ! I can understand their anxiety. It is natural for them to feel sorry that Delhi slipped out of their hands. But if they continue like this New Delhi will also slip out of their hands.

Sir, what attitude the ruling party adopts towards national problems may be seen in States where it is in the opposition. It is easy to advise us in the opposition to behave well and see that our opposition is constructive, but Congressmen will have to act upon their own advice where they are the opposition party.

AN HON. MEMBER : They are doing that.

SHRI VAJPAYEE : No, they are not. In Delhi they are calling the Lt. Governor a Jan Sanghi. In this very Delhi Shri Vidya Charan Shukla, Minister of State in the Home Ministry, is patting such elements on the back. If the Delhi Administration removes huts near the Irwin Hospital the propaganda is made that those living in the huts were Muslims and the Jan Sangh is removing them for communal reasons. The Delhi Administration removed the huts on the directive of the Lt. Governor. The Lt. Governor talked to Shri Fakhruddin Ali Ahmed, Mir Mushtaq Ahmed and other Muslim leaders of Delhi. With their support and cooperation it was decided to remove the huts but the Minister of State telephoned high officials of the Delhi Administration asking why the huts were removed, why the displaced people were not being resettled in Shri Vijay Kumar Malhotra's constituency ?

SHRI V.C. SHUKLA : This is not at all true.

SHRI VAJPAYEE : I am prepared to prove it. The Minister of State should not descend so low. He should express regret over his behaviour. A Jan Sangh leader was also sitting with the person he telephoned. I hope nobody sitting in the Home Minister's place would make such attempts to spread communalism.

There is one more example of the Home Ministry. In 1947 a person migrated to Pakistan. He became a citizen of Pakistan. But he returned to claim the property left behind in Delhi. The Administration lodged a complaint against him with the Court. He was arrested and jailed. On November 8, 1965 the Punjab High Court declared him a Pakistani citizen. He was directed to leave for Pakistan. But the Home Ministry allowed him to stay on. The Ministry even nominated him to the Delhi Waqf Board. Can a Pakistani be nominated to the Delhi Waqf Board ? As some Congressmen of Delhi are connected with him they persuaded the Home Ministry to nominate a Pakistani to the Waqf Board. Is Shri Chavan prepared to inquire into this matter ? I am not in the habit of leveling false charges. I do not believe in saying things that cannot be substantiated. This individual is still a member of the Delhi Waqf Board, although he has been declared a Pakistani citizen by the Punjab High Court.

Sir, Comrade Dange says the Naxalbari problem is a peasant problem created by the hunger for land. I do not think this is the right description of the Naxalbari situation. The landless' hunger for land. The common man wants a change. It is natural for those who did not get a share of prosperity 20 years after independence to get restless. But it was open to the West Bengal Government to end its apathy in Naxalbari. If there is fallow land the State Government could have taken steps to distribute it. If it was not possible to hold a session of the Legislative Assembly it could have issued an ordinance for the purpose. But it did not happen. What happened if Naxalbari deserves to be condemned. This is not just a question of peace and order. Actually national unity and democracy are in danger there. If it is a matter of land reforms why demolish bridges ? If it is a question of distributing land to the landless why have people's courts ? These courts are conducting cases and giving death sentences. A man who was thus sentenced was found with his heads severed.

We are not in favour of Central intervention in West Bengal at this time. We are not in favour of promulgating President's Rule in West Bengal. At the same time we shall not tolerate attempts to cover up the situation there. The whole country must know what is happening in West Bengal.

Sir, are we right only when we agree with Congressmen ? We too have our own assessment of what step should be taken when. You may not agree with our assessment.

DR. SUSHILA NAYAR (Jhansi) : There we agree with you.

SHRI VAJPAYEE : An attck on a Congress member of Parliament was sought to be connived at by saying that the attackers may have been goondas. He lost his watch and his fountain pen. I would like to know—who were those who demonstrated against the meeting that was held in Calcutta on July 2 to express the people's sentiments against China ? Who tried to attack the meeting ? Those who had come with bombs ? That meeting was held by us, so we could not be the attackers. The attackers were shouting slogans of 'Mau Tse-tung Zindabad'. If anyone in India now raises the slogan of Mao Tse-tung Zindabad it is certainly a danger signal for the country's future. Comrade Dange was talking of the arrival of the American army. It is also said that there are some supporters of the U.S. in the country. But when Pakistan and the U.S. entered into a military alliance and the whole country expressed anger at American policy not one citizen of India was found shouting 'Johnson Zindabad' or 'Eisenhower Zindabad'. We cannot shelter such elements in our country.

We are politically at war with such elements, and we have to win this political battle, but if the Home Ministry joins the conspiracy to topple non-Congress governments its view of right and wrong will grow dim., and knowingly or unknowingly it will play into the hands of elements that want to finally change the soul and nature of India.

There can be a difference of opinion on economic and social questions. There can also be a difference of opinion on whether or not we should continue privy purses but there must be no difference on our determination to preserve the independence and sovereignty of India. We shall neither become China's lackeys nor allow the nation's honour to be auctioned in the market place of Washington.

Comrade Dange has criticised Mao Tse-tung. He is not present in the House, otherwise I would have asked him—what philosophy of life produced Mao Tse-tung ? That philosophy of life is not acceptable to us. We believe in economic equality. Exploitation must end. But should not our democracy endure ? Should not violence be given up in this country ? I am sorry to say that in their zeal to appear revolutionary some Congress members use the same language, adopt the same style that they want to oppose in the final analysis. You cannot oppose communism by becoming communists. We have heard of a worshipper of Shiv becoming Shiv himself, but we do not want to see those disclaiming communism becoming communists.

We have a certain way of working. Even if we have to end privy purses we do not have to call the princes traitors. Let us praise their contribution to national unity and forge ahead into the future. Is even Sardar Patel's contribution being set at naught ? If we call the princes traitors that tarnishes Sardar Patel's image, as he had compromised with their so-called treachery. If we call the Birlas devils because of the Birla empire the Congress government too cannot have a clean face as it sheltered those devils for 20 years. So future policies should be decided upon. They should be progressive. They should fulfil the people's sentiments. But they should not pull down any person or class. Do not put a blot on the country's history. Do not forget that there are also good points in individuals. Our way of life, our Indianness lies in forging ahead, by opposing the bad points and accepting the good points in people. This way clashes with communism, so it should not be given up in the name of revolution.

SHRI D.C. SHARMA (Gurdaspur) : Your party has joined the Communists in forming government.

SHRI VAJPAYEE : I would like to say something. If we joined the Communists, the Communists are a separate party, but the Congress has itself been infiltrated by the Communists.

Sir, one more thing. This debate has discussed releasing Sheikh Abdullah. Whether he is released or not is not that important, what is really important is whether the country wants to stand firm by the Jammu and Kashmir policy adopted so long. There is a debate going on in New Delhi, and emphasis is being laid on a review of the Jammu and Kashmir problem. It is argued that it should not remain a part of India for all subjects. We should accept a political compromise that would agree to Jammu and Kashmir's remaining a part of India for only three subjects. I want to warn against this sort of thinking—the people of the country will not tolerate turning the clock back. The tide of time will not be allowed to be turned back. The sacrifice we have made to keep Jammu and Kashmir in India will not be allowed to go waste. If you want to progress in the right direction abrogate Article 37 of the Constitution. Sheikh Abdullah can be helped if he wants to serve Jammu and Kashmir as a citizen of India, with loyalty to the Indian Constitution and as a loyal son of mother India, but so long as his thoughts do not change it would be dangerous to release him. I am sure the Home Minister is wise enough not to get into such a dangerous position. Thank you.

Double Standards in Governors' Discretionary Powers

Sir, Shri Y.B. Chavan today occupies the seat that was once occupied by Shri Vallabhbhai Patel. The Sardar saved India from breaking apart by unifying 500 princely states and his name has gone down in history as the initiator of India's unity. Sometimes I wonder how future historians would describe Shri Chavan. Today the country stands on the edge of a break-up. Attempts are being made to weaken the Centre. States were originally provinces and were formed mainly for administrative convenience, but now they are being so equipped that cannot help the country's unity. If is time for us to think deeply over the challenges to national unity and territorial integrity, to find out the causes, and treat them with intelligence.

Volatile Situation in Telangana

Sir, the situation in Andhra is extremely volatile. The Telangana problem has been allowed to become so big that it is getting out of control. Surprisingly enough some officials of the Home Ministry have been sent to solve it. This problem cannot be solved by bureaucrats. It is also not a problem of rupees-annas-and-pies now. It is necessary to create confidence in the minds of the people of Telangana. The whole of Andhra has to be enthused to work unitedly to solve our own difficulties. It is a political problem. The leadership has failed to find a political solution to a political problem.

I fail to understand why the Chief Minister of Andhra does not resign. He can send his resignation to the Congress President. Andhra today needs some shock treatment that would agitate and rouse the heart of the people and prevent the youngmen from treading the path of suicide. For this some step that would re-establish the people's confidence is called for. Those who are demanding a separate Telangana are reasoning but those who want to keep Telangana within Andhra seem to want to stick to power.

Sir, I have read in the papers today—this House and the whole country would be happy if you could use your influence and prestige and solve the problem of Andhra. The Congress leadership is on test today. Challenges will have to be met and solutions found with intelligence and firmness.

There are some other danger areas too that need attention. One is Jammu. The report of the Gajendragadkar Committee has been received, and there should be no delay in implementing its recommendations. No one can charge Dr. Gajendragadkar with communalism or narrowness. But if his

Lok Sabha on March 31, 1969 on the functioning of the Home Ministry

recommendations are shelved resentment will smoulder. If prompt steps are not taken for its removal it will assume explosive proportions. Will the officials of the Home Ministry go to Jammu only when the situation becomes explosive ? Can the Home Minister not take the Chief Ministers into confidence and take steps for resolving the difficulties created by an imbalance in economic development ? Has the Central leadership become helpless ? Has the power struggle impeded the capacity to take effective steps ? This is not the way to do justice by the country.

The Rajasthan Scenario

Sir, the opposition party in Rajasthan is agitated over the implementation of the Beri Commission's recommendations. I do not approve of anybody staging a *dharna* in the Legislative Assembly. Unfortunately, the people of my party are also participants in it. But this commission was set up by the Government. At that time an assurance was given to the High Court by the Advocate General that the commission's recommendations would be implemented. But now the Government is dragging its feet and giving a chance to the people to feel upset. Cannot the Home Minister invite the Rajasthan Chief Minister and the leaders of the opposition parties and talk this over ? Shri Chavan is not only the Home Minister, he has also another position in the national life. If he invites the Rajasthan Chief Minister and opposition leaders and try for a solution through consensus and for a diffusion of the situation, I feel the Chief Minister would listen to him and we would also be able to persuade opposition leaders to listen to reason. But today there is no one who can bring them together. There is no one to link, but there are those who would break, no one to allay passions but there are those that would incite them. It is as if leaders at the centre have been struck by paralysis. I am sorry to say this, but the truth will have to be told, however bitter it may be.

Serious thought should be given to Centre-State relations. We have a federal constitution and this is the source of many ailments. It is not unnatural if there is some tussle between the Centre and the States in a federal constitution, but it should be resolved within the parameters of the Constitution. Both the Central and State Governments should act in accordance with the Constitution. But during the past two years has the Centre obeyed the letter and the spirit of the Constitution ? Is it not true that the Centre has adopted different standards in different situations and at different times ?

Government's Double Standards

Governors' powers are currently being discussed. I remember that when the Madhya Pradesh matter arose two years ago Home Minister Shri Chavan had clearly stated that apart from three articles in the Constitution—239 (2), 200 and 356—Governors have no discretionary powers in other matters. He referred to Shri Servai, but did he act upon it ? There is recently a question in Madhya Pradesh. I want to present it in the House and I call upon the

Home Minister to clarify the position in his reply. Can a Chief Minister who has lost the confidence of the House advise the Governor to dissolve the Legislative Assembly and is the Governor bound by that advice ? My answer is—no. A Chief Minister who has lost the trust of the House does not have the power to force the Governor to do this. But I know Shri Chavan's position. When, two years ago, after remaining in minority Shri D.P. Mishra told the Governor to dissolve the Legislative Assembly, this question had also been raised in the House and the Home Minister had said—even a Chief Minister who has lost the confidence of the House and is in minority has the right to advise the Governor and the Governor will have to abide by that advice. But when Raja Naresh Chandra Singh said so the rule did not apply to him.... *(Interruption)*....

SHRI SHEO NARAIN (Basti) : He was not even an elected member of the House. He did not face the House. What does Shri Vajapyee want ?

SHRI VAJAPYEE : It is not a question of whether a person was elected or not. Even an unelected person can remain Chief Minister for 6 months *(Interruption)*....

I am raising a limited question. I am ready to admit that Raja Naresh Chandra did not have a majority, but can a Chief Minister who does not have a majority demand the dissolution of the Legislative Assembly ?

A HON. MEMBER : The Governor will decide that.

SHRI VAJPAYEE : That is what I am saying. Different Governors are acting differently. In Bihar Shri Bhola Paswan Shastri said dissolve the Assembly and it was done, but in Haryana the Governor dismissed Rao Birendra Singh's Cabinet although he had a majority. At one place a Cabinet was dismissed on the ground of defections, while in Madhya Pradesh a government was formed on the ground of defections. Let not the Home Minister say the opposition too brings about defections. We do it, and you too do it, in such a situation we are all exposed. But it is not a question of political parties, it is a question of the definition of the Constitution. The time has come to define the Governor's discretionary powers. Governor Dharma Vir refused to read some portions of the address prepared by the Cabinet. The address is given under Section 175, which is not included in the Sections in which, as the Home Minister says, the Governor has discretionary powers. Still the Home Minister has supported the Governor. And in Punjab Governor Shri Pavte read the address as prepared by the Cabinet.

SHRI Y.B. CHAVAN, Home Minister : He may have used his discretion... *(Interruption)*....

SHRI VAJPAYEE : Can the Governors separately determine their own discretion ? Is this proper ? No, there is no discretion in Section 175. I shall read again and remind the Home Minister of what he has said. I quote Shri Chavan. He has used his words very carefully. He speaks with a sense of responsibility, and he does so even when he says different things at different times. He had said :

> "The Constitution is very clear on this point. The Governor of a State is the constitutional head excepting three articles. I have referred to the

latest scholarly edition of the Constitution published by Shri Seervai, the Advocate-General of Maharashtra, and he has said that only under three articles the Governor of a State functions as an agent of the President. They are articles 239 (2), 200 and 256. Except under these three articles the Governor of a State functions as an agent of the President. They are articles 239(2), 200 and 356. Except under these three articles the Governor functions as the constitutional head."

Shri Chavan adds :

"When an advice is given by the Chief Minister to a Governor the question is whether the Governor is bound by his advice or not. My answer to that is that he is bound to accept that advice."

I wish ....

SHRI CHAVAN : Please read the last statement again.

SHRI VAJPAYEE : "When an advice is given by the Chief Minister to a Governor the question is whether the Governor is bound by his advice or not. My answer to that is that he is bound to accept that advice."

SHRI CHAVAN : I never said "defeated."

SHRI VAJPAYEE : Who was defeated ? Raja Naresh Chandra was not. The Home Minister is distorting facts.

But if anyone was defeated it was Pandit D.P. Mishra. You had spoken in connection with him.

Important Constitutional Issue

I am raising an important constitutional issue. I do not want to win a point for the party. What happened in the past may be forgotten, but for the future the provisions of the Constitution must be clear-cut and unambiguous. We cannot have one rule for Governor Dharma Vir and another rule for Governor Pavte. We cannot have one standard for Pandit D.P. Mishra and another for Raja Naresh Chandra. This is not the way to protect the limits of the Constitution. I cannot understand why the Home Minister cannot accept the proposal of setting up an Inter-State Council. The framers of the Constitution have provided for such a Council to resolve Centre-State differences or differences among the States. It would be constituted under the Constitution. Today we have different governments in different states, with different interests and different complexions. We have changed over from a one-party age to a multi-party age. Now the Centre will not only have to do justice, it will have to seem to do justice. At the same time the States will not be allowed to transgress the Constitution. If the President were to nominate an Inter-State Council it would discuss and resolve controversial matters. I would like to know what objection the Home Minister has to setting up such a council.

Central Government Employees

I would like to discuss one more question. It is related to Central employees. That day Shri V.C. Shukla, Minister of State in the Ministry of Home, had declared that arrangements were being made to reinstate all employees except for a few dozens. But I learn that cases against those reinstated have not been taken back. Now if it has been decided to take them back without action against them....(*Interruption*).... They have not yet been reinstated but orders are being given. If these orders are honestly implemented....(*Interruption*).... the situation would be that the employees will continue in office and their cases would continue in Court. I am showing practical difficulties. When you sacked some employees and instituted cases against them you had also taken substitutes for them. Now if you take back the employees the substitutes will be out of work and the employees will have to be present in court. Whenever the Government does anything it does it gracelessly. If any step is to be taken it should be taken with firmness and with a large heart. I am not ready to accept that Shri Chavan cannot have a large heart if he wants to. I would like the cases against the employees to be taken back. Most of them deal with breaking Section 144. It is also said that Section 144 was infringed within the office. I was recently in Trivandrum where the employees of Kerala met me. They have not yet been taken back. New difficulties are being created for employees working in the Auditor-General's Office. It is not possible that the Home Minister is not aware of the situation in the Gol. Dakkhana here. So if you have taken one decision, take one sep forward and take the decision to take back all employees. If anybody has committed a serious offence there can be departmental action against him, but it is necessary to free the employees from the police and court cases. The spirit in which the steps are being taken calls also for a decision to take back the cases. I am not talking of cases where violence has been proved, but in the case of those who have been involved in court cases for breaking Section 144, in Clause 5 of the Ordinance serious thought should be given to take them back.

Communal Riots

One final thing. Communal riots are taking place n the country. Whenever they take place my party's name is linked to them. We had demanded an inquiry into the riot at Ranchi. The inquiry was made and the inquiry commission's report has also been presented. The commission headed by Justice Raghubar Dayal has stated that the riot was not planned by the Bharatiya Jan Sangh. The Government had received this report even before the mid-term elections, but it was suppressed, it was not allowed to be publicised. Now that the report has been received I would like to draw the Home Minister's attention to those who are objecting to it. An Hon. member of this House made a speech saying that the report of the Raghubar Dayal Commission is a partisan report, a bureaucratic report. It is partisan because it has absolved the Jan Sangh, but it would have been right if it had cast aspersons on us.

I call upon the Hon. Minister to state his position clearly on matters agitating the people's mind. Further, everyone will agree that we should have a secular state. It should have no scope for discrimination on grounds of religion, language or province. But does communalism mean severing our links with our traditions ? Does communalism mean we should turn our back on our culture ?

Are Hindu Customs Anti-secular ?

Prime Minister Smt. Indira Gandhi went to launch a ship built in India. She performed the ceremony by breaking a coconut. Communal papers objected to this by saying a coconut cannot be broken in a secular state. It is a Hindu custom, so breaking a coconut should be stopped.

Our revered President attended Sardar Vallabhbhai Patel's anniversary. He garlanded Sardar Patel's picture and stood before it with folded hands. Some newspapers wrote a Muslim President should not garland a picture and fold his hands before it, as these are Hindu customs. I say this is not the custom of any particular mode of workship. It is a part of the culture that has grown out of the soil of this country and we cannot break with it. These are some questions on which the political parties, the Home Minister and the Prime Minister should make their position clear.

Untouchability

I now refer to a big event. Dr. Karan Singh was on a visit to Patna, and I congratulate him on the speech he made there. But I was grieved to see him say that untouchability is a part of the Hindu religion. We are not prepared to accept that. Untouchability is a sin, a blot, a blemish. We shall not be able to hold our head high in the world so long as this blot is not washed off. I do not believe Hindu shastras support untouchability. Any definition of the shastras that says so is wrong. I shall go a still further and say if God comes down and asks us to accept untouchability I am not prepared to accept such a God. But I know God cannot say so, and his devotees too should not say so.

Sir, we had set up a committee under Shri Elia Perimal to go into the condition of Harijans and tribals (*Interruption*).

SHRI B. SHANKARANAND (Chikodi) : Only Hinduism recognises untouchability and no other religion in the world does it.

MR. SPEAKER : It is a good point that he is making. Do not spoil it.

SHRI VAJPAYEE : The Government of India had set up a Committee to go into the condition of Scheduled Castes and Scheduled Tribes. Shri Elia Perimal was its Chairman. Its report was presented to the President on January 26, Republic Day. But it has still not seen the light of day. Why is it not tabled on the floor of the House ? Why is it not shown to us ? If the Government is considering it that can be done also after publishing it. We will certainly have to think about the condition of Harijans and tribals. The question of integration is not only the question of bringing Hindus and Muslims together. It is also a question of bringing North and South together. The question of giving an important place to Harijans and Tribals in the nation's life is also a question of integration. The National Integration Council should hold a special meeting to consider the condition of Harijans and tribals. We would have to assure this class of society by our example that we are prepared to treat them as our equals. If necessary, we shall fight blind superstition for this. If necessary, we shall smash old customs for this.

This is an age of logic, an age of science. Even while preserving spirituality we will have to break down the barriers between man and man. We need a national campaign for this and the Home Minister should launch it. But he cleverly keeps saying only a few words, and hesitates when the country hopes for an initative by him. He should give up this hesitation and discharge his responsibility towards the nation. Where national problems are concerned, all parties will extend support. At least we assure our support.

Bhiwandi Riots

Now Hindus will not Take a Beating

Sir, with your permission I stand to initiate a discussion on the situation created in various parts of the country by communal disturbances. Today I would like to do some plain-speaking. This is not the time for goody goody things. The situation is serious. The nation's unity is at stake. The nation's boat is heaving on the high seas of communalism. The waters are rising up to our heads. The need of the hour is some serious thinking and plain speaking.

Sir, it is a matter of coincidence that Bhiwandi is in Maharashtra. It is also a matter of coincidence that there is an 'Indicate' Government in office in Maharashtra. But these coincidences have no direct relationship with the disturbances there. There can be a Bhiwandi in any State of India and a communal conflagration can spread under any Government. In Bihar there was a communal disturbance in Chaibasa, but there is an Indicate Government there. There were nearly 70 communal riots in that State even under President's Rule. In Bengal there were nearly 25 communal disturbances when a joint front was in power. Sparks of communalism were lighted in Calcutta, Howrah, Telanipara, Jagatdal, and there was loss of life and property. The other day in April, a procession of small children in Chamrajnagar in Mysore was attacked by 300 goondas in an organised manner. Before this riots have occurred in Chikmagalur, Ramnagar, Chennapathan. Currently there is a Syndicate Government in Mysore. I repeat that communal riots can take place anywhere, any time and under any government. So sacrificing the Gujarat government if there is a riot in Ahmedabad, taking the Indicate Government of Maharashtra to task if there is a riot there may be necessary to some extent, but it does not solve the problem.

The Government of Gujarat made mistakes and we pointed our finger at it. We shall also refer in the House to the mistakes of the Government of Maharashtra. But all I want to say is that communal riots are not a party matter. In the conditions prevailing in the country today a disturbance may occur at any place. The people are in such a state of mind that anywhere they may resort to violence and arson and break law and order. We will have to take down partisan blinkers to look at these riots. I wish Comrade Dange does so, and I am happy he has done it. We have to rise above party interests. We have to forget votes and care for the nation.

Lok Sabha on May 14, 1970 while initiating discussion on the situation created by communal tension in the country

The Question of Communalism

After the riots in Ahmedabad it was demanded that the Gujarat government must resign. I do not include my united socialist friends among those who made the demand. Whom I mean should be clear. They are not demanding the Maharashtra Government's resignation. Was what flowed in Ahmedabad was blood and what flowed in Bhiwandi water ? Will there be different standards for measuring communalism ? Were they not Indians who died in Ahmedabad, Bhiwandi and Jalgaon ? Can we not rise above partisan interests even on this question of national importance ? Can we not act with the nation's unity in view ? This discussion will show what attitude this House, the parties represented in it, and their spokesmen adopt towards this important problem. We must face the truth. However harsh and terrible it may be, we will have to reveal it. No whitewash will do. Nobody's sin may be covered up.

The first question is, who starts these riots...(*Interruption*) ....The second question is, why are they started. The third is, why do they spread ? And the fourth question is, what short term and long term steps need to be taken to prevent them ? About who starts them I do not want to say anything, but I have the report prepared by the Home Ministry. With your permission I could place it on the floor of the House. The National Integration Council has set up a subcommittee to consider the problem of communalism. Shri Nath Pai was a member of it. The Government of India had prepared a report for it in which major riots in the country during the past year and a half had been recounted and their reasons discussed. 23 riots took place during this period and according to the Home Ministry's report 22 of them were started by members of what is called the minority community. This report has not yet been published, but it should be.

These 23 riots include riots in Calcutta, Nagpur, Aurangabad, Cuttack as well as some other parts of the country. I take it that the report of the Home Ministry is based upon reports received from the State governments. But the reports of the State Governments should be based upon facts, and the facts proclaim loudly enough that these riots were started by some of our Muslim friends.

Who Wants Riots ?

When I say some Muslim friends I am setting apart other Muslims. Not all Muslims want communal riots. There are also patriots and peace-loving people among Muslims. Those who toil and take care of their families do not want to play with fire and violence. But there is certainly a section of Muslims—and this needs to be said without mincing words—that wants to bring communalism into the country. Let us not make the mistake of covering up facts. There is certainly a class that kindles the fire of riots. This is not my personal opinion, this is what the report says.

After this report was ready there was a riot in Indore on June 2, when master Chandgi Ram's procession of 300 people was sought to be stopped in a Muslim mohalla. This is also the Home Ministry's report. Then there was a riot in Jagatdal, where processions of Durga and Mahavir were stoned from a mosque. Later there was a riot in Choubasa, where a Ram Naomi procession was attacked with bombs.

Now I come to Bhiwandi. Bhiwandi is 35 miles away from Bombay. It has a Muslim majority. For many years one of our Muslim brethren has been the Chairman of the municipality there. There is nothing objectionable in it. There is frequently some tension in Bhiwandi on occasions like Ganesh festival and Shivaji Jayanti. Since the last couple of years, when Congress leaders of Maharashtra decided to participate in Shivaji Jayanti function with great enthusiasm our Muslim brethren of Bhiwandi also changed their attitude. Perhaps they thought Shivaji is a national hero, we should also participate in his Jayanti. The people of Bhiwandi welcomed this. But this time a few days before the function 30, 35, 37 leading Muslims of Bhiwandi tried to put some conditions on the procession.

Why ? Where they the people who were to decide if the Shivaji Jayanti procession should be taken out or not ? Were they the people to decide the route of the procession ? Were they to decide what slogans were to be raised ?

The Conditions of Bhiwandi

I am surprised—and also sorry—to see that Home Minister Shri Chavan—he is not present in the House, he is on sick bed— stated in the Rajya Sabha that those conditions were proper. He should not have said so. Could any self-respecting society accept these conditions ? And what were those conditions ? One was that the procession would not carry a saffron flag. Was not the saffron flag the flag of Shivaji Maharaj ? Was there no flag in this country before the tricolor ? Can we think of Gandhiji without the tricolor ? Pandit Jawaharlal Nehru's picture in the Central Hall has the tricolour in the background. If we cannot think of Gandhiji without the tricolour we can also not think of Shivaji Maharaj without the *Bhagwa*.

And why are Muslims against the *Bhagwa* ? Does Islam say saffron is a bad colour ? Does the Quran say the saffron colour should be opposed ? Had the Constituent Assembly decided after independence that the *Bhagwa* should be India's flag would the Muslims have revolted ? Still the condition was put in Bhiwandi that there should be no *Bhagwa* flag in the procession. And Shri Chavan, who claims to have inherited the heritage of Shivaji Maharaj, says the conditions were right. Sahyadri had come to the defence of the Himalayas, but how low it has fallen ! The demand to separate Shivaji Maharaja's flag from the Shivaji Jayanti procession can never be accepted. And I am happy that the Marathis of Bhiwandi—small as they are in number—declined to accept this condition.

The second condition was that *Gulal* must not be sprinkled. Why ? *Gulal* is the symbol of love. We sprinkle *Gulal* when we are happy. *Gulal* has no connection with a religion. When I was in Ahmedabad there was a procession of one lakh people and they coloured me all red with *Gulal*. It was a political procession. Should anyone object if a little *Gulal* was used in a Shivaji Jayanti procession ?

Another condition was—we shall decide the route of the procession. A meeting of the two parties was called, which the municipal Chairman did not attend. Those prominent Muslims who had put out a statement also did not come for the meeting. However, later it was said we are taking back our conditions. Now I feel this taking back of the conditions was a drama, a fraud which was meant to put the Hindus off their guard and confuse the Government of Maharashtra. And this purpose was served.

What were the Slogans ?

Now it is said that there was a disturbance in the procession because some people raised unauthorised slogans. What were those unauthorized slogans ? How many people raised them ? According to newspaper reports they were a handful. In a procession of 10-15 thousand people there could be some people who raised slogans that were apart from the slogans decided upon. I can also understand resentment about them. The few Muslims who participated in the procession could have left it. If they very much resented the slogans they could have expressed their resentment by holding a peaceful strike in Bhiwandi the next day. They could have approached the Maharashtra Government and demanded action against people raising such slogans. But they used the slogans as an excuse to attack the procession. When the procession went into the narrow street of the fish market.... (*Interruption*)....

SHRI SITA RAM KESRI (Kastikhar) : What were those slogans ?

SHRI VAJPAYEE : I do not know. The Government should find out. I would like to know what they were. But an attack on a procession cannot be allowed simply because wrong slogans were raised. In Ahmedabad too wrong slogans were raised—*"Jo Islam se takarayega woh choor choor ho jayega"*, but no one attacked that procession. No one can be allowed be take the law in his hands.

But the procession was attacked and fires were started in many places in the city of Bhiwandi. The attack and the arson took place at the same time... (*Interruption*)... Ismail Sahib asks, who started the fires ? I would like to tell him that they were started in Hindu localities. I can give their names, but that is not necessary. It is clear that the attack on the procession was pre-planned and things had been collected. The plan was to burn down the mohalla when the people went to participate in the procession.

Bhiwandi Plunged in Darkness

There are other proofs of the advance plan. The rioters cut off the water connection, plunged Bhiwandi into darkness by cutting the power connection, and cut off telephone communication. Fire brigade engines that went to put out the fire were attacked with stones and bombs. When a fire engine came from Kalyan its driver was struck in the chest with a spear and it could not reach Bhiwandi. Can all these things be done without planning ?

The weapons that were seized—they can be seen at the Bhiwandi police station—included newly-made spacers and molotov cocktails which could set the whole city on fire.

Our friends in the Congress have not escaped damage. Bhiwandi is a big centre of handlooms and powerlooms. The factories belonging to Congressmen have been reduced to ashes. One Dr. Acharya had a 12-bed hospital and 88 per cent of his patients were Muslims. That hospital too was reduced to ashes.

The question is, what did the Government of Maharashtra do about it ? Bhiwandi is 35 miles away from Bombay. Did the Government of Maharashtra not know that there was tension in the town, some prominent citizens had put conditions on the Shivaji Jayanti procession, and that people had become agitated because of them ? Could the government not have jailed those 35 or 37 citizens ? Could it not have made arrangements for the procession ? Home Minister Shri Chavan says 700 policemen were on duty there. Do you know they had no rifles ? When policemen were later sent from Bombay they too were not given rifles. And yet they were ordered to open fire. Bullets made of what could they fire ? The Government of Maharashtra will have to say why they were not given rifles. Firing was ordered, but there were no guns to fire.

Minister Asleep

The Chief Minister Shri Vasantrao Naik himself took 24 hours to reach Bhiwandi. On the seventh opposition leaders tried to contact the Chief Minister on the phone but they could not succeed. Then a phone call was made to Shri Kalyanrao Patil, Minister of State in the Home Department. The reply was that the Minister was asleep. Bhiwandi was burning but the Minister of Maharashtra was literally sleeping. Is this how communalism will be eradicated ?

I want to know why the army was not sent into Bhiwandi. If it could be sent to Jalgaon, why not to Bhiwandi ? If it had been sent, and if the homes reportedly storing arms had been searched, we would not have witnessed the terrible scene we saw in Bhiwandi. But the Government of Maharashtra was apathetic, it failed to do its duty, it took things causally, it is guilty of fatal apathy.

Along with Bhiwandi there was a riot in Jalgaon. It is said there was a gambling den in a Muslim mohalla, and it all started from there. In Pahar there was a riot because a saffron flag on a temple was removed. Those who removed it were goondas. It is not necessary to say to what community they belonged. The police were present and the flag was removed in their presence. After this there was trouble in Goregaon too. On the 5th a truck laden with people came there. They threatened and terrorized the people and said there would be a riot on Shivaji Jayanti day. The police took no action against them too.

The riots of Bhiwandi were preplanned. One more proof of this is available in the daily *Loksatta*. It is a Marathi newspaper and not a paper of our party.

On May 11 its Bhiwandi correspondent filed a report according to which a shopkeeper told him—the letter is in Marathi, I am paraphrasing it in Hindi—he has a rationing shop in a certain Mohalla. He said one day before the disturbance, on May 6, members of a certain religion lifted rations in large quantities from his shop—enough for 8 days. So he suspected there would be some trouble on the 7th. Clearly those who lifted the rations knew something was going to happen on the 7th.

Home Minister's Tears

Our newspapers have also reported what arrangements the Government made after the riots started. Shri Chavan went to Bhiwandi. That was right. I praise him for that. But I did not appreciate the fact that Shri Chavan began to weep when there was a riot in Maharashtra but there were no tears in his eyes when there was a riot in Ahmedabad. I understand his sorrow. But the Home Minister of India should express his reaction as a national leader, not as a leader of Maharashtra. We went to Bhiwandi and was addressing a meeting when a man came running and said—run, run, 17-18 people are coming to kill me with spears, they have set fire to my restaurant. A restaurant was torched in broad daylight just 20 feet away where Shri Chavan was speaking. It is true Shri Chavan rushed, the police also rushed with him, but by then the restaurant had been reduced to ashes.

Sir, there is one more incident. The disturbance started on Friday night. Goondas collected. They had bombs and molotov cocktails. When the people telephoned the police, five policemen arrived, but when they saw 200 goondas had collected they took to their heels. People saw them running away, and when they were stopped the policemen said—we too have lives to lose, can we fight with sticks, we should have guns and there should be bullets in the guns. I doubt if the Maharashtra Government really wants to stop these communal riots from spreading.

Now the question is, why are these riots started ? I agree our Muslim brethren lose more in the riots. There is greater loss of life and property among them. But it does not become the Home Minister to say so in the Rajya Sabha. Had he not said so I would not have referred to it. The Home Minister said Muslims of Bhiwandi have suffered the most. Children and women have died. Have only Muslims died ? I say his statement is beyond the truth. On the night of the 7th more Hindus died. And even supposing the statement is true, shall he now start giving community-wise figures of those who died ? Newspapers are not permitted to report how many Hindus died and how many Muslims. But the Home Minister lost his balance and made a statement that has evoked an intense reaction in Maharashtra. It has created a wave of resentment all over Maharashtra. Hindus are unhappy because he made a wrong statement, and the Muslims are unhappy because they suffered heavily. He should not have made such a statement.

Three Reasons of Riots

But the question is, why are riots started ? I call upon the House to think about this. I have not yet reached any conclusion. Some Muslims start the riot—knowing that they may lose life and property. There could be three reasons of why they start riots—one reason may be that our Muslim brethren have concluded that now there is no place for them in India, no guardian for them, so it is better to die fighting than to live. This may be one reason.

Another reason may be that some Muslims are connected with Pakistan and indulge in rioting at Pakistan's behest. Pakistan wants to tarnish our image. Hindus are being driven out of Pakistan. If atrocities are committed on Muslims in India Pakistan would get the opportunity of making propaganda against India.

The third and most important reason seems to be that some Muslim leaders do not want Muslims to merge with the national mainstream. They do not want Muslims to join different political parties on the basis of ideology. They do not want Muslims to become Communists or Congressmen or Jan Sanghis. They want Muslims to remain aloof and under the leadership of fundamentalist Maulavis. So they are ready even to fling people into fire to establish their leadership.... (*Interruption*)...... Yes, the Muslim League had done this. That history is being repeated. We will have to think about these reasons .... (*Interruption*).... Sir, the issue is not whether Muslims riot or not. This is the Home Ministry's report. Figures speak for themselves. They are burning figures. You cannot connive at the truth. We will have to think about these reasons.

A Riot : Action and Reaction

There is one more question. It is argued—even if Muslims start riots—suppose the Jagannath temple in Ahmedabad was attacked—why did people take revenge ? Suppose the Ram Naomi procession in Chaubasa was attacked with bombs, why did the Hindus get angry ? Suppose a couple of Muslims create a disturbance, why are the innocent made to pay for it ? I agree the innocent should not be punished. I agree the feeling of revenge is not good. We cannot allow any individual to take the law in his hands. But will this rule apply only to Hindus ? Will it not apply to Muslims ? Is throwing a bomb on a Ram Naomi procession a personal quarrel ? Is attacking a Shivaji procession a personal quarrel ? And along with these clashes fires were set at various places. We must understand two things. Whatever the reason, our Muslim brethren are getting more and more communal, and as a reaction Hindus are getting more and more aggressive. Nobody made the Hindus aggressive .... (*Interruption*).... If you want to give the credit for this to us we are willing to take it. But Sir, Hindus will no more take a beating in this country. The tradition of taking a beating went on for 700-800 years. Hindus will not start. Hindus will not initiate. Hindus will not kindle the fire with their own hands....(*Interruption*).... Yes, I am speaking as an Indian. Sir, that is why I said in the beginning that my submission to those who want to fight communalism is that you cannot fight communalism by ignoring Muslim communalism. If you promote Muslim communalism the other feeling will run high. Communalism is like a double-edged sword, it acts both ways....(*Interruption*)....

DR. MAITREE BASU (Darjeeling) : Thank God I am not a Hindu.

SHRI VAJPAYEE : Had you been a Hindu it would have been a matter of shame for the Hindu Society.... (*Interruption*)....

SHRI RANDHIR SINGH (Rohtak) : A Hindu does not talk like this. This is very wrong.

SHRI Y.P. MANDAL (Samastipur) : Today you have shown your true form. You have used very low language .... This is the language of communalism.... (*Interruption*)....

SHRI KANWAR LAL GUPTA (Delhi Sadar) : Sir, it would be better if you silence them. Otherwise not even their Prime Minister would be able to speak. We shall see how she speaks .... (*Interruption*)....

MR. DEPUTY SPEAKER : All the other hon. members who are interrupting will have their chance to speak and they can refute the arguments of Mr. Vajpayee. They should listen to him now.

SHRI RAMAVTAR SHASTRI (Patna) : One should not talk about women like this.

SMT. INDIRA GANDHI, the Prime Minister : I do not like to interrupt and I have always advised members on all sides of the House to listen to whoever is speaking. If I have done so on this occasion it was to point out to Hon. member Shri Vajpayee that he was using this opportunity to say things which will deeply hurt all minorities .... (*Interruption*)....

SHRI VAJPAYEE : It is a matter of opinion.

SMT. INDIRA GANDHI : I shall take only one second more to say.... (*Interruption*)..... I am indeed expressing my opinion.

SHRI KANWAR LAL GUPTA : These people are responsible for these riots ... (*Interruption*).... We do not agree with this mentality of yours. This mentality is responsible for the .... (*Interruption*)....

SMT. INDIRA GANDHI : I am perfectly entitled to say that his speech is going to create a bad atmosphere in the country. I am certainly entitled to draw the hon. member's attention to that. It is not only a question of Muslims. It is a question of Sikhs, Buddhists, Jains, Christians and all other minorities.... (*Interruption*)... as also of Harijans and backward communities.

SHRI VAJPAYEE : I am not yielding; the hon. Prime Minister did not raise any point of order.

AN HON. MEMBER : We do not accept that he speaks on behalf of all Hindus.

SHRI KANWARLAL GUPTA : The Prime Minister has no right to interfere in this .... (*Interruption*).

SHRI RABI RAY : In this House we are all Indians neither Hindus, nor Muslims.

SHRI N.K.P. SALVE (Betul) : Is it chivalrous to address the other Hon. lady member like that ? Would you do it to your sister ? The basic question is because we enjoy certain immunity are we completely free to cast off all decorum and are we free from the law of decency ? Is he entitled to call the lady what he said ?

SHRI VAJPAYEE : Sir, I am sorry....

SHRI DHIRESWAR KALITA (Gauhati) : Sir, on a point of order.

MR. DEPUTY SPEAKER : He is not yielding. Let him finish his speech. All right. What is your point of order ?

SHRI DHIRESWAR KALITA : The point of order is this. This is a very serious question. It may incite riots in our own country. So I want to say that that portion of his speech should be expunged.

MR. DEPUTY SPEAKER : It is your opinion. Now, only without being tense, can the debate continue ? Mr. Vajpayee, please conclude.

SHRI VAJPAYEE : Sir, I have not said anything. This is not the first time I stand in the House to speak. No member of this House can say I have made a speech that would incite passions .... *(Interruption)*.....

SHRI R.S. YADAV (Barabanki) : I think Shri Vajpayee has been somewhat carried away, but he did not mean it. What he said about the Hon. member should be expunged.

SHRI VAJPAYEE : Nothing should be expunged.

SHRI S.A. DANGE (Bombay Central South) : I want all those words to remain. I do not want any expunction .... *(Interruption)*....

MR. DEPUTY SPEAKER : Order, order.

SHRI VAJPAYEE : Sir, I do not think I have said anything in my speech that would incite passions. If the lady feels I have said something insulting about her I am wiling to take it back .... *(Interruption)*.... If someone says I am not a Hindu what is objectionable in my saying in reply 'it is good that you are not a Hindu ? .... *(Interruption)*....

SHRI RANDHIR SINGH : We are all brothers, whether Hindu or Muslim. All are Indians.

SHRI VAJPAYEE : Sir, as I was saying, communalism cannot be fought by promoting Muslim communalism .... *(Interruption)*.... Keep quiet, madam, you did not feel ashamed to join hands with the Muslim League .... *(Interruption)*.....

SMT. TARAKESWARI SINHA : Smt. Indira Gandhi joined hands with the Muslim League in Kerala ....*(Interruption)*.....

SMT. INDIRA GANDHI : Now it is all the more clear that you are with the Jan Sangh.

SMT. TARAKESWARI SINHA : You too joined hands with the Muslim League to form the Government....*(Interruption)*....

SHRI VAJPAYEE : Sir, what will happen to me in a quarrel between two ladies ? ....*(Interruption)*....

SMT. INDIRA GANDHI : I am not speaking as a woman or as a lady; I am speaking with great indignation on behalf of the Indian nation ....*(Interruption)*....

SHRI VAJPAYEE : You are heading a minority Government. You resign and get out ....*(Interruption)*.... One who broke her own party is talking of the nation.

I would like to make it clear again that when I said Hindus are becoming aggressive it was not my intention to justify that aggressiveness ....*(Interruption)*.... Listen to me, and understand. I went to Ahmedabad, where riots had taken place, and asked people not to take the law in their own hands. My speeches are proof of this. In today's speech I have said I do not approve of the sentiment of revenge. But one cannot close one's eyes to the situation. The situation is that Muslims are becoming more and more communal and Hindus more and more aggressive ....*(Interruption)*.... We must understand both these dangers and take steps to remove them.

Wherever there is a riot the name of the Jan Sangh is dragged in ....*(Interruption)*.... The Raghuvar Dayal Commission's report has been received and it says the Jan Sangh had no hand in the riots in Ranchi ....*(Interruption)*....

MR. DEPUTY SPEAKER : We have allotted 3 hours. I am not shutting you out, but I am putting it to the House. We have taken about 40 minutes. I am just drawing your attention to it.

SHRI KANWAR LAL GUPTA : Tell the Prime Minister not to disturb.

SHRI VAJPAYEE : Sir, communalism has been very much made a ploy for votes. I would like to warn political parties that now they would not even get votes by playing up Muslim communalism ....*(Interruption)*.... The Muslim league in Kerala. ....*(Interruption)*....

SHRI RANDHIR SINGH : All this is a drama for votes ....*(Interruption)*....

SHRI VAJPAYEE : In Kerala the Muslim League is addicted to power. My friend Shri Chandrajit Yadav from Sultanpur says the candidate from Muslim Majlis may get all Muslim votes ....*(Interruption)*....

SHRI CHANDRAJEET YADAV (Azamgarh) : What you say is wrong. You present everything wrongly. You also present Indian culture and Indian civilisation wrongly ....*(Interruption)*....

SHRI VAJPAYEE : Now you are going back on your words. Is this your morality ? Yesterday you had yourself said ....*(Interruption)*....

How to Fight Communalism

The question is, how do we want to fight communalism ? The Bharatiya Jan Sangh believes in the ideal of a secular state ....*(Interruption)*.... This is not a laughing matter. Those who have entered into an alliance with the Muslim League should not have the temerity to make charges against us. Those who live in glass houses should not throw stones at others. Their government rests on the support of the Muslim League and they call us communalists. Those who choose candidates for elections on the basis of communalism are calling us communalists. Those who get India into the Rabat Conference and humiliate it are calling us communalists ....*(Interruption)*....

The Bharatiya Jan Sangh has never said there should be discrimination on the basis of communalism in the country. We want neither discrimination nor partiality. We have accepted equal citizenship laid down in the Constitution. The doors of the Bharatiya Jan Sangh are open to all Indian citizens. But if a Muslim enters Jan Sangh posters appear in Delhi calling him a kafir. The language the Muslim League used against Mulana Azad and other nationalist Muslims is now being used against Muslims joining the Jan

Sangh. This is not the way to fight communalism ....(*Interruption*).... I want to conclude.

The question is, what should be done to tackle communal disturbances ? There are some long-term measures. We will have to take this question out of politics and solve it on a national level. The Prime Minister had initiated the National Integration Council, but it was made a weapon of propaganda against the Bharatiya Jan Sangh. This Council should be expanded. Currently it does not include the Organisation Congress, the Swatantra Party, the Samyukta Socialist Party ....(*Interruption*).... The Prime Minister should create an atmosphere for all nationalist parties to come together ....(*Interruption*).... and adopt concrete steps to solve the problem of communalism.

Who is, and Who should be, in the National Integration Council

It is also necessary that nationalist leaders like Shri M.C. Chagla, Shri Hamid Dalwai, Dr. Jeelany and Shri Anwar Dehlavi should be included in the National Integration Council. Whom the Prime Minister should include depends upon her. But is she prepared to say anything about Muslim communalists ? It is known to all that in Bhawandi the Tamir-i-Millat had vitiated the atmosphere. But did anyone name it ? The Shiv Sena is being critcised and it should be....(*Interruption*).... We too are being dragged in. Not that we are bothered. We are not here at the Prime Minister's pleasure, we are here inspite of her. We too represent the people of the country ....(*Interruption*).... But when there is the question of some Muslim communal organisation their lips are sealed. What is the Jamiat-ul-Ulema doing ? What is the Jamait-Islami doing ? What did the Tamir-e-Millat do in Bhiwandi ? But is there anyone to speak about it ?....(*Interruption*)....

It is also necessary to institute judicial inquiries where communal riots take place. Passions would have cooled down if the Maharashtra Government had promptly ordered a judicial inquiry. But they said they would make a magisterial inquiry and so the people had to agitate for a judicial inquiry. Conduct a judicial inquiry wherever a riot takes place and implement its recommendations.

I complain that the Maharashtra Government did not implement the recommendations of the Integration Council. The intelligence department was not strengthened. The police were not readied for preventing riots. What is happening with the Raghuvar Dayal Commission's recommendations ? A commission was set up for Ahmedabad and a Commission has been set up for Bhiwandi. But will the recommendations of all these commissions be thrown into the waste paper basket ? Will every problem be tested on the touchstone of politics ? Since the partition of the Congress the nexus between communalists and communists is on the increase and they have the Prime Minister's blessings. This is the reason why communalism is growing.

I have nothing to say to my communalist friends, but to those who are patriots in the Congress and those whose voice of conscience had awakened in the presidential election I put a question—are you ready to look at the problem of communalism in its reality ? Are you ready to solve it as a national problem ? The situation is serious, the country stands at the brink of destruction. We must rise above the politics of votes to look at this problem. If we have made a mistake, show it to us, we are ready to correct it. If Jan Sangh workers were at fault in Bhiwandi we are ready to take action against them. We shall correct them. But what is the position with other parties ? We will have to do some introspection, we will have to search our souls, and we will have to launch countrywide campaign to solve the problem of communalism on a national level. The longer we delay the more this problem would worsen, and then there will neither be democracy in this country nor will your dreams of establishing socialism be fulfilled.

SMT. INDIRA GANDHI, Prime Minister : Sir, I am not speaking just to score points. In the past I have never interrupted any Hon. member while he was speaking. I have done it this time because in the first place I felt it deeply, and secondly because I have the courage of conviction. In my opinion the Hon. member has done a great disservice to the country and its minorities. This is such a serious occasion and this subject is so delicate that taking up his axioms could prove still more dangerous. I have no intention of doing so. So far as the other points and figures are concerned Shri Shukla will reply later.

Shri Vajpayee has used this occasion mainly to attack Muslims and all minorities in general. He has proclaimed with his hand raised in the old Hitler style. I know what he said and what words he used, as I was present at that time.

SHRI KANWAR LAL GUPTA : You had taken training.

SMT. INDIRA GANDHI : What training I took is the business of the Indian people, not yours. I do not know the words Shri Vajpayee used, but he has challenged me for something. I would like to tell him that I have never shirked a challenge, and never will. We should face the Indian people.

SHRI VAJPAYEE : The Prime Minister should not lose control over herself.

SMT. INDIRA GANDHI : I am not losing control over myself. I am only saying this with all emphasis. I am not given to losing control over myself.

SHRI VAJPAYEE : I am also ready to face any type of challenge.

SMT. INDIRA GANDHI : Please do not talk like that. I am used to Shri Vajpayee and his party attacking me. Even in public statements they demean me by levelling baseless charges. They charged the Home Minister because he spoke frankly and with great sorrow. Actually Shri Vajpayee tried to extract something else from all this. He even tried ....*Interruption*.... Shri Gupta, please understand that I am going to say what I want to say. What you said by way of interruption is irrelevant .... you have to understand this right now ....

What happened in Delhi and the riots elsewhere were all lumped together, which is very sad. And no one among us wants to escape the responsibility. I cannot say definitely, but we should face the facts. Shri Vajpayee asked why these riots start. Are these small incidents, where a stone was thrown and a riot started ? A riot may flare up when somebody kills somebody else for the first time. It can also be caused by the atmosphere created by speeches like the one we heard today. It is this atmosphere that starts the disturbance.

And this is not a new thing. It is also not the first thing that it has happened. It is perhaps a coincidence that when people connected with the RSS or Jan Sangh go somewhere riots erupt in the surrounding areas, after some time. I do not know if this is a coincidence, but for me and for people who think about it this is certainly a strange coincidence. I think the Hon. member has been rightly advised to examine the situation and find out why these things happen.

It is very easy to level a charge against somebody. But there can be a better way to tackle the situation. I am not saying this is just impossible. I have not studied it, which is mainly why I am going there. Possibly something more could be done there. There is always scope for improvement. I do not know what advance information the Government had. But there is no doubt that since this particular party got some seats in this House and in the assemblies it is raising this poisonous topic still more openly. While Shri Vajpayee was speaking some Hon. members shouted that some of his comments should be expunged. I am happy they were not. I want them to remain on record so that future generations could see the real thinking of the Jan Sangh—not the forceful Hindi that Shri Vajpayee uses from time to time, but the truth behind the words. Today we saw naked Fascism behind those words.

A lot of time was given to Shivaji. There would be no one in the country, let alone in the House, who would not have respect for Shivaji. But using his name for fanning the flames of communalism is not doing justice to him.

SHRI V. KRISHNAMURTHY : It is an offensive act.

SMT. INDIRA GANDHI : Communalism is bad, whether of Hindus or Muslims or Sikhs. It is also not true that whenever it flared up we have not strongly condemned it. Whenever a Muslim organisation or individual used inflammatory words we criticised it. But this does not mean we cannot criticise the wrong things said by members of the majority community. As I have already said people of the majority community have a special responsibility in the areas where they live. They are not just people but people with a special responsibility. As Hindus are in much greater in numbers than Muslims, Christians and other minorities in this country they have a special responsibility. But it is also possible that at some places other people may be the majority .... At some places it may be the Sikhs, they have a greater responsibility towards other minorities. They may be Hindus or Muslims or somebody else. Similarly in Kashmir Muslims are in the majority. They have a similar responsibility there—of seeing that Hindus live in peace and security. This emphasis only shows that Hindus are not ready for all this. The atmosphere in the country has become poisonous. Now we know such thoughts are being instilled in the minds of people. It is true that not all people are good, but there are also good people whose responsibility it is to meet such adverse circumstances. In the event of such an unfortunate incident we must try to help those in difficulties. We must think of how we can prevent such things from happening again. But missing such events to level charges against people is to strike a blow at minorities. And if they repeat the same behaviour at other places it would be all the more wrong.

We all know that such incidents begin with small things. Why do they think of them on such a big scale at all ? Shri Vajpayee said in Ahmedabad that people should not take the law in their hands. But for me the rest of his speech looked as if he was emphasising one point—we shall not do all this. What does this mean ? It means 'we shall take the law in our hands, we shall take action, we must take steps'. What else does it mean ?

SHRI VAJPAYEE : I had not said so.

SMT. INDIRA GANDHI : This is what I understood the speech to mean. If that was not the meaning I hope he would clarify what it means and tell people not to do so. His own people are not doing so.

SHRI VAJPAYEE : But the Congress can do it. Members of the Congress party can do it.

SMT. INDIRA GANDHI : So far as I know, there was a lot of commotion there. I may be wrong, but so far as I can understand he was short of giving notice that he and his party were going to do some special things. If this reaction meant there should be riots and lives of minorities be endangered it is very bad. They are on this path. This is what I could understand from his speech.

SHRI MANOHARAN : The whole trouble is that Shri Vajpayee is unmarried.

SMT. INDIRA GANDHI : Unfortunately married people in his party are no better. Actually they are very bad.

As I said Shri Vajpayee did not do justice to Shivaji's memory. He has also done injustice to our old philosophy. Tradition does not include depriving the minorities of their rights. Actually the *smritis* state that our country opened its doors to all people who were unhappy in their own country. In the past we have opened our doors to people of all other religions and other customs and given them protection. We do so even today.

So the Hon. member is presenting a very different concept of India before the world. This is a bad thing. This concept is not in accordance with tradition. Actually the Jan Sangh ....*Interruption*...... I hope Shri Vajpayee does not think I am giving him so much importance ....*Interruption*......

SHRI VAJPAYEE : Shri Manoharan may have that complaint.

SMT. INDIRA GANDHI : I am not criticizing this party as a party. But it has two main aspects—the first communal aspect, and the second is still more dangerous—it is that of deliberately distorting history. This is being done. Books are being written to change our well-known history. This is most dangerous for us.

AN. HON. MEMBER : Indianisation.

SMT. INDIRA GANDHI : I have already referred to the underlying idea. It is connected with the atmosphere created in the House and in the country. Shri Vajpayee just declared the Muslims started the riots. He asked, why ? And he himself gave the answer—because they feel they cannot live in India. So they are launching this deadly battle. This is the cause. That is what I could understand from his speech.

SHRI VAJPAYEE : This is one reason ....*Interruption*...

SMT. INDIRA GANDHI : All right, it is one of the reasons ....*Interruption*....

SHRI VAJPAYEE : I had said so. There is nothing wrong in it. It is being objected to. ....*Interruption*....

SMT. INDIRA GANDHI : No objection is being raised.

I would like the Hon. member to read some of the speeches made by members of his party who have said exactly this that the Muslims cannot live in India unless they are Indianised.

SHRI VAJPAYEE : Now, it is my turn to challenge the Prime Minister. Let her produce a single speech, and I am prepared to take action against that Jan Sangh leader.

SHRI SHASHI BHUSHAN : Shri Golwalkar and Hon. Shri Balraj Madhok said so.

SMT. INDIRA GANDHI : Shri Golwalkar said ....*Interruption*....

They say that they are distinct from the RSS. We do not think that they are distinct. Certainly not I am told, I am not absolutely sure, that the members who have joined certain Governments on behalf of the Jan Sangh have been members of the RSS. I think there are any number of speeches which can be produced on these lines.

SHRI VAJPAYEE : Show a single one.

SMT. INDIRA GANDHI : Why one, we will show the whole thing. They were all presented in the National Integration Council. We'll show them all.

SHRI VAJPAYEE : Talk of the Jan Sangh, the Jan Sangh.

SMT. INDIRA GANDHI : Talk about whom ?

SHRI VAJPAYEE : I am talking about you, not about the Jamaiat-ul- Ulema. Otherwise you will get into difficulties. You have seen what speeches the leaders of the Jamaiat-ul-Ulema were making.

SMT. INDIRA GANDHI : We oppose all such speeches, whatever the community or organisation the people making them may belong. There is no doubt in this, and we have never hesitated to say so.

As I said earlier, whenever such a thing has been brought to my notice I have always spoken about it in private and in public meetings and elsewhere. On no occasion have I mentioned only one party if another party was also doing similar things.

One small point. The hon. members opposite call themselves the old Congress but on no occasion do they hesitate to dissociate themselves from many of the things which were done when they were with us....*Interruption*....

Sushila perhaps came late. She does not know what I have said. I have no intention of talking about a particular incident.

DR. SUSHILA NAYAR (Jhansi) : What is it you mean by saying so ?

SMT. INDIRA GANDHI : I do not want you to do it, but you do it. You know yourself. Why should I waste the time of the House ? I merely wanted to draw their attention. I am sure they all know what I am talking about.

DR. SUSHILA NAYAR : Political speech.

SMT. INDIRA GANDHI : I am making a speech, what has every body else done ? What did Mr. Vajpayee make ? Was it not a political speech ? (*Interruption*).

I am talking about a situation. What I am saying goes much deeper than what happened merely in Bhiwandi or Jalgaon or Ahmedabad. All these things form part of an atmosphere that is created. This is what I am trying to say, and I think it is extremely important that all Members of Parliament, as indeed all Indian citizens, think about these things far more deeply. You will be given all the facts about this. Chavanji has given the facts as known on the first day, and Shuklaji will give you whatever has come to our knowledge since then. But it is time for us not to regard these happenings merely as isolated incidents that take place, incidents which we debate. It is time to realize that it is this kind of communal thinking, these speeches and articles which come out in newspapers which are creating this atmosphere, and it is no use just getting up and saying. "You prove that we did it."

SHRI R.S. YADAV : Please explain what you are going to do.

SMT. INDIRA GANDHI : Action required by the situation there will certainly be taken.

SHRI R.S. YADAV : The House should know what you think.

SHRI PILOO MODY : I appreciate what the Prime Minister is saying, but she goes on saying the same thing. What I would like to know is what her contribution is to the positive aspects of a programme which will depress this communalism and put it underground.

SMT. INDIRA GANDHI : I think Mr. Piloo Mody has entirely missed the point of what I have said. We do not want to put this underground. On the contrary I welcome Mr. Vajpayee's speech because we feel that for the first time he has come over ground as far as this question was concerned. We do not want to put it underground. We wanted it to be overground and we want to fight it with all the strength at our command. This is not something which can be solved with a speech ....*Interruption*.... Shri Mody knows nothing about the Indian people. I happen to know them much better than him. I do not wish to take the time of the House any more ....*Interruption*. I am not yielding now to anybody. Shri Yadav asked what steps would be taken. There are no new steps in that sense. People have suffered and we have to see firstly what relief has to be given immediately and what we can do on a slightly long-term basis. There is already an enquiry going on and it will come to its conclusions but I admit that I do not know how much such enquiries help. Any way, it is necessary to have them and I am glad that there is one. Now, apart from the question of relief and so on, we must all get together and see how we can present this kind of atmosphere growing, how we can go down to the people, village by village and mohalla by mohalla to create that type of neighbourly feeling which in the last analysis is the only protection. The police can help in a particular situation but ultimately it is only one's neighbours who can be of real help. It is only the atmosphere in the country that can prevent this kind of rioting and senseless attacks on people. It is not just a question of whether somebody threw a stone, why should not people get angry ? That is where you judge the maturity of the people. If people had done something wrong, by all means catch the guilty. But you do not catch the guilty. In fact the guilty are the first to get away and it is only the innocent who are looted and murdered.

Bhiwandi a Warning and a Challenge

Sir, it would have been better if you had given me the opportunity to speak after the Home Minister. I admit that Rule 143 does not provide for a reply, but this discussion has gone on for a long time. Many things have been said that need to be replied to. However, I accept your ruling.

THE CHAIRMAN : You wrote for a personal explanation, so I am giving you a chance.

SHRI VAJPAYEE : The Home Minister is still to reply. That day he was not in the House; he was ill. Perhaps I criticised him very harshly. But I would like to clarify one point in that connection. When I said that Shri Chavan wept at the time of riots in Maharashtra but was not similarly affected by the riots of Gujarat perhaps I wrongly created the impression that he considers himself more as the leader of Maharashtra and does not have the same feeling or affection for other parts of the country. I had submitted that we will have to rise above party considerations to look at the problem of communalism. That the Syndicate should be criticised for the riots in Ahmedabad because it is in power there and we should not feel about it while we should be more affected by all the riots in Maharashtra, where the Indicate is in power... (*Interruptions*)

SHRI NAMBIAR (Tiruchirappalli) : On a point of order, Sir, is it a second speech or personal explanation ?

SHRI SHEO NARAIN : Are you the Master of the House ?

SHRI VAJPAYEE : And that was the context in which I said my words should not be misconstrued.

Not only that, the Prime Minister had deliberately presented my speech in a distorted form.

SHRI SHASHI BHUSHAN : Sir, why is he getting this extra time ?

MR. SPEAKER : Will you please sit down ?

SHRI VAJPAYEE : Sir, the Prime Minister said ....

SMT. INDIRA GANDHI, Prime Minister : Have you received a written copy of his personal explanation in advance, Sir ?

SHRI VAJPAYEE : Sir, what objection does the Prime Minister have ?

SMT. INDIRA GANDHI : No objection. I wanted to know.

MR. SPEAKER : Mr. Vajpayee said that he wanted to make a personal explanation. It is not a speech. It is a personal explanation. I have allowed it. The Prime Minister wants to know whether I have received a written copy in advance. No.

Lok Sabha on May 30, 1970 during discussion on points raised after the speech on May 14, 1970 on the Bhiwandi incidents

SHRI VAJPAYEE : Sir, you have given permission. I have the right to remove the misunderstanding that has been created about my speech.

The Prime Minister said :

"Shri Vajpayee has used this occasion to launch an attack on the Muslims in particular and, I think, all minorities."

There has been no reference to 'all minorities' in this discussion. Where did these minorities come from ? Does my speech refer to minorities ? Sir, I have not even held all Muslims responsible in my speech. Can this truth be falsified ? I would like to draw your attention and the attention of the House to what I had said. Sir, look at portions of my speech. Has not the Prime Minister heard it ? I had said not all Muslims want riots, there are patriots among Muslims too, there are peace-loving people among Muslims too—people who toil and care for their families. They do not want to play the game of violence and arson. But the Prime Minister dragged in all Muslims — and not only all Muslims but also Jains, Buddhists, Sikhs, Harijans and backward classes, and tried to create the impression that I am against all minorities, and she is the only champion of the minorities in this country.

The Prime Minister may have seen Shri Frank Moraes's article titled 'exploiting the minorities', in which he has appealed to her — for God's sake do not indulge in the exploitation of the minorities.

Sir, I have been charged with inciting the passions of Hindus through my speeches. Is this the only place for me to do that ? ... (*Interruptions*) ...

SHRI SHASHI BHUSHAN : You fan the flames of communalism everywhere.

SHRI VAJPAYEE : Can I not make speeches outside the House ? By your grace thousands of people come to listen to me. I have recently visited the Home Minister's constituency — Satara, Sholapur, Karad, Ahmednagar — and let him make inquiries through the intelligence department and say if there was anything objectionable in the speeches I made there. I never said anything that would create tension. So quite a few members might have wondered why I spoke like this in the House that day. Sir, I spoke deliberately. I did not threaten. I wanted to warn. Heed the warning. If this Lok Sabha does not heed this warning adverse effects in the country cannot be prevented. This is not a threat.

SOME HON. MEMBERS : It is.

SHRI VAJPAYEE : Sir, this is a warning. Can we prevent Hindu communalism from growing by compromising with Muslim communalism ? We cannot. So if you decide to fight at all, decide to fight communalism of both types; we are with you. But that day the Prime Minister did not say a single word about the Tamir-i-Millat. She was silent on the Shiv Sena. We refused to make an alliance with the Shiv Sena in Bombay. We could have made it, and Shiv Sena leader Shri Bal Thackeray said it was a passing thought (*Interruptions*).

SHRI MADHU LIMAYE (Monghyr) : Sir, I have a point of order.

SHRI SHASHI BHUSHAN : Sir, this is not a personal explanation. I too would like to reply to him.

MR. SPEAKER : You may give a personal explanation on specific matters, do not say anything beyond that.

SHRI KANWAR LAL GUPTA : Why is the Prime Minister impatient ? Why does she not allow him to speak ? Do not be impatient. Listen to him.

SHRI MADHU LIMAYE : Sir, there would be a controversy without any reason if nobody is prepared to voluntarily abide by the rules. You have permitted Shri Vajpayee to give a personal explanation, but I do not see any word of personal explanation in this. He is replying to a discussion. If you have the right to reply you may do so, I do not mind, but the procedure of personal explanation should not be misused. I know Shri Vajpayee always interrupts on such matters. I never speak, because I want to give members an opportunity to speak... (*Interruptions*) ... I am not taking revenge on Shri Vajpayee, I always like to give a chance, but after all there has to be a procedure. All this controversy would not have arisen if he had given his personal explanation in writing and business conducted according to procedure. I hold that rules should be observed.

MR. SPEAKER : I quite agree. So long I saw ......

SHRI VAJPAYEE : Permit me to reply to the discussion. You did not do so.

MR. SPEAKER : There is no question of a discussion here.

SHRI VAJPAYEE : Why not ?

MR. SPEAKER : I gave you an opportunity for a personal explanation, but so far you have not made any statement.

SHRI M.L. SONDHI (New Delhi) : Sir, you may hear my point of order. Let me make a brief submission on this.

MR. SPEAKER : Let me first reply to the first point of order.

SHRI M.L. SONDHI : This is a connected matter.

MR. SPEAKER : I shall listen to it later on.

SHRI M.L. SONDHI : You do give an opportunity whenever a point of order is raised to enable a few members to bring their points of view. And this has happened on many occasions when Shri Madhu Limaye is holding his point of order.

MR. SPEAKER : You are the only gentleman who will go on like this. This is the last time that I want to avoid this headache.

SHRI M.L. SONDHI : You may please hear me before making this remark.

MR. SPEAKER : First I want to reply to this point of order.

SHRI M.L. SONDHI : I am only claiming my right.

MR. SPEAKER : I say there is no right. Please sit down. Let me reply to the first point of order. What is all this wasting of time ? The point of order raised by Shri Madhu Limaye is fully justified. I am sorry that I could not trace that request of his. Please confine yourself to the personal explanation and not enter into a regular debate.

SHRI VAJPAYEE : I am not entering into a debate. I said I did not say this in my speech. The Prime Minister has put words in my mouth. I did not threaten, I wanted to warn. Is this not a personal explanation ? ....

MR. SPEAKER : There is a lot of difference. You entered into a debate.

SHRI VAJPAYEE : There will be some debate and the Home Minister is still to reply.

MR. SPEAKER : Give your statement in brief.

SMT. INDIRA GANDHI : I too want to reply.

SHRI VAJPAYEE : I have invited the Prime Minister to a public debate with me on communalism on All India Radio. The people will decide.

MR. SPEAKER : This cannot be a personal explanation.

SHRI VAJPAYEE : But repeating things that I did not say, ignoring the facts I presented and raising a fright, trying to project oneself as the champion of the minorities — this is not the way to fight the problem. Bhiwandi is a warning, Bhiwandi is a challenge. People of this country will have to pay heed to this warning, they will have to accept this challenge. But the first condition for this is that we will have to take this problem out of party politics. Is the Prime Minister ready to do so ? Her speech says she is not. She misrepresented my speech. Thank you.

Conspiracy to Circumscribe Fundamental Rights

Sir, with your permission I beg to raise a point of order.

I stand to oppose the Bill Shri Ram Niwas Mirdha seeks to table. Normally a Bill is not opposed at the stage of tabling. But in the present circumstances we have no option but to oppose it right now. My objection is constitutional, procedural as well as political. I submit that this Bill is unconstitutional, undemocratic and strikes at the people's rights. It seeks an unlimited concentration of power in the Government's hands for suppressing the opposition. The Constitution provides for the fundamental right of citizens "to assemble peaceably and form associations or unions. This is our fundamental right. It is true that the Constitution puts some constraints on it. One such limit is that if an association works against the sovereignty and integrity of the nation it may be declared illegal. This was the purpose of Parliament passing the Unlawful Activities Act. Its purpose was to declare those parties unlawful whose purpose is to hand over any part of India to any foreigner. But the present Bill transgresses the parameters of the Constitution and tramples upon the right to form associations. This Bill is not in accordance with the Constitution. It is unconstitutional. When the Government was asked in the House as well as outside it if it was thinking of declaring any organisation illegal, the Government spokesman had said that the Constitution did not allow them to do so. But now the Constitution was being set aside and a conspiracy hatched to pass a law by which organisations could be put out of existence.

This Bill has two parts. One relates to an amendment to Section 153 (A) of the Indian Penal Code. Please permit me to read the Section :

> "Whoever, by words either spoken or written, or by signs or by visible representations or otherwise, promotes or attempts to promote, on grounds of religion, race, language, caste or community or any other ground whatsoever, feelings of enmity or hatred between different religions, racial or language groups or castes or communities and which disturbs or is likely to disturb the public tranquillity shall be punished with imprisonment which may extend to three years or with fine or with both."

This means that this clause will apply to individuals, not organisations. If any individual indulges in the spread of hatred among individuals on the basis of religion, language etc. and creates tension he becomes liable for

Lok Sabha on September 3, 1970 during discussion on the Indian Penal Code Amendment Bill

punishment with imprisonment upto three years. So long this law was limited to individuals, but not its scope is being expanded. Parties, political as well as non-political, are being brought within its ambit, and the Government is arming itself with powers to declare them illegal.

Sir, there was a clause like this when the Unlawful Activities Bill was tabled in this House. At that time Shri Y.B. Chavan was piloting the Bill. It was sent to the Select Committee. The Committee had given the opinion — which later the House supported — that this Bill for declaring organisations illegal should be limited to those that wanted to hand over any Indian territory to another country and those that wanted to work against the country's sovereignty and territorial integrity. I am not aware of the circumstances in which this Bill is being presented. The Plebiscite Front could have been declared unlawful under the Unlawful Activities Act, and the House is entitled to know why that was not done. Does the Plebiscite Front want Jammu and Kashmir to secede from India ?

Naxalite Infiltration

There is another and still more serious problem facing the country. It is the Naxalites, who declare the President of China to be the President of India, who say the Chinese way is their way, who are collecting arms, breaking the law and indulging in political murders. You will be surprised and also grieved to learn that Naxalite activities have even entered our armed forces. A few days back Naxalite posters were found pasted in 36 ships of the Navy. These included the INS Vikrant. The posters were pasted in one day on 36 ships at the same time. Are we to understand that the Naxalites have penetrated those working on these ships ? What action is being taken against them ? The Air Force too is being penetrated by Naxalites. In this regard the House is not being taken into confidence. News is being suppressed. The news of the recent crash of an Air Force plane flying out of the Halwara air base was suppressed, because the crash had been caused by sabotage. According to information in my possession Naxalite activities are suspected to be responsible for the recent danger to an Indian Airlines plane in Assam.

The country's territorial integrity, independence and democratic structure are currently in danger from the Naxalites. The Prime Minister had given the assurance in the Consultative Committee to the Home Ministry that a law would be made against the Naxalites, but where is that law ? There is no law against the Naxalites, and now a law is being made which will not leave any party out of its ambit. Let our DMK friends beware, as they too can be arrested under Section 153 A. The Akali Dal, the Depressed League, any party... (*Interruption*)... the RSS and Bharatiya Jan Sangh are all included...(*Interruptions*)...

SHRI O.P. TYAGI (Moradabad) : All except the Chinese agents. (*Interruptions*].

SHRI VAJPAYEE : In Maharashtra the Shiv Sena, with whom the ruling Congress has an alliance, can also be included. The point is, what is the propriety of bringing forward this Bill ? Why did the Prime Minister not call an all-party meeting before presenting it ? After all what is secularism ? Who will decide who is communal ? Is the Muslim League communal or not ? Are those having an alliance with it communal or not ? Are those spreading the League all over the country through such an alliance guilty of conspiring against the country's integrity or not ? Will the right to decide this be given to the government — that government which is a minority government ? It had been demanded that an independent tribunal be set up to define communalism, but it was not accepted, because the Government wants to assume powers that can strike at its opponents. This House is not prepared to equip the Government with such powers, because the powers that were given were not used and those that have been demanded can be misused. So I would call upon the Minister to take this Bill back, otherwise the House will have to reject it right at this stage. Thank you.

Conquer Hearts, not Buildings

Sir, I have been deeply distressed to hear the speeches of the members of the ruling party. What happened on Jantar Mantar Road deserves to be condemned, and justifying it, saying it was right, making speeches in this House in support of the rowdyism that took place there compounds that sin all the more. Sir, no honest Congressman can support what happened there. I have talked to many eminent people outside the House—it is not necessary to name them—and they agree that what had happened should not have happened. Are we going to fight over buildings ? On the one hand the ruling Congress claims that the people are with it, it has a brute majority in the House, the Supreme Court has ruled in its favour, and on the other, it is fighting for the building on Jantar Mantar Road. Law-makers have become law-breakers. Those who expect discipline of the people have made a lowly demonstration of indiscipline. Those charged with setting up a regime of law and the Constitution have initiated the beginning of the end of it. Can anyone support this ?

Even supposing the Organisation Congress was in wrongful possession, a tenant in wrongful possession cannot be dispossessed by the landlord these days. Court permission for it has to be obtained, and even then the police have to do the job. But here you broke in forcibly and misbehaved with senior leaders.

SHRI H.K.L. BHAGAT : On a point of order. When the Speaker permitted this motion he made it absolutely clear that the circumstances resulting in the Jantar Mantar episode would not be discussed as they are *sub judice*. But Shri Vajpayee is directly discussing them. He is speaking against the clear instructions of the Speaker. The Speaker also said that if these were discussed he would stop the discussion.

MR. DEPUTY SPEAKER : I should expect everybody to observe that direction, but I do not think it has been observed by many. All I can do is to appeal to members to be dignified and restrained in their observations. We have heard some very constructive speeches in the midst of this confusion and indignation.

I would request everybody to cooperate in this.

SHRI K.S. CHAVDA (Patna) : This side observes the rules, while that side does not.

SHRI VAJPAYEE : Sir, how can facts be falsified ? Can anyone deny that No. 7 Jantar Mantar Road was in the possession of Organisation Congress in the past ? You may argue that after the Supreme Court verdict they should have

Lok Sabha on November 16, 1971 during discussion on the Calling Attention Motion on failure of police during violent demonstration on Jantar Mantar Road in New Delhi

surrendered it of their own accord. But if they were not in possession why was it necessary for you to go there at all ? No one can deny that you went there to drive them out and during that you misbehaved with Organisation Congress leaders. Do you want us to doubt the bonafides of Shri Sadiq Ali ? He was with you till yesterday. We have seen him as a leader of the Organisation Congress and as a leader of the freedom struggle. But now he is on a hungerstrike and is being ridiculed. If the ruling party behaves like this with their own colleagues one can well imagine how it will behave with its opponents.

The ruling party has given an opportunity to those who do not believe in the Constitution and in democracy to stand up in this House and declare that whatever they are doing is right. The excuse is being trotted out that they were invited by workers in the building and they accepted the invitation.

Sir, I have a servant at home. He is a poor man, and the gentlemen sitting there have the power to buy him. If they do so and make him write a letter I fear they may well take over No. 1 Feroze Shah Road. They are arguing that they went there at the invitation of the workers there. Shri Malaviya is arguing like that, the ruling party is arguing like that. I am sorry to see not a single member stood up to say what happened was wrong, it happened in an excess of enthusiasm, it should not have happened.

Occupying Buildings at Cost of Values

Yesterday the Prime Minister appealed to the people of the country for unity. Yesterday the Prime Minister appealed to political parties for cooperation. Is this the way to secure cooperation ? Is this the way to strengthen the people's commitment to democracy ? Shri Malaviya was talking of values. What values ? No value is protected by forcibly occupying a building. This is the beginning of fascism in the country. And remember, the demon you are rousing will devour you. Enemies of democracy are playing this game. Till the other day we had thought that such things happened only in West Bengal and the whole House condemned it, but now this is happening in the capital of the country, under the very nose of the Central Government and in the presence of a passive police.

Yesterday the police were active. Where was their passivity while teargassing the Akalis ? When it comes to shooting at peaceful Satyagrahis the police of Delhi do not bother about maintaining peace. The House has not forgotten, nor the country, how opposition parties were treated during demonstrations at Patel Chowk. The police could have intervened, they could have stopped those who forced their way in, but the police were rendered inactive, law and order were rendered ineffective, and now even the voice of conscience is not heard in the House. There is still a ray of hope—I do not know why the Prime Minister is not in the House. I do not know if she has expressed her displeasure. But reports have appeared in the press and I have also talked to some senior leaders. They too did not approve of it, but no one is speaking out. Everyone's lips are sealed. This is not good for the future of the country. The newspapers have written—and they are not Jana Sangh papers—'Ego of Power'—*Hindustan Times*; 'Shameful Act'—*Times of India*; 'Shameful'—*Indian Express*

I quote a portion from today's *Indian Express* :

> "The action of the political hooligans who took the law into their own hands ignoring the judgment of the Supreme Court in effect constitutes contempt of the highest judicial tribunal in this country. The perpetrators of this mischief cannot be allowed to get off unscathed. Public opinion irrespective of the party should unreservedly condemn this outrage. If not condemned it will mark the beginning of the end of law and order in this country."

Sir, what a lie to say that RSS men were protecting Jantar Mantar! They see the RSS everywhere. Kansa saw Krishna everywhere. Had RSS men been there you would not have been able to break in. I went there with three members of Parliament, but the police did not let me go in. When member of Parliament Shri Virendra Agrawal went there supporters of the Indicate, of the Indian National Congress, beat him up and tore his coat.

Twist by Congressmen at Jantar Mantar

This has recently happened at Jantar Mantar. I have seen the so-called supporters of the Congress dancing the twist after occupying Jantar Mantar. When did these twist dancers come into the Congress ? They were not doing their twist, they were twisting the Congress, they were twisting democracy. Do not rouse the devil, protect some values even in the struggle for power. Nothing is lost yet. You can leave Jantar Mantar. You have taken No. 5 Rajendra Prasad Road. You can take any building you want. You are the power. But if you misuse power, if power goes to your head, if you openly flout the people's opinion the future of the country would not be safe in your hands at this time of crisis. I would also appeal to the Prime Minister to tell her colleagues to leave Jantar Mantar. When you rule over the hearts of the people do not fight over buildings. The country is fighting a big battle. There is danger on the border. Fight Yahya Khan, do not fight Sadiq Ali. Liberate Bangladesh, not Jantar Mantar Road. But those who are eager to deal with Yahya Khan are forcing Sadiq Ali to go on hunger strike. This is a mistake. It will have to be paid for. An offence is committed, which calls for repentance. But justifying its propriety, levelling false charges against the RSS and saying that I went there with RSS men would not take away from the seriousness of your offence. The mistake made can still be corrected and the atmosphere in the country prevented from worsening. Thank you.

Concentration of Power

Sir, four months have passed since the Government of India's cease-fire after the 13-day war with Pakistan. Except for stray incidents all is quiet on the western front. Our eastern region has also become secure due to the creation of Bangladesh. In such circumstances there is no propriety in continuing the Emergency. Now that the din of war has died down fundamental rights should be restored. Doors of the Court should be opened for the citizens. Before the elections the Government had itself been ready to limit the Emergency to border areas. Now we see no reason even to continue it even in border areas.

Repeal Emergency

Sir, the Government had clearly assured that Defence of India Rules will not be used for actions where common law is available. It is regrettable that despite this assurance State Governments took recourse to it to deal with struggles of employees and workers. In this very New Delhi, under the nose of the Central Government it was declared that Defence of India Rules would be used to suppress the struggle of the Food Corporation employees. Once the Government acquires extraordinary powers it is not willing to return to normalcy. Common law is capable of dealing with any situation. In my opinion the time has come to lift the Emergency. Last year, while replying to the discussion on the Home Ministry's demands for grants the Prime Minister had said — I quote her :

> "Every political party, therefore, needs to examine seriously whether its faith in democracy is a durable one and not a mere tactic to undermine democracy through violent means. Can all parties represented in Parliament not join together to combat this violence and those who believe in it, instead of trying to battle amongst ourselves, each blaming the other ?"

The sentiments that inform this speech did not come into practice. Can it be denied that in West Bengal the ruling party adopted the same tactics that it is now condemning ? The same tactics when it is calling upon the whole country to fight ? What Shri Bhogendra Jha, spokesman for the Communist Party said yesterday strengthens my charge that Marxist methods were adopted to fight the Marxists. I quote him :

> "Our friend Shri Jyoti Basu has spoken on West Bengal on the occasion of the last election. What he said was one-sided, because they were paid

Lok Sabha on April 26, 1972 during discussion on the occasion of the demands for grants of the Ministry of Home Affairs in the same coin, somewhat wrongly, in view of their own people's conduct some time back.

I had hoped he would condemn such conduct—not only what only the Congress party did, but would give an assurance etc.".

Shri Bhogendra Jha is connected with the party that has an alliance with the ruling party.

SHRI D.N. TIWARI (Gopalganj) : There is no alliance.

SHRI VAJPAYEE : Shri Bhogendra Jha says in Bengal the Congress Party too gave more importance to means than to ends. In that case what is the difference between the Marxist Party and the Congress Party ? Is violence good ? Is it proper to reply to political violence with political violence ? If this argument is taken to its logical conclusion is not communal violence in reply to communal violence justified ? Will there be different yardsticks for violence ? On the one hand there are appeals to eschew violence, on the other there is adoption of the same methods for a few seats—this does not speak of a firm belief in democracy.

Booth Capturing

I am talking of a few seats because the ruling party would have won in West Bengal even if it had not adopted these methods. The situation had changed, the creation of Bangladesh and the defeat of Pakistan had left a lasting imprint on the hearts and minds of the people. But the ruling party had no confidence either in the people or in its own victory. Hence such methods were adopted as none in this House can justify. Does anyone have the courage to say what was done in Bengal was right ?

SHRI SATPAL KAPUR : The people did the right thing.

SHRI VAJPAYEE : Don't talk about the people. Talk about yourself (*Interruption*). It is not a matter of Bengal alone. Yesterday Shri D.N. Tiwari, a senior member of the ruling party, made a speech in the House. He is not only an Hon. member of Parliament, he also holds an important position in the ruling party. On reading his speech I was happy on the one hand and unhappy on the other. Happy because he showed the courage to tell the truth. But unhappy because what we used to say and what was ignored by dubbing it propaganda is not propaganda but the reality, and this is not a blot for any one party, it is a blot for the whole country. I quote Shri D.N. Tiwari.

> "In previous elections in Bihar there used to be bogus voting and impersonation. But now there is no question of one person going in place of another. Rather, some people raid a booth and capture it. This is what happened in 1967. In the mid-term election some 10-20 people surrounded a booth and raided it. Corruption grew so much that the presiding officer and the polling officer were bribed with a couple of hundred rupees and then they did nothing."

I also quote what Shri Tiwari added with a heavy heart :

> "Democracy is in danger. There was such large-scale corruption in the 1972 election that an inquiry is called for. Things went to such an extent

that the presiding officer himself captured the booth and stamped the ballot papers."

Similar thoughts have been expressed by another senior member from Bihar, Shri Vibhuti Mishra. He is not present in the House. His article has been published today by a leading Hindi daily of New Delhi. In such circumstances can elections be called impartial and free ? It is not only the opposition party that is demanding an inquiry. All those who have a conscience and who care for the future of democracy are naturally concerned about the tendencies seen in this election (*Interruption*).

Sir, democracy is basically a moral system. If the game is not played by the rules people may lose faith in democracy. I repeat the demand that we should have an all-party parliamentary committee which could suggest how to prevent such irregularities in future elections and also conduct a proper inquiry into the irregularities that have taken place this time. It is not only a question of one party. Pandit D.N. Tiwari said—and it may be true—that had there been no booth-capturing more candidates of the ruling party could have won. Whatever the case, it is necessary to stop booth-capturing. This problem should be given serious thought and necessary steps for the future considered (*Interruption*).

Sir, the incident of a Jan Sangh worker in Rajasthan being shot by the police is heart-rending. Yesterday I received a letter from his widow. Shri Om Prakash Rajoria, advocate and a member of the Gwalior Municipal Corporation went to Dholpur for propaganda against the Congress. He was seated in a jeep, which was flying a flag. At midnight the police shot him at the railway crossing near Dholpur city. It is said they shot him because they thought he was a dacoit. What inquiry will there be ? The police officer involved in the killing has not yet been transferred. The widow writes : "It is a month and a half since the killing, but neither have those responsible for it been suspended, nor any action taken. On the other hand senior police officer Shri Narain Singh, S.P., Bharatpur, and Raja Khera Station Officer Shri Rajvir Singh are daily harassing our eye-witnesses and telling them not to tell the truth but depose as they are told."

The dead cannot return. The widow cannot get her husband back, nor the orphaned children their father, but we must have a guarantee that in future no lives will be taken to ensure victory on the basis of political hatred. No one should try to play this thing down by saying it was just one case. Why should there be one case ? Why should political murder be resorted to ?

Unprincipled Defections

Sir, the Prime Minister had made one more point while replying to the discussion last year. I quote her :

> "The other point which is of concern to the entire country is that of unprincipled defections. We fully share the concern for this malady in our body politic and we are determined to take steps to check it."

One year is over, but no step has been taken. The Government cannot escape responsibility by saying that it did not get the cooperation of the opposition parties. Are all steps taken in consultation with the opposition ? When there is no will to do anything an attempt is being made to exploit the differences in the opposition parties. Nobody stopped the Government from an unilateral cease-fire, so who is stopping it from unilateral steps against defection ? Big steps can be taken unilaterally, while it is necessary to consult the opposition in small matters. Opposition parties have clearly expressed the view that defection should be declared illegal. It is not enough to say that a defector will not be made a minister for a certain period. It is not necessary to make him a minister at all. He can be made chairman of some commission. Many individuals had been discarded in the last election to the Lok Sabha, today they have become members of some commission or the other and are actually better off than present members. When one looks at them one sometimes feels that membership has no value. It is better to lose an election and be made chairman of some commission.

Sir, the ruling party has a vested interest in defections. The elections took place, a thumping victory was won. (*Interruption*). You have selfish interest, that is why an attempt was made to buy over Jan Sangh members with a bribe of two lakh rupees each. Make an impartial inquiry. We are prepared to prove it ....

SHRI B.P. MAURYA (Hapur) : This is wrong, this is wrong ...

SHRI VAJPAYEE : During the Rajya Sabha election the Congress fielded one candidate in excess in Madhya Pradesh in relation to the right number in proportion to the strength of its members in the Legislative Assembly. That candidate could not have won without defection. He was a capitalist and a relative of Chief Minister Sethi. Did the ruling party not know that he could not win without defection, without selling his soul ? But the ruling party tried to prevent a possible Jan Sangh win at one place by fielding one more candidate. It is a different thing that the attempt did not succeed. Not everything in the world can be bought. Not everyone has a price tag. The same game was played in Uttar Pradesh. Defection is vitiating and distorting democracy.

Sir, in the current post-election situation hope is being expressed that opposition parties will cooperate in the task of reconstruction. But this call for cooperation rings hollow when one sees how the cooperation extended during war time was exploited for winning elections.

Yesterday some members asked what was wrong in calling the Prime Minister a leader. 'Shri Vajpayee had also said in the House that she is a leader.' I submit I did not say so. I shall repeat what I said. This is the proceedings of the House, not a document of my own writing :

> "We hope the responsibility of changing the course of history vests in these hands. The Prime Minister has come forward to provide leadership to the country in this hour of crisis. We want victory for the country and we want to create a new history under the Prime Minister's leadership."

There is no talk of a leader here.

SOME HON. MEMBERS : There is more than that.

SHRI VAJPAYEE : Maybe more, but no talk of a leader. But that was the broadcast on All India Radio and was even reported in the press. I did not refute it, because I did not want to divide the country in war time.

SHRI B.P. MAURYA : That is your greatness.

SHRI VAJPAYEE : I am not sorry I praised, but I am sorry she did not live up to that praise.

Centre-State Relations

Winning an election is one thing, proving your greatness by conduct is another. Success is one thing, greatness another, I do not want to go deeper into this controversy, but one thing is clear. The Prime Minister cannot escape her responsibility in the discussion on Centre-State relations. In the election speeches she told the people—if you want development for this region vote for my party. Is it an offence to vote for an opposition party ? Did the people do wrong if they voted for the opposition ? Will they be punished for this by not developing their region ? Is this the way to preserve the country's unity ?

SHRI SATPAL KAPUR : This is wrong. This is misleading.

SHRI VAJPAYEE : There are people here who will reply on your behalf. After the elections the demand is growing that States should have more powers. The way All India Radio is being misused I feel one day somebody may demand a separate radio for the State.

Concentration of Power

Power has become concentrated in New Delhi. This is not good for the growth of democracy. Power should be decentralised. Decentralisation only upto the State level is not good. Power should be distributed up to the level of Corporation, Zila Parishad and Panchayat. At present the Panchayat, Zila Parishad, Municipality, Corporation are all puppets in the hands of State Governments. The Central Government is nothing but the Prime Minister and the Prime Minister alone. One more thing and I shall conclude.

Shri G.K. Reddy, a prominent journalist, writes :

> "The whole system of government at the Centre is such that almost the entire range of decisions relating to politics or personnel has to be taken or at least approved by the Prime Minister who is always hard-pressed for time. As a result, she is often obliged to put off decisions until the last moment, whether in relation to a Cabinet reshuffle, appointment of Governors, selection of Service Chiefs, posting of Ambassadors or promoting senior officials to key positions in the Government."

The Prime Minister is Prime Minister, Home Minister, Information and Broadcasting Minister, Minister for Atomic Energy. All intelligence agencies have been brought together. I would like to say forcefully that in this election the intelligence department found out which Congress candidate would be useful and who is working against the Congress. Intelligence reports were called for this.

Eradication of Corruption

Many Hon. Members have discussed corruption and how it can be eradicated. But if we have to eradicate corruption from the services, model behaviour on the part of political leaders would be needed. As the Sanskrit saying goes—"*Maha jano gatah sa panthah* "—people follow the way of eminent persons. If Gangotri is soiled the Ganga at Prayag cannot be pure.

Are not the charges against the Haryana Chief Minister proved ? Can the Attorney-General's view not be invited on them ? I fail to understand why the Prime Minister lets her name be dragged through that dirt. It was stated in the House today that an inquiry is not being made because the Chief Minister of Haryana can even touch New Delhi with his corruption. I say hand over this matter over to the Attorney-General.

Yesterday charges were also levelled against a Minister of Andhra Pradesh in the House. And those who made them belonged to the ruling party, not the opposition. Now that the Prime Minister has acquired power, let her eradicate corruption, make democracy a success in the country, and set healthy conventions. It is not enough to win elections. Along with elections it is necessary to strengthen the physical and moral foundation of the nation. Can we prove ourselves up to this task ?

SHRI K.C. PANT, Minister of State in the Ministry of Home Affairs : Sir, I listened very carefully to the debate both yesterday and today and while listening to the debate I was reminded of the great events we had seen in the year gone by. These events have been historical events. They had posed one of the most difficult challenges we have faced as a nation after independence. All the events in Bangladesh, which I need not recount, and the presence of ten million refugees in our country certainly posed a great challenge to us as a nation and to our leadership. Sir, it is a matter of great satisfaction that this country has emerged from this test with flying colours and with added confidence. Listening to Shri Vajpayee, I was surprised that he also repeated what many members of the opposition are prone to say, that we won the elections because of this victory. Would Vajpayee have been happy if we had lost the war so that the Jan Sangh might have won the elections ?

SHRI VAJPAYEE : Otherwise we would not have co-operated with you. It is hitting below the belt.

SHRI K.C. PANT : I thought he had struck me below the belt and I was replying to that. The elections were held .....

SHRI VAJPAYEE : So you are not better than me.

Why Object to Vande Mataram

Sir, before taking up the demands of the Home Ministry I would like to pay my humble homage to those Jawans and Officers of the Border Security Force who gave their lives in the 1971 Indo-pak war and in Bangladesh's war of independence. The Border Security Force has done commendable work at this hour of crisis. It is our duty to pat them on the back and make proper arrangements for the education and housing of their children. I had an opportunity to visit their Training Centre at Tekanpur near Gwalior. The training arrangements are excellent but their education and accommodation need to be improved. The Home Ministry should attend to it.

The Home Ministry has to look after the domestic front. According to the introduction to the report of the Home Ministry the subjects covered by its jurisdiction are the country's internal security in general, maintaining and strengthening the rule of law, assisting the States in maintaining public order, administering Union Territories, and Centre-State relations. Clearly preserving the country's unity is a major function of the Home Ministry.

We have now an explosive situation in the country. In Assam there were widespread disturbances on the question of language, and the Government could not discharge even its primary responsibility of protecting life, property and honour. In Andhra a widespread people's agitation is going on and many repressive measures are being resorted to for suppressing it, but that is not the real solution of the problems. There is a wave of discontent all over the country. The tendency to settle issues in the streets is on the increase. A small incident, an ordinary movement assumes violent proportions. The Home Ministry has regrettably failed to do its duty in this matter. If the people's frustration is not remedied in time, if discontent is allowed to get concentrated and if prompt action is not taken on legitimate demands the people's anger may explode in an unhealthy manner and endanger the democratic process. So a basic change in the Government's attitude is called for.

Aligarh University

Yesterday there was a lot of discussion on the Aligarh University, making Urdu the second official language, and the unfortunate communal riots in many areas. My party's name was also dragged in and ridiculous charges hurled against us. We firmly believe that those indulging in communal rioting should be firmly dealt with, to whatever community they may belong. Full compensation should be given for the damage caused in a riot. But it is

Lok Sabha on March 29, 1973 during discussion on the demands for grants of the Ministry of Home Affairs

also necessary to go into the basic cause of the riots. We had hoped that after Pakistan was partitioned, it could not remain one on the basis of religion—on which basis it had come into being as a free State, the atmosphere in India would also undergo a change and there would be no conflict or demand for special rights on the basis of religion, but it seems we have not learnt anything from the partition of Pakistan and the liberation of Bangladesh. Attempts are still going on to incite people on the basis of religion. Recently, on March 10-11, a conference was held in Delhi in which speeches were made. One person said—I quote : "That Indira whom we seated on the *'Takht'* (throne) we can also put on the *'Takhta'* (hanging platform)". The following couplet was also recited :

"Sarfaroshi ki tamanna ab hamare dil mein hai.
Dekhna hai jor kitna baju-e katil mein hai."

'We are out to woo martyrdom, we shall see how strong the killer's arm is'.

About Shri Fakhruddin Ali Ahmed they said his name contains the letters *Kha* and *Ra,* and if the two are put together it becomes *'Khara'*, an ass. Abusive words were used against him. Shri Nurul was called Namak Haram. Those who attended this conference included Shri Shamim's leader Sheikh Abdullah.

SHRI S.A. SHAMIM (Srinagar) : Shri Piloo Mody on your right was also present.

SHRI VAJPAYEE : I am not concerned with people on my right and left.

SHRI S.A. SHAMIM : I too have no leader. I am my own leader.

SHRI VAJPAYEE : You are your own leader and also your own follower. You have neither a leader nor a follower.

SHRI S.A. SHAMIM : That is why I am speaking honestly.

SHRI ISHAQ SAMHALI (Amroha) : Dr. Faridi has said we will get the Jan Sangh's cooperation.

SHRI VAJPAYEE : Dr. Faridi has also said the Jan Sangh is not at all ready for cooperation (*Interruption*).

Why is the communal atmosphere in the country deteriorating ? Why does a section of the Muslim society say in Bombay we are not prepared to say Vande Mataram ? Vande Matram is not anti-Islamic. When believers in Islam recite the Namaz do they not bow their heads to the 'pak' soil of this country ?

SHRI S.A. SHAMIM : That is for Khuda.

SHRI VAJPAYEE : But the head is touched to the ground, we eat the food this soil produces. It is the soil that gives us shelter in our final moments. Are there no national anthems in other countries ?

SHRI S.A. SHAMIM : The national anthem is Jana Gana Mana.

SHRI VAJPAYEE : This is the very misunderstanding of yours that I would like to remove.

SHRI S.A. SHAMIM : Do it as fast as you can.

SHRI VAJPAYEE : You had said the same thing yesterday. I have the proceedings of the Constituent Assembly with me. This is the statement made by the Chairman on 24.1.1950 regarding the National Anthem :

"MR. PRESIDENT : There is one matter which has been pending for discussion, namely, the question of the National Anthem. At one time it was thought that the matter might be brought before the House and a decision taken by the House by way of a Resolution. It has been said that instead of taking a formal decision by means of a resolution it is better if I make a statement with regard to the National Anthem. Accordingly I make this statement.

The composition consisting of the words—music known as Jana Gana Mana is the National Anthem of India subject to such alternations in one word as the Government may authorise as the occasion arises, and the song Vande Mataram which has played a historic part in the struggle for Indian freedom shall be honoured equally with Jana Gana Mana and shall have equal status with it.... (*Applause*). I hope this will satisfy the members."

The trouble in Bombay started when students of Urdu Madrasas refused to stand up to sing Vande Mataram on January 26.

SHRI EBRAHIM SULAIMAN SAIT (Kozhikode) : Force was used.

SHRI VAJPAYEE : Force is not used on anyone.

SHRI S.A. SHAMIM : They said those who will not recite will be killed. The school was closed....

SHRI VAJPAYEE : Sir, can anyone imagine that —

PROF. MADHU DANDAVATE (Rajapur) : Mr. Speaker, Sir, I committed a mistake. Instead of President, I said 'Jawaharlal Nehru'. I am requesting Shri Vajpayee to make that correction. When I quoted this resolution, by mistake instead of 'President' I said 'Jawaharlal Nehru'.

SHRI R.S. PANDEY (Rajnandgaon) : Vande Mataram is the prayer of the motherland.

SHRI S.A. SHAMIM : There are other songs also.

SHRI JYOTIRMOY BOSU (Diamond Harbour) : Whether you agree or disagree, this is a democratic way of saying.

SHRI VAJPAYEE : Nobody can be allowed to disagree on such issues.

Tomorrow they may say we will not bow before the Tricolour because we bow before Allah. Every man living in India will have to bow before the tricolour (*Interruption*).

Sir, patriotism does not have different meanings.

SHRI S.A. SHAMIM : Yes, it does. According to you Muslims are not patriots. According to us everyone living in Hindustan is a patriot.

SHRI VAJPAYEE : Had we thought so we would not have elected a Muslim to the Jammu-Kashmir Legislative Assembly from Pandit Prem Nath Dogra's constituency which has a two per cent Muslim population. The Congress has fielded a Hindu candidate and the propaganda was made that the Jan Sangh gave a Hindu seat to a Muslim and yet the people voted for us.

SHRI S.A. SHAMIM : Many such Hindus would be found in the Muslim League.

SHRI VAJPAYEE : Hindus would be found in the Muslim League ? And you would not be found in Bharatiya Jan Sangh ?

SHRI S.A. SHAMIM : May Khuda give me death before that.

SPEAKER : Why do you get so hot ?

SHRI VAJPAYEE : Sir, let us close this unfortunate controversy over Vande Mataram. The Muslim League raised it. And it did not remain confined to the League. Shri Khandvani, leader of the Congress Party in the Bombay Corporation, also sided with them. Now the Prime Minister says the victory of communal forces in the Bombay Corporation is causing riots there. But who gave life to communalism by forming a government in Kerala in alliance with the Muslim League ? What is the need of the Muslim League in independent India ? Parties should have their doors open for all. But instead of condemning the Muslim League a government is formed in league with it. The Prime Minister feels unhappy when that the same Muslim League opposes Vande Mataram and wins in Bombay. You will have to eat the bitter fruits of the seeds you sowed. I would even say communalism is like a double-edged sword. You cannot fight the communalism of other classes by encouraging Muslim communalism.

Now the Aligarh matter is being brought forward. Why is this dust being raised all over the country in the name of Aligarh ? They say the Muslim character of the Aligarh University should be preserved. What does Muslim character mean ? Muslims do not live only in India, they are there in Bangladesh and also in many countries of the world. Will all their universities have the same character ? Will or will not the university be coloured by the soil on which it stands ? Will it or will it not represent the hopes and aspirations of the society in which the university functions ?

Of course, I have no objection if anyone says it should teach Islam. That arrangement is present there. If it is necessary to arrange instruction in Muslim theology that too can be done. But making it only a minority institution would not be acceptable. There is no question of the Aligarh University having a Muslim character. In India every university should be Indian in character. This is as much applicable to the Hindu University as to Aligarh. Every university should be Indian in character. There can be no opposition to arrangements for the study of different religions and philosophies.

Democratise Universities

However, there is one aspect of the university with which I differ. It is that in every university the government is assuming more and more powers.

SHRI S.A. SHAMIM : What are minority rights ?

SHRI VAJPAYEE : Minority rights are nothing. There are minority rights in respect of language, there are minority rights for study of Islam, minority rights do not say a university in India will have only Muslim professors. Let this House have an open debate on what Muslim character means ....

SHRI SARJOO PANDE : But you support Aligarh.

SHRI ISHAQ SAMHALI : You are even going to become its life member.

SHRI VAJPAYEE : We do not support. Sir, this Maulana Sahib is both in the Communist Party as well as in the Jamjat-ul-Ulema. He is on both sides. The

Communist Party does not believe in Islam. It does not believe in religion, but the Maulana Sahib is also a Maulana of the Jamjat-ul-Ulema. He is playing both sides.

SHRI ISHAQ SAMHALI : Why does it bother you ?

SHRI VAJPAYEE : I am not bothered. I am showing your true colours.

Sir, I submit that universities should be democratised. If Aligarh has a nominated academic council that is wrong.

SHRI B.P. MAURYA (Hapur) : Aligarh should be taken last. Others should be taken first.

SHRI VAJPAYEE : Look, there is no first and last. Actually we are demanding a Bill for the Banaras University. You know we are demanding it. We are not in favour of more nominated members in the Academic Council and in the Executive Council and of the Visitor having extraordinary powers. Democratise all universities. To those who are pleading for Aligarh I say do not talk of the minority character of Muslims, talk of autonomy. You are not doing that.

Recently Shri Nurul Hasan visited Aligarh University but he was not allowed to eat. Shoes were thrown at his car. Is this the way to express a difference of opinion ? Those who are taking up the Aligarh matter should define Muslim character. Let the House and the country finally make up their mind on this.

Place of Urdu

The other thing is about Urdu. Yesterday Maulana Isaq Samhali said the Jan Sangh is also now supporting Urdu as the second official language for the sake of winning elections. Where did he hear this ?

SHRI ISHAQ SAMHALI : You said so at the Town Hall of Mordabad.

SHRI S.A. SHAMIM : At seven o'clock in the evening on the 25th.

SHRI VAJPAYEE : Sir, the newspaper report did not say the Town Hall. It said I said so at a workers' meeting. I refuted it. I denied that I was in favour of making Urdu the second official language. I agree that Urdu has been born in India, Urdu is an Indian language, and Urdu should prosper. In Jammu-Kashmir Urdu occupies the position of the official language. No one has opposed this. But we do not agree that Urdu is the language of the Muslims only. Full facilities should be given for learning Urdu, writing books in Urdu should be encouraged, and if there are any representations in Urdu an attempt should be made to reply to them in Urdu as far as possible. And this does not apply to Urdu alone. Our Constitution says the government should try to arrange to respond to a petition in the same language. If anyone wants his education in Urdu medium I have no objection.

But making Urdu the official language is not so simple. The demand to make it the second official language is motivated by communal reasons, by the politics of separation. You will have to make a rule for making a language the second official language, you will have to decide what percentage of people in a particular state speak a particular language for making it the official language. It is not a question of Urdu alone. In Assam there is the question of Bengali, in Punjab there is also the question of Hindi. Are you going to have one rule for Urdu and another for other languages ? This is not possible.

I submit the reasons for making Urdu the subject of an agitation do not include a desire for its development. The motive behind it is to gather all Muslims under the banner of Urdu and revive the pre-partition politics of the Muslim League type. We disagree with it. I say if you decide to make Urdu the official language there will be a mini-Pakistan in every office.

After all do all Muslims in Uttar Pradesh speak Urdu ? Does the Muslim living in Braj not speak Braj ? Does the Muslim living in Avadh not speak Avadhi ? But those Muslim League members who have been elected from Kerala and who cannot speak Urdu are advocating Urdu under the impression that Urdu is the language of Muslims. This is precisely what Jinnah had said—Hindus and Muslims are different, their languages are different. This is a wrong point of view. Leave it, then Urdu will get all the official facilities that you want. But do not make Urdu an instrument of politics.

I would also like to tell my Congress friends that elections in Uttar Pradesh are approaching. It is natural to want to win seats. Every party wants it. But the country is bigger than the vote (*Interruption*). We now see before us the consequences of the secret compromise you made with Faridi before the last election. The assurances secretly given were not fulfilled, so Shri Faridi is now vexed. Do not make the question of Muslims and Urdu a party matter. Let us sit together and fashion a national policy in this matter. Otherwise, we see that Pakistan is vivisected, Bangladesh is vivisected, Bangladesh became independent, while in India the Muslim League is growing, communalism is growing. There is a great responsibility on Shri Dixit. He occupies the seat that once Sardar Patel occupied. He should take some inspiration from Sardar Patel. He should also acquire some political acumen from Rajaji. He will have to follow the courage and administrative ability of Shri Pant. If in this hour of crisis he can take the ship of state out of the whirlpool and reach it to the haven of security and peace his Home Ministership will have succeeded. Otherwise he will not only drown the Home Ministry in the whirlpool but create difficulties for the country that would endanger democracy.

SPEAKER : I hope I can speak to you in Urdu.

SHRI VAJPAYEE : I too like Urdu very much. In fact I love Urdu *'Shairi'* (poetry).

SPEAKER : A person who is single (*'gair-shadishuda*) is always in love (*'fida'*) with Urdu *Shairi*.

Protectors Became Predators

I congratulate the *Indian Express* on bringing to light this barbaric incident, which has on the one hand forced us to bow our heads in shame, but on the other served public interest by showing that in the year 1980 and in this land of Lord Buddha and Mahatma Gandhi such inhuman atrocities are still being perpetrated without check. For this we need an alert, free and fearless press.

The administration may make mistakes .... In a democracy the government may become absolute, officials may transgress their powers, the common man may be subjected to excesses, but there is a provision of checks and balances in the administration, in which the press also has a place. I am sorry to say what happened in Bihar raises doubts whether the press there would be allowed to be free and secure.

Sir, I would like to know if, on August 23, 1980 the Government sent a secret circular to all district magistrates saying the press should not get such news, and if it does get it it should be prevented from going out. The Hon. Minister should find out about this.

DEPUTY SPEAKER : There are no two opinions on this. The entire House is agitated over this incident. Let us know the facts and we will act accordingly. (*Interruption*).

Supreme Court Judgment

SHRI VAJPAYEE : The Minister has admitted in his statement that one of the unfortunate people who were blinded in Bhagalpur jail had submitted a petition to the District Judge, Bhagalpur on July 6, 1980. The Minister should clarify why the Bihar Government did not take notice of this matter at that time. They are referring to the Supreme Court. I have a Supreme Court judgement with me—*Sunil Batra* versus *Delhi Administration*—which proved this. I quote :

> "All orders issued by the magistrate of the district, if expressed in terms requiring immediate compliance, be forthwith obeyed and a report made as prescribed in the said sub-section to the Inspector-General."

It further states as follows :

> "The District Magistrate must remember that in this capacity he is judicial officer and not an executive head and must function as such independently of the prison executive. To make prisoners' rights in correctional institutions viable, we direct the District Magistrate concerned to inspect the jails in the district once every week, receive complaints from individual prisoners, and enquire into them

Lok Sabha on December 1, 1980 during the discussion on the blinding of some suspected criminals in Bihar immediately. If he is too preoccupied with urgent work, paragraph 42 enables him to depute a magistrate subordinate to him to visit and inspect the jail. What is important is that he should meet the prisoners separately, if they have grievances. The presence of warders or officials will be inhibitive and must be avoided. He must ensure that his enquiry is confidential although subject to natural justice and does not lead to reprisals by jail officials. The rule speaks of the record of the result of each visit and inspection. This empowers him to enquire and pass orders."

A complaint was made and a petition filed on July 6. Did the magistrate or district magistrate with whom the petition was filed visit the jail ? Did they try to find out from the prisoners what happened to them ? Was this not brought to the notice of the State Government ?

Later, petitions were again filed on July 30, after which the Inspector-General of Prisons went there. The I.G. Bhagalpur also went. They met the Commissioner and also talked to the D.I.G. The S.P. was present during the talk. Had all these officers conspired to keep the State Government in the dark ? If not, why did the State Government not get information about this ?

Sir, you have seen the Supreme Court judgement. But when the petition was filed with the Sessions Judge he forwarded it to the Chief Magistrate. The Chief Magistrate sent it to the public prosecutor in October, and the public prosecutor sent it to the Police Superintendent. Citizens were blinded. Is this not 'eye for an eye' justice ? Was this not an attempt to enforce the law and justice of the 19th century ? Their crime was to be proved in court. The job of the police was to maintain law and order. But protectors became predators.

One of the persons who were blinded said it would have been better if he had been shot dead, everything would have been over in an instant and he would not have had to pass a whole life-time in a world of darkness. Who is going to restore his eye-sight ?

What difficulty does the minister have in ordering a judicial inquiry ? It is said the C.I.D. is inquiring into the event. The C.I.D. is a part of the same cruel establishment. It is our own establishment, but this matter cannot be left to it.

Why is no action being taken against those senior officers who are involved in this ? The S.P. has not been arrested while junior officers have been arrested. And even that information has been given today, as they knew there would be commotion in the House. But what is the role of senior officers in all this ? And where is that doctor, that so-called doctor, who was called and who pierced the eyes and put acid in them ? That doctor is nowhere to be found. Why are big officers being let off ? Place the medical report on the floor of the House. Why is it difficult for the Government to set up a parliamentary committee ?

Such incidents can be prevented in future only if Government machinery is at least against their repetition.

This is not a matter for the State. India is a signatory to a covenant in which we have promised the world that we shall not allow torture in our country. And don't say the Bihar Assembly has set up a Committee, so Parliament does not come into the picture. This matter will tarnish India's image in the world. What will we say if somebody asks questions in the United Nations, in the Human Rights Commission ?

This matter should be viewed with maximum seriousness. Shri Mhalgi has rightly said that it should not be given a political colour. Actually the Chief Minister of Bihar should have owned moral responsibility and resigned. Then he could have been persuaded to take his resignation back. But he did not do even that. This is a time for introspection. We do not want to score a debating point. This may also be happening in some other State. It is the responsibility of the House to see that such things don't happen again. We want to know what the Government is going to do about it. Thank you.

National Consensus on National Issues

Sir, in the course of the present discussion many members of the ruling party have talked of cooperation with opposition parties. Along with the talk of cooperation charges have also been levelled.

Did not the opposition parties join hands with the ruling party and pass a unanimous resolution in this House during the reservation agitation in Gujarat, when the agitationists took to the streets and the unity of the whole society was jeopardised ?

Had we wanted it, we could have exploited the reservation agitation for party benefit (*Interruption*). Shri Maniram Bagri is second to none in opposition, but it was he who suggested the unanimous passing of a resolution. I say this to stress that even the staunchest opponent has a constructive point of view.

Opposition parties are participating in tripartite talks for solving the problem of foreigners in Assam. You are in power, the headache is yours, but what do you care if Assam is in flames ? But we cannot adopt such an attitude, we do care, and that is why the opposition parties are extending their cooperation for a satisfactory solution of this problem.

Joint efforts are needed for solving national problems. But where is the atmosphere for that ? Was it necessary for the Prime Minister to look down upon the Janata Government's achievements while presenting her new 20-point programme ? She even said the country was about to break up in the two years of the Janata Government. No slogan of Khalistan was raised during these two years, nor had the Meenakshipuram incident taken place.

SHRI MADHAVRAO SCINDIA : There was a responsible opposition then.

SHRI VAJPAYEE : We know what sort of a responsible opposition there was. And we see how responsibly the government party behaves where it is in the opposition.

There cannot be different standards of behaviour. We were discussing Jammu and Kashmir, we too have raised our voice against the discrimination against Ladakh and Jammu. But will a violent agitation be incited in Ladakh and Kishtwar ? The Information Ministry organised a film festival in Calcutta, but a group of young men belonging to the ruling party created a disturbance in Netaji Sadan. If we do that it would be said that we are given to violence and we do not believe in democracy. But in Ladakh government offices may be set on fire, in Calcutta buses may be torched because fares have gone up due to diesel prices going up, your supporters may disrupt a film festival, and yet nobody will condemn them.

Lok Sabha on March 24, 1982 during discussion on the functioning of the Home Ministry

After 1947 we had evolved a national consensus to speed up the process of economic and social change in the country. That consensus has kept the country one so far. I regret it is now breaking down. The depressed class is no more willing to compromise with injustice. I appreciate the feelings of our Harijan brethren. In Meenakshipuram they said to me you cannot give us land, you cannot give us work, but at least stop calling us abusive names. Even that we have not been able to do.

When 'excesses' were committed on Harijans in the regime of the Janata Party they were 'excesses'. Are they not excesses now ? Did you not exploit those excesses at that time ? You had taken advantage of the incidents on Belchhi and Narainpur to stand the governments of the opposition party in the dock. The Prime Minister herself visited Narainpur. Reports asked her if she had come to reap political benefit as there was an opposition government in Uttar Pradesh. She replied, if our opponents make a mistake why should we not exploit it ? Now the situation has changed.

Time-bound Programme Needed

I repeat a national consensus is needed on the question of justice to Harijans and tribals. The Home Minister should call a meeting of the National Integration Council to consider this problem. A time-bound programme should be fixed. Just now Shri Venkatasubhaiah was talking about the National Integration Council. For how long has it not met ? It was set up and locked away in a cupboard. There is a committee on Communalism (*Interruption*). I am not on it, neither is Shri Chandra Shekhar. Shri Chavan was taken from the opposition. But, if I am not mistaken, what has the Committee done ? You can trot out figures to prove that communal incidents have gone down. But what happened in Kanyakumari is an alarm bell. Nowhere in the country had so much bitterness been created between Christians and Hindus to date. I am not making a charge, and a counter-charge will not be the answer. Today what is at stake is not some individual's future or some party's destiny but the unity and integrity of the country.

I call for an effort to evolve a broad national consensus on national issues. But for that the limitations of democratic institutions will have to be preserved. If the Governor's decisions always favour the ruling party it will not redound to the prestige of the institution of Governor. What happened in Kerala and Assam ? You dissolved the Assam Legislative Assembly. I am worried about the future. Now elections will have to be held in Assam. So long the assembly in Assam was suspended, not dissolved. The question of foreigners in Assam is not yet solved. Still the assembly was dissolved in order to prevent a candidate of the opposition getting elected to the Rajya Sabha. The Kerala Legislative Assembly could also have lasted some more days. The way every Rajya Sabha seat is being fought makes me wonder of a plan for a basic change in the constitution is under way. Let the Home Minister refute this.

In the past too a code of conduct for Governors had been discussed at a Governors' conference. You may say, why did you not do it when you were in power ? But the people removed us in the hope that you will do better than us. We could not pass an anti-defection law. We wanted to, but could not, because some people of our party were talking of defecting. But what is your difficulty ? I was on a visit to Goa. When elections were held there no Congress-I candidate was elected, all Congress-U candidates were elected, but now there is a Congress-I government there. Overnight it was revived. Would the heavens have fallen if Goa had not had your government ? But, no, a tendency of intolerance is raising its head. They want the opposition of opposition parties, but they are not ready for elections. I am sorry about what Shri Venkatasubbaiah has said about Delhi—for two years there is no metropolitan council here, no municipal corporation.

Delhi's Plight

Bureaucrats are presiding over the fate of the people of Delhi. There is no one to listen to their complaints. Where will they go ? To whom will they talk ? It is said we will have to think afresh about the structure of Delhi. Why had the process of thinking stopped for two years ? Keep thinking but also continue with elections. An experts' committee is being set up, but its terms of reference are not clear. Shri Tytler says we had given an assurance that we would set up an assembly. If you have given an assurance, fulfil it. Promises are for keeping. I feel inspired by Gyaniji, who is sitting in front of me. But no time limit has been set for submitting a report to the experts' committee.

When will the experts' committee submit a report ? You are setting up a committee for Old Delhi but what about the rest of Delhi ? I have also been elected from Delhi. But even I am not being taken into confidence as a member of Parliament. The Lt. Governor is touring the area with Congress MPs, but he will not accompany me.

What is the position of Delhi ? The bus service is running at a loss. The loss was Rs. 17 crores in 1979-80, Rs. 45 crore in 1980-81, and Rs. 60 crores in 1981-82. The fleet consists of 2626 buses, worth Rs. 40 crores while the loss is Rs. 60 crores. And still there are no facilities for the travelling public.

What is the position with DESU ? In 1978 it was second in rank in power generation in India. It had an average of 200 MW per day, but now this has come down to 150. The loss was Rs. 13 crores in 1979-80, Rs. 38 crores in 1980-81 and Rs. 50 crores in 1981-82. Since June 1980 DESU has no General Manager. The other day my friend Shri Bhagat had raised this question. Delhi is under the Centre's jurisdiction. There is no legislative assembly in Delhi. There is a multiplicity of authorities in Delhi. Delhi's issues cannot be represented in Parliament. Why are you delaying the appointment of a general manager ? But nobody cares for Delhi.

The result is that Delhi's rations have been cut down. In 1978 20 kg. of wheat was available per head. In 1980 this came down to 12 and in 1982 to 10. Labourers have to eat wheat, but they are given rice. Karnataka has complained that the people there want rice but receive wheat. The

Government claims there has been record production, then why cut down rations ?I have heard that the Lt. Governor has sent a report that the law and order situation in Delhi has deteriorated, so elections cannot be held for the time being. Table this report in the House. Why are elections in Delhi being avoided ? Is it because you fear defeat ?

SHRI B.N. SINGH, Minister for Parliamentary Affairs : We shall win.

SHRI VAJPAYEE : Then hold the election.

Election in States

There will be no election in Garhwal. In Assam there are 12 vacant Lok Sabha seats. The voters of Assam will not get the chance to elect their representatives. Elections are yet to take place in Jammu and Kashmir, Himachal Pradesh, Haryana and West Bengal. Sir, they know these States will not be in a good position, so Karnataka is being talked about and elections in Andhra are also being discussed.

While Shri Venkatasubbaiah was speaking I interrupted him. He too wanted to go to Andhra. My friend Shri Anjaiah was well off at the Centre, he was a Minister of State. When he was on his way to Andhra, I asked him, "Why are you going to Andhra ?" He said, "I have been promoted."

AN HON. MEMBER : You proved a bad influence.

SHRI VAJPAYEE : That day I said—is it promotion or demotion ?

Peons Better than Chief Ministers

How was he removed ? The Chief Minister's post has been devalued. The Chief Minister will of course belong to your party, but if you use your powers to humiliate him you will weaken the institution of Chief Minister. There could have been another way of removing him. In a meeting in Andhra I said the Chief Minister is being removed like a peon. Upon this a peon wrote me a protest letter. He said—'How can you compare the Chief Minister with us ? We are permanent, the Chief Minister is temporary. No one can remove us without a show-cause notice.' I had to apologise. I said publicly—'I have insulted peons, I apologise.'

Corruption Charges

Corruption is being discussed a lot. Those is power have to be responsible. Antulay was not removed when his case came before Parliament. The Court removed him. But corruption is not merely a legal point. There is also a moral aspect to it. Charge sheets of corruption are being given to the President and the governors of many States against the Chief Ministers and governments there. I would like to place before the House an example of how these charge-sheets are being played with by the Centre.

There was an unstarred question on December 9, 1981, which was answered by Shri Venkatasubbaiah. It related to charges levelled by the legislators of Madhya Pradesh against the Government there. Shri Venkatasubbaiah said :

"The charges in the representation made by Shri Sunderlal Patwa and others were sent to the Chief Minister of Madhya Pradesh according to the procedure laid down for comments. They were received some days back and are being examined."

This is Shri Venkatasubbaiah's reply on December 9, 1981. But Home Minister Gyani Zail Singh went on a tour of Madhya Pradesh on December 8, 1981. At the airport he was asked. "What happened to the charge sheet ?" His reply was reported by All India Radio. I quote the bulletin—

"In reply to a question during a talk with press reporters at Khandwa yesterday the Central Home Minister said—all charges of corruption levelled against Shri Arjun Singh, Chief Minister of Madhya Pradesh and his Government were found false and baseless.'

This is the Home Minister's reply. It was reported by the Radio on December 8 that he gave this reply on December 7. And on December 9 his own junior colleague says in the House that an inquiry is on. Corruption is not an internal affair of the Congress Party.

Yesterday one lakh people gave a memorandum to the Governor of Bihar against the Council of Ministers of the State. Bihar has a Chief Minister who issued his own order to take back the case against himself. He is charged with conspiracy. I would like to know—who will make the inquiry ? Decide upon an agreed procedure which will be applicable to all parties and for all time. This game of saying one thing while in office and another while in the opposition has gone for too long. You have also been in the opposition and can again go into opposition. Even today you are in the opposition in many states. But if you want to protect democracy you will have to give up violence. There will have to be consensus on the creation of a just social order and there will have to be a code of conduct. Can the Home Minister do this ? If he can he will prove himself worthy of the position he occupies, otherwise history will say about him—he was given a chance, but he lost it.

Home Minister Not at Home

Sir, the Home Ministry's report for 1982-83 is before me. It makes one feel that it is not a report on the internal situation in the country but a fable. The report says, 'during the year under review the law and order situation was under control.' It adds, 'the student front was in general normal.' It further adds, 'on the labour front too, apart from the strike of textile workers, no special tendency was noticed.'

What country does this report describe ? Does it relate to the internal situation in the country ? Or does it picture some never-never-land ? If all's well in the country and if our house is in the order it should be in, what do we have to worry about ? But speeches of ruling party members show anxiety. The Prime Minister's speech also shows it. However that anxiety is nowhere reflected in this report. The Prime Minister has given a new slogan — *'Shram eva jayate'*, 'toil alone triumphs'. I think the Home Minister's slogan is *'Bhram eva jayate'*, delusion alone triumphs. It is not necessary to place the truth before the House. It is necessary to cover up reality. Such a report cannot serve any purpose.

No one can deny that the situation in Punjab is serious. On April 4 firing was done at 12 places, many people were killed by police bullets, and there was heavy damage to property. Violence and killing have been going on in Punjab for a long time. But what does the report say ? Apart from 'stray' incidents the situation in Punjab was peaceful in general. The Home Minister may say the events of April 4 took place later. But is it not true that so far more than 30 people have been killed by the extremists ? Were those incidents 'stray' because they were killed one or two at a time ?

I am glad the Punjab Government has decided on a judicial inquiry into the events of April 4. Truth has no fear. If the demonstrators resorted to stone-throwing and firing on April 4 their doings will also come to light. My friends are present here. We three, Shri Harikesh Bahadur, Shri Bhogendra Jha and myself visited Malerkotla and Kupkalan. I am sorry the Punjab Government has misled the Home Minister. The Home Minister misled the House on the basis of the Punjab Government's report. The Punjab Government keeps the Home Minister in the dark and the Home Minister keeps the House in the dark. In Malerkotla people did not die in a stampede. We have visited the hospital and seen that they died of police bullets. What space was there for a stampede at the cross-roads ? What is the population of Malerkotla ? How many people out of that population were participating

Lok Sabha on April 11, 1983 during discussion on demands for grants of the Ministry of Home Affairs

in the demonstration ? People may have run when the police fired. But it is not true that five people died in the stampede. Who are those who were wounded by police bullets and are lying in the hospital ? In Kupkalan the police set the farmers' tractors and trolleys on fire. Burnt bicycles are still lying there. Will the farmers torch their own tractors ? The State Bank there was not looted. Municipal trucks standing there were not torched. There is a transformer there, but it was not smashed. The villagers told us—and we are ready to believe—that the police themselves set fire to their jeep and the police station.

A Congress candidate who was contesting the Lok Sabha election against Shri Barnala came to see us. He said he saw the police torching tractors and trolleys with his own eyes. Have even Congressmen in Punjab started making wrong statements ? But I am happy you have ordered a judicial inquiry. The inquiry should have comprehensive terms of reference. Setting up a commission would be still more useful if it could go into why the Government has not been able to apprehend the extremists and others involved in the killing.

There should also be a judicial inquiry into the events in Assam. No one can deny that people have been killed there in large numbers. The leaders of the movement have written to all members of Parliament and demanded that they should stress an inquiry for unmasking the forces responsible for the massacre. I know I will be criticised on Assam. If my speeches incited the people of Assam I am ready to stand in the dock. My friend Shri F.H. Mohsin is not present. On the basis of the published report of my speech he was trying to show that my speech in Jorhat on the 18th caused the massacre of Muslims in Nellie on the 17th. The massacre of Nellie took place on the 17th, my speech in Jorhat was on the 18th. I had compared the situation in Punjab and Assam.

SHRI P. VENKATASUBBAIAH : He did not mention about Nellie.

SHRI VAJPAYEE : He did not mention about Nellie! But he blamed me for all the massacre.

SHRI P. VENKATASUBBAIAH : The disaster that your speech had.

SHRI VAJPAYEE : I delivered my speech on 18th. Nellie massacre took place on 17th. Did it have retrospective effect ?

SHRI NIHAR RANJAN LASKAR, Minister of State in the Ministry of Home Affairs : It had its effect later also.

Students' Challenge

SHRI VAJPAYEE : The boys have given a challenge. I quote a portion of their letter :

> "The imposition of the election resulted in burning of villages, killing of thousands of lives and looting of property. After perpetration of the fraud, a calculated attempt has been now made to cover up the forces behind the massacres. We are throwing a challenge to the Government. Till February 10, 1983 violence was limited to state violence only and one must look into the reasons for sudden eruption of group violence

from February 11, 1983, with barely three days left for the imposed poll. Let the government send a team of honest, courageous and upright group of intelligence officers and let the government take the opposition parties into confidence in this regard. The team must unearth the forces behind the incident at Chimera and the carnage in Gohpur, which occurred almost simultaneously and had fallouts in Nellie and other places. Let it be a comprehensive enquiry. One thing more. The state IGP of Intelligence must not be associated in any way with such an enquiry. This is a necessary precondition to unearth the truth. Can you imagine that in an election meeting a candidate belonging to a particular party was holding a gun in one hand and the mike in the other, and he was inciting the gathering to take to arms at the right moment ? Was February 11, 1983, the right moment ? Ghani Khan Choudhury appealed to the foreigners to build a 'new' Assam. Was February 11, 1983, the beginning of the process ?

We have thrown a challenge to the Central Government. Will it be accepted to set the record right ? The Central Government and the contesting political parties have nothing to oppose in instituting such an enquiry if they very well know that their hands are clean."

Sir, in Assam maximum areas are being handed over to the Army. But there is no peace. Leaders of the agitation have suspended it. That suspension has not been adequately welcomed by the Government. They are bad if they agitate, they are bad even if they stop agitating. My friend Shri Chitta Basu says the agitationist leaders should not be given the status they were given. What was that status ?

SHRI CHITTA BASU : Respectability.

SHRI VAJPAYEE : They should receive respectability.

SHRI CHITTA BASU : Why ?

SHRI VAJPAYEE : That is my opinion. Will you not talk to those who are agitating ?

I support Shri Santosh Mohan Dev's view that talks with agitationist leaders should be resumed. But so long as the present government is in office normalcy cannot return to Assam. The administrative inquiry that has been ordered is not enough. A commission headed by a Supreme Court judge should be set up to inquire into the whole course of events in Assam.

SHRI MANIRAM BAGRI (Hissar) : That is right.

SHRI VAJPAYEE : What does truth have to fear ? We are ready for an inquiry. I have with me a tape of the speech by Shri Abdul Ghani Khan Choudhury, in which he said if you kill one man of ours we will kill two of yours.

SHRI SANTOSH MOHAN DEV : I also have tapes of your speeches.

SHRI VAJPAYEE : Place them before the commission.

SHRI ERA ANBARASU (Chengalpattu) : What happened to your statement when you said, 'Let Brahmaputra be flooded with blood ?'

SHRI VAJPAYEE : I did not say it. I denied. But Shri A.B.A. Ghani Khan Choudhury did not deny the allegation. The allegation was made in the Rajya Sabha.

PROF. K.K. TEWARY (Buxar) : He also denied.

SHRI VAJPAYEE : He did not deny.

SHRI ERA ANBARASU : Even if he has said so it is only to scare away those people who had been creating violence there.

SHRI VAJPAYEE : Now you are justifying his statement (*Interruption*).

The country did not face such a crisis during the last 35-36 years as it faces today.

The crisis is not only that the impartiality of the judiciary is being questioned, an attempt is being made to muzzle the press, Parliament has been devalued, governors have become puppets in the hands of the Centre. The Government is not interested in laying down any guidelines for governors. If there were guidelines how would Governors be able to serve the selfish ends of the party in power ? So they were given the freedom to act according to their sweet will in the name of discretion, but this sweet will was always expected to favour the ruling party.

The Real Danger

The danger is not only that all power is now concentrated in Delhi, and even in Delhi in the hands of one family. The danger is not that corruption has become institutionalised.

This danger is of course there and serious thought will have to be given to it, but the biggest crisis is that the people are losing faith in their future, their hopes for tomorrow are wilting. Despair, uncertainty and doubt are clouding their minds. Whether it is an individual or a community, the majority or the minority—all are worried. They all feel they are in great difficulties.

I would clarify this still further. The other day Shri Ram Vilas Paswan was speaking. Expressing the sorrows of Harijans and tribals he made a point that can touch anyone's heart strings. But is it not strange that a section is emerging among the higher castes that is asking—how long will the tribals, scheduled castes and scheduled tribes get loan facilities ? This class is not only emerging it is becoming vocal.

SHRI K.K. TEWARY : This is your party's class.

SHRI VAJPAYEE : They are all in our party. All good people are sitting over there, then why all these problems ? (*Interruption*).

Tiwariji, had the problem been so simple you would have solved it. It is complex. Now please do not interrupt. Pay attention to what I say.

Sir, you may recollect that there was a big agitation in Gujarat over reservations in medical colleges. I had raised my voice in favour of reservation—even at the cost of popularity. But the doctors who came to see me asked—if our ancestors have committed some sin how long will we pay for it ? Today the scheduled castes are unhappy, the scheduled tribes are unhappy, the upper castes are also complaining. We are entangled in a strange situation.

The communal situation has deteriorated so much, but the Home Ministry's report is trying to play it down too. Forty-five members of

Parliament have given a memorandum to the Prime Minister warning her that the Muslim minority is losing faith in the impartiality of the administration. It added that excesses are being perpetrated against it and says, "today the victim is being projected as aggressor and as a rebel and as a traitor."

The coming together of 45 members of different parties on some question is an important event. I certainly regret that if the Muslim community has a complaint it should become necessary for all Muslim members to come together to place it before the Government. Can their own parties, whichever they are, not fight for their legitimate interests ? If Muslim MPs come together on a Muslim problem will not Hindu MPs start coming together on a Hindu problem ? Do Hindus have no complaints in this country ? Are not Hindus being discriminated against in Jammu and Kashmir ?

SHRI MANIRAM BAGRI : In Punjab too.

SHRI VAJPAYEE : In Punjab too the Hindu is unhappy. Then should Hindu MPs come together to voice the complaints of Hindus ?

I have seen the memorandum presented by the 45 MPs. There are some very good things in it. For example, it says if a communal riot does not stop within 24 hours stringent action should be taken. Whether the Hindus do the riot or the Muslims it should be firmly suppressed. But now it is not so simple. Muslims—a section among them—believe that they have no future in India. On the other hand, a section among Hindus feels the Muslims are going the wrong way and trying to create the pre-1947 atmosphere. The gulf is widening. Both things cannot be true. But the number of those believing in both is on the increase. Whose failure is this ?

SHRI MANIRAM BAGRI : The Government's.

SHRI VAJPAYEE : That day the Chairman said in the House that Hindus and Sikhs are branches of the same tree. Now there is a clash between these branches. In Punjab many Hindus feel they are being treated highhandedly, while a big section among Sikhs feels discriminated against.

The seriousness of this crisis of confidence can be measured by the fact that the people have started losing faith even in the security forces. In Meerut serious charges have been made about the conduct of the PAC. I do not know how far they are true, but the Muslims of Meerut say they do not want the PAC and demand the deployment of the Border Security Force and the Central Reserve Police instead. In Punjab the Akalis are demanding the removal of the Central Reserve Police. On the other hand, the Hindus say they do not trust the Punjab constabulary.

In Assam the Bengali-speaking population and other people from Bangladesh complain against the Assam Police, while the Asamiyas, the old inhabitants of Assam, complain against the CRP. In Assam there was recently a skirmish between the CRP and the Assam Police and some people were killed. Fortunately everyone trusts the Army. The Government should not take it away all too frequently from the task of guarding the frontiers and press it into service for maintaining law and order. The prestige of the Army should be maintained. But if you use it again and again for maintaining law and order one day the Army would also become an object of criticism.

The National Crisis

There are also other examples of the national crisis I discussed. People sitting at the Centre feel that attempts are being made to weaken the Centre. On the other hand the states feel that they have been reduced to *municipalities*. The ruling party feels the only business of the opposition is to criticise the Government and hinder its working. The opposition feels the Government does not even want its concrete cooperation for problem-solving by taking it into confidence on every issue, let alone respect it.

Today it is not a question of any one class, any one party. The basic question is, how can this national crisis of confidence be resolved ? There is a growing gulf between Hindus and Muslims, Hindus and Sikhs, the higher castes and the scheduled castes, the tribals and the plains-dwellers, the ruling party and the opposition. How can it be bridged ? The Home Ministry has the responsibility of the home. Without setting our house in order we cannot speed up economic progress, nor maintain our respect in the world. The quarrels within the home that were taking place so far have now brought things to such a pass that the home may burn down, but the Home Ministry rests in peace in North Block (*Interruptions*).

You rang the bell at a very wrong time. I was going to support the demands for grants, now I will have to oppose. The situation is that God is in his heaven, all's under control in India and the Home Ministry's interest is in the grants. What will happen to this country ?

The National Integration Council has set up a Committee to prepare a code of ethics. Political parties should do some soul-searching. A section of Muslims decided on a satyagraha to save the country and the people and their leader general Shah Nawaz Khan corresponded with the Prime Minister. What attitude of the Prime Minister did that correspondence reveal ? Such a thing by one community is not wrong because it would produce a reaction in another community but because the BJP will exploit it. I quote a portion of the Prime Minister's letter :

> "Any satyagraha of the kind you have in mind and however peaceful you may think it will be, will be regarded as a direct hit at the Congress. In Bengal and Tripura our main opposition are the Marxists. But in the rest of India only the Jan Sangh, now the BJP, can be benefited if we are weakened. Do you not know the views of the BJP and RSS ?"

Do not talk about the complaints of Muslims. Muslims should not raise their voice for justice. She did not say some complaints are right, some are wrong, do not repeat the wrong ones, steps are being taken to remove the right ones.

Sir, if the Prime Minister has not written such a letter it is a matter of happiness for me. I do not have her letter.

PROF. K.K. TEWARY : Then why are you raising this ?

SHRI VAJPAYEE : Sir, I also do not have the memorandum given by 45 Muslim members, but it has been fully reproduced in the papers. Can it not be quoted ? If I am quoting it out of context you may put it in the right context.

PROF. K.K. TEWARY : I will do it.

SHRI VAJPAYEE : The Home Minister can produce a copy. My submission is that rousing one communalism is not the way to fight another communalism. Communalism can be fought on the basis of nationalism and secularism. We believe in a system in which there is neither discrimination nor impartiality on the basis of religion.

SHRI G.L. VYAS (Bhilwara) : Since when did this become your policy ?

SHRI VAJPAYEE : Since the time you were sent from Rajasthan to Delhi.

One more point—corruption. It is being discussed a lot. Now even the Government has admitted its prevalence. Saying this is a global phenomenon is not the end of it. What happened to the Lokpal Bill ? The Government is committed to it. A Lokpal Bill was brought in 1968. Later the Lok Sabha was dissolved and the Bill lapsed. In 1971 it was again brought forward but was kept hanging till 1977. The Janata Government had certainly tried sincerely to pass it as quickly as possible, but the Government itself went out of office.

SHRI G.L. VYAS : The Janata Government did not make any effort.

SHRI VAJPAYEE : Now it is three years since this Government came into power. Where is that Lokpal Bill ? A vigilance commission has been set up for employees. I have every annual report of that commission. When a Bill about the vigilance commission was tabled in Parliament the then Home Minister Shri Gulzarilal Nanda had said — a vigilance commissioner will not be appointed to any government post after retirement. But Shri Subimal Dutt was made High Commissioner to Bangladesh. Shri R.K.Trivedi was made Chief Election Commissioner. The Vigilance Commission's report can be the subject of discussion in the House. The Vigilance Commission is connected with corruption in the services. In many important matters the Government did not accept the Vigilance Commission's report. The Vigilance Commission said action should be taken against officers, but the Government did not accept the recommendations. It wrote to the Commission to change its recommendations. The Commission again repeated its recommendations, the matter was circumvented, and action was closed.

V PREVENTIVE DETENTION

Preventive Detention Encourages Authoritarianism

Sir, there are three main problems before us when we think about extending the period of the Preventive Detention Act. The first : Is it just and proper to keep an individual in jail without trial ? Is it in accordance with the rule of law in a democracy ? The second : Is there a situation in the country that would justify equipping the Government with the special powers envisaged in this Act ? The third : Does the experience of the past seven years show that the Government has used this Act with due consideration, only where it was needed to be used and only to the proper extent ?

So far as principles are concerned no one will agree that it is in accordance with the concept of democracy to keep a person in preventive detention without our trial or to arrest him without showing a cause. Rule of law means every individual has the right to enjoy his freedom so long as he does not infringe a common law. This is why no civilised country has law of preventive detention without trial. A democracy can have no place for such a law. This law that is in operation in the country for the past seven years strikes at the roots of democracy, suppresses civil liberties, destroys personal freedom, and is a blot on the Indian Republic. It is a matter of shame for the Government and challenge for the people of India.

I shall not take the time of the House in repeating what the late Pandit Motilal Nehru once said and what Pandit Jawaharlal Nehru, the Prime Minister today, said. In 1929 the British brought forward a Public Security Bill that related only to foreigners and provided for their detention without trial, but even that Bill for foreigners the late Pandit Motilal Nehru shot down, saying he could not support anybody's detention without trial. Pandit Jawaharlal Nehru had also agreed in 1936 that a government that resorts to detention without trial has no right to remain in office.

It may be argued that times have changed. Yesterday's opponents have become today's rulers. Seats have changed but the principles cannot. Personal freedom is as precious today as it was even when we were not independent, and any step that seeks to take it away should be opposed as firmly. A foreign government can be pardoned for making a law that does not respect our

Lok Sabha on December 10, 1957 regarding the Bill relating to extension of period of the Preventive Detention Act

freedom. But in independence we cannot let the government make a law that does not become it. But it is argued that the situation has changed. Today in this country at one place Brahmins are threatened with death, at another there is talk of burning the Constitution and at a third there is a controversy over language. But are these conditions serious enough to require a law like this to tackle them ? Is there an emergency in the country ? Has an emergency been declared in Madras ? Today the country does not have a crisis before it. We do not even have a war with Pakistan, we have a cease-fire, and Congress leaders say Pakistan is our friend. The *Mantra* of *Panch Sheel* is being chanted and doves of peace are being released into the sky. And if there is no danger, against what supposed danger is this weapon being prepared ? We have a big country and a big population. In such a big country some controversies will naturally be there. Where there are many vessels they are bound to bump into one another and make noise. Further, the Government and the ruling party cannot escape the responsibility of the situation prevailing in Madras or Punjab. The Congress has reached the seat of power with the backing and support of those very people who are today talking of burning the Constitution or killing Brahmins in Tamilnadu and Madras. It was these very people who were backing the Congress during the elections. They made speeches from Congress platforms. They openly supported today's Chief Minister of Madras. Now they are asking for their pound of flesh. They are asking for the price of the support they gave to the Congress. Hence this talk of burning the Constitution.

The Congress is also responsible for what is happening in Punjab. One may differ with the movement there, but if we go into its background we will find that the Congress party's secret understanding stands against the Congress. I may say—and Lala Achint Ram has agreed — that the Hindus of Punjab have lost faith in the Congress. Why ? Did the Bharatiya Jan Sangh try for it ? The reason is that the way the Congress entered into an understanding with the Akalis made the Hindus feel that the Congress is ignoring them. A brave youth of Punjab had to risk his life and go on a hunger strike for a copy of the agreement, and then at last the so-called regional formula was published. You cannot suppress the opposition to that formula with the Preventive Detention Act. Suppression will fan the flames all the more. If the suppression of the British could not suppress the Congress, the suppression of the Congress will also not be able to suppress the Arya Samaj and its colleagues. People fight and go to jail only when it is impossible for them to remain out of jail.

In Punjab 113 persons were taken into preventive detention. I object to the way Shri Datar gave the figures yesterday. In all 113 people were taken into preventive detention, out of whom 80 were let off by the advisory board. Why ? Because the charges against them were false. On this occasion I do not want to repeat all those charges to which my friends have referred. But I would like to mention the case of Shri Shyam Sundar Katiar of Rohtak. He was charged with addressing a public meeting in Rohtak on August 9. But on that day he was in jail. Then how could he make a speech ?

Another and similar case is that of Mahashay Krishna, founder-manager of *Veer Arjun* and *Pratap*, who was also taken into preventive detention. He was charged with participating in a secret meeting in Jalandhar in May 1956 and after this meeting riots broke out in Punjab. When he read about this charge in jail he wrote to his family that he did not visit Jalandhar at all in May. Detenus' letters are censored. When this letter was read by the censor there was consternation in the Punjab Government Secretariat. Later Mahashay Krishna made another correction — that he visited Jalandhar not in 1956 but in 1957. However he did not make any change about the riots. Actually there was no riot in Punjab after May 1957. Mahashay Krishna said even if I participated in a secret meet it cannot remain secret, because I am quite hard of hearing. If I have to say something I would have to speak so loudly that no secrecy would remain. Everybody knows this, but perhaps your intelligence people do not. The result was that he was put in jail.

Yesterday the advisory board received a lot of praise here. But would any State Government delay the setting up of an advisory board as much as the Punjab Government did ? The result was that there were people who had to remain in jail for 60 to 80 days before they were set at liberty by the advisory board. Justice Khosla of the Punjab advisory board has resigned. Why ? Reveal the reasons for it, which you have covered up. I suspect the resignation is due to interference with the functioning of the courts in Punjab. If that is not so, let the Home Ministry clarify the position. The advisory board cannot go to the bottom of the causes given for preventive detention. It is handicapped, it is not effective. I again recollect the late Pandit Motilal Nehru's speech on the Punjab Security Act. He said : "You may have an advisory Council or you may have a privy council, but neither will you be able to do anything so long as there is no right of argument, no right of cross-examining witnesses, no right to go to the bottom of a charge".

In such circumstances I would repeat that this law has been openly misused. It gives the powers that be the authority that endangers democracy.

I have no hesitation in saying that the happenings in Punjab are a warning for the whole country. The Home Minister should take it like that. I would even say if there is any one individual in Punjab who should be put in jail under preventive detention, it is Chief Minister Pratap Singh Kairon, who has revived memories of Hitler. But he is being patted on the back and praised to the skies, and a law is being made which, in his hands, would surely put an end to the freedom of the people of Punjab. I do not support, either in principle or in practice, the incarceration of any person without trial. In my opinion the common laws of the country are enough. If there is danger for the country you can declare an emergency, and if Parliament is not in session you can issue an ordinance. If the common laws are not enough you can amend them, but there is no need to bring in a black law like this.

One thing more. Yesterday the Home Minister said offences are going down, to which Communist Party leader Shri Dange replied. 'Offences have gone down because there is no Preventive Detention Act. Some parties have changed their policies and as a result offences are going down.' I think both these things are right. In these changed circumstances there is no propriety in extending the period of this old Act, and that too for three long years. Sardar Patel had proposed extension for one year. Now it is being extended for three years. This is uncalled for. If we want to build an atmosphere of cooperation for national reconstruction we cannot build it on this Prevention Detention Act. The country's plans require the cooperation of all parties. But if you want our cooperation with a sword hanging over our heads there can be no national reconstruction. There is still time. By withdrawing this black law the Government can show that it really wants our cooperation. Thank you.

Preventive Detention is Misused Against Jana Sangh

Sir, the Bill to extend the period of the Preventive Detention Act by three years is fresh proof of the fact that the Government is not willing to give up the special powers it acquired during the Emergency. Circumstances change, but the Government is not prepared to shed the armaments it has collected.

Shri Datar's speech does not indicate any special situation that would justify the preventive detention law. And even if Chinese activities have created a special situation on the northern border the Prime Minister and the Home Minister have already declared that a separate Bill will be tabled on the floor of the House to meet that situation. When the Government proposes to bring forward a bill to control propagandas relating to the border and when it may possibly also be supported, what is the propriety of extending the period of the Preventive Detention Bill ? This has not yet been made clear. The Minister of State has also claimed that this Bill will not be used for ending political opposition. I dispute this claim and I call upon the Home Ministry to collect information about how the Preventive Detention Act has been used against Jan Sangh workers in Bengal for the last three years. In 1956 three prominent workers of the Jan Sangh were taken into preventive detention on September 14. In 1958 the Organising Secretary of the party was detained, and the same day he was released. After one year another secretary was arrested. I would like to draw your attention to the causes given for the arrest. One was that they were making propaganda against the Nehru-Noon Pact. Can that be a reason for preventive detention ? Today the whole of West Bengal has unitedly raised its voice against the implementation of the Nehru-Noon Pact. Then will you take the whole of Bengal into preventive detention ?

SHRI S.M. BANERJI : There aren't enough jails, otherwise they would do it.

SHRI VAJPAYEE : For fear that this reason alone may be rejected by the High Court as baseless one more reason has also been added, which I am going to quote. Shri Ram Prasad Das was on his way to New Delhi to attend a meeting of the All-India Working Committee of the Jan Sangh, when he was arrested one day before it, I quote the charge levelled against him :

> "That you intend to proceed to Delhi on 9th October 1958 and that you are likely to instigate plans which may adversely affect the personal security of the Prime Minister of India."

SHRI TYAGI : It is a serious charge.

Lok Sabha on December 2, 1960 regarding the Bill relating to the Extension of Period of Preventive Detention Act

SHRI VAJPAYEE : I know it is a very serious charge, but can the Home Minister swear with his hand on his heart that a person coming here to participate in the All-India Working Committee of the Jana Sangh would imperil the Prime Minister's safety or would conspire against his life ? And if that is possible why was he alone arrested ? You could have arrested the whole Working Committee. If you think we do not have even that much respect for the Prime Minister I suggest you ban the Bharatiya Jan Sangh—or at least take us into confidence and tell us who in the Jan Sangh is against the Prime Minister's safety. We will take action against him. We shall put him out of the party. There was a conspiracy against the life of the Prime Minister of the country and we were not even told about it—And look at the fun of it—one year later that person was released. If he was hatching a plot you can still prosecute him and punish him. But that is not being done. Finally the case went to the High Court and the Court said release him forthwith. But the High Court's verdict was not obeyed. Even after the verdict that person was kept in jail for four months. I quote some lines from the verdict of the Calcutta High Court :

> "As successive Secretaries of the Jan Sangh appear to have been arrested and detained for long periods, although nothing untoward appears to have occurred, we have no doubt that the Government will consider the question of releasing the detenu as soon as possible."

This is the recommendation of the Calcutta High Court—I shall not call it a verdict. The Government should have honoured this recommendation, but even after this recommendation of the High Court the person is kept in jail for four months. Later he was released. Is this not misuse of the Preventive Detention Act ? If you think there are elements that would endanger the country's peace and security prosecute them openly, put a stop to their objectionable activities, but preventing their legitimate activities under cover of the preventive detention law can never be justified. I am against the use of the Preventive Detention Act against any person, whether he is Sheikh Abdullah or Master Tara Singh. It is not good to detain anybody without trial. If there are elements and forces which would jeopardise the country's independence and security, which are acquiring arms from abroad, which are working as fifth columns, you can make a separate law of treason for them. But no one can justify this sort of political misuse of the Preventive Detention Act.

I call upon the Home Minister to inquire into the way in which this Act has been used in West Bengal against Jan Sangh workers and tell us whether our workers are at fault. If they are in the wrong we shall take action against them. But you want to take action only on the police report.

Sir, I would place before you an example of a police report. In one report the ground given was that on a certain day you addressed a meeting at the Jan Sangh office and said all Muslims should be driven out of West Bengal. Now this particular worker says he was not present at the meeting at all, and the Vice-President of the West Bengal Jan Sangh, who is a Muslim gentleman, says he was present at the meeting and no such thing was said at it. Now who is telling the truth ? In such a situation will you detain anybody for a year on a police report ? Such examples disprove the Government's claim that it does not misuse this Act. Before extending the period of the Act the Government should explain to us, take the House into confidence, and tell us what condition prevails in the country that requires it to equip itself with the power to detain such people without trial. Shri Datar's speech does not indicate any such condition. Possibly Pandit Pant may throw some light in this regard, but I would remind him too that the Preventive Detention Act is no way to end any party. If that is what you want to do you will have to adopt other ways for it and you will have to obtain the people's trust in them. By detaining people like this the Congress is getting unpopular. And for those Congress members who have supported this Bill I have a warning — the day is not far off when those opposing the Act within the Congress organisation will also be taken into preventive detention by the Congress Government. Thank you.

Government Heading for Absolutism

Sir, I stand to oppose this Bill. As a member of the Joint Select Committee I and my colleagues had tried to see that this Bill could not lead to misuse of powers by the Government and fundamental rights given by the Constitution could be protected. But we did not succeed.

The Joint Select Committee was given an ass and its job was to make it a horse. But the result is that we have now a mule. Now this mule may be all right for bearing the burden of the Home Ministry, but if the Home Minister thinks that they can mount this mule to fight the battle of the nation's sovereignty and integrity I beg to differ with it.

We will have to bear in mind the circumstances in which this Bill was introduced. There was a party in Madras which talked of breaking away from India. In view of that challenge the National Integration Council set up a committee under Sir C.P. Ramaswamy Aiyar. The Home Minister claims that the present Bill is being introduced on its recommendations. The Home Minister will also admit that there is no such challenge in the South. The party that had raised the slogan of an independent Tamilnadu has given up the idea. It is now in power on the strength of the people's mandate. What crisis does the Home Minister now face that requires it to assume these special powers ?

As for the rebel Nagas who want to separate from India, the Government of India is having talks with them. On the one hand talks are being held with the rebels and on the other Parliament is asked for powers with which the Government could fight such elements. If the Government is inclined for talks asking for powers like this does not mean anything. Clearly these powers will not be used against the rebel Nagas with whom talks are in progress.

Nor will these special powers be used against that class in Jammu and Kashmir which has a nexus with Pakistan and wants to change the constitutional position of Jammu and Kashmir. Recently the Government of India has removed the restraints placed on Mirza Afzal Beg. The speech he made in Srinagar after that is a challenge to the rest of India's relationship with Kashmir. Are the demands made in that speech not a danger signal for the territorial integrity and sovereignty of the country ? It was with that danger in view that he had been arrested, but now the situation is that he has been released. The restrictions placed on Sheikh Abdullah have also been relaxed and one should not be surprised if he is completely freed in a few days' time.

Lok Sabha on December 18, 1967 during discussion regarding Unlawful Activities Bill

It is to be said — and it is being said that Kashmir's accession to India is not final, the Kashmir question may be opened again, and it should be discussed together by the people of Pakistan, Jammu and Kashmir and India. Will the Government place restrictions on such elements after the passing of this Bill ? And if restrictions are to be placed why remove them now ?

I am not in favour of keeping anybody in jail without trial. Personal freedom should be respected. But there is confusion in the Government's mind. There is a difference between its precept and practice. I am unable to understand the purpose behind this Bill — perhaps the House too is unable to do so.

We are told the Emergency is ending; it will be in force only in border areas, and in the rest of India the citizens will be restored the right to enjoy fundamental rights and approach the Supreme Court if they are infringed. But how did the Government behave when the Emergency was in force and it had powers ? Does the Government not have the power to declare the Plebiscite Front in Srinagar illegal ? Can the Government not declare it to be illegal if it wants to do so ? Even without this Bill the Government has that power because of the Emergency. But the Government did not use it. Then why ask for new powers ?

Autocratic Manners

We fear these powers would be misused. A couple of days ago the Home Minister has also indicated in what autocratic manner his mind works. A Congress member asked about the RSS and the Home Minister replied, 'the RSS is some sort of political organisation and we have asked Central Government employees not to join it.' Who gave the Government the right to declare any organisation political ?

SHRI Y.B. CHAVAN : It is inherent.

SHRI VAJPAYEE : Wonderful. It is inherited.

The Minister says the Government has the right to declare any organisation political and now it wants the power to declare any organisation illegal. One power is inherent, and the other it wants Parliament to give it.

SHRI Y.B. CHAVAN : It is one thing to consider political and another to declare illegal. For that a tribunal has to be faced.

SHRI VAJPAYEE : The Government is not ready to face a tribunal. The relevant article has a proviso that in view of a prevailing situation the Government may declare any organisation illegal without approaching the tribunal.

SHRI CHAVAN : But later it will have to approach.

SHRI VAJPAYEE : I shall come to that later.

The Government has decided that the RSS should be considered a sort of political party, but does the Home Minister know that two High Courts in the country have struck down action taken against government servants in this respect ? Does the Home Minister know the verdict of the Rajasthan High Court ? The verdict is that the RSS is a cultural organisation and no employee can be removed from employment for participating in it. What tribunal is the Home Minister talking about ?

In what direction is the Home Minister's mind working ? Any challenge to the country's territorial integrity and sovereignty must be firmly dealt with. But if the Government cannot do that it is not because it does not have the powers. It is because it does not have guts. It has a 'backbone of banana'. There are talks with rebel Nagas, there are secret talks with Sheikh Abdullah, but there is clearly the discriminatory policy of misusing government powers against those who want to work for the country's reconstruction in accordance with their own perceptions within the borders of the country.

The Bill says it will be an offence under the law for any one to work for the secession of any part of the country and also to talk of handing over Indian territory to others. But the Government is itself ceding Indian territory to others and not even consulting Parliament is considered necessary for it. Government officials can gift away Indian territory in consultation with or without consulting Ministers. That won't be illegal under this law. Now it is argued that if acquiring territory comes within sovereignty, ceding territory also comes within it. Is the Government not ready even for a system in which agreements involving cessation of territory would not come into force without Parliament's approval ?

But here we have freedom for officials and Ministers to work against the sovereignty and integrity of the country. However if any political party engages in any such activity it can be declared illegal. We do not want any party to work like that. But if a member of the ruling party says we should make a compromise with Pakistan by handing over to it one-third of Kashmir that is under its control will he be liable to be prosecuted under this Bill ? The Home Minister needs to clear this point.

I am not talking about Prime Minister Nehru. He had once publicly made this offer to Pakistan, but when Pakistan did not accept it he withdrew it. But does this Bill prevent the government from proceeding towards an agreement in which we offer to leave our right on one-third Kashmir and hand it over to Pakistan ? The information I receive causes concern. There are some secret talks going on in Delhi with Sheikh Abdullah, and not even the Home Ministry knows about it.

If my information is not wrong some confidential correspondence is going on between Sheikh Abdullah and the Prime Minister and in it some offers are being made to Sheikh Abdullah. I would like to make one thing clear. The process of integrating Jammu and Kashmir with the rest of India is going on and has scope for continuing. This process will not be allowed to be reversed. No one will have the right to put the clock back. The people of India will not agree that the Jammu and Kashmir valley be given more autonomy and some agreement on the lines of Sikkim or Bhutan be made with Sheikh Abdullah. If such an agreement is made can this Bill stop the government from making it ? It will not.

In his speech the Home Minister talked of divisive forces. He said the Bill is being brought forward against divisive forces. I can understand it if anyone wants any Indian territory to break away. I can understand if anyone wants to give it to China, Pakistan or some third country. But these divisive forces which endanger the national integration of the Prime Minister's and Home Minister's concept — this talk creates doubts in our minds. There is no accepted definition of national sovereignty and national integrity yet. So we had said in the Joint Select Committee that the word 'territorial' should be joined to 'integrity'. But this proposal was rejected on the grounds of the constitution. I would say except for cession and cessation every challenge should be met on the political level. The Home Minister also agrees that such forces cannot be tackled with law alone. Then why do you want to assume such powers by law ?

This Bill should be limited only to cession and secession. The dangers to the country's sovereignty and integrity that you think may arise should be dealt with on the political level. No one fires a gun to kill a mosquito. Linguism, provincialism and other small selfish interests are raising their head in the country. Our faith in democracy, our faith in the people of the country — the faith by which they were swearing while speaking on the Official Language Bill — should have the capacity to deal with such dangers. For that the government does not need to assume autocratic powers. This Bill will be acceptable to us if the Home Minister is willing to make some more amendments in it, otherwise I would demand its withdrawal, our party is not prepared to accept it. Thank you.

Smuggling on the Rise—Ordinance No Solution

Sir, I move :

"This House disapproves the Maintenance of Internal Security (Amendment) Ordinance, 1974 (Ordinance No. 11 of 1974) promulgated by the President on September 17, 1974"

I table the following resolution :

"This House disapproves of the Presidential order issued on the 16th November 1974 under Clause (1) of Article 359 of the Constitution suspending citizens' right to move any court with respect to orders of detention under Maintenance of Internal Security Act, 1971 for the enforcement of the rights conferred by Article 14, Article 21 and clauses (4), (5), (6) and (7), of Article 22 and also suspending all proceedings pending in any Court for the enforcement of the aforesaid rights with respect to orders of detention under the Maintenance of Internal Security Act."

Sir, today's newspapers have prominently reported that in many major cities smugglers have again started their activities. It has been reported that after lying low for some weeks smugglers have again speeded up their activities in a number of important cities. According to a countrywide survey those smugglers who were hiding because of the arrest of some people have again come into the open and started their activities.

Smuggling is like the tip of an iceberg. What is not seen is much more than what is unseen. It would be wrong to think that a mere 500 or 600 people would be able to spread a network of smuggling all over the country. The Government has amended the Security Act in order to arrest some smugglers. This amendment has been made by an ordinance. When Parliament was not in session the Government used the power to issue an ordinance and changed the Security Act with it. But it was not changed enough. Those smugglers who were arrested under the Security Act began to be released by some courts. The Government did not think about why the courts were releasing them. It tried to put all the blame on the courts and promulgated an ordinance to prevent detained smugglers from approaching the courts under Article 359 of the Constitution.

An emergency was declared in the country on December 31, 1971. Pakistan had attacked India. It is December 2, 1974 today. Three years have passed. We restored occupied territory to Pakistan, returned the POWs and made

Lok Sabha on December 2-3-1974 while moving the resolution seeking disapproval of the Maintenance of Internal Security (Amendment) Ordinance, 1974

agreements in Shimla and Delhi for normalising the situation. Even trade relations have begun between the two countries. Then what is the propriety in continuing the emergency ? And yet it is being continued. Under it the smugglers are at first detained under MISA, and when in some cases the courts restored personal freedom on the test of justice the Government issued a Presidential ordinance and deprived the smugglers of their fundamental rights. I would like to make it clear that we are in favour of the strictest action against smugglers. Smuggling is an anti-national activity and a smuggler is a traitor to the country. But even treason invites legal action against it. We still have rule of law in the country, not the law of the jungle. I charge that this Government does not want to take action against smugglers under the common law. The whole country demands that smugglers be produced in courts and prosecuted. All proof against them in the possession of the Government should be produced. Those political leaders and customs as well as police officers under whose protection smugglers were indulging in smuggling should also be exposed and made to share the smugglers' severest punishment. But the Government is not willing to produce them in court and prosecute them. It is in favour of their preventive detention leisure. Sir, you are a lawyer and have just returned from the U.N.O. You have a fresh mind and a fresh intellect. Please use that fresh intelligence in this matter as well. Preventive detention is meant for preventing a person from doing something in future. It is not meant to be punishment for old sins. Is the purpose only to prevent the detained smugglers from smuggling ? Will smuggling end with the arrest of 600 people ? Should they not be punished for the smuggling that they did in the past ? How will their preventive detention do that ? But the fact is the Government does not want to punish them.

Preventive Detention—How Long ?

Sir, the use of MISA against smugglers is a mockery of action under the common law. Smuggling is an offence. The Government should have the power to tackle it under the common laws. If these laws are inadequate they could be strengthened. For that the Government could approach the House. This House will not hesitate to give the Government the necessary powers for ending smuggling. But a Presidential ordinance was issued under section 359. Section 359 will continue so long as there is Emergency. But how long will the Emergency continue ? Is smuggling a foreign aggression now which cannot be fought without declaring an emergency ? At present an Emergency is continuing. I suspect that the Government either wants to continue the Emergency indefinitely or to jail smugglers for some days and then release them. Otherwise what is the need for issuing an ordinance under the Emergency to prevent smugglers from going to court ? When the Emergency is over, the ordinance is inoperative and the smugglers go to court, what will the Government do ?

Sir, the Law Commission had considered this matter many years ago. Its 47th report states :

"We have carefully considered this question and have given due consideration to the general tenor of the majority decision in Dhillon's case and the obiter observations made by Chief Justice Sikri who spoke for the majority in the said case. Our considered opinion is that, on the whole, it would be advisable for the Government to secure constitutional amendment enlarging the contents of Item 9 in List I of the Seventh Schedule. We accordingly suggest that Item 9 of List I may be amended so as to read as follows —

> "Preventive Detention for reasons connected with Defence, Foreign Affairs, the Security of India, the effective realisation of duties of Customs and Excise, or the conservation of Foreign Exchange; persons subjected to such detention."

Smuggling Continues while Government Sleeps

This was the Law Commission's report. Smuggling continued while the Government slept, and continued to undermine the country's economy. There was smuggling worth Rs. 1000 crores to Rs. 1200 crores in the country every year. At first gold was smuggled in. By introducing Gold Control the Government accomplished the task of robbing small goldsmiths of their daily bread, but it did not take strict action against smugglers of gold. It is true that gold smuggling has now declined, as gold prices have gone up in the international market. But now in addition to gold cloth is coming in, as also jewellery, watches, transistors. According to Government figures the quantity of smuggled goods seized by the authorities is going up. Its price is going up. This means smuggling has been continually going up during the past years. In 1971 goods worth Rs. 8.50 crores were seized, in 1972 worth Rs. 11.50 crores, in 1973 worth Rs. 14.50 crores and in the first eight months of 1974 goods worth Rs. 17 crores were seized. And the volume of goods not seized was bigger than goods seized.

These seized goods worth Rs. 17 crores include textiles worth Rs. 11.50 crores, watches worth a crore and gold worth two and a half lakh rupees. This is a new pattern of smuggling.

Sir, smugglers run their own reserve bank.

SHRI MOOLCHAND DAGA (Pali) : How do you know this ?

SHRI VAJPAYEE : Dagaji, in some matters we are *'Antaryami'*. This is an open secret. Shri Wagh, the Officer appointed for anti-smuggling operations, has admitted in an interview to the press that smugglers run their own reserve bank. A newspaper of Bombay even published the address of the bank, but the police have not yet raided it.

Parallel Government of Smugglers

This year the matter of smugglers was raised in the House in a very explosive manner when Shri Ganesh, former Minister of State in the Finance Ministry, stated in a press interview that smugglers are running a parallel government, they have their own telephone network, they listen in on customs officers' phone calls, and they have political contacts with high-ups.

Later a Congress member, Dr. V.K.R.V. Rao, had demanded a statement on the subject by way of a calling attention motion. Shri Ganesh had also said he would undertake a satyagraha against smugglers. But when the matter arose in the House Shri Ganesh became a little less loud. He even named three smugglers. I congratulate him. It is a matter of regret that when the House is discussing this matter he is not in the House — not even in the Finance Ministry. He has been discarded. He should have been rewarded, but he has been punished. Is that because what he said put the Government into difficulties ? Is that because his revelations put the Government in the dock ? Why was he shifted from the Finance Ministry ?

SHRI OM MEHTA : He had made the *'Shri Ganesh'* (beginning).

SHRI VAJPAYEE : But you turned Ganesh into a mouse. *'Vinayakam prakurvano rachayamasa vanaram'* — you were out to make a 'Vinayak' (Lord Ganesh) but made a 'vanar' (monkey). You made a mouse out of Ganesh and sent him to another Ministry.

SHRI OM MEHTA : He rides a mouse.

SHRI VAJPAYEE : This same mouse took him to another ministry. That mouse does not go as he says, it goes as the Prime Minister says.

It is not a question of smugglers alone. It is a question of the system, not of individuals. Haji Mastan was a coolie, how did he become a *'Crorepati'* ? 'Who made Yusuf a prince out of a pauper ? How did *'Malishwala Bakhia'* turn into 'Maharaj Bakhia' ? Narang was a small *'pheriwala'* till 1950, eking out a livelihood by exchanging German silver utensils for old pots and pans. How did he become wealthy ? How did starving Lalit become 'Maha Seth' Lalit ? How did this strange thing happen ? Who is responsible for it ?

The question is — how did smuggling start, who nurtured it, how it covered the whole country, who surrendered the whole system into its hands, who crowned it with a parallel government, who forced political leaders to fall at its feet.

SHRI RAM GOPAL REDDY (Nizamabad) : The Hon. Member should not speak like that.

SHRI VAJPAYEE : Is smuggling possible without official cooperation, without a nexus with Government officials ? Customs, excise, foreign exchange control, income tax officers, sales tax officers, the police, the intelligence department — all are in this cesspool, and the biggest thing is that political leaders sheltered smugglers. In short smuggling is foreign trade that goes on without government sanction. It is done in many ways. One is under-invoicing, the other over-invoicing, and the third way is that when NRIs send money home, smugglers' agents take it there in foreign exchange and deliver it at home in rupees. This robs the Reserve Bank of that much foreign exchange and smugglers get it for their anti-national activities. When foreign tourists come here foreign exchange is purchased from them at a higher rupee rate and this money is put to use for smuggling activities. Antique sculptures, stone edicts and artefacts of historical importance are smuggled out of India and the foreign exchange thus earned is used for smuggling. Licences are acquired with the help of some MP or minister for firms that exist only on paper. They send things to bogus firms abroad and also earn foreign exchange.

The question is how to stop all this. If the Government proposes a genuine campaign against smuggling and if it girds up its loins to act stringently against smuggling we shall cooperate with it. But we are not ready to believe in this campaign. Were only 600 people engaged in smuggling, and will smuggling end by taking them into preventive detention ?

Recently I had motored down to Cannanore. On the way there is a place called Kasargod. It is a coastal region. Kasargod is a major smuggling centre. When the leading smuggler there, Kalatra Abdul Kadir Haji — Haji Abdullah was arrested —

SHRI OM MEHTA : Which Abdullah ?

SHRI VAJPAYEE : Let not Shri Om Mehta worry. Not Sheikh Abdullah. Both hail from Kashmir and worry for each other. When Haji Abdullah was arrested everything was quiet in Kasargod for a few days, but then activities started again. He owns the Platinum Cinema and the Saphire Cinema there. He also owns a petrol pump. When there was a literary conference there he was chairman of the reception committee. When he was arrested he was also allowed to meet the press, when he said :

> "The President of India who has honoured me as one of the exporters last year has served me with an arrest warrant. It is an irony. I am an honest man and my earnings are all through honest means."

Today it is because of him that the Kerala Government is in power. He is a part of the Kerala nexus.

DEPUTY SPEAKER : We will now take up the statutory Resolution on the Maintenance of Internal Security (Amendment) Ordinance, the motion on the Presidential order and the Conservation of Foreign Exchange and Prevention of Smuggling Activities Bill. Shri Atal Bihari Vajpayee will continue his speech.

SHRI VAJPAYEE : Sir, I demand that a high-power committee headed by a High Court judge be set up to investigate the nexus between smugglers and political leaders and government officers.

The Prime Minister and his government now claim that a courageous step has been taken by acting against smugglers. The fact of the matter is that the Government has whitewashed the crimes of the smugglers. The proceedings of Parliament from 1970 to 1974 are testimony to the fact that members again and again raised the question of the nexus between political leaders and smugglers and every time the Government gave evasive answers. There was no inquiry into the conduct of political leaders, smugglers were treated leniently, they were given passports and 'P' forms, the Reserve Bank gave them foreign exchange and when smugglers were arrested arrangements were made to release them quickly on bail.

I have with me the report of Lok Sabha proceedings of April, 1970. Shri George Fernandes had asked :

> 'Had the regional passport officer at Bombay declined to issue a passport to Haji Mastan ? Was he later given a passport ? On whose

recommendation ? Does the Government know that at present Mastan is in jail on charges of smuggling ? Will the Government cancel his passport ?

The reply given by Shri Surendra Pal Singh, Deputy Minister for Foreign Affairs, was as follows —

'Haji Mastan Mirza's passport application was rejected in 1961 and 1963. On November 7, 1966 he was issued a passport for one year on the basis of a good conduct certificate given by the Governor of Gujarat. On September 23, 1969 the Directorate of Revenue Intelligence, New Delhi, had reported that on July 19, 1969 Customs Officers of Bombay had seized smuggled goods from Mastan's residence. He was arrested on July 20 and released later on bail.

At that time Shri Nityanand Kanungo was Governor of Gujarat. The certificate he gave recommending a passport was as follows :

"I know Shri Haji Mastan through Shri Akhtar Sayyad of Bombay as an Indian citizen with a good character history. He wishes to visit Aden to look after his relatives. As it is necessary for him to travel early the necessary documents may be provided for him.'

When my friend Shri Madhu Limaye raised this matter on March 18 the Government said an inquiry was going on. Later Shri Kanungo said his signature was forged. Then it was demanded in the House that if Haji Mastan prepared forged documents he should be prosecuted for forgery. But the Bombay Presidency Magistrate gave the decision...

SHRI MADHU LIMAYE (Banka) : And the High Court supported it.

SHRI VAJPAYEE : That Shri Kanungo's signature was genuine, not forged. How could a notorious smuggler succeed in securing the Governor's certificate ?

Not only that, Haji Mastan Mirza was given a telephone connection in the special category. This matter too was raised by Shri George Fernandes on April 2,1970. The question was as follows :

'Is it true that a person named Haji Mastan, residing at Baitul Sarur, 61/IX Warden Road, Bombay-26, was given a telephone connection (no. 359358) as a social worker in the free category (special) ?

Who recommended him for this category ? Did the Bombay telephone department inquire into Haji Mastan's social service ? Is it true that in the past he was denied a telephone connection in the free category ? Why did the Bombay telephone department change its decision ?

The reply given by the then Minister of State for Information and Broadcasting was as follows :

"Yes, the following had recommended :

1. Adam Adil, MLA.
2. V.M. Yagnik, Minister for Prohibition, Government of Maharashtra.
3. Bhagwandas K. Ashar, President, B. Ward, Zilla Congress Committee.
4. T.P. Karimsha, Vice-President, Maharashtra Mazdoor Sabha, Bombay.
5. M.A. Khatal, Municipal Councillor."

These include quite eminent personalities. While the House was discussing this matter (*Interruptions*) ... Shri Niti Raj Singh of the Congress had put a question. He was in the Council of Ministers so long, but he is not in it now. His question was —

> 'Does the Government know that those officers who are charged with preventing it actually promote it ?'

He added —

> 'In the BOAC gold case an officer changed the original report and re-wrote almost one-fourth of it. I place the report on the floor of the House. It is a 22-page report.'

The Speaker had then said it was not necessary to place it on the floor, ask your question. Then he asked —

> 'Did the Directorate of Revenue Intelligence change the original report as well as a smaller report and rewrote one-fourth of it ?'

There was no reply to this question.

AN HON. MEMBER : From what newspaper are your reading ?

SHRI VAJPAYEE : From the same newspaper that has been discussed at length — the opposition. But I do not depend upon newspapers alone. If you want it I can even read it out to you from the proceedings of the House.

If political leaders keep protecting smugglers and smugglers claim friendship with them, if smugglers work for political leaders during elections and keep getting good conduct certificates from them stringent action will never be taken against them.

There is a 67-year-old smuggler of Bombay by name Shri Krishna Budh Gowda. He has made a representation to the High Court against his detention and attached a certificate to it. This certificate is by Shri H.R. Gokhale and is as follows :

> "It gives me great pleasure to say that Shri K.B. Gowda worked for me during the mid-term poll. He is a hard-working and a loyal worker. He proved to be of assistance in the last election. I wish him well."

SHRI MADHU LIMAYE : Did the Indira wave consist of such people ?

SHRI VAJPAYEE : This was during the 1971 mid-term elections. The certificate was given immediately after the elections. That time too he was involved in smuggling. Two years ago the police had tried to catch him while unloading smuggled goods on the sea coast. His henchmen beat up the customs people and made away with two lorries laden with goods. Gowda was charged with murder but the charge could not be proved. The police did not try to prove it. He was released and surfaced as an active worker in the Law Minister's election.

The question is, how could the smugglers succeed in amassing wealth of crores of rupees ? Look at their mansions, look at the number of their cars, look at their opulent life-style, look at the Cinema houses under their ownership ...

AN HON. MEMBER : Look at the swimming pools.

SHRI VAJPAYEE : And look at their flooring of glass, under which there is a room.

SHRI MADHU LIMAYE : Don't go below that.

SHRI VAJPAYEE : I won't, Shri Limaye can. I am prohibited.

Is it not the job of the income tax people to inquire where all this wealth came from ? Ram Narang purchased the Ambassador Hotel for Rs. 76 lakhs. Was he asked where the money came from ? He did it very cleverly. Without paying estate duty he bought controlling interest in Sultan Brothers. Narang could successfully evade stamp duty of seven lakh rupees. No income tax was paid, nor estate duty, nor wealth tax. But could the income tax people not have asked where the wealth came from ?

The smuggler in the news in Kerala these days is known for charity. He has built mosques. He has erected a big mosque near Kasargod, in which he has built a tower. Nobody goes there to recite Namaz. That tower has been built as a look-out, to keep a watch on ships passing by. The Government of India has prepared a documentary film on smuggling. When this mosque was shown in the documentary a big hue and cry was raised in Kerala. (*Interruptions*) ...

AN HON. MEMBER : Not for a temple ?

SHRI VAJPAYEE : Maybe for a temple too. But we have no objection if a temple is shown in the documentary. But what did the Kerala Government do ? It stopped the screening of the documentary prepared by the Government of India. Smugglers are not only running the Government of Kerala, they are also making the Government of India dance to their tune.

It is not only a question of the income tax department. Customs officials are also involved. As I said yesterday, I travelled from Mangalore to Cannanore. The entire sea coast on the west lies unprotected. Cannot the Central Reserve Police be deployed ? Can the Border Security Force not be put to the task of breaking up the smugglers' network ? I say even the Navy could be used to scuttle ships that smuggle goods into our country and break up our economy. But the Border Security Force can be used in Bihar, the Central Reserve Police can be used for gunning down innocent people, it cannot be used for fighting smugglers.

Now smugglers are being arrested under MISA and some of them are being set free. So a President's ordinance was issued. A High Court releases a smuggler when the grounds for detention are either vague or indefinite. Who is responsible for keeping the grounds vague and indefinite ? There is a nexus between officials and smugglers. Detention grounds are deliberately kept deficient. Then the court will have to do its duty. If the grounds are vague and indefinite, the court will release them under the Constitution. Issuing a President's ordinance is not the way to stop them. Was any action taken against those who do the detaining ? Was any officer asked why the grounds were vague ?

What is the position with MISA now ? There was the case of Shri Ram Bahadur Rai, a student leader of Bihar, before the Supreme Court. The District Magistrate charged him with wanting to conduct a Gujarat-type movement in Bihar. He was asked—what do you mean by a Gujarat-type movement ?

He said it is a matter of common sense. On this Justice Chandrachud said—these days commonsense has become quite uncommon.

One person was released by the Supreme Court because he was charged with rubbing off an anti-Naxalite slogan on his wall. Is even cleaning a wall an offence ? Does that make him a Naxalite ? But he was taken into detention on that ground, and the Supreme Court released him. Justice Aiyar says : if these special powers are used like this the executive's capacity to produce proof will be weakened still further. I quote a portion of Justice Aiyar's verdict :

> "The potential executive tendency to shy at courts for prosecution of ordinary offences and to rely generally on the easier strategy of subjective satisfaction is a danger to the democratic way of life".

SHRI SHAMIM AHMED SHAMIM (Srinagar) : He seems to be a reactionary judge.

SHRI VAJPAYEE : He is the same judge who was a Minister of Kerala, Shri Krishna Aiyar is very progressive.

SHRI SHAMIM : He might have become reactionary later. It does not take time.

SHRI DINEN BHATTACHARYA (Srirampur) : He is an uncommitted judge.

SHRI VAJPAYEE : The House also knows that when Haji Mastan Mirza's matter came before a magistrate in Bombay his defence lawyer was the late Shri Mohan Kumaramangalam......

SHRI SHAMIM : He was a lawyer. If you were a lawyer you would have done the same.

SHRI VAJPAYEE : I would have been happy if it were not so.

SHRI DINEN BHATTACHARYA : He is not right reactionary but wrong reactionary.

SHRI S.A. SHAMIM : The lawyers did take objection.

SHRI K.P. UNNIKRISHNAN (Badagara) : What exactly are you trying to prove ?

SHRI SHAMIM : I am charging you of having taken money from smugglers. I will give you details.

SHRI VAJPAYEE : Come out with proof.

SHRI K.P. UNNIKRISHNAN (Badagara) : Even in his professional capacity he has not appeared. That is a fact. You are trying to play politics.

SHRI M. GOPALA REDDY (Nizamabad) : Have the people of your party made the charge that Abdullah was funded by Mastan ?

SHRI VAJPAYEE : Sir, it is being said when we talk of protecting fundamental rights...

SHRI RAJA KULKARNI (Bombay North-East) : Whose fundamental rights ?

SHRI VAJPAYEE : Every citizens's fundamental rights. When there is talk of that it is also said smugglers should be proceeded against under common legal action. If necessary that law could be strengthened further. But the Government cannot be given such blanket powers. Today these powers are being misused. Any district magistrate can arrest anybody on suspicion and jail him by calling him a smuggler.

Protection to Smugglers

Recently a matter came to me from Mathura. A Customs Officer went to arrest a person and asked for Rs. 25,000. He declined. Just then a police party on patrolling duty reached there, on which the customs official ran away, living their documents there. All those documents are with me. They include the intelligence report, what the district magistrate has written, as also a letter of the Chief Secretary to the Government of Uttar Pradesh, which says this person is suspected to be involved in gold smuggling. But the report also states that no gold was found during the raid. But there is suspicion. Then can you arrest on suspicion. Can you lock up on suspicion. Can you rob the person of his freedom on suspicion ? Don't you require proof ? Is it not the Government's responsibility to provc guilt in the court ? When we say so they say we are saving smugglers. That is why I had to discuss political connections and to name the late Mohan Kumaramangalam. I would be happy if I am wrong.

When we fight for fundamental rights we are charged with wanting to save smugglers. I would like to make it clear that we are in favour of strict action against smugglers, but this ordinance does not serve that purpose. Hence our demand for a high power commission that would go into the smugglers' connections with political leaders and the bureaucracy and decide upon effective action against them.

I am talking of ordinances. I am against ordinances issued by the President and I want the Finance Minister to let them lapse. I want him to withdraw the ordinance and come forward with a comprehensive Bill providing for strict action against all economic offences. As yet no smuggler's property has been confiscated. Those who were arrested are enjoying themselves in Yervada jail...

SHRI K.P. UNNIKRISHNAN : Will you agree for a change in the Constitution in respect of property ?

SHRI VAJPAYEE : The Constitution has already been changed. Powers have already been obtained from Parliament...

SHRI K.P. UNNIKRISHNAN : I am asking you.

SHRI VAJPAYEE : You are asking me. I am not the Finance Minister. I am not the Prime Minister of this country. You have the majority.

Sir, is this matter awaiting our consent ? Do they act only on our approval ? Do they not do to what we say 'no' ? We say place the CBI report on the table. Are you ready ?

We demand that the Government should have the legal power to confiscate smugglers' property, and if it approaches the House for it we shall support it. But the Finance Minister has told the consultative committee that a constitutional amendment is not necessary for this. Still they will not take over anybody's property. Rather, their wealth will be accepted for fighting elections. The same old deals are going on with detained smugglers.

I may also tell about Punjab. It is good that Sardar Darbara Singh reminded me. The Punjab Chief Minister has said — I know about the political leaders who are involved in smuggling, but I will not tell, because it is not in public interest. But the Chief Minister is not taking action against them. We want that stringent action be taken and the matter of smuggling exposed ....

SHRI DARBARA SINGH (Hoshiarpur) : He said let anyone show which Minister is involved in smuggling. He has challenged this.

SHRI VAJPAYEE : Then you too, Darbara Singh, can tell.

SHRI DARBARA SINGH : You know more about all things.

SHRI VAJPAYEE : I would call upon the Minister not to placate solving the serious problem of smuggling by taking *ad hoc* steps. Special powers do not last for ever. We have to eradicate smuggling. For this we need effective steps. This ordinance does not serve that purpose. Thank you.

Hoarders will Prosper Despite
MINI-MISA

Sir, I move the following resolution :

"This House disapproves the Prevention of Blackmarketing and Supply of Essential Commodities Ordinance, 1979 (No. 10 of 1979) promulgated by the President on October 5, 1979."

Sir, this ordinance was promulgated on October 5. At that time a caretaker government was in office. We had hoped that the present government would make an auspicious beginning, but *"Pratham grase makshika patah"* 'Things soured right at the beginning.'

Once they were in office, black laws like preventive detention were not long in coming. This ordinance was in effect for the last three months. Has it been able to control price rise during this period ? Could profiteering and blackmarketing be controlled ? Did hoarding end ? I know the Commerce Minister will say the State Governments declined to act upon this law, but that is not the whole truth ...

SHRI V.C. JAIN (Barmer) : That is quite true. I can tell about the Rajasthan Government—they did not act upon it.

SHRI HARISH RAWAT (Almora) : The Andhra Pradesh Government is sincerely implementing it.

SHRI VAJPAYEE : I am talking of Delhi. Delhi is a Union Territory. The responsibility of implementing this law in Delhi did not rest with the Delhi Administration, which is in the Janata Party's hands. It was the Central Government's responsibility, for it relates to law and order.

In Delhi 8 people were arrested under this ordinance. Some people were charged with blackmarketing, some were arrested for blackmarketing in edible oils, and some were charged with gambling. But the charges were so loose that the Lt. Governor, who is the Administrator, withdrew all of them except for one person. He is an appointee of the Central Government.

SHRI MANORANJAN BHAKTA (Andaman and Nicobar Islands) : He was appointed by the Janata Party.

SHRI VAJPAYEE : If all officers appointed by the Janata Party were no good you will have to remove thousands of officers to implement this law, and I feel a beginning in this direction has been made...(*Interruptions*).

Sir, did they also appoint the Chief Election Commissioner ? Is it proposed to remove him too ?

Lok Sabha on February 1-2-1980 while moving a resolution seeking approval of the Prevention of Blackmarketing and Supply of Essential Commodities Ordinance No. 10 of 1979

I would request the Minister to look at the facts about one matter that remains in Delhi. When it went to the advisory board, which included a High Court judge it opined that there should be no detention in the case. It is not that the ordinance has not been implemented, but there is a difference of opinion between us on what stringent action is necessary against anti-national activities and heinous crimes like profiteering, hoarding, blackmarketing which, as everyone agrees, should be severely dealth with ...(*Interruptions*).

I shall give another example. This law was enforced in Uttar Pradesh too, because the Lok Dal was in power in Uttar Pradesh as well as the Centre. (*Interruptions*).

If you give me enough time I shall reply to every question, but your bell will go off and I would be silenced. These people are new-comers to the House. I can understand their enthusiasm, but it would be better if enthusiasm is accompanied by some restraint. You will also get your chance, and then you may have your say.

Sir, I would like to know if this ordinance was implemented or not in Andhra. If it was how far did it help to stabilise prices ? The House would like to have the figures on this. The Minister should collect them. I too have had the opportunity to tour Hyderbad and many other parts of Andhra during the elections. I would like to tell you that in point of price rise there is no difference between Delhi and Andhra. Detaining anybody without trial in peacetime is against individual freedom and cannot be supported. A meeting of the International Commission of Jurists had taken place in Bangkok, which was attended by India. I quote the opinion expressed in that meeting :

> "Save during a period of public emergency threatening the life of the nation, no person of sound mind shall be deprived of his liberty except upon a charge of a specific offence and preventive detention without trial shall be contrary to the rule of law".

SHRI HARISH RAWAT : In that meeting Shri Ram Jethmalani or people of his thinking many have represented India.

SHRI VAJPAYEE : You do not know, they were your own representatives at the time.

We want to maintain rule of law, and only within that framework should we curb anybody's personal freedom. It is not enough to talk of the democratic ideal, the process too should be democratic. Recently the Supreme Court has given a historic judgment in *Smt. Maneka Gandhi's case.* It is that freedom may be denied only by procedure of law, but that procedure should also be fair. The objectives of the Bill state that the Essential Commodities Act, 1955 has been given teeth in accordance with the 47th report of the Law Commission. Now a person may be punished with seven years' imprisonment. But the experience now is that this punishment is not enough and the law needs to be made still stricter. In that case the Essential Commodities Act may be amended. If the Criminal Procedure Code needs to be changed that can be resorted to. We shall help you in that, because preventing black marketing, profiteering and smuggling cannot be the object of any one party; it is our national objective. However we have to look to what steps are being taken to achieve that objective.

One more thing. I have been a member of this House in the past. There are many new members, and I welcome them, but I remember the assurances that were given when MISA came into effect. We had given the Government unlimited powers without a discussion. It was a time of national crisis. At such a time there could not be a division of the House or of the country. The Government had clearly assured that MISA will not be used against political opponents. But the Emergency was declared and we were arrested under the same MISA.

SHRI C.P.N. SINGH (Padrauna) : You broke the rule of law by creating a special court.

SHRI VAJPAYEE : We did nothing anti-national. There was nothing anti-national in demanding the Prime Minister's resignation. If we had committed an offence we should have had the right to approach the Court. We were deprived of that right. So we cannot trust such assurances. We have the last three months' experience before us.

One more thing. When the present government was formed it had declared that it will not work with a feeling of vengeance. It had expressed a desire for cooperation. But what has happened in the last 15 days proves that (*Interruptions*) ... if any new proof is required to show that the present government is not willing to give up the feeling of revenge...

SHRI C.P.N. SINGH : Give an example.

SHRI VAJPAYEE : C.B.I. official Shri N.K. Singh is an instance in point. (*Interruptions*). He was asking me for an example.

SHRI C.P.N. SINGH : There is a case against Shri N.K. Singh for the last two and a half years.

SHRI G.L. VYAS : Sir, how we know Shri Atal Bihari Vajpayee's inner thoughts.

DEPUTY SPEAKER : There is a privilege motion before the Speaker.

SHRI VAJPAYEE : They wanted me to cite an example. I gave it. Let them not interrupt. I will not embarrass them.

SHRI EDUARDO FALEIRO (Mormugao). Please embarrass us. What about the Mini-MISA ?

SHRI VAJPAYEE : Sir, the ordinance that is becoming law has cast the net wide. It will not only bring blackmarketeers and profiteers into its orbit but will also strike at trade union rights. Even if labour leaders conduct a peaceful struggle to get legitimate demands of the labour accepted they can be charged with interfering with the supply and distribution of production of some essential commodity and land in jail.

SHRI HARISH RAWAT : The largest number of them was jailed during the Janata Party's administration. What do you have to say about that ?

SHRI C.P.N. SINGH : The Economic Bureau says there was maximum industrial unrest in 1979.

PROF. MADHU DANDAVATE : If there is going to be a free debate in this House ? Is a Leader of his stature going to be obstructed like this every minute ? Let us know that.

SHRI C.P.N. SINGH : Mr. Chairman, Sir, this is an accusation made against us (*Interruptions*).

DEPUTY SPEAKER : Order, Order.

SHRI C.P.N. SINGH : Prof. Dandavate is making an accusation against us and so I seek your protection. This is conjecture. Under what rule can he make accusations ?

SHRI BAPUSAHEB PARULEKAR (Ratnagiri) : Under what rule does he say this ?

DEPUTY SPEAKER : Order, please. The hon. member wants some clarifications from you.

SHRI VAJPAYEE : I am prepared to give any clarification he wants from me.

SHRI C.P.N. SINGH : Mr. Deputy Speaker, Sir, he said that the workers would be prosecuted by this Government. If you see the *Economic Review*, from 1978 to 1979, there was maximum industrial unrest in this country and production fell to the detriment of this country during the Janata rule.

SHRI VAJPAYEE : What clarification does he want ?

DEPUTY SPEAKER : That is all right. You may carry on.

SHRI VAJPAYEE : While replying to the points raised when the Bill was being tabled in the House and Commerce Minister had said two things. He had said there is COFEPOSA. It too has provision for preventive detention. The old Janata Government had not cancelled that law,and on that basis they want to justify this Act. I say this law relates to blackmarketing, profiteering, hoarding, and we have remedies for these illnesses in the country. Proof can be obtained in the country and offenders can be successfully prosecuted in court and punished under the Essential Commodities Act—if necessary by strengthening it. People detained under COFEPOSA are suspected of smuggling but proof for it is not available within the country. But this cannot be an adequate basis for introducing this Act.

The other, and more serious, thing he said is that this is an enabling provision. State Governments have to implement it. Whether or not they do so, it falls within State autonomy. If they do not implement it they will become unpopular, they will lose the people's confidence.

AN HON. MEMBER : They have lost it.

SHRI VAJPAYEE : No. Don't forget what happened in Kerala.

SHRI G.L. VYAS (Bhilwara) : Talk about yourself.

SHRI VAJPAYEE : I am talking about you. Shri Pranab Mukherji has given a veiled threat : "I would humbly and most respectfully remind him..." He was reminding Shri Jyotirmoy Bosu : "...That he should forget that there is a weak Government at the Centre. We know our competence, how, within our area of competence, to make a State Government agree to abide by a provision."

SHRI PRANAB MUKHERJEE : Within our area of competence.

SHRI VAJPAYEE : It is hardly a week that they are here. They should know that this is federal polity. You will practise co-existence with State Governments, whatever their colour or complexion.

This Bill empowers the Police Commissioner and the Deputy Commissioner to issue detention orders. There is a strong possibility that this power will be misused. Delhi now has a new Police Commissioner who was involved in some cases during the Janata Government days.

SHRI C.P.N. SINGH (Padrauna) : They were false cases. The High Court has given its judgement on them. This should be removed from the proceedings.

SHRI VAJPAYEE : I did not say anything about the judgement. I only said in those days he was involved in many cases.

SHRI C.P.N. SINGH : On a point of order. Sir, the Hon. Member has cast aspersions on the judgement of Delhi High Court. Is that permissible ?

SHRI RAVINDRA VARMA : He has not done that.

MR. DEPUTY SPEAKER : I think he has not done that; there is no point of order.

SHRI C.P.N. SINGH : He said that there were false cases against him. The old Government had instituted these cases. The Hon. member is aware of the fact that those cases were false and that is why the High Court has acquitted the person concerned.

MR. DEPUTY SPEAKER : He never said anything about the judgement. When an Hon. Member is speaking in this House, you note down all the points that he makes. You will have your own time, sufficient time. And when you get a chance or on behalf of your party when you get a chance, you reply to him. That would help you; that would help me also.

SHRI G.L. VYAS : False cases were made out. He is referring to cases dismissed by the Court. It was they who filed those cases.

MR. DEPUTY SPEAKER : When you get a chance to speak on this resolution you reply to them. Suppose you rise every time. When you are speaking, if another member from this side interrupts, your attention will be diverted.

SHRI VAJPAYEE : They do not want a fair debate in this House.

MR. DEPUTY SPEAKER : Please listen to him and note down all the points, when you speak, you reply to him. That is the parliamentary procedure. (*Interruptions*)

SHRI RAVINDRA VARMA : This is not possible. I can raise a point of order.

SHRI VAJPAYEE : If such an individual is Delhi's Police Commissioner and is given the right to deprive the citizens of their personal freedom there is a strong possibility that ...

AN HON. MEMBER : I say you are trying to frighten us by speaking loudly.

SHRI VAJPAYEE : I am not yielding. I am not yielding. The question is whether I will be allowed to continue or not. Let that question be decided once and for all.

SHRI G.L. VYAS : If they have given notice we can speak about Bhinder, otherwise not.

SHRI K.R. GOPAL (Kota) : Do they want to prevent the debate from continuing ?

SHRI VAJPAYEE : Sir, either you control them... (*Interruptions*).

SHRI CHANDRAJIT YADAV (Azamgarh) : In spite of your appeal, Sir, they are not listening.

MR. DEPUTY SPEAKER : You allow him to speak. You reply to him when your turn comes. It would be proper. We have no time (*Interruptions*). Order, Order.

SHRI VAJPAYEE : Let it be decided once and for all.

SHRI BAPUSAHEB PARULEKAR (Ratnagiri) : On a point of order.

MR. DEPUTY SPEAKER : There is a point of order. All of you please sit down. (*Interruptions*) .

SHRI BAPUSAHEB PARULEKAR : I am on a point of order. You have called me, Sir. I would like to invite your attention to rule 349(ii) which says :

> "Whilst the House is sitting, a member—(ii) Shall not interrupt any member while speaking by disorderly expression or noises or in any other disorderly manner."

All these learned friends here are behaving in a disorderly manner.

MR. DEPUTY SPEAKER : You address me, and do not show your fingers towards them.

SHRI BAPUSAHEB PARULEKAR : It says here that no member shall interrupt any member while he is speaking by disorderly expression or noises or in any other disorderly manner (*Interruptions*).

MR. DEPUTY SPEAKER : I accept this rule and we will see that all the sections of the House will faithfully implement this rule.

SHRI C.P.N. SINGH : Including the Janata Party.

MR. DEPUTY SPEAKER : I said, all the sections will faithfully implement this rule.

SHRI C.P.N. SINGH : This resolution says :

> "This House disapproves of the Prevention of Blackmarketing and Maintenance of Supplies of Essential Commodities ...."

But the Hon. member has been talking about Delhi Police and the appointment of the Police Commissioner. Is it relevant ? (*Interruptions*).

SHRI VAJPAYEE : Sir, I think my friends have not read this, Clause 3(2) of this Bill says—

> "Any of the following officers namely, district magistrates, Commissioners of Police, wherever they have been appointed, may also, if satisfied as provided in sub-section (1) exercise the powers to detain any person."

Here the Police Commissioner's conduct can be discussed. (*Interruption). There is a strong possibility that the Act would be used against those businessmen who have political differences with the party in power.*

AN HON. MEMBER : Those who help you.

SHRI VAJPAYEE : Yes, those who have supported the Janata Party or some other opposition party (*Interruption*).

Sir, District Magistrates are also being given powers (*Interruption).*

The Government should withdraw this Bill. The people are with you. You have secured a thumping majority. You are riding a wave. Then why use such a thunderbolt against minor blackmarketeers ? (*Interruption*). The business community is with the ruling party. This week's *Saptahik Hindustan* has published an article by Shri Basheshar Nath Gotewala, in which he wrote that all businessmen are with the Congress and they had gone in force to Chikmagalur to make Smt. Indira Gandhi victorious. You could invite those businessmen and explain things to them. If this is really against businessmen you could take advantage of the new atmosphere.

AN HON. MEMBER : This is against blackmarketeers and hoarders.

SHRI VAJPAYEE : Do members of Parliament engage in blackmarketing ?

SHRI P. SHIV SHANKAR, Minister of Law : Very objectionable remarks my friend has made. I would request him to withdraw them.

SHRI RAVINDRA VARMA : Nothing objectionable. He is asking a question.

SHRI P. SHIV SHANKAR : He cannot say that Members of Parliament indulge in blackmarketing (*Interruption*).

SHRI VAJPAYEE : I did not say that. You did not follow (*Interruptions*).

MR. DEPUTY SPEAKER : If he had said that he includes himself also.

SHRI P. SHIV SHANKAR : He cannot include others.

MR. DEPUTY SPEAKER : What did you say ?

SHRI VAJPAYEE : I did not say that.

MR. DEPUTY SPEAKER : Please clarify it.

SHRI VAJPAYEE : I was put a question. Then I put a counter-question, whether Members of Parliament indulge in blackmarketing. This is not objectionable.

SHRI P. SHIV SHANKAR : That is objectionable.

SHRI VAJPAYEE : I did not say that Members of Parliament are indulging in blackmarketing. No. The hon. Law Minister is expected to be more alert and more intelligent.

SHRI P. SHIV SHANKAR : I am trying to be more alert.

SHRI VAJPAYEE : Maybe because of the language, he did not follow me.

Sir, I would like to repeat the proposal that if the Government amends the Essential Commodities Act and the Criminal Procedure Code to extend the period of custody for persons engaged in such offences. We would support such amendments. Actually what the Government want to prevent is the quick release of such persons on bail. A person arrested on a charge of murder is kept in police custody or judicial custody and is released only on court orders. The same method can be adopted also in the case of those engaged in anti-social activities. If necessary, the common law may be strengthened, but we do not want to give to this government powers under the Preventive Detention Act, as it harbours a feeling of vengeance (*Interruption*). So I appeal to the House...

SHRI C.P.N. SINGH : The Shah Commission, the special courts — was that not revenge ?

SHRI VAJPAYEE : We had set up commissions. Offenders were free to approach the court. We did not jail anybody without trial, and that is what you want to do.

SHRI G.L. VYAS : You have committed the sin nobody did. You drove out and jailed a person elected to Parliament.

SHRI VAJPAYEE : Even there our Congress friends had made the beginning. An elected member of Parliament was driven out. It was you, not we, who had done this first. The Hon. member does not know about it.

Smt. Indira Gandhi had said we do not want to dig out old matters, we want to face the challenges of the '80s. Is this black act the way to face these challenges ?

As it is, you are knowingly or unknowingly congratulating the old governments. At least you approved of one thing we did. But we did not doubt the bonafides of the caretaker government. There was no apprehension that it would misuse power. Still we had opposed, because for us it is a matter of principle. But so far as your bonafides are concerned, in view of what we saw in the last fifteen days we cannot give you this power.

I demand that the House approve this resolution :

MR. DEPUTY SPEAKER : Motion moved.

> "This House disapproves of the Prevention of Blackmarketing and Maintenance of Supplies of Essential Commodities Ordinance 1979 (Ordinance No.10 of 1979) promulgated by the President on the 5th October, 1979."

Reply

SHRI VAJPAYEE : Sir, the Commerce Minister has not been able to give a satisfactory reply to the points I had raised while demanding disapproval of this ordinance, which were supported by other Opposition members who spoke after me. He, however, did some mud-slinging at Lok Dal members. He has charged that the Lok Dal has changed its attitude. Sir, the Lok Dal changed its attitude because the Government changed.

AN HON. MEMBER : Lok Dal or *'daldal'* ?

SHRI VAJPAYEE : Will or will not the Government misuse a law ? This should be the test for such laws. Before judging a government's conduct or before forecasting its future we will have to look at the past of that government (*Interruption*). So it is not necessary to say that the gentlemen who are sitting in front of us have a terrible past (*Interruption*)... Even after an assurance to the contrary MISA was misused.

AN HON. MEMBER : All hoarders talk of a terrible past.

SHRI VAJPAYEE : This Act gives wide powers to government officers. Yesterday too I had referred to this. The Minister cannot escape by saying that detention is only for 12 days, then the case would go to the advisory board.

I had given an example of Delhi. There were 8 arrests. Seven were released by the Administrator and the eighth case went to the advisory board. It released him. But in that case for those who remained in jail for 10, 12 or 20 days who is responsible for their loss of freedom and prestige and for the social blot on their name ?

Now this power is being given to the District Magistrate or Police Commissioner. On whose report will the Police Commissioner act ? He cannot personally look into every case. Some sub-inspector at a police station or Tehsil Officer will forward a case and on the basis of it the district magistrate or police commissioner will issue detention orders. They may well be cancelled later. But the individual will lose his freedom (*Interruption*).

MR. SPEAKER : This is a matter worth thinking about. You are all Hon. Members of the House, but you are quarrelling among yourselves. This does not become us. You should listen.

SHRI VAJPAYEE : I agree with you, Sir. This is not at all right. At least it should not happen when I am speaking.

MR. SPEAKER : This applies to all.

SHRI VAJPAYEE : The Minister said it takes time to dispose of matters under the Essential Commodities Act. He gave the example of West Bengal and also blamed the State Government. But after all through whom will this preventive detention law be enforced ? Will the district magistrate work under the State Government or the Central Government ? Will the Police Commissioner be under the State Government or will the Central Government order him directly ?

Sir, for this you will have to trust the State governments, you will have to take their cooperation. For cooperation you will have to prepare the right atmosphere. The Minister has denied that he gave a threat. He says it will be "within the area of competence". How can you force State Governments to implement preventive detention within the area of competence ? It is another matter that you may act vengefully in other fields.

Yesterday too I had referred to this point but the Minister did not give any reply. There can be no two opinions that strict action should be taken against blackmarketeers, hoarders and profiteers, but this Bill has not been limited to businessmen. Attempts are also being made to strike at trade union rights. Even if the labour goes on strike for something legitimate they would have to go to jail for obstructing production. Is that necessary ?

AN HON. MEMBER : You are twisting this.

SHRI VAJPAYEE : If I am twisting it the Hon. Minister could accept the amendment that Shri Indrajit Gupta has tabled in this connection. Our doubts are not baselsss. That is not because the government is now in your hands. You could have sent this Bill to the Select Committee. There can be consultation between the government party and the opposition on this amendment in the Essential Commodities Act. If it is necessary to amend the Criminal Procedure Code that too could be considered. But it seems that apart from detention you have no effective means of checking rising prices. The Commerce Minister should admit that prices go up when there is less production and scarcity, blackmarketing prospers and the hoarding instinct grows strong.

AN HON. MEMBER : This was your philosophy.

SHRI VAJPAYEE : This is not a matter of philosophy, it is pure economics, but they cannot understand it (*Interruption*). Some long-term and short-term measures will have to be adopted for checking inflation. But if you have only the weapon of the detention law as a short-term measure I fear this purpose will not be served.

Before deciding what is being hoarded you will first have to determine the extent to which one can collect. For deciding whether profiteering is going on you will have to determine prices of the commodities. While fixing prices you will have to bear in mind that if a commodity is not available in the open market you will have to make it available to the people at fixed prices. If prices are fixed but supplies are not available commodities will disappear into the blackmarket and whatever little may be available would also become unavailable. All this economic process is quite complex.

SHRI HARISH RAWAT : We know our job.

SHRI VAJPAYEE : You are fresh here, you do not know anything.

SHRI HARISH RAWAT : What you know has been proved during the last two and a half years.

SHRI C.P.N. SINGH : Hon'ble Sir, you moved all over the world and in the process forgot India.

SHRI VAJPAYEE : I may forget India, but India cannot forget me, and I am present here to pester you (*Interruption*). There is still time. Let the Minister think about it calmly. There is no difference of opinion on basic matters. There should be stringent action against social offenders.

The Opposition has made the offer that necessary amendments should be carried out in the Essential Commodities Act and the Criminal Procedure Code and an agreed solution evolved that would get the support of all sections of the House. Why can you not accept this offer ? The police report will go to the judicial magistrate. If the judicial magistrate rules that the defendant should be kept in custody there would be no objection. We have tabled an amendment to that effect. Even in a case of murder judicial custody is ordered by the judicial magistrate, not the Police Commissioner, nor even the district magistrate. You could accept this amendment and find a way that we can all tread together. Otherwise we would have to block the way. Thank you.

National Security Ordinance— Another MISA

Sir, I move the following resolution :

"This House disapproves of the National Security Ordinance 1980 (No. 11 of 1980) promulgated by the President on September 22, 1980."

Sir nineteen ordinances were issued in the last 10 months. Yesterday we set our stamp of approval on one ordinance and today another is before us for consideration. The Constitution gives the power to issue ordinances but this power is being misused. Under the articles of the Constitution it is the responsibility of the President to satisfy himself that in the prevailing situation there is no option but to issue an ordinance, but the ordinances that have now been promulgated spread their orbit from national security to preservation of forests. Could the forest preservation ordinance not have waited ? Could not the Government have waited for a meeting of the House for it ? But we have now a rule of ordinances and everyday Parliament has an ordinance before it. Actually a national security ordinance would not have been necessary after the ordinance that was passed yesterday. You gave the powers of the judicial magistrate to the executive magistrate and now all laws come within the limitation that if an executive magistrate, who is a government officer, thinks that any person can be asked for bail in order to prevent him from some offence, he can do so. He can also jail that person if proper bail is not forthcoming. Bail regulations have been made stricter. What was the need of this National Security Ordinance ? What happened on September 22, 1980 that made the Government lose its sleep and decide to strike at personal freedom ? When the National Security Bill comes up for clause-by-clause consideration the question will be raised—what is the difference between the defence of India, the security of India and the security of state that have been discussed in this ordinance ? It would be natural to ask—what is the difference between the defence of India and the security of India ? And if there is a difference between the two what is the difference between the 'Security of India' and the 'Security of the State' ? But ordinances are being drafted in a hurry and they are being implemented in a still greater hurry. The Government is not prepared to wait even for a session of Parliament. Sir, as I see it, this is being done to cover up their failures on all fronts (*Interruption*).

When I say, I see but I do not mean with my own eyes. Sir, they want me to see, but with their eyes.

Lok Sabha on December 10, 1980 while moving the resolution seeking disapproval of National Security Ordinance, 1980

When failures are discussed our friends see red. If you have not failed, if all's well in the country, prices are going down, essential commodities are adequately available in the market, if there is full security of life and property, and if lamb and lion lie together what is the need for a National Security Act ? Our opponent friends cannot sit on two stools at the same time. If conditions have improved in 10 months this ordinance is not necessary. If conditions have deteriorated you have brought forward this ordinance for muzzling the people's voice against the deterioration.

India is a participant to the Universal Declaration of Human Rights. According to Article 9 of that Declaration no person can be arbitrarily arrested or detained. We have also said in Article 51(3) of our Constitution that we shall abide by international laws. But by this ordinance we are transgressing them. Today's newspapers have published a report of International Amnesty. When it was written they did not know how fast conditions in India have deteriorated. The report says the provision for preventive detention for prevention of blackmarketing and supply of essential commodities is not proper. But when they look at the National Security Ordinance they would feel that India is progressing fast on the highway of denial of democratic rights.

Sir, the framers of our Constitution had provided that no person is to be arrested without showing cause or kept in jail without trial. But in view of the then prevailing situation detention had been provided for in the Constitution. But it seems a temporary arrangement is being made permanent. When the then Home Minister Sardar Patel introduced the Preventive Detention Bill in Parliament for the first time he had said that he could not sleep for nights. History is repeating itself. Now Sardar Zail Singh is the Home Minister. Sardar Patel could not sleep in nights before introducing the Bill, but Sardar Zail Singh is so happy on introducing the ordinance that he has started sleeping even by day. Attacking individual freedom, limiting individual freedom, may be justified in war time, but not in peace time.

DEPUTY SPEAKER : This is also an attack on the individual liberty of sleeping.

DR. SUBRAMANIAM SWAMY : It is not objectionable. The Home Minister is not here. It is he who has to execute the order.

DEPUTY SPEAKER : He has come now.

SHRI VAJPAYEE : Checking individual freedom is not a small thing. If the Government has reached the conclusion that the situation cannot be controlled by using the common law or means it has failed to control the situation and wants to acquire special powers. Why are they needed ? Look at the statement on the objectives of the Bill. It can satisfy nobody.

The district magistrate and the Police Commissioner are being given the power of detention. We have Police Commissioner's Raj in Delhi and people are being taken into detention. I have copies of the orders. The Police Commissioner is too busy to go into every case and satisfy himself before depriving somebody of his freedom. There are cyclostyled copies of the order, in which the names are just filled in. The Police Commissioner does not have the time even to sign. One copy is signed, then the signature is cyclostyled on other orders, and people are being deprived of their freedom on the authority of these cyclostyled signatures.

Sir, we were in jail for 19 months under MISA. When MISA was introduced the assurance was given that it would not be used against political opponents, but what actually happened ? The Home Minister also gives the same assurance, but it has no value. In Uttar Pradesh opposition leaders were detained under this black Act. In Gujarat those participating in the anti-price rise agitation were arrested. If they had committed an offence they should be prosecuted. If they have broken the peace the law will deal with them. But there is no proof, no witness, no defence, no appeal. We are going back to the Rowlatt Act days of the British Raj. In Madhya Pradesh the Collector of Indore District had stated that some people were habitual offenders ....

SHRI RAM PYARE PANIKA (Robertsganj) : In Madhya Pradesh their government detained people under MISA. Throw light on the circular you had sent out.

SHRI VAJPAYEE : I shall throw light and also some darkness on you.

District officials had recommended the detention of some people on the ground that they were goondas, but the State Government did not accept the recommendation, because a by-election was coming up and the help of goondas was needed for winning it. The Chief Minister gave a statement saying 'we wanted to think a hundred times before depriving a person of his freedom.' If the Madhya Pradesh Chief Minister wants to think a hundred times the Centre's Home Minister should think a thousand times. But he is not ready to do that.

In Allahabad, Uttar Pradesh, a person was detained on the charge that on a certain date he was indulging in a certain activity, when actually he was in jail on that date. How could be commit an offence if he was in jail, and if he was not committing an offence how could he be detained ?

AN HON. MEMBER : He could be an RSS expert at disguise (*'Bahurupee'*)

SHRI VAJPAYEE : Beware, there are some on that side too. Why does the Government hesitate to approach the courts ? If an arrested person is not produced before a magistrate within 24 hours there would be murders like that of Rajan in Kerala, there would be cases of blinding, as in Bhagalpur. After all when you issue a detention order you are expected to have some material on which you base or if that material, that cause, is good enough for detention why should there be any objection to show it to the detained person ? But on reading the order of Delhi I can tell you why. One order says you are a habitual offender, so the Government has decided to detain you. Don't you have any law against offenders ? Can you not put an offender in the dock ? Why is the Government not prepared to weigh itself in the scales of justice ?

One can think about limiting individual freedom in an extraordinary situation like danger on the borders in war time or jeopardy for India's independence or territorial integrity. But even there I would say that, seeing how the Government has misused MISA, even in times of national crisis we would certainly think a couple of times before giving special powers to this Government. Once bitten, we are twice shy. In 1971 the Bangladesh crisis was exploited to get MISA passed in this House. The opposition had raised no objection. Later when a leader of Shri Jayaprakash Narayan's stature was taken into detention the Attorney-General of India had stated in the Supreme Court that even if the police shot down somebody no one could object. Can we forget that old history ? What new situation has arisen today ? I ask again, why do you feel the need for this black Act ? I quote what Lord Simon had said : "To arrest a person without telling him as to why he is being arrested is the law of tyrant and that of slaves." This is not a National Security Ordinance, this is a National Slavery Ordinance. Your bonafides are suspect in our eyes. In view of how you are misusing power we cannot give you this special power.

SHRI R.P. PANIKA : What happened in Madhya Pradesh during your government ?

SHRI VAJPAYEE : He keeps saying the Janata Party too wanted to implement it. If you remember, a Bill was introduced in the days of the Janata Party Government, but due to public pressure and pressure of the party it had to be withdrawn. We would like to see how much pressure the Congress Party shows. But Congress Party members are demanding the Emergency.

SHRI VASANT SATHE, Minister for Information and Broadcasting : That is not true. It was withdrawn because of greed for power, because there was dissension.

SHRI VAJPAYEE : Our opponents cannot even understand that the complaint against the Janata Government is not of harshness but of softness. We did not detain our opponents.

SHRI R.P. PANIKA : People do not like those who are soft, so they removed these people.

SHRI VAJPAYEE : So they have decided to be harsh.

SHRI PANIKA : The Bill is in accordance with the people's aspirations.

SHRI VAJPAYEE : I would like to know what aspirations of the people this Bill would fulfil. There is a conflagration of popular discontent in the country, and you cannot put it out by detaining thousands of people. Assam is burning for the past ten months. The problem of Assam cannot be solved by calling in the army. If the farmers do not get the right price for their produce they will agitate.

MR. DEPUTY SPEAKER : Order, please. Any member interrupting should know this. If he wants to interrupt the Speaker, Shri Vajpayee, first he must yield. Then only you can put the thing. If he does not yield you cannot interrupt. Everyone of you gets up so often.

SHRI VAJPAYEE : You know, I am not yielding.

MR. DEPUTY SPEAKER : That is why from here you have gone there.

SHRI VAJPAYEE : Sir, in a democracy there is full freedom for expression of opposition in a peaceful manner. If farmers ask for a proper price for their sugarcane, raise their voice for thirty rupees a quintal—(*Interruption*)—they have the right not to sell their cane to the mills.

SHRI VASANT SATHE : Perhaps *'Rasta Roko'* is also included in the expression of opposition.

SHRI VAJPAYEE : Shri Vasant Sathe knows that in Maharashtra leaders of his party are also participating in the *Rasta Roko* agitation.

SHRI VASANT SATHE : Not a single one.

SHRI VAJPAYEE : The Chief Minister of Uttar Pradesh has announced that if anyone tells the farmers not to sell cane to sugar mills such leaders would be jailed under the National Security Ordinance (*Interruption*) .

AN HON. MEMBER : He said about obstructing the farmers.

SHRI VAJPAYEE : Look at the clauses of this ordinance. Look at the law that had been passed before this in the name of essential commodities. This 'defence of India' and 'Security of India' are so wide that no activity can escape them.

The Foreign Hand

One more strange thing. This says if anyone tries to adversely affect the country's foreign relationship he too could be proceeded against. In my opinion if there is someone who is really trying to vitiate foreign relations it is, first and foremost, Home Minister Gyani Zail Singh, who sees a foreign hand in everything, every disturbance. When he was asked why don't you act against the foreign hand he says the foreign hand is invisible, then how can we act ? If you cannot see the foreign hand how do you know it is foreign or Indian ? When the Home Minister talked of the foreign hand in Moradabad Smt. Indira Gandhi did not deny it. At first she kept silent on it, but her colleagues kept talking of the foreign hand, and the official spokesman kept his mouth shut. When the Prime Minister went to Moradabad she said "there is no foreign hand, there is foreign interference." What sort of a government is this that tolerates foreign interference ? And what is the difference between 'foreign hand' and 'foreign interference' ? It is to cover up their failures that at times they talk of a foreign hand, at times put the blame on the opposition and at times point their finger at the international situation. But this won't do now.

For ten months they have been saying that things have gone so bad in the Janata regime that it will take time to put them right. People began to ask how much time ? So to shut them up they have now brought forth the National Security Ordinance. You cannot speak, you cannot open your mouth, your freedom will be in the hands of the police. The Police Commissioner cannot look everywhere in Delhi. So it will be the Station House Officer who will decide who is to be detained. We saw in the Emergency that bribes were demanded by threatening people with detention. People were terrorised. The Government is going in the same direction.

The Advisory Board

When the ordinance was promulgated we were asked to read clause 9(2), which says there will be an advisory board. It was also said that the Chairman of the board will be appointed in consultation with the Chief Justice of India, and it will have two members, who will be either sitting judges or retired judges. The Bill now before us has changed this. I know the Law Minister or the Home Minister will say the Janata Government did not issue the notification required under the 44th amendment, but why did you not take note of this before issuing the ordinance ?

The ordinance and the Bill are two different things. In many States advisory boards have been set up under the Conservation of Foreign Exchange and Prevention of Smuggling Act, and under the Prevention of Blackmarketing and Maintenance of Supplies of Essential Commodities Act, but under the National Security Bill the government can appoint any advocate with ten years' practice to the boards to be set up under it. The advisory board will be manned by selected people. As it is, efforts are being made to man the high courts and the Supreme Court with judges of their choice. There are vacancies and it is argued that sitting judges cannot be spared because of the arrears in the high courts. If that is so increase the number of judges. But we saw yesterday and we see today again that the Government does not want to face the court. Yesterday the judicial magistrate's powers were given to the executive magistrate. By differentiating between the ordinance and the Bill and by exploiting the deficiency that a notification was not issued the Government is trying to set up boards that it could man with the people of its choice. In order that cases going to such boards could be disposed of detenus will not have the right to legal aid. In Delhi there are cases in which the detention orders are in English but the person on whom it is served does not know English. He cannot consult a lawyer. Then how will he defend himself ? All this means concentration of all power, an unrestrained administration, denial of individual freedom, a blow at the powers of the judiciary, and the creation of an atmosphere of danger to India's security so that personal freedom has no importance.

Foreign Relations

Sir, the Government has denied this and said it does not want any confrontation with Pakistan, rather, it wants to strengthen friendly relations. I welcome this pronouncement. These days Russian leaders are on a visit to our country. We are old friends, our friendship with them has stood the test of time, we should strengthen that friendship. At the same time we should also tell them that what they did in Afghanistan was not right, and if they are going to do the same thing in Poland that too won't be right .... (*Interruption*). But I am not raising this point here. Talks are going on for normalising our relations with China. Nepal and Bangladesh are our friends. Then where is the danger to India's security ? There is certainly tension within the country. Social tension and economic disparity are growing. Tensions would certainly rise if there is backwardness and inequality, and we have not been able to do justice to any class or region in the past 33 years.

But opening the doors of jails is not the way to resolve those tensions. For that you have to open the doors to people's hearts.

Contrary to Constitution's Spirit

I submit that this ordinance is contrary to the spirit of the Constitution of India. It also gives a lie to your claim that you were elected with the people's support. It further falsifies your claim that all's well in the country. This is an alarm bell. Today the power to detain people is being acquired, tomorrow complete usurpation of fundamental rights would be attempted. This is not an attempt to bring in an emergency by the back door, this is dictatorship boldly walking the highway. I am sorry to see that the job of doing this has fallen on the Home Minister. As I said earlier, Sardar Patel could not sleep nights before bringing in the Detention Act, but Gyani Zail Singh would find it easy to sleep even by day when all of us are behind bars. Thank you.

Ordinance Became Law, but Status Quo Continued

Madam, I move the following resolution :

"This House disapproves of the National Security (Amendment) Ordinance, 1987 promulgated by the President on June 9, 1987."

Madam, in the first place this ordinance should not have been promulgated at all, but it was promulgated—promulgated in an unnecessary form, and now it is being given the form of a law. This is utterly unnecessary. According to the statement accompanying the Bill, Punjab and Chandigarh have been declared disturbed areas, but there has been no improvement in the situation there. The law and order situation has been continuously deteriorating. President's Rule was imposed to check the deterioration. Despite it the situation does not seem to have come under control.

The essence of the ordinance promulgated is Clause 14-A. It was struck down by the Division Bench of the Punjab High Court, but there was an appeal to the Supreme Court. It has ordered suspension. What the final verdict will be no one knows. But the Government is not waiting for it. In the meanwhile, it promulgated the ordinance on June 9. At present this ordinance is in force in Punjab. Action is being taken under it. Has the situation in Punjab improved ? Even the Government cannot reply to this question in the affirmative.

The fact of the matter is that the ordinance is meant for acquiring powers to make the detention law still harsher. I am not raising here the basic question of how proper a detention law is in a free and democratic country that has a written constitution with a separate guarantee for fundamental rights. However this question will arise every time the period of the detention act is extended or it is made stricter. Since 1950 we have been discussing how far it is proper to arrest a citizen of a free country without showing cause and keeping him in prison without trial. Sardar Vallabhbhai Patel was Home Minister when the provision for detention was included in the Constitution. Today too we have a Sardar as Home Minister—Sardar Buta Singh. That time Sardar Patel could not sleep for two nights. Sardar Buta Singh cannot spare time even to attend the House. But this debate goes on and it will go on. Our friend Shri Chidambaram made a speech in the Lok Sabha in the course of which he said :

Rajya Sabha on August 26, 1987 while moving the resolution seeking disapproval of the National Security (Amendment) Ordinance, 1987

> "I believe that we must have a day when there would be full scope for personal liberty and freedom without having recourse to the law of Preventive Detention."

I respect his feelings. At least on the emotional level he agrees that the detention law is not good and should not be there, and a time will come when this black law would not be needed. When will that time come ?

The Punjab Situation

Madam, in Punjab there was also a time when Article 14(A) was not in operation. It did not exist from April 1986 to June 9, 1987. Had the law and order situation in Punjab deteriorated greatly at that time ? Were the police so hampered in the performance of duty that they could not discharge it ? It is true that this law was in existence, was effective, during the days of the Barnala government. But when the High Court struck it down, Article 14(A) was not in operation in Punjab. If we could do without it then why can't we do without it now ? If we look at this Bill that is being brought forward on the basis of an ordinance we would say that at the most this ordinance is a matter of days.

It says the law that is valid for four months will be valid for four months and two weeks, the clause that had been enforced for four weeks would be in force for five months, and the one that was in force for twelve months would now be in force for twenty-four. Has the law and order situation in Punjab deteriorated so little that the people there depend only on so many restrictions ? Will the police become effective if the Bill changes 15 days to 20 days ? Will the law and order machinery be able to challenge terrorism ? I know the thinking behind such amendments, such bills. Terrorism is an old problem in Punjab. Steps have also been taken to deal with it. Punjab and Chandigarh have been declared disturbed areas and other laws have also been passed. Is the law ineffective because the police have to do a job in 10 days for which they are demanding 15 days ? Is the House now going to give those 15 days ? Is this such a simple thing ? Is this a matter of days ?

In Punjab the police department has been strengthened. The police force has been provided with modern equipment. Now there should be no delay in sending information from the districts to Chandigarh. The whole of Punjab has been made the area of operations. But will the conflagration in Punjab be put out only by promptly giving facilities to the police ? It seems that whenever the situation in Punjab goes from bad to worse the government finds itself helpless, it approaches the House and the country for more powers. Are the powers it already has insufficient ? Are they being properly used ? Will the problem be solved only by changing the number of days in them ?

Madam, we did not hesitate to give the Government the powers it asked for Punjab. But what is the situation even after that ? For the present only Chandigarh and Punjab have been declared disturbed areas. Can the Minister of State in the Ministry of Home Affairs assure the House, assure me, that it would not become necessary to declare any more areas as disturbed ?

Territorists have stepped up their activities in Delhi. In Delhi they indulged in mass killings, killed people selectively, but they have not yet been apprehended. No one has been detained. Then what will you achieve by extending detention from 10 days to 15 ? The extremists have now covered Haryana. They are succeeding in spreading their activities and the Government has no weapon but this ordinance. Is there a shortage in the Government's armoury ? If not, then it does not have a clear perception, does not have the political will and no determination to solve the Punjab problem with far-sightedness and on the basis of morality.

An objection is raised when Bharatiya Janata Party demands that if paramilitary forces cannot control the situation in Punjab there should be no hesitation in calling for the Army's assistance. Yesterday I saw an article by Shri Satpal Dang, a respected leader of the Communist Party and of Punjab. He lives in Punjab. He is moving from village to village and fighting the terrorists. Workers of Bharatiya Janata Party are also trying to organise the people of Punjab including Hindus and Sikhs against the terrorists. But it is not easy for the rest of the country to understand what the people of Punjab are going through. Shri Dang writes in his article :

> "Possibly the strength of the paramilitary forces in the State is not adequate. If that is so, why are not more battalions being requisitioned ? If they were not available why not take the help of the army ? No answers are forthcoming. Nor is this all. As yet, no reaction has been forthcoming from the authorities to the plan of the extremists to capture all guardwaras and to use their resources for killing."

Extremists have acquired control on the Golden Temple precincts. Persons called A-grade extremists go into the Golden Temple, consult and plan the next day's killings, and leave. According to recent reports extremists are equipping themselves with the most modern weapons. There were such suspicions in the past too. Have they succeeded in getting helicopters ? Are they trying to get missiles ? Terrorism is now assuming the form of guerilla warfare. Can this type of ordinance fight it — an ordinance that talks of extending 10 days to 20, 20 days to 25 and 25 to 30 ? Instead of acquiring more powers the Government should use its present powers properly.

Army's Help for Fighting Terrorists

An all-out campaign is needed against terrorists. It should be launched with all might, and if necessary the help of the Army should be taken. At the same time the situation of discord in Punjab should end. The Government must say why Shri Prakash Singh Badal is under detention. If he has committed an offence, prosecute him. We differed with him. He had come to Parliament House and met opposition members. We gave him a piece of our mind. But what is the propriety in keeping him in jail ? How many people have been detained in Punjab ? In Britain terrorists can be prosecuted. In Punjab connected terrorists can be punished. In the U.S. cases can be conducted and punishment meted out. But there is no case so far against the terrorists who are in the Jodhpur jail for the past so many years. How will guilt or innocence be proved ? In his reply the Home Minister should tell us how many people are in detention in Punjab. He should also give the ground on which they were detained. What is Shri Prakash Singh Badal charged with ? There should be no objection to talking with people who are willing to give up violence and to solve the problem within the Constitution of India, within the unity and integrity of the country. But talks cannot succeed unless the terrorists are taught a lesson. The ordinance you are bringing forward for that is not enough. It needs a new strategy, and the people's cooperation would also be needed for its success. But once people feel confident that you are ready to crush the terrorists and will take any step required for it you will get the people's cooperation too. But with the Bill you have introduced, with the Ordinance you have promulgated, we can do nothing but oppose it.

Reply

Sir, the discussion on my motion is coming to a close. The ruling party has not given any satisfactory reply to the objections I had raised. Perhaps the Hon. Minister may throw some light on them in his reply to the full debate I had asked a simple question—Had the situation in Punjab worsened further because 14(A) was not in operation in the period from April 1986 to June 9, 1987 ? Why was it necessary to introduce it ? The second thing is this — the period is being extended from 5 to 10 days, 10 days to 15 for giving more time to the police and for administrative convenience, but if it is true that the administration has been strengthened, the police have become alert, if the administration and the police have become more active, the period should have been shortened rather than extended. Or are we going to extend this efficiency of the administration and the police—something on which some members have thrown light ? The Hon. Minister had made it clear that the advisory board is functioning. It has released many people in Punjab—but after they were kept in jail for three months. Now they will be kept in jail for 6 months. If the State Government arrests people indiscriminately, if they remain in jail, and if, while in jail, they come into contact with such elements that if they were not committing offences while outside they would start doing so after coming out of jail, that would not be a very good thing. Should it not be a matter of concern for us if an individual is robbed of his freedom for three months ? Now that period is being extended to 6 months.

Sir, my submission is — take the harshest possible steps, but do not adopt methods that would create new terrorists. I talked to Director-General Ribeiro. When I asked him, are you in favour of having President's Rule in Punjab for a long time, he said, 'no', because I know that people cannot raise their voice against excesses if they do not have their representatives at the lower levels, and the police force could also go the wrong way, as we are going to equip it with more powers. Are new powers really necessary ?

It is good that Sardar Buta Singh is present. There was a massacre at Jagdev Kalan on August 6-7. Twelve persons of 4 families were killed. They all belonged to the same religion. So far as killing is concerned the terrorists do not make religious distinctions. That day we all condoled with the Home

Minister. His family had to become a target. But I have come to know that there was a police post at Jagdev Kalan. On July 25, the residents protested against its removal. On July 27 it was removed. On August 6-7 the massacre took place. What law will cure this deficiency ? How will you solve this problem ? Two persons are suspected to be involved in the Jagdev Kalan massacre. They were not arrested. I do not know if they have been arrested. The General Secretary of our party went from Amritsar to Jagdev Kalan. There was a red alert in Punjab, he saw no patrol on the way. The terrorists moved about in the village for 45 minutes, raising slogans, but the police post that was nearby had been removed. They said we are not far away, call us if you need us. The Police did not come. How will this Bill solve these problems ?

Sir, I repeat it is necessary to eradicate terrorism, and you get and will get the cooperation of the whole House for it. But the way you are going about it — is it not creating new terrorists ? If people come to feel increasingly that excesses are being committed against them, if they have been left to the tender mercies of the police, that they are put in the dock without caring if they are guilty or innocent, that they are being looked at with suspicion, how can you achieve the objective of putting terrorism apart and securing the cooperation of the rest of the society against the terrorists ? I hope the Hon. Minister will throw light on these points in his reply. Thank you.

Release Advani Immediately

Mr. Speaker, Sir, I am not raising a matter relating to any State. It is an issue relating to two Hon'ble members of this House. At the moment, I do not want to go into the public excitement that had been caused due to the arrest of Shri L.K. Advani and Shri Vinay Katiyar and sending them to jail due to which we had to take a decision of remaining outside the House. They were to be produced in the court at Lucknow yesterday, but it was not done. The lawyers argued the case and the judge gave his judgement that they should be released. However, I have just now received a message on telephone from Renukoot that in spite of the judge's clear order they have not been released so far. In fact they should have been released during the night itself, so that they could reach Delhi in the morning and attend the House. But it appears that the Government of Uttar Pradesh is bent upon committing contempt of the court. It is not only a case of contempt but also of breach of privilege of the members. When they have been released by the Court, who can keep them behind bars? And, is it not against the Constitution and all democratic norms to keep them in jail ?

Mr. Speaker, Sir, the order of the Court must be obeyed; I would like you to intervene in the matter and they should be provided facility to come to Delhi immediately. Please issue this direction to the Central Government so that the members may attend the House. There are three or four days left for the present session to end. We also are eager to attend the sittings of the House. But, we may be forced to walk out of the House again if Shri L.K. Advani and Shri Katiyar are not released. Thank you.

Lok Sabha on December 21, 1993 on the arrest of Shri Advani and Shri Katiyar

VI Centre-State Relations

Dictatorial Attitude of Communists in Kerala

Sir, for the first time in the history of the world the Communist Party had come to power in Kerala by democratic means. This was a golden opportunity for them to give the lie to the charge—acquired due to foreign ancestors—by their conduct that for them democracy is not a means of ending democracy but a powerful, effective and permanent means for a change in the social structure.

But the Communist administration in Kerala for 27 months has made it clear that democracy and communism cannot co-exist. It has also been revealed that they are *status-quo-ists* and great hypocrites. The world may progress greatly, circumstances may change radically, but the Communist Party will not stop chanting dictatorship of the proletariat. And dictatorship of the proletariat means dictatorship of the party of the proletariat, and of course the party of the proletariat can only be the Communist Party, none else.

Sir, I charge that in Kerala the Communist Party is working for the establishment of dictatorship. Democracy means the government of the people, for the people, by the people. But I had been to Kerala during the days of the agitation. What I saw and heard led me to conclude that Kerala does not have a government of the people, but a government of, for and by the communist party. I charge that the Communist Party has not yet accepted the Constitution with all its articles. When the Chief Minister of Kerala assumed power he issued a message in the name of the people in which he pleaded helplessness about not being able to do what he wanted to do. Why is he helpless ? I quote his own words :

> "The administration of the problem state is a job; it is indeed difficult. The real difficulty is the fact that he and his colleagues have to work within the framework of the system which includes several regulation and procedures which are not to their liking."

The Constitution of India contains restraints that prevent democracy from changing into dictatorship and the Chief Minister of Kerala dislikes these limitations. Although his protestations were democratic his conduct was

Lok Sabha on August 20, 1959 on the resolution relating to dismissal of the Communist Government in Kerala and imposition of President's Rule in the State

quite the opposite. What are the restraints that the Constitution places on the administration ? The first is that there has to be a dividing line—a *Laxman Rekha*—between party and government. If anyone crosses that line it would lead to the abduction of the Sita of democracy by the obliterated. The independence of the judiciary was interfered with, and that was not all. Cell courts were set up which could issue summonses.

Some friends here have been criticising Congress administrations. I am also not a very great fan of the Congress and our Congress friends are aware of the fact that in this very Delhi they joined hands with us to defeat the Congress. But in spite of being a critic of the Congress I have no hesitation in saying that what happened during the Communist administration in Kerala has not yet happened in the thirteen States ruled by the Congress. In no State were cell courts set up. 14-year-old-boys were not banished from their homes, no parents were told to marry their daughters to communists, and no one who disobeyed a cell court was stabbed. This is possible only under a dictatorship, and in Kerala the Communist party is proceding in that direction.

The Communists' new police policy has been praised a lot here. I think this new police policy is based on Lenin's April thesis. It is said it is in the interest of labour and peasants. But I have seen in Kerala that whenever there was a problem of labourers either not connected with the communist party or opposed to it the policy of non-interference by the police was given the go-by and the police intervened. The Communist police beat up students with *lathis* and fired on labourers. It is clear that this new police policy was adopted for strengthening the communist party. There are instances where the Government did not concede the demands of anti-communist factory-workers' unions. And these factories did not all belong to capitalists, there is also a Government of India undertaking in Kerala. There was some disturbance there.

Discrimination between Labour and Labour in Kerala

The communists staged a *Dharna* there, saying they won't let the workers go in, and the police just watched. Was it a capitalist's industry ? It was a public sector undertaking, but when the workers were prevented by the *Dharna* from entering, the police did not interfere. What happened in Sitaram Mill ? What happened in the Government printing press ? The police intervened where the interests of the communist party were affected, but it was rendered ineffective where opponents and their unions were suppressed. During my tour I asked a worker— this is a workers' government—then how is it that you are opposed do it ? He replied—I am not a member of the Communist union, so I slept on a footpath. One day I was told that I would not be allowed to sleep there if I did not join the communist union, and if I did not listen I would be dealt with with a knife. This is the story of a labourer. Not all workers were protected in Kerala. Had they been, such a big agitation would not have arisen.

It has been repeatedly said that this movement was not launched by some party, it was the people's movement and parties joined it later. Had they not done so the people's tide would have carried them away. The people took a stand not for the protection of landlordism but for the preservation of the Constitution of India. Sir, in Uttar Pradesh the Congress Government finished two million landlords.

AN HON. MEMBER : Only in words.

SHRI VAJPAYEE : There was no movement there. The communist party could not take the people along with it, so it was expected of the Prime Minister that he would advise the people to stop the agitation. The communist party forgets that the Prime Minister is a great democrat. When the people are aroused no democrat can say no to their demands if they are right. He asked the communists to resign. Many communist members have spoken, but none has said why they are sticking to power. I sometimes wonder if they stuck to the chair or the chair stuck to them, and the President's declaration was required to separate the two. Had they some respect for the Prime Minister they would have said to him—it is wrong to talk of resignation, but we will do it for your sake. This would have redounded to the Communist party's prestige, but they did not have the moral courage to give up power, and ask people to elect them if they had done something for the people. So they did not resign.

Centre Protected Democracy

What could the Central Government then do ? Had it not done anything in the face of the murder of democracy in Kerala the Constitution would have proved ineffective. But I am happy it proved effective. If there is any attack on democracy we can meet it. The Centre's intervention in Kerala proves this. But the delay has given scope for delusions about the communists in the people's mind.

As yet it is not clear if the Centre's intervention is due to the communists' working for breaking the Constitution or because of the people's movement. In my opinion the government should not have waited for the people's movement. It should have intervened when the communists were transgressing the Constitution, murdering democracy, discriminating between citizen and citizen, ending equality in them and setting up dictatorship with the aid of democracy. But I can understand the Centre's difficulty. The Centre has a Congress government, Kerala has a Communist government. There was also some fear of international reaction, some consideration of what people would say. Any way, better late than never. I support the action taken which, though delayed, is in the right direction.

Shri Dange says the Prime Minister's chariot, that was riding above the ground has now come down to earth. I say the communist party could get the opportunity to entrench itself in the soil of the country precisely because the Prime Minister's chariot was riding above it. If now it has really come down to earth the communist party cannot have its feet on the ground, it will have to go underground. There can be no greater friend of the communist party than the Prime Minister. But when it is in the interest of the communist party they make much of him, when anything is against its interests they denigrate him. When, after the firing at Ankamali, the Governor issued a statement directly charging the opposition with violence the communists were very happy and he was an ideal Governor for them. Now that the Governor's report blames the Communist Party for breaking the Constitution the same Governor has now become a fallen person for them. Now they are not willing to take him into confidence. Such double standards won't do.

Communism will never Succeed in Kerala

The Communist administration in Kerala has proved that the communist party cannot work the democratic system, not even if it wants to. In Mahabharat Duryodhana says—I know what I am doing is wrong, but my mind itself is such that I cannot do the right thing. The communist party cannot work within the Constitution of India so long as it does not give up dictatorship of the proletariat, does not give up its belief in class struggle and does not stop looking abroad for inspiration. Not only in Kerala, in any State of the country a communist government, if it comes to power, would work against the Constitution. Shri Dange has made this clear. He has not repented over what happened in Kerala. He has thrown a challenge—a challenge to the Central Government that has unseated the communist government and a challenge for the House. The challenge is—if we get elected again, we'll do the same thing again. I say the House needs to ponder seriously over one point— when a party openly wants to break the constitution, has actually broken it with its conduct, should it have the freedom to capture power by winning elections under the Constitution ?

Two more points, and I shall finish. Shri Dange had referred to the Mahabharat. I too recollect an incident in the Mahabharat. The war between the Kauravas and the Pandavas was going on, and Karna's chariot had sunk in the ground. Arjun was prepared to kill him but Karna called out, saying don't you know morality, justice, *Dharma* ? Arjun replied, where was *Dharma* when Draupadi was being disrobed in Duryodhana's Court, where was *Dharma* when the plot was hatched to burn the Pandavas alive in a house of lac ?

Now the communists are talking of democracy, of justice. I ask them, where was democracy, where was the Constitution when they took up arms in Telangana after independence ? Why talk of Telangana ? As you know, Sir, it has been proved that recently in Punjab the communist party has promoted violence against the betterment levy. Courts were entered and overrun, and they claimed they were fighting for specific issues. I say the people of Kerala were also fighting for a specific issue and they said those who do not believe in democracy had to go.

People of Kerala Deserve Congratulations

The people of Kerala deserve to be congratulated. The brave people of Kerala have shown the country the way. I hope in future too they will give a fitting reply to the communist party. But the House and the Central Government need to seriously consider this—should or should not the communist party be allowed to enjoy democratic facilities when it cannot adopt and tread the path of democracy ?

One last thing. Now that President's Rule has been promulgated our Communist friends are charging—and Shri Narayanan Kutty charged that day—that a temple has been demolished. When asked where, he at first said in Trichur district, then he took back his words and said it was in Ernakulam.

I wrote to the people of my party at the places he named and asked them to find out the truth. I have pictures of the places about which charges were made. They show no temple was demolished and it is all false. But now the communists have stood up as the champions of Hindus. At least in this one respect the President's proclamation has proved of benefit. Still I would like to say that the charges so far levelled about the Hindu temples in Kerala are false and I hope no one would be taken in by them.

With these words I support the resolution. Thank you.

Why Avoid Kerala Elections

Sir, I had no intention of speaking on this Bill, but during the discussion some things were said that have prompted me to do so. General elections should take place in Kerala soon. It is not necessary to extend President's Rule there any more. It is true that the people of Kerala are fed up with political parties and their factionalism, but will never be content under President's Rule and Parliament will never be able to do justice by Kerala. Delhi has the Centre's administration. We cannot solve even Delhi's problems so it would be vain to hope that sitting in Delhi, thousands of miles away, the Central Government would be able to solve the problems of Kerala. The people of Kerala....

SHRI MAHAVIR PRASAD BHARGAVA : The people of Kerala were very happy, Vajpayeeji.

SHRI VAJPAYEE : I too have been to Kerala. I was not with you.

SHRI M.N. GOVINDAN NAIR : The Britishers also, just like you people, often said that the Indians were very happy under the British rule.

SHRI VAJPAYEE : The people of Kerala want a return to democracy, and there should be no delay in this. It is to be highly regretted that the timing of the elections in Kerala is being considered from the point of view of the partisan interests of the Congress. If the Congress party gets organised today, elections can be held tomorrow...

SHRI BHUPESH GUPTA : Congress party and its astrogers....

SHRI VAJPAYEE : ... and if the Congress party is not organised the elections can be avoided. This is a terrible situation. If democracy is made synonymous with one party the people would lose faith in it. I am also unhappy that the Governor of Kerala cares more for the interests of the Congress and less for the interests of Kerala. I had said in the House that when he was appointed he wanted an assurance from the Central Government that he would go to Kerala as Governor only when President's Rule was promulgated there. He was not willing to go during the functioning of the Legislative Assembly and a democratic administration. He went there when President's Rule was promulgated. But as the President's representative the Governor's job is to discharge his constitutional responsibility, not to get involved in party politics. Whether the Congress party is united or not, whether it finishes itself in internecine fighting, whatever his affection for the Congress, he cannot behave in a partisan manner so long as he occupies the position of Governor and is responsible for the administration of Kerala.

Rajya Sabha on December 7, 1965 during discussion on Money Bill in relation to Kerala

Governor Involved in Party Politics

But I am sorry to see that he is involved in party politics, and this has vitiated the whole political atmosphere of Kerala. The Governor lives in Kerala, but his heart is in Saharanpur. I wish the Hon. Minister places before the House the number of times Shri Ajit Prasad Jain visited Saharanpur since he became Governor of Kerala. He is cultivating his constituency. He visits Saharanpur to inaugurate a school and to open a small bridge on some road. I do not know if a Governor needs the President's permission to leave station. He is a public servant, he has been appointed as the administrative head there. If he visits Saharanpur every now and then he cannot discharge his responsibilities towards Kerala. If he wants to fight the election in Saharanpur he may do so, but then he should give up the Governorship of Kerala.

If President's Rule is to go on we want a person who would not get involved in party politics but pay attention to Kerala's industrial progress. Kerala is educationally quite advanced but equally backward industrially. The people of Kerala would be grateful for President's Rule if Kerala became economically developed during it. In the past too good plans were prepared on paper during President's Rule, but they were not implemented. That mistake should not be repeated.

Propaganda against Defence of India Rules

One more thing. Some of my friends have complained that Defence of India Rules have been misused. I would not enter into that, but I would like to place a case before the House where I would like to know why Defence of India Rules were not used. That is Shri Namboodiripad's case. He is openly carrying on propaganda against gold bonds and calling upon the people not to participate in the war effort. Shri Namboodiripad is my friend, he is very good on the personal level, but his politics, his propaganda, is hindering the nation's war effort, and you are allowing such a person to indulge in any type of propaganda. The nation is in a crisis, and nothing should be said that would break the people's morale. But he carries on his propaganda without check, and neither does the Kerala administration take any action, nor does Shri Nanda, who has been criticised so much. If Defence of India Rules exist, should they make an exception to anybody ? If yes, why ? Thank you.

Governors Becoming Dictators

Sir, Indian democracy is passing through a delicate phase. This is a testing time for the Central government. It is also a test for our federal Constitution. For the past 20 years a single party had the monopoly of power at the Centre and in the States. Now that monopoly is broken. Earlier the problems arising between the Centre and the States were being ironed out at the Congress party level. But now there is a Congress Government at the Centre and non-Congress governments in eight States. During the past 20 years no thought was devoted to what problems would arise from the constitutional point of view, and from the viewpoint of setting healthy democratic traditions. In the last general elections the country has made a democratic revolution. In eight States the Congress has had to lose power. Now our Constitution will be on test. Now we will have to set healthy traditions and show that for us the country comes before party. From now on establishing and nurturing healthy democratic traditions is important.

Sir, it is not a question of Shri Nityanand Kanungo, it is not even a question of saving or breaking the Government of West Bengal. Men may come and men may go, democratic governments will come and go in this country. The question, in this hour of test, is whether we will strengthen democracy, or will we weaken it ?

The Constitutional Position

Sir, we have a federal Constitution under which the Governor occupies an important place. It is true that he is the Centre's representative, but he is also the head of the State to which he is appointed. It is said he should be the link between the two. But he can prove to be that link only when he is forced to act in accordance with the Constitution. He can become that link only when he can gain and maintain the trust of both the Centre and the State.

Our Constitution is clear. The Governor cannot be given the powers that we have denied even to the President. It is argued that the Governor can convene the Legislative Assembly in his discretion and also dissolve it in his discretion. In my opinion that was not the intention of the framers of the Constitution. The matters in which the Governor can use his discretion have been made quite clear. There is scope for his discretion in deciding who should be called to form the government after an election. The Governor can also use his discretion in accepting or rejecting a Bill passed by the State's Legislative Assembly. If a Governor is nominated to a post by law—for instance to that of vice-chancellorship of a universit —he can use his

---

Lok Sabha on November 15, 1967 on the rights and responsibilities of Governors of States

discretion in the use of the vice-chancellor's powers. But calling the session of the Legislative Assembly without consulting the Chief Minister does not fall within the purvey of his authority.

I was surprised at the dangerous decisions taken at the recent Governors' conference in New Delhi. According to newspaper reports Governors have decided to use their dis cretion without any restraint. I quote a portion of the report :

> "Where a government which has lost its majority refuses to face the legislature, the Governor should call any other person commanding a majority to form a Government."

Who will decide whether the government has gone into a minority ? Will this be decided in the Raj Bhavan or in the Legislative Assembly ?

SHRI A.K. SEN : In the Legislative Assembly. Call the Assembly.

SHRI VAJPAYEE : If the decision is to be taken by the Legislative Assembly who will convene its session ? Every one agrees that it is for the Cheif Minister to do so. Then it is argued if the Chief Minister refuses to do so, what should the Governor do ? Sir, the Constitution clearly lays down that the interval between two sessions of the Legislative Assembly should not be more than 6 months. The Assembly should meet within 6 months. If a situation prevails in which the Congress party thinks six months to be an excessive period it could introduce a Bill for amendment to the Constitution—even though it had a major role in framing it. The period could be out down from six months to three. But so long as the Constitution is unchanged the Legislative Assembly should meet within six months. In this respect nothing can be imposed on the Chief Minister. It is for the Legislative Assembly to decide if the government is in a minority or not. This decision cannot be left to the Governor... (*Interruption*) . As for Madhya Pradesh I would like to point out that the Government had fallen during the session of the Assembly,... .

AN HON. MEMBER : What is happening in Haryana ?

SHRI VAJPAYEE : Have patience. I am prepared to reply to every question. I am shortly coming to Haryana too.

In their recent conference the Governors decided that in case a Chief Minister does not call the meeting of the Legislative Assembly the Governor can invite a person who, in his opinion, commands a majority, to form the Government. Suppose such a person is invited, the Legislative Assembly meets, and his government does not get a majority, what then would the Governor's position be ? Loyalties are changing—the Home Minister says parties are changed four times in a week. In such a situation suppose the Governor of West Bengal concludes that the present government is in a minority but by the time the Legislative Assembly meets it gains a majority, his position would become ridiculous. Obviously, therefore, so far as the question of convening the Assembly is concerned the Governor will have to act only on the advice of the Chief Minister.

This is the constitutional position. But it is not only a constitutional question. It is also political. We would not want any Chief Minister to function in a minority. The democratic requirement is that he should face a trial of strength in the Assembly as early as possible, and I want the Chief Ministers of West Bengal and Haryana to prove their majority in a like manner. (*Interruptions*). We are not a part of the West Bengal Government. A member had been elected (*Interruptions*) who was bought over by the Congress party. When I say he was bought over by the Congress party my Congress friends look happy. We support the Government in Haryana. We are not a part of the Government there, but we have told the Chief Minister that a meeting of the Legislative Assembly should be called as soon as possible. There is a by- election on December 3, but that cannot be an excuse for postponing the Assembly meeting. Similarly in West Bengal procurement cannot be an excuse for doing so, but the West Bengal Chief Minister has refused to call the Assembly. He is calling the meeting on December 16. It should also be urged that this meeting should be called as early as possible, but this urging should be on the political level. The Governor cannot be allowed to become a mini dictator. Let no party do any such thing as to serve its amends which would make it responsible for setting a dangerous tradition in the way of the development of Indian democracy. Today the Congress is in power at the Centre but not in West Bengal. Tomorrow this situation could change. So let us look at the problem from the viewpoint of wider interests of democracy, not of partisan ends. The letter and the spirit of the Constitution will have to be preserved and respected.

Assembly Speaker Ignored

I am surprised to see that so far as the question of calling a meeting of the Legislative Assembly is concerned the Speaker is nowhere in the picture. Members should traditionally have the right—if necessary this could be made a rule—to approach the Speaker with a sufficient majority and call for a meeting of the Assembly. Then the Speaker could consult the Chief Minister and convene the Assembly without bringing the Governor into the picture and then the meeting could find out where the majority lies. But for 20 years those who are now talking of setting conventions ignored the Speaker of the Legislative Assemblies. Now they want to bring the Governor into the picture, because they believe he will carry out New Delhi's wishes.

Sir, for the past eight months non-Congress governments have been functioning in eight States. Is there a single instance where the Governor's decision went in favour of a non-Congress party ? (*Interruptions*). How is it that every time the decision has favoured the Congress party, whether it is in Madhya Pradesh or in Rajasthan ? Now it is the turn of Bengal. The Governor is the President's representative and a link between the Centre and the State. Is he a respected individual occupying an important position under a federal constitution or is he a puppet dancing to New Delhi's tunes — a puppet for whom the people can have no respect ? We need to think seriously about this.

Appointment of Governors

It is said the Lok Sabha should approve the appointment of Governors. My friend Shri Nath Pai has also sent a Bill to this effect. I do not agree with it. Approval of the Lok Sabha would mean approval of the majority party. What would be the stamp of approval of the Lok Sabha ? It would really be the decision of the majority party. We will not walk into this trap. And if the Lok Sabha is to approve, names will be considered, merits will be discussed, old sins will be revealed and new charges levelled. The person who will finally become the Governor will already be in shreds.

There is also another proposal. It is that the Central Government should appoint the Governor in consultation with the Leader of the Opposition. In the circumstances that prevail today this proposal too does not look practical.

Thirdly, it is argued that the President does not have to consult the Central Government while appointing a Governor; he can use his discretion. I have my doubts about this. Where the President can use his discretion and where he cannot is yet to be made clear. The late Dr. Rajendra Prasad had initiated a debate on the President's powers. The majority opinion was that the President should act on the advice of the Central Government. Now if Governors are to be appointed by the President on the advice of the Central Government we will have to think afresh. As I said in the beginning, the Governor will be the Centre's representative but he will also be the head of State. Is it not possible for the Central Government to place two or three names before the Chief Ministers ? There could be a panel and the Chief Minister could pick one from it. Of course I do not want that a person solely of the State Government's choice be made the Governor.

For instance if the West Bengal Government wants Shri Nirmal Chandra Chatterjee to be made Governor of West Bengal that would be a loss to the Lok Sabha and so we would not advise it.

SHRI N.C. CHATTERJEE : I shall never want to be a candidate for the post.

SHRI VAJPAYEE : But if the Bihar Government says we do not want Shri Nityanand Kanungo will the Governor be foisted ? If the Bihar Government says we won't cooperate what will the Governor do in the Raj Bhavan ? Democracy is a delicate plant and needs to be nurtured gently. The Centre should take everybody with it while forging ahead. If the Centre thinks it is a non-Congress government and in those States it is in the opposition democracy will be in peril.

Have Faith In Bengal

We do not like many things that are happening in West Bengal. We were the first to raise in this House the matter of armed insurgency in Naxalbari. We have opposed a Gherao. We cannot tolerate some people in West Bengal raising slogans of Mao tse-Tung. But do not make the mistake of equating some people with the whole of West Bengal. This is the same Bengal that gave the clarion call of 'Vande Mataram', a call with which people embraced martyrdom. This is the same Bengal that produced Netaji, whose slogan of 'Jai Hind' inspired the whole country. This is the same Bengal that produced a gem of a person like Dr. Mukherjee. Just one wrong step by the Centre would lend strength to elements who have no faith in democracy, who want to change the government at gun-point. The battle is political and the decision will have to be on the political level. A minority government will have to face the people. There may be delay in democracy but there cannot be denial. The mills of democracy grind slow, but they grind exceedingly well. This House and this Government should have faith in the people of Bengal. They will fight such elements. They have the right to fight them. It is the duty of the rest of India to fight them.

If the Government in some State does not function according to the Constitution or if the law and order situation has broken down the Centre can intervene. If the situation demands such intervention anywhere, it is in Jammu-Kashmir. But, as my friend Shri Nath Pai has put it, the government of Jammu & Kashmir is in the hands of those who are friends of those in power in New Delhi. The Congress has still to realise that it must learn to sit in the opposition in those eight States that do not have Congress governments. At a time when democratic conventions are finally emerging central Congress leaders must observe them scrupulously. The whole situation needs to be seriously considered before taking a decision. Thank you.

Rampant Misuse of Article 356

Sir, I move the resolution as follows :

"The House regrets that the report sent by the Governor to the President on April 10,1968, in which it was recommended that the announcement about dissolving the State Legislative Assembly and holding mid-term elections, laid on the table of the House on April 16, 1968, be rejected, as the Samyukta Vidhayak Dal had a majority in the State Legislative Assembly and its leader should have been invited to form the government."

If there is to be a discussion on the motion and the resolution at the same time it may also be moved and I can speak later.

MR. SPEAKER : The Home Minister may move his resolution.

SHRI VAJPAYEE : I think thee is no separate discussion on the motion and the resolution.

SHRI Y.B. CHAVAN, Home Minister : I shall formally move the resolution. I shall move it but speak later on. Let him have his say now.

SHRI S.M. BANERJEE (Kanpur) : May I submit that there is a mistake in the order ? First, the resolution should have been put in and then only this motion. But the two have appeared in the reverse order.

MR. SPEAKER : Shri A.B. Vajpayee is prepared to speak now on his motion. So let not the Hon. member worry about it. Afterwards the Home Minister will move his resolution.

SHRI VAJPAYEE : Sir, on the one hand, democracy has been murdered in the State and we have gathered here for the post-mortem. On the other, a non-Congress government has been victimised by the Centre's duplicity and conspiracy and we are here to express our anger.

Sir, this is the fourth time in the past twelve months that the Central Government has misused Article 356 to smother regional autonomy and misused its powers for selfish partisan interests. First it was Rajasthan, then Haryana, then West Bengal, and now the Prime Minister's Uttar Pradesh. These are all links in the same chain, it is all the same willful story. It is the story of the centre's undemocratic behaviour. It is the story of the Governor's misuse of his office and partial conduct. It is the story of open disdain of the Constitution of India. It is the story of a blow at the very basis of the Indian Republic. It is the story of the tragic end of democracy in the country after the Fourth General Elections. The House needs to give serious thought to this story.

Lok Sabha on April 18, 1968 while moving the motion and resolution regarding President's Rule in Uttar Pradesh

When, during the framing of the Constitution the Constituent Assembly was considering Article 356 on August 3 and 4, 1947, Dr. Kunzru had raised an objection and said that the Central Government should not have the power to see if the government in a State was or was not functioning in accordance with the provisions of the Constitution. He had agreed that in the event of foreign aggression or domestic subversion or widespread disturbances the Centre could intervene in the States and take over the administration. But whether the government functions or does not function according to the Constitution is a very vague thing. Dr. Kunzro had said this provision should not be included in the Constitution. The Constituent Assembly had discussed this matter and one question was raised—if there is a multiplicity of parties in a State and if they cannot form a stable government should the Central government have the power to deprive the people of that region of their right to have a democratic government ? I quote a portion of what Dr. Kunzro said :

> "If there is a multiplicity of parties in any province, we may not welcome it. But is that fact by itself sufficient to warrant the Central Government's interference in the provincial administration ? There are many parties in some countries making ministeries unstable. Yet the Governments of these countries are carried on without any danger to their security or existence. It may be a matter of regret if too many parties exist in a province and they are not able to work together or arrive at an agreement on important matters in the interests of their province. But however regrettable this may be, it will not justify, in my opinion, the Central Government in intervening and making itself jointly with Parliament responsible for the Government of the province concerned."

What Dr. Ambedkar had said in reply to Dr. Kunzru's objection is worth remembering. There were questions and answers during the discussion and Dr. Kunzru had clearly asked :

> "May ask my hon. friend to make one point clear ? Is it the purpose of article 278"

The article in the Draft Constitution was as follows :

> "and article 278 (A) to enable the Central Government to intervene in provincial affairs for the sake of good government of a province ? :
>
> "DR. AMBEDKAR : No, No. The Central Government is not given that authority.
>
> "PANDIT KUNZRU : Or only when there is such misgovernment in the province as to endanger the public peace or...."

I also quote Dr. Ambedkar's reply :

> "In regard to the general debate which has taken place, it has been suggested that these articles are liable to be abused. I may say that I do not altogether deny that there is a possibility of these articles being abused or employed for political purposes. But that objection applies to every part of the Constitution which gives power to the Centre to override the provinces. In fact, I share the sentiments expressed by my hon. friend Mr. Gupta yesterday that the proper thing we ought to

expect is that the article will never be called into operation and they would remain a dead letter."

Dr. Ambedkar, who had played a decisive role in framing the Indian Constitution, had said provisions like article 356 would never be used, there will never be a need to use it. I do not want to go into the history of the past 18 years, when this article was used 12 times to unseat State governments and impose President's Rule. A point to be noted here is that only on 2 out of these 12 occasions did the use of this article adversely affect the Congress party's interests. On the remaining 10 occasions the article was used specifically for preventing opposition parties from forming the government. After the fourth general elections this is the fourth time that this article has been used. Every time an attempt is made to bring the Congress to power if it is not in power and to remove an opposition party from power if it is in power.

Assembly Dissolved when Opposition in Majority

The beginning was with Rajasthan. The Congress was not in a position to form a majority, so the Rajasthan Legislative Assembly was suspended. The moment the Congress could form the majority the Assembly was revived and the Congress was enthroned.

But the process of suspending the Legislative Assembly was not adopted in Haryana. There a non-Congress Cabinet was in a majority. It was not defeated in the Assembly, it was not even given the chance to try its strength. It was given no warning about improving its conduct, the Legislative Assembly was dissolved dictatorially, and the non-Congress government unseated. I do not want to enter into a discussion on how the West Bengal Governor behaved and how the West Bengal Government was functioning. There could be a difference of opinion on that matter. But no Governor can be given the power to dismiss a democratically elected government without giving it an opportunity to test its strength in the Assembly. The West Bengal Governor's conduct also opened the way to power for the Congress, the way that prevented opposition parties from coming to power.

The latest example is that of Uttar Pradesh. What was the situation there ? The Governor's report, on the basis of which the Central Government took this decision, is ridiculous. That report was given on April 10. What was the situation in Uttar Pradesh on April 10 ? All parties in the Samyukt Vidhayak Dal had accepted Shri Harishchandra Singh as their leader.

AN HON. MEMBER : Wrong.

AN HON. MEMBER : Not all parties.

SHRI VAJPAYEE : A delegation of the SVD had called upon the Governor and told him—invite Shri Harishchandra Singh to form a government, we are with him. The Bharatiya Kranti Dal was a party to this decision. A delegation of nine opposition parties had called on the Governor. If the Governor was not sure about the SVD's majority he could have invited the Congress party to form a government.

SHRI SHEO NARAIN (Basti) : Should have.

SHRI VAJPAYEE : Why did he not invite ? SVD leaders had demanded that the Congress, which was in a minority, should declare the names of those SVD legislators who, it claimed, had gone over to the Congress and given it a majority. The Congress party did not heed this demand. This I can understand, because there were really no such legislators. Their signatures had been obtained through coercion or inducement. Had their names been revealed they would not have been able to stand the shame.

Will the process of defection be engineered from the Raj Bhavan ? Imagine, Sir, Parliament is in session and some opposition members call on the President and say to him—the Indira Gandhi Government has lost its majority, because 20, or 22 or 30 Congress members have given us in writing that they are willing to join us...

AN HON. MEMBER : They will never get that chance.

SHRI HUKAM CHAND KACHCHWAI : They will get it soon.

SHRI VAJPAYEE : ...Then what will be the situation ? I am giving an example. On such an occasion will the President or the Governor of a State have the right to decide the majority or otherwise just on the basis of their saying so, without those names being declared ? This is a very dangerous policy that is being adopted. It can have terrible consequences.

If any one wants to defect he should do so openly. He should have the courage to face the people. Only when we advise defectors to have the courage to face the people will our democracy gain strength.

AN HON. MEMBER : What happened in Madhya Pradesh ?

SHRI VAJPAYEE : But the Governor of Uttar Pradesh did not do so. He claims he tried to form a stable government but could not. What does this stable government mean ? If one party has 51 members and the opposition has 49 whom will the Governor invite to form the Government ? A majority even of one is a majority, and the Governor or the President will have to go by it. Stability is a matter of the future. The Governor has to decide in the present. What government would last only the future can tell. It is possible that there could be injustice to somebody and the Governor may deny the right to form a government to those who are currently in the majority.

Another thing that needs to be decided is whether the fate of governments would be decided in the Raj Bhavan or in the Legislative Assemblies. The Home Minister may say the situation changed when the Governor suspended the Assembly and he would have to decide which party could form the government.

Even the Governor admits that the SVD had a majority.

Choudhary Charan Singh resigned because of differences within the SVD, but that did not end the SVD's majority. It chose Shri Ramchandra Vikal as the alternate leader.

AN HON. MEMBER : After how many days ?

SHRI VAJPAYEE : After three days.

Why did the Governor not invite him to form the government ?

Choudhary Charan Singh resigned on the 17th and Shri Ramchandra Vikal was elected on the 21st. The Governor said something very strange. I quote a portion of what he said on February 22 :

> "Given a reasonable time, a reorientation of political affiliations may emerge in the State Assembly, which might enable the formation of a stable Government without the necessity of another general election."

The Governor wanted to avoid mid-term elections. He had admitted that mid-term elections are expensive and the people of the State should not be put in this difficult position. So he suspended the Assembly. He wanted to give the parties an opportunity to marshal their strength in such a manner that the State could have a popular government. What was it that happened on April 10 ? The fact of the matter is that the parties that had drifted apart a little had come closer on April 10, SVD was united. Everyone agreed on Shri Harishchandra Singh's name.

Sir, I charge that the Governor of Uttar Pradesh broke the oath he took while assuming the post of Governor. According to the oath every Governor has to protect the Constitution and the law to the best of his ability and to dedicate himself to the service and welfare of the people. The Governor of Uttar Pradesh is guilty of breaking this oath. Instead of acting as the constitutional head of the State he has preferred to get mired in the bog of party politics and has acted with partiality. Can you imagine a Governor writing a letter to the leader of the 'opposition party' before deciding who should be made Chief Minister, asking—do you believe in the Fourth Five-Year Plan, are you prepared to marshal resources for it, and are you prepared to maintain the continuity of policies ? The type of letter that the Governor wrote to Shri Harishchandra Singh is a very serious matter.

Governor Imposed Conditions on Potential Chief Minister

No Governor can be given the power to impose conditions on a Chief Minister before he takes oath of office or to bind him to certain policies. This is totally against the democratic process. This is a blow at democracy. But the Governor of Uttar Pradesh wrote a letter to Shri Harishchandra Singh and tried to impose such conditions on him. Surprisingly enough when the same Governor wrote to Shri Chandrabhanu Gupta he did not emphasise the marshaling of resources for the fourth Five-year Plan and the maintenance of continuity of policies.

I would like the Home Minister to clarify whether he supports the writing of such a letter by a Governor. Sir, in this whole affair it is not only the Governor who is to blame, the Congress Government at the Centre is also guilty. The Governor made his recommendation under article 356 and sent his report. The Constitution does not give the Governor the power to break it. The Governor can only advise the President. It was open to the Central government to return the Governor's report for reconsideration. It was also open to the Central Government not to agree with the report. Before taking such a severe step, which neither the Congress wanted nor the opposition parties, the Central government could be formed in the State democratically it would have to think of something else. But the Central government did not think it necessary. SVD leaders came to Delhi, went to the Rashtrapati Bhavan and even had a discussion with the Prime Minister. They were prepared to prove a majority of 229 members on their side. They were prepared to be counted. But the Central Government did not allow such an opportunity.

Assembly Dissolved, Speaker Continues

What is surprising is that the Governor recomended that the Speaker of the Uttar Pradesh Assembly should continue, and the Central Government accepted the recommendation. The Legislative Assembly was dissolved, members newly elected to the Legislative Council would not be able to take oath, they would not receive their salaries, but the Speaker of the Assembly that was dissolved would continue in office. Then why was the Speaker of Haryana continued ? Was it because the Speaker of the Uttar Pradesh Assembly was a Congressman while the Speaker of Haryana belonged to the opposition ? Was it compulsory for the Central Government to accept this recommendation of the Governor ? Let the Home Minister reply. But he cannot reply, he will try to whitewash and say, this conduct is all right, because it has pleased neither Congressmen nor the opposition. If the test of doing the right thing is that it should displease everybody there would be no standard of popularity in a democracy.

SHRI Y.B. CHAVAN : This does not prove partiality.

SHRI VAJPAYEE : I shall show partiality too.

Had it been proved in Uttar Pradesh that a Congress Government could be formed and would continue the Central government would not have taken the harsh step of dissolving the Assembly. What makes me unhappy is that the Assembly had to fall a victim to the factionalism prevailing within the Congress. When Chaudhary Charan Singh said there should be mid-term elections the Governor did not agree, because he wanted to see if the Congress could form a government with the help of defectors. When the Congress did not get the opportunity he thought it fit to dissolve the Legislative Assembly rather than give SVD a chance of forming a government.

This is not only partiality, in Uttar Pradesh we see the naked dance of factionalism that is worse than partiality. Some Central Congress Ministers do not want Chandra Bhanu Gupta to become Chief Minister. So this drama of impartiality is being enacted.

Sir, recently a conference of Speakers of the country's legislative assemblies was held under the Chairmanship of the Speaker of the Lok Sabha. Some important decisions were taken in this conference. I would like the Home Minister to say if he is prepared to accept the decisions of a conference called by the Lok Sabha Speaker. I quote a portion of Dr. Sanjiva Reddy's speech :

> "A ministry which has lost its majority in the Assembly after the session is over may continue in office until another session is summoned, and if it fails to summon a House within a reasonable period, the remedy

which I have suggested in the preceding para will apply; that is to say, that the majority of members may force the Chief Minister to summon the Assembly on a date suggested by them".

A resolution passed in the conference on that basis says :

"The question whether a Chief Minister has lost majority in the Assembly or not should at all times be decided by the Assembly."

This is a very important decision.

SHRI Y.B. CHAVAN : How does it apply here ?

SHRI VAJPAYEE : The Home Minister may ask how it is applicable to Uttar Pradesh. I am explaining that. Whether a government would last or not should it be decided in the Legislative Assembly or should it be left to the Governor's sweet will ?

AN HON. MEMBER : Was there a government there ? The government had resigned and was out of office.

SHRI VAJPAYEE : The government had not vacated by resigning. It was Choudhary Charan Singh who had resigned. This thing is applicable to Uttar Pradesh in the sense that after the Chief Minister had resigned the majority party's representative was not invited to form the government, and an attempt was made behind the back of the Assembly to decide who had the majority. And even if this question is separated from Uttar Pradesh what had happened in West Bengal ? Is the Home Minister ready to set such conventions for the future ? The Congress is in for a big disappointment if it thinks it can regain its lost popularity by misusing the Governors' posts and making them puppets.

In the Hyderabad convention it was decided to finish non-Congress governments. In accordance with that conspiracy non-Congress governments are being toppled one by one. But this will not regain the people's affection for the Congress. There have been three by-elections to the Lok Sabha. In all three of them the Congress has been defeated. It should see the writing on the wall. It should listen to the underground rumblings within the country.

Sir, mid–term elections are a very expensive affair. Has the Central government considered the fact that subjecting one State after another to this expensive process would make democracy a slave of money rather than strengthen it ? Those parties which come to power with the people's mandate and which consider it a treason to accept foreign funds are at present in a very serious situation. How can they raise the resources for fighting elections ? On the one hand we are talking of bringing in socialism and ten– point programmes are being announced. On the other hand, such polices are being adopted as would increase the influence of money. From this point of view too the decision to dissolve the Legislative Assembly and order mid–term elections is wrong. This does not mean we are afraid of the election. We are ready for it. I can guarantee that if elections are held the Congress would win lesser seats than it has at present. But the question is, do we or do we not want our democratic, federal Constitution to succeed ? This House will have to answer this question. I appeal to the House to accept my resolution and restrain the Home Minister, so that he dare not strike at democracy in any State in future. Thank you.

Governor's Political Illness

Sir, with your permission I raise the matter of Madhya Pradesh in the House under Rule 370. After West Bengal, a constitutional drama is being enacted in Madhya Pradesh. There is a basic question here, and it is this—will the fate of the Madhya Pradesh government be decided by the Governor or by the elected representatives of the Madhya Pradesh Assembly ? Will it be decided in the Raj Bhavan or in the Vidhan Sabha Bhavan ? The Madhya Pradesh Assembly is at present in session. There is no question of holding the session or not. The SVD has a thumping majority in it. The Assembly is in session, but the opposition party, the Congress, did not have the courage to have a trial of strength. The SVD chose a new leader. In this connection the SVD leader in the Assembly called on the Governor, but the Governor had gone to bed. Whenever there are changes in the Central Council of Ministers, whenever departments are changed the President is woken up and persuaded to administer the oath even at night but they did not wake up the Governor of Madhya Pradesh .... (*Interruption*) .... clearly the Governor was in deep sleep. I will not discuss the propriety or impropriety of the Centre's representative in the States and the constitutional head slumbering like this. When he woke up the next morning he should have accepted the change of leadership and called the newly elected leader to form the government. But he said he wanted three days' time. He also said this government could continue as a caretaker government. There is no question of a caretaker government, because the government is in office, only the leader was changed. The Governor could have administered the oath of Chief Ministership to the new leader and told him to conduct the government, and that government could face the Assembly. If the Congress has a majority in Madhya Pradesh it could prove its strength in the Assembly and unseat the SVD government. But calling the government a caretaker government and giving the Congress an opportunity for horse-trading in the Assembly is against the Constitution. This is how democracy had been demolished. I am sorry to say that the Governor of Madhya Pradesh is not discharging his responsibility. I would quote a portion from the editorial in today's *Statesman*. Whether or not the M.P. Governor's illness is political has become a topic of discussion. On the one hand he is ill, and on the other, as I learn from information received from Bhopal, Mrs. Reddy is working as the acting Governor. She is talking to Congress members and getting reports on loss or gain in Congress strength. I do not know what provision in the Constitution

Lok Sabha on March 12, 1969 while raising a discussion on Madhya Pradesh Governor's action with regard to the formation of Ministry

gives the Governor's wife this power. The *Statesman* has echoed the people's feelings. I quote :

> "Suspicions that Mr. Reddy's illness may be more political than physical are bound to be expressed, especially in view of the wayward nature of politics in Madhya Pradesh. To delay the formation of the Ministry for three days and to keep the constitutional machinery in the State in deep freeze for this period is undesirable in any case, whether it helps the Congress Party to wean away SVD members or vice versa. If Mr. Reddy's health does not permit him to function, someone else should be asked to act in his place."

If the Governor is really ill it is the function of the Centre to arrange for another Governor. But the Governor cannot be given the power to decide the fate of the government in the Raj Bhavan and even suspend the Legislative Assembly. The Governor says this is a caretaker government. The Speaker says, how can a caretaker government reply ? A new government can be formed and it can prove its strength on the floor of the House. If it is in a minority it will be swept aside. Has the Home Minister acquired any information about the Governor's position in Bhopal ? Has he consulted the Governor ? Has the Governor been given any directive ? In view of the Governor's illness is the Home Minister thinking of sending another Governor ? Or is it that what is happening in Bhopal is all a conspiracy of the Home Ministry ? Let the Home Minister make things clear to the House. Thank you.

Chief Minister on Hunger-Strike!

Sir, in this House we have been discussing the problems of the whole country, but surprisingly enough our friends oppose a discussion on West Bengal. They had demanded a discussion on the events in Ahmedabad. Is Ahmedabad within the country but West Bengal out of it ? (*Interruptions*). West Bengal is still a part of India. Perhaps some friends may be trying to take it out of the country, but we shall never let their designs succeed. (*Interruptions*). A very strange situation has been created. The Chief Minister of a State .... (*Interruptions*) ....

MR. SPEAKER : The Hon. Member may please sit down.

SHRI HUKAM CHAND KACHCHWAI (Ujjain) : Sir, please restrain these people, otherwise we are ready to deal with them. (*Interruptions*).

SHRI VAJPAYEE : Sir, the raising of the West Bengal matter here is being opposed. This only means that those who are opposing it want to cover up their sins. (*Interruptions*).

SHRI P. RAMAMURTI : We are prepared to discuss it; let there be a proper discussion. Who wants to cover what ? ...(*Interruptions*).

SHRI VAJPAYEE : It is strange that our friends are ready for a discussion but not for a calling attention motion. A matter that can be discussed can also be the subject of a calling attention motion.

The power of the House is quite clear. There is a strange situation in West Bengal. It is an extraordinary thing in the history of our democracy that the Chief Minister of a State should go on a hunge-strike as a protest against the chaos and violence prevailing in his own state. (*Interruptions*).

SHRI S.N. SINGH (Varanasi) : He is an old Congressman. (*Interruptions*).

SHRI O.P. TYAGI (Moradabad) : Sir, silence this Hon. member.

SHRI VAJPAYEE : In his statement the Home Minister has referred to a statement issued by the Bengal Congress. I would like to refer to a document published by the Bengal Congress. Is or is not the Home Minister aware of the facts stated in this document ?

Chaos in West Bengal

According to this document there were 378 murders in West Bengal during the period from February end to October 4. (*Interruptions*). Of these 200 murders were political (*Interruptions*). The number of the wounded was 673. According to the document 292 complaints were filed with the police, but the police took no action (*Interruptions*).

Lok Sabha on December 3, 1969 during discussion on the situation arising from West Bengal Chief Minister's hunger-strike

In the 24-Parganas alone the court passed 202 strictures against the police. Three policemen were also fined. More than a thousand cases were withdrawn. According to the document there were 367 gheraos till August 551 strikes and 73 lock-outs which caused a loss of 61.59,787 man hours.

There is one more event that the House should note. When some people were sentenced to death in the Alipur court slogans were raised in the court and the judge was not allowed to work. These are facts revealed by people who are in power in West Bengal. Is the Home Minister prepared to make an extensive statement on the situation in West Bengal, so that the House and the country could be taken into confidence on what is happening there ?

We have taken an oath to protect the country's Constitution. The West Bengal Governor has taken the oath to protect the Constitution in West Bengal and conduct the administration according to law. Has the Home Minister or the Central government called for a report from the West Bengal Governor ? The Governor can do so under the Constitution. If it did not call for a report, why ? And, is the Home Minister ready to call for it ?

In Haryana the Governor dismissed the government there on the ground that the Ayaram– Gayaram syndrome had endangered democracy. The West Bengal Governor dismissed the Government because it was not ready to call a meeting of the Legislative Assembly on the date proposed by him. What does the Government propose to do about it ?

Central Government Mere Spectator

The question is, will the Central government be a silent spectator of this whole situation ? What is happening in West Bengal has imperilled the security and integrity of the country and the rule of law. Political killings are taking place, in the labour field the policy of finishing opponents is being adopted, and the police are sought to be controlled by a party.

Our friends are talking of victory in the recent by-election there. We have won a by-election there. (*Interruptions*).

SHRI S.N. SINGH : You caused Hindu-Muslim riots in Jammu.

SHRI VAJPAYEE : And in West Bengal these people caused Hindu-Muslim riots in Jagatdal.

SHRI P. RAMAMURTI : That is what I object to. You are allowing this Member ....(*Interruptions*).

MR. SPEAKER : Please ask that hon. member not to interfere from there like that.

SHRI VAJPAYEE : In West Bengal Indira Congress leader Shri S.S. Ray has said during the election that policemen wearing red handkerchiefs around their necks were present at polling stations. (*Interruptions*).

SHRI H.N. MUKERJEE : He has said something about not permitting references which were undesirable or unwarranted. Is this the way one functions ? Are we to expect from the Chair this kind of thing being allowed ? You told us you would not permit any unwarrantable references, and likewise he is going on continuously making parliamentarily unwarrantable references.

SHRI VAJPAYEE : Can I not say that policemen wearing red handkerchiefs were taken to polling stations in order to influence the election ? Can the Home Minister contradict this ? (*Interruptions*).

SHRI H.N. MUKERJEE : Are you allowing these things to go on record ? Is this how the country is going to be told about it! It is unparliamentary. (*Interruptions*). On a point of order. I want your ruling, Sir, Mr. Vajpayee is making observations which go against the spirit of what you said : that you would not permit such things. I want you to go into the record and see. Would you permit this sort of thing to be publicised to the country ? That is entirely out of order (*Interruptions*). I want you to examine the record. Does it accord with what you said earlier that you would not allow references which would be unwarrantable ? Please examine the record. (*Interruptions*). I am a stranger to *zahbartasti*.

SHRI VAJPAYEE : But not your opponents in West Bengal.

Sir, it is the Centre's responsibility to see that elections are fair and conducted properly, and if the police are used in an election—here I am not quoting the statement by some worker of my party but by the leader of the Indira Gandhi Legislature Party. The Home Minister may refute this if he wants to, but in the situation that has been created in West Bengal I again call on the Home Minister to give an extensive statement on it and call for a report from the Governor. Is he ready to do so ? When the Governor's report is received it could be tabled in the House.

SHRI Y.B. CHAVAN : As far as the situation in West Bengal is concerned, it is one which always causes concern in the mind of everybody here. But at the same time, we have to go into this matter carefully. The Chief Minister himself has taken cognizance of the situation there and is trying to deal with it politically because the main problem is the atmosphere that is created there and for that, he is preparing the people for a certain action.

AN HON. MEMBER : What is that action ?

SHRI Y.B. CHAVAN : I think it is much better that you ask the Chief Minister about it. His effort seems to be to go in that direction. There are two alternatives open to the Chief Minister. One is the constitutional, administrative action which he can take as Chief Minister in a legal way. The other is political action. He has chosen the political method. I think he needs our support and sympathy.

SHRI VAJPAYEE : Sir, what happened to my questions ? I had said two things—will the Home Minister give a full statement on the situation in West Bengal and will he ask the West Bengal Governor to send his report ?

Governors Centre's Puppets!

Sir, it is a matter of coincidence that on October 2, birth anniversary of Mahatma Gandhi democracy was murdered in Uttar Pradesh, and today, on Smt. Indira Gandhi's birthday, we are doing its postmortem. I say postmortem because in the end the ruling party's plans to instal its government in Uttar Pradesh were shattered. Parties believing in nationalism democracy and socio-economic justice triumphed there. The Prime Minister met her waterloo to in her home State. Now we have to consolidate the victory and strike down similar efforts to usurp power.

There are many significant aspects to the Uttar Pradesh affair. Governor Reddi has propounded a new and dangerous doctrine. This is not the question of any one party it is related to the future of parliamentary democracy. They tried to distinguish between one party's Chief Minister and the Chief Minister of a united government. They say the Chief Minister of a united government cannot say that those Ministers who have lost his confidence should resign or the Governor should relieve them of their office. This is an attempt to rewrite the Constitution of India. The Constitution does not distinguish between a single party government and a multi-party government. So long as a Chief Minister is the Chief Minister—whether he is in a minority or in a majority, whether he is the Chief Minister of one party or many parties—he has the right to make anyone a minister and relieve any minister of his office.

Sir, what would have been the situation if, after the division in the Congress Dr. Ram Subhag Singh, Shri Poonacha and Shri Jaisukh Lal Hathi had refused to resign ? Would the President have said Smt. Indira Gandhi is now in a minority and so should resign ? No President can say so. No Governor should also say so A reference has been made to the United Kingdom. Look up Ivor Jennings' *Cabinet Government*. He has given instances of minority governments in 1839 and 1931. Even then the advice given by the then Prime Minister to the King or Queen was accepted. The Attorney–General's advice will shatter the whole democratic structure to smithereeens. If the Chief Minister or Prime Minister does not have the right to choose or remove his Minister there can be no such thing as collective responsibility. I remember that the Constituent Assembly had discussed this problem at length. I quote Ambedkar :

> "No person shall be retained as member of the Cabinet if the Prime Minister says that he shall be dismissed."

Lok Sabha on November 19, 1970 during discussion on the Motion regarding the conduct of the Governor in Uttar Pradesh

The same thing applies to the Chief Minister. There is no question here of whether the Chief Minister is in a majority or minority.

Cycle of Events

The cycle of events is as follows. On the 24th Choudhary Charan Singh asked for the Congress Ministers' resignations. One of those whose resignations were demanded was also a Minister belonging to the Bharatiya Kranti Dal. What should have happened is that those ruling Congress Ministers who had lost the Chief Minister's confidence should have voluntarily vacated office. This was the way of morality and the demand of decency. But, Sir, shamelessness crossed limits. This will go down in history. To the eternal shame of the ruling party the process of parliamentary democracy will always bear the blot that the party withdrew its support but its Ministers continued in the Council of Ministers. I ask again—would Dr. Ram Subhag Singh have been praised if he had continued in the cabinet even after severing relations with the Prime Minister ? But now no one in the ruling party says a word about the conduct of the Ministers of his party. In Uttar Pradesh the constitution has not only been demolished, political morality has also been done away with.

But I was talking about Governor Reddy. Till September 27 he looked upon Choudhary Charan Singh as the Chief Minister. When the Congress withdrew its support on the 24th the Governor did not say, the support is withdrawn, now you are in a minority, so resign. He kept thinking. The 25th came and went, the 26th came and went, and on the 27th he took away Congress Ministers' departments at the instance of Choudhary Charan Singh. Clearly he agreed on that day that Choudhary Charan Singh had the majority, that he was the Chief Minister. If on the 27th Choudhary Charan Singh was the Chief Minister departments could be taken away at his behest and if the Governor could issue a directive to that effect why could he not accept the advice to relieve Congress Ministers of their posts ?

It is also wrong to say that the promise of Bharatiya Jan Sangh and Organisation Congress to extend support to Choudhary Charan Singh came later. Sir, look at the Governor's report—I am surprised at how a person occupying the responsible position of Governor could give such a ridiculous report. Page 4 of the report says —

> "Till the writing of this report, none of the political parties has given any specific indication that it will support any new Government headed by Shri Charan Singh."

This report is dated the 29th Page 5 says at the start :

> "On the 26th September Shri Madho Prasad Tripathy, leader of the Jan Sangh Legislature Party, and Shri Girdhari Lal, leader of the Organisation Congress Legislature Party wrote to me extending their support to the present Government headed by Shri Charan Singh."

On the 26th Choudhary Charan Singh had majority support, the number of members was 255, information was sent to the Governor in writing, but the Governor did not accept that majority.

Sir, when Choudhary Charan Singh was invited to become Chief Minister he was the leader of one party, that party did not have a majority, the ruling Congress supported it later. But here two parties give their support in writing. The Samyukta Socialist Party said the fate of the ministry would be decided in the Assembly. The meeting was to be held on the 6th. Choudhary Singh was ready to call the meeting on the 31st or the 1st, but the Governor did not wait.

Governor's Important Position

The Constitution has given an important position to the Governor. He is the head of State, the President's representative, and a link between the Centre and the State. He has to preserve and protect the Constitution of India. But will the Governors act accordingly ? They act differently in the same set of circumstances. In Rajasthan Dr. Sampoornanand did not agree that a majority could be formed with the help of independents. That was his discretion. In Haryana, Governor Shri Chakravarty dismissed Rao Birendra Singh because, in his opinion, defections were taking place. Shri Dharma Vir dismissed the Government of West Bengal because although Shri Ajay Mukherji was willing to call the Assembly he wanted some time and the Governor had no power to force him to do so. Punjab Governor Shri Pavte adopted another yardstick. Lucknow has a different drama altogether. What is all this ?

Will the Governors be given the freedom to use their discretion at will ? Will the Governors flout the Constitution in the same name of discretion ? Will they destroy democratic process ? Will Governors act as the Centre's puppets in the name of discretion ? If they do the federal Constitution of India will be in danger. Now there will be one party's government at the Centre and different parties' governments in the States. There will also be differences between those governments. The Governors will have to mete evenhanded justice. They will have to maintain the pre- eminence of the Constitution. But in all these cases, from Jaipur to Lucknow, the Governors used the right to discretion in different ways, but the result was the same—the ruling party stood to gain, those who sit on this side were the losers. Why ?

The Warning

Sir, Shri Hanumanthaiah is not present in the House, but he had given a warning when article 356 was being discussed in the Constituent Assembly. I now pity him. We hear a lot of discussion on the Attorney–General's opinion, but we do not know what the Law Ministry's opinion is. That time Shri Hanumanthaiah had said —

> "This is what article 365 (6) has to do, but in supporting this article I wish to sound a note of warning. Let those people who think that they are making hay while the sun shines take note of the future also. If this article is worked, as we have apprehended, in the interest of the classes or the communities that have taken hold of the Government of India,

the people will not keep quiet. That will be the starting of trouble to break the much sought after Indian unity and Indian nationalism;

Today Shri Hanumanthaiah's warning resounds in our ears. As Law Minister he may well not repeat his warning, but it is as valid today. If we have to keep India one, if we have to make a success of democracy Governors will have to conduct themselves as impartial constitutional heads.

Sir, it is also a matter of great surprise that when the Governor sent his report to the President he did not care to consider it. At least we have no proof to show that he tried to understand the other party's point of view. He was abroad, but the opposition leaders sent him a telegram there too Choudhary Charan Singh's cable was with him, he was requested to wait a few days and take his decision on returning to Delhi. The Assembly was to meet on October 6, but on October 6 it was put into suspended animation and Choudhary Charan Singh's Ministry removed. The heavens would not have fallen if the President had waited for three days. On his return after 96 hours he could have reviewed the whole situation. Just now Shri Dev quoted from Dr. Ambedkar's speech. I would like to repeat the quote.

> "I hope the President who is endowed with this power will take proper precautions before actually suspending the administration of the Province".

This was the hope of Dr. Ambedkar, the father of the Constitution, but Dr. Ambedkar had no idea that the government in New Delhi would pass into the hands of those people who would tear up the Constitution into shreds for keeping power in their hands or for keeping Uttar Pradesh under their control.

Sir, surprisingly by enough Governor Reddi says Choudhary Charan Singh did not have a majority. Then did Pandit Kamlapati Tripathi have it ? My sympathies are with Shri Tripathi. It seems the stars do not favour his becoming Chief Minister. But if the majority was not with Choudhary Charan Singh Kamalapati Tripathi could have been invited to become Chief Minister and he could have formed the government. Why was the Legislative Assembly put into suspended animation ? That was done because the Governor wanted to give the Congress the chance to purchase members. Pandit Kamlapati Tripathi did not have a majority and the Governor knew this but he gave time to form a majority and buy souls in the market place of Lucknow—Use temptation or terror or any other means but Uttar Pradesh must not slip out of hands. I regret that the Governor became a part of this conspiracy. He not only earned personal infamy he even brought the Governor's office into disrepute.

The office of Governor has now become a subject of controversy and there is a demand that it be done away with. Our DMK friends are demanding that the Governor's powers be pruned. Why did this situation arise ? Because the Centre made Governors as pawns on the chess-board of politics. The result is that the very office of Governor has come into danger.

Prime Minister's Dictatorial Tendencies

Saying anything about the Central government's attitude in this whole matter is like water on a duck's back. When we say the present administration is acquiring dictatorial attitudes and when we say this government will do anything for keeping power in its hands it is such events that are before our eyes. I am sorry the Prime Minister is not present in the House. Whenever we say she is adopting a dictatorial attitude she becomes displeased.

SHRI S.M. BANERJI : Because you assume a vexed form on seeing her.

SHRI VAJPAYEE : When the ruling Congress, when it was an undivided party, did not accept the Prime Minister's opinion for the office of President, the Prime Minister broke up the party. When the Rajya Sabha turned down the Bill on privy purses and special privileges of the princes the Prime Minister got it done by an executive order. And when the Prime Minister could not succeed in openly seating Pandit Kamlapati Tripathi on the throne in Uttar Pradesh she flouted the Constitution, misused the office of Governor, and got the Uttar Pradesh Government dissolved. There are dictatorial tendencies which we oppose. Is this because the Prime Minister has the support of the Right Communist Party in this ? That is the only *'Dal'* (party) in the country that has supported the U.P. Governor's conduct.

SHRI S.M. BANERJI : That is because it does not want to sink into a *'Daldal'* (bog).

SHRI VAJPAYEE : It is because they have sunk in the bog right up to their necks. But now the time has come to clarify the Governors' right to discretion in unambiguous terms. There should be no different yardsticks for measuring them. I do not want to read out the relevant article of the Constitution, but it is quite clear on the right to discretion. Accepting or not accepting any Minister's resignation is not for the Governor, it is for the Chief Minister. There should be constitutional guidelines on the discretionary powers of Governors, which would indicate how they should behave in what circumstances and whether there should be uniformity in their conduct.

Secondly, matter of the appointment of Governors should be reconsidered. One way would be what my friend Shri Nath Pai's Bill proposes—that the appointment could be approved by Parliament. Another would be to set up a panel, for which even opposition parties could be consulted, and a Governor appointed from that panel. They should not be mere puppets of the ruling party but real protectors of the Constitution.

Thirdly, in the whole matter of Uttar Pradesh, Attorney-General Shri Niren De has not conducted himself in accordance with his exalted position. He gave the advice what the Central Government wanted. The Governor should not have accepted that advice, and Shri Niren De should also not have given it. Shri De should resign, and if he does not, the Central Government should honourably retire him. Such a person would certainly land the Central Government in a pit, and as in the case of Uttar Pradesh, you would again have to suffer defeat if you received such wrong advice. So far as this resolution is concerned we are with you and I hope the House will also accept it.

SHRI SANT BUX SINGH (Fatehpur) : Mr. Chairman, Sir, while Shri Atal Bihari Vajpayee's eloquence was beautiful, his facts and observations were not equally beautiful. He criticised the Attorney-General without realising that the Attorney-General was merely advocating the opinion which Shri Atal Bihari Vajpayee's party itself had put up in the Punjab. On much flimsier grounds, in the Punjab, the Jan Sangh had advocated, when it came to the resignation of a few Ministers, that the Governor ought to dismiss the Chief Minister. When this opinion comes from the Jan Sangh, it is then fair.

SHRI VAJPAYEE : It is wrong. That was the stand of the Punjab Jan Sangh. But the Central Jan Sangh did not accept it (*Interruptions*).

SHRI SANT BUX SINGH : Thank you.

SHRI VAJPAYEE : Are you prepared, on behalf of your party, to say like this ?

SHRI SANT BUX SINGH : I am not speaking on behalf of Shri Vajpayee's party. I will come to the stand that our party took, I would urge that the condemnation that had been indulged in this House about the opinion of the Attorney-General has been extremely unfair. I sat here for the last two hours hoping to hear somebody say something worth-while by quoting books on the Constitution, and constitutional precedents, whereby it would be established that the Attorney-General gave a wrong opinion. The Attorney-General's opinion was based primarily on his reply to two points, the first of which was, could the Chief Minister dismiss the Ministers, and secondly, should the Chief Minister be allowed to continue in the given situation. Now, both Shri Charan Singh and Shri Atal Bihari Vajpayee have quoted Jennings in support of their opinion that Ministers can be dismissed. Le me tell Shri Atal Bihari Vajpayee that Jenning's book is clear. Lord Salisbury, writing to Queen Victoria in 1890, has said that there has not been a single case of the dismissal of a Minister. For months in this country we have gone on with this argument that a Chief Minister has the right to dismiss a Minister. I would like to put it to the great constitutionalists of this House and I would also like to put it to the greatest legal luminaries in this country who have spoken, to produce before this country a single case where a Minister has been dismissed. There is not one case that could be found in world history.

SHRI VAJPAYEE : In Vindhya Pradesh, one Minister was dismissed.

SHRI RAM KISHAN GUPTA (Hissar) : In Punjab also.

Article 356 and Uttar Pradesh

Sir, when the Indian Constitution was framed its framers had no idea that article 356 would be so misused. Under article 356 the centre can take over the administration of any state provided conditions are created there in which the government of that State cannot be conducted in accordance with the provisions of the Constitution.

Clearly the Centre can intervene in the event of a constitutional crisis. Had a constitutional crisis developed in Uttar Pradesh ? Even our Congress friends say the ruling Congress had 272 members with it; it had a tremendous majority in the Assembly, and the Chief Minister had the confidence of the ruling party. There was no constitutional crisis in Uttar Pradesh. If there was a crisis at all, it was in the ruling party. A crisis in the ruling party is not a constitutional crisis. But the Constitution was used to extricate the ruling party from the crisis of its own making. President's Rule was imposed, and now strange arguments are being put forward to justify it.

I am forced to say that from many points of view the Governor's letter is ridiculous. I respect him. He was my colleague in the Rajya Sabha. He left party politics before accepting Governorship. But he says in his letter that President's Rule be temporarily imposed in Uttar Pradesh. What does this mean ? You may say he said 'Temporary' because President's Rule could be ended when it would become possible to form a government. This means when the quarrels within the ruling party would be over ...

SHRI D.N. TIWARI : No, when you come into a majority.

SHRI VAJPAYEE : Let not Tiwariji be in such a hurry.

Governor's Certificates

When the ruling party puts its house in order, when its infighting is over the Governor would oblige it by putting it in power. Had the framers of the Constitution kept this role of a Governor in mind while framing article 356 ? Has the Governor, who governs a State, become a puppet in the hands of a particular party ? Should a Governor's conduct be subject to objection ? Not only this, the Governor has fulsomely praised Shri Kamlapati Tripathi, congratulated him on good administration, and placed him on a high pedestal for his resignation.

I would like to know if the government was working well under Kamlapati Tripathi's leadership, if everything was green in Uttar Pradesh, and if even the Governor was so attracted by this greenery that he broke the restraints of his position and made the mistake of conferring a certificate on

Lok Sabha on August 8, 1973 during the discussion on imposition of President's Rule in Uttar Pradesh

a Chief Minister who was being forced out, why was it necessary to remove that Chief Minister, why was he forced to become a martyr ? Shri Tripathi was not willing to resign, he was forced to do so.

A reference has been made to the PAC affair. That affair was over and it had been followed by a statement by Shri Tripathi in which he said he would not resign. There was a summons to Delhi and confabulations and pressure politics were in operation. He was told to sever his relationship with some colleagues. Perhaps it was feared that a sinking ship would drown everybody, so Shri Tripathi's ship was scuttled. And for this helplessness he is being praised. But it is not the Governor's job to issue certificates.

Sir, if the Congress party was not in a position to conduct the government despite its majority it was the constitutional duty of the Governor to invite the opposition to form the government. Whether that government could last or not could have been decided in the Assembly, not in the Raj Bhavan. The fate of governments would not be decided in the Governor's room but in the Legislative Assembly. If the government could not function it would fall; then nobody could have pointed a finger at the Governor and charged him with partiality. But the Governor says—we added up the figures and saw that the government could not have functioned. If it is the figure that counts even the Congress party with its figure of 272 could not have a government that could function, and it was said that the party that could not have a functioning government made a sacrifice. The opposition should at least have been given a chance.

One more thing. If Shri Tripathi resigned, the opposition was not in a position to form the government, and President's Rule was to be imposed, then why was the Assembly not dissolved ? The Assembly has been kept in suspended animation. Now what Hanuman will bring *Sanjivani* to revive it ? From where will this *Sanjivani* come ? Is it locked up in the Home Ministry ? What is the reason for not dissolving the Assembly ? This means the door has been kept open for a party that could not conduct a government to again come to power ...

SHRI K.D. MALAVIYA (Dumariganj) : You have a narrow outlook.

SHRI VAJPAYEE : Now that Shri Malaviya has spoken, he has spoken from a wide viewpoint.

The Legislative Assembly was not dissolved. Now it is said Uttar Pradesh will have a popular government again before October. Clearly it has been admitted that the Government had become unpopular, but it is no doll's play to impose President's Rule when you want it and lift it when you don't want it. This is misuse of the Constitution. This is flouting of democratic conventions. Parliamentary democracy cannot be conducted like this.

Since the Prime Minister came to power President's Rule was imposed 22 times in the past seven and a half years under article 356. This was done not because the government did not go on as per the Constitution, but in order to extricate the ruling party from its own difficulties, to save the leadership from the charges being levelled at it, and to serve party ends. For this purpose the Constitution is flouted and democratic values thrown to the winds.

The PAC Incident

Sir, a reference has been made to the PAC incident. The Home Minister has also said something. My party is not in favour of allowing armed forces—whether it is the army or the armed police—to form trade unions. We cannot allow them to organise trade unions, but we should recognise their association and keep the door open for consideration of their problems. They are also a part of our society. Circumstances also affect them. They too can have complaints about their service conditions. I shall give an instance. PAC Jawans do overtime according to rules. They also get overtime allowance, but the rule is that this allowance cannot exceed Rs. 10 per month. Should overtime not be related to the allowance ? He may stand for hours, he may attend the Prime Minister's meetings in plain dress to augment the audience, he may be motivated to suppress people's movements...

SHRI UMA SHANKAR DIXIT, Home Minister : Don't say that, Sir. We respect you. You think carefully before you speak. I request you, I pray to you...

SHRI VAJPAYEE : This is not a charge of my own making. The PAC people have publicly made this charge. As a matter of fact I did not know about it, but the secret has been revealed that PAC personnel are sent on security duty in plain clothes. If the Prime Minister is a popular leader armed paraphernalia is not necessary for her security. Think carefully about what I am saying.

Sir, do you know that PAC Jawans are used for looking after officer's buffaloes ? I can name places where PAC Jawans not only do that but sell milk in the market and hand over the income to the officers. Will this continue ? Are PAC officers not to blame ? State intelligence people were keeping the centre informed about PAC discontent for three months, and today it is said intelligence has failed. I have personally met intelligence officers. The Home Ministry has levelled charges against some political parties. I call for an inquiry into the PAC incident by a Supreme Court judge. How could such a big incident take place ? Who is responsible for it ? What party had a hand in it ? This is not an ordinary situation, so facts should be brought to light. The politics of charges and counter-changes cannot be allowed in this matter. A Supreme Court judge should inquire into the PAC incident in the light of the charge made by the Home Ministry, so that it could be found out how the PAC was forced to cross its limitations like this.

Dissolve Assembly and Hold Election

Sir, there is President's Rule in Uttar Pradesh. The Legislative Assembly should be immediately dissolved and elections held. It is not good to have an atmosphere of uncertainty about the elections. There is no question of forming a new government in October. If the ruling party comes to power by winning the election under somebody's influence it would misuse government machinery still more. So setting up a puppet government again would be playing with the Constitution still more. Elections should be held immediately. But government must function in Uttar Pradesh so long as elections are not held. There is a drought in many areas. The situation is not as bad as before, thanks to the late monsoon, but do not be under the illusion that it is good. Because of the crops that have been destroyed the next 3-4 months would be quite difficult. Relief works are being closed down. Workers come together but the centre has stopped its grant, labourers are returning home, and this has worsened the situation (*Interruptions*) . Those who have work in the fields will not be included in relief work. Foodgrain is selling for Rs. 180 a quintal. Restraints have been imposed in districts. (*Interruptions*). I am talking of test work because the people should have purchasing power.

Sir, there is no reason for stopping relief work. Work can be found out that can go on even during rains. You will have to find such work, otherwise people will die of hunger in large numbers. Then along with the drought there is the problem of floods. There are floods in some areas. Arrears are being collected, bullocks are being auctioned, students are being forced to pay fees. These problems will have to be considered sympathetically, and I say the bureacracy that is really governing under the Governor's control in President's Rule does not show a sympathetic attitude.

Strange Love for Urdu

One more thing and I shall finish. There are some things happening in Uttar Pradesh that the Governor is doing only with the election in view. I told him so when I met him yesterday, and I say so in the House also. Sir, you will be surprised to learn that a 'Minimal test' has been recently introduced for fifth grade students before their final examination. It is for Hindi and arithmetic. If a student gives the test for Hindi and arithmetic he is required to secure 60 marks in arithmetic. But if a student gives the test in arithmetic and Urdu he would need to secure only 40 marks. I cannot understand this. This is the state's direction. Can there be discrimination between students on the basis of Urdu and Hindi ? There is no objection to Urdu forging ahead and people learning it, but those students who take Urdu require a lesser number of marks to pass while those who take Hindi require more! (*Interruptions*). I am speaking with a sense of responsibility. You are not right.

Secondly, Urdu teachers are appointed even where there are no students for Urdu. How is this ? After all our rules are clear, the commission's report clear-ly says that a teacher should be arranged if one class has ten students and the whole class has 40. This should be strictly adhered to (*Interruptions*). As for Sanskrit you can learn it too. Why drag in Brahmins ? Urdu should first have students and then teachers. It is not that the teachers should be in place first and then they should collect students. This does not show love for Urdu. Election politics is at work here. For God's sake do not do everything with the election in view. If you do wrong things today for winning the election those wrong things would create difficulties for you tomorrow.

Finally, I would say that now that we have President's Rule in Uttar Pradesh the Centre should launch an all-out campaign for the development of the State, especially of eastern Uttar Pradesh and Bundelkhand. Now there is no administrative laxity, no official lethargy. Now we can work together, plans for economic development can be chalked out, and the centre can go ahead with their implementation. Then President's Rule could be said to be having borne some fruit, otherwise it would be felt that the ruling party misused the Constitution in order to save itself in a crisis. This misuse will not prove helpful for democracy. That is all that I have to say. Thank you.

Anger in Bihar

Sir, during this discussion my party and personally I have been repeatedly criticised. I do not claim that we are infallible. For example what happened in Saharsa is to be condemned. Whoever person of our party was involved in that incident, his conduct is objectionable. We have called for his explanation, and if we find his involvement we shall take action on the party level. But I would request my Congress friends to go deeply into what happened in Bihar. They should not look for scapegoats. They should not look for excuses to cover up their failure. They should not get entangled in the process of levelling charges for political benefit. A political party cannot do what happened in Gujarat and is happening in Bihar. Not even all political parties together can do it. The people are angry. They are about to rebel. The common man is losing his patience. Everything is in short supply. Prices are kissing the skies. The gulf of disparity is widening and the administration is mired in corruption from head to toe.

SHRI N.P. YADAV : Wrong.

SHRI VAJPAYEE : The movement in Bihar has just begun, but I have with me a statement issued by a Congress MLA on September 11, 1973. I quote a couple of lines from it :

> "SHRI JAI NARAYAN : The State Congress is full of corrupt and discredited leaders. He charged the Government with functioning as a private concern of the Ministers and officers."

We do not say so. There are people in the Congress too who feel the administration is not going on as it should. Nothing can be done in Government offices these days without giving bribes. It is natural that this should vex the common man, it is even necessary. During the last discussion I had said that this is not the failure of a party, this is a failure of the whole system. The people are losing faith in democracy. The people do not face bullets just to incite anybody. If it is we who are doing what is happening in Bihar, then we are quite powerful. But we are not. In Gujarat we are in no position at all. But there the Government was forced to resign. The Gujarat Legislative Assembly had to be dissolved, because the people of Gujarat got angry. And now the anger of the people of Bihar is being roused. Try to go to its causes. Can anyone deny that Bihar is backward economically and socially ? It is surprising that Bihar, rich in natural resources but steeped in poverty, had not got angry yet. It is no surprise that it is now angry. I would like to tell what the Governor of Bihar says on September 21, 1973; the

---

Lok Sabha on April 11, 1974 during discussion on the situation in Bihar

agitation took place later. A correspondent of the *Hindu* interviewed him and asked about the crash employment programme of Rs. 37 lakhs. What did Shri Bhandare say ? —

> "There is no crash programme in Bihar. There is only one programme in the State, and that is crush programme."

When do Demands Become Legitimate ?

This was before the agitation. Harassed by unemployment, the students flared up. Now it is being said, Congress members are saying, other friends are saying, that the students' demands are legitimate. Since when did they become legitimate ? Is it not true that these says demands become legitimate only when people take to the streets over them ? If the demand for change in the educational system is proper what is the way to get it accepted ? All Congress members of this House say the educational system is faulty. Who will change it ? If the government is not ready to change it will the students suffer their future to be plunged in darkness ? I congratulate the students of Bihar on launching an agitation for their legitimate demands. It is true that the agitation should be peaceful. But I would like to distinguish between constitutional and extra-constitutional methods. Our Constitution does not provide for satyagraha. It also does not provide for requesting anyone on bended knees to resign. It is not within the Constitution to ask for the dissolution of the Bihar Legislative Assembly. But once, when the people of Kerala got engry, the Kerala Legislative Assembly was dissolved.

SHRI BHOGENDRA JHA : In Kerala there was no power. The dismissal came from above.

SHRI VAJPAYEE : What Shri Bhogendra Jha says about Kerala he does not say about Bihar. There cannot be two yardsticks for Kerala and Bihar.

Sir, the fact of the matter is that even logical and just demands are not heeded so long as the people do not come on to the streets to support them. When the railway employees threatened a strike Shri Lalit Narain Mishra became willing to discuss bonus, otherwise he was not ready....

SHRI L.N. MISHRA, Railway Minister : I was always ready. I said repeatedly that I was ready for discussion.

SHRI VAJPAYEE : You had said there would be no bonus, there will be no talks on bonus.

SHRI L.N. MISHRA : You may look up the proceedings.

SHRI VAJPAYEE : What I say is that the people have now lost faith in peaceful means. It should be re-established. This is not a matter of charges and counter-charges. What are you doing to re-establish this faith ?

Sir, the Home Minister says in his statement —

> "I sincerely hope that all sections of the House would join in my earnest appeal to the students and others in Bihar, Gujarat and elsewhere to eschew violence and cooperate wholeheartedly in maintenance of peace and harmony and in upholding the basic values of our democratic society."

What the Students Say ?

In my opinion there is no difference between what the students of Bihar are saying and what the Home Minister says. I quote a portion of what the students say :

> "The present government of Bihar is murderous, it should go. But merely changing the Ministry is not our objective. We do not aim at changing the government or even at electing a new Legislative Assembly. Our aim is to change their character. If democratic values got destroyed, if democratic processes get corrupted democratic institutions become playthings. That is the situation today. Hence democracy has become a formal mask behind which corruption, loot and the demon of terror are hidding their faces. Our aim is to make adult franchise a reality, to organise the people's might behind democratic values, processes and institutions because it is only such democratic might that can demolish the demon of corruption, dearness and unemployment and grant security and self-respect to every citizen. Our battle is a battle for changing the present hideous form of economic, social and political life, a battle for equipping the people with their right and their might."

SHRI H.K. SINGH : This is your draft.

SHRI VAJPAYEE : If this is my draft no substance is left in the blame you have put on me. The students of Bihar are fighting for big objectives. The government would have to seriously think about how to bring about basic changes in the structure of the country.

I would ask my Congress friends—If the Government does not heed the legitimate demand for changing the educational system should the students just sit quietly ? Now they won't sit— this is the change that has come about, and the Prime Minister has contributed much in bringing it about. Now the people will no longer suffer in silence. Now the deprived, the oppressed, the exploited, the Dalit will not compromise with the present. You have roused a tide of expectations, now if you do not fulfil those expectations they would turn into a rebellion in the streets—this is what is happening today.

In her speech at Chandigarh on December 29,1970 the Prime Minister had said—if poverty increases, disparity increases, people will take to violence, they would come out on the streets. That is what is happening today. Those who have sown the wind should prepare to reap the whirlwind.

Attack on 'Searchlight'

One event in what happened in Bihar has not yet come fully to light. The Government has not yet ordered an inquiry into the attack on the *Searchlight.* This is a matter of the freedom of the press. Our party is being held responsible for the Bihar happenings. But what is the truth ? A few days back the editor of the *Searchlight* was here. He addressed a press conference. I quote a portion from the press report :

"The burning down of the office and press of the *Searchlight* was a deep-laid conspiracy against an outspoken newspaper; S.K. Rau, its Editor, said here today.

He said the complicity of the State Government in the conspiracy was clear from the facts that the police were not ordered to take action against the mob and the fire-brigade services were not available even on the day after the arson.

Mr. Rau was emphatic that the mischief-mongers were neither students nor the Anand Margis. He also excluded the R.S.S. and the Jan Sangh.

He said the Bihar CPI was particularly unhappy because of the criticism it got." (*Interruptions*) .

SHRI BHOGENDRA JHA : Mr. Rau is himself a Jan Sanghi...

SHRI VAJPAYEE : Sir, the editor of the *Searchlight* has demanded an inquiry and also said that if an inquiry commission were set up he would place more facts before it. I would like to know if the Government is prepared to set up a commission for inquiring into the attack on the *Searchlight* and the arson.

The other thing is about Gaya. Many things have been said, but I have before me a statement by Shri Mudrika Prasad Singh, ex-MP. He is a Congressman and a responsible person. According a press reports:

> " He told reporters here today that about 40 to 50 persons were killed in indiscriminate police firings at Gaya on April 12, according to a general public belief.

He said that for 48 hours the entire people of Gaya were under house arrest. The patrolling armed forces announced every five-minutes that anybody coming out of his house would be shot dead".

Here the Home Minister's statement is proved wrong. Further.

> "Mr. Singh said that according to official figures only 8 persons were killed in the police firing. But God alone knew how many people were killed. But the fact remained that several bodies were whisked away in police vans. The bodies were also dragged up to a considerable distance. The clots of blood on several roads spread over a distance of 20 ft bore testimony to it.
>
> He said that the police opened fire near the post office, Jain Mandir, Wool House, Kiran Cinema, Sabji Market, Motimahal and at other places. The body of a 12-year boy was found abandoned in the river Falgu.
>
> The students' agitation, he said, was most peaceful. It was spontaneous. There was a mass upsurge among the people as well. The work in all the Government offices had been totally paralysed by offering *dharna* which had been most peaceful. There was no physical obstruction by the students.
>
> He said that the local officials had conspired to resort to firings only to teach a lesson to the students and the people of Gaya. Although the firings were opened at 3 P.M. he had secret information that the conspiracy was hatched at 9 in the morning on that day."

This is not the statement of some opposition member. It is the statement of Shri Mudrika Prasad Singh, an ex-MP of the Congress. Congress members say the dead do not include students. Does this not mean the agitation was not limited to students but people in general had participated in it on a large scale ? Has this not become a people's agitation ? Is it not true that the police misbehaved with women ?

SHRI U.S. DIXIT : This is not true.

SHRI VAJPAYEE : Did you go to see ? I would request Shri Dixit not to reply only on what the Bihar Government says but make an inquiry on the Centre's behalf. Misbehavior with women is not a matter of any one party. If this charge is false it is all the more reason why the Government should have no objection to a judicial inquiry. Facts will come to light, wheat will be separated from the chaff, and those who are making false allegations will be exposed. There was firing in Bihar, so many people were killed, the *Searchlight* was attacked—why is the Government afraid of inquiring into all these things ?

I am sorry to see that during this discussion an attempt has been made to drag in even Shri Jaya Prakash Narayan's name. Those who do not deserve to sit at his feet are today flinging mud at him.

There can be a difference of opinion with Shri Jaya Prakash, but no one can doubt his patriotism. Democracy is a means, not an end. Shri Jaya Prakash has the full right to say that there is need for a basic change in the present democratic structure. But this is no reason for anyone to say... (*Interruptions*).

Tyranny will be overcome

Bihar is burning, the streets of Bihar are red with blood, the Government is bent on tyranny. People can be killed with bayonets, but it is not possible to sit on bayonets. I would conclude with a portion from a ghazal by Sahir Ludhianvi

"Julm phir julm hai barhta hai to mit jata hai,
Khoon phir khoon hai, tapkega to jam jayega.
Tum jis khoon ko maqtal mein dabana chaha,
Aaj woh kucha o bazar mein aa nikla hai.
kahin Shola, kahi nara, kahin patthar ban kar
Khoon chalta hai to rukta nahin sangino se,
Sar uthta hai to dabata nahi aaino se
Julm ki baat hi kya, julm ki aukat hi kya,
Julm bas julm hai aagaj se anjam tak
Khoon phir khoon hai, Sau shakl badal sakta hai.
Aisi shakl ki mitao to mitaye na bane.
Aise nare ki dabao to dabaye na bane."

'Tyranny is tyranny, the more it grows, the more it destroys itself.
Blood is blood, if it flows it will harden
The blood that you wanted to stem.

That blood now flows through lanes and the market place.
It is a flame here, a slogan there, a stone elsewhere.
When blood is on the move, bayonets cannot stop it.
When the head rises, it cannot be made to bow.
What is tyranny ? What is its power ?
Tyranny is tyranny, from concept to consequence.
Blood is blood, and can take on a hundred forms.
A form that you cannot demolish however you try.
A flame that you cannot put out however hard you blow.
A voice you cannot muzzle howsoever hard you suppress.

Instead of solving problems with police brutality, build bridges with the students, with the new generation. Rebuild the bridge that lies broken between the government and the opposition. Your credibility is over. Try to restore it. Blaming us will not solve the problem. It is not a question of any one party, it is the question of the whole country. Gujarat was a warning, that warning is being repeated in Bihar. If we do not need it the whole country will go up in flames, and the conflagration will consume us all. Thank you.

Terror in Tripura

Sir, I move a motion calling attention to a matter of urgent public importance and request the Home Minister to give a statement on the following :

"Declaration of two districts of Tripura as disturbed areas due to incidents of large-scale violence and large numbers of casualties due to them."

SHRI ZAIL SINGH, Home Minister : Sir, as the Hon. members knew, because of serious incidents of violence taking place in Tripura on June 7, I visited it on June 11 in the company of my colleagues, the Commerce Minister and the Deputy Minister, Civil Supplies. According to information available with the State Government 315 people were killed, hundreds injured, houses were torched in more than 100 villages, and more than one lakh people rendered homeless, who have been accommodated in relief camps. Some people fear that there has been even greater loss of life and property.

I and my colleagues surveyed the areas where violence had taken place and saw that fires were still burning in many of the villages. We also visited some relief camps and the Agartala Hospital, where nearly 500 people have been admitted, and listened to their tragic and heartrending tales. We sympathised with them and assured them that the government was greatly concerned in this matter, that it would make every effort to bring the guilty to book, and extend all help to those who have become victims of violence. During the visit to Agartala we also met representatives from various regions.

For the present nothing definite can be said about these incidents of violence but one thing is clear, which is that tensions between various groups were increasing. One of the reasons for this is the definite impact of the Assam agitation. It appears that militant and anti-social elements tried to exploit the situation.

The Central Government assured the State Government full help to tackle the situation, and assistance was accordingly started. Armed and para-military forces were immediately despatched. They have been air-lifted and are in position in the interior. The State Government has so far taken about 715 persons into custody. However tension still prevails and the situation needs careful watching.

Sir, with your permission, I would like to convey sympathies to those families that have suffered loss of life and property due to these incidents of violence.

Lok Sabha on June 12, 1980 while moving the Calling Attention Motion on disturbed conditions in Tripura

A Massacre

SHRI VAJPAYEE : Sir, we have listened to the Home Minister's statement with great attention. What has happened in Tripura is extraordinary. It would be no exaggeration to call it a massacre. It is extrarodinary that in independent India so many people should get killed and so many uprooted from their homes. What is still more tragic, large numbers of those who have been uprooted include those who had been already uprooted once and came to this country to settle down. They have again become refugees in their own country.

On behalf of the House the Home Minister has paid respects to the departed, prayed for peace to their souls, and condoled with their families. I join him in this.

Disturbance on such a large scale are possible only after elaborate preparations. Since when were these preparations going on ? From where did the rioters get arms ? How true are the press reports that they were receiving arms from foreign sources ?

Before this too news had come that a 'Tripura Sena' has been set up there which talks of liberating Tripura and bringing about secession through the medium of an armed rebellion. On the one hand it is said that it has an alliance with the Mizo National Front, on the other it is claimed that its people are receiving military training in Chittagong Hill Tracts.

The Home Minister has linked the Assam agitation with this and said this is one of the reasons. It is possible that the Assam agitation may have had a reaction, but the Hon. Minister will admit that the situation in Tripura was deteriorating for years. I was looking up old press clippings. I have with me an article published in the *Indian Express* of May 9, 1968. I will quote a portion from it—I shall not take much time.

> "Dark clouds portending imminent storm are gathering on the political horizon of Tripura : unawaited influx of Bengal Hindus from East Pakistan, consequent disturbance of the demographic equilibrium and growing pressure on land, acute food shortage, increasing unemployment, complete neglect of the backward and hill areas, shocking apathy of an indolent but all-powerful bureaucracy have created an explosive situation in this highly vulnerable region."

After this some political steps were taken in Tripura which gave the people a chance of representative government. However the tribals thought their existence was in danger, perhaps their identity itself would be finished.

Tribal Autonomy

Is it true that the present government in Tripura wanted to set up autonomous districts in tribal areas. They should have councils, and those councils should conduct the administration of their districts. An Act was also prepared for this, the President had given it his assent, but it could not come into force perhaps because the matter is pending in the High Court.

What I want to know is, why was no step taken earlier for a political solution of the whole problem ?

Now the first duty is to maintain law and order. So action will have to be taken against those who collected arms, used them and were responsible for large-scale violence. But it is important that there should be complete accord between the Centre and the Tripura Government. Selfish politics must not be allowed to intervene. Sometimes Congress-I friends demand that the Tripura Government should be dismissed, as it could not maintain law and order. I would like the Hon. Minister to say if the Government is thinking on these lines.

No the first duty is to maintain law and order. So action will have to be taken against those who collected arms, used them and were responsible for large-scale violence. But it is important that there should be complete accord between the Centre and the Tripura Government. Selfish politics must not be allowed to intervene. Sometimes Congress-1 friends demand that the Tripura Government should be dismissed, as it could not maintain law and order. I would like the Hon. Minister to say if the Government is thinking on these lines.

SHRI BHAGWAT JHA AZAD (Bhagalpur) : What if the massacre continues ?

SHRI VAJPAYEE : If it does the Central and State governments could jointly take steps. If you dismiss the State government the whole situation will go from bad to worse, and there would be no possibility of improving it. Or you may say it is necessary to dismiss the State Government because it is not assisting in the maintenance of law and order; rather, it is hindering it.

Tripura's Double Problem

Secondly, it was not clear why the Hon. Minister took the Commerce Minister with him on his tour—it was a very short tour, but it was good that he went immediately. He may have his own reasons, I do not know, But economically Tripura has been ignored. In the prevailing circumstances elaborate economic development plans cannot be chalked out or discussed. It is possible that he may have taken him along to help him, as Shri Pranab Mukherji could assist in talking to Bangla-speaking people. The Home Minister may have secured his help in this. The Tripura problem has two aspects—one is to end violence and establish peace, and secondly to assure the tribals that even if people have come in and settled in large numbers, thus reducing their population, their interests and their life-style would be protected. But I have not seen any such statement of the Home Minister published in the newspapers. He has said in a statement that Tripura's problem is not economic. But Tripura's problem is economic as well as protection of the tribals' existence. As I said such a big massacre was possible only after elaborate preparations. Then what was the government's intelligence doing ? The Chief Minister of Tripura was on a visit to Delhi (*Interruptions*) . States have their CID, and we know about them, but what was the Centre's intelligence doing ? Did or did not the Central Government have full information about this ? Did it have an inkling that such a big massacre was going to take place ? In his statement the Minister has talked of militant and anti-social elements. Who are these elements ? (*Interruptions*). A Congress member talked of the RSS, but I am happy to see that in the current discussion on the Afghanistan problem the Foreign Minister did not hold the RSS responsible. Who are these militants in Tripura, and with whom are they connected ? Funds and arms are coming in from abroad. Are they attempted to be stopped ? And by what time, in the Home Minister's opinion, would the situation be brought under control ?

SHRI ZAIL SINGH : Sir, Hon'ble Shri Vajpayee has said many things. He ended with questions, but I am grateful to him for the points he has made.

Rajiv-Lal Denga Accord

Sir, the Mizoram agreement to which the Home Minister has referred in his statement is not an agreement, it is a surrender by the Government. What is definite is that under the agreement the insurgents will surrender their arms. How many arms is not definite. There is no assurance that all arms will be surrendered. What is clear is that the Government of India surrendered before the insurgents.

Sir, this is a wrong agreement, done at the wrong time and in the wrong manner. The Home Minister is fully connected with the events in Punjab. In Punjab a decisive battle is being fought against the extremists by the Jawans of the Police, the Border Security Force and the Central Reserve Police who are staking their lives to free the country from the danger posed by the extremists. At such a time in Mizoram an agreement has been made that will encourage them. The extremists, who are young, misled boys, will now be told that if Mizoram with a population of less than five lakh can become a separate State on a handful of Mizos taking up arms and waging a long battle, why cannot Punjab be made a separate nation by killing innocent people, having a regime of massacre, and taking foreign help ? Sir, was it necessary to make this agreement at this time ? Is it the aim to secure plaudits for one agreement after another ? Talks with Shri Lal Denga have been going on for years. They were going on even during the Janata Government. But the Home Minister knows that the point on which the talks broke down was Lal Denga's insistence on the condition that the agreement should provide for his being given power in Mizoram without elections. The Janata Government said that could not be, if you want to come to power give up arms, take to peace, contest elections, if you get a majority you can come to power. The present agreement has a political agreement between Shri Lal Denga and Shri Arjun Singh behind it. What that political settlement is we do not know. The Hon. Minister did not even think it necessary to place a copy of that settlement on the floor of the House. We have it. But it should have been placed on the Table of the House.

Will Lal Denga Become Chief Minister Without Elections ?

Sir, how did the Government accept the condition to remove the elected Government in Mizoram ? Even if that Government belonged to the ruling party that does not give the ruling party the right to remove an elected government.... (*Interruptions*).... I would like to say to the lady that this is a

Rajya Sabha on July 21, 1986 during discussion on the Calling Attention Motion regarding the merits and demerits of the Mizoram Agreement

rather serious matter. I am also good at interruptions.... (*Interruptions*) Now Lal Denga will become the Chief Minister and elections will be held after that. Why was Lal Denga not made to accept the condition that he should fight elections ? This too is surrender. Right from now differences have started on the danger and definitions of the agreement. The statements that Lal Denga has given before and after the agreement are a danger signal for us.

Lal Denga says "Mizoram was never a part of India." Does the Government accept this ? When a journalist asked Lal Denga what would happen if the agreement was not implemented he said Mizoram would secede from India. It is true that in a later statement he attempted some whitewash. Insurgency has been going on in Mizoram for so many days. Lal Denga was out of the country, and it is not known if he is an Indian citizen or not. He calls Mizoram a separate nation, the Mizo National Front. Has the Government paid attention to his statements ? Has he been asked to explain ? My other friends have raised this question, so I do not want to repeat it, but why did the Government flatly turn down the idea of a Greater Mizoram ? The Government of India does not make a commitment in an agreement. Then why was it necessary for the Prime Minister to call a conference of Chief Ministers of big States in Aizwal ? No one will accept Greater Mizoram, but Lal Denga will not leave it. When Lal Denga talks of Greater Mizoram after becoming Chief Minister will a new crisis arise in that part of the country ? Why was he not plainly told to give up Greater Mizoram ? Lal Denga said Mizoram has secured greater autonomy than Kashmir. Kashmir has a special status, but the status of Mizoram will be more special than special. Jammu and Kashmir cannot trade, but Mizoram's right to trade is included in the agreement. Border trade in locally produced and grown agricultural commodities could be allowed under a scheme to be formulated by the Central Government.

House Kept in Dark About Conditions of Agreement

I charge that in the agreement with Lal Denga you are going to give him some concessions about which the House cannot be told, about which the country is not being taken into confidence. With what countries does he want to trade ? It is the same countries from which he brings in arms. What will happen behind the scene? Can the Home Minister say something about this with confidence ? It is true that the Central Government will have control, the Centre has approved, but why this talk of trade ? It is true the wording is "could be allowed." Whatever you have allowed, say it frankly. Otherwise you will come to grief. That has been happening with many agreements.

Problem of the Chakmas

And what will happen to the Chakmas ? There are thousands of Chakmas living in Mizoram. They are Buddhists, not Christians. The Mizo National Front wants to bring forth a Christian State. It is true that they have kept it a somewhat separate point in the Constitution. The Chakmas have a district and a district council. Lal Denga wants to do away with that council. It is true that the Home Minister's statement as well as the agreement state that the rights of the minorities will be protected. But that will be the Mizo Government's responsibility. If you intervene there will be a complaint against the interference. Will the Government think about setting up a Union Territory for the Chakmas ? Mizoram was also a hill district, then it was upgraded, and now it is a State. A State with a population of less than five lakh. It will have a separate high court, a separate university. How will you prevent such demands from arising in other parts of the country ? The 'Inner Line' also needs to be explained. You do not require a permit to go to Jammu and Kashmir. If this provision is meant for the protection of tribals the Home Minister will have to give a statement saying it will not be misused. After all we want to bring the people of Mizoram into the national mainstream. Their special interests must be protected. A feeling of separateness, of being a separate people, must not be allowed to grow.

Who Surrendered Arms ?

One more thing—who are the people who have surrendered arms in Mizoram ? What countries give them sanctuary ? What guarantee is there that all arms will be surrendered ? How will the Government verify if all the arms they have are surrendered ? And will the Government also make an agreement with the country that gives them sanctuary that it should stop doing so as it was making an agreement with them ?

I would like to have one more clarification—the agreement and the Home Minister's statement have no reference to amnesty. The way Shri Lal Denga defines it makes it clearly sound as if not only those in jail will be freed and resettled, but those who have left India, who are involved in violence, and who may have killed scores of people would also be freed under this agreement. They would also be honoured. If that is so what will its reaction be in Punjab ? The Home Minister should think about it. I would like to know the position in this regard. Thank you.

Statehood for Uttaranchal and Vananchal

The Case of Uttaranchal

Mr. Chairman, Sir, I rise to support the Resolution moved by my Hon. friend Shri Jagat Vir Singh Drona, not only because our party programme includes the demands for a separate 'Uttaranchal' and separate 'Vananchal' but also because it is the demand of the local people in the real sense. This demand is not politically motivated, rather it is to fulfil the requirements of economic development. As some members have pointed out, the States were recognised on language basis at the time of independence. At that time language was the main basis and it was but natural. If people speaking the same language remain in a single administrative unit, their development becomes easy and their cultural identity is strengthened. It was done so a long time ago. Now it appears that States formed on lingustic basis are too big to be administered properly, and their development is blocked. Their administration is also not smooth. Now the demand being raised is to accelerate the pace of development and run the administration properly. Small States would be helpful for this purpose. The proposal for the small States should be taken into consideration from this point of view. It is a wrong conception as has been pointed out just now by my Hon. friend that it would weaken the country. Really, the formation of small States would be helpful in the development of the country. Mr. Chairman, Sir, you belong to Punjab. Had Himachal not been separated....

MR. CHAIRMAN : Vajpayeeji, I come from Haryana.

SHRI VAJPAYEE : Haryana also has the same experience. Had Himachal not been separated, had there not been separate existence of Haryana, it would have lagged behind in the race of progress though it was a part of Punjab. It reduces the bitterness.

SHRI JAGMEET SINGH BRAR : Mr. Chairman, Sir, I am on a point of order. Shri Vajpayee has made a correct statement. I would like to point out one thing in particular that under the Chief Ministership of Shri Pratap Singh Kairon the areas of Haryana and Himachal Pradesh made equal development in the united Punjab. In fact, so far as I know major development took place upto Kullu and Lahaul Spiti. All this was done under the leadership of Pratap Singh Kairon....

MR. CHAIRMAN : Sardar Jagmeet Singhji, had it been so, Haryana would not have come into being.

Lok Sabha on March 5, 1993 during discussion on the Resolution regarding creation of New States

SHRI VAJPAYEE : Mr. Chairman, Sir, you have made my work easy. You may please tell him that such matters cannot be raised under point of order, if he wants to say something he should do so in the form of a speech. I thought that I had misbehaved or violated some rule and there will be a demand to expunge my speech.

MR. CHAIRMAN : Vajpayeeji, the youths of today are agitated. They want to say something.

SHRI VAJPAYEE : Mr. Chairman, Sir, it is also a wrong notion that if Uttaranchal is formed then Uttar Pradesh would be divided and if Vananchal is formed Bihar would be divided. Somebody would also say that if Bihar is to be divided, it should be done on his dead body. There is no question of division. The question is of reorganisation, it will be a division if any part is seceded from the country.

Mr. Chairman, Sir, if new districts can be formed, commissonaries can be set up, then new States can also be formed though it is somewhat a lengthy procedure. However that would be within the country, within the political set up and under the Constitution. There is no question at all to weaken to country and divide it. The Uttar Pradesh Assembly has already passed a resolution in favour of the formation of Uttaranchal. The Resolution was forwarded to the Centre but the Congress Party being the ruling party at Centre did not pay any attention to the Resolution. The Uttar Pradesh Legislative Assembly has since been dissolved. Mr. Chairman, Sir, the Assembly could have been revived even after the dismissal of the State Government. Now there will be elections again and the Uttaranchal issue will be a major election issue. We should get full support on this issue. The ruling side will be in loss again. Therefore, my submission is that Uttaranchal should be formed before the elections are held. At least we will lose on this point. Of course, other points will remain there. I am making a concrete suggestion. I am talking of their good. There is no loss in forming a separate State of Uttaranchal.

Mr. Chairman, Sir, backward areas demand attention. The resources should be utilised properly and there should be convenience of administration. In view of all this, Uttaranchal has a very strong case.

Vananchal

So far as, Vananchal is concerned, I would like to request the members from Jharkhand that for the present, they should accept the demand of a separate State consisting of Chhota Nagpur and Santhal Parganas, if they want to include some part of Bengal, Orissa and Madhya Pradesh in it, they will face opposition from all sides. Shri Singh Deo is not going to part with any part of Orissa.

SHRI SURAJ MANDAL (Godda) : He wants to come. Sambalpur is his area, he wants to come to Talcher.

SHRI VAJPAYEE : He want to come or you want him to come.

Mr. Chairman, Sir, the change in the borders of several States will create a lot of problems. Santhal Parganas and Chhota Nagpur combined together become a geographical unit and these are backward also. They have also been exploited....(*Interruptions*).... We are with you, but the difficulty is that they never fight for it consistently. Be with us and fight, only then something can be achieved.

Development Boards

Mr. Chairman, Sir, when a mass movement acquires momentum, several suggestions are given to mislead it. One such suggestion was of development board. You may remember when the demand for a Vidarbha State started gaining ground, it was suggested to have a development board, but Shri Shankarrao Chavan did not allow it to be formed. There was another demand of a separate State of Telangana in Andhra Pradesh. When such demands are politically motivated, they do not get public support for long. Even if they get support for a short time they do not achieve their goals. I would like to submit that these issues should be considered in view of development of these areas and convenience of administration. I do not agree that a pandora's box will be opened, if the States are reorganised again and this Government does not want to open that box. This Government has already opened a number of other such boxes. I do not think that any new box will get opened if these demands are accepted. A Commission should be constituted and its terms of reference should be very clear. Is it not necessary to reshape the political map of this country in view of administrative convenience and economic development ? The Commission should submit its recommendations within a fixed time period, but the formation of Vananchal and Uttaranchal should not be stopped on the pretext of constituting a Commission. If just to avoid the demands of these States, a Commission is constituted, this will be injustice to the States and this will only increase the resentment. At present, the people are demanding peacefully and I would like to tell my friends from Vananchal area that they should not allow to turn this movement violent. Violence and democracy should not go side by side. This applies to all of us including myself. It applies to the Congress also wherever it is in opposition. If Congress becomes violent in Calcutta and preaches non-violence to us in Delhi, it won't work. This will not help improve the situation, but will make it worse, it appears that the country is disintegrating. The norms should be one for all. I would request that while replying, the Hon. Minister should make clear his stand on Vananchal and Uttaranchal. These States should be formed and if it is thought necessary, a proposal for the constitution of a Commission to becide the question of entire reorganisation should be brought forward. We will welcome that proposal, but there should not be delay in the formation of Uttaranchal and Vananchal States.

Central Government's Apathy to Problems of Delhi

Mr. Speaker, Sir, it is a matter of great regret that our four colleagues could not attend the sitting of the House today. I am referring to the absence of Messrs Madan Lal Khurana, Kalka Das, Tara Chand Khandelwal and Baikunth Lal Sharma "Prem." The House is in session. Naturally, in ordinary course, they should have been here. They had been tirelessly airing the woes of Delhiites, but when there was no response from the Government they were forced to undertake today a fast for 72 hours in Chandni Chowk, outside this House.

The Central Government had stressed the point that the Octroi system would be abolished in Delhi. In a way, justification for its abolition could be understood; but at the same time it was also decided that the loss that would accrue to the Municipal Corporation of Delhi thereby will be compensated by the Central Government. This comes to Rs. 45 crores in a year. However, not a single paisa has been granted to the M.C.D. since January 1, 1993. Rs. 25 to 30 crores should have been paid by now. Hon'ble Home Minister's attention was drawn towards it repeatedly, but nobody bothers to look at the woes of Delhiites.

Delhi is the capital of India, but what is the position of availability of electricity in Delhi, how much shortage of water is here ? During this summer and in the rainy season, the sufferings undergone by the people of Delhi had never been experienced before. Roads are full of pot holes and the Corporation has issued an order that all allotments of money should be cancelled and no expenditure should be incurred without permission. Tenders have been pending for the last two years, the development activity in Delhi is at a standstill, there is no electricity, no water. Red Line buses do ply, but they are contributing in taking people from here to the other world. That is another story.

Home Minister Must Make Statement

Sir, you may please direct the Home Minister to make a statement in the House about Delhi and announce the amount that should be paid in lieu of the Octroi. I want your intervention in this matter. There is no Legislative Assembly in Delhi and the bureaucracy is ruling the roost. The Bill has been passed, but the Legislative Assembly has not been constituted. Parliament

Lok Sabha on August 18, 1993 about the 72-hour fast undertaken by BJP M.Ps from Delhi regarding the problems of Delhi

has no time for the affairs of Delhi and if it has got the time let us see which members of which Party support this demand of mine ?

Mr. Speaker, I think the issue is quite important. The Government should make a statement on this.

SHRI LAXMI NARAYAN PANDE: In the morning, Hon'ble Speaker had given a direction to the Government to make a statement about Delhi affairs. When is it going to be made ?

SHRI VAJPAYEE: You might perhaps recall, I had raised this matter during the Zero Hour. Four Lok Sabha members are on fast. The Central Government has to compensate Delhi for the loss of Octroi. Hon'ble Speaker had given direction to the Home Minister to make a statement, but that is not forthcoming. Has the Minister of Parliamentary Affairs informed the Minister of Home Affairs ? I had a talk with the Home Minister. He told me that he had no knowledge that he has to make a statement. It means that the Minister of Parliamentary Affairs has not done his duty well. The statement must come today before the House rises.

SHRI VAJPAYEE : Sir, I understand that the Minister of State in the Ministry of Home Affairs is ready with a statement on Delhi. If that is so, you may ask for the statement to be made first and the reply can come afterwards.

VII KASHMIR TANGLE

Withdraw Kashmir Issue from U.N.

MR. DEPUTY SPEAKER : Motion moved :

"This House is of opinion that on account of the failure of the United Nations Organisation to call upon Pakistan to vacate aggression in Kashmir the Government should withdraw its complaint from the United Nations Organisation as a measure of protest."

SHRI VAJPAYEE : I beg to move :

In the resolution—

From the words "should withdraw its complaint from the United Nations Organisation as a measure of protest" *substitute* :

"Should have its complaint in the U.N.O. dropped as a measure of protest (3)

4. I beg to move the following amendment :

In the resolution, *add* at the end, "and independently of the U.N.O. explore avenues to cause vacation of aggression" (4)

MR. DEPUTY SPEAKER : The resolution and amendments Nos 3 and 4 of Shri Vajpayee are before the House.

SHRI VAJPAYEE : Mr. Deputy Speaker, Sir, let me explain the amendments moved by me. I think the resolution moved by Shri Tariq cannot be accepted even though the government may wish to do so, because the issue once referred to the United Nations Organisation cannot perhaps be withdrawn technically. The Government can, if it so desires, refuse to discuss the issue further. Earlier also, when this demand to withdraw the Kashmir issue from U.N.O. was made, our Prime Minister had spoken of the technical objection that an issue once referred to U.N.O. cannot be withdrawn.

The U.N. Failed in its Obligations

I have moved this amendment keeping in mind the difficulty that we may not be able to withdraw the issue, but if that is not possible we may try that the question of Jammu and Kashmir may not be taken up for consideration by the United Nations. There is reason also for this demand. The United Nations has failed to do justice to India in regard to the question of Kashmir. It is common knowledge that Pakistan committed aggression in Jammu and Kashmir. The U.N. representative who visited Kashmir had also admitted

Lok Sabha on April 22, 1960 while moving amendments to the motion regarding withdrawal of the Kashmir issue from the UNO

that Pakistan invaded Kashmir. In spite of that, U.N.O. did not perform its duty which it should when one country is invaded by another country. And when we compare Kashmir with Korea—South Korea was attacked by North Korea—we find that when this matter was referred to U.N.O. within 24 hours North Korea was declared an aggressor and steps were taken to defend South Korea.

However, on the complaint made by India, no step was taken by U.N.O. Even after looking at the aggression this body, which is responsible for maintaining world peace, remained inactive and the Kashmir issue became an issue of cold war. Who committed the aggression and who was the victim, these questions were overlooked and the Kashmir issue became a pawn on the chess-board of international politics between the United States and the Soviet bloc. I think it was a mistake on the part of our Government to refer the Kashmir issue to the United Nations Organisation; in fact, there was no need to refer it to U.N. We could have resolved it or should have tried to resolve it ourselves. And it was being resolved also. Our troops were forging ahead, defeating the Pakistani forces in the battlefield. But when we were moving from one victory to another our Government entered into a cease-fire agreement, that is to say, that fetters of a cease-fire were used to shackle our winning forces. This resulted in one-third of Kashmir being still under Pakistani occupation.

We have not been defeated on the battleground. India has not been defeated in war, we have been defeated in the treaty. The history of treaties and agreements has brought no credit to us. Had our Government not committed itself to a cease-fire agreement the entire Kashmir would have been ours; but we committed a mistake.

Story of Kashmir—A Story of Blunders

The policy of the Government of Kashmir is a long story of blunders. Jammu and Kashmir wanted to accede to India earlier. But our Government did not agree to it. When Pakistan attacked it, and there was no other option left, only then did we integrate Jammu and Kashmir with India. There was no need to commit ourselves to a plebiscite. But our Prime Minister made an offer for a plebiscite at the instance of Lord Mountbatten. The people of Kashmir and even the Ruler of Jammu and Kashmir were in favour of full accession. They were ready to accede to India in the same manner as the other princely States had done. But we committed a blunder by making an offer for a plebiscite. However, this offer of plebiscite was not made to Pakistan; it was for the people of Jammu and Kashmir. Pakistan has no *locus standi* in this matter. When Pakistan is not prepared to give the right of self-determination to Pakhtoonistan I do not understand how it could demand it for Jammu and Kashmir. Jammu and Kashmir has become an integral part of India and I do not think there could be any change in it. Individuals may come and go, governments may be formed and unformed, but Jammu and Kashmir would remain an integral part of India and would adorn the head of Mother India.

My submission is that since we did not get justice in the United Nations Organisation there is no point in raising this issue in that forum. If this issue is raised by others, I do not think we will be promoting India's interests by taking part in it. Yes, I would welcome any other measures outside the United Nations Organisation for undoing the aggression committed by Pakistan against Jammu and Kashmir. But such an effort should be confined to pushing out the aggressor, not anything else. Thank you.

End Incongruous Status

Mr. Deputy Speaker, Sir, I beg to move :

"This House is of the opinion that the incongruous status of Jammu and Kashmir State should come to an end, because it has a separate Constitution, a separate Head of State and a separate flag in spite of this State being an integral part of India, and this State should be brought fully at par with other States of India, and for this purpose the House recommends that all necessary steps such as abrogation of Article 370, be initiated forthwith."

Sir, just now we have made a pious resolve of changing the name of Madras State to Tamilnadu. Tamilnadu is situated in the far south where the Indian Ocean washes the feet of Mother India. In Tamilnadu is situated Kanya Kumari, deeply immersed in the meditation of Lord Shiva, who has his abode in the Himalayas, from times immemorial. I now want to take the House from Kanyakumari to Kashmir. In fact discussion on Tamilnadu as well as on Kashmir on the same day brings before us the entire panorama of India.

Jammu and Kashmir is an integral part of India. But Jammu and Kashmir still has a separate Constitution of its own. Jammu and Kashmir is an indivisible part of India, but it has separate citizenship. We call Kashmir the crown of Mother India, the gem of the crown. But the Kashmir State has its separate flag. What is the reason for this ?

If the Constitution of India is suitable for all other States of India is it not suitable for Jammu and Kashmir ? If the citizenship of India is a matter of pride and respect for fifty crores of its citizens why is it not a matter of pride for forty lakh people of Jammu and Kashmir ?

Our tricolour flag is dear to the entire country and is a sinecure of all eyes. But Kashmir has a separate flag of its own besides the Indian tricolour. When the flags of all princely States have become things of the past there is no reason, no propriety in having a separate flag only for Jammu and Kashmir.

The question is how long will this dual system continue in India ? How long will this uncertainty remain ? Where there is a dual system there is uncertainty. Where there is uncertainty there is separation, there is cession. We are not tired of declaring day in and day out that Jammu and Kashmir is a part of India like other States, but we are making some discrimination against Jammu and Kashmir which this House should take into consideration.

Lok Sabha on November 22, 1968 while moving the resolution seeking abrogation of Article 370 of the Constitution relating to Jammu and Kashmir

Is is not amazing that a Jawan of India, a brave youth of our armed forces, who could sacrifice his life to save Jammu and Kashmir and to protect its land cannot settle in Jammu and Kashmir, he cannot purchase land in Jammu and Kashmir ? Is it not strange that this Parliament has no right to call for the accounts of the amount of hard-earned income of the people of India which can be frittered away like water in Jammu and Kashmir ? So far only one case has come in the court and the judgement given by the court was that the President of India was not the 'subject' of Jammu and Kashmir, therefore, he cannot purchase land there.

Princes have gone, the crowns of Maharajas have been thrown away, but in Jammu and Kashmir the talk of ruler and subject still goes on. On the basis of separate citizenship the so-called subjects of that State get facilities that the rest of our countrymen are deprived of.

Why this Discrimination ?

When the Constitution was being framed and article 370 was under discussion, what was said in the Constitutent Assembly at that time requires reiteration in brief. I would like to invite your kind attention as well as that of the House to the fact that article 370 is provided under the "temporary and transitional provisions." A part of our Constitution relates to temporary and transitional provisions and article 370 comes under that. It is, therefore, evident that this article is temporary and transitional. It cannot become a permanent part of the Indian Constitution.

When Dr. N. Gopalaswami Ayyangar was speaking on article 370 Maulana Hasrat Mohani asked why this discrimination against Jammu and Kashmir. I agree with his point that article 370 constitutes a discrimination against Jammu and Kashmir. I would like to quote Dr. Gopalaswami Ayyangar's reply :

> "This discrimination against Kashmir has arisen due to its special position. This particular State was not prepared for such treatment. All of us hope here that Jammu and Kashmir would also slowly become eligible for such treatment as has been provided in the case of other States."

Dr. Ayyangar's Announcement

When Dr. Ayyangar announced that in due course Kashmir State would also accede in the same manner as other princely States the Constituent Assembly reverberated with the sound of clappings. The Constitutent Assembly wanted to keep article 370 a temporary provision and to declare it infructuous at the earliest opportunity.

On November 27, 1963 in reply to a question by my friend Shri Shastri, Shri Nehru had said—I quote :

> "Our opinion is that Article 370 is transitional, *i.e.* temporary, as provided."

He again repeated it in English at the request of another member. I quote him again :

> "This House should remember that article 370 is a transitional regional arrangement. This does not form a permanent part of the Constitution. It would continue as its part so long as it is there."

Our former Minister of External Affairs, Shri Chagla, after presenting our case about Kashmir very firmly, ably and in a scholarly manner before the United Nations had stated that under the circumstances there was no place left for article 370, and it must be abrogated.

The present Chief Minister of Jammu and Kashmir, Shri Sadiq too has been in favour of abolition of article 370. On November 28, 1963 he said in a statement that a wall has been erected between Jammu and Kashmir and the rest of India due to article 370. He had also stated that in order to realise full integration it was necessary to remove this wall. Even after becoming Chief Minister, while speaking at the meeting of the Congress Parliamentary Party on March 1 and May 1 and May 20, Shri Sadiq had expressed his opinion in favour of abrogation of article 370.

The former Chief Minister of Jammu and Kashmir, Bakshi Ghulam Mohammed, who is present in the House, has already spoken in favour of abrogation of article 370. I do not know what he would say today.

SHRI GHULAM MOHAMMED BAKSHI : Same that I have said earlier.

SHRI BHATTACHARYA : Bakshi Saheb speaks with one voice.

SHRI VAJPAYEE : Several people have changed, but a change in somebody, a change in the opinion of someone cannot change the process of history. Neither could the intentions of the framers of the Constitution be changed, nor could the needle of the clock be turned back.

Strange Article

Some strange things have been provided in article 370. The first is :

> "The provisions of article 238 would not apply to Jammu and Kashmir."

Today nobody knows about article 238. It related to B category States. Those States were abolished and with them article 238 also came to an end. Again, article 370 refers to 'Dominion of India'. India is no more a Dominion. India has become a Republic. Article 370 also refers to Maharajas of Kashmir. But now there is no Maharaja in Kashmir. There is a Governor there like other states. Thus in all these matters this article has become ineffective and infructuous.

Article 370 itself provides the procedure for its abrogation. The framers have laid down in this connection—I quote :

> ".....The President may, by public notification, declare that this article shall cease to be operative or shall be operative only with such exceptions and modifications and from such date as he may specify."

Article 370 empowers the President to declare by an order that this article will not apply or apply only in a few cases.

It is right that as per provisions of the Constitution it should be done in consultation with the State Government. The Government is responsible to the Legislature of Jammu and Kashmir and its consent would be necessary for this change.

My only objective in bringing this resolution is that this House may express its intention, its desire and declare by an order of the President that the time has now come to make article 370 infructuous.

The President has issued many orders under this article, by which Jammu and Kashmir has come closer to the rest of India in administrative, economic matters, etc. The jurisdiction of the Supreme Court now extends to Jammu and Kashmir and the Election Commission of India supervises the elections there. Economic integration has been brought about. Thus several developments have taken place in the direction of full integration. These are good things and we welcome them. But my submission is that the time has now come to do it in one go, at one stroke.

Psychological Barrier

A psychological barrier stands between Jammu and Kashmir and the rest of India today. This barrier creates a situation of uncertainty in Jammu and Kashmir. This barrier strengthens the anti-Indian elements. This barrier constitutes an obstacle in the way of integration. It is time now to remove this psychological obstacle so that Jammu and Kashmir may occupy its respectful and equal place in the Republic of India like other States.

I am unable to understand why so much stress is being laid on maintaining the special status of Jammu and Kashmir. The conditions under which a special status was mooted for Jammu and Kashmir exist no more. A Constitutent Assembly for Jammu and Kashmir was constituted which took a final decision to merge Jammu and Kashmir with India. If a particular person was not present in that Constituent Assembly the decision of that Assembly cannot be changed. Once Jammu and Kashmir became a part of India it must be brought at par with other States in the country.

Special Status Antithesis of Equality

But it is being said that the special status of Jammu and Kashmir must be maintained. Do those who say so not exhibit communalism ? Why should the special status of Jammu and Kashmir be maintained ? Why should it not be brought on par with other States ? The very same people who complain that they have become second class citizens in India also talk of maintaining the special status of Jammu and Kashmir. We want that all must have equal status, must enjoy equal rights, must have equal freedom and equal opportunities. Equality and special status cannot go together.

A few days back a Conference was held in Srinagar. In that Conference contradictory statements were made. But it is argued that one good outcome of that Conference is that it became clear that the issue of Jammu and Kashmir would be resolved within the Indian Union. Does that mean that the issue of Jammu and Kashmir could have been resolved by taking it out of the Indian Union ? Will this House and this Government permit it ? Nobody can take

Jammu and Kashmir out of India, and the Government which shows any slackness in this matter will not be able to stand the wrath of public opinion.

The question is, do we want to reverse the constitutional process that has already undergone with regard to Jammu and Kashmir ? Do we want to go back to 1953 ? Do we want to continue this discrimination and partisanship in the name of special status ? My submission is that such a demand is anti-national. This is an affront to democracy. I cannot understand how those who are raising slogans against communalism could advocate special status for Jammu and Kashmir, because by maintaining special status only communalism develops. Moreover, it causes discrimination against the people of Jammu and Kashmir.

Explosive Situation

What is the situation today in Jammu and Kashmir ? The internal situation in the State is explosive. There is a lull before the storm. The Pakistani infiltrators are active in the valley. A few days back an attempt was made to loot the rifles of N.C.C. A section of youth is becoming restive. The teachers who have gone there from Aligarh are imparting education that nurtures separatist tendencies. Pro-Pakistani elements are openly inciting the people. Pictures of President Ayub Khan could be seen at every place. At times lorries carrying our Army Jawans are stoned. The Jawans are insulted. Looking at the difficult conditions in which our Jawans are working there, they deserve our appreciation. They are performing their duty towards the nation patiently in spite of provocation.

I want to give some instances about the law and order situation prevailing there. In 1965, during the Pakistani attack, some local people and Pakistani infiltrators had attacked a well-known post in Udhampur district, killing 13 Jawans of the Punjab Police. Several people were arrested. Some of them were prosecuted. But nobody could be convicted. The blood of the Jawans of Punjab Police is calling even today. But nobody is there to listen.

During the last five years there have been cases of arson at 200 places in Jammu and Kashmir. A loss of ten crores of rupees has been caused as a result of it. Nobody knows who the arsonists are. The Government has failed to trace them.

During the Arab-Israel conflict two churches were burnt down in Srinagar, property worth lakhs was looted. But nobody was punished.

During the movement by Kashmiri pandits people were killed, injured, houses were set on fire. But nobody could be punished.

We read reports every day about the arrests of spies and fifth columnists. Just now we have learnt that a big gang of spies has been busted. But instead of prosecuting them they are kept under detention in jails and during detention they are treated like political leaders.

Infiltrators Become Legislators

Is it not surprising that an officer who had helped Pakistani infiltrators during 1965 has now become a member of the State Legislature ? This officer was previously posted as Block Development Officer in Poonch. When Pakistan attacked, he disappeared and when Pakistan constituted a Revolutionary Council he became its member. When our troops drove away the Pakistanis this gentleman reappeared on the scene. He was redrafted into service. The Special Commissioner had complained against him. Investigations were on. But the State Government withdrew the case. And after six months he became a member of the State Legislature. The man who had gone with the Pakistanis, who was a member of the Revolutionary Council set up by Pakistan, is now a member of the State Legislature.

In 1965, 75,000 people had left for Pakistan. They are now coming back. Some people are coming after getting training in guerilla warfare. At that time Nandaji was Minister of Home Affairs and Shri Chavan was Defence Minister. They had stated at that time that all those who had gone to Pakistan would not be allowed to return indiscriminately. They will be screened so that undesirable elements may not enter India and endanger our security. But there are no arrangements for screening. The arrangements that exist are being misused against patriotic people. Those who had migrated to Pakistan are returning again.

Rewarding Those who Helped Pakistan

It is surprising that the citizens of Jammu and Kashmir who were looted and harassed by Pakistanis are being given assistance of Rs.120 only per family by the government while those who had migrated to Pakistan but are now returning are being paid Rs. 600 per family.

Rewarding those who helped Pakistan and ignoring those who remained faithful to India—how long will such things go on without recognising who is a friend and who is a foe ? Can we strengthen the security of Jammu and Kashmir in this manner ? Can pro-India elements in the valley feel encouraged by this ?

Mr. Chairman, Sir, the economic situation in the State was causing much concern. So far the State has received from the Centre more than Rs.300 crores as grants, loan and as financial assistance. Today the situation is that the State is neither in a position to pay any instalments towards repayment of the debt nor in a position to pay the interest on the loan. The State's contribution to the Five Year Plans is going down continuously. In the course of the First Five Year Plan Jammu and Kashmir had contributed 27 per cent of its share. During the Second Five Year Plan its share came down to 12 per cent, and it plummeted to a meagre 6 per cent in the Third Plan. The State's Fourth Five Year Plan is proposed to be of Rs. 225 crores. But the State of Jammu and Kashmir says that it cannot make any contribution to it. The entire amount has to be met by New Delhi.

Jammu and Kashmir is a part of India. Nobody, therefore, minds spending money there. We have shed our sweat and blood in defending Jammu and Kashmir. We are also spending money for Jammu and Kashmir and in future too we will be spending money there. But who will check that the money being spent in Jammu and Kashmir is spent properly ? Does Parliament have no right to exercise a check over the amount spent by the Centre ? What is the hitch in exercising such a check ? If there is any hitch it should be removed. We should get an opportunity to examine whether the amount paid by us is being properly spent or not.

Corrupt and Weak Administration

Mr. Speaker, Sir, there is need to have a strong, capable and clean administration in this State which is facing a two-pronged attack. But its present administration is weak, lethargic and corrupt. Appointments in the Government are not made on the basis of merit but on the basis of political, communal and regional considerations. Posts are not created to fulfil the needs of the administration, but to provide jobs to the rulers' close relatives.

Mr. Speaker, Sir, you will be surprised to know that the total number of tehsils in Jammu and Kashmir State is 32, but the number of Tehsildars is about 75 and that of Naib Tehsildars 100 ! I am unable to understand what so many Tehsildars do ! It is said that two swords cannot remain in one scabbard, and you can easily imagine how two Tehsildars will be working in one Tehsil in Jammu and Kashmir.

The total income of the State is Rs. 16 crores, but Rs. 20 crores are being spent on salaries of employees alone ! In 1947 there were 10,000 employees, but in 1963-64 their number increased to 66,000 and in 1967-68 to 91,000. The entire income of the State is spent on salaries. Wherefrom would money come for the development of the State ? We will have to make arrangements to ensure that at least the money which we are giving is spent properly.

Recently an instance has come to light showing how appointments are made. A professor has been appointed in the Medical College in the grade of Rs.1000-1500. The claim of the senior professor has been rejected. So far no professor was recruited directly there. They were promoted from assistant professors. But a gentleman alighted from a plane at the airport on September 29, 1968. He was a relative of a big leader of the State. He was appointed professor. And it is surprising that this gentleman had gone abroad to study medicine at State expenses, but he did not come back straight to India. He first went to Pakistan, tried to get a job there for full one year, but having failed to get a job in Pakistan he came to Srinagar where he was straightaway appointed a professor.

The assistant professor's claim was overlooked. Can such methods help in raising the morale of the employees and officials ? Will it make them more dutiful ? If there is no justice nobody would like to do his job properly.

Mr. Speaker, Sir, recently our President has recruited 25 officers to I.A.S. and I.P.S. at the recommendation of the State Government. But at the time of selection of the officers neither their merit nor their qualifications were taken into account. Even seniority was not counted in the appointments. There is one officer among them who was an accused in the Kashmir Conspiracy Case, but now he has become an I.A.S. officer.

Some of the I.A.S. officers are not even graduates. I know of at least two who are only matriculates. If no degree is required now for I.A.S. I would welcome it, but non-requirement of a degree must not apply only to Kashmir. If degrees are required throughout the country, but in Kashmir matriculates are made I.A.S. officers nobody can support it. I await to see the ingenuity with which the Home Minister would defend it.

Concrete Suggestions

Mr. Speaker, Sir, now I want to conclude my speech. My demand is that the President should declare article 370 infructuous by using the powers under the same article with the consent of the State Government. This could be done by an order of the President, but it is a matter of regret that it has not been done so far. This must be done now. It is high time this was done. There is need to bring a psychological change in the State, and the process for this change should commence from New Delhi. The President can initiate action in the matter.

Secondly, the Constitution of India should apply to Kashmir *in toto*. Jammu and Kashmir is an integral part of India and we cannot discriminate against it, we cannot deprive the people of Jammu and Kashmir of the fundamental rights provided in the Indian Constitution, nor from the dignity and pride of being an Indian citizen. In order to provide equal rights to those people it is essential to remove this psychological barrier and to apply the Indian Constitution there *in toto*.

My third demand is that an All-Party Committee should be constituted to examine how the money provided by the Centre so far to Jammu and Kashmir has been spent. This examination is also necessary so that the amount to be granted in future may be spent on industrial as well as the economic development of the State.

My fourth demand is that the government should make an unequivocal announcement that until Sheikh Abdullah and his colleagues call themselves Indian citizens, until they accept Jammu and Kashmir as an integral and inalienable part of the Indian Union, and until they declare Pakistan an aggressor no negotiations of any kind should be held with them.

My fifth demand is that the policy of discrimination against Jammu and Ladakh, the policy that is being pursued in spite of the Gajendragadkar Commission that looked into it, must end. The interests of Jammu and Ladakh should not be ignored in employment, economic planning and industrial development.

Some people are raising the slogan of autonomy for Jammu. We regarded this slogan as dangerous. A demand for reorganisation of Jammu and Kashmir on the basis of language could be made. Those who reorganised Punjab on the basis of language cannot stop that process from moving further to Jammu and Kashmir. But in my opinion as well as in the opinion of my party to talk about reorganisation of Jammu and Kashmir on the basis of language at this juncture would be inviting danger to national interest. But if justice is not meted out to Jammu and Ladakh regionalism would get encouragement.

It is also essential to make an attempt for planned industrial development of Jammu and Kashmir. No central project has been undertaken there so far. Jammu and Kashmir is a part of India for the last 20 years. We have given Rs. 300 crores to Jammu and Kashmir but no Central project has been undertaken there. It has been in the air for the last so many days that a telephone factory is likely to be set up there. We want to know how long will this take. What would be its cost and how many people would be provided jobs in it. An attempt should be made through a planned policy to promote handicrafts and cottage industries in Jammu and Kashmir. Youths are coming out after completing their education. When they remain unemployed they could be easily incited. There is need to provide them with opportunities for work.

We have passed the Unlawful Activities Act. Now nobody can talk about secession of any part of India. Any organisation which talks in that strain can be declared unlawful. I am unable to understand why this law has not been made applicable so far to Jammu and Kashmir. Those who live in this country but want secession of some part of it are guilty under the law and should be treated as such.

Complaint by Sheikh

Mr. Speaker, Sir, when Sheikh Abdullah visited Delhi he took the trouble to see me. He complaind that Indian democracy extends upto the Madhavpur post, at the most upto the Banihal Pass, but it has not reached the Kashmir Valley. I replied to him what I thought was appropriate.

SHRI Y.B. CHAVAN, Minister of Home Affairs : What was your reply ?

SHRI VAJPAYEE : I told him, Sheikh Saheb, when you were at the helm of affairs democracy could not even cross the post of Madhavpur. At that time a permit was required to enter Madhavpur. I agree with you that Indian democracy must reach the Kashmir Valley. Citizens should have fundamental rights. Freedom of the citizens must not be curtailed. Nobodoy should try to suppress genuine differences. It is essential that those parties that are working in India should work in Jammu and Kashmir too.

But today the situation is such that section 144 is always in force there. Pro-Pakistani elements have full freedom to play their games, but parties having loyalty to India cannot work there. It is true that after the charge was taken over by Mr. Sadiq there is some improvement in the situation, but it has improved only to some extent and there is need to bring about a change in that situation.

The people of Jammu and Kashmir should understand that on the one hand there is the Indian Republic, where there is freedom of speech, freedom of writing and freedom of association, where the Government could be changed peacefully, where you can experience the pride and joy of being a partner in the development of a great nation and on the other side there is Pakistan where in the name of basic democracy, freedom of the people has been strangulated, where the place for leaders of the opposition parties is not in Parliament but in jail.

The people of Jammu and Kashmir should understand this difference between India and Pakistan and it is our duty to make them understand this difference. I know that the Muslims of Jammu and Kashmir do not want to go to Pakistan, except a handful of them, but there is a section among them that wants to keep the bogey of Pakistan alive. We have to remove this bogey and convince the people of Jammu and Kashmir that they are equal partners in the Republic of India.

But to achieve this all discriminatory barriers must be removed. All elements dividing us psychologically must be brought to an end. Therefore, I have demanded abrogation of article 370 through my resolution so that Jammu and Kashmir may not only remain an integral part of India constitutionally, which it is today, but its people may also enjoy their rights as citizens of India and perform their duty. I am confident that the House would support my resolution and the government would also get an opportunity to express its views in this regard. Thank you.

Article 370 Discriminates Kashmiris

Mr. Speaker, Sir, I am grateful to the House for showing interest in my Resolution which makes a suggestion for abrogation of article 370 of the Constitution. But that is not the only demand made in the Resolution. I would like to read out a portion of it :

> ".....this State should be fully brought at par with the other States of India and for this purpose the House recommends that all necessary steps such as abrogation of article 370 be initiated forthwith."

However, the entire debate has centred around article 370. From one point of view this is good. Repeated discussions about it help this House and the country to make up their mind. From that point of view this discussion should be welcome.

I am amazed to listen to certain speeches during the discussion. This is not the first time when a plea has been made in the House for the abrogation of article 370. My friend Shri Prakash Vir Shastri had presented a Bill before this House in 1964 with the same objective. I have moved only a Resolution in the form of a recommendation. Had his Bill been adopted it would have been mandatory. Speaking on that Bill my friend Shri S.M. Banerjee, who is not present in the House, had said that article 370 should be abrogated. Shri Sarju Pandey had also spoken on it. I want to quote from Shri Pandey's speech :

> "Therefore I want to say that if you want to do something about Kashmir, then today the right type of Resolution has come. It should have come much earlier, but let it be done now."

This is from the speech of Shri Sarju Pandey delivered in 1964.

I also want to quote the words of Shri Bannerji :

> "Even after so many years no reason has been given in the House about not abrogating article 370."

Professor Mukherji is not present in the House at the moment. It is a pleasure to listen to his speech. He is a learned man. But today I was surprised and felt sorry to listen to his speech. It appears that the policy of the Communist Party has changed. Was the change brought about as a result of change in the policy of the Soviet Union ? If it is consequent upon that change the House must ponder over it seriously.

What was right in 1964 cannot become wrong in 1968. If it was justified, essential and in the wider interest of the country and Jammu and Kashmir to abrogate article 370 in 1964 it could not be said today that article 370 should not be abrogated. Dr. Lohia had voted in favour of Shri Prakash Vir Shastri's Bill and Shri Madhu Limaye had also voted in its favour. I am reminding my

---

Lok Sabha on December 6, 1968 while replying to the discussion on his Resolution seeking abrogation of article 370 of the Constitution

friend Shri S.M. Joshi about this. He has said that he agrees with the spirit of my Resolution, but the work of national integration is very difficult, we will have to do it slowly.

There can be no Limited Secession

My submission is that the work of national integration is a continuous process. This involves winning the hearts and minds of the people. And my objective in bringing this Resolution is the same—that article 370, which creates doubts in the minds of the people, must be made infructuous. On the one hand, there is the special status of the State, and on the other this article discriminates against the people of that State.

I want to warn those people who are in favour of limited accession of Jammu and Kashmir to India that the people of Jammu and Kashmir would not like limited accession. They do not want to forego their right to approach the Supreme Court. They would like free and fair conduct of elections. If the citizens of Jammu and Kashmir do not get the rights which are enjoyed by every citizen of India they would resent it and raise their voice against it.

I am indebted to Bakshi Saheb who has referred to me the case of a Government employee there. I want to ask, can such a thing happen in any other State of India ? If an employee does the work of the Employees' Association would he be given notice ? There is one Shri Abdul Hamid Afridi, Deputy Excise Commissioner, who says :

> "It has come to my notice that you are playing an active role in the activities of the Low Income Group Employees' Federation. A strict watch was being kept on your activities as a result of which the undersigned and myself have come to the conclusion that you hardly pay any attention and time to Governmental work, because you are more inclined to these activities. Some of my colleagues have informed me that they have seen you pasting posters of the said Federation on the walls of houses and shops."

Do the employees of Jammu and Kashmir have no right to form associations ? Has action to be taken against them for this ?

SHRI NAMBIAR : They are doing this work here. They are doing this here for the employees of the Central Government. Its counterpart is there. They are like brother and sister... (*Interruptions*).

House Empowered to Recommend Deletion of Article 370

SHRI VAJPAYEE : The situation is bad here, but not that bad. Even the Minister of Home Affairs would not support that if somebody is seen pasting posters he should be served with a notice. The employees of Jammu and Kashmir should not be treated in this manner. It is necessary to take some steps with a view to stopping such activities and for that I had made the suggestion that article 370 be abrogated. The President can do it by issuing an order. I admit this should be done with the consent of the State Government. But this House can make its recommendation, can express its opinion that the time has now come to abrogate article 370, which was a transitional and temporary provision of the Constitution. I regret to say that the Minister of Home Affairs wants to put off the entire question by describing this article as a bridge. Perhaps he has not understood the intention of the framers of the Constitution. If article 370 would be considered a bridge between Kashmir and India... (*Interruptions*).

SHRI Y.B. CHAVAN : I have not said that this is a bridge between Kashmir and India. I had said this constituted a bridge on the basis of which several articles of the Constitution were applied one after the other—a constitutional bridge for Jammu and Kashmir.

SHRI VAJPAYEE : The intention of the framers of the Constitution was quite clear—that article 370 was for some time only. Pandit Nehru had said that this article would erode itself. Does this mean that it would continue to exist ? You can say that the time has not yet come to rescind it completely, but it is unimaginable that article 370, which is a temporary provision, could be made permanent.

SHRI Y.B. CHAVAN : Nobody has done so.

SHRI VAJPAYEE : And it should not be done also. Now it is said that the same situation continues as was prevalent when the Constitution was framed. One-third portion of Jammu and Kashmir continues to be under the occupation of Pakistan. The case of Kashmir was under consideration of the Security Council. If this situation did not change and in the meanwhile we abrogate article 370, Pakistan will make a hue and cry.

Appeasement of Pakistan

I want to ask, are we continuing with this article 370 for appeasement of Pakistan ? It makes a hue and cry whenever you extend a new law there. Pakistan will always shout, but if the caravan of India's national integrity stops at Pakistan's shouting that would be the most unfortunate day for India. We cannot accept Pakistan as a party in the matter of Jammu and Kashmir.

My submission is that today this case is before the Security Council. Pakistan is trying to open it afresh and it is, therefore, essential to remove that psychological barrier which divides the people of Kashmir from us. Had the case of Kashmir not been before the Security Council, had Pakistan not made repeated attempts to raise that issue again and again, had some international powers not shown their unintelligent inclination to pat Pakistan in this case, perhaps there would have been no need to raise this demand. The case is before the Security Council and Pakistan has been making mischief creating a situation of uncertainty. To meet that situation we can take a step of abrogating article 370.

I shall finish after making one more point. Now Kashmir is no more a princely State. The Maharaja of Kashmir is present in this House to serve the Republic of India after being elected by the votes of the people. Nobody wants to bring monarchy to Kashmir again. Zamindari has been abolished in Kashmir and nobody wants to reestablish it there. So far as the question of purchase of land is concerned whether the restriction on this is reasonable or not is a different question. But, for that article 370 is not necessary.

Outsiders cannot purchase land in Arunachal. There is ban on the purchase of land belonging to tribals in Chhota Nagpur. But the Constitution of India need not be distorted for that as the work can be done by a Deputy Commissioner. We do not want that the people may go in very large numbers to purchase land in Jammu and Kashmir. But if there is fear of land being purchased arrangements could be made in that regard. The continuance of article 370 should not be supported on that ground.

No Two-Nation or Three-Nation Theory

It is a basic fact that the people of Kashmir have merged with us of their own free will. I am prepared to welcome Sheikh Abdullah who stood up against the two-nation theory of Qaid-e-Azam Jinnah. But sometimes I feel that a three-nation theory is now being propounded in Kashmir. He had fought the two-nation theory, but today he is describing Kashmir as a separate nation. My submission is that Kashmir cannot be a separate nation.

Do you know that so far as the purchase of land is concerned even people belonging to Jammu are not allowed to purchase land in the Kashmir Valley ? I have a name with me, that of Dr. J.R. Sethi. He is an eye specialist. He wanted to live in Kashmir after constructing his house. He asked for allotment of land for that purpose, but it was refused. He was allotted land in Jammu.... (*Interruptions*).

SHRI GHULAM MOHAMMED BAKSHI : Vajpayeeji, this is wrong.

SHRI VAJPAYEE : This is a fact. Apart from this I would like to draw the attention of the House to the fact that twenty thousand refugees had entered Jammu in 1947 from West Punjab. Please note that twenty thousand refugees had gone to Jammu from West Pakistan and settled there, but even today they have no franchise. Our own poeple have been made stateless in their own country. Indian citizens who were expelled from Pakistan, and are now settled in Jammu and Kashmir cannot cast their votes in elections. If you want to support this situation we will not tolerate it.

When Pakistan captured Muzaffarabad, twenty thousand Hindus, including Sikhs, were forced to leave their homes. The Hindus of Muzaffarabad reached Srinagar. Muzaffarabad was a part of Kashmir Province. The people from Muzaffarabad came to Srinagar, but they were not allowed to settle in Srinagar and were pushed to Jammu. We are not putting forth a communal demand. Communal behaviour is being shown in Jammu and Kashmir. Our officers who go to Jammu and Kashmir on official duty, officers who are appointed by the Minister of Home Affairs cannot cast their votes there. Their names cannot be included in the voters' list there. How long will this situation continue ? The question is not that of purchase of land, the question is of dismantling the walls of discrimination, to remove the psychological barriers that have been created. I admit this cannot be accomplished through passing of law alone, but sometimes the need to put the seal of law also arises..... (*Interruptions*).

SHRI ABDUL GHANI DAR : Army and police cannot rule the State.

SHRI VAJPAYEE : Nobody wants to rule by Army and Police. But those who praise Pakistan while living in India and who want to cede a portion of India to Pakistan would not be tolerated and if need be they would have to be dealt with with the help of Army and Police as well. After all why do we maintain the Army and the Police ?

Objective of Resolution

Mr. Speaker, Sir, my only objective in bringing this Resolution was to make up the mind of the House, to make up the mind of the country, and to bring the problems of Jammu and Kashmir before this House. The Minister of Home Affairs is very clever. He avoided many questions so cleverly. The people of Jammu and Kashmir want a clean, honest and strong administration. We put Sheikh Abdullah at the helm of affairs earlier. Today Sheikh Abdullah is not there. After him came Bakshi Ghulam Mohammed, but now he is an Hon'ble Member of this House. After Bakshi Saheb Sadiq became the Chief Minister of Jammu and Kashmir. I want to ask why this change is occurring so often ? One comes, another goes away; after all, why this confusion there ?

SHRI CHAVAN : It is happening everywhere.

SHRI VAJPAYEE : There is a difference. We have to understand this difference. It is happening everywhere, but when there is a change in the Chief Minister at other places it does not become an international issue. When Chief Ministers assume charge at other places Pakistan does not get a handle to malign India. If there is a change in the Chief Ministers at other places it does not create uncertainity in the minds of the people. Therefore, New Delhi will have to ponder over it seriously and do something to provide an honest and good administration in order to stabilise the situation in Jammu and Kashmir and to fully satisfy those people who have thrown their lot with India so that they may lead their lives with dignity and equality in a democratic India.

Several Hon'ble members have appealed to me not to insist on voting on this Resolution. I bow to the good wishes of the House and seek your permission to withdraw the Resolution. Thank you.

Abrogate Article 370

Sir, I beg to move that

> "The Bill further to amend the Constitution of India be taken into consideration."

Mr. Chairman, Sir, I have moved this Bill to amend article 370 of the Constitution. Bills to this effect have been moved in every Lok Sabha. If you glance through the Constitution of India you will find that article 370 has been included in that part of the Constitution which has been called by the framers of the Constitution as 'temporary and transitional'. Part XXI of the Constitution is temporary and transitional. From the title itself it is clear that the articles and clauses under this Part were included in the Constitution due to some special circumstances and the framers of the Constitution wanted that these provisions should not become permanent parts of the Constitution.

I remember when this article was being discussed in the Constitutent Assembly Maulana Hasrat Mohani had asked why Jammu and Kashmir was being discriminated against by including article 370. Of course, this article does not give any special concession to Jammu and Kashmir. But it discriminates against the citizens of that State. It does not allow them to come on par with the citizens of the rest of the country and that is why Maulana Hasrat Mohani had asked why this discrimination against Jammu and Kashmir. I want to quote from the reply given by Dr. Gopalaswami Ayyangar. He stated:

> "This discrimination is due to the special conditions in Kashmir. That particular State is not to yet ripe for this kind of intervention. It is the hope of everybody here that, in due course, even Jammu and Kashmir will become ready for the same sort of integration as has taken place in the case of other States."

Those Hon'ble members who were members of the old Lok Sabha might recall that whenever the question of abrogation of article 370 was raised during the time of Pandit Jawaharlal Nehru he also used to say that with the passage of time this article would also vanish. He also stated that this article was temporary. I remember he had once said that this would gradually erode. Pandit Nehru was clear is his mind that article 370 would not remain a part of our Constitution permanently. But 21 years have passed since the Constitution was adopted, and this article is still there. If you look at this article you will find how unnecessary and useless this article has become. I quote :

Lok Sabha on November 19, 1971 while moving the Constitution (Amendment) Bill seeking deletion of article 370 from the Constitution

"Notwithstanding anything in this Constitution,

(a) the provisions of article 238 shall not apply in relation to the State of Jammu and Kashmir."

Article 238 is now no more in the Constitution. That Article has been dropped, because it related to class 'B' States. 'B' class States have disappeared from our map. They have no existence in the Constitution any more, nor is article 238 found in the Constitution now.

But this reference to Article 238 still continues in article 370. It is further stated in article 370 that :

"(b) the power of Parliament to make laws for the said State shall be limited to :

(1) those matters in the Union List and the Concurrent List which, in consultation with the Government of the State, are declared by the President to correspond to matters specified in the Instrument of Accession governing the accession of the State to the Dominion of India as the matters with respect to which the Dominion Legislature may make laws for that State."

At that time India was referred to as a Dominion. Now our country is fully independent. Today India is not a Dominion, but in article 370 the reference to Dominion continues. In this article there is a mention of Maharaja of Kashmir while royalty has been abolished in Kashmir. Previously there was a Sadar-e-Riyasat, but now there is a Governor like in other States. But if any student looks into this article in the Constitution of India he would be unable to understand why it still continues.

Now a question could be asked as to why this insistence on removing this article. The first and foremost reason is that this article stands like a psychological barrier between Jammu and Kashmir and the rest of India. Why should a particular State have a special status ? On the one hand, we say that Jammu and Kashmir is an integral part of India and there can be no two opinions about it, but on the other we have given it a special status. There is a Union List in the Constitution. This House can make laws about the subjects given under the Union List. But this is not the position with regard to Jammu and Kashmir. Recently we have passed the Twenty-Fourth Amendment to the Constitution and that amendment was supported on the ground that it established the supremacy of this House. It was stated that this House is supreme, that this House is even above the Supreme Court. But so far as the question of Jammu and Kashmir is concerned this House is not above the Legislature of Jammu and Kashmir. Why this contradiction ? That is the reason why I have brought this amendment. It is now time to make it clear that so far as the question of subjects given in the Union List is concerned there would be no need to consult the Government of Jammu and Kashmir while framing laws about these subjects.

I do not know why such an amendment is not being brought forward from the Government side. It is true that there has been a change in the situation since the Constitution was framed : Jammu and Kashmir has come closer to the rest of India; the Auditor-General can audit the accounts there; the

Election Commission's authority has been extended to the Jammu and Kashmir State; and several other social welfare measures are being applied to Jammu and Kashmir. But in spite of that the fact cannot be forgotten that article 370, which was a temporary and transitional provision, still remains in the Constitution and it has become a cause of separation of Jammu and Kashmir from the rest of India. It is also provided in article 370 that if any law has to be enforced in Jammu and Kashmir it would be done in consultation with the Legislature of that State. The Constituent Assembly was formed later. It decided in favour of a merger with India. That was the decision of the people, which is irrevocable. Jammu and Kashmir is an integral part of India. But no change has been effected in article 370. I want that this change should be brought about. This process of change should have been initiated by providing that we are giving full authority to Lok Sabha to enact laws in this House regarding subjects included under the Union List.

The Psychological Barrier

I had spoken of a psychological barrier. This barrier is not only psychological but to some extent physical as well. No citizen of India can purchase land in Jammu and Kashmir. Our President too had to face a lot of difficulty when he required land for a post office, because in Jammu and Kashmir only its 'subjects' are allowed to purchase land there. The word subject still continues to be used. Royalty has been abolished, but subjects continue. Whose subjects ? Jammu and Kashmir is a part of the Indian Republic. But an old tradition continues, words and phrases are being repeated. Instead of removing the barrier it is being strengthened. It is being supported on the ground that if others are given the right to purchase land there the capitalists of India would go and purchase the entire land of Jammu and Kashmir. What a ridiculous idea ! Article 370 is not necessary in the Constitution for this purpose. The purchase of land could be banned. I am talking of the Union List. The other matters would be left for the State Government. It can pass legislation and the right to purchase land or its denial would be under the jurisdiction of the State Government. However, I am of the opinion that every citizen of India should have the right to settle down, purchase land and start his or her business in any part of India. This is essential for emotional integration.

There is also an economic aspect about Jammu and Kashmir. We find that the industrial development of the State has not been as it should be. The enormous amount of money given to the State Government has also not been spent properly. The Central Government could not set up big projects in Jammu and Kashmir. It is now heard that a telephone factory is going to be set up in Srinagar at a cost of one or two lakh rupees. Education is free there. The youth are studying and coming out of the universities. They require employment. Industrialisation is necessary to create employment. If capital and other resources are not available in the State capital could be invested there from India. Today nobody is prepared to invest money there. There are obstacles. Article 370 obstructs it.

Economic Development Vital

The pace of industrial development is not as fast as it should have been. Therefore, there is discontent among the educated section of the society and demonstrations are held from place to place. But anti-national elements take advantage of this discontent in Jammu and Kashmir. We should not forget that. If students go on strike, fight for their reasonable demands, or ask for employment the neighbouring Pakistan presents the issue in an anti-India manner. It presents every issue in an anti-India way. These problems exist in other parts of the country as well, but we will have to pay special attention to Jammu and Kashmir. We will have to accelerate the pace of economic development there. Power generation could be accelerated. There are certain aspects which could have been looked into by the Central Government, but it did not pay attention to it. I do not want to go into all that and this is also not the subject-matter of my Bill. All that I am saying is that so far as Jammu and Kashmir is concerned abrogation of article 370, which separates the rest of India from Jammu and Kashmir, must be considered seriously and the process must start now. I want to quote the amendment I have given notice of and what method I have suggested therein :

> "Notwithstanding anything in the Constitution the power of Parliament to make laws for the State of Jammu and Kashmir shall be limited to ....."

Limitation will be still there as before. But at present we cannot legislate without the concurrence of the Government of Jammu and Kashmir even about subjects given under the Union List. I want this to be abolished.

> (a) the **matter** in the Union List, and
>
> (b) such other matters in the Concurrent and State List which, with the concurrence of the State, the President may specify.
>
> *Explanation* : For the purpose of this article the Government of the State means the Governor of Jammu and Kashmir acting on the advice of the Council of Ministers of the State for the time being in office."

I have given one more amendment. For the present we may give authority to Parliament to legislate about the subjects under the Union List, but after January 26, 1972 article 370 should be abrogated; it should be made inoperative. The provision to make it inoperative has been made under this very article. I want to quote :

> "Notwithstanding anything in the foregoing provisions of this article, the President may, by public notification, declare that the article shall cease to be operative only with such exceptions and modifications and from such date as he may specify."

The President, if he so desires, may make the entire article inoperative. This would require the concurrence of the State Government of Jammu and Kashmir. But I do not think they will have any objection to giving their concurrence.

Today Jammu and Kashmir is facing a danger. The neighbouring country has an eye on it. It is quite possible that it may disturb the peace in the valley again by sending infiltrators. But the people of Jammu and Kashmir have full faith in the unflinching support of the entire people of India. The brave Jawans of our Army are ready to sacrifice their lives to protect Jammu and Kashmir. If our Jawans can sacrifice their lives for the sake of Jammu and Kashmir can't they have the right to purchase land there ?

If this Parliament can sanction an amount of more than three hundred crores rupees during the last twenty years for the development of Jammu and Kashmir can't it legislate for Jammu and Kashmir in regard to the subjects under the Union List ?

So far it was said that this case was pending before the United Nations Organisation. Pakistan goes on raising it off and on. We should not touch article 370, we should allow it to get eroded gradually. Now the position is that Pakistan has no right to speak on the question of Jammu and Kashmir. The people of Jammu and Kashmir are now aware what kind of treatment is being meted out by the military rulers of Pakistan to the inhabitants of East Bengal who have been in Pakistan since its inception, and a majority of whom are Muslims. I do not think that in view of this any sensible person in Jammu and Kashmir would like to say that he would prefer to be kicked under the boots of the Pakistani military dictatorship, leaving the status of equality prevailing in Indian democracy.

Withdraw Kashmir Issue from U.N.

Therefore it is essential that we should withdraw the question of Jammu and Kashmir from the United Nations Organisation. We should end whatever uncertainty remains about it. Pakistan has no claim over it. Pakistan is an aggressor in Jammu and Kashmir. The whole world knows what is the position of one-third of Kashmir occupied by Pakistan. In comparison to that Jammu and Kashmir forms a part of India in spite of so many shortcomings and uncertainties. It has made progress. There is democracy. The people have decided their own fate. Free and fair elections are held and their own representatives are running the administration there. Their representatives are also sitting in this Parliament. I think the time has come to abrogate article 370. Article 370 should be made inoperative from January 26 next and, before that, we should accept this amendment today providing that so far as the Union List is concerned this House will have the power to legislate about it.

I hope that this House would accept this Bill of mine and Chaudhary Saheb will also give a reply which would be to the liking of the Opposition. Thank you.

A Legacy Inherited

Mr. Speaker Sir, the clock has turned full circle. The wheel of time has brought such drastic changes that those who used to oppose introduction of adjournment motions before 25th June, 1975, are now placed in the position of introducing such motions while those who used to introduce them have become competent to successfully reply to these adjournment motions.

When Dr. Karan Singh was making his speech I was reminded of Karna of Mahabharat. During the battle, when the chariot of Karna got stuck in the earth, and an arrow started piercing his body he remembered *dharma*. He pleaded that to attack an unarmed person was against *dharma*. Arjun was in a fix for a while. But Lord Krishna, who was his charioteer said : "It does not become Karna to mention *dharma*. Where was his *dharma* when the Pandavas were deprived of their kingdom by defeating them in a gamble through treachery ? Where was *dharma* when Draupadi was disrobed in a full court ? Where was *dharma* when effort was made to burn the Pandavas alive in the house of lac" ? I want to ask Dr. Karan Singh, where was the democracy in the name of which he was speaking when the Congress Government at the Centre dismissed the duly elected DMK Government in Tamil Nadu, casting all principles aside and throwing the Constitution into a waste-paper basket ?

AN HON'BLE MEMBER : Do you want to do the same thing ?

SHRI VAJPAYEE : I am coming to that also. A mention was made during the debate ....

SHRI K. MAYATHEVAR : Sir, I rise on a point of order. The Hon. Minister of External Affairs here referred to the Tamil Nadu Government. I say that it was dismissed by the then Governor because of corruption charges.

MR. SPEAKER : There is no point of order. Will you please sit down ?

SHRI VAJPAYEE : Leave Tamil Nadu. Take Orissa. Well, when we talk of Kashmir, we can't help remembering Kanyakumari. After all, both are parts of India. What happened in Orissa ? In 1973 our friend Biju Patnaik got majority in the Legislative Assembly. The majority members were paraded before the Governor. But at the instance of the Centre the Governor did not give to the majority the opportunity to form the Government on the plea that it would not be stable. The Governor of Orissa took a decision in his discretion on the ground of stability. Can the Governor of Jammu and Kashmir not take a discretion ? Will there be different standards ?

Lok Sabha on March 29, 1977 as Minister of External Affairs while replying to the discussion on the adjournment motion regarding the situation in Jammu and Kashmir

Separate Constitution of J & K was Opposed

Sir, Jammu and Kashmir has a separate Constitution. According to it if the Governor is satisfied that the Government cannot be run in accordance with the provisions of the Constitution he can dissolve the Assembly. I want to clarify that in Jammu and Kashmir it is not President's Rule but Governor's Rue that is provided. This Constitution has been framed by those who are today finding in it a hurdle in their way. Our thinking is clear. When we were in the opposition we demanded that Jammu and Kashmir should not have a separate Constitution and that the Constitution of India should be made fully applicable there. Under the separate Constitution what is applicable to other States of India is not applicable to Jammu and Kashmir. Do our Congress friends now want to forget the special status of Kashmir ?

Sir, on 3rd March, 1975 when a discussion on an agreement with Sheikh Saheb took place this is what the then Prime Minister said :

> "This new political understanding is worthy of a person of Sheikh Abdulla's long record of service to the people and our cherished values. About 40 years ago Sheikh Abdulla became the foremost leader of the Kashmir people's fight against feudalism and he made his struggle a part of the larger national struggle for freedom and secularism".

He had showered more praises on Sheikh Saheb. But nobody at that time had thought about how many people were with Sheikh Abdulla. The whole State was then under the grip of his personality. When he was inclined towards the Congress party he was big, he was tall, he could carry everybody with him. When the Congress Party saw that Sheikh Abdulla was not prepared to toe their line the mistake of expressing no-confidence in him in the name of stability of the State was committed.

I want to ask, when elections were being held in the country, a new Government was to be installed, and the country was passing through a period of transition, why was the decision to withdraw confidence in Sheikh Abdulla taken ? There is a crooked move behind it. Efforts are being made to create disorder in Kashmir in order to put hurdles in the way of the new Government formed with the people's backing. When there was confidence in Sheikh Abdulla for so long, could not that confidence have remained for some more time ? (*Interruptions*).

Kashmir is a National Issue

I do not want to make a mention of the special status of Jammu and Kashmir in the Constitution, but you will agree that one-third of the State is under Pakistani occupation and UN observers are still present in the State. Everybody will agree that the question of Kashmir must not be looked at from party point of view. It is a national issue. Heavens would not have fallen if a decision about Jammu and Kashmir was taken in consultation with the new Government when it was formed. But that patience was not shown. Having been defeated in elections they started malicious moves. A situation has been created which can put the entire country in a difficult position. I want to appeal to the veteran leaders of the Congress Party, for God's sake do not do anything in Kashmir which may become a headache for us because you are more experienced, you claim to be more secular, you always put emphasis on being more nationalist. That headache will not be a headache for the Government, but for the entire country, and the people will never forgive the Congress Party for that.

Mr. Speaker, Sir, the only way to retrieve the situation is to go in for elections. Let the people of Jammu and Kashmir express their opinion in free and fair polls. The elections should be held as early as possible. But why do you hesitate to go to the people ? Shri Qureshi has said that no single individual is big enough. There is no doubt that after the people's decision there is no single big individual left now. Those days have now gone (*interruptions*). We have never supported the personality cult, nor ever will. We have never accepted any individual as a symbol of India and will never do so. You have done the right thing by moving an adjournment motion on the question of Jammu and Kashmir, but you should have the grace to respect the spirit in which our leader has admitted it. I want that senior leaders of the Congress Party and our party may sit together and not let a situation created in Kashmir which could be exploited by international vested interests. I am sure a spirit of doing some good to the country will awaken in the minds of our Congress friends.

SHRI MUHAMMED SHAFI QURESHI : You should have said this earlier—it was better to have consulted us before the Prime Minister gave his advice to the Governor.

SHRI VAJPAYEE : This situation would not have been created if our Congress friends had consulted us before withdrawing their confidence in Sheikh Abdulla. However, what had to happen has happened, I do not want to go into that. But for future I want to say that the policy of Kashmir should be decided jointly. Our Government will make efforts in that direction, but it has to be seen how far the Congress Party is prepared to come up after its defeat in the elections.

I want to make one point before concluding my speech. When I was in the opposition I was demanding abrogation of article 370. But we were criticised that we did not respect the sentiments of the people of Jammu and Kashmir. Today the same article 370 of the Constitution has become a reason for imposing Governor's rule over Kashmir. However I would like to make it clear that the new Government will not take any unilateral decision to make any changes in article 370; any decision will be taken after ascertaining the views of the people of Jammu and Kashmir. Thank you.

Distortion in U.N. Report

SHRI CHITTA BASU (Barasat) : Sir, I call the attention of the Minister of External Affairs to the following matter of urgent public importance and request that he may make a statement thereon :

> "Reported distortion of facts about Jammu and Kashmir appearing in a recent report of the U.N. Study Panel and the reaction of the Government thereto."

SHRI VAJPAYEE, Minister of External Affairs : Mr. Speaker, Sir, a Study by Mr. Hector Gros Espiell, Special Rapporteur, appointed in 1974 by the U.N. Sub-Commission on Prevention of Discrimination and Protection of Minorities, the final report on which was presented to the Sub-Commission in 1976, contains a list of 30 territories "still awaiting settlement as regards the implementation of United Nations resolutions concerning the right to self-determination of peoples under colonial or alien domination". Surprisingly, Jammu and Kashmir has also been included in this list.

When this Study came up for discussion at the 34th Session of the Commission of Human Rights, held in February-March this year, the leader of Indian Delegation, Shrimati Vijaya Laxmi Pandit, expressed strong reservation to it in the following words. I quote :

> "I must admit that my delegation was astonished to find that integral part of the sovereign Republic of India has been included in the list given in para 230 of the report. I wish to enter the strong reservation of my delegation in this connection."

Thereafter, our reservation was recorded as a footnote to the Study.

Subsequently, when this report was circulated as a document of the current session of the General Assembly, our delegate again expressed deep concern over this wrong delineation and entered our strong reservation, reiterating that Jammu and Kashmir is legally and constitutionally an integral part of India.

When the resolution on the Universal Realisation of the Right of Peoples of Self-determination was put up for final voting in the General Assembly, the Indian delegate again took exception to that part of the resolution which takes note of this document.

The Government of India deplore and strongly reject the unwarranted inclusion of Jammu and Kashmir in the list of territories under colonial or alien domination. The matter is being taken up with the U.N. Secretary-General.

Lok Sabha on December 6, 1978 as Minister of External Affairs while replying to the Calling Attention Motion regarding Reported Distortion of Facts about Jammu and Kashmir in a recent Report of the U.N. Study Panel

SHRI CHITTA BASU : Sir, I am thankful to the Hon. Minister for the forthright statement that he has made and I think, he would also agree with me that the issue of Jammu and Kashmir is of crucial significance for relations between India and Pakistan. So far as Pakistan is concerned, it has all along been asking to keep this question alive. Apart from the reference as mentioned in the United Nations document cited earlier, Pakistan had been harping on the issue since its very beginning. The House knows that Mr. Aga Shahi, Foreign Affairs Adviser to Pakistan, mentioned the Kashmir issue in his U.N. speech on October 19, 1978. Speaking on racial discrimination and self-determination in the Social and Humanitarian Commitee the Pakistani delegate also made a reference to it and unfortunately clubbed Jammu and Kashmir with Palestine and South Africa. Very recently the Pakistani ambassador in India is reported to have said that a just and honourable settlement of this issue, Jammu and Kashmir, will not only promote good relations but also ensure social progress. Very recently the Pakistani President is also reported to have made this observation, namely, "Unless Kashmir issue is solved, any headway made in other fields in Indo-Pakistan relations would not prove fruitful and meaningful". He made this statement on 28 November. The Government of India's position is clear and unambiguous, namely, Kashmir belongs to India politically, constitutionally and legally.

I may now draw the attention of the Hon. Minister to a statement made by him which was reported in *Tribune* of September 20, 1978, as follows :

> "He is opposed to the Simla Pact only because he had felt it would not bring permanent peace. This he feared because the Kashmir question has been left unresolved; now he was proceeding for permanent peace between the two countries."

This statement is very significant according to me. Having regard to this comment made by him and in the context described by me earlier, may I know from the Hon. Minister whether he has got any other steps for winning permanent friendship and peace between the two countries, India and Pakistan, short of the settlement of the issue of Kashmir.

Secondly, pending the winning of permanent peace between these two countries, may I know whether the Government considers it desirable to take the following steps, namely the policy of rapprochement between the two countries, India and Pakistan, specially railway traffic between the two countries, expedition of the new trade agreement between the two countries and opening a Consul in Karachi ?

SHRI VAJPAYEE : Mr. Speaker, Sir, I thought my friend Shri Chitta Basu will confine himself to the subject matter of the Calling Attention. What I said in Chandigarh and whether there will be further increase in trade between India and Pakistan, while that is an important matter, it is not fully relevant to the subject under discussion.

As the Hon. member has rightly pointed out, Jammu and Kashmir is an integral part of India. There is no question of any right of self-determination being involved. In fact, the only question which is yet to be settled is the continued illegal occupation by Pakistan of two-fifths of Kashmir. It is surprising that the Special Rapporteur included Jammu and Kashmir under the heading "Colonial and alien domination". When we pointed out this anomaly, this travesty of truth, he came out with a clarification that he included Jammu and Kashmir because some resolutions of the United Nations are outstanding in regard to Jammu and Kashmir. Here again the United Nations General Assembly have not adopted any resolution on Kashmir; neither has the Committee on Decolonisation. There was a resolution by the Security Council under the heading "India Pakistan Question". So the Special Rapporteur had no business to include Jammu and Kashmir here. We have made our strong reservation and we are approaching the Secretary-General. We will see that Jammu and Kashmir is deleted from this pernicious list, which has nothing to do with the actual facts.

Our stand in regard to colonisation is well known. We stand for decolonisation. We have offered our unstinted and unqualified support, material, moral and political, to those people who are still struggling against the last vestiges of colonialism in Southern Africa. But to equate Jammu and Kashmir which is part and parcel of India with these colonies is malicious.

AN HON. MEMBER : Preposterous.

SHRI VAJPAYEE : All right, preposterous.

DR. KARAN SINGH (Udhampur) : Mr. Speaker Sir, Jammu and Kashmir has a long history behind it. Our ancestors had established this State nearly 120 years ago. It has been a unique State from the plains of Jammu to the hills of Gilgit and Chitral and from Poonch to Ladakh. It has been an inseparable part of India's culture. I would say that it has been the crown of India.

I slightly differ from my friend, Shri Chitta Basu, when he says Jammu and Kashmir belongs to India; it is India. It is not a bit of property, it is not a necklace or a gold throne which belongs to A or B. Jammu and Kashmir has been a part of India through the centuries, and today also it is a part of India.

The External Affairs Minister has said that the mention of self-determination and colonial and alien domination in the U.N. document is absolutely intolerable. But I would like to point out one more thing. The Prime Minister is present here. I want to quote from the statement of Pakistan President General Zia made on 28th November :

> "During the last thirty years many governments came to power in Pakistan, but they had one common factor, that they fully supported the right of self-determination for the people of Jammu and Kashmir. He added that this was a solid commitment which in no case could diminish with the passage of time.

Recalling M.A. Jinnah, he said, "he had described Jammu and Kashmir as the lifeline of Pakistan and asked how Pakistan can forget it".

History is witness that whenever the internal situation in Pakistan has deteriorated it has raised the bogey of Kashmir to divert the attention of its people. The situation is again deteriorating there now. There is danger of turmoil taking place on the issue of Mr. Bhutto, and the rulers of Pakistan are again trying to rake up the bogey of Kashmir.....

In this context I want to put two or three questions. Firstly, about the UN document, the Hon'ble Minister has said that it should be revised, that the reference to Kashmir in it should be expunged and that he has taken up the matter with the UN Secretary-General. But I would like to know what other steps he proposes to take so that it is expunged at the earliest and this blame of alien and colonial domination is wiped away from the face of India. We are not prepared to tolerate this blasphemy. The United Nations should be clearly told it should be revised and the revised document should be placed there. What are you doing for this ?

Secondly, I want to know the reaction of the Government to the recent statement of General Zia. Did our Foreign Minister convey to Pakistan through our ambassador there or by calling the Pakistani ambassador in Delhi that we do not like these kinds of things and if any attempt was made to use India in the deteriorating situation of Pakistan we will strongly oppose it ?

Thirdly, will it be made clear as to what steps you are taking to recapture the 84,000 sq. miles of land in Kashmir which is under foreign occupation ? As somebody said, it is not a party matter. I entirely agree with that. The question of the nation's interests and existence is involved and no partisan policy should enter into this question. We want to know what policy the Minister of External Affairs proposes to follow in this respect.

SHRI VAJPAYEE : Mr. Speaker, Sir, I congratulate Shri Karan Singh for his eloquent and inspiring speech.....

SHRI VASANT SATHE : You are no less.

SHRI VAJPAYEE : In tune with him I want to reiterate that Jammu and Kashmir is not only an integral part of India but the future of India is inseparably linked with Jammu and Kashmir. It is not merely a piece of land for us, it is a symbol of certain ideals. Jammu and Kashmir became a part of India under the same procedure under which other princely States had joined India. The people of Jammu and Kashmir decided of their own free will to bind their destiny with India. No document of the United Nations can change this fact by misrepresentation, nor can it wash out the ideals of which Jammu and Kashmir is a symbol. We are taking this matter very seriously.

Situation Gradually Deteriorated

I would, however, like to say that this kind of thing is going on in one form or the other since 1973. In 1974, for the first time, a document appeared in which Jammu and Kashmir was mentioned. I am trying to find out as to why this matter was not taken up at that time. I have not so far been able to recover anything from the records on the strength of which I could say that we raised the objection and the situation gradually went on deteriorating.

In 1977, when this matter first came up at the level of the Governments, Smt. Vijaya Lakshmi Pandit projected India's views. Some clarification was given in the special report but, as I told Shri Chitta Basu in my initial reply, we cannot be satisfied with that clarification. In 1973 Tibet was included in those areas that are called Alien Dominion. This time Tibet was taken out from it. But Jammu and Kashmir is still there. I am inquiring into why it is so. We will have to first look seriously where the bungling has taken place in our Ministry before taking it up with the Secretary-General of UN. We must have been careless somewhere and accepted the reference of Jammu and Kashmir in that document. But we are alert now and want to raise this issue seriously.

SHRI VASANT SATHE : Let Tibet be included in it.

SHRI VAJPAYEE : If Shri Sathe asks his party first and then gives his opinion I am ready. Dr. Karan Singh has referred to the speech of Zia-ul-Haq. I agree with him that the rulers of Pakistan have used the issue of Jammu and Kashmir to divert the attention of their people. But the history of the last 30 years is also witness to the fact that this effort has failed, that Pakistan had to lose Bangladesh. Bangladesh, which was once East Pakistan, has now emerged as a free country. If the rulers of Pakistan made yet another misadventure in defiance of the interests of their people the results are not going to be good for them.

Kashmir is a Bilateral Issue

The Prime Minister had talks with General Zia-ul-Haq at Nairobi. When I went to Islamabad I had made the position of India clear to Pakistan on the issue of Kashmir. The Simla Agreement provided for talks on the Kashmir issue. That means Kashmir is a bilateral issue and no reference should now be made to the United Nations Resolution. Much water has flowed down the rivers of India and Pakistan since the passing of resolutions by the Security Council of the United Nations. Pakistan has accepted in the Simla Agreement that it will talk on this issue and when I was asked as to when we will be prepared for talks I said we could talk from that very day.

If Pakistan insists that the matter relates to that part of Kashmir which has merged with India, then our position is absolutely clear, that the matter relates to that part which has been forcibly occupied by Pakistan. Whenever talks are held Pakistan would be asked to vacate its aggression. But I also want to point out that they are trying to play with fire by raising the question of self-determination for Kashmir. Let the rulers of Pakistan ponder on what they have done in the matter of self-determination in their own country. They should think over it with a cool mind. I do not want to say anything more on this matter.

Dr. Karan Singh has warned that we should be cautious. I think we are watchful. While doing our best to improve relations with Pakistan we are keeping our security arrangements strong and are fully capable of replying to any challenge that may be thrown at us although our stand has been that all matters should be solved through talks.

As Dr. Karan Singh said, we have nothing but good wishes for Pakistan in our hearts. We do not want Pakistan to break up. We want Pakistan to be stable and to prosper. But if it plays with fire we cannot save it from the consequences.....

SHRI SAUGATA ROY : I can understand Mr. Jyotirmoy Bosu's reservations about China. I think the Foreign Minister will not have the same reservations.

I want to say this. While we have been trying to develop good relations with Pakistan that should be on the basis of the Simla Agreement. The Foreign Minister is a good orator. He sometimes goes out of his way in making statements. He said that we are prepared to discuss Kashmir. We should not be prepared to discuss Kashmir, because, that is not the Government's position, to discuss it. But the Foreign Minister is on record saying that we are prepared to discuss Kashmir. And, Sir, had it not been for his stomach ailment Mr. Atal Bihari Vajpayee would have been called Shuttle Bihari Vajpayee in this country, shuttling like a shuttlecock from one capital to another. What is all this ? I want to ask the Foreign Minister about one thing. In the context of the continuing design by the Anglo-U.S. imperialism and Pakistan and China to maintain their belligerant attitude towards India, may I know whether the Government will reconsider its attitude of overfriendly relationship with neighbours including visit by the Foreign Minister, and Information and Broadcasting Minister, Shri Lal Krishna Advani to Pakistan, the proposed visit to China, the proposed visit to Nepal and so on ? May I know whether this is being reconsidered in view of the fact that this conspiracy goes on to take out Kashmir from the body of India, of which it is in integral part.

SHRI VAJPAYEE : Sir, the House is going to discuss the International Situation and the Government of India's Foreign Policy on the 11th. I thought that my friend Mr. Saugata Roy—I would not call him Tataghat Roy—would keep his powder dry for that day.

Today we are discussing a specific issue. I am prepared to answer any charge about Government of India having a weak-kneed policy. The charge is baseless. It is without any foundation. We entered into an agreement with Pakistan on Salal project without making any new concessions to them. I would like to tell Mr. Chavan that you wanted to have an agreement with Pakistan on a particular basis and we entered into an agreement on that very basis.

Criticism Welcomed

We are discussing foreign policy and Dr. Karan Singh said that Kashmir is a national issue. Cannot we evolve a broad national consensus on international affairs and the policy of the Government of India ? We welcome criticism, but criticism should not be politically motivated. I am not interested in image-building.... (*Interruptions*).

SHRI VAYALAR RAVI (Chirayankil) : What about your agreement with Kathmandu ? You have given a free access to Calcutta port by Nepal; it is very dangerous.

SHRI VAJPAYEE : In regard to Nepal also....(*Interruptions*).

AN HON. MEMBER : What about Farakka project agreement ?

SHRI VAJPAYEE : We have discussed the Farakka agreement; we are prepared to have discussion again, if necessary.

MR. SPEAKER : Let us confine ourselves on Kashmir.

SHRI VAJPAYEE : But they have not confined themselves to Kashmir.

MR. SPEAKER : But you can.

SHRI VAJPAYEE : Yes, I can. In that case, I have nothing more to add to what I have already said. Thank you.

Hijacking of Aircraft

Mr. Speaker, Sir, I am sorry that even an issue like this on which the entire House is worried and on which the whole nation should stand united to meet the challenge is dividing us. It is creating excitement among us. If Shri Fernandes had sought for an information, he should have directly sought the same and the Government should have been ready to provide the same.

Mr. Speaker, Sir, the aircraft belonged to Government of India, Mr. Azad is the Minister in-charge, but the worry is because of lack of security at airports. Where from had that terrorist hijacker come ? If he hailed from Kashmir Valley, was he alone ? Or, were there other people also with him ? It is difficult to seek clarification about all the news reports that have been published, but they are causing apprehensions in the minds of the people.

Mr. Speaker, Sir, we would like that some senior Minister, who is also connected with the internal security of the country, should explain as to how this hijacking of the aircraft took place in the present situation that is prevailing in the Kashmir Valley. I would also like to tell my friend Shri George Fernandes that every citizen, including even the terrorist, has a right to life. Even he has a right to life, and a right to seek protection as a citizen, as a human being, even though he made 140 people hostages and kept them in the jaws of death for long hours. We should not lose our balance of mind on such an issue just because we are sitting in the Opposition. Therefore, Sir, I would request you to ask the Government to make a statement. The situation in Kashmir Valley is causing much concern to the House. The Police personnel of the State are coming on the road with arms, knocking at the doors of the United Nations Organisation and it appears that the Government does nothing except to watch helplessly. What kinds of initiatives were being taken there ? What was the objective behind changing the Governor ? What is happening in Kashmir Valley. Cannot the Prime Minister call the Opposition and talk to them....*(Interruptions)*.

SHRI PAWAN KUMAR BANSAL (Chandigarh) : What are you discussing ?

SHRI VAJPAYEE : We are discussing a matter of urgent public importance. (*Interruptions*).

SHRI VAJPAYEE : Mr. Speaker, I am sorry to say that this attitude is not proper....

MR. SPEAKER : You are in such a defensive position. You are in strong position.

SHRI VAJPAYEE : And they are more in number, they are running the Government, they will not even let us speak ? (*Interruptions*).

Lok Sabha on April 26, 1984 while demanding statement from the Government on hijacking of plane in Kashmir Valley

SHRI VAJPAYEE : Is the situation prevailing in Kashmir Valley not a matter of concern for you ? (*Interruptions*).

MR. SPEAKER : Mr.Bansal, please sit down.... (*Interruptions*).

MR. SPEAKER : You should not obstruct. That is all. The only thing that you should do is not to obstruct him.

SHRI VAJPAYEE : Mr. Speaker, the highjacker had come from Kashmir. He is a member of a banned organisation. How did he succeed in reaching here ? Were other people also with him ? Where was he staying in Delhi ? Has the worsening situation in Kashmir any connection with this episode ? All these things can be linked, I can do so, but do not try to gag me and I think you are also concerned about the situation in Kashmir (*Interruptions*).

MR. SPEAKER : Why are you obstructing him ? Let him speak. You are unnecessarily complicating the matter. (*Interruptions*).

MR. SPEAKER : I will decide whether it is orderly or not.

SHRI VAJPAYEE : Mr. Speaker, I have not been able to understand what our Congress friends want ? The members of the Congress Party were just now asking me as to what do we want ? We want that you should resign and go away.

Doda-A Disturbed Area

Mr. Speaker, Sir, the Minister of Home Affairs is aware of the situation in Doda. Government's attention has been drawn time and again about the situation prevailing in Doda. We have met the Prime Minister in this connection.

Sir, Doda is an important area. If Doda is cut off we will have no link or connection left with the Kashmir Valley. That is why the militants are concentrating their activities now around Doda. They are continuously trying to expel Hindus from there by creating terror among the people. The terrorists arrest the people, kill them by subjecting them to excesses, mutilate them and call their relatives and in full view of the crowds take out the pieces of flesh from their dead bodies and throw them at the faces of their children. Such kinds of incidents are taking place in this country. A military cantonment should be set up at Bhadrawah. This matter has been pending for years. When we meet we are told that there should be a cantonment. But who will give the land for it, who will pay for it, that is not being settled and the people are losing their lives. The people are ready to fight the terrorists with arms, but you do not supply arms to them. You are providing them protection. The House must consider this matter. We are being told again and again that during this special session let us not bother about what is happening in Doda and devote our entire energy on how to curtail the powers of the Election Commission. We are ready to participate in that debate too, although not for curtailing its powers but in restraining it. But about the situation in Doda, you may kindly direct the Home Minister to give a detailed and unambiguous statement. We will thereafter demand a discussion on it in the House. This is not a matter to be overlooked.

MR. SPEAKER : Would you like to respond ?

SHRI S.B. CHAVAN : Sir, I do not have the exact information with me just now, but so far as my information goes, Government is seriously considering whether we should declare the Doda area as a Disturbed Area. Once we declare this as a Disturbed Area, then the army gets all the special powers which are under that Act. So, we are seriously considering it. But the exact position I would not be able to tell at this stage.

SHRI LAL K. ADVANI (Gandhinagar) : We had met the Prime Minister eight days ago about this matter and had given him the facts in detail.

MR. SPEAKER : The most important thing he has said is that they are going to declare it as a Disturbed Area.

Lok Sabha on June 14, 1994 on the worsening situation in Doda under Special Mention after the Question Hour

SHRI LAL K. ADVANI : That was one of the demands. It is being delayed. If a special session can be called for this purpose, can't it be called to discuss Doda ?

MR. SPEAKER : That is an assurance on the floor of the House.

SHRI LAL K. ADVANI : Sir, I would plead with you that this is a matter on which he can take a decision by day after tomorrow.

MR. SPEAKER : No, no.

SHRI LAL K. ADVANI : Why not ? At least let us know what the Government proposes to do.

SHRI VAJPAYEE : Please direct them to make a detailed statement about the situation in Doda, because this is not a matter limited to declaration of Doda as a Disturbed Area only. There are certain other questions also which have been agitating the minds of the people. They have been demanding an increase in the strength of the security forces.

MR. SPEAKER : I shall discuss this matter..... (*Interruptions*).

SHRI VAJPAYEE : Terrorists are sitting on the mountains. You cannot face the terrorists from the plains unless helicopters are used to force them to get down the hills or they are killed.

VIII ASSAM AND PUNJAB

Assam—Strategically Important

Sir, today, when the House is discussing the difficult situation in Assam, elected representatives from Assam, except for Kachar, are not present here. Twelve seats are lying vacant. A strategically important region of the country is unrepresented in the House.

Just now our friend said the people of Assam have come to feel that New Delhi neglects them. Steps for the economic development of this region were not taken as quickly as its importance required. As a result the people of Assam consider themselves neglected, exploited and cursed.

Along with the economic crisis Assam now faces a new crisis—it can be called the demon of numbers. The population of the whole country increases at a rate of 24 per cent, but in Assam it increases at the rate of 34 per cent. In 1971 alone Assam's population increased by 26 lakhs. This cannot be called natural growth.

Chief Election Commissioner Shri Shakdher had also admitted the seriousness of the situation. I quote what he had said while addressing a conference of electoral officers in Ootacamund in October 1978 :

> "The influx has become a regular feature. I think that it may not be a wrong assessment to make on the basis of this increase of 34.95 per cent between the two censuses that the increase that is likely to be recorded in 1991 census would be more than 100 per cent over the 1961 census. In other words, a stage would be reached when the State may have to reckon with the foreign nationals who may in all probability have sizeable percentage, if not the majority population in the State."

The crisis of Assam is the crisis of its identity. Assam has its own language, nature is generous, there is a rich culture, there are rich natural resources, but the Assamese fear that they will become a minority in their own house. It is essential to remove this fear. This movement that is going on in Assam for the last 4-5 months is not being conducted by any political party, it is a people's movement. It is not even against a particular linguistic group or religious community. There is only one feeling at the bottom of it—how to keep Assam a region of Assamese-speaking people.

Some incidents that took place during this agitation deserve the Government's attention. There is President's Rule in Assam, the Legislative

---

Lok Sabha on February 2, 1980 on the Assam problem

Assembly is in suspended animation, the administration is being conducted under the Centre's supervision. It is necessary to have a judicial inquiry in the recent firing in Duliaganj. According to Government sources 5 people have died, but there are all sorts of rumours in Assam. I too had a chance to visit Assam, and saw that these rumours are misleading the people. It should not be impossible to find out how many have died. Was it necessary to resort to firing ? Was it impossible to control the situation without using the amount of force that was actually used ? These questions need to be answered. The Government says five people died. The people say the figure is much higher. Seventy one people are missing. The newspapers of Assam paint a really grim picture. I demand a judicial inquiry in the Duliganj firing. The Central government should take early steps in this matter.

Incidents of violence have taken place on a large scale in north Kamrup. People have died and thousands are languishing in camps. The army was called in to control the situation there. It would have been better if the army had not been brought in. The situation should have been controlled with the help of the Central Reserve Police or the Border Security Force. I had an opportunity to visit that region. There are complaints of excesses against the Jawans of the army, and it is most regrettable that those who have complained include women. This situation should be avoided. Some steps are also necessary to pacify the people's anger in this respect.

Representatives of student organisations of Assam have come here at the Prime Minister's invitation. I hope the talks will lead to some solution that could pacify the feelings of the people of Assam. Two or three steps need to be taken.

Dangerous Influx of Foreigners

The influx of foreign nationals into Assam must stop. The border adjoining Bangladesh must be strictly administered. I know there are practical difficulties in this. We have been discussing this for the last 30 years but have not been able to do anything. The people of Assam are losing their patience, the youth are getting angry. If timely steps are not taken a section of them may pass into the hands of anti-national elements. I do not agree with my friend Shri Mukherji that this agitation is secessionist. The agitationists are Indians and patriots, and want Assam to remain an integral part of India. But a section of the youth could say if nobody listens to us we may adopt a way that would not be a way of non-violence.

Who are foreign nationals ? This must be decided. They should not be given a place in the electoral rolls. If they are there they should be taken out. The people of Assam say lakhs of people have been included in the electoral rolls. This situation came into focus for the first time when there was the question of a by-election on the death of Shri Patwari. An examination of the electoral rolls revealed that a certain constituency had 70,000 foreign nationals. When 20,000 names out of the list were deleted there was an agitation. Nobody wants to drive out Indian citizens from there, and they should not be driven out. Those who live in Assam are residents and citizens of Assam, whatever their language or religion. Their rights, life and dignity should be protected.

But how can those who are foreign citizens live in Assam ? How can they vote ? How can they use their franchise to form the government ? It is necessary to identify them and take them out.

Early steps are necessary for the economic improvement of Assam. I agree we have not yet been able to lay a broad-gauge line there. A small strip joins Assam. There is pressure from Bangladesh. China is also there. So early steps need to be taken in this regard.

A point about forming a new government. If we are really to solve the Assam problem an all-party government should be formed there, if that is possible. I know it is very difficult. But if we think the situation in Assam is explosive, if we think Assam can affect the integrity and security of the country, all political parties should rise above differences and handle the problem as a national problem, and, if possible, form an all-party government in order to solve it. Thank you.

Assam Neglected

Sir, for how long will the voice of Assam not be heard in this House ? How long will the game of imposing and lifting President's Rule and forming and breaking governments in Assam go on ? Twelve seats from Assam are lying vacant in the Lok Sabha. The Legislative Assembly of Assam has lost the people's trust. But the government is not in a position to hold elections. It would not be proper to blame the youth for this. The youth of Assam deserve to be congratulated not only because they are fighting to save Assam but also because their struggle is for saving the unity and integrity of the whole of India. The Assam agitation is against foreigners, not against Indians who have gone there from other States. This agitation is not against Bangla-speaking residents of Assam, nor against Muslims. But no country can allow unchecked entry of foreigners inside its borders. If the Assam problem is not the problem of foreigners why did the Government want 1971 to be the cut-off year ?

It is certainly a problem of foreigners. While I am speaking here infiltration is going on. And this infiltration is not confined to Assam now. People from Bangladesh are entering the border districts of Bihar and Bengal in large numbers. They are not coming only in search of employment. Those who come in search of employment do not get their passports changed. They do not make clandestine efforts to get into the voters' lists. They are coming with a purpose in mind, and we must understand that purpose.

We should have friendly relations with Bangladesh, but Bangladesh must not shift its burden on to our shoulders. It is also time to tell the minority community in Bangladesh that they should fight for their rights in Bangladesh and not run to India in every difficulty. It is true that we had given some assurances at the time of partition, but no country can keep its borders open for ever. The Government admits that those who have come after 1971 should be identified, their names struck off the voters' lists, and they should be sent where they came from. Ten years have passed since 1971. Now we are in 1981. How many foreigners came within this period ? Were they identified ? Have their names been taken out of voters' lists ? When these questions are raised the answer given is that this cannot be done so long as the agitation goes on. In the meanwhile the agitation had calmed down. A government was formed. The agitationists had even suspended the agitation. The Government will have to prove its bona fides— does it have the will to drive out the foreigners and prevent their entry in future ?

Lok Sabha on December 21, 1981 on the anti-foreigner agitation in Assam

Problem of Credibility

The problem of Assam is the problem of credibility. The youth do not want power. There have been moves to get them into the government's party, but they have rejected those moves. They do not want to become MLAs, they have no ambition to become MPs. The whole problem of Assam is the creation of power-hungry leaders. They have their eyes shut while lakhs of foreigners are flooding Assam. You must understand the feelings of the youth. For the present Assam is a part of the national mainstream. It is not necessary to repeat what has happened in Mizoram. In Manipur the youth are fighting with rifles. Nagaland is already in a turmoil. There is an explosive situation in the whole North East region. Do we want that the patriotic youth of Assam should also fall into the hands of secessionist elements ? Sir, I ask the Government to explain what has happened there since, November 10. The Government says talks are going on. There were 14 rounds of talks, but at times the agitationists get the impression that the Government is extending the talks just to wear them out, so that the agitation dies its own death and the problem remains where it was. Suppose the youth agree to something here and change on returning to Gauhati, — they do not have the experience of conducting movements. It is easy to launch an agitation but difficult to withdraw it. The youth need sympathy. There are elements among them that want to drag them towards excess. Suppose the youth went back on what they had agreed to here and planned a rally in Gauhati on November 10, what was the need to ban the rally ? I too have been to a rally in Gauhati a few days ago, and there was no disturbance at that time. The agitationists could also have had their rally. But the BSF had a show of strength and said no rally would be allowed. The excuse made was that if the agitationists were allowed to hold a meeting similar permission would have to be given to the Minority Association, which wanted to hold a meeting the same day. The Minority Association could have been given permission for the next day. What the minorities of Assam say should also be heeded and their legitimate interests safeguarded. We have also told the agitationists' leaders that we do not approve of the violence that has taken place during the agitation and of the harassment of minorities, nor do we support these things. But by and large the agitation is peaceful and patriotic. It is for India's integrity, not for Assam's secession.

But how are we behaving there ? The rally was not permitted, but there were seven meetings of the agitationists, which were attended by thousands of people. The whole city came to a halt. But suppression began. The BSF set up camp at Judges Field. Propaganda was made on the Radio—in the 1.10 bulletin—that a bomb had exploded there. Later the Chief Secretary was made to say it was not a bomb but a *similar explosion.* Later it was found that it was just a ball of paper. In Assam you have destroyed the credibility of All India Radio. This is not the way to treat the people of Assam.

Movement Touched All

November 14 was Pandit Nehru's birth anniversary. The children of Gauhati assembled at a separate place, they did not participate in the official function. It was not compulsory to participate in the function. Even the children have anti–foreigner feelings. This movement has touched all—small children, men and women, men of letters, labourers, employees. This question touches everybody's nerve. For us this is not a question of votes, but I have realised to some extent the pain of the people of Assam. They think they will become strangers in their house, they will become a minority. Assam has a language of its own a life-style of its own, centuries old traditions of its own. Should these not be protected ? Try to remove the fear in their minds. But you are beating up people, jailing them and resorting to suppression.

Sir, do the people not have the right to observe a peaceful Bandh ? But when a call for Bandh was given in Gauhati on the 19th and 20th, action was taken against those shop-keepers who refused to open their shops. Can the police force people to open shops ? Who will be responsible if they are looted ? If the shop-keepers are in sympathy with the agitationists who can stop them ? But four prominent businessmen were arrested there and were externed from Gauhati district. The result was that the Bandh continued still further.

The employees are not with you. Why was it necessary to enforce the Essential Services and Maintenance Act there ? I read Shri Makwana's speech in the Rajya Sabha. The employees are with the agitation. Now who will keep up the power supply ? Why are the employees with the agitation ? They fear being removed from service. Action has been taken against them. But somewhere in their heart there is the feeling that the agitation is meant for preserving their identity, preserving their existence.

The bandh was a total success. The Government tried to keep buses and trucks moving, but there was no one to board them. On 14th November, the police tried to break up the children s rally. You cannot suffer the opposition of even small children, and you expect the people of Assam to be with you. This is not the way to have them with you. On 14th November, a 13-year-old boy was killed by CRP bullets in Dheeng. One boy was killed but the whole of Assam was wounded. Look at the incident on November 28. There was a bomb explosion in the agricultural office. I want to know from Shri Makwana who was arrested in this connection. Is it not true that a person named Maqtab Ali, who was arrested, is connected with the All Assam Minorities Association ? Is it not possible that some people would bring about bomb explosions to bring a bad name to the agitation ? I do not want to go into who incited such elements. I know the whole story of how efforts were made to bring a bad name to the Assam agitation at the time of Shri Sarin's visit during President's Rule. On November 29 the CRP and BSF attacked the veterinary camp of the agricultural university. Forty-nine boys staying at the hostel were arrested. They were not brought to jail. For 24 hours they were detained in a bus. They were given neither water nor food, nor were they allowed to get down for natural functions. You repeated the events that had taken place in the Gauhati University a year before.

(Shri Gulshan Ahmed in the Chair)

Government's Intentions Suspect

Sir, I know the agitationists have adopted a stiff attitude. They do not trust the Government s sincerity about solving their problem. The opposition is ready to contribute. But try sincerely. When Pt. Narain Dutt Tiwari visits Assam it is not for considering what concrete plans could be chalked out for removing Assam s backwardness, but to see how a government could be formed, how alienated MLAs working in tea plantations could be brought back into the fold. Anwar Taimur had formed a government but it could not last. You cannot imagine here the damage done by that government. A government working on communal policies cannot bring solace to Assam's soul. Communal policies could not save Assam, but the suppression would cause an explosion that would make Assam another Nagaland. So stop suppression, do not try to form a government, talk with the Assam agitationists as soon as possible, and hold elections there immediately. Under President's Rule it would be easy to resolve the problem. A government that is formed there sidelines this issue. Smt. Anwara Taimur had done the same. She said the foreigners' problem is a central matter, her responsibility is to maintain law and order. The MLAs hostel in Assam has been made into a fortress. And still there was an explosion there. Police dogs were brought to the hostel for investigation. They sniffed the place—and do you know where they went ? They headed in the direction of the Chief Minister's bungalow. I do not know what happened to the investigation. It was halted. The dogs lost the way. Even a dog is deluded when it goes towards the Chief Minister's directive. A selfish human being can do that, not a loyal animal. I do not want to repeat. We do not want to derive political benefit from the situation. I want to reassure this House with all sincerity. But the way you are trying to solve the problem of Assam is not the way. The youth could be invited for talks. No one is inciting them. They do not even want to talk to political parties. They know that political parties care for votes, not for Assam. They are good young men, young men of character. The country should be proud of them. But you said these agitationists want to take Assam out of the country, and told the army to suppress them. And the army brought out a bulletin — I do not quite remember its number—saying the Assam agitation is unpatriotic. For God's sake do not involve the Army in this. The political battle will continue. Let us try to understand the feelings of the people of Assam and solve their problem.

'Gardania' Passport

There is surely no difference of opinion after 1971. I know about those that have come in after 1971 and have been sent back. This is the test of the

Government s bona fides. We must also understand that Bangladesh will not take back anybody. Shri Makwana said somewhere that 200-250 people were externed. Press people asked, where ? He said don't ask that. They may have been driven out at one place but may have come in at another. This went on. I know it is difficult to protect the border. But not so difficult that for 34 years it would not be protected at all. Since Shri Nanda's times I have been raising the problem of Assam in the House for 25 years. He had assured that there would be wired fencing. It was not put up. The border was not closed. Posts were not increased. When I was Foreign Minister a matter had come up before me. I was told the regular passport that was issued was all right, but there is another type of passport in operation on the India-Bangladesh border. It is called the *'Gardania'* passport. I asked, what is *'Gardania* passport' ? They said— it is not necessary to have a passport. If you want to cross the border just reach there, pass some money to the sentry posted there, whether of Assam Rifles or the Border Security Force. He catches you by the neck (*'gardan'*) and gives you a push—and you are in Bangladesh without a passport. This is still going on. We could not stop it. We could not create confidence in the people of Assam. Do we want to throw Assam into the hands of the extremists ? Do not make this mistake. The people of Assam also feel that they are neglected. The state is economically backward. There is petroleum in Assam and the agitationists have been charged with causing a loss of thousands of rupees by not allowing petroleum to be taken out. But if oil could not be taken out it does not mean it was destroyed. It is not a fruit to rot if not plucked in time. Oil is safe in the ground, you can take it out later. But the people of Assam ask— what about the thousands of cubic metres of gas that is being flared every day ? We cannot use that gas. The Barauni refinery is developed, tea auctions take place in Calcutta. Assam gets a lesser royalty. We have built six bridges on the Ganga but there are only two bridges on the Brahmaputra so far. Economic problems get linked up with psychological problems. We have still time to solve them. The Prime Minister included the opposition parties in the talks. This was good. But she thought of them only when talks looked like breaking down. This is not good. I asked Gyaniji— why did you invite us when the talks were obstructed ? He replied—what was the need of calling you when the talks were going on well ?

"Dukh mein sumiran sab karey, sukh mein karey na koi ? jo sukh mein sumiran karey to dukh kahey ko hoi ?" 'Everybody remembers You in unhappiness, nobody remembers You in happiness. If one remembers You in happiness, why would there be unhappiness ?' We do not claim to be God, but the problem of Assam is a national problem, it should not be made a party problem. The Assam problem is a real problem. Take steps to solve it, take the youth with you, isolate the extremists, take the people of Assam with you.

Assam Left in the Lurch

The people of Assam have not forgotten what Prime Minister Shri Jawaharlal Nehru had said on the Radio in 1962 when the invading Chinese were knocking at the door of the country. They say when you were in difficulties you were ready to leave us in the lurch, the rest of the country did not care for us.

Let us realise their pain and try to solve this national problem. A way can be found, but stop suppression. It is possible that if this suppression continues the youth may refuse to come for talks.

Tell your officials that the people need to be persuaded to come to the right path. If efforts are made the problem of Assam can also be solved. But it depends upon those who are sitting there. Thank you.

Mockery of Elections in Assam

Sir, the drama which was being enacted in Assam and which finally turned into a tragedy, came to an end yesterday, but killings still continue. I have received a news report this morning, which says : "A big crowd attacked settlements near Tejpur. At least 100 people were killed and 2000 are lying wounded in hospital."

The Prime Minister is in Assam today. I do not know what areas she will tour. When she visited Assam in connection with an election campaign she chose only those regions where people migrating from Bangladesh or East Pakistan have settled down in large numbers.

Should the Prime Minister not have visited other regions ? Further, I would like Congress members to read the type of speeches she made. We are in the opposition we have no sense of responsibility we want to set the country on fire, we are not patriots. All patriotism has been monopolised by those sitting on that side. But then you should have talked responsibly in Assam.

What sort of speech Shri Abdul Ghani Khan Choudhary made has been talked about. Was it necessary for the Prime Minister to address a meeting at Malegaon, which has a large number of Bengali-speaking people instead of at Judges' Field ? She was speaking in Assamese but began in Bengali and did not conclude with Jai Hind. The Prime Minister of India concluded her speech with Khuda Hafiz. What does it mean ? I have no quarrel with Khuda Hafiz. But is this the way to maintain goodwill and communal unity by talking like this at election time ? The Prime Minister wore a *mekhla* (waist-band) on her visit, spoke Bangla and said Khuda Hafiz instead of Jai Hind. This is the Prime Minister's reality....

PROF. K.K. TEWARY (Buxar) : Does it behove you talking about the Prime Minister like this ? This is a serious debate.

SHRI VAJPAYEE : I am not yielding.

Sir, no Congress member stood up to protest when the patriotism of the leaders of opposition parties was being challenged. Truth is bitter. The Prime Minister will herself reply. The Home Minister is present here... (*Interruptions*).

CHAIRMAN : Please address the Chair. Do not talk directly.

SHRI VAJPAYEE : Everyone knows that people speaking different languages and following different religions live in Assam. There are also tribals there. But I shall quote the type of speeches the Prime Minister made :

Lok Sabha on February 21, 1983 during discussion on the conditions in Assam

"Harijans, Muslims and women are being attacked by the opposition to embarrass the Government, as they are supporting me."

Who is attacking Harijans ? Is it the opposition people ? Who is attacking Muslims and women ? Is it the opposition people ?

The reason why we oppose the Prime Minister is that she wants to create the illusion that women, Muslims and Harijans in this country can be saved only at the Prime Minister's hands and nobody else's.

Prime Minister's Assurance

The Prime Minister said in a meeting in Gauhati that nobody will be sent out of Assam. Let her deny that she said so. I have looked up the *Hindustan Times* of February 13. The Prime Minister had made a speech on February 12—

"Should we give a false promise that they will be removed, when we know that they will not be removed ?"

No one will be removed from Assam. No one will be removed even if he is a foreigner. Are there no foreigners in Assam ? If there are no foreigners why did talks go on for three years ? Has not the Government itself agreed that those who have come in after 1971 will be identified and their names struck off the voters' lists ? Does the Government feel bound by this agreement ? Has this obsession—I call it an obsession—about holding elections on the 1979 electoral rolls—not set Assam on fire ? If the Prime Minister does not give up this obsession her name will go down as the destroyer of the country. (*Interruptions*).

What is the meaning of holding the elections on the basis of the 1979 electoral rolls ? Do they not include people who have come after 1971 ? Can foreigners vote ? Eight lakh youth of Assam attained the age of 21 in 1980 they cannot vote, but foreigners can!

Will elections held on the basis of such electoral rolls represent or strengthen democracy ? In the entire election the propaganda was being made that foreigners will not be removed.

Sir, I have toured many regions of Assam. Congress members should not make this a party problem. All this bloodshed in Assam reminds me of 1947. If we are guilty, hang us, but the feeling that the people of Assam have come to acquire is not the making of any political party.

Just now Prof. Samar Mukherji admitted that the employees of Assam are not ready to take part in the elections. The employees fear loss of job, they fear their families would starve. They were under full police watch. But now the employee in Assam is opposing the election even at the risk of losing his job, because he feels that if the election takes place on the basis of electoral rolls prepared on the basis of foreigners, Assam would lose its separate culture, separate life-style, separate identity.

There has been a massacre. Who killed whom is not important. I never said rivers of blood will flow, but they are flowing. Today the Home Minister did not say how many people have died. There is nobody to count the bodies.

I visited Gohpur on the 16th. There were disturbances there on the 12th. The Deputy Commissioner did not go to Gohpur. The Deputy Commissioner of the district did not go to see the massacre, neither did the special S.P. On the 16th I asked the O.C. and the Additional Superintendent there—how many died ? The reply was—we have no information.

SHRI ANAND GOPAL MUKHOPADHYAY : Excuse me Vajpayeeji, what is your definition of foreigners ?

SHRI VAJPAYEE : I will come to it. Sir, he has put a very pertinent question.

SHRI ANAND GOPAL MUKHOPADHYAY : For Assam and for Kashmir.

SHRI VAJPAYEE : Foreigners are not to be defined by me. A foreigner has to be defined according to the Constitution and according to the law. Who am I to define ?

What happened at Gohpur

Sir, let me finish with Gohpur. I shall also come to that later. You took a battalion of one lakh there for holding the election, and still after the killings the O.C. was complaining to me, saying—we have 70 people, a small contingent of the Border Security Force has come, we cannot save the people. When the Deputy Commissioner was contacted and asked why he did not go when hundreds of houses were torched and dead bodies were lying in the jungle, he replied—my job is to hold elections, to save lives is not the job of the Government. It is the ruling party's job to climb the ladder of power by building the mansion of elections on a heap of corpses. (*Interruptions*). This is not the story of Gohpur alone. Shri Mukherji does not know that the quarrel of Gohpur is not a quarrel between those who want the election and those who don't. These scheduled tribes do not have the vote. They were raising slogans of Udayachal Zindabad and Indira Gandhi Zindabad. Congress leaders told Kachari Scheduled tribes—let the 20th pass, these Assamese will be driven across the railway line right up to the Brahmaputra river (*Interruptions*). Look at another example. Election was held for a seat near Dispur. Village Kshetri was set on fire on the 13th. The village was burning from 10.00 to 2.00 o' clock. On the 11th itself the villagers had complained in writing, but no arrangements were made. The whole village burnt down. Later the police arrested some people, but they were released because the Congress candidate said they are our voters, they are going to vote for them, let them go. In Gohpur too tribals caught indulging in arson were released at the police station. When I asked why they were released the reply was—they had assured they will not do anything. Such a big incident of violence occurred, but there were no arrests. Had we incited the people we should have been arrested. There was not a single person in the lock-up. The slogans raised in the Kshetri village near Dispur were like this : "We'll not let Indira Gandhi to die. We'll not let foreigners to be removed." What does this mean ? Even after this we would have understood if you had held an election. What took place is not an election. In Assam democracy has been killed (*Interruptions*).

A party of Bharatiya Janata Party visited 10 polling booths. They are located in the city in the Majo constituency,—at Hajo Higher Secondary School, Barcha Puril Lower Primary School, Hajo Burta Lower Primary School. When our party reached these centres at one o'clock there were no polling booths. We searched for them, we thought they had been shifted, but they had not been shifted. The presiding officers had loaded the whole polling station in their jeeps and buses. The ballot papers, the ballot boxes and the presiding officers—they were all in the bus. When they were asked what was happening they replied—nobody turned up for voting, so we are not required to sit till 3.30, we are going. Is this an election or an apology of an election ? Doctors were given the power to accept nominations. Police officers went from house to house and collected nomination papers. There was no police to save the life of the common man. But on the same day there was a large contingent of armed police outside the Congress candidate's house. The candidate had to be protected. I do not object to that, but should the citizens be left unprotected ? Had the Assam Government not completely abdicated its responsibility ? There was indiscriminate firing and elections were held at gunpoint.

Sir, I visited Titavar near Jorhat. There had been firing there the previous day. Four people had died in the firing and the dead included a person named Ataur Rehman. Those people who want to give the whole agitation a communal colour are not doing the right thing. That person was with the agitationists. There are many Muslims in Assam who have been living there since before and who sincerely feel people are coming in unchecked from Bangladesh and they should not. Why do you consider them to be against the agitation ? But I was saying something else, for 40 hours the police did not remove the bodies of those killed in the firing. Even in a war between two independent countries all arrangements are made for the treatment of the wounded. The dead are not dishonoured. But you were so busy with the election that bodies lay rotting.

I visited the hospitals at Gauhati and Dibrugarh. There were lines upon lines of wounded people and the doctors said they had no anti-gangrene syrup. A week before I had told the Home Minister in the meeting of the Consultative Committee : It is necessary to resort to firing, but it is not necessary to treat the wounded. I have with me a list of medicines given to me by doctors. People are dying because of shortage of medicines. Can any Congress member justify such a situation with his hand on his heart ? Even supposing the agitationists were in the wrong or people of the opposition parties had misled them, those wounded by police bullets are Indian citizens. Will you consider such a citizen an enemy because, in your opinion, he is going the wrong way ? Today the Home Minister said he is sending medicines. Could they not have been sent before this ? Tons upon tons of bread can be sent for those sent on election duty, but medicines cannot. The people of Assam are our own people and today we have condoled their death. The Prime Minister has gone there to express her sympathies, I ask you, why were there no medicines ?

Doctor prevented

You will be surprised to know—doctors in Dibrugarh told me there has been firing but the police did not bring in the dead. We have an ambulance standing by and we want to take it into the villages but the district officer said you cannot go. The doctors of Gauhati approached the High Court on this question and the High Court said there could be no such restraint. But when the doctors went there the next day the officials stopped them and said, don't go into the villages, don't care if people die. Those who oppose the Congress Government will have to pay for the opposition with their lives! (*Interruptions*).

Sir, elections should be free and fair. Shri Shiv Shankar is present here. Basic features include free and fair elections. Was the situation in Assam conducive to free and fair elections ? Forget the electoral rolls of 1979, although they too could have been changed. That time too Shri S.L. Shakdher had first of all raised this question. During a strike at Mangaldoi it was found that in a single Lok Sabha constituency there were 45,000 people whose citizenship was doubtful.

PROF. MADHU DANDAVATE : For administrative failures why are you asking them now ?

SHRI VAJPAYEE : Was a complete inquiry not called for after this ? Was an inquiry made ? Why were judicial tribunals not set up ? Why were attempts not made to strike out the names of foreigners ? Here in New Delhi a foreign woman's name had come into the voters' list. If this is possible here what may be happening in Assam, where for 35 years attempts have been made to bring in foreigners ? This can be easily imagined.

I charge the ruling party—you do not care for the country's unity. You do not care for Assam. You care only for votes. you want to save your vote bank, you want to increase it. I am going to say something that may possibly make you shout.

Brigadier Kale's Testimony

A riot had taken place in Gauhati in 1968. It was a matter of the oil refinery. There was a lot of fighting and arson and the army was called. Brigadier Kale was in command. Justice Sen of the Calcutta High Court was appointed to inquire into what happened after the army was called. Brigadier Kale appeared before the commission and made a statement saying—when I picked up my phone to talk during the riot I overheard a Central Minister telling a Minister of the State to let the riot continue for two hours more. This was Brigadier Kale's statement before Justice Sen. Justice Sen asked the names to be given in writing and two names were given on a piece of paper. The Government has suppressed that report. I would like it to be tabled in the House. Who was this Central Minister ? This was not a political leader's charge. Brigadier Kale was an army officer. Who in Delhi was saying carry on the riots in Gauhati ? What Minister in Gauhati was reluctant in stopping the riot at the behest of Delhi ? This is not a recent matter. The people of

Assam are frightened. I do not want to go into whether it is right or wrong. Get rid of the notion that everybody—men, women, children, workers, traders, government servants—was doing whatever he was doing because of somebody's incitement. Only then can you reassure them.

I agree that it is not for me to define foreigner, the Constitution will do it, the law will do it. But will a foreigner become a citizen only because he has succeeded in getting his name included in the voters' list ? I agree that some assurances had been given to refugees from Bangladesh. But the assurance was not that they would all be settled in Assam. The assurance was that India would come to their help. There is rest of India apart from Assam. The people of Assam complain—why are they all coming here ? They say, what will happen to us ? Will we become strangers in our house ? Hence the slogan 'Assam Mata'. That does not mean they do not raise slogans of *'Bharat Mata ki Jai'*. They say that too. Our States have their own speciality, their own variety. I have been to Andhra—there they call Andhra a nation, not a state. But they use a Telugu word that is used for State. They do not say Andhra is a separate nation. In Maharashtra they say *'Priya amucha ek Maharashtra desh ha'*—'this Maharashtra is our beloved country.' You may say, talk of *Rashtra* (the nation), not Maharashtra. Every one is aware of the situation in Nagaland. There is unrest in Mizoram. Manipur is gradually going under the control of rowdy elements. There is no peace in Tripura. There is peace only in the Brahmaputra valley. The people there are peaceful, they want to protect their language and their culture, but they do not want to cede from the country.

Do not try to cut them off from the country by calling them separatists. Possibly there may be some elements among them who might have concluded that nobody would listen to them on the basis of democracy. They may also have concluded that political leaders care for the vote, not for the country—neither for any part of it nor for the whole of it. Do you want all people of Assam valley to pass into their grasp ? Do you want to hand over the whole situation to the extremists ? What will be the consequence ? We clearly told the agitationist leaders that we were against violence. Shri Choudhary, who is present here, knows this. I want to refute the charge that we did not condemn the violence of Gauhati. Many people of Gauhati had attended my meeting. I talked to the Governor and he said 'Vajpayeeji, you are the first person to come here and say there should be no violence, you are doing a good thing'. (*Interruptions*).

Do you also know what happened to local leaders ? Why were Shri Mahanto and Shri Bhrigu Kumar Phukan arrested on getting down from the plane at Gauhati airport ? They had come to Delhi for talks and were returning. They had not committed an offence in Delhi and there was no question of committing an offence at the airport. Those who come for talks are not arrested. This is the tradition. But they were arrested and the people there become leaderless. The situation of 1942 was created.

Cycle of Violence and Coercion

Now go deep into the matter. When did the violence start ? The first incident took place in Gohpur on the 12th. Who incited it ? What feelings were roused all over Assam by the speeches of the Prime Minister and Shri Abdul Ghani Khan Choudhary ? The people of Assam thought there was no future for them. The people coming from Bangladesh thought—who can put us out ? The Government is backing us, Delhi Darbar is backing us, the police are backing us. You can see how the police are behaving. An armed skirmish between the CRP and the police of Assam is an ordinary event. Will you tell how many people died ? We too have some figures. I do not want to create a sensation in the country by placing them before you here. But who created such a situation ? Did we incite the CRP ? Did we incite the Assam Police ? Can the CRP beat up anybody passing by the street ? Can it fire indiscriminately ?

Sir, I have the name of a place written down with me. The people there were not prepared to vote. The CRP did firing there and people are still lying in hospital. We have their statements with us. This is what the CRP did. I have a photograph of Jorhat with me and I am ready to place it on the floor of the House. In the picture you can see a CRP man dragging a person for casting his vote (*Interruptions*). This is a photograph, this is not a joke. You are laughing, you should feel sorry that voters were carted in government vehicles. Is it not prohibited to use government vehicles for elections ? Will democracy be strengthened if voters are coerced and firing is resorted to for securing votes ?

I have with me a verdict of the Gauhati High Court. I would like to quote a portion of it here. It relates to how our security forces behaved. This verdict is dated January 28 not February but January 28. Somebody had complained to the High Court that these forces were behaving like occupation forces. I place the High Court's observation before the House :

> "We find sufficient force in the contention of the learned counsel for the petitioners of the allegations made in the petition that it is in fact a kind of aggression by the forces of the Government against the innocent members of the public. Those who wield so much force and power in performing their duties, we feel that it is the obligation of those in charge and responsible for ensuring the personnel perform their duties, to keep them under check, control and restraint by issuing necessary, appropriate and proper direction and in all contingencies they should specifically be told to honour human dignity."

The Home Minister says the High Court, the Supreme Court dismissed the case relating to the election. You were yourself not willing to postpone the election. You could have done that. The Constitution could have been amended for that purpose. We were prepared to vote. You can say you decided you will not postpone elections, but don't say the opposition could also decide not to talk with you. You may claim you consult the opposition for solving every problem. We are ready to give our opinion, also to give our cooperation, but for God's sake don't tell lies. Accept the responsibility of the wrong that is happening. If anything good happens the Prime Minister is prepared to take the credit. But who will accept the responsibility for the rivers of blood that are flowing in Assam ? Who will expiate that sin ? (*Interruptions*). Will we cleanse it ? We are cleaning up you too. But the people of Assam will not wash away your sins.

Electoral Rolls Challenged

Sir, the 1979 electoral rolls were challenged in High Court and it was argued that elections could not be held on their basis. The High Court asked for the rolls. The Advocate– General was asked to produce them by 4 o'clock. At 4 o'clock the Advocate– General said they would be produced at 10 o'clock the next morning. When the High Court sat the next day at 10 o'clock the election notification promulgated at midnight was produced. Then the High Court said our hands were bound. At that time neither could the High Court do anything, nor the Supreme Court.

Election Commission's Duties

But I must regretfully say that it is not the job of the Election Commission to see if there would be a constitutional vacuum. It did not do its duty. It promulgated a notification before a bench of the High Court gave its verdict. It is the job of the Election Commission to see that elections should be free and fair. If it thinks that is not possible in the prevailing circumstances, it is for the Election Commission to say that Election should not be held. The Election Commission is an autonomous institution under the Constitution. I do not like anybody criticising the Election Commission. But one by one you have made democratic institutions targets of attack. The Supreme Court is being packed with judges who, in your opinion, would decide in your favour. (*Interruptions*). The Election Commission too has been made an object of controversy (*Interruptions*).

SHRI JAMIL RAHMAN (Kishanganj) : Sir, I am on a point of order. Nothing should be said against the Supreme Court which is not a party here. (*Interruptions*). He has cast an aspersion on the Supreme Court. He has said : Such people are rewarded as would help the Government.

SHRI VAJPAYEE : Sir, does it not tarnish the Supreme Court when a Supreme Court image accepts the Congress-I's candidates ?

SHRI JAMIL RAHMAN : Vajpayeeji, I respect you, but that will not be good on your part to say that.

SHRI JAGDISH TYTLER (Delhi Sadar) : Sir, I am on a point of order. The reference about the kind of judges who have come to Supreme Court .... (*Interruptions*) .... should be deleted.

MR. CHAIRMAN : I will examine it.

SHRI VAJPAYEE : Sir, I had said the Government is trying to bring in judges who it thinks will give verdicts in its favour. What is objectionable in that ? Do I not have the right to ask about Bahrul Islam who had given a good character certificate to Jagannath Mishra ? (*Interruptions*). At first he was in the Congress, then he went to the Supreme Court, now he is back in the Congress. It seems as if there is nobody in the country except Bahrul Islam.

There is another thing I want to say—an independent judiciary is the foundation of democracy (*Interruptions*).

Is he on a point of order ? He is not an ordinary member. He is a Minister.

SHRI H.K.L. BHAGAT, Minister of State, Ministry of Information and Broadcasting : I am Parliamentary Minister also.

His reference to the Supreme Court judges, who are working, reflection on them and criticism of those judges, is unfair. He is not expected to raise that matter. And from a man of his stature! From Mr. Vajpayee, I did not expect that. It is very unfair.

Unfair on your part Mr. Vajpayee, to say this. Supreme Court judges, the first thing for you to criticise them! You can say many things of Dr. Mishra, anything you like, but for you to make reflection on the Supreme Court judges is not correct, not fair. You know the rules.

SHRI VAJPAYEE : I did not cast any reflection on the judges. I am criticising the Government.

SHRI RASHID MASOOD : Sir, Shri Vajpayee has only said (*Interruptions*) that the Government wants to seat such people (*Interruptions*). He has not said Supreme Court judges are bad.

SHRI H.K.L. BHAGAT : It is very wrong. It is absolutely against law. You know the rules. It is very unfortunate (*Interruptions*).

MR. CHAIRMAN : Mr. Bhagat, if there is anything wrong, that will be taken out of the proceedings.

PROF. MADHU DANDAVATE : If Cabinet Minister starts raising point of order, the next stage will come when point of order will be from the Chair.

MR. CHAIRMAN : I can assure you I would not be there.

SHRI VAJPAYEE : Sir, I am about to finish. I say the Government has to thank itself for the situation that now prevails because of its forcing elections on Assam. Tyranny cannot enable elections to be held nor a government to function. What sort of an election is this when opposition parties are not allowed to hold meetings.

SHRI A.B. DEO (Ajmer) : Just now you said you addressed a big meeting.

SHRI VAJPAYEE : That was one place. I am citing the instance of another place.

SHRI A.B. DEO : Sir, he is misleading the House.

SHRI H.K.L. BHAGAT : Mr. Deputy Speaker, I raised a point of order. While speaking Shri Vajpayee cast aspersion on the Supreme Court Judge. That must not go on record.

MR. DEPUTY SPEAKER : I think the Chair has already ruled that he will go through the proceedings.

SHRI VAJPAYEE : I did not cast any aspersion on any Supreme Court judge. I am within my rights to criticise Bahrul Islam. He is a candidate in the election.

SHRI H.K.L. BHAGAT : You made a reference to the Supreme Court judge.

SHRI VAJPAYEE : Yes, he was a judge.

MR. DEPUTY SPEAKER : We will go through the records (*Interruptions*).

MR. DEPUTY SPEAKER : In such a discussion instead of replying every now and then, the next speaker from the ruling party, I think he may be Shri Tewary, will note down all the points and if you do not agree he will counter them. That will be the proper procedure. Yes, Mr. Vajpayee (*Interruptions*).

SHRI VAJPAYEE : What I want to say is, those parties which were contesting the elections and which ......

SHRI P. SHIV SHANKAR, Minister of Energy : I hope what my friend while sitting has said has not gone on record.

MR. DEPUTY SPEAKER : Any remark by a member while sitting will not go on record. That is our rule.

SHRI VAJPAYEE : It will not go on record. But why do you listen to such things in the first place ?

Sir, my submission is, the conditions of an election are use of the right to vote in an atmosphere free from fear. It is true that this right was challenged by both sides, but is it not the job of the Government to act upon its decision ?

In Gauhati I was allowed to hold a meeting, but not in Tejpur, nor in Titabar, nor also in Dibrugarh. Here is a letter from the District Magistrate of Dibrugarh addressed to the vice-president, Dibrugarh Committee :

> "With reference to your above mentioned application, I regret that it is not possible to give permission for the public meeting on 17th February, 1983 in view of the present law and order situation."

Meetings cannot be held because of the law and order situation, but elections can. As we had boycotted elections we had the right to explain to the people why we had boycotted them and which parties had not done so. I would also call upon the leaders of the parties which are participating in the elections to explain the difficulties they had to face. I again ask, was it necessary to hold elections ? Could they not have been postponed ? During the Emergency the life of the Lok Sabha was extended from five years to seven and that was not done after consulting us, but after putting us in jail. That time the question of the Opposition's opinion was not raised.

The Prime Minister says, and the Home Minister repeated this morning, that there is a difference of opinion in the Opposition. That is so, and that is why we are separate. But we were prepared to give you the votes you required for a two-thirds majority in the Rajya Sabha. You did not amend the Constitution, so the responsibility of the massacre that took place in Assam after diciding not to amend the Constitution and after forcing elections on Assam lies on your shoulders. The hands of this Government are dyed red with the blood of the innocent people of Assam (*Interruptions*).

You cannot escape your blame by blaming Opposition parties. I do not know what is going to happen in Assam. The people have received a wound in the heart that will not be healed. Still we have to try. One way is to cancel the present elections. I do not know how that can be done, but these elections should be cancelled.

Foreigners' Problem Remains

These elections have not solved the foreigners' problem. It has become still more complex. So I have proposed an all-party committee for Assam. Let us forget our differences. Let us have a true assessment of what has happened in Assam. If we are guilty we shall accept the blame and if the Prime Minister and the Congress Party are guilty they should do the same.

I know the people of Assam. There are Bengali-speaking people, and also refugees from Bangladesh. As I have said it is not Government's international commitment to settle all refugees in Assam and make them citizens at one stroke. It is also not the commitment that they would be made voters before making them citizens (*Interruptions*).

SHRI SATYASADHAN CHAKRABORTY : This is a dangerous statement. What do you mean ? Are the refugees not the citizens of India ? (*Interruptions*).

SHRI VAJPAYEE : I am talking the sense which you may not understand.

SHRI SATYASADHAN CHAKRABORTY : Are the refugees not Indian citizens ? Can they be dispersed like cattle (*Interruptions*).

SHRI JAGDISH TYTLER : Tomorrow, about all those people, who have come from Pakistan and West Pakistan like us, he will say they are foreigners. (*Interruptions*).

SHRI VAJPAYEE : I want your protection.

DEPUTY SPEAKER : He is going to conclude now. Order please. Acharya Bhagwan Dev has taken more time than him.

SHRI VAJPAYEE : Had not Pakistanis from Sindcome into Rajasthan after 1971 ? Had it not become necessary to pass a citizenship law for them ? Can you make anyone a citizen with an executive order ? An executive order was issued in 1965 which said whoever comes from East Pakistan is a citizen. This is not in consonance with the Constitution. I know that those who were forced by circumstances to come had no refuge but India.

AN HON. MEMBER : That was a policy decision.

SHRI VAJPAYEE : Amend the Constitution to implement a policy decision. How can you do it without that ? The assurance given to those who came was that they would be given shelter in India. There was no assurance that the whole burden would be laid on Assam.

SHRI CHITTA BASU (Barasat) : That was a policy decision. (*Interruptions*) :

DEPUTY SPEAKER : Let him express his own views. If you want to oppose his views, you can reply to him when your chance comes after he completes his speech.

SHRI VAJPAYEE : Sir, I say there is no other way to solve the whole problem but to have talks.

DEPUTY SPEAKER : It is time to conclude now. If you are going to conclude, they are not going to interrupt. That is why I am asking you to conclude.

SHRI VAJPAYEE : These people have derailed me so many times. I shall now conclude.

Finally, I appeal for applying the healing balm to the wounded soul of Assam. Every tear of the citizens of Assam needs to be wiped. We are carrying out a post–mortem here. I am of the opinion that elections could have been postponed. You are of the opinion that they could not have been postponed. So now what next ? You held the elections, you paid a heavy price for them. What next ? Are these elections going to solve the foreigners problem ? Those who boycotted the elections will not accept the government that will now be formed in Assam. There has been such massive non-cooperation that it would be difficult to assess it. The government's curfew is not enforced, the agitationists' curfew is. I have already said, and I repeat, that employees are prepared to leave their jobs to participate in the agitation, the youth are prepared to die, women and children are prepared to fight. Accept the fact there is a strong feeling that is agitating the minds of these people. Do not ridicule that feeling. Do not dub it secessionist. The process of talks with them should resume. If this House, if all of us could make some contribution, so far as my party is concerned, we shall certainly be willing to participate. Thank you.

Assam Agitation Deep-rooted

Sir, after flying at summit level for seven days we have come down to the earth of reality today. For seven days attempts were made to hide the reality of Assam from the people. Television was ordered not to show any disturbing news about Assam. Those newspapers which...

SHRI M. RAM GOPAL REDDY (Nizamabad) : Sir, the same day the Summit conference was going on, the *Indian Express* had reported that there was starvation in Assam, while on the other hand guests were arriving from abroad. This is the position of our country.

SHRI VAJPAYEE : Sir, I am talking about television, not of the *Indian Express*.

MR. DEPUTY SPEAKER : He is only speaking about television. Government will reply; please do not interrupt.

SHRI VAJPAYEE : I shall also come to papers. Copies of papers published photographs of the Assam carnage— *India Today, Sunday, Ravivar*—were all bought over at five-star hotels where foreign guests stay so that they should not fall into their hands!

SHRI M. RAM GOPAL REDDY : Then why are you talking about that ?

SHRI VAJPAYEE : The customs stopped two foreign journals—*Time* and *Newsweek*. I ask you, if photographs are not published will the world think nothing happened there ? And if the world thinks so and you delude yourself you will be answerable to the people of Assam. You will have to face them. They cannot be suppressed. The situation cannot be falsified. Blood will speak and it is innocent blood. The Government is responsible for that blood, it will not be silenced.

Sir, what are the results of the elections ? We had advised against holding elections. We are ready to cooperate in the matter of amending the Constitution. But I do not wish to go into that controversy now. The results of the elections—the results that have come in after the open misuse of the administrative machinery, after making the election a joke—prove that the agitation in Assam is not limited to the valley, but limited to big people; its roots have gone quite deep.

I would like to place some figures before the House. Elections did not take place in 17 constituencies. I shall later go into why they did not take place, but 17 Assembly seats are lying vacant. What is the percentage of voting where seats were contested ? It was less than 15 per cent on 46 seats. In the tea plantation constituency—where it is said tea plantation workers are not with the agitation—the voting percentage is 16. In the Schedule Tribes constituencies the total voting percentage is 30. This is where propaganda is

Lok Sabha on March 4, 1983 during discussion on the Calling Attention Motion on the extraordinary events in Assam

made that all tribes are against the agitation because the agitationists want to uproot the tribals. In only 40 Assembly seats voting was normal.

Elections were not held for 17 seats in a Legislative Assembly of 126 seats. The matter of why there were no elections in 17 seats had gone to the court. The Election Commissioner was made a party to it. Shri Ganesan gave an affidavit, which is with me —

> "The poll in the remaining assembly and Parliamentary constituencies has been adjourned because of the abnormal situation prevailing in the constituencies concerned."

If election could be postponed that time in 17 constituencies, then, according to the letter written by the Election Commission, they could have been postponed at other places too. I would ask the Hon. Minister to look well in his cupboard. If the file on diesel oil in the Government's possession can go missing, so can the letter written by the Election Commission.

Polling took place there on the 14th. In 62-63 seats what was going to happen came to be known the same day. Riots had started. On the 12th a riot started in Tejpur. The same time a riot also started in Nabagaon. About the polling on the 14th you say it could not be stopped because the Constitution required it and we had to go by the Constitution. But after the polling on the 14th the constitutional obligation was fulfilled. The Chief Election Commissioner was of the opinion that elections should be postponed. Who insisted that they should not be ? If in 17 constituencies elections could be postponed because of abnormal conditions they could have been postponed in more constituencies as well. But everyone stood his ground.

Non-voters Included All Religions and Classes

Remove the notion from your mind that only people from the Brahmaputra valley or those who have gone from the Kanyakubja region were with this agitation. Do not spread this rumour. Brahmins boycotted this election in large numbers. Muslims already living in Assam have sided with the agitation on a large scale. They did not go to vote. Bengalis is sided with it in large numbers. They did not go to cast their votes. It is wrong to say that those who were frightened did not go to vote and those who were not did. Everyone settled in Assam—whether Hindus or Muslims, Bengalis, tea plantation workers or Marwaris felt that Assam was getting a raw deal. People crossing over from the border without check should be checked.

SHRI M. RAM GOPAL REDDY : Are they still coming ?

SHRI VAJPAYEE : They are still coming.

We are being taunted that elections had also taken place in 1977 but no objection had then been raised to the government that was formed. Then it was said elections also took place in 1979 and a ministry was formed in the State. Then they ask, if you have no objection to the electoral rolls of 1977-78 why do you object to the electoral rolls of 1979 ?

Sir, those who say such things perhaps do not know the whole truth. There is a difference in the voters' list of 1977-78 and that of 1979. Nearly 8 lakh voters have been added. I have figures with me, and I could present them all if you give me the time. For instance in Nabagaon voters increased by 32.18 per cent as compared to the voters' list of 1977 and 1978. How did this happen ? I am not asking for a reply at this time. Figures speak. My friend Shri Santosh Mohan Dev has also read out some figures. Leave Kachar district, where the polling was 32 per cent. Leaving aside the polling for the seats in Kachar the general polling has been very small.

For every seat the number of voters had increased. I was told that in the Dubri assembly constituency 12,000 voters were added as compared to 1978. How did they increase ? What was the process used for increasing the voters ? Were the voters counted. Were objections invited ? An increase of 6.7 lakh voters is not an ordinary thing. Are these the names of those who attained 21 and became lawfully entitled to vote ? Who will inquire into whose names they are ? I would also ask the parties which took part in the elections—did they know the fact that the electoral rolls of 1979 were not the same on the basis of which polling had taken place in 1977 and 1978 ?

Why Military Control Over Assam ?

Thirdly, we have handed over Assam to the army. Is it martial law there ? It is not, then how is the army discharging its responsibility there ? According to the Act under which the army was sent it could carry out a search on suspicion and could make an arrest without a warrant. Dr. Barua, Director of the Research Laboratory at Jorhat, and 10 other scientists were arrested. What is the charge against them ? "Waging war against the State."

Did they declare war on the state ? Shri Ramesh Kumar, a member of the national executive of the Bharatiya Janata Party was arrested merely because he went to the police station to complain that there were no police arrangements in the surrounding villages. He was locked up under section 302 and beaten up. A retired additional judge was arrested. Such indiscriminate arrests are being made there.

Sir, the Home Minister should take note of what the Gauhati High Court has said in the matter of the army that was before it. The Court said if the army is used under the present law it cannot resort to firing. Is it true that the Court has restrained the army from firing ? Why did the Government not try so far to remove that restraint ? What will be the result if the army is attacked by mischief-makers and if it is restrained from firing ? Can peace not be established in Assam without the army ? Are the Border Security Force and the CRP not enough for this ? Do we want the situation in Assam to normalise or to deteriorate ? If there are indiscriminate arrests things will worsen.

There are definite charges, definite complaints, against the Assam Police and the CRP. I am not blaming the whole force. The complaints are serious. Is there anybody to inquire into them! Just a single constable's wrong act could set the whole place on fire. The situation cannot normalise if charges of rape are levelled and they are not inquired into.

Sir, Assam has a government only in name. It does not have the right to rule. It does not have the people's mandate. Ministers cannot step out on the street, they cannot meet people.

Helicopters Galore

Smt. Vajpayee was moving about under police guard, I was moving without it. There was a helicopter at her disposal. Sir, there have been a lot of complaints about helicopters. Who were to fly in helicopters ? How many helicopters were flying ? It has been charged that helicopters air-dropped weapons and petrol. These charges should be inquired into. The Government has refuted the charge, but a mere refutation is not enough. How many helicopters were there during the election ? Who were authorized to use them ? When there was a fire on the 17th somebody said they saw a helicopter. Whose helicopter was it ? To date licensed arms are being kept at places where polling did not take place. Arms are not kept where polling took place.

Sir, I cannot describe the plight of the relief centres. I know it is a humanitarian problem. It is not a question of Hindu, Muslim, Bengali, Assamese. If there is a foreigner he too should be treated justly. But is this government doing justice. ?

As yet there are not adequate food arrangements at the refugee camps. There is the danger of an epidemic spreading. The monsoon starts in April. At many places refugees are lying in the open. I have personally been to Nalli, and spoke to people there. I wish they were sent home soon, but how can they go if there is no security ? On whose assurance will they go ? Twenty one new posts were opened. In my opinion that is not enough. The army cannot be deployed for an indefinite period. Then can there be a sense of security ?

The Home Minister was there yesterday and the day before. He could have invited local citizens to meet him during that period. He could have applied ointment to the wounds. It may be all right for the government to make a helicopter trip, talk to refugees and officers, and return to Gauhati, but it does not become Prakash Chandra Sethi.

Governor has Lost Credibility

Yesterday I suggested in Gauhati that a citizens' committee should be set up for assistance, but that was not done. The Governor has lost the trust of the people. No one is prepared to talk to the Chief Minister. But relief will have to be taken to the people. A beginning could have been made yesterday. Shri Sethi could have invited all citizens and said—let bygones be bygones, let us make a new beginning. People should be given relief, they should be settled, and then all problems of Assam settled. But is this happening ? Where is the determination to take all people with you ? The decision is to rule at gun-point.

The first mistake was to hold the elections. The second was to keep that government in office, and the third is to put all the blame on poor Vajpayee.

If that gives you any satisfaction I am prepared to take the whole blame. But do not give me the eminence I do not deserve. Our strength there is next to nothing, but we visit Assam time and again. Not for any political benefit—there will be no political benefit. We go to Assam because we want to tell them—you are not alone in your battle, you are not fighting for Assam alone, you are fighting for the whole of India, and we are with you. This thing will later help in keeping Assam with the rest of India. The type of speech Smt. Bajpai gave will not help to maintain unity. Did she inquire about the pamphlet to which she referred ?

DR. RAJENDRA KUMARI BAJPAI : It is with me.

SHRI VAJPAYEE : It is in Hindi, I have not seen it. They tried to get it printed during the election days. It is not a pamphlet of AASU.

PROF. MADHU DANDAVATE : Sir, please stop this civil war between the Vajpayees.

MR. DEPUTY SPEAKER : Civil war between the two Vajpayees ?

DR. RAJENDRA KUMARI BAJPAI : I have not learnt cutting a throat and shedding tears.

SHRI VAJPAYEE : There are many things you have not yet learnt. You will learn a lot of things in Smt. Indira Gandhi's court.

Sitting in Delhi and playing politics is one thing, going to Assam and solving problems is another. I do not want to blame, but if this attitude continues the situation in Assam will not normalise. When things go bad you may well blame us, but history will prove you guilty. Thank you.

Linguistic Division of Punjab

Madam, I stand to oppose this Bill. Not because I am opposed as a matter of principle to a constitutional provision for including any part of a State in a Union Territory or for reorganising a Union Territory, but I am forced to oppose it because of the context in which this Bill has been presented.

It has been decided to reorganise Punjab. The Congress Working committee had also resolved that a Punjabi-speaking State be made out of the present Punjab. The decision was not to take some part out of it and join it to Himachal Pradesh. In fact there is no question of addition of a part to Himachal Pradesh, because a Hindi-speaking region is made out of the same Punjab and that Hindi-speaking region can be added to Himachal.

SOME HON. MEMBERS : It is the Pahari-speaking region.

SHRI VAJPAYEE : There is no Pahari-speaking region. Himachal's language is Hindi. Pahari is a dialect, not a language and Pahari is not in the 14 languages of the Constitution. I respect it as a dialect and I want it to prosper. But it has not been decided to form States on the basis of dialects. Otherwise many people in Bihar would demand States and it would be difficult to stop them. I submit the situation of taking away any part out of present Punjab and joining it to Himachal Pradesh could have been avoided, and even maintaining the decision to establish a Punjabi State, the need to bring forward such a Bill could have been avoided. But this Bill has been presented and we are told a part will be added to Himachal Pradesh.

Chandigarh is being made a Union Territory. It has created this controversy. I do not want to go into the wider question of the division of Punjab. There will be separate Bills for that and the House will have the opportunity to consider them. I am against the division of Punjab because I hold that language alone cannot be the basis of reorganisation of States. Language is an important element, it will have to be considered, but we would get into difficulties if we reorganise only on the basis of language, endangering security, creating administrative difficulties and spreading the communal poison. I ask you a question—is this government, is this House ready to apply the principle of language also to Jammu and Kashmir ? Can we imagine the consequences of doing so ? Jammu and Kashmir do not have the same language. Jammu's language is akin to that of Himachal Pradesh, not of the Kashmir Valley, but because of historical reasons Jammu and Kashmir are together. And we want them to remain together, because that is in the interest of the nation, even if not in the interest of language. Was it not

Rajya Sabha on August 24, 1966 during discussion on the Resolution opposing the Constitution Amendment Bill regarding reorganisation of Punjab

in the national interest that Punjab should remain one ? What is the need to make a small border State smaller ?

Linguistic Problems

So far as language is concerned there was no hindrance to the development of Punjabi. Punjabi was taught in Haryana too, although it is not Haryana's language. If the principle of linguistic states is to be accepted does it mean the area of the language should be restricted, or does it rather mean it should be further widened for administrative and educational purposes ? But by bowing before a communal demand the Government has opened Pandora's box. Now one cannot say where this thing will end. Now we have controversies in Bombay, Maharashtra, Mysore. The demand for a separate Vidarbha is gaining strength. And there is also a demand in Jammu that it should be joined to Himachal.

SHRI SHEEL BHADRA YAJI : In Assam too.

SHRI VAJPAYEE : In Assam too the demand for a separate hill state will gain strength. Will the country be divided into small bits ? Will India suffer Balkanisation ? From this point of view I am opposed to the division of Punjab, but even if it had to be divided there was no need to join any part of it to Himachal Pradesh. What is the language of the region that has been so joined ? This is a matter of great controversy. Many people say their language is Hindi because they do not want to live in a Punjabi State. Why ? People want to leave Punjabi Suba and go to Haryana go to Himachal. The demand in Pathankot is getting stronger. As for Una tahsil the commission too has written that Una's language is Hindi, still it should go to the Punjabi State because the Anandpur Sahib Gurudwara is in Una. I cannot understand this at all. If division, reorganisation is to take place on the basis of language Una tahsil should go to Himachal Pradesh, even if the Anandpur Sahib Gurudwara goes to Himachal Pradesh. Is Himachal some foreign country, not our territory ? Will a region be divided on the basis of a Gurudwara ? I am really surprised that the Shah Commission should say such a thing. Guru Gobind Singh was born in Patna. He is our Guru too, not only the Guru of the Sikhs. We all revere him. But should Una remain in the Punjabi State because the Anandpur Sahib Gurudwara is in Una ? The Shah Commission may well think so, but Una's language is Hindi.

Chandigarh

Madam, the decision on Chandigarh has led to increased discontent.

SHRI ARJUN ARORA (U.P.) : The people of Chandigarh are happy.

SHRI VAJPAYEE : The people of Chandigarh are happy because they escaped going into the Punjabi Suba, but the people of Haryana are not happy. I say, when the Commission gave Chandigarh to Haryana why did the government not accept that decision ? The Law Minister may say the decision on Chandigarh was not unanimous and Shri Dutt had appended a note of dissent. But it was a majority decision. Still the people of Haryana are prepared to swallow the bitter pill of Chandigarh remaining a Union

Territory and its being the common capital of both new States. But had the commission recommended that Chandigarh should go to the Punjabi Suba would the Central Government have shown the courage of taking it out of the Punjabi State and making it the common capital of both States ? The people of Haryana complain that there was injustice done to them in the past and there is injustice being done to them now. But if the Government says that during the agitation against the creation of Punjabi Suba we had given the people certain assurances about maintaining the maximum common links between the two States, such as a common Governor, common boards for power, irrigation, water, and it is for the fulfilment of those assurances that we are making Chandigarh a common capital, the argument could be accepted. But the Government does not talk about more common links. Would only Chandigarh be the common capital! Would there be no common Governor ? The position regarding some links need to be clarified. It is true the Akali Dal is threatening that it would not recognise such common links, but will the Government buckle down before just one party and not think of the feelings of other parties, of the needs of the country and of the future ?

Punjabi versus Hindi versus Urdu

One more thing. My friend Shri Bhupesh Gupta is not present here. He has referred to the census of 1961. It is true that in that census Punjabi-speaking people wrote down Hindi as their mother tongue. But there are also people who are non-Sikhs and wrote Punjabi as their mother tongue. I have figures with me, but I would not take the time of the House. It would be wrong to say that every non-Sikh in Punjab wrote Hindi as the mother-tongue, and no one wrote Punjabi as their mother-tongue, but it is also true that lakhs put down Hindi as their mother tongue. They say we speak Punjabi but we never wrote Gurmukhi, Punjabi is our dialect not our language, we speak Punjabi at home and outside, but when it comes to writing we write in Hindi, actually Urdu is used in Punjab, people have been writing in Urdu. We cannot forget that when Swami Dayanand led the Hindi movement in Punjab it was against Urdu, not against Punjabi. It was an expression of nationalism, not a rejection of other languages of India. At that time there was no Gurmukhi; it was not current. At that time the quarrel was not Hindi versus Punjabi, it was Hindi versus Urdu. At that time Hindi became current in Punjab.

Need to Keep Punjab One

I hope the Government will decide about the reorganisation of Punjab after taking these suggestions into consideration apropos the Bill it is now introducing. I oppose the division of Punjab, but I also want that the reorganisation of States should not promote communal animus. Punjab should remain one, more necessary than that is that people living in Punjab should remain one. The integrity of the land is important but the unity of the children of that land is even more important. This is why the agitation going on in Punjab against Punjabi Suba was suspended after some assurances because we feel it would assume a communal form if it continued longer. But this does not mean we accept the division of Punjab very enthusiastically. When we look at the problem from the national perspective doubts arise in our mind and we hope the Government will make the maximum efforts to remove them.

Madam, this Bill is going to amend the Constitution and give the Government the power to add the territory of any State to a Union Territory. The point is, if a big part of Punjab is to be added to Himachal Pradesh, why keep Himachal as a Union Territory, why not give it full statehood ?

Secondly, this constitutional amendment does not give the Legislative Assemblies the power by which the President will be required to consult them about their existence. Legislative Assemblies of other States have that right, but the assemblies of Union Territories have been denied it. In my opinion this is not doing justice to legislative assemblies of Union Territories and to their people.

Why not Give Chandigarh to Haryana ?

So far as the question of Chandigarh is concerned, I would say when the Commission had made a majority recommendation that Chandigarh should go to Haryana was it necessary for the Government to change it ? Would the Government have dared to change the majority recommendation if it had been that Chandigarh should go to Punjabi Suba ? Injustice has been done to Haryana. Still I am in favour of Chandigarh as the common capital of both States, because there are many things that have to remain together. Even after political reorganisation the geography of Punjab cannot be changed. Canals and rivers cannot be changed. The things that have got mixed up in the life of Punjab cannot be divided. But the way Punjab has been divided lends strength to the demand for other small States, and it would be difficult for the Government to avoid such demands.

Still I hope the Government will sincerely act upon its assurances about maintaining the maximum accord. Thank you.

Constitutional Crisis in Punjab

Sir, under Rule 193 I raise a discussion on the statement made by the Home Minister regarding Punjab. It is a matter of regret that this is based upon information obtained from the Gill Government. The statement does not have more value than the statement by an offender—an offender who not only distorts the truth to hide his sin but also does not hesitate to resort to untruth.

What happened in the Punjab Legislative Assembly on March 18 ? Some truths are beyond doubt and there is no difference of opinion about them. One of them is that that day police personnel were called into the Assembly in mufti. It is also beyond doubt that they were called there on a directive from the Chief Minister. When the meeting began the police personnel in white were hiding behind the benches at the back. Before the Speaker's arrival the police had taken position in hiding.

SHRI VIBHUTI MISHRA (Motihari) : Were you there to see ?

SHRI VAJPAYEE : Neither were you there to see.

Now it is claimed they were Watch and Ward people. Had that been so they should have risen when the Speaker entered the chamber. But according to eye-witnesses they were hiding behind the benches and when opposition parties raised a point of order they filed out. They waited in the lobby for orders from the Chief Minister and the DIG, CID.

Does a Chief Minister have the power to invite the police into the Assembly ? After all who is the master of the House ? Is it the Speaker or the Chief Minister ? Sir, who is the master in this House ? Are you the master or is the Prime Minister the mistress ? Can the police be invited here on the Prime Minister's orders ?

For the last 20 years we have parliamentary democracy in India. We are proud of the fact that as compared to neighboring countries we have kept the torch of democracy burning. Some undesirable happenings have also taken place in this process of parliamentary democracy. But never before in the history of Indian democracy have the events in Punjab on March 18 taken place.

The Punjab Legislative Assembly is in Chandigarh. Chandigarh is a Union Territory. But the whole police force of Punjab was concentrated in Chandigarh, and by calling it within the Assembly arrangements were made to demolish democracy. This is a blot on the fair face of the Indian republic. It is an alarm bell for the future of democracy. We must listen to it and, as the highest democratic institution, we must do our duty in this situation.

Lok Sabha on March 21, 1968 while raising discussion on the statement made by the Home Minister regarding constitutional developments in Punjab

"Operation Gill"

Even before the Assembly's meeting on March 18 preparations for "Operation Gill" were complete. The Chief Minister had started arresting opposition legislators. On March 16-17 four MLAs were arrested and warrants were issued against more than twenty. Some of them approached the Speaker and sought protection. On March 18 a meeting took place at the Speaker's residence in the morning and it was decided to conduct the day's proceedings peacefully. But when opposition MLAs complained that there were warrants against them, they would not be allowed to enter, police goondas were being collected there and they would hinder the business of the House, the Speaker reassured them and said they could accompany him in his car and there would be no difficulty.

You will be surprised and also angry to know that the police stopped the Speaker's car and declined to let it proceed. The Speaker was himself at the wheel. The police opened the doors of the car and tried to drag out the members riding with him... (*Interruptions*) ... It is different matter that the car did not stop and the Speaker went into the Assembly with the MLAs.

Another meeting was held inside the Assembly at 1.00 o'clock and it was decided to conduct the business of the House with dignity and discipline. It was also decided that those who wished to raise points of order could do so peacefully, and that the Speaker's ruling would be final and acceptable to all.

Speaker's Powers

Now it is asked—does the Speaker have the power to declare an ordinance issued by the Governor to be illegal, and can members of the Legislative Assembly challenge such an ordinance ? This matter will have to be decided in the light of the rules of procedure of the Punjab Legislative Assembly. Whether or not the Governor issued the ordinance in accordance with the Constitution will also have to be considered. The Constitution empowers the Governor to issue an ordinance, but that power can be used only when neither House is in session. In Punjab both the Houses were in session and opposition members of Punjab claim—and there is truth in the claim—that the Governor's directive to prorogue the Assembly was effective from March 18, not March 14.

The Home Minister may argue that the directive to prorogue became effective from the day the Governor signed it. In this connection I would like to place before you Rule 7 of the rules and regulations of the Punjab Legislative Assembly —

"When a session of the Assembly is prorogued the Secretary shall issue a notification in respect thereof in the Gazette and inform the members".

SHRI Y.B. CHAVAN, Home Minister : The Hon. member should read it carefully to understand what it means.

SHRI VAJPAYEE : For the Hon. Minister's information I read again ...

SHRI Y.B. CHAVAN : It is not a question of reading it again. We should understand what it means.

SHRI VAJPAYEE : I have nothing to say if he alone understands what it means. It is possible that I may have been at the back when God distributed intelligence, but I was not absent.

SHRI S.M. BANERJI (Kanpur) : I say you were the first, I was there.

Governor's Powers

SHRI VAJPAYEE : Sir, was it enough for the Governor to sign or should the members also be informed about it ? Can the Home Minister deny that the members got the information on March 18 ? And the rule is clear—mere publication of the notification in the gazette is not enough. Members should also have information about it. That the members did not know about the proroguing of the Assembly means the Governor's notification about it is open to challenge and opposition members of the Punjab Legislative Assembly have challenged it. How can the ordinance be issued when the Assembly is in session ? It was on this basis that it was challenged in the meeting of March 18. A controversy has also been raised on whether a directive by the Governor—even when issued under the Constitution—can be challenged or not. Here too we have to look up the rules of the Punjab Legislative Assembly. I would like to draw your attention to Rule 112(1) :

> "A point of order shall relate to the interpretation or enforcement of these rules or such articles of the Constitution as regulate the business of the House and shall raise a question which is within the cognizance of the Speaker."

Business Rules

If directives issued under the Constitution relate to the business of the Assembly they too can be made subjects of points of order. The Speaker is free to give his ruling on them. Its finality cannot be questioned, and the Speaker of the Punjab Legislative Assembly has ruled that the Assembly stands prorogued from March 18. An ordinance issued on March 14 does not bind the House or the members. For more than a couple of hours the Assembly conducted a discussion quite peacefully. The Speaker gave his final ruling and left. But the drama that was played out in the Assembly after that was shameful for democratic India. No other Assembly has witnessed such a shameful scene. Many members have overstepped their rights and many unseemly incidents have taken place, but what happened that day was extraordinary, it crossed all limits. Sir, it cannot be denied that employees of the Assembly Secretariat were forcibly brought to the Assembly by the police. It can also not be denied that the Secretary of the Assembly Secretariat was dragged by the Chief Minister to the Speaker's chamber. He was forced to work under police guard. A ladder was brought to enable the police to enter. Now it is argued that the ladder was brought because they wanted to remove Gandhiji's picture from where it hung. I can understand why they wanted to remove Gandhiji's picture, because they were afraid they could not murder democracy right in the presence of his picture. But what was the need of removing it ? The ladder was brought for the use of the police. Members of opposition parties were beaten up and dragged. More than 200 police goondas entered the Legislative Assembly dressed in plain clothes and they misbehaved with members of opposition parties.

And within 15 minutes the budget was passed. In this regard too the Punjab Assembly has rules that are similar to ours. The budget is to be passed in two parts. In the first place there should be a general discussion on it, and secondly all demands for grants should be individually passed. The House may change this procedure. If it wants, the House may mix the general discussion and the discussion on the demands for grants. But that day nothing happened in the Punjab Assembly with the consent of the House. Everything was done forcibly by the police, everything was done by brute force, killing democracy in the process. The budget that was passed that day cannot be considered to have been passed.

Puppet Deputy Speaker

Sir, the Deputy Speaker has authenticated it. This is the same Deputy Speaker who did not stand up, who kept sitting, when information was received about a no-confidence motion against the Speaker. The Chief Minister said to him, why are you sitting ? Stand up—and the Deputy Speaker stood up. Sir, imagine a Deputy Speaker standing up to support a no-confidence motion against the Speaker.

Then the Deputy Speaker is forced into the seat, the drama of passing the budget is played out under his supervision, and then it is signed and forwarded to the Legislative Council. I regret the Home Minister is not prepared to admit that no Deputy Speaker is authorized to authenticate a Money Bill. Article 199(4) of the Constitution is quite clear on this point. They ask, what would happen if the Speaker becomes unconscious ?... (*Interruptions*) .... Perhaps they want to know, if the Speaker loses consciousness what Hanuman would bring Sanjivani ? And they say the Deputy Speaker is that Hanuman. I am afraid the Home Minister had either not consulted the Law Ministry, or if he has, he has been given wrong advice. If the Speaker is not in place the Appropriation Bill will not go to the Legislative Council as a Money Bill, it will go as an ordinary Bill After all, what is the purpose of a money Bill ? The purpose is to allow the Legislative Council to consider it within a certain parameter. But if this right can be given to the Deputy Speaker it will also have to be given to the members of the panel of Chairmen. Then it can also be given to other members. This was not the intention of the framers of the Constitution. The Home Minister should tell us if the Punjab Legislative Council considered the Appropriation Bill a Money Bill. If it has, it is wrong and its decision can be challenged in a court of law.

I would like to make one more demand. It is not a question of the Assembly, it is also a question of Parliament. Such a situation can arise here as well. What will happen then ? Sir, if you are not available to authenticate will the Deputy Speaker have the right ? I demand that the Home Minister call the Attorney-General to the House. The question whether the Deputy Speaker has the power to authenticate a Money Bill should be decided once for all. Under article 199 of the Constitution only the Speaker can do so.

SHRI Y.B. CHAVAN : May I intervene ? For your information, I have never said that the Deputy Speaker has a right. I said that this matter is not yet clear to me. This is the position I have taken. I have not taken that position. I said that this right of certificate is personal to the Speaker is a view which I do not entirely share yet. This was the statement I had made.

SHRI VAJPAYEE : Sir, this means the Home Minister too has his doubts.

SHRI CHAVAN : Yes.

SHRI VAJPAYEE : Then the way to remove the doubt is to call that Attorney–General to the House, take his advice ...

SHRI CHAVAN : What is the need of calling him here ?

SHRI VAJPAYEE : Why not call him here ?

SHRI CHAVAN : If we have not done anything here why call him ?

SHRI VAJPAYEE : This is not a question of the Punjab Legislative Assembly alone. It is a complicated constitutional matter, which may be raised elsewhere too. No doubt should be allowed to remain in this respect. So it would be good to take the decision, to take the final decision, after calling the Attorney– General and taking his opinion.

Serious Consequences

Sir, they may say if the opposition in Punjab is not satisfied and if it claims the budget has not been passed properly the doors of the Court are open for it. This is true. But I ask you—if the Court gives its verdict after March 31, and if it rules that the budget that is considered passed has not been passed, what will be the consequence ? Has the Home Minister imagined the serious consequences that would flow from it ? The whole economic structure will be affected, and the Government will totter. So the Central Government should not turn its face away from its responsibility by just saying "You are free to go to Court."

Sir, it is a question of the Constitution, a question of law, a question of facts and a question also of morality. Should a Chief Minister who can call the police into the Assembly be allowed to continue in office ? Does not morality, the Constitution, democracy require that he should be dismissed ? This is a day of test for the morality of the party that is supporting the Chief Minister to continue in office. Its democratic professions have today become a matter of test for the people. So far as the Constitution is concerned it is clear, and even while differing with the Punjab Speaker's conduct I would say he acted within the orbit of the Constitution. There can be a difference of opinion on whether it was right or wrong. but it has been given a constitutional form. But the later conduct is against the Constitution, against democracy, it is a fall from morality and a blow at democracy.

Fresh Mandate Needed

Sir, after the general elections the ruling Congress party lost its monopoly on power. The people's faith in the vote went up, democratic forces rallied together, but the events that have taken place after the general elections have created doubts about the future of democracy. Former Punjab Chief Minister Sardar Gurnam Singh had petitioned to the Governor saying instead of forcing this minority government on the people the Assembly should be dissolved and fresh elections held to give the people a chance to show what they feel, and the disturbances in the State began the very day the Governor turned down this petition. The Congress leaders sitting pretty at the Centre have sown thorns in the path to democracy by foisting a minority government on the people, but one day these same thorns with tear their garments apart. Democracy is in danger, we will have to protect it with all our might, and it is the duty of members sitting in this House to come forward to do so. In Punjab there is only one way to do so—no other way is left. It is to dissolve the Legislative Assembly, impose President's Rule, and give the people a chance to express their opinion by way of fresh elections. Democracy can be saved in Punjab only if Congress leaders at the Centre are prepared to go this way.

Finally, I will conclude with a quotation from an editorial in the *Hindustan Times* :

> "Sir, if worse is not to happen, the Lachchman Singh Gill Government should be dismissed straightaway, President's rule imposed on the State and mid-term elections held after a cooling-off period. How long are the people of Punjab to suffer a Ministry that will use any instrument—mass arrests on flimsy, technical charges, even forcible ejection of opposition members from the Assembly Chamber to perpetuate itself in office ?"

Further it states

> "Latter day politics in Punjab began as a reaction against the autocratic rule of late Sardar Pratap Singh Kairon. The behaviour of those in office today in Punjab makes the Kairon regime seem highminded by comparison. That is the measure of their fall."

This is the limit of a downfall, but the fall of Punjab cannot leave New Delhi unaffected. If the gods in Delhi do not wake up the cycle of events in Punjab will sweep even New Delhi into its vortex, and then democracy in the country may face such a serious crisis that we would find it difficult to overcome it. There is still time. The Centre needs to rouse its conscience and take all steps firmly.

Do not Alienate Patriotic Sikhs

Sir, the purpose of this adjournment motion is to condemn the Government's failure in solving the serious problem of Punjab. The purpose of the Bill is also to haul the State Government for the continually deteriorating law and order situation in Punjab. After all, whose responsibility is it to solve the problem ?

The Opposition has extended cooperation for solving the problem. Can the Home Minister deny this ? For the past some days the Prime Minister's speeches make it appear as if the opposition is wholly responsible for the deterioration in the situation. I quote what the Home Minister had said in this House on March 4 :

> "I must express my thanks to the leaders of the Opposition in Parliament for their participation and their valuable contribution to the tripartite talks. We will continue to seek solution in that spirit and we will continue to solicit the help and support of the Opposition leaders and parties to find out an amicable solution."

But these days a regular campaign has been launched against the Opposition. The Prime Minister says Opposition leaders say one thing when they meet her and another when they meet Akali leaders. What does this charge mean ? Let her name a leader. Let her explain his double-talk. If the Opposition's bona fides are suspect there cannot be cooperation. What type of answers has the Prime Minister given ? I shall quote from a newspaper :

> "Lucknow, 18th May
> To the suggestion of the Janwadi Party leader Chandrajit Yadav that the Akali Dal demands which have not so far been accepted by the Government should be referred to a Supreme Court Judge, Mrs. Gandhi retorted : how would it look if the entire government was handed over to the court ?"

Congress members have just said they are bound by the Court's verdict.

SHRI BUTA SINGH : Political problems will have to be solved by political parties.

SHRI CHANDRAJEET YADAV (Azamgarh) : Now the Punjab Governor also say that it should go to the Supreme Court both the water and territorial issues.

Punjab not a Party Problem

SHRI VAJPAYEE : Opposition parties are being charged with double-talk. The Home Minister thanks the Opposition parties for their cooperation, but

---

Lok Sabha on July 26, 1983 during discussion on the adjournment motion on Punjab

the Prime Minister condemns them. When the non-cooperation talks between the Akali Dal and the Congress government failed the opposition was invited to get involved. But when the talks started the opposition was not included, because our friends in the Congress thought it was a domestic matter between them and the Akali Dal. They thought they would deal with it, there was no need to take other parties of Punjab into confidence, no need to conduct talks on a national level, the problem would be solved. But when it was not solved leaders of the opposition were invited. My friend Shri Indrajit Gupta is present here and he knows that when tripartite talks were decided upon. I was not ready. I had reservations. I had learnt a lesson from my experiences on Assam. When talks begin to fail or when the Government decides not to compromise it blames the opposition parties.

Is it not true that as a result of the tripartite talks differences of opinion narrowed down and the Akalis agreed that a reference to the Anandpur Sahib resolution was not necessary in the setting up of the commission for considering Centre-State relations ? Is it not true that the Akalis were prepared to give up their claim over Himachal Pradesh, a large part of Haryana and Ganganagar in Rajasthan ? Is it not true that they agreed not to touch the agreement with Rajasthan so long as the problem of the division of water is not solved ? Is this not progress ? Shri Sethi himself said in his statement that there was progress in some matters and talks would be conducted on others :

> "As you know, the Government has been having a series of discussions on the demands of the Shiromani Akali Dal in which some progress has already been made, but some need to be discussed further."

SHRI R.L. BHATIA : Are they firm on that ? Is the Akali Dal firm ?

SHRI VAJPAYEE : That is exactly what I am asking Shri Sethi.

If he invited the Akalis for talks again why did he leave the opposition parties out ? I quote what he wrote to Sant Longowal :

> "It would be appropriate to resume the talks directly. I, therefore, invite you to meet me in Delhi."

Why was it not necessary at that time to take the opposition parties into confidence ? We would be quite happy if you solved the problem through direct talks. But if you cannot solve the matter why are you blaming us for your failure ?

What is the situation in Punjab today ? Is there a government there ? Are life and property safe in Punjab ? Every day people are getting killed. The unfortunate and terrible danger of a Hindu- Sikh confrontation has arisen. Who lighted the spark at Patiala ? Who gave the call for a Punjab bandh on behalf of the Hindu Suraksha Samiti ? Why is there no Hindu Suraksha Samiti in Haryana ? I can understand it if there is a controversy between Haryana and Punjab and a Samiti is set up to put forth Haryana's point of view. But from whom are the Hindus of Haryana in danger ?

AN HON. MEMBER : From the BJP.

No Khalistan

SHRI VAJPAYEE : Wrong. It is false. Don't play with the fate of the country like this. Who does not want unity and integrity ? Has not the Akali Dal kept itself aloof from the Khalistan demand ? No one except a handful of Sikhs wants Khalistan. The Sikhs are patriots. I have talked with people in England, in many countries of Europe, and in America. Those who support Khalistan cannot enter a Gurudwara in New York, nor in London. Everywhere my meetings were attended by a large number of Sikhs. I said there would be no Khalistan. They said, who wants it ? We do not demand Khalistan. But today we look upon every Sikh with suspicion. Do they not feel it ? In foreign countries Sikhs told me we love India but when we come to India we are looked at with suspicions are detained, there is an additional inspection of our passports. What if some Sikh has a Canadian passport ? The colour of the passport does not change the colour of blood and of the heart. We are deliberately talking of Khalistan. I would like to repeat that there would be no compromise on the question of Khalistan. The country will not be allowed to be partitioned again. But who is asking for a division ? We have raised a nightmare and it will be sought to be exploited in the next election. This is not the way to serve the country. Why can you not normalise the situation in Punjab ? It is true that the Akalis should strongly condemn violence, killings and terrorism. They are condemning. It is true that criminals should not get shelter in Gurudwaras. But what are the Punjab police and the administration doing ? People are getting killed, policemen are getting killed. Who killed Atwal ? The CBI is inquiring into it. What is the result ? Who was that Brigadier ? Who was that IPS Officer ? Whenever an agreement is likely to take place in Punjab some such murder is committed. Who is behind this ? What happened in Patiala was repeated in Jalandhar. The Sodal temple is a place of an old controversy. The matter is *sub judice*. The Court has withheld its verdict as there would be no new construction there. The police are guarding the place for 24 hours. Then how did construction take place there on the night of June 23 ? A big platform was built and a 125-foot high 'Nishan Sahib' was planted. What were the police doing ? Are the police under control of the Punjab government ? Is the government of Punjab under the control of the Chief Minister ? Sardar Darbara Singh is a nationalist Sikh, but he is not an administrator. The Punjab Government has failed in its primary duty of protecting life and property. A parcel full of bombs was sent to the office of the *Pratap*. How was it that in no post office was the parcel checked ?

Threats have been received at the office of the *Pratap* in the past too. The parcel went directly into the hands of the employees. We have metal detectors at Parliament House. There are no such arrangements in Punjab. The employees opened the parcel. Two people died, which increased the tension. The Punjab police fired on the mourners. The Nihangs were given full freedom. Change the government in Punjab. It is necessary to cleanse the administration in Punjab. Government decisions are known to the offenders beforehand. People who are not loyal to the country have infiltrated the

Punjab administration. Screen them. Establish law and order there. What can Opposition parties do in this ?

SHRI C.M. STEPHEN : Infiltrators from where ?

SHRI VAJPAYEE : Mr. Stephen, you did not follow me as to what I had said.

SHRI C.M. STEPHEN : I have perfectly followed.

SHRI VAJPAYEE : Not from Bangladesh.

SHRI C.M. STEPHEN : From inside I know.

I demand President's Rule

SHRI VAJPAYEE : I demand that President's Rule be imposed in Punjab if it is necessary to do so. Khalistan is not in America, if there is at all some idea of Khalistan it is in Punjab due to your failure. Deal with it strictly, then continue talks for solving the political problems. But what the Prime Minister is doing is not the way to keep talks going.

The Prime Minister says who am I to give land to Haryana ? She says, is this my land ? When Chandigarh was given to Punjab whose was it ? Why was the award given ? Why was it not said, let the court decide ? Berubari was given, Tin Bigha was given, whose land was that ?

Who said give the land of Haryana to Punjab ? I thought all land was India's. I said in Punjab, and I also said in Haryana that I was not worried so long as Chandigarh is in India. Can no way be found to iron out whatever differences remain ? But if the Government proposes tripartite talks I will have to think twice before joining them. We are not ready to be abused, we have sincerely tried to make the talks successful. Now our integrity is being challenged. I too suspect that the Government does not want to solve the Punjab problem till the next election. The Government wants conflict, not cooperation, tension, not goodwill. The government has its eyes on the coming elections, not on national unity. How long will this game go on ?

I would also like to tell the Akali Dal something. It has decided to suspend action till August 15. I welcome the decision, but I would like to go one step further. In view of the situation that prevails in Punjab they should suspend their agitation indefinitely. A conflict between Hindus and Sikhs would be most unfortunate for the country's life.

No one can say when Punjab will be on fire. The people of Punjab are patriotic and workers of political parties are behaving with restraint, but things can go bad. Riots have taken place at three places. I would like to appeal to the Akali Dal. The Government will not listen, they want the Chair. A campaign may be launched in Punjab after the agitation is suspended and Hindu-Sikh unity is established.

Ask the country

I say to the Akali Dal—don't ask the Prime Minister for anything, ask Haryana for what you want. Ask the country. Create goodwill in Haryana. The Prime Minister says why were the Akalis silent in 1977 ? It was not because they were going to get a share in the power. That you too are ready to give them. You are even ready to make Sardar Prakash Singh Badal Chief Minister (*Interruptions*).

But the Akali Dal rejected the proposal. It said that before any change of government the Assembly must be suspended for six months. You were not ready for that.

You say you do not want an alliance. You are not willing to share power. I shall accept it if you say so, but for us the problem of Punjab is not only the problem of sharing power.

In 1977 the Akalis were satisfied. Today there is a crisis of confidence among them. It was created after 1980. The way the Centre goes on, the way the Home Ministry is conducted, the way the Congress interfered with the Gurudwara elections, and the way Bhindranwale was propped up to checkmate the Akalis in the elections to the Gurudwaras in Delhi—all this has created doubts in the minds of the Akalis.

SHRI BUTA SINGH, Minister for Parliamentary Affairs : The Gurudwara elections had taken place in your regime.

SHRI VAJPAYEE : There was no trouble in those elections.

SHRI BUTA SINGH : Vajpayeeji, you know quite well that the whole Punjab Government had come down for the election campaign. The Chief Minister had come and also all ministers.

SHRI VAJPAYEE : Delhi's Lt. Governor had specially called college principals and told them whom to vote for. When I levelled this charge Gyaniji said the Lt. Governor is also a Sikh, even if a Mona Sikh (*Interruptions*).

The Prime Minister herself said there were no problems when the Centre was with us. If there are problems at the Centre now, it is your failure. There were also non-Janata governments in those days, but there was no conflict. And now the Prime Minister says non-Congress governments, non-Congress States are bent on a confrontation with the Centre (*Interruptions*).

Is asking for more powers for the States coliding with the Centre ? We too want more powers for the States in economic matters. If this country breaks it won't be because of the use of regional parties, it will break because executive concentration of power at the Centre will weaken national unity.

I wanted to tell the Sikhs something.

'Kaum' not Nation

They use the word *'Kaum'* for the Sikhs. I do not object to its use, for *'Kaum'* means community. But they write 'nation' in English. This creates a misunderstanding. Today I got a book by Sant Longowal which uses the word 'nation'. We have not accepted the two-nation theory, we shall not accept a multi-nation theory. Nationalism cannot be based on religion. The Pakistan that came into being on the basis of religion was divided and Bangladesh separated. Iran and Iraq are fighting with each other. People believing in many religions may live in one nation, and people believing in one religion may live in many nations. So there can be no question of accepting a Sikh nation. But now the Akalis have given a new twist. They say :

"The repeated affirmations currently being made by the Sikhs that 'They are a Nation' must be seen in this context".

What is the context ?

He has quoted Pandit Nehru. Then he has talked of article 25. It says Sikhs are called Hindus and Hindu Personal Law applies to them. Now the Akali Dal says amend article 25, take Sikhs out of the definition of Hindus, and make a separate personal law for them. I do not know if there is a separate Sikh personal law. So far there is not. Now perhaps they want to make it. The Directive Principles in the Constitution say the whole country will have one personal law. This has not been implemented yet because we do not want to forcibly impose a personal law on anybody. But so far as the Sikhs are concerned the whole social structure and the entire provision of law are such that they are an inseparable part of us. If today a Harijan becomes a Sikh, he does not lose the concessions he gets because of his being a Harijan. But if he embraces Islam or becomes a Buddhist he loses them. He does not lose them on becoming a Sikh because we hold that Sikhs are our own people, they are a part of the Hindu family. Do the Akalis want to destroy this ?

Don't Divide Families

The second question I would like to put to them is this. There can be a Hindu boy and a Sikh boy in the same family. A girl may have come in from a Sikh family and a boy may have married into a Sikh family. If there are different personal laws will different personal laws apply to different people in the same family ? Will not the families break down ? They now fear people may give up being Sikhs. Maybe another fear may arise—that people may be forced to remain Sikh. I submit that this decision should be left to the individual. What religion, what sect he follows is his personal matter. This talk of separate personal law makes me somewhat unhappy. The Sikhs are a sect and I bow before it. It has a tradition of martyrdom. The history of the world does not have such a tradition of sacrifices. But Guru Gobind Singh never talked of being separate. Originally, Sikhs were called Nanak Panthis. Guru Gobind Singh Maharaj said :

Akhil Vishwa mein Khalsa panth gaiey,
Jagey dharma Hindu sakal Bhand bhaajey.

'The Khalsa Panth and the Hindu Dharma resound throughout the world.'

Now the Akalis in search of an identity say they are not Hindus. I shall accept that, but I shall say to them, are you not Indians ? This is enough. The situation in Punjab can still be improved, provided the Congress concentrates on solving the problem rather than on the elections. But I have no such hope, so we seek to condemn the Government. Thank you.

Massacre Continues in Punjab

Sir, the promulgation of President's Rule in Punjab is a fresh example of how even the right step becomes ineffective if it is delayed. It would have been possible for the people of Punjab to come out of the crisis it now faces and it would have been possible for the country to overcome the worry that now surrounds it on all sides if President's Rule had been imposed a year ago or if the Darbara Singh Ministry had been replaced by a more effective government.

Lala Jagat Narain was killed on December 11, 1981. Since then killings have continued unchecked. Extremists stepped up their activities, the administration's morale plummeted, a sense of insecurity kept spreading in Punjab, and the final culmination was on October 6 when innocent people travelling by bus from Amritsar to Delhi were forced out of the bus at Dhalwa near village Nurpur of Kapurthala and gunned down. Before the Dhalwa massacre seven people who went for a morning walk near Jagraon were also similarly killed.

These killings are different from previous killings in Punjab. Previously the extremists' targets were either Nirankaris or police officers—and among them Sikhs were in a majority. Selected people were made the targets. But matters were kept hanging because there they were Hindus. There was no such madness before. Was the Government waiting for this day ? It is quite clear that the Darbara Singh government could not control the situation. Chief Minister Darbara Singh himself complained that he was not being allowed to work, that the Centre keeps interfering in everything.

Now there is a direct rule of the Centre. President's Rule was promulgated on October 7. We have declared Punjab a disturbed area. The police have been given special powers. Preparations are also being made to use the army. Why did things go so bad ? My time is limited. I was looking up the old proceedings. When the matter of Lala Jagat Narain's murder was raised in the House on September 11, 1981 the Home Minister said a handful of people want to create a disturbance and the opposition is blowing it up. He taunted us by saying we were doing so to derive political benefit. How did things come to such a pass in two years ?

What is happening now after the imposition of President's Rule ? I would like to quote the former Chief Minister's opinion in this matter. Shri Darbara Singh talked to a correspondent of *Dinman* and portions of the question-answers are given here.

Lok Sabha on November 16, 1983 while moving a Calling Attention Motion, and participating in the discussion, on the resolution seeking approval of the Proclamation providing for Prsident's rule in Punjab State

Shri Darbara Singh was asked if the situation had improved after the imposition of President's Rule. He replied, 'In my opinion, no. Rather it has deteriorated.' What of so many arrests that are being made ? Darbara Singh replied, what is new about it ? They are all offenders who should have been already arrested by the police. They are now being arrested. He added, 'there might hardly be an extremist among them'. He may no longer be the Chief Minister now, but he was once, and he is a responsible person of the ruling party. If we criticise we may be blamed, but if Shri Darbara Singh says something he must be saying it with due thought.

I ask the Home Minister—how many extremists have been arrested. They include smugglers or anti-social elements like thieves and goondas. How many of them are extremists ? The Home Minister should take the House into confidence about the total strength of the extremists.

Training camps are being discussed a lot. Hundreds of people are participating in them. Whether it is Jammu & Kashmir or Uttar Pradesh or Himachal Pradesh, if hundreds of people are taking training in camps the Government cannot save itself from the blame.

Bring out White Paper on Punjab

Sir, I would like the Government to publish a White Paper. It should mainly contain two things. Who are the extremists ? With what political party are they connected ? With which political leaders are they connected ? Who established Dal Khalsa ? Who received the support and cooperation of Sant Bhindranwale and his colleagues in the 1980 elections ? Sardar Santokh Singh was killed in Delhi. So far as I know the police do not have any clue so far. I do not know if the police have given any authorized information. This Sardar Santokh Singh was on Bhindranwale's side. He delivered a very provocative speech in Mehta Chowk. The White Paper should also throw light on the role of foreign forces. I regret to see that the Prime Minister said during Question Hour today that the cases cannot be proved in Court. No one tells you to prove in court. But take this court into confidence. If Khalistani training camps are going on in Pakistan all talk of normalizing relations with Pakistan should cease.

If they invite citizens and train them there cannot be normal relations, let alone friendship. When I visited Peking I told the Chinese leaders that they were supplying Nagas with weapons, then how can our relations improve ? The Chinese replied, that was in the past, now it won't be there. Was this matter raised with Pakistan on a diplomatic level ? Why does the Government not take the House into confidence ? I have not had an opportunity to ask a supplementary on the reply given today. The question was in connection with the CIA.

Reported Training of Punjab Extremists by Foreign Countries

"Whether it is a fact that recently Islamabad is said to have encouraged some of its own people to cross into India in the garb of Sikhs and indulge in terrorism."

A : Government has seen the news item."

What is this reply of the Hon. Minister ?

It is now being openly said in Punjab that those who forced the people out of the bus on October 6 and killed them could not have been Sikhs. It is true that there are extremists among the Sikhs too. But it is said the killers were foreigners. Has the Government been able to nab them ? Has a single agent, a single individual been caught who, it can be confidently said, was sent by Pakistan ?

Where Did the Killers Come From ?

You do not answer even that question. The reply given was—we have received some reports and we are investigating. You do not even say—we have definite information that some foreign forces are active, but we cannot place all the facts before the House because it would not be in the public interest to do so. The Prime Minister just said matters cannot be proved in court. But things could be explained to us, we could be taken into confidence.

The Prime Minister had made a statement to the effect that the roots of Khalistan are in the United States of America. She visited the U.S. after that. Was the matter raised with President Reagan ? Was he asked what connection the U.S. Government had with Khalistan ? If not, is all this being said for public consumption ?

Today the Home Minister has replied that search for arms has been going on for a month but only two hundred and twenty-five weapons have been seized. How many of them are Pakistani arms and how many are Chinese ? If they are, tell us. Take the House into confidence (*Interruptions*).

Bring out a While Paper. You have all the information. Today's newspapers have published a statement by the Governor of Punjab and you cannot avoid it by saying he does not know, the Centre does. The Governor of Punjab is not a statesman. Shri Sharma is not there. He has been transferred to Calcutta. While appointing him it was not taken into account that he was going to a State like Punjab. He was to be removed from here. Where should he be sent ? Send him to Punjab. Even at that time the situation was getting worse. It is true that there was a ministry there. But at that time the need was for a Governor who could advise the Chief Minister and maintain the morale of the services. But Shri Sharma had to be removed, so where should he be sent ? To Punjab. Now Shri B.D. Pandeya has come. He is an experienced person. But he should have full freedom to act. I can understand the appointment of an advisor if a political leader is the Governor and President's Rule is imposed. But what is the need of advisors for an able administrator like Shri Pandeya ? Does not Punjab have an administration ? Four advisors have gone there. All of them are behaving as if they are ministers. Every one goes to Amritssar. There everyone goes to bow before Darbar Sahib. It is not enough to go to Darbar Sahib, it is also necessary to go to Durgiana Mandir. They give a statement that the police would not enter the Golden Temple. One of them even issued a statement saying Guru Nanak Niwas is a part of the Golden Temple. We know it is separate. There was a road between the two in the past. It was a thoroughfare. Later it was closed in. Who is this advisor who says such things ? Perhaps his name is Jagat Pati. If you make Jagat Pati Punjab Pati you will get into difficulties. Tell the advisor to sit and work in the Secretariat.

It is necessary to turn the whole Punjab administration upside down. Sardar Nihal Singhwala is not present. Yesterday he said that in the days of the Janata and Akali Dal regimes dangerous elements had entered the police. If they entered in our regime how is it that they are still in place in the three and a half years of your regime ? What were you doing for three and a half years ?

The citizens of Punjab are apprehensive. They cannot take their complaints to the police station, nor can they trust the police. There is a crisis of confidence. This is not only an administrative matter. Many of our Sikh brethren in Punjab feel injustice is being done to them. Even Sikhs living abroad think so. I am not going into whether it is right or wrong on their part of think so. On the other hand the non-Sikhs feel they have been reduced to the status of second class citizens. Not both these things can be true. But a strange psychological condition has come into being which cannot be cured by President's Rule alone, by giving more powers to the police alone.

Bhindranwale Pampered

One thing we must understand well. Things would not have come to such a pass if the problems of Punjab had not been kept hanging. What is the Centre now going to do ? One day the Home Minister said we are ready to talk with the Akalis. It is good if the agitation has been suspended, but that is not our condition. Let them come for talks. The opposition people say suspend the agitation. It is being exploited by the extremists to spread their dangerous activities, but you are calling them for talks even if the agitation is not taken back. I ask you—what is the ruling party's connection with the extremists ? In the Bombay session of the Congress not a word was spoken against Bhindranwale. A specific demand for the dismissal of the elected Chief Minister of Jammu & Kashmir, by naming him, was made, but not one delegate said arrest Bhindranwale.

SHRI S.L. VYAS (Bhilwara) : Many people did.

SHRI VAJPAYEE : The services and government officers are under pressure and their moral is breaking. It is very necessary to shore it up. Some people here are demanding that a parallel government be set up. A parallel government is already functioning there. Those Government officers who do their duty are mentioned by name. Then they get going after their lives. The Government is unable to save the officers. Then their wives go to the Golden Temple, present petitions in Bhindranwale's court, wail before him and pray that their husband or their brother be let off.

This is a clipping from the *Hindustan Times*. These days our Congress friends have great affection for the *Hindustan Times*, so I have brought a clipping from that newspaper :

Officer Begs Bhindranwale for His Life

> A senior police officer, whose name is understood to have been included in the hit list, is reported to have visited Guru Nanak Niwas to beg for his life. According to official and Golden Temple sources, the police officer is a senior superintendent of police who, with two Akali leaders, met the Sikh militant leader, Mr. Jarnail Singh Bhindranwale in Guru Nanak Niwas.
>
> The official sources say that the police officer was in plain clothes and with two Akali leaders, including one member of the suspended Vidhan Sabha and another Sarpanch......

The Golden Temple sources say that the three of them went to Mr. Bhindranwale and begged for the exclusion of the name of the Senior Police Officer from his hit list. The sources say that Mr. Bhindranwale smiled and said nothing."

SHRI R.L. BHATIA (Amritsar) : That was refuted later.

SHRI VAJPAYEE : Refuted by whom ?

SHRI R.L. BHATIA : By the Director– General of Police that no Police Officer went there.

SHRI VAJPAYEE : He has found out the name.

SHRI R.L. BHATIA : When you are making an allegation....

SHRI VAJPAYEE : I am not making an allegation. This has not been denied.

SHRI R.L. BHATIA : It has been denied.

SHRI VAJPAYEE : Who denied it ? How am I to know it ? The denial should have been published in this paper. Officers' wives went and they returned blessing him.

SHRI R.L. BHATIA : You are saying she went. I say she never went.

SHRI VAJPAYEE : The Government should take stringent steps to maintain law and order. There can be no difference of opinions in that. But it is not only an administrative matter. Who is trying to bring politics into this ? The Prime Minister has levelled a charge against the Opposition parties.

> "New Delhi, August 10 : Mrs. Gandhi lashed out at the Opposition for, what she thought, their inconsistent stand on the Punjab problem. She said the Opposition spoke one thing to the Government and something quite different to the Akalis."

Inclusion of Opposition for Talks

Sir, the Prime Minister also said something else. She said the Punjab problem worsened because we included the Opposition parties in the talks. We did not say include us. I had my reservations on the day it was being considered whether or not Opposition parties should be included. The Home Minister is present in the House. I had said in the light of the experience of the Opposition parties in Assam we do not want to talk with you, you may talk with the Akalis. If there are tripartite talks in future Opposition parties will have to think a hundred times about them.

If talks fail Opposition parties are blamed. The Home Minister himself said in this House that Opposition parties played a constructive role. He also admitted differences have decreased. I have read his statement of Ratlam, in which he said Bharatiya Janata Party and Lok Dal are not cooperating with us, other Opposition parties are. Then solve the problem with their cooperation.

I shall place my demands in brief. Dissolve the Assembly. Secondly appoint a high-power commission to investigate the charge of discrimination and find out who are being discriminated against. Include the complaints of other people too in this. Inquire into discrimination in the services, in trade and in the armed forces. If there is discrimination against anybody it must be removed.

Thirdly, innocent people are getting killed in Punjab. The killers have weapons but the citizens are unarmed. Decide to give licenced arms liberally in Punjab. People are still complaining that those who should get licences for self-protection do not get arms.

One thing more. The Government should make up its mind about what it wants to do. If you want to keep things hanging till the next elections you may do so. But it would be a dangerous game with the country. The greater the delay the more the situation will deteriorate. You may not have tripartite talks, you may not invite Akalis for talks, but you should declare your intentions and act upon them. Do not keep the matters of Chandigarh and Abohar hanging. Do not worry about what will happen in the elections in Haryana. If you really care for the country's unity and want to take the cooperation of all for the country's security, do what is right. But do not procrastinate. The cycle is moving. Minds that were clean a month ago are now vitiated. If this process is not stopped there will be dire consequences. Thank you.

Punjab : From Bad to Worse

Sir, this is not the first time in the last few years that this House is liscussing the situation in Punjab against a serious background. The House ıas continuously been discussing the violence in Punjab, the extremism, the nixing of religion and politics, the failure of the Government to control the situation, its inefficiency and its helplessness. But as days pass things are going from bad to worse and the situation is getting out of control. It is not a question of political parties deriving political benefit. Sometimes there is great apprehension about India's unity and integrity.

On February 28 the Home Minister had made a statement on the situation in Haryana and Punjab. I quote a portion from it : "I would like to assure the House that the Government will take every possible step to end cruel violence, whatever that cost."

This is a statement of February 28, and on March 28 Shri Manchanda, Chairman of the Delhi Gurudwara Prabandhak Committee, was killed in this very Delhi, the Capital of India, not in the dark of night but in broad daylight, not in a lonely corner but in a crowded street.

Shri Manchanda's name was on the hit list. He had been given a guard. Look at the daring of the killers. They killed Manchanda and left without being caught. They must surely have been pursuing him. What was the Government doing ?

The fire of Punjab has reached the capital. Manchanda was connected with the government party. The government could not protect him too.

On April 1 the Home Minister surrendered before the Akalis in respect of article 25. He did not think it necessary even to inform the opposition parties, let alone take them into confidence. This is not the first time that when religious demands were accepted opposition parties were ignored and the announcement made in Gurudwaras.

Shri Seth may say Parliament was not in session, the Akalis were going to step up their agitation on April 2, and he had no option but to make the announcement. But could opposition leaders not have been contacted on the phone ?

It had been decided to observe an *'Azad Panth'* week. Before agreeing to amend article 25 did you ask the Akalis what freeing the *Panth* meant ? From whom did it want to be free ? Was it freedom from India, or freedom from Hindus ? Is it not free today ? The *Panth* came into being for the protection of the country and the religion.

Lok Sabha on April 4, 1984 during discussion on the growing violence in Punjab

Article 25

I do not know what talks took place with the Akali Dal. The Home Minister said in his statement that on March 18 the Government received a letter from the Akali Dal. What did it say ? Has the Akali Dal given the assurance that after the amendment of article 25 they would not raise the demand for a separate personal law ? Why did the Home Minister place before the Akali Dal the point about seeking Supreme Court advice on article 25 ? Article 25 is an article which, according to many friends including Sikh scholars and Sikh legal experts, accepts a separate power and a separate identity of Sikhism. A verdict of the Supreme Court of 1965 says :

> "The definition of Hindu is expanded for the special purpose of sub-clause (b) of Clause 2 of article 25 and for no other."

Under article 25 Sikhs have the right to wear a kirpan and move about with it.

It recognises a separate Sikh sect. Dalits and Harijans embracing Sikhism are today entitled to all special facilities. Was the Akali Dal asked if they want all these concessions to be withdrawn ?

What, after all, was the hurry with article 25 ? But the Government got frightened of what would happen on April 2 and surrendered.

The Sikh Students' Federation has been declared illegal. Clearly the Government must have reasons for doing so. But the Federation has thrown a challenge—they said we shall close all roads of Moga and not allow any buses to pass. Hundreds of people staged a *Dharna*. All work came to a halt. They demanded that all those who have been arrested should be released. Those who were under arrest were got released at the police station and taken away and those who remained were released on bail. Before surrendering in Delhi the Government surrendered in Punjab. But if an organisation is declared illegal and yet its members openly throw section 144 to the winds but the Government cannot arrest them what was the need of declaring it illegal ? The Home Minister did not even ask the Akalis—why did you not raise this matter before ? The question of article 25 was never raised in the tripartite talks. And now you are going to the extent of burning the Constitution. We will think about it. But by not doing so they accepted this point. What was the result ? I had said in Ahmedabad that the appeasement policy will not prove useful. The very next day Bharatiya Janata Party leader Shri Harbans Lal Khanna was killed in Amritsar. He had been the target of killers. There had already been an attempt to kill him but he had escaped. He was given a gunman. The gunman had a stengun. The killers came with pistols, first killed the gunman, took his stengun and with it killed Shri Harbans Lal Khanna. This means the killers knew how to use a stengun.

SHRI INDRAJIT GUPTA (Basirhat) : They have had very good training.

SHRI VAJPAYEE : How many such killers are there in Punjab ? Where do they receive training ? What is Mr. Kao, the Government's security advisor, doing ? When Opposition members of Parliament go abroad RAW agents are set behind them. What danger does this Government face from us ? When I went to the U.S. a RAW Officer was set behind me. He had been appointed in my days. I knew him. When I complained to the Prime Minister the Prime Minister said he was not trailing me, he was just looking after me.

Intelligence Department Breaking Down

The intelligence department of this Government is breaking down. The whole appartus is getting scattered. The morale of the services has broken down. What is happening in Punjab ? Harbanslal Khanna was killed there. He fully believed in Hindu–Sikh unity. But he was a courageous man. His murder will not silence his voice. We too will not be silenced. But the killers struck again. Religious fanatics made a person like Dr. Tiwari a victim. His wife comes from a Sikh family. This murder is madness. A person who seeks to keep the country one, the society one, to keep Hindus and Sikhs one, is sought to be silenced. Dr. Tiwari's killers had gone to him as his disciples. There was a time when disciples gave their life for their Guru in this country. Now those who take like go as disciples.

Yesterday we discussed if the House should adjourn. Rules were quoted. Can we not mourn his death, can we not adjourn because Shri Tiwari was a member of the other House ? He was connected with the Congress Party. He had organised a world Punjabi conference. He was a scholar of Punjabi. This murder is a challenge to the whole government. Does the Government have the courage, the firmness to face this challenge ? If you have decided to surrender why let the matter hang so long ? The Government has still not said what solution of the Punjab problem it has in mind. The Government has four alternatives before it. I do not want to repeat them. Time is short. Apply the 1970 award, entrust all controversies including Chandigarh to a new commission, entrust the division of Chandigarh between Punjab and Haryana and the remaining problems to a commission, and fourthly implement whatever is acceptable to both Haryana and Punjab. If both agreed, how far is the Central Government involved ?

You are in power. It is your responsibility to solve problems. Why do you not want to solve it ? Announce the solution of the Punjab problem that you think proper, and implement it unilaterally. But you will not do that. You will accept religious demands unilaterally. You will make the announcement on article 25 unilaterally.

I have also a complaint about the Akali Dal. They did not listen to the Opposition parties on article 25. Bharatiya Janata Party, Lok Dal have not fully supported the Akali Dal. But the Akali Dal did not take into confidence even those parties that have supported it. It made an agreement with the Government. It withdrew the 'Azad Panth' week. I am happy about that. But will this stop here ? Will there not be more demands after this ? I again ask—was personal law discussed ? Were concessions for Scheduled castes and Dalits who become Sikhs discussed ? What will happen to violence, murder and extremism ? Will things continue as at present ?

In the dark night of violence and murder in Punjab today we still see some small lamps of humanity, affection and Hindu-Sikh camaraderie fighting the darkness. Those Hindus who left villages through fear and went to the city were taken back by the Sikhs of the same village. This tragic situation has still not enveloped all villages. But the situation will deteriorate if the Government is unable to discharge its primary responsibility of protecting every citizen.

No Faith in Police

The people of Punjab have lost faith in the police of Punjab. When the funeral procession of Shri Harbanslal Khanna was taken out people became angry at the very sight of the police. The CRP is given a welcome wherever it goes. This is a most tragic situation. It is not healthy. But this situation will have to be faced. The Punjab police should be removed from critical areas and the CRP should be increased in strength, although its morale is not as high as it should be. At one place a bank was being looted and the CRP just stood by, saying why should we risk our life ? This Government cannot save us, it cannot save members of Parliament, it cannot save Opposition leaders, then who will give his life for such a government ? From where to where have you brought the country!

Gun Licences

In this very House the Home Minister had announced that arms licences would be liberally issued to peaceful unarmed citizens of Punjab. Now there are heaps of licence applications in every district, but what officer would risk his life by issuing them ? Let the Home Minister find out. Now Government people say Shri Bhairon Dutt Pande was considered a strong administrator but he proved weak (*Interruptions*). Now we will be made the scapegoat. Recall him, the people of Bengal are ready to take him back. Send Shri Sharma to Bihar, but not as Governor (*Interruptions*).

Sir, Shri Bhinder, Inspector-General of Police of Punjab, should also be recalled. There are serious complaints about him too. In Punjab we have officers—whether Hindu or Sikh—who do not have an iota of communalism in their mind. Today secularism is being challenged. If we cannot keep the services in Punjab aloof from the poison of communalism the secular structure of this country will not survive.

The Prime Minister is not present in the House. She came for a little time. We were obliged.

PROF. N.G. RANGA : You were yourself an important Minister. You know how difficult it is to be always in the House. She was here with us. Why do you make a point about her presence ?

AN HON. MEMBER : It is the duty of the Prime Minister to be present here.

PROF. MADHU DANDAVATE : Because Prof. Ranga has raised the issue, let me clarify when debate on such a sensitive issue took place Shri Morarji Desai made it a point to remain present in the House throughout.

PROF. N.G. RANGA : There were certain engagements ......

SHRI VAJPAYEE : All engagements should have been cancelled.

PROF. N.G. RANGA : You did not give notice of your time.

SHRI VAJPAYEE : She is not only the Prime Minister but is the Leader of the House (*Interruptions*).

PROF. N.G. RANGA : The Home Minister is here. Why to make a big point out of it ?

SHRI VAJPAYEE : I warn you—do not play with the situation in Punjab any more. I read in the papers today that the whole of Punjab has been declared a dangerously disturbed area. Whaty is this *'dangerously disturbed'* ? At first it we a disturbed area now it is dangerously distrubed. What does it mean in law ? The Bill you have tabled is titled. 'Punjab Disturbed Areas Bill, 1983'. Did the newspapers add 'dangerously' on their own or did you tell them ?

PROF. MADHU DANDAVATE : Is it a composite mistake ?

SHRI VAJPAYEE : These are small things, but they reveal how useless this government is.

Minister Uninformed

I shall tell you about an incident. Shri Tiwari was hit by a bullet and went to hospital. Shri Advani, member of the Rajya Sabha, rang up Shri Sethi to inquire about Shri Tiwari's condition. This was at 9.30 in the morning. Shri Sethi said Shri Tiwari was out of danger. Shri Advani went to the airport to go to Amritsar, where he learnt that Shri Tiwari had died. Does even the Home Minister get full information or not ? Is it not true that the Home Ministry is ignored and decisions are taken elsewhere ? Who are these people who decide ? The Punjab situation has not improved, the problem is not solved and already old officers of the Home Ministry have been transferred. I would not have complained if shifting them would have improved matters. But it seems the Government's policy is to let things drift. This policy of yours succeeded to some extent in Assam, but it won't succeed in Punjab.

PROF. N.G. RANGA : No that is no correct.

SHRI VAJPAYEE : Sir, efforts need to be made to solve the Punjab problem on a national level. For that talks are necessary. But before that peace and order should be fully established in Punjab. For this the Government must take stern steps. I do not understand why the opposition is asked—what is your solution ? You have the government in your hands, you have the power to make and change laws, the administration goes by your directives, the police force is in your hands and will go by your word—and we are asked for a solution. But whenever we offer a solution it is exploited for political ends.

Why get so cross with Bhindranwale's name ? It is an open secret that in the 1980 election he had worked for the Congress party. It is also a known fact that in the elections to the Gurdwara Prabandhak Committee Bhindranwale's colleagues had fought them in cooperation with the Congress. Who informs Bhindranwale of all the decisions that the Government takes ? He came to Delhi but was not arrested. The Prime Minister gave an interview to a weekly of Bombay but did not say a word against Bhindranwale. When she gave an interview to a weekly of Delhi she said we are ready to meet both Sants, Longowal as well as Bhindranwale. If you can find a solution by doing so, do meet them, but for God's sake solve the Punjab problem. Coming generations will never forgive you. I again say to you, do not make this a party matter. The opposition's attitude has been constructive, cooperative. But when you need cooperation you take it, when it does not benefit you, you ignore us while taking decisions. We won't complain if even those decisions bring peace. But Punjab is burning. Any moment something might happen that would put the whole country's existence and future on the line. Before that, Oh ! rulers of Delhi, take heed. Know your duty. If you cannot discharge your duty the Prime Minister should call a meeting of the Congress Parliamentary Party, tender her resignation in it, and ask the party to elect a new leader.

The Army in Harmandir Sahib

Let this Exception not Become a Practice

Sir, in the beginning I would like to congratulate those army officers and Jawans who freed Sri Harmandir Sahib, the Sikhs' holiest shrine and a place of reverence for all Indians, from the extremists and re-established its sanctity by risking as well as sacrificing their precious lives.

The army was entrusted a very difficult and delicate task. It should be congratulated for discharging that responsibility with skill and courage. But we must not lose sight of the fact that the army is primarily organised and equipped to fight foreign enemies. Using it against our own countrymen is a very unpleasant step, and we should avoid it as far as possible.

I would like to say two things about military action in Harmandir Sahib. The first is that this was the first occasion when the army was sent into any religious shrine, and it should be the last. Never again should a situation be allowed to develop when it would become imperative for us to send the army into a religious place for action against our own countrymen. After all looking after internal security is the job of the police. The Central Reserve Police can go to the assistance of the police. The help of the Border Security Force may also be taken. In Punjab all these three forces failed. Why ? Why did things come to such a pass that the army had to be called ? Punjab had a government that had to be dismissed. The Legislative Assembly is not dissolved but it is in suspended animation. The administration was crippled. The police became partisan. The society was divided. Hearts were separated by a gulf. Even *'Roti-Beti'* relationship could not prevent that gulf from widening.

Governor Pande and Bhinder have resigned. This has raised new questions. Against how many officers action was taken in Punjab ? How many officers have been charged with colluding with the extremists ? The White Paper is silent on this.

It was the Opposition parties that first demanded a White Paper. We wanted a White Paper that would bring to light the full true story of the rise of extremism in Punjab. Everyone knows that the Akali agitation began later, extremism raised its head first. The White Paper has also accepted this.

The White Paper does not tell the whole truth. Why did extremism rise in Punjab ? Why was it not contained ? Why were things allowed to come to such a pass ?

Sir, it is not enough to blame the officers. It is the political leaders who are to blame. It is the powers that be who are to blame.

Lok Sabha on July 25, 1984 on the White Paper issued in relation to Punjab

Who Made Bhindranwale a Hero ?

Before 1980 no one knew about Bhindranwale. He was a small 'Granthi' of village Bhinder who taught Guru Bani. How did he come on to the political stage ? How did he become the initiator of extremism ? The decision to send in the army was taken on June 5-6, 1986. I am talking of 1980. Nirankari Baba was killed. The murder was the result of a conspiracy. It took place in Delhi. Delhi's Lt. Governor Shri Jag Mohan wrote a "Secret, most immediate" D.O. to Punjab Chief Minister Darbara Singh on September 5, 1980. This D.O. number 287/L.G./80 said the CBI is inquiring into Nirankari Baba's murder. Notices were issued against 20 people. Non-bailable warrants were also issued against some people. But the letter complained of the non-cooperation of the Punjab police. I quote a portion of the letter :

> "Evidence has been collected to the effect that all the twenty persons against whom notices have been issued and the three persons against whom warrants have been issued either belong to Sant Bhindranwale Jatha or are his close associates/relatives and are holding under his protection. That was the reason for requesting local police of District Amritsar to have the notices served and the warrants executed. Two more fresh non-bailable warrants are being obtained against the persons mentioned in the annexure. CBI are also in the process of issuing notices u/s 160 Cr. P.C. to Sant Jarnail Singh Bhindranwale."

Then the letter complains—let alone acting on notices issued by the CBI from here they are not even returned to us and we are sending a man to collect them.

The White Paper refers to the fact that Bhindranwale was arrested. But it does not tell that he was released. It is said so at a later place but not where it should be. Former Chief Minister Darbara Singh made a forceful speech in the Rajya Sabha yesterday. He knows Pakistan conducts camps to train the extremists. The former Chief Minister knows, but the former Foreign Minister does not. Chief Minister Darbara Singh says he is ready to provide proof. Then why is it not included here ? If the Home Secretary of India can name Pakistan why is the Home Minister of India reluctant to do so ? I shall discuss this question later, not now.

What happened on June 5 and 6 is not a glorious story. I have congratulated the army because they risked their lives. The army has to obey a political directive. But today those who gave that political directive are in the dock. Why was this situation allowed to develop ? Why was Bhindranwale not arrested on September 5, 1980 ? He was later arrested on the basis of reasons described in Jag Mohan's letter but was released. Bhindranwale said I would be arrested at such and such a place and such and such a time, and before getting arrested I shall take a bath at the Golden Temple. Police Officers took him there for the bath. He was arrested and let off. After Nirankari Baba's murder the Government did not arrest even his relatives and colleagues. Who made Bhindranwale a hero ? The Akalis are not innocent. But the Government's job was expected of the Akali's. The Prime Minister told Opposition leaders the Akalis did not tell us arms were being collected in the

Golden Temple. Prof. Madhu Dandavate asked, did the Government know ? The Government would know if the Akalis tell them arms are being stockpiled in the Golden Temple, otherwise not.

The Akalis should have condemned the misuse of the Golden Temple. They should have openly come out against the extremists. I have a complaint about my Akali friends. But does that absolve the Government of its responsibility ? Bhindranwale visited Delhi. Who were those two Central Ministers who touched his fect here ?

PROF. K.K. TEWARY : That is wrong.

SHRI VAJPAYEE : It is true. Bhindranwale went up to Bombay and returned from there.

MR. DEPUTY SPEAKER : Please sit down, Mr. Anbarasu. Please sit down. You can reply when you get a chance. Please sit down. This is an important discussion. Let us have a clam discussion.

PROF. MADHU DANDAVATE : The Opposition has a right to expose facts and we will do it ruthlessly.

MR. DEPUTY SPEAKER : Please let us have a calm discussion.

SHRI ERA ANBARASU : Let him name the Minister who has done it.

AN HON. MEMBER : He should withdraw those words.

MR. DEPUTY SPEAKER : Mr. Anbarasu, he has not mentioned the name of any Minister. Why are you insisting! If you do not agree with him you can reply to him later.

SHRI KRISHNA DUTT SULTANPURI : He wants the names of those two ministers.

SHRI VAJPAYEE : If I reveal those names they will shout all the more. They are shouting so much even when I don't tell the names. If I take one name which they may say cannot be mentioned here....

MR. DEPUTY SPEAKER : Mr. Vajpayeeji, what you said is all right. Go ahead (*Interruptions*). Please, this is an important issue.

Army Role

SHRI VAJPAYEE : Sir, the army may be called to assist the civil administration. But the army should assist the civil administration, not conduct the civil administration. What is happening in Punjab ? The whole Punjab government is in the hands of the army. Is this necessary ? Is this desirable ? Is this a proper tradition that you are setting ?

Sir, a journalist was locked up in curfew for 60 hours in Amritsar. He was then told to go to Delhi and get a pass from the Deputy Commissioner. When he went to the Deputy Commissioner for the pass he was given it but was told to get it countersigned also by the army officer there. Why ?

President's Rule has been imposed at many places. The army has been called at many places to assist the civil administration, but nowhere has it happened that army officers were included in the Governor's advisors and entrusted important department like law and order and justice.

AN HON. MEMBER : Even before Punjab this has happened at many places.

MR. DEPUTY SPEAKER : Please, order.

SHRI VAJPAYEE : The matter of *Kar Seva* in the Golden Temple has now come up. I thought the *Kar Seva* would be conducted in such a way that the Prime Minister's announcements about applying the healing touch would be fulfilled. But everyone knows how it is going on. This is not the way to apply the healing balm to the wound. This is the way of deepening the wound. But I am saying something else.

When talks about the *Kar Seva* were held with the leaders of the Shiromani Gurudwara Prabandhak Committee Governor Satarwala did not represent the Government side. The acting Army Chief was called and General Oberoi was brought into the picture. Could not Governor Satarwala have done this job ?

But this thing does not stop here. The epidemic has spread upto Jammu & Kashmir, when, on that unfortunate day Jammu & Kashmir Governor Shri Jag Mohan...

SHRI ARIF MOHAMMED KHAN, Minister of State for Energy : Are we discussing Jammu & Kashmir now ?

SHRI VAJPAYEE : I can make a reference. I shall make it. They kept referring to Kashmir.

MR. DEPUTY SPEAKER : He will reserve his arguments for that discussion.

SHRI VAJPAYEE : It is a passing reference.

SHRI SATYA SADHAN CHAKRABORTY : Under what rule can you say this ?

SHRI VAJPAYEE : How can you debar any mention on J & K ?

Sir, I say the army is being misused. When the Governor of Jammu & Kashmir called on the Chief Minister to resign as he has lost his majority the Area Commander of the army was sitting with the Governor.

SHRI ARIF MOHAMMED KHAN : This is an absolute lie.

SHRI VAJPAYEE : What are you taking ? I am speaking with a sense of responsibility.

ACHARYA BHAGWAN DEO (Ajmer) : Sir, tell him to talk on Punjab, not on Kashmir.

MR. SPEAKER : You are not going to teach me anything. Sit down.

Acharyaji, sit down. You should realise that there is such a thing as decorum. Kashmir is not an outside matter. If there is any unparliamentary talk, any allegation I shall check it. But if anyone is presenting an argument you may refute it. This is the thing. Now sit down.

SHRI SATYA SADHAN CHAKRABORTY : You please go through the records. He has used the word lie.

MR. SPEAKER : I will go through the records.

SHRI ARIF MOHAMMED KHAN : Sir, I am trying to explain. Hon'ble Shri Vajpayee is a senior member. When he says something I cannot even imagine calling it a lie.

MR. DEPUTY SPEAKER : That is what I say. All India is included.

SHRI VAJPAYEE : Sir....

MR. DEPUTY SPEAKER : It is the same thing. It does not matter,—whether it is Ram or it is Laxman.

SHRI VAJPAYEE : Sir, it is nearly a month and a half since the army was sent into the Golden Temple, but extremists continue to be active in Punjab and the killings continue. A Central Minister told me—you will again say, give the name. He said 500 extremists are moving about, in search of prey.

AN HON. MEMBER : In Delhi ?

MR. DEPUTY SPEAKER : Wherever—go on.

SHRI VAJPAYEE : Delhi is included in it. But only 'Go Sevakas' are going to your place. You, Tripathiji, have no cause for worry.

The situation before sending the army into the Golden Temple was that the extremists were inside and the police outside. Now the situation is that the army is inside and the extremists outside.

Extremism has acquired a new dimension. The Bhakra Canal was cut twice, a plane was hijacked even after the military action.

AN HON. MEMBER : From where ?

SHRI VAJPAYEE : It was from a part of the country.

SHRI HARIKESH BAHADUR : You people got it done.

SHRI ARIF MOHAMMED KHAN : I am on my legs. He is a senior member. Let me explain my position. Shri Vajpayee is not only a responsible person, he is also a senior member of this House.

If Shri Vajpayee is saying this on the basis of personal information I would not dare to say he is wrong. If I had to refute I would have done it later. But this is published in the papers. I say what the newspapers have published is quite wrong.

Secondly, we are discussing Punjab at present, not Kashmir.

MR. DEPUTY SPEAKER : All right, let it go. A reference may be made. Sometimes it is Karnataka, sometimes Punjab, sometimes Kashmir. It does not matter much.

SHRI VAJPAYEE : Sir, we are discussing a national crisis here. A national crisis includes Punjab, and it also includes Jammu and Kashmir.

Sir, I cannot say if the number of extremists has gone up or down. Extremists were killed, they were caught, but sending the army into the Golden Temple has strengthened the ideological base of extremes. Whether you accept it or not is another matter. The society is now divided into two camps as if there has been polarization. Most Hindus cannot understand. Most Hindus cannot understand why their Sikh brethren are so annoyed. They did not themselves prevent the misue of the Golden Temple, they allowed arms to be collected and the offenders to collect. When action was taken why did they get angry ?

MR. DEPUTY SPEAKER : Where did the Sikhs do it ?

SHRI VAJPAYEE : On the other hand the Sikh community cannot understand why the whole Sikh society was being penalised and humiliated when only a handful of extremists were at fault.

AN HON. MEMBER : Absolutely wrong.

SHRI VAJPAYEE : Sir, I am talking about their feelings.

PROF. MADHU DANDAVATE : It is their assessment.

SHRI VAJPAYEE : Do they have the monopoly for patriotism ? We too love this country.

ACHARYA BHAGWAN DEO (Ajmer) : You give them encouragement. You have encouraged them.

SHRI VAJPAYEE : Sir, that is not true. I am prepared to give proof.

SHRI G.S. NIHALSINGHWALA : The word Sikh should not be used. Akali should be used.

SHRI SANTOSH MOHAN DEV : Why should he be allowed to speak ? He is not a Sikh. Do you mean to say that he is a Sikh ?

SHRI VAJPAYEE : They do feel that the military action in the Golden Temple has humiliated them.

SHRI SANTOSH MOHAN DEV : No.

SHRI VAJPAYEE : I did not say, all Sikhs think so.

PROF. MADHU DANDAVATE : Who is Shri Khushwant Singh ? He is a member of the Congress (I).

MR. SPEAKER : I am on my legs. Please sit down. Do not shout at each other. Please sit down. Whe I am on my legs you must sit down. I must say certain things. This is the highest forum. We have to be very responsible. There can be different ways of thinking, and different thoughts but they must not be expressed in such a way that they would pose a danger for the country. You can refute the allegations. I am very ashamed of this behaviour. You have to differentiate between certain things. This was action against certain individuals, not against a community. We must not allow this to be exploited, otherwise what will the coming generations say ?

PROF. MADHU DANDAVATE : Sir, please do not express your political views when you are in the Chair.

MR. SPEAKER : If this is a political opinion, if I have said anything political, I withdraw my words. I do not want to say anything political. I want to say only what concerns the future of this country. This is the only thing that I am concerned with. I don't want to say anything. If I am misunderstood I am sorry for it.

I say for God's sake don't do anything that would sow such seeds. That is all I have to say.

SHRI RAM VILAS PASWAN : Sir, you had asked the Government from the Speaker's chair long ago to take action.

MR. SPEAKER : Sit down.

SHRI RAM VILAS PASWAN : You had asked the Government two years ago to take action, but no action was taken.

MR. SPEAKER : For God's sake sit down.

PROF. K.K. TEWARY : Sir, what Prof. Dandavate has said is deplorable and is a very serious reflection on the Chair.

PROF. MADHU DANDAVATE : I don't want to claim certificates. I stand for certain principles.

MR. SPEAKER : I don't want to impose myself on this House. I only want to say that I don't want to impose my political will or political thinking on this House. This House is too competent to take care of itself. It was only my personal thinking. I wanted to say only for the posterity of the country and its future. If any of my friends wants to take objection, I don't want to intervene, please carry on.

SHRI SOMNATH CHATTERJEE : Sir, it is a very important debate. Members should listen and they should not disturb in this manner. Why can't they listen with a sense of responsibility ?

SHRI VAJPAYEE : Sir, my friends would perhaps not have been so upset if they had heard me out. I was going to say that many people have felt relief because of the military action. They should not be considered anti-Sikh or anti-Panth.

MR. SPEAKER : Same thing.

SHRI VAJPAYEE : I was also going to say that we should not make the mistake of considering all those who were against sending in the army to be Khalistanis. Passions are running high. So the Prime Minister had to talk of a healing touch. But where is the healing touch ? There were two occasions for it. One was the publication of this White Paper. One could have understood it if there had been sincerity in it and if it had revealed even unpleasant facts that would have stood the Government in the dock.

Sir, I had demanded the publication of a White Paper on the question of China. Pandit Jawaharlal Nehru was the Prime Minister. The White Paper that was published on India-China relations contained a letter which proved that China had invaded our borders. However the Parliament was not told about it, as Panditji said it would exacerbate feelings and we should first resolve the problem through talks. On the basis of the letter I told Pandiji—you kept the country in the dark, you made a mistake, and Nehruji said—yes, I made a mistake, I admit my mistake. You require a large heart to admit a mistake. This White Paper is incomplete. I again say the White Paper does not mention the failure of the administration—which includes the State Government and the Central Government—to bring to book Bhindranwale and the forces responsible for the rise of extremism in Punjab in 1980, 1981, 1982 and 1983. When I say this am I acting against the country ?

What Happened in Secret Meetings ?

Secret meetings were mentioned. Yesterday it was said if secret meetings were not to be disclosed they should have been kept secret. Now that they have been made public tell us what happened in them. And not all secret meetings have been mentioned here. There is no reference to the efforts made by Sardar Swaran Singh. Has the Congress Party disowned even Sardar Swaran Singh ? Did he make any efforts or did he not ? There was a meeting in which representatives of the Akali Dal and the Finance Minister took part. Different Ministers have talked in different ways. That meeting had reached agreement on the division of Chandigarh. The Prime Minister was on a visit to NewYork. It was decided to confirm the decision on her return. But nothing happened later. I ask—what happened on May 26 ? This was the last meeting after which military action took place. What happened in it ? Yesterday too I had asked—why are you keeping us in the dark ? Now we are told the Akalis were not ready for any compromise. What was discussed that day ? Was it said on behalf of the Government that Chandigarh would be given to Punjab and some surrounding villages should go to Haryana ? Did the Akalis reject this proposal too ? The Akalis say—no, we had accepted it. What is the truth ? The Prime Minister told leaders of opposition parties—the Akalis were raising the matter of the Yamuna, of sharing the waters of the Yamuna. The Akalis say—we are not such fools, we were talking about riparian rights. The Yamuna flows through Haryana, how can we talk of the Yamuna ? The Prime Minister also said the Akalis insisted that the Government should send the Anandpur Sahib resolution to the Sarkaria Commission while the Government says the Commission has been set up, you may send it. This too the Akalis deny. You may say don't trust the Akalis, trust the Prime Minister. It is easy for Congress Members to say so, but we do not believe so, So I say—reveal what happened in the secret meeting.

One more thing. I have already mentioned what Shri Darbara Singh said in the Rajya Sabha yesterday. The White Paper is silent on foreign contacts—who were the supporters of Khalistan ? There is a rumour going around which I want clarified by the Home Minister, but the Home Minister is not present, nor the Prime Minister....

White Paper Silent on Training of Extemists in Pakistan

Sir, the former Chief Minister of Punjab has said he has proof that the extremists were trainined in the use of arms in Pakistan. Does the Central Government also have that proof ? If it has, why is it not included in this White Paper ? Was this matter raised with Pakistan at the diplomatic level any time ? When was it done, and in what form ? If Pakistan trains Indian citizens to use arms for a revolt in India it is indulging in hostile activities. In such a situation there can be no talks with Pakistan. Then why a no-war pact ? Then how can there be talks on promoting commercial and cultural contacts ? When we decided to normalise relations with China we plainly told them—you have been supplying arms to Nagas and training them in their use, are you going to stop this or not ? China said—that is an old thing, let it go. We are engaged in love-talk with Pakistan. Shri Bhagat has recently been there. He has feasted on Shahi Kofta and Biryani and returned praising Pakistani hospitality. Our former Foreing Minister had taken the Foreign Minister of Pakistan to the Maldives in a plane. This was after the hijacking. These double standards cannot go on, this duplicity cannot go on. If Pakistan is hatching a conspiracy to break India the Prime Minister should tell us everything. Come, take the leaders of the opposition parties into confidence. When I met the Prime Minister after the military action she did not say anything about this. The Home Secretary said Pakistan has a hand in it. The White Paper is silent on it.

I want to ask one more thing—why was June 5 chosen for the military action ? June 4 was Guru Angad Devji's Jyoti-Jyot festival. People in large numbers had come from the villages for Darshan in the Gurudwara, for a holy dip and for listening to Guru Bani and *Sabad Kirtan*. Many innocent people were killed. Our sympathies are with them. We paid our tributes to them yesterday. But could their death not have been avoided ? It is now argued that June 5 was necessary because the Government had learnt from high level foreign sources that if the army was not sent in on June 5 an independent Khalistan would be declared from Harmindar Sahib and it would be recognised by some Arab and some Western countries.

SHRI G.S. NIHALSINGHWALIA : Twenty people were killed inside by bullets on the first and the second and they were to launch an agitation on the third.

MR. DEPUTY SPEAKER : Sit down, I shall allow you to speak.

SHRI VAJPAYEE : Sir, some newspapers are mentioning KGB. Did they get the news from Russia ? I do not know how far this is true, but if it is true, speak out plainly and take the House into confidence.

Sir, I would like to say something about the *Kar Seva*. It is most unfortunate that this should become a matter of controversy. We thought what has happened has happened. The army took action to free Harmandir Sahib from the extremists, in which the Akal Takht was damaged. Now according to the tradition of the Sikh Panth it should be reconstructed and all people should participate in Kar Seva for the purpose. But this thing also became a controversial matter. I would like to know why the talks with Baba Kharag Singh broke down. Is it true that the Government had agreed to withdrawing the army except at the 'Toshakhana' and the 'Darshani Dyodhi' ? What is there in the Toshakhana ? Is it necessary to keep the army there ? Why is it necessary to keep the army at the Darshani Dyodhi ? Protect the temple and prevent the entry of illegal persons into it. How can arms be allowed in ? The Gurudwara Prabandhak Committee says we had agreed that only traditional arms, that is swords and kirpans, would be allowed in, not any other weapons. They also agreed that no offenders would be given shelter. Who is this Baba Santa Singh ? I am not saying anything against him. If Baba Santa Singh is most useful for conducting *Kar Seva* why were talks first held with Baba Kharag Singh ? Has any agreement been reached with Baba Santa Singh ? Have any assurances been given to Baba Santa Singh about how Gurdwaras would be managed in future ? Is it not true that there are police cases against Baba Santa Singh too ?

Sir, after the military action we saw a sant brought on the T.V. He criticised Sant Bhindranwale strongly. I thought the was a man of courage. But a few days later we read in the papers that he was arrested. A cane of arms has been seized from his place. I am not making a speech to lay blame. (*Interruptions*).

Sir, I shall now conclude. It is not very good for the powers that be that even 36 years after independence, 36 years after partition, there is still a question-mark on the country's unity. It is not good that we are still not a nation. Pakistan came into being on the basis of religion, it got divided. We did not make religion our basis. We said our country will be secular. It will believe in all religions. And yet India is on the brink of division. Are only the Akalis responsible for this and is the Prime Minister as innocent as a child ?

The Prime Minister says she is ready to take poison. But it is Amrit that has gone to her share, the others will drink poison. What I say is, for God's sake don't make the country's unity a political issue, an electoral issue. Do not play with it. Forget what has happened and make a fresh start. How long will the army remain in the Golden Temple and how long will censorship continue in Punjab ? You cannot deploy the army at any place at every step. If the country remains one it will not be due to any one party, not due to any one individual, not due to any one family. If the country remains one it will be due to the patriotism of the 70 crore people of the country. Thank you.

Tragedy In Faridkot

Sir, I join the Hon. Minister in condemning the killing but I would like to seek a few clarifications. Sir, our warning that a slight fall in the activities of terrorists should not make the Government or the security forces complacent was not heeded. After intensification in the anti-terrorist campaign by the security forces in Amritsar and Gurdaspur it was expected that the terrorists would strike at some other place. Four districts of Punjab are posing problems. Apart from Gurdaspur and Amritsar the two other districts are Kapurthala and Ferozepur. This bus was coming from Amritsar. Innocent passengers belonging to one community—were taken out of the bus. This is a selective killing with the purpose to incite the people, but the killing was done in Kapurthala district. (*Interruptions*). Yes, it was in Faridkot district. I stand corrected. I would like to know whether there was any security guard with the bus. The bus was coming from Muktsar. It was passing through Faridkot district. I do not know whether buses are still allowed to ply in Punjab without security guards.

Secondly, I would like to know where did these terrorists board the bus ? Did they board the bus at Muktsar itself ? Was there any checking ? They came with pistols. They were armed. Why were they not prevented from boarding the bus ?

Thirdly, Sir, is there any patrolling of the main roads, thoroughfares ? This is one of the main roads in Punjab. If my information is correct the deluxe bus was to come to Delhi. That is why we have been demanding deployment of the army. Even now for patrolling purposes the army can be utilised. The Government has been patting its own back by claiming that the terrorists are on the run. I know this is too serious a matter and I do not want to say things which might hurt our friends on the opposite side, but obviously there is somebody masterminding the entire operation. While you concentrate on Amritsar and Gurdaspur, they strike in other districts.

Sir, I join in the Minister's appeal that there should be perfect communal harmony. That is what the terrorists do not want. But these killings must stop and I would like to have satisfactory replies from the Hon. Minister about the small points which have led to this bigger tragedy. In Krishnanagar only ten persons were killed and here in this case the number of those killed is 13. This is the highest number so far.

Rajya Sabha on July 25, 1986 during discussion on the Statement made by the Minister of State in the Ministry of Home Affairs regarding the massacre in Faridkot district

Killings Continue

Sir, the whole country has been stricken with grief at what happened in Muktsar on July 25. The people are upset, they are angry. About three years ago there had been a similar massacre in Punjab. On October 5, 1983 innocent people travelling by bus were similarly made to get down at Dhilwan and massacred. For three continuous years this has been going on in Punjab. Blood flows in Punjabi veins and tears flow in Punjabi eyes. Violence and killing are playing the dance of death in Punjab.

Sir, this time we are not asking for the dismissal of the Barnala Government, although three years ago the Darbara Singh Government had been dismissed after the massacre at Dhilwan.

SHRI DARBARA SINGH (Punjab) : I had resigned myself.

SHRI VAJPAYEE : We are neither demanding the resignation of the Barnala Government nor asking the Government to dismiss it. If it is necessary we shall demand the resignation of the Barnala Government. If necessary we shall even demand the resignation of the Central Government. After all how long will these massacres continue ?

Sir, that day the discussion centred on whether those who were killed belonged to one community or both communities. Shri Chidambaram is not present in the House. At first he stated that it was one community. This is in his written statement. The statement was made in the evening. Could not the Government find out for 12 hours if those who died belonged to one community or both ? And if it did not know what was the need to make this an issue ? While Shri Chidambaram was reading his statement he read out a chit saying "I learn from the Home Minister that those who died belonged to both communities." Papers in Punjab and news agencies say they belonged to one community. Now we are told there were also those of the other community but they were clean shaven. Again we are told "they were wounded but not dead." I ask you—if they belong to both communities does that mitigate the sin, the crime, of the terrorists ? Perhaps this incident was brought about with the intention of inciting people's passions when the news spread all over the country that people of one particular community were killed. But the damage has been done, because you had stated at 6 o'clock that people of the other community had also been killed while newspapers and news agencies reported that they were people of one community. Are even 12 hours not enough for this Government to get true news ?

Rajya Sabha on July 28, 1986 during discussion on the statement made by the Minister of State in the Ministry of Home Affairs on massacre in Faridkot district

Home Minister's Silence

Sir, even today the Home Minister's statement is silent on some important points. Was there a security guard onboard the bus ? No. Was there anyone to inspect at the point where the passengers boarded the bus at Muktsar ? No. Is it true that they had a walkie-talkie with them ? Where did the tractor come from ? How did they run away ?

Sir, we have been demanding for months—and we had to stage a Satyagraha to press the demand—that there should be no hesitation in calling the Army to patrol border districts. But this was made a prestige issue both in Delhi and Chandigarh. Finally you had to call the Army. It had to be called not only in Punjab but also in Delhi. Had the Army been called beforehand the massacre at Muktsar could perhaps have been avoided. But the Centre did not give advice. At present the Barnala Government is not in a position to ignore the Centre's advice. The Barnala Government is in a minority. It continues in office on the support of the Congress party. Yesterday Barnala was in Delhi. Shri Buta Singh told him it is not good to be in Delhi, go back. He went back. (Alarm bell)

Sir, I would like to have some more time. In fact, the House should be given an opportunity to have a full debate. The matter is so important and the situation so grave that just seeking clarifications won't do. So please give me some more time.

Sir, it was good that the Army was called. Give it patrolling duty. Had there been patrolling on the roads that day this incident would not have taken place. Muktsar is one of the affected districts. It was also known that if the terrorists were chased in Amritsar and Gurdaspur they would strike at places of their choice. They would strike fiercely, because they are currently feeling harassed by the action being taken against them. But no preventive action was taken.

Sir, what happened in Delhi was tragic. As a resident of Delhi I feel ashamed. Yesterday I saw burnt-out Gurdwaras, demolished temples, and mosques were also stoned. The atmosphere in Delhi has become vitiated. It is poisoned. Since innocent people were killed in the 1984 riots in Delhi the gulf in the city has widened. Yesterday the Home Minister had gone on a round, he may know. I have also gone around disturbed areas. The whole society has been divided into two camps. Who will bring them together ?

Tale of Woe

The Tilak Nagar incident could have been avoided. You had 24 hours. The Central Government is in the dock. The Central Government is directly responsible for Delhi. The Muktsar incident took place in the morning. You had a full day with you. Even before this there had been tension in Tilak Nagar. A clash was about to take place in Uttam Nagar. In Tilak Nagar there are 150-200 refugees from Punjab who have settled there. They are camping in temples. For two months we have been saying—don't let them live in temples, shift them elsewhere, settle them. People visit temples. The refugees from Punjab tell them their tale of woe. Perhaps they may be exaggerating. The atmosphere in Tilak Nagar was hotting up. At night there was no police bandobast. Could night curfew not have been imposed ?

The Home Minister may say there were full arrangements. But they were not adequate. (*Interruptions*) Buta Singhji, understand this. This is not a question of the Opposition and the Government. The Tilak Nagar incident could have been avoided. Two police officers went there in the morning. I have their names. One is Deol, D.C.P. and the other Thakur, A.C.P. Women were staging a *Dharna* there and the road was closed. Things should not have not been allowed to come to such a pass. They were persuaded to leave. But at that time the police officers used language that upset the whole thing. This led to incidents at many places all together.

There is an old quarrel between the Harijans and the Sikhs who have been settled there. It was in 1984 that this quarrel had taken root. People uprooted by the 1984 riots had been given houses there. These houses had been built for the Harijans of the area. It was even inaugurated as a Harijan colony. I know those who had been settled there after the riots of 1984 had been uprooted because of our misdeeds, and settling them is also our responsibility. But the feeling remained in the minds of the Harijans that houses built for them were given to other people. This resentment is entrenched in their mind. The Harijans there are in a poor plight. It is a filthy area and there are no drains. Ten houses were set on fire there. They cannot be called houses, they are huts. Could the Government not have made arrangements to settle them ? Could their houses not have been given to them ? This thing has been going on since 1984.

But Delhi keeps every issue hanging fire. In Delhi responsibility has been divided. There is no central cell of power that could decide things.

Administration has Failed

There was delay in imposing a curfew. It could have been imposed quickly. It was not enforced after it was announced. Delhi should conduct a high-level inquiry into the whole affair. The administration has failed in this. That failure should be investigated so that such a mistake may not be repeated in future.

The atmosphere has become explosive. There is a quarrel between two boys in Hauz Kazi, in the Jama Masjid area. One of them is a Hindu and the other a Muslim. One of them is drunk. The police take him away. Why has the Hindu boy arrested ? Hindu policemen gherao the police station. The boy was drunk. In the present situation people have become blind. This will have to be fought on a political level. Political leaders will have to acquire the habit of talking plainly and listening to plain talk.

Sir, we called for a *Bandh*. But really speaking this is not a *Bandh*, there is a general strike, because essential commodities are exempt from it. There were no disturbances in Delhi when the *Bandh* was called. We could have recalled the call for the *Bandh*, but had we done so the various small organisations and committees that have come up in and around Delhi would have called for a *Bandh*. People were getting incited, they were going the wrong way. The situation could have worsened. In Ghaziabad we had not called for a *Bandh*, but it took place. In Gujarat we did not participate in the call for a *Bandh*. An organised *Bandh* is a safety valve for anger. We have accepted the responsibility of maintaining peace. But if the Congress can participate in the *Bandh* in Punjab, in Chandigarh, why not in Delhi ? Is it because it is in the opposition in Punjab and in power in Delhi ?

DEPUTY CHAIRMAN : Kindly confine to seeking clarification now. A large number of speakers are there.

SHRI VAJPAYEE : Sir, I would like to know this from the Home Minister. He will say, 'You are referring to the Congress (I). I am the Home Minister of the country. I have nothing to do with the Congress (I).' But the *Bandh* question was raised by my friend here.

SHRI BUTA SINGH : You are speaking a foreign language that I cannot understand.

SHRI VAJPAYEE : In Punjab the Congress, CPI, CP(M) had participated in the *Bandh* and it was peaceful. Here too I had invited you to participate in the *Bandh*, but you did not .... (*Interruptions*)

SHRI BUTA SINGH : Sir, I shall give the clarification on this, but a senior leader like Shri Vajpayee should understand one thing—was the atmosphere that prevailed in Delhi for the last couple of days the same as in Punjab ? In Punjab all people shared in the grief. Had it been the same here the same thing would have happened here too. What happened here yesterday is still continuing, and your *Bandh* came in the midst of it. This was an additional burden.

SHRI VAJPAYEE : Sir, I still await an explanation. I have already said and I repeat—will the Government try to find out the deficiencies that were found in the arrangements this time ? After all the Home Minister had announced that he is going to call a meeting of the National Integration Council .... (*Interruptions*) ....

AN HON. MEMBER : The House is on fire.

SHRI VAJPAYEE : If the House is on fire a fire brigade is needed, and we will also have to arrange for a continuous water supply to it ....(*Interruptions*)....

SHRI N.K.P. SALVE (Maharashtra) : Shri Vajpayee is a very mature leader, full of the national spirit. I would like to know one thing—how proper, how justified, was it for you to call for a *Bandh* when the Government was in difficulties ? Shri Vajpayee has to explain this here.

SHRI VAJPAYEE : Sir, if the *Bandh* was proper in Punjab, a *Bandh* in which the Congress had participated, CPI had participated, CP(M) had participated ....(*Interruptions*) .... then how could a *Bandh* in Delhi be wrong ?

How Long Barnala Be Supported ?

Madam, the Home Minister has admitted in his speech that since October there has been a sudden spurt in terrorist activities, but he has not thrown light on why this has been so. If there is a massacre in Punjab every other day it would be futile to hope that the situation is improving or will improve.

It would also not be true to say that having been surrounded by security forces the terrorists have stepped up their activities in sheer desperation. The stepped-up activity is in accordance with a plan. Steps are being taken with deliberation. People are being killed selectively. At the same time there are also massacres.

The Security forces have given a good account under the leadership of Director General Rebeiro. The Punjab Police have also contributed. But according to Rebeiro only one-third of the 'A' grade terrorists have been caught or killed, two-thirds still remain. A large number of 'B' plus' grade have also not yet been caught.

I think the number of terrorists is increasing and Shri Rebeiro is not taking this increase into account. According to reports terrorists are crossing over from Pakistan in large numbers. The Government has not been able to stop this influx despite its claim of having sealed the border. I shall come to this later.

Situation Deteriorating

What is more serious, the deterioration in the political situation in Punjab during the past few months has encouraged more youths to join the ranks of the terrorists. The Akali Dal is divided. Those who fell out did so on the delicate issue of sending the police into the Darbar Sahib. When Shri Badal was asked what he would have done if he were the Chief Minister and terrorists had made Gurudwaras their bases he had no answer. But he made this an issue and he went so far that he openly aligned with the terrorists. He began attending the Bhog ceremony of the killers. This damaged the atmosphere in Punjab, and what Rebeiro accomplished was largely set at naught.

The Punjab Government also showed laxity. Leaders of the United Akali Dal went from village to village making poisonous propaganda, praising the killers, and giving them saropas. They openly threatened that they would kill the Prime Minister. But no action was taken against them. They were not caught. When this matter was raised in Punjab they said this is a locust

Rajya Sabha on November 11, 1986 during discussion on the Calling Attention Motion regarding the situation in Punjab

swarm, let it pass. Wherever they went they sowed seeds of poison, they spread sparks of fire.

In the rural areas, especially in the Gurdwaras, dangerous propaganda is being made, and Ragis and singers are at it day and night. Unfortunately the country's martyrs are divided. Poisonous propaganda is being made in buses. And when the Akali Dal got divided on an issue relating to religion the political atmosphere deteriorated still further.

I am sorry to say, I shall have to ask the Home Minister to give me a plain answer. It is not enough to say we have helped the Punjab Government in the past and we are helping them even now. Then why is the situation deteriorating ? Or are you also satisfied that the situation is improving ? Madam, it is meaningless to say the terrorists are on the run. It is the Home Minister who has to run when terrorists kill innocent people. We go from Delhi. The terrorists are coming in from Pakistan, going into villages from the cities and stepping up their activities where they are not active. Terrorists never stay at one place. It is in their nature to keep moving. They do not make Camps, do not build castles. Let us not labour under the illusion that the terrorists are running. The situation in Punjab has worsened, and the Centre cannot escape the responsibility for it.

I want to ask a straight question—does the Centre want to keep the Barnala Government or does it not want ? Barnala does not have his own majority. He is in power on the strength of the Congress party's majority. Shri Bhandare is not present in the House. He was saying in this House we should speak with one voice on the problem of Punjab.

Punjab Congress has One View, Centre's Congress has Another

I would say to Shri Bhandare that the Congress party is itself not prepared to speak with one voice. The Punjab Congress says one thing, leaders at the Centre say something else. I have a statement with me, dated Gurdaspur, November 10, in which Punjab Congress (I) President Beant Singh has charged the Barnala Government with sacrificing fundamental principles of politics for sticking to power. Beant Singh says the Barnala Government is trying to fly without wings. He said that so far 700 people had fallen victims to the terrorists. He repeated the charge that some Ministers are sheltering terrorists. Then Shri Beant Singh also said we shall not form a joint Government with the Akalis in Punjab as in Jammu and Kashmir, because the Congress is a secular party and it cannot have an alliance with a communal party. I do not know if Sardar Beant Singh considers the Muslim League a communal party or not. How far does he approve of making a person of the Ittehad-ul-Muslimeen the Mayor of Hyderabad and backing that Ittehad-ul ?

But I want to know—what is the Centre's policy ? Is it being decided to remove Barnala ? The reports coming in indicate that political instability is spreading in Punjab. Shri Barnala is himself shaken. Are you thinking of bringing in Sardar Balwant Singh who has talked of a corridor with Pakistan ? It is said Sardar Balwant Singh and Shri Arjun Singh, who have come into the Central Council of Ministers, are thick. Or is it someone else you are thinking of bringing in ? Are you looking at Amarender Singh ?

The Home Minister's statement contains a sentence that indirectly praises him. I would also praise his statement. It would be good if he moves away from Badal. If all those who are fighting terrorism come together we would welcome that. But there should be no delay in this. Punjab has a different situation as compared to Jammu and Kashmir. Don't keep things hanging. If you do that the terrorists will be encouraged and the administration will lose heart. The battle you are fighting with the terrorists will have to be fought for long. Does the Centre have a policy on Punjab ?

If Pakistan has a Hand, Expose It

There is another thing I want to ask. We have been hearing for years that terrorists are coming from Pakistan. Pakistan is being named and we are told Pakistan is giving them arms and training. I have seen a reply by Shri Chidambaram. He has said we have drawn Pakistan's attention on nine occasions. If anyone asks him what will you do next he will reply we are waiting for the tenth occasion. How long will this go on ? I wish the Home Minister pays attention to what Shri Rebeiro has said. When he was asked about Pakistan's involvement he said Pakistan is giving small arms and now his information is that Pakistan is selling arms. I say to the Home Minister, you have the documents, you have the proof, take us into confidence, show the documents and the proof to Pakistan's friends, unmask Pakistan, talk plainly to Pakistan and tell them if you do not stop providing arms and training to the terrorists there would be no talks for normalising relations with you. Can the Government not do this ? Madam, I want to know one thing. In the last session loud appeals were made to our patriotism and a resolution was introduced under article 249 of the Constitution. Speaking on the resolution the Home Minister made some remarkable points. He had tried to place all the blame on others and said there was not enough will power. I quote him :

> "There has to be a political will, there has to be a determination, and there has to be an adequate organisational set-up in the field itself which is committed, which is prepared to die for the security and integrity of the country. It is that thing which is lacking."

He was pointing his finger at the State Government. So the Centre said we want special powers, we want to seal the border in all strictness, we want to acquire some special powers in the matter of the police, administration, the courts, the jail. Some Opposition parties did not cooperate with the Government in this, but we did, and Shri Jaswant Singh, a member of our party, had said in his speech we are giving you powers, now do not make excuses from here onwards.

The Home Minister also said other things in his speech. I quote the questions he raised :

> "My three questions to the leadership of the Opposition are : Are they aware that a suitation exists which is of national importance ? My simple

question is this. Are they convinced that there is a situation which is of national importance in the border areas ? Secondly, if there is such a situation, are they satisfied that the manner in which the situation is presently being tackled is satisfactory, and, thirdly, if not, then what is the avenue left ? Are we to be spectators ? Are we to be standing and watching innocent people being butchered day in and day out, people being driven out from their hearths, people being sent out of the State ? These are the three questions. Unfortunately, no Hon. leader of the Opposition has answered these questions."

Now I will ask the Home Minister just one question—you got the powers you wanted Parliament to give you, now what is wanting ? What is lacking ? A question was asked—what happened about article 249 ? The reply given was—we are consulting the States, we are thinking. This means it is not a serious matter, there is no need for a prompt decision. When the Government demanded these powers we asked them—what will you do if the Punjab Government does not cooperate ? We were told if steps need to be taken for the security of the country they would be taken despite the Punjab Government. But now they say the Barnala Government does not listen. The Barnala Government is in power on your votes. Withdraw your support to it, let it fall if it cannot stand. But I do not think the Barnala Government will not listen to this. But after securing powers from Parliament when it came to taking steps you broke out in a sweat. If will power is lacking anywhere it is lacking in this Government. It does not have a clear mind. Punjab is again being made a chessboard of party politics and factional politics within the party. How long will this game go on ?

Madam, there are also some other questions that I would like to ask. It is being repeatedly said that we have to alienate the terrorists in Punjab, so it is necessary to implement the agreement. I would ask the Home Minister — when, during a foreign tour, she was once asked about this she said we were lax about implementing the Punjab agreement because the Barnala Government itself did not want it to be promptly implemented. Is this true ? If it is the Barnala Government, then it will have to explain. I would not have minded if Chandigarh had been given to Punjab on January 26. The Canal should have been built by August 15, but it was not. But now I do not see any direct connection between terrorism and implementation of the Punjab agreement. The agreement is self-contradictory, it contains internal contradictions, it has been drafted in a hurry, and I doubt if the Government will be able to force its implementation with its eyes on the politics of Haryana. But even if the agreement is implemented the Badal faction will say our demand is for implementing the Anandpur resolution, there will be no agreement on anything less than that, and the terrorists will say something else. There is an extremist group among them, which has linked itself with Khalistan. How can it be brought back ? I agree with my friends that the innocent among those who have been kept in jail for two years without trial and punishment should be released and those convicted should be sentenced.

VICE–CHAIRMAN (Smt. Kanak Mukherji) : Your 15 minutes are over. Please conclude now.

SHRI VAJPAYEE : Madam, it is a matter of Punjab and you know we people are connected with it.

VICE–CHAIRMAN (Smt. Kanak Mukherji) : Still be brief.

Punjab Wants to Know Names of Culprits of Delhi Riots

SHRI VAJPAYEE : There is also the question of deserters from the Army. Those who ran away from the Army were called deserters, not mutineers. What is the position about them ? Shri Barnala has claimed that some deserters have also been released. How many ? What is the position of the detenus in Jodhpur jail ? The Home Minister should take the House into confidence on this. The Government has done nothing for those who have become refugees from Punjab and are wandering around in Delhi. This is an explosive situation. It is necessary to pacify them. Sikhs from other States should be prevented from going to Punjab. Publication of the report of the Ranganath Mishra Commission has been demanded, I would like to join those making that demand. Actually I have heard that even the President is not being shown this report. I do not know how far this is true. But if the report is true and if even he is not being shown how can we ask for it ? But I doubt if those whose hands are red with the blood that flowed in Delhi's riots can successfully solve the Punjab problem. Someone has to take the blame for Delhi's riots. Someone will have to be punished.

Whenever we go to Punjab and talk of Hindu-Sikh brotherhood some questions are thrown at us. They ask, where were you when hundreds of Sikhs were being killed after Indiraji's assassination ? We reply to them in our own way, because we were not among the killers, but this Government is certainly in the dock. You set up a commission to inquire into the riots, although it was set up late and it was not allowed to function properly, but now don't suppress its report. Attention also needs to be paid to the people who are being killed on the border in the name of 'fake encounters.' Director General Rebeiro says whatever is happening on the border is being done by the Border Security Force, he is not connected with it. According to him the police could not be accused of killing innocent people. He also said those killed in village Dera Baba Nanak had really come from Pakistan. But why should the Government object to an inquiry if there are such incidents ? Sometimes security forces may commit excesses. In a situation like Punjab we can understand some excesses, but if you fall into a habit you will encourage a new terrorism even while suppressing the existing terrorism. We must not forget this. Thank you.

President's Rule at Wrong Time

Sir, there is nothing worth opposing in the Bill that is before the House for consideration. There can be a difference of opinion on the matter of President's Rule. But once it is imposed Parliament's taking over law-making powers and setting up an advisory committee of members of Parliament in this regard is a step in the right direction.

Sir, it is true that the matter of imposing President's Rule in Punjab was linked with elections in Haryana. President's rule was imposed later. It was imposed at a wrong time. What General Arora was saying is right. Before imposing President's rule the Barnala Government was compared with Maharaja Ranjit Singh's administration. A certificate of good conduct was given to the Barnala Government at the Jallianwala Bagh in Amritsar through a Central Minister. Then how did the Barnala Government suddenly become worth dismissal ? Actually President's rule should have been imposed on the day the Akali Government of Barnala lost its majority in the Legislative Assembly. It was in power on Congress support. Had the Congress party withdrawn its support and had it become necessary to promulgate President's rule in Punjab for want of a majority the Congress party would not now be in the dock.

There is also another aspect. President's rule was imposed at the wrong time. With the consent and knowledge of the Centre Jain Muni Shri Sushil Kumar had visited the Golden Temple to hold talks with different classes, different groups. Recently I met him in New York. He said we were about to reach some conclusion when President's rule was imposed and I had to return to Amritsar. What is the position in this regard ?

During the Barnala Government's time it had become impossible to control terrorism, because even against the Chief Minister's wishes some ministers of the Barnala Government had linked up with the terrorists. Barnala could not control them. The situation was deteriorating. In the name of social reform violence and killing had spread so much in Punjab that it had become difficult for people to live there. One achievement of President's rule that we will have to admit is that this business of what clothes women should wear, what people should do what business, which was going on in the name of social reform came to a stop. But terrorist activities have gone up. After Punjab it is Haryana and Delhi. Delhi is centrally administered. At first there was a massacre in Greater Kailash, and later two prominent leaders of Bharatiya Janata Party were gunned down in Kalkaji in broad daylight in front of their homes in the capital of India. When the Greater Kailash incident

Rajya Sabha on August 17, 1987 during discussion on the setting up of an Advisory Committee of members of Parliament after imposition of President's Rule in Punjab

took place the Government was warned that terrorists were setting up new bases in South Delhi, Chandigarh, Mohali. No effective preventive action was taken. The killers have not yet been caught. The terrorists' objective is clear.

I agree that in Punjab the pressure on them has increased. But if they can cause incidents at other places and go free an atmosphere conducive to their objectives would build up. Their intentions are clear—to bring about riots between Hindus and Sikhs, to create an atmosphere for driving non-Sikhs out of Punjab. Reports are now coming in that non-Sikhs are again leaving Punjab. Cannot the Army be called to assist the Punjab Police and paramilitary forces in the three districts that are contiguous to Pakistan, where the terrorists have concentrated their activities ? I am not asking for military rule in Punjab. In Delhi the Army was put on alert. In Meerut it took out a march. In Ahmedabad too the Army was required. It is very important to stem the outflow of people. But people have migrated from Punjab and if they spread to other parts of the country, if they again camp in Delhi the atmosphere would get vitiated. I would like to congratulate the people of Delhi. Even after the killing of Shri Sethi and Shri Munjal they showed patience. There was not a single incident of revenge. What do you expect of the people ? From the ramparts of the Red Fort the Prime Minister called for the people's cooperation. How is this cooperation expected ? The President has also made an appeal. I agree that tackling terrorism is everyone's task. But what can the common man do in this ? Is it not the Government's responsibility to check violent incidents ? I agree that President's rule is not the solution to the Punjab problem. It is neither possible nor is it the responsibility of Governor Ray or Director General Rebeiro to find a political solution for Punjab. Their responsibility is limited to checking terrorism from spreading, controlling it, to checking violence and killing.

Why No Safety Belt in Punjab ?

When the House had passed a resolution under article 249 will the Government say why a safety belt was not created in Punjab ? Yesterday the Prime Minister gave an interview to some newspaper and again complained that arms are coming in from Pakistan, there are bases in Pakistan. Why do you not stop the arms inflow and stop people from coming in after taking training ? Why was the proposal for a safety belt put in cold storage ? At first they said the Barnala Government was against it, and we do not want to have a safety belt in the face of that Government's opposition. But now the Barnala Government is not in power. The Centre is running the administration. Now have the safety belt. It is needed in Rajasthan, it is needed in Gujarat.

The Prime Minister is right in saying that arms are coming in, drugs are coming in, infiltration is going on. But the Government did not implement that resolution. I had visited Chandigarh. I could not meet Governor Shri Ray, but I met Director General Shri Rebeiro. I asked him, there are reports of innocent people being killed in encounters, are they wrong ? We must also not forget that terrorists are killing innocent people. But it is not good that the police should kill innocent people. I asked him, what will you do if such charges are made ? He said I have personally visited a hundred villages. He goes to a village, calls a meeting and asks, is any young man of the village missing ? Has any young man been killed in an encounter ? According to Shri Rebeiro in a hundred villages he did not meet a single person who supported the report that at some places people have been killed wrongly.

SARDAR J.S. AURORA : On a point of order, Sir —

THE VICE-CHAIRMAN (Shri Jagesh Desai) : How can there be a point of order now when he is speaking ?

SARDAR J.S. AURORA : There is a point of order. How do you say that there is no point of order ? A statement has been made about Mr. Rebeiro, I only want to say that in a meeting with the Governor one Mr. Kripal Singh, who is an MLA, said that fifteen innocent people had been killed and that he could give the names of those persons. But Mr. Rebeiro never asked for those names ....

THE VICE-CHAIRMAN (Shri P.K. Bansal) : He should have given those names .... It was his duty to give those names if he happened to have them with him.

SHRI VAJPAYEE : We agree that the problem of Punjab is not only the problem of law and order. It is a problem of the protection of the unity and integrity of the country. It cannot be solved on the strength of the police alone. But how can efforts to find a political solution make progress so long as violence and killings continue ? Recent events in Amritsar, the way even the Akal Takht Jathedar Shri Ragi had to leave Akal Takht and Amritsar, the way Khalistan slogans have been raised—all these indicate that the terrorists are bent upon a confrontation. We have no alternative but to meet their challenge, and in meeting that challenge we all have to give maximum cooperation. (*Interruptions*) Bhajanlalji, please do not say anything. The politics that Bhajanlal played after the bus massacre in Haryana was low politics.

SHRI BHAJAN LAL, Minister for Environment : How ? Sir, Atalji has very angrily said I played this sort of politics. I would like to clarify a little. When I came to know was it not my duty to go to the spot of the incident ? It is my district, my village where the incident took place. It is my area. So I went there in my personal capacity. His colleagues, who are in power in Haryana, charged that Bhajanlal has a hand in the incident. Then should I not challenge them ? Even today I give a challenge—let any Supreme Court or High Court Judge inquire into this, and if this charge is proved Bhajanlal will renounce politics for ever. If not, he should resign. Even today I say this. If anyone makes an accusation against me do I not have the right to speak ?

SHRI VAJPAYEE : The charge against Shri Bhajanlal is not that he brought about the bus massacre. I have not made any charge against him. You have no hand in it, but you ....

SHRI BHAJANLAL : You said so repeatedly.

SHRI VAJPAYEE : But people connected with Shri Bhajanlal were involved in the violence that took place later.

SHRI BHAJANLAL : That too is wrong. You have said a baseless thing. It would not be a good thing for me to say the BJP, the Lok Dal and you have a hand in it. Let us not talk about Congress, Lok Dal or BJP, let us talk against those who are responsible. What did the Lok Dal people do at the time of their victory rally ? They indulged in looting, they even dishonoured women, they looted boxes and handcarts of the poor. This sort of thing only Lok Dal people can do, not the Congress.

SHRI VAJPAYEE : We did not defend what happened that time. But the Haryana Government had been recently elected to power, and it was when they inherited power that suddenly so many people were killed in the bus incident. It was a sudden attack. But in retaliation a political campaign was launched against the Haryana Government, and that too by a Central Minister. I would have had no cause to complain if Shri Bhajanlal were not a Central Minister.

SHRI BHAJANLAL : You are a senior member. It does not become you to say such a thing. I respect you. I have done nothing. I have reluctantly replied to whatever they said.

SHRI VAJPAYEE : Sir, I was just continuing with my speech. I would not have mentioned Shri Bhajanlal. I have my own *Bhajan* in the morning. I have no need to mention Shri Bhajanlal in the House.

SHRI BHAJANLAL : Please speak on, and suggest how the very bad conditions in Punjab can be improved. Suggest how things can be corrected.

SHRI VAJPAYEE : Sir, is it not a suggestion when I suggested setting up a safety belt ? Is it not a suggestion when I say the Army's help should be taken in three districts ? Is it not a suggestion when I say defence teams should be set up in every village in order to organise the people of Punjab, arms should be given to those who wanted to fight terrorism, but care should be taken to see that they do not fall into wrong hands ? Our worker was killed there just yesterday. There are no arms, no licences. The police cannot fight terrorism everywhere. The people want to fight but they do not have arms. Arms are expensive, and they do not have licences. Why are defence teams not being set up in every village ? The Governor is trying to visit the maximum number of places. He is working hard. But that is not enough. I agree with my friends that maximum amount of people's cooperation needs to be secured in this battle. For this we should come together in Punjab and talk. President's rule cannot go on for ever. One day it will come to an end and Punjab will again have an elected Government. We too want it. But so long as terrorist violence continues, so long as selective killings and massacres do not stop I cannot understand how a political solution of this problem is possible. Thank you.

IX JUDICIARY AND FUNDAMENTAL RIGHTS

Independent Judiciary
Bedrock of Democracy

Sir, I did not propose to participate in this discussion. But the speeches I have heard have encouraged me to say a few words. It cannot be denied that the present Bill of Dr. Karni Singh has been motivated by an apprehension about what is happening at present. He fears that the independence of the judiciary will either be ended or controlled. But it is not only Dr. Karni Singh who has this fear. It is widely spread within and without this House. Its basis is the debate in the ruling party that the judiciary should be committed. No one will disagree with the way our friend has defined 'Committed.' It is quite natural and essential that the judiciary be committed to democratic ideas and our judges committed to constitutional principles. We all swear by the Constitution and we have to implement the directives contained in the Constitution. But the Constitution was framed in 1950. The Republic was declared in 1950. But 'commitment' is not being discussed since 1950. 'Commitment' is a new word. And the discussion is not limited to it. They ask about the judges' class character. Are we now giving into what family a judge is born in ? Are we going into his family tree ? And if he belongs to the middle class or he is a bourgeois judge. Then he cannot do justice to the working class.

All this thinking is totally against our tradition and our philosophy. In this country we developed a philosophy which enjoys a person occupying a judge's seat to keep the scale even and not bind himself to any selfish interest. So when a religious debate took place between Shankaracharya and Mandan Mishra, Mandan Mishra's wife was made the judge. Shankaracharya did not object out of fear that her verdict would go in Mandan Mishra's favour. The concept that originated as *'Panch Parameshwar'* developed into an impartial judiciary.

Independence of the Judiciary in the Dock

Now the impartiality of the judiciary is being questioned. Read the Law Commission's report. Judges are not appointed on merit alone, their caste,

Lok Sabha on August 4, 1972 on the Constitution Amendment Bill by Dr. Karni Singh regarding independence of the Judiciary

their religion is also made a basis. When a Chief Minister gives his advice in this respect he takes many things into consideration. I do not think it is necessary to bring the Chief Minister or the Prime Minister into the picture. I am not saying this out of lack of confidence in them. A system should be so devised that there would be no scope for misuse.

By talking of commitment some members of the ruling party are only promoting the fear that in this country every person will have to be committed to the ruling party—whether a judge or a newspaper or a civil servant. After all, in a democracy the ruling party may change, the people may elect another party to power. Of course we must be firmly committed to democratic ideals. This commitment is necessary and understandable.

The feeling of fear that has prompted this Bill needs to be removed, and I trust the Hon. Minister's reply to this discussion will do so. He should also advise members of his party that they have now a thumping majority, there is no need for a discussion on commitment, and that they would achieve what they are committed to.

If the Supreme Court gives its verdict against bank nationalisation it becomes reactionary, but when the same Supreme Court rules that President Giri's election is legal it comes in for praise. It is the same Supreme Court, but when it rules in favour of the Government it is progressive, forward-looking, committed, but if it rules against the Government the judge is bourgeois, his class character will have to be inspected, and it would be necessary to go into what family he is born in. Is this the test for Supreme Court verdicts ? Is this the test for the judiciary's decisions ? This thinking is vitiated, distorted and dangerous for democracy. It will have to be given up. The judiciary should always be independent and impartial, and when I say 'should be' it should not only 'be,' it should also be 'seen to be' and there should be no debate that would create the apprehension that attempts are made to influence the judges.

Give Rights to Judges, Not Favours

Whether or not retired judges should be appointed to some commission is also an important question. I know many of them are retired but not tired. They remain to serve, and could be appointed to some commission. Their learning and their qualities could be made use of. But there is no restraint in this. A judge the Government likes gets commission after commission, and one whom the Government does not so much like is seen going into *Sanyas*. One procedure for this could be like this—a panel of retired High Court and Supreme Court Judges could be formed and appointments could be made from it. It is not necessary to leave anyone included in it. They will be given commissions according to their order. Then they will see that they will not be given a commission as a Government favour, that their being considered for a commission will not depend upon their giving verdicts in favour of the Government. Their services will be availed of as and when necessary. So it is important to appoint judges from a panel. And, if the Government is not prepared for this, give them such a salary, such a pension that it would not be necessary to take up a job after retirement. Only then can they preserve their independence and impartiality. Thank you.

Supersession in Supreme Court

Government Wants Committed Judiciary

Sir, when I was listening to Shri Mohan Kumaramangalam an Urdu couplet came to my mind :

Kapra sada gala ho to mumkin nahin rafoo,
Seetey the astin gareban phat gaya.
Barey gunah barh gaye ujre gunah se,
Dhone se aur damaney eema chikat gaya."

> "If a cloth is worn out it can not be mended. If you sew the sleeve the whole garment gets torn. If you hide an offence it comes all the more to light. If you wash a blot, it sticks still more firmly."

MR. SPEAKER : I am happy you too speak Urdu.

SHRI VAJPAYEE : When we began to discuss this important topic we were told it was an unimportant matter, it is not a big thing to supersede three Supreme Court Judges and appoint a junior Judge to the position of Chief Justice, there are other important problems before the country, and it is not necessary to spend so much time on this matter. But the discussion we had and the speech that Shri Mohan Kumaramangalam made make it clear that this is not merely a question of any person becoming the Chief Justice, it is not even a question of denying three senior Judges of their rights, it is a question of whether or not the judiciary in this country would remain independent, whether or not democracy will survive in this country.

Shri Mohan Kumaramangalam's speech has strengthened the doubts and objections about the new Chief Justice's appointment that have been expressed by the Opposition Parties here and by the lawyers' associations and intellectuals outside Parliament. The Law Minister Shri Gokhale has sought to apply the ointment of the Law Commission's recommendations to the injuries caused to the independence and sanctity of the judiciary by the appointment of a junior Judge as Chief Justice after superseding three senior judges. But his friend Shri Kumaramangalam has rubbed salt on the wound. He has plainly said that the Government wants committed Judges. Shri Kumaramangalam has said Judges' philosophy and outlook would be taken into account while appointing them. He also asks—

> "It is not good that we should have as Chief Justice of India a man who will help to put an end to this period of confrontation ?"

Shri Kumaramangalam wants that such a person should be appointed as would end the confrontation that is continuing between the Government and the Supreme Court for the past six years.

Lok Sabha on May 4, 1973 during the discussion regarding Appointment of Chief Justice of India

He also says we want judges "... who can effectively work and help us in the Supreme Court."

Judges as Government Agents

What is the meaning of helping the Government ? In many cases the Government is a party to the matter. I am told in 80 per cent the Government is a party to the matter. There may be a conflict not only between individual and individual but also between individual and Government. An individual has to knock on the doors of the Supreme Court when individual freedom is in danger, when fundamental rights are hijacked. When the guarantee of personal dignity given in the Constitution is thrown to the winds. Are the present Judges of the Supreme Court there to help the Government ? Can those whose philosophy, whose outlook is in accord with the Government's philosophy and the Government's outlook protect the Constitution, protect individual freedom, and save fundamental rights ?

Shri Mohan Kumaramangalam is now talking of philosophy. Did this party and this Government have no philosophy before he came ? Has he given it for the first time ? Does the Constitution by which the Judges are asked to swear have no philosophy ? Were the framers of the Constitution devoid of any philosophy ? Did they not want economic progress ? Were they not committed to the principle of social justice ?

They were, but at the same time they were also committed to the independence of the judiciary. Hence the provision in the Constitution that the President will appoint the Judges. They cannot be removed till the age of 65. Their salaries would be drawn from the Consolidated Fund of India and Parliament cannot make any cuts in them. No Judge can be removed by Government order. The Constitution has laid down a special procedure for it, according to which members of both Houses of Parliament will have to submit a memorandum to the President and then action will be taken on it and a Judge removed. Do these provisions for the independence of the judiciary not mirror a philosophy ? Do they not have some basic thinking behind them ? Did the fathers of the Constitution not want a confluence of individual freedom and economic equality ? Did that not want the country to progress economically ? Did they not want disparity to go down and exploitation to end ? At the same time the protection of individual freedom was mainly entrusted to the Supreme Court.

Judges as Yes-men

Now they say Supreme Court Judges should be the Government's yes-men. Shri Mohan Kumaramangalam says a confrontation has been going on for six years. Now he hopes the confrontation would end. Does this mean the person who was made Chief Justice was told that he would be made Chief Justice on this condition alone ? Was he told he was not to give any decision against the Government ? Can Shri Mohan Kumaramangalam forecast what the Chief Justice will do in this matter ? Has the Chief Justice given any assurance in advance ? No guarantee can be given of what Judge will give what verdict.

I do not want to say anything against the Chief Justice. He is a respected Judge, but those three Judges who were superseded are also respected Judges. Much has been said about them. I was looking up the proceedings of the Supreme Court. I have before me a judgement of Justice Ray, who was a Judge of the Calcutta High Court. The matter of Haridas Mundhra was before him. Mundhra had been freed after three years in jail. He wanted to take over all shares of Hunggerford Turner Morrison and Company. At that time Mundhra had only 49 per cent shares. But he had an agreement with Hunggerford by which he could also buy up all the remaining 51 per cent shares. But Turner Morrison Company refused to part with their shares. Mundhra went to Court. The matter was heard by Justice Ray. He gave a judgement by which there was no need for Mundhra to pay Turner Morrison Company Rs. 80,60,000 to acquire the remaining shares. By his judgement Justice Ray gave Mundhra rights to 100 per cent shares without any payment. The matter went to Justice Masood. Justice Masood vacated the stay order. The matter also went to the Supreme Court. Justice K.S. Hegde and Justice K.K. Mathew heard the appeal. I quote a portion from their judgement that relates to Justice Masood :

> "The learned Judge then found that Mundhra was not keen in paying purchase money and getting transfer of 51 per cent shares for the reason that the injunction granted by the Court in the decree suit No. 600 of 1961, restraining the appellant from voting except in accordance with the instructions of Mundhra made him virtually the owner of 100 per cent shares in Turner Morrison, and if without paying any amount for 51 per cent shares of Turner Morrison he got control of Turner Morrison, it was to his interest not to pay anything to the appellant."

This is the case that Justice Ray had heard. I place this fact before you. I am not accusing Justice Ray. But can this not be construed to mean that Justice Ray gave a verdict that benefited Mundhra ? But I am not levelling a charge. (*Interruptions*) Will Justice Ray be evaluated on the basis of this judgement ? Will a Supreme Court Judge be deprived of his seniority on the basis of some judgement that he may have given against the Government ? Will the Government only appoint yes-men as Judges ?

SHRI SHASHI BHUSHAN (South Delhi) : That is why we have brought you into the Opposition.

SHRI VAJPAYEE : We did not come by your favour. We have come in spite of you. (*Interruptions*)

SHRI SHASHI BHUSHAN : It was by the Rajmata's favour that you came.

SHRI VAJPAYEE : Sir, I am surprised to see that the Prime Minister did not think it necessary to participate in this discussion.

SHRI S.M. BANERJI (Kanpur) : In this country Bharat was given the kingdom even when Ram was older.

SHRI VAJPAYEE : These latter-day Bharats want to rule themselves instead of on behalf of the Sandals.

But the Prime Minister thought it fit to mention this matter in the Phul Bagh meeting in Kanpur instead of in Parliament. She has referred to President Roosevelt. I can understand the Prime Minister's ambition to be on the same level as President Roosevelt. But this matter will be decided by historians not by her sycophants or her wrong advisors.

Wrong Example

It is wrong to give President Roosevelt's example. President Roosevelt was the President of the U.S., where the appointment of Judges is approved by the Senate. There have been many instances where the Senate rejected the President's nomination and the President had to send it another name. There is no such procedure in India. Then again, President Roosevelt's Council of Ministers did not have any members who were once communists and still talked of scientific communism. His party did not have people who discussed Judges' class character. His Council of Ministers also did not have senior members who did public mud-slinging at Judges, but when there was fear of a suit of defamation retracted their statement and did a whitewash.

England has also been mentioned and Australia and Canada have also been referred to. I would like to place a quotation from Churchill before the House :

> "The principle of the complete independence of the judiciary from the executive is the foundation of many things in our Island life. It is perhaps one of the deepest gulfs between us and all forms of totalitarianism. The Judge has not only to do justice between man and man but he also—and this is one of his most important functions—has to do justice between the citizens and the State."

But if there is a conflict between an individual and the State how will committed Judges give a judgement ? (*Interruptions*).

Government Philosophy

The question is not only about the Judges' commitment. This matter does not end here. Now the demand is being raised that the Judges should have the same social philosophy as the Government party. Tomorrow the Chief Election Commissioner would be expected to have the Government party's philosophy. (*Interruptions*). Along with the Chief Election Commissioner there would be the question of the Chairman of the Union Public Service Commission. Then this will be taken into account also when appointing Judges for going into firing incidents. Then will this rule also apply to the armed forces ? Will the appointment of the Army Chief ....

SHRI VASANT SATHE (Akola) : Let the Hon. Member at least not add falsehood to what Shri Kumaramangalam has said. When did Shri Kumaramangalam say it should be our party's philosophy ? Let the Hon. Member point out the sentence.

SHRI VAJPAYEE : Whose philosophy is Shri Mohan Kumaramangalam talking about ?

SHRI PILOO MODY (Godhra) : I agree what he did not talk about the Party's philosophy. He talked about his master's philosophy. His party had never held that philosophy.

SHRI VASANT SATHE : He talked about the philosophy that is enshrined in our Constitution ....(*Interruptions*).

SHRI VAJPAYEE : If Shri Sathe is talking about the philosophy of the Constitution this Constitution was not made yesterday. It was made in 1950. All appointments of Judges made so far were made according to the Constitution and all Judges were loyal to the Constitution. Whatever judgements they made were tested on this Constitution.

There can be a difference of opinion on Supreme Court judgements. The Supreme Court could reconsider its own judgements. Is it not a matter of surprise that the announcement of the new Chief Justice's appointment was done the same day the Supreme Court gave a good judgement on fundamental rights—good from the Government's point of view ? The announcement was made on the radio after the court rose for the day, and the Chief Justice was sworn in before the Supreme Court sat the next day. What was the need to do this in the dark of the night ? Why was this secretly done ?

Yesterday it was revealed that the Government did not show the etiquette to take the retiring Chief Justice into confidence, nor did it think it necessary to do so. I have a quotation from Dr. Ambedkar. But what need is there now to quote Dr. Ambedkar ? Now it is time for Mohan Kumaramangalam. Dr. Ambedkar had said :

> "It seems to me that in the circumstances in which we are today it would be dangerous to leave the appointments to be made by the President without any kind of reservation or limitation, that is to say, merely on the advice of the executive of the day. Similarly, it seems to me that to make every appointment subject to the concurrence of the Legislature is also not a very suitable provision. Apart from its being cumbrous, it also involves the possibility of the appointment being influenced by political pressure and political considerations. The draft article, therefore, steers a middle course. It does not make the President the supreme and the absolute authority in the matter of making appointments. It does not also import the influence of the Legislature. The provision in the article is that there should be consultation of persons who are *ex hypothesi* well qualified to give proper advice in matters of this sort."

Dr. Ambedkar did not say only the Council of Ministers will discuss. The President is not a puppet, he is not just a stamping machine. The President could consult the retiring Chief Justice. He could consult the Chief Justices of High Courts. (*Interruptions*). But I have come to know that the President was pressurised into superseding three Judges and appointing Justice Ray as Chief Justice. Is this in accordance with the spirit of the Constitution ? Is this in accordance with Dr. Ambedkar's declaration ?

It is clear that the Constitution is now being thrown to the winds, a blow is being struck at the root of the judiciary. The Government is now bent upon demolishing fundamental rights. No one is opposed to rapid economic progress of the country. But the Government wants to make the Supreme Court a scapegoat to hide its failures on the economic front. Has the Supreme Court prevented the Government from taking steps that would bring down dearness ? Has the Supreme Court prevented the Government from including the right to work in fundamental rights ? In the *Golak Nath* case a restriction of fundamental rights was prevented, not an expansion. Had the Government so wished it could have included the right to work among fundamental rights. It would have guaranteed a livelihood for every individual, and if he did not get work it would have provided for a dole. No provision was made in the Constitution for this. The Supreme Court did not hinder this.

Parliament Higher or Supreme Court ?

Now the question is again being raised—is the Parliament higher or the Supreme Court ? I say the Parliament is high in its field and the Supreme Court in its field. The Constitution of India is higher than both and the people of India higher than the Constitution. If the Government feels that the present Constitution hinders rapid socio-economic change it can change it. If the Government so wishes it can make Parliament take a decision to set up a new Constituent Assembly, and that Constituent Assembly can even frame a new Constitution. But when laws are made the matter of deciding their validity or otherwise would have to be left to the Supreme Court and its decision will have to be accepted gracefully. If the Government differs with it there are ways to change it too. But packing the Supreme Court with yes-men is not the way. The result of this will be that only a Judge who always agrees with the Government and decides in its favour will become Chief Justice.

SHRI S.A. SHAMIM (Srinagar) : He would be more a *'Chamcha'* than a Judge.

SHRI VAJPAYEE : Will this protect the Constitution ? Will it protect democracy ?

Principle of Seniority

Sir, I would like to demand that the Government accept the principle of seniority in the appointment of the Chief Justice. My friend Shri Jagannath Rao had also pointed out that there was no rule, on norm. Will the Government be allowed to act without restraint in this matter ? If the rule of seniority is not acceptable to you there should be some other method which would prevent the person whose right you disregard from feeling that you are superseding him for political reasons and want to humiliate him. Actually it would be good to apply the rule of seniority, and so far it was applied. Justice Imam's was a different case. He was not in good health, so Gajendragadkar was made the Chief Justice. Yesterday the Law Minister said he could cite many instances where a senior Judge was superseded by a junior. There may be such cases. But in those cases the Government did not talk about a committed judiciary. At that time there was no Mohan Kumaramangalam to guide the Government. At that time the Government's bona fides were not suspect. The basic problem today is that we suspect the Government's bona fides.

What philosophy will prevail in this country ? We have believed in *'Panch Parameshwar'* here. Whoever the person, whatever the party he is connected with, whatever class he comes from, once he occupies the seat of justice he will give up all temptations and decide the truth. This is this country's tradition. I shall give an example.

There was going to be a religious debate between Jagat Guru Adi Shankaracharya and Mandan Misra. The question arose—who will be the judge in a confrontation between two scholars ? Mandan Mishra's wife was made the judge. Shankaracharya did not object. He did not say to Mandan Misra, she is your wife, she will decide in your favour. He did not question her class character. Shankaracharya said once she becomes the judge she will decide on the basis of facts even if she is your wife. This has been this country's tradition. In this country we have the tradition of Jehangir's justice. But Mohan Kumaramangalam does not believe in that tradition. He does not believe in the tradition that has ripened on the banks of the Ganga. He believes in the tradition that has grown by the Volga. He cannot look at an individual apart from politics. Can an individual not be impartial ?

SHRI S.M. BANERJI : You should get married, then we'll make your wife a judge.

SHRI VAJPAYEE : Sir, when I enter into a religious debate with him he may make his wife the judge. I will have no objection.

Strike an Accord

I would now like to close. An individual could be selfless, impartial and free from temptation. An individual will rise above ground level, give up all selfish interests and give his decision. We want such a judiciary. We will have to develop such a judiciary. We will have to strike an accord between individual freedom and economic capacity. Shri Mohan Kumaramangalam wants only economic capacity, not individual freedom. We want both. This is the basic difference. This difference is not about three Judges. It is the difference between democracy and dictatorship. It is the difference between the Yogi and the Commissar. It is the difference between the Mahatma and Marx. It is the difference between democracy and Mohan Kumaramangalam.

Anti-democratic Dogma

I would like the Law Minister to clarify. It would have been better if the Prime Minister had come to the House and explained if the philosophy propounded by Shri Mohan Kumaramangalam is the Congress Party's philosophy. Has the Congress Party discussed it at any time ? If Judges are to be appointed on the basis of philosophy the Socialist Forum has a separate philosophy and the Forum is in eternal sleep in its grave, while the Nehru Forum has a separate philosophy and this Forum is sobbing. What philosophy will the Judges reflect ? The States will have different Governments. Will the Chief Justices of those High Courts represent the philosophy of those parties ? The philosophy they have propounded is anti-democratic, it strikes at the independence of the judiciary, it will destroy democracy, and so we have decided to fight against it—both inside the House and outside.

Sir, I thank all those Hon. Members who expressed their opinion on my Bill. I would like to remind the House that this Bill had been tabled in 1971, and in its objectives I had stated that at that very time the apprehension had arisen that in the name of an enlightened judiciary the Government would or may take steps that would strike at the independence and impartiality of the judiciary. Later events have strengthened this fear.

Sir, a point that was made against this Bill is—what would happen if the seniormost Judge is made the Chief Justice but he is physically or mentally incapacitated ? There has been such an instance and everybody knows that that Chief Justice had voluntarily resigned. But it can be argued, and it has been argued—what if somebody refuses to resign ? I say the way out of such situation is not to take over unlimited powers for appointing the Chief Justice. There is a way, and it has been provided for in the Constitution. The provisions for the Union Public Service Commission contain Section 310(3), which reads :

> "Notwithstanding anything in Clause (1), the President may by order remove from office the Chairman or any other member of a Public Service Commission if the Chairman or such other member, as the case may be,—is in the opinion of the President, unfit to continue in office by reason of infirmity of mind or body."

The Constitution provides that if a person cannot discharge his responsibility properly he may be removed by the President.

SHRI A.K.M. ISHAQUE (Basirhat) : They stand on totally different footings : one is Public Service Commission and the other is Chief Justice of Supreme Court.

SHRI VAJPAYEE : I am replying to the argument about what is to be done if a Judge is mentally or physically incapable. I say decide to appoint the seniormost Judge as the Chief Justice, and along with it empower the President to remove him if he is mentally or physically infirm.

SHRI A.K.M. ISHAQUE : He cannot remove them without impeachment.

SHRI VAJPAYEE : This is where the Constitution needs to be amended.

It has been accepted for the last 25 years that the Chief Justice should be accepted on the basis of seniority. Here I would like to quote from *"The Constitutional Law of India"* by Shri H.M. Seervai, who is a friend of the Law Minister. In the chapter on the Union Judiciary he says :

> "The provisions for the appointment of the Chief Justice of the Supreme Court and the Chief Justices of High Courts do not call for any discussion since, by convention, the seniormost Judge is appointed as the Chief Justice. The convention is based on the view that, on the whole, the interests of judicial administration are better served by eliminating the exercise of discretionary power in the appointing authorities than by the search for the best man."

This is Shri Seervai's opinion. From the inception of the Constitution till a few months ago the Government shared it, but afterwards it gave up the convention of making the seniormost Judge the Chief Justice.

Government Wants Unlimited Powers

The speech the Law Minister has made indicate that he wants unlimited powers in respect of the Chief Justice's appointment. Hence my amendment, which seeks to bind the Government to making only the seniormost Judge the Chief Justice.

According to my friend Shri Mishra's interpretation of the Constitution the Chief Justice is included in 'Judge,' so useful advice should be taken in his appointment. If the Law Minister accepts this interpretation there would be no need of my Bill. (*Interruptions*). The Constitution is not clear about making the seniormost Judge the Chief Justice, there is ambiguity, and they are exploiting it. I say this thing should be made quite clear.

On this point those who say it is wrong to say that we did not do consultation on the Chief Justice's appointment also say that we did not consult in any matter. According to them before retirement the Chief Justice used to write letters to the Government, and make recommendations about who should succeed him. I think this is not a fact. I know about one case. When Chief Justice Kania was about to retire and there was a proposal about appointing an outsider as Chief Justice all Supreme Court Judges had opposed it and threatened to resign. If they were not consulted how did they come to know that an outsider was coming and the seniormost Judge was not going to be made Chief Justice ?

I did not want to discuss the affidavit registered by the Government with the Delhi High Court, but as it is being discussed I shall also say something. I was surprised to read the document which says : "The Government denies that the Judges who have been superseded were eminent Judges."

They were Supreme Court Judges. You had made them Supreme Court Judges. You had made them after considering their merit. It is a different matter that they were not made Chief Justice, but does that mean that just in order to support your stand you will file an affidavit with the High Court saying those Judges were not eminent Judges ?

SHRI A.K.M. ISHAQUE : He was not so eminent as to become the Chief Justice.

SHRI VAJPAYEE : You have not read the affidavit at all.

This is most objectionable. The Law Minister has considered the Joint Secretary's affidavit as his own affidavit and this has been mentioned in it. This has strengthened the feeling that you wanted to penalise the superseded Judges for giving their verdict against the Government in the case of fundamental rights. I am surprised to see that the Law Minister did not think it proper to say a word about the late Shri Mohan Kumaramangalam's speech. My friend Shri Sathe said the Judges should have the same philosophy as that of the Constitution. Had this been said that very day all this quarrel would not have arisen. But Shri Mohan Kumaramangalam said we want Judges who would help the Government, who would be forward-looking. What does forward-looking mean ? Commenting on this Chief Justice Hidayatullah had remarked : a forward-looking Judge or a Judge looking forward to whether or not he gets a place on some commission after retirement ? But the Law Minister is completely silent on this point. In his reply to this discussion he replied to other points but he was silent on whether the Government wants Supreme Court Judges and the Chief Justice to be committed to the ruling party's philosophy or to the philosophy of the Constitution.

SHRI H.R. GOKHALE : I have said it so many times.

SHRI VAJPAYEE : Please say it once more.

SHRI H.R. GOKHALE : I have said it so many times.

SHRI VAJPAYEE : The Law Minister has referred to what the Attorney General has said in the Supreme Court. Let him not quote Justice Hegde. I have brought a copy of All India Reporter and would like to quote from this judgement.

SHRI H.R. GOKHALE : I have read it.

SHRI VAJPAYEE : I am reading from the A.I.R. Report. It says :

> "The respondents claim that Parliament can abrogate fundamental rights such as freedom of speech and expression, freedom to form associations or unions and freedom of religion. They claim that democracy can even be replaced and one-party rule established. Indeed, short of repeal of the Constitution, any form of Government with no freedom to the citizens can be set up by Parliament by exercising its power under Article 368."

Government Intentions Suspect

Sir, when it is said on behalf of the Government that there is no question of enhancing the Parliament's prestige it makes the Government's intentions still more suspect. This Parliament is elected on different issues. But the Law Minister was equating the Parliament with the people when he spoke. The Law Minister will recollect that when the Constitution Amendment Bill came before the House I had said that if you want to abrogate or abridge fundamental rights take an opinion poll, take a referendum, but it would be wrong to say that Parliament, which is elected every five years and which is elected on different issues, can destroy the very soul of the Constitution. Whether fundamental rights should be abridged or expanded is never made an election issue.

SHRI H.R. GOKHALE : This was placed in the manifesto.

SHRI VAJPAYEE : But your manifesto laid emphasis on *Garibi Hatao* and not abrogation of Fundamental Rights.

So I had said that if you want the people's opinion on this, say to them—we want to smother the freedom of expression, do you agree ?

Sir, I say the Parliament is limited within its orbit. It will forsake its representative character the day it decides to change democracy into dictatorship, the day it tries to demolish the citizens' fundamental rights. If you want to do such a thing you should go to the people, you should convene a Constituent Assembly, you should frame a new Constitution, but a House elected for five years on certain issues cannot change the bases of the Constitution.

But this power is being claimed under Article 368. This power has been challenged, and I congratulate those Judges who ruled that Parliament cannot change the basic character of the Constitution. No one can change India's democracy into a monarchy. The day the Parliament does so it will not remain Parliament. But why was such a thing was said on behalf of the Government ? Why did the Attorney-General have to say something in the Supreme Court that you did not mean ? I am not an *'Antaryami'*, so I do not know what's really in your mind, but what you say strengthens suspicion. You had something in mind, so you said Parliament has the power to destroy democracy if it wants to do so. No one has given the Parliament this power.

SHRI M. RAM GOPAL REDDY (Nizamabad) : I can place all the belongings in my house, in the market place, but I do not do so.

SHRI VAJPAYEE : Sir, this is neither Hon. Shri Reddy's *'Makan'* (house) nor his *'dukan'* (shop). This is India's highest representative body. Within its sphere it is independent. The Supreme Court is independent in its sphere and this House will have to accept the Supreme Court's interpretation of the Constitution. If the Parliament so wishes it can amend the Constitution. But that amendment will have to submit to the Court. Perhaps that is why you want Supreme Court Judges to be yes-men. I want to close the door on that. Accept the point about making the seniormost Judge the Chief Justice. If there is some deficiency then one more amendment can also be made saying that if a Chief Justice is infirm in body or mind, as has also been done in the case of the Comptroller and Auditor-General ....

SHRI MOOL CHAND DAGA (Pali) : What if his ideas are third-rate ?

SHRI VAJPAYEE : Then how did he reach the Supreme Court ? If you can take him upto the Supreme Court can you not make him the Chief Justice ? (*Interruptions*) And who will decide if that is so ? Will it be the powers that be ?

Implement Directive Principles

Our Directive Principles say there would be separation of the executive and the judiciary. That day Congress members were making forceful speeches, saying that Directive Principles are higher than Fundamental Rights. The late Mohan Kumaramangalam had said the same thing. If that is really so include the Directive Principles in Article 19. Include the directive principle of giving an unemployment allowance, include the directive principle of having a common civil code, make the directive principle of banning cow slaughter a fundamental right. But when fundamental rights are abridged you swear by directive principles, and when the question of implementing the principles comes up you say they are not justiciable. Whose system is this ? Is it the Supreme Court's or this House's or the Constitution's ?

It is argued that Supreme Court Judges do not care for the Directive Principles. This is stupid. You have yourself written into the Constitution that Directive Principles are not justiciable. (*Interruptions*) If the Government and the House wants directive principles to be put into practice and to make it compulsory for Supreme Court Judges to give their judgements in accordance with Directive Principles the Constitution can be amended and they can be included in the Chapter on Fundamental Rights. We shall support it. Bring in the amendment. But you won't do it. Sometimes you become advocates of fundamental rights, sometimes supporters of directive principles. But all in all your actions would strike a blow at the independence of the judiciary and create doubts about the future of Indian democracy. The Law Minister's speech does not remove our misgivings. Rather, they have been strengthened. Hence I stress my Bill. It should be passed. Thank you.

Appointment of Chief Justice—Amend the Constitution

Sir, I move that a Bill for further amendment of the Constitution of India be taken into consideration. Under this Bill I have proposed amendment to Article 124. It relates to the Union's Judiciary. I quote :

124. (1) There shall be a Supreme Court of India consisting of a Chief Justice of India and, until Parliament by law prescribes a larger number, of not more than seven other Judges.

(2) Every Judge of the Supreme Court shall be appointed by the President by warrant under his hand and seal after consultation with such of the Judges of the Supreme Court and of the High Courts in the States as the President may deem necessary for the purpose and shall hold office until he attains the age of sixty-five years :

Provided that in the case of appointment of a Judge other than the Chief Justice, the Chief Justice of India shall always be consulted.

I propose that the following be added after Article 124, Clause (1) :

"The Senior-most Judge of the Supreme Court of India shall be the Chief Justice of India."

So far the Constitution is silent on the appointment of the Chief Justice. It states that the President will consult the Chief Justice on the appointment of Judges, but it is silent on who will be consulted on the appointment of the Chief Justice. Perhaps this is so because the fathers of the Constitution thought that in respect of appointment of the Chief Justice a healthy convention would be followed, that the senior-most Judge would become the Chief Justice. But from the time a debate on a committed judiciary began in the country, people's courts began to be demanded, and the attitude of putting Parliament above the Constitution and the country began to gain strength, we began to suspect that the Government would appoint Chief Justice not on the basis of any healthy tradition but on political considerations.

I had given notice of this Bill on May 20, 1971. At that time what was going to happen in the Supreme Court in the future could not have been imagined. But there was certainly a doubt. Dark shadows could be seen on the horizon that created an apprehension in my mind that this Government may not hesitate to strike at the independence and impartiality of the judiciary. Hence the notice of this Bill. Its objectives have been stated thus :

Lok Sabha on August 24, 1973 while moving his Constitution Amendment Bill regarding appointment of the senior-most Judge of the Supreme Court as Chief Justice of India

"The object of this constitutional amendment is to ensure the impartiality of the Supreme Court of India. The present constitutional position gives the Government unlimited power in the appointment of the Chief Justice of India. This power may undermine the independence and impartiality of the highest organ of the judiciary, as the Government can fill the vacancies by appointing persons sharing their political views. Therefore, the amendment provides that only the senior-most Judge of the Supreme Court becomes the Chief Justice of India."

The apprehension has now become a reality. A junior Judge of the Supreme Court has been appointed Chief Justice, superseding three senior Judges. I do not want to go into personalities. And that is not the purpose of this discussion. Whoever occupies the seat of justice is worthy of our reverence.

But the question is, will there not be some procedure for appointing the Chief Justice ? So long it was said there is a tradition that the senior Judge will become the Chief Justice. This tradition was observed from the first year of independence to date — except for one exception when Justice Imam could not become Chief Justice in spite of being senior, because of physical disability. But in all other cases the principle of seniority was observed. However this time an exception has been made. The arguments put forward in defence of this exception are not only ridiculous, they have also unmasked the Government's intentions. The Law Minister is present in the House. He has removed the cobwebs from the report presented by the Law Commission in 1958 and presented it to the House. He says that the Law Commission has recommended that seniority need not be the only basis for appointment of the Chief Justice. The Law Commission included Justice Chagla too. Recently addressing the Lawyers' Association he said that the devil quotes *scriptures*, but he does not quote them wrongly.

Law Commission's Report Not Quoted Rightly

But in this same House the Law Commission's report is not quoted rightly. The Law Commission has also said that if you want a convention that the Chief Justice will not be appointed on the basis of seniority alone you should first make such a declaration, establish such a convention, so that in future appointments no one would feel he is ignored or victimised or penalised for his opinions. It would have been another matter if you had accepted this right after 1958 and if this convention had got established. The Government slept over the Law Commission's report for decades, much water flowed under the bridge, months changed into years, and suddenly the Government remembered the Law Commission's report when it decided to deny three senior Judges of their right. But I quote what the Law Commission says :

"Above all a person of sturdy independence and a towering personality who would, on the occasion arising, be the watchdog of the independence of the judiciary."

Such a person should be the Chief Justice. The Law Commission did not say the Chief Justice should be efficient or capable. The Government cannot accept one part of the Law Commission's report and reject another. It cannot swallow the sweet and spit out the bitter. That cannot be. The Law Commission's report cannot be divided into parts. If you accept the Law Commission's point of view that a Judge should be such that he would protect the independence and impartiality of the judiciary, that he should not be influenced by the Government, what was the need of standing up in this House and propounding a new philosophy according to which a person should be such that he would help the Government, that he would be forward-looking ?

I was reading Justice Hidayatullah. He has made a nice joke. He said should it be forward-looking or looking forward ? Not a forward-looking Judge but a Judge who will be a yes-men and look forward to what he would get. What does forward-looking mean ?

What has the Chief Justice promised ?

It was also said in the House that a Judge's philosophy should be the same as that of the Government, it should be the same social philosophy. The late Mohan Kumaramangalam is no more with us. I shall not quote him wrongly. It won't forget what he said that day in the House. He is no more in our midst. We miss him. But it cannot be denied that he said everything plainly and the Government was unmasked. At least I would praise his honesty. I disagree with his thinking, I am opposed to it, I consider his thinking detrimental to democracy, but he said quite fearlessly that they wanted a Judge who would put an end to the confrontation between the Supreme Court and the Parliament. Has the Chief Justice promised that this confrontation would be ended ?

The Law Minister visited Chandigarh a few days back. There he said the philosophy of the Judges should be the same as the philosophy of the Constitution. But is there not an internal discrepancy between what he says and the late Shri Mohan Kumaramangalam's reply ? We agree that the philosophy of the Judges should be the same as the philosophy of the Constitution. A Judge swears by the Constitution. He has to do justice without fear or favour. But the late Mohan Kumaramangalam did not talk of the philosophy contained in the Constitution. There would have been no quarrel if he had said that. He said we want a Judge who would help the Government. If the Judge helps the Government who would do justice by citizens going in appeal against the Government ? It has been repeated in the House that more than 60 per cent cases are against the Government. They will go on increasing, because the Government is taking more and more economic and social fields under its control and power is getting concentrated.

An individual may have a complaint. His fundamental rights may be transgressed. Then he has to knock on the doors of the Court. But if the Judge who sits there is sitting there for helping the Government the individual cannot get justice, individual freedom will not be preserved, and fundamental rights will not be protected.

The Government Must Clarify Its Position

I wanted a refutation of this in the House, but it has not been refuted. A whitewash has been attempted. Sardar Darbara Singh says it is only a matter of words and they are doing justice to Shri Mohan Kumaramangalam's memory. But the difference is not in words, it is a difference in thinking, a difference in philosophy. That is why this Bill gives an opportunity to the Government to clarify its position. What does the Government want ?

It may be argued that once we write it down in the Constitution that only a senior Judge will be made the Chief Justice no exception at all would be possible. What would happen if another case like that of Justice Imam comes up ? I submit if such a case comes up again the concerned individual will voluntarily resign and quit; no exception need be made for them. But the Government cannot be given unlimited powers on this basis.

Recently there was an all-India convention of lawyers in Delhi. It was organised by the Supreme Court Bar Association. Many members of the Law Commission attended it. They have nothing to do with party politics. But they were all worried about the independence of the judiciary. They demanded that the Government should have a clear mind on the subject.

When the Constitution was being framed Dr. Ambedkar had said this matter could not be left to the executive. Then whose opinion will be taken ? There was also a suggestion that there should be a panel, that panel should recommend names, and one of them should become the Chief Justice. I would have no objection if the Law Minister sets up any such system, but the present position cannot be accepted.

Is it not surprising that even the retiring Judge did not know who was to succeed him ? The retiring Chief Justice was not shown even common etiquette. The Government knew he was about to retire, then why was the decision not taken in time ? Why was it not announced beforehand ? Why was it done at the eleventh hour ?

I read one more thing in Justice Hidayatullah's speech. He said he thought Justice Shelat would become Chief Justice. Justice Hidayatullah says they would joke about it : "Hello, Shelat ! What about taking me to your swearing in ceremony ?"

—And he would call him Vacation Judge. But things happened the opposite way. Justice Hidayatullah make this revelation :

> "I learnt of the supersession of the three Judges and the appointment of Mr. Justice Ray at 11 o'clock on the 25th. The news came to me from Calcutta. It is a most remarkable thing that the announcement took place at 3.30 in the afternoon of the day and I knew about it at 11 in the morning."

SHRI H.R. GOKHALE, Minister of Law : Whose speech is it ?

SHRI VAJPAYEE : This is the speech of the former Chief Justice Mr. Hidayatullah. The news came from Calcutta. The official announcement came later. The news came in the morning. The retiring Judge was kept in the dark. Why ?

The other question raised in the Bar Association's conference was that the Government withheld the announcement about the Chief Justice so long as it did not learn about the Supreme Court's decision on fundamental rights. Is it not true that those three Judges who did not rule in favour of the Government were sidelined and deprived of their seniority ? Is this the way to enhance the prestige of the judiciary ? Is this the way to give the people the confidence that their fundamental rights would be protected, that the Supreme Court would do justice by them ?

This is not a question of only three Judges. I have also no complaint about the Chief Justice. He may be a good person. I am talking about a principle. I am stressing the development of a system. This thing cannot be permanently left in the Government's hands. The Government will have to be bound by certain limitations, and this Bill is an effort in that direction. It could be written down in the Constitution that the senior Judge would become the Chief Justice.

There is another argument—what if the senior Judge is not capable ? I would ask in return—if he was not capable how did he reach the Supreme Court ? Are there no requirements of capacity to reach the Supreme Court ? If a person can become Supreme Court Judge can he not become the Chief Justice ? And can anyone say the three superseded Judges were not capable or did not have the capacity to take decisions and provide leadership ?

But the Government wants yes-men as Judges. So it does not want to bind itself with any rule, any convention and any procedure. My Bill is an attempt in this direction and I wish the House considers it and gives its opinion. Thank You.

Fundamental Rights

Convene A New Constituent Assembly

Sir, I stand to oppose Shri Nath Pai's Bill. My opposition is basic, and so I have informed the Law Minister that no member of our party would be on the Select Committee being set up by him.

The Supreme Court has given a historic judgement. Realising its importance and acting upon it would strengthen our republic. The present discussion relates to whether Parliament is supreme or not. In my opinion the way this question has been raised would not take us to the right conclusion. In some matters Parliament is supreme. But if we think of all the three—Parliament, the Executive and the Judiciary—and the Constitution divides the powers of the three and demarcates separate fields for them—no one should hesitate to accept that the Constitution is supreme and the Parliament, the Judiciary and the Executive have to function within it.

It is true that Parliament has been given the power to amend the Constitution. But the fathers of the Constitution did not want to make its amendment easy. Had that been their intention they would not have laid down the condition of a two-thirds majority. Common law can be changed by majority. But no amendment in the Constitution is possible without a two-thirds majority. The only purpose of the fathers of the Constitution behind this was to ensure that the Constitution could not be amended easily. I was surprised to see that Shri Mulla tried to distort even this point of a two-thirds majority in his favour. In fact the point about a two-thirds majority strengthens the argument that an amendment in the Constitution should not be easy, and it should be still more difficult to amend and especially to abridge the portion on fundamental rights, which is the main part of the Constitution and on which our democratic structure stands.

Fundamental Rights

India is a republic. So the Constitution which the people of India have made and given to themselves gives us fundamental rights, fundamental freedoms. These rights may change with the times. But they should not be abridged without at least consulting the people to whom they have been given. I am surprised to see that members are not willing to go back to the people on this point. Those members who claim to be progressive should

Lok Sabha on July 7, 1967 during discussion on Shri Nath Pai's Constitution Amendment Bill regarding Parliament's rights to abridge on fundamental rights in the context of the Supreme Court judgement in Golak Nath's case

certainly have no difficulty in securing a fresh mandate of the people on this question.

The people's opinion was invited on whether Goa should merge in Maharashtra or remain separate. The letter of the Constitution does not include taking a public poll. But we developed a new process. The case of Goa has proved that public opinion received in such matters may differ from the opinion expressed in the election. The general elections in Goa led to the formation of a different type of Government. So I submit the Supreme Court's suggestion to convene a new Constituent Assembly is a revolutionary proposal. This Parliament should accept it. In a special matter, and especially in a matter where we are going to abridge the people's freedoms and rights, we should be ready to invite a fresh opinion of the people.

SHRI SHEO NARAIN : Who will constitute the Assembly ?

SHRI VAJPAYEE : The new constituent assembly will be convened with the approval of this Parliament. The President of the Republic will call it. It will consider this matter afresh. It will be elected on the basis of adult franchise. For those who talk of the supremacy of Parliament I have a question—can this Parliament abridge the right of adult franchise if it so wishes ? It cannot. And the day it will try to abridge the right of adult franchise either the issue will be settled on the streets or a fresh mandate of the people for such a basic change would become necessary.

I am happy with this judgement of the Supreme Court. There has been delay, but it is the right judgement, a historic judgement, and a revolutionary judgement. In the *Berubari case* we had hoped that the Supreme Court would rule that Parliament cannot cede any part of Indian territory to any foreigner. Can Parliament give to China the territory that has gone under Chinese control in the name of Supremacy ?

ACHARYA J.B. KRIPALANI : It did so.

SHRI VAJPAYEE : I would say to Acharyaji, not yet. But I do not want to discuss that here. The Supreme Court's judgement is quite clear on fundamental rights and the final decision on this should be left to the people.

Call New Constituent Assembly

One more thing. The new Constituent Assembly would be more revolutionary in form. Actually the old Constituent Assembly had not been elected on adult franchise. This Parliament should not take into its hands the task to end the fundamental freedoms and rights that we acquired through that assembly. But those who are opposed to convening a Constituent Assembly need not fear about property rights. The new Constituent Assembly will be a couple of steps ahead in that respect. If the country has really changed, if the people have changed, and if the new system is to be reflected in our rights and in our Constitution the new Constituent Assembly will go forward in the matter of property rights, not backward. So those who argue that the matter of property rights should be decided by the Parliament, not by the Constituent Assembly, have either not understood the mind of the country or are afraid of seeking the people's mandate on any issue. I do not agree with them. We should respect the Supreme Court's judgement. If we initiate action to change it we would be setting a very wrong tradition. I submit that we should respect that decision and prepare to call a Constituent Assembly in accordance with the procedure suggested by the Supreme Court. Thank you.

People's Mandate Necessary for Abridging Fundamental Rights

Sir, apart from the Prime Minister three lawyers have participated in the discussion on this Bill. But none of this *'Trimurti'* has been able to explain satisfactorily why we should be reluctant to approach the citizens if we want to end their fundamental rights. Yesterday I had given the example of the Maharashtrawadi Gomantak Party that won the election in Goa. The people of Goa placed power in their hands. But when it came to merging Goa in Maharashtra and the people's opinion was sought the people changed their verdict.

SHRI S.S. DESHMUKH (Parbhani) : Non-Goans had voted.

SHRI VAJPAYEE : Sir, saying now that these people voted and that time those people voted is no argument. Can any one rule out the possibility that the people may vote differently on different issues ? In a general election the people may decide one way, but when it comes to abridging fundamental rights they may react in a different way. So I say, those who believe in the people, who swear by the people's sovereignty and who accept that Parliament is supreme but the people are even higher should have no hesitation in approaching the people. I am sorry to see that in this discussion I was accused of talking of a referendum in order to prevent the passage of this Bill or to divert the people's attention. To accuse is not to argue. An accusation can be answered by a counter-accusation. I can accuse the Government of bringing forward this unnecessary Bill in order to cover up its failure in respect of Bangladesh. The Golak Nath verdict came in 1967. For three years you did not think of stepping up the process of economic and social change ....

SHRI Y.B. CHAVAN, Finance Minister : We were preparing.

SHRI VAJPAYEE : It is quite a few months since you won the election. During this period you could have sent the matter to the Supreme Court and secured its opinion or you could have brought forward a Bill in the first session of the Lok Sabha. But I do not want to express lack of confidence in your intentions, nor do I want you to criticise my intentions. Abridgement of fundamental rights is not an ordinary matter. The people have the right to be consulted before any such abridgement.

Yesterday Shri S.S. Ray also spoke during this discussion. I am sorry I was not present in the House at the time. But I read his speech today. He said I am not married, but had I been married 20 years ago I could have had many

Lok Sabha on August 4, 1971 during discussion on the Constitution (Twenty-fourth Amendment) Bill relating to Parliament's power to amend or abridge Fundamental Rights

wives, while now I cannot have more than one wife. What he meant is that the right to have wives is changing, it is changing for me, perhaps it is also changing for S.S. Ray, but the right to have more than one wife is not changing for Moin-ul Huq.

You talk of the Directive Principles of the Constitution. They state the country should have a common civil code. This matter will be tested after this Bill is passed.

SHRI. R.S. PANDEYA (Rajnandgaon) : For the protection of the minorities their systems should be protected.

SHRI VAJPAYEE : I agree that rights change and the right to property is also dependent on the society. It is not absolute. There was a time when the wife was considered a piece of property but she is now an equal partner, and our philosophy of life, our culture, has never rejected change. Different *'Smritis'* (codes) have been written and different rights defined. When we discussed *'Shashwat Dharma'* (eternal law) we also emphasised *'Yug Dharma'* (the law of the age), and if the law of the age expects that the right to property should be restricted no one can deny it. But I oppose because although my not being able to have more than one wife can be the subject matter of a joke it does not strengthen Shri Siddhartha Shankar Ray's argument. The problem is, he is Siddhartha, while I go by *'Yathartha'* (reality). He wants to prove (*'siddha'*) his meaning (*'artha'*) while I want to point to the reality (*'yathartha'*) of the country. And reality requires that you approach the people for their opinion.

I agree that times change and we too should change with them. Shri Siddhartha Shankar Ray also changed. I remember the day Shri Ray stood in opposition to Shri Moin-ul Huq in the *Assam Tribune* case. I would not like to repeat what he said that time. Now his position has changed. Now Shri Ray and Shri Choudhary are sitting on the same bench. So no one is against a change, but we have to see if that change is good for the people or not. There is *'Preya'* (pleasing) and there is *'Shreya'* (beneficial). Anything may be done for cheap popularity, but even in the midst of temporary, momentary passions we must have the courage to protect enduring values. It seems we are worshipping *'Preya'* and giving up *'Shreya.'* Otherwise no one should object to a referendum on abridging fundamental rights. The Law Minister says this is not practicable. When so many crores of people vote for the ruling party they are good, but when it comes to accepting my proposal for a referendum they becomes *'Sankhyasur'*—the devil of numbers.

We have so many *asuras* in the country and among them is also a *'Sankhyasur.'* If there are crores of people their opinion can be taken. If the Election Commission can make a mid-term poll possible within a month and a half for the convenience of the Prime Minister, for the convenience of the ruling party, why cannot a referendum on a basic subject be held within a month ? It should be. It would be a way to arouse the people, a way to involve them in politics, and also a way to arrive at decisions on important issues by enlightening them. So I say if you do not agree to a referendum you are afraid of approaching the people, there is fear in your heart. There are doubts. If you do not have doubts there is still time. The proposal for a referendum could be accepted. Then we would be fully with this Bill. Thank you.

Compensation for Acquired Property

Sir, I would have reacted to this Constitution Amendment Bill differently if its purpose had been only to remove the legal difficulties created by the Supreme Court judgement in the matter of bank nationalisation. By passing article 31(1)(2) of the Constitution in 1955 we have provided that if any property is compulsorily taken over or acquired such acquisition cannot be challenged on the ground that the legal compensation for it is not adequate.

In the matter of bank nationalisation the Supreme Court tried to go behind this decision. The need was to take a corrective step. We cannot accept a system in which the Government could be forced to pay hundred per cent compensation for taking over expensive property. Then the very purpose of taking over the property would be defeated. But we will have to differentiate between property and property. We cannot weigh a *'karorimal'* (millionaire) and a *'kaurimal'* (pauper) on the same scale. There are crores of people in this country whose property is just a hut or a couple of bighas of land or a small shop. Should they not get full compensation if it is necessary to take over their property for public purposes ?

If an ex-serviceman invests five thousand rupees, which he has earned in his lifetime by the sweat of his brow, in some company by way of its shares, if that is all his wealth, if he depends upon it in the evening of his life would it be in accordance with justice for the State to give him only nominal cash—not compensation, cash—on the Governmentalisation of that company ? If a widow deposits all her life's savings in a bank and secures her livelihood, and if it is her only means of livelihood, will the Government not act generously while taking it over ? Will she not be given full compensation ? I demand that this Bill should make it clear that if the Government takes over property below the maximum ceiling for public purposes, whether it is in the rural areas or in the city, its compensation would be paid at market rates.

There are maximum land holding laws in all States. It is a different matter that they are not implemented. I shall come to that later. If land below the maximum ceiling is taken over full compensation should be paid for it. These days an animated debate is going on over fixing a ceiling for urban property. One by one the State Governments are shifting this responsibility to the Centre. I do not know if they are doing so to avoid the responsibility or if they want uniformity in the relevant laws. I submit the Government should make it clear in this Bill that if any urban property below the maximum

Lok Sabha on December 1, 1971 during discussion on the Constitution (Twenty-fifth Amendment) Bill

ceiling is taken over—whether it is land or house, shop or a small factory—its full value will be given to the owner.

The Law Minister should not try to cancel out my proposal by saying that the maximum limit for urban property is not yet fixed. He should also not say that such a provision would be made when a law is made. It is not a question of details, it is a question of principles. The ruling party is committed to fixing a limit to urban property. By and large a limit of five lakhs has been mentioned. My party is in favour of bringing down this limit to three lakhs ....(*Interruptions*)

SHRI SHASHI BHUSHAN (South Delhi) : It has been increased by one lakh. It has been increased by one lakh since return from Ghaziabad to Delhi.

SHRI VAJPAYEE : If you do not read newspapers well that is not my fault. What I said in Ghaziabad means construction investment of two lakh and a separate price for the land—the two together do not exceed three lakh. But if you are not prepared to accept our proposal you may at least incorporate your own proposal about a limit of five lakhs in this Bill and say that full compensation would be paid for acquired property worth five lakhs or more.

SHRI PILOO MODY : You made it three lakhs, so now they will have to make it two lakhs. Then it will be your turn and you can make it one lakh.

SHRI VAJPAYEE : The result would be that Shri Mody will have no property left.

The most objectionable part of this Bill is the provision for ending all fundamental rights of the citizens in the name of implementing Directive Principles of State Policy. If there was only the question of correcting the situation created by the Supreme Court's judgement apropos bank nationalization there was no need to introduce clause 31 C.

The framers of the Constitution meant that fundamental rights are above Directive Principles. Fundamental Rights had the Supreme Court's protection. For their protection the citizen could go to court against the State. Shri K.T. Shah had tabled an amendment which sought to make the Directive Principles of State Policy justiciable so that their implementation could be demanded in a court of law. This amendment had not been accepted. According to Articles 37 provisions of Directive Principles of State Policy could not be enforced by any court. I remember that when under clause 48 some States passed laws prohibiting the slaughter of cows and calves and other milch and draught cattle they were struck down on the ground that although they were in accordance with the Directive Principles they deprived butchers of their right to make a living.

SHRI FRANK ANTHONY (Nominated—Anglo-Indian) : We got it done.

SHRI VAJPAYEE : But now it is difficult to get it done.

I have that verdict of the Supreme Court. On behalf of the other party Shri Frank Anthony ....

SHRI K. NARAYANA RAO : I am not sure whether Mr. Vajpayee is correct on that point.

SHRI PILOO MODY : If you are not sure, why don't you sit down ?

SHRI VAJPAYEE : After 20 years the clock has gone full circle. Directive Principles are dominating Fundamental Rights. I do not mind that, but I fail to understand why Fundamental Rights unconnected with property are being attacked for implementing article 39 (B) and (C), which deal with the ownership and control of property and prevention of detrimental concentration of property and means of production. Freedom of speech and expression, the right to peaceful and unarmed assembly, the freedom to form associations, and the fundamental right to unrestrained movement in India and to settle in any part of India are also being struck a blow.

The arguments that the Law Minister put forward yesterday for not accepting the Law Commission's recommendations do not hold water at all. They cannot satisfy anybody. Shri Gajendragadkar is the Chairman of the Law Commission. No one can accuse him of being reactionary. He too wants economic and social change in the society. He also wants the pace of change to be stepped up. The Law Commission also includes a member—I do not know how far this is true—who is considered to be a communist in ideology.

SHRI S.M. BANERJI : Good.

Law Commission's Recommendations

SHRI VAJPAYEE : And yet the Law Commission has made a very intelligent recommendation. It said that if you want to apply two directive principles of the Constitution—articles 39(B) and (C) it would be enough to include article 19 (1) (f) and (g), the rest of the fundamental rights need not be touched. What is the reply to that ? Shri Mohan Kumaramangalam would say there was the *Indian Express* case. He would refer to the daily *'Sakal.'* The *'Searchlight'* case would also be dragged in. The price-page schedule may be mentioned. Is it not possible that if the matter again went to the Supreme Court it might change its opinion ? The Supreme Court has been changing its opinion. In the present atmosphere in the country and in view of the Parliament's desire for change it may be hoped that the Supreme Court would give a decision that would establish a balance between the freedom of the press and the rights of small newspapers. But the Law Commission says if even after this there is any difficulty in your way you may bring forward another amendment. I wish the Law Minister takes pains to understand this properly.

I quote from the Law Commission's report :

> "In our opinion the purpose which article 31C has in mind would be effectively achieved if, instead of referring to article 19(1) as a whole, reference is made to article 19(f) and (g). It is these two clauses that are likely to be contravened by legislation contemplated by article 31C, and if a provision is made that no law passed with a view to implementing the policy enunciated in article 39 (B) and (C) contravenes, *inter alia,* article 19(1)(f) and (g), that would serve the purpose in view."

It also adds :

> "Freedom of speech and expression of opinion means not only freedom of speech and expression which is in conformity with the philosophy of the establishment, but more particularly freedom of speech and freedom

of the establishment, but more particularly freedom of speech and freedom of opinion which dissents from the philosophy of the establishment. This position no democrat can dispute."

In a democracy—if it is not a people's democracy as in Communist countries—Governments may change, the majority may change. In Britain yesterday's Prime Minister, Shri Harold Wilson, is today's Leader of the Opposition. Those who are in the Opposition today may be in power tomorrow. I am talking of a principle. But these people want to remain there till doomsday. That is the purpose of this Bill.

The question is not of accelerating the flow of economic and social change. It is deeper. What, after all, is the reason for attacking all Fundamental Rights ? The Law Minister could not convince the House of its propriety, nor could Shri Mohan Kumaramangalam create the confidence—despite all his arguments—that the Government really wants to acquire only as much right as is necessary in the present situation.

The proposed press Bill reveals the Government's intention. It gives a glimpse of the Government's mind. No one is satisfied with the press industry's present position. But transferring all powers to some Joint Secretary of Company Law Administration in the name of public trustee is to Governmentalise the press by the back door. How the draft Bill got into the press is also a mystery. The Bill is not yet before the Parliament. We know nothing about it. But it is published in the papers and is being debated. Now it is said it is not the Bill, just a working paper. But it shows in what direction the mind of the powers that be is working.

Foundation of Democracy

Not only the courage to suffer opposition but the generosity to respect it is the foundation of democracy. Where there is intolerance, bigotry and the willingness to dub Opposition as treachery, democracy ends and dictatorship begins.

Sir, the Law Minister claims that the road to the economic and social reconstruction of the country would be opened with this Bill. A new era would begin. Was this way closed so long ? Who closed it ? Whose gift is this Constitution ? Who had the responsibility of working this Constitution during the past 23-24 years of independence ? It is also wrong to say that in every matter the court proves as a hindrance. In respect of land reform the Parliament, passed a Constitution amendment that prevented land reform laws from being challenged in court. Can any member of the ruling party say land reform laws were honestly implemented ? Why not ? Why was there no extra land for distribution among the landless ? Why was it not distributed ? Now they say the land ceiling would be lowered. I do not know if even after that land would be left for distribution among the landless.

It is not only a question of changing the Constitution. It is also a question of changing man. We have to bring about a change in the human being. What have we done to make him more in industrious, more dutiful and more selfless ? Shri Gokhale has announced that the Government would intervene more and more in commerce and industry. The Government means the bureaucracy, which is useless, corrupt, heartless, apathetic to public welfare and self-centred.

What is the position of public enterprises today ? What does yesterday's report in *Hindustan Times* say loud and clear ? How much irregularity was there in the recent purchase of wheat from the farmers ? In issuing licences there is no limit to partiality. Where is public good ? Who cares for it ? All steps are taken for strengthening the ruling party's position and for collecting election funds.

A recent instance comes to my mind. Shri Gujral is present here. There is a ban on building ten-storey buildings in New Delhi. There are ten applications lying in the Secretariat. Permission can be granted for a donation of two and a half lakh rupees.

SHRI I.K. GUJRAL, Minister of State in the Ministry of Works & Housing : I want to make a categorical statement that no application is pending. I must say that the opposition to bringing discipline in New Delhi's growth has come from his party, because they are mixed up with multi-millionaires.

SHRI VAJPAYEE : Sir, the Jan Sangh does not have a majority in New Delhi. The New Delhi Municipality is a nominated body, and I am ready to prove that ten applications for permission to build multi-storeyed buildings are pending ....

SHRI I.K. GUJRAL : I challenge him. If he can prove it I shall resign, otherwise he will have to resign.

SHRI VAJPAYEE : I accept the challenge.

SHRI PILOO MODY : Sir, this is a most unfair challenge. Here he will have to fight a Lok Sabha seat and there he will only have to get nominated to the Rajya Sabha.

SHRI VAJPAYEE : Sir, I am surprised ....

SHRI R.S. PANDEYA (Rajnandgaon) : Sir, what is your ruling on this ? A big thing has been said. He said he would resign ....

SHRI VAJPAYEE : Sir, what I say is I am prepared to prove.

SHRI I.K. GUJRAL : Do it, do it.

SHRI VAJPAYEE : I say you should find out from your department.

SHRI I.K. GUJRAL : Sir, you have alleged that in order to collect funds for the party ....

SHRI VAJPAYEE : No, you have refuted that applications are pending ....

SHRI I.K. GUJRAL : Yes, I refute that too. I stick to whatever I have said. If Shri Vajpayee cannot prove it, he will have to pay for it.

SHRI R.S. PANDEYA : Sir, I suggest that a committee should be appointed to go into it and place all the facts before you so that you may come to a decision as to who should resign.

SHRI VAJPAYEE : Sir, I am surprised to see that the Government party has secured a two-thirds majority in the election, some members of the Telangana Praja Samiti have also defected and joined the ruling party, and yet the Government party is at the mercy of some Opposition parties for this Bill. When they threatened the Government changed its attitude. Have you ever seen in this House that when an amending Bill is on the floor of the House, the Law Minister has given notice of amendments in that Bill and then those amendments are themselves amended, as is being done now ? Had the Law Minister given notice of the amendments without thinking ? Did it not have the Government's support ?

AN HON. MEMBER : We have an open mind.

SHRI VAJPAYEE : You have a vacant mind. This is not proof of an open mind. Yesterday Shri Gokhale referred to Mahatma Gandhi and Shri Mohan Kumaramangalam swears by Marx. Are the ways of Mahatma Gandhi and Marx the same ? Is there no dividing line between the Yogi and the Commissar ? Does India want to eliminate economic disparity by sacrificing individual freedom ? Do we want to make a monster out of the State ? Do we want to concentrate all power in the hands of the State in order to prevent the concentration of wealth and of economic means in the hands of the individual ?

The ruling party has expressed its belief in a socialistic pattern of society. What is this socialistic pattern ? I quote from the Second Five Year Plan :

> "The socialist pattern of society is apt to be regarded as some fixed or rigid pattern. It is not rooted in any doctrine or dogma. Each country has to develop according to its own genius and tradition."

What is India's genius ? What is India's tradition ? We will have to achieve a confluence of individual freedom and economic equality. We will have to accord the rights of the individual with public good. This Bill does not achieve that accord. It acquires more powers than necessary, and there is full possibility of their misuse. I call upon the Hon. Minister to accept our amendment. Declare that people with small property are out of this Bill. It is not necessary to attack all Fundamental Rights. Fundamental Rights from (a) to (e) in article 19 (1) should be left untouched. Further thought may be given to it if necessary and if required for public good. It is not necessary to cover them in the Bill. Thank you.

Postal Bill : Infringement of Fundamental Rights

Sir, the very first thing I would like to say is that now that this Bill is about to be passed the Communication Minister Shri Arjun Singh should have been present in the House. Where is he ? What is he doing ? Today he is not there even in the Lok Sabha, so he must certainly have been present in the Parlok Sabha. Sir, perhaps he has not come because this is a very unpleasant job, so he has entrusted it to Shri Santosh Mohan Dev. Sir, I move an amendment that the authority to intercept anyone's mail should be obtained from a judicial magistrate instead of a Government officer. What objection does the Government have to bringing in a judicial magistrate in this? Even the Government officer is a junior one—a sub-divisional inspector—authorized by the Central Government by general or special order. I have moved that 'Central Government' should be replaced by 'magistrate.' Sir, you will agree that it is a very serious matter to acquire the power to stop, seize or destroy anyone's correspondence. When we write a letter and put a stamp on it we mail it with the confidence that it will reach the addressee. Now if you want to intercept it on the way you should at least take care to see that this is not left to the whims of officials. I repeat I have no complaint about postal employees. Intelligence officers of the Home Ministry sit in the post offices. They take away our correspondence in the morning and we get it half an hour or an hour late. Our letters are being screened. Are we anti-national ? I repeat, are we anti-national ? Do we pose a danger to the country's unity ?

SMT. PRITIBHA SINGH : You did the same thing during the Janata Party's regime.... (*Interruptions*)

SHRI VAJPAYEE : That is not true.

SMT. PRITIBHA SINGH : It is true, quite true. As you have examples we too have examples.

SHRI VAJPAYEE : Then you admit you do it .... (*Interruptions*)....

SMT. PRITIBHA SINGH : Whether we are doing it or not, you were doing it.... (*Interruptions*)....

Interception Must Stop

SHRI VAJPAYEE : Sir, we did not do it. If we did, it was wrong. We did it, so we are sitting here. And if you do it you will also have to come here.... (*Interruptions*).... What I say is, this should stop. This is not a party matter. We complained to Shri Mirdha about telephone tapping. We took all documents with us. We told him telephones of members of the ruling party

Rajya Sabha on December 10, 1986 during discussion on the Indian Post Office (Amendment) Bill

are being tapped, the telephone of the Chief Justice is being tapped, the telephone of the President of India is being tapped. I would like to tell the lady that this is not the question of a party.

SHRI SANTOSH MOHAN DEV : I have to censor the letters, Sir.

MR. CHAIRMAN (Shri H. Hanumanthappa) : You have already made the commitment that you will not censor Atal Bihariji's mail.

Safeguard Needed

SHRI VAJPAYEE : Sir, a safeguard is needed. You may approach a judicial magistrate for the authority to intercept mail. This should not be left to a postal officer. It would be misused. There is apprehension about that. The Minister should consider my suggestion.

SHRI SANTOSH MOHAN DEV : Sir, the suggestion given by Atal Bihari Vajpayeeji is not acceptable to me because whatever we have done, we have done after taking the views of the Law Commission and the Law Ministry also. The suggestion that he has given could have been a better one but, unfortunately, it is very time–consuming. Now it is not acceptable and I regret it very much. (*Interruptions*)....

THE VICE-CHAIRMAN (Shri H. Hanumanthappa) : Now I shall put the amendment moved by Mr. Atal Bihari Vajpayee to vote. The question is :

"That at page 3, line 4-5, for the words 'the Central Government' the words 'the Chief Judicial Magistrate' be substituted."

The motion was negatived.

THE VICE-CHAIRMAN (Shri H. Hanumanthappa) : There are two amendments by Mr. Atal Bihari Vajpayee.

SHRI VAJPAYEE : Sir, I move :

"That at page 6, —

(a) line 8, the words of 'public safety or tranquillity' be deleted.

(b) lines 9-12 the words 'friendly relations with foreign States or public order or for preventing incitement to the commission of any offence or on the occurrence of any public emergency' be deleted."

"That at page 6, *after* line 15 the following provisos be inserted namely :

'Provided that the person or the association of persons whose postal articles are to be intercepted or detained shall be so informed in writing along with the reasons for doing so.

Provided further that a panel of retired High Court Judges presided over by a sitting judge of a High Court will have to be satisfied beforehand that any act done with regard to specific individuals or institutions or associations of any kind is in the interest of the sovereignty, integrity and security of India."

Sir, the Hon. Minister has repeatedly reiterated that he has taken out the proviso of this clause, for which he deserves to be thanked. That proviso was against Fundamental Rights, and it could not have stood a challenge in court. He has also referred to the report of the Law Commission. It is true that now orders will be given in writing, and later they can be challenged in Court. My point is, you will acquire the powers to intercept mail and will do it. You will intercept the mail not only of individuals but also of organisations. You are also acquiring the powers to destroy that mail. But you are giving the concession that the individual may later approach the Court. The purpose of my amendment is that you should approach a High Court Judge before taking action. A panel could be set up for this and it could be told—we have reasons to believe that the correspondence we are going to intercept is being used against the security, integrity and unity of the country. Normally there should be no law like this. It is a different matter if there is an emergency and Fundamental Rights are suspended.

Sir, the second point I want to make is this—will those who really want to work against the interests of the country use your postal services for correspondence ? I would like to know how many matters like this there are in which the Government has acquired the powers to intercept the mail. What is being done today is being done without authority. Now if you do it you will have to give in writing. Will this not be a warning for them ? Will those involved in anti-national activities not change their *modus operandi* ? They will not be trapped. This will be used against political opponents. So I call upon the Minister to consider my amendment. I would not have objected to the Law Commission's report, but I fail to understand all these things :

> "... If satisfied that it is necessary or expedient so to do in the interests of public safety or tranquillity, the sovereignty and integrity of India, the security of the State, friendly relations with foreign States or public order or for preventing incitement to the commission of any offence...."

Empower Judges

Can steps not be taken in this matter under the other law ? It is not enough to write down "in the interest of sovereignty, integrity and security." But I am not stressing that point. My amendment is that the government put a provision as follows :

> "Provided that the person or the association of persons whose postal articles are to be intercepted or detained shall be so informed in writing along with the reasons for doing so.
>
> "Provided further that a panel of retired High Court Judges presided over by a sitting Judge of a High Court will have to be satisfied before hand that any act to be done with regard to specific individuals or institutions or associations of any kind is in the interest of sovereignty, integrity and security of India."

I want to bring in High Court Judges in this panel. Now you cannot say Judges do not care for the sovereignty, integrity and security of the country. I cannot accept the argument that there would be delay in acquiring powers. You want to take a serious step against fundamental rights. You should have no objection to securing permission from a panel of Judges. But if you do not accept this your intentions would be suspect. The Hon. Minister may complain that we are beginning on a note of suspicion. As my friend Shri Advani said this whole Bill rests on suspicion, on doubt. You have doubts about the people of India, and about us.

Government Cannot Veto Constitutional Amendment

The Constitution (Forty-fourth Amendment) Act of 1979 received the assent of the President on September 30, 1979. All the provisions of the Act except clause 3 dealing with preventive detention were brought into force by Government notifications.

Clause 3 of the Act amended clauses 4 and 7 of article 22 of the Constitution. This amendment ensures that the case of the detenues will be considered fairly and objectively as the Advisory Board is required to be constituted on the recommendation of the Chief Justice of the High Court. It is to consist of a sitting judge of the High Court as the Chairman and two sitting or retired Judges of the High Court as members instead of the Advisory Board consisting of persons qualified to be High Court Judges as was provided earlier. Secondly, the period within which reference to Advisory Board had to be made was reduced from 3 months to two months.

The Constitution Bench of the Supreme Court in its judgement on December 28, 1981 had passed strictures on the Government for its failure to comply with the constituent will of the Parliament. In fact, the Government is guilty of contempt of Parliament.

It is amazing that a Constitution Amendment Act passed by Parliament and given assent to by the President in 1979 has not yet been fully implemented. Even the above-mentioned judgement of the Supreme Court has failed to move the Government in this important matter concerning personal liberty.

I urge the Government to bring into force clause 3 of the Act without any further delay by issuing the necessary notification. The Government cannot be allowed to exercise vote on an Constitution Amendment Act that has been passed by Parliament and to which the President has given his assent. Thank you.

Rajya Sabha on March 3, 1988 during discussion on the Calling Attention Motion regarding non-implementation of the Constitution (Forty-fourth Amendment) Act, 1979

X ELECTIONS

Let Kashmiri's Elect Their MPs

Madam, I stand to welcome this Bill. It is a matter of happiness that those Union Territories for which members of the Lok Sabha were so long nominated will now have representatives elected by the people. They should certainly have this right. But while according the right of direct election to the Lok Sabha to these territories we must not forget that there are some large areas from where Lok Sabha members are not directly elected. I am talking of Jammu and Kashmir. The electorate there should get the opportunity to elect their representatives in the Lok Sabha at an early date. The Government has assured us that the Government of Jammu and Kashmir will be making its recommendation in this regard. But so far no recommendation has been received. I feel that although there is a special situation in Jammu and Kashmir the democratic process should not halt and the people there should be given the right to elect their representative directly.

I agree with Shri Loknath Mishra that there is no propriety in keeping Dadra and Nagar Haveli separate. In fact Goa, Daman and Diu should also be merged with adjoining territories. I cannot understand why Dadra and Nagar Haveli should remain separate. It is true that Dadra and Nagar Haveli were the first territories that we freed from the grip of Portuguese colonialism, but a long time has elapsed, and a bad effect of keeping separate is that separateness generates some selfish interests which hinder merger of that area with any other area. The Hon. Minister says there is a population of 57,000 and it has a Panchayat. Can this Parliament not do justice by it ? I do not object to the fact that we are giving them the right to elect a representative, but if it is separate it should have a representative in the Lok Sabha, even if the electorate is small.

All our States do not have the same number of voters for a Lok Sabha constituency. There are more voters per constituency in big States, where the population is denser than in small States or in States with a lesser population. From this point of view there should be no objection to allotting one seat to Dadra and Nagar Haveli. But what is the reason for keeping Dadra and Nagar Haveli separate ? We have just passed a Bill for Goa, Daman and Diu. In every session of Parliament bills keep coming in instalments. Today we are considering the services there, tomorrow it may be about adjoining States,

---

Lok Sabha on December 11, 1965 during discussion on the Representation of the People (Amendment) Bill, 1965

and then there would be the problem of the integration of services there. I hope the Hon. Minister will clarify why Dadra and Nagar Haveli is being kept separate.

Andaman and Nicobar Islands

So far as Andaman and Nicobar is concerned I do not agree with my friend. It cannot be joined to any State. It is surrounded by sea. It has a special position. Had our friend visited it he would perhaps not have asked such a question.

SHRI J.L. HATHI : He has been there, and that is why he asks.

SHRI VAJPAYEE : He says he has not been there.

SHRI J.L. HATHI : Then it is all right.

SHRI VAJPAYEE : If he has not been there I can understand it. I can understand the fact that he does not have enough information. But it would be very good for the people of Andaman and Nicobar to directly elect their representative to the Lok Sabha, and they should certainly have the opportunity to do so. We have to bring the people up to our level, and education in democracy is not possible without democratic rights. If some of us feel we cannot give them the right to vote till they are fit to use it I say democracy itself is an educative process and the people would be fit to use a right only when they are given that right. From this point of view the proposed arrangement is good.

But in the present conditions efforts need to be made to strengthen our relationship with Andaman and Nicobar. At present we have only a weekly flight there, and even that is via Rangoon, not direct. Andaman and Nicobar is our territory and has great strategic importance. In view of the situation that is developing in South-East Asia its importance has grown all the more. But administratively we have not been able to bring it as close as we should. It is true that Andaman and Nicobar and the rest of India are separated by the sea, and the means of communication in the archipelago are difficult, but we should develop more such means.

It is also necessary that all parties should be given some special facilities to work there. I have no doubt that the election there would be free and fair, as they would be held under the auspices of our Election Commission. But other parties will have to be given some facilities so that they can work and do their propaganda there. It would be difficult for me to say right now what concrete form those facilities should have, but the Government will have to think about it.

With these words I support the Bill. Thank you.

Vagaries of Electoral System

MR. DEPUTY SPEAKER : Now we take up the further discussion of the resolution moved by Shri Atal Bihari Vajpayee.

SHRI VAJPAYEE : Sir, free and fair elections are the basis of democracy, but it is a matter of regret that elections in India are getting more and more corrupt. Firstly, the influence of money in elections is increasing. Secondly, the administrative machinery is being openly misused for election purposes. The law has put a ceiling on a candidate's election expenses, a limitation, which is Rs. 35,000 for the Lok Sabha and, with some variation, Rs. 12,000 for the Legislative Assembly. But everyone knows this limit is observed more in the breach. Political parties can spend as much as they want on elections. Apart from my party there would hardly be a political party that may be approaching the people at large for fund collection. But elections cannot be fought on that alone. Now moneybags have to be tapped for the election of most candidates of all parties. By law companies cannot donate to political parties, but political parties can collect funds. Obviously this is No. 2 money. There is no accounting of this money.

According to Dr. Sethi's calculations about Rs. 100 crores are spent on elections to the Lok Sabha, Legislative Assemblies, the Presidential election etc. in India. He says this is bigger than the election expenditure in the U.S. You can easily imagine how much black money those elements that give Rs. 100 crores to political parties for fighting elections may be making in return.

Incidents of misuse of the administrative machinery are not only on the increase, this misuse is acquiring new forms. After the last elections there were many election petitions in which Tribunals and High Courts had to rule that Returning Officers tampered with ballot papers to oblige candidates, and wrongly rejected nomination papers. When Shri Sen-Verma was Chief Election Commissioner he had said at Ooty that if the Returning Officer did not do his duty impartially elections could not be kept free, but surprisingly enough under the law action can be taken against Government employees only in their personal capacity. If a candidate uses a Government employee's influence or authority for his own ends his election may be declared void. Possibly the employee may also be punished. But when the ruling party makes an organised attempt to tamper with or corrupt the voters by misuse of the administrative machinery there is no provision against it under the law. From this point of view the law is very much restricted. I quote the conditions :

Lok Sabha on March 1, 1974 during discussion on the resolution on free and fair elections

"... obtaining, procurement or abetting or attempting to obtain or procure any assistance for the furtherance of a candidate's election from any Government servant."

Unequal Battle

But when the entire Government machinery becomes active for helping the ruling party an election does not remain an equal battle. Opposition parties are forced to face heavy odds in such a battle. This House has often opined during discussions that during elections Ministers should not have the right to use Air Force planes, helicopters and other vehicles. The Joint Select Committee set up for amendment in election law also went into this, but the majority report was that misuse of Government resources should be stopped by consensus among political parties, and a convention developed so that such resources are not misused. The ruling party is not ready to check this corruption by law.

No one can object to the Prime Minister's tours during election days. But she does not tour as Prime Minister, she tours as the leader of her party, so there is no reason why Air Force planes should be made available to her, helicopters should fly with her in formations, the PWD should arrange the dais, and seating arrangements should be the responsibility of the police. Other parties are put to big loss as these facilities are not made available to them. Even Chief Ministers and other Ministers are seen using helicopters and planes. The Chief Minister of Uttar Pradesh uses a helicopter to go to Unnao, which is 13 miles from Kanpur. Not many people may come there to listen to him, but they certainly throng for a look at the helicopter. This sort of misuse of resources creates anger in the people and a sense of helplessness in the Opposition. It feels that the election battle is not an equal battle, and once a party gets into power it will do anything to keep it. So far as a convention is concerned, what has the Government done to develop it ? Was a meeting of representatives of political parties called ? Was an attempt made to find an agreed solution ? Misuse of the administrative machinery is distorting the whole election.

Influence of Money Power

So far as the question of increasing influence of money on elections is concerned there can be no two opinions that it should not be so. The Wanchoo Committee had also discussed this question, and I quote the conclusion it reached :

"We are of the opinion that in our country also the Government should finance political parties. We recommend that reasonable grants-in-aid should be given by the Government to national political parties and suitable criteria should be evolved for recognising such parties and determining the extent of grant-in-aid to each of them. For according recognition to a political party for this purpose, it should be registered under the Societies Registration Act, 1860 and its yearly accounts are audited and published within a prescribed time. Irrespective of the decision of Government on the question of financing political parties, we recommend that the parties be required to get their accounts audited and published annually."

The Joint Select Committee had considered the suggestion that the Government should bear the maximum election expenditure and had recommended that an experts' committee be set up for this. Why was it not set up ? Are important recommendations of a Joint Select Committee meant for decorating Government shelves ? Why does the Government not take them seriously ? The time has come to decide who will bear election expenses ? Will it be the candidate or the political party or the Government ? Students of political science will remember those days when a candidate in England had to pay from his pocket to make ballot boxes and set up polling booths. But those days are over. Now the feeling is gathering in all democratic countries that the Government should bear election expenses. I do not know the position of other parties. For us it is difficult to field an honest, poor man. Whether he will win or not is another matter. But first we have to ask him how much he can spend. (*Interruptions*) I have already discussed parties. If this burden is placed on parties they will approach moneybags, and politics would become the handmaid of the wealthy. Then it cannot be an instrument of the good of the people. Then you cannot discuss socialism.

Yesterday the Prime Minister expressed her thoughts in this connection in the Rajya Sabha. She said if the Government bears the expenses it would mean a lot of money. Ours is a big country. This is a good thing. It is a matter of pride that we are the world's biggest democracy. Then shall we allow democracy to be struck at the roots because there will be a little more expenditure ?

Not a Big Expense

We have made some calculations. Taking into consideration the expenditure limit of Rs. 35,000 for the Lok Sabha and Rs. 12,000 for Legislative Assembly if the candidates who could save their deposits in the Fourth General Election were reimbursed their expenses the Government would have had to spend Rs. 5 crores for the Lok Sabha and Rs. 10 crores for Legislative Assemblies. The Lok Sabha has 515 seats. There were 2,364 candidates in the Fourth General Elections. Out of them 1204 lost their deposits. 1160 candidates remained. If you calculate according to Rs. 35,000 it does not become a big sum. The Legislative Assemblies have 3,453 seats. They were contested by 15,472 candidates. But only 800 could save their deposits. If we pay them legally fixed expenses under no circumstances does the expenditure exceed Rs. 10 crores.

Even now our election expenditure comes to about Rs. 22 crores. The expenditure on preparing electoral rolls is Rs. 3.45 crores, on Parliamentary elections Rs. 7.41 crores and on Assembly elections Rs. 10 crores. These are Election Commission figures and I think spending Rs. 15 crores more for the sake of democracy is not a bad bargain. As it is, democracy is an expensive process. Where there are no parties and one man rules there is no question of election expenses. Election expenses are also small where only one party contests the election and other parties cannot. But we have deliberately adopted Parliamentary democracy. We give the electorate the right to choose their representatives after a fixed interval of time. But money must not vitiate this right, money must not distort the election process.

The Wanchoo Committee report has referred to many Western countries such as West Germany. I quote :

> "In this connection, it my be pertinent to refer to the manner in which this problem has been tackled in countries like West Germany and Japan. In West Germany, political parties are financed by the Government on the basis of the votes polled by them at the preceding election. In Japan, Government finances the election expenses of the national parties on the basis of the size of the constituency and also gives financial assistance for research and party publicity."

If other countries can adopt this system there is no reason why we cannot.

Defective Anglo-American System

Election law also needs another basic amendment. That too was considered by the Joint Select Committee. The current system in our country is the majority system, the first-past-the-post system. The horse that falls behind even by a hair's breadth is not taken into account. This is the Anglo-American system. Many countries of the world have rejected this system, because it is very strange. Sometimes a candidate bagging 30-40 per cent votes is declared elected. In the last election a certain candidate was declared elected even when he lost his deposit because other candidates polled still less votes. How can such a candidate claim to represent the majority in a constituency ? This system is a gamble. A slight change in the voters' views can substantially distort the election results. I would like to give an example.

In the Lok Sabha elections the ruling party got 44.99 per cent votes in 1952, 47.78 per cent in 1957, 44.73 per cent in 1962, 40.82 per cent in 1967 and 44 per cent in 1971, but it got 70 per cent more seats.

It is not a question of the Congress Party alone. Let not our Congress friends be under the impression that this system will always work to their advantage. It can go against them too. I can give an example of that also. In 1962 the Congress got 45.26 per cent votes in Tamil Nadu. In return it got 30 out of 41 seats. In 1967 it got 4 per cent less votes, but the number of its seats came down from 30 to 3. A mere 4 per cent decrease in the votes made such a big difference in seats.

Delhi is another example which affects both the ruling party and us. In Delhi the ruling party got 50 per cent votes in 1962 and walked away with all seats. In 1967 there was a slight decrease in the vote—it got 38 per cent vote, but it got only one seat, while we got six.

In West Bengal the Congress got 41.1 per cent votes and the United Front got 41.36 per cent. But in spite of this approximate parity the Congress got less seats. In 1969 there was a slight increase in the Congress vote—it got

41.31 votes. The United Front vote also increased to 41.98 per cent, but the Congress seats decreased from 127 to 55.

When I was analysing the election results of Britain I found at one place that the Conservative Party lost its majority in the House of Commons by only 4 per cent votes and its position became serious. Is this election system good ? Does it properly represent the people's mind ? Should it not be changed ? The Joint Select Committee has recommended that this majority system should be replaced by the List System and has suggested that this should be considered.

SHRI SATISH CHANDRA (Bareilly) : This is not our recommendation.

SHRI VAJPAYEE : I know you opposed it and then it was decided that an experts' committee would go into it. The Joint Select Committee has recommended that experts should consider this matter. Who will decide upon these experts ? Thank you.

Election Process Needs Cleansing

Sir, the Hon. Minister's reply has somewhat surprised me. He used selected convenient recommendations of the Joint Select Committee to cancel out certain points in this resolution, but he rejected the inconvenient ones. The Joint Select Committee had recommended the setting up of an experts' committee to consider the possibility of a List System. That committee is yet to be set up. While the Government has to set it up the Minister expresses the opinion that the List System is not suitable for the country. Does this mean that the Government has made up its mind on the recommendation about setting up such a committee for the List System, as recommended by the Joint Select Committee in which the Minister was personally present and in which the ruling party had a majority, and has thrown its recommendations in the waste paper basket ?

The other point is about Radio. The Minister said that in this matter an agreement could not be reached with political parties. Who proved a hindrance to such an agreement ? Is it not true that the ruling party used the veto to reject the Election Commissioner's proposal ? The Congress party said no formula that gave equal radio time to other parties along with the Congress was acceptable to them. This time it was the job of the Election Commission to invite political parties for consultations in this regard, but it did not take any initiative in the matter. Political parties were not consulted before the elections. The ruling party kept using the radio for itself.

Thirdly, the Wanchoo Committee's recommendation was rejected on the ground that a lot of money would have to be spent....

SHRI D.P. DHAR Planning Minister : You were going to have your own radio—what happened to it ?

SHRI VAJPAYEE : Preparations for it are going on. If you do not give equal time to all on the radio our radio will come into the field.

SHRI S.M. BANERJI : But these days the people are fed up with speeches. When a speech begins they shut off the radio.

SHRI VAJPAYEE : We shall also play Lata Mangeshkar's songs.

THE CHAIRMAN : Last time he had said we are starting B.B.C.—Bajpai Broadcasting Corporation.

SHRI VAJPAYEE : I did not say, you said.

Democracy Not a Cheap Process

Sir, will the Wanchoo Committee's recommendation about giving Government funds to political parties be rejected simply because it would

Lok Sabha on March 15, 1974 while replying to the discussion on the resolution regarding free and fair elections

mean paying out more money ? Is democracy a cheap process ? Will we hesitate to spend some money for the good health of democracy ? The figures I had given were about candidates who would be able to save their deposits, but even if we accept the Minister's figures Rs. 8 crores would be spent for the Lok Sabha and Rs. 16 crores for Legislative Assemblies. This is not a very big amount. Even now we are spending more than Rs. 22 crores for the Lok Sabha and Assembly elections. If politics is to be saved from moneybags and if elections are to be cleansed Rs. 16 crores is not a very big expense. The country should be willing to make it. I can understand it if, there is any objection apart from this. But Rs. 18 crores is not a big expense for proper elections. But even this the Minister did not accept.

I was surprised to learn that the Minister does not agree with making the Election Commission multi-member. He knows that the responsibilities of the Election Commission have increased, it has to perform quasi-judicial functions, but it has only one member. I had raised a fundamental question about his appointment. Why should not the system of his appointment be such as would leave no scope for objection ? It is possible. After all we have provided in the Lok Ayukta and Lok Pal Bill that the President would make the appointment in consultation with the Chief Justice of the Supreme Court and the Leader of the Opposition would also be consulted before the appointment. Can we not adopt this procedure in respect of the Chief Election Commissioner's appointment ? We can decide to make a retired Judge of the Supreme Court the Chief Election Commissioner, and we can also decide not to give him any other employment after retirement. I had given an example of this. The former Chief Election Commissioner was Law Secretary, then he came into the Election Commission, and after leaving it again became a member of the Law Commission. I am not taking an objection to any individual as such. I differ with the appointment procedure. A multi-member commission would be able to discharge its responsibility properly, its decisions would be more just, and it can also create greater confidence in the people's mind about itself.

Change The System

I regret my Congress friends did not discuss this resolution with the same feeling with which it was moved. I would remind them that it was moved before the elections in Uttar Pradesh and Orissa. We are concerned with changing the system. Any party can profit from it. The present system can prove advantageous to any party. But when we talk of the system it does not become at least for senior members to say—let us have an example, let us have a model. I do not claim my party is as pure as driven snow. But the present process forces every party to do objectionable things that vitiate the Ganga of democracy. In it there is no question of my providing a model or your providing it. The question is of the system—if the system is changed ways would open up for good conduct for all political parties.

Just now an Hon. senior member elected from Punjab was levelling false and mischievous allegations against the Bharatiya Jan Sangh that in Uttar

Pradesh it gave money to the Muslim League. I had challenged the Prime Minister to prove the charge—if it is proved I am ready to resign from the Lok Sabha. Can you prove this charge ? I want the House to set up a Committee to inquire into this charge. During the elections saying such things is understandable. But the elections are over and the results have come in. Let not victory go to your head. Making such charges in the House is immoral. If you have proof, produce it. Those who formed the Government in Kerala in league with the Muslim League are charging us with making an alliance with it. There is nothing wrong with forming a Government in alliance with somebody, but this is being said by way of a charge, and this charge is being levelled by those who have already committed this sin. They are making this charge not because it is true but because they want to cover up their own sins.

Impeccable Arrangements Needed

In my speech I did not make any attempt to give the colour of party politics to this resolution. The irregularities committed in elections can prove a hindrance for any party. We want that there should not be irregularities and election arrangements should be impeccable. I know counting is going on in the Saharanpur constituency. It is true that the Muslim League candidate was ahead by 400 votes, when there was a power failure, and when power returned....

SHRI D.P. DHAR : Then it must have been a lightning strike.

SHRI VAJPAYEE : The lightning struck the Muslim League. You take away electricity and you also cause it to fail. The result was that the Muslim League candidate was declared defeated.

Just now the member from Orissa was recounting what happened in the Chief Minister's constituency there. There too lightning struck. This lightning strikes Opposition parties. This is a mystery.

MR. CHAIRMAN : Perhaps the lightning knows.

SHRI VAJPAYEE : If there are complaints like this they cannot be rejected by saying they are complaining because they lost. First it was the leader of the Muslim League who said it in the House. Then Shri Mohanty said it. When two Hon. members of this Hon. House say something like this I cannot ignore it. I have to take notice of it, and the ruling party should also take notice of it. If there are irregularities like this they should be inquired into. We have to keep democracy alive, make it strong, make it full of vitality, but so long as elections are not fully free and fair democracy cannot work. I call upon the Law Minister to accept my resolution, otherwise I shall call upon the House to pass it. Thank you.

MR. CHAIRMAN : Now, I take the Resolution of Mr. Vajpayee.

Mr. Vajpayee, are you withdrawing the Resolution after the spirit in which it has been considered ?

SHRI VAJPAYEE : After the unsatisfactory reply of the Hon. Minister, there is no question of withdrawing the Resolution.

MR. CHAIRMAN : The question is :

"This House expresses concern over the growing influence of money-power and abuse of official machinery in elections and in order to ensure free and fair elections directs the Government—

(i) recognised political parties be given election grants as recommended by the Wanchoo Committee;

(ii) recommendations of the Joint Committee on Amendments to Election Law regarding equal radio time for recognised political parties, making of Election Commission a multi-member body, reducing voting age to 18 years, and examination by high-power committee of feasibility of adopting List System, be implemented;

(iii) Ministers be prohibited from using official machinery such as aircrafts, helicopters, vehicles and other facilities except on terms of parity with other recognised political parties; and

(iv) counting of votes be conducted booth-wise."

The motion was negatived.

Presidential Election Vitiated

Sir, I have requested your permission to say a few things in this regard. The point that has been raised is constitutionally and legally very important. It is to be regretted that instead of making an official statement in Parliament Government spokesmen say in the press that even if elections to the Legislative Assemblies in Gujarat and Pondicherry do not take place, the President's election will take place in August. I call upon the Law Minister to make a statement in this regard in the House.

As my friend Shri Madhu Limaye has said, this is not a question of a few vacancies. If Legislative Assemblies do not exist in some States there will not be a full electoral college that is required for electing the President. I would place before you an example of the consequence of this incompleteness. In the last Presidential election the tussle was between Shri Giri and Shri Sanjiva Reddy. Shri Giri had won with 14,650 voting units. The voting value of Gujarat MLAs is 20,000 voting units. Now if the Assembly does not exist there its members cannot take part in the President's election. This can substantially affect the election. At the same time it will not do justice to the members of the Legislative Assembly, and it will also vitiate the whole Presidential election.

I do not want the President's tenure to be increased, although there is provision for this in the Constitution, and Shri Madhu Limaye has also referred to it. But the Delimitation Commission could be asked to hurry up with the delimitation of constituencies as early as possible and hold elections in Gujarat and Pondicherry. These elections could be held before the President's election in August. There is no other way. Currently the Delimitation Commission is touring the whole country. It has recently discussed Madhya Pradesh with members of Parliament. It could be told to take up the task of delimitation in Gujarat and Pondicherry first. If it is immediately taken up it could be finished and elections held.

Entire Gujarat Left Out

But if the Government has made up its mind not to care for Legislative Assemblies it would be setting a dangerous tradition. It is true the Congress had a majority in the Gujarat Assembly. But a situation may arise where one party may be in power at the centre and other parties in the States. In such a situation if the election approaches near the party ruling at the Centre may use article 356 to dissolve those assemblies whose members, it may fear, may

Lok Sabha on April 23, 1974 regarding Presidential Election without full Electoral College

not vote for it. That would shatter our federal Constitution to pieces. Such a wrong convention should not be set.

So I support this resolution and request that under article 143 Supreme Court's opinion should be solicited for removing doubts in this regard. The matter should be sent to the Supreme Court, its opinion obtained and the Law Minister should make an official statement, so that we may discuss this matter if necessary.

MR. SPEAKER : I will send all these points raised by both of you to the Law Minister as well as the Home Minister so that they might examine them and come out with a statement.

SHRI MADHU LIMAYE : But the papers say ... They are trying to influence public opinion.

MR. SPEAKER : I do not know what is coming in the Press. The points raised here were vital points and they will be forwarded to the Hon. Ministers.

SHRI MADHU LIMAYE : The Law Minister is treating us with contempt. In many matters he does not reply—not even after a month's notice.

SHRI VAJPAYEE : The papers have said—

> "The Union Government has no intention of postponing the next Presidential election, which will be held in August as scheduled."

MR. SPEAKER : Now that you have raised the objections, these will be conveyed to them and they will be asked to come before the House with their views about this matter.

Right to Recall Elected Representatives

Sir, I stand to support this Bill. The right to recall elected representatives had been proposed at the time of framing of the Constitution, but it was not accepted. Since then, however, much water has flown under the bridge. Since then we have amended the Constitution 32 times. We live in revolutionary times. The Lok Sabha will have to be moulded in accordance with the changing times. Does democracy mean that the voter should have the right to elect his representative once in five years but he cannot see what that elected representative is doing for five years ? Sir, accountability is the foundation of democracy. Eternal vigilance is the price of liberty. Then should not the people remain alert for five years for the protection of democracy ? Should the people sleep for 4 years and 364 days and wake up for one day to exercise their vote ? Should not the people see if the representatives elected by them are working properly or not ? What should be done if they get elected for *'seva'* (service to the people) but acquire *'meva'* (wealth) ? Should the people watch in silence if they are elected for *'kam'* (work) but make *'daam'* (money) instead of work ?

SHRI M. RAM GOPAL REDDY : Vajpayeeji, we work.

SHRI VAJPAYEE : Then you will not be recalled. You can rest assured. But if Shri Tulmohan Ram, who gets elected as the people's representative, engages in an open scandal on licences, pockets thousands of rupees, brings Parliament into disrepute and besmirches his own name should the people who elected him not have the right to recall him ? The Congress Party is not willing to take action against Shri Tulmohan Ram. It is not willing even to suspend him, let alone remove him. Then will the people have no right ? Will they just watch for five years ? Democracy cannot mean this. Democracy does not mean the right to vote just once in five years. The elected representative should be responsible to the people, should be seen to be responsible to the people.

Sir, it is a matter of principles—should there be a right to recall an elected representative ? Switzerland is a small country, so its example cannot be applied. Soviet Russia is a big country, so its example cannot be applied. It is a communist country too, so its example cannot be applied. Then why don't you introduce something new in democracy ? The situation that currently prevails in our country is unique in the world. Politics has been vitiated and the people are coming out on to the streets. (*Interruptions*). We are bringing them. But why are some of our people coming out ? Because you have

Lok Sabha on November 15, 1974 during discussion on the Constitution (Amendment) Bill about voters' right to recall elected representatives by C.K. Chandrappan.

become useless. How can people express their discontent ? The Gujarat Legislative Assembly had to be dissolved. It is true that Shri Chandrappan's party had backed him then, but now it is not supporting him in Bihar. I do not want to enter this controversy, but if there is a right to recall there can be voting, so that more such occasions do not arise. If there is a right to recall it will act as a restraint on the elected representative, it will force him to be responsible to the people. At present he seems to think—who can remove me for five years ? This is not the sign of a living democracy. We should move away from traditional democracy and accept this amendment for a living, alert democracy. We should equip the people with the right to recall elected representatives, so that they can be stopped from coming on to the streets. Then controversial issues could be solved democratically in consultation with the people and corrupt members could be brought back to the right path. I am willing to go to the extent of saying that if you so wish you may make an amendment to the effect that 50 per cent vote should be required for recall. So far you can get elected on 32 per cent, on 44 per cent, but make recall a little difficult. Make it unacceptable so long as there is not 50 per cent voting.

But it must be admitted that this will promote a sense of responsibility among members of Parliament and others. The people would also experience the benefit of keeping an eye on them. So far the people think that once you elect somebody you cannot remove him, whatever he does, and the representative thinks he is free to do whatever he likes. I do not know whether the Hon. Minister or Madam is going to give the reply, but I would counsel against haste. You should do a little consultation.

DR. SAROJINI MAHISHI, Minister of State for Law: We are doing it.

SHRI VAJPAYEE : I have learnt just today that you have an open mind. The Government has not so far taken any decision in this matter. It is the demand of the Communist Party, so be careful while rejecting it. For, the memorandum given by the Communist Party in Bihar also includes the right to recall. They will be annoyed if you reject the demand and then you will be in difficulties.

Accept this in principle. Shri Chandrappan has also said that Parliament may pass a law about how this can be implemented, and at that time we can go into details. The election law needs to be amended. The Prime Minister says on the one hand that she is ready for a debate and on the other hand that the List System cannot be made applicable to India. If you have made up your mind what is left to discuss ? She has also said that proportional representation is not practicable for India. If what is current is alone practicable it means there is no scope for amending the electoral process. So I say, don't make haste, take a little time, and accept such Constitution amendments as would make the Constitution an elastic document capable of meeting the needs of the times. Thank you.

Bills De-linking Religion from Politics

Mr. Deputy Speaker, Sir, I am on a point of order, the Hon. Minister of Home Affairs has moved two motions in the House. Both the motions have the same intent. I would like to know whether the Hon. Minister of Home Affairs is going to take up the motion that was introduced on Friday or the motion which has been enlisted in the List of Business for today. If he does not want to take up the motion that was introduced on Friday, what is the position thereof ? It has been included in the List of Business. It will form a part of record. The Hon. Minister of Home Affairs has introduced this motion in a haste. Private Members' Business was in progress. Shrimati Bhattacharya was in the Chair. The Hon. Minister of Home Affairs came hurriedly, read out the motion hastily and left the House immediately.

Mr. Deputy Speaker, Sir, please go through the language of the motion, is such a mistake expected from the Hon. Minister of Home Affairs ?

> "Madam Chairman, I give notice of my intention to move the following Motion during the current session of the Lok Sabha....

Its language is not correct. Why was Shri Chavan in such a haste? I feel that the Hon. Speaker should have asked him as to why he was in such hurry.

Mr. Deputy Speaker, Sir, the Hon. Speaker might have said that he came hurriedly, created a hue and cry and left it in a mess. But I would like to know as to what will be the fate of this motion ? Will the motion introduced on Friday be hanging fire in this manner ? Is the Hon. Minister of Home Affairs withdrawing it ? If so, I would like to deal with the second motion.

SHRI S.B. CHAVAN : Sir, I would like to explain that that day the kind of motion which was moved by me, was not a regular motion. It was just an intention to move. I was not sure that it had to be in a particular form. I understand the Hon. Leader of the Opposition raising the point. I withdraw my earlier motion. That is why I am now suggesting a new motion that is in regular form. That is the position.

SHRI RANGARAJAN KUMARAMANGALAM, The Minister of State in the Ministry of Science and Technology : It was been rightly pointed out by the Leader of the Opposition. What was moved on that day was to inform the House of the intention to move. That is different from moving a resolution. And that is not done. What you are saying is correct. Nobody can disagree with your point of order that normally a written notice is given to the Speaker and it is not done in the House. Therefore, I personally think that this should not be misunderstood beyond that and now the motion that is being moved is a proper motion that proper notice has been given to the Speaker and

Lok Sabha on August 3, 1993 during discussion on the Motion to refer the Constitution (Eightieth Amendment) Bill to Joint Committee

brought to the House. There is no question of withdrawing the motion because the motion itself was not moved. *(Interruptions)*

SHRI RAM NAIK (Bombay North) : I am on another point. If this is the position and is going to be accepted, I have given amendments to that motion which was before us earlier. *(Interruptions)*

SHRI RANGARAJAN KUMARAMANGALAM : He could not have given an amendment. *(Interruptions)*

SHRI RAM NAIK : So, at least, my amendment and probably Atalji's amendment also should be regularised. Otherwise, it will be odd ....*(Interruptions)*.... What I want to say is that though the amendments are based on whatever was decided on that day, they should be regularised.

MR. CHAIRMAN : How can there be an amendment to intentions?

SHRI S.B. CHAVAN : I beg to move.

"That the Bill further to amend the Constitution of India be referred to a Joint Committee of the Houses consisting of 15 members, 10 from this House, namely : Shri Lal Krishna Advani, Shri E. Ahamed, Shri Pawan Kumar Bansal, Shri Somnath Chatterjee, Shri P. Chidambaram, Shri George Fernandes, Shri Nurul Islam, Shri K.M. Mathew, Shri Vilas Muttemwar, Kum. Vimla Verma and 5 from Rajya Sabha;

that in order to constitute a sitting of the Joint Committee the quorum shall be one-third of the total number of members of the Joint Committee;

that the Committee shall make a report to this House by the 16th August, 1993;

that in other respects the Rules of Procedure of this House relating to Parliamentary Committees shall apply with such variations and modifications as the Speaker may make; and

that this House do recommend to Rajya Sabha that Rajya Sabha do join the said Joint Committee and communicate to this House the names of 5 members to be appointed by Rajya Sabha to the Joint Committee."

MR CHAIRMAN : Motion moved :

"That the Bill further to amend the Constitution of India be referred to a Joint Committee of the Houses consisting of 15 members, 10 from this House....

SHRI RAM NAIK : Was any notice not given in this regard ?

SHRI S.B. CHAVAN : I have given notice earlier also that I have changed one of the names given earlier. The Hon. Speaker said that it was not necessary and if I wanted to furnish any information, I should do so while reading it out.

SHRI VAJPAYEE : I beg to move :

"1. That in the Motion :

(i) *for* 'consisting of 15 members, 10 from this House.'

substitute 'consisting of 30 members, 20 from this House.'

(ii) *after* '(10) Kum. Vimla Verma' insert

Shri Rasheed Masood, Shri Bhogendra Jha, Shri Sobhanadreeswara Rao Vadde, Shri Ebrahim Sulaiman Sait, Shri Guman Mal Lodha, Shri P.G.

Narayan, Shri Jangbir Singh, Shri Mohan Rawale, Smt. Dil Kumari Bhandari, Shri Abdul Ghafoor'.

(iii) *for* "and 5 from Rajya Sabha'

substitute 'and 10 from Rajya Sabha'

2. That in the motion :

for 'by the 16th August, 1993;'

substitute 'by the first day of the next session.'

for 'names of members'

substitute 'names of 10 members' "

Mr. Chairman, Sir, I object to the Motion moved by the Hon. Minister of Home Affairs. The first is about the composition of the committee. Never before in the annals of parliamentary history had a Joint Select Committee been constituted comprising 15 members only. 10 members from this House and 5 members from the other have been taken. If there is any precedence, I would like to request the Hon. Minister of Home Affairs or Shri Bhardwaj to trace it out and do us honour. After all, what was the need of making the size of the committee so small ? As a result thereof the political parties could not be represented commensurate with their strength in the House. I would like to make a reference to the book of Shri Kaul and Shakdher in this connection. Because their views are very clear. I quote :

> "The composition of a Select or a Joint Committee reflects the strength of the various parties and groups in the House(s) and in this sense, the Committee is a microcosm of the House or Houses."

Composition of the Joint Committee is Defective

What is the position of various political parties in this Committee ? First, I would like to state that many parties have been excluded from this Committee. It seems as if they do not have any existence at all. All they have to say is they do not have any existence at all and they have no say on this important Bill. Is it a correct procedure ? After all, this Bill is important, having a far-reaching effect. It seeks to amend the Constitution. The Representation of the People Act is also being amended. While going through its various clauses it appears that we are gradually proceeding towards the days of Emergency. Any organization can be declared unlawful and the nomination of any candidate can be cancelled at the time of filling nomination papers. Today morning we have elaborately discussed the arbitrary manners of an officer of the Election Commission. Through this Bill, we are giving a free hand to thousands of election officers and Returning Officers to act arbitrarily. Should the august House not be given an opportunity to hold a discussion on such an important Bill ? But the Hon. Minister will say that he had given the House such an opportunity. It was decided to refer it to a Select Committee. But has it been discussed with anybody as to what would be its composition ? Ten members are to be taken from the Lok Sabha in the Committee. Out of this 6 belongs to the Congress party. There are only 240 members of the Congress and they send 6 representatives. The Bharatiya Janata Party has 119 members. Our Party will be represented by only one member. One member is there because there cannot be less than one. They have been very kind to exclude small parties ....(*Interruptions*).... The representatives of Telugu Desam, the A.G.P., the C.P.I., the A.I.A.D.M.K. have not been included in it. The representative of the break-away group of Janata Dal (A) has also not been taken. Should not they have an opportunity to put up their viewpoint in the Committee. What have been the criteria in the composition of the Committee ? ....(*Interruptions*)

Mr. Chairman, Sir, the Constitution of the Committee is not merely a formality of you are to set up this Joint Parliamentary Committee just for name, we will be compelled to review our stance on the entire Committee. Again, it is being asked to submit its report immediately. But how early ? Mr. Chatterjee, this must be viewed seriously. How can it be done? ....(*Interruptions*).... We are ready to cooperate, but this time the House is in session. It is difficult to convene meetings during session days. Sitting of the J.P.C. are held. We have been entrusted with holding separate meetings of the Standing Committees also. Suppose, the committee wants to elicit opinion of some more persons and seeks their evidence for which it will require time not for delaying the matters but for the sake of democracy, will not be we have it for this purpose. The Hon. Minister of Home Affairs wants to overlook this committee and make it redundant. Mr. Chairman, Sir, therefore, I have brought forward amendments. Please expand the Committee. it should be constituted in such a manner that it comprises representatives of all the parties in the House. The representatives of other parties also should be included. If the representatives of the Congress Party are in proportion to its strength in this House, I have no objection. Also, the extension of the term of the Committee should also be considered and they should take the House into confidence. But if they are bent upon their arbitrariness, we will have to retaliate in our own way.

MR. CHAIRMAN : Have you moved your amendments ?

SHRI VAJPAYEE : Yes, Sir, I have moved amendment nos. 1, 2 and 4.

SHRI RAM NAIK (Bombay North) : I beg to move that in the Motion:

For "by the 16th August 1993" substitute "by the first week of the Winter Session 1993"

MR CHAIRMAN : The other motion is also identical, so both can be discussed together.

SHRI H.R. BHARDWAJ, The Minister of State in the Ministry of Law, Justice and Company Affairs : I beg to move :

> "That the Bill further to amend the Representation of the People Act, 1951 be referred to a Joint Committee of the Houses consisting of 15 members, 10 from this House, namely :
>
> Shri Lal Krishna Advani, Shri E. Ahamed, Shri Pawan Kumar Bansal, Shri Somnath Chatterjee, Shri P. Chidambaram, Shri George Fernandes, Shri Nurul Islam, Shri K.M. Mathew, Shri Vilas Muttemwar, Kumari Vimla Verma and 5 from Rajya Sabha;

that in order to constitute a sitting of the Joint Committee the quorum shall be one-third of total number of members of the Joint Committee;

that the Committee shall make a report to this House by the 16th August, 1993;

that in other respects the Rules of Procedure of this House relating to Parliamentary Committees shall apply with such variations and modifications as the Speaker may make; and

that this House do recommend to Rajya Sabha that Rajya Sabha do join the said Joint Committee and communicate to this House the names of 5 members to be appointed by Rajya Sabha to the Joint Committee"

MR CHAIRMAN : Motion moved :

SHRI VAJPAYEE : Mr. Chairman Sir, the Hon. Home Minister had a proposal to constitute a single committee in place of the existing two committees set up for two Bills. Hence I have given one amendment. We want to increase the number of members. I would like to read the amendment if you permit.

(i) *for* "consisting of 15 members, 10 from this House."

substitute "consisting of 30 members, 20 from this House."

(ii) *after* "(10) Kum. Vimla Verma" *insert*

Shri Rasheed Masood, Shri Bhogendra Jha, Shri Sobhanadreeswara Rao Vadde, Shri Ebrahim Sulaiman Sait, Shri Guman Mal Lodha, Shri P.G. Narayan, Shri Jangbir Singh, Shri Mohan Rawale, Smt. Dil Kumari Bhandari, Shri Abdul Ghafoor.

(iii) *for* "and 5 from Rajya Sabha."

"and 10 from Rajya Sabha"

2. That in the motion,—

for "by the 16th August, 1993;"

substitute "by the first day of the next session;"

4. *for* "names of 5 members"

substitute "names of 10 members"

SHRI SOMNATH CHATTERJEE : Additional ?

SHRI VAJPAYEE : Yes, I would like that it should be 10 members so that the total number of members is 30.

SHRI SURYA NARAYAN YADAV (Saharsa) : In this also you have left out JD(A).

SHRI VAJPAYEE : My amendment is that ten members from Rajya Sabha should be included and instead of 16th August, I have submitted that the report should be presented on the first day of the next session....

SHRI S.B. CHAVAN, The Minister of Home Affairs : Mr. Chairman, Sir, I quite appreciate the views expressed by the Leader of the Opposition. When this Bill was being introduced, in the initial stage itself, some Hon. members had raised the point that it should be referred to the Joint Select Committee. They should be given fifteen days' time so that within that period they will be able to complete their job.

After the new system had been introduced, normally, the Bill is referred to the Standing Committee which would go into the different clauses which are contained in this Bill. Since it was the wish of some of the Hon. members that this is a Bill on which they would like to have a wider kind of discussion and they wanted some time for discussing it in the Joint Select Committee, we gave them time and we said that this Bill should be passed within this session itself. I quite agree with the Hon. Leader of the Opposition that if some more members are accommodated, it would be better. I have no objection in agreeing to this proposal, provided, the Leader of the Opposition gives me an undertaking that this Bill would be passed during this Session itself. If that is agreed to, I have no objection in expanding even the number of members. But I cannot agree for postponing the submission of the report of the Committee till the first week of the next session. That will go against the very reason as to why we are trying to bring about this Bill.

Sir, if the Hon. Leader of the Opposition is prepared to concede that within 15 days' time, I will also give a concession for two or three more days viz. up to 16th August they will submit the report to the House so that we succeed in passing this Bill. That would be better. This is the only request I am making to the Leader of the Opposition.

Time Frame Cannot Be Rigid

SHRI VAJPAYEE : Mr. Chairman, Sir, the Committee will give due consideration to the desire of the Government but you cannot bind a Committee to present a report within a stipulated time and I also do not want to bind the Committee. (*Interruptions*)

SHRI S.B. CHAVAN : Then, Sir, I cannot agree.

SHRI VAJPAYEE : There is no need to link the two issues, that of constitution of the Committee and fixing the time limit. Do you think that we will accept the Committee which consists of six members from Congress party alone? You are not giving proper representation to even the Bharatiya Janata Party. We will have to decide whether to participate in the proceedings of the Committee or not.

DR. CHANDRA JEET YADAV (Azamgarh) : Mr. Chairman Sir, please do not decide in haste. It is a serious matter. In my view, the Hon. Home Minister has brought it in a haste but you please do not decide it in a hurry. You please obtain the opinion of the House through voting. It is really a serious matter. I think that the objections raised by Hon. Atal Bihari Vajpayee on the very first day and during the presentation of the amendments, are quite appropriate. So I would like to say that outcome of this Bill will be disastrous. It seems that the Hon. Home Minister has not gone through this bill due to paucity of time. I would like to say that it is not the proper way to amend the Constitution.

SHRI LAL K. ADVANI (Gandhinagar) : Mr. Chairman Sir, I am not discussing the objectives of this Bill. The Rules provide that when a motion of reference is made to the Select Committee one can speak about the contents of the Bill also.

Why the established conventions for the constitution of Select Committees are being violated ? The Hon. Minister of Home Affairs has to give answer to this query. If a Select Committee is constituted from one House, it should comprise 30-35 members as per the guidelines compiled by Kaul and Shakdher. They further state that it represents a microcosm of the House.

So a Select Committee comprises 30-35 members and so far as the question of a Joint Committee is concerned, they say : "As a rule it should be of 45 members." There should thus be 30 members from this House and 15 members from the other House. This is the usual thing. They explain the reasons thereof in the following words :

> "The composition of a Select Committee or a Joint Committee reflects the strength of the various parties and groups."

It cannot be admitted; it cannot be of the kind that the motion contains today. Their representation is six whereas the strength of the ruling party is less than half in the House. So, they should have only 4 members, not more than five at any rate. For the remaining five also, there should be a balance.

Shri Atal Bihari Vajpayee's suggestion for taking 30 : 10 members has been accepted but fixing a time limit amounts to restricting the Committee's function and that too at Shri Vajpayee's instance. I can only say that reasonable time should be given as suggested by Shri Chandra Jeet Yadav. The reasonable time would be the first day of next session.

It is very necessary that the session is summoned so early that we get a period of 20-25 days for discussion. In this connection Select Committee is a question not merely of political expediency, it is a question of the traditions of the House. For this, being the Speaker of the august House, you should ask the Government to apply established conventions, established traditions codified in the form by Kaul and Shakdher. Why should they be defaulted by the Government ? The Government should not do so. The Government should adhere to these traditions and accept the proposals made by the Leader of the Opposition.

SHRI SOMNATH CHATTERJEE (Bolpur) : So far as the number of members in the Committee is concerned, I do not object to it. It can be increased. I have no objection. A later date should be fixed during this session and if the Committee feels that it cannot do it then we can always come to the House, there is no final bar. But we are keen that in this session this Bill should be taken up for consideration. This is our submission.

SHRI GEORGE FERNANDES (Muzaffarpur) : Mr. Chairman, Sir, I would like to make few submissions in this regard. When a proposal to introduce the Bill was mooted, we had opposed it giving detailed reasons and I don't think there is any need to repeat all these points. We were already apprehensive of their intention. Our doubts were strengthened when they proposed 6 members from their side and only 4 members from the majority side. I think that communalism is only a pretext to bring forward this Bill. It is a direct infringement of Fundamental Rights guaranteed by the Constitution. There is no need to repeat the intentions of the ruling party. Though stress is being laid on communalism, it is a clear case of infringement of Fundamental Rights. The intentions of the Government become very clear with their proposal for the constitution of the Committee. They want to have majority representation in the Committee and introduce the Bill on the basis of the recommendation of their majority in the Committee. But it requires two-thirds majority as it is a Constitution (Amendment) Bill. The

Government wants to get the Bill passed by making this sort of manipulations and violate our Fundamental Rights. Their thinking is wrong. The amendment moved by Atalji to increase the strength of the Committee should be accepted by the Government by increasing the number of members. The Government should not lay down any conditions for this. This is my submission to the Government.... This is a very serious matter. While sticking to the rules for the formation of the Committee, we expect that you will also help us by asking them to give up the intentions with which they have moved the Bill.

SHRI VIJOY KUMAR YADAV (Nalanda) : Members from all the political parties should be taken in it. This is wrong.

MR. CHAIRMAN : I think there is so much difference, that if the expanded Committee is being agreed upon, the time limit which the Home Minister is suggesting may be accepted because that is not final. If it is not practicable, if the Committee has not completed the report, the House also gives extension of time. I do not think that there is any difference of opinion on this. The point is, if what is expanded is acceptable, ultimately as it is a Constitution (Amendment) Bill unless there is a two-thirds majority in the House it cannot be passed and the other Bill depends only upon the Constitution (Amendment) Bill. I would like to clarify. Therefore, instead of asking for deletion, if he does not press for Amendment No. 3 then, I think that a way out can be found out.

SHRI S.B. CHAVAN : The first point I want to respond relates to the misgivings which have been expressed by Hon. members Shri George Fernandes and Shri Chandra Jeet Yadav. In spite of the fact that on the other day I had made it absolutely clear, that we are proposing to use it only for misuse of religion for political purposes. As regards the rest of the provisions certainly the Committee can delete what is not required. I have stated that on that day itself. But still Shri George Fernandes goes on saying as if we have interest in taking away the Fundamental Rights of the citizens of this country. I do not think that it is correct.... 'Misuse of religion for political purposes' is the main aim of this Bill.

SHRI SOMNATH CHATTERJEE : That should be the main and only object.

SHRI SURYA NARAYAN YADAV : Please make your intentions clear.

SHRI S.B. CHAVAN : Our intention is very clear but your intentions have turned ill, for which we can do nothing. You are trying to view things in a distorted way which we do not mean at all. Our purpose is that for the continuance of politics, communalism should not be used in it. We do not have any other motive. We find that many armies are being raised which try to silence the voice of the poor. You delete all other provisions, I have no objection, then my intentions would be clear to you. Please withdraw your second amendment. If the Committee feels after its sitting that more time is required, it can think of further extension. But one thing I must say that it will be our all out effort to have the Bill passed during this session.

MR. CHAIRMAN : Are you in agreement with that ? All right, then I will put it to vote. Shall I put all the amendments together to vote, or one by one ?

SHRI VAJPAYEE : What about the constitution of the Committee.

SHRI S.B. CHAVAN : I agree to your proposal.

SHRI VAJPAYEE : There is no need to have an understanding with me. There are other Hon. members also in the House.

SHRI S.B. CHAVAN : I accept the amendments brought by you.

SHRI VAJPAYEE : Kindly tell the names of members of which parties are participating in it. Please postpone this motion. You can bring it in the evening or tomorrow.

SHRI S.B. CHAVAN : The names which you have given are acceptable to me. Do you accept them or not ? ....I was surprised that Shri Vajpayeeji had proposed the name of Shri Sulaiman Sait. This is a good thing. We welcome it.

SHRI VAJPAYEE : Whose name ?

SHRI S.B. CHAVAN : When you proposed the name of Shri Sulaiman Sait, I said that it is worth welcoming. A good atmosphere is being created.

SHRI VAJPAYEE : I have given his name because there are only two members of the Muslim League in the House who have taken interest in this matter....

SHRI CHANDRA JEET YADAV (Azamgarh) : You have given his name deliberately.

SHRI VAJPAYEE : Yes, I have given his name deliberately. One member of the Muslim League is already in the Committee so take the other member also.

SHRI CHANDRA JEET YADAV : You have given his name after a careful thought.

SHRI VAJPAYEE : If you have accepted the names given by me it is a good thing.

SHRI SURYA NARAYAN YADAV (Saharsa) : Shri Vajpayee has played the role of the Leader of Opposition very well. The ruling party has failed in its duty.

SHRI MADAN LAL KHURANA (South Delhi) : Now you have accepted it.

SHRI S.B. CHAVAN : Mr. Speaker, Sir, he has not accepted what I said....

SHRI MADAN LAL KHURANA : We accept it....

SHRI S.B. CHAVAN : Shri Vajpayeeji does not accept it.

SHRI MADAN LAL KHURANA : He has accepted and it is for Hon. Speaker....

SHRI VAJPAYEE : I accept the names mentioned here.

SHRI S.B. CHAVAN : No Congress(I) member figures in the list given by you. After hearing you, I thought that the names of Congress(I) members would certainly figure in it but not even a single Congress(I) member's name has figured in it.

SHRI SOMNATH CHATTERJEE : Sir, may I suggest one thing ? Let the Home Minister come with a revised list at 5.30 p.m. today.... (*Interruptions*)

SHRI S.B. CHAVAN : We can revise the names if he is prepared for this kind of a thing. I will again come to the House at 5.30 p.m. today after revising the names.

THE CHAIRMAN (Shri Sharad Dighe) : At that time, I hope, he will not press for his Amendment no. 2.

SHRI S.B. CHAVAN : Sir, he has to take a decision on that.

SHRI VAJPAYEE : Do not make it conditional. I will not accept any condition.

MR. CHAIRMAN : Then, it comes to the same thing.

SHRI VAJPAYEE : You have the majority. If you want you can accept it. The Hon. Home Minister has accepted that if the Committee is of the conclusion that the time should be extended, then it can be done.

SHRI S.B. CHAVAN : Time and again I have said that if the Committee would emphasize that a particular Bill should be passed in the current session, it would be done. If the Committee feels that it is impossible to report on some points of the Bill in the current session, in such a situation they can present the facts before the House during the next session and we can go accordingly.

SHRI S.B. CHAVAN : Sir, at 5.30 p.m. I will give you the revised names.

MR. CHAIRMAN : This discussion is postponed till 5.30 p.m.

Election Commission's Ultimatum

Mr. Speaker, Sir, the Minister of Home Affairs said that a statement would be made in the House. The statement should present a clear picture. The Chief Election Commissioner has raised many issues. He has raised the issue of Tripura, he has alleged that the action was not taken in Tripura as was decided by the Election Commission. He further arraigns that the Central Government is not ready to comply with the suggestions put forth by the Election Commission with regard to deploying of the paramilitary forces in Tamil Nadu, where bye-elections are going to be held.

Mr. Speaker, Sir, a perusal of all the papers sometimes shows as if the Election Commission has given an ultimatum to the Government. But the Election Commission states that the Government has stopped him from carrying out his duties and now it amounts to a total confrontation. I want to quote from the contents of the reply to the letter written by the Ministry of Home Affairs. The Commission has referred to some excerpts of the letter and later made remarks thereon. I quote :

> "The challenge in the above letter set forth by the Ministry of Home Affairs to the Commission's authority and prerogative to ask for the deployment of the staff under article 329 of the Constitution is now open and total. Hardly anything has been left unsaid in that letter as regards the stand of the Government of India in the matter. This challenge is fraught with the most perilous consequences for the future of democratic elections in India and if the open attempt to subjugate the Election Commission under the executive, is allowed to go unchallenged, it will destroy the very roots of India's democracy. The constitutional position of the Election Commission will be nullified, rendering it incapable of performing its fundamental function of securing the services of the staff required for conducting fair and free elections."

Congress Party Responsible for Deadlock

Mr. Speaker, Sir, the Constitution empowers the Chief Election Commissioner to monitor the elections, to provide guidance regarding the elections and the message enshrined in the Constitution is that the election should be held. It is the duty of the Election Commission to hold the elections. Now a deadlock has arisen where Election Commission is refusing to hold elections, not only for the present but it has given an ultimatum for the future also. The Congress party is being repeatedly grilled for this. I would like to quote another excerpt from the order of the Election Commission.

Lok Sabha on August 3, 1993 during discussion regarding orders by the Chief Election Commissioner

> "It is an irony of fact that the Commission's request and direction to deploy Central Police forces in the above mentioned two constituencies in my State of Tamil Nadu was issued after taking into consideration *inter alia* demand of members of Parliament, most of whom belong to the very party which runs the executive Government at the Centre, and the demands are also supported by the Leader of the Legislative Assembly; the Government of that very party at the Centre is now telling the Commission that it has no authority to make such a request and direction.

Parliament is also being held responsible. Allegations are being levelled against Members of Parliament also. Mr. Advani and we want your guidance as to how should we start a discussion on this issue.

MR. SPEAKER : I will see.

A Way Out Must Be Found

SHRI VAJPAYEE : Mr. Speaker, Sir, we would like to hear the Attorney-General and would like to give a chance to the Government also to defend themselves. A way out must be found to resolve this deadlock. We would wait for the statement which is going to be made in the evening and if this statement proves to be an eye-wash, then we will set our course of action. Thank you.

Can't the Bill to Separate Religion from Politics be Deferred?

Mr. Speaker, Sir, I have to raise a point of order. I have been a member of Parliament for over thirty years and the procedure has been that Bills are introduced and then referred to a Select Committee or circulated for eliciting public opinion thereon. A Select Committee was constituted in this connection, not at the instance of the Government, but on our insistence. A difference of opinion has arisen in regard to its membership, because the Government was emphasizing that since the Bill had to be passed immediately, the period prescribed for the Select Committee fell short. Shri George Fernandes is sitting here and our friend from Telugu Desham Party Shri Padmanabham is also present. Both of them were members of the Select Committee. They have written in their note that the Select Committee was not given time for consideration, that everything was done in haste; and today suddenly we are hearing from the mouth of the Home Minister that the discussion on the Bill be deferred.

Mr. Speaker, Sir, I do not think that there is any provision in the rules for deferment. The Home Minister has not moved any motion before the House for its circulation to elicit public opinion thereon. There is no such motion before the House. What is before the House ? A request by the Home Minister that since they cannot get it through...well, if they can't get it through then why did they bring it here ? Why did you not give full time for the consideration of the Bill ? But I will not go into these details. I will speak separately on its merits and Shri Advani would also like to speak on it. I have raised only a point of order as to what is this deferment ? Under what rule has this been done ?

SHRI VAJPAYEE : Mr. Speaker, Sir, when I spoke in the beginning I had confined myself to the point of order. However, many things have been said in the House thereafter. We are not against deferment, but it should be done under some procedure. It should conform to the rules. The Government has got stuck up in the mess created by itself. Those upon whom the Government was perhaps depending for taking it out of this mess did not help the Government. It is no use showing anger against the Opposition parties.

Mr. Speaker, Sir, Shri Chavan has also referred to 6 December events of the demolition of Babri structure]. If you just go through the old statements, Prime Minister Shri P.V. Narasimha Rao had announced in the Congress session at Tirupati before December 6 that he would frame such a law. The

Lok Sabha on August 24, 1993 on the statement made by the Home Minister regarding deferment of the Bill on Separation of Religion from Politics

incident of December 6 occurred afterwards. A top-most leader of the ruling party had tried for the withdrawal of the registration of the Bharatiya Janata Party.

Mr. Speaker, Sir, if the popularity of the Bharatiya Janata Party is increasing day by day, if more and more people are getting attracted towards our party, then the ruling party and the friendly parties should ponder over the reason behind this increasing popularity. Both these Bills have been brought here with the intention to defame us. Those who are opposed to us including many from the intelligentsia as well as the newspapers, have criticized these Bills, because both these Bills are undemocratic and unconstitutional and strike at the basic structure of the country. Religion should not be misused during the elections, I am using the word religion, and we have made a suggestion in this connection and even have given notice of amendment. However, the people do not understand, and when you talk about religion, the people derive another meaning from it. When you translate it into Hindi as *"Dharma,"* it creates difficulties. There is no difference of opinion on this question that communal feelings must not be incited, but do not talk of *dharma*. *Dharma* is comprehensive and actually denotes righteousness. *Dharma* unites, *Dharma* comes naturally, *Dharma* is duty—*"Dharma Chakra Pravartanaya"* (In order to establish righteousness) ....(*Interruptions*)

DR. KARTIKESHWAR (Balasore): Who accepts it ?

SHRI VAJPAYEE : Sir, as a speaker, my *dharma* (duty) is to speak the right thing and his *dharma* (duty) is to listen silently as a listener. He should observe his *dharma* (duty).

Mr. Speaker, Sir, there are so many laws in the country and we have also been stressing this point that there are so many laws in the country which provide that any kind of feelings of hatred should not be incited. However, this law provides only for use of religion. (*Interruptions*)

SHRI VAJPAYEE : Yes, Shri Shukla, a debate is taking place. It cannot be that a debate does not take place. It cannot be allowed that you emit poison against us and we do not even get an opportunity to reply to that.

MR. SPEAKER : I am allowing you.

Who is Congress to Preach Us

SHRI VAJPAYEE : No, Mr. Speaker, how did the question of 6 December arise ? They are sermonising us, but who supported the partition of the country on religious grounds ? Who are the people responsible for the division of the country ? Who is responsible for setting up a theocratic state in the neighbourhood ? Who have been hob-nobbing with the Muslim League ? Who has demanded votes in the name of establishing a Christian Government in Mizoram ? These are the people who are putting us in the dock. We are prepared to reply to that.

Mr. Speaker, Sir, please excuse me, I got excited, but things are being done which cause excitement.

MR. SPEAKER : We will have a regular later on. Not at this stage.

SHRI VAJPAYEE : Mr. Speaker, Sir, you will recall that I had put a proposal in the House that the Bill be referred to a Select Committee and the Home Minister had put a rider that the Bill must be returned early. We wanted that the Election Commissioner be called before the Select Committee, but it was rejected. Two former Election Commissioners had criticized the Bill and the people were not given time ....

MR. SPEAKER : We will have a regular debate later on.

SHRI VAJPAYEE : But, Mr. Speaker, please let me reply to the points already made.

MR. SPEAKER : I am not shutting it out totally. (*Interruptions*)

MR. SPEAKER : Unless Shri Vajpayee yields, I cannot allow you. Please sit down.

SHRI VAJPAYEE : Mr. Speaker, I want to make a submission to you that....(*Interruptions*)

SHRI VAJPAYEE : Sir, will they not allow me to speak ? (*Interruptions*)

MR. SPEAKER : Unless Shri Vajpayee yields, I cannot have the benefit of hearing Mr. Patra.

SHRI VAJPAYEE : Mr. Speaker, I will sit down if you ask me.

MR. SPEAKER : I am allowing you. Shri Sharad Yadav if you will interrupt, it will only prolong the matter.

SHRI SHARAD YADAV : Mr. Speaker, I bow to your ruling. As you said he will say everything still be according to the rules and within limits! Some people have made that point.

SHRI VAJPAYEE : What do you mean by some people have made that point ?

MR. SPEAKER : He is not referring to you only.

SHRI SHARAD YADAV : He is going in so much detail that a reply would become necessary after that. That means that the debate might commence today itself. But it cannot be possible.

MR. SPEAKER : That is why I am saying you be very brief.

SHRI SHARAD YADAV : Mr. Speaker, we should also be given an opportunity to have full say.

MR. SPEAKER : You may please sit down. Even if you have become the Leader, you will have to listen to me. If I think it necessary, I will give time. But only when I deem it necessary.

SHRI VAJPAYEE : Mr. Speaker, we have been demanding from the beginning that more time is required for the consideration of this Bill. Different points of view should be presented before the Parliament and the Parliamentary Committee, but everything was done hastily at that time and now a discussion is being avoided.

MR. SPEAKER : We will find it out.

SHRI VAJPAYEE : My socialist friends should not be angry. Dr. Lohia used to talk of co-ordination between religion and politics. He had said that "short-term religion is politics and long-term politics is religion." I am not quoting Gandhiji, I am talking of Dr. Lohia.

MR. SPEAKER : We will have a full-fledged discussion, Vajpayeeji.

SHRI VAJPAYEE : Mr. Speaker, things which have been said today in the House....

MR. SPEAKER : This would prolong debate.

SHRI VAJPAYEE : I do not want to prolong it. I want to submit to you, as I told you in the beginning, I do not want to digress. But our friends, who have failed today in extending support to the Government, have to give an explanation. They could give their explanation, but what was the need to involve us ? But now it has become clear that we were the target and hence this talk of religion is going on, not that of caste. There is already a law for this purpose, but according to the law your election could be set aside only after you have been declared elected. However, these people do not want to allow us to fight the elections and want to banish us by enacting a law on the strength of their majority. We are prepared to fight it out. Let us go to the people. However, Mr. Speaker, Sir, we held a rally and it was blacked out by the T.V. (*Interruptions*)

SHRI VAJPAYEE : You clarify it.

MR. SPEAKER : I will do everything.

SHRI VAJPAYEE : Under which rule does this deferment come ? Till what time will it continue ?

MR. SPEAKER : I cannot say till what time it will continue.

SHRI VAJPAYEE : You may direct the Home Minister to bring a motion formally for the circulation of the Bill to elicit public opinion thereon which the House may consider it.

Thoughtlessness In Calling Parliament's Special Session

Mr. Speaker, Sir, I have been connected with Parliament since 1957, sometimes as a member of Lok Sabha, at other times as a member of Rajya Sabha. I have seen several governments formed by the Congress Party, but I have never before come across such naivety as was exhibited today.

Sir, this is a special session. We are being reminded repeatedly that this special session has been summoned to amend the Constitution, so much so that we have been debarred from raising other questions. Sir, we have been emphasizing from the beginning that there must be a general consensus for amending the election law. The Election Commission is not an individual, it is an institution. It is not enough to carry the majority with you to take a decision in this matter. Sir, you might recall that in the meeting held in your Chamber I had asked Shri Vidya Charan Shukla whether he was going to take a decision on the basis of majority and his reply was in affirmative. Yesterday too, the question of majority was raised. You did not calculate whether two-thirds majority would be available or not. Even if you had succeeded in procuring two-thirds majority that decision of Parliament in a matter like election reforms would not have been justified.

T.N. Seshan has Shaken the Electoral Process

Which party does not want election reforms ? There is no party which does not want to cooperate with you in the matter of election reforms. On the other hand, our complaint is that the decision on the Goswami Committee Report has been pending for the last four years, the use of money power and muscle power is increasing, polling booths are being attacked, there is extravagance in expenditure. The Government should amend the laws relating to these matters, but they have not paid any attention to it. The present Chief Election Commissioner is taking interest in these matters, although we do not agree with all the things he is doing. However, this time when I visited various places during the bye-elections, I found that the walls were not painted. The number of posters has been reduced and lesser number of banners are visible. The Ministers are using private vehicles and keep the Government vehicle at bay lest it may be seen by Seshan. A single person has shaken the entire system and that is why the public has given its unstinted support to him, but

Lok Sabha on June 14, 1994 during the uproarious scenes created as a result of Government's decision not to introduce the Constitution Amendment Bill brought forward in order to curtail the powers of the Chief Election Commissioner

you are holding a special session for amending the Constitution in order to curtail his powers.

You have not done your calculations in counting of numbers. Until this morning, we have been saying that such Bills should not have been brought forward. Mr. Speaker, Sir, you are a witness to it. At least the Government should have listened to your advice because you have always been stressing the point that in important matters like this, some sort of general consensus should be arrived at. It is a great failure of the Government that it could not manage to gather majority behind it. One can say that it does not know even counting. But even if it had been in a position to get two- thirds majority, that would not have been conducive to strengthening the electoral process or raising the dignity of this House.

Parliament Deceived

Mr. Speaker, Sir, what would happen now ? The purpose for which this special session was summoned has been completely defeated and it is given to Shri Bhardwaj to perform the last rites. That was perhaps God's will, may be something good comes out of it. This word 'withdrawal' printed on the Bill was not a misprint; I had thought that it was a printer's devil. You had deliberately said that you have come to seek its withdrawal. This amounts to making a mockery of the House. The Government has treated the Parliament in such a shabby manner several times, which does not enhance the dignity of Parliament. But today, it has crossed all limits. The Government has put all decorum aside. The House has been deceived. We would like to know who is going to take the punishment for this. A way could have been found this morning to do it gracefully and with honour, if the Government was honest about it. But it could not even do this much. The Minister is talking of consensus. But he is not helpful in creating the atmosphere which was required to reach a consensus. A situation of anti-climax has been created before the House. Who will be punished for it ? It would be better if the Government tenders its resignation.

Mr. Speaker, Sir, there is no need to further continue this special session. You may adjourn the session *sine die*. The work for which we had assembled here is no more to be done, let us devote ourselves to other things. In future, a session of the Parliament should be called after careful thought. If this Government cannot muster the requisite number of Members in its support then it has no moral right to stay in power. Thank You.

XI EDUCATION

Controversy in Aligarh University

Sir, by cut motion No. 367 I have regretted the fact that the President has not appointed a committee to inquire into the affairs of the Aligarh University. When the Education Minister was speaking at the start, the House had hoped that he would perhaps announce the Government's decision that the President has decided to inquire into the affairs of the Aligarh University. But his speech ended with appeals and no indication was given about what the Government proposed to do. In my opinion when it has become impossible for the Chatterji Committee to inquire into the affairs of the University and when its members have resigned their membership no option is left for the Central Government except for the President announcing the setting up of a committee to go into the University's affairs.

I feel that more serious allegations than those made in this House can be made in respect of the Aligarh University. But I was surprised to see that a lady member of the Communist Party tried to give a communal colour to this affair. If a member of the House criticises the Aligarh University he is not motivated by communalism to do so, and I know my friend Shri Prakash Vir Shastri. His criticism should be taken in the spirit in which he has drawn the attention of the House to some irregularities about the Aligarh University. The word Muslim is attached to the name of the Aligarh University, so every Hindu criticising the university is assumed to be doing so with a communal feeling—nothing can be more communal than thinking like this. That day I was surprised to see during the half hour discussion that even those occupying ministers' seats were swept away in the current of communalism, interrupted the speaker and said things that did not show secularism. If there are any irregularities in the Aligarh University—and the Education Minister has admitted that there are irregularities, they have been there for the last ten years—one may well ask why there was no inquiry so far. If the officials of the University were proving a hindrance in the way of an inquiry a powerful committee should have been set up which could have torn apart the covering and brought the facts to light despite such hindrance. No link of a university with irregularities, corruption and suspicious behaviour can do credit to the university or to the country. There is no Hindu-Muslim question here. There has also been criticism of the Vice-Chancellor of the Hindu University in this

Lok Sabha on February 15, 1960 while participating in the discussion on the demands for grants of the Ministry of Education

House, but at that time no one said it was communally motivated, so I do not think there is any communalism involved when the Vice-Chancellor of the Aligarh University is criticised. Is it not true that the Vice-Chancellor of the Aligarh University was once dismissed from a job on grounds of moral turpitude ? I call on the Education Minister to refute this charge.

MR. DEPUTY SPEAKER : I would like to remind the Hon. member that I had in the past requested him, when he was speaking, not to mention individual personalities but speak generally on the general condition there. If you charge any specific individual it would create difficulties for him. This should not happen in the House.

SHRI VAJPAYEE : I agree with you, but in this discussion some such things have been said....

MR. DEPUTY SPEAKER : If there is a complaint should there not be an inquiry ?

SHRI VAJPAYEE : I agree with you, but I would like to know—without citing names—if it is not true that engineering equipment worth eight lakhs rupees that had been imported from abroad for the Aligarh Muslim University was exported to Pakistan after it reached Bombay, and if it is not true....

SHRI JAMAL KHWAJA : Does the Hon. member know that when he speaks here in the Lok Sabha he should speak with some responsibility ?

SHRI VAJPAYEE : I am speaking with the fullest sense of responsibility.

SHRI JAMAL KHWAJA : He is alleging that the equipment which was brought for the Aligarh Muslim University was exported to Pakistan, and the implication was that it was done by the Vice-Chancellor. Does he realise the meaning of his statement ?

MR. DEPUTY SPEAKER : I hope the Hon. member has satisfied himself with the veracity of the statement.

SHRI VAJPAYEE : I submit I have levelled a charge in all seriousness, and if the President appoints an inquiry committee I am prepared to submit proof. This charge was also published in the newspapers, but it was not refuted.

SHRI JAMAL KHWAJA : May I point out, Sir....

MR. DEPUTY SPEAKER : Order, order. I can only make it clear to the Hon. member that whenever he makes an allegation he must be sure of the grounds, he must be sure that it is true and that he has taken all measures to see that there is truth in it. That is all I can ask the Hon. member to do. I cannot stop him.

SHRI JAMAL KHWAJA : Sir, may I point out that those papers which published these reports have printed an apology, an unqualified apology in connection with this charge which had been most irresponsibly and unfortunately levelled against the Vice-Chancellor ? Does the Hon. member know that those very papers which published these reports have published an unqualified apology to the Vice-Chancellor ? The Vice-Chancellor was thinking of taking legal action against those persons. But when they came to know of it they published an unqualified apology. I really pity the ignorance of the Hon. member who does not know the facts.

SHRI VAJPAYEE : I know the facts. I am in possession of the papers in this matter.

MR. DEPUTY SPEAKER : According to the Hon. member the papers which had published these reports had offered an unqualified apology. He should take note of that also.

SHRI VAJPAYEE : What I am saying is that those papers that had apologised had levelled a charge against the Vice-Chancellor, which I do not want to repeat here, and the apology is in connection with that apology....

MR. DEPUTY SPEAKER : If despite this the Hon. member wants to say without maintaining names he can certainly do so. If in spite of this he wants to take responsibility he can speak about it. That will depend upon him.

SHRI VAJPAYEE : I also want to say something more about the Engineering College. The Centre had deputed Shri Mangal Rai to act as the Principal of the Engineering College. Why did he decline to do so ? What situation did he see in the College that made it impossible for him to work there ?

There is nothing new in the way Communist speakers have supported the Aligarh University in this discussion. Communists and communalists have joined hands in the way the University is being managed. When there is some disturbance in the Banaras University Communist Party members stand up and expose it and demand Government action....

SMT. RENU CHAKRAVARTTY : On a point of explanation, Sir, he can say whatever he likes, but I do not think he even followed what I said. I never, at no stage, supported any corruption or anything that was wrong. All that I said was that the terms of reference should include a fight against communalism and that is something, I suppose, which he does not like.

SHRI VAJPAYEE : The lady member should also bear in mind the speech the spokesman of the Communist Party made in the Rajya Sabha. What Communist Party papers are writing can also not be forgotten. In addition, the way Shri Khwaja was supporting the Vice-Chancellor there in his speech today and the way Communist members were backing him also provide some indications....

SMT. RENU CHAKRAVARTTY : What indications, may I know ? These communalists think they can fling about any sort of charges about anybody.

MR. DEPUTY SPEAKER : But could the Hon. member tell me what I should do ? That is my difficulty. If there is freedom of speech for everybody, unless he misuses or abuses it, I have to allow him. What shall I do if that be his inference or his conclusion ?

SMT. RENU CHAKRAVARTTY : The conclusion is all right. He must factually prove it. There are no facts at all.

SHRI VAJPAYEE : I would like to present facts about what I am saying. I have with me a copy of the M.A. Political Science paper of the Aligarh University. I have also taken my M.A. with Political Science. The Political Science that is taught in Aligarh University is not Political Science but Marxism. I too have some knowledge about it. Out of 13 questions in the Political Science paper 9 are about communism. I have 9 questions, which I would like to read out. They are as follows :

"Comment on any three of the following :

(J) Let a hundred gardens bloom, let a hundred philosophies contend. (Mao)"

The others are all like that.

"Briefly discuss the chief factors that contributed to the development of capitalism from its establishment in the sixteenth century to the time of Karl Marx."

"Carefully examine the analytical argument by which Karl Marx tries to prove that the basis of capitalism is the exploitation of labour."

"The knell of capitalist private property sounds, the expropriators are expropriated."

"Carefully examine the arguments by which Karl Marx tried to prove that the development of capitalism would inevitably lead to socialism through a proletarian revolution."

"What does V.I. Lenin tell us about the origin and working of finance capital in the world's most industrialised states ?"

This whole paper is like that.

"Explain carefully the Communist theory of the State which Lenin has expounded in his *State and Revolution.*"

"Carefully estimate the achievements of Chairman Mao as a political thinker. What do you understand by the term 'Thought of Mao Tse-tung ?"

"Trace the chief stages in the development of the Socialist programme in China since the establishment of the People's Republic in 1949."

MR. DEPUTY SPEAKER : A study can be undertaken even for the sake of criticism.

SMT. RENU CHAKRAVARTTY : He does not know that.

SHRI VAJPAYEE : That is not a paper on Marx's philosophy. This whole paper is on political thought, in which 9 questions out of 13 deal only with Marxism. I am not saying there are professors teaching at Aligarh Muslim University who are working for the Communist Party. And at the time of the agitation in Kerala, Professors at the Aligarh Muslim University had published a statement condemning it. I fail to understand how the agitation in Kerala and the Professors at Aligarh Muslim University are connected. A branch of the People's Publishing House is located at the Aligarh Muslim University and Professors are open Communist Party card-holders. I am saying this because it is not baseless to say that there is an alliance between the Communists and the Communalists.

SMT. RENU CHAKRAVARTTY : Are we to take it that card-holders of the Communist Party cannot be members of the University ? I myself was a professor at Calcutta.

MR. DEPUTY SPEAKER : The Hon. member may be allowed to proceed.

SHRI VAJPAYEE : Therefore, Sir, I would say that if any objectionable activities, any activities not in accordance with the level of a university go on in a university—whether Hindu is attached to its name or Muslim—the Central Government should intervene. The Education Minister has not made clear what the Government proposes to do in this matter. The reaction of the University to the half-hour discussion in the House has made it clear that a committee appointed by the University will not be allowed to know all the facts. Now it is said, that the Education Minister should name the members of the Committee after telling the Vice-Chancellor. I pity the Education Minister. I am sorry that his integrity is being doubted. Now the only way out is for the President to appoint an Inquiry Committee that would bring the facts to light and redeem the prestige of the Aligarh University. We want a good name for all universities in the country. We want them to have the people's confidence. But our universities are falling from their high standards. But the criticism of the Aligarh University cannot be discarded merely on the ground that those making it are communalists. All facts should be investigated and the truth brought to light.

Manufacture of Hindi Typewriters

I have given one more cut motion by which I have drawn the Education Minister's attention to the manufacture of Hindi typewriters. If we want to gradually replace a foreign language with our own we would certainly need Hindi typewriters. But this matter has been hanging fire for several years, because those entrusted with Devnagari script reform at first could not take any decision, and if they took one they could not remain firm on it. Consequently there has been no progress with the manufacture of Hindi typewriters. Now that they have taken a decision there should be no more delay in manufacturing Hindi typewriters. The Education Ministry may say that that is the job of the Commerce and Industry Ministry. This may be so from the point of view of allocation of administrative responsibilities. But the fact is, so long as we do not have a Hindi typewriter Hindi will not be current in official business, and it is the Ministry's responsibility to see that we make progress in this direction.

One more thing. Acharya Kripalani has made forceful logical points regarding our educational system. 13 years have passed since the country became independent, but the educational system that we used to criticise remains the same. Even now we criticise it. From the President to the Education Minister they all show the deficiencies in the system but they do not change it. This education is not taking the the country's youth in the right direction. It does not develop their character fully. It has gone backward from the culture of the soil. This education does not build character, it does not lend dignity to labour. It does not produce patriots. The time has come to change this educational system. The Education Minister should think about it. Thank you.

Faulty Educational System, Cause of Students' Discontent

Sir, members of Parliament have to some extent lost their moral right to consider the discontent among students and to advise them. After the way members of both this Houses behave, the way the Speaker is disregarded, and after the scenes we witness in Parliament advising students to respect their elders, obey their teachers and observe discipline looks like a joke. This House, this Parliament, this Government, the older generation could not provide the right leadership to students. We should accept our failure, and if we want to improve the students and bring them to the right path we must begin with ourselves.

Student-Police Confrontation

I do not go into the broad form of the problem. It cannot be denied that the educational system is faulty and that we could not change it in the twenty years of independence. This is most unfortunate. It neither makes life nor provides a means of livelihood. But this is not the reason for the discontent among the students. This educational system has been going on for 20 years, but never before have so many disturbances taken place as during this year. The proportion between the students and the teachers has gone up higher than in the past; it is going up every year. At the same time it would not be right to say that this is the reason of the disturbances. The reasons are economic, social, political but I do not want to go into them. The problem is immediate. It has been caused by a confrontation between the students and the police. The biggest problem is how to prevent such a confrontation. All agitations and disturbances that have taken place this year were caused by student-police clashes. In Delhi Law students launched an agitation and have complained of police excesses. This had a chain reaction. As a reaction there were agitations at other places as well. If the students are asked what their demands are they have no demands other than that there should be judicial inquiries in firings, arrested students should be released, and some arrangements should be made to redress their complaints. I call upon this House and the Education Minister to consider how a collision between the students and the police could be prevented.

Where Does the Campus Begin and End ?

Now it is argued that the police should not enter the campus except at the invitation of the Vice-Chancellor. May I know if these Vice-Chancellors have

Rajya Sabha on November 9, 1966 during the discussion on Calling Attention Motion regarding widespread discontentment among students

any law and order machinery of their own ? Harvard University has its own police, while other Universities of the world have their proctors and prefects. These are not some professors who are caught hold of and entrusted with this job. It is not done like that, separate people, who are non-academic and who maintain discipline, are employed for this. If the occasion calls for it they control the students. Our universities have no such arrangements. And then you say the police should not enter the campus. I say let us define a campus. Where does the Delhi University's campus begin and where does it end ? Delhi has no campus. If a bus is torched in front of a college it is the campus, the police cannot go there. But if a bus is set on fire the police will have to go there, they should go there. I am not in favour of considering students a privileged class. If they are within the campus and go by their professors' or the Vice-Chancellor's discipline the police would normally not be required to intervene, but when they cross the boundary they are like other citizens.

I have a complaint against Shri Chagla. He has said something in his statement. It is a good statement and it has presented all aspects of the problem. That it would not be acted upon is another matter. But he has said that when the police have to deal with students they should bear in mind that they are dealing with the most sensitive class of the society. Should the police confine this attitude only to the students ? Should it deal with other classes with a feeling of revenge ? I say the police should have the same attitude towards all sections of the society, all citizens and that attitude itself should be sensitive.

SHRI AKBAR ALI KHAN : Because of young age....

SHRI VAJPAYEE : That is a wrong thing. What is young age ? I am younger in age as compared to you. Let us not bring in this the matter of age. So long as they are inside the university, inside the colleges, and are bound by the discipline of the university they are students, they are young and their mistakes may be connived at. Once they come out on the street and take the law in their hands they should be punished like any other law-breaker.

Vice-Chancellors Taking Interest in Condemning Police

Sir, I am surprised to see that for the past some days some Vice-Chancellors are issuing statements condemning the police. The Vice-Chancellor of Delhi University has also said something which has given the students the impression that they have been saved. The Vice-Chancellor of Magadh University has also said something that has made the students feel that he is with them in criticising the police. And the latest Vice-Chancellor is Shri R.K. Nehru. The police should be criticised if they do something that merits criticism. But I warn that the tendency to praise the army for everything and to criticise the police for everything is growing in the country. This is not a good attitude. I know the police make mistakes. That day I myself said in the House that what happened in Delhi would not have happened if tear gas shells had not landed on the dais. I know how the police of Rohtak arrested the Jan Sangh MLA and beat him up in the lock-up. He was the people's elected representative and when I went to see the

Superintendent, the police officer who had ordered the beating, he said that was because he tried to run away. Sir, this MLA is so fat that he would not be able to run even if he wanted to.

SHRI CHANDRA SHEKHAR (U.P.) : Is he perhaps the MLA from Swami Rameshwaranand's constituency ?

SHRI VAJPAYEE : I am not talking about him.

SHRI CHANDRA SHEKHAR : Not his constituency ?

SHRI VAJPAYEE : No, he has been elected from Karnal, I am talking of Rohtak. Swamiji has recently been put in jail. Why are they after him ? Sir, I was saying....

MR. DEPUTY CHAIRMAN (Shri M.P. Bhargava) : It is about time....

SHRI VAJPAYEE : Sir, I am being interrupted. I am not responsible for that.

SHRI CHANDRASHEKHAR : Sir, let him speak. He is speaking well.

SHRI VAJPAYEE : Just you wait.

Police versus Army

Sir, the attitude of criticising the police for everything is not good. The police should be criticised if they behave like that, but I cannot accept criticism of the police for everything and praise of the army for everything. I can see the ill-effects of this. The police discharge their duty under great difficulties. They have their own problems. Sometimes they too need to be patted on the back, though not for what happened on Monday.

SHRI SYED AHMED (M.P.) : Even for that.

SHRI VAJPAYEE : That day too I had said at first the police acted mildly, but later they went out of control. Sir, I do not want to talk much about Delhi. When firing is resorted to, they shoot either to disperse the crowd or to kill. Do members of the House know that among those killed by bullets day before yesterday some were shot in the head, some in the chest ! I have yet to see somebody who was shot below the belt. It is a different matter that the dead bodies of those killed were not handed over to their relatives. I do not want to link that matter with this, but please accept my point when I say that we should conduct the police properly in order to make them discharge their responsibility.

One more thing. Shri Chagla has rightly said that students' agitations are launched with the feeling that the Government can be overcome, can be bent, an agitation can force the Government to give in, and if the agitation is violent this Government would give in quickly. This feeling has spread throughout the country, not only among students, it is there in every political party, in every section of the society, and the Government cannot escape responsibility for this. Threats of self-immolation are held out, and then the Government changes its decision. I hope that with Andhra the Government will stop changing decisions under threat.

SHRI AKBAR ALI KHAN : No, no, not threats. But it should do justice.

SHRI V.M. CHORADIA : Are they not the same as threats ?

SHRI AKBAR ALI KHAN : After the expert opinion of the consortium it is not right to say so. There is injustice. It should be redressed.

When Will Cow-slaughter Stop?

SHRI VAJPAYEE : Even if there is injustice the proper method should be adopted. If you do not think of the means this will happen in every case. This demand for a ban on cow-slaughter has arisen after independence. A crore and a half have put their signatures and said they wanted it. There is a Directive Principle in the Constitution about this. Gandhiji also wanted a ban on cow slaughter. But it was not stopped. Then an agitation was launched and letters were sent in the name of Chief Ministers. Outside people think that the Government buckles down before an agitation, so an agitation is required. And people also think the Government has greater listening power at the time of elections, so agitations take place at election time. If the Central Government stops keeping problems hanging in mid-air, gives up the habit of shutting up problems in a snake box, decides to crush snake's hood on the spot, does not do injustice, does not keep problems hanging, the atmosphere in the country can change. But when the Government invites rebel Nagas to Delhi and engages in love-talk with them, when after the boundary of Maharashtra was demarcated it sets up a commission to decide the boundary controversy between Mysore and Maharashtra, and when it is making temporary agreements for garnering votes in the elections, it is no wonder that the feeling should arise in the country that it understands only the language of agitations. This atmosphere should be changed.

Sir, the country is passing through a critical situation. No political party —even the ruling party—would be able to exploit this situation even if it wants to. The only result would be that they would go down into the pit and take the country with them. There is a smell of rebellion in the country, in the air. Now is the time for political parties to sit down together. Whatever my friend Shri Bhupesh Gupta and Shri Raj Narain say political parties should keep their hands off students. They should study politics, discuss politics, if they are major they may even vote, but we cannot allow our schools, our temples of learning, to be turned into political cockpits. But not only the opposing parties, even the ruling party is responsible. Who should be blamed ?

We are all now naked in this *Hamam* (public bath), hence there is greater cause for worry about the country's future. Somewhere we will have to draw a line, and if we don't, anarchy will swallow us. There will be no democracy, no Opposition parties, and even this Government will be in danger. If the students' agitation opens our eyes I would say they have done a good thing even while taking a wrong step by opening the eyes of their elders. Thank you.

Include Education In Concurrent List

Sir, By this Bill Shri Samant has demanded the inclusion of 'Education' in the Concurrent List. It is not the first time that this demand has been made in the House. Parliament has often laid stress on it. If we want to determine a national policy on education and if we want to get it effectively implemented in the States, Education cannot be left within the powers of the States alone. This matter had also come up in the National Integration Council and the Council had also felt that steps should be taken in this direction and the States should be prepared for it. But the State Governments are not willing to give up their powers. They do not care so much for education as for the appointment of teachers and the discrimination they can practice in it. They can reward somebody and award somebody, and they do not want the Centre to have any powers in this matter even under the Concurrent List. But now, apart from Tamil Nadu, we have Congress Governments in most States. Where there are no Congress Governments the Congress at the Centre is ruling through the President. This is the time for change and for bringing Education into the Concurrent List. Has the Government really considered this issue ? And if it has, what has it concluded ?

State Governments are preparing text books that have no uniformity in them. At places text books are detrimental to the feeling of national unity. Quite a few text books are preaching narrowness and bigotry, but the Central Government cannot intervene, because it is a State subject. I have gone through the discussion in the Constituent Assembly. There too this subject had been discussed. There are many fields where the Central Government too should have a say. Further, keeping it in the Concurrent List means we are not taking out this subject from the State List but we are giving the Central Government the power to consider it if necessary and determine a policy or make a law.

In my opinion this Bill is useful, good and necessary, and it should be accepted. But no private member's Bill or Constitution Amendment Bill can be passed unless this strong majority makes up its mind and decides to cooperate with us. So what I want to know is what has the Government decided ? Thank you.

Lok Sabha on July 27, 1973 on the Constitution Amendment Bill by Shri S.C. Samant for inclusion, of 'Education' in Concurrent List (List III) of the Constitution

Where is the New Education Policy ?

Sir, today is the final day of the session. Could we not have found time before this to discuss an important subject like education ? In the presence of members who can be counted on fingers we are considering a new document presented by the Government. The first document was the 'Challenge of Education.' Along with the presentation of the document the Education Ministry itself disappeared. In its place has arisen the Human Resources Development Ministry. This programme of action is under it—a document of 204 pages. I have tried to find a programme of action in it. The first document of action enumerated the faults in the education system. No one is unaware of the faults. A commission was set up under the Chairmanship of Dr. Radhakrishnan, a second commission was set up under the Chairmanship of Dr. Kothari. The whole country is familiar with the distortions and deficiencies in the present education policy, but where is the new education policy ? Is opening a school in every district the essence of the policy ? I shall discuss this later.

When the Prime Minister talked of a new education policy in his first broadcast on January 5, 1985 a wave of hope had arisen in the country. She repeated the same assurance on August 15. But there has been no effort at modernization of the education policy. It seems the Government has come to the conclusion that no basic change in the educational system is called for. If this is the conclusion, this is the essence, the goal of changing the mindset of the country by changing the education system will not be achieved. But this is a wide-ranging subject. I do not want to go into it for the present.

But, Sir, I would like to read out a portion of the programme of action:

> "The Programme of Action" is meant to provide an indication of the nature of actions which will be needed in order to implement the directions of the policy. It provides a broad strategy within which detailed scheme will be subsequently drawn up. It will also facilitate the preparatory work which will be required before such schemes can be worked out fully and put into operational form."

The discussion has been going on for two years. The title is 'Programme of Action.' What is the programme ? Will there be an unending discussion ? And even after an unending discussion the basic questions will remain unanswered !

Rajya Sabha on August 22, 1986 during discussion on the resolution regarding the programme of National Education Policy

Same Education—Yes or No ?

Sir, a basic question is, will every citizen of the country have the same education or not ? Will the present disparity in the educational field continue ? The so-called public schools are private schools. Will the son of a poor citizen of the country go to a tent school of the Delhi Municipal Corporation, and will the son of a rich man, a big man, receive education in private schools called public schools ? Should not education be equal for all ? How will the level of small schools, schools for the children of the poor, rise ? Who will pay attention to them ?

We had hoped the Education Minister would take steps for bringing equality in education.

Sir, the Varna system must go. But the Education Minister has established a new Varna, a new category, the fifth category of Navodaya Vidyalaya. Now there is one more category. Who will go there ? How many will go ? Will the Navodaya Vidyalaya not become a new cause for friction ? What will happen to the other schools ? Will there be no 'uday,' a new awakening, in them ? Will it be 'ast'—the setting ? They will not be 'nava'—new. They will be old.

500 crore rupees are going to be spent on Navodaya Schools. I am happy to see the Human Resources Development Minister has assured that now there will be no shortage of funds for education. I do not know how this assurance will be fulfilled. But I want to bind him to this assurance. What I am worried about is, even before I question him about his promise about giving full funds and he is in a position to reply he may be shunted from this Ministry and given another charge. These days it is difficult to say who will last where and how long. Shri Pant was the Education Minister. He wrote me a letter and the day I got it I learnt he was no more connected with the education department, he will now dig mines.

Operation Blackboard

But it is a very good thing if funds can be arranged for education. In this matter the whole House will give support and cooperation to the Human Resources Development Minister. But a time-bound programme is necessary for this. Operation Blackboard is being discussed a lot. 40 per cent schools do not have a blackboard. When will these blackboards come ? Is there any timebound programme for this ? How much will it cost ? I had hoped the Ministry would come up with some figures.

41.5 per cent primary schools do not have blackboards. 72 per cent schools do not have libraries and 53 per cent schools do not have playing grounds. 10 per cent villages do not have a school. Two-thirds population is illiterate.

Illiteracy and poverty have a deep connection. Through the 20-Point Programme the Prime Minister wants to strike at poverty. At the same time you will also have to strike at poverty. This document discusses a different type of schools for those children who are forced to work to maintain their poor families and cannot go to school in time. There will be a separate arrangement for them. What will be its form ? Who will bear that responsibility ? On what scale will funds be required for them ? I know everything cannot be done at one time. A time-bound programme will be required. I had hoped the House would be taken into confidence while it is discussing the subject.

There is one thing about Navodaya Schools. 75 per cent of the boys will be from rural areas. If the school is located in a backward area and if a district in that area contains two or three cities will the same condition still apply ? The children will be paid expenses. They will be provided with accommodation. The whole educational expense will be borne. In itself the plan is not bad, but I fear it will promote inequality.

Three-Language Formula

Secondly, this is being opposed on the ground of the three- language formula. I cannot understand this. Some people are in favour of Navodaya Schools because they will teach in three languages, while others are opposed to them for the same reason. Kalpanathji, you were not present here. There was a terrible speech here. It was said in the other House that Hindi has no grammar. The example given was that 'table' and 'chair' have the same gender. I do not want to go into that controversy, but this document does not lay down a clear policy even in respect of what the medium of instruction should be. The mother-tongue should be the medium of instruction, but what should it be where the mother-tongue and the official language are not the same ? There is a difficulty coming up in Assam. Sir, even you are connected with the border dispute between Maharashtra and Karnataka. This question has come to the fore. The mother-tongue should be the medium of instruction. The highest education should be given in the mother-tongue. But it cannot be denied that the Hindi region could not sincerely implement the three-language formula. How can we ask the people of the South to learn Hindi, speak Hindi ? If lakhs of people in the Hindi States became fluent in Tamil, Telugu, Malayalam and Kannada the opposition to Hindi will go down to some extent. But Navodaya Schools should not lead to these language quarrels. It is necessary to persuade those States to be with us. But the Central Government will have to think about the language problem keeping in mind those States where the mother-tongue and the official language are different.

Minorities' Rights

Thirdly, the Constitution has given the minorities the right to conduct and manage their own schools, but not the right to mismanage them. Do teachers in schools by minorities not have the right to demand proper salaries ? Should their conditions of service not be the same ? But teachers are removed from service, injustice is done to them, employees are dismissed and they cannot go to court because it is a minority institution. The minorities got their rights, but those rights should not be used to create a new inequality in the educational field. The Central Government will have to give serious thought to this matter. How ridiculous it is that in West Bengal schools run by the

Ramakrishna Mission had to go to Court and say they are minority institutions in order to preserve their autonomy ! Hindus have become a minority in this country. The Arya Samaj had to do the same thing in Punjab. How far will this dividing line go ? The right to mismanage should not be included in this. If necessary the Government could amend the Constitution, and I think the House will support you in this.

Uniformity of Syllabus

One more thing. A national syllabus is being discussed. Education is a concurrent subject. The States will chalk out their own education policy and also implement it, but somewhere there should be uniformity in the syllabus. But what is the form of that national syllabus ? How will it prove an effective instrument for the all-round development of personality ? No guidance for the future on this is provided in this document.

Finally, the focal point of education is the teacher.

"Shikshak aisa chahiye jo Shikshit hoi,
Janam janam ko morcha pal mein darey khoy."

Now we do not have such teachers, nor such disciples. But so long as we do not improve the condition of teachers, so long as we do not give them status in society the country cannot progress. These days teachers are going on strike. Delhi's teachers are fighting. The Chattopadhyaya Commission was set up, it made its recommendations, they were not implemented. The Pay Commission also thought about it, but gave nothing. Now teachers are on strike, students are wandering about the streets and members of Parliament are discussing a new education policy. Just now an MP from Bihar has given me a chit saying classes are held for hardly 60 days during the whole year. Schools are closed. Teachers have no interest. They are involved in their economic problems. If we put aside funds for education we should also improve the teachers' condition. We should place education on a high pedestal.

I agree there should be a general consensus among political parties on not making educational centres cockpits of politics. Bharatiya Janata Party is ready for this. Is the Congress also ready ?

SHRI KALPANATH RAI : Uttar Pradesh is.

SHRI VAJPAYEE : It is not.

SHRI KALPANATH RAI : It is quite ready.

SHRI VAJPAYEE : If you are, take the lead. Election to the Delhi University Union is about to take place. It is like the general elections. (*Interruptions*). We began later, you began first. The very first was the Communist Party. It began with the Students' Federation. (*Interruptions*) Listen to me. When I was a student I was connected with the Students' Federation. The Students' Congress came later. After that we set up Vidyarthi Parishad. But I say let us think about this matter afresh. If students and teachers are interested in politics they may take part in it, but there must be no distraction in education. Centres of education, temples of Goddess Saraswati, must not become dens of party politics. A national consensus will have to be developed for this. The

Prime Minister should take the lead in this. But the Prime Minister is unable to take the initiative in many matters.

An Hon'ble member had raised the question of reservations. It had become quite fierce in Gujarat at the time of elections. The Prime Minister had said we will arrive at a consensus after consulting all parties and then decide upon a policy. That consensus was not arrived at. Now there is a new controversy in Andhra Pradesh about reservations. There are some national issues on which there has to be a national consensus, otherwise the country will not be able to take the right decisions. In my opinion education is one such issue. Thank you.

XII LANGUAGE POLICY

People's Rule in People's Language

Sir, it is my misfortune that my mother-tongue is Hindi. Had I been born in some non-Hindi province it would have been better. For, then if I had said something in favour of Hindi it would have been given more weight.

The decision to adopt Hindi was not taken by those speaking Hindi alone. The voice of Hindi was first heard in non-Hindi provinces—Swami Dayanand, Mahatma Gandhi or the leaders of Bengal did not speak Hindi. Hindi became a programme of our struggle for independence, and it was included in the 14-point programme. In the first Draft of the Constitution it had been decided to give English a period of five years, but at the urging of Shri Gopalaswamy Iyengar, Shri Alladi Krishnaswamy Aiyar and Shri T.T. Krishnamachari the period was extended from five years to fifteen. Hindi numbers were internationalised, and instead of calling Hindi the national language it was called the official language. That time non-Hindi provinces did not oppose Hindi. The provisions in the Constitution were opposed either by Rajrishi Purushottam Das Tandon, who did not want English, or the late Maulana Azad, who wanted Hindustani in place of Hindi, but the South did not raise its voice against Hindi. But what did we do in 15 years ? Had we arranged for the teaching of Hindi, as the Constituent Assembly had decided and as was written down in the Constitution, the situation we see today would not have arisen. But the Centre could not introduce Hindi in Madras. The Government of Madras did not make Hindi compulsory. The compulsion was done away with. It was no more compulsory even to pass the examination. The teaching of Hindi thus became a joke.

Self-immolation in Madras Against Hindi

Two members of the South spoke. They say they are not against Hindi, the people of the South are learning Hindi. Let us be honest. How many people are learning Hindi and how many are learning English ? Is it not true that every year the number of students learning English is bigger and those learning Hindi smaller ? This proportion will always remain. Let us not delude ourselves. I am against forcing Hindi on any non-Hindi province. We are greatly grieved by what happened in Madras. Nothing can be more shameful than self-immolation against the country's language fifteen years after the establishment of democracy. The world is laughing at us. But I

Rajya Sabha on February 22, 1965 during discussion on the Government's Language Policy

would like to respect the feelings of those who immolated themselves. It is another matter that they died in opposition to Hindi although Hindi has not been forced on them.

In Madras Hindi will not be used for official purposes, Hindi will not be the medium of instruction. How many people join Central Services ? Even those have also burnt themselves to death who did not know English. How did they come to have love for English ? Surprisingly enough those who burnt themselves to death were found to be carrying notes saying they were immolating themselves in opposition to the imposition of Hindi. The whole body was charred but not the note. It was kept there later. Who incited people to commit suicide should be investigated. A DMK leader was with me on a visit to Viet Nam, where he saw Buddhists immolating themselves. It would not be surprising if he took inspiration from there and incited ingorant, innocent people to commit the heinous act of suicide.

English a Hindrance to Development of Indian Culture

We do not want Hindi to replace any regional language. So long as English continues Tamil will not develop, Bengali will not prosper. English is not only the enemy of Hindi, it is a hindrance in the development of every Indian language and in the development of our culture. But my saying so is not enough. If those speaking Tamil do not think their language will not get its due place if English continues, I cannot convince them. I have only one prayer to them—if you want to continue English, do so, continue English till eternity, but Rajaji went to the extent of saying that it should go on "Yavat chandra diwakar"—till the sun and the moon shine. English should continue till the waters of the Ganga and the Yamuna flow. But English is the sign of our slavery. We are not against English. English is a rich language. People should learn it. And why only English ? Let them learn French, German, Russian. Those of our students who go to these countries on scholarships acquire working knowledge of those languages in six months. So those who want to use English for official purposes, education etc. may do so, but they should accept Acharya Vinoba Bhave's third principle—English will not be forced on Hindi provinces.

How Long Will English Be Forced On Hindi Provinces ?

This agitation should make one thing clear, and I say to the Government : You may take any step you want to appease the non-Hindi people, but for God's sake stop the imposition of English on Hindi provinces. We do not want English in Hindi provinces. The Gujarat Government has arranged that English will be taught from the eighth standard. Then what business did the Central Education Minister have to go to Ahmedabad and tell them to teach English from the fifth standard, not the eighth ? If the Gujaratis do not want to learn English why should the Centre use force in its favour ? We do not want to impose Hindi but we will not allow English to be imposed. English will not continue in Hindi provinces. In official business, in education, in the university, in the railways, in posts and telegraphs, in the armed forces—

everywhere we shall remove English. Not because we hate English, but because if English continues democracy would become a joke, if English continues India will not make progress. The people's rule should go on in the people's language. English continues even in Uttar Pradesh, in Bihar, in Rajasthan because everybody looks to New Delhi, everybody takes inspiration from Delhi. If New Delhi cannot have Hindi in other provinces it will not have the right to have English in Hindi provinces.

I would like to make a suggestion. If our non-Hindi friends are not willing to accept Hindi as the link language their saying so only in Madras and New Delhi is not enough. Shri Atulya Babu may say in Parliament we have accepted Hindi and say in Bengal Hindi will not be imposed. Shri Kamraj may say in Raipur we should have Hindi but in a meeting of Syndicate members he would fan the flames of the anti-Hindi agitation. This double-talk must stop. Say honestly we shall not accept Hindi. Decide which language you accept. I call upon those who are non-Hindi speaking to hold a meeting and decide in it that Hindi will not be the link language, Hindi will not be the official language, we shall have the language we decide upon. If they all together decide upon a language, we Hindi-speaking people will show you that in 15 years we have learnt it and you may impose it on Hindi-speakers. But remove English. But they do not decide upon any language, they do not allow Hindi to function, and they want to impose English on us.

The Job-Language Relationship

I would like to give one more suggestion. It is said that the problem is about jobs. What will be the future of our children? English is used for the Union Public Commission. It had been recommended in the past that along with English the knowledge of Hindi and another regional language should be made compulsory for every candidate. Hindi States do not yet have the three-language formula. They should do so. But so long as a South Indian language is not necessary for a job no one will learn it. A candidate for a Union Public Service Commission must compulsorily know an Indian language in addition to his mother-tongue. The non-Hindi people may dicide what language other than Hindi it should be. We will accept if they choose Urdu. We will accept if they decide upon Punjabi. But let them decide upon a language and make it compulsory for boys from the Hindi States. If they want the jobs they will learn it, but jobs cannot be allowed to stop the country's cultural development. How many people join the Central services ? If necessary fix a quota of jobs in proportion to the population. If you want it, deny jobs in the Central services to Hindi people for ten years.

We shall persuade the Hindi people. But 'heads I win, tails you lose' won't do. It is not good to create an atmosphere endangering national unity for the sake of jobs. So we will have to look at this problem on a higher level. How much effort, time and money are spent on learning English ? My friend Shri Govind Reddy said the standard of English is falling. This is because the atmosphere has changed. Children start primary and secondary education in their mother-tongue and then English is imposed upon them. This is happening not only in Hindi States but also in non-Hindi ones. Tamil did not get the place in Madras that it should have, nor Bengali in Bengal. Not because Hindi has become the official language, but because English still dominates there. Only two per cent people know English. Will they for ever rule over the 98 per cent who do not know English ? Two per cent are the high caste people and they want to exploit the 98 per cent.

The decision to bring Indian languages is a revolutionary decision, but if it endangers the nation's unity the non-Hindi States may continue English, but we shall not let it continue in Patna, in Jaipur, in Lucknow.

SHRI N.M. ANWAR : But let it continue in Delhi. Delhi belongs to all.

SHRI VAJPAYEE : About Delhi let me say one thing. The Hindi that is the official language was born in Delhi itself.

SHRI N.M. ANWAR : Let it be.

SHRI VAJPAYEE : Hindi is not my mother tongue. At home I speak Brij. Some speak Maithili, some Bhojpuri....

SHRI N.M. ANWAR : Some Urdu.

SHRI VAJPAYEE : ....We left our dialect and adopted Hindi. Now you are asking us to leave that too. In what language should the administration of Delhi be conducted ? In the language of the people of Delhi, of course. The Chief Commissioner of Delhi says Delhi is Union Territory, so the Union's language policy will apply to it.

SHRI N.M. ANWAR : The Union belongs to all. It belongs to the people of all languages.

SHRI BHUPESH GUPTA : Tripura also has Hindi.

SHRI VAJPAYEE : This means the administration of Delhi should be conducted in the regional language. What is the regional language of Delhi ? It is Hindi.

AN HON. MEMBER : Punjabi.

SHRI VAJPAYEE : No objection, if Punjabi goes on along with Punjabi. Urdu too. But not English....

SHRI N.M. ANWAR : English too.

SHRI VAJPAYEE : ....The Home Ministry should give a clear directive in this respect. You may continue English in the Central Government but English will not be allowed in the Delhi Administration.

I do not want to threaten, but if there can be an agitation in Madras passions can be incited at other places too. Do not test our patriotism. We want the nation's unity. Those who want to preserve it through English do not understand the meaning of national unity. Real national unity will come about when Indian languages attain their due place. And if Indian languages get their due position at every place there will be no difference of opinion on the link language. As yet we do not have Tamil in Madras, we do not have Bengali in Bengal, so it is possible to incite the people there against Hindi. Once the common man there realises that two per cent English-knowing people are raising anti-Hindi slogans in order to keep them slaves, English won't remain. English won't go from New Delhi. If English has to go it will go from Madras, it will go from Bengal. Now the clock will have to be turned the other way. Hindi provinces have to do the full job. I hope Maharashtra also, Gujarat also will cooperate in not letting English continue. Thank You.

Justice to Sindhi Welcome

Sir, I stand to support and welcome this Bill. Even if after a long delay, we are now correcting the continuing injustice to the Sindhi language.

Sindhi is one of our national languages. India's soul speaks through Sindhi. The protection and development of Sindhi is a part of the protection and development of our country's cultural development. The question is, why could Sindhi not get its due place for twenty years of independence ? When I was first elected to this House in 1957 I had tabled a non-official Bill demanding that Sindhi be included in the Eighth Schedule. But at that time this demand was not accepted. At other places too I had raised this demand, but perhaps Sindhi's star had not then risen. I am happy that it has risen today.

I would say it is not enough to give the Sindhi language a place in the Constitution. That place should be given and it is being given. But Sindhi has no territory of its own. It will not be the official language of any province. From this point of view Sindhi is a refugee. It is necessary to give it official patronage. And as Sindhi is not the language of any one State we would have to make it the language of the whole country.

SHRI S.N. DWIVEDI (Kendrapara) : It should be made the link language.

SHRI VAJPAYEE . The Central Government will have to be particular about discharging its responsibility in this matter. The Central Government will have to arrange that Sindhi literature develops, Sindhi newspapers get an adequate share of advertising and Sindhi men of letters are honoured by the administration. Those States where Sindhi-speaking people have settled down in large numbers will also have to do justice by Sindhi. Where Sindhi can rightfully find a place in the educational system that place should be given to it. The Information Ministry should also use Sindhi for broadcasts not only in India but also in order to reach across the border. Today the feelings of the Sindhi people are being fulfilled. It is a matter of happiness. Our feelings too are being fulfilled. I speak Hindi. But Sindhi is my *'Mousi'* (aunt) and I respect Sindhi as much as Hindi. All Indian languages are sisters, and we want that they should all develop. From that point of view this Bill is welcome. I congratulate the Hon. Minister. Perhaps this thing was not done so long because it was waiting to be done by him. Thank you.

Lok Sabha on April 7, 1967 during discussion on the Constitution (Twenty-First Amendment) Bill seeking inclusion of Sindhi in the Eighth Schedule to the Constitution

Hindi Should Be Centre's Language

Sir, I was reminded of the England of 1650 as I listened to Shri Frank Anthony. Two languages were current in England in those days — French and Latin. All laws were made in French and all higher education was in Latin. The arguments that were then put forward for continuing French and Latin and for not allowing English to be brought in are the same that are being given today for continuing English in India.

Sir, what is surprising is that in 1650 those who opposed English in England were doctors, lawyers, intellectuals and those who had a vested interest in French and Latin. They had once called English a 'barrack language.' With great difficulty I have found a book titled, *'Triumphs of the English Language'* and brought with me. Its author is one Mr. Jones. This book is not available in our library.

AN HON. MEMBER : Where did you get it ?

SHRI VAJPAYEE : I got it from the British High Commission's library. Through you I would like to place a portion from it before the House. In 1650 a petition had been presented to the British Parliament. I will read out what the petition said :

> "That considering it a Badge of our slavery to a Norman conqueror, to have our Laws in the French tongue, and it is little less than brutish vassalage to be bound to walk by laws which the people cannot know, that therefore all the laws and Customs of this Realm be immediately written in our mother-tongue without any abbreviation of words."

The House should also take note of the decision that the British Parliament took in the matter. This decision is dated November 22, 1650.

> "Parliament thinks it fit to declare and enact and the present Parliament hereby declares and enacts in its right that all report books and judicial verdicts and laws of the realm be translated in the English language : And after January 1, 1651 all reports of court verdicts and all other books of law to be published will be in English."

In England too they had to fight for the introduction of English.

SHRI MANOHARAN : That is a unitary state. We have a federal structure.

SHRI VAJPAYEE : I shall discuss that too.

In England too it was argued that if doctors studied in English patients would die, English is not fit to become a medium for law and education. But the people of England proudly decided to introduce English, and they developed it so much that we have fallen in love with it, and we do not want to give it up. My mother-tongue is Hindi.

Lok Sabha on December 12, 1967 on the occasion of amendment bill and resolution on official language

SHRI N. SRIKANTAN NAIR : Mine is not.

SHRI VAJPAYEE : Sometimes I think it is my misfortune. Because Hindi is my mother-tongue I have to listen to things that I would not dream of saying to people speaking other languages. It was not Hindi people who decided to make Hindi the Centre's official language. We were not there in the Constituent Assembly. The high place that was accorded to Hindi in the Constituent Assembly before it became the official language was given to it by non-Hindi people. The Constituent Assembly just put its stamp of approval on it. This Parliament may change the Constitution if it wants to. If Parliament wants to make all Indian languages the languages of the Centre we shall not oppose it, rather we shall welcome it.

Hindi has no quarrel with any Indian language. It wants to see all Indian languages developed. But it was the Constituent Assembly's decision that Hindi should be the Centre's language. At the time of that decision the Draft Constitution had proposed only five years for the use of English. Later the period was extended to fifteen years in view of the difficulty for non-Hindi people.

SHRI J.B. KRIPALANI : That was the stupidity.

SHRI VAJPAYEE : Acharyaji is right. That was a mistake. Some people are of the opinion—and there may be truth in it—that if English was to go it should have gone at one stroke. Removing English gradually is difficult. But in view of the people's difficulties it was decided to continue it for fifteen years.

Our Southern friends were not dissatisfied with this decision. The period of fifteen years was satisfactory for Shri Alladi Krishnaswamy Ayer, Shri Gopalaswamy Iyengar and Shri T.T. Krishnamachari. If anybody was dissatisfied with the constitutional provision it was not the non-Hindi people, but Rajrishi Purushottam Das Tandon, who did not want international numerals, or Maulana Azad, who wanted Hindustani instead of Hindi. But people speaking non-Hindi languages or Southern languages were not dissatisfied.

Constituent Assembly's Intention

As Chairman of the Constituent Assembly Dr. Rajendra Prasad has said we have taken a delicate decision about language. We will have to implement it from year to year, month to month, week to week and minute to minute. But the Central Government thought—or those in the Central Government who had the power to implement the language policy thought—that a change may be attempted after fourteen years and eleven months had passed. When 1965 dawned the country reached the conclusion that English cannot yet be removed and arrangements need to be made to continue it still further.

A law was made in 1963. The assurances of Pandit Nehru that are mentioned were given by him in reply to a non-official resolution of Shri Frank Anthony in August-September 1959. I would like to place those assurances before you, as they are discussed a lot. But the time has also come to understand what those assurances really were. Pandit Nehru had said :

"English will continue as an associate language and I would not take it away till I was asked to take it away by the non-Hindi speaking areas."

SHRI NAMBIAR : Non-Hindi speaking areas do not want it to be taken away now. We will tell you when we are ready; don't be in a hurry.

SHRI VAJPAYEE : The assurance was that English will continue along with Hindi. The assurance was not that only English will continue. Is English continuing today along with Hindi ? English continues today, not Hindi. And after this Bill Hindi will fall into still greater disuse.

The President had issued some directives about the use of Hindi, one of which was that Hindi would be the medium for Union Public Service Commission examinations. This should have been done after 1965. Why did it not take place ? We want that along with Hindi other Indian languages should also become the medium of instruction and such a demand has been made. In 1954 the Congress Working Committee had passed a resolution saying that along with Hindi other Indian languages should also be the medium of examinations for Central Services. In 1960 the Home Ministry also issued a directive like that, but Indian languages were not made the medium of examination.

Why This Bill ?

Why was it necessary to bring forward this Bill ? This Bill is unnecessary. This Bill is unconstitutional. This Bill is being introduced with the intention of keeping English as the official language of India till eternity. If this Bill is passed it will block the way of progress of Indian languages. I have just said that Pandit Nehru's assurances were fulfilled in 1963. Then why was it necessary to introduce this Bill ? It is said that Shri Shastri had also given some assurances. What were they ? Why was it necessary to give them ? English is being used after 1963. In the Act of 1963 there is no time limit for the use of English. It can continue as long as we want it. There is no restraint on the use of English. That was Pandit Nehru's assurance. That was Shri Shastri's assurance. Then why was it necessary to introduce this Bill ? Sir, you can see that the DMK is not satisfied with this Bill. Even my friend Shri Frank Anthony is not satisfied. The Marxist Communists are also not satisfied. So far as we people are concerned we are not at all satisfied with this Bill....

SHRI MANOHARAN : Because assurances have been completely diluted, we are not satisfied.

SHRI NAMBIAR : We can take it as a compromise Bill. The Marxist Communists are prepared to take this Bill without any dilution as a compromise Bill. Anything diluted we do not accept.

SHRI VAJPAYEE : I do not know. Just now we heard Shri Ramamurthi. I do not know whether the Marxist Communists are going to speak in two voices.

Sir, I can understand the position of the DMK. Their field of activity is limited to Madras. And what they say in Madras they say also in New Delhi. They say what they mean. I can appreciate their feelings too. But I have a complaint about other all-India parties. I was very much grieved to listen to the speech of Praja Socialist Party leader Shri Surendra Nath Dwivedi.

SHRI MANOHARAN : Is it a crime that he spoke in Hindi ?

SHRI VAJPAYEE : He is my elder. He spoke in Hindi. He is older than I am. He is more experienced. He also said some amendments are necessary in this Bill. But the tone of his speech was such as to strike at the Hindi-speaking people. We never opposed Oriya. We never opposed Tamil. Our DMK friends called All India Radio Vanoli. They translated Satyameva Jayate into Tamil. We did not criticise it. If Tamil replaces English we will welcome that. On the other hand if Hindi replaces English they too should welcome that. I do not know Tamil but I love it and I hope they will also have the same love for other Indian languages.

Hindi Not Given Equal Status

Sir, it would be wrong to think that this Bill seeks to give equal status to Hindi and English. Say honestly that there will be bilingualism in this country. Everybody agrees that gradually the use of Hindi should grow, and everyone will agree that in the present conditions in the country there should honestly be bilingualism between Hindi and English. Does this Bill provide for that ? It does not give equal status to Hindi. Rather it has been given a lower position. This is not an honest Central bilingual policy. This is not a compromise. This is a surrender before the Anglophils. We are ready for a compromise. We know that the country's unity is the bigger thing and language is its instrument. We would not want to do anything that would jeopardise the country's unity. But providing for the use of English for all time to come is not the way to save the country's unity.

SHRI PILOO MODY : Then what is the way ?

SHRI VAJPAYEE : I'll show.

Sir, no one can deny and Acharya Kripalani also said that the British used Hindi in the armed forces. The army has people from all the States, all places, but Hindi was used there. In 1947 Indian languages were used right up to the High Court in Madhya Bharat, Rajasthan and even in Hyderabad. I come from Madhya Bharat. The Madhya Bharat High Court used to deliver its judgements in Hindi. In Hyderabad Urdu was used. After 1947, after independence, English was introduced there. Hindi had to take the back seat. Even when the Constitution was made attempts were made to continue English. In 1963 a Bill was introduced to continue English still further. And now in 1967 there is again a Bill in support of English and we are told—we are told every time—that now Hindi will come forward, now hindrance in the way of Hindi will be removed, now there will be no restraint on Hindi.

Sir, I am connected with the Party that has all along said we should do away with English once for all. We should use Indian languages. But we are willing to compromise on the question of language. We want to establish a national consensus. We want that a formula that would satisfy all regions should be evolved. I would like to assure my non-Hindi friends with all force at my command that we do not want to force Hindi on them. But they should not force English on us. They may use English, and those who want to use Hindi should have the freedom to do so. This Bill does not provide for that. It does not give equal status to Hindi and English. It hinders working in both languages. It gives prominence to English. It gives a lower position to Hindi.

Sir, when the British occupied Delhi they gave currency to a slogan—"*khalk khuda ka, mulk Badshah ka, aur hakumat Angrez Bahadur ki.*" If this Bill is passed in this form what will be the consequence ? There rule will be that of the people, Hindi will be the official language, but it will be English that will be in use. Hindi in name, English in reality. I do not know what amendments the Home Minister proposes to bring up in this Bill. If any amendments are to come up the House should be quickly taken into confidence. We would be willing to accept this amendment if it would bring accord between both the languages, both the points of view. The first thing is that if Hindi is used its translation in English should not be required. Either we use both languages for all work, we also do in English what we do in Hindi and vice versa, or we give employees the freedom to work either in English or in Hindi. What does this Bill provide ? If you use Hindi for work you will be asked to supply an English translation. Then will it be a penalty to work in Hindi ? Will double the time have to put in if work is done in Hindi ?

SHRI NAMBIAR : Because we do not know Hindi. So we want a translation. Why can't you tolerate that much ? We do not know your blessed Hindi....

SHRI VAJPAYEE : You could not tolerate even my speaking ? I am not yielding. Please sit down.

SHRI NAMBIAR : He wants tolerance from us. Yet he is against giving even the English translation....

MR. SPEAKER : I would request Shri Nambiar to resume his seat.

SHRI V. KRISHNAMOORTHY : He is not yielding even for interruption and yet he speakes of tolerance to the non-Hindi speaking people....

They would not allow us ....

SHRI NAMBIAR : If they do not allow, we have a right to live in India and we live despite their nepotism.

MR. SPEAKER : Order, Order.

SHRI VAJPAYEE : Sir, let not my friend Shri Nambiar be annoyed. Who is challenging their right to live in India ? If he has to put a question I shall wind up and then he may ask. When their leader Shri Ramamurthi was speaking, we did not interrupt him, nobody interrupted him.

SHRI NAMBIAR : I put a very simple question. I did not heckle him. I am not in that habit.

SHRI VAJPAYEE : Sir, I request you not to include this time in my time.

I have already said that those who do not know Hindi and want to work in English may do so. But those who want to work in Hindi should not be compulsorily required to furnish an English translation. Both languages should be equal. How can this be opposed ? Secondly, how and where will the translation be arranged ? Government servants are being taught Hindi since Hindi was decided upon as the Centre's language. Lakhs of employees have learnt Hindi, many knew Hindi already. Some non-Hindi employees are also issuing orders in Hindi and I have their names and copies of those orders. I do not want to take the time of the House by reading them out. Now if there has to be a translation it should be done, if necessary, where the letter goes. If there are people who know Hindi where the letter goes the translation may not be required at all. But if there are people working in English they should have full freedom to do so. Is the Government going to accept an amendment that the translation should be arranged at the destination of the letter and working in both languages should be allowed ?

Why Knowledge of English Compulsory for Job ?

Sir, the second point is that the proposed Bill makes knowledge of English compulsory for a job, but not knowledge of Hindi. We do not want Hindi to be compulsory nor English to be compulsory. Actually all Indian languages should be the medium of examination, and if the Central Government has not made such arrangements it is responsible for promoting envy and hatred among Indian languages. At least there should be no delay in making all Indian languages the medium of examination. But so long as that is not done the arrangement should be such that the option of using Hindi or English as the medium should be left to the candidate.

SHRI PILOO MODY : What about English ?

SHRI VAJPAYEE : You do not understand, you do not listen.

SHRI PILOO MODY : I am trying, my friend.

SHRI VAJPAYEE : If you try you will understand.

One more thing that needs to be done is that every year a report on how much progress has been achieved in respect of Hindi should be placed before the House. The country should be informed about it. Sir, what is the position today ? In 1967 we are facing a new India. Crores of youth have appeared on the national scene after getting education in their mother-tongue. Crores of people have acquired the right to vote, have realised its importance. Due to industrialisation people are coming into cities from the villages. We will have to take these changed circumstances in India into consideration while deciding about the official language. Today students of the Hindi region are upset. It would be wrong to think that somebody has incited them. They are upset because they think their future is dark. They are taking education in their mother-tongue. In those regions English has been made an optional language. Now if English is made compulsory for Central examinations it would be impossible for them to pass. For them this has become the question of their future. The House should identify itself with their feelings and then look at this problem.

I would also like to say this about the non-Hindi regions—if Tamil is used in Madras, Marathi is used for administration in Bombay, if Bengali is the medium of instruction and administration in Calcutta will English keep hanging on in New Delhi like Trisanku ? If Indian languages make progress, if Indian languages are used for official purposes, we will have to decide upon some language or the other for contact purposes in New Delhi. There is no question of imposing that language, it is developing on its own. it will take its place on its own.

Sir, I submit that this Bill is against the Constitution. My friend Shri Manoharan said just now that ours is a federation, not a unitary State. I agree with him. Our is a federal Government, not unitary, but the Constitution has made a distinction between the powers of the Centre and the States. There are some matters in which the Centre and the States can jointly pass laws. But there are some matters in which the Centre has supreme power and there are others in which the State has the final say. The matter of the official language falls within the parameter of the Centre. It is the Centre that has to decide the official language, and if the States are to be made a party to this decision that is not possible with the present form of the Government.

I remember Pandit Nehru was speaking after Shri Frank Anthony's speech. When Shri Anthony interrupted him and asked, does this Bill have any assurance for the non-Hindi people ? When he added there was no guarantee Pandit Nehru got annoyed ....

SHRI S.M. BANERJI : He said sit down.

SHRI VAJPAYEE : Pandit Nehru did not use such language even when angry. I would like to read out a portion of the Parliament's proceedings of April 24, 1963. It is in English, so please excuse me.

> "SHRI FRANK ANTHONY : May I know — I am not questioning the motives of the Prime Minister—how the Bill reflects his assurance ? How are the non-Hindi speaking people going to be consulted ?
>
> SHRI JAWAHARLAL NEHRU : I do not see how this Bill was going to say anything about the consultation of non-Hindi speaking people.
>
> SHRI FRANK ANTHONY : Why not ?
>
> SHRI JAWAHARLAL NEHRU : I say, according to my thinking, it is quite absurd and unconstitutional."

When Parliament decides about the Centre's official languages it may keep in mind all Indian languages and the people speaking them, but Parliament cannot leave this decision to the States.

Why is Centre Lame in Respect of Hindi ?

Sir, is it not surprising that Parliament can change the borders of any State if it wants, it can restrict or expand the borders of any State if it wants, it can change the name of any State if it wants. It may consult the State Legislative Assembly, but it need not accept the opinion. But this Bill provides that if even one State says that the Centre should use English the Centre will have to do so. This Parliament cannot abdicate its powers in favour of somebody else. Just one single State cannot be given the veto in respect of the Centre's official language.

One more thing. So far as the powers of the Lok Sabha and Rajya Sabha are concerned this Bill diminishes the Lok Sabha's powers. We may take any decision about the official language, we may take it with a majority, then that decision will go to the Rajya Sabha for approval. The Rajya Sabha may approve it or reject it. Then the Constitution provides for a joint sitting, where the final decision will be taken with a simple majority. But this Bill says, ask all State Legislative Assemblies and then get it passed by the Rajya Sabha too. I do not think the House can accept this. This is not a question of language alone. It is also a question of the Centre's authority and the House's supremacy. The Central Government should think about this.

Whatever my friends from Madras may say I have no hesitation in saying that Mysore, Andhra and Kerala are not opposed to Hindi. The other day Shri Nijalingappa said in his speech that Hindi was being taught there.

SHRI N. SREEKANTAN NAIR : Who told you ? I come from that State.

SHRI NAMBIAR : Are we to believe the Member from Kerala, or the Member from U.P. ? About Kerala, I think Mr. Sreekantan Nair can speak better than the Hon. member.

SHRI VAJPAYEE : Arrangements to teach Hindi are being made in Kerala, Andhra and Mysore. Madras is the only State where the all-India decision on language has not been accepted. Our friends from Tamil Nadu say they will propagate Hindi voluntarily. I agree with them. Whenever anything is imposed it is opposed. But the Constituent Assembly's decision was not an imposition. If we decide something and if we accept that decision and act according to it can it be called imposition ?

I agree that Hindi should not be forcibly propagated. But I have a letter that tells a very sorry tale. It is from Shri M.K. Ramakrishnan, Hindi teacher, Tagore Memorial Hindi School, Madurai.

SHRI MANOHARAN : I can produce a lot of letters like this.

SHRI VAJPAYEE : There are ten Hindi schools in Madurai. They are connected with the Dakshin Bharat Hindi Prachar Sabha. They teach Hindi and conduct examinations in Hindi. But the students and teachers are greatly upset these days. They have sent a telegram to the President and the Prime Minister. I quote a portion of that telegram :

> "Our institution is spreading Hindi for the last 20 years purely on a voluntary basis. We are preparing them for the various examinations conducted by the Dakshin Bharat Hindi Prachar Sabha, Madras. At present there are about 100 students in our institution, both boys and girls.
>
> "We hope you are aware that the Madras State Anti-Hindi Council suddenly gave an intimation that Hindi Prachar Sabha must be closed down and no theatre should screen Hindi films. Later, on the advice of our Chief Minister, Thiru C.N. Annadurai, they withdrew that."

SHRI SEZHIYAN : Mr. Annadurai is very tolerant. Is there one Tamil Prachar Sabha in U.P. ? Is there one Malayalam Prachar Sabha in M.P. ? You do not worry about any other language.

MR. SPEAKER : Please wind up now.

SHRI VAJPAYEE : I would like to quote one more portion.

> "But now at Madurai, some students have formed as members into an association and on 15.10.1967 they went in a group and forcibly got letters from some Theatre proprietors promising they would not screen any Hindi film."

The letter adds that those who are trying to propagate Hindi voluntarily are being hindered.

SHRI AMBAZHAGAN : It is also a voluntary objection.

SHRI VAJPAYEE : I say if we really mean to bring Hindi to the Centre it is not necessary to pass such a Bill. With such a Bill Hindi will go backward and the supremacy of English will continue. So I demand the recall of this Bill.

The Prime Minister says that this Bill is a compromise from both points of view. I have just said it is not a compromise. It is a surrender to English, it is an attempt to continue English for ever. We shall not be a party to this attempt. We are ready for a compromise. We are willing to give up the demand for the immediate removal of English. We want equal status for Hindi and English. We want full freedom for employees knowing Hindi and English to work in that language. A letter should be translated at the destination. There should be no restraint on the use of Hindi among Central Ministries and within the Secretariats. Then we are ready to withdraw our opposition. We are ready for a compromise. Whether other people are ready for it or not they should show it by their behaviour by amending this Bill.

Prime Minister Intervenes

SMT. INDIRA GANDHI, Prime Minister : Sir, I will not take much time of the House. I would like to say only a few words.

After religion language is one thing that excites the feelings of loyalty and passion. We saw a lot of passion in the House, and even outside the House we saw many activities that may be called passion. As Shri Vajpayee said, it is possible that students are worried about their livelihood.

But the question is, what is the purpose of language ? Many members said —yesterday I listened to many speeches—that it is for communication, for understanding each other, for our daily work, for increasing our knowledge, for bringing people together....

SHRI J.B. KRIPALANI : Also for fighting.

SMT. INDIRA GANDHI : All these are the functions of language. It is also meant for equally sharing with people the treasure house of thought. But what do we see today ? Language is becoming a barrier between one man and another. As Acharya Kripalani said, it has become the medium of fighting. This is a sad state of affairs. Language blends science with thought —or it should—and so it should bring about unity. The question before us is how to demolish the barriers that exist.

SHRI PILOO MODY : By moratorium.

SMT. INDIRA GANDHI : Whether a moratorium will break down barriers or strengthen them is a point for consideration. I agree that this will not stop what is happening outside, rather it will increase it. When we take up something it is good to finish it then and there. If we drag on something it can have the opposite result.

I would like to ask a question—in what country was language the product of politics ? English is a big language, it has spread to many countries and it has reached a high level. Was it made by Whitehall missiles ? Or was it strengthened by English poets, writers, dramatists and even traders who moved all over the world ? Let us not think that language is made or it grows because of Government work and without it it will be finished. The official languages in our country were suppressed, so it was natural that during the freedom struggle and even after independence people should have special feelings about them and they should want to develop them. It is not the question of a feeling alone, though I agree that too is important for the country. Our friend Shri Mody says poverty is being increased. It is not a question of increasing it. The question is that because of poverty and backwardness many people did not get opportunities in education, in jobs and in many other things that a few of us got. I know these people can be educated only in their mother-tongue. And hence it is necessary that in all States education should be given in the mother-tongue and the classes that were so long suppressed should be given the opportunity to acquire education, to have a place in the sun, and to benefit from the development of the country.

But how did Hindi come in ? In some countries like Belgium two languages are in use. In Switzerland and Yugoslavia there are three or four languages. We have fifteen. And that is not surprising, as our country is that much bigger. We are earnestly striving for the development of all these languages. People there should get education in them, and official business should also be conducted in them.

I know everyone is agreed on this. But the Centre cannot conduct its business in 15 languages, however dear they may be to us. Even if we respect every language it is not possible to work in so many languages. So it was thought that one language should become the national link and Hindi was selected as that language. Now I know this certainly creates a difficulty for those whose mother-tongue is not Hindi. Some friends from the South say Hindi is not a developed language. But how will it develop so long as people do not speak it, learn it, do not take it forward ? So we were telling them to help us in that too. A language can make progress only through its use. But I would say to my other friends—use not only in Government offices but outside too. More people should learn it, and books should be translated into it. Why are we apart from the rest of the world and why were we completely so before independence ? It was because we were completely in the dark about what was happening in the rest of the world and about new thinking, whether it was science or technology. So long as we remain cut off like this we cannot develop our language however hard we may try. The States have separate regional languages and there will be a separate link language or central language.

Three Reforms Necessary in Language Policy

There is certainly some inequality because of this. We must accept it. So I would like to know if the Hon. Minister would make three reforms in his Bill so that this complaint is largely removed. First I would say neither the knowledge of Hindi nor that of English should be compulsory for a candidate appearing for an examination. Secondly, when you are going to conduct examinations in the languages that are contained in the Eighth Schedule why did you provide for English here ? And thirdly, if there are doubts about jobs can the Hon. member think of quotas too ? Statewise .... (*Interruptions*) .... they are laughing today, but I can say with all force at my command that in order to remove people's doubts you will have to finally do so for some time. Then is the Hon. Minister willing to make three reforms in this resolution.

SHRI VAJPAYEE : Sir, the original resolution said that knowledge of Hindi will not be essential. Now an amendment has been brought in—which the Home Minister is willing to accept—that knowledge of Hindi or English will not be compulsory. Knowledge of either would be enough. My submission is, if all regional languages are being made the medium of examination is it not possible for us to arrange that the candidate should write his paper in his mother-tongue, but after selection he must acquire knowledge of Hindi and English before appointment ? ....(*Interruptions*).... Why are you making a din ? Be quiet and listen. ....(*Interruptions*).... Sir, should I speak or not ? I shall sit down if you say so. I shall sit down if they do not want to listen.

The Home Minister said if the three-language formula did not work well he may have to think about making one other Indian language compulsory for Hindi-speaking candidates. In this connection I would like to remind him that when a Parliamentary Committee was set up with Rajrishi Tandon and Seth Govind Das as members they had said that if the burden is to be equalised candidates from the Hindi-speaking region could have a compulsory paper in another Indian language, they would not oppose any such arrangement. We do not have more facilities as compared to our friends from the South, but when Indian languages are going to become the medium of instruction is prior knowledge of English or Hindi necessary ? Can we not arrange that after selection and before appointment the candidate may learn either Hindi or English as per his choice ? Thank you.

Indian Languages in Technical Fields

Mr. Speaker, Sir, with your permission, I rise to raise a matter of urgent public importance. The Government is openly violating the resolutions passed by Parliament. Even the directives issued by the President are not being followed. So much so that when my friend Shri Sharad Yadav raised the question of making Indian languages as the medium of examinations held by the Union Public Service Commission on December 13, 1993 in the House, even you had intervened and observed that "Both the Houses have passed the Resolution; it means that the entire Parliament has passed the Resolution." And you had expressed the desire that it should be followed. Shri Vidyacharan Shukla was speaking on that day and he had also assured that the directives would be followed. I want to quote him :

> "There are Resolutions of both the Houses of Parliament which have been accepted by the Government. There is a Presidential directive also on this matter."

Then he said that he would call the meeting of the Leaders and shall take a decision about it. This matter has been pending for years. Why should the Indian languages not be made the medium of examinations held by the Union Public Service Commission ? Could we not teach subjects like Medicine, Engineering etc. through the medium of Indian languages ? Could answer papers in Indian languages not be correctly evaluated ? If the Government needed preparations in this regard, then how much time, how many years do they require ?

Mr. Speaker, Sir, I want that this matter should be taken up seriously. The question whether English should be compulsory is also connected with it. Somebody could say that there is need to retain English in the country. However, need and compulsion are different things. They should be separated from each other. Today, Indian languages are not the medium of all the examinations resulting in wastage of several geniuses. Many youths cannot participate in the administration because they do not know English.

We are trying to ensure participation of backward classes in the administration, but English is causing hindrance in it. We are not against English. Those who want to read English in this country, let them do so. Its use is permissible in the administration as a link language. But it is not fair to make it compulsory. This was not the intention of the framers of the Constitution.

Mr. Speaker, Sir, I will like you to intervene in the matter and ask the Government to give a straightforward answer.

Lok Sabha on May 12, 1994 regarding making Indian languages as the medium of Examinations held by the Union Public Service Commission

MR. SPEAKER : I will allow one or two members to speak. (*Interruptions*) Very briefly you can mention, please.

SHRI VIDYACHARAN SHUKLA, Minister of Water Resources and Minister of Parliamentary Affairs : First of all, I would like to make a small correction in what the Hon. Leader of the Opposition has said. He said that in the UPSC we are not using Indian languages as the medium of examination, which is not correct, we are using all the Indian languages as the medium of examination in UPSC already.

SHRI VAJPAYEE : It is not so for engineering, or medicine; that is the problem.

SHRI VIDYACHARAN SHUKLA : Please listen to me.

SHRI VAJPAYEE : Sir, I will never misinform the House. I have never done it.

SHRI VIDYACHARAN SHUKLA : I am only giving my information, as I have. May be, if I have to correct myself, I will do so later.

MR. SPEAKER : Shri Vajpayee is asking about engineering and medicine. (*Interruptions*). All Right. We will find out.

SHRI VIDYACHARAN SHUKLA : I will correct it myself.

SHRI L.K. ADVANI (Gandhinagar) : Mr. Speaker, Sir, perhaps the House may not be aware that a similar situation was prevailing in England where Engineering and Medicine were not allowed to be taught through English medium and there were political devotees who insisted on bringing English, which brought about the present situation.

SHRI VIDYACHARAN SHUKLA : We all know that in Britain also in the beginning for several centuries the French language was being used, not English, because of the colonial rule of the French over that country. We all know it. It is not unknown to us.

MR. SPEAKER : Please hear little carefully what he is saying.

XIII SOCIAL PROBLEMS

Social Reform by Law

MR. DEPUTY SPEAKER : Motion moved.

"That the Bill to provide for the Restraint on *Sanyas Diksha* of a child be taken into consideration."

SHRI VAJPAYEE : Sir, I submit this Bill is against articles 25 and 28 of the Constitution. According to article 25 all citizens have equal right to freedom of thought and religious belief and of practice and propagation of religion. This Bill provides for prevention of initiation of minors into *Sanyas.*

The mover has admitted that this system prevails among Jains and Buddhists. It has become an inseparable part of these sects. Whether it is good or bad, whether it should continue or not is another matter, and there could be a difference of opinion on it. But this practice has prevailed for centuries in Jain and Buddhist sects which are parts of the big family of the Hindu religion. But this Government which claims to be secular and this House which is bound by Fundamental Rights accepted by the Constitution cannot claim the right to make a law that strikes at these integral practices of the Buddhist and Jain sects.

Not Within Parliament's Power

Sir, this Bill covers a wide area. Explaining the definition of *sanyas* given in the Bill the mover said every *Sanyasi, Yati, Muni,* Suri, Yogi, Bairagi, Mahant, Chela and *Brahmachari* is covered by it. A *Brahmachari* has also been included in the Bill. I submit—the mover has agreed—that *Brahmacharya* (celibacy) is the first *Ashram* (stage) of our *Ashram* system. And obviously if anyone is to be made a *Brahmachari* that is possible only when he is unmarried. Only a boy can be a *Brahmachari,* not an old man. A *Brahmachari* can be an unmarried man, not a married person or a widower. Now if a boy below 18 is prevented from getting initiated into *Brahmacharya* it would be against the rites enjoined in the *Ashram* system. If any individual below 18 wants to be initiated into *Brahmacharya,* if he wants to centralise his physical properties, if he wants to leave home according to ancient times and devote himself to the pursuit of knowledge it would be an offence under this Bill. It is not within the powers of this House to make such an arrangement.

Lok Sabha on April 3, 1959 during discussion on a Private Member's Bill seeking restraint on Child Sanyas

Secondly, Hindu *Dharma* (religion) believes in *Karma* (action), in its fruit, in re-birth. At least in our country it is not unnatural to believe that due to merit acquired in previous births a person may turn away from materialism and lean towards spirituality from childhood. There are examples of many great men who renounced the world at a young age and accepted a spiritual bond. They have the right, they have the freedom to break their bond with the world and relate to God from their very childhood. This Bill strikes at the individual freedom of persons who have a leaning towards such natural spirituality. The House has no power to do so.

Spirit of Constitutional Provision

One more and final point. The question is, is no decision to be taken about those who are minor ? I say the fathers of the Constitution had given full thought to this too. If a student is studying in a school that runs on Government grants where religious instruction is arranged, who will decide if that minor student should attend or not attend such instruction ? The framers of the Constitution left this matter to the guardians of the minor. I would like to read out the relevant article. Article 28(2) says :

> "No person attending an educational institution recognised by the state and receiving Government aid may be required to attend religious instruction given in such an institution or to attend religious practices in such an institution or in a place connected with it so long as that person or, if necessary, his guardian has not given his consent."

I would like to draw your attention to the spirit of this article. If the final decision on whether or not a minor should attend religious instruction has been left to the guardian this Bill would go against the spirit of this article. This article strikes out the freedom of the individual and is against the constitutional provision relating to a guardian's decision about a minor.

Sir, I would request you to give your own decision in this matter.

MR. DEPUTY SPEAKER : According to the tradition of this House the Chair has never taken the responsibility of ruling on whether a Bill or any other thing is in accordance with the Constitution or is *ultra vires*. It has been left to the House to accept or reject the Chair's opinion if and when it is given. In accordance with this tradition I decline to take this responsibility and leave it to the members to do as they please.

SHRI VAJPAYEE : Sir, then I would like to speak on this again.

MR. DEPUTY SPEAKER : I wanted myself that you should speak and so gave you time first. Well, now you may speak. May I know how many members would like to speak on this ?

(Many Hon. members stood up)

MR. DEPUTY SPEAKER : As many people wish to speak I think everyone should speak for five minutes.

SHRI VAJPAYEE : Those who are against should be given more time.

MR. DEPUTY SPEAKER : All right.

Change Public Opinion

SHRI VAJPAYEE : Even if the unconstitutional aspect of this Bill is not taken into account and even if one thinks from the practical point of view the first question that confronts us is, is the system of bringing about social reform through legislation right ? Is it practical ? Is it desirable ? And does it produce the expected result ? I submit this practice cannot be eradicated by law alone so long as public opinion is not enlightened and those to be affected by the Bill are not acquainted with the undesirability of initiating children into *Sanyas*. You may make a law but you will not be able to implement it. You may provide for punishment, but the feeling for social reform should come from the heart. They should be gradually prepared through propaganda to give up this practice. I am sorry to say no arrangement for enlightening public opinion was made before introducing this Bill. This matter is coming up in the House for the first time and provision is made for making the initiation of boys and girls into *Sanyas* a punishable offence. Further, even those boys and girls who have already been initiated have been covered by this Bill before its becoming law. They would also be put in the dock and punished. If this Bill is really inspired by the spirit of social reform it should not provide for punishment for those who have already taken *Sanyas*.

Act Cautiously

Sir, we must act very cautiously before interfering with and striking at social bodies that have been connected with religion for centuries. India is a religious country. Due to changing times some distortions have crept into that religion and those traditions. I do not advocate the continuance of those distortions. We should amend and change our religious practices in keeping with the demands of modern times, but that change should not begin with Parliament, with the law and the police, with the court and punishment. We have to motivate the religious institutions that can change religion, the Rishis and Munis who can actually influence and change public opinion. We should prepare their mind and do this thing gradually. As the mover has said no one is forcibly made a *Sanyasi*. He said there was a *Brahmachari* but later it was found that he had four children. May I ask how this Bill would stop this ?

These days we see many people in white clothes doing black deeds, but law cannot stop them. Now if we want to stop this the weapon of law is not the way, the way is to change the society's thinking, to change the people's mind. This task of changing the people's mind should not begin here. Actually public opinion should be changed outside and it should culminate here. Reform should not begin with Parliament, with the law, it should begin outside, and when the ground for reform is ready Parliament should put the stamp of approval on it in the form of a law. Enlightening public opinion should precede law. This Bill puts the cart before the horse. It goes against social conventions. This is impractical, undesirable and unconstitutional, and I would request the mover to withdraw it.

Dowry Will Go Not by Law Alone

Sir, I welcome the spirit in which this Bill has been presented before the Lok Sabha. No thinking person can support the dowry system. It has become a curse for us. It is an indication of the pitiable plight of the women in the Indian society. It is an index of the man's selfishness. It is a sign of our social backwardness. Everyone will agree that this custom of sale and purchase of brides and grooms must be removed from the roots.

But the question is, what is the right way to eradicate this vicious custom, which has distorted our culture down the ages ? The Law Minister has agreed in his speech that social evils cannot be eradicated by law alone, and if we consider the experience with laws that have so far been passed for removing social evils we would reach the conclusion that if the people are not enlightened, if there is no expression of an enlightened public opinion, if there is no social awakening such laws merely decorate the shelves. They are unable to fulfil our objective of basic social transformation.

In this connection the Law Minister has referred to the child marriage ordinance. I say it may be possible to book those engaged in a child's marriage at the time of the marriage, but how practicable would it be to arrest them at the time of giving or receiving dowry if there is no complaint from either side ? And he would not complain if he himself wants to give or take it. If a third party complains it would be a big problem for him to marshal witnesses. So we must admit there would be practical difficulties in implementing this law. How can they be removed ?

SHRI MAHAVIR TYAGI (Dehradun) : Boys will go into the black market.

SHRI VAJPAYEE : There is also another objection. I know there is a section of Brahmins where there are less girls and more boys. There the girl's side does not have to pay dowry. On the other hand the boy's side has to pay it.

SMT. RENU CHAKRABARTY (Basirhat) : This Bill covers that too.

SHRI VAJPAYEE : My objection is that the Bill would cover them, but the result would be that many boys will remain unmarried.

SMT. SAHODARA RAI : Only those who have a deficiency in them engage in such transactions, not others.

SHRI VAJPAYEE : If we think that this law with all its clauses may well stop this business at the time of marriage but giving gifts by the back door would begin. But do not say that you will look into the position of the girl's side after the marriage takes place and if dowry is not openly demanded....

SHRI TYAGI : —and when the father would die.

Lok Sabha on August 5, 1959 during discussion on the Dowry Prohibition Bill

SHRI VAJPAYEE : Many things will be looked at and attempts made to make the classes of the law ineffective even after it is passed to continue the giving and taking of money. But what I say should not be taken to mean that I am a supporter of the dowry system. I have already said that this custom should be eradicated, but for that it is not a law that is required first, it is social awakening. I charge that those who criticise the dowry system remain silent in this respect when it comes to bringing about a change in their own social and family life. All their activities are limited to politics, they are oriented towards attainment of power, and those who attain it only care for keeping it. But when the problem of social reforms comes up in the Lok Sabha we assume the mantle of sentinels of social reform and its alert advocates. The responsibility of creating the right atmosphere for social reform lies on all political parties, on people's representatives and also on the Government, but this responsibility has not been discharged so far.

Anti-dowry Movement

The Information Ministry could prepare a film against the dowry system. Non-official organisations which receive Government aid, like Bharat Sevak Samaj, Yuvak Samaj or the various student bodies could also be motivated to launch an anti-dowry movement. But we did not do this, instead we came up with a law. This is putting the cart before the horse. Making a law leads to a different feeling. We come to feel that our responsibility is over, we do not have anything more to do.

In respect of laws regarding untouchability I find that before making a law efforts were made to enlighten the society on this matter. Now this does not happen. Now social workers feel there is a law and it is a cognisable offence, now it is for the police to look into it, why should we care ? If social reform laws are made without social awareness they slow down the efforts for social reform.

Social reform organisations think our job is over, a law has been passed, now what is left for us to do ? This is not a good situation for the country. Even if a law is passed it cannot be implemented so long as the society and every individual is not alert. Actually I wanted the Law Minister to throw light on how the anti-dowry laws passed by two States were implemented there and what their experience has been.

Laws were made in Bihar and Andhra. After the passing of this Bill those laws will become infructuous. What is the experience of these two States ? Has the dowry system been really checked by law ? If the law is in force and reforms continue to be talked about and the dowry custom also continues this would not be a healthy situation. The test of social reform is not the growing number of laws. We should not just pass laws and think that the society is making progress. The Government as well as non-official organisations motivated by the Government will have to work for it.

So I propose that this Bill be publicised for popular awakening. We should take this Bill to the people—not for finding out if the people are in its favour or not but for ensuring that once it becomes law the people would cooperate in its implementation. This law cannot become effective so long as the people do not themselves come forward to implement it. What steps is the Government taking to bring about this social awakening ?

SHRI C.P. BHATTACHARYA : Awakening has been generated.

SHRI VAJPAYEE : A lady member said that the sum of Rs. 2000 that has been fixed is too big, it should be decreased. But if it is big for someone it may be small for someone else. My objection is not what is given to the bride. We can understand it if the bride's parents want to give something as *'kanyadan'* for the future happiness of their daughter. But if there is no cut in the overhead expenses in marriages these days it would mean continuing the dowry system in another form. How many people should be in the *Barat* ? But if, on the one hand, you disallow accepting more than two thousand rupees but allow that 500 people may come in the *Barat*, their railway fare should be paid for, and everyone of them should be given 10 rupees by way of *Dakshina* as well as a shawl as a parting gift, the bride's side would be squeezed dry and the law would not be able to intervene.

So this thing is not as simple as it is made out to be. After all this is a question of reforming the society. There are complexities in the social structure and the law cannot meet these complexities. It only gives cosmetic treatment. Perhaps by passing this law against dowry the Government wants a pat on the back for taking a step ahead in social reform. Doing so would be ignoring this serious problem. Its seriousness has not been fully assessed. If this law prevents only the dowry given and taken at the time of marriage but giving and receiving go on after marriage this law would not be very useful.

It was just now said that the police should step in, it should be made a cognisable offence. This sounds fine but I can fully appreciate the Government's difficulty in this. What will happen if the Government takes cognisance but it does not get a witness and the case falls through ? So I want to know the experience of those two States in this matter. Our Law Minister has made an emotional speech. We agree with the feeling that the evil custom of dowry is a blot on the fair face of our nation, but the question is, how can we wash it off ? The clauses of this Bill cannot fully remove this blot.

AN HON. MEMBER : They can to some extent.

Welfare of Scheduled Castes

This Constitution Amendment Bill is before us for consideration. By this bill the reservation given to Scheduled Castes and Scheduled Tribes in Parliament and Legislative Assemblies in the States is being extended by ten years. Actually this Bill is an admission of the fact that during the past 20 years we could not assimilate our Scheduled brethren into the rest of the society. When the Constitution was framed and reservation was provided for them it was hoped that it would be possible to assimilate the Scheduled Castes and Tribes into the society, they would stand on their feet and no reservation would be necessary for them. But this hope was belied and in 1959 we extended the reservation provision by ten years. Now it is being extended further by ten years.

In the situation that prevails today and we cannot close our eyes to reality—our Scheduled brethren need reservation. But the question is not only of giving representation in Parliament or legislatures, even after twenty years of such representation we have not been able to remove the backwardness of these oppressed classes. So it is necessary that along with passing a Bill for providing reservation we should also try to bring them up to the level of the rest of the society by giving them special concessions in the social field and to prepare them to fully exploit the educational facilities that we have given them.

It would not be right to say that untouchability has grown. We do not want to blow up the situation. At the same time I am against playing it down. Education has spread, industrialisation has expanded, people have migrated from villages to cities in large numbers, and as a result of all this the bonds of untouchability have loosened a little. But it is a matter of regret that the social reform movement that was going on in the country before independence, the effort that was being made for public enlightenment, the programme of Harijan uplift that was included in Gandhiji's constructive programmes fell into neglect once power came into our hands and once we attained *Swaraj*. Now whenever atrocities on Harijans are discussed everyone agrees on the necessity of launching an all-India campaign to end social discrimination. In the last session the Home Minister had also promised that with the cooperation of all parties he would initiate such a campaign. But no work has been done in that direction. It needs to be done.

I would like to clarify the stand of my party. We do not believe in untouchability. The Varna system may have had its uses at one time, today

Lok Sabha on December 9, 1969 during the discussion on the Constitution 23rd Amendment Bill relating to Reservations for Scheduled Castes

it has no relevance. A system that distinguishes between man and man, sets up a barrier between man and man, makes one individual higher and another lower by accident of birth is an inhuman system, a non-Hindu system and is against the law of God. We are not prepared to accept it. But saying so is not enough. It is necessary to give facilities to Scheduled brethren in the economic field. We have fixed a proportion for them in jobs. But they and others do not get jobs in that proportion. There should be an amendment in this Bill according to which an officer unable to recruit according to the prescribed proportion will have to note in his file the reasons for his inability. So far it was not necessary to give the reasons. We have reserved jobs but jobs are not available. We have not yet been able to remove the attitude of social discrimination in them. In this regard the educational facilities that we have provided have not been fully exploited.

Anglo-Indian Nomination

But there is one thing in this Bill that I would like to oppose. It is about our Anglo-Indian friends. I wish Shri Frank Anthony was here ....(*Interruptions*) .... he has come. This is a very important point, I am quoting from Shri Frank Anthony's book *"British Betrayal in India"* .... (*Interruptions*) .... I regret Shri Govinda Menon observed in his speech about the recommendations of the Sub-Committee on Minorities that the Anglo-Indians should also have nomination. But he forgot to mention that the Sub-Committee had accepted this recommendation only when Sardar Patel intervened. The Sub-Committee was initially against any right to nomination. I quote a portion from Shri Frank Anthony's book :

> The Minorities Sub-Committee started first with the case of the Anglo-Indians. Immediately I was opposed by Sidhwa, one of the two Parsee representatives. He said that he would oppose any Anglo-Indian representation as a nationalist Parsee, whatever that may have meant. He further said that if the Anglo-Indians were given representation, it would not only mean fantastic weightage but it would encourage the Parsees also to seek similar representation. The fight was long, grim and bitter. The case of no other minority occupied so much time. Every section of the community was opposed to giving the community any representation because they said it could not be justified either by principle or logic."

Shri Frank Anthony has also admitted that Dr. Mukherji, the representative of Indian Christians, was the biggest opponent of this. The question is, why should there be nomination in Lok Sabha ? I can understand nomination in the Rajya Sabha if Anglo-Indians representatives do not get elected to the Lok Sabha. But they do, Shri Piloo Mody is here. Shri Masani is here. Their number is small but they have joined hands with political parties here. They have mixed with the people and have been elected as their representatives. There is no reason why we should accept the principle of nomination in Lok Sabha.

Secondly, when nomination power was given for ten years even Shri Frank Anthony said—I again quote ... please give me time, do not be so harsh on the very first day .... (*Interruptions*) ....

DEPUTY SPEAKER : Your time is over. Please conclude.

SHRI VAJPAYEE : Sir, this is very difficult. This is an important Bill. The House may devote more time to it if it so wishes. But if you will not allow speaking, if you will not allow clarifying even a single point what is the need for a discussion ? We could have voting without it.

DEPUTY SPEAKER : The business of the House is fixed by the House, not by me, but by the Speaker and the whole House.

SHRI VAJPAYEE : I was quoting Shri Frank Anthony. He has himself admitted that no minority can always function under a communal label. I quote him :

> "Everywhere the minority will look forward to the time, sooner or later, when it will take its place not under any communal label or designation but as part and parcel of the whole Indian community."

Sardar Patel also said we are giving ten years, this is a notice. As Anglo-Indians were given many facilities under the British rule they cannot be placed in Scheduled Castes. They did not get concessions, so there was reservation for them. Anglo-Indians do not get more concessions, so reservation was provided. But there is no propriety in continuing this nomination, and I wish Shri Frank Anthony himself says we do not want nomination, we are prepared to be elected by the people. Thank you.

Untouchability Law and Social Awakening

Sir, this Bill is proof of the fact that during the past 22 years our efforts to end untouchability have failed, and now it has become necessary to stiffen relevant laws still further. When our Constitution was framed in 1950 we had made a declaration in article 17 of it. The declaration was :

> "Untouchability has been ended and its practice in any form is prohibited. Practice of any uneligibility due to untouchability will be an offence punishable by law."

The framers of the Constitution declared that untouchability was at an end, but the mere declaration did not end untouchability. A law was also passed to end it. But now even that law seems insufficient. Will the Hon. Minister tell us how many people were prosecuted all over the country for practicing untouchability in contravention of the existing law, and how many of them were punished ? Is it not true that it is very difficult to prove such cases in Court ? Untouchability is a punishable offence. The police need not wait for a complaint to be lodged. It can intervene on its own. But even the police include people who believe in untouchability, even those who do justice in such cases in the court have untouchability ingrained in their cultural influences. This is why law cannot eradicate this evil. No one can be against your stiffening of the penalty under law. I also do not think it necessary to make any changes in the recommendations of the Elaiperumal Committee. If you are going to stiffen it, stiffen it still further. But we would be making a mistake if we think we have put an end to untouchability by merely passing a law. Untouchability is a sin. We are atoning for this sin for hundreds of years. But this sin is not yet at an end. To some extent untouchability is practiced even in the United States. It is worse than racial discrimination based on pigmentation. In it discrimination is practiced on how fair or dark your skin is. But here everyone has the same colour skin, the same features, the same blood flows through their veins, and yet there is discrimination on the basis of birth. This is against humanity. This is against Indian philosophy, even against our religion.

Need for Social Awakening

I do not agree with those who equate untouchability with the Varna system. In Vedic times the Varna system was not based on birth. The same father had sons belonging to different Varnas, but they all lived together, ate

Lok Sabha on May 23, 1972 during discussion on the Untouchability (Offence) Amendment and Miscellaneous Provisions Bill

together. There were also inter-marriages. But later this system got vitiated and we have to remove the evil that crept into it. Today we do not need the Varna system on the basis of birth or on any other bases. Now we all belong to the same Varna. So along with the passage of a law we need a social revolution. The current of revolution that flowed till 1947 got blocked after the advent of freedom. Swami Dayanand, Mahatma Gandhi, Dr. Babasaheb Ambedkar brought about an awakening. They roused the people and filled their hearts with the spark of rebellion. They made them feel the present order must change, no one must be considered high and no one low. But once independence came we thought it would be enough to pass a law. This decelerated our pace towards social awakening.

The House may pass this law but a countrywide campaign for the eradication of untouchability needs to be launched on a social level. You know that even today Harijan students are not allowed to sit on the matting, Harijan villagers cannot wear chappals, they cannot sit on horseback at weddings, their women cannot wear ornaments. Even in the Central Secretariat there is a separate Surahi for Harijan employees and no attempt has been made to end this system. Everyday news comes of Harijan women being stripped naked and paraded through the market place. There is a boycott of Harijans near Poona. The Scheduled Castes Commissioner's report is full of such instances. All these events should stir the mind of the society. Along with law we need a nationwide campaign on the non-political level.

I will conclude with a suggestion. The National Integration Council that has been set up is so far involved only in the problem of communalism. It may tackle it, but I suggest that the National Integration Council should hold a special meeting to consider the problems of Scheduled Castes and Tribes and a campaign should be launched all over the country with the cooperation with all parties. Let us fix the target to fashion an India free of untouchability at the end of five years. It is necessary to draw a line in this matter. Let us change the circumstances and let us also change the mindset. We cannot do this with law alone.

Along with it social awakening is called for. But the Hon. Minister does not even mention a need for social awakening in his speech. The presence of members in the House too does not provide evidence of realisation of the seriousness of the subject. The subject merited the Prime Minister's presence in the House. He should have assured ....

DEPUTY SPEAKER : He is yet to make a speech.

SHRI VAJPAYEE : The Hon. Minister did make a speech while moving the Bill for consideration. He could have said many things. I will wait for his speech. Thank you.

Increasing Atrocities on Harijans

Sir, we are discussing an important national issue. It cannot be denied that during the past some years atrocities on Harijans have increased. The figures collected by the Home Ministry support the fact that there has been a substantial increase in the incidents of burning Harijans alive, torching their houses, unauthorized occupation of their lands, and otherwise humiliating and harassing them. In 1969 the number of such events all over the country was 441, in 1970, 483 and in 1971, 623. The figures for the periods January 1971 to October 1972 indicate that there were a total of 1971 incidents that involved individual violence. In all there were 6195 incidents, out of which 3524 incidents were caused by Harijan-High Caste clash. These figures tell a very sorry tale.

This is not a question of any one party. This is also not a battle between the Government and the Opposition. Therefore I said in the beginning that this is a national problem. We will have to go into the various aspects of it and then to solve it satisfactorily.

The Social Aspects

The social aspect of this problem is familiar to all. For centuries a system has prevailed in this country in which one man has been considered inferior to another, considered untouchable on the basis of birth. This is a sin of the Varna system.

AN HON. MEMBER : This system was made by the Brahmins.

SHRI VAJPAYEE : Who made it is not the question. Whoever made it, it is wrong. That it still continues is shameful for the country. In the rural areas these barriers of discrimination still stand. The Constitution has declared untouchability as a punishable offence, attempts are being made to stiffen anti-untouchability laws, and yet determination is being practiced between man and man. We need a national campaign to solve this problem.

In the days of the freedom struggle non-official efforts were going on in this direction. The Arya Samaj did significant work for removal of untouchability. The constructive programme under the leadership of Mahatma Gandhi tried to bridge this gap. But once power came into hands non-official efforts came to a halt. Now no non-official efforts are made to rouse the soul of the society and motivate the high castes to atone for this. These efforts are necessary. The Home Minister is reviving the National Integration Council and its initial meeting is to be held tomorrow. We could decide in it to launch a national campaign with the cooperation of all classes

Lok Sabha on August 23, 1973 during discussion on atrocities on Harijans

and all parties which could prove an effective instrument for ending social aspects of discrimination and untouchability.

But it is not only a social problem, it is also an economic problem. It is true that even after earning money a person considered low by birth cannot get a respectable place in the society. This is a social curse. But if they are landless—a majority of such persons are Harijans—if they have no means of livelihood, if their handicrafts have fallen backward because of progress in science and technology and are even dying down because they cannot stand competition, these people are also faced with an economic crisis. This crisis cannot be resolved by giving them equal representation in jobs—which we have not been able to give so far. Their industries should be safeguarded and changed in conformity with modern conditions so that they can stand competition in the market. This economic aspect needs also to be attended.

Reservations Not Forever

The principle behind reservation is that only equal opportunity is not enough. The backward will have to be brought up to a higher level by giving them special concessions. Then alone can they last in the race. Otherwise an opportunity means nothing for a Dalit or the oppressed. If we cannot stand everybody taking part in the race in line the race will not be run according to rules. This is why reservation has been advocated. But reservation should lead to immediate progress. We must not get the feeling that these crutches are for ever.

The Political Aspect

Now a political aspect of this problem is coming to light. It is very serious. This is not just a clash between Brahmins and Harijans. It is a clash, but it is also assuming other forms. In various regions and various fields the class in power, the group or sub-caste in power is stepping up its atrocities because it does not want to give up the power that has remained in its hands for centuries. On the other hand Harijans have woken up, are recognising their rights and have started sharing power. I would like to give an example. In Haryana the struggle is not between Brahmins and Harijans, it is between Jats and Harijans. My Jat friends should not get annoyed. I am not saying this to annoy them. I could give the example of Maharashtra. In Maharashtra the struggle is not between Brahmins and Harijans. Those who are Marathas, those who are Kshatriyas, those who are in a majority, those who are influential in the villages, those who dominate the Government....

AN HON. MEMBER : Jats are Shudras only.

SHRI VAJPAYEE : No, that is wrong. The question is not what they are but what they think they are.

AN HON. MEMBER : The Jatavas are Shudras, not the Jats.

SHRI VAJPAYEE : Now Harijans want to contest Panchayat elections, they want to become the Pradhan. They want to share power. This is a natural desire and also necessary. They should get a share in it. But those who had the monopoly of power do not want to share it either on the social level or even the political level, whether it is in Maharashtra or in Uttar Pradesh. This is the political aspect that is coming into focus, and it needs to be considered. This problem cannot be solved by only differentiating between high caste and Harijan. In whatever fields a particular group dominates it will have to be persuaded to share power, otherwise democracy will lose all meaning.

The Administrative Aspect

There is also a fourth aspect to this, and it is administrative incidents of excesses are on the increase. While it is a symbol of social awakening it is also proof of social change. While they cause a sense of anxiety they also rouse the hope that Harijans are no longer prepared to take it lying down. Now they will raise their voice, they will speak out, and they will fight for their rights. Perhaps they may have to face being burnt alive, but even if it comes to that their burning bodies would create a light in which those who burn them will see their face and hang their head in shame. This is a good sign, but our administrative apparatus has failed this test. It is true that the Home Minister has sent directives, the Prime Minister has held a conference of Chief Ministers, and attempts have been made to fix local officials' responsibility. But incidents take place, they are not immediately reported, and, as Shri Nawal Kishore has rightly said, many more incidents remain in the dark than coming to light, as there are no reports. Those who report are threatened. If there is a report the matter is settled in the name of a compromise. The offenders are saved, those who should be punished go scot free. The police do not discharge their responsibility. The officials are also not vigilant. In the ultimate analysis their conduct betrays the class to which they belong. Hence the stress on recruitment in the services in large numbers. They should be placed in important positions where they may not practice partiality but where they could resent injustice. At present we have not been able to create such resentment, such anger, so we should try for it. Incidents must be immediately reported. Look at Bihar. The Bihar Government woke up when the matter was raised in the Assembly. In the Bawra incident even those in power were involved. So a social boycott was imposed on those Harijans who had embraced Buddhism. They cannot drink water, they cannot work in the fields, they are lying outside the village. This atrocity is being perpetrated in an organised manner. But the Government machinery did not budge, because this machinery was influenced by those who had a direct hand in the incident.

So on the one hand a decision has to be taken on the political level and on the other the administrative apparatus needs to be strengthened. It will have to be activated. The most stringent action will have to be taken, and those officials who do not do their duty, who delay action, whose conduct shows that they have been deliberately negligent, deliberately careless, will have to be meted severe punishment. Everyone must come to know that the Government at the Centre or those in power in the States will not tolerate any laxity in this matter. We can do this job only by making the administration efficient.

Strengthening of Commissioner for SC and ST Necessary

One more thing and I shall conclude. In the Constitution we have provided for a Commissioner for Scheduled Castes and Scheduled Tribes. He submits his report. The report is delayed. If and when it does come we do not get a chance to discuss it. If we do get a chance we cannot extract from it what we want. Now the Commissioner's difficulty is that his administrative structure all over the country has been demolished. Now how can he get information ? How can he receive information when an incident takes place ? In the past he had separate offices in the regions. He could visit them, call for information and get an immediate report. The Home Ministry should think about this. It is necessary to strengthen his position. The Scheduled Castes and Tribes Commissioner should be given a machinery that would activate sources from New Delhi, that would bring the truth to light if the State Government is lax or if the local official fails to do his duty. Then the House could consider it. We should work for this as well.

Now I would wind up. As I said in the beginning, this is a national problem. The time, the energy and the resources we spent for national unity were spent for the unity that was limited to Hindu-Muslim, we neglected Harijans and *Vanvasis*. This was not good. We have no time to lose. Sometimes I feel it would be easier to close the gap between the rich and the poor than between the high caste and the Harijan, and so long as this equation does not change the country will not move. This relationship must basically change. This must be considered a national issue. The politics of votes will go on, the clashes between parties will go on for ever, even charges and countercharges can be accepted as a part of democracy. But there are certain problems on which the whole nation must come together, make up its mind and launch its efforts; otherwise we would never be able to fulfil our dream of making a new India where there is no discrimination on the basis of birth, on the basis of caste, on the basis of race. This is the test. This problem is the test of whether we do what we say. I feel this discussion will express a determination that would inspire us to forge ahead in this direction. Thank you.

Do Not Politicise Reservations

Sir, I had hoped that the reservation problem would be put in the proper perspective and the House would repeat the decision to extend the reservation period by 10 years that the legislatures and Parliament had taken only a few months ago. It is necessary for this House to repeat the decision that reservations in services and in educational institutions is a national policy, the House is bound by this policy, and it is necessary to implement it strictly. But I do not see any unanimous resolution being proposed.

SOME HON. MEMBERS : The Resolution is coming.

SHRI VAJPAYEE : This matter of the ruling party cannot be left to the Opposition parties. You have a two-thirds majority. You have power in your hands.

AN HON. MEMBER : This is politics.

SHRI VAJPAYEE : If you see politics in this you can never understand the difference between national policy and political policy.

Sir, my problem is, if a proposal is coming—and it is coming—what would I say ?

SHRI INDRAJIT GUPTA (Basirhat) : Don't spring a Resolution on us suddenly, without letting us see the draft. Everybody wants a Resolution, a unanimous Resolution. But don't suddenly produce a Resolution and say, "Pass it."

SHRI VAJPAYEE : And if a resolution is coming there is no need to make a speech. Move the resolution.

To Blame is Not to Solve the Problem

We have not been consulted in drafting a Resolution. Sir, they want to spring a surprise.

Sir, today I do not want to get entangled in charges and counter-charges. To blame is not to solve the problem. Looking for a scapegoat will not lead us anywhere. If you level a charge I can make a counter-charge. I do not also want to say that that day Shri Makwana tried to mislead the House. I do not want to say it.

We did not receive information about the meeting Sarvodaya leaders had called in Ahmedabad. The Lok Dal was not even invited. One of our workers had died and all people had gone to his funeral. The Sarvodaya leaders announced in the meeting that the Bharatiya Janata Party people could not be contacted and the Lok Dal people were not invited. And yet Shri Makwana levelled this sort of charge in the House. This thing makes us so sad.

AN HON. MEMBER : Don't say it.

Lok Sabha on March 18, 1981 during discussion on the situation arising out of the agitation regarding reservation of jobs for Scheduled Castes and Tribes

SHRI VAJPAYEE : All right, I won't say.

There is no reason for the doctors of post-graduate medical courses in Gujarat to keep their agitation going. I had said so to doctors in Ahmedabad. When I called on the Chief Minister he clearly said the carry-forward system has been abandoned, the interchangeability system has been abolished. The Gujarat Government even said that if a deserving student is denied a seat because of reservation of seats for students of Scheduled Castes and Tribes they would make additional seats available.

Practical Difficulties May be Resolved

This may create some practical difficulties later on, but I told the doctors to resolve them with the Government.

SHRI A.K. ROY (Dhanbad) : Do you support the steps of the State Government ?

SHRI VAJPAYEE : Yes, I do support them.

SHRI A.K. ROY : We do not support it. This is nothing but a surrender.

SPEAKER : Please speak on.

SHRI VAJPAYEE : I shall certainly do so.

When the Government accepted all these points there was no propriety in continuing the agitation. But I think it has passed from the hands of the medical students.

School students came to tell me that the BJP policy in this matter is not right. I asked them, what do you have to do with reservation ? Some of them said our examinations are approaching and we want them postponed, if the agitation grows the examinations will be postponed, maybe we would be declared passed without exams. This is childishness, but it is a dangerous game.

There are some complaints about how the reservation policy has been implemented, and those complaints should be looked into.

For instance even in post-graduate medical courses there is reservation in only 9 States, not in the rest.

Reservation in Post-graduate Medical Courses

I say this matter is not limited to Gujarat, as an Hon. member said just now, and as I also heard in the speech the other day. I know the Congress party is in a difficult position in respect of those who are to benefit from reservation. There are members even in the present ruling party who may ask, why did you put an end to the interchangeability, to the carry-forward system introduced by the Janata Government ? You may keep seats vacant and fill them up when there are students from Scheduled Castes and Tribes. If they say so there is weight in it too.

What will happen if the States that do not have reservation for post-graduate medical courses also start demanding that it should be done as in the other 9 States ? What will be the reaction then ?

On the other hand, what will happen if the demand arises elsewhere for the ending of interchangeability and carry-forward if it can be done in Gujarat ?

So do not look at the Gujarat problem alone. I am also not prepared to look at it as a matter of seats alone. The whole reservation system rests—has rested—on and began with the fact that the whole society is one, some of our brethren have remained neglected for centuries, have remained depressed and oppressed, and now we have to do justice to them, and there should be no objection if, in the process, a little injustice is done to those who have remained ahead for centuries, we will have to pay this price for maintaining the unity of the society.

The doctors who are agitating in Gujarat are good people, they are young people, I do not want to criticise them, but I failed to convince them that there should be no objection if one out of 22 Registrars belongs to the Scheduled Castes. Convincing upper caste employees working in the Central Secretariat is proving difficult.

Problem has Divided All

This problem has divided all parties. Those who live in glass houses should not throw stones at others. This problem has divided all parties and all trade unions. It is striking at the roots of our social unity, and the nation's integrity is in danger.

People are describing the present crisis as a crisis of civilisation. Why do they do so ? Is this crisis economic or political ?

AN HON. MEMBER : Crisis of civilisation.

SHRI VAJPAYEE : Civilisational crisis and crisis of civilisation—they are the same thing.

PROF. MADHU DANDAVATE : The translation is the same.

SHRI VAJPAYEE : Even in difficult days, in the times of foreign invasions, when we were in bondage and when the society was undermined by evil customs, we could maintain a sense of confidence, camaraderie and attachment. That attachment is coming to an end, that confidence is going to pieces. This is not a question of a few seats, a few jobs. Once trust is lost no system, no law, no rule can restore it. It is only on that trust that people walk in unison and the society forges ahead.

So we need to reaffirm the determination to continue reservation. But we need to take the new generation into confidence, to convince it, to place statistics before it. The dimension of the problem is not at the post-graduate level at all. The medical students there said to me how can those who are not capable of teaching teach us ? I said will standards fall if a new teacher of Scheduled Castes joined all the other teachers ? This is not possible.

AN HON. MEMBER : People are getting admission in colleges by giving donations.

SHRI VAJPAYEE : They are coming by donations. In Ahmedabad the candidates of trustees of the municipal corporation are coming. They are coming by money, not by merit. We have no objection at all in our minds about them. But we are losing the realisation that they are our brothers, the flesh of our flesh and the blood of our blood, we would let a little injustice to be done to ourselves but not give them scope for complaint.

This is not a game of politics. I wish the Prime Minister were present in the House. She is making very balanced statements. But I shall give an example of how they are construed where passions are roused :

> "Dr. Murgesh Vaishnav, President of the Action Committee of the agitating medicos, welcomed Mrs. Gandhi's statement in Delhi that meritorious students should not suffer due to reservation. Dr. Vaishnav said, 'we would like to congratulate her for taking a bold stand on the reservation issue'."

This is the leader of the agitationists. He finds the Prime Minister's statement supportive of his stand. The Scheduled Castes and Tribes find it supportive.

SHRI JAGJIVAN RAM (Sasaram) : No, we do not look at it as supportive. It is a very dangerous statement.

SHRI VAJPAYEE : I submit this problem will not be solved by just being clever. It will not be solved by putting the blame on somebody. If we are going to give us all the credit....

AN HON. MEMBER : Then we are prepared to take it.

SHRI VAJPAYEE : No, we do not merit it, nor are we convinced. If we are convinced we will say it loud and clear. We have not come into politics for votes, we have not compromised principles for power. But we are convinced that justice will have to be done to the backward. But how to convince the new generation ? There is a communication gap and the Government has failed to bridge it.

Figures Speak

Look at the statistics. I have Reserve Bank figures with me. No one seems to understand the problem. Look at the figures of the Reserve Bank, the Central Bank of India, the Punjab National Bank, the State Bank—the percentage should be fifteen there, but nowhere is it greater than even one per cent. Whom should we blame ? And do you know what is happening in the banks ? Their managements say we have an agreement with the trade unions. And not all trade unions are conducted by the RSS or by JP, there are also other friends who conduct trade unions. On this they say there is an agreement between the trade unions and the management, so do not get involved in whether reservation is applied or not. This thing divides even trade unions.

How many students are there in medical colleges ? But our young people do not understand that injustice has been done for centuries. They say, all right, injustice has been done for centuries, but we did not do it, so why should we suffer ? They do not have a fellow-feeling, they do not have a pain in the heart, and if we have lost anything in these thirty-three years it is this pain, it is this camaraderie. It is the misfortune of all problems that they have been politicised. The country is divided into parties and parties are getting divided into castes. Not only the country, not only the parties, even hearts have been divided.

Man an Economic Being

It is not enough to say big things here in the House. Who will fight the battle outside ? I agree that one party cannot. So far this matter has been limited to educational institutions. Now the employees of Gujarat are making demands. When they are asked, is there a complaint about recruitment they say we can put up with it in recruitment but we cannot understand this business of promotion—our junior becomes our senior. I too could not satisfy them. Reservation is understandable in recruitment. Even in respect of promotion the Supreme Court has ruled that it is right and we are implementing it. But the employee in the office says this is not proper. You may bring them up to the level by giving them concessions, but once they are equal to others, leave it at that. He who is capable of going ahead will go ahead. They show me the roster and ask, who will be the deputy secretary five years hence ? I say, do not worry about who becomes the deputy secretary, let him become, after all he is our brother. But this is an economic question, a question of bread and butter. Man has become such an economic being that nationalism, social unity, brotherhood, camaraderie, love, affection—these values do not appeal to anybody. In this we have failed.

There was a reference to Sarvodaya leaders just now. Not that they have not criticised. But they too have their limitations. Politics has overcome all. In every matter what political leaders say, goes. When did we consult Sarvodaya people ? Now that there is a crisis in Gujarat we have remembered them. But when it comes to morality in politics no one listens to Sarvodaya people. Then it becomes a shameful game of power. Now organisations are breaking down one by one, conventions are dying down one by one, traditions are getting trampled upon one by one. Those who are in power want to remain in power, and those who are in the Opposition want to exploit such opportunities for what they are worth. But our Congress friends should not complain about this. Uttar Pradesh had a Lok Dal Government. There was a disturbance in Narainpur, atrocities were committed on Harijans, and women were involved. Prime Minister Smt. Indira Gandhi went to Narainpur. When she was coming out after meeting the women a press reporter asked, can it be said you have come to exploit the mistake of the Lok Dal Government that is in power here ? The Prime Minister replied, if the Opposition makes a mistake why should we not exploit it ? This was her reply. Now our workers show us that reply and say, you will not understand politics, Smt. Gandhi knows how to play politics. When during the Janata regime reservation was applied to backward classes the Congress Party did not openly support it. They kept silent. Even now the statements that are being made are quite clever—a little on this side, a little on that. Look, I tell you, this won't do. This country will not run on cleverness, it will run on character, it will run on values. You do not have to fear, you are in a majority, you have the power, but you will have to take courage in your hands to take a decision. And for that you will have to be willing to take everyone with you. The way the reservation policy is being implemented may create some problems, and I have referred to them.

That day the Communist Party member Shri Bhogendra Jha had introduced a Bill, a non-official Bill—he is not of the BJP, and there is no question of his being of the RSS—and in that Bill he said along with education and the socially backward pay a little attention also to the economically backward. Does poverty depend only upon caste ? Is not poverty just poverty ? You may not have any reservation for it, but at least give some concessions for it, we do not think of those who are poor, those who are beggars.

Then should we have reservation in promotion too ? This should also be considered. No one can say the reservation that has gone on for 33 years has not benefited anybody, but we have also to look to whether those who should get the benefit get it. Are only some people benefiting from it while the rest are being deprived of it ?

All these points are such that all should come together, discuss them and arrive at a political consensus. But this has to do with the Prime Minister, and the Prime Minister is not present in the House, so this discussion has no meaning.

Increasing Atrocities on Adivasis

Harijans and *Vanvasis* have been discussed in this House time and again. We have been raising their problems. Replies have also been given. But never before has a reply been given that was as incomplete, insufficient and objectionable as the reply given today to this calling attention motion. I was going through old proceedings. A question had been asked in this regard on September 9, 1981. In his reply the then Home Minister had admitted that there has been an increase in the atrocities on Harijans and *Vanvasis* in 10 States. He had named those States and given figures. At the end of today's speech we were told that information was received about a total of 6751 incidents in 1983, but these figures do not cover all States. So the figures do not cover all States and whatever figures there are not complete. Then what can we discuss ? I want to know the State-wise figures. During his speech the Home Minister said the figures have gone down. I have before me a statement by two Harijan MLAs of Bihar, in which they have said according to Government records that there were 1948 incidents of excesses on Harijans in 1980-81, 2008 in 1981-82, and in 1983 the figure may be still higher. On what basis does the Minister say the incidence of such events has gone down ? He mentioned a case. Please look at the Hindi statement. It starts like this : "Reported" killing of some tribals in the Katihar district of Bihar...the killing is 'reported'....

SHRI RAMAVATAR SHASTRI : This translation is wrong 'Reported' or '*Kathit*' ?

SHRI VAJPAYEE : 'Reported' has been translated as "*Kathit*". This is wrong. Just now the Minister has admitted that there has been killing, four people have been killed, and here it says "*Kathit hatya.*"

MR SPEAKER : This is a technical translation.

SHRI VAJPAYEE : And this information is not complete. Even now it is not clear as to who made the attack. According to reports it was done in collaboration with those who came from Bangladesh. Why does the Minister want to hide this ?

He has talked about guidelines. He has just repeated what Gyaniji had said in the House in 1980. Has the Minister looked at the recommendations of the Parliamentary Committee on the Welfare of Scheduled Castes and Scheduled Tribes ? It says :

> "The Committee are not satisfied with the reply of the Government. By issuing guidelines to the State Governments the Central Government cannot absolve themselves of the constitutional responsibility under

Lok Sabha on August 3, 1983 during discussion on the Calling Attention Motion regarding atrocities on Harijans and Tribals and the recent reported killings of 9 Tribals in Bihar article 46 which makes abundantly clear that it is the responsibility of the Central Government to protect the Scheduled Castes and Scheduled Tribes from social injustice and all forms of exploitation."

The Committee added that a constitutional amendment is required for this. What is the Minister's reaction to this ?

A terrible incident of atrocity on Tribals took place at Gua in Bihar on June 1. I quote a portion of the newspaper report on this :

"On June 1 in the afternoon Mr. Verma entered Gua bazar with the five arrested allegedly tied to the rear of the jeep, had them tied to poles with heads hanging down and had them beaten. Twelve lathis broke in the process, the last one to handle the beating was said to be Mr. Verma himself."

There is a report against the DSP. I can understand arresting offenders, but I cannot understand tying them to jeeps and dragging them along. Does the Minister know about this ? Has the Centre called for information on this ? How long will such atrocities be perpetrated on Tribals ?

Atrocities Increasing Everywhere

I have a report from Tamilnadu. So far 26 Harijans have died in police custody in North Arcot and Dharmapuri. Atrocities were committed on them, needles were thrust in their nails, and their bodies were branded. The Civil Liberties Union has prepared a report on this. Do you know anything about it ?

In Andhra 4 Harijans were burnt alive in a village on January 5. This happened after the elections. Congress people tried hard to derive political benefit from it. A judicial inquiry was instituted. Has its report been received ?

Belchhi, Pipra, Parasbigha are in Bihar. Dehuli, Sardulpur, Rampura are in Uttar Pradesh. Massacres of Harijans took place at these places. Does the Government know what is happening there now ?

I am not talking about those who were arrested. I have a report saying the police were deployed in a certain village. They are committing atrocities on women there. Assurances about roads, power supply and hospitals were given but not fulfilled. There was a lot of noise at the time in these villages but what action was taken later ?

Does the Centre's Home Ministry have a cell to supervise if public declarations are implemented or not ?

Sir, I am concluding before my time is up. I had asked about the villages. The DSP had tied the Tribals to jeeps and beaten them up. Do you have any information about that ? No, you do not have any information.

Who Forced the Harijans to Dance ?

Madam, it is unfortunate if such incidents take place in any part of the country. If they are presented in the House with a political colour their seriousness would diminish. I have also a report on what happened in Shivpuri. The Home Minister of the State Government himself visited the village, and carried out an investigation.... (*Interruptions*).

DEPUTY CHAIRMAN : Please speak on.

SHRI VAJPAYEE : How can I speak if a lady interrupts me ?

DEPUTY CHAIRMAN : Atalji, if one lady is interrupting you another is asking you to speak.

SHRI VAJPAYEE : You are not a lady, you are the Chair.

Madam, according to my information those who forced the Harijans to dance and committed an excess are connected with the Congress....

SHRI KAPIL VERMA (U.P.) : There they say now that the BJP is in power, we cannot expect anything else....

SHRI VAJPAYEE : That was why I said in the beginning if BJP had not been mentioned....(*Interruptions*).... you did not mention, you are very sober. But please transfer a little of your thoughtfulness there too. I quite agree that if there is an excess on Harijans anywhere in this country, whatever the Government, this House has cause for worry. The Home Minister should be asked to collect information about this and place it before the House. It is not proper to name parties. I can mention your name and you can name my party. Nothing would come out of that .... (*Interruptions*)....Madam, there should be a way of talking....(*Interruptions*).

DEPUTY CHAIRMAN : He is a senior member of the House. Let him speak. When you spoke you were given permission to speak. Now let him present his point of view. The Chair has to take the final decision. Sit down quietly.

SHRI P. SHIV SHANKAR, Leader of the Opposition : Both are unmarried ....(*Interruptions*)....

SHRI VAJPAYEE : Madam, that is why the married cannot understand our sorrow. I support the demand that the Home Minister collect all facts about this incident and place them before the House, after which the House could discuss them. If necessary, blame could be apportioned. If you say that right from the beginning there is a change of Government in Madhya Pradesh but in Madhya Pradesh the people have changed the Government, it was not your pleasure that changed it. They say because there is a new Government Harijans cannot expect a better deal. What does this mean ?

Rajya Sabha on March 27, 1990 during discussion on the killing of Scheduled Caste woman in Shivpuri region of Madhya Pradesh

SHRI KAPIL VERMA : Those people say the Congress Government has been changed. We don't say so. (*Interruptions*)

SHRI VAJPAYEE : That is wrong. Those who did the beating were Congressmen. Ask them, I am asking you.

Madam, I say again, if we adopt this point of view towards atrocities on Harijans and minorities we cannot open up the way to do justice by them. Whoever may be to blame....(*Interruptions*) I can threaten you. You are yourself a threat from head to toe. You are threat incarnate. I am not threatening, I am talking sense. I say such matters should not be given a political colour. Whoever is in power, strict action should be taken in such matters and all facts presented before the House. Thank you.

Anti-Reservation Agitation

Government Responsible for Youths' Self-immolation

Madam, we have gathered here for a special session of Parliament. This session has been called for passing a Bill about a constitutional amendment regarding Punjab. Clearly the situation in Punjab is serious and is not conducive to holding elections. I am happy however that the Congress party has decided to support a constitutional amendment Bill in this regard. This is a step in the right direction. It would have been better if it had not kept up uncertainty in this matter. But better late than never.

But this discussion is taking place on another subject, not only because the Bill will first be passed by the Lok Sabha and then come here. What will we do in the meantime ? So let us discuss the Mandal Commission. Actually the present discussion is taking place under very serious circumstances. The situation is explosive, the situation is delicate. I would not be exaggerating if I say that Independent India had never before been faced with such a situation. Our youths, young boys and girls are immolating themselves, playing with their lives. Self-immolation is new to the North even if it may be familiar to the South. There is certainly something that touches the innermost recesses of their heart. We must try to find what that is.

From Jammu all over the North a chain of self-immolations has been formed in the towns and cities. In some States it is more, in some less. We all know that the student agitation has no single leadership, no particular body. I have not yet received proof showing that anyone is deliberately preparing students for self-immolation, but the boys are playing with their lives. When a boy studying in the eighth standard, for whom it is not yet definite if he will have to go in for a job, who may set up a business of his own, for whom entering the Central Services is a dream, commits self-immolation it becomes necessary to study in depth the problem of why he does it. If anyone dies in self-immolation it creates a situation in the society in which mental balance cannot be maintained. Let us face this situation.

Opportunities Be Given to the Backward

We have backward classes in the society. They are educationally backward, socially backward. We have a very unequal society, there is no equality in it. Inequality has been categorised here. In the absence of equality in education this inequality is growing. This is a separate aspect, and this is not the time to go into it at length. In this society, where there is no equality

Rajya Sabha on October 1, 1990 during discussion on the concern over students' self-immolation on the question of reservations

of opportunity, where inequality has entrenched itself due to birth and caste, education is not equal. (*Interruptions*)

Those who have been backward for centuries will have to be given some special opportunities, some special facilities.

We have a clear point of view on this, not only now but from the time we have been in politics. Shri Malaviya referred to our manifesto just now. What we have written in our manifesto we wrote after mutual consultation. Shri Solanki is present here. He had to face a big agitation in Gujarat. This agitation divides the country, divides the castes, divides the parties. Is the Janata Dal untouched by it ? It is a very delicate matter.

What should have happened is that even on the question of social justice a general consensus should have been formed. It could have been done. But for that the ruling party should have formed a consensus within itself. The question arises in my mind again and again—it was your affair. Our manifesto too mentions it. Shri Malaviya was reminding us of 1977. I do not want to go into past things. A commission had been set up under the chairmanship of Shri Kakasaheb Kalelkar. Its recommendations were also received. After touring the whole country Kaka Kalelkar had also concluded that this would amount to opening Pandora's box. In 1977, when we were in the Janata Party. I was a Minister—the party decided to set up another commission. Why ? The founding fathers of the Constitution had clearly said that there should be concessions. But in 1977 the Janata Party decided upon a review. It wanted a general consensus. So a commission was set up. It is true that this thing was hanging fire for so many years. It was also discussed from time to time. In general the opinion expressed in the House was that the recommendations of this commission should be implemented. But why August 7 ? Was there some *muhurtam*, some auspicious moment ? Does this have any background ? This question has to be answered, because people say this has been done for political reasons. It was done because infighting was going on in the Janata Dal. This may be wrong, but the question remains, why the 7th ?

In a democracy it is not enough to do the right thing. You must also do it the right way. This is very important. This is a question of ends and means. It is true that the Prime Minister at least informed my party. We were informed. (*Interruptions*)

SHRI JADHAV : (*Interruptions*)

SHRI VAJPAYEE : Jadhav Saheb, "*tumhi gappa basa*" —You be quiet, what am I saying ? Am I indulging in '*Bharh*' ? (non-sense) Madam, he said '*Bhumika,*' attitude, so I had to look for such a word, so I said '*Bharh.*' It is not a good parliamentary term. Those from Maharashtra are objecting to it, so I shall not use it again.

As I was saying, we were informed. They say we had it in our manifesto and so we did not have to be informed much about it and I accept that. But it would have been better if there were consultations. At least so far as my party is concerned we would have certainly cooperated. We have said this right from the beginning. I would like to read out from our manifesto. Please give me time. I am being attacked from both sides.

DEPUTY CHAIRMAN : Why do you sit in the middle ?

SHRI JAIPAL REDDY : He likes to be sandwiched from both sides.

SHRI VAJPAYEE : Those going by the middle path are pushed from both sides.

SHRI S.D. SINGH : Madam, had I been in his place I would have said because you are sitting in front of us....

DEPUTY CHAIRMAN : Come and take his seat.

SHRI VAJPAYEE : Madam, Shri Shankar Dayal Singh may say he is married, I am a bachelor, I cannot say so.

DEPUTY CHAIRMAN : Atalji, I too cannot say, because I too am married.

SHRI VAJPAYEE : Madam, this is our election manifesto. We had said this when there was an agitation in Gujarat, in Bihar, in Uttar Pradesh, and at that time we had decided upon a policy. We had reiterated it in our election manifesto. I quote it in full.

> "It is Bharatiya Janata Party's view that this problem should be considered without any partiality and with an open mind. So Bharatiya Janata Party recommends that—
>
> 1. Reservation for Scheduled Castes and Scheduled Tribes should continue as before.
> 2. In general there should also be reservations for backward classes on the basis of the Mandal Commission's report.
> 3. As poverty is an important cause of backwardness reservation should be arranged for other castes too on economic criteria."

Madam, I want to say here that we will not oppose reservations for the economically underprivileged, whatever their caste, class or religion. But if religion is made the basis it will create a new controversy. And I do not want to bring that in here.

This is our manifesto. We fought the election on its basis, we are bound by it. Now the Government party may say they are bound by their manifesto. But we belong to a supporting party, so if the two manifestoes clash, if there is some difference between them can we not sit together and resolve the difference through mutual consultation ? I know the Government is in a hurry, and so it made this announcement. Even while making the announcement if you had looked at Pramod Mahajan's clarification you would have seen that we had said both things—economic criteria should be the basis, for backward classes. Pardon me, our policy is different from that of the Congress. The Congress has now seen the light. (*Interruptions*) no, if it has not, that is also very good, but if it has, it is still better. We all agree that backward classes should get concessions and the poorest among them should get priority. I have the Karpoori Thakur formula with me. Karpoori Thakur was a leader of backward classes. But he was backward even among the backward. He had a different pain, a different ache. So he had found out a new way.

It is true that was done after the agitation and even after it complete peace did not prevail. But it was an effort. This is not even an attempt. According to a report Karpoori Thakur had given priority to the most backward classes among the other backward classes in Bihar; Backward 8 per cent, most backward 12 per cent, Scheduled Castes 14 per cent, Scheduled Tribes 10 per cent, Women 3 per cent, economically backward 3 per cent. Our Marxist friend has referred to this. We could have advanced further on the basis of this formula, we could have exchanged thoughts, we could have taken the people with us, and we could have prepared a background. But steps were taken in haste and the people were not fully informed about the result.

Reservation Limitations Were Made Clear

Our Janata Dal friends will admit that when the agitation became a little stronger I appealed to the youth and told them there was no propriety in continuing the agitation after the clarifications that were made. What were those clarifications ? They were that reservation will not apply to technical institutions, it will not apply to education, it will not apply to promotion, it will not apply to defence services, and that this matter is left to the States, they will decide what to do.

I thought this clarification was enough. It would satisfy the youth. Now it is certainly my complaint that if this package had been offered on the very first day and if the Prime Minister had declared—which he did later—that five to ten per cent reservation for the economically depressed would be considered and if an announcement to this effect had been made the same day it would have been better. But that was not done. As a result the whole picture did not become clear.

When clarifications were called for, a reference was made about Pramod Mahajan's clarification. Later that was also given up. It was made to mean that all those below the poverty line should be sent to Parliament and State Legislatures.

This is a different matter. This is a matter of jobs. It is directly related to the youth. And the situation also worsened because job opportunities are getting restricted. Recruitment to Central services had been closed down from the times of the previous Government itself.

Where are the Jobs ?

Where are the jobs that are being fought for? Where are the jobs that you are going to give ? We are told there would be three million new jobs. Very good, but all this controversy would not have been there if the whole thing could have come as a package, and the Government's determination to implement the Mandal Commission's recommendations as well as the election-time promise to include the right to work in the fundamental rights could have been added. I know this is also an election promise. Many promises have been made in the elections, but they are all meant for being fulfilled in the whole period of five years. It is not that all promises are instantly kept. If there is any difficulty that they create should not time be spent to go deep in them ? This was not done. Consequently difficulties increased.

Madam, Shri Malaviya has referred to 1977. I have already referred to it. He also asked Bharatiya Janata Party why it is adopting double standards. He says you are talking of the Court but not in the matter of the Rama Janmabhoomi temple. Then why talk of it here ?

We are talking about it to save the situation from getting more explosive. The youth are looking to the Court with hope. If the Court gives a stay—of course it is for the Court to give its decision—but do not drag the Rama Janmabhoomi issue in this. I could ask you—all right, we have double standards, but do you also have double standards ?

AN HON'BLE MEMBER : Both have double standards.

SHRI VAJPAYEE : The fact of the matter is that they have no standard at all. Friends, if you are going to interrupt....(*Interruptions*) All right, leave it, I am talking about this particular matter, not in general....

SHRI S.S. AHLUWALIA : Double Roti....

SHRI VAJPAYEE : Now who can attain Shri Ahluwalia's standard? It is an exceptional standard. I cannot even touch it.

Madam, you may say this is in the hands of the Supreme Court. But what is the Attorney-General going to say there ?

SHRI JAIPAL REDDY : We are going to oppose the stay.

SHRI S.S. AHLUWALIA : Is he the Law Minister ?

SMT. MARGARET ALVA : You are an official spokesman outside, not inside the House.

What is Communication Gap ?

SHRI VAJPAYEE : All right, now that the Government has clarified its position others will also find it easier to decide. There is one more aspect to it. Now we are told in a general way that there is some communication gap. Not everyone was consulted, there was some communication gap. The youth did not understand us, there was some communication gap. They still do not understand us, there is some communication gap. Why do they not understand ? Or is it that you are talking about a communication gap because you do not even want to reveal your objective and you could not show the efficiency, the intelligence, that was required to implement this. You want to cover up that too, and hence the communication gap.

Madam, a communication gap is not new for India. It is there from the time of the Ramayana. King Dasharath could not tell Kaikeyi that he had decided to make Ram the king and she had to accept his decision. A communication gap was created. Manthara said the opposite thing and the Ramayana happened. Ram had to go into exile. In the Mahabharata too there was a communication gap. Kunti told Karna that he was a Pandav, but she did not tell the Pandavas that he was their brother....

SHRI DIPEN GHOSH : Vajpayeeji, that was a desperate communication gap. Had there not been such a communication gap, there would not have been Mahabharata.

SHRI VAJPAYEE : That is why (*Interruptions*) you have made my job easy. This so-called communication gap, is it really sudden, accidental, or is it deliberate ? I....(*Interruptions*)....there is a gap here.

I do not know what this situation is. Madam, we are sad. Backward youth are quiet today, but if they feel that justice to them is so much opposed they have a right to think so. So far as members of the Council of Ministers are concerned they should show some more responsibility. Those who are in power have a greater responsibility. They may even have to drink poison. There must be restraint in their speech, there must not be incitement in their conduct. The nation's fortunes are in your hands, and this country on fire—these self-immolating youth—this is not an event to change history. My friend Shri Paswan should understand that history is not changed this way. At least in this country there is a tradition for changing history. We shall change history under Mahatma Gandhi's leadership, but there must be no violence. But perhaps Janata Dal has decided that it will not follow Mahatma Gandhi, it will follow Dr. Ambedkar.

I respect Dr. Ambedkar .... (*Interruptions*) Yes, I respect Dr. Ambedkar. But both Mahatma Gandhi and Dr. Ambedkar are parts of this country's tradition. But when the Prime Minister assumed power and addressed the nation the address did not mention Mahatma Gandhi. (*Interruptions*) Pardon me, I am not belittling him. Mahatma Gandhi had an art, a technique, with which to change society. He went on changing society. He kept changing even influenced people, and he changed them. The questions is, are social justice and social unity contradictory ? Can there not be an accord between the two ? Is social assimilation necessary for bringing about social justice ? It should not be. The other day the Prime Minister said, the question before me is, shall I stick to the decision I have taken or shall I stick to power, so I am ready to give up power. All right, but do not look at this question like this. We do not want the Prime Minister to step down. We also do not want that there should not be social justice, but we hope for a morality where social justice should also be there and at the same time social integrity should also not break up, some youth should not take the extreme step of committing suicide under stress of emotion. This is a tough task, and we will have to measure up to it. But this tough task is not being tackled. Easy alternatives are being chosen. The result is the crisis that faces the country. We must come together and think together to resolve this crisis.

The All-Party Meeting

Pardon me, there was an all-party meeting. In that meeting all were agreed on two points : there should be reservation for backward classes, and talks should be held with the students. The process of talks with the students was not promptly initiated. There was delay. There were no self-immolations then. The students were prepared to talk. But no talks were held then. Perhaps that was because you thought the storm that was raging would die down. We too did not think the situation would take such a dangerous turn. Had a discussion begun at that time things would not have gone sour. I know when you will discuss things you will discuss them with an open mind. But these contradictory statements have also queered the pitch. I know the party in power has its own difficulties. But if you say we are ready for talks and if you also say our decision remains what is there to talk about ? At the same time what Janeshwar Mishra says is also true—if we say we cancel our decision what is there to talk about ? We cannot very well say we have cancelled our decision, come, let's talk. They will say you did a very good thing, now we are going home.

Students Could Be Shown the Right Way

This is the difficulty. There is no easy way out of it. But students could be brought to the right path, and our effort should be to do so. It would have been easier if the Supreme Court had given a stay, an atmosphere could have been formed, some way could have been found. The reservation you have given for backward classes could have continued and the doubts in other people's mind could also have been dispelled. But no diplomacy is in evidence. This makes me sad. We are a supporting party. We do not have power in our hands. We can advise. But if every piece of advice is looked at from a partisan point of view, and if you think—Bharatiya Janata Party people have been snared, they lost Himachal Pradesh, in Delhi Shri Khurana's clothes were torn up, there is an agitation everywhere, they have lost their upper-caste vote, the backward were never with them—if this is the way you think, it is not a fruitful way, it is not a constructive way. I am not making accusations. At places there is a feeling—good, BJP people are in difficulties, let them suffer. If this is the test of your behaviour with colleagues and supporters the supporters would also have to think about it. You will also find yourself in difficulties.

I do not look at this question from the election point of view. I would also say to my friends in the party in power—do not think about who has how many votes, if we do this we can capture the whole vote bank and we shall race straight to Red Fort. Do not think like that. Something very big is at stake. It is not only power, it is not only the Government. The youth are asking questions and I have no answers. I am saying this in all sincerity. Punjab is burning, Kashmir is in the enemy's jaws, the situation in Assam is deteriorating, people are harassed by prices. Possibly all these problems are together affecting the youths' minds. People ask us too—Punjab is burning, the country is on fire and you are busy with Rath Yatra. They ask us this and we have given them a satisfactory reply in our own way. But it would not be good if in the meanwhile those in power create a new controversy. We know it was not the intention but Pandora's box has been opened and all sorts of creatures are crawling out. Find out a way to put them in the box. In this we are ready to help. So let no one talk in challenging tones. That will not help because this question is linked with the stability of the society. It is true it is an unequal society. There is exploitation. But remove exploitation in such a way that social unity is maintained and a permanent gulf is not created.

I would also tell the Opposition—your point of view on Punjab is constructive, I commend it. You could have decided not to cooperate, elections could have taken place. It would not have been good if elections had taken place in Punjab at this time. I know that your party too is not one on the Mandal question. Do not try to derive temporary political benefit. We are in loss, and we stick to our stand even at the cost of political loss, because we too believe in social justice and we too have no doubt in our mind about social unity. We should bring about social equality and there should also be integration. He who can achieve both these difficult tasks will write his name on the face of time in golden letters. The game of power will go on, but I do not know where it will lead us. Thank you.

Use of the word "Harijan"

Mr. Speaker, Sir, I would like to invite your attention to a matter of urgent public importance. Is the use of the word "Harijan" going to be regarded in this country as a criminal offence ? One can understand if our brethren belonging to the Scheduled Castes complain that they should not be known by the nomenclature "Harijan," because there is no mention of the word "Harijan" in the Constitution. However, the controversy that has arisen now about the word "Harijan" is very unfortunate. Gandhiji had popularised the use of the word "Harijan," but before that the great poet of Hindi Bhartendu Harishchandra had said, this about the Muslims : *Un Mussalman Harijan par kotin Hindu vaariye*

(Crores of Hindus could be sacrificed for those Muslims who are devotees of Hari (God Vishnu).) Gandhiji brought out a journal titled *"Harijan."* Some State Governments had expressed the view that the word "Harijan" denoted an inferior position and hurts the feeling of equality in the society. It is, therefore, not used in official business, but if anybody uses it in practice and puts the word "Harijan" as a suffix to his name; is he going to be penalised for that ? Will it be in consonance with our national tradition ?

Mr. Speaker, Sir, I am not raising this question keeping in mind certain particular individual or a particular State, but I want that this question must be discussed and, therefore, I have deliberately raised this question. I do not know what would be the reaction in the country but I want the House to spare some time for discussing it.

Special mention made in Lok Sabha on April 28, 1994 regarding the use of the word "Harijan"

XIV RELIGION

Misuse of Places of Worship

Sir, I stand to support this resolution, though I wish the mover reconsiders bringing places of pilgrimage within its purview. So far as the question of preventing the misuse of places of worship for political propaganda is concerned there can be no two opinions, and if we want to preserve the secular form of the Indian republic the time has come to take a final decision in this respect. In view of the circumstances in which the country was partitioned and of the evil effects of that partition which we have not yet been able to forget we have to prevent the repetition of events that strike at the secular form of the Indian republic and incite communal passions again.

Mixing up Politics and Religion

We have established a secular state. A natural corollary of this is that politics and religion should be kept apart. Those who link politics with religion or religion with politics do not believe in the principle of secularism, however long a speech they may give against communalism and however long a resolution they may pass in a conference. Attempts are again afoot to mix politics and religion. If they are not checked communalism will again raise its head in the country and our independence and national unity will be in great peril.

We have chosen the democratic way and any sect has the freedom to form a political party, openly contest elections, and consider economic and cultural problems. Why is it necessary to launch an agitation for that in temples or Mosques or Gurdwaras or Churches ? I was surprised to see Shri Sarhadi give the example of Jehangir's times. Time has passed. This is true not only for our Sikh brethren. In the past too all freedom struggles were linked with religion, but now there is no propriety in linking a mode of worship with politics. Of course if there is any difficulty in worshipping in a temple or a Gurdwara or if the Government is adopting any discriminatory policy in purely religious matters it could be considered. But if *fatwas* regarding elections are issued from Mosques, a political and communal agitation for a separate State is conducted from Gurdwaras, Churches are made the centre of separatist activities, and if then, as a result, people start going to temples

Lok Sabha on February 17, 1961 while participating in the discussion on the Resolution regarding preventing misuse of places of worship for political propaganda

for political activities, it cannot be supported. It is thirteen years since the country was partitioned ....

SHRI NAWAL PRABHAKAR (Outer Delhi) : RSS meetings take place in temples.

SHRI VAJPAYEE : The RSS is not a political party and I would say if that is so that too is wrong and should be stopped. And when I support this resolution the RSS too will not escape. Hon. members of the Congress should have the moral courage to support this resolution. But they cannot do so. They may give speeches against communalism, but at election time they compromise with communal elements. They talk of nationalism but cannot sacrifice partisan interests. This is why even thirteen years after independence communalism is growing, and it will not be removed so long as we refuse to adopt an attitude of compromise about it. Whatever the place of worship, it should not be allowed to conduct political parties there. Some people have just asked, what is a political activity, what is its definition ? The Central Government has made a rule that its employees cannot take part in politics. They are not bothered about this difficulty with definition. Any Government employee taking part in political activities is punished. And if there is indeed any difficulty about definition it could be considered. People's opinion could be invited and an acceptable definition prepared, which would include attainment of political power, or contesting political elections without restraining cultural and religious rights in any way.

Places of Worship Must Not Become Political Bases

Therefore it is necessary that all should concur with the basic spirit of this resolution. I cannot accept that politics may continue in places of worship because political activities cannot be defined. I would like that as a matter of principle we should agree that places of worship should not be made political bases. After that we could consider what sort of law we could make for it, what its definition should be, and what its purview. We can sit together and seriously think about it. No nationalist can connive at the present peril to national unity, and this peril has many forms. Let us not tolerate the communalism of any community, whether it is a minority or a majority. All rules apply equally to all. But we see that in Punjab the police cannot enter a Gurdwara but in Chandigarh the police can enter an Arya Samaj Mandir. If there are rules they should be the same for all. Recently entry into an Arya Samaj Mandir was prevented in Jalandhar, but are not Gurdwaras being used for months for conducting a communal agitation ?

That restraint has been lifted and I welcome it. I do not support conducting political activities in Arya Samaj Mandirs. I say no one should have the right to conduct such activities, whether it is a Gurdwara or a temple or any other religious place. We must have a firm and stringent policy on this. If we do not have it we cannot translate into reality our dream of establishing a secular State.

If we do not learn even from the partition of the country, if we do not keep politics away from religion, if we do not have a law that reflects public opinion on this, merely saying we should enlighten the public will not mean much. How much was public opinion enlightened on the Hindu Code Bill ? The Hindu Code Bill came into being, but there is no civil code as yet. The police cannot enter Gurdwaras, they can enter an Arya Samaj Mandir. *Fatwas* for winning elections can be issued in Mosques, and foreign missionaries can hatch plots to destroy national unity in Churches, and all these things are being tolerated. If we do not open our eyes to these dangers even now we cannot protect our independence and our nationhood.

This is not a resolution, this is a test for the Government. It is as if every Congressman's nationalism is being challenged. If they want that politics should not enter communalism they should support this resolution, otherwise it would be said that they talked of national unity but did nothing for it. Thank you.

Cow Protection Agitation

Where are the Missing Bodies

Madam, we are considering the statement made by Shri Jaisukhlal Hathi on November 10 regarding the events on November 7. This statement says 8 people died by police bullets and 41 were wounded. He gave the names of five of the dead. They are Shri Ram Rakha, Swami Ajudhyanand, Shri S.K. Jain, Shri Jagan Nath and Constable Shri Jai Prakash. Why did he not give the name of Shri Jhumarmal Asopa of Jodhpur ? He said three persons could not be identified. Does he know that Shri Jhumarmal Asopa's son went to the Willingdon Hospital at 10.30 at night and saw his father's dead body ? There were 16 other dead bodies there. Shri Jhumarmal's identity card was found on his body. He was a retired officer of the Railways and his identity card had his name and 'Jodhpur' written on it. His identity card, spectacles and wallet had been taken to the doctor. His son said I have identified my father's body, it should be handed over to us. The doctor said come in the morning, you will get it. When he went in the morning he said there was no dead body there. He wrote a letter to Smt. Indira Gandhi and I have in my possession the photostat copy of a chit written by the doctor at Willingdon Hospital. When he went to the doctor the next morning and said to him—'you told me to come for the body in the morning' the doctor sent him to a 'Sister.' The doctor wrote to the Sister—"Sister, please tell this gentleman who has taken the body of Mr. Jhumarmal." This is written by a doctor of the Willingdon Hospital. The Hospital's register contains the names of 17 people whose dead bodies were lying there. One of the 17 was Shri Jhumarmal Asopa. Where have those 17 bodies gone ? Where is Shri Jhumarmal's body ? Why was it not handed over to his family ? If the number of the dead was 8 where did the 17 dead bodies at the Willingdon Hospital come from ? Who will answer this question ? Will even information of dead bodies be withheld in a democracy ? Will they be burnt in an electric crematorium in the dark of the night ? I warn Home Minister Shri Chavan that this matter of dead bodies is very serious. Look at it after linking it to the demonstration on the 7th. If we are responsible for the demonstration of the 7th, if we have made some mistake we are ready to atone for our sins. But he who died was somebody's father, somebody's son, somebody's husband. You did not hand over his dead body to his family. Not only that, you kept the House in the dark, the country in the dark. I am prepared to produce that person and I would ask the Home Minister to seize the register of the Willingdon Hospital. It contains

Rajya Sabha on November 16, 1966 during discussion on the Statement on the death occurring during the procession of cow-protection agitators near the Parliament House due to police mismanagement

the names of 17 people who died. Then how did Shri Hathi say 8 people died ? Then why did Shri Hathi say Shri Jhumarmal Asopa did not die ? Who gave him that information ?

The Demonstration

Madam, it is being said that that day's demonstration was organised by the Bharatiya Jan Sangh and the RSS. How I wish we had done that ! Even before this we have organised demonstrations in the capital and no incidents took place during those demonstrations. Had we organised this demonstration the tragic event of November 7 would not have happened. What is a matter of regret is that it was not our demonstration but attempts are being made to malign us. Madam, the demonstration was organised by the All-Party Go-Raksha Maha Abhiyan Samiti.

SHRI M.P. BHARGAVA (U.P.) : It contained your people.

SHRI VAJPAYEE : Bharatiya Jan Sangh is not included in the Samiti. No political party is included in it. Yes, my people participated in it. My people have full freedom to do so, but it would be wrong to say that we had organised the demonstration. Do you know that the Chairman of the Go-Raksha Maha Abhiyan Samiti is Shri Prabhudutt Brahmachari ? Do you know that the Sadguru of the Namdhari Sikhs is its Vice-Chairman and Shri Hanuman Prasad Poddar its Treasurer ? It includes the Jains, the Arya Samaj, the Sanatan Dharma, the Sikh Sect. Even a batch of Muslims had participated in the procession. It was led by Master Nuruddin, whom the police have locked up.

Madam, the question is, did the police take necessary action ? The organisers of the demonstration had given the assurance that there would be no disturbance and they wanted to keep their assurance. But it was the responsibility of the police to catch the Goondas of Delhi. When we, the Jan Sangh, organised a demonstration on the occasion of Kutch nearly 400-450 Goondas had been arrested. How many Goondas had been arrested this time ? The Home Minister should find out. He should also find out why the police allowed the people to gather at the barracks built to the left of Parliament House before reaching in front of Parliament House. Those people were not connected with the demonstration, those people were not a part of the demonstration and those people had occupied the barracks even before the demonstration. We are trying to find out who they were. They had a loudspeaker too. In the permission given to the Secretary, All-Party Go Raksha Maha Abhiyan Samiti it was written that there would be no loudspeaker with the procession, but the Delhi Police saw that the people standing at the barracks had a loudspeaker. The slogans that were raised from the dais were—"Ban cow-slaughter. We have come peacefully to get our demands accepted." But the people on the barracks were raising other slogans. Jain Muni Shri Sushil Kumar requested them with folded hands—'do not raise this slogan. It is not authorized. Only the slogans we have decided upon will be raised.' But they did not listen. And they were in the forefront of those who indulged in stone-throwing. Who were those people and how were they allowed to collect ? I would also like to know who those people were who attacked Shri Kamraj. This is a matter for investigation. Do not level charges indiscriminately. If Shri Kamraj's house was attacked first and the demonstrators had dispersed due to police firing they must have gone later and set the fire, not before.

SHRI SHEEL BHADRA YAJI : It was before.

SHRI VAJPAYEE : Wrong. The Lt. Governor of the Delhi Administration has given the time table. Do not walk with your eyes closed.

Madam, if it is proved that Jan Sangh people indulged in violence, Jan Sangh people set cars on fire, I am prepared for any penalty. I shall sever connection with the Jan Sangh. I shall renounce politics. I cannot stay in a party that practices violence. But if you do not give us a chance to explain it would be an injustice to us, and we shall not tolerate injustice. (*Interruptions*). Please listen, give me a chance. If the demonstration went to Shri Kamraj's bungalow, Shri Ashok Mehta's bungalow was before that, and so was Shri T.N. Singh's. Were the demonstrators angry only with Shri Kamraj, not with Shri Ashok Mehta, not with Shri T.N. Singh ?

DEWAN CHAMAN LAL : Ashok Mehta is not the President.

SHRI VAJPAYEE : The security force should find out who those people were. Were they the demonstrators or were they some other people ? We are trying to find out, and if you help us we can. If our people are among them we shall punish them. But convince us that they were our people.

Madam, one thing I would like to say and I have said it that day too. It is that that day I was not allowed to address the demonstrators. On the dais a Sadhu forcibly took the mike from my hands. Who was that Sadhu ? At first he was sitting below the dais and he was creating a disturbance during the Jain Muni's speech. Later the demonstrators had caught hold of him and handed him over to the police. But later that Sadhu again came on to the dais. And he struck me on the head and took away the loudspeaker from my hands. How was he released from police custody ? Where is he now ? I went to the jail to look for him, because I know him by face, but he is not in police lock-up, nor in jail. Was he a man of the police ? Was he a man of the Delhi Administration ? Or was he a man who wanted to malign Shri Nanda ?

This matter is not as simple as it looks. That Sadhu should be produced.

Madam, 20-25 Sadhus, including Nagas, collected at the gate of Parliament House. Somewhere else we were trying to pacify the crowd. Had the police arrested those 20-25 Sadhus there would not have been that type of disturbance. But they were not arrested. Why ? Why was a tear gas shell lobbed on to the dais when those on the dais were trying to maintain peace ? Swami Rameshwaranand's speech was followed by that of Seth Govind Das and Shri Prakash Vir Shastri, but when I rose to speak that Sadhu caught hold of me. Had that Sadhu not been there and had 20-25 Sadhus not been allowed to collect at the gate of Parliament House this incident would not have happened. But the police lobbed a tear gas shell at the dais and cut wires. Had the police declared the crowd to be an illegal assembly ? Had the police given a chance to the crowd to disperse before teargasing it, before lathi-charging it ? Was a warning given before the firing ? Is there no law in this country, no respect for law ? The crowd was not warned, the crowd was not given a chance to disperse, and the dais was tear-gased, which made the crowd think there was a plot to kill the leaders seated on the dais. There were lakhs of people in the demonstration. They had come with one feeling in their hearts. They had come to knock on the doors of Parliament. They had come to get their demands accepted democratically. There may be a difference of opinion about their demand. Someone may say it is not proper to ban cow-slaughter by law. But it does not become the Government to say so when it can enforce prohibition by law. But instead of respecting the feelings of the people who came, there was tear gas smoke on the dais, which made people think there is a disturbance, there is a fire on the dais and their leaders are in danger.

Secondly, after loudspeaker wires were cut and the leaders left the dais who was to control the crowd ? Who made the crowd leaderless ? Some elements exploited the situation, set fire, damaged cars. Madam, believe me, the cars that were burnt down included three cars of Jan Sangh workers, the scooters that were burnt also included our workers' scooters. Did we torch our own cars ? Did we set our own scooters on fire ? We do not believe in such things. This is not the way we work. So there should be a judicial inquiry into the whole thing. Milk and water must be separated. Truth has no fear. If we are responsible for the whole disturbance you should rather welcome an inquiry. You will get an opportunity of wielding the sword on us at election time.

Madam, believe me, leaders and workers of the Jan Sangh who were not even present in Delhi that day have been put in jail. Prof. Balraj Madhok, All-India President of our party, was in Bombay on the morning of November 7 and came to Delhi by plane. He had not participated in the procession. He was not present on the dais. He reached Parliament House after the firing. He is in jail. Last night Mr. Advani, leader of our party in the Metropolitan Council, was arrested. Had he been a participant in the event of November 7 he would have been arrested before that. If he has been arrested because of our protest on November 13 there was no need to wait for two days. He was arrested and taken away last night. Even our office Secretary, who is a typist, an employee, and who had no connection with the party, was arrested and taken away. Indiscriminate arrests were made.

SHRI B.P. SINGH (Bihar) : Students.

SHRI NIRANJAN VERMA (M.P.): You have not even seen.

SHRI VAJPAYEE : We are inciting students ? This is the kind of intelligence Congress members are providing. If the Government depends upon such intelligence....

SHRI ARJUN ARORA (U.P.) : This is the intelligence of one member of the Congress.

SHRI VAJPAYEE : If this is the condition of Congress members' intelligence what will be the plight of small employees ?

Madam, these indiscriminate arrests must stop. Now there is no apprehension of breach of peace in Delhi. At least there is no question of our breaking the peace. Then why are these people being arrested ? Why is a storm being whipped up against the Jan Sangh ? Is it because the growing popularity of the Jan Sangh is causing worry to Congress leaders ? If the unfortunate events of November 7 are sought to be exploited for political vendetta the Congress Government and its ministers will not have the face to ask for the Opposition's cooperation on the food crisis. If you exploit the events of November 7 we shall also exploit the food crisis. Then where will the country go ?

Madam, the new Home Minister has taken charge of the Home Ministry at a critical juncture. This can now be used also for marshalling the scattered strength of the country, as also for overcoming internal and external dangers. At the same time it can be exploited to suppress the Opposition, to trample upon it.

Judicial Enquiry Demanded

You will be surprised, a newspaper named *'Patriot'* has put words in my mouth and reported that I said at the dais 'avenge blood with blood'. I could not even speak there. I had only said, "Brothers and sisters, I congratulate you on coming here in such large numbers." Can I say avenge blood with blood ? This *'Patriot'* paper, which claims to be progressive, has written this. There is a weekly named *'Link.'* It wrote Mr. Golwalkar was present on the dais. Mr. Golwalkar was in Yeotmal. The speech he gave that day has been published. But *'Link'* saw him on the dais. Many people have been seeing many things. But this country cannot be governed this way. Democracy cannot also be saved this way.

What happened on November 7 could have been avoided. What happened was unfortunate. Violence should be condemned. Violence should be boycotted. A day before I was in Nagpur and I had said at a public meeting that if we do not boycott violence, if we do not give up violence in public life our independence would be endangered and this democracy will change into mobocracy. Could I and my party incite violence ? But I would say one thing. If an attempt is made to derive political benefit from the events of November 7 as a political party we will oppose it in a peaceful manner. Putting us behind the bars will not put an end to the popularity of the Jan Sangh. The weapon of repression can only suppress people's feelings.

Madam, I demand again that the events of November 7 be fully inquired into. There should be a judicial inquiry and a Supreme Court Judge or High Court Judge appointed for it. Then all problems would be revealed. We are ready to stand in the dock. But do not try to hang us without giving us a chance of defence. For we shall fight to the death—and are ready to die fighting. Thank you.

Parliamentary Delegation to Ayodhya— A Wrong Precedent

SHRI VAJPAYEE : Mr. Speaker, Sir, it is a matter of regret that I was not present in the House, when the Ayodhya issue was raised. But, from the newspaper reports, I came to know that there was an uproar over the Ayodhya issue. Just now Shri Indrajit Gupta referred to the Ayodhya issue and perhaps the Hon. Minister of Home Affairs has made an announcement to the effect that a delegation should be sent to Ayodhya. I am also a member of the Standing Committee of the National Integration Council and at the Council's meeting it was decided that a delegation of the Council can visit Ayodhya if it so desires. But, under the present circumstances, in the aftermath of all these heated arguments done for the sake of it the visit of a Parliamentary delegation would be unusual, something unprecedented. If the House .... (*Interruptions*)

Mr. Speaker, Sir, the Hon. Minister of Information can collect the necessary information. If you remember correctly, in the President's Address, it was mentioned with regard to Ayodhya that the Union Government is maintaining a strict vigil, but the Home Ministry failed in its duty, when some incidents occurred there, despite its strict vigil. The Ministry of Home Affairs could have collected the necessary information. It is being posted of the latest situation by the Government of Uttar Pradesh but that information is being suppressed. It is our charge that the House is not being informed in the proper way and at the proper time. (*Interruptions*)

SHRI SAIFUDDIN CHOUDHURY : Why are you backtracking now ? (*Interruptions*)

SHRI VAJPAYEE : If the matter is of getting acquainted with the facts, then the Hon. members who wish to visit Ayodhya are welcome to do so.

SHRI INDRAJIT GUPTA (Midnapore) : The Chief Minister has not raised any objection.

SHRI VAJPAYEE : The Chief Minister has no objection, but I have. This is a matter of setting a precedent. The issue involved here is not limited to Ayodhya alone. Will delegations visit all those places, where ever there is a dispute. (*Interruptions*)

MR. SPEAKER : That day, you were not present.

SHRI VAJPAYEE : It is my misfortune that I was not here.

MR. SPEAKER : Let me tell you that when a demand for a visit by a delegation was made, it was said that there is no question of a Parliamentary

Lok Sabha on March 27, 1992 during discussion regarding sending a Parliamentary Delegation to Ayodhya

delegation, but the Hon. members are free to accompany the N.I.C. delegation, if they desire so.

SHRI VAJPAYEE : When a decision regarding the visit of the N.I.C. delegation was taken....

SHRI NITISH KUMAR (Barh) : That day, Advaniji did not oppose the decision.

SHRI VAJPAYEE : Does it mean that I cannot object to it ? (*Interruptions*) I may be allowed to make my point.

MR. SPEAKER : Yes, please. (*Interruptions*)

MR. SPEAKER : Not like this. If you have said something, he too may be allowed to make his point. That day also, you had said that anyone can go there. Vajpayeeji, is also reiterating the same thing. It's one and the same.

SHRI MRUTYUNJAYA NAYAK (Phulbani) : Sir, I need a clarification from Vajpayeeji.

SHRI VAJPAYEE : I am not yielding. (*Interruptions*)You allow me to complete what I want to say.

MR. SPEAKER : Please take your seats.

SHRI VAJPAYEE : Mr. Speaker, Sir, the Chief Minister has welcomed the visit of such a delegation. It is evident from this that the State Government is not suppressing any fact pertaining to Ayodhya....

SHRI INDRAJIT GUPTA : They should not suppress it but from your statement an impression is being created that the State Government wants to suppress some facts. (*Interruptions*)

SHRI VAJPAYEE : If the Hon. member want to visit Ayodhya with this attitude, which is reflected in the constant interruptions, then I do have objections to their visit. If the delegation is visiting Ayodhya with preconceived notions and the idea that the Centre will have to intervenes in U.P., then this visit will only worsen the situation and we cannot support it. What kind of things are being discussed in the House ? Don't I have the right to speak in this House....(*Interruptions*)

SHRI MUKUL BALKRISHNA WASNIK (Buldana): The situation in Ayodhya has come to such a pass that even if a member wants to visit the place, he cannot do so.

Home Minister's Threat to U.P. Government

SHRI VAJPAYEE : Mr. Speaker, Sir, just now Comrade Indrajit Gupta said that he would like to get acquainted with the facts. I know him for a very long time. If any delegation wants to visit the place, to get acquainted with the facts, then it should go with an open mind. The discussions that took place in the House and the manner in which I am being interrupted is not indicative of an open mind....(*Interruptions*) Please allow me to complete what I want to say.

Mr. Speaker, Sir, the Hon. Minister of Home Affairs has issued a threat to the U.P. Government, in the House. He has mentioned article 356 in this regard. It has also been mentioned that if necessary, the Central Government will take over the disputed site. I wonder, under which law this will be done ?

If this is the attitude of the Union Government, then how will the visit serve any purpose ? It aimed at strengthening the case for implementing article 356....

SHRI INDRAJIT GUPTA : Why are you saying this ? The interruptions are not aimed at you. Rather, they are opposing the Chief Minister's move.

SHRI VAJPAYEE : Opposing ? Our Chief Minister has nothing to hide. He is doing it openly. He has welcomed the visit. But I myself and many others are worried. You will have to think over it. (*Interruptions*)

MR. SPEAKER : I am not constituting the Committee. It is just that some Hon. members want to visit the site, as a decision to this effect was taken at the N.I.C. meeting. So, they are going. If anyone else wishes to do so, he too can go. He said only this much, nothing more. He did not ask me to constitute the Committee.

SHRI VAJPAYEE : Mr. Speaker, Sir, I would like to ask you a question. If a similar situation develops in any other State, will this visit to Ayodhya be looked upon as a precedent, as a convention ? Large scale killings have taken place in Bihar. (*Interruptions*)

SHRI SHARAD YADAV (Madhepura) : Mr. Speaker, Sir, I am on a point of order. I may be allowed to speak after him. (*Interruptions*)

MR. SPEAKER : All of you, please take your seats. I am on my feet. (*Interruptions*)

SHRI RAM VILAS PASWAN (Rosera) : Mr. Speaker, Sir, more killings have taken place in U.P. as compared to Bihar. Let the Hon. Minister of Home Affairs check for the facts in his report. We would like to challenge this charge and prove that Uttar Pradesh has witnessed killings, three times more than the killings in Bihar, ever since the formation of the Kalyan Singh Government in the State....(*Interruptions*).... They have turned U.P. into a mini Punjab !

SHRI MADAN LAL KHURANA (South Delhi) : Five thousand people have been killed in Bihar. (*Interruptions*)

SHRI VAJPAYEE : Mr. Speaker, Sir, I would like to complete what I want to say. My intention was not to raise any controversy. I did not know that the mere mention of Bihar would create such an uproar. (*Interruptions*)

SHRI RAM VILAS PASWAN : Atalji, people belonging to the Scheduled Castes have been imprisoned in Uttar Pradesh. (*Interruptions*)

In Uttar Pradesh poor people and young men belonging to Scheduled Castes have been put behind the bars for the past three months... you have turned Uttar Pradesh into mini Pubjab....(*Interruptions*)

SHRI MADAN LAL KHURANA : Shri Ishwar Choudhury of our party, who was killed, also belonged to Scheduled Caste. (*Interruptions*)

MR SPEAKER : Please take your seats. (*Interruptions*)

SHRI DEVENDRA PRASAD YADAV : The killings in Uttar Pradesh are taking place unabated. (*Interruptions*)

MR. SPEAKER : Why are you talking to each other ? Please sit down. You never resume your seat unless I raise my voice. What is this ? You must have observed the position of the presiding officer, whenever such contentious issues are raised in the House and the manner in which the discipline of the House is undermined. It is also our responsibility to keep in mind the ramifications of such heated arguments, outside the Parliament.

All the Hon. members have presented their views in very decent manner. My humble submission to you is that it is not a question of victory or defeat on any specific issue. This relates to the sensitivity, unity and integrity of our country. Keeping all these things in mind I feel that this august House of the country will hold a discussion on it. You do not take sides with anyone. Let us keep facts before the House. I feel it essential to ensure that the sentiments of anyone are not hurt.

SHRI VAJPAYEE : Mr. Speaker, Sir, I am really pained. This has not been settled anywhere. I was in Bangalore where I read in newspapers about the invitation extended by Kalyan Singhji. After all I am a senior member of this House and I feel that there should not be any doubts about my concern towards maintaining unity and goodwill in our country. If there is any doubt about it, it is very unfortunate. Mr. Speaker, Sir, if this sort of a feeling arise in my mind then....

SHRI SHARAD YADAV : There is no doubt, please speak further.

Efforts Made to Give the Dispute a Communal Colour

SHRI VAJPAYEE : Mr. Speaker, Sir, will it be treated as a precedent ? We will discuss it frankly. Today the issue is on Ayodhya. Ayodhya is in U.P. and B.J.P. Government is in power. There is some dispute over reconstruction of temple in Ayodhya. An effort has been made to give that dispute a communal colour. This is the background of that issue, whereas the N.I.C. has taken a decision on a different background. Shri Indrajit Gupta was present there.

SHRI INDRAJIT GUPTA : What was the background ?

SHRI VAJPAYEE : The background was that you come to Ayodhya with a goodwill, go round Ayodhya and have *darshan* of Lord Rama. The U.P. Government will make full arrangements for your visit. You go there and see as to whether there is tension or not....(*Interruptions*)

SHRI SHARAD YADAV : Mr. Speaker, Sir have *darshan* of Lord Rama there and Ravana and Sita here.

SHRI VAJPAYEE : I want Shri Gulam Nabi Azad and the Hon. Home Minister to go there. There has always been a demand that the Home Minister should visit Punjab and Kashmir. I would request the Union Home Minister to visit Ayodhya first....(*Interruptions*) The Home Minister should go there and find out the facts himself and thereafter present those facts before this House in the right perspective and not with threats. These threats will never be tolerated. In case you go with preconceived ideas which I am afraid you have already conceived then it will not serve any fruitful purpose. Earlier it used to be stated that we want to demolish the mosque, now it is claimed that we want to demolish the temples.... (*Interruptions*)

Threat Will Not be Tolerated

Mr. Speaker, Sir, we neither want to demolish the mosque nor are we in favour of demolishing the temple. Whatever is happening in Ayodhya is all in accordance with legal provisions. The High Court has not created any obstructions in it....(*Interruptions*) Now in case you want to create some obstruction by going there, it can't be helped. Mr. Speaker, Sir, they might be aware that some members of Parliament of the other House had gone to Ayodhya. I do not want to name them. (*Interruptions*) No when Kalmadiji went to Ayodhya, riots took place because he delivered provocative speeches there. Here also they delivered provocative speeches. I do not know what will be said there when they visit that place and how much provocative the speeches will be. However, my submission is whether we are going to find out facts or spoil the situation. I am not in favour of any committee visiting that place or in favour of a delegation of leaders paying a visit with political motives. It will not benefit anyone. I myself am a member of the Standing Committee and by virtue of my being a member of that Committee I would not like to go there at present. If at all I go there I would like to go alone. You accompany me. But do remember one thing that in case you decide to send a delegation to Ayodhya then it will set a precedent, then we will insist that you should send such delegations to other States also. (*Interruptions*) No, I cannot give any threat to West Bengal.

SHRI SAIFUDDIN CHOUDHURY : There is no such situation like Ayodhya in West Bengal. In case the situation prevailing in any of the States is similar to that of Ayodhya it should be the responsibility of the Parliament to ensure that delegation is sent there.

SHRI VAJPAYEE : Mr. Speaker, Sir, what is the situation in Ayodhya ?

SHRI MUKUL BALKRISHNA WASNIK : In view of the development that are taking place in Ayodhya, a Parliamentary Committee should go there. (*Interruptions*)

SHRI VAJPAYEE : The Hon. Home Minister has made a statement here. He has stated that there is no tension in Ayodhya. Did the Home Minister state that communal hatred is prevailing in Ayodhya at present ? The present situation in Ayodhya is a historical one. The parties which are present in this House have made no contribution in sorting out the Ayodhya issue amicably and through mutual dialogues.

SHRI E. AHMED (Manjeri) : Why don't you advise the Chief Minister of Uttar Pradesh not to go ahead with the demolition ? (*Interruptions*)

Law Treats Ayodhya Separately

SHRI VAJPAYEE : A law has been passed in this House. In that law it has been said that all the religious places shall be protected. However, Ayodhya has been left out of its purview.

SHRI BHOGENDRA JHA (Madhubani) : Only Babri Masjid and Ram Janma Bhoomi have been left out in Ayodhya.

SHRI ANBARASU ERA (Madras Central) : The same subject is being discussed for the last one week. There are thousands of people starving without food.

MR. SPEAKER : I will allow you.

SHRI VAJPAYEE : Mr. Speaker, Sir, the law that has been passed was brought in by the Central Government and all other parties had endorsed it. Under that law, Ayodhya has been granted the status of special category place of worship. After enacting that law, what had the Government and this House done to resolve the Ayodhya issue. When Shri Chandra Shekhar was the Prime Minister. *(Interruptions)*

SHRI SYED SHAHABUDDIN (Kishanganj) : This is a total misrepresentation of facts.

SHRI VAJPAYEE : Mr. Speaker, Sir, when Chandra Shekharji was the Prime Minister he had convened a meeting between Babri Masjid Action Committee and Ram Janma Bhoomi Samiti. Documents were exchanged and the issue had started moving towards a definite direction. *(Interruptions)*

SHRI NITISH KUMAR : Mr. Speaker, Sir, whether the discussion is based on the issue as to whether the committee should go there or not or Shri Vajpayee ji is supposed to narrate the entire episode in detail as he is doing.

SHRI VAJPAYEE : I will say what I want to say. *(Interruptions)*

Mr. Speaker, Sir, in case I am not interrupted frequently I will complete what I want to say, very soon. *(Interruptions)*

MR. SPEAKER : Please sit down. Mr. Vajpayee has said that he will finish quickly in case he is not interrupted. As such please resume your seats.

SHRI SHARAD YADAV : Mr. Speaker, Sir, we have no objection to Mr. Vajpayee's continuing to speak but at the same time we should also be allowed to comment on what he is saying.

SHRI VAJPAYEE : The new Government or in other words the Government headed by Shri Narasimha Rao instead of making any progress in the matter further to the exchange of documents has passed a legislation and they are sitting quietly. Now what is happening in Ayodhya ? Nothing is happening, only the ground is being cleared. *(Interruptions)*

Mr. Speaker, Sir, tourists visit Ayodhya in large numbers. They are expected to come on the forthcoming occasion of 'Ram Navami.' Lakhs of tourists come. *(Interruptions)* In case the Uttar Pradesh Government takes some initiative for development of tourism or for providing some amenities to tourists, the High Court has no objection to it and those who plead for abiding by the judgement of the Court should remember that the High Court has not objected to anything happening in Ayodhya. *(Interruptions)*

Let Home Minister Visit Ayodhya and Submit Factual Report

Mr. Speaker, Sir, I am suggesting a way out. My submission is that the Home Minister may go to Ayodhya, collect facts and after coming back may take the House into confidence and only thereafter should take a decision about the necessity to send a committee or delegation to Ayodhya.

Bomb Explosion in Ayodhya

Mr. Speaker, Sir, three issues have been raised in this discussion, all of them connected to Ayodhya. One issue is about the damage caused to the Masjid in bomb explosion in Faizabad. We are having contact with the U.P. Government.

Mr. Speaker, Sir, the entire House is the target of a bomb explosion and especially during the month of Ramzan if any Masjid is made the target of a bomb, then it is a serious matter and very disturbing....(*Interruptions*)....

Mr. Speaker, Sir, Faizabad is such a city, where even during Kar Sewa, no Masjid was damaged in any way. This is a record.

SHRI RAM VILAS PASWAN (Rosera) : At that time the Government was alert....(*Interruptions*)....

SHRI VAJPAYEE : At that time, no Masjid was damaged, this is very remarkable....(*Interruptions*)

Now you have come from Faizabad to Ayodhya, when I go to Ayodhya you will come to Faizabad....(*Interruptions*)....

Mr. Speaker, Sir, according to my information and as some Hon. members have said that there is a Masjid at the side of the main road in Kasaibara Mohalla. Today in the morning, 10 minutes before the Namaz a bomb exploded at 4.45 a.m. That bomb blast caused a one metre wide hole in the wall of backyard of that mosque and three nearby houses suffered partial damage. Nearby two people were sleeping in a hut and one of them sustained minor injury due to falling of a brick. The reconstruction work of mosque has begun and the mosque is being reconstructed. The House will be glad to know that strict security measures have been taken there and the situation is under control.

Mr. Speaker, Sir, I agree that certain elements may try to create tension in Ayodhya....(*Interruptions*) That attempt is wrong. Our Chief Minister himself had invited the delegation. Why are you bothered about our participation in it ? You visit Ayodhya, you are most welcome. You will be given a red carpet welcome. You can even offer prayers, if you want, otherwise you can return. Our perception regarding the nature and composition of the delegation is different, but the State Government is keen to receive a delegation. Recently, I had gone to Lucknow. We had talks with the Chief Minister and we even contacted the Home Ministry. The Chief Minister was of the opinion that it would be better if the delegation visits the State once the month of Ramzan is over and Id is celebrated peacefully in an atmosphere of goodwill. I have repeatedly told my respected friend, who call me 'Gurudev' that he has

Lok Sabha on March 31, 1992 while participating in the discussion regarding the Bomb explosion in Ayodhya

become more knowledgeable than me. He has raised the issue of the visit of Shri Mulayam Singh and his companions.

SHRI CHANDRA SHEKHAR (Ballia) : Shouldn't I have raised it ?

SHRI VAJPAYEE : There's nothing wrong in raising that matter, but they shouldn't have gone there at all, in the first instance.

SHRI CHANDRA SHEKHAR : And when they went there, you should have got them beaten up ?

Mulayam Singh Visit Ill-timed

SHRI VAJPAYEE : No, it is incorrect, Chandra Shekharji, the details of the incident are with me. They were on their way to Faizabad, after holding demonstrations before the collectorate. Shri Mulayam Singh has been the Chief Minister of Uttar Pradesh. I need not repeat the condition of Ayodhya, during his tenure as Chief Minister. His presence could have incited the people of Ayodhya and therefore he was stopped en route and asked to convey his message to the people from there only. As I mentioned earlier, he was told not to take the trouble of going there. He did not pay heed to it and was consequently stopped and in the process some scuffle took place. I have the details of the incident with me. (*Interruptions*)

Now if I mention the number of policemen injured in the process, you will say that I am echoing the figures given by the Uttar Pradesh Government. But if you are taking a stand on the basis of the information provided by Shri Mulayam Singh Yadav, we stand by the statement of Shri Kalyan Singh.

SHRI CHANDRA SHEKHAR : Mr. Speaker, Sir, reproducing the statement is a different thing, but if you want to prove that the misconduct of the State Government was correct, then you are most welcome to do so. (*Interruptions*)

SHRI VAJPAYEE : I don't want to prove any such thing. Chandra Shekharji, please don't level such allegations.

SHRI CHANDRA SHEKHAR : Mr. Speaker, Sir, during my tenure also, I used to tell the Government of that time that the partymen of other parties should not be maltreated. But if Shri Atal Bihariji says, that he has no objection, if the State Government maltreats respectable people and sets such precedent then it is alright....(*Interruptions*)

Sir, does it behove them to repeatedly mention the name of Shri Mulayam Singh ?

MR. SPEAKER : No, not at all.

SHRI CHANDRA SHEKHAR : But the leaders present in the House do not utter a single word in his defence. Mulayam Singh has his own standing in politics and he doesn't owe it to anyone. It seems that the formation of the State Government for the first time has gone into your head, but don't let it make you live under any illusion. (*Interruptions*)

Sir, I would like to reply to these things as well. Such talks are not acceptable. (*Interruptions*)

SHRI SHANKER SINGH VAGHELA (Godhara) : They are trying to disintegrate this country.

MR. SPEAKER : Please, keep it in mind that such discussions taking place in the House help in solving serious problems. Therefore, please see to it that you don't utter any such thing....

KUMARI UMA BHARTI (Khajuraho) : It was Shri Chandra Shekhar who raked up this issue.

MR. SPEAKER : No, he also didn't say any such thing. You please try to understand what Shri Vishwanath Pratap Singh and Shri Atal Bihari Vajpayee have to say. (*Interruptions*)

SHRI RAM VILAS PASWAN (Rosera) : They will start disturbing the moment any leader rises to speak.

MR. SPEAKER : Such interruptions won't serve any purpose. All these senior leaders by expressing their opinion are contributing towards a solution to this problem. So, please don't take any such action which may hinder this process.

SHRI SOMNATH CHATTERJEE (Bolpur) : Sir, I would like to know whether the Congress Party or the treasury bench has anything to say on this; not a single Congress member has spoken on this. (*Interruptions*)

MR. SPEAKER : Let us be kind to them. They are helping you by just keeping quiet. (*Interruptions*).... If you speak, it will only create problems. So please let Shri Vajpayee speak. (*Interruptions*). There were members who wanted to speak, but I did not allow them. Let us not be so unkind to them. (*Interruptions*).

SHRI VAJPAYEE : Mr. Speaker, Sir, I won't make any reference to Shri Mulayam Singh, because he is not present in the House.

MR. SPEAKER : You did't make any reference to him earlier also. Others did it.

SHRI VAJPAYEE : But he was leading those people who were going to Ayodhya. Thus, if I do not mention his name, I shall be doing injustice to him. That's why I said that he has an important role in this episode. I am sure that if he had asked Shri Chandra Shekhar whether the time was conducive for him to visit Ayodhya, the latter would have advised him against it and told him that the B.J.P. workers will take advantage of his visit, and create problems to defame him.

MR. SPEAKER : You are not serious.

SHRI VAJPAYEE : Mr. Speaker, Sir, we offer our regrets, if the police has committed any excesses there. It is regrettable if some Hon. members got injured in the scuffle. We would ask the Uttar Pradesh Government to order an inquiry into the incident. They should have checked any excessive use of force.

Sir, there is no prohibition on visiting Ayodhya and nobody wants to prevent people from visiting Ayodhya but if somebody is determined on taking a mob alongwith him, then certainly the responsibility of maintaining law and order in the city rests on the shoulders of the State Government. If it doesn't fulfil its obligations, then attempts would be made to bring it to the dock. After all, a mosque adjacent to the site in Faizabad has been damaged and moreover, it's the month of Ramzan. (*Interruptions*) There is lot of hustle bustle during night time. At such a time, the damage caused to a mosque is a matter of concern and needs to be given a serious thought. But, even then attempts are being made to put the State Government in an embarrassing situation. (*Interruptions*) Now again they have started interrupting.

SHRI INDRAJIT GUPTA : You don't entertain the idea of a delegation visiting Ayodhya.

SHRI VAJPAYEE : No, the State Government would welcome the visit of a delegation.

SHRI INDRAJIT GUPTA : But, that day you had opposed the idea. Shri Chandra Shekhar tried hard to solve the problem.

SHRI VAJPAYEE : Shri Chandra Shekhar has raised a very important question as to what step the Union Government is taking to solve the Ayodhya issue through a dialogue ? What has it done so far ? When Shri Chandra Shekhar was the Prime Minister, he found a way to make both the sides involved in the Ayodhya tangle, sit across the table and talk. That day, I mentioned this. But, that day perhaps the gravity of the situation did not dawn upon them. When both the sides sat across the table and exchanged documents, it seemed that the differences were narrowing down and the solution was not very far. I feel that if we had made further progress in that direction, we could have thrashed out a solution, through dialogue. But, the Union Government did not make any endeavour in that direction. They just passed a law on maintaining the *status quo* of the shrines, except Ayodhya. The Union Government has not taken any concrete step, aimed at bringing about a lasting solution to the dispute at Ayodhya. In the President's Address, it was stated that a close watch is being kept on the situation. Is it enough to simply keep a watch on the situation ? In Hindi, the term *Kadi Nazar* has been used, while in English, the term 'close watch' has been used. I fail to understand the difference. Is the Centre only going to see or will it do something about ? What is the role of the Centre ? When the Home Minister is asked, he has no information about it. He is not getting proper information. God knows what has happened to this Government ....(*Interruptions*)

Cartoons are being drawn on the Home Minister about his capabilities. The delegation can go. We have no objection about it. But we have problems. We don't want to start a wrong tradition by participating in it. It became clear here as to how wrong traditions are being started. Our friends from Bihar said that Shri Sahi has been murdered so a parliamentary delegation should be sent there....(*Interruptions*)

SHRI RAM VILAS PASWAN : It was said from both the sides.

SHRI VAJPAYEE : You were right. Only this will happen if a practice of sending parliamentary delegation is started. If someone will object about the delegation it will be said that he wants to hide something. Let's send a delegation. You leave for Ayodhya and we will leave for Patna. But let us fix the place of our meeting. Mr. Speaker, Sir, this House is our meeting place.

MR. SPEAKER : May be you can go on the same train.

SHRI VAJPAYEE : This House is the meeting place. I am sorry that I have to make a departure from the conventions. Is it not possible to raise an issue peacefully in this House and express one's own views forcefully ? ....(*Interruptions*) Neither we are able to make them understand nor you.

MR. SPEAKER : He is saying it for everyone.

SHRI VAJPAYEE : Sometimes it becomes difficult for me to sit here. When some outsider criticises our behaviour, we raise an issue of breach of privilege. When they find us like this, why can't they say anything about us ? There should be a system in this House. I have complaint against the Government also. When the proceedings of the House started today and the External Affairs Minister had already resigned, the Government should have stated about the resignation of the External Affairs Minister before the question was raised by anyone. There would have been no uproar, no problem in the House. How the External Affairs Minister behaved has become clear to the world. How the Parliamentary Affairs Minister behaved has become clear to us. The Home Minister is standing in the dock. The Government is in critical condition. Take care of it.

MR. SPEAKER : Shri Vajpayee has already told me whatever he wanted to say. I know about it.

Why Politics is Played from Places of Worship ?

Mr. Speaker, Sir, I should be given an opportunity to give a personal clarification. I did not want to take part in this discussion. Even now, it is not my desire because we want to hear the Prime Minister's reply. But can the discussion not take place in an atmosphere of peace, I have till now failed to understand....(*Interruptions*)

There are many serious questions before this country. These questions are such that will determine the future of the country. But this seriousness is not reflected in our discussion. There is a difference between heat and light....(*Interruptions*)

They are saying that you should not look ahead of you, you should look back. If we look back, it will be said that we do not look towards the future, we are not forward but backward looking. We are not only looking forward and backward but we are looking towards left as well.

My friend who just spoke, referred to my interview in 'Hello Zindagi' but it was an incomplete reference.* I had said that if the politics in this country is played from Masjid, from the Church, from the Gurudwara, then it cannot be stopped from reaching the door of the temple. There can be a discussion on it whether it is correct or wrong. But those who took politics to the Gurudwara, to the Mosque, are the people who go to the Mosque during elections to take orders from the Imam. We do not go.... (*Interruptions*)

I have never been to any Shankaracharya till today to seek blessings during elections. During the elections, I had gone to one area. I got the opportunity to meet one Shankaracharya. The newsmen asked me as to what sort of talk I had with him, whether I sought blessings for the party ? I said, no, I asked for the blessings for the country. Parties may exist, they may not exist, but the country must exist.

Communalism is Communalism

Mr. Speaker, Sir, if the Congress party in Mizoram seeks votes in the name of installing a Christian Government and writes so in its election manifesto, on that day Shri Arjun Singhji was saying that we had opposed it internally, but that opposition is not enough. I also keep on opposing many things in

* Shri Rashid Masood had said : "Vajpayeeji, is sitting, I wanted to congratulate him for the interview he had given on the T.V. "Hello Zindagi" where he said that this country is going to disintegrate when politics is being played from temples.

Personal clarification in the Lok Sabha on July 17, 1992 during the debate on Ram Janmabhoomi-Babri Masjid Dispute the party. But if they seek vote in the election in the name of installing a Christian Government in Mizoram, it will not do. You sought votes on this plank. This matter is pending in the Supreme Court since long. I can present this manifesto. One sided action will not do, there can be no one-sided battle against fundamentalism. Encouraging communalism on the one hand and fighting it on the other cannot go together.

The Congress Party talked about minority communalism for the first time in the Tirupati conference. I wished to congratulate you for this, but you will say that they are in collusion with each other, that is why I am not extending my congratulations. This has been said for the first time. Was the country not partitioned because of minority communalism....(*Interruptions*) Mr. Speaker, Sir, my difficulty is that I am not able to speak when I am interrupted...(*Interruptions*) Sir, I was talking about Tirupati. In Tirupati it was said for the first time that minority communalism is existing, but even for this the majority communalism was held responsible. There was nothing like majority communalism in this country.

Mr. Speaker Sir, my request is that if communalism is to be fought against, if the feeling of nationalism is to be created in its true sense, if communalism is to be rooted out, then there cannot be different yardsticks to measure communalism. If we want to curb narrow mindedness then we must fight it out whenever it is seen. If you compromise with communalism for the sake of securing votes then tendency to compromise with other types of communalism will grow.

SHRI RAM VILAS PASWAN : We will fight out evil with evil means.... (*Interruptions*)

Danger of Casteist Politics

SHRI VAJPAYEE : He is advising us to be good even in such an atmosphere. They are spreading casteism throughout the country....(*Interruptions*) Mr. Speaker Sir, I do not want to start a verbal dual with him but throughout the country he is saying that the President is Brahmin, Vice-President is Brahmin and the Prime Minister is also a Brahmin.

SHRI RAM VILAS PASWAN : That is what I am saying even today.

SHRI VAJPAYEE : He has stated that the leader of the Opposition is also a Brahmin. I did not know the caste of Shri Advani. We never go into the caste. Mr. Speaker, Sir, is it not another way to spread venom ? If we want to discuss the problems and want to solve the problems sincerely then we must go on making efforts in this direction.

As far as verdict of the court is concerned, Uttar Pradesh Government should implement it but the people, who themselves enacted a new legislation keeping aside the verdict of the Supreme Court in Shahbano case and amended the Constitution, should not give sermon to us. Thank you.

XV OTHER IMPORTANT ISSUES

Wild Charges by M.O. Mathai, Prime Minister Nehru's Secretary

Sir, I rise to seek your leave to raise a matter involving breach of privilege of the House. Shri M.O. Mathai, former Special Assistant to the Prime Minister in the course of his letter to the Prime Minister has made certain remarks which constitute a serious breach of privilege of this august House. The remarks are as follows :

> "But the ever-mounting tendency in our Parliament and our Press to attack public servants without caring to verify facts is having a devastatingly demoralising effect. Under such deplorable conditions very few self-respecting persons will care to enter Government service or public life."

May I submit in this connection that Shri Mathai has made a wild charge against this House. Let us consider the implications of what he has said. He has accused the House—(An Hon. Member : You also)—of a growing tendency to attack public servants without even caring for facts. I think this House is seized with a matter of another privilege motion when the Chief Minister of Kerala accused some members of this House. But, now the whole House has been accused. And that letter has been circulated by the Press Information Bureau of the Government of India and with the permission of the Prime Minister who is the Leader of the House and is expected to safeguard the dignity and honour of this House. I appreciate the frankness with which the Hon. Prime Minister during his Press Conference accepted that a mistake was committed and Shri Mathai caught him in a wrong mood, in an angry mood. I do not know on how many occasions the Prime Minister was caught by Shri Mathai in a wrong mood. He is also reported to have said that he has been committing foolish things. I think this is the most foolish thing that Shri Mathai has committed. Without going into the merits of the case....

MR. SPEAKER : Order, order. The Hon. member will note that under rule 225 it is said :

Lok Sabha on February 10, 1959 while raising the question of privilege regarding Shri M.O. Mathai's remarks in his letter to Prime Minister Pandit Jawaharlal Nehru

"...before the list of business is entered upon, call the member concerned, who shall rise in his place and, while asking for leave to raise the question of privilege, make a short statement relevant thereto."

The general conduct of Shri Mathai is not in question here. If he had not made that statement, he would not be a subject before the House at all. It is only with respect to the statement, and he has said enough.

If he wants to say anything more with respect to the statement, how the statement in the press ought to be accepted as genuine or any further remarks that this amounts to a contempt of the House and so on, they are allowed. After that, I shall hear if there is any opposition to this and follow the rest of the procedure. Only one question can be raised at a time.

SHRI VAJPAYEE : I think the statement is quite clear, self-evident, and it amounts to a breach of privilege of this House, and I request you and the House to take into consideration the breach that has been committed.

SHRI H.N. MUKHERJEE (Calcutta Central) : May I bring to your notice that I also gave notice of a motion.

SHRIMATI PARVATHI KRISHNAN (Coimbatore) : I have also given notice.

SHRI H.N. MUKHERJEE : Would you allow me to make a statement under rule 225 as you pointed out ? I feet that....

MR. SPEAKER : Under rule 225 not more than one question shall be raised at the same sitting. Shri Vajpayee has raised this question. If all the others relate to the same matter, I am not going to allow each one of them to speak on this particular matter.

SHRI BRAJ RAJ SINGH (Ferozabad) : The same question has been raised by many members.

SHRI SURENDRANATH DWIVEDY (Kendrapara) : A motion of privilege has been tabled by me.

MR. SPEAKER : Because the other questions are of the same nature and only one can be allowed, I have allowed Shri Vajpayee. It is goes through, the other questions will be barred, and all Hon. members will not have an opportunity to speak at this stage, whatever may happen later on. If leave is granted, a motion has to be made later under rule 226, and on that Hon. members will have the right to speak, not at this stage. Therefore, is there any opposition to this ?

SHRIMATI RENU CHAKRAVARTTY (Basirhat) : May I make a submission ? On a prior occasion, the House will remember, it is not one person who spoke on the subject.

SHRI TANGAMANI (Madurai) : So many members were allowed.

SHRIMATI RENU CHAKRAVARTTY : Various people were allowed to submit their positions on the question, and I am not quite clear as to what your ruling particularly means on this occasion.

MR. SPEAKER : What I said was this. Even now I shall bear the objection under rule 225. Thereafter, if leave is granted, Hon. members will have an opportunity, as many of them as I consider necessary and who want to speak on this question and throw light upon this matter. I will certainly do so.

SHRI V.P. NAYAR (Quilon) : The objection can be raised after hearing our case.

MR. SPEAKER : Let us go strictly by the rules.

SHRI H.N. MUKHERJEE : May I ask one thing ? Would you please let us have our say because we gave notice of the motion also, after the Prime Minister has spoken in this matter, because before the 25 members are asked to rise in their seats the House has got to make up its mind to a certain extent in regard to the relevancy of the matter at all ? After the Prime Minister has spoken, would you please let us have our say if we wish to make our submissions ?

MR. SPEAKER : It is only one person that can be called upon to speak on this occasion.

SHRIMATI PARVATHI KRISHNAN : There are other aspects of the matter.

MR. SPEAKER : I am concerned now with Shri Vajpayee's privilege motion. There may be a number of privilege motions. I am not ruling them out now. Let us see what happens to this motion and if a similar matter is sought to be raised in the same session, this having been disposed of, the other matters cannot come up, but so far as Hon. members who are interested in this subject are concerned, they might have tabled similar motions. I shall give them an opportunity if this matter is taken up. That is all that can be done at this stage. Let me ascertain if this is opposed.

SHRI H.N. MUKHERJEE : Even before the Prime Minister speaks, there might be certain points which he ought to bear in mind before he tells the House his reaction in the matter. He has already spoken to a press conference. I do not know how far that was proper when the Parliament was to meet but now when he is going to address the House, is it not better that he listens to some of us because we have also taken the responsibility of sending notice of this motion ?

SHRI JAIPAL SINGH (Ranchi West—Reserved—Sch. Tribes) : I humbly submit that if you were to interpret the rule as you are trying to do now, you are making a preemptive bid as they call it in Bridge. Various Hon. members have tabled this motion; the motions seem to be similar, but their approach may be dissimilar in each case. So, the Hon. Prime Minister will not have an opportunity to reply to what the other people have in mind. The motions may be similar, but the approach of each motion might be different. So, in fairness to the Prime Minister, it is only necessary that the various approaches be heard first.

Take my own case, I feel it is not a slander against members of the House. I say it is a direct charge against you in the Chair, that you have not been conducting the business of the House in the manner you should have, that you have permitted members of Parliament to say things without verification. That is why....

MR. SPEAKER : I am really sorry. While we are very anxious to guard our rights and protect them against any attacks or onslaughts, let us also be very strict and proceed according to the rules.

SHRI V.P. NAYAR : Sir, may I say that the prohibition in the rule is against only raising more than one question; there is no prohibition against more than one member raising the same question.

MR. SPEAKER : There is only one question that is raised. Hon. members will see rule 225 :

> "The Speaker, if he gives consent....and before the list of business is entered upon, call the member concerned, who shall rise in his place and, while asking....

I have asked Shri Vajpayee to state it. He has done so.

SHRI H.N. MUKHERJEE : I have also tabled a motion.

MR. SPEAKER : If he has also done so, it is not at this stage that I will call upon him. If leave is granted under rule 225, I will give him an opportunity because he has tabled a similar motion.

SHRI JAWAHARLAL NEHRU, Prime Minister and Minister of External Affairs : Mr. Speaker, Sir, the Hon. member has raised, as he has put it, a question of privilege involving a contempt of the House. Now, I should like to distinguish, if I may, between an impropriety and a question of privilege.

Speaking for myself, I think that the wording referred to is regrettable and not proper. That is a different matter. And, as a matter of fact, I am given to understand that Shri Mathai some time ago addressed you on this question expressing his deep regret that in a moment of whatever it was he wrote something without ever intending anything against the dignity of this House.

What I am suggesting is that we must not get mixed up between two things—the impropriety of a thing or the undesirability of something written, and the question of privilege. Of course, they are two separate things. Personally I regret that this was written and Shri Mathai : as I said, I understand, also expressed his deep regret for it. I do not myself see, apart from the question of impropriety, where the question of privilege comes in into this matter—on that point only—and because there was some....

SHRI V.P. NAYAR : He also said he had no intention.

SHRI JAWAHARLAL NEHRU : I am merely expressing, because, naturally, when this matter was referred to rather casually, I did not even know it was coming up now; otherwise, I would have perhaps brought up some papers in this connection, because, when I heard that this was going to come up, I was interested to find out some precedents previously as to how such a thing is dealt with, and so I had the matter enquired into from a parliamentary, constitutional and legal point of view to satisfy myself, and that satisfied me at any rate that anything like this could not be considered a breach of privilege or contempt of the House. I am merely stating this fact for the knowledge of the House. I do not venture to give any opinion myself except to say that apart from the impropriety of it I do not myself see where any breach of privilege comes in in the remarks made. It certainly does not apply to the House or, as one Hon. member has said, to you, Sir. It says—I have not got even the words before me at the present moment ; I have no papers, but I remember the words . . . .

SHRI GORAY (Poona) : Shall I quote ?

SHRI JAWAHARLAL NEHRU : But I remember the words namely that there is a growing tendency in Parliament for remarks or statements to be made without due inquiry. I do not think that . . . .

SHRI JAIPAL SINGH : And the Chair permits the remark, by implication. (*Interruptions*)

MR. SPEAKER : He said :

> "But the ever-mounting tendency in our Parliament and our Press to attack public servants without caring to verify facts is having a devastatingly demoralising effect."

SHRI JAWAHARLAL NEHRU : If I may say so, the answer to the Hon. member is this. I do not wish to enter into any argument in this matter. I would only make my submission, the submission I had made to you, that while these remarks are unfortunate and regrettable, and for my part, I regret them, and Mr. Mathai also is deeply sorry, as he has expressed it to you, Sir, yet, so far as the question of privilege is concerned, I do not think that is raised, and as far as I know, whenever something even much stronger than this has been said on these lines, it has been held elsewhere that no question of privilege is raised. I merely make this submission to you; it is for you to decide.

SHRI SURENDRANATH DWIVEDY : Does it mean that the Press Information Bureau is also absolved of its responsibility ? They have also committed a breach of privilege. (*Interruptions*)

MR. SPEAKER : Order, order. There is nothing more. Let us now proceed with this.

SHRI H.N. MUKHERJEE : I would beg of you to let me have my say in regard to this matter.

MR. SPEAKER : No Hon. member will be prevented from having his say legitimately. The Hon. member will kindly resume his seat. Under the rules, I have to ask if leave is objected to. That is what the Prime Minister says. Is it not so ?

SHRI JAWAHARLAL NEHRU : I do not know about objection. I am merely placing certain things before you. It is not for me to object, and I would not like to object or to agree. I am merely placing certain considerations before you for you to decide.

MR. SPEAKER : It is for the House to object, under the rules. It is true that Mr. Mathai has sent me a letter stating that :

"I enclose a copy of a letter from our Law Minister . . . ."

SHRI V.P. NAYAR : Law Minister ?

MR. SPEAKER : If you consider it appropriate, please place these papers before . . .

> "If the Lok Sabha in its wisdom decides that I have been responsible for casting aspersions on Parliament, I should like to state that it was never my intention, and I willingly express my deep regret . . . .(*Interruptions*)

I am not disposing of anything hurriedly.

> "As a citizen, I am interested, in upholding the supremacy of Parliament in India, particularly at a time when the . . ."

SOME HON. MEMBERS : Oh, oh. (*Interruptions*)

MR. SPEAKER : There is just one more sentence.

"...parliamentary system has broken down in some of our neighbouring countries."

That is all.

Now, 25 Hon. members must rise in their seats to say that they are in favour of leave being granted. How many Hon. members are in favour ?

(More than 25 Members rose in their seats)

MR. SPEAKER : Now, any objection ? *(Interruptions)*

SOME HON. MEMBERS : There is no objection to this.

MR. SPEAKER : I take it as an objection; the Hon. Prime Minister says that this does not amount to a breach of privilege. Therefore, I have asked Hon. members. Now, leave is granted.

The further step is under rule 226 which reads :

"If leave under rule 225 is granted, the House may consider the question and come to a decision or refer it to a Committee of Privileges on a motion made either by the Member who has raised the question of privilege or by any other member."

It is open now to the member raised it or to any other member to ask this House to dispose of it itself or send it to the Committee of Privileges. In either case, I would only ask the House to consider this letter that I have read. (*Interruptions*). It is not as if everybody should go on talking.

SHRI V.P. NAYAR : How does it absolve him ?

MR. SPEAKER : I am not saying anything now. What is the next motion now ?

SHRI NAUSHIR BHARUCHA (East Khandesh) : I am moving that the matter be referred to the Privileges Committee for a report.

SHRI BRAJ RAJ SINGH : I move that the House itself do decide and call Mr. Mathai to the Bar of the House.

SHRI JAWAHARLAL NEHRU : I only wish to say that I do not oppose this [Shri Vajpayee's] Motion, that is, the Motion to refer this matter to the Committee of Privileges.

I ventured to express my opinion that so far as I could understand it, there was no breach of privilege. But since this Motion has been admitted by you, I think the right course would be to send it to the Committee of Privileges for them to consider it fully.

Mr. Speaker, it is not quite clear to me whether there are two motions before the House or three. Raja Mahendra Pratap's suggestion ....(*Interruptions*)

AN HON. MEMBER : There is no motion.

MR. SPEAKER : He raised a point of order.

SHRI JAWAHARLAL NEHRU : You were pleased to say, Sir, that there were three motions. (*Interruptions*) May I be spared gestures from the other side, Sir ? I was enquiring of the Speaker. I can understand his language; he need not enforce it by gestures.

MR. SPEAKER : Though Raja Mahendra Pratap raised it as a point of order, in substance he wanted the proceedings to be dropped. I wanted to treat it as a substantive motion....(*Interruptions*) Order, order. He has not subsequently followed it up. He could have easily said that he wanted these proceedings should be dropped. He did not follow it up and therefore, I am not placing it before the House.... (*Interruptions*)

[Some Hon. Members rose.]

MR. SPEAKER : I have called the Hon. Prime Minister. (*Interruptions*)

SHRI JAWAHARLAL NEHRU : I am not going to give into anybody. Since Raja Mahendra Pratap's suggestion has not taken the form of a definite proposal, I need not say anything about it. But, I would like to say this that in a matter of this kind, as has been rightly pointed out, it should not be treated as a party matter or group matter. I have ventured to say it on an earlier occasion. Some words of mine have been quoted. I would say that when a considerable section of the House has a feeling that something should be done, it is hardly a matter for a majority to override those wishes. I look upon it from this point of view. Therefore, when a number of members of this House felt this way, I immediately agreed to a reference of this question to the Privileges Committee of the House and at that stage any suggestion to drop this matter would, I think, not be a right one because it would almost appear that an attempt was made somehow to hush matters or hide matters. It is not a good thing for such an impression to be created. Therefore, I would have opposed Raja Mahendra Pratap's proposal to drop this at this stage.... (*Interruptions*)

MR. SPEAKER : Order, order, Hon. members must follow the English. He says : "I would have opposed."

SHRI JAWAHARLAL NEHRU : As things are, I think the proper course is to send it to the Committee of Privileges.

There is another proposal that has been made. I do not even understand it in the sense how things are to be done in the House. I think it would be otherwise too, not only unnecessary but not very desirable. After all the dignity of the House may suffer in various ways and it may suffer even by attaching too great an importance to trivial matters. It is not merely a question of another person or other persons saying. What other persons say may affect the dignity of the House but how we treat it also affects the dignity of the House . . . .

I support this reference to the Privileges Committee but, quite apart from this, for the future, I may submit that it is a matter of maintaining the dignity of the House by not attaching too much importance to every odd word that some outsider says.

RAJA MAHENDRA PRATAP : I believe the Hon. Prime Minister is too liberal. We do not accept his views here. I ask for a division and I hope you will all agree that this should be dropped.

MR. SPEAKER : Order, order.

Raja Mahendra Pratap rose....(*Interruptions*)

MR. SPEAKER : Order, order. The Hon. member is irrepressible. I am exceedingly sorry. The other motion is for reference to the Committee of Privileges. The question is :

"That the attention of the House having been drawn by some Honourable members on February 10th, 1959, to a letter written to the Prime Minister by his Special Assistant Shri M.O. Mathai and made public on January 17, 1959 through Press release by the Prime Minister's Secretariat and the Press Information Bureau of the Government of India in which the said Shri M.O. Mathai, *inter alia,* remarks :

> "But the ever-mounting tendency in our Parliament and our Press to attack public servants without caring to verify facts is having a devastatingly demoralising effect. Under such deplorable conditions very few self-respecting persons will care to enter Government service or public life."

The House resolves that the matter be referred to the Committee of Privileges for investigation and report whether the above mentioned remarks of Shri M.O. Mathai made public through the Prime Minister's Secretariat and the Press Information Bureau of the Government of India constitute an adverse reflection on the dignity of the Members of Parliament and the Speaker of the Lok Sabha and whether they constitute a contempt of Parliament and also to recommend what further steps the House may take in the matter."

(The motion was adopted)

Parliament's Session Outside Delhi

Sir, I shall state the thought behind the amendment that I had tabled. When my friend Shri Prakash Vir Shastri moved this resolution perhaps he had no idea that this discussion would assume the form it has taken. The thought that motivated the introduction of this resolution in the House did not envisage the raising of a new controversy between North and South. Our country has attained political unity after a thousand years and it is now necessary to strengthen the roots of that unity. It is true that this mansion of unity stands on the foundation of our culture, but if we want to strengthen this unity in the political field we might have to take steps that seem necessary in the present context and in view of the country's expanse.

The Hon'ble President has for the last some years decided to celebrate Independence Day in the South, and the whole country has applauded this decision to go out of Delhi once a year and visit some other State, so that the people there may come into direct contact with him and realise that our unity is an enduring unity, practical unity which we can experience every moment.

I think this is the feeling behind the desire for holding a session of the Lok Sabha outside Delhi. It is not a question of changing the capital. Delhi will remain the capital. It was here that the *'killi'* (nail) was put in the ground, so it became Dilli. That nail is still buried here. No attempt is being made to take it out, and no attempt should be. The only question is, is it possible for us to hold a session of the Lok Sabha in Bangalore or Hyderabad ?

It cannot be denied that people beyond Vindhyachal will welcome such a session. At the same time it can also not be denied that there are many economic and practical difficulties in holding a session there. But it would not be proper to reject this proposal simply because of practical and economic difficulties, because they are not insurmountable. It is possible that in the near future we may not be able to hold a Lok Sabha session anywhere outside Delhi, but it could be possible in the future, and if the Ministry of Parliamentary Affairs takes interest and acts promptly we might be able to do so in the near future. As it is, there are many States in the country where sessions are held in the winter at one place and in the summer at another. The Jammu and Kashmir Legislative Assembly sits in Srinagar in the summer and in Jammu in the winter. The Bombay Legislative Assembly also used to sit at Poona. There is also an example in the Congress regime where Madhya Bharat was one State but it had two capitals, one at Gwalior, another at Indore. I do not know if they were following in the footsteps of Muhammed

Lok Sabha on Nov. 20, 1959 while speaking on the Resolution regarding holding a session of Parliament at Hyderabad or Bangalore

Tuqhlaq, but it was there. I do not understand it when my Congress friends oppose this.

AN HON. MEMBER : That is why that State came to an end.

SHRI VAJPAYEE : So let us try to resolve the difficulties. But there are emotions linked with this question, and we cannot ignore them.

In view of the colour the discussion has now assumed it would not be right to dismiss this matter summarily by saying transporting members would be difficult, there would not be an assembly house, and where will we sit ?

It could also be argued that if the Government could not provide all facilities to members even in 12 years how will it be possible to do so in Hyderabad or Bangalore ? There is force in such arguments. But the feeling behind this resolution should be respected. It should be acknowledged that this is being proposed in order to strengthen the country's unity, not for serving any political purpose. There is absolutely no need of talking about raising a new barrier between North and South. But we know our country is very big. When we read about its vastness in literature we feel very good, but when we have to move in this big country we have to face big difficulties.

The need is to bring about many such opportunities as would enable our fellow countrymen in distant parts to feel that all parts are being cared for. And although my amendment has been cancelled I trust the Minister will accept the suggestion to set up a committee to consider this matter.

That Committee should collect all sorts of figures and also consider how the difficulties in the way could be solved. And if that committee concludes even after considering those circumstances that this is not possible the House should also have no difficulty in accepting it. But if this resolution is summarily rejected that would have a bad effect on the people in some parts of the country, and we must guard against that. Thank you.

Remove the Disease and Its Causes

Sir, while considering the Health Ministry's demands for grants it is natural that we would think about the reasons for the deficiency in health services in the country as well as about the insufficient facilities for eradication of the diseases. After food, clothing and shelter arrangements for medical treatment are most necessary. Our seers and *Rishis* had envisaged a Bharat where all would be free of disease—*"serve santu niraamayah."*

This was how they had indicated this state. I do not have enough time at my disposal, but I must say that progress in this direction has not been satisfactory. To date medical facilities are extremely limited. Even in the cities, let alone the villages, it has not been possible to make the best possible treatment available to the common man. If we take Delhi alone and TB figures alone we would see that there are at least 25,000 TB patients in Delhi, but there are only 1200 hospital beds. The shortage can be easily estimated. Even in the capital of India we cannot give these facilities and we cannot even separate the 25,000 TB patients. They live in the midst of the people and spread the disease. Not only we cannot provide them beds, we cannot even segregate them. This is just an indication of how much we have done in this direction.

Now that we are on Delhi let me say one thing more. There are many hospitals in Delhi but there is no Central arrangement for them. Some hospitals are directly connected with the Central Government, some are managed by the Delhi Administration, while some fall within the field of the Delhi Municipal Corporation. Because of lack of centralised management the people of Delhi have not been able to derive adequate benefit from these hospitals. I hope all these hospitals would be managed from one source.

A hospital for cancer treatment has been set up in Delhi. This is a step in the right direction. The management of this hospital, however, complains that its fund allocation is not enough. It should be somewhat increased.

Adulteration Main Reason of Disease

A more important thing than medical treatment is to create conditions that would prevent the rise of disease. I am sorry to say that the Health Ministry has completely failed to take this aspect into consideration. It is necessary to combat a disease when it spreads, but more important is to prevent it from spreading. This aspect of the health problem has not been taken into consideration. The number of doctors is not in proportion to the population and there is no possibility of this deficiency being made up in the near future.

Lok Sabha on April 6, 1960 during discussion on the demands for grants of the Ministry of Health

Medical treatment facilities are also inadequate. There are no doctors in the villages. Those who are doctors do not want to go there. So if we look only to contain diseases the Government cannot win this race with its limited resources. So along with combating diseases efforts are also required to prevent their rise. For this checking adulteration of food-stuffs is very necessary. This is not the time to describe how adulteration of food articles goes on in Delhi right under the nose of the Central Government, but everything is adulterated and it enters our body by way of food. Howsoever we may increase the number of doctors, howsoever we may increase medical facilities, it would be difficult, if not impossible to check the spread of diseases if we do not check food adulteration.

In this connection, I would like to say something about the Government arrangements for drinking water in the villages. This report also refers to a Central Government plan for providing drinking water in the villages. Alongwith it there are also three other projects. One of them is the arrangements under the community development block. There are also local development works that arrange for the villages. And thirdly drinking water arrangements are also made from the economic assistance that the Home Ministry gives to members of our Scheduled Castes and Tribes. But there is no accord among these three plans, and potable water is still not available in thousands of villages although a total outlay of Rs. 50-60 crores was earmarked for this purpose in the First and Second Plans. When the Planning Commission was asked if it could specify the number of villages where the residents do not get potable water it could not do so. The Central Government also does not have such figures. We are chalking out big development plans, but clean drinking water for the villages is a primary need, upon which prevention of diseases depends to a large extent. Desirable progress has not yet been possible in this direction. According to the 1951 census there were 5 lakh 50 thousand villages. In 1948 a health survey and development committee was set up, and in 1949 an environmental hygiene committee was set up, but beyond making general recommendations they did not consider any concrete plan.

Funds for Tap, Not for Well

About the funds that the Ministry of Health gives for drinking water I would like to point out that money is given for tap water but not if a village people want to dig a well. There was a case near Delhi, which was brought to the Prime Minister's attention. Villagers wanted money for digging a well for drinking water but the Health Ministry said the money was reserved only for those villages where water is supplied by tap, not by well. This is a strange situation. It is very good if you want to take water everywhere by pipe. It would be welcome. But if your resources are limited and if you cannot provide tap water everywhere you should give for well-digging the money that is lying with you. In many villages the funds provided for drinking water arrangements under five year plans were not spent. Very little money was also spent under community development and out of the funds earmarked by the Home Ministry for the Scheduled Castes. There are still thousands of villages that have no drinking water. The Rajasthan Government had set up a committee under the chairmanship of the Hon. member Shri Harishchandra Mathur to assess the shortage of drinking water in the villages of the State and to see how it could be made up. Such Committees should be set up in all States, and the Health Ministry should take the initiative in the matter. Provision of clean water in the villages should be given priority and provision of potable water to villages in India should be made the Third Five Year Plan's target.

Where is Delhi's Master Plan ?

Sir, the Home Ministry is responsible for preparing a master plan for Delhi. That Ministry's report makes some reference to this matter. We have been hearing about this master plan for years. But that plan is not yet before the people. I do not think the Central Government has any clear idea of Delhi's future development. Every year there is an increase of one lakh in Delhi's population and we require housing in that proportion. But one effect of the Government's taking over 34,000 acres of land in Delhi has been that house construction has stopped. Instead of the Government building houses the building of houses by others has stopped. Now the Government should say how it will use the land it has taken over. It has been estimated that at least Rs. 300 crores would be needed to develop the land. Is the Central Government prepared to spend this amount for Delhi's development ? And if the Government cannot develop all the land it has taken over why was it taken over ? House building has stopped and Delhi needs houses. So make your plan quickly and place it before the people. It has been alleged that the plan gets changed in the official files. The area that was shown as the green belt in the Master Plan was changed to residential, and this has enabled some builders and some people in high positions in Delhi to earn lakhs of rupees, because the green belt was bought cheaply but after changing it to residential area it will be sold at high prices.

Colonisers Lined Their Pockets, Buyers Left High and Dry

There is a set-up called Delhi Land Finance. Its activities should be investigated and it should be found out how much land it purchased over the years and how it has sold it. Colonisers in Delhi bought land cheaply and sold it at high prices to people who were not in the know of things, who needed houses, and who longed for land. And those who bought the land are suffering. The colonisers washed their hands of the affair after buying the land cheaply and selling it dearly, but the land that was bought by the people from them passed into the Government's hands.

MR. DEPUTY SPEAKER : I too am one of them.

SHRI VAJPAYEE : Then I think the Health Minister will consider the matter seriously.

The land that has been taken over includes some *Bastis* (settlements) that have been approved by the Delhi Municipal Corporation or by the Delhi

Development Authority or whose layout has been approved by Shahdara or other local bodies. Such lands have also been taken over. What will be the future of these settlements ? Will the houses that have come up be demolished ? Will those people who have settled down be uprooted ? Will those settlements that have been approved by any local body, including the municipality, corporation or development authority, also be demolished ? The Central Government is mum on this point, and as a result the people are having all sorts of doubts. They fear their houses may be demolished and they may be uprooted. The Health Minister should take this opportunity to set the people's mind at rest.

Neglect of Indian Medical System

The Government has adopted a regrettable attitude towards the Indian medical system. Allopathy is modern science and no one would deny that it should develop and serve the people of India in treating ill health. But however hard we try we will not be able to make allopathic treatment available to every citizen of the country. I do not want to go into whether it is good or not, though there is a great difference of opinion on that. But even supposing for a moment that this facility should be available to all, can we arrange it ? In my opinion an Indian born and bred in the soil of this country would not respond as readily to the allopathic system as he would to the Indian system of cure. Allopathy suppresses a disease, it does not eradicate it. As against this Ayurveda is the science of life. It not only cures disease, it teaches how to prevent disease. But the Government has not yet decided upon a policy in this respect. Many committees have been set up, and they have submitted their reports. But they are gathering dust on the shelves in the Home Ministry. I would not be surprised if the Home Minister announces one more committee to consider the reports of these committees. Committees have been set up and they have given you their views. Now the Government should extend maximum facilities to indigenous systems like Ayurveda, the Yunani system, nature cure and homoeopathy, so that they could reach up to the villages of India. The Government does not have a proper attitude in this matter. It has scope for improvement. Thank you.

Government Misusing Attorney-General

Sir, I call the attention of the Home Minister to the following of urgent public importance and request him to make a statement on it :

> "The reported decision of the Congress Party to consult the Attorney-General on the Madhya Pradesh High Court's order in respect of Shri D.P. Mishra."

SHRI Y.B. CHAVAN, Minister of Home Affairs : The Central Government have taken steps to obtain the advice of the Attorney-General on the constitutional and legal issues involved in the question whether, in view of the orders passed by the High Court of Madhya Pradesh in the election case involving Shri D.P. Mishra, the Governor, Madhya Pradesh, could invite Shri D.P. Mishra, the present Leader of the Congress Party in Madhya Pradesh Legislative Assembly, to form the Ministry. The Governor has also wished to obtain the opinion of the Attorney-General on this matter. There is no question of the Congress Party seeking the advice of the Attorney-General.

SHRI MADHU LIMAYE (Monghyr) : Not true. Wrong. He is a very clever man.

SHRI VAJPAYEE : Sir, I was surprised as well as sad to listen to the Home Minister's statement. A meeting of the Congress Parliamentary Board was held on the 20th, in which it was decided to consult the Attorney-General before taking a decision about Shri D.P. Mishra. The Congress President told the press about this decision. I quote the *Indian Express* :

> "The Congress President, Mr. S. Nijalingappa, told newsmen that the Board wanted to get the Attorney-General's opinion about Mr. Mishra."

Other papers have also published similar reports. It is not necessary to repeat all of them. On publication of this report we approached you and said we wanted to challenge the propriety of this action. The Congress Parliamentary Board may take any decision about Pandit D.P. Mishra, but it cannot consult the Attorney-General of India. The Attorney-General is not meant for advising any party. He can advise the Government of India and Parliament. When this matter was raised the Home Minister decided that the Parliamentary Board's decision had put the Congress Party into difficulties, and so the Government of India should now consult the Attorney-General.

What is the Propriety ?

When was the decision that the Government of India should consult the Attorney-General taken ? On what date ? At what hour ? Was it taken before the Congress Parliamentary Board's decision on the 20th ? And if it was, why

***Lok Sabha** on March 22, 1969 while raising a Calling Attention Motion on the reported decision of the Congress Party to consult the Attorney-General on Madhya Pradesh High Court's order in respect of Shri D.P. Mishra*

was the House not taken into confidence ? The Home Minister did not accept the short-notice questions and calling attention motions that we had given notice of in this regard, because he thought the Congress Parliamentary Board had not yet decided about it. But now the Home Minister says the Attorney-General is being consulted on the basis of the Government of India's decision. I want to know when this decision was taken.

Secondly, what is the propriety of the Government of India consulting the Attorney-General about Pandit D.P. Mishra ? Pandit Mishra is a citizen of India.

AN. HON. MEMBER : An ordinary citizen.

ANOTHER HON. MEMBER : A disqualified citizen.

SHRI VAJPAYEE : His election was held void. The Madhya Pradesh High Court set it aside on grounds of corrupt practices. Where does the Central Government come into the picture in this ? He may become the Chief Minister or not, the Governor of Madhya Pradesh may invite him to form the Government or not, the Central Government does not come into it. Will the Central Government take such advice if the High Court's decision went against some other citizen ? Is the Central Government's decision based upon the Governor's decision ? I say the Central Government is misusing the position of the Attorney-General to decide about an individual belonging to its party. There is no reason for such misuse. What is the propriety of such a decision by the Central Government ? Will the Central Government be willing to do so in future about any citizen of the country ? If there is a question about a person of my party becoming or not becoming Chief Minister will we be able to consult the Attorney-General through the Government of India ?

Constitutional Propriety and Political Morality

It is not only a matter of law. It is also a question of constitutional propriety and political morality. The Madhya Pradesh High Court has annulled an individual's election on grounds of resorting to corrupt practices. The High Court's stay order says Pandit D.P. Mishra may sit in the Legislative Assembly, but he cannot participate in the proceedings, he cannot vote. Is the Attorney-General's advice being sought for use against the High Court's decision ?

SHRI N.K.P. SALVE (Betul) : Are we people going to determine this ?

SHRI VAJPAYEE : Sir, now that the Home Minister has admitted that the Attorney-General is being consulted I would like to repeat my request to you that the House discuss this matter and the Attorney-General be summoned before it. Under article 88 of the Constitution the Attorney-General can come to the House, can acquaint it with his thoughts and can be questioned. Even the Governor of Madhya Pradesh does not have the right to consult the Attorney-General. He can consult the Advocate-General but not the Attorney General. If the Attorney-General is to be consulted it should be done through the Central Government. I pray to you to accept our request that the Attorney-General be summoned to the House.

MR. SPEAKER : Before the Hon. Minister answers I want to say something. Shri Vajpayee also wrote to me about that. There are four ways of calling the Attorney-General. Attorney-General can come if he wants to. The Government can call him if they want some clarification.

SHRI NATH PAI (Rajapur) : We want (*Interruptions*).

MR SPEAKER : I said there are four ways. I have mentioned only two. Why do you shut me out ? The other way is, if the House wants, they may call him. (*Interruptions*) I say, if the House wants, they may call him. When I say, House, no shouting should take place. One is, he can himself come; the second, the Government can call him; and the third, the House can call him. There is a fourth way. I am coming to the fourth possibility. If the Speaker is in doubt about some legal aspect he can call. But now the Speaker is not involved in this. I am sitting here as Speaker now. If the Speaker is involved in any legal point where he has to give a ruling or something where he is in doubt, or where he has to give some sort of judgement naturally this can be done. But here there is no point on which I am asked to give any ruling here.

There is a controversy about Attorney-General being called by the Congress Party which we are discussing now ....(*Interruptions*) Hon. Members should hear me now ....

SHRI PILOO MODY (Godhra) : We shall keep quiet if you just phone him up.

MR. SPEAKER : The point that is now before the House is about the Congress Party or the Congress President asking for the opinion of the Attorney-General. The other things such as whether Shri D.P. Mishra will be Chief Minister or not are not before the House at all now. We are not discussing the question now. The question is whether the Congress Party can call the Attorney-General to give his opinion. That is the point now before the House. Therefore the question of my calling the Attorney-General does not arise. If the House wants it can call him at any time it likes.

SHRI S.M. BANERJEE (Kanpur) : Then I move that the Attorney-General be called to this House.

SHRI SHEO NARAIN (Basti) : If the House wants, and not if the Opposition wants.

MR. SPEAKER : There is no motion now before me. When it comes we shall consider it.

SHRI C. NAIDU (Chittoor) : On a point of order. Anybody has got a right to consult the Attorney-General in his private capacity. There is no bar to the Attorney-General being called to work for anybody. The Congress Party has got a right to consult him.

MR SPEAKER : There is no point of order. Now, the Home Minister may reply.

SHRI Y.B. CHAVAN : I really do not understand the controversy in this matter, because when the Governor himself expressed a desire to consult the Attorney-General....

But when an intricate constitutional and legal issue is raised, shall I not as a member of the House, and shall I not as an Indian citizen expect that he should consult a proper legal authority ? What is wrong about it ? The Attorney-General is certainly entitled to give his opinion and Government of India are entitled to get an opinion of the Attorney-General. It is wrong to say that the Governor has to consult only the Advocate-General, and it is improper for him to get the opinion of the Attorney-General. The question has been why the Government of India decided to consult the Attorney-General on a situation developing in the State, where a constitutional issue was likely to be raised.

SHRI VAJPAYEE : Sir, my questions have not been answered. I want to know —when, on what date, was the decision to consult the Attorney-General taken ? Is it true that it was taken after the Congress Parliamentary Board's decision ?

SHRI Y.B. CHAVAN : No. You may believe me if you want to. If you want to doubt that is up to you.

I discussed this matter with the Law Minister on the 19th instant. I do not remember exactly when the Parliamentary Board's meeting took place. I may tell my hon. friend this : if he wants to believe it he may believe it, otherwise not. In the Parliamentary Board I did say that in these matters the Government would like to be guided by the Attorney-General, and naturally when the Governor also expressed a desire to consult the Attorney-General, the Attorney-General came to be mentioned in the Parliamentary Board; he came to be mentioned only in this context.

SHRI VAJPAYEE : Sir, the Home Minister says he discussed the matter. I am not talking about the discussion. Is it or is it not the Government of India's decision that the Attorney-General be consulted ? There is no question of a discussion in some private-meeting.

SHRI Y.B. CHAVAN : I told him that I discussed it with the Law Minister on the 19th instant.

SHRI VAJPAYEE : On what date was the decision taken ? Is there any noting on the file ?

MR. SPEAKER : He must have taken the decision on the 19th perhaps.

SHRI S. KANDAPPAN (Mattur) : Why did he not take the House into confidence ?

SHRI VAJPAYEE : Sir, I had asked one more question—has the Home Ministry or the Government of India given thought to the constitutional propriety and political morality involved in the matter of Shri D.P. Mishra ? Is the Central Government bent upon making a corrupt person Chief Minister ?

SHRI Y.B. CHAVAN : I do not understand this. If he afraid that the Attorney-General .... (*Interruptions*)

SHRI N.K.P. SALVE : Point of order. Atalji has said a corrupt person ....

SHRI RABI RAY (Puri) : The High Court has said.

SHRI N.K.P. SALVE : Sir, my point of order is this—we can understand if Hukamchand Kachchwai says something like this. Baburao Patel has called him Tarzan in his journal. Does he not know how isolating it is to call somebody Tarzan ? We all have respect for Atalji. He presents his point of view in moderation. He says we want to make a corrupt person the Chief Minister. Whether he is corrupt or not is yet to be decided by the Supreme Court .... (*Interruptions*)

AN. HON. MEMBER : He is corrupt so long as the Supreme Court does not give its decision .... (*Interruptions*)

SHRI N.K.P. SALVE : Sir, I request that Atalji's remark about his being corrupt be expunged.

MR. SPEAKER : Will Hon. Members kindly sit down now ? I thought the word *'bhrashtachar'* was used for ....(*Interruptions*)

May I request all Hon. Members to resume their seats ? Shri N.K.P. Salve wanted my ruling on the point he had raised ....

SHRI N.K.P. SALVE : I want your ruling.

MR. SPEAKER : I am giving my ruling. I thought that the word *'bhrashtachar'* meant corruption or something like that. I do not know so much of Hindi ....

Pandit Deen Dayal Upadhyaya's Murder

Sir, I call the attention of the Minister for Home Affairs to the following subject of urgent public importance. I am happy he has recovered his health and returned to the House. I request that he make a statement on the following :

> "The demand made by more than 70 Members of Parliament that a judicial commission equipped with adequate and effective powers be set up to find out the facts regarding the murder of Shri Deen Dayal Upadhyaya, former President of Jan Sangh."

SHRI RABI RAY (Puri) : The Government should accept this demand.

SHRI Y.B. CHAVAN, Minister of Home Affairs : Sir, Government have received a copy of the joint statement dated June 22, 1969 issued by members of Parliament belonging to various political parties in which a demand was made that a judicial commission with investigative powers should be appointed to bring to book persons guilty of the murder of Shri Deen Dayal Upadhyaya. The statement was issued after the Special Sessions Judge, Varanasi, in his judgement dated June 9, 1969, had acquitted the two accused persons of the charge of murder of Shri Upadhyaya, while convicting one of them on a charge of stealing his belongings and sentencing him to 4 years' imprisonment.

It will be recalled that in a statement made in this House on February 14, 1968, I had informed the House that it was at the request of the Chief Minister, Uttar Pradesh that it had been decided to entrust the investigation to the Central Bureau of Investigation. It was, therefore, necessary to forward the judgement to the Government of Uttar Pradesh so that they may consider the question of filing an appeal against the acquittal of the two accused persons. The decision of the State Government is awaited.

The House will appreciate that notwithstanding the deep anxiety felt by a large section of the House it would not be possible for me to say anything more at this stage about the future course of action which can be determined only after we know the decision of the State Government. I may, however, assure the House that we are most anxious that no responsible section of public opinion should have reason to feel that all that is possible is not done to find out the facts.

Lok Sabha on July 29, 1969 while raising a Calling Attention Motion regarding the murder of Pandit Deen Dayal Upadhyaya

Patience has a Limit

SHRI VAJPAYEE : I was slightly disappointed with the Home Minister's statement. So far we have shown a lot of patience in this matter. But patience has a limit. At first we were told that Pandit Deen Dayal Upadhyaya died in a railway accident. Then a case was made up saying his killers were thieves and they killed him for robbing him. Sir, at that very time we had said Shri Upadhyaya could not be killed with the motive of robbery. There are some reasons behind this murder, and they should be brought to light.

We also gave some leads to the CBI but kept silent under the impression that the whole thing is *sub judice*. In the opinion of some of our friends we should not have done so. But now the time has come to break our silence and I ask the Home Minister when the Special Judge at Varanasi has clearly ruled that the two persons accused of murder be set free why should the appointment of a judicial commission be delayed ? I read out a portion of the verdict.

> "The evidence of murder not having been proved against the accused, the problem of truth about the murder still remains."

Can the truth be found on appeal ? Can new witnesses be produced in the appeal ? Can new proofs be submitted in the appeal ? The Special Judge said he has his limitations and he is not in a position to find out if the murder was done for political reasons or other reasons. I quote a portion of the verdict in that regard too :

> "Whether the motive for this crime was political is not a point directly involved in the case, but this obviously is a question very much linked up with identity of the killers. Theoretically, even if the accused were the killers, they might have been acting as the agents of a political group and it is always difficult to prove the negative. Nonetheless, once the killers are found the problem of motivation can be more confidently sorted out."

Can the murderer be found in the appeal ? I fear that in the appeal even the punishment of the accused, who has been convicted of felony and sentenced to four years' imprisonment, may be commuted. The Home Minister should know that asking the U.P. Government to appeal because the case is weak, keeping the matter hanging, filing an appeal to escape the decision to set up a judicial commission—all this is not the way to do justice in this case.

Sir, some questions are still unanswered. Who committed the murder ? Where was it committed ? The Special Judge at Varanasi says it is difficult to say :

> "The evidence on record does not prove Shri Upadhyaya to have been alive at Varanasi."

The whole CBI case is that he was murdered after Varanasi. The accused boarded the train at Rajghat station. The Judge says there is no proof that he was alive in Varanasi. Then again, where did the five-rupee note found in his pocket come from ? The CBI has not been able to unravel this mystery. Why ?

Thirdly, was he killed in the compartment or was his body placed on the railway track after the murder ? The Judge says he believes and there is reason to believe that the murder took place in the compartment. There were blood stains on the pillow. The bed sheet has not been recovered yet. The towel was found, but it has not yet been examined.

The railway conductor was not produced to give testimony. The Judge also said if death was caused by his striking against something—and he struck against a railway's pole—the body would not have been found in the position in which it was found. The Court has ruled that the body was tampered with.

I ask the Home Minister when the whole affair is full of so many mysteries, when a majority of the people of the country are agitated over the whole thing and when our workers are about to lose their patience what is the reason for delaying the appointment of a high-powered committee ? Even after the U.P. Government's decision the Central Government can decide to set up a high-powered commission. I would like to know why the Home Minister is delaying a decision.

SHRI Y.B. CHAVAN : I understand the strength of the feelings of the Hon. member and I share them. But the matter does not end there, because it would be rather a very embarrassing situation if the State Government decides to go in appeal before the HIgh Court. When the matter is being considered by another judicial body, should another judicial commission go into it ? This is, really speaking, the issue. The Government of India are not the party in this matter to take a decision whether an appeal should be made or not. Whatever examination we made of the judgement has been forwarded to the State Government and that Government with the advice of its legal advisers would take a certain decision in the matter. It would not take long. In case it decides to go in appeal, then the fact must be admitted, whether one likes it or not, that a further judicial opinion will have to be expected. This is the legal position. Even then, I have certainly taken note of the strength of the feelings of his party, not only of his party ....

SHRI RANGA (Srikakulam) : All parties.

SHRI Y.B. CHAVAN : All parties. I was going to say the same thing. It is not a question of whether it is the leader of one party or other. The matter involves the death of a leader of a political party and it is the responsibility of everyone of us to do the needful. I would merely plead for patience with the Government of India in this matter.

SOME HON. MEMBERS : How long ?

SHRI VAJPAYEE : Sir, one thing is not clear. The Minister for Home Affairs said if the U.P. Government decides to go in appeal—and I think it cannot do so without asking the Central Government—it would be difficult to set up a commission. Can I not put this in reverse order and say if the Central Government decides to set up a commission it would not be necessary for the U.P. Government to file an appeal ?

SHRI Y.B. CHAVAN : I do not think that would be a right method to adopt.

SHRI VAJPAYEE : Why not ?

SHRI Y.B. CHAVAN : Because going in appeal against a certain judgement is certainly a logical course to follow in the first instance.

SHRI VAJPAYEE : I had asked if other things would be found out in the appeal. Will new witnesses be produced ? Will new proofs be submitted ? The Home Minister has been a lawyer, he should tell us.

SHRI Y.B. CHAVAN : I am certainly a lawyer. But I do not look at this matter as a case to be argued. This is not a legalistic point of view and argument. My point of view was to share their feelings. I can certainly argue this point, but I won't do so. I am not arguing here like a lawyer, I am arguing like a person who is sensitive to the feelings of the people of the country.

Privy Purse and Special Privileges

Sir, some newspapers of Delhi are publishing an advertisement these days, showing the picture of a person but not his face, and the advertisement asks, who is this person whose annual income is equal to Rs. 4 lakh 48 thousand ? Who is this person whose income is 848 times the income of the average Indian citizen ? Who is this person whose income is two and a half times the income of the highest official of any company ?

Is this person some old king ? Is this person being given this annual income because of some merit of his ancestors ? This is no king, he claims to be a servant of the people. This is no feudal lord, he blows the trumpet of socialism. Old kings are being brought to an end, the glitter of crowns is merging in the history of the past, but those who swear by socialism on the national stage are creating new kings and queens. What will happen to their special privileges ?

Sir, this Bill was moved by Shri Y.B. Chavan. These days he graces the Finance Ministry instead of the Home Ministry. Big changes are being discussed, this too is a sign of change. Shri Chavan had said this Bill is being introduced because the concept of monarchy, the privy purses of princes and their special privileges do not accord with the concept of an egalitarian society. May I know since when did this accord come to an end ? The Constitution of India was framed in 1950. In that Constitution our freedom fighters retained those provisions that are now sought to be removed. I can understand the position of Com. Dange, who was against privy purses from the very beginning. There are also other parties that opposed this even at the time of the framing of the Constitution. But when their arguments were rejected, Sardar Patel's morality was accepted, and the patriotism of the princes was respected, what had the fathers of the Constitution — whose heirs the honourable ladies and gentlemen sitting in front of me claim to be — thought when they made this provision in the Constitution ? For 20 years they gave the privy purses and accepted the special privileges. Before 1967 the ruling party did not talk of ending privy purses. Were the mysteries of socialism suddenly revealed in 1967 ? Did the tidal wave of change arise only in 1967, when the ruling Congress was demolished in nine States and the people rejected the Congress ?

What change is being talked of ? Change is necessary. We too advocate change, but to date a link of our freedom struggle has been that along with change tradition should also continue. Dange's change is different—it is a change in which Stalin's grave can be dug up, in which mentioning

Lok Sabha on September 1, 1970 during discussion on the Constitution (Twenty-fourth Amendment) Bill, 1970 seeking abolition of Privy Purses of the former Princes

Khrushchev's name can be declared a sin. But India will not have that type of change. Coming generations will remember Sardar Patel, who roused the princes' patriotism, and they will also respect the princes who, taking inspiration from Sardar Patel's morality, merged their States.

Princes are in the Ruling Party Too

Sir, have the people demanded that the privy purses of princes should be stopped, their special privileges ended ? (*Interruptions*) Is it the demand of those people who elect these very princes to this House ? On the question of ending privy purses Rajmata Scindia of Gwalior had challenged them to take an opinion poll. The Government did not have the courage to do so. If the people want that privy purses should end they could be asked about it. Those people elect princes, there are princes even in the ruling party and they have defeated old Congressmen too. From the point of view of votes their victory is commendable. If popularity is the test we would have to honestly admit that in spite of good, bad, all sorts of persons, the princes of today are more popular than present day leaders. This popularity has been proved by elections .... (*Interruptions*) ....

Sir, I accept the necessity of change in the country, but what should be the process of change ? It shows the moral insolvency of the Government that it could not persuade the princes. If the people really want to end privy purses, if values have changed, if a new age is on the way, if the wave of change is dashing against the rock of time, princes cannot ignore the call of change. But is there anyone to arouse their patriotism, arouse their loyalty to modern values ? What Sardar Patel could achieve no one can do today. What we lack is not the princes, what we lack is those who can persuade the princes. We do not lack Mavlas, we lack Chhatrapati Shivaji, we do not lack Bhamashahs who would sacrifice their all at the instance of Pratap, we lack Maharana Pratap.

Abolition for Political Reasons

The reason for this is clear. It is thought today that an end to privy purses is being advocated for political reasons. For 20 years you kept giving privy purses. So long as the princes were with the ruling Congress those princes were also good, as pure as snow, they were servants of the people, paying privy purses princes was also proper, keeping a promise was good—"*pran jaye par vachan na jaye,*" a promise was to be kept at the cost of life. But in 1967 for the first time the princes dared to oppose the Congress—at least some of them. A majority of them is still there, and those who won elections with the support of princes are also on that side. But in 1967 they showed a little courage. Immediately old agreements are thrown into the waste paper basket, Sardar Patel's prestige is thrown into the dust, the slogan of socialism is raised, and it is claimed times have changed. Times changed in 1967, not in 1962, and could times not wait till 1970 ?

Sir, I say it is a matter of only four crores of rupees. The Prime Minister is willing to pay compensation, although Shri Dange does not approve even of that. Today privy purses are being ended at the instance of Shri Dange, tomorrow the Government will have to surrender on the question of compensation, still Shri Dange will not be satisfied. Demands will continue. I would like to prophesy that in her quest for cheap popularity the Prime Minister may even lose her position.

On getting pierced by the sharp barbs of a few Young Turks she has broken off talks with the princes and hung a sword over their heads by accepting this Bill. Sir, talks were going on, the princes were willing to arrive at a compromise through talks, but no self-respecting person could be made to come to an agreement at gun-point, and I congratulate the princes on their refusal to act against self-respect. But is this a democratic process ? Is this the way to protect democratic values of life ? On the one hand talks are conducted, and on the other a sword is being hung over their heads.

Sir, you were present in this House this morning. Now if this Bill is passed —I trust it will not be passed—all power will be concentrated in the hands of the Government, and the Prime Minister, who is also Home Minister, will hold talks with the princes. No one knows who will get how much compensation, what talks will take place, what promises will be extracted, what moves will take place on the chess-board of politics. Why this hunger for concentrating power in your hands ? Is there not politics behind this ? Can the Government not take the House into confidence on compensation ? But if you do that it would be difficult to get this Bill passed, because those whose cooperation is needed for supporting the Bill have just now clarified the position.

Wrong to Despise the Patriotism of Princes

Comrade Dange said a funny thing. He said that if the princes so wished they could serve like Maharaja Karan Singh. If they serve in Indiraji's court they are good, if they dare to oppose Indiraji they will be threatened with stoppage of privy purses and an attempt would be made to malign their whole history. This is not the time to go into history, but can anyone forget that just one Nizam jeopardised the whole of India by deciding not to merge in the Indian federation ? What would have happened if other princes had done the same ? Can we also forget that the merger of Jammu and Kashmir in India is also the result of a prince's instrument of accession ? There are good princes and bad princes, but despising the patriotism of princes is not the way to enhance the prestige of this House. Can we protect the democratic values of life, about which we talk, like this ?

Can anyone deny that there have been treaties with princes ? Can they be broken in this unilateral manner ? Have you thought of the consequences of breaking these treaties ? Have you thought of the reaction in Bhutan and Sikkim ? Sikkim too has a monarch who is tied to us with treaties. The King of Bhutan is similarly bound. If you break your treaties with your princes unilaterally will that not create doubts in their minds ? I have received news from Bhutan. When one of our Ministers went to Bhutan the King of Bhutan said to him—you people are unreliable, you my break your treaty with us any time, so we are going to the United Nations. If you nominate us we will go through you, otherwise we shall ask some other power to nominate us and will become a member of the United Nations. This is the reaction we have aroused in Bhutan. We want to keep Bhutan with us. In the clash between India and Communist China we want to keep Bhutan's loyalty with us. We want to keep Bhutan and Sikkim in the democratic camp, but if we behave with our princes like this we cannot motivate those kings to keep their promises to India.

The Example of Gwalior

At the time of merger of States the princes could have secured still more concessions for themselves if they had wanted to. I know the example of Gwalior. The Maharaja there paid fifty crore rupees in cash into the Central exchequer. Could he not have kept that money with him ? But today their patriotism is being challenged.

SHRI SONAWANE (Pandharpur) : Where did that money come from ?

SHRI VAJPAYEE : Our friend Shri Sonawane asks where the money came from. It came from where it comes to you. It is not that Old Kings got money from the skies and today's princes got it from *'Gangajali.'* But he paid fifty crore rupees into the Central exchequer because the country stood on the brink of change. The British wanted to divide the country into 500 bits. Pakistan was hatching a conspiracy. The role that the princes played at such a time should be evaluated in history and this House should also express its appreciation of it.

I think there is still time. The problem of privy purses and special privileges can be amicably solved through talks. But an atmosphere conducive to talks will have to be created. The princes cannot be inspired to make more sacrifices by hanging the sword of the Bill on their heads and by threatening them with passing the Bill. For that this Bill will have to be rejected and new talks will have to be held with the princes.

I fail to understand why the princes should not have the freedom to approach the Supreme Court if their special privileges are being taken away and their privy purses stopped. This thing cannot stand any test. Every citizen of this country is equal. Every citizen has the right to seek justice in a court. You are ending inequality on the one hand but creating it on the other. This makes it clear that ending inequality is not your purpose. Your purpose may be to punish some princes or to gain cheap popularity of socialism.

So far as the money is concerned, even the amount of four crore rupees is going to decrease every year. Every death decreases the privy purse amount. Now the amount has come down by half. It is going to decrease still further. No one can imagine that such a small sum of four crores will shore up the people's fortune. Obviously this is not a very big question.

It seems these cheap and inconsequential matters are being raised because of failure to bring about a fundamental change. They can become a political platform but they cannot strengthen the roots of democracy, nor can they enhance the prestige of the Constitution. Swearing by the same change by which others are swearing I would say members of this House must now do some introspection. Has the conscience that had awakened at the time of the presidential election gone to sleep ? It is now argued that there is no question of conscience in the matter of privy purses because it is a matter of money. I would not repeat the reply that Shri Bhanu Prakash Singh gave, but I would like to say to the Prime Minister—if there is a conscience and if it awakens it will not awaken only at your command. If there is a conscience and it awakens it will awaken where there is injustice, where there is inequality, and this House will reject this Bill. Thank you.

Conspiracy to Kill JP ?

We have ourselves called on Shri Jayaprakash Narayan and he said he was hit with a stick. I quote a portion of the statement by his office.'

> "Why should so many men have been injured in trying to protect me if the CRP men had no orders to hit me ?"

And he has said :

> "On the 4th November after the lathi charge, there seems to have been a dozen or more newspapermen who had made anxious-enquiries if my injury was serious, I had said to everyone of them that the lathi blow that I had received on my left shoulder was a light one because its main force had been absorbed by the arm of Nanaji Deshmukh, who, seeing the lathi coming towards me, tried to ward it off...."

Shri Jayaprakash's statement is that he was hit with a stick. But the Home Minister's statement is different (*Interruptions*) ....

SHRI JYOTIRMOY BOSU (Diamond Harbour) : Shri Jayaprakash Narayan got three injuries.

MR. SPEAKER : Order, please, I have not called him. Kindly sit down, all of you.

SHRI VAJPAYEE : We visited Patna for on-the-spot information about what happened on November 4. We also met Shri Jayaprakash Narayan there. He was directly asked if he was hit with a stick. He said—yes, I was hit with a stick, but I did not get a hard blow because Shri Nanaji Deshmukh caught the blow on his arm and he was wounded in the arm.

Whatever Shri Jayaprakash said has been published in the papers. I have brought a statement signed by him. The Minister may not believe the papers but he will have to believe this statement. I had read out a portion of this statement. Now I shall read out another :

> "Whether the lathi was directly aimed at me or had hit me accidentally, as the Prime Minister has suggested, should be better known to the Central Government because it was the CRP men who were wielding the lathis. The 'accidental' theory seems hard to believe, however, because no less than five persons, including Nanaji, were injured while protecting me. Among them was Mr. Ali Haider, convenor of the Gaya Jana Sangharsh Samiti, who received a nasty blow on his head. He is still in the hospital. Among them also was a student who was thrown to the ground and trampled upon by the CRP men, as a result of which he vomited quite a lot of blood.

Lok Sabha on November 15, 1974 during discussion on the Home Minister's statement regarding assault by police on Shri Jayaprakash Narayan on November 4, 1974

Among them were also two security men detailed by the Bihar Government to look after my safety. Why should so many men have been injured in trying to protect me if the CRP men had no orders to hit me ? Something more than equivocation is needed to answer this question."

Shri Jayaprakash adds :

"Mr. Brahmananda Reddy wanted the facts from me. Accordingly I have stated them above. What he does with them is his concern. On my part, all I wish to say is that I do not want his or anybody's apologies. The Congress has long passed the limits of the descencies and courtesies of a civilised public life."

Actually we have concluded that not only beating with lathis was arranged, an attempt was made even to kill Shri Jayaprakash ....(*Interruptions*) ....What I say is right. I do not know if New Delhi had a hand in the plot. But we have talked to the security people and to the CRP people. Hundreds of lathi blows were aimed at Shri Jayaprakash, how did this happen .... (*Interruptions*) ....

MR. SPEAKER : Order, please, the Minister is there.

SHRI VAJPAYEE : Those who killed Mahatma Gandhi ended on the gallows or were sentenced with transportation for life, but those who attacked Shri Jayaprakash Narayan with lathis are yet to be brought to book. And they are not going to escape. You cannot take Mahatma Gandhi's name and defend the attack on Shri Jayaprakash Narayan.

My friend Shri Jyotirmoy Bosu is witness. The securityman placed by the Government for Shri Jayaprakash Narayan's security had drawn a pistol to frighten the CRP people. He said—'do not strike with lathis. I have been placed at Shri Jayaprakash Narayan's disposal for his security. If anything happens to him I won't be able to show my face.' We are prepared to prove this. The identity card of the guard appointed by the Government for Shri Jayaprakash Narayan's security was forcibly taken away from him, and he was beaten with a lathi. Whenever he tried to save Shri Jayaprakash Narayan he was felled to the ground. So he had to draw his pistol.

Shri Jayaprakash Narayan does not want the apology. But if the Home Minister has a conscience that wants to say something, if the Prime Minister has a conscience that is awake, let it speak. If there is no conscience we have nothing to say. This matter should be referred to the Privileges Committee, because the Minister has misled the House.

Deaths in Police Custody

Sir, incidents of killing innocent people in police custody are on the increase in Delhi. Delhi is a Union Territory. Delhi does not have a Legislative Assembly. Such matters come up in Parliament. I wanted to raise this matter that very day, but, pardon me, I was not allowed to do so. What happened has surpassed the incidents of deaths in custody so far. I quote from a newspaper :

> "A young man named Mahendra of Jwala Nagar, Shahdara died in Loknayak Jayaprakash Narayan Hospital today due to merciless beating by the police. A policeman received a knife wound in the incident. A magisterial inquiry in the event has been ordered."

It is said that on August 16, Janmashtami day, a policeman was drinking in the company of some people at Circular Road, Jwala Nagar. Under the influence of alcohol there was a fight and somebody attacked the policeman with a knife. The event proved a calamity for the residents of Circular Road. The police went there on the night of August 17 and arrested 39 people including 8 women. They were all beaten badly at the police station. Even the women were not spared. They were misbehaved with. The police beat Govind and Rakesh so badly that their hands and feet broke. Their limbs are in plaster. But this was not enough for the police. They were looking for two youths named Mahendra and Ramkumar. They say these two are the real culprits. Catch them at any cost. Mahendra's family was so much pressurised that his father Sitaram himself took his son to the Vivek Vihar Police Station and handed him over to the Station Officer R.K. Tyagi. They also tracked down Ramkumar. At the Police Station Mahendra and Ramkumar were mercilessly beaten. They both became unconscious and were admitted in the General Hospital, Shahdara, but in view of their serious condition they were shifted to the Jayaprakash Narayan Hospital. There Mahendra died at 2 o'clock in the afternoon. This is the report of August 25.

Sir, it is true that a magisterial inquiry has been ordered in the whole matter. Action has also been taken against some policemen. But the question is, when interrogation techniques have advanced so much how proper is it to apprehend an innocent person on suspicion of his having committed a crime and to beat him to death ? How far does it become the capital city of Delhi ? More such incidents have taking place in Delhi. Delhi is a model for the whole country. If a policeman drinks on Janmashtami day, gambles when drunk, gets into a quarrel and gets stabbed, then action should be taken against the attacker, but to round up all residents of the colony and

Rajya Sabha on August 8, 1987 during discussion on the Calling Attention Motion regarding the killing of innocent people in police custody in Delhi

misbehave with women is something that has upset the people of Delhi. I wanted to raise the matter the same day, but, Sir, pardon me, it is difficult to raise even such an important matter in this House. When a matter concerning Delhi needs to be raised, the Chair and those occupying the Chair should always bear in mind that Delhi has not been given a Legislative Assembly because Parliament sits here. Where can we voice the grievances of the people of Delhi ? I thank you for giving me an opportunity to speak.

The Bhopal Gas Tragedy

Madam, there has been an agreement between the Union Carbide Corporation and the Government. It is about the people affected by the Bhopal Gas Tragedy. We are discussing it today. This was decided on February 14. February 14, 1989 will be remembered as an unfortunate day. It reminds us of December 3, 1984. That day, rather that night between the 2nd and the 3rd a plant set up by a multinational company began to spew poisonous gas, as a result of which the beautiful city of Bhopal became a gas chamber and thousands of people died. Thousands are still affected by the gas. Children and women fell victims. This was not an accident, it was a massacre.

But on the 14th a 4-year-old legal battle came to a dramatic and mysterious end. It would have been a different matter if there had an out-of-court settlement between Union Carbide and the Government. Disputes are settled like that. But an agreement should be an agreement. The agreement with Union Carbide is not an agreement, it is a surrender. The Government bent on its knees before Union Carbide. National interests have been surrendered. Salt has been rubbed on the wounds of the sufferers. What was the need to bring the Supreme Court into this ? You could have made an agreement with Union Carbide. Union Carbide is a well known multi-national company. There is a big power behind it. It has a worldwide network. Our leaders go to the USA and accept its hospitality. Its guest house in Bhopal has become a rest house for our political leaders. Union Carbide has a strong hold. Union Carbide has a long reach. You could have made an agreement with it outside the Court.

Interim Compensation

The matter of interim compensation had gone to the Supreme Court. The Trial Judge at Bhopal had awarded Rs. 350 crores as interim compensation. But when the matter went to the High Court the amount was reduced from Rs. 350 crores to Rs. 250 crores. The Government went in appeal to the Supreme Court. The Supreme Court had to decide the interim compensation. But instead of the interim compensation the Supreme Court gave the final verdict. The Supreme Court is supreme. The Supreme Court is within the Constitution. But it too has its own process. This matter was heard for many days. The Attorney-General read out from big tomes, and it looked as if the case would go on. But that day the Judges adjourned for lunch and when

Rajya Sabha on February 22, 1989 during discussion on the Bhopal Gas Tragedy

they returned the Chief Justice gave the verdict, which both Union Carbide and the Government of India accepted. (*Interruptions*)

SHRI MADAN BHATIA (Nominated) : Madam, on a point of order. May I respectfully submit when the Honourable member started his speech he was perfectly within his rights but the last sentence which he uttered was a gross reflection on a Judge of the Supreme Court and must be expunged.

DEPUTY CHAIRMAN : Whether somebody raised a valid point of order or not, if I cannot hear what he is saying how am I going to give a ruling on that ?

SHRI MADAN BHATIA : I am submitting to say that the Honourable member said that the Judges rose for lunch and they came and the Chief Justice announced the judgement ....

DEPUTY CHAIRMAN : There is no point of order.

SHRI MADAN BHATIA : It is a reflection on the conduct of the judiciary. It is a loaded insinuation.

DEPUTY CHAIRMAN : I don't think that there is any point of order. It is a statement of fact that the Judges rose for lunch and he came back and he gave the order. That is very simple. Let us not find anything between the lines. If he says something objectionable we are there to take note of it.

SHRI VAJPAYEE : Madam, I am making the Government my target. The Government is in the dock. That is why I said in the beginning it would have been better if this had been an out-of-court settlement. We would not have even needed to mention the Supreme Court. But the agreement has been made in the presence of the Court. Therefore it is necessary to say that the case that was going on for so many days has come to a dramatic end. When the verdict was given the Supreme Court had the faces of Union Carbide and the Government of India before it. The faces of Union Carbide representatives were fair and good-looking. The Government of India's face was the face of the Attorney-General, bearing the holy 'Tripund' mark. It was a respondent face. But the Court did not have the face of the Bhopal gas sufferers before it. It did not have before it the face of the sufferer who lost his entire family in the tragedy, the sufferer whose life has become worse than death. I know our friend will say the Government had acquired the power to represent all gas sufferers. An ordinance was issued, and the ordinance was made into a law. The Government of India had become *'mai-baap,'* the provider, the sustainer. But the facts that have so far come to light do not even indicate that the Government of India and its representatives told the Supreme Court that an agreement is being made, some proposals have been received and we want to chance to consult the sufferers. We do not know who were consulted. Secondly, where did this figure of Rs. 705 crores come from ? How did the Government fix this figure ? Why Rs. 705 crores, why not Rs. 700 crores ?

SHRI L.K. ADVANI (M.P.) : It came from a computer.

SHRI VAJPAYEE : Why not 750 crores ?

SHRI P. UPENDRA : This is in dollars.

SHRI VAJPAYEE : I am coming to dollars too. The dollar is also like this. The dollar too is no round figure, it goes end on. It is clear that in camera negotiations were going on between the Government and the Union Carbide. No objection to that. I repeat it is better to have an out-of-court settlement and avoid a long-drawn legal battle. But if this agreement had to be made it could have been made four years ago. It was certainly possible in 1986. But that time the Government was demanding $ 3.1 million, and now what is the sum settled ? Why did this situation come about ? After all what is the calculation, what is the argument, behind this Rs. 705 crores ? On what basis was this figure worked out ? This House, the people of this country, have the right to know this. The Government must explain. I do not want to say anything against the prestige of the Supreme Court Judges. But the Government must explain—why this Rs. 705 crores ? Is it not a random figure ? Just now Shri Advani said this was a computer game. The computer was working and it stopped at 705, so it was 705. Madam, this is not a Churhat lottery. It depends upon who is working the computer. But I have reliable information that at first Union Carbide was ready to pay 600 million dollars. I can quote from a book. I have also some personal experience in this and I shall refer to it too.

The book is titled *"The Killing Wind—Inside Union Carbide and the Bhopal Catastrophe."* Its author is Don Khurtzmann. What he has written in the book is revealing. He is not a writer to put the Government of India into difficulties. There is also no reason for him to be sympathetic to the multi-nationals. He has written on the basis of personal information. This book was published in mid-1987. I quote :

> "Whatever happened, Mr. Anderson was determined not to offer a sum that would exceed the amount covered by insurance and bank loans and this would mean a ceiling of about six hundred million."

This is on page 200.

SHRI L.K. ADVANI : This even insurance was going to pay. They were ready to pay that.

SHRI VAJPAYEE : Yes. In this Union Carbide was not going to lose anything. It is true that like a miserly capitalist Union Carbide began with 100 million. Take a hundred million, after all Indians have died, what are Indian lives worth ? In this unfortunate country life is cheap and leaders' conscience is also cheap. Carbide started with 100 million dollars. Then it went up. It reached 240 million. But the Government did not accept that, and the Government did the right thing. Then Union Carbide came to 350 million. But when the matter came before the New York Judge the Government of India's lawyer Michael Siresi said it was "completely unacceptable." 350 million cannot be accepted. According to this book, whose author is a reputed writer, the Government of India's lawyer told the New York Judge "it is a sellout," 350 million will not be accepted. This is a bargain. We have been sold out. I ask you, is this wrong ?

The agreement the Government of India has now made cannot be called proper. If interest is added to the 350 million dollars offered us in 1986 it would reach 470 million. Now we have accepted it. Why ?

I shall recount a personal experience. During the last four years I got the chance to visit the U.S. twice. A relative of mine lives in Denbury there. Denbury is the Union Carbide headquarters. Many Indians also work in Union Carbide plants. From them the Union Carbide may have learnt about my arrival in Denbury, and some of them came to see me. That was the first time we met. They again called on me on my second visit and they plainly said there has to be an out-of-court settlement, otherwise we'll keep the matter hanging. Now we have added the thing about sabotage. We will drag the thing on for so long that you will lose patience, so there should be an outside settlement. You should persuade your Government. I said I am in the Opposition. I am not a Government man, how can I persuade the Government ? Tell me, how far are you ready to go ? You will be surprised to hear, they said we are prepared to pay 600 million right now. We shall fully compensate the medical expenses of those in hospital. If necessary we shall take them to the U.S. We can go upto 1000 million.

On my return I passed on this information to those to whom I should give it. At that time the Government did not make an agreement. The legal battle went on for long. Now I do not want to go over the affidavits that the Government has filed in Court. They show the Government encouraged the fighting out of the matter in the U.S. In the U.S. we will get compensation. In the U.S. there is a higher price on human life. In the U.S. the trial will be by jury.

Betrayal of Third World

Madam, the Government has not only disappointed the sufferers of the gas tragedy, it has not only bargained away the nation's interest, it has also betrayed the entire Third World. Developing countries of the Third World were looking at the Union Carbide affair. Multi-national companies have spread there too. They are taking fertilizers there. These countries need fertilizers. They are hungry, they need food, they need to increase food production. These companies have spread their network there. They do not know what sort of poisons are being used there, neither do we know the full story. Along with M.I.C. what other things or elements were there ? Was there cyanide or not ? When doctors began the treatment it was revealed that Union Carbide had not only kept the country in the dark, it even kept the Government in the dark. The Third World countries were watching what was happening in this matter. Union Carbide and other companies are busy making profits. (*Interruptions*) Union Carbide has one more plant in the U.S. Are the safety arrangements there and in India the same ? Anderson said yes. This is wrong. Their factory there is computerized. Were some accident about to happen there it would have been automatically taken care of. What was the arrangement in Bhopal ? If I quote from the Government of India's affidavit — the tank was built wrongly, there was no proper maintenance for it, it was not equipped for storage of volatile liquids. The whole story is with me. And the Government of India did this so that Union Carbide could be put in the dock. Of course, this was the right thing to do. It is also true that officers of the State Government as well as the Central Government are involved in it. If the Union Carbide plant did not have security and safety arrangements why did not the employees and officers of the Madhya Pradesh Government pay attention ? Why did the Government of India not care ?

The Cover Up

Or is it that this agreement has been made in order to cover up the whole affair ? Now the Supreme Court has given its decision. All claims, all liabilities are finished, all criminal claims finished, all libel suits finished, everything is over. The way the Government made the agreement has caused widespread discontent. When the Government acquired the power to represent the gas victims it should have contacted them. The Government should have had some accord with the victims' feelings. I could not see any such indication during the Supreme Court hearing.

Madam, once the case of Sri Ram Fertilizers had gone to the Supreme Court. In the Supreme Court's verdict Justice Bhagwati had made some points. Now it was expected that as there was a precedent and as the Union Carbide case was similar the Supreme Court would follow the same procedure. But I regret to say that procedure was not followed.

Not a Matter of Politics

Madam, I am now about to conclude. I do not claim to be a legal expert, a legal expert like Shri Bhandare is sitting opposite me. I had certainly read Law but I left it after doing the Previous. That was not because I could not have passed Final but because I could not get a chance to do the Final. I am not speaking as a lawyer, I am speaking as a layman, and I agree with you that this is not a matter of politics, not a matter of party politics, but the Government decided upon such a big thing on such a small bargain. Now the gas victims are knocking on the doors of the Court. Yesterday they went to the Supreme Court. Today they are sitting at the Boat Club. I do not want to go into how the Rs. 705 crores will be distributed, what the arrangement for this is, whether it will reach the victims at all or go into the pockets of middlemen. That is a different story.

Court Should Reconsider

One more thing and I shall sit down. I request that the highest court of India, which is the protector of the people's rights, reconsider the whole issue. Even the Government of India should not interfere in this. We do not mind that there was an agreement, but the agreement was made the wrong way and it is of the wrong type.

This is not the way to make an agreement. Certainly not in a democracy. There should be accountability of the Government and also accountability of the judicial system. Now there is a question-mark in the people's mind—what is this that has happened ? From where did this figure of 705 crores come ? When Union Carbide was willing to pay more an agreement was not made on the ground that there was a lot of noise. Then will this agreement be changed if there is a lot of noise against it ? Is this how the Government of India will take decisions ? I say so long as the Supreme Court does not reconsider the issue this amount of 705 crore is an interim amount. It should be used for rehabilitation. It is interim, not final, neither should it be final. Thank you.

Indira Gandhi Assassination Enquiry and Government Hiding Facts

Sir, I have read both parts of the report very carefully. Now you want a discussion in the House on it. You will want and the House too will want that whatever discussion takes place should be meaningful, it should not be mere words. Now in this report Shri Thakkar has referred to some people, held some people responsible, but he has also recommended that there should be further investigation. The Government says we have investigated. The House is being informed about the result of the investigation. But the Government is not willing to take the House into confidence on the basis on which the results were arrived at, neither is it willing to take the country into confidence on this. This is not a matter of report. This has become a matter of the Government's credibility. At first they said the report will not be presented. The law was cited. That law was passed in a hurry. But later the report was presented. Now on reading it I do not think there is anything in it that required the report to be suppressed. It was all right so long as the matter was going on, but even Justice Thakkar has not said the report should be suppressed for ever. Home Minister Shri Buta Singh is present here. At first he was justifying the non-presentation of the report, and now in the same way he is justifying its presentation. Politics changes colours, but I had no idea the Home Minister would change colours so fast.

Sir, all attempts were being used to hold a certain person responsible, but now all attempts are being applied to prove that the same person is innocent. What is all this ? Does it not create a doubt in the public mind ? What do you want to hide ? I am sorry to say—I am not saying this in anger—if those people are to be prosecuted, if there was a conspiracy to assassinate Indiraji and if some people are involved in it we would want that they are brought to book. The Prime Minister's assassination was a terrible tragedy, but a Government that could not protect its Prime Minister will have to answer every question. Or is it that the Government is covering up its own sins ? Against 22 officers the Thakkar Commission .... (*Interruptions*) .... The Thakkar Commission has made recommendations against 22 officers.

CHAIRMAN : Listen, officers and the Government are different.

SHRI VAJPAYEE : Whose officers are they ? Are they not officers of the Government ?

CHAIRMAN : If an officer commits a murder can the Government be held responsible ?

Rajya Sabha on April 4, 1989 during discussion on the Report of the Thakkar Commission regarding assassination of Shrimati Indira Gandhi

SHRI VAJPAYEE : Sir, whose responsibility was it to ensure the Prime Minister's security ?

SHRI BUTA SINGH : Mr. Chairman, Sir, may I request Vajpayeeji to listen to me just for a moment. When I entered the House I was listening to Shri Gurupadaswamyji who was speaking on behalf of the whole Opposition. I listened to this sentence. Now, it has come from the leader of every Opposition party. I am very sure, you will give the opportunity because every party has now started speaking. (*Interruptions*) Had it been only representative of the whole Opposition, the thing would have been different. They are now not only on the limited issue. Shri Vajpayee and prior to that Shri Upendra, have gone into matters which are the subject matter of the report. Therefore, I think this side of the House also requires your consideration and I hope that the members of this side also would be allowed to remark on the points made by the Opposition members.

SHRI VAJPAYEE : If anyone from the ruling party wants to speak he is welcome as this is a matter for the whole House, not of the ruling party and the Opposition.

SHRI MADAN BHATIA (Nominated) : Sir, I am on a point of order. I am respectfully submitting that either they participate in the debate on the report or they confine themselves to the objections which they have raised that they will not participate in the debate unless all the documents are placed on the Table of this Hon. House. I am respectfully submitting that they have gone into the merits of the report. So we are entitled to discuss this report, and now they are trying to run away from the discussion on the report. We are challenging them to discuss the report. Let them discuss the report. (*Interruptions*) Why do they want to run away from the discussion ? (*Interruptions*)

SMT. RENUKA CHOWDHARY (A.P.) : We are not going to convert this House into a court-room. (*Interruptions*)

SHRI MADAN BHATIA : I challenge them to come forward and debate the report. They cannot be permitted to take two stands .... (*Interruptions*) .... Either they say, they do not want to participate in the debate .... (*Interruptions*) .... They should make their position clear. (*Interruptions*) ....

SHRI V. ARUNACHALAM (Tamil Nadu) : The Government has no guts to place all the materials on the Table of the House. We are not running away. (*Interruptions*).

SHRI MADAN BHATIA : I am on my legs. I have been permitted. (*Interruptions*)....

MR. CHAIRMAN : Mr. Bhatia, listen to me. Mr. Vajpayee will not go into the merits of the report. (*Interruptions*) ....

SHRI MADAN BHATIA : They are running away from the debate and the cat is out of the bag. Their political game is out. They have no sympathy for Mrs. Indira Gandhi whom they persecuted, whom they tried to involve in the murder of L.N. Mishra.

They tried to implicate her in the murder of L.N. Mishra. They did not succeed because ....

SHRI P. SHIV SHANKAR, Minister of Human Resource Development : Sir, may I make one submission ? (*Interruptions*)....

DR. G. VIJAYA MOHAN REDDY (Andhra Pradesh) : It is most irresponsible. What is this ? (*Interruptions*)

SHRI P. SHIV SHANKAR : May I make this submission ?

MR. CHAIRMAN : Order, Please.

SMT. RENUKA CHOUDHARY : Fight the election now, we'll see....

SHRI P. SHIV SHANKAR : Sir, I thought I should make one submission.

SHRI ANAND SHARMA (H.P.) : For politicising the departed leader's assassination ....

MR. CHAIRMAN : Sit down. Leader of the House is speaking.

SHRI VAJPAYEE : Mr. Chairman, have you ruled out the earlier point of order raised ?

SHRI P. UPENDRA : His point of order is there. He has not completed.

SHRI P. SHIV SHANKAR : I am also on a point of order.

MR. CHAIRMAN : Please let me hear, Shri Shankarji (*Interruptions*) .... You people, please sit down, let us hear him .... (*Interruptions*)

SHRI N.E. BALARAM (Kerala) : He is a lawyer. He is raising a point of order.

SHRI MADAN BHATIA : My objection has been upheld by the Hon. Chairman.

SHRI P. SHIV SHANKAR : My submission is very simple. My submission is that according to the business slated for today, immediately after the laying of papers on the Table, the Government motion about the report of the Union Public Service Commission has to be taken up. I presume that you were pleased to allow them to make some mention. The submission is that if it is a case where they would like to go into the merits of the Sarkaria Commission Report .... (*Interruptions*) I am sorry. Thakkar Commission Report. (*Interruptions*) Would you please sit down ? Why do you jump up like a frog without any reason ? (*Interruptions*). If it is a case where they would like to go into the merits of the Thakkar Commission Report, as some members have started doing, we should take up that issue first. You may please give a ruling on this. Either you take up that issue first or you take up the other issue, the matter which has been half way through, that is, the Union Public Service Commission Report. Either we take up that and proceed with it and then we take up the Thakkar Commission Report which is already there. Or if they would like to discuss the Thakkar Commission Report we are prepared for that. But then, if it is a case of going into the merits, then we must also be allowed to say something. Mr. Vajpayee started expatiating on the merits of the Thakkar Commission Report. If that be so, then let us go ahead with the Thakkar Commission Report straight away. You may kindly permit us. We have no objection about taking it up.

SHRI M.S. GURUPADASWAMY : May I clarify the position, Sir ?

MR. CHAIRMAN : Just a minute. The Deputy Chairman and myself permitted you only on a limited point, about the rest of the documents. So, about that you can say anything and that too, in short, because .... (*Interruptions*)

You people are making too much noise. What is the use of this ? I have said you people will also speak on it .... (*Interruptions*) .... I permitted these people who want to speak ....

SHRI JAGESH DESAI (Maharashtra) : Every day they say the same thing ....

SHRI VAJPAYEE : I am not going into the merits and demerits of the report that has been presented. I want to assure the House ....

SHRI SATPAL MITTAL (Nominated) : He is not going into the sin the Government wants to hide. Even while saying the Government wants to hide something Shri Vajpayee is not going into the demerits.

SHRI VAJPAYEE : What I say is for any meaningful discussion a full report is necessary. At the same time the report referred to in this report is required to be placed. After all the Thakkar Commission made recommendations against 22 officers ....

SHRI JAGESH DESAI : He is raising the same point .... (*Interruptions*) They are raising their same point ....

SHRI V.M. JADHAV (M.S.) : Sir, they are repeating the same thing .... (*Interruptions*)

CHAIRMAN : Wherever there is a reference to something else as Report, that I permitted in the case of Advaniji and everybody. But if you go to the question of officers, which officer etc ....

SHRI VAJPAYEE : No.

CHAIRMAN : Then it becomes discussion on the Report and, as the Leader of the House has said, we can have a discussion on the report itself. If you like, we can change the order.

SHRI VAJPAYEE : I want to ask why you have made it impossible for us to participate in the discussion ?

SHRI BHAJANLAL : How is that ?

CHAIRMAN : You have not presented the other documents.

SHRI VAJPAYEE : They have not presented the other documents and they have also not presented the other report. The Government has two types of reports based on the Thakkar Commission's report. Imagine what you would have done had you been in my place.

CHAIRMAN : I would not have gone into the merits. I would have remained on my points.

SHRI VAJPAYEE : What is objectionable is that the Opposition had placed before you the suggestion in all seriousness that if there is any material that cannot be divulged in public interest the Opposition could look at it in your chamber.

AN HON'BLE MEMBER : The same point was made yesterday.

SHRI VAJPAYEE : Cannot what was said yesterday be said today ? At the time of the Tulmohan affair I was a member of the Lok Sabha. At that time it was decided that the Opposition could go through secret files. At that time the Opposition was shown a secret file and I was one of those who saw it. At that time the Government trusted the Opposition. It was a corruption matter. Here the whole country is concerned and wants those involved in the killing of the Prime Minister to be punished. But you are not prepared to trust us.

SHRI N.K.P. SALVE (Maharashtra) : That is not so. That is wrong.

SHRI BUTA SINGH : You can trust Kehar Singh and Satwant Singh but not the Government.

SHRI MADAN BHATIA : Sir, I want to raise a point of order ....

SOME HON. MEMBERS : No, no.

SHRI MADAN BHATIA : Sir, with your permission I want to raise a point of order.

SHRI VAJPAYEE : Mr. Chairman, did you hear what the Home Minister said ? Sir, I want to say ....

MR. CHAIRMAN : You have given the example of Tulmohan Ram's case. This is a tradition. If the Government wishes it can benefit from it, it can take the Opposition into confidence. But it is not doing so. This strengthens the suspicion that the Government wants to hide something.

SHRI DIPEN GHOSH : There is something fishy.

SHRI VAJPAYEE : This is not in the interest of the Government, this is also not in the interest of the whole affair. We want the Government to place the facts it has before the country and before the House. If that is not proper take the House into confidence.

MR. CHAIRMAN : After this *'Hitopadesh,'* sage counsel, what is your opinion ?

SHRI VAJPAYEE : Sir, there are still some more speakers. There is consensus of opinion.

Ekata Yatra

Mr. Speaker, Sir, we do not understand the reason of the hue and cry over the Ekata Yatra of Dr. Joshi, the President of Bharatiya Janata Party. It would have been better if the Hon. friend had ascertained the facts before stating anything here. No weapons are being carried with that Yatra. It is neither possible nor it is conducive to do so. One should not just believe in rumours and repeat the same in the House. On the basis of rumours no allegation should be made. Government should not be asked to allow discussion on it. We are ready for the discussion on the Ekata Yatra. But why are all the parties exercised over this Yatra. (*Interruptions*)

SHRI VILAS MUTTEMWAR (Chimpur) : What is the need of this Yatra ?

SHRI VAJPAYEE : Every party implements its programmes. There is no reason to be excited over the Bharatiya Janata Party's national unity and integration programme.

SHRI VILAS MUTTEMWAR : This is just a *Vibhahjan Yatra.*

SHRI VAJPAYEE : Is it wrong to say that the entire country from Kashmir to Kanyakumari is one ? Is uttering of *VANDE MATRAM* wrong ? Is it wrong to repeat the resolution that India cannot be allowed to be divided further at any cost ? Our Yatra is not against any class or community. I do not see any reason that it would create tension in any sphere. The Ayodhya issue has been mentioned my Hon. colleagues must realise that this Yatra is for the unity and not for any controversy. (*Interruptions*) Now they do not allow me to speak.

No riot had even occurred during Shri Advani's Yatra.... (*Interruptions*) But Shri Joshi's Yatra is different from the controversial issue of Ayodhya which has unfortunately divided the people of the country on the line of religion. But the same cannot be said about the Kashmir issue. The issue of the country's unity and integrity is not related to any particular community only. Is it objectionable to say that Kashmir is an integral part of India ? Mr. Speaker, Sir, who has stopped them to take out any such Yatra, they too used to take out *'Sadbhavana Yatra.'* For them it is 'Sadbhavana' but if we do so, it becomes *'durbhavana.'* This double-standard is not possible.

SHRI P.M. SAYEED (Lakshadweep) : We did not carry weapons with us but you did. (*Interruptions*)

SHRI VAJPAYEE : I was willing to participate in the yesterday's meeting. Advaniji was to go to Madurai so he was in a hurry. Had I got invitation, I would have certainly participated in that meeting. (*Interruptions*) Later on it

Lok Sabha on December 11, 1991 during discussion regarding the Ekata Yatra of Dr. Murli Manohar Joshi, President of the Bharatiya Janata Party

was known that the invitation letter was despatched from the Prime Minister's House. But anyway I did not get that. (*Interruptions*) Had I been invited earlier, I would have very much participated and put forward our party's views in that meeting. But by convening the meeting at the last moment it was wrong to expect from any party that it would cancel its pre-scheduled programme. (*Interruptions*)

SHRI K.P. UNNIKRISHNAN : Dr. Joshi wrote to the Prime Minister on the 6th.

SHRI VAJPAYEE : Is Dr. Joshi's invitation to the Prime Minister to come to Srinagar along with members of other parties on the 26th January to hoist National flag after attending the Republic Day ceremony in Delhi objectionable ? To isolate the BJP the Prime Minister (*Interruptions*) If other parties think that they are no one side and all those parties are on the other side BJP a distinct party, we do not care for that. We cannot compromise on the issue of the country's unity and integrity. One may look at our slogans....

SHRI SRIKANT JENA (Cuttack) : Are you going to have a full scale debate on that ? (*Interruptions*)

SHRI VAJPAYEE : Our slogans unite the people. They do not divide them. I have no objection to a full scale debate. (*Interruptions*)

MR. SPEAKER : Please take your seat. Listen to me what I say Loknathji. Why are you standing ? What is this ? The questions are being raised and answered by themselves from different seats. I think this issue has diverted the attention of the people of the country as well as this House. An Hon. member has made his submission on this. And now when Shri Vajpayee is delivering his speech, other Hon. members are interrupting him. I will give chance to you all. But let a party finish its turn. Please do not rise to speak. Give your name if any of you want to speak on this. (*Interruptions*)

SHRI VAJPAYEE : Mr. Speaker, Sir, I would like to request you to allow the Hon. members to speak first because we will be their target. Hence, I would like to speak later on.

MR. SPEAKER : I will give you chance to clarify if I find any allegation in their speeches.

SHRI VAJPAYEE : For taking political mileage and creating misunderstanding this discussion will be central upon us. So please either allow me or allow any of my colleagues to speak later on. (*Interruptions*)

MR. SPEAKER : I will give you chance if it is required.

SHRI VAJPAYEE : Mr. Speaker, Sir, I would like to suggest to hold a full-fledged discussion on this in the Zero-Hour....(*Interruptions*)

MR. SPEAKER : Please take your seat. The same will happen even if a detailed discussion is held.

SHRI CHANDRAJEET YADAV : How can a detailed discussion take place on this ?

MR. SPEAKER : Chandrajeetji, please sit down. Time is being provided to you to express your views on whatever is taking place here. You may express just your views. It is not a question-answer session. However, if discussion is held in detail, then he who begins it will certainly reply to the necessary questions. (*Interruptions*)

SHRI SRIKANT JENA : I am not interested in this discussion.

MR. SPEAKER : You may not be interested but the House is interested. Yes I am allowing you, Shri Atal Bihari Vajpayee. (*Interruptions*)

MR. SPEAKER : Shri Atal Bihari Vajpayee, please continue. (*Interruptions*)

SHRI VAJPAYEE : Mr. Speaker, Sir, I would like to know whether you are allowing a discussion on it or not.... (*Interruptions*)....I have no objection if there is no discussion on it in the House.

MR. SPEAKER : I will just consult. (*Interruptions*)

SHRI GHULAM NABI AZAD, Minister of Parliamentary Affairs : We are not for any discussion as far as this particular subject is concerned. (*Interruptions*)

MR. SPEAKER : The Minister wants to make a statement.

SHRI GHULAM NABI AZAD : As far as this subject is concerned, we are not for any discussion. I do not know what Shri Atal Bihari Vajpayee is talking. I am just mentioning about the discussion. We are not for any discussion....

SHRI MADAN LAL KHURANA (South Delhi) : Mr. Speaker, Sir, please allow a discussion on it....(*Interruptions*)

SHRI VAJPAYEE : Allow me to speak, Sir.

MR. SPEAKER : Is it necessary ? (*Interruptions*)

SHRI VAJPAYEE : Allegations have been made against us. So clarifications, will have to be given. I am saying two or three things....

SHRI K.P. UNNIKRISHNAN : Will you extend the same courtesy to everybody ?

SHRI VAJPAYEE : This allegation is baseless that there is some nexus between BJP and Congress. As a member of the main Opposition party, I am carrying out my responsibilities. It has also been alleged that the Ram Temple in Ayodhya was opened as a consequence of nexus between the two parties. It was not the decision of the Government but of the court to open the lock of the temple. It has also been said that the demand to abrogate article 370 is against patriotism....(*Interruptions*)

MR. SPEAKER : Why are you going into detail ? What is the link between article 370 and the Yatra ?

SHRI VAJPAYEE : No. They have said....

MR. SPEAKER : It is not a detailed discussion.

SHRI VAJPAYEE : Mr. Speaker, Sir, when Pandit Jawahar Lal Nehru was alive and was our Prime Minister then I had moved a resolution in this House for abrogating the article 370. That was discussed in the House and the Communist members had also supported it. (*Interruptions*)

SHRI A. CHARLES : Sir, they have no respect for the Constitution of India.

SHRI VAJPAYEE : No. I am not yielding.

Mr. Speaker Sir, Pandit Nehru had said that article 370 was losing its relevance and one day it would not have any relevance at all. He did not say that article 370 would continue for ever nor did he say that on the basis of article 370 Kashmir was a part of India. Today, these things are being said. There may be difference of opinion, whether the demand to abrogate a article 370 should be raised at this time or not. This may be your opinion. But in our opinion by keeping article 370 in the statute book for so many years we had raised a psychological wall between Kashmir and the rest of the country. We have been its result so you please do not object to the authenticity of this question. We are ready to hold discussion on article 370. Now, it is said that the *Yatra* should be suspended, Mr. Speaker Sir, Shri Ram Vilas Paswan can go on a *Nyay Yatra*....

MR. SPEAKER : We are discussing the law and order situation and can also discuss it.

SHRI VAJPAYEE : But I am to give a personal clarification. Our friend Shri Rangarajan has said....

SHRIMATI GEETA MUKHERJEE (Panskura) : Sir, he has referred to the Communist members. So, I have a right to reply.

MR. SPEAKER : If, by doing so, every member is given permission, then how this House will run ? (*Interruptions*)

SHRI VAJPAYEE : Mr. Speaker, Sir, I was not waiting for any invitation for tomorrow's meeting but I received a phone call and Mr. Azad, who is sitting here told me that I had been invited for the meeting so he asked me if I would be coming or not. I said that I had not received the invitation. Then I went to see the Hon. Vice-President since that appointment was already fixed. Therefore, I was not waiting for the invitation.

Mr. Speaker Sir, I would like to suggest that let us all go together to Srinagar on 26th January to hoist the flag. After completing the programme here in Delhi on 26th January, all the leaders of the political parties can go to Srinagar. The Government can make this programme. We want to go and if you accompany us then we will be glad.

Protest Walk-out Against T.V. Blackout of BJP Rally

Mr. Speaker, Sir, you allow only one member to raise one issue but as you are aware there are certain important issues on which more than one member want to express their views. I had apprised the Minister of Information about the issue raised by Shri Khurana just now. I had requested him to be present in the House at 12.00 O'Clock and give his clarification when this matter is raised before the House. His work is to broadcast news, but in broadcasting, news discrimination is made. No news was broadcast about the meeting held yesterday and which was a historical meeting and was attended by a large number of people beyond expectations and at which a Bill was to be considered which is now under consideration of Parliament. Sir, you may please summon the Hon'ble Minister in the House and direct him to give clarifications.... The Hon'ble Minister has also now come. Yesterday a meeting of the Bharatiya Janata Party was held in Delhi which was totally blacked out by the Television. Is this the policy of the Television ? Shri V.P. Singh too has decided to stay away from Delhi on the question of social justice. That was also an important function and the Doordarshan did not think it necessary to show it. Sir, you may please seek an explanation from the Hon'ble Minister about it.

The second point I want to make is about posters. I agree with your observation that there can not be cross-questioning during the Zero Hour, but the difficulty is that you had made certain reservations in regard to the issue of objectionable Ramayana posters and action was also taken thereon and I think the discussion on the matter ended on that day. If that matter had not been raised today, there would have been no need to reply to that. My friend Shri Chatterjee was saying that that was written in a Jatak story, but was it necessary to exhibit it in Ayodhya through a poster ? (*Interruptions*)....

It is not a question of history. Several incidents have been mentioned in history and many things have been written in several books.

SHRI NIRMAL KANTI CHATTERJEE (Dumdum) : You stopped different versions of Ramayana. You broke diplomatic relations with Indonesia.

SHRI VAJPAYEE : If an opportunity was given to one of our members to present the other side then I think so much heat would not have been created.

MR. SPEAKER : Shri Vajpayee, I have objection to it. On the first issue raised by you, if the Hon'ble Minister wants to say anything I can allow that. But a subject was discussed here, the members had expressed their views thereon,

Lok Sabha on August 23, 1993 regarding blacking out of BJP Public Meeting on Doordarshan

and after that I also said that such posters should not be displayed. The Government took action and the poster was removed. Now if you want to prolong that matter unnecessarily and bring it before the country, that is another matter.

If you desire to have a discussion on it, if Shri Vajpayee wanted to speak on it or any other responsible leader wanted to say something on it, I would have given an opportunity. But if everybody would speak on it, then a discussion take place on it and no purpose is served by having a discussion like this. Therefore, after everything has been done, after discussion has taken place, action has been initiated, there is no meaning in having a discussion again since it would only result in allegations and counter-allegations.

SHRI VAJPAYEE : Mr. Speaker, Sir, I agree with your observation that once a matter has been discussed, it should not be discussed again, but it has been referred to again.

MR. SPEAKER : All right, I am trying to control it, but there is no need to prolong it in this way.

SHRI VAJPAYEE : All right, then we will raise this matter during the consideration of the Bill.

MR. SPEAKER : Yes, you can raise it, you can talk about it, nobody can prohibit you, but I would like to say that if any member tries to browbeat all the time then....

SHRI VAJPAYEE : Mr. Speaker, none of our members want to browbeat, nor do we believe in browbeating.

MR. SPEAKER : We have full faith in you.

SHRI VAJPAYEE : The ruling party is threatening us that they would deprive us from fighting the elections.

SHRI SAIFUDDIN CHOWDHARY (Katwa) : I want to congratulate Shri Vajpayee for telling that he agrees with it.

SHRI K.P. SINGH DEO, Minister of State for Information and Broadcasting : The Hon. Leader of the Opposition has raised two points. As far as the BJP rally is concerned, I am told it has been shown this morning.

SHRI VAJPAYEE : Was it shown this morning ?

SHRI K.P. SINGH DEO : Let me finish. It is because there was no request to cover it yesterday. This is what I have been told by the Department. But I will have to enquire.

As far as the second one is concerned, I will enquire and let you know.

There was no request to cover the rally. No rally was covered and it was shown this morning because the tapes were not available readily.

SHRI VAJPAYEE : Mr. Speaker, Sir, our office did inform the TV people and suppose the information is not sent and some public event takes place, then can't the TV people go there of their own accord to cover it ? Will the TV men have to be called by sending an invitation ? The information was sent from this side as well....

MR. SPEAKER : This is wrong. The reply which he could give has been given by him and he has stated that he would tell you after enquiry. He cannot add anything more now.

SHRI VAJPAYEE : He is misleading the House. Our office had informed them. Moreover, it is not necessary to inform them. It was not shown yesterday evening, but was shown only this morning. He has done a great favour to us. We are not prepared to accept this favour. The Hon'ble Minister must apologize for the mistake, otherwise we will have to walk-out of the House. We are expressing our protest.

Tributes

Pandit Govind Ballabh Pant

Sir, unshakeable as the Himalayas and deep as the sea, Pandit Govind Ballabh Pant was among those great personalities of India whose lives will ever inspire coming generations. Whether it was in struggle or in peace, he always led the nation successfully. At first at the State level and then at the national level he presented an ideal before us with his exceptional genius, deep scholarship and skill in administration, and spent every moment of his life and every atom of his physical being in the dedicated service of the nation. His life will be like a beacon for us.

His great contribution in the attainment of freedom and in making it everlasting will be a memorable part of history. Paying my tributes to him in all humility I pray to the Almighty to give us the strength to complete his unfinished task.

(Lok Sabha, March 7, 1961).

Dr. Rajendra Prasad

Sir, I pay respectful tributes to Rajendra Babu, whom death has taken away from our midst but whose fair name will ever be stamped on the face of time.

In his thinking and feeling, words and way of life, in his style and form Dr. Rajendra Prasad was the ever-new symbol of India's ancient culture. His life, which was a blend of learning and humility, authority and courtesy, the hardness of the diamond and the softness of a petal will continue to inspire future generations.

He was *Ajatshatru*—he had no enemy in the world. His heart was full of equal respect for those belonging to all parties as well as those of all views and principles. He was close to everyone and in his presence we felt one was in the presence of a sage. Even after attaining high office, pride did not touch him. He brought the atmosphere of the Sadaqat Ashram even to the Rashtrapati Bhavan. He remained dispassionate, unaffected, untouched like King Janak.

After King Bharat it was in his life that we saw the ideal of dispassion in practice. With him an era comes to an end. A tradition linking the past with the present is coming to a close.

Let us pray to the Almighty to give us the strength to bear this bolt from the blue, and to build the Bharat of his dreams so that we can repay his debt.

(Rajya Sabha, March 1, 1964).

Pandit Jawaharlal Nehru

Sir, a dream has been shattered, a song silenced, a flame has vanished in the infinite. It was the dream of a world without fear and without hunger, it was the song of an epic that had the echo of the Gita and the fragrance of the rose. It was the flame of a lamp that burnt all night, fought with every darkness, showed us the way, and one morning attained Nirvana.

Death is certain, the body is ephemeral. The golden body that yesterday we consigned to the funeral pyre of sandalwood was bound to end. But did death have to come so stealthily ? When friends were asleep and guards were slack we were robbed of a priceless gift of life. Bharat Mata is stricken with grief today—she has lost her favourite prince. Humanity is sad today—it has lost its devotee. Peace is restless today—its protector is no more. The down-trodden have lost their refuge. The common man has lost the light in his eyes. The curtain has come down. The leading actor on the stage of the world displayed his final role and taken the bow.

In the Ramayana Maharshi Valmiki has said of Lord Rama that he brought the impossible together. In Panditji's life we see a glimpse of what the great poet said. He was a devotee of peace and yet the harbinger of revolution, he was a devotee of non-violence but advocated every weapon to defend freedom and honour.

He was an advocate of individual freedom and yet was committed to bringing about economic equality. He was never afraid of a compromise with anybody, but he never compromised with anyone out of fear. His policy towards Pakistan and China was a symbol of this unique blend. It had generosity as well as firmness. It is unfortunate that this generosity was mistaken for weakness, while some people looked upon his firmness as obstinacy.

I remember I once saw him very angry during the days of the Chinese aggression when our Western friends were trying to prevail upon us to arrive at some compromise with Pakistan on Kashmir. When he was told we would have to fight on two fronts if there was no compromise on the Kashmir problem he flared up and said we would fight on both fronts if necessary. He was against negotiating under any pressure.

Sir, the freedom of which he was the general and protector is today in danger. We have to protect it with all our might. The national unity and integrity of which he was the apostle is also in danger today. We have to preserve it at any cost. The Indian democracy he established, and of which he made a success is also faced with a doubtful future. With our unity, discipline and self-confidence we have to make this democracy a success. The leader is gone, the followers remain. The sun has set, now we have to find our way by the light of the stars. This is a highly testing time. If we all could dedicate ourselves to the great ideal of a mighty and prosperous India that could make an honourable contribution to world peace for ever, it would indeed be a true tribute to him.

The loss to Parliament is irreparable. Such a resident may never grace Teen Murti again. That vibrant personality, that attitude of taking even the opposition along, that refined gentlemanliness, that greatness we may not again see in the near future. In spite of a difference of opinion we have nothing but respect for his great ideals, his integrity, his love for the country and his indomitable courage.

With these words I pay my humble homage to that great soul.

(Rajya Sabha, May 29, 1964).

Dr. Ram Manohar Lohia

Sir, one by one the beacons of the old generation are falling down. One by one our guides are turning away from us. One by one our oarsmen are leaving the ship of the nation in midstream and disappearing into eternity. Our heads bow in reverence and our hearts fill with gratitude towards all those who fought for freedom all their life, whose youth burned like a flame behind the bars and flowered in the midst of thorns of hardship, who made Herculean efforts to bring the Ganga of freedom down to earth, who contributed to the resurgence of a free India to the best of their ability.

I received the news of Dr. Lohia's death in Bangkok. Shri Solanki of the Swatantra Party and Ch. Ram Sevak of the Congress were with me. For a moment we became speechless and bereft of our senses, as if struck by a bolt. We had never thought that this warrior struggling on every front, this general giving a clarion call to everyone to fight every injustice and every privation, and this leader who could turn every circumstance the way he wanted on the strength of his indomitable self-confidence and capacity would lose the battle of life so soon. Perhaps there was something wrong in his treatment. Perhaps cruel death showed no mercy.

Dr. Lohia was a great patriot, one of the foremost leaders of the freedom struggle, a basic thinker and an individual with a revolutionary vision. His personality was unique, many-faceted and many-splendoured. He was himself a subject of controversy and took interest in raising new controversies. He was a rebel in life. It was as if rebellion was a part of his nature. He tried to give a new direction to the life of the nation, he was the harbinger and organiser of a new regime, a new dispensation. One may disagree with his opinions, but the fire that burnt in his heart for the down-trodden and the oppressed could not but scorch and light up whoever came near him.

Sir, Dr. Lohia is no more. His place may never be filled up. In the life of the nation his absence will always be felt. Dr. Lohia has left this world—that Dr. Lohia who opposed governmentalisation in spite of being a socialist, who attacked not only traditional moneybags but also official ones, who shot barbs of criticism and sarcasm not only at old maharajas but also new ones, who gave the *'Angrezi Hatao'* call, who held those disdaining Indian languages guilty of cutting *Bharat Mata's* (Mother India's) tongue, and who insisted on calling Everest 'Sagarmatha' and NEFA Urvasiam. Dr. Lohia has turned his back on us—that Dr. Lohia who always did plain speaking, who never forgave even his own comrades and yet who embraced everyone, and who tried to take everyone with him. He has shuffled off his mortal coil, but his name lives for ever. We have received from him the legacy of the many dreams he dreamt—the dream of a great and mighty India, the dream of bringing India and Pakistan together in a confederation, the dreams of a free Tibet and a free Paktoonistan, the dream of ending all discrimination based on caste, race and family, and the dream of a place of pride for Indian languages. These dreams are today our legacy. If we strive to transform them into reality that would be our real tribute to him.

(Lok Sabha, November 13, 1967).

Pandit Deen Dayal Upadhyaya

Sir, we are gathered in the shadow of grief. The wound that is still green is that of Shri Deen Dayal Upadhyaya's passing away. He was not a member of Parliament, but if any one individual could be given the credit for those Bharatiya Jana Sangh members of Parliament who are sitting in this and the other House, if any one could be given the credit for fashioning the Jana Sangh, fostering it and leading it to success, it is Upadhyayaji. A very simple person to look at, he was a basic thinker, a skilled organiser and a farsighted leader. The quality of taking everyone with him that he exhibited in his life would prove a guiding star for coming generations. He got a high education but did not take up a job. He did not bind himself with family ties. Every atom of his physical being and every moment of his life he dedicated to crowning *Bharat Mata* with glory.

The circumstances in which he met his end are heart-rending. It would not be proper to say he was the victim of railway accident. This is against the facts. His dead body was found a little distance away from Mughalsarai railway station on the way from Lucknow to Patna. Had he died in an accident his body would not have been found in a supine position, a sheet would not have been found on it, and a fifty-rupee note would not have been found in his hand. All wounds on his body indicate that he did not die in a railway accident. There are some other reasons for his death. They should be investigated. The Government of Uttar Pradesh is making inquiries. There is need for a high-level investigation by the Central Government. The body was seen at 3.45 a.m., but it was not brought on to the platform. Why ? He had a ticket in his pocket. There was a reservation slip. It could have been found out that he was on his way from Lucknow to Patna. But the employees at the Mughalsarai station did not do their duty. Had one of our workers not reached there by chance his body would have been declared unclaimed and sent for the last rites. It is not the question of just a leader, it is the question of the security of life of a citizen. It is also the question of safety of railway passengers. It is necessary to unravel all the mysteries surrounding his death. An attempt needs to be made to go to the bottom of this matter, so that there is no such tragedy in future, no party may have to suffer the loss of its priceless leader, and no one may have the opportunity to point his finger to political reasons in future.

Sir, we associate ourselves with what you, the Prime Minister and Acharya Ranga have said. So far as I am concerned I see darkness. For me the light has gone out. Whoever came into Shri Upadhyaya's contact will miss his restrained speech, his far-sightedness, his thinking for the whole country and his attitude of taking everyone with him. For us the void created by his departure will never be filled, but for the sake of the nation we must try to see that such tragedies do not recur.

(Lok Sabha, February 12, 1968).

Shri Nath Pai

Sir, death is the nature of the physical being. Still the heart is shaken when comrades on the path of struggle like Shri Nath Pai meet an untimely end, and the ephemeral nature of life exhibits itself in all its awesome form.

It is indeed difficult to imagine the Lok Sabha without Shri Nath Pai. The news could not be easily believed. It is really difficult to imagine that such a personality would depart from our midst so soon. He had a heart burning with the flame of patriotism, a mind full of freedom for humanity, an unshakeable faith in equality and greatness. He was ever ready for a struggle but generously willing for a compromise. He was a wizard with words and had the capacity to sway millions. He could demolish the opposition with the sharp barbs of logic, sarcasm and satire, but he never stopped to strike. Whenever a debate slackened and the interest of the House flagged Shri Nath Pai could be counted upon to infuse life into it. The discussion would ascend to a higher level. He had made a deep study of the Constitution, had given comprehensive thought to rules and regulations, and he could present his point of view in a manner that contained not only trenchant criticism but a visible effort to win the opponent to his view. The whole House, the whole country, especially the youth—we all grieve at his passing away. Our words cannot adequately express the grief we feel.

Our hearts naturally go out to his family. In Shri Nath Pai we have lost a promising politician.

(Lok Sabha, March 23, 1971).

Dr. K.M. Munshi

Dr. Kanhaiyalal Maneklal Munshi had become an institution even during his lifetime. Even if he had not entered politics, had not become an administrator he would have become immortal in the history of this country and in world literature as a great man of letters. He was a legal luminary and an eminent educationist, and his effort to develop and immortalise Indian culture and Indian literature by founding the Bharatiya Vidya Bhavan will always be remembered as a cherished part of our history. His death has created a void in our public life that can never be filled up.

(Lok Sabha, March 23, 1971).

Shri C. Rajagopalachari

Sir, in Rajaji's passing away modern India has lost a sage. He was gifted with a unique genius. From time to time his personality was put to the test, and every time it shone with greater splendour. As a great patriot, an able administrator, a scholar of Indian culture and a propounder of Indian philosophy Rajaji would be looked upon as one of the greatest men of the century. With his death one more link between the present and the past generation has snapped. Rajaji remained the man of action till the last moment of his life and stood firm on his convictions. He did not try to cover up differences. His pen and his speech were given to sarcasm, but he never levelled low charges on his opponents. He never doubted anybody's integrity. During his last days he accepted the fact that there was scope for a difference of opinion, but he stood firm by his beliefs and gave strength to the voice of dissent, which is important for democracy. Our public life has been left the poorer by his passing away. Hardly would we be able to fill the void his death has created.

I pay my humble tribute to him on my behalf and on behalf of my party.

(Lok Sabha, February 19, 1973).

Shri Jagjivan Ram

Mr. Chairman, I wholly agree with the Leader of the House that with the demise of Babuji an era has come to an end. The last link between the past and the present that existed between the present and past politics is broken. A great freedom fighter is gone. A nature player of the political stage has left us. The ablest administrator of independent India is no more. The House looks somewhat forlorn in the absence of that astute Parliamentarian.

Born in a small village of Bihar in a Dalit family, the child, who no sooner had opened his eyes inherited the curse and bane that which along with the caste which was victimised for centuries because of old disparities and discriminations. He gradually won them over and established himself at the centre of the national arena and then continued to be the focus of attention for decades.

While this fact reveals the greatness of the man, it also shows that our society is dynamic, even though its progress may be slow. Babuji imparted dignity to every position he occupied and lent grace to every assembly he attended. He had to swallow a great deal of bitterness in his life, but always extended the warmth of cordiality to every one. A fire burnt in his heart against disparities, and sometimes the sparks flew here and there. Nevertheless, he made a significant contribution in building up national unity, social amity and goodwill. His contribution in making the country self-sufficient in foodgrain production and in the war of liberation of Bangladesh will ever be remembered. Public life will not be the same without him.

Sir, I am sorry to state that the last moments of his life got engulfed in controversy. The broadcast of the news of his death by All India Radio, then its denial, Prime Minister's dash from the airport to the hospital to see him without adequate security arrangements and thereafter flying to Mauritius—all this has become a matter of public gossip. There can be no doubt that if the Prime Minister had postponed his Mauritius visit in view of the imminent end of Babuji, no misunderstanding would have been created in Mauritius. And the people there would not have taken it otherwise, since relations between our two countries are very cordial.

So many days have gone by since the passing away of Babuji. Could the Government not have come forward with a statement in regard to the questions raised in public ? I do not want to raise a controversy ....(*Interruption*).

AN HONOURABLE MEMBER : You have already raised a controversy.

SHRI VAJPAYEE : I am perfectly within my rights.

MR. CHAIRMAN : The Chair is on its legs. All of you will please resume your seats. Please, please, please, all of you. (*Interruptions*) .... I am sorry that Atal Bihariji has raised it in this meeting. He could raise it in any other meeting. I, therefore, request him to conclude his speech.

SHRI VAJPAYEE : Mr. Chairman, I am sorry that I said so. Maybe I said it because I am a new entrant. Or, probably the Members of this House have so far not known me due to which they are taking it ill. But you will have to hear these things for the next six years .... (*Interruption*).

SHRI VAJPAYEE : Sir, I accept your ruling, but I am not a new member to this House .... (*Interruptions*) I am not a new Member to Parliament ...... (*Interruptions*).... They have committed an impropriety. They should have made a public statement on that question.

MR. CHAIRMAN : I agree with you, Mr. Vajpayee. But my point is, this is not the occasion to raise it. If you wanted to raise it, I would have given you another opportunity. That is all I am saying.

SHRI BUTA SINGH, Minister of Home Affairs : Mr. Chairman ....

MR. CHAIRMAN : Now he is concluding. Please sit down.

SHRI BUTA SINGH : I only wanted to say that the BJP....

MR. CHAIRMAN : No explanations. This is not the time to make a complaint or give an explanation.

SHRI VAJPAYEE : Sir, our tributes to Babuji ....

SHRI SURESH KALMADI (Maharashtra) : ....(*Interruptions*).... maiden speech should not be interrupted.

SHRI JAGDAMBI PRASAD YADAV : Enough is enough. No more interruptions.

MR. CHAIRMAN : These things will not go on record. Now Mr. Vajpayee, I would request you to please conclude..

SHRI. VAJPAYEE : Mr. Chairman, concluding my submission, I have to say that the best tribute to Babuji will be to give impetus to the work of building an equitable India of his dreams. He fought with disparities throughout his life and because of these disparities he could not get to the position he should have. (*Interruption*) .... Sir, I am ready to face any interruption but, as per convention ....

SHRI A.G. KULKARNI (Maharashtra) : When he is concluding, he should not be disturbed. You have opposed a convention just now. He will conclude. Why should they disturb him ? It is not at all necessary, my dear friends.

SHRI JAGDAMBI PRASAD YADAV : Why are the Congress Members hurt by these things ?

MR. CHAIRMAN : This is not the occasion to indulge in this kind of cross-talk. Please. He is concluding. I would request all the members just to allow Mr. Atal Bihari Vajpayee to conclude his speech ...... (*Interruptions*)......

SHRI VAJPAYEE : Sir, I want to conclude, but perhaps my friends do not want it. If I have said something that has hurt them, I regret it. But, I assure you, I did not mean it.

Sir, in the end, I would like to say that so long as we do not build a society free from discrimination and committed to social justice, our tributes to Babuji would remain incomplete.

(Rajya Sabha, July 27, 1987).

Chaudhary Charan Singh

Madam, one by one we are losing the great personalities of the older generation. Hardly had we recovered from the shock of Shri Jagjivan Ram's sad demise when Chaudhary Charan Singh's death has created a great void in our public life. As the leader of the House and other friends have observed, Chaudhary Sahib will be remembered for long as a leading freedom fighter, an able administrator and a vigorous champion of the backward classes, especially of the peasantry.

We can call Chaudhary Sahib the representative of rural India, its spokesman, its living image. In his feelings and his speech, in his apparel and in his food he represented the real India.

Sometimes it appeared—and it was said on the basis of his economic thinking—that he wanted to take India backward, but this criticism had no substance. His economic thinking rooted in the soil. At least in north India Chaudhary Sahib presented an alternative way of thinking in respect of giving priority to agriculture, making the peasant the owner of the land, and solving the basic problem of unemployment by spreading a network of small and cottage industries. We may disagree with that way of thinking, but we could not but be impressed by the sincerity and vigour with which he worked, with how he collected newspaper clippings and how he indicated his point with a 10-year-old clipping that he would fish out of his collection.

Under the leadership of Pandit Govind Ballabh Pant he firmly implemented land reforms in Uttar Pradesh, made the tiller the owner of the land and successfully carried out demarcation of land holdings. And when the collective farming resolution came up at the Nagpur Congress Chaudhary Sahib rose in defence of the farmers' rights and challenged Pandit Nehru. He was not against co-operation in agriculture in principle but against collective farming, and finally the Party had to give it up.

It is true that his economic thinking was not as effective as it should have been. It is a bitter truth that the Chaudhary Charan Singh of Bharat was not fully accepted by India. He always felt the pain of it.

But the aspect of him that I liked best was that of the social reformer. He was a follower of Swami Dayanand and a staunch Arya Samajist. He felt that the caste system based upon birth was the biggest cause of India's slavery. He fought it all his life and was sometimes saddened that he was perhaps not accepted because he came from a backward community. But this is wrong. We gave him the highest office. He was inspired by Gandhiji and motivated by Sardar Patel.

One of those who were close to him told me that when he became Prime Minister an industrialist took a bag containing Rs. 25 lakhs in cash to his place. He not only returned the money but asked the man to leave his place. He was not in favour of fighting elections with industrialists' money. He preserved cleanliness and purity of life. That is something scarce these days.

We all grieve over his death. We share the grief of Smt. Gayatri Devi, their son and the family.

(Rajya Sabha, July 27, 1987).

Shri Rajiv Gandhi

Sir, death is the nature of the physical being. Birth and death are inseparably linked. But when death is not natural, when it does not come in the category described by the Gita as a change of old clothes, when it comes as a bolt from the blue, when it transforms a blooming flower of life into the ashes of a funeral pyre, when it is the consequence of a conspiracy and the result of a plot one simply does not know how to keep courage, how the family can bear such a cruel blow of fate. The dastardly assassination of Shri Rajiv Gandhi is a blow at the essence of our nation, it is a blot on Indian democracy. Once again our great civilisation and ancient culture have become objects of ridicule. Rarely may there be a country in the world that talks so much about non-violence. And yet there may scarcely be a country in the world where political leaders are killed like this. This chain of violence and assassination must end.

Sir, I saw Shri Rajiv Gandhi in many forms. Not at very close quarters but neither from very far. I saw him as a courteous pilot, then as a brother grieving over his brother, then as a son mourning over his mother, then as Prime Minister at the pinnacle of power, and then as a defeated general resolutely standing his ground. Some people thought that with the defeat of the Congress and with his losing Prime Ministership Shri Rajiv Gandhi may relinquish politics. But he was a fighter, he fought. He bore many blows and gave equally powerful blows in turn. He was a man of courage. As the Prime Minister said, when he met, he met with a smile, he observed all etiquette, and spoke sweetly. When there was a difference of opinion he tried to explain and he tried to understand. Sometimes he was ready for discussions in meetings with Opposition parties and presented his viewpoint forcefully. It is true that we had differences. In politics that is natural, to an extent even necessary. But Shri Rajiv Gandhi did not allow such differences of opinion to sour personal relationship. I am specially indebted to him. I had once fallen ill. Perhaps Shri Fotedar told him I should go abroad for treatment.

He called me and immediately made arrangements. It was a small thing, but it was something that touched the heart. So long as Indian democracy has this mutual respect and affection it can gather the strength to face an assault by murderers. The day we doubt each other's bona fides the future of India would be plunged into darkness.

Shri Rajiv Gandhi has departed from our midst. His dastardly assassination has highlighted the grave calamities that already beset the country on all sides. We have to meet these challenges. I do not want to make a political speech on this occasion, tomorrow has been fixed for that. Tomorrow there will be a discussion on who the killer was and what forces are responsible.

Shri J.R.D. Tata

Shri J.R.D. Tata would remain immortal not only as a recipient of Bharat Ratna, but also as a father of Indian industry. I would not like to call him as a leading industrialist; he was the father of industrialisation. Shri Tata had become industrialisation incarnate in this country. There is no need to make a comparative evaluation with other industrialists, nevertheless, Shri Tata had a unique personality and his work has no parallel and he would be remembered as the initiator of industrialisation in India. His personality was not confined to industry alone. As the Prime Minister said, his feet were firmly set on the ground, though he used to fly high in the sky. He had his own dreams about this country, even though one might differ with his dreams. He had an abiding interest in family planning and he always put in his efforts in that direction. His contribution to the public life makes Shri Tata into a class by himself. With his passing away an era has come to an end, to say so would not be an exaggeration.

We have to go ahead fast on the path of industrialisation, but profit should not be the sole motive. Inspiration for the development of the country should be at the root of it and a glimpse of it appears in the works of Shri Tata.

Mr. Speaker, I associate myself and my Party with what you and the Prime Minister have said and offer my humble tribute to all my late colleages.

(Lok Sabha, December 2, 1993).

Shri Morarji Desai

Mr. Speaker, Sir, according to Vedic philosophy a person should live as long as hundred years and it seemed that Morarji Bhai was goig to achieve this goal. But death willed otherwise. He could not complete the century of his life and death removed him from this world for all time to come. When we were celebrating his birth anniversary, it appeared that some ominous glance afflicted him, otherwise a person who had crossed 99 years of his life should have had no difficulty for living for a few days more.

With the death of Morarji Bhai an era has come to an end. A strong link between the past and the present has broken for ever. In a way his life span of 100 years depicted the entire history of modern India. Whereas it contains the joyous moments of attainment of our independence, it also reminds of our sufferings in prison, the agony of partition of the country as well as challenges before the divided country to march ahead on the part of development. Our leaders of those times did endeavour to fulfil their obligations to the best of their abilities and Morarji was one of them. He had a dominant personality. Certain characteristics of his nature often created some wrong notions in those people who failed to understand the very special person in him. He was a man of strong conviction. Sometimes his firmness was interpreted as obstinacy. Probably it was due to his inner moral strength, unflinching belief in God and deep commitment to his duty. The life of Morarjibhai was in fact a manifestation of the precept that one should do one's duty and accept the outcome without grudge. He held various offices and whatever responsibilities he shouldered he did his best to discharge them boldly.

He had the honour and the opportunity to serve the country as Prime Minister. I was a witness to the day when he became the Prime Minister and also when he resigned from that office. He displayed a rare control over his emotions. Victory did not inflict his ego, nor was he seen drowned in sorrow when he had to relinquish his Prime Ministership. He succeeded in bringing about marked improvement in relations with our neighbouring countries. He was the only statesman to be the recipient of the highest official award from India and as well as Pakistan.

He frankly expressed his views and always insisted on truth. Morarjibhai did not subscribe to the saying that one should not speak out the truth if it creates bitterness. We had differences with him on a number of important issues. For example, he did not approve of the liberation of Goa by military force; we disagreed with him on this point. We supported the integration of Sikkim as a right step lest the Sikkim became a base of anti-India conspiracy. Morarjibhai could hardly digest this point of view. Similarly there were several other issues on which we did not see eye to eye. I cannot narrate them all because of paucity of time. He always expressed his point of view with transparent honesty but once the decision was taken he would abide by it. He believed in discipline and also expected others to maintain discipline. As a Prime Minister he always fond to meet the people. Whenever he gave me an appointment to meet him, I did not had to wait for more than 15 minutes at the most. When I once asked him the secret about the time he could spare to meet so many people, he told me that he woke up very early and disposed of all the files right away.

In fact he had ample time to meet any visitors. That is why he had built up a massive public base. His death has created a deep void in our public life which may not be filled in hundred years to come.

(Lok Sabha, April 24, 1995).

The Best Parliamentarian Award For Shri Atal Bihari Vajpayee

The Bharat Ratna Pandit Govind Ballabh Pant Award, 1994 instituted by the Govind Ballabh Pant Memorial Society was conferred on Shri Atal Bihari Vajpayee by the Hon'ble Prime Minister Shri P.V. Narasimha Rao at a function in the Central Hall of the Parliament House at New Delhi on August 17, 1994. The speeches made on the occasion are reproduced below.

SHRI K.C. PANT

Hon'ble Mr. Vice-President, Hon'ble Prime Minister, Hon'ble Speaker of Lok Sabha, distinguished guests, Ladies and Gentlemen, I welcome you all here in this historical hall of Parliament House on behalf of the Govind Ballabh Pant Memorial Society and on my own behalf. The presence of Hon'ble Vice-President has lent dignity to this occasion. We are grateful to him.

We are thankful to the Hon'ble Prime Minister, who from his busy schedule found time for the function. He will shortly be conferring the Award of the Best Parliamentarian of today. This is the second such Award. He had conferred the first Award to Shri Indrajit Gupta. The Govind Ballabh Pant Memorial Society has received liberal co-operation from the Hon'ble Speaker of Lok Sabha right from the beginning in giving shape to the programme of conferring the Best Parliamentarian Award. He was gracious enough to accept the Chairmanship of the Jury for which we are particularly beholden to him. The credit of selecting the award winner in a non-partisan manner and without any political prejudice goes to the Jury.

The Govind Ballabh Pant Memorial Society was constituted about 30 years ago. On that occasion, Pandit Jawahar Lal Nehru observed :

> "Pandit Govind Ballabh Pant is enshrined in the hearts of our countrymen...as one of the greatest parliamentarians and administrators the country has produced...."

During these three decades, this Memorial Society has performed many functions, but none of them was such as would focus on the parliamentary life of Pandit Pant. Today's programme is one such step to fulfil this lacuna. Panditji's association with the people's representative bodies has been long and useful, from Kashipur Municipal Board and Nainital District Board to the Constituent Assembly. He played a prominent role in Uttar Pradesh as well as at the Centre, both as a member of the Opposition and of the ruling party. His conduct in all these bodies matched the highest values and ideals of democracy. He had an abiding faith in maintaining dignity, decorum and order in the House and preserving its honour. It is but natural to take note of these qualities while selecting the Parliamentarian for the Award that is being conferred in his memory.

I would like to put before you some of the thoughts of Pantji, which he had expressed in Lok Sabha, and which are even more relevant today :

> "We have the privilege of belonging to a great country but a country cannot be great simply because of its 'big nation' size. It is the unity of the people and it is their persuit of common ideals that give a country its strength."

In his view unity did not mean uniformity. In his own words,

> "The essence of democracy lies in giving the maximum freedom to every section that is consistent with the unity, integrity and progress of the country for its own development and for the satisfaction of all its aspirations and sometimes even its vagaries."

One more quotation is timely :

> "Democracy cannot function unless we exercise tolerance and discipline. Without these, no democracy howsoever wise the people be can produce adequate results."

Rules are essential for Parliament, but Parliament cannot function with lifeless rules. It is natural that the majority and the minority may have their own viewpoints. Even the existence of difference of opinion to a certain extent within the political parties should not be surprising.

Ours is a vast country. There are many creeds, castes and communities, differing geographical conditions and economic and social inequalities. There is conflict of interests at various levels. All these find their expression in Parliament, and it should be so. However, after all the heat that is generated in it, the Parliament must necessarily take some decision, because the work of the country cannot stop. At times it appears that the wheel of the parliamentary cart has stuck up in the quagmire of differences of opinion. At such times, all eyes move on to those members of Parliament who have a wide outlook, whose thinking is pacific, whose basic style of functioning is one of tolerance towards other's opinion. Such parliamentarians are found both in the ruling party as well as the Opposition, the Parliament cannot do without them.

Today this award is being conferred on Shri Atal Bihari Vajpayee. His faith in parliamentary democracy is undisputable. In 1978, when he was a Minister, he said this in Lok Sabha :

> "This House is a temple of democracy for me. I have tried to follow and preserve the dignity of this House for the last 20 years. When I used to sit in the Opposition, even then I was of the view that the House must run smoothly and the decisions should be taken here on the basis of debate, without casting aspersions on one's integrity. I held that view while I was on that side, I hold the same view when I am on this side...."

Atalji has been in Parliament for about four decades. During this period, he has carved a niche for himself by his oratorical skill, refined language and disciplined and dignified behaviour. His genius as a parliamentarian is recognised by all. He has shown time and again his capacity to rise above narrow conflicts, keeping the interest of the country above everything.

In the end, I would like to recall some words of Atalji in which I find a reflection of Pantji's ideas. He said :

> "Discussion should have grace, the standard must remain high. I have never hit below the belt. I do not regard my opponent as an enemy, nor do I wish anybody to regard me as his enemy. There will be genuine differences of opinion in politics, there will be conflict of ideas, but tolerance is the corner stone of democracy."

I have been in Parliament with Atalji for several decades, and therefore, it is no formality to say that I am particularly happy in extending him my hearty congratulations on this occasion. Thank you.

SHRI SHIVRAJ V. PATIL (Speaker of Lok Sabha)

We express our gratitude to the Hon'ble Vice-President and Hon'ble Prime Minister and welcome them on behalf of the Bharat Ratna Govind Ballabh Pant Memorial Society and Institute of Constitutional and Parliamentary Studies and on my own behalf for gracing this function. We are grateful to all the Hon'ble Ministers, Members of Parliament, Ambassadors, Officers, Journalists and other distinguished guests who have been kind enough to attend this function and extend our hearty welcome to them.

This Award is being conferred here for the second time. The first Award was conferred on Shri Indrajit Gupta. The Second is being conferred on Shri Atal Bihari Vajpayee. Shri Atal Bihari Vajpayee has preserved the dignity of this Award by accepting it and honouring our decision for which we are grateful to him and welcome him here.

Bharat Ratna late Pandit Govind Ballabh Pant was a great freedom fighter, administrator, parliamentarian and a profound thinker. Pantji underwent great suffering for the sake of the country. He was one of those freedom fighters who brought freedom to this country. He contributed to the reconstruction of the country with great skill and farsightedness. Even today we hear many stories about his eloquence and parliamentary skill. He used to speak in measured tones and touching words. His thoughts were deep and lofty. They emerged from Indian history, Indian culture, Indian philosophy, universal common sense and freedom struggle. They reflected the past, present and future.

They were wide-ranging, ubiquitous and good for all times. It is but proper that it has been decided to give this Award every year in the memory of this great son of India. We would like to congratulate the Institute for this and express our thanks to it. Such ceremonies are an attempt to pay our gratitude both to the person in whose memory the Award has been instituted as well as the person on whom it is conferred. A picture of their parliamentary skill, ability, presence of wit, boldness of their grit, vision and farsightedness comes before other members of Parliament, who can emulate them and take advantage from their qualities. And in that lies the usefulness of the Award.

Shri Vajpayee's language is idiomatic and sweet, poetic, inspiring, simple and at times full of soft satire. His words have a dynamism. They have a flow that brings to the fore variety of facts and the truth in his own style. People inside and outside Parliament are eager to listen to the music of his words, his thoughts and his arguments. Even between the pauses of his words and expressions there is some meaning, an argument, a melody. The listeners want to have a taste of it and they relish it.

Shri Vajpayee does not speak mere words, but words that are meaningful and thoughtful. His skill to express his thoughts in minimum of words is admirable. His thoughts work as a link between the past, the present and the future. Modern ideas are acceptable to him. He wants to give due respect to the original pristine ideas. What comes out of the admixture of both, is more true and important. Shri Vajpayee's philosophy is broad-based and reflects maturity. Shri Vajpayee's qualities and ability, thoughts and philosophy have been enhancing the dignity, the power and the utility of Parliament and we believe will continue to do so.

The dignity, efficiency and prestige of Parliament depends upon its rules and regulations and our Constitution. At the same time it also depends upon those who work there. Rules and regulations are necessary, but there is also the need to have the people who know these rules and have the ability and capacity to interpret them and use them. A mix of these qualities gives to it its outer and inner form, its structure and its basic strength. This function can be performed by an individual, by the entire Parliament and by the society. Our endeavour should be that this goes on and this can be done through such attempts. It is a matter of gratification that you have come here to co-operate in that attempt.

Bharat Ratna Pandit Govind Ballabh Pant Award is being conferred by the Leader of the House on the Leader of the Opposition in the presence of all of you and to which the Presiding Officers are witness for being the best Parliamentarian and Shri Vajpayee is accepting it. It is a sign of maturity of our parliamentary system. This sincerity of purpose is indicative of boldness of thought, large-heartedness and maturity of the Prime Minister and Shri Vajpayee. In this lies our true dignity and strength. Let this maturity, boldness and broad mindedness, wherein there is room for everyone, in which nobody is regarded as alien, prevail for ever. This is our prayer.

On this occasion, we pray for a long and healthy life to Shri Vajpayee so that he may continue to serve the Parliament, the country and the world. Thank you.

Shri P.V. Narasimha Rao (Prime Minister of India)

Revered Hon. Vice-President, Hon. Speaker, Hon. Members of Parliament, the National Bharat Ratna Pandit Govind Ballabh Pant Award is very thoughtful initiative of the Govind Ballabh Pant Memorial Society to honour this great Parliamentarian, statesman and national leader. This honour serves two noble objectives. It keeps alive the memory of Pandit Pant in his role as one of the leading parliamentarians to our country and also encourages parliamentarians to emulate him.

Pandit Pant in many ways was one of the most experienced parliamentarians of this generation. He had a rich experience of working in the U.P. Council even before independence. He was the Leader of the Swaraj Party of U.P. Council from 1923 to 1930. Later, he became the Deputy Leader of the Party in the Central Assembly. He thus had experience as a parliamentarian both in the Opposition and in Government. In both these roles, he revealed his skilful grasp of this forum. He was a forceful speaker who believed in swaying his audience not by rhetoric but by the force of argument and logic. His parliamentary skills as Chief Minister of U.P. and as the Union Home Minister were respected even by his friends and critics.

Pandit Pant's faith in the parliamentary process extended beyond the floor of the House. He believed in freedom of thought and expression and in the need for resolving all issues through a process of discussion and debate. Even political issues between India and Britain could be settled through non-violent means. This interactive process of resolving disputes did not attempt any prejudices based on religion or caste.

Pandit Pant held progressive views on social reforms and on the freedom of religion. He realised that prejudices and passions aroused in the name of religion and caste resulted in the faculties of reason and understanding getting clouded. The parliamentary process suffers a severe setback in such an environment.

Shri Atal Bihari Vajpayee is one of the most outstanding parliamentarians of our time. For sheer longevity of experience, he has few peers. He has been a member of one House or the other almost continuously since 1957. He has never been a mere member of the Central Hall. He has a very good knowledge of parliamentary rules and procedure and a razor sharp intellect and wit that is almost tailor-made for parliamentary debate. He has used these often with compelling effect.

We have always sat on opposite sides of the Well. I have always found his interventions intellectually stimulating. His long years in the Opposition have found his faculties of pleasant satire and critical comment to perfection. We all admire his oratorical skills and listen very attentively to him. Even from his position in the Opposition, he has shown that on occasions of national achievement, he is large-hearted and emotionally responsive. I remember the occasion, the great emotion packed occasion when he called Indira Gandhi, "Durga and Kali." I think that moment has hardly been surpassed since.

Atalji's knowledge of international relations and his experience as Minister for External Affairs have made him one of the leading experts in international diplomacy in the world today. Multilateral diplomacy is itself an extension of the parliamentary process to the international arena.

His performances as Leader of our Delegation at the meeting of the Commission on Human Rights in Geneva this year was an illustration of his diplomatic skills as well as of his commitment to the parliamentary system, which ensures that our country puts up a united front abroad on national issues.

His political convictions run deep but in the true parliamentary spirit. He operates within the parameters of the democratic process. He is willing to listen to other persons' views and has an unshakable faith in the need for ensuring that all disputes should be resolved through discussion. Whether in Parliament or outside, his adherence to high norms and behaviour is worthy of the highest parliamentary tradition and commands the respect of one and all. Young parliamentarians and aspirants would do well to pick up from him the art of conducting a debate and containing differences in a parliamentary system.

I congratulate Atal Bihariji once again and thank him for having received this Award from my, more or less, sinful hands. I wish him a long life and a successful career and we all wish him well in his further enlightening the House, enlightening the nation and perhaps enhancing the prestige of the country and the parliamentary system, which is what I think he has done so well so far. Thank you very much.

SHRI ATAL BIHARI VAJPAYEE

Hon'ble Vice-President, Hon'ble Prime Minister, Hon'ble Speaker, Shri Krishna Chandraji Pant, Shrimati Pant, Shri Bansal, Hon'ble Ministers and Hon'ble fellow Members of Parliament, I am at a loss to find words on this occasion. In fact, it is an occasion of that nature. But on such occasions, while it is difficult to speak out, it is also difficult not to say something. It is easy to speak in commendation ceremonies of others, but difficult to find words when the programme relates to oneself. I am grateful to Hon'ble Vice-President, to Hon'ble Prime Minister, to Hon'ble Speaker of the Lok Sabha, members of the Jury and members of Pandit Govind Ballabh Pant Memorial Society who have selected me for conferment of this prestigious Award.

I realise my limitations. I am aware of my shortcomings. The Jury must have selected me for this Award overlooking my inadequacies goodwill tends to overshadow. Ours is an unique country. Apply vermilion to a stone and it becomes worthy of being worshipped and bowed before.

Last year this honour was conferred on my senior Parliament colleague Comrade Indrajit Gupta. He was the fittest person for this Award from all angles. This cannot, however, be said about me. Now that this Award is being given to me, I am afraid it may be construed by someone that I am after him.

I have had the privilege of watching from close quarters the most revered Pandit Govind Ballabh Pant. I had the good fortune of coming in contact with him, first in Lucknow and then in Delhi. When he was busy in restructuring Uttar Pradesh into a modern State, I was working as a journalist at Lucknow and I used to pen down his achievements.

His laudable deeds matched with his personality. He will always be remembered for his great erudition, witticisms and repartees in parliamentary debates, the qualities which have just now been mentioned by the Hon'ble Speaker. His capacity to judge a person and the events correctly, his penetrating farsight, his quality to reconcile and harmonise contradictory views and his role in the struggle for independence as well as in reconstructing the country can never be forgotten. I feel honoured to receive this prestigious Award associated with his name.

When Pantji came to the Centre, I was a Member of Parliament either in Rajya Sabha or in Lok Sabha. That was a very difficult period and an explosive situation had developed due to reorganisation of States. The language controversy had also erupted. But Pandit Pant resolved these problems through his skill, ability and statesmanship. If I am not wrong, it was he who salvaged India from the mess that the country was engulfed in after the proposal of plebiscite in Jammu and Kashmir. He declared in unambiguous terms that the people of Kashmir had already given their verdict that they had decided to merge with India, and so the question of holding plebiscite again did not arise. Pakistan did not accept the proposals and the time did not stop for Pakistan, for the wheel of time never stops.

When I first became a member of Lok Sabha in 1957, Pandit Jawaharlal Nehru was the Prime Minister. He was also the Leader of the House. He used to attend the sittings of the House regularly, remained present in the House, contributed to the discussions, intervened in the proceedings if need arose and carried the Opposition with him. He gave full respect to the Speaker. His mere presence enhanced the dignity of the House. Everybody felt encouraged and inspired to play a constructive role in the House. I vividly remember an incident of that period which comes to my mind like a flash of lightning. Panditji had a faithful assistant in Shri M.O. Mathai. Shri Mathai had made certain comments on the behaviour of Members of Parliament. Naturally, the matter was raised in the House. All the parties in the House took objection to his comments. Notices of Motions for breach of privilege were sent to the Speaker. The question of contempt of the House was raised. The Speaker accepted the Motion given notice of by me. Pandit Nehru was present in the House. Addressing the Speaker he said that it does not appear to be a matter of breach of privilege, this may be an impropriety and that aspect should also be taken into consideration. But the House was not prepared for this. The Opposition also did not like it. Pandit Nehru sensed the mood of the House and gauged the strong feelings of the Opposition. He immediately accepted the proposal to refer the matter to the Committee of Privileges. I am quoting the words uttered by Pandit Nehru at that time :

> "When a considerable section of the House was feeling that something should be done, it is hardly a matter for the majority to override those wishes. Suggestion to drop this matter would I think not be a right one because it almost appears that an attempt was made somehow to hush matter or hide matters. It is not a good thing for such an impression to be created."

Democracy is not a play of 51 and 49. Democracy is basically a moral system. The House or the Parliament is not even a small court of law where dissection of words takes place. It is a political platform—I am not using the word political in its narrow sense, but in a wider sense—where hopes, aspirations and frustrations of 90 crores of people of this country should be reflected and echoed.

The Constitution and the laws are important in their own way, but if democracy is reduced to a mere skeleton or is turned into a ritual and its vital energy is dissipated then difficulties arise. It is the responsibility of all of us not to allow dissipation of that vital energy.

Just two days back, we celebrated our Independence Day anniversary. We have taken a pledge to preserve our independence at all costs. We want to take our country to prosperity. We unitedly face the external challenges. But there is need to take care that our internal democratic institutions are not devalued or eroded. The credibility of the people's representatives should not be lowered. The faith in the democratic institutions should not diminish. The plant of our democracy has strong roots, but they should not be allowed to grow hollow while the foliage above is increasing. That is the duty cast upon us.

I thank you all once again from the core of my heart. I have accepted the Award today from the Prime Minister's hands, which is sure to become a topic for comments. However, one cannot escape from it. I remember when I was elected to Parliament for the first time I was not given time to speak. I used to sit on the back benches. Once I wanted to speak on the motion on foreign policy moved by Pandit Nehru in the House, he moved such motion every year and had it discussed regularly. I was also keen to say something on it, but the Speaker said there was no time, that our party was very small, and so I should keep quiet. I walked out in protest. The practice of walk out still goes on. It is a different matter that the walk outs have now become rather long. However, a walk out is a democratic procedure, it has become a part and parcel of the parliamentary conduct. It is better to remain outside rather than get into the House and disturb its proceedings. That the members should not remain outside for a long period is another thing, but sometimes non-co-operation become necessary. Mahatma Gandhi had shown the path of non-co-operation, there should be no objection on treading that path, but that path should end in Parliament.

This is an era of democracy. This wave is sweeping across the world. India is the largest democracy of the world. The entire world is watching us. We cannot make the mistake of failing at this hour of the test. I express my gratitude once again from the core of my heart that I shall try my best to make my conduct worthy of this honour. Whenever I falter, the Pant Award may continue to caution, tell me not to commit the mistake of wavering from the path. Thank you very much.

SHRI K.R. NARAYANAN **(Vice-President of India)**

Respected Prime Minister, respected Speaker, respected Shri K.C. Pant, respected Shri Atal Bihari Vajpayeeji, Hon. Ministers and Hon. Members of

Parliament, it is a great pleasure and privilege for me to preside over this ceremony to present this year's Pandit Govind Ballabh Pant Award for the Best Parliamentarian to Shri Atal Bihari Vajpayee.

We had a galaxy of great parliamentarians in our country. Our freedom movement was interspersed by constitutional and parliamentary struggle and by direct mass action through non-violent means. Pandit Govind Ballabh Pant was one of the versatile giants of this period, who distinguished himself in the parliamentary arena and made heroic sacrifices in the field of direct action. After independence he emerged as a parliamentarian *par excellence*, while devoting his energies in creative action for the building up of modern India. His superb command of language, his debating skill and his wit and humour made him the role model of an eminent parliamentarian. The institution of the Best Parliamentarian Award is a fitting memorial to him and an inspiration to those who are chosen to receive it from year to year.

I am glad that it has been decided to bestow this year's Award on Shri Atal Bihari Vajpayee. He is a parliamentarian in the mould of Pandit Govind Ballabh Pant. We have seen him now for 37 years in the parliamentary forum through momentous events and grave crises. On all such occasions, he made his impact on Parliament and the country through his overpowering reasoning and overflowing eloquence. His debating skill, his witticisms and repartees and his poetic language made his speeches forceful and delightful. He is one of those who used Parliament as an educational forum as well as a political weapon and enhanced the prestige of the parliamentary institution.

In 1987, Shri Vajpayee observed on the floor of the Rajya Sabha that however long the political career of a person might be, one did not know the real pulse of politics without an association with the Rajya Sabha. He has had experience of both Houses and in that sense he is the complete parliamentarian and still growing having returned to the Lok Sabha, from what he called the 'Parlok Sabha.'

Winston Churchill was once asked what he valued most in his life. His answer was : "two simple letters which come as suffix to my name, Winston Churchill, M.P." I believe, our MPs also value this suffix in the same way. To be elected as a representative of the people is an honour and a trust. It is also a position of power if only one knows how to use it in the forum of Parliament. I believe that a single well-reasoned, well articulated speech in Parliament will have more effect within and outside the House than a hundred demonstrations.

While addressing the All India Conference of Presiding Officers in 1992, Shri Vajpayee criticised those members who become too much publicity conscious and exhorted them to make quality speeches which can draw the attention of the public and the Press : "The speech should be," he said, and I quote :

> "such as can be read in the next Session as well. The speech should be such as can be read in the other House too. And some of the speeches should be such as could be read by the next generation as well."

This is the ideal that the best parliamentarian of the year has set before us.

A good speech is not merely an eloquent speech. The eloquence must reflect the mood of the people and the need of the nation. It must also try to mould the thinking of the people and suggest or at least hint at some approach to the solution of the problem at hand. Shri Vajpayee's parliamentary speeches are marked not only by a debating skill but also by substance.

Among many pronouncements on national and international issues that he made, I should here refer to one instance only, concerning the lot of the lowliest and the lost in our society. In 1988, there was a massacre of Harijans at a place in Jahanabad, in which all the men were killed but the womenfolk spared. Vajpayeeji speaking in the Rajya Sabha said that he had enquired why that has happened, he said :

> "I got a reply that the murderers wanted that only the menfolk should be killed and when the women would cry by beating their breasts they will enjoy the scene. How cruel is it ? Is it not beastly ? Does it behove a civilised society ? Are we really civilized ?"

Vajpayeeji said that the entire might of the machinery of Government should be used to deal with such situations. In this context he made one suggestion, that at the viva voce examination for I.A.S. and I.P.S. selections the candidates should be asked if they believed in the Varna system. "If an officer believes in caste or varna and a man being high or low by birth, then he cannot do justice. Such an officer cannot maintain law and order during caste strife." In that speech he touched upon a cardinal problem in our society which can be expanded to apply to other types of social strife that recur in our country.

No description of Atalji as a parliamentarian can be complete without reference to his role as a member of the Government. His parliamentary experience, his power of reasoning, and his eloquence stood him in good stead when he was Foreign Minister of India from 1977 to 1979. I had the good fortune to work under his direction in the People's Republic of China during a part of this period. The late Girilal Jain in an article once compared him to Nehru saying that Nehru was his model.

We know that Shri Atal Bihari Vajpayee had differences with Nehru and 'blasted' him in Parliament on his foreign policy. But in his foreign policy he followed his footprints, as admitted by Shri Vajpayee himself. But he followed him in his own way with a touch of originality. Of Nehru he once remarked :

> "He may have committed mistakes. Who has not ? But he gave dignity and sophistication to India's political life and culture and enriched them."

One may say that Shri Vajpayee himself has given and is giving dignity and sophistication to India's political life, particularly to India's parliamentary life.

Shri Vajpayee once recalled that Nehru introduced him to Khrushchev in New York as a 'bright young parliamentarian.' Today a bright young parliamentarian of the early 'sixties is before us as the Best Parliamentarian.

May I conclude, by congratulating Shri Atal Bihari Vajpayee on his richly deserved Award of the Best Parliamentarian and by wishing him all the best in the years to come ? Thank you.

Index